Reutter's
The Law of Public
Education

EIGHTH EDITION

by

Charles J. Russo
Panzer Chair in Education and Adjunct Professor of Law
University of Dayton

Foundation Press
2012

THOMSON REUTERS

© 1970, 1976, 1985, 1994, 2004 FOUNDATION PRESS

© 2006, 2009 THOMSON REUTERS/FOUNDATION PRESS

© 2012 By THOMSON REUTERS/FOUNDATION PRESS

> 1 New York Plaza, 34th Floor
>
> New York, NY 10004
>
> Phone Toll Free 1–877–888–1330
>
> Fax 646–424–5201
>
> foundation–press.com

Printed in the United States of America

ISBN 978–1–60930–070–8

Mat #41188704

To Debbie:
With all of my love, now, always, and forever

PREFACE

As with past editions, the Eighth Edition of *Reutter's The Law of Public Education* is designed to provide basic knowledge of the law relating to public education in the United States. The textual material covers key principles of law applicable to public education. This edition incorporates important recent developments into the conceptual framework that has been present since the First Edition was published in 1970. The most notable change in this edition is that the original Chapter 13 on student rights has been divided into two separate chapters. Chapter 13 now covers student due process, discipline, and sexual harassment while Chapter 14 focuses on student free speech. The last two chapters, on special education and school desegregation, have been renumbered accordingly.

The Eighth Edition includes citations to more than 400 new cases since 2008 along with substantive discussions of many of these disputes. The volume also adds a variety of new opinions in its 123 case excerpts even as I have culled a few older cases and replaced selected opinions with more up-to-date judgments. While older cases remain, I have retained those that are still good law to provide a sense of how longstanding precedent is in selected areas.

New case excerpts review developments in such key areas as whether a school board could be liable for the off-campus death of a student in Chapter 7; a variety of issues dealing with teacher rights in Chapters 9, 10, and 11; the Supreme Court's recent opinion on strip searches of students in Chapter 13; and two cases on student use of the Internet in Chapter 14, one in which educators were able to discipline a student for its misuse and another in which the student prevailed in the face of attempted discipline. Citations throughout the book continue to include references to West's *Education Law Reporter*, thereby making it easier for instructors, students, practitioners, and other readers to locate cases.

The more than 4,400 cases cited in the footnotes to the Eighth Edition, plus those in the notes-on-cases were selected as the most authoritative and representative illustrations of the law. These cases are included in order to enhance the book's usefulness both as a teaching tool and a reference volume that provides a starting point for further research. Moreover, while recognizing that they are of extremely limited precedential value at best, this edition includes a small number of citations to cases from WESTLAW and the Federal Appendix, referring to these disputes typically for their underlying novel issues rather than for their holdings as substantive points of law. Except for Chapter 1, which is designed for those who are unfamiliar with the general operation of the law and American legal system, each chapter focuses on the legal aspects of an area in education law. Insofar as there is some necessary overlapping between and among the chapters, the

Table of Contents and the Index help users to locate needed information more readily.

The cases at the end of the chapters provide opportunities to examine judicial reasoning on major issues. The cases were edited to improve their readability by deleting material unimportant to themes of Education Law, yet to preserve flavor as well as continuity. Omissions from the opinions, except for citations, are marked. Cases were selected for their precedential value based on the substantive questions that they addressed and collectively to illustrate judicial thinking in a manner intended to enhance readers' understanding of the issues and principles that they examined. Where possible, the text continues to rely on cases from the United States Supreme Court. Except for chapters 2 and 16, on the Supreme Court's jurisprudence with regard to the Religion Clauses of the First Amendment and desegregation respectively, which present cases chronologically since doing so provides a better sense of the development of the Court's thinking, cases generally appear in the same order as they are discussed in the text.

The Eighth Edition analyzes and synthesizes judicial interpretations of constitutions, statutes, regulations, and litigation in an objective manner while avoiding personal value judgments. I have continued the approach of Professors Reutter and Hamilton in hoping that readers will concern themselves ultimately not only with what the law is, but with what it should be. Since making intelligent legal decisions depends on knowledge of the law itself, I hope that this book will provide instructors, students, practitioners, and other readers with the information that will help them to make the best judgments possible.

ACKNOWLEDGMENTS

As with any book of this magnitude, there are many people to be thanked. I would like to thank individuals in five different groups. First, I would like to thank Professor E. Edmund Reutter for the confidence he displayed in offering me the opportunity to work on a book that meant so much to him and his good friend Professor Hamilton. I greatly appreciate the chance to keep the book current and hope that I have "made him proud."

Second, I would like to thank the professionals at Foundation Press, led by its Editor in Chief, Mr. John Bloomquist, in Eagan, Minnesota, for his support through the process of writing and editing. Thanks, too, to Senior Acquisitions Editor Mr. Robb Westawker and Production Manger, Ms. Roxy Birkel, at Foundation's headquarters for their invaluable assistance in preparing the manuscript for publication. It has been a pleasure working with all of these professionals. Needless to say, I look forward to continuing to work together on future editions.

Third, I would like to express my deep gratitude to friends (listed alphabetically) who offered many useful comments in voluntarily serving as reviewers of selected portions of the text: Dr. Frank Brown, Carey Boshamer Professor of Education, University of North Carolina at Chapel Hill, School of Education; Dr. Allan G. Osborne, Jr., retired Principal, Snug Harbor Community School, Quincy, MA; Dr. Ralph Sharp, Associate Professor and School Administration Program Director, East Central University, Ada, Oklahoma; and Mr. William E. Thro, University Counsel & Associate Professor of Government, Christopher Newport University. I greatly appreciate all of the assistance that these dedicated professionals provided in freely giving of their time and expertise by graciously making helpful suggestions and comments on the content of the materials that they reviewed since their efforts assisted me to focus on the chapters they read.

I would again like to extend a special note of thanks to Dr. Ralph Sharp who continues to go well above and beyond the call of professional duty, demonstrating true friendship, virtually from the moment that I started working with the Fifth Edition, for his constant support as he read, and we discussed, a variety of issues pertaining to topics in the book. A special thanks, too, to Mr. Bill Thro, who has prepared the Teacher's Edition for this volume. The first time that there is such a tool, it is sure to be of value to adopters.

Fourth, at the University of Dayton, I would like to thank Dr. Kevin J. Kelly, Dean, and Dr. Dan Raisch, former Associate Dean, of the School of Education and Allied Professions (SOEAP), as well as Dean Paul McGreal in our School of Law. In addition, I would be remiss if I did not offer special thanks to Rev. Joseph D. Massucci, my former Chair in the Department of Educational Leadership and Dr. Dave Dolph, my current Chair. The support of these friends helped to make the writing process easier. I would also like to thank Mr. Jeff Greenley, University of Dayton School of Law, class of 2012, for his tremendous assistance in checking all of the citations and for proofreading the book. Thanks, too, to Dr. Michael Jernigan, a former doctoral student of mine at the University of Dayton for proofreading significant portions of the text. Further, I would like to thank Ms. Nancy Crouchley in the SOEAP at the University of Dayton for her gracious assistance in proofreading the text. A special thanks is in order for my assistant, Ms. Elizabeth Pearn in the SOEAP at the University of Dayton for her outstanding help proofreading the entire text and preparing the manuscript for publication.

Last, and certainly not least, keeping in mind the often-cited maxim of Supreme Court Justice Joseph Story, that the law "is a jealous mistress and requires a long and constant courtship," I would like to take this opportunity to express my undying love and devotion to my wife, Debbie, our daughter Emily, our son David, and his wife Li Hong, for allowing me to take the time away from our family life during the years that I have worked on this book. I would also like to thank Debbie for her loving and generous assistance in helping with many facets of the book. I am truly blessed to have such a wonderful, loving family.

November 2011

SUMMARY OF CONTENTS

TABLE OF CONTENTS

TABLE OF LEGAL TOPICS ILLUSTRATED BY CASES

TABLE OF CASES

Principal cases are in bold type. Non-principal cases are in roman type. References are to Pages.

REUTTER'S
THE LAW OF PUBLIC
EDUCATION

CHAPTER 1

LEGAL FRAMEWORK FOR PUBLIC EDUCATION

INTRODUCTION

Public school boards in the United States, which are arms of their states, have the duty to prepare children to become productive members of society.[1] Before discussing the legal issues arising in public elementary and secondary schools, it is important to acknowledge the large and ever-growing body of law directing the actions of educational officials. It is also worth noting that Education (or School) Law, as this area of study is known, is but one part of a larger body of law dealing with governmental operations influencing the daily responsibilities of educators. This chapter begins with a brief discussion of the common law, examines the sources and types of laws in the American legal system, and reviews how they impact daily school operations.

THE COMMON LAW

In medieval England, legal scholars and practitioners devoted a great deal of time and attention to "discovering" the law, based on the notion that the laws of nature were available to deal with problems if only they could be found.[2] As the modern study of law emerged, lawyers and academics analyzed judicial decisions in order to uncover the widely held view of the natural law. Contemporaneously, professional communities in London, the Inns of Court, which Winston Churchill described as "half colleges, half law schools . . . produced annual law reports or Year Books"[3] that judges began to treat as authoritative. In this way, common law, also referred to as judge made law, the basis for precedent, which was "discovered" as a result of litigation, stood in contrast to the enacted laws or statutes in England.[4]

---

1. For a history of urban education, with a focus on the "one best system" for educating all children, *see* DAVID B. TAYAK, THE ONE BEST SYSTEM: A HISTORY OF URBAN AMERICAN EDUCATION (1974).

2. BLACKSTONE'S COMMENTARIES (circa 1760) embraced this belief; the Declaration of Independence shares this approach.

3. 1 WINSTON S. CHURCHILL, HISTORY OF THE ENGLISH SPEAKING PEOPLES 176–177 (1956).

4. England still does not have a written constitution.

The legal system in the United States, sometimes referred to as the Anglo–American system of jurisprudence, evolved out of English common law. As customs became accepted bases of conduct, they were distilled into principles that courts enunciated in specific cases. These judicial pronouncements formed English and, later, American common law.

Insofar as courts tended to follow their earlier decisions, the doctrine of *stare decisis*, literally, "to abide by," also referred to as precedent or *res judicata*, literally, "a matter judged," emerged. *Stare decisis* stands for the proposition that once a court has resolved an issue, the question is ordinarily not revisited. However, as a flexible principle, *stare decisis* permits the judiciary to revisit issues such as where the Supreme Court's opinion in *Brown v. Board of Education (Brown)*[5] repudiated the pernicious doctrine of "separate but equal" from *Plessy v. Ferguson*,[6] a case involving accommodations in public railway cars, and explicitly extended to schools in *Gong Lum v. Rice*.[7] By relying on precedent, which stands for the proposition that a majority ruling of the highest court in a jurisdiction is binding on all lower courts in that jurisdiction, judges instilled a degree of certainty in legal proceedings. In other words, by basing their judgments on the collected wisdom of earlier cases, judges did not have to "re-invent the wheel" whenever new, or seemingly new, legal issues arose. Rather, by applying precedent, judges can turn to older judicial opinions in resolving disputes, thereby granting parties a measure of predictability in evaluating the outcome of their cases.

As noted, most of American law is heavily indebted to the common law. Among the many areas in civil law that evolved from common law are the rights and duties of parents in caring for their children; the authority of school officials to act *in loco parentis*, literally, "in place of the parents," when dealing with students; the elements of contracts; the essentials of torts; the principles of land ownership; and a myriad of other legal concepts. Accordingly, the fundamental principles governing many aspects relating to the daily operation of public schools are not the result of statutory or constitutional provisions but exist by virtue of the common law.

CIVIL LAW

It is important to keep in mind that while the primary focus of Education Law in general, and this book in particular, is civil law, it is helpful for readers to get a better understanding of the nature of civil law.[8] In discussing civil law, it is useful to examine it in contrast to what it is not, criminal law, even though criminal law is beyond the scope of this book.

---

5. 347 U.S. 483, 74 S.Ct. 686, 98 L.Ed. 873 (1954). [Case No. 116]

6. 163 U.S. 537, 16 S.Ct. 1138, 41 L.Ed. 256 (1896).

7. 275 U.S. 78, 48 S.Ct. 91, 72 L.Ed. 172 (1927).

8. Unless otherwise noted, the book focuses exclusively on civil law.

Civil law and criminal law differ in three significant ways. The first difference between civil law and criminal law deals with the parties. As reflected by the vast majority of cases in this book, in disputes involving civil law the parties are ordinarily private individuals exclusively or private individuals and the state, in and through state or local school boards or other educational agencies, or their employees as arms of the government, in disagreements over civil law. In this context, civil law is defined as disputes that are not criminal in nature. On the other hand, in cases involving criminal law, the state brings its weight to bear against individuals who violated criminal statutes. Unlike civil law, which is a combination of common law and statute, whether an act is criminal is defined exclusively by statute since there is no such thing as a common law criminal violation.

The second difference between civil law and criminal law is the measure of damages. In civil law, the measure of damages, or relief sought, can be legal and/or equitable. Legal damages, which seek restitution, typically money to put individuals in the positions that they would have been but for the damages they experienced, most commonly appear in cases dealing with negligence, breaches of contracts, and/or employment disputes involving requests for back pay and benefits. Equitable damages, which are far more commonly sought in disputes dealing with Education Law, usually involve requests for judicial orders, or writs of mandamus, directing public officials to do something such as end segregated public schooling, provide an appropriate education for children with disabilities, or stop limiting student rights to free speech. In addition, particularly in employment situations, plaintiffs can seek both legal and equitable relief.[9] In cases involving criminal law, the penalties are most commonly incarceration or fines for wrongdoing.

The final difference between civil law and criminal law is the burden of proof. In civil cases, the plaintiffs, or parties initiating the litigation, must prove that defendants are liable by a preponderance of the evidence. This means that ordinarily plaintiffs must provide evidence that is accorded greater weight than that presented by defendants. As described by the Supreme Court of Iowa, "[a] preponderance of the evidence is the evidence 'that is more convincing than opposing evidence' or 'more likely true than not true.' It is evidence superior in weight, influence, or force."[10] Further, in some civil cases, where experience demonstrates the need for greater certainty, courts may rely on the intermediate standard of "clear and convincing evidence," which is more than a preponderance but less than beyond a reasonable doubt; this applies in such admittedly non-education

---

9. Of course, when individuals have been harmed by the criminal acts of others, they may also have suffered civil losses in connection with obtaining medical care and missing work. When plaintiffs have incurred such losses, they can file civil suits after the state has proceeded with criminal charges. It is better for injured parties to pursue civil remedies after the completion of criminal litigation because if defendants are adjudged guilty criminally, then plaintiffs can ordinarily proceed directly to the damages stage since the higher burden of proof in criminal cases is conclusive proof of civil liability. Conversely, plaintiffs cannot rely on not guilty verdicts in civil proceedings just as findings of liability are inadmissible in criminal court due to the different burdens of proof.

10. *Martinek v. Belmond–Klemme Community School Dist.*, 772 N.W.2d 758 [249 Educ. L. Rep. 390] (Iowa 2009), *reh'g denied* (2009). (internal citations omitted) [Case No. 77]

types of disputes as those seeking to have individuals declared as mentally incompetent and patent law. Conversely, in criminal cases, in order for states to establish that individuals who are accused of crimes are guilty, they must meet the "beyond a reasonable doubt" standard of proof.

THE FEDERAL CONSTITUTION

Simply stated, the United States Constitution is the law of the land. Put another way, all federal statutes and regulations, state constitutions, state laws and regulations, ordinances of local governmental units, and school board rules are subject to the Constitution as interpreted by the Supreme Court and other judicial bodies. In addition to serving as the source of American law, the Constitution creates three co-equal branches of the federal government, each of which is discussed further in the following sections.

Article I of the United States Constitution identifies Congress as the legislative body charged with the responsibility of "making" law. Article II explains the role of the President, the chief executive, who exercises the authority to enforce the laws passed by Congress, chiefly through regulations promulgated by various federal departments and agencies. Article III describes the powers of the courts, which are responsible for interpreting the law. As a democratic republic, state constitutions in the United States, which are supreme in their own jurisdictions as long as they do not vary from or contradict the Federal Constitution, create governmental systems reflecting the structure of the federal government and operate in essentially the same manner as their federal counterparts.

In identifying the duties of the federal government, and distinguishing those from the responsibilities of state governments, four types of powers can be delineated in the United States Constitution: enumerated, implied, reserved, and concurrent. Article I, Section 8, contains the enumerated powers that only the federal government can exercise;[11] among these powers are "to provide for the common Defence [sic] and general welfare of the United States ... [t]o regulate Commerce with foreign Nations, and among the several States ... [t]o coin Money, and regulate the value thereof ... [t]o promote Post Offices ..., [and] [t]o constitute Tribunals inferior to the Supreme Court."

Over time, the second set of powers, implied powers, those reasonably necessary to effectuate the express authority of the federal government, emerged. For example, in providing for minting of coins and other currency, the federal government has the implied authority to create the Department of Treasury and such bureaucracies as it deems necessary to exercise this responsibility.

---

11. *See* THE FEDERALIST No. 45 at 292 (James Madison) (Clinton Rossiter ed., 1961). "The powers delegated by the proposed Constitution to the federal government are few and defined."

As discussed below under the Tenth Amendment, the third set of powers, reserved, are those not delegated to the United States by the Constitution nor prohibited by it to the States or to the people. From the perspective of the study of Education Law, the most important reserved power is education because despite its coverage of a wide area of powers, duties, and limitations, the Constitution is silent with regard to education, thereby rendering it a responsibility of individual states. The earliest federal enactment addressing schooling is the Northwest Ordinance of 1787, which encouraged the creation of schools as the means of education.[12]

The final type of power, concurrent, is shared by both the federal and state governments. The most noteworthy example of a concurrent power is taxation, insofar as both levels of government can tax residents.

School-related litigation generally involves relatively few sections of the Constitution. The amendments protecting individual rights are the sections of the Constitution impacting most dramatically on schools. The restrictions on Congressional power and the States that most frequently come before the courts are Article I, Sections 8 and 10, as well as the First, Fourth, Fifth, and Fourteenth Amendments.

One key provision of Article I, Section 8, is the Commerce Clause, which the Supreme Court has applied with interesting results. For example, in *Katzenbach v. McClung*,[13] a non-school case, the Court broadly interpreted Congressional authority under the Civil Rights Act of 1964 in helping to eliminate racial discrimination in restaurants. After generally deferring to Congressional authority pursuant to the Commerce Clause since 1937,[14] for the first time in almost sixty years, in *United States v. Lopez*,[15] the Court struck down a federal law, the Gun–Free School Zones Act, on the basis that Congress exceeded its authority in relying on the Commerce Clause in attempting to limit the flow of guns into public schools. Five years later, in *United States v. Morrison*,[16] albeit set in higher education, the Court again struck down a federal law, the Violence Against Women Act, after a student was viciously raped by three members of her university's football team, on the ground that it did not involve interstate commerce. In a telling comment on the relationship between the Court and Congress reflecting part of the difference between members of the Court who are strict constructionists and those who engage in judicial activism, a topic that is discussed a bit more below, Chief Justice Rehnquist's majority opinion observed that "[d]ue respect for the decisions of a coordinate

---

12. According to Article 3 of the Northwest Ordinance, "Religion, morality, and knowledge, being necessary to good government and the happiness of mankind, schools and the means of education shall forever be encouraged." SOUL OF AMERICA: DOCUMENTING OUR PAST, VOL. I: 1492–1870 at 86 (Robert C. Baron ed., 1994).

13. 379 U.S. 294, 85 S.Ct. 377, 13 L.Ed.2d 290 (1964).

14. Starting with *NLRB v. Jones & Laughlin Steel Corp.*, 301 U.S. 1, 57 S.Ct. 615, 81 L.Ed. 893 (1937), the Court afforded Congress considerably greater latitude in regulating conduct and transactions under the Commerce Clause than under its earlier case law.

15. 514 U.S. 549, 115 S.Ct. 1624, 131 L.Ed.2d 626 [99 Educ. L. Rep. 24] (1995).

16. 529 U.S. 598, 120 S.Ct. 1740, 146 L.Ed.2d 658 [144 Educ. L. Rep. 28] (2000). The Court explained that "[g]ender-motivated crimes of violence are not, in any sense of the phrase, economic activity.... We accordingly reject the argument that Congress may regulate noneconomic, violent criminal conduct...." *Id.* at 613.

branch of Government demands that we invalidate a congressional enactment only upon a plain showing that Congress has exceeded its constitutional bounds."[17]

CONTRACTS CLAUSE

Early in American history, political leaders recognized the importance of preserving the integrity of contracts. The Framers of the Constitution realized that unless contractual agreements could be relied on without possible subsequent modifications or abrogation by state laws, the national economy could neither progress nor develop. To this end, Article I, Section 10 provides in part that "no State shall . . . pass any . . . law impairing the obligation of contracts."

Article I, Section 10 is involved when state legislatures seek to change teachers' tenure rights, salaries, or retirement benefits to the possible detriment of individuals who acquired vested status under the law. In analyzing legal disputes of this type, one of the important considerations that courts must take into account is whether relationships between public school officials and educators are contractual. If relationships are contractual, such as under collective bargaining agreements, then school boards or state officials may not make changes without the risk of having violated Article I, Section 10 of the Constitution.

SPENDING CLAUSE

As noted below, Congress retains the authority to enact laws under the general welfare clause of Article I, Section 8[18] by offering funds for purposes that it deems to serve the public good, including education. If states accept federal funds, they are bound by whatever conditions Congress has attached to the legislation. If challenged, federal courts must be satisfied that conditions pass constitutional musters. In 1987, Congress expanded its authority by defining a "program or activity" as encompassing "all of the operations of [an entity] any part of which is extended Federal financial assistance."[19] This broad general prohibition covers "race, color or national origin,"[20] "sex,"[21] and "otherwise qualified handicapped individuals,"[22] categories of increasing importance in schools.

---

17. *Id.* at 607.

18. According to this section, "The Congress shall have Power to . . . provide for . . . [the] general welfare of the United States."

19. Civil Rights Restoration Act, 20 U.S.C.A. § 1687.

20. 42 U.S.C.A. § 2000d [known as Title VI, its designation in the Civil Rights Act of 1964]. This statute is in the Appendix.

21. 20 U.S.C.A. § 1681 [known as Title IX, its designation in the Education Amendments of 1972]. Key provisions from this statute are in the Appendix.

22. 29 U.S.C.A. § 794 [known as Section 504, its designation in the Rehabilitation Act of 1973]. This statute is in the Appendix.

THE BILL OF RIGHTS

In the process leading to the ratification of the Federal Constitution in 1789, thereby replacing the ineffective Articles of Confederation, some of the Framers feared that they may have created a federal government that, unless its powers were restricted, might have ignored the civil rights of individual citizens. In order to offer a counterbalance to the authority of the federal government, and help with the ratification of the Constitution, its Framers proposed ten amendments, comprising the Bill of Rights that served to guarantee personal rights.

The Bill of Rights was ratified and added to the United States Constitution in 1791. The process for amending the Constitution is in Article V. The following discussion highlights the amendments that are most relevant for education.

First Amendment

The First Amendment was adopted to ensure personal freedoms or civil rights in declaring that "Congress shall make no law respecting an establishment of religion, or prohibiting the free exercise thereof; or abridging the freedom of speech, or of the press; or the right of the people peaceably to assemble, and to petition the Government for a redress of grievances."

Both religion clauses of the First Amendment, dealing with the establishment and free exercise of religion, have been subject to vast amounts of litigation. While the First Amendment relates solely to Congress, the Supreme Court extended its protection to the States through its interpretation of the Fourteenth Amendment.[23] As discussed primarily in Chapter 2, these clauses have been involved in two categories of cases involving schools: those overseeing the use of public funds to aid students in religiously affiliated non-public schools and those concerning a wide array of prayer and/or religious activities in public schools.

Parties in educational disputes regularly invoked the First Amendment's freedom of speech clause since the 1960s. Most of the litigation over the free speech rights of students and teachers substantively involved expression, whether spoken, written, or symbolic. On the other hand, the amount of litigation devoted to the rights of assembly and petition and the derivative right of association in connection with employee organizations such as unions to engage in concerted actions designed to influence educational policies, especially those affecting working conditions, has decreased in recent years.

Fourth Amendment

The Fourth Amendment forbids unreasonable searches and seizures, asserting that warrants "describing the place to be searched, and the persons or things to be seized" can be issued only "upon probable cause," a

---

23. *Cantwell v. State of Conn.*, 310 U.S. 296, 303, 60 S.Ct. 900, 903, 84 L.Ed. 1213 (1940). *But see Barron v. Mayor and City Council of Baltimore*, 32 U.S. 243, 8 L.Ed. 672 (1833) (holding that the Bill of Rights was inapplicable to the states because its history indicated that it was limited in force to the federal government).

high standard that ordinarily applies in criminal, rather than civil, cases. The Fourth Amendment has been contested in well over three hundred school cases since the Court first applied it in an educational setting in *New Jersey v. T.L.O.*[24] Additionally, the Fourth Amendment is sometimes mentioned in connection with the right of privacy, a concept that is also associated with the notion of liberty in the Fourteenth Amendment.

Tenth Amendment

Since education is not mentioned in the Constitution, it is a function of the States under the Tenth Amendment: "[t]he powers not delegated to the United States by the Constitution, nor prohibited by it to the States, are reserved to the States respectively, or to the people."

The Constitution's silence with regard to education should not be interpreted as meaning that it does not affect schooling. Beginning largely with *Brown*, the Supreme Court, soon to be followed by lower federal courts, acknowledged that constitutional rights, such as equal protection under the Fourteenth Amendment, have a major impact on schooling. Consequently, as the courts and Congress have taken a more active role in education, the number of cases involving federal Constitutional issues, particularly under the Fourteenth Amendment, and statutory questions increased dramatically since *Brown*.

Eleventh Amendment

The Eleventh Amendment reads that "[t]he Judicial power of the United States shall not be construed to extend to any suit in law or equity, commenced or prosecuted against one of the United States by Citizens of another State, or by Citizens or Subjects of any Foreign State."

The adoption of the Constitution "did not disturb States' immunity from private suits, thus firmly enshrining this principle in our constitutional framework"[25] The widespread acceptance of the proposition "that the Constitution would not strip the States of sovereign immunity"[26] can be seen in the reaction to *Chisholm v. Georgia (Chisholm)*,[27] wherein the Supreme Court held that private citizens from one State could sue another State.[28] Almost immediately, Congress passed, and the States ratified, the Eleventh Amendment, effectively overturning *Chisholm* and restoring a concept derived in part from the common-law tradition coupled with constitutional design.

The Eleventh Amendment's being facially limited to the "provisions of the Constitution that raised concerns during the ratification debates and

---

24.   469 U.S. 325, 105 S.Ct. 733, 83 L.Ed.2d 720 [21 Educ. L. Rep. 1122] (1985). [Case No. 96]

25.   *Federal Maritime Comm'n v. South Carolina State Ports Auth.*, 535 U.S. 743, 752, 122 S.Ct. 1864, 152 L.Ed.2d 962 (2002).

26.   *Alden v. Maine*, 527 U.S. 706, 716, 119 S.Ct. 2240, 144 L.Ed.2d 636 (1999).

27.   2 U.S. 419, 2 Dall. 419, 1 L.Ed. 440 (1793).

28.   The Court explicitly acknowledged that *Chisholm* was wrong. *See Federal Maritime Comm'n*, 535 U.S. at 752–53; *Alden,* 527 U.S. at 721–22.

... *Chisholm* ...''[29] aside, it confirms the broader notion that States are immune from suit. The Eleventh Amendment also bars suits against a variety of entities, including corporations created by the federal government,[30] and applies in such important venues for education as state courts[31] and federal administrative proceedings.[32]

As broad as sovereign immunity is, it is not absolute since it permits five exceptions. First, under extraordinary circumstances, Congress may abrogate the sovereign immunity of States[33] but must do so explicitly.[34] Second, States may waive their sovereign immunity.[35] Third, by invoking the jurisdiction of the federal courts, States expose themselves to the equivalent of compulsory counterclaims that do not exceed the amounts or differ in kind from the relief they seek.[36] Fourth, federal courts generally may order state officials, in their official capacities, to conform their conduct to federal law.[37] Finally, "States, in ratifying the Constitution, did surrender a portion of their inherent immunity by consenting to suits brought by sister States or by the Federal Government."[38]

Fourteenth and Fifth Amendments

According to Section 1 of the Fourteenth Amendment:

All persons born or naturalized in the United States, and subject to the jurisdiction thereof, are citizens of the United States and of the State wherein they reside. No State shall make or enforce any law which shall abridge the privileges or immunities of citizens of the United States; nor shall any State deprive any person of life, liberty, or property, without due process of law; nor deny to any person within its jurisdiction the equal protection of the laws.

---

29. *Alden v. Maine*, 527 U.S. 706, 723, 119 S.Ct. 2240, 144 L.Ed.2d 636 (1999).

30. *Smith v. Reeves*, 178 U.S. 436, 20 S.Ct. 919, 44 L.Ed. 1140 (1900).

31. *Alden v. Maine*, 527 U.S. 706, 712, 119 S.Ct. 2240, 144 L.Ed.2d 636 (1999).

32. *Federal Maritime Comm'n v. South Carolina State Ports Auth.*, 535 U.S. 743, 760, 122 S.Ct. 1864, 152 L.Ed.2d 962 (2002).

33. *Fitzpatrick v. Bitzer*, 427 U.S. 445, 96 S.Ct. 2666, 49 L.Ed.2d 614 (1976). *But see Seminole Tribe of Fla. v. Florida*, 517 U.S. 44, 116 S.Ct. 1114, 134 L.Ed.2d 252 (1996) (affirming that Congress lacked authority under the Indian Commerce Clause to abrogate the States' Eleventh Amendment immunity).

34. *Dellmuth v. Muth*, 491 U.S. 223, 109 S.Ct. 2397, 105 L.Ed.2d 181 [53 Educ. L. Rep. 792] (1989) (noting that insofar as Congress can abrogate States' immunity only by making its intention unmistakably clear in a statute's language, it did not do so under the then Education for All Handicapped Children's Act, now the Individuals with Disabilities Education Act). However, Congress essentially overturned this decision in the statute. *See* 20 U.S.C.A. § 1403(a): "A State shall not be immune under the 11th amendment to the Constitution of the United States from suit in Federal court for a violation of this chapter."

35. *College Sav. Bank v. Florida Prepaid Postsecondary Educ. Expense Bd.*, 527 U.S. 666, 119 S.Ct. 2219, 144 L.Ed.2d 605 [135 Educ. L. Rep. 362] (1999).

36. *See, e.g., Oklahoma Tax Comm'n v. Citizen Band Potawatomi Indian Tribe of Okla.*, 498 U.S. 505, 111 S.Ct. 905, 112 L.Ed.2d 1112 (1991).

37. *Ex parte Young*, 209 U.S. 123, 28 S.Ct. 441, 52 L.Ed. 714 (1908); *Frew ex rel. Frew v. Hawkins*, 540 U.S. 431, 124 S.Ct. 899, 157 L.Ed.2d 855 (2004).

38. *Federal Maritime Comm'n v. South Carolina State Ports Auth.*, 535 U.S. 743, 752, 122 S.Ct. 1864, 152 L.Ed.2d 962 (2002).

The first clause of Section 1 of the Fourteenth Amendment defines citizenship, specifying privileges shared by citizens of the United States and other persons. The last two clauses of Section 1 have widespread applicability to public education. The next-to-last clause in Section 1, the Due Process Clause, has perhaps been applied more frequently than any other provision of the Constitution with regard to schooling. The final clause, the Equal Protection Clause, has also received wide attention in educational disputes.

Enacted in 1868, the Fourteenth Amendment applies to the States. The Fifth Amendment pursuant to which, in part, "[n]o person shall ... be deprived of life, liberty, or property, without due process of law ..." applies to the federal government. The Supreme Court recognized the difference between the Fifth and Fourteenth Amendments when, on the same day that it struck down segregated schooling in *Brown* under the Equal Protection Clause of the Fourteenth Amendment, it relied on the Due Process Clause of the Fifth Amendment in invalidating the practice in *Bolling v. Sharpe* (*Bolling*),[39] a dispute which originated in Washington, D.C. The Court applied the Fifth, rather than the Fourteenth, Amendment in *Bolling* since public schools in Washington, D.C., are under the control of Congress and hence the federal government.

Due process includes a pair of distinct aspects that may be viewed as the two sides of a coin. Substantive due process addresses the rights of Americans whether under the Constitution or specific legislative or regulatory enactments. Under this concept, laws must have both purposes within the legitimate power of government and be rationally related to achieving those goals. In other words, as reflected in the ensuing discussion of equal protection, substantive due process protects individuals against grossly unfair acts of government. Procedural due process concerns the decision-making process applicable in evaluating whether public officials violated the law. Pursuant to this provision, those purporting to implement laws must apply basic fairness. More specifically, individuals who may suffer deprivations must be informed of what they are accused and must be offered the opportunity to defend their actions before fair and impartial third-party decision makers.

Individuals who have substantive due process rights, such as tenured teachers, are entitled to procedural due process. Conversely, individuals, such as non-tenured teachers, who lack substantive due process rights are not entitled to procedural due process unless it is conferred on them by collective bargaining contracts or state law.

At the heart of equal protection is the notion that individuals or groups that "are similarly situated should be treated alike."[40] Put another way, all within a classification must be accorded the same rights and privileges while being subjected to the same duties. Per se classifications are subject to closer examination, must be based on differences relevant to the subject, and cannot be prohibited by law.

---

39. 347 U.S. 497, 74 S.Ct. 693, 98 L.Ed. 884 (1954). [Case No. 116]

40. *Cleburne v. Cleburne Living Ctr.*, 473 U.S. 432, 439, 105 S.Ct. 3249, 87 L.Ed.2d 313 (1985).

Under equal protection analysis, the general constitutional test for acceptability of criteria for classifications is whether they are rationally related to legitimate governmental purposes.[41] There is a very strong, but rebuttable, presumption that criteria established through the legislative process are constitutional.[42] It is difficult for plaintiffs to succeed if courts apply this test.

At the other end of the continuum, when legislation or acts of governmental officials or bodies allegedly infringe on fundamental rights (such as those mentioned explicitly in the United States Constitution including freedom of religion or speech or that are implicitly there as declared by the Supreme Court), or disadvantage members of suspect classes by categorizing individuals based on constitutionally "suspect" factors such as race or legislatively protected categories (such as age in some situations), the courts apply the "strict scrutiny" test and are unlikely to uphold classifications unless they are based on compelling justifications.[43] Suspect classes are clearly defined groups in need of extraordinary protection from the majoritarian political process since they have been subjected purposefully to unequal treatment or are relegated to positions of virtual political powerlessness. Under strict scrutiny analysis, the burden shifts to the government to demonstrate a compelling need for such classifications. Even if restrictions are permissible, they must be as narrowly drawn as possible. When courts apply the so-called compelling interest test, governmental classifications or actions are likely to fail.

Classifications such as illegitimacy and gender fall into a third, in-between, category and continue to be subject to heightened judicial scrutiny. In limited circumstances, the Supreme Court adopted an intermediate standard of review that is not as difficult for the government to meet as the compelling interest test but which involves less deference to legislation than the rational relations test. Under this test, the Court refuses to uphold classifications unless they bear "substantial relationships" to "important" governmental interests.[44]

As noted, the Supreme Court interpreted the First Amendment, for example, as applying to the States through the Fourteenth Amendment.[45]

---

41. The Supreme Court declared that " . . . if a law neither burdens a fundamental right nor targets a suspect class, we will uphold the legislative classification so long as it bears a rational relation to some legitimate end." *Romer v. Evans*, 517 U.S. 620, 632, 116 S.Ct. 1620, 134 L.Ed.2d 855 [109 Educ. L. Rep. 539] (1996).

42. *See Hazelwood School Dist. v. Kuhlmeier*, 484 U.S. 260, 273, 108 S.Ct. 562, 98 L.Ed.2d 592 [43 Educ. L. Rep. 515] (1988) [Case No. 105] " . . . [w]e hold that educators do not offend the First Amendment by exercising editorial control over the style and content of student speech in school-sponsored expressive activities so long as their actions are reasonably related to legitimate pedagogical concerns."

43. For a notorious example of a case wherein the Supreme Court allowed a race-based classification to survive strict scrutiny, *see Korematsu v. United States*, 323 U.S. 214, 65 S.Ct. 193, 89 L.Ed. 194 (1944) (upholding the internment of Japanese–Americans during World War II based on their ancestry).

44. The case that comes closest to applying this standard in a school setting was *Plyler v. Doe*, 457 U.S. 202, 102 S.Ct. 2382, 72 L.Ed.2d 786 [4 Educ. L. Rep. 953] (1982), *reh'g denied*, 458 U.S. 1131, 103 S.Ct. 14, 73 L.Ed.2d 1401 (1982), even though the majority did not clearly indicate that it was applying this test. [Case No. 82]

45. *See Cantwell v. State of Conn.*, 310 U.S. 296, 303, 60 S.Ct. 900, 903, 84 L.Ed. 1213 (1940).

As a result, restrictions under the First and Fourteenth Amendments must be considered along with limits on state constitutions when examining the validity of state laws or local school board policies. In a specific example on the interplay between constitutional provisions dealing with the funding of non-public schools, a major area of controversy, courts must consider both the First and Fourteenth Amendments. In *Everson v. Board of Education*,[46] the plaintiff unsuccessfully raised the Fourteenth Amendment's prohibition against using public funds for private purposes. The Court pointed out that the First Amendment's bar is against using public funds for religious purposes, a subcategory of private purposes.[47] The Court has applied the Fourteenth Amendment in a wide range of educational disputes such as those dealing with the rights of parents to direct the education of their children,[48] teachers who are subject to dismissal,[49] student discipline,[50] and racial segregation.[51]

FEDERAL STATUTES AND REGULATIONS

Pursuant to the Tenth Amendment, education is a constitutional power reserved to the States.[52] Even so, Congress retains the authority to enact laws under the General Welfare Clause of Article I, Section 8,[53] by offering funds for purposes that it deems to serve the public good. Beginning in the 1960s, Congress enacted a series of statutes such as the Civil Rights Act of 1964[54] which subject public school systems to its anti-

---

46. *Everson v. Board of Educ.*, 330 U.S. 1, 67 S.Ct. 504, 91 L.Ed. 711 (1947), *reh'g denied*, 330 U.S. 855, 67 S.Ct. 962, 91 L.Ed. 1297 (1947). [Case No. 1]

47. *See* the discussion of *Lemon v. Kurtzman*, 403 U.S. 602, 91 S.Ct. 2105, 29 L.Ed.2d 745 (1971) and its progeny in Chapter 2. [Case No. 6]

48. *See, e.g., Meyer v. Nebraska*, 262 U.S. 390, 43 S.Ct. 625, 67 L.Ed. 1042 (1923).

49. *See, e.g., Cleveland Board of Education v. Loudermill*, 470 U.S. 532, 105 S.Ct. 1487, 84 L.Ed.2d 494 [23 Educ. L. Rep. 473] (1985), *on remand*, 763 F.2d 202 [25 Educ. L. Rep. 158] (6th Cir.1985), *on remand*, 651 F.Supp. 92 [37 Educ. L. Rep. 502] (N.D.Ohio 1986), *aff'd*, 844 F.2d 304 [46 Educ. L. Rep. 523] (6th Cir.1988), *cert. denied*, 488 U.S. 941, 109 S.Ct. 363, 102 L.Ed.2d 353 (1988), *cert. denied*, 488 U.S. 946, 109 S.Ct. 377, 102 L.Ed.2d 365 [50 Educ. L. Rep. 15] (1988). [Case No. 75]

50. *See, e.g., Goss v. Lopez*, 419 U.S. 565, 95 S.Ct. 729, 42 L.Ed.2d 725 (1975). [Case No. 94]

51. *See, e.g., Brown v. Board of Educ.*, 347 U.S. 483, 74 S.Ct. 686, 98 L.Ed. 873 (1954). [Case No. 116]

52. *Epperson v. State of Ark.*, 393 U.S. 97, 104, 89 S.Ct. 266, 21 L.Ed.2d 228 (1968) [Case No. 6] ("By and large, public education in our Nation is committed to the control of state and local authorities. Courts do not and cannot intervene in the resolution of conflicts which arise in the daily operation of school systems and which do not directly and sharply implicate basic constitutional values. On the other hand, '[t]he vigilant protection of constitutional freedoms is nowhere more vital than in the community of American schools' (internal citations omitted).")

53. According to this section: "The Congress shall have Power to ... provide for ... [the] general welfare of the United States."

54. 42 U.S.C.A. § 2000e–2a [popularly known as "Title VII," its designation in the Civil Rights Act of 1964, made applicable to public schools in 1972]. Portions of this statute are in the Appendix.

discrimination in employment provisions that have had a profound effect on public education.[55]

Many of the federal statutes with a direct and substantial impact on public education make federal funds available to state and local governments conditioned on their observing specified rules for the use of the money. By way of illustration, in order to receive funding for special education under the Individuals with Disabilities Education Act (IDEA),[56] states, in and through state and local educational agencies or school boards, must develop detailed procedures to identify children with disabilities and offer each qualified child a free appropriate public education in the least restrictive environment. Chapter 15 examines the IDEA in detail.

In another example of federal involvement in education, as part of the reauthorization of the Elementary and Secondary Education Act of 1965, in 2002 Congress enacted the No Child Left Behind Act (NCLB), perhaps the most controversial federal education statute ever.[57] Pursuant to the NCLB's far-ranging provisions, states that receive federal financial assistance must take steps to improve academic achievement among students who are economically disadvantaged; assist in preparing, training, and recruiting "highly qualified" teachers (and principals); provide improved language instruction for children of limited English proficiency; make school systems accountable for student achievement, particularly by imposing standards for adequate yearly progress for students and districts; require school systems to rely on teaching methods that are research based and that have been proven effective; and afford parents better choices while creating innovative educational programs, especially if local school systems are unresponsive to their needs. To date, federal trial courts have refused to allow parents and private service providers who are opposed to the NCLB's provisions[58] the right to file private rights of action.[59] Amid considerable controversy over its future as this book heads to press, elements of the NCLB are examined in Chapter 9, on teachers, and in Chapter 12 on curricular issues including accountability.

Courts have also responded to claims that the NCLB is an unfunded mandate. The federal trial court in Connecticut granted the United States Department of Education's (DOE) motion for summary judgment, essen-

---

55. Federal statutes, which consist of fifty titles, are published in the United States Code, abbreviated U.S.C. The unofficial version, the United States Code Annotated, published by Thomson–West, abbreviated U.S.C.A., includes useful annotations, or brief summaries of all cases that have cited federal statutes. In addition to WESTLAW and LEXIS, both of which are available by subscription, federal statutes can be found in a variety of on-line Web sites. *See*, *e.g.*, http://www.gpoaccess.gov/uscode (official Web site of the Government Printing Office); http://thomas.loc.gov/home/bills_res.html (official Web site of the Library of Congress).

56. 20 U.S.C.A. §§ 1400 *et seq*. *See* Chapter 14 for a full discussion of this far-reaching statute. Portions of this statute are in the Appendix.

57. 20 U.S.C.A. §§ 6301 *et seq*. Portions of this statute are in the Appendix.

58. The courts rejected claims by parents and private service providers, respectively. *See Association of Community Org. v. New York*, 269 F.Supp.2d 338 [179 Educ. L. Rep. 661] (S.D.N.Y. 2003); *Fresh Start Academy v. Toledo Bd. of Educ.*, 363 F.Supp.2d 910 [197 Educ. L. Rep. 275] (N.D.Ohio 2005).

59. *See, e.g., Blakely v. Wells*, 380 Fed.App'x 6, 8 [260 Educ. L. Rep. 605] (2d Cir. 2010), citing *Horn v. Flores*, 557 U.S. 433, ___, n. 6174, 129 S.Ct. 2579, 2598, n. 6, 174 L.Ed.2d 406 [245 Educ. L. Rep. 572] (2009) ("NCLB does not provide a private right of action"); *Watson v. Washington Twp. of Gloucester County Pub. School Dist.*, 413 Fed.Appx. 466 [267 Educ. L. Rep. 116] (3rd Cir. 2011).

tially dismissing the state's claim that the NCLB violated its own unfunded mandate provisions, the Spending Clause, and the Tenth Amendment.[60] The court later reached the same outcome as to the remainder of the claim which alleged that the DOE violated the Administrative Procedures Act (APA) in rejecting Connecticut's two proposed amendments over the timing and method of assessment of children who needed special education and were classified as Limited English Proficiency students.[61] The court explained that although it refused to address the merits of the underlying NCLB claims, the DOE did not act arbitrarily or capriciously pursuant to the APA in rejecting the plans. Similarly, the Seventh Circuit affirmed the dismissal of a similar claim alleging that the NCLB and the IDEA are legally incompatible.[62] The court determined that the statutes simply did not conflict with one another.

The Sixth Circuit initially reached the opposite result, holding that insofar as a school board and educational associations had standing, their suit against the DOE could proceed under the Spending Clause based on the claim that they need not meet the requirements of the NCLB since federal funding was insufficient to cover increased costs of compliance.[63] After an en banc panel[64] vacated its original order subject to a rehearing, an evenly divided court upheld the dismissal of claims that the NCLB was an unfunded mandate.[65] The First Circuit subsequently reached the same outcome in rejecting a claim that the NCLB was an unfunded mandate.[66]

Regulations promulgated by the DOE and other agencies afford the executive branch the opportunity to enforce statutes by carrying out their full effect.[67] In other words, while statutes set broad legislative parameters with regard to such areas as compulsory attendance, regulations permit administrative agencies to fill in necessary details concerning the amount of time that children must be in class and the subject matter that they need to study in order to satisfy the law. Regulations are thus presumptively valid and must be treated like acts of Congress.

STATE CONSTITUTIONS

60. *Connecticut v. Spellings*, 2007 WL 329118 (D. Conn. 2007). For the earlier ruling in this dispute, *see Connecticut v. Spellings*, 453 F.Supp.2d 459 [214 Educ. L. Rep. 186] (D. Conn.2006).

61. *Connecticut v. Spellings*, 549 F.Supp.2d 161 [233 Educ. L. Rep. 209] (D.Conn.2008).

62. *Board of Educ. of Ottawa Twp. High School Dist. 140 v. Spellings*, 517 F.3d 922 [230 Educ. L. Rep. 159] (7th Cir.2008).

63. *School Dist. of the City of Pontiac v. Spellings*, 512 F.3d 252 [228 Educ. L. Rep. 651] (6th Cir.2008).

64. An en banc panel, literally, "in the bench" is one consisting of all judges in a court or circuit.

65. *School Dist. of City of Pontiac v. Secretary of the U.S. Dep't of Educ.*, 584 F.3d 253 [249 Educ. L. Rep. 654] (6th Cir. 2009), *cert. denied*, ___ U.S. ___, 130 S.Ct. 3385, 177 L.Ed.2d 302 (2010).

66. *Connecticut v. Duncan*, 612 F.3d 107, 259 Educ. L. Rep. 18 (2d Cir. 2010), *cert. denied*, ___ U.S. ___, 131 S.Ct. 1471, 179 L.Ed.2d 360 (2011).

67. Federal regulations are published in the Code of Federal Regulations, abbreviated C.F.R. In addition to WESTLAW and LEXIS, both of which are available by subscription, federal statutes can be found in a variety of on-line Web sites. *See, e.g.,* http://www.gpoaccess.gov/cfr/index.html (official Web site of the Government Printing Office).

Subject to the supremacy of the United States Constitution and federal statutes, state constitutions form the basic law of individual states. The primary function of state constitutions is to restrict the powers of state legislatures, which have complete, or plenary, authority subject to federal law or state constitutions. State constitutions may require legislatures to perform specified acts, most notably for the purpose of this book such as establishing public educational systems and may forbid other acts such as using a state's credit to support private ventures.

State constitutions typically deal with many of the same matters as their federal counterpart, particularly in the areas of church-state relations and individual freedoms. Consistent with equal protection analysis, states may place more, but not fewer, limits on governmental relations whether with regard to religious bodies, teachers, and/or students than the Federal Constitution mandates.

Insofar as state constitutions are direct products of their people, no legislatures have sole power to amend state constitutions. Indeed, since legislatures are creatures of their constitutions, they lack the power to amend the constitutions that give them their existence. Procedures for amending state constitutions are found within their provisions. Normally, amending constitutions is a slow process due to the importance of deliberation before changes can be made in such fundamental legal documents.

State Statutes and Regulations

State statutes are an abundant source of laws impacting public schools.[68] The courts consistently describe the power of state legislatures over their public school systems as plenary. This, of course, is true only in a relative sense. As discussed above, state legislatures are subject to the limitations of federal law and of state constitutions as they apply to education, just as is the case with legislation covering other agencies and segments of society. When agencies that are charged with the administration, or implementation, of statutory provisions act, their interpretations are generally accorded judicial deference unless they are clearly erroneous, fraudulent, in bad faith, an abuse of discretion, or arbitrary.[69]

Public school systems, and many other governmental agencies, have become so complex that it is difficult to oversee their administration in detail through specific legislative enactments. The law is settled that state and local boards of education, administrators, and teachers have the authority to adopt and enforce reasonable rules and regulations to ensure the smooth operation and management of schools. As such, rules and

---

68. State statutes and regulations are published in state publications and on-line Web sites that appear under a variety of titles.

69. *Commonwealth, Dep't of Educ. v. Empowerment Bd. of Control of Chester–Upland School Dist.*, 938 A.2d 1000 [228 Educ. L. Rep. 793] (Pa.2007).

regulations are subject to the same constitutional limitations as statutes passed by legislative bodies. Moreover, it is possible that teachers who develop their own rules for classroom management can violate the civil rights of students. For example, if it is unconstitutional for Congress or state legislatures to enact laws violating the free speech rights of students, it is equally impermissible for teachers to do so by creating rules limited to their classrooms. Of course, nothing prohibits teachers from enacting rules that comply with the law. It is also important to note that legislation or rule-making on any level cannot conflict with higher authorities. For instance, local school boards cannot require parents and/or students to pay fees for tuition if state law prohibits the practice.[70]

THE COURTS

IN GENERAL

Constitutional provisions, statutes, and regulations are not self-executing. Rather, they merely permit or require respective government agencies, including educational systems, to engage in or avoid specific actions. If individuals or bodies affected by provisions think that they are being improperly implemented, they may turn to the courts for relief. Since the judiciary cannot act on its own initiative, the courts can intervene only when parties initiate litigation, giving birth to a real case or controversy.

The duty of the courts is to interpret the law. Absent statutory guidance, or if regulations are unclear, courts apply common law. Since common law is a judicial creation, the courts may adjust it to changing circumstances. Where statutes are at issue, the task of the courts is to uncover, as far as possible, the intent of the legislative bodies that enacted the laws. In many cases, courts must try to impute to the legislature intent that they believe lawmakers would have had if the matter had been called to their attention. In reaching their judgments, the courts cannot avoid taking economic, political, social, educational, and perhaps other implications of the cases before them into consideration.

The role of judges and their latitude in interpreting constitutions, statutes, and regulations has caused a great deal of controversy. Two schools of thought have emerged in this regard. On the one hand are those who maintain that judges should stay close to the original texts by interpreting them consistent with the intent of those who wrote them, thereby engaging in judicial restraint. On the other hand are those who believe that judges are free to interpret the law based on their own beliefs, thereby engaging in judicial activism.[71] Not surprisingly, this debate often plays itself out in legal battles involving education.

---

70. *Nagy v. Evansville–Vanderburgh School Corp.*, 844 N.E.2d 481 [207 Educ. L. Rep. 311] (Ind.2006) (striking down a mandatory student services fee), *on subsequent appeal*, 870 N.E.2d 12 [221 Educ. L. Rep. 845] (Ind.Ct.App.2007) (reversing the denial of the parents' request for attorney fees), *transfer denied*, 891 N.E.2d 35 (Ind.2008). [Case No. 89]

71. The first section in Chapter 2 includes a brief discussion of original intent with regard to religion.

As with the rest of the legal system, the American judiciary operates at both the federal and state levels. The most common judicial feature is a three-tiered system with trial courts, intermediate appellate courts, and courts of last resort, most commonly named supreme courts.

FEDERAL COURTS

According to Article III, Section 1 of the United States Constitution, "[t]he judicial Power of the United States, shall be vested in one supreme [sic] Court, and in such inferior Courts as the Congress may from time to time ordain and establish." Federal litigation typically begins in trial courts, properly known as United States District Courts, before possibly proceeding to Circuit Courts of Appeal and the Supreme Court.

Congress can create federal jurisdiction as it sees fit. Plaintiffs ordinarily have recourse to the federal courts when there are disagreements over provisions in the Federal Constitution, federal statutes, federal regulations, or when there is diversity of state residence between litigants.[72]

Since the 1960s one provision has perhaps most profoundly affected public education, and other governmental functions, by serving as a basis for suits in federal courts. This statute, 42 U.S.C. section 1983, commonly known as section 1983 originated as the Civil Rights Act of 1871,[73] a law which was designed to provide a remedy for those whose federally protected civil rights, most notably freed slaves during Reconstruction, were violated. Insofar as plaintiffs can recover monetary awards and attorney fees[74] pursuant to section 1983, it offers protection to those whose civil rights have been violated by school officials. Under this far-reaching statute:

> Every person who, under color of any statute, ordinance, regulation, custom, or usage, of any State or Territory, subjects, or causes to be subjected, any citizen of the United States or other person within the jurisdiction thereof to the deprivation of any rights, privileges, or immunities secured by the Constitution and laws, shall be liable to the party injured in an action at law, suit in equity, or other proper proceeding for redress.

Under section 1983, students or educators who claim the deprivation of federal constitutional or statutory rights, based on the actions of school

---

72. In suits based on diversity,

"(a) ... district courts shall have original jurisdiction of all civil actions where the matter in controversy exceeds the sum or value of $75,000, exclusive of interest and costs, and is between—

(1) citizens of different States;

(2) citizens of a State and citizens or subjects of a foreign state;

(3) citizens of different States and in which citizens or subjects of a foreign state are additional parties; and

(4) a foreign state, defined in section 1603(a) of this title, as plaintiff and citizens of a State or of different States." 28 U.S.C.A. § 1332.

73. The statute was originally known as section 1983 of the Klu Klux Klan Act of April 20, 1871, "An Act to Enforce the Provisions of the Fourteenth Amendment to the Constitution of the United States, and for other Purposes."

74. 42 U.S.C.A. § 1988.

officials or by operation of laws or regulations, can seek to invoke federal jurisdiction. This means that plaintiffs can have federal courts address the validity of laws or regulations while adjudicating complaints where federal jurisdiction might otherwise have been difficult to establish. Even so, section 1983 does not require federal courts to resolve all suits in which parties allege that they suffered from unconstitutional deprivations since federal constitutional or statutory questions must exist in substance, not in mere allegations or hypothetical questions.

Federal District Courts

Federal trial courts of general jurisdiction have few limits on the types of cases that they may hear.[75] Each state contains at least one federal trial court for a total of eighty-nine federal districts in the fifty states; by including the courts in Puerto Rico, the Virgin Islands, the District of Columbia, Guam, and the Northern Mariana Islands, the number of federal trial courts increases to ninety-four.[76] In special circumstances, if parties sought to enjoin the enforcement of state statutes on the ground that they violated the Federal Constitution,[77] disputes were resolved by special panels composed of three federal district court judges[78] that could have been appealed directly to the Supreme Court.[79]

Federal Circuit Courts

For appeals in the federal judicial system, the United States is divided into eleven numbered federal circuit courts of appeal, commonly referred to as circuit courts, plus the District of Columbia Circuit.[80] A thirteenth court,

---

75. Published opinions of federal trial courts can be found in the Federal Supplement, abbreviated F. Supp., now in its second series, F.Supp.2d. In addition to WESTLAW and LEXIS, federal cases can be found in a variety of on-line Web sites. *See, e.g.,* www.uscourts.gov (official Web site of the federal judiciary); http://www.supremecourtus.gov (official Web site of the Supreme Court).

76. The list of federal district courts is located at 28 U.S.C.A. §§ 81–131.

77. 28 U.S.C.A. § 1253.

78. Such a three member panel was involved in *Goss v. Lopez,* 419 U.S. 565, 95 S.Ct. 729, 42 L.Ed.2d 725 (1975). [Case No. 94]

79. Chief Justice John Roberts *2011 Year–End Report on the Federal Judiciary* revealed that

"[t]otal case filings in the district courts grew 2% to 367,692."

http://www.supremecourt.gov/publicinfo/year-end/2011year-endreport.pdf at 13.

The Report also specified that "[c]ivil filings in the U.S. district courts grew 2% to 289,252 cases. Fueling this growth was a 2% increase in federal question cases (i.e., actions under the Constitution, laws, or treaties of the United States in which the United States is not a party in the case), which resulted mainly from cases addressing civil rights, consumer credit, and intellectual property rights. Cases filed with the United States as a party climbed 9%.... Although criminal case filings (including transfers) remained stable (up by 12 cases to 78,440), the number of criminal defendants increased 3% to set a new record of 102,931."

http://www.supremecourt.gov/publicinfo/year-end/2011year-endreport.pdf at 14.

80. Published opinions of federal circuit courts appear in the Federal Reporter, abbreviated F., now in its third series, F.3d. Cases not selected for publication in F.3d are included in the Federal Appendix, abbreviated Fed.Appx. Cases in the Fed.Appx. are of limited precedential value.

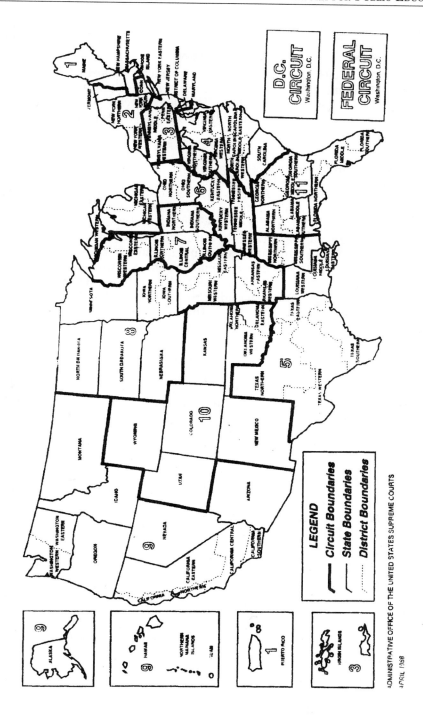

the Federal Circuit, has appellate jurisdiction over patents, federal governmental contracts, federal merit system protection, trademarks, and international trade. (See map on page 19.)

Rulings of circuit courts, which are ordinarily heard by three-judge panels, are binding on federal trial courts in the states within their jurisdiction and persuasive elsewhere.[81] Under special circumstances, all judges in a circuit review cases in en banc hearings.[82] Appeals from circuit courts go to the Supreme Court.[83]

The Supreme Court

As noted, pursuant to Article III, Section 1 of the United States Constitution, "[t]he judicial Power of the United States, shall be vested in one supreme [sic] Court...."[84] Yet, it was not until *Marbury v. Madison*[85] that the Supreme Court asserted its authority to review decisions of the other branches of government. This nine-member body is primarily an appellate court.[86] The Court can summarily affirm lower court rulings or dismiss appeals for lack of substantial federal questions rather than decide cases with full opinions after examining the complete record of lower court proceedings, reviewing written briefs that have been submitted by the litigants and other interested parties and hearing oral arguments.

The Supreme Court has discretion to review rulings of lower federal courts and state high courts[87] involving federal constitutional, statutory, or regulatory issues. When the Court agrees to hear an appeal, it issues a writ of *certiorari*, literally, "to be informed of." In order for the Court to grant *certiorari*, abbreviated as *cert.*, a minimum of four justices must typically agree to hear an appeal.[88] When a case is resolved, the Court's opinion

81. A list of the states composing each circuit is set forth in 28 U.S.C.A. § 41.

82. *See, e.g., Newdow v. U.S. Congress,* 328 F.3d 466 [176 Educ. L. Rep. 44] (9th Cir. 2003), *rev'd,* 542 U.S. 1, 124 S.Ct. 2301, 159 L.Ed.2d 98 [188 Educ. L. Rep. 17] (2004), *reh'g denied,* 542 U.S. 961, 125 S.Ct. 21, 159 L.Ed.2d 851 (2004) (wherein the Ninth Circuit refused a request for an en banc panel to reconsider a ruling over the constitutionality of the words 'under God' in the Pledge of Allegiance). [Case No. 15]

83. Chief Justice John Robert's *2011 Year–End Report on the Federal Judiciary* revealed that "[f]ilings in the regional courts of appeals fell 1.5% to 55,126. http://www.supremecourt. gov/publicinfo/year-end/2011year-endreport.pdf at 14.

84. Published opinions of the Supreme Court can be found in the United States Reports, abbreviated U.S., published by the Supreme Court; the Supreme Court Reporter, abbreviated S.Ct., published by West; and Lawyer's Edition, abbreviated L.Ed., published by Lawyer's Cooperative Publishing Company, now in its second series.

85. 5 U.S. (1 Cranch) 137, 2 L.Ed. 60 (1803).

86. The Court has original jurisdiction, meaning that a case can begin there in limited circumstances. Among the areas over which Article III, Section 2, identifies as being in the Court's original jurisdiction are "[c]ases affecting Ambassadors ... other public Ministers and Consuls ... to Controversies between two or more States...."

87. 469 U.S. 325, 105 S.Ct. 733, 83 L.Ed.2d 720 [21 Educ. L. Rep. 1122] (1985), for example, was an appeal from the Supreme Court of New Jersey. [Case No. 96]

88. The long-standing so-called "Rule of Four" is a judicial, rather than a legislative, creation even though Congress may have had it in mind in enacting the Judiciary Act of 1925. Previously, in 1890, Congress created *certiorari,* or discretionary review, in 26 Stat. 826, Sections 4–6.
Still, some Justices have disagreed on how strictly the rule applies. *See, e.g., Harris v. Pennsylvania Railroad Co.,* 361 U.S. 15, 24, n.2, 80 S.Ct. 22, 4 L.Ed.2d 1 (1959) (Douglas, J., concurring) "When the Act of February 13, 1925 (43 Stat. 936), which broadened our *certiorari* jurisdiction, was before the Congress, Mr. Justice Van Devanter, speaking for the

authoritatively enunciates federal law on the matter while usually explaining the rationale for its judgment.[89]

STATE COURTS

States have their own judicial systems established by their constitutions and legislatures; these systems vary in organization and degree of complexity.[90] State judicial systems generally include a number of inferior courts such as small claims and county courts; these courts exercise limited jurisdiction that is expressly delineated in the laws under which they were created. All states have trial courts of general jurisdiction and at least one level of appellate review. However, there is little consistency in the names that states apply to their various levels of court. Most states have two levels of appellate courts. As in the federal system, the first level of review, generically referred to as intermediate appellate courts, is typically before a panel of three judges. The highest state courts are generically referred to as courts of last resort. In states with two levels of appeal, the absolute right of appeal for some cases is only to the intermediate appellate court; most other appeals are by the leave of the court.

State courts are, of course, bound by the United States Constitution and must apply it in their decisions, which, under limited circumstances, are subject to review by the Supreme Court. On matters of state law, state

---

Court, made explicit that the 'rule of four' governs the grant of petitions for *certiorari*. He testified before the Subcommittee of the Senate Judiciary Committee as follows:.... if there were five votes against granting the petition and four in favor of granting it, it would be granted, because we proceed upon the theory that when as many as four members of the court, and even three in some instances, are impressed with the propriety of our taking the case the petition should be granted. This is the uniform way in which petitions for writs of *certiorari* are considered.' Hearings on S. 2060, Feb. 2, 1924, 68th Cong., 1st Sess., p. 29. *And see* Hearings on H.R. 8206, Dec. 18, 1924, 68th Cong., 2d Sess., p. 8;" *Ohio ex rel. Eaton v. Ohio*, 360 U.S. 246, 247, 79 S.Ct. 978, 3 L.Ed.2d 1200 (1959) (Brennan, J., voting to note probable jurisdiction, in a separate memorandum) "... if four Justices or more are of opinion that the questions presented by the appeal should be fully briefed and argued orally, an order noting probable jurisdiction or postponing further consideration of the jurisdictional questions to a hearing on the merits is entered;" *Burrell v. McCray*, 426 U.S. 471, 472, 96 S.Ct. 2640, 48 L.Ed.2d 788 (1976) (per curiam, Stevens, J., concurring) "... it is my understanding that at least one Member of the Court who voted to grant certiorari has now voted to dismiss the writ; accordingly, the action of the Court does not impair the integrity of the Rule of Four." *But see Rogers v. Missouri Pacific Railway Co.*, 352 U.S. 500, 529 (Frankfurter, J., dissenting) "The 'rule of four' is not a command of Congress. It is a working rule devised by the Court as a practical mode of determining that a case is deserving of review, the theory being that if four Justices find that a legal question of general importance is raised, that is ample proof that the question has such importance."

89. Chief Justice John Robert's *2011 Year–End Report on the Federal Judiciary* revealed: The total number of cases filed in the Supreme Court decreased from 8,159 filings in the 2009 Term to 7,857 filings in the 2010 Term, a decrease of 3.7%. The number of cases filed in the Court's *in forma pauperis* docket decreased from 6,576 filings in the 2009 Term to 6,299 filings in the 2010 Term, a 4.2% decrease. The number of cases filed in the Court's paid docket decreased from 1,583 filings in the 2009 Term to 1,558 filings in the 2010 Term, a 1.6% decrease. During the 2010 Term, 86 cases were argued and 83 were disposed of in 75 signed opinions, compared to 82 cases argued and 77 disposed of in 73 signed opinions in the 2009 Term.

http://www.supremecourt.gov/publicinfo/year-end/2011year-endreport.pdf at 13.

90. Published opinions of state courts are located in a variety of sources both in print and electronically. The most widely available source is West's National Reporter System which divides the United States into seven regions: Atlantic, North Eastern, North Western, Pacific, South Eastern, Southern, and South Western; each is in at least its second series.

courts are parallel to their federal counterparts. State courts' interpretations of federal law are subject to review only by the Supreme Court.

Insofar as education is a state function and federal courts exist for federal matters, most educational controversies are handled by state courts. Absent substantial federal questions, cases are tried in state courts. If substantial federal questions are involved with state questions, cases may be heard in either state or federal courts. The increased emphasis on civil rights and liberties, coupled with the use of section 1983, has led to increasing numbers of education cases being filed in federal courts. When federal courts examine cases involving both state and federal law, they must follow interpretations of state law made by the state courts within which they sit.

JUDICIAL PROCEDURES

The procedures of federal and state courts are a complex amalgam of statutes, rules, and common law. Yet, since some basic principles are generally consistent, an overview of these procedures can help readers to have a better understanding of Education Law.

Civil suits start when plaintiffs, the parties initiating litigation, file summonses and complaints or, as these joint documents are called in some jurisdictions, petitions, alleging the facts in dispute. These documents are designed to allege that harm has occurred, that laws are being or were violated, or that officials or agencies are not or have not performed their specified legal duties. The parties initiating actions thereby seek judicial relief, whether legal or equitable damages or a combination of the two. Plaintiffs may, for example, ask courts to find that boards of education broke contracts and that aggrieved employees may receive monetary damages for their losses of salary and orders returning them to their jobs. Alternatively, if parents challenge the actions of school boards for allegedly failing to provide educational programming for their children, they may seek orders to obtain services. If plaintiffs seek to require public officers or agencies to perform nondiscretionary duties, their object is to seek writs of mandamus. If agencies or individuals allegedly are engaged in illegal activities, plaintiffs may ask courts to grant injunctions ordering the parties to discontinue the illegal acts.

Plaintiffs may also seek injunctions to preserve the legal status quo by preventing contemplated actions. Courts may grant preliminary or temporary injunctions, pending the full adjudication of disputes. Courts typically grant temporary injunctions when plaintiffs can show that they will suffer irreparable harm if relief is not granted at once, that there are reasonable probabilities or substantial likelihoods of prevailing on the merits, that the threatened injuries outweigh the potential harm that injunction would impose on defendants, and that the public interest will not suffer. While judicial reasoning on motions for preliminary injunctions may be instructive on the law, they cannot ultimately apply the law to the facts until they are fully set forth at a trial. Courts issue permanent injunctions after trials on the merits, meaning that both sides have had the opportunity to address the substance of the underlying issues.

Insofar as Article 3, Section 2 of the Constitution requires courts to resolve real cases or controversies,[91] the judiciary does not ordinarily decide hypothetical cases or provide advisory opinions.[92] Not only must there be genuine controversies, but plaintiffs must have individualized legal interests, or standing over disputed points.[93] Common law precedent grants taxpayers who wish to sue standing when they challenge local school board expenditures. Merely being taxpayers under common law generally does not grant standing to sue state-level or federal agencies.[94] Absent statutory authorization, individuals filing suit solely to contest state or federal expenditures must allege some individualized harm, not simply injuries that all citizens or taxpayers would suffer.

When plaintiffs challenge statutes or regulations, they may be questioned either on their faces or as applied. Facial challenges involve claims that provisions are completely invalid and incapable of any legal application. In these cases, courts are not required to examine the facts of actual instances of alleged unlawfulness. When challenges are on statutes or regulations as applied, courts must consider their impact in specific situations.

As disputes head to trial, they pass through a variety of stages. During the pleadings, the plaintiffs initiate litigation by having summonses and complaints served on defendants. These documents are designed to inform defendants about the nature of claims along with enough information to allow them to prepare defenses along with statements of what the plaintiffs seek in the form of damages. Defendant can respond by admitting, denying, or raising new (counter) claims in whole or in part. This stage can go through several rounds of exchanges before the parties move on to the next level of pre-trial activity, discovery.

Once the parties have informed each other of what disputes are about through the pleadings, cases proceed to discovery. During discovery, the parties seek to narrow the disputed issues for trial. In this way, if the parties agree that a teacher's contract was terminated on a specific date, then they can so stipulate and focus on other issues such as the reason for the school board's action. Attorneys ordinarily rely on two tools in discovery: interrogatories and depositions. Interrogatories consist of a series of

---

91. This section reads, "[t]he judicial Power shall extend to all Cases, in Law and Equity, arising under this Constitution, the Laws of the United States, and Treaties made, or which shall be made, under their Authority;...."

92. *See, e.g., State v. Self,* 155 S.W.3d 756, 761 [195 Educ. L. Rep. 1019] (Mo.2005) ("... a constitutional controversy cannot be manufactured in the trial court or on appeal in order to obtain an advisory opinion") (reversing a mother's conviction for knowingly or purposely failing to cause her daughter to attend school regularly). *But see Advisory Opinion to the Attorney Gen.,* 824 So.2d 161 [169 Educ. L. Rep. 449] (Fla.2002) (offering an advisory opinion upholding the constitutionality of a ballot initiative amending the state constitution to require funding of universal pre-kindergarten programs).

93. *See, e.g., Elk Grove Unified School Dist. v. Newdow,* 542 U.S. 1, 124 S.Ct. 2301, 159 L.Ed.2d 98 [188 Educ. L. Rep. 17] (2004), *reh'g denied,* 542 U.S. 961, 125 S.Ct. 21, 159 L.Ed.2d 851 (2004) (holding that a father's challenge to the words "under God" in the Pledge of Allegiance could not proceed because he lacked standing). [Case No. 15]

94. For such a case, *see Arizona Christian School Tuition Org. v. Winn,* ___ U.S. ___, 131 S.Ct. 1436, 179 L.Ed.2d 523 [265 Educ. L. Rep. 855] (2011), *on remand,* 658 F.3d 889 (9th Cir. 2011) (reiterating that being a taxpayer does not provide standing to seek relief in federal court).

written questions prepared by the attorneys of both sides of disputes that each party must answer. Depositions are oral statements made in the presence of the attorneys. Depositions can allow parties to refresh their memories of events before trial since a fair amount of time may pass between the time that suits are filed and when they are litigated. Depositions can also serve as the basis by which to challenge the accuracy of witnesses' testimony or to introduce the evidence if witnesses are unavailable to appear either due to death or because they are unable, or unwilling, to attend and courts lack the authority to compel their appearances.

Judges can dismiss complaints before trial if they determine that allegations, if eventually proven, would not have legally entitled plaintiffs to the relief requested. Additionally, judges may terminate trials if, after plaintiffs presented their evidence, they are convinced that even if the evidence were accepted as true, it did not prove their cases. If plaintiffs pass these two hurdles, the defense attorneys have opportunities to present their versions of the cases.

Before cases can proceed to trial, judges must make two important determinations. First, judges must consider whether plaintiffs have raised allegations that, if proven, would entitle them to relief on claims for which relief can be granted, also known as establishing a *prima facie* case, literally, "at first sight" or "on the face of it." Second, judges must evaluate whether there are genuine disputes over material issues of fact. If judges are satisfied that plaintiffs have met their burdens, then cases can proceed to trial. In the event that judges are convinced that plaintiffs failed to meet their initial burden, and that no genuine issue of fact remain, then they typically grant defendants' motions for summary judgment essentially dismissing the claims. Motions for summary judgment are generally filed before matters head to trial, asking courts to resolve issues without having to engage in actual trials.

Once disputes go to trial, plaintiffs bear the ultimate burden of proof. At trial, after plaintiffs meet their initial burden, the burden may shift to the defendants to counter the initial arguments by raising other points. For instance, if the attorney representing a group of teachers who are contesting a school board's refusal to renew their probationary contracts can argue that their having engaged protected First Amendment activity such as trying to form a union was a substantial factor in its action, then its lawyer must show that the board would have reached the same outcome even if the teachers had not taken part in the protected activity.

The two key "players" at trials are the juries and judges.[95] Juries, often referred to as triers of fact,[96] make findings of fact in evaluating what occurred and apply them to the law as interpreted by judges, sometimes called triers of law, reaching conclusions that culminate in judgments and

---

95. According to Article II, Section 2 of the Constitution, the President "shall nominate and by and with the Advice and Consent of the Senate, shall appoint ... Judges of the supreme [sic] Court, and all other officers of the United States...." Depending on state and local law, some judges are elected while others are appointed.

96. The jury selection process involves attorneys for both the plaintiff and defendant questioning individuals to evaluate their ability to be impartial. This process, which is often referred to as "voir dire," literally "to speak the truth," is designed to select impartial jurors.

decrees specifying the outcome of the litigation. Federal trial courts and some state trial courts hand down written opinions explaining their rationales. Although only the parties to specific cases are bound by trial court rulings,[97] opinions become part of the common law, indicating what the outcomes of similar disputes are likely to be unless there are material differences between the suits.

At least one level of appeal is generally available for all civil cases. The parties bringing appeals are generally known as appellants or petitioners; opposing parties are typically referred to as appellees or respondents. On appeal, appellants attempt to demonstrate that lower courts erred either in their findings of fact, conclusions of law, or both. As to facts, parties may claim that judges improperly admitted evidence, misinterpreted testimony and exhibits, and/or otherwise incorrectly conducted trials. As to questions of law, parties may claim that judges applied the wrong law or misconstrued the law in some fashion in reaching judgments.

Appellate courts neither hear witnesses nor consider issues that were not raised at trial. Rather, they review the written records of lower court proceedings, including the testimony of witnesses, examine briefs, and usually hear oral arguments of both parties. As part of the appellate process, both parties submit written arguments known as briefs to the judges in support of their positions. In many cases, most notably at the Supreme Court, parties interested in the outcomes of cases can submit so-called *amicus curiae*, literally, "friend of the court," briefs seeking to sway the judges in their favor.

Appellate courts can affirm, reverse, vacate, modify and/or remand earlier judgments. In remanding, or sending cases back to lower courts for further action, appellate panels can direct lower courts to modify their previous decisions or, in cases involving remands to trial courts, can order them to re-try disputes in their entirety. On questions of fact, appellate courts must accept the findings of trial courts unless they are clearly erroneous. Appellate panels must accept the evidence from trial courts that observed the parties and witnesses, while appellate courts are limited to evidence in the written records that they review. As to conclusions of law, appellate courts owe no deference to the reasoning of trial courts and may disagree on the meaning of laws.

The opinions of the majority of judges in appellate cases become precedent, the law of the case that is controlling within jurisdictions. Judges who agree with the ultimate outcome but who do not support all of the reasoning in majority opinions may file concurring opinions. Judges may also file dissenting opinions that justify their reasons for disagreeing with the majorities. Once majorities of judges agree on opinions, regardless of the margin of a vote, they become precedent in given jurisdictions. For

---

97. Class actions involve one or more representatives of a "class" bringing suit on behalf of all members of the group. If courts permit cases to proceed as class actions, the outcomes are binding on all members of the classes. In order to maintain class actions, plaintiff classes must assert claims that are typical of their classes, the question(s) of law must be common to all members, getting all members of the classes into suits individually must be impracticable, and plaintiff classes must adequately protect the interests of all members of the classes.

example, rulings of the Supreme Court are binding on all lower courts while decisions of state supreme courts are binding only in those states.

On occasion, judges include gratuitous statements in their analyses addressing rules of law or legal principles that are not directly involved in the resolution of cases. Insofar as these remarks, known as *obiter dictum*, literally, "a remark by the way," or *dictum* (*dicta*, in plural) are of no precedential value, judges, lawyers, and students of the law must be careful to distinguish between such voluntary, non-binding comments and a case's holding or rule of law. Although dicta is of no precedential value, it can be useful as a form of non-binding judicial perspectives.

The opinions of appellate courts typically indicate the point or points of law on which they agree, or disagree, with lower courts. The higher courts are in the judicial hierarchy, the more authoritative their opinions. Lower courts are bound by the orders and opinions of higher courts in their jurisdictions. At common law, opinions of courts in one jurisdiction, although not binding precedent on courts in other jurisdictions, are persuasive or non-binding on points that are not treated by their legislatures. Decisions of federal circuit courts are binding on federal trial courts within their jurisdictions and persuasive elsewhere. Although some members of the Supreme Court have occasionally,[98] but not universally,[99] sought to apply international law in their opinions, this issue is beyond the scope of this book.

Insofar as there is ultimately only one answer to questions of federal law, the Supreme Court usually grants *certiorari* to resolve disagreements between and among the circuits.[100] Each time courts cite opinions approvingly, the weight of those cases on the issues increases. In the uncommon situation of pluralities, where less than a majority of judges agrees on the same rationale in a case, the earlier judgments remain in place for the parties but the outcome is not binding on other litigants or in other jurisdictions.[101]

---

98. For cases applying international law, *see, e.g., Lawrence v. Texas*, 539 U.S. 558, 123 S.Ct. 2472, 156 L.Ed.2d 508 (2003) (invalidating a law that made it a crime for two persons of the same sex to engage in specified intimate sexual conduct as unconstitutional as applied to adult males who participated in a consensual act of sodomy in the privacy of their home); *Roper v. Simmons*, 543 U.S. 551, 125 S.Ct. 1183, 161 L.Ed.2d 1 (2005) (relying in part on the influence of international law in invalidating the imposition of the death penalty).

99. For cases rejecting the application of international law, *see, e.g. Sosa v. Alvarez–Machain*, 542 U.S. 692, 124 S.Ct. 2739, 159 L.Ed.2d 718 (2004) (unanimously rejecting the wholesale incorporation of customary international law into American federal court adjudications under the Federal Torts Claim Act); *Sanchez–Llamas v. Oregon*, 546 U.S. 1001, 126 S.Ct. 620, 163 L.Ed.2d 503 (2006) (refusing to accept the interpretation of the International Court of Justice as applied to the Vienna Convention on Consular Relations).

100. *Compare, e.g., Sherman v. Community Consol. School Dist. 21 of Wheeling Twp.*, 980 F.2d 437 [79 Educ. L. Rep. 396] (7th Cir.1992), *cert. denied*, 508 U.S. 950, 113 S.Ct. 2439, 124 L.Ed.2d 658 (1993) (upholding the constitutionality of the Pledge of Allegiance) with *Elk Grove Unified School Dist. v. Newdow*, 542 U.S. 1, 124 S.Ct. 2301, 159 L.Ed.2d 98 [188 Educ. L. Rep. 17] (2004), *reh'g denied*, 542 U.S. 961, 125 S.Ct. 21, 159 L.Ed.2d 851 (2004) (initially striking down the words "under God" in the Pledge as psychologically coercive). [Case No. 15]

101. For plurality decisions, *see, e.g., Mitchell v. Helms*, 530 U.S. 793, 120 S.Ct. 2530, 147 L.Ed.2d 660 [145 Educ. L. Rep. 44] (2000) (upholding the constitutionality of Chapter 2 of Title I, now Title VI, of the Elementary and Secondary Education Act, a far-reaching federal law permitting the loan of instructional materials including library books, computers, television sets, tape recorders, and maps, to non-public schools); *Regents of the Univ. of Cal. v.*

Once the highest courts in jurisdictions render their judgments, their opinions become *res judicata*, literally, "a matter judged," such that parties cannot return the disputes to court for further litigation. This is true not only for specific court systems, but also between state and federal courts when one system has addressed an issue. Further, *res judicata* bars any attempt to relitigate the same claims under different theories of recovery.

POSTSCRIPT

To the extent that this volume, and all legal writings, rely on the legal system of citation, this brief postscript is designed for students who may be taking their first law course and, as such, are unfamiliar with legal citations.

Prior to being published in bound volumes, most cases are available in slip opinions from a variety of loose-leaf services and from electronic sources. Statutes and regulations are available in similar readily accessible formats. Legal materials are also available online from a variety of sources, most notably WESTLAW and LEXIS-NEXIS. State laws and regulations can generally be accessed online.

Supreme Court cases can be located in a variety of sources. The official version of Supreme Court cases is the United States Reports (U.S.). The same opinions appear in two unofficial versions, West's Supreme Court Reporter (S.Ct.) and the Lawyer's Edition, published by Lawyers Cooperative Publishing Company, now in its second series (L.Ed.2d). The advantage of the unofficial versions of cases, and statutes, described below, is that in addition to the entire text of the Court's opinions, publishers provide valuable research tools and assistance, in the forms of headnotes that facilitate the efforts of attorneys, educational practitioners, and students of the law as they engage in legal research.

Federal appellate cases are published in the Federal Reporter, now in its third series (F.3d). Cases that are not chosen for publication in F.3d are printed in the Federal Appendix (Fed.Appx.); cases that appear in the Federal Appendix are of no precedential value. Federal trial court rulings are in the Federal Supplement, now in its second series (F.Supp.2d). State cases are published in a variety of publications, most notably in West's National Reporter system, which breaks the country up into seven regions: Atlantic, North Eastern, North Western, Pacific, South Eastern, South Western, and Southern, all of which are in the second or third series.

The official version of federal statutes is the United States Code (U.S.C.). As with Supreme Court cases, West publishes an unofficial, annotated version of federal statutes, the United States Code Annotated (U.S.C.A.). The final version of federal regulations can be found in the Code

---

Bakke, 438 U.S. 265, 98 S.Ct. 2733, 57 L.Ed.2d 750 (1978) (permitting a medical school admissions policy that was designed to increase minority enrollment to remain in place).

of Federal Regulations (C.F.R.). As with cases, state statutes and regulations are published in a variety of sources.

As imposing as they may appear, legal citations are easy to read. The first number in citations indicates the volume numbers where the cases, statutes, or regulations are located; the following abbreviation refers to the books or series of volumes in which the materials are located; the second number refers to the page on which cases begin or the section numbers of statutes or regulations; the last part of citations, set off by parentheses, typically includes the names of the courts,[102] and the year in which disputes were resolved.

The following brief illustrations of how to read citations for cases, statutes, and regulations should help to clarify this material. The citation for *Brown v. Board of Education*, the Supreme Court's ruling calling for equal educational opportunities for all children by ending segregation based on race, 347 U.S. 483, 74 S.Ct. 686, 98 L.Ed. 873 (1954), reveals that it can be found in volume 347 of the United States Reports, the Court's official version, starting at page 483. *Brown* can also be located in volume 74 of West's Supreme Court Reporter, beginning on page 686, and volume 98 of the Lawyer's Edition, starting on page 873. Of course, *Brown* was decided in 1954. For all other courts, abbreviated versions of their names also appear with the date.

Turning to a statute, the Individuals with Disabilities Education Act (IDEA), 20 U.S.C.A. §§ 1400 *et seq.*, can be found in Title 20 of the United States Code starting at section 1400. The IDEA's regulations are located at 300 C.F.R. §§ 300.1 *et seq.*, meaning that they are in title 300 of the Code of Federal Regulations, beginning at section 300.1. State statutes and regulations follow a similar pattern.

---

102. As noted below, an exception applies to the Supreme Court since the name of the reporter is self-identifying.

CHAPTER 2

CHURCH–STATE RELATIONS IN EDUCATION

INTRODUCTION

The First Amendment was added to the United States Constitution in 1791 as part of the Bill of Rights. Yet, the Supreme Court did not address a case involving religion and public education on the merits of a First Amendment claim until 1947 in *Everson v. Board of Education (Everson)*.[1] In the years since *Everson*, the Court has resolved more cases dealing with the religion clauses of the First Amendment than any other subject in Education Law. Further, the Court refused to review or affirmed without opinion many lower court cases and resolved disputes in other realms of church-state relations with implications for public education.[2]

According to the sixteen words of the religion clauses of the First Amendment, "Congress shall make no law respecting an establishment of religion, or prohibiting the free exercise thereof." Since the First Amendment explicitly prohibits only Congress from making laws establishing religion, in 1940, the Supreme Court applied the First Amendment to the states through the Fourteenth Amendment in *Cantwell v. Connecticut*.[3] Individuals are thus afforded the same rights in suits against the federal or state governments with regard to the establishment of religion.

In addressing First Amendment religion cases, the Supreme Court created confusion over the appropriate judicial standard. Initially, the

---

1. 330 U.S. 1, 67 S.Ct. 504, 91 L.Ed. 711 (1947), *reh'g denied*, 330 U.S. 855, 67 S.Ct. 962, 91 L.Ed. 1297 (1947). [Case No. 1]

2. *See, e.g., Employment Div., Dep't of Human Resources of Or. v. Smith (Smith)*, 494 U.S. 872, 886, 110 S.Ct. 1595, 1600, 108 L.Ed.2d 876 (1990), *reh'g denied*, 496 U.S. 913, 110 S.Ct. 2605, 110 L.Ed.2d 285 (1990); *on remand*, 799 P.2d 148 (Or.1990) (upholding the dismissal of drug counselors who ingested peyote as part of a sacramental ritual in the Native American Church, a legally organized religious movement that was recognized by the federal government, ruling that generally applicable, religion-neutral laws that have the effect of burdening a particular religious practice need not be justified by a compelling government interest); *City of Boerne v. Flores*, 521 U.S. 507, 117 S.Ct. 2157, 138 L.Ed.2d 624 (1997) (striking down the Religious Freedom Restoration Act because, in creating a statutory remedy based on the free exercise test that was essentially eliminated in *Smith*, Congress exceeded the enforcement provision of Section 5 of the Fourteenth Amendment).

3. 310 U.S. 296, 60 S.Ct. 900, 84 L.Ed. 1213 (1940) (striking down the convictions of Jehovah's Witnesses for violating a statute against the solicitation of funds for religious, charitable, or philanthropic purposes without prior approval of public officials). *See also Barron v. Mayor and City Council of Baltimore*, 32 U.S. 243, 8 L.Ed. 672 (1833) (holding that the Bill of Rights was inapplicable to the states since its history revealed that it was limited to the federal government).

Justices created a two-part test in *School District of Abington Township v. Schempp* and *Murray v. Curlett*[4] to review the constitutionality of prayer and Bible reading in public schools. The Court subsequently expanded this two-part test into the tripartite Establishment Clause standard in *Lemon v. Kurtzman* (*Lemon*),[5] a dispute involving government aid to religiously affiliated non-public schools.

When the Court applies the *Lemon* test in cases involving aid and religious activity, its failure to explain how, or why, it had become a kind of "one-size fits all" measure leaves lower courts, lawyers, commentators, and school officials seeking clarity. This confusion emerges because the Court has failed to offer adequate explanations of how the tripartite test, the first two prongs of which originated in companion cases addressing Bible reading and prayer while the third part emerged in a case dealing with tax exemptions for churches, fit together.

Confusion over the meaning of the Establishment Clause is exacerbated because as membership on the Supreme Court changes, its jurisprudence on the status of state aid to non-public schools and religious activity in public schools, however broadly these terms are construed, is subject to modification. For example, in *Agostini v. Felton*,[6] a case permitting the on-site delivery of educational services for poor students who attended religiously affiliated non-public schools, the Court modified the *Lemon* test by reviewing only its first two parts, purpose and effect, while recasting entanglement as one criterion in evaluating a statute's effect when the state provides aid to students who attend religiously affiliated non-public schools. Moreover, in *Lee v. Weisman*,[7] a case prohibiting prayer at public school graduation ceremonies, the Court enunciated the psychological coercion test when reviewing prayer in schools while in *Lynch v. Donnelly*,[8] a non-school case on the inclusion of a Nativity scene in a Christmas display on public property, a plurality of the Court discussed what Justice O'Connor described as the endorsement test when dealing with religious activity in public settings.

Appeals to history over the original intent of the Establishment Clause fail to provide clear answers, stemming largely from the fact that close ties between religion and government began during the colonial period. In fact, up until the Revolutionary War, there "... were established churches in at least eight of the thirteen former colonies and established religions in at least four of the other five."[9]

Rather than engage in a lengthy discussion of the different approaches to the Establishment Clause, suffice it to say that two major camps emerged at the Supreme Court and throughout the judiciary: separationists and accommodationists. On the one hand are supporters of the Jeffersoni-

4. 374 U.S. 203, 83 S.Ct. 1560, 10 L.Ed.2d 844 (1963). [Case No. 4]

5. 403 U.S. 602, 91 S.Ct. 2105, 29 L.Ed.2d 745 (1971). [Case No. 7]

6. 521 U.S. 203, 117 S.Ct. 1997, 138 L.Ed.2d 391 [119 Educ. L. Rep. 29] (1997). [Case No. 11]

7. 505 U.S. 577, 112 S.Ct. 2649, 120 L.Ed.2d 467 [75 Educ. L. Rep. 43] (1992). [Case No. 10]

8. 465 U.S. 668, 687, 104 S.Ct. 1355, 1366, 79 L.Ed.2d 604 (1984).

9. *Engel v. Vitale*, 370 U.S. 421, 428 n. 5, 82 S.Ct. 1261, 8 L.Ed.2d 601 (1962).

an[10] metaphor calling for erecting a "wall of separation" between church and state,[11] language that does not appear in the Constitution; this is the perspective most often associated with the Supreme Court over the past fifty plus years.[12] On the other hand, accommodationist maintain that the government is not prohibited from permitting some aid or serving the needs of children under the Child Benefit Test or from accommodating the religious preferences of parents who send their children to non–public schools.

This book focuses on federal, not state, law. Even so, it is important to recognize that developments at both levels often overlap. In other words, while many cases arise under state law, such as vouchers in Cleveland, Ohio,[13] they are often ultimately resolved on the basis of the Federal Constitution. It is thus worth noting that the Federal Constitution is more open to some forms of aid to religious schools than its state counterparts, a distinction that emerged during the latter part of the Nineteenth Century.

The push for separation between church and state received a boost on December 7, 1875, when President Grant, in his final State of the Union address, called for a constitutional amendment "forbidding the teaching [of religion in public schools] ... and prohibiting the granting of any school funds, or school taxes or any part thereof, either by legislative, municipal, or other authority, for the benefit or in aid, directly or indirectly, of any religious sect or denomination...."[14]

---

10. The metaphor of the "wall of separation" comes from Thomas Jefferson's letter of January 1, 1802, to Nehemiah Dodge, Ephraim Robbins, and Stephen S. Nelson, A Committee of the Danbury Baptist Association. 16 WRITINGS OF THOMAS JEFFERSON 281 (Andrew Adgate Lipscomb & Albert Ellery Bergh, eds. 1903). Jefferson wrote:

Believing with you that religion is a matter which lies solely between man and his God ... I contemplate with sovereign reverence that act of the whole American people which declared that their legislature should "make no law respecting an establishment of religion, or prohibiting the free exercise thereof," thus building a wall of separation between church and state.

The Supreme Court first used the term in *Reynolds v. United States,* 98 U.S. 145, 164, 25 L.Ed. 244 (1878) (rejecting a Free Exercise Clause challenge to a federal polygamy statute).

11. The metaphor of the "wall of separation" traces its origins to Roger Williams who coined the term more than 150 years before Thomas Jefferson used it in his letter to the Danbury Baptist Convention. Roger Williams, Mr. Cotton's Letter Lately Printed, Examined and Answered (1644), reprinted in 1 THE COMPLETE WRITINGS OF ROGER WILLIAMS 392 (1963) ("and when they have opened a gap in the hedge or wall of Separation between the Garden of the Church and the Wilderness of the world....").

12. Supreme Court Justices have adopted widely different perspectives on the "wall." *See, e.g., McCreary County, Ky. v. American Civil Liberties Union of Ky.,* 545 U.S. 844, 890, 125 S.Ct. 2722, 162 L.Ed.2d 729 (2005) (Scalia, J., dissenting) (striking down a public display of the Ten Commandments) noting that "a majority of the Justices on the current court ... have, in separate opinions, repudiated the brain-spun *Lemon* test that embodies the supposed principle of neutrality between religion and irreligion." *But see* Justice Souter's majority opinion, *id.* at 861: "[d]espite the intuitive importance of official purpose to the realization of Establishment Clause values, the Counties ask us to abandon *Lemon's* purpose test, or at least to truncate any enquiry into purpose here. Their first argument is that the very consideration of purpose is deceptive: according to them, true 'purpose' is unknowable, and its search merely an excuse for courts to act selectively and unpredictably in picking out evidence of subjective intent. The assertions are as seismic as they are unconvincing."

13. *See Zelman v. Simmons–Harris,* 536 U.S. 639, 649, 122 S.Ct. 2460, 153 L.Ed.2d 604 [166 Educ. L. Rep. 30] (2002). [Case No. 14]

14. 4 CONG. REC. 175 (1875) (annual message of the President of the United States). Near the end of his address he reiterated that "[n]o sectarian tenets shall ever be taught in any

Following the lead of President Grant, former Congressman, and then Senator, later unsuccessful Presidential candidate, James K. Blaine of Maine introduced a constitutional amendment in 1875 designed to have prevented aid from going to schools "under the control of any religious sect,"[15] then code for Roman Catholic schools. While the Amendment failed to win passage in 1876, most states adopted Blaine-type constitutional provisions that place substantial limits on the relationship between religious institutions and state governments.[16] Despite this early concern over the interplay between religion and education, another half-century would pass before the Supreme Court addressed its first cases in this contentious arena, initially reviewing disputes under the Fourteenth Amendment, and did not accept a case on the merits of such a claim until *Everson* in 1947.

PRE-HISTORY

Prior to the emergence of its modern Establishment Clause jurisprudence in *Everson*, the Supreme Court examined two cases significantly impacting religiously affiliated non-public schools and their students. In both cases, the Court relied on the Due Process Clause of the Fourteenth Amendment rather than the Establishment Clause.

PIERCE V. SOCIETY OF SISTERS

The first, and arguably more far-reaching, of the Supreme Court's two early cases on religion and education was *Pierce v. Society of Sisters of the Holy Names of Jesus and Mary (Pierce)*.[17] In *Pierce*, the proprietors of a Roman Catholic school and secular school, the Hill Military Academy, challenged a voter-approved initiative in Oregon calling for the enactment of a new compulsory attendance law. The law required all "normal" students, meaning those who did not need what would today be described

---

school supported in whole or in part by the State, nation, or by the proceeds of any tax levied upon any community." *Id.* at 181.

15. The entire proposed Amendment read:

No State shall make any law respecting an establishment of religion or prohibiting the free exercise thereof; and no money raised by taxation in any State for the support of public schools, or derived from any public fund therefore, nor any public lands devoted thereto, shall ever be under the control of any religious sect, nor shall any money so raised or lands so devoted be divided between religious sects or denominations.

See 4 CONG. REC. 205 (1875) (Blaine's statement submitting a proposed constitutional amendment to Congress).

16. Thirty seven states, plus the Commonwealth of Puerto Rico, have Blaine-type language in their constitutions. *See, e.g.*, ALASKA CONSTIT. ART. VII, § 1; CAL. CONSTIT. ART. XVI, § 5; COLO. CONSTIT. ART. IX, § 7; FLA. CONSTIT. ART. I, § 3; HAW. CONSTIT. ART. X, § 1; MICH. CONSTIT. ART. I, § 4; MO. CONSTIT. ART. IX, § 8; NEB. CONSTIT. ART. VII, § 11; N.Y. CONSTIT. ART. XI, § 3; OKLA. CONSTIT. ART. II, § 5; PA. CONSTIT. ART. III, § 29; TEX. CONSTIT. ART. I, § 7; VA. CONSTIT. ART. IV, § 16; WIS. CONSTIT. ART. I, § 18. For a discussion of the Blaine Amendment, *see Mitchell v. Helms*, 530 U.S. 793, 828–29, 120 S.Ct. 2530, 2551–52, 147 L.Ed.2d 660 [145 Educ. L. Rep. 44, 65–66] (2000), *reh'g denied*, 530 U.S. 1296, 121 S.Ct. 15, 147 L.Ed.2d 1039 (2000), *on remand sub nom. Helms v. Picard*, 229 F.3d 467 [148 Educ. L. Rep. 32] (5th Cir. 2000).

17. 268 U.S. 510, 45 S.Ct. 571, 69 L.Ed. 1070 (1925). [Case No. 81]

as special education, between the ages of eight and sixteen who had not completed the eighth grade, to attend public schools. After a federal trial court enjoined enforcement of the statute, the Court affirmed in favor of the schools.

In its unanimous opinion, the Supreme Court ruled that enforcement of the statute would have seriously impaired, if not destroyed, the profitable features of the schools' businesses and greatly diminished the value of their property. Although recognizing the power of the state "reasonably to regulate all schools, to inspect, supervise, and examine them, their teachers and pupils . . . ,"[18] the Court focused on the schools' property rights under the Fourteenth Amendment. The Court grounded its judgment on the realization that the schools sought protection from unreasonable interference with their students and the destruction of their business and property. The Court also decided that while states may oversee such important features as health, safety, and teacher qualifications relating to the operation of non-public schools, they could not do so to an extent greater than they did for public schools.

Along with serving as a kind of Magna Carta protecting the right of non-public schools to operate, the Supreme Court included important language about parental rights, acknowledging that "[t]he child is not the mere creature of the state; those who nurture him and direct his destiny have the right, coupled with the high duty, to recognize and prepare him for additional obligations."[19] The Court thus affirmed the unconstitutionality of the compulsory attendance law because it "unreasonably interfere[d] with the liberty of parents and guardians to direct the upbringing and education of children under their control."[20]

COCHRAN V. LOUISIANA STATE BOARD OF EDUCATION

Cochran v. Louisiana State Board of Education (Cochran)[21] involved a statute under which all students received free textbooks, regardless of where they attended school. A taxpayer unsuccessfully challenged the law as a violation of the Fourteenth Amendment by taking private property through taxation for a non-public purpose. As in *Pierce*, the Supreme Court resolved the dispute based on the Due Process Clause of the Fourteenth Amendment rather than the First Amendment's Establishment Clause.

Unanimously affirming the judgment of the Supreme Court of Louisiana since the students, rather than their schools, were the beneficiaries of the law, the Justices were satisfied that the statute served a valid secular purpose. In so doing, the Supreme Court presaged the Child Benefit Test that would emerge in *Everson v. Board of Education*.[22] As discussed below,

---

18. *Id.* at 534.

19. *Id.* at 535.

20. *Id.* at 534–535.

21. 281 U.S. 370, 50 S.Ct. 335, 74 L.Ed. 913 (1930).

22. 330 U.S. 1, 67 S.Ct. 504, 91 L.Ed. 711 (1947), *reh'g denied*, 330 U.S. 855, 67 S.Ct. 962, 91 L.Ed. 1297 (1947). [Case No. 1]

while the Supreme Court has consistently upheld similar textbook provisions, state courts have struck them down under their own constitutions.[23]

THE COURT'S MODERN ESTABLISHMENT CLAUSE JURISPRUDENCE: STATE AID TO STUDENTS WHO ATTEND RELIGIOUSLY AFFILIATED NON-PUBLIC SCHOOLS

The Supreme Court's modern Establishment Clause jurisprudence with regard to state aid in the context of K–12 education, sometimes referred to as parochiaid, evolved through three phases. During the first phase, which began in 1947 with *Everson v. Board of Education*,[24] and ended in 1968 with *Board of Education of Central School District No. 1 v. Allen*,[25] the Court enunciated the Child Benefit Test, a legal construct permitting publicly funded aid because it assists children rather than their religiously affiliated non-public schools. The years between the Court's 1971 judgment in *Lemon v. Kurtzman*[26] and *Aguilar v. Felton*[27] in 1985, the second phase, were static with regard to the Child Benefit Test as the Court largely refused to move beyond the limits it created in *Everson* and *Allen*. The Court's 1993 ruling in *Zobrest v. Catalina Foothills School District*[28] breathed new life into the Child Benefit Test, allowing it to enter a phase that extends to the present. The following sections examine the primary topics and cases involving state aid to religiously affiliated non-public schools and their students.

TRANSPORTATION

Everson v. Board of Education[29] stands out as the first Supreme Court case on the merits of the Establishment Clause and education. At issue in *Everson* was a statute from New Jersey permitting local school boards to make rules and enter into contracts for student transportation. After a local board, acting pursuant to the statute, authorized reimbursement to parents for the money they spent on bus fares sending their children to Catholic schools, a taxpayer filed suit claiming that the law was unconstitutional in two respects: first, in an approach not unlike the plaintiff's

---

23. *See, e.g., People ex rel. Klinger v. Howlett*, 305 N.E.2d 129 (Ill.1973); *Gaffney v. State Dep't of Educ.*, 220 N.W.2d 550 (Neb.1974); *Paster v. Tussey*, 512 S.W.2d 97 (Mo.1974), *cert. denied*, 419 U.S. 1111, 95 S.Ct. 785, 42 L.Ed.2d 807 (1975); *Bloom v. School Comm. of Springfield*, 379 N.E.2d 578 (Mass.1978); *California Teachers Ass'n v. Riles*, 176 Cal.Rptr. 300 (Cal.1981); *In re Advisory Opinion*, 228 N.W.2d 772 (Mich.1975); *Fannin v. Williams*, 655 S.W.2d 480 (Ky.1983); *Matter of Certification of a Question of Law from U.S. Dist. Ct., Dist. of S.D.*, 372 N.W.2d 113 [26 Educ. L. Rep. 1232] (S.D.1985).

24. 330 U.S. 1, 67 S.Ct. 504, 91 L.Ed. 711 (1947), *reh'g denied*, 330 U.S. 855, 67 S.Ct. 962, 91 L.Ed. 1297 (1947). [Case No. 1]

25. 392 U.S. 236, 88 S.Ct. 1923, 20 L.Ed.2d 1060 (1968). [Case. No. 5]

26. 403 U.S. 602, 91 S.Ct. 2105, 29 L.Ed.2d 745 (1971). [Case No. 7]

27. 473 U.S. 402, 105 S.Ct. 3232, 87 L.Ed.2d 290 [25 Educ. L. Rep. 1022] (1985).

28. 509 U.S. 1, 113 S.Ct. 2462, 125 L.Ed.2d 1 [83 Educ. L. Rep. 930] (1993).

29. 330 U.S. 1, 67 S.Ct. 504, 91 L.Ed. 711 (1947), *reh'g denied*, 330 U.S. 855, 67 S.Ct. 962, 91 L.Ed. 1297 (1947). [Case No. 1]

unsuccessful argument in *Cochran*, he alleged that the law authorized the state to take the money of some citizens by taxation and bestow it on others for the private purpose of supporting non-public schools in contravention of the Fourteenth Amendment; second, he charged that the statute was one "respecting an establishment of religion" since it forced him to contribute to support church schools in violation of the First Amendment.

A closely divided Supreme Court affirmed the statute's constitutionality. The Court flatly rejected the plaintiff's Fourteenth Amendment argument since it found that facilitating secular education is clearly a public purpose. As to the First Amendment, the Justices declared that neither a state nor the federal government could aid one religion, all religions, or prefer one religion over another. The Court added that no tax, large or small, could be levied to support any religious activity or institution. Permitting the statute to remain in effect, the Court reasoned that the First Amendment did not prohibit a state from extending general benefits to all of its citizens without regard to their religious beliefs as it placed student transportation in the same category of other public services such as police, fire, and health protection. Justice Black's majority opinion introduced the Jeffersonian metaphor into the lexicon of the Court's First Amendment jurisprudence, writing that: "[t]he First Amendment has erected a wall between church and state. That wall must be kept high and impregnable. We could not approve the slightest breach."[30]

Following *Everson*, states must choose whether to provide publicly funded transportation to students who attend religiously affiliated non-public schools. As might have been anticipated, lower courts, relying on state constitutional provisions, reached mixed results on this issue. Some cases prohibited states from providing transportation to students in religious schools in determining that doing so violated their constitutions.[31] For instance, a federal trial court in Iowa,[32] relying on the state constitution, prohibited a board of education from offering transportation to a student who attended a religious school outside of its boundaries.

The Eighth Circuit, in a case from South Dakota, affirmed that a local board could discontinue providing transportation to students who attended a religiously affiliated non-public school within its boundaries unless the children were being transported to athletic, musical, speech, or other interscholastic contests because state law did not obligate it to do so.[33] The court posited that the students and their parents lacked standing since they failed to ask school officials to reinstate bus service or to show that their

---

30. *Id.* at 18.

31. *See, e.g. Visser v. Nooksack Valley School Dist. No. 506*, 207 P.2d 198 (Wash.1949). *McVey v. Hawkins*, 258 S.W.2d 927 (Mo.1953); *Matthews v. Quinton*, 362 P.2d 932 (Alaska 1961), *cert. denied*, 368 U.S. 517, 82 S.Ct. 530, 7 L.Ed.2d 522 (1962); *Board of Educ. for Indep. School Dist. No. 52 v. Antone*, 384 P.2d 911 (Okla.1963); *Epeldi v. Engelking*, 488 P.2d 860 (Idaho 1971), *cert. denied*, 406 U.S. 957, 92 S.Ct. 2058, 32 L.Ed.2d 343 (1972); *Luetkemeyer v. Kaufmann*, 364 F.Supp. 376 (W.D.Mo.1973), *aff'd*, 419 U.S. 888, 95 S.Ct. 167, 42 L.Ed.2d 134 (1974).

32. *Americans United for Separation of Church and State v. Benton*, 413 F.Supp. 955 (S.D.Iowa 1975).

33. *Pucket v. Hot Springs School Dist. No. 23–2*, 526 F.3d 1151 [232 Educ. L. Rep. 628] (8th Cir.2008).

doing so would have been futile since the board indicated that it would provide busing again when it clarified an issue dealing with insurance. Further, a trial court in New York confirmed that the State Commissioner of Education did not exceed his authority in prohibiting a local board from providing free transportation to children who attended private pre-kindergarten classes.[34] The court agreed with the commissioner that the statute dealing with student transportation to school did not authorize local boards to provide it to children in private pre-kindergarten classes.

Conversely, the federal trial court in Connecticut[35] and the First Circuit, in a dispute from Rhode Island,[36] both of which explicitly rejected the case from Iowa, along with the Supreme Court of Pennsylvania[37] permitted students from religiously affiliated non-schools to receive transportation beyond district lines. Also, the Supreme Court of Kentucky affirmed the constitutionality of a statute allocating funding for students who attended non-public elementary schools because the plan impermissibly aided religiously affiliated and other non-public schools.[38]

In *Wolman v. Walter (Wolman)*,[39] the Supreme Court addressed the related question of transportation for field trips. At issue was a statute from Ohio permitting the use of public funds to provide transportation for field trips for children who attended religiously affiliated non-public schools. The Court invalidated the law because insofar as field trips were oriented to the curriculum, they were in the category of instruction rather than non-ideological secular services such as transportation to and from school.

Most recently, an appellate court in Indiana affirmed that a state statute did not obligate local boards to provide free shuttle service from public middle schools to the non-public schools that children attended.[40] Rather, the court decreed that the law only required boards to have drivers pick the students up from the non-public schools near the district's regular school bus routes and drop them off at public middle schools nearest to their non-public schools.

TEXTBOOKS

Following the lead of *Cochran*, albeit under the First, rather than the Fourteenth, Amendment, in *Board of Education of Central School District*

---

34. *Board of Educ. of Lawrence Union Free School Dist. Number 15 v. McColgan*, 846 N.Y.S.2d 889 [226 Educ. L. Rep. 993] (2007).

35. *Cromwell Property Owners Ass'n v. Toffolon*, 495 F.Supp. 915 (D.Conn.1979).

36. *Members of Jamestown School Comm. v. Schmidt*, 699 F.2d 1 [9 Educ. L. Rep. 70] (1st Cir.1983), *cert. denied*, 464 U.S. 851, 104 S.Ct. 162, 78 L.Ed.2d 148 (1983).

37. *Pequea Valley School Dist. v. Commonwealth of Pa. Dep't of Educ.*, 397 A.2d 1154 (Pa.1979), *appeal dismissed for want of a substantial federal question*, 443 U.S. 901, 99 S.Ct. 3091, 61 L.Ed.2d 869 (1979).

38. *Neal v. Fiscal Court, Jefferson County*, 986 S.W.2d 907 [133 Educ. L. Rep. 624] (Ky.1999).

39. 433 U.S. 229, 97 S.Ct. 2593, 53 L.Ed.2d 714 (1977).

40. *Roman Catholic Archdiocese of Indianapolis v. Metropolitan School Dist. of Lawrence Twp.*, 945 N.E.2d 757 [266 Educ. L. Rep. 469] (Ind. Ct. App. 2011).

No. 1 v. Allen *(Allen)*,[41] *the Supreme Court affirmed the constitutionality of a statute from New York directing local school boards to loan books to children in grades seven to twelve who attended non-public schools.*[42] *The law did not mandate that the books had to be the same as those used in the public schools but did require titles to be approved by local board officials before they could be adopted. Relying largely on the Child Benefit Test, the Court observed that the statute's purpose was not to aid religion or non-public schools and that its primary effect was to improve the quality of education for all children.*

Subject to the delivery of services to individual students as in *Zobrest v. Catalina Foothills School District*,[43] *Allen* represented the outer limit of the Child Benefit Test for large groups of children prior to the Supreme Court's ruling in *Agostini v. Felton*,[44] discussed below. The Justices upheld like textbook provisions in *Meek v. Pittenger*[45] and *Wolman*, both of which are also examined in more detail below.

SECULAR SERVICES AND SALARY SUPPLEMENTS

In its most significant case involving the Establishment Clause and education, *Lemon v. Kurtzman (Lemon)*,[46] the Supreme Court struck down a statute from Pennsylvania calling for the purchase of secular services and a law from Rhode Island designed to provide salary supplements for teachers in non-public schools. The Pennsylvania statute empowered the superintendent of education to purchase specified secular educational services from non-public schools. Officials directly reimbursed the non-public schools for their actual expenditures for teacher salaries, textbooks, and instructional materials. The superintendent had to approve the textbooks and materials, which were restricted to the areas of mathematics, modern foreign languages, physical science, and physical education. In Rhode Island, officials had the authority to supplement the salaries of certificated teachers of secular subjects in non-public elementary schools by directly paying them amounts not in excess of fifteen percent of their current annual salaries; their salaries could not exceed the maximum paid to public school teachers. The supplements were available to teachers in non-public schools where average per pupil expenditures on secular education were less than in public schools. In addition, the teachers had to use the same materials as were used in public schools.

Invalidating both statutes, the Supreme Court enunciated the tripartite standard destined to become known as the *Lemon* test. In creating this

---

41.   392 U.S. 236, 88 S.Ct. 1923, 20 L.Ed.2d 1060 (1968). [Case No. 5]

42.   *Board of Educ. of Cent. School Dist. No. 1, Towns of East Greenbush v. Allen,* 273 N.Y.S.2d 239 (N.Y.Sup.Ct.1966), *rev'd,* 276 N.Y.S.2d 234 (N.Y.App.Div.1966), *aff'd,* 281 N.Y.S.2d 799 (N.Y.1967), *probable jurisdiction noted,* 389 U.S. 1031, 88 S.Ct. 767, 19 L.Ed.2d 819 (1968).

43.   509 U.S. 1, 113 S.Ct. 2462, 125 L.Ed.2d 1 [83 Educ. L. Rep. 930] (1993).

44.   521 U.S. 203, 117 S.Ct. 1997, 138 L.Ed.2d 391 [119 Educ. L. Rep. 29] (1997). [Case No. 11]

45.   421 U.S. 349, 95 S.Ct. 1753, 44 L.Ed.2d 217 (1975).

46.   403 U.S. 602, 91 S.Ct. 2105, 29 L.Ed.2d 745 (1971). [Case No. 7]

measure, the Court added a third prong, dealing with excessive entanglement, from *Walz v. Tax Commission of New York City*,[47] which upheld New York State's practice of providing state property tax exemptions for church property used in worship services,[48] to the two-part test it created in *Abington v. Schempp*. The Court wrote that:

> Every analysis in this area must begin with consideration of the cumulative criteria developed by the Court over many years. Three such tests may be gleaned from our cases. First, the statute must have a secular legislative purpose; second, its principal or primary effect must be one that neither advances nor inhibits religion; finally, the statute must not foster "an excessive government entanglement with religion."[49]

Addressing entanglement and state aid to religiously affiliated institutions, the Court noted that three further factors came into consideration: "we must examine the character and purposes of the institutions that are benefitted, the nature of the aid that the State provides, and the resulting relationship between the government and religious authority."[50]

As part of its analysis, the Supreme Court reviewed its prior cases on the relationship between church and state in education, concluding that total separation was unnecessary. The Court was concerned that the relationship in *Lemon* was too close since the religious schools, which constituted an integral part of the mission of the Catholic Church, involved substantial religious activities. Catholic schools were the sole beneficiaries in Rhode Island and were virtually so in Pennsylvania.

The *Lemon* Court distinguished aid for teachers' salaries from secular, neutral, or non-ideological services, facilities, or materials. Recalling *Allen*, the Court remarked that teachers have a substantially different ideological character than books. In terms of potential for involving faith or morals in secular subjects, the Justices feared that while the content of a textbook is ascertainable, a teacher's handling of a subject matter is not. The Court also noted the inherent conflict when teachers who work under the direction of religious officials are faced with separating religious and secular aspects of education. The majority decided that the restrictions and oversight necessary to ensure that teachers avoid non-ideological perspectives give rise to impermissible entanglement. The Court contended that an ongoing history of government grants to non-public schools suggests that these programs were almost always accompanied by varying measures of control. According to the Court, weighing which expenditures of church-

---

47. 397 U.S. 664, 90 S.Ct. 1409, 25 L.Ed.2d 697 (1970).

48. For more recent cases with differing results over whether religious institutions were entitled to tax exemptions, *see Episcopal School of Cincinnati v. Levin*, 884 N.E.2d 561 [231 Educ. L. Rep. 452] (Ohio 2008) (affirming that the planned use of real property as a school qualified for a tax exemption); *Faith Builders Church v. Department of Revenue of State*, 882 N.E.2d 1256 [230 Educ. L. Rep. 355] (Ill.App.Ct.2008), *appeal denied*, 889 N.E.2d 1115 (Ill. 2008) (denying a tax exemption to a church where the operation of a preschool was more characteristic of a commercial day care center than a facility used primarily for religious purposes).

49. *Lemon v. Kurtzman*, 403 U.S. 602, 612–613, 91 S.Ct. 2105, 29 L.Ed.2d 745 (1971) (internal citations omitted). [Case No. 7]

50. *Id.* at 615.

related schools were religious and which were secular created an impermissible intimate relationship between church and state.

In what has developed into a kind of "catch–22" situation, programs typically passed *Lemon's* first two prongs only to have had excessive entanglement serve as the basis for invalidating various forms of aid to students in religiously affiliated non-public schools. The difficulty was exacerbated due to the realization that even though the first two parts of the *Lemon* test were developed in the context of prayer cases and the third in a non-educational context, the Supreme Court applied its tripartite standard widely in disputes involving aid to non-public schools and their students.

TUITION REIMBURSEMENTS TO PARENTS

Two months after *Lemon*, the Pennsylvania legislature enacted a statute permitting parents whose children attended non-public schools to request tuition reimbursement. The same parent as in *Lemon* challenged the new law as having the primary effect of advancing religion.[51] In *Sloan v. Lemon (Sloan)*,[52] the Supreme Court affirmed that the law impermissibly singled out a class of citizens for a special economic benefit. The Justices thought it plain that this was unlike the "indirect" and "incidental" benefits flowing to religious schools from programs aiding all parents by supplying bus transportation and secular textbooks for their children. The Court commented that transportation and textbooks were carefully restricted to the purely secular side of church-affiliated schools and did not provide special aid to their students.

The Supreme Court expanded *Sloan's* rationale in a case from New York, *Committee for Public Education and Religious Liberty v. Nyquist (Nyquist)*.[53] The Justices decreed that even though the grants went to parents rather than to school officials, this did not compel a different result. The Court was of the view that insofar as parents would have used the money to pay for tuition and the law failed to separate secular from religious uses, the effect of the aid unmistakably would have provided the desired financial support for non-public schools. The majority rejected the state's argument that parents were not simply conduits because they were free to spend the money in any manner they chose since they paid the tuition and the law merely provided for reimbursements. The Court ascertained that even if the grants were offered as incentives to have parents send their children to religious schools, the law violated the Establishment Clause regardless of whether the money made its way into the coffers of the religious institutions.

INCOME TAX BENEFITS

Another section of the same New York statute in *Nyquist* aided parents via income tax benefits. Under the law, parents of children who attended

---

51. *Lemon v. Sloan*, 340 F.Supp. 1356 (E.D.Pa.1972).

52. 413 U.S. 825, 93 S.Ct. 2982, 37 L.Ed.2d 939 (1973).

53. 413 U.S. 756, 93 S.Ct. 2955, 37 L.Ed.2d 948 (1973).

non-public schools were entitled to income tax deductions as long as they did not receive tuition reimbursements under the other part of the statute. The Supreme Court invalidated this provision in pointing out that in practice there was little difference, for purposes of evaluating whether the aid had the effect of advancing religion, between a tax benefit and a tuition grant. The Court based its judgment on the notion that under both programs qualifying parents received the same form of encouragement and reward for sending their children to non-public schools.

In *Mueller v. Allen* (*Mueller*),[54] the Supreme Court upheld a statute from Minnesota granting all parents state income tax deductions for the actual costs of tuition, textbooks, and transportation associated with sending their children to K–12 schools. The statute afforded parents deductions of $500 for children in grades K–6 and $700 for those in grades seven to twelve. The Justices distinguished *Mueller* from *Nyquist* primarily because the tax benefit at issue was available to all parents, not only those whose children were in non-public schools, and the deduction was one among many rather than a single taxpayer expense. Conceding the legislature's broad latitude to create classifications and distinctions in tax statutes, and that the state could have been considered as gaining a benefit from the plan since it promoted an educated citizenry while reducing the costs of public education, the Court was convinced that the law satisfied all three of *Lemon's* prongs. Interestingly, the Court paid scant attention to the fact that insofar as the public schools were essentially free, the expenses of parents whose children attended them were at most minimal and that about ninety-six percent of the taxpayers who benefitted had children who were enrolled in religious schools.

The first of a trilogy of cases dealing with the procedural aspects of tax credits arose in Arizona where a statute authorizing a tuition tax credit which allowed state income taxpayers who voluntarily contributed money to a "student tuition organizations (STOs)" to receive dollar-for-dollar tax credits of up to $500 of their annual tax liability. In turn, the STOs create voucher programs granting scholarships to students who attend primarily non-public schools. In *Arizona Christian School Tuition Organization v. Winn*,[55] a closely divided Supreme Court rejected a challenge to the constitutionality of a tax credit program. Without addressing the merits of the tax credits, the Court rejected the claim of taxpayers that the program violated the Establishment Clause. Instead, the Court upheld the constitutionality of the program because the taxpayers lacked standing since any financial benefit to religion was due to private choices rather than governmental action as to how the funds were spent.

In the second case, the Supreme Court of Oregon determined that insofar as a draft title of a ballot initiative designed to grant state income tax credits to parents of children in grades K–12 was inadequate because it failed to address its goal adequately, it had to be modified before it could be

---

54.   463 U.S. 388, 103 S.Ct. 3062, 77 L.Ed.2d 721 [11 Educ. L. Rep. 763] (1983). [Case No. 8]

55.   ___ U.S. ___, 131 S.Ct. 1436, 179 L.Ed.2d 523 [265 Educ. L. Rep. 855] (2011), *on remand*, 658 F.3d 889 (9th Cir. 2011).

submitted to voters.[56] Finally, the Sixth Circuit affirmed a grant of summary judgment in favor of a school board in Kentucky in a dispute over whether a resident could gain access to its Web site in an attempt to gather information while seeking to garner support for a pending law designed to institute tax credits for students in non-public schools, regardless of whether they were religiously affiliated or home schooled.[57] The court agreed that the taxpayer lacked the right to access the information on the Web site since the board's advocacy of defeating the pending bill was government speech not creating a limited open forum requiring it to include opposing points of view.

REIMBURSEMENTS TO RELIGIOUSLY AFFILIATED NON-PUBLIC SCHOOLS

In another aspect of *Nyquist*, the Supreme Court invalidated the statute's maintenance and repair provision for non-public schools since it placed almost no restrictions on how funds were used.[58] The Justices wrote that insofar as it was clear that the government is forbidden from erecting buildings in which religious activities are conducted, it may not pay to renovate them when they fall into disrepair.

On the same day as it handed down *Nyquist*, in another case from New York, the Supreme Court applied essentially the same rationale in *Levitt v. Committee for Public Education and Religious Liberty (Levitt)*,[59] invalidating a statute allowing the state to reimburse non-public schools for expenses incurred while administering and reporting test results as well as other records. Since there were no restrictions on the use of the funds, such that teacher-prepared tests on religious subject matter were seemingly reimbursable, the Court discerned that the aid had the primary effect of advancing religious education because there were insufficient safeguards in place to regulate how the monies were spent.[60]

In *Wolman v. Walter*,[61] the Supreme Court upheld a law from Ohio permitting reimbursements for religious schools using standardized tests and scoring services. The Justices distinguished these tests from the ones in *Levitt* since the latter were neither drafted nor scored by non-public school personnel. The Court also reasoned that the law did not authorize payments to church-sponsored schools for costs associated with administering the tests.

The Supreme Court revisited *Levitt* in *Committee for Public Education and Religious Liberty v. Regan*[62] after the New York State legislature modified the law. Under its new provisions, the statute provided reimburse-

---

56. *Terhune v. Myers*, 154 P.3d 1284 [217 Educ. L. Rep. 964] (Or.2007).

57. *Page v. Lexington County School Dist. No. 1*, 531 F.3d 275 [234 Educ. L. Rep. 538] (4th Cir.2008).

58. 413 U.S. 756, 93 S.Ct. 2955, 37 L.Ed.2d 948 (1973).

59. 413 U.S. 472, 93 S.Ct. 2814, 37 L.Ed.2d 736 (1973).

60. *See also New York v. Cathedral Acad.*, 434 U.S. 125, 98 S.Ct. 340, 54 L.Ed.2d 346 (1977), *on remand*, 403 N.Y.S.2d 895, 374 N.E.2d 1246 (1978) (striking down a successor law providing reimbursements to religious schools for record keeping and testing).

61. 433 U.S. 229, 97 S.Ct. 2593, 53 L.Ed.2d 714 (1977).

62. 444 U.S. 646, 100 S.Ct. 840, 63 L.Ed.2d 94 (1980).

ments to non-public schools for the actual costs of complying with state requirements for reporting on students and for administering mandatory and optional state-prepared examinations. Unlike the statute in Ohio, this law directed that the tests were to be graded by personnel in the non-public schools that were, in turn, reimbursed for these services. In addition, the law created accounting procedures to monitor reimbursements. The Justices recognized that the differences between the statutes were permissible since scoring essentially objective tests and recording their results along with attendance data offered no significant opportunity for religious indoctrination while serving secular state educational purposes. The Court added that the accounting method did not create excessive entanglement since the reimbursements were equal to the actual costs.

INSTRUCTIONAL MATERIALS AND EQUIPMENT

In *Meek v. Pittenger* (*Meek*),[63] the Supreme Court reviewed the constitutionality of loans of instructional materials, including textbooks and equipment, to religiously affiliated non-public schools in Pennsylvania. The Court upheld the loans of textbooks, but invalidated parts of the law dealing with periodicals, films, recordings, and laboratory equipment as well as equipment for recording and projecting in interpreting the statute as having the primary effect of advancing religion due to the predominantly religious character of participating schools. The Justices were troubled since the only statutory requirement imposed on the schools to qualify for the loans was that their curricula had to offer the subjects and activities mandated by the commonwealth's board of education. The Court stated that the church-related schools were the primary beneficiaries and that the massive aid to their educational function necessarily resulted in aid to their sectarian enterprises as a whole.

The Supreme Court reached similar results in *Wolman v. Walter* (*Wolman*)[64] in upholding a statute from Ohio which specified that textbook loans were to be made to students or their parents, rather than directly to their non-public schools. The Justices struck down a provision designed to allow loans of instructional equipment including projectors, tape recorders, record players, maps and globes, and science kits. Echoing *Meek*, the Court invalidated the statute's authorizing the loans based on its fear that insofar as it would have been impossible to separate the secular and sectarian functions for which these items were being used, the aid inevitably provided support for the religious roles of the schools.

In *Mitchell v. Helms*,[65] a case from Louisiana, the Supreme Court expanded the boundaries of permissible aid to religiously affiliated non-public schools. A plurality upheld the constitutionality of Chapter 2 of Title I, now Title VI, of the Elementary and Secondary Education Act (Chapter

---

63.   421 U.S. 349, 95 S.Ct. 1753, 44 L.Ed.2d 217 (1975).

64.   433 U.S. 229, 97 S.Ct. 2593, 53 L.Ed.2d 714 (1977).

65.   530 U.S. 793, 120 S.Ct. 2530, 147 L.Ed.2d 660 [145 Educ. L. Rep. 44] (2000), *reh'g denied*, 530 U.S. 1296, 121 S.Ct. 15, 147 L.Ed.2d 1039 (2000), *on remand sub nom. Helms v. Picard*, 229 F.3d 467 [148 Educ. L. Rep. 32] (5th Cir.2000).

2),[66] a federal law permitting the loans of instructional materials such as library books, computers, television sets, tape recorders, and maps to non-public schools. The Court relied on the fact that *Agostini v. Felton*, discussed below, modified the *Lemon* test by reviewing only its first two parts while recasting entanglement as one criterion in evaluating a statute's effect. Since the purpose part of the test was not challenged, the plurality believed it necessary only to consider Chapter 2's effect, concluding that it did not foster impermissible indoctrination because aid was allocated pursuant to neutral secular criteria that neither favored nor disfavored religion and was available to all schools based on secular, nondiscriminatory grounds. In its rationale, the plurality explicitly reversed those parts of *Meek* and *Wolman* that were inconsistent with its analysis on loans of instructional materials.

AUXILIARY SERVICES

In *Meek v. Pittenger*,[67] the Supreme Court struck down a statute that allowed public school personnel to provide auxiliary services on-site in religiously affiliated non-public schools. In addition, the Justices banned the delivery of remedial and accelerated instructional programs, guidance counseling and testing, and services for children who were educationally disadvantaged. The Court asserted that it was immaterial that the students would have received remedial, rather than advanced, work since the required surveillance to ensure the absence of ideology would have given rise to excessive entanglement between church and state.

The Supreme Court reached a variety of results in *Wolman v. Walter*.[68] Along with upholding the textbook loan program, the Court permitted the state to supply non-public schools with state-mandated tests while allowing public school employees to go on-site to perform diagnostic tests to evaluate whether students needed speech, hearing, and psychological services. The Justices also permitted public funds to be spent providing therapeutic services to students from non-public schools as long as they were delivered off-site. The Court prohibited the state from loaning instructional materials and equipment to schools or from using funds to pay for field trips for students in non-public schools.

Zobrest v. Catalina Foothills School District[69] signaled a dramatic shift in the Supreme Court's Establishment Clause jurisprudence. At issue was a school board's refusal to provide a sign-language interpreter, under the Individuals with Disabilities Education Act,[70] for a deaf student in Arizona who transferred to a Catholic high school. After the Ninth Circuit affirmed that such an arrangement would have violated the Establishment Clause,[71] the Court disagreed. The Justices viewed the interpreter as providing

---

66. 20 U.S.C.A. §§ 7301–73.

67. 421 U.S. 349, 95 S.Ct. 1753, 44 L.Ed.2d 217 (1975).

68. 433 U.S. 229, 97 S.Ct. 2593, 53 L.Ed.2d 714 (1977).

69. 509 U.S. 1, 113 S.Ct. 2462, 125 L.Ed.2d 1 [83 Educ. L. Rep. 930] (1993).

70. 20 U.S.C.A. §§ 1400 *et seq.*

71. 963 F.2d 1190 [75 Educ. L. Rep. 178] (9th Cir.1992).

neutral aid to the student without offering financial benefits to his parents or school and there was no governmental participation in the instruction because the interpreter was only a conduit to effectuate the child's communications. The Court relied in part on *Witters v. Washington Department of Services for the Blind*,[72] wherein it upheld the constitutionality of extending a general vocational assistance program to a man who is blind as he studied to become a clergyman at a religious college.[73] The Supreme Court of Washington subsequently interpreted its state constitution as forbidding such use of public funds and the Supreme Court refused to hear an appeal.[74]

The next year the Supreme Court considered a case where the New York State legislature created a school district which had the same boundaries as those of a religious community in an attempt to accommodate the needs of parents of children with disabilities who wished to send them to a nearby school with programs designed to honor their religious practices. After all three levels of the state court system struck the statute down as violating the Establishment Clause, in *Board of Education of Kiryas Joel Village School District v. Grumet*,[75] the Court affirmed that the law was unconstitutional. The Justices agreed that the creation of the district deprived it of a means to review such state action for the purpose of safeguarding the principle that the government should not prefer one religion to another or religion to no religion. The Court explained that while a state may accommodate a group's religious needs by alleviating special burdens, it stepped over the line, especially since the board could have offered an appropriate program at one of its public schools or at a neutral site near one of the village's religious schools.

Days after the Supreme Court struck down the statute, the New York State legislature amended the law in an attempt to eliminate the Establishment Clause problem. Even so, the Court of Appeals of New York struck down the revised statute because it violated the Establishment Clause insofar as it had the effect of advancing one religion.[76]

The Eighth Circuit, in a case from Minnesota, accommodated the religious beliefs of parents who objected to the use of technology in public education. The court permitted what was essentially a special public school

---

72. 474 U.S. 481, 106 S.Ct. 748, 88 L.Ed.2d 846 [29 Educ. L. Rep. 496] (1986).

73. *But see Locke v. Davey*, 540 U.S. 712, 124 S.Ct. 1307, 158 L.Ed.2d 1 [185 Educ. L. Rep. 30] (2004) (invalidating a program from Washington designed to provide a scholarship for a student who pursued a degree in pastoral theology where program rules prohibited the release of funds to pay for individuals who wished to study for the ministry). The Tenth Circuit reached the opposite outcome in *Colorado Christian Univ. v. Weaver*, 534 F.3d 1245 [235 Educ. L. Rep. 68] (10th Cir.2008) (striking down a scholarship program for college and university students who attended in-state non-public institutions for violating both the Establishment and Free Exercise Clauses by excluding "pervasively sectarian" schools).

74. *Witters v. State Comm'n for the Blind*, 771 P.2d 1119 [53 Educ. L. Rep. 278] (Wash.1989), *cert. denied*, 493 U.S. 850, 110 S.Ct. 147, 107 L.Ed.2d 106 (1989).

75. 512 U.S. 687, 114 S.Ct. 2481, 129 L.Ed.2d 546 [91 Educ. L. Rep. 810] (1994).

76. *Grumet v. Cuomo*, 659 N.Y.S.2d 173, 681 N.E.2d 340 [119 Educ. L. Rep. 603] (1997); *Grumet v. Pataki*, 697 N.Y.S.2d 846 [139 Educ. L. Rep. 986] (1999), *cert. denied*, 528 U.S. 946, 120 S.Ct. 363, 145 L.Ed.2d 284 (1999).

to operate without the use of technology since it was satisfied that the local board did not improperly endorse religion.[77]

SHARED FACILITIES AND SHARED TIME

Conflicts have arisen when officials in public and non-public schools entered into cooperative arrangements. The extent to which these arrangements are permissible is an unresolved question since there is a disagreement among jurisdictions on whether public and non-public schools can share facilities, engage in shared time, and/or operate dual enrollment programs. The key issues in these disputes are whether public funds are used for religious purposes and whether religious influences are present in public schools.

When dealing with the use of public funds in religious schools, disputes occur after local school boards lease part or all of church-owned buildings. In a pair of cases separated by forty years, the Supreme Court of Nebraska invalidated a leasing program where part of a building was used by a religious school in light of the garb and devotional attitude of the sisters who taught there, the instructions and services that a local priest offered in classrooms and the chapel, and insignia in the building created an environment reflecting Catholic beliefs.[78] In the second case, the court observed that a public school board may use or lease classrooms in a church or other building affiliated with a religious organization for public school purposes if the property is under the control of public school officials and the instruction is secular.[79] In citing the latter case from Nebraska, the Supreme Court of Georgia affirmed that an arms-length commercial contract under which a public school system leased classroom space from a church did not violate the Establishment Clause of the state constitution.[80] The court pointed out that insofar as the purpose of the lease was to permit the public school system to establish and operate a kindergarten in a non-sectarian environment, the payments did not constitute an unconstitutional form of monetary aid to the church.

Questions involving shared time or dual enrollment depend largely on the wording of compulsory education statutes relating to religion and education. In an early case, the Supreme Court of Pennsylvania posited that a student who attended a religious school could not be denied the opportunity to enroll in a manual training course in a local public school.[81] More than fifty years later, an appellate court in Illinois upheld an experimental program which allowed students who otherwise would have been eligible for full-time enrollment in public high schools to attend

---

77. *Stark v. Independent School Dist., No. 640*, 123 F.3d 1068 [121 Educ. L. Rep. 41] (8th Cir.1997), *reh'g and suggestion for reh'g en banc denied* (1997), *cert. denied*, 523 U.S. 1094, 118 S.Ct. 1560, 140 L.Ed.2d 792 (1998).

78. *State ex rel. Pub. School Dist. No. 6, Cedar County v. Taylor*, 240 N.W. 573 (Neb.1932). *See also Zellers v. Huff*, 236 P.2d 949 (N.M.1951) (prohibiting the use of facilities where many direct and indirect religious influences were present in schools).

79. *State ex rel. School Dist. of Hartington v. Nebraska State Bd. of Educ.*, 195 N.W.2d 161 (Neb.1972), *cert. denied*, 409 U.S. 921, 93 S.Ct. 220, 34 L.Ed.2d 182 (1972).

80. *Taetle v. Atlanta Indep. School Sys.*, 625 S.E.2d 770 (Ga.2006).

81. *Commonwealth ex rel. Wehrle v. School Dist.*, 88 A. 481 (Pa.1913).

classes there on a part-time basis and take other courses in a religious school.[82] Rather than rely on the First Amendment, the court rooted its judgment in the fact that the local board had the power to experiment in an educational program that applied to all non-public schools, not just ones that were religiously affiliated. The court was of the opinion that the state's compulsory education law did not specify that all classes had to take place in one location. Shortly thereafter, the Supreme Court of Missouri adopted a contrary position with regard to the state's compulsory education law.[83] In its order, the court questioned procedures whereby public funds were used to send speech teachers into religious schools to provide speech therapy and to allow some of these students to go to public schools to receive speech therapy during the regular class day. The court prohibited public school personnel from going into religious schools while invalidating the practice of permitting their students to travel to public schools. The court interpreted the state's compulsory education law as stipulating that the school day had to be of a set length and that it had to be spent entirely in one type of school.

The Supreme Court of Michigan discussed shared time in relation to a state constitutional amendment prohibiting financial aid to students or their non-public schools. The court upheld the program in clarifying that if teaching took place on leased premises or in non-public schools, services had to be provided only under conditions appropriate for public schools.[84] The court maintained that ultimate and immediate control of subject matter, personnel, and premises had to be under the direction of public school officials, and the courses had to be open to all eligible students. The federal trial court in Rhode Island, summarily upheld by the First Circuit, reached a like outcome in refusing to invalidate a leasing agreement because it did not violate the *Lemon* test.[85] Federal trial courts in New Hampshire[86] and Kentucky[87] struck down dual-enrollment plans intended to have permitted boards to lease space in religious schools and have teachers selected by public school officials teach secular subjects in the non-public schools.

More than a decade after the Supreme Court of Michigan upheld the state constitutional amendment on shared time, officials in Grand Rapids created an extensive program. The program increased to the point where publicly paid teachers conducted ten percent of classes in religious schools and a substantial number of them had worked in the religious schools. The Sixth Circuit decreed that the plan violated the Establishment Clause.[88] On

---

82. *Morton v. Board of Educ.*, 216 N.E.2d 305 (Ill.App.Ct.1966).

83. *Special Dist. for Educ. and Training of Handicapped Children v. Wheeler*, 408 S.W.2d 60 (Mo.1966).

84. *In re Proposal C.*, 185 N.W.2d 9 (Mich.1971).

85. *Thomas v. Schmidt*, 397 F.Supp. 203 (D.R.I.1975), *aff'd*, 539 F.2d 701 (1st Cir.1976).

86. *Americans United for Separation of Church and State v. Paire*, 359 F.Supp. 505 (D.N.H.1973).

87. *Americans United for Separation of Church and State v. Board of Educ.*, 369 F.Supp. 1059 (E.D.Ky.1974).

88. *Americans United for Separation of Church and State v. School Dist. of City of Grand Rapids*, 718 F.2d 1389 [14 Educ. L. Rep. 40] (6th Cir.1983).

further review, in *School District of City of Grand Rapids v. Ball* (*Ball*),[89] the Supreme Court affirmed that the released time program failed all three prongs of the *Lemon* test. Moreover, the Court invalidated an after school community education program in which teachers from religious schools worked part-time for the local public school board, instructing students in their own buildings.

On the same day that it resolved *Ball*, the Supreme Court addressed a case from New York City over the constitutionality of permitting public school teachers to provide remedial instruction under Title I of the Elementary and Secondary Education Act of 1965 (Title I)[90] for specifically targeted children, who were educationally disadvantaged, on-site in their religiously affiliated schools. After a federal trial court refused to enjoin the program and the Second Circuit invalidated it, a divided Supreme Court, in *Aguilar v. Felton* (*Aguilar*),[91] agreed. Even though the New York City Board of Education (NYCBOE) developed safeguards to ensure that public funds were not spent for religious purposes, the Court struck it down based solely on the fear that a monitoring system might have created excessive entanglement of church and state.

In *Agostini v. Felton* (*Agostini*),[92] the Supreme Court took the unusual step of dissolving the injunction it upheld in *Aguilar* twelve years earlier. In a major shift in its jurisprudence, the Court reasoned that the Title I program did not violate any of the three standards that it used to consider whether state aid advanced religion since there was no governmental indoctrination, there were no distinctions between recipients based on religion, and there was no excessive entanglement. The majority ruled that a federal program designed to provide supplemental, remedial instruction and counseling services to disadvantaged children on a neutral basis is not invalid under the Establishment Clause when the assistance is provided on-site in religiously affiliated non-public schools pursuant to a program containing safeguards such as those that the NYCBOE implemented. Perhaps the most significant development in *Agostini* was that the Court modified the *Lemon* test by reviewing only its first two parts, purpose and effect, while recasting entanglement as one criterion in evaluating a statute's effect.

In a case with a broad resemblance to *Agostini*, the Circuit Court for the District of Columbia found that the federally chartered AmeriCorps Education Awards Program (EAP), a nationwide community service program, did not violate the Establishment Clause even though some participants taught religion and secular subjects in religious schools.[93] The court

---

89.   473 U.S. 373, 105 S.Ct. 3216, 87 L.Ed.2d 267 [25 Educ. L. Rep. 1006] (1985).

90.   In an earlier case involving the Elementary and Secondary Education Act, the Supreme Court concluded that public school officials could not use federal funds under the Act to provide on-site instruction for educationally deprived children in their religiously affiliated non-public schools. *Wheeler v. Barrera,* 417 U.S. 402, 94 S.Ct. 2274, 41 L.Ed.2d 159 (1974).

91.   473 U.S. 402, 105 S.Ct. 3232, 87 L.Ed.2d 290 [25 Educ. L. Rep. 1022] (1985).

92.   521 U.S. 203, 117 S.Ct. 1997, 138 L.Ed.2d 391 [119 Educ. L. Rep. 29] (1997). [Case No. 11]

93.   *American Jewish Congress v. Corporation for Nat'l and Community Serv.*, 399 F.3d 351 [195 Educ. L. Rep. 733] (D.C.Cir.2005), *cert. denied*, 546 U.S. 1130, 126 S.Ct. 1132, 163 L.Ed.2d 927 [205 Educ. L. Rep. 573] (2006).

pointed out that the EAP was permissible because it was a government program that was neutral toward religion while providing aid directly to a broad class of citizens who, in turn, directed government assistance to religious schools entirely on their own genuine and independent private choices. The court added that the program was constitutional because no objective observer who was familiar with the full history and context of the EAP would have viewed the aid that the religious institutions received as carrying the imprimatur of governmental endorsement.

VOUCHERS

Vouchers have generated controversy with courts reaching mixed results in disputes over their constitutionality. The Supreme Court of Wisconsin upheld a program to offer vouchers to students who attended religiously affiliated non-public schools.[94] At the same time, state[95] and federal[96] appellate courts in Maine upheld laws including non-sectarian schools but specifically excluding religiously affiliated non-public schools from taking part in tuition vouchers programs. Subsequently, Maine's highest court upheld a statute prohibiting the use of either state[97] or municipal[98] general funds to pay tuition for children who attended religiously affiliated non-public schools. Earlier, the Supreme Court of Vermont affirmed the unconstitutionality of a state law intended to provide reimbursements to parents for tuition for religiously affiliated non-public schools.[99] Still, it was not until a dispute from Ohio made its way to the Supreme Court that vouchers assumed center stage.

The Ohio General Assembly, acting pursuant to a desegregation order, enacted the Ohio Pilot Project Scholarship Program (OPPSP) to assist children in Cleveland's failing public schools.[100] The main goal of the OPPSP, which contains significant anti-discrimination provisions, was to permit an equal number of students to receive vouchers and tutorial assistance grants while attending regular public schools. Another part of the law provided greater choices to parents and children via the creation of community (known as charter schools elsewhere) and magnet schools while a third section featured tutorial assistance for children.

---

94. *Jackson v. Benson*, 578 N.W.2d 602 [126 Educ. L. Rep. 399] (Wis.1998), *cert. denied*, 525 U.S. 997, 119 S.Ct. 466, 142 L.Ed.2d 419 (1998). *See also Thomas More High School v. Burmaster*, 704 N.W.2d 349 [202 Educ. L. Rep. 793] (Wis.Ct.App.2005), *review denied* (2005) (affirming that the program applied only to non-public schools in Milwaukee).

95. *Bagley v. Raymond School Dep't*, 728 A.2d 127 [134 Educ. L. Rep. 226] (Me. 1999), *cert. denied*, 528 U.S. 947, 120 S.Ct. 364, 145 L.Ed.2d 285 (1999).

96. *Strout v. Albanese*, 178 F.3d 57 [135 Educ. L. Rep. 398] (1st Cir.1999), *cert. denied*, 528 U.S. 931, 120 S.Ct. 329, 145 L.Ed.2d 256 (1999).

97. *Anderson v. Town of Durham*, 895 A.2d 944 [207 Educ. L. Rep. 978] (Me.2006), *cert. denied*, 549 U.S. 1051, 127 S.Ct. 661, 166 L.Ed.2d 512 (2006).

98. *Joyce v. State of Maine*, 951 A.2d 69 [234 Educ. L. Rep. 175] (Me.2008).

99. *Chittenden Town School Dist. v. Department of Educ.*, 738 A.2d 539 [138 Educ. L. Rep. 858] (Vt.1999).

100. OHIO REV. CODE ANN. §§ 3313.974 *et seq.*

In an initial challenge, the Supreme Court of Ohio upheld the OPPSP[101] but severed the part of the law affording priority to parents who belonged to religious groups supporting sectarian institutions. In interpreting the OPPSP as having violated the state constitutional requirement that every statute have only one subject, the court struck it down. The court stayed enforcement of its order to avoid disrupting the then current school year. The General Assembly of Ohio quickly re-enacted a revised statute.

A federal trial court in Ohio, relying largely on *Nyquist,*[102] enjoined the operation of the revised statute as a violation of the Establishment Clause.[103] A divided Sixth Circuit, also applying *Nyquist*, affirmed that the OPPSP had the impermissible effect of advancing religion.[104]

In *Zelman v. Simmons–Harris* (*Zelman*), the Supreme Court reversed the judgment of the Sixth Circuit and upheld the constitutionality of the OPPSP. Relying on *Agostini*, the Court began by considering "whether the government acted with the purpose of advancing or inhibiting religions [and] whether the aid has the 'effect' of advancing or inhibiting religion."[105] Conceding the lack of a dispute over the program's valid secular purpose in providing programming for poor children in a failing school system, the Court examined whether it had the forbidden effect of advancing or inhibiting religion. The Justices were satisfied that the voucher program was constitutional because, as part of the state's far-reaching attempt to provide greater educational opportunities in a failing school system, it allocated aid on the basis of neutral secular criteria that neither favored nor disfavored religion, was made available to both religious and secular beneficiaries on a nondiscriminatory basis, and offered assistance directly to a broad class of citizens who directed the aid to religious schools based entirely on their own genuine and independent private choices. The Court was untroubled by the fact that most of the participating schools were religiously affiliated because parents chose to send their children to them insofar as surrounding public schools refused to take part in the program. The Court conceded that most of the students went to religiously affiliated schools not as a matter of law but because they were unwelcomed in the public schools. The majority also indicated that insofar as the Ohio program differed greatly from the one in *Nyquist,* the lower courts misplaced their reliance on it. The Court concluded that in light of an unbroken line of cases supporting true private choice that provided benefits directly to a wide range of needy private individuals, its only choice was to uphold the voucher program.

Post–*Zelman* litigation challenging vouchers has focused on state constitutional grounds since they are typically more stringent than under their federal counterpart. In a case that began before *Zelman* reached the Supreme Court, an appellate court in Florida[106] initially upheld vouchers

---

101. *Simmons–Harris v. Goff*, 711 N.E.2d 203 [135 Educ. L. Rep. 596] (Ohio 1999).

102. 413 U.S. 756, 93 S.Ct. 2955, 37 L.Ed.2d 948 (1973).

103. *Simmons–Harris v. Zelman*, 72 F.Supp.2d 834 [140 Educ. L. Rep. 243] (N.D.Ohio 1999).

104. *Simmons–Harris v. Zelman*, 234 F.3d 945 [149 Educ. L. Rep. 691] (6th Cir.2000).

105. 536 U.S. 639, 649, 122 S.Ct. 2460, 153 L.Ed.2d 604 [166 Educ. L. Rep. 30] (2002). [Case No. 14]

106. *Bush v. Holmes*, 767 So.2d 668 [147 Educ. L. Rep. 1125] (Fla.Dist.Ct.App.2000), *review denied*, 790 So.2d 1104 (Fla.2001).

for students who attended religious schools. In the aftermath of *Zelman*, an intermediate appellate court in Florida interpreted the no-aid provision of the state constitution as prohibiting the state from providing indirect benefits to "sectarian" schools due to their having received tax dollars through the voucher program.[107] On further review, the Supreme Court of Florida agreed that the voucher system violated the state constitution's requirement of a uniform system of free public schools.[108] In a related claim, the Eleventh Circuit affirmed that under a voucher program available only to children who attended failing schools, the state of Florida had no duty to pay for students to attend non-public schools.[109]

In other cases, the Supreme Court of Colorado affirmed that a program requiring school boards to pay a portion of locally raised tax revenues to parents with children who performed unsatisfactorily in public schools, which in turn required the parents to pay those funds to non-public schools with special programs designed for those students, violated the local control provisions of the state constitution.[110] In addition, the First Circuit affirmed that a law in Maine, which stipulated that only non-sectarian non-public schools were eligible to participate in a program permitting students to receive public funds to attend K–8 schools, did not violate equal protection because a rational relationship existed between the statute and the state's legitimate interests.[111] The court rejected the parental claim that such a judgment would have infringed on their free exercise of religion by impermissibly interfering with their fundamental right to choose religious education for their children. Also, the Supreme Court of Arizona upheld a voucher program for children with disabilities and who were in foster care since the funds were earmarked for students making them the true beneficiaries under the law.[112]

The Supreme Court of Utah, in a case failing to reach the merits of the issue, refused to grant a writ to sponsors of both a voucher law and a referendum on the statute challenging the ballot title of the referendum.[113] In being satisfied that the referendum ballot title was neither patently false nor biased, the court refused to modify its wording. Eventually, voters rejected a law that would have enacted the most comprehensive voucher program in the United States.[114]

---

107. *Bush v. Holmes*, 886 So.2d 340 [193 Educ. L. Rep. 938] (Fla.Dist.Ct.App.2004).

108. *Bush v. Holmes*, 919 So.2d 392 [206 Educ. L. Rep. 756] (Fla.2006).

109. *Children A & B ex rel. Cooper v. Florida*, 355 F.Supp.2d 1298 [195 Educ. L. Rep. 889] (N.D.Fla.2004), *aff'd sub nom. Cooper v. Florida*, 140 Fed.Appx. 845 [201 Educ. L. Rep. 111] (11th Cir.2005).

110. *Owens v. Colorado Congress of Parents, Teachers and Students*, 92 P.3d 933 [189 Educ. L. Rep. 395] (Colo.2004).

111. *Eulitt ex rel. Eulitt v. Maine, Dep't of Educ.*, 386 F.3d 344 [192 Educ. L. Rep. 651] (1st Cir.2004).

112. *Cain v. Horne*, 202 P.3d 1178 [242 Educ. L. Rep. 435] (Ariz. 2009).

113. *Snow v. Office of Legislative Research and General Counsel*, 167 P.3d 1051 [224 Educ. L. Rep. 447] (Utah 2007).

114. Erik W. Robelen, *Utah's Vote Raises Bar on Choice: Voucher Program's Defeat May Lead to Strategy Shift*, EDUC. WEEK, Nov. 14, 2007, at 1.

THE COURT'S MODERN ESTABLISHMENT CLAUSE JURISPRUDENCE: RELIGIOUS ACTIVITIES AND PUBLIC SCHOOLS

Unlike its evolving jurisprudence with regard to aid to students and their religiously affiliated non-public schools, the Supreme Court's attitude toward school-sponsored prayer and religious activity in public education has remained constant. Starting with *Engel v. Vitale*,[115] the Court has had an essentially unbroken line of cases prohibiting school-sponsored prayer and religious activities in public schools.

RELEASED TIME

Permitting public school officials to release children during the class day to allow them to receive religious instruction reached the Supreme Court twice. The first challenge arose in Champaign, Illinois, where members of the Jewish, Roman Catholic, and Protestant faiths formed a voluntary association and obtained approval from the local board for a cooperative plan to offer religion classes to children whose parents agreed to have them take part in the program. The students were released from their public schools and their religion instructors notified their regular teachers if they were absent. The courses were taught in regular classrooms, in three separate groups, by a Jewish rabbi, Catholic priests, and Protestant teachers. Students who did not attend religious instruction had to go to other places in their schools to pursue their secular studies.

In *People of State of Illinois ex rel. McCollum v. Board of Education of School District No. 71, Champaign County (McCollum)*,[116] the Supreme Court invalidated the program. The Court pointed out not only that tax-supported buildings were being used to disseminate religious doctrine but also that public school officials gave religious groups invaluable, albeit impermissible, aid in helping them by providing students for their classes via the state's compulsory education machinery.

The Supreme Court next considered the constitutionality of a different type of released time program. A statute from New York permitted officials to release students from their public schools so that they could attend religious classes at other locations. Opponents of the program viewed it as basically no different from the one in *McCollum,* arguing that the weight and influence of public schools was used to support a program of religious instruction because officials kept records with regard to which children were released while the remaining students had to stay in school even though regular classes were halted so that their peers could attend released time classes.

In *Zorach v. Clauson (Zorach)*,[117] the Supreme Court upheld the constitutionality of the program, agreeing that state officials can accommodate the religious wishes of parents by releasing their children at their request. Unlike *McCollum*, the Court was satisfied that the practice was

---

115. 370 U.S. 421, 82 S.Ct. 1261, 8 L.Ed.2d 601 (1962).

116. 333 U.S. 203, 68 S.Ct. 461, 92 L.Ed. 649 (1948). [Case No. 2]

117. 343 U.S. 306, 72 S.Ct. 679, 96 L.Ed. 954 (1952). [Case No. 3]

permissible since public schools were not used for religious instruction. The Court commented that this disagreement was one of the degrees of separation of church and state. The Court analogized that released time was not unlike acceptable arrangements and excuses for students who were absent for religious reasons.[118]

The Second Circuit, almost fifty years after *Zorach*, rejected a challenge to another released time program from New York that a mother filed on behalf of her children, neither of whom took part in the activity. Under the program, parents who wished to have their children participate were released from classes early so that they could receive instruction at nearby religiously affiliated non-public schools. Students who did not take part in the program remained in school classrooms but did not engage in organized activities until the participants returned. Affirming a grant of summary judgment in favor of the school board, the court determined that the program passed Establishment Clause analysis because it did not use public funds or on-site religious instruction, was purely voluntary, and educators did not bring any specific coercion or pressure to bear on non-participants.[119]

In South Carolina, the federal trial court rejected a challenge to a released time program granting students academic credit for participating in religious studies.[120] The court upheld the constitutionality of the program because it passed all three prongs of the *Lemon* test insofar as it did not have an impermissible religious motive, its principal effect did not advance religion, and it did not create excessive entanglement because it granted students credit without regard to a particular religion or denomination.

USE OF THE BIBLE

Long a staple resource in American education,[121] the landscape with regard to the use of the Bible in public schools shifted dramatically in light of the companion cases of *School District of Abington Township v. Schempp* and *Murray v. Curlett* (*Abington*),[122] suits originating in Pennsylvania and Maryland respectively. In *Abington*, the Supreme Court found that prayer and Bible reading, as part of the opening of a school day, violated the Establishment Clause. The Court indicated that insofar as the Bible was a sectarian document, the First Amendment dictated governmental neutrality with regard to religious matters based on the premises that the state

---

118. New York City's Public Schools continue to permit released time. *See Regulation of the Chancellor, A–630, Religious Accommodation of Students*, available at http://docs.nycenet. edu/docushare/dsweb/Get/Document–27/A–630.pdf

119. *Pierce ex rel. Pierce v. Sullivan West Cent. School Dist.*, 379 F.3d 56 [191 Educ. L. Rep. 36] (2d Cir.2004).

120. *Moss v. Spartanburg County School Dist. No. 7*, 775 F. Supp.2d 858 [269 Educ. L. Rep. 531] (D.S.C. 2011).

121. For apparently the first case involving the Bible in public schools, *see Board of Educ. of Cincinnati v. Minor*, 23 Ohio St. 211 (Ohio 1872) (upholding a board's vote to discontinue Bible reading in public schools).

122. 374 U.S. 203, 83 S.Ct. 1560, 10 L.Ed.2d 844 (1963). [Case No. 4]

could not aid any or all religions and that all have the right to choose personal courses with reference to religion, free of any state compulsion. The Court posited that it consistently recognized that the First Amendment withdrew all legislative power from the government respecting religious beliefs or their expression.

In creating a measure to evaluate the constitutionality of prayer and Bible reading in public schools, the Supreme Court declared that "[t]he test may be stated as follows: what are the purpose and the primary effect of the [legislative] enactment? ... [T]o withstand the strictures of the Establishment Clause there must be a secular legislative purpose and a primary effect that neither advances nor inhibits religion."[123] Perhaps in an attempt to allay concerns that it was anti-religious, the Court added in dicta that nothing in its opinion forbade the secular study of the Bible in public schools in appropriate contexts such as literature or history. The Court wrote:

> It certainly may be said that the Bible is worthy of study for its literary and historic qualities. Nothing we have said here indicates that such study of the Bible or of religion, when presented objectively as part of a secular program of education, may not be effected consistently with the First Amendment.[124]

Following *Abington*, controversies continue over the place, if any, of the Bible in public school curricula.[125] For instance, the Fifth Circuit disapproved a "Bible as Literature" course taught essentially from a Christian religious perspective as part of fundamentalist and/or evangelical doctrine.[126] The court also noted that the state-approved textbook did not contain a discussion of the Bible's literary qualities. Other courts suggested guidelines under which the Bible could have been studied, including using fully certificated teachers who are employed in the same manner as other staff, vesting complete control of course content and materials in school boards, supervising courses to assure objectivity in teaching, and forbidding such classes from being mandatory.[127]

The Eighth Circuit affirmed the unconstitutionality of a program in Arkansas allowing students to leave their regular classrooms to learn about the Bible in voluntary sessions during school hours.[128] The classes were taught by volunteers who did not act on behalf of any church and students did not receive course credit for participating. In sidestepping whether the

---

123. *Id.* at 222.

124. *Id.* at 225. Justice Brennan's concurrence added that "[t]he holding of the Court today plainly does not foreclose teaching about the Holy Scriptures or about the differences between religious sects in classes in literature or history ...," *Id.* at 300.

125. *See, e.g., Roberts v. Madigan,* 921 F.2d 1047 [64 Educ. L. Rep. 1038] (10th Cir.1990), *cert. denied,* 505 U.S. 1218, 112 S.Ct. 3025, 120 L.Ed.2d 896 (1992) (preventing a teacher from silently reading a Bible during class time).

126. *Hall v. Board of School Comm'rs of Conecuh County,* 656 F.2d 999 (5th Cir.1981).

127. *Wiley v. Franklin,* 497 F.Supp. 390 (E.D.Tenn.1980); *Crockett v. Sorenson,* 568 F.Supp. 1422 [13 Educ. L. Rep. 290] (W.D.Va.1983).

128. *Doe v. Human,* 725 F.Supp. 1503 [57 Educ. L. Rep. 888] (W.D.Ark. 1989), *aff'd,* 923 F.2d 857 [65 Educ. L. Rep.714] (8th Cir.1990), *cert. denied,* 499 U.S. 922, 111 S.Ct. 1315, 113 L.Ed.2d 248 (1991).

classes were primarily religious or secular, the court viewed the program as having had the principal effect of advancing Christianity.

A federal trial court in Mississippi forbade a school board from offering a Bible-study class taught in a rotation with music, physical education, and library classes or one purportedly to teaching the history of the Middle East as violating the Establishment Clause.[129] Similarly, opponents challenged a school board's adoption of a two-semester Bible history course, with time equally divided between the Old and New Testaments, even though it already had a comparative religion class. A federal trial court in Florida permitted the Old Testament class to proceed but enjoined the course on the New Testament based on its belief that the plaintiffs were likely to prevail on the merits of their claim that it violated the Establishment Clause.[130] The Sixth Circuit affirmed that a board in Tennessee's fifty-one year practice of permitting students from a local Christian college to teach weekly religion classes that presented the Bible as religious truth during the regular school day for students in grades K–5 violated the Establishment Clause because it failed all three parts of the *Lemon* test as an unconstitutional establishment of religion.[131]

PRAYER IN SCHOOL

Generally

In *Engel v. Vitale*,[132] the Supreme Court accepted its first case involving school prayer. At issue was a prayer composed by the New York State Board of Regents for suggested use in public schools to inculcate moral and spiritual values in students. When a local school board adopted the prayer as part of a policy that required its daily recitation in class, parents challenged its doing so even though the policy included a provision that permitted parents to request that their children be exempted from taking part as long as they did so in writing. The prayer was: "Almighty God, we acknowledge our dependence upon Thee, and we beg Thy blessings upon us, our parents, our teachers and our country."[133]

Reversing earlier judgments in favor of the school board, the Supreme Court ruled that the daily recitation of prayer was a religious activity inconsistent with the Establishment Clause. The Court devoted a significant portion of its opinion reviewing the history of state-sponsored prayer in the Anglo–American system of government from Sixteenth Century England through the Colonial Period, asserting that "[t]here can be no doubt that New York State's prayer program officially establishes the religious beliefs embodied in the Regents' prayer."[134]

---

129. *Herdahl v. Pontotoc County School Dist.*, 933 F.Supp. 582 [112 Educ. L. Rep. 131] (N.D.Miss.1996).

130. *Gibson v. Lee County School Bd.*, 1 F.Supp.2d 1426 [127 Educ. L. Rep. 85] (M.D.Fla. 1998).

131. *Doe v. Porter*, 370 F.3d 558 [188 Educ. L. Rep. 100] (6th Cir.2004).

132. 370 U.S. 421, 82 S.Ct. 1261, 8 L.Ed.2d 601 (1962).

133. *Id.* at 422.

134. *Id.* at 430.

In its rationale, the Supreme Court observed that the First Amendment's Establishment and Free Exercise Clauses forbid different types of governmental encroachment against religion. The Justices maintained that insofar as the Establishment Clause, unlike the Free Exercise Clause, does not depend on any direct government compulsion, public officials violate it by enacting laws establishing an official religion regardless of whether their actions coerce non-believers. The Court feared that even absent overt pressure, placing the power, privilege, and support of the government behind a particular religious belief ran the risk of asserting indirect coercion on others, especially minorities, to conform to the officially approved religion. The Court decided that insofar as the Founders considered religion to be "too personal, too sacred, too holy, to permit its 'unhallowed perversion' by a civil magistrate,"[135] state-sponsored prayer was contrary to their original intent in drafting the First Amendment.

The following year, the Supreme Court barred the use of prayer (and Bible reading) as part of opening exercises in public schools in *Abington,* discussed in the previous section. Twenty years would pass before the Court returned to the question of prayer in public schools on the merits.

In the interim, lower courts addressed prayer in a variety of circumstances. The Second Circuit upheld a principal in New York's prohibiting students from reciting prayers before eating a mid-morning snack.[136] The Seventh Circuit barred the use of a prayer in Illinois that did not include the word "God"[137] even though school assemblies were voluntary and leaders of the student council had requested permission to begin them with a prayer. Also, the Supreme Court of New Jersey invalidated a board policy intended to allow students, immediately prior to the formal opening of school, to join in a voluntary religious exercise in a gymnasium where a student volunteer would select, and read, the remarks of the chaplain of the Congressional Record to the gathered assembly.[138] The court viewed this procedure as no different from reading prayers directly from a religious source.

As to voluntary school prayer, the Supreme Judicial Court of Massachusetts ordered an end to a local school committee's plan for voluntary prayer instituted in accord with a statute permitting students to participate in such activities before the beginning of the school day if their parents approved.[139] During that same year, the Third Circuit struck down a program, adopted at the urging of students and parents in Pennsylvania, to permit voluntary nondenominational prayer and Bible reading because it

---

135. *Id.* at 432.

136. *Stein v. Oshinsky,* 348 F.2d 999 (2d Cir.1965), *cert. denied,* 382 U.S. 957, 86 S.Ct. 435, 15 L.Ed.2d 361 (1965).

137. *DeSpain v. DeKalb County Community School Dist.,* 384 F.2d 836 (7th Cir.1967), *cert. denied,* 390 U.S. 906, 88 S.Ct. 815, 19 L.Ed.2d 873 (1968).

138. *State Bd. of Educ. v. Board of Educ. of Netcong,* 270 A.2d 412 (N.J.1970), *cert. denied,* 401 U.S. 1013, 91 S.Ct. 1253, 28 L.Ed.2d 550 (1971).

139. *Commissioner of Educ. v. School Comm. of Leyden,* 267 N.E.2d 226 (Mass.1971), *cert. denied,* 404 U.S. 849, 92 S.Ct. 85, 30 L.Ed.2d 88 (1971). *See also Kent v. Commissioner of Educ.,* 402 N.E.2d 1340 (Mass.1980).

was state action.[140] A decade later, the Fifth Circuit struck down the same kind of statute from Louisiana[141] while the Eleventh Circuit argued that it was unconstitutional for teachers in Alabama to engage in prayer absent a board policy or state statute motivating their activities.[142] The court wrote that insofar as the school board was aware of the activities and took no steps to stop them, it, in effect, ratified the teachers' conduct.

When a school board in Arkansas knowingly permitted a band teacher to conduct prayer and religious activities at school functions, the Eighth Circuit held it liable for attorney fees incurred in obtaining an injunction to stop the practice.[143] In a case from Georgia, the Eleventh Circuit barred a plan designed to have not only allowed representatives of the student government to make a random selection of invocation speakers from non-clergy volunteers but which would also have permitted ministers to offer invocations prior to the start of high school football games.[144] In like manner, the Fifth Circuit affirmed that school employees in Texas could neither initiate nor lead students in prayer before and after athletic practices and competitions.[145]

Prayer at Graduation and Other Activities

After not addressing a case on point in twenty years, the Supreme Court examined school-sponsored prayers in public schools in a dispute from Rhode Island. At issue was whether a religious leader, here a rabbi, could offer prayers as part of an official school graduation ceremony incident to a board policy that permitted principals to invite members of the clergy to offer non-sectarian prayers. In addition, the principals gave speakers guidelines for prayers on civic occasions prepared by an inter-faith organization. Students were not required to attend the graduation ceremony in order to receive their diplomas.[146]

In *Lee v. Weisman* (*Lee*),[147] a divided Supreme Court affirmed the unconstitutionality of school-sponsored graduation prayer. Sidestepping the *Lemon* test, the Justices based their judgment on two major points. First, the Court thought that prayer was unacceptable because the state, through

---

140. *Mangold v. Albert Gallatin Area School Dist.*, 438 F.2d 1194 (3d Cir.1971).

141. *Karen B. v. Treen*, 653 F.2d 897 (5th Cir.1981), *aff'd without written opinion*, 455 U.S. 913, 102 S.Ct. 1267, 71 L.Ed.2d 455 (1982).

142. *Jaffree v. Wallace*, 705 F.2d 1526 [11 Educ. L. Rep. 51] (11th Cir.1983), *aff'd as to this issue*, 466 U.S. 924, 104 S.Ct. 1704, 80 L.Ed.2d 178 (1984).

143. *Steele v. Van Buren Pub. School Dist.*, 845 F.2d 1492 [46 Educ. L. Rep. 572] (8th Cir.1988).

144. *Jager v. Douglas County School Dist.*, 862 F.2d 824 [50 Educ. L. Rep. 694] (11th Cir.1989), *cert. denied*, 490 U.S. 1090, 109 S.Ct. 2431, 104 L.Ed.2d 988 (1989).

145. *Doe v. Duncanville Indep. School Dist.*, 70 F.3d 402 [104 Educ. L. Rep. 1032] (5th Cir.1995).

146. For a case with a twist concerning graduation ceremonies, *see Doe 3 ex rel. Doe 2 v. Elmbrook School Dist.*, 658 F.3d 710 [273 Educ. L. Rep. 710] (7th Cir. 2011) (affirming that allowing a public school board to conduct graduation ceremonies and related events in a rented Christian church did not coerce participation in religion, endorse its beliefs, or excessively entangle religion and the state in violation of the Establishment Clause).

147. 505 U.S. 577, 112 S.Ct. 2649, 120 L.Ed.2d 467 [75 Educ. L. Rep. 43] (1992). [Case No. 10]

school officials, played a pervasive role in the process both by selecting who would pray and by directing its content. Second, the Court feared that such governmental activity could result in psychological coercion of students. The Court was of the opinion that insofar as the students were a captive audience who may have been forced, against their wishes, to participate in ceremonies, they were not genuinely free to be excused from attending.

On the same day that the Supreme Court struck down *Lee*, it vacated and remanded without comment a case from the Fifth Circuit dealing with graduation prayer.[148] The major difference between the cases was that in the one from Texas, members of a high school's senior class, not school officials, selected volunteers to deliver non-sectarian, non-proselytizing prayers at their graduation. On remand, the Fifth Circuit followed the dissent in *Lee,* narrowly interpreting it as precluding only school-sponsored prayers.[149] The Court refused to hear an appeal, thereby leaving the door open to additional controversy.

Following *Lee*, the circuit courts remained divided over student-sponsored prayer at graduation ceremonies. Both the Third and Ninth Circuits struck down student-sponsored prayer while the Fifth and Eleventh Circuits upheld its use. The Ninth Circuit initially invalidated student-sponsored prayer in Idaho on the ground that insofar as school officials ultimately controlled the ceremony, they could not permit students to choose whether to pray at graduation.[150] The Supreme Court avoided the controversy by vacating the judgment as moot and remanding with instructions to dismiss, apparently since the students had graduated.[151] Shortly thereafter, the Fifth Circuit allowed part of a statute from Mississippi permitting student-sponsored prayer at graduation to remain in effect but struck down portions of the law allowing students to initiate non-sectarian, non-proselytizing prayer at compulsory and non-compulsory events.[152] The same court eventually invalidated a law from Louisiana granting officials the authority to allow an opportunity, at the start of each day, for students and teachers desiring to do so to observe a brief time in prayer or meditation as a violation of the Establishment Clause.[153]

The Third Circuit affirmed that a policy of permitting student-led prayer at a public high school graduation ceremony in New Jersey violated

---

148. *Jones v. Clear Creek Indep. School Dist.*, 930 F.2d 416 [67 Educ. L. Rep. 89] (5th Cir.1991), *cert. granted, vacated, and remanded*, 505 U.S. 1215, 112 S.Ct. 3020, 120 L.Ed.2d 892 [75 Educ. L. Rep. 108] (1992).

149. *Jones v. Clear Creek Indep. School Dist.*, 977 F.2d 963 [78 Educ. L. Rep. 42] (5th Cir.1992), *reh'g denied*, 983 F.2d 234 (5th Cir.1992), *cert. denied*, 508 U.S. 967, 113 S.Ct. 2950, 124 L.Ed.2d 697 (1993).

150. *Harris v. Joint School Dist. No. 241*, 41 F.3d 447 [95 Educ. L. Rep. 892] (9th Cir.1994).

151. *Cert. granted, judgment vacated with directions to dismiss as moot*, 515 U.S. 1154, 115 S.Ct. 2604, 132 L.Ed.2d 849 [102 Educ. L. Rep. 34] (1995).

152. *Ingebretsen v. Jackson Pub. School Dist.*, 88 F.3d 274 [110 Educ. L. Rep. 942] (5th Cir.1996), *cert. denied sub nom. Moore v. Ingebretsen*, 519 U.S. 965, 117 S.Ct. 388, 136 L.Ed.2d 304 (1996).

153. The Fifth Circuit affirmed that a statute permitting verbal prayer in school was unconstitutional. *Doe v. School Bd. of Ouachita Parish*, 274 F.3d 289 [160 Educ. L. Rep. 17] (5th Cir.2001).

the Establishment Clause.[154] The court viewed the board's having retained significant authority over the ceremony as meaning that prayer could not have been treated as promoting the free speech rights of students. After first upholding a board policy from Idaho designed to allowed a minimum of four graduating students to offer an address, poem, reading, song, musical presentation, prayer, or other presentation at their commencement based on neutral secular criteria,[155] the Ninth Circuit vacated its earlier judgment because a parent lacked standing to challenge the policy since the students graduated.[156]

In two different cases from California, the Ninth Circuit affirmed that school officials could refuse to allow students to deliver sectarian prayers or proselytizing valedictory addresses. In the first, the court added that the prohibition did not violate the students' free speech rights.[157] In the second, the court agreed that when officials denied a student's request to include religious proselytizing comments in his salutatorian commencement address, they did not violate his rights to freedom of religion, speech, or equal protection.[158]

The issue of prayers at high school football games re-emerged in Texas where parents and students challenged two board policies permitting student volunteers to pray at graduations and football games. A federal trial court upheld both policies as long as the prayers were non-sectarian and non-proselytizing. The Fifth Circuit affirmed that prayer at graduation had to be non-sectarian and non-proselytizing but reversed in striking down the policy permitting prayers at football games.[159] Even though the board appealed on both forms of prayer, the Supreme Court opted to address only prayer at the football games,[160] thereby leaving the split between the circuits over student-led graduation prayer in place.

In *Santa Fe Independent School District v. Doe (Santa Fe)*,[161] a closely divided Supreme Court affirmed that the policy permitting student-led prayers prior to the start of high school football games violated the Establishment Clause. In *Santa Fe*, the Justices primarily relied on the

154. *American Civil Liberties Union of N.J. v. Black Horse Pike Reg'l Bd. of Educ.*, 84 F.3d 1471 [109 Educ. L. Rep. 1118] (3d Cir.1996).

155. *Doe v. Madison School Dist. No. 321*, 147 F.3d 832 [127 Educ. L. Rep. 607] (9th Cir.1998).

156. *Doe v. Madison School Dist. No. 321, reh'g granted, opinion withdrawn*, 165 F.3d 1265 [132 Educ. L. Rep. 67] (9th Cir.1999), *vacated*, 177 F.3d 789 [135 Educ. L. Rep. 387] (9th Cir.1999).

157. *Cole v. Oroville Union High School Dist.*, 228 F.3d 1092 [147 Educ. L. Rep. 878] (9th Cir.2000), *cert. denied sub nom. Niemeyer v. Oroville Union High School Dist.*, 532 U.S. 905, 121 S.Ct. 1228, 149 L.Ed.2d 138 (2001).

158. *Lassonde v. Pleasanton Unified School Dist.*, 320 F.3d 979 [173 Educ. L. Rep. 778] (9th Cir.2003), *cert. denied*, 540 U.S. 817, 124 S.Ct. 78, 157 L.Ed.2d 34 (2003).

159. *Doe v. Santa Fe Indep. School Dist.*, 168 F.3d 806 [132 Educ. L. Rep. 687] (5th Cir.1999).

160. 528 U.S. 1002, 120 S.Ct. 494, 145 L.Ed.2d 381 [140 Educ. L. Rep. 21] (1999).

161. 530 U.S. 290, 120 S.Ct. 2266, 147 L.Ed.2d 295 [145 Educ. L. Rep. 21] (2000). [Case No. 12]

endorsement test[162] rather than the psychological coercion test. Put another way, the Court reviewed the status of prayer from the perspective of whether its being permitted at football games was an impermissible governmental approval or endorsement of religion rather than as a form of psychological coercion subjecting fans to values and/or beliefs other than their own. In striking the policy down, the Justices rebuffed the board's three main claims. First, it rejected the board's contention that the policy enhanced the free speech rights of students. Second, the Court disagreed with the board's stance that the policy was neutral on its face. Third, the majority rebuffed the board's defense that a legal challenge was premature since prayer had not been offered at a football game under the policy. In a related dispute, the Fifth Circuit affirmed that a high school student and her parents lacked standing to challenge the constitutionality of a board policy prohibiting religious references in public address system messages broadcast prior to football games because they could not demonstrate any adverse effect from the judgment.[163]

Controversy remains after *Santa Fe*. In another case from Texas, a federal trial court decided that a recent high school graduate had standing to challenge a school board's policy of allowing the graduating classes at its high schools to vote on whether to permit students to recite a prayer at commencement ceremonies in light of his allegation that he was forced to vote on whether to have an invocation.[164] The court also thought that parents who claimed direct injuries on behalf of themselves and their minor children who attended the older siblings' graduation had standing in light of the direct harm that they suffered. The court rejected the claim of parents acting on behalf of their children who merely attended school in the district and might someday graduate from one of the high schools because they lacked standing. The court maintained that mere abstract knowledge of the existence of the policy was insufficient to confer standing absent evidence that the parents or students participated in or were directly exposed to the voting and invocations.

In two earlier cases, the Eleventh Circuit upheld student-initiated prayer in school settings. In Alabama, parents questioned a statute permitting non-sectarian, non-proselytizing student-initiated prayer at school-related assemblies, sporting events, graduation ceremonies, and other school events. According to the court, the board's allowing genuinely student-initiated religious speech in school and at school-related events did not violate the Establishment Clause and had to be permitted as a form of free speech. The court acknowledged that while the students' religious speech could not be state supervised, it was subject to time, manner, and place restrictions.[165] On remand after the Supreme Court summarily vacated its judgment, the Eleventh Circuit responded that the injunction, which prevented the board from permitting any prayer in a public context at

---

162. The endorsement test, which asks whether the purpose of a governmental action is to endorse or approve of a religion or religious activity, first arose in *Lynch v. Donnelly*, 465 U.S. 668, 687, 104 S.Ct. 1355, 1366, 79 L.Ed.2d 604 (1984) (O'Connor, J., concurring).

163. *Ward v. Santa Fe Indep. School Dist.*, 393 F.3d 599 [194 Educ. L. Rep. 488] (5th Cir.2004).

164. *Does 1–7 v. Round Rock Indep. School Dist.*, 540 F.Supp.2d 735 [231 Educ. L. Rep. 235] (W.D.Tex.2007).

165. *Chandler v. James*, 180 F.3d 1254 [136 Educ. L. Rep. 201] (11th Cir.1999), *request for en banc reh'g denied*, 198 F.3d 265 (11th Cir.1999), *cert. granted, judgment vacated and remanded sub nom. Chandler v. Siegelman*, 530 U.S. 1256, 120 S.Ct. 2714, 147 L.Ed.2d 979 [146 Educ. L. Rep. 622] (2000).

school functions, was over-broad because it equated all student religious speech in public contexts at schools with speech supported by the state.[166] The court was of the opinion that officials cannot prohibit genuine student-initiated religious speech nor apply restrictions, on its time, place, and manner, which exceed those on secular speech.[167]

A superintendent in Florida issued a memorandum for high school graduation ceremonies in response to a request from students who wished to have some type of brief opening and/or closing messages by classmates. The guidelines afforded students the chance to direct their own messages without being monitored or reviewed by school officials. When speakers at ten of seventeen high school graduation ceremonies delivered some form of religious message, other students unsuccessfully challenged the practice as an establishment of religion and an infringement on their free exercise of religion. A federal trial court entered a judgment in favor of the board. On appeal, the Eleventh Circuit initially reversed in favor of the students[168] but was overruled by an en banc panel.[169] The Supreme Court vacated and remanded[170] for further consideration in light of *Santa Fe*. The Eleventh Circuit reinstated its original judgment since it was satisfied that the policy did not facially violate the Establishment Clause insofar as it had the secular purposes of not only affording graduating students the opportunity to direct their graduation ceremonies but also of permitting students the opportunity to exercise their freedom of expression.[171] In a case with the opposite result, the Ninth Circuit affirmed that educators did not violate a student's right to the free exercise of religion in requiring him to delete religious proselytizing comments from a commencement address.[172]

The Tenth Circuit affirmed that school officials in Colorado did not violate the First Amendment rights of a student in requiring her to make an e-mail apology to attendees at her graduation ceremony.[173] Officials disciplined the student for ignoring the principal's instructions by delivering a speech during the ceremony mentioning her Christian faith and encouraging listeners to explore Christianity before she could receive her diploma. The court held that educators did not impinge or burden the student's right to free exercise of religion because they had the authority to

---

166. *Chandler v. Siegelman*, 230 F.3d 1313 [148 Educ. L. Rep. 138] (11th Cir.2000), *suggestion for reh'g en banc denied, Chandler v. Siegelman*, 248 F.3d 1032 [153 Educ. L. Rep. 528] (11th Cir.2001).

167. *Cert. denied sub nom. Chandler ex rel. Chandler v. Siegelman*, 533 U.S. 916, 121 S.Ct. 2521, 150 L.Ed.2d 694 (2001).

168. *Adler v. Duval County School Bd.*, 174 F.3d 1236 [134 Educ. L. Rep. 790] (11th Cir.1999).

169. *Adler v. Duval County School Bd.*, 206 F.3d 1070 [142 Educ. L. Rep. 773] (11th Cir.2000).

170. *Adler v. Duval County School Bd.*, 531 U.S. 801, 121 S.Ct. 31, 148 L.Ed.2d 3 [148 Educ. L. Rep. 31] (2000).

171. *On remand, opinion reinstated, Adler v. Duval County School Bd.*, 250 F.3d 1330 [154 Educ. L. Rep. 80] (11th Cir.2001), *cert. denied*, 534 U.S. 1065, 122 S.Ct. 664, 151 L.Ed.2d 579 (2001).

172. *Lassonde v. Pleasanton Unified School Dist.*, 320 F.3d 979 [173 Educ. L. Rep. 778] (9th Cir.2003).

173. *Corder v. Lewis Palmer School Dist. No. 38*, 566 F.3d 1219 [244 Educ. L. Rep. 994] (10th Cir. 2009), *cert. denied*, ___ U.S. ___, 130 S.Ct. 742, 175 L.Ed.2d 515 [252 Educ. L. Rep. 26] (2009).

regulate school sponsored speech. The court also rejected the student's claim that her having had to apologize was compelled speech because their actions were related to the legitimate pedagogical concern of learning to respect school rules, courtesy, and discipline.

On the other hand, a divided Supreme Court of Montana ruled that educational officials violated the First Amendment free speech, but not religious, rights of a former student when they sought to limit the content of her proposed valedictory speech because they opposed her references to religion in her prepared remarks.[174] Reversing an earlier judgment to the contrary, the court held both that the student's appeal was not moot even though she graduated and that her passing references to God and Christ could not reasonably have interpreted as the school board's having endorsed her beliefs.

Employee and Board Prayer

In a variation on the prayer at football games theme, the Third Circuit held that a school board policy prohibiting a coach in New Jersey from participating in student-initiated team prayer was not constitutionally vague or over-broad and that his bowing his head and kneeling with his team while the athletes prayed violated the Establishment Clause.[175] The court decreed that insofar as the coach's actions during the prayers did not address a matter of public concern, they failed to trigger his rights to freedom of speech, academic freedom, freedom of association, or due process.

A second case involving employees' prayer was litigated in Michigan with the Seventh Circuit affirming that a school board did not violate the First Amendment rights of a guidance counselor who prayed with students, advocated abstinence, and disapproved of contraception when it chose not to renew her contract.[176] The court explained that in not renewing the counselor's employment contract due to her behavior, rather than her Christian beliefs, the board was within its rights in limiting her actions since she lacked the ability to offer uncontrolled expressions that varied from established curricular content.

In an older case from Indiana, the Seventh Circuit affirmed that pursuant to a board policy that officials consistently applied to prohibit the use of school facilities for religious activity, teachers lacked a right to conduct regularly scheduled prayer meetings for themselves before students arrived for class.[177] The court emphasized the board's concern that

---

174. *Griffith v. Butte School Dist. No. 1*, 244 P.3d 321 [262 Educ. L. Rep. 1019] (Mont. 2010).

175. *Borden v. School Dist. of Twp. of E. Brunswick*, 523 F.3d 153 [231 Educ. L. Rep. 583] (3d Cir.2008), *cert. denied*, 555 U.S. 1212, 129 S.Ct. 1524, 173 L.Ed.2d 656 [242 Educ. L. Rep. 21] (2009).

176. *Grossman v. South Shore Pub. School Dist.*, 507 F.3d 1097 [227 Educ. L. Rep. 109] (7th Cir.2007).

177. *May v. Evansville–Vanderburgh School Corp.*, 787 F.2d 1105 [31 Educ. L. Rep. 727] (7th Cir.1986).

permitting such meetings to take place could have caused controversies that were not related to work.

Three federal circuits agreed that prayer at school board meetings is unconstitutional. In a case from Delaware, the Third Circuit held that the legislative prayer exception enunciated by the Supreme Court in *Marsh v. Chambers*,[178] had the primary effect of advancing religion and the disputed policy excessively entangled the board with religion.[179] Earlier, a teacher in Ohio sued his board for opening its sessions in such a manner. The Sixth Circuit invalidated the practice as unconstitutional since students were often involved in the meetings and hearings in a variety of settings.[180] The court refused to treat the meetings as being subject to the legislative prayer exception because they were an integral component of the public school system. In a similar dispute from California, the Ninth Circuit found that teachers had standing to sue and that their school board violated the Establishment Clause by allowing prayers "in the name of Jesus" at its meetings.[181] However, in a long running case from Louisiana, a federal trial court denied cross-motions for summary judgment on the status of board prayer since issues of fact remained over whether the policy justifying it was valid within the parameters of the legislative exemption.[182]

A novel question arose in Nebraska where a school board member recited the Lord's Prayer at a commencement ceremony. Under the threat of litigation, the board dropped the proposed invocation and benediction from the ceremony. Even so, the board member, acting on his own initiative, included the prayer as part of his remarks. A divided Eighth Circuit affirmed that the board was not liable since the individual who recited the prayer did so on his own accord in opposition to the board's collectively refusing to include it in the ceremony.[183]

At issue in Arkansas was whether school officials could start mandatory in-service training sessions and faculty meetings with prayer. In response to a challenge by a teacher and a part-time bus driver who objected to the prayers, the Eighth Circuit affirmed that the practice violated the Establishment Clause since it constituted government endorsement of religion.[184]

---

178. 463 U.S. 783, 103 S.Ct. 3330, 77 L.Ed.2d 1019 (1983) (permitting prayer at the start of legislative sessions in Nebraska).

179. *Doe v. Indian River School Dist.*, 653 F.3d 256 [272 Educ. L. Rep. 44] (3d Cir. 2011).

180. *Coles ex rel. Coles v. Cleveland Bd. of Educ.*, 171 F.3d 369 [133 Educ. L. Rep. 392] (6th Cir.1999), *petition for reh'g en banc denied*, 183 F.3d 538 (6th Cir.1999).

181. *Bacus v. Palo Verde Unified School Dist. Bd. of Educ.*, 52 Fed.Appx. 355 [172 Educ. L. Rep. 24] (9th Cir.2002).

182. *Doe v. Tangipahoa Parish School Bd.*, 631 F. Supp.2d 823 [248 Educ. L. Rep. 151] (E.D. La. 2009). For the earlier litigation, *see Doe v. Tangipahoa Parish School Bd.*, 473 F.3d 188 [215 Educ. L. Rep. 539] (5th Cir.2006).

183. *Doe ex rel. Doe v. School Dist. of the City of Norfolk*, 340 F.3d 605 [180 Educ. L. Rep. 39] (8th Cir.2003).

184. *Warnock v. Archer*, 380 F.3d 1076 [191 Educ. L. Rep. 620] (8th Cir.2004), *reh'g and reh'g en banc denied, on remand*, 397 F.3d 1024 (8th Cir.2005).

PERIODS OF SILENCE

Lower federal courts disagreed on whether brief periods of silence before the start of school involves religion. The federal trial court in Massachusetts dismissed a challenge to such a law, interpreting it as neither having violated the First Amendment nor the students' right to free exercise of religion.[185] The court thought that the law did not prohibit or inhibit the parental right to guide and instruct their children with regard to religion. Moreover, after a federal trial court in Tennessee struck down such a statute, the Sixth Circuit vacated and remanded its judgment.[186] Shortly thereafter, the federal trial court in New Mexico invalidated a law authorizing local boards to permit a moment of silence because it lacked a secular purpose.[187]

In its first case on the merits of such a dispute, the Supreme Court reviewed a law from Alabama authorizing a period of silence at the start of the school day for "meditation or voluntary prayer." In *Wallace v. Jaffree*[188] the Court examined the bill's legislative history, including the purpose of the sponsors to return voluntary prayer to the public schools and its preamble, concluding that it lacked a secular purpose. Subsequently, after lower federal courts struck down a statute from New Jersey as unconstitutional, the Court dismissed an appeal without reaching the issue on the merits.[189] The Court ruled that the former speaker of the state general assembly and former president of the state senate who intervened in and took part in the litigation to uphold the law's constitutionality could no longer participate in the suit since they lacked standing by virtue of having lost their leadership positions.

Four circuit courts upheld statutes permitting silence in schools. The Eleventh Circuit affirmed that a statute from Georgia allowing a moment of silent reflection in school was constitutional since it passed all three prongs of the *Lemon* test.[190] The Fourth Circuit upheld a law from Virginia mandating a minute of silence in schools including the word "pray" in listing an unlimited range of permissible mental activities.[191] The court affirmed that the statute did not violate the Establishment Clause because even though it had two purposes, one clearly secular and the other an accommodation of religion, it did not run afoul of the *Lemon* test's requirement of only a secular purpose. The court reasoned that the statute neither advanced nor hindered religion and did not result in the state's

---

185. *Gaines v. Anderson*, 421 F.Supp. 337 (D.Mass.1976). *See also Opinion of the Justices*, 108 N.H. 97, 228 A.2d 161 (1967) (holding that a law requiring a period of silence for meditation did not violate the First Amendment).

186. *Beck v. McElrath*, 548 F.Supp. 1161 [7 Educ. L. Rep. 156] (M.D.Tenn.1982), *judgment vacated, appeal dismissed sub nom. Beck v. Alexander*, 718 F.2d 1098 (6th Cir.1983).

187. *Duffy v. Las Cruces Pub. Schools*, 557 F.Supp. 1013 [9 Educ. L. Rep. 1206] (D.N.M. 1983).

188. 472 U.S. 38, 105 S.Ct. 2479, 86 L.Ed.2d 29 [25 Educ. L. Rep. 39] (1985).

189. *Jurisdiction dismissed sub nom. Karcher v. May*, 479 U.S. 1062, 107 S.Ct. 946, 93 L.Ed.2d 995 [38 Educ. L. Rep. 416] (1987), *appeal dismissed*, 484 U.S. 72, 108 S.Ct. 388, 98 L.Ed.2d 327 [42 Educ. L. Rep. 1062] (1987).

190. *Bown v. Gwinnett County School Dist.*, 112 F.3d 1464 [118 Educ. L. Rep. 28] (11th Cir.1997).

191. *Brown v. Gilmore*, 258 F.3d 265 [155 Educ. L. Rep. 1031] (4th Cir.2001), *cert. denied*, 533 U.S. 1301, 122 S.Ct. 1, 150 L.Ed.2d 782 (2001).

becoming excessively entangled with religion. The Fifth Circuit reached a like result in a case from Texas, affirming that a law calling for a minute of silence following the recitation of the Pledge of Allegiance during which students may, if they choose, reflect, pray, meditate, or engage in any other silent activity that is unlikely to interfere with or distract others was constitutional because it satisfied all three prongs of the *Lemon* test.[192] Subsequently, the Seventh Circuit reversed an earlier order to the contrary in upholding the Illinois Silent Reflection and Student Prayer Act.[193] The court ruled both that the law was neither unconstitutionally vague nor did it advance or inhibit religion.

STUDENT-INITIATED RELIGIOUS ACTIVITY

In an early dispute, the Supreme Court chose not to review a case that upheld a school board's refusal to allow students to conduct voluntary communal prayer meetings in school immediately before the start of the academic day.[194] Previously, the Second Circuit viewed such a prohibition as not infringing on students' rights to the free exercise of religion, speech, or equal protection since educational officials had a compelling interest to remove any indication of their sponsoring religious activities in public schools.

A week before it chose not to hear an appeal in the case in the preceding paragraph, in *Widmar v. Vincent (Widmar)*,[195] the Supreme Court determined that when officials at a state university in Missouri made its facilities generally available for activities of registered student groups, they could not close them to other groups based on the religious content of their speech. Relying on the framework of freedom of speech, the Justices recognized that insofar as over one hundred registered student groups used the facilities, officials created a forum for the exchange of ideas and thus could not bar access to it solely because of the content of the speech. The Court expressly distinguished the case from those involving religious activities in public grade schools, observing that facilities in those settings are generally not used as open fora while university students are less impressionable than young children.

The Supreme Court next refused to review a case from Texas wherein the Fifth Circuit invalidated a board policy of permitting students to gather at a school with supervision for voluntary religious meetings close to the beginning or end of the day.[196] The court wrote that the policy implied recognition of religious activities and meetings as an integral part of a school's extracurricular program along with implicit approval of educational officials.

---

192. *Croft v. Governor of Texas*, 562 F.3d 735 [243 Educ. L. Rep.550] (5th Cir. 2009).

193. *Sherman ex rel. Sherman v. Koch*, 623 F.3d 501 [261 Educ. L. Rep. 527] (7th Cir. 2010), *cert. denied*, ___ U.S. ___, 132 S.Ct. 92, 181 L.Ed.2d 22 (2011).

194. *Brandon v. Board of Educ. of Guilderland Cent. School Dist.*, 635 F.2d 971 (2d Cir.1980), *cert. denied*, 454 U.S. 1123, 102 S.Ct. 970, 71 L.Ed.2d 109 (1981).

195. 454 U.S. 263, 102 S.Ct. 269, 70 L.Ed.2d 440 [1 Educ. L. Rep. 13] (1981).

196. *Lubbock Civil Liberties Union v. Lubbock Indep. School Dist.*, 669 F.2d 1038 [2 Educ. L. Rep. 961] (5th Cir.1982), *cert. denied*, 459 U.S. 1155, 103 S.Ct. 800, 74 L.Ed.2d 1003 (1983).

Spurred on in large part by *Widmar*, in 1984 Congress enacted the Equal Access Act.[197] The Act mandates that officials in public secondary schools receiving federal financial assistance and permitting non-curriculum related student groups to meet during non-instructional time cannot deny access to groups due to the religious, political, philosophical, or other content of their speech. The Act allows officials to exclude groups if their meetings materially and substantially interfere with the orderly conduct of school activities.

The Supreme Court upheld the Equal Access Act in *Board of Education of Westside Community Schools v. Mergens (Mergens)*.[198] Relying on statutory interpretation, the Court decided that Congress maintained that most high school students could recognize that allowing a religious club to function in school does not imply the endorsement of religion. Since Congress did not define "non-curriculum related," the Court thought it necessary to do so in order to evaluate the status of some student groups. The Court observed that insofar as a variety of existing clubs failed to satisfy the criteria, the religious group was entitled to meet in school. Insofar as only four Justices agreed that the Equal Access Act passed Establishment Clause muster, the Court left the door open to more litigation in a line of cases that treat religious expression as a hybrid that protects the rights of religious groups to express their opinions as a form of free speech.[199]

Circuit courts have extended the scope of the Equal Access Act to allow students to select leaders who comply with a club's religious standards;[200] to meet during lunch time[201] and during a school's morning activity period at which attendance was taken;[202] to have access to funding and fund-raising activities, a school yearbook, public address system, bulletin board, school supplies, school vehicles, and audio-visual equipment;[203] and to broadcast a video promoting the club during morning announcements.[204]

At least one court rejected the claim that a school board created a limited open forum designed to permit members of a religious club to make announcements involving prayers and Bible readings before classes on a school's public address system; the court did permit voluntary student prayer before school to continue.[205] After the Ninth Circuit initially upheld

---

197.   20 U.S.C.A. §§ 4071 *et seq.* This statute is in the Appendix.

198.   496 U.S. 226, 110 S.Ct. 2356, 110 L.Ed.2d 191 [60 Educ. L. Rep. 320] (1990). [Case No. 9]

199.   *See, e.g., Rosenberger v. Rector and Visitors of Univ. of Va.*, 515 U.S. 819, 115 S.Ct. 2510, 132 L.Ed.2d 700 [101 Educ. L. Rep. 552] (1995).

200.   *Hsu v. Roslyn Union Free School Dist.*, 85 F.3d 839 [109 Educ. L. Rep. 1145] (2d Cir.1996), *cert. denied*, 519 U.S. 1040, 117 S.Ct. 608, 136 L.Ed.2d 534 (1996).

201.   *Ceniceros v. Board of Trustees of the San Diego Unified School Dist.*, 106 F.3d 878 [116 Educ. L. Rep. 82] (9th Cir.1997).

202.   *Donovan ex rel. Donovan v. Punxsutawney Area School Bd.*, 336 F.3d 211 [179 Educ. L. Rep. 48] (3d Cir.2003).

203.   *Prince v. Jacoby*, 303 F.3d 1074 [169 Educ. L. Rep. 85] (9th Cir.2002), *cert. denied*, 540 U.S. 813, 124 S.Ct. 62, 157 L.Ed.2d 27 (2003).

204.   *Krestan v. Deer Valley Unified School District No. 97, of Maricopa County*, 561 F.Supp.2d 1078 [235 Educ. L. Rep. 361] (D.Ariz.2008).

205.   *Herdahl v. Pontotoc County School Dist.*, 933 F.Supp. 582 [112 Educ. L. Rep. 131] (N.D.Miss.1996).

the board's refusal to recognize a club in light of its proposed requirement that voting members express their faith in the Bible and in Jesus Christ because officials feared that it violated the district's non-discrimination policies,[206] an en banc panel reversed in favor of the organizers.[207] The court found that although the board did not violate either the Equal Access Act or the club's First Amendment rights by applying its non-discrimination policy to the disputed provision, a question of fact was present as to whether educators acted appropriately in refusing to grant the club an exemption from the policy based on its Christian character or the content of the speech of its members.

In an unanticipated application of the Equal Access Act, the Eighth Circuit,[208] along with federal trial courts in Indiana,[209] Florida,[210] and Kentucky,[211] agreed that school officials could not deny Gay/Straight Alliance clubs the opportunity to use school facilities. Federal trial courts in Texas[212] and Colorado[213] reached the opposite result. Since these cases did not involve religion, they are discussed in Chapter 14.

The status of the Equal Access Act may be in some doubt in light of the Supreme Court's analysis in *Christian Legal Society v. Martinez.*[214] The Court affirmed that officials at a public law school in California had the authority to implement a policy requiring an on-campus religious group to admit all-comers from the student body, including those who disagree with its beliefs, as a condition of becoming a recognized student organization. On remand, the Ninth Circuit rejected the group's remaining claim on the basis that organizational leaders failed to preserve their argument that law school officials selectively applied the policy for appeal.[215]

ACCESS TO SCHOOL FACILITIES BY NON-SCHOOL RELIGIOUS GROUPS

A controversy in New York arose when a school board, acting pursuant to a state statute, enacted a policy that permitted it to make its facilities

---

206. *Truth v. Kent School Dist.*, 499 F.3d 999 [224 Educ. L. Rep. 652] (9th Cir.2007).

207. *Truth v. Kent School Dist.*, 524 F.3d 957 [232 Educ. L. Rep. 70] (9th Cir.2008).

208. *Straights and Gays for Equality v. Osseo Area Schools–Dist. No. 279*, 540 F.3d 911 [236 Educ. L. Rep. 173] (8th Cir.2008).

209. Gay–Straight Alliance of Yulee High Sch. v. School Bd. of Nassau County, 602 F. Supp.2d 1233 [243 Educ. L. Rep.301] (M.D. Fla. 2009); *Franklin Central Gay/Straight Alliance v. Franklin Twp. Community School Corp.*, 2002 WL 32097530 (S.D.Ind.2002), *reconsideration denied*, 2002 WL 31921332 (S.D.Ind.2002).

210. *Gonzalez v. School Bd. of Okeechobee County*, 571 F.Supp.2d 1257 [237 Educ. L. Rep. 291] (S.D.Fla.2008).

211. *Boyd County High School Gay Straight Alliance v. Board of Educ. of Boyd County, Ky.*, 258 F.Supp.2d 667 [177 Educ. L. Rep. 211] (E.D.Ky.2003). This case spawned litigation in which a student unsuccessfully sought to be excluded from diversity training which focused on diversity and equity issues including discussion of anti-gay harassment. *See Morrison v. Board of Educ. of Boyd County*, 521 F.3d 602 [231 Educ. L. Rep. 527] (6th Cir.2008), *cert. denied*, 555 U.S 1171, 129 S.Ct. 1318, 173 L.Ed.2d 586, [242 Educ. L. Rep. 20] (2009).

212. *Caudillo v. Lubbock Indep. School Dist.*, 311 F.Supp.2d 550 [187 Educ. L. Rep. 564] (N.D.Tex.2004).

213. *Palmer High School Gay/Straight Alliance v. Colorado Springs School Dist. No. 11*, 2005 WL 3244049 (D.Colo.2005).

214. ___ U.S. ___, 130 S.Ct. 2971, 177 L.Ed.2d 838 (2010).

215. *Christian Legal Soc'y v. Wu*, 626 F.3d 483 [262 Educ. L. Rep. 398] (9th Cir. 2010).

available to an array of social and civic groups. When the board refused to rent a facility to a religious group which sought to show a film series on child-rearing, lower courts ruled in its favor.[216]

On appeal, in a rare unanimous judgment in *Lamb's Chapel v. Center Moriches Union Free School District (Lamb's Chapel)*,[217] the Supreme Court reversed in favor of the religious group. In a hybrid situation wherein it treated religious speech as a form of free speech, the Justices essentially extended *Mergens'* rationale. The Court ruled that in light of the board's having created a limited open forum, it violated the free speech rights of the group by engaging in viewpoint discrimination.

Eight years later, a dispute erupted when officials in another school system in New York refused to permit a non-school-sponsored club to meet during non-class hours so that members and moderators could discuss child-rearing along with character and moral development from a religious perspective. While forbidding the religious club from meeting, officials allowed three other groups to gather because although they addressed related topics, they did so from secular perspectives. On further review of orders in favor of the board,[218] the Supreme Court agreed to hear an appeal to resolve a split in the lower courts since the Eighth Circuit[219] had upheld the right of the same kind of club in Missouri to use school facilities for its meetings.[220]

In *Good News Club v. Milford Central School (Milford)*,[221] the Supreme Court reversed in favor of the club. The Court reasoned not only that the board violated the Club's rights to free speech by engaging in impermissible viewpoint discrimination when it refused to permit it to use school facilities for its meetings, which were not worship services, but also that such a restriction was not justified by fears of violating the Establishment Clause.

The Second Circuit, in a long-running dispute in New York City,[222] held that forbidding religious worship services from taking place in public school facilities was a content-based exclusion. The court was satisfied that the policy did not constitute viewpoint discrimination but was an acceptable content-based exclusion in light of the board's reasonable concern that

---

216. *Lamb's Chapel v. Center Moriches Union Free School Dist.*, 770 F.Supp. 91 [69 Educ. L. Rep. 787] (E.D.N.Y.1991), *aff'd*, 959 F.2d 381 [73 Educ. L. Rep. 915] (2d Cir.1992).

217. 508 U.S. 384, 113 S.Ct. 2141, 124 L.Ed.2d 352 [83 Educ. L. Rep. 30] (1993), *on remand*, 17 F.3d 1425 [89 Educ. L. Rep. 783] (2d Cir.1994). [Case No. 37]

218. 21 F.Supp.2d 147 [130 Educ. L. Rep. 678] (N.D.N.Y.1998), *aff'd*, 202 F.3d 502 [141 Educ. L. Rep. 475] (2d Cir.2000).

219. *Good News/Good Sports Club v. School Dist. of the City of Ladue*, 28 F.3d 1501 [92 Educ. L. Rep. 1148] (8th Cir.1994), *cert. denied*, 515 U.S. 1173, 115 S.Ct. 2640, 132 L.Ed.2d 878 (1995).

220. *See also Daugherty v. Vanguard Charter School Acad.*, 116 F.Supp.2d 897 [148 Educ. L. Rep. 208] (W.D.Mich.2000) (permitting a "Moms' Prayer Group" to use a Parents' Room for ninety minutes once a week since other groups were allowed to do so).

221. 533 U.S. 98, 121 S.Ct. 2093, 150 L.Ed.2d 151 [154 Educ. L. Rep. 45] (2001). [Case No. 13]

222. For the first reported case in this litigation, *see Bronx Household of Faith v. Community School Dist. No. 10*, 127 F.3d 207 [121 Educ. L. Rep. 892] (2d Cir.1997), *cert. denied sub nom. Bronx Household of Faith v. Board of Educ. of City of N.Y.*, 523 U.S. 1074, 118 S.Ct. 1517, 140 L.Ed.2d 670 (1998), *leave to file for reh'g denied*, 524 U.S. 934, 118 S.Ct. 2337, 141 L.Ed.2d 708 (1998).

permitting the services to occur would have violated the Establishment Clause.[223]

A case involving a teacher and a Good News Club arose in South Dakota. The Eighth Circuit affirmed that school officials violated the teacher's free speech rights by refusing to allow her to join after school meetings of a Good News Club. The court reversed an earlier order allowing the teacher to meet with the club only at schools other than where she taught. Viewing the teacher's after-school activity as private speech, the court explained that her involvement did not put the board at risk of violating the Establishment Clause.[224]

In a case with a different take on the issue of access, an atheist mother unsuccessfully challenged a school board's policy of allowing the Boy Scouts to make in-school membership presentations during lunch breaks pursuant to a community access policy. The mother alleged that permitting the Scouts to seek members violated a state law against discrimination based on religion in public schools in light of their belief in a deity. The Supreme Court of Oregon, in finding that the policy allowing the Scouts to make the presentations did not violate the law because they neither differentiated among students nor mentioned religion in their talks, remanded for further consideration in light of its analysis.[225]

On a related topic, courts agree that if school boards permit their facilities to be made available to non-profit organizations, they may not charge higher fees to religious groups. The Fourth Circuit posited that a board regulation in Virginia, which allowed officials to charge churches an escalating rate for the use of facilities, discriminated both against religious speech and interfered with or burdened the church's right to speak and practice its religion.[226]

Another aspect of access emerged in Tennessee when a federal trial court invalidated the practice of allowing a group called "Praying Parents" to use a school's newsletter to engage in such practices as communicating with teachers and other parents, gathering to pray around the school's flagpole, and having a National Day of Prayer in the cafeteria.[227] In response to a claim from objecting parents, the court was satisfied both that they had standing and that issues of fact existed as to whether officials

---

223. *Bronx Household of Faith v. Board of Educ. of City of New York*, 650 F.3d 30 (2d Cir.2011), *cert. denied*, ___ U.S. ___, 132 S.Ct. 816, ___ L.Ed.2d ___ (2011).

224. *Wigg v. Sioux Falls School Dist. 49–5*, 382 F.3d 807 [192 Educ. L. Rep. 15] (8th Cir.2004), *reh'g and reh'g en banc denied* (2004).

225. *Powell v. Bunn*, 142 P.3d 1054 [212 Educ. L. Rep. 893] (Or.2006).

226. *Fairfax Covenant Church v. Fairfax County School Bd.*, 17 F.3d 703 [89 Educ. L. Rep. 763] (4th Cir.1994), *cert. denied*, 511 U.S. 1143, 114 S.Ct. 2166, 128 L.Ed.2d 888 (1994). *See also Shumway v. Albany County School Dist. No. One Bd. of Educ.*, 826 F.Supp. 1320 [84 Educ. L. Rep. 989] (D.Wyo.1993).

227. *Doe v. Wilson County School Sys.*, 524 F.Supp.2d 964 [228 Educ. L. Rep. 231] (M.D.Tenn.2007). *See also Doe v. Wilson County School* Sys., 564 F.Supp.2d 766 [236 Educ. L. Rep. 306] (M.D.Tenn.2008) (adding that although the activities of the parental group violated all three prongs of the *Lemon* test, the board was not liable because it was unaware of the constitutional violations since the parents and the school's principal failed to follow the policies as written).

violated the Establishment Clause.[228] The same court later invalidated a board policy designed to limit the parent group from placing religious posters in the school lobby and hallway leading to the cafeteria.[229] The court explained that once the board created a limited open forum, it could not restrict the content of parental speech.

OTHER RELIGIOUS INFLUENCES

RELIGIOUS MUSIC

Controversy has arisen over the use of religious music, especially at graduation ceremonies. In a dispute from Utah, the Tenth Circuit affirmed the dismissal of a student's complaint that officials violated her rights under the Establishment and Free Exercise Clauses by permitting her school's choir to sing Christian religious music, including the song, "The Lord Bless You and Keep You."[230] Previously, the Fifth Circuit ruled that permitting a school choir to adopt the same song as its theme song did not violate the Establishment Clause since there were legitimate secular reasons for doing so because it was useful to teach students to sight read and sing a cappella; the practice did not advance or endorse religion; and not permitting the choir to adopt the song would have demonstrated hostility rather than neutrality toward religion.[231]

On the other hand, the Ninth Circuit affirmed that a superintendent in Washington did not violate a high school student's rights to freedom of religion or speech in prohibiting her wind ensemble from performing an instrumental version of *Ave Maria* at her graduation due to concerns that it could have been interpreted as endorsing religion.[232] Similarly, the Third Circuit affirmed the rejection of a father's claim that a board policy in New Jersey forbidding the use of religious music in holiday celebrations was unconstitutional because it reflected the impermissible message of governmental disapproval of and hostility toward religion.[233] Earlier, a federal trial court in Florida enjoined the playing of a country music song about

---

228. *See also Doe v. Wilson County School Sys.*, 2008 WL 4372959 (M.D. Tenn. 2008) (while conceding that the plaintiffs were the prevailing party, the court reduced their award for attorney fees to $100,221.24 since they did not succeed on all of their claims).

229. *Gold v. Wilson County School Bd. of Educ.*, 632 F.Supp. 771 [248 Educ. L. Rep. 190] (M.D. Tenn. 2009).

230. *Bauchman v. West High School*, 132 F.3d 542 [122 Educ. L. Rep. 1133] (10th Cir.1997), *cert. denied*, 524 U.S. 953, 118 S.Ct. 2370, 141 L.Ed.2d 738 (1998).

231. *Doe v. Duncanville Indep. School Dist.*, 70 F.3d 402 [104 Educ. L. Rep. 1032] (5th Cir.1995).

232. *Nurre v. Whitehead*, 580 F.3d 1087 [249 Educ. L. Rep. 76] (9th Cir. 2009), *cert. denied*, ___ U.S. ___, 130 S.Ct. 1937, 176 L.Ed.2d 399 (2010).

233. *Stratechuk v. Board of Educ., South Orange–Maplewood School Dist.*, 587 F.3d 597 [250 Educ. L. Rep. 907] (3d Cir. 2009), *cert. denied*, ___ U.S. ___, 131 S.Ct. 72, 178 L.Ed.2d 24 (2010).

God in America where doing so would have violated the Establishment Clause.[234]

FLAG SALUTE—PLEDGE OF ALLEGIANCE

Amid controversy over the constitutionality of requiring students to salute the American flag and recite the Pledge of Allegiance, a practice tracing its origins to 1892, the Supreme Court initially chose not to address the question on its merits in *Johnson v. Town of Deerfield*,[235] summarily affirming an order refusing to enjoin a statute from Massachusetts directing students to recite the pledge. A year later, in *Minersville School District v. Gobitis (Gobitis)*,[236] the Court rejected the claim of Jehovah's Witnesses in Pennsylvania who argued that requiring their young to salute the flag was equivalent to forcing them to worship an image contrary to their core religious beliefs. The Court concluded that the students had to participate in the pledge.

In the face of significant criticism of *Gobitis*, the Supreme Court revisited the question of the pledge when Jehovah's Witnesses and others challenged the constitutionality of a state regulation requiring students to participate or risk being charged with insubordination and expulsion. As in *Gobitis*, the Jehovah's Witnesses argued that the pledge violated their rights to religious freedom. In *West Virginia State Board of Education v. Barnette (Barnette)*,[237] the Justices, torn between the conflict over the limits of state power and individual rights, ruled that students could not be compelled to salute the flag. The Court was convinced that requiring children to salute the flag exceeded constitutional limits on governmental power because doing so invaded the individual's sphere of intellect and spirit that is protected by the First Amendment.

Almost a quarter of a century later, the Supreme Court of New Jersey addressed whether Black Muslim children who refused to participate in the pledge could be excluded from public school when they claimed that doing so violated their religious beliefs.[238] Educators excluded the students in light of their contention that the beliefs were motivated as much by politics as by religion, rejecting their claim of "conscientious scruples" since the two were closely intertwined with their racial aspirations. Although not resolving whether the students' refusal to salute the flag was religious or political, the court ordered their reinstatement in pointing out that they stood respectfully at attention during the pledge and were not disruptive.

---

234. *S.D. v. St. Johns County School Dist.*, 632 F. Supp.2d 1085 [248 Educ. L Rep. 215] (M.D. Fla. 2009).

235. 25 F.Supp. 918 (D.Mass.1939) (refusing to enjoin a statute requiring students to recite the pledge), *aff'd*, 306 U.S. 621, 59 S.Ct. 791, 83 L.Ed. 1027 (1939), *reh'g denied*, 307 U.S. 650, 59 S.Ct. 832, 83 L.Ed. 1529 (1939). *See also Leoles v. Landers*, 192 S.E. 218 (Ga.1937), *appeal dismissed*, 302 U.S. 656, 58 S.Ct. 364, 82 L.Ed. 507 (1937); *Gabrielli v. Knickerbocker*, 82 P.2d 391 (Cal.1938), *appeal dismissed, cert. denied*, 306 U.S. 621, 59 S.Ct. 786, 83 L.Ed. 1026 (1939).

236. 310 U.S. 586, 60 S.Ct. 1010, 84 L.Ed. 1375 (1940).

237. 319 U.S. 624, 63 S.Ct. 1178, 87 L.Ed. 1628 (1943).

238. *Holden v. Board of Educ., Elizabeth*, 216 A.2d 387 (N.J.1966).

Maryland's high court[239] and the Fifth Circuit,[240] in a case from Florida, struck down requirements that would have had students who objected to the flag salute stand while their classmates recited the pledge. In neither of these cases had school officials offered students the option of leaving their rooms. Even where students had the option of either leaving a room or standing silently during the pledge, the Second Circuit held that school officials in New York could not discipline a child who remained quietly seated.[241] The court declared that forcing students to stand could no more be required than the pledge and that having individuals leave rooms during its recitation might have been viewed as a punishment for not participating. The court emphasized that there was no evidence that the student was disruptive or interfered with the rights of others.

Another dispute from New York involved the rights of a nine-year-old with a disability who refused to stand during the pledge. While not reaching the merits of the claim, a federal trial court refused to grant the school board's motion for summary judgment over whether the child was punished for refusing to participate in the pledge.[242] Moreover, a former high school student in Alabama sued his principal and others for violating his rights to free speech for punishing him since he raised his fist during the recitation of the pledge. The student was given a choice of a paddling or a detention which would have delayed his receiving his diploma at graduation. On further review of a grant of summary judgment in favor of school officials, the Eleventh Circuit reversed and remanded.[243] According to the court, since genuine issues of material fact remained over whether the student was punished for failing to say the pledge, in violation of his clearly established right to be free from compelled speech, his case should not have been dismissed.

In a controversy over the inclusion of the words "under God" in the pledge, which we added in 1954 when President Eisenhower signed a law making the addition official,[244] the Seventh Circuit affirmed that school officials in Illinois could lead the pledge, including the contested phrase, as long as students were free not to participate.[245] The court interpreted the use of the phrase in the context of the secular vow of allegiance as patriotic or ceremonial expression rather than religious speech. Conversely, after the Ninth Circuit affirmed that a school board in California violated the Establishment Clause by having students recite the words "under God" in the pledge,[246] the Supreme Court intervened. In *Elk Grove School District*

239. *State v. Lundquist*, 278 A.2d 263 (Md.1971).

240. *Banks v. Board of Public Instruction of Dade County*, 314 F.Supp. 285 (S.D.Fla.1970), aff'd, 450 F.2d 1103 (5th Cir.1971).

241. *Goetz v. Ansell*, 477 F.2d 636 (2d Cir.1973).

242. *Rabideau v. Beekmantown Cent. School Dist.*, 89 F.Supp.2d 263 [143 Educ. L. Rep. 202] (N.D.N.Y.2000).

243. *Holloman ex rel. Holloman v. Harland*, 370 F.3d 1252 [188 Educ. L. Rep. 620] (11th Cir.2004).

244. 4 U.S.C.A. § 4.

245. *Sherman v. Community Consol. School Dist. 21 of Wheeling Twp.*, 980 F.2d 437 [79 Educ. L. Rep. 396] (7th Cir.1992), *cert. denied*, 508 U.S. 950, 113 S.Ct. 2439, 124 L.Ed.2d 658 (1993).

246. *Newdow v. United States Congress*, 292 F.3d 597 [166 Educ. L. Rep. 108] (9th Cir.2002), 328 F.3d 466 [176 Educ. L. Rep. 44] (9th Cir.2003), *cert. granted sub nom. Elk*

v. Newdow *(Newdow),*[247] *the Court sidestepped the merits of the constitutionality of the words "under God," resolving the dispute on the ground that the non-custodial father lacked standing to challenge the policy, thereby leaving the door open for future litigation.*

The Third Circuit, in the first post-*Newdow* appellate case involving the pledge, affirmed that a statute from Pennsylvania, directing officials to provide for its recitation or the singing of the national anthem each morning and to notify the parents of students who declined or refrained from doing so, constituted viewpoint discrimination in violation of the First Amendment.[248] The court also indicated that requiring private schools to provide for recitation of the pledge or national anthem at the beginning of each school day violated their First Amendment right to freedom of expressive association.

In a dispute from Virginia that was put on hold in light of *Newdow,* the Fourth Circuit rejected the claim of a father who alleged that the daily recital of the pledge in school forced his children to worship a secular state. The court was satisfied that the voluntary daily recitation of the pledge did not violate the Establishment Clause since it did not have a religious purpose or effect and did not create excessive government entanglement with religion insofar as even though it is a religious statement, it is largely a patriotic expression.[249] At the same time, the court ruled that the non-attorney father could not litigate his *pro se* claim.[250] Within a month, a federal trial court in California, relying on the case from the Ninth Circuit that the Supreme Court vacated as moot in *Newdow,* granted the plaintiffs' request to prevent students from reciting the words "under God" in the pledge as a violation of the Establishment Clause.[251] On further review, the dispute was apparently laid to rest[252] when a divided Ninth Circuit upheld the pledge since neither state law nor the board policy required students to participate in its recitation.[253]

Grove Unified School Dist. v. Newdow, 540 U.S. 945, 124 S.Ct. 384, 157 L.Ed.2d 274 [182 Educ. L. Rep. 34] (2003).

247.   542 U.S. 1, 124 S.Ct. 2301, 159 L.Ed.2d 98 [188 Educ. L. Rep. 17] (2004), [Case No. 15] *reh'g denied,* 542 U.S. 961, 125 S.Ct. 21, 159 L.Ed.2d 851 (2004).

248.   *Circle Schools v. Pappert,* 381 F.3d 172 [191 Educ. L. Rep. 629] (3d Cir.2004).

249.   *Myers v. Loudoun County Pub. Schools,* 418 F.3d 395 [200 Educ. L. Rep. 581] (4th Cir.2005).

250.   In another dispute involving the same parent, a federal trial court in Virginia granted the school board's motion for summary judgment when officials refused to print an advertisement that he sought to include in an athletic program. The court agreed that the board could exclude the advertisement because the names of the Web sites that he sought to include in it in opposition to what he described as "civil religion" could be rejected as vulgar. *Myers v. Loudoun County School Bd.,* 500 F.Supp.2d 539 [223 Educ. L. Rep. 786] (E.D.Va.2007).

251.   *Newdow v. Congress of U.S.,* 383 F.Supp.2d 1229 [201 Educ. L. Rep. 915] (E.D.Cal. 2005).

252.   For another such case, *see Freedom from Religion Foundation v. Hanover School Dist.,* 665 F. Supp.2d 58 [252 Educ. L. Rep. 779] (D.N.H. 2009) (applying both the *Lemon* and coercion tests in upholding a state law requiring local school boards to set aside time for the daily recitation of the pledge).

253.   *Newdow v. Rio Linda Union School Dist.,* 597 F.3d 1007 [254 Educ. L. Rep. 544] (9th Cir. 2010).

At issue in Florida was a local board policy, enacted pursuant to a state law, requiring students to recite the pledge unless they were excused from doing so by the written consent of their parents. Even if students were excused, the law and board policy required them to stand at attention during the recitation of the pledge.[254] The court invalidated the statute both on its face and as applied. On further review, in distinguishing the case at bar from *Barnette*, the Eleventh Circuit reversed and upheld the law, describing it as "largely a parental-rights statute"[255] that, in requiring parents to be notified if their children do not participate in the pledge, effectuated their constitutional right to control the education of their children. The court did invalidate the part of the law requiring students to stand during the pledge.

STUDENT BELIEFS

In the nexus between student beliefs and curricular control, the courts generally upheld the actions of school officials if they are able to demonstrate their reliance on legitimate pedagogical reasons. For example, the Sixth Circuit affirmed that a student in Tennessee could not write a biography about Jesus as a historical figure since she failed to follow her teacher's directions in completing the assignment.[256] Previously, the same court agreed that officials in Michigan did not violate a second-grader's First Amendment rights to freedom of religion in preventing her from showing a videotape of herself singing a proselytizing religious song to classmates during show-and-tell.[257] The court maintained that educators had the legitimate pedagogical purpose of avoiding a situation where other children or their parents would have been offended by the song's religious content.

The Eleventh Circuit affirmed that a high school principal in Florida did not violate a student's First Amendment rights to free speech or free exercise of religion by requiring her to remove religious messages from a mural she painted as part of a school-wide beautification project.[258] The court ruled that insofar as the project was under the direction of a teacher, and officials had no intention of creating a public forum, they could regulate the content of the student's speech because it was part of a school-sponsored activity.

---

254. *Frazier v. Alexandre*, 434 F.Supp.2d 1350 [210 Educ. L. Rep. 1123] (S.D.Fla.2006).

255. *Frazier v. Winn*, 535 F.3d 1279 [235 Educ. L. Rep. 737] (11th Cir.2008), *reh'g en banc denied*, 555 F.3d 1292 (11th Cir. 2009), *cert. denied sub nom. Frazier v. Smith*, ___ U.S. ___, 130 S.Ct. 69, 175 L.Ed.2d 25 (2009).

256. *Settle v. Dickson County School Bd.*, 53 F.3d 152 [100 Educ. L. Rep. 32] (6th Cir.1995), *cert. denied*, 516 U.S. 989, 116 S.Ct. 518, 133 L.Ed.2d 426 (1995).

257. *DeNooyer v. Livonia Pub. Schools*, 799 F.Supp. 744 [77 Educ. L. Rep. 1182] (E.D.Mich.1992), *aff'd sub nom. Denooyer v. Merinelli*, 1 F.3d 1240 [85 Educ. L. Rep. 39] (6th Cir.1993), *reh'g denied, opinion superseded without published opinion*, 12 F.3d 211 [88 Educ. L. Rep. 551] (6th Cir.1993), *cert. denied*, 511 U.S. 1031, 114 S.Ct. 1540, 128 L.Ed.2d 193 (1994).

258. *Bannon v. School Dist. of Palm Beach County*, 387 F.3d 1208 [193 Educ. L. Rep. 78] (11th Cir.2004), *reh'g and reh'g en banc denied*, 125 Fed.Appx. 984 (11th Cir.2004), *cert. denied*, 546 U.S. 811, 126 S.Ct. 330, 163 L.Ed.2d 43 [202 Educ. L. Rep. 26] (2005).

In a dispute from Michigan, a student sued school officials after they refused to permit her to participate in a panel discussion involving clergy and religious leaders on homosexuality and religion because they disagreed with her message and sought to ensure that only one point of view was presented. The court found that officials violated the student's rights because they violated all three parts of the *Lemon* test.[259] The court thought that the panel lacked a secular purpose because it had an overtly religious character by virtue of its being made up of clergy and religious leaders, some of whom wore religious garb. The court wrote that insofar as the panel was created to communicate a religious perspective on homosexuality, it had the primary effect of advancing religion. The court concluded that the panel violated the Establishment Clause because school officials became excessively entangled with religion since they selected the clergy participants, vetted their views, afforded them the use of school facilities and a captive student audience, and censored the plaintiff's speech based on her religious beliefs.

Two federal appellate courts considered the religious expression rights of younger students. The Third Circuit affirmed that school officials in New Jersey could prohibit a first-grader from reading a religious story to classmates and from placing a religious poster on a school wall.[260] Still, the court permitted the plaintiffs to amend their complaint about the poster. In the second case, parents of a kindergarten child in New York filed suit after a teacher refused to display their son's entire poster. When directed to illustrate ways to save the environment, the child selected and cut out pictures from a magazine with the help of his mother, arranging them on a poster. In response to the teacher's question about who the man with outstretched arms was, he responded that it was Jesus, "the only way to save the world."[261] On being told that the poster was unacceptable due to "religious" reasons, the child and his mother created a second poster. The second poster also depicted a robed man but included people picking up and recycling trash along with children holding hands encircling the world. After a federal trial court granted the educators' motions for summary judgment, the Second Circuit reversed in favor of the parents on the free speech claim. The court reasoned that insofar as the assignment was curriculum related, the teacher could reject the child's work as unresponsive to the assignment. Even so, the court reversed in favor of the parents on the free speech claim because genuine issues of fact remained as to whether the reasons proffered by the educators for censoring the poster constituted viewpoint discrimination since they may not have excluded secular images that were equally non-responsive. The court affirmed that when officials folded the child's unresponsive poster before displaying it so that the robed religious figure was not visible, they did not violate the Establishment Clause.

---

259. *Hansen v. Ann Arbor Pub. Schools*, 293 F.Supp.2d 780 [183 Educ. L. Rep. 825] (E.D.Mich.2003).

260. *C.H. ex rel. Z.H. v. Oliva*, 226 F.3d 198 [148 Educ. L. Rep. 585] (3d Cir.2000), *cert. denied sub nom. Hood v. Medford Twp. Bd. of Educ.*, 533 U.S. 915, 121 S.Ct. 2519, 150 L.Ed.2d 692 (2001).

261. *Peck ex rel. Peck v. Baldwinsville Cent. School Dist.*, 426 F.3d 617, 621 [202 Educ. L. Rep. 512] (2d Cir.2005).

On a related matter, the Third Circuit affirmed that school officials in New Jersey did not violate the Establishment Clause rights, among others, of a mother by prohibiting her from reading selections from the Bible to her son's kindergarten class as part of a "show and tell" activity.[262] The court maintained that in light of the age and impressionability of the children who were present, and the possibility that the students might have viewed her as an authority figure, educational officials voiced a legitimate concern over the perception of endorsement of religion in violation of the Establishment Clause.

As to extracurricular activities such as sports practices[263] and graduation ceremonies,[264] the few courts addressing the issue agreed that school officials did not have to reschedule events in order to accommodate the religious beliefs of students. However, the Supreme Court of Oregon affirmed that granting the request of parents and student-athletes who attended a religiously affiliated secondary school to adjust the schedule of a basketball tournament so that they would be excused from playing on their Sabbath would not have violated the Establishment Clause.[265] If anything, the court explained that modifying the schedule to accommodate those with differing religious beliefs would have advanced the values served by the Establishment Clause and that any burdens that the change may have imposed on others such as increased ticket prices and inconvenience did not entail government sponsorship or entanglement with religion.

In what can only be described as an unusual case involving religion and extracurricular activities, the Sixth Circuit rejected a parental claim that the use of the "Blue Devil" as a school mascot violated the Establishment Clause.[266] The court affirmed that the charge lacked merit since no reasonable observer would have believed that the "Blue Devil's" principal or primary effect was to advance or inhibit religion or that its use was meant to endorse or disapprove any religious choice.

RELIGIOUS GARB

Students

The courts seem to agree that educators must devise less restrictive alternatives to preventing students from wearing religious garb to school.[267] The Ninth Circuit affirmed that officials violated the rights of Sikh stu-

---

262. *Busch v. Marple Newton School Dist.*, 567 F.3d 89 [244 Educ. L. Rep. 1023] (3d Cir. 2009), *cert. denied*, ___ U.S. ___, 130 S.Ct. 1137, 175 L.Ed.2d 991 (2010).

263. *Keller v. Gardner Community Consol. Grade School Dist. 72C*, 552 F.Supp. 512 [8 Educ. L. Rep. 271] (N.D.Ill.1982).

264. *Smith by Smith v. Board of Educ., North Babylon Union Free School Dist.*, 844 F.2d 90 [46 Educ. L. Rep. 518] (2d Cir.1988).

265. *Nakashima v. Oregon State Bd. of Educ.*, 185 P.3d 429 [232 Educ. L. Rep. 944] (Or.2008).

266. *Kunselman v. Western Reserve Local School Dist.*, 70 F.3d 931 [105 Educ. L. Rep. 43] (6th Cir.1995).

267. *See also Isaacs v. Board of Educ. of Howard County, Md.*, 40 F.Supp.2d 335 [134 Educ. L. Rep. 166] (D.Md.1999) (granting a school board's motion for summary judgment when a student relied on the First Amendment right to free speech in seeking to wear a head wrap to school to celebrate her cultural heritage).

dents by trying to prevent them from wearing ceremonial daggers under their clothes.[268] The court decided that officials overstepped their authority absent a showing that a total ban on weapons was the least restrictive alternative way to promote campus safety.

In a case from Texas overlapping with issues of grooming, the Fifth Circuit invalidated a board policy which forbade male students from having their hair touch their ears. The policy would have required a student who is a Native American to wear his long hair in a bun on top of his head or in a braid tucked into his shirt. Affirming an order in favor of the student, the court held that in light of his sincere religious belief in wearing his hair visibly long, the policy would have imposed a substantial burden on his right to the free exercise of religion.[269] In an earlier case overlapping with issues of dress, when students wore rosaries to school as necklaces, a federal trial court in Texas ruled that educators violated their First Amendment right to pure speech because rosaries were a form of religious expression.[270]

Teachers

Many older cases addressed whether teachers in public schools could wear distinctive religious garb. The disputes often arose over whether Roman Catholic nuns could wear their habits while teaching in public schools.[271] In an early case, the Supreme Court of Pennsylvania affirmed the authority of a local school board to hire Catholic nuns as teachers and to permit them to teach in their habits.[272] Shortly thereafter, the state legislature enacted a law specifically designed to prevent teachers from wearing dress or insignia indicating membership in religious orders while at work. In deferring to legislative authority, the same court also upheld a law banning nuns from teaching in their habits.[273]

The Supreme Court of Oregon, in a case involving a teacher who became a Sikh and wore white clothes and a white turban while teaching, posited that she was subject to a state legislative ban on religious dress while performing her teaching duties.[274] In dicta the court acknowledged

---

268. *Cheema v. Thompson*, 67 F.3d 883 [104 Educ. L. Rep. 57] (9th Cir.1995).

269. *A.A. ex rel. Betenbaugh v. Needville Indep. School Dist.*, 611 F.3d 248 [258 Educ. L. Rep. 955] (5th Cir. 2010). For an earlier case reaching the same result, *see Alabama and Coushatta Tribes of Texas v. Trustees of the Big Sandy Indep. School Dist.*, 817 F.Supp. 1319 [82 Educ. L. Rep. 442] (E.D. Tex. 1993), *remanded by* 20 F.3d 469 [90 Educ. L. Rep. 579] (5th Cir. 1994).

270. *Chalifoux v. New Caney Indep. School Dist.*, 976 F.Supp. 659 [121 Educ. L. Rep. 751] (S.D.Tex.1997).

271. In a related matter, at least one court affirmed that the fact that nuns simply turned their earnings over to their religious superiors was not a justification for barring them from serving as public school teachers. *See Gerhardt v. Heid*, 267 N.W. 127 (N.D.1936).

272. *Hysong v. School Dist. of Gallitzin Borough*, 30 A. 482 (Pa. 1894). *See also Rawlings v. Butler*, 290 S.W.2d 801 (Ky. 1956).

273. *Commonwealth v. Herr*, 78 A. 68 (Pa.1910). *See also O'Connor v. Hendrick*, 77 N.E. 612 (N.Y.1906); *Zellers v. Huff*, 236 P.2d 949 (N.M.1951).

274. *Cooper v. Eugene School Dist. No. 4J*, 723 P.2d 298 [34 Educ. L. Rep. 614] (Or.1986), *appeal dismissed*, 480 U.S. 942, 107 S.Ct. 1597, 94 L.Ed.2d 784 (1987).

that such a prohibition would not have applied to incidental elements such as a cross or Star of David or to ethnic or cultural dress.

Two other cases reached mixed results. The Supreme Court of Mississippi ascertained that school officials could not dismiss a teacher who was a member of the African Hebrew Israelites out of Ethiopia faith for insubordination when she wore a religious head wrap to school.[275] Yet, the Third Circuit, relying on the statute discussed two paragraphs earlier, rejected the claim of a female Muslim teacher in Pennsylvania who adhered to the religious conviction that she should, when in public, cover her entire body except her face and hands.[276]

Whether educators can wear religious symbolism seems to depend largely on their size and obviousness. The federal trial court in Connecticut granted a school board's motion for summary judgment in a dispute where officials directed a substitute teacher either to cover a t-shirt with the message "Jesus 2000" on it or to go home and change into other clothes.[277] The court was of the opinion that administrators did not violate the teacher's First Amendment rights to the free exercise of religion or free speech. Conversely, a federal trial court in Pennsylvania granted an instructional assistant's motion for a preliminary injunction after she was suspended for refusing to remove or conceal a small cross she regularly wore on a necklace, as required by her school board's religious affiliations policy.[278] The court agreed that the policy violated the Free Exercise Clause since its being directed only at religious exercise and symbolic expression made it impermissibly content and viewpoint based.

DISTRIBUTION OF PROSELYTIZING MATERIALS/ RELIGIOUS LITERATURE IN SCHOOLS

In an early case, the Supreme Court of New Jersey was of the view that where school officials enacted a generally applicable policy for all student groups, they could impose reasonable time, manner, and place restrictions on the ability of students to distribute religious literature such as Gideon Bibles[279] or proselytize in schools. Amid considerable controversy over the distribution of religious materials and literature in schools, courts, even within the same jurisdiction, have reached conflicting results.

The Third,[280] Seventh,[281] and Eighth[282] Circuits, along with federal trial courts, agreed that students cannot hand out religious newspapers,[283]

---

275. *Mississippi Employment Securities Comm'n v. McGlothin,* 556 So.2d 324 [58 Educ. L. Rep. 859] (Miss.1990), *cert. denied,* 498 U.S. 879, 111 S.Ct. 211, 112 L.Ed.2d 171 (1990).

276. *United States v. Board of Educ. for School Dist. of Philadelphia,* 911 F.2d 882 [62 Educ. L. Rep. 460] (3d Cir.1990).

277. *Downing v. West Haven Bd. of Educ.,* 162 F.Supp.2d 19 [157 Educ. L. Rep. 112] (D.Conn.2001).

278. *Nichol v. ARIN Intermediate Unit 28,* 268 F.Supp.2d 536 [179 Educ. L. Rep. 315] (W.D.Pa.2003).

279. *Tudor v. Board of Educ. of Borough of Rutherford,* 100 A.2d 857 (N.J.1953), *cert. denied,* 348 U.S. 816, 75 S.Ct. 25, 99 L.Ed. 644 (1954).

280. *Walz ex rel. Walz v. Egg Harbor Twp. Bd. of Educ.,* 342 F.3d 271 [180 Educ. L. Rep. 115] (3d Cir.2003), *cert. denied,* 541 U.S. 936, 124 S.Ct. 1658, 158 L.Ed.2d 356 (2004) (forbidding the distribution of pencils with religious messages attached to them).

281. *Berger v. Rensselaer Cent. School Corp.,* 982 F.2d 1160 [80 Educ. L. Rep. 68] (7th Cir.1993), *cert. denied,* 508 U.S. 911, 113 S.Ct. 2344, 124 L.Ed.2d 254 (1993); *Muller by Muller*

advertisements about activities,[284] or invitations to such events as alternatives to Halloween parties[285] or religious meetings[286] where the activities were motivated by religious objections as long as officials enunciated appropriate time, manner, and place restrictions about the distribution of non-school materials at school.[287]

The Sixth Circuit affirmed that a fifth-grader in Michigan could not sell pipe-cleaner candy cane Christmas tree ornaments that he made as part of a school project if they were attached to religious cards promoting Jesus.[288] The court observed that the principal did not violate the student's free speech rights because insofar as the activity was school-sponsored, he had greater latitude to restrict the child's behavior.[289] The court interpreted the principal's action as being reasonably related to legitimate pedagogical concerns of neither offending other students nor their parents and not subjecting young children to unsolicited religious promotional messages that might have conflicted with what they were taught at home.

The Third,[290] Fourth,[291] Fifth,[292] Sixth,[293] Seventh,[294] and Ninth[295] Circuits, along with federal trial courts in New York[296] and Washington,[297]

---

v. Jefferson Lighthouse School, 98 F.3d 1530 [113 Educ. L. Rep. 1085] (7th Cir.1996), *cert. denied*, 520 U.S. 1156, 117 S.Ct. 1335, 137 L.Ed.2d 495 (1997) (prohibiting the distribution of Bibles).

282. *Victory Through Jesus Sports Ministry Found. v. Lee's Summit R–7 School Dist.*, 640 F.3d 329 [267 Educ. L. Rep. 466] (8th Cir. 2011), *reh'g and reh'g en banc denied* (2011); *Roark v. South Iron R–1 School Dist.*, 573 F.3d 556 [246 Educ. L. Rep. 723] (8th Cir. 2009).

283. *Thompson v. Waynesboro Area School Dist.*, 673 F.Supp. 1379 [43 Educ. L. Rep. 138] (M.D.Pa.1987); *Hemry v. School Bd. of Colorado Springs School Dist. No. 11*, 760 F.Supp. 856 [67 Educ. L. Rep. 142] (D.Colo.1991). *But see Rivera v. East Otero School Dist. R–1*, 721 F.Supp. 1189 [56 Educ. L. Rep. 861] (D.Colo.1989) (permitting a student to distribute a religious newsletter).

284. *Krestan v. Deer Valley Unified School Dist. No. 97, of Maricopa County*, 561 F.Supp.2d 1078 [235 Educ. L. Rep. 361] (D.Ariz.2008).

285. *See, e.g., Guyer v. School Bd. of Alachua County*, 634 So.2d 806 [90 Educ. L. Rep. 961] (Fla.Dist.Ct.App.1994), *review denied without published opinion*, 641 So.2d 1345 (Fla.1994), *cert. denied*, 513 U.S. 1044, 115 S.Ct. 638, 130 L.Ed.2d 544 (1994); *Johnston–Loehner v. O'Brien*, 859 F.Supp. 575 [94 Educ. L. Rep. 167] (M.D.Fla.1994).

286. *Muller by Muller v. Jefferson Lighthouse School*, 98 F.3d 1530 [113 Educ. L. Rep. 1085] (7th Cir.1996), *cert. denied*, 520 U.S. 1156, 117 S.Ct. 1335, 137 L.Ed.2d 495 (1997).

287. *Pounds v. Katy Indep. School Dist.*, 517 F.Supp.2d 901 [226 Educ. L. Rep. 829] (S.D.Tex.2007).

288. *Curry ex rel. Curry v. Hensiner*, 513 F.3d 570 [229 Educ. L. Rep. 30] (6th Cir.2008), *reh'g and reh'g en banc denied* (2008).

289. *See also Edwards v. United States*, 249 F.R.D. 25 (D.Conn.2008) (dismissing a mother's *pro se* challenge to her being prevented from distributing candy canes to her oldest child's class while talking about the Bible during regular school hours).

290. *Child Evangelism Fellowship of N.J. v. Stafford Twp. School Dist.*, 386 F.3d 514 [192 Educ. L. Rep. 670] (3d Cir.2004).

291. *Child Evangelism Fellowship v. Montgomery County Pub. Schools*, 457 F.3d 376 [211 Educ. L. Rep. 591] (4th Cir.2006). *See also Peck v. Upshur County Bd. of Educ.*, 155 F.3d 274 [129 Educ. L. Rep. 77] (4th Cir.1998) (while finding that a neutral board policy permitting non-students to disseminate Bibles and other religious materials in school during class hours did not violate the Establishment Clause, striking it down as applied to elementary school students).

292. *Doe v. Duncanville Indep. School Dist.*, 70 F.3d 402 [104 Educ. L. Rep. 1032] (5th Cir.1995) (ruling that a student and her father lacked standing to challenge the practice of distributing Bibles in school since she was not in a class where they were given out and the board did not expend any funds in the process).

permitted groups and/or single students to distribute religious materials in schools since doing so did not violate the Establishment Clause. These courts generally recognized the presence of safeguards in place such as educators reviewing materials to ensure that they were not proselytizing and that information was sent home to parents who could choose whether their children would participate in the activities.

More recently, the Fifth Circuit reached a split decision in a dispute from Texas that arose in part because school officials searched the bags of students, confiscating pencils with religious messages on them. While the court held that students had the right to distribute the pencils, it granted the educators' motions for qualified immunity because it thought that the law on this issue had not been clearly established.[298] In a similar case, the federal trial court in Massachusetts granted a Bible study club's request to enjoin a policy against distributing items at school including candy canes with religious messages attached to them because the group's private expressive religious actions were not disruptive.[299] The court suggested that students who might have been offended by the candy canes with religious messages were free to decline them since they were not coerced into accepting the gifts.

PUBLIC RELIGIOUS DISPLAYS ON SCHOOL GROUNDS

In its only case directly involving schools, *Stone v. Graham,*[300] the Supreme Court noted that posting the Ten Commandments in classrooms, even if they were purchased with private funds, violated the Establishment Clause. The Court's brief per curiam opinion ascertained that the Kentucky statute requiring the posting lacked a secular purpose, emphasizing that the Ten Commandments were not integrated into the school curriculum. The Court was unpersuaded by a small notation on the postings to the effect that the Commandments were part of the fundamental legal code of Western Civilization and the common law of the United States.

---

293. *Rusk v. Crestview Local School Dist.*, 379 F.3d 418 [191 Educ. L. Rep. 84] (6th Cir.2004).

294. *Sherman v. Community Consol. School Dist. 21,* 8 F.3d 1160 [87 Educ. L. Rep. 57] (7th Cir.1993), *cert. denied,* 511 U.S. 1110, 114 S.Ct. 2109, 128 L.Ed.2d 669 (1994) (affirming that the distribution of Boy Scout materials did not violate the Establishment Clause).

295. *Hills v. Scottsdale Unified School Dist. No. 48,* 329 F.3d 1044 [176 Educ. L. Rep. 557] (9th Cir.2003), *cert. denied,* 540 U.S. 1149, 124 S.Ct. 1042, 157 L.Ed.2d 1042, 184 Educ. L. Rep. 23 (2004). *But see Culbertson v. Oakridge School Dist.,* 258 F.3d 1061 [155 Educ. L. Rep. 1085] (9th Cir.2001) (rejecting the claim that distribution of Good News Club permission slips would have violated the Establishment Clause).

296. *M.B. ex rel. Martin v. Liverpool Cent. School Dist.,* 487 F.Supp.2d 117 [221 Educ. L. Rep. 79] (N.D.N.Y.2007).

297. *See also Daugherty v. Vanguard Charter School Acad.,* 116 F.Supp.2d 897 [148 Educ. L. Rep. 208] (W.D.Mich.2000).

298. *Morgan v. Swanson,* 659 F.3d 359 [273 Educ. L. Rep. 524] (5th Cir. 2011).

299. *Westfield High School L.I.F.E. Club v. City of Westfield,* 249 F.Supp.2d 98 [175 Educ. L. Rep. 506] (D.Mass.2003).

300. 449 U.S. 39, 101 S.Ct. 192, 66 L.Ed.2d 199 (1980), *reh'g denied,* 449 U.S. 1104, 101 S.Ct. 904, 66 L.Ed.2d 832 (1981), *on remand,* 612 S.W.2d 133 (Ky.1981).

Debate continues to rage over the Ten Commandments in school settings. A federal trial court in Kentucky granted a student's request to enjoin officials from displaying the Ten Commandments and other religious documents, pointing out that she had a strong likelihood of success on the merits of her claim.[301] Two cases from the Sixth Circuit reached results consistent with non-school cases on point.[302] In the first, the court affirmed an injunction against a board in Ohio's displaying stone monuments inscribed with the Ten Commandments at a high school since the plaintiffs had standing to file suit and the board failed to establish a secular purpose for the display.[303] In the second case, the Sixth Circuit rejected modifications to displays in a county courthouse and public school in Kentucky including a variety of documents along with the Ten Commandments such as the full text of the Magna Carta, the Declaration of Independence, and a Biblical citation. The court decided that the display violated the Establishment Clause because it had the effect of advancing religion.[304] This latter case ultimately made its way to the Supreme Court but was limited to a review of the dispute involving the courthouse.

In two non-school cases, the Supreme Court reached mixed results. In the first, *McCreary County, Kentucky v. American Civil Liberties Union of Kentucky*,[305] the Court, focusing on the fact that officials erected, and modified, the display at the county courthouse three times since putting it up in 1999, affirmed that it violated the Establishment Clause largely because it failed *Lemon's* secular purpose test. Conversely, in *Van Orden v. Perry*,[306] a plurality affirmed that a display of the Ten Commandments including seventeen monuments and twenty-one historical markers commemorating the state's history spread out over the twenty-two acres of the Texas State Capitol was constitutional. In eschewing the *Lemon* test, the plurality essentially thought that including the Ten Commandments in the display was constitutional because even though they continue to have religious significance, the monument was a far more passive display than in *Stone*.

Shortly after the Supreme Court resolved its cases on the Ten Commandments, the Eighth Circuit rejected a challenge to the presence of a

---

301. *Doe v. Harlan County School Dist.*, 96 F.Supp.2d 667 [144 Educ. L. Rep. 503] (E.D.Ky.2000).

302. *See, e.g., Indiana Civil Liberties Union v. O'Bannon*, 259 F.3d 766 (7th Cir.2001), *cert. denied*, 532 U.S. 1058, 121 S.Ct. 2209, 149 L.Ed.2d 1036 (2001) (prohibiting a monument on the grounds of the statehouse including the Ten Commandments); *Books v. City of Elkhart*, 235 F.3d 292 (7th Cir.2000), *cert. denied*, 532 U.S. 1058, 121 S.Ct. 2209, 149 L.Ed.2d 1036 (2001) (forbidding a monument on the lawn of a city's municipal building that was inscribed with the Ten Commandments); *Suhre v. Haywood County*, 131 F.3d 1083 (4th Cir.1997) (banning a display of the Ten Commandments in a county courtroom); *Glassroth v. Moore*, 229 F.Supp.2d 1290 (N.D.Ala.2002) (proscribing a monument engraved with the Ten Commandments in a courthouse).

303. *Baker v. Adams County/Ohio Valley School*, 86 Fed.Appx. 104 [184 Educ. L. Rep. 745] (6th Cir.2004), *cert. denied*, 545 U.S. 1152, 125 S.Ct. 2989, 162 L.Ed. 910 (2005).

304. *American Civil Liberties Union v. McCreary County, Ky.*, 354 F.3d 438 [184 Educ. L. Rep. 67] (6th Cir.2003), *cert. granted*, 543 U.S. 924, 125 S.Ct. 310, 160 L.Ed.2d 221 [192 Educ. L. Rep. 631] (2004) (also forbidding the posting of the Ten Commandments in a county courthouse).

305. 545 U.S. 844, 125 S.Ct. 2722, 162 L.Ed.2d 729 (2005).

306. 545 U.S. 677, 125 S.Ct. 2854, 162 L.Ed.2d 607 (2005).

long-standing granite monument in a city park that was donated by a civic organization and had been displayed without objection for decades.[307] In explaining that the words on the monument faced away from the park and that the Ten Commandments had undeniable historic meaning along with their religious significance, the court ruled that its simply having religious content or promoting a message consistent with a religious doctrine did not run afoul of the Establishment Clause. Subsequently, the Tenth Circuit reversed an injunction that denied a religious group's request to erect a monument in a public park where the Ten Commandments were already displayed in asserting that this amounted to an infringement on its right to free speech.[308] On appeal in *Pleasant Grove City v. Summum*,[309] the Supreme Court unanimously reversed in holding that insofar as the group's desire to place a permanent monument in a public park was a form of governmental speech, officials could deny the request without having to have their action subjected to strict scrutiny review.

When dealing with other kinds of displays at schools, courts also reached mixed results.[310] In a case involving the school from the tragic shootings in Columbine, Colorado, the Tenth Circuit held that a tile painting/installation project sponsored by the board as part of the building's reconstruction was school-sponsored speech.[311] As such, the court allowed officials to exercise editorial control under the First Amendment because their actions were reasonably related to legitimate pedagogical concerns. The court added that officials could exclude bricks from a walkway in front of the school bearing inscriptions containing Christian messages and/or referring to Jesus.[312] Conversely, a federal trial court in Virginia granted a parental motion for summary judgment where a board ordered the removal of bricks decorated with Latin crosses while allowing those with secular symbols to remain in place in a school's walkway of fame.[313] The court viewed the actions of school officials who removed only bricks with religious symbols as constituting impermissible viewpoint discrimination.[314]

---

307. *ACLU Neb. Found. v. City of Plattsmouth*, 419 F.3d 772 (8th Cir.2005).

308. *Summum v. Pleasant Grove City*, 499 F.3d 1170 (10th Cir. 2007).

309. 555 U.S. 460, 129 S.Ct. 1125, 172 L.Ed.2d 853 (2009).

310. *Washegesic v. Bloomingdale Pub. Schools*, 33 F.3d 679 [94 Educ. L. Rep. 32] (6th Cir.1994), *reh'g and suggestion for reh'g en banc denied* (1994), *cert. denied*, 514 U.S. 1095, 115 S.Ct. 1822, 131 L.Ed.2d 744 (1995) (directing officials to remove a portrait of Jesus that was painted by a graduate and which hung in a school hall as violating the Establishment Clause).

311. *Fleming v. Jefferson County School Dist. R–1*, 298 F.3d 918 [167 Educ. L. Rep. 649] (10th Cir.2002), *as amended on denial of reh'g and reh'g en banc* (2002), *cert. denied*, 537 U.S. 1110, 123 S.Ct. 893, 154 L.Ed.2d 783 (2003).

312. *See also Seidman v. Paradise Valley Unified School Dist. No. 69*, 327 F.Supp.2d 1098 [191 Educ. L. Rep. 175] (D.Ariz.2004) (rejecting parents' motion for summary judgment in a suit against a board for violations of their First and Fourteenth Amendment rights over their having to remove the word "God" from the proposed inscription "God Bless Quinn We Love You Mom and Dad," and a similar inscription for their daughter that would have appeared on wall tiles on an interior school wall).

313. *Demmon v. Loudoun County Pub. Schools*, 342 F.Supp.2d 474 [193 Educ. L. Rep. 497] (E.D.Va.2004).

314. *See also Anderson v. Mexico Acad. and Cent. School*, 186 F.Supp.2d 193 [162 Educ. L. Rep. 262] (N.D.N.Y.2002), *remanded sub nom. Kiesinger v. Mexico Acad. & Cent. School*, 56

CURRICULAR ELEMENTS

Consistent with dicta in *Abington v. Schempp* that "[t]he holding of the Court today plainly does not foreclose teaching about the Holy Scriptures or about the differences between religious sects in classes in literature or history ...,"[315] the judiciary has reached mixed results over the place of religion in public school curricula. Courts have yet to devise a test to evaluate the balance between teaching about religion and the teaching of religion in public schools.

In an early case, the Supreme Court of New Hampshire upheld the practice of displaying plaques, containing the words "In God We Trust,"[316] that were visible in each classroom. The court treated the display as acceptable because it was the national motto that appeared on coins and currency,[317] on public buildings,[318] and in the national anthem.

The Ninth Circuit affirmed the dismissal of challenge from parents who questioned the use of curricular materials on Islam.[319] The materials included a simulation unit on Islamic culture in a social studies course that, among other things, required students to wear identification tags displaying their new Islamic names, dress as Muslims, memorize and recite an Islamic prayer that has the status of the Lord's Prayer in Christianity as well as other verses from the Uur'an, recite the Five Pillars of Faith, and engage in fasting and acts of self denial.[320] Without addressing the merits of the claims, the court determined that the activities "were not ... 'overt religious exercises' that raise[d] Establishment Clause concerns."[321]

Turning to a different issue, courts are reluctant to allow teachers to use supplemental materials with religious content. A federal trial court in

Fed.Appx. 549 [173 Educ. L. Rep. 709] (2d Cir.2003) (remanding for a review of the entire record where the trial court decided that a board's exclusion of the plaintiffs' bricks from the walkway in front of school because their inscriptions contained Christian messages and/or referred to "Jesus" violated their right to free speech by engaging in viewpoint discrimination but did not violate the Establishment Clause).

315. *School District of Abington Twp. v. Schempp and Murray v. Curlett*, 374 U.S. 203, 300, 83 S.Ct. 1560, 10 L.Ed.2d 844 (1963). [Case No. 4]

316. *Opinion of the Justices*, 228 A.2d 161 (N.H.1967).

317. *See also Aronow v. United States*, 432 F.2d 242 (9th Cir.1970) (affirming that the phrase "In God We Trust" on American currency and coins as well as in the national anthem had nothing to do with the establishment of religion). For cases rejecting similar challenges, see, *e.g.*, *O'Hair v. Murray*, 588 F.2d 1144 (5th Cir.1979), *cert. denied sub nom. O'Hair v. Blumenthal*, 442 U.S. 930, 99 S.Ct. 2862, 61 L.Ed.2d 298 (1979); *Newdow v. Lefevre*, 598 F.3d 638 (9th Cir. 2010), *cert. denied*, ___ U.S. ___, 131 S.Ct. 1612, 179 L.Ed.2d 501 (2011).

318. *See also Lambeth v. Board of Comm'rs of Davidson County*, 407 F.3d 266 (4th Cir.2005), *cert. denied*, 546 U.S. 1015, 126 S.Ct. 647, 163 L.Ed.2d 525 (2005) (affirming that the inscription "In God We Trust" on a county government center did not violate the Establishment Clause).

319. *Eklund v. Byron Union School Dist.*, 154 Fed.Appx. 648 (9th Cir.2005), *cert. denied*, 549 U.S. 942, 127 S.Ct. 86, 166 L.Ed.2d 252 (2006).

320. *Eklund v. Byron Union Sch. Dist.*, 2006 WL 1519184 (Appellate Petition, Motion and Filing) (U.S. 2006). *Petition for a Writ of Certiorari* (No. 05–1539) at 3–13.

321. *Eklund v. Byron Union Sch. Dist.*, 154 Fed.Appx. 648 (9th Cir.2005) (internal citations omitted), *quoting Brown v. Woodland Joint Unified Sch. Dist.*, 27 F.3d 1373, 1382 [92 Educ. L. Rep. 828] (9th Cir.1994) (affirming that a curricular program which asked children to discuss witches or create poetic chants and pretend they were witches or sorcerers did not require them to practice the "religion" of witchcraft in violation of Establishment Clause or California Constitution).

California largely rejected the claims of an elementary school teacher that officials violated his rights by prohibiting him from using religious materials in class and talking about religion with his students.[322] The court added that if the plaintiff could prove that officials permitted other similarly situated teachers to include religious expression in their lessons and supplemental handouts but prevented him from doing so, he would have had evidence to present a case that they violated his right to equal protection. On the flip side, the federal trial court in Maine denied a school board's motion for summary judgment where a history teacher filed suit claiming that officials forbade him from providing instruction about non-Christian religions and directed him to include only references to Christianity.[323] The court was convinced that in light of remaining material issues of fact as to whether officials yielded to pressure from parents who did not want the teacher to offer information about religions other than Christianity, the case should have proceeded to trial.

In a case from California, a federal trial court rejected the claim of an organization which disagreed with the manner in which state curricular standards addressed Hinduism.[324] In granting the state's motion for summary judgment, the court noted both that the group lacked standing and that the standards passed Establishment Clause analysis because the process under which they were developed satisfied all three parts of the *Lemon* test.

A case overlapping with religious celebrations arose in Delaware where the mother of a Muslim elementary school child raised a variety of claims. The federal trial court rejected the school board's motion for summary judgment since genuine issue of fact remained as to whether a fourth-grade teacher's use of Christmas readings violated the student's rights under the State Constitution's Preference Clause, essentially the equivalent of the Federal Free Exercise Clause, or Equal Protection Clause of the Fourteenth Amendment and whether school officials were entitled to qualified immunity for the alleged violations of the child's rights.[325] The court granted the board's motion for summary judgment with regard to the claim that the teacher's reading from a textbook that brought up religion in discussing events of 9/11 on the basis that this did not violate child's rights under the State Constitution's Preference Clause.

Religious Celebrations

Considering the vast amount of litigation dealing with religion in public schools, it is surprising that the Supreme Court has yet to address a case directly on the place of religious celebrations in schools. The closest that the Court came to this contentious topic was when it twice addressed public displays involving Christmas in non-school cases.

---

322. *Williams v. Vidmar*, 367 F.Supp.2d 1265 [198 Educ. L. Rep. 292] (N.D.Cal.2005).

323. *Cole v. Maine School Admin. Dist. No. 1*, 350 F.Supp.2d 143 [195 Educ. L. Rep. 130] (D.Me.2004).

324. *California Parents for the Equalization of Educ. Materials v. Noonan*, 600 F. Supp.2d 1088 [243 Educ. L. Rep.96] (E.D. Cal. 2009).

325. *Doe v. Cape Henlopen School Dist.*, 759 F. Supp.2d 522 [266 Educ. L. Rep. 812] (D. Del. 2011).

In *Lynch v. Donnelly*,[326] a plurality of the Supreme Court upheld the inclusion of a Nativity scene in a Christmas display on public property relying largely on the endorsement test. *County of Allegheny v. American Civil Liberties Union*,[327] the second case, involved two displays. The first display was of a creche in a county courthouse including an angel bearing a banner with the message *Gloria in Excelsis Deo*, literally, "Glory to God in the Highest," along with a sign stating that the scene was donated by a private religious organization. The second display, which was located outside of an office building owned by the city and county, consisted of a forty-five-foot Christmas tree, an eighteen-foot menorah, and a sign proclaiming the city's salute to liberty during the holiday season. The Court affirmed that the first display had the impermissible effect of endorsing religion.[328] As to the second display, the Court was satisfied that insofar as the Christmas tree and menorah were placed in the broader context of the season and did not endorse a particular religious faith, it passed constitutional muster.

Turning to religious celebrations in schools, the Eighth Circuit upheld a set of guidelines that a school board in South Dakota developed for use in connection with religious observances, most notably Christmas and other holidays.[329] The guidelines permitted objective discussion of both religious and secular holidays. The court indicated that explanations of historical and contemporary values relating to holidays; short-term use of religious symbols as examples of religious heritages; and integration of music, art, literature, and drama with religious themes could be included in curricula as long as they were presented objectively as a traditional part of the cultural and religious heritages of holidays. In affirming that curricular material asking children to discuss witches or create poetic chants and directing them to pretend they were witches or sorcerers did not require students to practice the religion of witchcraft in violation of the Establishment Clause or the California Constitution, the Ninth Circuit went so far in dicta as to suggest that "a reenactment of the Last Supper or a Passover dinner might be permissible if presented for historical or cultural purposes."[330]

In another case examining holiday commemorations, a federal trial court in Pennsylvania addressed a situation where school officials permitted a "Winter Holiday" display including information on Chanukah and Kwanzaa, but nothing on Christmas other than a parody of a traditional

---

326. 465 U.S. 668, 104 S.Ct. 1355, 79 L.Ed.2d 604 (1984).

327. 492 U.S. 573, 109 S.Ct. 3086, 106 L.Ed.2d 472 (1989).

328. *See also American Civil Liberties Union of New Jersey v. Schundler*, 168 F.3d 92 (3d Cir.1999) (affirming that a display of a menorah and a Christmas tree in front of a city hall violated the Establishment Clause; also allowing a display consisting of a creche, a menorah, and a Christmas tree, along with plastic figures of Santa Claus, Frosty the Snowman, a red sled, Kwanzaa symbols, and two signs explaining that the exhibit was part of a series of displays that the city erected throughout the year to celebrate the cultural and ethnic diversity of its residents, to remain since it was virtually indistinguishable from the ones in *Lynch* and *ACLU* cited in the two previous footnotes).

329. *Florey v. Sioux Falls School Dist. 49–5*, 619 F.2d 1311 (8th Cir.1980), *cert. denied*, 449 U.S. 987, 101 S.Ct. 409, 66 L.Ed.2d 251 (1980).

330. *Brown v. Woodland Joint Unified School Dist.*, 27 F.3d 1373, 1380, n.6 [92 Educ. L. Rep. 828] (9th Cir.1994).

Christmas hymn that the plaintiff, a youth minister, found offensive.[331] The court rejected the plaintiff's challenge, responding that the display did not offend the Establishment Clause by favoring one religion over another. Subsequently, the Second Circuit upheld a policy of the New York City Board of Education that permitted seasonal displays of a menorah along with a star and crescent but not a manger scene or creche.[332] The court maintained that insofar as the policy had the perceived secular purpose of promoting pluralism and respect for diversity, did not have the principle or primary effect of advancing or inhibiting religion, and did not excessively entangle church and state, it passed Establishment Clause muster.

Courts reached mixed results with regard to Good Friday, the day commemorating the death of Christ. The Seventh Circuit affirmed that a law from Illinois making Good Friday a paid holiday for teachers and closing schools violated the Establishment Clause since it was a purely sectarian holiday unaccompanied by any secular rituals.[333] In the first of three cases reaching the opposite result, the Seventh Circuit later affirmed that Indiana's recognition of Good Friday as a legal holiday for state employees did not violate the Establishment Clause since its doing so was based on secular justifications including the provision of a spring holiday that were supported by evidence and did not constitute a sham.[334] The court explained, for example, that the state's actions were justified because Good Friday occurred during a time period in which there would be over four months without a holiday and over thirty percent of schools in the state were closed on that day. The court noted that the recognition of Good Friday neither had the principal effect of advancing religion nor represented an endorsement of religion. The Fourth[335] and Sixth[336] Circuits also upheld the status of Good Friday as a legal holiday.

Evolution

Judicial controversy over the origins of humankind in public schools first arose in the so-called "Scopes Monkey Trial." At issue was a challenge to a state law forbidding the teaching of evolution since doing so contradicted the literalist Biblical interpretation of creation in Genesis. After a

---

331. *Sechler v. State College Area School Dist.*, 121 F.Supp.2d 439 [149 Educ. L. Rep. 141] (M.D.Pa.2000). For a case in a non-school setting, *see Spohn v. West*, 2000 WL 1459981 (S.D.N.Y.2000) (dismissing the claim of a Christian worker in a public hospital that a display of Jewish, but not Christian, religious symbols during the December holiday season violated his First Amendment rights under the Establishment Clause).

332. *Skoros v. City of N.Y.*, 437 F.3d 1 [206 Educ. L. Rep. 525] (2d Cir.2006), *cert. denied*, 549 U.S. 1205, 127 S.Ct. 1245, 167 L.Ed.2d 74 (2007).

333. *Metzl v. Leininger*, 57 F.3d 618 [101 Educ. L. Rep. 112] (7th Cir.1995).

334. *Bridenbaugh v. O'Bannon*, 185 F.3d 796 (7th Cir. 1999), *cert. denied*, 529 U.S. 1003, 120 S.Ct. 1267, 146 L.Ed.2d 217 (2000).

335. *Koenick v. Felton*, 190 F.3d 259 [138 Educ. L. Rep. 100] (4th Cir.1999), *cert. denied*, 528 U.S. 1118, 120 S.Ct. 938, 145 L.Ed.2d 816 (2000) (affirming the rejection of a retired teacher's claim that a Maryland statute providing for public school holidays on the Friday before Easter through the Monday after Easter violated the Establishment Clause).

336. *Granzeier v. Middleton*, 173 F.3d 568 (6th Cir.1999) (affirming that closing courts and offices in a county courthouse and administration building on Good Friday along with posting a sign on the courthouse door containing a picture of a four-inch high crucifix with the image of Christ did not violate the Establishment Clause).

substitute science teacher agreed to confess to having violated the law even though post-trial evidence suggests that he did not do so, he was fined $100 as part of a plan to get the case to a higher court. While leaving the statute that made teaching evolution a crime in place, in *Scopes v. State*,[337] the Supreme Court of Tennessee reversed the teacher's conviction because the judge improperly assessed a fine that could only have been imposed by a jury. Officials followed the court's advice and did not take any further action in light of its comment that there was "nothing to be gained by prolonging the life of this bizarre case."[338]

The Supreme Court considered a challenge to a 1928 law from Arkansas forbidding the teaching of evolution in state-supported schools in *Epperson v. Arkansas*.[339] The Court invalidated the statute for failing to comply with the recently created judicial test from *Abington*. The Court held that the statute was unconstitutional since it attempted to blot out a particular scientific theory due to its supposed conflict with the literal Biblical account of creation. A federal trial court then struck down another law from Arkansas that would have required providing balanced treatment for instruction on Biblical notions of creation if evolution was included in the curriculum.[340]

A second Supreme Court case on the origins of humankind arose in Louisiana where a statute prohibited the teaching of "evolution-science" in public elementary and secondary schools unless accompanied by instruction on "creation-science." In *Edwards v. Aguillard*,[341] the Court invalidated the law as unconstitutional because it violated the first prong of the *Lemon* test since it lacked a secular purpose. The Court was of the opinion that the legislation impacted the science curriculum by reflecting a religion-based view that either banished the theory of evolution from the classroom or added the presentation of a religious viewpoint that rejects evolution entirely.

In another case from Louisiana, a school board adopted a resolution disclaiming the endorsement of evolution after it failed to introduce "creation-science" into its curriculum as a legitimate scientific alternative to evolution. Parents successfully challenged the disclaimer under the Establishment Clause in both the federal and state constitutions.[342] The Fifth Circuit affirmed that the disclaimer was unacceptable because it did not promote the articulated objective of encouraging informed freedom of belief or critical thinking while advancing the purposes of disclaiming orthodoxy of belief and of reducing offense to the sensibilities of any student or parent. In like fashion, a federal trial court in Georgia held that a board's ordering officials to place stickers on biology textbooks, proclaiming that

---

337. *Scopes v. State*, 289 S.W. 363 (Tenn.1927).

338. *Id.* at 367.

339. 393 U.S. 97, 89 S.Ct. 266, 21 L.Ed.2d 228 (1968). [Case No. 6]

340. *McLean v. Arkansas Bd. of Educ.*, 529 F.Supp. 1255 [2 Educ. L. Rep. 685] (E.D.Ark. 1982).

341. 482 U.S. 578, 107 S.Ct. 2573, 96 L.Ed.2d 510 [39 Educ. L. Rep. 958] (1987).

342. *Freiler v. Tangipahoa Parish Bd. of Educ.*, 185 F.3d 337 [137 Educ. L. Rep. 195] (5th Cir.1999), *reh'g en banc denied*, 201 F.3d 602 [141 Educ. L. Rep. 458] (5th Cir.2000), *cert. denied*, 530 U.S. 1251, 120 S.Ct. 2706, 147 L.Ed.2d 974 (2000).

evolution was a theory, not fact, and inviting students to approach material in their books with open minds, study it carefully, and give it critical consideration, violated the Establishment Clause by impermissibly favoring religion. On appeal, the Eleventh Circuit vacated and remanded in favor of the board on the basis that it needed additional evidentiary inquiries and new findings of fact before proceeding.[343]

As the newest battleground in disputes over the origins of humankind, a federal trial court in Pennsylvania invalidated a school board policy on the teaching of intelligent design in a high school biology class. The policy would have required students to hear a statement mentioning intelligent design as an alternative to Darwin's theory of evolution. The court invalidated the policy as unconstitutional since it both amounted to an endorsement of religion in violation of the Establishment Clause and violated the *Lemon* test because its primary purpose was to change the biology curriculum to advance religion along with having the primary effect of imposing a religious view perspective into the biology course.[344]

Disputes have also arisen over whether educators can be required to teach about evolution. An appellate court in California rejected the claim of a teacher that officials violated his right to free speech in directing him not to talk about religion during the school day because he refused to teach about evolution.[345] Also, an appellate court in Minnesota upheld a board's reassigning a teacher to a different biology course when he refused to teach about evolution.[346]

A novel question including a teacher's criticism of a student's belief in creationism arose in California. The Ninth Circuit affirmed the denial of the student's claims against a teacher who described religion as "superstitious nonsense"[347] in addition to demonstrating hostility to religion in general and to Christianity in particular. In granting the teacher's motion for qualified immunity because the law was not clearly established, the court rejected the student's request for declaratory and injunctive relief as moot because he graduated from high school. The court added that judicial intervention would have been inappropriate since educators need to have "leeway to challenge students to foster critical thinking skills and develop their analytical abilities."[348]

---

343. *Selman v. Cobb County School Dist.*, 449 F.3d 1320 [210 Educ. L. Rep. 51] (11th Cir.2006).

344. *Kitzmiller v. Dover Area School Dist.*, 400 F.Supp.2d 707 [205 Educ. L. Rep. 250] (M.D.Pa.2005).

345. *Peloza v. Capistrano Unified School Dist.*, 37 F.3d 517 [94 Educ. L. Rep. 1159] (9th Cir.1994), *cert. denied*, 515 U.S. 1173, 115 S.Ct. 2640, 132 L.Ed.2d 878 (1995).

346. *LeVake v. Independent School Dist. No. 656*, 625 N.W.2d 502 [153 Educ. L. Rep. 356] (Minn.Ct.App.2001), *review denied* (2001), *cert. denied*, 534 U.S. 1081, 122 S.Ct. 814, 151 L.Ed.2d 698 (2002).

347. *C.F. v. Capistrano Unified School Dist.*, 654 F.3d 975, 982 [272 Educ. L. Rep. 169] (9th Cir. 2011).

348. *Id.* at 988.

[CASE NO. 1]   CONSTITUTIONALITY OF PROVIDING TRANSPORTATION TO STUDENTS WHO ATTEND NON–PUBLIC SCHOOLS

EVERSON v. BOARD OF EDUCATION OF EWING TOWNSHIP

Supreme Court of the United States, 1947.
330 U.S. 1, 67 S.Ct. 504, 91 L.Ed. 711.

■ MR. JUSTICE BLACK delivered the opinion of the Court.

A New Jersey statute authorizes its local school districts to make rules and contracts for the transportation of children to and from schools. The appellee, a township board of education, acting pursuant to this statute authorized reimbursement to parents of money expended by them for the bus transportation of their children on regular busses operated by the public transportation system. Part of this money was for the payment of transportation of some children in the community to Catholic parochial schools. These church schools give their students, in addition to secular education, regular religious instruction conforming to the religious tenets and modes of worship of the Catholic Faith. The superintendent of these schools is a Catholic priest.

. . .

The only contention here is that the State statute and the resolution, in so far as they authorized reimbursement to parents of children attending parochial schools, violate the Federal Constitution in these two respects, which to some extent, overlap. First. They authorize the State to take by taxation the private property of some and bestow it upon others, to be used for their own private purposes. This, it is alleged, violates the due process clause of the Fourteenth Amendment. Second. The statute and the resolution forced inhabitants to pay taxes to help support and maintain schools which are dedicated to, and which regularly teach, the Catholic Faith. This is alleged to be a use of State power to support church schools contrary to the prohibition of the First Amendment which the Fourteenth Amendment made applicable to the states.

First. The due process argument that the State law taxes some people to help others carry out their private purposes is framed in two phases. The first phase is that a state cannot tax A to reimburse B for the cost of transporting his children to church schools. This is said to violate the due process clause because the children are sent to these church schools to satisfy the personal desires of their parents, rather than the public's interest in the general education of all children. This argument, if valid, would apply equally to prohibit state payment for the transportation of children to any non-public school, whether operated by a church, or any other non-government individual or group. But, the New Jersey legislature has decided that a public purpose will be served by using tax-raised funds to pay the bus fares of all school children, including those who attend parochial schools. The New Jersey Court of Errors and Appeals has reached the same conclusion. The fact that a state law, passed to satisfy a public need, coincides with the personal desires of the individuals most directly affected is certainly an inadequate reason for us to say that a legislature has erroneously appraised the public need.

. . .

It is much too late to argue that legislation intended to facilitate the opportunity of children to get a secular education serves no public purpose. The same thing is no less true of legislation to reimburse needy parents, or all parents, for payment of the fares of their children so that they can ride in public busses to and from schools rather than run the risk of traffic and other hazards incident to walking or "hitchhiking." Nor does it follow that a law has a private rather than a public purpose because it provides that tax-raised funds will be paid to reimburse individuals on account of money spent by them in a way which furthers a public program. Subsidies and loans to individuals such as farmers and home owners, and to privately owned transportation systems, as well as many other kinds of businesses, have been commonplace practices in our state and national history.

. . .

Second. The New Jersey statute is challenged as a "law respecting an establishment of religion." The First Amendment, as made applicable to the states by the Fourteenth, commands that a state "shall make no law respecting an establishment of religion, or prohibiting the free exercise thereof." These words of the First Amendment reflected in the minds of early Americans a vivid mental picture of conditions and practices which they fervently wished to stamp out in order to preserve liberty for themselves and for their posterity. Doubtless their goal has not been entirely reached; but so far has the Nation moved toward it that the expression "law respecting an establishment of religion," probably does not so vividly remind present-day Americans of the evils, fears, and political problems that caused that expression to be written into our Bill of Rights. Whether this New Jersey law is one respecting the "establishment of religion" requires an understanding of the meaning of that language, particularly with respect to the imposition of taxes. Once again, therefore, it is not inappropriate briefly to review the background and environment of the period in which that constitutional language was fashioned and adopted.

. . .

The "establishment of religion" clause of the First Amendment means at least this: Neither a state nor the Federal Government can set up a church. Neither can pass laws which aid one religion, aid all religions, or prefer one religion over another. Neither can force nor influence a person to go to or to remain away from church against his will or force him to profess a belief or disbelief in any religion. No person can be punished for entertaining or professing religious beliefs or disbeliefs, for church attendance or non-attendance. No tax in any amount, large or small, can be levied to support any religious activities or institutions, whatever they may be called, or whatever form they may adopt to teach or practice religion. Neither a state nor the Federal Government can, openly or secretly, participate in the affairs of any religious organizations or groups and vice versa. In the words of Jefferson, the clause against establishment of religion by law was intended to erect "a wall of separation between Church and State."

... New Jersey cannot consistently with the "establishment of religion" clause of the First Amendment contribute tax-raised funds to the support of an institution which teaches the tenets and faith of any church. On the other hand, other language of the amendment commands that New Jersey cannot hamper its citizens in the free exercise of their own religion. Consequently, it cannot exclude individual Catholics, Lutherans, Mohammedans, Baptists, Jews, Methodists, Nonbelievers, Presbyterians, or the members of any other faith, *because of their faith, or lack of it,* from receiving the benefits of public welfare legislation. While we do not mean to intimate that a state could not provide transportation only to children attending public schools, we must be careful, in protecting the citizens of New Jersey against state-established churches, to be sure that we do not inadvertently prohibit New Jersey from extending its general State law benefits to all its citizens without regard to their religious belief.

Measured by these standards, we cannot say that the First Amendment prohibits New Jersey from spending tax-raised funds to pay the bus fares of parochial school pupils as a part of a general program under which it pays the fares of pupils attending public and other schools. It is undoubtedly true that children are helped to get to church schools. There is even a possibility that some of the children might not be sent to the church schools if the parents were compelled to pay their children's bus fares out of their own pockets when transportation to a public school would have been paid for by the State. ... Similarly, parents might be reluctant to permit their children to attend schools which the state had cut off from such general government services as ordinary police and fire protection, connections for sewage disposal, public highways and sidewalks. Of course, cutting off church schools from these services, so separate and so indisputably marked off from the religious function, would make it far more difficult for the schools to operate. But such is obviously not the purpose of the First Amendment. That Amendment requires the state to be a neutral in its relations with groups of religious believers and non-believers; it does not require the state to be their adversary. State power is no more to be used so as to handicap religions, than it is to favor them.

This Court has said that parents may, in the discharge of their duty under state compulsory education laws, send their children to a religious rather than a public school if the school meets the secular educational requirements which the state has power to impose. It appears that these parochial schools meet New Jersey's requirements. The State contributes no money to the schools. It does not support them. Its legislation, as applied, does no more than provide a general program to help parents get their children, regardless of their religion, safely and expeditiously to and from accredited schools.

The First Amendment has erected a wall between church and state. That wall must be kept high and impregnable. We could not approve the slightest breach. New Jersey has not breached it here.

Affirmed.

NOTES

1. The dissent argued that it was impossible to select the cost of transportation from among other expenses associated with education and characterize it as not aiding non-public schools because, where needed, it is "as essential to education as any other element" of the total cost. Did the majority respond to this point? If so, how?

2. In concurring opinions in *Engel v. Vitale* and *School District of Abington Township v. Schempp*, Justice Douglas wrote that in retrospect he agreed with the dissenters. Had he initially voted with the dissent, how might this have changed the face of church-state relations?

[CASE NO. 2]   CONSTITUTIONALITY OF VOLUNTARY RELIGIOUS INSTRUCTION IN PUBLIC SCHOOLS

PEOPLE OF THE STATE OF ILLINOIS EX REL. McCOLLUM v. BOARD OF EDUCATION OF SCHOOL DISTRICT 71, CHAMPAIGN COUNTY

Supreme Court of the United States, 1948.
333 U.S. 203, 68 S.Ct. 461, 92 L.Ed. 649.

■ Mr. Justice Black delivered the opinion of the Court.

. . .

. . . In 1940 interested members of the Jewish, Roman Catholic, and a few of the Protestant faiths formed a voluntary association called the Champaign Council on Religious Education. They obtained permission from the Board of Education to offer classes in religious instruction to public school pupils in grades four to nine inclusive. Classes were made up of pupils whose parents signed printed cards requesting that their children be permitted to attend; they were held weekly, thirty minutes for the lower grades, forty-five minutes for the higher. The council employed the religious teachers at no expense to the school authorities, but the instructors were subject to the approval and supervision of the superintendent of schools. The classes were taught in three separate religious groups by Protestant teachers, Catholic priests, and a Jewish rabbi, although for the past several years there have apparently been no classes instructed in the Jewish religion. Classes were conducted in the regular classrooms of the school building. Students who did not choose to take the religious instruction were not released from public school duties; they were required to leave their classrooms and go to some other place in the school building for pursuit of their secular studies. On the other hand, students who were released from secular study for the religious instructions were required to be present at the religious classes. Reports of their presence or absence were to be made to their secular teachers.

The foregoing facts, without reference to others that appear in the record, show the use of tax-supported property for religious instruction and the close cooperation between the school authorities and the religious council in promoting religious education. The operation of the state's compulsory education system thus assists and is integrated with the program of religious instruction carried on by separate religious sects. Pupils compelled by law to go to school for secular education are released in part from their legal duty upon the condition that they attend the religious classes. This is beyond all question a utilization of the tax-established and tax-supported public school system to aid religious groups to spread their faith. And it falls squarely under the ban of the First Amendment (made applicable to the States by the Fourteenth) as we interpreted it in *Everson v. Board of Education.* There we said: "Neither a state nor the Federal Government can set up a church. Neither can pass laws which aid one religion, aid all religions, or prefer one religion over another. Neither can force or influence a person to go to or to remain away from church against his will or force him to profess a belief or disbelief in any religion. No person can be punished for entertaining or professing religious beliefs or disbeliefs, for church attendance or nonattendance. No tax in any amount, large or small, can be levied to support any religious activities or institutions, whatever they may be called, or whatever form they may adopt to teach or practice religion. Neither a state nor the Federal Government can, openly or secretly, participate in the affairs of any religious organizations or groups, and vice versa. In the words of Jefferson, the clause against establishment of religion by law was intended to erect 'a wall of separation between Church and State.'" The majority in the *Everson* case, and the minority as shown by quotations from the dissenting views, ... agreed that the First Amendment's language, properly interpreted, had erected a wall of separation between Church and State. They disagreed as to the facts shown by the record and as to the proper application of the First Amendment's language to those facts....

To hold that a state cannot consistently with the First and Fourteenth Amendments utilize its public school system to aid any or all religious faiths or sects in the dissemination of their doctrines and ideals does not, as counsel urge, manifest a governmental hostility to religion or religious teachings. A manifestation of such hostility would be at war with our national tradition as embodied in the First Amendment's guaranty of the free exercise of religion. For the First Amendment rests upon the premise that both religion and government can best work to achieve their lofty aims if each is left free from the other within its respective sphere. Or, as we said in the *Everson* case, the First Amendment has erected a wall between Church and State which must be kept high and impregnable.

Here not only are the state's tax-supported public school buildings used for the dissemination of religious doctrines. The State also affords sectarian groups an invaluable aid in that it helps to provide pupils for their religious classes through use of the state's compulsory public school machinery. This is not separation of Church and State.

The cause is reversed and remanded to the State Supreme Court for proceedings not inconsistent with this opinion.

Reversed and remanded.

NOTES

1. Note that the Court quoted with approval from *Everson* on the point of the unconstitutionality of government aid to all religions.

2. Do you think the Court would have reached the same result if the children who attended religion classes were dismissed from school?

3. On remand from the Fifth Circuit's having vitiated a volunteer school counseling program that involved the use of clergy because it violated the Establishment Clause by advancing religion and by creating excessive entanglement, a federal trial court in Texas agreed that the program failed the neutrality test of *Lemon v. Kurtzman. Oxford v. Beaumont Independent School Dist.*, 224 F.Supp.2d 1099 [171 Educ. L. Rep. 182] (E.D. Tex. 2002).

[CASE NO. 3] CONSTITUTIONALITY OF "RELEASED TIME" FOR RELIGIOUS INSTRUCTION

ZORACH v. CLAUSON

Supreme Court of the United States, 1952.
343 U.S. 306, 72 S.Ct. 679, 96 L.Ed. 954.

■ MR. JUSTICE DOUGLAS delivered the opinion of the Court.

New York City has a program which permits its public schools to release students during the school day so that they may leave the school buildings and school grounds and go to religious centers for religious instruction or devotional exercises. A student is released on written request of his parents. Those not released stay in the classrooms. The churches make weekly reports to the schools, sending a list of children who have been released from public school but who have not reported for religious instruction.

This "released time" program involves neither religious instruction in public school classrooms nor the expenditure of public funds. All costs, including the application blanks, are paid by the religious organizations. The case is therefore unlike *McCollum v. Board of Education*. . . .

It takes obtuse reasoning to inject any issue of the "free exercise" of religion into the present case. No one is forced to go to the religious classroom and no religious exercise or instruction is brought to the classrooms of the public schools. A student need not take religious instruction. He is left to his own desires as to the manner or time of his religious devotions, if any.

There is a suggestion that the system involves the use of coercion to get public school students into religious classrooms. There is no evidence in the record before us that supports that conclusion. The present record indeed tells us that the school authorities are neutral in this regard and do no more than release students whose parents so request. If in fact coercion were used, if it were established that any one or more teachers were using their office to persuade or force students to take the religious instruction, a wholly different case would be presented. . . .

Moreover, apart from that claim of coercion, we do not see how New York by this type of "released time" program has made a law respecting an establishment of religion within the meaning of the First Amendment. There is much talk of the separation of Church and State in the history of the Bill of Rights and in the decisions clustering around the First Amendment. There cannot be the slightest doubt that the First Amendment reflects the philosophy that Church and State should be separated. And so far as interference with the "free exercise" of religion and an "establishment" of religion are concerned, the separation must be complete and unequivocal. The First Amendment within the scope of its coverage permits no exception; the prohibition is absolute. The First Amendment, however, does not say that in every and all respects there shall be a separation of Church and State. Rather, it studiously defines the manner, the specific ways, in which there shall be no concert or union or dependency one on the other. That is the common sense of the matter. Otherwise the state and religion would be aliens to each other—hostile, suspicious, and even unfriendly. Churches could not be required to pay even property taxes. Municipalities would not be permitted to render police or fire protection to religious groups....

We would have to press the concept of separation of Church and State to these extremes to condemn the present law on constitutional grounds. The nullification of this law would have wide and profound effects. A Catholic student applies to his teacher for permission to leave the school during hours on a Holy Day of Obligation to attend a mass. A Jewish student asks his teacher for permission to be excused for Yom Kippur. A Protestant wants the afternoon off for a family baptismal ceremony. In each case the teacher requires parental consent in writing. In each case the teacher, in order to make sure the student is not a truant, goes further and requires a report from the priest, rabbi, or the minister. The teacher in other words cooperates in a religious program to the extent of making it possible for her students to participate in it. Whether she does it occasionally for a few students, regularly for one, or pursuant to a systematized program designed to further the religious needs of all the students does not alter the character of the act.

We are a religious people whose institutions presuppose a Supreme Being. We guarantee the freedom to worship as one chooses. We make room for as wide a variety of beliefs and creeds as the spiritual needs of man deem necessary. We sponsor an attitude on the part of government that shows no partiality to any one group and that lets each flourish according to the zeal of its adherents and the appeal of its dogma. When the state encourages religious instruction or cooperates with religious authorities by adjusting the schedule of public events to sectarian needs, it follows the best of our traditions. For it then respects the religious nature of our people and accommodates the public service to their spiritual needs. To hold that it may not would be to find in the Constitution a requirement that the government show a callous indifference to religious groups. That would be preferring those who believe in no religion over those who do believe. Government may not finance religious groups nor undertake religious instruction nor blend secular and sectarian education nor use secular institutions to force one or some religion on any person. But we find no constitutional requirement which makes it necessary for government to be hostile to religion and to throw its weight against efforts to widen the effective scope of religious influence. The government must be neutral when it comes to competition between sects. It may not thrust any sect on any person. It may not make a religious observance compulsory. It may not coerce anyone to attend church, to observe a religious holiday, or to take religious instruction. But it can close its doors or suspend its operations as to those who want to repair to their religious sanctuary for worship or instruction. No more than that is undertaken here.

This program may be unwise and improvident from an educational or a community viewpoint. That appeal is made to us on a theory, previously advanced, that each case must be decided on the basis of "our own prepossessions." Our individual preferences, however, are not the constitutional standard. The constitutional standard is the separation of Church and State. The problem, like many problems in constitutional law, is one of degree.

In the *McCollum* case the classrooms were used for religious instruction and the force of the public school was used to promote that instruction. Here, as we have said, the public schools do no more than accommodate their schedules to a program of outside religious instruction. We follow the *McCollum* case. But we cannot expand it to cover the present released program unless separation of Church and State means that public institutions can make no adjustments of their schedules to accommodate the religious needs of the people. We cannot read into the Bill of Rights such a philosophy of hostility to religion.

Affirmed.

NOTES

1. The Supreme Court of Wisconsin, in a case involving an amendment to the state constitution permitting released time, rejected a claim that later Supreme Court cases superseded *Zorach. See State ex rel. Holt v. Thompson*, 225 N.W.2d 678 (Wis.1975). The Fourth, *Smith v. Smith*, 523 F.2d 121 (4th Cir.1975), *cert. denied*, 423 U.S. 1073, 96 S.Ct. 856, 47 L.Ed.2d 83 (1976), and Ninth, *Lanner v. Wimmer*, 662 F.2d 1349 [1 Educ. L. Rep. 138] (10th Cir.1981), Circuits rebuffed similar challenges to *Zorach's* viability.

2. Do you think that released time is a sound pedagogical practice?

[CASE NO. 4]   CONSTITUTIONALITY OF THE BIBLE AND THE LORD'S PRAYER IN PUBLIC SCHOOLS

SCHOOL DISTRICT OF ABINGTON TOWNSHIP v. SCHEMPP, MURRAY v. CURLETT

Supreme Court of the United States, 1963.
374 U.S. 203, 83 S.Ct. 1560, 10 L.Ed.2d 844.

■ Mr. Justice Clark delivered the opinion of the Court.

. . . These companion cases present the issues in the context of state action requiring that schools begin each day with readings from the Bible. While raising the basic questions under slightly different factual situations, the cases permit of joint treatment. In light of the history of the First Amendment and of our cases interpreting and applying its requirements, we hold that the practices at issue and the laws requiring them are unconstitutional under the Establishment Clause, as applied to the States through the Fourteenth Amendment.

. . . The Commonwealth of Pennsylvania by law, . . . requires that "At least ten verses from the Holy Bible shall be read, without comment, at the opening of each public school on each school day. Any child shall be excused from such Bible reading, or attending such Bible reading, upon the written request of his parent or guardian." The Schempp family, husband and wife and two of their three children, brought suit to enjoin enforcement of the statute. . . .

The appellees Edward Lewis Schempp, his wife Sidney, and their children, Roger and Donna, are of the Unitarian faith and are members of the Unitarian Church in Germantown, Philadelphia, Pennsylvania, where they . . . regularly attend religious services. . . .

On each school day at the Abington Senior High School between 8:15 and 8:30 a.m., while the pupils are attending their home rooms or advisory sections, opening exercises are conducted pursuant to the statute. The exercises are broadcast into each room in the school building through an intercommunications system and are conducted under the supervision of a teacher by students attending the school's radio and television workshop. Selected students from this course gather each morning in the school's workshop studio for the exercises, which include readings by one of the students of 10 verses of the Holy Bible, broadcast to each room in the building. This is followed by the recitation of the Lord's Prayer, likewise over the intercommunications system, but also by the students in the various classrooms, who are asked to stand and join in repeating the prayer in unison. The exercises are closed with the flag salute and such pertinent announcements as are of interest to the students. Participation in the opening exercises, as directed by the statute, is voluntary. The student reading the verses from the Bible may select the passages and read from any version he chooses, although the only copies furnished by the school are the King James version, copies of which were circulated to each teacher by the school district. During the period in which the exercises have been conducted the King James, the Douay and the Revised Standard versions of the Bible have been used, as well as the Jewish Holy Scriptures. There are no prefatory statements, no questions asked or solicited, no comments or explanations made and no interpretations given at or during the exercises. The students and parents are advised that the student may absent himself from the classroom or, should he elect to remain, not participate in the exercises. . . .

At the first trial Edward Schempp and the children testified as to specific religious doctrines purveyed by a literal reading of the Bible "which were contrary to the religious beliefs which they held and to their familial teaching." The children testified that all of the doctrines to which they referred were read to them at various times as part of the exercises. Edward Schempp testified at the second trial that he had considered having

Roger and Donna excused from attendance at the exercises but decided against it for several reasons, including his belief that the children's relationships with their teachers and classmates would be adversely affected. . . .

. . .

The wholesome "neutrality" of which this Court's cases speak . . . stems from a recognition of the teachings of history that powerful sects or groups might bring about a fusion of governmental and religious functions or a concert or dependency of one upon the other to the end that official support of the State or Federal Government would be placed behind the tenets of one or of all orthodoxies. This the Establishment Clause prohibits. And a further reason for neutrality is found in the Free Exercise Clause, which recognizes the value of religious training, teaching and observance and, more particularly, the right of every person to freely choose his own course with reference thereto, free of any compulsion from the state. This the Free Exercise Clause guarantees. Thus, as we have seen, the two clauses may overlap. As we have indicated, the Establishment Clause has been directly considered by this Court eight times in the past score of years and, with only one Justice dissenting on the point, it has consistently held that the clause withdrew all legislative power respecting religious belief or the expression thereof. The test may be stated as follows: what are the purpose and the primary effect of the enactment? If either is the advancement or inhibition of religion then the enactment exceeds the scope of legislative power as circumscribed by the Constitution. That is to say that to withstand the strictures of the Establishment Clause there must be a secular legislative purpose and a primary effect that neither advances nor inhibits religion. . . .

Applying the Establishment Clause principles to the cases at bar we find that the States are requiring the selection and reading at the opening of the school day of verses from the Holy Bible and the recitation of the Lord's Prayer by the students in unison. These exercises are prescribed as part of the curricular activities of students who are required by law to attend school. They are held in the school buildings under the supervision and with the participation of teachers employed in those schools. . . .

. . . Nor are these required exercises mitigated by the fact that individual students may absent themselves upon parental request, for that fact furnishes no defense to a claim of unconstitutionality under the Establishment Clause. Further, it is no defense to urge that the religious practices here may be relatively minor encroachments on the First Amendment. . . .

It is insisted that unless these religious exercises are permitted a "religion of secularism" is established in the schools. We agree of course that the State may not establish a "religion of secularism" in the sense of affirmatively opposing or showing hostility to religion, thus "preferring those who believe in no religion over those who do believe." We do not agree, however, that this decision in any sense has that effect. In addition, it might well be said that one's education is not complete without a study of comparative religion or the history of religion and its relationship to the advancement of civilization. It certainly may be said that the Bible is worthy of study for its literary and historic qualities. Nothing we have said here indicates that such study of the Bible or of religion, when presented objectively as part of a secular program of education, may not be effected consistent with the First Amendment. But the exercises here do not fall into those categories. They are religious exercises, required by the States in violation of the command of the First Amendment that the Government maintain strict neutrality, neither aiding nor opposing religion....

The place of religion in our society is an exalted one, achieved through a long tradition of reliance on the home, the church and the inviolable citadel of the individual heart and mind. We have come to recognize through bitter experience that it is not within the power of government to invade that citadel, whether its purpose or effect be to aid or oppose, to advance or retard. In the relationship between man and religion, the State is firmly committed to a position of neutrality. Though the application of that rule requires interpretation of a delicate sort, the rule itself is clearly and concisely stated in the words of the First Amendment....

It is so ordered.

NOTES

1. In the trial court, the father of the Schempp family testified that he refused to request that his children be excused from the morning exercises because he thought they would have been labeled "odd." Was the father's concern justified?

2. In *Engel v. Vitale*, the Supreme Court struck down a policy calling for the recitation of a "non-denominational" prayer at the beginning of each school day. Is there a different constitutional issue raised when a prayer is formulated by school officials rather than their requiring the Lord's Prayer?

[CASE NO. 5]   CONSTITUTIONALITY OF PROVIDING TEXTBOOKS TO STUDENTS IN NON–PUBLIC SCHOOLS

BOARD OF EDUCATION OF CENTRAL SCHOOL DISTRICT NO. 1 v. ALLEN

Supreme Court of the United States, 1968.
392 U.S. 236, 88 S.Ct. 1923, 20 L.Ed.2d 1060.

■ MR. JUSTICE WHITE delivered the opinion of the Court.

A law of the State of New York requires local public school authorities to lend textbooks free of charge to all students in grades seven through 12; students attending private schools are included. This case presents the question whether this statute is a "law respecting the establishment of religion or prohibiting the free exercise thereof," and so in conflict with the First and Fourteenth Amendments to the Constitution, because it authorizes the loan of textbooks to students attending parochial schools. We hold that the law is not in violation of the Constitution.

Until 1965, § 701 of the Education Law of the State of New York, McKinney's Consol. Laws, c. 16, authorized public school boards to designate textbooks for use in the public schools, to purchase such books with public funds, and to rent or sell the books to public school students. In 1965 the Legislature amended § 701, basing the amendments on findings that the "public welfare and safety require that the state and local communities give assistance to educational programs which are important to our national defense and the general welfare of the state." Beginning with the 1966–1967 school year, local school boards were required to purchase textbooks and lend them without charge "to all children residing in such district who are enrolled in grades seven to twelve of a public or private school which complies with the compulsory education law." The books now loaned are "textbooks which are designated for use in any public, elementary or secondary schools of the state or are approved by any boards of education," and which—according to a 1966 amendment—"a pupil is required to use as a text for a semester or more in a particular class in the school he legally attends." . . .

Everson v. Board of Education is the case decided by this Court that is most nearly in point for today's problem. . . .

Of course books are different from buses. Most bus rides have no inherent religious significance, while religious books are common. However, the language of § 701 does not authorize the loan of religious books, and the State claims no right to distribute religious literature. Although the books loaned are those required by the parochial school for use in specific courses, each book loaned must be approved by the public school authorities; only secular books may receive approval. The law was construed by the Court of Appeals of New York as "merely making available secular textbooks at the request of the individual student," supra, and the record contains no suggestion that religious books have been loaned. Absent evidence we cannot assume that school authorities, who constantly face the same problem in selecting textbooks for use in the public schools, are unable to distinguish between secular and religious books or that they will not honestly discharge their duties under the law. In judging the validity of the statute on this record we must proceed on the assumption that books loaned to students are books that are not unsuitable for use in the public schools because of religious content.

The major reason offered by appellants for distinguishing free textbooks from free bus fares is that books, but not buses, are critical to the teaching process, and in a sectarian school that process is employed to teach religion. However, this Court has long recognized that religious schools pursue two goals, religious instruction and secular education. In the leading case of *Pierce v. Society of Sisters*, the Court held that although it would not question Oregon's power to compel school attendance or require that the attendance be at an institution meeting State-imposed requirements as to quality and nature of curriculum, Oregon had not shown that its interest in secular education required that all children attend publicly operated schools. A premise of this holding was the view that the State's interest in education would be served sufficiently by reliance on the secular teaching that accompanied religious training in the schools maintained by the Society of Sisters. Since *Pierce,* a substantial body of case law has confirmed the power of the States to insist that attendance at private schools, if it is to satisfy state compulsory-attendance laws, be at institutions which provide minimum hours of instruction, employ teachers of specified training, and cover prescribed subjects of instruction. Indeed, the State's interest in assuring that these standards are being met has been considered a sufficient reason for refusing to accept instruction at home as compliance with compulsory education statutes. . . .

Underlying these cases, and underlying also the legislative judgments that have preceded the court decisions, has been a recognition that private education has played and is playing a significant and valuable role in raising national levels of knowledge, competence, and experience. Americans care about the quality of the secular education available to their children. They have considered high quality education to be an indispensable ingredient for achieving the kind of nation, and the kind of citizenry, that they have desired to create. Considering this attitude, the continued willingness to rely on private school systems, including parochial systems, strongly suggests that a wide segment of informed opinion, legislative and otherwise, has found that those schools do an acceptable job of providing secular education to their students. This judgment is further evidence that parochial schools are performing, in addition to their sectarian function, the task of secular education.

Against this background of judgment and experience, unchallenged in the meager record before us in this case, we cannot agree with appellants either that all teaching in a sectarian school is religious or that the processes of secular and religious training are so intertwined that secular textbooks furnished to students by the public are in fact instrumental in the teaching of religion. This case comes to us after summary judgment entered on the pleadings. Nothing in this record supports the proposition that all textbooks, whether they deal with mathematics, physics, foreign languages, history, or literature, are used by the parochial schools to teach religion. No evidence has been offered about particular schools, particular courses, particular teachers, or particular books. We are unable to hold, based solely on judicial notice, that this statute results in unconstitutional involvement of the State with religious instruction or that § 701, for this or the other reasons urged, is a law respecting the establishment of religion within the meaning of the First Amendment. . . .

The judgment is affirmed.

NOTES

1.   Justice Douglas' dissent declared that there is nothing ideological about a bus, school lunch, public nurse, or scholarship. However, he thought that textbooks go to the very heart of education in non-public schools. Is this a valid distinction?

2.   The Supreme Court struck down a program that would have furnished textbooks to students who attended non-public schools that had racially discriminatory policies. *Norwood v. Harrison*, 413 U.S. 455, 93 S.Ct. 2804, 37 L.Ed.2d 723 (1973).

3.   The Court affirmed, without a written opinion, a case from New Jersey invalidating a plan which allowed parents whose children attended non-public schools to be reimbursed for purchasing secular textbooks. *Public Funds for Pub. School v. Marburger*, 358 F.Supp. 29 (D.N.J.1973), *aff'd*, 417 U.S. 961, 94 S.Ct. 3163, 41 L.Ed.2d 1134 (1974). The Court maintained that reimbursement was

unconstitutional since it applied exclusively to parents whose children were enrolled in non-public, primarily religious, schools. Previously, the Court refused to hear an appeal wherein the Supreme Court of Oregon held that a state law that authorized free textbooks for students who were enrolled in a religiously affiliated non-public school violated the state constitution. *Dickman v. School Dist. No. 62C, Oregon City, Clackamas County*, 366 P.2d 533 (Or.1961), *cert. denied sub nom. Carlson v. Dickman*, 371 U.S. 823, 83 S.Ct. 41, 9 L.Ed.2d 62 (1962).

[CASE NO. 6]   CONSTITUTIONALITY OF STATUTE FORBIDDING TEACHING OF EVOLUTION

EPPERSON v. STATE OF ARKANSAS

Supreme Court of the United States, 1968.
393 U.S. 97, 89 S.Ct. 266, 21 L.Ed.2d 228.

■ MR. JUSTICE FORTAS delivered the opinion of the Court.

I

This appeal challenges the constitutionality of the "anti-evolution" statute which the State of Arkansas adopted in 1928 to prohibit the teaching in its public schools and universities of the theory that man evolved from other species of life....

The Arkansas law makes it unlawful for a teacher in any state-supported school or university "to teach the theory or doctrine that mankind ascended or descended from a lower order of animals," or "to adopt or use in any such institution a textbook that teaches" this theory. Violation is a misdemeanor and subjects the violator to dismissal from his position.

The present case concerns the teaching of biology in a high school in Little Rock. According to the testimony, until the events here in litigation, the official textbook furnished for the high school biology course "did not have a section on the Darwinian Theory." Then, for the academic year 1965–1966, the school administration, on recommendation of the teachers of biology in the school system, adopted and prescribed a textbook which contained a chapter setting forth "the theory about the origin . . . of man from a lower form of animal."

Susan Epperson, a young woman who graduated from Arkansas' school system and then obtained her master's degree in zoology at the University of Illinois, was employed by the Little Rock school system in the fall of 1964 to teach 10th grade biology at Central High School. At the start of the next academic year, 1965, she was confronted by the new textbook (which one surmises from the record was not unwelcome to her). She faced at least a literal dilemma because she was supposed to use the new textbook for classroom instruction and presumably to teach the statutorily condemned chapter; but to do so would be a criminal offense and subject her to dismissal....

. . . Only Arkansas, Mississippi, and Tennessee have such "anti-evolution" or "monkey" laws on their books. There is no record of any prosecutions in Arkansas under its statute. It is possible that the statute is presently more of a curiosity than a vital fact of life in these States. Nevertheless, the present case was brought, the appeal as of right is properly here, and it is our duty to decide the issues presented.

II

At the outset, it is urged upon us that the challenged statute is vague and uncertain and therefore within the condemnation of the Due Process Clause of the Fourteenth Amendment. The contention that the Act is vague and uncertain is supported by language in the brief opinion of Arkansas' Supreme Court. That court, perhaps reflecting the discomfort which the statute's quixotic prohibition necessarily engenders in the modern mind, stated that it "expresses no opinion" as to whether the Act prohibits "explanation" of the theory of evolution or merely forbids "teaching that the theory is true." Regardless of this uncertainty, the court held that the statute is constitutional.

. . .

In any event, we do not rest our decision upon the asserted vagueness of the statute. On either interpretation of its language, Arkansas' statute cannot stand. It is of no moment whether the law is deemed to prohibit mention of Darwin's theory, or to forbid any or all of the infinite varieties of communication embraced within the term "teaching." Under either interpretation, the law must be stricken because of its conflict with the constitutional prohibition of state laws respecting an establishment of religion or prohibiting the free exercise thereof. The overriding fact is that Arkansas' law selects from the body of knowledge a particular segment which it proscribes for the sole reason that it is deemed to conflict with a particular religious doctrine; that is, with a particular interpretation of the Book of Genesis by a particular religious group. . . .

Judicial interposition in the operation of the public school system of the Nation raises problems requiring care and restraint. Our courts, however, have not failed to apply the First Amendment's mandate in our educational system where essential to safeguard the fundamental values of freedom of speech and inquiry and of belief. By and large, public education in our Nation is committed to the control of state and local authorities. Courts do not and cannot intervene in the resolution of conflicts which arise in the daily operation of school systems and which do not directly and sharply implicate basic constitutional values. On the other hand, "The vigilant protection of constitutional freedoms is nowhere more vital than in the community of American schools," and "This Court will be alert against invasions of academic freedom. . . ." As this Court said in *Keyishian v. Board of Regents*, the First Amendment "does not tolerate laws that cast a pall of orthodoxy over the classroom." . . .

There is and can be no doubt that the First Amendment does not permit the State to require that teaching and learning must be tailored to the principles or prohibitions of any religious sect or dogma. In *Everson v. Board of Education*, this Court, in upholding a state law to provide free bus service to school children, including those attending parochial schools, said:

"Neither [a State nor the Federal Government] can pass laws which aid one religion, aid all religions, or prefer one religion over another." ...

In the present case, there can be no doubt that Arkansas has sought to prevent its teachers from discussing the theory of evolution because it is contrary to the belief of some that the Book of Genesis must be the exclusive source of doctrine as to the origin of man. No suggestion has been made that Arkansas' law may be justified by considerations of state policy other than the religious views of some of its citizens. It is clear that fundamentalist sectarian conviction was and is the law's reason for existence. Its antecedent, Tennessee's "monkey law," candidly stated its purpose: to make it unlawful "to teach any theory that denies the story of the Divine Creation of man, as taught in the Bible, and to teach instead, that man has descended from a lower order of animals." Perhaps the sensational publicity attendant upon the *Scopes* trial induced Arkansas to adopt less explicit language. It eliminated Tennessee's reference to "the story of the Divine Creation of man" as taught in the Bible, but there is no doubt that the motivation for the law was the same: to suppress the teaching of a theory which, it was thought, "denied" the divine creation of man....

The judgment of the Supreme Court of Arkansas is reversed.

NOTES

1. The Supreme Court of Mississippi struck down the last anti-evolution statute in *Smith v. State*, 242 So.2d 692 (Miss.1970). Subsequently, Tennessee enacted a statute prohibiting the use of any textbook that discussed evolution unless there were a disclaimer that the doctrine was only a theory and not scientific fact as to the origin of man. The statute required the inclusion of the Genesis version of creation, if any version at all was included, while permitting it alone to be printed without the disclaimer. Also, the statute declared "the Holy Bible shall not be defined as a textbook, but is hereby declared to be a reference work, and shall not be required to carry the disclaimer." The Sixth Circuit declared the statute unconstitutional because it gave a preferential position to the Biblical version of creation. *Daniel v. Waters*, 515 F.2d 485, 487 (6th Cir.1975).

2. Several state legislatures have discussed including intelligent design in public school curricula. What do you think about this approach?

[CASE NO. 7]   CONSTITUTIONALITY OF REIMBURSEMENTS TO NON–PUBLIC SCHOOLS

LEMON v. KURTZMAN, EARLEY v. DiCENSO

Supreme Court of the United States, 1971.
403 U.S. 602, 91 S.Ct. 2105, 29 L.Ed.2d 745.

■ MR. CHIEF JUSTICE BURGER delivered the opinion of the Court.

These two appeals raise questions as to Pennsylvania and Rhode Island statutes providing state aid to church-related elementary and secondary schools. Both statutes are challenged as violative of the Establishment and Free Exercise Clauses of the First Amendment and the Due Process Clause of the Fourteenth Amendment.

Pennsylvania has adopted a statutory program that provides financial support to non-public elementary and secondary schools by way of reimbursement for the cost of teachers' salaries, textbooks, and instructional materials in specified secular subjects. Rhode Island has adopted a statute under which the State pays directly to teachers in non-public elementary schools a supplement of 15% of their annual salary. Under each statute state aid has been given to church-related educational institutions as well as other private schools. We hold that both statutes are unconstitutional.

I

The Rhode Island Statute

The Rhode Island Salary Supplement Act was enacted in 1969. It rests on the legislative finding that the quality of education available in non-public elementary schools has been jeopardized by the rapidly rising salaries needed to attract competent and dedicated teachers. The Act authorizes state officials to supplement the salaries of teachers of secular subjects in non-public elementary schools by paying directly to a teacher an amount not in excess of 15% of his current annual salary. As supplemented, however, a non-public school teacher's salary cannot exceed the maximum paid to teachers in the State's public schools, and the recipient must be certified by the state board of education in substantially the same manner as public school teachers.

In order to be eligible for the Rhode Island salary supplement, the recipient must teach in a non-public school at which the average per-pupil expenditure on secular education is less than the average in the State's public schools during a specified period. Appellant state Commissioner of Education also requires eligible schools to submit financial data. If this information indicates a per-pupil expenditure in excess of the statutory limitation, the records of the school in question must be examined in order to assess how much of the expenditure is attributable to secular education and how much to religious activity.

The Act also requires that teachers eligible for salary supplement must teach only those subjects that are offered in the State's public schools. They must use "only teaching materials which are used in the public schools." Finally, any teacher applying for a salary supplement must first agree in writing "not to teach a course in religion for so long as or during such time as he or she receives any salary supplements" under the Act....

The District Court concluded that the Act violated the Establishment Clause, holding that it fostered "excessive entanglement" between government and religion. In addition two judges thought that the Act had the impermissible effect of giving "significant aid to a religious enterprise." We affirm.

The Pennsylvania Statute

. . .

The statute authorizes appellee state Superintendent of Public Instruction to "purchase" specified "secular educational services" from non-public schools. Under the "contracts" authorized by the statute, the State directly reimburses non-public schools solely for their actual expenditures for teachers' salaries, textbooks, and instructional materials. A school seeking reimbursement must maintain prescribed accounting procedures that identify the "separate" cost of the "secular educational service." These accounts are subject to state audit. The funds for this program were originally derived from a new tax on horse and harness racing, but the Act is now financed by a portion of the state tax on cigarettes.

There are several significant statutory restrictions on state aid. Reimbursement is limited to courses "presented in the curricula of the public schools." It is further limited "solely" to courses in the following "secular" subjects: mathematics, modern foreign languages, physical science, and physical education. Textbooks and instructional materials included in the program must be approved by the state Superintendent of Public Instruction. Finally, the statute prohibits reimbursement for any course that contains "any subject matter expressing religious teaching, or the morals or forms of worship of any sect."

. . .

The court granted [Pennsylvania's] motion to dismiss the complaint for failure to state a claim for relief. It held that the Act violated neither the Establishment nor the Free Exercise Clauses, Chief Judge Hastie dissenting. We reverse.

II

In *Everson v. Board of Education* this Court upheld a state statute which reimbursed the parents of parochial school children for bus transportation expenses. There Mr. Justice Black, writing for the majority, suggested that the decision carried to "the verge" of forbidden territory under the Religion Clauses. Candor compels acknowledgement, moreover, that we can only dimly perceive the lines of demarcation in this extraordinarily sensitive area of constitutional law.

The language of the Religion Clauses of the First Amendment is at best opaque, particularly when compared with other portions of the Amendment. Its authors did not simply prohibit the establishment of a state church or a state religion, an area history shows they regarded as very important and fraught with great dangers. Instead they commanded that there should be "no law *respecting* an establishment of religion." A law may be one "respecting" the forbidden objective while falling short of its total realization. A law "respecting" the proscribed result, that is, the establishment of religion, is not always easily identifiable as one violative of the Clause. A given law might not *establish* a state religion but nevertheless be one "respecting" that end in the sense of being a step that could lead to such establishment and hence offend the First Amendment.

In the absence of precisely stated constitutional prohibitions, we must draw lines with reference to the three main evils against which the Establishment Clause was intended to afford protection: "sponsorship, financial support, and active involvement of the sovereign in religious activity."

Every analysis in this area must begin with consideration of the cumulative criteria developed by the Court over many years. Three such tests may be gleaned from our cases. First, the statute must have a secular legislative purpose; second, its principal or primary effect must be one that neither advances nor inhibits religion; finally, the statute must not foster "an excessive government entanglement with religion."

III

. . .

Our prior holdings do not call for total separation between church and state; total separation is not possible in an absolute sense. Some relationship between government and religious organizations is inevitable. Fire inspections, building and zoning regulations, and state requirements under compulsory school attendance laws are examples of necessary and permissible contacts. . . .

In order to determine whether the government entanglement with religion is excessive, we must examine the character and purposes of the institutions which are benefitted, the nature of the aid that the State provides, and the resulting relationship between the government and the religious authority. . . . Here we find that both statutes foster an impermissible degree of entanglement.

(a) Rhode Island program

. . .

The church schools involved in the program are located close to parish churches. This understandably permits convenient access for religious exercises since instruction in faith and morals is part of the total educational process. The school buildings contain identifying religious symbols such as crosses on the exterior and crucifixes, religious paintings and statues either in the classrooms or hallways. Although only approximately 30 minutes a day are devoted to direct religious instruction, there are religiously oriented extracurricular activities. Approximately two-thirds of the teachers in these schools are nuns of various religious orders. Their dedicated efforts provide an atmosphere in which religious instruction and religious vocations are natural and proper parts of life in such schools. Indeed, as the District Court found, the role of teaching nuns in enhancing the religious atmosphere has led the parochial school authorities to attempt to maintain a one-to-one ratio between nuns and lay teachers in all schools rather than permitting some to be staffed almost entirely by lay teachers.

On the basis of these findings the District Court concluded that the parochial schools constituted "an integral part of the religious mission of the Catholic Church." The various characteristics of the schools make them "a powerful vehicle for transmitting the Catholic faith to the next generation." This process of inculcating religious doctrine is, of course, enhanced by the impressionable age of the pupils, in primary schools particularly. In short, parochial schools involve substantial religious activity and purpose.

The substantial religious character of these church-related schools gives rise to entangling church-state relationships of the kind the Religion

Clauses sought to avoid. Although the District Court found that concern for religious values did not inevitably or necessarily intrude into the content of secular subjects, the considerable religious activities of these schools led the legislature to provide for careful governmental controls and surveillance by state authorities in order to ensure that state aid supports only secular education.

The dangers and corresponding entanglements are enhanced by the particular form of aid that the Rhode Island Act provides. Our decisions from *Everson* to *Allen* have permitted the States to provide church-related schools with secular, neutral, or non-ideological services, facilities, or materials. But transportation, school lunches, public health services, and secular textbooks supplied in common to all students were not thought to offend the Establishment Clause. We note that the dissenters in *Allen* seemed chiefly concerned with the pragmatic difficulties involved in ensuring the truly secular content of the textbooks provided at state expense.

In *Allen* the Court refused to make assumptions, on a meager record, about the religious content of the textbooks that the State would be asked to provide. We cannot, however, refuse here to recognize that teachers have a substantially different ideological character than books. In terms of potential for involving some aspect of faith or morals in secular subjects, a textbook's content is ascertainable, but a teacher's handling of a subject is not. We cannot ignore the dangers that a teacher under religious control and discipline poses to the separation of the religious from the purely secular aspects of precollege education. The conflict of functions inheres in the situation. . . .

We do not assume, however, that parochial school teachers will be unsuccessful in their attempts to segregate their religious beliefs from their secular educational responsibilities. But the potential for impermissible fostering of religion is present. The Rhode Island Legislature has not, and could not, provide state aid on the basis of a mere assumption that secular teachers under religious discipline can avoid conflicts. The State must be certain, given the Religion Clauses, that subsidized teachers do not inculcate religion—indeed the State here has undertaken to do so. To ensure that no trespass occurs, the State has therefore carefully conditioned its aid with pervasive restrictions. An eligible recipient must teach only those courses that are offered in the public schools and use only those texts and materials that are found in the public schools. In addition the teacher must not engage in teaching any course in religion.

A comprehensive, discriminating, and continuing state surveillance will inevitably be required to ensure that these restrictions are obeyed and the First Amendment otherwise respected. Unlike a book, a teacher cannot be inspected once so as to determine the extent and intent of his or her personal beliefs and subjective acceptance of the limitations imposed by the First Amendment. These prophylactic contacts will involve excessive and enduring entanglement between state and church.

. . .

(b) Pennsylvania program

The Pennsylvania statute also provides state aid to church-related schools for teachers' salaries. The complaint describes an educational system that is very similar to the one existing in Rhode Island. According to the allegations, the church-related elementary and secondary schools are controlled by religious organizations, have the purpose of propagating and promoting a particular religious faith, and conduct their operations to fulfill that purpose. Since this complaint was dismissed for failure to state a claim for relief, we must accept these allegations as true for purposes of our review.

As we noted earlier, the very restrictions and surveillance necessary to ensure that teachers play a strictly non-ideological role give rise to entanglements between church and state. The Pennsylvania statute, like that of Rhode Island, fosters this kind of relationship. Reimbursement is not only limited to courses offered in the public schools and materials approved by state officials, but the statute excludes "any subject matter expressing religious teaching, or the morals or forms of worship of any sect." In addition schools seeking reimbursement must maintain accounting procedures that require the State to establish the cost of the secular as distinguished from the religious instruction.

The Pennsylvania statute, moreover, has the further defect of providing state financial aid directly to the church-related schools. This factor distinguishes both *Everson* and *Allen,* for in both those cases the Court was careful to point out that state aid was provided to the student and his parents—not to the church-related school.... The history of government grants of a continuing cash subsidy indicates that such programs have almost always been accompanied by varying measures of control and surveillance. The government cash grants before us now provide no basis for predicting that comprehensive measures of surveillance and controls will not follow. In particular the government's post-audit power to inspect and evaluate a church-related school's financial records and to determine which expenditures are religious and which are secular creates an intimate and continuing relationship between church and state.

IV

A broader base of entanglement of yet a different character is presented by the divisive political potential of these state programs. In a community where such a large number of pupils are served by church-related schools, it can be assumed that state assistance will entail considerable political activity. Partisans of parochial schools, understandably concerned with rising costs and sincerely dedicated to both the religious and secular educational missions of their schools, will inevitably champion this cause and promote political action to achieve their goals. Those who oppose state aid, whether for constitutional, religious, or fiscal reasons, will inevitably respond and employ all of the usual political campaign techniques to prevail. Candidates will be forced to declare and voters to choose. It would be unrealistic to ignore the fact that many people confronted with issues of this kind will find their votes aligned with their faith.

Ordinarily political debate and division, however vigorous or even partisan, are normal and healthy manifestations of our democratic system of government, but political division along religious lines was one of the principal evils against which the First Amendment was intended to protect. The potential divisiveness of such conflict is a threat to the normal political process. To have States or communities divide on the issues presented by state aid to parochial schools would tend to confuse and obscure other issues of great urgency. We have an expanding array of vexing issues, local and national, domestic and international, to debate and divide on. It conflicts with our whole history and tradition to permit questions of the Religion Clauses to assume such importance in our legislatures and in our elections that they could divert attention from the myriad issues and problems which confront every level of government. The highways of church and state relationships are not likely to be one-way streets, and the Constitution's authors sought to protect religious worship from the pervasive power of government. The history of many countries attests to the hazards of religion intruding into the political arena or of political power intruding into the legitimate and free exercise of religious belief. . . .

The potential for political divisiveness related to religious belief and practice is aggravated in these two statutory programs by the need for continuing annual appropriations and the likelihood of larger and larger demands as costs and populations grow. . . .

V

. . .

Finally, nothing we have said can be construed to disparage the role of church-related elementary and secondary schools in our national life. Their contribution has been and is enormous. Nor do we ignore their economic plight in a period of rising costs and expanding need. Taxpayers generally have been spared vast sums by the maintenance of these educational institutions by religious organizations, largely by the gifts of faithful adherents.

The merit and benefits of these schools, however, are not the issue before us in these cases. The sole question is whether state aid to these schools can be squared with the dictates of the Religion Clauses. Under our system the choice has been made that government is to be entirely excluded from the area of religious instruction and churches excluded from the affairs of government. The Constitution decrees that religion must be a private matter for the individual, the family, and the institutions of private choice, and that while some involvement and entanglement is inevitable, lines must be drawn. . . .

The judgment of the Rhode Island District Court in No. 569 and No. 570 is affirmed. The judgment of the Pennsylvania District Court in No. 89 is reversed, and the case is remanded for further proceedings consistent with this opinion.

NOTES

1. On the same day that it ruled in *Lemon*, the Supreme Court upheld the constitutionality of the Higher Education Facilities Act of 1963 which made construction grants available to institutions of higher education, including church related colleges and universities. In *Tilton v. Richardson (Tilton)*, 403 U.S. 672, 91 S.Ct. 2091, 29 L.Ed.2d 790 (1971), the Court reasoned that while the section of the law that limited recipients' obligation not to use federally-financed facilities for sectarian instruction or religious worship to twenty years unconstitutionally allowed a contribution of property of substantial value to religious bodies, that section was severable. However, the Court was satisfied that the remainder of the statute did not violate the First Amendment. In upholding the remainder of the law, the Court distinguished *Tilton* from *Lemon* insofar as in *Tilton*, indoctrination was not a substantial purpose or activity of church-related colleges since the student body was not composed of impressionable children, the aid was non-ideological, and there was no excessive entanglement where the grants were one-time and single-purpose. Two years later, in *Hunt v. McNair*, 413 U.S. 734, 93 S.Ct. 2868, 37 L.Ed.2d 923 (1973), the Court decided that insofar as religion was not pervasive in the institution, South Carolina was free to issue revenue bonds to benefit the church-related college because it did not guarantee them with public funds. Later, the Supreme Court of California ruled that agreements facilitating the issuance of tax-exempt bonds to finance the construction of a conduit that would benefit a private Christian school and two Christian universities did not violate the Establishment Clause because all of the institutions offered broad curricula in secular subjects and the secular classes consisted of information and course work that was neutral with respect to religion. *California Statewide Communities Development Auth. v. All Persons Interested in Matter of Purchase Agreement*, 152 P.3d 1070 [216 Educ. L. Rep. 895] (2007).

2. In his concurrence in *Lamb's Chapel v. Center Moriches Union Free School Dist.*, 508 U.S. 384, 398, 113 S.Ct. 2141, 124 L.Ed.2d 352 [83 Educ. L. Rep. 30] (1993), *on remand*, 17 F.3d 1425 [89 Educ. L. Rep. 783] (2d Cir.1994). [Case No. 37], Justice Scalia employed a caustic description of the *Lemon* test: "Like some ghoul in a late-night horror movie that repeatedly sits up in its grave and shuffles abroad, after being repeatedly killed and buried, *Lemon* stalks our Establishment Clause jurisprudence once again, frightening the little children and school attorneys of Center Moriches Union Free School District." What do you think of this characterization?

[CASE NO. 8]   CONSTITUTIONALITY OF INCOME TAX DEDUCTION FOR EDUCATIONAL EXPENSES

MUELLER v. ALLEN

Supreme Court of the United States, 1983.
463 U.S. 388, 103 S.Ct. 3062, 77 L.Ed.2d 721 [11 Educ. L. Rep. 763].

■ JUSTICE REHNQUIST delivered the opinion of the Court.

. . .

Minnesota, by a law originally enacted in 1955 and revised in 1976 and again in 1978, permits state taxpayers to claim a deduction from gross income for certain expenses incurred in educating their children. The deduction is limited to actual expenses incurred for the "tuition, textbooks and transportation" of dependents attending elementary or secondary schools. A deduction may not exceed $500 per dependent in grades K through six and $700 per dependent in grades seven through twelve.

Today's case is no exception to our oft-repeated statement that the Establishment Clause presents especially difficult questions of interpretation and application. . . .

One fixed principle in this field is our consistent rejection of the argument that "any program which in some manner aids an institution with a religious affiliation" violates the Establishment Clause. For example, it is now well-established that a state may reimburse parents for expenses incurred in transporting their children to school, *Everson v. Board of Education*, and that it may loan secular textbooks to all schoolchildren within the state, *Board of Education v. Allen*.

Notwithstanding the repeated approval given programs such as those in *Allen* and *Everson*, our decisions also have struck down arrangements resembling, in many respects, these forms of assistance. In this case we are asked to decide whether Minnesota's tax deduction bears greater resemblance to those types of assistance to parochial schools we have approved, or to those we have struck down. Petitioners place particular reliance on our decision in *Committee for Public Education v. Nyquist*, where we held invalid a New York statute providing public funds for the maintenance and repair of the physical facilities of private schools and granting thinly disguised "tax benefits," actually amounting to tuition grants, to the parents of children attending private schools. As explained below, we conclude that § 290.09(22) bears less resemblance to the arrangement struck down in *Nyquist* than it does to assistance programs upheld in our prior decisions and those discussed with approval in *Nyquist*.

The general nature of our inquiry in this area has been guided, since the decision in *Lemon v. Kurtzman*, by the "three-part" test laid down in that case:

> "First, the statute must have a secular legislative purpose; second, its principle or primary effect must be one that neither advances nor inhibits religion . . .; finally, the statute must not foster 'an excessive government entanglement with religion.'"

While this principle is well settled, our cases have also emphasized that it provides "no more than [a] helpful signpost" in dealing with Establishment Clause challenges. With this *caveat* in mind, we turn to the specific challenges raised against § 290.09(22) under the *Lemon* framework.

Little time need be spent on the question of whether the Minnesota tax deduction has a secular purpose. Under our prior decisions, governmental assistance programs have consistently survived this inquiry even when they have run afoul of other aspects of the *Lemon* framework. This reflects, at least in part, our reluctance to attribute unconstitutional motives to the states, particularly when a plausible secular purpose for the state's program may be discerned from the face of the statute.

A state's decision to defray the cost of educational expenses incurred by parents—regardless of the type of schools their children attend— evidences a purpose that is both secular and understandable. An educated populace is essential to the political and economic health of any community, and a state's efforts to assist parents in meeting the rising cost of educational expenses plainly serves this secular purpose of ensuring that the state's citizenry is well-educated. Similarly, Minnesota, like other states, could conclude that there is a strong public interest in assuring the continued financial health of private schools, both sectarian and non-sectarian. By educating a substantial number of students such schools relieve public schools of a correspondingly great burden—to the benefit of all taxpayers. ...All these justifications are readily available to support § 290.09(22), and each is sufficient to satisfy the secular purpose inquiry of *Lemon*.

We turn therefore to the more difficult but related question whether the Minnesota statute has "the primary effect of advancing the sectarian aims of the non-public schools." In concluding that it does not, we find several features of the Minnesota tax deduction particularly significant. First, an essential feature of Minnesota's arrangement is the fact that § 290.09(22) is only one among many deductions—such as those for medical expenses and charitable contributions—available under the Minnesota tax laws. Our decisions consistently have recognized that traditionally "[l]egislatures have especially broad latitude in creating classifications and distinctions in tax statutes," in part because the "familiarity with local conditions" enjoyed by legislators especially enables them to "achieve an equitable distribution of the tax burden." ...

Other characteristics of § 290.09(22) argue equally strongly for the provision's constitutionality. Most importantly, the deduction is available for educational expenses incurred by *all* parents, including those whose children attend public schools and those whose children attend non-sectarian private schools or sectarian private schools. ... "[T]he provision of benefits to so broad a spectrum of groups is an important index of secular effect."

In this respect, as well as others, this case is vitally different from the scheme struck down in *Nyquist*. There, public assistance amounting to tuition grants, was provided only to parents of children in *non-public* schools. This fact had considerable bearing on our decision striking down the New York statute at issue; we explicitly distinguished both *Allen* and *Everson* on the grounds that "In both cases the class of beneficiaries included *all* schoolchildren, those in public as well as those in private schools." Moreover, we intimated that "public assistance (*e.g.,* scholarships) made available generally without regard to the sectarian-non-sectarian or public-non-public nature of the institution benefited," might not offend the Establishment Clause. We think the tax deduction adopted by Minnesota is more similar to this latter type of program than it is to the arrangement struck down in *Nyquist*. Unlike the assistance at issue in *Nyquist,* § 290.09(22) permits *all* parents—whether their children attend public school or private—to deduct their children's educational expenses.... [A] program, like § 290.09(22), that neutrally provides state assistance to a broad spectrum of citizens is not readily subject to challenge under the Establishment Clause.

We also agree with the Court of Appeals that, by channeling whatever assistance it may provide to parochial schools through individual parents, Minnesota has reduced the Establishment Clause objections to which its action is subject. It is true, of course, that financial assistance provided to parents ultimately has an economic effect comparable to that of aid given directly to the schools attended by their children. It is also true, however, that under Minnesota's arrangement public funds become available only as a result of numerous, private choices of individual parents of school-age children. For these reasons, we recognized in *Nyquist* that the means by which state assistance flows to private schools is of some importance: we said that "the fact that aid is disbursed to parents rather than to . . . schools" is a material consideration in Establishment Clause analysis, albeit "only one among many to be considered." It is noteworthy that all but one of our recent cases invalidating state aid to parochial schools have involved the direct transmission of assistance from the state to the schools themselves. The exception, of course, was *Nyquist,* which, as discussed previously, is distinguishable from this case on other grounds. Where, as here, aid to parochial schools is available only as a result of decisions of individual parents no "imprimatur of State approval" can be deemed to have been conferred on any particular religion, or on religion generally.

. . . The Establishment Clause of course extends beyond prohibition of a state church or payment of state funds to one or more churches. We do not think, however, that its prohibition extends to the type of tax deduction established by Minnesota. The historic purposes of the clause simply do not encompass the sort of attenuated financial benefit, ultimately controlled by the private choices of individual parents, that eventually flows to parochial schools from the neutrally available tax benefit at issue in this case.

Petitioners argue that, notwithstanding the facial neutrality of § 290.09(22), in application the statute primarily benefits religious institutions. Petitioners rely . . . on a statistical analysis of the type of persons claiming the tax deduction. They contend that most parents of public school children incur no tuition expenses, and that other expenses deductible under § 290.09(22) are negligible in value; moreover, they claim that 96% of the children in private schools in 1978–1979 attended religiously affiliated institutions. Because of all this, they reason, the bulk of deductions taken under § 290.09(22) will be claimed by parents of children in sectarian schools. Respondents reply that petitioners have failed to consider the impact of deductions for items such as transportation, summer school tuition, tuition paid by parents whose children attended schools outside the school districts in which they resided, rental or purchase costs for a variety of equipment, and tuition for certain types of instruction not ordinarily provided in public schools.

We need not consider these contentions in detail. We would be loath to adopt a rule grounding the constitutionality of a facially neutral law on annual reports reciting the extent to which various classes of private citizens claimed benefits under the law. Such an approach would scarcely provide the certainty that this field stands in need of, nor can we perceive principled standards by which such statistical evidence might be evaluated . . . .

Thus, we hold that the Minnesota tax deduction for educational expenses satisfies the primary effect inquiry of our Establishment Clause cases.

Turning to the third part of the *Lemon* inquiry, we have no difficulty in concluding that the Minnesota statute does not "excessively entangle" the state in religion. The only plausible source of the "comprehensive, discriminating, and continuing state surveillance" necessary to run afoul of this standard would lie in the fact that state officials must determine whether particular textbooks qualify for a deduction. Making decisions such as this does not differ substantially from making the types of decisions approved in earlier opinions of this Court. In *Board of Education v. Allen*, for example, the Court upheld the loan of secular textbooks to parents or children attending non-public schools; though state officials were required to determine whether particular books were or were not secular, the system was held not to violate the Establishment Clause. . . .

For the foregoing reasons, the judgment of the Court of Appeals is Affirmed.

NOTES

1. Should it have mattered that ninety-six percent of the children in non-public schools in Minnesota attended religious schools?

2. An appellate court in Illinois upheld a tax credit of up to $500 for educational expenses incurred on behalf of a qualifying pupil in grades K–12 at any state public or non-public school that complies with various state laws. The court rejected arguments that the credit had the effect of advancing religion not only because the majority of non-public schools are religiously affiliated but also because eighty-two out of the state's 102 counties do not have any non-sectarian schools. Should these two facts have made a difference? *Griffith v. Bower*, 747 N.E.2d 423 [153 Educ. L. Rep. 938] (Ill. App. Ct. 2001), *appeal denied*, 755 N.E.2d 477 (Ill. 2001).

[CASE NO. 9]   THE EQUAL ACCESS ACT AND STUDENT GROUPS

BOARD OF EDUCATION OF WESTSIDE COMMUNITY SCHOOLS v. MERGENS

Supreme Court of the United States, 1990.
496 U.S. 226, 110 S.Ct. 2356, 110 L.Ed.2d 191 [60 Educ. L. Rep. 320].

■ JUSTICE O'CONNOR delivered the opinion of the Court, except as to Part III.

This case requires us to decide whether the Equal Access Act, 20 U.S.C.[A.] §§ 4071–4074, prohibits Westside High School from denying a student religious group permission to meet on school premises during noninstructional time, and if so, whether the Act, so construed, violates the Establishment Clause of the First Amendment.

I

. . .

Students at Westside High School are permitted to join various student groups and clubs, all of which meet after school hours on school premises. The students may choose from approximately 30 recognized groups on a voluntary basis....

There is no written school board policy concerning the formation of student clubs. Rather, students wishing to form a club present their request to a school official who determines whether the proposed club's goals and objectives are consistent with school board policies and with the school district's "Mission and Goals"—a broadly worded "blueprint" that expresses the district's commitment to teaching academic, physical, civic, and personal skills and values.

In January 1985, respondent Bridget Mergens ... requested permission to form a Christian club at the school. The proposed club would have the same privileges and meet on the same terms and conditions as other Westside student groups, except that the proposed club would not have a faculty sponsor. According to the students' testimony at trial, the club's purpose would have been, among other things, to permit the students to read and discuss the Bible, to have fellowship, and to pray together. Membership would have been voluntary and open to all students regardless of religious affiliation.

... The school officials explained that school policy required all student clubs to have a faculty sponsor, which the proposed religious club would not or could not have, and that a religious club at the school would violate the Establishment Clause. In March 1985, Mergens appealed the denial of her request to the Board of Education, but the Board voted to uphold the denial....

II

A

In *Widmar v. Vincent,* we invalidated, on free speech grounds, a state university regulation that prohibited student use of school facilities " 'for purposes of religious worship or religious teaching.' " In doing so, we held that an "equal access" policy would not violate the Establishment Clause under our decision in *Lemon v. Kurtzman.* In particular, we held that such a policy would have a secular purpose, would not have the primary effect of advancing religion, and would not result in excessive entanglement between government and religion. We noted, however, that "[u]niversity students are, of course, young adults. They are less impressionable than younger students and should be able to appreciate that the University's policy is one of neutrality toward religion."

In 1984, Congress extended the reasoning of *Widmar* to public secondary schools. Under the Equal Access Act, a public secondary school with a "limited open forum" is prohibited from discriminating against students who wish to conduct a meeting within that forum on the basis of the "religious, political, philosophical, or other content of the speech at such meetings." Specifically, the Act provides:

"It shall be unlawful for any public secondary school which receives Federal financial assistance and which has a limited open forum to deny equal access or a fair opportunity to, or discriminate against, any students who wish to conduct a meeting within that limited open forum on the basis of the religious, political, philosophical, or other content of the speech at such meetings."

A "limited open forum" exists whenever a public secondary school "grants an offering to or opportunity for one or more non-curriculum related student groups to meet on school premises during non-instructional time." "Meeting" is defined to include "those activities of student groups which are permitted under a school's limited open forum and are not directly related to the school curriculum." "Non-instructional time" is defined to mean "time set aside by the school before actual classroom instruction begins or after actual classroom instruction ends." Thus, even if a public secondary school allows only one "non-curriculum related student group" to meet, the Act's obligations are triggered and the school may not deny other clubs, on the basis of the content of their speech, equal access to meet on school premises during non-instructional time.

The Act further specifies that "[s]chools shall be deemed to offer a fair opportunity to students who wish to conduct a meeting within its limited open forum" if the school uniformly provides that the meetings are voluntary and student-initiated; are not sponsored by the school, the government, or its agents or employees; do not materially and substantially interfere with the orderly conduct of educational activities within the school; and are not directed, controlled, conducted, or regularly attended by "non-school persons." "Sponsorship" is defined to mean "the act of promoting, leading, or participating in a meeting. The assignment of a teacher, administrator, or other school employee to a meeting for custodial purposes does not constitute sponsorship of the meeting." If the meetings are religious, employees or agents of the school or government may attend only in a "non-participatory capacity." Moreover, a State may not influence the form of any religious activity, require any person to participate in such activity, or compel any school agent or employee to attend a meeting if the content of the speech at the meeting is contrary to that person's beliefs.

Finally, the Act does not "authorize the United States to deny or withhold Federal financial assistance to any school" or "limit the authority of the school, its agents or employees, to maintain order and discipline on school premises, to protect the well-being of students and faculty, and to assure that attendance of students at the meetings is voluntary."

B

The parties agree that Westside High School receives federal financial assistance and is a public secondary school within the meaning of the Act. The Act's obligation to grant equal access to student groups is therefore triggered if Westside maintains a "limited open forum"—*i.e.,* if it permits one or more "non-curriculum related student groups" to meet on campus before or after classes.

Unfortunately, the Act does not define the crucial phrase "non-curriculum related student group." Our immediate task is therefore one of statutory interpretation. We begin, of course, with the language of the statute. The common meaning of the term "curriculum" is "the whole body of courses offered by an educational institution or one of its branches."... . Any sensible interpretation of "non-curriculum related student group" must therefore be anchored in the notion that such student groups are those that are not related to the body of courses offered by the school. The difficult question is the degree of "unrelatedness to the curriculum" required for a group to be considered "non-curriculum related."

The Act's definition of the sort of "meeting[s]" that must be accommodated under the statute sheds some light on this question. "[T]he term 'meeting' includes those activities of student groups which are ... not *directly related* to the school curriculum." (emphasis added). Congress' use of the phrase "directly related" implies that student groups directly related to the subject matter of courses offered by the school do not fall within the "non-curriculum related" category and would therefore be considered "curriculum related."

The logic of the Act also supports this view, namely, that a curriculum-related student group is one that has more than just a tangential or attenuated relationship to courses offered by the school. Because the purpose of granting equal access is to prohibit discrimination between religious or political clubs on the one hand and other non-curriculum-related student groups on the other, the Act is premised on the notion that a religious or political club is itself likely to be a non-curriculum-related student group. It follows, then, that a student group that is "curriculum related" must at least have a more direct relationship to the curriculum than a religious or political club would have.

Although the phrase "non-curriculum related student group" nevertheless remains sufficiently ambiguous that we might normally resort to legislative history, we find the legislative history on this issue less than helpful. ...

We think it significant, however, that the Act, which was passed by wide, bipartisan majorities in both the House and the Senate, reflects at least some consensus on a broad legislative purpose. The committee reports indicate that the Act was intended to address perceived widespread discrimination against religious speech in public schools, and, as the language of the Act indicates, its sponsors contemplated that the Act would do more than merely validate the status quo. The committee reports also show that the Act was enacted in part in response to two federal appellate court decisions holding that student religious groups could not, consistent with the Establishment Clause, meet on school premises during noninstructional time. A broad reading of the Act would be consistent with the views of those who sought to end discrimination by allowing students to meet and discuss religion before and after classes.

In light of this legislative purpose, we think that the term "non-curriculum related student group" is best interpreted broadly to mean any student group that does not *directly* relate to the body of courses offered by the school. In our view, a student group directly relates to a school's curriculum if the subject matter of the group is actually taught, or will soon be taught, in a regularly offered course; if the subject matter of the group concerns the body of courses as a whole; if participation in the group is required for a particular course; or if participation in the group results in academic credit. We think this limited definition of groups that directly relate to the curriculum is a commonsense interpretation of the Act that is consistent with Congress' intent to provide a low threshold for triggering the Act's requirements.

For example, a French club would directly relate to the curriculum if a school taught French in a regularly offered course or planned to teach the subject in the near future. A school's student government would generally relate directly to the curriculum to the extent that it addresses concerns, solicits opinions, and formulates proposals pertaining to the body of courses offered by the school. If participation in a school's band or orchestra were required for the band or orchestra classes, or resulted in academic credit, then those groups would also directly relate to the curriculum. The existence of such groups at a school would not trigger the Act's obligations.

On the other hand, unless a school could show that groups such as a chess club, a stamp collecting club, or a community service club fell within our description of groups that directly relate to the curriculum, such groups would be "non-curriculum related student groups" for purposes of the Act. The existence of such groups would create a "limited open forum" under the Act and would prohibit the school from denying equal access to any other student group on the basis of the content of that group's speech. Whether a specific student group is a "non-curriculum related student group" will therefore depend on a particular school's curriculum, but such determinations would be subject to factual findings well within the competence of trial courts to make.

Petitioners contend that our reading of the Act unduly hinders local control over schools and school activities, but we think that schools and school districts nevertheless retain a significant measure of authority over the type of officially recognized activities in which their students participate. First, schools and school districts maintain their traditional latitude to determine appropriate subjects of instruction. To the extent that a school chooses to structure its course offerings and existing student groups to avoid the Act's obligations, that result is not prohibited by the Act. On matters of statutory interpretation, "[o]ur task is to apply the text, not to improve on it." Second, the Act expressly does not limit a school's authority to prohibit meetings that would "materially and substantially interfere with the orderly conduct of educational activities within the school." The Act also preserves "the authority of the school, its agents or employees, to maintain order and discipline on school premises, to protect the well-being of students and faculty, and to assure that attendance of students at meetings is voluntary." Finally, because the Act applies only to public secondary schools that receive federal financial assistance, a school district seeking to escape the statute's obligations could simply forego federal funding. Although we do not doubt that in some cases this may be an unrealistic option, Congress clearly sought to prohibit schools from discriminating on the basis of the content of a student group's speech, and that obligation is the price a federally funded school must pay if it opens its facilities to non-curriculum-related student groups. . . .

C

... Petitioners contend that all of these student activities [cited as being non-curriculum-related] are curriculum-related because they further the goals of particular aspects of the school's curriculum.... Subsurfers [scuba diving] furthers "one of the essential goals of the Physical Education Department—enabling students to develop lifelong recreational interests." Chess "supplement[s] math and science courses because it enhances students' ability to engage in critical thought processes." ...

To the extent that petitioners contend that "curriculum related" means anything remotely related to abstract educational goals, however, we reject that argument. To define "curriculum related" in a way that results in almost no schools having limited open fora, or in a way that permits schools to evade the Act by strategically describing existing student groups, would render the Act merely hortatory....

Rather, we think it clear that Westside's existing student groups include one or more "non-curriculum related student groups." Although Westside's physical education classes apparently include swimming, counsel stated at oral argument that scuba diving is not taught in any regularly offered course at the school. Based on Westside's own description of the group, Subsurfers does not directly relate to the curriculum as a whole in the same way that a student government or similar group might. Moreover, participation in Subsurfers is not required by any course at the school and does not result in extra academic credit. Thus, Subsurfers is a "non-curriculum related student group" for purposes of the Act.... The record therefore supports a finding that Westside has maintained a limited open forum under the Act....

The remaining statutory question is whether petitioners' denial of respondents' request to form a religious group constitutes a denial of "equal access" to the school's limited open forum. Although the school apparently permits respondents to meet informally after school, respondents seek equal access in the form of official recognition by the school. Official recognition allows student clubs to be part of the student activities program and carries with it access to the school newspaper, bulletin boards, the public address system, and the annual Club Fair. Given that the Act explicitly prohibits denial of "equal access ... to ... any students who wish to conduct a meeting within [the school's] limited open forum" on the basis of the religious content of the speech at such meetings, we hold that Westside's denial of respondents' request to form a Christian club denies them "equal access" under the Act.

Because we rest our conclusion on statutory grounds, we need not decide—and therefore express no opinion on—whether the First Amendment requires the same result.

III

Petitioners contend that even if Westside has created a limited open forum within the meaning of the Act, its denial of official recognition to the proposed Christian club must nevertheless stand because the Act violates the Establishment Clause of the First Amendment, as applied to the States through the Fourteenth Amendment. Specifically, petitioners maintain that because the school's recognized student activities are an integral part of its educational mission, official recognition of respondents' proposed club would effectively incorporate religious activities into the school's official program, endorse participation in the religious club, and provide the club with an official platform to proselytize other students.

. . .

Accordingly, we hold that the Equal Access Act does not on its face contravene the Establishment Clause. Because we hold that petitioners have violated the Act, we do not decide respondents' claims under the Free Speech and Free Exercise Clauses. For the foregoing reasons, the judgment of the Court of Appeals is affirmed.

It is so ordered.

NOTES

1. Eight Justices agreed that the Equal Access Act did not violate the Establishment Clause. Even so, the plurality could not render a majority opinion on this point.

2. In the plurality opinion, four Justices agreed that it was rational for Congress to make the determination left open by the Court in *Widmar v. Vincent*, namely that secondary school students are capable of distinguishing between State-initiated, school-sponsored, or teacher-led religious speech and student-initiated and led religious speech. What do you think?

3. If the Equal Access Act were to be repealed, could school boards prevent students from organizing Christian clubs? Would boards be obliged to recognize Christian Clubs?

[CASE NO. 10]   PRAYER AT A PUBLIC SCHOOL GRADUATION CEREMONY

LEE v. WEISMAN

Supreme Court of the United States, 1992.
505 U.S. 577, 112 S.Ct. 2649, 120 L.Ed.2d 467 [75 Educ. L. Rep. 43].

■ JUSTICE KENNEDY delivered the opinion of the Court.

School principals in the public school system of the city of Providence, Rhode Island, are permitted to invite members of the clergy to offer invocation and benediction prayers as part of the formal graduation ceremonies for middle schools and for high schools. The question before us is whether including clerical members who offer prayers as part of the official school graduation ceremony is consistent with the Religion Clauses of the First Amendment, provisions the Fourteenth Amendment makes applicable with full force to the States and their school districts.

I

A

Deborah Weisman graduated from Nathan Bishop Middle School, a public school in Providence, at a formal ceremony in June 1989. She was about 14 years old.... Acting for himself and his daughter, Deborah's father, Daniel Weisman, objected to any prayers at Deborah's middle school graduation, but to no avail. The school principal, petitioner Robert E. Lee, invited a rabbi to deliver prayers at the graduation exercises for Deborah's class....

It has been the custom of Providence school officials to provide invited clergy with a pamphlet entitled "Guidelines for Civic Occasions," prepared by the National Conference of Christians and Jews. The Guidelines recommend that public prayers at non-sectarian civic ceremonies be composed with "inclusiveness and sensitivity," though they acknowledge that "[p]rayer of any kind may be inappropriate on some civic occasions." The principal gave Rabbi Gutterman the pamphlet before the graduation and advised him the invocation and benediction should be non-sectarian.

. . .

The school board (and the United States, which supports it as *amicus curiae*) argued that these short prayers and others like them at graduation exercises are of profound meaning to many students and parents throughout this country who consider that due respect and acknowledgment for divine guidance and for the deepest spiritual aspirations of our people ought to be expressed at an event as important in life as a graduation. We assume this to be so in addressing the difficult case now before us, for the significance of the prayers lies also at the heart of Daniel and Deborah Weisman's case....

II

These dominant facts mark and control the confines of our decision: State officials direct the performance of a formal religious exercise at promotional and graduation ceremonies for secondary schools. Even for those students who object to the religious exercise, their attendance and participation in the state-sponsored religious activity are in a fair and real sense obligatory, though the school district does not require attendance as a condition for receipt of the diploma.

This case does not require us to revisit the difficult questions dividing us in recent cases, questions of the definition and full scope of the principles governing the extent of permitted accommodation by the State for the religious beliefs and practices of many of its citizens. For without reference to those principles in other contexts, the controlling precedents as they relate to prayer and religious exercise in primary and secondary public schools compel the holding here that the policy of the city of Providence is an unconstitutional one. We can decide the case without reconsidering the general constitutional framework by which public schools' efforts to accommodate religion are measured. Thus we do not accept the invitation of petitioners and *amicus* the United States to reconsider our decision in *Lemon v. Kurtzman*. The government involvement with religious activity in this case is pervasive, to the point of creating a state-sponsored and state-directed religious exercise in a public school. Conducting this formal religious observance conflicts with settled rules pertaining to prayer exercises for students, and that suffices to determine the question before us.

The principle that government may accommodate the free exercise of religion does not supersede the fundamental limitations imposed by the Establishment Clause. It is beyond dispute that, at a minimum, the Constitution guarantees that government may not coerce anyone to support or participate in religion or its exercise, or otherwise act in a way which "establishes a [state] religion or religious faith, or tends to do so." The State's involvement in the school prayers challenged today violates these central principles.

That involvement is as troubling as it is undenied. A school official, the principal, decided that an invocation and a benediction should be given; this is a choice attributable to the State, and from a constitutional perspective it is as if a state statute decreed that the prayers must occur. The principal chose the religious participant, here a rabbi, and that choice is also attributable to the State. The reason for the choice of a rabbi is not disclosed by the record, but the potential for divisiveness over the choice of a particular member of the clergy to conduct the ceremony is apparent.

Divisiveness, of course, can attend any state decision respecting religions, and neither its existence nor its potential necessarily invalidates the State's attempts to accommodate religion in all cases. The potential for divisiveness is of particular relevance here though, because it centers around an overt religious exercise in a secondary school environment where, as we discuss below, subtle coercive pressures exist and where the student had no real alternative which would have allowed her to avoid the fact or appearance of participation.

The State's role did not end with the decision to include a prayer and with the choice of clergyman. Principal Lee provided Rabbi Gutterman with a copy of the "Guidelines for Civic Occasions," and advised him that his prayers should be non-sectarian. Through these means the principal directed and controlled the content of the prayer. Even if the only sanction for ignoring the instructions were that the rabbi would not be invited back, we think no religious representative who valued his or her continued reputation and effectiveness in the community would incur the State's displeasure in this regard. It is a cornerstone principle of our Establishment Clause jurisprudence that "it is no part of the business of government to compose official prayers for any group of the American people to recite as a part of a religious program carried on by government," and that is what the school officials attempted to do.

Petitioners argue, and we find nothing in the case to refute it, that the directions for the content of the prayers were a good-faith attempt by the school to ensure that the sectarianism which is so often the flashpoint for religious animosity be removed from the graduation ceremony. The concern is understandable, as a prayer which uses ideas or images identified with a particular religion may foster a different sort of sectarian rivalry than an invocation or benediction in terms more neutral. The school's explanation, however, does not resolve the dilemma caused by its participation. The question is not the good faith of the school in attempting to make the prayer acceptable to most persons, but the legitimacy of its undertaking that enterprise at all when the object is to produce a prayer to be used in a formal religious exercise which students, for all practical purposes, are obliged to attend. . . .

The First Amendment's Religion Clauses mean that religious beliefs and religious expression are too precious to be either proscribed or prescribed by the State. The design of the Constitution is that preservation and transmission of religious beliefs and worship is a responsibility and a choice committed to the private sphere, which itself is promised freedom to pursue that mission. . . .

These concerns have particular application in the case of school officials, whose effort to monitor prayer will be perceived by the students as inducing a participation they might otherwise reject. Though the efforts of the school officials in this case to find common ground appear to have been a good-faith attempt to recognize the common aspects of religions and not the divisive ones, our precedents do not permit school officials to assist in composing prayers as an incident to a formal exercise for their students. And these same precedents caution us to measure the idea of a civic religion against the central meaning of the Religion Clauses of the First Amendment, which is that all creeds must be tolerated and none favored. The suggestion that government may establish an official or civic religion as a means of avoiding the establishment of a religion with more specific creeds strikes us as a contradiction that cannot be accepted.

The degree of school involvement here made it clear that the graduation prayers bore the imprint of the State and thus put school-age children who objected in an untenable position. We turn our attention now to consider the position of the students, both those who desired the prayer and she who did not.

To endure the speech of false ideas or offensive content and then to counter it is part of learning how to live in a pluralistic society, a society which insists upon open discourse towards the end of a tolerant citizenry. And tolerance presupposes some mutuality of obligation. It is argued that our constitutional vision of a free society requires confidence in our own ability to accept or reject ideas of which we do not approve, and that prayer at a high school graduation does nothing more than offer a choice. . . . This argument cannot prevail, however. It overlooks a fundamental dynamic of the Constitution.

The First Amendment protects speech and religion by quite different mechanisms. Speech is protected by insuring its full expression even when the government participates, for the very object of some of our most important speech is to persuade the government to adopt an idea as its own. The method for protecting freedom of worship and freedom of conscience in religious matters is quite the reverse. In religious debate or expression the government is not a prime participant, for the Framers deemed religious establishment antithetical to the freedom of all. The Free Exercise Clause embraces a freedom of conscience and worship that has close parallels in the speech provisions of the First Amendment, but the Establishment Clause is a specific prohibition on forms of state intervention in religious affairs with no precise counterpart in the speech provisions. The explanation lies in the lesson of history that was and is the inspiration for the Establishment Clause, the lesson that in the hands of government what might begin as a tolerant expression of religious views may end in a policy to indoctrinate and coerce. A state-created orthodoxy puts at grave risk that freedom of belief and conscience which are the sole assurance that religious faith is real, not imposed.

. . .

As we have observed before, there are heightened concerns with protecting freedom of conscience from subtle coercive pressure in the elementary and secondary public schools. Our decisions in *Engel v. Vitale* and *School District of Abington Tp. v. Schempp* recognize, among other things, that prayer exercises in public schools carry a particular risk of indirect coercion.... What to most believers may seem nothing more than a reasonable request that the nonbeliever respect their religious practices, in a school context may appear to the nonbeliever or dissenter to be an attempt to employ the machinery of the State to enforce a religious orthodoxy....

... Research in psychology supports the common assumption that adolescents are often susceptible to pressure from their peers towards conformity, and that the influence is strongest in matters of social convention.... [T]he government may no more use social pressure to enforce orthodoxy than it may use more direct means....

There was a stipulation in the District Court that attendance at graduation and promotional ceremonies is voluntary. Petitioners and the United States, as *amicus,* made this a center point of the case, arguing that the option of not attending the graduation excuses any inducement or coercion in the ceremony itself. The argument lacks all persuasion. Law reaches past formalism. And to say a teenage student has a real choice not to attend her high school graduation is formalistic in the extreme. True, Deborah could elect not to attend commencement without renouncing her diploma; but we shall not allow the case to turn on this point. Everyone knows that in our society and in our culture high school graduation is one of life's most significant occasions. A school rule which excuses attendance is beside the point. Attendance may not be required by official decree, yet it is apparent that a student is not free to absent herself from the graduation exercise in any real sense of the term "voluntary," for absence would require forfeiture of those intangible benefits which have motivated the student through youth and all her high school years. Graduation is a time for family and those closest to the student to celebrate success and express mutual wishes of gratitude and respect, all to the end of impressing upon the young person the role that it is his or her right and duty to assume in the community and all of its diverse parts.

The importance of the event is the point the school district and the United States rely upon to argue that a formal prayer ought to be permitted, but it becomes one of the principal reasons why their argument must fail. Their contention, one of considerable force were it not for the constitutional constraints applied to state action, is that the prayers are an essential part of these ceremonies because for many persons an occasion of this significance lacks meaning if there is no recognition, however brief, that human achievements cannot be understood apart from their spiritual essence. We think the Government's position that this interest suffices to force students to choose between compliance or forfeiture demonstrates fundamental inconsistency in its argumentation. It fails to acknowledge that what for many of Deborah's classmates and their parents was a spiritual imperative was for Daniel and Deborah Weisman religious conformance compelled by the State. While in some societies the wishes of the majority might prevail, the Establishment Clause of the First Amendment is addressed to this contingency and rejects the balance urged upon us. The Constitution forbids the State to exact religious conformity from a student as the price of attending her own high school graduation. This is the calculus the Constitution commands.

The Government's argument gives insufficient recognition to the real conflict of conscience faced by the young student. The essence of the Government's position is that with regard to a civic, social occasion of this importance it is the objector, not the majority, who must take unilateral and private action to avoid compromising religious scruples, here by electing to miss the graduation exercise. This turns conventional First Amendment analysis on its head. It is a tenet of the First Amendment that the State cannot require one of its citizens to forfeit his or her rights and benefits as the price of resisting conformance to state-sponsored religious practice. To say that a student must remain apart from the ceremony at the opening invocation and closing benediction is to risk compelling conformity in an environment analogous to the classroom setting, where we have said the risk of compulsion is especially high. Just as in *Engel v. Vitale* and *School District of Abington Township v. Schempp*, we found that provisions within the challenged legislation permitting a student to be voluntarily excused from attendance or participation in the daily prayers did not shield those practices from invalidation, the fact that attendance at the graduation ceremonies is voluntary in a legal sense does not save the religious exercise. . . .

We do not hold that every state action implicating religion is invalid if one or a few citizens find it offensive. People may take offense at all manner of religious as well as nonreligious messages, but offense alone does not in every case show a violation. We know too that sometimes to endure social isolation or even anger may be the price of conscience or nonconformity. But, by any reading of our cases, the conformity required of the student in this case was too high an exaction to withstand the test of the Establishment Clause. The prayer exercises in this case are especially improper because the State has in every practical sense compelled attendance and participation in an explicit religious exercise at an event of singular importance to every student, one the objecting student had no real alternative to avoid. . . .

For the reasons we have stated, the judgment of the Court of Appeals is

Affirmed.

NOTES

1. Rabbi Gutterman's prayers were:

INVOCATION: "God of the Free, Hope of the Brave: For the legacy of America where diversity is celebrated and the rights of minorities are protected, we thank You. May these young men and women grow up to enrich it. For the liberty of America, we thank You. May these new graduates grow up to guard it. For the political process of America in which all its citizens may participate, for its court system where all may seek justice we thank You. May those we honor this morning always turn to it in trust. For the destiny of America we thank You. May the graduates of Nathan Bishop Middle School so live that they might help to share it. May our aspirations for our country and for these young people, who are our hope for the future, be richly fulfilled. AMEN."

BENEDICTION: "O God, we are grateful to You for having endowed us with the capacity for learning which we have celebrated on this joyous commencement. Happy families give thanks for seeing their children achieve an important milestone. Send Your blessings upon the teachers and administrators who helped prepare them. The graduates now need strength and guidance for the future, help them to understand that we are not complete with academic knowledge alone. We must each strive to fulfill what You require of us all: To do justly, to love mercy, to walk humbly. We give thanks to You, Lord, for keeping us alive, sustaining us and allowing us to reach this special, happy occasion. AMEN." *Lee* at 581–582.

"God" appears twice and "lord" once in the 252 words of prayer. Justice Blackmun's concurrence noted that the phrase in the Benediction, "We must each strive to fulfill what you require of us all, to do justly, to love mercy, to walk humbly" conveys a Judeo–Christian message that was clearly borrowed from the Prophet Micah at Chapter 6, verse 8. (Blackmun, J., concurring), at 604, note 5. Similarly, Justice Souter's concurrence feared that the reference from Micah "embodies a straightforwardly theistic premise" (Souter, J., concurring), at 617.

What do you think about these prayers?

2. In a caustic dissent, Justice Scalia, joined by Chief Justice Rehnquist and Justices White and Thomas, wrote:

I find it a sufficient embarrassment that our Establishment Clause jurisprudence regarding holiday displays has come to "requir[e] scrutiny more commonly associated with interior decorators than with the judiciary." But interior decorating is a rock-hard science compared to psychology practiced by amateurs. A few citations of "[r]esearch in psychology" that have no particular bearing upon the precise issue here, cannot disguise the fact that the Court has gone beyond the realm where judges know what they are doing. The Court's argument that state officials have "coerced" students to take part in the invocation and benediction at graduation ceremonies is, not to put too fine a point on it, incoherent. *Lee v. Weisman*, 505 U.S. 577, 636, 112 S.Ct. 2649, 120 L.Ed.2d 467, 75 Educ. L. Rep. 43, (Scalia, J., dissenting).

3. The Sixth and Seventh Circuits, in cases involving public universities in Tennessee and Indiana, respectively, upheld prayer at graduation ceremonies. The courts essentially agreed that the prayers did not violate the Establishment Clause because they did not involve young students and attendance was voluntary. *Tanford v. Brand*, 104 F.3d 982 [115 Educ. L. Rep. 339] (7th Cir.1997), *cert. denied*, 522 U.S. 814, 118 S.Ct. 60, 139 L.Ed.2d 23 (1997); *Chaudhuri v. State of Tenn.*, 130 F.3d 232

[122 Educ. L. Rep. 573] (6th Cir.1997), *cert. denied*, 523 U.S. 1024, 118 S.Ct. 1308, 140 L.Ed.2d 473 (1998). Are these fair distinctions?

[CASE NO. 11]   TITLE I SERVICES AND STUDENTS IN RELIGIOUSLY AFFILIATED NON–PUBLIC SCHOOLS

AGOSTINI v. FELTON

Supreme Court of the United States, 1997.
521 U.S. 203, 117 S.Ct. 1997, 138 L.Ed.2d 391 [119 Educ. L. Rep. 29].

■ JUSTICE O'CONNOR delivered the opinion of the Court.

In *Aguilar v. Felton* this Court held that the Establishment Clause of the First Amendment barred the city of New York from sending public school teachers into parochial schools to provide remedial education to disadvantaged children pursuant to a congressionally mandated program. On remand, the District Court for the Eastern District of New York entered a permanent injunction reflecting our ruling. Twelve years later, petitioners—the parties bound by that injunction—seek relief from its operation. Petitioners maintain that *Aguilar* cannot be squared with our intervening Establishment Clause jurisprudence and ask that we explicitly recognize what our more recent cases already dictate: *Aguilar* is no longer good law. We agree with petitioners that *Aguilar* is not consistent with our subsequent Establishment Clause decisions and further conclude that, on the facts presented here, petitioners are entitled under Federal Rule of Civil Procedure 60(b)(5) to relief from the operation of the District Court's prospective injunction.

I

In 1965, Congress enacted Title I of the Elementary and Secondary Education Act of 1965 to "provid[e] full educational opportunity to every child regardless of economic background" (hereinafter Title I). Toward that end, Title I channels federal funds, through the States, to "local educational agencies" (LEA's). The LEA's spend these funds to provide remedial education, guidance, and job counseling to eligible students. An eligible student is one (i) who resides within the attendance boundaries of a public school located in a low-income area and (ii) who is failing, or is at risk of failing, the State's student performance standards. Title I funds must be made available to all eligible children, regardless of whether they attend public schools, and the services provided to children attending private schools must be "equitable in comparison to services and other benefits for public school children."

An LEA providing services to children enrolled in private schools is subject to a number of constraints that are not imposed when it provides aid to public schools. Title I services may be provided only to those private school students eligible for aid, and cannot be used to provide services on a "school-wide" basis. In addition, the LEA must retain complete control over Title I funds; retain title to all materials used to provide Title I services; and provide those services through public employees or other persons independent of the private school and any religious institution. The

Title I services themselves must be "secular, neutral, and non-ideological" and must "supplement, and in no case supplant, the level of services" already provided by the private school.

Petitioner Board of Education of the City of New York (hereinafter Board), an LEA, first applied for Title I funds in 1966 and has grappled ever since with how to provide Title I services to the private school students within its jurisdiction. Approximately 10% of the total number of students eligible for Title I services are private school students. Recognizing that more than 90% of the private schools within the Board's jurisdiction are sectarian, the Board initially arranged to transport children to public schools for after-school Title I instruction. But this enterprise was largely unsuccessful. Attendance was poor, teachers and children were tired, and parents were concerned for the safety of their children. The Board then moved the after-school instruction onto private school campuses, as Congress had contemplated when it enacted Title I. After this program also yielded mixed results, the Board implemented the plan we evaluated in *Aguilar v. Felton*.

That plan called for the provision of Title I services on private school premises during school hours. Under the plan, only public employees could serve as Title I instructors and counselors. Assignments to private schools were made on a voluntary basis and without regard to the religious affiliation of the employee or the wishes of the private school. As the Court of Appeals in *Aguilar* observed, a large majority of Title I teachers worked in non-public schools with religious affiliations different from their own. The vast majority of Title I teachers also moved among the private schools, spending fewer than five days a week at the same school.

Before any public employee could provide Title I instruction at a private school, she would be given a detailed set of written and oral instructions emphasizing the secular purpose of Title I and setting out the rules to be followed to ensure that this purpose was not compromised. Specifically, employees would be told that (i) they were employees of the Board and accountable only to their public school supervisors; (ii) they had exclusive responsibility for selecting students for the Title I program and could teach only those children who met the eligibility criteria for Title I; (iii) their materials and equipment would be used only in the Title I program; (iv) they could not engage in team teaching or other cooperative instructional activities with private school teachers; and (v) they could not introduce any religious matter into their teaching or become involved in any way with the religious activities of the private schools. All religious symbols were to be removed from classrooms used for Title I services. The rules acknowledged that it might be necessary for Title I teachers to consult with a student's regular classroom teacher to assess the student's particular needs and progress, but admonished instructors to limit those consultations to mutual professional concerns regarding the student's education. To ensure compliance with these rules, a publicly employed field supervisor was to attempt to make at least one unannounced visit to each teacher's classroom every month.

In 1978, six federal taxpayers—respondents here—sued the Board in the District Court for the Eastern District of New York. Respondents sought declaratory and injunctive relief, claiming that the Board's Title I program violated the Establishment Clause. The District Court permitted the parents of a number of parochial school students who were receiving Title I services to intervene as codefendants. The District Court granted summary judgment for the Board, but the Court of Appeals for the Second Circuit reversed.... In a 5-to-4 decision, this Court affirmed on the ground that the Board's Title I program necessitated an "excessive entanglement of church and state in the administration of [Title I] benefits." On remand, the District Court permanently enjoined the Board "from using public funds for any plan or program under [Title I] to the extent that it requires, authorizes or permits public school teachers and guidance counselors to provide teaching and counseling services on the premises of sectarian schools within New York City."

The Board, like other LEA's across the United States, modified its Title I program so it could continue serving those students who attended private religious schools. Rather than offer Title I instruction to parochial school students at their schools, the Board reverted to its prior practice of providing instruction at public school sites, at leased sites, and in mobile instructional units (essentially vans converted into classrooms) parked near the sectarian school. The Board also offered computer-aided instruction, which could be provided "on premises" because it did not require public employees to be physically present on the premises of a religious school.

It is not disputed that the additional costs of complying with *Aguilar's* mandate are significant. Since the 1986–1987 school year, the Board has spent over $100 million providing computer-aided instruction, leasing sites and mobile instructional units, and transporting students to those sites. Under the Secretary of Education's regulations, those costs "incurred as a result of implementing alternative delivery systems to comply with the requirements of *Aguilar v. Felton*" and not paid for with other state or federal funds are to be deducted from the federal grant before the Title I funds are distributed to any student. These "*Aguilar* costs" thus reduce the amount of Title I money an LEA has available for remedial education, and LEA's have had to cut back on the number of students who receive Title I benefits. From Title I funds available for New York City children between the 1986–1987 and the 1993–1994 school years, the Board had to deduct $7.9 million "off-the-top" for compliance with *Aguilar*. When *Aguilar* was handed down, it was estimated that some 20,000 economically disadvantaged children in the city of New York and some 183,000 children nationwide would experience a decline in Title I services.

In October and December of 1995, petitioners—the Board and a new group of parents of parochial school students entitled to Title I services—filed motions in the District Court seeking relief under Federal Rule of Civil Procedure 60(b) from the permanent injunction entered by the District Court on remand from our decision in *Aguilar*. Petitioners argued that relief was proper ... because the "decisional law [had] changed to make legal what the [injunction] was designed to prevent." Specifically, petitioners pointed to the statements of five Justices in *Board of Education of Kiryas Joel Village School District v. Grumet* calling for the overruling of *Aguilar*. The District Court denied the motion.... The Court of Appeals for the Second Circuit affirmed.... We granted certiorari and now reverse.

II

The question we must answer is a simple one: Are petitioners entitled to relief from the District Court's permanent injunction under Rule 60(b)? Rule 60(b)(5), the subsection under which petitioners proceeded below, states:

"On motion and upon such terms as are just, the court may relieve a party ... from a final judgment [or] order ... [when] it is no longer equitable that the judgment should have prospective application."

In *Rufo v. Inmates of Suffolk County Jail*, we held that it is appropriate to grant a Rule 60(b)(5) motion when the party seeking relief from an injunction or consent decree can show "a significant change either in factual conditions or in law." A court may recognize subsequent changes in either statutory or decisional law. A court errs when it refuses to modify an injunction or consent decree in light of such changes.

Petitioners point to three changes in the factual and legal landscape that they believe justify their claim for relief under Rule 60(b)(5). They first contend that the exorbitant costs of complying with the District Court's injunction constitute a significant factual development warranting modification of the injunction. Petitioners also argue that there have been two significant legal developments since *Aguilar* was decided: a majority of Justices have expressed their views that *Aguilar* should be reconsidered or overruled; and *Aguilar* has in any event been undermined by subsequent Establishment Clause decisions....

Respondents counter that, because the costs of providing Title I services off site were known at the time *Aguilar* was decided, and because the relevant case law has not changed, the District Court did not err in denying petitioners' motions. Obviously, if neither the law supporting our original decision in this litigation nor the facts have changed, there would be no need to decide the propriety of a Rule 60(b)(5) motion. Accordingly, we turn to the threshold issue whether the factual or legal landscape has changed since we decided *Aguilar*.

We agree with respondents that petitioners have failed to establish the significant change in factual conditions required by *Rufo*. Both petitioners and this Court were, at the time *Aguilar* was decided, aware that additional costs would be incurred if Title I services could not be provided in parochial school classrooms....

We also agree with respondents that the statements made by five Justices in *Kiryas Joel* do not, in themselves, furnish a basis for concluding that our Establishment Clause jurisprudence has changed.... The views of five Justices that the case should be reconsidered or overruled cannot be said to have effected a change in Establishment Clause law.

In light of these conclusions, petitioners' ability to satisfy the prerequisites of Rule 60(b)(5) hinges on whether our later Establishment Clause cases have so undermined *Aguilar* that it is no longer good law. We now turn to that inquiry.

III

A

In order to evaluate whether *Aguilar* has been eroded by our subsequent Establishment Clause cases, it is necessary to understand the rationale upon which *Aguilar*, as well as its companion case, *School District of Grand Rapids v. Ball* rested.

In *Ball*, the Court evaluated two programs implemented by the School District of Grand Rapids, Michigan. The district's Shared Time program, the one most analogous to Title I, provided remedial and "enrichment" classes, at public expense, to students attending non-public schools. The classes were taught during regular school hours by publicly employed teachers, using materials purchased with public funds, on the premises of non-public schools. The Shared Time courses were in subjects designed to supplement the "core curriculum" of the non-public schools. Of the 41 non-public schools eligible for the program, 40 were " 'pervasively sectarian' " in character—that is, " 'the purpos[e] of [those] schools [was] to advance their particular religions.' "

The Court conducted its analysis by applying the three-part test set forth in *Lemon*. . . . The Court acknowledged that the Shared Time program served a purely secular purpose, thereby satisfying the first part of the so-called *Lemon* test. Nevertheless, it ultimately concluded that the program had the impermissible effect of advancing religion.

The Court found that the program violated the Establishment Clause's prohibition against "government-financed or government-sponsored indoctrination into the beliefs of a particular religious faith" in at least three ways. First, drawing upon the analysis in *Meek v. Pittenger*, the Court observed that "the teachers participating in the programs may become involved in intentionally or inadvertently inculcating particular religious tenets or beliefs.". . . .

The presence of public teachers on parochial school grounds had a second, related impermissible effect: It created a "graphic symbol of the 'concert or union or dependency' of church and state," especially when perceived by "children in their formative years." . . .

Third, the Court found that the Shared Time program impermissibly financed religious indoctrination by subsidizing "the primary religious mission of the institutions affected." . . .

The New York City Title I program challenged in *Aguilar* closely resembled the Shared Time program struck down in *Ball*, but the Court found fault with an aspect of the Title I program not present in *Ball*: The Board had "adopted a system for monitoring the religious content of publicly funded Title I classes in the religious schools." Even though this monitoring system might prevent the Title I program from being used to inculcate religion, the Court concluded, as it had in *Lemon* and *Meek*, that the level of monitoring necessary to be "certain" that the program had an exclusively secular effect would "inevitably resul[t] in the excessive entanglement of church and state," thereby running afoul of *Lemon's* third prong. In the majority's view, New York City's Title I program suffered from the "same critical elements of entanglement" present in *Lemon* and *Meek*: the aid was provided "in a pervasively sectarian environment . . . in the form of teachers," requiring "ongoing inspection . . . to ensure the absence of a religious message." Such "pervasive monitoring by public authorities in the sectarian schools infringes precisely those Establishment Clause values at the root of the prohibition of excessive entanglement." The Court noted two further forms of entanglement inherent in New York City's Title I program: the "administrative cooperation" required to implement Title I services and the "dangers of political divisiveness" that might grow out of the day-to-day decisions public officials would have to make in order to provide Title I services.

Distilled to essentials, the Court's conclusion that the Shared Time program in *Ball* had the impermissible effect of advancing religion rested on three assumptions: (i) any public employee who works on the premises of a religious school is presumed to inculcate religion in her work; (ii) the presence of public employees on private school premises creates a symbolic union between church and state; and (iii) any and all public aid that directly aids the educational function of religious schools impermissibly finances religious indoctrination, even if the aid reaches such schools as a consequence of private decisionmaking. Additionally, in *Aguilar* there was a fourth assumption: that New York City's Title I program necessitated an excessive government entanglement with religion because public employees who teach on the premises of religious schools must be closely monitored to ensure that they do not inculcate religion.

B

Our more recent cases have undermined the assumptions upon which *Ball* and *Aguilar* relied. To be sure, the general principles we use to evaluate whether government aid violates the Establishment Clause have not changed since *Aguilar* was decided. For example, we continue to ask whether the government acted with the purpose of advancing or inhibiting religion, and the nature of that inquiry has remained largely unchanged. Likewise, we continue to explore whether the aid has the "effect" of advancing or inhibiting religion. What has changed since we decided *Ball* and *Aguilar* is our understanding of the criteria used to assess whether aid to religion has an impermissible effect.

1

As we have repeatedly recognized, government inculcation of religious beliefs has the impermissible effect of advancing religion. Our cases subsequent to *Aguilar* have, however, modified in two significant respects the approach we use to assess indoctrination. First, we have abandoned the presumption erected in *Meek* and *Ball* that the placement of public employees on parochial school grounds inevitably results in the impermissible effect of state-sponsored indoctrination or constitutes a symbolic union between government and religion. . . .

Second, we have departed from the rule relied on in *Ball* that all government aid that directly assists the educational function of religious schools is invalid....

... [U]nder current law, the Shared Time program in *Ball* and New York City's Title I program in *Aguilar* will not, as a matter of law, be deemed to have the effect of advancing religion through indoctrination. Indeed, each of the premises upon which we relied in *Ball* to reach a contrary conclusion is no longer valid. First, there is no reason to presume that, simply because she enters a parochial school classroom, a full-time public employee such as a Title I teacher will depart from her assigned duties and instructions and embark on religious indoctrination, any more than there was a reason in *Zobrest* to think an interpreter would inculcate religion by altering her translation of classroom lectures. Certainly, no evidence has ever shown that any New York City Title I instructor teaching on parochial school premises attempted to inculcate religion in students....

As discussed above, *Zobrest* also repudiates *Ball's* assumption that the presence of Title I teachers in parochial school classrooms will, without more, create the impression of a "symbolic union" between church and state.... We do not see any perceptible (let alone dispositive) difference in the degree of symbolic union between a student receiving remedial instruction in a classroom on his sectarian school's campus and one receiving instruction in a van parked just at the school's curbside. To draw this line based solely on the location of the public employee is neither "sensible" nor "sound" and the Court in *Zobrest* rejected it.

Nor under current law can we conclude that a program placing full-time public employees on parochial campuses to provide Title I instruction would impermissibly finance religious indoctrination. In all relevant respects, the provision of instructional services under Title I is indistinguishable from the provision of sign-language interpreters under the IDEA. Both programs make aid available only to eligible recipients. That aid is provided to students at whatever school they choose to attend. Although Title I instruction is provided to several students at once, whereas an interpreter provides translation to a single student, this distinction is not constitutionally significant. Moreover, as in *Zobrest*, Title I services are by law supplemental to the regular curricula. These services do not, therefore, "reliev[e] sectarian schools of costs they otherwise would have borne in educating their students."

.   .   .

We are also not persuaded that Title I services supplant the remedial instruction and guidance counseling already provided in New York City's sectarian schools. Although Justice SOUTER maintains that the sectarian schools provide such services and that those schools reduce those services once their students begin to receive Title I instruction, his claims rest on speculation about the impossibility of drawing any line between supplemental and general education, and not on any evidence in the record that the Board is in fact violating Title I regulations by providing services that supplant those offered in the sectarian schools. We are unwilling to speculate that all sectarian schools provide remedial instruction and guidance counseling to their students, and are unwilling to presume that the Board would violate Title I regulations by continuing to provide Title I services to students who attend a sectarian school that has curtailed its remedial instruction program in response to Title I. Nor are we willing to conclude that the constitutionality of an aid program depends on the number of sectarian school students who happen to receive the otherwise neutral aid. *Zobrest* did not turn on the fact that James Zobrest had, at the time of litigation, been the only child using a publicly funded sign-language interpreter to attend a parochial school.

What is most fatal to the argument that New York City's Title I program directly subsidizes religion is that it applies with equal force when those services are provided off campus, and *Aguilar* implied that providing the services off campus is entirely consistent with the Establishment Clause. . . .

2

Although we examined in *Witters* and *Zobrest* the criteria by which an aid program identifies its beneficiaries, we did so solely to assess whether any use of that aid to indoctrinate religion could be attributed to the State. A number of our Establishment Clause cases have found that the criteria used for identifying beneficiaries are relevant in a second respect, apart from enabling a court to evaluate whether the program subsidizes religion. Specifically, the criteria might themselves have the effect of advancing religion by creating a financial incentive to undertake religious indoctrination. This incentive is not present, however, where the aid is allocated on the basis of neutral, secular criteria that neither favor nor disfavor religion, and is made available to both religious and secular beneficiaries on a nondiscriminatory basis. Under such circumstances, the aid is less likely to have the effect of advancing religion.

In *Ball* and *Aguilar*, the Court gave this consideration no weight. Before and since those decisions, we have sustained programs that provided aid to all eligible children regardless of where they attended school. . . .

Applying this reasoning to New York City's Title I program, it is clear that Title I services are allocated on the basis of criteria that neither favor nor disfavor religion. The services are available to all children who meet the Act's eligibility requirements, no matter what their religious beliefs or where they go to school. The Board's program does not, therefore, give aid recipients any incentive to modify their religious beliefs or practices in order to obtain those services.

3

We turn now to *Aguilar's* conclusion that New York City's Title I program resulted in an excessive entanglement between church and state. Whether a government aid program results in such an entanglement has consistently been an aspect of our Establishment Clause analysis. We have considered entanglement both in the course of assessing whether an aid program has an impermissible effect of advancing religion and as a factor separate and apart from "effect." Regardless of how we have characterized the issue, however, the factors we use to assess whether an entanglement is "excessive" are similar to the factors we use to examine "effect." That is, to assess entanglement, we have looked to "the character and purposes of the institutions that are benefited, the nature of the aid that the State provides, and the resulting relationship between the government and religious authority." Similarly, we have assessed a law's "effect" by examining the character of the institutions benefited and the nature of the aid that the State provided. Indeed, in *Lemon* itself, the entanglement that the Court found "independently" to necessitate the program's invalidation also was found to have the effect of inhibiting religion. Thus, it is simplest to recognize why entanglement is significant and treat it—as we did in *Walz*— as an aspect of the inquiry into a statute's effect.

Not all entanglements, of course, have the effect of advancing or inhibiting religion. Interaction between church and state is inevitable and we have always tolerated some level of involvement between the two. Entanglement must be "excessive" before it runs afoul of the Establishment Clause. . . .

The pre-*Aguilar* Title I program does not result in an "excessive" entanglement that advances or inhibits religion. As discussed previously, the Court's finding of "excessive" entanglement in *Aguilar* rested on three grounds: (i) the program would require "pervasive monitoring by public authorities" to ensure that Title I employees did not inculcate religion; (ii) the program required "administrative cooperation" between the Board and parochial schools; and (iii) the program might increase the dangers of "political divisiveness." Under our current understanding of the Establishment Clause, the last two considerations are insufficient by themselves to create an "excessive" entanglement. They are present no matter where Title I services are offered, and no court has held that Title I services cannot be offered off campus. Further, the assumption underlying the first consideration has been undermined. In *Aguilar*, the Court presumed that full-time public employees on parochial school grounds would be tempted to inculcate religion, despite the ethical standards they were required to uphold. Because of this risk pervasive monitoring would be required. But after *Zobrest* we no longer presume that public employees will inculcate religion simply because they happen to be in a sectarian environment. Since we have abandoned the assumption that properly instructed public employees will fail to discharge their duties faithfully, we must also discard the assumption that pervasive monitoring of Title I teachers is required. There is no suggestion in the record before us that unannounced monthly visits of public supervisors are insufficient to prevent or to detect inculcation of religion by public employees. Moreover, we have not found excessive entanglement in cases in which States imposed far more onerous burdens on religious institutions than the monitoring system at issue here.

To summarize, New York City's Title I program does not run afoul of any of three primary criteria we currently use to evaluate whether government aid has the effect of advancing religion: It does not result in governmental indoctrination; define its recipients by reference to religion; or create an excessive entanglement. We therefore hold that a federally funded program providing supplemental, remedial instruction to disadvantaged children on a neutral basis is not invalid under the Establishment Clause when such instruction is given on the premises of sectarian schools by government employees pursuant to a program containing safeguards such as those present here. The same considerations that justify this holding require us to conclude that this carefully constrained program also cannot reasonably be viewed as an endorsement of religion. Accordingly, we must acknowledge that *Aguilar*, as well as the portion of *Ball* addressing Grand Rapids' Shared Time program, are no longer good law.

C

The doctrine of stare decisis does not preclude us from recognizing the change in our law and overruling *Aguilar* and those portions of *Ball* inconsistent with our more recent decisions.... As discussed above, our Establishment Clause jurisprudence has changed significantly since we decided *Ball* and *Aguilar*, so our decision to overturn those cases rests on far more than "a present doctrinal disposition to come out differently from the Court of [1985]." We therefore overrule *Ball* and *Aguilar* to the extent those decisions are inconsistent with our current understanding of the Establishment Clause.

Nor does the "law of the case" doctrine place any additional constraints on our ability to overturn *Aguilar*. Under this doctrine, a court should not reopen issues decided in earlier stages of the same litigation. The doctrine does not apply if the court is "convinced that [its prior decision] is clearly erroneous and would work a manifest injustice." In light of our conclusion that *Aguilar* would be decided differently under our current Establishment Clause law, we think adherence to that decision would undoubtedly work a "manifest injustice," such that the law of the case doctrine does not apply.

IV

We therefore conclude that our Establishment Clause law has "signifi-cant[ly] change[d]" since we decided *Aguilar*. We are only left to decide whether this change in law entitles petitioners to relief under Rule 60(b)(5). We conclude that it does. Our general practice is to apply the rule of law we announce in a case to the parties before us. We adhere to this practice even when we overrule a case....

... we see no reason to wait for a "better vehicle" in which to evaluate the impact of subsequent cases on *Aguilar's* continued vitality. To evaluate the Rule 60(b)(5) motion properly before us today in no way undermines "integrity in the interpretation of procedural rules" or signals any departure from "the responsive, non-agenda-setting character of this Court." Indeed, under these circumstances, it would be particularly inequitable for us to bide our time waiting for another case to arise while the city of New York labors under a continuing injunction forcing it to spend millions of dollars on mobile instructional units and leased sites when it could instead be spending that money to give economically disadvantaged children a better chance at success in life by means of a program that is perfectly consistent with the Establishment Clause.

For these reasons, we reverse the judgment of the Court of Appeals and remand the cases to the District Court with instructions to vacate its September 26, 1985, order.

It is so ordered.

NOTES

1. Note how the composition of the Supreme Court can affect the outcome of a case. In *Aguilar*, Justice O'Connor authored a scathing dissent in favor of permitting the on-site delivery of aid. In *Agostini* she authored the majority opinion.

2. In *Aguilar* the Court modified the *Lemon* test, at least as it applies to state-aid to students in religiously affiliated non-public schools test, reviewing only its first two parts, purpose and effect, while recasting entanglement as one criterion in evaluating a statute's effect. Does this make sense?

[CASE NO. 12]   PRAYER AT PUBLIC SCHOOL SPORTING EVENTS

SANTA FE INDEPENDENT SCHOOL DISTRICT v. DOE

Supreme Court of the United States, 2000.
530 U.S. 290, 120 S.Ct. 2266, 147 L.Ed.2d 295 [145 Educ. L. Rep. 21].

■ JUSTICE STEVENS delivered the opinion of the Court.

Prior to 1995, the Santa Fe High School student who occupied the school's elective office of student council chaplain delivered a prayer over the public address system before each varsity football game for the entire season. This practice, along with others, was challenged in District Court as a violation of the Establishment Clause of the First Amendment. While these proceedings were pending in the District Court, the school district adopted a different policy that permits, but does not require, prayer initiated and led by a student at all home games. The District Court entered an order modifying that policy to permit only non-sectarian, non-proselytizing prayer. The Court of Appeals held that, even as modified that . . . the football prayer policy was invalid. We granted the school district's petition for certiorari to review that holding.

I

The Santa Fe Independent School District (District) is a political subdivision of the State of Texas, responsible for the education of more than 4,000 students. . . . The District includes the Santa Fe High School, two primary schools, an intermediate school and the junior high school. Respondents are two sets of current or former students and their respective mothers. One family is Mormon and the other is Catholic. The District Court permitted respondents (Does) to litigate anonymously to protect them from intimidation or harassment.

Respondents commenced this action in April 1995 and moved for a temporary restraining order to prevent the District from violating the Establishment Clause at the imminent graduation exercises. In their complaint the Does alleged that the District had engaged in several proselytizing practices, such as promoting attendance at a Baptist revival meeting, encouraging membership in religious clubs, chastising children who held minority religious beliefs, and distributing Gideon Bibles on school premises. They also alleged that the District allowed students to read Christian invocations and benedictions from the stage at graduation ceremonies, and to deliver overtly Christian prayers over the public address system at home football games.

On May 10, 1995, the District Court entered an interim order addressing a number of different issues. With respect to the impending graduation, the order provided that "non-denominational prayer" consisting of "an invocation and/or benediction" could be presented by a senior student or students selected by members of the graduating class. The text of the prayer was to be determined by the students, without scrutiny or preapproval by school officials. References to particular religious figures "such as Mohammed, Jesus, Buddha, or the like" would be permitted "as long as the general thrust of the prayer is non-proselytizing."

In response to that portion of the order, the District adopted a series of policies over several months dealing with prayer at school functions. The policies enacted in May and July for graduation ceremonies provided the format for the August and October policies for football games. The May policy provided: " 'The board has chosen to permit the graduating senior class, with the advice and counsel of the senior class principal or designee, to elect by secret ballot to choose whether an invocation and benediction shall be part of the graduation exercise. If so chosen the class shall elect by secret ballot, from a list of student volunteers, students to deliver nonsectarian, non-proselytizing invocations and benedictions for the purpose of solemnizing their graduation ceremonies.' " The parties stipulated that after this policy was adopted, "the senior class held an election to determine whether to have an invocation and benediction at the commencement [and] the class voted, by secret ballot, to include prayer at the high school graduation." In a second vote the class elected two seniors to deliver the invocation and benediction.

In July, the District enacted another policy eliminating the requirement that invocations and benedictions be "non-sectarian and non-proselytising," but also providing that if the District were to be enjoined from enforcing that policy, the May policy would automatically become effective. The August policy, which was titled "Prayer at Football Games," was similar to the July policy for graduations. It also authorized two student elections, the first to determine whether "invocations" should be delivered, and the second to select the spokesperson to deliver them. Like the July policy, it contained two parts, an initial statement that omitted any requirement that the content of the invocation be "non-sectarian and non-proselytising," and a fallback provision that automatically added that limitation if the preferred policy should be enjoined. On August 31, 1995, according to the parties' stipulation, "the district's high school students voted to determine whether a student would deliver prayer at varsity football games.... The students chose to allow a student to say a prayer at football games." A week later, in a separate election, they selected a student "to deliver the prayer at varsity football games."

The final policy (October policy) is essentially the same as the August policy, though it omits the word "prayer" from its title, and refers to "messages" and "statements" as well as "invocations." It is the validity of that policy that is before us.

The District Court did enter an order precluding enforcement of the first, open-ended policy.... Both parties appealed.... The Court of Appeals majority agreed with the Does.

We granted the District's petition for certiorari, limited to the following question: "Whether petitioner's policy permitting student-led, student-initiated prayer at football games violates the Establishment Clause." We conclude, as did the Court of Appeals, that it does.

II

The first Clause in the First Amendment to the Federal Constitution provides that "Congress shall make no law respecting an establishment of religion, or prohibiting the free exercise thereof." The Fourteenth Amendment imposes those substantive limitations on the legislative power of the States and their political subdivisions. In *Lee v. Weisman* we held that a prayer delivered by a rabbi at a middle school graduation ceremony violated that Clause. Although this case involves student prayer at a different type of school function, our analysis is properly guided by the principles that we endorsed in *Lee*....

In this case the District first argues that this principle is inapplicable to its October policy because the messages are private student speech, not public speech. It reminds us that "there is a crucial difference between government speech endorsing religion, which the Establishment Clause forbids, and private speech endorsing religion, which the Free Speech and Free Exercise Clauses protect." We certainly agree with that distinction, but we are not persuaded that the pregame invocations should be regarded as "private speech."

These invocations are authorized by a government policy and take place on government property at government-sponsored school-related events. Of course, not every message delivered under such circumstances is the government's own. We have held, for example, that an individual's contribution to a government-created forum was not government speech. Although the District relies heavily on *Rosenberger* and similar cases involving such forums, it is clear that the pregame ceremony is not the type of forum discussed in those cases. The Santa Fe school officials simply do not "evince either 'by policy or by practice,' any intent to open the [pregame ceremony] to 'indiscriminate use,' ... by the student body generally." Rather, the school allows only one student, the same student for the entire season, to give the invocation. The statement or invocation, moreover, is subject to particular regulations that confine the content and topic of the student's message....

Granting only one student access to the stage at a time does not, of course, necessarily preclude a finding that a school has created a limited public forum. Here, however, Santa Fe's student election system ensures that only those messages deemed "appropriate" under the District's policy may be delivered. That is, the majoritarian process implemented by the District guarantees, by definition, that minority candidates will never prevail and that their views will be effectively silenced.

Recently, in *Board of Regents of University of Wisconsin System v. Southworth*, we explained why student elections that determine, by majority vote, which expressive activities shall receive or not receive school benefits are constitutionally problematic: "To the extent the referendum substitutes majority determinations for viewpoint neutrality it would undermine the constitutional protection the program requires. The whole theory of viewpoint neutrality is that minority views are treated with the same respect as are majority views. Access to a public forum, for instance, does not depend upon majoritarian consent. That principle is controlling here." Like the student referendum for funding in *Southworth*, this student election does nothing to protect minority views but rather places the students who hold such views at the mercy of the majority. Because "fundamental rights may not be submitted to vote; they depend on the outcome of no elections," the District's elections are insufficient safeguards of diverse student speech.

In *Lee*, the school district made the related argument that its policy of endorsing only "civic or non-sectarian" prayer was acceptable because it minimized the intrusion on the audience as a whole. We rejected that claim by explaining that such a majoritarian policy "does not lessen the offense or isolation to the objectors. At best it narrows their number, at worst increases their sense of isolation and affront." Similarly, while Santa Fe's majoritarian election might ensure that most of the students are represented, it does nothing to protect the minority; indeed, it likely serves to intensify their offense. Moreover, the District has failed to divorce itself from the religious content in the invocations. It has not succeeded in doing so, either by claiming that its policy is " 'one of neutrality rather than endorsement' " or by characterizing the individual student as the "circuit-breaker" in the process. Contrary to the District's repeated assertions that it has adopted a "hands-off" approach to the pregame invocation, the realities of the situation plainly reveal that its policy involves both perceived and actual endorsement of religion. In this case, as we found in Lee, the "degree of school involvement" makes it clear that the pregame prayers bear "the imprint of the State and thus put school-age children who objected in an untenable position."

The District has attempted to disentangle itself from the religious messages by developing the two-step student election process. The text of the October policy, however, exposes the extent of the school's entanglement. The elections take place at all only because the school "board has chosen to permit students to deliver a brief invocation and/or message." The elections thus "shall" be conducted "by the high school student council" and "[u]pon advice and direction of the high school principal." The decision whether to deliver a message is first made by majority vote of the entire student body, followed by a choice of the speaker in a separate, similar majority election. Even though the particular words used by the speaker are not determined by those votes, the policy mandates that the "statement or invocation" be "consistent with the goals and purposes of this policy," which are "to solemnize the event, to promote good sportsmanship and student safety, and to establish the appropriate environment for the competition."

In addition to involving the school in the selection of the speaker, the policy, by its terms, invites and encourages religious messages. The policy itself states that the purpose of the message is "to solemnize the event." A religious message is the most obvious method of solemnizing an event. Moreover, the requirements that the message "promote good citizenship" and "establish the appropriate environment for competition" further narrow the types of message deemed appropriate, suggesting that a solemn, yet nonreligious, message, such as commentary on United States foreign policy, would be prohibited. Indeed, the only type of message that is expressly endorsed in the text is an "invocation"—a term that primarily describes an appeal for divine assistance. In fact, as used in the past at Santa Fe High School, an "invocation" has always entailed a focused religious message. Thus, the expressed purposes of the policy encourage the selection of a religious message, and that is precisely how the students understand the policy. The results of the elections described in the parties' stipulation make it clear that the students understood that the central question before them was whether prayer should be a part of the pregame ceremony. We recognize the important role that public worship plays in many communities, as well as the sincere desire to include public prayer as a part of various occasions so as to mark those occasions' significance. But such religious activity in public schools, as elsewhere, must comport with the First Amendment.

The actual or perceived endorsement of the message, moreover, is established by factors beyond just the text of the policy. Once the student speaker is selected and the message composed, the invocation is then delivered to a large audience assembled as part of a regularly scheduled, school-sponsored function conducted on school property. The message is broadcast over the school's public address system, which remains subject to the control of school officials. It is fair to assume that the pregame ceremony is clothed in the traditional indicia of school sporting events, which generally include not just the team, but also cheerleaders and band members dressed in uniforms sporting the school name and mascot. The school's name is likely written in large print across the field and on banners and flags. The crowd will certainly include many who display the school colors and insignia on their school T-shirts, jackets, or hats and who may also be waving signs displaying the school name. It is in a setting such as this that "[t]he board has chosen to permit" the elected student to rise and give the "statement or invocation."

In this context the members of the listening audience must perceive the pregame message as a public expression of the views of the majority of the student body delivered with the approval of the school administration. In cases involving state participation in a religious activity, one of the relevant questions is "whether an objective observer, acquainted with the text, legislative history, and implementation of the statute, would perceive it as a state endorsement of prayer in public schools." Regardless of the listener's support for, or objection to, the message, an objective Santa Fe

High School student will unquestionably perceive the inevitable pregame prayer as stamped with her school's seal of approval.

The text and history of this policy, moreover, reinforce our objective student's perception that the prayer is, in actuality, encouraged by the school. When a governmental entity professes a secular purpose for an arguably religious policy, the government's characterization is, of course, entitled to some deference. But it is nonetheless the duty of the courts to "distinguis[h] a sham secular purpose from a sincere one."

According to the District, the secular purposes of the policy are to "foste[r] free expression of private persons ... as well [as to] solemniz[e] sporting events, promot[e] good sportsmanship and student safety, and establis[h] an appropriate environment for competition." We note, however, that the District's approval of only one specific kind of message, an "invocation," is not necessary to further any of these purposes. Additionally, the fact that only one student is permitted to give a content-limited message suggests that this policy does little to "foste[r] free expression." Furthermore, regardless of whether one considers a sporting event an appropriate occasion for solemnity, the use of an invocation to foster such solemnity is impermissible when, in actuality, it constitutes prayer sponsored by the school. And it is unclear what type of message would be both appropriately "solemnizing" under the District's policy and yet non-religious.

Most striking to us is the evolution of the current policy from the long-sanctioned office of "Student Chaplain" to the candidly titled "Prayer at Football Games" regulation. This history indicates that the District intended to preserve the practice of prayer before football games. The conclusion that the District viewed the October policy simply as a continuation of the previous policies is dramatically illustrated by the fact that the school did not conduct a new election, pursuant to the current policy, to replace the results of the previous election, which occurred under the former policy. Given these observations, and in light of the school's history of regular delivery of a student-led prayer at athletic events, it is reasonable to infer that the specific purpose of the policy was to preserve a popular "state-sponsored religious practice."

School sponsorship of a religious message is impermissible because it sends the ancillary message to members of the audience who are nonadherents "that they are outsiders, not full members of the political community, and an accompanying message to adherents that they are insiders, favored members of the political community." The delivery of such a message— over the school's public address system, by a speaker representing the student body, under the supervision of school faculty, and pursuant to a school policy that explicitly and implicitly encourages public prayer—is not properly characterized as "private" speech.

III

The District next argues that its football policy is distinguishable from the graduation prayer in *Lee* because it does not coerce students to participate in religious observances. Its argument has two parts: first, that there is no impermissible government coercion because the pregame messages are the product of student choices; and second, that there is really no coercion at all because attendance at an extracurricular event, unlike a graduation ceremony, is voluntary.

The reasons just discussed explaining why the alleged "circuit-breaker" mechanism of the dual elections and student speaker do not turn public speech into private speech also demonstrate why these mechanisms do not insulate the school from the coercive element of the final message. In fact, this aspect of the District's argument exposes anew the concerns that are created by the majoritarian election system. The parties' stipulation clearly states that the issue resolved in the first election was "whether a student would deliver prayer at varsity football games," and the controversy in this case demonstrates that the views of the students are not unanimous on that issue.

One of the purposes served by the Establishment Clause is to remove debate over this kind of issue from governmental supervision or control. We explained in *Lee* that the "preservation and transmission of religious beliefs and worship is a responsibility and a choice committed to the private sphere." The two student elections authorized by the policy, coupled with the debates that presumably must precede each, impermissibly invade that private sphere. The election mechanism, when considered in light of the history in which the policy in question evolved, reflects a device the District put in place that determines whether religious messages will be delivered at home football games. The mechanism encourages divisiveness along religious lines in a public school setting, a result at odds with the Establishment Clause. Although it is true that the ultimate choice of student speaker is "attributable to the students," the District's decision to hold the constitutionally problematic election is clearly "a choice attributable to the State."

The District further argues that attendance at the commencement ceremonies at issue in *Lee* "differs dramatically" from attendance at high school football games, which it contends "are of no more than passing interest to many students" and are "decidedly extracurricular," thus dissipating any coercion. Attendance at a high school football game, unlike showing up for class, is certainly not required in order to receive a diploma. Moreover, we may assume that the District is correct in arguing that the informal pressure to attend an athletic event is not as strong as a senior's desire to attend her own graduation ceremony.

There are some students, however, such as cheerleaders, members of the band, and, of course, the team members themselves, for whom seasonal commitments mandate their attendance, sometimes for class credit. The District also minimizes the importance to many students of attending and participating in extracurricular activities as part of a complete educational experience. As we noted in *Lee*, "[l]aw reaches past formalism." To assert that high school students do not feel immense social pressure, or have a truly genuine desire, to be involved in the extracurricular event that is American high school football is "formalistic in the extreme." We stressed in *Lee* the obvious observation that "adolescents are often susceptible to pressure from their peers towards conformity, and that the influence is strongest in matters of social convention." High school home football games are traditional gatherings of a school community; they bring together students and faculty as well as friends and family from years present and past to root for a common cause. Undoubtedly, the games are not important to some students, and they voluntarily choose not to attend. For many others, however, the choice between whether to attend these games or to risk facing a personally offensive religious ritual is in no practical sense an easy one. The Constitution, moreover, demands that the school may not force this difficult choice upon these students for "[i]t is a tenet of the First Amendment that the State cannot require one of its citizens to forfeit his or her rights and benefits as the price of resisting conformance to state-sponsored religious practice."

Even if we regard every high school student's decision to attend a home football game as purely voluntary, we are nevertheless persuaded that the delivery of a pregame prayer has the improper effect of coercing those present to participate in an act of religious worship. For "the government may no more use social pressure to enforce orthodoxy than it may use more direct means." As in *Lee*, "[w]hat to most believers may seem nothing more than a reasonable request that the nonbeliever respect their religious practices, in a school context may appear to the nonbeliever or dissenter to be an attempt to employ the machinery of the State to enforce a religious orthodoxy." The constitutional command will not permit the District "to exact religious conformity from a student as the price" of joining her classmates at a varsity football game.

The Religion Clauses of the First Amendment prevent the government from making any law respecting the establishment of religion or prohibiting the free exercise thereof. By no means do these commands impose a prohibition on all religious activity in our public schools. Indeed, the common purpose of the Religion Clauses "is to secure religious liberty." Thus, nothing in the Constitution as interpreted by this Court prohibits any public school student from voluntarily praying at any time before, during, or after the school day. But the religious liberty protected by the Constitution is abridged when the State affirmatively sponsors the particular religious practice of prayer.

IV

Finally, the District argues repeatedly that the Does have made a premature facial challenge to the October policy that necessarily must fail. The District emphasizes, quite correctly, that until a student actually delivers a solemnizing message under the latest version of the policy, there can be no certainty that any of the statements or invocations will be religious. Thus, it concludes, the October policy necessarily survives a facial challenge.

This argument, however, assumes that we are concerned only with the serious constitutional injury that occurs when a student is forced to participate in an act of religious worship because she chooses to attend a school event. But the Constitution also requires that we keep in mind "the myriad, subtle ways in which Establishment Clause values can be eroded,"

Lynch, and that we guard against other different, yet equally important, constitutional injuries. One is the mere passage by the District of a policy that has the purpose and perception of government establishment of religion. Another is the implementation of a governmental electoral process that subjects the issue of prayer to a majoritarian vote.

The District argues that the facial challenge must fail because "Santa Fe's Football Policy cannot be invalidated on the basis of some 'possibility or even likelihood' of an unconstitutional application." Our Establishment Clause cases involving facial challenges, however, have not focused solely on the possible applications of the statute, but rather have considered whether the statute has an unconstitutional purpose. Writing for the Court in *Bowen*, the Chief Justice concluded that "[a]s in previous cases involving facial challenges on Establishment Clause grounds, we assess the constitutionality of an enactment by reference to the three factors first articulated in *Lemon v. Kurtzman....* which guides '[t]he general nature of our inquiry in this area.' Under the Lemon standard, a court must invalidate a statute if it lacks 'a secular legislative purpose.' " It is therefore proper, as part of this facial challenge, for us to examine the purpose of the October policy.

... [T]he text of the October policy alone reveals that it has an unconstitutional purpose. The plain language of the policy clearly spells out the extent of school involvement in both the election of the speaker and the content of the message. Additionally, the text of the October policy specifies only one, clearly preferred message—that of Santa Fe's traditional religious "invocation." Finally, the extremely selective access of the policy and other content restrictions confirm that it is not a content-neutral regulation that creates a limited public forum for the expression of student speech. Our examination, however, need not stop at an analysis of the text of the policy.

This case comes to us as the latest step in developing litigation brought as a challenge to institutional practices that unquestionably violated the Establishment Clause. One of those practices was the District's long-established tradition of sanctioning student-led prayer at varsity football games. The narrow question before us is whether implementation of the October policy insulates the continuation of such prayers from constitutional scrutiny. It does not. Our inquiry into this question not only can, but must, include an examination of the circumstances surrounding its enactment. Whether a government activity violates the Establishment Clause is "in large part a legal question to be answered on the basis of judicial interpretation of social facts.... Every government practice must be judged in its unique circumstances...." Our discussion in the previous sections demonstrates that in this case the District's direct involvement with school prayer exceeds constitutional limits.

The District, nevertheless, asks us to pretend that we do not recognize what every Santa Fe High School student understands clearly—that this policy is about prayer. The District further asks us to accept what is obviously untrue: that these messages are necessary to "solemnize" a football game and that this single-student, year-long position is essential to the protection of student speech. We refuse to turn a blind eye to the context in which this policy arose, and that context quells any doubt that this policy was implemented with the purpose of endorsing school prayer.

Therefore, the simple enactment of this policy, with the purpose and perception of school endorsement of student prayer, was a constitutional violation. We need not wait for the inevitable to confirm and magnify the constitutional injury. In *Wallace*, for example, we invalidated Alabama's as yet unimplemented and voluntary "moment of silence" statute based on our conclusion that it was enacted "for the sole purpose of expressing the State's endorsement of prayer activities for one minute at the beginning of each school day." Therefore, even if no Santa Fe High School student were ever to offer a religious message, the October policy fails a facial challenge because the attempt by the District to encourage prayer is also at issue. Government efforts to endorse religion cannot evade constitutional reproach based solely on the remote possibility that those attempts may fail.

This policy likewise does not survive a facial challenge because it impermissibly imposes upon the student body a majoritarian election on the issue of prayer. Through its election scheme, the District has established a governmental electoral mechanism that turns the school into a forum for religious debate. It further empowers the student body majority with the authority to subject students of minority views to constitutionally improper messages. The award of that power alone, regardless of the students' ultimate use of it, is not acceptable. Like the referendum in *Board of Regents of University of Wisconsin System v. Southworth*, the election mechanism established by the District undermines the essential protection of minority viewpoints. Such a system encourages divisiveness along religious lines and threatens the imposition of coercion upon those students not desiring to participate in a religious exercise. Simply by establishing this school-related procedure, which entrusts the inherently nongovernmental subject of religion to a majoritarian vote, a constitutional violation has occurred. No further injury is required for the policy to fail a facial challenge.

. . . To properly examine this policy on its face, we "must be deemed aware of the history and context of the community and forum." Our examination of those circumstances above leads to the conclusion that this policy does not provide the District with the constitutional safe harbor it sought. The policy is invalid on its face because it establishes an improper majoritarian election on religion, and unquestionably has the purpose and creates the perception of encouraging the delivery of prayer at a series of important school events.

The judgment of the Court of Appeals is, accordingly, affirmed.

It is so ordered.

NOTES

1.   In granting *certiorari* in this case, the Court sidestepped the key question of prayer at public school graduation ceremonies. Should the Court have accepted this question in light of all of the conflicting results in the circuit courts?

2.   In a scathing dissent, in *Santa Fe* at 318, Chief Justice Rehnquist, joined by Justices Scalia and Thomas, accused the Court of "bristl[ing] with hostility to all

things religious in public life." The dissent viewed the issue in *Santa Fe* as student, not government, speech where, unlike *Lee's* having a prayer delivered by a rabbi under the direction of a school official, the policy allowed students to select or create prayers. The dissent added that if students had been selected on wholly secular criteria, such as public speaking skills or social popularity, they could have delivered religious messages that would likely have passed constitutional muster. What do you think?

[CASE NO. 13] ACCESS RIGHTS OF RELIGIOUS GROUPS TO USE PUBLIC SCHOOL FACILITIES

GOOD NEWS CLUB v. MILFORD CENTRAL SCHOOL

Supreme Court of the United States, 2001.
533 U.S. 98, 121 S.Ct. 2093, 150 L.Ed.2d 151 [154 Educ. L. Rep. 45].

■ JUSTICE THOMAS delivered the opinion of the Court.

This case presents two questions. The first question is whether Milford Central School violated the free speech rights of the Good News Club when it excluded the Club from meeting after hours at the school. The second question is whether any such violation is justified by Milford's concern that permitting the Club's activities would violate the Establishment Clause. We conclude that Milford's restriction violates the Club's free speech rights and that no Establishment Clause concern justifies that violation.

I

The State of New York authorizes local school boards to adopt regulations governing the use of their school facilities. In particular, N.Y. Educ. Law § 414 enumerates several purposes for which local boards may open their schools to public use. In 1992, respondent Milford Central School (Milford) enacted a community use policy adopting seven of § 414's purposes for which its building could be used after school. Two of the stated purposes are relevant here. First, district residents may use the school for "instruction in any branch of education, learning or the arts." Second, the school is available for "social, civic and recreational meetings and entertainment events, and other uses pertaining to the welfare of the community, provided that such uses shall be nonexclusive and shall be opened to the general public."

Stephen and Darleen Fournier reside within Milford's district and therefore are eligible to use the school's facilities as long as their proposed use is approved by the school. Together they are sponsors of the local Good News Club, a private Christian organization for children ages 6 to 12. Pursuant to Milford's policy, in September 1996 the Fourniers submitted a request to Dr. Robert McGruder, interim superintendent of the district.... The next month, McGruder formally denied the Fourniers' request on the ground that the proposed use—to have "a fun time of singing songs, hearing a Bible lesson and memorizing scripture,"—was "the equivalent of religious worship." According to McGruder, the community use policy, which prohibits use "by any individual or organization for religious purposes," foreclosed the Club's activities.

In response to a letter submitted by the Club's counsel, Milford's attorney requested information to clarify the nature of the Club's activities. The Club sent a set of materials used or distributed at the meetings and the following description of its meeting:

> The Club opens its session with Ms. Fournier taking attendance. As she calls a child's name, if the child recites a Bible verse the child receives a treat. After attendance, the Club sings songs. Next Club members engage in games that involve, inter alia, learning Bible verses. Ms. Fournier then relates a Bible story and explains how it applies to Club members' lives. The Club closes with prayer. Finally, Ms. Fournier distributes treats and the Bible verses for memorization.

McGruder and Milford's attorney reviewed the materials and concluded that "the kinds of activities proposed to be engaged in by the Good News Club were not a discussion of secular subjects such as child rearing, development of character and development of morals from a religious perspective, but were in fact the equivalent of religious instruction itself." In February 1997, the Milford Board of Education adopted a resolution rejecting the Club's request to use Milford's facilities "for the purpose of conducting religious instruction and Bible study."

In March 1997, petitioners, the Good News Club, Ms. Fournier, and her daughter Andrea Fournier (collectively, the Club), filed an action under 42 U.S.C.[A.] § 1983 against Milford.... The Club alleged that Milford's denial of its application violated its free speech rights under the First and Fourteenth Amendments, its right to equal protection under the Fourteenth Amendment, and its right to religious freedom under the Religious Freedom Restoration Act of 1993.

The Club moved for a preliminary injunction to prevent the school from enforcing its religious exclusion policy against the Club and thereby to permit the Club's use of the school facilities. On April 14, 1997, the District Court granted the injunction. The Club then held its weekly after school meetings from April 1997 until June 1998 in a high school resource and middle school special education room. In August 1998, the District Court vacated the preliminary injunction and granted Milford's motion for summary judgment.... The Club appealed, and a divided panel of the ... Second Circuit affirmed.... There is a conflict among the Courts of Appeals on the question whether speech can be excluded from a limited public forum on the basis of the religious nature of the speech.... We granted certiorari to resolve this conflict.

II

The standards that we apply to determine whether a State has unconstitutionally excluded a private speaker from use of a public forum depend on the nature of the forum. If the forum is a traditional or open public forum, the State's restrictions on speech are subject to stricter scrutiny than are restrictions in a limited public forum. We have previously declined to decide whether a school district's opening of its facilities pursuant to N.Y. Educ. Law § 414 creates a limited or a traditional public forum. Because the parties have agreed that Milford created a limited public forum when it opened its facilities in 1992 we need not resolve the issue here. Instead, we simply will assume that Milford operates a limited public forum.

When the State establishes a limited public forum, the State is not required to and does not allow persons to engage in every type of speech. The State may be justified "in reserving [its forum] for certain groups or for the discussion of certain topics." The State's power to restrict speech, however, is not without limits. The restriction must not discriminate against speech on the basis of viewpoint, and the restriction must be "reasonable in light of the purpose served by the forum."

III

Applying this test, we first address whether the exclusion constituted viewpoint discrimination. We are guided in our analysis by two of our prior opinions, *Lamb's Chapel* and *Rosenberger*. In *Lamb's Chapel*, we held that a school district violated the Free Speech Clause of the First Amendment when it excluded a private group from presenting films at the school based solely on the films' discussions of family values from a religious perspective. Likewise, in *Rosenberger*, we held that a university's refusal to fund a student publication because the publication addressed issues from a religious perspective violated the Free Speech Clause. Concluding that Milford's exclusion of the Good News Club based on its religious nature is indistinguishable from the exclusions in these cases, we hold that the exclusion constitutes viewpoint discrimination. Because the restriction is viewpoint discriminatory, we need not decide whether it is unreasonable in light of the purposes served by the forum . . . .

Milford has opened its limited public forum to activities that serve a variety of purposes, including events "pertaining to the welfare of the community." Milford interprets its policy to permit discussions of subjects such as child rearing, and of "the development of character and morals from a religious perspective." For example, this policy would allow someone to use Aesop's Fables to teach children moral values. Additionally, a group could sponsor a debate on whether there should be a constitutional amendment to permit prayer in public schools and the Boy Scouts could meet "to influence a boy's character, development and spiritual growth." In short, any group that "promote[s] the moral and character development of children" is eligible to use the school building.

Just as there is no question that teaching morals and character development to children is a permissible purpose under Milford's policy, it is clear that the Club teaches morals and character development to children. For example, no one disputes that the Club instructs children to overcome feelings of jealousy, to treat others well regardless of how they treat the children, and to be obedient, even if it does so in a non-secular way. Nonetheless, because Milford found the Club's activities to be religious in nature—"the equivalent of religious instruction itself," it excluded the Club from use of its facilities.

Applying *Lamb's Chapel*, we find it quite clear that Milford engaged in viewpoint discrimination when it excluded the Club from the after school forum. In *Lamb's Chapel*, the local New York school district similarly had adopted § 414's "social, civic or recreational use" category as a permitted use in its limited public forum. The district also prohibited use "by any group for religious purposes...."

Like the church in *Lamb's Chapel*, the Club seeks to address a subject otherwise permitted under the rule, the teaching of morals and character, from a religious standpoint. Certainly, one could have characterized the film presentations in Lamb's Chapel as a religious use, as the Court of Appeals did. And one easily could conclude that the films' purpose to instruct that " 'society's slide toward humanism ... can only be counter-balanced by a loving home where Christian values are instilled from an early age' " was "quintessentially religious." The only apparent difference between the activity of *Lamb's Chapel* and the activities of the Good News Club is that the Club chooses to teach moral lessons from a Christian perspective through live storytelling and prayer, whereas *Lamb's Chapel* taught lessons through films. This distinction is inconsequential. Both modes of speech use a religious viewpoint. Thus, the exclusion of the Good News Club's activities, like the exclusion of Lamb's Chapel's films, constitutes unconstitutional viewpoint discrimination.

Our opinion in *Rosenberger* also is dispositive. In *Rosenberger*, a student organization at the University of Virginia was denied funding for printing expenses because its publication, Wide Awake, offered a Christian viewpoint. Just as the Club emphasizes the role of Christianity in students' morals and character, Wide Awake " 'challenge[d] Christians to live, in word and deed, according to the faith they proclaim and ... encourage[d] students to consider what a personal relationship with Jesus Christ means.' " Because the university "select[ed] for disfavored treatment those student journalistic efforts with religious editorial viewpoints," we held that the denial of funding was unconstitutional....

Despite our holdings in *Lamb's Chapel* and *Rosenberger*, the Court of Appeals, like Milford, believed that its characterization of the Club's activities as religious in nature warranted treating the Club's activities as different in kind from the other activities permitted by the school. The "Christian viewpoint" is unique, according to the court, because it contains an "additional layer" that other kinds of viewpoints do not. That is, the Club "is focused on teaching children how to cultivate their relationship with God through Jesus Christ," which it characterized as "quintessentially religious." With these observations, the court concluded that, because the Club's activities "fall outside the bounds of pure 'moral and character development,' " the exclusion did not constitute viewpoint discrimination.

We disagree that something that is "quintessentially religious" or "decidedly religious in nature" cannot also be characterized properly as the teaching of morals and character development from a particular viewpoint. What matters for purposes of the Free Speech Clause is that we can see no logical difference in kind between the invocation of Christianity by the Club and the invocation of teamwork, loyalty, or patriotism by other associations to provide a foundation for their lessons. It is apparent that the unstated principle of the Court of Appeals' reasoning is its conclusion that any time religious instruction and prayer are used to discuss morals and character, the discussion is simply not a "pure" discussion of those issues. According to the Court of Appeals, reliance on Christian principles taints moral and character instruction in a way that other foundations for thought or viewpoints do not. We, however, have never reached such a conclusion. Instead, we reaffirm our holdings in *Lamb's Chapel* and *Rosenberger* that speech discussing otherwise permissible subjects cannot be excluded from a limited public forum on the ground that the subject is discussed from a religious viewpoint. Thus, we conclude that Milford's exclusion of the Club from use of the school, pursuant to its community use policy, constitutes impermissible viewpoint discrimination.

. . .

IV

Milford argues that, even if its restriction constitutes viewpoint discrimination, its interest in not violating the Establishment Clause outweighs the Club's interest in gaining equal access to the school's facilities. In other words, according to Milford, its restriction was required to avoid violating the Establishment Clause. We disagree. We have said that a state interest in avoiding an Establishment Clause violation "may be characterized as compelling," and therefore may justify content-based discrimination. However, it is not clear whether a State's interest in avoiding an Establishment Clause violation would justify viewpoint discrimination. We need not, however, confront the issue in this case, because we conclude that the school has no valid Establishment Clause interest.

We rejected Establishment Clause defenses similar to Milford's in two previous free speech cases, *Lamb's Chapel* and *Widmar*. In particular, in *Lamb's Chapel*, we explained that "[t]he showing of th[e] film series would not have been during school hours, would not have been sponsored by the school, and would have been open to the public, not just to church members." Accordingly, we found that "there would have been no realistic danger that the community would think that the District was endorsing religion or any particular creed." Likewise, in *Widmar*, where the university's forum was already available to other groups, this Court concluded that there was no Establishment Clause problem.

The Establishment Clause defense fares no better in this case. As in *Lamb's Chapel*, the Club's meetings were held after school hours, not sponsored by the school, and open to any student who obtained parental consent, not just to Club members. As in *Widmar*, Milford made its forum available to other organizations. The Club's activities are materially indistinguishable from those in *Lamb's Chapel* and *Widmar*. Thus, Milford's reliance on the Establishment Clause is unavailing.

Milford attempts to distinguish *Lamb's Chapel* and *Widmar* by emphasizing that Milford's policy involves elementary school children. According to Milford, children will perceive that the school is endorsing the Club and will feel coercive pressure to participate, because the Club's activities take place on school grounds, even though they occur during non-school hours. This argument is unpersuasive.

First, we have held that "a significant factor in upholding governmental programs in the face of Establishment Clause attack is their neutrality towards religion." Milford's implication that granting access to the Club would do damage to the neutrality principle defies logic. For the "guarantee of neutrality is respected, not offended, when the government, following neutral criteria and evenhanded policies, extends benefits to recipients whose ideologies and viewpoints, including religious ones, are broad and diverse." The Good News Club seeks nothing more than to be treated neutrally and given access to speak about the same topics as are other groups. Because allowing the Club to speak on school grounds would ensure neutrality, not threaten it, Milford faces an uphill battle in arguing that the Establishment Clause compels it to exclude the Good News Club.

Second, to the extent we consider whether the community would feel coercive pressure to engage in the Club's activities, the relevant community would be the parents, not the elementary school children. It is the parents who choose whether their children will attend the Good News Club meetings. Because the children cannot attend without their parents' permission, they cannot be coerced into engaging in the Good News Club's religious activities. Milford does not suggest that the parents of elementary school children would be confused about whether the school was endorsing religion. Nor do we believe that such an argument could be reasonably advanced.

Third, whatever significance we may have assigned in the Establishment Clause context to the suggestion that elementary school children are more impressionable than adults, we have never extended our Establishment Clause jurisprudence to foreclose private religious conduct during non-school hours merely because it takes place on school premises where elementary school children may be present.

None of the cases discussed by Milford persuades us that our Establishment Clause jurisprudence has gone this far. . . .

Fourth, even if we were to consider the possible misperceptions by schoolchildren in deciding whether Milford's permitting the Club's activities would violate the Establishment Clause, the facts of this case simply do not support Milford's conclusion. There is no evidence that young children are permitted to loiter outside classrooms after the school day has ended. Surely even young children are aware of events for which their parents must sign permission forms. The meetings were held in a combined high school resource room and middle school special education room, not in an elementary school classroom. The instructors are not schoolteachers. And the children in the group are not all the same age as in the normal classroom setting; their ages range from 6 to 12. In sum, these circumstances simply do not support the theory that small children would perceive endorsement here.

Finally, even if we were to inquire into the minds of schoolchildren in this case, we cannot say the danger that children would misperceive the endorsement of religion is any greater than the danger that they would perceive a hostility toward the religious viewpoint if the Club were excluded from the public forum. This concern is particularly acute given the reality that Milford's building is not used only for elementary school children. Students, from kindergarten through the 12th grade, all attend school in the same building. There may be as many, if not more, upperclassmen than elementary school children who occupy the school after hours. . . .

We cannot operate, as Milford would have us do, under the assumption that any risk that small children would perceive endorsement should counsel in favor of excluding the Club's religious activity. We decline to employ Establishment Clause jurisprudence using a modified heckler's veto, in which a group's religious activity can be proscribed on the basis of what the youngest members of the audience might misperceive. . . . There are countervailing constitutional concerns related to rights of other individuals in the community. In this case, those countervailing concerns are the free speech rights of the Club and its members. . . . And, we have already found that those rights have been violated, not merely perceived to have been violated, by the school's actions toward the Club.

We are not convinced that there is any significance in this case to the possibility that elementary school children may witness the Good News Club's activities on school premises, and therefore we can find no reason to depart from our holdings in *Lamb's Chapel* and *Widmar*. Accordingly, we conclude that permitting the Club to meet on the school's premises would not have violated the Establishment Clause.

V

When Milford denied the Good News Club access to the school's limited public forum on the ground that the Club was religious in nature, it discriminated against the Club because of its religious viewpoint in violation of the Free Speech Clause of the First Amendment. Because Milford has not raised a valid Establishment Clause claim, we do not address the question whether such a claim could excuse Milford's viewpoint discrimination.

The judgment of the Court of Appeals is reversed, and the case is remanded for further proceedings consistent with this opinion.

NOTE

1. In a similar case from Louisiana, wherein the Supreme Court vacated and remanded the Fifth Circuit's judgment in light of *Milford. Campbell v. St. Tammany's School Bd.*, 533 U.S. 913, 121 S.Ct. 2518, 150 L.Ed.2d 691 [154 Educ. L. Rep. 73] (2001), *on remand*, 300 F.3d 526 [168 Educ. L. Rep. 128] (5th Cir.2002), a federal trial court granted the group's request to use school facilities. *Campbell v. St. Tammany Parish School Bd.*, 2003 WL 21783317 (E.D.La.2003).

[CASE NO. 14]   PUBLIC FUNDS FOR VOUCHERS TO RELIGIOUSLY AFFILIATED NON–PUBLIC SCHOOLS

ZELMAN v. SIMMONS–HARRIS

Supreme Court of the United States, 2002.
536 U.S. 639, 122 S.Ct. 2460, 153 L.Ed.2d 604 [166 Educ. L. Rep. 30].

■ CHIEF JUSTICE REHNQUIST delivered the opinion of the Court.

The State of Ohio has established a pilot program designed to provide educational choices to families with children who reside in the Cleveland City School District. The question presented is whether this program offends the Establishment Clause of the United States Constitution. We hold that it does not.

There are more than 75,000 children enrolled in the Cleveland City School District. The majority of these children are from low-income and minority families. Few of these families enjoy the means to send their children to any school other than an inner-city public school. For more than a generation, however, Cleveland's public schools have been among the worst performing public schools in the Nation. In 1995, a Federal District Court declared a "crisis of magnitude" and placed the entire Cleveland school district under state control. Shortly thereafter, the state auditor found that Cleveland's public schools were in the midst of a "crisis that is perhaps unprecedented in the history of American education." The district had failed to meet any of the 18 state standards for minimal acceptable performance. Only 1 in 10 ninth graders could pass a basic proficiency examination, and students at all levels performed at a dismal rate compared with students in other Ohio public schools. More than two-thirds of high school students either dropped or failed out before graduation. Of those students who managed to reach their senior year, one of every four still failed to graduate. Of those students who did graduate, few could read, write, or compute at levels comparable to their counterparts in other cities.

It is against this backdrop that Ohio enacted, among other initiatives, its Pilot Project Scholarship Program. The program provides financial assistance to families in any Ohio school district that is or has been "under federal court order requiring supervision and operational management of the district by the state superintendent." Cleveland is the only Ohio school district to fall within that category.

The program provides two basic kinds of assistance to parents of children in a covered district. First, the program provides tuition aid for students in kindergarten through third grade, expanding each year through eighth grade, to attend a participating public or private school of their parent's choosing. Second, the program provides tutorial aid for students who choose to remain enrolled in public school.

The tuition aid portion of the program is designed to provide educational choices to parents who reside in a covered district. Any private school, whether religious or nonreligious, may participate in the program and accept program students so long as the school is located within the boundaries of a covered district and meets statewide educational standards. Participating private schools must agree not to discriminate on the basis of race, religion, or ethnic background, or to "advocate or foster unlawful behavior or teach hatred of any person or group on the basis of race, ethnicity, national origin, or religion." Any public school located in a school district adjacent to the covered district may also participate in the program. Adjacent public schools are eligible to receive a $2,250 tuition grant for each program student accepted in addition to the full amount of per-pupil state funding attributable to each additional student. All participating schools, whether public or private, are required to accept students in accordance with rules and procedures established by the state superintendent.

Tuition aid is distributed to parents according to financial need. Families with incomes below 200% of the poverty line are given priority and are eligible to receive 90% of private school tuition up to $2,250. For these lowest-income families, participating private schools may not charge a parental co-payment greater than $250. For all other families, the program pays 75% of tuition costs, up to $1,875, with no co-payment cap. These families receive tuition aid only if the number of available scholarships exceeds the number of low-income children who choose to participate. Where tuition aid is spent depends solely upon where parents who receive tuition aid choose to enroll their child. If parents choose a private school, checks are made payable to the parents who then endorse the checks over to the chosen school.

The tutorial aid portion of the program provides tutorial assistance through grants to any student in a covered district who chooses to remain in public school ... The number of tutorial assistance grants offered to students in a covered district must equal the number of tuition aid scholarships provided to students enrolled at participating private or adjacent public schools.

The program has been in operation within the Cleveland City School District since the 1996–1997 school year. In the 1999–2000 school year, 56 private schools participated in the program, 46 (or 82%) of which had a religious affiliation. None of the public schools in districts adjacent to Cleveland have elected to participate. More than 3,700 students participated in the scholarship program, most of whom (96%) enrolled in religiously affiliated schools. Sixty percent of these students were from families at or below the poverty line. In the 1998–1999 school year, approximately 1,400 Cleveland public school students received tutorial aid. This number was expected to double during the 1999–2000 school year.

The program is part of a broader undertaking by the State to enhance the educational options of Cleveland's schoolchildren in response to the 1995 takeover [t]hat includes programs governing community and magnet schools. Community schools are funded under state law but are run by their own school boards, not by local school districts. These schools enjoy academic independence to hire their own teachers and to determine their own curriculum. They can have no religious affiliation and are required to accept students by lottery. During the 1999–2000 school year, there were 10 start-up community schools in the Cleveland City School District with more than 1,900 students enrolled. For each child enrolled in a community school, the school receives state funding of $4,518, twice the funding a participating program school may receive.

Magnet schools are public schools operated by a local school board that emphasize a particular subject area, teaching method, or service to students. For each student enrolled in a magnet school, the school district receives $7,746, including state funding of $4,167, the same amount received per student enrolled at a traditional public school. As of 1999, parents in Cleveland were able to choose from among 23 magnet schools, which together enrolled more than 13,000 students in kindergarten through eighth grade. . . .

In 1996, respondents, a group of Ohio taxpayers, challenged the Ohio program. . . . The Ohio Supreme Court rejected respondents' federal claims, but held that the enactment of the program violated certain procedural requirements of the Ohio Constitution. The state legislature immediately cured this defect, leaving the basic provisions discussed above intact.

In July 1999, respondents filed this action . . . seeking to enjoin the reenacted program on the ground that it violated the Establishment Clause. . . . In August 1999, the District Court issued a preliminary injunction barring further implementation of the program, which we stayed pending review by the Court of Appeals. In December 1999, the District Court granted summary judgment for respondents. In December 2000, a divided panel of the Court of Appeals affirmed . . . finding that the program had the "primary effect" of advancing religion in violation of the Establishment Clause. The Court of Appeals stayed its mandate pending disposition in this Court. We granted certiorari, and now reverse the Court of Appeals.

The Establishment Clause of the First Amendment . . . prevents a State from enacting laws that have the "purpose" or "effect" of advancing or inhibiting religion. . . . There is no dispute that the program challenged here was enacted for the valid secular purpose of providing educational assistance to poor children in a demonstrably failing public school system. Thus, the question presented is whether the Ohio program nonetheless has the forbidden "effect" of advancing or inhibiting religion.

To answer that question, our decisions have drawn a consistent distinction between government programs that provide aid directly to religious schools and programs of true private choice, in which government aid reaches religious schools only as a result of the genuine and independent choices of private individuals. While our jurisprudence with respect to the constitutionality of direct aid programs has "changed significantly" over the past two decades, our jurisprudence with respect to true private choice programs has remained consistent and unbroken. Three times we have confronted Establishment Clause challenges to neutral government programs that provide aid directly to a broad class of individuals, who, in turn, direct the aid to religious schools or institutions of their own choosing. Three times we have rejected such challenges.

In *Mueller,* we rejected an Establishment Clause challenge to a Minnesota program authorizing tax deductions for various educational expenses, including private school tuition costs, even though the great majority of the program's beneficiaries (96%) were parents of children in religious schools. We began by focusing on the class of beneficiaries, finding that because the class included "all parents," including parents with "children [who] attend non-sectarian private schools or sectarian private schools," the program was "not readily subject to challenge under the Establishment Clause." Then, viewing the program as a whole, we emphasized the principle of private choice, noting that public funds were made available to religious schools "only as a result of numerous, private choices of individual parents of school-age children." This, we said, ensured that " 'no imprimatur of state approval' can be deemed to have been conferred on any particular religion, or on religion generally." We thus found it irrelevant to the constitutional inquiry that the vast majority of beneficiaries were parents of children in religious schools. . . .

In *Witters,* we used identical reasoning to reject an Establishment Clause challenge to a vocational scholarship program that provided tuition aid to a student studying at a religious institution to become a pastor. Looking at the program as a whole, we observed that "[a]ny aid . . . that ultimately flows to religious institutions does so only as a result of the genuinely independent and private choices of aid recipients. . . ."

Five Members of the Court, in separate opinions, emphasized the general rule from *Mueller* that the amount of government aid channeled to religious institutions by individual aid recipients was not relevant to the constitutional inquiry. Our holding thus rested not on whether few or many recipients chose to expend government aid at a religious school but, rather, on whether recipients generally were empowered to direct the aid to schools or institutions of their own choosing.

Finally, in *Zobrest,* we applied *Mueller* and *Witters* to reject an Establishment Clause challenge to a federal program that permitted sign-language interpreters to assist deaf children enrolled in religious schools . . . we stated that "government programs that neutrally provide benefits to a broad class of citizens defined without reference to religion are not readily subject to an Establishment Clause challenge. . . ." we observed that the program "distributes benefits neutrally to any child qualifying as 'disabled.' " Its "primary beneficiaries," we said, were "disabled children, not sectarian schools."

We further observed that "[b]y according parents freedom to select a school of their choice, the statute ensures that a government-paid interpreter will be present in a sectarian school only as a result of the private decision of individual parents." Our focus again was on neutrality and the principle of private choice, not on the number of program beneficiaries attending religious schools. . . .

Mueller, Witters, and *Zobrest* thus make clear that where a government aid program is neutral with respect to religion, and provides assistance directly to a broad class of citizens who, in turn, direct government aid to religious schools wholly as a result of their own genuine and independent private choice, the program is not readily subject to challenge under the Establishment Clause. A program that shares these features permits government aid to reach religious institutions only by way of the deliberate choices of numerous individual recipients. The incidental advancement of a religious mission, or the perceived endorsement of a religious message, is reasonably attributable to the individual recipient, not to the government. . . .

We believe that the program challenged here is a program of true private choice, consistent with *Mueller, Witters,* and *Zobrest,* and thus constitutional. As was true in those cases, the Ohio program is neutral in all respects toward religion. It is part of a general and multifaceted undertaking by the State of Ohio to provide educational opportunities to the children of a failed school district. It confers educational assistance directly to a broad class of individuals defined without reference to religion, *i.e.,* any parent of a school-age child who resides in the Cleveland City School District. The program permits the participation of all schools within the district, religious or nonreligious. Adjacent public schools also may participate and have a financial incentive to do so. Program benefits are available to participating families on neutral terms, with no reference to religion. The only . . . preference [is] for low-income families, who receive greater assistance and are given priority for admission. . . .

There are no "financial incentive[s]" that "ske[w]" the program toward religious schools. Such incentives "[are] not present . . . where the aid is allocated on the basis of neutral, secular criteria that neither favor nor disfavor religion, and is made available to both religious and secular beneficiaries on a nondiscriminatory basis." The program here in fact creates financial disincentives for religious schools, with private schools receiving only half the government assistance given to community schools and one-third the assistance given to magnet schools. Adjacent public schools, should any choose to accept program students, are also eligible to receive two to three times the state funding of a private religious school. Families too have a financial disincentive to choose a private religious school over other schools. Parents that choose to participate in the scholarship program and then to enroll their children in a private school (religious or nonreligious) must copay a portion of the school's tuition. Families that choose a community school, magnet school, or traditional public school pay nothing. . . .

Respondents suggest that even without a financial incentive for parents to choose a religious school, the program creates a "public perception that the State is endorsing religious practices and beliefs." But we have repeatedly recognized that no reasonable observer would think a neutral program of private choice, where state aid reaches religious schools solely as a result of the numerous independent decisions of private individuals, carries with it the *imprimatur* of government endorsement. The argument is particularly misplaced here since "the reasonable observer in the endorsement inquiry must be deemed aware" of the "history and context" underlying a challenged program. Any objective observer familiar with the full history and context of the Ohio program would reasonably view it as one aspect of a broader undertaking to assist poor children in failed schools, not as an endorsement of religious schooling in general.

There also is no evidence that the program fails to provide genuine opportunities for Cleveland parents to select secular educational options for their school-age children. Cleveland schoolchildren enjoy a range of educational choices: They may remain in public school as before, remain in public school with publicly funded tutoring aid, obtain a scholarship and choose a religious school, obtain a scholarship and choose a nonreligious private school, enroll in a community school, or enroll in a magnet school. That 46 of the 56 private schools now participating in the program are religious schools does not condemn it as a violation of the Establishment Clause. The Establishment Clause question is whether Ohio is coercing parents into sending their children to religious schools, and that question must be answered by evaluating all options Ohio provides Cleveland schoolchildren, only one of which is to obtain a program scholarship and then choose a religious school.

Justice SOUTER speculates that because more private religious schools currently participate in the program, the program itself must somehow discourage the participation of private nonreligious schools. But Cleveland's preponderance of religiously affiliated private schools certainly did not arise as a result of the program; it is a phenomenon common to many American cities. Indeed, by all accounts the program has captured a remarkable cross-section of private schools, religious and nonreligious. It is true that 82% of Cleveland's participating private schools are religious schools, but it is also true that 81% of private schools in Ohio are religious schools. To attribute constitutional significance to this figure, moreover, would lead to the absurd result that a neutral school-choice program might be permissible in some parts of Ohio, such as Columbus, where a lower percentage of private schools are religious schools, but not in inner-city Cleveland, where Ohio has deemed such programs most sorely needed, but where the preponderance of religious schools happens to be greater. . . .

Respondents and Justice SOUTER claim that even if we do not focus on the number of participating schools that are religious schools, we should attach constitutional significance to the fact that 96% of scholarship recipients have enrolled in religious schools. They claim that this alone proves parents lack genuine choice, even if no parent has ever said so. We need not consider this argument in detail, since it was flatly rejected in *Mueller*, where we found it irrelevant that 96% of parents taking deductions for tuition expenses paid tuition at religious schools. Indeed, we have recently found it irrelevant even to the constitutionality of a direct aid program that a vast majority of program benefits went to religious schools. The constitutionality of a neutral educational aid program simply does not turn on whether and why, in a particular area, at a particular time, most private schools are run by religious organizations, or most recipients choose to use the aid at a religious school. . . .

This point is aptly illustrated here. The 96% figure upon which respondents and Justice SOUTER rely discounts entirely (1) the more than 1,900 Cleveland children enrolled in alternative community schools, (2) the more than 13,000 children enrolled in alternative magnet schools, and (3) the more than 1,400 children enrolled in traditional public schools with tutorial assistance. Including some or all of these children in the denominator of children enrolled in nontraditional schools during the 1999–2000 school year drops the percentage enrolled in religious schools from 96% to under 20%. The 96% figure also represents but a snapshot of one particular school year. In the 1997–1998 school year, by contrast, only 78% of scholarship recipients attended religious schools. The difference was attributable to two private nonreligious schools that had accepted 15% of all scholarship students electing instead to register as community schools, in light of larger per-pupil funding for community schools and the uncertain future of the scholarship program generated by this litigation. Many of the students enrolled in these schools as scholarship students remained enrolled as community school students, thus demonstrating the arbitrariness of counting one type of school but not the other to assess primary effect. . . .

Respondents finally claim that we should look to *Committee for Public Ed. & Religious Liberty v. Nyquist* to decide these cases. We disagree for two reasons. First, the program in *Nyquist* was quite different from the program challenged here. *Nyquist* involved a New York program that gave a package of benefits exclusively to private schools and the parents of private school enrollees. Although the program was enacted for ostensibly secular purposes, we found that its "function" was "unmistakably to provide desired financial support for non-public, sectarian institutions. . . ." The program thus provided direct money grants to religious schools. It provided tax benefits "unrelated to the amount of money actually expended by any parent on tuition," ensuring a windfall to parents of children in religious schools. It similarly provided tuition reimbursements designed explicitly to "offe[r] . . . an incentive to parents to send their children to sectarian schools." Indeed, the program flatly prohibited the participation of any public school, or parent of any public school enrollee. Ohio's program shares none of these features.

Second, were there any doubt that the program challenged in *Nyquist* is far removed from the program challenged here, we expressly reserved judgment with respect to "a case involving some form of public assistance (*e.g.*, scholarships) made available generally without regard to the sectarian-non-sectarian, or public-non-public nature of the institution benefited." That, of course, is the very question now before us, and it has since been answered, first in *Mueller*, then in *Witters*, and again in *Zobrest*. To the extent the scope of *Nyquist* has remained an open question in light of these later decisions, we now hold that *Nyquist* does not govern neutral educational assistance programs that, like the program here, offer aid directly to a broad class of individual recipients defined without regard to religion.

In sum, the Ohio program is entirely neutral with respect to religion. It provides benefits directly to a wide spectrum of individuals, defined only by financial need and residence in a particular school district. It permits such individuals to exercise genuine choice among options public and private, secular and religious. The program is therefore a program of true private choice. In keeping with an unbroken line of decisions rejecting challenges to similar programs, we hold that the program does not offend the Establishment Clause.

The judgment of the Court of Appeals is reversed.

It is so ordered.

NOTES

1. The dissenters, led by Justice Stevens' raising the specters of "the Balkans, Northern Ireland, and the Middle East," *Zelman v. Simmons–Harris*, at 686, voiced concerns about divisiveness and religious strife based on the majority's upholding the voucher program. Is Justice Stevens' fear well-founded? Can you distinguish the situation in the United States and those three locations?

2. Given the narrowness of the vouchers statute at issue, since it was developed exclusively for Cleveland as part of a school desegregation suit, are similar programs likely to withstand constitutional challenges? Are constitutional challenges more likely to succeed in federal or state courts?

[CASE NO. 15] THE CONSTITUTIONALITY OF THE WORDS "UNDER GOD" IN THE PLEDGE

ELK GROVE UNIFIED SCHOOL DISTRICT v. NEWDOW

Supreme Court of the United States, 2004.
542 U.S. 1, 124 S.Ct. 2301, 159 L.Ed.2d 98 [188 Educ. L. Rep. 17].

■ JUSTICE STEVENS delivered the opinion of the Court.

Each day elementary school teachers in the Elk Grove Unified School District (School District) lead their classes in a group recitation of the Pledge of Allegiance. Respondent, Michael A. Newdow, is an atheist whose daughter participates in that daily exercise. Because the Pledge contains the words "under God," he views the School District's policy as a religious indoctrination of his child that violates the First Amendment. A divided panel of the Court of Appeals for the Ninth Circuit agreed with Newdow. In light of the obvious importance of that decision, we granted certiorari to review the First Amendment issue and, preliminarily, the question whether Newdow has standing to invoke the jurisdiction of the federal courts. We conclude that Newdow lacks standing and therefore reverse the Court of Appeals' decision.

I

"The very purpose of a national flag is to serve as a symbol of our country," and of its proud traditions "of freedom, of equal opportunity, of religious tolerance, and of good will for other peoples who share our aspirations." As its history illustrates, the Pledge of Allegiance evolved as a common public acknowledgement of the ideals that our flag symbolizes. Its recitation is a patriotic exercise designed to foster national unity and pride in those principles. The Pledge of Allegiance was initially conceived more than a century ago. As part of the nationwide interest in commemorating the 400th anniversary of Christopher Columbus' discovery of America, a widely circulated national magazine for youth proposed in 1892 that pupils recite the following affirmation: "I pledge allegiance to my Flag and the Republic for which it stands: one Nation indivisible, with Liberty and Justice for all." In the 1920's, the National Flag Conferences replaced the phrase "my Flag" with "the flag of the United States of America."

In 1942, in the midst of World War II, Congress adopted, and the President signed, a Joint Resolution codifying a detailed set of "rules and customs pertaining to the display and use of the flag of the United States of America." . . . This resolution, which marked the first appearance of the Pledge of Allegiance in positive law, confirmed the importance of the flag as a symbol of our Nation's indivisibility and commitment to the concept of liberty.

Congress revisited the Pledge of Allegiance 12 years later when it amended the text to add the words "under God." The House Report that accompanied the [1954] legislation observed that, "[f]rom the time of our earliest history our peoples and our institutions have reflected the traditional concept that our Nation was founded on a fundamental belief in God." The resulting text is the Pledge as we know it today: "I pledge allegiance to the Flag of the United States of America, and to the Republic for which it stands, one Nation under God, indivisible, with liberty and justice for all."

II

Under California law, "every public elementary school" must begin each day with "appropriate patriotic exercises." The statute provides that "[t]he giving of the Pledge of Allegiance to the Flag of the United States of America shall satisfy" this requirement. The Elk Grove Unified School District has implemented the state law by requiring that "[e]ach elementary school class recite the pledge of allegiance to the flag once each day." Consistent with our case law, the School District permits students who object on religious grounds to abstain from the recitation.

In March 2000, Newdow filed suit in the United States District Court for the Eastern District of California against the United States Congress, the President of the United States, the State of California, and the Elk Grove Unified School District and its superintendent. At the time of filing, Newdow's daughter was enrolled in kindergarten in the Elk Grove Unified School District and participated in the daily recitation of the Pledge. Styled as a mandamus action, the complaint explains that Newdow is an atheist who was ordained more than 20 years ago in a ministry that "espouses the religious philosophy that the true and eternal bonds of righteousness and virtue stem from reason rather than mythology." The complaint seeks a declaration that the 1954 Act's addition of the words "under God" violated the Establishment and Free Exercise Clauses of the United States Constitution, as well as an injunction against the School District's policy requiring daily recitation of the Pledge. It alleges that Newdow has standing to sue on his own behalf and on behalf of his daughter as "next friend."

The case was referred to a Magistrate Judge, whose brief findings and recommendation concluded, "the Pledge does not violate the Establishment Clause." The District Court adopted that recommendation and dismissed the complaint on July 21, 2000. The Court of Appeals reversed and issued three separate decisions discussing the merits and Newdow's standing.

In its first opinion the appeals court unanimously held that Newdow has standing "as a parent to challenge a practice that interferes with his right to direct the religious education of his daughter." . . . On the merits, over the dissent of one judge, the court held that both the 1954 Act and the School District's policy violate the Establishment Clause of the First Amendment.

After the Court of Appeals' initial opinion was announced, Sandra Banning, the mother of Newdow's daughter, filed a motion for leave to intervene, or alternatively to dismiss the complaint. She declared that although she and Newdow shared "physical custody" of their daughter, a state-court order granted her "exclusive legal custody" of the child, "including the sole right to represent [the daughter's] legal interests and make all decision[s] about her education" and welfare. Banning further stated that her daughter is a Christian who believes in God and has no objection either to reciting or hearing others recite the Pledge of Allegiance, or to its reference to God. Banning expressed the belief that her daughter would be harmed if the litigation were permitted to proceed, because others might incorrectly perceive the child as sharing her father's atheist views. Banning accordingly concluded, as her daughter's sole legal custodian, that it was not in the child's interest to be a party to Newdow's lawsuit. On September 25, 2002, the California Superior Court entered an order enjoining Newdow from including his daughter as an unnamed party or suing as her "next friend." That order did not purport to answer the question of Newdow's Article III standing.

In a second published opinion, the Court of Appeals reconsidered Newdow's standing. . . . The court noted that Newdow no longer claimed to represent his daughter, but unanimously concluded that "the grant of sole legal custody to Banning" did not deprive Newdow, "as a non-custodial parent, of Article III standing to object to unconstitutional government action affecting his child." The court held that under California law Newdow retains the right to expose his child to his particular religious views even if those views contradict the mother's, and that Banning's objections as sole legal custodian do not defeat Newdow's right to seek redress for an alleged injury to his own parental interests.

On February 28, 2003, the Court of Appeals issued an order amending its first opinion and denying rehearing en banc. The amended opinion omitted the initial opinion's discussion of Newdow's standing to challenge the 1954 Act and declined to determine whether Newdow was entitled to declaratory relief regarding the constitutionality of that Act. Nine judges dissented. . . . We granted the School District's petition for a writ of certiorari to consider two questions: (1) whether Newdow has standing as a non-custodial parent to challenge the School District's policy, and (2) if so, whether the policy offends the First Amendment.

III

In every federal case, the party bringing the suit must establish standing to prosecute the action. "In essence the question of standing is whether the litigant is entitled to have the court decide the merits of the dispute or of particular issues." The standing requirement is born partly of " 'an idea, which is more than an intuition but less than a rigorous and explicit theory, about the constitutional and prudential limits to the powers of an unelected, unrepresentative judiciary in our kind of government.' "

The command to guard jealously and exercise rarely our power to make constitutional pronouncements requires strictest adherence when matters of great national significance are at stake. Even in cases concededly within our jurisdiction under Article III, we abide by "a series of rules under which [we have] avoided passing upon a large part of all the constitutional questions pressed upon [us] for decision." Always we must balance "the heavy obligation to exercise jurisdiction," against the "deeply rooted" commitment "not to pass on questions of constitutionality" unless adjudication of the constitutional issue is necessary.

Consistent with these principles, our standing jurisprudence contains two strands: Article III standing, which enforces the Constitution's case or controversy requirement; and prudential standing, which embodies "judicially self-imposed limits on the exercise of federal jurisdiction." The Article III limitations are familiar: The plaintiff must show that the conduct of which he complains has caused him to suffer an "injury in fact" that a favorable judgment will redress. Although we have not exhaustively defined the prudential dimensions of the standing doctrine, we have explained that prudential standing encompasses "the general prohibition on a litigant's raising another person's legal rights, the rule barring adjudication of generalized grievances more appropriately addressed in the representative branches, and the requirement that a plaintiff's complaint fall within the zone of interests protected by the law invoked." . . .

One of the principal areas in which this Court has customarily declined to intervene is the realm of domestic relations. Long ago we observed that "[t]he whole subject of the domestic relations of husband and wife, parent and child, belongs to the laws of the States and not to the laws of the United States." So strong is our deference to state law in this area that we have recognized a "domestic relations exception" that "divests the federal courts of power to issue divorce, alimony, and child custody decrees." We have also acknowledged that it might be appropriate for the federal courts to decline to hear a case involving "elements of the domestic relationship," even when divorce, alimony, or child custody is not strictly at issue . . . Thus, while rare instances arise in which it is necessary to answer a substantial federal question that transcends or exists apart from the family law issue, in general it is appropriate for the federal courts to leave delicate issues of domestic relations to the state courts.

As explained briefly above, the extent of the standing problem raised by the domestic relations issues in this case was not apparent until August 5, 2002, when Banning filed her motion for leave to intervene or dismiss the complaint following the Court of Appeals' initial decision. At that time, the child's custody was governed by a February 6, 2002, order of the California Superior Court. That order provided that Banning had "sole legal custody as to the rights and responsibilities to make decisions relating to the health, education and welfare of'' her daughter. The order stated that the two parents should '' 'consult with one another on substantial decisions relating to' '' the child's '' 'psychological and educational needs,' '' but it authorized Banning to '' 'exercise legal control' '' if the parents could not reach '' 'mutual agreement.' ''

That family court order was the controlling document at the time of the Court of Appeals' standing decision. After the Court of Appeals ruled, however, the Superior Court held another conference regarding the child's custody. At a hearing on September 11, 2003, the Superior Court announced that the parents have "joint legal custody," but that Banning "makes the final decisions if the two ... disagree."

Newdow contends that despite Banning's final authority, he retains "an unrestricted right to inculcate in his daughter—free from governmental interference—the atheistic beliefs he finds persuasive." The difficulty with that argument is that Newdow's rights, as in many cases touching upon family relations, cannot be viewed in isolation. This case concerns not merely Newdow's interest in inculcating his child with his views on religion, but also the rights of the child's mother as a parent generally and under the Superior Court orders specifically. And most important, it implicates the interests of a young child who finds herself at the center of a highly public debate over her custody, the propriety of a widespread national ritual, and the meaning of our Constitution.

The interests of the affected persons in this case are in many respects antagonistic. Of course, legal disharmony in family relations is not uncommon, and in many instances that disharmony poses no bar to federal-court adjudication of proper federal questions. What makes this case different is that Newdow's standing derives entirely from his relationship with his daughter, but he lacks the right to litigate as her next friend. . . .

Newdow's parental status is defined by California's domestic relations law. Our custom on questions of state law ordinarily is to defer to the interpretation of the Court of Appeals for the Circuit in which the State is located. In this case, the Court of Appeals, which possesses greater familiarity with California law, concluded that state law vests in Newdow a cognizable right to influence his daughter's religious upbringing. The court based its ruling on two intermediate state appellate cases holding that "while the custodial parent undoubtedly has the right to make ultimate decisions concerning the child's religious upbringing, a court will not enjoin the non-custodial parent from discussing religion with the child or involving the child in his or her religious activities in the absence of a showing that the child will be thereby harmed." Animated by a conception of "family privacy" that includes "not simply a policy of minimum state intervention but also a presumption of parental autonomy," the state cases create a zone of private authority within which each parent, whether custodial or non-custodial, remains free to impart to the child his or her religious perspective.

Nothing that either Banning or the School Board has done, however, impairs Newdow's right to instruct his daughter in his religious views. Instead, Newdow ... wishes to forestall his daughter's exposure to religious ideas that her mother, who wields a form of veto power, endorses, and to use his parental status to challenge the influences to which his daughter may be exposed in school when he and Banning disagree. The California cases simply do not stand for the proposition that Newdow has a right to dictate to others what they may and may not say to his child respecting religion. [The California cases] . . . are concerned with protecting " 'the fragile, complex interpersonal bonds between child and parent,' " and with permitting divorced parents to expose their children to the " 'diversity of religious experiences [that] is itself a sound stimulant for a child.' " The cases speak not at all to the problem of a parent seeking to reach outside the private parent-child sphere to restrain the acts of a third party. A next friend surely could exercise such a right, but the Superior Court's order has deprived Newdow of that status.

In our view, it is improper for the federal courts to entertain a claim by a plaintiff whose standing to sue is founded on family law rights that are in dispute when prosecution of the lawsuit may have an adverse effect on the person who is the source of the plaintiff's claimed standing. When hard questions of domestic relations are sure to affect the outcome, the prudent course is for the federal court to stay its hand rather than reach out to resolve a weighty question of federal constitutional law. There is a vast difference between Newdow's right to communicate with his child—which both California law and the First Amendment recognize—and his claimed right to shield his daughter from influences to which she is exposed in school despite the terms of the custody order. We conclude that, having been deprived under California law of the right to sue as next friend, Newdow lacks prudential standing to bring this suit in federal court.

The judgment of the Court of Appeals is reversed.

It is so ordered.

NOTES

1. Justices Kennedy, Souter, Ginsburg, and Breyer joined Justice Stevens' opinion as to standing. Three members of the Supreme Court concurred separately. Chief Justice Rehnquist's concurrence was joined by Justice O'Connor and in part by Justice Thomas. Justice O'Connor and Justice Thomas wrote separate concurrences in which they would have granted the father standing and would have upheld the Pledge on its face. In light of his critical comments about this case as it was pending, Justice Scalia did not take part in its consideration or decision.

2. In limiting its decision to standing, the Court avoided the issue of whether the words "under God" are ceremonial (or civic) deism, representing the place that religion has played in American history or a form of impermissible establishment of religion. What do you think?

CHAPTER 3

STATE-LEVEL ENTITIES

INTRODUCTION

Under the Tenth Amendment to the United States Constitution, education is a function of the state, rather than the federal, government. Thus, absent federal restrictions on their authority, legislatures have plenary, or full, power over education subject only to the limits present in state constitutions, typically through their departments of education. As reflected in this chapter, courts ordinarily uphold legislative control to oversee duties and responsibilities between and among state, intermediate, and local educational agencies. Since their authority over public education is plenary, legislatures may change educational systems as they deem appropriate.

ESTABLISHMENT AND ALTERATION OF SCHOOL DISTRICTS

IN GENERAL

School districts and their governing bodies, usually called school boards, boards of education, or in a limited number of jurisdictions, school committees, are state agencies[1] acting independently of local governments and municipalities.[2] In this way, local boards are "creatures of the state" designed by legislatures to carry out their state constitutional mandates to educate the children entrusted to their care.[3] As "creatures of the state which can only be formed, dissolved, or altered in accordance with"[4] state law, school boards have only the power and authority that they are granted by their state legislatures.[5]

---

1. *Department of Fin. v. Commission on State Mandates*, 134 Cal.Rptr.2d 237 [176 Educ. L. Rep. 894] (Cal.2003).

2. *City of Manchester School Dist. v. City of Manchester*, 843 A.2d 966 [186 Educ. L. Rep. 449] (N.H.2004).

3. *See, e.g., State ex rel. School Dist. of City of Independence v. Jones*, 653 S.W.2d 178 [12 Educ. L. Rep. 582] (Mo.1983); *Plum Borough School Dist. v. Schlegel*, 855 A.2d 939 [191 Educ. L. Rep. 416] (Pa.Cmwlth.Ct.2004).

4. *Pocantico Home & Land Co. v. Union Free School Dist. of Tarrytowns*, 799 N.Y.S.2d 235, 239 [200 Educ. L. Rep. 300] (N.Y.App.Div.2005), *appeal dismissed*, 806 N.Y.S.2d 167 (N.Y.2005).

5. *See, e.g., National Educ. Ass'n–Wichita v. Unified School Dist. No. 259, Sedgwick County*, 674 P.2d 478 [15 Educ. L. Rep. 948] (Kan.1983); *Academy of Charter Schools v.*

Acting pursuant to their plenary power, state legislatures can set district boundaries,[6] abolish local school units, and/or redistrict states regardless of pre-existing boundaries[7] by means of detachment, annexation, dissolution, consolidation[8] (sometimes referred to as regionalization[9] or mergers[10]) or a combination of methods.[11] States can also set specific procedures with which landowners must comply when challenging reorganizations to combine districts[12] or schools.[13] As long as a court can clearly identify what parcel of property is involved in a consolidation, it is likely to uphold a merger even if there are deficiencies in a petition of transfer.[14] In addition, as illustrated by a case from the Supreme Court of South Dakota, when homeowners petition to move from one district to another, school officials are free to combine requests covering essentially the same tract of land as long as their actions are not arbitrary and capricious.[15]

The Supreme Court of Illinois, in a detachment and annexation case, followed the general rule in cautioning that such a petition should only be granted when there is an overall benefit to the annexing system and a detachment outweighs the detriment to the detaching district and its surrounding community.[16] More than a decade later, an appellate court in Illinois permitted an annexation where there was no substantial detriment to either district and the educational benefit to the family involved would have been considerable since the mother taught in the annexing system and most of the friends of the family's children lived there.[17] Similarly, in deferring to the discretion of the state board of education, the Supreme Court of North Dakota affirmed an annexation where the transfer of a

---

Adams County School Dist. No. 12, 32 P.3d 456 [157 Educ. L. Rep. 896] (Colo.2001), *reh'g denied*; *Pucket v. Hot Springs School Dist. No. 23–2*, 526 F.3d 1151, 1157 [232 Educ. L. Rep. 628] (8th Cir.2008).

6. *See, e.g., Sherwood School Dist. 88J v. Washington County Educ. Serv. Dist.*, 6 P.3d 518 [146 Educ. L. Rep. 879] (Or. Ct. App. 2000).

7. *Moore v. Board of Educ. of Iredell County*, 193 S.E. 732 (N.C.1937); *Opinion of the Justices*, 246 A.2d 90 (Del.1968); *Rose v. Council for Better Educ.*, 790 S.W.2d 186 [60 Educ. L.Rep. 1289] (Ky.1989).

8. *Friends of Lake View School Dist. No. 25 v. Beebe*, 578 F.3d 753 [248 Educ. L. Rep. 86] (8th Cir. 2009).

9. *Board of Educ. of Borough of Englewood Cliffs v. Board of Educ. of Borough of Tenafly*, 788 A.2d 729 [161 Educ. L. Rep. 542] (N.J.2002).

10. *Kings Mountain Bd. of Educ. v. North Carolina State Bd. of Educ.*, 583 S.E.2d 629 [179 Educ. L. Rep. 499] (N.C.Ct.App.2003), *writ denied, review denied*, 588 S.E.2d 476 (N.C.2003).

11. *Charleston School Dist. No. 9 v. Sebastian County Bd. of Educ.*, 778 S.W.2d 614 [56 Educ. L. Rep. 1340] (Ark.1989).

12. *Nicholson v. Red Willow County School Dist. No. 0170*, 699 N.W.2d 25 [199 Educ. L. Rep. 934] (Neb.2005).

13. *Wallace v. Iowa State Bd. of Educ.*, 770 N.W.2d 344 [247 Educ. L. Rep. 914] (Iowa 2009).

14. *Koch v. Cedar County Freeholder Bd.*, 759 N.W.2d 464 [240 Educ. L. Rep. 908] (Neb. 2009).

15. *Pruchniak v. School Bd. of Elk Point–Jefferson School Dist. No. 61–7*, 691 N.W.2d 298 [194 Educ. L. Rep. 946] (S.D.2004).

16. *Carver v. Bond/Fayette/Effingham Reg'l Bd. of School Trustees*, 586 N.E.2d 1273 [72 Educ. L. Rep. 967] (Ill.1992).

17. *Dukett v. Regional Bd. of School Trustees*, 795 N.E.2d 945 [180 Educ. L. Rep. 859] (Ill.App.Ct.2003).

smaller parcel of territory than was originally at issue would have had a less significant impact on the budgets of two local school boards.[18] The same court later affirmed that economic factors may be valid considerations for a school board to take into account when reviewing petitions for minor boundary changes.[19]

In California, an appellate court considered whether state law required a school board to admit children who lived on a property situated partly within its geographic boundaries. Where a family's property straddled the boundary line between two districts, and only twenty-six percent was located in the receiving system, the court affirmed that the family's home was within that system.[20] The court rejected the board's claim that "in" the district should have been interpreted as meaning that the property was entirely within the boundaries of the receiving system.

A dispute in Pennsylvania involved a mother who lived in a rented apartment with her children in one district but owned a house in the neighboring school system. An appellate court, distinguishing between domicile and residence for the purpose of school attendance, ruled that insofar as the mother and children lived mostly in the house, it was their domicile.[21] The court declared that the mother and her children could not rely on the apartment as their residence since allowing them to do so would have resulted in "school-shopping."

Unless required by state constitutions[22] or statutes,[23] state and local officials do not need consent from district residents before redistricting. In fact, even if residents vote against boundary changes, legislatures can still proceed with consolidations.[24] A dispute over the input of district residents involved the attempt of two towns to withdraw from regional school systems. When the towns sought to withdraw from their school administrative units after obtaining the required public input, the state commissioner of education refused to set a date for the municipal vote without revisions to the withdrawal agreement. Town officials unsuccessfully argued that insofar as they only had to prepare a withdrawal agreement for voters, negotiations over remaining matters could follow, rather than precede, voter approval. In deferring to the authority of the commissioner, the Supreme Judicial Court of Maine concluded that state officials did not have

---

18. *New Town Public School Dist. No. 1 v. State Bd. of Pub. Educ.*, 650 N.W.2d 813 [169 Educ. L. Rep. 412] (N.D.2002). *See also Johnson v. Lennox School Dist. No. 41–4*, 649 N.W.2d 617 [168 Educ. L. Rep. 491] (S.D.2002).

19. *Kirby v. Hoven School District No. 53–2*, 686 N.W.2d 905 [192 Educ. L. Rep. 252] (S.D.2004).

20. *Katz v. Los Gatos–Saratoga Joint Union High School Dist.*, 11 Cal.Rptr.3d 546 [186 Educ. L. Rep. 916] (Cal.Ct.App.2004).

21. *Paek v. Pen Argyl Area School Dist.*, 923 A.2d 563 [220 Educ. L. Rep. 726] (Pa.Cmwlth. Ct.2007) (noting that after the parents of the children divorced, their father died in a car accident).

22. *Fisher v. Fay*, 122 N.E. 811 (Ill.1919).

23. *Petition of 2,952 Registered Voters of Wayne County, In Opposition to Reorganization of Wayne County School Dist.*, 574 So.2d 619 [65 Educ. L. Rep. 991] (Miss.1990).

24. *Fruit v. Metropolitan School Dist. of Winchester*, 172 N.E.2d 864 (Ind.1961).

to set a date for the vote on the withdrawal agreement until town and district officials completed an acceptable agreement.[25]

If legislatures authorize local school boards to petition for boundary changes, they may do so despite the wishes of voters.[26] Even so, legislatures may not change boundaries in ways designed to violate the Federal Constitution as, for example, when modifications deliberately impacted adversely on the racial balance of students,[27] impeded a remedy for de jure segregation,[28] or intentionally helped a religious group.[29] Where statutes provide for alterations of districts by means of elections, courts strictly enforce procedural matters before voters can go to the polls. Once elections are over, courts intervene only on showings of fraud or that alleged procedural violations prevented voters from giving full expression of their wills.[30]

The Supreme Court of Kansas, in a dispute over a school board's challenge to orders of the state superintendent of public instruction to transfer part of its territory to other districts, affirmed that even though a board is a legal body that may sue or be sued, it lacked the authority to file suit questioning the boundaries or the validity of the organization of another district.[31] The court explained that such a suit can be brought only in the state's name by duly authorized state officers. In like fashion, the Supreme Court of Minnesota affirmed that the state school boards association lacked standing to contest the constitutionality of a consolidation statute because its interests were those of its members who could not bring such a suit.[32] The Supreme Court of Nebraska also affirmed the dismissal of an action by local school board members who attempted to sue as individuals rather than members of a board in order to avoid precedent with regard to a transfer of parcels of property.[33] The court characterized the board's efforts as a facade.

Since states create political subdivisions such as municipal corporations[34] and school boards[35] in order to better facilitate governmental actions, these entities lack substantive rights under the Federal Constitution that they may invoke against their creators. Yet, courts may consider challenges by local boards if there are substantial allegations that legislatures used unconstitutional means to effect boundary changes.[36] Insofar as

---

25. *Town of Eagle Lake v. Commissioner, Dep't of Educ.*, 818 A.2d 1034 [174 Educ. L. Rep. 1017] (Me.2003).

26. *Kosmicki v. Kowalski*, 171 N.W.2d 172 (Neb.1969).

27. *Akron Bd. of Educ. v. State Bd. of Educ. of Ohio*, 490 F.2d 1285 (6th Cir.1974).

28. *Wright v. Council of City of Emporia*, 407 U.S. 451, 92 S.Ct. 2196, 33 L.Ed.2d 51 (1972).

29. *Board of Educ. of Kiryas Joel Village School Dist. v. Grumet*, 512 U.S. 687, 114 S.Ct. 2481, 129 L.Ed.2d 546 [91 Educ. L. Rep. 810] (1994).

30. *Eriksen v. Ray*, 321 N.W.2d 59 (Neb.1982).

31. *Unified School Dist. No. 335 v. State Bd. of Educ.*, 478 P.2d 201 (Kan.1970).

32. *Minnesota Ass'n of Pub. Schools v. Hanson*, 178 N.W.2d 846 (Minn.1970).

33. *In re Plummer Freeholder Petition*, 428 N.W.2d 163 [48 Educ. L. Rep. 973] (Neb.1988).

34. *Williams v. Mayor and City Council of Baltimore*, 289 U.S. 36, 53 S.Ct. 431, 77 L.Ed. 1015 (1933).

35. *Triplett v. Tiemann*, 302 F.Supp. 1239 (D.Neb.1969).

36. *Hall v. City of Taft*, 302 P.2d 574 (Cal.1956).

such unusual claims would not be questioning the basic power of legislatures to create, alter, or abolish school districts, courts could address the merits of the contentions.

CHARTER SCHOOLS

Generally

The charter school movement began in 1991 when Minnesota enacted the first statute authorizing their creation.[37] To date, forty states plus the District of Columbia and Puerto Rico have adopted laws permitting the creation of charter schools.[38] Charter schools, which are public schools of choice, are typically operated as not-for-profit institutions by private groups either independently or occasionally in conjunction with public institutions such as universities, continue to survive challenges to their constitutionality.[39] Since charter schools must initially be approved pursuant to state law, even though they operate locally, they are discussed here rather than in Chapter 4.

Along with having the power to create school districts, subject to judicial review,[40] state legislatures can create[41] and fund[42] innovative forms of public[43] schooling[44] such as charter schools[45] while providing them with

37. MINN. STAT. ANN. § 124D.10.

38. http://www.charterschoolcenter.org/resource/measuring-model-ranking-state-public-charter-school-laws.

39. *See, e.g., Council of Organizations and Others for Educ. About Parochiaid v. Governor,* 566 N.W.2d 208 [120 Educ. L. Rep. 265] (Mich.1997); *In re Grant of Charter School Application of Englewood on Palisades Charter School,* 753 A.2d 687 [145 Educ. L. Rep. 431] (N.J.2000). *See also State ex rel. Ohio Congress of Parents and Teachers v. State Bd. of Educ.,* 822 N.E.2d 809 (Ohio 2005) (accepting a challenge to the constitutionality of Ohio's charter, or community, school program).

40. *See Gwinnett County School Dist. v. Cox,* 710 S.E.2d 773 [268 Educ. L. Rep. 983] (Ga. 2011) (invalidating the statute creating charter schools on the basis that they were not "special" within the meaning of the state constitution).

41. *Boulder Valley School Dist. v. State Bd. of Educ.,* 217 P.3d 918 [249 Educ. L. Rep. 430] (Colo. Ct. App. 2009), *cert. denied,* 2009 WL 3165618 (Colo. 2009) (upholding a law creating charter schools that are unaffiliated with local boards).

42. For an interesting case on funding, *see Alternatives Unlimited v. Ohio Dep't of Educ.,* 949 N.E.2d 117 [268 Educ. L. Rep. 516] (Ohio Ct. Cl. 2011) (affirming that the State Department of Education was liable for breach of contract damages in the form of lost profits when it refused to pay the operator costs associated with educating the children who attended the school).

43. As political subdivisions of the state, the Sixth Circuit affirmed that community schools, as they are known there, are barred from filing due process claims against the state. *Greater Heights Acad. v. Zelman,* 522 F.3d 678 [231 Educ. L. Rep. 570] (6th Cir.2008). *But see Knapp v. Palisades Charter High School,* 53 Cal.Rptr.3d 182 [215 Educ. L. Rep. 957] (Cal.Ct.App.2007), *modified on denial of reh'g* (2007), *review denied,* (2007), *cert. denied.,* 552 U.S. 888, 128 S.Ct. 255, 169 L.Ed.2d 149 (2007); *New York Charter Schools Ass'n v. DiNapoli,* 886 N.Y.S.2d 74 [249 Educ. L. Rep. 806] (N.Y.2009); *LTTS Charter School v. C2 Constr.,* 288 S.W.3d 31 [247 Educ. L. Rep. 531] (Tex. Ct. App. 2009), *reh'g overruled* (2009) (agreeing that charter schools are not public agencies within the meaning of state law).

44. *See Moreau v. Avoyelles Parish School Bd.,* 897 So.2d 875 [197 Educ. L. Rep. 463] (La.Ct.App.2005), *writs denied,* 904 So.2d 704, 705 (La.2005) (declaring that no statute requires local boards to fund charter schools since doing so is a state responsibility).

45. For a dispute over another type of innovation, *see Wake Cares v. Wake County Bd. of Educ.,* 660 S.E.2d 217 [231 Educ. L. Rep. 951] (N.C.Ct.App.2008) (affirming that the state

facilities reasonably equivalent to those used by public schools.[46] This means that depending on variations in state laws, charter schools are ordinarily entitled to receive funds proportionate to those expended for the education of similar student populations on a per pupil basis.[47] Along this line of thought, an appellate court in North Carolina posited that state law required educational officials to fund a charter school using the same method as they applied to public schools.[48] However, in a related suit involving the same charter school, another appellate court in North Carolina affirmed that it was not entitled to funding from the capital outlay funds of county boards of education.[49] Conversely, an appellate court in New Jersey rejected a challenge to a state statute which funded charter schools at ninety percent of the rate of traditional public schools while forbidding them from receiving state facilities funds.[50] The court agreed that the law did not violate the equal protection rights of students in the charter schools because the restriction was minor and was justified by the need to reduce diversion of scarce resources from traditional public schools. Further, where officials at a charter school designed to provide assistance to families involved in home schooling failed to comply with a statutory requirement that at least half of its teachers have appropriate teaching licenses, an appellate court in Oregon affirmed an order of the State Superintendent of Public Instruction denying it funding.[51] Moreover, the Ninth Circuit pointed out that for-profit charter schools are ineligible for federal grants from state educational agencies that receive monies under the Elementary and Secondary Education Act.[52] Still, states lack the automatic power to subject charter schools to public audits absent express legislative authorization.[53]

Charter schools, the number of which is typically specified by state law,[54] operate under contracts,[55] or charters, usually granted by local and/or

General Assembly authorized a local board to establish year-round public schools), *temporarily stayed, appeal dismissed, review allowed, aff'd*, 675 S.E.2d 345 (N.C. 2009).

46. *See, e.g., California School Bds. Ass'n v. California Bd. of Educ.*, 119 Cal.Rptr.3d 596 [263 Educ. L. Rep. 268] (Cal.Ct.App. 2010).

47. *Baltimore City Bd. of School Comm'rs v. City Neighbors Charter School*, 929 A.2d 113 [223 Educ. L. Rep. 250] (Md.2007). *But see Jenkins v. Kansas City Missouri School Dist.*, 516 F.3d 1074 [229 Educ. L. Rep. 414] (8th Cir.2008), *reh'g and reh'g en banc denied* (2008) (affirming that the state could not be required to use funds designed to desegregate public schools for a charter school).

48. *Sugar Creek Charter School v. Charlotte–Mecklenburg Bd. of Educ.*, 673 S.E.2d 667 [242 Educ. L. Rep. 479] (N.C. Ct. App. 2009), *appeal dismissed, review denied*, 687 S.E.2d 296 (N.C. 2009).

49. *Sugar Creek Charter School v. State*, 712 S.E.2d 730 [270 Educ. L. Rep. 317] (N.C. Ct. App. 2011).

50. *J.D. v. Davy*, 2 A.3d 387 [259 Educ. L. Rep. 709] (N.J. Super. Ct. App. Div. 2010).

51. *Coquille School Dist. 8 v. Castillo*, 159 P.3d 338 [220 Educ. L. Rep. 885] (Or.Ct.App. 2007).

52. *Arizona State Bd. for Charter Schools v. United States Dep't of Educ.*, 464 F.3d 1003 [213 Educ. L. Rep. 114] (9th Cir.2006).

53. *New York Charter Schools Ass'n v. DiNapoli*, 886 N.Y.S.2d 74 [249 Educ. L. Rep. 806] (2009).

54. *See, e.g., Taos Mun. Schools Charter School v. Davis*, 102 P.3d 102 [194 Educ. L. Rep. 415] (N.M.Ct.App.2004), *cert. denied* (2004) (pointing out that state law stipulates that there can be no more than fifteen charter schools), *overruled on jurisdictional grounds in Smith v.*

state boards of education.[56] Applicants for charters may have limited rights of appeal if their applications are denied.[57]

Depending on state legislation, groups of parents as well as not-for profit[58] or for-profit entities[59] may form charter schools anew or can convert them from existing public schools.[60] Either way, faculty and staff at charter schools are public employees who typically cannot be assigned to charter schools without their consent. In addition, faculty and staff at charter schools are ordinarily covered by operative collective bargaining agreements and other state laws.[61]

In return for being exempted from many state laws,[62] charter schools are accountable for the academic achievement of their students. While charters vary in duration, they typically range from three to five years in length.[63] When contracts expire, depending on state law, charter granting entities can renew or terminate agreements.

Charter schools, although free from many state rules with regard to staff and curricular issues, are still subject to general state laws. In such a case, the Supreme Court of Pennsylvania affirmed that insofar as officials at a charter school had to comply with a Right-to-Know Act, they had to disclose information about the school's financial status because insofar as it performed an essential governmental function, it was an agency covered by the law.[64] Further, the Ninth Circuit affirmed that operators of a charter

---

City of Santa Fe, 171 P.3d 300 (N.M.2007) (addressing a statute dealing with the drilling of domestic water wells).

55. For a discussion of charters as contracts along with an examination of state statutes on point, *see Foreman v. Chester–Upland School Dist.*, 941 A.2d 108, 121, note 7 (Smith–Ribner, J., dissenting), [229 Educ. L. Rep. 712] (Pa.Cmwlth.Ct.2008), *appeal granted*, 951 A.2d 264 (Pa.2008).

56. *See, e.g., Board of Educ. of School Dist. No. 1 in City and County of Denver v. Booth*, 984 P.2d 639 [137 Educ. L. Rep. 1109] (Colo.1999) (holding that the State Board of Education did not unconstitutionally infringe on a local school board's control of instruction in ordering approval of a charter application).

57. *Berkley Elementary School Advisory Council v. School Bd. of Polk County*, 826 So.2d 364 [170 Educ. L. Rep. 405] (Fla.Dist.Ct.App.2002).

58. *See, e.g., Brookwood Presbyterian Church v. Ohio Dep't of Educ.*, 940 N.E.2d 1256 [263 Educ. L. Rep. 931] (Ohio 2010) (denying a charter application from a not-for-profit church on the basis that it was not an "education oriented entity").

59. *West Chester Area School Dist. v. Collegium Charter School*, 812 A.2d 1172 [172 Educ. L. Rep. 855] (Pa.2002).

60. *See, e.g.,* Ohio Rev. Code Ann. § 3314.02 (referring to charter schools as community schools).

61. *But see Northern Kane Educ. Corp. v. Cambridge Lakes Educ. Ass'n*, 914 N.E.2d 1286 [249 Educ. L. Rep. 800] (Ill. App. Ct. 2009), *appeal denied*, 924 N.E.2d 456 (Ill. 2010) (finding that insofar as charter schools were exempt from enumerated state laws, the labor relations board lacked the jurisdiction to grant teachers union status). However, the state legislature repudiated this decision in enacting 2009 Ill. Laws Act 96–0104, S.B. 1984, defining charter schools as educational employers subject to the State Labor Relations Board.

62. *See, e.g., Ohnesorge v. Winfree Acad. Charter School*, 328 S.W.3d 654 [263 Educ. L. Rep. 437] (Tex.Ct. App. 2010) (exempting a charter school from the state's Whistleblower Protection Act since it was not a public school district within the meaning of the law).

63. *Missouri v. Williamson*, 141 S.W.3d 418 [191 Educ. L. Rep. 899] (Mo.Ct.App.2004), *reh'g denied* (2004) (noting that a charter was good for five years as a matter of law and that officials lacked an entitlement to judicial review of a school board's refusal to renew a charter).

64. *Zager v. Chester Community Charter School*, 934 A.2d 1227 [226 Educ. L. Rep. 109] (Pa.2007).

school in Idaho and two of the teachers could not use religious documents as text books because doing so would have violated a provision in the state constitution against using religious books or documents in public schools.[65]

Use of Real Property

In terms of land use, a case from New York addressed whether a charter school should have been granted a variance to construct and operate a facility in an area of a city zoned for commercial use. In modifying an earlier order in favor of the school's operators, an appellate court affirmed that provisions in the city's zoning ordinance that resulted in the wholesale exclusion of educational uses from commercial areas was unconstitutional on its face.[66] The court remanded for a consideration of whether the school should have been granted a permit in light of the city's entitlement to impose reasonable conditions directly related to public health, safety, and welfare in a manner consistent with its police authority. Subsequently, the Supreme Court of Hawaii ruled that organizers of a charter school had to obtain a special use permit so that they could operate a special farm within the state's land use agricultural district.[67]

A state tax commissioner sought further review of an order reversing its denial of a tax exemption for real property that its owner leased for profit to operators of a charter school. Reversing in favor of the tax commissioner, the Supreme Court of Ohio ruled that insofar as the entity that owned the property leased it for profit, even though it was used as a public school, it was not entitled to the exemption it sought.[68]

Applications and Revocations

Prior to receiving charters, organizers must submit detailed plans about how schools are to function.[69] In a manner resembling the way in which non-public schools function, the goal of charter schools is to permit officials to operate schools free of many of the regulations that apply to traditional public schools. Organizers and parents are thus free to develop the missions, programs, and goals for their schools, all of which are aimed at enhancing student achievement.

Not surprisingly, litigation has emerged over the denial of applications to operate charter schools. The Supreme Court of South Carolina affirmed

---

65. *Nampa Classical Acad. v. Goesling*, ___ Fed.Appx. ___, 2011 WL 3562954 (9th Cir. 2011).

66. *Albany Preparatory Charter School v. City of Albany*, 818 N.Y.S.2d 651 [210 Educ. L. Rep. 1238] (N.Y.App.Div.2006).

67. *County of Hawaii v. Ala Loop Homeowners*, 235 P.3d 1103 [258 Educ. L. Rep. 794] (Haw. 2010).

68. *Anderson/ Maltbie v. Levin*, 937 N.E.2d 547 [261 Educ. L. Rep. 1066] (Ohio 2010). For a similar case, *see In Re Appeal of Collegium Found.*, 991 A.2d 990 [255 Educ. L. Rep. 301] (Pa. Cmwlth. Ct. 2010), *appeal denied*, 13 A.3d 481 (Pa. 2010) (holding that insofar as the property used by a public charter school was leased from a for-profit entity, it was disqualified from a real estate tax exemption).

69. *Shelby School v. Arizona State Bd. of Educ.*, 962 P.2d 230 [128 Educ. L. Rep. 1254] (Ariz.Ct.App.1998) (determining that organizers do not have a constitutional right to open charter schools).

that where a county board of education failed to meet the statutory requirements for the denial of an application, the operators should have been granted the charter.[70] Further, officials in Pennsylvania successfully challenged a local board's denial of their application to create a charter school.[71] An appellate court affirmed that the local school board failed to prove that the organizers were unable to comply with commonwealth law where officials from the charter school created a proposed governance structure, identified the possible location of the facility, provided a detailed curriculum and objectives, and submitted an adequate faculty and professional development plan.

Of course, if local school boards have the authority to approve or deny applications to form charter schools, they must act in good faith. In the first of two cases from Florida, an appellate court affirmed that where a local board denied an application based on unsupported assumptions about the quality of the education that it might have provided and its concerns about the applicants' lack of capital funding or use of operational dollars, the state board of education had the authority to overrule its action.[72] The court declared that in denying the charter application, the local board failed to act in good faith because it did not provide a legally sufficient reason for doing so. Another appellate court affirmed that the Florida Department of Education had the authority to grant a charter despite the state constitutional provision which grants local school boards control over schools within their boundaries.[73] The court agreed that the local board lacked good cause to deny the charter based on alleged deficiencies in the areas of student assessment and accountability, promotion of students, finance, and class size.

When a charter school applicant's proposal failed to comply with state law, the Supreme Court of Illinois refused to disturb an earlier order rejecting it since the initial action was not clearly erroneous.[74] In a novel question, the Supreme Court of South Carolina ruled that an applicant for a charter school was not entitled to damages for rent reimbursement and student stipends from a local school board insofar as absent an approved application, the plaintiff was not operating a charter school.[75]

In other cases on the denials of charter applications, the Supreme Court of Wyoming addressed a dispute where whether the applicants sought to operate a school in violation of a provision in the statute forbidding schools from opening if their sole purpose was to avoid school closures or consolidations. In remanding, the court held that insofar as the

---

70. *Lee County School Dist. Bd. of Trustees v. MLD Charter Sch. Acad. Planning Comm.,* 641 S.E.2d 24 [216 Educ. L. Rep. 955] (S.C.2007).

71. *Carbondale Area School Dist. v. Fell Charter School,* 829 A.2d 400 [179 Educ. L. Rep. 833] (Pa.Cmwlth.Ct.2003).

72. *School Bd. of Osceola County v. UCP of Cent. Fla.,* 905 So.2d 909 [200 Educ. L. Rep. 421] (Fla.Dist.Ct.App.2005), *review denied,* 914 So.2d 954 (Fla.2005).

73. *School Bd. of Volusia County v. Academies of Excellence,* 974 So.2d 1186 [230 Educ. L. Rep. 114] (Fla.Dist.Ct.App.2008), *review dismissed,* 981 So.2d 1200 (Fla.2008). [Case No. 16]

74. *Comprehensive Community Solutions v. Rockford School Dist. No. 205,* 837 N.E.2d 1 [203 Educ. L. Rep. 318] (Ill.2005).

75. *James Acad. of Excellence v. Dorchester County School Dist. Two,* 657 S.E.2d 469 [230 Educ. L. Rep. 82] (S.C.2008).

local board's initial denial was unsupported by a finding that the applicants intended to avoid obeying the statute, it had to act anew on the application.[76] Also, the Supreme Court of Oklahoma affirmed a grant of summary judgment in favor of a rejected applicant who sought to compel a local board to agree to binding arbitration pursuant to the state's Dispute Resolution Act.[77] The court ruled that the statute was inapplicable since it did not authorize the school's organizers to compel the board to proceed to binding arbitration. Moreover, the Supreme Judicial Court of Massachusetts affirmed that the commonwealth board of education's rejection of a charter school application was not subject to judicial review because it did not act in an adjudicatory proceeding.[78]

At the other end of the process, as litigation emerges with regard to the revocations of charters for cause, courts reach mixed results. For example, the Supreme Court of Florida,[79] along with appellate courts in Florida,[80] Massachusetts[81] and Wisconsin,[82] upheld the revocation of charters where organizers failed to satisfy statutory standards while a panel in Pennsylvania refused to adopt such an approach.[83] An appellate court in California went so far as to declare that in light of questions about a charter school's effectiveness, due process did not require an evidentiary hearing in the presence of a neutral fact finder before a county board of education revoked its charter.[84]

Non–Discrimination Provisions and Charter Schools

Insofar as charter schools remain subject to federal and state[85] anti-discrimination laws, they must be open, without cost, to all children, including students with disabilities and must pay for their programming

---

76. *Laramie County School Dist. No. 2 v. Albin Cats Charter School*, 109 P.3d 552 [196 Educ. L. Rep. 971] (Wyo.2005).

77. *Pentagon Acad. v. Independent School Dist. No. 1*, 82 P.3d 587 [184 Educ. L. Rep. 589] (Okla.2003).

78. *School Comm. of Hudson v. Board of Educ.*, 863 N.E.2d 22 [217 Educ. L. Rep. 697] (Mass.2007).

79. *School Bd. of Palm Beach County v. Survivors Charter School*, 3 So.3d 1220 [242 Educ. L. Rep. 962] (Fla. 2009) (permitting immediate termination of a charter due to fiscal mismanagement).

80. *School Bd. of Palm Beach County v. Survivors Charter Sch.*, 3 So.3d 1220 [242 Educ. L. Rep. 962] (Fla. 2009).

81. *Commonwealth v. Roxbury Charter High Pub. School*, 865 N.E.2d 1183 [219 Educ. L. Rep. 251] (Mass.App.Ct.2007), *review denied*, 871 N.E.2d 492 (Mass. 2007).

82. *Johnson v. Burmaster*, 744 N.W.2d 900 [229 Educ. L. Rep. 859] (Wis.Ct.App.2007), *review denied*, 749 N.W.2d 662 (Wis. 2008).

83. *Ronald H. Brown Charter School v. Harrisburg City School Dist.*, 928 A.2d 1145 [222 Educ. L. Rep. 810] (Pa.Cmwlth.Ct.2007).

84. *Today's Fresh Start v. Los Angeles County Office of Educ.*, 128 Cal.Rptr.3d 822 [269 Educ. L. Rep. 638] (Cal.Ct.App. 2011).

85. *But see Mosaica Educ. v. Pennsylvania Prevailing Wage Appeals Bd.*, 925 A.2d 176 [221 Educ. L. Rep. 737] (Pa.Cmwlth.Ct.2007), *appeal denied*, 953 A.2d 543 (Pa. 2008) (deciding that a management company was not obligated to comply with a prevailing wages statute for employees who worked on a school renovation project since the job did not involve "public work" within the meaning of the law).

such as homebound instruction.[86] In Pennsylvania, an appellate court rejected a local board's claim that a charter school designed for students who were gifted impermissibly discriminated on intellectual ability.[87] The court affirmed not only that charter schools may limit admissions by specialty areas but also that officials demonstrated sustainable parental support, the presence of an adequate financial plan, and appropriate physical facilities.

A dispute arose in New Jersey when officials at two charter schools transferred students with special needs to private schools without consulting their local boards and sought to be reimbursed for their expenses. The federal trial court granted the charter schools' motion for summary judgment on the basis that the Individuals with Disabilities Education Act (IDEA) does not grant local boards private rights of action to dispute the placements of students from charter schools unless the parties first exhaust administrative remedies by means of due process hearings.[88] In a second case from New Jersey, an appellate court remanded a suit for a hearing over whether a charter school's practices, such as its admissions lottery, waiting list, sibling preference list, and withdrawal policy, all of which were designed to increase its enrollments, exacerbated a local district's racial imbalance.[89]

In Massachusetts, the federal trial court ruled that officials did not violate the needs of a special education student who was evaluated under a competency-based system.[90] The court concluded that the evaluation met the IDEA's dictates since the child's teacher had flexibility in considering whether he mastered the subject matter through use of tests, discussions, or other methods and simply passed or failed him without awarding letter or number grades. The court rejected a parental claim that officials should have modified the school's grading system to accommodate their son because they allegedly received insufficient input regarding his progress to decide whether they should have requested that he be provided with additional assistance.

Where a hearing officer granted a special education student's request for a formula-based compensatory education award, her charter school unsuccessfully sued her and her mother.[91] In rejecting the school's motion for summary judgment, the federal trial court in the District of Columbia decided that there was no reason to disturb the award of 375 hours of tutoring since it was reasonably calculated to close the two year grade level

---

86. *Golden Door Charter School v. State–Operated School Dist. of City of Jersey City, Hudson County,* 948 A.2d 716 [233 Educ. L. Rep. 372] (N.J.Super.Ct.App.Div.2008).

87. *Central Dauphin School Dist. v. Founding Coalition of Infinity Charter School,* 847 A.2d 195 [187 Educ. L. Rep. 665] (Pa.Cmwlth.Ct.2004), *appeal denied,* 860 A.2d 491 (Pa.2004).

88. *Asbury Park Bd. of Educ. v. Hope Acad. Charter School,* 278 F.Supp.2d 417 [181 Educ. L. Rep. 494] (D.N.J.2003).

89. *In re Red Bank Charter School,* 843 A.2d 365 [186 Educ. L. Rep. 405] (N.J.Super.Ct.App.Div.2004), *certification denied,* 852 A.2d 193 (N.J.2004).

90. *Claudia C–B v. Board of Trustees of Pioneer Valley Performing Arts Charter School,* 539 F.Supp.2d 474 [231 Educ. L. Rep. 89] (D.Mass.2008).

91. *Mary McLeod Bethune Day Acad. Pub. Charter School v. Bland,* 555 F.Supp.2d 130 [234 Educ. L. Rep. 91] (D.D.C.2008).

gap that the child experienced because officials failed to provide her with an appropriate education under the IDEA.

On a different issue involving the IDEA, in the first of two cases from the District of Columbia concerning charter schools and attorney fees, the federal trial court granted a parent's motion to recover fees.[92] According to the court, the statutory cap on attorney fees was inapplicable to charter schools since it only covered disputes involving schools operated by the board of education. In the second dispute, the court found that even though a student prevailed in a due process hearing, she was not entitled to recover attorney fees because in dropping out of school, her relationship with the board was unchanged.[93] The court maintained that awarding fees would have been wasteful since the litigation failed to contribute to the student's welfare.

Depending on state law, local boards may be required to provide transportation for children to and from their charter schools.[94] However, the Seventh Circuit affirmed that insofar as students at an independent public charter school were not similarly situated to those who attended other schools in a local district because they had longer school days and five weeks of summer classes, officials did not violate the equal protection rights of the children in the charter school.[95] The court reasoned that insofar as the charter school operated wholly independently of the board, it was more akin to an autonomous school district than an individual school, thereby permitting officials to exclude the students from their statutory busing duty. In like manner, the Supreme Court of Connecticut agreed that state law did not require a local board to provide transportation services to under-aged children who attended kindergarten in charter schools.[96]

Delegation of Legislative Power

Legislatures can use their discretion to create or abolish school districts. Yet, since legislatures are seldom able to make the necessary surveys to evaluate the most effective plans for forming districts, they ordinarily enact general laws establishing policies for creating systems and delegating authority to lower officials or bodies to execute their directives as long as they do not do so "understandingly or advantageously."[97] Under this principle, a county board of education may act as an agent of the legislature with power circumscribed by an enabling statute. Statutory interpretation of laws empowering agencies is thus a judicial question over whether

---

92. *Brown v. Barbara Jordan P.C.S.*, 539 F.Supp.2d 436 [231 Educ. L. Rep. 85] (D.D.C. 2008).

93. *E.M. v. Marriott Hospitality Pub. Chartered High School*, 541 F.Supp.2d 395 [231 Educ. L. Rep. 728] (D.D.C.2008).

94. *Moreau v. Avoyelles Parish School Bd.*, 897 So.2d 875 [197 Educ. L. Rep. 463] (La.Ct.App.2005), *writs denied*, 904 So.2d 704, 705 (La.2005); *Mosaica Acad. Charter School v. Commonwealth Dep't of Educ.*, 813 A.2d 813 (Pa.2002).

95. *Racine Charter One v. Racine Unified School Dist.*, 424 F.3d 677 [202 Educ. L. Rep. 40] (7th Cir.2005).

96. *Board of Educ. of the Town of Hamden v. State Bd. of Educ.*, 898 A.2d 170 [209 Educ. L. Rep. 281] (Conn.2006).

97. *Hill v. Relyea*, 216 N.E.2d 795, 797 (Ill.1966).

officials exceeded or misinterpreted their authority.[98] Still, courts typically do not consider whether agency actions are in the best interests of areas since this is a legislative prerogative.[99] Delegation aside, legislatures cannot avoid their constitutional duties by delegating their power to local officials. In such a case, the Supreme Court of California directed state officials to prevent a local board from ending its school year six weeks early due to financial difficulties on the basis that they had to further the state's policy of ensuring uniform education for all children.[100]

A fundamental principle of American government is the separation of powers of the legislative, executive, and judicial branches. Put another way, one branch of the government cannot encroach on the prerogatives of another. Since each branch is charged with specific powers, one may not divest itself of its authority or delegate it to the others. An unconstitutional delegation of power thus occurs "when the Legislature confers upon an administrative agency the unrestricted authority to make fundamental policy determinations."[101] This separation of powers at the state level does not present a question of federal constitutional law.[102]

Courts purportedly adhere to the principle of separation of powers but differ by degree on how far legislatures can go in delegating authority to subordinate agencies or officials over the formation and alteration of school districts. The basic inquiry is how much detail legislatures have placed in statutes guiding administrative actions.

State courts provide guidelines for legislatures in reviewing the constitutionality of delegation of authority. Following the general rule, the Supreme Court of Pennsylvania ordered its legislature to provide "adequate standards which will guide and restrain the exercise of the delegated administrative functions"[103] in reorganizing school districts. In like fashion, the Supreme Court of Kansas interpreted its constitution as permitting the legislature to authorize the state superintendent to establish unified school districts and disorganize others if either elections had been conducted approving such creations or local boards petitioned for such actions.[104] Conversely, the Supreme Court of Illinois struck down a statute as an unconstitutional delegation of authority where the legislature left the formation of high school districts up to county superintendents without providing guidelines for their creation and efficient operations on such topics as area, assessed valuation, number of students, and size.[105] The court viewed the law as not uniformly applicable in similar situations and territories since it was subject to different attitudes of county superinten-

98. *Brandon Valley Indep. School Dist. No. 150 v. Minnehaha County Bd. of Educ.*, 181 N.W.2d 96 (S.D.1970).

99. *Thorland v. Independent Consol. School Dist.*, 74 N.W.2d 410 (Minn.1956).

100. *Butt v. State*, 15 Cal.Rptr.2d 480 [79 Educ. L. Rep. 1039] (Cal.1992).

101. *Clean Air Constituency v. California State Air Resources Bd.*, 114 Cal.Rptr. 577, 586 (Cal.1974).

102. *Highland Farms Dairy v. Agnew*, 300 U.S. 608, 57 S.Ct. 549, 81 L.Ed. 835 (1937).

103. *Chartiers Valley Joint Schools v. County Bd. of School Directors*, 211 A.2d 487, 493 (Pa.1965).

104. *Tecumseh School Dist. v. Throckmorton*, 403 P.2d 102 (Kan.1965).

105. *Kenyon v. Moore*, 122 N.E. 548 (Ill.1919).

dents and to variations within counties if superintendents left their offices. Another appellate court in Illinois upheld the state board's granting a waiver to Chicago's school board over the physical education standards in the state curriculum in order to make room for increased requirements in mathematics, science, and foreign languages. The court affirmed that the waiver was not an unconstitutional delegation of legislative authority since it simply excused the board from compliance with a portion of the law for a period of time.[106]

Uniformity does not necessarily mean sameness. Rather, uniformity means that the bases of classification should be clear and reasonable in relation to statutory subject matter and purposes. By way of illustration, the Supreme Court of Iowa upheld the constitutionality of a law providing for the reorganization of school districts based on whether there was a resident average daily attendance of at least 300.[107] The court found that if there were a reasonable ground for a classification and if it operated equally on all within the same class, it achieved constitutional uniformity.

IMPAIRMENT OF OBLIGATIONS OF CONTRACTS

The legislative right to create, alter, or abolish school districts is subject to the limitation that their actions not conflict with Article I, Section 10 of the Federal Constitution's prohibition against enacting laws impairing the obligation of contracts. Still, it is important to keep in mind that state subdivisions do not have contracts between themselves and their legislatures that can be impaired by boundary adjustments. The Supreme Court reiterated this point in a case involving redistricting, *Attorney General of the State of Michigan ex rel. Kies v. Lowrey*.[108] Since the law passed muster under the state constitution, the Court observed that it did not violate the Federal Constitution.

A second case from Michigan exemplifies how a constitutional bar against the impairment of contracts can arise.[109] A statute provided that where school district territory was annexed to another system, the remaining portion was liable for bonds issued for lands and buildings located on the original district. Due to a boundary change, the amount of property on which a tax could have been levied to meet bond obligations was lessened. The state high court struck the law down as an unconstitutional impairment on the obligations of a contract of bondholders since it relieved a considerable part of the territory, which was in the district when the bonds were issued, from payment without making a provision for payment from other sources. Maine's highest court also invalidated a law specifying that towns detached from districts which had outstanding bonds would be liable

---

106. *Reece v. Board of Educ. of City of Chicago*, 767 N.E.2d 395 [166 Educ. L. Rep. 283] (Ill.App.Ct.2002).

107. *Becker v. Board of Educ.*, 138 N.W.2d 909 (Iowa 1965).

108. 199 U.S. 233, 26 S.Ct. 27, 50 L.Ed. 167 (1905).

109. *Board of Educ. of City of Lincoln Park v. Board of Educ. of City of Detroit*, 222 N.W. 763 (Mich.1929).

only if the reorganized systems were unable to pay after levies on their assets.[110]

PRE-EXISTING ASSETS AND DEBTS

When school districts are reorganized or dissolved, legislatures can distribute assets and liabilities in any manner not affecting existing contracts. Absent statutory provisions for the disposition of property, most courts agree that property belongs to the district in which it is located when a change is made. In one such case, the Supreme Court of New Hampshire determined that the undisposed of property of a dissolved district vested in the cooperative system that assumed the functions of the original board.[111] In so doing, the court rejected the argument of officials from the local town that the municipality should have been awarded the disputed property.

As discussed earlier, school property does not belong to local boards in the sense that legislatures or courts are prohibited from transferring it to other districts. In other words, property belongs to the states that maintain it in trust for boards to use in providing education for the children who live within their boundaries. The fact that property is located in another district after a boundary change does not relieve the original system of its liability to pay for indebtedness incurred in connection with it since the original system remains an entity regardless of how its size may have changed.[112] This doctrine is based on the theory that no board owns property in the true sense of the word by binding itself to pay for it because it incurs liability for state, not local, purposes. Instead, residents must be aware that legislatures may change district boundaries and that school buildings or other facilities may be located in other systems.

The Supreme Court dismissed an appeal from Washington's highest court for want of a substantial federal question in a case over the constitutionality of a statute that transferred property financed by bonds issued by local school boards to the state board that dealt with community colleges.[113] In allowing the statute to remain in place, the Court was of the opinion that the legislature expressly reaffirmed all contracts between local boards and their bondholders.

While legislatures may provide for the division of school board property and the apportionment of debts when a part of their territory and property are transferred to other districts, their failure to do so does not invalidate reorganization statutes. Absent such a provision, most courts follow the common law rule which leaves property where it is and a debt on the original debtor.[114] As illustrated by a case from the Supreme Court of Illinois, this approach can create hardships.[115] The court noted that a

---

110. *Canal Nat. Bank v. School Admin. Dist. No. 3*, 203 A.2d 734 (Me.1964).

111. *In re Beauregard*, 859 A.2d 1153 [193 Educ. L. Rep. 266] (N.H.2004).

112. *People ex rel. Raymond Community High School Dist. v. Bartlett*, 136 N.E. 654 (Ill.1922).

113. *Moses Lake School Dist. No. 161 v. Big Bend Community College*, 503 P.2d 86 (Wash.1972), *appeal dismissed*, 412 U.S. 934, 93 S.Ct. 2776, 37 L.Ed.2d 393 (1973).

114. *Pass School Dist. v. Hollywood City School Dist.*, 105 P. 122 (Cal.1909).

115. *People ex rel. Raymond Community High School Dist. v. Bartlett*, 136 N.E. 654 (Ill.1922).

county clerk could not have been required to extend a tax for the payment of bonded indebtedness that was incurred before a district was divided against detached territory. Consequently, the remaining board incurred a much larger tax burden than contemplated when the debts were created.

Most states have statutes addressing financial difficulties that arise when changes are made in district boundaries as legislatures attempted to provide for equitable divisions of debts. While these laws are frequently attacked on a variety of grounds, a case from the Supreme Court of Michigan reveals that these statutes are uniformly sustained.[116] The court maintained that a statute which required a receiving district to pay the debts of a sending board in proportion to the value of the detached property did not violate the constitutional inhibition against taking property without due process.

Absent controlling constitutional provisions, legislatures have almost unlimited authority to provide for the payment of debts in old school districts. Laws typically provide that designated agencies such as local school boards must make equitable distributions of an old district's assets and debts. While the issue of what constitutes an equitable distribution is a question of fact, the statutes survived constitutional challenges.[117] The Supreme Court of Wyoming rejected such a challenge to a state law mandating that in a reorganization of districts, a county committee had the power to allocate equitably the assets and debts affected by its plan. In brushing aside a claim that the statute violated a state constitutional provision against the creation of new debts without a vote of those who were to be affected, the court upheld the statute in agreeing that it concerned the division of existing debts instead of the creation of new ones.[118] The court interpreted the statute as meaning that there must be a bona fide allocation of debts to any area relative to the benefits it received from additional assets accrued in a reorganization.

Other aspects of the distribution of financial assets and liabilities have faced judicial scrutiny. As demonstrated by a case from the Supreme Court of Missouri, the failure of state officials to consult with voters in a school district that had a surplus in its treasury before it was consolidated did not violate the state or federal constitutions.[119] In addition, an appellate court in Ohio upheld an arrangement whereby taxpayers of a receiving district in a consolidation plan were taxed on their property for payment of the indebtedness of the old school system.[120]

EXERCISE OF DISCRETION

The agencies designated to pass on the alteration or consolidation of districts must exercise discretion that is neither arbitrary nor unreason-

---

116. *School Dist. No. 3 of Bloomfield Twp. v. School Dist. of City of Pontiac*, 246 N.W. 145 (Mich.1933).

117. *Rapp v. Bethel–Tate Consol. School Dist.*, 16 N.E.2d 224 (Ohio Ct.App.1937).

118. *Lund v. Schrader*, 492 P.2d 202 (Wyo.1971).

119. *State ex rel. Bilby v. Brooks*, 249 S.W. 73 (Mo.1923).

120. *Rapp v. Bethel–Tate Consol. School Dist.*, 16 N.E.2d 224 (Ohio Ct.App.1937).

able. In such a situation, the Supreme Court of South Dakota recognized that taxpayers could seek judicial review of an order of the state agency with the power to alter school district boundaries.[121] Insofar as the committee exceeded its statutory authority, the court asserted that the change it ordered had to be annulled.

Legislatures must designate bodies to examine district boundaries and cannot leave matters completely to the desires of individual residents. For instance, the Supreme Court of Kansas decreed that the state statute which permitted landowners to exclude their property from school districts by exercising their own will was unconstitutional as an impermissible delegation of legislative power.[122] In concluding that "all things being equal," the desires of the residents may be considered, though, an appellate court in Illinois was of the view that officials had to consider petitions from residents as long as they complied with statutory and constitutional safeguards prior to acting.[123]

The Supreme Court of Nebraska invalidated a statute which conferred the authority to change district boundaries without notice or an opportunity for a hearing from property owners to county superintendents of schools, clerks, and boards of education. The court viewed this arrangement as a violation of the Fourteenth Amendment's Due Process Clause.[124] While some statutes require hearings before districts can be altered, state agencies are not bound to follow their results. When this occurs, courts typically examine the results of hearings to assure that basic facts were presented and that viewpoints were not suppressed.

Courts may be inclined to overlook procedural irregularities in reorganization proceedings. Even so, a case from the Supreme Court of Illinois demonstrates that proposals must be presented adequately.[125] State law dictated that prior to hearings on proposed reorganizations, officials had to submit maps depicting the districts involved to county boards along with information on the probable effects of the changes. The court invalidated a proceeding at which a board secretary's map consisted merely of a drawing of rectangles while his financial report only showed assessed valuations, amounts levied and expended, and the amount of state aid claims. Invalidating the proposed plan as inadequate, the court indicated that the secretary did not offer information on tax rates or indebtedness, that there was no testimony to supplement the scanty data in his report, and that there was unsatisfactory testimony on educational conditions in one of the districts.

Where the state legislature enacted a scheme for the decentralization of the New York City public school system, it established general criteria

---

121. *Elk Point Indep. School Dist. No. 3 v. State Comm'n on Elementary and Secondary Educ.*, 187 N.W.2d 666 (S.D.1971).

122. *State ex rel. Jackson v. School Dist. No. 2*, 34 P.2d 102 (Kan.1934).

123. *Burnidge v. County Bd. of School Trustees of Kane County*, 167 N.E.2d 21 (Ill.App.Ct. 1960).

124. *Ruwe v. School Dist. No. 85 of Dodge County*, 234 N.W. 789 (Neb.1931).

125. *Crainville School Dist. v. County Bd. of School Trustees*, 177 N.E.2d 248 (Ill.App.Ct. 1961).

including one that each subdistrict should have 20,000 students. When the city board of education issued a tentative decentralization plan for Manhattan containing six districts, some of them had far less than the statutorily prescribed number of students. Following the prescribed hearing on the plan, the board developed a scheme to have five districts in Manhattan. On further review, the state's highest court invalidated the plan and ordered further hearings because it was substantially different from the one used at the hearings.[126] The court added that the districts proposed at the hearing did not meet the legislative mandate for the number of students. More recently, an appellate court in California upheld a writ against a law that would have essentially reorganized the Los Angeles school system by transferring the board's power to the superintendent while granting the mayor the authority to ratify the superintendent's appointment.[127] The court affirmed that insofar as voters have the right to choose whether their board is elected or selected, the statute violated state constitutional principles that they must approve changes in board control of city charters.

According to the Supreme Court of Iowa, even where a proposed merger of districts met statutory requirements, the state education agency was not obligated to grant its approval.[128] The court affirmed that the agency could reject the proposed merger if its action was supported by legally sufficient reasons.

POWERS OF A STATE EDUCATION AGENCY

IN GENERAL

Each jurisdiction has a central education agency, the limits and authority of which are delineated in its constitutions and statutes. Other than Minnesota and Wisconsin,[129] all jurisdictions have state-level boards of education which have general authority over public schools. All jurisdictions have chief state school officers, usually called state superintendents of schools or state commissioners of education, with the authority to implement board directives.[130] State-level agencies also have staff members who carry out these bodies' day-to-day functions. In general, state boards are charged with policymaking one level below the legislature, the execution of which is under the direction of the chief state school officer.[131] In most jurisdictions, intermediate educational agencies, typically at the county

---

126. *Tinsley v. Monserrat*, 308 N.Y.S.2d 843 (1970).

127. *Mendoza v. California*, 57 Cal.Rptr.3d 505 [219 Educ. L. Rep. 116] (Cal.Ct.App.2007).

128. *Armstrong–Ringsted Community School Dist. v. Lakeland Area Educ. Agency*, 597 N.W.2d 776 [136 Educ. L. Rep. 1048] (Iowa 1999).

129. http://www.nasbe.org/index.php/web-links/2–state-boards.

130. *Bailey v. Truby*, 321 S.E.2d 302 [20 Educ. L. Rep. 980] (W.Va.1984); *Abbott by Abbott v. Burke*, 575 A.2d 359 [60 Educ. L. Rep. 1175] (N.J.1990).

131. *See, e.g., New Haven v. State Bd. of Educ.*, 638 A.2d 589 [90 Educ. L. Rep. 236] (Conn.1994).

level, operate between state and local boards. While the duties and powers of intermediate units vary widely, they are generally assigned specific responsibilities to operate within their geographical boundaries.

The two most common methods of selecting members of state boards of education are appointments by the governor and popular elections. At least one state, Ohio, applies a hybrid approach since it has eleven elected members and eight who are appointed by the governor.[132] In a limited number of jurisdictions, state board members get their posts ex officio because they were elected to other governmental posts.[133] The method of selecting members of state boards generally is not critical in relation to their legal powers.

Chief state school officers can be appointed by state boards of education, popularly elected, or appointed by governors. Where chief state school officers are elected, statutes, or occasionally constitutional provisions, usually delineate their powers. Where the state constitution authorized the legislature to provide for the election of a state superintendent of public instruction, it enacted a law directing the state board to elect this official to serve both as its head and as chief executive of the state department of education. When challenged, the Supreme Court of Oregon invalidated the law as unconstitutional.[134] The court rejected the argument that the state board's having selected a professional was a more desirable method of identifying the superintendent than a popular election. The court interpreted the constitutional provision calling for an election to mean one by state voters, not the state board. The court thought that while the statute providing for election of the superintendent by the state board was unconstitutional, the present superintendent, who was in office prior to being appointed by the governor, did not have to vacate the office.

In a second case from Oregon, a dispute arose over the powers of the state superintendent in relation to those of the state board of education concerning average class loads per teacher. While the state board wished to raise the class load, the superintendent claimed that insofar as his office was identified in the constitution, the legislature could delegate this authority only to him and not to the appointed board. The Supreme Court of Oregon disagreed, contending that insofar as the constitutional creation of the title of superintendent of public instruction was neither a limitation nor a prohibition on the legislative power to create the board, it had the authority to adopt and enforce rules as it saw fit.[135]

The Constitution of Idaho directs the legislature to create a state board of education with general supervisory power over the state's public schools. In the face of a challenge, the state supreme court struck down an act that would have divided jurisdiction among three bodies: a council governing higher education, a council governing public schools, and a board comprised

---

132. OHIO REV. CODE ANN. §§ 3301.01–02.

133. Again, in Ohio, as an illustration, the Chairs of the state Senate and House Committees dealing primarily with education are non-voting ex officio members of the state board. OHIO REV. CODE ANN. § 3301.01(B)(2).

134. *State ex rel. Musa v. Minear*, 401 P.2d 36 (Or.1965).

135. *State Bd. of Educ. v. Fasold*, 445 P.2d 489 (Or.1968).

of both councils to oversee public educational endeavors not falling directly under either of the councils.[136] The court wrote that insofar as the constitution plainly required a single board, the legislature and governor were powerless to change that basic structure. Similarly, the Supreme Court of Wyoming reasoned that where a statute empowered the state board to adopt rules and exceptions governing the certification of teachers and administrators, it, not the chief state school officer, had the final say in a disagreement over the rules.[137] Further, the Supreme Court of New Jersey emphasized that the commissioner and the state board did not share equal status as administrative decision makers since the latter had ultimate authority in this area.[138]

Conflicts frequently develop due to a lack of clarity or specificity in constitutional or statutory language. In such a case, the Third Circuit affirmed that the power to formulate a school calendar resided in a territorial board of education, not the department of education even though the latter was designated as the collective bargaining agent for the territory.[139] The court relied on the board's more expansive general powers in resolving the matter while suggesting that a legislative response would have been desirable.

DELEGATION OF LEGISLATIVE POWER TO THE STATE EDUCATION AGENCY

The general principle of separation of powers is often invoked in challenges to rules and regulations of state agencies and officials. As long as legislatures provide reasonably adequate standards governing delegations, the courts are generally content not to interfere.[140] In such a case, the Court of Appeals of Maryland upheld a contract that the state board of education entered into with a private company to operate schools that failed to meet student performance standards.[141] The court explained that in light of the concept of legislative ratification, which permits governmental entities to engage in actions that they may not be expressly authorized to perform, the legislators ratified the board's action in agreeing that a private company can be the employer of teachers in failing schools.

If a legislative power is non-delegable, the issue of an administrative regulation's reasonableness is usually not addressed. The Supreme Court of Nebraska considered the principle of separation of powers in a dispute over a statute expressly granting the state superintendent the authority to formulate rules and regulations for high schools to collect free high school tuition money.[142] The court struck the statute down as an unconstitutional

---

136. *Evans v. Andrus*, 855 P.2d 467 [84 Educ. L. Rep. 522] (Idaho 1993).

137. *Wyoming State Dep't of Educ. v. Barber*, 649 P.2d 681 [5 Educ. L. Rep. 1272] (Wyo.1982).

138. *Probst v. Board of Educ. of Borough of Haddonfield, Camden County*, 606 A.2d 345 [74 Educ. L. Rep. 137] (N.J.1992).

139. *Virgin Islands Joint Bd. of Educ. v. Farrelly*, 984 F.2d 97 (3d Cir.1993).

140. *Ward v. Scott*, 93 A.2d 385 (N.J.1952).

141. *Baltimore Teachers Union v. Maryland State Bd. of Educ.*, 840 A.2d 728 [184 Educ. L. Rep. 910] (Md.2004). [Case No. 17]

142. *School Dist. No. 39 of Washington County v. Decker*, 68 N.W.2d 354 (Neb.1955). [Case No. 18]

delegation of authority in violation of the principle of separation of powers since the legislature failed to provide the superintendent with a sufficiently definite policy framework within which to act.

At the same time, in light of the increasing complexity of schools, courts recognize that guidelines cannot be too specific. Since the separation of powers doctrine was not intended to confine legislatures to the alternatives of virtual inaction or the imposition of rigidly inflexible laws that would have distorted rather than promoted their objectives, broad guidelines consistent with legislative plans generally meet constitutional standards.[143] Yet, laws delegating power must not be so vague as to reduce their operational meanings to becoming almost totally dependent on the subjective discretion of administrative boards or officers. In an illustrative case, the Supreme Court of Connecticut affirmed the invalidity of granting local boards the power to expel students for conduct that was inimical to the best interests of schools.[144]

The issue of delegation of authority to a state superintendent developed in an unusual way in Illinois at the time when it did not have a state board. Where the superintendent of public instruction followed legislative directives in preparing regulations as to minimum requirements for student health and safety, including school construction, a local board contested whether it would have to comply with the rules. The board alleged that the directives amounted to an unconstitutional delegation of legislative power. Acknowledging that judicial yardsticks measuring the delegation of powers must vary according to the nature of specific issues, the state's highest court upheld the legislature's ability to delegate this authority to the superintendent.[145] The court also examined the limits set by the superintendent, declaring that he exceeded the legislative intent to establish minimum standards. In conceding that the legislature had not given the superintendent unfettered power to set his own standards of excellence, the court decided that the rules he created were invalid because they were considerably more stringent than other well-recognized norms for school construction.

Ramifications of the delegation of authority to a state board of education constitute less of a problem than to state superintendents of education. In Ohio, for example, after a local board received a warning that a high school failed to meet several minimum standards, it challenged the state board's authority to revoke the school's charter. An appellate court, although expressing its sympathies for the local board, believed that the state board had the power to enforce the law requiring high schools to meet minimum state requirements.[146] The court rejected the local board's raising the issue of the improper delegation of authority on the basis that it was not the "real question" because the legislature had almost unlimited power

---

143. *Schreiber v. County Bd. of School Trustees*, 198 N.E.2d 848 (Ill.1964).

144. *Mitchell v. King*, 363 A.2d 68 (Conn.1975).

145. *Board of Educ. of City of Rockford v. Page*, 211 N.E.2d 361 (Ill.1965).

146. *Board of Educ. of Aberdeen–Huntington Local School Dist. v. State Bd. of Educ.*, 189 N.E.2d 81 (Ohio Ct. App.1962).

which it could delegate to any agency it created as long as it retained the ability to withdraw that power.

Whether the state legislature delegated authority to its state board of education arose in a suit over rules promulgated to enforce, ultimately through fund cut-offs, a statute requiring boards to eliminate de facto segregation in local districts. The Supreme Court of Illinois held that the rules exceeded the authority of state education officials since a statute specifically treating the matter placed responsibility in the hands of local boards and directed the state attorney general to provide for their enforcement.[147] The court remarked that the legislative provision empowering the state board to promulgate rules for establishing and maintaining free schools was limited by the legislation pertaining to de facto segregation and means to correct the problem. Shortly thereafter, another dispute arose in Illinois over the state board's ability to withhold funds for a program for gifted students due to alleged racial segregation in a district. The state's highest court ascertained that the state board lacked the authority to withhold funds and that no federal law gave it the power to do so.[148]

A dispute in North Carolina involved a charge that the state board of education exercised powers regarding teacher certification without legislative standards or guidelines. In rejecting this claim, the state's highest court noted that the state constitution conferred this power on the state board subject to legislative limitation and revision.[149] The court was convinced that insofar as the legislature had not acted, the board retained the power to regulate teacher qualifications. The court commented that delegation of powers comes into play in relation to legislative, not constitutional, powers. The same court later heard a case involving the effect of legislation on a state board rule that sought to prevent local boards from contracting with a private company to provide daily twelve-minute television news programs containing two minutes of commercial advertising. The state board long had the statutory power to adopt textbooks while other laws directed local boards to adopt written procedures used in selecting supplementary materials that were consistent with the textbooks. Shortly after the state board enacted the new rule, the legislature amended the supplementary materials statute to grant local boards complete control over the matter. In concluding that the legislature abrogated the state board's rule, the court observed that insofar as public policy was in the province of the legislature, it did not violate the constitutional rights of students or anyone else.[150]

As illustrated by a case from Iowa, the separation principle is not restricted to the powers of agencies exercising state-wide authority. Where

---

147. *Aurora East Pub. School Dist. No. 131 v. Cronin*, 442 N.E.2d 511 [8 Educ. L. Rep. 85] (Ill.1982).

148. *Board of Educ. of City of Peoria, School Dist. No. 150 v. Sanders*, 502 N.E.2d 730 [36 Educ. L. Rep. 835] (Ill.App.Ct.1986), *appeal denied*, 508 N.E.2d 208 [39 Educ. L. Rep. 1183] (Ill.1987), *cert. denied*, 484 U.S. 926, 108 S.Ct. 290, 98 L.Ed.2d 250 [42 Educ. L. Rep. 1060] (1987).

149. *Guthrie v. Taylor*, 185 S.E.2d 193 (N.C.1971).

150. *State v. Whittle Communications*, 402 S.E.2d 556 [66 Educ. L. Rep. 1299] (N.C.1991), *reh'g denied*, 404 S.E.2d 878 (N.C.1991).

state law gave county boards the ability to set the boundaries of reorganized school districts, the state's highest court rejected the charge that the legislature reposed absolute, unregulated, and undefined discretionary powers of a legislative nature in the county boards.[151] In the opinion of the court, the fact that standards for the action of county boards were statutorily prescribed, namely that educational conditions in the areas should be studied and that hearings were to be conducted on petitions for district reorganization, was a sufficient statement of the legislative policy under which the boards were authorized to act. The court emphasized that life has become so complex that for the legislature to enact laws in detail covering many governmental services would not only have been impractical, but impossible. The court concluded that many matters must be left to administrative agencies.

Legislatures may confer powers of local regulation on municipal corporations without violating the separation of powers principle. Under this theory, since local boards are recognized as quasi-municipal corporations, state officials may properly grant them the powers of local self-governance.[152] Even so, delegated powers must not conflict with overarching state laws. In such a case, an appellate court in California invalidated a provision in a city charter on tenure for school administrators and supervisors because it conflicted with state statutes.[153] The court found that the charter's having been enacted prior to the conflicting statutes was of no consequence.

The different legal effects of a legislature's enacting a policy and a state board's doing so under legislatively delegated powers is well illustrated in connection with modifying teacher certification requirements. As discussed in Chapter 9, it is well settled that individuals who possess certificates do not have contracts and that requirements for retention or renewal are subject to change. When the state board of education attempted to reduce the length of existing five-year certificates, the Supreme Court of Rhode Island enjoined it from doing so.[154] The court distinguished the case at bar from one resolved a short while earlier in Connecticut[155] since the source of the changes was the state board, not the legislature.

ADMINISTRATIVE POWERS

The generality of statutes related to the powers of state education agencies has generated a great deal of litigation over the extent of their authority. Statutes commonly provide that state superintendents, state boards, or both have general supervision and control over state school systems. Whether general statutes confer specific powers is subject to judicial review. While state educational officials can enact reasonable rules

---

151. *Wall v. County Bd. of Educ.*, 86 N.W.2d 231 (Iowa 1957).

152. *American Fed'n of Teachers v. Yakima School Dist. No. 7*, 447 P.2d 593 (Wash.1968).

153. *Whisman v. San Francisco Unified School Dist.*, 150 Cal.Rptr. 548 (Cal.Ct.App.1978).

154. *Reback v. Rhode Island Bd. of Regents for Elementary and Secondary Educ.*, 560 A.2d 357 [54 Educ. L. Rep. 1213] (R.I.1989).

155. *Connecticut Educ. Ass'n v. Tirozzi*, 554 A.2d 1065 [52 Educ. L. Rep. 604] (Conn.1989).

directing the operation of public schools, whether specific rules or actions are reasonable is subject to judicial review.[156]

A case from the Supreme Court of Illinois reflects the general rule as to the administrative authority of state educational officials. A statute gave the chief state school official the authority to act as the legal adviser of all school officers with the ability to offer his opinion on any question arising under the state's school laws. The court was satisfied that the law neither encroached on the judiciary's power to regulate the practice of law nor removed the common law powers of the attorney general which did not extend beyond acting as adviser to executive officers, boards, and departments of the state government.[157]

Maryland's highest court considered the extent of a general grant of power when a local school board passed a resolution requiring it to send the fingerprint cards of its employees to the local police for review.[158] In upholding the state board's power in the face of a challenge by a local board, the court relied on the general statutes that gave the former control and supervision on the basis that this mandate afforded it the final word on matters concerning educational policy or administration. The court maintained that insofar as screening employees was an administrative concern, it lay within the power of the state board.[159] In a suit over a busing contract, the same court affirmed that the state board has the authority to set educational policies for public schools and to adopt by-laws by which its dictates are carried out.[160]

The Supreme Court of Washington examined a dispute over whether the state board of education could deny accreditation to a proposed high school even though the local board responsible for its operation met all state requirements. In upholding the state board's denial of accreditation in part because there was no need for the school since adequate facilities existed in a neighboring district, the court asserted that the legislature did not intend for accreditation to be granted automatically to every school that met the state board's minimum standards.[161] When the board applied essentially the same rationale in denying accreditation to another new school, a different local board claimed that it did not properly consider a report and recommendations from the state superintendent.[162] The court disagreed with the local board, arguing that the recommendations were only advisory and that a review of the board's minutes revealed that it did not ignore the report which contained caveats along with serious, unanswered questions about fiscal responsibility. In noting that accreditation

---

156. *Board of Educ. of Plainfield v. Cooperman*, 523 A.2d 655 [38 Educ. L. Rep. 607] (N.J.1987).

157. *Board of Educ., School Dist. No. 142, Cook County v. Bakalis*, 299 N.E.2d 737 (Ill.1973).

158. *Wilson v. Board of Educ. of Montgomery County*, 200 A.2d 67 (Md.1964).

159. *See also Henry v. Earhart*, 553 A.2d 124 [51 Educ. L. Rep. 959] (R.I.1989).

160. *Chesapeake Charter v. Anne Arundel County Bd. of Educ.*, 747 A.2d 625 [142 Educ. L. Rep. 994] (Md.2000).

161. *State ex rel. DuPont–Fort Lewis School Dist. No. 7 v. Bruno*, 384 P.2d 608 (Wash. 1963).

162. *DuPont–Fort Lewis School Dist. No. 7 v. Bruno*, 489 P.2d 171 (Wash.1971).

was a qualification for participation in activities receiving state funds in addition to recognition of academic proficiency, the court emphasized that the state board exercised its fiscal and academic responsibility.

In a case from New York, a state law provided that funds for construction of school buildings would not be paid to boards that were scheduled for reorganization unless the commissioner of education certified that the allocations would not have impeded reorganization. When voters in two districts which were to be merged rejected the proposal by decisive margins, one of the boards unsuccessfully applied for a certificate of non-impedance and for an apportionment of state aid for the construction of a new music room. In its suit against the commissioner, an appellate court rejected the local board's claim that the funds could have been used after the commissioner approved the reorganization.[163] The court was persuaded that the issue was whether the use of state funds to improve existing facilities that were slated to become part of a reorganized district would have impeded reorganization. The court upheld the statute, which left the decision on whether such aid would impede reorganization to the discretion of the commissioner, as a valid delegation of authority.

Where a statute provided for a state subsidy for capital outlays, a school board purchased land to develop into an athletic facility. When the commissioner of education refused to grant the aid on the ground that the project was not covered by the statute, the board filed suit. In directing the commissioner to fund the project, the Supreme Judicial Court of Maine posited that insofar as the law invited a broad interpretation, it would exercise the traditional liberal policy of an expansive interpretation of the concept of educational purposes and needs.[164]

In a case where the state constitution granted general supervisory powers over education to the state board, the Supreme Court of Kansas found that this provision empowered it to require local boards to adopt policies, which were to be reviewed by a local attorney and filed with it, regulating student and employee conduct.[165] Conversely, as to a school district organization, the same court decreed that the state board's failure to follow legislative guidelines meant that its action was arbitrary as a matter of law.[166]

Interpreting provisions in its constitution relating to powers of the boards of the commonwealth and local school systems, the Supreme Court of Virginia pointed out that the former lacked the authority to require the latter to submit disputes between themselves and non-supervisory employees to binding arbitration.[167] The court distinguished the power of general supervision vested in the state-level board from the supervision of schools vested in local boards. The court determined that giving the common-

---

163. *Siegel v. Allen*, 255 N.Y.S.2d 336 (N.Y.App.Div.1965).

164. *City of Westbrook v. Logan*, 227 A.2d 793 (Me.1967).

165. *State ex rel. Miller v. Board of Educ. of Unified School Dist. No. 398, Marion County (Peabody)*, 511 P.2d 705 (Kan.1973).

166. *State ex rel. Dix v. Board of Educ.*, 578 P.2d 692 (Kan.1978).

167. *School Bd. of City of Richmond v. Parham*, 243 S.E.2d 468 (Va.1978).

wealth's board the authority it claimed would have rendered the constitutional grant of power to local boards for supervision of schools meaningless.

The Supreme Court of Pennsylvania upheld the right of the commonwealth's board of education to promulgate mandatory system-wide regulations covering a wide range of aspects of student discipline.[168] In rejecting a claim that the board exceeded its power, the court thought that the legislature's granting the board the authority to make regulations carrying out its duties was an essential element of the educational process included in its mandate to set standards governing school programs.

If legislation is specific, state boards cannot deviate from their prescriptions. Where a state statute provided for a minimum of 175 days each school year, the Supreme Court of Wyoming indicated that the state board lacked the authority to approve an experimental four-day week for a local district that would have resulted in a 144–day school year.[169] The court added that the alternative schedule, which had been in operation for about seven months, may have jeopardized state-aid entitlements since the number of days required was set by law.

The increasing complexity of legal matters in education has prompted courts to interpret the powers of state administrative officers broadly. The Supreme Court of New Jersey, for example, held that insofar as the powers of its state commissioner of education are more extensive than in other jurisdictions, a commissioner may have to act on matters that some commissioners apparently preferred not to consider on their own initiatives. The court explained that the commissioner was responsible for making an independent judgment over the non-retention of an administrator, not merely considering whether a local school board's actions were arbitrary, capricious, or the result of prejudice.[170] The court was of the view that its order did not interfere with the commissioner's policy of allowing local boards to select their own solutions in the first instance but that on appeal, he would have had to substitute his judgment rather than simply disapprove a local board's action and remand a dispute for further action. The court reaffirmed, extending this notion in a case involving de facto segregation, expressly directing the commissioner to take whatever steps appeared appropriate to correct a problem that a local board was not alleviating.[171]

In a case involving racial balances, at issue was the commissioner's quasi-judicial finding that the proposed establishment of a new high school in a virtually all-white community, which had sent its students to a school in a district with a mixed racial population, would have resulted in an increased racial imbalance in the one school and the creation of a virtually all-white school in the neighboring community.[172] The one district completely encircled the other and the two were closely interrelated by com-

---

168. *Girard School Dist. v. Pittenger*, 392 A.2d 261 (Pa.1978).

169. *Johnston v. Board of Trustees, School Dist. No. 1 West, Sheridan County*, 661 P.2d 1045 [10 Educ. L. Rep. 832] (Wyo.1983).

170. *In re Masiello*, 138 A.2d 393 (N.J.1958).

171. *Booker v. Board of Educ., Plainfield*, 212 A.2d 1 (N.J.1965).

172. *Jenkins v. Township of Morris School Dist.*, 279 A.2d 619 (N.J.1971).

mercial and transportation patterns since there was considerable interdependency in municipal public services. Although the commissioner wrote that he lacked the authority to intervene, the Supreme Court of New Jersey adopted a contrary view. Citing the previous cases, the court contended that where the legislature granted the commissioner broad powers, it would not permit him the administrative narrowing of duties that resulted in a disavowal of both power and responsibility. The court acknowledged that the commissioner had the power to direct the continuance of the sending-receiving relationship between the districts after the expiration of the present contract, to order the boards to proceed with suitable steps toward regionalization, and to order a merger if he was convinced that doing so was necessary to fulfill the state's educational and school desegregation policies.[173]

As far-reaching as their powers may be, state officials and agencies cannot retrospectively approve local board actions involving individual rights. Such a case arose where a state law did not specify the teaching areas within which one could have earned tenure. Over the years, the courts recognized administrative rules of the commissioner and state department providing for "horizontal" tenure such as for kindergarten, elementary, and secondary schools as well as for some specified special subjects rather than "vertical" tenure such as in English, social studies, and mathematics. In the face of a challenge to one of the commissioner's unreviewed orders, which declared that tenure areas could be created by administrative action at the district level, subject only to his ad hoc retrospective approval, the Court of Appeals of New York stated that such a view was erroneous.[174] The court commented that insofar as the commissioner failed to furnish standards for local boards, he undermined the purposes of the tenure statute because boards could easily have manipulated the standard in withholding or withdrawing tenure from teachers. According to the court, while the statute did not prohibit vertical tenure, the legislature or board of regents had to clarify the extent to which this could be done before rules could be put into effect.

A more recent case highlights the discretion that a system-wide board exercises over teacher licenses. The Supreme Judicial Court of Massachusetts affirmed that the commonwealth's board of education could promulgate regulations requiring mathematics teachers in under-performing schools to pass assessment tests prior to licensure.[175] The court remarked that insofar as the regulations were rationally related to the commonwealth's interest in having high-quality mathematics teachers in schools where student performances in the commonwealth-wide student mathematics assessment were low, they did not violate the educators' rights to equal protection rights under either the federal or commonwealth constitutions.

---

173. *See also Board of Educ. of Borough of Englewood Cliffs v. Board of Educ. of Borough of Tenafly*, 788 A.2d 729 [161 Educ. L. Rep. 542] (N.J.2002).

174. *Baer v. Nyquist*, 357 N.Y.S.2d 442 (N.Y.1974).

175. *Massachusetts Fed'n of Teachers v. Board of Educ.*, 767 N.E.2d 549 [164 Educ. L. Rep. 393] (Mass.2002).

Enforcement of Administrative Powers

The enforcement of administrative powers and the penalties that state-level agencies may invoke against non-compliance frequently leads to litigation. Among the penalties that state officials can impose for non-compliance are the denial of accreditation, revocation of teaching certificates, and the removal of local school board members from office in the face of substantial proof of dereliction. The need for evidence is particularly true where, as in the overwhelming majority of districts, board members are popularly elected. This principle was illustrated in a case where the Supreme Court of Kentucky upheld the removal of members of a local county board for misconduct in office.[176] The board members violated state law by awarding a construction contract without the prior approval of the chief state school officer by voting to purchase storage tanks for more than $10,000 without seeking competitive bids and for purchasing more than $10,000 worth of equipment from one member's brother. The same court later declared that the legislature did not exceed its authority in enacting a law empowering the commonwealth's board to remove individuals for causes not enumerated in the Constitution of Kentucky since it was vested with authority to consider the eligibility of board members.[177] The court refused to uphold the removal of board members for perceived inadequacy with regard to their efforts to apprise themselves of their district's financial condition.

When dealing with the removal of local school board members, legislatures are not under the same restrictions as subordinate agencies such as state boards of education. This issue arose in a challenge to the constitutionality of a law abolishing the incumbent board in New York City and ordering the mayor to appoint a new one under a different system. The state's highest court sustained the new law on the basis that the legislature had the power to abolish an office it created or modify its term even if doing so curtailed an incumbent's unexpired term.[178] In a second case from New York, an appellate court affirmed that the commissioner of education had the statutory authority to remove local school board members for violations of law or neglect of duty.[179] The court cautioned that this express power did not impose an overseer invested with veto power to substitute his or her opinions for those of local board members.

If school systems fall into chaos, state education officials may have the implied power to intervene. In the first of a trilogy of cases from New Jersey, the state's highest court affirmed the appointment of a monitor general to supervise activities in a district that was "in an abysmal state due almost entirely to the mismanagement and incompetence of the members of the local board of education."[180] In a second dispute involving the takeover of a district due to poor management, an appellate court affirmed

---

176. *State Bd. for Elementary and Secondary Educ. v. Ball*, 847 S.W.2d 743 [81 Educ. L. Rep. 633] (Ky.1993).

177. *Hale v. Combs*, 30 S.W.3d 146 [148 Educ. L. Rep. 1084] (Ky.2000).

178. *Lanza v. Wagner*, 229 N.Y.S.2d 380 (N.Y.1962), *cert. denied*, 371 U.S. 901, 83 S.Ct. 205, 9 L.Ed.2d 164 (1962).

179. *Verbanic v. Nyquist*, 344 N.Y.S.2d 406 (N.Y.App.Div.1973).

180. *Matter of Board of Educ. of Trenton*, 431 A.2d 808, 809 (N.J.1981).

that while officials violated the rights of administrators and an auditor in terminating their contractual rights, the plaintiffs were not entitled to compensation for lost vacation time.[181] In the third case, an appellate court affirmed the removal of an elected board and the district's being taken over by the state where there was undisputed evidence of nepotism and misbehavior by board members.[182] Also, the Supreme Court of California ruled that state officials had the duty to intervene when a board planned to close a district due to financial problems.[183] While interpreting state law as not requiring a takeover of operations, the court agreed that even if state officials resisted acting, they could not avoid the state's ultimate responsibility.

As exemplified by a case from the Supreme Court of Pennsylvania, if a legislature enacts a takeover law, it must be clear that it is not aimed at a particular district.[184] The court upheld a takeover statute allowing mayors in specified cities to assume control over failing school systems. The court was satisfied that the law violated neither equal protection nor a prohibition against special laws and did not interfere with any branch of the mayor-council optional form of government. Moreover, in a dispute from Louisiana, an appellate panel affirmed that insofar as a statute transferring failing schools to a recovery school district did not violate the Contracts Clause of either the Federal or state constitution, the trial court properly dismissed challenges to its validity.[185]

Challenges to the authority of state officials and boards can arise from their attempts to control the actions of local boards by withholding state funds. In general, courts are reluctant to approve the cutting off of funds as a means of ensuring compliance with state policies. This is particularly true if state-level authorities do not afford boards opportunities to be heard and/or to correct objectionable practices before being denied aid. If officials clearly violate financing laws, courts may order the withholding of public funds pending compliance. Where a law over teacher salaries was unambiguous, the Supreme Court of Arkansas ordered the state department of education to withhold funds from a board that it had permitted to avoid compliance with the statute.[186]

In an early case, the Supreme Court of Wisconsin resolved a disagreement over whether the state superintendent could withhold funds in order to enforce state regulations in a dispute over his attempt to require a local board to abandon an antiquated school building and replace it with one that was satisfactory.[187] Where state law called for the appointment of a

---

181. *Caponegro v. State Operated School Dist. of City of Newark, Essex County,* 748 A.2d 1208 [143 Educ. L. Rep. 562] (N.J.Super.Ct.App.Div.2000).

182. *Contini v. Board of Educ. of Newark,* 668 A.2d 434 [105 Educ. L. Rep. 1108] (N.J. Super. Ct. App. Div. 1995), *certification denied,* 678 A.2d 713 (N.J.1996).

183. *Butt v. State,* 15 Cal.Rptr.2d 480 [79 Educ. L. Rep. 1039] (Cal.1992).

184. *Harrisburg School Dist. v. Zogby,* 828 A.2d 1079 [179 Educ. L. Rep. 412] (Pa.2003).

185. *United Teachers of New Orleans v. State Bd. of Elementary and Secondary Educ.,* 985 So.2d 184 [234 Educ. L. Rep. 1044] (La.Ct.App.2008).

186. *Junction City School Dist. v. Alphin,* 855 S.W.2d 316 [83 Educ. L. Rep. 1193] (Ark.1993).

187. *State ex rel. School Dist. No. 8, Town of Wauwatosa v. Cary,* 163 N.W. 645 (Wis.1917).

building inspector and permitted the withholding of state funds to enforce the superintendent's orders, the board succeeded in forcing him to allot it the district's share of state funds despite its failure to comply with the building inspector's order. The court emphasized that insofar as other sections of the law placed the power to build schools in the hands of local boards, the state superintendent could not assume this responsibility by attempting to withhold funds to enforce state regulations. An early case supporting the withholding of state aid by a chief state school officer involved a statute that permitted the denial of funds until a board provided suitable facilities with convenient access to its students. The Supreme Court of New Jersey interpreted the law as requiring local boards to provide transportation to students who lived more than two miles from school.[188]

Conversely, a dispute arose in Texas where a state law stipulated that a county superintendent's salary and expenses were to be paid from local district funds. In addition, the law made the state superintendent responsible for the general superintendency of business relating to the state's public schools. A controversy arose when a board refused to contribute its share to a county superintendent and the state superintendent sought to impound part of its allocated funds to cover this expense. An appellate court granted the local board's request for mandamus in ascertaining that the state superintendent lacked the power to interfere with the legally prescribed course of state funds that were allocated to its treasury.[189]

In later cases, the Supreme Court of Illinois[190] and an appellate panel in Ohio[191] approved the withholding of funds from boards that did not comply with state transportation laws. In another case, the Supreme Court of Ohio ordered the state superintendent to grant a one-day waiver of required instruction to a school system when not doing so would have cost it $750,000 because of a mid-winter closure due to a strike by school personnel.[192]

QUASI-JUDICIAL POWERS

Ordinarily, courts resolve disputes involving the rights of individuals or organizations. Yet, in many jurisdictions selected controversies may, or must, be resolved by administrative agencies acting in quasi-judicial fashion. At the state level, quasi-judicial authority may rest in the hands of state superintendents, state boards, or other legislatively approved authorities such as local superintendents.[193] Adjudications of administrative agencies are binding on the parties. Absent state constitutional, statutory, or

---

188. *Board of Educ. of West Amwell Twp. v. State Bd. of Educ.*, 135 A. 664 (N.J.1927).

189. *Austin Indep. School Dist. v. Marrs*, 41 S.W.2d 9 (Tex.Com.App.1931).

190. *Board of Educ., School Dist. No. 142, Cook County v. Bakalis*, 299 N.E.2d 737 (Ill.1973).

191. *In re Resolution*, 385 N.E.2d 295 (Ohio Ct.App.1978).

192. *State ex rel. Cleveland Bd. of Educ. v. State Bd. of Educ. of Ohio*, 464 N.E.2d 137 [17 Educ. L. Rep. 932] (Ohio 1984). [Case No. 19]

193. *Strother v. Board of Educ. of Howard County*, 623 A.2d 717 [82 Educ. L. Rep. 557] (Md.Ct.Spec.App.1993).

regulatory provisions to the contrary, the courts usually permit state agencies and officers latitude in developing procedures such as the form of hearings and over the admissibility of evidence.

Even in states where administrative review is available, agencies may not hear all cases. As such, it is important to consider what disputes may, or must, be referred for review before petitioners have recourse to the courts. Another question remains over the scope of judicial review and whether it must be a trial de novo or a review of the record and, if the latter, what standard applies. Illustrations of quasi-judicial functioning of state education agencies follow.

In New York, parties can appeal educational disputes to the state commissioner or directly to the courts. Appeals to the commissioner are final subject to judicial review on the limited question of whether, on the record, the commissioner's action was arbitrary or lacked a rational basis.[194] Courts in New York agreed that the commissioner's judgment can substitute for that of other education authorities, including local school boards and hearing panels.[195] If matters primarily involve the meaning of constitutional or statutory provisions, the courts are likely to examine the commissioner's action more closely.[196] If an issue of educational policy is linked with a constitutional question such as academic freedom, the scope of judicial review remains limited.[197] Reflecting the general rule that the judiciary defers to administrative agencies, courts in New York agreed that where the regulations governing appeals to the commissioner provide for the review of affidavits and exhibits rather than evidentiary hearings, this approach did not violate due process.[198]

In a state with a different approach, Rhode Island allows its commissioner of education to conduct evidentiary hearings on complaints before rendering decisions de novo.[199] Unlike New York, Rhode Island provides for appeals of most of the commissioner's actions to the state board before the courts can assume jurisdiction. In such instances, the courts review cases based on the facts as provided by the commissioner and reviewed by the board unless they are unsupported by evidence in the record.[200] The fact that a record may contain additional evidence to support contrary conclusions is irrelevant.[201] For instance, the Supreme Court of Rhode Island

---

194. *Gundrum v. Ambach*, 448 N.Y.S.2d 466 [3 Educ. L. Rep. 1075] (N.Y.1982).

195. *Board of Educ. of City of N.Y. v. Allen*, 188 N.Y.S.2d 515 (N.Y.1959); *Conley v. Ambach*, 472 N.Y.S.2d 598 [16 Educ. L. Rep. 576] (N.Y.1984). [Case No. 20]

196. *Ross v. Wilson*, 127 N.E.2d 697 (N.Y.1955).

197. *Malverne Union Free School Dist. v. Sobol*, 586 N.Y.S.2d 673 [76 Educ. L. Rep. 1124] (N.Y.App. Div.1992), *appeal withdrawn*, 591 N.Y.S.2d 141 (N.Y.1992).

198. *Forrest v. Ambach*, 463 N.Y.S.2d 84 [11 Educ. L. Rep. 590] (N.Y.App.Div.1983), *appeal dismissed*, 468 N.Y.S.2d 1028 (N.Y.1983); *Akshar v. Mills*, 671 N.Y.S.2d 856 [125 Educ. L. Rep. 802] (N.Y.App.Div.1998), *leave to appeal dismissed*, 683 N.Y.S.2d 172 (N.Y.1998), *reargument denied*, 688 N.Y.S.2d 495 (N.Y. 1999).

199. *Slattery v. Cranston School Comm.*, 354 A.2d 741 (R.I.1976).

200. *Campbell v. School Comm. of Coventry*, 21 A.2d 727 (R.I.1941).

201. *Brown v. Elston*, 445 A.2d 279 [4 Educ. L. Rep. 211] (R.I.1982).

maintained that where a statute expressly vested a power in a local board, the commissioner could not substitute his judgment for its.[202]

In New Jersey, the state commissioner can resolve educational disputes with further review possible by the state board of education. While state law calls for evidentiary hearings, exhaustion of statutory remedies prior to seeking judicial review is not absolute since, in a far-ranging opinion, the state's highest court declared that the requirement is a policy of convenience and discretion rather than of law.[203] The court was satisfied that while the judiciary may intervene without waiting for other tribunals to act, it generally leaves educational matters to the disposition of state education officials.[204]

The legislature of Texas provides for review of school disputes through appeals to the state commissioner and the state board of education. The courts in Texas appear to agree that parties must exhaust administrative remedies before resorting to judicial review[205] but make a major exception regarding tax matters which can be taken directly to court without recourse to the central agency.[206] Texas law also permits an initial resort to the courts where there are undisputed facts and the only issue is a pure question of law.[207] In reviewing an adjudication of the state board, courts in Texas not only apply the common rule that an action must be upheld if it is supported by substantial evidence but also do not consider whether they would have reached the same result.[208] This rule applies to orders of the state board, not of local boards or the commissioner since the latter are subordinate administratively.[209] Less common in Texas is requiring trial courts to accept testimony from the parties along with examining the records of state-level administrative bodies.[210]

At issue in Maryland was whether the state board of education was required to hear appeals from county boards since the chief state school officer lacked a quasi-judicial role. Even though a statute provided for such a route, the state board claimed that it did not have to accept all requests for review. In rejecting the state board's interpretation of the statute, the court suggested that the board's argument over the fiscal implications that such a workload would have imposed on it had to be addressed by the legislature.[211]

---

202. *Exeter–West Greenwich Reg'l School Dist. v. Pontarelli*, 460 A.2d 934 [11 Educ. L. Rep. 559] (R.I.1983).

203. *Redcay v. State Bd. of Educ.*, 25 A.2d 632 (N.J.1942).

204. *See also Laba v. Board of Educ. of Newark*, 129 A.2d 273 (N.J.1957); *In re Masiello*, 138 A.2d 393 (N.J.1958).

205. *Ball v. Kerrville Indep. School Dist.*, 504 S.W.2d 791 (Tex.Civ.App.1973); *see also Sanchez v. Huntsville Indep. School Dist.*, 844 S.W.2d 286 [80 Educ. L. Rep. 736] (Tex.Ct.App. 1992).

206. *City of Dallas v. Mosely*, 286 S.W. 497 (Tex.Civ.App.1926).

207. *Alvin Indep. School Dist. v. Cooper*, 404 S.W.2d 76 (Tex.Civ.App.1966); *Calvin V. Koltermann, Inc. v. Underream Piling Co.*, 563 S.W.2d 950 (Tex.Civ.App.1977).

208. *Board of Trustees of Crystal City Indep. School Dist. v. Briggs*, 486 S.W.2d 829 (Tex.Civ.App.1972).

209. *Temple Indep. School Dist. v. State Bd. of Educ.*, 493 S.W.2d 543 (Tex.Civ.App.1973).

210. *Wylie Indep. School Dist. v. Central Educ. Agency*, 488 S.W.2d 166 (Tex.Civ.App. 1972).

211. *Board of Educ. of Garrett County v. Lendo*, 453 A.2d 1185 [8 Educ. L. Rep. 686] (Md.1982).

JUDICIAL REVIEW OF ACTIONS OF STATE-LEVEL AGENCIES

IN GENERAL

As a general rule, the courts are inclined to allow state education officials discretion in creating and enforcing rules,[212] going so far as to note that state commissioners have primary jurisdiction to hear and resolve all controversies arising under state school laws.[213] To this end, an appellate court in Maryland recognized that insofar as the power conferred on the state board gave it the authority to have the last word on disagreements over the administration of public schools, the judiciary had limited power to interfere.[214] As noted, courts ordinarily do not intervene in disputes involving state agencies unless allegations include, for example, claims that their actions implicated a constitutional claim;[215] violated a specific law;[216] exceeded their general powers;[217] acted arbitrarily, capriciously, or unreasonably;[218] or were not based on substantial evidence.[219]

The courts are more likely to examine quasi-judicial rather than administrative actions. In *Board of Education of Hendrick Hudson Central School District v. Rowley*, the Supreme Court, conceding that the judiciary is ill-equipped to act as a kind of "super" school board in evaluating complex factors affecting education, cautioned judges not to substitute their views of proper educational methodology for that of competent school officials. The Court observed that "[w]e previously have cautioned that courts lack the 'specialized knowledge and experience' necessary to resolve 'persistent and difficult questions of educational policy. . . .' Therefore, once a court determines that the requirements of the Act have been met, questions of methodology are for resolution by the States [through school

---

212. *See, e.g., Ware v. Valley Stream High School Dist.*, 551 N.Y.S.2d 167 [58 Educ. L. Rep. 1242] (N.Y.1989); *Kletzkin v. Board of Educ. of Borough of Spotswood, Middlesex County*, 642 A.2d 993 [91 Educ. L. Rep. 1025] (N.J.1994); *Morton Community Unit School Dist. No. 709 v. J.M.*, 152 F.3d 583 [128 Educ. L. Rep. 972] (7th Cir.1998), *cert. denied*, 526 U.S. 1004, 119 S.Ct. 1140, 143 L.Ed.2d 208 (1999).

213. *Bower v. Board of Educ. of City of East Orange*, 694 A.2d 543 [119 Educ. L. Rep. 176] (N.J.1997).

214. *Hurl v. Board of Educ. of Howard County*, 667 A.2d 970 [105 Educ. L. Rep. 565] (Md.Ct.Spec.App.1995).

215. *Pinckney v. Board of Educ. of Westbury Union Free School Dist.*, 920 F.Supp. 393 [108 Educ. L. Rep. 664] (E.D.N.Y.1996); *Brownsville Area School Dist. v. Student X*, 729 A.2d 198 [134 Educ. L. Rep. 534] (Pa.Cmwlth.Ct.1999), *appeal denied*, 745 A.2d 1225 (Pa.1999).

216. *Yaw v. Walla Walla School Dist. No. 140*, 722 P.2d 803 [34 Educ. L. Rep. 296] (Wash.1986); *Fairbanks North Star Borough School Dist. v. NEA–Alaska*, 817 P.2d 923 [70 Educ. L. Rep. 223] (Alaska 1991).

217. *Petition of Dunlap*, 604 A.2d 945 [73 Educ. L. Rep. 993] (N.H.1991).

218. *Petition of Dunlap*, 604 A.2d 945 [73 Educ. L. Rep. 993] (N.H.1991); *Dennery v. Board of Educ. of Passaic County Reg'l High School Dist. No. 1, Passaic County*, 622 A.2d 858 [81 Educ. L. Rep. 945] (N.J.1993).

219. *Pushay v. Walter*, 481 N.E.2d 575 [26 Educ. L. Rep. 1194] (Ohio 1985); *Brownsville Area School Dist. v. Student X*, 729 A.2d 198 [134 Educ. L. Rep. 534] (Pa.Cmwlth.Ct.1999), *appeal denied*, 745 A.2d 1225 (Pa.1999).

officials]."[220] At the same time, the Supreme Court of Wyoming reasoned that "the courts are always open to correct arbitrary, capricious, or fraudulent action taken by an administrative official or board."[221] The one condition to this rule is that as long as important rights are not extinguished, legislatures can provide for review of different decisions by different paths to the courts.[222]

RULES AND THEIR ENFORCEMENT

The extent of rule-making authority of administrative agencies under general grants of power is sometimes subject to litigation. While generalizations are difficult, at least two courts have addressed this issue. The Supreme Court of Montana presented two criteria for considering whether administrative regulations are inconsistent with legislative intent. The court held that regulations are unauthorized if they "engraft additional and contradictory requirements on the statute" or if they "engraft additional, noncontradictory requirements on the statute which were not envisioned by the legislature."[223] The Supreme Court of Washington, albeit in a case from higher education, posited that rules may fill in gaps in legislation if they are "necessary to the effectuation of a general statutory scheme," acknowledging that administrative rules adopted pursuant to legislative grants of authority should be upheld if they are "reasonably consistent with the statute[s] being implemented."[224]

Courts ordinarily agree that state agencies can resolve matters that fall within their jurisdiction. Even so, considerable difficulty ensues if power is based on a generalized statute. When reviewing the authority of state officials, the courts often maintain that the powers of their offices extend only to educational, not legal, matters. Yet, constitutional rights as to person and property, not to mention statutory interpretations, are often inextricably intertwined with educational considerations. The more cases one reads on the distinction between legal and educational matters, the more involved the differentiation becomes. Since the courts have the final word as to whether matters are educational or legal, their judgments often influence the course of education on substantive issues.

In the face of a presumption that administrative officers or bodies exercised their power properly, the burden of proof is generally on the parties challenging administrative actions.[225] Not surprisingly, the courts typically do not pass on the wisdom of discretionary acts of state or local officials,[226] limiting themselves to legal considerations. At most, if courts

---

220. 458 U.S. 176, 208, 102 S.Ct. 3034, 73 L.Ed.2d 690 [5 Educ. L. Rep. 34] (1982). [Case No. 110]

221. *School Dists. Nos. 2, 3, 6, 9, and 10 v. Cook*, 424 P.2d 751, 755 (Wyo.1967).

222. *Board of Educ. of Armstrong High School Dist. No. 225 v. Ellis*, 328 N.E.2d 294 (Ill.1975).

223. *Bell v. Department of Licensing*, 594 P.2d 331, 333 (Mont.1979).

224. *Green River Community College, Dist. No. 10 v. Higher Educ. Personnel Bd.*, 622 P.2d 826, 828 (Wash.1980).

225. *Steubenville v. Culp*, 38 Ohio St. 18 (Ohio 1882).

226. *See, e.g., Board of Educ. of Indep. School Dist. No. 92 of Pottawatomie v. Earls*, 536 U.S. 822, 838, 122 S.Ct. 2559, 153 L.Ed.2d 735 [166 Educ. L. Rep. 79] (2002), *on remand*, 300

invalidate orders, they can require further administrative actions consistent with their decrees.

Another relevant generalization is that if statutes outline procedures for solving problems or securing redress within the executive branch, the courts usually require parties to exhaust administrative remedies before asserting jurisdiction. Still, if a federal constitutional or statutory right is involved, the Supreme Court decided that section 1983 is available to provide "immediate access to the federal courts notwithstanding any provision of state law to the contrary."[227]

Occasionally, state boards or chief state school officers fail to carry out their duties. If duties are ministerial, or mandatory, such as dealing with apportioning state funds, parties can seek writs of mandamus to require performance.[228] Where duties involve elements of discretion, it is up to the judiciary to set liabilities for harm flowing from nonperformance. In an example of the latter, the Sixth Circuit affirmed that where Ohio's State Board of Education failed to discharge its responsibilities to halt intentionally segregative practices in Cleveland, it had to share in the costs of desegregating its schools.[229]

A good example of judicial review of state-level activity involved the Tennessee Secondary School Athletic Association (TSSAA), a not-for-profit membership corporation funded largely through gate receipts from interscholastic sports events, organized to regulate interscholastic high school sports in public and private schools. Even though no school was forced to join, about eighty-four percent of the state's public high schools and fifty-five private schools were members. Under the TSSAA's bylaws, member schools were represented by their principals or faculty members who had votes in selecting members of its governing bodies. The TSSAA sets membership standards and student eligibility rules and has the power to penalize any member school that violates those rules. Half of the TSSAA's meetings took place during official hours at public schools.

When the TSSAA penalized a private school for violating a recruiting rule, the school sued it and its executive director under section 1983, claiming that it engaged in state action in violation of the First and Fourteenth Amendments. In *Brentwood Academy v. Tennessee Secondary School Athletic Association*,[230] the Supreme Court ruled in favor of the private school. Rejecting the TSSAA's arguments to the contrary, the Court found that its regulatory activity was state action due to its pervasive interaction with public school officials. The Court found that insofar as the

---

F.3d 1222 [168 Educ. L. Rep. 581] (10th Cir.2002). [Case No. 112] ("In upholding the constitutionality of the [drug testing] Policy [at issue], we express no opinion as to its wisdom. Rather, we hold only that Tecumseh's Policy is a reasonable means of furthering the School District's important interest in preventing and deterring drug use among its schoolchildren.").

227. *Patsy v. Board of Regents of the State of Fla.*, 457 U.S. 496, 504, 102 S.Ct. 2557, 73 L.Ed.2d 172 (1982).

228. *Board of Educ. of Iron Mt. v. Voelker*, 259 N.W. 891 (Mich.1935).

229. *Reed v. Rhodes*, 662 F.2d 1219 [1 Educ. L. Rep. 120] (6th Cir.1981).

230. 531 U.S. 288, 121 S.Ct. 924, 148 L.Ed.2d 807 [151 Educ. L. Rep. 18] (2001), *on remand*, 262 F.3d 543 [157 Educ. L. Rep. 467] (6th Cir.2001), *reh'g en banc denied, cert. denied*, 535 U.S. 971, 122 S.Ct. 1439, 152 L.Ed.2d 382 (2002).

TSSAA would virtually not have existed but for the support it received from the public schools and their officials, it had to be viewed as a public institution.

On remand, the Sixth Circuit affirmed that the anti-recruiting rule, which prohibited high school coaches from recruiting middle school athletes, was a content-based regulation of speech that violated the school's First Amendment rights since it was insufficiently narrowly tailored to serve a permissible purpose.[231] The court also agreed that TSSAA's board violated the school's right to due process because it improperly considered ex parte evidence in imposing sanctions pursuant to the rule. On further review in *Tennessee Secondary School Athletic Association v. Brentwood Academy*,[232] the Supreme Court reversed in favor of the TSSAA. The Court reasoned that the rule did not violate the First Amendment since the school voluntarily joined the association and agreed to abide by its policies. The Court added that the TSSAA did not violate the school's due process rights because prior to imposing the sanction, the TSSAA conducted an investigation and a hearing that the school not only had notice of but at which it was represented by counsel and had the opportunity to adduce evidence, none of which was excluded. In its analysis, the Court rejected the school's claim that the TSSAA acted improperly when its full board, acting ex parte, heard from investigators and other witnesses concerning a separate incident in which a basketball coach, who was not one of the school's employees, encouraged a middle school basketball player to attend the school. The Court concluded that the coach's allegations were unlikely to have increased the severity of the penalties it received.

HEARINGS

If statutes require administrative bodies to convene hearings before acting, courts typically examine the manner in which they are conducted in order to ensure that they complied with due process. It is, then, vital to distinguish two basic types of hearings: legislative or rule-making and quasi-judicial or adversarial.

The purpose of legislative hearings is to convey information and opinions to decision-making bodies. Even though there is no constitutional requirement that rule-making agencies conduct hearings before acting, statutes frequently grant them discretion as to whether hearings are necessary to clarify the positions of the parties.[233] In addition, there is typically no legal duty for these bodies to do any more than listen to the views expressed because they have the power to act as they see fit.

Quasi-judicial hearings are required where precise determinations of fact and law are needed. These kinds of hearings implicate constitutional

---

231. *On remand, Brentwood Acad. v. Tennessee Secondary School Athletic Ass'n,* 304 F.Supp.2d 981 [186 Educ. L. Rep. 180] (M.D.Tenn.2003), 442 F.3d 410 [207 Educ. L. Rep. 554] (6th Cir.2006), *reh'g and reh'g en banc denied.*

232. 551 U.S. 291, 127 S.Ct. 2489, 168 L.Ed.2d 166 [220 Educ. L. Rep.39] (2007). [Case No. 21]

233. *State of Cal., Dep't of Educ. v. Bennett,* 843 F.2d 333 [46 Educ. L. Rep. 52] (9th Cir.1988).

due process because liberty or property rights are involved. The most common cases in these categories, as reflected in Chapters 11 and 13 of this book, respectively, pertain to the dismissals of teachers and student for disciplinary infractions. In these situations, the courts require minimal procedures, but do not expect administrative bodies to comply with the same procedural strictness as in judicial settings.

State boards may employ hearing officers to conduct quasi-judicial hearings and offer recommendations. While state bodies can reject findings or conclusions of hearing officers, they still must review the transcripts of hearings before acting.[234] Once officials review the evidence, they will have satisfied due process. In rejecting a claim to the contrary, the Supreme Court, in *Morgan v. United States*,[235] a non-school case, found it unnecessary for officials who are responsible for reaching an ultimate decision to be present when evidence is received.

Absent statutory specifications as to how hearings are to be conducted, and if the subject matter is essentially one of policy formulation or application, instead of individual rights, the presumption is in favor of legislative-type hearings.[236] By way of illustration, the Supreme Court of Oregon pointed out that a judicial-type hearing was not necessary where a legislatively created district boundary board conducted a hearing on proposed changes once it provided the requisite notice.[237] The chairman of the hearing board reviewed the stipulations governing its ability to act on petitions for annexation, after which members of the audience were invited to express their perspectives about the proposed change, all of which were recorded in the board's minutes. Once the hearing was completed, the board made the requested boundary changes. The court rejected a challenge to the board's vote on the ground that it did not make formal findings on such issues as the effect that the proposed changes would have had on the ability of districts to provide mandated educational programs since the statute did not require it to do so.

The Supreme Court of Wisconsin affirmed that for a non-judicial hearing, the only issues subject to judicial review are whether a board acted within its jurisdiction and whether its order was arbitrary and/or capricious.[238] The court noted that a board action is arbitrary and capricious when it lacks a rational base, is unreasonable when all facts and opinions are considered, or when it is the result of an unconsidered, wilful, and irrational choice of conduct rather than the result of a winnowing and sifting process. The court decided that the board was not limited to considering facts in the record since it was free to utilize other information within its knowledge. The court remarked that even though a board member expressed a general view on a controversial matter such as a

234. *Board of Educ. of Melrose Mun. Schools v. New Mexico State Bd. of Educ.*, 740 P.2d 123 [40 Educ. L. Rep. 1279] (N.M.Ct.App.1987).

235. 298 U.S. 468, 56 S.Ct. 906, 80 L.Ed. 1288 (1936).

236. *Johnson v. Schrader*, 507 P.2d 814 (Wyo.1973).

237. *School Dist. No. 7 of Wallowa County v. Weissenfluh*, 387 P.2d 567 (Or.1963).

238. *Joint School Dist. No. 2 v. State Appeal Bd.*, 266 N.W.2d 374 (Wis.1978).

school district reorganization plan, this did not bar the individual from participating in the board's action.

[CASE NO. 16]   REVIEWING CHARTER SCHOOL APPLICATIONS

SCHOOL BOARD OF VOLUSIA COUNTY
v. ACADEMIES OF EXCELLENCE

Florida District Court of Appeals, 2008.
974 So.2d 1186 [230 Educ. L. Rep. 114], *review dismissed*, 981 So.2d 1200 (Fla.2008).

■ PALMER, C.J.

The motion for rehearing and for rehearing en banc filed by the School Board of Volusia County is denied. However, the prior opinion of this court, dated November 30, 2007 is withdrawn, and we substitute the following in its place.

The School Board of Volusia County (School Board) appeals the final order entered by the State of Florida, Department of Education (State Board), reversing the School Board's denial of the charter school application filed by Academies of Excellence (Academies). Determining that the record contains competent, substantial evidence to support the State Board's decision, we affirm.

Academies applied to the School Board for permission to open a charter elementary school in Volusia County, Florida. Pertinent to this appeal, in the application the following information was set forth:

L.   Student Performance Standards

. . .

4.   To be considered as meeting student performance standards, students must perform at Level 3 and above on the mathematics and reading sections of the Florida Comprehensive Assessment Test.

5.   Students who score at or above the 25th percentile on norm-referenced tests are considered to have demonstrated acceptable student performance standards.

Additionally, as part of the finance portion of the application, Academies indicated that it expected to initially enroll 450 students.

The School Board held a hearing to consider Academies' application. During the hearing, Dr. Chris Colwell, Deputy Superintendent for Instruction Services, testified that Academies' application failed to set a goal for itself of attaining an A, B, C, or D grade in terms of success of the school. He stated that a specific stated goal was required and appropriate. Next, Colwell took issue with Academies' standard that "students who score at or above the 25th percentile on norm referenced tests are considered to have demonstrated acceptable student performance standards." He testified that the standard was lower than the standards held by public schools in Volusia County and lower than the standards that would be expected by the State of Florida.

Bill Kelly, Jr., Deputy Superintendent of Finance, opined that Academies' application lacked evidence of sound financial planning. Specifically,

Kelly found Academies' enrollment projection of 450 students in the first year of operation to be unreasonable. Based on the unreasonable enrollment figure, Kelly stated that Academies' budget revenues were overstated. Kelly also stated that Academies was understating its capital budget by one million dollars for facilities and land costs.

At the conclusion of the hearing, the School Board denied Academies' application. Specifically, the School Board concluded that Academies' application failed to meet the standards for minimal acceptance in the areas of student assessment/accountability and finance/class size requirements.

Academies appealed the School Board's ruling to the State Board of Education. The Charter School Appeals Commission conducted a hearing on the matter. During that hearing, Kathleen Schoenberg, attorney for Academies, argued that Academies' application properly addressed the statutory requirement regarding student assessment and that the argument over finances was just a difference of opinion between the School Board and Academies.

Ted Doran, attorney for the School Board, argued that Academies had failed for the fourth time to produce an application sufficient statutorily to proceed to the next level. Dr. Colwell testified that Academies' failure to include a school goal in its application made Academies unaccountable for its performance under the Governor's A–Plus Plan. Further, Colwell stated that it was unacceptable that Academies considered the 25th percentile to be an acceptable level of student performance. However, he did indicate that Academies had admitted that this figure on their application was a typographical error and that the figure should have been 51st percentile instead of 25th percentile.

In response, Schoenberg stated that Academies mistakenly omitted a sentence stating that the school's goal was to be an "A" school. However, she argued that omission of that one sentence was not enough to make the entire application deficient.

The Commission asked the parties whether there was a specific requirement that a school grade be part of the application. Colwell admitted that the application template did not include such a requirement and Schoenberg stated that the statute does not require the school to include a school grade as one of its goals.

At the conclusion of the comments on student assessment/accountability, the Commission voted that the School Board had competent, substantial evidence to support its finding that the application was statutorily deficient in the area of student assessment/accountability. However, immediately thereafter, the Commission voted that the School Board's finding that the application was statutorily deficient in the area of student assessment/accountability was not good cause for denial. After more discussion, the Commission voted that the School Board did not have competent substantial evidence to support its finding that the application was statutorily deficient in the areas of finance/class size requirements. Subsequently, the Commission voted to recommend to the State Board that Academies' appeal be granted.

The Commission's recommendations were submitted to the State Board. The State Board conducted a hearing during which it considered whether to accept the Commission's recommendation to overturn the decision of the School Board and to grant Academies' application. . . . Subsequently, the State Board issued a written order upholding the findings and recommendations of the Commission. This appeal timely followed.

The School Board challenges the State Board's final order, claiming first that the Board deviated from the record below and improperly created its own record during the appeal process. Specifically, the School Board argues that the School Board and Academies were bound by the record developed before the School Board and thus it was error for the parties to add new evidence during the appeal process. We reject this argument because both the School Board and Academies presented, without any objection, testimony before the Commission regarding the issues of student assessment/accountability and finance/class size requirements. Additionally, the School Board did not raise any objections to the comments made during the State Board meeting regarding the 25th percentile promotion rate, nor did the School Board raise the argument before the State Board that it now raises on appeal. Accordingly, the School Board failed to preserve this issue for our review.

In a related argument, the School Board claims that the State Board improperly conducted a *de novo* review of the evidence by accepting testimony at the State Board hearing. Again, this argument was not properly preserved for our review.

The School Board further argues that the State Board's order must be reversed because it fails to include a fact-based justification for the Board's decision. We disagree.

Section 1002.33(6)(e)1. & 5. of the Florida Statutes (2005) provides:

1002.33. Charter schools

. . .

(6) Application process and review.

Beginning September 1, 2003, applications are subject to the following requirements:

. . .

(e) 1. A Charter School Appeal Commission is established to assist the commissioner and the State Board of Education with a fair and impartial review of appeals by applicants whose charter applications have been denied, whose charter contracts have not been renewed, or

. . .

. . .

5. Commission members shall thoroughly review the materials presented to them from the appellant and the sponsor. The commission may request information to clarify the documentation presented to it. In the course of its review, the commission may facilitate the postponement of an appeal in those cases where additional time and communi-

cation may negate the need for a formal appeal and both parties agree, in writing, to postpone the appeal to the State Board of Education. A new date certain for the appeal shall then be set based upon the rules and procedures of the State Board of Education. *Commission members shall provide a written recommendation to the state board as to whether the appeal should be upheld or denied. A fact-based justification for the recommendation must be included.* The chair must ensure that the written recommendation is submitted to the State Board of Education members no later than 7 calendar days prior to the date on which the appeal is to be heard. Both parties in the case shall also be provided a copy of the recommendation.

§ 1002.33(6)(e)1. & 5., Fla. Stat. (emphasis added [in original]). The statute clearly states that the Commission, not the State Board, must include a fact-based justification for its recommendation. Therefore, the failure of the State Board to include a fact-based justification for its decision does not constitute reversible error.

The School Board next challenges the State Board's final order, claiming that the School Board's basis for denying Academies' charter school application constituted good cause because Academies' application was unsound in student assessment/accountability and finance/class size requirements. The School Board claims that, because the Commission found that Academies' application was statutorily deficient in the area of student assessment/accountability, the Commission erred in concluding that this deficiency was not good cause for denial of Academies' application. We disagree.

While Academies admitted at the hearing before the Commission that it had mistakenly omitted a sentence from its application that should have said the school's goal was to be an "A" school, a representative from the School Board also admitted that the application template did not include a requirement that one of the goals include a school grade. Section 1002.33(6)(a) of the Florida Statutes also contains no such requirement, and the Florida charter schools standard application includes no such requirement. Therefore, competent substantial evidence supports the Commission's conclusion that the School Board did not have good cause to deny Academies' application on that basis.

Next, the School Board argues that the Commission erred in concluding that the School Board did not have good cause to deny Academies' application based on statutory deficiencies in Academies' basis for promotion of students. Specifically, the School Board argues that Academies' could not promote students based on reaching the 25th percentile. This issue was extensively discussed at the meeting before the Commission. Academies indicated that it was willing to correct this language. Academies' willingness to rectify the situation appeared to be the reason that the Commission concluded that this error on Academies' application was not good cause to deny the application. Based on the testimony and argument presented at the hearing, the Commission had sufficient evidence before it to properly conclude that, although Academies' application was statutorily deficient, such a deficiency was not good cause for denial of the application when Academies recognized the problem and was willing to correct it.

The School Board also argues that the Commission erred in concluding that the School Board did not have competent substantial evidence to support its finding that Academies' application was statutorily deficient in the area of finance/class size requirement. We again disagree. The record demonstrates that Academies rebutted the reasons the School Board gave for denying its application, and the evidence demonstrated that many of the School Board's reasons for denial were based on opinion. Also, a School Board representative admitted that Academies' budget was correct if it could achieve its estimated enrollment number.

Finally, the School Board challenges the State Board's final order, claiming that the order which was entered pursuant to section 1002.33 of the Florida Statutes conflicts with, and thereby violates, the School Board's constitutional authority under Article IX, section 4(b), of the Florida Constitution, to operate, control and supervise public schools, and its authority under Article IX, section 1(a), of the Florida Constitution, to make adequate provision for a uniform and high quality system of free public schools. Specifically, the School Board argues that, because the act of operating and controlling all free public schools in Volusia County is conferred exclusively on the School Board, section 1002.33(6)(c) is unconstitutional because it permits the State Board to open a charter school.

. . .

Section 1002.33(6)(c) does not permit the State Board to open a charter school. Rather, the statute permits the State Board to approve or deny a charter application after it completes an extensive review process. Granting a charter application is not equivalent to opening a public school. The approval of an application is just the beginning of the process to open a charter school. Once the charter application has been granted, the school board still has control over the process because the applicant and the school board must agree on the provisions of the charter. A school board can also cause a charter to be revoked or not renewed. Furthermore, under the Constitution of Florida, while the school board shall operate, control and supervise all free public schools within their district the State Board of Education has supervision over the system of free public education as provided by law.

AFFIRMED.

NOTES

1. Did the State Board usurp the authority of local school officials?

2. What is the impact of charter schools on public education in your district? State?

[CASE NO. 17]   AUTHORITY OF A STATE BOARD TO CONTRACT
WITH A PRIVATE, FOR–PROFIT CORPORATION TO OPERATE A
SCHOOL

BALTIMORE TEACHERS UNION, AMERICAN FEDERATION OF TEACHERS, LOCAL 340, AFL–CIO v. MARYLAND STATE BOARD OF EDUCATION

Court of Appeals of Maryland, 2004.
840 A.2d 728 [184 Educ. L. Rep. 910].

■ ELDRIDGE, J.

Baltimore Teachers Union, American Federation of Teachers, Local 340, AFL–CIO, filed in the Circuit Court for Baltimore City a complaint for a declaratory judgment and injunctive relief, alleging that the Maryland State Board of Education lacked statutory authority to enter into a contract with Edison Schools, Inc. for the operation and management of three Baltimore City public elementary schools. The Circuit Court held that the State Board acted within its statutory authority conferred by the General Assembly. Before argument in the Court of Special Appeals, the Union filed in this Court a petition for a writ of certiorari. We granted the petition and shall affirm.

I

Governance of the Maryland public school system is two-tiered. The Maryland State Board of Education is the head of the State Department of Education.... Twenty-three county boards of education and the New Baltimore City Board of School Commissioners (the "New Board") operate as the statutory heads of the twenty-four local public school systems. The State Board is charged with the general supervision of the Maryland public schools, including the development and implementation of educational policies. The State Board is authorized to adopt rules and regulations for the administration and enforcement of the education law. In 1993, the Board promulgated regulations establishing public school performance standards that were adopted and codified in the Code of Maryland Regulations (COMAR). Regulation .01 establishes the scope of the regulations and regulation .02 is the definition section. The student performance areas tracked by the State are set forth in regulation .03. Regulation .04 establishes the standards that apply to the student performance areas. Regulation .05 sets out the reporting requirements, and the mandate that each public school develop a school improvement plan is set forth in regulation .06.

The regulations further set forth a two-phased process for public schools that fail to meet the prescribed student performance standards. Regulations .07 and .08 describe "local reconstitution" where, if a school fails to meet all standards at a level of satisfactory or better in the student performance areas, the State Board may require the overall program and management of a school to be placed under the direct control of the local school board. By February 2000, the State Board had ordered 97 schools throughout Maryland to be placed under local reconstitution. Of these, 83 schools were in Baltimore City.

If a school under local reconstitution fails to show sufficient improvement, regulation .10 provides for "state reconstitution" by which the State Board determines the overall program and management of the school. In 1999, the State Board reconstituted three of the lowest performing public elementary schools in Baltimore City.... Student performance remained stagnant at these elementary schools despite being under local reconstitution for at least three years. No more than 10% of the students at the schools had met the State's standard in all student performance areas in any year since 1993 when the school performance regulations were adopted.

The State Board examined the feasibility of closing one or more of the underperforming elementary schools. The Board determined that any closure would result in increased transportation costs and the transfer of students to other low performing public schools already under local reconstitution. The Board concluded that the most viable option was to contract out the operation and management of the three schools to a third party. Following a request for proposals in accordance with the State procurement procedure, the State Board and the New Board entered into a "Contract for the Operation and Management of Schools Under State Reconstitution in Baltimore City" with Edison Schools, Inc., for a term of five years. The contract with Edison was approved by the Maryland Board of Public Works on March 22, 2000.

Edison is a private company specializing in the management of public schools. It operates under contracts with local school districts and boards of charter schools. Pursuant to its contract with the State Board, Edison is required to provide the three public elementary schools with curriculum and curriculum development, instructional services, instructional and support personnel, teaching tools, special education and related services, educational services with limited or no English proficiency, and other services which may be necessary. Edison serves as the employer of all employees hired for the elementary schools and is responsible for providing management and professional development for all personnel working in the three schools. Edison has the power to hire, assign, discipline, and dismiss all personnel hired at the schools.

The Baltimore Teachers Union initiated the present action in the Circuit Court for Baltimore City against the State Board and the New Board....

The State Board and the New Board filed motions to dismiss the complaint for lack of standing. Alternatively, the State Board moved for summary judgment, maintaining that the Board acted within the scope of its statutory authority by promulgating the challenged regulations and contracting with a private vendor for the operation of the three elementary schools. The Union filed a cross-motion for summary judgment. Edison filed a motion to intervene which was unopposed. Following a hearing, the Circuit Court issued an order declaring that the Union had standing, that the challenged regulations were within the State Board's statutory authority, and that the two Boards were statutorily authorized to enter into the contract.

The Union filed a notice of appeal to the Court of Special Appeals, and the State Board filed a cross-appeal on the standing issue. Prior to argument in the intermediate appellate court, the Union filed in this Court a petition for a writ of certiorari which we granted. The petition presented the single question of whether the challenged regulations and contract were authorized by the General Assembly.

II

As a threshold matter, we must first consider whether the Baltimore Teachers Union had standing to challenge the reconstitution regulations and the Edison contract. . . .

. . . we hold that the Union has demonstrated that, as the designated collective bargaining representative of Baltimore City Public School employees, it has standing to maintain the present judicial action.

III

Turning to the merits of the case, Baltimore Teachers Union argues that COMAR exceed[s] the statutory authority of the Maryland State Board of Education, and that the State Board's contractual delegation of the operation and management of the reconstituted schools illegally grants powers to Edison which are vested exclusively in the New Board. While the State Board exercises general supervisory authority, the Union argues that the State Board lacks statutory authority to take over the basic functions of the local boards. The Union contends that there exists "no statute which directly and without equivocation authorizes the State Board" to turn over a public school to a third party and place it under the sole control of a private business.

We need not and shall not decide whether the State Board was statutorily authorized to adopt the reconstitution regulations in 1993. Even if the State Board lacked the statutory authority to promulgate the reconstitution regulations in 1993, subsequent enactments by the General Assembly remove any doubt as to the statutory authorization for the State Board's actions. The General Assembly has passed legislation which confirms and ratifies the State Board's power to issue the reconstitution regulations and to enter into third party contracts pursuant to those regulations. The legislation makes clear that the General Assembly knew of and approved of the State Board's exercise of its statutory authority to contract with Edison for the operation and management of the three public elementary schools.

The principle of legislative ratification is well-established in the law. In the situation where a governmental entity takes action which may or may not be statutorily authorized, but where the appropriate legislative body later ratifies that action, the ratification clearly validates the action prospectively and, in the absence of constitutional limitations, may validate the action retroactively. As Justice Harlan stated for the Supreme Court long ago, "it is not perceived why subsequent legislative ratification is not, in the absence of constitutional restrictions upon such legislation, equivalent to original authority." This Court has also recognized "that whatever a legislative body 'may authorize in prospect, it may adopt and validate in retrospect, so long as there is no interference with vested rights.' "

In 1997, the General Assembly directed the New Board to take actions necessary to "[i]mprove the status of schools that are subject to a State reconstitution notice." In 1999 the General Assembly passed legislation regarding stipends for classroom teachers and, in doing so, distinguished between a local school board as an employer and a private employer of a teacher in a reconstituted school. Section 6–306(b)(4) mandates that a classroom teacher holding an advanced professional certificate, who teaches in a public school identified by the State Board "as a reconstitution school, a reconstitution-eligible school, or a challenge school, shall receive a stipend from the State in the amount of $2,000 for each year that the teacher performs satisfactorily in the classroom." This language is in contrast to subsection (b)(2) that authorizes a stipend from the State for a classroom teacher "who is employed by a [local] board and who holds a certificate issued by the National Board for Professional Teaching Standards."

The General Assembly enacted legislation in 2000 protecting the pension rights of teachers previously employed by the local boards, working for a third party contractor operating a school under the reconstitution regulations. The statutory provisions specifically reference "an employee of the New Baltimore City Board of School Commissioners or another county board of education" who is "hired by a third-party contractor to work in a school that is reconstituted by order of the Maryland State Board of Education." The statute authorizes public school employees, whether vested or not in the retirement system, who are hired by a private contractor operating a school under state reconstitution, to withdraw their accumulated retirement or pension benefits without penalty, to receive service credit for the time employed with the private contractor, and to purchase up to five years of service credit at the employee rate for the period of employment with a third party contractor in a reconstituted school.

The 1997, 1999 and 2000 legislation demonstrates the General Assembly's awareness and approval that the State Board would be entering into contracts with private vendors in accordance with the reconstitution regulations. The statutory language directly references schools "subject to a State reconstitution notice" in addition to those schools "identified by the State Board as a reconstitution school, reconstitution-eligible school, or a challenge school." The language distinguishes between teachers "employed by a [local] board" and those who teach "in a public school identified by the State Board as a reconstitution school" for purposes of stipends and bonuses. The legislation affirmatively makes provisions to protect the pension rights of school teachers employed by third party contractors.

Given the language incorporating the reconstitution regulations and protecting the retirement benefits of those working in reconstituted schools, it is clear that the General Assembly recognized that the employer of a teacher in a public school under State reconstitution may be a private employer, and, thus, it is reasonable to infer legislative ratification of the regulations. As the Circuit Court correctly observed, "the General Assembly has considered and ... countenanced and condoned the [Board's] authority to enter into a third party contract." The General Assembly has clearly ratified the reconstitution regulations.

IV

The Union in its brief before this Court, for the first time in this case, argues that the challenged regulations and the Edison contract violate Article VIII, § 1, of the Maryland Constitution.

As earlier mentioned, the Union in its Circuit Court complaint emphasized that the "claims in this action are solely a matter of statutory law." In its complaint, cross-motion for summary judgment, and memoranda filed in the Circuit Court, the Union never raised a constitutional issue. The Circuit Court's memorandum and its declaratory judgment made no mention of a constitutional issue, as the Union had raised no such issue. The Union's certiorari petition did not present a constitutional issue....

Since the constitutional issue raised in the Union's brief was not raised in the trial court, we shall decline to address it. It is particularly important not to address a constitutional issue not raised in the trial court in light of the principle that a court will not unnecessarily decide a constitutional question.

.... The challenged action in the case at bar was ratified and authorized by the General Assembly.

JUDGMENT AFFIRMED, WITH COSTS.

NOTES

1. One member of the court conceded that the union had standing to proceed but disagreed with the outcome. The judge argued that the majority did not answer whether the Maryland State Board of Education had the authority to compel a local board to privatize a public school, permitting a private, for-profit corporation to control the school's staff and curriculum.

2. Should state boards have the authority to permit the privatization of underperforming public schools?

[CASE NO. 18] DELEGATION OF LEGISLATIVE POWERS TO CHIEF STATE SCHOOL OFFICER

SCHOOL DISTRICT NO. 39 OF WASHINGTON COUNTY v. DECKER

Supreme Court of Nebraska, 1955.
68 N.W.2d 354.

■ CHAPPELL, JUSTICE.

Plaintiff, School District No. 39 of Washington County, generally known as Rose Hill School District, is a rural Class II school district conducting both elementary and ninth and tenth high school grades in Washington County. It brought this action in equity to enjoin the enforcement of Rule III–3 of Section B, "Criteria for Approved Schools" promulgated as of July 1, 1952, by defendant Freeman Decker, then Superintendent of Public Instruction, under purported authority granted him by the last sentence of section 79–307, R.R.S.1943. Such section provides: "The Superintendent of Public Instruction shall prescribe forms for making all reports and regulations for all proceedings under the general school laws of the state. *He shall also formulate rules and regulations for the approval of all high schools for the collection of free high school tuition money.*" (Italics supplied.)

Rule III–3 also provides: "The teacher-pupil ratio for high school (grades 9–12) shall not be less than 1–5."

On May 12, 1953, defendant had removed plaintiff's high school from the list of approved schools for the school year 1953–1954 because its teacher-pupil ratio was "1–4 which is less than the minimum standards" required by Rule III–3. Concededly, such removal made plaintiff ineligible for collection of free high school tuition for nonresident pupils, deprived it of exemption from the free high school tax levy together with the right to be considered for accreditation status, and, as stated by defendant, "so far as our records are concerned, there is no high school in Rose Hill."

Insofar as important here, plaintiff sought injunctive relief primarily upon the ground that the last sentence of section 79–307, R.R.S.1943, was an unconstitutional and invalid delegation of legislative authority and power to an executive or administrative officer of the state. In other words, plaintiff contended that Rule III–3 was invalid and unenforceable because such statute granted defendant authority to "formulate rules and regulations for the approval of all high schools for the collection of free high school tuition money" without therein or otherwise in any statute in pari materia therewith providing any legislative numerical limitations, standards, rules, or criteria for the guidance of defendant in so doing. . . .

As disclosed by the record, defendant admitted that there is no magic in the ratio of 1–5 required by Rule III–3, and that it could as well have been higher or lower, but should be higher. As a matter of fact, defendant also admitted that there are only eight ninth and tenth grade high schools left in Nebraska, but that in the recent past he had waived the ratio of 1–5 for two or three other like high schools in Washington County because they had prospects for more students in the future, or had suggested the possibility of reorganization.

Thus the Superintendent of Public Instruction has been delegated a free hand without legislative limitations or standards to make or change at will any numerical ratio or standard required for approval of high schools for the collection of free high school tuition money when it would have been a simple matter for the Legislature, which had the power and authority, to have incorporated limits and standards in the statute. As a consequence, without questioning the motives or ability of the Superintendent of Public Instruction, there might well be approval of some high schools upon one standard and a withholding of approval from others by a qualification of such standard or by virtue of another. Thus, defendant had arbitrary power over the life or death of all high schools in this state and the preservation or destruction of their property and the grant or denial of free high school revenue, dependent upon the granting or refusal of approval.

Article II, section 1, Constitution of Nebraska provides: "The powers of the government of this state are divided into three distinct departments, the legislative, executive and judicial, and no person or collection of persons being one of these departments, shall exercise any power properly belonging to either of the others, except as hereinafter expressly directed or permitted."

As said in 42 Am.Jur., Public Administrative Law, § 45, p. 342, citing authorities from many states: "It is a fundamental principle of our system of government that the rights of men are to be determined by the law itself, and not by the let or leave of administrative officers or bureaus. This principle ought not to be surrendered for convenience, or in effect nullified for the sake of expediency. However, it is impossible for the legislature to deal directly with the host of details in the complex conditions on which it legislates, and when the legislature states the purpose of the law and sets up standards to guide the agency which is to administer it, there is no constitutional objection to vesting discretion as to its execution in the administrators.... A statute which in effect reposes an absolute, unregulated, and undefined discretion in an administrative body bestows arbitrary powers and is an unlawful delegation of legislative powers. The presumption that an officer will not act arbitrarily but will exercise sound judgment and good faith cannot sustain a delegation of unregulated discretion." ...

... We have considered the question of constitutionality in the light of the presumption of validity to which a legislative act is entitled. Nevertheless, we conclude that the last sentence of section 79–307, R.R.S. 1943, ... [unconstitutionally] delegates legislative authority to the Superintendent of Public Instruction....

Reversed and remanded with directions.

NOTES

1. The line of demarcation between the ability of chief state school officers to legislate, which is unconstitutional, and their authority to formulate reasonable rules and regulations is unclear. Do you agree with the court's placing the power to classify districts on the legislative side of the line?

2. From an educational view, was the regulation that the superintendent promulgated a sound one?

3. Do you think it likely the regulation that precipitated this case would have withstood judicial scrutiny if the legislature had indicated that one of the items that the superintendent could have taken into account was the student-teacher ratio?

[CASE NO. 19]   MANDAMUS AGAINST CHIEF STATE SCHOOL OFFICER

STATE EX REL. CLEVELAND BOARD OF EDUCATION v. STATE BOARD OF EDUCATION OF OHIO

Supreme Court of Ohio, 1984.
464 N.E.2d 137 [17 Educ. L. Rep. 932].

■ PER CURIAM.

This action in mandamus was brought by the Cleveland Board of Education to compel respondent, the State Board of Education of Ohio and its superintendent, Dr. Franklin B. Walter, to waive one day of required instruction in the Cleveland Public School System for the 1983–1984 school year.

On January 11, 1984 and January 12, 1984, members of the Unity Unions employed by the Cleveland Board of Education engaged in a work stoppage. These were primarily custodial employees whose duties included operating the boilers in the schools and other maintenance functions. On the days in question, the temperature in Cleveland ranged from 5°F to 18°F. Considering the lack of personnel to operate the heating systems and maintain the buildings, relator's superintendent closed the schools for those two days.

As a result of the closing of school on these two days, the Cleveland Public Schools will have been open for instruction one day less than required by R.C. 3313.48 if the regularly scheduled school year is not extended. The make-up day of instruction is currently scheduled for June 19, 1984, which Relator alleges will cost $750,000.

Relator initially sought a waiver of two days of instruction from respondent which was denied. Relator's request for an adjudication hearing pursuant to R.C. 119.07 and 119.09 was granted. A hearing was held and on May 24, 1984, the state superintendent issued his final order denying the requested waiver.

On May 25, 1984, this action in mandamus was filed seeking the issuance of a writ to compel respondent to waive the one day of instruction. (It is conceded that relator has available an appeal to the court of common pleas from its R.C. Chapter 119 appeal. However, in view of the fact that this dispute concerns whether the schools will be open on June 19, 1984, it would be impossible for relator to obtain the relief requested through that appeal process.) . . .

■ PER CURIAM. The sole issue presented is whether relator is entitled to the waiver of one day of required instruction as requested. The waiver of the minimum school year requirements is governed by R.C. 3317.01(B) which provides in relevant part:

> . . . This requirement shall be waived by the superintendent of public instruction if it had been necessary for a school to be closed because of disease epidemic, hazardous weather conditions, damage to a school

building, or other temporary circumstances due to utility failure rendering the school building unfit for school use,....

For the reasons that follow, we conclude that relator is entitled to the waiver of one day of instruction due to "other temporary circumstances due to utility failure rendering the school building unfit for school use" under R.C. 3317.01(B). We note first that no argument was made nor evidence presented to suggest that relator's superintendent acted imprudently in closing the schools. The utilities were inoperable, creating a genuine concern for the welfare of the students if classes were held. We sympathize with respondent's concern that too lenient enforcement of minimum school year requirements will erode the protections they afford to Ohio's public school students. However, the purpose of the minimum school year is to provide guidelines to insure that public schools offer quality education. We cannot conclude that one day of instruction will improve the quality of education offered in the Cleveland Public Schools this year, particularly when the one day will cost relator $750,000.

In so holding, we expressly reject relator's contention that the reason for the utility failure is irrelevant in determining whether a waiver is appropriate under R.C. 3317.01(B). We find simply that the reasons for the utility failure herein do not justify requiring relator to schedule a make-up day of instruction at a cost of $750,000. This expenditure can only adversely affect relator's students in the long run, with no practical benefit in return.

Accordingly, the writ is allowed.

NOTES

1. The common law writ of mandamus is designed to compel performance of a non-discretionary duty. Did the superintendent's decision not to grant the waiver clearly fit in that category?

2. Why was this case decided by the state's highest court without its having gone through the lower courts first?

3. With whom do you agree, the superintendent or the court?

[CASE NO. 20] JUDICIAL REVIEW OF DECISION OF CHIEF STATE SCHOOL OFFICER

CONLEY v. AMBACH

Court of Appeals of New York, 1984.
472 N.Y.S.2d 598, 460 N.E.2d 1083 [16 Educ. L. Rep. 576].

MEMORANDUM.

The authority of the Commissioner of Education to review the findings of a hearing panel ... [in connection with charges against a tenure teacher] includes the right to annul the decision of the panel on the ground of bias or partiality of the panel chairman. The standard by which the determination of the commissioner in the exercise of such authority is to be judged on judicial review is whether his determination "was made in violation of lawful procedure, was affected by an error of law or was arbitrary and capricious or an abuse of discretion". The operative test in this instance is whether the commissioner's determination to annul the decision of the hearing panel was arbitrary and capricious.

His determination was made on the ground that, during the course of the proceedings before the panel, its chairman accepted a remunerative position with the New York State United Teachers (NYSUT) as one of eight arbitrators available to hear disputes between NYSUT and its professional employees, without disclosure thereof to the board of education until subsequent to the close of the hearings. This employment, coupled with the circumstance that counsel for NYSUT represented the teacher at the hearings, was found to raise a sufficient question as to the impartiality of the chairman (or the appearance thereof) as to warrant vacatur of the decision of the panel. Although no direct relationship between the chairman and one of the parties to the proceeding was revealed, there was shown to have been an undisclosed connection between the chairman and counsel for the teacher. This connection alone, without any showing of actual partiality or impropriety on the part of the chairman (of neither of which is there any suggestion in this record), constituted a rational basis for the commissioner's action. Accordingly, his determination of annulment was not arbitrary or capricious and must be sustained.

The commissioner had no authority, however, to impose the prescriptions that he did on the further conduct of the hearings. Specifically, he had no authority to direct the selection of the new chairman of the panel by the parties; the statute mandates that the third member of the panel shall be chosen by mutual agreement of the other two panel members.

Additionally, inasmuch as portions of the evidence at the hearings consisted of conflicting testimony of live witnesses, the credibility and persuasive force of which testimony might not be susceptible to adequate evaluation on the basis of a reading of the transcript only, it was an abuse of discretion, in view of the key role played by the chairman of the hearing panel as its only impartial member, to order the determination of the reconstituted panel to be based only "upon the record already established". This is not to say that portions or all of the transcript of the first hearings cannot be employed by the new panel in making its determination; it is to say only that, absent agreement of the parties and the new chairman, the commissioner cannot order that the consideration of the new panel be confined to the record already established. . . .

Order modified, with costs to petitioner, and matter remitted to Supreme Court, Albany County, with directions to remand to the commissioner for further proceedings in accordance with the memorandum herein and, as so modified, affirmed.

NOTES

1. The hearing panel found the teacher to be at fault on two of thirteen charged specifications and recommended a $300 fine. When the board appealed, the commissioner annulled the panel's action, but the trial court overturned the

commissioner's action. The appellate court reinstated the commissioner's order, holding that as chief educational officer of the state, he had the authority to adopt higher ethical standards for disclosure than might have existed in commercial or other arbitration situations. What do you think about this?

2. In a unanimous opinion, New York's highest court rejected any notion suggesting that the appearance of bias did not exist where a board's appointee to a hearing panel sought and obtained an additional $100 per-diem fee from it, an arrangement unknown to the teacher, her attorney, or other panel members. The court thus upheld the annulment of the panel's split decision calling for the teacher's dismissal and the board's acceptance thereof. The panel conducted forty-six days of hearings, after which the chair and the board's appointee voted for dismissal, with the teacher's appointee disagreeing on the major charges and recommending only a letter of reprimand and caution. The court concluded that an entirely new hearing panel would have to consider the charges. *Syquia v. Board of Educ. of Harpursville Cent. School Dist.*, 591 N.Y.S.2d 996 [80 Educ. L. Rep. 182] (N.Y.1992).

[CASE NO. 21] "JUDICIAL REVIEW OF THE AUTHORITY OF A STATE ATHLETIC ASSOCIATION"

TENNESSEE SECONDARY SCHOOLS ATHLETIC ASSOCIATION v. BRENTWOOD ACADEMY

Supreme Court of the United States, 2007.
551 U.S. 291, 127 S.Ct. 2489, 168 L.Ed.2d 166 [220 Educ. L. Rep. 39].

■ JUSTICE STEVENS announced the judgment of the Court....

The principal issue before us is whether the enforcement of a rule prohibiting high school coaches from recruiting middle school athletes violates the First Amendment. We also must decide whether the sanction imposed on respondent for violating that rule was preceded by a fair hearing.

I

Although this case has had a long history, the relevant facts may be stated briefly. The Tennessee Secondary School Athletic Association (TSSAA) is a not-for-profit membership corporation organized to regulate interscholastic sports among its members, which include some 290 public and 55 private high schools in Tennessee. Brentwood Academy is one of those private schools.

Since the early 1950's, TSSAA has prohibited high schools from using "undue influence" in recruiting middle school students for their athletic programs. In April 1997, Brentwood's football coach sent a letter to a group of eighth-grade boys inviting them to attend spring practice sessions. The letter explained that football equipment would be distributed and that "getting involved as soon as possible would definitely be to your advantage." It was signed "Your Coach." While the boys who received the letter had signed a contract signaling their intent to attend Brentwood, none had enrolled within the meaning of TSSAA rules. All of the boys attended at least some of the spring practice sessions. As the case comes to us, it is settled that the coach's pre-enrollment solicitation violated the TSSAA's anti-recruiting rule and that he had ample notice that his conduct was prohibited.

TSSAA accordingly sanctioned Brentwood. After proceeding through two layers of internal TSSAA review, Brentwood brought this action against TSSAA and its executive director in federal court under 42 U.S.C.[A.] § 1983. As relevant here, Brentwood made two claims: first, that enforcement of the rule was state action in violation of the First and Fourteenth Amendments; and second, that TSSAA's flawed adjudication of its appeal had deprived the school of due process of law. The District Court granted relief to Brentwood, but the Court of Appeals reversed, holding that TSSAA was a private voluntary association that did not act under color of state law. We granted certiorari and reversed, holding that the District Court was correct on the threshold issue On remand, the Sixth Circuit sent the case back to the District Court, which once again ruled for Brentwood. TSSAA appealed, and the Court of Appeals affirmed over one judge's dissent. The majority held that the anti-recruiting rule is a content-based regulation of speech that is not narrowly tailored to serve its permissible purposes. It also concluded that the TSSAA Board improperly considered *ex parte* evidence during its deliberations, thereby violating Brentwood's due process rights.

We again granted certiorari and we again reverse.

II

The First Amendment protects Brentwood's right to publish truthful information about the school and its athletic programs. It likewise protects the school's right to try to persuade prospective students and their parents that its excellence in sports is a reason for enrolling. But Brentwood's speech rights are not absolute. It chose to join TSSAA, an athletic league and a state actor invested with a three-fold obligation to prevent the exploitation of children, to ensure that high school athletics remain secondary to academics, and to promote fair competition among its members. TSSAA submits that these interests adequately support the enforcement against its member schools of a rule prohibiting coaches from trying to recruit impressionable middle school athletes. Brentwood disagrees, and maintains that TSSAA's asserted interests are too flimsy and its rule too broad to support what the school views as a serious curtailment of its constitutional rights. Two aspects of the case taken together persuade us that TSSAA should prevail.

A

The anti-recruiting rule strikes nowhere near the heart of the First Amendment. TSSAA has not banned the dissemination of truthful information relating to sports, nor has it claimed that it could. Our cases teach that there is a difference of constitutional dimension between rules prohibiting appeals to the public at large and rules prohibiting direct, personalized communication in a coercive setting.

Ohralik v. Ohio State Bar Assn. nicely illustrates the point. In *Ohralik,* we considered whether the First Amendment disabled a state bar association from disciplining a lawyer for the in-person solicitation of clients. The lawyer argued that under our decision in *Bates v. State Bar of Ariz.,* which invalidated on First Amendment grounds a ban on truthful advertising relating to the "availability and terms of routine legal services," his solicitation was protected speech. We rejected the lawyer's argument, holding that the "in-person solicitation of professional employment by a lawyer does not stand on a par with truthful advertising about the availability and terms of routine legal services, let alone with forms of speech more traditionally within the concern of the First Amendment." We reasoned that the solicitation ban was more akin to a conduct regulation than a speech restriction. . . .

Drawing on these examples, we found that the "[i]n-person solicitation by a lawyer of remunerative employment is a business transaction in which speech is an essential but subordinate component," the prohibition of which raised few (if any) First Amendment problems.

Ohralik identified several evils associated with direct solicitation distinct from the harms presented by conventional commercial speech. Direct solicitation "may exert pressure and often demands an immediate response, without providing an opportunity for comparison or reflection;" its goal "may be to provide a one-sided presentation and to encourage speedy and perhaps uninformed decisionmaking;" and it short circuits the "opportunity for intervention or counter-education by agencies of the Bar, supervisory authorities, or persons close to the solicited individual." For these reasons, we concluded that in-person solicitation "actually may disserve the individual and societal interest, identified in *Bates,* in facilitating 'informed and reliable decisionmaking.' "

We have since emphasized that *Ohralik's* "narrow" holding is limited to conduct that is " 'inherently conducive to overreaching and other forms of misconduct.' " And we have not been chary of invalidating state restrictions on solicitation and commercial advertising in the absence of the acute risks associated with in-person legal solicitation. In our view, however, the dangers of undue influence and overreaching that exist when a lawyer chases an ambulance are also present when a high school coach contacts an eighth grader.

After all, it is a heady thing for an eighth-grade student to be contacted directly by a coach—here, "Your Coach"—and invited to join a high school sports team. In too many cases, the invitation will come accompanied with a suggestion, subtle or otherwise, that failure to accept will hurt the student's chances to play high school sports and diminish the odds that she could continue on to college or (dream of dreams) professional sports. Such a potent entreaty, playing as it does on youthful hopes and fears, could well exert the kind of undue pressure that "disserve[s] the individual and societal interest . . . in facilitating 'informed and reliable decisionmaking.' " Given that TSSAA member schools remain free to send brochures, post billboards, and otherwise advertise their athletic programs, TSSAA's limited regulation of recruiting conduct poses no significant First Amendment concerns.

B

Brentwood made a voluntary decision to join TSSAA and to abide by its antirecruiting rule. Just as the government's interest in running an effective workplace can in some circumstances outweigh employee speech rights, so too can an athletic league's interest in enforcing its rules sometimes warrant curtailing the speech of its voluntary participants. This is not to say that TSSAA has unbounded authority to condition membership on the relinquishment of any and all constitutional rights. As we recently emphasized in the employment context, "[s]o long as employees are speaking as citizens about matters of public concern, they must face only those speech restrictions that are necessary for their employers to operate efficiently and effectively." Assuming, without deciding, that the coach in this case was "speaking as [a] citize[n] about matters of public concern," TSSAA can similarly impose only those conditions on such speech that are necessary to managing an efficient and effective state-sponsored high school athletic league.

That necessity is obviously present here. We need no empirical data to credit TSSAA's common-sense conclusion that hard-sell tactics directed at middle school students could lead to exploitation, distort competition between high school teams, and foster an environment in which athletics are prized more highly than academics. TSSAA's rule discourages precisely the sort of conduct that might lead to those harms, any one of which would detract from a high school sports league's ability to operate "efficiently and effectively." For that reason, the First Amendment does not excuse Brentwood from abiding by the same anti-recruiting rule that governs the conduct of its sister schools. To hold otherwise would undermine the principle, succinctly articulated by the dissenting judge at the Court of Appeals, that "[h]igh school football is a game. Games have rules." It is only fair that Brentwood follow them.

III

The decision to sanction Brentwood for engaging in prohibited recruiting was preceded by an investigation, several meetings, exchanges of correspondence, an adverse written determination from TSSAA's executive director, a hearing before the director and an advisory panel composed of three members of TSSAA's Board of Control, and finally a *de novo* review by the entire TSSAA Board of Directors. During the investigation, Brentwood was notified of all the charges against it. At each of the two hearings, Brentwood was represented by counsel and given the opportunity to adduce evidence. No evidence offered by Brentwood was excluded.

Brentwood nevertheless maintains that its due process rights were violated when the full TSSAA board, during its deliberations, heard from witnesses and considered evidence that the school had no opportunity to respond to. Some background is necessary to understand the claim. One of the matters under investigation was whether an Amateur Athletic Union basketball coach named Bart King had pushed talented middle school students—including a basketball star named Jacques Curry—to attend Brentwood. Brentwood consistently maintained that King had no affiliation with the school and no authority to act on its behalf. Nevertheless, the initial decision by TSSAA's executive director, as well as the subsequent decision by the director and the advisory panel, declared Curry (as well as several other players) ineligible to play for Brentwood.

As it had in earlier stages of the case, in Brentwood's final appeal to the TSSAA Board, the school offered live testimony from Curry and an affidavit from King denying the alleged recruiting violations. Once Curry had testified, Brentwood's counsel advised the board that King was available to answer any questions, but did not call him as a witness. After reviewing the evidence, the board found that Brentwood had committed three specific violations of its rules, none of which appeared to involve either King or Curry, and it reinstated Curry's eligibility. As a penalty for the three violations, the board put Brentwood's athletic program on probation for four years, excluded the boys' basketball and football teams from tournament playoffs for two years, and imposed a $3,000 fine.

During its deliberations, the board discussed the case with the executive director who had presided at the earlier proceedings and two TSSAA investigators, none of whom had been cross-examined. The investigators also provided handwritten notes to the board detailing their investigations; Brentwood never received those notes. The District Court found that the consideration of the *ex parte* evidence influenced the board's penalty decision and contravened the Due Process Clause. The Court of Appeals accepted that finding, as well as the conclusion that the evidence tainted the fairness of the proceeding. TSSAA now maintains that the lower courts erred.

We agree. Even accepting the questionable holding that TSSAA's closed-door deliberations were unconstitutional, we can safely conclude that any due process violation was harmless beyond a reasonable doubt. To begin with, it is hard to believe that the King allegations increased the severity of the penalties leveled against Brentwood. But more importantly, Brentwood's claim of prejudice rests on the unsupported premise that it would have adopted a different and more effective strategy at the board hearing had it been given an opportunity to cross-examine the investigators and review their notes. Despite having had nearly a decade since the hearing to undertake that cross-examination and review, Brentwood has identified nothing the investigators shared with the board that Brentwood did not already know. Perhaps that is why Brentwood never explains what a more effective strategy might have looked like. Brentwood obliquely suggests it might have had King testify at the hearing, but it gives no inkling of what his testimony would have added to the proceedings. We are not inclined to speculate on its behalf.

IV

We accordingly reverse the judgment of the Court of Appeals and remand the case for further proceedings consistent with this opinion.

It is so ordered.

NOTES

1.   Do you agree with the Supreme Court? Put another way, how should the judiciary view relationships between state athletic associations and non-public schools?

2.   Should schools, public or non-public, be able to recruit players for athletic teams?

3.   Have interscholastic sports taken on a life of their own that conflicts with academic programming in schools? What can or should school officials and/or parents do about this?

CHAPTER 4

LOCAL SCHOOL BOARDS: POWERS AND PROCEDURES

INTRODUCTION

Education was a primary concern in America from the earliest days of colonial New England. To this end, in 1642, a Massachusetts law directed "certain chosen men of each town to ascertain from time to time, if parents and masters were attending to their educational duties; if the children were being trained in learning and labor and other employments."[1] After five years, community leaders abandoned the law since it did not mandate the creation of public schools.

A second law, passed in 1647, was more successful. The "ye old deluder" statute, so-called because it was designed to combat Satan's desire to delude people into ignorance of scriptures in order to lead them more easily to damnation, required all towns with more than fifty households to establish and maintain schools.[2] The law also called for fines of officials in towns where leaders did not follow the law. While this law was not strictly complied with only a decade after its enactment, it did introduce the legal principle that education is a function of local government. Officials in Connecticut enacted virtually the same law in 1650.[3] In 1693, leaders in Connecticut further solidified local control over education by implementing another law directing town selectmen to operate schools and to impose taxes to support them if so directed by votes of residents at town meetings.[4] Similar laws were soon in effect throughout New England.

In early America, public education was a function of local government, administered by town meetings and then town selectmen. Yet, since selectmen were responsible for all town agencies, not just education, they often delegated authority for such tasks as choosing new teachers or supervising

---

1. SOUL OF AMERICA: DOCUMENTING OUR PAST, VOL. I: 1492–1870 at 19 (Robert C. Baron ed., 1994).

2. DOCUMENTS OF AMERICAN HISTORY, VOL. I: TO 1898 at 29 (Henry Steele Commager, ed., 7th ed., 1965). Retaining its original spelling, the statute begins: "It being one chiefe project of ye ould deluder, Satan, to keepe men from the knowledge of ye Scriputures,.... [i]t is therefore ordred, yt evry towneship ... [with 50 households shall] forthwith appoint one ... to teach all such children ... to write & reade [and] whose wages shall be paid eithr by ye parents or mastrs of such children, or by ye inhabitants in genrall...."

3. LAWRENCE A. CREMIN, AMERICAN EDUCATION: THE COLONIAL EXPERIENCE, 1607–1783 at 181–182 (1970).

4. CHARLES E. REEVES, SCHOOL BOARDS: THEIR STATUS, FUNCTIONS AND ACTIVITIES at 19 (1954, reprinted 1969).

the construction of new school buildings. When it became necessary for selectmen to delegate more of their duties relating to education, in 1721 they appointed the first permanent school committee in Boston. This action marked the beginning of the process of separating school governing bodies from other local governmental entities.[5]

The first federal document to mention education was the Northwest Ordinance, adopted in 1787. According to Article III of the Ordinance, "religion, morality, and knowledge, being necessary to good government and the happiness of mankind, schools and the means of education shall forever be encouraged."[6] This language greatly influenced state constitutions in the American Midwest and is evident today as states grant plenary powers to local school boards.

The colonial practice of local control carried over into the new American republic. In 1789, a Massachusetts law authorized the creation of separate school committees. Later that year, a statute from Boston called for the election of a twelve-member committee to serve as a separate governing body over public schools.[7] In 1798, Massachusetts recognized the committees as separate governing bodies; selectmen or other town officials were sometimes members of the board. In 1826, legislators amended the law to ensure that the committees were independent of other governmental bodies.[8] In this way, the process begun over a century earlier was brought to completion in New England before spreading throughout the country.

POWERS IN GENERAL

GENERALLY

As noted in Chapter 3, local school boards are "creatures of the state" with powers defined by law. Even so, the evolution of American public education is characterized by broad judicial interpretations of implied powers of local school officials.[9] The Supreme Court acknowledged this point in *San Antonio Independent School District v. Rodriguez*,[10] commenting that local school boards have the authority to tailor educational needs to their communities. Judicial deference to local boards, as long as they do not act in "unreasonable, arbitrary, capricious or unlawful manner[s],"[11]

---

5. *Id.* at 17.

6. BARON, *supra* note 1, at 86.

7. Raymond E. Callahan. *The American Board of Education, 1789–1960.* In UNDERSTANDING SCHOOL BOARDS 19 (Peter J. Cistone, ed. 1975).

8. REEVES, *supra* note 4, at 20.

9. *Michigan Educ. Ass'n v. Secretary of State*, 801 N.W.2d 35, 52 [269 Educ. L. Rep. 842] (Mich. 2011) ("[S]chool districts and school officers have only such powers as the statutes expressly or impliedly grant to them.") (internal citations omitted).

10. 411 U.S. 1, 93 S.Ct. 1278, 36 L.Ed.2d 16 (1973).

11. *Sherwood Nat'l Educ. Ass'n v. Sherwood–Cass R–VIII School Dist.*, 168 S.W.3d 456, 460 [201 Educ. L. Rep. 394] (Mo.Ct.App.2005), *reh'g and/or transfer denied* (Mo.Ct.App.2005), *transfer denied* (Mo.2005).

has encouraged freedom and experimentation out of proportion to that suggested by the legal structure of public education.

Creative school boards typically introduce new practices in what may be described as exercises of latent implied powers. If practices are unchallenged, or survive judicial scrutiny, they may spread until they are generally accepted. In an overwhelming number of cases involving new educational practices, local boards have prevailed, usually on the basis that these initiatives are desirable ways of achieving broad legislative and/or educational goals. The earliest, and perhaps most dramatic, example of this process was the extension of a common school system to include high schools when the Supreme Court of Michigan's acceptance of this practice in the "Kalamazoo case" meant that educators could initiate similar reforms in other states.[12]

Insofar as most locales are home to both school boards and local governments, relations between the two often result in litigation even though both entities are separate. That is, even if the boundaries of municipal units and school districts are coterminous, their affairs are supposed to remain separate.[13] While so-called "home rule" charters, which allow municipalities the exclusive right to enact legislation addressing local needs, do not diminish the power of states to regulate education,[14] such authority must typically yield to municipal home rule provisions governing the same subject matter such as school budgets. In such a case, the Supreme Court of Connecticut held that a municipality and local school board could jointly discharge their responsibilities to ensure that an education budget met general state requirements to address the needs of the town's children.[15] Even so, as reflected by a case from the Supreme Court of New Hampshire, municipalities must not exceed the scope of their authority in attempting to turn independent school boards into city departments.[16]

A recent example of an on-going conflict over the ability of a school board to experiment arose in California. A federal trial court rejected the claim of a non-profit organization which alleged that a board's having chartered Waldorf Schools as part of a voluntary desegregation plan violated the Establishment Clause because they taught anthrosophy, an approach to life apparently based on the teachings of Dr. Rudolf Steiner, that constituted a religion.[17] In granting the board's motion for judgment on partial findings, the court was satisfied that the schools did not violate the

---

12. *Stuart v. School Dist. No. 1 of Village of Kalamazoo*, 30 Mich. 69 (Mich. 1874).

13. *State ex rel. Harbach v. Mayor of City of Milwaukee*, 206 N.W. 210 (Wis.1925).

14. *School Comm. of the Town of Winslow v. Inhabitants of the Town of Winslow*, 404 A.2d 988 (Me.1979).

15. *Board of Educ. of the Town and Borough of Naugatuck v. Town and Borough of Naugatuck*, 843 A.2d 603 [186 Educ. L. Rep. 420] (Conn.2004).

16. *City of Manchester School Dist. v. City of Manchester*, 843 A.2d 966 [186 Educ. L. Rep. 449] (N.H.2004). *See also Forsberg v. Kearsarge Reg'l School Dist.*, 940 A.2d 251 [229 Educ. L. Rep. 684] (N.H.2007), *reh'g denied* (2008) (affirming that voters' method of adopting a budget complied with the state's home rule statute).

17. *PLANS v. Sacramento City Unified School Dist.*, 752 F. Supp.2d 1136 [265 Educ. L. Rep. 1077] (E.D. Cal. 2010). For the earliest reported litigation in this dispute, *see PLANS v. Sacramento City Unified School Dist.*, 319 F.3d 504 (9th Cir. 2003).

Establishment Clause because anthrosophy was not a comprehensive system of belief and worship, did not address deep and imponderable matters, and did not have formal and external signs associated with traditional religions.

DIMENSIONS OF BOARD AUTHORITY

Ministerial or Mandatory Authority

School boards must perform ministerial or mandatory functions. If boards fail to exercise their ministerial duties, they and their members may face liability. Ministerial duties allow for little or no choice concerning whether or how they are to be performed. Laws relating to mandatory board duties typically include such obligations as adopting bylaws and rules to discharge their duties, setting tax rates, hiring superintendents and other school personnel, purchasing sites on which to build schools, prescribing courses of instruction and textbooks, and enforcing compulsory education laws.[18]

Boards cannot delegate their authority to act in matters that legislatures specifically assigned to them such as hiring personnel. At the same time, "school boards are limited in their employment decisions in that such decisions must be reasonable, in the best interests of the students, and not arbitrary or capricious."[19] Still, since it is impractical, if not impossible, for boards to be involved actively in the process of hiring all new teachers, they must rely on their administrative staff to make recommendations about job applicants. As such, even if approval is a mere formality, boards must act on recommendations from school officials. Boards may delegate the performance of purely ministerial functions such as procuring and recording a deed to property that it purchased to one or more of its members.[20] In light of the emergence of school-based decision making as well as new working relationships between boards and building-level management councils on personnel, budgetary, and curricular matters,[21] it will be interesting to observe what changes transpire in relations between boards and their staffs.

Discretionary Authority

Discretionary powers afford school boards the authority to act on nonmandatory duties that arguably account for the larger part of their actions. Examples of discretionary power include the right to expand the size of a

---

18. *See, e.g.,* ARIZ. REV. STAT. ANN. §§ 15–341 *et seq.,* COLO. REV. STAT. ANN. §§ 22–32–101 *et seq.,* FLA. STAT. ANN. §§ 1001.42 *et seq.,* 105 ILL. COMP. STAT. ANN. 5/14–6.01, KY. REV. STAT. ANN. § 160.290, LA. REV. STAT. ANN. §§ 17.81.01 *et seq.,* MICH. COMP. LAWS ANN. §§ 380.1131 *et seq.,* MISS. CODE ANN. § 37–7–301, N.M. STAT. ANN. § 22–5–4, TEX. EDUC. CODE ANN. § 28–11 App., UTAH CODE ANN. § 53A–1a–501.6.

19. *Board of Educ. of County of Randolph v. Scott,* 617 S.E.2d 478, 484 [201 Educ. L. Rep. 365] (W.Va.2005).

20. *Looney v. Consolidated Indep. School Dist.,* 205 N.W. 328 (Iowa 1925).

21. For two extensive statutes of this type, *see* 105 ILL. COMP. STAT. ANN. 5/34–2.1 *et seq.,* KY. REV. STAT. ANN. § 160.345.

school's professional staff, whether to accept federal aid for school programs, whether to offer extracurricular activities, and/or whether to adopt curricular standards that are more stringent than state guidelines. As discussed earlier, as long as boards properly exercise their discretionary power by not acting arbitrarily or capriciously, the courts are reluctant to interfere with their decisions.

As litigation demonstrates, the fine line between mandatory and discretionary duties can be easily blurred. Put another way, boards ordinarily treat issues related to extracurricular activities as discretionary duties. Since it is difficult to imagine what schools would be like if schools failed to offer a variety of programs for students, extracurricular activities are essentially rendered mandatory board duties.

To the extent that it is impossible to foresee, or legislate on, all emerging issues in schools, the courts agree that along with their express powers, local boards may exercise their authority "by necessary implication"[22] in ways enabling them to perform their duties. Here it is important to note that while boards have implied powers related only to education, not general governmental concerns, they must be careful not to exceed their authority. In such a case, the Supreme Court of Pennsylvania found that a local board exceeded its implied power in providing funds to help combat juvenile delinquency since this was not part of a school's program.[23] Yet, almost thirty years later, a federal trial court held that the Pennsylvania legislature explicitly superseded this earlier judgment in upholding the legality of a condom distribution program in high schools.[24] More recently, the Supreme Court of South Dakota reiterated the general rule about the authority of boards to act when legislatures expressly grants them power that could necessarily have been implied by statute. Yet, the court affirmed that a local board exceeded its authority when it reimbursed two private citizens for the legal fees they incurred in their private legal action to overturn a decision of a school election recount board.[25] The court explained that the board was not authorized to reimburse individuals for private legal fees.

When in doubt, the courts, applying common law, are inclined to reject the existence of implied powers since boards have no inherent authority. Case law reveals that while courts typically do not deviate from this principle, they interpret implied powers broadly, seeming to have become even more open to this notion in recent years. As illustrated by a case from the Supreme Court of Arkansas, a board cannot enlarge its powers if doing so conflicts with state law. Where a state law provided for annual contracts

---

22. *D.O.F. v. Lewisburg Area School Dist. Bd. of School Directors*, 868 A.2d 28, 33 [196 Educ. L. Rep. 263] (Pa.Cmwlth.Ct.2004).

23. *Barth v. School Dist. of Philadelphia*, 143 A.2d 909 (Pa.1958).

24. *Parents United for Better Schools v. School Dist. of Philadelphia Bd. of Educ.*, 978 F.Supp. 197 [122 Educ. L. Rep. 155] (E.D. Pa. 1997), *aff'd*, 148 F.3d 260 [127 Educ. L. Rep. 670] (3d Cir.1998).

25. *In re Writ of Certiorari as to Wrongful Payments of Attorney Fees made by Brookings School Dist. School Bd.*, 668 N.W.2d 538 [180 Educ. L. Rep. 301] (S.D.2003).

for teachers, the court decided that a local board could not offer an employment agreement to a teacher that exceeded the statutory limit.[26]

The judicial rule that local boards possess both express and implied powers is essentially one of expedience as a basis for sustaining apparently sound board actions. If courts apply statutes strictly, they can limit the implied powers of boards but may have the undesired effect of restricting educational experimentation. In these situations, empowering statutes can be changed to bring powers in question within the scope of the express authority of boards. By the same token, if legislatures disagree with judicial extensions of the implied powers, they can restrict or withdraw board authority by enacting new laws.

Clearly, boards must exercise their authority in accord with statutory and common law procedures. A key common law principle in this regard is that delegated powers may not be further delegated by the persons or bodies to whom they were originally delegated. Even if not required to do so, boards may seek advice from committees, employees, consultants, students, and the public but must then make final decisions since they have no power to diminish their authority even if they wish to do so. In such a dispute, an appellate court in Florida indicated that a hiring committee was merely advisory since the final decision whether to employ an applicant rested with the board and superintendent.[27]

Nondelegable Authority

It is often unclear whether the powers to execute matters are nondelegable or whether acts constitute improper delegations. The latter problem is similar to that of delegation of legislative power discussed in Chapter 3.[28] Legislatures can substantially clarify the rules of delegation through specific statutes on board powers while the judiciary can evaluate the boundaries of legislative delegation.

School boards must retain their nondelegable powers even where collective bargaining contracts are enforceable since boards can no more bargain away their powers than they can unilaterally impose their will.[29] Where collective bargaining statutes specifically cover matters in relation to other laws applicable to how boards function, the question of delegability may be answered implicitly, if not explicitly.

Questions of delegation of school board authority to administrators frequently arise when plaintiffs seek to have actions nullified. To this end, where a school board overturned a superintendent's approval of a teacher's transfer in light of its interpretation of its bargaining agreement, the Supreme Court of Wyoming ruled that if the provision placed final authority over transfers in the hands of the superintendent, it would have been

---

26. *Nethercutt v. Pulaski County Special School Dist.*, 475 S.W.2d 517 (Ark.1972).

27. *Knox v. District School Bd. of Brevard*, 821 So.2d 311 [167 Educ. L. Rep. 971] (Fla.Dist.Ct.App.2002).

28. *See Reece v. Board of Educ. of City of Chicago*, 767 N.E.2d 395 [166 Educ. L. Rep. 283] (Ill.App.Ct.2002).

29. *Dayton Classroom Teachers Ass'n v. Dayton Bd. of Educ.*, 323 N.E.2d 714 (Ohio 1975).

forced to excise that portion of the contract as invalid since the assignment of teachers was a discretionary, nondelegable board duty.[30] Similarly, the Supreme Court of Washington invalidated a board policy authorizing a superintendent to place a teacher on probation and to impose a monetary sanction.[31] The court pointed out that even if a policy is negotiated with a professional organization, the result would have been a nullity because only boards can set working conditions.

School boards can delegate ministerial functions to execute their decisions or to act on their behalf. Where a statute required boards to notify teachers in writing of their intent not to renew their employment contracts, the Supreme Court of South Dakota affirmed that a letter conveying this message that was signed only by a superintendent did not violate the law.[32] The court contended that only a strained construction would have suggested that the board lacked the ability to have the superintendent transmit the information. Further, where a school board had the long-standing practice of sending all summonses naming it as defendant to the receptionist of its law department, who accepted them on its behalf, the Supreme Court of Illinois affirmed that this was a lawful delegation of the authority to accept service.[33]

Giving substantial weight to the principle of nondelegability, the Court of Appeals of New York observed that when questions of arbitrability arose in a collective bargaining contract, absent a clear, unequivocal agreement to the contrary, a board did not intend to refer the dispute to that forum.[34] The same court also posited that a board could not bargain away its right to inspect teacher personnel files.[35]

Boards are generally empowered to adopt policies establishing procedures for exercising their nondelegable powers. These procedures may have the effect of curtailing the exercise of board powers for a while, but courts generally do not treat agreeing to procedural parameters as constituting illegal delegation. For example, the highest court in Massachusetts asserted that a school committee can bind itself for a limited period in order to observe specified criteria in disapproving personnel transfers that were approved by the superintendent.[36]

The question of illegal delegation of school board powers has been unsuccessfully raised in cases seeking to invalidate rules of state athletic or activities associations. The Supreme Court of South Dakota, in upholding a law that expressly permitted boards to join groups regulating interscholastic activities, emphasized that a board was not required to join.[37] If a board

---

30. *Diefenderfer v. Budd*, 563 P.2d 1355 (Wyo.1977).

31. *Noe v. Edmonds School Dist. No. 15 of Snohomish County*, 515 P.2d 977 (Wash.1973).

32. *Cutshaw v. Karim*, 256 N.W.2d 566 (S.D.1977).

33. *Sarkissian v. Chicago Bd. of Educ.*, 776 N.E.2d 195 [170 Educ. L. Rep. 327] (Ill.2002).

34. *Acting Superintendent of Schools of Liverpool Cent. School Dist. v. United Liverpool Faculty Ass'n*, 399 N.Y.S.2d 189 (N.Y.1977).

35. *Board of Educ., Great Neck Union Free School Dist. v. Areman*, 394 N.Y.S.2d 143 (N.Y.1977).

36. *Bradley v. School Comm. of Boston*, 364 N.E.2d 1229 (Mass.1977).

37. *Anderson v. South Dakota High School Activities Ass'n*, 247 N.W.2d 481 (S.D.1976).

joined the organization, the court maintained that it, in effect, ratified the association's rules and made them its own.

In addition, school boards may contractually limit selected powers for periods of time. Unless bound by contracts or the common law doctrine of promissory estoppel, boards can change policies as they see fit in the interests of carrying out their duties.[38]

RULES AND REGULATIONS IN GENERAL

Local boards have the implied power to make and enforce reasonable rules and regulations designed to ensure efficient school operations. Since the question of reasonableness is often a question of fact, and board rules pertain to a wide range of subjects, many cases involved discussions of whether boards acted properly. Insofar as most courts have adopted the rule of presumptive validity that boards acted reasonably, the burden of proof is ordinarily on parties contesting rules. The judicial presumption in favor of board rules is premised on the role of the courts as being designed to ensure that boards do not exercise their discretion arbitrarily or unreasonably rather than set educational policy.

A substantial part of the common law of education is derived from situations in which courts review the actions of local school officials. It is clear that most matters requiring the attention of these officials can only be dealt with locally. Statutes may thus specify that children are eligible to enter school at age six, but this could mean that on the day they reach six, at the beginning of the school year in which they reach six, or at various other points. The Supreme Court of Montana addressed the reasonableness of entrance cut-off dates where a state law directed officials to open schools to all children between the ages of six and twenty-one. Here a local board rule stipulated that only children who were the age of six prior to November 15 could be admitted to first grade at the beginning of the school year in September. The court upheld the board's ability to prevent a child who was born in late November because it exercised sound educational judgment in adopting a rule that did not conflict with the purpose of the law.[39]

As highlighted by a case from New Jersey, local rules cannot be contrary to statutes such as where the state's highest court struck down a retirement incentive because of the impact that it would have had on the state system.[40] Regardless, it is not always clear whether regulations conflict with legislation. For instance, provisions in board policies that are out of line with state-level prescriptions for teacher tenure are unenforceable since local boards cannot bind themselves to re-employ probationary teachers who received favorable evaluations[41] or to submit to arbitration

---

38. *Michie v. Board of Trustees of Carbon County School Dist. No. 1*, 847 P.2d 1006 [81 Educ. L. Rep. 581] (Wyo. 1993). [Case No. 22]

39. *State ex rel. Ronish v. School Dist. No. 1 of Fergus County*, 348 P.2d 797 (Mont.1960).

40. *Fair Lawn Educ. Ass'n v. Fair Lawn Bd. of Educ.*, 401 A.2d 681 (N.J.1979). [Case No. 23]

41. *Leonard v. Converse County School Dist. No. 2*, 788 P.2d 1119 [59 Educ. L. Rep. 534] (Wyo.1990).

over the nonrenewal of their contracts.[42] Further, the Supreme Court of Illinois declared that a board could not avoid or alter a statutory provision with regard to full-time service during a teacher's probationary period even if motivated by a shortage of funds.[43] In a second case from Illinois, an appellate court applied this principle even though a local board approved tenure status for some teachers six years before a case involving the issue arose.[44] Moreover, where a state-level system of conducting disciplinary hearings for tenured teachers included a pay scale for the members of the hearing panel, an appellate court was of the opinion that a local board lacked the authority to augment the per diem stipend of its appointee.[45]

School officials must administer board rules fairly. As such, the First Circuit determined that where a school committee allowed a group that opposed busing to achieve desegregation to use its internal distribution system to disseminate information about its perspective, it had to permit the same access to those who supported busing.[46] In like fashion, an appellate court in Illinois affirmed that where a board used a mailing list to communicate with parents about a referendum, officials had to make the list available to others who wished to express their views on the matter.[47] Also, where a board created a pressroom for members of the media to cover its meetings, a federal trial court in Florida remarked that it had to articulate the existence of a compelling interest before it could deny access to it to representatives of the teacher union's in-house publication.[48]

In a case reaching the opposite outcome, the Sixth Circuit affirmed a grant of summary judgment in favor of a school board in Kentucky in a dispute over whether a resident could gain access to its Web site and other information in an attempt to gather information while seeking to garner support for pending legislation that was designed to institute tax credits for students in non-public schools, regardless of whether they were religiously affiliated, and who were home schooled.[49] The court agreed that the taxpayer lacked the right to access the information on the Web site since the board's advocacy of defeating the pending bill was government speech that did not create a limited open forum requiring it to include opposing points of view.

SCHOOL BUILDING SITES, STANDARDS, AND ZONING

In carrying out major responsibilities, as long as boards comply with state law, they have implied power to select and purchase school sites.

---

42. *Mindemann v. Independent School Dist. No. 6 of Caddo County*, 771 P.2d 996 [53 Educ. L. Rep. 270] (Okla.1989).

43. *Johnson v. Board of Educ. of Decatur School Dist.*, 423 N.E.2d 903 (Ill.1981).

44. *Evans v. Benjamin School Dist. No. 25*, 480 N.E.2d 1380 [26 Educ. L. Rep. 753] (Ill.App.Ct.1985).

45. *Syquia v. Board of Educ. of Harpursville Cent. School Dist.*, 591 N.Y.S.2d 996 [80 Educ. L. Rep. 182] (1992).

46. *Bonner–Lyons v. School Comm. of City of Boston*, 480 F.2d 442 (1st Cir.1973).

47. *Wood v. School Dist. No. 65*, 309 N.E.2d 408 (Ill.App.Ct.1974).

48. *United Teachers of Dade v. Stierheim*, 213 F.Supp.2d 1368 [168 Educ. L. Rep. 347] (S.D.Fla.2002).

49. *Page v. Lexington County School Dist. No. 1*, 531 F.3d 275 [234 Educ. L. Rep. 538] (4th Cir.2008).

Under this principle, where procedures for erecting and paying for school buildings are spelled out, local boards lack the power to enter agreements to lease buildings with arrangements for future purchases.[50] At the same time, neither may boards discharge all attendance personnel where only these employees are statutorily authorized to enforce compulsory education requirements.[51]

A case from Connecticut illustrates how taxpayer challenges to board actions in selecting school sites are often litigated based on the charge that they abused their discretion.[52] The taxpayers did not claim that the board's action was tainted by fraud or corruption or that it was illegal in the sense that it was procedurally irregular. Rather, the taxpayers' only claim was that the board should have been enjoined because its action constituted a gross abuse of discretion. The court refused to consider the arguments that other sites were more desirable, specifying that it is not for the judiciary to say how many alternative methods of accomplishing a desired result must be investigated or considered before officials embark on a course of action.

Two disputes over zoning involved the Religious Land Use and Institutionalized Persons Act (RLUIPA). Under RLUIPA, "[n]o government shall impose or implement a land use regulation ... that imposes a substantial burden on the religious exercise of a person, including a religious assembly or institution, unless the government demonstrates that imposition of the burden ... (A) is in furtherance of a compelling governmental interest; and (B) is the least restrictive means of furthering that compelling governmental interest."[53] The Second Circuit ruled that in New York a village's denial of a religious school's request for a special use permit violated RLUIPA since it substantially burdened the school's religious exercise insofar as officials lacked alternatives to meet the institution's religious needs.[54] After an appellate court decided that a township board violated the rights of a religious school that sought to open a day care center, the Supreme Court of Michigan vacated its judgment. The high court declared that on remand the court had to consider whether the denial of the variance imposed a "substantial burden" on the school's religious exercise such that it "coerce[d] individuals into acting contrary to their religious beliefs," meaning that " '[a] mere inconvenience or irritation' " or "something that simply makes it more difficult in some respect to practice one's religion does not constitute a 'substantial burden.' "[55]

A case over whether a board complied with state law included a disagreement over whether officials could exchange school property for privately-owned land without conducting a public auction. The Supreme

---

50. *Haschke v. School Dist. of Humphrey in County of Platte*, 167 N.W.2d 79 (Neb.1969).

51. *Geduldig v. Board of Educ. of City of N.Y.*, 351 N.Y.S.2d 167 (N.Y.App.Div.1974).

52. *McAdam v. Sheldon*, 216 A.2d 193 (Conn.1965).

53. 42 U.S.C.A. §§ 2000cc(a)(1)(A), (B).

54. *Westchester Day School v. Village of Mamaroneck*, 504 F.3d 338 [226 Educ. L. Rep. 595] (2d Cir.2007).

55. *Shepherd Montessori Ctr. Milan v. Ann Arbor Charter Twp.*, 739 N.W.2d 664 [224 Educ. L. Rep. 926] (Mich.Ct.App.2007), *judgment vacated*, 746 N.W.2d 105, 106 (Mich.2008), citing *Greater Bible Way Temple of Jackson v. City of Jackson*, 733 N.W.2d 734 (Mich.2007).

Court of Wyoming affirmed that even though the state constitution prohibited the "sale" of school lands without a public auction, it did not forbid an "exchange" of such real property.[56] The court was of the opinion that where there was not a clear constitutional prohibition against the transaction, the legislature properly exercised its power to authorize exchanges of school lands for private lands of equal value.

The Supreme Court of Indiana rejected a claim that school board members were unduly influenced by recommendations from university consultants.[57] One or more of the board members who were originally opposed to the establishment of a single high school were apparently convinced otherwise after seeing the results of a survey advising such a course of action. In commenting favorably on its seeking the services of the university faculty, the court upheld the board's action.

In New Mexico, where a recall of school board members was constitutionally permitted for malfeasance or misfeasance in office or for violations of the oath of office, the state's highest court halted a recall election over a choice of the site for a new high school.[58] In recognizing that the site had a number of disadvantages that were listed in the petition, the court affirmed that the charge was without merit since malfeasance in connection with a recall vote had to evince an improper motive.

Administrative agencies that have fiscal relationships with school officials lack the ability to dispute locations of school buildings absent specific authority to do so. In such a case, the Supreme Court of Tennessee explained that the authority invested in non-school bodies for general fiscal approval of school expenditures did not extend to the location of buildings.[59]

In Pennsylvania, an appellate court considered whether city officials could withhold their approval for an addition to a school under a zoning code since they believed that the board was overbuilding.[60] In ascertaining that the board complied with all zoning and building requirements other than obtaining conditional-use approval, the court stressed that a municipality may not interfere with a board's power to locate a school facility in a district. While acknowledging that building styles and sizes, assignment patterns, and transportation arrangements are beyond a municipality's power to regulate, the court added that the board had to make a properly documented application for permits as required of all other developers. Further, the Supreme Court of Pennsylvania affirmed that a zoning board could limit the use of a district's athletic fields to school-related activities.[61] The court upheld the rejection since the zoning board already granted the

---

56. *Director of the Office of State Lands & Investments v. Merbanco*, 70 P.3d 241 [177 Educ. L. Rep. 558] (Wyo.2003).

57. *Cooper v. Huntington County Community School Corp.*, 232 N.E.2d 887 (Ind.1968). *See also Christian v. Geis*, 225 N.W.2d 868 (Neb.1975).

58. *CAPS v. Board Members*, 832 P.2d 790 [75 Educ. L. Rep. 1211] (N.M.1992).

59. *Mosier v. Thompson*, 393 S.W.2d 734 (Tenn.1965).

60. *School Dist. of Pittsburgh v. City of Pittsburgh*, 352 A.2d 223 (Pa.Cmwlth.Ct.1976).

61. *Hazleton Area School Dist. v. Zoning Hearing Bd.*, 778 A.2d 1205 [156 Educ. L. Rep. 1136] (Pa. 2001).

board an exception to construct the fields in an area zoned for residential use.[62]

The extent to which school boards must comply with local building and zoning codes varies from one jurisdiction to another. The Supreme Court of Washington addressed the crucial considerations in reviewing whether a board was bound by a municipal building code.[63] According to the court, the major point was whether the state preempted the field of regulating school construction since it developed detailed and comprehensive standards in this regard. The court found that the state had not deprived the municipality of jurisdiction over selected aspects of school construction even though it could have done so. The court rejected as illusory the claim that requiring a board to conform to the municipal building code would lead to permitting municipalities to interfere with the operation, management, and control of public schools. In like manner, the Supreme Court of Pennsylvania held that a board had to comply with a local zoning ordinance which required it to provide off-street parking when it erected a new building.[64] Conversely, the Supreme Court of Michigan examined whether a school construction plan should have been altered to take local ordinance requirements regarding parking, setback, storm water control, and environmental issues into account. The court affirmed that insofar as state law granted the superintendent of public instruction exclusive jurisdiction over school construction and site plans, boards were immunized from local zoning ordinances.[65] Previously, an appellate court in New Jersey believed that a board was not subject to municipal regulations covering such matters as height, setbacks, and parking.[66]

If a school board's selection of a site is subject to voter approval in a referendum, a question can arise as to how much information educational officials must voluntarily give to the public. Where board members, an architect, and school building contractor were indicted for allegedly failing to disclose conditions of the subsurface at a building site, an appellate court in New Jersey dismissed the charge of misconduct in office absent evidence that the defendants were accused of corruption.[67] The court was convinced that in making a policy decision to build the school after it considered the facts, the board had no legal duty to make all of the details available to the public.

---

62. *See also Mitchell v. Zoning Hearing Bd. of the Borough of Mount Penn*, 838 A.2d 819 [184 Educ. L. Rep. 420] (Pa.Cmwlth.Ct.2003), *reargument denied* (2004) (affirming that a trial court properly limited special exceptions about the accessory use of a gymnasium and auditorium for elementary school students and that the use of the facilities by all other children in the district was not authorized because it was not incidental to the proposed elementary school).

63. *Edmonds School Dist. No. 15 v. City of Mountlake Terrace*, 465 P.2d 177 (Wash.1970).

64. *School Dist. of Philadelphia v. Zoning Bd. of Adjustment*, 207 A.2d 864 (Pa.1965).

65. *Charter Twp. of Northville v. Northville Pub. Schools*, 666 N.W.2d 213 [178 Educ. L. Rep. 943] (Mich.2003).

66. *Murnick v. Board of Educ. of City of Asbury Park*, 561 A.2d 1193 [55 Educ. L. Rep. 189] (N.J.Super.Ct.App.Div.1989).

67. *State v. Lally*, 194 A.2d 252 (N.J.Super.Ct.Law Div.1963).

SCHOOL BOARD MEMBERSHIP

GENERALLY

Regardless of whether legislatures provide for school board members to be appointed[68] or elected,[69] they are state, not local, officers since education is a statewide responsibility.[70] Once in office, board members owe a fiduciary duty[71] to the public and remain there under the auspices of, and may have their powers extended or limited by, the discretion of state legislatures since, as noted, they possess only those powers invested in them by their legislatures.[72] Moreover, as exemplified by a case from the Supreme Court of Georgia, absent statutory term limits, there are no restrictions on how many times board members can be reelected.[73]

State legislatures set qualifications for school board membership. Reflective of the rule that legislatures cannot adopt unconstitutional criteria, the Supreme Court, in *Turner v. Fouche*,[74] rejected ownership of real property in a district as a qualification. In one instance, where state law did not specify a minimum age to become a board member, an appellate court in New Jersey stated that the statute implied that candidates had to be old enough to vote.[75]

Legislatures may not only set eligibility requirements[76] such as district residency,[77] prohibiting teachers from serving on boards in the districts where they work,[78] and/or imposing anti-nepotism requirements for members,[79] but can also change the methods of selecting members even if an incumbent is removed in the process.[80] In a dispute over residency, an

---

68. *Ham v. The Mayor, Aldermen and Commonalty of the City of N.Y.*, 70 N.Y. 459 (N.Y.1877) (holding that even where board members were appointed by a mayor, they were not municipal officials).

69. At least one federal court ruled that there is no fundamental right to have an elected school board. *Hawkins v. Johanns*, 88 F.Supp.2d 1027 [143 Educ. L. Rep. 169] (D.Neb.2000).

70. *State ex rel. Walsh v. Hine*, 21 A. 1024 (Conn. 1890); *Landis v. Ashworth*, 31 A. 1017 (N.J.1895).

71. *See Roslyn Union Free School Dist. v. Barkan*, 926 N.Y.S.2d 349 [269 Educ. L. Rep. 694] (N.Y.2011) (affirming that a six-year statute of limitations applied where a board unsuccessfully filed charges, including breach of fiduciary duty, against a former member).

72. *Michigan Educ. Ass'n v. Secretary of State*, 801 N.W.2d 35 [269 Educ. L. Rep. 842] (Mich. 2011). *See also Packer v. Board of Educ. of Town of Thomaston*, 717 A.2d 117 [129 Educ. L. Rep. 400] (Conn.1998).

73. *Dyal v. Pope*, 660 S.E.2d 725 [232 Educ. L. Rep. 483] (Ga.2008).

74. 396 U.S. 346, 90 S.Ct. 532, 24 L.Ed.2d 567 (1970).

75. *Vittoria v. West Orange Bd. of Educ.*, 300 A.2d 356 (N.J.Super.Ct.App.Div.1973).

76. *Unified School Dist. No. 501, Shawnee County, Kan. v. Baker*, 6 P.3d 848 [146 Educ. L. Rep. 902] (Kan.2000).

77. *Ben Hill County Bd. of Educ. v. Davis*, 510 S.E.2d 826 [132 Educ. L. Rep. 1017] (Ga.1999).

78. *State ex rel. Pryor ex rel. Jeffers v. Martin*, 735 So.2d 1156 [136 Educ. L. Rep. 1100] (Ala.1999); *Unified School Dist. No. 501, Shawnee County, Kan. v. Baker*, 6 P.3d 848 [146 Educ. L. Rep. 902] (Kan.2000).

79. *Commonwealth ex rel. Stumbo v. Crutchfield*, 157 S.W.3d 621 [196 Educ. L. Rep. 984] (Ky.2005); *Grizzle v. Kemp*, 634 F.3d 1314 [265 Educ. L. Rep. 895] (11th Cir. 2011).

80. *Lanza v. Wagner*, 229 N.Y.S.2d 380 (1962), *appeal dismissed*, 371 U.S. 74, 83 S.Ct. 177, 9 L.Ed.2d 163 (1962).

appellate court in Louisiana affirmed the rejection of a challenge to a candidate's qualification to run for a board based on the claim that he was not actually domiciled in the parish the preceding year. Reiterating the presumption against a change of domicile unless an individual makes a clear statement to do so, the court agreed that the candidate was qualified since he spent eighty percent of his time at his residence in the parish and otherwise met the criteria to establish a household.[81] In another case on membership, an appellate court in Connecticut, in a long-running suit, affirmed a provision in an amendment to a town charter that allowed its mayor to serve automatically on its school board.[82] The court noted that insofar as a state statute specifically allowed such an alteration, the mayor could serve on the board.

A key condition for membership is that if legislatures choose to have elected school boards, they cannot limit the rights of district residents to vote absent compelling reasons for doing so. In *Kramer v. Union Free School District No. 15*,[83] the Supreme Court struck down a statute from New York designed to limit voting to individuals who were otherwise eligible to cast ballots in state and federal elections based on whether they owned or leased taxable real property within a district or were parents or custodians of children enrolled in the local public schools.

REMOVAL OF BOARD MEMBERS

Absent inappropriate factors such as race, legislatures may set the conditions under which board members can be removed from office pursuant to recall elections[84] or where districts are experiencing financial and academic difficulties.[85] Of course, board members can be removed for dereliction of duty,[86] criminal misconduct even if it was committed in a state other than where an individual serves,[87] and/or conflict of interest.[88] For example, the Supreme Court of New Jersey affirmed a local board's removal of one of its members who, along with his wife, requested a special education due process hearing against it on behalf of his son due to a

---

81. *Knott v. Angelle*, 846 So.2d 825 [177 Educ. L. Rep. 741] (La.Ct.App.2003).

82. *Board of Educ. of Town and Borough of Naugatuck v. Town and Borough of Naugatuck*, 800 A.2d 517 [166 Educ. L. Rep. 659] (Conn.Ct.App.2002), *aff'd on other grounds*, 843 A.2d 603 [186 Educ. L. Rep. 420] (Conn.2004).

83. 395 U.S. 621, 89 S.Ct. 1886, 23 L.Ed.2d 583 (1969). *See also Hussey v. City of Portland*, 64 F.3d 1260 (9th Cir.1995), *cert. denied*, 516 U.S. 1112, 116 S.Ct. 911, 133 L.Ed.2d 843 (1996); *Mixon v. State of Ohio*, 193 F.3d 389 [139 Educ. L. Rep. 59] (6th Cir.1999).

84. *See, e.g.*, CAL. GOV'T CODE §§ 1770(b), (f); LA. REV. STAT. ANN. § 42:1411; MD. CODE ANN., EDUC. § 3–108; MICH. STAT. ANN. § 168.316; N.J. STAT. ANN. § 18A:12–3; N. M. STAT. ANN. § 22–7–13; N.Y. EDUC. LAW § 2559; OHIO REV. CODE ANN. § 3.07; OR. REV. STAT. ANN. § 332.030(1)(f).

85. *McKnight v. Hayden*, 65 F.Supp.2d 113 [139 Educ. L. Rep. 333] (E.D.N.Y.1999).

86. *In re Removal of Kuehnle*, 830 N.E.2d 1173 [200 Educ. L. Rep. 310] (Ohio Ct.App. 2005).

87. *Caldwell v. Owens*, 781 So.2d 895 [152 Educ. L. Rep. 891] (La.Ct.App.2001).

88. The Supreme Court rejected a challenge to a conflict of interest law, ruling that forbidding a legislator who had a conflict of interest about a proposed statute from advocating its passage or failure during legislative debate was a reasonable time, place, and manner limitation under the First Amendment. *Nevada Comm'n on Ethics v. Carrigan*, ___ U.S. ___, 131 S.Ct. 2343, 180 L.Ed.2d 150 (2011).

conflict of interest.[89] The court noted that not all potential disagreements require the removal of board members since the conflict of interest statute is silent about disputes where individuals have concerns about the education of their own children. Even so, the court held that the fact-sensitive nature of the case demanded the board member's removal because it called into question his ability to perform his duties. The court concluded that insofar as the public could have lacked confidence in the board member's ability to perform his duties in light of his having sought to advance his personal interest, he could be removed from office.

On a different aspect of dealing with the removal of board members, the Supreme Court of New Mexico agreed that where a recall petition sufficiently alleged that members violated the state's Open Meetings Act and was not based solely on political or personal motives, a recall vote could proceed.[90] On the other hand, when a board sought to remove its chairperson, the Supreme Court of Connecticut reversed in his favor in deciding both that the board's bylaws required that he be afforded reasonable notice as to whether his removal was for cause and that this included the chance to present a defense.[91]

As highlighted in a case from New York, even if it is not as a result of a recall election, a board member may be entitled to a name clearing hearing where allegations leading to removal may harm one's reputation. The Second Circuit ruled that a board member who was removed from office for allegedly sprinkling voodoo dust in front of the door of a school official was entitled to a pre-deprivation hearing before removal to consider whether the chancellor of schools violated her liberty interest under the Fourteenth Amendment.[92]

When recall elections occur, judicial review functions as it does in connection with regular elections,[93] including the requirement of providing a member who is subject to removal with notice.[94] In one case, the Supreme Court of Washington affirmed the rejection of a petition for a recall election of members of a local board based on the allegation that they failed to prevent a school closure, to conduct hearings on the proposed closure, and to prevent the sale of school property. The court concluded that the charges were without merit since the board acted only after taking a proper vote and the sale was following through on an existing contract.[95]

---

89.   *Board of Educ. of the City of Sea Isle v. Kennedy*, 951 A.2d 987 [234 Educ. L. Rep. 188] (N.J.2008). [Case No. 24]

90.   *Doña Ana County Clerk v. Martinez*, 124 P.3d 210 [204 Educ. L. Rep. 380] (N.M.2005).

91.   *LaPointe v. Board of Educ. of the Town of Winchester*, 878 A.2d 1154 [200 Educ. L. Rep. 790] (Conn.2005).

92.   *Velez v. Levy*, 401 F.3d 75 [196 Educ. L. Rep. 76] (2d Cir.2005).

93.   *Johnson v. Maehling*, 597 P.2d 1 (Ariz.1979).

94.   *State ex rel. Ragozine v. Shaker*, 772 N.E.2d 1192 [167 Educ. L. Rep. 909] (Ohio 2002).

95.   *In re Recall Charges Against Seattle School Dist. No. 1 Directors*, 173 P.3d 265 [228 Educ. L. Rep. 482] (Wash.2007).

SCHOOL BOARD PROCEDURES

IN GENERAL

Insofar as local school boards are legal entities only as a whole, their members lack individual authority to act independently on behalf of their districts.[96] In order for board actions to be binding, they must occur in legally convened meetings.[97] If board members individually sign documents, their doing so is invalid if boards repudiate their actions when they meet.[98]

Where a collective bargaining agreement provided that if a school committee and its teachers' association would abide by an arbitrator's award, they were to use that method of dispute resolution to overcome their differences. When a committee refused to accede to an arbitrator's award on the basis that its chair lacked the authority to bind it, the Supreme Judicial Court of Massachusetts agreed.[99] The court reasoned that neither the bargaining agreement nor the application that the committee chair signed agreeing to arbitration committed it to such a course of action since this could only have been done by a majority vote of the whole committee.

Absent statutes to the contrary, school boards can develop and adopt procedural rules for their meetings.[100] If neither boards nor legislatures establish guidelines, the rules of parliamentary procedure, which flow from general principles of common law, govern board meetings.[101] As illustrated by an early case from Kentucky, legislatures can require boards to adopt rules and bylaws. The court affirmed that insofar as this kind of law clothes board rules with the effect and force of the statutory provisions authorizing them, actions to the contrary are void.[102]

The Court of Appeals of New York addressed whether a school board could reconsider its dismissal of a probationary secretary since the resolution calling for it to do so lacked the needed majority vote when it was initially addressed even though it was reintroduced and adopted at the next meeting. The court rejected the secretary's argument that the initial vote rendered the matter *res judicata*, explaining that *res judicata* applies to judicial, not administrative, actions.[103]

---

96. *Bender v. Williamsport Area School Dist.*, 475 U.S. 534, 106 S.Ct. 1326, 89 L.Ed.2d 501 [30 Educ. L. Rep. 1024] (1986).

97. For an example of a statute codifying the power, or lack thereof, of individual board members, *see* 105 ILL. COMP. STAT. 5/10–16.5 "Oath of Office: . . . I shall recognize that a board member has no legal authority as an individual and that decisions can be made only by a majority vote at a public board meeting; . . . ."

98. *State ex rel. Steinbeck v. Treasurer of Liberty Twp.*, 22 Ohio St. 144 (Ohio 1871).

99. *Sheahan v. School Comm. of Worcester*, 270 N.E.2d 912 (Mass.1971).

100. *Ex parte Etowah County Bd. of Educ.*, 584 So.2d 528 [69 Educ. L. Rep. 981] (Ala.1991); *Iversen v. Wall Bd. of Educ.*, 522 N.W.2d 188 [94 Educ. L. Rep. 499] (S.D.1994).

101. *McCormick v. Board of Educ.*, 274 P.2d 299 (N.M.1954).

102. *Montenegro–Riehm Music Co. v. Board of Educ.*, 145 S.W. 740 (Ky.1912).

103. *Venes v. Community School Bd. of Dist. 26*, 402 N.Y.S.2d 807 (N.Y.1978).

Notice of Meetings

As noted, school boards may take official action only at legal meetings. In order for board meetings to be legal, common law requires that all of their members must be given notice unless sessions are regular ones whose dates were set by law.[104] In the case of regular meetings, members and officials are charged with notice of the dates on which they are to take place.

The purpose of the notice requirement for special meetings is to ensure that all board members have the opportunity to attend. If board meetings could be conducted by parts of boards without notice to their remaining members, the public might be deprived of part of its representation. Of course, the presence of all members is not essential to the legality of meetings since only a quorum is required. In this way, notice is designed to afford, as far as possible, each member the opportunity to attend. The public is also ordinarily entitled to notice that a special board meeting is to take place.[105] If notice to the public lacks specificity, as demonstrated by a judgment of the Supreme Court of Wisconsin, a meeting can be declared void.[106] The court decided that the notice the board provided failed to describe its planned subject matter, relating to a new master contract for employees, was inadequate.

Courts interpret notice requirements strictly. Not only does the public have the right to have all board members made aware of meetings, but individual members have a right to be notified.[107] Where statutes impose requirements for special meetings, which are typically different from those for regular meetings, they must be followed.[108] In such a case, the Supreme Court of New Hampshire affirmed that if special meetings are called to raise or appropriate funds, at least one-half of eligible voters must cast ballots.[109]

Absent statutory requirements for notice of special meetings, the general rule is that boards lack authority to act if any members are not present unless all have had reasonable notice and an opportunity to attend. A reasonable time before such notice must be given means that members must have sufficient time to prepare and know of the times and places of meetings.[110]

An older case from Iowa highlights the types of circumstances that may render it unnecessary to give notice to all board members. Where a dispute arose over the hiring of a superintendent at a contested meeting, and board membership changed, members sought to annul his contract.

---

104. *Twitchell v. Bowman*, 440 P.2d 513 (Wyo.1968).

105. *Rampello v. East Irondequoit Cent. School Dist.*, 653 N.Y.S.2d 469 (N.Y.App.Div. 1997).

106. *Buswell v. Tomah Area School Dist.*, 732 N.W.2d 804 [220 Educ. L. Rep. 859] (Wis.2007).

107. *Elsemore v. Inhabitants of Town of Hancock*, 18 A.2d 692 (Me.1941).

108. *Katterhenrich v. Federal Hocking Local School Dist. Bd. of Educ.*, 700 N.E.2d 626 [129 Educ. L. Rep. 776] (Ohio Ct.App.1997), *appeal not allowed*, 684 N.E.2d 707 (Ohio 1997).

109. *Bedford Chapter–Citizens for a Sound Economy v. School Admin. Unit No. 25–Bedford School Dist.*, 867 A.2d 414 [195 Educ. L. Rep. 913] (N.H.2004), *reh'g denied* (2005).

110. *Green v. Jones*, 108 S.E.2d 1 (W.Va.1959).

The board members argued that the superintendent was hired at an illegal meeting since one member did not receive notice. Evidence revealed that the absent member was in California on the day of the meeting and had been there for months. The court affirmed that insofar as the member would have been unable to attend even if he had notice, the meeting at which the superintendent was hired was legal.[111]

If, despite the lack of notice, all board members attend and participate in meetings, actions cannot be invalidated for lack of notice.[112] This applies the common sense rule that if all members are present, the purpose of the notice requirement is met. Even if all board members are present at special meetings that convened without proper notice, should members refuse to act, any actions will be of no effect.[113]

Local board members cannot, by private agreement, waive the right to receive notice. To this end, even if a three-member board agrees that two of its members can act to bind the third in his or her absence, even with providing prior notice, any action at such a meeting is invalid.[114] When regular meetings are postponed, common law only requires notice be given to those who were absent from the meetings at which the new date was set.[115] If meetings continue on other days, it is unnecessary to send notice of their continuance to members who were absent.[116]

Voting

In order for board meetings to be legal, a quorum is necessary.[117] Under common law, a quorum is a simple majority.[118] For a board action to be legal, absent a statute specifying otherwise, a majority vote of a quorum is required.[119] Legislatures may specify different numerical votes to transact specific items of business.[120]

School board members can generally vote in any manner they wish such as raising their hands, secret ballots, or voice votes, subject only to the general rule that they cannot operate arbitrarily or fraudulently. Boards may even adopt one form of voting on some topics and another on others at the same meeting. For instance, since nothing in common law prohibits

---

111. *Consolidated School Dist. of Glidden v. Griffin*, 206 N.W. 86 (Iowa 1925).

112. *Hanna v. Wright*, 89 N.W. 1108 (Iowa 1902).

113. *Johnson v. Dye*, 127 S.W. 413 (Mo.Ct.App.1910). *See also Knickerbocker v. Redlands High School Dist.*, 122 P.2d 289 (Cal.Ct.App.1942).

114. *School Dist. No. 22 v. Castell*, 150 S.W. 407 (Ark.1912).

115. *Keyes v. Class "B" School Dist. No. 421 of Valley County*, 261 P.2d 811 (Idaho 1953).

116. *Barnhart Indep. School Dist. v. Mertzon Indep. School Dist.*, 464 S.W.2d 197 (Tex.Civ. App.1971).

117. *Konovalchik v. School Comm. of Salem*, 226 N.E.2d 222 (Mass.1967).

118. *East Poinsett County School Dist. No. 14 v. Massey*, 876 S.W.2d 573 [91 Educ. L. Rep. 723] (Ark.1994).

119. *State ex rel. Mason v. Mayor and Aldermen of the City of Paterson*, 35 N.J.L. 190 (N.J.1871); *F.T.C. v. Flotill Products*, 389 U.S. 179, 88 S.Ct. 401, 19 L.Ed.2d 398 (1967).

120. *Board of School Trustees of South Vermillion School Corp. v. Benetti*, 492 N.E.2d 1098 [32 Educ. L. Rep. 242] (Ind.Ct.App.1986).

boards from doing so, they can vote by secret ballot on some questions and by voice vote on others. Some states dictate that specified board actions can only take place by roll-call votes.[121] Since this requirement is usually treated as mandatory, actions taken by any other form of voting are not legally binding.[122] Where state law directed boards to act only by roll-call votes, an appellate court in Colorado invalidated a principal's reassignment since the board failed to vote in this manner.[123] Conversely, a year earlier, the Supreme Court of Pennsylvania decided that insofar as the statutory requirement of a recorded roll-call vote for teacher appointments was not mandatory, a board's failure to comply did not automatically invalidate the contracts at issue since doing so would have been unconscionable.[124]

A case from the Supreme Court of Arkansas is consistent with the rule that even if an illegal voting procedure is well-intentioned and of long standing, it cannot be validated. At issue was a superintendent's practice of getting the approval of three board members over the employment and dismissal of teachers. Pursuant to this arrangement, the whole board did not consider these actions. The court found that insofar as the board's dismissal of a teacher was a nullity under the circumstances, it had to pay her salary until the end of the contract period.[125]

Questions arise about the legal effects of members' refraining from voting on issues that are properly before boards since those who are part of quorums are obligated to vote. Members who thus refrain from voting are regarded as acquiescing in board actions.[126] Since abstentions are not counted in evaluating whether majorities voted for motions, if seven members are present, with three voting in favor, two voting against, and two not voting, resolutions are considered passed absent statutory requirements of affirmative votes of majorities of all present or of majorities of entire boards.[127]

Voting rules for boards are firmly established at common law. Even so, disputes continue to arise over the application of voting rules. A case from Missouri involved the legality of a meeting about an election that two members of a three-person board attended. The third member declined to attend since he opposed calling the election. When the board president, who favored calling the election, presented the petition to the member who was present, and the latter refused to vote, the president cast his vote in favor of the proposition and called the election. In upholding the vote, an appellate court indicated that insofar as only one member of the board actually voted, this did not render the election invalid because when a

121. *See, e.g.,* ALASKA STAT. § 14.20.180 (dismissal or non-retention of teachers); IOWA CODE ANN. § 279.13 (automatic continuation of teacher contracts).

122. *Ready v. Board of Educ.,* 17 N.E.2d 635 (Ill.App.Ct.1938).

123. *Robb v. School Dist. No. RE 50(J),* 475 P.2d 30 (Colo.Ct.App.1970).

124. *Mullen v. Board of School Directors of DuBois Area School Dist.,* 259 A.2d 877 (Pa.1969).

125. *Farris v. Stone County School Dist. No. 1,* 450 S.W.2d 279 (Ark.1970).

126. *Payne v. Petrie,* 419 S.W.2d 761 (Ky.1967).

127. *Bunsen v. County Bd. of School Trustees,* 198 N.E.2d 735 (Ill.App.Ct.1964).

member sits silently by during a call for a vote, such a person is regarded as acquiescing in, rather than opposing, the measure.[128]

If members who do not wish to vote on measures actually withdraw from meetings, thereby resulting in the lack of quorums, boards cannot act under normal circumstances as long as the withdrawals are genuine.[129] In such a case, where three trustees stepped away from the part of the room where the rest of the board was in order to take places among the observers, the Supreme Court of Indiana affirmed that they could not change from trustees to mere spectators when they had an opportunity to vote with the others.[130] In agreeing that the trustees could not use such a procedural maneuver to thwart a vote, the court found that the action of the three voting members was valid, in effect, by a vote of three-to-none with three abstentions.

In another case involving a three-person board, one member proposed an action that the second opposed and the third supported before becoming incapacitated. The Supreme Court of Minnesota affirmed that insofar as the third member did not fulfill his obligation to vote, the general rule that main motions are voted on in the order in which they are made applied.[131] The first motion, in effect, passed by a vote of one-to-zero with two abstentions. However, some states require an affirmative vote of a fixed percent of all members or of all of those present on specified matters. In these situations, a blank ballot or a refusal to vote is not considered an acquiescence to the will of the majority.[132]

Local school boards cannot change the common law on basic procedures for voting without legislative permission. If boards adopt formal rules to this effect, they are generally invalid since their customary procedures are irrelevant because local bodies cannot make rules in derogation of the law over counting ballots and determining majorities.[133] By way of illustration, the Supreme Court of Wisconsin declared that a local board lacked the authority to change the common law rule concerning a quorum even though a statute authorized it to establish its own procedural rules.[134] The court added that where the legislature conferred a power on a board that it could exercise without the legislature's providing the number of members necessary to act, the common law rule prevailed and a majority of a board quorum may act lawfully. While recognizing that the legislature could either have changed the rule or empowered a local board to modify its own rules, the court wrote that, absent a controlling provision, the common law principle that a majority of a whole body is necessary to constitute a quorum applied.

---

128. *Mullins v. Eveland*, 234 S.W.2d 639 (Mo.Ct.App.1950).

129. *Levisa Oil Corp. v. Quigley*, 234 S.E.2d 257 (Va.1977).

130. *State ex rel. Walden v. Vanosdal*, 31 N.E. 79 (Ind.1892).

131. *Edwards v. Mettler*, 129 N.W.2d 805 (Minn.1964).

132. *Forbis v. Fremont County School Dist. No. 38*, 842 P.2d 1063 [79 Educ. L. Rep. 665] (Wyo.1992).

133. *Murdoch v. Strange*, 57 A. 628 (Md.1904).

134. *Endeavor–Oxford Union Free High School Dist. v. Walters*, 72 N.W.2d 535 (Wis.1955).

An appellate court in New Jersey rejected a board's claim that it was bound by a bylaw specifying a two-thirds vote of its full membership to close and sell a school building since state law only required a roll-call majority of full membership.[135] The court forbade the sale because another bylaw required two public meetings for adoption of such a matter.

Occasionally, it turns out that after school boards acted, one of their members was ineligible to serve. During challenges to the elections of members or to individuals' continuing eligibility to serve, boards cannot suspend operations pending judicial resolution. Under these circumstances, questions arise as to the validity of board actions. Board members whose eligibility is subsequently rejected are considered "de facto members" with regard to board actions during the pendency of ultimately successful challenges. A case from Kentucky illustrates a situation where a board appointed a superintendent to a new term that was to begin seven months later, when his current contract expired, to the post of board secretary. Since a vote of a de facto member was necessary to approve the second action, an appellate court reiterated the general rule that a contract made by a board pending ouster proceedings against a member would normally not be retroactively invalidated if it depended on the vote of a member who was ultimately removed.[136] Relying on the fact that there was no necessity to act on the contract renewal or appointment as board secretary so far in advance of the expiration of the two contracts, the court reached the opposite result, observing that the vote of the de facto member could not be counted.

Public Nature of Meetings

Courts uniformly uphold statutes requiring school board meetings to be open to the public.[137] Open meeting laws typically direct boards to give reasonable advanced public notice of the time and place of their sessions in part so that the public may attend and speak.[138]

Once participants are present, officials cannot unreasonably limit their rights to speak. For example, the Supreme Court of New Jersey affirmed that a board president violated the free speech rights of a father when he cut off the latter's critical comments about an athletic coach only thirty seconds after the parent began to voice his concerns.[139] Yet, a year earlier the Sixth Circuit upheld a board policy in Tennessee that refused to permit parents of high school football players to make repeat appearances at its next meeting.[140] The court affirmed that insofar as the policy was content-

---

135. *Matawan Reg'l Teachers Ass'n v. Matawan–Aberdeen Reg'l School Dist. Bd. of Educ.*, 538 A.2d 1331 [45 Educ. L. Rep. 1123] (N.J.Super.Ct.App.Div.1988). [Case No. 25]

136. *Board of Educ. of McCreary County v. Nevels*, 551 S.W.2d 15 (Ky.Ct.App.1977).

137. *See, e.g., Kavanaugh v. West Sonoma County Union High School Dist.*, 129 Cal. Rptr.2d 811 [173 Educ. L. Rep. 171] (Cal.2003); *McComas v. Board of Educ. of Fayette County*, 475 S.E.2d 280 (W.Va.1996).

138. *Rauert v. School Dist. 1–R of Hall County*, 555 N.W.2d 763 [114 Educ. L. Rep. 628] (Neb.1996).

139. *Besler v. Board of Educ. of West Windsor–Plainsboro Reg'l School Dist.*, 993 A.2d 805 [256 Educ. L. Rep. 826] (N.J. 2010).

140. *Lowery v. Jefferson County Bd. of Educ.*, 586 F.3d 427 [250 Educ. L. Rep. 542] (6th Cir. 2009).

neutral and left parents alternative means to voice their complaints, it passed constitutional muster.

Of course, if a school board conducts an open meeting, it cannot selectively exclude participants. In such a case, an appellate court in New York affirmed that a board could not exclude teachers, as members of the public, from the open part of the meeting at which it voted to terminate their contracts.[141]

Whether boards have complied with state open meeting laws is not always easy to evaluate since there are two legal issues to consider: that the public is permitted to be present and that records of meetings are then made available. This reflects the position that the term "public" is relative, rather than absolute, in describing board meetings. A good example of this principle occurred in California where a board met briefly in open session, adjourned for about an hour, reconvened in executive session, and met again in open session to terminate the contracts of teachers who challenged the session on the basis that it did not meet the statutory requirement of being public. An appellate court affirmed that the meeting was legal even though the board met in an executive session that excluded the public.[142] The court asserted that the board could convene in executive session to discuss matters affecting teachers' contracts as long as it took its final action in an open session.

Another case involving an executive session arose when a former school administrative assistant sued a school board's attorney who acted as its secretary *pro tem* during an executive session in connection with disagreements that she had with officials over the operations of the district's special education programs. The Supreme Court of New Jersey ruled that although the attorney was not entitled to protection under the state statute providing for indemnification to any person holding any office, position, or employment under a board's jurisdiction, he was entitled to coverage to the extent he was sued in his capacity as the board's secretary *pro tem*.[143]

If a school board violates an open meetings law, it may have the opportunity to correct its mistake. In such a case, the Supreme Court affirmed that where a board met in an emergency meeting to accept the resignation of the district superintendent but voted to ratify its action in an open session as part of its next regularly scheduled meeting, it had rectified its error.[144]

Entire school board meetings need not be open to the public. Only those parts of meetings at which boards take final actions must be open.[145] In such a case, the Supreme Court of Minnesota affirmed that it is essential

---

141. *Goetschius v. Board of Educ. of Greenburgh Eleven Union Free School Dist.*, 664 N.Y.S.2d 811 [122 Educ. L. Rep. 764] (N.Y.App.Div.1997).

142. *Alva v. Sequoia Union High School Dist.*, 220 P.2d 788 (Cal.Ct.App.1950).

143. *Sahli v. Woodbine Bd. of Educ.*, 938 A.2d 923 [228 Educ. L. Rep. 781] (N.J.2008).

144. *Katz v. South Burlington School Dist.*, 970 A.2d 1226 [244 Educ. L. Rep. 673] (Vt. 2009).

145. *Jewell v. Board of Educ., Duquoin Community Unit Schools, Dist. No. 300*, 312 N.E.2d 659 (Ill.App.Ct.1974).

for board meetings to be conducted in public places located within the territorial confines of their districts.[146] The court invalidated a board meeting that convened in a private office at the county seat, twenty miles from the district. In like fashion, an appellate court in Florida pointed out that board members who attended a workshop at the state's school boards convention that met more than 100 miles from its headquarters in another county violated state law because it did not afford citizens a reasonable opportunity to attend.[147] Earlier, absent a specific statute, the Supreme Court of Utah concluded that "unless matters were of such a delicate nature or of the type where public policy dictates nondissemination, the meeting itself should be open to the public and press."[148]

Boards typically discuss personnel[149] and other sensitive matters such as litigation[150] in executive or closed sessions, reconvening to vote in public.[151] Even so, states typically limit the use of executive sessions since they are exceptions to the rule that government business should be conducted in public.[152] Accordingly, the Supreme Court of Louisiana forbade a closed board session where there was an advanced call, an agenda, a polling of members' views, and a recording of what occurred.[153] The Supreme Court of Colorado also barred closed gatherings of board members at which they talked about matters prior to voting on them without engaging in public discussions.[154] States can dispense with the obligation of boards to take minutes in executive sessions as long as they take final votes in public.[155]

The Supreme Judicial Court of Massachusetts considered a case where more than ninety individuals applied for a superintendency and a screening committee selected sixteen for interviews. The school committee reviewed

---

146. *Quast v. Knutson*, 150 N.W.2d 199 (Minn.1967).

147. *Rhea v. School Bd. of Alachua County*, 636 So.2d 1383 [91 Educ. L. Rep. 780] (Fla.Dist.Ct.App.1994).

148. *Conover v. Board of Educ. of Nebo School Dist.*, 267 P.2d 768, 771 (Utah 1954).

149. *See, e.g., Fairchild v. Liberty Indep. School Dist.*, 597 F.3d 747 [254 Educ. L. Rep. 503] (5th Cir. 2010); *Nuzzi v. St. George Community Consol. School Dist. No. 258*, 688 F.Supp.2d 815 [256 Educ. L. Rep. 268] (C.D. Ill. 2010).

150. *See, e.g., Soter v. Cowles Publishing Co.*, 174 P.3d 60 [228 Educ. L. Rep. 528] (Wash.2007) (affirming that a board did not have to release information about a student's death even though the parties reached a settlement without litigation). *But see Trib Total Media v. Highlands School Dist.*, 3 A.3d 695 [260 Educ. L. Rep. 283] (Pa. Cmwlth. Ct. 2010), *appeal denied*, 24 A.3d 865 (Pa. 2011) (forbidding a board from invoking the protection of a closed executive session to prevent reporters from attending a discussion about possible litigation over a tax assessment since it allowed representatives of a local shopping plaza to be present).

151. *Hanover School Dist. No. 28 v. Barbour*, 171 P.3d 223 [227 Educ. L. Rep. 274] (Colo.2007) (ruling that notice to a probationary teacher whose contract was not being renewed was insufficient since the board acted in a closed session).

152. *See, e.g.,* KY. REV. STAT. ANN. § 61.800, "Legislative Statement of Policy:" "The General Assembly finds and declares that the basic policy of KRS 61.805 to 61.850 is that the formation of public policy is public business and shall not be conducted in secret and the exceptions provided for by KRS 61.810 or otherwise provided for by law shall be strictly construed."

153. *Reeves v. Orleans Parish School Bd.*, 281 So.2d 719 (La.1973).

154. *Bagby v. School Dist. No. 1, Denver*, 528 P.2d 1299 (Colo.1974).

155. *Kyle v. Morton High School*, 144 F.3d 448 [126 Educ. L. Rep. 651] (7th Cir.1998).

candidates at a public meeting, not by name, but by assigned numbers, selecting five finalists. Although the school committee released the names of the finalists and interviewed each at a public meeting, it refused to disclose the names of other candidates. The court affirmed that the open meeting statute required the school committee to release the names of the sixteen finalists along with the minutes of the meeting where their credentials were discussed.[156] While conceding the possibility that disclosure might have invaded the privacy of candidates, the court decreed that whether doing so reduced the effectiveness of hiring procedures was a question best left for the legislature. Almost thirty years later, the Supreme Court of South Carolina reached the same outcome in affirming that a state statute required a board to disclose the names of all five candidates for a job as superintendent rather than only the two who were interviewed.[157]

A question arises as to discussions occurring at informal gatherings of school board members. The Eighth Circuit affirmed that an informal conversation between a superintendent and board members in Missouri over a construction contract did not violate the state's open meetings law since there was no quorum present, no formal vote was taken or recorded, and the meeting had not been planned to discuss the issue.[158] In like fashion, a federal trial court in Tennessee contended that a gathering at the superintendent's house before the start of a regular board meeting did not violate state law because even though he may have spoken with some members about public business, he did not discuss matters individually or in a group with all of them or even about the same topics.[159] Previously, a federal trial court in Illinois was of the opinion that while board members and other school officials were present at a political rally, their discussion of public policy issues unrelated to schools did not violate the state's open meetings law.[160] On the other hand, the Supreme Court of Appeals of West Virginia affirmed that a gathering at which four of five board members were present the day before they voted on school closings and consolidations violated state law.[161] The court determined that the gathering constituted a meeting because even though those present did not follow formalities and had no intent to violate the law, it gave the superintendent the advantage in persuasion and coalition building for proposals that passed with little discussion the following day.

At common law it is unnecessary to publish an agenda in advance when all board members have proper notice. Generally, matters that can be considered at regular meetings may be acted on at special sessions.[162] If boards issue agendas in advance, this does not waive their right to amend

156. *Attorney General v. School Comm. of Northampton*, 375 N.E.2d 1188 (Mass.1978).

157. *New York Times Co. v. Spartanburg County School Dist.*, 649 S.E.2d 28 [222 Educ. L. Rep. 876] (S.C.2007).

158. *Hanten v. School Dist. of Riverview Gardens*, 183 F.3d 799 [136 Educ. L. Rep. 761] (8th Cir.1999).

159. *Bundren v. Peters*, 732 F.Supp. 1486 [59 Educ. L. Rep. 733] (E.D.Tenn.1989).

160. *Nabhani v. Coglianese*, 552 F.Supp. 657 [8 Educ. L. Rep. 276] (N.D.Ill.1982).

161. *McComas v. Board of Educ. of Fayette County*, 475 S.E.2d 280 (W.Va.1996).

162. *Moore v. City Council of City of Perry*, 93 N.W. 510 (Iowa 1903).

them at meetings.[163] If state law requires boards to release agendas prior to meetings, they cannot transact any other business[164] even if members had not planned to add new issues.[165] Where a local board refused to allow a citizen to place an item on the agenda for its monthly meeting the Supreme Court of Georgia held that he was not entitled to a writ of mandamus compelling it to do so insofar as it acted pursuant to its discretionary authority.[166]

Once they enter executive sessions, boards lack the authority to act on matters that were not identified in open meetings with proper notice. In such a case, the Supreme Court of Kentucky voided a variety of a board's personnel actions.[167] The court interpreted the open meeting law as requiring the board to identify a specific subject of discussion for a closed session and to limit its discussions to that topic.

A dispute involving open meetings that overlapped with board committees arose in Florida where access to hiring interviews was at issue. Where there was a vacancy for a principal of a middle school, a superintendent appointed a committee of board employees to join her in interviewing and ranking candidates based on their performances in the interviews. A parent alleged that this committee was a governmental board that performed official acts of interviewing and recommending job candidates. An appellate court denied the parent's request for an injunction, positing that the committees served in fact-finding, advisory capacities and that the ultimate hiring decision was made by the district superintendent and board.[168]

Board Records

As with meetings, official board minutes and other records are open to public inspection under state open records or sunshine laws.[169] Still, not every board document is subject to open records laws since those generated pursuant to investigations that can result in litigation are generally exempt from disclosure.[170] A practical aspect of this issue arose over whether a board clerk's notes were "public writings" subject to disclosure. The Supreme Court of Utah ascertained that while the notes were not available

---

163. *Crifasi v. Governing Body of Oakland*, 383 A.2d 736 (N.J.Super.Ct.App.Div.1978); *Unified School Dist. No. 407 by Boatwright v. Fisk*, 660 P.2d 533 [10 Educ. L. Rep. 392] (Kan.1983).

164. *Santa Barbara School Dist. v. Superior Ct.*, 118 Cal.Rptr. 637 (Cal.1975).

165. *Barrett v. Lode*, 603 N.W.2d 766 [140 Educ. L. Rep. 763] (Iowa 1999).

166. *James v. Montgomery County Bd. of Educ.*, 661 S.E.2d 535 [232 Educ. L. Rep. 973] (Ga.2008).

167. *Floyd County Bd. of Educ. v. Ratliff*, 955 S.W.2d 921 [122 Educ. L. Rep. 873] (Ky.1997).

168. *Knox v. District School Bd. of Brevard*, 821 So.2d 311 [167 Educ. L. Rep. 971] (Fla.Dist.Ct.App.2002).

169. As noted by former Supreme Court Justice Louis Brandeis, "[s]unlight is said to be the best of disinfectants; electric light the most efficient policeman," *Other People's Money* 62 (National Home Library Foundation ed. 1933), cited in *Buckley v. Valeo*, 424 U.S. 1, 67, note 80, 96 S.Ct. 612, 658, 46 L.Ed.2d 659 (1976).

170. *Seifert v. School Dist. of Sheboygan Falls*, 740 N.W.2d 177 [226 Educ. L. Rep. 286] (Wis.Ct.App.2007).

for public inspection, the final transcribed minutes, awaiting only approval and placement in the board's records, were subject to public review.[171] In a different context, an appellate court in New Jersey affirmed that handwritten minutes that a board secretary took during an executive session were not subject to disclosure.[172] The court explained that insofar as the notes were essentially a memory aid for the secretary, and were of no value to anyone else, they were not public records subject to disclosure.[173]

If boards do not act in executive sessions, there is apparently no need for minutes.[174] If boards do act in executive sessions, the minutes of their regular meetings must record not only that they convened but must also include references to the subject matter and a record of their final actions or votes.[175] In Maine, a dispute arose over whether a school committee properly entered into an executive session to discuss budgets and budget proposals as well as whether the materials it generated were subject to disclosure. The state's highest court ruled that documents the officials prepared for use during the executive session and notes that individuals made during it were not subject to public examination under the state's Freedom of Access Act since the public was legitimately excluded from the meeting.[176]

Courts have upheld tape recording[177] and videotaping[178] of regular board meetings. In New York, an appellate court was of the view that permitting parents to videotape a meeting was both consistent with the legislative intent of the state's open meeting laws and that while boards may reasonably regulate use of cameras to ensure that they do not interfere with meetings, they may not directly prohibit their use.[179] Previously, an appellate court in Louisiana affirmed that a board could prevent one of its members from tape recording an executive session based on the confidential nature of the material that it was to discuss.[180]

---

171. *Conover v. Board of Educ. of Nebo School Dist.*, 267 P.2d 768 (Utah 1954).

172. *O'Shea v. West Milford Bd. of Educ.*, 918 A.2d 735 [217 Educ. L. Rep. 861] (N.J.Super.Ct.App.Div.2007).

173. *See also Education Law Ctr. v. New Jersey Dep't of Educ.*, 966 A.2d 1054 [242 Educ. L. Rep. 831] (N.J. 2009) (holding that records relating to a school finance suit were not subject to release because they included factual components that were entitled to deliberative-process protection under the Open Public Records Act).

174. *State ex rel. Zinngrabe v. School Dist. of Sevastopol*, 431 N.W.2d 734 [50 Educ. L. Rep. 181] (Wis.Ct.App.1988).

175. *Gersen v. Mills*, 737 N.Y.S.2d 137 [161 Educ. L. Rep. 930] (N.Y.App.Div.2002).

176. *Blethen Maine Newspapers v. Portland School Comm.*, 947 A.2d 479 [232 Educ. L. Rep. 886] (Me.2008).

177. *Belcher v. Mansi*, 569 F.Supp. 379 [13 Educ. L. Rep. 318] (D.R.I.1983); *Mitchell v. Board of Educ. of Garden City Union Free School Dist.*, 493 N.Y.S.2d 826 [27 Educ. L. Rep. 1201] (N.Y.App.Div.1985).

178. *Maurice River Twp. Bd. of Educ. v. Maurice River Twp. Teachers Ass'n*, 475 A.2d 59 [17 Educ. L. Rep. 537] (N.J.Super.Ct.App.Div.1984); *Hain v. Board of School Directors of Reading School Dist.*, 641 A.2d 661 [91 Educ. L. Rep. 234] (Pa.Cmwlth.Ct.1994).

179. *Csorny v. Shoreham–Wading River Cent. School Dist.*, 759 N.Y.S.2d 513 [177 Educ. L. Rep. 490] (N.Y.App.Div.2003).

180. *Dean v. Guste*, 414 So.2d 862 [5 Educ. L. Rep. 1300] (La.Ct.App.1982), *writ denied*, 414 So.2d 862 (La.App. 1982), *cert denied sub nom. Dean v. St. Bernard Parish School Bd.*, 459 U.S. 1070, 103 S.Ct. 489, 74 L.Ed.2d 632 (1982).

School officials often defend attempts to keep records from the public based on privacy concerns even though boards serve the public. The common law inquiry, augmented by widespread freedom of information statutes, is whether the desired materials would invade someone's privacy and, if so, whether the individual's privacy concern outweighs the public interest served by disclosure. Since presumptions favor disclosure, the courts seem to be in complete agreement that salary data must be disclosed.[181] For example, the highest court of Massachusetts believed that the public records statute required disclosure of absentee records of teachers when they only revealed the dates and generic classifications of their absences.[182]

A more recent case illustrates how the use of technology has impacted board records. The Supreme Court of Wisconsin, in a case of first impression, rejected an attempt by teachers to enjoin their school board from completing a request under the state's sunshine laws for the e-mails they sent over a six-week period. Reversing an earlier order to the contrary, the court held that insofar as the disputed personal e-mails were neither work-related nor concerned board activities, they were not subject to disclosure.[183] The court explained that simply writing, sending, and receiving messages on board-owned computers did not qualify them as records under the state's sunshine laws. In another case involving e-mail, the Supreme Judicial Court of Massachusetts ruled that electronic deliberations between members of a school committee were subject to disclosure.[184] The court explained that even though some of the e-mail messages between members of the school committee and its chair discussing the professional competence of the superintendent did not involve a quorum, they had to be disclosed because they had the effect of circumventing the requirements of the commonwealth's open meeting law.

As demonstrated by a case from the Supreme Court of Oregon, school boards cannot adopt policies if they conflict with state open records laws. Where a board promised confidentiality of names and addresses to teachers it employed during strikes, the court struck its action down because such a blanket policy thwarted the legislative intent to have records of public bodies open to the public unless there was an individualized reason not to do so.[185]

The adequacy of board records is another source of litigation as courts are unable to agree whether failure to keep records invalidates actions that should have been recorded. Of course, a great deal depends on the nature of the underlying actions. Courts recognize that it may be unreasonable to

181. *Mans v. Lebanon School Bd.*, 290 A.2d 866 (N.H.1972); *Hastings and Sons Pub. Co. v. City Treasurer of Lynn*, 375 N.E.2d 299 (Mass.1978).

182. *Brogan v. School Comm. of Westport*, 516 N.E.2d 159 [43 Educ. L. Rep. 362] (Mass.1987).

183. *Schill v. Wisconsin Rapids School Dist.*, 786 N.W.2d 177 [258 Educ. L. Rep. 735] (Wis. 2010).

184. *District Attorney for Northern Dist. v. School Comm. of Wayland*, 918 N.E.2d 796 [251 Educ. L. Rep. 898] (Mass. 2009).

185. *Guard Pub. Co. v. Lane County School Dist. No. 4J*, 791 P.2d 854 [60 Educ. L. Rep. 973] (Or.1990).

require all board actions to be recorded in official minutes books in order to be legal. The Supreme Court of Iowa thus affirmed that a law requiring an official record of board proceedings in connection with designating students whose tuition should be paid in another district was only directory.[186] The court upheld the board's vote absent a formal record because there was other evidence substantiating its action.

If records must be kept, courts do not always require them to provide all of the details. Yet, "minutes certainly should be prepared promptly and be made available to the public within a reasonable time."[187] The minimum requirement for records is to show that boards acted. In such a case, where there was enough information in board records to provide a full understanding of a bond sale, the Supreme Court of Montana refused to invalidate a transaction even though it agreed that more details would have been desirable.[188]

The official records of school board meetings are prima facie evidence of their actions. While oral testimony cannot be used to enlarge or restrict information that is in records,[189] it may be able to fill in omissions or to clarify a record if it is not clear on its face.[190] As occasionally happens, when officials realize that records are incorrect, boards may amend them to convey events accurately.[191]

A novel case involving board records arose in Pennsylvania. The Third Circuit affirmed that the opinion of a school board member about a teacher's having improperly touched her grand-niece, coupled with her exaggerations about the conduct of others involved in the incident, was not protected by the Fourteenth Amendment right to privacy.[192] Even though the information was leaked to the press, the court agreed that the board member's claim, that the disclosure caused harm to her reputation, problems with her family, and the loss of both emotional peace of mind and income, lacked merit.

Use of Committees

Just as individual members lack authority to act for boards, so, too, committees have no power to act for whole boards. This aside, it is often necessary, and sometimes desirable, to have small groups complete fact-finding and preliminary work rather than have entire boards do so. When this happens, committees must report back to their boards so that they can

---

186. *School Dist. of Soldier Twp. v. Moeller,* 73 N.W.2d 43 (Iowa 1955).

187. *In re Removal of Kuehnle,* 830 N.E.2d 1173, 1194 [200 Educ. L. Rep. 310] (Ohio Ct.App.2005).

188. *Elliot v. School Dist. No. 64–JT,* 425 P.2d 826 (Mont.1967).

189. *Lewis v. Board of Educ. of Johnson County,* 348 S.W.2d 921 (Ky.1961); *Tuscaloosa City Bd. of Educ. v. Roberts,* 440 So.2d 1058 [14 Educ. L. Rep. 857] (Ala.1983); *Cross v. Commonwealth ex rel. Cowan,* 795 S.W.2d 65 [62 Educ. L. Rep. 1246] (Ky.Ct.App.1990).

190. *Spann v. Joint Boards of School Directors,* 113 A.2d 281 (Pa.1955); *Knutsen v. Frushour,* 436 P.2d 521 (Idaho 1968).

191. *State v. Board of Educ. of Bath–Richfield Local School Dist.,* 218 N.E.2d 616 (Ohio 1966).

192. *Malleus v. George,* 641 F.3d 560 [268 Educ. L. Rep. 71] (3d Cir. 2011).

act. Since they cannot act independently, it is not surprising that an appellate court in New York affirmed that board subcommittees and ad hoc committees were not subject to the state's open meetings law.[193] Of course, boards cannot permit committees to take final actions on matters that they must consider as a whole. Thus, committees cannot be charged with such duties as selecting building sites and contracting to have schools built[194] or rescinding contracts with consultants.[195]

Allegations have surfaced that school boards perfunctorily adopted committee recommendations without proper deliberations, a charge that is difficult to prove. The Supreme Court of New Jersey rejected a charge that board members failed to engage in due deliberation in a dispute over a contract for desks.[196] The court held that while the board had to act as a whole, the fact that a committee conducted negotiations and reported back to it was sufficient to render the contract valid.

Whether entire boards must participate in all phases of activities is unclear since the failure of all members to be present throughout sessions can lead to challenges. Generally, absent statutes to the contrary, quorums may act for whole boards. However, where state law required a "full board" to be present at hearings for teachers who are not tenured, the Supreme Court of Rhode Island ruled that all members had to attend.[197] Further, an appellate court in Pennsylvania upheld the commonwealth board of education's use of a panel to hear a case on school district reorganization where the whole board reviewed the record before acting.[198] Four years earlier, the Supreme Court of Minnesota reasoned that a board had implied power to employ a hearing examiner to conduct hearings with no board members present.[199] The court observed that the examiner heard the evidence, summarized the facts, and offered conclusions but did not render a judgment on the merits, did not recommend how the matter should have been resolved, and took no part in the board's decision-making process.

SCHOOL ELECTIONS

GENERALLY

One way in which the public can participate in school operations is through elections. Since elections may be on whatever matters legislatures

---

193. *Jae v. Board of Educ. of Pelham Union Free School Dist.*, 802 N.Y.S.2d 228 [202 Educ. L. Rep. 766] (N.Y.App.Div.2005), *leave to appeal denied*, 816 N.Y.S.2d 749 (N.Y.2006).

194. *Kinney v. Howard*, 110 N.W. 282 (Iowa 1907).

195. *School Dist. No. 1 of Silver Bow County v. Driscoll*, 568 P.2d 149 (Mont.1977).

196. *State v. Board of Educ.*, 51 A. 483 (N.J.1902).

197. *Jacob v. Board of Regents for Educ.*, 365 A.2d 430 (R.I.1976).

198. *Independent School Dist. Comprised of Western Portions of Hamlin and Sargeant Twps., McKean County v. Commonwealth, State Bd. of Educ.*, 417 A.2d 269 (Pa.Cmwlth.Ct. 1980).

199. *Whalen v. Minneapolis Special School Dist. No. 1*, 245 N.W.2d 440 (Minn.1976).

choose, the procedures by which they occur are subject only to restrictions of the Federal and state constitutions. In addition, elections for school board members may differ from those on bond issues or other matters while special elections may be subject to restrictions not placed on regular elections. If elections lack legislative authority or violate the material provisions of the law they are nullities.

It all but goes without saying that school board elections must be fair. In one case, an appellate court in Texas affirmed an order invalidating an election and calling for a new vote where there was sufficient evidence that irregularities materially affected the outcome.[200] The court agreed that the election should have been voided since current board members and school administrators allowed unauthorized persons to serve as election judges and clerks.

A case from Minnesota addressed when school board elections can take place. An appellate court affirmed that a board could schedule its elections in even-numbered rather than odd-numbered years since the legislation granted local officials the discretion to select when they can occur as long as they had transition plans in place.[201]

Petitions for Elections

Election procedures are usually set in motion when candidates file their petitions. Statutes usually require petitions to contain the signatures of specified numbers or percentages of electors in districts and must be presented to the designated officers or boards that are authorized to call elections. Whether the calling of elections is ministerial or discretionary depends on state law. Even where it is discretionary, courts may order elections to proceed if they think that officials abused their discretion.[202]

Officials who are designated to act on election petitions are responsible for evaluating both whether the signers are legal electors and whether their signatures are genuine since the mere recital in petitions that signers are legal electors is insufficient evidence of that fact.[203] In some states, officers or agencies that must act on petitions may rely on the affidavits of those who circulated them that signatures are genuine, that those who signed are electors, and that signatories did so before the filing deadline.[204]

State law may require individuals who sign petitions to provide their addresses so as to allow officials to establish their identities.[205] Absent a statutory requirement that signatures be compared, the failure to do so is

200. *Gonzalez v. Villarreal*, 251 S.W.3d 763 [232 Educ. L. Rep. 499] (Tex.Ct.App.2008), *review dismissed* (2008), *reh'g overruled* (2008), *reh'g of petition for review denied* (2008).

201. *Houck v. Eastern Carver County Schools*, 787 N.W.2d 227 [259 Educ. L. Rep. 220] (Minn.Ct.App.2010).

202. *Gibson v. Winterset Community School Dist.*, 138 N.W.2d 112 (Iowa 1965).

203. *People ex rel. Anderson v. Community Unit School Dist. No. 201*, 129 N.E.2d 28 (Ill.App.Ct.1955).

204. *Burns v. Kurtenbach*, 327 N.W.2d 636 [8 Educ. L. Rep. 434] (S.D.1982).

205. *Board of Educ. of Rich Twp. High School Dist. No. 227, Cook County v. Brown*, 724 N.E.2d 956 [144 Educ. L. Rep. 553] (Ill.App.Ct.1999), *appeal denied*, 731 N.E.2d 762 (Ill.2000), *cert. denied*, 531 U.S. 958, 121 S.Ct. 383, 148 L.Ed.2d 295 (2000).

no basis for striking names from petitions.[206] The primary saving grace protecting school boards from having elections invalidated due to inadequate petitions is that the validity of signatures may not be attacked for the first time after elections occurred. The Supreme Court of Nebraska applied this rule where a party sought to enjoin a board from asserting its control over territory.[207] An opponent challenged the board by claiming that where one person who signed the petition was not a qualified voter, if his name were struck from the petition it would not have had the requisite number of signatures. The court dismissed the claim without hearing evidence since the opponent questioned the validity of the petition collaterally insofar as he filed suit for another purpose, namely about the board's taking on new territory.

Opponents challenged a petition dealing with district consolidations, alleging that some individuals signed on Sunday, others were not signed in the presence of the circulator, and persons signed for others. The Supreme Court of Michigan refused to invalidate the election even in conceding the general rule that before an election takes place public officials must follow the exact provisions of the state law if a party files suit over their enforcement.[208] The court declared that if an election is contested after it is over, statutory requirements are to be treated as directory unless the law specifies that noncompliance is a fatal defect or renders the result doubtful.

Questions about the legality of one's signing for another occur most often with spouses. The question is typically whether the general rule of signature ratification or adoption applies on school petitions. The general rule is that a person who ratifies or adopts a signature placed there by another is bound by the same. The Supreme Court of Missouri applied this rule where evidence showed that a husband authorized his wife to sign his name on a petition.[209] The court observed that generally no particular mode or form of authorization is necessary to authorize one person to sign another's name to a legal document and that oral permission is sufficient unless a statute requires the authority to be in writing.

Assuming that petitions are signed validly, questions arise as to the right of signers to withdraw their names. Clearly, there must be a cutoff point beyond which signatures may not be withdrawn since petition procedures could not operate effectively. At common law, signers of petitions may always withdraw before they are presented to the agencies or officers designated by law to receive and act on the documents.

Courts agree that names may not be withdrawn from petitions after they are filed with the proper agencies or officers even if they had not been acted on.[210] For example, the Supreme Court of North Dakota refused to allow individuals to withdraw their names from a petition about re-opening a school after it was filed.[211] The court pointed out that once the petition

206. *Johnson v. Maehling*, 597 P.2d 1 (Ariz.1979).

207. *Cacek v. Munson*, 69 N.W.2d 692 (Neb.1955).

208. *Richey v. Board of Educ. of Monroe County*, 77 N.W.2d 361 (Mich.1956).

209. *State ex rel. Kugler v. Tillatson*, 312 S.W.2d 753 (Mo.1958).

210. *Zilske v. Albers*, 29 N.W.2d 189 (Iowa 1947).

211. *Judson PTO v. New Salem School Bd.*, 262 N.W.2d 502 (N.D.1978).

was accepted as sufficient, the school board was not empowered to permit withdrawals. According to the court, since there was no statutory provision for a hearing on such petitions, the filing was equivalent to the board's acting because the law required schools to be re-opened. Other courts permitted signers to withdraw their names at any time before boards acted on petitions. In such a case, the Supreme Court of Nebraska refused to restrict a citizen's ability to withdraw his name from a petition when the statutes forbade his doing so and when no consideration seemed to require such a restriction.[212] The court asserted that permitting individuals to withdraw from petitions before they were acted on was calculated to discourage hasty presentations of petitions without full disclosure of the merits of the underlying questions. Similarly, an appellate court in Illinois was satisfied that individual names can be withdrawn from petitions after action on them has begun, but before final disposition, and can lead to the termination of procedures if insufficient numbers of names remain on petitions.[213]

In the jurisdictions with provisions preventing the removal of signatures other than under unusual circumstances, such as having signed due to duress or misrepresentation, state law governs.[214] Even after petitions are accepted, names may be withdrawn in the face of evidence that signers were induced to do so by fraud, misrepresentation, or misapprehension. Usually, withdrawals under these circumstances may be made only by leave of the courts or other bodies with jurisdiction over the proceedings.[215]

Cases have also arisen on the flip side of the question, namely over adding names. In such a dispute, the Supreme Court of Nebraska remarked that the rules governing the withdrawal of names from petitions apply to their being added.[216] The court specified that even though the deadline for signing passed, names could be added before the petition was filed.

The Supreme Court of Ohio reviewed two cases about petitions. In the first, the court wrote that adding a name to a petition after a board of elections found that it was valid did not violate the statutory proscription against altering, correcting, or adding to petitions once they were filed.[217] The court decided that insofar as the challenge did not involve fraud, deception, or undue influence in the petitioning process, and the purpose of the statute was to prevent changes between the time when a petition was filed and addressed, there was no reason to render it invalid. The second case addressed whether noncompliance with a law prohibiting the signing of another's name on an election petition with the knowledge and permission of the circulator invalidated only the individual signature or an entire petition. The court rejected the latter approach, stating that absent evidence that the word ''knowingly'' in the statute meant more than its

---

212. *State ex rel. Larson v. Morrison*, 51 N.W.2d 626 (Neb.1952).

213. *Konald v. Board of Educ. of Community Unit School Dist. 220*, 448 N.E.2d 555 [10 Educ. L. Rep. 1150] (Ill.App.Ct.1983).

214. *State ex rel. Muter v. Mercer County Bd. of Educ.*, 175 N.E.2d 305 (Ohio Ct.App.1959).

215. *In re Mercersburg Indep. School Dist.*, 85 A. 467 (Pa.1912).

216. *Retzlaff v. Synovec*, 132 N.W.2d 314 (Neb.1965).

217. *State ex rel. Carson v. Jones*, 263 N.E.2d 567 (Ohio 1970).

ordinary meaning, it would enforce the common understanding of the word.[218]

Notice of Elections

Notice requirements for school elections vary widely. Among the common specifications are publication of notice for a set number of days or weeks prior to the dates of elections and posting notices in public places. At the very least, notice must inform voters about an election's purpose, its date, where and when they can vote, and when the polls open and close.

The adequacy of notice is often challenged because it contained omissions or errors. The proper wording of election notices is one of considerable nicety, especially with regard to bond elections. In bond elections, the terminology of notice should be detailed enough to enable voters to understand the nature of propositions while providing brief descriptions of the underlying projects[219] and their costs[220] along with being sufficiently broad to avoid unduly restricting boards in using the proceeds.

A case from Ohio illustrates the effect of an error in notice. State law required bond election notices to declare the amount of proposed issues, their purpose, the maximum term of the bonds, and the estimated additional tax rate, expressed in dollars and cents for each one hundred dollars of valuation and in mills for each dollar of valuation. Due to an error, the notice omitted the amount of the annual tax levy in mills, a portion of the issue's purpose, and the amount of the annual tax levy was stated as being 3.2 rather than .32, the proper rate. An appellate court rejected the claim that the errors rendered the result invalid absent evidence that the election was widely publicized in the district.[221] Acknowledging that newspaper articles described the needs of the schools, the amount of the bond issue, and its proposed uses, the court was satisfied that voters received notice through other media. In like fashion, the Supreme Court of Missouri rejected a claim of inadequacy in the face of a charge that three of five notices were not in public places because although they were on school property, they were inaccessible to the public.[222] The court rebuffed the allegation that those who entered the schools to read the notices would have been trespassers because there would not have been an unauthorized entry. The court also rejected the argument that having three notices set back from a street rendered them improper since it interpreted the law as not requiring a public place to be near a street.

In a dispute examining notice from a different perspective, the Supreme Court of Georgia reversed in favor of a school board member who challenged the validity of a referendum that purportedly was designed to

218. *State ex rel. Dennis v. Miller*, 274 N.E.2d 459 (Ohio 1971).

219. *Borough of Brentwood v. Department of Community Affairs*, 657 A.2d 1025 [100 Educ. L. Rep. 204] (Pa.Cmwlth.Ct.1995).

220. *Simonetti v. Commonwealth, Dep't of Community Affairs*, 651 A.2d 626 [96 Educ. L. Rep. 623] (Pa.Cmwlth.Ct.1994).

221. *State ex rel. Bd. of Educ. of the Plain Local School Dist. v. McGlynn*, 135 N.E.2d 632 (Ohio Ct.App.1955).

222. *Montgomery v. Reorganized School Dist. No. 1*, 339 S.W.2d 831 (Mo.1960).

provide an opportunity for then-current members to remain in office.[223] The court held that insofar as the referendum, which did not inform voters that their approval would have shortened the terms of some board members by two years, failed to comply with the law prohibiting the abolition of elective office or shortening or lengthening their terms without the approval of local voters, it was invalid.

As highlighted in a case from the Supreme Court of Utah, alleged misadvice to electors through notices can lead to litigation. Where a school board distributed a brochure explaining a bond election and its purpose, parts of it were printed in newspapers in conjunction with, but not as a part of, the statutory notice. After the election, due to cost underestimates, the board sought to use more money for one project and thus did not allocate the funds for all of the projects specified in the brochure. The court refused to enjoin the readjusted building program in declaring that the usual rule was that if a board publishes notice pursuant to a law that binds it, collateral statements or explanatory materials are not binding.[224] While refusing to base its order on the status of the brochure, the court upheld the board's reasonable power to re-allocate bond money following the election since it did not engage in deceit, fraud, or corruption.

Courts tend to interpret election laws as preserving voters' choices.[225] Mere irregularity of notice or failure to give notice for the full time prescribed by statute is generally not fatal to the validity of elections if voters knew that it was coming and an issue was generally known in a district, if a comparatively full vote was cast, and if the irregularity did not mislead voters to their disadvantages. Courts ordinarily treat notice requirements as directory unless laws clearly indicate a legislative intent that elections are to be rendered invalid if statutory requirements are not fulfilled or unless there is a gross irregularity.[226] An example of the latter occurred where the resolution calling for a bond election indicated that a set sum of money was to be voted on for school purposes. The Supreme Court of New Mexico affirmed that due to the lack of precision in the wording in the notice, it failed to advise the electorate of the actual purpose of the proposed bond issue.[227] While conceding that the notice did not have to include details of proposed uses of the funds, the court thought that it had to be less broad than the wording as it appeared.

Ballots

Assuming that elections are called legally, specified officials are charged with preparing ballots. The usual requirement of secret ballots ordinarily applies to school elections. When, by accident or design, elections

---

223. *Burton–Callaway v. Carroll County Bd. of Elections*, 619 S.E.2d 634 [202 Educ. L. Rep. 869] (Ga.2005).

224. *Ricker v. Board of Educ. of Millard County School Dist.*, 396 P.2d 416 (Utah 1964).

225. *Abts v. Board of Educ. of School Dist. Re–1 Valley in Logan County*, 622 P.2d 518 (Colo.1980).

226. *Eustace v. Speckhart*, 514 P.2d 65 (Or.Ct.App.1973); *Wright v. Board of Trustees of Tatum Indep. School Dist.*, 520 S.W.2d 787 (Tex.Civ.App.1975).

227. *Board of Educ. of City of Aztec v. Hartley*, 394 P.2d 985 (N.M.1964).

are conducted in ways that destroy the secrecy of ballots, they can usually be invalidated.[228]

The strong public interest in secret ballots and the right of voters not to reveal how they voted aside, there are exceptions to the exercise of this right. If investigations establish that individuals were ineligible to vote, and if it appears that the results of elections could have been changed by their votes, then persons may be required to disclose how they voted. Since this requirement is designed to purge elections of illegal votes, the right to secret ballots may, in such situations, have to give way to the public interest in proving that all voters were qualified.[229]

If requirements are designed to ensure the integrity of the election process, then they are usually treated as mandatory. Thus, the failure of election officials to follow provisions covering duplicate ballots when originals are damaged can lead to having ballots invalidated, even if it means disenfranchising voters who cast them. In such a case, an appellate court in Illinois invalidated ballots even though there were no allegations of impropriety and officials claimed that the damaged ballots and duplicates could easily have been matched.[230] The court was of the view that insofar as the provisions in the election code were mandatory, officials had to apply them strictly in order to contribute substantially to the integrity of the election process.

Individuals have challenged elections where ballots were not worded in such a fashion as to provide voters with a clear choice between alternative propositions. In cases involving charges that ballots contained more than one proposition, courts have ruled that the language of ballots must be plain, understandable, and subject to only one interpretation. These cases have led to the creation of what is referred to as the "single proposition" rule. This rule is designed to prevent including two or more unrelated propositions on one ballot, thereby compelling voters to accept an undesirable proposition in order to obtain a desirable one. In order to constitute a single proposition or question, there must be a natural relationship between the objects covered on ballots so that they form one whole plan.

Turning to examples, the Supreme Court of Montana affirmed that it was unnecessary to have separate petitions to transfer elementary and school territories since a single petition clearly identified the intent to transfer both parcels of land.[231] Earlier, the Supreme Court of Illinois determined that "constructing" and "equipping" schools can be treated as a single purpose since the terms were not so unrelated as to require separate propositions.[232] Similarly, the Supreme Court of Minnesota posited that in order to constitute duplicity of subject matter in violation of the state constitution's single-proposition requirement, a ballot must embrace

---

228. *Corn v. Blackwell*, 4 S.E.2d 254 (S.C.1939).

229. *Wehrung v. Ideal School Dist. No. 10*, 78 N.W.2d 68 (N.D.1956). [Case No. 26]

230. *Larson v. Board of Educ. of Bement Community School Dist. No. 5, in Piatt and Champaign Counties*, 455 N.E.2d 866 [14 Educ. L. Rep. 561] (Ill.App.Ct.1983).

231. *McKirdy v. Vielleux*, 19 P.3d 207 [151 Educ. L. Rep. 627] (Mont.2000).

232. *Carstens v. Board of Educ. of East Alton–Wood River Community High School Dist.*, 187 N.E.2d 682 (Ill.1963).

"two or more dissimilar and discordant subjects which cannot reasonably be said to have any legitimate connection."[233] The court upheld a bond issue that was designed to permit a board to acquire and better its schools on the basis that it satisfied the single-proposition rule. Previously, the same court struck down a proposition that read, "[s]hall the Independent Consolidated School District No. 1 of Stevens County issue bonds in the sum of $400,000 for the erection of a new schoolhouse and/or expansion, improvement, and equipment of its schoolhouses?"[234] as violating the single-proposition rule. The court maintained that this question contained three alternative proposals: erect a new school building, improve equipment and expand existing buildings, or a combination of new construction and improvements. The court concluded that this ballot's vice was that the three-part question made it impossible to evaluate whether a majority of voters agreed to authorize any of the proposals since they could not have approved their choices without also voting for the alternatives.

When elections are completed, propositions as worded on ballots are binding. While the full text of propositions does not have to be on ballots, what is printed must clearly identify the issues and their chief features in words of plain meaning.[235] As demonstrated by a case from the Supreme Court of Oregon, agreements that are not parts of resolutions are usually unenforceable. At issue was whether an agreement signed by school board members in the districts involved in a consolidation was binding on the newly created board since some voters had the understanding that the agreement was to be incorporated into the reorganization plan. Five years after accepting the agreement that no school would have been changed, moved, or consolidated without approval of electors in its attendance area, the voters in the new district passed a bond issue for just one high school. The court affirmed that insofar as the agreement was not incorporated in the plan, the alleged misadvice did not invalidate the election and its binding effect on the district.[236]

Voter Qualifications

Those who meet the qualifications for casting ballots are known as electors. Those who actually cast ballots are voters. Although the terms are often used synonymously, the difference can be important. For instance, some statutes require pre-set percentages of electors to approve specified items.[237] Absent such express provisions, measures are carried by a majority of voters.

---

233. *Buhl v. Joint Indep. Consol. School Dist. No. 11*, 82 N.W.2d 836, 839 (Minn.1957).

234. *Green v. Independent Consol. School Dist. No. 1*, 68 N.W.2d 493, 494 (Minn.1955).

235. *Wright v. Board of Trustees of Tatum Indep. School Dist.*, 520 S.W. Civ. App.1975).

236. *Grant v. School Dist. No. 61, Baker County*, 415 P.2d 165 (Or.1966), *cert. denied*, 385 U.S. 1010, 87 S.Ct. 717, 17 L.Ed.2d 547 (1967). [Case No. 27]

237. *See, e.g.*, ARK. CODE ANN. § 6–13–615(a)(2) ("The petitions calling for such an issue [namely, electing board members] to be placed on the ballot shall be signed by not less than ten percent (10%) of the qualified electors of the district, based upon the total number of registered voters in the district."); FLA. STAT. ANN. § 105.035(3) ("(3) Each candidate for election to ... the office of school board member shall obtain the signature of a number of

Constitutional and statutory provisions on voter eligibility exist in all states. While the requirements vary slightly, a common element is residence both per se and for a specified minimum period before elections. Whether individuals are residents when seeking to vote or have been district residents for sufficient periods of time is not always a simple matter. The fact that persons may be physically present in districts does not necessarily constitute being residents for voting purposes. At the same time, absences from districts, even for substantial periods of time, may not necessarily disqualify individuals from voting. Whether individuals are residents depends on an array of factors because some courts equate residence for voting purposes with "domicile," or permanent places of abode, since persons may only have one of the latter.

A case from the Supreme Court of North Dakota illustrates the rule that one does not lose residence for voting purposes merely because a family moves from a district, enrolls its children in schools outside of it, and a parent accepts a position elsewhere.[238] The court decided that where a voter intended to return to the first district, and evidence revealed that he was only living in the second temporarily, he remained a resident of the first for voting purposes.

Statutes requiring persons to reside in districts for set periods of time before becoming eligible to vote are subject to strict scrutiny. In *Dunn v. Blumstein*,[239] the Supreme Court affirmed that bona fide residents could not be required to live in locations for three months prior to voting. The Court suggested that a period of thirty-days appeared to be ample to complete administrative tasks related to checking on residence and preventing voter fraud. While some state courts have adopted a thirty-day rule,[240] the Court upheld a fifty-day requirement.[241]

In setting special qualifications for school elections, their validity depends on whether they constitute inconsistent classifications subject to strict scrutiny. In *Kramer v. Union Free School District No. 15*,[242] the Supreme Court struck down a provision from New York which sought to restrict voting in specified districts essentially to parents of children enrolled in the public schools and owners or lessees of taxable real property and their spouses. On the same day, the Supreme Court invalidated a statute from Louisiana allowing only "property taxpayers" to vote in an election called to approve the issuance of public utility bonds.[243] More recently, the Tenth Circuit upheld a law from Utah limiting voters in a special election about consolidation of school systems to those who lived

---

qualified electors equal to at least 1 percent of the total number of registered electors of the district, circuit, county, or other geographic entity represented by the office....").

238. *Wehrung v. Ideal School Dist. No. 10*, 78 N.W.2d 68 (N.D.1956). [Case No. 26]

239. 405 U.S. 330, 92 S.Ct. 995, 31 L.Ed.2d 274 (1972).

240. *Torres v. Laramie County School Dist. No. 1*, 506 P.2d 817 (Wyo.1973), *cert. denied*, 414 U.S. 990, 94 S.Ct. 342, 38 L.Ed.2d 229 (1973).

241. *Marston v. Lewis*, 410 U.S. 679, 93 S.Ct. 1211, 35 L.Ed.2d 627 (1973).

242. 395 U.S. 621, 89 S.Ct. 1886, 23 L.Ed.2d 583 (1969). *See also Hussey v. City of Portland*, 64 F.3d 1260 (9th Cir.1995), *cert. denied*, 516 U.S. 1112, 116 S.Ct. 911, 133 L.Ed.2d 843 (1996); *Mixon v. State of Ohio*, 193 F.3d 389 [139 Educ. L. Rep. 59] (6th Cir. 1999).

243. *Cipriano v. City of Houma*, 395 U.S. 701, 89 S.Ct. 1897, 23 L.Ed.2d 647 (1969).

within the boundaries of a proposed new district.[244] In so ruling, the court refused to apply strict scrutiny analysis since it was convinced that the law was rationally related to the legitimate state interest in limiting voting on district matters to those who will live within the new school systems.

One Person One Vote Principle

Courts generally apply the one person, one vote principle to school board elections.[245] Pursuant to this principle, qualified voters must be given equal opportunities to participate in elections.[246] However, courts have examined the principle of one person, one vote in connection with other types of situations in school board elections. In *Sailors v. Board of Education of Kent County*,[247] the Supreme Court affirmed that the principle was inapplicable to county boards chosen by delegates from local boards. In not contesting the elections of the latter, opponents challenged the fact that each local board had one delegate, regardless of how many people lived in a district. The Court noted that the system was basically appointive, rather than elective, and that county boards performed essentially administrative rather than legislative functions. The Court acknowledged that insofar as the choice of members of the county board was based on appointment and not election, and since no election was required for nonlegislative officers, the principle of one person, one vote was inapplicable.

Emphasizing its rationale in the preceding case with regard to the dichotomy between appointive and elective boards, the Supreme Court, in *Hadley v. Junior College District of Metropolitan Kansas City, Missouri*,[248] found that when members of an elected body are chosen from separate districts, the arrangement must be such that, to the extent practicable, equal numbers of voters can vote for proportionally equal numbers of officials. In so deciding, the Court struck down a statute permitting component public school boards to create consolidated junior college districts.

On another matter, states may require more than simple majority votes to pass bond referenda. Although such an arrangement mathematically gives more weight to negative votes, the Supreme Court was satisfied that such a situation did not violate the Fourteenth Amendment. In *Gordon v. Lance*,[249] the Court pointed out that the Constitution requires more than majority votes on certain matters. The Court contended that as long as provisions do not discriminate against a group of voters who can be identified by inappropriate criteria such as race or wealth, they do not violate the right to equal protection. Further, the Supreme Court of New

---

244. *City of Herriman v. Bell*, 590 F.3d 1176 [252 Educ. L. Rep. 72] (10th Cir. 2010).

245. The phrase apparently originated in *Reynolds v. Sims*, 377 U.S. 533, 558, 84 S.Ct. 1362, 12 L.Ed.2d 506 (1964).

246. *English v. Board of Educ. of Town of Boonton*, 301 F.3d 69 [168 Educ. L. Rep. 590] (3d Cir.2002), *cert. denied*, 537 U.S. 1148, 123 S.Ct. 852, 154 L.Ed.2d 851 [173 Educ. L. Rep. 40] (2003).

247. 387 U.S. 105, 87 S.Ct. 1549, 18 L.Ed.2d 650 (1967).

248. 397 U.S. 50, 90 S.Ct. 791, 25 L.Ed.2d 45 (1970).

249. 403 U.S. 1, 91 S.Ct. 1889, 29 L.Ed.2d 273 (1971).

Hampshire ruled that a change in the super-majority voting requirement necessary to authorize the issuance of bonds did not violate the state constitutional requirement that called for a referendum to change the charter or form of government.[250] The court ascertained that the change did not violate equal protection because insofar as voters in some districts operated under distinctly different forms of government than others, not all voters and districts were similarly situated.

The Supreme Court of Illinois nullified a decentralization arrangement under which the state legislature created local school councils for each school and granted them substantial governmental powers.[251] According to the law, each council was to consist of ten elected members: six parents chosen by parents, two residents of the school area elected by residents, and two teachers elected by the school staff. The court rejected the notion that parents were to elect six council members based on the claim that they had a greater interest in the school than qualified voters who did not have children in the schools or that parents had any special competence to select council members of quality. In invalidating the law, the court emphasized that each council had broad powers for all members in its attendance zone.

A mother questioned the method of selecting members of the New York City Board of Education. The board consists of one appointed member from each of the five borough school boards and two others named by the mayor. Since the five boroughs have vastly different populations, the mother claimed that the system violated the principle of one person, one vote. A federal trial court rejected the mother's claim, holding that this principle only applies to elected, not appointed, representatives such as school board members.[252] In a second case from New York, members of a high school district unsuccessfully complained that a board's appointing members from residents of a larger feeder district meant that they received the same number of appointees as did the other smaller districts. The court granted the board's motion to dismiss, reiterating that the principle of one person, one vote applies only when officials are elected, not appointed.[253]

In New Jersey, an appellate court rejected the claim that a statute mandating the elimination of districts not operating schools and merging them with systems that did so was not a violation of the equal protection principle of one person, one vote.[254] The court upheld the law in explaining both that voters in the eliminated district lacked a right to permanent representation on the newly consolidated board and all votes in the resulting at-large district counted as much as those of any other voter.

---

250. *McGraw v. Exeter Region Co-op. School Dist.*, 765 A.2d 710 [150 Educ. L. Rep. 769] (N.H.2001).

251. *Fumarolo v. Chicago Bd. of Educ.*, 566 N.E.2d 1283 [65 Educ. L. Rep. 1181] (Ill.1990).

252. *Cohanim v. New York City Bd. of Educ.*, 204 F.Supp.2d 452 [166 Educ. L. Rep. 158] (E.D.N.Y.2002).

253. *Vernet v. Bellmore–Merrick Cent. High School Dist.*, 343 F.Supp.2d 186 [193 Educ. L. Rep. 726] (E.D.N.Y.2004), *aff'd without published opinion*, 155 Fed.Appx. 32 (2d Cir.2005). [Case No. 28]

254. *Borough of Rocky Hill v. State*, 21 A.3d 657 [268 Educ. L. Rep. 911] (N.J. Super. Ct. Chanc. Div. 2010).

Finally, in a case with application to school finance, members of a local school board unsuccessfully challenged a county board's rejection of budgets and tax rates that it had approved. Affirming in favor of the county board, the Supreme Court of South Carolina observed that it did not dilute the local board's voting rights in violation of equal protection and the principle of one person, one vote because both boards provided services for students in the district that the local board served.[255]

Use of School Funds for Board Elections

At best, election notices can contain only brief statements of their purposes. Since the ability of voters to make informed judgments depends on the completeness of their knowledge and understanding of the propositions at issue, local boards have the implied power, if not the duty, to disseminate relevant information about elections. Accordingly, boards can make reasonable expenditures designed to inform voters.

A different issue is present when boards seek to use school monies to advocate their views. When boards abandon their functions of providing information on both sides of issues and use school funds to advocate favorable votes, they may exceed their authority. The Supreme Court of New Jersey, in reaching this result in a case involving a brochure containing a request to "vote yes," thought that it did not mean to imply that the board was restrained from advocating the adoption of its plan in ways other than those involving expenditures of public funds.[256] The court suggested that the board could finance public meetings and radio or television broadcasts as long as views on both sides of the issue were freely expressed.

The Supreme Court of California reasoned that insofar as governmental neutrality in elections is a "fundamental precept of this nation's democratic electoral process,"[257] public funds could not be used to lobby to promote a position. In like fashion, the Tenth Circuit affirmed that a city and school board improperly spent money to help defeat a proposed amendment to the Colorado Constitution that would have mandated voter approval of all acts resulting in tax increases.[258] The court was of the view that a statute permitting contributions to campaigns only involving issues in which the state's political subdivisions have an official concern did not provide the city and board with the authority to spend money on the campaign to oppose the proposed amendment.

Two cases from New York reveal differing judicial attitudes, even in the same state, as to how far school officials may go in encouraging voters to support proposals. The state's highest court affirmed that "vote yes" to "help protect our school facilities and the quality of education in our District" exceeded the boundaries that were reasonably necessary to edu-

---

255. *Burriss v. Anderson County Bd. of Educ.*, 633 S.E.2d 482 [211 Educ. L. Rep. 1047] (S.C.2006).

256. *Citizens to Protect Pub. Funds v. Board of Educ. of Parsippany–Troy Hills Twp.*, 98 A.2d 673 (N.J.1953). [Case No. 29]

257. *Stanson v. Mott*, 130 Cal.Rptr. 697, 705 (Cal.1976).

258. *Campbell v. Joint Dist. 28–J*, 704 F.2d 501 [10 Educ. L. Rep. 132] (10th Cir.1983).

cate voters about budget and bond-issue proposals.[259] Conversely, an appellate court declared that expressions of opinion in district publications, including characterizations of a bond issue as a critical initiative that would build the future of the community's children's, was not impermissible advocacy.[260]

[CASE NO. 22] POWER OF BOARD TO CHANGE POLICY—
PROMISSORY ESTOPPEL

MICHIE v. BOARD OF TRUSTEES

Supreme Court of Wyoming, 1993.
847 P.2d 1006 [81 Educ. L. Rep. 581].

■ MACY, CHIEF JUSTICE.

. . .

Dr. Michie served as an elected member of the Board of Trustees from 1981 to December 1988. In the fall of 1984, the Board of Trustees requested the school superintendent to investigate whether the board members could legally participate in the school district's insurance plan. The superintendent contacted the school attorney for a legal opinion.

At a Board of Trustees meeting held on October 11, 1984, the school attorney opined that the board members could participate in the insurance plan without violating [a Wyoming statute barring compensation for school trustees] as long as each participant paid his own premium. The superintendent also informed the board members that participation in the insurance plan would not be limited to their terms on the Board of Trustees. The minutes reflect that the Board of Trustees took the following action:

> Smith then moved to allow board members to be put on the group insurance program at their own expense. Motion seconded by Michie and carried.

Dr. Michie canceled his family's health insurance policy shortly after the aforestated action was taken and enrolled under the school district's insurance plan effective December 1, 1984. John Smith enrolled sometime later.

Dr. Michie and Mr. Smith did not serve on the Board of Trustees after 1988. On March 23, 1989, the then-elected Board of Trustees voted unanimously to disallow participation by all board members, past or present, in the school district's insurance plan. . . .

The Michies filed a complaint against the Board of Trustees in the United States District Court for the District of Wyoming on April 3, 1991. . . .

The federal district court ruled in its summary judgment order that the Michies could not maintain their 42 U.S.C.[A.] § 1983 action because

---

259. *Phillips v. Maurer*, 499 N.Y.S.2d 675, 676 [31 Educ. L. Rep. 200] (N.Y.1986).

260. *Karpoff v. Mills*, 744 N.Y.S.2d 725 (N.Y.App.Div.2002), *leave to appeal denied*, 752 N.Y.S.2d 588 (N.Y.2002).

they possessed no property right, under either contract law or equity, to continue to participate in the school district's insurance plan. The court made this ruling upon determining: (1) that the 1989 Board of Trustees effectively voided the alleged contract because the Michies failed to demonstrate that it was either "reasonably necessary or of a definable advantage" to the school district; and (2) that equitable remedies, being discretionary in nature, do not give rise to legal rights cognizable under 42 U.S.C.[A.] § 1983. The court accordingly granted a summary judgment in favor of the Board of Trustees on the Michies' breach-of-contract and 42 U.S.C.[A.] § 1983 claims. It also dismissed the Michies' promissory estoppel . . . [claim], without prejudice, for lack of subject matter jurisdiction.

The Michies renewed their promissory estoppel claim against the Board of Trustees by filing a complaint in state district court on January 13, 1992. . . .

The Michies concede on appeal that the federal district court determined that they did not have an enforceable contract with the school district because any contract which might have existed was effectively voided by the 1989 Board of Trustees. They contend, however, that the state district court erred as a matter of law by granting a summary judgment on their promissory estoppel claim, apparently on this basis. The Michies argue that an enforceable contractual obligation is not an element of a promissory estoppel claim.

We agree that a claim for promissory estoppel is not dependent upon the existence of a promise which is enforceable under traditional contract principles. By definition, promissory estoppel is an equitable remedy for detrimental reliance upon a promise which does not rise to the level of a formal contract. As explained in Restatement (Second) of Contracts § 90(1) (1981):

A promise which the promisor should reasonably expect to induce action or forbearance on the part of the promisee or a third person and which does induce such action or forbearance is binding if injustice can be avoided only by enforcement of the promise. The remedy granted for breach may be limited as justice requires.

This Court has recognized that promissory estoppel may be used as an affirmative cause of action. The elements which must be proved in a promissory estoppel action are:

"(1) a clear and definite agreement; (2) proof that the party urging the doctrine acted to its detriment in reasonable reliance on the agreement; and (3) a finding that the equities support the enforcement of the agreement."

Whether elements one and two exist are questions for the finder of fact. Whether element three is satisfied is decided as a matter of law by the court.

In the instant case, the Michies contend that they presented evidence to satisfy each promissory estoppel element. We agree, however, with the state district court that the Michies failed to demonstrate "the existence of a contract or enforceable promise." ... [W]e understand the court's summary judgment order to be founded upon simple deductive reasoning: If it is against public policy to enforce an extended-term governmental contract, it is also against public policy to enforce an extended-term governmental promise embodied in the contract.

In [a prior case] this Court directly addressed the issue of whether extended-term governmental contracts are voidable as a matter of public policy.... On appeal, this Court stated:

> [A]n agreement extending beyond the term of the contracting authority ... may be voidable by the government or void upon attack by a third party if, under the facts and circumstances, the agreement is not reasonably necessary or of a definable advantage to the city or governmental body. The issue when raised is decided as a matter of law, and the burden of evidence of the actual facts defining convenience and necessity devolve either upon the non-governmental contracting party when attacked by the government or upon the third party who separately might attack the validity of the contract....

The public policy underlying the rule ... is straightforward: A governing body should not be able to deprive its successor in interest of discretion to act for the public good. We believe that this policy applies not only to extended-term governmental contracts but also to extended-term governmental promises which do not constitute formal contracts. Accordingly, both are voidable absent a showing of reasonable necessity or definable advantage. The Michies were not able to satisfy this requirement in federal court and are collaterally estopped from attempting to do so now. The equities of this case do not support the application of the doctrine of promissory estoppel against the Board of Trustees. The Board of Trustees was entitled to a summary judgment as a matter of law.

Affirmed.

NOTES

1. Although school boards, as corporate bodies, are not affected by changes in membership, successor boards (with new members or with old members who change their minds) are not powerless to change course. Consider the court's articulation of this common law principle as it relates to contracts.

2. An appellate court in Ohio held that even though a superintendent, based on conversations with individual board members, promised that two nonresident students would be able to attend local schools by paying tuition until they graduated, the arrangement was unenforceable since only the board could enter into a binding contract. The court concluded that the fact that the students attended for four years did not create a basis for promissory estoppel against the board. *Walker v. Lockland City School Dist. Bd. of Educ.*, 429 N.E.2d 1179 [2 Educ. L. Rep. 203] (Ohio Ct. App.1980).

[CASE NO. 23]   POWER OF BOARD TO OFFER RETIREMENT INCENTIVE

FAIR LAWN EDUCATION ASSOCIATION v. FAIR LAWN BOARD OF EDUCATION

Supreme Court of New Jersey, 1979.
401 A.2d 681.

■ PASHMAN, J.

In this case we are called upon to assess the validity of an Early Retirement Remuneration Plan (ERR) agreed to by the Fair Lawn Board of Education (Board) and the Fair Lawn Education Association (Association)—the majority representative of the Board's teaching employees. For the reasons to be given below, we conclude that the particular plan here at issue: (1) lacks statutory authorization; (2) contravenes this Court's holdings in [2 cases]; and (3) is preempted by the comprehensive statutory scheme relating to the operation of retirement benefits. Consequently, that plan cannot be implemented.

On July 1, 1976, the Association and the Board entered into a collective agreement covering the 1976–1977 and 1977–1978 school years. Article VI of that agreement set forth the provisions of the ERR plan whose legality is here in dispute. Under the terms of the contract, teachers between the ages of 55 and 64 who retired prior to September 1, 1977 would receive an additional payment in the amount of $6,000 upon leaving the Board's employ. Instructors retiring after the start of the 1977–1978 school year were also entitled to remuneration over and above their normal pension. The value of their benefit, however, was dependent upon age, with those relinquishing their positions at an earlier age receiving a larger bonus. The sums to be paid ranged from $500 for a 64–year–old teacher to $6,000 for retiring instructors aged 55 to 57. Four payment options—including lump sum and various installment alternatives—were provided. The goals underlying the adoption of this plan were twofold: (1) to "reward loyalty and long years of service," and (2) to encourage early retirements in order that tenured teachers could be replaced by younger, less experienced instructors whose salary levels would be much lower. . . .

On June 24, 1977, the Association filed suit in the Chancery Division seeking both a declaration that the ERR plan was valid and specific performance of its terms. The Board—named as sole defendant—joined the Teachers' Pension and Annuity Fund (TPAF) as third-party defendant. The pleadings and arguments below demonstrate that of these parties, the Board and the Association are in fact aligned in interest, and that TPAF is the only opponent of the plan. . . .

I

Local boards of education are creations of the State and, as such, may exercise only those powers granted to them by the Legislature—either expressly or by necessary or fair implication. We must therefore determine whether local boards have been delegated the authority to make payments to employees which are unrelated to services rendered for the sole purpose of inducing early retirement.

The trial court held that authorization for the plan could be found in two statutory provisions: N.J.S.A. 18A:27–4 (a local board may set the "terms and tenure of employment, ... salaries and time and mode of payment thereof ...") and N.J.S.A. 34:13A–5.3 (public employers and their employees may negotiate concerning "terms and conditions of employment"). We disagree.

N.J.S.A. 18A:27–4 does not confer upon local boards an unlimited power to negotiate all types of financial benefits for their teaching employees. Rather, the statute's use of the word "salaries" indicates that the Legislature intended to grant boards the power to set the "time and mode of payment" only of compensation which bears some relation to the rendition of past or present services. Under the ERR plan here at issue, payments are geared to age, not service. Moreover, the sums to which instructors are entitled decrease as length of service increases. It is thus clear that the parties to this contract intended to reward early retirement rather than the amount and quality of the work that a particular teacher had performed. As such, these payments are not authorized by N.J.S.A. 18A:27–4.

Nor are the payments called for by the ERR plan authorized by the Employer–Employee Relations Act, N.J.S.A. 34:13A–1 *et seq.* That statute does not enlarge the areas in which the Board has been delegated the responsibility to act. Rather, it merely recognizes the right of public employee representatives to negotiate with the Board over matters which, in the absence of negotiation, could have been set unilaterally by the Board. As such, the provisions of the Employer–Employee Relations Act do not operate to confer authority upon the Board to agree to compensation schemes which bear no relation to the amount and quality of the services which its teaching employees have rendered.

We therefore conclude that the Board has not been delegated the power to agree to or make the payments called for by the ERR plan here at issue. These payments, being unrelated to service, do not constitute "compensation" or "customary fringe benefits" with respect to which negotiation is permissible. Consequently, Article VI of the parties' collective agreement is *ultra vires* and unenforceable.

II

. . .

[The court reviewed two prior decisions (involving nonschool public employees) in which it had enunciated the principle that "actions taken by a state agency which may substantially affect retirement age and thus the actuarial assumptions of a statutory pension system are impermissible unless clearly and unequivocally authorized by the legislature."]

III

It is axiomatic that a municipality may not act in an area which the Legislature has preempted. In deciding whether a particular municipal activity has been preempted, the Court must determine whether the Legislature intended its action to preclude the exercise of local authority. . . .

In assessing the legislative intent, the primary factor to be considered is whether the municipal action adversely affects the legislative scheme. . . . [ERR's] adverse effect upon the comprehensive legislative scheme has been fully documented. . . . Hence, its existence stands " 'as an obstacle to the accomplishment and execution of the full purposes and objectives' of the Legislature[.]" . . .

. . .

Although we are not unsympathetic to the desire of local boards of education to reduce their expenses, sanction for plans such as the one at issue must come from the Legislature. That branch of government has determined that preservation of the TPAF's fiscal integrity is presently to be accorded paramount concern. We are not at liberty to reassess the policy judgment which it has made. Absent clear and unequivocal statutory authority, ERR plans such as Fair Lawn's may not be established. . . .

Accordingly, the judgment of the Appellate Division is affirmed.

NOTES

1. From an educational viewpoint, do you think the plan that was struck down had merit?

2. The court lists three bases for invalidating the plan in the first paragraph. Are they independent of each other?

3. Could a local school board pay teachers who retire a lump sum for unused sick leave days? Could the state legislature permit local boards to offer financial incentives for early retirement?

[CASE NO. 24] REMOVAL OF A LOCAL SCHOOL BOARD MEMBER FOR CONFLICT OF INTEREST

BOARD OF EDUCATION OF THE CITY OF SEA ISLE CITY v. KENNEDY

Supreme Court of New Jersey, 2008.
951 A.2d 987 [234 Educ. L. Rep. 188].

■ JUSTICE LaVECCHIA delivered the opinion of the Court.

This appeal involves the interplay between the School Ethics Act (SEA), *N.J.S.A.* 18A:12–21 to –34, and *N.J.S.A.* 18A:12–2. *N.J.S.A.* 18A:12–2 prohibits board of education members from having a direct or indirect interest in any claim against their board. The SEA operates in complementary fashion. It also addresses conflicts of interest for school board members and prohibits, among other things, certain representational activities that would put a board member in a position inconsistent with that of his or her board. However, the SEA contains an exemption that allows "any school official, or members of his immediate family, [to] represent [ ] himself, or themselves, in negotiations or proceedings concerning his, or their, own interests."

In this matter, a board member had filed a special education due process request with the State Director of Special Education Programs on behalf of his son. Relying on *N.J.S.A.* 18A:12-2's prohibition against a member having an interest in an inconsistent claim against the board, the Commissioner of Education ordered the board member's removal from office. The State Board of Education affirmed the Commissioner's determination, as did the Appellate Division. We granted certification to consider whether a statutory conflict exists between *N.J.S.A.* 18A:12-2's statement of qualifications for board of education office and the SEA's exemption in *N.J.S.A.* 18A:12-24(j).

We conclude that the two statutes can, and must, be harmonized. Otherwise, an important and vital group of citizens—parents of special education pupils—might be effectively precluded from participation on local boards of education for fear that they must give up the ability to address educational issues that may arise in connection with their children's specialized programs. We hold that not all controversies and disputes that occasionally may erupt between the parents of special education pupils and local school districts concerning a child's educational program should require a sitting board of education member's removal from office. A more nuanced analysis must be undertaken when a board member's removal is sought for having pursued his or her child's due process rights to an appropriate special education program. That said, we agree with the Commissioner's determination that, in this matter, removal was necessary and appropriate because of the concrete, pecuniary aspects to the dispute between the parties. We therefore affirm the judgment of the Appellate Division, as modified by this opinion.

Petitioner William J. Kennedy (Kennedy) was elected to his first three-year term on the Sea Isle City Board of Education in 2001 and was appointed to serve as president by his colleagues on the board. His term ended abruptly when, on June 29, 2003, he resigned. Immediately thereafter, Kennedy and his spouse, individually and on behalf of their minor son, M.K., filed a request with the New Jersey Department of Education (Department) for a hearing concerning their son's special education program. Their petition for a due process hearing was filed against the Sea Isle City Board of Education (Board), the entity responsible for providing special education services to M.K., who had been diagnosed with an autism spectrum disorder. The Kennedys' petition asserted that their son's individualized educational program (IEP) failed to satisfy his educational needs, in violation of the Individuals with Disabilities Education Act. . . .

Just prior to the parties' settlement of the IEP dispute, Kennedy again was elected, on April 20, 2004, to the Board for a three-year term to commence on April 28, 2004. As noted, on April 27th, the day before Kennedy's new term of office was to start, the Kennedys and the Board finalized the terms of the IEP settlement and signed the agreement that ended their litigation. Kennedy served on the Board uneventfully for purposes of this appeal until March 2005. However, on March 1 and 2, 2005, while he was serving again as the Board's president, Kennedy and his spouse, individually and on behalf of their son, filed two, virtually identical, letter applications requesting a due process hearing and an emergent hearing with the Department of Education, State Director of the Office of Special Education Programs.

The Kennedys' petitions broadly claimed that, through numerous acts and omissions, the Board materially breached the terms of the April 27, 2004, settlement agreement. . . .

Kennedy's applications for relief prompted the Board immediately to file with the Commissioner of Education a petition of appeal seeking a declaratory ruling that the Kennedy applications created a conflict of interest with the Board that was incompatible with Kennedy's continued Board membership. The Commissioner transferred the Board's request for declaratory relief, as well as the due process applications for enforcement of the April 27, 2004, settlement, to the Office of Administrative Law where the matters were assigned to an administrative law judge (ALJ). The ALJ issued an Initial Decision, dated May 16, 2005, finding Kennedy's conduct to be permissible pursuant to *N.J.S.A.* 18A:12–24(j) because the due process requests were designed to protect the educational rights of Kennedy's child. . . .

In a Final Decision dated June 30, 2005, the Commissioner, however, rejected the ALJ's recommendation and held that Kennedy's actions created a disqualifying conflict of interest under *N.J.S.A.* 18A:12–2. As noted, the . . . order that Kennedy be removed from office was affirmed by the State Board of Education and by the Appellate Division. The Appellate Division specifically rejected Kennedy's argument that the Legislature, in creating the exemption found in *N.J.S.A.* 18A:12–24(j), impliedly repealed *N.J.S.A.* 18A:12–2. The panel viewed the two statutes as operating "in separate spheres" and concluded that the exemption found in *N.J.S.A.* 18A:12–24(j) comes into operation for those board members who remain qualified as board members.

II.

Petitioner, Kennedy, asserts essentially the same arguments that he advanced below. He contends that, in enacting *N.J.S.A.* 18A:12–24(j), the Legislature clearly meant for board members to be able to represent their personal interests in "negotiations and proceedings" involving their school boards. However, by treating *N.J.S.A.* 18A:12–2 as an ongoing and absolute requirement for sitting board members, the Commissioner rendered *N.J.S.A.* 18A:12–24(j) inapplicable for board members. Therefore, petitioner claims that the administrative agency's determination defies legislative intent.

Petitioner argues that the two statutes should be construed together, which would make either of two interpretations possible. . . .

Taking the other tack, the Board urges deference to the agency's interpretation of its own statutes. More specifically, the Board contends that the unambiguous language of *N.J.S.A.* 18A:12–2 requires Kennedy's removal because it establishes an ongoing prohibition against conflicts of interest between a board member and the Board. The Board argues that *N.J.S.A.* 18A:12–2 serves an important preventative purpose, helping to avoid situations in which specific conflicts are likely to arise. Further, the

Board argues that *N.J.S.A.* 18A:12–2 was not repealed by *N.J.S.A.* 18A:12–24(j), because the latter statute neither references the earlier statute nor purports to address the qualifications needed to maintain board membership. Accordingly, the Board urges us to affirm the determinations below, which found that *N.J.S.A.* 18A:12–2 imposes an ongoing qualification requirement for board members.

With that, we turn to the statutory provisions at issue.

III.

A.

Our goal when construing a statute is to discern and fulfill the Legislature's intent.... If the language is clear, then the interpretative process will end without resort to extrinsic sources. We look to extrinsic evidence if a plain reading of the enactment leads to more than one plausible interpretation. Among the sources that inform us is the long-standing meaning ascribed to the language by the agency charged with its enforcement. In the final analysis, the polestar of the inquiry is the intent of the drafters.

Other important principles also instruct our analysis. When attempting "to discover the legislative intent, the statute must be read in light of the old law, the mischief sought to be eliminated and the proposed remedy." Also, "[a]cts in *pari materia* as well as related acts not strictly in *pari materia,* should be examined." In accordance with those principles then, we begin our analysis in this statutory construction case by examining the plain language of the statute relied on by the Commissioner.

B.

N.J.S.A. 18A:12–2, codified in a section of the school laws described as "Qualifications" for office for members of local boards of education, is titled "Inconsistent interests or office prohibited." It provides,

> No member of any board of education shall be interested directly or indirectly in any contract with or claim against the board, nor, in the case of local and regional school districts, shall he hold office as mayor or as a member of the governing body of a municipality, nor in the case of county special services school districts and county vocational school districts, shall he hold office as a member of the governing body of a county.

Thus, in rather plain language, the statute sets out clear prohibitions against board members having inconsistent claims against the board, interests in contracts with the board, and specific office-holding. Another provision, *N.J.S.A.* 18A:12–2.1, fixes a time-certain application for that qualification for office, as well as all other statutorily required qualifications. Before assuming the duties of office, board members must take and subscribe to an oath that they possess all qualifications for office. Plainly, the Legislature intended that no one be permitted to commence their service in office as a local board of education member without swearing that he or she meets all qualifications for office at the time of taking office.

The next logical question is whether the plain language of *N.J.S.A.* 18A:12–2's qualification for office requires immediate and automatic removal when any type of claim arises during a member's term. *N.J.S.A.* 18A:12–2 is silent about removal from office. In related provisions in Title 18A, however, the legislative answer is express and unequivocal.

Against that series of clear legislative pronouncements, we find it textually uncertain whether the Legislature meant for removal of a seated school board member to be similarly absolute, and immediately required, whenever the member has an interest in any kind of claim that may arise during the course of the member's term. The Legislature certainly could have included such a requirement, because it knew how to impose immediate removal in the related statutes. The Legislature also spoke clearly and forcefully in requiring no inconsistent claims as a condition for assuming office as a board member. However, a qualification to assume office does not necessarily equate to a required forfeiture of office when a like issue arises during the term of a sitting member. Because neither *N.J.S.A.* 18A:12–2 nor *N.J.S.A.* 18A:12–3, the related statute establishing removal grounds, state that inconsistent claims are an automatic basis for removal, we can only conclude that some ambiguity surrounds the question.

We have no doubt that having an inconsistent claim can be additional cause for removal, but the question is whether removal is the only remedy when a board member has an interest in a claim against the board. That the Commissioner of Education, who historically has heard petitions to remove a sitting board of education member for alleged conflicts of interest, generally has concluded that the claims which have arisen have required a board member's removal does not compel the conclusion that removal is the only course of action. Indeed, the Commissioner has stated his willingness to engage in fact-sensitive, case-specific analyses in respect of a member's direct or indirect interest in alleged "inconsistent" claims and contracts.

On its face, *N.J.S.A.* 18A:12–2 mandates that no board member may serve who has filed a claim against the board of education on which he sits. Case law has further established that any such claim must be examined on a case-by-case basis in arriving at a determination as to whether the circumstances in the matter demonstrate that the board member would benefit in a substantial and material way from said claim. If so, the statute should be applied and the board member disqualified from serving on said board.

Accordingly, the Commissioner's decisions examining claims by board members have discussed the relevance of determining whether the member was pursuing a claim in the public interest rather than "personal aggrandizement and enrichment," and such other considerations as whether the claim giving rise to the conflict of interest promised "substantial and material benefit" to the claimant. We note further that, in one decision, the Commissioner specifically rejected the argument that *N.J.S.A.* 18A:12–2 requires automatic disqualification for "any" claim against a board.

In sum, we find that the Commissioner's applications of *N.J.S.A.* 18A:12–2 demonstrate a willingness to engage in a careful examination of a board member's asserted conflicting interest in a claim against a board and, further, to find that not all claims in which a board member has an interest constitute a "substantial conflict" requiring removal from office as the sole remedy. . . .

With enactment of the SEA, the Legislature declared its intention "to ensure and preserve public confidence" in local school board members, *N.J.S.A.* 18A:12–22, by providing local board members with advance guidance on ethical conduct so that such members might conduct their personal affairs appropriately and within the bounds ethically expected. *N.J.S.A.* 18A:12–24(j). The SEA considered the advocacy interests of board members and recognized a limited need to except board members from an absolute prohibition from pursuing their family members' interests in "negotiations and proceedings" involving the board. Read broadly, the later-enacted SEA could contradict *N.J.S.A.* 18A:12–2's interest in prohibiting substantial conflicting claims that pit a board member's interest in a claim against the interests of the board. Implied repealers are not favored, however, and would require that we find the later-enacted statute to be utterly inconsistent or repugnant to the earlier.

We need not do so here for the two statutes are readily capable of being harmonized. The Legislature's authorization of a board member's ability to pursue resolution of some personal issues, interests, or disagreements with a school district through negotiations and even "proceedings" is not repugnant to the earlier recognition by the Commissioner that not all "claims" against a board will require disqualification and removal from office under *N.J.S.A.* 18A:12–2. We view the SEA's exemption as a legislative expansion of that previously recognized, limited case-law exception to the rule against inconsistent claims. Certainly, we perceive no direct statutory conflict between the two statutes. The reconciliation of the two statutes will unfold based on fact-sensitive analyses for substantial and deeply antagonistic interests that would call into question a board member's ability to perform public duties and the public's confidence in that ability of the member to perform his or her office, notwithstanding the advancement of a personal interest through negotiations or a "proceeding."

The Legislature's exemption allowing participation in certain "proceedings" must be taken into account by the Commissioner in removal actions based on *N.J.S.A.* 18A:12–2's prohibition against inconsistent claims. We recognize that that shall require careful case development. As a matter of fairness, the Court should provide the public with advice and guidance. The Legislature has recognized the value of such advance notice about the parameters of acceptable behavior, specifically noting that the more guidance that school board members receive, the better for them and for the public that they serve.

We conclude that a board member should not be removed from office merely because he or she has advanced any claim "in a proceeding" against a school district involving that individual or an immediate family member's interests. Substantial, disqualifying conflicts of interest should be identified either by type of claim, *i.e.* specific monetary claims by the member or a family member as in a tort claim, or by type of proceeding. Because, as the

Legislature recognized, board member conflicts of interest can implicate the authority of both the Commissioner of Education and the SEC, the two agencies with related and overlapping authority here should consult and attempt to harmonize their approaches on these important matters. Ultimately, however, the line between acceptable and prohibited activities by board members, in respect of the advancement of personal or a family member's interests in proceedings against a board of education, may be resolved through the prism of a fact-specific inquiry.

We therefore turn once again to the setting of this case. Although the instant matter is technically moot in that Kennedy's term of office is long over, the present controversy provides a vehicle through which guidance may be provided to school boards, their members, the Commissioner, and the SEC. We occasionally will decide matters where the issue is of substantial importance, likely to reoccur, but capable of evading review. Accordingly, we shall address the merits of this allegedly disqualifying claim advanced by Kennedy, on behalf of his son, in a special education due process hearing request against the board on which he served.

IV.

By way of background, the delivery of special education services to handicapped children is governed by both federal and state law....

. . .

Our analysis must begin with the recognition that both board and parent are held to have a common interest in the resolution of an appropriate education for the child. Indeed, this Court explained that concerns about such matters as the allocation of the burden of proof in special education proceedings have less importance because of their shared interest in getting the "right" educational programming and placement for the child.

In that setting, the adversary nature of the proceedings should yield to obtaining the right result for the handicapped child.... [W]e believe the obligation of parents at the due-process hearing should be merely to place in issue the appropriateness of the IEP. The school board should then bear the burden of proving that the IEP was appropriate.

. . .

The Commissioner should examine the nature of the dispute and establish a more careful and fact-specific explanation of when a conflict over a child's educational program becomes so substantial that removal from office is required. That said, when a due process claim includes a request for specific monetary relief, we believe that a line has been crossed and a substantial conflict between a board member and the board can be found to exist.

Such a request arose in this action where the due process petition forwarded to the State Director included a demand for payment to Kennedy's spouse for services that she had provided to her son. We cannot reconcile that claim for substantial monetary relief with a board member's continued service on a local board. For that reason, we have no hesitancy in approving the relief ordered in this matter. Indeed, we note, as did the Appellate Division below, that the due process demand in issue gave rise to escalating federal litigation between the parties, which continues to date as far as we understand. Finally, we commend to the Commissioner, for her considered judgment, whether a set of guidelines might be developed so that parents of students might better understand the limits imposed on them should they choose to run for office on their local board of education.

V.

The judgment of the Appellate Division is affirmed, as modified by this opinion.

NOTES

1. The decision here was unanimous.

2. What do you think of this case? Is it fair for school board members to not be able to challenge the actions of educators when they seek to protect the rights of their children with disabilities?

[CASE NO. 25]   VOTING PROCEDURES OF BOARDS

MATAWAN REGIONAL TEACHERS ASSOCIATION v. MATAWAN–ABERDEEN REGIONAL SCHOOL DISTRICT BOARD OF EDUCATION

Superior Court of New Jersey, Appellate Division, 1988.
538 A.2d 1331 [45 Educ. L. Rep. 1123].

■ BRODY, J.A.D.

The issue in this appeal is whether a local school board may lawfully adopt a plan, which includes the closing and sale of a school building, by a majority vote of its full membership after consideration at a single public meeting even though its bylaws require adoption by a 2/3 vote of its full membership after consideration at two public meetings. We hold that the board is not bound by the bylaw that limits the authority of the majority, but is bound by the bylaw that requires two public meetings for adoption of the plan.

The dispute arose when the nine members of the Matawan–Aberdeen Regional School District Board of Education (the board) voted 5 to 4 to reorganize the school district by adopting "Plan C" (the plan). The cornerstone of the plan is the closing and sale of a school and an administration building in the Borough of Matawan. Closing the school requires relocating students and changing the range of classes in the remaining schools. Adoption of the plan is a matter of substantial local public interest. Petitioners are the union that represents board employees, and 92 resident-taxpayers of the district.

An administrative law judge (ALJ) summarily dismissed the claim that the bylaws barred adoption of the plan. The Commissioner of Education and the State Board of Education affirmed the ALJ's summary dismissal for the reasons he had expressed.

The relevant bylaws provide the following:

No policy shall be adopted by the Board until it has received a vote of the full Board at two public meetings. . . .

Bylaws shall be adopted, amended or repealed by a 2/3 vote of the full Board.

Local boards of education "may exercise only those powers granted to them by the Legislature—either expressly or by necessary or fair implication." *Fair Lawn Educ. Ass'n v. Fair Lawn Bd. of Educ.* Boards derive the authority to adopt bylaws from N.J.S.A. 18A:11–1c, which provides that a local board shall

Make, amend and repeal rules, not inconsistent with this title or with the rules of the state board, for its own government and the transaction of its business and for the government and management of the public schools and public school property of the district and for the employment, regulation of conduct and discharge of its employees. . . .

Boards derive the authority to govern and manage the district from N.J.S.A. 18A:11 d, which provides that a local board shall

Perform all acts and do all things, consistent with law and the rules of the state board, necessary for the lawful and proper conduct, equipment and maintenance of the public schools of the district.

N.J.S.A. 18A:111 is silent with respect to the number of votes necessary to adopt rules and to govern and manage the district. It must be assumed that by its silence the Legislature intended the common-law rule to apply, i.e., a majority vote of the members of the board constituting a quorum shall be sufficient. At common law, a majority of a public body constitutes a quorum. Thus the Legislature has empowered a majority of the majority of a local board to adopt bylaws and conduct the board's business.

We reject the argument that the Legislature has merely established a minimum number of affirmative votes necessary for local board action, which the board may increase in its bylaws to assure a broader consensus. Depriving the majority of its authority and responsibility to govern in favor of a broader consensus carries the risk of inaction where action is warranted. There may be actions which should be taken with the affirmative votes of an enhanced majority because of their overwhelming importance or because they constitute a departure from the norm. The Legislature has provided for such particular instances by requiring the vote of an enhanced majority. A relevant example is the statute that prohibits a local board from selling school lands except "by a recorded roll call majority vote of its full membership." N.J.S.A. 18A:205. That requirement was met here.

We conclude that the Legislature has preempted a local board's authority to strike the balance between requiring a broad consensus for action and the attendant risk of inaction. We arrive at this conclusion because striking that delicate balance is a matter of major governmental importance calling for uniform treatment throughout the State and is a subject on which the Legislature has acted in many specific instances by requiring an enhanced majority.

Our holding conforms to long-standing precedent in this State. In *Barnert v. Paterson*, the court held:

> When the charter of a municipal corporation or a general law of the state does not provide to the contrary, a majority of the board of aldermen constitute a quorum, and the vote of a majority of those present, there being a quorum, is all that is required for the adoption or passage of a motion or the doing of any other act the board has power to do.
>
> Under the twenty-third section of the charter, the board is given power "to establish its own rules of procedure." But I do not think that under this power it was designed to confer upon this board the adoption of a rule changing either the general law or any special provision in the charter. Power to make such rules and by-laws was inherent in the corporation without this provision. Such by-laws must be in accordance with the charter or the general rules of law. The charter is silent and the general law requires a majority vote. . . .

By contrast, the bylaw requiring that action on non-emergent matters of policy be considered at two public meetings does not conflict directly or indirectly with any statute. Its purpose is not to remove the responsibility and authority to act from those members of a local board who are authorized by state law to act. Rather, its purpose is to assure that those having that responsibility and authority act only upon due deliberation after notice to the public and interested third parties. Our courts have long compelled public bodies to adhere to such bylaws.

In *Eggers v. Newark*, a Board of Street and Water Commissioners adopted an ordinance during the meeting at which it was introduced despite a bylaw that required publication between the first and second readings. The commissioners purported to suspend the bylaw by unanimous consent. The court held that the bylaws had been duly adopted pursuant to statute and therefore "constituted the working regulations governing [the Board's] action so far as not regulated by higher authority of the statute." . . .

In *Hicks v. Long Branch Commission*, the Court set aside a special appropriation because, in violation of the Commission's bylaws, each commissioner's vote was not recorded. The Court said,

> The standing rules, adopted by ordinance under the express authority of the charter, as before stated, provide that "on every vote relating to any special appropriation the yeas and nays shall be taken and recorded." This rule was as binding upon the commission and its members as any statute or other law of the commonwealth. Its importance is manifest. It is designed to secure, in matters relating to the public funds, deliberate action on the part of each commissioner, and immediate as well as permanent public evidence thereof, readily accessible to the voters of the municipality, on which their representatives may be held responsible.

The binding effect of bylaws designed to give the public notice before official action is taken was reaffirmed by the Court in *Erie R.R. Co. v. Paterson* where a Board of Public Works adopted an ordinance at a meeting held on a date not scheduled in its bylaws. In setting aside the ordinance the Court cited the language in *Eggers* with approval.

In the absence of any statute to the contrary, the board's bylaw requiring two public meetings to adopt the plan is binding. We must therefore set aside the resolution that purported to adopt the plan at a single meeting. Our determination renders moot the other issues that have been raised in this appeal.

Reversed.

NOTES

1. This case illustrates an important distinction between procedural rules that lower government bodies must follow and those that cannot be enacted absent state legislation.

2. Contemplate the rationale expressed in *Eggers v. Newark* and *Hicks v. Long Branch Commission* (quoted in the case) that served as basis of the opinion. How does it serve the long-range interests of a democratic government?

[CASE NO. 26]   RESIDENCE FOR VOTING PURPOSES— DISQUALIFIED VOTERS

WEHRUNG v. IDEAL SCHOOL DISTRICT NO. 10

Supreme Court of North Dakota, 1956.
78 N.W.2d 68.

■ GRIMSON, JUDGE.

On the 14th day of October 1955, the Ideal School District No. 10, of McKenzie County, North Dakota, held an election to determine whether to issue negotiable bonds in the amount not exceeding $120,000. A notice of said election was duly published and at said election 480 votes were cast in favor of issuance of the bonds and 237 were cast against it. The vote in favor was more than the required 66 2/3 percent of the voters who had voted. As a result the proposition of issuing the bonds was declared carried. In due time seven taxpayers of Ideal School District No. 10 commenced a contest of the election alleging that the election had been conducted illegally and that many illegal votes were cast. They prayed that the officers of the district be enjoined from proceeding further and that the election be declared null and void. The contestees deny the illegality of the election. A hearing was duly had in district court and judgment entered sustaining the election. The contestants appealed to this court and ask for a trial de novo.

There are several issues but appellants summarize them under three points as follows:

"1. Permitting, or requiring, an unqualified voter to disclose how he voted.

"2. Permitting people, not qualified voters of the district, to vote.

"3. Permitting the voters of the First Addition to the Wold Addition in the townsite of Watford City to vote claiming that Addition was not legally annexed to the Ideal School District."

As to the first point the contestants and appellants presented 12 witnesses who were examined as to their legal qualifications to vote at that election. When the witnesses were examined as to how they voted at this election the court informed those whom it found to be qualified voters that they did not need to disclose that fact unless they wished to do so. In *Torkelson v. Byrne*, this court held the qualified elector cannot be compelled to disclose for whom he voted. However, this privilege of secrecy is entirely a personal one and the voter himself may waive his privilege and testify for whom he voted.

Two voters were found to be disqualified to vote in this election. As to those two voters the court ruled they would have to disclose how they voted. In *Hanson v. Village of Adrian*, the court held:

"Having proven that the contestees voted without right, it is proper by competent evidence to ascertain how they voted, so as to purge the election of the illegal vote."

The court was clearly right in requiring the disqualified voters to disclose how they voted and to deduct their votes from the total. As it happened one voted for and the other against the bonds so that the result was not changed, and more than 66 2/3rds percent remained in favor of bonds.

On the next point the contestants and appellants object to the ruling of the court holding several of the challenged voters were qualified to vote. They especially question the votes of Earl Quale and his wife. Mr. Quale testified that he had a home in Watford City located in Ideal School District No. 10; that for more than a year while he had no work in Watford City he had been living temporarily in Arnegard, renting his home in Watford City because he needed the income from the rent to save his home from foreclosure; that even though his children went to school at Arnegard during that time he always intended to come back to make Watford City his permanent home; that he now has work there and is waiting until his tenant finds another place to move into, so that he can bring his family back to his home; that he never voted in Arnegard. Other witnesses were cross-examined as to their residence and disclosed that even though they temporarily worked on a farm or other places, they had a home in Watford City and always intended to return there and never voted anywhere else.

Residence is the place where one lives when not called elsewhere for labor or other special purposes and to which on such occasions he returns. There can be only one residence and it cannot be lost until another is gained. It can be changed only by union of act and intent. The testimony of the witnesses whose residence in Watford City was questioned was that they had homes in Watford City and intended to return there and did return when occasion arrived. They had no intent of obtaining a residence anywhere else. Residence is a question of fact in which the intention of the party enters as an important element. Under the testimony those witnesses had a residence in Watford City of sufficient length of time to become qualified electors. The district court so found and the evidence supports such finding....

. . .

The judgment of the district court is affirmed.

NOTES

1.   Do you agree with the rationale for the rule that qualified voters cannot be compelled to disclose for whom they voted, but disqualified voters can be so compelled? *See Corn v. Blackwell,* 4 S.E.2d 254 (S.C.1939), wherein officials inadvertently had ballots printed and numbered consecutively from one up to hundreds. The ballots were then cast in such a manner as to render it easy to determine how each person voted. The court held that insofar as this destroyed the secrecy of the ballot, the election results had to be invalidated.

2.   Compare the legal concept of residence for purpose of voting with that of residence for tuition-free attendance in public schools.

[CASE NO. 27]   MISADVICE TO ELECTORS IN SCHOOL ELECTION

GRANT v. SCHOOL DISTRICT NO. 61, BAKER COUNTY

Supreme Court of Oregon, 1966.
415 P.2d 165.

■ DENECKE, JUSTICE.

This is a declaratory judgment proceeding brought because of a controversy concerning the formation of an Administrative School District and the acts of such District.

Under the provisions of what is now ORS 330.505 *et seq.*, the Baker County School Reorganization Committee proposed an Administrative School District, in effect consolidating several school districts in the northeastern part of the county. The residents of Eagle Valley, the area of one of the school districts, were apprehensive that the proposed district would cause them to lose their high school and that one high school, to serve the entire district, would be built in the more populous Pine Valley. At a public hearing on the proposed new district, called pursuant to the school reorganization statute, a document was referred to which commenced, "To Whomsoever It May Concern." It was signed by the directors and clerks of all the districts proposed to be in the new Administrative District. It provided, among other things, as follows: "That no school be changed, moved or consolidated without the approval of the patrons in the attendance area which that school serves."

The complaint filed by plaintiffs as representatives of the residents of Eagle Valley alleges that the Eagle Valley residents "were advised that said agreement [the above-quoted statement] would be incorporated in the school district reorganization plan." The "said agreement" was not in fact incorporated in the school reorganization plan. Plaintiffs further allege that because of their belief that they would continue to have their own high school until they approved a change, they voted in favor of the new Administrative District.

About five years after the new Administrative District was formed, a majority of the voters of the new district passed a bond issue for one high school for the entire district, to be built in Pine Valley.

The plaintiffs sought a declaration that the defendant Administrative District had no right to move the school without obtaining the consent of the Eagle Valley voters.

The trial court held against the plaintiffs and we affirm its ruling.

Art. VIII, 3, of the Oregon Constitution, vests the state legislature with the responsibility for public education.

The legislature has provided that a bond issue is passed and binding upon the entire district if it is approved by a majority of the voters in the entire district.

That legislative command is binding upon the new district. The alleged misadvice to the Eagle Valley voters cannot change or limit that legislative command. See [cases] holding that misrepresentations made during a campaign by public officials will not vitiate an election.

Affirmed.

NOTES

1. In common business transactions, misrepresentations relied on by others to their detriment are grounds for invalidating the transactions. Should the same rule apply to elections?

2. The Supreme Court of Arizona affirmed that an election to rescind a bond issue that was approved at a prior election was valid as long as officials had not sold any bonds. The court acknowledged that other courts were divided on the question. *Members of Bd. of Educ. of Pearce Union High School Dist. v. Leslie*, 543 P.2d 775 (Ariz.1975).

3. Massachusetts' highest court invalidated an election where, contrary to statute, an unsuccessful candidate for reelection to a school committee was unintentionally not designated as an incumbent while others were properly identified. *Rizzo v. Board of Election Comm'rs of Revere*, 525 N.E.2d 409 [47 Educ. L. Rep. 685] (Mass.1988). Is this reasonable? Fair?

[CASE NO. 28] ONE PERSON, ONE VOTE APPLIES ONLY TO ELECTED POSITIONS

VERNET v. BELLMORE–MERRICK CENTRAL HIGH SCHOOL DISTRICT

United States District Court, Eastern District of New York, 2004.
343 F.Supp.2d 186 [193 Educ. L. Rep. 726] *aff'd without published opinion*, 155 Fed.Appx. 32 (2d Cir.2005).

■ PLATT, DISTRICT JUDGE.

Defendant Bellmore–Merrick High School District ("Bellmore–Merrick") moves, prior to serving its answer, to dismiss Plaintiff Stephen P. Vernet's ("Mr. Vernet") complaint ... on the ground that the exact same claims were decided by this Court thirty years ago in favor of Bellmore–Merrick.

Mr. Vernet brings this action under 42 U.S.C.[A.] § 1983, and invokes the jurisdiction of this Court under 28 U.S.C.[A.] §§ 1331 and 1343.

Jurisdiction is further invoked under 28 U.S.C.[A.] §§ 2201 and 2202 as Mr. Vernet is seeking a declaratory judgment.

. . .

For the following reasons, Bellmore–Merrick's motion is GRANTED.

Facts

Bellmore–Merrick is organized under New York Education Law § 1901. Bellmore–Merrick oversees the administration of two middle schools and three high schools located in the Town of Hempstead, Nassau County. . . .Bellmore–Merrick is composed of four Union Free School Districts ("UFSD"). The respective populations of the four USFD's vary widely: . . . .

The four districts govern the elementary schools that feed into two middle schools and three high schools which make up the Bellmore–Merrick school district. The UFSD's, i.e. the elementary schools, are each governed by a school board consisting of members elected by the residents of each Union Free School District: . . . .

Each school board, acting separately for their own UFSD's, then appoints two of its members to serve on the Bellmore–Merrick school board which governs the middle and high schools. The residents of the four UFSD's do not vote directly for the individuals who serve on the Bellmore–Merrick school board.

Mr. Vernet claims that the current practice of allowing each UFSD to select two of its members to serve on the Bellmore–Merrick school board despite a disparity in the number of residents within each UFSD, violates the "one man, one vote" principle and the Equal Protection Clause of the 14th Amendment. Mr. Vernet contends the individual votes of residents in each of the UFSD are "diluted" because each UFSD has the same number of members selected to represent their community on the Bellmore–Merrick school board.

Standard

In deciding a motion to dismiss under FED. R. CIV. P. 12(b) the Court is required to accept as true all factual allegations in the complaint and to consider documents attached to and incorporated by reference in the complaint. In a Rule 12(b)(6) motion to dismiss for failure to state claims upon which relief may be granted, Bellmore–Merrick bears the burden of showing that even if Mr. Vernet's allegations are accepted as true, and all reasonable inferences are drawn in Mr. Vernet's favor, Mr. Vernet is still not entitled to relief.

Discussion

I. *Defendant's Argument: The Decision in Rosenthal v. Board of Education Mandates Dismissal of Plaintiff's Action.*

Bellmore–Merrick's sole reason for dismissal of Mr. Vernet's claims is grounded in the *stare decisis* impact of a 1974 decision by this Court involving the same claims and defendant. [In *Rosenthal*] . . . the Court considered whether the process by which board members are chosen to serve on the Bellmore–Merrick school board violated the "one man, one vote" principle and was therefore unconstitutional. The Court held that the two-tiered method of choosing board members was an appointive vice elective process and that the "one man, one vote" principle only applied in cases where "the officials whose election is challenged must have been elected by popular vote."

II. *Plaintiff's Response*

a. *Rosenthal mislabeled the Bellmore–Merrick school board selection process as an appointive governing body.*

Mr. Vernet concedes that "(i)n *Rosenthal*, the Second Circuit properly recognized the 'one man, one vote' principle only applies to elective bodies."

Mr. Vernet argues that although the Second Circuit correctly reaffirmed the Supreme Court's holding that the "one person, one vote" principle does not apply where officials are appointed, the Bellmore–Merrick school board only *appears* to be an appointed governing body. Mr. Vernet alleges that the term appointment is merely a label misapplied to the Bellmore–Merrick school board selection process and argues that discovery should be permitted to substantiate this allegation.

Mr. Vernet, however, fails to allege any facts in his complaint whatsoever to support his contention that the Bellmore–Merrick school board selection process is anything other than appointive in nature. Mr. Vernet challenges whether the *Rosenthal* Court properly defined the Bellmore–Merrick school board's selection process on the grounds that the "plaintiff in *Rosenthal* did not conduct an evidentiary exploration of the issue of elective versus appointive nature of the [Bellmore–Merrick school board]."

The Court of Appeals for the Second Circuit convened the *Rosenthal* three Judge panel specifically for the task of deciding whether the Bellmore–Merrick school board selection process was appointive or elective. The three Judge panel determined that the nature of the Bellmore–Merrick school board selection process was appointive in nature. Included in the Court's analysis was testimony from the then President of the Bellmore–Merrick school board concerning the functions of the school board. The Court also reviewed New York Education Law § 1901. Mr. Vernet provides no reason for this Court to doubt that the *Rosenthal* three Judge panel would have come to a different conclusion today considering the two tier selection process remains—as Mr. Vernet concedes—unchanged.

Mr. Vernet further alleges that he has learned, through his own research, that members of the Bellmore–Merrick school board "are voted upon by motion in open meetings of the Union Free School District Boards of Education." Mr. Vernet does not describe the research he conducted. Moreover, Mr. Vernet's complaint is devoid of any factual allegations related to such research. He further questions whether the names of those selected to be on the Bellmore–Merrick school board are "discussed" and whether "general campaigning" occurs during UFSD meetings. Mr. Vernet asks this Court to permit further discovery in the hopes of substantiating these questions on the grounds that "all of these events and more are indicative of an election."

Naturally board members wishing to be appointed to a position of increased responsibility would not simply sit on their hands and wish for an appointment. Even if it were true that members of the individual UFSD's campaigned amongst their colleagues to be selected to the Bellmore–Merrick school board, that fact would not change the essential appointive nature of the selection process. The key factor in deciding whether the Bellmore–Merrick school board selection process violates the principle of one person, one vote, is whether the board members selected to serve on the Bellmore–Merrick school board are popularly elected: "The emphasis we put on popular election as the test echoes the Supreme Court's recognition that the crucial factor in the application of Fourteenth Amendment considerations to any apportionment scheme is that the officials whose election is challenged must have been elected by popular vote."

b. *The current structure of the Bellmore–Merrick Central High School District supports a weighted voting system and is therefore unconstitutional.*

Mr. Vernet's other argument is that the current selection process of the Bellmore–Merrick school board supports a weighted voting system. Mr. Vernet contends that his ability to participate in the selection of members to the Bellmore–Merrick school board is diluted because his more populous UFSD has an equal number of members on the Bellmore–Merrick school board as do the smaller UFSD's. Mr. Vernet asks the Court to compare the facts of this case to *Jackson v. Nassau County Board of Supervisors*, in which a group of residents in Nassau County challenged the make-up of the Nassau County Board of Supervisors on the grounds that the more populous Town of Hempstead had more weighted votes than the other, smaller towns, and that such practice was unconstitutional.

At the time the Court in *Jackson* evaluated the political process in Nassau County, the Nassau County Board of Supervisors were elected from each of the five towns within Nassau County using a weighted voting system. This method of voting gave supervisors from more populous towns more voting power when deciding issues before the Board. The Court determined that this process was unconstitutional on the grounds that i) the "one man, one vote" applied to local governmental agencies; ii) the United States Supreme Court had rejected weighted voting; and iii) the formula by which votes were distributed amongst the towns in Nassau County created a standard deviation between the actual population and the weighted votes which was impermissibly large and thereby violated the one person, one vote requirement.

Bellmore–Merrick responds that *Jackson* is distinguishable form the case at bar because representatives on the Nassau County Board of Supervisors were popularly elected. In this case there exists a two-tiered system in which the Bellmore–Merrick school board members are not popularly elected but appointed by school boards which are popularly elected. Bellmore–Merrick asserts that under the holding of *Rosenthal* it does not matter in a two-tiered selection process that the members of the local boards who make the appointments to the second tier were themselves popularly elected.

This Court agrees with Bellmore–Merrick that *Rosenthal* and *Warden* provide the requisite *stare decisis* effect to stave off Mr. Vernet's challenges to the appointive nature of the Bellmore–Merrick school board and his claim that residents' votes within the UFSD's are diluted. *Jackson* is distinguishable because in that case the residents of Nassau County directly elected members to the Board of Supervisors whereas in the case at bar, the Bellmore–Merrick's school board members are appointed.

The result is the same even if this Court applied the holding in *Jackson* to the first tier of the Bellmore–Merrick school board selection process. The individual UFSD's do not meet as a single governing unit unlike the now dismantled Nassau County Board of Supervisors. The weight of one resident's vote is equal to any other vote within the Bellmore, North Bellmore, Merrick or North Merrick school districts when choosing representatives for their applicable UFSD. Neither the first or second tier of the Bellmore–Merrick school board selection process involves the unconstitutional practice of weighted voting as described by the Court in Jackson.

Conclusion

Mr. Vernet seems to suggest that the issue of diluted voting was a new inequity in the American political landscape discovered by the Court in the *Jackson* case: "Until the mid–1990s the courts tolerated an illegal weighted voting system which violated the 'one man, one vote' principle." In fact, the *Rosenthal* Court specifically discussed the issue of weighted voting in its analysis of the Bellmore–Merrick school board selection process: "If plaintiff did in fact vote for the members of the [Bellmore–Merrick school board] representing his union free school district, his vote would be diluted in violation of the one man, one vote principle." The Court instead held that the Bellmore–Merrick school board was appointive in nature and so like Mr. Rosenthal's claims thirty years ago, Mr. Vernet's contention that his vote as a resident within the Bellmore–Merrick school district is diluted has no merit. Despite Mr. Vernet's frustrations with New York Education Law § 1901 and the Bellmore–Merrick school board selection process, nothing presented by Mr. Vernet in his complaint persuades this Court that the holding in *Rosenthal* should be disturbed.

Accordingly, Defendant Bellmore–Merrick's motion pursuant to FED. R. CIV. P. 12(b)(6) to dismiss Plaintiff Mr. Vernet's complaint is hereby GRANTED.

SO ORDERED.

NOTES

1.   Do you agree with the court?

2.   Should local school board members be appointed or elected?

[CASE NO. 29]   POWER OF BOARD TO EXPEND FUNDS TO
ADVOCATE FAVORABLE VOTE

CITIZENS TO PROTECT PUBLIC FUNDS v. BOARD
OF EDUCATION OF PARSIPPANY–TROY
HILLS TOWNSHIP

Supreme Court of New Jersey, 1953.
98 A.2d 673.

■ WILLIAM J. BRENNAN, JR., J.

. . . Defendant proposed a program for enlarging several school buildings and to issue bonds in the amount of $560,000 to finance the first half of the program. There being existing debt limitations, approval of the proposal, as required by R.S. 18:5–86 . . . was first obtained from the State Commissioner of Education and the Local Government Board before the proposal was submitted, as is also required by that statute and as was in any event required by R.S. 18:7–73, N.J.S.A., to a referendum vote at an election held December 2, 1952 when the proposal was adopted by a vote of 875 to 542. However, the defendant board did not prior to that election submit the proposed building expansion plans to the local planning board for approval as to "location, character and extent thereof," according to R.S. 40:55–7, as amended. . . .

When the building program was authorized by resolution adopted August 27, 1952, the 1952–1953 school budget included an appropriation captioned "Current expenses, administrative, architecture fees, preliminary." Some $358.85 of this appropriation was spent by defendant for "printing, artist's work and postage" to print and circulate an 18–page booklet entitled "Read the Facts Behind the Parsippany–Troy Hills School Building Program." All but one page of the booklet depicts in graphic form, effectively illustrated to arrest the reader's attention, such facts as the growth of the grade school population (from 1945, doubled, and by 1956 to be tripled), the inadequacies of existing facilities, the proposed immediate additions, with architectural sketches, to two schools, other expansions planned to be deferred until 1955, the aggregate and annual costs, principal and interest, of the immediate program and the effect upon taxes of such cost. However, there also appears on the cover and on two of the pages "Vote Yes," and "Vote Yes–December 2, 1952," and an entire page which, except for an accompanying sketch, we reproduce:

"What Will Happen if You Don't Vote Yes?"

"Double Sessions"

"This will automatically Cheat your child of 1/3 of his education (4 hours instead of 6).

"Yearly school changing and hour long Bus rides will continue for many children.

"Morning Session (8:30–12:30) Children will leave home 1/2 hour earlier.

"Afternoon Session (12:30–4:30) Children will return home 1 1/2 hours later (many after dark).

"Children in some families would be attending different sessions (depending upon grade).

"Transportation costs will increase (could double) with 2 sets of bus routes per day.

"Temporary room rentals will continue ($4,000 per year).

"Double use of equipment will necessitate more rapid replacement.

"Note: Operating expenses will continue to rise as the enrollment increases (more teachers, more supplies and equipment for children. This Will Be So Whether We Build Or Not.)"

On December 1, the day before the referendum election, radio station WMTR broadcast a 15–minute panel discussion of the proposed building program as one of the station's "public interest" programs. The panel was composed of a member of the defendant board of education and two members of a citizens advisory committee which assisted the board in the formulation of the building program. The superintendent of schools, with the approval of the board's president, advised the principals of the several schools equipped with public address systems or radios that school children in grades four to eight might be permitted to hear the broadcast. According to the numerous affidavits of teachers offered to support defendant's motion for dismissal, some turned on the program and others did not, the reception was unsatisfactory in many instances and the broadcast for that reason was not heard, many children paid no attention to it, and the reaction of at least one class was why "do we have to listen to this sort of thing." And it appears without contradiction that the panel discussion was purely informative as to the scope of the building program and that there was no exhortation to vote affirmatively for the proposed bond issue at the referendum election the next day. . . .

The contention that there was error in the denial of a declaratory judgment as to the legality of the expenditures for the printing and distribution of the booklet, and the exposure of school children to the radio broadcast is premised solely upon the assertion that the same things may be done or attempted by the defendant board in connection with the balance of the building program upon its submission to the electorate for adoption. It was conceded on the oral argument that the actions under attack, if improper, would not suffice to invalidate the election already held. But the actions taken, it is admitted, had particular relation only to the proposal before the electorate on December 2, 1952, and for aught that appears they seem to have spent their force. The booklet on its face shows that it is not intended for use in connection with future plans for complet-ing the balance of the expansion program. Plainly, then, any issues as to both the booklet and the radio broadcast are moot and the resolution of new, or even similar, issues as to other actions attempted by the defendant for a similar purpose in the future must await the event. . . .

There is no express statutory provision authorizing the expenditure by boards of education of public funds in the manner done by the defendant board for the printing and distribution of the booklet. The power, however, within the limits hereafter stated, is to be found by necessary or fair implication in the powers expressly conferred by R.S. 18:7–77.1, N.J.S.A., which enumerates the permissible items which may be included in the annual budget, and more particularly as incident to "(b) the building, enlarging, repairing or furnishing of a schoolhouse or schoolhouses."

The power so implicit plainly embraces the making of reasonable expenditures for the purpose of giving voters relevant facts to aid them in reaching an informed judgment when voting upon the proposal. In these days of high costs, projects of this type invariably run into very substantial outlays. This has tended to sharpen the interest of every taxpayer and family man in such projects. Adequate and proper school facilities are an imperative necessity, but the large additional tax burden their cost often entails concerns taxpayers that they be obtained with the maximum economy of cost. At the same time the complexities of today's problems make more difficult the task of every citizen in reaching an intelligent judgment upon the accommodation of endurable financial cost with the acknowledged need for adequate education. The need for full disclosure of all relevant facts is obvious, and the board of education is well qualified to supply the facts. But a fair presentation of the facts will necessarily include all consequences, good and bad, of the proposal, not only the anticipated improvement in educational opportunities, but also the increased tax rate and such other less desirable consequences as may be foreseen. If the presentation is fair in that sense, the power to make reasonable expenditure for the purpose may fairly be implied as within the purview of the power, indeed duty, of the board of education to formulate the construction program in the first instance. And the choice of the media of communication to give such facts, whether by the use of a booklet, as in this case, radio broadcast, newspaper advertising, or other means, is within the discretion, reasonably exercised, of the board of education. The booklet under attack here, in 17 of its 18 pages, fairly presents the facts as to need and the advantages and disadvantages of the program, including the tax effect of its cost, and if it stopped there, none could fairly complain that the reasonable expenditure made for its preparation and distribution was without the scope of the implied power.

But the defendant board was not content simply to present the facts. The exhortation "Vote Yes" is repeated on three pages, and the dire consequences of the failure so to do are over-dramatized on the page reproduced above. In that manner the board made use of public funds to advocate one side only of the controversial question without affording the dissenters the opportunity by means of that financed medium to present their side, and thus imperilled the propriety of the entire expenditure. The public funds entrusted to the board belong equally to the proponents and opponents of the proposition, and the use of the funds to finance not the presentation of facts merely but also arguments to persuade the voters that only one side has merit, gives the dissenters just cause for complaint. The expenditure is then not within the implied power and is not lawful in the absence of express authority from the Legislature.

. . .

We do not mean that the public body formulating the program is otherwise restrained from advocating and espousing its adoption by the voters. Indeed, as in the instant case, when the program represents the body's judgment of what is required in the effective discharge of its responsibility, it is not only the right but perhaps the duty of the body to endeavor to secure the assent of the voters thereto. The question we are considering is simply the extent to and manner in which the funds may with justice to the rights of dissenters be expended for espousal of the voters' approval of the body's judgment. Even this the body may do within fair limits. The reasonable expense, for example, of the conduct of a public forum at which all may appear and freely express their views pro and con would not be improper. The same may be said of reasonable expenses incurred for radio or television broadcasts taking the form of debates between proponents of the differing sides of the proposition. It is the expenditure of public funds in support of one side only in a manner which gives the dissenters no opportunity to present their side which is outside the pale.

We acknowledge that the limits here pronounced are not suggested in the decision of the former Court of Errors and Appeals in *City Affairs Committee of Jersey City v. Board of Com'rs of Jersey City*. We are persuaded, however, that simple fairness and justice to the rights of dissenters require that the use by public bodies of public funds for advocacy be restrained within those limits in the absence of a legislative grant in express terms of the broader power....

Judgment affirmed.

NOTES

1. Employees can spend school funds to draw up building plans, and in most jurisdictions, for educational and architectural consultants. Is it logical to prevent these same officials from spending funds to urge the acceptance of their proposed plans?

2. If school officials work diligently with community participation to develop a proposal for school improvement, is strict neutrality as regards to its acceptance clearly in the public interest? How can board members work for its acceptance within the bounds of this decision?

3. The Supreme Court of Mississippi cited this case as the most thorough discussion of permissible expenditures by public bodies. The court maintained that board members were personally liable for flagrantly unauthorized expenditures, including paying campaign workers and having a fish fry, in support of a school bond referendum. *Smith v. Dorsey*, 599 So.2d 529 [75 Educ. L. Rep. 692] (Miss. 1992).

CHAPTER 5

SCHOOL FINANCE

INTRODUCTION

As reflected by the Supreme Court's first ever case involving elementary and secondary schools, *Springfield Township v. Quick* (*Quick*),[1] financing public education is ordinarily a joint enterprise of state and local school boards even if the relationship between these two bodies does not always operate smoothly. The *Quick* Court held that state officials in Indiana did not violate the rights of a township when they allocated funds from the state treasury by considering how much money that township schools had available under a federal law.

Relatively little of the litigation on finance as it impacts local school systems addresses state-level concerns. Cases involving states typically examine constitutional mandates and legislative limits on how resources to pay for public education are raised and/or allocated, often resulting in judicial orders calling for the creation of new funding plans.[2] In the process, school finance cases seem to take on lives of their own, requiring multiple rounds of litigation before returning to legislatures.[3] In light of questions over how state and local boards pay for schooling, this chapter focuses on raising and distributing funds for public education.

THE SCHOOL TAX

POWER TO LEVY

As discussed in Chapter 3, school boards are creatures of the state designed to implement state constitutional mandates dealing with public education. This means that the legislatures that create school boards not only set tax rates but also have the authority to identify which properties

---

1. 63 U.S. 56, 22 How. 56, 16 L.Ed. 256 (1859).

2. *See, e.g., Robinson v. Cahill*, 303 A.2d 273 (N.J.1973), *cert. denied*, 414 U.S. 976, 94 S.Ct. 292, 38 L.Ed.2d 219 (1973); *Edgewood Indep. School Dist. v. Kirby*, 777 S.W.2d 391 [56 Educ. L. Rep. 663] (Tex.1989); *Rose v. Council for Better Educ.*, 790 S.W.2d 186 [60 Educ. L. Rep. 1289] (Ky.1989).

3. *See, e.g., DeRolph v. State*, 677 N.E.2d 733 [116 Educ. L. Rep. 1140] (Ohio 1997). This litigation resulted in more than ten reported opinions, with the state supreme court culminating judicial involvement, at least for the time being, *sub nom. State v. Lewis*, 786 N.E.2d 60 [174 Educ. L. Rep. 1073] (Ohio 2003), and returning the dispute to the state legislature.

are to be taxed and which are exempt from taxation.[4] Further, boards may exercise only those powers that legislatures confer on them, whether expressly or impliedly, and may be granted fiscal powers in a variety of ways, even in the same jurisdiction.[5]

The authority of local boards to establish and operate schools does not include the implied power to levy taxes, which, with the exception of Michigan,[6] is ordinarily based on the value of real property within districts.[7] Accordingly, boards have no inherent power to tax.[8] Rather, since taxation is a special power that legislatures must specifically confer on subordinate governmental agencies, even when boards may levy taxes for specific purposes, they lack constitutional rights to do so.[9]

In delegating their taxing powers, both as to kinds and rates, legislatures can limit the ability of lower bodies, such as school boards, to tax as long as taxing authorities include elected officials. Since legislatures and local school boards are bound by state constitutional tax limits,[10] the courts do not permit even indirect exceptions.[11] Legislatures cannot delegate their power to levy taxes to appointed bodies unless they set clear limits on the extent of transferred powers.[12] As long as legislative delegations specify the purposes and maximum amounts or rates for taxes, they are likely to be upheld.[13] Under these arrangements, courts are ordinarily satisfied that legislatures have set taxes and are merely granting discretion to local administrators in their implementation. Even so, legislatures run the risk of violating the separation of powers doctrine if they permit local legislators to approve tax rate increases imposed by county school boards.[14]

Turning to illustrative cases, a dispute arose in Chicago over the school board's ability to prepare its own budget even though it depended on city officials to levy taxes. The Supreme Court of Illinois rejected the claim that the city's levying taxes was an unlawful exercise of power under the state constitution, pointing out that the statutory language authorizing the levy

---

4. *School Dist. of City of Monessen v. Farnham & Pfile Co.*, 878 A.2d 142 [200 Educ. L. Rep. 250] (Pa.Cmwlth.Ct.2005).

5. *Pirrone v. City of Boston*, 305 N.E.2d 96 (Mass.1973).

6. MICH. COMP. LAWS ANN. § 388.1620. *See also DeRolph v. State*, 754 N.E.2d 1184, 1212–13 [156 Educ. L. Rep. 1290] (Ohio 2001) (Douglas, J., concurring) (discussing Michigan's approach).

7. *State v. Campbell County School Dist.*, 32 P.3d 325 [157 Educ. L. Rep. 366] (Wyo.2001).

8. *Marion & McPherson Ry. Co. v. Alexander*, 64 P. 978 (Kan.1901) [Case No. 30]; *Frazier v. State By and Through Pittman*, 504 So.2d 675 [39 Educ. L. Rep. 417] (Miss.1987); *Unified School Dist. No. 229 v. State*, 885 P.2d 1170 [96 Educ. L. Rep. 258] (Kan.1994), *cert. denied*, 515 U.S. 1144, 115 S.Ct. 2582, 132 L.Ed.2d 832 (1995).

9. *Edgewood Indep. School Dist. v. Meno*, 917 S.W.2d 717 [108 Educ. L. Rep. 1310] (Tex.1995).

10. *Hurd v. City of Buffalo*, 355 N.Y.S.2d 369 (1974).

11. *Bethlehem Steel Corp. v. Board of Educ. of City School Dist. of Lackawanna*, 406 N.Y.S.2d 752, 378 N.E.2d 115 (1978), *appeal dismissed*, 439 U.S. 922, 99 S.Ct. 303, 58 L.Ed.2d 315 (1978).

12. *Wilson v. School Dist. of Philadelphia*, 195 A. 90 (Pa.1937); *Crow v. McAlpine*, 285 S.E.2d 355 [1 Educ. L. Rep. 1004] (S.C.1981).

13. *Minsinger v. Rau*, 84 A. 902 (Pa.1912); *Village of W. Milwaukee v. Area Bd. of Vocational, Technical and Adult Educ.*, 187 N.W.2d 387 (Wis.1971).

14. *Gunter v. Blanton*, 192 S.E.2d 473 (S.C.1972).

was framed in the conjunctive, joining the board and city.[15] The court reasoned that insofar as the board had to complete all preliminary steps before adopting a budget, and no school taxes would have been forthcoming if the city council had not passed an ordinance levying one, the board did not levy the tax. Previously, the Supreme Court of Tennessee held that where the legislature set the rate by which the amount of tax was deduced from events occurring within a year, this was a direct exercise of taxing power rather than a permissible delegation to school officials.[16] The Supreme Court of Delaware also upheld a legislative grant of power to the state board of education to impose a tax on reorganized districts to cover payments for bonded indebtedness.[17]

Insofar as education is a state rather than a local function, school taxes are state, not local, funds even if they are levied by local boards. As highlighted by a case from Kansas, state officials may compel local boards to operate schools that function pursuant to specified standards even if district residents do not agree with such arrangements.[18] In like manner, Maryland's highest court agreed that a board may be required to issue bonds to raise funds to erect a school where voters had not consented to the plan.[19] Other courts ruled that if taxes are levied for special purposes, the funds must be used only for those purposes.[20] Funds remaining after goals are achieved may be distributed as legislatures permit.[21]

Absent statutory or constitutional provisions to the contrary, such as where the Constitution of Kentucky permitted a sheriff's commission to do so,[22] when municipal bodies collect taxes levied by school boards, they are entitled to the entire proceeds.[23] On a related point, an appellate court in Pennsylvania affirmed that a tax collector was not entitled to additional compensation for collecting a district's real estate taxes. The collector unsuccessfully argued that insofar as the applicable statute only required him to collect taxes passed by an ordinance, not a school board resolution, he was entitled to extra remuneration for his efforts. The court noted that while both resolutions and ordinances are vehicles by which political subdivisions may levy and collect taxes, and boards were limited to the former, boards had no other means to direct elected officials to collect their taxes.[24] Still, a municipality is not permitted to assess a school board's collection fee or retention of accrued interest.[25]

---

15. *Latham v. Board of Educ. of the City of Chicago*, 201 N.E.2d 111 (Ill.1964).

16. *Kee v. Parks*, 283 S.W. 751 (Tenn.1926).

17. *Opinion of the Justices*, 246 A.2d 90 (Del.1968).

18. *State v. Freeman*, 58 P. 959 (Kan.1899).

19. *Revell v. City of Annapolis*, 31 A. 695 (Md.1895). [Case No. 31]

20. *Thomas v. Board of Educ., County of McDowell*, 261 S.E.2d 66 (W.Va.1979); *Lind v. Rockland School Dist. No. 382*, 821 P.2d 983 [71 Educ. L. Rep. 946] (Idaho 1991) (adding that board spending is limited to the amount authorized in an election).

21. *Douglas Indep. School Dist. No. 3 of Meade and Pennington Counties v. Bell*, 272 N.W.2d 825 (S.D.1978).

22. *Marshall v. Commissioner ex rel. Hatchett*, 20 S.W.3d 478 [145 Educ. L. Rep. 797] (Ky.Ct.App.2000).

23. *New Orleans v. Fisher*, 180 U.S. 185, 21 S.Ct. 347, 45 L.Ed. 485 (1901).

24. *Plum Borough School Dist. v. Schlegel*, 855 A.2d 939 [191 Educ. L. Rep. 416] (Pa.Cmwlth.Ct.2004).

Courts generally permit land developers to be charged impact fees to pay for needed facilities to accommodate changes in civic services occasioned by developments with school boards often being the sole beneficiaries. For example, the Supreme Court of California decided that the use of a local fee resulting in a board's being the sole beneficiary did not violate equal protection.[26] In addition, the Supreme Court of Florida agreed that an arrangement of this type did not violate the state constitutional mandate for a uniform system of free schools.[27]

IRREGULAR LEVIES

Where state laws require local agencies and school boards to follow established procedures in levying taxes, their failure to do so can give rise to questions over the validity of taxes. The validity of taxes in the face of irregularities depends on whether courts interpret statutory collection provisions as mandatory or discretionary. If courts believe that legislatures intended statutory steps to be conditions precedent to the validity of taxes, they are treated as mandatory. Courts are confronted with the alternatives of invalidating irregularly levied taxes and perhaps causing financial chaos for school systems or treating them as valid and imposing hardships on taxpayers. Courts also usually agree that taxes are valid if irregularities are minor and do not deprive taxpayers of substantial rights.

If it appears that irregularities deprive taxpayers of a voice over whether taxes should be levied, courts are disposed to treat statutory provisions as mandatory. This situation arises most often in disputes over notice of elections addressing taxes because unlike the dates of general elections, which are fixed by law, the dates of levies are set by local school boards. Courts agree that the electorate is bound to take note of elections set by law such that local notice is treated as merely a reminder. When dealing with levies, since voters have no notice of elections except as provided by their local boards, courts are more likely to treat statutory notice as mandatory.[28] If evidence reveals that residents knew of elections and had the opportunity to vote, or that providing notice would not have changed the results, the courts leave the results in place.[29]

When school boards do not use funds for the express purposes for which they are collected, taxpayers have rights of redress. In such a case, the Supreme Court of Georgia affirmed that a board improperly used the proceeds from a special purpose local option sales tax for educational

---

25. *State ex rel. School Dist. of Springfield R–12 v. Wickliffe*, 650 S.W.2d 623 [11 Educ. L. Rep. 735] (Mo.1983), *Grand Rapids Pub. Schools v. City of Grand Rapids*, 381 N.W.2d 783 [30 Educ. L. Rep. 888] (Mich.Ct.App.1985).

26. *Candid Enterprises v. Grossmont Union High School Dist.*, 218 Cal.Rptr. 303 [27 Educ. L. Rep. 950] (Cal.1985).

27. *St. Johns County v. Northeast Fla. Builders Ass'n*, 583 So.2d 635 [69 Educ. L. Rep. 636] (Fla.1991).

28. *Roberts v. Murphy*, 86 S.E. 545 (Ga.1915).

29. *Shelton v. School Bd.*, 142 P. 1034 (Okla.1914).

purposes.[30] Where the board sought to raise $75 million for technology, with $59 million allocated to buy laptop computers for all middle and secondary school students in the district, the court agreed that it could not do so. The court held that the board could not use the proceeds for laptop computers since the resolution before voters was on whether funds could be used for designated capital outlay projects, including system-wide technology improvements in all schools, not computers for students. The same court subsequently affirmed that the proposed use of school tax funds to pay for a redevelopment project for historical rail segments encircling the urban core of a city violated state constitutional restrictions on expenditures of such funds since doing so was neither necessary nor incidental to public education.[31]

In a different situation, the Supreme Court of Iowa affirmed that school boards lacked the authority to use their property tax levies to pay fuel costs for their transportation services programs.[32] The court explained that the levies could not be used in this manner since the fuel services program allowing the boards to pay a set price for fuel, along with a risk management fee applied to the difference between the guaranteed price and actual cost of fuel they received, did not constitute an insurance agreement. The court refused to treat the program as one for insurance because it did not protect the boards against the risk of loss that allowed them to levy taxes to pay the costs of the fuel services programs.

RATE OF LEVY

Once school board officials formulate budgets, they must levy taxes to raise funds. In order to establish tax rates, officials must make estimates of revenues, sometimes raising more funds than anticipated. Generally speaking, boards cannot use their taxing powers to establish surpluses. Even so, the Supreme Court of Illinois reached different results in two cases separated by sixty-seven years. In the first, the court invalidated a levy by a local board that was designed to accumulate a fund to be used at some time in the future to build a school.[33] Conversely, the court rejected a claim that a tax levy was illegal since it was allegedly excessive.[34] The court acknowledged that although boards may not levy taxes beyond their needs, and thereby unnecessarily accumulate funds, they need not wait until money is actually required to pay outstanding obligations before levying taxes. Previously, the Supreme Court of Nebraska upheld a levy intended to have generated a small surplus if all of the funds had been collected.[35] The court pointed out that possible fluctuations in the amounts of expenses and revenues made it necessary for the board to estimate the sums that it would have needed.

---

30. *Johnstone v. Thompson*, 631 S.E.2d 650 [210 Educ. L. Rep. 817] (Ga.2006).

31. *Woodham v. City of Atlanta*, 657 S.E.2d 528 [230 Educ. L. Rep. 87] (Ga.2008).

32. *Iowa Ass'n of School Bds. v. Iowa Dep't of Educ.*, 739 N.W.2d 303 [224 Educ. L. Rep. 904] (Iowa 2007).

33. *Cleveland, C., C. & St. L. Ry. Co. v. People*, 69 N.E. 832 (Ill.1904).

34. *People ex rel. Sweet v. Central Ill. Pub. Serv. Co.*, 268 N.E.2d 404 (Ill.1971).

35. *C. R. T. Corp. v. Board of Equalization*, 110 N.W.2d 194 (Neb.1961).

When a county school board increased the tax rate to almost twice that of the prior year, taxpayers sought to enjoin its action as an abuse of discretion. The board countered that the levy was necessary due to uncertainty over the continued availability of federal funds. The Supreme Court of Georgia, observing that the funds that the board hoped to raise were about equal to the money ordinarily expected from the federal source, refused to grant the injunction.[36]

A dispute arose between a municipality and a school board when the former sought to compel the latter to spend an accumulated surplus before remitting the taxes that it was required to collect for schools. In directing the municipality to remit the taxes, an appellate court in New Jersey indicated that the board was entitled to maintain a reasonable surplus in order to meet unforeseen contingencies.[37] The court added that insofar as the state commissioner of education created a procedure for reviewing board budgets, a municipality could not impose its own limits.

In a case that had become moot, the Supreme Court of South Dakota determined that although it approved a school board's transfer of one year's surplus general funds to capital outlay funds,[38] there was a substantial difference when it did so for three years.[39] The court prevented the board from acting in the second situation since it feared that officials could have circumvented the requirement of obtaining voter approval for funding large building programs.

TAXPAYER REMEDIES FOR ILLEGAL TAXATION

Ordinarily, individuals who voluntarily pay taxes are unable to recover their funds based on the theory that insofar as they are presumed to know the law, and paid their taxes knowing of their invalidity, they could not claim ignorance as a ground on which to recoup their payments.[40] Occasionally, individual taxpayers or groups of taxpayers in class action suits,[41] challenge their having paid taxes under laws that were invalidated for one reason or another. In these kinds of cases, questions arise as to the rights of taxpayers to recover their funds. For instance, where a school board incorrectly assessed real property, an appellate court in Pennsylvania

---

36. *Watkins v. Jackson*, 179 S.E.2d 747 (Ga.1971).

37. *Board of Educ. of Borough of Fair Lawn v. Mayor and Council of Borough of Fair Lawn*, 362 A.2d 1270 (N.J.Super.Ct.Law Div.1976), *aff'd*, 380 A.2d 290 (N.J.Super.Ct.App.Div.1977).

38. *Blumer v. School Bd. of Beresford Indep. School Dist.*, 237 N.W.2d 655 (S.D.1975).

39. *Anderson v. Kennedy*, 264 N.W.2d 714 (S.D.1978).

40. *Cornell v. Board of Educ. for High School Dist. No. 99*, 3 N.E.2d 717 (Ill.App.Ct.1936). *See also Montour School Dist. v. Township of Collier*, 944 A.2d 113 [230 Educ. L. Rep. 667] (Pa.Cmwlth.Ct.2008) (affirming that a board was not entitled to recoup real estate taxes it paid to another township and local board).

41. *Frank v. Barker*, 20 S.W.3d 293 [146 Educ. L. Rep. 933] (Ark.2000).

directed officials to refund the difference to the aggrieved retirement center.[42]

The general rule with regard to the recovery of improperly paid taxes is inapplicable when remittances are made under duress or compulsion such as an imminent threat of seizure of the property. Payments that are made after protests are insufficient to render them involuntary such that parties can claim that they made payments under duress.[43] Yet, some jurisdictions recognize that payments are made under protest for the purposes of possible recovery.[44] In addition, a court can distinguish between a taxing authority's erroneous and illegal conduct, permitting recovery in the latter situation.[45]

Cases often turn on whether courts believe that the public interest should be protected by requiring individual taxpayers to bear the losses for mistaken or illegal collections of funds. The courts rely on the notion that when public agencies make commitments on the assumption that the funds paid into their treasuries would have remained available, the common good could suffer a great hardship if agency funds are depleted by having to make repayments. While there is some conflict in case law, the rule of non-recovery is still widely applied, especially where a taxing authority's failure was due to an error or to exceeding a power that was unclear beforehand.[46] Even so, it seems settled that the collection of illegal taxes may be enjoined.[47]

As demonstrated by a case from Texas, while taxpayers can enjoin the collections of illegal taxes, illegality is not necessarily a defense in a suit for delinquent taxes. The dispute arose when taxpayers, who did not protest a taxing scheme when it was instituted, refused to pay the tax and attempted to defend their behavior by attacking the illegality of the system when they were sued. In dismissing the claim, an appellate court declared that the taxpayers failed to meet their burden of proving that they suffered substantial financial losses due to the failure of city and board officials to assess their property legally since it was insufficient to show that officials used an illegal system of rendering and assessing taxes.[48]

In a second case from Texas, an appellate court ruled that a school taxing authority's failure to include personal property on a tax roll was not a basis for enjoining an assessment of real property. The court rejected the argument that leaving personal property off of tax rolls required officials to levy higher taxes on real property in order to raise the revenue for school operations. The court was of the view both that the omission was simply an unchallenged custom and that the taxpayers failed to show that the new

---

42. *Nottingham Vill. Ret. Ctr. Assoc., LP v. Northumberland County Bd. of Assessments,* 885 A.2d 93 [203 Educ. L. Rep. 303] (Pa.Cmwlth.Ct.2005).

43. *Wilson v. School Dist. of Philadelphia,* 195 A. 90 (Pa.1937).

44. *McDonough v. Aylward,* 500 S.W.2d 721 (Mo.1973); *Jenkins by Agyei v. State of Mo.,* 967 F.2d 1248 [76 Educ. L. Rep. 42] (8th Cir.1992), *cert. denied,* 506 U.S. 1033, 113 S.Ct. 811, 121 L.Ed.2d 684 (1992).

45. *Niagara Mohawk Power Corp. v. City School Dist. of City of Troy,* 464 N.Y.S.2d 449 [12 Educ. L. Rep. 450] (N.Y.1983).

46. *Gulesian v. Dade County School Bd.,* 281 So.2d 325 (Fla.1973).

47. *Shaffer v. Carter,* 252 U.S. 37, 40 S.Ct. 221, 64 L.Ed. 445 (1920).

48. *City of Houston v. McCarthy,* 371 S.W.2d 587 (Tex.Civ.App.1963).

approach would have resulted in substantial changes in taxes.[49] Similarly, the Supreme Court of Wyoming found that the state legislature could have limited school funding taxes to property taxes even though nothing prohibited it from imposing other taxes or creating new methods of raising revenues.[50]

Taxpayers cannot claim entitlements to tax adjustments because they allegedly do not receive equal shares of benefits.[51] The Supreme Court of New Hampshire applied this principle in interpreting a century-and-a-half-old statute which permitted town governments to abate the taxes of those who claimed to have been aggrieved by tax assessments.[52] The court declared that the plaintiff's claim lacked merit since he was not personally aggrieved by the statute insofar as the town allowed for a limited real estate tax abatement to those who paid for the education of their high school-aged children outside of the district.

APPORTIONMENT OF STATE SCHOOL FUNDS

Funds collected by local boards are state monies that may, subject to constitutional restrictions, be spent in any manner that legislatures deem to be in the best interest of their states. Statewide taxes to raise money for school purposes, then, are constitutional even if their proceeds are distributed so that less-wealthy districts get more state aid than wealthier ones. Opponents of this approach claim that such legislation deprives some citizens of property without due process of law, that it violates the constitutional prohibition against unequal taxation, and that it results in taxation for a private purpose. The courts have consistently rejected these claims in firmly upholding the validity of laws designed to equalize educational opportunities.[53]

Taxes need not be spent in the districts where they are collected. Yet, the manner of apportioning state funds has caused considerable legal difficulty. Some state constitutions specify distribution plans for funds while others identify only goals or purposes. In a case addressing such a distinction, the Supreme Court of Illinois upheld the statutory language that "the state has the primary responsibility for financing the system of public education"[54] as a purpose not requiring state officials to supply more than half of needed funds to local school boards.

Constitutional apportionment plans address only those funds specified in their provisions. If it is permissible to create funds that are separate and

---

49. *Kirkpatrick v. Parker*, 406 S.W.2d 81 (Tex.Civ.App.1966).

50. *State v. Campbell County School Dist.*, 32 P.3d 325 [157 Educ. L. Rep. 366] (Wyo.2001).

51. *Union Refrigerator Transit Co. v. Kentucky*, 199 U.S. 194, 26 S.Ct. 36, 50 L.Ed. 150 (1905).

52. *Barksdale v. Town of Epsom*, 618 A.2d 814 [80 Educ. L. Rep. 132] (N.H.1992).

53. *Sawyer v. Gilmore*, 83 A. 673 (Me.1912) [Case No. 32]; *State ex rel. Woodahl v. Straub*, 520 P.2d 776 (Mont.1974).

54. *Blase v. State*, 302 N.E.2d 46, 47 (Ill.1973).

distinct from those covered by state constitutions, the monies may be distributed as legislatures dictate. To this end, Connecticut's highest court asserted that although public funds could not be used to transport children to non-public schools, non-constitutional funds could be used.[55] On the other hand, if all money coming into a state's coffers for school purposes automatically becomes part of the constitutional fund, it cannot be distributed except in accordance with the constitutional plan.

Where the state constitution provided for distribution based on student populations, and the legislature set up a program focusing on the measure of needs in school systems, the Supreme Court of Michigan invalidated the statute as unconstitutional.[56] In another case from Michigan, where the constitution prevented officials from "reducing the state financed proportion of the necessary costs of any existing activity or service required of units of local government by state law,"[57] the same court held that the provision covered categorical aid for specific courses required by state officials such as driver education and special education but did not cover general aid to schools. The court subsequently interpreted this provision as not covering a board's share of Social Security payments for school employees.[58]

When officials planned to impose a levy on all taxable property within a county's boundaries, and the proceeds were to be distributed to school systems based on their needs, opponents challenged the proposed tax. The opponents claimed that the tax violated the constitutional provision that taxes had to be uniform on the same class of persons within the territorial limits of the taxing authority. The Supreme Court of Idaho upheld the levy, positing that insofar as it was on all taxable property in the county, there was no lack of uniformity because financial need provided a rational basis for distributing educational funding.[59] The court was satisfied that even though the proceeds were not distributed equally throughout the county, its uniformity was not destroyed as long as receipts were apportioned fairly in an effort to equalize educational standards.

At issue in Georgia was a law permitting specified types of school boards to receive financial aid based on calculations of property values that were one-third higher than they were in actuality. The record revealed that the law had the effect of reducing state contributions to these systems while proportionately increasing aid to less-wealthy districts. The state's highest court upheld the statute, maintaining that insofar as its key feature was that it sought to help all schools, it required all boards to do their best before receiving state supplements to secure the minimum level of funding. The court commented that although the system was imperfect, since the

---

55. *Snyder v. Town of Newtown*, 161 A.2d 770 (Conn.1960).

56. *Board of Educ. of City of Detroit v. Fuller*, 218 N.W. 764 (Mich.1928).

57. *Durant v. State Bd. of Educ.*, 381 N.W.2d 662, 666 [30 Educ. L. Rep. 870] (Mich.1985).

58. *Schmidt v. Department of Educ.*, 490 N.W.2d 584 [78 Educ. L. Rep. 517] (Mich.1992).

59. *Board of Trustees of Joint Class A School Dist. No. 151 v. Board of County Comm'rs of Cassia County*, 359 P.2d 635 (Idaho 1961).

idea was commendable, it could not be "shackled by legalistic theories and hair splitting."[60]

In a novel question dealing with contributions to pay for the cost of public education, Maine's highest court affirmed the rejection of a claim from an island town and its residents challenging a law intended to prohibit them from withdrawing from a school district even though no school-aged children lived in the community during the academic year.[61] The court explained that the appeal was moot due to legislative action changing the law by eliminating the provision designed to have allowed towns to withdraw from school districts. The court rejected an accompanying equal protection claim because the law was rationally related to the legitimate governmental purpose of enacting legislation dealing with public education.

Another funding case involved a suit by a school board which sought to recover fees from a neighboring district where part of the first board's personal property tax revenue was mistakenly paid to the second for four years due to a taxpayer's error. The Supreme Court of Ohio affirmed that the plaintiff board could not recover the proceeds under the theory of unjust enrichment since a statutory mechanism was in place to prevent and correct such an error.[62]

LITIGATION OVER STATE FUNDING FORMULAS

The 1970s ushered in a wave of litigation challenging school financing systems tolerating markedly uneven per-pupil expenditures in local districts. This litigation is almost evenly split as challenges have succeeded in about half of the states where plaintiffs questioned systems of funding public education.[63]

In *Serrano v. Priest* (*Serrano I*),[64] the opinion of the Supreme Court of California generated more reaction than any other state court case on school finance. At the core of *Serrano I* was the court's perspective that a funding scheme, which rendered the quality of a child's education dependent on a school district's wealth, invidiously discriminated against the poor in violation of the Equal Protection Clause of the Fourteenth Amendment and the state constitution. The court believed that the wealth of districts was the basis for substantially different per-pupil expenditures as reflected by examples of systems with high property values which, with low tax rates, spent much more per child than others with high tax rates and lower property valuations. The court was also troubled by the fact that the state's financial aid program fell far short of equalizing discrepancies such that of the $355 per child state guarantee for students in elementary

---

60. *Rice v. Cook*, 150 S.E.2d 822, 824 (Ga.1966).

61. *Town of Frye Island v. State*, 940 A.2d 1065 [229 Educ. L. Rep. 706] (Me.2008).

62. *Board of Educ. of the N. Olmsted City School Dist. v. Board. of Educ. of the Cleveland Mun. School Dist.*, 844 N.E.2d 832 [207 Educ. L. Rep. 325] (Ohio 2006).

63. For a list of cases from courts of last resort addressing school funding, *see* note 4 following *San Antonio Indep. School Dist. v. Rodriguez.* [Case No. 33]

64. 96 Cal.Rptr. 1241 (Cal.1971).

schools, $125 was distributed on a flat basis regardless of a district's wealth, thereby actually widening the gap in some instances between rich and poor school systems. In discussing education as a fundamental interest to both individuals and society, the court applied strict scrutiny in striking down the system of financing education for failing to serve a compelling state interest. Although the United States Supreme Court essentially repudiated *Serrano I's* analysis under the Federal Constitution a year and one-half later, the Supreme Court of California ultimately reaffirmed its initial judgment on the basis of the state constitution.[65]

Shortly after *Serrano I*, a federal trial court embraced its analysis in striking down Texas' system of school funding based on equal protection analysis. The court directed officials to change the taxing and financing system but stayed its order for two years to give the legislature time to redress the situation.[66]

On further review in *San Antonio Independent School District v. Rodriguez (San Antonio)*,[67] its only case on school finance, the Supreme Court reversed in favor of Texas. At the outset, even though it conceded that the wealth discrimination before it was unlike any of the forms of wealth discrimination it previously reviewed, the Court ruled that the proper Fourteenth Amendment standard was the rational basis test rather than strict scrutiny. The Court decreed that its prior cases in which it invalidated wealth classifications, individuals or groups constituting a class who suffered from discrimination had two distinguishing characteristics: "because of their impecunity they were completely unable to pay for some desired benefit, and as a consequence, they sustained an absolute deprivation of a meaningful opportunity to enjoy that benefit."[68] In contrast, in *San Antonio*, the Court did not think that anyone was completely deprived of educational opportunities under the statewide minimum foundation program that was financed by state and local revenues. If anything, the Court found that the amount that local boards contributed to the program illustrated their relative taxpaying ability measured by assessable property. The Court further recognized that local boards could supplement the foundation program by levying additional property taxes.

In *San Antonio*, the Supreme Court rejected the plaintiffs' claim that the system was discriminatory since per-child expenditures demonstrated an inverse variation with the wealth of families. According to the Court, the data did not support the allegation that the poorest families were clustered in the poorest-property districts. Importantly, the Court rejected the argument that education is a fundamental right, writing that the key to "fundamental" is not in "comparisons of the relative societal significance of education as opposed to subsistence or housing" or "by weighing whether education is as important as the right to travel" since the answer lies "in assessing whether there is a right to education explicitly or

---

65. *Serrano v. Priest (II)*, 325 Cal.Rptr. 345 (Cal.1976), *cert. denied*, 432 U.S. 907, 97 S.Ct. 2951, 53 L.Ed.2d 1079 (1977), opinion supplemented by 141 Cal.Rptr.2d 315 (Cal.1977).

66. *Rodriguez v. San Antonio Indep. School Dist.*, 337 F.Supp. 280 (W.D.Tex.1971).

67. 411 U.S. 1, 93 S.Ct. 1278, 36 L.Ed.2d 16 (1973). [Case No. 33]

68. *Id.* at 20.

implicitly guaranteed by the Constitution."[69] The Court emphasized that "[e]ducation, of course, is not among the rights afforded explicit protection under our Federal Constitution. Nor do we find any basis for saying it is implicitly so protected."[70]

The *San Antonio* Court ascertained that the state's desire to retain a degree of local educational autonomy met the rational basis test. Although admitting that reliance on local property taxation for school revenues provided less freedom of choice with respect to expenditures for some districts, the Court remarked that the existence of inequalities in the manner in which a state achieves its goal is not alone a sufficient basis for vitiating an entire system. In a "cautionary postscript," the Justices referred to the need for expertise and deliberation in resolving matters of educational finance, expressing its concern about the consequences of a judicially imposed change. In concluding, the Court reiterated that while its action should not have been viewed as approval of the status quo, "ultimate solutions must come from the lawmakers and from the democratic pressures of those who elect them."[71]

Following *San Antonio*, school finance remains the province of state courts, ordinarily under the equal protection clauses of state constitutions. State supreme courts order changes to financing systems when discrepancies vary greatly between and among districts, where lower ends are very low, where plans for distributing financial aid do little to help poor districts or increase the variations between richer and poorer districts, and/or where state mandates impede local boards from providing education of reasonable quality. The courts typically grant legislatures time to redesign their plans.

Turning to a brief historical review of state litigation, the Supreme Court of New Jersey eschewed the influence of *San Antonio*, striking down the state's method of financing schools as violating the state constitutional provision calling for a thorough and efficient system of free public schools due to discrepancies in dollar input per pupil.[72] In this initial round of litigation, the court was not satisfied by the fact that state aid covered only twenty-eight percent of operating expenses, some of which was distributed regardless of local taxpaying ability. Connecticut's highest court invalidated a similar state aid plan in applying strict scrutiny under general state constitutional provisions.[73]

The Supreme Court of Washington, focusing on the unique words "paramount duty" and "ample provision" in its state constitutional mandate for education, interpreted these terms as requiring the legislature to make regular tax sources available for a basic program of schooling.[74] The Supreme Court of Arkansas invalidated the state's system of distributing funds as completely irrational because it actually increased inequities

---

69. *Id.* at 33.

70. *Id.* at 35.

71. *Id.* at 59.

72. *Robinson v. Cahill*, 303 A.2d 273 (N.J.1973), *cert. denied*, 414 U.S. 976, 94 S.Ct. 292, 38 L.Ed.2d 219 (1973).

73. *Horton v. Meskill*, 376 A.2d 359 (Conn.1977).

74. *Seattle School Dist. No. 1 of King County v. State*, 585 P.2d 71 (Wash.1978).

among districts.[75] The same court later reached the identical outcome.[76] On the other hand, as one of the courts that sustained its financing system, the Supreme Court of Oregon,[77] relying on *San Antonio*, agreed that the state's interest in local control, the fact that a minimum educational program was available in all districts, and that important services other than education relied largely on local property taxes, provided adequate justification to leave the system intact.

Mandating that the test for a fundamental right under the Federal Constitution was inappropriate under a state constitution, the Supreme Court of Ohio upheld the state's financing system as a rational way of meeting the constitutional mandate for a "thorough and efficient system of common schools."[78] This court, in litigation discussed below, reached a different result. Maryland's highest court reached the same outcome as the original case from Ohio under a similarly worded constitutional education provision.[79] In dicta, the court suggested that the state's school finance plan would have been constitutional even under heightened scrutiny.

One aspect of a case from New York presented a new challenge to the state's system of finance: the plan discriminated against large city school districts for an array of reasons including special non-education demands on the property, diminished purchasing power of municipal education dollars, and larger concentrations of pupils with special needs. In upholding the system, the Court of Appeals of New York stipulated that the state was long regarded as a leader in public education, that it was third in the nation in per-pupil expenditures, and that it was a legislative function to allocate funds among services, certainly in the absence of gross and glaring inadequacy, which had not been shown to exist due to the financing system.[80] As with Ohio, more recent litigation, discussed below, reached the opposite result. Other states that rejected challenges to their systems of financing schools included Georgia[81] and Illinois.[82]

In a novel approach, Wisconsin tried to remove property wealth as a factor in school funding. The plan embodied the notion of establishing a ratio for each district between equalized value of real estate per student within a system and a statewide amount. Under the plan, districts were to be equalized in power to finance education. The new formula purportedly provided equal tax dollars for educational purposes from equal tax effort regardless of disparities in tax bases with some property-wealthy districts

---

75. *Dupree v. Alma School Dist. No. 30 of Crawford County*, 651 S.W.2d 90 [11 Educ. L. Rep. 1091] (Ark.1983).

76. *Lake View School Dist. No. 25 of Phillips County v. Huckabee*, 91 S.W.3d 472 [173 Educ. L. Rep. 248] (Ark.2002).

77. *Olsen v. State*, 554 P.2d 139 (Or.1976).

78. *Board of Educ. of City School Dist. of Cincinnati v. Walter*, 390 N.E.2d 813 (Ohio 1979) (citing Art. 6, § 2 of the state constitution).

79. *Hornbeck v. Somerset County Bd. of Educ.*, 458 A.2d 758 [10 Educ. L. Rep. 592] (Md.1983).

80. *Board of Educ., Levittown Union Free School Dist. v. Nyquist*, 453 N.Y.S.2d 643 [6 Educ. L. Rep. 147] (N.Y.1982), *appeal dismissed*, 459 U.S. 1139, 103 S.Ct. 775, 74 L.Ed.2d 986 (1983).

81. *McDaniel v. Thomas*, 285 S.E.2d 156 [1 Educ. L. Rep. 982] (Ga.1981).

82. *Blase v. State*, 302 N.E.2d 46 (Ill.1973).

receiving no state aid due to their using tax rates to raise more than the state-guaranteed amount. The overages were to go into the general state fund to be distributed to property-poor districts. The court invalidated the plan, deciding that the legislature could not compel a board to tax its residents for the direct benefit of another or for the sole benefit of the state.[83] The same court eventually upheld the state's funding system as adequate.[84]

The Supreme Court of Texas applied a like rationale in disapproving a legislative plan designed to comply with its mandate to change the state's method of financing public schools.[85] The court noted that local property tax revenues for education were not subject to state redistribution. However, the court suggested that the state could redistrict and thereby alter the local tax bases of school districts. The court then decided that the state's system of taxation for funding public schools violated the state constitution's prohibition against state-wide ad valorem taxes.[86] Although it conceded that it was a close question, the court was convinced that the state provided sufficient money to fund schools within the meaning of the state constitution's requirements for an adequate, efficient, and suitable public school system, remanding the issue to the state legislature.

A second case dealing with ad valorem taxes was litigated in Louisiana where an appellate court upheld their use to help fund the "Recovery School District" that was created to help educate students who attended failing schools.[87] The court rejected the claim that allowing funds that would otherwise have been allocated to parish school systems would have violated the state constitutional requirement that parish school systems receive equitable funding for their students because the state board had the authority to dispense funds as it saw fit.

The Supreme Court of New Jersey re-entered the school finance arena seventeen years after its original case, reasoning that the legislative response that it originally upheld on its face[88] was unconstitutional as applied to poor urban districts.[89] The court thus called for a revamping of the state's financing system to assure substantial equality in educational funding between poor urban districts and property rich systems. The court required the level of funding to be adequate in order to provide for the special educational needs of the disadvantaged districts. As the litigation continued, the court issued a series of judgments clarifying its initial

---

83. *Buse v. Smith*, 247 N.W.2d 141 (Wis.1976).

84. *Kukor v. Grover*, 436 N.W.2d 568 [52 Educ. L. Rep. 241] (Wis.1989), *reconsideration denied*, 443 N.W.2d 314 (Wis.1989).

85. *Edgewood Indep. School Dist. v. Kirby*, 804 S.W.2d 491 [66 Educ. L. Rep. 496] (Tex.1991).

86. *Neeley v. West Orange–Cove Consol. Indep. School Dist.*, 176 S.W.3d 746 [204 Educ. L. Rep. 793] (Tex.2005).

87. *Triplett v. Board of Elementary and Secondary Educ.*, 21 So.3d 401 [250 Educ. L. Rep. 1157] (La. Ct. App. 2009).

88. *Robinson v. Cahill*, 303 A.2d 273 (N.J.1973), *cert. denied*, 414 U.S. 976, 94 S.Ct. 292, 38 L.Ed.2d 219 (1973).

89. *Abbott by Abbott v. Burke*, 575 A.2d 359 [60 Educ. L. Rep. 1175] (N.J.1990).

order,[90] finally calling on the legislature to provide appropriate funding for boards in future budgets.[91]

The Supreme Court of Kentucky emphasized the quality of education along with calling for more parity in access to funds by local school boards. The court bluntly stated that "Kentucky's entire system of common schools is unconstitutional. . . . This decision applies to the statutes creating, implementing and financing the *system* and to all regulations, etc., pertaining thereto."[92] Not long thereafter, the Supreme Judicial Court of Massachusetts applied Kentucky's goals in broadly outlining that commonwealth's constitutional duty to educate its students. The provision, first adopted in 1780 while Massachusetts was still a colony, directed its legislature to "cherish . . . public schools and grammar schools in the towns."[93]

More recently, the highest courts of Arkansas,[94] Kansas,[95] Montana,[96] New Hampshire,[97] New York,[98] Ohio,[99] Tennessee,[100] and Vermont[101] struck down their systems of funding while the Supreme Court of Colorado agreed

---

90. *See, e.g., Abbott by Abbott v. Burke*, 643 A.2d 575 [92 Educ. L. Rep. 545] (N.J.1994); 693 A.2d 417 [118 Educ. L. Rep. 371] (N.J.1997), *appeal after remand*, 710 A.2d 450 [126 Educ. L. Rep. 258] (N.J.1998); *opinion clarified*, 751 A.2d 1032 [145 Educ. L. Rep. 427] (N.J.2000); 748 A.2d 82 (N.J.2000), *order clarified*, 790 A.2d 842 [162 Educ. L. Rep. 407] (N.J.2002), *modified in part*, 852 A.2d 185 (N.J. 2004), *modified*, 857 A.2d 173 (N.J.2004).

91. *Abbott ex rel. Abbott v. Burke*, 20 A.3d 1018 [268 Educ. L. Rep. 328] (N.J. 2011).

92. *Rose v. Council for Better Educ.*, 790 S.W.2d 186, 215 [60 Educ. L. Rep. 1289] (Ky.1989) (emphasis in original).

93. *McDuffy v. Secretary of Executive Office of Educ.*, 615 N.E.2d 516, 557 [83 Educ. L. Rep. 657] (Mass.1993).

94. *Lake View School Dist. No. 25 of Phillips County v. Huckabee*, 91 S.W.3d 472 [173 Educ. L. Rep. 248] (Ark.2002). Based on allegations that the state failed to satisfy an earlier order to provide an adequate and substantially equal education for all students, the court reopened the litigation. The court rejected the state's argument that its earlier release of jurisdiction required the parties to file a new case. *Lake View School Dist. No. 25 of Phillips County, Arkansas v. Huckabee*, 210 S.W.3d 28, [215 Educ. L. Rep. 1198] (Ark.2005), *mandate stayed*, 220 S.W.3d 645 [220 Educ. L. Rep. 383] (Ark.2005), *mandate deferred*, 243 S.W.3d 919 [229 Educ. L. Rep. 953] (Ark.2006), *mandate issued*, 257 S.W.3d 879 [235 Educ. L. Rep. 690] (Ark.2007).

95. *Montoy v. State*, 102 P.3d 1160 [194 Educ. L. Rep. 439] (Kan.2005), *republished with concurring opinion*, 120 P.3d 306 [202 Educ. L. Rep. 319] (Kan.2005), *opinion supplemented*, 112 P.3d 923 [198 Educ. L. Rep. 703] (Kan.2005).

96. *Columbia Falls Elementary School Dist. No. 6 v. State*, 109 P.3d 257 [196 Educ. L. Rep. 958] (Mont.2005). Previously, the same court invalidated the state's system of funding as violating the state constitutional guarantee of equal educational opportunities for all children. *Helena Elementary School Dist. No. 1 v. State*, 769 P.2d 684 [52 Educ. L. Rep. 342] (Mont.1989), *opinion amended*, 784 P.2d 412 [57 Educ. L. Rep. 1374] (Mont.1990) (postponing the effect of the initial judgment to allow the legislature and governor's office time to implement a satisfactory system of funding).

97. *Claremont School Dist. v. Governor*, 703 A.2d 1353 [123 Educ. L. Rep. 233] (N.H.1997), *reh'g denied, motion to vacate stay denied*, 725 A.2d 648 [133 Educ. L. Rep. 161] (N.H.1998). The court subsequently denied a challenge to the constitutionality of the new funding scheme in *Londonderry School Dist. SAU #12 v. State of N.H.*, 958 A.2d 930 (N.H.2008).

98. *Campaign for Fiscal Equity v. State of N.Y.*, 769 N.Y.S.2d 106 [183 Educ. L. Rep. 970] (N.Y.2003). For an unsuccessful companion case involving the city of Rochester, *see Paynter v. State of N.Y.*, 765 N.Y.S.2d 819 [181 Educ. L. Rep. 757] (N.Y.2003).

99. *DeRolph v. State*, 677 N.E.2d 733 [116 Educ. L. Rep. 1140] (Ohio 1997). *See also State v. Lewis*, 786 N.E.2d 60 [174 Educ. L. Rep. 1073] (Ohio 2003).

100. *Tennessee Small School Systems v. McWherter*, 91 S.W.3d 232 [172 Educ. L. Rep. 1044] (Tenn.2002).

101. *Brigham v. State*, 692 A.2d 384 [117 Educ. L. Rep. 667] (Vt.1997).

that parents presented a justiciable claim that the state's funding scheme was unconstitutional.[102] The highest courts in Alabama,[103] Alaska,[104] Indiana,[105] Missouri,[106] Oregon,[107] South Carolina,[108] South Dakota,[109] Wisconsin,[110] and Wyoming[111] reached opposite results in upholding their state systems of funding. Further, the high courts in Nebraska[112] and Oklahoma,[113] along with an intermediate appellate panel in Texas,[114] rejected challenges as nonjusticiable political questions.[115]

Courts continue to review school finance cases that have yet to reach the merits of their claims. For example, the Supreme Court of Connecticut affirmed that taxpayers who sought a declaratory judgment challenging the state's funding statute, which required each town to contribute to a district's educational expenses based on per pupil cost of education, lacked standing absent proof that they would have suffered actual injuries.[116] A plurality of the same court later decided that insofar as a challenge to the state's system of funding was subject to judicial review, the dispute had to be remanded for a trial on the merits.[117] Along the same line, the Supreme Court of Nebraska affirmed that a local board could not intervene in a challenge to the constitutionality of the state's school funding system on the basis of its speculative allegation that it would have been harmed due to any loss of funding. The court thus rejected the claim as insufficient to present a direct legal right permitting it to take part in the suit.[118]

102. *Lobato v. State of Colorado*, 218 P.3d 358 [249 Educ. L. Rep. 881] (Colo. 2009).

103. *Alabama, Ex parte James*, 836 So.2d 813 [174 Educ. L. Rep. 487] (Ala.2002).

104. *Matanuska–Susitna Borough School Dist. v. State*, 931 P.2d 391 [116 Educ. L. Rep. 401] (Alaska 1997).

105. *Bonner v. Daniels*, 907 N.E.2d 516 [245 Educ. L. Rep. 412] (Ind. 2009).

106. *Committee for Educ. Equality v. State*, 294 S.W.3d 477 [249 Educ. L. Rep. 926] (Mo. 2009).

107. *Pendleton School Dist. 16R v. State*, 200 P.3d 133 [241 Educ. L. Rep. 423] (Or. 2009).

108. *Abbeville County School Dist. v. State*, 515 S.E.2d 535 [135 Educ. L. Rep. 833] (S.C.1999).

109. *Davis v. South Dakota*, 804 N.W.2d 618 [273 Educ.L.Rep. 411] (S.D. 2011).

110. *Vincent v. Voight*, 614 N.W.2d 388 [146 Educ. L. Rep. 422] (Wis. 2000).

111. Wyoming, *Campbell County School Dist. v. State*, 181 P.3d 43 [232 Educ. L. Rep. 394] (Wyo.2008).

112. *Nebraska Coalition for Educ. Equity and Adequacy v. Heineman*, 731 N.W.2d 164 [219 Educ. L. Rep. 761] (Neb.2007).

113. *Oklahoma Educ. Ass'n v. Oklahoma*, 158 P.3d 1058 [220 Educ. L. Rep. 360] (Okla.2007).

114. *Hendee v. Dewhurst*, 228 S.W.3d 354 [222 Educ. L. Rep. 880] (Tex.Ct.App.2007), *review denied* (2007), *reh'g overruled* (2007), *appeal after remand sub nom.*, 253 S.W.3d 320 (Tex.Ct.App.2008), *reh'g overruled* (2008), *petition stricken* (2008).

115. *But see New York State Ass'n of Small City School Dist. v. New York*, 840 N.Y.S.2d 179 [222 Educ. L. Rep. 830] (N.Y.App.Div.2007) (allowing the state school board association to challenge funding on its own behalf but not in the name of individual members).

116. *Seymour v. Region One Bd. of Educ.*, 874 A.2d 742 [198 Educ. L. Rep. 645] (Conn.2005), *cert. denied*, 546 U.S. 1016, 126 S.Ct. 659, 163 L.Ed.2d 526 (2005).

117. *Connecticut Coalition for Justice in Educ. Funding v. Rell*, 990 A.2d 206 [254 Educ. L. Rep. 874] (Conn. 2010).

118. *Douglas County School Dist. 0001 v. Johanns*, 694 N.W.2d 668 [196 Educ. L. Rep. 949] (Neb.2005).

In a related matter, two state high courts denied attorney fees to prevailing school boards in litigation over funding public education. The Supreme Court of Ohio affirmed that insofar as a board had more than 500 employees, it was ineligible to recover attorney fees even though it prevailed in a dispute with its state counterpart over how funds were calculated.[119] In addition, the Supreme Court of Oregon upheld the denial of attorney fees to a board since the relief it obtained failed to vindicate an important constitutional right applicable to all citizens.[120]

School Bonds

In General

Absent express statutory authority, school boards operate on cash bases, meaning that they meet current expenses out of tax proceeds of former years or other funds.[121] Other boards operate on deficit bases, indicating that they lack adequate cash reserves and rely on levies from current years to meet their expenses.[122] Either way, the duties of state officials include ensuring that local boards manage educational appropriations wisely while encouraging them to avoid having deficits and directing them to pay those that can be promptly eliminated.[123] At this point, it is important to recall that although boards have no implied authority to borrow money, they may be able to issue bonds[124] or other negotiable instruments[125] to improve their cash flow. Even when legislatures permit boards to borrow funds, this right is strictly construed. For instance, if legislatures grant boards the power to borrow money or issue bonds for specific purposes, those funds can be applied only to that purpose.[126]

Statutes authorizing boards to issue bonds typically include detailed procedures and prerequisites including time periods within which challenges must be filed.[127] When challenged, questions usually arise over the validity of bonds if school officials fail to comply exactly with procedures. The general rule is that if it appears that legislative intent was for

---

119. *Cincinnati City School Dist. Bd. of Educ. v. State Bd. of Educ. of Ohio*, 913 N.E.2d 421 [248 Educ. L. Rep. 473] (Ohio 2009).

120. *Pendleton School Dist. 16 R v. State*, 217 P.3d 175 [249 Educ. L. Rep. 417] (Or.2009).

121. *Conn v. Middlebury Union High School Dist. No. 3*, 648 A.2d 1385 [95 Educ. L. Rep. 300] (Vt.1994); *Clay v. Independent School Dist. No. 1 of Tulsa County*, 935 P.2d 294 [117 Educ. L. Rep. 756] (Okla.1997).

122. *In re County Collector of Du Page County for Judgment for Taxes for Year 1993*, 718 N.E.2d 164 [144 Educ. L. Rep. 364] (Ill.1999).

123. *Maryland State Bd. of Educ. v. Bradford*, 875 A.2d 703 [199 Educ. L. Rep. 298] (Md.2005).

124. *G.I.S. Venture v. Novak*, 902 N.E.2d 744 [242 Educ. L. Rep. 309] (Ill.App.Ct.2009).

125. *Hewitt v. Board of Educ.*, 94 Ill. 528 (Ill.1880).

126. *State ex rel. Howard v. Crawford*, 16 P.3d 473 [150 Educ. L. Rep. 496] (Okla.Civ.App. 2000).

127. *Snell v. Johnson County School Dist. No. 1*, 86 P.3d 248 [185 Educ. L. Rep. 1063] (Wyo.2004); *de Koning v. Mellema*, 534 N.W.2d 391 [101 Educ. L. Rep. 1106] (Iowa 1995).

procedures to be conditions precedent to the validity of bond issues, the failure to comply renders bonds invalid. On the other hand, there is a strong judicial inclination to uphold bond issues if it appears that irregularities did not deprive taxpayers of substantial rights[128] or did not affect the outcome of elections.[129] If school boards comply with procedural requirements to secure bond funding to pay for construction, their actions are likely to survive challenges.[130] In such a case, when a legislature enacted new procedural requirements for bonds after an earlier version was struck down, taxpayers unsuccessfully challenged the use of bond funds that were secured under old standards. The Supreme Court of Wyoming pointed out that insofar as the bonds were approved while the previous regulations remained in place, the amended statutes governing the new bonding procedures did not apply retroactively.[131]

Controversies can arise in connection with the requirement that notice of elections must be published a specified number of days before elections can occur. If electors have adequate notice, signified by a majority's having appeared and cast ballots, and the result could not have been affected by the shorter notice, elections are likely to be sustained.[132] In an illustrative case, the Supreme Court of New Hampshire upheld the validity of a bond issue against the charge that there were defects in the report that school officials had to submit to the state.[133] The court acknowledged that the acts of town meetings should be liberally construed and, if they fell within the authorized power of town officials, minor distinctions would not be allowed to defeat the voters' intent. Since the information required in the report received wide publicity otherwise, and was discussed in public meetings, the court concluded that officials substantially complied with the law. Later, the First Circuit affirmed that a state law from New Hampshire, which required a lower voter percentage in districts using an official ballot system for bond approvals, as opposed to those that relied on town meetings to gain acceptance, did not violate equal protection.[134] The court found this approach to be acceptable because it was rationally related to the legitimate governmental interest of ensuring that residents could vote.

Another source of difficulties for school boards arises when officials publish information about bond elections but wish to deviate from their initial statements. The Supreme Court of Utah discussed this issue in a case where taxpayers sought to prevent a board from proceeding with a building plan after it published a notice of a bond election and printed

---

128. *Ganske v. Independent School Dist. No. 84*, 136 N.W.2d 405 (Minn.1965).

129. *Abts v. Board of Educ. of School Dist. Re-1 Valley in Logan County*, 622 P.2d 518 (Colo.1980).

130. *See, e.g., Nicholson v. Red Willow County School Dist. No. 0170*, 699 N.W.2d 25 [199 Educ. L. Rep. 934] (Neb.2005).

131. *Snell v. Johnson County School Dist. No. 1*, 86 P.3d 248 [185 Educ. L. Rep. 1063] (Wyo.2004).

132. *State ex rel. School Dist. No. 2 v. March*, 189 N.W. 283 (Neb.1922).

133. *Hecker v. McKernan*, 196 A.2d 38 (N.H.1963).

134. *Walker v. Exeter Region Co-op. School Dist.*, 284 F.3d 42 [162 Educ. L. Rep. 701] (1st Cir.2002); *See also Opinion of the Justices*, 765 A.2d 706 [150 Educ. L. Rep. 765] (N.H.2001); *McGraw v. Exeter Region Co-op. School Dist.*, 765 A.2d 710 [150 Educ. L. Rep. 769] (N.H.2001).

explanatory brochures that were distributed to the public while other parts were published in newspapers in connection with, but not as part of, the notice. The brochure explained that the funds were to be spent under the two main categories of elementary and secondary schools. The bond issue passed, but when the projected costs in the preliminary estimate for the high school proved to be too low, the board proposed to use a much greater proportion of the fund for its construction, leaving a relatively smaller amount for the elementary school. The court rejected the claim that the revised proposal was a breach of faith in recognizing that the board had latitude carrying out its goal of providing the best school system in the most efficient and economic way.[135]

A more recent case from California reached the opposite result when taxpayers were unable to enjoin their school board from constructing a new gymnasium. In rejecting the taxpayers' claim that the board did not provide enough specificity as to the projects that were to be funded, an appellate court affirmed that the bond proposal satisfied the state constitutional requirement that it include a list of the facilities projects to be funded and authorized funding of a gymnasium even though it was not identified on the ballot itself.[136] The court declared that the board's placing the project list, which included the gymnasium, in the resolution, coupled with a discussion of the list in the ballot's pamphlet, more than met the requirements of state law.

Where a state statute raised the maximum rate of interest to be paid on school bonds, a question emerged as to whether the higher rate applied to bonds authorized by an election occurring prior to the law's passage. The Supreme Court of Kansas affirmed that the higher rate applied since bonds are not considered as issued until they are actually delivered or put into circulation.[137] In ruling that the law in effect at the time of the issuance became part of the bond contract, the court decided that the statute was not rendered retroactive when applied to bonds which were not issued as of the statute's effective date.

As exemplified by a case from Iowa, when taxpayers dispute the results of school bond elections, courts expect challengers to comply strictly with procedural requirements. The state's highest court thus affirmed the rejection to a challenge over whether a local board received the required sixty percent voter approval for a bond where the plaintiff failed to file a petition bond within the specified twenty days called for by state statute.[138]

LIABILITY ON ILLEGAL BONDS

Insofar as bonds that are issued contrary to law are void, investors cannot recover their losses. Even so, since illegality is often not discovered

---

135. *Ricker v. Board of Educ. of Millard County School Dist.*, 396 P.2d 416 (Utah 1964).

136. *Committee for Responsible School Expansion v. Hermosa Beach City School Dist.*, 48 Cal.Rptr.3d 705 [212 Educ. L. Rep. 822] (Cal.Ct.App.2006).

137. *Baker v. Unified School Dist. No. 346, County of Linn*, 480 P.2d 409 (Kan.1971).

138. *In re AHST Community School Dist. Pub. Measure "B" Election*, 735 N.W.2d 605 [221 Educ. L. Rep. 868] (Iowa 2007).

until after boards have received and spent the funds derived from bond sales, an issue arises as to whether bondholders must bear the losses or may recover their investments.

Some courts permit recovery in quasi-contract for the value of the benefit conferred on boards subject to the exception that they must have had authority to issue valid bonds in the first place.[139] In other words, if bonds are invalid due to boards' lack of power to issue them, bondholders cannot recover any expected benefits; bondholders may be able to reclaim unspent funds that boards retain or can try to recover property purchased with their investments if they can trace it to specific property and recovery does not seriously injure other board property or disrupt orderly school management. If boards lack authority to issue bonds, the courts usually refuse to find that there were implied contracts in favor of bondholders since doing so would deprive boards of the very protection that statutes were designed to afford.

SCHOOL DISTRICT WARRANTS

School warrants are orders drawn against board funds, or, if laws specifically permit, against funds to be collected within statutorily defined periods. Unlike bonds, warrants are not designed to run for a number of years since they are not negotiable instruments.

Since investors are charged with notice of illegalities in the issuance of instruments, they purchase them at their own risk.[140] The reason is clear: if innocent purchasers were not afforded protection, boards would be able to spend district funds illegally by issuing negotiable warrants and taxpayers would lack recourse. Public policy requires individuals who deal with boards to assume responsibility for the legality of warrants rather than open the way to possible depletion of school funds through the issuance of illegal warrants.

In an illustrative case, the Supreme Court of New Hampshire reviewed a dispute over the content of a warrant. The court affirmed that state laws granting governing bodies or school boards broad discretion to determine the number, format, and content of articles that they place on warrants do not afford them unfettered discretion to do so if another statute sets restrictions on the format of warrant articles.[141]

---

139. *Geer v. School Dist. No. 11*, 111 Fed. 682 (8th Cir.1901).

140. *Kellogg v. School Dist. No. 10*, 74 P. 110 (Okla.1903).

141. *In re Inter Lakes School Bd.*, 780 A.2d 1275 [157 Educ. L. Rep. 747] (N.H.2001).

LIMITATIONS ON DISTRICT INDEBTEDNESS

IN GENERAL

States typically impose constitutional or statutory limits on the amount of debt that local school boards can incur. The question of what constitutes indebtedness has generated judicial conflict. According to the majority position, net, not gross, indebtedness is the appropriate measure in evaluating whether boards can incur additional debt.[142] Net indebtedness is that which remains after deducting board assets that are available for the payment of existing debts from the total of all outstanding debts, including cash on hand, taxes levied, and other available assets. Assets do not actually have to be applied to pay for debts but only need to be available. Further, contracts for current expenses are not considered indebtedness while funds on hand to meet them are not treated as assets. Put another way, even though boards may have reached their legal debt limits, they may still levy taxes for current operating expenses.[143]

Courts adopting the minority view refuse to apply the net indebtedness test, maintaining that even though assets may be on hand to pay debts, they remain until they are paid.[144] This perspective may appear more logical and more nearly in accord with the commonly accepted understanding of debt, but greatly restricts boards from financing their operations.

Borrowed funds are not considered debts if the monies are from revenue, rather than general obligation, bonds. Individuals who own revenue bonds must depend entirely on income produced by the ventures that their monies finance. Generally, while school boards may not issue revenue bonds, states may do so. The Supreme Court of Michigan rejected a plan designed to apply the state constitutional debt limit to bonds that the state sought to issue to generate funds to loan to boards with large operating deficits.[145] Under the plan, the payments of principal and interest would have been made by local school boards, and, if they defaulted, by the state from its aid payments due the boards. The court conceded that regardless of how the plan was presented, the state was the borrower even though repayment would have been made primarily by residents of school districts and that the bonds were, in effect, general obligation bonds subject to the state constitutional debt limit.

If it appears to be to the advantage of school boards to enter into contracts for periods of years for supplies or services, most courts agree that these agreements are legal even if the funds extend board indebtedness beyond legal limits. In these instances, contracts usually provide that payments are to be made annually from accrued funds such that the amounts falling due each year should equal the indebtedness incurred, not the total identified in contracts.[146] While this rule is ordinarily restricted to contracts for goods or services and is not extended to those for construc-

---

142. *Rettinger v. School Bd. of City of Pittsburgh*, 109 A. 782 (Pa.1920).
143. *Grant v. City of Davenport*, 36 Iowa 396 (Iowa 1873).
144. *Angola Brick & Tile Co. v. Millgrove School Twp.*, 127 N.E. 855 (Ind.Ct.App.1920).
145. *In re Advisory Opinion Constitutionality of P.A. 1 and 2*, 211 N.W.2d 28 (Mich.1973).
146. *La Porte v. Gamewell Fire–Alarm Telegraph Co.*, 45 N.E. 588 (Ind.1896).

tion, the Supreme Court of Indiana applied it to a lease agreement between a board and a public corporation set up for school construction.[147]

At issue in another case was whether a contested bond issue would have exceeded constitutional debt limits. At the time of the bond vote, a school board had the cash on hand to pay the principal of the outstanding debt. The Supreme Court of New Hampshire posited that the sum on hand could have been subtracted from the outstanding authorized indebtedness, thereby bringing the amount of the bond issue within the legal debt limit.[148]

In a third case dealing with limits on bond indebtedness, the Supreme Court of New Jersey interpreted the school funding provision of the state constitution as authorizing state-backed school bonds without reference to its debt limitation clause.[149] The court affirmed that in allowing the state to guarantee local debt, the school fund language advanced the constitutional guarantee of providing each student with a thorough and efficient education.

As highlighted by a case from the Supreme Court of South Carolina, special problems can occur when districts are reorganized. The court evaluated the validity of bonds issued by the board in a consolidated district that succeeded to the property, rights, and obligations of the systems it was formed out of when they ceased to exist as separate entities. The court was of the view that the consolidated board's debt was limited to the constitutional maximum of eight percent of the property value that had been placed on each of the constituent districts.[150]

Where district boundaries and counties or cities are coterminous, and each has a debt limit, an issue can arise as to the relationship between their debt limits. In such a case, a school board was only able to raise about $300,000 out of the needed $800,000 due to its constitutional debt limit. Pursuant to a provision in the state constitution which permitted a county to sell bonds for a corporate purpose, it sold $500,000 worth of bonds and turned the proceeds over to the board. Opponents argued that insofar as the bond sale was not for a corporate purpose since the board had the duty to operate its schools, the effect of turning over the proceeds indirectly permitted educational officials to incur a debt beyond the system's constitutional limit. However, pursuant to the state constitution, the legislature could not authorize counties to levy taxes or issue bonds except for specified purposes, one of which was education. In treating the latter provision as express constitutional justification for the authorization, the Supreme Court of South Carolina was satisfied that this did not exceed the debt limit because the common boundary of the county and board notwithstanding, they were separate and distinct corporate entities subject to different debt limitations.[151]

147. *Teperich v. North Judson–San Pierre High School Bldg. Corp.*, 275 N.E.2d 814 (Ind.1971), *cert. denied*, 407 U.S. 921, 92 S.Ct. 2462, 32 L.Ed.2d 806 (1972).

148. *Hecker v. McKernan*, 196 A.2d 38 (N.H.1963).

149. *Lonegan v. State*, 809 A.2d 91 [171 Educ. L. Rep. 266] (N.J.2002), *clarification denied*, 807 A.2d 189 (N.J.2002).

150. *Boatwright v. McElmurray*, 146 S.E.2d 716 (S.C.1966).

151. *Grey v. Vaigneur*, 135 S.E.2d 229 (S.C.1964).

SHORT-TERM BORROWING

Short-term borrowing is usually necessary due to emergencies, board failures to collect anticipated revenues, and/or board desires to implement programs deemed immediately necessary or desirable for the welfare of the schools for which funds are presently unavailable. As with individuals or businesses, situations may arise in which it is advisable to borrow money for short periods rather than operate strictly on cash bases. Aware of this reality, statutes generally permit short-term borrowing subject to various restrictions. Yet, in most situations, short-term borrowing is not considered an implied board power.[152]

Constitutional or statutory debt limits apply equally to short and long-term borrowing. Anticipation of revenues is limited since it would be poor business and educational practice to permit boards to commit district revenues for unreasonable periods in advance. It is conceivable that absent such limitations, future school operations could be rendered difficult, if not impossible. The most common restriction is that boards cannot anticipate revenues in excess of those of the fiscal year in which anticipations are made. The purpose of this restriction is to prevent boards from continuing to increase their non-bonded debts.

When legislatures grant boards authority to borrow money, state laws usually specify procedures that they must strictly follow. While the authority to borrow does not ordinarily include the ability to issue negotiable instruments of indebtedness, there are cases to the contrary. For example, the Supreme Court of Florida maintained that where a statute permitted borrowing but did not specify the procedure to be followed, a board had the implied authority to execute its evidence of indebtedness in accord with standard business practices.[153]

In operating schools, boards may sometimes accumulate such large debts that attempting to pay them off entirely in a single year would strain their budgets. This leads to a consideration of whether boards can fund indebtedness and arrange for their payments over relatively short periods of time. Some statutes permit boards to issue bonds under such circumstances, but only after votes of district residents at potentially considerable expense. If boards can fund existing debts by relying on the use of short-term loans, they can avoid large amounts of expenses. As such, state laws often allow boards to fund their obligations in this way.

A question that school boards often face in connection with funding obligations is whether doing so constitutes the creation of new indebtedness which extends their total debt beyond statutory or constitutional limits or beyond that which they can incur during a single year. Since courts typically agree that funding present obligations does not create new debt, the validity of obligations must be viewed in light of the financial status of boards when they incurred the original debts, not as of the dates of funding.[154]

---

152. For an exception *see Logan v. Board of Pub. Instruction for Polk County*, 158 So. 720 (Fla.1935).

153. *Board of Pub. Instruction for Bay County v. Barefoot*, 193 So. 823 (Fla.1939).

154. *Citizens Bank v. Rowan County Bd. of Educ.*, 118 S.W.2d 704 (Ky.1938).

BUDGETARY PROCEDURES

In order for school officials to plan more carefully, state laws require them to prepare budgets of proposed expenditures. Detailed provisions vary but include such requirements as having budgets itemized and published as well as being subject to public hearings, reviewing agencies, and procedures for transferring funds from some budgetary items to others.

When reviewing agencies seek to exert measures of control over school expenditures or when taxpayers challenge budgets, these disputes are subject to judicial review. Attempts by reviewing agencies or taxpayers to modify board expenditures are generally unsuccessful unless they can demonstrate that applicable statutes make it clear that they can do so. The judicial attitude is ordinarily that insofar as boards are responsible for school operations, they must be free to consider how and where expenditures are made, subject only to constitutional debt limitations. The major exception seems to arise when schools are fiscally dependent on municipal governments. In these cases, with courts liberally interpreting board powers, they present budgets to municipal authorities who may reduce their totals or eliminate items not required by state law and not placed in their province.[155] Under this form of organization, boards are not restricted to adherence to particular items in a budget as long as they do not attempt to spend more than the total amount appropriated to support schools.[156]

Where voters rejected an item in a proposed school budget that would have provided for four teacher aides, the board rehired the one aide it previously employed and paid her under an appropriation for the salaries of school district officials. In upholding the board's action, the Supreme Court of New Hampshire asserted that the board had the power to transfer the voter-approved funds and that the action of the voters could not have been interpreted as a retroactive disapproval of the aide's employment.[157]

The Supreme Court of Georgia, in upholding a contract for a field house, interpreted the requirement in state law that no funds shall be disbursed by local school boards except in accordance with budgets filed with the state board.[158] Recognizing that not every expenditure had to be a line item in the budget, the court affirmed that insofar as the board had a balance of unobligated funds in excess of the planned expenditure, it acted within its power.

As illustrated by a case from the Supreme Court of Utah, claims that educational officials failed to provide sufficient itemization in budgets are

---

155. *Ring v. Woburn,* 43 N.E.2d 8 (Mass.1942); *Carroll v. City of Malden,* 320 N.E.2d 843 (Mass.Ct.App.1974).

156. *Leonard v. School Comm. of Springfield,* 135 N.E. 459 (Mass.1922). *See also Lynch v. City of Fall River,* 147 N.E.2d 152 (Mass.1958); *Warwick School Comm. v. Gibbons,* 410 A.2d 1354 (R.I.1980).

157. *Ashley v. Rye School Dist.,* 274 A.2d 795 (N.H.1971).

158. *Concerned School Patrons & Taxpayers v. Ware County Bd. of Educ.,* 263 S.E.2d 925 (Ga.1980).

generally unsuccessful. Where state law required school budgets to be itemized, a taxpayer challenged a published budget consisting of ten classifications of accounts, each of which was further subdivided into sixty items. After the budget was approved, officials further divided it into more than 1,500 accounts, leading the court to affirm its validity as sufficiently itemized in compliance with state law.[159]

In a dispute over whether broad classifications constituted adequate itemization to the state as to the purposes for which expenditures were to be made, the Supreme Court of Arizona observed that a total of forty-one sub-items in six categories was sufficient.[160] In another aspect of the case, the court commented that while a school board could transfer funds among sub-items in each of the six general categories, it could not transfer funds among the general categories.

Courts adhere to the rule that funds raised by taxation for one purpose cannot be diverted to another.[161] In an illustrative case, where a school board made a budgetary transfer from its general to its capital outlay fund, the Supreme Court of South Dakota upheld the transfer on the grounds that there was no evidence that the transferred money was raised by local tax levies and the amount was less than that derived from sources other than local taxes.[162] The Supreme Court of Idaho also determined that setting monies aside from a fund designed to purchase notes to pay for defaulted school bonds did not violate the state constitution since they were part of a common scheme to increase the flexibility of the management of the state's school endowment fund.[163]

On another matter, current tax revenues cannot be used to pay obligations that accrued during previous school years. Unless budgets permit boards to use current funds for old debts, such payments can be enjoined.[164] At the same time, at least one court thought that if a past debt had been paid, a request for an injunction would have been moot.[165]

SCHOOL FINANCE AND MUNICIPAL AUTHORITIES

As boards seek sufficient funds to operate schools, they often encounter difficulties with local government agencies such as city councils. Since state legislatures grant powers both to boards and municipalities, they may establish methods of finance which either keep the two operations completely separate or have them intertwined.

---

159. *Tuttle v. Board of Educ. of Salt Lake City*, 294 P. 294 (Utah 1930).

160. *Isley v. School Dist.*, 305 P.2d 432 (Ariz.1956).

161. *School Dist. No. 2 v. Jackson–Wilson High School Dist.*, 52 P.2d 673 (Wyo.1935).

162. *Stene v. School Bd. of Beresford Indep. School Dist., No. 68*, 206 N.W.2d 69 (S.D.1973).

163. *Idaho Endowment Fund Investment Bd. v. Crane*, 23 P.3d 129 [153 Educ. L. Rep. 973] (Idaho 2001).

164. *Warren v. Sanger Indep. School Dist.*, 288 S.W. 159 (Tex.Com.App.1926).

165. *Rawson v. Brownsboro Indep. School Dist.*, 263 S.W.2d 578 (Tex.Civ.App.1953).

The power of state legislatures to require city authorities to issue bonds to raise money to build schools was at the heart of a leading, albeit older, case from Maryland. The state's highest court reasoned that the legislature had the power to direct city authorities to create a debt for a school building.[166] Legislatures can also set minimum sums that city officials must raise for school purposes and can require them to do so without discretion.[167] Further, a legislature can require city officials to allocate a specified percent of a total budget to a financially dependent school board.[168]

Where a city sought to enjoin construction of a high school until the board received approval from a referendum, the Supreme Court of Pennsylvania was of the opinion that granting one governmental unit standing to sue due to a hypothetical threat to property tax revenues would have meant that neither could have effectively functioned since each could have challenged the other's actions.[169] In addition, the court rejected the city's argument that it could sue on behalf of its taxpayers who lacked standing.

The Supreme Court of Alaska addressed a different aspect of municipal and school board power where a home rule borough sought to require a neighboring school system to participate in centralized accounting without the statutorily required board approval. At issue was the validity of an ordinance from a home rule borough that conflicted with a state statute. The court acknowledged that it previously adopted a local activity rule as a method of resolving impasses between state statutes, which was designed to further specific policies and municipal ordinances that directly or collaterally impeded such implementation, depending on whether the matters were statewide or local concerns. The court wrote that the state constitutional provision, which vested power in the legislature to establish and maintain a system of public schools, was decisive because state control was not diminished by the legislature's having delegated selected functions to local boards. The court thus concluded that the board could not be required to take part in centralized accounting.[170] Thirty years later the Supreme Court of Alaska remarked that a state law conferring authority on municipal assemblies to appropriate school budgets did not pre-empt a home rule municipality charter which granted a mayor veto power over a school budget even though the law was silent as to the mayor's role in the appropriations process.[171]

The preceding cases should not be interpreted as meaning that statutes absolutely prohibit municipalities from approving appropriations for educational purposes. Still, absent laws clearly granting this power to municipalities, courts generally agree that school boards have independent authority to calculate the amount of money needed for schools while munici-

---

166. *Revell v. City of Annapolis*, 31 A. 695 (Md.1895). [Case No. 31]

167. *City of Louisville v. Commonwealth*, 121 S.W. 411 (Ky.1909).

168. *Board of Educ. of City School Dist. of City of N.Y. v. City of N.Y.*, 394 N.Y.S.2d 148 (N.Y.1977).

169. *City of Hazleton v. Hazleton Area School Dist.*, 276 A.2d 545 (Pa.1971).

170. *Macauley v. Hildebrand*, 491 P.2d 120 (Alaska 1971).

171. *Municipality of Anchorage v. Repasky*, 34 P.3d 302 [158 Educ. L. Rep. 822] (Alaska 2001).

palities must levy, collect, and turn over tax proceeds without question.[172] Moreover, municipal or county units that collect taxes ordinarily can retain a share for administrative expenses unless statutorily forbidden to do so[173] or keep accrued interest on collected school taxes.[174] If municipal bodies violate this rule and improperly retain expenses for collecting taxes, boards can recover the funds even if the former spent them.[175]

Municipal or county tax collectors sometimes collect more money than school boards request due to difficulties in accurately predicting the exact amount of money taxes are likely to produce. In one such case, Maryland's highest court held that a board was entitled to the funds.[176] The court ruled that insofar as state law directed county boards to submit proposed budgets to county officials, their obligation was to levy taxes and distribute the proceeds to boards.

Where a school committee included a provision in the collective bargaining agreement with its teachers to create a procedure intended to fund payments to a health and welfare fund, a city whose boundaries were contiguous with those of the district claimed that the committee's power to set compensation for its employees did not include making payments to third persons for their benefit. The Supreme Judicial Court of Massachusetts disagreed, believing that the payments to the fund were acceptable because they were modest in amount and intelligent in purpose while having no different impact on the city than direct payments to teachers.[177]

Courts may occasionally require municipal governing bodies and/or school boards to expend funds to implement their orders. For instance, the Second Circuit, while conceding that it would have been better to direct a fiscally dependent school board in New York operating under a desegregation decree to supply details regarding expenditures of additional funds that it claimed to have needed from a city, nevertheless upheld an order that a city council add a specific sum to the board's budget.[178]

A more recent dispute arose over a town's proposed amendment to its home rule charter in relation to educational budgeting. The Supreme Court of Connecticut ascertained that although providing education is a statewide responsibility, since the procedure pursuant to which the town adopted its budget was a local issue, its funding board and the local school board could work together to pass a budget satisfying the state's requirements as to educating the town's children.[179]

---

172. *Board of Educ. of Town of Stamford v. Board of Finance of Town of Stamford*, 16 A.2d 601 (Conn.1940).

173. *Coleman v. Kiley*, 225 S.E.2d 273 (Ga.1976).

174. *State ex rel. School Dist. of Springfield R–12 v. Wickliffe*, 650 S.W.2d 623 [11 Educ. L. Rep. 735] (Mo.1983).

175. *Venhaus v. Board of Educ. of Pulaski County*, 659 S.W.2d 179 [14 Educ. L. Rep. 598] (Ark.1983).

176. *Board of Educ. of Montgomery County v. Montgomery County*, 205 A.2d 202 (Md. 1964).

177. *Kerrigan v. City of Boston*, 278 N.E.2d 387 (Mass.1972).

178. *Arthur v. Nyquist*, 712 F.2d 809 [12 Educ. L. Rep. 656] (2d Cir.1983), *cert. denied*, 466 U.S. 936, 104 S.Ct.1907, 80 L.Ed.2d 456 (1984).

179. *Board of Educ. of the Town and Borough of Naugatuck v. Town and Borough of Naugatuck*, 843 A.2d 603 [186 Educ. L. Rep. 420] (Conn.2004).

ALIMENTATION OF SCHOOL FUNDS

State statutes create procedures on the manner of distribution and amounts of funds to be received by local school boards, depending on which agencies distribute the monies. In some jurisdictions, since boards within specific classes are entitled to set amounts of funds, public officials lack discretion as they exercise purely ministerial duties. In jurisdictions granting discretion for distributing funds subject to only broad restrictions, courts typically do not intervene absent charges that officials acted in bad faith or unreasonably.[180]

Difficulties arise when state officials either fail, or refuse, to make payments to boards or questions arise as to how the amounts of funds are calculated. Where state law required the state superintendent of public instruction to apportion equalization funds to boards by a set date, the Supreme Court of Michigan upheld a city school board's request for a mandamus order compelling him to do so.[181]

State laws typically provide that proceeds from fines, forfeitures, and other specified sources become part of school funds. The Constitution of North Carolina stipulates that "[c]lear proceeds of all penalties and forfeitures and all fines collected in the several counties for any breach of penal or military laws of the state shall be faithfully appropriated for establishing and maintaining the free public schools in the several counties of the state."[182] The state's highest court invalidated a statute permitting judicial clerks to earn five percent commissions on all such funds in deciding that insofar as the term "clear proceeds" meant "total sums collected," no subtractions were permitted.[183] On remand, a trial court ruled that another provision of the state constitution requires all punitive fines, penalties, and forfeitures collected by state agencies to be placed in the state's general fund to provide for the needs of public education. In enforcing its earlier order, the court commented that the civil penalties that the state agencies collected pursuant to its ruling belonged to and should be paid to the state's public schools.[184]

In disputes over alimentation, courts clearly insist that there should be no interference with the way in which spending agencies disburse funds since they typically reject administrative attempts to hinder such distributions absent express authority. The courts recognize that school operations could be rendered impossible if funds can be tied up pending the resolution of every question raised by officials who are part of the alimentation

---

180. *State ex rel. King v. Board of Educ. of Russell County*, 108 So. 588 (Ala.1926).

181. *Board of Educ. of Iron Mountain v. Voelker*, 259 N.W. 891 (Mich.1935).

182. *Board of Educ. of Guilford County v. City of High Point*, 197 S.E.191, 192 (N.C.1938) (citing ART. IX, § 5 of the state constitution).

183. *North Carolina School Bds. Ass'n v. Moore*, 614 S.E.2d 504 [199 Educ. L. Rep. 456] (N.C.2005) (interpreting ART. IX § 7 of the state constitution).

184. *North Carolina School Bds. Ass'n v. Moore*, 2008 WL 4485538 (N.C.Super.Ct.2008).

process. To this end, the Supreme Court of Wisconsin found that the disbursement of school aid was a ministerial function once officials discovered the facts and were satisfied that boards met the state standards.[185] The court held that the initial discretionary authority of state-level officials did not transform the mandatory aid payments into departmental funds that were incurred in the execution or administration of a programmatic responsibility subject to reductions by the state's chief fiscal officer.

It is important to distinguish between legislative authorizations and appropriations of funds. Appropriations allocate funds for authorized programs. If there is only an authorization, the Supreme Court of Michigan explained that a school board could not pursue funds through a mandamus action against the state.[186] After state officials set aside insufficient funds to pay intermediate school boards the amounts to which they were entitled, the same court upheld the state's board's having reduced each system's allocation by the percentage needed to conform to the appropriation.[187]

Where a statutory definition of exceptional children included those who were gifted and talented, a statute required state-level officials to reimburse boards for costs of special education. When a board refused to establish a program for the gifted until it received the money, the Supreme Court of Pennsylvania noted that insofar as the receipt of public funds was not a condition precedent, the board had to establish the program on its own, after which time it could seek a writ of mandamus if officials failed to meet their ministerial duty of allocating funds.[188] Similarly, the Supreme Judicial Court of Massachusetts pointed out that a local school committee could not refuse to provide special education services for qualified children on the basis that it refused to comply with an unfunded mandate.[189] The court decided that even if the statutes and regulations pertaining to special education were unfunded mandates, the committee was only entitled to a declaration that they were ineffective, not to reimbursement of the monies it spent.

In a case involving a novel, albeit unsuccessful, defense, when Chicago's board operated schools for fewer than the state-mandated minimum number of days due to a teacher strike and a shortage of funds, it challenged the state's adjusting the amount of its financial aid. The Supreme Court of Illinois rejected the board's argument that the strike was "an act of God" that rendered its compliance with state law impossible.[190] Instead, the court suggested that the board should have directed its plea for forgiveness to the legislature. In like manner, the Supreme Court of Pennsylvania upheld reductions in aid to districts remaining open for fewer

---

185. *School Dist. of LaFarge v. Lindner*, 301 N.W.2d 196 (Wis.1981).

186. *Board of Educ. of Oakland Schools v. Porter*, 221 N.W.2d 345 (Mich.1974).

187. *Board of Educ. of Oakland Schools v. Superintendent of Pub. Instruction*, 257 N.W.2d 73 (Mich.1977).

188. *Central York School Dist. v. Commonwealth, Dep't of Educ.*, 399 A.2d 167 (Pa. Cmwlth.Ct.1979).

189. *City of Worcester v. The Governor*, 625 N.E.2d 1337 [88 Educ. L. Rep. 227] (Mass. 1994).

190. *Cronin v. Lindberg*, 360 N.E.2d 360 (Ill.1976).

than the required number of days due to teacher strikes.[191] Conversely, the Supreme Court of Montana reasoned that state statutes were so vague and uncertain that penalizing a board for not offering classes on a specified number of days due to a teacher strike was impermissible.[192]

The power of governors to reduce state aid to education is partly a statutory question and partly a constitutional one involving the separation of powers. Massachusetts' highest court indicated that statutes authorizing the governor to make reductions did not cover education aid since the funds were not administered by an agency under the control of the governor or one of the governor's secretaries.[193] The court added that constitutional issues of significance would have been worthy of attention had it been unable to resolve the case on the basis of the statutory wording. More recently, an appellate court in New Jersey upheld the authority of the governor to issue an executive order withholding funds from school boards for the remainder of a fiscal year.[194] In rejecting the argument that the governor violated the separation of powers provision in the state constitution, the court affirmed that the financial emergency granted him an exception to the applicable state law.

FEDERAL FUNDS

The Supreme Court has interpreted the general welfare clause in the Federal Constitution as authorizing Congress to spend money for the educational benefit of the people of the United States as long as the primary purpose is regulation or control.[195] To this end, as discussed in Chapter 1, if Congress offers aid to states primarily for educational purposes, such as to educate children with disabilities, it may attach conditions that become contractual when state officials accept the monies.[196] In addition, Congress can require states that accept federal funds to submit assurances of compliance forms[197] and may recover misspent funds.[198] Before states are bound to comply with conditions, there must be clear Congressional intent that such conditions are present so that officials can knowingly choose whether to accept the funds.[199]

---

191. *School Dist. of Pittsburgh v. Commonwealth, Dep't of Educ.*, 422 A.2d 1054 (Pa.1980).

192. *Missoula High School Legal Defense Ass'n v. Superintendent of Pub. Instruction*, 637 P.2d 1188 [1 Educ. L. Rep. 1293] (Mont.1981).

193. *Town of Brookline v. Governor*, 553 N.E.2d 1277 [60 Educ. L. Rep. 181] (Mass.1990).

194. *Perth Amboy Bd. of Educ. v. Christie*, 997 A.2d 262 [258 Educ. L. Rep. 325] (N.J.Super.Ct.App.Div.2010).

195. According to this provision, "[t]he Congress shall have Power To.... provide for the ... general Welfare of the United States," U.S. CONST. ART. I, § 8. *See United States v. Butler*, 297 U.S. 1, 56 S.Ct. 312, 80 L.Ed. 477 (1936), *Helvering v. Davis*, 301 U.S. 619, 57 S.Ct. 904, 81 L.Ed. 1307 (1937).

196. *See, e.g.,* Individuals with Disabilities Act, 20 U.S.C.A. §§ 1400 *et seq.*

197. *Grove City College v. Bell*, 465 U.S. 555, 104 S.Ct. 1211, 79 L.Ed.2d 516 [15 Educ. L. Rep. 1079] (1984).

198. *Bell v. New Jersey and Pa.*, 461 U.S. 773, 103 S.Ct. 2187, 76 L.Ed.2d 312 [11 Educ. L. Rep. 30] (1983).

Conditions that are attached to federal funds must not be unconstitutional. If conditions are imposed as administrative regulations, they must not exceed an agency's authority. For example, the Court of Appeals for the District of Columbia declared that the Secretary of Agriculture exceeded his rule making authority by barring the sale of foods in schools that competed with those provided in the federally subsidized school breakfast and lunch program.[200] Yet, the court upheld restrictions on the sale of "junk foods" in schools on the basis that Congress authorized such a limit for the purpose of promoting consumption of nutritious foods.

Impacted school areas, those with populations that are substantially enlarged by the attendance of children of federal employees, but which lose school tax revenues because the federal government is exempt from property taxes, receive funds according to a formula. When officials deducted a substantial amount of impact aid that a local board would have received from the state, the federal trial court in New Mexico decreed that this violated the Supremacy Clause of the Federal Constitution[201] since federal financial relief did not reach local taxpayers to the extent Congress contemplated.[202] The court invalidated the plan since the purpose of the federal law was to aid local boards, not provide compensation for the state.

A more recent case from New Mexico dealing with impact aid involved an unsuccessful challenge by two school boards to an order of the United States Secretary of Education certifying that the state's aid program equalized expenditures for local districts. This order permitted the state to factor in the receipt of impact aid payments when making its own aid distributions to those boards. In rejecting the boards' claim that state officials erred in calculating aid, the Tenth Circuit maintained that insofar as the Department of Education's construction of the disparity standard was permissible, its interpretation was entitled to judicial deference.[203]

On further review in *Zuni Public School District No. 89 v. Department of Education*,[204] a closely divided Supreme Court rejected the claim of the school boards that the federal regulation interpreting the funding formula at issue in the federal Impact Aid Act unfairly deprived them of resources. In affirming that the regulation was a reasonable method of carrying out the Congressional statutory purpose of excluding statistical outliers, the

---

199. *Pennhurst State School and Hosp. v. Halderman*, 451 U.S. 1, 101 S.Ct. 1531, 67 L.Ed.2d 694 (1981).

200. *National Soft Drink Ass'n v. Block*, 721 F.2d 1348 [15 Educ. L. Rep. 32] (D.C.Cir. 1983).

201. Under this Clause, "[t]his Constitution, and the Laws of the United States which shall be made in Pursuance thereof; and all Treaties made, or which shall be made, under the Authority of the United States, shall be the supreme Law of the Land; and the Judges in every State shall be bound thereby, any Thing in the Constitution or Laws of any State to the Contrary notwithstanding." U.S. Const. art. VI, § 2.

202. *Shepheard v. Godwin*, 280 F.Supp. 869 (E.D.Va.1968).

203. *Zuni Pub. School Dist. No. 89 v. United States Dep't of Educ.*, 393 F.3d 1158 [194 Educ. L. Rep. 515] (10th Cir.2004), *vacated in en banc hearing*, 437 F.3d 1289 (10th Cir.2006), *cert. granted*, 548 U.S. 941, 127 S.Ct. 36, 165 L.Ed.2d 1013 (2006).

204. 550 U.S. 81, 127 S.Ct. 1534, 167 L.Ed.2d 449 [218 Educ. L. Rep. 24] (2007), *reh'g denied*, 551 U.S. 1110, 127 S.Ct. 2931, 168 L.Ed.2d 257 (2007). [Case No. 35]

Court noted that the Act allows the United States Department of Education to identify school systems that should be "disregarded" by looking to the numbers of their students and their size in addition to per-pupil expenditures. Interpreting the regulation as falling within the scope of the statute's plain language, the Justices thought that insofar as the law is concerned about both students and school systems, the "disregard" instruction can include the distribution of ranked populations consisting of students or school systems weighed by enrollees, not merely of unweighed systems. The Court acknowledged that no statistician disagreed with the opinion that the language could have been interpreted in this manner.

Courts do not necessarily presume that the Supremacy Clause permits federal legislation to supersede state power absent Congressional intent to do so. Applying this rule, the Tenth Circuit upheld a finance plan that treated districts differently from each other as long as all received special federal funds connected with a community's having been identified as a federally owned and managed installation for atomic research and development.[205] The record revealed that the government transferred ownership of schools it built to a newly created board and continued to provide it with financial grants. The court distinguished this situation from that in impact aid cases where the aid was supplementary, explaining that there was no such intent in the atomic-energy-community legislation, remarking that when the plan to finance the community originated, there was nothing to supplement.

Previously, a school board in North Carolina that enrolled large numbers of children whose parents were connected with the federal government, regardless of whether they were in the military, charged tuition for non-domiciliary enrollees, officials disputed the cutbacks in federal impact aid that it faced. The Fourth Circuit invalidated the plan on contractual and constitutional grounds.[206] The court premised its contractual rationale on the board's having accepted federal aid for school construction that was available both to systems experiencing substantial enrollments of children whose parents were connected with the federal government and which promised to make the facilities which were still in service equally available to these students as well as children of local families. The court's constitutional analysis relied on the Supremacy Clause, concluding that the tuition charges were in effect a tax designed to discriminate against individuals who were connected with the federal government and, by extension, against the federal government.

The following year, the Supreme Court applied the Supremacy Clause in invalidating a statute from South Dakota that would have required local governments to distribute federal payments in lieu of taxes to compensate for the loss of tax revenues from federally administered national parks and wilderness areas in the same way that they distributed general tax revenues.[207] The Court interpreted Congressional intent as wishing to permit

---

205. *Los Alamos School Bd. v. Wugalter*, 557 F.2d 709 (10th Cir.1977), *cert. denied*, 434 U.S. 968, 98 S.Ct. 512, 54 L.Ed.2d 455 (1977).

206. *United States v. Onslow County Bd. of Educ.*, 728 F.2d 628 [16 Educ. L. Rep. 717] (4th Cir.1984).

207. *Lawrence County v. Lead–Deadwood School Dist. No. 40–1*, 469 U.S. 256, 105 S.Ct. 695, 83 L.Ed.2d 635 [21 Educ. L. Rep. 1111] (1985).

units of local government to choose how to use the money unfettered by state intervention.

[CASE NO. 30]   POWER OF BOARD TO LEVY TAXES

MARION & McPHERSON RAILWAY CO. v. ALEXANDER

Supreme Court of Kansas, 1901.
64 P. 978.

■ CUNNINGHAM, J.

The plaintiff in error in this action seeks to enjoin the collection of all taxes levied for school purposes in school district No. 79, Marion County, Kan., in excess of 2 per cent on the taxable property owned by it in said district. A graded school district, No. 79, had been organized, identical in boundaries and inhabitants with school district No. 79; such organization being authorized by article 7, c. 92, of the General Statutes of 1889. That article generally provided for the organization of union or graded schools, its principal sections being as follows: Section 107 provides for the selection of a board of directors by the graded school district, and that such board shall consist of a director, clerk, and treasurer. Section 108 directs that such board of directors shall, in all matters relating to the graded school, possess all the powers and discharge all the like duties of boards of directors in other districts. Section 109 provides that the union districts thus formed shall be entitled to an equitable share of the school funds, to be drawn from the treasurer of each district so uniting, in proportion to the number of children attending the said graded school for each district. Section 110: "The said union district may levy taxes for the purpose of purchasing a building or furnishing proper buildings for the accommodation of the school or for the purpose of defraying necessary expenses and paying teachers, but shall be governed in all respects by the law herein provided for levying and collecting district taxes." Section 111 provides certain duties for the clerk of the union district in relation to reports, and that the district treasurer shall apportion the amount of school moneys due the union district, and pay the same over to the treasurer of the union district on order of the clerk and director thereof. Section 112, that the clerk of the union district shall make report to the county superintendent, and discharge all the duties of clerk in like manner as the clerk of the district. Section 113, that the treasurer of the district shall perform all the duties of treasurer as prescribed in the act in like manner as the district treasurer. Section 115, that any single district shall possess power to establish graded schools in like manner and subject to the same provisions as two or more districts united. Section 28 of the same chapter (being the section which gives the general power for levying district taxes) provides: "The inhabitants qualified to vote at a school meeting, lawfully assembled, shall have power: ... To vote a tax annually not exceeding two per cent on the taxable property in the district, as the meeting shall deem sufficient for the various school purposes, and distribute the amount as the meeting shall deem proper in the payment of teachers' wages, and to purchase or lease a site."

These are all the sections which afford light for the solution of the question involved. From these, it is contended by plaintiff in error that while the inhabitants of one or more school districts may form a union or graded district, and create machinery to run the same and to maintain any and all schools therein, the total levy "for the various school purposes" cannot exceed 2 per cent on the taxable property in any one district annually. It is contended by the defendants in error that the various sections quoted, conferring as they do upon the various members of the graded school district board all the powers of like officers of ordinary district boards, and erecting a separate entity for the purpose of managing a separate school, and conferring upon that entity the power to levy taxes as found in section 110, give the power to such graded school district to make within its bounds an additional levy not to exceed 2 per cent; that is, that it may levy as much as the original school district may, and this in addition to what the original district levies, and not that the total of both levies must be the limit fixed in section 28. The court below took this view of the question. In this we do not agree. We think that by section 28 the entire levy may not exceed 2 per cent; and we are strengthened in this conclusion by the language of section 109, which says that a union district shall be entitled to "an equitable share of the school funds," and also by that in section 111,"the district treasurer shall apportion the amount of school money due the union district and pay the same over to the union district." The law fixes the time for holding the annual meetings of the union or graded districts in June, while the annual meetings of school districts occur in July. All these provisions, taken together, indicate that it was the purpose of the legislature that, while the first meeting that of the graded district could suggest the levy desired for graded school purposes, the last one only possessed the power to vote the tax which for "the various school purposes" could not in any one year exceed 2 per cent. Or, at least, there must be such harmony in the action of both bodies that the aggregate levy may not exceed the limit found in section 28. We may say that the question is not one entirely free from doubt, but can hardly believe that the legislature would have left it in that condition, had its purpose been to confer the right to so largely increase the burden of taxation. The authority to levy taxes is an extraordinary one. It is never left to implication, unless it is a necessary implication. Its warrant must be clearly found in the act of the legislature. Any other rule might lead to great wrong and oppression, and when there is a reasonable doubt as to its existence the right must be denied. Therefore to say that the right is in doubt is to deny its existence.

The levies sought to be enjoined are those for the years 1894 and 1895, and our conclusion is that the judgment of the district court must be reversed, and it be directed to make the injunction perpetual, enjoining all of the defendants from collecting all of said school taxes in excess of 2 per cent All the justices concurring.

All justices concurring.

NOTES

1. "The power of the board of education of a non-high school district to levy taxes is statutory. The language granting that power is to be strictly construed and will not be extended beyond the plain import of the words used." *People ex rel. Smith, County Collector v. Wabash Railway Co.*, 28 N.E.2d 119, 122 (Ill.1940).

2. Generally, boards may not levy taxes to build up surpluses beyond fixed percents, set by legislatures, of current expenses. The Supreme Court of Nebraska found that although a reasonable contingency was permissible, a tax levy creating a surplus of fifty percent of a budget was excessive. *Kissinger v. School Dist. No. 49 of Clay County*, 77 N.W.2d 767 (Neb.1956). What do you think?

[CASE NO. 31]   POWER OF STATE TO REQUIRE LOCAL ISSUE OF BONDS

REVELL v. MAYOR, ETC., OF ANNAPOLIS

Court of Appeals of Maryland, 1895.
31 A. 695.

■ ROBINSON, C.J.

The act of 1894, c. 620, provides for the erection of a public school building in the city of Annapolis, and, to pay for the same, it authorizes and directs the school commissioners of Anne Arundel county to borrow money, not exceeding the sum of $20,000, on bonds to be indorsed by the county commissioners; and for the same purpose it directs that the city of Annapolis shall issue bonds to the amount of $10,000, and that said bonds shall be issued without submitting the question of their issue to the voters of said city. The city of Annapolis has refused to issue the bonds as thus directed by the act, and the question is whether the legislature has the power to direct that the city authorities shall issue bonds to raise money to be applied to the erection of a public school building in said city. This power is denied, on the broad ground that it is not competent for the legislature to compel a municipal corporation to create a debt or levy a tax for a local purpose, in which the state has no concern, or to assume a debt not within the corporate powers of a municipal government. If the correctness of this general proposition be conceded for the purposes of this case, we do not see how it affects in any manner the validity of the act now in question. We cannot agree that the erection of buildings necessary for the public schools is a matter of merely local concern, in which the state has no interest. In this country the people are not only in theory, but in practice, the source of all governmental power, and the stability of free institutions mainly rests upon an enlightened public opinion. Fully recognizing this, the constitution declares that it shall be the duty of the legislature "to establish throughout the state a thorough and efficient system of free public schools, and to provide, by taxation or otherwise," for their maintenance and support.... And the legislature has accordingly established a public school system, and has provided for its support by state and local taxation. It cannot be said, therefore, that the erection of buildings for public school purposes is a matter in which the state has no concern; nor can we agree that the creation of a debt for such purposes is not within the ordinary functions of municipal government. What is a municipal corporation? It is but a subordinate part of the state government, incorporated for public purposes, and clothed with special and limited powers of legislation in regard to its own local affairs. It has no inherent legislative power, and can exercise such powers only as have been expressly or by fair implication delegated to it by the legislature.... The legislature may, at its pleasure, alter, amend, and enlarge its powers. It may authorize the city authorities to establish public schools within the corporate limits, and direct that bonds shall be issued to raise money for their support, payable at intervals during a series of years. There is no difference in principle between issuing bonds and the levying of a tax in one year sufficient to meet the necessary expenditure. It would be less burdensome to the taxpayers to issue bonds payable at intervals than to levy a tax to raise $10,000 in any one year. This, however, is a matter of detail, within the discretion of the legislature, and over which the courts have no control.

If the legislature has the power to direct the city authorities to create a debt for a public school building, the exercise of this power in no manner depends upon their consent or upon the consent of the qualified voters of the city. We recognize the force of the argument that the question whether a municipal debt is to be created ought to be left to the discretion and judgment of the people who are to bear the burden. We recognize the fact that the exercise of this power by the legislature may be liable to abuse. But this abuse of a power is no argument against its exercise. The remedy, however, in such cases, is with the people to whom the members of the legislature are responsible for the discharge of the trust committed to them. It is a matter over which the courts have no control....

... It follows from what we have said that the judgment sustaining the demurrer in this case must be overruled. Judgment reversed.

NOTES

1. When school boards fail to carry out their duties to the satisfaction of local communities, are residents justified in seeking legislative action to accomplish their wishes?

2. To what extent is special legislation justified to cope with problems not generally present in a state?

[CASE NO. 32] POWER OF STATE TO RAISE AND DISTRIBUTE SCHOOL FUNDS

SAWYER v. GILMORE

Supreme Judicial Court of Maine, 1912.
83 A. 673.

■ CORNISH, J.

This bill in equity is brought to enjoin the Treasurer of State and his successors in office from collecting a tax assessed under the provisions of chapter 177 of the Public Laws of 1909....

The case comes up on report, and by stipulation the only question raised and to be considered is the constitutionality of the chapter above referred to under the state and federal Constitutions.

Chapter 177 of the Public Laws of 1909, the statute in question, reads as follows:

"Section 1. A tax of one and a half mills on a dollar shall annually be assessed upon all of the property in the state according to the valuation thereof and shall be known as the tax for the support of common schools. . . .

"Sec. [sic] 3. One-third of this fund shall be distributed by the Treasurer of State on the first day of January, annually, to the several cities, towns and plantations according to the number of scholars therein, as the same shall appear from the official returns made to the state superintendent of public schools for the preceding year, and the remaining two-thirds of said fund shall be distributed by the Treasurer of State on the first day of January, annually, to the several cities, towns and plantations, according to the valuation thereof as the same shall be fixed by the state assessors for the preceding year." . . .

Objections . . . are raised to the manner of distribution. . . .

The first objection is that this act imposes an unequal burden of taxation upon the unorganized townships of the state, because, while the fund is created by the taxation of all the property in such townships as well as upon the property in the cities, towns, and plantations, no provision is made for the distribution of any part thereof to such townships, but it is all apportioned among the cities, towns, and plantations. The townships are omitted. In other words, while four subdivisions of the state are made to contribute to the fund, only three are permitted to share in the financial benefits.

This objection, however, is without legal foundation. The Legislature has the right under the Constitution to impose an equal rate of taxation upon all the property in the state, including the property in unorganized townships, for the purpose of distributing the proceeds thereof among the cities, towns, and plantations for common school purposes, and the mere fact that the tax is assessed upon the property in four municipal subdivisions and distributed among three is not in itself fatal. . . .

. . . The fundamental question is this: Is the purpose for which the tax is assessed a public purpose, not whether any portion of it may find its way back again to the pocket of the taxpayer or to the direct advantage of himself or family. Were the latter the test, the childless man would be exempt from the support of schools and the sane and well from the support of hospitals. In order that taxation may be equal and uniform in the constitutional sense, it is not necessary that the benefits arising therefrom should be enjoyed by all the people in equal degree, nor that each one of the people should participate in each particular benefit. Laws must be general in their character, and the benefits must affect different people differently. This is due to difference in situation. . . . In a Republic like ours each must contribute for the common good, and the benefits are received not directly in dollars and cents, but indirectly in a wider diffusion of knowledge, in better homes, saner laws, more efficient administration of justice, higher social order, and deeper civic righteousness. . . .

But the plaintiff further attacks the method of distribution as unconstitutional because it is made, not according to the number of scholars, as is the school mill fund, but one-third according to the number of scholars and two-thirds according to valuation, thus benefiting the cities, and richer towns more than the poorer.

But that result is not the test of constitutionality. Inequality of assessment is necessarily fatal, inequality of distribution is not, provided the purpose be the public welfare. The method of distributing the proceeds of such a tax rests in the wise discretion and sound judgment of the Legislature. If this discretion is unwisely exercised, the remedy is with the people, and not with the court. Such distribution might be according to population, or according to the number of scholars of school age, or according to school attendance, or according to valuation, or partly on one basis and partly on another. The Constitution prescribes no regulation in regard to this matter, and it is not for the court to say that one method should be adopted in preference to another. We are not to substitute our judgment for that of a co-ordinate branch of the government working within its constitutional limits. The distribution of the school mill fund of 1872 has resulted in inequality. That distribution has been, and continues to be, based on the number of scholars, thereby benefiting the poorer towns more than the richer, because they receive more than they pay, and in the opinion of the justices before cited that method is deemed constitutional. The act under consideration apportions the newly created common school fund one-third according to the number of scholars and two-thirds according to the valuation as fixed by the state assessors, thereby benefiting the richer towns more than the poorer, producing inequality in the other direction, but we are unable to see why this method is not equally constitutional with the other. Both taxes are assessed for the same admittedly public purpose, both promote the common welfare, and the fact that the Legislature has seen fit to distribute the two on different bases is not fatal to the validity of either. It may be that the two methods taken together produce a more equal distribution than either operating alone. In any event, the Legislature has adopted both methods, and both must stand or fall together. . . .

Our conclusion therefore is that chapter 177 of the Public Laws of 1909 violates neither the state nor the federal Constitution, and the must therefore be:

Bill dismissed, with costs.

NOTES

1. This same court previously upheld the School Mill Act of 1872 which was the first in the state to impose a tax on property devoted to the maintenance of common schools. *Opinion of the Justices*, 68 Me. 582 (1878).

2. Is the court's appraisal of the benefits of public education sound? To what extent should public services be supported by its users? Does the answer depend on a particular service?

[CASE NO. 33]   CONSTITUTIONALITY OF STATE FINANCE PLAN IN
RELATION TO EQUALITY OF EDUCATIONAL OPPORTUNITY

SAN ANTONIO INDEPENDENT SCHOOL
DISTRICT v. RODRIGUEZ

Supreme Court of the United States, 1973.
411 U.S. 1, 93 S.Ct. 1278, 36 L.Ed.2d 16.

■ MR. JUSTICE POWELL delivered the opinion of the Court.

This suit attacking the Texas system of financing public education was
initiated by Mexican–American parents whose children attend the elementary and secondary schools in the Edgewood Independent School District,
an urban school district in San Antonio, Texas. They brought a class action
on behalf of schoolchildren throughout the State who are members of
minority groups or who are poor and reside in school districts having a low
property tax base.... The complaint was filed in the summer of 1968 and a
three-judge court was impaneled in January 1969. In December 1971 the
panel rendered its judgment in a per curiam opinion holding the Texas
school finance system unconstitutional under the Equal Protection Clause
of the Fourteenth Amendment.... For the reasons stated in this opinion,
we reverse the decision of the District Court.

I

The first Texas State Constitution, promulgated upon Texas' entry
into the Union in 1845, provided for the establishment of a system of free
schools. Early in its history, Texas adopted a dual approach to the financing
of its schools, relying on mutual participation by the local school districts
and the State....

Recognizing the need for increased state funding to help offset disparities in local spending and to meet Texas' changing educational requirements, the state legislature in the late 1940's undertook a thorough
evaluation of public education with an eye toward major reform. In 1947,
an 18–member committee, composed of educators and legislators, was
appointed to explore alternative systems in other States and to propose a
funding scheme that would guarantee a minimum or basic educational
offering to each child and that would help overcome interdistrict disparities
in taxable resources. The Committee's efforts led to ... establishing the
Texas Minimum Foundation School Program. Today, this Program accounts for approximately half of the total educational expenditures in
Texas.

The Program calls for state and local contributions to a fund earmarked specifically for teacher salaries, operating expenses, and transportation costs. The State, supplying funds from its general revenues, finances
approximately 80% of the Program, and the school districts are responsible—as a unit—for providing the remaining 20%. The districts' share,
known as the Local Fund Assignment, is apportioned among the school
districts under a formula designed to reflect each district's relative taxpaying ability. The Assignment is first divided among Texas' 254 counties

pursuant to a complicated economic index that takes into account the relative value of each county's contribution to the State's total income from manufacturing, mining, and agricultural activities. It also considers each county's relative share of all payrolls paid within the State and, to a lesser extent, considers each county's share of all property in the State. Each county's assignment is then divided among its school districts on the basis of each district's share of assessable property within the county. The district, in turn, finances its share of the Assignment out of revenues from local property taxation.

The design of this complex system was twofold. First, it was an attempt to assure that the Foundation Program would have an equalizing influence on expenditure levels between school districts by placing the heaviest burden on the school districts most capable of paying. Second, the Program's architects sought to establish a Local Fund Assignment that would force every school district to contribute to the education of its children but that would not by itself exhaust any district's resources. Today every school district does impose a property tax from which it derives locally expendable funds in excess of the amount necessary to satisfy its Local Fund Assignment under the Foundation Program. . . .

The school district in which appellees reside, the Edgewood Independent School District, has been compared throughout this litigation with the Alamo Heights Independent School District. This comparison between the least and most affluent districts in the San Antonio area serves to illustrate the manner in which the dual system of finance operates and to indicate the extent to which substantial disparities exist despite the State's impressive progress in recent years. Edgewood is one of seven public school districts in the metropolitan area. Approximately 22,000 students are enrolled in its 25 elementary and secondary schools. The district is situated in the core-city sector of San Antonio in a residential neighborhood that has little commercial or industrial property. The residents are predominantly of Mexican–American descent: approximately 90% of the student population is Mexican–American and over 6% is Negro. The average assessed property value per pupil is $5,960—the lowest in the metropolitan area—and the median family income ($4,686) is also the lowest. At an equalized tax rate of $1.05 per $100 of assessed property—the highest in the metropolitan area—the district contributed $26 to the education of each child for the 1967–1968 school year above its Local Fund Assignment for the Minimum Foundation Program. The Foundation Program contributed $222 per pupil for a state-local total of $248. Federal funds added another $108 for a total of $356 per pupil.

Alamo Heights is the most affluent school district in San Antonio. Its six schools, housing approximately 5,000 students, are situated in a residential community quite unlike the Edgewood District. The school population is predominantly "Anglo," having only 18% Mexican–Americans and less than 1% Negroes. The assessed property value per pupil exceeds $49,000, and the median family income is $8,001. In 1967–1968 the local tax rate of $.85 per $100 of valuation yielded $333 per pupil over and above its contribution to the Foundation Program. Coupled with the $225 provided from that Program, the district was able to supply $558 per student.

Supplemented by a $36 per-pupil grant from federal sources, Alamo Heights spent $594 per pupil.

Although the 1967–1968 school year figures provide the only complete statistical breakdown for each category of aid, more recent partial statistics indicate that the previously noted trend of increasing state aid has been significant. For the 1970–1971 school year, the Foundation School Program allotment for Edgewood was $356 per pupil, a 62% increase over the 1967–68 school year. Indeed, state aid alone in 1970–1971 equaled Edgewood's entire 1967–1968 school budget from local, state, and federal sources. Alamo Heights enjoyed a similar increase under the Foundation Program, netting $491 per pupil in 1970–1971. These recent figures also reveal the extent to which these two districts' allotments were funded from their own required contributions to the Local Fund Assignment. Alamo Heights, because of its relative wealth, was required to contribute out of its local property tax collections approximately $100 per pupil, or about 20% of its Foundation grant. Edgewood, on the other hand, paid only $8.46 per pupil, which is about 2.4% of its grant. It appears then that, at least as to these two districts, the Local Fund Assignment does reflect a rough approximation of the relative taxpaying potential of each.

Despite these recent increases, substantial interdistrict disparities in school expenditures found by the District Court to prevail in San Antonio and in varying degrees throughout the State still exist. And it was these disparities, largely attributable to differences in the amounts of money collected through local property taxation, that led the District Court to conclude that Texas' dual system of public school financing violated the Equal Protection Clause. The District Court held that the Texas system discriminates on the basis of wealth in the manner in which education is provided for its people. Finding that wealth is a "suspect" classification and that education is a "fundamental" interest, the District Court held that the Texas system could be sustained only if the State could show that it was premised upon some compelling state interest. On this issue the court concluded that "[n]ot only are defendants unable to demonstrate compelling state interests . . . they fail even to establish a reasonable basis for these classifications." . . .

This, then, establishes the framework for our analysis. We must decide, first, whether the Texas system of financing public education operates to the disadvantage of some suspect class or impinges upon a fundamental right explicitly or implicitly protected by the Constitution, thereby requiring strict judicial scrutiny. If so, the judgment of the District Court should be affirmed. If not, the Texas scheme must still be examined to determine whether it rationally furthers some legitimate, articulated state purpose and therefore does not constitute an invidious discrimination in violation of the Equal Protection Clause of the Fourteenth Amendment.

II

A

The wealth discrimination discovered by the District Court in this case, and by several other courts that have recently struck down school-financing laws in other States, is quite unlike any of the forms of wealth discrimination heretofore reviewed by this Court. Rather than focusing on the unique features of the alleged discrimination, the courts in these cases have virtually assumed their findings of a suspect classification through a simplistic process of analysis: since, under the traditional systems of financing public schools, some poorer people receive less expensive educations than other more affluent people, these systems discriminate on the basis of wealth. This approach largely ignores the hard threshold questions, including whether it makes a difference for purposes of consideration under the Constitution that the class of disadvantaged "poor" cannot be identified or defined in customary equal protection terms, and whether the relative—rather than absolute—nature of the asserted deprivation is of significant consequence. Before a State's laws and the justifications for the classifications they create are subjected to strict judicial scrutiny, we think these threshold considerations must be analyzed more closely than they were in the court below.

The case comes to us with no definitive description of the classifying facts or delineation of the disfavored class. Examination of the District Court's opinion and of appellees' complaint, briefs and contentions at oral argument suggests, however, at least three ways in which the discrimination claimed here might be described. The Texas system of school financing might be regarded as discriminating (1) against "poor" persons whose incomes fall below some identifiable level of poverty or who might be characterized as functionally "indigent," or (2) against those who are relatively poorer than others, or (3) against all those who, irrespective of their personal incomes, happen to reside in relatively poorer school districts. Our task must be to ascertain whether, in fact, the Texas system has been shown to discriminate on any of these possible bases and, if so, whether the resulting classification may be regarded as suspect.

The precedents of this Court provide the proper starting point. The individuals, or groups of individuals, who constituted the class discriminated against in our prior cases shared two distinguishing characteristics: because of their impecunity they were completely unable to pay for some desired benefit, and as a consequence, they sustained an absolute deprivation of a meaningful opportunity to enjoy that benefit. In *Griffin v. Illinois* and its progeny, the Court invalidated state laws that prevented an indigent criminal defendant from acquiring a transcript, or an adequate substitute for a transcript, for use at several stages of the trial and appeal process. The payment requirements in each case were found to occasion de facto discrimination against those who, because of their indigency, were totally unable to pay for transcripts. And the Court in each case emphasized that no constitutional violation would have been shown if the State had provided some "adequate substitute" for a full stenographic transcript.

Likewise, in *Douglas v. California*, a decision establishing an indigent defendant's right to court-appointed counsel on direct appeal, the Court dealt only with defendants who could not pay for counsel from their own resources and who had no other way of gaining representation. Douglas provides no relief for those on whom the burdens of paying for a criminal defense are relatively speaking, great but not insurmountable. Nor does it deal with relative differences in the quality of counsel acquired by the less wealthy....

Only appellees' first possible basis for describing the class disadvantaged by the Texas school-financing system—discrimination against a class of definably "poor" persons—might arguably meet the criteria established in these prior cases. Even a cursory examination, however, demonstrates that neither of the two distinguishing characteristics of wealth classifications can be found here. First, in support of their charge that the system discriminates against the "poor," appellees have made no effort to demonstrate that it operates to the peculiar disadvantage of any class fairly definable as indigent, or as composed of persons whose incomes are beneath any designated poverty level. Indeed, there is reason to believe that the poorest families are not necessarily clustered in the poorest property districts. A recent and exhaustive study of school districts in Connecticut concluded that "[i]t is clearly incorrect ... to contend that the 'poor' live in 'poor' districts.... Thus, the major factual assumption of *Serrano*—that the educational financing system discriminates against the 'poor'—is simply false in Connecticut." Defining "poor" families as those below the Bureau of the Census "poverty level," the Connecticut study found, not surprisingly, that the poor were clustered around commercial and industrial areas—those same areas that provide the most attractive sources of property tax income for school districts. Whether a similar pattern would be discovered in Texas is not known, but there is no basis on the record in this case for assuming that the poorest people—defined by reference to any level of absolute impecunity—are concentrated in the poorest districts.

Second, neither appellees nor the District Court addressed the fact that, unlike each of the foregoing cases, lack of personal resources has not occasioned an absolute deprivation of the desired benefit. The argument here is not that the children in districts having relatively low assessable property values are receiving no public education; rather, it is that they are receiving a poorer quality education than that available to children in districts having more assessable wealth. Apart from the unsettled and disputed question whether the quality of education may be determined by the amount of money expended for it, a sufficient answer to appellees' argument is that, at least where wealth is involved, the Equal Protection Clause does not require absolute equality or precisely equal advantages. Nor indeed, in view of the infinite variables affecting the educational process, can any system assure equal quality of education except in the most relative sense....

For these two reasons—the absence of any evidence that the financing system discriminates against any definable category of "poor" people or that it results in the absolute deprivation of education—the disadvantaged class is not susceptible of identification in traditional terms.

As suggested above, appellees and the District Court may have embraced a second or third approach, the second of which might be characterized as a theory of relative or comparative discrimination based on family income. Appellees sought to prove that a direct correlation exists between the wealth of families within each district and the expenditures therein for education. That is, along a continuum, the poorer the family the lower the dollar amount of education received by the family's children.

The principal evidence adduced in support of this comparative-discrimination claim is an affidavit submitted by Professor Joel S. Berke of Syracuse University's Educational Finance Policy Institute....

Professor Berke's affidavit is based on a survey of approximately 10% of the school districts in Texas. His findings ... show only that the wealthiest few districts in the sample have the highest median family incomes and spend the most on education, and that the several poorest districts have the lowest family incomes and devote the least amount of money to education. For the remainder of the districts—96 districts composing almost 90% of the sample—the correlation is inverted, i.e., the districts that spend next to the most money on education are populated by families having next to the lowest median family incomes while the districts spending the least have the highest median family incomes. It is evident that, even if the conceptual questions were answered favorably to appellees, no factual basis exists upon which to found a claim of comparative wealth discrimination.

This brings us, then, to the third way in which the classification scheme might be defined-district wealth discrimination. Since the only correlation indicated by the evidence is between district property wealth and expenditures, it may be argued that discrimination might be found without regard to the individual income characteristics of district residents. Assuming a perfect correlation between district property wealth and expenditures from top to bottom, the disadvantaged class might be viewed as encompassing every child in every district except the district that has the most assessable wealth and spends the most on education. Alternatively ... the class might be defined more restrictively to include children in districts with assessable property which falls below the statewide average, or median, or below some other artificially defined level.

However described, it is clear that appellees' suit asks this Court to extend its most exacting scrutiny to review a system that allegedly discriminates against a large, diverse, and amorphous class, unified only by the common factor of residence in districts that happen to have less taxable wealth than other districts. The system of alleged discrimination and the class it defines have none of the traditional indicia of suspectness: the class is not saddled with such disabilities, or subjected to such a history of purposeful unequal treatment, or relegated to such a position of political powerlessness as to command extraordinary protection from the majoritarian political process.

We thus conclude that the Texas system does not operate to the peculiar disadvantage of any suspect class. But in recognition of the fact that this Court has never heretofore held that wealth discrimination alone provides an adequate basis for invoking strict scrutiny, appellees have not relied solely on this contention. They also assert that the State's system impermissible interferes with the exercise of a "fundamental" right and that accordingly the prior decisions of this Court require the application of the strict standard of judicial review. It is this question—whether education is a fundamental right, in the sense that it is among the rights and liberties protected by the Constitution—which has so consumed the attention of courts and commentators in recent years.

B

In *Brown v. Board of Education*, a unanimous Court recognized that "education is perhaps the most important function of state and local governments." What was said there in the context of racial discrimination has lost none of its vitality with the passage of time.... This theme, expressing an abiding respect for the vital role of education in a free society, may be found in numerous opinions of Justices of this Court writing both before and after *Brown* was decided.

Nothing this Court holds today in any way detracts from our historic dedication to public education. We are in complete agreement with the conclusion of the three-judge panel below that "the grave significance of education both to the individual and to our society" cannot be doubted. But the importance of a service performed by the State does not determine whether it must be regarded as fundamental for purposes of examination under the Equal Protection Clause....

... It is not the province of this Court to create substantive constitutional rights in the name of guaranteeing equal protection of the laws. Thus, the key to discovering whether education is "fundamental" is not to be found in comparisons of the relative societal significance of education as opposed to subsistence or housing. Nor is it to be found by weighing whether education is as important as the right to travel. Rather, the answer lies in assessing whether there is a right to education explicitly or implicitly guaranteed by the Constitution.

Education, of course, is not among the rights afforded explicit protection under our Federal Constitution. Nor do we find any basis for saying it is implicitly so protected. As we have said, the undisputed importance of education will not alone cause this Court to depart from the usual standard for reviewing a State's social and economic legislation. It is appellees' contention, however, that education is distinguishable from other services and benefits provided by the State because it bears a peculiarly close relationship to other rights and liberties accorded protection under the Constitution. Specifically, they insist that education is itself a fundamental personal right because it is essential to the effective exercise of First Amendment freedoms and to intelligent utilization of the right to vote....

We need not dispute any of these propositions. The Court has long afforded zealous protection against unjustifiable governmental interference with the individual's rights to speak and to vote. Yet we have never presumed to possess either the ability or the authority to guarantee to the citizenry the most effective speech or the most informed electoral choice. That these may be desirable goals of a system of freedom of expression and of a representative form of government is not to be doubted. These are indeed goals to be pursued by a people whose thoughts and beliefs are freed from governmental interference. But they are not values to be implemented by judicial intrusion into otherwise legitimate state activities.

Even if it were conceded that some identifiable quantum of education is a constitutionally protected prerequisite to the meaningful exercise of either right, we have no indication that the present levels of educational expenditures in Texas provide an education that falls short. Whatever merit appellees' argument might have if a State's financing system occasioned an absolute denial of educational opportunities to any of its children, that argument provides no basis for finding an interference with fundamental rights where only relative differences in spending levels are involved and where—as is true in the present case—no charge fairly could be made that the system fails to provide each child with an opportunity to acquire the basic minimal skills necessary for the enjoyment of the rights of speech and of full participation in the political process.

Furthermore, the logical limitations on appellees' nexus theory are difficult to perceive. How, for instance, is education to be distinguished from the significant personal interests in the basics of decent food and shelter? Empirical examination might well buttress an assumption that the ill-fed, ill-clothed and ill-housed are among the most ineffective participants in the political process, and that they derive the least enjoyment from the benefits of the First Amendment. . . .

C

It should be clear, for the reasons stated above and in accord with the prior decisions of this Court, that this is not a case in which the challenged state action must be subjected to the searching judicial scrutiny reserved for laws that create suspect classifications or impinge upon constitutionally protected rights.

We need not rest our decision, however, solely on the inappropriateness of the strict-scrutiny test. A century of Supreme Court adjudication under the Equal Protection Clause affirmatively supports the application of the traditional standard of review, which requires only that the State's system be shown to bear some rational relationship to legitimate state purposes. This case represents far more than a challenge to the manner in which Texas provides for the education of its children. We have here nothing less than a direct attack on the way in which Texas has chosen to raise and disburse state and local tax revenues. We are asked to condemn the State's judgment in conferring on political subdivisions the power to tax local property to supply revenues for local interests. In so doing, appellees would have the Court intrude in an area in which it has traditionally deferred to state legislatures. . . .

Thus, we stand on familiar grounds when we continue to acknowledge that the Justices of this Court lack both the expertise and the familiarity with local problems so necessary to the making of wise decisions with respect to the raising and disposition of public revenues. . . .

In addition to matters of fiscal policy, this case also involves the most persistent and difficult questions of educational policy, another area in which this Court's lack of specialized knowledge and experience counsels against premature interference with the informed judgments made at the state and local levels. . . . On even the most basic questions in this area the scholars and educational experts are divided. Indeed, one of the major sources of controversy concerns the extent to which there is a demonstrable correlation between educational expenditures and the quality of education—an assumed correlation underlying virtually every legal conclusion drawn by the District Court in this case. Related to the questioned relationship between cost and quality is the equally unsettled controversy as to the proper goals of a system of public education. And the question regarding the most effective relationship between state boards of education and local school boards, in terms of their respective responsibilities and degrees of control, is now undergoing searching re-examination. The ultimate wisdom as to these and related problems of education is not likely to be divined for all time even by the scholars who now so earnestly debate the issues. In such circumstances, the judiciary is well advised to refrain from imposing on the States inflexible constitutional restraints that could circumscribe or handicap the continued research and experimentation so vital to finding even partial solutions to educational problems and to keeping abreast of ever-changing conditions. . . .

III

. . .

In its reliance on state as well as local resources, the Texas system is comparable to the systems employed in virtually every other State. . . .

. . . While assuring a basic education for every child in the State, it permits and encourages a large measure of participation in and control of each district's schools at the local level. In an era that has witnessed a consistent trend toward centralization of the functions of government, local sharing of responsibility for public education has survived. . . .

The persistence of attachment to government at the lowest level where education is concerned reflects the depth of commitment of its supporters. . . .

Appellees do not question the propriety of Texas' dedication to local control of education. To the contrary, they attack the school-financing system precisely because, in their view, it does not provide the same level of local control and fiscal flexibility in all districts. Appellees suggest that local control could be preserved and promoted under other financing systems that resulted in more equality in educational expenditures. While it is no doubt true that reliance on local property taxation for school revenues provides less freedom of choice with respect to expenditures for some districts than for others, the existence of "some inequality" in the manner in which the State's rationale is achieved is not alone a sufficient basis for striking down the entire system. It may not be condemned simply because it imperfectly effectuates the State's goals. Nor must the financing system fail because, as appellees suggest, other methods of satisfying the State's interest, which occasion "less drastic" disparities in expenditures, might be conceived. Only where state action impinges on the exercise of fundamental constitutional rights or liberties must it be found to have chosen the least restrictive alternative. . . .

IV

In light of the considerable attention that has focused on the District Court opinion in this case and on its California predecessor, *Serrano v. Priest*, a cautionary postscript seems appropriate. It cannot be questioned that the constitutional judgment reached by the District Court and approved by our dissenting Brothers today would occasion in Texas and elsewhere an unprecedented upheaval in public education. Some commentators have concluded that, whatever the contours of the alternative financing programs that might be devised and approved, the result could not avoid being a beneficial one. But, just as there is nothing simple about the constitutional issues involved in these cases, there is nothing simple or certain about predicting the consequences of massive change in the financing and control of public education. Those who have devoted the most thoughtful attention to the practical ramifications of these cases have found no clear or dependable answers and their scholarship reflects no such unqualified confidence in the desirability of completely uprooting the existing system.

The complexity of these problems is demonstrated by the lack of consensus with respect to whether it may be said with any assurance that the poor, the racial minorities, or the children in overburdened core-city school districts would be benefitted by abrogation of traditional modes of financing education....

... We hardly need add that this Court's action today is not to be viewed as placing its judicial imprimatur on the status quo. The need is apparent for reform in tax systems which may well have relied too long and too heavily on the local property tax. And certainly innovative thinking as to public education, its methods, and its funding is necessary to assure both a higher level of quality and greater uniformity of opportunity. These matters merit the continued attention of the scholars who already have contributed much by their challenges. But the ultimate solutions must come from the lawmakers and from the democratic pressures of those who elect them.

Reversed.

NOTES

1. Was *San Antonio* an attempt to use the judiciary to accomplish what was essentially a legislative function? What are the ramifications of this question in terms of education, politics, and social policy?

2. What does, or should, "fundamental" mean when used in connection with rights. Why is the designation of a right as fundamental so important?

3. What does "equality of educational opportunity" mean? Is, or can, it be measured by expenditures? Are there judicially manageable standards by which it can be assessed? Must jurisdictions endeavor to provide "equality of educational opportunities?"

4. As reflected below, school finance litigation has produced almost equal results as to the constitutionality of state funding formulas.

UPHOLDING FINANCE PLANS

Alabama, *Ex parte James*, 836 So.2d 813 [174 Educ. L. Rep. 487] (Ala.2002); Alaska, *Matanuska–Susitna Borough School Dist. v. State*, 931 P.2d 391 [116 Educ. L. Rep. 401] (Alaska 1997); Colorado, *Lobato v. State of Colorado*, 218 P.3d 358 [249 Educ. L. Rep. 881] (Colo. 2009) (rejecting challenge as nonjusticiable); Connecticut, *Seymour v. Region One Bd. of Educ.*, 874 A.2d 742 [198 Educ. L. Rep. 645] (Conn.2005), *cert. denied*, 546 U.S. 1016, 126 S.Ct. 659, 163 L.Ed.2d 526 (2005) but allowing another challenge to proceed, *Connecticut Coalition for Justice in Educ. Funding v. Rell*, 990 A.2d 206 [254 Educ. L. Rep. 874] (Conn.2010); Florida, *Coalition for Adequacy and Fairness in School Funding v. Chiles*, 680 So.2d 400 (Fla.1996), *reh'g denied* (1996); Georgia, *McDaniel v. Thomas*, 285 S.E.2d 156 [1 Educ. L. Rep. 982] (Ga.1981); Idaho, *Idaho Schools for Equal Educational Opportunity v. Evans*, 850 P.2d 724 [82 Educ. L. Rep. 660] (Idaho 1993); Illinois, *Blase v. State*, 302 N.E.2d 46 (Ill.1973); Indiana, *Bonner ex rel. Bonner v. Daniels*, 907 N.E.2d 516 [245 Educ. L. Rep. 412] (Ind. 2009); Louisiana, *Louisiana Ass'n of Educators v. Edwards*, 521 So.2d 390 [45 Educ. L. Rep. 905] (La.1988), *superseded by constitution amendment as stated in Charlet v. Legislature of State of La.*, 713 So.2d 1199 [128 Educ. L. Rep. 510] (La.Ct.App.1998), *writ denied*, 730 So.2d 934 (La.1998), *reconsideration not considered*, 734 So.2d 1221 [136 Educ. L. Rep. 635] (La.1999); Maine, *School Admin. Dist. No. 1 v. Commissioner*, 659 A.2d 854 [101 Educ. L. Rep. 289] (Me.1995); Maryland, *Hornbeck v. Somerset County Bd. of Educ.*, 458 A.2d 758 [10 Educ. L. Rep. 592] (Md.1983); Massachusetts, *Hancock v. Commissioner of Educ.*, 822 N.E.2d 1134 [195 Educ. L. Rep. 591] (Mass.2005) (refusing to adopt the recommendation of a specially assigned superior court judge that the system of funding failed to satisfy its duty under the Massachusetts Constitution to educate the state's children adequately); Michigan, *Milliken v. Green*, 212 N.W.2d 711 (Mich.1973); Minnesota, *Skeen v. State*, 505 N.W.2d 299 (Minn.1993); Missouri, *Committee for Educ. Equality v. State*, 294 S.W.3d 477 [249 Educ. L. Rep. 926] (Mo. 2009); Nebraska, *Nebraska Coalition for Educational Equity and Adequacy v. Heineman*, 731 N.W.2d 164 [219 Educ. L. Rep. 761] (Neb.2007) (affirming that a challenge was a nonjusticiable as a political question); Oklahoma, *Oklahoma Educ. Ass'n v. Oklahoma*, 158 P.3d 1058 [220 Educ. L. Rep. 360] (Okla.2007) (dismissing a challenge for lack of justiciability as a political question); *Pendleton School Dist. 16R v. State*, 200 P.3d 133 [241 Educ. L. Rep. 423] (Or. 2009); Pennsylvania, *Danson v. Casey*, 399 A.2d 360 (Pa. 1979); Rhode Island, *City of Pawtucket v. Sundlun*, 662 A.2d 40 [102 Educ. L. Rep. 235] (R.I.1995); South Carolina, *Abbeville County School Dist. v. State*, 515 S.E.2d 535 [135 Educ. L. Rep. 833] (S.C.1999); South Dakota, *Davis v. South Dakota*, 804 N.W.2d 618 [273 Educ.L.Rep. 411] (S.D. 2011); Virginia, *Scott v. Commonwealth*, 443 S.E.2d 138 [91 Educ. L. Rep. 396] (Va.1994); Wisconsin, *Vincent v. Voight*, 614 N.W.2d 388 [146 Educ. L. Rep. 422] (Wis.2000); Wyoming, *Campbell County School Dist. v. State*, 181 P.3d 43 [232 Educ. L. Rep. 394] (Wyo.2008).

INVALIDATING FINANCE PLANS

Arizona, *Roosevelt Elementary School Dist. No. 66 v. Bishop*, 877 P.2d 806 [93 Educ. L. Rep. 330] (Ariz.1994); Arkansas, *Lake View School Dist. No. 25 of Phillips County v. Huckabee*, 91 S.W.3d 472 [173 Educ. L. Rep. 248] (Ark.2002), 210 S.W.3d 28 [215 Educ. L. Rep. 1198] (Ark.2005), *mandate stayed*, 220 S.W.3d 645 [220 Educ. L. Rep. 383] (Ark.2005), *mandate deferred*, 243 S.W.3d 919 [229 Educ. L. Rep. 953] (Ark.2006), *mandate issued*, 257 S.W.3d 879 [235 Educ. L. Rep. 690] (Ark.2007); California, *Serrano v. Priest*, 96 Cal.Rptr. 601, 487 P.2d 1241 (1971); Kansas, *Montoy v. State*, 102 P.3d 1160 [194 Educ. L. Rep. 439] (Kan.2005), *republished with concurring opinion*, 120 P.3d 306 [202 Educ. L. Rep. 319] (Kan.2005), *opinion supplemented*, 112 P.3d 923 [198 Educ. L. Rep. 703] (Kan.2005); Kentucky, *Rose v. Council for Better Educ.*, 790 S.W.2d 186 [60 Educ. L. Rep. 1289] (Ky.1989); Massachusetts, *McDuffy v. Secretary of Executive Office of Educ.*, 615 N.E.2d 516 [83 Educ. L. Rep. 657] (Mass. 1993); Montana, *Columbia Falls Elementary School Dist. No. 6 v. State*, 109 P.3d 257 [196 Educ. L. Rep. 958] (Mont.2005); New Hampshire, *Claremont School Dist. v. Governor*, 703 A.2d 1353 [123 Educ. L. Rep. 233] (N.H. 1997), *but see Londonderry School Dist. SAU #12 v. State of N.H.*, 958 A.2d 930 (N.H.2008) (rejecting a challenge to the new funding scheme); New Jersey, *Robinson v. Cahill*, 303 A.2d 273 (N.J.1973), *cert. denied*, 414 U.S. 976, 94 S.Ct. 292, 38 L.Ed.2d 219 (1973); New York, *Campaign for Fiscal Equity v. State of N.Y.*, 769 N.Y.S.2d 106 [183 Educ. L. Rep. 970] (N.Y. 2003), *see also New York State Ass'n of Small City School Dist. v. New York*, 840 N.Y.S.2d 179 [222 Educ. L. Rep. 830] (N.Y.App.Div.2007) (finding that the state school board association could challenge funding on its own behalf but not in the name of individual members); North Carolina, *Hoke County Bd. of Educ. v. State of N.C.*, 599 S.E.2d 365 [190 Educ. L. Rep. 661] (N.C.2004); North Dakota, *Bismarck Pub. School Dist. No. 1 v. State By and Through N.D. Legislative Assembly*, 511 N.W.2d 247 [88 Educ. L. Rep. 1184] (N.D.1994) (while the court ruled that the funding statute was unconstitutional, it lacked the super-majority needed to vitiate the law); Ohio, *DeRolph v. State*, 677 N.E.2d 733 [116 Educ. L. Rep. 1140] (Ohio 1997); Tennessee, *Tennessee Small School Systems v. McWherter*, 91 S.W.3d 232 [172 Educ. L. Rep. 1044] (Tenn.2002); Texas, *Edgewood Indep. School Dist. v. Kirby*, 777 S.W.2d 391 [56 Educ. L. Rep. 663] (Tex.1989); *see also Neeley v. West Orange–Cove Consol. Indep. School Dist.*, 176 S.W.3d 746 [204 Educ. L. Rep. 793] (Tex.2005), *Hendee v. Dewhurst*, 228 S.W.3d 354 [222 Educ. L. Rep. 880] (Tex.Ct.App.2007), *reh'g overruled* (2007) (rejecting a claim that school funding was a political issue); Vermont, *Brigham v. State*, 692 A.2d 384 [117 Educ. L. Rep. 667] (Vt.1997); Washington, *Seattle School Dist. No. 1 of King County v. State*, 585 P.2d 71 (Wash.1978); West Virginia, *Pauley v. Kelly*, 255 S.E.2d 859 (W.Va.1979).

[CASE NO. 34]   POWER OF A BOARD TO USE UNOBLIGATED FUNDS

CONCERNED SCHOOL PATRONS AND TAXPAYERS v. WARE COUNTY BOARD OF EDUCATION

Supreme Court of Georgia, 1980.
263 S.E.2d 925.

■ BOWLES, JUSTICE.

This controversy arose when the Board of Education of Ware County adopted a resolution authorizing a contract to construct a field house/physical education/athletic facility for a school. Plaintiffs, as taxpayers and patrons of the school system, brought a suit in the superior court of that county seeking to enjoin the action of the board. . . .

. . . A permanent injunction was denied. Plaintiffs appeal to this court. We affirm.

Art. VII, Sec. I, Par. I of the State Constitution (Code Ann. 2–4901) provides for a system of common schools in the state. Art. VIII, Sec. VII, Par. I (Code Ann. 2–5501) providing for local taxation for education reads in part as follows: "The fiscal authority of each county shall annually levy a school tax for the support and maintenance of education, not greater than twenty mills per dollar as certified to it by the county board of education, upon the assessed value of all taxable property within the county located outside any independent school system or area school district therein. . . . School tax funds shall be expended only for the support and maintenance of public schools, public education, and activities necessary or incidental thereto, including school lunch purposes. . . ." The legislature in keeping with constitutional provisions adopted an Act known as "Adequate Program for Education in Georgia Act." The Act specifically recognizes the development of good physical and mental health as a part of the educational process. Additionally, [a section] provides for a course in health and physical education. [Another section] provides: "The county boards of education shall have the power to purchase, lease, or rent school sites, build, repair or rent schoolhouses, purchase maps, globes, and school furniture and make all arrangements necessary to the efficient operation of the school. . . . In respect to the building of schoolhouses, the said board of education may provide for the same by a tax on all property located in the county and outside the territorial limits of any independent school system." Plaintiffs have made no constitutional attack on any pertinent statute.

We conclude that boards of education do have lawful authority to provide for and construct physical education facilities which may incidentally include a field house or related athletic facility.

Although no funds of a county board of education can be disbursed except in accordance with a budget filed with the State Board of Education, this does not mean that every expenditure must be a line item in the budget submitted. With respect to the year in question, the Ware County Board of Education had a beginning balance of unobligated or uncommitted funds in excess of the amount of the proposed expenditure for the athletic facility. Unobligated funds included in the budget may be used by a board of education for any purpose provided by statute, within the constitutional parameters of our state educational system. The unobligated funds on hand may have been accumulated as a result of thrift practiced by the board with respect to any prior year's budget. There is no contention on the part of the plaintiffs that any millage has been determined or levied by county authorities with respect to any year in excess of the 20 mills limitation included in the Georgia Constitution (Code Ann. § 25501). . . .

Plaintiffs' petition was filed after the millage for the year had been determined and assessed. (And we suspect by December largely paid.) The issue involved is one of authority by the board of education to spend tax money already collected, not the power to levy a tax for a designated purpose.

The obligation incurred by the board of education regarding the expenditure of accumulated funds on hand at the time of the execution of the contract, which were sufficient for the purpose, was not an attempt to bind a succeeding board of education to a future obligation. A board of education may incur a lawful obligation to pay for the purchase or construction of a facility where sufficient funds are on hand for that purpose, even though the construction contract may not be fully completed before the end of the term of some or all of the members of that body.

The trial court did not err in finding in favor of the defendants.

Judgment affirmed.

NOTES

1. What was the major reason this case was brought? The building of athletic facilities, as an implied power of local boards, seemed well settled a half century earlier. *See, e.g., McNair v. School Dist. No. 1*, 288 P. 188 (Mont.1930).

2. Note the issue of board authority that the court identified in the next to last full paragraph of its opinion. What is the difference in theory? In practice?

[CASE NO. 35]   FEDERAL AID TO LOCAL SCHOOL BOARDS

ZUNI PUBLIC SCHOOL DISTRICT NO. 89
v. DEPARTMENT OF EDUCATION

Supreme Court of the United States, 2007.
550 U.S. 81, 127 S.Ct. 1534, 167 L.Ed.2d 449 [218 Educ. L. Rep. 24].

■ JUSTICE BREYER delivered the opinion of the Court.

A federal statute sets forth a method that the Secretary of Education is to use when determining whether a State's public school funding program "equalizes expenditures" throughout the State. The statute instructs the Secretary to calculate the disparity in per pupil expenditures among local school districts in the State. But, when doing so, the Secretary is to "disregard" school districts *"with per-pupil expenditures . . . above the 95th percentile or below the 5th percentile of such expenditures . . . in the State."* (emphasis added).

The question before us is whether the emphasized statutory language permits the Secretary to identify the school districts that should be "disregard[ed]" by looking to the *number of the district's pupils* as well as to the size of the district's expenditures per pupil. We conclude that it does.

I

A

The federal Impact Aid Act provides financial assistance to local school districts whose ability to finance public school education is adversely affected by a federal presence. Federal aid is available to districts, for example, where a significant amount of federal land is exempt from local property taxes, or where the federal presence is responsible for an increase in school-age children (say, of armed forces personnel) whom local schools must educate. The statute typically prohibits a State from offsetting this federal aid by reducing its own state aid to the local district. If applied without exceptions, however, this prohibition might unreasonably interfere with a state program that seeks to equalize per-pupil expenditures throughout the State, for instance, by preventing the state program from taking account of a significant source of federal funding that some local school districts receive. The statute consequently contains an exception that permits a State to compensate for federal impact aid where "the Secretary [of Education] determine[s] and certifies . . . that the State has in effect a program of State aid that *equalizes* expenditures for free public education among local [school districts] in the State." (emphasis added).

The statute sets out a formula that the Secretary of Education must use to determine whether a state aid program satisfies the federal "equaliz[ation]" requirement. The formula instructs the Secretary to compare the local school district with the greatest per-pupil expenditures to the school district with the smallest per-pupil expenditures to see whether the former exceeds the latter by more than 25 percent. So long as it does not, the state aid program qualifies as a program that "equalizes expenditures." More specifically the statute provides that "a program of state aid" qualifies, *i.e.,* it "equalizes expenditures" among local school districts if, "in the second fiscal year preceding the fiscal year for which the determination is made, the amount of per-pupil expenditures made by [the local school district] with the highest such per-pupil expenditures . . . did not exceed the amount of such per-pupil expenditures made by [the local school district] with the lowest such expenditures . . . by more than 25 percent."

The statutory provision goes on to set forth what we shall call the "disregard" instruction. It states that, when "making" this "determination," the "*Secretary shall . . . disregard [school districts] with per-pupil expenditures . . . above the 95th percentile or below the 5th percentile of such expenditures.*" (emphasis added). It adds that the Secretary shall further:

> "take into account the extent to which [the state program reflects the special additional costs that some school districts must bear when they are] geographically isolated [or when they provide education for] particular types of students, such as children with disabilities."

B

This case requires us to decide whether the Secretary's present calculation method is consistent with the federal statute's "disregard" instruction. The method at issue is contained in a set of regulations that the Secretary first promulgated 30 years ago. Those regulations essentially state the following:

When determining whether a state aid program "equalizes expenditures" (thereby permitting the State to reduce its own local funding on account of federal impact aid), the Secretary will first create a list of school districts ranked in order of per-pupil expenditure. The Secretary will then identify the relevant percentile cutoff point on that list on the basis of a specific (95th or 5th) percentile of *student population*—essentially identifying those districts whose students account for the 5 percent of the State's total student population that lies at both the high and low ends of the spending distribution. Finally the Secretary will compare the highest spending and lowest spending school districts of those that remain to see whether they satisfy the statute's requirement that the disparity between them not exceed 25 percent.

The regulations set forth this calculation method as follows:

"[D]eterminations of disparity in current expenditures ... per-pupil are made by—

"(i) Ranking all [of the State's school districts] on the basis of current expenditures ... per pupil [in the relevant statutorily determined year];

"(ii) Identifying those [school districts] that fall at the 95th and 5th percentiles of the total number of pupils in attendance [at all the State's school districts taken together]; and

"(iii) Subtracting the lower current expenditure ... per pupil figure from the higher for those [school districts] identified in paragraph (ii) and dividing the difference by the lower figure."

The regulations also provide an illustration of how to perform the calculation:

"In State X, after ranking all [school districts] in order of the expenditures per pupil for the [statutorily determined] fiscal year in question, it is ascertained by counting the number of pupils in attendance in those [school districts] in ascending order of expenditure that the 5th percentile of student population is reached at [school district A] with a per pupil expenditure of $820, and that the 95th percentile of student population is reached at [school district B] with a per pupil expenditure of $1,000. The percentage disparity between the 95th percentile and the 5th percentile [school districts] is 22 percent ($1000 − $820 = $180/$820)."

Because 22 percent is less than the statutory "25 percent" requirement, the state program in the example qualifies as a program that "equalizes expenditures."

C

This case concerns the Department of Education's application of the Secretary's regulations to New Mexico's local district aid program in respect to fiscal year 2000. As the regulations require, Department officials listed each of New Mexico's 89 local school districts in order of per-pupil spending for fiscal year 1998. (The calculation in New Mexico's case was performed, as the statute allows, on the basis of per-pupil *revenues,* rather than per-pupil *expenditures.* For ease of reference we nevertheless refer, in respect to New Mexico's figures and throughout the opinion, only to "per-pupil expenditures.") After ranking the districts, Department officials excluded 17 school districts at the top of the list because those districts contained (cumulatively) less than 5 percent of the student population; for the same reason, they excluded an additional 6 school districts at the bottom of the list.

The remaining 66 districts accounted for approximately 90 percent of the State's student population. Of those, the highest ranked district spent $3,259 per student; the lowest ranked district spent $2,848 per student. The difference, $411, was less than 25 percent of the lowest per-pupil figure, namely $2,848. Hence, the officials found that New Mexico's local aid program qualifies as a program that "equalizes expenditures." New Mexico was therefore free to offset federal impact aid to individual districts by reducing state aid to those districts.

Two of New Mexico's public school districts, Zuni Public School District and Gallup–McKinley County Public School District (whom we shall collectively call Zuni), sought further agency review of these findings. Zuni conceded that the Department's calculations were correct in terms of the Department's own regulations. Zuni argued, however, that the regulations themselves are inconsistent with the authorizing statute. That statute, in its view, requires the Department to calculate the 95th and 5th percentile cutoffs solely on the basis of the number of school districts (ranked by their per-pupil expenditures), without any consideration of the number of pupils in those districts. If calculated as Zuni urges, only 10 districts (accounting for less than 2 percent of all students) would have been identified as the outliers that the statute instructs the Secretary to disregard. The difference, as a result, between the highest and lowest per-pupil expenditures of the remaining districts (26.9 percent) would exceed 25 percent. Consequently, the statute would forbid New Mexico to take account of federal impact aid as it decides how to equalize school funding across the State.

A Department of Education Administrative Law Judge rejected Zuni's challenge to the regulations. The Secretary of Education did the same. Zuni sought review of the Secretary's decision in the Court of Appeals for the Tenth Circuit. Initially, a Tenth Circuit panel affirmed the Secretary's determination by a split vote (2 to 1). Subsequently, the full Court of Appeals vacated the panel's decision and heard the matter en banc. The 12–member en banc court affirmed the Secretary but by an evenly divided court (6 to 6). Zuni sought certiorari. We agreed to decide the matter.

II

A

Zuni's strongest argument rests upon the literal language of the statute. Zuni concedes, as it must, that if the language of the statute is open or ambiguous—that is, if Congress left a "gap" for the agency to fill— then we must uphold the Secretary's interpretation as long as it is reasonable. For purposes of exposition, we depart from a normal order of discussion, namely an order that first considers Zuni's statutory language argument. Instead, because of the technical nature of the language in question, we shall first examine the provision's background and basic purposes. That discussion will illuminate our subsequent analysis in Part II–B, *infra*. It will also reveal why Zuni concentrates its argument upon language alone.

Considerations other than language provide us with unusually strong indications that Congress intended to leave the Secretary free to use the calculation method before us and that the Secretary's chosen method is a reasonable one. For one thing, the matter at issue—*i.e.*, the calculation method for determining whether a state aid program "equalizes expenditures"—is the kind of highly technical, specialized interstitial matter that Congress often does not decide itself, but delegates to specialized agencies to decide.

For another thing, the history of the statute strongly supports the Secretary. Congress first enacted an impact aid "equalization" exception in 1974. The exception originally provided that the "ter[m] ... 'equaliz[ing] expenditures' ... shall be defined by the [Secretary]." Soon thereafter, in 1976, the Secretary promulgated the regulation here at issue defining the term "equalizing expenditures" in the manner now before us. As far as we can tell, no Member of Congress has ever criticized the method the 1976 regulation sets forth nor suggested at any time that it be revised or reconsidered.

The present statutory language originated in draft legislation that the Secretary himself sent to Congress in 1994. With one minor change (irrelevant to the present calculation controversy), Congress adopted that language without comment or clarification. No one at the time—no Member of Congress, no Department of Education official, no school district or State—expressed the view that this statutory language (which, after all, was supplied by the Secretary) was intended to require, or did require, the Secretary to change the Department's system of calculation, a system that the Department and school districts across the Nation had followed for nearly 20 years, without (as far as we are told) any adverse effect.

Finally, viewed in terms of the purpose of the statute's disregard instruction, the Secretary's calculation method is reasonable, while the reasonableness of a method based upon the number of districts alone (Zuni's proposed method) is more doubtful. When the Secretary (then Commissioner) of Education considered the matter in 1976, he explained why that is so.

Initially the Secretary pointed out that the "exclusion of the upper and bottom 5 percentile school districts is based upon the accepted principle of statistical evaluation that such percentiles usually represent *unique* or *noncharacteristic* situations."(emphasis added). That purpose, a purpose to exclude statistical outliers, is evident in the language of the present statute. The provision uses the technical term "percentile"; it refers to cutoff numbers ("95th" and "5th") often associated with scientific calculations; and it directly precedes another statutory provision that tells the Secretary to account for those districts, from among the middle 5th to 95th percentile districts, that remain "noncharacteristic" in respect to geography or the presence of special students (such as disabled students).

The Secretary added that under the regulation's calculation system the "percentiles" would be "determined on the basis of numbers of pupils and not on the basis of numbers of districts." He said that to base "an exclusion on numbers of districts" alone "would act to apply the disparity standard in an unfair and inconsistent manner among States." He then elaborated upon his concerns:

> "The purpose of the exclusion is to eliminate those anomalous characteristics of a distribution of expenditures. In States with a small number of large districts, an exclusion based on percentage of school districts might exclude from the measure of disparity a substantial percentage of the pupil population in those States. Conversely, in States with large numbers of small districts, such an approach might exclude only an insignificant fraction of the pupil population and would not exclude anomalous characteristics."

To understand the Secretary's first problem, consider an exaggerated example, say a State with 80 school districts of unequal size. Suppose 8 of the districts include urban areas and together account for 70 percent of the State's students, while the remaining 72 districts include primarily rural areas and together account for 30 percent of the State's students. If the State's greatest funding disparities are among the 8 urban districts, Zuni's calculation method (which looks only at the number of districts and ignores their size) would require the Secretary to disregard the system's 8 largest districts (*i.e.,* 10 percent of the number 80) even though those 8 districts (because they together contain 70 percent of the State's pupils) are typical of, indeed characterize, the State's public school system. It would require the Secretary instead to measure the system's expenditure equality by looking only to noncharacteristic districts that are not representative of the system as a whole, indeed districts accounting for only 30 percent of the State's pupils. Thus, according to Zuni's method, the Secretary would have to certify a state aid program as one that "equalizes expenditures" even if there were gross disparities in per-pupil expenditures among urban districts accounting for 70 percent of the State's students. By way of contrast, the Secretary's method, by taking into account a district's size as well as its expenditures, would avoid a calculation that would produce results so contrary to the statute's objective.

To understand the Secretary's second problem consider this very case. New Mexico's 89 school districts vary significantly in respect to the number of pupils each contains. Zuni's calculation system nonetheless forbids the Secretary to discount more than 10 districts—10 percent of the total number of districts (rounded up). But these districts taken together account for only 1.8 percent of the State's pupils. To eliminate only those districts, instead of eliminating districts that together account for 10 percent of the State's pupils, risks resting the "disregard" calculation upon a few particularly extreme noncharacteristic districts, yet again contrary to the statute's intent.

Thus, the history and purpose of the disregard instruction indicate that the Secretary's calculation formula is a reasonable method that carries out Congress' likely intent in enacting the statutory provision before us.

B

But what of the provision's literal language? The matter is important, for normally neither the legislative history nor the reasonableness of the Secretary's method would be determinative if the plain language of the statute unambiguously indicated that Congress sought to foreclose the Secretary's interpretation. And Zuni argues that the Secretary's formula could not possibly effectuate Congress' intent since the statute's language literally forbids the Secretary to use such a method. Under this Court's precedents, if the intent of Congress is clear and unambiguously expressed by the statutory language at issue, that would be the end of our analysis. A customs statute that imposes a tariff on "clothing" does not impose a tariff on automobiles, no matter how strong the policy arguments for treating the two kinds of goods alike. But we disagree with Zuni's conclusion, for we believe that the Secretary's method falls within the scope of the statute's plain language.

That language says that, when the Secretary compares (for a specified fiscal year) "the amount of per-pupil expenditures made by" (1) the highest-per-pupil-expenditure district and (2) the lowest-per-pupil-expenditure district, "the Secretary shall . . . disregard" local school districts "with per-pupil expenditures . . . above the 95th percentile or below the 5th percentile of such expenditures in the State." The word "such" refers to "per-pupil expenditures" (or more precisely to "per-pupil expenditures" in the test year specified by the statute). The question then is whether the phrase *"above the 95th percentile . . . of . . . [per pupil] expenditures"* permits the Secretary to calculate percentiles by (1) ranking local districts, (2) noting the student population of each district, and (3) determining the cutoff point on the basis of districts containing 95 percent (or 5 percent) of the State's students.

Our answer is that this phrase, taken with absolute literalness, limits the Secretary to calculation methods that involve "per-pupil expenditures." But it does not tell the Secretary which of several different possible methods the Department must use. Nor does it rule out the present formula, which distributes districts in accordance with per-pupil expenditures, while essentially weighting each district to reflect the number of pupils it contains.

Because the statute uses technical language (*e.g.,* "percentile") and seeks a technical purpose (eliminating uncharacteristic, or outlier, districts), we have examined dictionary definitions of the term "percentile."
. . .

These definitions, mainstream and technical, all indicate that, in order to identify the relevant percentile cutoffs, the Secretary must construct a distribution of values. That distribution will consist of a "population" ranked according to a characteristic. That characteristic takes on a "value" for each member of the relevant population. The statute's instruction to identify the 95th and 5th "percentile of such expenditures" makes clear that the relevant *characteristic* for ranking purposes is per-pupil expenditure during a particular year. But the statute does not specify precisely what *population* is to be "distributed" (*i.e.,* ranked according to the population's corresponding values for the relevant characteristic). Nor does it set forth various details as to how precisely the distribution is to be constructed (as long as it is ranked according to the specified characteristic).

But why is Congress' silence in respect to these matters significant? Are there several *different* populations, relevant here, that one might rank according to "per-pupil expenditures" (and thereby determine in several *different* ways a cutoff point such that "*n* percent of [that] population" falls, say below the percentile cutoff)? We are not experts in statistics, but a statistician is not needed to see what the dictionary does not say. No dictionary definition we have found suggests that there is any *single* logical, mathematical, or statistical link between, on the one hand, the characterizing data (used for ranking purposes) and, on the other hand, the nature of the relevant population or how that population might be weighted for purposes of determining a percentile cutoff.

Here, the Secretary has distributed districts, ranked them according to per-pupil expenditure, but compared only those that account for 90 percent of the State's pupils. Thus, the Secretary has used—as his predecessors had done for a quarter century before him—the State's *students* as the relevant population for calculating the specified percentiles. Another Secretary might have distributed districts, ranked them by per-pupil expenditure, and made no reference to the number of pupils (a method that satisfies the statute's *language* but threatens the problems the Secretary long ago identified). A third Secretary might have distributed districts, ranked them by per-pupil expenditure, but compared only those that account for 90 percent of total pupil expenditures in the State. A fourth Secretary might have distributed districts, ranked them by per-pupil expenditure, but calculated the 95th and 5th percentile cutoffs using the per-pupil expenditures of all the individual *schools* in the State. A fifth Secretary might have distributed districts, ranked them by per-pupil expenditure, but accounted in his disparity calculation for the sometimes significant differences in per-pupil spending at different grade levels.

Each of these methods amounts to a different way of determining which districts fall between the 5th and 95th "percentile of per-pupil expenditures." For purposes of that calculation, they each adopt different populations—students, districts, schools, and grade levels. Yet, linguistically speaking, one may attribute the characteristic of per-pupil expenditure to each member of any such population (though the values of that characteristic may be more or less readily available depending on the chosen population). Hence, the statute's literal language covers any or all of these methods. That language alone does not tell us (or the Secretary of Education), however, which method to use.

Justice SCALIA's claim that this interpretation "defies any semblance of normal English" depends upon its own definition of the word "per." That word, according to the dissent, "connotes ... a single average figure assigned to a unit the composite members of which are individual pupils." In fact, the word "per" simply means "[f]or each" or "for every." Thus, nothing in the English language forbids the Secretary from considering expenditures *for each* individual pupil in a district when instructed to look at a district's "per-pupil expenditures." The remainder of the dissent's argument, colorful language to the side, rests upon a reading of the statutory language that ignores its basic purpose and history.

We find additional evidence for our understanding of the language in the fact that Congress, in other statutes, has clarified the matter here at issue thereby avoiding comparable ambiguity. For example, in a different education-related statute, Congress refers to "the school at the 20th percentile in the State, *based on enrollment,* among all schools *ranked by the percentage of students at the proficient level.*" (emphasis added). In another statute fixing charges for physicians services, Congress specified that the maximum charge "shall be the 50th percentile of the customary charges for the service *(weighted by the frequency of the service)* performed by nonparticipating physicians in the locality during the [prior] 12–month period." (emphasis added). In these statutes Congress indicated with greater specificity how a percentile should be determined by stating precisely not only which data values are of interest, but also (in the first) the population that is to be distributed and (in the second) the weightings needed to make the calculation meaningful and to avoid counterproductive results. In the statute at issue here, however, Congress used more general language (drafted by the Secretary himself), which leaves the Secretary with the authority to resolve such subsidiary matters at the administrative level.

We also find support for our view of the language in the more general circumstance that statutory "[a]mbiguity is a creature not [just] of definitional possibilities but [also] of statutory context." That may be so even if statutory language is highly technical. After all, the scope of what seems a precise technical chess instruction, such as "you must place the queen next to the king," varies with context, depending, for example, upon whether the instructor is telling a beginner how to set up the board or telling an advanced player how to checkmate an opponent. The dictionary acknowledges that, when interpreting technical statistical language, the purpose of the exercise matters, for it says that "quantile," "percentile," "quartile," and "decile" are "terms [that] can be modified, though not always very satisfactorily, to be applicable to ... a large sample ranked in ascending order."

Thus, an instruction to "identify schools with average scholastic aptitude test scores below the 5th percentile of such scores" may vary as to the population to be distributed, depending upon whether the context is one of providing additional counseling and support to *students* at low-performing schools (in which case the relevant population would likely consist of students), or one of identifying unsuccessful learning protocols at low-performing schools (in which case the appropriate population may well be the schools themselves). Context here tells us that the instruction to identify school districts with "per-pupil expenditures" above the 95th percentile "of such expenditures" is similarly ambiguous, because both students and school districts are of concern to the statute. Accordingly, the disregard instruction can include within its scope the distribution of a ranked population that consists of pupils (or of school districts weighted by pupils) and not just a ranked distribution of unweighted school districts alone.

Finally, we draw reassurance from the fact that no group of statisticians, nor any individual statistician, has told us directly in briefs, or indirectly through citation, that the language before us cannot be read as we have read it. This circumstance is significant, for the statutory language is technical, and we are not statisticians. And the views of experts (or their absence) might help us understand (though not control our determination of) what Congress had in mind.

The upshot is that the language of the statute is broad enough to permit the Secretary's reading. That fact requires us to look beyond the language to determine whether the Secretary's interpretation is a reasonable, hence permissible, implementation of the statute. For the reasons set forth in Part II–A, *supra,* we conclude that the Secretary's reading is a reasonable reading. We consequently find the Secretary's method of calculation lawful.

The judgment of the Tenth Circuit is affirmed.

It is so ordered.

NOTE

Justice Scalia's scathing dissent, at 108, in which Chief Justice Roberts and Justice Thomas joined, declared that ". . . today's decision is nothing other than the elevation of judge-supposed legislative intent over clear statutory text" (at 108). He added "[w]hy should we suppose that in matters more likely to arouse the judicial libido-voting rights, antidiscrimination laws, or environmental protection, to name only a few—a judge in the School of Textual Subversion would not find it convenient (yea, *righteous!*) to assume that Congress *must* have meant, not what it said, but what he knows to be best?" *Id.* at 119. With whom do you agree, the majority or the dissent?

CHAPTER 6

Use of School Funds and Property

Introduction

State constitutions and statutes cannot cover all uses of school funds.[1] Accordingly, courts are frequently asked to interpret general grants of power and apply them in cases over the implied spending ability of local boards. How cases are resolved often depends on what courts consider desirable public policy. What may be a proper use of school funds or property in one state may be improper in another. Further, since what may be improper at one time may be acceptable later, courts are increasingly deferential in interpreting board powers over the use of school property.

Transportation of Students

Absent express legislative authority, such as under the Individuals with Disabilities Education Act,[2] or state law, some courts refused to permit school boards to allocate funds to transport children.[3] In addition, courts tend to interpret transportation laws narrowly, adopting the view that the basic responsibility for getting children to and from school lies with their parents. This judicial attitude may be affected by the realization that paying for transportation is relatively expensive and does not contribute directly to education per se. For example, the Supreme Court of Michigan, in an older case, held that even under a statute which granted school boards the power "to do all things needful and necessary for the maintenance, prosperity and success of the schools of the district and the promotion of the thorough education of the children thereof,"[4] a board lacked the authority to allocate funds for transportation.

---

1. In a case highlighting how state constitutions cannot address all aspects of the use of funds for public education, the Supreme Court of Oklahoma invalidated a "gist," or summary on a ballot petition, as failing to provide a clear description of an initiative as requiring local boards to use a minimum of sixty-five percent of their operational expenditures on classroom instruction. The court ruled that the gist was flawed since it failed to discuss legislative sanctions for non-conforming boards and the possibilities of waivers from the state superintendent. *In re Initiative Petition No. 384*, 164 P.3d 125 [222 Educ. L. Rep. 407] (Okla. 2007).

2. 20 U.S.C.A. § 1401(26)(A).

3. *See, e.g., Harwood v. Dysart Consol. School Dist.*, 21 N.W.2d 334 (Iowa 1946); *Ex parte Perry County Bd. of Educ.*, 180 So.2d 246 (Ala. 1965).

4. *Township School Dist. of Bates v. Elliott*, 268 N.W. 744, 744 (Mich. 1936).

In its only case involving transportation of students not involving religion[5] or race,[6] *Kadrmas v. Dickinson Public Schools*,[7] the Supreme Court upheld the constitutionality of a statute from North Dakota authorizing non-reorganized school boards to charge a user fee not exceeding the actual cost of transporting children to school. The Court acknowledged that insofar as the state constitution did not require boards to transport all students, educational officials had no duty to provide it free of charge. The Court rejected an equal protection challenge against charging only parents of children in non-reorganized districts, positing that social and economic legislation can be overturned only if it is completely irrational. In recognizing that the legislature acted out of its desire to encourage voters to adopt plans for reorganization, the Court affirmed that where a suspect class was not discriminated against and the law did not infringe on a fundamental right, it was not subject to strict scrutiny. Four years later, the Supreme Court of California affirmed that a law permitting boards to charge the same kinds of fees did not violate the equal protection clause of the state constitution.[8]

If legislation does not require boards to transport students, officials may discontinue providing service at any time. Where boards lacked funds to offer transportation, two appellate court rulings in Michigan agreed that they were not required to continue to make it available.[9]

The Third Circuit upheld the policy of a school board in Pennsylvania offering only one-way transportation for kindergarten children. The court found that insofar as the law at issue did not require boards to provide kindergarten or transportation for students in public schools, and its action was rationally based on not wishing to employ drivers or engage buses at midday, officials did not violate the Federal Constitution.[10] Following remand, the Third Circuit again rejected a federal trial court's attempt to exercise jurisdiction based on its argument that insofar as the board had power to transport children to and from school, the general purposes of transportation would not have been served by providing it only one way.[11] More recently in Pennsylvania, parents of children who attended a private, half-day kindergarten unsuccessfully sued their board for offering full-day

---

5. *See, e.g., Everson v. Board of Educ.*, 330 U.S. 1, 67 S.Ct. 504, 91 L.Ed. 711 (1947), *reh'g denied*, 330 U.S. 855, 67 S.Ct. 962, 91 L.Ed. 1297 (1947). [Case No. 1]

6. *See Swann v. Charlotte–Mecklenburg Bd. of Educ.*, 402 U.S. 1, 91 S.Ct. 1267, 28 L.Ed.2d 554 (1971). [Case No. 118]

7. 487 U.S. 450, 108 S.Ct. 2481, 101 L.Ed.2d 399 [47 Educ. L. Rep. 383] (1988).

8. *Arcadia Unified School Dist. v. State Dep't. of Educ.*, 5 Cal.Rptr.2d 545 [72 Educ. L. Rep. 1137] (Cal.1992).

9. *Sutton v. Cadillac Area Pub. Schools*, 323 N.W.2d 582 [6 Educ. L. Rep. 187] (Mich. Ct. App.1982); *Lintz v. Alpena Publ. Schools of Alpena and Presque Isle Counties*, 325 N.W.2d 803 [7 Educ. L. Rep. 411] (Mich. Ct. App. 1982).

10. *Shaffer v. Board of School Directors of Albert Gallatin Area School Dist.*, 687 F.2d 718 [6 Educ. L. Rep. 487] (3d Cir.1982), *cert. denied*, 459 U.S. 1212, 103 S.Ct. 1209, 75 L.Ed.2d 449 (1983).

11. *On remand, Shaffer v. Board of School Directors of Albert Gallatin Area School Dist.*, 570 F.Supp. 698 [13 Educ. L. Rep. 731] (W.D. Pa. 1983), *rev'd*, 730 F.2d 910 [17 Educ. L. Rep. 9] (3d Cir.1984).

kindergarten while discontinuing midday busing.[12] The court pointed out that insofar as bus service was discretionary, officials only had to provide it during regular school hours. In New York, a trial court confirmed that the State Commissioner of Education did not exceed his authority in prohibiting a local board from providing free transportation to children who attended private pre-kindergarten classes.[13] The court agreed with the commissioner's determination that the statute dealing with student transportation did not authorize local boards to provide transportation to students in private pre-kindergarten classes.

Other legislatures permitted or required transportation for students, regardless of where they attended school. Even so, as reflected by an early case from Iowa, when a legislature grants boards such authority, it is typically strictly construed.[14] At issue was a law directing boards to transport specified students to and from school. In response to a challenge to a board's practice of transporting students to school-sponsored events outside of the district, the court decided that the statute did not give the board the discretion to expand its power in this way. The Supreme Court of Utah reached a different outcome in ruling that a board was required to transport students at district expense if their presence was required at after school activities.[15] Distinguishing between students who took part in the extracurricular activities and those who attendance was not required because they were spectators, the court added that the board could not offer the latter free transportation. The Supreme Court of North Carolina subsequently observed that boards could contract for transportation to bring athletic teams and bands to and from scheduled events.[16]

The judiciary has reached mixed results over the duty of boards to provide transportation to children who attend religiously affiliated non-public schools, a topic that is also discussed in Chapter 2. In *Everson v. Board of Education*,[17] the Supreme Court upheld the constitutionality of a statute from New Jersey which permitted local boards to make rules and contracts to transport children to and from their religiously affiliated non-public schools. Moreover, the Supreme Court of North Dakota, without reaching the constitutional question, wrote that state law did not entitle local boards to be reimbursed for transporting "pupils" to non-public schools.[18] Under state law, the court interpreted "pupil" as a "public school enrollee" and "school" as a "public school." In like fashion, the Supreme Court of Kentucky reasoned that allocating funds to transport students to

---

12. *Crowe v. School Dist. of Pittsburgh*, 805 A.2d 691 [169 Educ. L. Rep. 314] (Pa. Cmwlth. Ct. 2002), *appeal granted without opinion*, 815 A.2d 1043 [173 Educ. L. Rep. 897] (Pa. 2003).

13. *Board of Educ. of Lawrence Union Free School Dist. Number 15 v. McColgan*, 846 N.Y.S.2d 889 [226 Educ. L. Rep. 993] (N.Y.Sup.Ct.2007).

14. *Schmidt v. Blair*, 213 N.W. 593 (Iowa 1927).

15. *Beard v. Board of Educ. of N. Summit School Dist.*, 16 P.2d 900 (Utah 1932).

16. *State ex rel. N.C. Utilities Comm. v. McKinnon*, 118 S.E.2d 134 (N.C. 1961).

17. 330 U.S. 1, 67 S.Ct. 504, 91 L.Ed. 711 (1947), *reh'g denied*, 330 U.S. 855, 67 S.Ct. 962, 91 L.Ed. 1297 (1947). [Case No. 1]

18. *Dickinson Pub. School Dist. No. 1 v. Scott*, 252 N.W.2d 216 (N.D. 1977).

non-public elementary schools, including institutions that were religiously affiliated, was not an unconstitutional form of aid.[19]

In a case with mixed results, the Eighth Circuit, in a dispute from South Dakota, affirmed that a local board could discontinue providing transportation to students who attended a religiously affiliated non-public school within its boundaries unless they were being transported to athletic, musical, speech, or other interscholastic contests because state law did not obligate it to do so.[20] The court maintained that the students and their parents lacked standing since they failed to ask school officials to reinstate bus service or to show that doing so would have been futile because the board expressed its intention of providing busing again when it clarified an issue dealing with insurance. Most recently, an appellate court in Indiana affirmed that a state statute did not obligate local boards to provide free shuttle service from public middle schools to the non-public schools that children attended.[21] Rather, the court decreed that the law only required the boards to have drivers pick the students from the non-public schools up near the district's regular school bus routes and drop them off at public middle schools nearest to their non-public schools. This topic is covered in more detail in Chapter 2.

Instead of transporting students, some states permit boards to reimburse parents for the cost of bringing their children to school. The Supreme Court of Kansas upheld a board's paying a mileage rate to parents who lived in out-of-the-way locations rather than providing bus transportation.[22] The court was persuaded that this complied with the statutory requirement of providing or furnishing transportation. Where a mileage rate was reasonable, the Supreme Court of Washington was of the opinion that parents were not entitled to compensation for their time, vehicle depreciation, and actual fuel costs.[23]

Courts generally defer to the discretion of school boards to furnish transportation for purposes within their powers unless educational officials act arbitrarily. For instance, the Supreme Court of Tennessee rejected a claim from parents that their son should have been transported to a school nearer to their home since the board offered him transportation to a more distant school.[24] The court upheld the board's willingness to send the child to the closer school, without transportation, as a valid exercise of its discretion.

Conflicts arise when laws authorizing transportation do not specify how far students must be transported. In such a case, the Supreme Court of Connecticut reviewed a law requiring local boards to transport children

---

19. *Neal v. Fiscal Ct., Jefferson County*, 986 S.W.2d 907 [133 Educ. L. Rep. 624] (Ky. 1999).

20. *Pucket v. Hot Springs School Dist. No. 23–2*, 526 F.3d 1151 [232 Educ. L. Rep. 628] (8th Cir.2008).

21. *Roman Catholic Archdiocese of Indianapolis v. Metropolitan School Dist. of Lawrence Twp.*, 945 N.E.2d 757 [266 Educ. L. Rep. 469] (Ind. Ct. App. 2011).

22. *State ex rel. Stephan v. Board of Educ. of Unified School Dist. 428, Barton County, Ks.*, 647 P.2d 329 [5 Educ. L. Rep. 251] (Kan. 1982).

23. *State ex rel. Rosenberg v. Grand Coulee Dam School Dist.*, 536 P.2d 614 (Wash. 1975).

24. *Davis v. Fentress County Bd. of Educ.*, 402 S.W.2d 873 (Tenn. 1966).

as long as doing so was "reasonable and desirable."[25] When a board denied
parental transportation requests due to the presence of traffic hazards
between their homes and the schools their children attended, the court
upheld an order of the state board directing its local counterpart to offer
transportation. The court explained that the children were entitled to
transportation since their safety had to be taken into consideration. The
Supreme Court of Rhode Island later reached a like outcome where state
law required boards to provide transportation for students who lived far
enough away from school as to make regular attendance impractical.[26]
Earlier, the same court asserted that laws requiring boards to transport
public school students "to and from school" applied to children who
attended non-public schools. The court noted that the law did not obligate
boards to transport children to their out-of-district religious schools since it
interpreted legislative intent as contemplating that children be transported
to schools, regardless of whether they were public or non-public, located
within district boundaries.[27] Also, where a state law required boards to
transport students from non-public schools up to ten miles beyond district
boundaries as long as children in public schools were transported to district
schools, the Supreme Court of Pennsylvania declared that a board did not
have to transport resident children who attended public schools in other
districts on a tuition basis.[28]

The Supreme Court of California interpreted a school board's refusal
to provide transportation to children in an inaccessible part of the district
as an abuse of discretion.[29] The court rejected the board's claim that
providing transportation would have been too costly, that it would have led
to requests from families in other areas, and that buses would have had
difficulty operating on the narrow roads in the area. The court concluded
that insofar as the students who were from a poor family would have been
unable to get to school without transportation, and the board had the
financial resources available, it could have purchased a new, smaller bus to
bring the children to school. In addition, on three occasions, the Supreme
Court of Appeals of West Virginia agreed that transportation must be
provided for all children.[30]

A related concern involves the power of school boards generally to set
routes, times, and places for bus stops. Boards are unlikely to be liable for
injuries that students suffer while waiting for transportation as long as bus
stops are not located in unreasonable or dangerous locations.[31] As long as
the distances from their home is reasonable, children can be required to

25. *Town of Waterford v. Connecticut State Bd. of Educ.*, 169 A.2d 891, 894 (Conn. 1961).

26. *Brown v. Elston*, 445 A.2d 279 [4 Educ. L. Rep. 211] (R.I. 1982).

27. *Chaves v. School Comm. of Town of Middletown*, 211 A.2d 639 (R.I. 1965).

28. *Babcock School Dist. v. Potocki*, 466 A.2d 616 [14 Educ. L. Rep. 117] (Pa. 1983).

29. *Manjares v. Newton*, 49 Cal.Rptr. 805 (Cal.1966).

30. *Shrewsbury v. Board of Educ., County of Wyo.*, 265 S.E.2d 767 (W. Va. 1980); *Pauley v. Bailey*, 324 S.E.2d 128 (W. Va. 1984); *Collins v. Ritchie*, 351 S.E.2d 416 [36 Educ. L. Rep. 1002] (W. Va. 1986).

31. *See, e.g., Hackler By and Through Hackler v. Unified School Dist. No. 500, of Kansas City*, 777 P.2d 839 [55 Educ. L. Rep. 311] (Kan. 1989); *Moshier v. Phoenix Cent. School Dist.*, 605 N.Y.S.2d 581[88 Educ. L. Rep. 200] (N.Y.App. Div. 1993), *order aff'd*, 615 N.Y.S.2d 872 (N.Y.1994).

walk to bus stops.[32] However, an appellate court in Illinois remarked that students cannot be required to walk to pickup points that are a distance from their homes that is equal to the one beyond which transportation must be furnished.[33]

INSURANCE

As demonstrated by a case from the Supreme Court of Alabama, the implied power of local boards to insure school property appears to be settled. The court affirmed that a state law requiring trustees to care for the property and look after the general interests of schools granted them such power.[34] Other jurisdictions have extended board duties to include insurance for all of the vehicles they own or permit employees to operate.[35] In an illustrative case, the Supreme Court of Kentucky, overruling a statute and case law to the contrary, decreed that a statute authorizing boards to provide for liability and indemnity insurance against the negligence of drivers or operators of school buses or other vehicles that they own or operate did not waive their governmental immunity from suit.[36]

Difficulties can arise when boards seek to insure school property as part of mutual benefit associations based on reciprocal contracts designed to provide benefits to members as a matter of right. This kind of insurance does not call for the payment of set premiums and pro-rates losses among members in such a way that boards may be subject to heavy, unspecified losses. Where a board's contingent insurance liability was unlimited, the Supreme Court of Idaho invalidated its purchase.[37] Yet, where the amount of contingent liability was set at a stated maximum, the Supreme Court of Wyoming upheld its validity.[38] The court commented that the board's liability was not dispositive of the policy's constitutionality since it depended on the ultimate liability in relation to the premium charged by ordinary fire insurance companies. The related practice of self-insurance, whether for property or employees, remains common in many jurisdictions.[39]

---

32. *Flowers v. Independent School Dist. of Tama*, 16 N.W.2d 570 (Iowa 1944).

33. *People ex rel. Schuldt v. Schimanski*, 266 N.E.2d 409 (Ill. App. Ct. 1971).

34. *American Ins. Co. v. Newberry*, 112 So. 195 (Ala. 1927).

35. *See, e.g., Mortara v. Cigna Property & Cas. Ins. Co.*, 811 A.2d 458 (N.J. Super. Ct. App. Div. 2001), *aff'd*, 811 A.2d 404 (N.J. 2002).

36. *Grayson County Bd. of Educ. v. Casey*, 157 S.W.3d 201 [196 Educ. L. Rep. 975] (Ky. 2005) (invalidating *Taylor v. Knox County Board of Educ.*, 167 S.W.2d 700 (Ky. 1942), *Board of Educ. of Rockcastle County v. Kirby*, 926 S.W.2d 455 [111 Educ. L. Rep. 1046] (Ky. 1996), and KY. REV. STAT. § 160.310).

37. *School Dist. No. 8 v. Twin Falls County Mutual Fire Ins. Co.*, 164 P. 1174 (Idaho 1917).

38. *Burton v. School Dist. No. 19*, 38 P.2d 610 (Wyo. 1934).

39. *See, e.g., Christensen v. Milbank Ins. Co.*, 658 N.W.2d 580 [174 Educ. L. Rep. 1087] (Minn. 2003) (noting that state law authorized a self-insurance pool); *Bass v. New Hanover County Bd. of Educ.*, 580 S.E.2d 431 (N.C. Ct. App. 2003) (citing state law as permitting local boards to establish joint agencies to administer self-insurance programs to pay claims and judgments).

Local boards can purchase group life, health, and disability insurance for their employees. Since state statutes and collective bargaining contracts typically obligate school boards to do so, it is unlikely that the judiciary would disagree with the Supreme Court of New Mexico's decree that "securing of group insurance for the teachers enables the board of education to procure a better class of teachers, and prevents frequent changes in the teaching force."[40]

When school boards provide group health insurance benefits for staff, some employees probably receive more valuable benefits than others. In such a case, a state law in California authorized a board to purchase insurance while another required equal pay for men and women with equivalent certificates who performed like duties. An appellate court contended that a board did not have to provide insurance coverage in a way that would have required it to revise its salary schedules to give the same monetary equivalent to similarly situated employees.[41] The court cited administrative difficulties of calculating cash equivalents for everyone, observing that whether family benefits were to be included was within a board's discretion.

In a case from Michigan involving a different type of insurance, the Sixth Circuit affirmed that a school board was not covered by the terms of its liability insurance coverage when it settled a racial discrimination claim filed by a group of its employees.[42] The court agreed that the policy was inapplicable because the insurance policy expressly included provisions stipulating that it could not be used in cases involving racial discrimination.

CONFLICTS WITH BUSINESS

Disputes have arisen over school enterprises, most notably cafeterias and the sale of books and school materials[43] which may conflict with business interests in local communities. The courts refuse to treat the fact that private enterprises may suffer when school boards conduct these kinds of operations in schools as dispositive of whether public funds or property may be used in this manner. Rather, in evaluating whether boards can permit activities to proceed, the courts examine a venture's primary purpose. As witnessed by the relative dearth of litigation, the law is settled that as long as school enterprises are designed to serve student needs instead of earning profits or to destroy private businesses,[44] boards may continue with such activities.

---

40.   *Nohl v. Board of Educ.*, 199 P. 373, 374 (N.M.1921).

41.   *Sheehan v. Eldredge*, 84 Cal.Rptr. 894 (Cal.Ct.App.1970).

42.   *Ann Arbor Pub. Schools v. Diamond State Ins. Co.*, 236 Fed.Appx. 163 [224 Educ. L. Rep. 670] (6th Cir.2007).

43.   For a more detailed discussion relating to textbooks and course materials, *see* Chapter 12.

44.   *See, e.g., Hailey v. Brooks*, 191 S.W. 781 (Tex.Civ.App.1916).

When boards create school cafeterias to serve students, with prices set simply to cover the cost of operations, the courts uniformly uphold their authority to act.[45] In a leading case, the Tenth Circuit affirmed that insofar as a board in Colorado operated a cafeteria that was for the benefit of the student body, and did not serve a private mercantile purpose, it acted lawfully.[46] The Supreme Court of Washington agreed that a board could allow students to operate a cafeteria and use the profits to pay for costs associated with extracurricular activities.[47]

As to the sale of supplies, the Supreme Court of Wisconsin affirmed that a school board could sell them to students at cost since doing so aided successful school operations.[48] Earlier, the same court ascertained that if a dealer could prove that a board permitted principals to conduct stores in their buildings, which sold school books, stationery, and supplies to students at a profit, it would enjoin them from doing so.[49] Conversely, a year earlier, the Supreme Court of Michigan enjoined a board from purchasing and selling books to students even though doing so was more convenient and economical than through local dealers.[50] Subsequently, an appellate court in Illinois affirmed that a board exceeded its authority in imposing a fifteen percent handling charge on books it sold to students.[51]

SPECIAL EQUIPMENT AND SERVICES

SPECIAL ITEMS

The implied power of local school boards to purchase materials and equipment that are reasonably necessary to conduct curricular activities now seems beyond genuine dispute.[52] As highlighted by the different approaches taken by the courts in Massachusetts, Pennsylvania, Oklahoma, and Michigan, the judiciary has not always agreed on purchases of special items for small numbers of students that are made without express statutory authority.

In an early case, the Supreme Judicial Court of Massachusetts invalidated a school committee's purchase of uniforms and accessories for a basketball team as exceeding its power since the uniforms were not supplies under a commonwealth statute.[53] The court posited that when

---

45. *Krueger v. Board of Educ.*, 274 S.W. 811 (Mo. 1925).

46. *Goodman v. School Dist. No. 1, City and County of Denver*, 32 F.2d 586 (8th Cir.1929).

47. *Hempel v. School Dist. No. 329 of Snohomish County*, 59 P.2d 729 (Wash. 1936).

48. *Cook v. Chamberlain*, 225 N.W. 141 (Wis. 1929).

49. *Tyre v. Krug*, 149 N.W. 718 (Wis. 1914).

50. *Kuhn v. Board of Educ. of Detroit*, 141 N.W. 574 (Mich. 1913).

51. *Hamer v. Board of Educ. of Twp. High School Dist. No. 113, County of Lake*, 367 N.E.2d 739 (Ill. App. Ct. 1977).

52. *Commercial State Bank of Shepherd v. School Dist. No. 3 of Coe Twp., Isabella County*, 196 N.W. 373 (Mich. 1923).

53. *Brine v. City of Cambridge*, 164 N.E. 619 (Mass. 1929).

subjects such as manual arts and cooking were added to the curriculum, the legislature expressly permitted boards to purchase and loan these necessary items to students, but it had not done so for athletic teams.

On the other hand, where a statute authorized school boards to purchase furniture, equipment, textbooks, school supplies, and other items for school use, it did not refer to athletic supplies and equipment. The Supreme Court of Pennsylvania affirmed that this statute, together with one authorizing boards to provide gymnasiums and playgrounds, was broad enough to cover athletic supplies and equipment even though they were not specifically mentioned.[54] A year later, the Supreme Court of Oklahoma interpreted a state law as permitting a board to purchase band uniforms. The court noted that insofar as the law granted the board the ability to incur the expenses necessary to carry out its express authority, and had already organized a course in instrumental music, the purchase was appropriate.[55] Using a similar rationale, fifty years earlier, the Supreme Court of Michigan was of the view that insofar as a board had the authority to include music in a school's curriculum, it could purchase a piano for use in such classes.[56]

As to other items, an appellate court in Michigan affirmed that a board could use its funds to require students and staff to carry identification cards in school. The court observed that the board could use competitive bidding to select one company to take the photographs and could grant it the exclusive right to take pictures and sell them to students on school premises.[57] Also, the Fourth Circuit agreed that a board in Virginia could select an "official photographer" for the school yearbook even though it received a portion of the profits from the sale of portraits since students were not required to make any purchases.[58] Further, the Supreme Court of Georgia thought that a board could select one company to conduct its band recruitment program since students were not required to buy or rent instruments from that firm.[59] At the same time, an appellate court in Louisiana upheld a board's practice of allowing a salesperson of a jewelry company selected by a committee of faculty and students to sell class rings on school premises since no one was required to buy one.[60]

LEGAL SERVICES

Absent state statutes to the contrary requiring school boards to use the services of specified government counsel,[61] courts have upheld their implied power to select and pay for legal services of their own choosing.[62] As

---

54. *Galloway v. School Dist. of Borough of Prospect Park*, 200 A. 99 (Pa.1938).

55. *Excise Bd. of Kay County v. Atchison, T. and S.F. Ry. Co.*, 91 P.2d 1087 (Okla.1939).

56. *Knabe v. Board of Educ. of West Bay City*, 34 N.W. 568 (Mich.1887).

57. *LaPorte v. Escanaba Area Pub. Schools*, 214 N.W.2d 840 (Mich.Ct.App.1974).

58. *Stephen Jay Photography v. Olan Mills*, 903 F.2d 988 [60 Educ. L. Rep. 748] (4th Cir.1990).

59. *Ken Stanton Music v. Board of Educ.*, 181 S.E.2d 67 (Ga.1971).

60. *Givens Jewelers of Bossier v. Rich*, 313 So.2d 913 (La.Ct.App.1975).

61. *Denman v. Webster*, 73 P. 139 (Cal.1903).

62. *Arrington v. Jones*, 191 S.W. 361 (Tex.Civ.App.1917).

demonstrated by a case from New Jersey, a board's legal counsel must engage only in activities in its interest. A dispute arose when a superintendent sued a board president and individual members over an allegedly libelous letter that she addressed to him and sent to a local newspaper. An appellate court stated that a board resolution, purportedly approving the president's letter, was ineffective to convert the superintendent's personal action into a board matter that would have entitled her to have the board pay for her defense. The court pointed out that insofar as the board members who voted for the resolution did so in the course of performing their duties, they were entitled to reimbursement.[63] Even so, since the courts have recognized that it is not in the public interest to inhibit board members as they perform their duties, they liberally permit reimbursements for civil,[64] but not criminal,[65] litigation. On a related matter, an appellate court in Arizona held that a board could not use public funds to protect a board member's right to remain in office after he moved out of the district.[66]

Boards generally lack the implied power to pay attorney fees for employees who are sued in their individual, rather than in their official, capacities. To this end, a board's paying attorney fees would constitute an impermissible gift of public funds for a private purpose. Reiterating this principle, an appellate court in New York refused to order a board to pay the legal fees of a teacher who was exonerated on a criminal charge of sexual abuse of one of his students.[67] In a case reaching the same outcome, an appellate panel in Maryland decided that a statute requiring a board to furnish counsel for teachers who acted in official capacities was not triggered in a sex abuse case since a court or jury could not have concluded that a board authorized educators to engage in sexual abuse or harassment of their students.[68] As with board members, the Supreme Court of Rhode Island interpreted an indemnification statute that covered any claim, demand, or suit arising from employment as applying only to civil proceedings.[69]

---

63. *Errington v. Mansfield Twp. Bd. of Educ.*, 241 A.2d 271 (N.J. Super. Ct. App. Div. 1968).

64. *See, e.g., Miller v. Board of Trustees*, 970 P.2d 512 [131 Educ. L. Rep. 1114] (Idaho 1998), *cert. denied*, 526 U.S. 1159, 119 S.Ct. 2050, 144 L.Ed.2d 216 (1999); *Dunn v. Jurupa Unified School Dist.*, 94 Cal.Rptr.2d 529 [145 Educ. L. Rep. 1089] (Cal. Ct. App. 2000); *Brademas v. South Bend Community School Corp.*, 783 N.E.2d 745 (Ind. App. Ct. 2003).

65. *Powers v. Union City Bd. of Educ.*, 308 A.2d 71 (N.J. Super. Ct. Law Div. 1973), *aff'd*, 317 A.2d 373 (N.J. Super Ct. App. Div. 1974); *certification denied*, 325 A.2d 709 (N.J. 1974).

66. *Campbell v. Harris*, 638 P.2d 1355 [2 Educ. L. Rep. 277] (Ariz. Ct. App. 1981).

67. *Lamb v. Westmoreland Cent. School Dist.*, 533 N.Y.S.2d 157 [49 Educ. L. Rep. 952] (N.Y. App. Div. 1988), *appeal denied*, 539 N.Y.S.2d 298 (N.Y. 1989).

68. *Matta v. Board of Educ. of Prince George's County*, 552 A.2d 1340 [51 Educ. L. Rep. 953] (Md. Ct. Spec. App. 1989).

69. *Monti v. Warwick School Comm.*, 554 A.2d 638 [52 Educ. L. Rep. 153] (R.I. 1989).

MISCELLANEOUS USES OF FUNDS

Many cases address whether school boards have the implied power to spend money for specific purposes. The general rule is that boards can make expenditures to carry out their express, and reasonably implied, powers. If boards exceed their authority, the legal remedy for aggrieved parties is ordinarily to seek injunctions. While courts typically do not order the recovery of expenditures based on reasonable assumptions, board members or administrators may be liable for expenditures that were clearly unauthorized[70] even if they did not act with improper motives.[71] The following cases reflect the types of issues that arise.

The Supreme Courts of Ohio,[72] Pennsylvania,[73] and Vermont[74] agreed that school boards could build parking facilities pursuant to their general powers. On a different matter, two courts disagreed over whether boards had implied authority to purchase camp sites for children.[75] Still other courts ruled that boards could not build residences for staff[76] or purchase land for use in teaching agriculture under a statute authorizing them to acquire land for school buildings and playgrounds.[77] Moreover, an appellate court in New York allowed a board to hire architects to devise plans for the construction of school buildings.[78] An appellate court in Illinois also affirmed that a board had the implied power to employ a public relations consultant to serve as a liaison between the press and community.[79]

In a dispute from Massachusetts, the commonwealth's highest court permitted a school committee to reimburse board members for expenses they incurred attending a national convention for school boards.[80] According to the court, the members' attendance at the gathering satisfied the law's requirements since they could have secured information of value that would have improved service in the district. Previously, an appellate court in Kentucky upheld a board's implied power to pay for membership in the commonwealth's association for school boards.[81]

Boards often pay employees and/or provide benefits in order to settle claims dealing with their contracts. Clearly, abuses can occur when employees are offered money in exchange for resigning and/or not contesting adverse personnel actions. However, with the expense of litigation and the turmoil it can cause, settlements may be economically and educationally

---

70. *Smith v. Dorsey*, 599 So.2d 529 [75 Educ. L. Rep. 692] (Miss. 1992).

71. *Campbell v. Joint Dist. 28–J*, 704 F.2d 501 [10 Educ. L. Rep. 132] (10th Cir.1983).

72. *Wayman v. Board of Educ.*, 215 N.E.2d 394 (Ohio 1966).

73. *In re School Dist. of Pittsburgh*, 244 A.2d 42 (Pa. 1968).

74. *Patch v. Springfield School Dist.*, 989 A.2d 500 [253 Educ. L. Rep. 766] (Vt. 2009).

75. *Compare Wilson v. Graves County Board of Educ.*, 210 S.W.2d 350 (Ky. 1948) (denying such authority) with *In re Board of Pub. Instruction of Alachua County*, 35 So.2d 579 (Fla. 1948) (recognizing such power).

76. *Cf. Taylor v. Board of Pub. Instruction*, 26 So.2d 180 (Fla. 1946).

77. *Board of Educ. of City of Nickerson v. Davis*, 135 P. 604 (Kan. 1913).

78. *People ex rel. Kiehm v. Board of Educ.*, 190 N.Y.S. 798 (N.Y. App. Div. 1921).

79. *Ryan v. Warren Twp. High School Dist. No. 121*, 510 N.E.2d 911 [40 Educ. L. Rep. 896] (Ill. App. Ct. 1987). [Case No. 36]

80. *Day v. City of Newton*, 174 N.E.2d 426 (Mass. 1961).

81. *Schuerman v. State Bd. of Educ.*, 145 S.W.2d 42 (Ky. Ct. App. 1940).

prudent. Regardless, boards cannot make payments and, if questioned, simply claim that they exercised their discretion.[82]

INCOME FROM SCHOOL BOND ISSUES

As discussed in Chapter 5, school boards cannot issue bonds or borrow money absent express statutory authority to do so. Since the power to issue bonds is an extraordinary one, it may be exercised only for the express purposes set forth in authorizing statutes. The strictness with which courts interpret bonding authority is understandable in light of the fact that insofar as bonds are issued prospectively, they can obligate district taxpayers for long periods of time. The strict construction given to the language of bonding statutes and the propositions that are placed before voters assures, as far as possible, that the contemplated use of bonding power and bond proceeds will be for the designated purposes.

Where a state auditor refused to register bonds, a school board unsuccessfully challenged his refusal to act. The Supreme Court of Kansas found that insofar as the bonds were to be used for a new roof and to replace the heating and electrical systems, but since there were no structural changes to the building, the vote was illegal because the funds were for repairs rather than erecting and equipping a school.[83] Conversely, the Supreme Court of Wisconsin maintained that a statute which authorized bonding to erect or purchase a school building was sufficiently broad to cover lending for remodeling since such work involved more than repairs or minor changes to the structure.[84] The Supreme Court of North Carolina followed this rationale in affirming that additions to physical facilities necessarily implied acquisition of more land for a school.[85]

When school boards issue construction bonds, questions can arise as to what legally constitutes parts of buildings. The Supreme Court of Wyoming considered whether the term "building" included its equipment. In upholding the validity of a bond issue, the court noted that specified types of equipment may properly be considered parts of buildings that can be purchased with their proceeds.[86] The court wrote that equipment was limited to that which, when installed, became parts of buildings, such as heating systems, light fixtures, and laboratory desks which are firmly attached to the floor. The court added that even permanent equipment, which is akin to fixtures, should be placed in buildings during construction in order to fall within the provision of the bonding statutes. Further, an appellate court in New York rejected a suit by taxpayers who claimed that a bond proposal's inclusion of computers as equipment in renovated buildings

---

82. *Ingram v. Boone*, 458 N.Y.S.2d 671 [8 Educ. L. Rep. 1076] (N.Y. App. Div. 1983). [Case No. 37]

83. *School Dist. No. 6, Chase County v. Robb*, 93 P.2d 905 (Kan. 1939).

84. *Cotter v. Joint School Dist. No. 3 of Village of Plum City*, 158 N.W. 80 (Wis. 1916).

85. *Lutz v. Gaston County Bd. of Educ.*, 192 S.E.2d 463 (N.C. 1972).

86. *Jewett v. School Dist. No. 25 in Fremont County*, 54 P.2d 546 (Wyo. 1936).

violated constitutional provisions restricting indebtedness of local subdivisions.[87] The court affirmed that state laws prescribing a ten-year period of probable usefulness for computer systems did not prohibit the board from including computers as equipment within the proposal.

Occasionally, as school boards seek to utilize bond funds, they must do so in ways that differ from the wording of bonding propositions. In the first of two cases from Tennessee, the state supreme court affirmed that bond money spent constructing a high school gymnasium that elementary school children used regularly, especially during inclement weather, did not render the board's action illegal.[88] The court deemed that the use of the facility did not change its character as a gymnasium. Additionally, when a board realized that its cost estimates for a project were too low, and used the funds for only part of the proposed improvements, an appellate court in Tennessee upheld its action.[89] The court indicated that the board could spend funds as it judged best. An appellate court in Oklahoma agreed that a board did not have to spend bond proceeds in the precise amounts allocated to each specific project.[90] The court asserted that the board could use the funds on projects outlined in bond issue statements as long as the monies were spent in a manner consistent with the bond issue.

INCOME FROM SCHOOL ACTIVITIES

Based on their general authority to direct school activities, boards have the power and duty to control the income generated by these activities. Since the courts treat such income as school funds, a court in Pennsylvania reiterated the general rule that these monies should be deposited, dispersed, and audited in the same manner as funds derived from taxation or other sources.[91] In a second case from Pennsylvania, an appellate court upheld the validity of a law subjecting school activity funds to audits.[92] The court recognized that if funds arise from the use of school property and the services of board personnel, they are district funds that must be deposited in the board's official account and are subject to being audited.

In a dispute primarily over an ousted board member's possible illegal use of funds that were raised via vending machines, the Supreme Court of Kentucky addressed the nature of school activities funds.[93] The court rejected the former board member's claims that the monies from the machines were not school funds because they were raised by children for

---

87. *Friedman v. Board of Educ. of East Ramapo Cent. School Dist.*, 686 N.Y.S.2d 84 [133 Educ. L. Rep. 565] (N.Y. App. Div. 1999).

88. *Moody v. Williamson County*, 371 S.W.2d 454 (Tenn.1963).

89. *State ex rel. Miller v. Peacock*, 405 S.W.2d 478 (Tenn. Ct. App. 1965).

90. *State ex rel. Howard v. Crawford*, 16 P.3d 473 [150 Educ. L. Rep. 496] (Okla.Civ.App. 2000), *cert. denied* (Okla. Civ. App. 2000).

91. *In re German Twp. School Directors*, 46 Pa. D. & C. 562 (Pa.Com.Pl.1943).

92. *Petition of Auditors of Hatfield Twp. School Dist.*, 54 A.2d 833 (Pa.Super.Ct.1947).

93. *Commonwealth ex rel. Breckinridge v. Collins*, 379 S.W.2d 436 (Ky.1964).

various projects, that they belonged to classes or school-related organizations, and that they were kept separate from tax money. In ordering the board member's removal, the court declared that the monies from the vending machines were school funds subject to the board's full control.

A case from Texas reveals how school activity funds continue to generate litigation. The Fifth Circuit determined that insofar as a principal who resigned in the face of an accusation that she mismanaged school activities funds had not presented a matter of public concern in her letter to the board, she could not file suit for defamation.[94] The significance of this case is that although not directly discussing the matter, the court did not question the principle that the funds were public monies.

Insofar as school activity funds are school property, educators lack the authority to administer or dispose of these monies in manners not specified by law. Questions can thus arise as to whether administrators can maintain funds that are not under board control and, if so, what accounting is necessary. In a complex case, taxpayers sought to have a principal account for monies that students and high school teachers voluntarily raised, with no input from the board, over four years to pay for items such as athletic equipment and choir robes. The principal exercised sole control over the unaudited funds. When the case first reached the Supreme Court of South Carolina, it remanded for a consideration of whether the principal made a proper accounting and whether there was a genuine shortage.[95] The court avoided a discussion of the legal status of the funds since the board neither raised nor administered the money directly or indirectly. The same court subsequently affirmed that the taxpayers did not present any issues entitling them to relief.[96] While conceding that the principal's system of record keeping left much to be desired, the court was of the opinion that nothing in the record suggested that he personally profited from the funds entrusted to his care and no one was financially damaged as a result of his manner of handling the monies.

INCOME FROM GIFTS

School boards can generally accept gifts. When gifts are conveyed by wills, boards may not receive funds or property for designated purposes that they are barred from carrying out by impracticality, impossibility, or illegality. If goals simply cannot be achieved, such as granting awards for the highest grades in subjects that are no longer taught, the common law of testamentary charitable trusts, also known as the doctrine of *cy pres*, permits courts to designate other uses for the funds as long as they are close to the ones specified by the testators.

If accepting gifts would cause school boards to engage in illegal activities, such as where a trust discriminated based on gender and reli-

---

94. *Bradshaw v. Pittsburg Indep. School Dist.*, 207 F.3d 814 [143 Educ. L. Rep. 65] (5th Cir.2000), *reh'g denied*, (2000).

95. *Betterson v. Stewart*, 121 S.E.2d 102 (S.C.1961).

96. *Betterson v. Stewart*, 140 S.E.2d 482 (S.C.1965).

gion,[97] courts may be able to reform them by eliminating the offending restrictions. Of prime judicial concern is to execute the general charitable intent of testators. If the charitable intent of donors can be carried out simply by naming other administrators for wills, courts can apply the doctrine of deviation to implement changes in the administrative terms of trusts. Such situations could arise not only if boards were legally unable to serve as trustees but also if they were unwilling to do so for policy reasons.[98]

Uses of School Property

Uses in General

School buildings are state-owned property that do not belong to local boards even if they are paid for solely by local funds.[99] Taxpayers may have difficulty understanding this point since they are typically inclined to treat schools as their own because they were financed with "their" money. Even though school buildings are constructed for educational purposes, groups often use them for a variety of non-school activities. As might have been anticipated, whether and the extent to which school buildings may be used for non-school purposes has been widely litigated. Placing constitutional considerations aside for a moment, since legislative oversight for use of local school buildings is fairly scarce, "the care, custody, and control of all school property is the responsibility"[100] of local boards.

Permissible Uses and Conditions of Use

School buildings can be used for activities open to parents and the general public, even if officials charge attendance fees.[101] While uncertainty arises when activities are not school-related, if boards allow their facilities to be used in such a manner, they must be careful to ensure that activities neither interfere with school programs nor damage buildings.[102]

Other than their use as polling places, statutes rarely interfere with board discretion over the use of school buildings for non-school purposes. In a case dealing with a school's use as a polling place, the Eighth Circuit

---

97. *In re Certain Scholarship Funds*, 575 A.2d 1325 [61 Educ. L. Rep. 149] (N.H. 1990).

98. *Matter of Estate of Wilson*, 465 N.Y.S.2d 900 [13 Educ. L. Rep. 110] (N.Y. 1983).

99. *See, e.g., Pritchett v. County Bd. of School Trustees*, 125 N.E.2d 476 (Ill. 1955); *Bellevue School Dist. No. 405 v. Brazier Const. Co.*, 675 P.2d 232 [15 Educ. L. Rep. 995] (Wash. 1984), *reconsideration granted*, 680 P.2d 40 [17 Educ. L. Rep. 413] (Wash. 1984), *and adhered to on reh'g*, 691 P.2d 178 [21 Educ. L. Rep. 734] (Wash. 1984).

100. *Goldes v. City of N.Y.*, 797 N.Y.S.2d 102, 103 [199 Educ. L. Rep. 371] (N.Y. App. Div. 2005) (rejecting a claim of liability against a city in a personal injury action). *See also Lloyd v. Grella*, 611 N.Y.S.2d 799 [90 Educ. L. Rep. 1202] (1994), *reargument denied*, 616 N.Y.S.2d 482 (N.Y. 1994).

101. *Beard v. Board of Educ. of N. Summit School Dist.*, 16 P.2d 900 (Utah 1932).

102. *Merryman v. School Dist. No. 16*, 5 P.2d 267 (Wyo. 1931).

affirmed that officials did not violate the First Amendment rights of individuals who sought to collect signatures on an initiative petition drive as voting took place at a school in Missouri.[103] The court agreed that the response of school officials in calling the police, who arrested the plaintiffs for refusing to leave, was reasonable and not content-based in light of their safety concerns and disruption coupled with the fact that the petition circulators made no effort to seek or receive permission to be on school property.

California has long gone further than other states in providing statutory guidance for non-school use of buildings. State law created civic centers as designated public fora at all public school facilities and grounds that permit community groups to meet to discuss subjects of an educational, political, economic, artistic, and/or moral nature.[104] Pursuant to this statute, local boards must adopt reasonable rules dealing with the use of facilities as long as such use does not interfere with regular school purposes.

In apparently the earliest case under this statute, an appellate court in California upheld a board's authority to permit a dance in a school auditorium.[105] Other cases before the Supreme Court of California allowed boards to exclude a speaker who created a disturbance in other locations[106] and prospective users who refused to abide by a rule that required them to stipulate that they did not intend to put the property to an illegal use.[107] On the other hand, where a speaker wished to address the question of peace, the court rejected a board's claim that doing so would have violated its prohibited use of school buildings for sectarian, political, or partisan purposes.[108] The court later struck down the statutory requirement that those who applied for permission to use school buildings had to submit statements that they did not advocate the violent overthrow of the government and their groups were neither Communist nor Communist-front organizations.[109]

Courts are reluctant to permit private plaintiffs with common interests to interfere with school uses. For example, the Supreme Court of Kentucky rejected the claim of the owner of a private music hall that a board policy, which permitted a local civic organization to rent its gymnasium when not being used for school purposes, had an adverse impact on his business.[110] The court affirmed that the policy was constitutional because it was adopted pursuant to a statute. In addition, the Supreme Court of North Carolina affirmed that a suit by private day care providers, where a board

---

103. *Embry v. Lewis*, 215 F.3d 884 [145 Educ. L. Rep. 227] (8th Cir.2000), *reh'g and reh'g en banc denied*, (2000).

104. CAL. EDUC. CODE § 38131. *See also* 76 Op. Atty. Gen. 52, 4–20–93 (Cal.1993).

105. *McClure v. Board of Educ. of City of Visalia*, 176 P. 711 (Cal.Ct.App.1918).

106. *Payroll Guarantee Ass'n v. Board of Educ.*, 163 P.2d 433 (Cal.1945).

107. *American Civil Liberties Union of S. Cal. v. Board of Educ. of City of Los Angeles*, 379 P.2d 4 (Cal.1963), *cert. denied*, 375 U.S. 823, 84 S.Ct. 64, 11 L.Ed.2d 56 (1963).

108. *Goodman v. Board of Educ. of San Francisco*, 120 P.2d 665 (Cal.Ct.App.1941).

109. *American Civil Liberties Union of S. Cal. v. Board of Educ. of City of Los Angeles*, 10 Cal.Rptr. 647 (Cal. 1961), *cert. denied*, 368 U.S. 819, 82 S.Ct. 34, 7 L.Ed.2d 25 (1961).

110. *Hall v. Shelby County Bd. of Educ.*, 472 S.W.2d 489 (Ky. 1971).

opened an after school program of its own for children who were left
without supervision at the end of the school day and lasted until their
parents came home, lacked merit. In reasoning that the board charged
parents a nominal fee but covered the costs of the school's use and
volunteers conducted the program, the court agreed that the program met
the constitutional requirement that all expenditures of tax dollars be for
public purposes since the program's intent was to further educational
achievement of students.[111]

In the first of two cases from the Eighth Circuit involving dancing,
parents sought to have a board in Arkansas sponsor more than two dances
a year. The court rejected the parents' claim that dancing should have been
treated as a form of expression entitled to First Amendment protection.[112]
In refusing to interpret the First Amendment as covering social or recreational dancing, as opposed to dance before an audience as an art form, the
court explained that the board had the discretion to permit its facilities to
be used as it saw fit. In the second case, the court was unwilling to disturb
a long-standing board rule in Missouri that prohibited schools from being
used for dances.[113] Even though the board acted in response to a large
segment of the community which opposed social dancing on religious
grounds, the court affirmed that the policy did not violate the Establishment Clause since officials were free to use the facilities as they deemed
appropriate.

As much discretion as boards have to establish use policies, school
employees have no corresponding right to conduct unapproved meetings or
use facilities without getting permission from boards. Since disputes of this
kind, which typically involve constitutional questions, tend to overlap with
litigation on differentiating among users, the final cases in this section
serve as a segue to the next part of this chapter.

The Seventh Circuit, in a case from Indiana, affirmed that pursuant to
a board policy that officials consistently applied to prohibit the use of
school facilities for religious activity, teachers lacked a right to conduct
regularly scheduled prayer meetings for themselves before students arrived
for class.[114] The court remarked that its rationale was not related to costs
of electricity and maintenance or to the content of the meetings. The court
emphasized the board's concern that permitting such meetings to take
place could have caused controversies that were not related to work. The
court concluded that if some groups were permitted to meet, the board
could not bar others under the freedom of speech clause.

In the first of four cases involving unions, *Perry Education Association
v. Perry Local Educators' Association*,[115] the Supreme Court decreed that a

---

111. *Kiddie Korner Day Schools v. Charlotte–Mecklenburg Bd. of Educ.*, 285 S.E.2d 110 [1
Educ. L. Rep. 972] (N.C. App. 1981).

112. *Jarman v. Williams*, 753 F.2d 76 [22 Educ. L. Rep. 737] (8th Cir.1985).

113. *Clayton by Clayton v. Place*, 884 F.2d 376 [55 Educ. L. Rep. 920] (8th Cir.1989), *reh'g
denied*, 889 F.2d 192 (8th Cir.1989), *cert. denied*, 494 U.S. 1081, 110 S.Ct. 1811, 108 L.Ed.2d
942 (1990).

114. *May v. Evansville–Vanderburgh School Corp.*, 787 F.2d 1105 [31 Educ. L. Rep. 727]
(7th Cir.1986).

115. 460 U.S. 37, 103 S.Ct. 948, 74 L.Ed.2d 794 [9 Educ. L. Rep. 23] (1983).

school board can grant access to its intra-school system mail facilities to the exclusive bargaining representative of teachers while barring use by a rival union. In a like dispute, the Seventh Circuit rejected a challenge from board candidates in Illinois who claimed that a board violated their rights by permitting the union representing its teachers to use its internal mail system to communicate with members about a board election.[116] The court affirmed that insofar as the policy of allowing the union to use the mail system was viewpoint neutral and reasonable, it did not violate the First Amendment.[117] Also, the Supreme Court of Kansas affirmed that a board's denial of access to its mail system to an alternative teachers' association-union to distribute brochures through the system's internal mail system did not violate the First Amendment. Previously, where a statute in Maryland permitted boards to deny access to school property to those lacking lawful business there, the Fourth Circuit affirmed that a union representative could be barred from a school parking lot.[118] The court agreed that even though his presence was not disruptive, the board was free to exclude the representative since officials deemed that his solicitations were unrelated to the education of students and the parking lot had not become a public forum.

DIFFERENTIATING AMONG USES AND USERS

When reviewing the Free Speech Clause of the First Amendment, the Supreme Court has identified three different types of fora.[119] Under the first category, governmental power to regulate expression is most restricted on public properties that are traditional public fora such as parks, streets, and sidewalks. The government may "exclude a speaker from a traditional public forum 'only when the exclusion is necessary to serve a compelling state interest and the exclusion is narrowly drawn to achieve that interest.' "[120] Narrowly tailored content-neutral regulations as to time, place, and manner of expression can be enforced, but only if the governmental interest is significant and alternative channels of communication are open.

The same standard that applies in public fora governs "designated public fora," public property that the state has opened for public use as places for expressive activity.[121] The government can create such fora either by express policy or by substantial practice. In limited public fora, First

116. *Davidson v. Community Consol. School Dist. 181*, 130 F.3d 265 [122 Educ. L. Rep. 583] (7th Cir.1997).

117. *Unified School Dist. No. 233 Johnson County v. Kansas Ass'n of Am. Educators*, 64 P.3d 372 [174 Educ. L. Rep. 419] (Kan. 2003).

118. *Grattan v. Board of School Commr's of Baltimore City*, 805 F.2d 1160 [36 Educ. L. Rep. 56] (4th Cir.1986).

119. For discussions of forum analysis, *see Perry Educ. Ass'n v. Perry Local Educators' Ass'n*, 460 U.S. 37, 103 S.Ct. 948, 74 L.Ed.2d 794 [9 Educ. L. Rep. 23] (1983); *Hazelwood School Dist. v. Kuhlmeier*, 484 U.S. 260, 108 S.Ct. 562, 98 L.Ed.2d 592 [43 Educ. L. Rep. 515] (1988). [Case No. 105]

120. *Arkansas Educ. Television Comm'n v. Forbes*, 523 U.S. 666, 677, 118 S.Ct. 1633, 140 L.Ed.2d 875 (1998) (quoting *Cornelius v. NAACP Legal Def. & Educ. Fund., Inc.*, 473 U.S. 788, 800, 105 S.Ct. 3439, 87 L.Ed.2d 567 (1985)).

121. *Arkansas Educ. Television Comm'n v. Forbes, Id.*

Amendment protections provided to traditional public fora apply, but only to entities of a character similar to those the government admits to the fora. The government is not indefinitely bound to retain the open nature of limited fora.

A non-public forum, the third category of public property, such as a classroom,[122] "is not by tradition or designation a forum for public communication."[123] As such, non-public fora are subject to less rigorous scrutiny than traditional open or designated public fora. In these settings, the government can enforce regulations to reserve fora for their intended purposes, communicative or otherwise, but they "must be 'reasonable in light of the purpose served by the forum.' "[124] Limitations cannot be intended to suppress expression since public officials oppose viewpoints.[125] During the class day, schools are generally non-public fora. Once the class day is over, the type of fora that schools become depends on board policies and practices.

Access by Religious Groups

Given the place of religion in American life, it is not surprising that many suits have been litigated over religious speech. In *Heffron v. International Society for Krishna Consciousness*, the Supreme Court refused to grant religious organizations "rights to communicate ... superior to those of other organizations having social, political, or other ideological messages to proselytize."[126] The court thus rejected the religious group's challenge to a regulation of a state fair in Minnesota which required all solicitations, sales, and/or distributions of material to be from fixed locations. Rather than repeat material discussed in greater detail in Chapter 2, this section highlights key cases wherein religious groups sought access to public school facilities.

The Supreme Court reached a different result after religious speech received less protection than other forms of speech. In *Widmar v. Vincent*,[127] (*Widmar*) the Justices posited that university officials essentially created a forum for student use by making facilities available to over one hundred registered student organizations. The Court was of the view that officials could not bar a student organization that wished to conduct

---

122.   *See, e.g., Walz ex rel. Walz v. Egg Harbor Twp. Bd. of Educ.*, 342 F.3d 271 [180 Educ. L. Rep. 115] (3d Cir.2003), *cert. denied*, 541 U.S. 936, 124 S.Ct. 1658, 158 L.Ed.2d 356 (2004).

123.   *Perry Educ. Ass'n v. Perry Local Educators' Ass'n*, 460 U.S. 37, 46, 103 S.Ct. 948, 74 L.Ed.2d 794 [9 Educ. L. Rep. 23] (1983).

124.   *Good News Club v. Milford Cent. School*, 533 U.S. 98, 106–107 121 S.Ct. 2093, 150 L.Ed.2d 151 [154 Educ. L. Rep. 45] (2001) [Case No 13] (quoting *Cornelius v. NAACP Legal Defense and Educ. Fund*, 473 U.S. 788, 806, 105 S.Ct. 3439, 87 L.Ed.2d 567 (1985)); *Arkansas Educ. Television Comm'n v. Forbes*, 523 U.S. 666, 682, 118 S.Ct. 1633, 140 L.Ed.2d 875 (1998); *Rosenberger v. Rector and Visitors of Univ. of Va.*, 515 U.S. 819, 829, 115 S.Ct. 2510, 132 L.Ed.2d 700 [101 Educ. L. Rep. 552] (1995); *Lamb's Chapel v. Center Moriches Union Free School Dist.*, 508 U.S. 384, 392–93, 113 S.Ct. 2141, 124 L.Ed.2d 352 [83 Educ. L. Rep. 30] (1993), *on remand*, 17 F.3d 1425 [89 Educ. L. Rep. 783] (2d Cir.1994). [Case No. 38]

125.   *See, e.g., Cornelius v. NAACP Legal Defense and Educ. Fund*, 473 U.S. 788, 105 S.Ct. 3439, 87 L.Ed.2d 567 (1985).

126.   452 U.S. 640, 652–53, 101 S.Ct. 2559, 69 L.Ed.2d 298 (1981).

127.   454 U.S. 263, 102 S.Ct. 269, 70 L.Ed.2d 440 [1 Educ. L. Rep. 13] (1981).

religious meetings. As discussed more fully in Chapter 2, the Court distinguished *Widmar* from cases involving public schools on the bases that this was a forum available to many diverse groups and that university students are less impressionable than young children.

Many pre-*Widmar* cases involving access to school property by outside groups upheld prohibitions against religious use. Whether cases remain valid is cloudy because judicial opinions often did not record all of the facts or respond to some arguments that were important for the disposition of future cases. For instance, the Supreme Court of Pennsylvania upheld a rule that facilities could not be used for religious or sectarian purposes.[128] The court rejected a claim that a board violated equal protection by permitting non-religious uses and that its discretionary power to allow use of school facilities had to be exercised in full or not at all.

In the first post-*Widmar* case, the federal trial court in Kansas entered a judgment in favor of a church that was denied occasional use of school facilities for religious services. Pursuant to the policy, facilities were available for recognized community organizations whose activities were of general interest and who used the building for community purposes. Where the facilities were used by an array of groups, and there were no guidelines to distinguish between religious and non-religious meetings, the court reasoned that "[h]aving created a public forum, [the board] cannot exclude [the church group] from the forum because of the religious content of [the church group's] intended speech unless such exclusion is justified under applicable constitutional case law."[129]

Acting in large part in response to *Widmar*, Congress enacted the Equal Access Act.[130] According to the Act, any public secondary school that receives federal financial assistance, and that permits one or more non-curriculum-related student groups to meet on school premises during non-instructional time, cannot withhold such a privilege on the basis of the religious, political, philosophical, or other content of the speech at such meetings.

In *Board of Education of Westside Community Schools v. Mergens,*[131] a case from Nebraska, the Supreme Court upheld the Equal Access Act. Relying on statutory interpretation rather than the constitutional question, the Court was convinced that Congress thought that most high school students could recognize that allowing a religious club to function in school does not imply endorsement of religion. The Court's failure to address the constitutional dimensions of the Act has led to a line of cases treating

---

128. *McKnight v. Board of Pub. Educ.,* 76 A.2d 207 (Pa. 1950), *appeal dismissed,* 341 U.S. 913, 71 S.Ct. 737, 95 L.Ed. 1349 (1951).

129. *Country Hills Christian Church v. Unified School Dist. No. 512, Johnson County, State of Ks.,* 560 F.Supp. 1207, 1219 [10 Educ. L. Rep. 1006] (D. Kan.1983). *See also Grace Bible Fellowship v. Maine School Admin. Dist. No. 5,* 941 F.2d 45 [69 Educ. L. Rep. 210] (1st Cir.1991).

130. 20 U.S.C.A. §§ 4071 *et seq.* This statute is in the Appendix.

131. 496 U.S. 226, 110 S.Ct. 2356, 110 L.Ed.2d 191 [60 Educ. L. Rep. 320] (1990). [Case No. 9]

religious expression as a kind of hybrid wherein it protects a religious group's right to express its opinion as a form of free speech.[132]

Even after *Mergens*, it is clear that the Equal Access Act does not protect otherwise unlawful speech. In such a case, the Ninth Circuit held that a provision in the Act could not be interpreted as requiring school boards to approve meetings that are otherwise unlawful or to forbid religious meetings on the ground that use of school for them would have violated the state constitution.[133] The panel emphasized the Supreme Court's determination that the Act had to be read as effectuating a broad Congressional purpose and so remained in effect, thereby preempting state law. Other courts have looked beyond written policies to conduct and actions in evaluating whether fora are limited and, if so, to what subjects and/or classes of participants may use school facilities. Thus, when a school auditorium in New York was used for some fund-raising activities and for at least one Christmas program, the Second Circuit required access for another religious activity.[134]

The Supreme Court, in a rare unanimous judgment, in *Lamb's Chapel v. Center Moriches Union Free School District*,[135] reversed in favor of a religious group in New York. In a hybrid situation wherein it treated religious speech as a form of free speech, the Court ascertained that insofar as the board created a limited open forum, it violated the group's free speech rights by engaging in viewpoint discrimination. The Court pointed out that the board, which had a policy of allowing its facilities to be used for social, civic, and recreational meetings and entertainment when school was not in session, could not bar a church group from using them to show a six-part film series on family values from the Christian point of view. Relying on the Free Speech Clause, the Court observed that school officials misapplied a board policy which prohibited religious use of the property. The Court added that absent a restriction on the subject matter of the films, the board could not erect a bar based on the viewpoint to be expressed about that subject matter.[136]

Another dispute arose when officials in another school system in New York refused to permit a non-school sponsored club to meet during non-class hours so that members and moderators could discuss child-rearing along with character and moral development from a religious perspective. School officials permitted other youth groups to meet because even though they addressed related topics, they did so from secular perspectives. The

---

132. *See, e.g., Rosenberger v. Rector and Visitors of Univ. of Va.*, 515 U.S. 819, 115 S.Ct. 2510, 132 L.Ed.2d 700 [101 Educ. L. Rep. 552] (1995).

133. *Garnett v. Renton School Dist. No. 403*, 987 F.2d 641 [81 Educ. L. Rep. 704] (9th Cir.1993), *cert. denied*, 510 U.S. 819, 114 S.Ct. 72, 126 L.Ed.2d 41 (1993), *appeal after remand*, 21 F.3d 1113 [91 Educ. L. Rep. 31] (9th Cir.1994), *on remand*, 1994 WL 555397 (W.D. Wash. 1994) (granting a declaratory judgment and awarding attorney fees to the plaintiffs).

134. *Travis v. Owego–Apalachin School Dist.*, 927 F.2d 688 [66 Educ. L. Rep. 75] (2d Cir.1991).

135. 508 U.S. 384, 113 S.Ct. 2141, 124 L.Ed.2d 352 [83 Educ. L. Rep. 30] (1993), *on remand*, 17 F.3d 1425 [89 Educ. L. Rep. 783] (2d Cir.1994). [Case No. 38]

136. *See also Rosenberger v. Rector and Visitors of Univ. of Va.*, 515 U.S. 819, 115 S.Ct. 2510, 132 L.Ed.2d 700 [101 Educ. L. Rep. 552] (1995) (treating religious expression as a hybrid, protecting a religious group's right to express its opinion as a form of free speech).

Supreme Court agreed to hear an appeal to resolve a split in the lower courts since the Eighth Circuit[137] had upheld the right of the same kind of club in Missouri to use school facilities for its meetings.

In *Good News Club v. Milford Central School*,[138] the Supreme Court reversed in favor of the club.[139] The Court decided not only that the officials violated the club's rights to free speech by engaging in impermissible viewpoint discrimination in refusing to permit it to use school facilities for its meetings, which were not worship services, but also that such a restriction was unjustified by fears of violating the Establishment Clause.

The Second Circuit, in a long-running dispute in New York City, determined that forbidding religious worship services from taking place in public school facilities was a content-based exclusion.[140] The court was satisfied that the policy did not constitute viewpoint discrimination but was an acceptable content-based exclusion in light of the board's reasonable concern that permitting the services to occur would have violated the Establishment Clause.[141]

In Michigan, an appellate court affirmed the rejection of a challenge filed by an atheist father and his son who objected to a board's permitting the Boy Scouts to use school facilities.[142] The court ruled that the board's allowing the Boy Scouts to distribute their literature and collect their communications during class hours, and to hang posters in school hallways, did not implicate the state constitution's Establishment Clause since a wide array of groups were allowed to display posters and distribute literature as long as they met neutral qualifying criteria. The court held that the board's actions did not denote the group's religious aspect and neither school officials nor the board compelled students to take literature or incorporated it into the curriculum. Chapter 2 explores issues surrounding access to school facilities by religious groups in greater detail while Chapter 12 examines other questions that have arisen under the Equal Access Act.

Access by Non–Religious Groups

Moving away from religious uses, while school officials can close the door to all outside organizations, based on equal protection, once they make

137. *Good News/Good Sports Club v. School Dist. of the City of Ladue*, 28 F.3d 1501 [92 Educ. L. Rep. 1148] (8th Cir.1994), *cert. denied*, 515 U.S. 1173, 115 S.Ct. 2640, 132 L.Ed.2d 878 (1995).

138. 533 U.S. 98, 121 S.Ct. 2093, 150 L.Ed.2d 151 [154 Educ. L. Rep. 45] (2001). [Case No 13]

139. For an earlier ruling involving the Boy Scouts, *see Sherman v. Community Consol. School Dist. 21 of Wheeling Twp.*, 8 F.3d 1160 [87 Educ. L. Rep. 57] (7th Cir.1993), *cert. denied*, 511 U.S. 1110, 114 S.Ct. 2109, 128 L.Ed.2d 669 (1994).

140. For the first reported case in this litigation, *see Bronx Household of Faith v. Community School Dist. No. 10*, 127 F.3d 207 [121 Educ. L. Rep. 892] (2d Cir.1997), *cert. denied sub nom. Bronx Household of Faith v. Board of Educ. of City of N.Y.*, 523 U.S. 1074, 118 S.Ct. 1517, 140 L.Ed.2d 670 (1998), *leave to file for reh'g denied*, 524 U.S. 934, 118 S.Ct. 2337, 141 L.Ed.2d 708 (1998).

141. *Bronx Household of Faith v. Board of Educ. of City of N.Y.*, 650 F.3d 30 (2d Cir.2011).

142. *Scalise v. Boy Scouts of Am.*, 692 N.W.2d 858 [195 Educ. L. Rep. 961] (Mich. Ct. App. 2005), *appeal denied*, 700 N.W.2d 360 (Mich. 2005), *reconsideration denied*, 713 N.W.2d 252 (Mich. 2006), *cert. denied*, 547 U.S. 1163, 126 S.Ct. 2330, 164 L.Ed.2d 840 (2006).

facilities available, they must treat all similar groups similarly. To this end, boards can deny groups or individuals[143] access to their facilities in the face of evidence of clear and present dangers and/or that public disorders[144] and damage to buildings would have resulted from proposed uses. Still, boards cannot bar groups simply because they, or a part of the public, might be hostile to the opinions of groups as long as programs are not unlawful per se.[145] In an older case that remains relevant, the Court of Appeals of New York applied these principles when a school board sought to bar one of a series of concerts from taking place at its facilities since it was to feature a controversial performer who was critical of American foreign policy.[146] Even though the scheduled date for the concert had passed, the court found that the board impermissibly cancelled it because officials could not prohibit the singer from appearing due to its having disagreed with his views.

Statutes or ordinances preventing loitering on school grounds or in the vicinity of school buildings are increasingly common. Rules of this type are ordinarily acceptable as long as they are not overly vague or restrictive. In one such case, parents and their son sued school officials in Illinois claiming that their disciplining him for breaking an anti-loitering rule violated his rights to free speech, assembly, and due process and that it was unconstitutionally vague.[147] The Seventh Circuit affirmed a dismissal in favor of school officials in acknowledging both that the use of the term "loitering" in the rule did not render it unconstitutionally vague and that it did not violate his First Amendment guarantees of free speech and free assembly.

As important as parental input in the education of their children is, parents must observe limits when at school facilities. One such dispute involved a non-custodial father in Virginia who was barred from school facilities based on his pattern of verbal abuse and threatening behavior toward officials after his son was not selected for a high school basketball team. The Fourth Circuit affirmed that the father's suit was properly dismissed as insubstantial and frivolous.[148] In another case, a federal trial court in Texas granted a board's motion for summary judgment where a mother sought unauthorized access to monitor her son's class.[149] The court contended that officials did not deny the mother the right to voice her complaints about how her son was being treated when they asked her to

---

143. *See, e.g., In re Joseph F.*, 102 Cal.Rptr.2d 641 [149 Educ. L. Rep. 835] (Cal. Ct. App. 2000) (denying a hostile and belligerent student access to school).

144. *See, e.g., Local Organizing Comm., Denver Chapter, Million Man March v. Cook*, 922 F.Supp. 1494 [109 Educ. L. Rep. 223] (D. Colo. 1996); *Reeves v. Rocklin Unified School Dist.*, 135 Cal.Rptr.2d 213 [177 Educ. L. Rep. 414] (Cal. Ct. App. 2003).

145. *See, e.g., East High Gay/Straight Alliance v. Board of Educ.*, 81 F.Supp.2d 1166 [141 Educ. L. Rep. 776] (D. Utah 1999), 81 F.Supp.2d 1199 [141 Educ. L. Rep. 809] (D. Utah 1999); *East High School Prism Club v. Seidel*, 95 F. Supp.2d 1239 [144 Educ. L. Rep. 260] (D. Utah 2000); *Colin ex rel. Colin v. Orange Unified School Dist.*, 83 F.Supp.2d 1135 [142 Educ. L. Rep. 138] (C.D. Cal.2000) (agreeing that school officials could not deny clubs sponsored by gay and lesbian students the use of school facilities under the Equal Access Act).

146. *East Meadow Community Concerts Ass'n v. Board of Educ.*, 272 N.Y.S.2d 341 (N.Y.1966).

147. *Wiemerslage Through Wiemerslage v. Maine Twp. High School Dist. 207*, 29 F.3d 1149 [93 Educ. L. Rep. 64] (7th Cir.1994).

148. *Lovern v. Edwards*, 190 F.3d 648 [138 Educ. L. Rep. 118] (4th Cir.1999).

149. *Ryans v. Gresham*, 6 F.Supp.2d 595 [127 Educ. L. Rep. 862] (E.D. Tex. 1998).

leave the building since her presence was disruptive in her child's class-room. Moreover, the Seventh Circuit affirmed that part of a judgment that a divorced non-custodial father in Illinois lacked a constitutional right to be present on school grounds to monitor the school's protection of his children from bullies.[150] The court specified that the father's interests were out-weighed by those of the state, including the need of school officials to have autonomy. The court did reinstate that part of the father's claim which alleged that officials discriminated against him and other non-custodial parents.

DISPOSAL OF PROPERTY

Insofar as the implied powers of school boards to use property do not extend to its disposal, this subject is typically covered by statute.[151] Even so, disputes arise where statutory language over the disposal of unneeded school buildings is unclear.[152] If statutes fail to address property disposal, courts have not interfered with the discretion of boards unless they manifestly abused their power[153] and they were satisfied that officials acted in the best interests of their school systems.[154] At least one court agreed that a board could even sell unwanted property on an installment, rather than a cash, basis since it would have been unrealistic to expect developers to mortgage vacant lands while borrowing money for construction.[155] More-over, the authority of boards to manage and control their schools does not imply the power to sell or give away property. As such, boards cannot, in effect, give away real estate by leasing it for nominal sums, even for worthy causes such as leasing property to a community hospital for one dollar a year.[156]

Courts disagree on what can be done with buildings when they are no longer used for school purposes. For example, the Supreme Court of North Dakota indicated that a building where classes no longer met continued to serve school purposes and was not subject to reverter to the original grantor since it was used to store equipment and supplies.[157] Likewise, an appellate court in Illinois affirmed that a former school campus remained district property subject to state school, rather than county, building codes

---

150. *Crowley v. McKinney*, 400 F.3d 965 [196 Educ. L. Rep. 50] (7th Cir.2005), *cert. denied*, 546 U.S. 1033, 126 S.Ct. 750 163 L.Ed.2d 573 (2005).

151. *See, e.g., Whiteside v. Cherokee County School Dist. No. One*, 428 S.E.2d 886 [82 Educ. L. Rep. 270] (S.C. 1993); *Western Area Business and Civic Club v. Duluth School Bd. Indep. Dist. No. 709*, 324 N.W.2d 361 [6 Educ. L. Rep. 808] (Minn. 1982).

152. *Ross v. Wilson*, 308 N.Y. 605 (N.Y.1955). [Case No. 39]

153. Merely filing a suit seeking to enjoin a school closing does not prevent a board from selling the physical plant. *See Laurales v. Desha County School Dist. No. 4 of Snowlake*, 632 F.2d 72 (8th Cir.1980).

154. *Veal v. Smith*, 146 S.E.2d 751 (Ga. 1966).

155. *Singer Architectural Servs. Co. v. Doyle*, 254 N.W.2d 587 (Mich. Ct. App. 1977).

156. *Prescott Community Hosp. Comm'n v. Prescott School Dist.*, 115 P.2d 160 (Ariz. 1941).

157. *Ballantyne v. Nedrose Pub. School Dist. No. 4, Ward County*, 177 N.W.2d 551 (N.D. 1970).

even though the board rented it out to private entities which ran before and after school programs there.[158] Since schools also used the gymnasium about twice per month and officials stored property there, the court noted that these actions kept the building under the state standards. An appellate court in Texas reached the opposite result in contending that a building was no longer reserved "for school purposes only" when a board leased it to a city to use as a recreation center.[159] In returning the property to the original grantor, the court rejected the board's argument that it leased the building to prevent vandalism and keep it in good repair for eventual reopening as a school by focusing on language in the operative deed that required it to be used "for school purposes only."

Not all jurisdictions agree on the role of district residents when boards seek to dispose of real property. The Supreme Court of Iowa emphasized the mandatory nature of statutes covering the disposal of school property when it voided an attempted sale that was not in strict compliance with a law permitting boards to dispose of property valued up to a set amount without a vote of local residents.[160] Conversely, the Supreme Court of Virginia struck down a statute that required boards which wished to sell property to obtain a majority of votes from residents in a referendum, as an unlawful delegation of power to the electorate.[161] Yet, where a board sold a building that it had leased to a Catholic school following a referendum in which the majority of voters approved the transaction, the Supreme Court of Montana upheld the sale as a valid exercise of its authority.[162]

[CASE NO. 36]   BOARD POWER TO EMPLOY A CONSULTANT

RYAN v. WARREN TOWNSHIP HIGH SCHOOL DISTRICT NO. 121

Appellate Court of Illinois, 1987.
510 N.E.2d 911 [40 Educ. L. Rep. 896].

■ JUSTICE WOODWARD delivered the opinion of the court.

Defendant, Warren Township High School District No. 121 (hereinafter school district), appeals from a judgment entered for the plaintiff, Keith Ryan and against the school district in the amount of $1,975. On appeal, the school district contends that it lacked the authority under the School Code to contract for plaintiff's services, and that the contract was unenforceable because it violated the Election Interference Prohibition Act.

Plaintiff, the only witness in the case, testified that in September 1985, he was working as a public relations manager for Clausing and Company.

---

158. *County of Lake v. Board of Educ. of Lake Bluff School Dist. No. 65*, 761 N.E.2d 163 [161 Educ. L. Rep. 574] (Ill. App. Ct. 2001).

159. *Sewell v. Dallas Indep. School Dist.*, 727 S.W.2d 586, 587 [38 Educ. L. Rep. 1300] (Tex. Ct. App. 1987).

160. *Unification Church v. Clay Cent. School Dist.*, 253 N.W.2d 579 (Iowa 1977). *See also Davis v. Board of Educ. of Hewlett–Woodmere Union Free School Dist.*, 509 N.Y.S.2d 612 [36 Educ. L. Rep. 854] (N.Y. App. Div. 1986), *appeal denied*, 517 N.Y.S.2d 1028 (1987).

161. *Howard v. School Bd. of Alleghany County*, 122 S.E.2d 891 (Va. 1961).

162. *Good Schools Missoula v. Missoula County Pub. School Dist. No. 1*, 188 P.3d 1013 [234 Educ. L. Rep. 412] (Mont. 2008).

He was contacted by Dr. Paul Rundio, the superintendent of the school district, who requested a cost estimate of plaintiff's services. At that time, the school district had decided to raze Warren High School, which had been damaged by fire, and build a new school. However, community members who opposed the school district's plan instituted a lawsuit to block the destruction of the school. Dr. Rundio hired plaintiff to act as a liaison with members of the press and the community, to issue press releases, and to hold public meetings. The term of plaintiff's employment was from September to November 1985, prior to the school board elections.

Plaintiff submitted an itemized proposal and cost estimate totaling $5,000 to Dr. Rundio. Plaintiff was unaware of any public school board meeting adopting his oral contract negotiated with Dr. Rundio. The school district paid an interim bill for plaintiff's services in the amount of $3,200. On November 1, 1985, plaintiff submitted a second bill on the amount of $1,975 to the school district. When the school district refused payment, plaintiff filed this lawsuit.

. . .

The school district contends first that it did not have the authority to contract with plaintiff, so the contract is null and void.

Contracts entered into by a public body which are prohibited by an express provision of the law, or which under no circumstances could be legally entered into, are uniformly held to be *ultra vires* and void. While statutes granting powers to school boards must be strictly construed, a school board has the power expressly conferred and such powers as may be necessary to carry into effect those expressly granted. We conclude that the contract was not prohibited by an express provision of the School Code, and our interpretation of the School Code permits entering into the contract.

Implicit in the school district's power to hold regular and special meetings open to the public is the need to disseminate information to the public and receive feedback from the community. The School Code specifies that the school district should hold meetings where the members of the public are afforded an opportunity to question the board or to comment. Hiring a public relations consultant would enhance the school district's communication with the public especially where the parties described relations between them as "explosive" and "turbulent." Plaintiff arranged public meetings and tours of the old school and generally assisted the board in communicating with the public. Section 10–20.21 of the School Code contemplates the hiring of professionals and highly skilled individuals for their services, although a public relations consultant is not specifically listed. While we express no opinion regarding the board's judgment in hiring a public relations consultant, we conclude that the School Code does not prohibit entering into a contract with the plaintiff.

Defendant's reliance on *Evans v. Benjamin School District No. 25* for the proposition that the school district's actions are limited to the express provisions of the School Code is misplaced. The facts in *Evans* are distinguishable from the case at bar. At issue in *Evans* was the school board's power to grant tenure to a teacher. The teacher had not met the standards set out in section 24–11 of the Illinois School Code. The school district could not ignore the provision and grant tenure based on its own discretion. In this case, the legislature had not sought to provide specifications governing the hiring of consultants.

While the school district's actions were not void and *ultra vires,* no evidence exists establishing that the school district had voted to authorize an expenditure for plaintiff's fees. Section 10–7 of the School Code provides in relevant part:

> "On all questions involving the expenditure of money, the yeas and nays shall be taken and entered on the records of the proceedings of the board. . . .

Plaintiff testified that, to his knowledge, no meeting of the board occurred for the purpose of hiring him or approving the expenditure of his fees. By failing to call a meeting in order to authorize an expenditure for plaintiff's services, the school district irregularly contracted with the plaintiff. The parties do not dispute the trial court's finding that the board irregularly exercised its power in hiring the plaintiff.

Courts have distinguished between cases where the school district was utterly without the power to make a contract and cases in which it had the power, but exercised it in an irregular fashion. In the latter case, it is well settled that the conduct is merely voidable, and plaintiff may recover in *quantum meruit.* The rationale is as follows:

> Contracts entered into by a municipality which are expressly prohibited by law, and which under no circumstances can be entered into, are void and ultra vires. They may not be rendered valid thereafter by estoppel or ratification of the municipality. However, there is another class of municipality contracts, distinct from the void type heretofore referred to, wherein the municipality has the power to enter into the contract, but where a portion thereof may be beyond its power, or its power may have been irregularly exercised. As to this class of contracts, a municipality may not assert its want of authority, or power, or the irregular exercise thereof, where to do so would give it an unconscionable advantage over the other party. Municipal corporations, as well as private corporations and individuals, are bound by principles of common honesty and fair dealing.

Therefore, although the contract was irregularly entered into, plaintiff is entitled to be reimbursed for his services where the school district ratified the contract by accepting the services and by making the partial payment.

. . . [P]laintiff's services continued for several months with the board's full knowledge as all the members knew of the public meetings scheduled by the plaintiff, his helping them with interviews, and his discussion with them of ideas for various committees. In this case also, both parties agree that the hiring was done in an irregular fashion.

Defendant's final contention is that the contract is void since it violates the Election Interference Prohibition Act. Section 103 of that Act states as follows:

No public funds shall be used to urge any elector to vote for or against any candidate or proposition, or be appropriated for political or campaign purposes to any candidate or political organization. This provision shall not prohibit the use of public funds for dissemination of factual information relative to any proposition appearing on an election ballot. . . .

The school district alleges that the school board hired the plaintiff as a propagandist to market its decision within days of an election involving the very board members who hired the public relations consultant. Defendants, however, do not support their allegations with any specific facts. Further, even if the allegations were true, the plaintiff was only promoting the board's idea which was to build a new school rather that promoting the candidates themselves.

· · ·

Affirmed.

NOTE

Procedures for employing professionals not engaged in educational functions directly, such as architects, physicians, and lawyers, are generally not covered by competitive bidding statutes. Should they be?

[CASE NO. 37]   BOARD POWER TO PAY A SUPERINTENDENT TO RESIGN

INGRAM v. BOONE

New York Supreme Court, Appellate Division, 1983.
458 N.Y.S.2d 671 [8 Educ.L.Rep. 1076].

MEMORANDUM BY THE COURT. . . .

Petitioners are taxpaying residents of the Union Free School District #1 of the Town of Hempstead. . . . They have commenced the instant proceeding to review an agreement entered into between the board of education of the school district and the district superintendent, alleging it was violative of the statutory and constitutional law of this State.

In August, 1980 Dr. Oliver Lancaster contracted with the board of education to serve as superintendent of schools for a period of four years commencing July 1, 1980. Approximately one year later, in the fall of 1981, a dispute allegedly arose between the board of education and Dr. Lancaster concerning his performance as superintendent. The board entered into negotiations with Lancaster in an effort to obtain his resignation which negotiations culminated in a resolution proposed at a public meeting of the board held on December 17, 1981 whereby Dr. Lancaster would resign effective December 31, 1981, the school district would pay him a lump sum of $65,000 and the board would continue Dr. Lancaster's insurance under several policies until the termination date of his employment contract or until he received insurance coverage from another source, whichever date occurred first. The resolution was approved by a vote of four to zero with one abstention. Thereafter, a formal stipulation was executed and general releases were signed. By order to show cause dated December 31, 1981 petitioners instituted the instant proceeding in which they challenge the lawfulness of the subject agreement.

Petitioners had standing to commence this proceeding by virtue of section 1 of article VIII of the State Constitution which forbids gifts of public funds. However, the payment of public funds as damages for breach of a contractual obligation or in settlement of a contested claim is not prohibited by this constitutional provision. On the record before us, it is impossible to determine whether the payment to Dr. Lancaster can be construed as a settlement of a legitimate claim or whether it is, in fact, a gift of public moneys. A mere claim of exercise of discretion and judgment is not enough, in the absence of competent proof, to validate the payment. Accordingly, [the trial court] properly directed that a hearing on this question be held.

NOTES

1. The Supreme Court of New Mexico held that a school board was not required to conduct a hearing before it suspended its superintendent with full salary for the three months remaining in his contract. The court explained that this did not amount to a discharge for which a hearing would have been required. *Black v. Board of Educ. of Jemez Mountain School Dist. No. 53*, 529 P.2d 271 (N.M. 1974). What do you think?

2. The Supreme Court of Wyoming, in invalidating the purchase of the remainder of a superintendent's contract on the ground that the special board meeting was not properly called, commented that there was grave doubt about the matter. *Twitchell v. Bowman*, 440 P.2d 513 (Wyo.1968).

[CASE NO. 38]   ACCESS TO A SCHOOL BUILDING

LAMB'S CHAPEL v. CENTER MORICHES UNION FREE SCHOOL DISTRICT

Supreme Court of the United States, 1993.
508 U.S. 384, 113 S.Ct. 2141, 124 L.Ed.2d 352 [83 Educ. L. Rep. 30].

■ JUSTICE WHITE delivered the opinion of the Court.

Section 414 of the New York Education Law authorizes local school boards to adopt reasonable regulations for the use of school property for 10 specified purposes when the property is not in use for school purposes. Among the permitted uses is the holding of "social, civic and recreational meetings and entertainments, and other uses pertaining to the welfare of the community; but such meetings, entertainment and uses shall be non-exclusive and open to the general public." The list of permitted uses does not include meetings for religious purposes. . . .

Pursuant to § 414's empowerment of local school districts, the Board of Center Moriches Union Free School District (District) has issued rules and regulations with respect to the use of school property when not in use for school purposes. The rules allow only 2 of the 10 purposes authorized by § 414: social, civic, or recreational uses (Rule 10) and use by political organizations if secured in compliance with § 414 (Rule 8). Rule 7, however, consistent with the judicial interpretation of state law, provides that "[t]he school premises shall not be used by any group for religious purposes."

The issue in this case is whether, against this background of state law, it violates the Free Speech Clause of the First Amendment, made applicable to the States by the Fourteenth Amendment, to deny a church access to school premises to exhibit for public viewing and for assertedly religious purposes, a film dealing with family and child-rearing issues faced by parents today.

I

Petitioners (Church) are Lamb's Chapel, an evangelical church in the community of Center Moriches, and its pastor John Steigerwald. Twice the Church applied to the District ... to use school facilities to show a six-part film series.... A brochure provided on request of the District ... stated that the film series would discuss [a commentator's] views on the undermining influences of the media that could only be counterbalanced by returning to traditional, Christian family values instilled at an early stage. The brochure went on to describe the contents of each of the six parts of the series. The District denied the first application, saying that "[t]his film does appear to be church related and therefore your request must be refused." The second application for permission to use school premises for showing the film, which described it as a "Family oriented movie-from the Christian perspective," was denied using identical language.

[The District Court and the Court of Appeals ruled in favor of the school board.]

. . .

II

There is no question that the District, like the private owner of property, may legally preserve the property under its control for the use to which it is dedicated. It is also common ground that the District need not have permitted after-hours use of its property for any of the uses permitted by § 414 of the state education law. The District, however, did open its property for 2 of the 10 uses permitted by § 414. The Church argued below that because under Rule 10 of the rules issued by the District, school property could be used for "social, civic, and recreational" purposes, the District had opened its property for such a wide variety of communicative purposes that restrictions on communicative uses of the property were subject to the same constitutional limitations as restrictions in traditional public fora such as parks and sidewalks. Hence, its view was that subject-matter or speaker exclusions on District property were required to be justified by a compelling state interest and to be narrowly drawn to achieve that end. Both the District Court and the Court of Appeals rejected this submission, which is also presented to this Court. The argument has considerable force, for the District's property is heavily used by a wide variety of private organizations, including some that presented a "close question," which the Court of Appeals resolved in the District's favor, as to whether the District had in fact already opened its property for religious uses. We need not rule on this issue, however, for even if the courts below were correct in this respect—and we shall assume for present purposes that they were—the judgment below must be reversed.

With respect to public property that is not a designated public forum open for indiscriminate public use for communicative purposes, we have said that "[c]ontrol over access to a nonpublic forum can be based on subject matter and speaker identity so long as the distinctions drawn are reasonable in light of the purpose served by the forum and are viewpoint neutral." The Court of Appeals appeared to recognize that the total ban on using District property for religious purposes could survive First Amendment challenge only if excluding this category of speech was reasonable and viewpoint neutral. The court's conclusion in this case was that Rule 7 met this test. We cannot agree with this holding, for Rule 7 was unconstitutionally applied in this case. (Although the Court of Appeals apparently held that Rule 7 was reasonable as well as viewpoint neutral, the court uttered not a word in support of its reasonableness holding. If Rule 7 were to be held unreasonable, it could be held facially invalid, that is, it might be held that the rule could in no circumstances be applied to religious speech or religious communicative conduct. In view of our disposition of this case, we need not pursue this issue.)

The Court of Appeals thought that the application of Rule 7 in this case was viewpoint neutral because it had been and would be applied in the same way to all uses of school property for religious purposes. That all religions and all uses for religious purposes are treated alike under Rule 7, however, does not answer the critical question whether it discriminates on the basis of viewpoint to permit school property to be used for the presentation of all views about family issues and child-rearing except those dealing with the subject matter from a religious standpoint.

There is no suggestion from the courts below or from the District or the State that a lecture or film about child-rearing and family values would not be a use for social or civic purposes otherwise permitted by Rule 10. That subject matter is not one that the District has placed off limits to any and all speakers. Nor is there any indication in the record before us that the application to exhibit the particular film involved here was or would have been denied for any reason other than the fact that the presentation would have been from a religious perspective. . . .

The film involved here no doubt dealt with a subject otherwise permissible under Rule 10, and its exhibition was denied solely because the film dealt with the subject from a religious standpoint. The principle that has emerged from our cases "is that the First Amendment forbids the government to regulate speech in ways that favor some viewpoints or ideas at the expense of others." . . .

The District, as a respondent, would save its judgment below on the ground that to permit its property to be used for religious purposes would be an establishment of religion forbidden by the First Amendment. This Court suggested in *Widmar v. Vincent* that the interest of the State in avoiding an Establishment Clause violation "may be [a] compelling" one justifying an abridgment of free speech otherwise protected by the First Amendment; but the Court went on to hold that permitting use of University property for religious purposes under the open access policy involved there would not be incompatible with the Court's Establishment Clause cases.

We have no more trouble than did the *Widmar* Court in disposing of the claimed defense on the ground that the posited fears of an Establishment Clause violation are unfounded. The showing of this film would not have been during school hours, would not have been sponsored by the school, and would have been open to the public, not just to church members. The District property had repeatedly been used by a wide variety of private organizations. Under these circumstances, as in *Widmar,* there would have been no realistic danger that the community would think that the District was endorsing religion or any particular creed, and any benefit to religion or to the Church would have been no more than incidental. As in *Widmar,* permitting District property to be used to exhibit the film involved in this case would not have been an establishment of religion under the three-part test articulated in *Lemon v. Kurtzman.* The challenged governmental action has a secular purpose, does not have the principal or primary effect of advancing or inhibiting religion, and does not foster an excessive entanglement with religion.

The District also submits that it justifiably denied use of its property to a "radical" church for the purpose of proselytizing, since to do so would lead to threats of public unrest and even violence. There is nothing in the record to support such a justification, which in any event would be difficult to defend as a reason to deny the presentation of a religious point of view about a subject the District otherwise makes open to discussion on District property.

.   .   .

The Attorney General also argues that there is no express finding below that the Church's application would have been granted absent the religious connection. This fact is beside the point for the purposes of this opinion, which is concerned with the validity of the stated reason for denying the Church's application, namely, that the film sought to be shown "appeared to be church related."

For the reasons stated in this opinion, the judgment of the Court of Appeals is

Reversed.

NOTES

1. If church officials had wanted to conduct a prayer meeting or a religious service, should the board have permitted one to occur?

2. Consider how the lower courts erred in interpreting viewpoint neutrality. Can you distinguish between viewpoint and subject matter neutrality and/or discrimination?

[CASE NO. 39]   BOARD POWER TO DISPOSE OF SCHOOL PROPERTY

ROSS v. WILSON

Court of Appeals of New York, 1955.
308 N.Y. 605.

■ VAN VOORHIS, JUDGE.

The controversy in this proceeding concerns the sale of the schoolhouse which served common school district No. 1 of the Towns of Ellicott and Gerry, in Chautauqua County, before it was superseded by a central school district. This district had been known as the Ross Mills District. In February, 1953, the board of education of the recently formed central school district called a special meeting of the qualified voters of the former common school district to vote upon whether to close the school and sell the school property. Such procedure is required by subdivision 6 of section 1804 of the Education Law, which also provides that if the common school district schoolhouse is sold, the net proceeds be apportioned among the taxpayers of the common school district.

At the special meeting of the common school district called by the board of education in 1953, four propositions were submitted: (1) Should the school of the former common school district be closed? (2) Should the school property be sold to Ross Mills Church of God for $2,000? (3) Should the property be sold to Ross Grange No. 305 for $3,000? (4) Should the property be sold by public auction to the highest bidder? The notice stated that proposition number 1 would be voted upon, "and as many of the succeeding propositions as is necessary to dispose of the property". At the meeting, the proposal to close the school was carried. A motion was then made but declared out of order that the meeting should next ballot upon whether to sell the school property at public auction to the highest bidder. Then proposition number 2 was presented to the meeting to sell the school property to Ross Mills Church of God for $2,000. It was carried by a vote of 32 to 24. That ended the meeting.

The Commissioner of Education on appeal taken to him pursuant to section 310 of the Education Law sustained this action of the board of education. Thereupon this article 78 proceeding was instituted to review his determination, which was annulled by Special Term but reinstated by the Appellate Division upon the ground that decisions by the Commissioner of Education are final unless purely arbitrary, and that his decision could not thus be characterized in this instance inasmuch as subdivision 6 of section 1804 of the Education Law, pursuant to which this schoolhouse was sold, does not expressly state that it must be sold to the highest bidder upon the organization of a central school district. . . .

No question was raised that Ross Grange was financially able to pay $3,000 in cash for the property. In his opinion upholding the action of the school district, the Commissioner of Education placed his decision upon the following ground: "The type and character of the purchaser of such property after centralization is often a matter of vital import to the rural communities of this State. It is my opinion that the legislature fully intended to give the voters of component districts a choice as to the type of person or organization whom they wished to have literally in their midst. If the sale were to be mandated to be made to the highest bidder, it may well be that a 'saloon', filling station or other enterprise undesirable to a specific community might be forced upon it...." ...

In the conduct of private affairs, the problem sometimes arises whether a better price can be obtained upon the sale of property at private sale or at auction. In the case of a public body, such as a school district, the object to be achieved is likewise to realize the best price for the property, although the judgment of the Legislature must be followed concerning whether that purpose is more likely to be accomplished by public auction. But if the Legislature does not require a schoolhouse to be sold at public auction, it by no means follows from that circumstance that the Legislature intended to authorize the public officials charged with the administration of school property, or even the majority of qualified electors voting at a school district meeting, to sell the property for a smaller amount than has been offered with due formality by a proper purchaser for a lawful use.... If, as was intimated by the Commissioner of Education, a former school site might be used for a filling station, bar and grill or other enterprise undesirable to a specific community, zoning ordinances or other lawful regulatory measures should be adopted....

The amount of money involved is small, but the principle is important; the offer which was rejected was to pay 50% more for this schoolhouse than the one which was accepted. Bogert, writing on Trusts and Trustees, says (§ 745): "Whether the trustee should endeavor to sell by negotiation with possible buyers, or should put the property up at auction, depends upon the circumstances of the individual case. He should use the method which will, considering the place of sale and the type of property for sale, be apt to bring the best price." In the present situation, the Legislature has determined that it was not necessary to sell this property at auction, although that procedure would have been permissible, but the latitude allowed in the method of sale was designed to enable these public fiduciaries to adopt the method which in their judgment would bring the best price, and it was their duty to sell at the best price which it brought, not deliberately to select and to favor a buyer at a lower price than was otherwise obtainable. In the same section of Bogert it is also said: "A power to sell is not equivalent to a power to give away. If the trustee transfers for a merely nominal price or a wholly inadequate price, the sale may be set aside"....

... The direct result of what occurred is, in effect, to approve a contribution of $1,000 by the school district to the church....

This contribution by a common school district to a particular church is not made in aid of any educational activity conducted by the church, but operates as an outright gift of public funds to a church for its general church purposes. Even if the facts of the case did not present the special situation of the use of public money for the support of a religious establishment, neither a common school district meeting nor the district trustees are empowered to expend the resources of the school district for other than educational objects....

There is no power in either the board or the voters at a district meeting to pick and choose arbitrarily between purchasers, each desiring to use the property for lawful and proper purposes, or to transfer the funds or other property of the district in aid of one or to the disadvantage of another. In this instance, there is lack of power to use public funds to aid a church by discriminating against the grange. . . .

For the reasons mentioned, we think that there was a total lack of power in the school district to accept an offer of $2,000 from the Church of God of Ross Mills and at the same time to reject an equally bona fide offer of $3,000 from the grange. Although we respect the desire of the commissioner to uphold, if possible, the action taken by the district meeting, since the meeting lacked power to do what it did, the commissioner's confirmation was thus, in a legal sense, purely arbitrary, and thus reviewable in court. . . . The order appealed from should be reversed and the determinations of the Commissioner of Education and of the board of education approving the sale to the Church of God of Ross Mills should be annulled, with costs to appellants in this court and in the Appellate Division.

The order of the Appellate Division should be reversed and that of Special Term reinstated, with costs in this court and in the Appellate Division.

NOTES

1. At each of the three appellate steps there was a reversal.

2. The state commissioner of education sustained the board's action. Is this type of question an appropriate one for a chief state school officer?

CHAPTER 7

TORTS

INTRODUCTION

Torts, civil wrongs other than disputes involving contracts, arise when individuals suffer harm or loss due to the improper conduct of others. The major types of torts impacting on school boards, their members, employees, and students are negligence, where conduct unintentionally fails to meet an acceptable standard of care, thereby resulting in injury; intentional torts including assault, battery, false imprisonment, defamation, and intentional infliction of emotional distress; and strict liability, where injuries result due to the creation of unusual hazards and liability is imposed without fault. While the most frequent common law tort, negligence, has generated a significant body of case law, violations of civil rights constitute an expanding area of liability under 42 U.S.C. section 1983 (section 1983).[1]

DOCTRINE OF BOARD NON-LIABILITY

At common law, school boards are not liable for torts committed by their members, agents, or employees. In light of increasing dissatisfaction with this principle, many jurisdictions modified this doctrine legislatively and/or judicially.

Non-liability, or immunity, based on the common law principle that the state is sovereign and cannot be sued without its consent, has been supplemented by statute. In upholding the aggregate cap in the state's Governmental Immunity Act after two students were killed and three others were seriously injured in a car accident while returning from an out-of-state extracurricular debate tournament, the Supreme Court of Utah reiterated the general rule as to immunity. The court declared that "[t]he right to sue in tort a school district or any other governmental entity engaging in a governmental function does not qualify as . . . a fundamental right."[2]

The doctrine of non-liability applies to subordinate state agencies such as school boards under the theory that they are arms of the state carrying

---

1. This statute is in the Appendix.

2. *Tindley v. Salt Lake City School Dist.*, 116 P.3d 295 [200 Educ. L. Rep. 406] (Utah 2005).

out governmental functions.[3] Board immunity for tort liability is derived from the concept of sovereignty. Even so, many courts and states have identified grounds other than that "the sovereign can do no wrong" to support immunity. One basis for avoiding liability is that the law does not provide funds to pay for damages against boards since money raised for education may not be diverted to cover the costs of tort claims since such payments are not expenditures for school purposes. Another rationale is that when torts occur, boards cannot be liable if those who acted on their behalf exceeded the scope of their lawful authority. Board immunity for the acts of their employees is grounded in the notion that no master-servant or *respondeat superior* relationship exists that would render boards liable for the acts of their employees even if they act within the scope of their employment.

EXCEPTIONS TO DOCTRINE OF NON-LIABILITY

IN GENERAL

Immunity is a common law concept that is subject to statutory and judicial exceptions. Not surprisingly, statutory differences vary markedly from one jurisdiction to another. There is a great deal of controversy as to whether the legislative or judicial branches should make such changes. Since immunity has a lengthy history in the United States and has many ramifications, courts are reluctant to abandon it entirely. Courts that are unwilling to accept the concept of immunity in its entirety have recognized exceptions to the doctrine.

PROPRIETARY ACTS

A major exception to immunity occurs when courts impose liability on school boards and their employees for torts connected with their proprietary, but not governmental, functions.[4] This distinction emerges because governmental agencies serve dual capacities. In their governmental capacities boards exercise rights springing from sovereignty such that their acts are treated as political and governmental, thereby giving rise to immunity,[5] even if it is limited statutorily.[6] When boards or their employees perform proprietary functions that can be carried out by private persons, and that do not serve "the single and noble purpose ... [of] ... educating the children,"[7] they may face liability.

---

3. *See, e.g., Ex Parte Phenix City Board of Educ.*, 67 So.3d 56 [270 Educ. L. Rep. 923] (Ala. 2011) (reiterating that a board was entitled to constitutional immunity).

4. *But see Morningstar Water Users Ass'n v. Farmington Mun. School Dist. No. 5*, 901 P.2d 725, 729–30 [103 Educ. L. Rep. 443] (N.M.1995) (citing critiques from Justices Cardozo and Holmes about the advisability of continuing this distinction).

5. *See, e.g., Ledfors v. Emery County School Dist.*, 849 P.2d 1162 [82 Educ. L. Rep. 250] (Utah 1993); *Berler v. City of N.Y.*, 584 N.Y.S.2d 709 [75 Educ. L. Rep. 1166] (N.Y.Sup.Ct.App. Term 1992).

6. *Anderson v. Blankenship*, 790 F.Supp. 695 [75 Educ. L. Rep. 300] (E.D.Tex.1992).

Even courts that recognize the dichotomy between governmental and proprietary functions[8] do little more than classify acts in one category or the other. Due to this lack of judicial clarity, it is often difficult to evaluate under which category acts appear until courts have resolved disputes. In fact, legislative action may require the judiciary to differentiate between governmental and proprietary functions. For example, after the legislature enacted a law providing immunity where a state agency was discharging the governmental duty of highway construction, the Supreme Court of Michigan reasoned that the concept of "governmental functions," undefined in the statute, is a term of art used to describe "those activities of government which due to their public nature should not give rise to liability at common law."[9] The following cases illustrating the proprietary-governmental distinction highlight the challenge facing courts as they seek to distinguish between the two.

Claims often arise when individuals are injured while attending events at school facilities. The Supreme Court of Arizona intervened in a dispute where a spectator who was seriously hurt due to a faulty railing at a football game sued two school boards that rented a stadium from a third system. The court found that insofar as the third board charged a rental fee for the use of the stadium, thereby abandoning its governmental role and embarking on a proprietary activity, it was liable for the spectator's injuries.[10]

Conversely, where a spectator was injured when bleacher seats collapsed during a football game, the Supreme Court of Michigan expressly refused to follow the case from Arizona in denying the plaintiff's claim.[11] The court affirmed that insofar as the spectator was injured in a stadium owned by the home team, which did not intend to make a profit from its admission fee, it was merely promoting an educational activity that entitled it to immunity. Similarly, the Supreme Court of Virginia affirmed that where a board was statutorily authorized to lease school property, including the renting of its auditorium for concerts, it was not liable for injuries that a spectator sustained when she slipped and fell in an aisle since the board never abandoned its governmental capacity.[12] In defining the governmental-proprietary test as whether a function tended to promote the cause of education, the court was satisfied that leasing the auditorium for the concert was permissible since it stimulated and fostered student interest.[13]

---

7. *Allen v. Salina Broadcasting*, 630 S.W.2d 225, 227 [3 Educ. L. Rep. 779] (Mo.Ct.App. 1982).

8. *Boyd By and Through Boyd v. Gulfport Mun. Separate School Dist.*, 821 F.2d 308 [40 Educ. L. Rep. 112] (5th Cir.1987).

9. *Thomas v. State Highway Dep't*, 247 N.W.2d 530, 532 (Mich.1976).

10. *Sawaya v. Tucson High School Dist.*, 281 P.2d 105 (Ariz.1955).

11. *Richards v. School Dist. of City of Birmingham*, 83 N.W.2d 643 (Mich.1957).

12. *Kellam v. School Bd. of the City of Norfolk*, 117 S.E.2d 96 (Va.1960).

13. *See also Smith v. Board of Educ. of City of Marietta*, 167 S.E.2d 615 (Ga.Ct.App.1969) (affirming that the operation of a public school auditorium, primarily for the use and benefit of the public, was a governmental function even though the board may have received some incidental revenue from the rentals).

The Supreme Court of Kansas affirmed that a board engaged in a governmental function when it allowed its community room to be used for a county agricultural extension program.[14] In denying relief to a participant who fell and was injured in an unlighted stairway, the court decided that insofar as the use of the building was governmental, the only duty that the board owed users was to refrain from wilfully and wantonly causing them to be injured. An appellate court in Texas reached the same result in pointing out that a board was not liable for injuries that a spectator sustained when she slipped on bleachers while attending a play-off football game.[15] The court explained that the board's renting of its stadium to two other school systems was not a proprietary action insofar as doing so benefitted students in the state.

On the other hand, the Supreme Court of Pennsylvania determined that when a school board conducted a summer recreation program that was open to the general public, it took on a proprietary function.[16] The court noted that insofar as the board charged a fee for a program that it was not statutorily required to offer, and which could have been provided by a private firm, it was liable for injuries that a child sustained while participating in its activities. The same court eventually abolished the common law immunity of school boards.[17] Later, an appellate court in North Carolina ruled that officials were not liable for head injuries that a child suffered as a participant in a voluntary after school enrichment program for which there was a weekly fee.[18] The court remarked that insofar as the program was an undertaking traditionally provided by local government, staff members who were sued in their official capacities were entitled to immunity.

NUISANCES

Individuals who are injured due to the alleged failures of educators to keep school premises in safe conditions may file suit under an exception, recognized in some jurisdictions, which permits recoveries against boards for maintaining nuisances. While there is a lack of judicial clarity over the meaning of nuisance, courts have extended it to forms of annoyance or inconvenience that interfere with common public rights. A nuisance, in the words of the Supreme Court of Errors of Connecticut, "involves as an essential element that it can be the natural tendency of the act or thing complained of to create dangers and inflict injury upon person or property."[19] Since they may have their origins in negligence, it is sometimes difficult to decide which acts constitute nuisances.

Even though the responsibility for maintaining nuisances seems to be treated as an exception to the general rule of non-liability, the basis for this

---

14. *Smith v. Board of Educ. of Caney School Dist. No. 34*, 464 P.2d 571 (Kan. 1970).

15. *Fowler v. Tyler Indep. School Dist.*, 232 S.W.3d 335 [224 Educ. L. Rep. 513] (Tex. Ct. App. 2007), *review denied* (2007).

16. *Morris v. School Dist. of Township of Mount Lebanon*, 144 A.2d 737 (Pa. 1958).

17. *Ayala v. Philadelphia Bd. of Pub. Educ.*, 305 A.2d 877 (Pa. 1973).

18. *Schmidt v. Breeden*, 517 S.E.2d 171 [136 Educ. L. Rep. 1063] (N.C. Ct. App. 1999).

19. *Laspino v. City of New Haven*, 67 A.2d 557, 558 (Conn. 1949).

exception is unclear. Some courts believe that if officials of public agencies, such as school boards, mismanage the properties for which they are responsible, they are liable for damages to other persons or their property. Other courts have written that one explanation for the difference between liability for nuisance and non-liability for negligence is that in most situations boards may, by judicial decree, be required to abate nuisances without undue hardship on their part. If individuals sue boards for damages, the usual arguments in favor of immunity apply. To this end, an appellate court in Georgia affirmed that the same immunity that protected boards and their officials applied equally to claims in negligence and nuisance.[20]

Another possible factor contributing to school board liability is that nuisances usually impact property rights that the courts carefully guard. In older cases, courts agreed that the discharge of sewage into a stream[21] and the maintenance of a defective privy well on school property were nuisances.[22] Courts have since refused to find boards liable for creating nuisances where a student was injured in a woodworking class;[23] where piles of snow remained in a school playground after a parking lot was plowed;[24] and where a baseball field was constructed at an elementary school.[25]

Liability Insurance and Immunity

Courts are unable to agree on whether school boards waive their governmental immunity from tort liability by purchasing insurance. Some courts do not consider purchasing insurance a waiver of immunity for a variety of reasons.[26] For instance, an appellate court in North Carolina affirmed that when a board purchased liability insurance it did not waive its governmental immunity.[27] The court pointed out that the insurance policy expressly stipulated that the board was not waiving its immunity. On the flip side, although preserving district funds is the basic modern justification for retaining immunity, since this reason is at least weakened, if not

---

20. *Dollar v. Dalton Pub. Schools*, 505 S.E.2d 789 [130 Educ. L. Rep. 330] (Ga. Ct. App. 1998).

21. *Watson v. New Milford*, 45 A. 167 (Conn. 1900).

22. *Briegel v. City of Philadelphia*, 19 A. 1038 (Pa. 1890).

23. *Burke v. Austin Indep. School Dist.*, 709 F.Supp. 120 [52 Educ. L. Rep. 1046] (W.D. Tex. 1987).

24. *Hendricks v. Southfield Pub. Schools*, 444 N.W.2d 143 [55 Educ. L. Rep. 729] (Mich. Ct. App. 1989).

25. *Paredes v. City of North Bay Village*, 693 So.2d 1153 [118 Educ. L. Rep. 796] (Fla. Dist. Ct. App. 1997).

26. *See, e.g., Grayson County Bd. of Educ. v. Casey*, 157 S.W.3d 201 [196 Educ. L. Rep. 975] (Ky. 2005); *Crisp County School Sys. v. Brown*, 487 S.E.2d 512 [119 Educ. L. Rep. 722] (Ga. Ct. App. 1997); *Barr v. Bernhard*, 562 S.W.2d 844 (Tex.1978).

27. *Magana v. Charlotte–Mecklenburg Bd. of Educ.*, 645 S.E.2d 91 [220 Educ. L. Rep. 938] (N.C. Ct. App. 2007). *See also Lail ex rel. Jestes v. Cleveland County Bd. of Educ.*, 645 S.E.2d 180 [220 Educ. L. Rep. 941] (N.C. Ct. App. 2007).

obviated, when boards purchase insurance policies to protect their funds, other courts permit recovery up to the maximum of their coverage.[28]

In jurisdictions where immunity has not been limited, there appears to be no reason to purchase liability insurance to protect boards except, perhaps, in anticipation of judicial abrogation of the doctrine if it exists solely in common law. Absent statutes permitting boards to purchase insurance, such actions could constitute illegal expenditures of funds. In such a case, the highest court of West Virginia permitted a successor school board to recover premiums from an insurance company.[29] Where state law granted boards the authority to furnish transportation for children but did not authorize them to carry liability insurance on school buses, the court held that the original board made an improper expenditure since there was nothing against which the policy of indemnification could operate. The court concluded that the insurance company had to return the premiums to the board.

ABROGATION OF THE DOCTRINE OF NON-LIABILITY

JUDICIALLY

Courts have agreed that insofar as the rule of governmental immunity from tort liability was created judicially, they can abrogate it if legislatures remain silent. The Supreme Court of Illinois was the first to repudiate this doctrine in a personal injury suit filed on behalf of a student who was hurt due to the negligence of a school bus driver.[30] Having considered the history of immunity and the bases on which it rested, the court was of the opinion that the doctrine was no longer appropriate. In so doing, the court placed school boards in the same legal situation as private corporations that can be sued for injuries caused by the negligence of their officers, agents, or employees. However, the same court subsequently observed that the state legislature repudiated this order and set a maximum amount for such recoveries.[31]

Conversely, even after arguing that governmental immunity was unacceptable, the Supreme Judicial Court of Massachusetts refused to abrogate it because "the Legislature should be afforded an opportunity to do this by a comprehensive statute."[32] When the legislature refused to act, the court expressed its intent to abrogate the doctrine in the first appropriate case

---

28. *See, e.g., Brewer By and Through Brewer v. Independent School Dist. No. 1*, 848 P.2d 566 [81 Educ. L. Rep. 1093] (Okla.1993); *Crowell v. School Dist. No. 7 of Gallatin County*, 805 P.2d 522 [65 Educ. L. Rep. 919] (Mont.1991); *Brown v. Egan Consol. School Dist. No. 50–2*, 449 N.W.2d 259 [57 Educ. L. Rep. 1017] (S.D.1989).

29. *Board of Educ. of Raleigh County v. Commercial Cas. Ins. Co.*, 182 S.E. 87 (W.Va. 1935). *See also Awe v. University of Wyo.*, 534 P.2d 97 (Wyo. 1975).

30. *Molitor v. Kaneland Community Unit Dist. No. 302*, 163 N.E.2d 89 (Ill.1959), *cert. denied*, 362 U.S. 968, 80 S.Ct. 955, 4 L.Ed.2d 900 (1960).

31. *See Woodfield Lanes v. Village of Schaumburg*, 523 N.E.2d 36 (Ill.App.Ct.1988), *appeal denied*, 530 N.E.2d 267 (Ill.1988) (citing to the creation of the Illinois Tort Immunity Act).

32. *Morash and Sons v. Commonwealth*, 296 N.E.2d 461, 468 (Mass.1973).

following the end of the next legislative session unless that body "acted definitively as to the doctrine"[33] and planned to make the abrogation retroactive to the date of the case in which it first criticized the doctrine. Not surprisingly, the legislature enacted a law permitting some tort claims, excluding those involving the exercise of discretionary functions.[34]

LEGISLATIVELY

Legislatures have adopted a variety of approaches in modifying the doctrine of non-liability as some imposed liability for selected activities. To this end, "safe place" laws require owners of public buildings to construct and maintain them in a manner that they are safe for employees and others.[35] As reflected in some of the cases reviewed in this chapter, legislatures have completely abrogated the common law doctrine, thereby placing school boards on the same plane as individuals and private corporations.[36] For example, the Supreme Court of Ohio thought that pursuant to a former exception to sovereign immunity that expressly imposed liability, a board may be liable when the failure of one of its officials to report a teacher's sexual abuse of a minor, in violation of the state's reporting statute, proximately results in the teacher's sexually abusing another minor student.[37]

Some courts have abolished the general doctrine of non-liability but made exceptions precluding liability in specific activities such as those involving high degrees of discretion. By way of illustration, the Supreme Court of Georgia ruled that school board members and officials were entitled to immunity even though they failed to adopt a school safety plan under state law.[38] In a dispute where parents filed suit after their son was severely injured by a peer, the court explained that insofar as preparing the statutorily mandated safety plan was a discretionary, rather than a ministerial, act, neither the board nor officials could be liable for failing to act. However, where a school employee allowed a fourteen-year-old female to leave school with a middle aged man who falsely claimed to be her uncle and later raped her, an appellate court in Georgia refused to grant the educator's motion for official immunity.[39] The court held that insofar as the employee failed to perform her ministerial duty to ensure the student's safety, she was not entitled to immunity. Yet, the Supreme Court of Ohio held that when a player was injured in a baseball practice in a school

---

33. *Whitney v. City of Worcester*, 366 N.E.2d 1210, 1211 (Mass. 1977).

34. *See Cady v. Plymouth–Carver Reg'l School Dist.*, 457 N.E.2d 294 [14 Educ. L. Rep. 1091] (Mass. Ct. App. 1983).

35. *See, e.g.*, OHIO REV. CODE ANN. § 4167.09; WISC. STAT. ANN. § 101.11.

36. *See, e.g.*, *Granville v. Minneapolis Pub. Schools*, 732 N.W.2d 201 [220 Educ. L. Rep. 850] (Minn. 2007) (holding that a school board was not entitled to an immunity defense since the legislature had failed to revive the statute after it expired in 1974).

37. *Yates v. Mansfield Bd. of Educ.*, 808 N.E.2d 861 [187 Educ. L. Rep. 1005] (Ohio 2004).

38. *Murphy v. Bajjani*, 647 S.E.2d 54 [221 Educ. L. Rep. 904] (Ga. 2007). *See also Leake v. Murphy*, 644 S.E.2d 328 [220 Educ. L. Rep. 377] (Ga. Ct. App. 2007) (affirming that a board was not liable when a person with a hammer attacked a student in school since it had a school safety plan in place).

39. *Cotton v. Smith*, 714 S.E.2d 55 [270 Educ. L. Rep. 885] (Ga. Ct. App. 2011).

gymnasium, the board was not liable because the coach exercised his judgment and discretion in the use of equipment and facilities.[40]

Other legislatures have modified immunity by indirection through the operation of "save harmless" statutes.[41] These laws require school boards to defend, at their own expense, charges against staff arising out of damage claims for their allegedly tortious acts. Under such statutes, boards must pay judgments that may be recovered against employees who act within the scope of their duties. Still, boards and/or their employees may be covered by general legislation modifying governmental tort immunity.

BY THE SUPREME COURT FOR SECTION 1983 CASES

The Supreme Court handed down a series of judgments on the limits of immunity, the liability of board members, and, by extension, other school officials for constitutional torts under the extensive reach of section 1983. Section 1983, which became law as part of the Civil Rights Act of 1871,[42] was designed to provide a remedy for those whose federally protected civil rights, most notably freed slaves during Reconstruction, were violated. Insofar as plaintiffs can recover monetary awards and attorney fees[43] pursuant to section 1983, it offers protection to those whose civil rights have been violated by school officials.

In *Wood v. Strickland* (*Wood*), a case of first impression from Arkansas on the procedural due process rights of students who were subjected to long-term suspensions, the Supreme Court found that school board members may be sued under section 1983. The Court reasoned that granting board members absolute immunity from damages claims would have invalidated much of the promise of section 1983. The Court also considered the need for board members to exercise their "judgment independently, forcefully, and in a manner best serving the long-term interest of the school and the students."[44] Asserting that state courts permit damages claims for bad faith or malicious acts to proceed, the Justices recognized a federal cause of action against board members who act out with "ignorance or disregard of settled, indisputable law."[45] In softening the impact of its judgment, the Court added that board members could be liable for damages only if they "acted with such an impermissible motivation or with such disregard of the student's clearly established constitutional rights that his action cannot reasonably be characterized as being in good faith."[46] On remand, the

---

40.   *Elston v. Howland Schools*, 865 N.E.2d 845 [219 Educ. L. Rep. 242] (Ohio 2007).

41.   *See, e.g.,* CONN. GEN. STAT. ANN. § 10–236a; 14 DEL. CODE ANN. § 1095; 9; FLA. STAT. ANN. § 1012.85; 105 ILL. COMP. STAT. ANN. 5/34A–602; N.J. STAT. ANN. § 18A:12–20; MCKINNEY'S EDUC. LAW § 2561; 24 PA. STAT. ANN. § 24–2451.

42.   The statute was originally known as section 1983 of the Klu Klux Klan Act of April 20, 1871, "An Act to Enforce the Provisions of the Fourteenth Amendment to the Constitution of the United States, and for other Purposes."

43.   42 U.S.C.A. § 1988(b) addresses attorney fees.

44.   420 U.S. 308, 320, 95 S.Ct. 992, 43 L.Ed.2d 214 (1975), *reh'g denied*, 421 U.S. 921, 95 S.Ct. 1589, 43 L.Ed.2d 790 (1975), *on remand, sub nom. Strickland v. Inlow*, 519 F.2d 744 (8th Cir.1975). [Case No. 40]

45.   *Id.* at 321.

46.   *Id.* at 322.

Eighth Circuit decided that insofar as school officials violated the students' rights to due process, the case had to be returned to the trial court for further consideration.[47] In *Gebser v. Lago Vista Independent School District*,[48] the Court applied language that was similar to *Wood*, pointing out that educators can be liable for sexual harassment in schools only if they acted with deliberate indifference to allegations of which they were aware.

At issue in *Carey v. Piphus*[49] was whether board members in Illinois could have been liable for damages for violating the procedural due process rights of students who were suspended. The Supreme Court unanimously posited that although violations of procedural due process could trigger suits without proof of actual damages, alleged victims must prove damages in order to collect more than nominal awards if the behavior of school officials is ultimately justified. While conceding that the common law concept of compensatory damages for violations of legal rights applied to section 1983 cases, the Court specified that they could not be presumed in all circumstances solely on violations of due process.

The Supreme Court expanded the reach of section 1983 in *Monell v. Department of Social Services of City of New York (Monell)*,[50] a case challenging policies requiring employees who were pregnant to take unpaid leaves of absence before being required to do so for medical reasons. The Court decreed that insofar as local governments, including school boards, are "persons" under section 1983, they may be sued under its provisions. Since inconsistencies developed over the years, particularly in disputes involving school boards, the Justices re-examined the legislative history of section 1983, remarking that Congress did not intend to grant absolute immunity to local governmental bodies. The Court declined the opportunity to address whether local governments could be afforded some degree of immunity short of absolute immunity. Even so, the Court stated that local governments may not be sued for injuries that were inflicted solely by their employees or agents. Echoing the language of section 1983, the Court was of the view that public bodies can be liable only when their policies or customs inflict the injuries of deprivations of rights, privileges, or immunities secured by the Constitution and laws.

Two years later, the Supreme Court answered *Monell's* open question. Where a former police chief alleged that he was discharged in violation of his substantive and procedural due process rights, in *Owen v. City of Independence, Missouri*,[51] the Justices ascertained that local government officials were not entitled to qualified immunity based on good faith. The Court asserted that if constitutional violations committed in good faith

---

47. *Strickland v. Inlow*, 519 F.2d 744 (8th Cir.1975).

48. 524 U.S. 274, 118 S.Ct. 1989, 141 L.Ed.2d 277 [125 Educ. L. Rep. 1055] (1998). [Case No. 100]

49. 435 U.S. 247, 98 S.Ct. 1042, 55 L.Ed.2d 252 (1978). [Case No. 41]

50. 436 U.S. 658, 98 S.Ct. 2018, 56 L.Ed.2d 611 (1978).

51. 445 U.S. 622, 100 S.Ct. 1398, 63 L.Ed.2d 673 (1980). *See also Maine v. Thiboutot*, 448 U.S. 1, 100 S.Ct. 2502, 65 L.Ed.2d 555 (1980) (holding that officials who acted under color of state law violated the rights of parents in denying them aid to families with dependent children).

were not subject to damages claims, public officials could have thwarted section 1983's purposes. According to the Court, it was fairer to allocate financial burdens to the costs of government borne by all taxpayers than to allow the impact to fall solely on those whose rights were violated. The Court contended that insofar as doctrines of tort law changed significantly over the past century, views of governmental responsibility should reflect this evolution.

One result of the Supreme Court's reliance on the subjective "impermissible motivation" limit on qualified immunity in *Wood* was that it called for trials with the effect that insofar as section 1983 suits against school, and other public, officials could not be disposed of by summary judgment, the judiciary was becoming unduly burdened by insubstantial claims. Acknowledging this difficulty in *Harlow v. Fitzgerald*, a case from the District of Columbia over a civilian's allegedly unlawful discharge from working for the Air Force, the Justices eliminated the subjective standard. The Court left the objective standard in place which requires defendants to prove that they did not "violate clearly established constitutional or statutory rights of which a reasonable person would have known."[52] The Court was persuaded that officials who violate this objective standard are not entitled to immunity.

In a case that may have a significant impact on the application of section 1983, the Sixth Circuit affirmed that the Michigan Athletic Association's use of differential scheduling for girls' high school sports seasons, but not for male, violated equal protection.[53] On appeal, the Supreme Court vacated the Sixth Circuit's judgment[54] in light of *Rancho Palos Verdes v. Abrams* (*Abrams*).[55] In *Abrams*, the Court wrote that a petitioner could not file suit under section 1983 since the telecommunications statute at issue provided a remedy. On remand, the Sixth Circuit affirmed that Title IX did not provide the advocacy group challenging the rule with its exclusive remedy since the group's reliance on section 1983 to enforce the equal protection claim, rather than Title IX charge, negated its preclusion argument.[56] Since school boards are often sued under section 1983, even though other federal laws provide statutory remedies, the Sixth Circuit's judgment aside, if other courts follow *Abrams'* suggestion that plaintiffs cannot rely on section 1983 to file constitutional claims, it could have a major impact on school-related claims.

---

52. 457 U.S. 800, 818, 102 S.Ct. 2727, 73 L.Ed.2d 396 (1982).

53. *Communities for Equity v. Michigan High School Athletic Ass'n*, 377 F.3d 504 [190 Educ. L. Rep. 67] (6th Cir.2004).

54. *Michigan High School Athletic Ass'n v. Communities for Equity*, 544 U.S. 1012, 125 S.Ct. 1973, 161 L.Ed.2d 845 (2005).

55. *City of Rancho Palos Verdes, Cal. v. Abrams*, 544 U.S. 113, 125 S.Ct. 1453, 161 L.Ed.2d 316 (2005), *on remand*, 406 F.3d 1094 (9th Cir.2005).

56. *Communities for Equity v. Michigan High School Athletic Ass'n*, 459 F.3d 676 [212 Educ. L. Rep. 56] (6th Cir.2006), *cert. denied*, 549 U.S. 1322, 127 S.Ct. 1912, 167 L.Ed.2d 566 (2007).

REESTABLISHMENT OF NON-LIABILITY BY STATE STATUTE

After an initial wave of litigation abrogating immunity, state legislatures re-established at least portions of it for officials who act within the scope of their authority.[57] Yet, since the courts have the power to review legislative actions, tensions can arise between the two branches of government. While legislation ordinarily treats immunity directly, the Supreme Court of Alabama, conceding that the legislature is the appropriate body to make policy in the field of governmental immunity, ruled that it was conferred by a statute that empowered school boards to file suit but that did not mention that they were immune from liability if sued.[58]

The common law doctrine of non-liability of governmental bodies does not extend to employees.[59] Legislatures can still grant at least a measure of immunity to employees[60] and, even if they do not prevent suits against employees, can provide indemnification for monetary judgments if they are liable.[61]

On three occasions, the Supreme Court of Illinois interpreted legislation placing teachers squarely *in loco parentis* with regard to students and provided that boards were not liable for acts of employees unless the individuals were also at fault. Insofar as parents are liable to their children only in the case of wilful and wanton misconduct, the statute makes this the standard that plaintiffs must meet to establish teacher liability.[62] In later cases, the court declared that boards may be liable even if no *in loco parentis* relationship existed at the site of an injury such as where a person with a free pass to a football game was hurt when knocked to the ground by one of a large number of boisterous young people who were milling around[63] and where school officials allegedly provided a player with an inadequate and defective football helmet.[64]

NEGLIGENCE

IN GENERAL

Negligence is a common law tort involving fault when one's unintentional conduct breaches a duty of care and injures another person or

---

57. *See, e.g., Brown v. Wichita State Univ.*, 547 P.2d 1015 (Kan.1976); *English v. Newark Housing Auth.*, 351 A.2d 368 (N.J. Super. Ct. App. Div. 1976).

58. *Enterprise City Bd. of Educ. v. Miller*, 348 So.2d 782 (Ala. 1977).

59. *Baird v. Hosmer*, 347 N.E.2d 533 (Ohio 1976); *Sansone v. Bechtel*, 429 A.2d 820 (Conn. 1980).

60. *Kobylanski v. Chicago Bd. of Educ.*, 347 N.E.2d 705 (Ill.1976); *Barr v. Bernhard*, 562 S.W.2d 844 (Tex. 1978).

61. *Talmadge v. District School Bd. of Lake County*, 355 So.2d 502 (Fla.Dist.Ct.App.1978).

62. *Kobylanski v. Chicago Bd. of Educ.*, 347 N.E.2d 705 (Ill.1976).

63. *Tanari v. School Directors of Dist. No. 502, County of Bureau*, 373 N.E.2d 5 (Ill.1977).

64. *Gerrity v. Beatty*, 373 N.E.2d 1323 (Ill. 1978).

persons. In school settings, boards and their employees have the duty to protect students and others from reasonably foreseeable risks of harm. The duty of educators to supervise students, in particular, aside, neither boards nor teachers are insurers of student safety since most injuries in schools arise from what the law calls unavoidable, or pure, accidents, such as where one child unintentionally injured a classmate by kicking him in the ankle during a soccer game that they participated in as part of a physical education class.[65] Further, educators cannot reasonably be expected to supervise and control students continuously.[66] In such a case, an appellate court in California affirmed that a local board was not liable for the death of one child and the serious injuries that another sustained when an unlicensed motorist struck them as they passed through a marked cross-walk on the way to school.[67] The court ruled that absent officials' having assumed a specific responsibility for the students, the board was not liable for the harm that they suffered. While boards are responsible not only for students but also visitors to schools such as those making deliveries,[68] this section focuses primarily on the obligations that educational officials owe to students.

In order for school officials to be liable for negligence, injured parties must prove that educators failed to meet the elements of negligence: duty and the related concept of foreseeability, breach, injury, and causation. Moreover, school officials must have been unable to present a defense such as immunity, assumption of risk, and/or contributory/comparative negligence to help to reduce, or even eliminate, liability.

When reviewing the elements of negligence it is important to realize that they are not mutually exclusive. As such, many of the cases discussed in this chapter can be used to examine multiple points of law. Since the facts are essential in evaluating whether parties have breached their duties of care[69] and are negligent, the following discussion of exemplary cases helps to illustrate the array of issues dealing with student supervision in school settings.

DUTY

In the law of negligence, absent a legal relationship, one has no duty to act. However, if individuals voluntarily take on duties that they are under

---

65. *Paca v. City of N.Y.*, 858 N.Y.S.2d 772 [232 Educ. L. Rep. 913] (N.Y. App. Div. 2008). For like results involving other sports in gym classes, *see Knightner v. William Floyd Union Free School Dist.*, 857 N.Y.S.2d 726 [232 Educ. L. Rep. 346] (N.Y. App. Div. 2008) (dodgeball); *Odekirk v. Bellmore–Merrick Cent. School Dist.*, 895 N.Y.S.2d 184 [253 Educ. L. Rep. 840] (N.Y. App. Div. 2010) (floor hockey); *Acunia ex rel. Salgado v. New York City Dep't of Educ.*, 891 N.Y.S.2d 70 [251 Educ. L. Rep. 888] (N.Y. App. Div. 2009) (basketball).

66. *Mirand v. City of N.Y.*, 614 N.Y.S.2d 372 [92 Educ. L. Rep. 957] (1994).

67. *Cerna v. City of Oakland*, 75 Cal.Rptr.3d 168 [231 Educ. L. Rep. 389] (Cal. Ct. App. 2008), *reh'g denied* (2008), *review denied* (2008).

68. *Salerno v. North Colonie Cent. School Dist.*, 861 N.Y.S.2d 811 [234 Educ. L. Rep. 954] (N.Y. App. Div. 2008) (affirming a board's motion for summary judgment where an employee of a distribution company was allegedly injured while delivering bottled water to a high school).

69. *See Travis v. Bohannon*, 115 P.3d 342 [199 Educ. L. Rep. 942] (Wash. Ct. App. 2005) (reiterating the general rule that whether school officials satisfied the four elements of negligence was a question of fact for a jury).

no obligation to assume, they may be liable for failing to follow through. In a case of this type, an appellate court in New York affirmed the denial of a motion for summary judgment where a school nurse volunteered to assist a ten-year-old child who was injured when she fell in a school playground.[70] The court explained that once the nurse voluntarily intervened, she had the duty to act with reasonable care such that she could be subject to liability for not staying with the student to help support her as she waited for her mother to get her car so that she could bring her child to a hospital for treatment.

Educators who act within the scope of their duties whether in classrooms, at other schools in districts, or as part of co-curricular or extracurricular activities, whether on campus or off, have a duty to assist all students even if they do not know an individual child or group of students personally. This duty arises based on educators' legal relationships with their school boards and is not limited to children (or others) from the buildings where they work.

Given the significance of the element of duty, it is safe to say that most negligence cases can be viewed in the broad context of adequacy of supervision. In theory, since adequate supervision should prevent students from being injured as a result of reasonably foreseeable dangers, all school activities must be supervised depending on such factors as the nature of the events and the ages of the children who are involved.

The Supreme Court of California addressed the question of adequate supervision when a student who was injured while playing at school during the day died that night.[71] Even though responsibility for supervising that area was assigned to members of the physical education department, the department head left supervision to whomever was in the gymnasium office rather than create a formal schedule. The court determined that the teacher on duty was eating lunch and preparing for classes at a desk that faced away from the students and that a wall obscured his view of the area where they were playing. In finding that there was evidence from which a jury could have uncovered negligence, the court noted that the mere fact that a student's misconduct was the cause of the injury did not necessarily absolve the teacher from a charge of negligent supervision.[72] Also, an appellate court in Pennsylvania affirmed that where a student severely injured his hand during a woodshop class, and the school board characterized the teacher's conduct as negligent supervision, the child was entitled to monetary damages.[73]

Once the law recognizes the existence of a legal relationship, educators have the duty to anticipate reasonably foreseeable injuries or risks to students and take reasonable steps to try to protect them from harm. Since foreseeability is a highly flexible concept that varies based on students' ages

---

70. *Hilts v. Board of Educ. of Gloversville Enlarged School Dist.*, 857 N.Y.S.2d 292 [232 Educ. L. Rep. 304] (N.Y. App. Div. 2008).

71. *Dailey v. Los Angeles Unified School Dist.*, 87 Cal.Rptr. 376 (Cal. 1970).

72. *See also Sheehan v. St. Peter's Catholic School*, 188 N.W.2d 868 (Minn. 1971).

73. *Wells v. Harrisburg Area School Dist.*, 884 A.2d 946 [203 Educ. L. Rep. 288] (Pa. Cmwlth. Ct. 2005).

and physical conditions as well as the degree of danger inherent in situations, the law does not expect educators to foresee all harms that might befall children. Rather, educators are responsible for only those mishaps that can reasonably be anticipated or of which they are actually aware. In Florida, an appellate court illustrated this point in affirming that a school board was liable where a kindergarten student was sexually assaulted in the class bathroom.[74] The court agreed that educators breached their duty when they failed to warn a substitute teacher that the assaulting child had a history of developmental problems and sexually aggressive behavior or to instruct the substitute about pass procedures used to restrict more than one student at a time from occupying the bathroom. On the other hand, the Supreme Court of Montana affirmed that a board was not liable for injuries that a pedestrian sustained when she was struck by a car driven by a student as she jogged near a high school.[75] The court refused to impose liability on the board because officials were unaware of the fact that almost eighteen months earlier the student expressed great interest in getting a driver's license so that he could do horrible things to others since it did not owe the pedestrian a foreseeable duty of care.

Whether an act is foreseeable cannot be based on speculation. If school officials take reasonable precautions, and intervening acts that could not have been foreseen occur, they are unlikely to be liable. For example, where teachers could not have anticipated that students were going to pull chairs out from under peers as they attempted to sit down, courts have refused to impose liability.[76] Other courts refused to impose liability on school boards for events that were not foreseeable, such as where a student slipped and was injured during a classroom skit;[77] where a high school student was injured when he ran, or was pushed, into another participant during a "frisbee relay race" in a physical education class;[78] where students engaged in spontaneous fighting;[79] where a child who was not a member of a group threw rocks at and injured a student who was a participant in an after school program that gathered on a playground;[80] where a child suddenly

---

74. *Miami–Dade County School Bd. v. A.N., Sr.*, 905 So.2d 203 [199 Educ. L. Rep. 1003] (Fla. Dist. Ct. App. 2005), *review denied*, 915 So.2d 1196 (Fla. 2005).

75. *Emanuel v. Great Falls School Dist.*, 209 P.3d 244 [245 Educ. L. Rep. 492] (Mont. 2009).

76. *Boyer v. Jablonski*, 435 N.E.2d 436 [4 Educ. L. Rep. 596] (Ohio Ct. App. 1980); *Tomlinson v. Board of Educ. of Elmira*, 583 N.Y.S.2d 664 [74 Educ. L. Rep. 1262] (N.Y. App. Div. 1992).

77. *Jones v. Jackson Pub. Schools*, 760 So.2d 730 [145 Educ. L. Rep. 845] (Miss. 2000).

78. *Siegell v. Herricks Union Free School Dist.*, 777 N.Y.S.2d 148 [187 Educ. L. Rep. 983] (N.Y. App. Div. 2004).

79. *Hernandez v. Christopher Robin Acad.*, 714 N.Y.S.2d 518 [147 Educ. L. Rep. 1057] (N.Y. App. Div. 2000); *Johnsen v. Carmel Cent. School Dist.*, 716 N.Y.S.2d 403 [149 Educ. L. Rep. 592] (N.Y. App. Div. 2000); *Dadich v. Syosset High School*, 717 N.Y.S.2d 634 [150 Educ. L. Rep. 234] (N.Y. App. Div. 2000).

80. *Rinehart ex rel. Combs v. Boys & Girls Club of Chula Vista*, 34 Cal.Rptr.3d 677 [202 Educ. L. Rep. 246] (Cal. Ct. App. 2005). *See also Fotiadis v. City of N.Y.*, 853 N.Y.S.2d 591 [230 Educ. L. Rep. 395] (N.Y. App. Div. 2008) (affirming that a board was not liable where a student was injured on falling from a swing since the child disregarded his mother's instruction to attend a program and was hurt while he was not in the control and custody of school officials).

and spontaneously kicked a friend while the two were on a school play-ground;[81] where a child struck a peer as they exited a school bus[82] unless one child was clearly the aggressor and school officials failed to intervene;[83] and where a high school student injured his thumb when a classmate spontaneously held a door shut as he tried to pull it open.[84] At the same time, depending on the facts, not all courts agree on whether boards should be liable if children are injured while using playground equipment.[85]

While the requisite level of supervision may decrease before the opening of school days and after students are dismissed, once officials know, or reasonably should know, that children are present, they must take precautions to ensure their safety. In an older case, the Supreme Court of Washington affirmed that a board was liable for injuries that a nine-year-old sustained when an upright piano fell on her after the class day ended.[86] The court recognized that insofar as the sixty-year-old piano was in a position that it could easily have tipped over, and it was foreseeable that small children would try to move it, the board was liable. Similarly, where a board operated a breakfast program but provided only one teacher for the first half hour after it opened for the day, an appellate court in Louisiana decided that it was responsible for the injuries that a child sustained when she fell in the school's playground prior to the start of classes.[87] Further, where a principal was aware that students were playing football before classes began because he directed them to play in the location where a child was injured, the Supreme Court of Idaho found that a trial was necessary to consider whether he breached his duty to supervise the students.[88]

As reflected by a case from the Supreme Court of New Jersey, disputes arise over the duty of care when children are dismissed from school. The court reinstated a suit where parents alleged that educators breached their duty of care when, as part of an early dismissal, their nine year-old son was struck by a car a few blocks from school and paralyzed from the neck down.[89] The court was of the opinion that even though the child's parents ignored the fact that their son was subject to early dismissal, educators still had the duty to exercise reasonable care in supervising students by creating

---

81. *Van Leuvan v. Rondout Valley Cent. School Dist.*, 798 N.Y.S.2d 770 [200 Educ. L. Rep. 295] (N.Y. App. Div. 2005).

82. *Murnyack v. Rebon*, 801 N.Y.S.2d 658 [202 Educ. L. Rep. 275] (N.Y.App.Div.2005).

83. *Shoemaker v. Whitney Point Cent. School Dist.*, 750 N.Y.S.2d 355 [171 Educ. L. Rep. 903] (N.Y.App.Div.2002), *leave to appeal dismissed*, 757 N.Y.S.2d 820 [175 Educ. L. Rep. 662] (N.Y.2003).

84. *Rose ex rel. Rose v. Onteora Cent. School Dist.*, 861 N.Y.S.2d 442 [234 Educ. L. Rep. 255] (N.Y.App.Div. 2008).

85. For cases rejecting board liability *see, e.g., Navarra v. Lynbrook Pub. Schools*, 733 N.Y.S.2d 730 [159 Educ. L. Rep. 717] (N.Y.App.Div.2001); *Sinto v. City of Long Beach*, 736 N.Y.S.2d 700 [161 Educ. L. Rep. 594] (N.Y.App.Div.2002). For a case rejecting a board's motion for summary judgment, *see Lemos v. City of Poughkeepsie School Dist.*, 749 N.Y.S.2d 88 [171 Educ. L. Rep. 332] (N.Y.App.Div.2002).

86. *Kidwell v. School Dist. No. 300, Whitman County*, 335 P.2d 805 (Wash. 1959).

87. *Laneheart v. Orleans Parish School Bd.*, 524 So.2d 138 [46 Educ. L. Rep. 1266] (La. Ct. App. 1988).

88. *Bauer v. Minidoka School Dist. No. 331*, 778 P.2d 336 [55 Educ. L. Rep. 748] (Idaho 1989).

89. *Jerkins ex rel. Jerkins v. Anderson*, 922 A.2d 1279 [219 Educ. L. Rep. 998] (N.J. 2007).

dismissal supervision policies, providing notice to parents of the policies, and complying with them in monitoring students through dismissal.

Conversely, where a child called his mother on a cell phone as he left school and she waved to him from across the road, an appellate court in New York affirmed that the board was not liable when he was struck by a vehicle as he attempted to cross in the middle of a block, under her direction, rather than at a designated, supervised location on school grounds.[90] The court pointed out that insofar as the board did not owe a custodial duty of care to the student, it could not be liable for his injuries. Previously, where a student was struck by a car after being chased off of school grounds by a peer before classes started, he and his mother failed in their negligence action against the board.[91] The Supreme Court of Kansas affirmed that the student could not recover for negligence absent evidence that officials affirmatively assumed a duty to render services to protect or supervise him before classes began since he was not in their custody or control.

Litigation often arises when students throw objects around schools and school grounds.[92] Where a child was struck in the eye by a paper clip that another student shot from a rubber band, the Supreme Court of New Jersey reasoned that the principal was liable for his injuries.[93] The court maintained that insofar as the principal was present at school but had not created rules for students as they gathered before entering classes, had not assigned teachers or others to assist him in supervising children at that time, and was engaged in activities other than overseeing the children when the accident took place, he was liable.

The Supreme Court of Wyoming reached the opposite result in declaring that a school board and a teacher's aid were not liable where a seven-year-old was partially blinded by a small rock, which was thrown by a peer and bounced off a larger rock, while the children were at recess.[94] The court observed that insofar as the aid who was supervising the playground where the accident occurred walked by the students about thirty seconds before the mishap took place but did not see anything out of the ordinary, and the injury was not foreseeable, neither she nor the board could be liable. In like fashion, an appellate court in Ohio affirmed that a board was not liable for a first-grader's injuries after he was struck in the eye by a dirt-ball thrown by a fourth-grader since the older child's action was not foreseeable.[95]

---

90. *Vernali v. Harrison Cent. School Dist.*, 857 N.Y.S.2d 699 [232 Educ. L. Rep. 343] (N.Y.App.Div.2008).

91. *Glaser ex rel. Glaser v. Emporia Unified School Dist. No. 253*, 21 P.3d 573 [152 Educ. L. Rep. 795] (Kan.2001).

92. For a case where a pedestrian filed suit after she claimed to have been struck, and injured, by a book that was thrown out of a school window, *see Almonte v. City of N.Y.*, 826 N.Y.S.2d 741 [215 Educ. L. Rep. 1030] (N.Y.App.Div.2006) (affirming that a board was not liable where the plaintiff was unable to demonstrate that educators created a dangerous condition).

93. *Titus v. Lindberg*, 228 A.2d 65 (N.J.1967).

94. *Fagan v. Summers*, 498 P.2d 1227 (Wyo.1972).

95. *Allison v. Field Local School Dist.*, 553 N.E.2d 1383 [60 Educ. L. Rep. 191] (Ohio Ct.App.1988).

As reflected by two cases from New York, snowballs can create unique controversies. In the first, the state's highest court refused to impose liability on school officials for the injury a child sustained when he was struck by a snowball that was thrown on school property while he was returning from lunch recess.[96] The court acknowledged that while there was a school rule against throwing snowballs and the injured child's teacher warned students not to do so, the board was not liable because officials were unaware of any special danger and there was no proof that the teacher knew of other snowball throwing on the day of the incident. The court went so far as to comment that although no one grows up in New York without throwing, or being hit by, snowballs, it would have required educators to engage in intensive policing, almost child by child, to take all snowball throwing out of play activity. On the other hand, two years later, an appellate court in New York upheld a jury verdict of negligence in another snowball case.[97] In distinguishing its factual setting from the previous case, the court posited that educators knew, or should have known, of hard frozen snow or ice in the school yard that caused the child's injury. The court pointed out that there was evidence of inadequate supervision of the school yard when the child was injured by an iceball after becoming the target for a large number of students who gathered to play.

In a case overlapping with the section on sports and dangerous activities, when a sixteen-year-old female high school football player suffered serious internal injuries after being tackled cleanly by a player from the other team, she and her mother sued their school board for negligent supervision.[98] Even though it voiced its concern over the seriousness of the student's injuries, an appellate court in Maryland affirmed that the board did not have a duty to warn her or her mother of the risks posed by her voluntary participation in interscholastic football because the foreseeable risk of injury was normal and obvious.

As violence continues to rear its ugly head in and around school activities, parties increasingly file suit in attempts to render school officials liable for harm to students. For instance, the tragic shootings at Columbine High School in April 1999 that left fifteen people dead including a teacher and the two students who undertook the rampage, and injured others, gave rise to a series of unsuccessful lawsuits against the board and other public officials.[99]

Two cases illustrate the types of issues that educators face with regard to violence in and around schools. In Louisiana, the mother of a student who was shot and killed in a parking lot after a school-sponsored fund-

---

96. *Lawes v. Board of Educ. of City of N.Y.*, 266 N.Y.S.2d 364 (N.Y.1965).

97. *Cioffi v. Board of Educ. of City of N.Y.*, 278 N.Y.S.2d 249 (N.Y.App.Div.1967). *See also Thorne v. Burr*, 340 N.Y.S.2d 677 (N.Y.App.Div.1973).

98. *Hammond v. Board of Educ. of Carroll County*, 639 A.2d 223 [90 Educ. L. Rep. 256] (Md. Ct. Spec. App. 1994).

99. *See, e.g., Ruegsegger v. Jefferson County School Dist. R–1*, 187 F.Supp.2d 1284 [162 Educ. L. Rep. 796] (D.Colo.2001); *Rohrbough v. Stone*, 189 F.Supp.2d 1088 [163 Educ. L. Rep. 292] (D.Colo.2001), *reconsideration denied*, 189 F.Supp.2d 1144 (D. Colo.2002); *Schnurr v. Board of County Commr's*, 189 F.Supp.2d 1105 [163 Educ. L. Rep. 309] (D. Colo. 2001).

raising dance sued the board and the club where the event occurred over the alleged lack of security. An appellate court was satisfied that the board had not breached its duty of care since officials lacked the requisite degree of foreseeability that would have imposed a duty on them to provide additional security in the parking lot.[100] The court added that the club owner was not liable for the student's death since there was only slight foreseeability and gravity of harm from the criminal acts of a third party in the parking lot. Similarly, where a student was shot by an unknown assailant while leaving a dance at his high school cafeteria, an appellate court in New York affirmed a grant of summary judgment in favor of a board in his suit that sought to recover for his injuries.[101] The court agreed that the student's claim of inadequate supervision lacked merit since officials could not reasonably have foreseen that the shooting would take place.[102] Another appellate court in New York agreed that a student who was assaulted by a peer on his way home from school could not sue his board for failing to provide sufficient security to protect him from criminal activity since he was injured as he exited a subway and was not in the school's custody.[103]

In the first of two tragic cases, when a high school student with a history of truancy and drug abuse returned to school following a visit to the doctor but did not check back in, she was subsequently murdered in a premeditated act after she left campus without permission. The Supreme Court of Vermont, in the face of a wrongful death action filed by the deceased student's mother, affirmed a grant of summary judgment in favor of school officials.[104] The court explained that insofar as educators lacked the requisite notice or knowledge of the student's premeditated murder, it was not within the realm of foreseeable actions for which they could be liable. Similarly, the Supreme Court of Idaho affirmed the dismissal of charges in a case where a high school student was shot and killed by two of her male peers.[105] The court agreed that insofar as the risk of harm that the males presented to the deceased female was not foreseeable, the board did not have a duty to protect her from the shooting that occurred at night and off school grounds.

---

100. *Lee v. B & B Ventures*, 793 So.2d 215 [157 Educ. L. Rep. 428] (La. Ct. App. 2001), *writ denied*, 807 So.2d 236 (La. 2002).

101. *Jimenez v. City of N.Y.*, 738 N.Y.S.2d 380 [162 Educ. L. Rep. 500] (N.Y. App. Div. 2002). For other cases where school officials were not liable for the off-campus shooting deaths of students, *see, e.g., Hill v. Safford Unified School Dist.*, 952 P.2d 754 [124 Educ. L. Rep. 721] (Ariz. Ct. App. 1997); *Kindred v. Board of Educ. of Memphis City Schools*, 946 S.W.2d 47 [118 Educ. L. Rep. 1227] (Tenn. Ct. App. 1996).

102. *See also LaPage v. Evans*, 830 N.Y.S.2d 818 [217 Educ. L. Rep. 678] (N.Y. App. Div. 2007) (determining that where a fight on a school bus was unforeseeable neither the board nor the driver could be liable).

103. *Stagg v. City of N.Y.*, 833 N.Y.S.2d 188 [219 Educ. L. Rep. 203] (N.Y. App. Div. 2007).

104. *Edson v. Barre Supervisory Union #61*, 933 A.2d 200 [225 Educ. L. Rep. 959] (Vt. 2007).

105. *Stoddart v. Pocatello School Dist. #25*, 239 P.3d 784 [260 Educ. L. Rep. 925] (Idaho 2010). [Case No. 42]

BREACH

Two important elements must be taken into account when evaluating whether educators have breached their duty of care. The first relates to how educators performed, or failed to perform, their duties. More specifically, educators can breach their duties in one of two ways.[106] First, educators can breach their duties by not acting when they have duties to act; this is referred to as nonfeasance. Second, educators can breach their duties by failing to act properly when they have duties to act; this is known as misfeasance. In addition, where educators act improperly, or with evil intent, they commit malfeasance, an intentional tort, as in cases involving sexual misconduct with students.[107] Although malfeasance is mentioned here, it is important to keep in mind that it is an intentional tort, not an act of negligence. Additionally, if school officials are aware that employees are failing to meet their responsibilities, whether due to nonfeasance, misfeasance, or malfeasance, they, and their boards, may be liable for the tortious conduct of staff members.

The second major issue under breach is the appropriate standard of care educators must follow. In evaluating whether individuals have met the appropriate level of care, courts have adopted a common law standard of reasonableness. A flexible standard,[108] courts typically instruct juries to consider educators' behavior in light of the legal construct known as the reasonable person, also known as the reasonably prudent person.[109] While stopping short of establishing a clear hierarchy, based on education and years of experience working with children, reasonable teachers are likely to be expected to provide higher standards of care than reasonable persons but not to the same level of care as reasonable parents. In this way, courts have tried to create an objective standard requiring teachers to provide the same level of care as reasonably prudent professionals of similar education and background. This degree of care is ordinarily based on equivalent age, education, experience, maturity, and other relevant characteristics.

Cases involving sports highlight the need to apply the proper standard of care. When a high school football player who was being considered for an athletic scholarship to college broke his neck while correctly executing a block, the Court of Appeals of New York asserted that the coach should not have been judged under the same standard of care as a reasonably prudent parent.[110] The court indicated that insofar as the student voluntarily took

---

106. *See Lindberg ex rel. Conservator for Backlund v. United States*, 368 F.Supp.2d 1028, 1032 [198 Educ. L. Rep. 595] (D.S.D. 2005) ("negligence may be active or passive; it may consist of either doing something negligently or negligently failing to act.").

107. For a discussion of sexual harassment and misconduct involving students, *see* Chapter 13.

108. *See Simmons ex rel. Simmons v. Columbus County Bd. of Educ.*, 615 S.E.2d 69, 74 [199 Educ. L. Rep. 955] (N.C. Ct. App. 2005) (" 'The standard of due care is always the conduct of a reasonably prudent person under the circumstances. Although the standard remains constant, the proper degree of care varies with the circumstances.' "), citing *Bolkhir v. North Carolina State Univ.*, 365 S.E.2d 898, 900 [45 Educ. L. Rep. 393] (N.C. 1988).

109. This concept traces its origins to British common law, *Vaughan v. Menlove* (1837) 3 Bing. N.C. 468, 132 E.R. 490 (C.P.) (holding that Menlove's failure to exercise reasonable care led to the destruction of Vaughn's two cottages in a fire), where it was first identified as the "reasonable man" standard.

110. *Benitez v. New York City Bd. of Educ.*, 543 N.Y.S.2d 29 [54 Educ. L. Rep. 933] (N.Y. 1989). [Case No. 43]

part in the game, the coach met the less demanding standard of ordinary reasonable care. In addition, the court applied the defense of assumption of risk, concluding that insofar as the student-athlete voluntarily participated in the game and was aware of the possible risks involved, the coach was not liable.

In a like case, a high school football player sued his school board after his coaches, both of whom had teaching certificates and coaching endorsements, allowed him to return to a game in which he had suffered a concussion. The Supreme Court of Nebraska was of the view that the proper standard of care for the coaches was that of a reasonable person with a teaching certificate and coaching endorsement rather than the lower standard of the reasonable person who lacked such credentials.[111] The court remarked that insofar as coaches with coaching endorsements received specialized training in athletic injuries, including head injuries, they should have met the heightened standard of care. Following remand, the court ascertained that the coaches acted in accord with this higher standard since they evaluated the player several times before permitting him to return to the game and were familiar with the symptoms of a concussion.[112]

A second case from Nebraska involved a first-grade student who was injured while playing a game that his teacher had just taught his class. The state supreme court affirmed that the teacher failed to act in a way that a reasonably prudent person in her position should have because she did not provide direct supervision, even in the early portions of a game that the children were playing for the first time.[113]

INJURY

Before aggrieved parties can prevail in negligence actions, their injuries must be of the kind for which compensation can be awarded. For example, if a student who was running through a school hallway slipped and fell on water as it leaked from a drinking fountain that was accumulating on the floor for at least an hour, three factors need to be examined. The first question is whether school officials had a duty to keep the floor safe and clean. Assuming the obvious, that officials had such a duty, the question of foreseeability comes into play. Since officials should have foreseen that such an incident could have occurred, they should have had it cleaned up reasonably quickly. Second, the issue of the school's duty and possible breach, in terms of supervising the area, must be answered. The third concern is the nature of the child's injuries. If the child's only injury was a wet pair of pants, it is highly unlikely that his claim will proceed. However, if the child broke his leg on falling, there is a greater likelihood that this may be deemed an injury for which compensation can be awarded. Even so, in one such case illustrating the fact-specific nature of negligence cases, an

---

111. *Cerny v. Cedar Bluffs Junior/Senior Pub. School,* 628 N.W.2d 697 [155 Educ. L. Rep. 827] (Neb. 2001).

112. *Cerny v. Cedar Bluffs Junior/Senior Pub. School,* 679 N.W.2d 198 [187 Educ. L. Rep. 783] (Neb. 2004).

113. *Johnson v. School Dist. of Millard,* 573 N.W.2d 116 [123 Educ. L. Rep. 904] (Neb. 1998).

appellate court in New York ruled where it was raining or snowing for hours, and officials directed staff members to place a mat on a vestibule floor, a school board did not have a duty to cover the entire floor with mats and have the area mopped continuously where officials lacked actual or constructive notice that water was being tracked into the building.[114] The court thus dismissed the claim of a plaintiff who slipped and fell on a section of the wet floor.

Insofar as the existence of a physical harm is present in most of the cases discussed in this section, an unusual dispute from Louisiana exemplifies causation by focusing on the nature of an injury. An appellate court affirmed that a school board was liable for the emotional injuries that a kindergarten-aged child suffered when a physical education teacher told him that he hanged his friends with a jump rope.[115] The court thought that insofar as the evidence revealed that the child was a well-adjusted five-year-old before the teacher pretended that he hanged his friends to death with a jump rope while he was not present, he and his parents were entitled to damages for the emotional harm that he experienced.

CAUSATION

The final element in establishing liability for negligence is that school personnel must be the legal, or proximate cause, of injuries brought about by their breaches. Put another way, as situations evolve, the last person or group of persons in a temporal chain of events who could have taken steps to prevent injuries from occurring are typically considered as at least contributing to, if not actually the legal cause of, mishaps.

Litigation from New York demonstrates judicial analysis with regard to causation. When a student was stabbed by a peer while in her schoolyard three days after an earlier altercation, an appellate court in New York reversed an initial grant of summary judgment in favor of the board in a case combining issues of breach of duty and causation.[116] The court found that insofar as officials were on notice that such an incident might have occurred, their failure to act was the proximate cause of the student's injury. Conversely, a board challenged the denial of its motion for summary judgment in a case filed by a high school student who was assaulted in school after school hours by a former student. An appellate court in New York reversed in favor of the board on the ground that it was not liable absent a showing that the attack was foreseeable.[117] The court concluded not only that while there were previous trespassing incidents by former students after school hours, none involved physical violence against stu-

---

114. *Gonzalez–Jarrin v. New York City Dep't of Educ.*, 855 N.Y.S.2d 87 [231 Educ. L. Rep. 840] (N.Y. App. Div. 2008).

115. *Spears on Behalf of Spears v. Jefferson Parish School Bd.*, 646 So.2d 1104 [96 Educ. L. Rep. 884] (La. Ct. App. 1994). [Case No. 44]

116. *Walley v. Bivins*, 917 N.Y.S.2d 461 [264 Educ. L. Rep. 829] (N.Y. App. Div. 2011).

117. *Nossoughi v. Ramapo Cent. School Dist.*, 731 N.Y.S.2d 78 [157 Educ. L. Rep. 806] (N.Y. App. Div. 2001).

dents but also that any negligence by the school officials was not the proximate cause of the plaintiff's injuries.[118]

Insofar as two sets of circumstances, those involving athletics and off-campus activities, give rise to special concerns, these topics are addressed under their own headings.

ATHLETICS

It almost goes without saying that the greater the risk of injuries to students in activities such as interscholastic sports involving physical contact, the more carefully that school officials must provide supervision. Moreover, proper instruction before students engage in risky activities is particularly important.[119] Still, it is not essential for educators to instruct students about specific dangers of doing things that are clearly forbidden.[120]

An older case involved a physical education teacher's permitting two male students who were untrained in boxing to fight one round and part of another while he sat in the bleachers. When one of the students was fatally injured, an appellate court in New York affirmed that the teacher was liable both because he failed to teach them the proper principles of defense and since he was unable to supervise them properly from his seat in the bleachers.[121]

On the other hand, the Supreme Court of Missouri affirmed that when individuals are engaged in sports involving physical contact, such as wrestling, it is necessary to show in great detail what duty instructors failed to provide in damages actions.[122] The court decreed that general charges of failure to teach or designate rules are insufficient since plaintiffs must prove precisely how the omissions of educators led to the injuries that the children sustained or how the performance of omitted acts would have prevented the harm from occurring. In refusing to impose liability on the teacher, the court recognized that students who engage in activities such as wrestling are presumed to have assumed the risks inherent in the activity, a topic discussed below under the defenses to negligence.

A tragic case arose in Texas where parents claimed that school officials acted with deliberate indifference when their daughter died following the completion of a run during training activities for her high school basketball team.[123] The Fifth Circuit summarily affirmed an earlier order that since the parents failed to prove that educators acted with deliberate indifference

---

118. *See also Mastropolo v. Goshen Cent. School Dist.*, 837 N.Y.S.2d 236 [221 Educ. L. Rep.285] (N.Y. App. Div. 2007) (deciding that a student was the proximate cause of his own injury when he was injured as he jumped up and swung on pipes supporting a basketball backboard in knowing violation of school rules).

119. *Benitez v. New York City Bd. of Educ.*, 543 N.Y.S.2d 29 [54 Educ. L. Rep. 933] (N.Y. 1989) (also discussing assumption of risk). [Case No. 43]

120. *Payne v. North Carolina Dep't of Human Res.*, 382 S.E.2d 449 [55 Educ. L. Rep. 753] (N.C. Ct. App. 1989).

121. *La Valley v. Stanford*, 70 N.Y.S.2d 460 (N.Y. App. Div. 1947).

122. *Smith v. Consolidated School Dist. No. 2*, 408 S.W.2d 50 (Mo. 1966).

123. *Livingston v. DeSoto Indep. School Dist.*, 391 F.Supp.2d 463 [203 Educ. L. Rep. 665] (N.D. Tex. 2005), *aff'd*, 170 Fed.Appx 307 (5th Cir.2006).

to their daughter's well-being, the team's coach and trainer were entitled to qualified immunity.

Immunity as a defense aside, it is understandable that school officials seek to limit liability for student participation in activities that can cause injuries. As long as officials carefully craft release forms, courts are unwilling to impose liability.[124] At the same time, courts are likely to invalidate releases that are too broad or vague. For instance, the Supreme Court of Washington invalidated release forms that officials in different districts required students to sign before engaging in school-related activities such as interscholastic athletics. According to the court, the releases, which sought to protect the boards from all future negligence, violated public policy for a variety of reasons.[125] Similarly, an appellate court in New York invalidated a release form that was executed by parents of a child who participated in a youth wrestling activity which stipulated only that they absolved the president of the tournament and head coach of all risks beyond those inherent in wrestling.[126] The court affirmed that the release was void *ab initio* and did not bar their negligence action because it failed to limit liability plainly and precisely.

Educators must also provide adequate supervision at school-sponsored extracurricular activities. One of the most dramatic, albeit older, cases in this area arose when, as part of a club's initiation ceremony, a student who was subjected to an electric shock died. The Supreme Court of South Dakota contended that a teacher was personally liable since he actively participated in the initiation activities, even to the point of testing the electrical appliance.[127]

A dispute from New York illustrates how school officials have the duty to protect spectators at athletic events even if they occur off-campus; this case also serves as a segue to the next section. A high school student who was injured while watching a school-sponsored ice hockey game when a puck struck her in the nose filed a personal injury action against the rink owner and her school board claiming that the defendants breached their duty of care to keep her safe. On further review of the denial of the owner's motion for summary judgment, an appellate court in New York affirmed that the student's suit should have been able to proceed.[128] The court noted that genuine issues of material fact remained over whether the protective screening around the rink satisfied the owner's duty to protect the student and other spectators from flying pucks.

---

124. *Aaris v. Las Virgenes Unified School Dist.*, 75 Cal.Rptr.2d 801 [126 Educ. L. Rep. 350] (Cal. Ct. App.1998). *See also Sharon v. City of Newton*, 769 N.E.2d 738 [165 Educ. L. Rep. 742] (Mass. 2002).

125. *Wagenblast v. Odessa School Dist. No. 105–157–166J*, 758 P.2d 968 [48 Educ. L. Rep. 676] (Wash. 1988).

126. *Alexander v. Kendall Cent. School Dist.*, 634 N.Y.S.2d 318 [105 Educ. L. Rep. 262] (N.Y. App. Div. 1995).

127. *De Gooyer v. Harkness*, 13 N.W.2d 815 (S.D.1944).

128. *Guenther v. West Seneca Cent. School Dist.*, 796 N.Y.S.2d 465 [199 Educ. L. Rep. 363] (N.Y. App. Div. 2005).

OFF-PREMISES ACTIVITIES

The liability of school board personnel and/or boards for negligence depends on whether they have met their duty of care. The duty to supervise students on school grounds is clear. Efforts to extend the scope of duty beyond the premises are increasing. In this regard, it is important to emphasize that common law sets the duty of school officials as being coextensive with, and concomitant to, their physical custody and control over children.

Transportation

When boards provide transportation for children, since they owe students the highest duty of care,[129] their doing so in effect extends their boundaries via the bus to stops where students board and leave buses.[130] As can be expected, the use of school buses to transport students has generated litigation. As long as bus stops are not located in unreasonably dangerous places, boards are unlikely to be liable for injuries to children that occur there.[131] Boards also have no duty to ensure that students reach designated bus stops safely prior to the arrival of buses[132] and, as long as the distance from home is reasonable, children can be required to walk to bus stops.[133]

On homeward trips, bus drivers have the duty to see that children have crossed roads to the opposite sides of streets if necessary.[134] In such a case, an appellate court in Georgia rejected a board's motion for summary judgment in a mother's wrongful death action against it, the school bus driver, and the driver who struck and killed her daughter.[135] After the mother and other driver reached a settlement agreement, the court affirmed that material issues of fact existed as to whether the bus driver initiated the boarding procedure for children. In New York, parents of a student who was injured when he was struck by a car as he exited a bus sued the bus company, driver, and board. An appellate court affirmed that the bus company's failure to equip the vehicle as a school bus did not violate a law regulating school buses since it was inapplicable to a bus that was not used solely to transport students.[136]

Where a second-grade student, who was dropped off early by his school bus driver, died as a result of injuries that he sustained while attempting to

---

129. *Green v. Carlinville Community Unit School Dist. No. 1*, 887 N.E.2d 451 [233 Educ. L. Rep. 425] (Ill.App.Ct.2008), *appeal dismissed*, 897 N.E.2d 251 (Ill.2008).

130. *Pratt v. Robinson*, 384 N.Y.S.2d 749 (N.Y.1976).

131. *See, e.g., Hackler By and Through Hackler v. Unified School Dist. No. 500, of Kansas City*, 777 P.2d 839 [55 Educ. L. Rep. 311] (Kan.1989); *Moshier v. Phoenix Cent. School Dist.*, 605 N.Y.S.2d 581 [88 Educ. L. Rep. 200] (N.Y.App.Div.1993), *order aff'd*, 615 N.Y.S.2d 872 (N.Y.1994).

132. *Cavalier v. Ward*, 723 So.2d 480 [131 Educ. L. Rep. 1166] (La.Ct.App.1998), *writ denied*, 729 So.2d 1047 (La.1998).

133. *Flowers v. Independent School Dist. of Tama*, 16 N.W.2d 570 (Iowa 1944).

134. *Johnson v. Svoboda*, 260 N.W.2d 530 (Iowa 1977).

135. *DeKalb County School Dist. v. Allen*, 561 S.E.2d 202 [163 Educ. L. Rep. 1002] (Ga.Ct.App. 2002), *cert. denied*, (2002).

136. *Sigmond v. Liberty Lines Transit*, 689 N.Y.S.2d 239 [135 Educ. L. Rep. 218] (N.Y. App. Div. 1999).

climb into his house through a window, his parents sued the board for negligence. The Supreme Court of Ohio ruled that where a genuine issue of material fact existed as to whether the driver violated a state statute that prohibited school bus drivers from starting their vehicles until after the children leaving them have reached places of safety, the suit should have been able to proceed.[137]

In a case overlapping with field trips, the parents of first-graders and chaperones who were injured when the driver of a school bus lost control of his vehicle challenged a jury verdict in favor of the school and driver. Reversing in favor of the plaintiffs, an appellate panel in Indiana explained that the trial court erred in failing to instruct the jury that it reasonably could have inferred that the driver should not have lost control of his bus as much as he did on a clear, dry spring day.[138]

Field Trips

School-sponsored field trips require special supervisory precautions because educators typically take children to unfamiliar places. While there are no precise guidelines for field trips, a rule of thumb is that the younger students are, the greater the amount, and degree, of supervision that educators must provide. Of course, children with special needs require greater supervision.

When a sixth-grader was raped by acquaintances after she left the park where a class field trip occurred, the supervising teacher had left the park without her, stopped by her house, and returned to school. Although the teacher contacted the child's mother, she did not disclose the incident to school officials. The Court of Appeals of New York was convinced that the board was liable since evidence supported a jury's verdict that the rape was a foreseeable result of the danger created by the failure of educators to supervise the outing adequately.[139] Conversely, an appellate court in New York reversed the denial of a school board's motion for summary judgment in a case where a kindergarten child was injured on being thrown from a hay ride while on a field trip.[140] The court was satisfied that where forty children were accompanied by twelve adults, and one of the chaperones was seated next to the child who was tossed from her seat, the board did not breach its duty of supervision.

On a field trip to a zoo, a parent whose son was assaulted by children from another school sued the board for negligent supervision. The federal trial court in the District of Columbia rejected the board's motion to dismiss the claim on the basis that its staff owed a duty to supervise its

---

137. *Turner v. Central Local School Dist.*, 706 N.E.2d 1261 [132 Educ. L. Rep. 909] (Ohio 1999).

138. *Aldana v. School City of East Chicago*, 769 N.E.2d 1201 [165 Educ. L. Rep. 769] (Ind. Ct. App. 2002), *transfer denied*, 783 N.E.2d 699 (Ind. 2002).

139. *Bell v. Board of Educ. of the City of N.Y.*, 665 N.Y.S.2d 42 [122 Educ. L. Rep. 1031] (N.Y. 1997).

140. *David v. City of N.Y.*, 835 N.Y.S.2d 377 [220 Educ. L. Rep. 792] (N.Y. App. Div. 2007).

students in order to prevent foreseeable harm such as the type that befell the child.[141]

Open Campus Policies

Difficulties can arise when students are permitted, as part of open campus policies, to leave school. The Supreme Court of Connecticut held that immunity barred a negligence claim where a board policy permitted tenth, eleventh, and twelfth-grade students to leave campus during unscheduled times.[142] The court found that educators had no specific duty to supervise high school students at all times. An appellate court in Arizona reached a like result when parents of two children who were killed in a car accident challenged the failure of school officials to enforce their board's closed campus policy. The court affirmed that the board could not be liable because the failure of educators to enforce the policy did not breach their general duty to avoid exposing students to foreseeable, unreasonable risks of harm.[143]

Two courts in Louisiana reached different outcomes when students were molested on leaving school. In the first case, a twelve-year-old was sexually molested on her way home as she walked home through a known high crime area because she was not allowed to ride the after-hours school bus.[144] In rejecting the student's claim that the student was denied access to a telephone to arrange transportation home, the Supreme Court of Louisiana agreed that insofar as she had access to alternative means of transportation the board did not breach its duty of reasonable supervision.[145] Conversely, after a junior high school student checked herself out of school in violation of a board policy that authorized only the principal or vice-principal to allow children to leave during regular class hours, she was sexually molested by a stranger while walking home through a bad neighborhood. An appellate court affirmed that officials breached their duty since the scope of their supervisory responsibilities encompassed the foreseeable risk that a female student walking through a bad area might fall victim to a criminal who frequented the area.[146]

DEFENSES

Even if injured parties established that the elements of negligence are present, school boards and their employees have three primary defenses available to limit or eliminate liability. The defenses recognize that even though boards and officials have the duty to look after students, they

---

141. *Thomas v. City Lights School*, 124 F.Supp.2d 707 [150 Educ. L. Rep. 169] (D.D.C. 2000).

142. *Heigl v. Board of Educ. of Town of New Canaan*, 587 A.2d 423 [66 Educ. L. Rep. 674] (Conn. 1991).

143. *Tollenaar v. Chino Valley School Dist.*, 945 P.2d 1310 [121 Educ. L. Rep. 1154] (Ariz. Ct. App. 1997).

144. *S.J. v. Lafayette Parish School Bd.*, 41 So.3d 1119 [259 Educ. L. Rep. 353] (La. 2010).

145. For an earlier case reaching a similar outcome, *see Jackson v. Colvin*, 732 So.2d 530 [135 Educ. L. Rep. 296] (La. Ct. App. 1998).

146. *D.C. v. St. Landry Parish School Bd.*, 802 So.2d 19 [160 Educ. L. Rep. 686] (La. Ct. App. 2001), *writ denied*, 793 So.2d 169 (La. 2001).

cannot be accountable for all conceivable harms that befall the children in their care.

Immunity

As discussed above, immunity is the most frequent defense employed by school systems. Immunity is based on the common law principle, now supplemented widely by various statutes dealing with such aspects as recreational[147] and discretionary function[148] immunity, that the government, in and through its branches and departments such as school boards, cannot be liable for the tortious acts of their officers or employees. Immunity also protects school employees such as coaches[149] who act as agents of their boards.

Contributory/Comparative Negligence

Both contributory and comparative negligence are premised on the notion that parties played parts in causing their injuries. The difference between these similar sounding defenses, which now apply in an almost equal number of jurisdictions, is significant. Contributory negligence, which traces its origins in the United States back almost two hundred years,[150] completely bars individuals from recovering for their injuries if they contributed in any way to the harm that they suffered.[151]

As courts and legislatures acknowledged that the defense of contributory negligence led to inequitable results, an increasing number of jurisdictions adopted the standard of comparative negligence. Comparative negligence permits juries to apportion liability based on a percentage of relative fault between the parties to allow plaintiffs to recover for the harm that they suffered if they are not more than fifty percent liable.[152] Some states apply what is referred to as "pure comparative negligence" which permits plaintiffs to recover even if they contributed more than fifty percent to their injuries.[153]

In a related concern involving liability, issues arise as to the appropriate standard to apply when children contribute to their injuries. Rather

---

147. *See, e.g., Auman v. School Dist. of Stanley–Boyd*, 635 N.W.2d 762 [159 Educ. L. Rep. 321] (Wis.2001).

148. *See, e.g., Cooper v. Paulding County School Dist.*, 595 S.E.2d 671 [187 Educ. L. Rep. 1091] (Ga.Ct.App.2004); *Arteman v. Clinton Community Unit School Dist.*, 763 N.E.2d 756 [163 Educ. L. Rep. 913] (Ill.2002).

149. *See, e.g., Feagins v. Waddy*, 978 So.2d 712 [231 Educ. L. Rep. 986] (Ala.2007).

150. *Smith v. Smith*, 19 Mass. 621 (Mass.1825).

151. *See, e.g., Funston v. School Town of Munster*, 849 N.E.2d 595 [210 Educ. L. Rep. 438] (Ind.2006) (applying contributory, rather than comparative, negligence to governmental entities such as schools in Indiana).

152. *See, e.g., Siders v. Reynoldsburg School Dist.*, 650 N.E.2d 150 [100 Educ. L. Rep. 708] (Ohio Ct.App.1994); *Millus v. Milford*, 735 N.Y.S.2d 202 [160 Educ. L. Rep. 855] (N.Y.App.Div. 2001); *Johnson ex rel. Johnson v. Dumas*, 811 So.2d 1085 [163 Educ. L. Rep. 1049] (La.Ct.App. 2002); *Heuser ex rel. Jacobs v. Community Ins. Corp.*, 774 N.W.2d 653 [250 Educ. L. Rep. 766] (Wis.Ct.App.2009).

153. *But see Church v. Massey*, 697 So.2d 407 [120 Educ. L. Rep. 604] (Miss.1997) (criticizing an improper jury instruction on pure comparative negligence).

than expecting children to meet the same standard of care as adults, courts take their ages and physical conditions into account when the defense of comparative negligence is raised. As a general rule, courts agree that children between the ages of seven and fourteen[154] are incapable of negligence for their own behavior while those over the age of fourteen may be accountable on case-by-case bases. In such a case, an appellate court in Louisiana declared that a six-year-old child did not negligently cause his own injury even though he ran out into the street and into the side of a car while returning to school to wait for his mother.[155] The court observed that the six-year-old did not share in the fault for his injury since he acted in the manner that could have been expected of a child of his age.[156]

Assumption of Risk

Assumption of risk, which is also based on comparative fault, can reduce recoveries in proportion to the degree to which the conduct of plaintiffs contributed to their accidents if they voluntarily exposed themselves to known and appreciated risks of harm,[157] particularly in cases where students are hurt while participating in sports. In fact, as noted by the Court of Appeals of New York, in following the general rule, it had "not applied this doctrine outside of this limited context [of athletic and recreational activities] and it is clear that its application must be closely circumscribed if it is not seriously to undermine and displace the principles of comparative causation that the Legislature has deemed applicable to 'any action to recover damages for personal injury, injury to property, or wrongful death.' "[158] The court thus affirmed that the father of a student who was twelve years of age could proceed with his negligence claim to recover from injuries that the child sustained as he attempted to slide down a school bannister insofar as he had been left wholly unsupervised.

Before turning to cases involving sports, it is worth examining a dispute wherein an appellate court in Maryland applied the defense of assumption of risk in favor of a school board. Here a high school student, who deceived educational officials about her voluntarily leaving school without permission and was sexually assaulted by her uncle-in-law, sued it for negligent supervision.[159] The court affirmed that insofar as the student willingly left the building with her uncle and knew of his intentions when

---

154. *Simmons ex rel. Simmons v. Columbus County Bd. of Educ.*, 615 S.E.2d 69, 76 [199 Educ. L. Rep. 955] (N.C. Ct. App. 2005) (noting that "In North Carolina, children between the ages of seven and fourteen are presumed to be incapable of contributory negligence.").

155. *Sutton v. Duplessis*, 584 So.2d 362 [69 Educ. L. Rep. 968] (La. Ct. App. 1991).

156. *See also Lewis v. Dependent School Dist. No. 10 of Pottawatomie County*, 808 P.2d 710 [66 Educ. L. Rep. 1283] (Okla. Ct. App. 1990).

157. *See Murphy v. Steeplechase Amusement Co.*, 250 N.Y. 479, 482 (1929) ("*Volenti non fit injuria.* [literally, 'to a willing person it is not a wrong'] One who takes part in such a sport accepts the dangers that inhere in it so far as they are obvious and necessary, just as a fencer accepts the risk of a thrust by his antagonist or a spectator at a ball game the chance of contact with the ball.") (internal citations omitted).

158. *Trupia ex rel. Trupia v. Lake George Cent. Sch. Dist.*, 901 N.Y.S.2d 127, 129 [257 Educ. L. Rep. 812] (N.Y. 2010).

159. *Tate v. Board of Educ. of Prince George's County*, 843 A.2d 890 [186 Educ. L. Rep. 437] (Md. Ct. App. 2004).

she did so, her having assumed the risk of her injuries meant that she could not recover from the board.

Since assumption of risk is a far-reaching defense in cases involving sports, it is worth reviewing its application in specific examples. In New York, an appellate court affirmed that a cheerleader who was injured during practice could not recover from her school board since she assumed the risks of her sport and was practicing voluntarily under the supervision of her coach.[160] Another appellate court in New York ruled that where a ninth-grade student voluntarily participated in a basketball game in a schoolyard where a hole on the playing surface was clearly visible, he knowingly assumed the risk of injury such that the board was not liable for the injuries he sustained when he fell.[161]

In the first of two cases involving baseball, an appellate court in New York agreed that a board could not be liable for injuries that an experienced high school baseball player sustained when he was hit in the eye by a pitch from a batting machine after he asked the coach to increase the velocity of the pitches. The court conceded that insofar as the player understood what he was doing when he voluntarily participated in the activity, he could not recover for his injuries.[162] In the second dispute, an appellate court in New York decided that a coach, a former minor league player, who was injured when a foul ball that was hit into a dugout struck him in the face could not sue the city that owned the park because he assumed the risk of being there.[163] Other courts reached similar results in agreeing that assumption of risk prevented suits from continuing where plaintiffs were injured while participating in interscholastic baseball,[164] basketball,[165] cheerleading,[166] equestrienne activities,[167] field hockey,[168] football,[169] gymnastics,[170] ice hockey,[171] lacrosse,[172] soccer,[173] softball,[174] swimming,[175] track and field,[176] tennis,[177] wrestling,[178] and weightlifting.[179]

---

160. *Lomonico v. Massapequa Pub. Schools*, 923 N.Y.S.2d 631 [267 Educ. L. Rep. 323] (N.Y.App.Div.2011).

161. *Casey v. Garden City Park–New Hyde Park School Dist.*, 837 N.Y.S.2d 186 [221 Educ. L. Rep. 278] (N.Y.App.Div.2007).

162. *Harris v. Cherry Valley–Springfield School Dist.*, 760 N.Y.S.2d 768 [178 Educ. L. Rep. 470] (N.Y.App.Div.2003).

163. *Reyes v. City of New York*, 858 N.Y.S.2d 760 (N.Y.App.Div.2008).

164. *Godwin v. Russi*, 879 N.Y.S.2d 567 (N.Y.App.Div.2009).

165. *Lincoln v. Canastota Cent. School Dist.*, 861 N.Y.S.2d 488 [234 Educ. L. Rep. 258] (N.Y.App.Div.2008); *Ribaudo v. La Salle Instit.*, 846 N.Y.S.2d 209 [226 Educ. L. Rep. 974] (N.Y.App.Div.2007), *leave to appeal denied*, 862 N.Y.S.2d 469 (N.Y. 2008).

166. *Christian v. Eagles Landing Christian Acad.*, 692 S.E.2d 745 [256 Educ. L. Rep. 934] (Ga.Ct.App.2010); *DiGiose v. Bellmore–Merrick Cent. High School Dist.*, 855 N.Y.S.2d 199 [231 Educ. L. Rep. 842] (N.Y.App.Div.2008).

167. *Papa ex rel. Papa v. Russo*, 719 N.Y.S.2d 723 [150 Educ. L. Rep. 911] (N.Y.App.Div. 2001), *leave to appeal denied*, 757 N.Y.S.2d 817 (N.Y.2003).

168. *Sandler ex rel. Sandler v. Half Hollow Hills West High School*, 672 N.Y.S.2d 120 [125 Educ. L. Rep. 1330] (N.Y.App.Div.1998).

169. *Hammond v. Board of Educ. of Carroll County*, 639 A.2d 223 [90 Educ. L. Rep. 256] (Md.Ct.Spec.App.1994); *Benitez v. New York City Bd. of Educ.*, 543 N.Y.S.2d 29 [54 Educ. L. Rep. 933] (N.Y.1989). [Case No. 43]

170. *Weber v. William Floyd School Dist.*, 707 N.Y.S.2d 231 [144 Educ. L. Rep. 610] (N.Y.App.Div.2000).

171. *Greenberg by Greenberg v. North Shore Cent. School Dist. No. 1*, 619 N.Y.S.2d 151 [96 Educ. L. Rep. 206] (N.Y.App.Div.1994).

Courts are unwilling to apply the assumption of risk defense in school settings where a student was injured while stepping in a hole in front of his school while playing touch football;[180] coaches did not warn a student sufficiently about the dangers of diving into a pool;[181] students warmed up in a hazardous location prior to the start of a volleyball game;[182] coaches conducted a track practice in a high school hallway that unreasonably increased a student's risk of injury;[183] it was unclear whether teachers compelled a student who was injured in a relay race at school to participate in the event;[184] there was a concealed rut in the surface of a lacrosse field;[185] a coach lacked enough experience to provide adequate supervision to avoid injury to a cheerleader;[186] and teachers failed to provide adequate safety equipment for physical education classes dealing with such activities as in-line skating,[187] softball,[188] and volleyball[189] or interscholastic sports such as football.[190]

172. *Ciccone v. Bedford Cent. School Dist.*, 800 N.Y.S.2d 452 [201 Educ. L. Rep. 287] (N.Y. App. Div. 2005), *leave to appeal denied*, 810 N.Y.S.2d 416 (2005).

173. *Ballou v. Ravena–Coeymans–Selkirk School*, 898 N.Y.S.2d 358 [255 Educ. L. Rep. 948] (N.Y. App. Div. 2010).

174. *Hyde v. North Collins Cent. School Dist.*, 922 N.Y.S.2d 677 [266 Educ. L. Rep. 940] (N.Y.App. Div. 2011). *See also Navarro v. City of N.Y.*, 929 N.Y.S.2d 236 [271 Educ. L. Rep. 399] (N.Y.App.Div.2011) (involving an elective softball class).

175. *Aronson v. Horace Mann–Barnard School*, 637 N.Y.S.2d 410 [106 Educ. L. Rep. 1281] (N.Y.App.Div.1996) *leave to appeal denied*, 651 N.Y.S.2d 15 (N.Y.1996).

176. *Gerry v. Commack Union Free School Dist.*, 860 N.Y.S.2d 133 [233 Educ. L. Rep. 878] (N.Y.App.Div.2008) (involving a student-participant who was injured in a shot put event).

177. *Bendig v. Bethpage Union Free School Dist.*, 904 N.Y.S.2d 731 [258 Educ. L. Rep. 373] (N.Y.App.Div.2010).

178. *Lilley v. Elk Grove Unified School Dist.*, 80 Cal.Rptr.2d 638 [130 Educ. L. Rep. 1297] (Cal.Ct.App.1998).

179. *American Powerlifting Ass'n v. Cotillo*, 934 A.2d 27 [226 Educ. L. Rep. 83] (Md. 2007).

180. *Simmons v. Saugerties Cent. School Dist.*, 918 N.Y.S.2d 661 [265 Educ. L. Rep. 403] (N.Y.App.Div.2011).

181. *Kahn v. East Side Union High School Dist.*, 4 Cal.Rptr.3d 103 [180 Educ. L. Rep. 312] (Cal.2003).

182. *Gilbert ex rel. Gilbert v. Lyndonville Cent. School Dist.*, 730 N.Y.S.2d 638 [157 Educ. L. Rep. 283] (N.Y.App.Div.2001).

183. *Kane ex rel. Kane v. North Colonie Cent. School Dist.*, 708 N.Y.S.2d 203 [145 Educ. L. Rep. 1096] (N.Y.App.Div.2000).

184. *Smith v. J.H. West Elementary School*, 861 N.Y.S.2d 690 [234 Educ. L. Rep. 948] (N.Y.App.Div.2008).

185. *McGrath v. Shenendehowa Cent. School Dist.*, 906 N.Y.S.2d 399 [258 Educ. L. Rep. 1232] (N.Y.App.Div.2010).

186. *Larson v. Cuba Rushford Cent. School Dist.*, 912 N.Y.S.2d 827 [262 Educ. L. Rep. 584] (N.Y.App.Div.2010).

187. *Jackson v. Lawrence Pub. School Dist.*, 735 N.Y.S.2d 570 [160 Educ. L. Rep. 491] (N.Y.App.Div.2001). *But see Arteman v. Clinton Community Unit School Dist.*, 763 N.E.2d 756 [163 Educ. L. Rep. 913] (Ill. 2002) (refusing to impose liability for a rollerblading accident in a physical education class based on discretionary function immunity).

188. *Muniz v. Warwick School Dist.*, 743 N.Y.S.2d 113 [165 Educ. L. Rep. 731] (N.Y.App. Div.2002); *Zmitrowitz ex rel. Zmitrowitz v. Roman Catholic Diocese of Syracuse*, 710 N.Y.S.2d 453 [145 Educ. L. Rep. 760] (N.Y.App.Div.2000).

189. *Carson v. Baldwin Union Free School Dist.*, 910 N.Y.S.2d 117 [261 Educ. L. Rep. 730] (N.Y.App.Div.2010).

190. *Harvey v. Ouachita Parish School Bd.*, 674 So.2d 372 [110 Educ. L. Rep. 507] (La. Ct. App. 1996), *writ denied*, 681 So.2d 1260 (La. 1996).

EDUCATIONAL MALPRACTICE

Beginning in the 1970s, parents and others sought to render school boards liable for perceived educational shortcomings allegedly due to pedagogical errors committed while students were in schools. Malpractice is a term of art for negligence of professional personnel, usually those who work in a one-to-one relationship with clients such as physicians or lawyers. To date, all efforts to establish educational malpractice in regular education have failed[191] since it is "... a tort theory beloved of commentators, but not of courts."[192]

In the leading case on educational malpractice, parents charged that school officials improperly permitted their son, who could read only at the fifth-grade level, to graduate from high school. The student and his parents sought redress because even though he attended school for twelve years he was only qualified for jobs requiring little or no ability to read or write. An appellate court in California, in rejecting the suit, discussed at length the duty of care concept in the law of negligence.[193] The court reasoned that the claim was not actionable since it lacked a workable rule of care against which to measure the alleged conduct of educators, no injury within the meaning of the law of negligence, and no perceptible connection between the educators' conduct and the student's alleged injury. In other words, the court posited that the student's claims were too amorphous to be justiciable as negligence. The court also dismissed a charge of intentional misrepresentation because even though the student and his parents had the opportunity to do so, they were unable to allege facts proving the requisite element of reliance on the alleged misrepresentation.

Along with the reasons cited above, other courts have recognized the difficulties of measuring damages and the public policy considerations that the acceptance of such cases would, in effect, have positioned them as overseers of day-to-day operation of schools.[194] Courts have pointed out that insofar as aggrieved parents can seek redress through the administrative channels of local boards and state-level educational agencies, they are not

---

191. Since children with disabilities have statutorily protected rights, some courts have allowed such suits to proceed. *See, e.g., Snow v. State,* 469 N.Y.S.2d 959 (N.Y. App. Div. 1983), *aff'd,* 485 N.Y.S.2d 987 (N.Y. 1984); *M.C. on Behalf of J.C. v. Central Reg'l School Dist.,* 81 F.3d 389 [108 Educ. L. Rep. 522] (3d Cir.1996), *cert. denied,* 519 U.S. 866, 117 S.Ct. 176, 136 L.Ed.2d 116 (1996). *But see Suriano v. Hyde Park Cent. School Dist.,* 611 N.Y.S.2d 20 [90 Educ. L. Rep. 1163] (N.Y. App. Div. 1994).

192. *Ross v. Creighton Univ.,* 740 F.Supp. 1319, 1327 [62 Educ. L. Rep. 85] (N.D. Ill. 1990), *rev'd in part on other grounds,* 957 F.2d 410 [73 Educ. L. Rep. 352] (7th Cir.1992).

193. *Peter W. v. San Francisco Unified School Dist.,* 131 Cal.Rptr. 854 (Cal. Ct. App.1976).

194. For other representative cases, *see, e.g., McGovern v. Nassau County Dep't of Social Servs.,* 876 N.Y.S.2d 141 [243 Educ. L. Rep. 429] (N.Y. App. Div. 2009); *Simon v. Celebration Co.,* 883 So.2d 826 [192 Educ. L. Rep. 996] (Fla. Dist. Ct. App. 2004); *Key v. Coryell,* 185 S.W.3d 98 [207 Educ. L. Rep. 450] (Ark. Ct. App. 2004); *Hunter v. Board of Educ. of Montgomery County,* 439 A.2d 582 (Md. 1982) [Case No. 45]; *Donohue v. Copiague Union Free School Dist.,* 418 N.Y.S.2d 375 (N.Y. 1979).

helpless bystanders as school officials make decisions affecting the education of their children. Of course, as evidenced in the voluminous litigation on the tort of negligence, if specific acts of school employees directly, or intentionally, cause injuries to students, liability may apply.[195]

INTENTIONAL TORTS

ASSAULT AND BATTERY

These two intentional torts are discussed under the same heading since they are often closely related. At common law, assault is placing another in the reasonable apprehension of an immediate, unwanted touching.[196] Thus, if teachers threaten misbehaving children that they will walk to the back of classrooms and slap them the following day, the educators did not commit assault both because the threats were of future, rather than immediate contact, and since common law assault cannot be based on mere words. Moreover, parties must be aware that they are being assaulted.[197] For example, if a teacher throws an object at a group of students but misses them and hits a child who did not see it, the teacher may well have battered the child who was struck and assaulted the ones at whom the item was hurled. Battery, on the other hand, is the actual unconsented to touching.[198]

School boards and teachers can face civil (or criminal[199]) liability for assault and/or battery in cases involving corporal punishment and sexual misconduct involving students, topics that are covered in Chapter 13. In suits where students who are subjected to corporal punishment sue for battery, courts ordinarily do not award damages unless educators acted with legal malice, which an appellate court in Alabama defined as "the intentional doing of a wrongful act without just cause or excuse, either with an intent to injure the other party or under such circumstances that the law will imply an evil intent."[200]

A case from Tennessee involved charges of both assault and battery where a high school basketball player alleged that his coach subjected him to unreasonable corporal punishment by paddling him based on reports

---

195. For cases suggesting that educational malpractice might lie for intentional behavior, see, e.g., *B.M. by Burger v. State*, 649 P.2d 425 [5 Educ. L. Rep. 1265] (Mont.1982), *appeal after remand*, 698 P.2d 399 [24 Educ. L. Rep. 541] (Mont.1985). *But see Brantley v. District of Columbia*, 640 A.2d 181 [90 Educ. L. Rep. 658] (D.C.1994); *Doe v. Town of Framingham*, 965 F.Supp. 226 [119 Educ. L. Rep. 109] (D.Mass.1997).

196. RESTATEMENT (SECOND) OF TORTS § 21.

197. *Spacek v. Charles*, 928 S.W.2d 88 [112 Educ. L. Rep. 525] (Tex.Ct.App.1996).

198. RESTATEMENT (SECOND) OF TORTS § 13.

199. For a case involving criminal battery in a school setting, *see C.M.M. v. State*, 983 So.2d 704 [234 Educ. L. Rep. 441] (Fla.Dist.Ct.App.2008) (affirming a student's conviction where she battered a police officer who was assigned to work as a school resource officer and was engaged in the legal execution of his official duty).

200. *Hinson v. Holt*, 776 So.2d 804, 812 [151 Educ. L. Rep. 343] (Ala.Civ.App.1998), *citing Empiregas v. Feely*, 524 So.2d 626, 628 (Ala.1988).

from his teachers about his conduct while in class. The Sixth Circuit affirmed that insofar as the coach's use of corporal punishment was not unreasonable, he did not commit assault and battery in dealing with the student.[201]

In a case from Louisiana, an appellate court affirmed that a school board shared liability with a fifth-grader who committed a sexual assault on a third-grader and her younger sister while on a school bus.[202] Grounding its judgment in state common law rather than Title IX, the court held that where the bus driver, a board employee, conceded that she violated board rules on exiting the bus at a transfer point and that she could have prevented the assault that took place, the board was independently liable for the harm that befell the students.

FALSE IMPRISONMENT

False imprisonment occurs when individuals intentionally and unlawfully confine others against their wills, even if the others do not suffer physical harms.[203] Set out for perhaps the first time well over a century ago, the Supreme Court of Indiana recognized the authority of educators to detain students as a form of discipline as a defense to false imprisonment.[204] More than eighty years later, the Court of Appeals of New York relied on this case when a student was injured while attempting to climb out of a window as the bus driver proceeded to a police station because of damage that children did to the vehicle.[205] The court declared that even if a jury agreed that the driver falsely imprisoned the student, the child would have been unable to recover for his injuries if he acted unreasonably in attempting to climb out of the bus. When a bus driver became lost and was four hours late arriving at school, an appellate court in Florida affirmed that neither the driver nor school board was liable for false imprisonment because there was no intent to restrain the student, a special needs child, against his will.[206]

The Supreme Court of Iowa affirmed that a student did not establish a claim of false imprisonment when school officials sent him home on an unsupervised bus ride as discipline for violating rules while on a band trip in Texas.[207] The court maintained that this claim was without merit since the student willingly accompanied an educator to the bus station, boarded the vehicle without objection, and failed to produce evidence that he put up a fight to stay on the trip or to receive another punishment. Three years earlier, a federal trial court in Arkansas determined that a student who

201. *Nolan v. Memphis City Schools*, 589 F.3d 257 [251 Educ L. Rep. 533] (6th Cir.2009).

202. *Doe v. East Baton Rouge Parish School Bd.*, 978 So.2d 426 [231 Educ. L. Rep. 968] (La. Ct. App. 2007), *writ denied*, 978 So.2d 306 (La. 2008).

203. RESTATEMENT (SECOND) OF TORTS § 35.

204. *Fertich v. Michener*, 11 N.E. 605 (Ind. 1887).

205. *Sindle v. New York City Transit Auth.*, 352 N.Y.S.2d 183 (N.Y. 1973).

206. *School Bd. of Miami–Dade County, Florida v. Trujillo*, 906 So.2d 1109 [200 Educ. L. Rep. 910] (Fla. Dist. Ct. App. 2005), *reh'g denied* (2005).

207. *Ette ex rel. Ette v. Linn–Mar Community School Dist.*, 656 N.W.2d 62 [173 Educ. L. Rep. 662] (Iowa 2002).

disrupted a choir class and had to sit in the choir library for three periods lacked a claim for false imprisonment.[208] In remarking that the student was neither physically threatened nor forced to enter this room, and was able to do her homework there, the court concluded that she was not subject to false imprisonment because if she refused the teacher's order to enter the room, she would have been subjected to a harsher form of discipline. In addition, where parents in Missouri gave their informed consent to have their child placed in a private residential facility with full knowledge of its restrictions after he was arrested and charged with terroristic threatening and criminal mischief, the Eighth Circuit affirmed that they could not sue the school and a variety of other defendants for false imprisonment.[209]

Courts are willing to find that students were subjected to false imprisonment under egregious circumstances. In such cases, when a coach locked a football player in a locker room[210] and a teacher chained a student with poor attendance to a tree for an hour and one-half even though he claimed that it was a joke,[211] courts affirmed that the students presented viable claims.

DEFAMATION

Defamation involves the intentional, or at least negligent, unprivileged communication of a false statement to a third party that harms the reputation of the person being spoken about.[212] Spoken defamation is slander; written defamation is libel. Depending on the jurisdiction, some courts may go so far as to require that allegedly defamatory remarks contain objectively verifiable assertions of fact rather than mere opinions.[213]

School officials have three key protections at their disposal when dealing with defamation: truth, privilege, and opinion. If statements are true, and do not invade persons' rights to privacy, there can be no claims for defamation.[214] If there is a question of fact as to whether a statement is true, an area that overlaps with privilege, such a matter is ordinarily reserved for a jury. In an illustrative case, where a former director of technology in Iowa sued an associate superintendent over the latter's allegation that he was dangerous, the Eighth Circuit affirmed that whether

---

208. *Wallace v. Bryant School Dist.*, 46 F.Supp.2d 863 [135 Educ. L. Rep. 488] (E.D. Ark. 1999), *aff'd*, 208 F.3d 219 (8th Cir.2000).

209. *Blair v. Wills*, 420 F.3d 823 [201 Educ. L. Rep. 97] (8th Cir.2005), *reh'g and reh'g en banc denied* (2005).

210. *Newman v. Obersteller*, 915 S.W.2d 198 [107 Educ. L. Rep. 352] (Tex. Ct. App. 1996).

211. *Banks v. Fritsch*, 39 S.W.3d 474 [152 Educ. L. Rep. 379] (Ky. Ct. App. 2001).

212. RESTATEMENT (SECOND) OF TORTS § 558. *See also Harris ex rel. Harris v. Pontotoc County School Dist.*, 635 F.3d 685, 692 [265 Educ. L. Rep. 908] (5th Cir.2011) ("Defamatory statements must be made to a third party and not to the claimant.").

213. *See, e.g., Lifton v. Board of Educ. of City of Chicago*, 416 F.3d 571 [200 Educ. L. Rep. 39] (7th Cir.2005).

214. For statements reiterating this rule in dicta, *see, e.g., Goldberg v. Brooks*, 948 N.E.2d 1108 [268 Educ. L. Rep. 507] (Ill. App. Ct. 2011); *James v. DeGrandis*, 138 F.Supp.2d 402, 416 [153 Educ. L. Rep. 618] (W.D.N.Y. 2001).

the allegation was true was a proper matter for a jury to consider.[215] In another case, where a principal made derogatory comments about a seventy-year-old teacher with thirty-four years of experience, who served as head foreign languages teacher on a one-year renewable contract, while in a meeting with parents about her role as chaperone in an overseas trip, an appellate court in Massachusetts denied the school committee's motion for summary judgment.[216] The court ascertained that insofar as a genuine issue of material fact remained as to whether the principal's assessment of the teacher's performance was false, it rejected the committee's motion.

A case about the status of truth as a defense arose in Louisiana where a professional association of teachers sought review of a grant of summary judgment in favor of a union after it sued the latter for defamation. The association sued the union over the contents of a brochure that it distributed questioning the former's ability to meet the needs of its members. Reversing in favor of the association, an appellate court decided that where material issues of fact existed over the truth of the statements, the matter should have been permitted to proceed to trial.[217]

School officials may be entitled to the defense of privilege when charged with defamation. Put another way, statements such as recommendations or evaluations offering opinions supportable by some evidence and that are made to appropriate persons in the line of duty are not actionable since they are protected by privilege. In an early case, the Supreme Court of Nebraska reasoned that a letter from the state superintendent of schools to an administrator that described a teacher as unfit since he was under the influence of liquor was not actionable as defamation because it was sent in connection with the superintendent's official duties.[218]

Courts agreed that defamation suits were not actionable based on privilege where a superintendent investigated a board president and vice-president's use of a district credit card;[219] where a school director wrote a letter to a newspaper questioning whether a school business manager engaged in budgetary misconduct;[220] where the director of an early childhood education program remarked to television reporters about why some staff members had their employment terminated;[221] and where comments by a school board's attorney were made in response to questions from another lawyer on subject matter that ultimately resulted in litigation.[222]

---

215. *Smith v. Des Moines Pub. Schools*, 259 F.3d 942 [156 Educ. L. Rep. 56] (8th Cir.2001).

216. *Dragonas v. School Comm. of Melrose*, 833 N.E.2d 679 [201 Educ. L. Rep. 296] (Mass. App. Ct. 2005), *review denied*, 836 N.E.2d 1096 (Mass. 2005).

217. *Associated Professional Educators of La. v. Louisiana Fed'n of Teachers*, 981 So.2d 242 [232 Educ. L. Rep. 994] (La. Ct. App. 2008), *reh'g denied* (2008).

218. *De Bolt v. McBrien*, 147 N.W. 462 (Neb. 1914).

219. *Gallegos v. Escalon*, 993 S.W.2d 422 [135 Educ. L. Rep. 852] (Tex. Ct. App. 1999).

220. *Matta v. Burton*, 721 A.2d 1164 [131 Educ. L. Rep. 788] (Pa. Cmwlth. Ct. 1998), *appeal discontinued*, 736 A.2d 606 (Pa. 1999).

221. *Enriquez v. Khouri*, 13 S.W.3d 458 [142 Educ. L. Rep. 1102] (Tex. Ct. App. 2000).

222. *Lewis v. School Dist. #70*, 523 F.3d 730 [231 Educ. L. Rep. 631] (7th Cir.2008).

If statements are clearly opinions, such as where parents and students criticized teachers[223] or school officials[224] or where letter writers commented on the close relationship between a member of a school committee and a construction manager who was involved in a school project,[225] courts refused to impose liability. An exception arises if statements can reasonably be understood to be based on undisclosed defamatory underlying facts.[226] Perhaps the most notable case in this regard was *Milkovich v. Lorain Journal Company*, wherein a high school wrestling coach sued a newspaper for defamation when an editorial suggested that he committed perjury. In acknowledging that insofar as the statements about the coach were not opinions because they could have been proven to be true or false, the Supreme Court noted that "where a statement of 'opinion' on a matter of public concern reasonably implies false and defamatory facts regarding public figures or officials, those individuals [can recover damages if they] show that such statements were made with knowledge of their false implications or with reckless disregard of their truth."[227]

A key element of successful claims by school officials is proving that they suffered significant harm to their professional reputations. Mere hurt feelings are insufficient. By way of example, an appellate court in Louisiana affirmed that a principal was not liable for defamation when he wrote a letter to a superintendent recommending that a teacher not be re-employed and when he was overheard referring to her and another teacher as "nuts."[228] In failing to uncover anything defamatory in the letter, which, it suggested, would have been covered by privilege, the court thought that the principal's oral remarks were not slanderous because he made them in an informal conversation, and although unflattering, did not cause the teacher any harm. In another dispute, where a principal sued the man who had an affair with his wife for defamation, and the latter posted false rumors about him in an Internet chat room, an appellate court in Missouri affirmed a default judgment in favor of the plaintiff.[229] The court agreed that the rumors were defamatory since they harmed the principal's professional reputation.

In a dispute from Maryland, a high school teacher-coach who was suspended with pay and transferred when two female members of his cross-country team falsely accused him of sexual misconduct based on their desire to have a different coach, sued them and their parents for defamation. The state's highest court initially reinstated the claims, explaining that insofar as the students' complaints were not absolutely privileged despite the strong public opinion that they and their parents should be protected from suit for reporting his alleged sexual misconduct, the defama-

---

223. *Ansorian v. Zimmerman*, 627 N.Y.S.2d 706 [101 Educ. L. Rep. 366] (N.Y. App. Div. 1995).

224. *Nampa Charter School v. DeLaPaz*, 89 P.3d 863 [187 Educ. L. Rep. 1056] (Idaho 2004).

225. *Alves v. Hometown Newspapers*, 857 A.2d 743 [192 Educ. L. Rep. 215] (R.I. 2004).

226. *Baker v. Lafayette College*, 532 A.2d 399 [42 Educ. L. Rep. 598] (Pa. 1987).

227. 497 U.S. 1, 20, 110 S.Ct. 2695, 111 L.Ed.2d 1 [60 Educ. L. Rep. 1061] (1990).

228. *McGowen v. Prentice*, 341 So.2d 55, 56 (La. Ct. App. 1976).

229. *Scott v. LeClercq*, 136 S.W.3d 183 [189 Educ. L. Rep. 436] (Mo. Ct. App. 2004).

tion claim could have proceeded to trial in light of the harm that the teacher-coach suffered.[230] However, the same court subsequently held that the educator's claim was barred by absolute privilege.[231] The court was convinced that the teacher-coach's claim could not proceed since adequate procedural safeguards were in place to minimize the occurrence of defamatory statements in school administrative proceedings.

After a high school teacher in New York was suspended for showing an "R" rated movie to her class, she sued her principal for defamation for allegedly telling the board's attorney that she did so in violation of district policy. An appellate court affirmed a grant of summary judgment in favor of the defendants on the ground that the principal's alleged comment was protected by qualified privilege absent the teacher's ability to show that he spoke with malice.[232]

A case from the Supreme Court of New Jersey reveals how First Amendment concerns can be intertwined with defamation claims while serving as a segue to the next part of this section. The court affirmed that a teacher-chaperone could not sue another teacher with whom she shared duties while on a school trip after the latter sent their principal a letter discussing the plaintiff's alleged improprieties.[233] The court held that the letter was not actionable because to the extent that it involved a matter of public concern, namely student safety, it was entitled to substantial First Amendment protection absent a showing of actual malice by the letter writer.

Public Figures

Insofar as defamation is speech, some First Amendment considerations apply. In the interest of free discussion of matters of public concern, the Supreme Court treats public officials and public figures differently from private persons. In order for public officials to succeed in defamation claims, plaintiffs must prove that communicators acted with actual malice in making harmful and false statements that were known to be false or that defendants acted with reckless disregard for the truth.[234]

A case arose in this regard in California when an appellate court affirmed the rejection of a claim filed by the former superintendent of a system of charter schools who sued its officers for libel over their posting statements on the organization's Web site urging that he be investigated due to his alleged ties to a terrorist group.[235] The court agreed that where the alleged libel pertained to the former superintendent's role as a public official, he had to prove actual malice in order to prevail.[236] In another case,

---

230. *Flynn v. Reichardt*, 749 A.2d 197 [143 Educ. L. Rep. 585] (Md.Ct.App.2000).

231. *Reichardt v. Flynn*, 823 A.2d 566 [177 Educ. L. Rep. 357] (Md.Ct.App.2003).

232. *Clark v. Schuylerville Cent. School Dist.*, 902 N.Y.S.2d 707 [257 Educ. L. Rep. 1016] (N.Y.App.Div.2010).

233. *Rocci v. Ecole Secondaire Macdonald–Cartier*, 755 A.2d 583 [146 Educ. L. Rep. 283] (N.J.2000).

234. *New York Times Co. v. Sullivan*, 376 U.S. 254, 84 S.Ct. 710, 11 L.Ed.2d 686 (1964).

235. *Ghafur v. Bernstein*, 32 Cal.Rptr.3d 626 [200 Educ. L. Rep. 842] (Cal.Ct.App.2005).

236. *See also Jee v. New York Post Co.*, 688 N.Y.S.2d 49 [134 Educ. L. Rep. 551] (N.Y.App.Div.1999), *appeal denied*, 697 N.Y.S.2d 565 (N.Y. 1999) (affirming that a principal

an appellate court in Georgia affirmed that insofar as a former superintendent failed to demonstrate that members of a newspaper staff who reported
on a petition seeking his removal allegedly due to abusing his position acted
with actual malice, his claim was not actionable because he was a public
figure.[237]

Courts generally treat board members[238] and superintendents[239] as
public figures but are divided with regard to teachers,[240] principals,[241] and
coaches.[242] In such a dispute, an appellate court in South Carolina affirmed
that insofar as an assistant principal was not a public official who had to
prove actual malice on the part of a minister who used a racial slur in
connection with him while in the presence of others, he was entitled to
monetary damages.[243] Where a father led a campaign that apparently
resulted in the dismissal of a high school football coach while their two sons
competed for the same position, an appellate court in Illinois remanded the
dispute for trial since it was unclear whether the parent acted with actual
malice.[244] The court maintained that the timing of the father's critical
remarks about the coach to school board officials and a local newspaper
raised triable issues of fact as to whether he acted with actual malice.

A subcategory of public figures are limited-purpose public figures,
those who achieve fame or notoriety due to one specific incident or issue. In
such a case, as part of its lengthy opinion, a federal trial court in
Pennsylvania dismissed many, but not all, of the claims against a prominent television personality for defamation and other charges alleging that
the plaintiff, the former headmistress of a school she founded for girls in
South Africa, was aware of the alleged mistreatment of students by staff

---

who challenged a reporter's investigation and the credibility of individuals who provided him
with information could not sue for defamation absent evidence that the allegedly defamatory
statements were published with malice or that the reporter knew them to be false and
published them with reckless disregard for the truth).

237. *Atkins v. News Publishing Co.*, 658 S.E.2d 848 [230 Educ. L. Rep. 827] (Ga. Ct. App.
2008).

238. *Peavy v. Harman*, 37 F.Supp.2d 495 (N.D. Tex.1999). *But see Roberts v. Board of
Educ.*, 25 F.Supp.2d 866 [131 Educ. L. Rep. 128] (N.D. Ill.1998).

239. *Purvis v. Ballantine*, 487 S.E.2d 14 [119 Educ. L. Rep. 709] (Ga.Ct.App.1997).

240. For a case finding that a teacher was not a public official, *see Dec v. Auburn Enlarged
School Dist.*, 672 N.Y.S.2d 591 [126 Educ. L. Rep. 365] (N.Y.App.Div.1998). For cases
recognizing teachers as public officials, *see, e.g., Kelley v. Bonney*, 606 A.2d 693 [74 Educ. L.
Rep. 896] (Conn.1992); *Elstrom v. Independent School Dist. No. 270*, 533 N.W.2d 51 [100
Educ. L. Rep. 733] (Minn.Ct.App.1995); *Tweedall v. Fritz*, 987 F.Supp. 1126 [124 Educ. L. Rep.
122] (S.D.Ind.1997).

241. For cases affirming that principals were not public officials, *see Ellerbee v. Mills*, 422
S.E.2d 539 [78 Educ. L. Rep. 1104] (Ga.1992), *cert. denied*, 507 U.S. 1025, 113 S.Ct. 1833, 123
L.Ed.2d 460 (1993); *Beeching v. Levee*, 764 N.E.2d 669 [162 Educ. L. Rep. 938] (Ind. Ct. App.
2002). For cases affirming that while principals were public officials, defendants were not
liable for defamation since they did not act with reckless disregard for the truth in making
statements, *see Jordan v. World Pub. Co.*, 872 P.2d 946 [90 Educ. L. Rep. 1227] (Okla.Ct.App.
1994); *Palmer v. Bennington School Dist.*, 615 A.2d 498 [78 Educ. L. Rep. 881] (Vt. 1992).

242. *O'Connor v. Burningham*,165 P.3d 1214 (Utah 2007) (holding that insofar as a
basketball coach was not a public figure, he did not have to prove actual malice by parents
whose criticisms led to his dismissal).

243. *Goodwin v. Kennedy*, 552 S.E.2d 319 [157 Educ. L. Rep. 387] (S.C.Ct.App.2001).

244. *Myers v. Levy*, 808 N.E.2d 1139 [187 Educ. L. Rep. 952] (Ill.App.Ct.2004), *appeal
denied*, 823 N.E.2d 967 (Ill.2004).

members.[245] In interpreting the defendant's remarks as capable of having a defamatory meaning, the court refused to dismiss this claim since questions of fact remained as to whether the television personality had serious doubts about what she said about the former headmistress.

Intentional Infliction of Emotional Distress

Intentional infliction of emotional distress, although being raised with some regularity, is generally unsuccessful. In order to prevail on such claims, injured parties must establish that defendants acted intentionally or recklessly; that the conduct was extreme and outrageous; that the defendants' actions caused the plaintiffs severe emotional distress; that the conduct exceeded all possible bounds of decency; and that it was utterly intolerable in a civilized community.[246] For example, a federal trial court in Virginia granted a school board's motion for summary judgment where a kindergarten teacher filed suit for intentional or negligent infliction of emotional distress when she was suspended pending her undergoing a medical and psychiatric examination.[247] The court held that school officials did not violate the teacher's rights or engage in outrageous or intolerable conduct necessary to allow the emotional distress claims to proceed in light of evidence that her threatening behavior toward other employees had an unsettling effect on the school's staff.

Where a teacher was passed over for a coaching position in favor of a candidate who lacked a certificate, an appellate court in Ohio affirmed that the board's conduct did not constitute the extreme and outrageous conduct required to support an action for intentional infliction of emotional distress.[248] The court observed that the record revealed that the board used adequate standards in determining that the teacher was unqualified for the coaching position. Further, an appellate court in Texas affirmed that female high school students could not sue a television station for broadcasting part of a videotape that their band director made in an attempt to discover who was going through their belongings, but which showed them changing their clothes for, among other causes of action, intentional infliction of emotional distress and defamation.[249] The court refused to permit the suit to proceed since the broadcasts, which were on a matter of legitimate public concern, neither subjected the students to intentional infliction of emotional distress nor defamation.[250]

---

245. *Mzamane v. Winfrey*, 693 F.Supp.2d 442 [257 Educ. L. Rep. 296] (E.D.Pa.2010).

246. Restatement (Second) of Torts § 46 (1965). In rejecting such a claim in a case involving the picketing of the funeral of a soldier who was killed in Iraq, the Supreme Court specified that "a plaintiff must demonstrate that the defendant intentionally or recklessly engaged in extreme and outrageous conduct that caused the plaintiff to suffer severe emotional distress." *Snyder v. Phelps*, ___ U.S. ___, 131 S.Ct. 1207, 1215, 179 L.Ed.2d 172 (2011).

247. *Earley v. Marion*, 540 F.Supp.2d 680 [231 Educ. L. Rep. 224] (W.D.Va.2008), *aff'd*, 340 Fed.Appx 169 (4th Cir.2009).

248. *Katterhenrich v. Federal Hocking Local School Dist. Bd. of Educ.*, 700 N.E.2d 626 [129 Educ. L. Rep. 776] (Ohio Ct.App.1997), *appeal not allowed*, 684 N.E.2d 707 (Ohio 1997).

249. *Doe v. Mobile Video Tapes*, 43 S.W.3d 40 [153 Educ. L. Rep. 805] (Tex.Ct.App.2001).

250. *See also, e.g., Dollard v. Board of Educ. of Town of Orange*, 777 A.2d 714 [156 Educ. L. Rep. 273] (Conn.Ct.App.2001); *Stamper v. Charlotte–Mecklenburg Bd. of Educ.*, 544 S.E.2d 818 [152 Educ. L. Rep. 832] (N.C.Ct.App.2001).

An appellate court in Kansas affirmed that school officials were not liable for negligent infliction of emotional distress when a four-year-old child was inadvertently left on a bus after he fell asleep on the way to his preschool.[251] The court explained that the child's parents were unable to recover since the harms that their son allegedly suffered, including nightmares, anxiety, nervousness, physically shaking, acting-out, sleep difficulties, bed-wetting, a significant increase in his weight, and refusing to attend school were not compensable physical injuries for the purposes of their claim against the preschool that operated the bus.

In a tragic case from New York, an appellate court modified a jury verdict in favor of a mother who sued a school board for pain and suffering as well as for intentional infliction of emotional distress after her fourteen-year-old son drowned while on an eighth-grade field trip.[252] The court agreed that officials failed to supervise the student and did not realize that he was missing until after everyone had left the park, which closed at 5 P.M. School officials returned to the park at 9 P.M. to search for the child, but did not notify his mother until about 1 A.M. the next day, when maintenance workers discovered his body in a wave pool. In the intervening hours, even though the student's body was at the bottom of the pool, lifeguards used the pool for relay races and other activities. The court indicated that insofar as the mother failed to establish that she suffered a contemporaneous or consequential physical injury as required to support her claims of emotional distress over the death of her son, she could not recover on that claim.

Conversely, an appellate court in Florida reinstated a high school teacher's claim for intentional infliction of emotional distress against students who allegedly participated in the production and distribution of a newsletter in which the author threatened to kill her and rape her and all of her children.[253] The court was satisfied that the teacher presented a cause of action against the students for intentional infliction of emotional distress since their alleged behavior was so outrageous and extreme that it exceeded all bounds of decency.

[CASE NO. 40] LIABILITY FOR VIOLATING THE CIVIL RIGHTS OF STUDENTS

WOOD v. STRICKLAND

Supreme Court of the United States, 1975.
420 U.S. 308, 95 S.Ct. 992, 43 L.Ed.2d 214.

[The school board suspended three students for about three months, up to the end of their semester, for "spiking" the punch at a meeting of an extracurricular organization that parents and others students attended. Two students filed suit under section 1983 seeking, among other things,

---

251. *Ware ex rel. Ware v. ANW Special Educ. Co-op. No. 603*, 180 P.3d 610 [230 Educ. L. Rep. 803] (Kan. Ct. App. 2008).

252. *Maracallo v. Board of Educ. of the City of N.Y.*, 800 N.Y.S.2d 23 [200 Educ. L. Rep. 861] (N.Y. App. Div. 2005).

253. *Nims v. Harrison*, 768 So.2d 1198 [148 Educ. L. Rep. 518] (Fla. Dist. Ct. App. 2000).

damages against administrators and board members for allegedly violated their rights to due process. This excerpt is limited to the part of the case relating to liability of school officials.]

■ Mr. Justice White delivered the opinion of the Court....

The District Court instructed the jury that a decision for respondents had to be premised upon a finding that petitioners acted with malice in expelling them and defined "malice" as meaning "ill will against a person—a wrongful act done intentionally without just cause or excuse." In ruling for petitioners after the jury had been unable to agree, the District Court found "as a matter of law" that there was no evidence from which malice could be inferred.

The Court of Appeals, however, viewed both the instruction and the decision of the District Court as being erroneous. Specific intent to harm wrongfully, it held, was not a requirement for the recovery of damages. Instead, "[i]t need only be established that the defendants did not, in the light of all the circumstances, act in good faith. The test is an objective, rather than a subjective one."

Petitioners as members of the school board assert here, as they did below, an absolute immunity from liability under § 1983 and at the very least seek to reinstate the judgment of the District Court. If they are correct and the District Court's dismissal should be sustained, we need go no further in this case. Moreover, the immunity question involves the construction of a federal statute, and our practice is to deal with possibly dispositive statutory issues before reaching questions turning on the construction of the Constitution. We essentially sustain the position of the Court of Appeals with respect to the immunity issue.

The nature of the immunity from awards of damages under § 1983 available to school administrators and school board members is not a question which the lower federal courts have answered with a single voice. There is general agreement on the existence of a "good faith" immunity, but the courts have either emphasized different factors as elements of good faith or have not given specific content to the good-faith standard.

This Court had decided three cases dealing with the scope of the immunity protecting various types of governmental officials from liability for damages under § 1983. In *Tenney v. Brandhove*, the question was found to be one essentially of statutory construction. Noting that the language of § 1983 is silent with respect to immunities, the Court concluded that there was no basis for believing that Congress intended to eliminate the traditional immunity of legislators from civil liability for acts done within their sphere of legislative action. That immunity, "so well grounded in history and reason ...", was absolute and consequently did not depend upon the motivations of the legislators. In *Pierson v. Ray*, finding that "[t]he legislative record gives no clear indication that Congress meant to abolish wholesale all common-law immunities" in enacting § 1983, we concluded that the common-law doctrine of absolute judicial immunity survived. Similarly, § 1983 did not preclude application of the traditional rule that a policeman, making an arrest in good faith and with probable cause, is not liable for damages, although the person arrested proves innocent. Consequently the Court said: "Although the matter is not entirely free from doubt, the same consideration would seem to require excusing him from liability for acting under a statute that he reasonably believed to be valid but that was later held unconstitutional, on its face or as applied." Finally, last Term we held that the chief executive officer of a State, the senior and subordinate officers of the State's National Guard, and the president of a state-controlled university were not absolutely immune from liability under § 1983, but instead were entitled to immunity, under prior precedent and in light of the obvious need to avoid discouraging effective official action by public officers charged with a considerable range of responsibility and discretion, only if they acted in good faith. . . .

Common-law tradition, recognized in our prior decisions, and strong public-policy reasons also lead to a construction of § 1983 extending a qualified good-faith immunity to school board members from liability for damages under that section. Although there have been differing emphases and formulations of the common-law immunity of public school officials in cases of student expulsion or suspension, state courts have generally recognized that such officers should be protected from tort liability under state law for all good-faith, non-malicious action taken to fulfill their official duties.

As the facts of this case reveal, school board members function at different times in the nature of legislators and adjudicators in the school disciplinary process. Each of these functions necessarily involves the exercise of discretion, the weighing of many factors, and the formulation of long-term policy. "Like legislators and judges, these officers are entitled to rely on traditional sources for the factual information on which they decide and act." As with executive officers faced with instances of civil disorder, school officials, confronted with student behavior causing or threatening disruption, also have an "obvious need for prompt action, and decisions must be made in reliance on factual information supplied by others."

Liability for damages for every action which is found subsequently to have been violative of a student's constitutional rights and to have caused compensable injury would unfairly impose upon the school decision maker the burden of mistakes made in good faith in the course of exercising his discretion within the scope of his official duties. School board members, among other duties, must judge whether there have been violations of school regulations and, if so, the appropriate sanctions for the violations. Denying any measure of immunity in these circumstances "would contribute not to principled and fearless decision-making but to intimidation." The imposition of monetary costs for mistakes which were not unreasonable in the light of all the circumstances would undoubtedly deter even the most conscientious school decisionmaker from exercising his judgment independently, forcefully, and in a manner best serving the long-term interest of the school and the students. The most capable candidates for school board positions might be deterred from seeking office if heavy burdens upon their private resources from monetary liability were a likely prospect during their tenure.

These considerations have undoubtedly played a prime role in the development by state courts of a qualified immunity protecting school officials from liability for damages in lawsuits claiming improper suspensions or expulsions. But at the same time, the judgment implicit in this common-law development is that absolute immunity would not be justified since it would not sufficiently increase the ability of school officials to exercise their discretion in a forthright manner to warrant the absence of a remedy for students subjected to intentional or otherwise inexcusable deprivations.

. . . Absent legislative guidance, we now rely on those same sources in determining whether and to what extent school officials are immune from damage suits under § 1983. We think there must be a degree of immunity if the work of the schools is to go forward; and, however worded, the immunity must be such that public school officials understand that action taken in the good-faith fulfillment of their responsibilities and within the bounds of reason under all the circumstances will not be punished and that they need not exercise their discretion with undue timidity. . . .

The disagreement between the Court of Appeals and the District Court over the immunity standard in this case has been put in terms of an "objective" versus a "subjective" test of good faith. As we see it, the appropriate standard necessarily contains elements of both. The official must himself be acting sincerely and with a belief that he is doing right, but an act violating a student's constitutional rights can be no more justified by ignorance or disregard of settled, indisputable law on the part of one entrusted with supervision of students' daily lives than by the presence of actual malice. To be entitled to a special exemption from the categorical remedial language of § 1983 in a case in which his action violated a student's constitutional rights, a school board member, who has voluntarily undertaken the task of supervising the operation of the school and the activities of the students, must be held to a standard of conduct based not only on permissible intentions, but also on knowledge of the basic, unquestioned constitutional rights of his charges. Such a standard neither imposes an unfair burden upon a person assuming a responsible public office requiring a high degree of intelligence and judgment for the proper fulfillment of its duties, nor an unwarranted burden in light of the value which civil rights have in our legal system. Any lesser standard would deny much of the promise of § 1983. Therefore, in the specific context of school discipline, we hold that a school board member is not immune from liability for damages under § 1983 if he knew or reasonably should have known that the action he took within his sphere of official responsibility would violate the constitutional rights of the student affected, or if he took the action with the malicious intention to cause a deprivation of constitutional rights or other injury to the student. That is not to say that school board members are "charged with predicting the future course of constitutional law." A compensatory award will be appropriate only if the school board member has acted with such an impermissible motivation or with such disregard of the student's clearly established constitutional rights that his action cannot reasonably be characterized as being in good faith. . . .

The judgment of the Court of Appeals is vacated and the case remanded for further proceedings consistent with this opinion.

So ordered.

NOTES

1. Section 1983 grants rights of redress to individuals who had their civil rights violated by public officials. Do you agree that upholding the board's argument for absolute immunity would have denied much of section 1983's promise?

2. On remand, the Eighth Circuit held that insofar as officials violated the students' right to procedural due process, they were entitled to have their records cleared and to try to prove their claim of damages against individual board members. *Strickland v. Inlow*, 519 F.2d 744 (8th Cir.1975).

[CASE NO. 41] DAMAGES WHEN STUDENTS ARE DENIED DUE PROCESS PRIOR TO BEING SUSPENDED

CAREY v. PIPHUS

Supreme Court of the United States, 1978.
435 U.S. 247, 98 S.Ct. 1042, 55 L.Ed.2d 252.

■ Mr. Justice Powell delivered the opinion of the Court.

In this case, brought under 42 U.S.C.A. § 1983, we consider the elements and prerequisites for recovery of damages by students who were suspended from public elementary and secondary schools without procedural due process.... We ... hold that in the absence of proof of actual injury, the students are entitled to recover only nominal damages.

I

Respondent Jarius Piphus was a freshman at Chicago Vocational High School during the 1973–1974 school year. On January 23, 1974, during school hours, the school principal saw Piphus and another student standing outdoors on school property passing back and forth what the principal described as an irregularly shaped cigarette. The principal approached the students unnoticed and smelled what he believed was the strong odor of burning marihuana. He also saw Piphus try to pass a packet of cigarette papers to the other student. When the students became aware of the principal's presence, they threw the cigarette into a nearby hedge.

The principal took the students to the school's disciplinary office and directed the assistant principal to impose the "usual" 20–day suspension for violation of the school rule against the use of drugs. The students protested that they had not been smoking marihuana, but to no avail. Piphus was allowed to remain at school, although not in class, for the remainder of the school day while the assistant principal tried, without success, to reach his mother.

A suspension notice was sent to Piphus' mother, and a few days later two meetings were arranged among Piphus, his mother, his sister, school officials, and representatives from a Legal Aid Clinic. The purpose of the meetings was not to determine whether Piphus had been smoking marihuana, but rather to explain the reasons for the suspension. Following an unfruitful exchange of views, Piphus and his mother, as guardian *ad litem,* filed suit against petitioners in Federal District Court ... charging that Piphus had been suspended without due process of law in violation of the Fourteenth Amendment. The complaint sought declaratory and injunctive relief, together with actual and punitive damages in the amount of $3,000. Piphus was readmitted to school under a temporary restraining order after eight days of his suspension.

Respondent Silas Brisco was in the sixth grade at Clara Barton Elementary School in Chicago during the 1973–1974 school year. On September 11, 1973, Brisco came to school wearing one small earring. The previous school year the school principal had issued a rule against the wearing of earrings by male students because he believed that this practice denoted membership in certain street gangs and increased the likelihood that gang members would terrorize other students. Brisco was reminded of this rule, but he refused to remove the earring, asserting that it was a symbol of black pride, not of gang membership.

The assistant principal talked to Brisco's mother, advising her that her son would be suspended for 20 days if he did not remove the earring. Brisco's mother supported her son's position, and a 20–day suspension was imposed. Brisco and his mother, as guardian *ad litem,* filed suit in Federal District Court ... charging that Brisco had been suspended without due process of law in violation of the Fourteenth Amendment. The complaint sought declaratory and injunctive relief, together with actual and punitive damages in the amount of $5,000. Brisco was readmitted to school during the pendency of proceedings for a preliminary injunction after 17 days of his suspension.

... We granted certiorari to consider whether, in an action under § 1983 for the deprivation of procedural due process, a plaintiff must prove that he actually was injured by the deprivation before he may recover substantial "nonpunitive" damages.

II

42 U.S.C.A. § 1983, enacted as § 1 of the Civil Rights Act of 1871, 17 Stat. 13, provides:

> Every person who, under color of any statute, ordinance, regulation, custom, or usage, of any State or Territory, subjects, or causes to be subjected, any citizen of the United States or other person within the jurisdiction thereof to the deprivation of any rights, privileges, or immunities secured by the Constitution and laws, shall be liable to the party injured in an action at law, suit in equity, or other proper proceeding for redress.

The legislative history of § 1983, demonstrates that it was intended to "create a species of tort liability" in favor of persons who are deprived of "rights, privileges, or immunities secured" to them by the Constitution....

A

Insofar as petitioners contend that the basic purpose of a § 1983 damages award should be to compensate persons for injuries caused by the deprivation of constitutional rights, they have the better of the argument. Rights, constitutional and otherwise, do not exist in a vacuum. Their purpose is to protect persons from injuries to particular interests, and their contours are shaped by the interests they protect.

Our legal system's concept of damages reflects this view of legal rights. "The cardinal principle of damages in Anglo–American law is that of *compensation* for the injury caused to plaintiff by defendant's breach of duty." The Court implicitly has recognized the applicability of this principle to actions under § 1983 by stating that damages are available under that section for actions "found ... to have been violative of ... constitutional rights *and to have caused compensable injury....*"

The Members of the Congress that enacted § 1983 did not address directly the question of damages, but the principle that damages are designed to compensate persons for injuries caused by the deprivation of rights hardly could have been foreign to the many lawyers in Congress in 1871. Two other sections of the Civil Rights Act of 1871 appear to incorporate this principle, and no reason suggests itself for reading § 1983 differently. To the extent that Congress intended that awards under § 1983 should deter the deprivation of constitutional rights, there is no evidence that it meant to establish a deterrent more formidable than that inherent in the award of compensatory damages.

B

It is less difficult to conclude that damages awards under § 1983 should be governed by the principle of compensation than it is to apply this principle to concrete cases. But over the centuries the common law of torts has developed a set of rules to implement the principle that a person should be compensated fairly for injuries caused by the violation of his legal rights. These rules, defining the elements of damages and the prerequisites for their recovery, provide the appropriate starting point for the inquiry under § 1983 as well.

It is not clear, however, that common-law tort rules of damages will provide a complete solution to the damages issue in every § 1983 case. In some cases, the interests protected by a particular branch of the common law of torts may parallel closely the interests protected by a particular constitutional right. In such cases, it may be appropriate to apply the tort rules of damages directly to the § 1983 action. In other cases, the interests protected by a particular constitutional right may not also be protected by an analogous branch of the common law torts. In those cases, the task will be the more difficult one of adapting common-law rules of damages to provide fair compensation for injuries caused by the deprivation of a constitutional right.

... The purpose of § 1983 would be defeated if injuries caused by the deprivation of constitutional rights went uncompensated simply because the common law does not recognize an analogous cause of action. In order to further the purpose of § 1983, the rules governing compensation for injuries caused by the deprivation of constitutional rights should be tailored to the interests protected by the particular right in question—just as the common-law rules of damages themselves were defined by the interests protected in the various branches of tort law. We agree with Mr. Justice Harlan that "the experience of judges in dealing with private [tort] claims supports the conclusion that courts of law are capable of making the types of judgment concerning causation and magnitude of injury necessary to accord meaningful compensation for invasion of [constitutional] rights." With these principles in mind, we now turn to the problem of compensation in the case at hand.

C

The Due Process Clause of the Fourteenth Amendment provides:

> "nor shall any State deprive any person of life, liberty, or property, without due process of law; . . . ."

This Clause "raises no impenetrable barrier to the taking of a person's possessions," or liberty, or life. Procedural due process rules are meant to protect persons not from the deprivation, but from the mistaken or unjustified deprivation of life, liberty, or property. Thus, in deciding what process constitutionally is due in various contexts, the Court repeatedly has emphasized that "procedural due process rules are shaped by the risk of error inherent in the truth-finding process. . . ." Such rules "minimize substantively unfair or mistaken deprivations of" life, liberty, or property by enabling persons to contest the basis upon which the State proposes to deprive them of protected interests. . . .

The parties . . . disagree as to the . . . holding of the Court of Appeals that respondents are entitled to recover substantial—although unspecified—damages to compensate them for "the injury which is 'inherent in the nature of the wrong,'" even if their suspensions were justified and even if they fail to prove that the denial of procedural due process actually caused them some real, if intangible, injury. Respondents, elaborating on this theme, submit that the holding is correct because injury fairly may be "presumed" to flow from every denial of procedural due process. Their argument is that in addition to protecting against unjustified deprivations, the Due Process Clause also guarantees the "feeling of just treatment" by the government. They contend that the deprivation of protected interests without procedural due process, even where the premise for the deprivation is not erroneous, inevitably arouses strong feelings of mental and emotional distress in the individual who is denied this "feeling of just treatment." They analogize their case to that of defamation *per se,* in which "the plaintiff is relieved from the necessity of producing any proof whatsoever that he has been injured" in order to recover substantial compensatory damages.

Petitioners do not deny that a purpose of procedural due process is to convey to the individual a feeling that the government has dealt with him fairly, as well as to minimize the risk of mistaken deprivations of protected interests. They go so far as to concede that, in a proper case, persons in respondents' positions might well recover damages for mental and emotional distress caused by the denial of procedural due process. Petitioners' argument is the more limited one that such injury cannot be presumed to occur, and that plaintiffs at least should be put to their proof on the issue, as plaintiffs are in most tort actions.

We agree with petitioners in this respect. As we have observed in another context, the doctrine of presumed damages in the common law of defamation *per se* "is an oddity of tort law, for it allows recovery of purportedly compensatory damages without evidence of actual loss." . . . The doctrine has been defended on the grounds that those forms of defamation that are actionable *per se* are virtually certain to cause serious injury to reputation, and that this kind of injury is extremely difficult to prove. Moreover, statements that are defamatory *per se* by their very nature are likely to cause mental and emotional distress, as well as injury to reputation, so there arguably is little reason to require proof of this kind of injury either. But these considerations do not support respondents' contention that damages should be presumed to flow from every deprivation of procedural due process.

First, it is not reasonable to assume that every departure from procedural due process, no matter what the circumstances or how minor, inherently is as likely to cause distress as the publication of defamation *per se* is to cause injury to reputation and distress. Where the deprivation of a protected interest is substantively justified but procedures are deficient in some respect, there may well be those who suffer no distress over the procedural irregularities. Indeed, in contrast to the immediately distressing effect of defamation *per se,* a person may not even know that procedures *were* deficient until he enlists the aid of counsel to challenge a perceived substantive deprivation.

Moreover, where a deprivation is justified but procedures are deficient, whatever distress a person feels may be attributable to the justified deprivation rather than to deficiencies in procedure. But the injury caused by a justified deprivation, including distress, is not properly compensable under § 1983. This ambiguity in causation, which is absent in the case of defamation *per se,* provides additional need for requiring the plaintiff to convince the trier of fact that he actually suffered distress because of the denial of procedural due process itself.

Finally, we foresee no particular difficulty in producing evidence that mental and emotional distress actually was caused by the denial of procedural due process itself. Distress is a personal injury familiar to the law, customarily proved by showing the nature and circumstances of the wrong and its effect on the plaintiff. In sum, then, although mental and emotional distress caused by the denial of procedural due process itself is compensable under § 1983, we hold that neither the likelihood of such injury nor the difficulty of proving it is so great as to justify awarding compensatory damages without proof that such injury actually was caused. . . .

III

Even if respondents' suspensions were justified, and even if they did not suffer any other actual injury, the fact remains that they were deprived of their right to procedural due process. "It is enough to invoke the procedural safeguards of the Fourteenth Amendment that a significant property interest is at stake, whatever the ultimate outcome of a hearing...."

Common-law courts traditionally have vindicated deprivations of certain "absolute" rights that are not shown to have caused actual injury through the award of a nominal sum of money. By making the deprivation of such rights actionable for nominal damages without proof of actual injury, the law recognizes the importance to organized society that those rights be scrupulously observed; but at the same time, it remains true to the principle that substantial damages should be awarded only to compensate actual injury or, in the case of exemplary or punitive damages, to deter or punish malicious deprivations of rights.

Because the right to procedural due process is "absolute" in the sense that it does not depend upon the merits of a claimant's substantive assertions, and because of the importance to organized society that procedural due process be observed, we believe that the denial of procedural due process should be actionable for nominal damages without proof of actual injury. We therefore hold that if, upon remand, the District Court determines that respondents' suspensions were justified, respondents nevertheless will be entitled to recover nominal damages not to exceed one dollar from petitioners....

The judgment of the Court of Appeals is reversed, and the case is remanded for further proceedings consistent with this opinion.

It is so ordered.

NOTES

1. Insofar as procedural due process is considered an absolute right, its denial is actionable without proof of injury.

2. Why might an individual who violated a school rule file suit on the basis of procedural due process?

[CASE NO. 42]   NON–LIABILITY FOR THE OFF–CAMPUS DEATH OF A STUDENT

STODDART v. POCATELLO SCHOOL DISTRICT #25

Supreme Court of Idaho, 2010.
239 P.3d 784 [260 Educ. L. Rep. 925].

■ HORTON, JUSTICE.

This case arises from the shocking murder of Cassie Jo Stoddart (Cassie Jo) by Brian Draper (Draper) and Torey Adamcik (Adamcik) in September 2006. The Stoddart family (the Stoddarts), together with the Contreras Family (the Contrerases) (in whose house Cassie Jo was murdered), (collectively "the Plaintiffs") brought this suit, advancing claims against the Pocatello School District (the School District) for wrongful death, negligent and/or intentional infliction of emotional distress and for property loss and loss of property value. These claims are predicated upon the School District's alleged failure to take necessary action to protect Cassie Jo despite warnings that Draper and Adamcik planned a "Columbine-like" shooting.

The district court granted the School District's motion for summary judgment and entered judgment dismissing the action against the School District. The Plaintiffs have timely appealed from that judgment. We affirm.

I. FACTUAL AND PROCEDURAL BACKGROUND

On February 17, 2004, approximately two and a half years prior to Cassie Jo's murder, a student reported that Draper and another student, C.N., were planning a school shooting. The report was based upon statements made by C.N. in the course of repeated telephone conversations occurring on February 14, 2007, with two girls, G.D. and M.B. G.D. recorded a portion of one conversation in which C.N. stated, "going to have a school shooting on Tuesday, 17th, 2004." After G.D. brought the threat to the attention of officials at Irving Middle School, the principal and the School Resource Officer (SRO) called C.N. into the principal's office where he was confronted with the recording. C.N. denied any intention to bring a weapon to school or to participate in a school shooting. The SRO then went to Draper's home and interviewed Draper and his mother. Draper's mother checked her caller ID and found that three telephone calls had been placed from that phone to G.D. Draper stated that C.N. had made the recorded statement after G.D. "begged" him to repeat the statement about a school shooting. The following day, the principal and the SRO brought G.D., M.B., C.N. and Draper into the principal's office for a one-hour discussion of the matter. C.N. and Draper were warned and agreed not to make any such statements again, even in a joking manner.

Approximately one month later, another group of students reported that C.N. and Draper were planning a school shooting, this time to occur at a school dance. They reported that C.N. had stated that he, Draper, and another boy had made this plan at a previous dance and had walked through the dance pretending to shoot people. The principal and SRO interviewed C.N. C.N. initially denied any knowledge of the matter. As the interview continued, C.N. claimed that Draper and the other boy wanted to commit a school shooting at the next dance and that Draper and the other boy had walked through an earlier dance acting out a shooting, pretending to use firearms and identifying locations that could be used. C.N. stated that Draper was obsessed with Columbine and that Draper had "pictures of people with knives and guns and different killers hanging on the walls of his bedroom, as well as letters about the Columbine shooting incident." The SRO interviewed Draper about the matter, in the presence of the principal and Draper's mother. Draper claimed that he and the other boys had walked through the dance using imaginary paintball guns. Draper's mother denied that Draper had any posters on his wall depicting weapons or "evil looking pictures."

C.N. was referred for psychological counseling and transferred to an alternative school. The principal has since stated that, based on the disposition of the investigations, "we must have felt that [Draper] was not a threat." Draper's school disciplinary records did not mention either of the reports or the subsequent investigation.

In September 2006, another student, S.C., who was assigned to share a locker with Draper, found several notes between Draper and Adamcik. She viewed these notes as threatening and remembers the word "death" in them, but can remember little more about them. S.C. showed one of the notes to her mother that asked "when are we going to do this?" Her mother recalls seeing the note, although she does not recall its content. Because S.C. was upset, her mother encouraged her to bring the notes to the attention of school officials. S.C. brought the notes to the attention of the SRO and vice-principal who "dismissed [her] concerns."

On September 22, 2006, the same day Cassie Jo was murdered, Draper and Adamcik made a video recording of themselves talking about their plans to kill Cassie Jo and to carry out a Columbine-style shooting. That night, Draper and Adamcik entered the Contrerases' house and stabbed Cassie Jo to death. Draper and Adamcik were arrested, tried, and found guilty of Cassie Jo's murder.

On January 31, 2008, the Stoddarts and the Contrerases filed a complaint alleging that Draper and his parents, Adamcik and his parents, and the School District were liable to them for Cassie Jo's wrongful death, infliction of emotional distress, and property damage and loss of property value.

The School District moved for summary judgment, arguing that the School District did not owe Cassie Jo a duty of care under the circumstances, that the School District was immune from liability under I.C. § 6–904A, and that the School District was not jointly and severally liable for the acts of Draper and Adamcik.

Following a hearing, the district court issued a memorandum decision granting the School District's motion. The court found that because the murder occurred off school grounds and after school hours, the School District owed no duty to Cassie Jo at the time of her murder. The court further found that, even if the School District had a duty to supervise Cassie Jo or her killers, the immunity afforded the School District by I.C. § 6–904A would bar recovery. Finally, the court ruled that the School District would not be jointly and severally liable with the co-defendants for the damages suffered by the Plaintiffs. . . . The Plaintiffs now appeal the decision of the district court regarding duty and immunity; they do not challenge the district court's determination regarding joint and several liability.

II. STANDARD OF REVIEW

When reviewing a motion for summary judgment, this Court uses the same standard employed by the trial court when deciding such a motion. Summary judgment is proper "if the pleadings, depositions, and admissions on file, together with the affidavits, if any, show that there is no genuine issue as to any material fact and that the moving party is entitled to a judgment as a matter of law." "The burden is on the moving party to prove an absence of genuine issues of material fact." This Court views the facts and inferences in the record in favor of the non-moving party. Whether a duty of care exists is a question of law over which this Court exercises free review.

III. ANALYSIS

.... Because we conclude that the district court properly found that the School District owed no duty of care under the circumstances, we do not reach the question of immunity.

A. The Plaintiffs have failed to demonstrate a duty owed to Cassie Jo.

The Plaintiffs bring this suit under the Idaho Tort Claims Act. "The Act abrogates sovereign immunity and renders a governmental entity liable for damages arising out of its negligent acts or omissions." "The purpose of the ITCA is to provide 'much needed relief to those suffering injury from the negligence of government employees.' "

A cause of action for common law negligence in Idaho has four elements: "(1) a duty, recognized by law, requiring the defendant to conform to a certain standard of conduct; (2) a breach of that duty; (3) a causal connection between the defendant's conduct and the resulting injury; and (4) actual loss or damage." As the district court's summary judgment was based on the absence of a duty recognized by law, we too look only to the question of duty rather than going on to other questions such as legal causation.

The Plaintiffs argue that the district court erred because there were two sources from which the School District owed a duty to Cassie Jo. First, relying on the School District's common law duties and I.C. § 33–512(4), which expressly identifies a school district's duty to protect the health and morals of its students, they argue that the district court erred because the School District had a duty to safeguard its students from foreseeable harms because the danger to Cassie Jo arose on school grounds and during school hours. Second, the Plaintiffs argue that by conducting an investigation of Draper two and a half years prior to Cassie Jo's murder, the School District assumed a duty to investigate competently. They contend that a competent investigation would have allowed the School District to take appropriate action to protect Cassie Jo from the danger presented by Draper and Adamcik, and by failing to conduct a competent investigation, the School District breached its duty to Cassie Jo.

i. *A duty may exist where foreseeable harm arises on school grounds during school hours, even where the actual injury occurs off school grounds and after school hours.*

The district court found that neither I.C. § 33–512(4) nor the underlying common law special relationship between a school district and its students created a duty to care for students at the time of Cassie Jo's murder, which occurred at night, off school grounds. The court, relying on *Rife v. Long* (1995), stated that this Court "decided that when a student is not under the care, custody and supervision of a school, it is the parent's responsibility to take steps to protect the child from foreseeable risks of harm . . . ." We do not decide the case on those grounds. Other decisions from this Court, notably *Brooks v. Logan (Brooks I)* (1995) and *Hei v. Holzer* (2003), have recognized that a school district may owe a duty to its students, despite the fact that injury occurred off of school grounds and outside of school hours.

Brooks I involved a student who committed suicide off school grounds but had written about his suicidal tendencies in a journal as part of his English class assignments. This Court, basing its decision to remand on I.C. § 33–512(4), stated that "we must assume that the negligence occurred, if at all, while Jeff was attending school and [his teacher] failed to seek help. The result of the alleged negligence is the only element that did not take place on the school grounds." Describing the scope of the duty, the Court stated that I.C. § 33–512(4) "exemplifies the role of the state to the children in school, which is a role described as one in loco While this Court later found that the school district in *Brooks* was immune from suit under I.C. § 6–904A, the underlying question of whether the school district owed the student a duty was settled by *Brooks I.*

The School District argues that the holding of *Brooks I* was subsequently abrogated by statute with the enactment of I.C. § 33–512B. The statute provides that "[n]otwithstanding the provisions of section 33–512(4), Idaho Code, neither a teacher nor a school district shall have a duty to warn of the suicidal tendencies of a student absent the teacher's knowledge of direct evidence of such suicidal tendencies." Certainly, the passage of I.C. § 33–512B modified the *Brooks* holding regarding suicidal tendencies. However, we do not interpret the statute as abrogating all duties embodied in I.C. § 33–512(4) or limiting liability to injuries that occur on school grounds and during school hours. . . .

The *Hei* case involved a sexual relationship between a student over the age of majority and a teacher. The Court distinguished between the claims against the school district alleging that there was negligent supervision of Hei (the student) and those claims alleging negligent supervision of Holzer (the teacher). The Court found that a duty existed toward the student. However, the Court also found that only the claim based on the school district's supervision of the teacher could proceed because of the immunity conferred by I.C. § 6–904A.

Rife is not inconsistent with the proposition that the relevant inquiry is to the location of the negligence rather than the location of the injury. The *Rife* Court noted that in enacting I.C. § 33–512, "the legislature was addressing the need to properly supervise students during their required attendance at school, and mandating that the school district is responsible for any negligence occurring while the children are there." In *Rife,* where the relevant supervision would have occurred off school grounds and outside of school hours, the school district was under no duty to provide that supervision. Here, the Stoddarts argue that proper investigation during school hours would have prevented Cassie Jo's death, even though she was murdered off school grounds and after school hours. Based on the language of *Rife, Brooks I,* and *Hei,* we cannot say that the location of the injury is dispositive in determining whether the school district owed Cassie Jo a duty.

ii. The School District did not have a duty of care to prevent Cassie Jo's murder.

This Court has previously recognized a duty by school districts to take reasonable steps to guard against foreseeable harms faced by their students. *Brooks I* creates "a statutory duty which requires a school district to act reasonably in the face of foreseeable risks of harm." This case requires this Court to determine whether the scope of this general duty should be extended to require that a school district take reasonable steps to prevent a violent criminal act against a student by a fellow student away from school grounds and not in connection with a school-sponsored activity.

In *Rife,* this Court considered the question whether to extend the duty of care against the risk of reasonably foreseeable harm to a student while a student is in the custody of a school district to include a duty to see that students travel safely to and from school In declining to impose such a duty, this Court stated: Determining whether a duty will arise in a particular instance involves a consideration of policy and the weighing of several factors which include:

> [T]he foreseeability of harm to the plaintiff, the degree of certainty that the plaintiff suffered injury, the closeness of the connection between the defendant's conduct and the injury suffered, the moral blame attached to the defendant's conduct, the policy of preventing future harm, the extent of the burden to the defendant and consequences to the community of imposing a duty to exercise care with resulting liability for breach, and the availability, cost, and prevalence of insurance for the risk involved (citations omitted).

With respect to the foreseeability of the harm, this Court has stated:

> [F]oreseeability is a flexible concept which varies with the circumstances of each case. Where the degree of result or harm is great, but preventing it is not difficult, a relatively low degree of foreseeability is required. Conversely, where the threatened injury is minor but the burden of preventing such injury is high, a higher degree of foreseeability may be required.

In light of the lack of foreseeability of this crime and the enormous burden that would be imposed upon school districts if we were to find that a duty exists in this case, we conclude that no duty attached to the School District under these circumstances. Although we reach this conclusion, we do not suggest that the injury sustained in this case was "minor." We are fully conscious of the enormous loss suffered by the Stoddart family as a result of the brutal murder of Cassie Jo. Rather, despite the enormity of the harm involved in this case, our decision turns on the related considerations of foreseeability and the burdens a contrary decision would impose on school districts.

Normally, the foreseeability of a risk of harm, and thus whether a duty consequently attaches, is a question of fact reserved for the jury. Foreseeability is most commonly addressed when considering the question of proximate causation. However, in view of the district court's holding that the School District did not owe a duty of care to Cassie Jo under the circumstances of this case, and our acknowledgment that a school district generally owes a duty of care to protect its students from foreseeable risks of harm, we must determine whether the general duty attached, that is, whether injury sustained in this case was reasonably foreseeable.

"[W]hen the undisputed facts can lead to one reasonable conclusion, this court may rule upon the issue of foreseeability as a matter of law." We conclude that there is no genuine issue of material fact and that the danger to Cassie Jo was not foreseeable. There is nothing in the record that suggests that the School District received information during the 2004 investigation of Draper's and C.N.'s threat of a Columbine-style shooting that would provide notice that two and a half years later one of the two students involved would commit a murder that was not, in fact, a school shooting, but rather a prelude to a planned Columbine-style attack.

We do not suggest that school districts have no duty to take appropriate action, whether by school officials or by contacting law enforcement, when school officials become aware of specific information that a student or students may be the target of a violent crime, even if that crime does not occur on school grounds. However, whatever duty the School District owed to its students in 2004 did not include the duty of indefinitely monitoring Draper, which is effectively what the Plaintiffs are now arguing. In weighing the factors identified in *Rife,* we simply cannot impose such an enormous burden on school districts.

Nor did any duty arise, as the Plaintiffs argue, upon receiving the report and note from S.C. in 2006. Viewing the evidence most favorably to the Plaintiffs, S.C. relayed her concern that Adamcik and Draper had been exchanging notes that she viewed as threatening and provided a note that asked when are we going to do this? The notes did not identify Cassie Jo as the potential victim of a crime. Despite the terrible tragedy that occurred in this case, we are unable to conclude that Cassie Jo's murder was foreseeable, absent the benefit of hindsight. For these reasons, we affirm the district court's conclusion that the School District did not have a duty to take steps to prevent Cassie Jo's murder.

iii.   The School District did not assume a duty towards Cassie Jo in its 2004 investigation.

Plaintiffs also argue that the School District assumed a duty to competently investigate Draper in 2004. "If one voluntarily undertakes to perform an act, having no prior duty to do so, the duty arises to perform the act in a non-negligent manner." The Plaintiffs argue that the School District assumed a duty by conducting the investigation of Draper two and a half years before Cassie Jo's murder. "When a party assumes a duty by voluntarily performing an act that the party had no duty to perform, the duty that arises is limited to the duty actually assumed."

The Plaintiffs' claim is without merit. "[P]ast voluntary acts do not entitle the benefited party to expect assistance on future occasions, at least in the absence of an express promise that future assistance will be forthcoming." The investigation of the 2004 threats was not part of the "assistance" that would have been necessary to prevent Cassie Jo's murder. To the extent that there was an assumption of a duty by way of the investigation in 2004, that investigation concerned the threat by Draper to commit a school shooting then, with C.N. The School District did not assume an ongoing duty to monitor Draper's potential involvement in a future school shooting, much less a crime that might be committed away from school grounds. We therefore find that the School District did not assume any duty connected to the injury suffered by the Plaintiffs.

B. We do not reach the question of whether the district court erred in finding the School District immune from prosecution.

Because we find that the Plaintiffs have not demonstrated that the School District owed a duty to take steps to prevent Cassie Jo's murder, we affirm the grant of summary judgment on that ground and we do not reach the question of whether the School District has immunity ...

C. We deny the parties' requests for attorney fees under I.C. § 12–121.

Both the School District and the Plaintiffs request attorney fees under I.C. § 12–121. ... The Plaintiffs have not prevailed in this appeal and therefore are not entitled to an award of attorney fees. We are unable to find that the Plaintiffs have pursued this appeal frivolously. We therefore deny all parties' requests for attorney fees.

IV. CONCLUSION

We affirm the district court's grant of summary judgment dismissing the Plaintiffs' complaint against the School District. We deny the parties' requests for attorney fees. Costs to the School District.

NOTES

1. Do you think that the board should have been liable in this case?

2. Could anyone have done anything to have avoided this tragedy from occurring?

[CASE NO. 43]   STANDARD OF CARE, ASSUMPTION OF RISK

BENITEZ v. NEW YORK CITY BOARD OF EDUCATION

Court of Appeals of New York, 1989.
543 N.Y.S.2d 29 [54 Educ. L. Rep. 933].

■ BELLACOSA, JUDGE.

In this personal injury action seeking damages arising from a paralyzing high school football injury, the jury returned a verdict for plaintiff Benitez on four separate theories of negligence against the New York City Board of Education (Board) and its Public Schools Athletic League (PSAL). The Trial Justice granted a postverdict motion rejecting two of the four negligence theories. In a split decision, the Appellate Division affirmed the judgment for Benitez in the sum of $878,330 and subsequently granted the Board and PSAL leave to appeal.

We reverse and dismiss the complaint because plaintiff adduced insufficient evidence that defendants breached any duty of reasonable care which can be said to have proximately caused his injuries. A board of education, its subordinate employees and interscholastic athletic organizations must exercise only reasonable care to protect student athletes in sports competitions from injuries arising out of unassumed, concealed, or unreasonably increased risks. The trial court incorrectly resolved the duty/causation issue and did so under an erroneous higher duty of care instruction.

Benitez was a 19–year–old senior star athlete at George Washington High School (GW) when he suffered a broken neck in 1983 during a varsity football game against another Division A team, John F. Kennedy High School (JFK). GW had been placed in Division A prior to the 1982 season by the Football Committee of the PSAL. The PSAL determined, pursuant to established guidelines, that GW was better suited for Division A competition than the less competitive Division B league where GW had been dominant the three previous seasons. GW exhausted its administrative appeals, arguing throughout that Division A competition was "potentially dangerous to the safety and welfare of the team" and that the players might "suffer serious injuries". Before the start of the 1983 season, GW again sought to be assigned to Division B, citing among its grounds safety concerns and the injury toll suffered by the team during the 1982 season. Under PSAL administrative guidelines and because the injuries suffered by GW players were akin in number and degree with those of other Division A teams, this request for reassignment was also denied.

Following the 1983 denial, GW's coach advised the school's new principal to drop the football program but was told that such action would result in the barring of all GW athletic teams from interscholastic competition for the year. Prior to the 1983 GW–JFK game, the coach and the assistant principal in charge of physical education and health advised GW's principal that the game was a mismatch and should not be played because of the high risk of injury. The coach testified as a witness for plaintiff that, despite the principal's decision to play the season and the game, he viewed it as the coach's responsibility to pull a team off the field in the face of unsafe competition. He felt at the time it was unsafe for his team to be playing JFK; he knew his players were fatigued; he did not have the personnel to rest Benitez; and he was aware that injuries are most likely to occur when players are tired. He did not unilaterally cancel the game because he feared it might cost him his job.

Plaintiff Benitez had received numerous college football scholarship offers before his injury. He testified that he played football voluntarily and that he was fully trained by a qualified coach, particularly with respect to proper blocking techniques. His injury occurred with 1 minute and 17 seconds left in the first half of the game while correctly executing a block during a kick-off return by his team. Prior to his injury, he engaged, as was customary for him, in the great majority of plays for his team's offensive, defensive and special squads. Plaintiff conceded he was fatigued at the time of his injury but had not so informed his coach.

Benitez initiated this action against the Board, PSAL and City of New York alleging negligence in placing and retaining GW in Division A; allowing GW to play the JFK game in the face of an obvious mismatch; and allowing him to play virtually the entire first half of the game without adequate rest. Prior to submission of the case to the jury, the Trial Justice dismissed the case as against the City of New York. The court subsequently instructed the jury, over objection, that the defendants were obligated to exercise the same level of care "as a parent of ordinary prudence would exercise under the same circumstances."

The jury verdict in Benitez' favor apportioned 30% of the fault against him and 70% against the defendants. The Trial Justice granted, in part, a motion for a judgment notwithstanding the verdict and dismissed the causes relating to the placement and retention of GW in Division A, reasoning that these were discretionary determinations. Declining to direct a defendants' verdict on the remaining negligence theories, the Trial Justice stated: "[c]ertainly, the jury had a right to indicate that from the facts that were given, that they acted negligently in permitting him to play; particularly, if the coach indicated that he was fatigued. And, if he was playing him in a manner knowing that he was fatigued, certainly the jury could find that he was negligent in doing that."

In affirming, the Appellate Division majority reasoned that despite Benitez' voluntary participation and assumption of the risks inherent in football, the coach knew it was unsafe for Benitez to be playing full time, while tired, in a mismatched game and that the failure to rest him substantially increased the likelihood of injury and was its proximate cause. Additionally, the risk of injury was said to have been unreasonably enhanced by the "indirect compulsion" of the teacher-student relationship and the student's concern that he not jeopardize his college scholarship opportunities by removing himself from the game.

The dissenting Justice stated that the standard of care applicable to this situation was unsettled, but regardless of whether it was a "reasonable care" or a "prudent parent" standard, neither was breached in this case. Viewing fatigue and injury as risks inherent in football and assumed by plaintiff, the dissenter asserted that the assumption of risk defense was unrebutted. He rejected application of the "implied compulsion" theory as there was no evidence that the 19–year–old plaintiff was acting in other than a voluntary manner.

Leave was granted by the Appellate Division on a certified question which need not be answered, as the order appealed from finally determines the action. We reverse and dismiss the complaint.

The trial court erroneously instructed the jury that a school owes a student voluntarily competing in an interscholastic high school football game the more protective duty and standard of care of a prudent parent. In the context of wholly voluntary participation in intramural, interscholastic and other school-sponsored extracurricular athletic endeavors, we have required the exercise of the less demanding ordinary reasonable care standard.

To be sure, application of the personal injury principles of duty, breach and proximate cause in the context of sports injuries almost invariably includes a discussion also of assumption of risk. The common Latin aphorism cited in the cases translates as follows: one who consents to an act does not suffer a compensable injury. As Judge Cardozo put it in the "Flopper" amusement ride case, "[o]ne who takes part in such a sport accepts the dangers that inhere in it so far as they are obvious and necessary, just as a fencer accepts the risk of a thrust by his antagonist or a spectator at a ball game the chance of contact with the ball." As an integral part of athletic competitions, persons are generally held by their actual and implied consents to the risks of "injury-causing events which are known, apparent or reasonably foreseeable consequences of the participation." In this context, however, important legal distinctions are drawn between compulsory physical education courses and voluntary participation in interscholastic athletic activity as well as between professional and amateur status.

Assumption of risk in competitive athletics "is not an absolute defense but a measure of the defendant's duty of care." The policy underlying this tort rule is intended to facilitate free and vigorous participation in athletic activities. But even with professional athletes, it is "qualified to the extent that participants do not consent to acts which are reckless or intentional" Awareness of the risk assumed is to be assessed against the background of the skill and experience of the particular plaintiff, and in that assessment a higher degree of awareness will be imputed to a professional than to one with less than professional experience in the particular sport. Manifestly, a high school athlete, even an outstanding one, does not assume all the risks of a professional sportsperson, but neither does a 19–year–old senior star football player and college scholarship prospect fall within the extra protected class of those warranting strict parental duties of supervision.

... this court accepted a distinction between the circumstances of a physical education course, where participation is compulsory, and purely voluntary activity in interscholastic sports. We dismissed the complaint in that case in circumstances remarkably parallel to this case, albeit in a different sport—baseball. Players who voluntarily join in extracurricular interscholastic sports assume the risks to which their roles expose them but not risks which are "unreasonably increased or concealed." The distinction has continued validity and usefulness in correctly deciding this and like cases.

We hold that a board of education, its employees, agents and organized athletic councils must exercise ordinary reasonable care to protect student athletes voluntarily involved in extracurricular sports from unassumed, concealed or unreasonably increased risks.

On the record before us, we conclude as a matter of law that there was no showing of inherent compulsion and that Benitez' injury was not the consequence of a failed duty of care on the part of the defendants.

The theory of inherent compulsion provides that the defense of assumption of the risk is not a shield from liability, even where the injured party acted despite obvious and evident risks, when the element of voluntariness is overcome by the compulsion of a superior. Two factors are generally present to sustain a finding of liability on an inherent compulsion theory despite the injured party's knowledge of the risk, "a direction by a superior to do the act" and "an economic compulsion or other circumstance which equally impels" compliance with the direction. Though the risk is foreseen, an assurance of safety generally implicit in the supervisor's direction supplants the plaintiff's assumption of the risk by requiring action despite prudent cautionary concerns.

The coach undeniably supervised plaintiff, who may have feared that if he did not play or if he asked to be rested his athletic standing or scholarship opportunities might be jeopardized. However, there was no evidence at all that plaintiff was concerned about an unreasonably heightened risk of competition or that his coach directed him to disregard a risk he would not have otherwise assumed anyhow. While plaintiff testified he was tired, he acknowledged that he was participating voluntarily, that he did not inform his coach of his fatigue, and that he was playing without complaint under the same conditions as he had for the previous season and one half. In sum, plaintiff Benitez failed to present any evidence that he had no choice but to follow the coach's direction to play despite his concern over enhanced risk factors known by or communicated to the coach.

Moreover, while issues of proximate cause are generally fact matters to be resolved by a jury, "where only one conclusion may be drawn from the established facts ... the question of legal cause may be decided as a matter of law." Fatigue and, unfortunately, injury are inherent in team competitive sports, especially football. Benitez was concededly an excellent athlete, properly equipped and well-trained. He was playing voluntarily in the same manner as he had for the previous year and one half against Division A competition and had not requested rest or complained. Within the breadth and scope of his consent and participation, plaintiff put himself at risk in the circumstances of this case for the injuries he ultimately suffered. On his own proof, he thus failed to meet the burden of showing some negligent act or inaction, referenced to the applicable duty of care owed to him by these defendants, which may be said to constitute "a substantial cause of the events which produced the injury." The injury in this case, in sum, was a luckless accident arising from the vigorous voluntary participation in competitive interscholastic athletics.

Accordingly, the order of the Appellate Division should be reversed and the complaint dismissed, with costs. The certified question should not be answered as unnecessary.

NOTES

1. Following *Benitez*, courts in New York have applied the reasonably prudent parent standard for young children. *See Paragas v. Comsewogue Union Free Sch. Dist.*, 885 N.Y.S.2d 128 [248 Educ. L. Rep. 785] (N.Y.App.Div.2009) (affirming that although a board owed the higher standard to a six-year-old first-grader, it was not liable because it met its duty of care); *Doe v. Lorich*, 788 N.Y.S.2d 754 [195 Educ. L. Rep. 288] (N.Y.App.Div.2005) (allowing a case to proceed to trial where a principal failed to conduct an investigation into whether a teacher sexually abused a third-grade student on the issue of whether he acted with the same duty of care as a reasonably prudent parent); *Enright by Enright v. Busy Bee Playschool*, 625 N.Y.S.2d 453 [99 Educ. L. Rep. 1073] (N.Y.Sup.Ct.1995) (ruling that a jury was properly instructed that officials in a preschool owed children the duty of a prudent

parent rather than that of ordinary reasonable care). Is it wise applying a higher standard of care for young children?

2. Where school officials sent a fifteen-year-old ninth-grade student home alone from a band trip via a 1,100–mile cross-country bus trip, the Supreme Court of Iowa held that insofar as the law charged them with the care and control of children, they had to exercise the same standard of care as a parent of ordinary prudence under comparable circumstances. Do you agree? *Ette v. Linn–Mar Community School Dist.*, 656 N.W.2d 62 [173 Educ. L. Rep. 662] (Iowa 2002).

3. In addressing the significance of the defense of assumption risk, an appellate court in England, in *Regina (Hampstead Heath Winter Swimming Club and Another) v. Corporation of London and Another*, Queens Bench Division, [2005] 1 W.L.R. 2930, 2943, available at 2005 WL 959620, criticized "[t]he pursuit of an unrestrained culture of blame and compensation has many evil consequences and one is certainly the interference with the liberty of the citizen." The court described assumption of risk as the legal vehicle that opposes society's "imposing a grey and dull safety regime on everyone," in the sense that it affords people the opportunities to choose whether they wish to engage in risky activities. Do you agree with this sentiment?

[CASE NO. 44]   AN INJURY FOR WHICH COMPENSATION CAN BE AWARDED

SPEARS v. JEFFERSON PARISH SCHOOL BOARD

Court of Appeal of Louisiana, 1994.
646 So.2d 1104 [96 Educ. L. Rep. 884].

■ GOTHARD, JUDGE.

This appeal arises out of an action filed by the plaintiffs, Joyce and Samuel Spears individually and on behalf of their minor son, Justin, for injuries sustained while Justin was a kindergarten student at Woodland West Elementary School, a part of the Jefferson Parish School System. Liability of the defendant was established by a joint stipulation of the parties and the matter went to trial on the issue of quantum. In due course the trial court rendered judgment, accompanied by written reasons, in favor of the plaintiffs as follows:

Past treatment expenses
$5,498.00

Future treatment
$2,160.00

General damages—Justin
$100,000.00

Loss of Consortium Mr. and Mrs. Spears $5,000.00 each
$10,000.00

Total award
$117,658.00

Defendant appeals that judgment.

FACTS

On February 28, 1989, Justin Spears was a kindergarten student at Woodland West Elementary School. Because it was a rainy day, the students were seated on the floor of the Cafeteria watching a movie during their regularly scheduled Physical Education class under the supervision of Coach John Brooks and Coach Johnny Peyton. Justin and two of his friends began to be slightly disruptive. At that time Coach Brooks called the boys over to sit near him. The boys began to play with his hair and his ears. Coach Brooks told the boys that if they did not stop annoying him he would "kill them." Because the coach was experiencing management problems with the three boys, he took two of them into an adjacent office with him while he did some paperwork, leaving the rest of the class to watch the movie. Justin stayed behind talking to Coach Peyton. The boys began asking Coach Brooks how he would kill them. Coach Brooks told them he would probably tie the jump rope around their neck and push them off a chair in the office. Because Justin was talking to Coach Peyton during this discussion, Coach Brooks asked the boys if they wanted to play a trick on Justin and they agreed.

The testimony differs as to the events that followed, but it is clear that Coach Brooks led Justin to believe that his friends were dead. He told Justin he had hanged them by their neck with the jump rope, and at least one of the boys was lying on the floor pretending to be dead. When Justin saw the boy lying there he became upset and began to cry. Coach Brooks told Justin it was just a joke and that the boys were not really dead.

Plaintiffs introduced live testimony from Justin and both of his parents. They also introduced depositions from two psychologists who treated Justin. According to the evidence, Justin was a normal, well-adjusted five-year-old before the incident. However, in the weeks following the incident he began to exhibit infantile behavior. He refused to go to the bathroom alone and refused to wipe himself. He was afraid that Coach Brooks would come out of the mirror in the bathroom and harm him. Justin would no longer sleep in his own room. He became overly dependent on his mother and was not comfortable when she was out of sight.

Justin was treated by Dr. Lynne Shwery, a psychologist at Children's Hospital. Dr. Shwery testified at her deposition that she treated Justin from the time of the incident until he moved with his family to Virginia in June, 1991. She opined that Justin had "experienced an event that was outside the range of usual human experience and that would be markedly distressing to almost anyone." She diagnosed Justin as having Post–Traumatic Stress Disorder and explained that Justin was fearful and anxious. He had come to the realization that the world was not a safe place and that all adults could not be trusted.

From the time of the family's relocation to Virginia in 1991, Justin was treated by Dr. Tonya Fridy; that treatment was still on going at the time of trial. Dr. Fridy's professional diagnosis concurred with that of Dr. Shwery's. Additionally, Dr. Fridy stated that Justin had separation anxiety and social phobia disorder and would probably need three to five more years of therapy.

The defendant offered testimony from their own expert, Dr. Vincent Carbone. He conducted an evaluation of Justin and concluded that Justin was "a very anxious child who was very fearful of things in his environment," but Dr. Carbone did not agree that Justin was suffering from Post–Traumatic Stress Disorder.

After considering all of the evidence, the trial court rendered judgment in favor of plaintiff, accompanied by written reasons which included the finding that "this child has been effectively robbed of a normal, carefree childhood due to the careless actions of the coach."

In brief to this court the defendant assigns nine errors which can be placed into three arguments. First, it is argued that the trial court erred in its findings of fact concerning the magnitude of Justin's injuries and thus the award of damages is excessive. Second, it is argued that the award of loss of consortium to the parents is incorrect. The final argument concerns an evidentiary ruling on the defendant's assertion that Justin's parents failed to mitigate the damages.

When reviewing the factual findings of the trial court we are restricted by the manifest error standard of *Rosell v. ESCO*. Where there is conflicting testimony, reasonable inferences of fact should not be disturbed, even when the appellate court may feel its own evaluations and inferences are as reasonable as those of the trial court. Where there are two permissible views of the evidence, the fact finder's choice between them cannot be manifestly erroneous or clearly wrong. Further, when factual findings are based on credibility of witnesses, the manifest error/clearly wrong standard demands great deference to the trier of fact. The rule that questions of credibility are for the trier of fact also applies to the evaluation of expert testimony, unless the stated reasons of the expert are patently unsound. Here the opinions of experts are supported by sound reasons and there is ample support for the trial court's findings of fact. Consequently, we find no manifest error in the trial court's reliance on the expert testimony in its formulation of factual findings in this matter.

Our review of the amount awarded as general damages is subject to *Youn v. Maritime Overseas Corp.*, in which the [United States] Supreme Court, stated:

> ... an appellate court should rarely disturb an award of general damages. Reasonable persons frequently disagree about the measure of general damages in a particular case. It is only when the award is, in either direction, beyond that which a reasonable trier of fact could assess for the effects of the particular injury to the particular plaintiff under the particular circumstances that the appellate court should increase or reduce the award.

Given the circumstances of this case and the standard of review mandated by the Supreme Court, we do not find the trial court's award of general damages in the amount of $100,000.00 to Justin was an abuse of discretion. For the same reasons we cannot find that the award of $2,160.00 for future therapy was an abuse of discretion. Therefore, we will not overturn those portions of the judgment.

The defendant also complains of the award of $5,000.00 each to Justin's parents for loss of consortium. ... At trial the plaintiffs introduced evidence concerning the loss of consortium claim.

In reasons for judgment the trial court stated:

With respect to the claim for loss of consortium filed on behalf of Mr. and Mrs. Spears the Court believes that they personally have suffered heartache and anxiety as a result of the trauma to their child. The Spears have enjoyed little quality time alone because of Justin's need to be constantly in their physical presence. The Court believes that $5000.00 per parent is adequate to compensate them for their loss of consortium.

Defendant argues that the factual finding by the trial court does not warrant an award for loss of consortium, but rather, an award for mental anguish . . . which is precluded by the stipulation.

Loss of consortium in the context of the parent/child relationship means loss of the aid, assistance and companionship of the child, or loss of affection, society and service. We agree with the defendant's assertion that mental anguish suffered by the parents because of the injury to their son is not compensable in a loss of consortium claim. Further, we agree that the trial court was incorrect in awarding damages based on the reasons stated.

However, we find that the record contains evidence to support a claim for loss of consortium. It is clear from the record that the incident adversely affected the relationship between Justin and his parents. The child, who was developing normally before the incident, became a behavior problem as a direct result of defendant's actions. Injuries incurred by the child rendered the family life difficult afterward since Justin no longer wished to go on family outings. Consequently, we do not find error in the award on loss of consortium damages to the parents.

The final assignment of error concerns certain evidentiary rulings made by the trial court during the testimony of defense expert witness, Dr. Vincent Carbone. During that testimony the defendant attempted to show that the Spears were overprotective parents who projected their parental fears to Justin, making the injury worse than it might have been and slowing the child's recovery. The plaintiffs' counsel objected to this line of questioning, arguing that the evidence would be only relevant to show a failure to mitigate the damages or to establish causation. Plaintiffs' counsel further argued that since failure to mitigate damages is an affirmative defense and had not been pled, and causation was not at issue, the evidence was inadmissible. The trial court sustained the objection, but allowed the defendant to proffer the evidence.

On appeal defendant argues that the trial court erred in ruling that mitigation of damages is an affirmative defense and that the Spears did not fail to mitigate their damages. Also, defendant argues that the proffer offered at the end of the testimony disrupted the flow of the evidence and prejudiced the defense in the presentation of its case.

. . .

Because the trial court considered the mitigation to be a viable issue before the court and made a judgment based on a factual finding supported by evidence contained in the record, we cannot find error in the evidentiary rulings at trial or the finding the Spears did not fail to mitigate the damages. Nor do we find any merit to defendant's argument that the offer of the proffer at the end of the expert's testimony upset the flow of evidence to such an extent that it prejudiced the presentation of defendant's case. The defendant was allowed to offer all of the evidence it wished to offer and it was all considered by the trial court.

For the foregoing reasons the judgment of the trial court is affirmed. Costs are assessed to the appellant.

AFFIRMED

NOTES

1. What do you think about the outcome in this case? Is it fair?

2. What kind of professional development activities should school officials provide for teachers to avoid getting themselves into situations like this one?

[CASE NO. 45]   EDUCATIONAL MALPRACTICE

HUNTER v. BOARD OF EDUCATION OF MONTGOMERY COUNTY

Court of Appeals of Maryland, 1982.
439 A.2d 582 [2 Educ. L. Rep. 114].

■ DIGGES, JUDGE.

This case primarily presents the troubling but nevertheless important question, ... of whether an action can be successfully asserted against a school board and various individual employees for improperly evaluating, placing or teaching a student....

... The action was instituted ... shortly after Ross' sixteenth birthday. As best we can gather from the declaration, the parents ... complain that the school system negligently evaluated the child's learning abilities and caused him to repeat first grade materials while being physically placed in the second grade. It is alleged that this misplacement, which continued at least through grade school, generally caused the student to feel "embarrassment," to develop "learning deficiencies," and to experience "depletion of ego strength." ...

It is clear ... that the gravamen of petitioners' claim in this case sounds in negligence, asserting damages for the alleged failure of the school system to properly educate young Hunter, and we first focus our attention on this aspect of it. In so doing, we note that these so-called "educational malpractice" claims have been unanimously rejected by those few jurisdictions considering the topic.... These decisions generally hold that a cause of action seeking damages for acts of negligence in the educational process is precluded by considerations of public policy, among them being the absence of a workable rule of care against which the defendant's conduct may be measured, the inherent uncertainty in determining the cause and nature of any damages, and the extreme burden which would be imposed on the already strained resources of the public school system to say nothing of those of the judiciary. Thus ... where a high school graduate sought recovery in tort for a claimed inadequate education, the California court, viewing the problem as whether an actionable duty of care existed, noted that the "wrongful conduct and injuries allegedly involved in educational malfeasance" were neither comprehensible nor assessable within the judicial framework and explained as follows:

Unlike the activity of the highway or the marketplace, classroom methodology affords no readily acceptable standards of care, or cause, or injury. The science of pedagogy itself is fraught with different and conflicting theories of how or what a child should be taught, and any layman might—and commonly does—have his own emphatic views on the subject. The "injury" claimed here is plaintiff's inability to read and write. Substantial professional authority attests that the achievement of literacy in the schools, or its failure, is influenced by a host of factors which affect the pupil subjectively, from outside the formal teaching process, and beyond the control of its ministers. They may be physical, neurological, emotional, cultural, environmental; they may be present but not perceived, recognized but not identified.

We find in this situation no conceivable "workability of a rule of care" against which defendants' alleged conduct may be measured . . . no reasonable "degree of certainty that . . . plaintiff suffered injury" within the meaning of the law of negligence . . . , and no such perceptible "connection between the defendant's conduct and the injury suffered," as alleged, which would establish a causal link between them within the same meaning.

Although the just-articulated policy considerations alone sufficed to negate a legal duty of care . . . the court aptly identified additional, practical consequences of imposing such a duty upon the persons and agencies who administer our public educational system: . . . . [T]he New York Court of Appeals addressed the identical proposition . . . , but viewed the issue as presenting solely a question of public policy. . . . The New York court concluded that the action should not be permitted because to do so would "constitute blatant interference with the responsibility for the administration of the public school system lodged by [State] Constitution and statute in school administrative agencies." . . .

We find ourselves in substantial agreement with the reasoning employed by the [California and New York] courts, for an award of money damages, in our view, represents a singularly inappropriate remedy for asserted errors in the educational process. The misgivings expressed in these cases concerning the establishment of legal cause and the inherent immeasurability of damages that is involved in such educational negligence actions against the school systems are indeed well founded. Moreover, to allow petitioners' asserted negligence claims to proceed would in effect position the courts of this State as overseers of both the day-to-day operation of our educational process as well as the formulation of its governing policies. This responsibility we are loathe to impose on our courts. Such matters have been properly entrusted by the General Assembly to the State Department of Education and the local school boards who are invested with authority over them. . . .

. . .

JUDGMENT OF THE COURT OF SPECIAL APPEALS AFFIRMED IN PART AND REVERSED IN PART AND CASE REMANDED TO THAT COURT FOR THE ENTRY OF A JUDGMENT IN ACCORDANCE WITH THIS OPINION. COSTS TO BE DIVIDED EQUALLY BETWEEN THE PARTIES.

NOTES

1.   Widespread attempts to differentiate educational malpractice from negligence in order to avoid the centuries-old principles of negligence law have been uniformly unsuccessful. Is this wise?

2.   Should claims for educational malpractice be actionable? How would, or should, liability be assessed?

CHAPTER 8

Contractual Liability of School Boards and Employees

Introduction

The law of contracts clearly applies to public school boards.[1] Even so, since a detailed treatment of the nature of contracts is beyond the scope of this book, this chapter provides a brief overview of the law of contracts, an area that is generally well-settled, examining issues primarily other than those involving school employees.

Contracts Generally

The basic elements of contracts are mutual assent, reflected by offer and acceptance; consideration; legally competent parties; legal subject matter; and agreement in a form required by law. Mutual assent, which refers to a "meeting of the minds," signifies that parties must agree on such essential elements as the subject or subjects covered, price, and time of performance.[2] For example, where a teacher lied on her employment application to officials in a religiously affiliated non-public school, an appellate court in Louisiana held that insofar as her answers improperly induced them to hire her by causing them to believe she possessed principles that she lacked, her doing so vitiated their consent such that the parties had not entered into a valid contract insofar as there was no meeting of the minds.[3] In this regard, it is important to recognize that counteroffers, if made prior to acceptances, are rejections of original offers.[4] Thus, those who wish to accept offers should do so first unequivocally before making counteroffers which seek to modify the terms of offers.

---

1. *Perritt Ltd. Partnership v. Kenosha Unified School Dist. No. 1*, 153 F.3d 489 [128 Educ. L. Rep. 1023] (7th Cir.1998).

2. In what is a sign of the times with regard to the use of technology, one court ruled that "[a] contract is no less a contract simply because it is entered into via a computer." *Forrest v. Verizon Communications*, 805 A.2d 1007, 1010 (D.C. 2002).

3. *LaCross v. Cornerstone Christian Acad. of Lafayette*, 896 So.2d 105 [197 Educ. L. Rep. 451] (La. Ct. App. 2004), *writ denied*, 896 So.2d 1037 (La. 2005).

4. *Foster v. Ohio State Univ.*, 534 N.E.2d 1220 [51 Educ. L. Rep. 1344] (Ohio Ct. App. 1987).

Consideration, or that which each side pays for a promise or performance, is something of value, usually money or its equivalent in goods or services. Promises to make gifts or to perform gratuitous services are not contracts because they are not supported by consideration. In a broader sense, consideration is present if promisees, in return for promises, do anything legal which they are not required to do, or do not do something which they can legally do.

In one of the classic cases in the law of contracts, albeit not set in an educational context, the Court of Appeals of New York examined the parameters of consideration. The court affirmed that when a young man kept his promise to his uncle to refrain from drinking alcohol or using tobacco until he was twenty-one years of age in exchange for $5,000, the two entered into a contract since by refraining from doing something that he was legally free to do, he provided consideration in return for his promise.[5]

Legal competency in the context of school settings means that the parties must be authorized to enter into agreements. This stands for the proposition that contracts must be ones that boards have the legal ability to form and the other parties are empowered to enter. If contracts exceed board authority, referred to as acting *ultra vires*, literally, "beyond the powers," they are unenforceable. Legality of subject matter also refers to the fact that parties cannot create binding contracts if the contracts require them to perform acts that are prohibited by law.

Contracts must be in the proper form in order to be enforceable. In other words, even though oral contracts may be as binding as written ones, in order to be enforceable, specific types of contracts must be in writing. At the same time, under the parole evidence rule, absent evidence to the contrary such as memos suggesting that a key term such as price may change, since written agreements are intended to be treated as the final agreements between parties, courts refuse to permit individuals to modify their agreements by introducing contemporaneous oral statements that change the content of contracts.[6] Even if agreements are not contained on single pieces of paper, courts can accept that parties formed contracts by relying on multiple documents[7] as long as all essential terms are in writing and there are express references to other writings or connections between documents demonstrating that they relate to the same contracts.[8]

Individuals must be of legal age to enter into contracts. As to age, while minors, legally known as "infants," generally cannot enter into binding contracts, they can be expected to abide by agreements that they enter into in school settings such as those incident to training rules designed to maintain eligibility in order to participate in interscholastic

---

5. *Hamer v. Sidway*, 124 N.Y. 538 (N.Y.1891).

6. *Russell v. Halteman's Adm'x*, 153 S.W.2d 899 (Ky.1941).

7. *ICI Const. v. Orangefield Indep. School Dist.*, 339 S.W.3d 235 [268 Educ. L. Rep. 1021] (Tex.Ct.App.2011) (refusing to find that a contract had been formed).

8. *Mariani v. School Directors of Dist. 40, LaSalle County*, 506 N.E.2d 981 [39 Educ. L. Rep. 225] (Ill.App.Ct.1987), *appeal denied*, 515 N.E.2d 111 [43 Educ. L. Rep. 251] (Ill.1987).

sports[9] because "[i]f an infant enters into any contract subject to conditions or stipulations, he [sic] cannot take the benefit of the contract without the burden of the conditions or stipulations."[10] As expressed by the Supreme Court, minors cannot employ the infancy defense, meaning that they cannot try to rely on their age to escape contractual compliance, as "a sword to be used to the injury of others, although the law intends it simply as a shield to protect the infant from injustice and wrong."[11]

Under the common law principle known as the statute of frauds that has been made statutory in most jurisdictions,[12] four types of contracts that are important for schools must be in writing in order to be enforceable. First, agreements that, by their terms, cannot be performed within one year must be in writing.[13] Second, agreements to purchase or sell interests in real property must be in writing.[14] Third, contracts for the purchase of goods worth more than $500.00 must be in writing.[15] Fourth, promises to answer the debts of others, such as where school systems merge and newly created boards agree to pay the debts of their predecessors such as mortgages and salaries, must be in writing.[16]

If parties make mutual mistakes in written contracts, courts may correct, or reform, their errors or can invalidate agreements on the ground that the parties failed to achieve a meeting of the minds.[17] In such a case, where a secretary used the wrong form, stating that a superintendent was hired for one year, rather than two, the Supreme Court of Arkansas affirmed that a board could not subsequently claim that the agreement was for one year.[18] The court explained that insofar as the parties wished to enter into a two-year contract, having their signatures affixed to the wrong form did not change their intended agreement. If an error is unilateral, as

---

9.   *See, e.g., Schultzen v. Woodbury Cent. Community School Dist.*, 187 F.Supp.2d 1099 [162 Educ. L. Rep. 766] (N.D. Iowa 2002) (holding that a female student-athlete could not be punished more harshly than males for the same offense of smoking in violation of training rules).

10.   5 WILLISTON ON CONTRACTS § 9:14 (4th ed. 2007).

11.   *MacGreal v. Taylor*, 167 U.S. 688, 701, 17 S.Ct. 961, 42 L.Ed. 326 (1897).

12.   *See, e.g., Mays–Maune & Assoc. v. Werner Bros.*, 139 S.W.3d 201 [190 Educ. L. Rep. 1058] (Mo. Ct. App. 2004) (affirming that insofar as the statutory requirement calling for contracts to be in writing is mandatory, strict compliance is required in order to bind school boards).

13.   *See, e.g., Spectrum Benefit Options v. Medical Mut. of Ohio*, 880 N.E.2d 926 [229 Educ. L. Rep. 226] (Ohio Ct. App. 2007); *Kirschling v. Lake Forest School Dist.*, 687 F.Supp. 927 [47 Educ. L. Rep. 977] (D. Del. 1988); *Senghas v. L'Anse Creuse Pub. Schools*, 118 N.W.2d 975 (Mich. 1962). *But see Gens v. Casady School*, 177 P.3d 565 [229 Educ. L. Rep. 891] (Okla. 2008) (ruling that an oral agreement may be a continuing contract that extends for more than a year but not be within the statute of frauds if either party can terminate it at any time).

14.   *Board of Educ., Gadsden Indep. School Dist. No. 16 v. James Hamilton Const. Co.*, 891 P.2d 556 [98 Educ. L. Rep. 1037] (N.M. Ct. App. 1994), *cert. denied*, 890 P.2d 807 (N.M. 1995).

15.   *Double AA Builders, Ltd. v. Grand State Constr.*, 114 P.3d 835, 841 (Ariz. Ct. App. 2005).

16.   *American Cas. Co. of Reading, Pa. v. Devine*, 157 So.2d 661 (Ala. 1963); *Parsons v. Kelso*, 125 S.W. 227 (Mo. Ct. App. 1910).

17.   For perhaps the classic case on mutual mistakes, *see Sherwood v. Walker*, 33 N.W. 919 (Mich. 1887) (invalidating the sale of a cow where both the buyer and seller were unaware that she was pregnant, a situation that would have increased the purchase price greatly).

18.   *Hampton School Dist. No. 1 of Calhoun County v. Phillips*, 470 S.W.2d 934 (Ark. 1971).

where a moving company's bid to transport the contents of school was one-third of the amount that it billed a board, an appellate court decided that it could not recover for its mistake.[19] An appellate court in Minnesota reasoned that recovery was inappropriate absent evidence that board officials acted in any way to mislead or take advantage of the moving company since they made additional inquiries into the bid and confirmed the company's confidence in its offer.

BOARD AUTHORITY TO ENTER INTO CONTRACTS

The contractual liability of school boards depends in part on whether they had the authority to enter into agreements. As revealed by a case from Texas, once a board enters into a contract, its status with regard to potential liability may change. An appellate court affirmed that when a board exercised its authority to enter into a contract with a company to install synthetic turf on its football field, it waived its immunity from liability with respect to the company's breach of contract claim.[20]

In addition to the common law authority of boards to enter into contracts, they must comply with applicable statutory mandates.[21] In one case, a dispute arose over whether a county board of education violated state law by hiring private legal counsel rather than relying on the county's prosecuting attorney to handle its legal affairs. The Supreme Court of Appeals of West Virginia affirmed that the board could exercise discretion in choosing whether to use the services of the county prosecuting attorney or hire its own legal counsel.[22] In another case, four days before a new consolidated school district came into being, its board and one of the component systems entered into a new employment contract with the superintendent. When the new board tried to set aside the reorganization, it refused to honor the superintendent's contract. The Supreme Court of Colorado affirmed that the superintendent could not recover on the contract since the old board exceeded its authority in entering into the agreement.[23]

As noted, school boards are created to carry out state constitutional mandates to provide for public education. Boards have only those powers, including contractual ability, that legislatures expressly grant them along with those necessarily implied to enable them to carry out their express duties[24] such as entering into collective bargaining agreements.[25] As impor-

---

19. *A.A. Metcalf Moving & Storage Co. v. North St. Paul–Maplewood Oakdale Schools*, 587 N.W.2d 311 [131 Educ. L. Rep. 504] (Minn.Ct.App.1998).

20. *Longview Indep. School Dist. v. Vibra–Whirl*, 169 S.W.3d 511 [201 Educ. L. Rep. 403] (Tex.Ct.App.2005).

21. *Berkheimer Assoc. ex rel. North Coventry Twp. v. Norco Motors*, 842 A.2d 966 [185 Educ. L. Rep. 977] (Pa.Cmwlth.Ct.2004), *appeal dismissed*, 860 A.2d 125 (Pa.2004).

22. *Longwell v. Board of Educ. of the County of Marshall*, 583 S.E.2d 109 [179 Educ. L. Rep. 484] (W.Va.2003).

23. *Achenbach v. School Dist. No. RE–2, Brush*, 491 P.2d 57 (Colo.1971).

24. *National Educ. Ass'n–Wichita v. Unified School Dist. No. 259, Sedgwick County*, 674 P.2d 478 [15 Educ. L. Rep. 948] (Kan.1983); *Swinney v. Deming Bd. of Educ.*, 873 P.2d 238 [91 Educ. L. Rep. 347] (N.M.1994).

tant as it may be, the express power of boards to enter into contracts does not necessarily imply the ability to include clauses calling for arbitration of disputes growing out of construction contracts.[26]

A controversial topic with regard to board power involves agreements where they "contract out" services such as for food and maintenance to private companies in order to try to save money. In an illustrative case, the Supreme Court of Minnesota affirmed that a board could not unilaterally contract out food services work while a collective bargaining agreement remained in effect.[27] The Supreme Court of Vermont reached a similar result with regard to a board's attempt to contract out for custodial services.[28] Conversely, the Court of Appeals of New York ruled that a law permitting boards to subcontract services that the state's commissioner of education might have approved, such as printing, authorized them to subcontract out their printing services without subjecting themselves to operative collective bargaining agreements.[29]

Where statutes neither explicitly nor implicitly cover the manner in which boards must execute their functions, they may be able to contract out specified services.[30] However, if board personnel have performed the services under collective bargaining statutes, boards must bargain on the matters. In a disagreement over a food service program, the Supreme Court of Wisconsin affirmed that insofar as the same work would have had to have been completed either way, it had no choice but to reject a board's claim that a dispute was primarily related to the formulation or management of public policy that would have given a union undue control over its affairs.[31] In treating the dispute as one dealing with conditions of employment, the court observed that the board was not obligated to accept the union's proposal.

If a statute specifies the manner or form in which boards must enter into contracts, agreements created in any other way are invalid.[32] As such, where state laws require specified types of board contracts to be in writing, even though oral contracts for the same subject matter would have been valid if formed by individuals or private corporations, they are invalid.[33] As

---

25. *Savage Educ. Ass'n v. Trustees of Richland County Elementary Dist. No. 7*, 692 P.2d 1237 [22 Educ. L. Rep. 506] (Mont. 1984).

26. *W.M. Schlosser Co. v. School Bd. of Fairfax County, Va.*, 980 F.2d 253 [79 Educ. L. Rep. 382] (4th Cir.1992), *cert. denied*, 508 U.S. 909, 113 S.Ct. 2340, 124 L.Ed.2d 251 (1993).

27. *Independent School Dist. No. 88, New Ulm v. School Serv. Employees Union Local 284*, 503 N.W.2d 104 [84 Educ. L. Rep. 827] (Minn. 1993).

28. *Milton Educ. and Support Ass'n v. Milton Bd. of School Trustees*, 824 A.2d 605 [177 Educ. L. Rep. 410] (Vt. 2003).

29. *Vestal Employees Ass'n, NEA/NY, NEA v. Public Employment Relations Bd. of State of N.Y.*, 705 N.Y.S.2d 564 [143 Educ. L. Rep. 331] (N.Y.2000).

30. *Nassau Educ. Chapter of Civil Serv. Employees Ass'n v. Great Neck Union Free School Dist.*, 454 N.Y.S.2d 67 [6 Educ. L. Rep. 365] (N.Y.1982).

31. *Unified School Dist. No. 1 of Racine County v. Wisconsin Employment Relations Comm'n*, 259 N.W.2d 724 (Wis. 1977).

32. *Minor v. Sully Buttes School Dist. No. 58–2*, 345 N.W.2d 48 [16 Educ. L. Rep. 624] (S.D. 1984).

33. *Board of School Commr's of the City of Indianapolis v. State ex rel. Wolfolk*, 199 N.E. 569 (Ind.1936); *Richard D. Kimball Co. v. City of Medford*, 166 N.E.2d 708 (Mass. 1960). *But*

discussed below, other contracts that boards enter may have to be awarded to the lowest bidders.

School boards inevitably attempt, in good faith, to form contracts that turn out to be invalid due to their failure to follow statutory guidelines. Still, good faith does not validate illegal contracts.[34] In a closely related matter, most jurisdictions treat contracts as implying covenants of good faith and fair dealing.[35]

Insofar as laws restricting board powers to enter into contracts are designed to protect the public, the degree of protection that they afford depends on the strictness with which courts interpret applicable statutes. Where a law in California required boards to take official actions by formal votes at legally called public meetings, an appellate court interpreted it as meaning that a contract to purchase property for a school site could not be authorized in an executive session.[36] In a variation of this issue, an appellate court in Pennsylvania affirmed that while a formal recorded board vote is unnecessary, there must be solid proof of compliance with applicable laws before contracts become enforceable.[37] Another court in Pennsylvania warned that individuals or companies relying "on agreements with an agent of the school district without first obtaining approval by a vote of the majority of the members at a public meeting do so at their peril."[38]

As demonstrated by a case from Arizona, good intentions are irrelevant to contractual validity. An appellate court affirmed that a board was not contractually obligated to accept high school students tuition-free from another district based on an agreement that a predecessor board formed twenty-seven years earlier.[39] The court found that the contract was not only legislatively unauthorized, but impliedly prohibited by a statute that specified procedures for dealing with nonresident students.[40] On the other hand, where a state law did not require a board to obtain prior approval from voters, the Supreme Court of New Hampshire affirmed the ability of

see Burk v. Livingston Parish School Bd., 182 So. 656 (La.1938) (ordering a board to make full payment on an oral contract where the work was completed).

34. *Conners v. City of Lowell*, 140 N.E. 742 (Mass.1923).

35. *Christensen v. Kingston School Comm.*, 360 F.Supp.2d 212 [196 Educ. L. Rep. 854] (D. Mass. 2005); *Blanck v. Hager*, 360 F.Supp.2d 1137 [196 Educ. L. Rep. 872] (D.Nev.2005), *aff'd*, 220 Fed.Appx. 697 (9th Cir.2007). *But see Hispanic College Fund v. National Collegiate Athletic Ass'n*, 826 N.E.2d 652, 658 [197 Educ. L. Rep. 770] (Ind.Ct.App.2005), *transfer denied*, 841 N.E.2d 181 (Ind.2005) ("Indiana law does not impose a generalized duty of good faith and fair dealing on every contract.").

36. *Santa Monica Unified School Dist. v. Persh*, 85 Cal.Rptr. 463 (Cal.Ct.App.1970).

37. *Parents Against Abuse In Schools v. Williamsport Area School Dist.*, 594 A.2d 796 [69 Educ. L. Rep. 466] (Pa.Cmwlth.Ct.1991). *But see Hazleton Area School Dist. v. Krasnoff*, 672 A.2d 858 [107 Educ. L. Rep. 886] (Pa.Cmwlth.Ct.1996), *appeal denied*, 685 A.2d 548 (Pa. 1996) (requiring an affirmative vote of a majority of a board on a contract to increase its debt).

38. *Berkheimer Assoc. ex rel. N. Coventry Twp. v. Norco Motors*, 842 A.2d 966, 971 [185 Educ. L. Rep. 977] (Pa. Cmwlth. Ct. 2004), *appeal denied*, 860 A.2d 125 (Pa. 2004).

39. *Oracle School Dist. No. 2 v. Mammoth High School Dist. No. 88*, 633 P.2d 450 (Ariz. Ct. App. 1981).

40. *See also Public Improvements v. Board of Educ. of City of N.Y.*, 453 N.Y.S.2d 170 [5 Educ. L. Rep. 1231] (N.Y.1982) (refusing to invoke the rule of estoppel against a public agency).

two boards to enter into a three-year tuition agreement under which one board sent its students to a high school in the other district.[41] The court rejected a challenge from taxpayers who opposed the contract in determining that voters in the sending district ratified the agreement.

At issue in a dispute over the construction of a school administration center was whether a board authorized its president to sign the prime contract. An appellate court in Texas refused to void the contract in positing that a jury could have discovered the presence of authorization from such evidence as the minutes of the meeting at which the board accepted the prime contractor's low bid, testimony that the contractor did not perform any work until the architect approved it, and testimony from board members that officials made payments under the contract.[42]

Oral contracts can present special concerns. In one case, the Supreme Court of Ohio pointed out that a principal's oral promise to provide a teacher with a duty-free lunch period in exchange for her agreeing to teach journalism classes and serve as newspaper adviser was not binding on the board since he lacked the authority to enter into such an arrangement.[43] Earlier, an appellate court in Ohio indicated that a superintendent's oral representations to parents that if their children were accepted as students on a tuition basis, they would have been able to attend classes until graduation was not binding even though it was based on conversations with individual board members.[44] The court was of the opinion that the parties never entered into a contract since the board as a whole did not approve the agreement.

In a case with a different outcome, the Third Circuit affirmed that an oral contract between a school board and a construction firm in Pennsylvania was enforceable.[45] The court acknowledged that the board agreed to allow the company to bid on three building projects based on the drawings, specifications, and equipment lists that officials prepared. When the board withdrew the projects from bidding due to a lack of subsidies from the commonwealth, the company sought reimbursement for its services. A federal trial court rejected the board's claims that the agreement was not binding since it was made at a conference rather than a formal meeting and that only written contracts could be enforced against boards for this type of work.[46]

CONTRACTS EXTENDING BEYOND A BOARD'S TERM

41. *Foote v. Manchester School Dist.*, 883 A.2d 283 [202 Educ. L. Rep. 206] (N.H. 2005).

42. *Calvin V. Koltermann, Inc. v. Underream Piling Co.*, 563 S.W.2d 950 (Tex. Civ. App. 1977).

43. *Wolf v. Cuyahoga Falls City School Dist. Bd. of Educ.*, 556 N.E.2d 511 [61 Educ. L. Rep. 267] (Ohio 1990).

44. *Walker v. Lockland City School Dist. Bd. of Educ.*, 429 N.E.2d 1179 [2 Educ. L. Rep. 203] (Ohio Ct. App. 1980).

45. *Titan Environmental Constr. Sys. v. School Dist. of Philadelphia*, 421 F.Supp. 1289 (E.D. Pa. 1976), *aff'd without reported opinion*, 564 F.2d 90 (3d Cir.1977).

46. *See also Robert W. Anderson Housewrecking and Excavating v. Board of Trustees, School Dist. No. 25, Fremont County*, 681 P.2d 1326 [17 Educ. L. Rep. 1232] (Wyo. 1984).

Disputes arise over whether school boards can form contracts extending beyond their terms in office. As ongoing legal entities with changing memberships, boards have some ability to act prospectively. If this concept were carried to its logical conclusion, though, boards could deprive successor boards of a great deal of authority. Aware of the dangers inherent in such situations, courts consistently agree that boards do not have unlimited powers to bind their successors even if they enter into agreements with other governmental agencies.[47] Put another way, if new board members could repudiate actions of their predecessors, the resulting uncertainty and instability could lead to chaos. The courts carefully examine fact situations where it appears that either of these extremes has occurred.

Two cases involving contracts examine difficulties that arose when school boards exceeded their authority. Outgoing board members sought to grant a contract extension to a superintendent for an extra four-year term starting a year before the end of his current term. When new members disagreed, Kentucky's highest court declared that the old board lacked the authority to create a new term for the superintendent prior to the expiration of his time in office.[48] The court wrote that any other result would have made it possible for superintendents to secure the votes of the majority of board members, splice terms, and perpetuate their stays in office indefinitely, thereby defeating the right of the people to select, even if indirectly, successors. In like fashion, an appellate court in New Jersey affirmed that a board, which hired a superintendent for a two-year probationary term, could not, after eight-and a half months, grant him a three-year contract including tenure.[49] The court reviewed the board's proceedings, maintaining that it relied on an illegal modus operandi since the real reason for the change was that members of the majority block, mindful of a coming election, sought to grant the superintendent tenure while they could even though it meant shortening his probationary period by almost two-thirds.

The general rule appears to be that absent express or implied statutory limits on their authority, or if there is no fraud or collusion, boards can enter into contracts that extend for reasonable periods beyond their terms. In litigation on point, courts have reached mixed results. For example, according to an older case from the Supreme Court of Iowa, if a contract lies totally within the term of a succeeding board, it is invalid.[50] In other instances, courts have interpreted statutes as empowering boards, as ongoing legal bodies, to bind their successors even though the services would be

---

47. *See Greene County School Dist. v. Greene County*, 607 S.E.2d 881 [195 Educ. L. Rep. 349] (Ga. 2005) (affirming that insofar as a school board's agreement to convey property to a county in exchange for a reduction in the county's commission for collecting taxes for it was not a valid intergovernmental contract, it did not bind the subsequent board of commissioners).

48. *Board of Educ. of Pendleton County v. Gulick*, 398 S.W.2d 483 (Ky. 1966).

49. *Thomas v. Board of Educ. of Morris Twp.*, 215 A.2d 35 (N.J. Super. Ct. App. Div.1965), *aff'd*, 218 A.2d 630 (N.J. 1966).

50. *Independent School Dist. v. Pennington*, 165 N.W. 209 (Iowa 1917).

performed wholly within the terms of the new boards.[51] A party wishing to obviate a board's attempt to bind its successor must show that an agreement extending beyond the term of a contracting board is not reasonably necessary or offered no definable advantage.[52]

COMPETITIVE BIDDING

IN GENERAL

Most jurisdictions have laws, often with multiple versions addressing different bodies, requiring all or specified public contracts, including those for schools, to be subject to competitive bidding. Since these laws are typically designed "to 'guard against favoritism, improvidence, extravagance and corruption,' "[53] disappointed bidders generally lack standing to challenge adverse decisions absent claims that officials engaged in fraud, corruption, or other acts undermining the integrity of the process.[54]

The laws typically require school boards to award contracts to the "lowest responsible bidder"[55] or the "lowest and best bidder,"[56] with some states using both terms.[57] While most contracts for professional services[58] or repair services[59] are ordinarily not subject to competitive bidding, there are exceptions to this rule.[60]

The Supreme Court of Arizona addressed the nature of bids in relation to final contracts when a contractor sued a school board for breach after

---

51. *King City Union High School Dist. v. Waibel*, 37 P.2d 861 (Cal.Ct.App.1934).

52. *Michie v. Board of Trustees of Carbon County School Dist. No. 1*, 847 P.2d 1006 [81 Educ. L. Rep. 581] (Wyo. 1993).

53. *Oceanside Charter School v. New Jersey State Dep't of Educ. Office of Compliance Investigation*, 11 A.3d 864, 870 [263 Educ. L. Rep. 813] (N.J.Super.Ct.App.Div.2011), citing *M.J. Paquet v. New Jersey Dep't of Transp.*, 794 A.2d 141 (N.J.2002).

54. *Arnoldy v. Mahoney*, 791 N.W.2d 645 (S.D.2010).

55. *See, e.g.*, ALA. CODE 1975 § 16–2–8; WEST'S ANN. CAL. EDUC. CODE § 17060, IDAHO CODE § 33–601; 105 ILL. COM. STAT. ANN. 5/10–9; INDIANA CODE ANN. § 20–9.1–2–9; IOWA CODE ANN. § 260C.38; KAN. STAT. ANN. § 72–6760; LA. REV. STAT. ANN. § 15:1035; MINN STAT. ANN. § 123B.52; MISS. CODE ANN. § 37–41–31; MO. REV. STAT. ANN. 177.086; N.J. STAT. ANN. § 9:11–2; NEW MEXICO STAT. ANN. § 49–6–13; N.Y. MCKINNEY'S EDUC. L. § 305; OHIO REV. CODE ANN. § 3318.10; 24 PA. STAT. ANN. § 7–751; TEX. CODE ANN., EDUC. CODE § 44.033.

56. IND. CODE. ANN. § 5–16–1–1.9; KY. REV. STAT. ANN. § 162.070; MISS. CODE ANN. § 37–39–7; OHIO REV. CODE § 3381.11; TENN. CODE. ANN. § 49–2–203; W. VA. CODE ANN. § 10–4–3.

57. *See* Indiana, Mississippi, Ohio, and West Virginia, *id.*

58. *Cress v. State*, 152 N.E. 822 (Ind.1926); *Malloy v. Boyertown Area School Bd.*, 657 A.2d 915 [100 Educ. L. Rep. 198] (Pa.1995); *Shively v. Belleville Twp. High School Dist. No. 201*, 769 N.E.2d 1062 [167 Educ. L. Rep. 836] (Ill.App.Ct.2002), *appeal denied*, 786 N.E.2d 200 (Ill.2002); *B & C Electric v. East Baton Rouge Parish School Bd.*, 849 So.2d 616 [179 Educ. L. Rep. 539] (La. Ct. App. 2003).

59. *Tiger Air & Heat v. Jefferson Parish School Bd.*, 832 So.2d 324 [172 Educ. L. Rep. 1056] (La.Ct.App.2002), *writ denied*, 839 So.2d 35 (La. 2003).

60. *See, e.g., Motta v. Philipsburg School Bd. Trustees, Dist. #1*, 110 P.3d 1055 (Mont. 2005) (stating that insofar as an agreement to provide workshops for administrators, teachers, and other selected community members was a professional services contract, the board was required to advertise for bids and award it to the lowest responsible bidder).

the latter sought to cancel a bid before executing a final written agreement. The court decided that in light of the common law rule that a public agency that accepts a bid on a public contract is not bound until a formal contract exists, the board did not breach the agreement.[61]

Another question about competitive bidding arose when a local board agreed to an exclusive ten-year contract with a national soft drink company to provide vending machines to sell its products at a school. A competing company unsuccessfully alleged that insofar as it did not have the opportunity to bid for the contract, the board violated a state law that prohibits any "person" from regulating commerce to prevent competition in the sale of merchandise. The Supreme Court of Montana observed that the statute was inapplicable because the board was not a "person" engaged as a business.[62]

Competitive bidding statutes are designed to ensure, as far as possible, both that school boards do not become victims of wrongdoing and that they receive the most for their money. In this regard, the Supreme Court of Mississippi stipulated that bidding laws, which were born of experience, are designed to protect boards and taxpayers from permitting officials to favor one contractor over another at public expense.[63]

Where statutes prevent school boards from seeking separate bids for some kinds of contracts, courts are generally unwilling to waive such provisions. Since courts usually interpret statutory provisions designed to safeguard public funds strictly, non-conforming contracts are rendered void.[64]

Pre-qualification requirements for bidders such as descriptions of qualifications and posting bonds are generally treated as mandatory. Consequently, contracts lacking these elements are void. In a dispute from Louisiana, where officials at a company that placed a bid denied that they ever failed to complete a contract, the Fifth Circuit asserted that a board could disqualify the firm before awarding the project because it did not prequalify.[65] On another issue dealing with pre-qualifications, the Supreme Court of Nevada affirmed that when a local school board rejected a contractor's application for a renovation project, its only avenue of redress was an administrative appeal since state law did not permit private causes of actions.[66]

---

61. *Ry–Tan Const. v. Washington Elementary School Dist. No. 6*, 111 P.3d 1019 [198 Educ. L. Rep. 327] (Ariz. 2005).

62. *Montana Vending v. Coca–Cola Bottling Co. of Mont.*, 78 P.3d 499 [182 Educ. L. Rep. 345] (Mont. 2003).

63. *Beall v. Board of Supervisors*, 3 So.2d 839 (Miss. 1941).

64. *Buchanan Bridge Co. v. Campbell*, 54 N.E. 372 (Ohio 1899).

65. *Systems Contractors Corp. v. Orleans Parish School Bd.*, 148 F.3d 571 [127 Educ. L. Rep. 722] (5th Cir.1998). *See also Crest Const. Corp. v. Shelby County Bd. of Educ.*, 612 So.2d 425 [80 Educ. L. Rep. 1139] (Ala. 1992).

66. *Richardson Constr. v. Clark County School Dist.*, 156 P.3d 21 [218 Educ. L. Rep. 988] (Nev. 2007).

LOWEST RESPONSIBLE BIDDER

Disputes have arisen over school board difficulties evaluating what constitutes the "lowest responsible" or "lowest and best" bidders. While bidding laws typically require boards to provide due process to "unresponsive bidders,"[67] low bidders generally lack the right to sue[68] since the purpose of competitive bidding statutes is not to grant rights to bidders but to benefit taxpayers who can file suit to ensure statutory compliance.[69] As reflected by an appellate panel in Indiana, when a school "board is vested with discretionary power to enter into public contracts pursuant to competitive bidding, an honest exercise of such discretion will not be disturbed by the courts."[70] Boards that reject all bids must typically issue other bid notices in order to procure contractors or suppliers.[71]

When evaluating whether bidders are responsive, meaning that their bids conform in all respects to specifications of awarding authorities,[72] boards are free to consider factors beyond financial ability and can examine characteristics such as financial standing, general ability, experience, reputation, promptness, and quality of previous work.[73] For instance, the Supreme Court of Rhode Island posited that a school committee did not act unreasonably, in bad faith, or arbitrarily in awarding a contract to a bidder who did not submit the lowest bid.[74] The court was satisfied that the committee carefully considered factors such as the relative experience of bidders, expertise, qualifications, and quality of work in granting the contract to the bidder it considered to be superior where the criteria were sufficiently objective, measurable, and enunciated.

The Supreme Court of Georgia affirmed that when a school board voted to accept the bid of a contractor that corrected the deficiency of failing to provide a list of subcontractors, provisions in state law expecting "responsive" bidders to conform in all "material" respects to bid requirements did not mean that all bids had to meet every statement precisely in

67. *D.H. Williams Constr. v. Clovis Unified School Dist.*, 53 Cal.Rptr.3d 345 [215 Educ. L. Rep. 964] (Cal.Ct.App.2007), *reh'g denied* (2007), *review denied* (2007) (affirming that a bidder could change an unlicensed subcontractor where a board failed to provide it with due process).

68. *See Laidlaw Transit v. Anchorage School Dist.*, 118 P.3d 1018 [201 Educ. L. Rep. 714] (Alaska 2005) (affirming that where a matching bid was treated as responsive, an unsuccessful bidder had no right to sue). *But see Advance Elec. Co. v. Montgomery Twp. Bd. of Educ.*, 797 A.2d 216 [165 Educ. L. Rep. 243] (N.J.Super.Ct.App.Div.2002), *certification denied*, 807 A.2d 195 (N.J. 2002) (affirming that in light of the importance of bidding statutes for public school projects, an unsuccessful bidder may challenge a bid award by seeking to enforce the policy behind the law).

69. *Black Ash Servs. v. DuBois Area School Dist.*, 764 A.2d 672 [150 Educ. L. Rep. 228] (Pa.Cmwlth.Ct.2000).

70. *Gariup Const. Co. v. Carras–Szany–Kuhn & Assocs.*, 945 N.E.2d 227, 235 (Ind.Ct.App. 2011).

71. *Painting & Decorating Contractors of Am. v. Ellensburg School Dist.*, 638 P.2d 1220 [2 Educ. L. Rep. 271] (Wash. 1982).

72. *Bigley v. MSD of Wayne Twp. Schools*, 823 N.E.2d 278 [195 Educ. L. Rep. 935] (Ind.Ct.App.2004), *transfer denied*, 831 N.E.2d 742 (Ind.2005).

73. *Hibbs v. Arensberg*, 119 A. 727, 729 (Pa.1923). [Case No. 46] For a more recent case, *see Steingass Mechanical Contracting v. Warrensville Heights Bd. of Educ.*, 784 N.E.2d 118 [173 Educ. L. Rep. 981] (Ohio Ct.App.2003).

74. *H.V. Collins Co. v. Tarro*, 696 A.2d 298 (R.I.1997).

bid invitations.[75] At the same time, the Supreme Court of Pennsylvania was of the view that a board was not obligated to reject the low bidder that failed to meet the bid specification that its surety issue a bid bond with an "A–" rating or better.[76] The court added that insofar as the board had discretion to waive the defects and, on request, the contractor furnished a bond of required quality, the submission of a bid with a lower-rated surety did not give the contractor an impermissible competitive advantage over other bidders.

On matters of propriety and reputation, when a school board in New York feared that there was a link between a bidder and persons suspected of, and eventually indicted for, perjury in connection with bid rigging involving other public agencies, it was able to withhold a contract even though the party was the lowest bidder.[77] The court remarked that it was unnecessary to conduct a hearing for the rejected bidder before the disqualification. Other courts in New York contended that although a board may disqualify a bidder for engaging in bidding improprieties,[78] one may not exclude an individual who invoked the privilege against self-incrimination before a grand jury.[79] Another appellate court in New York confirmed that an individual with a prior criminal conviction was not a responsible bidder[80] while the Second Circuit affirmed that the New York City School Construction Authority did not violate the rights of a prospective low bidder whose company was subject to a criminal investigation.[81]

CONDITIONS OF BIDDING

Consistent with their own policies, state, and federal law, school boards are free to set conditions such as requiring prime contractors to perform a minimum percentage of work with their own employees.[82] In another type of pre-condition implicating constitutional concerns, the Eighth Circuit affirmed that insofar as a board in Missouri's preference for union labor, expressed in its construction bid specifications, did not transgress the constitutional right of non-union employees to associate freely, it did not violate the rights of a firm that was denied a contract even though it was the lowest bidder.[83] Earlier, the Supreme Court of Alaska thought that a borough's requiring successful bidders on a high school renovation project

---

75. *R.D. Brown Contractors v. Board of Educ. of Columbia County*, 626 S.E.2d 471 [206 Educ. L. Rep. 1022] (Ga.2006).

76. *Gaeta v. Ridley School Dist.*, 788 A.2d 363 [160 Educ. L. Rep. 847] (Pa.2002).

77. *Arglo Painting Corp. v. Board of Educ. of City of N.Y.*, 263 N.Y.S.2d 124 (N.Y.1965).

78. *Caristo Constr. Corp. v. Rubin*, 225 N.Y.S.2d 502 (N.Y.1962).

79. *Turley v. Lefkowitz*, 342 F.Supp. 544 (W.D.N.Y.1972), *aff'd*, 414 U.S. 70, 94 S.Ct. 316, 38 L.Ed.2d 274 (1973).

80. *Crescent Bus Corp. v. Board of Educ. of City of N.Y.*, 463 N.Y.S.2d 259 [11 Educ. L. Rep. 979] (N.Y. App. Div. 1983).

81. *John Gil Const. v. Riverso*, 7 Fed.Appx. 134 [157 Educ. L. Rep. 581] (2d Cir.2001).

82. *Valley Crest Landscape v. City Council*, 49 Cal.Rptr.2d 184 (Cal.Ct.App.1996); *Benjamin R. Harvey Co. v. Board of Educ., Spring Lake Heights School Dist.*, 817 A.2d 1023 (N.J. Super. Ct. Law Div. 2002).

83. *Hanten v. School Dist. of Riverview Gardens*, 183 F.3d 799 [136 Educ. L. Rep. 761] (8th Cir.1999).

to enter into a project labor agreement with local unions did not violate either the state constitution or its procurement code.[84] The court concluded that non-union contractors lacked a constitutionally protected right to equal protection to be free of bid specifications requiring participation in such agreements. More recently, an appellate court in Pennsylvania affirmed that a board could refuse to consider bids from non-union contractors since doing so was designed to ensure timely completion of the project by avoiding strikes and work stoppages.[85]

As reflected by a dispute from New Jersey, a board may require bidders to submit a financial statement.[86] An appellate court ascertained that where the lowest bidder was one of two, out of a total of twenty-six, bidders who failed to submit financial statements, it, and a taxpayer, lacked standing to sue.

If items are absent from lowest bids, some courts agree that they may still be accepted if the missing information is furnished before contracts are signed. Where the lowest bidder failed to submit a graphic representation of the schedule of work with a bid, but did so before the contract was awarded, the Supreme Judicial Court of Massachusetts was convinced that the contract was valid because when the bid was submitted, the missing information did not affect its total price.[87] In like fashion, appellate courts in New York agreed that a bidder's failure to include a certificate of non-collusive bidding did not render the lowest bid invalid,[88] and where a bid included a breakdown of unit prices rather than a total bid amount,[89] boards were free to grant them the contracts. Since then, the Supreme Court of South Carolina affirmed that a low bidder was entitled to correct a sealed bid on a $16,000,000 school construction project in order to add $613,000 for a roof buildup where the board's procurement code only prohibited corrections if they caused a bidder to have the low bid.[90] In conceding that the bidder had the low bid both before and after the correction and used the same bid amount from a roofing contractor as three other bidders, the court rejected the unsuccessful bidder's claim as without merit.

Prior to accepting bids, school boards typically expect the parties to sign the necessary paperwork. Where a low bidder failed to comply with the specifications of signing a bid, an appellate court in Washington affirmed that the company was not entitled to a writ of mandamus to require the

---

84. *Laborers Local No. 942 v. Lampkin*, 956 P.2d 422 [126 Educ. L. Rep. 437] (Alaska 1998).

85. *Sossong v. Shaler Area School Dist.*, 945 A.2d 788 [231 Educ. L. Rep. 378] (Pa.Cmwlth. Ct.2008), *reargument denied* (2008), *appeal denied*, 967 A.2d 962 (Pa. 2009).

86. *Albert F. Ruehl Co. v. Board of Trustees of Schools for Indus. Educ.*, 203 A.2d 410 (N.J.Super.Ct.Law Div. 1964).

87. *Gil–Bern Constr. Corp. v. City of Brockton*, 233 N.E.2d 197 (Mass.1968).

88. *Consolidated Sheet Metal Works v. Board of Educ.*, 308 N.Y.S.2d 773 (N.Y.1970).

89. *Daniel Finley Allen & Co. v. East Williston Union Free School Dist.*, 533 N.Y.S.2d 19 [49 Educ. L. Rep. 724] (N.Y.App.Div.1988). *See also Sweet Assoc. v. Gallman*, 318 N.Y.S.2d 528 (N.Y.App.Div.1971), *aff'd*, 328 N.Y.S.2d 857 (N.Y.1972) (permitting a board to break a bid down into separate bids in order to save money).

90. *Martin Engineering v. Lexington County School Dist. One*, 615 S.E.2d 110 [199 Educ. L. Rep. 963] (S.C.2005). [Case No. 47]

board to accept its bid.[91] The court explained that the board could not legally have accepted the bid since it was not binding without the signature. Subsequently, an appellate court in Louisiana applied the same principle where a board improperly accepted a bid from a corporation that failed to submit the specified corporate resolution authorizing the signing of the bid.[92] The court was persuaded that the requirement of proof of the resolution was necessary for the bid to be valid. In addition, boards can demand strict adherence to deadlines for filing bids. Appellate courts in New York[93] and Michigan[94] upheld board refusals to consider bids that were submitted two and five minutes late, respectively.

Bid laws commonly set maximum expenditure levels that may be made without bids.[95] Difficulties can arise when projects involve separate contracts, each totaling less than the amount required for competitive bidding, but, when combined, exceed the limit. If the purpose of breaking bids into separate contracts is to save money, as illustrated by a case before the Supreme Court of Utah, the judiciary is likely to rule in favor of boards.[96] Where a board awarded a construction contract but failed to include a sprinkler system in the bid due to the lack of funds, it rebid the cost of the sprinkler system and materials only, intending to use its own personnel for installation. The court affirmed that the board did not violate the state bidding statute since it proceeded in the most efficient and economical manner.

The extent to which administrative bodies can place restrictions on bidders may depend on a jurisdiction's public policy. In a dispute over whether a state building commission could include a provision requiring a contractor to pay a scale of minimum wages, the Supreme Court of Alabama decided that it lacked the authority to do so.[97] The court interpreted the law as delegating authority to the commission to do such things as designate the quality and nature of materials used and the quality of work. The court was of the opinion that the wage requirement would have violated the state's competitive bidding statute. Almost a quarter of a century later, the Supreme Court of Louisiana adopted a similar position when a board imposed such a requirement.[98] Yet, where the state legisla-

---

91. *A. A. B. Electric v. Stevenson Pub. School Dist. No. 303*, 491 P.2d 684 (Wash. Ct. App. 1971).

92. *Stafford Constr. Co. v. Terrebonne Parish School Bd.*, 560 So.2d 558 [60 Educ. L. Rep. 269] (La. Ct. App. 1990).

93. *George A. Nole & Son v. Board of Educ. of City School Dist. of Norwich*, 514 N.Y.S.2d 274 [38 Educ. L. Rep. 1075] (N.Y. App. Div. 1987).

94. *Great Lakes Heating, Cooling, Refrigeration and Sheet Metal Corp. v. Troy School Dist.*, 494 N.W.2d 863 [80 Educ. L. Rep. 238] (Mich. Ct. App. 1992).

95. *See, e.g., Committee to Keep Our Pub. Schools Pub. v. Schweiker*, 803 A.2d 869 [168 Educ. L. Rep. 412] (Pa. Cmwlth. Ct. 2002), *aff'd*, 838 A.2d 565 [183 Educ. L. Rep. 968] (Pa. 2003) (affirming that the School Reform Commission had the authority to suspend the statute requiring open bidding on all purchases of $10,000 or more for furniture, equipment, textbooks, and other school supplies).

96. *Utah Plumbing & Heating Contractors Ass'n v. Board of Educ.*, 429 P.2d 49 (Utah 1967). [Case No. 48]

97. *Wallace v. Board of Educ. of Montgomery County*, 197 So.2d 428 (Ala. 1967).

98. *Louisiana Associated Gen. Contractors v. Calcasieu Parish School Bd.*, 586 So.2d 1354 [70 Educ. L. Rep. 715] (La. 1991).

ture required employers to pay prevailing wages on public construction jobs, Maryland's highest court interpreted "lowest responsible bidder" as meaning "lowest responsible bidder utilizing the prevailing wage rate" in a locality.[99] Further, an appellate court in Ohio affirmed the dismissal of a challenge to a prevailing wage requirement for bidders on a construction project.[100] The court indicated that the plaintiffs lacked standing because they could not demonstrate that they suffered an actual injury as a result of its being included in the contractual provisions.

As revealed by the remainder of the cases in this section, courts have considered constitutional issues when dealing with bidding laws for public projects that can implicate school boards. The Supreme Court of Ohio affirmed that bids for public construction contracts can be required to include written assurances of employment nondiscrimination.[101] The court decreed that a bidder's failure to offer such assurances was a valid ground for rejecting the low bid. However, a federal trial court in California distinguished between the power of a state and a local board to institute affirmative action policies.[102] Where a board policy required bidders for general contracting jobs to be minority-owned or to utilize minority-owned businesses for at least twenty-five percent of their base bid amounts, the court interpreted the condition as violating the state law calling for contracts to be awarded to the lowest responsible bidder.

A federal trial court in New York invalidated a state law that required granting preferences to state citizens who were residents for a year prior to seeking employment on public construction projects.[103] The court found that the law was unconstitutional because it violated the equal protection rights of those who were denied jobs due to the lack of a compelling reason for treating resident aliens differently from citizens. In a brief memorandum opinion in *Lefkowitz v. C.D.R. Enterprises (Lefkowitz)*,[104] the Supreme Court summarily affirmed.

A year after *Lefkowitz*, in another non-education case, the Supreme Court struck down a statute from Alaska designed to have granted preferences to state citizens over those of other states without reaching the merits of the equal protection claim.[105] The Justices ruled that insofar as

---

99. *Demory Brothers v. Board of Pub. Works*, 329 A.2d 674, 679 (Md.1974). *See also Mortenson v. Leatherwood Constr.*, 137 S.W.3d 529 [189 Educ. L. Rep. 938] (Mo.Ct.App.2004).

100. *State ex. rel. N. Ohio Chapter of Assoc. Builders & Contractors v. Barberton City School Dist. Bd. of Educ.*, 935 N.E.2d 861 [261 Educ. L. Rep. 446] (Ohio Ct.App.2010), *appeal allowed*, 934 N.E.2d 354 (Ohio 2010), *motion to dismiss appeal denied*, 944 N.E.2d 1177 (Ohio 2011), *appeal dismissed as improvidently allowed*, 947 N.E.2d 1207 (Ohio 2011).

101. *Weiner v. Cuyahoga Community College Dist.*, 249 N.E.2d 907 (Ohio 1969), *cert. denied*, 396 U.S. 1004, 90 S.Ct. 554, 24 L.Ed.2d 495 (1970).

102. *Associated Gen. Contractors of Cal. v. San Francisco Unified School Dist.*, 431 F.Supp. 854 (N.D.Cal.1977), *aff'd*, 616 F.2d 1381 (9th Cir.1980), *cert. denied*, 449 U.S. 1061, 101 S.Ct. 783, 66 L.Ed.2d 603 (1980).

103. *C.D.R. Enterprises v. Board of Educ. of City of N.Y.*, 412 F.Supp. 1164 (E.D.N.Y. 1976).

104. 429 U.S. 1031, 97 S.Ct. 721, 50 L.Ed.2d 742 (1977).

105. *Hicklin v. Orbeck*, 437 U.S. 518, 98 S.Ct. 2482, 57 L.Ed.2d 397 (1978). *See also White v. Massachusetts Council of Constr. Employers*, 460 U.S. 204, 103 S.Ct. 1042, 75 L.Ed.2d 1 (1983).

the state's high rate of unemployment was not due to an influx of nonresidents, officials had little or no connection to much of the activity that the law covered. Conversely, in *Fullilove v. Klutznik*,[106] a plurality of the Court upheld a statute authorizing federal public works projects in a dispute from New York that granted preferences to businesses owned by racial minorities.

In *City of Richmond v. J.A. Croson Company*,[107] the Supreme Court struck down a plan from Virginia that was designed to set aside at least thirty percent of the dollar amounts of city government contracts for minority businesses. Applying strict scrutiny, the Court reasoned that among the plan's deficiencies were the lack of identified past discrimination in the construction industry to justify the "unyielding" racial quota and its being insufficiently narrowly tailored to remedy the effects of past discrimination. A year later, in a dispute from Washington, D.C., the Court upheld a preference policy for minority ownership of new radio or television stations in *Metro Broadcasting v. Federal Communications Commission*[108] as long as it could have been shown that it had a substantial relationship to an important Congressional interest. On the other hand, in *Adarand Contractors v. Pena*,[109] a subcontracting firm in Colorado that was denied the guardrail portion of a federal highway project successfully challenged the constitutionality of a program designed to offer contracts to disadvantaged business enterprises. The Court invalidated the program because its use of race was not sufficiently narrowly tailored to achieve a compelling governmental interest.

Along the same line, an appellate court in Florida noted that an unsuccessful bidder for a school board's eye vision care contract waived its right to contest the use of raced-based criteria in the request for proposals.[110] The court declared that insofar as the bidder failed to challenge the criteria within the set time of the publication of the specifications in a bid solicitation protest, its claim failed. Additionally, the Supreme Court of Indiana pointed out that a pool supplier could not challenge an award of public contract under the state's Public Purchasing Statute where it was neither a citizen nor taxpayer of the municipality.[111] The court acknowledged that under the statute at issue, only a citizen or a taxpayer of a municipality may challenge the award of a government contract.

MISTAKEN BIDS

Disputes arise when, after boards accept, or try to accept, mistaken bids, bidders refuse either to enter into contracts or to be bound by the terms of their agreements. Cases involving mistaken bids are governed by

---

106.   448 U.S. 448, 100 S.Ct. 2758, 65 L.Ed.2d 902 (1980).

107.   488 U.S. 469, 109 S.Ct. 706, 102 L.Ed.2d 854 (1989).

108.   497 U.S. 547, 110 S.Ct. 2997, 111 L.Ed.2d 445 (1990).

109.   515 U.S. 200, 115 S.Ct. 2097, 132 L.Ed.2d 158 (1995).

110.   *Optiplan v. School Bd. of Broward County*, 710 So.2d 569 [126 Educ. L. Rep. 550] (Fla. Dist. Ct. App. 1998).

111.   *Brownsburg Community School Corp. v. Natare Corp.*, 824 N.E.2d 336 (Ind. 2005).

the general rule of contract law that individuals (or boards) cannot accept bids (or offers) if they knew, or reasonably should have known, that they were mistaken. Although it might be argued that bidders should be responsible for their errors, some mistakes do not necessarily indicate carelessness. Rather, it is the common practice of bidders to wait until the latest possible time before submitting bids in order to take full advantage of last-minute changes in the cost and availability of labor and materials. Since subcontractors follow the same procedure, main contractors are often required to compute their bids hurriedly, with little opportunity to check all figures for accuracy, and under pressure to submit them before bid deadlines expire.

Where a clerical error led a firm to bid more than ten percent less than it should have, four days after the board accepted the bid, its officials sought to withdraw from the contract. The Supreme Court of Nebraska affirmed that under the circumstances, the firm could withdraw.[112] The court commented that the only loss that the board would have incurred was that which it sought to gain through taking undue advantage of the bidder. While the opinion is unclear as to whether the board actually knew of the mistake when it accepted the bid, the court believed that it was so low that board officials reasonably should have suspected that an error occurred and should have investigated that possibility before trying to enter into the contract.

A case from Louisiana highlights a unilateral mistake that a court refused to correct. A bakery sought to escape the consequences of non-performance of a contract with a school board primarily on the basis that its bid was mistaken because the manager of its local office overlooked the increase in the cost of flour. An appellate court rejected the company's claim that the board should have been aware of the error since its bid for supplying bread was nine cents a loaf lower than others. The court affirmed that insofar as the alleged error was in the judgment of company officials, not a mathematical calculation, the contract was binding.[113] Also, the court was unable to uncover any evidence that the board suspected an error in the bid.

In the first of two cases that segue into the next section, the Supreme Court of Ohio discussed the impact of submitting a bid bond with a bid.[114] The court determined that when a bid bond was in force, a school board could recover from the contractor that submitted the mistaken low bid. The court maintained that while the bid bond contract was separate from the offer, it became effective when the offer was accepted and remained in effect until the parties entered a performance contract. The court observed that excusing the bidder would have rendered the bid bond meaningless. Further, an appellate court in Oklahoma affirmed that it lacked the equitable power to relieve a contractor of the forfeiture of its bid bond once

---

112. *School Dist. of Scottsbluff v. Olson Constr. Co.*, 45 N.W.2d 164 (Neb. 1950).

113. *Caddo Parish School Bd. v. Cotton Baking Co.*, 342 So.2d 1196 (La. Ct. App. 1977).

114. *Board of Educ. v. Sever–Williams Co.*, 258 N.E.2d 605 (Ohio 1970), *cert. denied*, 400 U.S. 916, 91 S.Ct. 175, 27 L.Ed.2d 155 (1970).

company officials realized that it contained an error.[115] The court ascertained that the apparently successful bidder had to forfeit the bond pursuant to the state's competitive bidding statute if the contract was not executed even though company officials advised the board of the error in the bid and tried to withdraw it before the board awarded the contract.

WITHDRAWAL OF BIDS

If bids are withdrawn properly, bid bonds should be cancelled and contractors should not be obligated to enter into performance contracts. Where a bidder notified city officials that there was a substantial clerical error in a bid on the day bids were submitted and opened, school officials asked for, and promptly received, the work sheets that clearly revealed the error. When, after three weeks, the board still awarded the contract to the bidder to construct a junior high school based on the erroneous bid, New York's highest court affirmed that insofar as the bid was rescinded, the bid bond had to be cancelled because the contractor had no legal obligation to fulfill its bond.[116] The court was of the view that where the amount made enforcement of the contract unconscionable, the city should not have been permitted to enforce the bid.

An appellate court in Florida reached the opposite result where a bidder was unable to withdraw a bid after all bids were opened and the results announced, but before the school board accepted the bid. Even though no state law prevented the bidder from withdrawing, the court affirmed that there was a fundamental reason, grounded in public policy, forbidding it from permitting the bidder to do so.[117] The court expressed its concern that if a bidder could withdraw without justification or cause after bids were opened and the results announced, doing so could lead to the perpetration of frauds obviating the benefits of the state's bidding law.

Where a procedure is in place for withdrawing mistaken bids, bidders must comply with directions. If courts allowed mistaken bids to be withdrawn too easily, some bidders might try to manipulate the system in attempts to thwart the purposes of competitive bidding statutes. While bids are ordinarily treated merely as offers that may be withdrawn prior to acceptance, due to the public interest involved, states may impose restrictions on bidders' ability to withdraw bids.

In a case highlighting the need for bidders to comply with directions, a dispute arose where a public school building authority had a rule permitting bids to be withdrawn as long as a company representative personally appeared at its office with a written request to do so prior to the time set for their being opened. The Supreme Court of Pennsylvania refused to permit a bidder to withdraw where its bid was a great deal lower than

---

115. *J.D. Graham Const. v. Pryor Pub. Schools Indep. School Dist. No. 1, Mayes County,* 854 P.2d 917 [83 Educ. L. Rep. 1144] (Okla. Civ. App. 1993).

116. *City of Syracuse v. Sarkisian Bros.,* 451 N.Y.S.2d 945 [5 Educ. L. Rep. 216] (N.Y. App. Div. 1982), *aff'd,* 454 N.Y.S.2d 71 (N.Y. 1982).

117. *Hotel China & Glassware Co. v. Board of Pub. Instruction,* 130 So.2d 78 (Fla. Dist. Ct. App. 1961).

others.[118] The court posited that the bidder made no attempt to withdraw except via an unverified telegram that did not specify the reason for wishing to do so. In recognizing that the bidder's attitude was one of indifference and unconcern, the court found that due to concerns for the general welfare it could not condone such looseness in public contractual relations. The court thought that permitting the bidder to withdraw would not only have placed a premium on negligence but would also have opened the door for fraudulent conduct between bidders or between bidders and public bodies inviting bids.

CHANGING CONTRACTS LET ON BIDS

Under the law of contracts, both parties are bound and neither may escape all or any parts of agreements without the consent of the other. While parties are free to modify or amend their contracts as they wish, this rule is generally inapplicable to contracts between boards and bidders pursuant to competitive bidding laws. The reason for this variation is that if boards and bidders entering into competitive bid contracts can change them at will, they can circumvent the benefits that the laws are designed to afford. Even so, situations may arise wherein the public interest is best served by allowing boards and bidders to agree to limited contractual modifications.

Courts permit parties some flexibility in modifying contracts. In other words, modifications are typically acceptable if the changes are neither so extensive nor so great as to amount essentially to abandoning original agreements and entering into new ones. In such a case, an appellate court in Illinois affirmed that when a board acted in good faith in agreeing to contractual changes based on new data, judicial intervention was unwarranted.[119]

Applying the general rule of non-modification can be difficult since it can be a challenge in evaluating the substantiality of contractual changes. In the first of two cases exemplifying disputes in this regard, the Supreme Court of South Dakota considered a provision that permitted a board to authorize changes in a building contract as work progressed. As the building was under construction, the board wished to build a stage opening but did not advertise for bids. After the contractor agreed to build the opening for about an extra five percent of the original contract price, it unsuccessfully sought payment from the board. The court asserted that insofar as this change was not merely incidental, but constituted a supplemental agreement for independent work, and was made contrary to public policy requiring competitive bidding, the contractor could not claim that the board made an implied promise to pay for labor and materials.[120]

Where a board let a contract to erect five school buildings under competitive bids, the agreement provided an insufficient amount to pay for

---

118. *Modany v. State Pub. School Bldg. Auth.*, 208 A.2d 276 (Pa. 1965).

119. *Stahelin v. Board of Educ., School Dist. No. 4, DuPage County*, 230 N.E.2d 465 (Ill. App. Ct. 1967).

120. *Seim v. Independent Dist. of Monroe*, 17 N.W.2d 342 (S.D. 1945).

all of the construction. After the board and contractor agreed to eliminate one building and make other changes that reduced the contract's amount, a taxpayer enjoined the enforcement of the revised agreement. Maryland's highest court agreed that insofar as the variation in the general plan was so substantial that it constituted, for all intents and purposes, a new contract that was not let on competitive bids, it was invalid.[121] More than forty years later, the Supreme Court of Arkansas reached a like result. Where a general contractor made a unilateral error in a bid amounting to less than four percent of a contract, the court was satisfied that insofar as the magnitude of the error did not render the agreement unenforceable, the contractor was not entitled to rescission in light of its mistake.[122]

In Utah, the eventual low bidder on a school construction project submitted a contingency letter with its bid explaining that insofar as it had difficulty calculating the price and availability of materials, it would have to modify its fee accordingly as the information became available. Inexplicably, the letter remained unread until six weeks after the parties signed a contract. When the contractor tried to recover extra funds, the state's highest court refused its request since the original contract was valid.[123] The court contended that insofar as school officials read and accepted the bid, and the parties signed a contract that did not mention the contingency letter, the contractor was not entitled to recover additional funds for the increased cost of materials.

RECOVERY UNDER CONTRACTS

EXPRESS AND IMPLIED CONTRACTS

As an initial matter, it is settled law that school boards cannot form implied contracts if they lack the authority to enter into express contracts.[124] The concept of implied contracts is designed to permit boards to recover when they fail to follow statutory requirements rather than to exceed their powers. As courts have used the vehicle of implied contracts to remove a measure of the protection afforded by statutory requisites, it is a modification justly designed to alleviate the hardships on those who furnish goods or services to boards in good faith.

Even in cases where contracts are void, since boards often have received goods or services, questions arise as to whether suppliers are entitled to remedies. Typical remedies for breaches of contract are suits to determine damages based on the actual harm suffered and to enforce agreements for liquidated damages which set the amount of damages in advance as a contractual term.[125]

---

121.   *Hanna v. Board of Educ.*, 87 A.2d 846 (Md.1952).

122.   *Mountain Home School Dist. No. 9 v. T.M.J. Builders*, 858 S.W.2d 74 [84 Educ. L. Rep. 1174] (Ark.1993).

123.   *Jaye Smith Constr. Co. v. Board of Educ., Granite School Dist.*, 560 P.2d 320 (Utah 1977).

124.   *Reams v. Cooley*, 152 P. 293 (Cal.1915).

In addressing the question of damages, regardless of their form, it is important to distinguish among different kinds of contracts. Although the distinctions are sometimes less than clear, contracts fall into three classes. The first type of contract is one wherein parties expressly delineate their rights and duties, either orally or in writing. An implied-in-fact contract, the second type, "arises when the circumstances make it reasonably certain that an agreement was intended"[126] even though the parties did not reach an express agreement to enter into a contract. For example, when individuals accept goods or services under conditions showing that they were not meant to be gratuitous, courts often imply that insofar as the parties intended to enter into contracts, they were bound; these contracts are no less binding because they are implied. The difference between contracts that are express and implied-in-fact is the manner in which they are formed. In the former, contracts are formed by words; in the latter, by conduct.[127]

The third type of contract, implied-in-law, embraces so-called quasi-contracts.[128] These contracts are not contracts in the true sense of the word. Rather, these contracts are created by law for reasons of justice and equity, obligating parties that receive benefits from others that would have resulted in unjust enrichment if they were not required to pay. In some cases, the courts permit parties to recover as if they had entered into contracts. In such a case, the Eighth Circuit ruled that an architectural firm in Nebraska could recover the cost of services it rendered for a school board in Iowa.[129] Even though there was a disagreement over exactly how much was at issue, the court concluded that not allowing the firm to recover some of its expenses would have conferred an unjust enrichment on the board. Similarly, a year earlier the Supreme Court of Pennsylvania rejected a school board's claim that after a contractor recovered fees from a construction company on a contract that was struck down as illegal, it was entitled to the refund on the basis that the contractor would have gained an unjust enrichment.[130] The court affirmed that insofar as the claim was based in contract, the board could not allege that the contractor did garner an unjust enrichment. However, where a statute in Pennsylvania required an affirmative action of all board members before a contract could be

---

125. For a case involving liquidated damages, albeit in a non-public school, *see Barrie School v. Patch*, 933 A.2d 382 [225 Educ. L. Rep. 973] (Md. 2007) (upholding the general rule that the school was entitled to liquidated damages of tuition for a full academic year, with no duty to mitigate damages, where parents withdrew their child before the start of the year since the amount was a fair estimation of the school's loss). For another case affirming the validity of a liquidated damages clause for tuition, *see Turner v. Atlanta Girls' School*, 653 S.E.2d 380 [227 Educ. L. Rep. 357] (Ga. Ct. App. 2007).

126. *Manno v. St. Felicitas Elementary School*, 831 N.E.2d 1071, 1077 [200 Educ. L. Rep. 349] (Ohio Ct. App. 2005).

127. *Ryan v. Warren Twp. High School Dist. No. 121*, 510 N.E.2d 911 [40 Educ. L. Rep. 896] (Ill. App. Ct. 1987).

128. *Boyd v. Black School Twp.*, 23 N.E. 862 (Ind. 1890).

129. *Rambo Assoc. v. South Tama County Community School Dist.*, 487 F.3d 1178 [221 Educ. L. Rep. 50] (8th Cir.2007).

130. *Wilson Area School Dist. v. Skepton*, 895 A.2d 1250 [207 Educ. L. Rep. 1000] (Pa. 2006).

finalized, the Third Circuit ruled that a subcontractor was barred from filing a claim for unjust enrichment when the latter sought to recover additional expenses in light of delays that it experienced in finishing a moving project in the district's administrative offices.[131]

Classifying contracts is important since the measure of recovery is different in each category. In cases involving express contracts, recovery is based on the terms of the agreements. When dealing with implied-in-fact contracts, recovery depends on the reasonable value of goods or services rendered. By contrast, in express contracts, the stated amounts are generally recoverable regardless of whether they are reasonable, with courts holding parties to improvident agreements as long as they are not unconscionable or adhesion contracts and that they were freely formed. In disputes dealing with implied-in-fact contracts, since there are no set prices or agreements, the law does not imply promises to pay more than the reasonable value. In implied-in-law cases, then, the measure of recovery, if any is permitted,[132] is calculated based on the amount of benefit conferred on the parties receiving the property or services, not by their price or reasonable value.

Courts impose implied-in-law contracts on parties receiving benefits since the law considers it inequitable to enrich one party at the expense of another. If a party has not received a benefit, there can be no recovery regardless of market price or reasonable value. Since the courts often confuse implied-in-fact and implied-in-law cases, they can fail to apply the appropriate measure of recovery. Indeed, in many cases, it is difficult to tell whether courts are referring to contracts that are implied-in-fact or in-law or whether they are permitting recovery on implied or quasi-contracts. Unfortunately, courts tend to apply the terms "reasonable value" and "benefits received" more or less indiscriminately even though the terms or the amounts of recovery are not necessarily the same.

As long as such actions are not barred by sovereign immunity,[133] courts often apply the concept of *quantum meruit*, literally, "as much as it deserves," to disputes involving either type of implied contract, whether implied-in-fact or implied-in-law, as it historically pertained to quasi-contracts.[134] In such a case, the Supreme Court of Georgia ruled that when a contractor sued a school board, baseball coach, and booster's club to recover for the cost of a baseball hitting facility, the coach, who was the contact person in the transaction, was not liable for damages under *quantum meruit*.[135] The court noted that the coach could not be liable

---

131. *Wayne Moving & Storage of N.J. v. School Dist. of Philadelphia*, 625 F.3d 148 [262 Educ. L. Rep. 42] (3d Cir.2010).

132. For cases denying recovery under quasi-contracts, *see Strain–Japan R–16 School Dist. v. Landmark Sys.*, 51 S.W.3d 916 [156 Educ. L. Rep. 719] (Mo. Ct. App. 2001); *Mays–Maune & Assoc. v. Werner Bros.*, 139 S.W.3d 201 [190 Educ. L. Rep. 1058] (Mo. Ct. App. 2004).

133. *Harden v. Clarke County Bd. of Educ.*, 631 S.E.2d 741 [210 Educ. L. Rep. 824] (Ga. Ct. App. 2006) (affirming the denial of a *pro se* claim for additional compensation based on *quantum meruit*).

134. *See Alternatives Unlimited v. New Baltimore City Bd. of School Commr's*, 843 A.2d 252 [186 Educ. L. Rep. 341] (Md. Ct. Spec. App. 2004) (treating a *quantum meruit* claim as redundant to the extent that it was based on the theory of quasi-contract).

135. *Brown v. Penland Constr. Co.*, 641 S.E.2d 522 [217 Educ. L. Rep. 732] (Ga. 2007). [Case No. 49]

because he was entitled to immunity if it assumed that his discretionary actions were within the scope of his authority and that he did not act in a wilful, wanton, or malicious manner or with actual intent to cause injury. The court added that even if it assumed that the coach was acting outside of the scope of his duties, he was still not liable because the board, not the coach, accepted the benefits that the company bestowed and he had not made an implied promise to pay for the facility.

A case from Arkansas illuminates the interplay between implied contracts and *quantum meruit*. A superintendent signed a lease-purchase agreement for books and materials in excess of $113,000 with the understanding that he could use federal funds as payment. Although another administrator and the book salesman encouraged the superintendent to sign the contract, they both knew that federal funds could not be used to pay for the books. Since the school board was apparently unaware of the situation at its inception, students used the materials for at least a year. When company officials asked the board to pay for the materials, it refused, claiming that the superintendent exceeded his authority in entering into the contract. As a result, the board put the materials into storage and notified company officials to pick up their property. In concluding that neither party was without fault, the court decided that insofar as they formed an implied contract, *quantum meruit* applied.[136] The court thus gave the company the option of taking back the used books or having the board keep them in return for $13,500 in payment.

INVALID CONTRACTS IN GENERAL

Statutory requirements controlling school contracts are designed to protect boards and taxpayers. To this end, requirements specifying the types of contracts that must be in writing are intended to avoid misunderstandings that can easily arise under oral contracts. In like manner, competitive bidding laws are designed to ensure that goods and services can be procured at the lowest price possible and to guard against collusion at public expense. When boards receive benefits under contracts that are invalid due to their failure to meet statutory requirements, the courts are faced with the options of relaxing legal protections or permitting boards to retain benefits without compensating the other parties.

If school boards enter into express contracts that courts later invalidate, they can be liable under the theory of implied contracts for the reasonable value of the goods or services. The limitations against recovery are that the form or manner of entering into contracts cannot violate statutory restrictions, the ability of boards to form contracts, and/or public policy. Insofar as the application of this rule has caused courts considerable difficulty, they have reached varying results. The outcomes of cases often seem to turn on what courts consider to be the better public policy, strict enforcement of the statutory protections afforded boards or the equitable claims of aggrieved parties. Courts allowing recovery ordinarily agree that permitting boards to claim contractual invalidity while retaining benefits

---

136. *Responsive Environments Corp. v. Pulaski County Special School Dist.*, 366 F.Supp. 241 (E.D. Ark. 1973).

can be unconscionable.[137] Courts denying recoveries on implied contracts typically do so on the basis that reaching other outcomes would open the door to raids on school funds[138] or that they expect strict compliance with state contract law[139] since making exceptions runs the risk of nullifying the very protections that the law seeks to provide.

ULTRA VIRES CONTRACTS

The weight of authority is that parties cannot recover based on *quantum meruit* if the actions of school boards are *ultra vires*. The fact that most courts refuse to imply the existence of contracts where express agreements are *ultra vires* reflects the limit beyond which the judiciary refuses to go in sacrificing statutory protection to avoid hardships on those who acted in good faith by conferring benefits on boards. In denying recoveries, courts reason that individuals or companies dealing with boards are bound to know the limits of their contractual powers as statutory provisions define the limits of their authority.

Whether contracts are *ultra vires* is an issue that is not free from difficulty unless something is expressly prohibited by statute[140] or school boards set specific conditions precedent to their entering into valid contracts.[141] Courts ordinarily strike down contracts as *ultra vires* when boards make unauthorized expenditures,[142] violate specific statutory provisions,[143] exceed state constitutional debt limits,[144] or lack sufficient funds to pay for expenditures.[145] In considering whether contracts are *ultra vires*, courts may declare categorically that agreements are impermissible since laws addressing the scope of boards' contractual limits cannot be drawn so as to consider their specific authority in all conceivable transactions. In close cases it is difficult to know whether boards exceeded their contractual authority until disputes are litigated.

Where an architectural firm proceeded with work pursuant to a contract in excess of the amount of money covered by the appropriation, the Supreme Judicial Court of Massachusetts affirmed that insofar as the firm did so at its own risk, it could not recover even though it acted in good

---

137. *Burk v. Livingston Parish School Bd.*, 182 So. 656 (La. 1938).

138. *Oberwarth v. McCreary County Bd. of Educ.*, 121 S.W.2d 716 (Ky.1938); *Goodyear v. Junior College Dist. of St. Louis*, 540 S.W.2d 621 (Mo.Ct.App.1976).

139. *Strain–Japan R–16 School Dist. v. Landmark Sys.*, 51 S.W.3d 916 [156 Educ. L. Rep. 719] (Mo.Ct.App.2001).

140. *Board of Educ. v. Chicago Teachers Union, Local 1, Am. Fed'n of Teachers*, 326 N.E.2d 158 (Ill.App.Ct.1975).

141. *CADO Business Sys. of Ohio v. Board of Educ. of Cleveland City School Dist.*, 457 N.E.2d 939 [15 Educ. L. Rep. 358] (Ohio Ct.App.1983); *Ryan v. Warren Twp. High School Dist. No. 121*, 510 N.E.2d 911 [40 Educ. L. Rep. 896] (Ill.App.Ct.1987).

142. *Smith v. Dorsey*, 599 So.2d 529 [75 Educ. L. Rep. 692] (Miss.1992).

143. *Robert W. Anderson Housewrecking and Excavating v. Board of Trustees, School Dist. No. 25*, 681 P.2d 1326 [17 Educ. L. Rep. 1232] (Wyo.1984); *Swinney v. Deming Bd. of Educ.*, 873 P.2d 238 [91 Educ. L. Rep. 347] (N.M.1994).

144. *Moe v. Mallard County School Dist.*, 179 P. 980 (Utah 1919).

145. *School Dist. No. 9 Fractional of Waterford and Pontiac Twps. v. McLintock*, 237 N.W. 539 (Mich.1931).

faith.[146] Conversely, where school board members unanimously approved a contract with an architectural firm, encouraged it to begin work, and executed a written contract, an appellate court in Pennsylvania affirmed that it was not unlawful for the board to pay for work that was actually done before the contract was executed since there was no fraud involved.[147]

School boards in Kansas sued to cancel lease-purchase agreements for photocopying equipment once they experienced difficulty in obtaining service. An appellate court affirmed a grant of summary judgment in favor of the boards on the ground that the agreements were void and unenforceable because they failed to contain mandatory disclosures of such matters as the amount of capital cost required to purchase the items if paid in cash, annual average effective interest costs, and amount included in payments for service, maintenance, and insurance for other charges exclusive of capital and interest costs.[148] The court specified that when a contract is declared void for failing to comply with an express statutory requirement, it could not intervene to render the agreement, or part thereof, valid.

RATIFICATION OF INVALID CONTRACTS

School boards, like other corporate bodies, can act only through their agents. As such, some of the general rules governing agency relationships apply to agents of school boards. One rule of agency is that even when agents act outside of the scope of their duties, and their acts are not binding on their principals, the latter may ratify acts binding themselves as if the agents had the authority at the outset. This rule applies to board actions which, due to irregularities, were not binding or which were supposedly carried out by individuals acting on their behalf. The rule is subject to the exception that boards must have had the ability to act as they did because they cannot ratify *ultra vires* acts.[149]

When school boards ratify unauthorized acts, most courts do not require them to take formal steps since they accept that boards did so when they acted in ways consistent with the underlying agreements[150] or complied with statutory requirements. Yet, as revealed by a case from Pennsylvania, where only four, rather than the required five, board members approved a contract, an appellate court affirmed that it was unratified even though district officials made payments under the agreement.[151] Also, an appellate court in Kentucky judged that insofar as a board "must act

---

146. *Murphy v. City of Brockton*, 305 N.E.2d 103 (Mass.1973). *See also School Dist. No. One of Pima County v. Hastings*, 472 P.2d 44 (Ariz.1970).

147. *Kennedy v. Ringgold School Dist.*, 309 A.2d 269 (Pa.Cmwlth.Ct.1973).

148. *Unified School Dist. No. 207 v. Northland Nat'l Bank*, 887 P.2d 1138 [96 Educ. L. Rep. 1156] (Kan.Ct.App.1994).

149. *Arkansas Nat'l Bank v. School Dist. No. 99, Washington County*, 238 S.W. 630 (Ark.1922); *St. Paul Foundry Co. v. Burnstad School Dist. No. 31*, 269 N.W. 738 (N.D.1936).

150. *Frank v. Board of Educ.*, 100 A. 211 (N.J.Err. & App.1917). [Case No. 50]

151. *Grippo v. Dunmore School Bd.*, 365 A.2d 678 (Pa.Cmwlth.Ct.1976).

through its records," an entry in one's minutes could constitute ratification if a board would "bear a loss because [an agent] failed to perform his duty."[152]

The fact that school boards can retain benefits even when they are aware of the material facts in transactions does not necessarily constitute ratification if it is impossible for them to reject the benefits. If, for instance, improvements such as fixtures cannot be removed from school property, the fact that boards permit them to be used does not amount to ratification.[153] The basis for the rule is that if boards are obliged to refrain from using such improvements or are found to have ratified transactions, then school activities could be seriously disrupted. When dealing with non-permanent goods, such as school supplies and furniture, some courts, even in the same jurisdiction, disagree over whether board acceptance and use of these items means that they can be required to pay for such materials.[154]

Another issue concerns whether those who acted on behalf of boards were truly their agents. In these cases the parties claiming to be agents bear the burden of proof. In a dispute from North Carolina, a principal directed a salesperson to see a choral director who signed orders for decorative lamps to be used in fund-raising efforts. After the choral director stopped working for the board, the principal sent payment to the novelty company and returned the unsold lamps. Faced with a discrepancy in the amount of money that the principal sent, an appellate court rejected the company's claim to recover the money. The court affirmed that the board was not liable because insofar as it had not entered into the contract, and the principal lacked the authority to act on its behalf, it had not ratified the agreement.[155]

An appellate court in Louisiana took a different approach where a teacher who served as a class sponsor conferred with the principal before signing a contract for entertainment at a prom. When the principal discovered that the contract was for a sound system, not a live band, and deemed the arrangement inappropriate, he and the teacher informed the contractor that the company's services were unnecessary. In light of a term in the contract calling for payment if the contract was cancelled, an appellate court ruled that insofar as the principal had the implied authority to bind the board and properly delegated it to the teacher, the board was liable.[156]

---

152. *Ramsey v. Board of Educ. of Whitley County*, 789 S.W.2d 784, 786–787 [60 Educ. L. Rep. 1284] (Ky. Ct. App. 1990).

153. *Young v. Board of Educ.*, 55 N.W. 1112 (Minn. 1893); *Panther Oil and Grease Mfg. Co. v. Blount County Bd. of Educ.*, 134 So.2d 220 (Ala. Ct. App. 1961).

154. *A.H. Andrews Co. v. Delight Special School Dist.*, 128 S.W. 361 (Ark. 1910) (finding that a board's acceptance, and continued use, of school desks did not solve an irregularity in the execution of a contract). *See also Richards v. School Twp. of Jackson*, 109 N.W. 1093 (Iowa 1906). *But see First Nat'l Bank v. Whisenhunt*, 127 S.W. 968 (Ark. 1910) (affirming that a board's unauthorized purchase of maps was not ratified by their acceptance and use).

155. *Community Projects for Students v. Wilder*, 298 S.E.2d 434 [8 Educ. L. Rep. 521] (N.C. Ct. App. 1982).

156. *Hebert v. Livingston Parish School Bd.*, 438 So.2d 1141 [14 Educ. L. Rep. 237] (La. Ct. App. 1983).

Ratification renders contracts as valid as if they were formed strictly in accord with the authority of school boards. Most courts agree that boards cannot partially ratify agreements since they must approve actions either in whole or not at all. An older case exemplifies this general rule. Where a certificated teacher began working under a contract that a board knew was invalid, but paid part of his salary, an appellate court in Kansas maintained that its doing so ratified the contract for the entire employment period.[157]

In building projects, boards often rely on architects to inform them when performance contracts are complete. When a problem arose with a gymnasium floor before a new building was completed, the architect accepted the contractor's additional work as satisfactory. The board, relying on the architect's advice, made final payment unconditionally. When the contractor refused to honor a warranty that it would remedy defects that appeared within a year of final payment, the Supreme Court of Montana remarked that the board's issuing a final, unconditional payment constituted its ratification of the architect's acceptance of the floor.[158] The court decreed that if the floor was defective when accepted, the warranty was inapplicable since it only covered flaws that appeared within a year. The court added that the board lacked a remedy against the contractor because it waived its prior right not to accept the floor.

BOARD CONTRACTS AND CONFLICT OF INTEREST

School board members and employees must avoid conflicts of interest, a principle that has become statutory, constitutional, or both, in many jurisdictions.[159] Conflict of interest laws typically stipulate that it is unlawful for persons in public offices, including board members, to have pecuniary interests, either directly or indirectly, in contracts on which they may be called on to act or vote.

Perhaps the most challenging issue in cases dealing with conflicts of interest is deciding what constitutes an interest in a school contract. If board members entered into contracts with district officials to construct, furnish, or repair buildings or to provide supplies or services, there would be little doubt that these were conflicts of interest.

A more difficult situation occurs when corporations or companies in which board members or school employees have substantial interests enter into contracts with their boards. Since corporations are separate legal entities, distinct from their stockholders, the question becomes whether their interests equate to those of individual board members. In an early

157.   *Jones v. School Dist. No. 144*, 51 P. 927 (Kan. Ct. App. 1898).

158.   *Grass Range High School Dist. v. Wallace Diteman*, 465 P.2d 814 (Mont. 1970).

159.   *See, e.g.*, ARIZ. STAT. ANN. § 38–503; CAL. EDUC. CODE ANN. § 35233; KAN. STAT. ANN. § 754304; KY. REV. STAT. ANN. § 160.180; MICH. COMP. LAWS ANN. § 388.1769b; MISS. CODE ANN. § 25–4–105; N.J. STAT. ANN. § 18A:12–22; N.Y. MCKINNEY'S EDUC. L. § 2590–n; N.D. CENT. CODE § 15.1–07–17; S.D. CODIFIED LAWS § 6–1–1; WASH. REV. CODE ANN. § 42.52.030; W. VA. CODE § 6–6–7. *See also, e.g.*, GA. CONSTIT. ART. 1, § 2, Par. 1; MISS. CONSTIT. ART. 4 § 109.

case, the Supreme Court of Wisconsin agreed that a school treasurer violated the state's conflict of interest law when, after a contract had been let, he notified the contractor that a corporation in which he had a substantial interest could, and did, furnish a significant portion of the necessary building materials. When the corporation sued the contractor for the price of materials, the latter defended itself on the ground that the treasurer's interest in the corporation rendered the contract void.[160] The court held that this type of contract violated both the spirit and express provisions in the law.

The Supreme Court of South Dakota affirmed that a board's contract with a business that repaired a school bus was *ultra vires* as a conflict of interest where one of its members was a company shareholder, officer, and director.[161] In noting that the board could have used other firms to repair the bus, the court agreed that the board member, and two other persons associated with the company, had to reimburse the board.

Controversies often arise when school boards deal with employment contracts for spouses, family members, or prospective members, with most courts agreeing that such agreements are conflicts of interest. The Supreme Court of Kentucky upheld the constitutionality of an anti-nepotism law which prevented boards from hiring relatives of their members.[162] The court reasoned that either a board member, or her daughter, both of whom were long serving in the district, had to relinquish her position.[163] In a similar vein, the Supreme Court of Oklahoma originally ruled that a candidate whose wife was a teacher in a district was ineligible to run for the board under the state's anti-nepotism statute.[164] On rehearing, the court pointed out that the candidate, who was elected to the board pending the outcome of the case, could serve the remainder of his term in accordance with newly enacted provisions which suspended the operation of the anti-nepotism statute. In both instances, the courts agreed that the statutes did not violate the equal protection rights of the board members.

Within less than five weeks, the Supreme Court of Mississippi resolved two cases involving board members who were married to school employees. In the first, the court rejected a board member's claim that his voting against hiring his wife for a job as a teacher did not violate the state constitutional prohibition against having a direct or indirect interest in board contracts.[165] The court was of the view that insofar as it was the board member's interest in his wife's contract, not his vote, that was forbidden, they had to return her salary and pay a fine. Unlike the second

---

160. *Bissell Lumber Co. v. Northwestern Cas. & Sur. Co.*, 207 N.W. 697 (Wis. 1926).

161. *Ayres v. Junek*, 247 N.W.2d 488 (S.D. 1976).

162. *Chapman v. Gorman*, 839 S.W.2d 232 [78 Educ. L. Rep. 1128] (Ky. 1992).

163. For another case rejecting a challenge to Kentucky's nepotism statute, *see Craig v. Kentucky State Bd. for Elementary and Secondary Educ.*, 902 S.W.2d 264 [102 Educ. L. Rep. 356] (Ky. Ct. App. 1995) (affirming that statutory prohibitions against school board members influencing the hiring of school or district employees was not unconstitutionally vague or overly broad).

164. *Sharp v. Tulsa County Election Bd.*, 890 P.2d 836 [98 Educ. L. Rep. 424] (Okla. 1994).

165. *Waller v. Moore ex rel. Quitman County School Dist.*, 604 So.2d 265 [77 Educ. L. Rep. 1029] (Miss. 1992).

case, the court did not address the board member's ability to continue serving. Shortly thereafter, the court affirmed a grant of summary judgment on liability where a board member whose husband was a teacher in the district during her term on the board violated the state's public servant conflict of interest statute.[166] The court observed that the board member had to be removed from office and fined while her husband had to forfeit his job and salary because even though she did not vote for him, or influence others to do so, she violated the law.

The Supreme Court of Georgia reached the opposite result in affirming that the public trust provision of the state constitution did not preclude board members who were married to employees of a county school system from voting on matters affecting staff compensation and benefits.[167] The court acknowledged that the state constitution did not articulate a duty requiring board members to refrain from participating in such votes. Earlier, the Supreme Court of Virginia affirmed that a conflict of interest did not prevent a board from hiring the sister-in-law of one of its members since she was not a regular employee when he was appointed.[168]

In a related concern, the Supreme Court of Kansas interpreted state law as meaning that an individual could not serve as both a teacher and school board member in the same district.[169] Overturning an adjudication of the state government's ethics commission that this did not violate the conflict of interest statute, the court thought that permitting one person to operate in both capacities was inconsistent with the meaning and intent of the common law rule of incompatibility of office. Interestingly, the court did not explicitly rely on the state's conflict of interest law in reaching its judgment. Previously, the Supreme Court of Colorado indicated that a board policy precluding its members from teaching in the district, but permitting their spouses to do so, did not violate members' rights to equal protection.[170] The court agreed with the board that it could have believed that its conflict of interest policy should have encompassed members but not their spouses so as to avoid having to face complaints over incompatibility of interests. In another case involving an administrative directive rather than a state statute, an appellate court in Ohio affirmed that a board did not abuse its discretion in refusing to recommend the low bidder on a painting contract because the company was owned by one of its teachers.[171]

As reflected by two cases from New Jersey, conflict of interest disputes over real estate are not uncommon. In the first, an appellate court affirmed

---

166. *Towner v. Moore ex rel. Quitman County School Dist.*, 604 So.2d 1093 [77 Educ. L. Rep. 1056] (Miss. 1992).

167. *Ianicelli v. McNeely*, 527 S.E.2d 189 [143 Educ. L. Rep. 1073] (Ga. 2000).

168. *Williams v. Augusta County School Bd.*, 445 S.E.2d 118 [92 Educ. L. Rep. 686] (Va. 1994).

169. *Unified School Dist. No. 501, Shawnee County, Kan. v. Baker*, 6 P.3d 848 [146 Educ. L. Rep. 902] (Kan. 2000).

170. *Montrose County School Dist. Re–1J v. Lambert*, 826 P.2d 349 [73 Educ. L. Rep. 271] (Colo. 1992).

171. *Darnell Painting Co. v. Toledo Bd. of Educ.*, 669 N.E.2d 311 [111 Educ. L. Rep. 1354] (Ohio Ct. App. 1995).

that school board members could not be personally liable for one member's allegedly improper opposition to a development plan.[172] The plaintiff unsuccessfully claimed that the member opposed the plan due to concerns that it would have had an adverse impact on his adjacent property. A second court invalidated a vote over whether to build two adult-sized baseball fields with lighting towers on a school board's property.[173] Recognizing that two board members had direct and indirect personal interests in the outcome, the court concluded that the one who actually voted was ineligible to have done so under the state's conflict of interest law. The court thus invalidated the entire vote.

[CASE NO. 46]　LOWEST RESPONSIBLE BIDDER CHANGING CONTRACTS AFTER LETTING

HIBBS v. ARENSBERG

Supreme Court of Pennsylvania, 1923.
119 A. 727.

[At issue was whether a board could proceed under a contract which was let to a bidder other than the lowest bidder. The plaintiff also alleged that the contract was changed after it had been let. This is an appeal of a judgment in favor of the board]

■ KEPHART, J. . . .

It is averred, in the bill to restrain the school directors from awarding the contract to construct a badly needed school building in a school district in Fayette county, that the architect's plans and specifications do not fully state the kind, quality, and quantity of materials required. One special item reads:

> "The face brick . . . to be a thoroughly vitrified, wire-cut, face brick of such color as will be selected by the architect and school board; . . . to cost not more than $34.00 per thousand."

We see no reason why an intelligent bid could not be made on this item. Vitrified, wire-cut, face brick has a definite meaning; the contract preserved the right of inspection and rejection of materials; and there was little opportunity to slight the quality. If a certain make of brick had been selected, or several makes, we can readily see a charge of a different character might be presented.

That the directors later decided to use a little more expensive brick would not condemn the letting, or cause the directors to be liable for the increased price, or avoid the purchase. There was no such departure from the general purpose as would require reletting. Unforeseen contingencies or new ideas sometimes make it necessary to change the character or quality of material or a part of a structure from the original plans. A certain

---

172. *Lake Lenore Estates, Assoc. v. Township of Parsippany–Troy Hills Bd. of Educ.*, 712 A.2d 200 [127 Educ. L. Rep. 342] (N.J. Super. Ct. App. Div. 1998).

173. *Friends Retirement Concepts v. Board of Educ. Borough of Somerville*, 811 A.2d 962 [172 Educ. L. Rep. 340] (N.J. Super. Ct. Law Div. 2002) (it appears that the other board member did not vote on the resolution).

flexibility in the power of officials to take care of these matters is intended to be granted, that the law relating to public letting may not become an instrument of oppression through a too rigid construction. These officers must act honestly, reasonably, and intelligently, and a new departure must not so vary from the original plan or be of such importance as to constitute a new undertaking, which the act controls, and where fairness could only be reached through competitive bidding. Courts, however, will be slow to interfere unless it appears the officers are not acting in good faith....

... [But there were some] mistakes in the letting. The architect did not supply a sufficient number of copies of the plans and specifications for all those who expressed a wish to bid. Reputable contractors were deprived of the opportunity to submit prices. Competitive bidding could not be secured under these conditions. We cannot too strongly condemn the motives of some architects and public officials in following this practice; it opens the door to the grossest kind of fraud. A favored contractor, apprised in advance, may easily have the limited number of plans and specifications on file lifted by persons not bona fide bidders, or, through a combination none too infrequent, the favored contractor submits a price (the lowest) that is high enough to give an excessive profit and pays to other higher bidders a commission "or rake-off" as their part of the gain for participating in the combination. Of course, there are other methods. Officials must have on file enough sets of plans and specifications to supply those who demand them within a reasonable time prior to the day on which the bids are to be submitted. The time within which a request is made should be sufficient to enable the architect to furnish additional copies if those first furnished have been exhausted. The court was in error in passing over this fact as not being of sufficient consequence to restrain the work.

At the first meeting of the board, after the bids were submitted they were all deemed too high. A week later, at an adjourned meeting, the bid of the Republic Construction Company, fourth lowest bidder, was accepted by the vote of four of the directors. Two of the board were not present, and another, though present, did not vote....

The contract was awarded to the fourth lowest bidder without investigating the responsibility of the three lower bidders. This is contrary to the Act of July 10, 1919, which directs the contract be let to the lowest responsible bidder. The term "lowest responsible bidder" does not mean the lowest bidder in dollars; nor does it mean the board may capriciously select a higher bidder regardless of responsibility or cost. What the law requires is the exercise of a sound discretion by the directors. They should call to their assistance the means of information at hand to form an intelligent judgment. They should investigate the bidders to learn their financial standing, reputation, experience, resources, facilities, judgment and efficiency as builders. This was not done. The court below censures the board for omitting this important step, but it holds, inasmuch as they had ample knowledge of the successful bidder and the merit of its work, the contract could be awarded. This might do in private affairs, but will not pass when public funds are at stake; it is not the exercise of discretion. Though the directors were not bound in law to give the contract to the lowest bidder, who might be irresponsible, they were bound to investigate, and if a bidder measured up to the law's requirement as a responsible party, the board could not capriciously award the contract to another. Giving a bond alone does not make up for responsibility; we have too many bonding companies willing to indemnify almost anything. But there should be a sufficient reason, where a bidder is lowest and responsible, why the job was not given to him. And where such reason appears, the action of the board is generally conclusive. . . .

We have indicated in this opinion where we think the court below was in error in permitting the work to go ahead. On the record presented the school board was without authority to award the contract and bind the school district.

The decree of the court below is reversed, the bill is reinstated with a procedendo to issue the injunction as prayed for in the bill; costs to be paid by appellee.

NOTES

1. In *In re Scranton City School Dist. Audit*, 47 A.2d 288 (Pa. 1946), school board officials sought to divide a project involving an expenditure of $12,673.63 into a number of contracts, each less than $300 in amount, in order to have it completed in a short time and to save money. Under Pennsylvania law, contracts for less than $300 were not required to be let to the lowest responsible bid. The court struck the board's action down as violating the competitive bidding statute. Would you have reached the same outcome?

2. After a school board advertised for bids to supply milk and reserved the right to reject any of them, officials accepted a bid from a local firm even though it was $1,500 more than the lowest bid from a company located elsewhere. The court ruled that insofar as the competitive bid statute covered only construction supplies, the board's action was legal. *Gosselin's Dairy v. School Comm. of Holyoke*, 205 N.E.2d 221 (Mass.1965).

[CASE NO. 47]   PERMITTING A BID MODIFICATION

MARTIN ENGINEERING v. LEXINGTON COUNTY SCHOOL DISTRICT ONE

Supreme Court of South Carolina, 2005.
615 S.E.2d 110 [199 Educ. L. Rep. 963].

■ JUSTICE WALLER

We certified this case from the Court of Appeals pursuant to Rule 204(b), SCACR. At issue is whether Lexington County School District One (District) properly allowed Respondent Sharp Construction Company (Sharp), to amend its bid on the Lexington High School Additions and Renovations Project (Project). The circuit court granted District summary judgment, holding the correction was properly allowed. We affirm.

FACTS

In August 2003, District received bids for the Project. Sharp was the low bidder with a bid of $16,300,000.00. Appellant, Martin Engineering, was the second lowest bidder with a bid of $17,375,000.00. Immediately after the bids were opened, Sharp advised District it had inadvertently neglected to include a roofing subcontractor's bid in its overall bid. It requested to be allowed to correct its bid by adding the roofing cost, $613,500.00, to its bid. Alternatively, Sharp requested to withdraw its bid. District allowed Sharp to adjust its bid, resulting in an overall bid by Sharp of $16,913,500.00, some $461,500.00 less than Martin's bid. Martin filed a complaint in the circuit court seeking an injunction. The circuit court held the adjustment was properly allowed in compliance with District's Procurement Code and Regulations.

ISSUES

1. Did the circuit court err in holding District properly allowed the upward adjustment?

2. Did the court err in finding Sharp would suffer a substantial loss if it were not allowed to correct its bid?

1.   CORRECTION OF BID

District's Procurement Code, Article 2, Section 2–102 controls Competitive Sealed Bidding. In particular, section 2–102(10), "Correction or Withdrawal of Bids: Cancellation of Awards" states: Corrections or withdrawal of inadvertently erroneous bids before or after award, or cancellation of awards or contracts based on such bid mistakes may be permitted where appropriate. After bid openings, no change in bid prices or other provisions of bids prejudicial to the interest of the school district or fair competition will be permitted. A bidder must submit a written request to either correct or withdraw a bid to the school district. Each written request must document the fact that the bidder's mistake is clearly an error that will cause him substantial loss. In order to maintain the integrity of the competitive sealed bidding process, a bidder will not be permitted to correct a bid mistake after bid opening that would cause such bidder to have the low bid, unless the mistake, in the judgment of the school district, is clearly evident from examining the bid document: for example, extension of unit prices or errors in addition. All decisions to permit the correction of (sic) withdrawal of bids, or to cancel awards or contracts based on bids mistakes, will be supported by a written determination.

Martin contends that unless an error is clearly evident by examining the bid document itself, no correction is permissible. We disagree. It is patent from the language of § 2–102(10) that only a correction which *causes the bidder to have the low bid* [emphasis in original] requires the mistake be *clearly evident from examining the bid document*. On the other hand, where the bid correction does not *cause* the bidder to have the low bid, nothing in § 2–102 requires District to confine its review to the bid document itself.

Here, the item Sharp failed to include in its bid the bid of its roofing subcontractor, Watts. There was evidence that three different roofing contractors had utilized the identical roof bid from Watts in bidding on District's project. Moreover, Sharp had listed Watts as a sub-contractor in its bid. This evidence was in existence prior to the time the bids were opened. From this evidence, we find it was within District's discretion to determine that correction of Sharp's inadvertently erroneous bid was proper, and that the correction would not be prejudicial to the interests of the school district or fair competition.

Martin asserts the integrity of the bidding process and the need for fair competition require clear rules for post opening bid corrections. While we are not unmindful of the need to preserve the integrity of the bidding process, we find no violation of the rules in this case. Martin has not shown that the procedures followed by District render the upward correction unfair or unjust, nor has he demonstrated in what manner the correction was prejudicial to the District or to fair competition.

As noted by District's order in this case, "It is true that Sharp's omission of the price for the build-up roof was not apparent from the bid form itself. However, the mistake is clear, and the amount Sharp intended to bid for the roof is evident, by examining the roofing subcontractor's sub-bid, which was submitted to several of the bidders, including Sharp and Martin." We agree with the District that allowing the correction in this case neither jeopardized the integrity of the sealed bidding process, nor was it prejudicial to the interests of the District or fair competition. To the contrary, to accept Martin's argument that District must reject Sharp's bid and accept its bid, some $461,500.00 higher than Sharp's corrected bid, would clearly be prejudicial to the District requiring it to expend substantially more money.

Martin cites case law from other jurisdictions as supporting its claim that post-opening bid amendments are impermissible unless an error is readily apparent on the face of the bid. We find cases from other jurisdictions, addressing other state procurement codes, are simply inapplicable to District's procurement code.

2.   SUBSTANTIAL LOSS

Martin next asserts Sharp failed to produce evidence that the bid mistake would cause him "substantial loss" as required by section 2–102(10) ("each written request must document that the bidder's mistake is clearly an error that will cause him substantial loss"). Accordingly, Martin contends the circuit court erred in finding "it patently reasonable to determine that omitting $613,000 in this Project would constitute a substantial loss." We disagree.

It is uncontroverted that Sharp neglected to include $613,000.00 for the roof build up in its bid on the project. Although it is unclear precisely the extent to which this affects Sharp's overall profit margin, we find that $613,000.00 constitutes a substantial loss.

The circuit court's order granting District summary judgment is

AFFIRMED.

NOTES

1.   Do you think that the outcome in this case was fair?
2.   Should all contracts relating to public schools be let out for bids?

[CASE NO. 48]   USE OF REGULAR MAINTENANCE PERSONNEL IN
SCHOOL CONSTRUCTION

UTAH PLUMBING AND HEATING CONTRACTORS ASSOCIATION v. BOARD OF EDUCATION OF WEBER COUNTY SCHOOL DISTRICT

Supreme Court of Utah, 1967.
429 P.2d 49.

■ CROCKETT, CHIEF JUSTICE.

Plaintiffs, an organization of plumbing contractors and three other trade associations ... sued to enjoin defendant Weber County Board of Education from installing a sprinkling system on the Roy High School football field. Plaintiffs contend that the defendant's use of its own maintenance employees to put in the sprinkling system was a violation of Section 53111, U.C.A. 1953, which requires advertising for bids "[w]henever any schoolhouse is to be built" or any improvement constructed costing over $20,000. . . .

After the contract for the school had been awarded and construction was well under way, additional funds from the State became available. It was then that the School Board decided they should install the sprinkling system on the football field at the least possible cost. By advertising for bids for the materials only, and using their regularly employed maintenance people during their free time from other duties, the job could be done for approximately $3200, about $2700 of it for materials, which they purchased from the lowest bidder.

The position essayed by plaintiffs is that the board was obliged to consider the sprinkling system as part of the "building of the schoolhouse" which cost $2,600,000, and that it should have been included in the advertisements for bids for its construction; or alternatively, even though constructed later, it still must be considered as part of the entire project and advertised for bids.

. . . The powers of the Board of Education are derived from statute and consist only of those expressly granted or those reasonably implied as necessary to carry out the duties imposed upon it. A number of sections of our code grant authority to school boards for the construction and maintenance of facilities for the operation of public school systems. Under the heading, "Further Powers of Boards of Education," Section 53620 U.C.A. 1953, provides:

> Every board of education shall have power ... to construct and erect school buildings and to furnish the same, ... to purchase, exchange, repair and improve high school apparatus, books, furniture, fixtures and all other school supplies. It ... may do all things needful for the maintenance, prosperity and success of the schools, and the promotion of education; . . . .

The extensive discretion reposed in the school board by this section is apparent.

We are aware that in decisions construing the powers of school districts, the terms "school building" and "schoolhouse" are often given a broad meaning to encompass the entire functioning school plant, including athletic facilities. However, from this fact and the fact that under the grants of power to the board of education just referred to above, it has authority to construct and maintain athletic facilities, it does not necessarily follow that the sprinkling system in question must be regarded as coming within the language of Section 53111, first referred to above, requiring bids "[w]henever any schoolhouse is to be built." Whether it does or not may depend upon the circumstances. For example, it seems quite obvious that if the schoolhouse itself has already been built, the construction of some additional facility or improvement to the school plant, such as the installation of some additional blackboards, visual aid equipment, or of a sprinkling system in the athletic field, would not be within the meaning of the phrase "building a schoolhouse." If it were so, the school administration would often be hampered in adapting school buildings and facilities to changing needs such as supplying the deficiencies listed above in this very building with which we are concerned. This would be squarely contrary to the plain intent of Section 53620, above quoted which authorizes the Board to improve apparatus, books, furniture, fixtures and do all things needful for the maintenance, prosperity and success of the schools, and the promotion of education. . . .

The principle that the School Board may not fragment a building contract into separate units to avoid the requirement of bids nor otherwise circumvent the requirements of the statutes is sound. From what we have said it should be apparent that as we view the evidence there is a reasonable basis therein to substantiate the trial court's refusal to find that the defendant Board did so. On the other hand, the evidence supports its findings to the contrary. Pertinent to this issue is the fact that the Board did request bids on the pipe and materials and bought them from the lowest bidder. This is evidence of its good faith and its desire to properly and lawfully perform its duty in administering the school system in "the most efficient and economical" manner possible. It is our opinion that its initiative and frugality in the premises should be approved and commended, rather than censured.

· · ·

Affirmed. Costs to the defendant (respondent).

NOTES

1. While the judges disagreed over whether the association had standing, they agreed on the merits of the case.

2. What do you think about using regular board employees on school repair and construction projects? If the amount of money involved exceeds the amount that is required to be let on competitive bids, is your answer still the same? Put another way, should school boards consider the impact that such situations may have on local economies?

[CASE NO. 49]   CONTRACT DISPUTE OVER *QUANTUM MERUIT*

BROWN v. PENLAND CONSTRUCTION COMPANY

Supreme Court of Georgia, 2007.
641 S.E.2d 522 [217 Educ. L. Rep. 732], reconsideration denied.

■ MELTON, JUSTICE.

After some discussions with a number of people including Michael Brown, the former varsity baseball coach of Ridgeland High School, Penland Construction Company (PCC) constructed an indoor baseball hitting facility for the high school on land owned by the Walker County Board of Education (Board). When the Board refused to pay for the facility, PCC sued Brown, the Board, the school district, and the school's Athletic Boosters Club (Boosters Club). The defendants' motions for directed verdict were denied, and a jury awarded PCC $150,000, finding Brown, the Board, and the school district jointly and severally liable under a quantum meruit theory. The Court of Appeals affirmed. We granted certiorari to determine only whether the trial court erred by denying Brown's motion for directed verdict in which Brown argued that he was not liable to PCC under the doctrine of quantum meruit. For the reasons that follow, we reverse.

Quantum meruit operates on the theory that "when one renders service or transfers property which is valuable to another, which the latter accepts, a promise is implied to pay the reasonable value thereof." However, any suit against a public official in his or her individual capacity is barred by official immunity where the public official has engaged in discretionary acts that are within the scope of his or her authority, and the official has not acted in a wilful or wanton manner; with actual malice; or with the actual intent to cause injury. There is no allegation that Brown acted in a wilful, malicious, or wanton manner in his dealings with PCC, or with an actual intent to cause injury. Thus, assuming that Brown, as Ridgeland High's baseball coach, had the authority to act on behalf of the Board to create an implied agreement here, PCC's action for quantum meruit against him individually would be barred by official immunity.

Even if we assume that Brown was acting beyond the scope of his authority, however, PCC's quantum meruit action against Brown individually would still fail. It is undisputed that the alleged agreement here was for PCC to build a hitting facility that was to be approved by the Board and paid for by the Boosters Club. Thus, although PCC rendered a service that was valuable to the school, it was the Board, and not Brown, that accepted those services to create an implied promise of payment. Because Brown did not individually accept the services rendered by PCC, there was no implied promise created for Brown to personally pay for the hitting facility. As such, an action in quantum meruit seeking payment for construction of the facility would not lie against Brown.

Because there is no implied agreement requiring Brown to pay for the hitting facility, PCC's argument that Brown is liable for having received a personal benefit from the construction of the hitting facility goes to the question of unjust enrichment, and not quantum meruit. Nevertheless,

PCC's argument is without merit. The undisputed evidence reveals that Brown was merely plying his trade as a high school baseball coach in a facility that had been provided for the benefit of the school; not that he obtained some special personal benefit from the facility outside of his role as a high school coach. Specifically, the Board owns the land upon which the facility was built, and Brown does not; and Brown was paid by the school, not by individual students and athletes directly, for providing coaching services in the facility. In addition, any enhanced reputation conferred on the school's athletic program due to the existence of the hitting facility is a benefit conferred on the school, not on Brown as an individual, as this same "benefit" would be enjoyed by any baseball coach subsequently employed by the school. There is no evidence of record, but only speculation, that Brown's individual reputation was directly connected to, or for that matter enhanced by, PCC's construction of the hitting facility. To the contrary, the most that can be concluded from the record is that Brown's individual merit or lack thereof as a baseball coach is entirely unrelated to PCC's construction of the indoor hitting facility on school property. Accordingly, we reverse that portion of the Court of Appeals' opinion concluding that the trial court properly denied Brown's motion for a directed verdict.

Judgment reversed.

NOTES

1.   Would it have been fair to render the coach liable?

2.   "The doctrine of implied contract cannot be invoked to do rough justice and fasten liability where the legal requirements specifically prohibit." [sic] *Lutzken v. City of Rochester*, 184 N.Y.S.2d 483, 486 (N.Y.App.Div.1959).

[CASE NO. 50]   RATIFICATION OF AN INVALID CONTRACT

FRANK v. BOARD OF EDUCATION OF JERSEY CITY

Court of Errors and Appeals of New Jersey, 1917.
100 A. 211.

■ BLACK, J.

There is but a single question presented by the record in this case to be answered; viz., whether a municipal corporation is liable to pay for work done and materials furnished it by an unauthorized agent, when the municipality had the power to make a contract for such purposes. If so, whether an agency to purchase such supplies in fact can be implied from the acts and conduct of the parties and a ratification of the contract for such supplies be also implied from like acts and conduct. The application of elemental and well-recognized principles in the law of agency to the facts, as disclosed by the record in this case, leads us to answer these questions in the affirmative. . . .

The facts on which the ruling of the trial court was based are these: The above work and materials were actually furnished by the respondent to the appellant, by order of John T. Rowland, Jr., supervising architect of the appellant, except two items. He had been permitted by the appellant "for a number of years" to order labor and materials of the nature sued for in this case. His orders had been recognized by the appellant, and the amounts therefor had been paid by it. "Many previous orders of the same kind were duly paid for by the defendant," furnished by the respondent. The item of $46.70 for repairing motor generator was for labor, which was furnished by the respondent to the appellant by order of Charles C. Wilson, vice principal of the Jersey City high school, which was under appellant's control. All the items except the item of $5.00 for one pole tester were "emergency" work; i.e., they were furnished at the time the emergency existed, requiring immediate performance, and before a meeting of the appellant could be held to pass upon the necessity of doing the same and ordering it to be done.

The respondent had done other work and furnished materials of a similar character for the appellant under and by similar orders. Such work had been regularly paid for, in due course, by the appellant, when the bills for the same were presented without question as to the regularity of the requests or the authority of the said Rowland and Wilson. The work done and materials furnished, sued for in this suit, were done and furnished, relying on the fact that previous orders by Rowland and Wilson, under similar circumstances, had been paid for by the appellant. The respondent knew that this practice existed and was permitted to exist by the appellant. This practice had been so "for a number of years." The appellant knew that the work and materials had been furnished it by the respondent at or about the times they had been so furnished and it did not, until three years after the last work had been performed, deny the authority of the said Rowland and Wilson to order the work and materials. The appellant has had the use and benefit of the work so done and materials furnished. . . .

. . . [In a statute] there is express authority for the appointment of an agent, a business manager. The term is immaterial. A supervising architect or vice principal might just as well be called an agent or business manager. There is also the recognition by the legislature of the fact that the board of education probably could not act in many cases without appointing such agents, since the very necessity of some cases requires that such a board should act through agents. . . . It would be quite impracticable to require either a formal resolution for every possible small expenditure, or for the board to act by a majority in person. In the state of facts these orders under consideration are called "emergency" orders. . . .

The literature of the law of agency is rich in adjudged cases. The principles pertinent to the subject under discussion are these: An agency, as between individuals or business corporations, may be implied from prior habit, or from a course of dealings of a similar nature between the parties. The agency may be implied from the recognition or acquiescence of the alleged principal as to acts done in his behalf by the alleged agent, especially if the agent has repeatedly been permitted to perform acts like the one in question. But when it is implied, and in so far as it is implied, the power of the agent must be determined from no one fact alone but from all the facts and circumstances for which the principal is responsible. So ratification may be implied from any acts, words, or conduct on the part of the principal which reasonably tend to show an intention on the part of the principal to ratify the unauthorized acts or transactions of the alleged agent, provided the principal in doing the acts relied on as a ratification acted with knowledge of the material facts. The rule is particularly applicable where it appears that the principal has repeatedly recognized and affirmed similar acts by the agent. So a municipal corporation may ratify the unauthorized acts and contracts of its agents or officers which are within the scope of the corporate powers, but not otherwise. . . .

We think, as the board of education had the power, under the statute, to contract for the work done and material supplied in this case, there was created by conduct an implied agency, an agency in fact, on the part of Messrs. Rowland and Wilson, and further, that by implication the contracts of these unauthorized agents have been ratified by the acts and conduct of the school board.; hence it was not error for the trial court to direct a judgment in favor of the respondent and against the appellant.

The judgment will therefore be affirmed, with costs.

NOTES

1. In *Everett v. Board of Pub. Instruction of Volusia County*, 186 So. 209 (Fla.1939), a janitor sued to recover on a contract he formed with the principal of his school. Although the janitor was recommended for the job, the board appointed someone else even though its members knew that he rendered services under the contract and they did nothing to indicate that his services were unwanted. The court found that the janitor presented a cause of action in *quantum meruit*. Was this fair?

2. "School district officers cannot be permitted by the law to enter into a written contract with a teacher, none of them denying its validity for 10 weeks, or half the term, but recognizing it by making payments upon it, in which payments all join, and then, after the teacher, in the utmost good faith and reliance upon the contract, has taught that length of time, discharge him without cause, and plead in bar of payment under the contract that they never met and consulted, nor took corporate action in hiring him, or made any record in a book of the execution of the contract. It appears very clearly in this case that a majority of the school board assented to this contract in the first place, as evidenced by their executing it. It was afterward ratified by all three of them. It was not necessary that there should be a direct proceeding with the express intent to ratify. It may be done indirectly, and by acts of recognition or acquiescence, or acts inconsistent with repudiation or disapproval." *Crane v. Bennington School Dist.*, 28 N.W. 105, 107 (Mich.1886).

CHAPTER 9

TEACHER CERTIFICATION, EMPLOYMENT, AND CONTRACTS

INTRODUCTION

Laws governing the qualifications, employment, and contracts of teachers along with other school employees are primarily established at the state level. Even so, federal laws, especially in the area of anti-discrimination, have a major impact on the employment rights of educators in public schools. As such, this chapter reviews issues associated with the employment of educators, most notably teachers, in public schools.

TEACHER CERTIFICATION/ LICENSURE

GENERALLY

All jurisdictions have laws[1] requiring public school teachers to obtain certification or licenses[2] based on qualifications such as having completed professional preparation programs[3] and/or passing criminal background checks.[4] Whether referred to as certification or licensure, insofar as state endorsements are not contracts, mere possession of credentials does not satisfy the statutory definition of being a teacher since individuals must

---

1. *See, e.g.,* ALA. CODE 1975 §§ 16–23–1 *et seq.*; ALASKA STAT. §§ 14.20.010 *et seq.*; CAL. EDUC. CODE ANN. § 44203; 105 ILL. COMP. STAT. 5/21–0.01 *et seq.*; KY. REV. STAT. ANN. §§ 161.010 *et seq.*; MONT. CODE ANN. §§ 20–4–101 *et seq.*; N.Y. McKINNEY'S EDUC. LAW § 3001; OHIO REV. CODE ANN. §§ 3319.22 *et seq.*; 70 OKLA. STAT. ANN. § 6–106; PA. STAT. ANN. §§ 12–1201 *et seq.*; TEX. EDUC. ANN. § 21.041; WYO. STAT. ANN. §§ 21–7–501 *et seq.*

2. Amid debate over whether educators should receive permanent certification, or licenses, subject to regular renewal as in professions such as law or medicine, unless otherwise noted, this book uses the term certification to apply to both.

3. *Irizarry v. Anker,* 558 F.2d 1122 (2d Cir.1977) (upholding a board's refusal to go beyond a catalogue description in denying course credit to an applicant); *State ex rel. Thompson v. Ekberg,* 613 P.2d 466 (Okla.1980) (requiring a principal to have a masters degree). [Case No. 51]

4. *See, e.g.,* ARK. STAT. ANN. § 6–17–410; CAL. EDUC. CODE ANN. §§ 44339 *et seq.*; CONN. GEN. STAT. ANN. § 10–221d; KY. REV. STAT. ANN. § 160.380; MICH. COMP. LAWS ANN. § 380.1230a; MINN. STAT. ANN. § 122A.18; MISS. CODE ANN. § 37–13–89; OHIO REV. CODE ANN. § 3319.39; OR. REV. STAT. ANN. § 326.603; R.I. GEN. LAWS ANN. § 16–2–18.1; TENN. CODE. ANN. § 49–5–413; TEX. EDUC. ANN. § 22.083. For a case rejecting a challenge to background checks, *see Hilliard v. Ferguson,* 30 F.3d 649 [93 Educ. L. Rep. 116] (5th Cir.1994).

typically both possess valid certificates and perform statutory job duties.[5] Certification laws differ as to substantive requirements and procedures since legislatures vest varying amounts of discretion in state level boards and departments of education, chief state school officers, and local boards.

Certification requirements are subject to judicial scrutiny under federal and state anti-discrimination statutes and the Fourteenth Amendment. Since the right to engage in a legitimate occupation is a liberty interest, state officials can only deny individuals jobs if there are reasonable standards in place to protect public health, safety, and welfare.[6] Employment is also identified as a property right.[7] However, when the actions of educational agencies are rooted in the ministerial application of objective criteria, rather than the exercise of discretion, courts are reluctant to intervene on behalf of aggrieved teachers. In one such case, an appellate court in Pennsylvania dismissed the challenge of a teacher who failed the Praxis II test in Spanish Content Knowledge that was required for certification.[8] The court explained that insofar as the teacher lacked an expectation that she would have received a certificate, officials did not deprive her of any right or privilege, including the opportunity to litigate her disagreement. A year earlier, another appellate court in Pennsylvania upheld the denial of an administrative certificate to a teacher with only one year of experience where the applicable statute required a minimum of five years of professional experience and the completion of an approved graduate program of study.[9] The court refused to grant the teacher credit for her teaching experience at a charter school.

In a preliminary question, in *Ambach v. Norwick*, the Supreme Court upheld a statute from New York requiring individuals who wished to become public school teachers to be United States citizens. Recognizing that "[t]he importance of public schools in the preparation of individuals for participation as citizens, and in the preservation of the values on which our society rests, long has been recognized by our decisions . . . ,"[10] the Court wrote that a state may regard teachers as having an obligation to promote civic virtues and understanding in their classes. More recently, a federal trial court in Georgia reached the opposite result.[11] The court enjoined the enforcement of a state statute precluding aliens from public employment on the basis that it violated the Equal Protection Clause absent individualized findings that their remaining in their jobs would have undermined legitimate state interests.

---

5. *Sealey v. Board of Educ.*, 14 S.W.3d 597 [143 Educ. L. Rep. 1091] (Mo.Ct.App.1999), *reh'g denied* (1999). *See also Houston v. Nelson*, 147 S.W.3d 589 [193 Educ. L. Rep. 332] (Tex.Ct.App.2004).

6. *Meyer v. Nebraska*, 262 U.S. 390, 43 S.Ct. 625, 67 L.Ed. 1042 (1923).

7. *See, e.g., Leetham v. McGinn*, 524 P.2d 323 (Utah 1974); *Connecticut Educ. Ass'n v. Tirozzi*, 554 A.2d 1065 [52 Educ. L. Rep. 604] (Conn.1989).

8. *Dauer v. Department of Educ.*, 874 A.2d 159 [198 Educ. L. Rep. 621] (Pa.Cmwlth.Ct. 2005).

9. *Davenport v. Department of Educ.*, 850 A.2d 802 [188 Educ. L. Rep. 917] (Pa.Cmwlth.Ct. 2004).

10. 441 U.S. 68, 76, 99 S.Ct. 1589, 60 L.Ed.2d 49 (1979).

11. *Chang v. Glynn County School Dist.*, 457 F.Supp.2d 1378 [214 Educ. L. Rep. 668] (S.D. Ga. 2006).

On other basic matters, courts have refused to eliminate loyalty oaths,[12] residency requirements,[13] and mental and physical examinations for job candidates.[14] In California, an appellate court reviewed a law barring convicted felons from acquiring teaching credentials. Reversing in favor of an applicant for a credential, the court held that insofar as his conviction for discharging a firearm in a grossly negligent manner was reduced to a misdemeanor, and he was placed on probation, the statute did not bar him from seeking teacher certification.[15]

If candidates meet the legal standards for certification, state agencies may not arbitrarily reject their applications[16] or impose new conditions such as age requirements.[17] As reflected by an older case from Maryland, when the state legislature delegated its authority to an examining and certificating agency, the judiciary refused to become involved. The state's highest court denied a candidate's request for a writ of mandamus challenging the requirements that changed after he entered a preparation program.[18] The court noted that insofar as the state board could enact bylaws to effectuate the state's educational policies, it would not interfere and grant certification to a candidate who failed to meet the requirement of graduating in the upper four-fifths of his class and earn a grade of "C" or better in "practical teaching." As evidenced by a case from New York, where the qualifications for teaching certificates were clear and applicants lacking the basic requirements failed to correct their deficiencies by acquiring the necessary background, they were not entitled to receive certificates.[19]

A high profile case from New York City involved a challenge to the State Commissioner of Education's granting a waiver to the chief executive of a magazine company so that she could receive a "School District Leader Certificate" enabling her to serve as Chancellor of the public schools even though she had no prior experience in education and lacked a masters or higher degree.[20] A trial court determined that the Commissioner did not

---

12. *Gough v. State*, 667 A.2d 1057 [105 Educ. L. Rep. 584] (N.J. Super. Ct. App. Div. 1995). For earlier cases dealing with loyalty and loyalty oaths, *see* Chapter 10 at notes 109–121 and accompanying text.

13. *Wardwell v. Board of Educ. of City School Dist. of City of Cincinnati*, 529 F.2d 625 (6th Cir.1976); *Mogle v. Sevier County School Dist.*, 540 F.2d 478 (10th Cir.1976), *cert. denied*, 429 U.S. 1121, 97 S.Ct. 1157, 51 L.Ed.2d 572 (1977). For cases agreeing that teachers satisfied residency requirements necessary to keep their jobs, *see Gigliotti v. Bianco*, 919 N.Y.S.2d 641 [265 Educ. L. Rep. 1186] (N.Y. App. Div. 2011); *Krajkowski v. Bianco*, 925 N.Y.S.2d 735 [268 Educ. L. Rep. 502] (N.Y. App. Div. 2011).

14. *Sullivan v. River Valley School Dist.*, 197 F.3d 804 [140 Educ. L. Rep. 127] (6th Cir.1999), *cert. denied*, 530 U.S. 1262, 120 S.Ct. 2718, 147 L.Ed.2d 983 (2000) (also rejecting the applicant's claim that he was disabled under the Americans with Disabilities Act).

15. *Gebremicael v. California Comm'n on Teacher Credentialing*, 13 Cal.Rptr.3d 777 [187 Educ. L. Rep. 943] (Cal. Ct. App. 2004).

16. *Keller v. Hewitt*, 41 P. 871 (Cal.1895); *State ex rel. Hopkins v. Wooster*, 208 P. 656 (Kan.1922).

17. *State ex rel. Johnson v. Matzen*, 210 N.W. 151 (Neb. 1926).

18. *Metcalf v. Cook*, 178 A. 219 (Md.1935).

19. *Bhatt v. New York State Educ. Dep't*, 843 N.Y.S.2d 737 [224 Educ. L. Rep. 890] (N.Y. App. Div. 2007), *leave to appeal denied*, 859 N.Y.S.2d 392, 889 N.E.2d 79 (N.Y. 2008).

20. *Snyder v. New York State Bd. of Regents*, 919 N.Y.S.2d 770 [265 Educ. L. Rep. 1190] (N.Y. Sup. Ct. 2010).

abuse his discretion in granting the waiver since the candidate had training, background, and experience that were substantially equivalent to the
certification requirements for superintendents.[21]

In North Carolina, a dispute arose when the state board of education
adopted a regulation stipulating that all public school teaching certificates
would expire after five years and that educators who wished to renew their
credentials had to earn six units of credit during the five-year period
immediately preceding renewal. The Supreme Court of North Carolina
upheld the regulation since there was a reasonable basis for the belief of
state officials that the quality of teachers' classroom performances would
improve if they broadened or kept their knowledge up-to-date.[22] Similarly,
the Supreme Court of Connecticut affirmed that state officials could replace
the statutory scheme, which permitted teachers to receive certification for
life, revocable only for cause, with one conferring five-year renewable
certificates premised on successful completion of professional development
activities.[23] While acknowledging that teachers had constitutionally protected property interests in their certificates, the court decided that the new
system did not deprive them of due process. The court was satisfied that
insofar as the legislative goal of enhancing the quality of public education
was important, the plan was not unduly restrictive or onerous.

When school officials knowingly employed a woman to teach subjects
for which she lacked certification, and continually reassured her that this
was not a problem, they were still able to discharge her due to her lack of
qualifications. The Supreme Court of Wisconsin affirmed that insofar as
the teacher was responsible for being certified, and local administrators
could not waive the requirement, she was not entitled to equitable relief.[24]
In like fashion, an appellate court in New York confirmed that a school
board could discharge a teacher even after officials obtained permission
from the state department of education permitting him to continue to
remain on the job since he refused to complete course work toward
certification nine years after he was hired.[25] Another appellate court in
New York agreed that a teacher could be denied certification in earth
science since the biology course that he took failed to meet state requirements.[26] The Court of Appeals of New York reached a different outcome in
affirming that a teacher who taught for seven years and was awarded
tenure could not be denied a permanent certificate since she failed to
complete student teaching.[27] The court ruled that the commissioner of

---

21. Interestingly, Cathleen P. (Cathie) Black did not last long as Chancellor. *See* Michael
Barbaro, Sharon Otterman, & Javier C. Hernandez, *After 3 Months, Mayor Replaces Schools
Leader*, N.Y. TIMES, April 8, 2011 at A1.

22. *Guthrie v. Taylor*, 185 S.E.2d 193 (N.C. 1971), *cert. denied*, 406 U.S. 920, 92 S.Ct. 1774,
32 L.Ed.2d 119 (1972).

23. *Connecticut Educ. Ass'n v. Tirozzi*, 554 A.2d 1065 [52 Educ. L. Rep. 604] (Conn. 1989).

24. *Grams v. Melrose–Mindoro Joint School Dist. No. 1*, 254 N.W.2d 730 (Wis. 1977).

25. *Chapman v. Board of Educ. of Yonkers City School Dist.*, 394 N.Y.S.2d 52 (N.Y. App.
Div. 1977). *See also Smith v. Andrews*, 504 N.Y.S.2d 286 [37 Educ. L. Rep. 893] (N.Y. App.
Div. 1986), *appeal denied*, 513 N.Y.S.2d 1025 [38 Educ. L. Rep. 1136] (N.Y. 1987).

26. *Emminger v. Education Dep't of State of N.Y.*, 627 N.Y.S.2d 127 [100 Educ. L. Rep.
687] (N.Y. App. Div. 1995).

27. *Bradford Cent. School Dist. v. Ambach*, 451 N.Y.S.2d 654 [5 Educ. L. Rep. 189] (N.Y.
1982). *See also Matteson v. State Bd. of Educ.*, 136 P.2d 120 (Cal. Ct. App. 1943).

education did not abuse his discretion in waiving the student teaching requirement under the circumstances.

The Supreme Court of South Carolina relied solely on the denial of procedural due process in prohibiting the cancellation of a teaching certificate when a private testing agency notified the state department of education that a score should have been canceled.[28] The court found that the regulation providing for automatic invalidation was unconstitutional where the only evidence against the teacher was an unexplained note from the testing company.

The Fourth Circuit outlined the necessary steps to comply with Section 504 of the Rehabilitation Act of 1973 (Section 504)[29] and, by extension, the Americans with Disabilities Act (ADA),[30] when individuals with disabilities are unable to meet certification requirements. A candidate in Virginia who was diagnosed as having learning disabilities failed the communications skills portion of the National Teacher Examination (NTE), which is designed to measure academic achievement of teachers eight times, twice after she received special aids and more time to complete the test. Following lengthy litigation, the court determined that the teacher was entitled to a trial on the merits of whether she was otherwise qualified under Section 504.[31]

In an emerging issue, the No Child Left Behind Act (NCLB) requires school boards to hire teachers who are "highly qualified."[32] Matters are complicated because under the NCLB the standards vary depending on whether teachers are in regular or special education,[33] the level at which they teach, and whether individuals are experienced or new.

The first case on issues surrounding whether teachers are "highly qualified" was litigated in Connecticut. The federal trial court affirmed its preliminary order rejecting a claim by tenured teachers who challenged the state's new certification standards for teaching mathematics as a core subject.[34] The court ruled that the newer, more rigorous, standards did not violate the teachers' right to equal protection because the educators failed to compare themselves to others who were similarly situated.

THE NCLB AND HIGHLY QUALIFIED TEACHERS

In requiring school boards to hire teachers who meet its "Highly Qualified Teacher" (HQT) mandate, the NCLB directs local officials to create programs to improve the quality of teaching while instituting in-

---

28. *Brown v. South Carolina State Bd. of Educ.*, 391 S.E.2d 866 [60 Educ. L. Rep. 1004] (S.C. 1990). [Case No. 52]

29. 29 U.S.C.A. § 794(a). This statute is in the Appendix.

30. 42 U.S.C.A. §§ 12101 *et seq.* Portions of this statute are in the Appendix.

31. *Pandazides v. Virginia Bd. of Educ.*, 13 F.3d 823 [88 Educ. L. Rep. 963] (4th Cir.1994).

32. 20 U.S.C.A. § 7801(23) (dealing with teachers in regular education). This section of the statute is in the Appendix.

33. 20 U.S.C.A. § 1401(10) (dealing with teachers in special education). This section of the statute is in the Appendix.

34. *Buell v. Hughes*, 596 F. Supp. 2d 380 [242 Educ. L. Rep. 140] (D. Conn. 2009).

structional leadership development programs for principals and superintendents[35] along with offering high quality professional development programs for all staff.[36] The NCLB also requires local school boards to improve teacher quality by supporting professional development programs designed to focus on practices grounded in scientifically based research to prepare and recruit HQTs.[37] The NCLB grants state and local officials the flexibility to select the strategies that best meet their needs to improve teaching and learning. In return, local officials must demonstrate that their districts and/or schools have achieved adequate yearly progress by ensuring that all teachers in core academic subjects are HQTs.[38]

According to the NCLB, all students must be taught by HQTs in core academic subjects.[39] The NCLB's regulations stipulate that "[t]he term 'core academic subjects' means English, reading or language arts, mathematics, science, foreign languages, civics and government, economics, arts, history, and geography."[40]

The NCLB divides teachers who must become HQTs into two groups, those new to the profession and those who have been teaching. New "highly qualified" elementary teachers must meet two requirements. First, these teachers must have at least bachelors' degrees. Second, these teachers must demonstrate, by passing rigorous state, rather than federal, tests, that they have subject knowledge and teaching skills in reading, writing, mathematics, and other areas of basic elementary school curricula.[41] New middle and secondary HQTs must have at least bachelors' degrees and have demonstrated high levels of competency in each of the academic subjects in which they teach either by passing rigorous state tests in each of these subjects or successfully completing academic majors, graduate degrees, course work equivalent to undergraduate academic majors, or advanced certifications in credentialing in these areas.[42]

On the other hand, the NCLB requires experienced teachers to have at least bachelors' degrees, meet the requirements for those new to the profession, and have passed rigorous state tests or demonstrate competence in all of the academic subjects that they teach. These competencies must be based on high objective uniform standards that are set by states for grade appropriate academic subject matter knowledge and teaching skills; aligned with challenging state academic content and student academic achievement standards that have been developed in consultation with core content specialists, teachers, principals, and school administrators; created to offer objective, coherent information about individuals' attainment of content knowledge in the subjects they teach; applied uniformly to all teachers in the same academic subjects and grade levels throughout states; take into

---

35. 20 U.S.C.A. § 6301(1).

36. 20 U.S.C.A. § 6301(10).

37. *See, e.g.*, 20 U.S.C.A. § 6316(b)(3)(A).

38. 20 U.S.C.A. § 6301(1).

39. 20 U.S.C.A. § 6319(a)(2).

40. 34 C.F.R. § 200.55(b), 20 U.S.C.A. § 6319(a)(2).

41. 20 U.S.C.A. § 7801(23)(B)(i).

42. 20 U.S.C.A. § 7801(23)(B)(ii).

consideration, but not be based primarily on, the time the teachers were teaching in their academic subjects; are available to the public on request; and may involve multiple, objective measures of teacher competency.[43]

As applied to special education teachers, the HQT provisions require school officials to "take measurable steps to recruit, hire, train, and retain highly qualified school personnel to provide special education and related services"[44] for students with disabilities; similar rules apply to personnel who provide related services and paraprofessionals.[45] In order to be classified as HQTs, subject area teachers must not only be certified fully in special education or pass state-designed special education licensing examinations, but must also possess bachelors' degrees and demonstrate knowledge of each of the subjects for which they are the primary instructors.[46]

Pursuant to the provisions relating to special education, which apply the same deadlines as for regular teachers under the NCLB,[47] currently employed special education teachers must meet these standards even if they provide instruction in multiple subjects.[48] New special education teachers have up to two years after they are hired to become "highly qualified" in different subjects as long as they are fully certificated in at least one.[49] The Individuals with Disabilities Education Act (IDEA)[50] adds that teachers who satisfy its HQT requirements also qualify for this title under the NCLB.[51] Even so, the IDEA does not create a private right of action for parents to ensure that children are taught by HQTs.[52]

Funding and Support for Highly Qualified Teachers

The NCLB makes funds available to state and local school boards to offer activities to support HQTs. These provisions allow local officials to transfer up to fifty percent of their federal NCLB grant monies to Title I funds in order to target resources as they see fit.[53] Further, the federal government supports the development of teachers in such needed subject areas as mathematics, sciences, special education, and languages through such innovative programs as Troops for Teachers[54] and Transition to Teaching.[55]

Along with the NCLB, federal law offers student loan forgiveness of up to $5,000 for HQTs who serve for five consecutive complete school years in

---

43.   20 U.S.C.A. § 7801(23)(C).

44.   20 U.S.C.A. §§ 1412(a)(14)(C), (D).

45.   20 U.S.C.A. § 1412(a)(14)(B).

46.   20 U.S.C.A. § 1402(10)(B).

47.   20 U.S.C.A. § 1412(a)(14)(C).

48.   20 U.S.C.A. § 1401a(10)(D)(ii).

49.   20 U.S.C.A. § 1401a(10)(D)(iii).

50.   20 U.S.C.A. §§ 1400 *et seq.*

51.   20 U.S.C.A. § 1401a(10)(F).

52.   20 U.S.C.A. § 1412(a)(14)(E).

53.   20 U.S.C.A. § 6762(a)(2).

54.   20 U.S.C.A. §§ 6671 *et seq.*

55.   20 U.S.C.A. §§ 6681 *et seq.*

low-income schools.[56] Full-time secondary school HQTs in mathematics or science[57] or elementary or secondary school teachers whose primary responsibility is to provide special education for children with disabilities[58] may receive up to $17,500 in student loan forgiveness.

EXAMINATIONS FOR CERTIFICATES

Where state legislatures require candidates to take competitive examinations to earn certification, questions arise as to the appropriate procedures. In an early case, an appellate court in New York directed a testing firm to provide an unsuccessful candidate for a license as a high school department chair with model answers to essay questions and other parts of the examination.[59] The court thought that refusing to permit the candidate to review the standard against which his performance was measured was unreasonable.

A year later, New York's highest court refused to annul failure ratings in an interview test that was part of a licensing examination for elementary school principals who claimed that it lacked sufficiently objective standards.[60] The court was of the opinion that insofar as the skills necessary to become a principal cannot be adequately measured with precision, and the interview examination procedures were appropriate, they were sufficient. The same court also considered whether eligibility lists based on competitive examinations could be avoided in appointing elementary school principals who possessed characteristics that were deemed necessary in inner-city schools. In another case involving an experiment with decentralization and community involvement, the board of education created a post of "demonstration elementary school principal" in following its normal procedure and temporarily appointing candidates. The court overturned judgments that this approach violated the state's constitutional mandate of a merit system since it did not test for special qualifications.[61] The court pointed out that the principals could remain on the job pending the rapid development of criteria and bases for their assessment.

In a case from South Carolina on teacher testing,[62] the United States Supreme Court summarily upheld the use of the NTE. The Court reasoned that state educational officials could rely on the NTE since it was validated to test the qualifications of prospective educators.

The first of four cases from Texas saw the Fifth Circuit uphold the legislature's general power to require teacher candidates to pass a Pre-Professional Skills Test. The court dissolved a preliminary injunction

---

56. 20 U.S.C.A. §§ 1078–10(b), (c)(1).

57. 20 U.S.C.A. § 1078–10(c)(3)(A)(ii).

58. 20 U.S.C.A. § 1078–10(c)(3)(B)(ii).

59. *Schwartz v. Bogen*, 281 N.Y.S.2d 279 (N.Y. App. Div.1967).

60. *Nelson v. Board of Examiners of Bd. of Educ.*, 288 N.Y.S.2d 454 (N.Y. 1968).

61. *Council of Supervisory Ass'ns of Pub. Schools v. Board of Educ.*, 297 N.Y.S.2d 547 (N.Y. 1969).

62. *United States v. State of S.C*, 445 F.Supp. 1094 (D.S.C.1977), *aff'd, sub nom. National Educ. Ass'n v. United States*, 434 U.S. 1026, 98 S.Ct. 756, 54 L.Ed.2d 775 (1978).

against the test, ordering a trial on the merits of claims that it was both invalid and had a disparate impact on minority students. As part of its analysis, the court reiterated the basic rule that a state is "not obligated to educate or certify teachers who cannot pass a fair and valid test of basic skills necessary for professional training"[63] and that disparate impact alone did not violate the Fourteenth Amendment's Equal Protection Clause. Shortly thereafter, the Supreme Court of Texas upheld a statute that required teachers to pass a basic skills test in order to keep their certificates in the face of allegations that it impaired their contract rights.[64] The court rejected the argument that insofar as the test did not include a specific provision for hearings or avenues of appeal, it was a retroactive law that violated due process. The court emphasized that insofar as no contract was involved in the case of a license and because decertification was not automatic, it could be governed by the law covering revocation for cause. Subsequently, the Fifth Circuit affirmed both that statistical analysis provided by minority candidates who failed to pass Texas' compulsory certification test was inapplicable under Title VII of the Civil Rights Act of 1964,[65] discussed below, since they were not employees[66] and that neither the state nor the local school board acted with intent to discriminate when minority teachers were unable to pass the same test.[67]

In a controversy from Alabama over testing, the Eleventh Circuit vacated a consent decree stipulating that teacher certification examinations violated Title VII because they included impermissible racial bias against African Americans.[68] Also, the Ninth Circuit upheld the validity of the California Basic Educational Skills Test that all candidates are required to pass before they can teach or fill other positions in public schools in the face of a claim that it violated the rights of minority candidates.[69] The court maintained that the examination was constitutional because it used properly validated methods to show that it had a manifest relationship to teaching since it was job related to the extent that it actually measured skills, knowledge, or ability required for successful job performance.[70]

The most recent dispute on point has yet to be resolved on its merits. A class of educators sued the New York City Board of Education and State Department of Education under Title VII and state laws alleging that they violated the rights of African American and Latino teachers by requiring them to pass examinations to receive or retain their teaching licenses. In remanding an earlier order that the test was sufficiently job-related as

---

63. *United States v. LULAC*, 793 F.2d 636, 639 [37 Educ. L. Rep. 772] (5th Cir.1986).

64. *State v. Project Principle*, 724 S.W.2d 387 [37 Educ. L. Rep. 961] (Tex. 1987).

65. 42 U.S.C.A. §§ 2000 *et seq.* Portions of this statute are in the Appendix.

66. *Fields v. Hallsville Indep. School Dist.*, 906 F.2d 1017 [61 Educ. L. Rep. 442] (5th Cir.1990), *cert. denied*, 498 U.S. 1026, 111 S.Ct. 676, 112 L.Ed.2d 668 (1991).

67. *Frazier v. Garrison I.S.D.*, 980 F.2d 1514 [79 Educ. L. Rep. 420] (5th Cir.1993).

68. *Allen v. Alabama State Bd. of Educ.*, 164 F.3d 1347 [131 Educ. L. Rep. 920] (11th Cir.1999), *vacated*, 216 F.3d 1263 [146 Educ. L. Rep. 628] (11th Cir.2000).

69. *Association of Mexican–American Educators v. State of Cal.*, 231 F.3d 572 [148 Educ. L. Rep. 639] (9th Cir.2000).

70. *See also Feldman v. Board of Educ. of City School Dist. of City of N.Y.*, 686 N.Y.S.2d 842 [134 Educ. L. Rep. 262] (N.Y. App. Div. 1999) (affirming the termination of the licenses of teachers who failed the NTE).

clearly erroneous, the Second Circuit dismissed the state as a party on the basis that the New York City Board of Education alone was an employer that might have been subject to Title VII liability.[71]

A federal trial court in Massachusetts rejected the claims of teachers who were unable to pass a licensing examination.[72] In granting the commonwealth's motion to dismiss for failure to state a claim, the court held that the examination did not discriminate against applicants for whom English was a second language insofar as any alleged discrimination failed to rise to the level that it was purposeful and intentional.

In a case on the issue of disability and eligibility to take a test, the Third Circuit affirmed that a school board in Pennsylvania could not deny a woman who was blind the opportunity to take a qualifying examination for teachers.[73] The court posited that insofar as the right to take the examination arose under commonwealth law, the board violated the Fourteenth Amendment by arbitrarily creating the irrebuttable presumption that no person who was blind could qualify to teach. When the applicant was finally allowed to take, and pass, the examination, the court affirmed her entitlement to seniority as of the time she would have been employed but for the illegal postponement of her doing so.

A federal trial court in Minnesota, in another disagreement overlapping with the rights of the disabled, granted the state licensing board's motion for summary judgment in refusing to waive the mathematics section of an examination for a candidate with dyslexia.[74] The court noted that insofar as the mathematics portion of the test related to an essential job function, the candidate's inability to pass it meant that she was not an otherwise qualified individual who was entitled to protection under federal and state disability laws. In like fashion, a federal trial court in New York rejected the claim of a teacher that officials failed to accommodate her disability under the ADA.[75] Insofar as the teacher refused to take a required certification examination, the court held that she was not otherwise qualified for a job.

SUSPENSION–REVOCATION OF CERTIFICATES

State agencies have the authority to grant credentials and to revoke them for cause such as where one teacher assaulted a child[76] and another directed inappropriate and verbally abusive language at students[77] as long as their actions are not arbitrary or capricious.[78] Courts typically uphold

---

71. *Gulino v. Board of Educ. of N.Y. City,* 460 F.3d 361 [212 Educ. L. Rep. 106] (2d Cir.2006), *cert. denied,* 554 U.S. 917, 128 S.Ct. 2986, 171 L.Ed.2d 885 (2008).

72. *Alston v. Massachusetts,* 661 F.Supp.2d 117 [252 Educ. L. Rep. 196] (D. Mass. 2009).

73. *Gurmankin v. Costanzo,* 556 F.2d 184 (3d Cir.1977).

74. *Jacobsen v. Tillmann,* 17 F.Supp.2d 1018 [129 Educ. L. Rep. 1094] (D. Minn. 1998).

75. *Falchenberg v. New York City Dep't of Educ.,* 375 F.Supp.2d 344 [199 Educ. L. Rep. 813] (S.D.N.Y. 2005), *appeal dismissed* (2009).

76. *In re Appeal of Morrill,* 765 A.2d 699 [150 Educ. L. Rep. 758] (N.H.2001).

77. *Knight v. Winn,* 910 So.2d 310 [201 Educ. L. Rep. 989] (Fla. Dist. Ct. App. 2005), *reh'g denied* (2005).

78. *Von Gizycki v. Levy,* 771 N.Y.S.2d 174 [185 Educ. L. Rep. 325] (N.Y. App. Div. 2004).

the mandatory revocation or suspension of credentials when educators are convicted of specified crimes[79] such as driving under the influence of alcohol[80] or moral turpitude[81] or are indicted for possession of cocaine with intent to distribute[82] or welfare fraud.[83]

A case from Missouri reflects how narrowly the judiciary interprets the concept of moral turpitude. An appellate court reinstated the certificate of a teacher who was suspended for ninety-days after pleading guilty to a charge of second-degree child endangerment for leaving her three young children alone in her car for almost an hour when she went into a casino to gamble.[84] The court explained that the state board failed to prove that the teacher's conduct involved moral turpitude. Along the same line, an appellate court in Georgia ruled that the state's Professional Standards Commission exceeded its authority in imposing suspensions of a week on the licenses of two teachers who were married to each other for ethics violations because they failed to supervise a party that their daughter hosted at their home where under-aged drinking allegedly occurred.[85] The court held that there was no evidence that the teachers' conduct at their home impaired their ability to function professionally. Similarly, West Virginia's highest court decided that although a teacher beat his son in such a way that the child had welt marks on his left shoulder and back, his license could not be suspended due to the lack of a nexus between his misconduct and his professional duties.[86]

While not directly involving the revocation of a teacher's license for misconduct, a case from New Mexico presented an interesting question. After a teacher inappropriately touched a male child, his father sued various officials alleging that the defendants were liable for renewing the educator's license. The federal trial court granted the defendants' motion for summary judgment based on the defense of qualified sovereign immunity.[87] Reflective of the three previous cases in which the judiciary was reluctant to revoke licenses absent proof of misconduct, the court determined that although the teacher failed to disclose a previous allegation of inappropriate conduct with a child on an earlier renewal, since the results of an investigation of that claim produced insufficient evidence to revoke his license, the defendants could not be liable.

---

79. *Vogulkin v. State Bd. of Educ.*, 15 Cal.Rptr. 335 (Cal.Ct.App.1961).

80. *Broney v. California Comm'n on Teacher Credentialing*, 108 Cal.Rptr.3d 832 [256 Educ. L. Rep. 313] (Cal.Ct.App.2010).

81. *Bowalick v. Commonwealth*, 840 A.2d 519 [184 Educ. L. Rep. 903] (Pa.Cmwlth.Ct. 2004).

82. *Dupree v. School Comm. of Boston*, 446 N.E.2d 1099 [10 Educ. L. Rep. 336] (Mass.Ct. App.1983), *review denied*, 451 N.E.2d 1166 (Mass.1983).

83. *Perryman v. School Comm. of Boston*, 458 N.E.2d 748 [15 Educ. L. Rep. 533] (Mass.Ct.App.1983).

84. *Brehe v. Missouri Dep't of Elementary and Secondary Educ.*, 213 S.W.3d 720 [216 Educ. L. Rep. 973] (Mo.Ct.App.2007).

85. *Professional Standards Comm'n v. Peterson*, 643 S.E.2d 899 [219 Educ. L. Rep. 321] (Ga.Ct.App.2007).

86. *Powell v. Paine*, 655 S.E.2d 204 [228 Educ. L. Rep. 934] (W.Va.2007).

87. B.T. v. Davis, 557 F.Supp.2d 1262 [234 Educ. L. Rep. 917] (D.N.M.2007).

In an older case, the Second Circuit upheld an order of the commissioner of education that a local board not re-employ a tenured teacher from New York pending the revocation of his certification after he was convicted of, and served a prison term for, conspiring to promote bribery of public officials.[88] Moreover, an appellate court in Pennsylvania affirmed the revocation of a teacher's certificate based on a guilty plea to a charge of mail fraud.[89] Since the applicable statute required only that a teacher engage in a crime involving moral turpitude and did not mandate a pre-revocation hearing beyond establishing that such a crime was committed, the court was content that commonwealth officials acted within the bounds of their authority. According to another appellate court in Pennsylvania, an educator did not have to be convicted of a criminal offense before officials could revoke her certification for submitting false, and forged, information with a job application.[90] The court's rationale was consistent with the general rule that public school employees can be expected to meet higher standards of conduct than their peers in the private sector since there is no right to public employment.

An appellate court in Georgia permitted the state Professional Standards Commission to revoke an educator's certification for improperly coaching students on a standardized test.[91] The court referred to evidence that an instructional specialist identified portions of the examination he discovered in the teacher's classroom and admitted to using materials he could not have had other than during the hours when the test was administered as diagnostic measures for his students. Earlier, another appellate court in Georgia[92] affirmed the revocation of a coach-teacher's certification due to his role in a grade-changing scandal that sought to render ineligible players able to play football.

Litigation involving violent behavior by teachers and/or other educators has led to mixed results. Where a teacher from Georgia engaged in violent behavior, an appellate court upheld the six-month suspension of his license for violating the state's Code of Ethics.[93] The court agreed that insofar as the teacher was involved in two altercations on school property within four months, one with the cafeteria manager over food prices and the second after avoiding a car accident with a student, his uncontrolled anger and inappropriate behavior warranted a suspension because his actions seriously impaired his ability to function professionally. Another appellate court in Georgia upheld the one-year suspension of a superintendent's certificate for brandishing a firearm during a confrontation with a

---

88. *Pordum v. Board of Regents of State of N.Y.*, 491 F.2d 1281 (2d Cir.1974), *cert. denied*, 419 U.S. 843, 95 S.Ct. 74, 42 L.Ed.2d 71 (1974).

89. *Startzel v. Commonwealth, Dep't of Educ.*, 562 A.2d 1005 [55 Educ. L. Rep. 637] (Pa. Cmwlth. Ct. 1989).

90. *Nanko v. Department of Educ.*, 663 A.2d 312 [102 Educ. L. Rep. 1149] (Pa. Cmwlth. Ct. 1995).

91. *Professional Standards Comm'n v. Smith*, 571 S.E.2d 443 [171 Educ. L. Rep. 623] (Ga. Ct. App. 2002).

92. *Brewer v. Schacht*, 509 S.E.2d 378 [131 Educ. L. Rep. 1138] (Ga. Ct. App.1998).

93. *Professional Standards Comm'n v. Valentine*, 603 S.E.2d 792 [192 Educ. L. Rep. 978] (Ga. Ct. App. 2004), *cert. denied* (2004).

worker at a road construction site.[94] The court agreed with state officials that the superintendent's conduct constituted "good and sufficient cause" under the state's provisional standards and that the applicable statute was not unconstitutionally vague.

An appellate court in Arizona affirmed the revocation of a high school teacher's certificate after a series of incidents in which he displayed aggressive, threatening, and intimidating behavior at or involving teenagers or young children.[95] The court commented that although not all of the incidents resulted in criminal convictions, the plaintiff proved that he was unfit to teach. Conversely, the Supreme Court of Appeals of West Virginia upheld the reinstatement of a teacher's license after it was suspended because he beat his nine-year-old son.[96] The court was satisfied that insofar as the beatings that the educator imposed on his son were unrelated to his teaching and coaching duties, his license had to be reinstated.

Another major ground for the revocation of certification involves sexual misconduct and impropriety, especially with students. In such a case, the Supreme Court of New Hampshire affirmed the revocation of a teacher's certificate for lack of good moral character where he pled no contest for simple assault after being accused of inappropriate sexual contact with a thirteen-year-old female that he was tutoring in his home.[97] The court ascertained there was sufficient evidence of a nexus between the former teacher's outside conduct and his fitness and ability to teach.[98] An appellate court in Ohio also affirmed the revocation of a former art teacher's certificate by reason of unbecoming conduct.[99] While the teacher had an excellent professional reputation spanning thirty years, he engaged in sexual conduct in an adult bookstore and pled no contest to a charge of public indecency in an incident that received media attention and impacted his professional life. The court indicated that insofar as the teacher's actions created a nexus between his conduct and ability to teach when he solicited students to write letters on his behalf, the revocation of his certificate for at least two years was not unwarranted. In like fashion, an appellate court in Pennsylvania affirmed the revocation of a teacher's certificate in the face of a not-guilty verdict on criminal charges where he was accused of having improperly touched two male students.[100] The court observed that the criminal acquittal was not *res judicata* in the teacher's

---

94. *Professional Standards Comm'n v. Alberson*, 614 S.E.2d 132 [199 Educ. L. Rep. 437] (Ga. Ct. App. 2005).

95. *Winters v. Arizona Bd. of Educ.*, 83 P.3d 1114 [185 Educ. L. Rep. 354] (Ariz.Ct.App. 2004).

96. *Powell v. Paine*, 697 S.E.2d 161 [259 Educ. L. Rep. 237] (W.Va.2010).

97. *In re Appeal of Morrill*, 765 A.2d 699 [150 Educ. L. Rep. 758] (N.H.2001).

98. For other cases where teachers had their certificates revoked for engaging in sexual misconduct with students, *see, e.g., Groht v. Sobol*, 604 N.Y.S.2d 279 [87 Educ. L. Rep. 555] (N.Y. App. Div. 1993); *Howard v. Missouri State Bd. of Educ.*, 913 S.W.2d 887 [106 Educ. L. Rep. 942] (Mo.Ct.App.1995); *Welcher v. Sobol*, 642 N.Y.S.2d 370 [109 Educ. L. Rep. 896] (N.Y. App. Div.1996).

99. *Hoffman v. State Bd. of Educ.*, 763 N.E.2d 210 [161 Educ. L. Rep. 955] (Ohio Ct. App. 2001).

100. *Boguslawski v. Department of Educ.*, 837 A.2d 614 [183 Educ. L. Rep. 928] (Pa. Cmwlth. Ct. 2003).

being disciplined where the revocation was supported by substantial evidence. Further, an appellate court in Illinois affirmed the five-year suspension of an assistant principal's teaching and administrative certificates for immorality where he fathered a child with one of his fourteen-year-old students.[101]

In a case with a twist, the Supreme Court of Minnesota refused to reinstate posthumously the certification of a teacher who died while litigation was pending over his inappropriate sexual contact with a student.[102] The court believed that the teacher's due process rights were not violated with respect to collateral estoppel in his license revocation hearing as to whether he engaged in non-consensual sexual conduct with a student since there was little risk of an erroneous deprivation of his right and the state had an interest in expeditiously barring contact between students and teachers who may be dangerous to the well-being of children.

When faced with the difficult matter of revoking certificates, some courts refused to do so where penalties were disproportionate to the offenses[103] or, as exemplified below, when officials failed to protect the due process rights of teachers. Even as they exercise their authority to revoke certifications, state officials must establish cause[104] and institute appropriate procedural due process procedures since educators may have protected property interests in their certification.[105] Since revocation of their certifications deprives educators of employment, the courts carefully explore the procedures used in taking such steps. The considerations of required procedures before educators can be dismissed, discussed in Chapter 11, apply here, and must be augmented as warranted by the more serious penalty of the loss of certification.

As reflected in the next four cases, courts considered different procedural issues in conducting certificate revocation hearings. In a dramatic fact pattern, an appellate court in Wisconsin reinstated the licenses of a teacher-social worker who was acquitted of all criminal charges other than carrying a concealed weapon after she fatally shot her former son-in-law.[106] The court was of the view that the teacher's shooting of her son-in-law, in order to protect her daughter and granddaughters from threats he made on their lives, and her carrying of a concealed weapon, were not "immoral conduct" justifying the revocation of her licenses. The court decreed that

---

101. *Hayes v. State Teacher Certification Bd.*, 835 N.E.2d 146 [202 Educ. L. Rep. 259] (Ill. App. Ct. 2005), *appeal denied*, 844 N.E.2d 37 (Ill. 2005). The former assistant principal also faced dismissal and criminal proceedings.

102. *Falgren v. State Bd. of Teaching*, 545 N.W.2d 901 [108 Educ. L. Rep. 890] (Minn. 1996).

103. *See, e.g., Macks v. Department of Educ.*, 250 P.3d 394 [266 Educ. L. Rep. 504] (Or. Ct. App. 2011) (overturning the revocation of school bus driver's certificate for leaving four unwanted voice messages for a man with whom she was romantically involved since her actions failed to constitute an imminent threat of violence).

104. *Brown v. South Carolina State Bd. of Educ.*, 391 S.E.2d 866 [60 Educ. L. Rep. 1004] (S.C. 1990) [Case No. 52]; *Joyell v. Commissioner of Educ.*, 696 A.2d 1039 [119 Educ. L. Rep. 1078] (Conn. Ct. App. 1997).

105. *Scott v. Stewart*, 560 S.E.2d 260 (W. Va. 2001); *Gee v. Professional Practices Comm'n*, 491 S.E.2d 375 [121 Educ. L. Rep. 849] (Ga. 1997).

106. *Epstein v. Benson*, 618 N.W.2d 224 [147 Educ. L. Rep. 1059] (Wis. Ct. App. 2000).

the unconscionable pattern of delay and deception by officials in the state's department of public instruction on remand of an earlier judgment violated the teacher's rights to due process.

An appellate court in Pennsylvania reinstated the certificate of a teacher who was accused of engaging in sexual intercourse with a child under the age of eighteen and furnishing alcoholic beverages to persons under the age of twenty-one in the presence of her nine-year-old son.[107] The court contended that the Professional Standards and Practices Commission, in acting solely on the basis of an indictment, and the nature of the charges against her, violated the teacher's rights to due process by depriving her of a property interest without providing a meaningful pre- or post-deprivation hearing.

In California, an appellate court affirmed that a teacher who was being investigated for sexual misconduct with students lacked statutory or due process rights to obtain the addresses and other identifying information of the complainant and witnesses or to cross-examine them.[108] The court rejected the teacher's request for the material in declaring that his doing so would have exceeded the scope of protections afforded in the state statute dealing with such allegations.

An appellate court in New York affirmed the revocation of a teacher's certification for engaging in inappropriate conduct with male students even though he admitted to having done so only after a private investigator who worked for the board falsely told him that there was incriminating evidence of his behavior and that if he failed to admit it or if he sought counsel, the board would pursue a criminal conviction rather than merely seek his resignation.[109] The court specified that insofar as the revocation process was designed not to punish the teacher but to protect the welfare of his students, his admission of improper sexual activity could have been used as evidence supporting the removal of his certification.

In a later case from New York, an appellate court confirmed the one-year suspension of an educator's teacher and administrator certificates based on his admission that he had sexual relations with two of his former students shortly after they graduated from high school.[110] The court agreed that insofar as the teacher groomed the students for future sexual relationships prior to their graduations by affording them special treatment, his punishment was appropriate.

Educator Misuse of Technology and the Internet

Not surprisingly, technology and the Internet are increasingly involved in the revocation of certificates. An appellate court in Georgia upheld the

---

107. *Slater v. Pennsylvania Dep't of Educ.*, 725 A.2d 1248 [133 Educ. L. Rep. 521] (Pa.Cmwlth.Ct.1999).

108. *California Teachers Ass'n v. California Comm'n on Teacher Credentialing*, 4 Cal. Rptr.3d 369 [180 Educ. L. Rep. 239] (Cal.Ct.App.2003).

109. *Stedronsky v. Sobol*, 572 N.Y.S.2d 445 [68 Educ. L. Rep. 1089] (N.Y.App.Div.1991), *appeal denied*, 578 N.Y.S.2d 878 (N.Y.1991).

110. *Mudge v. Huxley*, 914 N.Y.S.2d 339 [263 Educ. L. Rep. 321] (N.Y.App.Div.2010).

revocation of a principal's certificate based on her behavior in connection with her investigation of, and response to, a video displaying a female student and two male peers engaging in oral sex with each other.[111] The court was satisfied that even though the penalty was harsher than an administrative law judge's recommendation that the principal receive at least a one-year suspension of her license, the action of the state's Professional Standards Commission was neither arbitrary nor capricious. The court maintained that insofar as the principal failed to investigate the video or to contact the students and their parents promptly along with her having misled both the parents and her supervisors as to her conduct, it would not substitute its judgment for that of the Commission.

An appellate court in Florida affirmed that a teacher's sending profanity-laced, sexually explicit material over the Internet directly to sixteen seventh-grade students warranted the permanent revocation of her certification as a penalty clearly authorized by statute.[112] The court added that the revocation was appropriate since it was not inconsistent with the past practice of the Education Practices Commission (EPC). Earlier, another appellate court in Florida affirmed the revocation of a teacher's certificate because he inappropriately accessed pornographic Internet sites on a school computer and battered his wife.[113] The court remarked that the EPC had the authority to revoke his certificate based on uncontroverted evidence in the complaint against the teacher.

CERTIFICATES IN RELATION TO CONTRACTS

Since educators lacking certification are not competent to enter contracts with school boards,[114] such agreements are of no legal effect.[115] In addition, as highlighted by a case from the Court of Appeals of New York, state laws typically prevent boards from using school funds to pay individuals who lack valid certificates.[116]

In an older case, Kentucky's highest court explained that a teacher who neither had certification nor was eligible for it since she had yet to reach her eighteenth birthday at the start of a school year was ineligible to receive a salary before she turned eighteen.[117] The court conceded that the board would have to pay her for the teaching she did after her birthday and

---

111. *Professional Standards Comm'n v. Adams*, 702 S.E.2d 675 [262 Educ. L. Rep. 1042] (Ga. Ct. App. 2010).

112. *Wax v. Horne*, 844 So.2d 797 [177 Educ. L. Rep. 699] (Fla. Dist. Ct. App. 2003).

113. *Stueber v. Gallagher*, 812 So.2d 454 [164 Educ. L. Rep. 496] (Fla. Dist. Ct. App. 2002). *But see Bowalick v. Commonwealth*, 840 A.2d 519 [184 Educ. L. Rep. 903] (Pa. Cmwlth. Ct. 2004) (declaring that a teacher who was convicted of assault over a domestic dispute with his wife was entitled to a hearing as to whether his behavior met the statutory definition of moral turpitude necessary to revoke his certification).

114. *Seamonds v. School Dist. No. 14, Fremont County*, 68 P.2d 149 (Wyo. 1937).

115. *Goose River Bank v. Willow Lake School Twp.*, 44 N.W. 1002 (N.D. 1890).

116. *Meliti v. Nyquist*, 391 N.Y.S.2d 398 (N.Y. 1976).

117. *Floyd County Bd. of Educ. v. Slone*, 307 S.W.2d 912 (Ky. 1957). *See also Flanary v. Barrett*, 143 S.W. 38 (Ky. 1912).

the receipt of her certification.[118] Later, an appellate court in New York was persuaded that it was appropriate to terminate a probationary teacher's full-time appointment since she lacked certification to serve as an elementary school counselor.[119] The court concluded that while the teacher did not receive the requisite notice that her contract was being terminated, she was ineligible for back pay since she was unqualified for the job she performed.

On the other hand, an appellate court in Pennsylvania stated that a teacher whose certificate expired and was not renewed due to "bureaucratic delays" could not be dismissed. However, where teachers are responsible for their lack of certification, boards may terminate their contracts.[120] In such a case, where a teacher was permitted to work temporarily after having passed an examination under a special act, the Supreme Judicial Court of Massachusetts affirmed that his school committee had the right not to renew his contract because he neither sought, nor obtained, certification.[121]

Where a teacher who taught fourth grade for eighteen years was offered a contract to teach seventh and eighth grades, she claimed that her board violated the state's tenure law since she was unqualified for those grades. The Supreme Court of South Dakota discerned, as a matter of law, that insofar as the teacher was qualified because her certificate encompassed the grades for which the board had the power to offer her an assignment, her refusal meant that her statutory rights expired.[122]

EMPLOYMENT

GENERALLY

As noted, teaching certificates attest that individuals have met the minimum state qualifications to apply for jobs in public schools. Certificates do not address the skill levels of candidates. Where state law requires educators to be certificated, local boards may neither employ staff who fail to meet this standard nor use school funds to pay such individuals.

Local boards may require teachers to have extra qualifications such as additional courses[123] or certifications[124] beyond what is required by law as long as they are neither arbitrary nor capricious, are reasonably related to

---

118. *See also Sorenson v. School Dist. No. 28*, 418 P.2d 1004 (Wyo.1966) (denying a salary for a teacher who lacked certification).

119. *Sullivan v. Windham–Ashland–Jewett Cent. School Dist.*, 628 N.Y.S.2d 454 [101 Educ. L. Rep. 1007] (N.Y. App. Div. 1995).

120. *Brubaker v. Community Unit School Dist. No. 16, Sangamon and Morgan Counties*, 360 N.E.2d 1228 (Ill. App. Ct. 1977).

121. *Luz v. School Comm. of Lowell*, 313 N.E.2d 925 (Mass. 1974).

122. *Collins v. Wakonda Indep. School Dist. No. 1*, 252 N.W.2d 646 (S.D. 1977).

123. *Montgomery County Bd. of Educ. v. Messer*, 79 S.W.2d 224 (Ky. 1935).

124. *Cowen v. Harrison County Bd. of Educ.*, 465 S.E.2d 648 [106 Educ. L. Rep. 383] (W. Va. 1995).

the jobs they seek, and are not barred by constitutional or statutory considerations.[125] For example, in *Harrah Independent School District v. Martin*,[126] the Supreme Court affirmed that a school board in Oklahoma had the right not to renew the contract of a teacher who was aware of, but refused to comply with, a policy, enacted pursuant to state law, requiring her to participate in continuing education requirements. Even so, in a dispute with constitutional ramifications, *Shelton v. Tucker*,[127] the Court held that a school board in Arkansas could not require job applicants to list the names of all organizations that they were members of because doing so would have unduly restricted their freedom of association.

Where state laws require boards to act on employee nominations by superintendents, they still retain the power to set qualifications. In such a situation, under a Florida statute which stipulated that a superintendent's recommendations could only be rejected for good cause, an appellate court affirmed that a board could refuse to appoint an administrator with a master's degree in business administration but lacked experience in either school finance or a school system.[128] Subsequently, when a superintendent refused to re-nominate a painter based on reasonable suspicion that he violated board policy by using drugs and rejected offers to provide help, another appellate court in Florida affirmed that the board need not re-hire the employee.[129] The court wrote that insofar as only the superintendent had the authority to nominate an individual, and had not done so, the board was not free to act.

DISCRIMINATORY EMPLOYMENT PRACTICES

Title VII of the Civil Rights Act of 1964 (Title VII)[130] is the most significant federal anti-discrimination statute dealing with employment. In relevant part, Title VII reads that:

It shall be an unlawful employment practice for an employer:

(1) to fail or refuse to hire or to discharge any individual, or otherwise to discriminate against any individual with respect to his compensation, terms, conditions, or privileges of employment, because of such individual's race, color, religion, sex, or national origin; or

(2) to limit, segregate, or classify his employees or applicants for employment in any way which would deprive or tend to deprive any individual of employment opportunities or otherwise adversely affect his status as an employee, because of such individual's race, color, religion, sex, or national origin.[131]

---

125. *See Pierce v. Indiana Dep't of Correction*, 885 N.E.2d 77 [231 Educ. L. Rep. 879] (Ind. Ct. App. 2008) (finding that the State Department of Correction could require all teachers in juvenile facilities to obtain licenses in special education since doing so did not interfere with the authority of the Department of Education).

126. 440 U.S. 194, 99 S.Ct. 1062, 59 L.Ed.2d 248 (1979). [Case No. 53]

127. 364 U.S. 479, 81 S.Ct. 247, 5 L.Ed.2d 231 (1960).

128. *Sinclair v. School Bd. of Baker County*, 354 So.2d 916 (Fla. Dist. Ct. App.1978).

129. *Cox v. School Bd. of Osceola County*, 669 So.2d 353 [107 Educ. L. Rep. 1066] (Fla. Dist. Ct. App. 1996).

130. 42 U.S.C.A. §§ 2000 *et seq.*

131. 42 U.S.C.A. § 2000e–2(a).

The Pregnancy Discrimination Act (PDA), enacted in response to two Supreme Court cases which upheld the denial of pregnancy-related benefits,[132] now incorporated into Title VII, prohibits discrimination "... on the basis of pregnancy, childbirth, or related medical conditions...."[133] In a case from Illinois, the Seventh Circuit affirmed a grant of summary judgment in favor of a school board when a special education teacher whose contract was not renewed alleged that officials discriminated against her due to her pregnancy.[134] The court refused to believe that there was even a pretext of discrimination due to pregnancy since the board needed to eliminate one job coupled with the fact that the plaintiff's evaluations revealed that she was the least effective probationary teacher in her school.[135]

Three other major federal laws forbid workplace discrimination. The Age Discrimination in Employment Act[136] protects workers who are forty or over. The ADA,[137] noted earlier, mirroring language of Section 504, requires employers to make reasonable accommodation for employees who are otherwise qualified to work. The Family and Medical Leave Act[138] provides a range of protections for employees who need to take time off to care for family members or themselves who are in need of medical attention.

A second category of statutes outlaws discrimination in programs receiving federal financial aid. The most notable of these is Title VI of the Civil Rights Act of 1964 (Title VI), according to which "[n]o person in the United States shall, on the ground of race, color, or national origin, be excluded from participation in, be denied the benefits of, or be subjected to discrimination under any program or activity receiving Federal financial assistance."[139] Disputes involving Titles VI and VII are often filed together. Another major federal law in this regard is Section 504, cited earlier, which forbids discrimination against individuals with disabilities. In addition, although Title IX of the Educational Amendments of 1972 (Title IX)[140] proscribes discrimination based on gender, it is beyond the scope of this chapter since it applies primarily to students, not employees. Since most

---

132. *Geduldig v. Aiello*, 417 U.S. 484, 94 S.Ct. 2485, 41 L.Ed.2d 256 (1974) (under the Fourteenth Amendment); *General Elec. Co. v. Gilbert*, 429 U.S. 125, 97 S.Ct. 401, 50 L.Ed.2d 343 (1976) (under Title VII).

133. 42 U.S.C.A. § 2000e(k).

134. *Silverman v. Board of Educ. of the City of Chicago*, 637 F.3d 729 [266 Educ. L. Rep. 618] (7th Cir.2011).

135. *See also Heaphy v. Webster Cent. School Dist.*, 761 F. Supp. 2d 89 [267 Educ. L Rep. 123] (W.D.N.Y. 2011) (rejecting a teacher's PDA claim where her contract was not renewed because of her poor performance evaluation).

136. 29 U.S.C.A. §§ 621 *et seq.* Portions of this statute are in the Appendix.

137. 42 U.S.C.A. §§ 12101 *et seq.* Portions of this statute are in the Appendix.

138. 29 U.S.C.A. §§ 2611 *et seq.*

139. 42 U.S.C.A. § 2000d. This statute is in the Appendix.

140. 20 U.S.C.A. § 1681. Portions of this statute are in the Appendix.

litigation involving employment focuses on Title VII, it receives the lion's share of attention in this chapter.

TITLE VII GENERALLY

The Supreme Court crafted two different tests for alleged discrimination in the workplace involving Title VII: disparate impact and disparate treatment, both of which can be present in the same claim. In *Griggs v. Duke Power Company (Griggs)*,[141] the Court interpreted Title VII as prohibiting not only overt discrimination, but also practices that appear to be fair in form but discriminatory in their impact. In other words, the Court proscribed what appear to be otherwise neutral criteria that are shown, often through reliance on quantitative data, to have a disparate impact on members of a particular group or class. At issue in *Griggs* was a power company in North Carolina's requirement that all of its employees have a high school education and perform satisfactorily on tests before being assigned to departments that had, in the past, practiced racial discrimination. In *Griggs*, the Justices struck down both of the company's requirements because they were unrelated to successful job performance and had a disparate impact on African Americans.[142] The Court ruled that Congress did not command that persons be hired simply since they were formerly subject to discrimination or because they were members of a minority group. Rather, the Court decided that employers had to remove artificial, arbitrary, or unnecessary barriers which discriminate on the basis of race or other impermissible classifications.

In setting forth its disparate impact standard, in *Washington v. Davis*,[143] the Supreme Court was of the opinion that while this theory serves as a sufficient basis on which to present a prima facie case of employment discrimination under Title VII, plaintiffs also must provide proof of intent to discriminate in order to prevail in equal protection claims. In a controversy over the use of written examinations for police officer candidates, the Court found that the test's disparate impact on minorities notwithstanding, it was not unlawful. The Justices upheld the use of examinations absent evidence that officials acted with a discriminatory purpose. The Court was satisfied that the positive relationship between the test results and training school performances of candidates was sufficient to validate their use even aside from their possible relationship to actual job duties as police officers. Since the dispute arose in Washington, D.C., the case was filed under the Fifth Amendment, which applies to the federal government, rather than the Fourteenth Amendment, which covers states.

The Supreme Court clarified the steps and burdens of proof in Title VII cases involving disparate treatment, wherein individuals allege treatment different from other similarly situated individuals, in *McDonnell*

---

141. 401 U.S. 424, 91 S.Ct. 849, 28 L.Ed.2d 158 (1971).

142. *But see United States v. State of S.C.*, 445 F.Supp. 1094 (D.S.C.1977), *aff'd sub nom. National Educ. Ass'n v. United States*, 434 U.S. 1026, 98 S.Ct. 756, 54 L.Ed.2d 775 (1978) (upholding the use of the NTE as a valid measure for evaluating teacher candidates).

143. 426 U.S. 229, 96 S.Ct. 2040, 48 L.Ed.2d 597 (1976).

Douglas Corp. v. Green (McDonnell Douglas).[144] In Title VII cases, plaintiffs must prove that employers acted with intent; they are not required to do so in disputes relying on the disparate impact theory. *McDonnell Douglas* was filed by a civil rights activist who, after engaging in disruptive and illegal activity as part of his protest against being dismissed by an airplane manufacturer, claimed that the firm's general hiring practices were racially motivated. Vacating and remanding in favor of the employee, the Court determined that Title VII did not restrict his right to sue to only those charges on which the Equal Employment Opportunity Commission (EEOC) had made findings of reasonable cause.

Based on the Supreme Court's Title VII jurisprudence in disputes claiming disparate treatment, the initial burden is on plaintiffs to establish prima facie cases of discrimination by filing claims with the EEOC within 180 days of when alleged unlawful employment practices occurred.[145] In a non-education case involving employee compensation that is beginning to impact schools, *Ledbetter v. Goodyear Tire and Rubber Co.*,[146] the Supreme Court affirmed that when calculating this 180–day time limit, an employer's initial "unlawful employment practice" occurs on the day when an employee's salary is set improperly, not when the individual received later paychecks.[147] However, this case was abrogated by the enactment of the Lilly Ledbetter Fair Pay Act of 2009 (FPA)[148] since Congress and the President agreed that the Court unduly restricted the time frames within which employees could file claims of wage discrimination. Insofar as FPA claims are likely to also involve the Age Discrimination in Employment Act, relevant litigation is reviewed later in this chapter under the heading "Statutory Protections."

When filing Title VII complaints, aggrieved parties must allege the existence of four or five elements, depending on whether the last two are merged into one or they are left as separate items. The elements are membership in a protected class; application for a position; qualification for the job; rejection; and an employer continues to seek applicants with the plaintiff's qualifications. These elements, with appropriate adaptations, constitute a prima facie case of discrimination for adverse personnel actions.

If plaintiffs establish prima facie cases, defendants must articulate legitimate, nondiscriminatory reasons for acting such as bona fide occupational qualifications. If defendants can do so, they must raise genuine issues of fact, thereby returning the burden to plaintiffs to prove that the

---

144. 411 U.S. 792, 93 S.Ct. 1817, 36 L.Ed.2d 668 (1973). *See also Texas Dep't of Community Affairs v. Burdine*, 450 U.S. 248, 101 S.Ct. 1089, 67 L.Ed.2d 207 (1981).

145. 42 U.S.C.A. § 2000e–5(e)(1). *See, e.g., Black v. Columbus Pub. Schools*, 211 F.Supp.2d 975 [168 Educ. L. Rep. 202] (S.D. Ohio 2002), *aff'd in relevant part*, 79 Fed.Appx. 735 [182 Educ. L. Rep. 785] (6th Cir.2003).

146. 550 U.S. 618, 127 S.Ct. 2162, 167 L.Ed.2d 982 (2007).

147. *But see O'Grady v. Middle Country School Dist. No. 11*, 556 F. Supp.2d 196 [234 Educ. L. Rep. 690] (E.D.N.Y. 2008) (refusing to dismiss a claim of age discrimination on the basis that each time the retired teacher received a payment from the board, the statute of limitations began to run anew).

148. 29 U.S.C. § 626.

explanations were pretexts.[149] As demonstrated by a case from the Eleventh Circuit, if a plaintiff files suit after having adjudicated a claim before the EEOC, one may bring only those claims that were included in the EEOC charge or that are likely, reasonably related, or growing out of such allegations.[150] Affirming that an applicant for a custodial position was properly dismissed, the court indicated that the rule was designed to afford both the EEOC and an employer the chance to settle a dispute while affording the latter fair notice of the conduct about which an individual is complaining.

As noted, plaintiffs often rely on statistics in trying to prove that defendants engaged in patterns or practices of employment discrimination. In these instances, gross statistical disparities among groups may constitute prima facie proof of patterns or practices of discrimination. Still, comparisons must be made by qualified professionals in the context of proper labor markets. Plaintiffs must also show that discrimination was the defendants' standard operating procedure, "the regular rather than the unusual practice."[151]

Employment actions need not be based solely on objective criteria. While the use of subjective criteria may provide evidence of discrimination, since it is not conclusive,[152] the same types of statistical analyses apply to results of subjective and objective methods,[153] both of which must be defensible even if they are not the best options available. Yet, overall or bottom-line results do not suffice as a defense against the use of discriminatory preliminary elements since "[t]he principal focus of [Title VII] is the protection of the individual employee, rather than the protection of the minority group as a whole."[154]

In the words of the Fourth Circuit, "Title VII is not a 'bad acts' statute."[155] If an act or policy impacts disproportionately on members of a protected group, it may run afoul of Title VII.[156] For instance, the Fourth Circuit directed a school board in Virginia to discontinue its practice of word-of-mouth hiring and hiring of relatives because insofar as most of its employees were predominantly white, this approach had a disparate impact on minorities.[157]

---

149. *See St. Mary's Honor Ctr. v. Hicks*, 509 U.S. 502, 113 S.Ct. 2742, 125 L.Ed.2d 407 (1993) (reiterating that plaintiffs bear the ultimate burden of proof in discrimination cases).

150. *Geldon v. South Milwaukee School Dist.*, 414 F.3d 817 [199 Educ. L. Rep. 625] (7th Cir.2005).

151. *International Brotherhood of Teamsters v. United States*, 431 U.S. 324, 336, 97 S.Ct. 1843, 52 L.Ed.2d 396 (1977).

152. *McCarthney v. Griffin–Spalding County Bd. of Educ.*, 791 F.2d 1549 [32 Educ. L. Rep. 910] (11th Cir.1986).

153. *Watson v. Fort Worth Bank and Trust*, 487 U.S. 977, 108 S.Ct. 2777, 101 L.Ed.2d 827 (1988).

154. *Connecticut v. Teal*, 457 U.S. 440, 453, 102 S.Ct. 2525, 73 L.Ed.2d 130 (1982).

155. *Holder v. City of Raleigh*, 867 F.2d 823, 828 (4th Cir.1989).

156. *See, e.g., Knight v. Hayward Unified School Dist.*, 33 Cal.Rptr.3d 287 [201 Educ. L. Rep. 275] (Cal. Ct. App. 2005) (reiterating the general rule in rejecting the claim that a health insurance company's refusal to pay for in vitro fertilization constituted disability discrimination because it applied equally to all).

157. *Thomas v. Washington County School Bd.*, 915 F.2d 922 [63 Educ. L. Rep. 76] (4th Cir.1990). [Case No. 54]

Occasionally, adverse employment actions are based on a number of factors, only one of which is illegal. In these so-called mixed-motive cases, once Title VII plaintiffs prove that illegal elements played a part in employment actions, defendants can prevail only by showing that they would have acted in the same way even if the forbidden considerations were not part of the decision-making process.[158] In a case with mixed motives and mixed results, the Eleventh Circuit recognized that while a school board in Alabama offered an affirmative defense as to why it chose not to hire an African American, he might have been entitled to damages if he could have shown that the board's action was based on racial discrimination.[159]

Rather than engage in an exhaustive discussion of disputes arising under Title VII, since the substantive analysis does not vary significantly from one case to another, the following headings review representative disputes from among the thousands of actions that have been litigated under this far-reaching statute. Many discrimination claims also can be filed under state statutes that are modeled after Title VII.

Race/National Origin

In *Hazelwood School District v. United States*,[160] the Supreme Court considered the relationship between Title VII and racial discrimination in teacher employment. The Justices thought that a federal trial court in Missouri misconceived the role of statistics in employment discrimination cases in its racial comparison of the district's teachers and students. The Court reasoned that the Eighth Circuit correctly concluded that the proper comparison should have been between the racial compositions of the teaching staff and the qualified public school teacher population in the labor market. Despite this, the Court vacated and remanded because the Eighth Circuit erred in substituting its judgment for that of the trial court in declaring that the board engaged in a pattern or practice of discrimination. The Court also directed the trial judge to determine the proper labor market area for comparison. Further, the Eighth Circuit remanded a dispute from Arkansas for a consideration of the relevant labor market in evaluating the propriety of the proportionality requirement that a federal trial court imposed on a school board in a class action discrimination suit filed by African American teachers.[161] The next year, the Fifth Circuit affirmed that African American teachers in Mississippi failed to prove that the board in a formerly segregated district had not discontinued its discriminatory employment practices where the percentages of black teachers

---

158. *See Price Waterhouse v. Hopkins*, 490 U.S. 228, 109 S.Ct. 1775, 104 L.Ed.2d 268 (1989), as modified by the Civil Rights Act of 1991. The Act provides that if employers prove that they would have taken the same actions absent the discriminatory factors, plaintiffs remain eligible for attorney fees and costs.

159. *Harris v. Shelby County Bd. of Educ.*, 99 F.3d 1078 [113 Educ. L. Rep. 1124] (11th Cir.1996).

160. 433 U.S. 299, 97 S.Ct. 2736, 53 L.Ed.2d 768 (1977).

161. *Scoggins v. Board of Educ. of Nashville, Ark. Pub. Schools*, 853 F.2d 1472 [48 Educ. L. Rep. 772] (8th Cir.1988).

increased over the time at issue and there was no evidence supporting their claim that they were subjected to discriminatory treatment.[162]

Since Title VII cases involving race and national origin often deal with all but identical issues, they are addressed together under this heading. Courts reviewed a variety of procedural and substantive disputes, more often than not entering judgments in favor of school boards. As to procedural matters, courts required individuals to file complaints in a timely manner;[163] dismissed allegations for failure to state claims in complaints that were much longer than they needed to be;[164] and clarified the standards for the admissibility of evidence.[165]

Courts allowed suits to proceed where employees presented prima facie cases of racial discrimination such as where an African American was dismissed for taking part in a protest over the firing of another African American[166] and when a white teacher with seventeen years of experience was demoted from the job as chair of her department in favor of an African American with less experience and seniority.[167] In a case involving national origin discrimination, a federal trial court in Ohio asserted that a custodian who was Mexican American presented a prima facie case where a supervisor made a series of derogatory remarks over a period of twenty-two years despite her having lodged unsuccessful complaints with her employer.[168]

On the other hand, the Seventh Circuit affirmed the rejection of a discrimination claim premised on national origin when officials reassigned a teacher of Hispanic origin from a high school to a middle school.[169] The court refused to treat the transfer as an adverse employment action where the teacher simply preferred working in the high school. Similarly, the First Circuit affirmed that the Department of Education in the Commonwealth of Puerto Rico did not discriminate based on national origin when officials refused to hire a teacher from Venezuela or to issue her a teaching certificate.[170] The court agreed that the teacher had not been subject to discrimination since she failed to prove that she was more qualified for a job or the certificate than when she applied initially.

---

162. *Quarles v. Oxford Mun. Separate School Dist.*, 868 F.2d 750 [52 Educ. L. Rep. 38] (5th Cir.1989).

163. *Black v. Columbus Pub. Schools*, 211 F. Supp.2d 975 [168 Educ. L. Rep. 202] (S.D. Ohio 2002), *aff'd*, 79 Fed.Appx. 735 [182 Educ. L. Rep.785] (6th Cir.2003).

164. *Bennett v. Schmidt*, 153 F.3d 516 [129 Educ. L. Rep. 32] (7th Cir.1998).

165. *Freeman v. Madison Metropolitan School Dist.*, 231 F.3d 374 [148 Educ. L. Rep. 629] (7th Cir.2000).

166. *Copeland v. Rosen*, 38 F. Supp.2d 298 [133 Educ. L. Rep. 885] (S.D.N.Y. 1999).

167. *Mohr v. Chicago School Reform Bd. of Trustees*, 99 F. Supp.2d 934 [145 Educ. L. Rep. 280] (N.D. Ill. 2000).

168. *Lagunovich v. Findlay City School Sys.*, 181 F. Supp.2d 753 [161 Educ. L. Rep. 458] (N.D. Ohio 2001). *See also Lewis v. State of Del. Dep't of Pub. Instruction*, 948 F.Supp. 352 [115 Educ. L. Rep. 683] (D. Del.1996). *But see Salvadori v. Franklin School Dist.*, 293 F.3d 989 [166 Educ. L. Rep. 454] (7th Cir.2002) (affirming that a Filipina teacher was unable to prove that her dismissal was pretextual where school officials offered evidence that she had not performed satisfactorily).

169. *Lucero v. Nettle Creek School Corp.*, 566 F.3d 720 [244 Educ. L. Rep. 965] (7th Cir.2009).

170. *Moron–Barradas v. Department of Educ. of Commonwealth of Puerto Rico*, 488 F.3d 472 [221 Educ. L. Rep. 502] (1st Cir.2007).

Examples of additional unsuccessful Title VII claims include cases where an African American employee was disciplined differently from a white worker who committed the same kind of offense but was unable to show that the board's action was a pretext for discrimination;[171] a superintendent had race neutral, non-pretextual reasons for terminating the contract of a principal who failed to carry out his duties and to maintain discipline in a school;[172] staff could not prove that other employees who used racial epithets were treated differently;[173] a superintendent's ill-advised remarks about Native Americans were insufficient to establish discriminatory intent in discharging a teacher who was late to work regularly;[174] and a minority applicant was not hired by an all-white interview team since she failed to establish a prima facie claim of disparate impact and her attorney misrepresented statistical data.[175]

Other cases wherein plaintiffs were unsuccessful concerned disputes such as where a white substitute teacher claimed that a board's refusal to hire her for a full-time job was motivated by race;[176] an applicant failed to present evidence to support her claim that she was not hired for a teaching position because she was both a Muslim and Lebanese;[177] an African American teacher failed to prove that she met a school board's legitimate performance expectations;[178] an African American applicant for a job as a purchasing clerk failed to demonstrate that she was qualified for the job;[179] a retired African American teacher was disciplined for having been arrested on gun charges while on sabbatical;[180] and an African American who served as an administrative assistant/registrar at a high school failed to establish a prima facie case of disparate treatment when she was released for poor job performance.[181]

Religion

Perhaps the Supreme Court's most important case involving the religious rights of public school employees is *Ansonia Board of Education v.*

---

171. *Silvera v. Orange County School Bd.*, 244 F.3d 1253 [152 Educ. L. Rep. 75] (11th Cir.2001), *cert. denied*, 534 U.S. 976, 122 S.Ct. 402, 151 L.Ed.2d 305 (2001), *reh'g denied*, 535 U.S. 1013, 122 S.Ct. 1598, 152 L.Ed.2d 513 (2002). *See also Conward v. Cambridge School Comm.*, 171 F.3d 12 [133 Educ. L. Rep. 367] (1st Cir.1999).

172. *Joseph v. New York City Bd. of Educ.*, 171 F.3d 87 [133 Educ. L. Rep. 380] (2d Cir.1999), *cert. denied*, 528 U.S. 876, 120 S.Ct. 182, 145 L.Ed.2d 154 (1999).

173. *Sims–Eiland v. Detroit Bd. of Educ.*, 173 F. Supp.2d 682 [159 Educ. L. Rep. 620] (E.D. Mich. 2001); *Daso v. The Grafton School*, 181 F. Supp.2d 485, 493 [161 Educ. L. Rep. 388] (D. Md.2002).

174. *Clearwater v. Independent School Dist. No. 166*, 231 F.3d 1122 (8th Cir.2000).

175. *Bennett v. Roberts*, 295 F.3d 687 (7th Cir.2002).

176. *Koszola v. Board of Educ. of City of Chicago*, 385 F.3d 1104 (7th Cir.2004).

177. *Raad v. Alaska State Comm'n for Human Rights*, 86 P.3d 899 (Alaska 2004).

178. *Shanklin v. Fitzgerald*, 397 F.3d 596 (8th Cir.2005), *reh'g denied* (2005), *cert. denied*, 546 U.S. 1066, 126 S.Ct. 807, 163 L.Ed.2d 636 (2005).

179. *Dixon v. Pulaski County Special School Dist.*, 578 F.3d 862 [248 Educ. L. Rep. 97] (8th Cir.2009).

180. *Bailey v. New York City Bd. of Educ.*, 536 F. Supp.2d 259 [230 Educ. L. Rep. 200] (E.D.N.Y. 2007).

181. *Samuel v. Williamsburg–James City County School Bd.*, 540 F. Supp.2d 667 [231 Educ. L. Rep. 216] (E.D. Va. 2008), *aff'd*, 293 Fed.Appx. 229 (4th Cir.2008).

Philbrook (Ansonia).[182] In *Ansonia* the Court interpreted Title VII as requiring school boards to make reasonable accommodations to meet the religious needs of teachers even if they are not the ones the educators sought. Where a teacher in Connecticut needed, on average, six days per school year to fulfill religious duties to his church by visiting hospital patients, he challenged his board's refusal to modify provisions in its collective bargaining agreement which permitted him to use only three of his eighteen paid days of leave to do so. The teacher asked the board either to permit him to use six days for his religious needs or to allow him to pay for his own substitute when absent. As the dispute continued, the teacher stopped taking unauthorized leave, scheduled required hospital visits on church holy days, and worked on holy days.

In *Ansonia* the Justices wrote that Title VII did not require the board to prove that the teacher's alternatives would have caused it an undue hardship. Rather, the Justices posited that once school officials offered the teacher a reasonable accommodation, even if it was unacceptable to him, they were not required to do anything else. The Supreme Court added that even if the teacher had to take days off without pay, the option other than using the three days stipulated in his contract, this had no direct impact on his employment status. On remand, the Second Circuit contended that, as administered, the bargaining agreement did not discriminate against the teacher on the basis of religion.[183]

Another case involving the nexus between the religious rights of teachers under the First Amendment and collective bargaining agreements arose in New York. An appellate court ascertained that a provision in a bargaining contract granting teachers a maximum of three days per year for religious observance was constitutional.[184] When board officials tried to have the teachers use personal time rather than the days allotted in the contract, the court commented that the provision did not offend the Establishment Clause because it neither impermissibly advanced religion by coercing union members to profess a religious belief nor imposed any requirements regarding which religious holidays might be invoked.

In the first of two other cases with resemblances to *Ansonia*, a federal trial court in Texas granted a school board's motion for summary judgment in a dispute filed by a former instructor. When the instructor refused to meet his job obligation of working at least one full weekend each month since his religious beliefs prevented him from doing so between sunset on Friday and Saturday, the board terminated his employment.[185] The court remarked that insofar as the board proved that requiring other employees to work in place of the instructor would have imposed an undue hardship on them, his claim was without merit.[186] Also, the Sixth Circuit affirmed

---

182.   479 U.S. 60, 107 S.Ct. 367, 93 L.Ed.2d 305 (1986).

183.   *Philbrook v. Ansonia Bd. of Educ.*, 925 F.2d 47 [65 Educ. L. Rep. 715] (2d Cir.1991), *cert. denied*, 501 U.S. 1218, 111 S.Ct. 2828, 115 L.Ed.2d 998 (1991).

184.   *Maine–Endwell Teachers' Ass'n v. Board of Educ.*, 771 N.Y.S.2d 246 [185 Educ. L. Rep. 327] (N.Y. App. Div. 2004).

185.   *Bynum v. Fort Worth Indep. School Dist.*, 41 F. Supp.2d 641 [134 Educ. L. Rep. 860] (N.D. Tex. 1999).

186.   *See also Favero v. Huntsville Indep. School Dist.*, 939 F.Supp. 1281 [113 Educ. L. Rep. 747] (S.D. Tex.1996), *aff'd without reported opinion*, 110 F.3d 793 (5th Cir.1997) (affirming

that a school board in Ohio did not violate Title VII by failing to accommodate a carpenter's religious observance of the Sabbath since such an adjustment, which would have permitted him to work on Sundays, rather than Saturdays, would have been an undue burden on the school system.[187] The court was of the view that the undue burden arose not only since the carpenter's collective bargaining agreement dictated that people working Sunday had to be paid double-time, while staff who worked on Saturday were only paid time-and-a-half, but also because even if he was only paid time-and-a-half for Sunday work, the board would have had to pay at least one other employee double-time to open the building. The court declared that insofar as this would have amounted to more than de minimis costs, it was sufficient to defeat the carpenter's religious accommodation claim.

A case from California addressed the extent to which public employees can express their religious preferences in the workplace. The Ninth Circuit invalidated a prohibition against permitting an employee of the state department of education to display religious materials on the interior walls of his cubbyhole at work.[188] The court observed that such a restriction was unnecessary to serve the department's interest in efficiency where there was no evidence of disruption in general or that any employee but the plaintiff engaged in the religious activity.

The Third Circuit reinstated the Title VII claim of a teacher at a charter school who alleged that she was retaliated against, in the form of not having her employment contract renewed due to her refusal to participate in a required "libations ceremony," apparently honoring ancestors, that conflicted with her Christian beliefs.[189] The court held that insofar as the teacher presented sufficient evidence to establish her claim, her case should not have been dismissed.

Claims of religious discrimination under Title VII often fail where school officials provide legitimate, non-discriminatory rationales for their actions. In such a case, a former high school paraprofessional sued his ex-principal, claiming that he was dismissed from his job in violation of his rights to practice his Islamic faith and due process.[190] In granting the principal's motion for summary judgment, a federal trial court in New York maintained that the plaintiff was unable to prove one of the elements of a prima facie case, that he performed his duties satisfactorily. The court pointed out that during the two years prior to his dismissal, the paraprofessional's evaluations revealed that he needed to improve and that he received verbal and written warnings along with two written reprimands for neglect of duty and insubordination. The court commented that the

---

that officials did not have to give bus drivers extra leave to participate in religious observances since this would have imposed an undue hardship on the board).

187. *Creusere v. Board of Educ. of City School Dist. of City of Cincinnati*, 88 Fed.Appx. 813 [185 Educ. L. Rep. 500] (6th Cir.2003), *cert. denied*, 541 U.S. 1074, 124 S.Ct. 2414, 158 L.Ed.2d 985 (2004).

188. *Tucker v. California Dep't of Educ.*, 97 F.3d 1204 [113 Educ. L. Rep. 102] (9th Cir.1996).

189. *Wilkerson v. New Media Technology Charter School*, 522 F.3d 315 [231 Educ. L. Rep. 560] (3d Cir.2008).

190. *Sharif v. Buck*, 338 F. Supp.2d 435 [192 Educ. L. Rep. 762] (W.D.N.Y. 2004), *aff'd*, 152 Fed.Appx. 43 (2d Cir.2005).

principal was not liable for violating the plaintiff's right to due process absent evidence of his personal involvement in the evaluation process since the collective bargaining only required the administrator to refer the matter to the board's department of human resources which had the duty to notify the employee about his dismissal. Similarly, the Seventh Circuit affirmed that a school board did not retaliate against a former employee who filed a discrimination claim based on religion.[191] The court was satisfied that insofar as the employee ignored warnings that he was violating board policy by giving gifts to students and offering to have dinner with them after school hours, officials had not violated Title VII.

Religious disputes have also arisen over instructional issues. For example, an appellate court in California rejected the claim of a teacher who alleged that officials violated his rights to free speech when they directed him not to talk about religion during the school day after he refused to teach about evolution.[192] An appellate court in Minnesota also affirmed a board's reassigning a teacher to teach a different biology course after he refused to teach about evolution.[193] In addition, the Seventh Circuit affirmed that school officials in Indiana did not violate an individual's rights when they removed his name from an approved list of substitutes because he insisted on presenting his own religious views in class.[194] Along the same line, a federal trial court in California largely rejected the claims of an elementary school teacher who alleged that officials violated his rights by not permitting him to use supplemental classroom materials with religious content and talking about religion with his students.[195] The court stated that if the plaintiff could prove that officials permitted others teachers to include religious expressions in their lessons and handouts but prevented him from doing so, then he would have had evidence to present a case that they violated his right to equal protection.

On a different matter, in cases not involving Title VII, the Ninth Circuit ruled that a school board in Idaho violated the religious rights of a principal when he was dismissed because he and his wife chose to home school their children.[196] The court interpreted the board's employment action as amounting to punishing the plaintiff for exercising his right to the free exercise of religion. Subsequently, the Sixth Circuit affirmed that a superintendent could be personally liable for refusing to hire a substitute teacher to a promised full-time position unless the applicant removed his child from a Catholic school and enrolled him in a public school.[197] Accord-

---

191. *Mohammed v. Racine Unified School Dist.*, 206 Fed.Appx. 543 [217 Educ. L. Rep. 146] (7th Cir.2006).

192. *Peloza v. Capistrano Unified School Dist.*, 37 F.3d 517 [94 Educ. L. Rep. 1159] (9th Cir.1994), *cert. denied*, 515 U.S. 1173, 115 S.Ct. 2640, 132 L.Ed.2d 878 (1995).

193. *LeVake v. Independent School Dist. No. 656*, 625 N.W.2d 502 [153 Educ. L. Rep. 356] (Minn. Ct. App. 2001), *review denied* (2001), *cert. denied*, 534 U.S. 1081, 122 S.Ct. 814, 151 L.Ed.2d 698 (2002).

194. *Helland v. South Bend Community School Corp.*, 93 F.3d 327 [111 Educ. L. Rep. 1108] (7th Cir.1996), *cert. denied*, 519 U.S. 1092, 117 S.Ct. 769, 136 L.Ed.2d 715 (1997).

195. *Williams v. Vidmar*, 367 F. Supp.2d 1265 [198 Educ. L. Rep. 292] (N.D. Cal. 2005).

196. *Peterson v. Minidoka County School Dist. No. 331*, 118 F.3d 1351 [120 Educ. L. Rep. 71] (9th Cir.1997), *opinion amended*, 132 F.3d 1258 (9th Cir.1997).

197. *Barrett v. Steubenville City Schools*, 388 F.3d 967 [193 Educ. L. Rep. 124] (6th Cir.2004), *cert. denied*, 546 U.S. 813, 126 S.Ct. 334, 163 L.Ed.2d 47 [202 Educ. L. Rep. 27] (2005).

ing to the court, the teacher not only had a protected constitutional right to liberty in directing the education of his son by sending him to the school of his choice, but also that the superintendent could be liable because this right was well-established when he acted as he did. A year earlier, the Fifth Circuit allowed the claims of a teacher whose superintendent refused to hire her as an assistant principal because her son attended a religious school to proceed to trial over whether he violated her right to educate her child as she saw fit.[198]

In Arkansas, a dispute involving religion took on a different twist where a teacher challenged not only a superintendent's practices of reciting prayers at mandatory teacher meetings and requiring staff to attend in-service sessions at a religious college where prayers were part of the meeting. The Eighth Circuit was persuaded that a trial court abused its discretion in prohibiting prayer at meetings only when the teacher attended.[199] The court directed school officials to permit the teacher to skip any in-service training sessions where prayers would be offered and ordered the board to end its endorsement of a particular religious message at meetings.

The Eighth Circuit affirmed that school officials violated the free speech rights of an elementary teacher in South Dakota by refusing to allow her to join a Good News Club that met after school. The court reversed an order that would have permitted the teacher to meet with the club, but only at schools other than where she taught. Holding that the teacher's after-school participation amounted to private speech, the court explained that the after-school participation did not put the board at risk of violating the Establishment Clause.[200]

Title VII and Religious Employers

In addition to protections applicable to workers in public schools, Title VII has special rules for religiously affiliated non-public schools. In fact, Title VII provides significant protection to religious employers since it permits them to set bona fide occupational qualifications including religion and allows them to limit hiring in key areas to members of their faiths.

Three major exemptions under Title VII are relevant to religious schools.[201] The first, and arguably most important exemption, deals with situations where "religion, sex, or national origin is a bona fide occupational qualification [BFOQ] reasonably necessary to the operations of that particular business or enterprise."[202] In such a case, the Sixth Circuit

---

198. *Barrow v. Greenville Indep. School Dist.*, 332 F.3d 844 [177 Educ. L. Rep. 922] (5th Cir.2003), *reh'g and reh'g en banc denied*, 75 Fed.Appx. 982 (5th Cir.2003), *on remand*, 2003 WL 21653871 (N.D. Tex. 2003), *cert. denied sub nom. Smith v. Barrow*, 540 U.S. 1005, 124 S.Ct. 547, 157 L.Ed.2d 411 (2003).

199. *Warnock v. Archer*, 380 F.3d 1076 [191 Educ. L. Rep. 620] (8th Cir.2004).

200. *Wigg v. Sioux Falls School Dist. 49–5*, 382 F.3d 807 [192 Educ. L. Rep. 15] (8th Cir.2004), *reh'g and reh'g en banc denied* (2004).

201. A fourth exemption in Title VII is that it is inapplicable to institutions with fifteen or fewer employees. Accordingly, Title VII has a limited impact on K–12 schools since, for the statute's purposes, these schools are typically considered part of the larger religious organizations to which they belong. 42 U.S.C.A. § 2000e(b).

202. 42 U.S.C.A. § 2000e–2(e)(1).

addressed the nonrenewal of the contract of a teacher in a Roman Catholic elementary school in Ohio who gave birth six months after getting married. Although pointing to language in the teacher's contract that "by word and example you will reflect the values of the Catholic Church,"[203] the court refused to uphold a grant of summary judgment in favor of the diocese. The Sixth Circuit returned the dispute to trial court for further consideration since it was uncertain whether the teacher's contract was not renewed solely due to her pregnancy.[204] Earlier, the same court upheld the dismissal of a suit filed by a former preschool teacher who claimed that she was fired due to her pregnancy.[205] The court affirmed that officials in the Christian school did not violate Title VII since the former teacher was unable to show that they applied the policy against premarital sex in a discriminatory manner.

A closely related second exemption applies to "a religious corporation, association, educational institution, or society with respect to the employment of individuals of a particular religion to perform work connected with the carrying on by such corporation, association, educational institution, or society of its activities."[206] This is sometimes referred to as the ministerial exception, with the burden of proof of the necessity of the BFOQ resting on employers, even if individuals are not ordained clerics. In order to apply this exception, religious institutions must be able to prove that staff members' teaching or other activities are so integrally related to furthering their spiritual and pastoral missions that their duties may be treated as ministerial.

In *Corporation of Presiding Bishops v. Amos (Amos)*[207] the Supreme Court upheld the constitutionality of the ministerial exception. Although *Amos* involved a custodian, the Court was of the opinion that the statute did not violate the Establishment Clause because earlier language, referring to an institution's "religious activities," was no longer in the law. As such, the Court extended the reach of the exemption to non-religious employment-related activities.

When a first-grade teacher in a Roman Catholic school was dismissed, she filed suit claiming that she had been subjected to age discrimination. Reversing an earlier order to the contrary, the Supreme Court of Wisconsin decided that insofar as the teacher's job was so closely linked to the religious mission of the school, she was covered by the ministerial exception such that she could not adjudicate her claim of age discrimination.[208]

---

203. *Cline v. Catholic Diocese of Toledo*, 206 F.3d 651, 656 (6th Cir.2000), *reh'g and reh'g en banc denied* (2000).

204. *See also Ganzy v. Allen Christian School*, 995 F.Supp. 340 (E.D.N.Y. 1998) (denying a motion for summary judgment entered on behalf of a Christian school in a dispute over whether the contract of an unmarried teacher was terminated due to her pregnancy).

205. *Boyd v. Harding Acad. of Memphis*, 88 F.3d 410 [110 Educ. L. Rep. 981] (6th Cir.1996).

206. 42 U.S.C.A. § 2000e–1.

207. 483 U.S. 327, 107 S.Ct. 2862, 97 L.Ed.2d 273 (1987).

208. *Coulee Catholic Schools v. Labor and Industry Review Comm'n, Dep't of Workforce Dev.*, 768 N.W.2d 868 (Wis. 2009).

As this book heads to press, the Supreme Court unanimously upheld the constitutionality of the ministerial exception, albeit as it has been extended under the ADA rather than Title VII. At issue was whether officials at a Lutheran elementary school in Michigan could dismiss a contract teacher who was also a commissioned minister in the church after she discharged. Reversing the Sixth Circuit's order to the contrary, in *Hosanna–Tabor Evangelical Lutheran Church and School v. Equal Employment Opportunities Commission,*[209] the Court ruled that despite the teacher's allegation that her primary duties were secular, the ministerial exception, which is soundly rooted in the First Amendment, precluded her ADA claim. In her ADA suit the teacher alleged that she was dismissed in retaliation for threatening to take legal action when she refused to resign in a dispute over whether she could return to work due to her health problems. Emphasizing that the First Amendment forbids the government from contradicting a church's determination who can act as its ministers, the Court reasoned that the ministerial exception thus applied to bar the teacher's claim even though she spent more than six hours of her seven-hour day teaching secular subjects, using secular textbooks while not incorporating religion into these materials; teachers at the school were not required to be "called" or members of the Lutheran faith in order to conduct religious activities as part of their jobs; and that the duties of contract teachers were identical to those lacking the title of minister.

On the same day that it handed down *Hosanna–Tabor,* the Supreme Court rejected two additional challenges involving the ministerial exception. In the first, the Director of the Department of Religious Formation unsuccessfully sued the Roman Catholic Diocese of Tulsa, Oklahoma, for gender and age discrimination after being dismissed from her position.[210] In the second, the Justices declined to hear the appeal in a dispute wherein a Director of Religious Education, who also taught mathematics classes, sued the Roman Catholic Diocese of Lansing after having alleged violations of the state's Whistleblowers' Protection Act and Civil Rights Act for retaliatory dismissal over charges unrelated to her duties as a religious educator.[211] The Court was satisfied that the employees could not proceed with their suits because they were subject to the ministerial exception.

The third exemption, which applies to institutions that are "in whole or in substantial part, owned, supported, controlled, or managed by a particular religious corporation, association or society, or if the curriculum of such school, college, university, or other educational institution . . . is directed toward the propagation of a particular religion,"[212] permits policies which allow hiring preferences for members of a particular faith. In such a case, albeit set in higher education, the Eleventh Circuit permitted a Baptist university to limit a faculty member's teaching assignments to

---

209. ___ U.S. ___, 131 S.Ct. 1783, 179 L.Ed.2d 653 (2011), rev'g, 597 F.3d 769 [254 Educ. L. Rep. 520] (6th Cir.2010), reh'g and reh'g en banc denied (2010).

210. *Skrzypczak v. Roman Catholic Diocese of Tulsa,* 611 F.3d 1238 (10th Cir.2010), *cert. denied,* ___ S.Ct. ___, 2012 WL 117541 (2012).

211. *Weishuhn v. Catholic Diocese of Lansing,* 756 N.W.2d 483 (Mich. Ct. App. 2008), *appeal after remand,* 787 N.W.2d 513 (Mich. Ct. App. 2010), *appeal denied,* 787 N.W.2d 507 [259 Educ. L. Rep. 836] (Mich. 2010), *cert. denied,* ___ S.Ct. ___, 2012 WL 117540 (2012).

212. 42 U.S.C.A. § 2000–(e)(2)(e).

undergraduate classes and prevent him from teaching in its divinity school due to religious differences that he had with his dean.[213] The court added that even though the university was no longer under the direct control of a religious governing body, it was entitled to the exemption because it was still substantially supported by that church.

Sex

Insofar as Title IX, which outlaws discrimination based on sex, is ordinarily applied to cases involving students, and is discussed in Chapter 13, employees must file suit pursuant to Title VII.[214] This may change in light of the Supreme Court's ruling in *Jackson v. Birmingham Board of Education*.[215] The Court permitted a male to proceed with his retaliation claim that he was removed as head coach of a girls' high school basketball team after he complained about the facilities available to his team. The Court held that Title IX created a private right of action for retaliation even in the absence of express Congressional intent to do so.[216]

In another expansion of the law, in a non-education case, *Burlington Northern and Santa Fe Railway v. White*,[217] the Supreme Court posited that Title VII's anti-retaliation protections in suits alleging discrimination based on gender are not limited to actions related to ultimate workplace employment decisions. The Court thus affirmed that officials violated the rights of a female forklift operator when they changed her job assignment in retaliation for her having complained about sexual harassment by her supervisor.[218] In another non-education case, the Supreme Court addressed a claim that a male was dismissed in retaliation for his fiancee's having filed a sex discrimination complaint against their common employer with the EEOC. In *Thompson v. North American Stainless*,[219] the Court decided that if the male could prove the charge, then he had a valid retaliation claim against the employer under Title VII.

Federal courts were not initially receptive to claims of sexual discrimination under Title VII.[220] As courts became open to such charges,[221] two

---

213. *Killinger v. Samford Univ.*, 113 F.3d 196 [118 Educ. L. Rep. 48] (11th Cir.1997). *See also Hall v. Baptist Memorial Health Care Corp.*, 215 F.3d 618 [145 Educ. L. Rep. 216] (6th Cir.2000) (granting the college's motion for summary judgment, thereby permitting the dismissal of an employee who was ordained by a church with a large gay congregation).

214. *Lakoski v. James*, 66 F.3d 751 [103 Educ. L. Rep. 652] (5th Cir.1995), *cert. denied*, 519 U.S. 947, 117 S.Ct. 357, 136 L.Ed.2d 249 (1996), *reh'g denied*, 519 U.S. 1035, 117 S.Ct. 598, 136 L.Ed.2d 525 (1996); *Gibson v. Hickman*, 2 F. Supp.2d 1481 [127 Educ. L. Rep. 173] (M.D. Ga. 1998).

215. 544 U.S. 167, 125 S.Ct. 1497, 161 L.Ed.2d 361 (2005), *on remand*, 416 F.3d 1280 (11th Cir.2005).

216. More than a year-and-one-half after the Supreme Court resolved this dispute, the teacher and school board reached a settlement in which the coach was reinstated to his position. *Coach in Title IX Case Wins Reinstatement*, EDUCATION WEEK, Dec. 6, 2006, at 14.

217. 548 U.S. 53, 126 S.Ct. 2405, 165 L.Ed.2d 345 (2006).

218. For a case that relied on the Supreme Court's precedent here, *see Easterling v. School Bd. of Concordia Parish*, 196 Fed.Appx. 251 [214 Educ. L. Rep. 1017] (5th Cir.2006) (reversing and remanding in favor of a physical education teacher who alleged that her board discriminated against her in retaliation for her having filed a claim over various aspects of her job).

219. ___ U.S. ___, 131 S.Ct. 863, 178 L.Ed.2d 694 (2011).

broad theories of discrimination emerged: hostile work environment and quid pro quo harassment. In claims filed under hostile work environment, which are more numerous than quid pro quo cases, plaintiffs must prove that employers' creation of hostile and offensive working environments result in intolerable conditions. In cases of quid pro quo harassment, plaintiffs must show that defendants engaged in unwelcomed conduct of a sexual nature that was directly connected to tangible aspects of the economic benefits of employment.

The Supreme Court addressed its first case on sexual discrimination in *Meritor Savings Bank FSB v. Vinson (Meritor)*.[222] In *Meritor*, a female bank employee in Washington, D.C., who went on sick leave and was fired, sued officials based on her supervisor's demands for sexual relations. The employee acquiesced to the supervisor's repeated demands and allowed herself to be subjected to other forms of inappropriate sexual conduct out of fear of losing her job. The Justices, discerning that Title VII is not limited to economic or tangible discrimination, affirmed that "[w]ithout question, when a supervisor sexually harasses a subordinate because of the subordinate's sex, that supervisor 'discriminate(s)' on the basis of sex"[223] and that "a claim of 'hostile environment' sex discrimination is actionable under Title VII."[224] In *Meritor*, the Court enunciated the five elements in a claim of sexual discrimination based on the existence of a hostile work environment, an offense that is ordinarily established by a series of incidents. While the same criteria also can apply in cases of quid pro quo harassment, since its parameters are more readily established than hostile work environment, discussion here is limited to the latter.

The first element in a hostile work environment sexual discrimination claim is that plaintiffs must belong to a protected category. Since most suits are filed by women, this element is satisfied on its face when women file claims. Second, plaintiffs must have been subjected to unwelcomed sexual harassment. In other words, "the conduct must be unwelcome in the sense that the employee did not solicit or incite it, and in the sense that the employee regarded the conduct as undesirable or offensive."[225] Third, the harassment must have been based on sex. This can be established in a variety of ways such as when "harassing behavior lack[s] a sexually explicit content but [is] directed at women and motivated by animus against women"[226] or by "behavior that is not directed at a particular individual or group of individuals, but is disproportionately more offensive or demeaning

---

220. *Barnes v. Costle*, 561 F.2d 983 (D.C. Cir.1977); *Corne v. Bausch & Lomb*, 390 F.Supp. 161 (D. Ariz.1975) *vacated by Corne v. Bausch and Lomb*, 562 F.2d 55 (9th Cir.1977); *Tomkins v. Public Serv. Electric & Gas Co.*, 568 F.2d 1044 (3d Cir.1977).

221. *See, e.g., Bundy v. Jackson*, 641 F.2d 934 (D.C. Cir.1981).

222. 477 U.S. 57, 106 S.Ct. 2399, 91 L.Ed.2d 49 (1986), *on remand sub nom. Vinson v. Taylor*, 801 F.2d 1436 (D.C. Cir.1986).

223. *Id.* at 64.

224. *Id.* at 73.

225. *Henson v. City of Dundee*, 682 F.2d 897, 903 (11th Cir.1982).

226. *Robinson v. Jacksonville Shipyards*, 760 F.Supp. 1486, 1522 (M.D. Fla. 1991).

to one sex.''[227] Fourth, the harassment must affect a term, condition, or privilege of employment to such a degree that it creates an abusive work environment. In other words, the harassment must be so pervasive as to alter working conditions to the point that, under the totality of the circumstances, it seriously affects the psychological well-being of plaintiffs. The fifth element is that employers knew or should have known of the harassment but failed to take prompt remedial action.

In *Harris v. Forklift Systems (Harris)*[228] the Supreme Court elaborated on the concept of harassment through an abusive work environment in response to questions that it left unanswered in *Meritor. Harris* was filed by a female executive in Tennessee who quit her job after the company president made inappropriate sexual comments to her about business dealings, suggesting that she must have engaged in sexual relations with a client in order to obtain a contract. In agreeing that the president's behavior was actionable, the Justices decided that whether an environment is hostile or abusive is to be determined by examining such factors as frequency and severity of the conduct as well as whether it was physically threatening or humiliating, rather than merely offensive utterances, and whether it unreasonably interfered with one's work performance. The Court thought that in order for employers to be liable under Title VII, abusive work environments need not seriously affect employees' psychological well-being or lead to tangible job losses. On remand, the Sixth Circuit and a federal trial court in Tennessee affirmed a judgment in favor of the employee.[229]

In *Oncale v. Sundowner Offshore Services (Oncale)*,[230] the Supreme Court addressed same-sex sexual harassment for the first time. The Court found that same-sex sexual harassment, involving a male roustabout on an eight-man platform crew in Louisiana who alleged that he was forcibly subjected to humiliating sex-related actions by some of his male co-workers in the presence of the rest of the crew and was physically assaulted and threatened with rape by another worker, was actionable under Title VII.[231]

Burlington Industries v. Ellerth (Burlington)[232] and *Faragher v. City of Boca Raton (Faragher)*,[233] handed down on the same day, involved similar factual circumstances dealing with retaliation. In *Burlington*, a woman in Illinois quit her sales job after a supervisor subjected her to constant sexual harassment. The Supreme Court framed the issue as whether "an employee who refuses the unwelcome and threatening sexual advances of a supervisor, yet suffers no adverse, tangible job consequences, can recover

---

227. *Id.* at 1522–1523.

228. 510 U.S. 17, 114 S.Ct. 367, 126 L.Ed.2d 295 (1993).

229. 14 F.3d 601 (6th Cir.1993), *on remand*, 1994 WL 792661 (M.D. Tenn. 1994).

230. 523 U.S. 75, 118 S.Ct. 998, 140 L.Ed.2d 201 (1998).

231. For a case of same sex harassment in a school setting, *see Madon v. Laconia School Dist.*, 952 F.Supp. 44 [116 Educ. L. Rep. 253] (D.N.H. 1996) (permitting a Title VII complaint to proceed against a principal but not the school board).

232. 524 U.S. 742, 118 S.Ct. 2257, 141 L.Ed.2d 633 (1998), *on remand*, 165 F.3d 31 (7th Cir.1998).

233. 524 U.S. 775, 118 S.Ct. 2275, 141 L.Ed.2d 662 (1998), *on remand*, 166 F.3d 1152 (11th Cir.1999).

against the employer without showing the employer is negligent or other-wise at fault for the supervisor's actions."[234] Answering in the affirmative, the Court indicated that employees who refuse unwelcomed and threaten-ing sexual advances from supervisors but suffer no adverse tangible job consequences may recover from employers without showing that they were negligent or otherwise at fault for the supervisors' actions. The Court asserted that employers may raise affirmative defenses to liability or damages claims which require them to show that they exercised reasonable care to prevent, and promptly correct, sexually harassing behavior and employees unreasonably failed to take advantage of preventive or corrective opportunities or to otherwise avoid harm. At the end of its analysis, the Court reflected that "[g]iven our explanation that the labels quid pro quo and hostile work environment are not controlling for purposes of establish-ing employer liability, [the plaintiff] should have an adequate opportunity to prove she has a claim for which Burlington is liable."[235]

In *Faragher*, a lifeguard at a city pool in Florida quit after supervisors created a sexually hostile work atmosphere by repeatedly subjecting her and other female lifeguards to uninvited and offensive touching, by making lewd remarks, and by speaking of women in offensive terms. The Justices agreed that although employers are subject to vicarious liability under Title VII for actionable discrimination by supervisors, employers may raise affirmative defenses that look to the reasonableness of their actions in seeking to prevent and correct harassing conduct along with the reason-ableness of the employees' conduct in trying to avoid harm. The Court declared that the city was vicariously liable to the lifeguard based on officials' failure to exercise reasonable care to prevent the supervisor's harassing behavior. On remand, the Eleventh Circuit reinstated a federal trial court ruling in favor of the lifeguard.[236]

Relying on *Faragher*, the Fourth Circuit believed that insofar as a principal in Virginia's assigning extra work to a school psychologist was not a tangible employment action that created a hostile work environment sufficient to give rise to impute board liability, it had no choice but to vacate an earlier judgment in her favor and return the dispute to a lower court for further action.[237] In like manner, a teacher in Florida sued a board, claiming that it was liable where a principal created a hostile work environment by making comments of a sexual nature to her on numerous occasions.[238] A federal trial court granted the board's motion for summary judgment, recognizing that it not only had a policy prohibiting sexual harassment but also that the teacher did not even file a complaint pursuant to its grievance procedures.

In *Clark County School District v. Breeden*, the Supreme Court ad-dressed whether a single incident can give rise to liability in a case

---

234. *Burlington* at 747.

235. *Id.* at 765–66.

236. *Faragher v. City of Boca Raton*, 166 F.3d 1152 (11th Cir.1999).

237. *Reinhold v. Commonwealth of Va.*, 151 F.3d 172 [128 Educ. L. Rep. 588] (4th Cir.1998).

238. *Masson v. School Bd. of Dade County, Fla.*, 36 F. Supp.2d 1354 [133 Educ. L. Rep. 489] (S.D. Fla. 1999).

involving retaliation for an allegedly sexually harassing remark. The dispute arose when a woman in Nevada who worked in a department that hired other staff filed suit for retaliation when she was transferred for complaining on learning that a supervisor made a sexually explicit comment about her to another person. In rejecting the woman's claim in a brief per curiam order, the Court decreed that "[n]o reasonable person could have believed that the incident recounted above violated Title VII's standards."[239]

Title VII claims for sexual discrimination permit courts to award such relief as back pay but ordinarily not reinstatement[240] or punitive damages.[241] Courts rejected Title VII claims where a complaint was not filed in a timely manner;[242] an assault complaint did not include sexual harassment;[243] and boards offered legitimate, non-discriminatory reasons for adverse employment actions.[244] However, where an employee unsuccessfully claimed that she was dismissed for participating in an internal investigation into rumors about sexual harassment, the Supreme Court reversed in her favor. In *Crawford v. Metropolitan Government of Nashville and Davidson County*,[245] the Court held that insofar as Title VII's anti-retaliation provision protects employees who speak out about discrimination not on their own initiative, but in response to questions during internal investigations by employers, her case had to be remanded to consider whether she was dismissed for speaking freely during the investigation.

A federal trial court in Louisiana addressed an uncommon situation involving the claim of gender discrimination under Title VII where a male was passed over in favor of a female for a job as a middle school assistant principal.[246] In rejecting the school board's motion for summary judgment, the court reasoned that genuine issues of material fact as to the qualifications of the male and the female who was hired and whether his sex was a motivating factor in the board's action precluded its motion for summary judgment. The court thought that the male presented evidence that he was interviewed by females only, that discrepancies existed as to the statements of one of the interviewees and one of his former principals, and that there

---

239. 532 U.S. 268, 271, 121 S.Ct. 1508, 149 L.Ed.2d 509 [152 Educ. L. Rep. 492] (2001), *reh'g denied*, 533 U.S. 912, 121 S.Ct. 2264, 150 L.Ed.2d 248 (2001), *on remand*, 258 F.3d 958 (9th Cir.2001).

240. *Prine v. Sioux City Community School Dist.*, 95 F. Supp.2d 1005 [144 Educ. L. Rep. 239] (N.D. Iowa 2000).

241. *Jonasson v. Lutheran Child and Family Servs.*, 115 F.3d 436 [118 Educ. L. Rep. 853] (7th Cir.1997) (also awarding compensatory damages); *Molnar v. Booth*, 229 F.3d 593 [148 Educ. L. Rep. 54] (7th Cir.2000).

242. *Cross v. Chicago School Reform Bd. of Trustees*, 80 F. Supp.2d 911 [141 Educ. L. Rep. 662] (N.D. Ill. 2000).

243. *Howard–Ahmad v. Chicago School Reform Bd. of Trustees*, 161 F. Supp.2d 857 [157 Educ. L. Rep. 588] (N.D. Ill. 2001).

244. *Jackson v. Delta Special School Dist. No. 2*, 86 F.3d 1489 [110 Educ. L. Rep. 574] (8th Cir.1996); *Robbins v. Jefferson County School Dist. R–1*, 186 F.3d 1253 [137 Educ. L. Rep. 489] (10th Cir.1999).

245. 555 U.S. 271, 129 S.Ct. 846, 172 L.Ed.2d 650 (2009).

246. *Louis v. East Baton Rouge Parish School Bd.*, 303 F. Supp.2d 799 [185 Educ. L. Rep. 938] (M.D. La. 2003).

was a significant difference between his qualifications and those of the woman who was selected for the job.

In a case involving a novel factual setting, the First Circuit reviewed a dispute where a female teacher in Puerto Rico was sexually harassed by one of her students. In ascertaining that while the teacher could have filed suit under Title IX, her claim was cognizable under Title VII.[247] The court rejected the defendants' motion for summary judgment over whether educational officials could have been liable due to the presence of remaining issues of fact. At the same time, the court granted the defendants' motion for summary judgment since the teacher failed to establish a prima facie case of Title VII retaliation in light of her forced resignation prior to the termination of her contract. The court acknowledged that the school's director was not entitled to qualified immunity from the teacher's suit.

Sexual Orientation

On a different matter related to classifications based on sex, even though it is a topic receiving a great deal of attention in the popular press, federal statutory law does not protect individuals based on their sexual orientation. However, courts have extended such protection to teachers. A federal trial court ruled that when school officials in Ohio discriminated against a teacher who is gay in not renewing his contract due to his sexual orientation, he was entitled to reinstatement on a two-year contract and an award of damages for back pay and emotional distress as well as attorney fees.[248] Moreover, a federal trial court in New York wrote that officials violated the equal protection rights of a teacher who was a lesbian by not protecting her from harassment by students.[249] Along with denying motions for qualified immunity for both the school board and principal, the court specified that the teacher was entitled to attorney fees.

The Tenth Circuit affirmed that a superintendent of schools in Wyoming was not liable for discrimination based on sexual orientation when the positions of two administrators who were gay were eliminated and they were not offered other jobs in the district.[250] The court decided that insofar as the superintendent was not the final policymaker with regard to hiring actions, he was entitled to qualified immunity because there was no clearly established line of judicial authority prohibiting adverse employment actions against individuals due to their sexual orientation when the board chose not to offer the plaintiffs other positions.

On the other hand, the Supreme Judicial Court of Maine entered a judgment in favor of a high school softball coach whose contract was not renewed allegedly for hazing players and subjecting them to verbal

---

247. *Plaza–Torres v. Rey*, 376 F. Supp.2d 171 [200 Educ. L. Rep. 166] (D. Puerto Rico 2005).

248. *Glover v. Williamsburg Local School Dist. Bd. of Educ.*, 20 F. Supp.2d 1160 [130 Educ. L. Rep. 661] (S.D. Ohio 1998).

249. *Lovell v. Comsewogue School Dist.*, 214 F. Supp.2d 319 [168 Educ. L. Rep. 749] (E.D. N.Y. 2002).

250. *Milligan–Hitt v. Board of Trustees of Sheridan County School Dist. No. 2*, 523 F.3d 1219 [231 Educ. L. Rep. 671] (10th Cir.2008).

abuse.[251] The court found that even though the plaintiff told the superintendent that other coaches hazed their players, his failure to act on the information raised a question of fact as to whether she was discriminated against because she was a lesbian.

An openly gay high school librarian with more than twenty years of experience successfully challenged his six-month suspension without pay, being reassigned to another school, and being required to attend counseling and training because he touched, whispered, and stood silently next to students in attempting to maintain order in a library. A trial court in New York annulled an arbitration award that imposed the penalties insofar as the record revealed that the male engaged in the same kind of conduct as a heterosexual female librarian who did not face charges and who was not required to attend counseling or training.[252] The court explained that the award subjected the librarian to discrimination based on his sexual orientation.

In another kind of dispute involving sexual orientation, the Eighth Circuit affirmed that a school board in Minnesota did not create a hostile work environment in permitting a male teacher who is transgendered to use a faculty restroom for women.[253] In rejecting the claim of a female faculty member, the court noted that she neither suffered an adverse employment action nor did the arrangement affect a term, condition, or privilege of her employment since she had convenient access to numerous other restrooms. The court affirmed that the teacher lacked a claim for religious discrimination since she failed to inform the board of her belief and she did not suffer an adverse employment action.

Genetic Information

The most recent federal antidiscrimination statute is the Genetic Information Nondiscrimination Act of 2008 (GINA).[254] GINA prohibits discrimination in health coverage and employment based on genetic information including facts about an individual's genetic tests or those of a family member or knowledge about any disease, disorder, or condition of a family member. GINA defines genetic tests as including analyses of human DNA, RNA, chromosomes, proteins, or metabolites detecting genotypes, mutations, or chromosomal changes. GINA excludes routine tests such as those dealing with complete blood counts or cholesterol. Insofar as GINA is so new, there is no recorded litigation to date.

According to Title I of GINA, it is illegal for health insurers or health plan administrators to request or require genetic information for individuals or their family members or to use such data to make decisions

---

251.   *Cookson v. Brewer School Dep't*, 974 A.2d 276 [246 Educ. L. Rep. 310] (Me. 2009).

252.   *Asch v. New York City Board/Dep't of Educ.*, 927 N.Y.S.2d 836 [269 Educ. L. Rep. 671] (N.Y. Sup. Ct. 2011).

253.   *Cruzan v. Special School Dist., No. 1*, 294 F.3d 981 [166 Educ. L. Rep. 492] (8th Cir.2002).

254.   122 Stat. 881, Pub. L. 110–233 (2008), codified at 26 U.S.C.A. § 9834; 42 U.S.C.A. §§ 300gg–53, 1320d–9; 42 U.S.C.A. §§ 2000–ff *et seq.*

concerning coverage, rates, or preexisting conditions. These protections apply only to health insurance and do not extend to life, disability, or long-term care insurance.

Title II of GINA prohibits discrimination against employees or applicants for employment based on genetic information. Title II forbids employers from using genetic information in making employment decisions while restricting them from obtaining genetic information.

As with other federal antidiscrimination laws, GINA applies to employers with fifteen or more employees and provides protections in any aspect of employment, including hiring, firing, wages, fringe benefits, job assignments, promotions, layoffs, training, and conditions of employment. Consistent with other antidiscrimination laws, GINA makes it unlawful to harass individuals because of their genetic information or to retaliate against individuals who file discrimination charges or participate in discrimination investigations or legal proceedings.

PRIVACY

Fourth Amendment Issues

As discussed in Chapter 13, the judiciary has focused considerably more attention on the privacy rights of students than teachers. The privacy rights of school employees are based on the Fourteenth Amendment's liberty clause which protects the bodily integrity of individuals and the Fourth Amendment's protection against unreasonable searches and seizures.

The Supreme Court has yet to address drug testing or searches of public school employees but has examined these questions in three non-school cases. *O'Connor v. Ortega*[255] involved the search of a doctor's locked office purportedly to conduct an inventory and to look for evidence that he allegedly sexually harassed two females. Officials at the public hospital also alleged that the doctor inappropriately disciplined a medical resident. In upholding the search, the Justices relied heavily on the reasonableness standard of *New Jersey v. T.L.O.*[256] The Court posited that hospital officials had the authority to enter a locked office at any time for business-related purposes such as conducting an inventory, looking for files or records, or investigating alleged acts of wrongdoing. The Court suggested that extending such searches to the personal property of employees, such as briefcases or purses, would have required reasonable suspicion.

The Supreme Court next reviewed companion cases involving public employees. In *Skinner v. Railway Labor Executives' Association*,[257] the Court permitted testing of railroad employees for drugs and alcohol after serious accidents even without showings of individualized suspicion. In

---

255. 480 U.S. 709, 107 S.Ct. 1492, 94 L.Ed.2d 714 (1987).

256. 469 U.S. 325, 105 S.Ct. 733, 83 L.Ed.2d 720 [21 Educ. L. Rep. 1122] (1985). [Case No. 96]

257. 489 U.S. 602, 109 S.Ct. 1402, 103 L.Ed.2d 639 (1989).

National Treasury Employees Union v. Von Raab,[258] the Court upheld the United States Customs Service's practice of drug testing employees who applied for promotions or transfers to drug interdiction positions that would have required them to carry firearms. In both cases, the Justices justified testing based on the government's compelling interest in ensuring railway safety and that front-line personnel in drug interdiction had unimpeachable integrity and judgment, respectively.

One of the more significant issues involving the privacy rights of teachers, and other school employees, involves their Fourth Amendment right to be free from unreasonable searches and seizures. Still, it is worth recalling that insofar as "[a] teacher's employment in the public schools is a privilege, not a right,"[259] absent language to the contrary in state statutes or collective bargaining agreements, boards have authority in defining their employees' privacy expectations with regard to drug testing. Not surprisingly, courts have reached mixed results over drug testing of teachers and other school employees.

As to suspicionless testing, in the first case handed down by a court of last resort, the Court of Appeals of New York struck down a board policy intended to subject all probationary teachers in a school district to urinalysis to detect potential drug abuse as a pre-condition to receiving tenure.[260] The court held that the policy violated the constitutional bar to unreasonable searches and seizures absent individualized suspicion.

Three years later, a federal trial court in Georgia reached the same result.[261] In enjoining a policy and invalidating an underlying statute as unconstitutional, the court explained that the state's sole rationale for requiring suspicionless drug testing for all applicants for state employment, namely its generalized interest in ensuring integrity of work force, was insufficiently compelling to outweigh the privacy rights of applicants for teaching and other positions even if they had diminished expectations of privacy under the Fourth Amendment. The Fifth Circuit eventually struck down a policy that would have required random drug testing of school employees, including teachers.[262] The court observed that the policy, which required testing for school employees who were injured on the job, violated the Fourth Amendment's prohibition against unreasonable searches since there was no special needs exception present to the requirement of individualized suspicion. The court was convinced that the policy was unacceptable because testing did not respond to an identified problem of drug use by employees and there was an insufficient nexus between worker injuries and drug use.

---

258.   489 U.S. 656, 109 S.Ct. 1384, 103 L.Ed.2d 685 (1989).

259.   *Board of Educ. of City of Los Angeles v. Wilkinson*, 270 P.2d 82, 85 (Cal. Ct. App. 1954).

260.   *Patchogue–Medford Congress of Teachers v. Board of Educ. of Patchogue–Medford Union Free School Dist.*, 517 N.Y.S.2d 456 [40 Educ. L. Rep. 917] (N.Y. 1987).

261.   *Georgia Ass'n of Educators v. Harris*, 749 F.Supp. 1110 [64 Educ. L. Rep. 122] (N.D. Ga. 1990).

262.   *United Teachers of New Orleans v. Orleans Parish School Bd.*, 142 F.3d 853 [126 Educ. L. Rep. 104] (5th Cir.1998).

On the other hand, the Sixth Circuit became the first federal appellate court to uphold suspicionless drug testing of teachers, reinstating a board policy in Tennessee requiring all individuals who wished to work in safety-sensitive positions to submit to testing as a pre-condition of employment.[263] In addition, the court upheld that part of the policy calling for drug testing based on reasonable suspicion and rejected alcohol testing of employees since the standards were much more stringent than they were for even drunk drivers.

A federal trial court in Kentucky later relied on the Sixth Circuit's precedent in denying a teacher's request for a preliminary injunction in a challenge to a school board's policy of random suspicionless drug testing of twenty-five percent of its employees.[264] The court pointed out that although the Sixth Circuit had not required evidence of a drug problem to justify such a policy, one had existed among staff and faculty. The court thought that the policy included sufficient procedural safeguards to protect teacher privacy. A variety of courts have upheld suspicionless drug testing of other school employees such as school bus attendants;[265] a mechanic's helper;[266] bus drivers following accidents resulting in bodily injury or $1,000 in property damage except where buses were struck when they were legally parked;[267] and custodians as well as other safety-sensitive school personnel in an elementary school.[268]

Conversely, two other courts invalidated suspicionless drug testing policies premised on the safety-sensitive nature of teaching. A federal trial court in West Virginia reasoned that absent a concern that a momentary lapse by teachers would place students at risk or a pervasive drug problem in the district, the proposed policy violated their privacy rights.[269] An appellate court in North Carolina explained that absent evidence of a drug problem with employees in their schools, a board's suspicionless drug and alcohol policy violated the protections present in the state constitution, it was unenforceable.[270]

In a case from Indiana, the Seventh Circuit upheld a school board requirement that a teacher submit to biweekly drug tests.[271] The court

263. *Knox County Educ. Ass'n v. Knox County Bd. of Educ.*, 158 F.3d 361 [130 Educ. L. Rep. 62] (6th Cir.1998), *cert. denied*, 528 U.S. 812, 120 S.Ct. 46, 145 L.Ed.2d 41 (1999).

264. *Crager v. Board of Educ. of Knott County*, 313 F. Supp.2d 690 [187 Educ. L. Rep. 892] (E.D. Ky. 2004).

265. *Jones v. Jenkins*, 878 F.2d 1476 [54 Educ. L. Rep. 1138] (D.C. Cir.1989) (permitting testing without probable cause).

266. *English v. Talladega County Bd. of Educ.*, 938 F.Supp. 775 [113 Educ. L. Rep. 291] (N.D. Ala. 1996). *See also Cox v. McCraley*, 993 F.Supp. 1452 [125 Educ. L. Rep. 456] (M.D. Fla. 1998) (upholding a policy requiring an employee who was on an annual contract to submit to a drug test, enter a drug assistance program, or resign after he was informed that officials had reasonable suspicion that he violated a board policy regarding drug and/or alcohol abuse).

267. *Cornette v. Commonwealth*, 899 S.W.2d 502 [101 Educ. L. Rep. 474] (Ky. Ct. App. 1995).

268. *Aubrey v. School Bd. of Lafayette Parish*, 148 F.3d 559 [127 Educ. L. Rep. 710] (5th Cir.1998).

269. *American Fed'n of Teachers–West Va. AFL–CIO v. Kanawha County Bd. of Educ.*, 592 F. Supp.2d 883 [241 Educ. L. Rep. 570] (S.D.W.Va. 2009).

270. *Jones v. Graham County Bd. of Educ.*, 677 S.E.2d 171 [245 Educ. L. Rep. 497] (N.C. Ct. App. 2009).

rejected the teacher's equal protection claim that an athletic director who was caught stealing from the school was treated more favorably than he was by not being required to take drug tests. The court determined that the difference was the presence of a law covering teachers who have felony drug convictions on their records.

The Eleventh Circuit affirmed the dismissal of a teacher in Georgia who refused to submit to suspicion-based urinalysis testing after a drug-sniffing dog alerted officials to the presence of marijuana in her car.[272] The court concluded that insofar as the board acted pursuant to a county-wide safe school plan which called for a drug free workplace, it had the authority to dismiss the teacher.

Non-suspicion based cases reached results in favor of school employees. An appellate court in Pennsylvania ordered the reinstatement of a school custodian with twenty-eight years of experience who was dismissed for using marijuana, following a work-related injury, while off-duty and off of school property.[273] The court ruled that the board lacked just cause to terminate the custodian's employment since her actions neither impacted school activities nor violated its substance abuse policy. Further, a federal trial court in Tennessee invalidated a random urinalysis testing policy as unreasonably intrusive; the board instituted the policy after two teachers were arrested for illegal drug activities.[274]

The Second Circuit, in a case from New York involving a search and seizure that serves as a segue for the next section, maintained that a teacher who was suspended with pay and reassigned to an administrative position after being charged with stalking a student with whom he was sexually involved nine years earlier had no expectation of privacy in his classroom or its contents.[275] In affirming a grant of summary judgment in favor of the school board, the court recognized that insofar as the teacher was suspended and asked to turn in his classroom keys, he had a diminished expectation of privacy. The court added that school officials had reasonable investigatory and non-investigatory grounds to search the teacher's classroom after he had been given two opportunities to remove personal items from the room.[276]

---

271. *Ott v. Edinburgh Community School Corp.*, 189 Fed.Appx. 507 [213 Educ. L. Rep. 976] (7th Cir.2006).

272. *Hearn v. Board of Pub. Educ.*, 191 F.3d 1329 [138 Educ. L. Rep. 662] (11th Cir.1999), *reh'g and suggestion for reh'g en banc denied*, 204 F.3d 1124 (11th Cir.1999), *cert. denied*, 529 U.S. 1109, 120 S.Ct. 1962, 146 L.Ed.2d 794 (2000).

273. *Loyalsock Twp. Area School Dist. v. Loyalsock Custodial Maint.*, 931 A.2d 75 [224 Educ. L. Rep. 299] (Pa. Cmwlth. Ct. 2007).

274. *Smith County Educ. Ass'n v. Smith County Bd. of Educ.*, 781 F.Supp.2d 604 [270 Educ. L. Rep. 769] (M.D. Tenn. 2011).

275. *Shaul v. Cherry Valley–Springfield Cent. School*, 363 F.3d 177 [186 Educ. L. Rep. 604] (2d Cir.2004).

276. For an interesting case, albeit from higher education, *see Biby v. Board of Regents, of Univ. of Neb. at Lincoln*, 419 F.3d 845 [201 Educ. L. Rep. 36] (8th Cir.2005) (affirming that officials did not violate any clearly established constitutional rights by conducting a warrantless search of an employee's computer for work-related materials).

Educator Workplace Privacy

A former teacher in New York City sought further review of the denial of her claims that school officials violated her right to privacy by disclosing that she suffered from fibromyalgia.[277] Although conceding a general right to privacy, the Second Circuit affirmed that the teacher lacked a constitutionally-protected right since the disclosure of her condition did not carry a social stigma and she was not subjected to discrimination once her illness became known.

In a privacy case where a defendant raised a novel defense, an appellate court in Texas rejected the claim of a former employee of a religiously affiliated non-public school who was indicted pursuant to a statute that prohibited school employees from engaging in sexual relations with students in the institutions where they work.[278] The court was satisfied that the statute did not infringe on a fundamental right to engage in adult consensual activity.

Federal trial courts reached mixed results in claims over the alleged release of the medical records of school employees. A federal trial court in Illinois granted a school board's motion to dismiss claims that educational officials violated a teacher's privacy rights by disclosing his personal medical information.[279] The court was of the opinion that school officials did not violate the plaintiff's rights in sending out a notice which stated that there was no reason for concern because an unidentified staff member was being treated for meningitis insofar as they did not release private medical information about the teacher. Conversely, a federal trial court in New York rejected a board's motion for summary judgment when a secretary claimed that officials violated her rights by disclosing her medical records to unauthorized personnel.[280] The court found that the disclosure clearly infringed on the secretary's rights to privacy and confidentiality.

A case from the Supreme Court of Wisconsin dealt with a teacher's alleged right to privacy and the release of information to a newspaper about a compact disc (or CD) containing pornographic images and Internet searches that he allegedly viewed and conducted on his school computer.[281] The court affirmed that insofar as state law did not prohibit the release of the information, the records were not exempt from disclosure.[282]

In Illinois, a federal trial court resolved a dispute with a twist in granting a school board's motion for judgment on the pleadings when

---

277. *Matson v. Board of Educ. of the City School Dist. of N.Y.*, 631 F.3d 57 [264 Educ. L. Rep. 541] (2d Cir.2011).

278. *Ex parte Morales*, 212 S.W.3d 483 [216 Educ. L. Rep. 711] (Tex. Ct. App. 2006).

279. *Levin v. Board of Educ. of the City of Chicago*, 470 F. Supp.2d 835 [217 Educ. L. Rep. 207] (N.D. Ill. 2007).

280. *Burns v. Cook*, 458 F. Supp.2d 29 [214 Educ. L. Rep. 1078] (N.D.N.Y. 2006).

281. *Zellner v. Cedarburg School Dist.*, 731 N.W.2d 240 [219 Educ. L. Rep. 281] (Wis. 2007).

282. *See also Cyr v. Madawaska School Dist.*, 916 A.2d 967 [217 Educ. L. Rep. 559] (Me. 2007) (upholding the denial of access to an unredacted copy of an investigative report when a superintendent refused to re-nominate a probationary teacher for a job).

special education teachers disputed its attempted installation of audio-visual recording equipment in their classrooms to help to protect vulnerable students who are physically and emotionally challenged from abuse.[283] According to the court, since the teachers lacked a reasonable expectation of privacy in their classrooms, the proposed monitoring system would not have violated their Fourth Amendment rights. Previously, a case with a like outcome arose in Pennsylvania when a school bus driver sued a board on a variety of charges, most notably alleging that officials violated his Fourth Amendment right to privacy after a video camera was installed on his vehicle, without his knowledge, to ensure student safety. In a case that was unreported for two years, a federal trial court noted that insofar as the camera was not located in a private area, and the driver had a diminished expectation of privacy, his claim was without merit.[284]

A case involving technology and privacy arose in Connecticut. The federal trial court permitted a principal's privacy claim against her superintendent to proceed since he accessed, opened, and read an email she sent to her attorney while on medical leave.[285] The court acknowledged that while officials could engage in routine maintenance and monitoring of the computer system, a question of fact remained as to whether the superintendent exceeded his authority.

STATUTORY PROTECTIONS AGAINST DISCRIMINATION

In addition to Title VII, teachers and other school employees have a variety of statutory protections safeguarding their rights in the workplace. Key statutes in this regard protect educators against discrimination based on age, disability, and the need to care for one's self and family members who are ill.

Age

Pursuant to the Age Discrimination in Employment Act (ADEA):

It shall be unlawful for an employer—

(1) to fail or refuse to hire or to discharge any individual or otherwise discriminate against any individual with respect to his compensation, terms, conditions, or privileges of employment, because of such individual's age;

(2) to limit, segregate, or classify his employees in any way which would deprive or tend to deprive any individual of employment opportunities or otherwise adversely affect his status as an employee, because of such individual's age; or

---

283. *Plock v. Board of Educ. of Freeport School Dist. No. 145*, 545 F. Supp.2d 755 [232 Educ. L. Rep. 708] (N.D. Ill. 2007).

284. *Goodwin v. Moyer*, 549 F.Supp.2d 621 [233 Educ. L. Rep. 257] (M.D. Pa. 2006).

285. *Brown–Criscuolo v. Wolfe*, 601 F. Supp.2d 441 [243 Educ. L. Rep. 245] (D. Conn. 2009).

(3) to reduce the wage rate of any employee in order to comply with this [law].[286]

Even in protecting workers over the age of forty, the ADEA permits employers to rely on seniority or BFOQs[287] in order to avoid liability. Since the protections afforded by Title VII and the ADEA are very much alike, judicial analyses often rely on analogous reasoning such that in order to be actionable, qualified employees must be over the age of forty, must have been treated less favorably than others not in the protected class, must have suffered an adverse employment action,[288] and must file suit within ninety-days of receiving right-to-sue letters from the EEOC.[289]

In a non-education case, *Gross v. FBL Financial Services*,[290] the Supreme Court clarified the parameters of ADEA claims based on disparate treatment. In holding that plaintiffs must prove that age was the "but for" cause of their having suffered adverse employment actions, the Court rejected the mixed motives theory in explaining that unlike general Title VII claims, the burden does not shift to employers to justify their actions.

As noted earlier, since *Ledbetter v. Goodyear Tire and Rubber Co.*[291] was abrogated by the enactment of the Lilly Ledbetter Fair Pay Act of 2009 (FPA),[292] litigation is beginning to emerge. The first case to apply the new provision in an educational context arose in Kansas.[293] A federal trial court rejected the claim of two classified school employees in noting that under the FPA amendment to the ADEA, the board's eliminating their positions and transferring them to lower-paying jobs was not an impermissible compensation decision or practice. The court added that the board's action did not extend the 300–day administrative limitations provision under the FPA insofar as the elimination of their positions were discrete employment actions of which they were aware and the reduction of their salaries was a known consequence of their changing jobs.

Once employees present prima facie cases, employers can seek to rebut them by providing legitimate non-discriminatory reasons for acting. In such a case, the Eighth Circuit affirmed that a school board in Iowa did not violate the ADEA in refusing to hire a forty-seven year-old teacher as a counselor, instead transferring her to a lower paying job.[294] The court

---

286. 29 U.S.C.A. § 623(a). Portions of this statute are in the Appendix.

287. 29 U.S.C.A. § 623(f).

288. *Widoe v. District No. 111 Otoe County School*, 147 F.3d 726 [127 Educ. L. Rep. 576] (8th Cir.1998); *Gavigan v. Clarkstown Cent. School Dist.*, 84 F. Supp.2d 540 [142 Educ. L. Rep. 179] (S.D.N.Y. 2000) (both finding that employees presented prima facie cases).

289. 42 U.S.C.A. § 2000e–5. For cases applying this statutory requirement, *see, e.g.*, *Bedden–Hurley v. New York City Bd. of Educ.*, 385 F. Supp.2d 274 [202 Educ. L. Rep. 656] (S.D.N.Y. 2005); *Williams v. East Orange Community Charter School*, 396 Fed.Appx. 895 [263 Educ. L. Rep. 515] (3d Cir.2010).

290. 557 U.S. 167, 129 S.Ct. 2343, 174 L.Ed.2d 119 (2009), *on remand*, 588 F.3d 614 (8th Cir.2009).

291. 550 U.S. 618, 127 S.Ct. 2162, 167 L.Ed.2d 982 (2007).

292. 29 U.S.C. § 626.

293. *Almond v. Unified School Dist.*, 749 F. Supp. 2d 1196 [265 Educ. L. Rep. 568] (D. Kan. 2010).

294. *Tusing v. Des Moines Indep. Community School Dist.*, 639 F.3d 507 [267 Educ. L. Rep. 65] (8th Cir.2011).

agreed that the board did not discriminate based on age since the teacher was not licensed as a school counselor.

Along the same line, in the first of two cases from New York, a federal trial court rejected the ADEA claim of a sixty-year-old school bus diver who had been dismissed.[295] The court pointed to the fact that board officials presented evidence garnered from interviews with students and their parents that they had concerns about the plaintiff's excessive speed when behind the wheel of the bus, reckless driving, and inappropriate interaction with children. Since officials articulated the legitimate non-discriminatory reason that a younger female teacher performed better on her interviews than a fifty-year-old male when both sought an administrative position in the district, a federal trial court in New York granted its motion for summary judgment in his case which claimed that they violated his rights under both the ADEA and Title VII.[296]

In a case reaching the opposite outcome, when a principal made derogatory statements about her role as a chaperone on an overseas trip, a seventy-year-old teacher with thirty-four years of experience who served as head foreign languages teacher on a one-year renewable contract challenged the abolition of her position so that the money spent on her salary could be used for other purposes. An appellate court in Massachusetts denied the school committee's motion for summary judgment.[297] The court thought that where genuine issue of material fact remained as to whether the principal's assessment of the teacher's performance, which also caused her to file a defamation action, was false and not a good faith review such that a discriminatory animus could have been inferred, the matter should have proceeded to trial. In another case involving an older teacher, the Seventh Circuit partially reversed in favor of a sixty-nine-year-old full-time substitute who was demoted to a job as a roving substitute.[298] The court held that an issue of fact existed as to whether the board's proffered reason for displacing the teacher, namely a decline in the enrollment in the high school program in which she taught combined with her being the least senior person in it, was a pretext for age discrimination.

As evidenced by a case from New York, if two employees are over the age of forty, as where a fifty-three-year-old coach was passed over in favor of a forty-three-year-old, individuals cannot claim the protection of the ADEA.[299] A federal trial court held that even though the coach presented a prima facie case, he failed to prove that the board's actions were a pretext for age discrimination.

295. *Stein v. Churchville–Chili Cent. School Dist.*, 760 F.Supp.2d 308 [266 Educ. L. Rep. 824] (W.D.N.Y. 2011).

296. *Brierly v. Deer Park Union Free School Dist.*, 359 F. Supp.2d 275 [196 Educ. L. Rep. 534] (E.D.N.Y. 2005).

297. *Dragonas v. School Comm. of Melrose*, 833 N.E.2d 679 [201 Educ. L. Rep. 296] (Mass. App. Ct. 2005), *review denied*, 836 N.E.2d 1096 (Mass. 2005).

298. *Filar v. Board of Educ. of the City of Chicago*, 526 F.3d 1054 [232 Educ. L. Rep. 613] (7th Cir.2008).

299. *Ranieri v. Highland Falls–Ft. Montomery School Dist.*, 198 F. Supp.2d 542 [165 Educ. L. Rep. 98] (S.D.N.Y. 2002).

In the first of a pair of non-school cases, the Supreme Court ruled that the ADEA authorizes aggrieved employees to sue under a "disparate-impact" theory of liability, which does not require them to prove that their employers engaged in intentional discrimination if they can show that they were adversely affected by the actions of the employers due to age. In *Smith v. City of Jackson, Mississippi*,[300] when city officials granted proportionately larger pay raises to younger police officers, older ones claimed that doing so violated the ADEA. On further review of dismissals in favor of the city, the Court decided that although the ADEA permits recoveries based on disparate impact, the officers could not have recovered since the city based its action on the statute's "reasonable factors other than age"[301] provision. On a different issue involving the ADEA and disparate impact, in *Meacham v. Knolls Atomic Power Laboratory*, the Justices decided that employers who are defending against age-related claims bear the burden of proof both as to production of evidence and persuasion in showing that their actions were based on "reasonable factors other than age."[302] The upshot is that, as discussed in the next paragraph, school boards that offer early retirements and/or shift personnel may have to be concerned with whether their actions have a disparate impact on employees who are protected by the ADEA.

Another controversial area involving the ADEA concerns benefits and early retirement incentive plans where age is a factor. The Supreme Court, in *General Dynamics Land System v. Cline*,[303] upheld a collective bargaining agreement's eliminating health care benefits for retired employees except for those who were fifty or older. In rejecting an ADEA claim by employees who were between the ages of forty and fifty, the Court reasoned that the ADEA did not stop employers from favoring older employees over younger workers. Other courts have invalidated plans that tied the amount of benefits to years of age.[304] Even so, the Eighth Circuit affirmed that a school system in Iowa violated the ADEA when it enacted a retirement-incentive plan which excluded employees who were over the age of sixty-five.[305] The court determined that a denial of benefits solely on age was inconsistent with the ADEA's purpose of prohibiting arbitrary age discrimination. Also, the federal trial court in Minnesota invalidated a board's early retirement plan since it provided early retirees lump sum payments that varied according to their ages.[306]

A procedural dispute involving the ADEA arose in New York. A federal trial court rejected a school board's motion to dismiss a retired teacher's

---

300.   544 U.S. 228, 125 S.Ct. 1536, 161 L.Ed.2d 410 (2005).

301.   29 U.S.C.A. § 623(f)(1).

302.   554 U.S. 84, 128 S.Ct. 2395, 171 L.Ed.2d 283 (2008).

303.   540 U.S. 581, 124 S.Ct. 1236, 157 L.Ed.2d 1094 (2004).

304.   *See Abrahamson v. Board of Educ. of Wappingers Falls Cent. School Dist.*, 374 F.3d 66 [189 Educ. L. Rep. 503] (2d Cir.2004); *Auerbach v. Board of Educ. of the Harborfields Cent. School Dist. of Greenlawn*, 136 F.3d 104 [123 Educ. L. Rep. 1142] (2d Cir.1998).

305.   *Jankovitz v. Des Moines Indep. Community School Dist.*, 421 F.3d 649 [201 Educ. L. Rep. 428] (8th Cir.2005).

306.   *Overlie v. Owatonna Indep. School Dist.*, 341 F. Supp.2d 1081 [193 Educ. L. Rep. 483] (D. Minn. 2004).

claim as untimely.[307] The court declared that the limitations period on the teacher's charge of age discrimination due to a change in benefits retriggered each time she received a payment of her health benefits cost under her retirement plan.

In *Kentucky Retirement Systems v. Equal Employment Opportunity Commission*,[308] a case that segues into the next section, the Supreme Court found that a retirement system did not violate the ADEA in differentiating between employees who sought benefits after completing the requisite number of years for eligibility rather than due to their disabilities. The Court was satisfied that allowing lesser benefits for those who retired due to disabilities did not violate the ADEA. The Justices explained that this approach was acceptable since it was designed to treat employees with disabilities as if they became disabled after, rather than before, they gained eligibility for regular retirement benefits. The Court wrote that any differential treatment was due to pension eligibility where age could have been taken into account since the regular retirement rules permissibly considered age in such a manner that it treated employees with disabilities as if they worked until when they were eligible for regular pensions.

Disability

As discussed in Chapter 15, federal law provides extensive protection for students with disabilities. Section 504, which covers both students and school employees as well as others who may be in schools such as parents and visitors, applies to those who have, had, or are believed to have had impairments that substantially limit major life activities.[309] Of course, school boards must be aware that employees or applicants had impairments before plaintiffs can proceed with legal actions against them in employment disputes.[310]

Individuals who are otherwise qualified, meaning that they are qualified despite their impairments, cannot be denied the benefits of, or participation in, programs receiving federal financial assistance as long as they can do so by means of reasonable accommodations.[311] Title I of the ADA prohibits discrimination by private sector employers with fifteen or more employees.[312] Title II of the Act applies to public accommodations, in

---

307. *O'Grady v. Middle Country School Dist. No. 11*, 556 F. Supp.2d 196 [234 Educ. L. Rep. 690] (E.D.N.Y. 2008).

308. 554 U.S. 135, 128 S.Ct. 2361, 171 L.Ed.2d 322 (2008).

309. 34 C.F.R. § 104.3(j)(2)(i) ("Major life activities means functions such as caring for one's self, performing manual tasks, walking, seeing, hearing, speaking, breathing, learning, and working.").

310. *See, e.g., Isaksson–Wilder v. New York State Div. of Human Rights*, 841 N.Y.S.2d 658 [223 Educ. L. Rep. 942] (N.Y. App. Div. 2007) (affirming that a school board was not liable for discrimination in refusing to hire a job applicant with a mental disability since those who did the hiring were unaware of her condition).

311. 34 C.F.R. § 104.12.

312. Congress enacted the ADA Amendments Act of 2008, 42 U.S.C.A. §§ 12102(1), (3)(A) explicitly abrogating the Supreme Court's holdings in *Sutton v. United Air Lines*, 527 U.S. 471, 119 S.Ct. 2139, 144 L.Ed.2d 450 (1999) (ruling that individuals whose physical or mental impairment are corrected through medication or other measures do not have impairments presently limiting major life activities) and *Toyota Motor Mfg., Ky. v. Williams*, 534 U.S. 184,

language mirroring that of Section 504, requiring reasonable accommodations for otherwise qualified individuals with the result that it is being used extensively in cases alleging employment discrimination just as disputes involving students are now more commonly filed under Section 504.[313]

When otherwise qualified employees allege discrimination based on disabilities, employers must make reasonable accommodations unless doing so would cause undue hardships. In response to requests for accommodations, then, employers can claim one of three defenses to avoid compliance: if making accommodations would result in "a fundamental alteration in the nature of [a] program;"[314] if they impose "undue financial burden[s];"[315] or if having individuals present creates a substantial risk of injury to themselves or others.[316]

In *School Board of Nassau County, Florida v. Arline (Arline),*[317] the Supreme Court first applied Section 504 in a K–12 setting when it affirmed that school officials violated a teacher's rights by discharging her due to recurrences of tuberculosis. In declaring that the teacher was otherwise qualified for the job, the Court enunciated a four-part test for use in cases involving contagious diseases; these elements consider the nature of the risk, its duration, its severity, and the probabilities that the disease will be transmitted and cause varying degrees of harm. On remand, a federal trial court in Florida agreed that insofar as the teacher was otherwise qualified, she was entitled to reinstatement and back pay,[318] typical remedies in such litigation.

---

122 S.Ct. 681, 151 L.Ed.2d 615 (2002) (interpreting the term "substantially limits" as meaning that impairments must prevent or severely restrict individuals from engaging in activities that are of central importance to most people's daily lives, emphasizing that the impact of impairments must be permanent or long-term in order to provide protection under the ADA). The amended Act broadens the definition of disability, making it easier for individuals to prove that they were victims of workplace discrimination, especially those who suffered from epilepsy, diabetes, cancer, multiple sclerosis and other ailments who were improperly denied protection insofar as their conditions could be controlled by medications or other measures. The Act specifically grants an exception so that employers may consider the mitigating effects of ordinary eyeglasses or contact lenses in evaluating whether visual impairments substantially limit major life activities. The Act also modifies Section 504 so that the definitions of disability and major life activities in both laws are identical.

In a case interpreting these provisions, the Sixth Circuit affirmed the denial of the claim of a former administrator alleging that she was reassigned to a teaching position because her board refused to regard her as having an impairment. The court refused to apply the amendment, which removed the requirement that claimants prove their being regarded as having an impairment applied only if a major life activity was at issue, could not be applied retroactively. *Milholland v. Sumner County Bd. of Educ.,* 569 F.3d 562 [246 Educ. L. Rep. 43] (6th Cir.2009).

313. *See, e.g., Temple v. Board of Educ. of City of N.Y.,* 322 F. Supp.2d 277 [189 Educ. L. Rep. 681] (E.D.N.Y. 2004) (rejecting a teacher's ADA claim that systemic lupus erythematosus was a physical impairment that substantially limited a major life function).

314. *Southeastern Community College v. Davis,* 442 U.S. 397, 410, 99 S.Ct. 2361, 60 L.Ed.2d 980 (1979) [Case No. 109]; *Alexander v. Choate,* 469 U.S. 287, 105 S.Ct. 712, 83 L.Ed.2d 661 (1985).

315. *Davis, id.* at 412.

316. *See School Bd. of Nassau County, Fla. v. Arline,* 480 U.S. 273, 287–88, 107 S.Ct. 1123, 94 L.Ed.2d 307 [37 Educ. L. Rep. 448] (1987). [Case No. 55]

317. *Id.*

318. *Arline v. School Bd. of Nassau County,* 692 F.Supp. 1286 [49 Educ. L. Rep. 195] (M.D. Fla. 1988).

In the first of a trilogy of cases from New York, a federal trial court rejected the ADA and Section 504 claims of a former cafeteria worker who alleged that her dismissal for giving food away to the child of a friend was a pretext for disability discrimination.[319] The court pointed out that insofar as the plaintiff had performed her job satisfactorily despite her learning disability, her claim lacked merit. A second federal trial court reached a similar outcome when a custodian who suffered from narcolepsy and sleep apnea claimed that his board violated the ADA in dismissing him from his job.[320] The court agreed that the board could terminate the custodian's employment because rather than refer to his illness, officials articulated a legitimate non-discriminatory reason in light of his misconduct and poor performance in fifteen of nineteen areas in which he was evaluated. In the third case, a federal trial court dismissed the claim of a guidance counselor who suffered from the learning disability, dyslexia, and dysgraphia, which affected her ability to write.[321] The court noted that insofar as the counselor resigned rather than allow herself to be denied tenure, her claim that school officials violated her rights under the ADA when they informed a possible employer about her writing ability did not qualify as retaliation under the law.

The federal trial court in New Hampshire denied the claims of a teacher with attention deficit-hyperactivity disorder, whose contract was not renewed, when he sought to be permitted to better control students by permitting them to listen to music and play games for up to half of class periods.[322] In rejecting the teacher's requested accommodations, the court agreed with the board that doing so would have proved that the plaintiff failed to perform the essential function of teaching students.[323]

On the other hand, the First Circuit permitted the claims of teachers in Puerto Rico who sought reduced class sizes as accommodations to their disabilities to proceed.[324] Reversing the denial of the claims, the court explained that insofar as the teachers received this accommodation in four of the past five years, they presented valid claims under the ADA and Section 504. Other courts allowed suits to proceed or entered judgments in favor of employees in disputes where an otherwise qualified employee needed rest periods during the day and a transfer to a school closer to home;[325] a room change due to rheumatoid arthritis;[326] a teacher needed

---

319. *Stephan v. West Irondequoit Cent. School Dist.*, 769 F. Supp. 2d 104 [268 Educ. L. Rep. 146] (W.D.N.Y. 2011).

320. *Sanzo v. Uniondale Union Free School Dist.*, 381 F. Supp.2d 113 [201 Educ. L. Rep. 503] (E.D.N.Y. 2005).

321. *Hanig v. Yorktown Cent. School Dist.*, 384 F. Supp.2d 710 [202 Educ. L. Rep. 156] (S.D.N.Y. 2005).

322. *Hess v. Rochester School Dist.*, 396 F. Supp.2d 65 [204 Educ. L. Rep. 518] (D.N.H. 2005).

323. For other cases agreeing that putting in a full day is an essential job requirement for teachers, *see Kurek v. North Allegheny School Dist.*, 233 Fed.Appx. 154 [223 Educ. L. Rep. 188] (3d Cir.2007); *Nunn v. Illinois State Bd. of Educ.*, 211 Fed.Appx. 502 [218 Educ. L. Rep. 144] (7th Cir.2006); *Ramirez v. New York City Bd. of Educ.*, 481 F. Supp.2d 209 [219 Educ. L. Rep. 632] (E.D.N.Y. 2007).

324. *Sepúlveda–Villarini v. Department of Educ. of Puerto Rico*, 628 F.3d 25 [263 Educ. L. Rep. 484] (1st Cir.2010).

325. *Young v. Central Square Cent. School Dist.*, 213 F. Supp.2d 202 [168 Educ. L. Rep. 264] (N.D.N.Y. 2002).

326. *Ross v. Board of Educ. of Prince George's County*, 195 F. Supp.2d 730 [164 Educ. L. Rep. 240] (D. Md. 2002).

the use of an accessible bathroom and keys to locked emergency doors due to her degenerative arthritis;[327] an injured groundskeeper challenged a board's refusal for reinstatement;[328] a teacher had paralyzed vocal cords;[329] and a teacher who was seriously hearing-impaired sought a full-time classroom aide to help him to preserve classroom discipline.[330]

Courts reached mixed results with regard to employees who suffered from cancer as the federal trial court in New Mexico permitted the claim of a former school administrator with breast cancer to proceed[331] while one in Missouri disagreed in refusing to treat it as a disabling impairment.[332] An appellate court in New York, relying in part on state law, affirmed that a teacher who had cancer surgery was not discriminated against on the basis of disability, or gender, since her condition had not limited a major life function.[333]

In an emerging medical issue, courts are split on carpal tunnel syndrome. The Ninth Circuit reversed in favor of a janitor in Nevada who alleged that a board violated his rights by not offering him the reasonable accommodation of making him a school safety officer before terminating his employment.[334] Conversely, a federal trial court in Connecticut rejected the claim of a part-time employee that a board refused to hire to a full-time job in light of her charge that officials discriminated against her due to her disability since it did not think that carpal tunnel syndrome substantially limited her major life activity of working.

Courts denied relief in a variety of cases including where teachers, staff members, and/or job applicants were alcoholics;[335] deaf;[336] had diabetes and noncancerous polyps;[337] had multiple sclerosis;[338] were schizophrenic;[339]

327. *Gordon v. District of Columbia*, 480 F. Supp.2d 112 [219 Educ. L. Rep. 493] (D.D.C. 2007).

328. *Johnson v. Paradise Valley Unified School Dist.*, 251 F.3d 1222 [154 Educ. L. Rep. 461] (9th Cir.2001).

329. *Chavez v. Waterford School Dist.*, 720 F. Supp.2d 845 [261 Educ. L. Rep. 636] (E.D. Mich. 2010), *reconsideration denied*, 2010 WL 3180388 (E.D. Mich. 2010).

330. *Henry v. Unified School Dist.*, 328 F. Supp.2d 1130 [191 Educ. L. Rep. 289] (D. Kan. 2004).

331. *Keller v. Board of Educ. of City of Albuquerque*, 182 F. Supp.2d 1148 [161 Educ. L. Rep. 507] (D.N.M. 2001) (also relying on the ADA).

332. *Treiber v. Lindbergh School Dist.*, 199 F. Supp.2d 949 [165 Educ. L. Rep. 136] (E.D. Mo. 2002).

333. *Sirota v. New York City Bd. of Educ.*, 725 N.Y.S.2d 332 [154 Educ. L. Rep. 263] (N.Y. App. Div. 2001).

334. *Wellington v. Lyon County School Dist.*, 187 F.3d 1150 [137 Educ. L. Rep. 890] (9th Cir.1999).

335. *Larkin v. Methacton School Dist.*, 773 F.Supp.2d 508 [269 Educ. L. Rep. 129] (E.D. Pa. 2011), *order issued*, 2011 WL 666277 (E.D. Pa. 2011).

336. *Adeyemi v. District of Columbia*, 525 F.3d 1222 [232 Educ. L. Rep. 570] (D.C. Cir.2008), *cert. denied*, ___ U.S. ___, 129 S.Ct. 606, 172 L.Ed.2d 464 (2008).

337. *Williams v. Brunswick County Bd. of Educ.*, 725 F. Supp.2d 538 [261 Educ. L. Rep. 980] (E.D.N.C. 2010), *aff'd*, 440 Fed.Appx. 169 (4th Cir.2011).

338. *Shepherd v. Chambers*, 794 N.W.2d 678 [264 Educ. L. Rep. 854] (Neb. 2011); *Nyrop v. Independent School Dist. No. 11*, 616 F.3d 728 [260 Educ. L. Rep. 57] (8th Cir.2010).

339. *Boyer v. KRS Computer and Business School*, 171 F. Supp.2d 950 [159 Educ. L. Rep. 117] (D. Minn.2001) (also rejecting a claim of alcoholism since the employee was sober for sixteen years).

sought to perform only light duties;[340] refused to undergo psychological testing despite being disruptive at school;[341] suffered from a disabling kidney disorder;[342] had cervical and spine injuries;[343] suffered arm and back pains along with chronic headaches;[344] had epilepsy and congenital fusion of two vertebrae;[345] experienced physical and psychological harms as a result of being attacked physically before starting work with a school board;[346] threatened to kill a group of students even though she claimed that her speaking out was the result of a documented head injury;[347] had an unspecified learning disability;[348] and suffered from osteoarthritis,[349] typically agreeing that requested accommodations were not reasonable, that conditions did not limit major life activities, or that individuals were not otherwise qualified.[350]

In the first case directly implicating the rights of a school employee with AIDS/HIV, a teacher challenged his school board's refusal to reinstate him to his job due to his illness. On further review of the denial of his request for an injunction, the Ninth Circuit reversed in favor of the teacher.[351] The court indicated that officials violated the teacher's rights under Section 504 absent adequate medical evidence that he would have passed the disease on to his students or coworkers and that the public fear of AIDS was an insufficient ground on which to deny his request to permit him to return to his job. In another case, the federal trial court in Puerto

---

340. *Hinson v. U.S.D. No. 500,* 187 F. Supp.2d 1297 [162 Educ. L. Rep. 801] (D. Kan.2002). *But see Butterfield v. Sidney Pub. Schools,* 32 P.3d 1243 [157 Educ. L. Rep. 929] (Mont.2001) (relying on Section 504's regulations and state law in deciding that a board acted improperly in refusing to reinstate a custodian with a back injury).

341. *Sullivan v. River Valley School Dist.,* 197 F.3d 804 [140 Educ. L. Rep. 127] (6th Cir.1999), *cert. denied,* 530 U.S. 1262, 120 S.Ct. 2718, 147 L.Ed.2d 983 (2000).

342. *Gammage v. West Jasper School Bd. of Educ.,* 179 F.3d 952 [136 Educ. L. Rep. 131] (5th Cir.1999).

343. *Francis v. Providence School Bd.,* 198 Fed.Appx. 18 [215 Educ. L. Rep. 40] (1st Cir.2006).

344. *Reifer v. Colonial Intermediate Unit 20,* 462 F. Supp.2d 621 [215 Educ. L. Rep. 713] (M.D. Pa. 2006).

345. *Chappell v. Butterfield–Odin School Dist.,* 673 F.Supp.2d 818 [253 Educ. L. Rep. 693] (D. Minn. 2009).

346. *Curcio v. Bridgeport Bd. of Educ.,* 477 F. Supp.2d 515 [218 Educ. L. Rep. 422] (D. Conn. 2007).

347. *Macy v. Hopkins County School Bd. of Educ.,* 484 F.3d 357 [219 Educ. L. Rep. 382] (6th Cir.2007), *cert. denied,* 552 U.S. 826, 128 S.Ct. 201, 169 L.Ed.2d 37 (2007).

348. *Falso v. Churchville–Chili Cent. School Dist.,* 547 F. Supp.2d 233 [233 Educ. L. Rep. 103] (W.D.N.Y. 2008), *aff'd,* 328 Fed.Appx. 55 (2d Cir.2009).

349. *Filar v. Board of Educ. of the City of Chicago,* 526 F.3d 1054 [232 Educ. L. Rep. 613] (7th Cir.2008) (also denying the board's motion for summary judgment on the teacher's ADEA claim).

350. *Falchenberg v. New York City Dep't of Educ.,* 375 F. Supp.2d 344 [199 Educ. L. Rep. 813] (S.D.N.Y. 2005), *appeal dismissed* (2009) (rejecting a teacher's ADA claim when she refused to take a certification test after officials failed to accommodate her dyslexia since her choosing not to do so meant that she was not otherwise qualified for a job).

351. *Chalk v. United States Dist. Ct. Cent. Dist. of Cal.,* 840 F.2d 701 [45 Educ. L. Rep. 58] (9th Cir.1988).

Rico dismissed the claim of a teacher with HIV who filed suit under the ADA alleging that his contract was not renewed due to his condition.[352] The court was convinced that officials relied on legitimate nondiscriminatory grounds that the teacher was frequently late for work and was unable to control students.

Family and Medical Leave Act

The Family and Medical Leave Act (FMLA) protects employees who may have to choose between job security and personal, and family, health concerns. Under the FMLA, school boards, as public agencies that employ fifty or more employees for each working day during each of twenty or more calendar workweeks in a current or preceding calendar year, must provide unpaid leave to eligible staff members for medical or child care purposes during set twelve-month periods.[353] In order to be covered by the FMLA, school employees, including part-time staff, must have worked for at least twelve months, providing at least 1,250 hours of service during the year immediately preceding the start of their leaves.[354]

Subject to any greater protections that they may have under other federal or state laws or collective bargaining agreements, school employees are entitled to twelve weeks of unpaid leave during any twelve-month period as provided for in the employer's FMLA policy.[355] If school board policies permit paid leave for fewer than twelve weeks, the remainder of leave may be without pay. School employees who have accrued paid vacation, personal, or family leave days may choose to or boards may require them to substitute these days for unpaid leave.[356] If leave plans do not allow for substitutions, then they are not permitted.[357] In creating one-year policies, boards may use the calendar year, any twelve-month leave period such as the fiscal year, a twelve-month span measured forward from the first FMLA leave date, or a rolling twelve-month period backward from the first FMLA leave date.[358]

Under the FMLA, school employees can request leaves under two broad categories. The first, child care, covers the birth, adoption, or foster care assumption of a child within twelve months of the event.[359] The second, a "serious health condition," covers the illness of a spouse, child, or parent, or one rendering an employee unable to perform job functions.[360] Educators who request leave must provide school officials with thirty-days

---

352. *Velez Cajigas v. Order of St. Benedict*, 115 F. Supp.2d 246 [147 Educ. L. Rep. 928] (D. Puerto Rico 2000).

353. 29 U.S.C.A. §§ 2611(4)(A)(I), (B).

354. 29 U.S.C.A. § 2611(2)(A).

355. 29 U.S.C.A. § 2612(a). *See Lyons v. North East Indep. School Dist.*, 277 Fed.Appx. 455 [235 Educ. L. Rep. 93] (5th Cir.2008) (affirming that a school board did not violate this provision in recalculating an employee's eligibility at the start of a new FMLA year).

356. 29 U.S.C.A. §§ 2612(d)(1), (2).

357. 29 C.F.R. § 825.207(b)(c).

358. 29 C.F.R. § 825.200(b).

359. 29 U.S.C.A. §§ 2612(a)(1)(A), (B).

360. 29 U.S.C.A. § 2611(11).

notice or as much as is practicable.[361] Staff members who seek leave for foreseeable treatments due to serious medical conditions must make reasonable efforts to schedule them so as not to cause undue disruptions to the operations of their employers.[362] School boards can waive this requirement.

As part of the certification that school boards may request from health care providers before granting leaves, staff members should include the date when the condition began, its likely duration, and a statement of inability to perform job functions as designated in a description given to the health care provider.[363] If dealing with care for a family member, this certification should include an estimate of how long it will take to provide care.[364] If school board officials doubt the validity of certifications, they may require staff members, at their own expense, to obtain second opinions.[365] If the two opinions conflict, boards may, at their expense, have employees submit to the opinion of a third health care provider that is mutually acceptable to both parties; this third evaluation binds both parties.[366]

The FMLA includes special rules for school personnel who work primarily in instructional capacities. Under these provisions, if teachers request intermittent or reduced schedule leaves for foreseeable medical care and would be absent for more than twenty percent of the total working days during leave periods, school systems have two options. Boards can either require teachers to take leaves for periods not to exceed the length of their planned treatments or may temporarily transfer them to other jobs with equivalent pay and benefits.[367]

Special rules also apply to leaves taken near the end of school terms. First, if teachers wish to begin leaves more than five weeks prior to the end of terms, boards may require them to wait until the end of the terms if the leaves are at least three weeks long and they would return to work during the three weeks before the end of the terms. Second, if teachers request leaves less than five weeks before the end of terms, boards may require them to wait until the end of the terms if their requested leaves are more than two weeks long and their returns would be during the two weeks prior to the end of the terms. Third, if requested leaves are less than three weeks before the end of terms and greater than five working days, boards may require teachers to take leaves that last until the end of the terms.[368]

The key protection available under the FMLA is that school employees who are returning from leaves must be restored to their same or equivalent positions with equivalent pay and benefits.[369] Under this provision, school employees are not entitled to additional seniority, employment benefits, or

---

361.   29 U.S.C.A. § 2612(e)(1).

362.   29 U.S.C.A. § 2612(e)(2).

363.   29 U.S.C.A. §§ 2613(b)(1–3).

364.   29 U.S.C.A. § 2613(b)(4)(A).

365.   29 U.S.C.A. § 2613(c).

366.   29 U.S.C.A. § 2613(d).

367.   29 U.S.C.A. § 2618(c).

368.   29 U.S.C.A. § 2618(d).

369.   For a case involving a teacher-coach's return to work, *see Gary Community School Corp. v. Powell*, 906 N.E.2d 823 [244 Educ. L. Rep. 763] (Ind. 2009) (ruling that a board had to return the plaintiff, a full-time teacher in the district, to his part-time coaching position when

any other rights, benefits, or positions that they would not have been entitled to but for taking leave.[370] If school board officials have good faith reasons to eliminate the jobs of individuals who are on leave, and do not act out of retaliation, then, subject to proving that they acted with proper motives, the positions can be terminated.[371]

Along with protecting school employees from being fired for asserting their rights,[372] the FMLA requires boards to make, keep, and preserve records demonstrating their compliance.[373] As part of this process, the Department of Labor has the right to conduct annual reviews of the FMLA records of school boards and may examine them more frequently if necessary to investigate alleged violations.[374] School boards that violate the FMLA may not only have to reinstate or promote employees but may also be liable for up to twelve weeks of wages, benefits, and reasonable attorney fees.[375]

In cases dealing with substantive issues, the Tenth Circuit affirmed that a former school employee's back injury was not a health condition entitled to coverage under the FMLA[376] while the Eleventh Circuit affirmed that officials did not improperly deny an employee's request for maternity leave since she was ineligible to ask for it.[377] Further, the Fifth Circuit affirmed that when a school board adjusted an employee's job description while she was on maternity leave, it did not violate the FMLA since the changes were minimal and intangible.[378] However, the Seventh Circuit affirmed that a former bookkeeper could sue members of her board and various officials in their individual capacities in a dispute where she claimed that she was a victim of retaliation because she took intermittent leave.[379] The court agreed that the suit could proceed since the bookkeeper offered direct evidence of the board's discriminatory motivation by establishing that she was treated less favorably than others who chose not to take FMLA leave after she returned to work even though she performed her job satisfactorily. Later, the Sixth Circuit decided that a reduction in a teacher's coaching stipend when he was out on medical leave did not violate the FMLA since the money was not part of his regular salary.[380] Also, the

---

he returned from FMLA medical leave since the 1,250 hour requirement applied to his overall service in the system, not just his coaching duties).

370.   29 U.S.C.A. § 2614(a)(3).

371.   29 U.S.C.A. § 2614(a)(3)(B).

372.   29 U.S.C.A. § 2615(b).

373.   29 U.S.C.A. § 2616.

374.   29 U.S.C.A. § 2616.

375.   29 U.S.C.A. § 2617.

376.   *Jones v. Denver Pub. Schools*, 427 F.3d 1315 [203 Educ. L. Rep. 76] (10th Cir.2005) (affirming the lack of coverage for a former employee's condition).

377.   *Walker v. Elmore County Bd. of Educ.*, 379 F.3d 1249 [191 Educ. L. Rep. 124] (11th Cir.2004) (affirming a grant of summary judgment in favor of a school board where a teacher claimed that officials denied her maternity leave under the FMLA).

378.   *Smith v. East Baton Rouge Parish School Bd.*, 453 F.3d 650 [210 Educ. L. Rep. 913] (5th Cir.2006).

379.   *Lewis v. School Dist. #70*, 523 F.3d 730 [231 Educ. L. Rep. 631] (7th Cir.2008).

380.   *Harris v. Metropolitan Gov't of Nashville and Davidson County*, 594 F.3d 476 [253 Educ. L. Rep. 538] (6th Cir.2010), *reh'g and reh'g en banc denied* (2010).

Supreme Court of Indiana affirmed that although a part-time coaching job failed to satisfy the FMLA's statutory minimum of more than 1,250 hours per year, since the total of hours applied to the plaintiff's overall service to the board, including his full-time teaching position, he was entitled to reinstatement to his coaching position on returning from a medical leave.[381]

As to procedural matters, the federal trial court in Oregon judged that the denial of a former administrator's claim under the ADA did not preclude a filing under the FMLA[382] while the Sixth Circuit affirmed that the Eleventh Amendment barred a public employee from suing her board.[383] In a case from Illinois, a federal trial court interpreted the separate definition of an employer in the FMLA that applied when litigation occurred at the local level as prohibiting suits against school officials in their individual capacities.[384]

PREFERENCES FOR VETERANS

Courts generally uphold reasonable laws designed to benefit veterans in light of the overriding public interest in rewarding those who sacrificed to defend the nation. Title VII also exempts such laws from scrutiny.

The Supreme Court rejected a challenge to preferences for veterans in public employment in *Personnel Administrator of Massachusetts v. Feeney* (*Feeney*).[385] The Court upheld a statute giving a lifetime preference in public employment to qualified veterans even though doing so resulted in preventing a disproportionate number of qualified women from attaining civil service positions. The court "noted that most states, as well as the federal government, give some sort of hiring preference to veterans."[386] Since courts are reluctant to offer such an absolute hiring preference or to extend the case's reach in situations involving classifications based on gender,[387] *Feeney's* precedential value is limited.

In a case limiting the reach of a preference law, an appellate court in Pennsylvania found that a statute did not cover a veteran who challenged an examination given by a school board.[388] According to the court, the law applied only to examinations administered by the Civil Service Commission. Earlier, another appellate court in Pennsylvania affirmed that the statute

381. *Gary Community School Corp. v. Powell*, 906 N.E.2d 823 [244 Educ. L. Rep. 763] (Ind. 2009).

382. *Bourgo v. Canby School Dist.*, 167 F. Supp. 2d 1173 [158 Educ. L. Rep. 314] (D. Or. 2001).

383. *Touvell v. Ohio Dept. of Mental Retardation and Development Disabilities*, 422 F.3d 392 (6th Cir.2005), *cert. denied*, 546 U.S. 1173, 126 S.Ct. 1339, 164 L.Ed.2d 54 (2006) (affirming that a former employee of a state agency could not sue under the FMLA alleging that officials interfered with her entitlement to leave for self-care).

384. *Lombardi v. Board of Trustees Hinsdale School Dist. 86*, 463 F. Supp.2d 867 [215 Educ. L. Rep. 836] (N.D. Ill. 2006).

385. 442 U.S. 256, 99 S.Ct. 2282, 60 L.Ed.2d 870 (1979), *on remand*, 475 F.Supp. 109 (D. Mass. 1979), *aff'd*, 445 U.S. 901, 100 S.Ct. 1075, 63 L.Ed.2d 317 (1980).

386. *Player v. Village of Bensenville*, 722 N.E.2d 792, 795 (Ill. App. Ct. 1999).

387. *White v. McGill*, 585 N.E.2d 945 [72 Educ. L. Rep. 346] (Ohio Ct. App. 1990).

388. *Zablow v. Board of Educ. of School Dist. of Pittsburgh*, 729 A.2d 124 [134 Educ. L. Rep. 526] (Pa. Cmwlth. Ct. 1999).

applied only to appointments, not promotions.[389] In a later case, an appellate court in Kansas affirmed that insofar as the state statute affording hiring preferences to veterans applied only to public agencies, it was inapplicable to not-for-profit employers.[390]

TEACHER CONTRACTS

IN GENERAL

Employment agreements between school boards and their teachers must conform to all general rules for contracts[391] except as they may be modified by state laws.[392] As with certificated employees who must be classified in a manner consistent with state law, contracts cannot supersede statutory requirements.[393]

Insofar as state laws grant school boards the authority to employ staff, they alone must exercise that function and may not delegate hiring to anyone,[394] including superintendents.[395] Of course, superintendents or individual board members may interview and recommend teachers, but boards retain the final hiring authority.[396] Additionally, where state law requires boards to obtain recommendations from superintendents before hiring teachers, they must do so.[397]

---

389. *Belle Vernon Area School Dist. v. Teamsters Local Union No. 782, Int'l Brothers of Teamsters*, 670 A.2d 1201 [106 Educ. L. Rep. 1203] (Pa. Cmwlth. Ct. 1996).

390. *Little v. State*, 121 P.3d 990 [202 Educ. L. Rep. 858] (Kan. Ct. App. 2005).

391. *Wright v. Mead School Dist. No. 354*, 944 P.2d 1 [121 Educ. L. Rep. 312] (Wash. Ct. App. 1997), *review denied*, 954 P.2d 277 (Wash.1998); *Wells v. Board of Trustees of Laramie County School Dist. No. 1*, 3 P.3d 861 [145 Educ. L. Rep. 785] (Wyo. 2000).

392. *Drain v. Board of Educ. of Frontier County School Dist. No. 46*, 508 N.W.2d 255 [87 Educ. L. Rep. 612] (Neb. 1993).

393. *Motevalli v. Los Angeles Unified School Dist.*, 18 Cal.Rptr.3d 562 [191 Educ. L. Rep. 838] (Cal. Ct. App. 2004), *review denied* (2004) (affirming the nonrenewal of the contract of a teacher with emergency certification who refused to cooperate with random weapons searches of students).

394. *McAndrew v. School Comm. of Cambridge*, 480 N.E.2d 327 [26 Educ. L. Rep. 404] (Mass. Ct. App. 1985).

395. *Fremont Re-1 School Dist. v. Jacobs*, 737 P.2d 816, 818–819 [40 Educ. L. Rep. 465] (Colo. 1987) (a school board "may delegate to subordinate officers and boards powers and functions which are ministerial or administrative in nature, where there is a fixed and certain standard or rule which leaves little or nothing to the judgment or discretion of the subordinate. However, legislative or judicial powers, involving judgment and discretion on the part of the municipal body, which have been vested by statute in a municipal corporation may not be delegated unless such has been expressly authorized by the legislature.").

396. *Fortney v. School Dist. of West Salem*, 321 N.W.2d 225 [4 Educ. L. Rep. 1281] (Wis.1982); *Crawford v. Board of Educ., Barberton City Schools*, 453 N.E.2d 627 [13 Educ. L. Rep. 475] (Ohio 1983); *Miotto v. Yonkers Pub. Schools*, 534 F. Supp.2d 422 [229 Educ. L. Rep. 660] (S.D.N.Y. 2008).

397. *Tripp v. Martin*, 79 S.E.2d 521 (Ga.1954); *Katterhenrich v. Federal Hocking Local School Dist. Bd. of Educ.*, 700 N.E.2d 626 [129 Educ. L. Rep. 776] (Ohio Ct. App. 1997) (affirming that a board's non-compliance with such a provision was harmless where the candidate was unqualified); *McCalister v. School Bd. of Bay County*, 971 So.2d 1020 [228 Educ. L. Rep. 994] (Fla. Dist. Ct. App. 2008).

Since employee contracts are governed by state laws,[398] staff members are bound to comply with statutory provisions because they are deemed incorporated into their contracts.[399] Perhaps the most common requirement for school contracts is that they must be in writing.[400] The rule of incorporation applies to local board policies, covered in the next section, and collective bargaining agreements[401] which can modify board policies.[402] Insofar as most statutory contract rights cover typical duties, regular employment provisions are inapplicable to extracurricular activities.[403]

As with other contracts, if school boards lack the authority to enter into agreements, they may not ordinarily ratify such agreements. Even if boards merely fail to comply with formalities in forming contracts, such as reducing them to writing, and state laws do not prohibit them from doing so, boards cannot use their own failure to follow the law to the disadvantage of teachers.[404]

Questions arise as to the relationships between the common law of contracts and statutes designed to protect employees against arbitrary and/or capricious board actions. Generally, statutes do not operate when employees act voluntarily, by intent or gross neglect, to remove themselves from coverage. In such a case, where a teacher failed to return his contract in a timely manner, an appellate court in Washington affirmed that it would not remedy his failure to do so.[405]

In a related matter, courts generally agree that contracts terminated by mutual agreement, as in voluntary resignations, are generally not covered by statutory procedures.[406] In these cases, when employees resign, since they are offering to dissolve existing contracts,[407] boards must accept

---

398. *Gere v. Council Bluffs Community School Dist.*, 334 N.W.2d 307 [11 Educ. L. Rep. 629] (Iowa 1983).

399. *School Comm. of Town of N. Kingstown v. Crouch*, 808 A.2d 1074 [171 Educ. L. Rep. 258] (R.I. 2002); *Zattiero v. Homedale School Dist. No. 370*, 51 P.3d 382 [167 Educ. L. Rep. 946] (Idaho 2002); *Hallissey v. School Admin. Dist. No. 77*, 755 A.2d 1068 [146 Educ. L. Rep. 293] (Me. 2000).

400. *See, e.g., Board of Educ. of Perry County v. Jones*, 823 S.W.2d 457 [72 Educ. L. Rep. 1190] (Ky. 1992). *But see Kirschling v. Lake Forest School Dist.*, 687 F.Supp. 927 [47 Educ. L. Rep. 977] (D. Del.1988) (upholding an oral agreement based on state law).

401. *Oregon School Employees Ass'n, Chapter 89 v. Rainier School Dist. No. 13*, 808 P.2d 83 [66 Educ. L. Rep. 1270] (Or.1991); *LaSorsa by LaSorsa v. UNUM Life Ins. Co. of Am.*, 955 F.2d 140 [72 Educ. L. Rep. 756] (1st Cir.1992); *Hunting v. Clark County School Dist. No. 161*, 931 P.2d 628 [116 Educ. L. Rep. 422] (Idaho 1997).

402. *Gilmore v. Bonner County School Dist. No. 82*, 971 P.2d 323 [132 Educ. L. Rep. 197] (Idaho 1999).

403. *State ex rel. Savarese v. Buckeye Local School Dist. Bd. of Educ.*, 660 N.E.2d 463 [106 Educ. L. Rep. 871] (Ohio 1996); *Cruse v. Clear Creek I.S.D.*, 976 F.Supp. 1068 [121 Educ. L. Rep. 972] (S.D. Tex. 1997).

404. *Flaherty v. Independent School Dist. No. 2144, Chisago Lakes Schools*, 577 N.W.2d 229 [125 Educ. L. Rep. 878] (Minn. Ct. App. 1998).

405. *Corcoran v. Lyle School Dist. No. 406, Klickitat County*, 581 P.2d 185 (Wash. Ct. App. 1978).

406. *Brinson v. School Dist. No. 431*, 576 P.2d 602 (Kan.1978); *Brown v. Board of Educ. of Morgan County School Dist.*, 560 P.2d 1129 (Utah 1977); *Upshaw v. Alvin Indep. School Dist.*, 31 F. Supp.2d 553 [132 Educ. L. Rep. 96] (S.D. Tex. 1999).

407. *Shade v. Board of Trustees of Redondo Union High School Dist. in Los Angeles County*, 70 P.2d 490 (Cal. Ct. App.1937).

their offers. As in other contractual situations, offers to resign can be withdrawn before being accepted[408] but ordinarily not after boards act.[409] If resignations are tendered orally when statutes require them to be in writing, they cannot be binding even if purportedly accepted by formal board resolutions. In a case that could also fit in the section on the nonrenewal of contracts, the Supreme Court of Arkansas held that remedies under the state's Teacher Fair Dismissal Act were inapplicable to an oral resignation.[410] The court reasoned that where a board's acceptance of a resignation did not amount to a nonrenewal, suspension, or other disciplinary action within the meaning of the statute, it was inapplicable.[411]

If submitted under coercion or duress such as where illegal pressures induced employees to behave in ways that they were unable to act freely, resignations may be invalid. If board officials merely suggest that employees should resign or threaten to pursue lawful courses of action, such as instituting dismissal proceedings, this does not constitute duress as long as employees have time and opportunities to deliberate before acting.[412]

Resignations may be transformed into constructive discharges if school officials deliberately make working conditions so intolerable that employees have no choice but to resign. Of course, employees bear the heavy burden of proving that officials intentionally engaged in specific and substantial deviations from normal operations that amounted to harassment. For example, the Eighth Circuit remarked that a teacher in South Dakota with years of satisfactory evaluations who was at the top of the pay scale was subjected to "an intense pattern of classroom observation, criticism, and evaluation"[413] that led to his constructive discharge due to his age. Conversely, where a teacher with a history of conflict with regard to the relationship that she and her son had with the board voluntarily resigned, a federal trial court in Texas stated that in doing so she waived her rights to due process in her claim for constructive discharge.[414] Other courts agreed that educators who resigned waived rights to recall in situations involving layoffs[415] and payments for unused sick leave.[416]

408. *Totevski v. Board of Educ. of Hempstead Pub. School Dist.*, 680 N.Y.S.2d 824 [131 Educ. L. Rep. 253] (N.Y. 1998).

409. *Schmitt v. Hicksville UFSD No. 17*, 606 N.Y.S.2d 761 [88 Educ. L. Rep. 1139] (N.Y. App. Div. 1994). *But see Pierce v. Douglas School Dist. No. 4*, 686 P.2d 332 [19 Educ. L. Rep. 716] (Or.1984) (recognizing that a board was not required to accept a teacher's resignation in order for it to become effective).

410. *Williams v. Little Rock School Dist.*, 66 S.W.3d 590 [162 Educ. L. Rep. 604] (Ark.2002).

411. On a different issue involving the same statute, an appellate court in Arkansas affirmed that its provisions were inapplicable to a substitute teacher because he did not occupy a position requiring a teaching license. *Harris v. Altheimer Unified School Dist.*, 227 S.W.3d 437 [222 Educ. L. Rep. 437] (Ark. Ct. App. 2006).

412. *Dusanek v. Hannon*, 677 F.2d 538, [4 Educ. L. Rep. 409] (7th Cir.1982), *cert. denied*, 459 U.S. 1017, 103 S.Ct. 379, 74 L.Ed.2d 512 (1982).

413. *Lee v. Rapid City Area School Dist. No. 51–4*, 981 F.2d 316, 328 [79 Educ. L. Rep. 748] (8th Cir.1992).

414. *Upshaw v. Alvin Indep. School Dist.*, 31 F. Supp.2d 553 [132 Educ. L. Rep. 96] (S.D. Tex. 1999).

415. *Tomiak v. Hamtramck School Dist.*, 397 N.W.2d 770 [36 Educ. L. Rep. 897] (Mich. 1986).

416. *Turnbough v. Mammoth Spring School Dist. No. 2*, 78 S.W.3d 89 [167 Educ. L. Rep. 492] (Ark. 2002). *But see Schwartz v. Gary Community School Corp.*, 762 N.E.2d 192 [161

Where school board officials agree to conditions in resignations, they may not then disavow what were, in effect, contractual agreements. As such, when a chief school administrator offered to resign in return for six months of salary, the Supreme Court of South Carolina ruled that a board could not then refuse to pay the money.[417]

The extent to which school boards may contract for payments to employees who agree to resign is unclear. Payments might be subject to challenges as illegal gifts in return for payments for services not rendered. On the other hand, payments could be described as settlements to avoid costly litigation.[418] In an illustrative case, the Eighth Circuit affirmed that a mother in Texas could not sue a school board in Nebraska for entering into a confidential settlement agreement with the teacher who molested her son and provided him with a positive letter of recommendation rather than terminate his contract.[419] The court rejected the notion that the behavior of board officials rose to the level of deliberate indifference so as to warrant liability under section 1983 when the teacher sexually molested the child in Texas.

In an egregious case that reached a different outcome, the Supreme Court of California was of the opinion that boards can be liable for providing good recommendations to undeserving employees.[420] When officials learned that an administrator allegedly sexually molested a student, they gave him a favorable letter of recommendation in exchange for his resignation. The administrator relied on the letter to obtain a job in another school system where he allegedly engaged in sexual misconduct with the student whose claim was at issue. The court reinstated the student's claim against the board that gave the administrator the good letter of recommendation.

As reflected by a case from Ohio, not all settlement provisions are upheld when disputed due to public policy. An appellate court voided a settlement agreement executed in connection with a resignation where a school board agreed not to disclose information about a teacher's pedophilia.[421]

BOARD POLICIES INCLUDED

School boards have implied, if not express, authority to adopt reasonable policies for employees. As long as local policies neither violate state or

---

Educ. L. Rep. 631] (Ind. Ct. App.2002) (declaring that a school board that incorrectly treated a school psychologist's letter as a resignation owed him pay for accumulated sick leave).

417. *Cain v. Noel*, 235 S.E.2d 292 (S.C.1977).

418. *Ingram v. Boone*, 458 N.Y.S.2d 671 [8 Educ. L. Rep. 1076] (N.Y. App. Div.1983).

419. *Shrum ex rel. Kelly v. Kluck*, 249 F.3d 773 [153 Educ. L. Rep. 600] (8th Cir.2001).

420. *But see Randi W. v. Muroc Joint Unified School Dist.*, 60 Cal.Rptr.2d 263 [115 Educ. L. Rep. 502] (Cal. 1997).

421. *Bowman v. Parma Bd. of Educ.*, 542 N.E.2d 663 [55 Educ. L. Rep. 707] (Ohio Ct. App. 1988).

federal law, especially when dealing with personnel evaluations,[422] they are incorporated, explicitly or by reference, into employment contracts and are upheld as long as they are reasonable. When teachers are not made aware of rules or policies by reference in their contracts or other means, boards may be unable to discipline them for violations absent proof that individuals knew of or should have known of them through due diligence.[423] In one such case, the Seventh Circuit affirmed the dismissal of a tenured teacher in Wisconsin who admitted that he knowingly violated board policy by using a school computer to search the Internet to access pornography.[424]

The Supreme Court has made it clear that while individuals lack a right to work for the state on their own terms, they do have a right not to be excluded or treated differently pursuant to provisions that are arbitrary or discriminatory.[425] Put another way, although no one has a right to public employment, individuals do have the right not to be excluded or treated differently for unconstitutional reasons. In such a case, the Supreme Court of Nebraska maintained that a teacher with twenty years of experience who took time off from work due to the illness, and eventual death of her mother, had not violated a board policy. The court concluded that insofar as the board's action "... was arbitrary and capricious at best, and reprehensible at worst,"[426] the teacher was entitled to reinstatement with back pay.

Problems may develop when school boards seek to bind teachers to regulations that they adopted after individuals were hired. Two older cases addressed disputes of this kind. The Supreme Court of California rejected a teacher's claim that a policy requiring staff to take graduate course work or have their pay reduced was inapplicable to her contract.[427] The court observed that board rules, which were in effect when the teacher's contract was renewed, were part of her agreement. The Supreme Court of Indiana, rejecting a teacher's request for a leave of absence to campaign for public office, asserted that if staff could be bound only by regulations that existed when their contracts were formed, conditions in districts would have to remain static for at least a year.[428] Other courts reached similar results.[429]

Along the same line, in *Harrah Independent School District v. Martin*,[430] the Supreme Court upheld the dismissal of a tenured teacher who refused to comply with a board's continuing education requirement which

---

422. *Baker v. Board of Educ., County of Hancock*, 534 S.E.2d 378 [147 Educ. L. Rep. 376] (W. Va. 2000).

423. *Miller v. South Bend Special School Dist. No. 1, McHenry County*, 124 N.W.2d 475 (N.D. 1963).

424. *Zellner v. Herrick*, 639 F.3d 371 [267 Educ. L. Rep. 55] (7th Cir.2011).

425. *Wieman v. Updegraff*, 344 U.S. 183, 73 S.Ct. 215, 97 L.Ed. 216 (1952); *Perry v. Sindermann*, 408 U.S. 593, 92 S.Ct. 2694, 33 L.Ed.2d 570 (1972).

426. *Drain v. Board of Educ. of Frontier County School Dist. No. 46*, 508 N.W.2d 255, 261 [87 Educ. L. Rep. 612] (Neb. 1993).

427. *Rible v. Hughes*, 150 P.2d 455 (Cal.1944).

428. *School City of East Chicago v. Sigler*, 36 N.E.2d 760 (Ind. 1941).

429. *See, e.g., Chatham v. Johnson*, 195 So.2d 62 (Miss.1967); *Wisconsin State Employees Ass'n v. Wisconsin Natural Resources Bd.*, 298 F.Supp. 339 (W.D. Wis. 1969).

430. 440 U.S. 194, 99 S.Ct. 1062, 59 L.Ed.2d 248 (1979). [Case No. 53]

expected staff with only bachelors' degrees to earn five semester hours of credit every three years. When the state legislature removed the penalty that teachers who did not comply with such policies could have their pay reduced, a board in Oklahoma afforded recalcitrant staff members the option of taking courses or facing dismissal. In upholding a teacher's dismissal, the Court commented that the policy was rationally related to the board's objective of enforcing the continuing education obligations of its staff.

As could have been expected, litigation occurs when educators seek to require school boards to make certain that their policies comply with state laws. In this regard, courts have addressed cases dealing with such issues as affording due process rights to all employees below the rank of superintendent[431] as well as entering judgments in favor of staff members where boards failed to comply with evaluation,[432] notice,[433] and due process[434] requirements. Courts also resolved cases in favor of boards such as where they agreed that officials did not have to provide a basketball coach with a formal evaluation of his performance before his coaching contract was not renewed;[435] a temporary teacher with statutory procedural rights;[436] or a superintendent with due process in terminating his contract.[437]

DUTIES COVERED BY IMPLICATION

Contracts vary greatly over the extent to which they specify teacher duties. Collective bargaining agreements tend to include more provisions than individual contracts but often fail to answer the difficult question of the implied duties. This section does not examine the myriad of cases surrounding the duty of teachers to provide adequate supervision of students since this topic is covered in Chapter 7.

In one of the first cases to consider the question, an appellate panel in New York affirmed, without its own rationale, a trial court's detailed analysis of the implied duties of teachers in relying substantially on a directive of the state commissioner of education.[438] In upholding rules which expected teachers to perform duties beyond classroom instruction,

---

431. *Small v. Board of Trustees, Glacier County School Dist. No. 9*, 31 P.3d 358 [156 Educ. L. Rep. 1434] (Mont.2001); *Cimochowski v. Hartford Pub. Schools*, 802 A.2d 800 [167 Educ. L. Rep. 799] (Conn. 2002).

432. *Bonilla v. Board of Educ. of City of N.Y.*, 728 N.Y.S.2d 69 [155 Educ. L. Rep. 1305] (N.Y. App. Div. 2001).

433. *Bentley v. School Dist. No. 025 of Custer County*, 586 N.W.2d 306 [130 Educ. L. Rep. 900] (Neb. 1998).

434. *Thomas v. Evangeline Parish School Bd.*, 733 So.2d 102 [135 Educ. L. Rep. 866] (La. Ct. App.1999), *writ denied*, 744 So.2d 626 (La. 1999).

435. *Board of Educ. of Erlanger–Elsmere School Dist. v. Code*, 57 S.W.3d 820 [158 Educ. L. Rep. 878] (Ky. 2001).

436. *Zalac v. Governing Bd. of Ferndale Unified School Dist.*, 120 Cal.Rptr.2d 615 [165 Educ. L. Rep. 277] (Cal. Ct. App. 2002).

437. *Milstead v. Jackson Parish School Bd.*, 726 So.2d 979 [133 Educ. L. Rep. 280] (La. Ct. App. 1998), *writ denied*, 742 So.2d 557 (La. 1999).

438. *Parrish v. Moss*, 106 N.Y.S.2d 577 (N.Y. Sup. Ct. 1951), *aff'd*, 107 N.Y.S.2d 580 (N.Y. App. Div. 1951).

the court wrote that school boards can only assign teachers to tasks related to their subject areas or those in their contracts such as supervising study halls or conducting student conferences. In clarifying that school officials could, for instance, assign English teachers to direct school plays, physical education teachers to coach intramural and interschool athletic teams, and band instructors to accompany students on band trips, they could not require mathematics teachers to coach athletic teams or compel teachers to perform janitorial duties or to drive school buses.[439] Consistent with collective bargaining agreements, and presaging arrangements that largely obviated, but did not totally eliminate, litigation over disputes in this regard, the court ascertained that boards could arrange for teachers to perform extra duties in return for more pay. As evidence of the impact of bargaining, the Supreme Court of New Hampshire acknowledged that a board committed an unfair labor practice in refusing to negotiate a salary scale for extracurricular positions since such compensation is a mandatory subject of negotiations.[440]

Disputes over co-curricular and extracurricular activities generated litigation, with mixed results, over the extent to which school boards can require educators to perform additional duties. The Supreme Court of Pennsylvania was of the view that a teacher could not be required to supervise a voluntary high school bowling club.[441] The court ruled that the teacher could not have been required to perform this duty since it was not sufficiently related to the school program. On the other hand, in a pre-bargaining case, an appellate court in Illinois affirmed that teachers could be required to supervise extracurricular activities in the evenings or on Saturdays at a rate of compensation lower than their regular salaries.[442] Another appellate court in Illinois has since affirmed that a teacher who was assigned an unreasonable number of extra duties could resign as volleyball coach while retaining her status as teacher along with other extracurricular activities.[443]

Having conceded that supervision of extracurricular activities was part of their duties, a trial court in New Jersey contended that the concerted resignations of teachers from these assignments constituted an illegal strike.[444] On further review, an appellate court noted that the question of whether the teachers had to perform the duties under their collective bargaining contract should have been referred to the state's Public Employment Relations Commission.[445] In the absence of bargaining, the Fifth

---

439. *See also McGrath v. Burkhard*, 280 P.2d 864 (Cal. Ct. App.1955) (rejecting the argument that extending implied duties to include such activities as attending athletic events required teachers to perform essentially police work).

440. *Appeal of Berlin Educ. Ass'n*, 485 A.2d 1038 [22 Educ. L. Rep. 192] (N.H. 1984).

441. *Pease v. Millcreek Twp. School Dist.*, 195 A.2d 104 (Pa. 1963).

442. *District 300 Educ. Ass'n v. Board of Educ. of Dundee Community Unit School Dist. No. 300*, 334 N.E.2d 165 (Ill. App. Ct. 1975).

443. *Lewis v. Board of Educ. of N. Clay Community Unit School Dist. No. 25*, 537 N.E.2d 435 [53 Educ. L. Rep. 596] (Ill. App. Ct. 1989).

444. *Board of Educ. of City of Asbury Park v. Asbury Park Educ. Ass'n*, 368 A.2d 396 (N.J. Super. Ct. Chanc. Div. 1976).

445. *Board of Educ. of City of Asbury Park v. Asbury Park Educ. Ass'n*, 382 A.2d 392 (N.J. Super. Ct. App. Div. 1977).

Circuit affirmed that a school board in Texas was justified in terminating the contract of a teacher for insubordination when he refused to collect tickets and to supervise students at high school football games.[446]

Another contentious topic is extra duty for special events such as open houses and parent-teacher conferences. An appellate court in Pennsylvania upheld the dismissal of a temporary teacher who refused to be present at an open house even though she knew that she was expected to attend.[447] The court thought that the teacher's unexplained refusal to take part in an event that was a significant part of the school program, since it brought parents to school to talk with teachers and to examine the work of their children, was a valid basis for her dismissal. West Virginia's highest court, in a case in which it did not consider whether a teacher's attendance at a parent-teacher conference was required or optional, indicated that even if it were optional, an educator had the duty to cooperate with school officials by informing them of reasons why she might not attend such an event.[448] The court was convinced that although a teacher could be disciplined for missing a parent-teacher conference, dismissal was too severe of a sanction. Yet, the Supreme Court of Colorado upheld a teacher's dismissal for a wide array of offenses, including missing parent-teacher conferences, on the ground of neglect of duty.[449]

Educators may also be expected to help in special circumstances. In an illustrative case, the Supreme Court of Iowa upheld the termination of a principal's contract when he refused to perform the duties of an attendance officer.[450] The court found that in interpreting "other duties" in state law and in the principal's contract, it could not be said that board officials exceeded their discretion in assigning him tasks ordinarily performed by attendance officers since "other duties" is not restricted to instructional activities.

NONRENEWAL OF TEACHER CONTRACTS

When contracts expire, they dissolve unless there are grounds on which renewals can be required such as if one party fails to perform a condition necessary for an agreement to be terminated properly. At the end of contract periods, since the parties are placed in essentially the same position that they were in before the agreements began, the nonrenewals of limited contracts can be distinguished from tenured or continuing contracts since they can be allowed to expire[451] for any lawful reason. Even so, state laws typically provide teachers whose contracts are about to be nonrenewed with notice. "The purpose underlying these notice provisions is to allow

---

446. *Blair v. Robstown Indep. School Dist.*, 556 F.2d 1331 (5th Cir.1977).

447. *Johnson v. United School Dist. Joint School Bd.*, 191 A.2d 897 (Pa. Super. Ct. 1963).

448. *Fox v. Board of Educ. of Doddridge County*, 236 S.E.2d 243 (W. Va. 1977).

449. *Board of Educ. of Jefferson County School Dist. R–1 v. Wilder*, 960 P.2d 695 [128 Educ. L. Rep. 378] (Colo. 1998).

450. *Gere v. Council Bluffs Community School Dist.*, 334 N.W.2d 307 [11 Educ. L. Rep. 629] (Iowa 1983).

451. *Vasquez v. Happy Valley Union School Dist.*, 72 Cal.Rptr.3d 15 [229 Educ. L. Rep. 159] (Cal. Ct. App. 2008).

teachers whose services are to be discontinued a period of time to seek other employment.''[452]

If teachers work under at-will employment contracts, school officials may dismiss them at any time.[453] When an at-will teacher engaged in criminal activity such as entering a guilty plea for driving a motor vehicle while under the influence of drugs or alcohol, the Supreme Court of Kentucky was unwilling to disturb the nonrenewal of her contract.[454]

Insofar as non-tenured teachers lack property interests in their jobs, they are not entitled to the same procedural protections as their tenured colleagues.[455] When dealing with tenure or continuing contracts, since employees have acquired substantive due process rights, they are entitled to procedural safeguards before they can be dismissed. Chapter 11 reviews the hearing requirements that are necessary in order to dismiss employees with tenure or continuing contracts.

The Supreme Court first examined the extent to which the Fourteenth Amendment's due process clause applied to the nonrenewal of the contracts of non-tenured educators in the context of companion cases from public institutions of higher education. Although these cases are set in higher education, they are important for educators in elementary and secondary schools because they help to set the parameters on the contractual rights of teachers and other staff members. *Board of Regents of State Colleges v. Roth (Roth)*[456] considered whether a non-tenured faculty member had a Fourteenth Amendment right to an explanation and a hearing when his contract was not renewed. In *Perry v. Sindermann (Perry)*,[457] the Court discussed the circumstances under which a public employee might gain the procedural rights of tenure absent an express statutory or contractual provision for such protection.

Roth was filed by a faculty member in Wisconsin who served under a one-year fixed contract. After the faculty member challenged the nonrenewal of his contract, the Supreme Court rejected his claim that he was entitled to a statement of reasons and a hearing in order to protect against having such decisions made based on improper motives. The Justices declared that the requirements of procedural due process apply only to deprivations of interests encompassed within the concepts of "liberty" and "property" in the Fourteenth Amendment since the "range of interests protected by procedural due process is not infinite."[458] The Court was satisfied that the nature of the interest at stake was the crucial factor as to whether it was constitutionally protected because, although the faculty member was not

452. *Vetter v. Board of Educ.*, 900 N.Y.S.2d 235, 236 [256 Educ. L. Rep. 343] (N.Y. 2010).

453. *Cape v. Greenville County School Dist.*, 618 S.E.2d 881 [202 Educ. L. Rep. 370] (S.C. 2005), *reh'g denied* (S.C. 2005).

454. *Commonwealth v. Solly*, 253 S.W.3d 537 [233 Educ. L. Rep. 486] (Ky. 2008).

455. *See, e.g., Pennycuff v. Fentress County Bd. of Educ.*, 404 F.3d 447 [197 Educ. L. Rep. 29] (6th Cir.2005), *reh'g and reh'g en banc denied* (2005); *Halfhill v. Northeast School Corp.*, 472 F.3d 496 [215 Educ. L. Rep. 251] (7th Cir.2006).

456. 408 U.S. 564, 92 S.Ct. 2701, 33 L.Ed.2d 548 (1972). [Case No. 56]

457. 408 U.S. 593, 92 S.Ct. 2694, 33 L.Ed.2d 570 (1972). [Case No. 57]

458. *Board of Regents of State Colleges v. Roth*, 408 U.S. 564, 570, 92 S.Ct. 2701, 33 L.Ed.2d 548 (1972). [Case No. 56]

rehired and remained free to seek another job, he did not suffer a deprivation of his liberty interest.

In *Roth*, the Supreme Court maintained that the faculty member did not suffer a harm to his liberty interest, which is at issue when an individual's reputation is at stake since university officials neither seriously damaged his standing in his community by making a charge, such as dishonesty, nor did they impose a stigma on him that prevented him from obtaining other employment in his field, circumstances that would have established the right to a hearing. As to property interests, the Court concluded that insofar as they do not derive from the Constitution but, rather, are created and defined by independent sources such as state law, the specific terms of the faculty member's contract did not secure any interest in his being employed beyond the one-year term of his contract.

Perry was filed by a faculty member who taught at three different colleges in the state system of Texas for ten consecutive years. Having served under four one-year contracts at a junior college, he challenged the nonrenewal of his contract, without a written explanation or a hearing, after he criticized policies of the state board of regents. At issue was whether the faculty member had a protected property interest in his job. The Supreme Court addressed the concept of property interest for due process purposes by clarifying that it could derive not only from express legislative or contractual wording but also from existing rules or understandings, as a kind of unwritten common law in a given university that some faculty have the equivalent of tenure. However, the Court also recognized that a claim of de facto tenure, which could be examined only at a hearing, must be more than a mere subjective expectancy of re-employment. The Court determined that although the faculty member might not have had tenure, since any lack of a contractual right to be rehired was immaterial where his claim that his contract was not renewed was based on his exercising his constitutional right to freedom of speech, he was entitled to the protection of due process.

The Supreme Court delineated the concept of liberty interests in *Bishop v. Wood*[459] wherein a police officer in North Carolina who was dismissed without a hearing filed suit after he was informed of the reasons in a private meeting. Along with the common stigma claim, the officer charged that the reasons for his dismissal were false. The Court, in upholding the officer's dismissal, affirmed that he did not suffer from an actionable stigma since the reasons were not made public until he filed suit. In addition, the Court believed that the false allegations did not require a hearing because insofar as the officer received the reasons in private, his reputation was not affected by their truth or falsity. The Court reasoned that the Constitution could not be interpreted as requiring federal judicial review of the many daily personnel actions that public officials make and that insofar as state law had not conferred a property right on the officer, the rejection of his liberty interest claim meant that he was left without a federal remedy.

---

459. 426 U.S. 341, 96 S.Ct. 2074, 48 L.Ed.2d 684 (1976).

A year later, in *Codd v. Velger*,[460] a brief per curiam order directing the Second Circuit to reinstate the judgment of a federal trial court in New York, the Supreme Court held that officials did not stigmatize a former police officer by placing material in his personnel file that was related to an apparent suicide attempt and releasing the file, with his permission, to a prospective employer. The Court emphasized that insofar as the purpose of hearings on stigmatization claims is to afford employees opportunities to refute the charges and clear their names, if the truth of a charge is not at issue, there is no constitutional need for hearings. The Court specified that employees are entitled to hearings only if employers create and disseminate false and defamatory impressions about individuals whose employment is terminated and that any harm that might have taken place was not occasioned by the lack of a hearing.

Due Process Rights of Non–Tenured Teachers

As could have been anticipated, many disputes have arisen when non-tenured employees sought to establish that they had property or liberty interests in their jobs entitling them to due process hearings. While liberty and property interests can arise in the same case,[461] as highlighted in the following review of representative litigation, these allegations usually appear separately. The fact that states require school board officials to provide reasons for the nonrenewal of contracts does not in itself create a federal right.[462] State procedural rights are enforceable in state courts which are empowered to interpret the existence and extent of rights allegedly created by state laws.[463] As evidenced by an order of the Supreme Court of Arkansas, when school boards meet their statutory duties of notice, courts are reluctant to interfere on behalf of teachers.[464]

Property rights granted by states are shaped by the procedures provided in legislation or state constitutional interpretations in evaluating such rights. For example, the Supreme Court of New Jersey granted teachers whose contracts were not renewed the right to be informed of reasons, suggesting that although these can be communicated at informal hearings, it would not place restrictions on the ability of boards to act as they saw fit.[465] In like fashion, the Supreme Court of Texas ruled that where a state statute stipulated that if the annual contracts of teachers were not renewed, boards had to notify them of the reasons for doing so along with opportunities for hearings since under these circumstance educators had

---

460.   429 U.S. 624, 97 S.Ct. 882, 51 L.Ed.2d 92 (1977).

461.   *Perez v. Denver Pub. Schools*, 919 P.2d 960 [111 Educ. L. Rep. 537] (Colo. Ct. App.1996); *Sickon v. School Bd. of Alachua County, Fla.*, 719 So.2d 360 [130 Educ. L. Rep. 944] (Fla. Dist. Ct. App. 1998); *Townsend v. Vallas*, 256 F.3d 661 [155 Educ. L. Rep. 142] (7th Cir. 2001).

462.   *Ryan v. Aurora City Bd. of Educ.*, 540 F.2d 222 (6th Cir.1976), *cert. denied*, 429 U.S. 1041, 97 S.Ct. 741, 50 L.Ed.2d 753 (1977).

463.   *Sigmon v. Poe*, 564 F.2d 1093 (4th Cir.1977).

464.   *Russell v. Watson Chapel School Dist.*, 313 S.W.3d 1 [258 Educ. L. Rep. 421] (Ark. 2009). [Case No. 58]

465.   *Donaldson v. Board of Educ. of N. Wildwood*, 320 A.2d 857 (N.J.1974).

protected property interests.[466] Earlier, the same court overturned the nonrenewal of a teacher's contract since the board's proffered reason was not on a list of eighteen specified in its policies.[467] If state laws require officials to notify teachers in person[468] or by a specific statutorily set date[469] about the nonrenewal of their contracts or that boards must make such decisions in open, rather than executive, sessions,[470] then courts typically reinstate them to their positions.

When legislatures create state-wide tenure systems, local boards cannot change their dimensions, whether by collective bargaining or other means. Thus, de facto tenure is not possible.[471] Put another way, a property right such as tenure can be based only on an affirmative act of government[472] by an authorized body such as a school board.[473] School employees usually lack property rights in their jobs unless they have statutory entitlements to them[474] such as under tenure provisions or unless changes in duties amount to demotions giving rise to procedural due process rights to hearings.[475]

Courts rejected claims that employees lacking tenure had property rights in an array of cases. Representative cases included those where contracts expired and were simply not renewed;[476] the contract of a probationary teacher was not renewed because he had a physical confrontation with one of his middle school students[477] while another did so since a probationary teacher rendered unsatisfactory performance;[478] and a board

---

466. *Grounds v. Tolar Indep. School Dist.*, 856 S.W.2d 417 [84 Educ. L. Rep. 559] (Tex. 1993).

467. *Seifert v. Lingleville Indep. School Dist.*, 692 S.W.2d 461 [26 Educ. L. Rep. 512] (Tex. 1985).

468. *Hoschler v. Sacramento City Unified School Dist.*, 57 Cal.Rptr.3d 115 [218 Educ. L. Rep. 613] (Cal. Ct. App. 2007), *review denied* (2007).

469. *See, e.g., Bentley v. School Dist. No. 025 of Custer County, Nebraska*, 586 N.W.2d 306 [130 Educ. L. Rep. 900] (Neb.1998); *Peoples v. San Diego Unified School Dist.*, 41 Cal.Rptr.3d 383, [207 Educ. L. Rep. 725] (Cal. Ct. App. 2006); *Hoschler v. Sacramento City Unified School Dist.*, 57 Cal.Rptr.3d 115 [218 Educ. L. Rep. 613] (Cal. Ct. App. 2007), *review denied* (2007).

470. *Hanover School Dist. No. 28 v. Barbour*, 171 P.3d 223 [227 Educ. L. Rep. 274] (Colo. 2007). *See also California Teachers Ass'n v. Vallejo City Unified School Dist.*, 56 Cal.Rptr.3d 712 [217 Educ. L. Rep. 890] (Cal. Ct. App. 2007).

471. *Ryan v. Aurora City Bd. of Educ.*, 540 F.2d 222 (6th Cir.1976), *cert. denied*, 429 U.S. 1041, 97 S.Ct. 741, 50 L.Ed.2d 753 (1977); *Meyr v. Board of Educ. of Affton School Dist.*, 572 F.2d 1229 (8th Cir.1978).

472. *Confederation of Police v. City of Chicago*, 547 F.2d 375 (7th Cir.1977).

473. *Castro v. New York City Bd. of Educ.*, 777 F.Supp. 1113 [71 Educ. L. Rep. 465] (S.D.N.Y. 1990), *aff'd without written opinion*, 923 F.2d 844 (2d Cir.1990), *cert. denied*, 498 U.S. 1099, 111 S.Ct. 992, 112 L.Ed.2d 1076 (1991).

474. *Ulichny v. Merton Community School Dist.*, 249 F.3d 686 [153 Educ. L. Rep. 573] (7th Cir. 2001).

475. *Smith v. Ouachita Parish School Bd.*, 702 So.2d 727 [122 Educ. L. Rep. 1069] (La. Ct. App. 1997), *writ denied*, 706 So.2d 978 (La. 1998).

476. *Corns v. Russell County Va. School Bd.*, 52 F.3d 56 [99 Educ. L. Rep. 761] (4th Cir.1995); *State ex rel. McGinty v. Cleveland City School Dist. Bd. of Educ.*, 690 N.E.2d 1273 [123 Educ. L. Rep. 1270] (Ohio 1998).

477. *Kirby v. Yonkers School Dist.*, 767 F.Supp.2d 452 [267 Educ. L. Rep. 675] (S.D.N.Y. 2011).

478. *Murnane v. Department of Educ. of City of N.Y.*, 919 N.Y.S.2d 24 [265 Educ. L. Rep. 738] (N.Y. App. Div. 2011).

chose not to renew the contract of a guidance counselor who prayed with students.[479]

As to liberty interests, it is difficult for employees to establish that they suffered from stigmas unless board members and/or school officials made public statements or released derogatory information about their employment status.[480] The constitutional requirement is that employees whose contracts are not renewed must prove that they were seriously harmed, not merely that they were rejected and deemed to be of insufficient merit for re-employment in the district. Even where statements have gone beyond internal channels, if they describe perceived professional weakness or unsatisfactory performance in general, they usually do not rise to the constitutional level since, as reflected in the following review, most courts agreed that a liberty interest is not at issue absent specific and substantial charges.

Courts refused to find that school officials acted in ways that stigmatized employees or that they were entitled to name-clearing hearings in cases where teachers were denied tenure[481] or when a teacher was not provided with reasons for being denied tenure.[482] Other cases involved charges of using ineffective teaching methods;[483] being reassigned to another school in a district in connection with testing irregularities;[484] being temporarily suspended pending the completion of a criminal investigation;[485] having a contract not renewed for refusing to take a drug test;[486] being absent frequently;[487] and hitting a student.[488] The Eighth Circuit decided that a superintendent in Missouri whose contract was terminated after his district lost its accreditation was not entitled to a name-clearing hearing when members of a special administrative board alleged that cheating went on in the system during his watch.[489] The court held that the alleged comment about cheating was not a direct assault on the plaintiff's honesty that created a level of stigma implicating a liberty interest in his reputation warranting a name-clearing hearing under procedural due process since it only questioned his performance in effectively overseeing

---

479. *Grossman v. South Shore Pub. School Dist.*, 507 F.3d 1097 [227 Educ. L. Rep. 109] (7th Cir. 2007).

480. *Hayes v. Phoenix–Talent School Dist. No. 4*, 893 F.2d 235 [58 Educ. L. Rep. 45] (9th Cir.1990).

481. *Calvin v. Rupp*, 471 F.2d 1346 (8th Cir.1973); *Meyr v. Board of Educ. of Affton School Dist.*, 572 F.2d 1229 (8th Cir.1978).

482. *Cato v. Collins*, 539 F.2d 656 (8th Cir. 1976).

483. *LaBorde v. Franklin Parish School Bd.*, 510 F.2d 590 (5th Cir.1975); *Shirck v. Thomas*, 486 F.2d 691 (7th Cir. 1973).

484. *Thomas v. Smith*, 897 F.2d 154 [58 Educ. L. Rep. 1114] (5th Cir. 1989).

485. *Strasburger v. Board of Educ., Hardin County Community Unit School Dist. No. 1*, 143 F.3d 351 [126 Educ. L. Rep. 577] (7th Cir.1998), *cert. denied*, 525 U.S. 1069, 119 S.Ct. 800, 142 L.Ed.2d 661 [132 Educ. L. Rep. 283] (1999).

486. *Cox v. McCraley*, 993 F.Supp. 1452 [125 Educ. L. Rep. 456] (M.D. Fla. 1998).

487. *Cohen v. Litt*, 906 F.Supp. 957 [105 Educ. L. Rep. 515] (S.D.N.Y.1995) (also unsuccessfully alleging violations of a property interest).

488. *Burton v. Town of Littleton*, 426 F.3d 9 [202 Educ. L. Rep. 86] (1st Cir. 2005) (also rejecting the teacher's ADEA claim).

489. *Stodghill v. Wellston School Dist.*, 512 F.3d 472 [228 Educ. L. Rep. 696] (8th Cir. 2008).

school operations without suggesting that he condoned or was even aware of the cheating.

On the other hand, courts agreed that the existence of stigmas entitled employees to name-clearing hearings in disputes over having one's name placed on an "Ineligible/Inquiry List;" wilful neglect of duty;[490] and responsibility for rapid deterioration of a school.[491] Other cases addressed situations where officials accused a teacher of fabricating or causing sex crimes involving students;[492] there were unjustified allegations of child abuse;[493] comments on an evaluation were so harsh that they would probably have convinced other boards not to hire an individual;[494] and a teacher was named on a registry of child abusers even after being cleared of all allegations.[495]

A related concern is the effect of including a constitutionally protected right as a factor in not renewing the contract of a non-tenured teacher. The Supreme Court addressed such a so-called mixed-motives case in *Mt. Healthy City Board of Education v. Doyle (Mt. Healthy).*[496] A teacher in Ohio with a record of being difficult in school claimed that a board violated his rights by not renewing his contract because he called a radio talk show and criticized a memo from his principal dealing with a faculty dress code. The Court rejected the Sixth Circuit's position that inclusion of a protected activity as a substantial part of the basis for the nonrenewal of the teacher's contract entitled him to reinstatement with back pay. The Court pointed out that the Sixth Circuit would have placed the teacher in a better position as a result of the exercise of his purportedly constitutionally protected conduct than he would have occupied had he done nothing. According to the Court, this meant that if teachers show that protected conduct about school matters is a substantial or motivating factor when boards choose not to renew contracts, boards must be given the opportunities to demonstrate that they would have taken the same action in not re-employing individuals but for their protected conduct. On remand, the Sixth Circuit ascertained that the board would not have renewed the teacher's contract regardless of whether he placed the call to the radio station.[497]

---

490. *Huntley v. Community School Bd. of Brooklyn, N.Y. School Dist. No. 14,* 543 F.2d 979 (2d Cir.1976), *cert. denied,* 430 U.S. 929, 97 S.Ct. 1547, 51 L.Ed.2d 773 (1977).

491. *Staton v. Mayes,* 552 F.2d 908 (10th Cir.1977), *cert. denied,* 434 U.S. 907, 98 S.Ct. 309, 54 L.Ed.2d 195 (1977).

492. *Burke v. Chicago School Reform Bd. of Trustees,* 169 F. Supp.2d 843 [158 Educ. L. Rep. 631] (N.D. Ill. 2001).

493. *Winegar v. Des Moines Indep. Community School Dist.,* 20 F.3d 895 [90 Educ. L. Rep. 580] (8th Cir.1994), *cert. denied,* 513 U.S. 964, 115 S.Ct. 426, 130 L.Ed.2d 340 (1994).

494. *Donato v. Plainview–Old Bethpage Cent. School Dist.,* 96 F.3d 623 [112 Educ. L. Rep. 624] (2d Cir.1996), *cert. denied,* 519 U.S. 1150, 117 S.Ct. 1083, 137 L.Ed.2d 218 (1997), *on remand,* 985 F.Supp. 316 [123 Educ. L. Rep. 617] (E.D.N.Y.1997).

495. *Matter of Allegations of Sexual Abuse at East Park High School,* 714 A.2d 339 [128 Educ. L. Rep. 302] (N.J. Super. Ct. App. Div. 1998).

496. 429 U.S. 274, 97 S.Ct. 568, 50 L.Ed.2d 471 (1977). [Case No. 59]

497. *Doyle v. Mt. Healthy City School Dist. Bd. of Educ.,* 670 F.2d 59 [2 Educ. L. Rep. 973] (6th Cir. 1982).

Some courts, in non-education cases, have suggested that parts of *Mt. Healthy* were superseded legislatively[498] while others, in educational disputes, chose not to extend it[499] or distinguished it away.[500] The Supreme Court applied *Mt. Healthy* in non-education cases[501] and one dispute involving education, *Givhan v. Western Line Consolidated School District* (*Givhan*).[502] On remand in *Givhan*, the Fifth Circuit affirmed that insofar as one motivating factor behind a school board in Mississippi's choosing not to rehire a teacher was her exercise of protected speech in criticizing school officials, it violated her rights since it would not have terminated her contract but for her having spoken out.[503] Subsequently, the First Circuit affirmed that although one motivating factor behind a school board in Maine's nonrenewal of a teacher's contract was her exercise of protected free speech, it did not violate her rights.[504] Additionally, the Third Circuit decided that a board in Pennsylvania might have been able to defeat a teacher's claim of malicious prosecution if officials could have proven that they would have dismissed her even in the absence of her exercising protected speech.[505]

[CASE NO. 51]   CONTRACT WITH AN UNCERTIFICATED PRINCIPAL

STATE EX REL. THOMPSON v. EKBERG

Supreme Court of Oklahoma, 1980.
613 P.2d 466.

■ SIMMS, JUSTICE:

Plaintiff appeals from a defendants' judgment in a taxpayer's suit brought ... by electors in the Vian School District of Vian, Oklahoma, to recover damages against the Vian School Board (Board) members ... for the wrongful hiring of Moxom as principal of the Vian High School.

Moxom was hired to serve as principal for the 1974–75 school year at a salary of $11,200 per year. Moxom did not have a standard master's degree as required for his certification by 70 O.S.Supp.1972, § subsection 9. The Board hired Moxom only after a representative of the State Department of Education, Ben Chapman, advised the Board that the degree requirement would be waived. Moxom was then working toward his master's degree, and the Board had little time in which to hire a principal before the school

---

498. *See N.L.R.B. v. Fluor Daniel*, 161 F.3d 953 (6th Cir. 1998) (suggesting that the Civil Rights Act of 1991, 42 U.S.C.A. § 2000e–2(m), superseded aspects of *Mt. Healthy* in Title VII cases). *See also Rivera v. United States*, 924 F.2d 948 (9th Cir. 1991).

499. *Zugarek v. Southern Tioga School Dist.*, 214 F. Supp.2d 468 [168 Educ. L. Rep. 756] (M.D. Pa. 2002).

500. *Belanger v. Madera Unified School Dist.*, 963 F.2d 248 [75 Educ. L. Rep. 118] (9th Cir. 1992), *cert. denied*, 507 U.S. 919, 113 S.Ct. 1280, 122 L.Ed.2d 674 (1993).

501. *Waters v. Churchill*, 511 U.S. 661, 114 S.Ct. 1878, 128 L.Ed.2d 686 (1994).

502. 439 U.S. 410, 99 S.Ct. 693, 58 L.Ed.2d 619 (1979).

503. *On remand*, 592 F.2d 280 (5th Cir.1979), *appeal after remand*, 691 F.2d 766 [7 Educ. L. Rep. 242] (5th Cir. 1982).

504. *Wytrwal v. Saco School Bd.*, 70 F.3d 165 [104 Educ. L. Rep. 1023] (1st Cir. 1995).

505. *Merkle v. Upper Dublin School Dist.*, 211 F.3d 782 [144 Educ. L. Rep. 83] (3d Cir. 2000).

year began. Moxom then served as principal for the school year, acquiring his master's degree sometime thereafter.

Appellant (plaintiff below) claims that the purported waiver of the certification requirement was ineffective, and therefore the appellees are liable for double the amount of the salary for the wrongful act of hiring an uncertified principal.

The trial court found the purported "waiver" or "permission" effective and gave judgment for the defendants.

70 O. S. Supp.1972, § 3–104, in its applicable provision, reads:

The control of the State Department of Education and the supervision of the public school system of Oklahoma shall be vested in the State Board of Education and, subject to limitations otherwise provided by law, the State Board of Education shall: . . .

9. Have full and exclusive authority in all matters pertaining to standards of qualifications and the certification of persons for instructional, supervisory, and administrative positions and services in the public schools of the state, and shall formulate rules and regulations governing the issuance and revocation of certificates. . . .

. . . Provided, further, that the requirements for a certificate for county superintendent of schools, district superintendent of schools and principal, shall include not less than a standard master's degree. . . .

Defendants claim that the State Board of Education's grant of full and exclusive authority in matters pertaining to qualifications allows it to waive the specific requirement of a master's degree for a principal, and that, in fact, this waiver is given routinely by [it].

A plain reading of the statute shows a legislative intent that no person is to be certified to be a principal unless he or she holds a standard master's degree. This is a specific exception to the general words of grant of authority, and as a rule, general words in a statute are limited by subsequent more specific terms. To hold otherwise and allow the State Board of Education discretion to ignore the requirement, would make the requirement meaningless. This Court will not presume the legislature has done a vain and useless act. Further, statutes must be interpreted to render every word and sentence operative, rather than in a manner which would render a specific statutory provision nugatory.

Finally, the grant of authority to the State Board of Education is specifically subject to limitations otherwise provided by law. The requirement that a principal hold a standard master's degree is one such limitation.

We hold, therefore, that the State Board of Education has no authority to waive the requirement of a master's degree for a certificate for a principal, and such purported waiver is of no effect.

Plaintiffs base the liability of the defendants on 70 O.S.1971, § 5–15, providing a recovery of double the amount of money wrongfully paid, specifically including money paid on an unlawful school employment contract. This statute is penal in nature and must be strictly construed.

The policy of this statute was discussed in [a case]:

The statutes above quoted determine the public policy of this state, which is that boards of education may not knowingly hire and pay uncertified teachers or superintendents or other employees, and if such is done, the members of such board shall be jointly liable for the return of the amount of public money thus expended.

Liability under the statute is only imposed where the Board "knowingly" hires a principal without certification. Under the facts presented, the Board could not reasonably have known that the waiver given was ineffective to satisfy the certificate requirement. We hold today that the requirement of a master's degree for a principal cannot be waived. This holding stands as notice to all school boards that any such purported waiver is of no effect, and that any money expended under such purported waiver is an unlawful expenditure that will subject the parties involved to liability under 70 O.S.1971, § 5–125.

Judgment of the trial court affirmed.

NOTES

1. The court did not discuss whether Mr. Chapman was an agent of the state department who was authorized to make statements on its behalf. Was it reasonable for the board to believe that he was its agent?

2. Can an agent bind his principal to violate the law? Was it clear that the waiver violated the law?

[CASE NO. 52] PROCEDURAL DUE PROCESS AND TEACHER CERTIFICATION

BROWN v. SOUTH CAROLINA STATE BOARD OF EDUCATION

Supreme Court of South Carolina, 1990.
391 S.E.2d 866 [60 Educ. L. Rep. 1004].

■ GREGORY, CHIEF JUSTICE.

This appeal is from a circuit court order affirming respondent's (Board's) invalidation of appellant's teaching certificate. We reverse and remand.

Appellant took the National Teacher's Examination (NTE) for elementary school teachers which is administered by Educational Testing Service (ETS). On March 28, 1987, ETS reported to the State Department of Education (Department) that appellant had achieved a passing score. The Department then issued appellant a teaching certificate valid through June 1990.

With certificate in hand, appellant applied for a teaching position with the Dorchester County School District No. 4. The superintendent of schools who interviewed appellant noted that her NTE scores were at the 78th percentile nationally, well above the required score of 50 percent. Because of this and other qualifications, appellant was offered a position as a second grade teacher. She performed satisfactorily on the job.

On January 25, 1988, the Department received a report from ETS stating simply that appellant's March 28, 1987, NTE scores had been "canceled" and directing the Department to "delete them from your records." The Department then advised appellant that because her NTE scores had been canceled, her teaching certificate was no longer valid and she could qualify for certification only upon presentation of a valid passing NTE score. At appellant's request, a hearing was scheduled and the invalidation was suspended until that time.

A hearing was held before the Teacher Recruitment, Training, and Certification Committee of the Board. The only evidence produced at the hearing to support invalidation of appellant's teaching certificate was the notification from ETS that her NTE scores had been canceled. The Committee recommended appellant's teaching certificate be invalidated and the Board affirmed that decision. On appeal to the circuit court, the Board's decision was affirmed and this appeal followed.

Appellant contends the regulation under which her teaching certificate was invalidated is unconstitutional because it violates her right to procedural due process. Reg. 43–59 provides:

If any testing company invalidates a test score, the State Board of Education shall accept that determination and, if a teaching certificate has been issued based upon the invalid score, shall automatically invalidate that certificate effective the date of receipt of notification of the score invalidity by the Office of Teacher Education and Certification.

The fourteenth amendment Due Process Clause requires procedural due process be afforded an individual deprived of a property or liberty interest by the State. The right to hold specific employment and the right to follow a chosen profession free from unreasonable governmental interference come within the liberty and property interests protected by the Due Process Clause. The liberty interest at stake is the individual's freedom to practice his or her chosen profession; the property interest is the specific employment. When the State seeks to revoke or deny a professional license, these interests are implicated and procedural due process requirements must be met. The State must afford notice and the opportunity for a hearing appropriate to the nature of the case.

Where important decisions turn on questions of fact, due process requires an opportunity to confront and cross-examine adverse witnesses. Procedural due process often requires confrontation and cross-examination of one whose word deprives a person of his or her livelihood. Moreover, the evidence used to prove the State's case must be disclosed to the individual so that he or she has an opportunity to show it is untrue.

We hold Reg. 43–59 unconstitutional because it does not provide for notice and an opportunity to be heard when the State deprives a teacher of his or her teaching certificate. The fact that appellant was granted a hearing as a matter of favor in this case does not save the regulation from constitutional attack under the Due Process Clause. Further, the hearing appellant was granted did not comport with procedural due process since the Board did not disclose any evidence substantiating cancellation of the

NTE scores in order to allow appellant the opportunity to contest the allegations against her.

The Board contends appellant cannot complain she was deprived of due process because she failed to avail herself of ETS procedure to contest the cancellation of her scores. On the record before us, however, ETS procedure does not provide for any hearing whereby appellant could confront her accusers. The Board further contends it could not obtain information from ETS regarding cancellation of appellant's scores absent her consent which she refused to give. The record, however, reveals no attempt by the Board to obtain information regarding cancellation of appellant's test scores from ETS. . . .

REVERSED and REMANDED.

NOTES

1.   Was the regulation struck down because it was flawed or due to the way in which it was implemented?

2.   Why do you think that ETS was unwilling to supply the state board with the information it needed?

[CASE NO. 53]   PROFESSIONAL GROWTH REQUIREMENT FOR TEACHERS

HARRAH INDEPENDENT SCHOOL DISTRICT v. MARTIN

Supreme Court of the United States, 1979.
440 U.S. 194, 99 S.Ct. 1062, 59 L.Ed.2d 248.

■ PER CURIAM.

Respondent Martin was employed as a teacher by petitioner School District under a contract that incorporated by reference the School Board's rules and regulations. Because respondent was tenured, Oklahoma law required the School Board to renew her contract annually unless she was guilty of, among other things, "wilful neglect of duty." The same Oklahoma statute provided for hearing and appeal procedures in the event of nonrenewal. One of the regulations incorporated into respondent's contract required teachers holding only a bachelor's degree to earn five semester hours of college credit every three years. Under the terms of the regulation, noncompliance with the continuing-education requirement was sanctioned by withholding salary increases.

Respondent, hired in 1969, persistently refused to comply with the continuing-education requirement and consequently forfeited the increases in salary to which she would have otherwise been entitled during the 1972–1974 school years. After her contract had been renewed for the 1973–1974 school term, however, the Oklahoma Legislature enacted a law mandating certain salary raises for teachers regardless of the compliance with the continuing-education policy. The School Board, thus deprived of the sanction which it had previously employed to enforce the provision, notified respondent that her contract would not be renewed for the 1974–1975 school year unless she completed five semester hours by April 10, 1974.

Respondent nonetheless declined even to enroll in the necessary courses and, appearing before the Board in January 1974, indicated that she had no intention of complying with the requirement in her contract. Finding her persistent noncompliance with the continuing-education requirement "wilful neglect of duty," the Board voted at its April 1974 meeting not to renew her contract for the following school year ...

. . .

The School District has conceded at all times that respondent was a "tenured" teacher under Oklahoma law, and therefore could be dismissed only for specified reasons. She was accorded the usual elements of procedural due process. . . .

... [R]espondent's claim is simply that she, as a tenured teacher, cannot be discharged under the School Board's purely prospective rule establishing contract nonrenewal as the sanction for violations of the continuing-education requirement incorporated into her contract.

The School Board's rule is endowed with a presumption of legislative validity, and the burden is on respondent to show that there is no rational connection between the Board's action and its conceded interest in providing its students with competent, well-trained teachers. Respondent's claim that the Board acted arbitrarily in imposing a new penalty for noncompliance with the continuing-education requirement simply does not square with the facts. By making pay raises mandatory, the state legislature deprived the Board of the sanction that it had earlier used to enforce its teachers' contractual obligation to earn continuing-education credits. The Board thus turned to contract nonrenewal, but applied this sanction purely prospectively so that those who might have relied on its past practice would nonetheless have an opportunity to bring themselves into compliance with the terms of the contracts. . . .

The School District's concern with the educational qualifications of its teachers cannot under any reasoned analysis be described as impermissible, and respondent does not contend that the Board's continuing-education requirement bears no rational relationship to that legitimate governmental concern. Rather, respondent contests "the permissibility of the classification by which [she] and three other teachers were required to achieve [by April 1974] the number of continuing education credits that all other teachers were given three years to achieve."

The Board's objective in sanctioning violations of the continuing-education requirement was, obviously, to encourage future compliance with the requirement. Admittedly, imposition of a penalty for noncompliance placed respondent and three other teachers in a "class" different from those teachers who had complied with their contractual obligations in the past. But any sanction designed to enforce compliance with a valid rule, whatever its source, falls only on those who break the rule. Respondent and those in her "class" were the only teachers immediately affected by the Board's action because they were the only teachers who had previously broken their contractual obligation. . . .

That the Board was forced by the state legislature in 1974 to penalize noncompliance differently than it had in the past in no way alters the equal protection analysis of respondent's claim. Like all teachers employed in the School District, respondent was given three years to earn five continuing-education credits. Unlike most of her colleagues, however, respondent refused to comply with the requirement, thus forfeiting her right to routine pay raises. Had the legislature not mandated salary increases in 1974, the Board presumably would have penalized respondent's continued refusal to comply with the terms of her contract by denying her an increase in salary for yet another year. The Board, having been deprived by the legislature of the sanction previously employed to enforce the continuing-education requirement, merely substituted in its place another, albeit more onerous, sanction. The classification created by both sanctions, however, was between those who had acquired five continuing-education credits within the allotted time and those who had not.

At bottom, respondent's position is that she is willing to forgo routine pay raises, but she is not willing to comply with the continuing-education requirement or to give up her job. The constitutional permissibility of a sanction imposed to enforce a valid governmental rule, however, is not tested by the willingness of those governed by the rule to accept the consequences of noncompliance. The sanction of contract nonrenewal is quite rationally related to the Board's objective of enforcing the continuing education obligation of its teachers. Respondent was not, therefore, deprived of equal protection of the laws.

The petition for certiorari is granted, and the judgment of the Court of Appeals is

Reversed.

NOTES

1. Should the teacher have been given more time to meet the requirement that she flaunted? The Court noted that she declined even to enroll in courses and in January said she made it known that she had no intention of complying.

2. School boards can make reasonable in-service requirements conditions of employment. *See Last v. Board of Educ. of Community Unit School Dist. No. 321*, 185 N.E.2d 282 (Ill. App. Ct.1962). Professional associations also advocate increased preparation for teachers. What do you think about this?

[CASE NO. 54] DISCRIMINATORY INITIAL EMPLOYMENT PRACTICES

THOMAS v. WASHINGTON COUNTY SCHOOL BOARD

United States Court of Appeals, Fourth Circuit, 1990.
915 F.2d 922 [63 Educ. L. Rep. 76].

■ BUTZNER, SENIOR CIRCUIT JUDGE

Thomas appeals a judgment of the district court that dismissed her action against the Washington County School Board, alleging racial discrimination in violation of Title VII of the Civil Rights Act of 1964. In her complaint Thomas sought remedies for two alleged violations of the Act: first, a teaching position and monetary relief for the Board's denial of employment and, second, injunctive relief to restrain the Board from continuing its hiring practices. We affirm the district court's dismissal of the hiring claim, vacate the judgment with respect to the omission of injunctive relief, and remand for further proceedings.

I

Thomas is a black woman who was raised and educated in Washington County, Virginia. She graduated cum laude from Emory & Henry College and shortly thereafter was certified by the Commonwealth of Virginia to teach social studies in secondary schools. In 1982, while in her final year of college, she applied for a teaching position in Washington County. Although she kept her application current, the Board failed to notify her of job openings on three separate occasions over a two year period. Those jobs were filled by white teachers.

One position was filled by someone more qualified than Thomas and another position was filled by someone transferring from another school within the county. It does not appear that there was any discrimination against Thomas in those instances. A third position, however, was filled by Mary Sue Smith, one of two white applicants interviewed for the position. Smith also graduated from Emory & Henry College with excellent grades, although not cum laude. She was the wife of a Washington County school teacher. She heard of the opening through word-of-mouth and was hired after having only one interview—the norm was three. Thomas heard of the vacancies after the Board filled them. She filed a complaint with the EEOC alleging racial discrimination. The EEOC issued a right to sue letter and this action followed.

The Board's evidence disclosed that Thomas's application was over-looked because the cover sheet indicated she had not yet been certified to teach. There was information within Thomas's file to indicate that she was certified, but apparently the file was not opened.

The district court found that the Board's failure to consider Thomas for the vacancies was a mistake rather than an act of intentional discrimination. This was a factual finding and is subject to review under a clearly erroneous standard. The court's finding of mistake was based largely on credibility determinations and is supported by the evidence. Consequently, it is binding upon us.

II

The district court did not grant Thomas's request for an injunction to require the Board to change its discriminatory hiring procedure. Instead the court admonished the Board:

As a practical matter, however, the defendant should seriously consider plaintiff's application the next time a position in her field becomes vacant. The defendant was successful in this case primarily because it showed that it was ignorant of plaintiff's credentials and qualifications. Defendant now knows that plaintiff is a qualified teacher and cannot plead ignorance again. The defendant should remember that it is still subject to Title VII and act accordingly.

Although Thomas is presently teaching in nearby Tennessee, she is, as the district court recognized, a prospective applicant for a teaching position in Washington County. Consequently, she is entitled to hiring practices that conform to the requirements of Title VII.

The legal premise for Thomas's claim is sound. Congress enacted Title VII "to achieve equality of employment opportunities" through the removal of "artificial, arbitrary, and unnecessary barriers to employment when the barriers operate invidiously to discriminate on the basis of racial or other impermissible classification." *Griggs v. Duke Power Co.* held that a plaintiff need not prove intentional discrimination, for Title VII also proscribes "practices that are fair in form, but discriminatory in operation." "The necessary premise of the disparate impact approach is that some employment practices, adopted without a deliberately discriminatory motive, may in operation be functionally equivalent to intentional discrimination."

The factual basis of Thomas's claim is disclosed by evidence that establishes that the Board has erected barriers that invidiously discriminate on the basis of race. The Washington County school system was desegregated in 1963. At that time there were six black elementary teachers. There remained six black elementary teachers and no black high school teachers until 1981 when Dennis Hill, following an EEOC complaint, was hired as a physical education teacher and coach for one of the high schools. He remained the only black high school teacher in the county schools. Apart from Hill, no black teacher was hired from 1975 until 1988, after this action was filed. In 1988, the superintendent, having learned that an elderly black teacher was retiring, requested Hill to recruit another black teacher. Wittingly or unwittingly, the Board has limited black teachers over the years to a rather rigid quota.

Between 1981 and 1988, at least 46 relatives of school employees were hired, including Smith. Notices of teaching vacancies are generally not advertised; they are posted in each school in the Washington County school system. Several black applicants testified that they learned of vacancies only after they had been filled. These policies and practices amount to nepotism and word-of-mouth hiring, which, in the context of a predominantly white work force, serve to freeze the effects of past discrimination.

Courts generally agree that, whatever the benefits of nepotism and word-of-mouth hiring, those benefits are outweighed by the goal of providing everyone with equal opportunities for employment.... Nepotism and word-of-mouth hiring constitute badges of discrimination in the context of a predominantly white work force.

Nepotism is not per se violative of Title VII. Given an already integrated work force, nepotism might have no impact on the racial composition of that work force. In such cases, nepotism, word-of-mouth hiring, and similar practices might simply amount to "bad acts" which discriminate against all outsiders without having any disparate impact on racial or religious minorities. "Title VII is not a 'bad acts' statute" and does not proscribe that type of discrimination. However, when the work force is predominantly white, nepotism and similar practices which operate to exclude outsiders may discriminate against minorities as effectively as any intentionally discriminatory policy.

Thomas proved the existence of "artificial, arbitrary, and unnecessary barriers to employment [that] operate invidiously to discriminate on the basis of racial ... classifications." Two of the Board's practices bear a causal relationship to her unsuccessful efforts to secure employment. They are the Board's practice of nepotism and the general practice of posting notice of vacancies only in the schools. Thomas did not learn of the vacancies until after they were filled. She is therefore entitled to injunctive relief to remedy these unlawful practices.

The district court's admonition, while well intentioned, fell short of affording the relief Title VII contemplates.... "The trial judge in a Title VII case bears a special responsibility in the public interest to resolve the employment dispute, for once the judicial machinery has been set in train, the proceeding takes on a public character in which remedies are devised to vindicate the policies of the Act, not merely to afford private relief to the employee." ...

The district court quite properly found that Thomas did not offer sufficient statistical evidence to prove discrimination under the disparate impact theory by the means of statistics. The county's population is 98.2% white and 1.8% black. Black teachers constitute only .5% of the secondary schools' faculties. The Board's policy of generally limiting its pool of applicants to county residents, coupled with the lack of proof of the number of qualified applicants living in the county, other than Thomas, made the data base inadequate for statistical purposes. However, although disparate impact cases usually focus on statistics, they are neither the exclusive nor a necessary means of proof. The paucity of statistics is no bar to the prospective injunctive relief Thomas seeks, for Thomas has proved by other means that the Board's hiring practices have a disparate impact on minorities and violate Title VII. She produced evidence of at least 46 cases of nepotism, a stipulation from the Board which revealed a practice of posting vacancies in schools and offices with public notice only in exceptional circumstances, and testimony from other black applicants which indicated they were not being given an opportunity to compete for teaching jobs, largely because the Board's practices of nepotism and word-of-mouth hiring kept them unaware of job openings.

III

We affirm the district court's judgment insofar as it denies Thomas's claim that the Board intentionally discriminated against her when it failed to hire her.

Thomas has shown that as a prospective applicant she is entitled to injunctive relief to conform the Board's hiring policies to Title VII. We vacate the district court's judgment insofar as it dismisses her complaint and remand the case for further proceedings.

The district court is directed to fashion an injunction requiring the Board to publicly advertise vacancies and fill them by a selection process that is not influenced by race. The district court should also prohibit the Board from giving preference to relatives of employees. The court should prescribe any other conditions that it deems proper to achieve equality of employment opportunities without regard to race for all qualified applicants certified by the state. The court may limit the injunction to a reasonable number of years.

Each side, having substantially prevailed on appeal, shall pay its own costs and one-half the cost of the appendix. On remand the district court should award to Thomas appropriate counsel fees and costs for services in both trial and appellate courts with respect to the grant of prospective injunctive relief.

AFFIRMED IN PART, VACATED IN PART, AND REMANDED

NOTES

1. The plaintiff was the catalyst for a substantial legal change in board practices but did not receive a tangible benefit.

2. Is there professional support for the hiring policies that were practiced in this case?

[CASE NO. 55]   EMPLOYMENT RIGHTS OF TEACHERS WITH DISABILITIES

SCHOOL BOARD OF NASSAU COUNTY, FLORIDA v. ARLINE

Supreme Court of the United States, 1987.
480 U.S. 273, 107 S.Ct. 1123, 94 L.Ed.2d 307 [37 Educ. L. Rep. 448].

■ JUSTICE BRENNAN delivered the opinion of the Court.

Section 504 of the Rehabilitation Act of 1973 prohibits a federally funded state program from discriminating against a handicapped individual solely by reason of his or her handicap. This case presents the questions whether a person afflicted with tuberculosis, a contagious disease, may be considered a "handicapped individual" within the meaning of § 504 of the Act, and, if so, whether such an individual is "otherwise qualified" to teach elementary school.

I

From 1966 until 1979, respondent Gene Arline taught elementary school in Nassau County, Florida. She was discharged in 1979 after suffering a third relapse of tuberculosis within two years. After she was denied relief in state administrative proceedings, she brought suit in federal court, alleging that the school board's decision to dismiss her because of her tuberculosis violated § 504 of the Act.

A trial was held in the District Court ... According to the medical records ... Arline was hospitalized for tuberculosis in 1957. For the next 20 years, Arline's disease was in remission. Then, in 1977, a culture revealed that tuberculosis was again active in her system; cultures taken in March 1978 and in November 1978 were also positive.

The superintendent of schools for Nassau County, Craig Marsh, then testified as to the school board's response to Arline's medical reports. After both her second relapse, in the spring of 1978, and her third relapse in November 1978, the school board suspended Arline with pay for the remainder of the school year. At the end of the 1978–1979 school year, the school board held a hearing, after which it discharged Arline, "not because she had done anything wrong," but because of the "continued reoccurence [sic] of tuberculosis." In her trial memorandum, Arline argued that it was "not disputed that the [school board dismissed her] solely on the basis of her illness. Since the illness in this case qualifies the Plaintiff as a 'handicapped person' it is clear that she was dismissed solely as a result of her handicap in violation of Section 504." The District Court held, however, that although there was "[n]o question that she suffers a handicap," Arline was nevertheless not "a handicapped person under the terms of that statute." The court found it "difficult ... to conceive that Congress intended contagious diseases to be included within the definition of a handicapped person." The court then went on to state that, "even assuming" that a person with a contagious disease could be deemed a handicapped person, Arline was not "qualified" to teach elementary school.

The Court of Appeals reversed, holding that "persons with contagious diseases are within the coverage of section 504," and that Arline's condition "falls ... neatly within the statutory and regulatory framework" of the Act. The court remanded the case "for further findings as to whether the risks of infection precluded Mrs. Arline from being 'otherwise qualified' for her job and, if so, whether it was possible to make some reasonable accommodation for her in that teaching position" or in some other position. We granted certiorari and now affirm.

II

In enacting and amending the Act, Congress enlisted all programs receiving federal funds in an effort "to share with handicapped Americans the opportunities for an education, transportation, housing, health care, and jobs that other Americans take for granted." To that end, Congress not only increased federal support for vocational rehabilitation, but also addressed the broader problem of discrimination against the handicapped by including § 504, an antidiscrimination provision patterned after Title VI of the Civil Rights Act of 1964. Section 504 of the Rehabilitation Act reads in pertinent part:

> "No otherwise qualified handicapped individual in the United States, as defined in section 706(7) of this title, shall, solely by reason of his handicap, be excluded from participation in, be denied the benefits of, or be subjected to discrimination under any program or activity receiving Federal financial assistance...." 29 U.S.C.[A.] § 794.

In 1974 Congress expanded the definition of "handicapped individual" for use in § 504 to read as follows:

> "[A]ny person who (i) has a physical or mental impairment which substantially limits one or more of such person's major life activities,

(ii) has a record of such an impairment, or (iii) is regarded as having such an impairment." 29 U.S.C.[A.] § 706(7)(B).

The amended definition reflected Congress' concern with protecting the handicapped against discrimination stemming not only from simple prejudice, but also from "archaic attitudes and laws" and from "the fact that the American people are simply unfamiliar with and insensitive to the difficulties confront[ing] individuals with handicaps." To combat the effects of erroneous but nevertheless prevalent perceptions about the handicapped, Congress expanded the definition of "handicapped individual" so as to preclude discrimination against "[a] person who has a record of, or is regarded as having, an impairment [but who] may at present have no actual incapacity at all."

In determining whether a particular individual is handicapped as defined by the Act, the regulations promulgated by the Department of Health and Human Services are of significant assistance. As we have previously recognized, these regulations were drafted with the oversight and approval of Congress; they provide "an important source of guidance on the meaning of § 504." The regulations are particularly significant here because they define two critical terms used in the statutory definition of handicapped individual. "Physical impairment" is defined as . . ."

"[A]ny physiological disorder or condition, cosmetic disfigurement, or anatomical loss affecting one or more of the following body systems: neurological; musculoskeletal; special sense organs; respiratory, including speech organs; cardiovascular; reproductive, digestive, genito-urinary; hemic and lymphatic; skin; and endocrine."

In addition, the regulations define "major life activities" as "functions such as caring for one's self, performing manual tasks, walking, seeing, hearing, speaking, breathing, learning, and working."

III

Within this statutory and regulatory framework, then, we must consider whether Arline can be considered a handicapped individual. According to . . . testimony . . . Arline suffered tuberculosis "in an acute form in such a degree that it affected her respiratory system," and was hospitalized for this condition. Arline thus had a physical impairment as that term is defined by the regulations, since she had a "physiological disorder or condition . . . affecting [her] . . . respiratory [system]." This impairment was serious enough to require hospitalization, a fact more than sufficient to establish that one or more of her major life activities were substantially limited by her impairment. Thus, Arline's hospitalization for tuberculosis in 1957 suffices to establish that she has a "record of . . . impairment" within the meaning of 29 U.S.C.[A.] § 706(7)(B)(ii), and is therefore a handicapped individual.

Petitioners concede that a contagious disease may constitute a handicapping condition to the extent that it leaves a person with "diminished physical or mental capabilities," and concede that Arline's hospitalization for tuberculosis in 1957 demonstrates that she has a record of a physical impairment. Petitioners maintain, however, that Arline's record of impairment is irrelevant in this case, since the school board dismissed Arline not because of her diminished physical capabilities, but because of the threat that her relapses of tuberculosis posed to the health of others.

We do not agree with petitioners that, in defining a handicapped individual under § 504, the contagious effects of a disease can be meaningfully distinguished from the disease's physical effects on a claimant in a case such as this. Arline's contagiousness and her physical impairment each resulted from the same underlying condition, tuberculosis. It would be unfair to allow an employer to seize upon the distinction between the effects of a disease on others and the effects of a disease on a patient and use that distinction to justify discriminatory treatment.

Nothing in the legislative history of § 504 suggests that Congress intended such a result. That history demonstrates that Congress was as concerned about the effect of an impairment on others as it was about its effect on the individual. Congress extended coverage, in 29 U.S.C.[A.] § 706(7)(B)(iii), to those individuals who are simply "regarded as having" a physical or mental impairment. The Senate Report provides as an example of a person who would be covered under this subsection "a person with some kind of visible physical impairment which in fact does not substantially limit that person's functioning." Such an impairment might not diminish a person's physical or mental capabilities, but could nevertheless substantially limit that person's ability to work as a result of the negative reactions of others to the impairment.

Allowing discrimination based on the contagious effects of a physical impairment would be inconsistent with the basic purpose of § 504, which is to ensure that handicapped individuals are not denied jobs or other benefits because of the prejudiced attitudes or the ignorance of others. By amending the definition of "handicapped individual" to include not only those who are actually physically impaired, but also those who are regarded as impaired and who, as a result, are substantially limited in a major life activity, Congress acknowledged that society's accumulated myths and fears about disability and disease are as handicapping as are the physical limitations that flow from actual impairment. Few aspects of a handicap give rise to the same level of public fear and misapprehension as contagiousness. Even those who suffer or have recovered from such noninfectious diseases as epilepsy or cancer have faced discrimination based on the irrational fear that they might be contagious. The Act is carefully structured to replace such reflexive reactions to actual or perceived handicaps with actions based on reasoned and medically sound judgments: the definition of "handicapped individual" is broad, but only those individuals who are both handicapped and otherwise qualified are eligible for relief. The fact that some persons who have contagious diseases may pose a serious health threat to others under certain circumstances does not justify excluding from the coverage of the Act all persons with actual or perceived contagious diseases. Such exclusion would mean that those accused of being contagious would never have the opportunity to have their condition evaluated in light of medical evidence and a determination made as to whether they were "otherwise qualified." Rather, they would be vulnerable to discrimination on the basis of mythology—precisely the type of injury

Congress sought to prevent. We conclude that the fact that a person with a record of a physical impairment is also contagious does not suffice to remove that person from coverage under § 504.

IV

The remaining question is whether Arline is otherwise qualified for the job of elementary schoolteacher. To answer this question in most cases, the district court will need to conduct an individualized inquiry and make appropriate findings of fact. Such an inquiry is essential if § 504 is to achieve its goal of protecting handicapped individuals from deprivations based on prejudice, stereotypes, or unfounded fear, while giving appropriate weight to such legitimate concerns of grantees as avoiding exposing others to significant health and safety risks. The basic factors to be considered in conducting this inquiry are well established. In the context of the employment of a person handicapped with a contagious disease, we agree with amicus American Medical Association that this inquiry should include ... "[findings of] facts, based on reasonable medical judgments given the state of medical knowledge, about (a) the nature of the risk (how the disease is transmitted), (b) the duration of the risk (how long is the carrier infectious), (c) the severity of the risk (what is the potential harm to third parties) and (d) the probabilities the disease will be transmitted and will cause varying degrees of harm."

In making these findings, courts normally should defer to the reasonable medical judgments of public health officials. The next step in the "otherwise-qualified" inquiry is for the court to evaluate, in light of these medical findings, whether the employer could reasonably accommodate the employee under the established standards for that inquiry.

Because of the paucity of factual findings by the District Court, we, like the Court of Appeals, are unable at this stage of the proceedings to resolve whether Arline is "otherwise qualified" for her job. The District Court made no findings as to the duration and severity of Arline's condition, nor as to the probability that she would transmit the disease. Nor did the court determine whether Arline was contagious at the time she was discharged, or whether the School Board could have reasonably accommodated her. Accordingly, the resolution of whether Arline was otherwise qualified requires further findings of fact.

We hold that a person suffering from the contagious disease of tuberculosis can be a handicapped person within the meaning of § 504 of the Rehabilitation Act of 1973, and that respondent Arline is such a person. We remand the case to the District Court to determine whether Arline is otherwise qualified for her position. The judgment of the Court of Appeals is

Affirmed.

NOTES

1. The Court first applied Section 504 in an educational dispute in *Southeastern Community College v. Davis*, 442 U.S. 397, 99 S.Ct. 2361, 60 L.Ed.2d 980 (1979). [Case No. 109]

2.   Was this decision wise? Was it safe for the school community?

[CASE NO. 56]   PROCEDURAL DUE PROCESS FOR NON-TENURED
FACULTY MEMBERS

BOARD OF REGENTS OF STATE COLLEGES v. ROTH

Supreme Court of the United States, 1972.
408 U.S. 564, 92 S.Ct. 2701, 33 L.Ed.2d 548.

■ MR. JUSTICE STEWART delivered the opinion of the Court.

In 1968 the respondent, David Roth, was hired for his first teaching job as assistant professor of political science at Wisconsin State University–Oshkosh. He was hired for a fixed term of one academic year. The notice of his faculty appointment specified that his employment would begin on September 1, 1968, and would end on June 30, 1969. The respondent completed that term. But he was informed that he would not be rehired for the next academic year.

The respondent had no tenure rights to continued employment.... There are no statutory or administrative standards defining eligibility for re-employment. State law thus clearly leaves the decision whether to rehire a non-tenured teacher for another year to the unfettered discretion of University officials.

. . .

The respondent ... brought this action in a federal district court alleging that the decision not to rehire him for the next year infringed his Fourteenth Amendment rights. He attacked the decision both in substance and procedure. First, he alleged that the true reason for the decision was to punish him for certain statements critical of the University administration, and that it therefore violated his right to freedom of speech. Second, he alleged that the failure of University officials to give him notice of any reason for nonretention and an opportunity for a hearing violated his right to procedural due process of law.

... The only question presented to us at this stage in the case is whether the respondent had a constitutional right to a statement of reasons and a hearing on the University's decision not to rehire him for another year. We hold that he did not.

I

The requirements of procedural due process apply only to the deprivation of interests encompassed within the Fourteenth Amendment's protection of liberty and property. When protected interests are implicated the right to some kind of prior hearing is paramount. But the range of interests protected by procedural due process is not infinite.

... [T]o determine whether due process requirements apply in the first place, we must look not to the "weight" but to the nature of the interest at stake. We must look to see if the interest is within the Fourteenth Amendment's protection of liberty and property....

Yet, while the Court has eschewed rigid or formalistic limitations on the protection of procedural due process, it has at the same time observed certain boundaries. For the words "liberty" and "property" in the Due Process Clause of the Fourteenth Amendment must be given some meaning.

II

"While this Court has not attempted to define with exactness the liberty ... guaranteed [by the Fourteenth Amendment] the term has received much consideration, and some of the included things have been definitely stated. Without doubt, it denotes not merely freedom from bodily restraint but also the right of the individual to contract, to engage in any of the common occupations of life, to acquire useful knowledge, to marry, establish a home and bring up children, to worship God according to the dictates of his own conscience, and generally to enjoy those privileges long recognized ... as essential to the orderly pursuit of happiness by free men." In a Constitution for a free people, there can be no doubt that the meaning of "liberty" must be broad indeed.

There might be cases in which a State refused to re-employ a person under such circumstances that interests in liberty would be implicated. But this is not such a case.

The State, in declining to rehire the respondent, did not make any charge against him that might seriously damage his standing and associations in his community. It did not base the nonrenewal of his contract on a charge, for example, that he had been guilty of dishonesty, or immorality. Had it done so, this would be a different case. For "[w]here a person's good name, reputation, honor or integrity is at stake because of what the government is doing to him, notice and an opportunity to be heard are essential." In such a case, due process would accord an opportunity to refute the charge before University officials. (The purpose of such notice and hearing is to provide the person an opportunity to clear his name. Once a person has cleared his name at a hearing, his employer, of course, may remain free to deny him future employment for other reasons.) In the present case, however there is no suggestion whatever that the respondent's interest in his "good name, reputation, honor or integrity" is at stake.

Similarly, there is no suggestion that the State, in declining to re-employ the respondent, imposed on him a stigma or other disability that foreclosed his freedom to take advantage of other employment opportunities. The State, for example, did not invoke any regulations to bar the respondent from all other public employment in State universities. Had it done so, this, again, would be a different case. For "[t]o be deprived not only of present government employment but of future opportunity for it is no small injury ..." The Court has held, for example, that a State, in regulating eligibility for a type of professional employment, cannot foreclose a range of opportunities "in a manner ... that contravene[s] ... due process," and, specifically, in a manner that denies the right to a full prior hearing. In the present case, however, this principle does not come into play.

To be sure, the respondent has alleged that the nonrenewal of his contract was based on his exercise of his right to freedom of speech. But this allegation is not now before us. The District Court stayed proceedings on this issue, and the respondent has yet to prove that the decision not to rehire him was, in fact, based on his free speech activities.

Hence, on the record before us, all that clearly appears is that the respondent was not rehired for one year at one University. It stretches the concept too far to suggest that a person is deprived of "liberty" when he simply is not rehired in one job but remains as free as before to seek another.

III

The Fourteenth Amendment's procedural protection of property is a safeguard of the security of interests that a person has already acquired in specific benefits. These interests—property interests—may take many forms.

Thus the Court has held that a person receiving welfare benefits under statutory and administrative standards defining eligibility for them has an interest in continued receipt of those benefits that is safeguarded by procedural due process. . . . Similarly, in the area of public employment, the Court has held that a public college professor dismissed from an office held under tenure provisions, *Slochower v. Board of Education*, and college professors and staff members dismissed during the terms of their contracts, *Wieman v. Updegraff*, have interests in continued employment that are safeguarded by due process. Only last year, the Court held that this principle "proscribing summary dismissal from public employment without a hearing or inquiry required by due process" also applied to a teacher recently hired without tenure or a formal contract but nonetheless with a clearly implied promise of continued employment.

Certain attributes of "property" interests protected by procedural due process emerge from these decisions. To have a property interest in a benefit, a person clearly must have more than an abstract need or desire for it. He must have more than a unilateral expectation of it. He must, instead, have a legitimate claim of entitlement to it. It is a purpose of the ancient institution of property to protect those claims upon which people rely in their daily lives, reliance that must not be arbitrarily undermined. It is a purpose of the constitutional right to a hearing to provide an opportunity for a person to vindicate those claims.

Property interests, of course, are not created by the Constitution. Rather, they are created and their dimensions are defined by existing rules or understandings that stem from an independent source such as state law—rules or understandings that secure certain benefits and that support claims of entitlement to those benefits. Thus the welfare recipients . . . had a claim of entitlement to welfare payments that was grounded in the statute defining eligibility for them. The recipients had not yet shown that they were, in fact, within the statutory terms of eligibility. But we held that they had a right to a hearing at which they might attempt to do so.

Just as the welfare recipients' "property" interest in welfare payments was created and defined by statutory terms, so the respondent's "property" interest in employment at the Wisconsin State University–Oshkosh was created and defined by the terms of his appointment. Those terms secured his interest in employment up to June 30, 1969. But the important fact in this case is that they specifically provided that the respondent's employment was to terminate on June 30. They did not provide for contract renewal absent "sufficient cause." Indeed, they made no provision for renewal whatsoever.

Thus the terms of the respondent's appointment secured absolutely no interest in re-employment for the next year. They supported absolutely no possible claim to entitlement to re-employment. Nor, significantly, was there any state statute or University rule or policy that secured his interest in re-employment or that created any legitimate claim to it. In these circumstances, the respondent surely had an abstract concern in being rehired, but he did not have a property interest sufficient to require the University authorities to give him a hearing when they declined to renew his contract of employment.

IV

Our analysis of the respondent's constitutional rights in this case in no way indicates a view that an opportunity for a hearing or a statement of reasons for nonretention would, or would not, be appropriate or wise in public colleges and universities. For it is a written Constitution that we apply. Our role is confined to interpretation of that Constitution.

We must conclude that the summary judgment for the respondent should not have been granted, since the respondent has not shown that he was deprived of liberty or property protected by the Fourteenth Amendment. The judgment of the Court of Appeals, accordingly, is reversed and the case is remanded for further proceedings consistent with this opinion. It is so ordered. Reversed and remanded.

NOTES

1. Specific charges and a hearing before removal constitute the heart of tenure protection. Had the Supreme Court upheld the lower courts in *Roth*, would any practical differences have remained between teachers who are tenured and those who have not yet achieved this status?

2. Based on *Roth*, public employees whose employment is not renewed at the end of their contracts may seek to come under its umbrella by alleging impairment of liberty or property interests. What do you think about such an approach?

[CASE NO. 57]   PROCEDURAL DUE PROCESS FOR NON-TENURED FACULTY MEMBERS, II

PERRY v. SINDERMANN

Supreme Court of the United States, 1972.
408 U.S. 593, 92 S.Ct. 2694, 33 L.Ed.2d 570.

■ Mr. Justice Stewart delivered the opinion of the Court.

From 1959 to 1969 the respondent, Robert Sindermann, was a teacher in the state college system of the State of Texas. After teaching for two years at the University of Texas and for four years at San Antonio Junior College, he became a professor of Government and Social Science at Odessa Junior College in 1965. He was employed at the college for four successive years, under a series of one-year contracts. He was successful enough to be appointed, for a time, the cochairman of his department.

During the 1968–1969 academic year, however, controversy arose between the respondent and the college administration. The respondent was elected president of the Texas Junior College Teachers Association. In this capacity, he left his teaching duties on several occasions to testify before committees of the Texas Legislature, and he became involved in public disagreements with the policies of the college's Board of Regents. In particular, he aligned himself with a group advocating the elevation of the college to four-year status—a change opposed by the Regents. And, on one occasion, a newspaper advertisement appeared over his name that was highly critical of the Regents.

Finally, in May 1969, the respondent's one-year employment contract terminated and the Board of Regents voted not to offer him a new contract for the next academic year. The Regents issued a press release setting forth allegations of the respondent's insubordination. But they provided him no official statement of the reasons for the nonrenewal of his contract. And they allowed him no opportunity for a hearing to challenge the basis of the nonrenewal.

. . .

I

The first question presented is whether the respondent's lack of a contractual or tenure right to re-employment, taken alone, defeats his claim that the nonrenewal of his contract violated the First and Fourteenth Amendments. We hold that it does not.

For at least a quarter century, this Court has made clear that even though a person has no "right" to a valuable governmental benefit and even though the government may deny him the benefit for any number of reasons, there are some reasons upon which the government may not act. It may not deny a benefit to a person on a basis that infringes his constitutionally protected interests—especially his interest in freedom of speech. For if the government could deny a benefit to a person because of his constitutionally protected speech or associations, his exercise of those freedoms would in effect be penalized and inhibited. This would allow the government to "produce a result which [it] could not command directly." Such interference with constitutional rights is impermissible. . . .

In this case, of course, the respondent has yet to show that the decision not to renew his contract was, in fact, made in retaliation for his exercise of the constitutional right of free speech. . . .

. . . The respondent has alleged that his nonretention was based on his testimony before legislative committees and his other public statements critical of the Regents' policies. And he has alleged that this public criticism was within the First and Fourteenth Amendment's protection of freedom of speech. Plainly, these allegations present a bona fide constitutional claim. For this Court has held that a teacher's public criticism of his superiors on matters of public concern may be constitutionally protected and may, therefore, be an impermissible basis for termination of his employment. . . .

II

The respondent's lack of formal contractual or tenure security in continued employment at Odessa Junior College, though irrelevant to his free speech claim, is highly relevant to his procedural due process claim. But it may not be entirely dispositive.

We have held today in *Board of Regents v. Roth* that the Constitution does not require opportunity for a hearing before the nonrenewal of a non-tenured teacher's contract, unless he can show that the decision not to rehire him somehow deprived him of an interest in "liberty" or that he had a "property" interest in continued employment, despite the lack of tenure or a formal contract. In *Roth* the teacher had not made a showing on either point to justify summary judgment in his favor.

Similarly, the respondent here has yet to show that he has been deprived of an interest that could invoke procedural due process protection. As in *Roth*, the mere showing that he was not rehired in one particular job, without more, did not amount to a showing of a loss of liberty. Nor did it amount to a showing of a loss of property.

But the respondent's allegations—which we must construe most favorably to the respondent at this stage of the litigation—do raise a genuine issue as to his interest in continued employment at Odessa Junior College. He alleged that this interest, though not secured by a formal contractual tenure provision, was secured by a no less binding understanding fostered by the college administration. In particular, the respondent alleged that the college had a de facto tenure program, and that he had tenure under that program. He claimed that he and others legitimately relied upon an unusual provision that had been in the college's official Faculty Guide for many years:

> "Teacher Tenure: Odessa College has no tenure system. The Administration of the College wishes the faculty member to feel that he has permanent tenure as long as his teaching services are satisfactory and as long as he displays a cooperative attitude toward his co-workers and his superiors, and as long as he is happy in his work."

Moreover, the respondent claimed legitimate reliance upon guidelines promulgated by the Coordinating Board of the Texas College and University System that provided that a person, like himself, who had been employed as a teacher in the state college and university system for seven years or more has some form of job tenure. Thus the respondent offered to prove that a teacher, with his long period of service, at this particular State College had no less a "property" interest in continued employment than a formally tenured teacher at other colleges, and had no less a procedural due process right to a statement of reasons and a hearing before college officials upon their decision not to retain him.

We have made clear in *Roth* that "property" interests subject to procedural due process protection are not limited by a few rigid, technical forms. Rather, "property" denotes a broad range of interests that are secured by "existing rules or understandings." A person's interest in a benefit is a "property" interest for due process purposes if there are such rules or mutually explicit understandings that support his claim of entitlement to the benefit and that he may invoke at a hearing.

A written contract with an explicit tenure provision clearly is evidence of a formal understanding that supports a teacher's claim of entitlement to continued employment unless sufficient "cause" is shown. Yet absence of such an explicit contractual provision may not always foreclose the possibility that a teacher has a "property" interest in re-employment. For example, the law of contracts in most, if not all, jurisdictions long has employed a process by which agreements, though not formalized in writing, may be "implied." Explicit contractual provisions may be supplemented by other agreements implied from "the promisor's words and conduct in the light of the surrounding circumstances." And, "[t]he meaning of [the promisor's] words and acts is found by relating them to the usage of the past."

A teacher, like the respondent, who has held his position for a number of years, might be able to show from the circumstances of this service—and from other relevant facts—that he has a legitimate claim of entitlement to job tenure. Just as this Court has found there to be a "common law of a particular industry or of a particular plant" that may supplement a collective-bargaining agreement, so there may be an unwritten "common law" in a particular university that certain employees shall have the equivalent of tenure. This is particularly likely in a college or university, like Odessa Junior College, that has no explicit tenure system even for senior members of its faculty, but that nonetheless may have created such a system in practice.

In this case, the respondent has alleged the existence of rules and understandings, promulgated and fostered by state officials, that may justify his legitimate claim of entitlement to continued employment absent "sufficient cause." We disagree with the Court of Appeals insofar as it held that a mere subjective "expectancy" is protected by procedural due process, but we agree that the respondent must be given an opportunity to prove the legitimacy of his claim of such entitlement in light of "the policies and practices of the institution." Proof of such a property interest would not, of course, entitle him to reinstatement. But such proof would obligate college officials to grant a hearing at his request, where he could be informed of the grounds for his nonretention and challenge their sufficiency.

Therefore, while we do not wholly agree with the opinion of the Court of Appeals, its judgment remanding this case to the District Court is affirmed.

Affirmed.

NOTE

How may *Perry* benefit teachers in states lacking tenure statutes?

[CASE NO. 58]   NON-REAPPOINTMENT OF A TEACHER

RUSSELL v. WATSON CHAPEL SCHOOL DISTRICT

Supreme Court of Arkansas (2009).
313 S.W.3d 1 [258 Educ. L. Rep. 421].

■ PAUL E. DANIELSON, JUSTICE.

Following our remand to the circuit court in this matter involving the Teacher Fair Dismissal Act (TFDA), *Watson Chapel Sch. Dist. v. Russell* (*Russell I*), appellant Bernice Martin Russell now appeals from the circuit court's order dismissing her complaint against appellee Watson Chapel School District (the District). In this appeal, Ms. Russell makes two assertions: (1) that the circuit court erred as a matter of law and made clearly-erroneous findings; and (2) that this court should not abandon its reasoning in *Hamilton v. Pulaski County School District*. We affirm the circuit court's order.

The preliminary facts in this matter were adequately set forth in our prior opinion. Suffice it to say, in 2002, the District's school board voted not to renew Ms. Russell's contract with the District. She then filed suit in the Jefferson County Circuit Court, alleging that the school board's action was void because the District failed to comply with the notice provision contained within the TFDA. The circuit court entered judgment in Ms. Russell's favor, finding that the notice provided to Ms. Russell was insufficient under section 6–17–1506(b)(2)(B). In addition, the circuit court awarded Ms. Russell $77,137 in contract damages.

The District appealed to this court, asserting, among other things, that the notice that was sent to Ms. Russell substantially complied with the TFDA. In examining this issue, we concluded that in order for a reviewing court to determine whether a notice of nonrenewal substantially complied with the TFDA, the circuit court must examine not only the notice of nonrenewal, but also any record of the school-board hearing made pursuant to Ark.Code Ann. § 6–17–1509(c)(4)....

In determining the sufficiency of the notice, a circuit court should examine a school district's notice within the context of what actually occurred during the school-board hearing. Furthermore, when a record of the hearing has been made pursuant to Ark.Code Ann. § 6–17–1509(c)(4), a circuit court must review the notice in conjunction with the hearing transcript and compare the evidence the school district presented to support the charges against the teacher with the actual defense that he or she was able to present as a counter to that evidence. To do otherwise, would undermine the clear intent of the General Assembly that a notice will be deemed sufficient if a "reasonable teacher can prepare a defense."

Accordingly, we reversed and remanded the matter, holding that the circuit court erred when it ruled on the sufficiency of the notice of nonrenewal without first examining the transcript of the school-board hearing. Specifically, we remanded to the circuit court for "a determination of the sufficiency of the nonrenewal notice based upon a full review of the evidence presented at the school-board hearing."

Upon remand, the circuit court scheduled a hearing, which was continued. The circuit court then received a letter from the District's counsel, which stated that he and Ms. Russell's counsel agreed that a hearing might be unnecessary and suggested that both parties submit simultaneous proposed findings of fact and conclusions of law. It does not appear from the record that any hearing was held, nor any proposed precedent filed. Nonetheless, the circuit court filed its order on May 2, 2008, in which it found that the District "did comply with the notice requirements of the Teacher Fair Dismissal Act (TFDA)." The circuit court, noting that it had reviewed the school-board transcript, delineated the reasons for nonrenewal contained in the notice and found that the "statements made during the hearing by [Ms. Russell] and on her behalf indicate[d] that [she] had the opportunity to review the documents presented by the [District] at the hearing and to defend against all issues raised in the notice." Accordingly, the circuit court ... dismissed Ms. Russell's cause. She now appeals.

Ms. Russell argues, as her first point on appeal, that the circuit court erred as a matter of law and made clearly-erroneous findings. She claims that the circuit court failed to follow this court's mandate and that she was left to "guesswork and speculation" as to the reasons for the nonrenewal recommendation. The District counters that viewing the record in its entirety, the circuit court's finding that the notice of nonrenewal was sufficient was not clearly erroneous. It contends that the circuit court had evidence before it that the notice of nonrenewal was adequate to allow Ms. Russell to prepare a defense and, for that reason, the circuit court's order should be affirmed.

Our standard of review in matters involving the TFDA is limited to whether the circuit court's decision was clearly erroneous. A finding is clearly erroneous when, although there is evidence to support it, the reviewing court on the entire evidence is left with a firm conviction that an error has been committed.Facts in dispute and determinations of credibility are within the province of the fact-finder.

The TFDA provides that a nonrenewal by a school district shall be void unless the school district substantially complies with the provisions of the Act. At issue in the instant case is whether the District substantially complied with the provisions of section 6–17–1506(b)(2)(B). We hold that it did.

In order for the District to have substantially complied with section 6–17–1506(b)(2)(B), the notice of recommended nonrenewal was required to include "a statement of the reasons for the recommendation, setting forth the reasons in separately numbered paragraphs so that a reasonable teacher can prepare a defense." Thus, the relevant inquiry is whether the notice of nonrenewal was sufficient such that *a reasonable teacher* could defend against the reasons given.

In *Russell I*, we held that, in determining the sufficiency of a notice of nonrenewal, a circuit court should examine a "school district's notice within the context of what actually occurred during the school-board hearing." We further observed that such a review must be conducted in order to determine whether a reasonable teacher could have prepared a defense. This is because the events of the hearing itself are at least some evidence of whether a reasonable teacher could defend.

Here, the circuit court, after reviewing the transcript of the school-board hearing, concluded that the notice of nonrenewal was sufficient based upon the fact that Ms. Russell was able to defend on all issues raised. While the circuit court did not base its conclusion on whether a reasonable teacher could defend, it is clear to this court that the circuit court's conclusion regarding the sufficiency of the notice of nonrenewal was not clearly erroneous. It is evident from a review of both the notice of nonrenewal and the school-board hearing that the notice substantially complied with the section 6–17–1506(b)(2)(B), such that a reasonable teacher could prepare a defense. Accordingly, we hold that the circuit court did not clearly err in finding that the notice of nonrenewal complied with section 6–17–1506(b)(2)(B).

For her second point, relying on *Hamilton v. Pulaski County School District*, Ms. Russell argues that her notice of nonrenewal lacked completeness. She contends that the notice of nonrenewal failed to comply with the statute as it relied on her personnel file and contained reasons based upon the generic reasons set forth in the statute, both of which she claims this court rejected as sufficient reasons in *Hamilton*. The District responds that *Hamilton* is distinguishable, in that the standard for the District at that time was strict compliance and that, in Ms. Russell's case, she received responses from the District to her requests for more information.

Ms. Russell's argument is without merit, as this court's decision in *Hamilton* was under a prior version of the statute. In *Hamilton*, this court considered the sufficiency of a teacher's notice of nonrenewal. There, we did observe that "teachers [were] entitled to rely on a simple and complete statement of reasons as to nonrenewal of their contracts." We further observed that "[m]ere recitation of the generic categories of inefficiency and noncompliance with written regulations and policies tells a teacher nothing about the reasons for nonrenewal" and that "[w]ithout that information, preparation for a hearing is well nigh impossible."

At that time, the General Assembly required that "[t]he notice of recommended nonrenewal of a teacher shall include a simple but complete statement of the reasons for such recommendation." However, in 1999, the General Assembly amended section 6–17–1506, deleting the "simple but complete" language and substituting "setting forth the reasons in separately numbered paragraphs so that a reasonable teacher can prepare a defense."

The language of section 6–17–1506(b)(2)(B) as it stands now simply cannot be construed the same as the former language of "simple but complete." It is clear that the General Assembly, by its amendment, did not intend for school districts to send a notice of nonrenewal with no basis whatsoever; however, it is also just as clear that the current language of the statute does not require the specificity previously required under the prior version of the statute. Instead, the contents of the notice must now only consist of reasons in separately numbered paragraphs such that a reasonable teacher can prepare a defense. In sum, our decision in *Hamilton* was based on prior law and not the reasonable-teacher standard, and Ms. Russell's reliance on that decision is misplaced.

For the foregoing reasons, we affirm the circuit court's order.

NOTE

Some states require school boards to provide teachers whose contracts are not renewed with explanations of their actions while others mandate that they do so only if they ask for reasons. What do you think of these two different approaches? Which do you prefer?

[CASE NO. 59]   NON-REAPPOINTMENT OF A TEACHER— PARTIALLY BASED ON AN UNCONSTITUTIONAL REASON

MT. HEALTHY CITY SCHOOL DISTRICT BOARD OF EDUCATION v. DOYLE

Supreme Court of the United States, 1977.
429 U.S. 274, 97 S.Ct. 568, 50 L.Ed.2d 471.

■ MR. JUSTICE REHNQUIST delivered the opinion of the Court.

Respondent Doyle sued petitioner Mt. Healthy Board of Education in the United States District Court for the Southern District of Ohio. Doyle claimed that the Board's refusal to renew his contract in 1971 violated his rights under the First and Fourteenth Amendments to the United States Constitution. After a bench trial the District Court held that Doyle was entitled to reinstatement with back pay. The Court of Appeals for the Sixth Circuit affirmed ...

Doyle was first employed by the Board in 1966. He worked under one-year contracts for the first three years, and under a two-year contract from 1969 to 1971. In 1969 he was elected president of the Teachers' Association, in which position he worked to expand the subjects of direct negotiation between the Association and the Board of Education. During Doyle's one-year term as president of the Association, and during the succeeding year when he served on its executive committee, there was apparently some tension in relations between the Board and the Association.

Beginning early in 1970, Doyle was involved in several incidents not directly connected with his role in the Teachers' Association. In one instance, he engaged in an argument with another teacher which culminated in the other teacher's slapping him. Doyle subsequently refused to accept an apology and insisted upon some punishment for the other teacher. His persistence in the matter resulted in the suspension of both teachers for one day, which was followed by a walkout by a number of other teachers, which in turn resulted in the lifting of the suspensions.

On other occasions, Doyle got into an argument with employees of the school cafeteria over the amount of spaghetti which had been served him; referred to students, in connection with a disciplinary complaint, as "sons of bitches"; and made an obscene gesture to two girls in connection with their failure to obey commands made in his capacity as cafeteria supervisor. Chronologically the last in the series of incidents which respondent was involved in during his employment by the Board was a telephone call by him to a local radio station. It was the Board's consideration of this incident which the court below found to be a violation of the First and Fourteenth Amendments.

In February of 1971, the principal circulated to various teachers a memorandum relating to teacher dress and appearance, which was apparently prompted by the view of some in the administration that there was a relationship between teacher appearance and public support for bond issues. Doyle's response to the receipt of the memorandum—on a subject which he apparently understood was to be settled by joint teacher-administration action—was to convey the substance of the memorandum to a disc jockey at WSAI, a Cincinnati radio station, who promptly announced the adoption of the dress code as a news item. Doyle subsequently apologized to the principal, conceding that he should have made some prior communication of his criticism to the school administration.

Approximately one month later the superintendent made his customary annual recommendations to the Board as to the rehiring of non-tenured teachers. He recommended that Doyle not be rehired. The same recommendation was made with respect to nine other teachers in the district, and in all instances, including Doyle's, the recommendation was adopted by the Board. Shortly after being notified of this decision, respondent requested a statement of reasons for the Board's actions. He received a statement citing "a notable lack of tact in handling professional matters which leaves much doubt as to your sincerity in establishing good school relationships." That general statement was followed by references to the radio station incident and to the obscene gesture incident.

The District Court found that all of these incidents had in fact occurred. It concluded that respondent Doyle's telephone call to the radio station was "clearly protected by the First Amendment," and that because it had played a "substantial part" in the decision of the Board not to renew Doyle's employment, he was entitled to reinstatement with back pay. The District Court did not expressly state what test it was applying in determining that the incident in question involved conduct protected by the First Amendment, but simply held that the communication to the radio station was such conduct. The Court of Appeals affirmed in a brief per curiam opinion.

Doyle's claims under the First and Fourteenth Amendments are not defeated by the fact that he did not have tenure. Even though he could have been discharged for no reason whatever, and had no constitutional right to a hearing prior to the decision not to rehire him, he may nonetheless establish a claim to reinstatement if the decision not to rehire him was made by reason of his exercise of constitutionally protected First Amendment freedoms.

That question of whether speech of a government employee is constitutionally protected expression necessarily entails striking "a balance between the interests of the teacher, as a citizen, in commenting upon matters of public concern and the interest of the State as an employer, in promoting the efficiency of the public services it performs through its employees." *Pickering v. Board of Education.* There is no suggestion by the Board that Doyle violated any established policy, or that its reaction to his communication to the radio station was anything more than an ad hoc response to Doyle's action in making the memorandum public. We therefore accept the District Court's finding that the communication was protected by the First and Fourteenth Amendments. We are not, however, entirely in agreement with that court's manner of reasoning from this finding to the conclusion that Doyle is entitled to reinstatement with back pay.

The District Court made the following "conclusions" on this aspect of the case:

"(1) If a non-permissible reason, e.g., exercise of First Amendment rights, played a substantial part in the decision not to renew—even in the face of other permissible grounds—the decision may not stand (citations omitted).

"(2) A non-permissible reason did play a substantial part. That is clear from the letter of the Superintendent immediately following the Board's decision, which stated two reasons—the one, the conversation with the radio station clearly protected by the First Amendment. A court may not engage in any limitation of First Amendment rights based on 'tact'—that is not to say that 'tactfulness' is irrelevant to other issues in this case."

At the same time, though, it stated that "in fact, as this Court sees it and finds, both the Board and the Superintendent were faced with a situation in which there did exist in fact reason ... independent of any First Amendment rights or exercise thereof, to not extend tenure."

Since respondent Doyle had no tenure, and there was therefore not even a state law requirement of "cause" or "reason" before a decision could be made not to renew his employment, it is not clear what the District Court meant by this latter statement. Clearly the Board legally could have dismissed respondent had the radio station incident never come to its attention. One plausible meaning of the court's statement is that the Board and the Superintendent not only could, but in fact would have reached that decision had not the constitutionally protected incident of the telephone call to the radio station occurred. We are thus brought to the issue whether, even if that were the case, the fact that the protected conduct played a "substantial part" in the actual decision not to renew would necessarily amount to a constitutional violation justifying remedial action. We think that it would not.

A rule of causation which focuses solely on whether protected conduct played a part, "substantial" or otherwise, in a decision not to rehire, could place an employee in a better position as a result of the exercise of constitutionally protected conduct than he would have occupied had he done nothing. The difficulty with the rule enunciated by the District Court is that it would require reinstatement in cases where a dramatic and perhaps abrasive incident is inevitably on the minds of those responsible for the decision to rehire, and does indeed play a part in that decision— even if the same decision would have been reached had the incident not occurred. The constitutional principle at stake is sufficiently vindicated if such an employee is placed in no worse a position than if he had not engaged in the conduct. A borderline or marginal candidate should not have the employment question resolved against him because of constitutionally protected conduct. But that same candidate ought not to be able, by engaging in such conduct, to prevent his employer from assessing his performance record and reaching a decision not to rehire on the basis of that record, simply because the protected conduct makes the employer more certain of the correctness of its decision.

This is especially true where, as the District Court observed was the case here, the current decision to rehire will accord "tenure." The long term consequences of an award of tenure are of great moment both to the employee and to the employer. They are too significant for us to hold that the Board in this case would be precluded, because it considered constitutionally protected conduct in deciding not to rehire Doyle, from attempting to prove to a trier of fact that quite apart from such conduct Doyle's record was such that he would not have been rehired in any event.

. . .

Initially, in this case, the burden was properly placed upon respondent to show that his conduct was constitutionally protected, and that this conduct was a "substantial factor"—or to put it in other words, that it was a "motivating factor" in the Board's decision not to rehire him. Respondent having carried that burden, however, the District Court should have gone on to determine whether the Board had shown by a preponderance of the evidence that it would have reached the same decision as to respondent's reemployment even in the absence of the protected conduct.

We cannot tell from the District Court opinion and conclusions, nor from the opinion of the Court of Appeals affirming the judgment of the District Court, what conclusion those courts would have reached had they applied this test. The judgment of the Court of Appeals is therefore vacated, and the case remanded for further proceedings consistent with this opinion.

NOTE

Should the First Amendment protect teachers from disciplinary actions for making phone calls to radio talk shows if they criticize their school boards or any district personnel by name?

CHAPTER 10

TERMS AND CONDITIONS OF TEACHER EMPLOYMENT

INTRODUCTION

In addition to the federal laws that were reviewed in the previous chapter, state statutes and regulations dealing with the terms and conditions of teacher employment have proliferated in such areas as salaries, personnel records, leaves, assignments and transfers, and collective bargaining. Amid considerable debate over its future, where state laws permit negotiations, bargaining statutes have had perhaps the broadest impact on teacher employment since they typically result in the development of policies influencing a range of issues involving the daily terms and conditions of the professional lives of educators. In light of these issues, this chapter examines a range of legal matters dealing with the terms and conditions of teacher employment.

SALARIES

IN GENERAL

Absent statutory constraints or constitutional prohibitions on their implied power to set salaries for staff, school boards are free to act as they deem appropriate.[1] Some legislatures have enacted laws directly or indirectly related to teacher salaries that restrict the power of local boards. Even so, since boards must adopt salary schedules and pay teachers commensurate with their education and experience, they have broad discretion in setting wages.[2] Courts have upheld the all but universal use of salary schedules, a practice that developed in Denver, Colorado, and Des Moines, Iowa, in 1921,[3] as long as classifications are reasonable and teachers with like training and experience who perform similar services are treated

---

1. *Hansen v. Board of Educ. of School Dist. No. 65*, 502 N.E.2d 467 [36 Educ. L. Rep. 827] (Ill. App. Ct. 1986).

2. *Osborn v. Harrison School Dist. No. 2*, 844 P.2d 1283 [80 Educ. L. Rep. 732] (Colo. Ct. App. 1992).

3. Martin H. Mailn & Charles Taylor Kerchner, *Charter Schools and Collective Bargaining: Compatible Marriage or Illegitimate Relationship?* 30 HARV. J. PUB. POL'Y 885, 909 (2007).

uniformly.[4]

PLACEMENT ON SALARY SCHEDULES

When school board officials place new teachers on salary schedules, they are ordinarily not obligated to grant them credit for experiences outside of their state public school systems.[5] Once salary policies are in place, school officials may not administer them in an arbitrary or discriminatory manner such as by making new rules retroactive.[6] Yet, as revealed by a case from the Supreme Court of South Dakota, a board had the authority to impose a term in a collective bargaining agreement that unilaterally allowed it to go over and above its salary schedule when it deemed it necessary to do so.[7]

If school officials grant teachers credit for past work, board policies usually do not require them to pay educators for experience that is not directly related to their jobs. For example, the Supreme Court of Arkansas rejected a teacher's claim that her board failed to pay her in accord with its salary schedule.[8] The court affirmed that the board, which hired the teacher as an elementary school counselor, could pay her based on her five years of teaching experience even though she worked in schools for seventeen years since she willingly signed a contract indicating that she was paid at this rate. Boards may grant credit for experiences other than teaching such as military service.[9]

When qualifications and performance are equal, teachers must be treated the same,[10] even granting them credit for past years of service following breaks in employment once they are placed on salary schedules.[11] In a case on equality of performance, an appellate court in South Carolina affirmed that when teachers who worked in the statewide prison school system were not compensated any differently than their counterparts in the regular public schools, they were entitled to salary supplements.[12]

Insofar as titles alone are not controlling, the Supreme Court of Minnesota agreed that regular teachers and those in a special vocational-technical school could be paid differently.[13] The Supreme Judicial Court of

---

4. *Adair v. Stockton Unified School Dist.*, 77 Cal.Rptr.3d 62 [232 Educ. L. Rep. 231] (Cal. Ct. App. 2008), *review denied* (2008).

5. *Howard Union of Teachers v. State*, 478 A.2d 563 [18 Educ. L. Rep. 929] (R.I. 1984); *Fry v. Board of Educ.*, 112 P.2d 229 (Cal. 1941).

6. *Aebli v. Board of Educ.*, 145 P.2d 601 (Cal. Ct. App.1944); *Board of Educ. of Katonah–Lewisboro Union Free School Dist. v. Ambach*, 432 N.Y.S.2d 661 (N.Y. App. Div. 1980).

7. *Sisseton Educ. Ass'n v. Sisseton School Dist. No. 54–8*, 516 N.W.2d 301 [91 Educ. L. Rep. 328] (S.D. 1994).

8. *Stone v. Mayflower School Dist.*, 894 S.W.2d 881 [98 Educ. L. Rep. 1108] (Ark. 1995).

9. *See North Plainfield Educ. Ass'n on Behalf of Koumjian v. Board of Educ. of Borough of N. Plainfield, Somerset County*, 476 A.2d 1245 [18 Educ. L. Rep. 334] (N.J. 1984).

10. *Vittal v. Long Beach Unified School Dist.*, 87 Cal.Rptr. 319 (Cal. Ct. App. 1970).

11. *Mifflinburg Area Educ. Ass'n ex rel. Ulrich v. Mifflinburg Area School Dist.*, 724 A.2d 339 [132 Educ. L. Rep. 507] (Pa. 1999).

12. *Abraham v. Palmetto Unified School Dist. No. 1*, 538 S.E.2d 656 [149 Educ. L. Rep. 909] (S.C. Ct. App. 2000), *reh'g denied* (2000).

13. *Frisk v. Board of Educ. of Duluth*, 75 N.W.2d 504 (Minn. 1956).

Massachusetts reached a similar outcome in noting that not all supervisors had to be paid in like fashion.[14] Later, the Supreme Court of Idaho affirmed that a board did not violate the rights of teachers who served as department chairpersons in refusing to pay them extra compensation.[15] The court acknowledged that insofar as the operative bargaining pact did not create employment contracts with individuals, they were not entitled to additional compensation solely by reason of the extra duty pay schedules in the master agreement.

Disputes also arise over substitute teachers. The Supreme Court of Ohio affirmed that a school board was statutorily required to pay long-term substitutes only the minimum pay on its salary schedule.[16] An appellate court in Pennsylvania struck down a provision in a bargaining agreement which required substitute teachers who were hired to full-time positions to give up all claims to salary schedule placements for any or all time spent as substitutes.[17] The court held that the provision violated a statute that required boards to give substitutes salary credits for long-term service if they are hired to work in the same districts where they served as substitutes. This is consistent with the general rule that bargaining agreements may not conflict with statutes.

BASES OF SALARY CLASSIFICATIONS

School boards may not differentiate salaries based on race, sex, or marital status. Still, boards may classify teachers for salary purposes as long as they do so based on grounds that are reasonable, natural, and based on substantial differences that are germane to their duties. As such, an appellate court in California affirmed that a board's professional growth policy, which covered activities that were separate and distinct from bona fide elements of teaching experience, violated the state law governing uniform salaries for teachers since it did not treat years of training and years of experience uniformly.[18]

Perhaps the most significant salary issue is pay raises. Courts generally uphold salary differences based on subjective judgments as long as applicable criteria are reasonably specific and relevant. For instance, a federal trial court in Illinois refused to exercise its jurisdiction where a teacher claimed that her superintendent failed to follow committee recommendations that she be granted a merit increase because others who were no more qualified than she received the increase and she did not receive any written reasons why she was not awarded a raise.[19] The court found that insofar as the

---

14. *Murphy v. School Comm. of Lawrence*, 73 N.E.2d 835 (Mass. 1947).

15. *Gilmore v. Bonner County School Dist. No. 82*, 971 P.2d 323 [132 Educ. L. Rep. 197] (Idaho 1999).

16. *State ex rel. Antonucci v. Youngstown City School Dist. Bd. of Educ.*, 722 N.E.2d 69 [140 Educ. L. Rep. 740] (Ohio 2000).

17. *Greater Johnstown School Dist. v. Greater Johnstown Educ. Ass'n*, 804 A.2d 680 [168 Educ. L. Rep. 843] (Pa. Cmwlth. Ct.2002), *appeal denied*, 812 A.2d 1231 (Pa. 2002).

18. *Wygant v. Victor Valley Joint High School Dist.*, 214 Cal.Rptr. 205 [25 Educ. L. Rep. 396] (Cal. Ct. App. 1985).

19. *Kanter v. Community Consol. School Dist. 65*, 558 F.Supp. 890 [10 Educ. L. Rep. 137] (N.D. Ill. 1982).

teacher lacked a legitimate expectation of a merit salary increase, she had neither a constitutionally protected property interest nor a right to procedural due process to standards defining merit or written reasons for her being denied a raise.

An appellate court in Arizona addressed another issue concerning merit or performance-based pay. The court affirmed the dismissal of the claims of non-teaching employees who sought to be included in their board's performance-based plan.[20] In light of a state statute applicable to teachers with valid certificates or individuals who are not teachers, the court agreed that the plaintiffs were ineligible to participate in the compensation plan because they were not teachers.

In the first of three cases wherein it resolved salary disputes, the Supreme Court of New Jersey reiterated the general rule that an annual pay raise based on meritorious service is not a matter of statutory right but is subject to denial for inefficiency or other good cause.[21] The court next decided that when a school board withheld salary increments from a teacher due to her unsatisfactory performance, she was not entitled to have them restored and returned to the board's salary schedule when she performed satisfactorily.[22] In the third case, the court ruled that while teacher evaluations are a managerial prerogative essential to the way in which boards discharge their duties, officials could not withhold a teacher's annual raise due to her excessive absences since an arbitrator determined that they did so for disciplinary, rather than educational, reasons.[23]

Recognizing that school boards have the authority to create extra incentives for teachers to receive raises,[24] courts have upheld policies awarding raises on items other than typical teaching duties. Among the cases in which courts upheld raises where where teachers were present seventy-five percent of a school year;[25] achieved scores in excess of the minimum on the National Teacher Examination;[26] and attained National Board certification.[27]

On the general question of extra pay for specified types of teachers, an appellate court in Louisiana affirmed that a school board was required to

---

20. *Reeves v. Barlow*, 251 P.3d 417 [267 Educ. L. Rep. 354] (Ariz. Ct. App. 2011).

21. *North Plainfield Educ. Ass'n on Behalf of Koumjian v. Board of Educ. of Borough of N. Plainfield, Somerset County*, 476 A.2d 1245 [18 Educ. L. Rep. 334] (N.J. 1984).

22. *Probst v. Board of Educ. of Borough of Haddonfield, Camden County*, 606 A.2d 345 [74 Educ. L. Rep. 137] (N.J. 1992).

23. *Scotch Plains–Fanwood Bd. of Educ. v. Scotch Plains–Fanwood Educ. Ass'n*, 651 A.2d 1018 [96 Educ. L. Rep. 984] (N.J. 1995). *See also Board of Educ. Twp. of Neptune in County of Monmouth v. Neptune Twp. Educ. Ass'n*, 675 A.2d 611 [115 Educ. L. Rep. 372] (N.J. 1996) (declaring that payments of fourth year salary increments after the expiration of a three-year contract violated state law).

24. *Weatherford v. Martin*, 418 So.2d 777 [6 Educ. L. Rep. 275] (Miss. 1982).

25. *Hunt v. Alum Rock Union Elementary School Dist.*, 86 Cal.Rptr. 663 (Cal. Ct. App. 1970).

26. *Newman v. Crews*, 651 F.2d 222 (4th Cir. 1981).

27. *Bailey v. Independent School Dist. No. I–29 of Cleveland County, Okla.*, 256 P.3d 57 [269 Educ. L. Rep. 332] (Okla. 2011) (acknowledging that teachers who achieved this milestone were entitled to an annual bonus but denying their claims that a local board had to pay withholding taxes on these monies).

pay special education teachers only a ten percent salary supplement for sixteen-days since a pre-existing clause in an amendment to their contract was inapplicable to their case.[28] The court reasoned that the amendment applied only to teachers who were employed when the contract went into effect.[29]

In addition to salary and medical benefits,[30] school boards may offer teachers other benefits. In apparently the only reported case on point, when faced with a shortage of qualified personnel, the Supreme Judicial Court of Massachusetts upheld a dependency-allowance plan for teachers who were the sole support of spouses or children.[31] Where a board permitted children of its non-resident faculty to attend school without paying tuition, New York's highest court affirmed that it could not unilaterally stop doing so.[32] The court indicated that the dispute was subject to arbitration under the collective bargaining agreement between the board and its teachers. Subsequently, the Eighth Circuit observed that a board policy in Arkansas of allowing children of certificated and administrative employees to attend school in the district even if they lived outside of it, but not allowing children of other non-resident employees to do so was rationally related to its desire to recruit or retain quality teachers and administrators.[33] The court was satisfied that the policy did not violate the equal protection rights of non-resident employees whose children were ineligible to attend schools in the district.[34]

CHANGES IN SALARY CLASSIFICATIONS

School boards and the unions of their employees can modify salary classifications and scales from one collective bargaining agreement to the next. While bargaining has certainly not eliminated salary disputes, they were arguably more common before the advent of negotiations. In *Phelps v. Board of Education*[35] the Supreme Court resolved a controversy from New Jersey over whether a board could reduce teacher salaries under a permis-

---

28. *Phillips v. Orleans Parish School Bd.*, 755 So.2d 353 [144 Educ. L. Rep. 446] (La. Ct. App. 2000), *writ denied*, 761 So.2d 547 (La. 2000).

29. *See also Weslaco Fed'n of Teachers v. Texas Educ. Agency*, 27 S.W.3d 258 [147 Educ. L. Rep. 730] (Tex. Ct. App. 2000) (affirming that teachers were not entitled to a local supplement they received the previous year when their board failed to adopt a salary schedule in a timely manner).

30. *See, e.g., Thiemann v. Columbia Pub. School Dist.*, 338 S.W.3d 835 [268 Educ. L. Rep. 572] (Mo. Ct. App. 2011) (reversing a motion for summary judgment in favor of a school board in a dispute over the amount of coverage an employee was entitled to under a group benefit plan).

31. *Cotter v. City of Chelsea*, 108 N.E.2d 47 (Mass. 1952).

32. *Board of Educ. of New Paltz Cent. School Dist. v. New Paltz United Teachers*, 407 N.Y.S.2d 632 (N.Y. 1978).

33. *Clayton v. White Hall School Dist.*, 875 F.2d 676 [53 Educ. L. Rep. 1107] (8th Cir. 1989).

34. As evidence that such arrangements continue, in an unpublished opinion the Supreme Court of Montana essentially agreed that a local board could provide a teacher with rental housing pursuant to her employment contract. The court affirmed that the teacher had to make restitution for past rent due and other fees once she was no longer a board employee. *Roberts v. Lame Deer School Dist. No. 6*, 264 P.3d 519 (Mont. 2011).

35. 300 U.S. 319, 57 S.Ct. 483, 81 L.Ed. 674 (1937). [Case No. 60]

sive statute that conflicted with a prohibition in the state's tenure law against reductions without following tenure procedures. The Court pointed out that insofar as the tenure law was a statement of legislative policy rather than a contract, the reductions for teachers were permissible because they were carried out in a nondiscriminatory manner.

In order to protect teachers, some states enacted statutes requiring boards to pay them the same amount as the previous year unless school systems make across-the-board pay cuts or individuals reduce their responsibilities.[36] Even where there is apparent mutual consent on salary reductions, school officials must follow state law. To this end, the highest courts in Arkansas,[37] Tennessee,[38] and Washington[39] agreed that teachers could sue to recover the full salary to which they were entitled even though they signed contracts agreeing to work for lower wages.

School boards cannot reduce salary schedules during school years[40] or for extra duty assignments. In an illustrative case on the latter point, an appellate court in California affirmed that a board could not unilaterally eliminate the stipend that it paid teachers who were required to make calls on absent students since, insofar as there was no material change in their duties, it sought, in effect, to reduce their pay impermissibly.[41]

Conflicts arise over changes in classifications of teachers or other educators on salary schedules. In such a case, an appellate court in California maintained that teachers who resigned or left their jobs at the end of a school year were not entitled to payment under the terms of a collective bargaining agreement which granted a one-time retroactive payment to individuals who retired or returned to work the following school year.[42] The court asserted that insofar as the agreement between the board and union excluded teachers who resigned or left voluntarily, and the payment was not salary for the purposes of the state's uniform salary law, they did not have their status changed impermissibly. Moreover, when an assistant principal was involuntarily transferred from one school to another and temporarily had her pay grade and salary reduced pursuant to a board policy calling for mandatory reductions for those subject to involuntary transfers, a federal trial court in Texas rejected her claim of pay discrimination.[43] The court treated the claim as one without merit since the board reinstated the assistant principal to her original salary after officials

---

36. See, e.g., 105 ILL. COMP. STAT. ANN. 5/24–11; KY. REV. STAT. ANN. § 161.760; OHIO REV. CODE ANN. § 3319.12. See also Pigue v. Christian County Bd. of Educ., 65 S.W.3d 540 [161 Educ. L. Rep. 1080] (Ky. Ct. App. 2001) (upholding the statute).

37. Marvel v. Coal Hill Pub. School Dist., 635 S.W.2d 245 [5 Educ. L. Rep. 667] (Ark. 1982). [Case No. 61]

38. McMinn County Bd. of Educ. v. Anderson, 292 S.W.2d 198 (Tenn. 1956).

39. Malcolm v. Yakima County Consol. School Dist. 90, 159 P.2d 394 (Wash. 1945).

40. Abraham v. Sims, 42 P.2d 1029 (Cal. 1935).

41. A.B.C. Fed'n of Teachers v. A.B.C. Unified School Dist., 142 Cal.Rptr. 111 (Cal. Ct. App. 1977).

42. California Teachers' Ass'n v. Governing Bd. of the Hilmar Unified School Dist., 115 Cal.Rptr.2d 323 [160 Educ. L. Rep. 449] (Cal. Ct. App. 2002).

43. Vicari v. Ysleta Indep. School Dist., 546 F. Supp.2d 387 [232 Educ. L. Rep. 805] (W.D. Tex. 2008), aff'd in part, 291 Fed.Appx. 614 [238 Educ. L. Rep. 588] (5th Cir. 2008) (addressing only the limited point that the pay supervisor was entitled to qualified immunity).

reinterpreted the policy and reimbursed her for the difference in compensation that she experienced.

Individuals who receive benefits erroneously are generally not entitled to continue to receive them once mistakes are discovered.[44] If the benefit is overpayment of salary, school boards can later deduct these sums from teachers' pay as long as the amounts are not substantial, no great hardship results, and doing so does not violate express contractual terms.[45]

PERSONNEL FILES

School boards must preserve personnel files for their employees. Since states have enacted Open Records Laws to make personnel files and other public materials available,[46] disputes have arisen over who has access to this information.

A major concern over the content of personnel files is whether teachers have the right to challenge the inclusion of uncomplimentary materials. The Court of Appeals of New York, echoing the widely accepted view, was of the opinion that school officials can place letters that are critical of teacher performance or conduct in their files without affording hearings since supervisors have the right and duty to do so.[47] The Tenth Circuit reached the same outcome in affirming that officials in Colorado could place a letter of reprimand in a teacher's file over inappropriate comments that he made in class about the behavior of students because the admonition was neither impermissibly vague nor broad.[48] The court added that the letter could be included because it was not subject to constitutional protection insofar as the teacher's speech was not a matter of public concern. Conversely, the Sixth Circuit directed officials in Ohio to remove a letter from a teacher's personnel file since it believed that they placed it there simply in retaliation for his protected union activities.[49]

In an extension of teachers' rights to challenge the correctness of items in their files that may be stigmatizing or that present barriers to future employment if they dealt with dismissals and are likely to be disclosed to future employers, the Second Circuit reiterated the general rule that educators have the right to name-clearing hearings.[50] However, the court

---

44. *Shoban v. Board of Trustees of Desert Ctr. Unified School Dist.*, 81 Cal.Rptr. 112 (Cal. Ct. App. 1969).

45. *Green Local Teachers Ass'n v. Blevins*, 539 N.E.2d 653 [54 Educ. L. Rep. 296] (Ohio Ct. App. 1987).

46. *See, e.g.*, ALA. CODE 1975 § 16–22–14; ARK. CODE ANN. § 6–17–1505; CAL. EDUC. CODE ANN. § 44031; FLA. STAT. ANN. § 1012.31; IDAHO CODE ANN. § 33–518; 20 ME. REV. STAT. ANN. § 13004; N.C. GEN. STAT. ANN. § 115C–319; N.D. CENT. CODE §§ 15.1–17–01 *et seq.*; OR. REV. STAT. § 342.850; VA. CODE ANN. § 22.1–295.1.

47. *Holt v. Board of Educ. of Webutuck Cent. School Dist.*, 439 N.Y.S.2d 839 (N.Y. 1981).

48. *Miles v. Denver Pub. Schools*, 944 F.2d 773 [69 Educ. L. Rep. 1060] (10th Cir. 1991).

49. *Columbus Educ. Ass'n v. Columbus City School Dist.*, 623 F.2d 1155 (6th Cir. 1980).

50. *Brandt v. Board of Co-op. Educ. Servs.*, 845 F.2d 416 [46 Educ. L. Rep. 548] (2d Cir. 1988).

thought that when the teacher in New York failed to prove that officials violated his protected liberty interest because stigmatizing allegations were removed from his personnel file, not allowing the records to be disclosed meant that there was no likelihood of any future disclosure of the stigmatizing charges. In a non-education case, the Supreme Court affirmed that while individuals may be able to file defamation claims under state law if false information is released, federal causes of action do not arise when premised solely on reputational injuries occurring due to the release of derogatory information when disputes are not in the context of discharges or the nonrenewals of contracts.[51]

The Supreme Court of Alabama addressed a novel question over whether state law allowed a hearing officer to examine evidence other than that which was contained in the file of a teacher who was dismissed.[52] The court decided that a hearing officer could consider material that was not in the teacher's personnel file since the plaintiff had introduced evidence not in his record arguing that he had been disciplined due to personal bias on the part of board officials.

Whether, and to whom, confidential information must be divulged is ordinarily resolved on a case-by-case basis in light of competing considerations.[53] The Supreme Court of North Dakota affirmed that under the state's Open Records Law, personnel files are public records available for inspection.[54] Further, the Supreme Court, in a case from higher education, *University of Pennsylvania v. Equal Employment Opportunity Commission (EEOC)*,[55] affirmed that a faculty member's confidential tenure files were subject to subpoena by the EEOC when it investigated discrimination claims. However, an appellate court in Louisiana refused to order the release of a teacher's tenure file.[56] The court explained that personnel files were an exception to the state public records act and could not be released without the express written consent of the individual who was involved or a judicial decree. Further, the Supreme Court of Pennsylvania affirmed an injunction blocking the release of the home addresses of teachers on the ground that its disclosure could have resulted in irreparable harm to their rights to privacy.[57]

In a case with a different focus, the Fifth Circuit rejected the claim of a teacher and her school board that the Family Educational Rights and Privacy Act (FERPA)[58] prevented officials from disclosing the contents of

51. *Siegert v. Gilley*, 500 U.S. 226, 111 S.Ct. 1789, 114 L.Ed.2d 277 (1991), *reh'g denied*, 501 U.S. 1265, 111 S.Ct. 2920, 115 L.Ed.2d 1084 (1991).

52. *Ex parte Webb*, 53 So.3d 121 [264 Educ. L. Rep. 949] (Ala. 2009).

53. *Berst v. Chipman*, 653 P.2d 107 [7 Educ. L. Rep. 437] (Kan. 1982).

54. *Hovet v. Hebron Pub. School Dist.*, 419 N.W.2d 189 [44 Educ. L. Rep. 1325] (N.D. 1988).

55. 493 U.S. 182, 110 S.Ct. 577, 107 L.Ed.2d 571 [57 Educ. L. Rep. 666] (1990).

56. *Gannett River States Publishing Corp. v. Monroe City School Bd.*, 8 So.3d 833 [244 Educ. L. Rep. 885] (La. Ct. App. 2009), *writ denied*, 10 So.3d 745 (2009).

57. *Pennsylvania State Educ. Ass'n ex rel. Wilson v. Commonwealth Dep't of Community and Economic Dev., Office of Open Records*, 981 A.2d 383 [249 Educ. L. Rep. 324], *aff'd*, 2 A.3d 558 (Pa. 2010).

58. 20 U.S.C.A. § 1232g.

her college transcript.[59] The court affirmed that FERPA was inapplicable because it covered the records of only students, not employees. Even assuming that the plaintiff had a recognizable privacy interest in her transcript, the court commented that it was outweighed by the public's interest in evaluating the competence of teachers.[60] An appellate court in Minnesota reached the same outcome in positing that while a union had standing to challenge the release of disciplinary information about teachers, its interest in non-disclosure was ultimately outweighed by the public's right to such information.[61]

Courts have reached mixed results in disputes over the privacy rights of job applicants. Appellate courts in Pennsylvania[62] and Indiana[63] agreed that boards did not have to release information about applicants. The court in Pennsylvania conceded that while applications might have been covered by a relevant statute, since the files included confidential information such as home addresses, social security numbers, and college transcripts, they were protected from disclosure. The court from Indiana interpreted its statute as applying only to present or former employees, not applicants. In a case that reached a different outcome, an appellate court in Ohio contended that the media could have access to the names, applications, and resumes of individuals who sought a superintendency on the ground that a board failed to present a good reason why the information should not have been released.[64] Similarly, the Supreme Court of South Carolina affirmed that where a state statute required school boards to release the names of not less than three job applicants, a newspaper was entitled to the names of all five of the semi-finalists for a position as superintendent rather than just those of the two final candidates.[65]

LEAVES

The Family and Medical Leave Act,[66] discussed in Chapter 9, ensures that school employees have a federally protected right to take time off from work to care for their own medical needs and/or those of their family members. Even though state laws and collective bargaining agreements

---

59. *Klein Indep. School Dist. v. Mattox*, 830 F.2d 576 [42 Educ. L. Rep. 70] (5th Cir.1987), *cert. denied*, 485 U.S. 1008, 108 S.Ct. 1473, 99 L.Ed.2d 702 [46 Educ. L. Rep. 27] (1988).

60. *See also Brouillet v. Cowles Publishing Co.*, 791 P.2d 526 [60 Educ. L. Rep. 638] (Wash. 1990) (affirming that FERPA did not prevent the disclosure of a teacher's records).

61. *Minneapolis Fed'n of Teachers v. Minneapolis Pub. Schools, Special School Dist. No. 1*, 512 N.W.2d 107 [89 Educ. L. Rep. 261] (Minn. Ct. App. 1994).

62. *Cypress Media v. Hazleton Area School Dist.*, 708 A.2d 866 [125 Educ. L. Rep. 527] (Pa. Cmwlth. Ct. 1998), *appeal dismissed*, 724 A.2d 347 (Pa. 1999).

63. *South Bend Tribune v. South Bend Community School Corp.*, 740 N.E.2d 937 [150 Educ. L. Rep. 253] (Ind. Ct. App. 2000).

64. *State ex rel. Dayton Newspapers v. Dayton Bd. of Educ.*, 747 N.E.2d 255 [153 Educ. L. Rep. 756] (Ohio Ct. App. 2000).

65. *New York Times Co. v. Spartanburg County School Dist.*, 649 S.E.2d 28, 29 [222 Educ. L. Rep. 876] (S.C. 2007).

66. 29 U.S.C.A. §§ 2611 *et seq.*

vary as to the extent to which teachers may take time off due to illness, it is well-established that they have rights to sick leave.[67]

Abuse of sick leave constitutes cause for disciplinary action against employees.[68] An appellate court in Pennsylvania ascertained that when two teachers used sick leave to go on a ski trip after school officials denied their requests for personal leave, the board had just cause to terminate their contracts.[69] On the other hand, an appellate court in Illinois affirmed that while a teacher abused her sick leave by using it to attend a professional conference, she could not be dismissed because her action was remediable.[70] The court explained that the teacher could not be fired since officials failed to provide her with written warnings to cease her behavior.

Before granting requests for medical leaves, school board officials may ask teachers for evidence from health care providers that they were ill, either as a matter of general policy[71] or where there is a question about their conditions.[72] Officials may also require teachers to undergo physical examinations to evaluate their health before returning to work.[73]

Details of sick leave policies are ordinarily negotiable, typically as a mandatory topic of bargaining,[74] as long as agreements do not violate federal or state law. When board policies provide various leaves, the resulting legal issues primarily deal with contractual interpretation. If educators do not take all of their sick leave, absent state statutes or bargaining provisions to the contrary, courts differ over whether they can be compensated for unused time. In cases focusing on disputes of this type, the Supreme Court of Arkansas affirmed that a teacher could not obtain payment for unused sick leave[75] while an appellate court in Indiana reached the opposite result in a dispute involving a school psychologist.[76]

Turning to maternity leave, an appellate court in Indiana affirmed that where state law granted teachers a right to request one-year leaves of absence following childbirth, a school board had to grant a teacher's

67. *Averell v. Newburyport*, 135 N.E. 463 (Mass. 1922).

68. *Reddick v. Leon County School Bd.*, 405 So.2d 757 [1 Educ. L. Rep. 464] (Fla. Dist. Ct. App. 1981); *Board of Educ. of Laurel County v. McCollum*, 721 S.W.2d 703 [36 Educ. L. Rep. 1026] (Ky. 1986).

69. *Riverview School Dist. v. Riverview Educ. Ass'n*, 639 A.2d 974 [90 Educ. L. Rep. 280] (Pa. Cmwlth. Ct. 1994), *appeal denied*, 655 A.2d 518 (Pa. 1995).

70. *Board of Educ. of Joliet Twp. High School Dist. No. 204 v. Illinois State Bd. of Educ.*, 770 N.E.2d 711 [167 Educ. L. Rep. 845] (Ill. App. Ct. 2002), *appeal denied*, 786 N.E.2d 180 (Ill. 2002).

71. *Crowston v. Jamestown Pub. School Dist. No. 1*, 335 N.W.2d 775 [12 Educ. L. Rep. 525] (N.D. 1983).

72. *Brown v. Houston Indep. School Dist.*, 763 F.Supp. 905 [67 Educ. L. Rep. 1175] (S.D. Tex. 1991), *aff'd without published opinion*, 957 F.2d 866 [73 Educ. L. Rep. 375] (5th Cir.1992), *cert. denied*, 506 U.S. 868, 113 S.Ct. 198, 121 L.Ed.2d 140 (1992).

73. *Strong v. Board of Educ. of Uniondale Union Free School Dist.*, 902 F.2d 208 [60 Educ. L. Rep. 379] (2d Cir.1990), *cert. denied*, 498 U.S. 897, 111 S.Ct. 250, 112 L.Ed.2d 208 (1990).

74. *See, e.g., Waterloo Community School Dist. v. Public Employment Relations Bd.*, 650 N.W.2d 627 [169 Educ. L. Rep. 402] (Iowa 2002).

75. *Turnbough v. Mammoth Spring School Dist. No. 2*, 78 S.W.3d 89 [167 Educ. L. Rep. 492] (Ark. 2002).

76. *Schwartz v. Gary Community School Corp.*, 762 N.E.2d 192 [161 Educ. L. Rep. 631] (Ind. Ct. App. 2002), *transfer denied*, 774 N.E.2d 518 (Ind. 2002).

request as long as she met the statutory requirements.[77] The court added that the teacher was entitled to take maternity leave even though she initially did not ask for a full year since she gave the board ample notice that she was requesting the entire amount available under the law. On a procedural matter, an appellate court in Texas reached a different outcome when a probationary teacher sued her board after officials refused to allow her to return to work following maternity leave. The court was of the view that insofar as material issues of fact existed as to whether the teacher was dismissed or voluntarily abandoned her position and whether she was physically able to return to work, she had to exhaust administrative remedies before filing suit.[78]

Teachers may also seek leave for personal, including religious,[79] and professional reasons such as sabbaticals. School boards retain discretion to grant or deny requests for leaves of absence.[80] Teachers must continue to meet professional requirements while on leave. In such a case, the Supreme Court of Colorado affirmed that a board could terminate the contract of a teacher who was on leave for sex-reassignment surgery since she allowed her license to lapse.[81]

More recently, the Supreme Court of North Dakota affirmed that a local board did not breach a teacher's modified contract when it refused to pay her for time she spent on unpaid leave even though classes were cancelled due to flooding.[82] The court pointed out that the board treated the teacher like all other employees who were on unpaid leave insofar as it refused to pay them for days on which the schools were closed.

As to sabbatical leaves, boards face potentially troublesome issues in evaluating eligibility and what positions teachers return to when they come back from leaves. Clearly, boards retain discretion in granting sabbaticals.[83] When teachers are scheduled to return to work, disputes arise over whether they are entitled to their exact same positions. Courts generally do not interpret the term "same position" as meaning the same exact academic job.[84]

If one party breaches a sabbatical contract, either teachers[85] or boards[86] can sue. Once teachers return from sabbatical leaves, they retain

---

77. *Board of School Trustees of Salem Community Schools v. Robertson*, 637 N.E.2d 181 [92 Educ. L. Rep. 962] (Ind. Ct. App. 1994).

78. *Mercedes Indep. School Dist. v. Munoz*, 941 S.W.2d 215 [117 Educ. L. Rep. 373] (Tex. Ct. App. 1996).

79. For a review of the use of leave time for religious purposes, *see* the discussion of *Ansonia Bd. of Educ. v. Philbrook*, 479 U.S. 60, 107 S.Ct. 367, 93 L.Ed.2d 305 [35 Educ. L. Rep. 365] (1986) at notes 182–183 and accompanying text in Chapter 9.

80. *Giordano v. Ambach*, 509 N.Y.S.2d 203 [36 Educ. L. Rep. 416] (N.Y. App. Div. 1986).

81. *Snyder v. Jefferson County School Dist. R–1*, 842 P.2d 624 [79 Educ. L. Rep. 632] (Colo. 1992).

82. *Godon v. Kindred Pub. School Dist.*, 798 N.W.2d 664 [267 Educ. L. Rep. 870] (N.D. 2011).

83. *Board of Educ. of Three Village Cent. Schools of Towns of Brookhaven and Smithtown v. Three Village Teachers' Ass'n*, 419 N.Y.S.2d 665 (N.Y. App. Div. 1979).

84. *Taube v. St. Charles Parish School Bd.*, 787 So.2d 377 [155 Educ. L. Rep. 976] (La. Ct. App. 2001).

85. *Cahill v. Board of Educ. of City of Stamford*, 444 A.2d 907 [4 Educ. L. Rep. 163] (Conn. 1982).

86. *Trumansburg Cent. School Dist. v. Chalone*, 449 N.Y.S.2d 92 [3 Educ. L. Rep. 720] (N.Y. App. Div. 1982).

the rights that they would have enjoyed had they remained in active service but do not gain enhanced rights.[87]

ASSIGNMENTS AND TRANSFERS

School boards have the discretion to assign teachers to individual schools since educators do not have rights to teach in specific buildings.[88] Since some states have established statutory or regulatory policies for employee transfers, school officials must comply with their mandates.[89] Absent state-level constraints, local boards, often subject to terms in collective bargaining agreements, have the discretion[90] to establish their own policies with regard to assigning, and transferring, teachers to similar positions[91] within their areas of certification[92] even if, for example, an individual is relieved of coaching responsibilities in the process.[93]

As long as school boards comply with their own rules, courts ordinarily do not intervene. In a dispute from New Jersey, an appellate court wrote that a board could involuntarily transfer a tenured teacher when it abolished his position and required him to teach different subjects within his area of certification.[94] The court specified that the board did not violate the teacher's rights since he did not suffer a loss in pay or other job benefits and was not singled out for the transfer on a prohibited basis.

In Indiana, a federal trial court granted a school board's motion for summary judgment when it transferred a teacher during an investigation over whether he behaved inappropriately with two female students.[95] The court remarked that insofar as officials provided the teacher with suitable employment, it did not force him to resign. The Seventh Circuit reached the same outcome in affirming that a board in Illinois did not violate the rights of a tenured physical education teacher when it temporarily transferred him to an administrative position, with full pay, pending an investi-

---

87. *Gardner v. State ex rel. Dep't of Educ.*, 844 So.2d 311 [176 Educ. L. Rep. 955] (La. Ct. App. 2003), *writ denied*, 847 So.2d 1280 (La. 2003).

88. *Gordon v. Nicoletti*, 84 F. Supp.2d 304 [142 Educ. L. Rep. 169] (D. Conn.2000); *Maupin v. Independent School Dist. No. 26*, 632 P.2d 396 (Okla. 1981).

89. *Ex parte Ezell*, 545 So.2d 52 [54 Educ. L. Rep. 1023] (Ala.1989), *on remand*, 545 So.2d 55 [55 Educ. L. Rep. 334] (Ala. Civ. App. 1989).

90. *Stevenson v. Lower Marion County School Dist. No. Three*, 327 S.E.2d 656 [23 Educ. L. Rep. 1101] (S.C. 1985).

91. *Thomas v. Smith*, 897 F.2d 154 [58 Educ. L. Rep. 1114] (5th Cir. 1989).

92. *Quarles v. McKenzie Pub. School Dist. No. 34*, 325 N.W.2d 662 [7 Educ. L. Rep. 401] (N.D. 1982); *Adlerstein v. Board of Educ. of City of N.Y.*, 466 N.Y.S.2d 973 [13 Educ. L. Rep. 836] (N.Y. App. Div.1983), *aff'd*, 485 N.Y.S.2d 1 [22 Educ. L. Rep. 1220] (N.Y. 1984).

93. *Jett v. Dallas Indep. School Dist.*, 798 F.2d 748 [34 Educ. L. Rep. 384] (5th Cir. 1986), *aff'd in part, remanded in part*, 491 U.S. 701, 109 S.Ct. 2702, 105 L.Ed.2d 598 [54 Educ. L. Rep. 30] (1989).

94. *Carpenito v. Board of Educ. of the Borough of Rumson*, 731 A.2d 538 [135 Educ. L. Rep. 567] (N.J. Super. Ct. App. Div. 1999).

95. *Tweedall v. Fritz*, 987 F.Supp. 1126 [124 Educ. L. Rep. 122] (S.D. Ind. 1997).

gation after one of his students drowned due to an apparent lack of supervision in the pool area.[96]

An older case reflects the general rule that teachers can be discharged for refusing to accept assignments in their areas of competence. When a physical education teacher who was relieved of his duties as football coach refused to continue to coach basketball, the Supreme Court of Pennsylvania upheld his dismissal.[97] More than sixty years later, an appellate court in Texas affirmed that when a tenured teacher refused to come to work for three months as a protest against being transferred, the board had cause to terminate her employment.[98]

Involuntary transfers are subject to heightened judicial scrutiny if they involve educators' exercises of their First Amendment rights. The Ninth Circuit addressed a controversy involving the transfer of a counselor of Mexican American ancestry who criticized board policies relating to the classification of Mexican American children since the tests were given in English. A federal trial court in Arizona maintained that while the transfer was impermissible since it was partially in retaliation for the counselor's exercise of her First Amendment rights, she lacked an entitlement to relief because she did not suffer a loss of pay or status. In remanding, the panel concluded that the counselor was entitled to a remedy, emphasizing that she had neither harassed school officials nor was insubordinate.[99] Previously, the Supreme Court of California invalidated the transfer of a teacher who was critical of, but complied with, board policies.[100]

Individuals in administrative positions may be reassigned to other jobs,[101] including those lower in the hierarchy,[102] or teaching,[103] ordinarily without hearings,[104] absent statutory or contractual provisions to the contrary. If, as with other school staff, state statutes provide detailed directives dealing with the demotion of administrators, officials must strictly apply the law.[105]

---

96. *Townsend v. Vallas*, 256 F.3d 661 [155 Educ. L. Rep. 142] (7th Cir. 2001).

97. *Appeal of Ganaposki*, 2 A.2d 742 (Pa. 1938).

98. *Miller v. Houston Indep. School Dist.*, 51 S.W.3d 676 [156 Educ. L. Rep. 708] (Tex. Ct. App. 2001), *reh'g overruled, review denied, reh'g of petition for review denied, cert. denied*, 535 U.S. 905, 122 S.Ct. 1203, 152 L.Ed.2d 142 (2002).

99. *Bernasconi v. Tempe Elementary School Dist. No. 3*, 548 F.2d 857 (9th Cir.1977), *cert. denied*, 434 U.S. 825, 98 S.Ct. 72, 54 L.Ed.2d 82 (1977).

100. *Adcock v. Board of Educ. of San Diego Unified School Dist.*, 109 Cal.Rptr. 676 (Cal. 1973).

101. *McCoy v. McConnell*, 461 S.W.2d 948 (Tenn. 1970).

102. *Scottsdale School Dist. v. Clark*, 512 P.2d 853 (Ariz. Ct. App. 1973).

103. *Love–Lane v. Martin*, 201 F. Supp.2d 566 [165 Educ. L. Rep. 526] (M.D.N.C.2002), *aff'd in relevant part, vacated in part, and remanded*, 355 F.3d 766 [184 Educ. L. Rep. 133] (4th Cir. 2004), *cert. denied*, 543 U.S. 813, 125 S.Ct. 49, 160 L.Ed.2d 18 [192 Educ. L. Rep. 301] (2004).

104. *Sharp v. Lindsey*, 285 F.3d 479 [163 Educ. L. Rep. 88] (6th Cir. 2002); *McCoy v. Lincoln Intermediate Unit No. 12*, 391 A.2d 1119 (Pa. Cmwlth. Ct.1978), *cert. denied*, 441 U.S. 923, 99 S.Ct. 2033, 60 L.Ed.2d 397 (1979).

105. *Edgar v. School Bd. of Calhoun County*, 549 So.2d 726 [56 Educ. L. Rep. 680] (Fla. Dist. Ct. App. 1989).

Disputes also arise over the free speech rights of principals, especially if their actions subject them to demotions. The Sixth Circuit affirmed that the free speech rights of a principal from Tennessee who was returned to a teaching job after he criticized his superintendent's position on a dress code were outweighed by the latter's need for a good working relationship with staff.[106] Further, the Seventh Circuit affirmed that a board in Wisconsin could demote a principal to assistant principal since, as a policymaking employee, her criticism of its attempts to gain additional state aid for disadvantaged students was not protected free speech.[107]

A final factor that is sometimes involved in teacher assignments is race. Since this topic is discussed in detail in Chapter 16, suffice it to say that the courts have reached mixed results in examining the role of race as a factor in transfers and reassignments in eliminating racial segregation.[108]

LOYALTY

LOYALTY OATHS

After World War II, loyalty oaths for teachers and other public employees proliferated. As provisions became increasingly extensive, they focused more on what teachers should have avoided doing rather than on what they should have done. Some oaths barred teachers from participating in outside groups while others contained stipulations requiring them to attest that they did not engage in specified activities before being hired. Oaths often included criminal penalties for making false statements and being rendered ineligible for teaching.

In its first case on point, *Wieman v. Updegraff*,[109] the Supreme Court unanimously invalidated a loyalty oath statute from Oklahoma primarily because it disqualified individuals from public employment if, during the preceding five years, they belonged to organizations deemed subversive, regardless of whether they knew of their character. In conceding that membership could have been innocent, the Court did not believe that public employees should have been punished for joining groups if they were unaware of their activities and purposes.

At issue in *Sweezy v. State of New Hampshire*[110] was a contempt conviction that had been entered against a guest speaker at a university

---

106. *Sharp v. Lindsey*, 285 F.3d 479 [163 Educ. L. Rep. 88] (6th Cir. 2002).

107. *Vargas–Harrison v. Racine Unified School Dist.*, 272 F.3d 964 [159 Educ. L. Rep. 459] (7th Cir. 2001), *cert. denied*, 537 U.S. 826, 123 S.Ct. 120, 154 L.Ed.2d 38 (2002).

108. *See, e.g., Wygant v. Jackson Bd. of Educ.*, 476 U.S. 267, 106 S.Ct. 1842, 90 L.Ed.2d 260 [32 Educ. L. Rep. 20] (1986), *reh'g denied*, 478 U.S. 1014, 106 S.Ct. 3320, 92 L.Ed.2d 728 [35 Educ. L. Rep. 20] (1986); *Jacobson v. Cincinnati Bd. of Educ.*, 961 F.2d 100 [74 Educ. L. Rep. 51] (6th Cir.1992), *cert. denied*, 506 U.S. 830, 113 S.Ct. 94, 121 L.Ed.2d 55 (1992). [Case No. 62]

109. 344 U.S. 183, 73 S.Ct. 215, 97 L.Ed. 216 (1952).

110. 354 U.S. 234, 77 S.Ct. 1203, 1 L.Ed.2d 1311 (1957), *reh'g denied*, 355 U.S. 852, 78 S.Ct. 7, 2 L.Ed.2d 61 (1957).

who refused to answer questions about his knowledge of political parties and their members. Although the dispute did not involve a loyalty oath per se, the Supreme Court vitiated the speaker's conviction because the questions were an invasion of his liberties in the areas of academic freedom and political expression.

In *Cramp v. Board of Public Instruction of Orange County, Florida*, the Supreme Court, again unanimously, invalidated an oath as unconstitutionally vague since it barred individuals from giving "aid, support, advice, counsel or influence to the Communist Party."[111] Although not questioning the state's power to safeguard the public service from disloyalty, the Court decreed that officials had to describe forbidden conduct in language that was sufficiently objective.

The Supreme Court, in *Elfbrandt v. Russell*,[112] introduced a new criterion for loyalty legislation from Arizona: officials could not impose penalties unless they could show that individual members of organizations joined them with the specific intent of furthering or participating in the groups' unlawful ends. Fearing that teachers might have been inhibited from participating in a variety of activities if the new criterion were not added, the Court held that to presume that members share in the unlawful aims of organizations to which they belong is an unconstitutional inference.

In *Knight v. Board of Regents of University of State of New York* (*Knight*),[113] the Supreme Court summarily upheld an oath that required individuals to support the federal and state constitutions while faithfully discharging their job duties. The trial court decided that insofar as the oath did not impose restrictions on political or philosophical expressions and was not unconstitutionally vague, the state had the authority to require educators to take the oath.

Citing *Knight* as the leading case, the Supreme Court, in a per curiam opinion, upheld a similar requirement from Florida in *Connell v. Higginbotham* since it demanded no more of public employees than was required of all state and federal officers. The Justices also agreed that the state could not summarily dismiss those who refused to pledge that they did "not believe in the overthrow of the government . . . by force or violence."[114]

In *Biklen v. Board of Education*,[115] the Supreme Court upheld the oath from *Knight* in a religious challenge from a teacher in New York. After a federal trial court was convinced that the state had a compelling interest in having teachers agree to support the federal and state constitutions, the Court affirmed, in a memorandum opinion, that insofar as a teacher had the opportunity to make the oath or affirmation and thus retain her

---

111.   368 U.S. 278, 281, 82 S.Ct. 275, 7 L.Ed.2d 285 (1961).

112.   384 U.S. 11, 86 S.Ct. 1238, 16 L.Ed.2d 321 (1966).

113.   269 F.Supp. 339 (S.D.N.Y.1967), *aff'd*, 390 U.S. 36, 88 S.Ct. 816, 19 L.Ed.2d 812 (1968). [Case No. 63]

114.   403 U.S. 207, 209, 91 S.Ct. 1772, 29 L.Ed.2d 418 (1971).

115.   333 F.Supp. 902 (N.D.N.Y.1971), *aff'd*, 406 U.S. 951, 92 S.Ct. 2060, 32 L.Ed.2d 340 (1972).

position, she was not entitled to a hearing before her contract was terminated.

In a plurality, *Cole v. Richardson*, the Supreme Court upheld an oath from Massachusetts which required individuals to "oppose the overthrow of the government of the United States of America or of this Commonwealth by force, violence or by any illegal or unconstitutional method."[116] The Court also unanimously sustained language obligating individuals to uphold and defend the federal and commonwealth constitutions since this only applied, rather than expanded, the obligation of the oath's first provision.

NEW YORK'S FEINBERG LAW

New York State enacted the Feinberg Law, which, although not requiring an oath, was designed to implement and enforce older statutes. The new law made membership in subversive organizations prima facie evidence of disqualification for employment in public schools, further requiring the Board of Regents, along with local boards, to file reports on teacher loyalty. In *Adler v. Board of Education* (*Adler*),[117] the Supreme Court upheld the facial constitutionality of the statute on the basis that if an organization had been declared subversive, and if employees were notified, they would have been free to choose between group membership and public employment.

After the Feinberg Law was extended to personnel of public institutions of higher learning, the state developed complex administrative procedures. However, in *Keyishian v. Board of Regents of University of State of New York*, the Supreme Court invalidated this system, including the Feinberg Law, its administrative regulations, and the two older statutes that it was enacted to implement, since "[t]he regulatory maze created by New York [wa]s wholly lacking in 'terms susceptible of objective measurement.' "[118] The Court ruled that unlike *Adler*, which involved a review of a declaratory judgment suit, it had yet to consider a charge of unconstitutional vagueness that had not been raised in the earlier case.

THE FIFTH AMENDMENT

During the 1950s, Congressional and state legislative investigative committees were common. When a congressional committee investigating Communist activities tried to question a faculty member at a public college in New York City, he refused to answer, pleading the Fifth Amendment's provision against self-incrimination. Even so, a section in the city charter provided that whenever employees utilized this privilege to avoid answering questions about their official conduct, their employment was automatically terminated. In *Slochower v. Board of Higher Education of New York City*,[119] the Supreme Court noted that the provision violated due process.

---

116.   405 U.S. 676, 677–78, 92 S.Ct. 1332, 31 L.Ed.2d 593 (1972).
117.   342 U.S. 485, 72 S.Ct. 380, 96 L.Ed. 517 (1952).
118.   385 U.S. 589, 604, 87 S.Ct. 675, 17 L.Ed.2d 629 (1967).
119.   350 U.S. 551, 76 S.Ct. 637, 100 L.Ed. 692 (1956).

Adding that it did not think that the faculty member had a right to teach in higher education, or that a proper inquiry might not have shown that dismissal was warranted, the Court found that a summary dismissal without a hearing violated due process.

Two years later, in *Beilan v. Board of Public Education, School District of Philadelphia*,[120] the Supreme Court upheld a teacher's dismissal for refusing to answer whether he had been an officer of the Communist Political Association in the previous eight years. Agreeing that he was insubordinate and lacked both frankness and candor, the Court contended that insofar as fitness to teach depends on a broad range of factors, of which classroom conduct is but one, the board had the authority to dismiss the teacher.

As evidence that the effects of anti-Communist investigations linger, an appellate court in New York affirmed that denial of a petitioner's request to access records of interviews.[121] The court conceded that although the transcripts of interviews about membership in the Communist Party were relevant to the work of the board of education, the privacy interests of the surviving subjects of the investigation and their relatives outweighed any interest in publishing the names of teachers that were in the disputed records.

COLLECTIVE BARGAINING

IN GENERAL

Modeled largely after the process in private sector industrial labor relations, collective bargaining is the vehicle whereby school boards and their employees negotiate over terms and conditions of employment, a term of art that emerged out of the National Labor Relations Act. Public sector bargaining received a big boost in 1958 when New York City permitted municipal employees to bargain collectively for the first time. In 1959, Wisconsin became the first state to mandate bargaining by public employees.[122] A brief strike by teachers in New York City in 1962 led to a wave of teacher activism[123] culminating in more than thirty states enacting statutes granting teachers the right to organize and bargain collectively with their school boards over terms and conditions of employment.[124]

---

120. 357 U.S. 399, 78 S.Ct. 1317, 2 L.Ed.2d 1414 (1958).

121. *Harbatkin v. New York City Dep't of Records and Information Servs.*, 924 N.Y.S.2d 80 [267 Educ. L. Rep. 783] (N.Y. App. Div. 2011).

122. GUS TYLER, WHY THEY ORGANIZE, IN EDUCATION AND COLLECTIVE BARGAINING: READINGS IN POLICY AND RESEARCH 19–20 (Anthony M. Cresswell & Michael J. Murphy eds. 1976).

123. CHARLES TAYLOR KERCHNER & DOUGLAS E. MITCHELL, THE CHANGING IDEA OF A TEACHER'S UNION 1 (1988).

124. *See, e.g.*, CAL. GOV'T CODE § 3540; COLO. REV. STAT. ANN. § 8–2–101; CONN. GEN. STAT. ANN. § 10–153a; DEL. CODE ANN. tit. 14, § 4001; IDAHO CODE ANN. § 33–1271; 115 ILL. COMP. STAT. ANN. 5/1; IND. CODE ANN. § 20–7.5–1–1; IOWA CODE ANN. § 20.1; KAN. STAT. ANN. § 75–4321; ME. REV. STAT. ANN. tit. 26, § 966; MD. CODE ANN., EDUC. §§ 4–312 *et seq.*; MICH. STAT. ANN. § 423.209; MINN. STAT. ANN. § 179.10; NEB. REV. STAT. ANN. § 81–1370; N.H. REV. STAT. ANN. §§ 273–A:1 *et seq.*;

The extent to which boards may engage in bargaining varies from one jurisdiction to the next. In fact, considerable controversy has erupted pursuant to changes that legislatures made in states such as Wisconsin[125] and Ohio[126] over the extent to which teachers and other public school employees may be able to bargain over the terms and conditions of their employment. How these disputes are resolved may well shape the future of collective bargaining in public education.

To the extent that state law permits them to do so, school boards and employee unions are free to enter into contracts created via legally approved bargaining processes on topics that are properly subject to negotiations. The Federal Constitution not only guarantees freedom of speech and association but also restricts the conditions that can be placed on public employees. While the First Amendment does not require boards to recognize or bargain with unions,[127] it does protect teachers who join labor organizations[128] and cannot discipline them for doing so or for engaging in protected union activities.

BARGAINING UNITS

In order to negotiate with their school boards, employee unions must organize bargaining units. Once local unions are organized, state-level public employment relations boards typically certify that, as a result of votes of eligible employees, they are recognized as the exclusive bargaining agents of their members.[129] Once boards recognize unions, negotiations are limited to sessions with the exclusive bargaining representatives of their employees.[130] As such, boards may not engage in direct dealings with teachers in which they bypass their unions to discuss terms and conditions of employment.[131]

N.J. Stat. Ann. § 34:13A–5.3; McKinney's Civil Serv. Law Ann. §§ 204 *ET SEQ.*; N.D. Cent. Code Ann. § 34–08–02; Ohio Rev. Code Ann. §§ 4117.01 *ET SEQ.*; Or. Rev. Stat. §§ 243.650 *ET SEQ.*; Pa. Stat. Ann. TIT. 24, § 11–1133; R.I. Gen. Laws Ann. §§ 28–9.3–1 *ET SEQ.*; S.D. Cod. Laws Ann. §§ 3–18–1 *ET SEQ.*; Vt. Stat. Ann. TIT. 16 §§ 1981 *ET SEQ.*; Wash. Rev. Code Ann. §§ 41.56.010 *ET SEQ.*

125. Wis. Stat. § 111.70. This statute survived a challenge in *State ex rel. Ozanne v. Fitzgerald*, 798 N.W.2d 436 (Wis. 2011).

126. OHIO REV. CODE ANN. §§ 4117.01 *et seq.* Since voters repudiated this law in a ballot initiative, presumably the matter heads back to the Ohio General Assembly. For news coverage, *see, e.g.,* Laura A. Bischoff & Lynn Hulsey, *Unions Celebrate Decisive Victory*, DAYTON DAILY NEWS, Nov. 9, 2011, at A1.

127. *See, e.g., Federacion de Maestros de Puerto Rico v. Acevedo–Vila*, 545 F. Supp.2d 219 [232 Educ. L. Rep. 648] (D. Puerto Rico 2008) (reiterating the general rule that public employees, such as teachers, who carry out traditional governmental functions, lack constitutional rights to organize, to engage in collective bargaining, to strike, and/or to participate in picketing).

128. *Stellmaker v. DePetrillo*, 710 F.Supp. 891 [53 Educ. L. Rep. 512] (D. Conn.1989).

129. *Appeal of Londonderry School Dist.*, 707 A.2d 137 [124 Educ. L. Rep. 948] (N.H. 1998).

130. *Independence–Nat'l Educ. Ass'n v. Independence School Dist.*, 162 S.W.3d 18 [198 Educ. L. Rep. 357] (Mo. Ct. App. 2005), *transfer denied* (2005), *on subsequent appeal*, 223 S.W.3d 131 [221 Educ. L. Rep. 398] (Mo. 2007).

131. *Board of Educ. of Region 16 v. State Bd. of Labor Relations*, 7 A.3d 371 [261 Educ. L. Rep. 993] (Conn. 2010).

On their part, unions have the duty to represent all employees in good faith[132] during and after bargaining, including individuals who are not members but must pay so-called agency or representation fees,[133] discussed below. In a case dealing with the duty of fair representation, an appellate court in Massachusetts affirmed that a union's refusal to pursue a former substitute teacher's grievances against her school was not a breach of its duty of fair representation.[134] The court held that absent evidence supporting the teacher's claim of bad faith against the union, her grievances were unfounded. Conversely, the Supreme Court of Connecticut affirmed that a union breached its duty of fair representation in connection with the dismissal of one of its members when its representative negotiated a settlement with the school board that was unfavorable to him but did not inform him of this fact.[135]

As a means of avoiding conflicts of interest, different bargaining units form around communities of interest such that teachers, typically referred to as professional staff, are in one unit, while other employees, usually referred to as classified staff, such as office workers and maintenance staff, are in another.[136] For instance, an appellate court in New York affirmed that a teachers' union did not have the duty to represent retired teachers since retired employees do not belong to the same community of interest as active employees.[137] At the same time, managerial or administrative and confidential employees who work in personnel offices with information and/or others involved in bargaining are usually not permitted to form unions.[138] In fact, the Supreme Court of Nebraska decided that a union violated state law when it tried to include principals and supervisors in the same unit.[139]

132. *See, e.g., Sutton v. Cleveland Bd. of Educ.,* 958 F.2d 1339 [73 Educ. L. Rep. 624] (6th Cir. 1992); *Fratus v. Marion Community Schools Bd. of Trustees,* 749 N.E.2d 40 [154 Educ. L. Rep. 642] (Ind. 2001); *Service Employees Int'l Union Local No. 150 v. Wisconsin Employment Relations Comm'n,* 791 N.W.2d 662 [262 Educ. L. Rep. 622] (Wis. Ct. App. 2010), *review denied,* 793 N.W.2d 69 (Wis. 2010).

133. *O'Brien v. City of Springfield,* 319 F. Supp.2d 90 [189 Educ. L. Rep. 142] (D. Mass. 2003).

134. *Saxonis v. City of Lynn,* 817 N.E.2d 793 [193 Educ. L. Rep. 309] (Mass. App. Ct. 2004), *review denied,* 822 N.E.2d 304 (Mass. 2005), *cert. denied,* 546 U.S. 819, 126 S.Ct. 350, 163 L.Ed.2d 59 (2005).

135. *Piteau v. Board of Educ. of City of Hartford,* 15 A.3d 1067 [265 Educ. L. Rep. 1115] (Conn. 2011).

136. *See, e.g., Neshannock Educational Support Professionals Ass'n v. Pennsylvania Labor Relations Bd.,* 22 A.3d 1103 [269 Educ. L. Rep. 264] (Pa. Cmwlth. Ct. 2011) (declaring that an accounts payable clerk could join the bargaining unit for non-professional staff because she was not a confidential employee).

137. *Baker v. Board of Educ., Hoosick Falls Cent. School Dist.,* 770 N.Y.S.2d 782 [184 Educ. L. Rep. 940] (N.Y. App. Div. 2004).

138. *Barrington School Comm. v. Rhode Island State Labor Relations Bd.,* 608 A.2d 1126 [75 Educ. L. Rep. 1130] (R.I. 1992); *Chicago Teachers Union v. Illinois Educ. Labor Relations Bd.,* 695 N.E.2d 1332 [127 Educ. L. Rep. 369] (Ill. App. Ct. 1998). *But see, e.g., Pennsylvania School Bds. Ass'n v. Commonwealth Ass'n of School Adm'rs,* 805 A.2d 476, 491 [169 Educ. L. Rep. 289, 304] (Pa. 2002).

139. *Papillion/La Vista Schools Principals and Supervisors Org. v. Papillion/LaVista Dist. No. 27,* 562 N.W.2d 335 [117 Educ. L. Rep. 736] (Neb. 1997).

SCOPE OF BARGAINING

Collective bargaining is subject to legislative control and judicial interpretation. Since statutes vary in scope and specificity, some refer only expansively to terms and conditions of employment while others leave gray areas requiring judicial interpretation.

Topics for bargaining can be classified into three broad categories.[140] Consistent with practices in private sector labor law, mandatory topics include such matters as salaries and other terms and conditions of employment. On the other hand, boards and unions are prohibited from engaging in managerial prerogatives such as setting staffing needs and curriculum. A third category of topics, those that are permissive, is most readily subject to judicial interpretation.

In a case demonstrating the difficulty in evaluating which of the three areas within which items for bargaining fit, the Supreme Court of Alaska explained that "logically and semantically it is nearly impossible to assign specific items"[141] beyond salaries, fringe benefits, number of hours worked, and amount of leave time to the categories of negotiable or non-negotiable. The court, in strongly suggesting that more specific guidance from the legislature would have been helpful, categorized fifty items which had been raised in the three cases it consolidated for review. The non-negotiable topics included relief from nonprofessional chores, class size and teacher load, personnel evaluation, and school calendar. Acknowledging the difficulty in seeking to place all topics neatly into these three sometimes overlapping categories, the following sections review major topics under each, highlighting judicial exceptions in various jurisdictions.

Mandatory Topics of Bargaining

In considering whether proposals are subject to mandatory bargaining, the Supreme Court of Iowa offered a two-part test.[142] First, the court pointed out that proposals had to fall within the meaning of subjects listed in the state's collective bargaining statute. Second, the court indicated that proposals could not be outside of the scope of bargaining. In light of its analysis, the court asserted that issues concerning staff who taught more than 300 minutes per day and pooling sick leave were mandatory topics while those dealing with evaluations and the time and place of wage payments were not subject to mandatory bargaining.[143]

---

140.   See *Colonial School Bd. v. Colonial Affiliate*, 449 A.2d 243 [6 Educ. L. Rep. 87] (Del. Super. Ct. 1982).

141.   *Kenai Peninsula Borough School Dist. v. Kenai Peninsula Educ. Ass'n*, 572 P.2d 416, 422 (Alaska 1977).

142.   For similar tests, see *In re Hillsboro–Deering School Dist.*, 737 A.2d 1098 [138 Educ. L. Rep. 447] (N.H. 1999); *Webster Educ. Ass'n v. Webster School Dist.*, 631 N.W.2d 202 [155 Educ. L. Rep. 1381] (S.D. 2001).

143.   *Waterloo Community School Dist. v. Pub. Employment Relations Bd.*, 650 N.W.2d 627 [169 Educ. L. Rep. 402] (Iowa 2002); *Kenai Peninsula Borough School Dist. v. Kenai Peninsula Educ. Ass'n*, 572 P.2d 416, 422 (Alaska 1977).

Beyond terms and conditions of employment, such as salaries[144] and fringe benefits,[145] over which boards are statutorily bound to bargain, courts agree that an array of topics are subject to mandatory negotiations. Among the items that courts have agreed are mandatory subjects of bargaining due to their impact on financial aspects of employment are a new policy requiring teachers to submit their lesson plans via the internet;[146] reimbursing teachers for graduate studies;[147] the impact of a smoke-free work environment;[148] holiday pay;[149] subcontracting of services;[150] early retirement incentives;[151] a reduction-in-force plan;[152] stipends for mileage and released time while serving on professional development committees;[153] a proposed dress code policy;[154] a merit system for hiring set forth in a bargaining agreement;[155] moving expenses for a new teacher;[156] teacher transfers and reassignments;[157] and whether a contract was subject to remain in effect until the parties negotiated a new agreement.[158]

Prohibited Topics of Bargaining

Among the topics that courts interpreted as beyond the power of school boards to bargain over are whether to consolidate the positions of two

144. *See, e.g., Fort Stewart Schools v. Federal Labor Relations Auth.*, 495 U.S. 641, 110 S.Ct. 2043, 109 L.Ed.2d 659 [60 Educ. L. Rep. 9] (1990) (affirming that proposals for salary, leave, and mileage reimbursement for teachers at schools owned and operated by the United States Army were mandatory subjects of bargaining); *Neshaminy Fed'n of Teachers Local Union 1417 v. Pennsylvania Labor Relations Bd.*, 986 A.2d 908 [252 Educ. L. Rep. 271] (Pa. Cmwlth. Ct. 2009).

145. *Secretary of Admin. & Finance v. Commonwealth Employment Relations Bd.*, 904 N.E.2d 468 (Mass. Ct. App. 2009) (dealing with parking fringe benefits).

146. *School Dist. of Indian River County v. Florida Pub. Employees Relations Comm'n*, 64 So.3d 723 [269 Educ. L. Rep. 418] (Fla. Dist. Ct. App. 2011).

147. *Barnett v. Durant Community School Dist.*, 249 N.W.2d 626 (Iowa 1977).

148. *Local 1186 of Council No. 4, AFSCME, AFL–CIO v. State Bd. of Labor Relations*, 620 A.2d 766 [81 Educ. L. Rep. 206] (Conn. 1993).

149. *Cadott Educ. Ass'n v. Wisconsin Employment Relations Comm'n*, 540 N.W.2d 21 [104 Educ. L. Rep. 1345] (Wis. Ct. App. 1995).

150. *Matter of Watkins Glen Cent. School Dist. (Watkins Glen Faculty Ass'n)*, 628 N.Y.S.2d 824 [101 Educ. L. Rep. 1022] (App. Div. 1995); *Morrisville School Dist. v. Pennsylvania Labor Relations Bd.*, 687 A.2d 5 [115 Educ. L. Rep. 29] (Pa. Cmwlth. Ct. 1996), *appeal denied*, 700 A.2d 445 (Pa. 1997).

151. *Ringgold School Dist. v. Ringgold Educ. Ass'n*, 694 A.2d 1163 [119 Educ. L. Rep. 190] (Pa. Cmwlth. Ct. 1997).

152. *Webster Educ. Ass'n v. Webster School Dist.*, 631 N.W.2d 202 [155 Educ. L. Rep. 1381] (S.D. 2001).

153. *Governing Bd. of Special Educ. Dist. of Lake County v. Sedol Teachers' Union, Lake County Fed'n of Teachers, Local 504, IFT–AFT, AFL–CIO*, 772 N.E.2d 847 [167 Educ. L. Rep. 886] (Ill. App. Ct. 2002), *appeal denied*, 786 N.E.2d 183 (Ill. 2002).

154. *Polk County Bd. of Educ. v. Polk County Educ.*, 139 S.W.3d 304 [190 Educ. L. Rep. 1072] (Tenn. Ct. App. 2004), *appeal denied* (2004).

155. *Walter v. Scherzinger*, 121 P.3d 644 [202 Educ. L. Rep. 844] (Or. 2005).

156. *Ekalaka Unified Bd. of Trustees v. Ekalaka Teachers' Ass'n*, 149 P.3d 902 [215 Educ. L. Rep. 1123] (Mont. 2006).

157. *Bonner School Dist. No. 14 v. Bonner Educ. Ass'n*, 176 P.3d 262 [229 Educ. L. Rep. 247] (Mont. 2008). *See also Lawrence County Educ. Ass'n v. Lawrence County Bd. of Educ.*, 244 S.W.3d 302 [229 Educ. L. Rep. 958] (Tenn. 2007) (noting that a collective bargaining agreement could modify the authority of school officials to transfer tenured teachers).

158. *Central City Educ. Ass'n v. Merrick City School Dist.*, 783 N.W.2d 600 [257 Educ. L. Rep. 1042] (Neb. 2010).

department chairs[159] or to abolish jobs;[160] assignments and transfer policies;[161] granting tenure;[162] withholding salary increments;[163] creating school
calendars;[164] appointing principals[165] and department heads;[166] and rework-
ing a board's organizational structure.[167]

The amount of time that teachers must work in inclement weather has
led to disputes, thereby serving as a segue into the next section on
permissive topics of bargaining. In a case with mixed results, an appellate
court in Indiana observed that although a board did not have the duty to
bargain over make-up days and adopting a policy on school closings, its
practice of issuing supplemental contracts to teachers for make-up days did
not elevate the subject of make-up days to the status of a mandatory topic
of bargaining.[168] The court also posited that the board's refusal to initiate
discussions with the union about make-up days and a school closing plan
was an unfair labor practice. Similarly, an appellate court in New Jersey
maintained that while a board did not have to negotiate over whether to
have class on days scheduled as recess days in order to make up for time
missed due to snow, the impact of the change was subject to bargaining.[169]

Permissive Topics of Bargaining

If topics are not excluded from bargaining, questions arise as to
whether they must be subject to negotiations. Although many disputes
begin in administrative proceedings, they are typically resolved by the
courts. In considering whether topics are subject to mandatory or permissive bargaining, some courts, rather than simply proclaiming matters
subject to mandatory bargaining, have suggested guidelines beyond such

---

159. *Dunellen Bd. of Educ. v. Dunellen Educ. Ass'n*, 311 A.2d 737 (N.J. 1973).

160. *School Comm. of Braintree v. Raymond*, 343 N.E.2d 145 (Mass. 1976).

161. *Blount County Educ. Ass'n v. Blount County Bd. of Educ.*, 78 S.W.3d 307 [167 Educ. L. Rep. 504] (Tenn. Ct. App. 2002). *See also School Dist. of Seward Educ. Ass'n v. School Dist.*, 199 N.W.2d 752 (Neb. 1972).

162. *Cohoes City School Dist. v. Cohoes Teachers Ass'n*, 390 N.Y.S.2d 53, 358 N.E.2d 878 (1976); *School Comm. of Danvers v. Tyman*, 360 N.E.2d 877 (Mass.1977); *Mindemann v. Independent School Dist. No. 6 of Caddo County*, 771 P.2d 996 [53 Educ. L. Rep. 270] (Okla. 1989).

163. *Board of Educ. of Twp. of Bernards v. Bernards Twp. Educ. Ass'n*, 399 A.2d 620 (N.J. 1979).

164. *Kenai Peninsula Borough School Dist. v. Kenai Peninsula Educ. Ass'n*, 572 P.2d 416 (Alaska 1977); *Montgomery County Educ. Ass'n v. Board of Educ. of Montgomery County*, 534 A.2d 980 [43 Educ. L. Rep. 720] (Md. 1987); *Public Employee Relations Bd. v. Washington Teachers' Union Local 6*, 556 A.2d 206 [52 Educ. L. Rep. 1075] (D.C. 1989).

165. *Berkshire Hills Reg'l School Dist. Comm. v. Berkshire Hills Educ. Ass'n*, 377 N.E.2d 940 (Mass. 1978).

166. *Maine School Admin. Dist. No. 61 Bd. of Dirs. v. Lake Region Teachers Ass'n*, 567 A.2d 77 [57 Educ. L. Rep. 940] (Me. 1989).

167. *State ex rel. Quiring v. Board of Educ. of Indep. School Dist. No. 173, Mountain Lake*, 623 N.W.2d 634 [152 Educ. L. Rep. 271] (Minn. Ct. App. 2001).

168. *Union County School Corp. Bd. of School Trustees v. Indiana Educ. Employment Relations Bd.*, 471 N.E.2d 1191 [21 Educ. L. Rep. 989] (Ind. Ct. App. 1984), *reh'g denied* (1985), *transfer denied* (1985).

169. *Piscataway Twp. Educ. Ass'n v. Piscataway Twp. Bd. of Educ.*, 704 A.2d 981 [123 Educ. L. Rep. 764] (N.J. Super. Ct. App. Div. 1998), *certification denied*, 718 A.2d 1214 (N.J. 1998).

basic restatements as conditions of employment, managerial prerogatives, and basic policy issues. The courts caution that these judgments must be made on case-by-case bases. In such a dispute, the Supreme Court of Kansas thought that the key was to consider "how direct the impact of an issue is on the well-being of the individual teacher, as opposed to its effect on the operation of the school system as a whole."[170] The Supreme Court of Pennsylvania set the test as "whether the impact of the issue on the interest of the employee in wages, hours and terms and conditions of employment outweighs its probable effect on the basic policy of the system as a whole."[171] Moreover, an appellate court in California offered a useful distinction in noting that permissive, or non-mandatory, topics are those neither covered by state statute nor identified by the judiciary.[172]

Among the permissive topics that courts have recognized are broad zipper clauses, which allow parties to renegotiate items in mid-contract;[173] drug testing;[174] the timing and effective dates of lay-offs;[175] and adoption of year-round schooling.[176] One of the more controversial topics of bargaining is class size since some jurisdictions treat it as excluded from bargaining[177] while others treat it as mandatory[178] or permissive.[179]

Teacher evaluations highlight differences between substance and procedure. Whether, and by whom, evaluations are carried out is usually considered to be a policy matter excluded from bargaining.[180] However, some courts treat the procedures used in the evaluation processes as subject to mandatory[181] bargaining while others view it as a permissive[182] topic.

---

170. *National Educ. Ass'n of Shawnee Mission v. Board of Educ. of Shawnee Mission Unified School Dist. No. 512*, 512 P.2d 426, 435 (Kan. 1973).

171. *Pennsylvania Labor Relations Bd. v. State College Area School Dist.*, 337 A.2d 262, 268 (Pa. 1975).

172. *South Bay Union School Dist. v. Public Employment Relations Bd.*, 279 Cal.Rptr. 135 [66 Educ. L. Rep. 357] (Cal. Ct. App. 1991).

173. *Central Dauphin School Dist. v. Central Dauphin Bus Drivers' Ass'n*, 996 A.2d 47 [257 Educ. L. Rep. 741] (Pa. Cmwlth. Ct. 2010) (affirming that impasse procedures applied to a mid-contract bargaining dispute); *Mt. Vernon Educ. Ass'n, IEA–NEA v. Illinois Educ. Labor Relations Bd.*, 663 N.E.2d 1067 [109 Educ. L. Rep. 305] (Ill. App. Ct. 1996).

174. *Drivers, Chauffeurs and Helpers Local Union No. 639 v. District of Columbia*, 631 A.2d 1205 [86 Educ. L. Rep. 283] (D.C. 1993).

175. *West Bend Educ. Ass'n v. Wisconsin Employment Relations Comm'n*, 357 N.W.2d 534 [21 Educ. L. Rep. 305] (Wis. 1984).

176. *Racine Educ. Ass'n v. Wisconsin Employment Relations Comm'n*, 571 N.W.2d 887 [122 Educ. L. Rep. 1281] (Wis. Ct. App. 1997).

177. *West Irondequoit Teachers Ass'n v. Helsby*, 358 N.Y.S.2d 720, 315 N.E.2d 775 (1974); *Kenai Peninsula Borough School Dist. v. Kenai Peninsula Educ. Ass'n*, 572 P.2d 416 (Alaska 1977).

178. *Decatur Bd. of Educ., Dist. No. 61 v. Illinois Educ. Labor Relations Bd.*, 536 N.E.2d 743 [52 Educ. L. Rep. 1153] (Ill. App. Ct.1989), *appeal denied*, 545 N.E.2d 107 (Ill. 1989).

179. *Fargo Educ. Ass'n v. Fargo Pub. School Dist. No. 1*, 291 N.W.2d 267 (N.D. 1980).

180. *Bethlehem Twp. Bd. of Educ. v. Bethlehem Twp. Educ. Ass'n*, 449 A.2d 1254 [6 Educ. L. Rep. 748] (N.J. 1982).

181. *Aplington Community School Dist. v. Iowa Pub. Employment Relations Bd.*, 392 N.W.2d 495 [34 Educ. L. Rep. 607] (Iowa 1986); *City of Beloit by Beloit City School Bd. v.*

RESTRAINTS ON BOARDS

In perhaps the most significant restraint on school boards and teachers in the realm of labor relations, the legislatures in North Carolina, Texas, and Virginia, expressly forbid collective bargaining between governmental units and employees.[183] The Supreme Court of Missouri, though, overturning its own sixty-year-old precedent to the contrary, decided that the state constitution grants public employees, including those in schools, the same right to organize and bargain collectively as their colleagues in the private sector.[184] Even so, boards may not dismiss or fail to rehire teachers solely due to their constitutionally protected union activities.[185] Likewise, consistent with provisions in state constitutions, boards cannot require teachers to identify whether they belong to various organizations, presumably including unions, as a condition of employment[186] or discriminate against those who are not union members in awarding benefits such as pay raises.[187]

So-called union shops, prevalent in the private sector and which typically require all employees to join unions within a set time after being

---

Wisconsin Employment Relations Comm'n, 242 N.W.2d 231 (Wis. 1976); Milberry v. Board of Educ. of School Dist. of Philadelphia, 354 A.2d 559 (Pa. 1976).

182. *Alton Community Unit School Dist. No. 11, Counties of Madison and Jersey v. Illinois Educ. Labor Relations Bd.*, 567 N.E.2d 671 [66 Educ. L. Rep. 397] (Ill. App. Ct. 1991); *In re Pittsfield School Dist.*, 744 A.2d 594 [141 Educ. L. Rep. 847] (N.H. 1999).

183. N.C. GEN. STAT. ANN. § 95–98, ("Any agreement, or contract, between the governing authority of any city, town, county, or other municipality, or between any agency, unit, or instrumentality thereof, or between any agency, instrumentality, or institution of the State of North Carolina, and any labor union, trade union, or labor organization, as bargaining agent for any public employees of such city, town, county or other municipality, or agency or instrumentality of government, is hereby declared to be against the public policy of the State, illegal, unlawful, void and of no effect"); *see also Winston–Salem/Forsyth County Unit of North Carolina Ass'n of Educators v. Phillips*, 381 F.Supp. 644 (M.D.N.C. 1974). TEX. GOV'T CODE ANN. § 617.002. ("(a) An official of the state or of a political subdivision of the state may not enter into a collective bargaining contract with a labor organization regarding wages, hours, or conditions of employment of public employees. (b) A contract entered into in violation of Subsection (a) is void. (c) An official of the state or of a political subdivision of the state may not recognize a labor organization as the bargaining agent for a group of public employees"). VA. CODE ANN. § 40.1–57.2 ("No state, county, municipal, or like governmental officer, agent or governing body is vested with or possesses any authority to recognize any labor union or other employee association as a bargaining agent of any public officers or employees, or to collectively bargain or enter into any collective bargaining contract with any such union or association or its agents with respect to any matter relating to them or their employment or service"); *see also Commonwealth v. County Bd. of Arlington County*, 232 S.E.2d 30 (Va. 1977).

184. *Independence–Nat'l Educ. Ass'n v. Independence School Dist.*, 223 S.W.3d 131 [221 Educ. L. Rep. 398] (Mo. 2007) (expressly rejecting *City of Springfield v. Clouse*, 206 S.W.2d 539 (Mo. 1947)).

185. *Fort Frye Teachers Ass'n v. SERB*, 809 N.E.2d 1130 [188 Educ. L. Rep. 433] (Ohio 2004) (remarking that the nonrenewal of a teacher's contract due to his union activities was an unfair labor practice); *Classroom Teachers of Dallas/Texas State Teachers Ass'n/National Educ. Ass'n v. Dallas Indep. School Dist.*, 164 F. Supp.2d 839 [157 Educ. L. Rep. 677] (N.D. Tex. 2001) (finding that anti-union threats, harassment, and illegal threats of dismissal did not amount to an adverse employment action); *Morfin v. Albuquerque Pub. Schools*, 906 F.2d 1434 [61 Educ. L. Rep. 470] (10th Cir. 1990); *Hickman v. Valley Local School Dist. Bd. of Educ.*, 619 F.2d 606 (6th Cir. 1980); *Durango School Dist. No. 9–R v. Thorpe*, 614 P.2d 880 (Colo. 1980).

186. *Shelton v. Tucker*, 364 U.S. 479, 81 S.Ct. 247, 5 L.Ed.2d 231 (1960).

187. *Benson v. School Dist. No. 1 of Silver Bow County*, 344 P.2d 117 (Mont. 1959).

hired, are either not permitted or expressly forbidden in public employment. As such, two issues, one on dues collection, the other on communications with members, arise as to how unions can interact with their members. The first of these two concerns relates to the collection of dues via employee "check-offs," on appropriate forms; this addresses the willingness of unions to permit their boards to collect the dues via payroll deductions before passing the funds on to the unions. Most states with collective bargaining statutes permit "dues check-offs" to assist unions in their activities.[188]

Fair Share Fees and Payroll Deductions

An important issue involving union activities deals with financial support for costs associated with bargaining, especially as expenses relate to individuals who exercise their right not to join organizations. In order to balance equities, unions can charge nonmembers agency or representation fees to pay their fair share for the services that they receive via their negotiated employment contracts. The Supreme Court has addressed various aspects of fair share arrangements in educational contexts on four separate occasions.

Abood v. Detroit Board of Education (Abood)[189] is the first Supreme Court case on agency fees in education. In *Abood*, the Court specified that the Constitution does not prohibit agency fee provisions in bargaining contracts as long as unions do not use these funds to support ideological activities that members and nonmembers oppose and that are unrelated to the process of negotiations. The Court explained that insofar as individuals who object to how their funds are being spent must notify unions of their concerns, they should do so in general terms so that they do not have to reveal their positions on particular matters.

Six years later, in a non-school case, the Supreme Court decreed that agency fees could be used for conventions, business meetings and occasional social activities, and publications that communicate about nonpolitical activities.[190] The Court also approved of advanced reductions of fees for nonmembers. At the same time, the Court forbade unions from using agency fees for organizing activities and litigation not connected to bargaining while disapproving the use of rebates in dealing with fees even if unions paid interest on these funds.

The Supreme Court next examined procedures established to effectuate the collection of dues in *Chicago Teachers Union, Local No. 1, AFT, AFL–CIO v. Hudson.*[191] The Court disapproved of a rebate system because it did

---

188. *But see City of Charlotte v. Local 660, Intern. Ass'n of Firefighters*, 426 U.S. 283, 96 S.Ct. 2036, 48 L.Ed.2d 636 (1976) (declaring that public employee unions do not have a constitutional right to "check-offs").

189. 431 U.S. 209, 97 S.Ct. 1782, 52 L.Ed.2d 261 (1977).

190. *Ellis v. Brotherhood of Railway, Airline and Steamship Clerks, Freight Handlers, Express and Station Employees*, 466 U.S. 435, 104 S.Ct. 1883, 80 L.Ed.2d 428 (1984).

191. 475 U.S. 292, 106 S.Ct. 1066, 89 L.Ed.2d 232 [30 Educ. L. Rep. 649] (1986), *on remand*, 922 F.2d 1306 [65 Educ. L. Rep. 81] (7th Cir. 1991), *cert. denied*, 501 U.S. 1230, 111 S.Ct. 2852, 115 L.Ed.2d 1020 (1991).

not avoid the risk that funds of nonunion members might have temporarily been used for improper purposes. Under this system the Court feared that the unions offered inadequate information to justify the amount of agency fees while not affording reasonably prompt answers about expenditures and fees by an impartial third-party decision maker.

In a case from Michigan involving a faculty union in a public institution of higher learning, *Lehnert v. Ferris Faculty Association*,[192] the Supreme Court considered which activities unions may charge to nonmembers. According to the Court, chargeable items must be germane to bargaining, must be justified by the government's vital policy interest in labor peace and avoiding "free riders," and must not significantly add to the burdening of free speech inherent in allowing an agency or union shop. The Court permitted a local union to bill nonmembers for costs associated with otherwise chargeable activities of its state and national affiliates even when those activities, such as for publications dealing not only with bargaining but with teaching and education generally, professional development, employment opportunities, and miscellaneous matters were neither political nor public in nature. The Court refused to permit the union to charge nonmembers for the costs of lobbying and general public relations activities.

The Ninth Circuit, in a case from California, reiterated that insofar as non-union members have an absolute right to be free from supporting speech with which they may disagree, unions must develop fair, prompt, and effective procedures to identify what sums individuals must pay and how their money is to be used.[193] State courts continue to apply similar analyses in upholding dues "check-off" provisions as long as adequate safeguards are in place.[194]

Turning to its fourth educational case on point, the Supreme Court further restricted the ability of unions to spend the fair share fees of nonmembers. In *Davenport v. Washington Education Association*, the Court unanimously held that "it does not violate the First Amendment for a State to require that its public-sector [teacher] unions receive affirmative authorization from a nonmember before spending that nonmember's agency fees for election-related purposes."[195] In vacating the judgment of the Supreme Court of Washington, the Justices decided that the statute violated the rights of nonmembers in requiring them to make express requests that their fees not be used to support activities with which they disagreed. The

---

192.   500 U.S. 507, 111 S.Ct. 1950, 114 L.Ed.2d 572 [67 Educ. L. Rep. 421] (1991).

193.   *Grunwald v. San Bernardino City Unified School Dist.*, 994 F.2d 1370 [83 Educ. L. Rep. 963] (9th Cir. 1993), *cert. denied*, 510 U.S. 964, 114 S.Ct. 439, 126 L.Ed.2d 373 (1993). *See also Mitchell v. Los Angeles Unified School Dist.*, 963 F.2d 258 [75 Educ. L. Rep. 126] (9th Cir. 1992), *cert. denied*, 506 U.S. 940, 113 S.Ct. 375, 121 L.Ed.2d 287 (1992) (stating that a union's opt out procedures to give dissenting nonunion employees opportunities to object to full agency fees protected their First Amendment rights).

194.   *Laborers Local No. 942 v. Lampkin*, 956 P.2d 422 [126 Educ. L. Rep. 437] (Alaska 1998); *Hayden v. Linton–Stockton Classroom Teachers Ass'n*, 686 N.E.2d 143 [122 Educ. L. Rep. 527] (Ind. Ct. App.1997); *Browne v. Wisconsin Employment Relations Comm'n*, 485 N.W.2d 376 [75 Educ. L. Rep. 502] (Wis. 1992), *reconsideration denied*, 491 N.W.2d 770 (Wis. 1992).

195.   551 U.S. 177, 191, 127 S.Ct. 2372, 2383, 168 L.Ed.2d 71 (2007). [Case No. 64]

Court essentially declared that nonmembers can continue to enjoy the benefits of union membership without having to support all union activities since such an approach more accurately reflects the support of members for the political activities of their unions.

In a related matter, the Ninth[196] and Tenth[197] Circuits struck down laws forbidding payroll deductions for union political advocacy on the ground that doing so violated the free speech rights of public employees, including teachers. On further review of the case from the Ninth Circuit, *Ysursa v. Pocatello Education Association*, (*Ysursa*), the Supreme Court ruled that the ban on public-employee payroll deductions for political activities at the local level was constitutional because it furthered Idaho's interest in separating the operation of government from partisan politics, noting that educational officials were "under no obligation to aid the Unions in their political activities."[198] In light of *Ysursa*, the Tenth Circuit reversed its earlier order and upheld the law from Utah which forbade state or local public employers from withholding voluntary political contributions from the paychecks of their employees.[199] Further, the Supreme Court of Michigan reached a like result in affirming that a payroll deduction plan designed to remit funds to a union's political action committee was an impermissible contribution under state law.[200]

Union Communications in Schools

The second important concern of unions is being able to communicate with members at their places of work, especially if rival groups seek access to the same people. In *Perry Education Association v. Perry Local Educators' Association*, a case from Indiana, the Supreme Court addressed "whether the First Amendment . . . is violated when a union that has been elected by public school teachers as their exclusive bargaining representative is granted access to certain means of communication while such access is denied to a rival union."[201] Responding that this was not a constitutional violation, the Court found that the privilege of exclusive access to intra-school system mail facilities was properly characterized as an appropriate restriction on the use of public property that was not, by designation or in fact, a general public forum or a limited public forum. Even if the mailing system were to be considered a limited public forum by virtue of its occasional use by groups such as the Cub Scouts and YMCAs, the Justices wrote that the First Amendment would require only that similar organizations be granted access. The Court did not agree that the rival union fell

---

196. *Pocatello Educ. Ass'n v. Heideman*, 504 F.3d 1053 (9th Cir. 2007), *cert. granted sub nom. Ysursa v. Pocatello Educ. Ass'n*, 552 U.S. 1294, 128 S.Ct. 1762, 170 L.Ed.2d 538 (2008).

197. *Utah Educ. Ass'n v. Shurtleff*, 512 F.3d 1254 (10th Cir. 2008).

198. 555 U.S. 353, 129 S.Ct. 1093, 1099, 172 L.Ed.2d 770 (2009), *on remand sub nom. Pocatello Educ. Ass'n v. Heideman*, 561 F.3d 1048 (9th Cir. 2009). [Case No. 65]

199. *Utah Educ. Ass'n v. Shurtleff*, 565 F.3d 1226 (10th Cir. 2009).

200. *Michigan Educ. Ass'n v. Secretary of State*, 801 N.W.2d 35 [269 Educ. L. Rep. 842] (Mich. 2011).

201. 460 U.S. 37, 44, 103 S.Ct. 948, 74 L.Ed.2d 794 [9 Educ. L. Rep. 23] (1983), *on remand*, 705 F.2d 462 (7th Cir. 1983).

into the category of groups entitled to access because insofar as the union had a unique function, the board acted rationally in the interest of labor peace by agreeing to limit access to the exclusive bargaining representative of its staff. The Court ascertained that the rival union was excluded not because of its views, but due to its status in relation to the board and its teachers. In asserting that the rival union had alternative channels of communication available such as bulletin boards, meeting rooms, and the United States mail in addition to its having had equal access to mailboxes during election periods, the Court was satisfied that the board did not violate its rights.

In *Texas State Teachers Association v. Garland Independent School District*[202] the Supreme Court summarily affirmed a judgment from the Fifth Circuit which maintained that insofar as a school board had not created either public or limited public fora in its schools or mail facilities, denying a teachers' organization access to them during school hours did not violate teachers' First Amendment rights because alternative means of communication were available. The Court thought that board policies purporting to deny faculty members the right to discuss teacher organizations during non-class time and preventing them from using school mail facilities to communicate about employee organizations were unconstitutional. More recently, the Supreme Court of California affirmed that insofar as teacher mailboxes were not public fora, a policy prohibiting a union from placing endorsements of candidates who were running for the school board in the mailboxes was a viewpoint-neutral regulation that satisfied First Amendment analysis since they were not places where the open exchange of ideas occurred.[203]

DISPUTE RESOLUTION

School boards and unions ordinarily resolve disputes over the administration of collective bargaining contracts through grievances that, depending on state laws and local contracts, may pass through various stages before being subject to arbitration. Arbitration is properly used to refer to the process whereby parties agree to be bound by the decision of a third party that they select. Since arbitration is an alternative to judicial review, when courts are content that arbitrators draw their judgments from the essence of the underlying bargaining agreements, more often than not they leave the adjudications in place, especially if plaintiffs fail to exhaust administrative remedies under collective bargaining agreements.[204] In evaluating whether terms and/or conditions in bargaining contracts are drawn from the essence of the agreements, courts often consider whether past practices between the parties impact the way in which contracts are implemented.[205]

---

202. 784 F.2d 1113 [30 Educ. L. Rep. 1108] (5th Cir.1986), *aff'd*, 479 U.S. 801, 107 S.Ct. 41, 93 L.Ed.2d 4 [34 Educ. L. Rep. 1004](1986).

203. *San Leandro Teachers Ass'n v. Governing Bd. of San Leandro Unified School Dist.*, 95 Cal.Rptr.3d 164 [245 Educ. L. Rep. 364] (Cal. 2009).

204. *See, e.g., Gazunis v. Foster*, 929 A.2d 531 [223 Educ. L. Rep. 293] (Md. 2007).

205. *See, e.g., Penns Manor Area School Dist. v. Penns Manor Area Educ. Support Personnel Ass'n*, 953 A.2d 614 [235 Educ. L. Rep. 465] (Pa. Cmwlth. Ct. 2008) (affirming that

Arbitration should not be confused with mediation, conciliation, fact-finding, or other forms of conflict resolution that do not culminate in legally binding outcomes. There is an important distinction between interest arbitration, which focuses on an agreement's terms, and rights or grievance arbitration that is concerned with a provision's application to an existing agreement. Grievance arbitration is prevalent in both the public and private sectors. While interest arbitration is virtually unused in the private sector, it constitutes one way to resolve impasses in the public sector when work stoppages, regardless of whether they are legally permissible, pose a danger to the public welfare. As described by Massachusetts' highest court, " 'interest' arbitration involves the settlement of the terms of a contract between the parties, whereas, in the more familiar 'grievance' arbitration, the subject is [sic] claimed violation or interpretation of the terms of an existing contract."[206]

As demonstrated by an opinion of the Supreme Court of New Jersey, the judiciary initially questioned the role of the public in the formulation and application of policy if arbitrators resolve too many matters related to bargaining. In a case restricting the scope of educational matters that were negotiable and/or arbitrable, the court mused that "[t]here would be little room for community involvement if agreements concerning educational policy matters could be negotiated behind closed doors and disputes concerning that agreement settled by an arbitrator who lacks public accountability."[207] The Supreme Court of Pennsylvania later illustrated how this concern lessened when it commented that a law which gave selected school administrators the right to bargain collectively and engage in binding arbitration was not an unlawful delegation of legislative powers.[208]

A case from the Court of Appeals of New York exemplifies how the issue of non-delegability of board power cannot be raised to stay the process where broad arbitration clauses are in collective bargaining contracts and arbitrators fashion sufficiently narrow remedies. Even though the ultimate decision on class composition is ordinarily up to a board's discretion, when a board summarily altered the make-up of a class, the court held that the dispute could proceed to arbitration since the bargaining agreement provided for this method of dispute resolution in disputes concerning proper contractual interpretation.[209]

Questions of lawful delegation of governmental power arise in connection with arbitration, especially interest arbitration. Courts do not agree whether the ultimate authority to craft contractual provisions with school boards can be placed in the hands of separate bodies created to resolve

---

past practices between the parties created a separate and enforceable term of employment which school board officials could not alter unilaterally).

206. *School Comm. of Boston v. Boston Teachers Union, Local 66, Am. Fed'n of Teachers,* 363 N.E.2d 485, 486 (Mass. 1977), *superseded by statute/rule, Marlborough Firefighters, Local 1714 v. City of Marlborough,* 378 N.E.2d 437 (Mass. 1978).

207. *Ridgefield Park Educ. Ass'n v. Ridgefield Park Bd. of Educ.,* 393 A.2d 278, 286–87 (N.J. 1978).

208. *Pennsylvania School Bds. Ass'n v. Commonwealth Ass'n of School Adm'rs,* 805 A.2d 476, 491 [169 Educ. L. Rep. 289, 304] (Pa. 2002).

209. *Babylon Union Free School Dist. v. Babylon Teachers Ass'n,* 579 N.Y.S.2d 629 [72 Educ. L. Rep. 988] (N.Y. 1991).

impasses. Where parties rely on interest arbitration, courts typically emphasize the need for enabling statutes to include standards and parameters circumscribing the focus and scope of the process.[210]

As to grievance arbitration, most courts have followed the lead of the highest court of Connecticut,[211] which was the first to uphold the power of a local board to enter into a contract with a teachers' association to arbitrate grievances. Boards, of course, can agree to arbitrate grievances only if statutorily empowered to do so. If boards voluntarily agree to arbitration in jurisdictions permitting them to do so, the results are usually binding as long as matters are properly delegable. At the same time, arbitration can generally only be initiated by parties to bargaining contracts, namely school boards and unions, rather than individuals who are covered by those agreements.[212]

In light of disagreements over the scope of arbitration, the Supreme Court of New Hampshire enunciated a three-part test for evaluating whether disputes are arbitrable. This test considers, first, if an issue is reserved to the exclusive authority of a school board; second, if a proposal primarily impacts terms and conditions of employment rather than managerial prerogatives; and third, if a proposal is incorporated into a bargaining agreement, neither the resulting contractual term nor the grievance process may interfere with the board's performance of its duty.[213] In the underlying dispute, the court ruled that the board did not engage in impermissible subcontracting by eliminating a teacher's job and offering band options to students outside of the school.[214]

Including grievance arbitration clauses in collective bargaining contracts has spawned a great deal of litigation. To the extent that arbitration developed in the private sector as a substitute for judicial review, and the parties voluntarily agree to its use, courts are reluctant to intervene in labor disputes. Consequently, absent contractual language to the contrary, in interpreting private sector labor agreements, the presumption has been that the parties agreed to arbitrate disputes, with doubts being resolved in favor of coverage.[215] The courts have largely transferred this perspective to the educational arena.[216] The judiciary broadly interprets general arbitration clauses in bargaining contracts, granting stays only where statutes

---

210. *City of Amsterdam v. Helsby*, 371 N.Y.S.2d 404 (N.Y. 1975).

211. *Norwalk Teachers' Ass'n v. Board of Educ.*, 83 A.2d 482 (Conn. 1951).

212. *Ray v. Brookville Area School Dist.*, 19 A.3d 29 [267 Educ. L. Rep. 731] (Pa. Cmwlth. Ct. 2011).

213. *In re Kennedy*, 27 A.3d 844 (N.H. 2011), *as modified on denial of reconsideration* (2011). [Case No. 66]

214. *In re Board of Educ. of Watertown City School Dist. (Watertown Educ. Ass'n)*, 688 N.Y.S.2d 463 [134 Educ. L. Rep. 984] (N.Y. 1999). Earlier, the New York Court of Appeals devised a two-part test with the first considering the "may they do so" test, addressing the subject matter of disputes and whether parties expressed a lawful intent to bargain and the second examining the "did they do so" test in reviewing whether the parties agreed to arbitrate grievances, acknowledging that this does not employ a presumption for or against arbitration.

215. *United Steelworkers of Am. v. Warrior & Gulf Navigation Co.*, 363 U.S. 574, 80 S.Ct. 1347, 4 L.Ed.2d 1409 (1960).

216. *See, e.g., Davis v. Chester Upland School Dist.*, 786 A.2d 186 [160 Educ. L. Rep. 170] (Pa. 2001).

have vested power solely in boards or where permitting the process to proceed would violate public policy.[217]

A case from New York examined the scope of an arbitrator's authority. An appellate court affirmed that an arbitrator could order a board to cease the unilateral implementation of a resolution changing health insurance providers that had been identified in a bargaining agreement since the award did not violate public policy.[218] Also, the court modified the order in finding that the arbitrator exceeded the scope of his authority in directing the board to reinstate teachers who were laid off since doing so exceeded the specifically enumerated limitations on his power.

When parties submit to arbitration, the scope of judicial review is limited. Since the parties have bargained for arbitrators' interpretations, the courts ordinarily do not deal with the merits of disputes. If the subject matter of grievances is arguably covered by a contract, whether petitioners are right or wrong is a question for arbitrators to evaluate.[219] Neither ambiguities as to coverage nor arbitrators' alleged errors of interpretation of law or fact, absent irrationality[220] or other impermissible grounds such as fraud, or bad faith, generally are subject to litigation. The courts review arbitration awards only to assure that they rationally draw their essence from bargaining agreements[221] and that remedies are not contrary to law or boards' managerial prerogative such as dismissing an employee for immorality where a teacher-coach sent love letters to students.[222] Arbitrators need to have flexibility in considering remedies. This fact is integral to the theory underlying the use of arbitration as a means of resolving disputes in the ongoing relationships between organized employees and management.[223] The parties, of course, may place contractual restrictions on remedies.

---

217. *Board of Educ., West Babylon Union Free School Dist. v. West Babylon Teachers Ass'n*, 438 N.Y.S.2d 291 (N.Y. 1981).

218. *Buffalo Teachers Fed'n v. Board of Educ. of City School Dist. of City of Buffalo*, 855 N.Y.S.2d 775 [231 Educ. L. Rep. 874] (N.Y. App. Div. 2008).

219. *United Steelworkers of Am. v. American Mfg. Co.*, 363 U.S. 564, 80 S.Ct. 1343, 4 L.Ed.2d 1403 (1960).

220. "An arbitrator's interpretation [must] be upheld if it can, in any rational way, be derived from the language and context of the agreement.... [R]eversal is not warranted even if a court believes that the decision, though rational, is incorrect." *Greater Johnstown Area Vocational–Technical School v. Greater Johnstown Area Vocational–Technical Educ. Ass'n*, 553 A.2d 913, 915 [51 Educ. L. Rep. 983] (Pa. 1989).

221. *See, e.g., Allegheny Valley School Dist. v. Allegheny Valley Educ. Ass'n*, 943 A.2d 1021 [230 Educ. L. Rep. 338] (Pa. Cmwlth. Ct. 2008) (affirming that an arbitration award allowing a teacher to use sick leave for a family member's medical appointment was rationally derived from the operative bargaining agreement); *School Dist. of City of Erie v. Erie Educ. Ass'n*, 873 A.2d 73 [197 Educ. L. Rep. 658] (Pa. Cmwlth. Ct. 2005) (ruling that an arbitration order that a board violated the bargaining agreement with its teachers by effecting unilateral changes in the terms and conditions of their employment by expecting individuals to teach physical education to students in their homerooms was rationally derived from the contract). *But see Flandreau Pub. School Dist. No. 50–3 v. G.A. Johnson Const.*, 701 N.W.2d 430 [200 Educ. L. Rep. 396] (S.D. 2005) (affirming that a trial court, not an arbitrator, had the authority to consider whether a dispute was subject to arbitration).

222. *Manheim Cent. Educ. Ass'n v. Manheim Cent. School Dist.*, 572 A.2d 31 [59 Educ. L. Rep. 445] (Pa. Cmwlth. Ct.1990), *appeal denied*, 582 A.2d 326 (Pa. 1990).

223. *See United Steelworkers of Am. v. Warrior & Gulf Navigation Co.*, 363 U.S. 574, 80 S.Ct. 1347, 4 L.Ed.2d 1409 (1960).

Among the issues that courts agreed were subject to arbitration dealt with disputes over whether a teacher could compel arbitration over his unresolved grievance even though his teaching certificate had expired;[224] class size provisions for special education classes;[225] to clarify an ambiguity over whether a matter was subject to arbitration;[226] whether a female teacher could return to work early from maternity leave;[227] a teacher's placement on a salary scale;[228] a teacher's voluntary transfer;[229] whether a union complied with time requirements for filing a grievance;[230] withholding a salary increment from a principal who was absent excessively;[231] whether employees could receive both early-retirement bonuses and payments for unused sick leave;[232] extra-duty assignments;[233] terminating a teacher's contract for failing to renew his certificate;[234] a proposed bumping system to be used as part of a reduction-in-force;[235] teachers' entitlements to the value of selected shares of stock that a board received due to the demutualization of its health insurer;[236] a board's mid-term contract termination of a custodian's employment;[237] eliminating a composition period for high school English teachers;[238] and terminating a social worker's contract.[239]

Other courts agreed that the placement of a letter in a teacher's personnel file that did not result in disciplinary proceedings against her;[240]

224. *Kalispell Educ. Ass'n v. Board of Trustees, Kalispell High School Dist. No. 5*, 255 P.3d 199 [269 Educ. L. Rep. 287] (Mont. 2011).

225. *New Britain Bd. of Educ. v. New Britain Fed'n of Teachers*, 754 F.Supp.2d 407 [266 Educ. L. Rep. 126] (D. Conn. 2010).

226. *Board of Educ. of Deer Park Union Free School Dist. v. Deer Park Teacher's Ass'n*, 909 N.Y.S.2d 738 [261 Educ. L. Rep. 721] (N.Y. App. Div. 2010).

227. *West Allegheny School Dist. v. West Allegheny Educ. Ass'n*, 997 A.2d 411 [258 Educ. L. Rep. 336] (Pa. Commw. Ct. 2010).

228. *Souderton Area School Dist. v. Souderton Area Educ. Ass'n*, 639 A.2d 904 [90 Educ. L. Rep. 275] (Pa. Cmwlth. Ct.1994), *appeal denied*, 655 A.2d 519 (Pa. 1994).

229. *Orleans Parish School Bd. v. United Teachers of New Orleans*, 689 So.2d 645 [116 Educ. L. Rep. 1320] (La. Ct. App.1997), *writ denied*, 692 So.2d 1091 (La. 1997).

230. *Dalton v. Schneider*, 667 N.Y.S.2d 523 [123 Educ. L. Rep. 860] (N.Y. App. Div. 1997).

231. *Edison Twp. Bd. of Educ., Middlesex County v. Edison Twp. Principals and Supervisors Ass'n*, 701 A.2d 459 [121 Educ. L Rep. 1075] (N.J. Super. Ct. App. Div.1997).

232. *United School Dist. v. United Educ. Ass'n*, 782 A.2d 40 [157 Educ. L. Rep. 782] (Pa. Cmwlth. Ct. 2001).

233. *Apollo–Ridge School Dist. v. Apollo–Ridge Educ. Ass'n*, 799 A.2d 911 [166 Educ. L. Rep. 275] (Pa. Cmwlth. Ct. 2002).

234. *Mount Adams School Dist. v. Cook*, 81 P.3d 111 [183 Educ. L. Rep. 1017] (Wash. 2003).

235. *School Comm. of Westport v. American Fed'n of State, County and Mun. Employees, Council 93, Local 2667*, 810 N.E.2d 848 [188 Educ. L. Rep. 962] (Mass. App. Ct. 2004).

236. *Region 14 Bd. of Educ. v. Nonnewaug Teachers' Ass'n*, 866 A.2d 1252 [195 Educ. L. Rep. 909] (Conn. 2005).

237. *Pascack Valley Bd. of Educ. v. Support Staff*, 933 A.2d 589 [225 Educ. L. Rep. 997] (N.J. 2007).

238. *North Providence School Comm. v. North Providence Fed'n of Teachers, Local 920, American Fed'n of Teachers*, 945 A.2d 339 [231 Educ. L. Rep. 339] (R.I. 2008).

239. *Walton v. Maine School Admin. Dist. 52*, 945 A.2d 1241 [231 Educ. L. Rep. 386] (Me. 2008).

240. *Hickey v. New York City Dep't of Educ.*, 903 N.Y.S.2d 362 [258 Educ. L. Rep. 359] (N.Y. App. Div. 2010), *aff'd*, 929 N.Y.S.2d 1 [270 Educ. L. Rep. 825] (N.Y. 2011).

whether a teacher should have been rehired as a basketball coach;[241] a disagreement over health insurance;[242] the nonrenewal of a teacher's contract;[243] a teacher's dismissal for not renewing his teaching certificate;[244] using a sick-leave bank for extended post maternity leave;[245] a school nurse's duty to dispense medication for students with special needs;[246] and selecting teachers to work during summer school[247] were not subject to arbitration. Another group of courts believed that arbitrators exceeded the scope of their authority in directing a board to negotiate the rate of compensation for teachers who had to work beyond the end of the school day;[248] ordering the reinstatement of a non-permanent teacher;[249] and a dispute over controversial reading materials.[250]

A final form of dispute resolution occurs when contract negotiations break down and neither party is willing to compromise. At this point, the parties can declare an impasse[251] and, depending on the jurisdiction, proceed to mediation and/or fact-finding.[252] When breakdowns occur following the expirations of contracts, courts fall into three groups. Courts in the first group agree that original agreements may be deemed to continue by the implied mutual assent of the parties[253] while those in the second declare that boards must continue to pay step increases to employees.[254] Courts in

241. *Franklin County Bd. of Educ. v. Crabtree*, 337 S.W.3d 808 [267 Educ. L. Rep. 409] (Tenn. Ct. App. 2010), *reh'g denied* (2010), *appeal denied* (2011).

242. *In re Massena Cent. School Dist.*, 918 N.Y.S.2d 228 [265 Educ. L. Rep. 390] (N.Y. App. Div. 2011).

243. *Warwick School Comm. v. Warwick Teachers' Union*, 705 A.2d 984 [123 Educ. L. Rep. 1228] (R.I. 1998).

244. *Mount Adams School Dist. v. Cook*, 81 P.3d 111 [183 Educ. L. Rep. 1017] (Wash. 2003).

245. *Pocantico Hills Cent. School Dist. v. Pocantico Hills Teachers Ass'n*, 694 N.Y.S.2d 417 [137 Educ. L. Rep. 759] (N.Y. App. Div. 1999), *leave to appeal denied*, 705 N.Y.S.2d 6 (N.Y. 2000).

246. *Woonsocket Teachers' Guild, Local 951, AFT v. Woonsocket School Comm.*, 770 A.2d 834 [153 Educ. L. Rep. 319] (R.I. 2001).

247. *Chicago Teachers Union, Local No. 1 Am. Fed'n of Teachers v. Illinois Educ. Labor Relations Bd.*, 778 N.E.2d 1232 [171 Educ. L. Rep. 539] (Ill. App. Ct. 2002), *appeal denied*, 787 N.E.2d 171 (Ill. 2003).

248. *Central Dauphin School Dist. v. Central Dauphin Educ. Ass'n*, 767 A.2d 16 [151 Educ. L. Rep. 532] (Pa. Cmwlth. Ct. 2001).

249. *North Miami Educ. Ass'n v. North Miami Community Schools*, 736 N.E.2d 749 [148 Educ. L. Rep. 445] (Ind. Ct. App.2000), *decision clarified on reh'g*, 746 N.E.2d 380 [153 Educ. L. Rep. 352] (Ind. Ct. App.2001), *transfer denied*, 761 N.E.2d 417 (Ind. 2001).

250. *School Admin. Dist. No. 58 v. Mount Abram Teachers Ass'n*, 704 A.2d 349 [123 Educ. L. Rep. 255] (Me. 1997).

251. For cases discussing impasse, *see, e.g., Mountain Valley Educ. Ass'n v. Maine School Admin. Dist. No. 43*, 655 A.2d 348 [98 Educ. L. Rep. 256] (Me.1995); *State ex rel. Boggs v. Springfield Local School Dist. Bd. of Educ.*, 694 N.E.2d 1346 [125 Educ. L. Rep. 1337] (Ohio 1998).

252. *See, e.g.,* OHIO REV. CODE ANN. § 4117.14(C) for a statute dealing with breakdowns in bargaining.

253. *State ex rel. Boggs v. Springfield Local School Dist. Bd. of Educ.*, 757 N.E.2d 339 [158 Educ. L. Rep. 435] (Ohio 2001), *reconsideration denied*, 761 N.E.2d 49 (Ohio 2002).

254. *Board of Trustees of Univ. of Me. Sys. v. Associated Colt Staff of Univ. of Me. Sys.*, 659 A.2d 842 [101 Educ. L. Rep. 279] (Me. 1995); *See also Cobleskill Cent. School Dist. v. Newman*, 481 N.Y.S.2d 795 [21 Educ. L. Rep. 645] (N.Y. App. Div. 1984).

the third group refuse to order boards to pay step increases.[255] The next section examines whether cessations in bargaining can lead to work stoppages or strikes.

STRIKES AND OTHER CONCERTED ACTIVITIES

Strikes have been fairly common in the private sector. Even so, courts and legislatures ordinarily frown on strikes by teachers and other public employees. In the earliest case on point, the Supreme Court of Errors of Connecticut, although conceding that educators had the right to bargain collectively, concluded that teacher strikes were illegal.[256] In addition to common law barriers against teacher strikes, as reflected by an order of an appellate court in Massachusetts,[257] courts have overwhelmingly sustained statutory prohibitions against strikes[258] absent express legislative permission authorizing work stoppages.[259] Some courts have thus granted teachers a qualified right to strike.[260]

In a case with a twist, an appellate court in Ohio considered the meaning of a strike. The court affirmed that when school bus drivers refused to be available to transport students to extracurricular activities since they did not have a duty to do so, their refusal to render this voluntary service could not be viewed as a strike.[261]

When teachers threaten to strike, courts typically use their discretion in evaluating requests for injunctions. The Supreme Court of Michigan was the first court to apply restraint in granting injunctions when it required a board to show that a strike would have resulted in "violence, irreparable injury, or breach of the peace" since injunctions on other grounds are "basically contrary to [state] public policy."[262] The Supreme Court of New Hampshire, while agreeing that strikes by public employees were illegal, followed the lead of Michigan and pointed out that an injunction should not have automatically been issued since it had to consider operational factors

---

255. *Board of Educ. of Twp. of Neptune in County of Monmouth v. Neptune Twp. Educ. Ass'n*, 675 A.2d 611 [115 Educ. L. Rep. 372] (N.J.1996). *See also Providence Teachers Union v. Providence School Bd.*, 689 A.2d 388 [116 Educ. L. Rep. 703] (R.I. 1997).

256. *Norwalk Teachers' Ass'n v. Board of Educ.*, 83 A.2d 482 (Conn.1951). *See also Pinellas County Classroom Teachers Ass'n v. Board of Pub. Instruction of Pinellas County*, 214 So.2d 34 (Fla. 1968).

257. *Commonwealth Employment Relations Bd. v. Boston Teachers Union*, 908 N.E.2d 772 [245 Educ. L. Rep. 991] (Mass. Ct. App. 2009), *review denied*, 914 N.E.2d 330 (Mass. 2009), *cert. denied*, ___ U.S. ___, 130 S.Ct. 1738, 176 L.Ed.2d 213 (2010). [Case No. 67]

258. *See, e.g., Anchorage Educ. Ass'n v. Anchorage School Dist.*, 648 P.2d 993 [5 Educ. L. Rep. 1010] (Alaska 1982); *Warwick School Comm. v. Warwick Teachers' Union, Local 915*, 613 A.2d 1273 [77 Educ. L. Rep. 861] (R.I. 1992); *Mountain Valley Educ. Ass'n v. Maine School Admin. Dist. No. 43*, 655 A.2d 348 [98 Educ. L. Rep. 256] (Me. 1995).

259. *Jefferson County Bd. of Educ. v. Jefferson County Educ. Ass'n*, 393 S.E.2d 653 [61 Educ. L. Rep. 765] (W. Va. 1990).

260. *Reichley v. North Penn School Dist.*, 626 A.2d 123 [83 Educ. L. Rep. 1030] (Pa. 1993); *Martin v. Montezuma–Cortez School Dist. RE–1*, 841 P.2d 237 [79 Educ. L. Rep. 256] (Colo. 1992).

261. *Shelby Ass'n of School Support, OEA/NEA v. Shelby City Bd. of Educ.*, 662 N.E.2d 37 [107 Educ. L. Rep. 980] (Ohio Ct. App. 1995).

262. *School Dist. for City of Holland v. Holland Educ. Ass'n*, 157 N.W.2d 206, 210 (Mich. 1968).

such as whether negotiations were conducted in good faith and whether recognized methods of settlement failed.[263] An appellate court in Minnesota, in revoking a temporary injunction in favor of a union on the ground that it failed to show irreparable harm, explained that any right the teachers had to strike matured when they filed the notice of intent to strike rather than when it was actually exercised.[264] In another case, the Supreme Court of Arkansas affirmed that taxpayers did not have a right to enjoin a strike by teachers absent a showing of irreparable harm.[265]

The courts can punish violations of judicial orders to end strikes by placing unions and their leaders in contempt even without jury trials.[266] When union officials violate court orders, they and their unions can be fined[267] and suffer the loss of dues "check-off" privileges.[268] Leaders can also be jailed for contempt.[269] Yet, statements that individuals intend to violate injunctions against strikes are not acceptable bases for contempt decrees.[270]

Teachers who participate in illegal strikes may face penalties including loss of pay,[271] perhaps having to reimburse boards for expenses caused incident to strikes,[272] and, as highlighted by the Supreme Court's judgment in a case from Wisconsin, *Hortonville Joint School District No. 1 v. Hortonville Education Association*,[273] the loss of their jobs. However, the Supreme Court of Colorado affirmed that where a strike by public school teachers was legal, their board could not recover for tortious interference with their contracts between it and other teachers.[274]

On the other hand, an appellate court in New Jersey refused to expunge the records of teachers who were incarcerated for between one and five days for refusing to comply with an injunction prohibiting them from

---

263. *Timberlane Reg'l School Dist. v. Timberlane Reg'l Educ. Ass'n*, 317 A.2d 555 (N.H. 1974).

264. *Central Lakes Educ. Ass'n v. Independent School Dist. No. 743, Sauk Centre*, 411 N.W.2d 875 [41 Educ. L. Rep. 1072] (Minn. Ct. App.1987).

265. *Wilson v. Pulaski Ass'n of Classroom Teachers*, 954 S.W.2d 221 [122 Educ. L. Rep. 334] (Ark. 1997).

266. *Rankin v. Shanker*, 295 N.Y.S.2d 625 (N.Y. 1968).

267. *Wilmington Fed'n of Teachers v. Howell*, 374 A.2d 832 (Del.1977); *Labor Relations Comm'n v. Fall River Educ. Ass'n*, 416 N.E.2d 1340 (Mass. 1981).

268. *Buffalo Teachers Fed'n v. Helsby*, 676 F.2d 28 [4 Educ. L. Rep. 14] (2d Cir. 1982).

269. *In re Block*, 236 A.2d 589 (N.J.1967). *See also Board of Educ. v. Newark Teachers Union, Local No. 481*, 276 A.2d 175 (N.J. Super. Ct. App.Div.1971), *cert. denied*, 404 U.S. 950, 92 S.Ct. 275, 30 L.Ed.2d 267 (1971).

270. *Board of Educ. of Brunswick City School Dist. v. Brunswick Educ. Ass'n*, 401 N.E.2d 440 (Ohio 1980).

271. *Board of Educ. of Marshallton–McKean School Dist. v. Sinclair*, 373 A.2d 572 (Del.1977).

272. *Passaic Twp. Bd. of Educ. v. Passaic Twp. Educ. Ass'n*, 536 A.2d 1276 [44 Educ. L. Rep. 1185] (N.J. Super. Ct. App. Div. 1987). *But see Franklin Twp. Bd. of Educ. v. Quakertown Educ. Ass'n*, 643 A.2d 34 [92 Educ. L. Rep. 525] (N.J. Super. Ct. App. Div. 1994) (reaching the opposite result).

273. 426 U.S. 482, 96 S.Ct. 2308, 49 L.Ed.2d 1 (1976).

274. *Martin v. Montezuma–Cortez School Dist. RE–1*, 841 P.2d 237 [79 Educ. L. Rep. 256] (Colo. 1992).

striking.[275] In a matter of first impression, the court determined that while its ability to expunge records was limited to criminal cases, even if it could have exercised such authority here, it would have not done so because the history of strikes in the district suggested the likelihood that another would occur in the near future.

Along with actual work stoppages, courts have granted orders forbidding teachers from engaging in such activities as mass resignations[276] and absences to protest labor issues,[277] treating these as equivalent to participating in strikes. In a related concern, since unions have engaged in picketing as a form of protest when dealing with labor issues, the practice has generated litigation. If employees picket solely to induce breaches of contracts[278] or to obstruct government functions,[279] they can be restrained. Courts do not enjoin informational picketing unless it can be shown that it is likely to be disruptive.[280]

The fact that picketing may be peaceful neither validates its use nor renders it legal when employees offer to perform essential services. In such a case, the Supreme Court of Illinois agreed that custodians could be enjoined from picketing since their behavior disrupted normal school operations.[281] The same court later affirmed that a judge could issue a temporary restraining order without notice or a hearing when striking teachers engaged in picketing.[282] The court indicated that the Constitution does not afford the same kind of freedom to those who communicate ideas by picketing as it does to those who do so via pure speech.

[CASE NO. 60]   SALARY REDUCTION–LEGISLATION IMPAIRING OBLIGATION OF CONTRACT

PHELPS v. BOARD OF EDUCATION

Supreme Court of the United States, 1937.
300 U.S. 319, 57 S.Ct. 483, 81 L.Ed. 674.

■ MR. JUSTICE ROBERTS delivered the opinion of the Court.

The people of New Jersey have ordained by their Constitution that the Legislature "shall provide for the maintenance and support of a thorough and efficient system of free public schools." In fulfillment of this command a comprehensive school law was adopted in 1903 by which boards of

---

275. *Board of Educ., Twp. of Middleton v. Middletown Teachers Educ. Ass'n*, 839 A.2d 159 [184 Educ. L. Rep. 433] (N.J. Super. Ct. Ch. Div. 2003).

276. *Board of Educ. of the City of N.Y. v. Shanker*, 286 N.Y.S.2d 453 (N.Y. App. Div. 1967).

277. *Pruzan v. Board of Educ. of City of N.Y.*, 217 N.Y.S.2d 86 (N.Y. 1961).

278. *Board of Educ. of Martins Ferry City School Dist. v. Ohio Educ. Ass'n*, 235 N.E.2d 538 (Ohio Com. Pl. 1967).

279. *State v. Heath*, 177 N.W.2d 751 (N.D. 1970).

280. *Board of Educ. of Danville Community Consol. School Dist. No. 118 v. Danville Educ. Ass'n*, 376 N.E.2d 430 (Ill. App. Ct. 1978).

281. *Board of Educ. v. Redding*, 207 N.E.2d 427 (Ill. 1965). *See also City of Pana v. Crowe*, 316 N.E.2d 513 (Ill. 1974).

282. *Board of Educ. v. Kankakee Fed'n of Teachers Local No. 886*, 264 N.E.2d 18 (Ill.1970), *cert. denied*, 403 U.S. 904, 91 S.Ct. 2203, 29 L.Ed.2d 679 (1971).

education were set up for cities, towns, and school districts throughout the state.... This general school law was amended by the Act of April 21, 1909, section 1 of which provided: "The service of all teachers, principals, supervising principals of the public schools in any school district of this state shall be during good behavior and efficiency, after the expiration of a period of employment of three consecutive years in that district, unless a shorter period is fixed by the employing board.... No principal or teacher shall be dismissed or subjected to reduction of salary in said school district except for inefficiency, incapacity, conduct unbecoming a teacher or other just cause, and after a written charge of the cause or causes shall have been preferred against him or her, ... and after the charge shall have been examined into and found true in fact by said board of education, upon reasonable notice to the person charged, who may be represented by counsel at the hearing."

An Act of February 4, 1933, premising that existing economic conditions require that boards of education be enabled to fix and determine the amount of salary to be paid to persons holding positions in the respective school districts, authorizes each board to fix and determine salaries to be paid officers and employees for the period July 1, 1933, to July 1, 1934, "notwithstanding any such person be under tenure;" prohibits increase of salaries within the period named; forbids discrimination between individuals in the same class of service in the fixing of salaries or compensation; and sets a minimum beyond which boards may not go in the reduction of salaries. On June 23, 1933, the board adopted a resolution reducing salaries for the school year July 1, 1933, to July 1, 1934, by a percentage of the existing salaries graded upward in steps as the salaries increased in amount, except with respect to clerks, the compensation of each of whom was reduced to a named amount....

The position of the appellants is that by virtue of the Act of 1909 three years of service under contract confer upon an employee of a school district a contractual status indefinite in duration which the legislature is powerless to alter or to authorize the board of education to alter. The Supreme Court holds that the Act of 1909 "established a legislative status for teachers, but we fail to see that it established a contractual one that the Legislature may not modify.... The status of tenure teachers, while in one sense perhaps contractual, is in essence dependent on a statute, like that of the incumbent of a statutory office, which the Legislature at will may abolish, or whose emoluments it may change."

This court is not bound by the decision of a state court as to the existence and terms of a contract, the obligation of which is asserted to be impaired, but where a statute is claimed to create a contractual right we give weight to the construction of the statute by the courts of the state. Here those courts have concurred in holding that the act of 1909 did not amount to a legislative contract with the teachers of the state and did not become a term of the contracts entered into with employees by boards of education. Unless these views are palpably erroneous we should accept them.

It appears from a stipulation of facts submitted in view of evidence that after a teacher has served in a school district under yearly contracts for three years it has not been customary to enter into additional further formal contracts with such teacher. From time to time, however, promotions were granted and salary raised for the ensuing year by action of the board. In the case of many of the appellants there have been several such increases in salary.

Although after the expiration of the first three years of service the employee continued in his then position and at his then compensation unless and until promoted or given an increase in salary for a succeeding year, we find nothing in the record to indicate that the board was bound by contract with the teacher for more than the current year. The employee assumed no binding obligation to remain in service beyond that term. Although the act of 1909 prohibited the board, a creature of the state, from reducing the teacher's salary or discharging him without cause, we agree with the courts below that this was but a regulation of the conduct of the board and not a term of a continuing contract of indefinite duration with the individual teacher.

The resolution of June 23, 1933, grouped the existing salaries paid by the board into six classes the lowest of which comprised salaries between $1200 and $1999; and the highest included salaries ranging between $4000 and $5600. The reduction in the lowest class for the coming year was 10 per cent; that in highest class 15 per cent. Salaries in the intermediate classes were reduced 11, 12, 13, and 14 per cent. It resulted that in some instances a teacher receiving the lowest salary in a given bracket would have his compensation reduced to a figure lower than the reduced compensation of one receiving the highest salary in the next lower bracket. From this circumstance it is argued that the board's action arbitrarily discriminated between the employees and so denied them the equal protection of the laws guaranteed by the Fourteenth Amendment.

We think it was reasonable and proper that the teachers employed by the board should be divided into classes for the application of the percentage reduction. All in a given class were treated alike. Incidental individual inequality resulting in some instances from the operation of the plan does not condemn it as an unreasonable or arbitrary method of dealing with the problem of general salary reductions or deny the equality guaranteed by the Fourteenth Amendment.

Judgments affirmed.

NOTES

1.   Note the Supreme Court's statement that although it was not bound by the judgment of a state court as to the existence and terms of a contract, it gave weight to its interpretation of the statute that was alleged to have created a contractual right.

2.   If legislatures can change the tenure status and retirement allowances of teachers at will, their rights appear to be flimsy. Are individual teachers or groups of teachers seriously threatened by precipitous legislative action in these areas?

[CASE NO. 61]   RIGHT OF TEACHER TO MINIMUM SALARY

MARVEL v. COAL HILL PUBLIC SCHOOL DISTRICT

Supreme Court of Arkansas, 1982.
635 S.W.2d 245 [5 Educ. L. Rep. 667].

■ HICKMAN, JUSTICE.

The question in this case is whether a full-time school teacher can be denied the minimum salary due to teachers because of a written contract for a lesser amount. The trial court found such a contract enforceable. We disagree and reverse.

Deborah Marvel had been a part-time librarian and teacher for the Coal Hill Public School District when her contract was negotiated for the 1979–1980 school year. She said that Mr. Nolan Williams, the superintendent of schools, told her she would serve as part-time librarian and part-time teacher but would receive the same salary that full-time teachers did. (She had been paid in the past as an aide, but was now to be paid as a teacher.) Williams refuted that. But the contract only provided for a salary of $9,800.00 and the minimum a full-time teacher with her experience would receive is $11,450.00. She accepted the position and signed the contract but chose to sue for the difference, which was $1,650.00, plus interest.

The parties disagreed as to whether Miss Marvel signed the contract under protest but that is irrelevant. It is not disputed that she was a "teacher" within the meaning of Ark. Stats. Ann. 80–1326 (Repl.1980), and performed all the duties of a full-time teacher. She performed the ancillary duties of all teachers such as hall monitor, attending ball games and faculty meetings. She kept grade, class planning and attendance records. In order to qualify as full-time, she was required to work six periods a day. She acted as a teacher five periods a day and as a librarian two periods. It is also undisputed that the school district filed with the State Department of Education a salary schedule, as required by Ark. Stats. Ann. 80–1324 and 80–850.7 (Repl.1980), and that her salary as a full-time teacher would have been $11,450.00.

The superintendent said the reason Miss Marvel was not paid the minimum salary is because the part of her salary for teaching remedial reading was Title I money (federal money) and the grant did not allow her to be paid more.

The trial court held that the contract did not violate Arkansas law which requires that school districts promulgate minimum salary schedules. . . . The court found that since she was paid fairly for librarian duties from general funds that the district complied with the law, and found further that Miss Marvel knowingly and freely entered into a binding agreement.

The trial court was wrong in its interpretation of the law. Miss Marvel was a full-time teacher and the district could not receive her services and refuse to pay her the minimum salary it paid other full-time teachers. Title

I provisions cannot be used to avoid Ark. Stats. Ann. 80—1327 and 80—850.7, which require each school district to set a schedule of minimum salaries and abide by it.

If the district's position were to prevail, then no teacher could be sure of equal treatment when he or she was hired or retained at least to the extent that a minimum salary would apply to all hired for full-time duties. The school district received the benefit of the services of a full-time teacher and it should not be allowed to manipulate the law to avoid its legal responsibility.

The judgment is reversed and the cause remanded for the court to enter judgment for the appellant.

NOTES

1. Accepting as true the superintendent's statements about the use of Title I money, there still was no prohibition against supplementing those salary funds with state or local money.

2. Why did the court not need to resolve the disagreement as to whether Ms. Marvel signed the contract under protest?

[CASE NO. 62] CONSTITUTIONALITY OF RACE–BASED TEACHER TRANSFER PLAN

JACOBSON v. CINCINNATI BOARD OF EDUCATION

United States Court of Appeals, Sixth Circuit, 1992.
961 F.2d 100 [74 Educ. L. Rep. 51], *cert. denied*,
506 U.S. 830, 113 S.Ct. 94, 121 L.Ed.2d 55.

■ ALAN E. NORRIS, CIRCUIT JUDGE.

Eight Cincinnati public school teachers and the Cincinnati Federation of Teachers ("CFT"), the union that represents them, brought suit in the district court challenging the teacher transfer policy adopted by the Cincinnati Board of Education ("Board") to ensure that the faculty of its schools reflects system-wide racial balance. After an evidentiary hearing, the district court concluded that the policy did not violate either plaintiffs' Fourteenth Amendment right to equal protection or the terms of the collective bargaining agreement ("CBA") negotiated by the CFT and the Board. Accordingly, the district court denied plaintiffs' request to enjoin the transfer policy. For the reasons outlined below, we affirm the judgment of the district court.

This dispute has its genesis in the 1970s, when concerted efforts to eradicate indicia of racial segregation within the Cincinnati public school system began. On January 14, 1974, the Board adopted a policy designed to ensure that the teaching staff of a given school approximated the racial balance of the teaching staff of the system as a whole. Shortly thereafter, the Board issued a statement indicating how this general policy would be implemented. Among other things, the statement provided that the percentage of black teachers in any school should not be five percent greater or less than the percentage of black teachers throughout the system. In order to implement this racial balance, the policy restricts the ability of some teachers to voluntarily transfer to other school buildings, and requires the reassignment of others. It is this portion of the policy which plaintiffs challenge.

In the same year that these efforts to balance the racial composition of the faculty were initiated, a group of school children and their parents filed a lawsuit against the Board, contending that the school system was unlawfully segregated. That suit was ultimately settled by the parties, and the district court adopted the settlement agreement as a consent decree. Paragraph 5 of the settlement agreement reads as follows:

The Cincinnati Board of Education currently has in force a policy which requires that the staff in each of its schools has a racial composition which is within 5% of the racial composition of the staff in the district as a whole. The Board shall maintain that policy in effect and take steps necessary to assure that it is enforced.

The CFT actively participated in the resolution of [the settled suit] and did not object to the maintenance of the staff racial balance policy. The position of the CFT is reflected in the CBA negotiated with the Board. Section 250, paragraph 1, of the CBA contains the following provision regarding teacher transfers: "Teacher requests for transfer will be honored if positions are available and the teacher is qualified for a particular vacancy, provided that the transfer is consistent with the racial balance of the staff."

We begin by noting that school authorities have broad discretion to implement educational policy. This authority includes the power to pre-scribe a ratio of white to minority students that reflects the composition of the overall school district, particularly when such a policy is implemented in order to prepare students for life in a pluralistic society. And we believe that this discretionary authority includes the power to assign faculty to achieve a racial ratio reflecting the racial composition of the system's teachers. The Supreme Court has recognized that the attainment of an integrated teaching staff is a legitimate concern in achieving a school system free of racial discrimination.

Here, the district court found that the policy adopted by the Board is race conscious in the sense that it allows the Board to determine the schools at which a teacher may teach solely on the basis of his or her race. However, the court went on to find that the policy is "specific race neutral in that there is no disparate impact as to race in its application. It is applied equally to both black and white teachers. In some instances, it will benefit or harm white teachers; in others, it will benefit or harm black teachers." We agree with that characterization. We are therefore unable to agree with plaintiffs' contention that the policy establishes preferences based on race that require us to examine the policy with strict scrutiny to determine whether it conflicts with guarantees afforded them under the Constitution.

Under analogous circumstances, the Court of Appeals for the Third Circuit offered these observations concerning the appropriate level of scrutiny to which such a policy should be subjected:

No case has suggested that the mere utilization of race as a factor, together with seniority, school need, and subject qualification, is prohibited. Since the classification is not preferential, it might most appropriately be reviewed for its rational relationship to a legitimate government objective, under which standard it would be patently valid. At most, since there is some element of racial classification, albeit not of preference, the appropriate level of scrutiny would be the intermediate level suggested by four members of the Court in *Bakke*, in which the classification was indeed preferential.

The appropriate question under that standard is whether the classification "serve[s] important governmental objectives" and is "substantially related to achievement of those objectives."

In our view, this intermediate level of scrutiny is the proper one, since the Cincinnati teacher transfer policy, like the policy challenged in Kromnick, does not prefer one race over another. Accordingly, we must determine whether the policy is substantially related to an important governmental objective. We believe the policy at issue meets that test. It was implemented to achieve a racially integrated faculty throughout the Cincinnati public school system. Not only is this a legitimate objective, it has been endorsed in the past by the CFT. In fact, section 250 of the CBA, which appellants mistakenly contend has been violated by the Board, expressly allows for the accommodation of such a transfer policy.

We therefore hold that plaintiffs have failed to demonstrate how their interest in selecting the schools to which they are assigned outweighs the Board's interest in fostering an integrated, pluralistic school system.

The judgment of the district court is affirmed.

NOTES

1.   What is your impression of the role of the union in pursuit of the claim of unconstitutionality in this case?

2.   Would this case serve as a precedent for resolving a dispute where a factor in an involuntary transfer was a teacher's sex, years of experience (age), or religion?

[CASE NO. 63]   CONSTITUTIONALITY OF TEACHERS' OATH

KNIGHT v. BOARD OF REGENTS OF THE UNIVERSITY OF THE STATE OF NEW YORK

United States District Court, Southern District of New York, 1967.
269 F.Supp. 339.

■ TYLER, DISTRICT JUDGE.

Plaintiffs are twenty-seven faculty members at Adelphi University, a private, non-profit institution of higher learning located in Garden City, New York and tax exempt under Section 420 of the New York Real Property Tax Law, McKinney's Consol.Laws, c. 50–A.

Section 3002 of the New York Education Law, ... requires every citizen teacher, instructor or professor in any public school or in any private school the real property of which is in whole or in part exempt from taxation to execute an oath. In pertinent part, Section 3002 reads as follows:

> Oath to support federal and state constitutions. It shall be unlawful for any citizen of the United States to serve as teacher, instructor or professor in any school or institution in the public school system of the state or in any school, college, university or other educational institution in this state, whose real property, in whole or in part, is exempt from taxation under section four of the tax law unless and until he or she shall have taken and subscribed the following oath or affirmation: "I do solemnly swear (or affirm) that I will support the constitution of the United States of America and the constitution of the State of New York, and that I will faithfully discharge, according to the best of my ability, the duties of the position of . . . (title of position and name or designation of school, college, university or institution to be here inserted), to which I am now assigned."

Although this statutory requirement dates back to 1934, through inadvertence Adelphi had not previously requested that its faculty members execute the oath. In October, 1966, however, upon being made aware of the statute, the administrative offices of Adelphi asked all the members of its teaching staff to sign and return the oath. Plaintiffs have refused to do so, instead bringing this action to enjoin the enforcement of the oath provision. . . .

So far as we can determine, the precise question of whether an oath such as that provided for by Section 3002 may constitutionally be required of teachers has not been ruled upon by the Supreme Court. That Court, however, has recently stated that Georgia's requirement that her legislators take a similar oath in no way impinges upon the First Amendment's protection of free speech. Moreover, the Court, in striking down so called "negative loyalty oath" requirements of the states, has never suggested that the First Amendment proscribes any form of oath or affirmation required of teachers.

. . .

Plaintiffs . . . urge that section 3002 suffers the vice of vagueness. In support of this theory, they rely upon the line of Supreme Court cases striking down "negative loyalty oaths" or "non-Communist oaths". As plaintiffs' counsel candidly conceded at oral argument, however, such oaths, which typically require an affiant to state that he is not now and has never been a member of certain organizations, present a very different problem.

The language of Section 3002 is simple and clear in its import. It requires no more than that the subscriber affirm that he will support the constitutions of the United States and the State of New York and that he will be a dedicated teacher. The statutory language of support of the constitutional governments can be substantially equated to that allegiance which, by the common law, every citizen was understood to owe his sovereign. . . . In our view, a state can reasonably ask teachers in public or tax exempted institutions to subscribe to professional competence and dedication.

Plaintiffs, conceding that it is constitutionally permissible to demand from public officials, federal and state, an oath or affirmation substantially the same as that set forth in Section 3002, suggest that different considerations apply to teachers. In sum, it is said that teachers' speech must be totally "free of interference". But, as may be implied from what has already been said, we interpret the statute to impose no restrictions upon political or philosophical expressions by teachers in the State of New York. A state does not interfere with its teachers by requiring them to support the governmental systems which shelter and nourish the institutions in which they teach, nor does it restrict its teachers by encouraging them to uphold the highest standards of their chosen profession. Indeed, it is plain that a state has a clear interest in assuring "... careful and discriminating selection of teachers" by its publicly supported educational institutions.

The plaintiffs' motion for an injunction pendente lite is denied, and defendants' motion to dismiss the complaint is granted. It is so ordered.

NOTES

1.   What was the legal basis for making the oath applicable to the faculty of private schools?

2.   Was this oath a threat to academic freedom?

[CASE NO. 64]   UNION RIGHTS TO COLLECT DUES FROM NON–MEMBERS

DAVENPORT v. WASHINGTON EDUCATION ASSOCIATION

Supreme Court of the United States, 2007.
551 U.S. 177, 127 S.Ct. 2372, 2383, 168 L.Ed.2d 71.

■ JUSTICE SCALIA delivered the opinion of the Court.

The State of Washington prohibits labor unions from using the agency-shop fees of a nonmember for election-related purposes unless the non-member affirmatively consents. We decide whether this restriction, as applied to public-sector labor unions, violates the First Amendment.

I

The National Labor Relations Act leaves States free to regulate their labor relationships with their public employees. The labor laws of many States authorize a union and a government employer to enter into what is commonly known as an agency-shop agreement. This arrangement entitles the union to levy a fee on employees who are not union members but who are nevertheless represented by the union in collective bargaining. The primary purpose of such arrangements is to prevent nonmembers from free-riding on the union's efforts, sharing the employment benefits obtained by the union's collective bargaining without sharing the costs incurred. However, agency-shop arrangements in the public sector raise First Amendment concerns because they force individuals to contribute money to unions as a condition of government employment. Thus, in *Abood v. Detroit Bd. of Ed.*, we held that public-sector unions are constitutionally prohibited from using the fees of objecting nonmembers for ideological purposes that are not germane to the union's collective-bargaining duties. And in *Teachers v. Hudson*, we set forth various procedural requirements that public-sector unions collecting agency fees must observe in order to ensure that an objecting nonmember can prevent the use of his fees for impermissible purposes. Neither *Hudson* nor any of our other cases, however, has held that the First Amendment mandates that a public-sector union obtain affirmative consent before spending a nonmember's agency fees for purposes not chargeable under *Abood*

The State of Washington has authorized public-sector unions to negotiate agency-shop agreements. Where such agreements are in effect, Washington law allows the union to charge nonmembers an agency fee equivalent to the full membership dues of the union and to have this fee collected by the employer through payroll deductions. However, § 42.17.760 (hereinafter § 760), which is a provision of the Fair Campaign Practices Act (a state initiative approved by the voters of Washington in 1992), restricts the union's ability to spend the agency fees that it collects. Section 760, as it stood when the decision under review was rendered, provided:

> "A labor organization may not use agency shop fees paid by an individual who is not a member of the organization to make contributions or expenditures to influence an election or to operate a political committee, unless affirmatively authorized by the individual."

Respondent, the exclusive bargaining agent for approximately 70,000 public educational employees, collected agency fees from nonmembers that it represented in collective bargaining. Consistent with its responsibilities under *Abood* and *Hudson* (or so we assume for purposes of these cases), respondent sent a "*Hudson* packet" to all nonmembers twice a year, notifying them of their right to object to paying fees for nonchargeable expenditures, and giving them three options: (1) pay full agency fees by not objecting within 30 days; (2) object to paying for nonchargeable expenses and receive a rebate as calculated by respondent; or (3) object to paying for nonchargeable expenses and receive a rebate as determined by an arbitrator. Respondent held in escrow any agency fees that were reasonably in dispute until the *Hudson* process was complete.

In 2001, respondent found itself in Washington state courts defending, in two separate lawsuits, its expenditures of nonmembers' agency fees. The first lawsuit was brought by the State of Washington, petitioner in No. 05–1657, and the second was brought as a putative class action by several nonmembers of the union, petitioners in No. 05–1589. Both suits claimed that respondent's use of agency fees was in violation of § 760. Petitioners alleged that respondent had failed to obtain affirmative authorization from nonmembers before using their agency fees for the election-related purposes specified in § 760. In No. 05–1657, after a trial on the merits, the trial court found that respondent had violated § 760 and awarded the State both monetary and injunctive relief. In No. 05–1589, a different trial judge held that § 760 provided a private right of action, certified the class, and stayed further proceedings pending interlocutory appeal.

After intermediate appellate court proceedings, a divided Supreme Court of Washington held that, although a nonmember's failure to object after receiving respondent's *"Hudson* packet" did not satisfy § 760's affirmative-authorization requirement as a matter of state law, the statute's imposition of such a requirement violated the First Amendment of the Federal Constitution. The court reasoned that this Court's agency-fee jurisprudence established a balance between the First Amendment rights of unions and of nonmembers, and that § 760 triggered heightened First Amendment scrutiny because it deviated from that balance by imposing on respondent the burden of confirming that a nonmember does not object to the expenditure of his agency fees for electoral purposes. The court also held that § 760 interfered with respondent's expressive associational rights under *Boy Scouts of America v. Dale,*. We granted certiorari.

II

The public-sector agency-shop arrangement authorizes a union to levy fees on government employees who do not wish to join the union. Regardless of one's views as to the desirability of agency-shop agreements, *see Abood,* it is undeniably unusual for a government agency to give a private entity the power, in essence, to tax government employees. As applied to agency-shop agreements with public-sector unions like respondent, § 760 is simply a condition on the union's exercise of this extraordinary power, prohibiting expenditure of a nonmember's agency fees for election-related purposes unless the nonmember affirmatively consents. The notion that this modest limitation upon an extraordinary benefit violates the First Amendment is, to say the least, counterintuitive. Respondent concedes that Washington could have gone much further, restricting public-sector agency fees to the portion of union dues devoted to collective bargaining. Indeed, it is uncontested that it would be constitutional for Washington to eliminate agency fees entirely. For the reasons that follow, we conclude that the far less restrictive limitation the voters of Washington placed on respondent's authorization to exact money from government employees is of no greater constitutional concern.

A

The principal reason the Supreme Court of Washington concluded that § 760 was unconstitutional was that it believed that our agency-fee cases, having balanced the constitutional rights of unions and of nonmembers, dictated that a nonmember must shoulder the burden of objecting before a union can be barred from spending his fees for purposes impermissible under *Abood*. The court reached this conclusion primarily because our cases have repeatedly invoked the following proposition: " '[D]issent is not to be presumed-it must affirmatively be made known to the union by the dissenting employee.' " The court concluded that § 760 triggered heightened First Amendment scrutiny because it deviated from this perceived constitutional balance by requiring unions to obtain affirmative consent.

This interpretation of our agency-fee cases extends them well beyond their proper ambit. Those cases were not balancing constitutional rights in the manner respondent suggests, for the simple reason that unions have no constitutional entitlement to the fees of nonmember-employees. We have never suggested that the First Amendment is implicated whenever governments place limitations on a union's entitlement to agency fees above and beyond what *Abood* and *Hudson* require. To the contrary, we have described *Hudson* as "outlin[ing] a *minimum* set of procedures by which a [public-sector] union in an agency-shop relationship could meet its requirement under *Abood*." (emphasis added). The mere fact that Washington required more than the *Hudson* minimum does not trigger First Amendment scrutiny. The constitutional floor for unions' collection and spending of agency fees is not also a constitutional ceiling for state-imposed restrictions.

. . .

B

Respondent defends the judgment below on a ground quite different from the mistaken rationale adopted by the Supreme Court of Washington. Its argument begins with the premise that § 760 is a limitation on how the union may spend "its" money, citing for that proposition the Washington Supreme Court's description of § 760 as encumbering funds that are lawfully within a union's possession. Relying on that premise, respondent invokes *First Nat. Bank of Boston v. Bellotti,* and related campaign-finance cases. It argues that, under the rigorous First Amendment scrutiny required by those cases, § 760 is unconstitutional because it applies to ballot propositions and because it does not limit equivalent election-related expenditures by corporations.

The Supreme Court of Washington's description of § 760 notwithstanding, our campaign-finance cases are not on point. For purposes of the First Amendment, it is entirely immaterial that § 760 restricts a union's use of funds only after those funds are already within the union's lawful possession under Washington law. What matters is that public-sector agency fees are in the union's possession only because Washington and its union-contracting government agencies have compelled their employees to pay those fees. The cases upon which respondent relies deal with governmental restrictions on how a regulated entity may spend money that has come into its possession without the assistance of governmental coercion of its employees. As applied to public-sector unions, § 760 is not fairly described as a restriction on how the union can spend "its" money; it is a condition placed upon the union's extraordinary *state* entitlement to acquire and spend *other people's* money.

The question that must be asked, therefore, is whether § 760 is a constitutional condition on the authorization that public-sector unions enjoy to charge government employees agency fees. Respondent essentially answers that the statute unconstitutionally draws distinctions based on the content of the union's speech, requiring affirmative consent only for election-related expenditures while permitting expenditures for the rest of the purposes not chargeable under *Abood* unless the nonmember objects. The contention that this amounts to unconstitutional content-based discrimination is off the mark.

It is true enough that content-based regulations of speech are presumptively invalid. We have recognized, however, that "[t]he rationale of the general prohibition ... is that content discrimination 'raises the specter that the Government may effectively drive certain ideas or viewpoints from the marketplace.' " And we have identified numerous situations in which that risk is inconsequential, so that strict scrutiny is unwarranted. For example, speech that is obscene or defamatory can be constitutionally proscribed because the social interest in order and morality outweighs the negligible contribution of those categories of speech to the marketplace of ideas. Similarly, content discrimination among various instances of a class of proscribable speech does not pose a threat to the marketplace of ideas when the selected subclass is chosen for the very reason that the entire class can be proscribed. Of particular relevance here, our cases recognize that the risk that content-based distinctions will impermissibly interfere with the marketplace of ideas is sometimes attenuated when the government is acting in a capacity other than as regulator. Accordingly, it is well established that the government can make content-based distinctions when it subsidizes speech. And it is also black-letter law that, when the government permits speech on government property that is a nonpublic forum, it can exclude speakers on the basis of their subject matter, so long as the distinctions drawn are viewpoint neutral and reasonable in light of the purpose served by the forum.

The principle underlying our treatment of those situations is equally applicable to the narrow circumstances of these cases. We do not believe that the voters of Washington impermissibly distorted the marketplace of ideas when they placed a reasonable, viewpoint-neutral limitation on the State's general authorization allowing public-sector unions to acquire and spend the money of government employees. As the Supreme Court of Washington recognized, the voters of Washington sought to protect the integrity of the election process, which the voters evidently thought was being impaired by the infusion of money extracted from nonmembers of unions without their consent. The restriction on the state-bestowed entitlement was thus limited to the state-created harm that the voters sought to remedy. The voters did not have to enact an across-the-board limitation on the use of nonmembers' agency fees by public-sector unions in order to vindicate their more narrow concern with the integrity of the election process. We said in *R.A.V.* that, when totally proscribable speech is at issue, content-based regulation is permissible so long as "there is no realistic possibility that official suppression of ideas is afoot." We think the same is true when, as here, an extraordinary and totally repealable authorization to coerce payment from government employees is at issue. Even if it be thought necessary that the content limitation be reasonable and viewpoint neutral, the statute satisfies that requirement. Quite obviously, no suppression of ideas is afoot, since the union remains as free as any other entity to participate in the electoral process with all available funds other than the state-coerced agency fees lacking affirmative permission. In sum, given the unique context of public-sector agency-shop arrangements, the content-based nature of § 760 does not violate the First Amendment.

We emphasize an important limitation upon our holding: we uphold § 760 only as applied to public-sector unions such as respondent. Section 760 applies on its face to both public-and private-sector unions in Washington. Since private-sector unions collect agency fees through contractually required action taken by private employers rather than by government agencies, Washington's regulation of those private arrangements presents a somewhat different constitutional question. We need not answer that question today, however, because at no stage of this litigation has respondent made an overbreadth challenge. Instead, respondent has consistently argued simply that § 760 is unconstitutional as applied to itself. The only purpose for which it has noted the statute's applicability to private-sector unions is to establish that the statute was meant to be a general limitation on electoral speech, and not just a condition on state agencies' authorization of compulsory agency fees. That limited contention, however, is both unconvincing and immaterial. The purpose of the voters of Washington was undoubtedly the general one of protecting the integrity of elections by limiting electoral spending in certain ways. But § 760, though applicable to all unions, served that purpose through very different means depending on the type of union involved: It *conditioned* public-sector unions' authorization to coerce fees from government employees at the same time that it *regulated* private-sector unions' collective-bargaining agreements. The constitutionality of the means chosen with respect to private-sector unions has no bearing on whether § 760 is constitutional as applied to public-sector unions.

· · ·

We hold that it does not violate the First Amendment for a State to require that its public-sector unions receive affirmative authorization from a nonmember before spending that nonmember's agency fees for election-related purposes. We therefore vacate the judgment of the Supreme Court of Washington and remand the cases for further proceedings not inconsistent with this opinion.

It is so ordered.

NOTES

1.   Are fair share fees fundamentally fair? Put another way, should teachers be required to pay such fees when they choose not to be union members?

2.   Does paying fair share fees compel individuals to support positions with which they may not agree?

[CASE NO. 65] THE CONSTITUTIONALITY OF MANDATORY
PAYROLL DEDUCTIONS FOR UNION DUES

YSURSA v. POCATELLO EDUCATION ASSOCIATION

Supreme Court of the United States, 2009.
555 U.S. 353, 129 S.Ct. 1093, 172 L.Ed.2d 770.

■ CHIEF JUSTICE ROBERTS delivered the opinion of the Court.

Under Idaho law, a public employee may elect to have a portion of his
wages deducted by his employer and remitted to his union to pay union
dues. He may not, however, choose to have an amount deducted and
remitted to the union's political action committee, because Idaho law
prohibits payroll deductions for political activities. A group of unions
representing Idaho public employees challenged this limitation. They conceded that the limitation was valid as applied at the state level, but argued
that it violated their First Amendment rights when applied to county,
municipal, school district, and other local public employers.

We do not agree. The First Amendment prohibits government from
"abridging the freedom of speech"; it does not confer an affirmative right
to use government payroll mechanisms for the purpose of obtaining funds
for expression. Idaho's law does not restrict political speech, but rather
declines to promote that speech by allowing public employee checkoffs for
political activities. Such a decision is reasonable in light of the State's
interest in avoiding the appearance that carrying out the public's business
is tainted by partisan political activity. That interest extends to government at the local as well as state level, and nothing in the First Amendment prevents a State from determining that its political subdivisions may
not provide payroll deductions for political activities.

I

Idaho's Right to Work Act declares that the "right to work shall not be
infringed or restricted in any way based on membership in, affiliation with,
or financial support of a labor organization or on refusal to join, affiliate
with, or financially or otherwise support a labor organization." As part of
that policy, the Act prohibits any requirement for the payment of dues or
fees to a labor organization as a condition of employment, but authorizes
employers to deduct union fees from an employee's wages with the employee's "signed written authorization." The Act covers all employees, "including all employees of the state and its political subdivisions."

Prior to 2003, employees could authorize both a payroll deduction for
general union dues and a payroll deduction for union political activities
conducted through a political action committee. In 2003, the Idaho Legislature passed the Voluntary Contributions Act (VCA). That legislation,
among other things, amended the Right to Work Act by adding a prohibition on payroll deductions for political purposes. That amendment provides:
"Deductions for political activities as defined in chapter 26, title 44, Idaho
Code, shall not be deducted from the wages, earnings or compensation of
an employee." The term "political activities" is defined as "electoral

activities, independent expenditures, or expenditures made to any candidate, political party, political action committee or political issues committee or in support of or against any ballot measure." Violations of § 44–2004(2) are punishable by a fine not exceeding $1,000 or up to 90 days of imprisonment, or both.

Shortly before the VCA was to take effect, plaintiff labor organizations sued the Bannock County prosecuting attorney, the Idaho secretary of state, and the Idaho attorney general in their official capacities, alleging that the ban on political payroll deductions was unconstitutional under the First and Fourteenth Amendments to the United States Constitution. The District Court ... struck down the VCA ... "to the extent that it applies to local governments and private employers," because the State had failed to identify any subsidy it provided to such employers to administer payroll deductions.

The state defendants appealed, contending that the ban on political payroll deductions may be constitutionally applied to local government employees ... therefore the only issue ... concerned application of the ban to local government employees.

The Court of Appeals agreed with the District Court that there was "no subsidy by the State of Idaho for the payroll deduction systems of local governments." The appellate court remarked that "the generalized lawmaking power held by the legislature with respect to a state's political subdivisions does not establish that the state is acting as a proprietor" with respect to local government employers. The court instead regarded the relationship between the State and its political subdivisions as analogous to that between the State and a regulated private utility. While "Idaho has the ultimate power of control over the units of government at issue," it did not "actually operat[e] or contro[l] the payroll deduction systems of local units of government." The court therefore applied strict scrutiny to Idaho's decision to prevent local government employers from allowing payroll deductions for political purposes, and held the statute unconstitutional as applied at the local level.

We granted certiorari and now reverse.

II

Restrictions on speech based on its content are "presumptively invalid" and subject to strict scrutiny. The unions assert that the ban on checkoffs for political activities falls into this category because the law singles out political speech for disfavored treatment.

The First Amendment, however, protects the right to be free from government abridgment of speech. While in some contexts the government must accommodate expression, it is not required to assist others in funding the expression of particular ideas, including political ones. "[A] legislature's decision not to subsidize the exercise of a fundamental right does not infringe the right, and thus is not subject to strict scrutiny."

The court below concluded, and Idaho does not dispute, that "unions face substantial difficulties in collecting funds for political speech without using payroll deductions." But the parties agree that the State is not constitutionally obligated to provide payroll deductions at all. While public-ly administered payroll deductions for political purposes can enhance the unions' exercise of First Amendment rights, Idaho is under no obligation to aid the unions in their political activities. And the State's decision not to do so is not an abridgment of the unions' speech; they are free to engage in such speech as they see fit. They simply are barred from enlisting the State in support of that endeavor. Idaho's decision to limit public employer payroll deductions as it has "is not subject to strict scrutiny" under the First Amendment.

Given that the State has not infringed the unions' First Amendment rights, the State need only demonstrate a rational basis to justify the ban on political payroll deductions. The prohibition is not "aim[ed] at the suppression of dangerous ideas," but is instead justified by the State's interest in avoiding the reality or appearance of government favoritism or entanglement with partisan politics. We have previously recognized such a purpose in upholding limitations on public employee political activities. Banning payroll deductions for political speech similarly furthers the gov-ernment's interest in distinguishing between internal governmental opera-tions and private speech. Idaho's decision to allow payroll deductions for some purposes but not for political activities is plainly reasonable.

Davenport [v. Washington Education Association] guides our resolution here. That case also involved a distinction based on the content of speech: Specific consent was required from nonunion members before agency fees charged to them could be used for election-related activities, but consent was not required with respect to agency fees used for other purposes. We rejected the unions' argument that this requirement violated the First Amendment because it turned on the content of the speech at issue. We recognized that the statute, rather than suppressing union speech, simply declined to assist that speech by granting the unions the right to charge agency fees for election activities. That decision was reasonable given the State's interest in preserving the integrity of the election process. We also concluded that the State did "not have to enact an across-the-board limitation ... to vindicate [its] more narrow concern."

Here the restriction is on the use of a checkoff to fund political activities, but the same analysis governs. Idaho does not suppress political speech but simply declines to promote it through public employer checkoffs for political activities. The concern that political payroll deductions might be seen as involving public employers in politics arises only because Idaho permits public employer payroll deductions in the first place. As in *Daven-port,* the State's response to that problem is limited to its source—in this case, political payroll deductions. The ban on such deductions plainly serves the State's interest in separating public employment from political activi-ties.

III

The question remains whether the ban is valid at the local level. The unions abandoned their challenge to the restriction at the state level, but contend that strict scrutiny is still warranted when the ban is applied to local government employers. In that context, the unions argue, the State is no longer declining to facilitate speech through its own payroll system, but is obstructing speech in the local governments' payroll systems. We find that distinction unpersuasive, and hold that the same deferential review applies whether the prohibition on payroll deductions for political speech is directed at state or local governmental entities.

"Political subdivisions of States—counties, cities, or whatever—never were and never have been considered as sovereign entities." They are instead "subordinate governmental instrumentalities created by the State to assist in the carrying out of state governmental functions." State political subdivisions are "merely . . . department [s] of the State, and the State may withhold, grant or withdraw powers and privileges as it sees fit." Here the Idaho Legislature has elected to withhold from *all* public employers the power to provide payroll deductions for political activities.

The State's legislative action is of course subject to First Amendment and other constitutional scrutiny whether that action is applicable at the state level, the local level, both, or some subpart of either. But we are aware of no case suggesting that a different analysis applies under the First Amendment depending on the level of government affected, and the unions have cited none. The ban on political payroll deductions furthers Idaho's interest in separating the operation of government from partisan politics. That interest extends to all public employers at whatever level of government.

In reaching the opposite conclusion, the Court of Appeals invoked our decision in *Consolidated Edison Co. of N.Y. v. Public Serv. Comm'n of N.Y.* In that case, we held that a state commission could not, consistent with the First Amendment, prohibit a privately owned electric utility from discussing controversial issues in its bill inserts. We ruled that the fact that the State regulated the utility did not authorize the prohibition. The Court of Appeals concluded that the same analysis applied here, and that "the State's broad powers of control over local government entities are solely those of a regulator, analogous to the [state commission's] regulatory power over [the private utility]."

That analogy is misguided. A private corporation is subject to the government's legal authority to regulate its conduct. A political subdivision, on the other hand, is a subordinate unit of government created by the State to carry out delegated governmental functions. A private corporation enjoys constitutional protections, but a political subdivision, "created by the state for the better ordering of government, has no privileges or immunities under the federal constitution which it may invoke in opposition to the will of its creator."

Both the District Court and the Court of Appeals found it significant that "there is no subsidy by the State of Idaho for the payroll deduction systems of local governments." The Court of Appeals emphasized that there was no evidence that "Idaho has attempted to use its asserted powers to manage the day-to-day operations of local government personnel." Given the relationship between the State and its political subdivisions, however, it is immaterial how the State allocates funding or management responsibilities between the different levels of government. The question is whether the State must affirmatively assist political speech by allowing public employers to administer payroll deductions for political activities. For the reasons set forth in this opinion, the answer is no.

. . .

The Court of Appeals ruling that Idaho Code § 44–2004(2) is unconstitutional with respect to local units of government is reversed.

It is so ordered.

NOTES

1. In light of changes that are occurring in many states with regard to bargaining and teacher unions, is *Ysursa* part of a larger challenge to the viability of unions?

2. Do you think that *Ysursa* will have much of an impact on how unions operate?

[CASE NO. 66]   ARBITRATION IN PUBLIC SECTOR LABOR CONTRACTS

IN RE KENNEDY

Supreme Court of New Hampshire, 2011.
27 A.3d 844, *as modified on denial of reconsideration* (2011).

■ CONBOY, J.

The petitioners, Matthew Kennedy and the Hinsdale Federation of Teachers (union), appeal the decision of the New Hampshire Public Employee Labor Relations Board (PELRB) denying their unfair labor practice claims against the respondent, the Hinsdale School District (school district). On appeal, the petitioners argue that the PELRB erred when it: (1) denied their claim that the school district had engaged in impermissible subcontracting; and (2) dismissed their claim that the school district violated its reduction-in-force policy. We affirm.

The administrative record supports the following facts. Kennedy was a music teacher in the Hinsdale Middle and High Schools for approximately ten years and a member of a bargaining unit represented by the union. The school district and the union were parties to a collective bargaining agreement (CBA), which contained a grievance procedure providing for, among other things, binding arbitration. The only matters excluded from the required grievance procedure were management prerogatives and teacher non-renewals.

Citing lack of student participation, the school district attempted to not renew Kennedy's employment for the 2008–2009 school year. This action was overturned by the state board of education on the grounds that the school district had failed to provide timely notice of non-renewal. On March 26, 2009, the school district again notified Kennedy that he was not being renewed due to declining enrollment.

Prior to Kennedy's non-renewal, the school district had two music teachers: Kennedy, who was in charge of the band program, and a second teacher who headed the choral program. This second teacher continues to be employed by the district. The history of the school's band program has been marked by steadily declining enrollment. In 1996, nearly seventy students participated in the band program. During the 2007–2008 school year, forty students participated. During the 2008–2009 school year, only twenty students participated in the band. Of these, five received credit, and fifteen participated on a "drop-in" basis, receiving no credit. Due to difficulties in rescheduling the band class after the petitioner's earlier nonrenewal was overturned, the union and the school district had agreed that the class would be held after the end of the normal school day. For the 2009–2010 school year, only fourteen students indicated interest in participating in band.

Prior to the commencement of the 2009–2010 school year, the school district eliminated the Hinsdale band program and entered into an agreement with Brattleboro (Vermont) High School whereby interested Hinsdale students could receive credit for participation in Brattleboro's music offerings, including band and choral programs, music theory electives, afterschool jazz band and madrigal groups, and music festival ensembles. The school district had previously entered into a similar arrangement for students to take vocational training courses at Brattleboro because of declining interest at Hinsdale. In addition, Hinsdale students could participate in the Winchester community band program, though not for credit. The school district also offered online music classes through the Virtual High School program.

The petitioners did not file a grievance concerning the school district's decision to not renew Kennedy's employment for the 2009–2010 school year. Rather, pursuant to RSA 189:14–a and RSA 189:14–b (Supp.2010), which set forth appeal procedures available to a teacher who has been nonrenewed, Kennedy appealed the decision to the Hinsdale School Board and, subsequently, to the state board of education. Each board affirmed the nonrenewal after a hearing.

The petitioners also filed an unfair labor practice complaint with the PELRB, alleging that the district had violated RSA 273–A:5, I (2010) by: (1) non-renewing Kennedy in retaliation for his union activity; (2) violating the school district's reduction-in-force policy in connection with Kennedy's termination of employment; and (3) outsourcing the school band program. After a hearing, the PELRB granted the school district's motion to dismiss the reduction-in-force claim, and denied the remaining claims. The petitioners appeal only the PELRB's rulings on their outsourcing and reduction-in-force claims.

The petitioners have the burden of proving that the PELRB's decision is clearly unreasonable or unlawful. The PELRB's findings of fact are deemed prima facie lawful and reasonable, and we will not disturb its order unless it is erroneous as a matter of law or we are satisfied by a clear preponderance of the evidence that it is unjust or unreasonable.

The petitioners first argue that the school district's action in replacing Kennedy's position with the Brattleboro offerings, the Winchester community band, and the Virtual High School constituted impermissible subcontracting. The school district asserts that it properly exercised its right to change its curriculum ... and the parties' CBA, which states that "educational policy, [and] the operation and management of schools ... are vested exclusively in the [school] [b]oard."

The Public Employee Labor Relations Act requires public employers and employee organizations to negotiate in good faith over the terms and conditions of employment. A public employer's unilateral change in a term or condition of employment is tantamount to a refusal to negotiate that term. "Terms and conditions" of employment are defined as wages, hours, and other conditions of employment "other than managerial policy within the exclusive prerogative of the public employer." Such managerial policy is defined in the Act as including, but not limited to, "the functions, programs, and methods of the public employer, including the use of technology, the public employer's organizational structure, and the selection, direction and number of its personnel, so as to continue public control of governmental functions."

While managerial policy may include position creation and elimination, employee wages and hours are a mandatory subject of negotiation.

The prerogatives afforded to management, however, do not include the right to substitute subcontracted work for bargaining unit work. In *Appeal of Hillsboro–Deering,* we held that "[w]hile the school district may have ... the management prerogative to change the amount or nature of the work performed by its bargaining unit, it [can]not lawfully terminate bargaining unit employees during the term of the CBA and subcontract with private companies to perform their work." We recognized that the employer's actions in replacing union employees with independent contractors to perform the same duties at reduced wages and benefits had "[i]n essence ... created a wholesale change in the bargained-for wages and hours of its employees." However, we also noted that a true layoff or reorganization is within managerial policy and is not subject to an unfair labor practice claim.

Relevant to our analysis here is the three-pronged test we have articulated for determining whether a particular proposal or action constitutes a mandatory subject of bargaining. First, "[t]o be negotiable, the subject matter of the [proposal] must not be reserved to the exclusive managerial authority of the public employer by the constitution, or by statute or statutorily adopted regulation." "Second, the proposal must primarily affect the terms and conditions of employment, rather than matters of broad managerial policy." "Third, if the proposal were incorporated into a negotiated agreement, neither the resulting contract provision nor the applicable grievance process may interfere with public control of governmental functions contrary to the provisions of RSA 273–A:1, XI [reserving matters of managerial policy to the employer]." Negotiation over the public employer's action is mandatory only if all three prongs are met.

Here, even assuming the first and third prongs of this test are satisfied, we cannot conclude that the second is satisfied; this is, we cannot conclude that the school district's action *primarily* affected the terms and conditions of employment, rather than matters of broad managerial policy.

Of significance is the fact that Kennedy's job duties were not simply transferred to an outside contractor. Thus, this case is distinguishable from *Appeal of City of Nashua,* in which we held that a school board's dismissal of unionized custodial workers and subsequent hiring of part-time employees to perform the same duties at reduced wages and benefits constituted an unfair labor practice. In so holding, we recognized that, because the actual job duties to be performed remained the same, the action was one that primarily affected wages and hours.

On the record before us, we agree with the PELRB's conclusion that the elimination of the Hinsdale band program was part of a reorganization within the district's managerial prerogative. As the PELRB noted, no outside contractor was hired to replace Kennedy as the Hinsdale band instructor. Moreover, the record supports the school district's conclusion that "the music program lack[ed] viability." A memorandum written by the Hinsdale Middle/High School principal noted that the limited performance opportunities offered to the band were of particular concern to the administration. For example, it was necessary for the band to be augmented with graduated students and members of the community in order to play at the 2008 graduation ceremony. Further, "a crucial factor in determining program viability" was a lack of participation in music offerings by high school freshmen and sophomores and middle school students, which indicated that interest was unlikely to rebound. Thus, the primary effect of the elimination of the band program was to alter the district's curricular offerings, not to transfer Kennedy's duties to another provider. Accordingly, we affirm the PELRB's decision on this issue.

The petitioners next argue the PELRB erred in dismissing their claim that the school district committed an unfair labor practice by terminating Kennedy's employment in violation of its reduction-in-force policy. They assert that the PELRB erred in determining that Kennedy's termination was a nonrenewal rather than a reduction-in-force (RIF), and that a remand is necessary because the PELRB did not address the question of whether it had jurisdiction over the reduction-in-force claim. In its dismissal motion, the school district argued that the PELRB lacked jurisdiction over the petitioners' reduction-in-force claim because the petitioners had failed to exhaust the required grievance procedure.

In granting the school district's motion to dismiss, the PELRB ruled that Kennedy's termination was a non-renewal, not a reduction-in-force. The board stated, "The [petitioners] themselves treated Mr. Kennedy's termination as a non-renewal by utilizing an appeal procedure under RSA 189:14–b, the 'nonrenewal appeal' statute, rather than filing a grievance as to the violation of the reduction-in-force policy, despite the fact that ... violations of the reduction-in-force policy are not expressly excluded from the contractual grievance procedure."

We have held that while the PELRB has primary jurisdiction over unfair labor practice claims under RSA 273–A:5, it does not generally have jurisdiction to interpret the CBA when the CBA provides for final binding arbitration. Absent specific language to the contrary in the CBA, however, the PELRB is empowered to determine as a threshold matter whether a specific dispute falls within the scope of the CBA. Thus, the PELRB is empowered to interpret the CBA to the extent necessary to determine whether a dispute is arbitrable.

We disagree with the petitioner's assertion that the PELRB did not reach the jurisdictional question. The PELRB found that "violations of the reduction-in-force policy are not expressly excluded from the contractual grievance procedure." We interpret this as a ruling that violations of the reduction-in-force policy are reserved to binding arbitration by the grievance procedure and, therefore, outside the PELRB's jurisdiction. We find no error in this ruling.

Accordingly, we do not conclude that the PELRB's decision is erroneous as a matter of law or that it is unjust or unreasonable.

Affirmed.

NOTES

1. Is arbitration an appropriate vehicle for resolving labor disputes in education?

2. Can you think of an alternative dispute resolution procedure in lieu of arbitration?

[CASE NO. 67] INJUNCTION AGAINST TEACHERS' STRIKE

COMMONWEALTH EMPLOYMENT RELATIONS BOARD v. BOSTON TEACHERS UNION

Appeals Court of Massachusetts, 2009.
908 N.E.2d 772 [245 Educ. L. Rep. 991] (Mass. Ct. App. 2009), *review denied*, 914 N.E.2d 330 (Mass. 2009), *cert. denied*, ___ U.S. ___, 130 S.Ct. 1738, 176 L.Ed.2d 213 (2010).

■ GRAHAM, J.

The Boston Teachers Union, Local 66, AFT, AFL–CIO (union), appeals from a judgment ordering it to pay $30,000 to the general fund of the Commonwealth, following an adjudication that the union was in contempt of an order of the Superior Court. In the order, the union was found to have violated the provisions of G.L. c. 150E, § 9A, which prohibits public employees and their unions from inducing, encouraging, or condoning a strike. The union contends that the judge's order, issued after the union set a date for a strike vote, but prior to the actual strike vote, violated the union members' rights under the First Amendment to the United States Constitution by imposing a prior restraint upon the union's right to free speech and assembly. We affirm.

Background. The union represents teachers and aides employed in Boston's public school system by the Boston School Committee (school committee). As the certified bargaining representative for public employees, the union's collective bargaining relationship is governed by G.L. c. 150E, §§ 1 et seq. (Act). The Commonwealth Employment Relations Board (board) is charged with administering and enforcing the Act.

General Laws c. 150E, § 9A(*a*), prohibits public employees and their organizations from engaging in a strike, and further provides that "no public employee or employee organization shall induce, encourage or condone any strike, work stoppage, slowdown or withholding of services by such public employees." General Laws c. 150E, § 9A(b), directs the board to prevent or correct violations of § 9A(a) as follows: "Whenever a strike occurs or is about to occur, the employer shall petition the [board] to make an investigation. If, after investigation, the [board] determines that any provision of paragraph (a) of this section has been or is about to be violated, it shall immediately set requirements that must be complied with, including, but not limited to, instituting appropriate proceedings in the superior court for the county wherein such violation has occurred or is about to occur for enforcement of such requirements."

The events leading to the Superior Court action began in December of 2006. The school committee and the union were parties to a collective bargaining agreement that expired on August 31, 2006. Since January, 2006, the parties had been involved in unsuccessful and acrimonious negotiations for a successor collective bargaining agreement. Convinced that the pressure of a pending strike vote was needed to motivate compromise by the school committee on terms of a new collective bargaining agreement, the union, on January 6, 2007, posted on its Web site an "emergency" "e-Bulletin" announcing a motion "[t]o place before the membership on February 14, 2007 for discussion, consideration, and debate by that body, in accordance with the bylaws, the question whether there should be a one-day strike on February 15, 2007 or on such other dates as may be chosen by the membership."

The e-Bulletin stated that the bargaining sessions over the previous twelve months "have not been productive" and that the parties "are still far apart on key issues"; described the school committee's proposal as "insulting to us"; and asserted that "[t]he school committee is apparently willing to foist the contract settlement on the new superintendent, using stall and crawl tactics." The e-Bulletin advised the union members that, in accordance with the motion, "over the next five weeks, we will be preparing for all exigencies that could result." It also scheduled "an emergency Area Captains meeting" for January 11, 2007, "an emergency, sign-in Building Representatives meeting" for February 1, 2007, and the strike vote meeting for February 14, 2007.

On January 7, 2007, the union president telephoned the Boston school superintendent and gave him a "heads up" about the February 14, 2007, strike vote and the February 15, 2007, strike date. Then, on January 11, 2007, the union advised its members by way of another e-Bulletin that on the previous day the membership had voted to approve the motion for "a strike vote to be taken" at the February 14, 2007, meeting. The e-Bulletin noted that the January 10, 2007, meeting "was [the] highest-attended membership meeting in over two years" and that the vote "was unanimous."

Meanwhile, the school committee, anticipating that union membership would authorize a strike, petitioned the board on January 9, 2007, to initiate an investigation pursuant to G.L. c. 150E, § 9A(b). The board conducted an investigation and held a hearing during which the parties had an opportunity to present evidence and examine witnesses. Following the investigation, the board concluded that although a strike vote had not yet been taken and approved by the union membership, the union's actions were "reasonably construed as constituting 'induce[ment], encourage[ment] or condon[ation of] any strike, work stoppage, slowdown or withholding of services by such public employees' " in violation of § 9A(*a*); and that a strike was "about to occur." Acting pursuant to § 9A(*b*), the board issued an order that required the union, its officers, and its executive board members, inter alia, to rescind and disavow their motion for a strike vote.

The union failed to comply with the board's order, and on January 31, 2007, the board held a compliance hearing. While the union appeared at the hearing, it offered no evidence that it had complied with any of the requirements of the board's order. The school committee presented the board with copies of e-Bulletins and union newspaper articles posted after the board had issued its order, which demonstrated the union's noncompliance with the board's order. One article quoted an executive board member: "waiting any longer is not an option." The article further noted that the members left a January, 2007, meeting "with a 'steely willingness to strike if the School Committee forces [their] hand.' " On February 6, 2007, the board issued a decision in which it found that the union had failed to comply with the board's order.

Superior Court proceedings. After the union failed to comply with the order, the board filed a complaint in the Superior Court seeking enforcement of its order. The school committee was allowed to intervene as a plaintiff. A judge of the Superior Court held an evidentiary hearing on February 12, 2007. The following day, the judge granted the board and the school committee a temporary restraining order. In his order, the judge found that the union had engaged in prohibited § 9A(*a*) activities, and found that a strike by the Union was "about to occur." He therefore (a) enjoined the union, its members, officers, and executive board members from engaging in or threatening a strike or work stoppage; (b) enjoined the union from inducing, encouraging, or condoning any strike or work stoppage; and (c) required the union, by 11:00 A.M. on February 14, 2007, to disavow, publicly, the motion for a strike vote, notify its members of the disavowal and the members' obligation to perform their duties and refrain from participating in a strike. The union was also required to inform the members of the provisions of §§ 9A(*a*) and (*b*) of G.L. c. 150E, and of the board's order.

On February 14, 2007, the day of the scheduled vote, the union sought a stay from the Superior Court. That motion was denied and the union immediately filed a motion for a stay with the single justice of this court under Mass.R.A.P. 6(a), as amended, 378 Mass. 930 (1979). On the afternoon of February 14, 2007, the single justice heard the motion and denied it.

No strike vote occurred on February 14, 2007, and there was no strike on February 15, 2007. Instead of providing the union membership with the notices set out in the judge's order, the union issued a "special" e-Bulletin dated February 14, 2007, in which it announced that "[t]he following motion passed the [union] membership this afternoon: To recess today's meeting to 2/28/07 and to defer, in light of recent developments, any discussion, consideration and debate on the Executive Board's December 20, 2006 motion to that meeting." This action prompted the board to return to the Superior Court and file a complaint for contempt.

After an evidentiary hearing, the judge found the union in contempt of his earlier order, and imposed a prospective "coercive fine" against the union. The union complied with the judge's order the following day, and later filed a timely appeal to this court.

Discussion. The union argues that the board prematurely and improperly concluded that a strike was "about to occur." The union further argues that the board has long held that the trigger for a determination that an employee organization is about to strike is when "certain conditions precedent have been satisfied such that it can be said that no further union action is necessary for a strike to commence."

The union acknowledges that, in the circumstances of this case, the board's ability to intervene before any actual strike is significantly impaired, but argues that such impairment is relatively minor, and that the board's investigation would be simplified because "it will be considerably easier for the employer-petitioner to prove its case if a strike has already commenced when a strike investigation hearing is convened." We are not persuaded. The purpose of the Act, set forth in clear and unequivocal language, is to allow the board to intervene in a labor dispute at a point where the board may set the requirements necessary to prevent an illegal strike that is about to occur.

The longstanding "actual vote" rule assumes that a public employer will have sufficient time to engage the process set forth in the Act once a strike vote has been held. That assumption is invalid in the particular circumstances of this case, and we therefore reject the interpretation of the statute suggested by the union because it would make the statute ineffective.

We conclude that the evidence before the board amply supported its conclusion that the union violated the provisions of § 9A(a) by encouraging and inducing a strike. That evidence included the e-Bulletins and articles from the union newspaper. A reasonable inference that the union was involved in encouraging a strike was warranted, if not compelled, by all of the evidence.

The union also alleges that the judge imposed a judicial prior restraint upon the union's exercise of protected speech and right to peaceful assembly guarantees in the First Amendment and in art. 16 of the Massachusetts Declaration of Rights by enforcing the board's alleged unconstitutional application of § 9A and issuing an injunction prohibiting the union "from gathering to discuss the merits of a strike and requiring it to disavow prior statements." We disagree. The union concedes, as it must, that there is no constitutional right of public employees to strike. In addition to barring strikes, § 9A also makes it unlawful for a public employee or union to "induce, encourage or condone" a strike.

The injunction issued by the judge imposed four requirements, namely, it enjoined the union, its executive board, and its members from engaging in or threatening a strike, and prohibited the union, its executive board, and its officers from inducing, encouraging, or condoning a strike; ordered them to disavow the executive board vote that scheduled the strike vote; required them to notify the members of their legal obligation not to engage in a strike; and required them to inform the members of the provision of § 9A and of the board's decision. The injunction placed no prior restraint upon the union to engage in public speech or debate, but rather prohibited it from engaging in actions that properly were prohibited under § 9A.

Moreover, to the extent that the conduct regulated by § 9A "includes both 'speech' and 'nonspeech' elements, the purpose of the statute is entirely unrelated to the suppression of free expression." The board has a substantial interest in preventing a strike by the union members, and "[a]ny incidental limitation of First Amendment freedoms" is justified.

Accordingly, the judgment is affirmed.

So ordered.

NOTES

1.   What are the pros and cons of granting public school teachers the right to strike?

2.   Can teachers bargain effectively if they lack the right to call for a strike? Can school boards bargain effectively if they cannot respond with lockouts?

CHAPTER 11

TEACHER TENURE, DISMISSAL, AND RETIREMENT

INTRODUCTION

At common law, the authority of school boards to hire teachers and other employees includes the right to dismiss them subject to constitutional, statutory, and/or contractual constraints. Even absent express contractual provisions identifying grounds for which educators may be discharged, common law permits dismissals for cause. What constitutes sufficient cause is, of course, a question of fact on a case-by-case basis.

The fact that legislatures grant school boards the right to employ teachers does not mean that they can act arbitrarily or capriciously. Teachers who comply with express and/or implied contractual conditions have the right to retain their jobs until their contracts expire or they retire. As such, it is important to keep in mind the critical distinction between board decisions not to renew the expired contracts of untenured teachers and discharging tenured faculty members.

After reviewing the significance and status of tenure statutes, this chapter focuses on dismissals primarily involving tenured teachers, including issues surrounding their free speech rights. When school boards terminate the employment of tenured teachers, they do so under two broad categories, for cause and not for cause, the latter typically referred to as a reduction-in-force. The final part of the chapter considers the rights of teachers who retire.

TENURE STATUTES

Most jurisdictions have enacted legislation granting school boards the non-delegable authority[1] to grant tenure,[2] sometimes referred to as con-

---

1. *Remus v. Board of Educ. for Tonawanda City School Dist.*, 727 N.Y.S.2d 43 [155 Educ. L. Rep. 759] (N.Y. 2001).

2. *See, e.g.*, ALASKA STAT. § 14.20.150; CAL. EDUC. CODE ANN. § 33123; GA. CODE ANN. § 20-2-242; 105 ILL. COMP. STAT. ANN. 5/2-3.47; MD. CODE ANN. EDUC. § 6-202; MICH. COMP. LAWS ANN. § 38.91; MONT. CODE ANN. § 20-6-711; N.J. STAT. ANN. § 18A:13-42; N.Y. EDUC. LAW § 3012-a; TENN. CODE ANN. § 49-2-203. *But see, e.g.*, ARK. CODE ANN. § 6-17-1503(b) ("This subchapter is not a teacher tenure law in that it does not confer lifetime appointment of teachers.").

tinuing contract status,[3] to teachers. Some jurisdictions also extend tenure rights to administrators[4] who meet statutory requirements by satisfactorily serving probationary periods.[5] Courts have long upheld the constitutionality of tenure laws,[6] acknowledging that they must be liberally construed in favor of educators since their purpose is to afford "protection [for] competent and qualified teachers in the security of their positions"[7] as well as to ensure them measures of protection from unjust dismissals.[8] To this end, courts tend to agree that educators do not waive their rights to tenure as teachers when they accept positions as administrators in the same district.[9]

In a case that it described as "highly unusual,"[10] an appellate court in New York affirmed that where a school board granted a teacher tenure in an improper area, the remedy was to return the dispute to the board so that officials could examine her lesson plans, evaluations, and in-class work in order to reclassify her into an accepted tenure area rather than terminate her employment. However, the state's highest court affirmed that where a probationary teacher who admitted consuming alcoholic beverages with students while serving as a chaperone during an overseas exchange program rejected her superintendent's offer to extend her probationary period for an extra year because the effective date of tenure had not yet occurred, the board could rescind its conditional tenure appointment and terminate her contract without having to meet the statutory guidelines otherwise applicable to a formal dismissal.[11]

School boards can confer tenure only by taking affirmative actions.[12] Accordingly, courts and states are unwilling to grant tenure by default or

---

3. *See, e.g.*, 105 Ill. Comp. Stat. Ann. 5/11D–10; Iowa Code Ann. § 279.15; Ohio Rev. Code Ann. § 4419.09(C); Okla. Stat. Ann. Title 70 § 6–101.

4. *Nelson v. Board of Educ. of Twp. of Old Bridge*, 689 A.2d 1342 [116 Educ. L. Rep. 1062] (N.J. 1997); *Bell v. Board of Educ. of Vestal Cent. School Dist.*, 472 N.Y.S.2d 899 [16 Educ. L. Rep. 894] (N.Y. 1984).

5. *Picogna v. Board of Educ. of Twp. of Cherry Hill*, 671 A.2d 1035 [107 Educ. L. Rep. 859] (N.J. 1996).

6. *Teachers' Tenure Act Cases*, 197 A. 344 (Pa.1938); *State ex rel. Bishop v. Board of Educ.*, 40 N.E.2d 913 (Ohio 1942).

7. *Sherwood Nat'l Educ. Ass'n v. Sherwood–Cass R–VIII School Dist.*, 168 S.W.3d 456, 459–60 [201 Educ. L. Rep. 394] (Mo. Ct. App. 2005), *reh'g and/or transfer denied* (2005).

8. *Palmer v. Louisiana State Bd. of Elementary and Secondary Educ.*, 842 So.2d 363 [175 Educ. L. Rep. 845] (La.2003); *State ex rel. Donah v. Windham Exempted Village School Dist. Bd. of Educ.*, 630 N.E.2d 687 [90 Educ. L. Rep. 367] (Ohio 1994).

9. *East Canton Educ. Ass'n. v. McIntosh*, 709 N.E.2d 468 [134 Educ. L. Rep. 284] (Ohio 1999), *reconsideration denied*, 711 N.E.2d 1015 (Ohio 1999), *cert. denied*, 528 U.S. 1061, 120 S.Ct. 614, 145 L.Ed.2d 509 (1999). *But see Pittman v. Chicago Bd. of Educ.*, 64 F.3d 1098 [103 Educ. L. Rep. 68] (7th Cir. 1995), *cert. denied*, 517 U.S. 1243, 116 S.Ct. 2497, 135 L.Ed.2d 189 (1996).

10. *Abrantes v. Board of Educ. of Norwood–Norfolk Cent. School Dist.*, 649 N.Y.S.2d 957, 959 [114 Educ. L. Rep. 608] (N.Y. App. Div. 1996), *leave to appeal denied*, 657 N.Y.S.2d 405 (N.Y. 1997).

11. *Remus v. Board of Educ. for Tonawanda City School Dist.*, 727 N.Y.S.2d 43 [155 Educ. L. Rep. 759] (N.Y. 2001).

12. *Ray v. Board of Educ. of Oak Ridge Schools*, 72 S.W.3d 657 [164 Educ. L. Rep. 954] (Tenn. Ct. App.2001), *appeal denied* (2001).

estoppel.[13] In an illustrative case, an appellate court in California upheld the denial of permanent status to a teacher who spent two years teaching under an emergency license.[14] The court agreed that state law was clear that time spent teaching under such a permit did not count toward permanent status except for teachers who were credentialed in other states. The court refused to intercede on behalf of the teacher and grant her tenure by estoppel since board officials had not misled her about the effect of teaching under an emergency permit. On the other hand, as reflected by a case from New York, where service as a regular substitute counted toward tenure, a teacher was entitled to tenure by estoppel.[15] Where state laws impose statutory requirements such as notice, some courts apply statutes strictly against boards with the result that teachers were awarded tenure because school officials failed to follow the law while others refuse to grant tenure under these circumstances.[16]

The general rule is that tenure statutes cover only those positions that are explicitly identified.[17] Strict interpretation of tenure statutes is evident in judicial refusal to extend their protection to supplementary positions such as coaching.[18] Consequently, when coaches are relieved of their duties but do not suffer the loss of tenure,[19] courts are unwilling to intervene on their behalf, especially where board actions are supported by just cause, even if evidence is grounded in hearsay as in a case from Iowa that upheld a coach's dismissal for his threatening and intimidating treatment of student-athletes along with his use of profanity.[20]

---

13. *But see Wood v. North Wamac School Dist. No. 186,* 899 N.E.2d 578 [240 Educ. L. Rep. 785] (Ill. App. Ct. 2008) (affirming that a one-year leave of absence could be counted toward the four year probationary period before receiving teacher tenure since state law required individuals to be employed for four consecutive terms but did not explicitly require them to teach during all four).

14. *Smith v. Governing Bd. of Elk Grove Unified School Dist.,* 16 Cal.Rptr.3d 1 [189 Educ. L. Rep. 814] (Cal. Ct. App. 2004), *review denied* (2004).

15. *Speichler v. Board of Co–Operative Educ. Servs., Second Superv. Dist.,* 659 N.Y.S.2d 199, 203 [119 Educ. L. Rep. 614] (N.Y. 1997) ("Tenure by estoppel results 'when a school board accepts the continued services of a teacher or administrator, but fails to take the action required by law to either grant or deny tenure prior to the expiration of the teacher's probationary term'") (internal citations omitted). For cases reaching the same result, *see also Brenes v. City of New York,* 733 F.Supp.2d 357 [263 Educ. L. Rep. 167] (E.D.N.Y. 2010); *Triana v. Board of Educ. of the City of N.Y.,* 849 N.Y.S.2d 569 [228 Educ. L. Rep. 879] (N.Y. App. Div. 2008).

16. *Compare Farrington v. School Comm. of Cambridge,* 415 N.E.2d 211 (Mass. 1981) (granting tenure under such circumstances) and *Matter of Zunic v. Nyquist,* 370 N.Y.S.2d 228 (N.Y. App. Div. 1975), *aff'd on opinion below,* 390 N.Y.S.2d 919 (N.Y. 1976) (granting a probationary teacher who did not receive the required statutory notice of dismissal back pay, but not reinstatement or tenure). *See also Sullivan v. Centinela Valley Union High School Dist.,* 122 Cal.Rptr.3d 871 [265 Educ. L. Rep. 1170] (Cal. Ct. App. 2011) (affirming the denial of a teacher's claim that he was entitled to tenure by estoppel since he failed to receive notice that he was not going to receive tenure).

17. *Frye v. Independent School Dist. No. 625,* 494 N.W.2d 466 [80 Educ. L. Rep. 210] (Minn. 1992); *Franson v. Bald Eagle Area School Dist.,* 668 A.2d 633 [105 Educ. L. Rep. 1125] (Pa. Cmwlth. Ct.1995), *appeal denied,* 677 A.2d 840 (Pa. 1996).

18. *Lagos v. Modesto City Schools Dist.,* 843 F.2d 347 [46 Educ. L. Rep. 60] (9th Cir. 1988), *cert. denied,* 488 U.S. 926, 109 S.Ct. 309, 102 L.Ed.2d 328 (1988); *Davis v. Russell,* 852 So.2d 774 [180 Educ. L. Rep. 963] (Ala. Civ. App. 2002); *Mignault v. Ledyard Pub. Schools,* 792 F.Supp.2d 289 [273 Educ. L. Rep. 212] (D. Conn.2011).

19. *Ex parte Dunn,* 962 So.2d 814 [224 Educ. L. Rep. 572] (Ala. 2007) (where a teacher was removed from his job as basketball coach for physically abusive discipline of student-athletes but did not suffer the loss of tenure in light of his overall good record as a school employee).

20. *Christopher v. Windom Area School Dist.,* 781 N.W.2d 904 [256 Educ. L. Rep. 911] (Minn. Ct. App. 2010), *review denied* (2010); *Board of Directors of Ames Community School Dist. v. Cullinan,* 745 N.W.2d 487 [229 Educ. L. Rep. 869] (Iowa 2008), *reh'g denied* (2008).

In *State ex rel. Anderson v. Brand (Brand)*,[21] the Supreme Court held that jurisdictions may make tenure contractual rather than place it on legislative status. The Court refused to allow a board in Indiana to repudiate a teacher's tenure where an unusually worded statute was repealed after she acquired tenure. In upholding the teacher's right to tenure, the Court suggested that the legislature could have changed the statute for prospective employees but not for those who were already covered by its original provisions.

Courts generally uphold legislative authority to change tenure laws based on the rationale that jurisdictions cannot permanently bind themselves to specific employment practices.[22] In such a case, the Supreme Court of Illinois upheld the legislature's elimination of tenure for principals in Chicago.[23] In a related dispute, the Seventh Circuit, echoing the Supreme Court's analysis in *Brand*, agreed that a legislature could rescind tenure even if it meant that principals who were returned to the least senior positions on the list of tenured teachers might lose their jobs.[24]

Insofar as statutes typically require teachers to work full-time for set periods of time, typically three or four years, before becoming eligible for tenure, questions arise about educators who served as substitute teachers. As with many areas, the courts reach mixed results. Some courts are reluctant to permit short-term service as substitutes[25] or time spent working under emergency status[26] to be credited toward meeting probationary periods prior to gaining tenure. In a case of first impression, an appellate court in New York affirmed that a substitute teacher could not accrue credit toward tenure for time spent under an intern certificate because he lacked a valid teacher's certificate.[27] Other courts made exceptions, refusing to preclude time spent as substitutes into account if educators rendered substantial service.[28]

[Case No. 68] *See also Samuelson v. LaPorte Community School Corp.*, 526 F.3d 1046 [232 Educ. L. Rep. 605] (7th Cir. 2008), *Lawrence County Educ. Ass'n v. Lawrence County Bd. of Educ.*, 244 S.W.3d 302 [229 Educ. L. Rep. 958] (Tenn. 2007), *Brown v. Simmons*, 478 F.3d 922 [216 Educ. L. Rep. 855] (8th Cir. 2007).

21. 303 U.S. 95, 58 S.Ct. 443, 82 L.Ed. 685 (1938).

22. *Morgan v. Potter*, 298 N.W. 763 (Wis. 1941), *cert. denied*, 314 U.S. 673, 62 S.Ct. 136, 86 L.Ed. 538 (1941). *See also Phelps v. Board of Educ.*, 300 U.S. 319, 57 S.Ct. 483, 81 L.Ed. 674 (1937).

23. *Fumarolo v. Chicago Bd. of Educ.*, 566 N.E.2d 1283 [65 Educ. L. Rep. 1181] (Ill. 1990).

24. *Pittman v. Chicago Bd. of Educ.*, 64 F.3d 1098 [103 Educ. L. Rep. 68] (7th Cir. 1995), *cert. denied*, 517 U.S. 1243, 116 S.Ct. 2497, 135 L.Ed.2d 189 (1996).

25. *Reis v. Biggs Unified School Dist.*, 24 Cal.Rptr.3d 393 [195 Educ. L. Rep. 261] (Cal. Ct. App. 2005); *Zalac v. Governing Bd. of Ferndale Unified School Dist.*, 120 Cal.Rptr.2d 615 [165 Educ. L. Rep. 277] (Cal. Ct. App. 2002), *review denied* (2002); *Emanuel v. Independent School Dist. No. 273, Edina School Dist.*, 615 N.W.2d 415 [146 Educ. L. Rep. 860] (Minn. Ct. App. 2000), *review denied* (2000). For older cases, *see Tyler v. School Dist. No. 1, City and County of Denver*, 493 P.2d 22 (Colo. 1972); *Hudson v. Independent School Dist. No. 77*, 258 N.W.2d 594 (Minn. 1977).

26. *Smith v. Governing Bd. of Elk Grove Unified School Dist.*, 16 Cal.Rptr.3d 1 [189 Educ. L. Rep. 814] (Cal. Ct. App. 2004), *reh'g and review denied* (2004).

27. *Berrios v. Board of Educ. of Yonkers City School Dist.*, 927 N.Y.S.2d 368 [269 Educ. L. Rep. 275] (N.Y. App. Div. 2011).

28. *See, e.g., Dees v. Board of School Comm'rs of Mobile County*, 57 So.3d 781 [266 Educ. L. Rep. 560] (Ala. Civ.App. 2010); *Dial v. Lathrop R–II School Dist.*, 871 S.W.2d 444 [89 Educ. L. Rep. 1033] (Mo. 1994).

TEACHER DISMISSAL

DISMISSAL FOR CAUSE GENERALLY

Statutes addressing tenure generally permit teacher contracts to continue without the need for express renewals. This obligates school boards to follow specified procedures when they wish to terminate the employment of tenured teachers. While procedures vary from one jurisdiction to another, they involve four basic elements: timely notice that dismissal is being contemplated, specification of charges, a hearing at which the allegations are examined and a judgment rendered on the record regarding a teacher's future employment. Most statutes also include provisions for appeals that often culminate in judicial review.

Tenure statutes typically permit the dismissal of tenured teachers only for specified grounds. Conversely, non-tenured teachers can have their employment terminated for any lawful reason[29] without hearings.[30] Recognizing that states employ a variety of terms for the same topics, the three sometimes overlapping grounds for which teachers can be dismissed for cause are insubordination, conduct unbecoming a professional, and incompetence. The overlapping nature of these bases for dismissal aside, when boards review specific charges, they cannot act on any others absent a phrase such as "other good and just cause" in applicable statutes. Although some states include the catch-all phrase "other good and just cause," described by an appellate court in Colorado as any action that "includes any cause bearing a reasonable relationship to a teacher's fitness to discharge her duties,"[31] this review focuses on the three major categories present in most laws.[32]

Legislatures retain the authority to enumerate the grounds for which tenured teachers may be discharged. In other words, local school boards may not add reasons of their own choosing. Even so, from a practical point of view, most courts give broad interpretations to such words as incompetence, immorality, and conduct unbecoming a teacher. Moreover, since teachers cannot be disciplined for exercising their constitutional rights such as First Amendment guarantees, this discussion includes a section on their rights to free speech.

---

29. *Shiers v. Richland Parish School Bd.*, 902 So.2d 1173 [198 Educ. L. Rep. 1009] (La. Ct. App. 2005), *writ denied*, 916 So.2d 1066 (La. 2005); *Haviland v. Yonkers Pub. Schools*, 800 N.Y.S.2d 578 [201 Educ. L. Rep. 667] (N.Y. App. Div. 2005).

30. *Von Gizycki v. Levy*, 771 N.Y.S.2d 174 [185 Educ. L. Rep. 325] (N.Y. App. Div. 2004).

31. *Fredrickson v. Denver Pub. School Dist.*, 819 P.2d 1068, 1073 [71 Educ. L. Rep. 274] (Colo. Ct. App.1991). *See also Spurlock v. Board of Trustees, Carbon County School Dist. No. 1*, 699 P.2d 270 [25 Educ. L. Rep. 577] (Wyo. 1985).

32. For a case involving all three of the major categories as well as other good and just cause, *see Ex parte Wilson*, 984 So.2d 1161 [234 Educ. L. Rep. 496] (Ala. 2007) (affirming an earlier order reversing and remanding a hearing officer's reinstatement of a teacher-cheerleading sponsor who, among other charges, operated a personal gymnastics business in her school, for a new hearing).

Tenure statutes, local board policies, and collective bargaining agreements often require school officials to warn teachers before they initiate disciplinary actions for remediable offenses. Absent specific provisions mandating remediation, boards are under no obligation to warn teachers and to offer them opportunities to correct their behavior.[33] In considering whether misconduct is remediable, an appellate court in Illinois applied a two-part test in examining whether a teacher's conduct "(1) has caused significant damage to students, the faculty, or the school and (2) could not have been corrected even if superiors had given the teacher the statutorily prescribed warning."[34] The court decided that where a tenured teacher's refusal to accept a classroom assignment was irremediable, the board could terminate his contract. When courts are convinced that misconduct can be corrected or punishments are disproportionate to offenses, they typically afford teachers opportunities to improve.[35]

As reflected by a case from New York, criminal conduct is treated as irremediable per se.[36] An appellate court thus vacated part of an arbitration award that would have reinstated a dean of students who was guilty of drug possession if he successfully completed a treatment program.[37] The court maintained that the reinstatement order was irrational and defied common sense since it would have returned the dean to a position administering a program that was designed to discourage students from using drugs.

Insubordination

In order to be subject to charges of insubordination, teachers must intentionally fail to comply with legitimate orders of supervisors or with valid policies of which they were, or reasonably should have been, aware.[38] The Supreme Court of Tennessee, for example, reasoned that a teacher could not be discharged for failing to return to duty when her superintendent ordered her to do so since she was medically unable to work due to stress, fear, and intimidation after a star basketball player failed her class.[39]

---

33. *Roberts v. Lincoln County School Dist. No. One*, 676 P.2d 577 [16 Educ. L. Rep. 331] (Wyo. 1984).

34. *Board of Educ. of City of Chicago v. Harris*, 578 N.E.2d 1244, 1248 [70 Educ. L. Rep. 156] (Ill. App. Ct. 1991), *appeal denied*, 584 N.E.2d 126 (Ill. 1991), *partially abrogated on a point not at issue here by Russell v. Board of Educ. of City of Chicago*, 883 N.E.2d 9 [230 Educ. L. Rep. 365] (Ill. App. Ct. 2007).

35. *See, e.g., Hall v. Board of Trustees of Sumter County School Dist. No. 2*, 499 S.E.2d 216 [125 Educ. L. Rep. 1362] (S.C. Ct. App. 1998), *reh'g denied* (1998); *Smith v. Board of Educ., Onteora Cent. School Dist.*, 633 N.Y.S.2d 625 [104 Educ. L. Rep. 1279] (N.Y. App. Div. 1995), *leave to appeal denied*, 642 N.Y.S.2d 858 (N.Y. 1996).

36. *McBroom v. Board of Educ., Dist. No. 205*, 494 N.E.2d 1191 [33 Educ. L. Rep. 404] (Ill. App. Ct. 1986).

37. *City School Dist. of City of N.Y. v. Campbell*, 798 N.Y.S.2d 54 [199 Educ. L. Rep. 908] (N.Y. App. Div. 2005).

38. *Sims v. Board of Trustees, Holly Springs, Mun. Separate School Dist.*, 414 So.2d 431 [4 Educ. L. Rep. 933] (Miss. 1982).

39. *McGhee v. Miller*, 753 S.W.2d 354 [47 Educ. L. Rep. 1228] (Tenn. 1988), *appeal after remand*, 785 S.W.2d 817 [59 Educ. L. Rep. 567] (Tenn.1990), *appeal after remand*, 837 S.W.2d 596 [78 Educ. L. Rep. 156] (Tenn. 1992).

When teachers are unaware of policies, or rules are unreasonable, courts agree that they cannot be dismissed for insubordination. In such a case, an appellate court in Illinois affirmed that a board could not dismiss a tenured teacher for scheduling a vacation during a winter break that the board cancelled due to a strike since she and others were unaware of this ad hoc rule.[40] While some courts treat a single incident as justifying a dismissal for insubordination,[41] others disagree, declaring that teachers must engage in persistent or continuing behavior before boards can terminate their employment.[42]

Among the array of reasons for which boards dismissed teachers for insubordination, four stand out: discipline, corporal punishment, sexual misconduct with students, and instructional issues such as refusing to comply with legitimate instructional methodologies and policies, including evaluations. A discussion of each of these topics follows.

Discipline: Courts addressed a variety of claims wherein teachers faced sanctions for alleged violations of laws and/or board policies when disciplining students. Where state law forbade cruelty to students, an appellate court in Illinois upheld a teacher's dismissal for using a cattle prod on a student since it was satisfied that this behavior met the statutory definition.[43] Further, an appellate court in Louisiana upheld a teacher's dismissal for brandishing a starter pistol to gain control over hostile students in positing that this was unacceptable conduct.[44] Similarly, an appellate court in Alabama upheld the dismissal of a teacher-principal who fired a shot into a floor as a scare tactic to break up a fight where board policy prohibited staff members from bringing firearms onto school property.[45] In a case reaching the opposite outcome, when a student in Louisiana who was armed with a large board seriously threatened a teacher, an appellate court believed that insofar as he acted reasonably in retrieving a gun from his car in order to protect himself when pursued, he should not have lost his job.[46]

Corporal punishment: Not surprisingly, the use of corporal punishment or force has generated litigation. When a primary school music teacher disregarded express directives from supervisors about the use of force in class and intentionally hit or tapped a student on the hand with a three-foot pointer, the Supreme Court of Colorado agreed that her school board

---

40. *Board of Educ. of Round Lake Area Schools Community Unit School Dist. No. 116 v. State Board of Educ.*, 685 N.E.2d 412 [121 Educ. L. Rep. 821] (Ill. App. Ct. 1997).

41. *Ware v. Morgan County School Dist. No. RE–3*, 748 P.2d 1295 [44 Educ. L. Rep. 778] (Colo. 1988); *Hall v. Board of Trustees of Sumter County School Dist. No. 2*, 499 S.E.2d 216 [125 Educ. L. Rep. 1362] (S.C. Ct. App. 1998), *reh'g denied* (1998).

42. *Sims v. Board of Trustees, Holly Springs, Mun. Separate School Dist.*, 414 So.2d 431 [4 Educ. L. Rep. 933] (Miss. 1982).

43. *Rolando v. School Directors of Dist. No. 125, LaSalle County*, 358 N.E.2d 945 (Ill. App. Ct. 1976).

44. *Myres v. Orleans Parish School Bd.*, 423 So.2d 1303 [8 Educ. L. Rep. 545] (La. Ct. App. 1982), *writ denied*, 430 So.2d 657 (La.1983), *reconsideration denied*, 433 So.2d 155 (La. 1983).

45. *Burton v. Alabama State Tenure Comm'n*, 601 So.2d 113 [76 Educ. L. Rep. 293] (Ala. Civ. App. 1992).

46. *Landry v. Ascension Parish School Bd.*, 415 So.2d 473 [4 Educ. L. Rep. 1361] (La. Ct. App. 1982), *writ denied*, 420 So.2d 448 (La. 1982).

could dismiss her for insubordination.[47] In like fashion, an appellate court in Tennessee affirmed the dismissal of a third-grade teacher who slapped students, placed her hands on their faces to get them to pay attention, and hit them on their heads with a soft-cover textbook.[48] The court noted that the teacher was insubordinate because she failed to follow instructions from her principal and assistant principal to refrain from placing her hands on her students.

On the other hand, an appellate court in Colorado rejected a school board's attempt to dismiss a tenured teacher who refused to comply with her principal's directive not to ever touch a student physically for disciplinary reasons.[49] The court pointed out that the teacher was not insubordinate when she intervened to stop two children who struck her while disrupting class because the principal's order would have unequivocally divested her of authority pursuant to a board policy. Moreover, the Supreme Court of Alabama ordered the reinstatement of a teacher who was about to be dismissed for using corporal punishment.[50] The court disagreed with the board's assessment that the teacher should have been dismissed when, in response to a disrespectful gesture from a student whom others described as difficult, she tapped him on the face. Subsequently, an appellate court in New York affirmed that in the face of insufficient evidence to support a finding that a teacher violated state regulations by improperly using physical force against a student, the penalty of dismissal was excessive and shocking to one's conscience.[51] However, where a bus escort in New York struck a child, and was not merely defending herself, during an altercation on a bus, an appellate court affirmed that her dismissal did not shock the conscience.[52]

Sexual misconduct with students: It almost goes without saying that when teachers or other staff members engage in sexual activity with students, they violate board policies, and the law, against sexual harassment, a topic explored later in this section and in Chapter 13. Even so, courts have upheld the dismissals of educators for insubordination in a variety of cases with sexual overtones such as spanking female teenagers and discussing explicitly sexual matters with them;[53] making sexually suggestive statements in class;[54] using sexually explicit materials;[55] touch-

---

47. *Board of Educ. of West Yuma School Dist. RJ–1 v. Flaming*, 938 P.2d 151 [118 Educ. L. Rep. 1202] (Colo. 1997).

48. *Ketchersid v. Rhea County Bd. of Educ.*, 174 S.W.3d 163 [203 Educ. L. Rep. 423] (Tenn. Ct. App. 2005), *appeal denied* (2005) (also affirming that the teacher was incompetent and inefficient).

49. *Fredrickson v. Denver Pub. School Dist.*, 819 P.2d 1068 [71 Educ. L. Rep. 274] (Colo. Ct. App. 1991).

50. *Ex parte Alabama State Tenure Comm'n*, 555 So.2d 1071 [58 Educ. L. Rep. 841] (Ala.1989), *on remand*, 555 So.2d 1075 [58 Educ. L. Rep. 845] (Ala. Civ. App. 1989).

51. *Weinstein v. Department of Educ. of City of N.Y.*, 798 N.Y.S.2d 383 [199 Educ. L. Rep. 916] (App. Div. 2005), *leave to appeal denied*, 812 N.Y.S.2d 35 (N.Y. 2006).

52. *Duncan v. Klein*, 832 N.Y.S.2d 188 [218 Educ. L. Rep. 645] (N.Y. App. Div. 2007).

53. *Penn–Delco School Dist. v. Urso*, 382 A.2d 162 (Pa. Cmwlth. Ct. 1978).

54. *Pryse v. Yakima School Dist. No. 7*, 632 P.2d 60 (Wash. Ct. App. 1981), *reviewed denied*, 96 Wash.2d. 1011 (Wash. 1981).

ing female students when explicitly warned not to do so;[56] pulling on a student's bra strap and intimidating her for reporting the incident;[57] offering to perform sex acts on students in adult education classes;[58] and directing an inappropriate sexual comment at a student.[59]

An appellate court in Arizona upheld a male teacher's dismissal for insubordination for lying and for refusing to cooperate with his school board's investigation of his relationship with a seventeen-year-old student.[60] In like manner, the Sixth Circuit affirmed that a board in Michigan could deny tenure to a female high school physical education teacher who had a sexual relationship with a student within nine months of the latter's graduation.[61] The court observed that the teacher repeatedly denied that she engaged in improper conduct with the student despite evidence to the contrary. Yet, where a school board waited more than seven years before attempting to terminate the contract of a teacher for allegedly sexually harassing a student, an appellate court in Louisiana affirmed his reinstatement with lost pay and benefits on the basis that waiting this long was fundamentally unfair.[62]

Instructional issues: An older case from the First Circuit illustrates difficulties that can arise when teachers seek to use ideas or language that may be offensive to others. After a teacher in Massachusetts assigned an article for classroom discussion that a psychiatrist wrote for a reputable publication that included a term for an incestuous son, the court decreed that he could not lose his job for insubordination.[63] While conceding that some regulation of classroom speech is proper, the court found that it was inappropriate to discipline the teacher both because he had insufficient notice that he could not use such material and since the word appeared in at least five books in the library.[64]

The Supreme Court of California was of the opinion that a teacher could not be dismissed for reading a story in class that he wrote and which contained language objectionable to school officials.[65] The court determined that the reading was only a single, good faith, incident as a teaching technique that was not barred by any school rule. Conversely, the Seventh

---

55. *Bernstein v. Norwich City School Dist. Bd. of Educ.*, 726 N.Y.S.2d 474 [154 Educ. L. Rep. 916] (N.Y. App. Div. 2001), *leave to appeal dismissed*, 733 N.Y.S.2d 375 [159 Educ. L. Rep. 710] (N.Y. 2001).

56. *Forte v. Mills*, 672 N.Y.S.2d 497 [126 Educ. L. Rep. 362] (N.Y. App. Div. 1998).

57. *Thibodeau v. Northeastern Clinton Cent. School Bd. of Educ.*, 833 N.Y.S.2d 294 [218 Educ. L. Rep. 961] (N.Y. App. Div. 2007).

58. *Capone v. Patchogue–Medford Union Free School Dist.*, 832 N.Y.S.2d 283 [218 Educ. L. Rep. 647] (N.Y. App. Div. 2007).

59. *Lackow v. Department of Educ. of City of N.Y.*, 859 N.Y.S.2d 52 [233 Educ. L. Rep. 845] (N.Y. App. Div. 2008).

60. *Welch v. Board of Educ. of Chandler Unified School Dist. No. 80 of Maricopa County*, 667 P.2d 746 [12 Educ. L. Rep. 1290] (Ariz. Ct. App. 1983).

61. *Flaskamp v. Dearborn Pub. Schools*, 385 F.3d 935 [192 Educ. L. Rep. 359] (6th Cir. 2004), *reh'g en banc denied*, 385 F.3d 935 (6th Cir. 2004).

62. *Leban v. Orleans Parish School Bd.*, 972 So.2d 376 [228 Educ. L. Rep. 1002] (La. Ct. App. 2007), *writ denied*, 976 So.2d 184 (La. 2008).

63. *Keefe v. Geanakos*, 418 F.2d 359 (1st Cir. 1969).

64. *See also Mailloux v. Kiley*, 448 F.2d 1242 (1st Cir. 1971).

65. *Lindros v. Governing Bd. of Torrance Unified School Dist.*, 108 Cal.Rptr. 185 (Cal. 1973), *cert. denied*, 414 U.S. 1112, 94 S.Ct. 842, 38 L.Ed.2d 739 (1973).

Circuit upheld the dismissal of a teacher in Illinois for distributing brochures to eighth-grade students referring to the pleasures of marijuana use
and encouraging them to free themselves of the moral environment of their
homes in order to experience a new sense of love and community.[66]

Courts agree that selected classroom behaviors are so clearly improper
that school boards need no specific rules before disciplining teachers. The
Sixth Circuit ruled that a board in Kentucky could dismiss a tenured
teacher for insubordination for showing a violent and sexually suggestive
movie, the content of which she never previewed or discussed, since it
lacked an educational purpose.[67] The court rejected the teacher's claim that
she engaged in protected First Amendment speech which others sometimes
rely on in alleging that they have rights to academic freedom.[68] An
appellate court in Arkansas affirmed that even absent a specific prohibition, a teacher could be dismissed for unprofessional conduct when she
offered to, but did not, sell raffle tickets to students in return for higher
grades.[69] Also, an appellate court in New York upheld a teacher's dismissal
for unprofessional conduct when she improperly disclosed words on a
standardized achievement test to her students.[70]

The judiciary tends to be unresponsive to claims of academic freedom
when teachers are charged with insubordination and/or inefficiency. Courts
rendered judgments against teachers who refused to follow directions with
regard to curricular activities;[71] course content;[72] supplemental reading
materials;[73] and the teaching of subjects dealing with love of country, the
flag, or other patriotic matters.[74] Additionally, courts limited the ability of
teachers to vent, or expound on their personal views, whether speaking
against the police following an automobile accident;[75] where proselytizing;[76]
or praying out loud in class.[77]

---

66. *Brubaker v. Board of Educ., School Dist. 149, Cook County, Ill.*, 502 F.2d 973 (7th
Cir.1974), *cert. denied*, 421 U.S. 965, 95 S.Ct. 1953, 44 L.Ed.2d 451 (1975).

67. *Fowler v. Board of Educ. of Lincoln County, Ky.*, 819 F.2d 657 [39 Educ. L. Rep. 1011]
(6th Cir. 1987), *cert. denied*, 484 U.S. 986, 108 S.Ct. 502, 98 L.Ed.2d 501 [43 Educ. L. Rep. 21]
(1987).

68. *See also Krizek v. Board of Educ. of Cicero–Stickney Twp. High School Dist. No. 201,
Cook County*, 713 F.Supp. 1131 [54 Educ. L. Rep. 491] (N.D. Ill. 1989) (involving a non-
tenured teacher).

69. *Gatewood v. Little Rock Pub. Schools*, 616 S.W.2d 784 (Ark. Ct. App. 1981).

70. *Altsheler v. Board of Educ. of Great Neck Union Free School Dist.*, 476 N.Y.S.2d 281
[17 Educ. L. Rep. 1199] (N.Y. 1984), *reargument dismissed*, 483 N.Y.S.2d 1026 [22 Educ. L.
Rep. 1237] (N.Y. 1984).

71. *In re Proposed Termination of James E. Johnson's Teaching Contract with Indep.
School Dist. No. 709*, 451 N.W.2d 343 [58 Educ. L. Rep. 1031] (Minn. Ct. App. 1990), *review
denied* (1990).

72. *Bradley v. Pittsburgh Bd. of Educ.*, 910 F.2d 1172 [62 Educ. L. Rep. 426] (3d Cir.
1990).

73. *Kirkland v. Northside Indep. School Dist.*, 890 F.2d 794 [57 Educ. L. Rep. 396] (5th
Cir. 1989), *cert. denied*, 496 U.S. 926, 110 S.Ct. 2620, 110 L.Ed.2d 641 (1990).

74. *Palmer v. Board of Educ. of City of Chicago*, 603 F.2d 1271 (7th Cir.1979), *cert. denied*,
444 U.S. 1026, 100 S.Ct. 689, 62 L.Ed.2d 659 (1980).

75. *Petrie v. Forest Hills School Dist. Bd. of Educ.*, 449 N.E.2d 786 [11 Educ. L. Rep. 618]
(Ohio Ct. App. 1982).

76. *La Rocca v. Board of Educ. of Rye City School Dist.*, 406 N.Y.S.2d 348 (N.Y. App. Div.
1978), *appeal denied*, 413 N.Y.S.2d 1025, 385 N.E.2d 1075 (1978), *appeal dismissed*, 413
N.Y.S.2d 1030 (N.Y. 1978).

Policies on student assessments and grading are integral to school operations. Although teachers assign grades, their power may be subject to restrictions. Courts seem to agree that teachers can be required to conform to reasonable rules and be evaluated on this aspect of their jobs.[78] West Virginia's highest court ascertained that an administrator's merely asking a teacher to re-evaluate a grade did not raise constitutional issues.[79]

Courts upheld the dismissals of tenured teachers for insubordination where individuals refused to follow directives not to leave classes unattended;[80] sign a supplement to a contract containing excerpts of board policies;[81] comply with guidelines to make timely reports on lost books and to retain final examinations;[82] obey rules such as getting approval for specified articles to appear in a school newspaper;[83] refuse to accept a student into a class;[84] perform hall duty;[85] implement a professional growth plan;[86] turn in lesson plans;[87] and discontinue a confrontational approach with supervisors in addition to claiming that she, not they, controlled both her curriculum and classroom methods.[88]

Other courts refuted board attempts to dismiss teachers for insubordination where educators refused to stop denigrating the ability of special education students;[89] refused to submit to a psychological examination not required by law for reinstatement;[90] took time off from work due to the illness, and eventual death, of her mother;[91] refused to request an unpaid medical leave of absence for evaluating her psychological fitness since her

---

77. *Fink v. Board of Educ. of Warren County School Dist.*, 442 A.2d 837 [3 Educ. L. Rep. 105] (Pa. Cmwlth. Ct.1982), *appeal dismissed*, 460 U.S. 1048, 103 S.Ct. 1493, 75 L.Ed.2d 927 [19 Educ. L. Rep. 21] (1983).

78. *Brown v. Wood County Bd. of Educ.*, 400 S.E.2d 213 [65 Educ. L. Rep. 608] (W. Va. 1990).

79. *Meckley v. Kanawha County Bd. of Educ.*, 383 S.E.2d 839 [56 Educ. L. Rep. 328] (W. Va. 1989).

80. *Gordon v. Lafayette County School Dist.*, 923 So.2d 260 [207 Educ. L. Rep. 800] (Miss. Ct. App. 2006).

81. *Sims v. Board of Trustees, Holly Springs, Municipal Separate School Dist.*, 414 So.2d 431 [4 Educ. L. Rep. 933] (Miss. 1982).

82. *Moffitt v. Batesville School Dist.*, 643 S.W.2d 557 [8 Educ. L. Rep. 877] (Ark. 1982).

83. *Nicholson v. Board of Educ. Torrance Unified School Dist.*, 682 F.2d 858 [5 Educ. L. Rep. 733] (9th Cir. 1982).

84. *Hatton v. Wicks*, 744 F.2d 501 [20 Educ. L. Rep. 400] (5th Cir. 1984). [Case No. 69]

85. *Lockhart v. Board of Educ. of Arapahoe County School Dist. No. 6*, 735 P.2d 913 [39 Educ. L. Rep. 349] (Colo. Ct. App. 1986).

86. *Hope v. Charlotte–Mecklenburg Bd. of Educ.*, 430 S.E.2d 472 [83 Educ. L. Rep. 481] (N.C. Ct. App. 1993).

87. *School Dist. No. 1, City and County of Denver v. Cornish*, 58 P.3d 1091 [171 Educ. L. Rep. 1028] (Colo. Ct. App. 2002).

88. *Barnes v. Spearfish School Dist. No. 40–2*, 725 N.W.2d 226 [214 Educ. L. Rep. 1231] (S.D. 2006).

89. *Chattooga County Bd. of Educ. v. Searels*, 691 S.E.2d 629 [255 Educ. L. Rep. 997] (Ga. Ct. App. 2010).

90. *In re Mary Silvestri's Teaching Contract with Indep. School Dist. No. 695*, 480 N.W.2d 117 [72 Educ. L. Rep. 1050] (Minn. Ct. App. 1992), *review denied* (1992).

91. *Drain v. Board of Educ. of Frontier County School Dist. No. 46*, 508 N.W.2d 255 [87 Educ. L. Rep. 612] (Neb. 1993).

wait for a dismissal hearing at which to defend herself was proper exercise of her procedural rights;[92] a board, rather than a hearing officer, terminated a teacher's contract;[93] and lacked sufficient evidence proving that a teacher failed to provide a fitness for duty report before she returned to work.[94]

CONDUCT UNBECOMING A TEACHER

"[T]eacher[s] serve[ ] as [ ] role model[s] for [their] students, exerting a subtle but important influence over their perceptions and values."[95] Most, if not all, courts agree with this statement of the Supreme Court, expecting the character and conduct of educators to be above that of persons who do not work in sensitive relationships with children. Accordingly, courts have upheld teacher dismissals for offenses variously referred to as conduct unbecoming an educator, immorality, and/or moral turpitude.[96]

In recent years there has been a trend recently toward affording teachers more freedom in their personal lives than in the more distant past. Still, it is difficult to draw a line between the rights of teachers as private citizens and as educators. The bottom line is that, generally speaking, the private lives of educators are their own business unless or until their actions impact on their professional lives. In one noteworthy area in this regard, the courts have long agreed that being an unwed mother does not per se constitute grounds for dismissal.[97]

Conduct unbecoming an educator, as with incompetence, is basically a term of art, its meaning shaped by contemporary concepts of improper personal conduct. Courts have thus refused to invalidate the term immorality as unconstitutionally vague as a ground for dismissal.[98] The Supreme Court of Pennsylvania, in often quoted language,[99] pointed out as much when it described immorality as "a course of conduct as offends the morals of the community and is a bad example to the youth whose ideals a teacher is supposed to foster and to elevate."[100] In the underlying dispute, the court

---

92. *Board of Educ. of City of Chicago v. Weed*, 667 N.E.2d 627 [111 Educ. L. Rep. 1306] (Ill. App. Ct. 1996).

93. *Board of Educ. of Community Consol. School Dist. No. 54 v. Spangler*, 767 N.E.2d 452 [166 Educ. L. Rep. 294] (Ill. App. Ct. 2002).

94. *Brawner v. Marietta City Bd. of Educ.*, 646 S.E.2d 89 [221 Educ. L. Rep. 370] (Ga. Ct. App. 2007).

95. *Ambach v. Norwick*, 441 U.S. 68, 78–79, 99 S.Ct. 1589, 60 L.Ed.2d 49 (1979).

96. For a case upholding the termination of a teacher's contract for moral turpitude where "misconduct compromised her ability to function in her job and constituted unacceptable behavior," *see Chaplin v. New York City Dep't of Educ.*, 850 N.Y.S.2d 425 [229 Educ. L. Rep. 202] (N.Y. App. Div. 2008).

97. *Andrews v. Drew Municipal Separate School Dist.*, 507 F.2d 611 (5th Cir.1975); *New Mexico State Bd. of Educ. v. Stoudt*, 571 P.2d 1186 (N.M.1977).

98. *Sullivan v. Meade Indep. School Dist. No. 101*, 530 F.2d 799 (8th Cir. 1976); *Weissman v. Board of Educ. of Jefferson County School Dist. No. R–1*, 547 P.2d 1267 (Colo. 1976); *Ross v. Robb*, 662 S.W.2d 257 [15 Educ. L. Rep. 606] (Mo. 1983).

99. *See, e.g., Kinniry v. Abington School Dist.*, 673 A.2d 429, 432 [108 Educ. L. Rep. 312] (Pa. Cmwlth. Ct. 1996).

100. *Horosko v. Mount Pleasant Twp. School Dist.*, 6 A.2d 866, 868 (Pa.1939), *cert. denied*, 308 U.S. 553, 60 S.Ct. 101, 84 L.Ed. 465 (1939).

reinstated a teacher who was dismissed due to her public behavior, which included playing dice with customers for drinks, in a bar that her husband owned.

In a case combining the elements of immorality and neglect of duty, the Supreme Court of Oregon affirmed the dismissal of a teacher with nineteen years of experience who had never been subject to prior disciplinary sanctions.[101] After the teacher argued with her estranged husband, she tried to commit suicide by taking prescription medications, ramming her car into her husband's, pushing the car into the house of his girlfriend, and causing significant damage to the home. In reversing an earlier order to the contrary, the court agreed that the board had a reasonable basis on which to terminate the teacher's employment.

Another case involved a variety of charges against a teacher who was fired for misconduct. The Supreme Court of Delaware affirmed that a school board did not abuse its discretion in dismissing a teacher for immorality and misconduct where its action was based on substantial evidence.[102] According to evidence in the record, among his misdeeds, the teacher coerced a student to transport him to a known drug market after midnight to purchase illegal drugs, accepted money for raising grades, and willfully and knowingly used inappropriate language at a school event.

If teachers are subject to discipline, school officials must prove that their behavior reduced their occupational effectiveness. Put another way, officials must prove that there is a rational nexus between teachers' inappropriate conduct and their professional duties to such an extent that it impairs or destroys their professional effectiveness.[103]

The Supreme Court of California identified factors in considering whether the behavior of teachers renders them unfit if activities occurred outside of school settings. The court addressed "the likelihood that the conduct may have adversely affected students or fellow teachers, the degree of such adversity anticipated, the proximity or remoteness in time of the conduct, the type of teaching certificate held by the party involved, the extenuating or aggravating circumstances, if any, surrounding the conduct, the praiseworthiness or blameworthiness of the motives resulting in the conduct, the likelihood of the recurrence of the questioned conduct, and the extent to which disciplinary action may inflict an adverse impact or chilling effect upon the constitutional rights of the teacher involved or other teachers."[104] Twenty-five years later, an appellate court in California explicitly applied these criteria in affirming the dismissal of a male teacher for sexually harassing female students.[105]

---

101. *Bergerson v. Salem–Keizer School Dist.*, 144 P.3d 918 [213 Educ. L. Rep. 822] (Or. 2006).

102. *Bethel v. Board of Educ. of Capital School Dist.*, 985 A.2d 389 [254 Educ. L. Rep. 873] (Del. 2009).

103. *Woo v. Putnam County Bd. of Educ.*, 504 S.E.2d 644 [129 Educ. L. Rep. 853] (W. Va. 1998).

104. *Morrison v. State Bd. of Educ.*, 82 Cal.Rptr. 175, 186 (Cal. 1969).

105. *Governing Bd. of ABC Unified School Dist. v. Haar*, 33 Cal.Rptr.2d 744 [94 Educ. L. Rep. 384] (Cal. Ct. App. 1994), *review denied* (1994).

In specific cases, the Supreme Court of Colorado affirmed the dismissal of a tenured teacher for immorality for violating board policy by drinking beer with students while acting in her official capacity as cheerleader sponsor.[106] The court agreed that insofar as the teacher knowingly violated the policy, the board could terminate her employment since her conduct had a direct bearing on her relationship to students and the school community. In another dispute involving alcohol, the Supreme Court of Iowa upheld a teacher's dismissal for allowing her son to have a party at her house at which he and others drank alcohol. After the students left the teacher's house, four of them were killed when the driver lost control of his car and it hit a tree. Among its reasons for affirming the teacher's dismissal, the court referred to her "unprofessional conduct in allowing students to use [her] property for a party where alcohol was illegally used by students ... failure to protect the safety and well-being of students, inability to be effective as a teacher, [being] a poor role model, and poor and ineffective leadership."[107]

A novel case was litigated in Missouri where an appellate court upheld the dismissal of a tenured teacher for immorality in light of her having tried to convince the incarcerated, non-English speaking, undocumented mother of an eleven-month-old who was facing deportation charges to give her child up for adoption to persons who were interested in having a child.[108] The court agreed that the teacher's lack of judgment in attempting to cover up her manipulation of a vulnerable mother while refusing to accept responsibility for her actions demonstrated that she was unfit for the job.

Courts usually concur that educator misbehavior in class or on school premises has enough of a relationship to their duties as to meet the nexus criterion as a matter of law, meaning without need for proof of connection. In such situations, courts have upheld the dismissals of teachers for making racially derogatory remarks to, or about, students in class[109] and for being rude to children.[110] Reflective of the typical judicial approach, the Supreme Court of Montana treated isolated remarks that were disrespectful to students such as calling one a "slob" for not paying attention and for being slumped down in her chair[111] as insufficient to justify dismissals.

The judiciary regularly upholds discipline of educators who engaged in inappropriate sexual contact with students, even for incidents that did not

---

106. *Blaine v. Moffat County School Dist. Re No. 1*, 748 P.2d 1280 [44 Educ. L. Rep. 763] (Colo. 1988).

107. *Walthart v. Board of Directors of Edgewood–Colesburg Community School Dist.*, 694 N.W.2d 740, 741–42 [197 Educ. L. Rep. 388] (Iowa 2005).

108. *Homa v. Carthage R–IX School Dist.*, 345 S.W.3d 266 [270 Educ. L. Rep. 902] (Mo. Ct. App. 2011), *transfer denied* (2011).

109. *Emri v. Evesham Twp. Bd. of Educ.*, 327 F. Supp.2d 463 [191 Educ. L. Rep. 142] (D. N.J. 2004); *Resetar v. State Bd. of Educ.*, 399 A.2d 225 (Md. 1979), *cert. denied*, 444 U.S. 838, 100 S.Ct. 74, 62 L.Ed.2d 49 (1979).

110. *Emri v. Evesham Twp. Bd. of Educ.*, 327 F. Supp.2d 463 [191 Educ. L. Rep. 142] (D. N.J. 2004) (the teacher also made racist remarks to students).

111. *Trustees of Lincoln County School Dist. No. 13, Eureka v. Holden*, 754 P.2d 506 [46 Educ. L. Rep. 1036] (Mont. 1988).

surface for years.[112] Among the actions involving sexuality that led to dismissals for conduct unbecoming are touching a student's breasts;[113] asking a student to touch her breasts in addition to a male teacher's touching his own genitals in front of her;[114] having sexual relations with a student;[115] exposing oneself on many occasions over four years to female students;[116] taking photographs of young girls surreptitiously and using them in a sexually gratifying manner;[117] engaging in sexual[118] and romantic[119] relations with students; hugging and allegedly trying to kiss a female student;[120] writing overtly sexual letters to female students;[121] placing a hand on a female student's knee;[122] and taking topless photographs of female students.[123]

Even if there are circumstances that may reduce the personally controllable reasons for inappropriate conduct, teachers can be dismissed for conduct unbecoming an educator. Courts have upheld dismissals for drug dependency derived from an effort to combat obesity[124] and for shoplifting possibly as a result of temporary mental instability.[125]

Turning to criminal behavior as a basis for dismissal, the Supreme Court of Alaska reiterated the general rule that there need not always be a separate nexus between the moral turpitude of educators and their fitness to perform their duties because they can be expected to meet a higher standard than non-educators. The court thus affirmed that a board had the authority to dismiss a teacher for engaging in a sexual relationship with a

112. *Toney v. Fairbanks North Star Borough School Dist., Bd. of Educ.*, 881 P.2d 1112 [95 Educ. L. Rep. 380] (Alaska 1994); *Waisanen v. Clatskanie School Dist.*, 215 P.3d 882 [248 Educ. L. Rep. 872] (Ore. Ct. App. 2009).

113. *In re Watt (East Greenbush Cent. School Dist.)*, 925 N.Y.S.2d 681 [268 Educ. L. Rep. 494] (N.Y. App. Div. 2011).

114. *Douglas v. New York City Bd./Dep't of Educ.*, 929 N.Y.S.2d 127 [270 Educ. L. Rep. 820] (N.Y. App. Div. 2011).

115. *Lehto v. Board of Educ. of Caesar Rodney School Dist.*, 962 A.2d 222 [240 Educ. L. Rep. 289] (Del. 2008) [Case No. 70]; State v. Hirschfelder, 242 P.3d 876 (Wash. 2010).

116. *Miller v. Grand Haven Bd. of Educ.*, 390 N.W.2d 255 [33 Educ. L. Rep. 1247] (Mich. Ct. App. 1986), *appeal denied* (1986).

117. *Montefusco v. Nassau County*, 39 F. Supp.2d 231 [134 Educ. L. Rep. 127] (E.D.N.Y. 1999).

118. *Toney v. Fairbanks North Star Borough School Dist.*, Bd. of Educ., 881 P.2d 1112 [95 Educ. L. Rep. 380] (Alaska 1994).

119. *Andrews v. Independent School Dist. No. 57*, 12 P.3d 491 [148 Educ. L. Rep. 1061] (Okla. Civ. App. 2000).

120. *Baltrip v. Norris*, 23 S.W.3d 336 [146 Educ. L. Rep. 573] (Tenn. Ct. App. 2000), *appeal denied* (2000).

121. *Board of Educ. of Sparta Community Unit School Dist. No. 140 v. Illinois State Bd. of Educ.*, 577 N.E.2d 900 [69 Educ. L. Rep. 846] (Ill. App. Ct. 1991).

122. *Rivers v. Board of Trustees, Forrest County Agricultural High School*, 876 So.2d 1043 [190 Educ. L. Rep. 731] (Miss. Ct. App. 2004).

123. *Dixon v. Clem*, 492 F.3d 665 [222 Educ. L. Rep. 580] (6th Cir. 2007).

124. *Martin v. Guillot*, 875 F.2d 839 [53 Educ. L. Rep. 1113] (11th Cir.1989).

125. *Board of Directors of Lawton–Bronson Community School Dist. v. Davies*, 489 N.W.2d 19 [77 Educ. L. Rep. 482] (Iowa 1992).

fifteen-year-old minor, years earlier in another state, even though his behavior did not result in a conviction.[126]

An appellate court in Louisiana affirmed that even though a tenured teacher completed probation after having pled guilty to charges of possessing marijuana and cocaine, and the criminal proceedings were dismissed, his school board could terminate his contract for moral turpitude.[127] The court asserted that even though the charges were dropped because the teacher completed probation, nothing changed the fact that he engaged in inappropriate behavior.[128]

Appellate courts in Pennsylvania[129] and Michigan[130] affirmed that tenured teachers could be dismissed following convictions for trafficking in counterfeit goods and embezzlement at a part-time job, respectively, since their actions negatively impacted their reputations in their school communities. Also, an appellate court in New York affirmed the dismissal of a tenured teacher who had prior convictions for fraud based on similar misconduct after she was convicted of grand larceny.[131] The court stated that insofar as the penalty was not so disproportionate to the offense so as to shock the conscience, there was no reason why the teacher should have been reinstated. Although apparently not involving a criminal conviction, another appellate court in New York relied on the shock the conscience rationale in upholding the dismissal of a tenured teacher. The court agreed that insofar as the teacher knowingly defrauded New York City of $98,000 in free tuition by enrolling her children in the public schools even though she did not live within city boundaries, dismissal was an appropriate penalty.[132]

A novel misuse of technology arose in California where a school board challenged an order of the State's Commission on Professional Competence reinstating a teacher it fired for posting graphic photographs of himself on an Internet site soliciting sex.[133] Reversing in favor of the board, an appellate court held that insofar as the teacher's immoral conduct rendered him unfit to teach, it had the discretion to terminate his employment.

---

126. *Toney v. Fairbanks North Star Borough School Dist., Bd. of Educ.*, 881 P.2d 1112 [95 Educ. L. Rep. 380] (Alaska 1994).

127. *Dubuclet v. Home Ins. Co.*, 660 So.2d 67 [103 Educ. L. Rep. 547] (La. Ct. App. 1995), *writ denied*, 664 So.2d 446 (La. 1995).

128. *See Board of Educ. of Hopkins County v. Wood*, 717 S.W.2d 837 [35 Educ. L. Rep. 824] (Ky. 1986) (dismissing a tenured teacher for smoking marijuana in his apartment with others, including two fifteen-year-old students, during the summer when school was not in session).

129. *Kinniry v. Abington School Dist.*, 673 A.2d 429 [108 Educ. L. Rep. 312] (Pa. Cmwlth. Ct. 1996).

130. *Satterfield v. Board of Educ. of the Grand Rapids Pub. Schools*, 556 N.W.2d 888 [114 Educ. L. Rep. 1192] (Mich. Ct. App. 1996).

131. *Green v. New York City Dep't of Educ.*, 793 N.Y.S.2d 405 [197 Educ. L. Rep. 714] (N.Y. App. Div. 2005), *leave to appeal denied*, 806 N.Y.S.2d 161 (N.Y. 2005), *reargument denied*, 810 N.Y.S.2d 419 (N.Y. 2005).

132. *Cipollaro v. New York City Dep't of Educ.*, 922 N.Y.S.2d 23 [266 Educ. L. Rep. 899] (N.Y. App. Div. 2011).

133. *San Diego Unified School Dist. v. Commission on Professional Competence*, 124 Cal.Rptr.3d 320 [267 Educ. L. Rep. 301] (Cal. Ct. App. 2011).

Incompetence/Neglect of Duty

Incompetence, sometimes referred to as neglect of duty, is a ground for dismissal in common law[134] as well as under most statutes. Abstractly, incompetence is a term of art lacking a precise definition that has been given a variety of meanings extending far beyond those related to subject matter, teaching methods, or preserving discipline, ordinarily over time rather than as a single event, that has not been rendered inappropriate for vagueness when boards seek to terminate the contracts of tenured teachers.[135] Insofar as there is a legal presumption that certificated teachers are competent, the longer they serve without documented difficulties, the stronger the presumption becomes. To this end, the burden of proof of incompetence or neglect of duty is on school officials who claim that teachers have failed to perform satisfactorily.

The Supreme Court of Nebraska ruled that the standard to be used in evaluating incompetence was not that of perfection, but, not unlike the reasonable educator in negligence cases, of performance required of others executing the same or like duties.[136] Almost twenty years hence the same court indicated that incompetence can be defined as demonstrated deficiencies or shortcomings in educators' knowledge in subject matter or administrative skills.[137] The court affirmed that a school board improperly dismissed a superintendent over claims that he erred in preparing drafts of budget documents and did not provide him with evaluations and notice of his alleged deficiencies.[138] Other courts agreed that tenured teachers must be given notice of their deficiencies and opportunities to improve.[139]

Failure to preserve student discipline is frequently offered as a cause for teacher dismissal due to incompetence.[140] For instance, an appellate court in Tennessee affirmed that a board could dismiss a tenured teacher for incompetence, inefficiency, insubordination, and neglect of duty in light of sufficient evidence that she failed to control her class, used questionable grading methods, and required extraordinary assistance from administrators and parents to enforce discipline.[141] Other dismissals for incompetence for inappropriate discipline included cases where a principal tied a child with a behavioral disorder to a desk, bound his ankles and wrists with duct tape, and left him in an open doorway in public view for about two hours[142]

---

134. *City of Crawfordsville v. Hays*, 42 Ind. 200 (Ind. 1873).

135. *California Teachers Ass'n v. Governing Bd.*, 192 Cal.Rptr. 358 [11 Educ. L. Rep. 574] (Ct. App. 1983), *cert. denied sub nom. Takahashi v. Governing Board of the Livingston Union School Dist.*, 465 U.S. 1008, 104 S.Ct. 1003, 79 L.Ed.2d 235 (1984); *Board of Educ. of W. Yuma School Dist. RJ–1 v. Flaming*, 938 P.2d 151 [118 Educ. L. Rep. 1202] (Colo. 1997).

136. *Sanders v. Board of Educ. of S. Sioux City Community School Dist. No. 11*, 263 N.W.2d 461 (Neb. 1978).

137. *Boss v. Fillmore County School Dist. No. 19*, 559 N.W.2d 448 [116 Educ. L. Rep. 380] (Neb. 1997).

138. *See also Sekor v. Board of Educ. of the Town of Ridgefield*, 689 A.2d 1112 [116 Educ. L. Rep. 1049] (Conn. 1997); *Ruchert v. Freeman School Dist.*, 22 P.3d 841 [153 Educ. L. Rep. 424] (Wash. Ct. App. 2001), *review denied*, 35 P.3d 381 (Wash. 2001) (addressing standards in evaluating whether tenure can be revoked for incompetence).

139. *Jones v. New York City Bd. of Educ.*, 592 N.Y.S.2d 441 [80 Educ. L. Rep. 700] (N.Y. App. Div.1993).

140. *Linstad v. Sitka School Dist.*, 963 P.2d 246 [129 Educ. L. Rep. 504] (Alaska 1998).

141. *Childs v. Roane County Bd. of Educ.*, 929 S.W.2d 364 [113 Educ. L. Rep. 505] (Tenn. Ct. App. 1996), *appeal denied* (1996).

142. *Sylvester v. Cancienne*, 664 So.2d 1259 [105 Educ. L. Rep. 1350] (La. Ct. App.1995), *writ not considered*, 666 So.2d 663 (La. 1996). *But see James v. Trumbull County Bd. of Educ.*,

and where a teacher bound one student with electrical cord and placed soap on the tongue of another.[143]

In preserving classroom decorum, teachers must apply board policies designed to limit student expression and/or their own instructional techniques. In a case from Missouri, the Eighth Circuit[144] upheld the dismissal of a teacher who permitted students to make videotapes including in excess of one hundred and fifty uses of profanity and racial slurs because she persistently violated board policy prohibiting such behavior.[145] Earlier, in Pennsylvania, when a tenured teacher disregarded directives to discontinue using a classroom management technique he developed, the Third Circuit affirmed that the board could terminate his contract.[146]

Evaluations of classroom performance have resulted in a fair amount of litigation. The general rule with regard to the substance of evaluations is that as long as they are based on professional criteria and are applied by competent evaluators, results are not subject to judicial review absent claims that low ratings are influenced by, or in retaliation for, teachers exercising their constitutional rights. In a case that failed to specify whether the teacher was tenured, an appellate court in New York refused to reverse two years of unsatisfactory evaluations where she received seven such ratings in one academic year and four in the next since the actions of officials were not arbitrary, capricious, or irrational.[147]

In expansive interpretations of evaluations, courts upheld the dismissals of tenured teachers due to the lack of student progress;[148] the inability to impart curricular knowledge as reflected in a high rate of failures;[149] and the combination of weak rapport with students and poor communication skills with parents.[150] In what was then a novel case involving evidence of incompetence or inefficiency, an appellate court in Texas affirmed that the

---

663 N.E.2d 1361 [109 Educ. L. Rep. 349] (Ohio Ct. App. 1995) (affirming that a tenured teacher could not be dismissed for wilful and persistent violations of board policy for placing hot sauce in the mouth of a student with multiple disabilities since officials failed to identify a rule that she violated).

143. *Johanson v. Board of Educ. of Lincoln County School Dist. No. 1*, 589 N.W.2d 815 [132 Educ. L. Rep. 916] (Neb. 1999).

144. *Lacks v. Ferguson Reorganized School Dist. R–2*, 147 F.3d 718 [127 Educ. L. Rep. 568] (8th Cir.1998), *suggestion for reh'g en banc denied*, 154 F.3d 904 (8th Cir.1998), *cert. denied*, 526 U.S. 1012, 119 S.Ct. 1158, 143 L.Ed.2d 223 (1999). [Case No. 71]

145. *See also Spurlock v. East Feliciana Parish School Bd.*, 885 So.2d 1225 [193 Educ. L. Rep. 626] (La. Ct. App. 2004), *writ denied*, 885 So.2d 591 (La. 2004) (affirming that where a tenured second-grade teacher was dismissed for the use of poor judgment in allowing children to simulate sex acts in her classroom, the board could not have created a policy addressing every possible act of wilful neglect of duty).

146. *Bradley v. Pittsburgh Bd. of Educ.*, 913 F.2d 1064 [62 Educ. L. Rep. 894] (3d Cir. 1990).

147. *Batyreva v. New York City Dep't of Educ.*, 854 N.Y.S.2d 390 [230 Educ. L. Rep. 713] (N.Y. App. Div. 2008).

148. *Whaley v. Anoka–Hennepin Indep. School Dist. No. 11*, 325 N.W.2d 128 [7 Educ. L. Rep. 206] (Minn. 1982).

149. *In re Proposed Termination of James E. Johnson's Teaching Contract with Indep. School Dist. No. 709*, 451 N.W.2d 343 [58 Educ. L. Rep. 1031] (Minn. Ct. App. 1990), *review denied* (1990).

150. *Raitzik v. Board of Educ. of City of Chicago*, 826 N.E.2d 568 [197 Educ. L. Rep. 685] (Ill. App. Ct. 2005).

use of videotapes in the evaluation process did not violate a teacher's right to privacy.[151] The court noted that affording the teacher access to the tapes, though not in edited form, sufficed as notice of evidence to be considered when the board initiated dismissal proceedings. Fifteen years later, an appellate court in Kentucky rejected a teacher's request that she be able to take part in an in camera review of videotapes of her performance that were made to monitor her behavior with her students after children complained that she treated them inappropriately.[152] The court remanded for additional consideration as to whether the teacher could examine the tapes in her official capacity as an educator who had a legitimate educational interest in viewing their content under the Family Educational Rights and Privacy Act.

Courts have upheld the dismissals of teachers and other school employees for a variety of offenses. Courts agreed that educators could be dismissed for being unable to define standards for a student assessment and not keeping records of the same;[153] failing to comply with special education paperwork requirements;[154] supervising a strip search of students;[155] having excessive absences;[156] telling dirty jokes to students and referring to another teacher in front of other pupils by a derogatory name;[157] and failing to prevent the loss or theft of more than $25,000 of gate receipts at a high school's athletic events.[158]

FREE SPEECH RIGHTS OF TEACHERS

Concerns arise about the employment status of teachers and other public employees who exercise their First Amendment rights to freedom of speech as private citizens. Beginning with *Pickering v. Board of Education of Township High School District (Pickering)*,[159] the Supreme Court has handed down a series of judgments designed to help clarify the parameters of this important topic.

At issue in *Pickering* was the attempt of a school board in Illinois to dismiss a teacher for writing a letter to a local newspaper which criticized its handling of a bond issue and its allocation of financial resources

---

151. *Roberts v. Houston Indep. School Dist.*, 788 S.W.2d 107 [60 Educ. L. Rep. 251] (Tex. Ct. App. 1990), *writ denied* (1990). [Case No. 72]

152. *Medley v. Board of Educ., Shelby County*, 168 S.W.3d 398 [201 Educ. L. Rep. 380] (Ky. Ct. App. 2004), *review denied* (2005).

153. *Davis v. Board of Educ. of City of Chicago*, 659 N.E.2d 86 [105 Educ. L. Rep. 1175] (Ill. App. Ct. 1995).

154. *Hellmann v. Union School Dist.*, 170 S.W.3d 52 [201 Educ. L. Rep. 955] (Mo. Ct. App. 2005).

155. *Rogers v. Board of Educ. of City of New Haven*, 749 A.2d 1173 [143 Educ. L. Rep. 968] (Conn. 2000).

156. *McKinnon v. Board of Educ. of N. Bellmore Union Free School Dist.*, 709 N.Y.S.2d 104 [145 Educ. L. Rep. 1100] (N.Y. App. Div. 2000) (also including a charge of misconduct).

157. *Oleske v. Hilliard City School Dist. Bd. of Educ.*, 764 N.E.2d 1110 [162 Educ. L. Rep. 958] (Ohio App. 2001), *appeal not allowed*, 761 N.E.2d 48 (Ohio 2002).

158. *Smith v. Bullock County Bd. of Educ.*, 906 So.2d 938 [200 Educ. L. Rep. 905] (Ala. Civ. App. 2004), *cert. denied* (2005).

159. 391 U.S. 563, 88 S.Ct. 1731, 20 L.Ed.2d 811 (1968). [Case No. 73]

between its educational and athletic programs. The Supreme Court identified the need to find the appropriate "[b]alance between the interests of the teacher, as a citizen, in commenting upon matters of public concern and the interest of the State, as an employer, in promoting the efficiency of the public services it performs through its employees."[160] In rejecting the board's claim that the letter was detrimental to the best interests of the schools, the Court wrote that the teacher's right to free speech was primary since this was a matter of public concern.

In *Pickering*, the Supreme Court examined a variety of factors which led it to rule in favor of the teacher. Along with recognizing that the teacher had the right to speak out on a legitimate matter of public concern as a private citizen, the Justices commented that he did not have a close working relationship with those he criticized, that his letter did not have a detrimental impact on the administration of the district, and that it did not negatively affect his regular duties. In deciding that the interests of the board and schools were not synonymous, the Court acknowledged that the public interest in having free and unhindered debate on matters of public importance was crucial. The Court added that insofar as "teachers are, as a class, the members of a community most likely to have informed and definite opinions as to how funds allotted to the operation of the schools should be spent,"[161] it was essential that they be able to speak freely on such questions.

The Supreme Court revisited the free speech rights of teachers eleven years later in *Mt. Healthy City Board of Education v. Doyle* (*Mt. Healthy*),[162] wherein it considered the effect of including a constitutionally protected right as a factor in not renewing the contract of a teacher who lacked tenure. The board chose not to renew the contract of a teacher who had a record of being difficult in school despite his claim that it violated his rights after he called into a radio talk show and criticized a memorandum from his principal dealing with a faculty dress code. The Court rejected the Sixth Circuit's finding that including a protected activity as a substantial part of the justification for the nonrenewal of a probationary teacher's contract entitled him to reinstatement with back pay. The Justices remarked that the Sixth Circuit would have placed the teacher in a better position as a result of exercising his protected speech than had he done nothing. The Court conceded that where a teacher shows that protected conduct about a school matter was a substantial or motivating factor where a board chooses not to renew a contract, it must be given the opportunity to show that it would have chosen not to re-employ in the absence of the protected conduct. On remand, the board reported that it would not have renewed the teacher's contract regardless of whether he placed the call to the radio talk show.[163]

---

160. *Id.* at 569.

161. *Id.* at 572.

162. 429 U.S. 274, 97 S.Ct. 568, 50 L.Ed.2d 471 (1977).

163. *Doyle v. Mt. Healthy City School Dist. Bd. of Educ.*, 670 F.2d 59 [2 Educ. L. Rep. 973] (6th Cir. 1982).

The Supreme Court returned to the issue of the free speech rights of teachers in *Givhan v. Western Line Consolidated School District* (*Givhan*).[164] The Court determined that the *Pickering* balancing test applies to teachers who express themselves during private conversations with their supervisors. When school officials decided against renewing the contract of a non-tenured teacher in Mississippi, she was informed that it was in response for, among other reasons, her allegedly making petty and unreasonable demands on the principal and addressing him in a manner variously described as insulting, hostile, loud, and arrogant. The teacher also complained that the board, which operated under a court-ordered desegregation plan, was racially discriminatory in its employment policies and practices. In refusing to reinstate the teacher, the Court reasoned that the Fifth Circuit erred in declaring that school officials were justified in not renewing her contract, suggesting that under *Mt. Healthy*, they may have had sufficient cause on other grounds that would have required further proceedings. The Court thought that under *Pickering*, the judiciary must consider working relationships of personnel as well as the contents of communications in evaluating whether private communications exceeded the scope of First Amendment protection.

At issue in *Connick v. Myers* (*Connick*),[165] was whether *Pickering* protects public employees who communicate their views about workplace matters to peers. At issue was a former assistant district attorney's challenge to her dismissal on the same day that she was scheduled for a transfer to another division because she circulated a questionnaire about office operations among staff. The Supreme Court distinguished *Givhan* in conceding that while the teacher's statements there involved issues of public concern, the attorney's were primarily based on an internal disagreement with her supervisors and the questionnaire interfered with the close working relationships in the office. In noting that the attorney's dismissal did not violate her rights, the Court established a two-step test to evaluate whether speech is entitled to First Amendment protections. First, the Court explained that the judiciary must consider whether the speech involved an issue of public concern by examining its content and form along with the context within which it was expressed. Second, the Justices posited that if speech does deal with a matter of public concern, the judiciary must balance employees' interests as citizens in speaking out on matters of public concern against those of employers in promoting effective and efficient public services. Almost a decade hence, in *Waters v. Churchill*,[166] a case from Illinois involving a nurse who criticized internal policies at a public hospital, a plurality of the Court reiterated that public employees who publicly dispute internal policies not dealing with matters of public concern may lack constitutional protection.

In a more recent application of *Connick's* principles, albeit again not in a school setting, in *Garcetti v. Ceballos* (*Garcetti*),[167] the Supreme Court,

---

164.   439 U.S. 410, 99 S.Ct. 693, 58 L.Ed.2d 619 (1979).

165.   461 U.S. 138, 103 S.Ct. 1684, 75 L.Ed.2d 708 (1983).

166.   511 U.S. 661, 114 S.Ct. 1878, 128 L.Ed.2d 686 (1994).

167.   547 U.S. 410, 126 S.Ct. 1951, 164 L.Ed.2d 689 (2006). [Case No. 74]

reversing an earlier order from the Ninth Circuit to the contrary, affirmed that insofar as a deputy district attorney's complaints about supervisors were not on matters of public concern, his speech lacked First Amendment protection. The underlying dispute involved a deputy district attorney's complaints about a supervisor, in a disagreement over a memorandum he wrote claiming that a police officer lied in an affidavit to secure a warrant, and which concluded that the affidavit made serious misrepresentations amounting to governmental misconduct. The Court held that insofar as public employees who speak out pursuant to their official duties are not doing so as citizens for First Amendment purposes, the Constitution is unavailable to insulate their communications from employer discipline. The Court added that insofar as the plaintiff spoke in his official capacity rather than as a private citizen when he wrote his memorandum, his comments were not protected by the First Amendment.

In cases involving free speech claims, plaintiffs must show that they presented prima facie cases of adverse employment actions as a result of exercising their rights. In making such a determination, the Tenth Circuit found that job descriptions are not the ultimate factor in evaluating whether teachers addressed matters of public concern.[168] The court remanded the claims of former teachers at a charter school for consideration of whether they were subjected to adverse employment actions because they exercised their right to free speech on matters of public concern relating to school operations.[169]

Examples of subjects that met the criterion of public concern include where a payroll clerk-typist was dismissed for repeatedly warning the superintendent about fraud and theft in her office and[170] school employees suffered adverse employment actions due to criticisms of or questions about a delay by officials in implementing federally mandated programs for students with disabilities.[171] Thier cases involved a medication policy;[172] a principal's failure to implement a school improvement plan;[173] a board's child abuse reporting policy;[174] a teacher's complaining about classroom safety, even though he expressed his views privately, through approved,

168. *Brammer–Hoelter v. Twin Peaks Charter Acad.*, 492 F.3d 1192 [222 Educ. L. Rep. 596] (10th Cir. 2007).

169. For other cases involving remands to consider whether speech involved matters of public concern, *see Morris–Hayes v. Chester Union Free City School*, 211 Fed.Appx. 28 [218 Educ. L. Rep. 141] (2d Cir. 2007); *Trujillo v. Albuquerque Pub. Schools*, 212 Fed.Appx. 760 [218 Educ. L. Rep. 162] (10th Cir. 2007).

170. *Ross v. Lichtenfeld*, 755 F. Supp.2d 467 [266 Educ. L. Rep. 173] (S.D.N.Y. 2010).

171. *Southside Pub. Schools v. Hill*, 827 F.2d 270 [41 Educ. L. Rep. 439] (8th Cir.1987).

172. *Johnsen v. Independent School Dist. No. 3 of Tulsa County*, 891 F.2d 1485 [57 Educ. L. Rep. 1154] (10th Cir. 1989).

173. *Harris v. Victoria Indep. School Dist.*, 168 F.3d 216 [132 Educ. L. Rep. 662] (5th Cir. 1999), *reh'g and reh'g en banc denied*, 336 F.3d 343 [179 Educ. L. Rep. 81] (5th Cir. 1999), *cert. denied*, 528 U.S. 1022, 120 S.Ct. 533, 145 L.Ed.2d 413 (1999).

174. *Calvit v. Minneapolis Pub. Schools*, 122 F.3d 1112 [120 Educ. L. Rep. 952] (8th Cir. 1997).

formal channels;[175] and allegations that officials treated students unequally based on the social status of their parents.[176]

Additional matters that were deemed to be of public concern included a secretary's questions about whether a board's awarding of a contract presented a conflict of interest;[177] a teacher's inviting a speaker to class to talk about industrial hemp;[178] the head of a bus drivers' union-like organization expressing her concerns about student safety due to overcrowding on buses and the lack of pre-trip inspections;[179] a school nurse's challenging a grossly unsatisfactory employment rating in retaliation for her advocating on behalf of students with disabilities in her district;[180] a physical therapist's complaining that her school board did not do enough to meet the educational needs of students with disabilities;[181] a secretary's responding to a question from a reporter over whether the school's principal resigned;[182] and a teacher's reporting financial improprieties by other school employees to her board.[183]

A case from Ohio highlights how the elements of a free speech claim come together. The Sixth Circuit affirmed that school officials retaliated against a teacher by not renewing her contract after she exercised her First Amendment right to free speech. At issue were parental complaints about the teacher's use of such novels as *Fahrenheit 451*, *To Kill a Mockingbird*, and *Siddhartha* even though the school board paid for the books and approved their use. The court identified the three elements of a First Amendment retaliation claim as whether an employee was engaged in a constitutionally protected activity, whether the employer's action caused an injury that would have been likely to chill a person of ordinary firmness from continuing it, and whether the employer's action was, at least in part, a response to the protected activity.[184] The court also applied the *Pickering–Connick* test which requires public employees to prove that if they engaged in speech, whether they were disciplined for addressing issues of public concern, and whether their interests outweighed those of their employers in ruling that the board acted inappropriately by not renewing the teacher's contract.

In many cases, courts refused to treat the speech of school employees as protected since it failed to involve matters of public concern and was

---

175. *Weintraub v. Board of Educ. of City of N.Y.*, 593 F.3d 196 [253 Educ. L. Rep. 17] (2d Cir. 2010), *cert. denied*, ___ U.S. ___, 131 S.Ct. 444, 178 L.Ed.2d 344 (2010).

176. *Corbett v. Duerring*, 780 F.Supp.2d 486 [270 Educ. L. Rep. 678] (S.D. W. Va. 2011).

177. *Kirchmann v. Lake Elsinore Unified School Dist.*, 67 Cal.Rptr.2d 268 [120 Educ. L. Rep. 523] (Cal. Ct. App. 1997).

178. *Cockrel v. Shelby County School Dist.*, 270 F.3d 1036 [158 Educ. L. Rep. 551] (6th Cir. 2001), *cert. denied*, 537 U.S. 813, 123 S.Ct. 73, 154 L.Ed.2d 15 [170 Educ. L. Rep. 458] (2002).

179. *Cook v. Gwinnett County School Dist.*, 414 F.3d 1313 [199 Educ. L. Rep. 637] (11th Cir. 2005).

180. *McGreevy v. Stroup*, 413 F.3d 359 [199 Educ. L. Rep. 593] (3d Cir. 2005).

181. *Ryan v. Shawnee Mission U.S.D. 512*, 416 F. Supp.2d 1090 [207 Educ. L. Rep. 120] (D. Kan. 2006).

182. *Salge v. Edna Indep. School Dist.*, 411 F.3d 178 [198 Educ. L. Rep. 807] (5th Cir. 2005).

183. *Peres v. Oceanside Union Free School Dist.*, 426 F.Supp.2d 15 [209 Educ. L. Rep. 151] (E.D.N.Y. 2006).

184. *Evans–Marshall v. Board of Educ. of the Tipp City Exempted Village School Dist.*, 428 F.3d 223 [203 Educ. L. Rep. 88] (6th Cir. 2005).

unrelated to their job duties. Among these cases were instances criticizing a superintendent[185] or a board's hiring of a superintendent;[186] questioning a school's policies with regard to class size;[187] challenging the nonrenewals of teaching[188] and coaching contracts;[189] complaining about unfavorable evaluation ratings;[190] questioning a board's passing an applicant over for a newly-created staff position in retaliation for speaking out about alcohol and drug use by school bus drivers;[191] referring to others by using such epithets as "ignorant and abusive," "mentally ill," "mindless criminals," and "alcoholic;"[192] questioning the accuracy of school attendance records;[193] challenging a board's tobacco policy;[194] claiming that officials created a racially hostile work environment;[195] and criticizing the quality of leadership and the education children received in a district.[196]

Other cases where courts rejected the claims of school employees concerned such matters as writing a letter to a local newspaper criticizing a hiring process;[197] failing to comply with procedures when administering state-wide standardized tests;[198] making an allegedly racist remark about immigration during class;[199] opposing a board policy designed to seek aid for disadvantaged students;[200] engaging in disruptive speech such as where a principal wrote a letter to and spoke critically about a superintendent's dress code policy;[201] circulating a survey among faculty members evaluating a school's administration and speaking critically of its quality at a school

---

185. *Burkybile v. Board of Educ. of Hastings–On–Hudson Union Free School Dist.*, 411 F.3d 306 [199 Educ. L. Rep. 26] (2d Cir. 2005), *cert. denied*, 546 U.S. 1062, 126 S.Ct. 801, 163 L.Ed.2d 628 (2005).

186. *Vukadinovich v. Board of School Trustees of Michigan City Area Schools*, 978 F.2d 403 [78 Educ. L. Rep. 269] (7th Cir. 1992), *cert. denied*, 510 U.S. 844, 114 S.Ct. 133, 126 L.Ed.2d 97 (1993).

187. *Cliff v. Board of School Commr's of City of Indianapolis*, 42 F.3d 403 [96 Educ. L. Rep. 365] (7th Cir. 1994), *reh'g and reh'g en banc denied* (1995).

188. *See, e.g., Padilla v. South Harrison R–II School Dist.*, 181 F.3d 992 [136 Educ. L. Rep. 728] (8th Cir.1999), *reh'g and reh'g en banc denied*, 192 F.3d 805 (8th Cir. 1999).

189. *Lancaster v. Independent School Dist. No. 5*, 149 F.3d 1228 [128 Educ. L. Rep. 67] (10th Cir. 1998).

190. *Fales v. Garst*, 235 F.3d 1122, 1124 [150 Educ. L. Rep. 41] (8th Cir. 2001).

191. *Wheeler v. Natale*, 178 F. Supp.2d 407 [160 Educ. L. Rep. 797] (S.D.N.Y. 2001).

192. *Farhat v. Jopke*, 370 F.3d 580, 586 [188 Educ. L. Rep. 108] (6th Cir. 2004).

193. *Brewster v. Board of Educ. of Lynwood Unified School Dist.*, 149 F.3d 971 [128 Educ. L. Rep. 50] (9th Cir. 1998), *cert. denied*, 526 U.S. 1018, 119 S.Ct. 1252, 143 L.Ed.2d 349 (1999).

194. *Hill v. Silsbee Indep. School Dist.*, 933 F.Supp. 616 [112 Educ. L. Rep. 150] (E.D. Tex. 1996).

195. *Wallace v. School Bd. of Orange County*, 41 F.Supp.2d 1321 [134 Educ. L. Rep. 879] (M.D. Fla. 1998).

196. *McCullough v. Wyandanch Union Free School Dist.*, 187 F.3d 272 [137 Educ. L. Rep. 505] (2d Cir.1999), *on remand*, 132 F. Supp.2d 87 [151 Educ. L. Rep. 874] (E.D.N.Y. 2001).

197. *Quick v. Bozeman School Dist. No. 7*, 983 P.2d 402 [137 Educ. L. Rep. 819] (Mont.1999).

198. *Rodriguez v. Laredo Indep. School Dist.*, 82 F.Supp.2d 679 [141 Educ. L. Rep. 1080] (S.D. Tex. 2000), *reconsideration denied*, 143 F. Supp.2d 727 [155 Educ. L. Rep. 177] (S.D. Tex. 2001).

199. *Sivek v. Baljevic*, 758 A.2d 473 [147 Educ. L. Rep. 203] (Conn. Super. Ct. 1999), *aff'd*, 758 A.2d 441 (Conn. App. Ct. 2000).

200. *Vargas–Harrison v. Racine Unified School Dist.*, 272 F.3d 964 [159 Educ. L. Rep. 459] (7th Cir. 2001), *cert. denied*, 537 U.S. 826, 123 S.Ct. 120, 154 L.Ed.2d 38 (2002).

201. *Sharp v. Lindsey*, 285 F.3d 479 [163 Educ. L. Rep. 88] (6th Cir. 2002).

board meeting;[202] sending inflammatory and disparaging letters to members of a board for years;[203] expressing one's political views in a middle school class;[204] trying to convert a school into a charter school;[205] sending memoranda to a school's office manager and principal questioning the handling of athletic funds;[206] and voicing support for a student walkout and demonstration over proposed changes in federal immigration policy.[207]

Where an award-winning kindergarten teacher was dismissed for sending unauthorized and inappropriate correspondence to parents and students, failing to grade report cards, and not completing other end-of-year tasks, the Seventh Circuit affirmed that officials did not retaliate against her for speech in which she criticized them for the early renewal of her principal's contract or over her proposal to restructure the kindergarten program.[208] The court concluded that when the teacher resigned following a demand that she produce a doctor's note after taking five consecutive sick days, the board did not constructively discharge her from her job.

The Fourth Circuit affirmed that a principal in Virginia did not violate the rights of a Spanish teacher who posted religious materials on a bulletin board in his classroom.[209] The court explained that insofar as the materials were curricular in nature and failed to address a matter of public concern, the teacher's actions were not protected speech. The court added that the board did not have to tolerate teacher speech that was inconsistent with its basic educational mission.

Two areas engendering controversy are the lifestyles and political activities of teachers. In a case involving lifestyle and sexual preferences,[210] the Second Circuit affirmed that under the *Pickering* balancing test, the New York City Board of Education's interest in the orderly operation of a high school outweighed a tenured teacher's interest in commenting on matters of public concern through his membership in the North American Man/Boy Love Association. The court reported that the association identified its primary goal as seeking to bring about a change in attitudes and laws governing sexual activity between men and boys while advocating the

---

202. *Levich v. Liberty Cent. School Dist.*, 361 F. Supp.2d 151 [197 Educ. L. Rep. 70] (S.D.N.Y. 2004).

203. *Jackson v. State of Alabama State Tenure Comm'n*, 405 F.3d 1276 [197 Educ. L. Rep. 499] (11th Cir. 2005).

204. *Calef v. Budden*, 361 F. Supp.2d 493 [197 Educ. L. Rep. 93] (D.S.C. 2005).

205. *D'Angelo v. School Bd. of Polk County, Fla.*, 497 F.3d 1203 [223 Educ. L. Rep. 598] (11th Cir. 2007).

206. *Williams v. Dallas Indep. School Dist.*, 480 F.3d 689 [217 Educ. L. Rep. 802] (5th Cir. 2007).

207. *Garcia v. Montenegro*, 547 F. Supp.2d 738 [233 Educ. L. Rep. 146] (W.D. Tex. 2008), *aff'd*, 326 Fed.Appx. 312 (5th Cir. 2009).

208. *Lifton v. Board of Educ. of City of Chicago*, 416 F.3d 571 [200 Educ. L. Rep. 39] (7th Cir. 2005).

209. *Lee v. York County School Div.*, 484 F.3d 687 [219 Educ. L. Rep. 413] (4th Cir. 2007), *cert. denied*, 552 U.S. 950, 128 S.Ct. 387, 169 L.Ed.2d 263 [225 Educ. L. Rep. 51] (2007).

210. For an earlier case, *see, e.g., National Gay Task Force v. Board of Educ. of the City of Oklahoma City*, 729 F.2d 1270 [16 Educ. L. Rep. 1035] (10th Cir. 1984), *aff'd by an equally divided Court*, 470 U.S. 903, 105 S.Ct. 1858, 84 L.Ed.2d 776 [23 Educ. L. Rep. 845] (1985) (permitting a teacher to be dismissed for "public homosexual conduct").

abolition of laws governing the age of consent for activities that limit freedom of expression, including child pornography laws. The court was of the opinion that the teacher's dismissal, even absent evidence that he engaged in any illegal or inappropriate conduct with students, based on disruption caused by public furor over his activities in the group, did not amount to impermissible "heckler's veto."[211] The court was satisfied that the board's action was not motivated by the desire to retaliate against the teacher for his membership in the association.

On the other hand, the federal trial court in Utah was convinced that school officials violated the equal protection and free speech rights of a teacher who was a lesbian by prohibiting her from discussing her sexual orientation outside of class since officials did not forbid other teachers from talking about their heterosexual orientations in this manner.[212] The court observed that the principal's refusal to assign the teacher to coach volleyball constituted retaliation for exercising her First Amendment rights such that officials had to offer her a contract for the job.[213] In a related dispute, the Supreme Court of Utah affirmed the dismissal of a case against the teacher which claimed that she violated the state constitution and statutes governing the conduct of teachers and psychologists by leading discussions of alternate lifestyles in a psychology course that she taught.[214] The court agreed that insofar as the statute did not create a private right of action, the taxpayers lacked standing to sue.

In another case about lifestyles, the Ninth Circuit affirmed that when a school board in California erected a bulletin board on which it provided information about Gay and Lesbian Awareness Month, a teacher lacked a First Amendment right to post material with a different perspective.[215] The court decided that insofar as the information was attributable to the board as an expression of its policy, it could properly exclude materials reflecting a different perspective.

When teachers become involved in situations with political connotations, boards cannot enforce rules prohibiting all types of political activities on school premises. In one case, a board unsuccessfully tried to stop a teachers' organization from circulating a petition that was addressed to state and local authorities protesting threatened cutbacks in educational expenditures. In language that relied on the then recently resolved *Tinker v. Des Moines Independent Community School District*,[216] the Supreme Court of California pointed out that the board could have prevented the teachers from acting only on a showing of a "clear and substantial threat to

---

211. *Melzer v. Board of Educ. of City School Dist. of City of N.Y.*, 336 F.3d 185, 198 [179 Educ. L. Rep. 32] (2d Cir. 2003), *cert. denied*, 540 U.S. 1183, 124 S.Ct. 1424, 158 L.Ed.2d 87 [185 Educ. L. Rep. 415] (2004).

212. *Weaver v. Nebo School Dist.*, 29 F. Supp.2d 1279 (D. Utah 1998).

213. *See also Glover v. Williamsburg Local School Dist. Bd. of Educ.*, 20 F. Supp.2d 1160 [130 Educ. L. Rep. 661] (S.D. Ohio 1998) (ordering a teacher's reinstatement with back pay where a board discriminated against him by not renewing his contract due to his sexual orientation).

214. *Miller v. Weaver*, 66 P.3d 592 [175 Educ. L. Rep. 334] (Utah 2003).

215. *Downs v. Los Angeles Unified School Dist.*, 228 F.3d 1003 [147 Educ. L. Rep. 855] (9th Cir. 2000), *cert. denied*, 532 U.S. 994, 121 S.Ct. 1653, 149 L.Ed.2d 636 (2001).

216. 393 U.S. 503, 89 S.Ct. 733, 21 L.Ed.2d 731 (1969). [Case No. 102]

order and efficiency"[217] in schools. The Second Circuit then upheld the right of a teacher in New York to wear a black armband in class as a protest against American involvement in Vietnam.[218] In another case the court agreed that a board in New York could not dismiss a teacher for refusing to participate in the flag-salute ceremony where she simply stood silently at attention during its recitation.[219] Also, Massachusetts' highest court maintained that requiring teachers to lead their classes in the Pledge of Allegiance would have violated their First Amendment rights.[220]

In a case that reached a different outcome involving political speech, the Seventh Circuit upheld a grant of summary judgment in favor of a school board in Indiana when it chose not to renew the contract of a probationary elementary school teacher who made her opposition to the war in Iraq known as part of a classroom discussion of current events.[221] While conceding that the war was a matter of public concern, the court explained that the teacher had the right to express herself as long as her doing so was not disruptive to school operations. However, the court affirmed that the First Amendment did not protect the teacher because she departed from the board's approved curriculum which allowed her to address controversies related to the war as long as she permitted students to speak out on all sides of the debate while keeping her opinion private. The court noted that the First Amendment does not permit educators in elementary and secondary schools who address captive audiences of students to cover topics or advocate perspectives if they deviate from approved district curricula.

A high profile case from New York City dealt with educator speech that had indirect political connotations. At issue were remarks by the former acting interim principal of a public high school that offered classes in Arab language and culture that led to a media firestorm. When a reporter "questioned her about the meaning of the Arabic word 'intifada,' [she] accurately explained that the root of the word means 'shaking off.' She also stated that the word has been associated with violence and the Palestinian/Israeli conflict and emphasized that she would never affiliate herself with an organization that condones violence."[222] In rejecting the plaintiff's claim that board officials terminated her employment in retaliation for exercising her First Amendment rights, the Second Circuit affirmed that a federal trial court did not abuse its discretion in rejecting her motion for a preliminary injunction requiring them to afford her a full and fair opportunity to be considered for the position of permanent principal. Relying on

---

217. *Los Angeles Teachers Union v. Los Angeles City Bd. of Educ.*, 78 Cal.Rptr. 723, 732 (Cal. 1969).

218. *James v. Board of Educ. of Cent. School Dist. No. 1, Addison*, 461 F.2d 566 (2d Cir.1972), *cert. denied*, 409 U.S. 1042, 93 S.Ct. 529, 34 L.Ed.2d 491 (1972).

219. *Russo v. Central School Dist. No. 1, Towns of Rush*, 469 F.2d 623 (2d Cir.1972), *cert. denied*, 411 U.S. 932, 93 S.Ct. 1899, 36 L.Ed.2d 391 (1973).

220. *Opinions of the Justices to the Governor*, 363 N.E.2d 251 (Mass. 1977).

221. *Mayer v. Monroe County Community School Corp.*, 474 F.3d 477 [215 Educ. L. Rep. 626] (7th Cir. 2007), *reh'g and reh'g en banc denied* (7th Cir. 2007), *cert. denied*, 552 U.S. 823, 128 S.Ct. 160, 169 L.Ed.2d 32 (2007)

222. *Almontaser v. New York City Dep't of Educ.*, 519 F.3d 505, 506–507 [230 Educ. L. Rep. 561] (2d Cir. 2008).

Garcetti, the court explained that when public employees such as the plaintiff speak out as part of their official duties, since their words are not protected, they can be subject to employer discipline The court added that even if the plaintiff's speech had been protected, her being removed from the interim position and not being considered for the permanent job was justified under *Pickering.*[223]

Other courts relied on *Garcetti* in refusing to protect speech where a former high school security specialist wrote a letter to officials about the inadequacy and inefficiency of safety policies in his district;[224] a teacher disagreed with administrators over instructional materials;[225] a teacher criticized an administrator for refusing to discipline a student who threw a book during class;[226] a teacher made an inappropriate comment about a student's ethnicity;[227] and a teacher accused a colleague of sexually harassing her step-daughter.[228]

In another aspect of political activities, the Supreme Court of Kentucky invalidated a provision in a comprehensive school reform act which prohibited school employees from participating in campaigns for the elections of local school board members. The court invalidated parts of the law in contending that they were unconstitutionally vague and overbroad because it was unclear which activities were forbidden.[229] Four years later, a federal trial court in Pennsylvania struck down a board policy designed to prevent teachers from engaging in political activities on district property at any time.[230] The court decreed that insofar as the policy would have violated the teachers' First Amendment rights by preventing off-duty educators from soliciting votes at official polling places located on school property, it was unconstitutional. Further, a federal trial court in New York upheld a board policy forbidding teachers from wearing political buttons in support of candidates to class.[231] The court agreed with the board's concern that it

---

223.   For another case citing *Garcetti,* see *Casey v. West Las Vegas Indep. School Dist.,* 473 F.3d 1323 [215 Educ. L. Rep. 604] (10th Cir. 2007) (ruling that a former superintendent who was demoted and fired failed to present a claim that she was retaliated against for exercising her rights to free speech in charging her school board with violating state and federal laws because she spoke out in the performance of her official duties).

224.   *Posey v. Lake Pend Oreille School Dist.,* 546 F.3d 1121 [238 Educ. L. Rep. 537] (9th Cir. 2008).

225.   *Evans–Marshall v. Board of Educ. of Tipp City Exempted Village School Dist.,* 624 F.3d 332 [261 Educ. L. Rep. 904] (6th Cir. 2010), *cert. denied,* ___ U.S. ___, 131 S.Ct. 3068, 180 L.Ed.2d 889 (2011). For related litigation in this dispute, see *Evans–Marshall v. Board of Educ. of the Tipp City Exempted Village School Dist.,* 428 F.3d 223 [203 Educ. L. Rep. 88] (6th Cir. 2005).

226.   *Weintraub v. Board of Educ. of City of N.Y.,* 593 F.3d 196 [253 Educ. L. Rep. 17] (2d Cir. 2010), *cert. denied,* ___ U.S. ___, 131 S.Ct. 444, 178 L.Ed.2d 344 (2010).

227.   *In re Watt (East Greenbush Cent. School Dist.),* 925 N.Y.S.2d 681 [268 Educ. L. Rep. 494] (N.Y. App. Div. 2011).

228.   *Condiff v. Hart County School Dist.,* 770 F.Supp.2d 876 [268 Educ. L. Rep. 797] (W.D. Ky. 2011).

229.   *State Bd. for Elementary and Secondary Educ. v. Howard,* 834 S.W.2d 657 [76 Educ. L. Rep. 1211] (Ky. 1992).

230.   *Castle v. Colonial School Dist.,* 933 F.Supp. 458 [112 Educ. L. Rep. 120] (E.D. Pa. 1996).

231.   *Weingarten v. Board of Educ. of City of N.Y.,* 680 F. Supp.2d 595 [255 Educ. L. Rep. 144] (S.D.N.Y. 2010).

remain neutral while not allowing teachers to influence students by wearing such buttons. The court rejected the argument that middle and secondary schools could distinguish between the views of individual teachers and the board.

The Supreme Court addressed a matter of speech that is related to employee rights of association and collective bargaining that was discussed in the previous chapter. In *Texas State Teachers Association v. Garland Independent School District*,[232] the Court summarily affirmed that board policies purporting to deny faculty members the right to discuss teacher organizations during non-class time and preventing them from using school mail facilities to mention employee organizations were unconstitutional.

In another issue involving the associational rights of school employees, the First Circuit affirmed that educational officials in Puerto Rico did not violate the rights of a former school director whose contract was not renewed allegedly due to her political affiliation.[233] The court agreed that the director failed to prove that her contract was not renewed on account of her political activities. Conversely, a federal trial court in Virginia ruled that when a principal was transferred to a central office job in retaliation for providing active support to a school board member's unsuccessful opponent in an election, she was entitled to awards of compensatory and punitive damages along with attorney fees.[234]

PROCEDURAL DUE PROCESS

In *Cleveland Board of Education v. Loudermill (Loudermill)*,[235] the Supreme Court ruled that absent exigent circumstances, wherein educators can be suspended with pay,[236] the Fourteenth Amendment requires school boards to provide individuals with property interests in their jobs, whether through tenure or unexpired contracts, to procedural due process, beginning with notice.[237] The Court specified that "tenured public employee[s]

---

232.   *Texas State Teachers Ass'n v. Garland Indep. School Dist.*, 784 F.2d 1113 [30 Educ. L. Rep. 1108] (5th Cir.1986), *aff'd*, 479 U.S. 801, 107 S.Ct. 41, 93 L.Ed.2d 4 [34 Educ. L. Rep. 1004] (1986).

233.   *Hatfield–Bermudez v. Aldanondo–Rivera*, 496 F.3d 51 [223 Educ. L. Rep. 531] (1st Cir. 2007).

234.   *Chadwell v. Lee County School Bd.*, 535 F. Supp.2d 586 [230 Educ. L. Rep. 38] (W.D. Va. 2008).

235.   470 U.S. 532, 105 S.Ct. 1487, 84 L.Ed.2d 494 [23 Educ. L. Rep. 473] (1985), *on remand*, 763 F.2d 202 [25 Educ. L. Rep. 158] (6th Cir.1985), *on remand*, 651 F.Supp. 92 [37 Educ. L. Rep. 502] (N.D. Ohio 1986), *aff'd*, 844 F.2d 304 [46 Educ. L. Rep. 523] (6th Cir.1988), *cert. denied*, 488 U.S. 941, 109 S.Ct. 363, 102 L.Ed.2d 353 (1988), *cert. denied*, 488 U.S. 946, 109 S.Ct. 377, 102 L.Ed.2d 365 [50 Educ. L. Rep. 15] (1988). [Case No. 75]

236.   *See Bauman v. Board of Educ. of Watkins Glen Cent. School Dist.*, 800 N.Y.S.2d 461 [201 Educ. L. Rep. 290] (N.Y. App. Div. 2005) (affirming that although a tenured principal was entitled to pay while suspended, the board had no duty to provide her with expired stipends for extra duty assignments because it was free to terminate those at any time).

237.   *See, e.g., Tweedall v. Fritz*, 987 F.Supp. 1126 [124 Educ. L. Rep. 122] (S.D. Ind. 1997) (judging that one day's notice was adequate for a teacher who was accused of touching students inappropriately).

[are] entitled to oral or written notice of the charges against [them], an explanation of the employer's evidence, and an opportunity to present [their] side of the story."[238]

Depending on state law, tenured teachers are not necessarily entitled to full pre-termination hearings as long as they are afforded opportunities to have hearings once they are dismissed.[239] As reflected by a case from the Supreme Court of South Carolina, as managerial employees, administrators are not ordinarily entitled to pre-dismissal hearings.[240] The court explained that although the former principal would have preserved her rights to a hearing had she been a teacher, she had no such protection under state law as an administrator.

In a controversial case from New York where teachers awaiting disciplinary hearings leading to their possible dismissals for cause, a federal court rejected a variety of claims.[241] Most notably for this heading, the court ruled that the board of education did not violate their rights to procedural due process since they continued to be paid while they were placed in the temporary assignment center awaiting their hearings.

As discussed in Chapter 9, since untenured (and/or non-certificated) teachers and other staff[242] lack the same property interests in their jobs, they are not entitled to identical procedural protections as their tenured colleagues unless granted, for example, by a collective bargaining agreement.[243] It should, then, not be surprising that jurisdictions have adopted statutes of varying degrees of particularity in establishing due procedures dealing with the dismissals of teachers.[244] Since courts strictly enforce statutory due process rights, the failure of school boards to comply ordinarily renders adverse employment actions invalid.[245] In emphasizing its importance, the Supreme Court, in a non-school case, *Morrissey v. Brewer*,[246] held that due process, which may not be as precise in its requirements

---

238. *Cleveland Board of Educ. v. Loudermill*, 470 U.S. 532, 546, 105 S.Ct. 1487, 84 L.Ed.2d 494 [23 Educ. L. Rep. 473] (1985). [Case No. 75]

239. *See, e.g., Baird v. Board of Educ. for Warren Community Unit School Dist.*, 389 F.3d 685 [193 Educ. L. Rep. 402] (7th Cir. 2004), *cert. denied*, 546 U.S. 811, 126 S.Ct. 332, 163 L.Ed.2d 45 (2005).

240. *Henry–Davenport v. School Dist. of Fairfield County*, 705 S.E.2d 26 [264 Educ. L. Rep. 440] (S.C. 2011).

241. *Adams v. New York State Educ. Dep't*, 752 F. Supp. 2d 420 [265 Educ. L. Rep. 993] (S.D.N.Y. 2010).

242. *Laurano v. Superintendent of Schools of Saugus*, 945 N.E.2d 933 [266 Educ. L. Rep. 494] (Mass. 2011) (affirming that a nurse who had yet to acquire professional teacher status was not entitled to a written notice of intent that her school committee was not renewing her contract).

243. *See, e.g., Lillibridge v. Meade School Dist. #46–1*, 746 N.W.2d 428 [230 Educ. L. Rep. 415] (S.D. 2008) (affirming that a Junior ROTC instructor was not entitled to a due process hearing as outlined in his collective bargaining agreement since he was not certificated).

244. *See, e.g.,* Ala. Code 1975 § 16–24–9; Ariz. Rev. Stat. Ann. § 15–539; Ark. Code Ann. § 6–17–1503; Colo. Rev. Stat. Ann. § 22–63–202; 105 Ill. Comp. Stat. Ann. 5/24–12; Kan. Stat. Ann. § 72–5438; N.Y. Educ. Law § 3020–a; Ohio Rev. Code Ann. § 3319.16; 24 Pa. Stat. Ann. § 11–1127; W. Va. Code Ann. § 18A–2–8.

245. *Jackson v. El Dorado School Dist.*, 48 S.W.3d 558 [155 Educ. L. Rep. 936] (Ark. Ct. App. 2001); *Neshaminy Fed'n of Teachers v. Neshaminy School Dist.*, 462 A.2d 629 [12 Educ. L. Rep. 807] (Pa. 1983).

246. 408 U.S. 471, 92 S.Ct. 2593, 33 L.Ed.2d 484 (1972).

as state law, and focuses on the issue of fairness, must be interpreted in light of factual contexts and different types of proceedings.

In another non-education case, *Mathews v. Eldridge*, the Supreme Court found that "identification of the specific dictates of due process generally requires consideration of three distinct factors: First, the private interest that will be affected by the official action; second, the risk of an erroneous deprivation of such interest through the procedures used, the probable value, if any, of additional or substitute procedural safeguards; and finally, the Government's interest, including the function involved and the fiscal and administrative burdens that the additional or substitute procedural requirement would entail."[247]

The Supreme Court's having stopped short of setting a precise formula for due process in *Loudermill* aside, at the core of procedural due process is notice and a hearing at which teachers have the chance to address the charges that they face. In most jurisdictions, initial hearings are conducted by local school boards, hearing officers, or state administrative agencies. While hearings need not conform to strict judicial processes,[248] evidence that might not be admitted in court may be admissible as long as it does not violate the fundamentals of fair hearings.[249] Whether hearings are adequate is ultimately a matter of judicial interpretation.

NOTICE

Teachers often challenge the adequacy of the notice of the charges they face. Clearly, teachers must be notified of all charges against them[250] with sufficient specificity,[251] including names, dates, facts, and/or other information that officials relied on in seeking to take adverse employment actions,[252] so that they can prepare responses.[253] Accordingly, the Supreme Court of Wyoming struck down a charge of inability to establish rapport with students as too vague.[254]

If charges against teachers involve a pattern of conduct, notice must include the time periods covered and the specifics.[255] At the same time,

---

247. 424 U.S. 319, 96 S.Ct. 893, 47 L.Ed.2d 18 (1976).

248. *Knox County Bd. of Educ. v. Willis*, 405 S.W.2d 952 (Ky.1966). [Case No. 76]; *Cope v. Board of Educ. of Town of W. Hartford*, 495 A.2d 718 [26 Educ. L. Rep. 699] (Conn. Ct. App. 1985).

249. *Carangelo v. Ambach*, 515 N.Y.S.2d 665 [39 Educ. L. Rep. 752] (N.Y. App. Div.1987), *appeal denied*, 522 N.Y.S.2d 109 [43 Educ. L. Rep. 756] (N.Y. 1987).

250. *Clark County School Dist. v. Riley*, 14 P.3d 22 [149 Educ. L. Rep. 615] (Nev.2000); *McDaniel v. Princeton City School Dist. Bd. of Educ.*, 45 Fed.Appx. 354 [169 Educ. L. Rep. 129] (6th Cir. 2002).

251. *Washington v. Independent School Dist. No. 625*, 590 N.W.2d 655 [133 Educ. L. Rep. 589] (Minn. Ct. App. 1999).

252. *Blackburn v. Board of Educ. of Breckinridge County*, 564 S.W.2d 35 (Ky. Ct. App. 1978).

253. *Cliff v. Board of School Commr's of City of Indianapolis*, 42 F.3d 403 [96 Educ. L. Rep. 365] (7th Cir. 1994), *reh'g and suggestion for reh'g en banc denied*, 42 F.3d 403 [96 Educ. L. Rep. 365] (7th Cir. 1994); *Rubin v. Lafayette Parish School Bd.*, 649 So.2d 1003 [97 Educ. L. Rep. 965] (La. Ct. App.1994), *writ denied*, 654 So.2d 351 (La. 1995).

254. *Powell v. Board of Trustees of Crook County School Dist. No. 1*, 550 P.2d 1112 (Wyo. 1976).

255. *Allen v. Texarkana Pub. Schools*, 794 S.W.2d 138 [62 Educ. L. Rep. 779] (Ark. 1990).

officials must provide teachers with notice far enough in advance of disciplinary proceedings so that they will have adequate time to prepare defenses.[256] Where state law required boards to give teachers written notice by a set date, the federal trial court in Vermont denied a board's motion for summary judgment in a suit by a non-tenured teacher who claimed that the oral notice that she received, almost two months late, was insufficient to terminate her employment.[257]

When statutes provide specifics with regard to notice, courts generally expect school officials to comply strictly with these requirements. When officials failed to comply with notice requirements, school employees have been reinstated as a matter of law[258] and may have been entitled to new contracts[259] and/or damages.[260] Where rights are limited by statute such as when employees are placed on administrative leave,[261] where they engage in behavior that exceeds the limits of their employment,[262] or where they have other remedies available under collective bargaining agreements,[263] notice may not be required.

HEARINGS

Loudermill clarified the minimum due process requirements that boards must provide for teachers with property interests in their employment before terminating their jobs. The Supreme Court specified that teachers are entitled to "[s]ome kind of hearing"[264] prior to discharge.[265] The Court indicated that informal pre-termination hearings need not be elaborate since post-termination hearings should follow at which educators could present their cases. The Seventh Circuit illustrated this principle in a case from Illinois when it affirmed that a board's failure to provide a principal with elaborate, trial-type rights, including the ability to cross-

---

256. *Clark County School Dist. v. Riley*, 14 P.3d 22 [149 Educ. L. Rep. 615] (Nev.2000) (affirming that four days notice was insufficient).

257. *Latouche v. North Country Union High School Dist.*, 131 F. Supp.2d 568 [151 Educ. L. Rep. 817] (D. Vt. 2001).

258. *Morrison v. Board of Educ. of Weatherford Pub. Schools*, 47 P.3d 888 [165 Educ. L. Rep. 810] (Okla. Ct. Civ. App. 2002), *cert. denied* (2002).

259. *State ex rel. Chapnick v. East Cleveland City School Dist. Bd. of Educ.*, 755 N.E.2d 883 [157 Educ. L. Rep. 302] (Ohio 2001).

260. *McDaniel v. Princeton City School Dist. Bd. of Educ.*, 45 Fed.Appx. 354 [169 Educ. L. Rep. 129] (6th Cir. 2002).

261. *Pavlik v. Chinle Unified School Dist. No. 24*, 985 P.2d 633 [138 Educ. L. Rep. 547] (Ariz. Ct. App. Div. 1999).

262. *Scro v. Board of Educ. of Jordan–Elbridge Cent. School Dist.*, 930 N.Y.S.2d 706 [271 Educ. L. Rep. 600] (N.Y. App. Div. 2011), *reargument denied*, 935 N.Y.S.2d 267 (N.Y. App. Div. 2011).

263. *Rich v. Montpelier Supervisory Dist. (Rich)*, 709 A.2d 501 [125 Educ. L. Rep. 736] (Vt. 1998); *Barrera v. Frontier Cent. School Dist.*, 672 N.Y.S.2d 218 [125 Educ. L. Rep. 1332] (N.Y. App. Div. 1998).

264. *Rich, Id.* at 542.

265. *See Rettie v. Unified School Dist.*, 167 P.3d 810 [224 Educ. L. Rep. 438] (Kan. Ct. App. 2007), *review denied* (2008) (ruling that while a tenured teacher whose employment was terminated because her teaching certificate expired lacked a right to a due process hearing, she could not be deprived of her property interest in continued employment).

examine witnesses, at his pre-termination hearing did not deprive him of due process because he lacked a protectable property interest in employment beyond the term of his contract.[266]

As to the nature of hearings, where statutes, contracts, or board policies require pre-termination hearings, they must ordinarily precede individuals' removals from the payroll.[267] Yet, the absence of full adversarial pre-termination hearings does not per se invalidate board actions. Along with providing employees appropriate notice of the charges they face, board officials must present all of the evidence they relied on so that teachers can respond.[268] While records of events are not automatically excluded from evidence if they occurred during previous school years, in order to be inadmissible, teachers must prove how the passage of time prejudiced their defenses such as when witnesses were unavailable or their memories were unclear.[269] If boards rely on past events, notice must inform teachers of their intent to do so.[270]

Hearings may be open to the public[271] or closed.[272] At hearings, educators can question witnesses[273] and be assisted by counsel[274] but are not entitled to unlimited time to make their cases.[275] Boards must make findings of fact based on the records[276] before them by relying on competent, probative, credible evidence.[277] While courts generally uphold administrative adjudications unless they are contrary to the manifest weight of

---

266.   *Head v. Chicago School Reform Bd. of Trustees*, 225 F.3d 794 (7th Cir. 2000).

267.   *Vanelli v. Reynolds School Dist. No. 7*, 667 F.2d 773 [2 Educ. L. Rep. 366] (9th Cir. 1982).

268.   *Haddock v. Board of Educ., Unified School Dist. No. 462, Cowley County*, 661 P.2d 368 [10 Educ. L. Rep. 405] (Kan. 1983).

269.   *Tomczik v. State Tenure Comm'n*, 438 N.W.2d 642 [53 Educ. L. Rep. 248] (Mich. Ct. App. 1989), *appeal denied* (1990).

270.   *Allen v. Texarkana Pub. Schools*, 794 S.W.2d 138 [62 Educ. L. Rep. 779] (Ark. 1990).

271.   *Gibson v. Caruthersville School Dist. No. 8*, 336 F.3d 768 [179 Educ. L. Rep. 84] (8th Cir. 2003), *reh'g and reh'g en banc denied* (2003) (referring to an open hearing).

272.   *Unke v. Independent School Dist. No. 147, Dilworth*, 510 N.W.2d 271 [88 Educ. L. Rep. 784] (Minn. Ct. App. 1994), *review denied* (1994) (declaring that a board violated the state's open meeting law by failing to close a meeting during a discussion of private information about a school counselor).

273.   *Gibson v. Caruthersville School Dist. No. 8*, 336 F.3d 768 [179 Educ. L. Rep. 84] (8th Cir.2003), *reh'g and reh'g en banc denied* (2003); *Lafferty v. Board of Educ. of Floyd County*, 133 F. Supp.2d 941 [152 Educ. L. Rep. 562] (E.D. Ky. 2001).

274.   *Gibson v. Caruthersville School Dist. No. 8*, 336 F.3d 768 [179 Educ. L. Rep. 84] (8th Cir.2003), *reh'g and reh'g en banc denied* (2003); *Coleman v. Reed*, 147 F.3d 751 [127 Educ. L. Rep. 583] (8th Cir. 1998), *reh'g and reh'g en banc denied* (1998).

275.   *Halpern v. Board of Educ. of City of Bristol*, 703 A.2d 1144 [124 Educ. L. Rep. 338] (Conn. 1997), *cert. denied*, 523 U.S. 1138, 118 S.Ct. 1842, 140 L.Ed.2d 1092 (1998). *See also Clark v. Board of Directors of School Dist. of Kansas City*, 915 S.W.2d 766 [107 Educ. L. Rep. 368] (Mo. Ct. App. 1996) (positing that although a board's imposing time limits during a hearing may have been unreasonable, its doing so did not prevent a tenured teacher from having a full and fair opportunity to rebut charges that he inappropriately disciplined students).

276.   *Harmon v. Mifflin County School Dist.*, 713 A.2d 620 [127 Educ. L. Rep. 916] (Pa. 1998); *Barnett v. Board of Educ. of Town of Fairfield*, 654 A.2d 720 [97 Educ. L. Rep. 1086] (Conn. 1995).

277.   *Jones v. Sully Buttes Schools*, 340 N.W.2d 697 [14 Educ. L. Rep. 809] (S.D. 1983); *Ross v. Springfield School Dist. No. 19*, 657 P.2d 188 (Or. 1982).

evidence, there is an increasing judicial tendency to examine the evidence in cases involving adverse employment actions.

Some jurisdictions permit trials de novo to review dismissals and grant courts original, rather than appellate, jurisdiction. In light of this fact, the adequacy of administrative hearings is not directly involved. Other jurisdictions provide that while judicial review is of the record of hearings, courts are empowered to make additional inquiries or take extra testimony in their discretion. In such a case, the Supreme Court of Kansas reasoned that the legislature may provide for an external hearing committee, rather than a local board, to have the authority to render a final judgment as to whether a tenured teacher was to be dismissed.[278] The court acknowledged that as long as a board can appeal a committee's action to a judge, its general power is not unconstitutionally impaired.

As with notice requirements, if statutes or board policies prescribe details for conducting hearings, they must be strictly followed or they are likely to be invalidated. Pursuant to statutory provisions or judicial orders,[279] when hearings are conducted before hearing officers rather than boards, teachers may be entitled to see, and respond to, reports before the meetings at which boards are to act.[280]

Issues often arise over the impartiality of board members or hearing officers when employees are subjected to adverse employment actions. The Supreme Court discussed impartiality in *Hortonville Joint School District No. 1 v. Hortonville Education Association*,[281] a dispute from Wisconsin wherein it upheld board authority to dismiss striking teachers. The Court emphasized that mere familiarity with the facts of a case in light of performing one's statutory duties did not disqualify the board members from acting as decision makers, especially since they did not have personal or official stakes in dismissing the teachers that would have disqualified them on due process grounds.

When seeking to disqualify decision makers, educators must meet the heavy burden of proving that board members or hearing officers are incapable of fairly judging controversies. Even where board members or hearing officers had some involvement in or knowledge of disputes, such as where boards are named in suits[282] or a hearing officer knew another hearing officer who presided over an earlier unrelated hearing involving a teacher who was faced with job dismissal,[283] courts typically reject claims

---

278. *Unified School Dist. No. 380, Marshall County v. McMillen*, 845 P.2d 676 [80 Educ. L. Rep. 1034] (Kan. 1993).

279. *Winston v. Board of Educ. of Borough of S. Plainfield*, 309 A.2d 89 (N.J. Super. Ct. App. Div. 1973), *aff'd*, 319 A.2d 226 (N.J.1974); *Powell v. Brown*, 238 S.E.2d 220 (W. Va. 1977).

280. *Buck v. Board of Educ. of City of N.Y.*, 553 F.2d 315 (2d Cir.1977), *cert. denied*, 438 U.S. 904, 98 S.Ct. 3122, 57 L.Ed.2d 1147 (1978).

281. 426 U.S. 482, 96 S.Ct. 2308, 49 L.Ed.2d 1 (1976).

282. *Green v. Clarendon County*, 923 F.Supp. 829 [109 Educ. L. Rep. 681] (D.S.C. 1996).

283. *See, e.g., Zrake v. New York City Dep't of Educ.*, 838 N.Y.S.2d 31 [221 Educ. L. Rep. 825] (N.Y. App. Div. 2007), *leave to appeal dismissed*, 849 N.Y.S.2d 28 (N.Y. 2007).

that they are unable to act impartially at full and fair hearings.[284] If employees can prove that board members are biased, then courts can find that they were deprived of their rights to due process.[285] In a related matter, a case from the Supreme Court of Rhode Island reiterated the general rule that hearing officers are entitled to quasi-judicial immunity when they act in their official capacities in disputes over teacher dismissals.[286]

REMEDIES FOR WRONGFUL DISCHARGE

Section 1983, discussed in greater detail in Chapter 7, permits individuals to seek redress for violations of their federally protected civil rights. Not surprisingly, school employees rely on section 1983 when filing suits against their boards for claims of unlawful dismissal. Since prevailing parties in civil rights cases can recover attorney fees,[287] section 1983 is an attractive vehicle for redress of adverse employment actions that can be linked to deprivations of federal constitutional and/or statutory rights.

School employees with property interests in their jobs who suffer adverse employment actions are entitled to recover for damages that they sustained just as if they were in breach of contract suits.[288] While the theory of contractual recovery is designed to place injured parties in the positions that they would have occupied but for the breaches, it requires them to mitigate damages. As happened in a case from Arkansas, where a school board breached the contract of a principal who obtained a new job at a higher salary in another school district, an appellate court affirmed that he was not entitled to recover damages because, by mitigating his damages, he did not suffer any loss.[289]

If teachers are unable to procure other jobs, they are entitled to recover the full back pay that they would have earned but for being discharged,[290] subject to mitigating their losses.[291] Even with the obligation to mitigate, teachers are not required to accept just any positions which may be offered. Rather, educators are obliged to accept only jobs of the

---

284. *Felder v. Charleston County School Dist.*, 489 S.E.2d 191 [120 Educ. L. Rep. 616] (S.C. 1997), *reh'g denied* (1997); *Riter v. Woonsocket School Dist. No. 55–4*, 504 N.W.2d 572 [85 Educ. L. Rep. 249] (S.D. 1993).

285. *Crump v. Board of Educ. of Hickory Admin. School Unit*, 392 S.E.2d 579 [60 Educ. L. Rep. 1259] (N.C. 1990), *appeal after remand*, 420 S.E.2d 462 [77 Educ. L. Rep. 555] (N.C. Ct. App. 1992) (denying supplemental relief in the form of back pay, front pay, reinstatement, and attorney fees), *dismissal allowed, review denied*, 424 S.E.2d 400 (N.C. 1992).

286. *Richardson v. Rhode Island Dep't of Educ.*, 947 A.2d 253 [232 Educ. L. Rep. 868] (R.I. 2008), *cert. denied*, 555 U.S. 1143, 129 S.Ct. 1011, 173 L.Ed.2d 303 (2009).

287. 42 U.S.C.A. § 1988. *See McDaniel v. Princeton City School Dist. Bd. of Educ.*, 45 Fed.Appx. 354 [169 Educ. L. Rep. 129] (6th Cir. 2002).

288. *Okebiyi v. Crew*, 757 N.Y.S.2d 299 [175 Educ. L. Rep. 648] (N.Y. App. Div. 2003).

289. *Larry v. Grady School Dist.*, 119 S.W.3d 528 [183 Educ. L. Rep. 270] (Ark. Ct. App. 2003).

290. *Grant v. Board of Educ. of City of Chicago*, 668 N.E.2d 1188 [112 Educ. L. Rep. 390] (Ill. App. Ct.1996), *appeal denied*, 675 N.E.2d 632 (Ill. 1996); *Farmer v. Kelleys Island Bd. of Educ.*, 630 N.E.2d 721 [90 Educ. L. Rep. 387] (Ohio 1994), *opinion clarified*, 638 N.E.2d 79 [93 Educ. L. Rep. 281] (Ohio 1994).

291. *Hosford v. School Comm. of Sandwich*, 659 N.E.2d 1178 [106 Educ. L. Rep. 313] (Mass. 1996).

same general character as they filled.[292] Moreover, teachers are not bound to accept work in other geographic locations even if the jobs are as good as or better than the ones from which they were discharged since individuals are not required to make sacrifices in mitigating damages.[293] In taking reasonable steps to avoid or minimize their losses, educators who are improperly discharged may have to accept offers from their boards for part-time teaching positions.[294] The burden of proof is on boards to show that teachers failed to make enough effort to mitigate damages.[295]

Insofar as educators who have been dismissed or suspended must make reasonable efforts to secure other jobs in order to help school boards reduce the flow of public funds incident to litigation, courts have upheld awards mitigating recoveries when they returned to work.[296] For example, an appellate court in California affirmed that a board was entitled to deduct the amount of money a teacher might have earned from an award of back pay when she returned to work from a compulsory leave after being arrested on drug charges and successful completion of a diversion program that led to the dismissal of the charges she faced.[297] In concluding that she made no effort to seek a teaching job during her suspension, even though she had valid credentials and an otherwise unblemished record in an area of high demand, the court rejected the teacher's claim that her perception that she was not hireable as an in sufficient basis to demonstrate futility in attempting to mitigate damages.[298]

Along with back pay, educators who have been improperly subjected to adverse employment actions have been reinstated to their previous positions with front pay[299] and their seniority rights protected.[300] Even so, not all courts agree that employees are automatically entitled to reinstatement,[301] especially where it would be not only disruptive but also destructive of a learning environment.[302]

---

292. *Selland v. Fargo Pub. School Dist. No. 1*, 302 N.W.2d 391 (N.D. 1981).

293. *Kenaston v. School Admin. Dist. No. 40*, 317 A.2d 7 (Me.1974); *Board of School Trustees of Baugo Community Schools v. Indiana Educ. Employment Relations Bd.*, 412 N.E.2d 807 (Ind. Ct. App. 1980).

294. *Gross v. Board of Educ. of Elmsford Union Free School Dist.*, 571 N.Y.S.2d 200 [68 Educ. L. Rep. 473] (N.Y. 1991).

295. *Assad v. Berlin–Boylston Reg'l School Comm.*, 550 N.E.2d 357 [58 Educ. L. Rep. 1008] (Mass.1990).

296. *Unzueta v. Ocean View School Dist.*, 8 Cal.Rptr.2d 614 [74 Educ. L. Rep. 1202] (Ct. App. 1992), *reh'g denied and opinion modified* (1992), *review denied* (1992); *Marshall School Dist. v. Hill*, 939 S.W.2d 319 [116 Educ. L. Rep. 1253] (Ark. Ct. App. 1997).

297. *Martin v. Santa Clara Unified School Dist.*, 125 Cal.Rptr.2d 337 [169 Educ. L. Rep. 609] (Cal. Ct. App. 2002), *review denied* (2002).

298. *See also California Teachers Ass'n v. Governing Bd. of the Golden Valley Unified School Dist.*, 119 Cal.Rptr.2d 642 [164 Educ. L. Rep. 818] (Cal. Ct. App. 2002), *review denied* (2002) (directing the trial court, on remand, to consider whether the teacher failed to mitigate damages by seeking other employment through the exercise of reasonable diligence).

299. *DePace v. Flaherty*, 183 F. Supp.2d 633 [161 Educ. L. Rep. 845] (S.D.N.Y. 2002); *Clark County School Dist. v. Riley*, 14 P.3d 22 [149 Educ. L. Rep. 615] (Nev. 2000).

300. *Harms v. Independent School Dist. No. 300, LaCrescent*, 450 N.W.2d 571 [58 Educ. L. Rep. 734] (Minn. 1990).

301. *Hicks v. Gayville–Volin School Dist.*, 668 N.W.2d 69 [179 Educ. L. Rep. 889] (S.D. 2003); *Mustafa v. Clark County School Dist.*, 157 F.3d 1169 [129 Educ. L. Rep. 990] (9th Cir. 1998); *Bowman v. Ferrell*, 627 So.2d 335 [87 Educ. L. Rep. 1107] (Miss. 1993).

When teachers breach their employment contracts, school boards may be entitled to damages. The Supreme Court of Montana affirmed that a board could recover liquidated damages from a teacher who breached his contract by informing officials that he would not return to work only two weeks before the start of the term.[303] The court indicated that the board was entitled to damages since the teacher failed to prove that the inclusion of such a clause in his contract was unconscionable.[304]

DISMISSAL NOT FOR CAUSE: REDUCTION-IN-FORCE

Most jurisdictions have statutes directly dealing with the abolition of teaching or other educational positions without fault on the part of individual employees. This practice is commonly referred to as reduction-in-force (RIF).[305] The grounds for RIF, the order in which employees are released, the right to "bump" others, and call-back rights are matters of state law subject to modifications by board policies and collective bargaining agreements.

GROUNDS FOR RELEASE

Unless school boards modify their RIF policies pursuant to collective bargaining agreements, this is an area controlled by statute. RIFs are most commonly statutorily authorized for declines in student enrollments,[306] financial exigencies,[307] elimination of positions or programs,[308] and board

---

302. *Jackson v. Delta Special School Dist. No. 2*, 86 F.3d 1489 [110 Educ. L. Rep. 574] (8th Cir.1996), *reh'g denied* (1996).

303. *Arrowhead School Dist. No. 75 v. Klyap*, 79 P.3d 250 [182 Educ. L. Rep. 915] (Mont. 2003).

304. For an earlier case with the same result, *see Bowbells Pub. School Dist. No. 14 v. Walker*, 231 N.W.2d 173 (N.D. 1975).

305. *See, e.g.,* ALASKA STAT. ANN. § 14.20.177; CAL. EDUC. CODE ANN. §§ 44955 *et seq.*; CONN. GEN. STAT. §§ 10–151 *et seq.*; GA. CODE ANN. § 20–4–35; HAW. REV. STAT. § 302A–609; 105 ILL. COMP. STAT. 5/24–12; KY. REV. STAT. ANN. § 161.800; LA. REV. STAT. ANN. § 17:81.4; MICH. COMP. LAWS § 38.105; N.J. STAT. ANN. § 18A:28–9; N.Y. EDUC. LAW §§ 3013 *et seq.*; OHIO REV. CODE ANN. § 3319.17; PA. STAT. ANN. Tit. 24 § 11–1124; R.I. GEN. LAWS § 16–13–6; UTAH CODE ANN. § 53A–8–107; WASH. REV. CODE § 28A.405.210; WIS. STAT. ANN. § 118.23.

306. *Willie v. Board of Trustees*, 59 P.3d 302 (Idaho 2002); *Nickel v. Saline County School Dist. No. 163*, 559 N.W.2d 480 [116 Educ. L. Rep. 393] (Neb. 1997).

307. *State ex rel. Quiring v. Board of Educ. of Indep. School Dist. No. 173, Mountain Lake, Minn.*, 623 N.W.2d 634 [152 Educ. L. Rep. 271] (Minn. Ct. App. 2001), *review denied* (2001); *Boner v. Eminence R–1 School Dist.*, 55 F.3d 1339 [100 Educ. L. Rep. 886] (8th Cir. 1995); *Impey v. Board of Educ. of Borough of Shrewsbury*, 662 A.2d 960 [102 Educ. L. Rep. 639] (N.J. 1995).

308. *State ex rel. Quiring v. Board of Educ. of Indep. School Dist. No. 173, Mountain Lake, Minn.*, 623 N.W.2d 634 [152 Educ. L. Rep. 271] (Minn. Ct. App.2001), *review denied* (2001). In a case with a twist, the Supreme Court of Louisiana affirmed that even though a school board could dismiss a shop teacher who brought a gun to school, he was entitled to back pay since the superintendent failed to notify him that the board eliminated the only class that he was certified to teach as part of a RIF. *Howard v. West Baton Rouge Parish School Bd.*, 865 So.2d 708 [185 Educ. L. Rep. 778] (La. 2004).

discretion.[309] Occasionally, boards rely on a combination of factors such as where the Supreme Court of Iowa upheld the termination of a principal's contact as part of a RIF due to declining enrollment, budgetary restrictions and problems, reduction of positions, and realignment of school organization.[310]

Courts generally defer to board discretion[311] on the good faith need for RIFs. If challenged, educational officials must prove that they carried out justifiable RIFs[312] in accord with applicable state laws,[313] their own policies,[314] and/or bargaining contracts.[315] In addition, courts expect policies to include descriptions of the criteria that boards rely on[316] and how they are weighed[317] in implementing RIFs. In such a case, the Supreme Court of Appeals of West Virginia ordered a board to re-employ teachers of hospital or home-bound students with disabilities when it realized that officials violated state law by eliminating their full-time jobs without showing any need to do so and replacing them with part-time hourly employees.[318] In another dispute, an appellate court in Oregon granted school custodians' request for a writ of mandamus challenging a board's plan to release all of them and contract out their jobs since it failed to justify its action as based on the good faith desire to improve services.[319]

ORDER OF RELEASE AND BUMPING

Once school boards determine that RIFs are necessary, the next step is to set the order of release. While RIFs are ordinarily based on seniority, since seniority rights are not derived from common law, they must be based

309. *Ballato v. Board of Educ. of Town of Stonington*, 633 A.2d 323 [87 Educ. L. Rep. 171] (Conn. Ct. App.1993), *certification denied*, 638 A.2d 37 (Conn. 1994).

310. *Martinek v. Belmond–Klemme Community School Dist.*, 772 N.W.2d 758 [249 Educ. L. Rep. 390] (Iowa 2009), *reh'g denied* (2009). [Case No. 77]

311. *State ex rel. Quiring v. Board of Educ. of Indep. School Dist. No. 173, Mountain Lake, Minn.*, 623 N.W.2d 634 [152 Educ. L. Rep. 271] (Minn. Ct. App. 2001).

312. *Borr v. McKenzie County Pub. School Dist. No. 1*, 560 N.W.2d 213 [116 Educ. L. Rep. 787] (N.D.1997); *Stone County School Bd. v. McMaster*, 573 So.2d 753 [65 Educ. L. Rep. 666] (Miss. 1990).

313. *Wood County Bd. of Educ. v. Smith*, 502 S.E.2d 214 [127 Educ. L. Rep. 1112] (W. Va. 1998); *Barnett v. Board of Educ. of Town of Fairfield*, 654 A.2d 720 [97 Educ. L. Rep. 1086] (Conn.1995).

314. *Chilson v. Kimball School Dist. No. 7–2*, 663 N.W.2d 667 [177 Educ. L. Rep. 1204] (S.D. 2003); *Gettysburg School Dist. 53–1 v. Larson*, 631 N.W.2d 196 [155 Educ. L. Rep. 1375] (S.D. 2001).

315. *State ex rel. Ohio Ass'n of Pub. School Emp./AFSCME, Local 4, AFL–CIO v. Batavia Local School Dist. Bd. of Educ.*, 729 N.E.2d 743 [144 Educ. L. Rep. 689] (Ohio 2000).

316. *Wilder v. Grant County School Dist. No. 0001*, 658 N.W.2d 923 [175 Educ. L. Rep. 328] (Neb.2003); *Zalac v. Governing Bd. of Ferndale Unified School Dist.*, 120 Cal.Rptr.2d 615 [165 Educ. L. Rep. 277] (Cal. Ct. App. 2002), *review denied* (2002).

317. *Nickel v. Saline County School Dist. No. 163*, 559 N.W.2d 480 [116 Educ. L. Rep. 393] (Neb. 1997).

318. *State ex rel. Boner v. Kanawha County Bd. of Educ.*, 475 S.E.2d 176 [112 Educ. L. Rep. 504] (W. Va.1996); *Wood County Bd. of Educ. v. Smith*, 502 S.E.2d 214 [127 Educ. L. Rep. 1112] (W. Va. 1998).

319. *Scherzinger v. Portland Custodians Civil Serv. Bd.*, 149 P.3d 142 [215 Educ. L. Rep. 460] (Or. Ct. App. 2006), *petition for review withdrawn*, 169 P.3d 1269 (Or. 2007) (Table).

on statutes or collective bargaining agreements.[320] Courts typically treat seniority as a rational, but not exclusive, criterion in selecting teachers for RIFs.[321] To this end, the Supreme Court of Nebraska upheld a board's retention of a tenured business education teacher with three years' experience rather than one who worked for six years due to the greater contribution that the former made to the school's extracurricular activities program.[322]

As evidenced by a case from the Court of Appeals of New York, the judiciary can interpret tenure statutes broadly to include seniority rights within the category of probationary teachers.[323] The court observed that insofar as merely abolishing positions is not equivalent to dismissals, boards must consider whether qualified employees are eligible for other positions.

Boards bear the burden of proving that positions are unnecessary when they are eliminated during RIFs.[324] However, boards are not usually required to interchange large numbers of courses or modify established positions to create jobs for teachers who were RIFed.[325] In evaluating seniority, absent modifications based on board policy or bargaining agreements, the first criterion is actual full-time service.[326] Beyond that, board methods must be reasonable and not prohibited by statute. For instance, where state law specified that teachers with less seniority within the tenure areas to be abolished were to be part of a RIF, an appellate court in New York invalidated a provision in a bargaining contract that would have allowed individuals to change their tenure areas voluntarily so that they could accrue seniority.[327] Subsequently, the Court of Appeals of New York extended the statutory seniority protections applicable to teachers to tenured teaching assistants.[328]

When tenured teachers lose their jobs as part of RIFs, non-tenured teachers typically cannot be retained in positions of the same kind nor may board policies grant them the status of tenured faculty.[329] In such a dispute, the Supreme Court of Pennsylvania wrote that the statutory prescription of

---

320. *Schoonmaker v. Capital Region Bd. of Co-op. Educ. Servs.*, 916 N.Y.S.2d 252 [264 Educ. L. Rep. 317] (N.Y. App. Div. 2011), *leave to appeal denied*, 922 N.Y.S.2d 273 (N.Y. 2011).

321. *Board of Educ. of County of Wood v. Enoch*, 414 S.E.2d 630 [73 Educ. L. Rep. 299] (W. Va. 1992).

322. *Dykeman v. Board of Educ. of School Dist. of Coleridge, Cedar County*, 316 N.W.2d 69 [2 Educ. L. Rep. 862] (Neb. 1982).

323. *Lezette v. Board of Educ., Hudson City School Dist.*, 360 N.Y.S.2d 869 (N.Y. 1974).

324. *Bauer v. Board of Educ., Unified School Dist. No. 452, Johnson*, 765 P.2d 1129 [50 Educ. L. Rep. 1255] (Kan. 1988).

325. *Peters v. Board of Educ. of Rantoul Twp. High School Dist. No. 193 of Champaign County*, 454 N.E.2d 310 [13 Educ. L. Rep. 1039] (Ill.1983); *Butler v. Board of Educ., Unified School Dist. No. 440, Harvey County*, 769 P.2d 651 [52 Educ. L. Rep. 332] (Kan. 1989).

326. *Schoenfeld v. Board of Co-op. Educ. Servs. of Nassau County*, 469 N.Y.S.2d 133 [14 Educ. L. Rep. 1062] (N.Y. App. Div.1983).

327. *Szumigala v. Hicksville Union Free School Dist. Bd. of Educ.*, 539 N.Y.S.2d 83 [52 Educ. L. Rep. 698] (N.Y. App. Div. 1989).

328. *Madison–Oneida Bd. of Co-op. Educ. Servs. v. Mills*, 790 N.Y.S.2d 619 (N.Y. 2004).

329. *Babb v. Independent School Dist. No. I–5 of Rogers County, Okla.*, 829 P.2d 973 [74 Educ. L. Rep. 977] (Okla. 1992).

seniority in RIF situations applies to positions as they exist.[330] In other words, the court decreed that incumbents of eliminated positions were entitled to retain jobs for which they were certificated even if those positions had been occupied by others with less seniority.

A controversial case involving the intersection of RIF, seniority, and affirmative action was days away from oral argument at the Supreme Court when the parties reached a settlement agreement. At issue was a dispute from New Jersey wherein a school board, mistakenly acting on its belief that its affirmative action program required it to terminate the contract of a white, rather than an African American, teacher based solely on race, dismissed the white woman even though the two had virtually identical credentials. The Third Circuit affirmed that the board's RIF plan, which was adopted to promote racial diversity rather than remedy discrimination or its past effects, violated the constitutional rights of non-minorities.[331]

Individuals who lose their jobs in RIFs are responsible to assure board officials that their certifications for other positions are valid when it is time for "bumping," a term of art that makes it possible for employees with more seniority, and the same credentials, to be able to save their jobs at the expense of less senior colleagues.[332] While it involved administrators, rather than teachers, a case from Minnesota illustrates this principle. An appellate court permitted a middle school principal with less seniority to preserve her job while a more senior elementary school principal was released as part of a RIF due to a job consolidation.[333] The court remarked that insofar as the more senior principal lacked the appropriate qualifications for the job under state law and was ineligible for the position that she was in, she was properly released as part of the RIF. According to the court, the board was not required to change job duties of remaining supervisory positions to accommodate the more senior principal. In another case, a tenured drafting teacher unsuccessfully alleged that his school board's failure to transfer him to a different job after his position was eliminated as part of a RIF constituted age discrimination. An appellate court in New York affirmed that officials acted properly in not offering the teacher a job in social studies or industrial arts since he was not tenured in those areas.[334] Additionally, the court was satisfied that the board eliminated the program for economic reasons, not age discrimination.

---

330. *Duncan v. Rochester Area School Bd.*, 571 A.2d 365 [59 Educ. L. Rep. 121] (Pa.1990). *See also Dallap v. Sharon City School Dist.*, 571 A.2d 368 [59 Educ. L. Rep. 124] (Pa. 1990).

331. *Taxman v. Board of Educ. of the Twp. of Piscataway*, 91 F.3d 1547 [111 Educ. L. Rep. 696] (3d Cir. 1996), *cert. granted*, 521 U.S. 1117, 117 S.Ct. 2506, 138 L.Ed.2d 1010 [122 Educ. L. Rep. 389] (1997), *cert. dismissed*, 522 U.S. 1010, 118 S.Ct. 595, 139 L.Ed.2d 431 [122 Educ. L. Rep. 570] (1997).

332. *Moe v. Independent School Dist. No. 696, Ely, Minn.*, 623 N.W.2d 899 [152 Educ. L. Rep. 288] (Minn. Ct. App.2001); *School Comm. of Westport v. American Fed'n of State, County and Mun. Employees*, 810 N.E.2d 848 [188 Educ. L. Rep. 962] (Mass. Ct. App. 2004) (involving paraprofessionals).

333. *Hinckley v. School Bd. of Indep. School Dist. No. 2167*, 678 N.W.2d 485 [187 Educ. L. Rep. 262] (Minn. Ct. App. 2004).

334. *Davis v. School Dist. of City of Niagara Falls*, 772 N.Y.S.2d 180 [185 Educ. L. Rep. 723] (N.Y. App. Div. 2004).

As highlighted by a case from Illinois, being eligible for certification is not the same as having certification. An appellate court affirmed that a teacher who eventually received certification was ineligible to "bump" a less senior teacher who was qualified.[335] Subsequently, the Supreme Court of Indiana affirmed that a board could retain a less than fully qualified staff member without tenure over a similarly situated tenured colleague where the former was closer to qualifying for the needed second certificate for a new position.[336]

An appellate court in New York affirmed the general rule that "bumping" rights applied only to those who were qualified for jobs, not for new positions. The court agreed that a teacher who lost her job as chair of a social studies department was not entitled to reinstatement to a district level position as chair of social studies.[337] In like fashion, the Court of Appeals of New York affirmed that a psychologist was not entitled to re-employment as an elementary school counselor since he lacked certification for the newly created position.[338] Also, the Supreme Court of South Dakota addressed a dispute where a policy that was incorporated into the collective bargaining agreement between a board and its teachers' union specified that seniority would have priority in RIFs if teachers had the necessary certification.[339] The court held that in light of the fact that a teacher with greater seniority lacked appropriate credentials, she could not "bump" into a position involving technology because "bumping" applies to positions that persons seek to move into rather than those from which they are "bumped."[340]

CALL BACK RIGHTS

Subject to board policy[341] and collective bargaining agreements, RIF statutes typically provide that the positions of certificated employees[342] who have been released cannot be filled until they have first been offered their jobs back.[343] State law may even specify how many months or years of

335. *Hancon v. Board of Educ. of Barrington Community Unit School Dist. No. 220*, 474 N.E.2d 407 [23 Educ. L. Rep. 192] (Ill. App. Ct. 1985), *appeal denied* (1985).

336. *Stewart v. Fort Wayne Community Schools*, 564 N.E.2d 274 [64 Educ. L. Rep. 893] (Ind.1990), *cert. denied*, 502 U.S. 856, 112 S.Ct. 169, 116 L.Ed.2d 133 (1991).

337. *Donato v. Board of Educ. of the Plainview–Old Bethpage Cent. School Dist.*, 729 N.Y.S.2d 187 [156 Educ. L. Rep. 291] (N.Y. App. Div. 2001).

338. *Davis v. Mills*, 748 N.Y.S.2d 890 [171 Educ. L. Rep. 323] (N.Y. 2002).

339. *Hanson v. Vermillion School Dist. No. 13–1*, 727 N.W.2d 459 [216 Educ. L. Rep. 635] (S.D. 2007).

340. *See also Dees v. Marion–Florence Unified School Dist. No. 408*, 149 P.3d 1 [215 Educ. L. Rep. 448] (Kan. Ct. App. 2006) (affirming that insofar as a tenured counselor from an elementary school was not qualified for a job in a high school, she could not "bump" her way into the other position).

341. *Brum v. Board of Educ. of Wood County*, 599 S.E.2d 795 [190 Educ. L. Rep. 1034] (W. Va. 2004).

342. *Greater Johnstown School Dist. v. Greater Johnstown Educ. Ass'n*, 647 A.2d 611 [94 Educ. L. Rep. 352] (Pa. Cmwlth. Ct. 1994).

343. *See Cook v. Board of Educ. of Eldorado Community Unit School Dist. No. 4*, 820 N.E.2d 481 [194 Educ. L. Rep. 922] (Ill. App. Ct. 2004) (deciding that a genuine issue of fact

seniority that individuals retain while on preferred eligibility, or call-back, lists.[344] Under preferred eligibility provisions, employees are usually called back to work in the order of seniority such that the first to be released from their jobs are the first to be called back.[345]

Two cases exemplify the significance of complying with statutory guidelines with regard to teacher eligibility under call-back provisions. If, as in California, state law requires teachers to have two years of experience in school systems before acquiring call-back rights, then those with less seniority have no rights to preferred eligibility for reinstatement.[346] In New York, an appellate court ordered a board to place a teacher on a preferred eligibility list even though once he was laid off as part of a RIF, his program was terminated and the board that took over dismissed him for unsatisfactory performance.[347] The court decided that the board could not consider the teacher's work after he was laid off in evaluating whether he met his statutory duty of providing faithful and competent service.

RETIREMENT

IN GENERAL

All jurisdictions have statutes addressing teacher retirement.[348] Fortunately, legal issues that were crucial in the early stages of the development of teacher retirement systems have been long settled as courts upheld their constitutionality[349] and the authority of retirement boards to act as they see fit in managing retirement funds.[350] Yet, litigation continues over eligibility for participation in state retirement systems and proposed changes in benefits.

In a case involving a preliminary question, the Supreme Court of Pennsylvania addressed what salary is included in the calculation of retire-

---

regarding how broadly the school board defined the category of positions in which a teacher's aide/library aide worked precluded her involuntary dismissal).

344. *Avila v. Board of Educ. of N. Babylon Union Free School Dist.*, 658 N.Y.S.2d 703 [119 Educ. L. Rep. 205] (N.Y. App. Div. 1997), *leave to appeal denied*, 666 N.Y.S.2d 563, 689 N.E.2d 533 (1997).

345. *Board of Educ. of County of Mercer v. Owensby*, 526 S.E.2d 831 [143 Educ. L. Rep. 1065] (W. Va.1999); *Fontaine v. Wissahickon School Dist.*, 658 A.2d 851 [100 Educ. L. Rep. 625] (Pa. Cmwlth. Ct. 1995), *reargument denied* (1995).

346. *California Teachers Ass'n v. Mendocino Unified School Dist.*, 111 Cal.Rptr.2d 879 [156 Educ. L. Rep. 1183] (Cal. Ct. App. 2001).

347. *Bojarczuk v. Mills*, 774 N.Y.S.2d 593 [186 Educ. L. Rep. 955] (N.Y. App. Div. 2004).

348. *See, e.g.*, ALA. CODE § 16–25–110; CAL. EDUC. CODE §§ 22100 *et seq.*; FLA. STAT. ANN. § 238.01; GA. CODE ANN. § 47–3–44; ILL. COMP. STAT. ANN. 5/16–106; KY. REV. STAT. ANN. §§ 161.220 *et seq.*; N.Y. EDUC. LAW § 501 § 501; OHIO REV. CODE ANN. §§ 3307.01 *et seq.*; OKLA. STAT. ANN. tit. 70 §§ 17–101 *et seq.*; PA. STAT. ANN. tit. 24 §§ 8102 *et seq.*; W. VA. CODE ANN. § 18–7A–1.

349. *Trumper v. School Dist. No. 55 of Musselshell County*, 173 P. 946 (Mont.1918); *Shinnick v. State*, 128 N.E. 91 (Ohio 1920); *School Dist. No. 1, Multnomah County v. Teachers' Retirement Fund Ass'n of School Dist. No. 1, Multnomah County*, 96 P.2d 419 (Or. 1939).

350. *Kraus v. Riley*, 80 P.2d 864 (Mont.1938); *Crawford v. Teachers' Retirement Fund Ass'n of School Dist. No. 1, Multnomah County*, 99 P.2d 729 (Or. 1940).

ment benefits. The court affirmed the denial of a request from teachers that the calculation of their retirement benefits include payments they received while working for their unions.[351] The court explained that the retirement code protected only those benefits that retirees would have been entitled to if they had remained working for school boards and did not include the amounts that they received above their regular salaries since doing so would have artificially enhanced their benefits.

The financial dimensions of teacher retirement systems include two elements: the amounts derived from employee contributions and those from employer contributions. The former is known technically as an annuity, the latter as a pension. Typical retirement systems call for deductions from employee salaries with public funds constituting the remainder necessary to provide for retirement allowances. In addition to provisions for retirement benefits, plans ordinarily cover other key areas such as death benefits for survivors.[352]

Except for changes in existing retirement plans, or where constitutional provisions may intrude, legislatures have plenary power to establish plans as they see fit. Local retirement systems typically preceded state-level programs in many jurisdictions.[353] Since local plans were often unsound actuarially and states have more economic ability to finance retirement plans than local boards, with the exception of a few large municipalities,[354] local plans were blended into state systems.

THE NATURE OF RETIREMENT BENEFITS

In its only case on point, *Dodge v. Board of Education*,[355] the Supreme Court examined legislation from Illinois providing for pensions for retired teachers that were paid entirely from tax funds. When the legislature reduced the allowance for all teachers, including those who had already retired, the Supreme Court of Illinois rejected their claim that this violated their contractual rights since no contract existed. The Court affirmed that insofar as the gratuitous payments were non-contractual, the teachers lacked vested rights to the funds. The substantial weight of authority is now against permitting the allowances of those already retired to be changed to their disadvantage.[356]

The legality of changes in modern retirement plans depends on whether arrangements are considered contractual. The general rule is that

---

351. *Kirsch v. Public School Employees' Retirement Bd.*, 985 A.2d 671 [252 Educ. L. Rep. 239] (Pa. 2009).

352. *Venet v. Teachers' Retirement Sys. of City of N.Y.*, 552 N.Y.S.2d 275 [59 Educ. L. Rep. 161] (N.Y. App. Div. 1990), *appeal denied*, 559 N.Y.S.2d 982 (N.Y. 1990); *Pepper v. Peacher*, 742 P.2d 21 [41 Educ. L. Rep.1107] (Okla. 1987) (holding that death benefits were not revoked by divorce where the name of the beneficiary was not changed).

353. *Board of Educ. of Louisville v. City of Louisville*, 157 S.W.2d 337 (Ky. 1941).

354. *Venet v. Teachers' Retirement Sys. of City of N.Y.*, 552 N.Y.S.2d 275 [59 Educ. L. Rep. 161] (N.Y. App. Div. 1990), *appeal denied*, 559 N.Y.S.2d 982 (N.Y. 1990).

355. 302 U.S. 74, 58 S.Ct. 98, 82 L.Ed. 57 (1937).

356. *Newcomb v. Ogden City Pub. School Teachers' Retirement Comm'n*, 243 P.2d 941 (Utah 1952).

legislation does not create contractual rights unless legislative intent to this effect is clear. In this way, retirement statutes have been regarded as expressions of legislative policy, subject to future change if circumstances warrant. At issue in an earlier case was a state constitutional provision which made retirement benefits contractual so that they could not be reduced by legislative action. When the state retirement board sought to adopt new mortality tables that would have reduced the benefits of members, the Court of Appeals of New York declared that this would have violated the state constitution.[357] In rejecting the claim that not permitting the changes would have bankrupted the system, the court pointed out that if that were to have been the case, then legislators would have had to provide the funds needed to pay the allowances of those who were already members. The same court later invalidated a statute that would have required the retirement system to invest funds in municipal bonds that were floated as part of a plan to alleviate a severe fiscal emergency in New York City.[358] The court noted that such an approach was unacceptable since it could have interfered with the integrity and security of the sources that paid for the protected benefits.

Later, the First Circuit contended that legislative changes to Maine's retirement system did not violate the contractual rights of teachers since they had not started receiving their pension benefits.[359] Also, the Supreme Court of Ohio upheld changes in the state's statutory classification that placed members into groups as non-retired and retired, asserting that teachers do not possess their contract rights until their pensions vest by operation of law.[360]

MEMBERSHIP ELIGIBILITY AND BENEFITS

Local school boards cannot adopt policies designed to contravene state retirement laws. If jurisdictions set eligibility requirements for retirement[361] including disability retirement[362] programs, local boards can neither deviate from these provisions nor institute incentive plans for early retirement that might threaten the actuarial soundness of systems.[363] Where plans provide exceptions for early retirement, system administrators must grant requests for benefits.[364]

Litigation has rendered mixed results over whether employees had sufficient notice when they seek to join retirement systems retroactively.

357. *Birnbaum v. New York State Teachers' Retirement Sys.*, 176 N.Y.S.2d 984 (N.Y. 1958).

358. *Sgaglione v. Levitt*, 375 N.Y.S.2d 79, 337 N.E.2d 592 (1975).

359. *Parker v. Wakelin*, 123 F.3d 1 [120 Educ. L. Rep. 966] (1st Cir. 1997), *cert. denied*, 523 U.S. 1106, 118 S.Ct. 1675, 140 L.Ed.2d 813 (1998).

360. *State ex rel. Horvath v. State Teachers Retirement Bd.*, 697 N.E.2d 644 [127 Educ. L. Rep. 1017] (Ohio 1998), *reconsideration denied*, 700 N.E.2d 334 (Ohio 1998), *cert. denied*, 525 U.S. 1179, 119 S.Ct. 1115, 143 L.Ed.2d 111 (1999).

361. *Herzig v. Board of Educ. of the Town of W. Hartford*, 204 A.2d 827 (Conn.1964).

362. *Shepherd v. Chambers*, 794 N.W.2d 678 [264 Educ. L. Rep. 854] (Neb. 2011); *State ex rel. Ackerman v. State Teachers Retirement Bd.*, 883 N.E.2d 445 [230 Educ. L. Rep. 730] (Ohio 2008).

363. *Fair Lawn Educ. Ass'n v. Fair Lawn Bd. of Educ.*, 401 A.2d 681 (N.J. 1979).

364. *Weddum v. Davenport Community School Dist.*, 750 N.W.2d 114 [232 Educ. L. Rep. 926] (Iowa 2008).

Whether employees can join retirement systems retroactively depends on the nature of the notice that they received. If board officials can show that employees received appropriate notice, individuals cannot join retroactively.[365] Conversely, if employees can prove that they did not receive appropriate notice, they can join public retirement systems at later dates.[366]

Turning to issues involving service credit in retirement systems, the Supreme Court of Wisconsin affirmed that two teachers who left their jobs and took separation benefits retained their membership rights in the state's system when they returned to work.[367] The court found that the teachers' service credit was sufficient to sustain their memberships as a matter of right. Also, where fifteen teachers failed to submit their request for purchasing out-of-state service credit in a timely manner, the Supreme Court of Vermont affirmed that insofar as they lacked a substantive right to such benefits, the State Teachers' Retirement had the discretion to deny their application.[368] Further, an appellate court in New York ruled that a teacher who retired at the end of a one-year leave of absence due to personal issues could not count his time off toward the calculation of his benefits.[369] Since the teacher's leave agreement was silent on this issue, the court was satisfied that he was not entitled to the additional benefits he requested.

In a related matter, courts in Massachusetts,[370] Ohio,[371] and Pennsylvania[372] denied individuals who taught in non-public schools opportunities to join their state retirement systems while another appellate court in Pennsylvania affirmed that commonwealth officials properly denied retirement credit to a member who worked with students from non-public schools in her capacity with a not-for-profit corporation.[373] In addition, an appellate court in Ohio affirmed that a teacher who worked as a part-time teaching assistant at a public university for two years was ineligible to purchase service credit.[374]

---

365.   *Liebert v. Board of Educ. for Scotia–Glenville Cent. School Dist.*, 704 N.Y.S.2d 352 [142 Educ. L. Rep. 477] (N.Y. App. Div. 2000), *leave to appeal denied*, 712 N.Y.S.2d 447 (N.Y. 2000); *Capone v. Board of Educ. of Lafayette Cent. School Dist.*, 697 N.Y.S.2d 895 [139 Educ. L. Rep. 1006] (N.Y. App. Div. 1999).

366.   *See, e.g., Serio v. Board of Educ. of Valley Stream Union Free School Dist. No. 13*, 703 N.Y.S.2d 232 [142 Educ. L. Rep. 465] (N.Y. App. Div. 2000); *Bettis v. Potosi R–III School Dist.*, 51 S.W.3d 183 [156 Educ. L. Rep. 329] (Mo. Ct. App. 2001).

367.   *Solie v. Employee Trust Funds Bd.*, 695 N.W.2d 463 [197 Educ. L. Rep. 798] (Wis. 2005).

368.   *Ahern v. Mackey*, 925 A.2d 1011 [221 Educ. L. Rep. 793] (Vt. 2007).

369.   *Kito v. Board of Educ. of William Floyd Sch. Dist.*, 867 N.Y.S.2d 152 [238 Educ. L. Rep. 843] (N.Y. App. Div. 2008).

370.   *Dube v. Contributory Retirement Appeal Bd.*, 733 N.E.2d 1089 [146 Educ. L. Rep. 414] (Mass. Ct. App. 2000). *But see Rosing v. Teachers' Retirement Sys.*, 936 N.E.2d 875 [261 Educ. L. Rep. 783] (Mass. 2010) (permitting a teacher in a non-public school funded in whole or in part by the commonwealth to purchase service credits).

371.   *State ex rel. State Teachers Retirement Bd. v. West Geauga Local School Dist. Bd. of Educ.*, 722 N.E.2d 93 [140 Educ. L. Rep. 743] (Ohio Ct. App.1998), *appeal allowed*, 705 N.E.2d 367 (Ohio 1999), *appeal dismissed as improvidently allowed*, 718 N.E.2d 928 (Ohio 1999).

372.   *Cain v. Public School Employees' Retirement Sys.*, 651 A.2d 660 [96 Educ. L. Rep. 632] (Pa. Cmwlth. Ct. 1994), *appeal denied*, 659 A.2d 560 (Pa. 1995).

373.   *Thorpe v. Public School Employees' Retirement Bd.*, 879 A.2d 341 [200 Educ. L. Rep. 814] (Pa. Cmwlth. Ct. 2005).

374.   *State ex rel. Palmer v. State Teachers Retirement Bd.*, 629 N.E.2d 1377 [89 Educ. L. Rep. 946] (Ohio Ct. App. 1993).

Courts reached mixed results with regard to military service as some have permitted veterans to purchase credit[375] while others disagreed.[376] The Supreme Court of Alaska added that the board of the state's teacher retirement service erred in granting service credit to two teachers who worked both outside of the state and with the Bureau of Indian Affairs.[377] Other courts reached opposite outcomes with regard to credit for out-of-state service as some granted it[378] but others refused to do so.[379] Still other courts granted substitute[380] and part-time[381] teachers eligibility to join retirement systems. Courts also rejected claims that independent contractors could join retirement systems[382] and that lump-sum buy-outs of employee contracts should have counted toward retirement benefits.[383]

On the flip side of seeking to buy into retirement systems, an appellate court in Utah affirmed that a charter school could not retroactively seek to be excluded from the state system.[384] The court agreed that the school was not entitled to retroactive exclusion from the system following the enactment of an opt-out amendment to the statute requiring charter schools that offer retirement benefits to participate in the state system since the change was prospective.

On a specific matter, in a non-education case, the Supreme Court struck down the practice of treating women differently from men regarding

---

375. *Dailey v. Public School Retirement Sys. of Mo.,* 707 F.Supp. 1087 [52 Educ. L. Rep. 582] (E.D. Mo.1989); *Morris v. Commonwealth, Pub. School Employees' Retirement Sys.,* 538 A.2d 1385 [45 Educ. L. Rep. 1131] (Pa. Cmwlth. Ct.1988), *appeal denied,* 557 A.2d 345 (Pa.1989); *Watkins v. Oldham,* 731 S.W.2d 829 [40 Educ. L. Rep. 551] (Ky. Ct. App.1987).

376. *Fishman v. Teachers' Retirement Sys.,* 408 N.E.2d 113 (Ill. App. Ct.1980), *cert. denied,* 452 U.S. 915, 101 S.Ct. 3048, 69 L.Ed.2d 418 (1981); *Newcomb v. New York State Teachers' Retirement Sys.,* 373 N.Y.S.2d 554 (N.Y. 1975).

377. *Bartley v. State, Dep't of Admin., Teacher's Retirement Bd.,* 110 P.3d 1254 [197 Educ. L. Rep. 849] (Alaska 2005), *reh'g denied* (2005).

378. *Weston v. Contributory Retirement Appeal Bd.* 923 N.E.2d 110 [254 Educ. L. Rep. 397] (Mass. App. Ct. 2010); *Hopkins v. Public School Employees' Retirement Bd.,* 674 A.2d 1197 [109 Educ. L. Rep. 271] (Pa. Cmwlth. Ct.1996).

379. *Day v. Public School Employees' Retirement Sys.,* 682 A.2d 398 [112 Educ. L. Rep. 1012] (Pa. Cmwlth. Ct. 1996) (denying retirement credit for an out-of-state maternity leave of absence which was neither certified by an out-of-state employer nor credited by its retirement system).

380. *Board of State Teachers Retirement Sys. of Ohio v. Cuyahoga Falls City School Dist. Bd. of Educ.,* 498 N.E.2d 167 [35 Educ. L. Rep. 266] (Ohio Ct. App. 1985).

381. *Madden v. Contributory Retirement Appeal Bd.,* 729 N.E.2d 1095 [144 Educ. L. Rep. 721] (Mass. 2000); *Hawes v. Public School Employees' Retirement Bd.,* 778 A.2d 1277 [156 Educ. L. Rep. 1147] (Pa. Cmwlth. Ct. 2001) (permitting service as a part-time teacher to count toward total service).

382. *Roesch v. Board of Educ. for Wayne–Finger Lakes Bd. of Co-op. Educ. Servs.,* 687 N.Y.S.2d 448 [134 Educ. L. Rep. 542] (N.Y. App. Div. 1999).

383. *Wallon v. New York State Teachers' Retirement Sys.,* 741 N.Y.S.2d 597 [164 Educ. L. Rep. 854] (N.Y. App. Div. 2002).

384. *Thomas Edison Charter School v. Retirement Bd.,* 189 P.3d 79 [234 Educ. L. Rep. 1000] (Utah Ct. App. 2008).

financial aspects of retirement.[385] In the context of public employment, the Court interpreted Title VII as barring the use of retirement plans designed to require women to contribute more than men for equal benefits. The Court was of the opinion that neither Title VII nor its judgment was intended to revolutionize the insurance and pension industries. Rather, the Court thought that it did not imply either that it would have been unlawful for employers to set aside equal retirement contributions for each of their employees and have retirees purchase benefits in the open market or that insurance companies would have been prevented from considering the composition of employers' work forces in calculating the costs of retirement and/or death benefit plans. The Court subsequently interpreted Title VII as prohibiting employers from offering their employees the option of receiving retirement benefits from one of an array of companies that they selected, all of which paid women lower monthly benefits than men who made the same contributions.[386]

In a case involving retirement benefits and lost investments, teachers and other school employees filed a variety of claims against their board and officials when the payroll deductions that they invested in the company that the board selected to manage their retirement savings plans lost money. An appellate court in New York affirmed that the save harmless provision in the contract dealing with the retirement savings plan that insulated the board and its officials from liability was acceptable since it neither offended public policy nor condoned gross negligence or intentional wrongdoing.[387]

CALCULATIONS OF BENEFITS

The fact that inflation can place retired educators in poor economic conditions beyond their control led to a relaxation of earlier prohibition against expenditures to raise retirement benefits. To this end, the Supreme Court of Wisconsin distinguished a moral duty from a gratuity,[388] defining the former as "an obligation which, though lacking in any foundation cognizable in law, springs from a sense of justice and equity ... but not from a mere sense of doing benevolence or charity."[389] Since the state statute authorized local boards to provide extra payments, the court indicated that they did not fall within the constitutional inhibition that applied only to the state treasury.

Modern courts have adopted an attitude toward retirement benefits that differs from the perspectives of their predecessors. Insofar as modern courts view retirement benefits as inducements to enter and remain in

---

385. *City of Los Angeles, Dep't of Water and Power v. Manhart*, 435 U.S. 702, 98 S.Ct. 1370, 55 L.Ed.2d 657 (1978).

386. *Arizona Governing Comm. for Tax Deferred Annuity and Deferred Comp. Plans v. Norris*, 463 U.S. 1073, 103 S.Ct. 3492, 77 L.Ed.2d 1236 (1983).

387. *Elmira Teachers' Ass'n ex rel. Martin v. Elmira City School Dist.*, 861 N.Y.S.2d 195 [234 Educ. L. Rep. 245] (N.Y. App. Div. 2008), *leave to appeal denied*, 868 N.Y.S.2d 601 (N.Y. 2008).

388. Although involving a pension for police officers not educators, the Supreme Court of North Dakota declared that "[a] pension plan is an added salary and compensation for services performed; it is not a gratuity." *Klug v. City of Minot*, 795 N.W.2d 906 (N.D. 2011) (affirming that officials could combine a police pension with city employee pension plans).

389. *State ex rel. Holmes v. Krueger*, 72 N.W.2d 734, 738 (Wis. 1955).

public service,[390] they treat them as property rights governed by statutes for employees with vested rights.[391] Even so, litigation continues over what salary and benefits that employees earned can be included in calculating their retirement benefits.

In the first of illustrative cases on point, the Supreme Court of Appeals of West Virginia agreed with two retirees who alleged that the board of the state's retirement system erred in refusing to include lump-sum payments for accumulated vacation pay in calculating their final average salaries for the purposes of computing their benefits.[392] The court reasoned that insofar as the rule that the board applied went into effect after the petitioners made their requests for benefits, it was inapplicable. On the other hand, when a board in New York granted a disproportionate salary increase to an administrator who was about to retire, an appellate court affirmed that officials of the state's retirement system had a rational basis for excluding this financial package in calculating his benefits.[393] Similarly, another appellate panel in New York affirmed that insofar as an administrator's two percent expense allowance was not compensation, it did not have to be included in calculating his average salary for retirement purposes.[394]

A novel case about the calculation of benefits arose in Illinois. An appellate court affirmed a reduction of a retired teacher's benefits by the amount of money that she received as extra pay while taking part in an illegal kickback scheme in her district.[395] The court agreed that insofar as the teacher received monies as part of an illegal scheme, these funds were not salary for the purposes of calculating her pension.

On the first of two practical questions about calculating retirement benefits, the Supreme Court of Georgia addressed the use of actuarial tables. The court ruled that state law required officials to employ adopted mortality tables both in determining valuation and in establishing actuarial equivalence between optional-allowance and maximum-benefit allowances for retirees.[396]

---

390. *Rosinski v. Teachers Retirement Ass'n Bd. of Trustees*, 495 N.W.2d 14 [80 Educ. L. Rep. 979] (Minn. Ct. App.1993).

391. *See, e.g., Tubbs v. State ex rel., Teachers' Retirement Sys. of Okla.*, 57 P.3d 571 [171 Educ. L. Rep. 360] (Okla. 2002) (permitting a pension to be divided after a divorce); *Pierce v. State*, 910 P.2d 288 (N.M.1995) (ascertaining that state retirement laws create vested property rights but not contract rights); *National Educ. Ass'n–R.I. by Scigulinsky v. Retirement Bd. of R.I. Employees' Retirement Sys.*, 972 F.Supp. 100 [120 Educ. L. Rep. 1006] (D.R.I. 1997), *vacated and remanded by National Educ. Ass'n–Rhode Island ex rel. Scigulinsky v. Retirement Bd. of Rhode Island Employees' Ret. Sys.*, 172 F.3d 22, 25 (1st Cir. 1999) (distinguishing the rights of vested and non-vested employees).

392. *Summers v. West Virginia Consol. Pub. Retirement Bd.*, 618 S.E.2d 408 [201 Educ. L. Rep. 774] (W. Va. 2005).

393. *Palandra v. New York State Teachers' Retirement Sys.*, 924 N.Y.S.2d 194 [267 Educ. L. Rep. 798] (N.Y. App. Div. 2011); *Holbert v. New York State Teachers' Retirement Sys.*, 840 N.Y.S.2d 655 [222 Educ. L. Rep. 838] (N.Y. App. Div. 2007).

394. *Maillard v. New York State Teachers' Retirement Sys.*, 870 N.Y.S.2d 567 [240 Educ. L. Rep. 371] (N.Y. App. Div. 2008), *leave to appeal denied*, 879 N.Y.S.2d 52 (N.Y. 2009).

395. *Adams v. Board of Trustees of Teachers' Retirement Sys. of Ill.*, 944 N.E.2d 789 [265 Educ. L. Rep. 1236] (Ill. App. Ct. 2011).

396. *Plymel v. Teachers Retirement Sys.*, 637 S.E.2d 379 [214 Educ. L. Rep. 862] (Ga. 2006).

A year later, the Sixth Circuit held that retirement incentives paid to teachers are subject to Federal Insurance Contributions Act (FICA), more commonly referred to as Social Security.[397] The court explained that these sums were subject to FICA because they are wages under the meaning of the law.

MEDICAL-HEALTH BENEFITS

As members of the "Baby Boom" generation start to retire, concerns are arising over costs associated with their medical and health benefits once they leave their jobs. The Supreme Court of Michigan rejected the claim of retired public school employees who challenged an increase in their prescription drug co-payments and the deductibles under the master health care plan as diminishing or impairing their accrued financial benefits.[398] The court responded that insofar as the statute establishing health care benefits for public school retirees did not create a contract between them and the state for the purposes of federal and state constitutional provisions prohibiting the impairment of contracts, such that these were not accrued financial benefits, their claim was without merit.

In like fashion, the Supreme Court of New Hampshire reviewed whether health care premiums could be treated as income in calculating retirement benefits. The court affirmed an adjudication of the state's retirement system that a local board's payments towards the cost of health insurance premiums for retired teachers pursuant to their collective bargaining agreements were not what it described as earnable compensation in the calculation of their retirement benefits.[399] The court thus agreed that the retired teachers were not entitled to reimbursement for costs they expended while working.

An appellate court in Massachusetts reached a different outcome on a related issue where retired teachers filed suit over their having agreed to pay a higher percentage of their medical costs while they were working. The court affirmed that insofar as paying increased costs for their health insurance premiums constituted what it interpreted as regular compensation, it could be included in calculating their retirement benefits.[400]

In a case of first impression involving health benefits, an appellate court in New York vacated an order denying benefits to the same-sex partner of a retired teacher.[401] The court observed that insofar as a change in state law required public agencies to provide full spousal benefits to same-sex couples who were validly married in other jurisdictions, the

---

397. *Appoloni v. United States*, 450 F.3d 185 [210 Educ. L. Rep. 83] (6th Cir. 2006), *cert. denied*, 549 U.S. 1165, 127 S.Ct. 1123, 166 L.Ed.2d 891 [216 Educ. L. Rep. 35] (2007).

398. *Studier v. Michigan Pub. School Employees' Retirement Bd.*, 698 N.W.2d 350 [199 Educ. L. Rep. 398] (Mich. 2005).

399. *In re Farmington Teachers' Ass'n*, 969 A.2d 422 [244 Educ. L. Rep. 149] (N.H. 2009). [Case No. 78]

400. *Olsen v. Teachers' Retirement Bd.*, 874 N.E.2d 492 [224 Educ. L. Rep. 402] (Mass. Ct. App. 2007).

401. *Funderburke v. State Dep't of Civil Serv.*, 854 N.Y.S.2d 466 [230 Educ. L. Rep. 717] (N.Y. App. Div. 2008).

retired teacher was entitled to medical benefits for his partner. In a second case from New York on health insurance, an appellate court affirmed that a retired teacher could change the terms of his coverage from an individual to a family plan to include his wife since doing so was consistent with the provisions of the bargaining agreement under which he procured his benefits.[402]

[CASE NO. 68]   NO RIGHT TO TENURE IN COACHING POSITION

BOARD OF DIRECTORS OF AMES COMMUNITY SCHOOL DISTRICT v. CULLINAN

Supreme Court of Iowa, 2008.
745 N.W.2d 487 [229 Educ. L. Rep. 869].

■ LARSON, JUSTICE.

The board of directors of the Ames Community School District terminated the coaching contract of Dennis Cullinan under the authority of Iowa Code sections 279.15–.19A (2003). Cullinan appealed to an adjudicator, pursuant to Iowa Code section 279.17, who reversed the termination. The board sought judicial review, the district court affirmed, and in a two-to-one decision, the court of appeals affirmed as well. On further review, we vacate the decision of the court of appeals, reverse the judgment of the district court, and remand.

I.   Facts and Prior Proceedings.

Dennis Cullinan was employed by the Ames Community School District in 1997 as both a high school social studies teacher and head boys' basketball coach. At the end of the 1997–98 school year, Cullinan's probationary status was extended for a year as the result of complaints the school administration had received regarding Cullinan's coaching-particularly his threatening and intimidating treatment of student-athletes and his use of profane language directed at the student-athletes. Five basketball players, including a returning letterman, quit during the season. A memo to Cullinan from the athletic director on April 14, 1998, in connection with the extension of his probation, stated:

You are hereby notified that major concerns with the Boys Basketball Program exist that must be addressed and corrected during 1998–99.

The memo stated that the school expected the [c]reation of a Less Threatening Environment for Players. Again, we must work to end the public perception that a few of your athletes have been threatened and intimated. There must not be any evidence that threats and intimidation are being used as a motivational tool in any manner. . . . It is expected that significant improvements in all areas will be realized during the next school year. As always, members of the District Athletic Administration will be continually available to offer any additional assistance necessary to help you tackle these important issues. (Emphasis added.)

---

402. *Bower v. Board of Educ., Cazenovia Cent. School Dist.*, 862 N.Y.S.2d 185 [235 Educ. L. Rep. 525] (N.Y. App. Div. 2008), *leave to dismiss appeal*, 872 N.Y.S.2d 57 (N.Y. 2008).

This memo essentially restated principles that were already emphasized by the Ames School District in both the parent-athlete handbook and
the coach's handbook . . . . .

. . .

Cullinan received a satisfactory written evaluation from the athletic
director in May 1999 and was offered a new contract for the 1999–2000
school year. No further concerns were raised regarding Cullinan's coaching
until the 2001–02 school year, when he became the subject of numerous
student and parent complaints. During the 2001–02 school year, captains of
the basketball team met with one of Cullinan's assistants and Cullinan
himself to complain about Cullinan's treatment of team members.

One player and his father filed seven harassment complaints, alleging
incidents of name-calling and profanity by Cullinan during the 2000–01
season. The athletic director investigated these complaints and found they
had merit, although they did not meet the harassment-policy requirement
that the acts complained of be "sexual [ ]or discriminatory in nature." The
results of the harassment investigation were considered by the administration as a part of a larger inquiry prompted by other parents' complaints
filed collectively on May 10, 2002. On that date, a packet of material was
delivered to the school administration entitled *"Parents of Ames High
Basketball Players vs. Dennis Cullinan."* The packet contained a copy of
the school's harassment policy and sixteen letters from fifteen families
outlining complaints primarily concerning Cullinan's demeanor toward
athletes, and the decreasing interest in the basketball program that resulted.

The authors of the letters stated in their summary of complaints that
their concerns were not based on playing time or Cullinan's lack of
basketball knowledge, were not about a single event, and were not about
the team's win/loss record. Rather, the parents stated that their concerns:

ARE about an environment that impacts young men's confidence, self
esteem and lives on and off the court.

ARE about long term behaviors over a number of years by Coach
Cullinan that creates a negative, hostile environment.

ARE about parents and athletes that are afraid to come forward for
fear of retribution or becoming the person with increased focus for
criticism by the coach.

ARE about young men who love basketball, who walk away because of
the environment.

ARE about a coach who advises injured players to not see a doctor,
because they may receive medical restrictions, rather than showing
concern for the health and well being of the athlete.

ARE about a coach who ignores the rules of the Iowa High School
Athletic Association setting a poor example for ethical behavior for the
young men.

ARE about a coach who can talk a good story, but cannot "walk the
talk."

In response to the "Parents v. Cullinan" complaints, Cullinan outlined his positive influence on the basketball program and provided several letters of support-primarily from fellow coaches familiar with Cullinan and his basketball program. The complaints and Cullinan's response were investigated by the athletic director, principal, and superintendent. On June 5, 2002, the athletic director summarized his conclusions and noted that Cullinan had not heeded the prior requirements set out in the 1998 probation-extension memo. The June 5 memo stated:

> What complicates the current concerns in our boys' basketball program even further is that issues about Mr. Cullinan's style and demeanor were addressed in a memorandum dated April 14, 1998, that was placed in his personnel file. . . .

This memo was followed by a memo from the assistant superintendent, Tim Taylor, to Cullinan dated July 2, 2002, outlining the administration's perceptions of Cullinan's performance and directing Cullinan to take corrective measures. This memo, compiled following discussions with the athletic director and the superintendent, stated:

> As you are aware, your professional judgment as an athletic coach is under constant scrutiny from students and parents as well. By failing to meet expectations you seriously jeopardize your credibility, place the district in an awkward situation, and tarnish your own reputation.

> The behavior in question is the alleged and perceived intimidation and emotional abuse and the alleged and perceived fear of retribution, by you, against student athletes under your control as members of the varsity boys basketball program. Such behavior is not consistent with our standards of conduct and is unacceptable. Several parents of athletes have stepped forward to express their belief that fear appears to be the main motivator used by you as a coach and because, in their opinion, no real relationship exists between the players and the head coach, it is in the best interests of their sons to not participate in the varsity basketball program in the future. These parents have also requested your immediate termination as Head Varsity boys Basketball Coach at Ames High. Of great concern is that this is not a "new" issue. A letter does exist in your personnel file and meetings for remediation of identical problems within the boys' basketball program are documented from 1998. The memo then included a plan of remediation. . . .

> . . .

Following this memo, Cullinan received a satisfactory year-end evaluation for the 2002–03 school year. However, the athletic director emphasized that the district would "continue to monitor and expect this coaching style to continue well into the future."

Unfortunately, Cullinan's coaching was again called into question on December 16, 2003, when Cullinan is alleged to have failed to comply with the July 2, 2002 directive prohibiting one-on-one "acute individual student-athlete corrections." Alex Thompson, a player, failed to follow Cullinan's coaching instructions during a game, resulting in a turnover. After the game, Cullinan sent an assistant to bring Thompson to him. It is undisputed that Thompson and Cullinan met in a hallway without parents or other adults present and out of earshot of the assistant coaches, in apparent violation of the administration's directive of July 2. Cullinan admitted he met with Thompson, but the tenor and purpose of the meeting is in dispute. Thompson claimed it was intimidating. Cullinan claims that the meeting was not corrective, and furthermore, the July 2 directive regarding one-on-one meetings was no longer in effect. Regardless of the purpose or tenor of the meeting, Thompson's parents complained about the meeting to the superintendent the next day.

The administration investigated, concluding Cullinan violated the directive and suspended him for two games without pay. On March 23, 2004, Michael McGrory, principal, wrote a memo to Cullinan following a meeting with the athletic director and Cullinan. The principal stated that "[t]he two main concerns during your terms as coach" were (1) "[d]evelopment of a team concept" and (2) "[c]reation of a less threatening environment for players." The memo continued:

Upon review of all the facts and circumstances during your tenure as head coach, it is apparent that you have not rectified the concerns to a satisfactory level. Due to your inability to make sufficient progress in the before mentioned concerns, I am recommending to the superintendent that your basketball coaching contract not be renewed.

On April 28, 2004, based on the principal's recommendation of termination and his own investigation, the superintendent recommended termination of Cullinan's coaching contract for "[f]ail[ing] to effectively lead the program [and f]ail[ing] to adequately remediate leadership deficiencies in [the] program." A hearing at Cullinan's request was held in June and July 2004, and the board voted unanimously to terminate Cullinan's coaching contract. Additional facts will be discussed as we apply them in the disposition of the case.

II.   Rules for Review of Termination Decisions.

Review of a school board's termination of a teacher's contract is for correction of errors at law. Under Iowa Code section 279.19A, the procedure for termination of coaching contracts is the same as for teachers' contracts.

Section 279.18 provides that, "[i]n proceedings for judicial review of the adjudicator's decision, the court shall not hear any further evidence but shall hear the case upon the certified record." On judicial review,

[t]he court may affirm the adjudicator's decision or remand to the adjudicator or the board for further proceedings upon conditions determined by the court. The court shall reverse, modify, or grant any other appropriate relief from the board decision or the adjudicator's decision....

The statute does not state which decision is to be reviewed by the court—the adjudicator's or the board's. However, it is clear under our case law that we review the board's findings, not those of the adjudicator.

A reviewing court must determine whether a school board's decision is supported by a preponderance of the competent evidence in the record. On review of the school board's decision, especially on issues of credibility, the court is obliged to give weight to the board's fact findings, although it is not bound by them.

Termination of a teaching or coaching contract may only be for "just cause." The legislature has not defined just cause; however, we have stated:

> Probably no inflexible "just cause" definition we could devise would be adequate to measure the myriad of situations which may surface in future litigation. It is sufficient here to hold that in the context of teacher fault a "just cause" is one which directly or indirectly significantly and adversely affects what must be the ultimate goal of every school system: high quality education for the district's students. It relates to job performance including leadership and role model effectiveness. It must include the concept that a school district is not married to mediocrity but may dismiss personnel who are neither performing high quality work nor improving in performance. On the other hand, "just cause" cannot include reasons which are arbitrary, unfair, or generated out of some petty vendetta.

In addition to these general principles for review of termination cases, two additional questions arise in this case. The first is what weight should be given to the hearsay evidence presented to the board, and the second is what should be the proper scope of the board's inquiry into just cause?

A.   Hearsay Evidence. It is clear that hearsay evidence is admissible in teacher termination cases. The question here is how much weight should be accorded such evidence, and that will depend upon a myriad of factors—the circumstances of the case, the credibility of the witness, the credibility of the declarant, the circumstances in which the statement was made, the consistency of the statement with other corroborating evidence, and other factors as well.

Using this multiple-factor test, we believe the hearsay evidence in this case bore sufficient indicia of reliability to be properly considered. The administrative reports and memoranda, while hearsay, had been drafted as part of the school administrators' official responsibilities. The parents' letters in the packet of May 10, 2002, were, in most cases, signed by the writers, and in all cases, the writers were identified in the letters. The writers were therefore subject to being called for questioning by Cullinan if he had doubts about the accuracy of the letters or the parents' motivations for writing them. In addition, the basketball players themselves were all identified in the letters and subject, if Cullinan had desired, to be called as witnesses as well. The players' statements were made under circumstances that tended to establish credibility.....

. . .

.... in this case, the players' statements were made by teenagers who were obviously distressed by the situation; they were made to trusted individuals, i.e., their parents; and they carried a consistent message—the players expressed the view that the coach was threatening and intimidating toward them.

We reject the argument that the board improperly considered the hearsay evidence. The termination statute and our cases make it clear that a board may consider such evidence in making its decision, and the evidence provided in this case bore sufficient indicia of reliability to be a part of the record.

B.   The Scope of the Board's Just–Cause Inquiry. It is true that the December 16, 2003 hallway incident involving Alex Thompson and Culli-nan, in which Cullinan allegedly violated the plan for remediation, was the spark that initiated the proceedings for termination. The parties, however, raise a question as to the scope of the board's just-cause inquiry: is it based exclusively on the events of December 16, as Cullinan appears to argue, or may the inquiry also include Cullinan's employment history predating December 16, as the board argues?

The adjudicator adopted a narrow scope of inquiry and limited the just-cause inquiry to the question of whether the December 16, 2003 incident violated the July 2002 remediation directive concerning one-on-one meet-ings. This is clear from his ruling in which he criticized the board for a "deliberate merging of the earlier incidents with the incident [on December 16], which triggered the termination at issue." The district court and the court of appeals appear to have adopted a narrow scope of inquiry as well and concluded that the December 16 incident was insufficient to constitute just cause.

We reject this narrow scope of the board's inquiry. While the board's termination order discussed the December 16 incident at length, its order made it clear that the termination was based on Cullinan's entire history with the district—not just the December 16 incident. The latter incident was, apparently, merely the proverbial straw that broke the camel's back. The superintendent listed two grounds for termination: "Failure to effec-tively lead the program [and] . . . [t]o adequately remediate leadership deficiencies in [the] program." The board concluded that both bases for termination had been established.

The attorney who conducted the hearing on behalf of the board rejected Cullinan's attempts to restrict the superintendent's evidence to the December 16 incident. She correctly ruled that, because failure to remedi-ate prior problems had been charged by the superintendent in his recom-mendation for termination, the board [had to go] back to see what hap-pened in the past to indicate whether or not the employee had knowledge of what was expected. I do believe that even 98 as well as 2002 is relevant for showing that, and so I'm going to rule that it is relevant for the board to consider what had been told to the coach in prior years.

The board's evidence included Cullinan's entire employment history, and its decision was based on his failure to remediate prior problems as well as the events of December 16. . . .

This broad scope of the just-cause inquiry is consistent with our case law. In *Sheldon Community School District Board of Directors v. Lundblad*, a teacher argued that the board could not consider incidents "long since resolved." We rejected that argument. . . .

. . .

In this case, Cullinan cannot credibly argue that he was caught by surprise by the board's consideration of his entire coaching career at the Ames High School, rather than limiting it only to the December 16 hallway incident. He was informed throughout his career about the need for respect toward athletes. These principles were continuously emphasized in the coach's and parents' manuals, the administration's memoranda to Cullinan explaining the grounds for extending his probation, and numerous complaints from parents and students during his career. Further, Cullinan was notified by the superintendent that one of the grounds for termination was Cullinan's failure to remediate preexisting problems. We conclude the board appropriately considered Cullinan's coaching history in deciding whether to terminate his coaching contract.

C. The Board's Just–Cause Determination. Cullinan asserts a number of arguments supporting his claim that the board did not have just cause to terminate his coaching contract, even considering his previous problems in the district. In order to determine whether the board's decision was justified by a preponderance of the evidence, we must address each of Cullinan's assertions, the board's evidence, and the holdings of the adjudicator and of reviewing courts.

First, Cullinan contends the December 16 hallway meeting with Alex Thompson was not sufficient just cause for termination. This contention is based, initially, on Cullinan's argument that the one-on-one meeting with Thompson did not violate any directive to which he was subject. Cullinan asserts that the prohibition against one-on-one meetings contained in the assistant superintendent's July 2 directive was not included in the remediation plan he drafted and to which he was subject. The board responds that Cullinan's remediation plan merely supplemented the July 2 directive, and thus, the provisions of both documents were in effect. We agree with the board that the administration's approval of Cullinan's remediation plan did not evidence an intent to allow one-on-one meetings between Cullinan and the student-athletes. Whether Cullinan's meeting with Thompson on December 16 qualified as a situation requiring the presence of another adult is another question.

The July 2 directive required acute individual student-athlete corrections . . . [to be] [d]one away from the group setting or directed to the group as a whole [or][d]one in the presence of an assistant coach or in the presence of a student's counselor or parent.

The athletic director testified at the board hearing that he had discussed the meaning of this requirement with Cullinan, and Cullinan understood what it meant, i.e., that he must not have one-on-one meetings with his student-athletes. The board credited this evidence and rejected Cullinan's version of the matter, based on his demeanor at the hearing. Additionally, the board credited Thompson's testimony that the meeting was intimidating. We give deference to the board's credibility findings. The board in its ruling stated it "specifically finds" that the December 16 event was an "acute individual correction" in violation of the July 2 directive. Even if that were not so, the board concluded, the incident "was intimidating and in violation of his earlier multiple warnings."

We need not decide whether Cullinan violated the July 2 directive. Contrary to the decision of the adjudicator and the reviewing courts, our detailed analysis of the record in this case shows that Cullinan's termination did not rise or fall on whether the December 16 hallway incident violated the July 2 directive. Whether or not the December 16 incident was alone sufficient to constitute just cause, it was certainly enough to trigger the termination proceeding and open the door to the board's consideration of Cullinan's failure to remediate the problems that have followed him throughout his career in the Ames district.

Next, Cullinan attacks the board's reliance on the parents' complaints contained in the "*Parents v. Cullinan*" packet. Cullinan argues these complaints lack merit because they are based on their sons' lack of playing time. He characterized the complaints as a parents' "conspiracy." The board rejected this argument, concluding that the parents' complaints about playing time, while considered, did not affect the termination decision. We agree with the board. First, Alex Thompson's complaint, which triggered the termination process, had nothing to do with playing time. Thompson was, in fact, a starter on the basketball team and a college recruit. Further, an examination of the parents' complaint letters reveal that, while playing time was mentioned, their primary complaint involved Cullinan's demeanor toward students and the damage it was doing to the basketball program. Also, some of the letters were from parents whose sons had already graduated and were therefore not concerned with playing time. The parents of one former player stated:

> Kyle's experience on the Ames High basketball team remains perhaps the darkest point in his life and one which he finds difficult to talk about. The most significant thing he took away from it was a vow never to be put down again.
>
>   . . . .

Other letters from parents of former players expressed the same complaints: intimidation, derogatory treatment, and profanity. Tim Taylor, the assistant superintendent and personnel director, testified that most of the parents' concerns reflect[ ] upon such things as intimidation, the use of profanity, effects upon student athletes' self-esteem, lack of team building and that there were concerns that the program was on shaky ground because kids were not having fun and not interested in coming out for basketball.

In response to the question of whether it was a playing-time issue, Taylor replied, "not at all." The superintendent pointed out that Cullinan's failure to remediate the problems the administration had notified him of presented a significant concern. . . . .

Further, the superintendent emphasized that the students themselves took the highly unusual step of meeting with the athletic director to express their concerns about a lack of excitement on the part of the players, which was attributed to Cullinan's coaching. This was the consensus of the administration's concerns expressed by two athletic directors, the principal, the assistant superintendent, and the superintendent. Clearly, the over-riding concern of the parents and the administration was not playing time, but rather "what was happening to our students."

. . .

When we consider the entire record, we conclude the superintendent established just cause by a preponderance of the competent evidence.

The adjudicator (but not the reviewing courts) also reversed the board's order on the ground it was "unreasonable and a clearly unwarrant-ed exercise of discretion." Because we have concluded that the termination was proper on just-cause grounds, it follows that the decision was not invalid as unreasonable or an abuse of the board's discretion.

We vacate the decision of the court of appeals, reverse the judgment of the district court, and remand for a district court order affirming the decision of the board.

DECISION OF COURT OF APPEALS VACATED; JUDGMENT OF DISTRICT COURT REVERSED; CASE REMANDED.

NOTES

1. Should supplemental positions such as serving as a coach be eligible for tenure?

2. Suppose that coaching was part of the teacher's regular assignment. Would this have been a legally significant difference?

3. Is it appropriate to rely on hearsay in administrative hearings incident to dismissals?

[CASE NO. 69]   RIGHT OF A TEACHER TO REFUSE TO ACCEPT A STUDENT

HATTON v. WICKS

United States Court of Appeals, Fifth Circuit, 1984.
744 F.2d 501 [20 Educ. L. Rep. 400].

■ JERRE S. WILLIAMS, CIRCUIT JUDGE.

This is an unusual case in which an established sixth grade teacher, under contract and who had taught sixth grade at the same school for ten years, was discharged for refusing to accept into her class a thirteen year old "disciplinary problem student" who chose her as his teacher in what the discharged teacher calls a "lineup" of the available teachers. The use of the word "lineup" to describe what actually occurred is, to some extent at least, a stigmatizing overstatement. Appellant Ethel Hatton was an estab-lished and qualified school teacher under contract to teach in the Columbus Municipal Separate School District, Columbus, Mississippi. She was called into the office of the principal of her school, appellee Marshall Wicks, together with two other available sixth grade teachers. Also present in the office was the thirteen year old male student and that student's mother. The principal asked the student which of the three teachers he would like to have as his sixth grade teacher, and he chose the appellant. The principal then stated that it was settled and the student would be in appellant's class. When the mother presented the thirteen year old boy for enrollment in appellant's class the next Monday, appellant refused to enroll him.

In the afternoon of the same day, appellant was summoned to appellee's office for a conference. When appellee told her at the conference that she was under an obligation to accept the student in her class, she indicated she would not do so and walked out of the meeting without further discussion.

Appellee later wrote her a letter granting her a conference with him, setting a date ten days later. She failed to appear at this conference. In the meantime the child had been assigned to another teacher.

Appellant was discharged for these two instances of what the principal and other school authorities call "insubordination." She was afforded hearings before the Superintendent of Schools, and the entire School Board, and then a review by the Department of Education of the State of Mississippi. All three of these tribunals upheld her discharge.

Five years later appellant brought this suit in the United States District Court under 42 U.S.C.[A.] § 1983 claiming substantive due process of law violations on the ground that the public school authorities did not have the constitutional right under the Fourteenth Amendment to discharge her under the facts outlined above. After a full trial, the district court held that there had been no constitutional violation in her discharge. We affirm.

There is no procedural due process of law challenge in this case. Appellant does not challenge the adequacy of the administrative hearings which she was given in accordance with Mississippi law. She challenges only the result of those hearings which upheld her discharge.

Appellant raises the question of whether there was "substantial evidence" in the administrative proceedings and in the district court to establish the existence of a constitutional due process violation. The issue is not one of "substantial evidence", however. The critical and controlling facts in this case are not in dispute at all. They are as reported above. The sole question which is before us, then, is whether the existence of these facts and these events constitutes a violation of appellant Hatton's civil rights under the due process of law clause of the Fourteenth Amendment. That question obviously is a question of law, a question of the interpretation and application of the Constitution. As such we are not bound to a clearly erroneous standard of review of the findings and conclusions of the district court.

No issue was raised concerning the motive for appellant's discharge. The finding, not disputed, is that appellant was discharged for insubordination for twice failing to accept the pupil in her class when ordered to do so by the principal. Thus we do not have the typical mixed motive case so we need not inquire whether or not she would have been discharged absent these circumstances. Neither party challenges the finding of the district court that the discharge was for the overt circumstances shown in this case.

Appellant takes the position that she could not be fired for "insubordination" because under Mississippi law insubordination requires "a constant or continuing intentional refusal to obey a direct or implied order, reasonable in nature and given by or with proper authority." Whether or not her actions constituted insubordination under the Mississippi law does not control this case. Mississippi cannot by defining "insubordination" or other grounds for discharge of teachers create or eliminate federal constitutional rights. The federal rights are independent of the state law. It is not amiss, however, to point out that her two refusals to accept this pupil into her class may constitute insubordination under the Mississippi definition.

Whether or not appellant was insubordinate under Mississippi law, the issue before this Court is whether she has established that her discharge under the admitted facts and circumstances of this case constituted a violation of her substantive due process right under the Fourteenth Amendment. The district court concluded that she had not established a violation of such a constitutional right, and we agree.

The action of the principal may have been somewhat unusual in giving this particular pupil the opportunity to choose which teacher he wished to have in the sixth grade. It should be pointed out, however, that such choice was under the supervision of the principal, who had ruled out two other teachers who otherwise would have been available because their classes were housed in temporary buildings outside the main school building, and the principal felt that this particular pupil might create less problems if he remained in the main school building. Further, while no one disputes appellant's claim that this particular pupil was a "disciplinary problem," he did not constitute such a serious problem that he could not attend regular school classes with other students. After appellant's refusal to accept this student, the student was assigned to another sixth grade class as a regular pupil in that class. Finally, the record reveals that the pupil had rational and sensible reasons for choosing the class of this particular teacher rather than the other two sixth grade teachers who accompanied appellant to the principal's office.

The record reveals that this particular student was being given an opportunity that students generally did not have. But we cannot quarrel with a conclusion of a school administrator that treating a particular student with such care might be to the advantage not only of the pupil but also of the other students in the school as well.

This discussion of the circumstances yields the constitutional answer. This Court would be intruding in the details of the administration of the school if it found a constitutional violation in this case. Appellant was not placed in a lineup. She and two other teachers were simply brought into the principal's room to enable this pupil to decide which class he wanted to go into for the sixth grade. The principal then directed that his choice be implemented, and appellant refused. Later when he attempted to talk to her about it again, she again refused and walked out on him. She makes no showing that she is entitled to any privilege over any other teacher who might have this pupil assigned to her or his classroom. There was not the slightest hint of racial, religious, or gender discrimination, or interference with her free speech or other personal rights. She was simply assigned a pupil for her class who had the right to be assigned to such a class. She refused the assignment twice and was discharged. It must be recognized that under these circumstances a teacher who refuses to carry out her or his obligations in this manner is "interfering with the regular operation of the schools," and is engaged in conduct which "materially and substantially impedes the operation or effectiveness of the educational program." Appellant's asserted section 1983 claim must fail.

AFFIRMED.

NOTES

1. Why do you think Hatton filed suit in federal court under section 1983 rather than state courts after losing before the state department of education?

2. Should there be any conditions under which a teacher can refuse to instruct a student? Consider the last paragraph of the opinion.

[CASE NO. 70]   TEACHER DISMISSAL–IMMORALITY

LEHTO v. BOARD OF EDUCATION OF THE CAESAR RODNEY SCHOOL DISTRICT

Supreme Court of Delaware (2008).
962 A.2d 222 [240 Educ. L. Rep. 289].

■ RIDGLEY, JUSTICE:

Appellant, Christopher Lehto, appeals from the decision of Appellee, Board of Education of the Caesar Rodney School District (the "Board"), terminating his employment as a teacher on grounds of immorality. Lehto appealed his dismissal to the Superior Court, which affirmed the decision of the Board. Lehto now appeals to this Court, arguing that there is insufficient evidence to support his dismissal. We find no merit in Lehto's appeal and affirm.

I.

Lehto was an art teacher at the Star Hill Elementary School ("Star Hill") in the Caesar Rodney School District in Camden, Delaware (the "District"), for eight years. In early 2007, Lehto became involved in a sexual relationship with a seventeen-year-old female (the "Student") who attended Polytech Senior High School in Woodside, Delaware. At the time, Lehto was thirty-four years old.

Lehto was previously the Student's teacher when she attended Star Hill. He became reacquainted with his former student in December 2006 when she began to come to the elementary school to pick up her younger sibling, who attended Star Hill at the time. The two soon began to speak on the phone and Lehto provided assistance to the Student with at least one school project.

The relationship became sexual in nature a few months later and Lehto and the Student engaged in several instances of sexual contact. On one occasion, Lehto called in sick and stayed home from work. During school hours, Lehto communicated with the Student and she came to his home during her lunch hour. They watched a movie and began to kiss, eventually moving to the floor where the Student's shirt was removed. The couple then moved to Lehto's bedroom where he fondled and licked the Student's breasts. They also engaged in "grinding", or simulated sexual intercourse, but the episode ended without Lehto and the student engaging in actual sexual intercourse.

Several other occasions of sexual contact occurred in a Wal–Mart parking lot after Lehto and the Student met for lunch. During these trysts, Lehto and the Student kissed and [he initiated inappropriate intimate touching].

Eventually, the Student told a friend about her relationship with Lehto and that friend told her parent, who informed the Delaware State Police. Lehto was charged with fourth degree rape based on the Student's age and his position as a person "in a position of trust, authority or supervision" over her. However, a *nolle prosequi* was entered on the charge on June 14, 2007 for lack of prosecutive merit.

On July 2, 2007, the Board notified Lehto of its intention to terminate his services as a teacher because of immorality and/or misconduct in office. At a hearing held on August 15, 2007, the District presented evidence through Detective Kevin McKay of the Delaware State Police, who had conducted the investigation of Lehto. Detective McKay had interviewed Lehto and the Student, both of whom detailed the numerous instances of sexual contact described above. In an effort to show that the relationship had not affected his job performance, Lehto presented evidence of his teaching evaluations, all of which had been positive. Lehto also presented proof that the State dismissed the rape charge initially filed against him.

On August 27, 2007, the Board issued its written decision terminating Lehto. The Board found that there was no factual dispute that the relationship between Lehto and the Student was of a sexual nature. It concluded that Lehto's conduct in initiating and engaging in a sexual relationship with a minor constituted immorality, violated the common mores of society, and provided just cause for his termination. The Board noted: "Such conduct certainly interferes with Mr. Lehto's important function of serving as a role model to the students in his school, and threatens the moral and social orientation of such students." The Board based its finding of immorality on the fact that the relationship "sends the wrong message to students of the District regarding appropriate relationships between teachers and students" and that "the referenced relationship evinces a serious lack of judgment that is far below the standard of such judgment acceptable for teachers employed by the Caesar Rodney School District."

Lehto appealed to the Superior Court, arguing that there was no substantial evidence in the record or any legal basis to support the Board's ruling. Particularly, Lehto focused on the fact that the Student did not attend a school within the District, that he did not engage in criminal activity, and that the affair had no impact on his professional duties. The Superior Court acknowledged that "[t]he definition of immorality does not lend itself to methodical application," and found that the Board's determination that Lehto could no longer serve as an effective role model to the students in his school because of his conduct was supported by substantial evidence. The Superior Court affirmed the Board's decision and this appeal followed.

II.

When reviewing an appeal from a decision of a board of education, we apply the substantial evidence review standard. "Substantial evidence has been defined as 'such relevant evidence as a reasonable mind might accept as adequate to support a conclusion.' " "If there was presented substantial and credible evidence to support the charges and a fair administrative hearing was had, the Superior Court cannot substitute its judgment for the judgment of the school authorities."

Immorality requires a nexus with fitness to teach

The Board terminated Lehto because of "immorality" pursuant to 14 *Del. C.* § 1411, which provides:

> Termination at the end of the school year shall be for 1 or more of the following reasons: Immorality, misconduct in office, incompetency, disloyalty, neglect of duty, willful [sic] and persistent insubordination, a reduction in the number of teachers required as a result of decreased enrollment or a decrease in education services. The board shall have power to suspend any teacher pending a hearing if the situation warrants such action.

Immorality is not defined in this statute, or anywhere else in 14 *Del. C.* ch. 14; however, in *Skripchuk v. Austin,* the Superior Court addressed the meaning of "immorality" as follows:

> Although there might be disagreement about the meaning of 'immorality' in some cases, by the very nature of the term, which refers to the common mores of society, one would expect broad agreement in most cases. Moreover, *the term will be construed in the context in which it appears in this chapter to refer to such immorality as may reasonably be found to impair the teacher's effectiveness by reason of his unfitness or otherwise.*

We adopt this definition for purposes of Section 1411.

Consistent with *Skripchuk,* a majority of courts have required that "a nexus exist between the off-duty conduct and a teacher's duties before allowing termination of the teacher based on immorality." An early decision in this area was *Morrison v. State Board of Education,* in which California's State Board of Education, acting pursuant to a state statute, revoked a teacher's "life diplomas" because he had engaged in "immoral conduct." The California Supreme Court ruled that the statute upon which the revocation was based was not unconstitutionally vague, but only to the extent that its terms—including "immoral conduct"—were construed to implicate only conduct that impacts the fitness to teach. Since *Morrison,* numerous courts have similarly interpreted analogous statutes to require a nexus. That nexus typically focuses "on how the conduct may affect the teacher's ability to teach," which includes "the teacher's ability to maintain discipline in the classroom, the effect the act will have on the teacher's students, and the attitudes of the teacher's [students'] parents." Additionally, "off-campus acts for which a teacher is being disciplined need not be limited to teacher-student interactions, but must relate to his/her fitness as a teacher and must have an adverse effect on or within the school community." We conclude that in cases involving termination for "immorality," this nexus test strikes a proper balance under Section 1411 for school boards to apply.

The nexus was sufficient to support Lehto's termination

The record demonstrates a sufficient nexus between the undisputed sexual relationship between Lehto and the Student and Lehto's fitness to teach. Lehto argues to the contrary and cites performance reviews that predate the public disclosure of his relationship. However, this argument discounts the sexual nature of his relationship with the Student that began in the school environment, that involved a minor sibling of another minor student who attended his school, and the public controversy which followed Lehto's arrest and the disclosure of the relationship.

Many decisions have upheld the termination of a teacher because of immorality based on a teacher's affair with a student. Although this case involves a sexual relationship with a minor who is a former, but not current, student, this distinction does not make a difference. Other jurisdictions have also considered the nexus between a teacher's fitness to teach and his sexual conduct outside of the school with a non-student who is a minor. Despite the lack of a direct connection with the classroom, these jurisdictions have found a nexus based on the effect of the conduct on the teacher's position as a role model and the parents' ability to trust the safety of their children to the school.

. . .

Here, part of Lehto's job as a teacher was to serve as a role model for his students. Because a teacher's interpersonal relationships are observed by and reflected in the conduct of students, teacher-student relationships must be kept within the bounds of acceptable conduct. If proven, Lehto's sexual contact with a minor directly related to his fitness to teach other minors and impacted the school community. There was a proper nexus between his alleged off-duty conduct and his fitness to teach.

The evidence was sufficient to support the Board's decision.

Our review for substantial evidence looks only for "such relevant evidence as a reasonable mind might accept as adequate" to support the Board's conclusion. Detective McKay's testimony, based on corroborating interviews with both Lehto and the Student, detailed Lehto's sexual relationship with a seventeen-year-old former student-a relationship initiated in the school environment where the Student's younger sibling was enrolled. The community learned of this relationship. The Board could reasonably conclude that the relationship itself threatened Lehto's "important function of serving as a role model to the students in his school...." Moreover, the public disclosure of that relationship permitted the Board to infer a significant detrimental impact on the school community if Lehto continued to teach, as Lehto's actions and his continuation in his position could reasonably undermine parents' confidence in both Lehto and the District.

The record also provided substantial evidence from which the Board could conclude that Lehto's actions in pursuing and engaging in this relationship "threaten[ed] the moral and social fabric of the school environment, . . . sen[t] the wrong message to students of the District regarding appropriate relationships between teachers and students" and "evince[ed] a serious lack of judgment that is far below the standard of such judgment acceptable for teachers employed by the Caesar Rodney School District." We conclude that there was substantial evidence to support the Board's decision that Lehto's relationship with the Student constituted immorality justifying dismissal under 14 *Del. C.* § 1411.

III.

The judgment of the Superior Court is AFFIRMED.

NOTES

1.   Did the teacher here have any legitimate basis for appeal.

2.   This action was limited to the civil issue of the teacher's dismissal. Should the teacher also have faced criminal charges?

[CASE NO. 71]   TEACHER DISMISSAL–INCOMPETENCE–NEGLECT OF DUTY, USE OF CONTROVERSIAL INSTRUCTIONAL APPROACH

LACKS v. FERGUSON REORGANIZED SCHOOL DISTRICT R–2

United States Court of Appeals, Eighth Circuit, 1998.
147 F.3d 718 [127 Educ. L. Rep. 568].

■ RICHARD S. ARNOLD, CHIEF JUDGE.

In this case Ferguson–Florissant Reorganized School District ("the school board") appeals the District Court's grant of summary judgment in favor of the plaintiff, Cecilia Lacks, on Lacks's claim under Missouri law that her termination by the board was not supported by substantial evidence. The school board also appeals a jury verdict in favor of Lacks on First Amendment and race discrimination claims. We reverse and remand for the entry of judgment in favor of the defendant school district. We hold, among other things, that a school district does not violate the First Amendment when it disciplines a teacher for allowing students to use profanity repetitiously and egregiously in their written work.

Cecilia Lacks began teaching at Berkeley Senior High School in the fall of 1992 after teaching at other schools in the same school district since 1972. Lacks taught English and journalism classes, and she sponsored the school newspaper. In October 1994, Lacks divided her junior English class into small groups and directed them to write short plays, which were to be performed for the other students in the class and videotaped. The plays written by the students contained profanity, including the repeated uses of

... [vulgar language and racial slurs]. When the plays were videotaped, these words were used more than 150 times in approximately forty minutes. Lacks later admitted that the plays contained an unusual amount of profanity, and one of her witnesses later described the use of profanity in the plays as "extreme," "disgusting," "upsetting," and "embarrassing." Lacks was aware of the content of the plays before they were performed, because she had previously reviewed at least one of the scripts and had attended rehearsals of the plays the day before. On October 10, the students performed their plays and were videotaped at the direction of Lacks. Two other school district employees were also present during the videotaping of the plays: Donna Clark, a part-time teacher, and Mike Minks, an audio-visual technician. Clark and Minks eventually received letters of reprimand from the school administration for allowing the students to use profanity.

The following January, as a result of complaints by one of Lacks's students, the existence of the videotapes came to the attention of Vernon Mitchell, the principal of Berkeley High School. Mitchell initiated an inquiry into the matter, and he and two school district administrators met with Lacks and her union representative twice over the next two weeks. During the investigation, the administrators learned that as part of a poetry-writing exercise, Lacks had permitted a student to read aloud in a classroom two of his poems which contained profanity and graphic descriptions of oral sex.

Following the investigation, Dr. Robert Fritz, the district superintendent, formally charged Lacks with "willful or persistent violation of and failure to obey [the school district's] policies" under Mo. Ann. Stat. § 168.114. Fritz alleged that Lacks violated several school board policies and recommended her termination by the school board. Lacks requested a hearing, and the school board heard testimony from Lacks and fifteen other witnesses over five evenings in early March 1995. The school board also examined numerous exhibits and viewed the videotaped performances of the students' plays. At the hearing, the school board narrowed its earlier allegations to one charge: violation of board policy 3043, which requires teachers to enforce the section of the Student Discipline Code which prohibits profanity. On March 23, the board issued a decision which found that Lacks was aware of the school board's policy preventing profanity, that she could have chosen teaching methods which prohibited profanity, and that her failure to do so constituted a "willful and persistent practice violative of Board policy to a degree that cannot be ... tolerated." Based on its findings, the school board terminated Lacks's teaching contract.

In May 1995, Lacks brought suit in a Missouri state court, seeking judicial review of the school board's decision under Mo. Ann. Stat. § 168.120. She also alleged that the school board violated her due process rights under the United States and Missouri Constitutions, violated her rights under the First Amendment and 42 U.S.C.[A.] § 1983, and discriminated against her on the basis of race in violation of Missouri law and Title VII of the federal Civil Rights Act. The school board removed the entire case to the District.... [which] granted the school board's motion to dismiss Lacks's due process claims for failure to state a claim upon which relief could be granted, but it denied the school board's motion to dismiss Lacks's First Amendment claim. The District Court also entered partial summary judgment in favor of Lacks on her claim for review of the school board's termination of her teaching contract. In its order, the District Court held that Lacks did not willfully violate board policy 3043, because she believed that profanity was permitted in the context of creative expression in the classroom. Accordingly, the District Court awarded Lacks reinstatement with back pay, attorneys' fees, and costs.

The parties proceeded to trial in November 1996 on Lacks's First Amendment and race discrimination claims. The school board moved for judgment as a matter of law at the close of Lacks's case and its own case, and the District Court denied the motion both times. The District Court submitted the case to the jury, which returned a verdict in favor of Lacks for $500,000 on the First Amendment claim and $250,000 on the race discrimination claim. The school board now appeals.

II

We can easily dispose of the school board's argument that the District Court improperly allowed the board to remove the case because it lacked jurisdiction to review the school board's decision ... we hold that the District Court properly allowed the school board to remove this case.

III

A

Under Missouri law, when a school board terminates a contract with a teacher under Mo. Ann. Stat. § 168.114, including termination for the willful or persistent violation of a school board regulation, the teacher may appeal the school board's decision to a state circuit court and seek judicial review of the school board's decision. The court must affirm the decision of the school board unless the decision (1) violates a constitutional provision; (2) is made in excess of statutory authority or jurisdiction; (3) is unsupported by "competent and substantial evidence upon the whole record"; (4) is made for any other reason unauthorized by law; (5) is made upon unlawful procedure or without a fair trial; (6) is arbitrary, capricious or unreasonable; or (7) involves an abuse of discretion. This scope of review is limited. The reviewing court must affirm the school board if the board "reasonably could have reached the decision it did." The court may not substitute its judgment of the evidence for that of the school board, and it must consider all evidence in the light most favorable to the decision of the board. The determination of the credibility of the witnesses is a function of the school board, not the reviewing court.

The District Court granted summary judgment in favor of Lacks because it found insufficient evidence in the record that Lacks "willfully or persistently" violated board policy 3043. The parties agree with the District Court that proof of "willful or persistent" violation is twofold: The school board must prove both an intent to act and an intent to violate or disobey a particular regulation. In other words, in order to prevail the school board must prove that Lacks violated the board policy prohibiting profanity, and that she knew that the board policy applied to the profanity used by her students. After a careful review of the evidence, we hold that the record contains sufficient evidence for the school board to have concluded that Lacks willfully violated board policy.

Lacks admitted that she allowed students to use profanity in the classroom in the context of performing the plays they had written and reading aloud the poems they had composed. At the hearing, and in her brief, Lacks defended this practice by arguing that she thought that the board's policy on profanity applied only to "student behavior" and not to students' creative assignments. She also argued that her teaching method, which she describes as the "student-centered method" and which she explained at length at the hearing, required her to allow her students creative freedom, which included the use of profanity. Lacks could not say with certainty that she would be able to teach at Berkeley High School if her students were not given the freedom to use profanity in their creative activities. As evidence that Lacks believed that the anti-profanity policy did not apply to students' creative assignments, the District Court noted that testimony at the hearing indicated some confusion within the school district as to whether reading aloud literature which contained profanity might violate the school board's prohibition on profanity. For example, Larilyn Lawrence, a curriculum coordinator for language arts at the school district, believed that a videotaped production of a play with students using profanity could fall within acceptable course parameters. On the other hand, Barbara Davis, the assistant superintendent for curriculum instruction, testified that teachers in the school district should not allow students to read aloud profanity contained in literary works.

The school board also heard testimony from Lacks's principal, Vernon Mitchell, that he told Lacks that profanity was not permitted in the school newspaper. Mitchell testified that he specifically spoke to Lacks in 1993 about profanity in the school newspaper, and told her that use of profanity in the newspaper was not allowed. Mitchell said that he had reviewed a draft of the newspaper and was concerned that the students were including profanity in the paper by writing "S blank blank T" and "F blank blank K" rather than writing every letter of the profane words. Mitchell testified that he discussed the use of profanity in the newspaper with Lacks "[t]wo or three times." Mitchell also noted that signs posted in Lacks's classroom read "No Profanity." When the board issued its opinion terminating Lacks's contract, it based its decision in part on its finding that Lacks had been warned about the use of profanity by Mitchell.

Lacks claimed that Mitchell never warned her about the use of profanity in the newspaper. However, under Missouri law, assessing the credibility of witnesses is the function of the school board, not the reviewing court. Because the school board heard testimony that Lacks was directly warned by the principal in her school that including "S blank blank T" and "F blank blank K" in the student newspaper violated the school board's profanity policy, the board could have reasonably found that Lacks knew that profanity was not allowed in students' creative activities. While Lacks did produce some evidence that confusion existed in the school district as to the profanity policy, and while she denied that she had been warned about it, we must read the record in the light most favorable to the school board's decision, together with all reasonable inferences.

The policy prohibiting profanity was explicit and contained no exceptions. It was not ambiguous. The board was free to find that Mitchell gave Lacks an express and particularized direction about the student newspaper. We think it was not unreasonable for the board to treat student writing for the newspaper and student writing for the class as alike. Isolated instances of profanity had been overlooked or tolerated in the past, but what went on in Lacks's classroom went far beyond the reading aloud of a novel containing the occasional "damn." The board might have chosen a lesser form of discipline, especially in view of Lacks's long and devoted service. It was not required to do so by law. We hold that the board's decision was reasonable and supported by substantial evidence on the record as a whole. The judgment in the plaintiff's favor on this claim must be reversed.

B

When the jury returned a verdict in favor of Lacks on her First Amendment claim, it provided answers to two interrogatories posed by the District Court's instructions. Under the District Court's instructions, answering "no" to either of the interrogatories allowed Lacks to prevail on the First Amendment claim. With respect to the first interrogatory—"Did [Lacks] have reasonable notice that allowing students to use profanity in their creative writing was prohibited?"—the jury answered "no." With respect to the second interrogatory—"Did defendant school district have a legitimate academic interest in prohibiting profanity by students in their creative writing, regardless of any other competing interests?"—the jury also answered "no." District Court subsequently entered judgment in favor of Lacks with respect to her First Amendment claim. We reverse and hold, as a matter of law, that the answer to both of those questions was "yes."

Lacks argued at trial and on appeal that she was acting as a facilitator for her students' speech, and that, under First Amendment law, she cannot be punished for not prohibiting her students' use of profanity unless she was provided with reasonable notice that profanity was prohibited in students' creative exercises, and unless the prohibition on profanity in creative activity served a legitimate academic interest. At least one court has held that, under the First Amendment, a school district must provide a teacher with notice as to what types of expression are prohibited in a classroom before it holds the teacher responsible for failing to limit that type of expression. We are satisfied that Lacks was provided with enough notice by the school board that profanity was not to be allowed in her classroom, whether in the context of a creative exercise or not. Lacks testified at trial that she understood that, under her contract with the school district, she was required to enforce the Student Discipline Code, and she testified that she was familiar with the rules and policies of the school board. The Student Discipline Code clearly prohibits profanity and obscene gestures, and it contains no exception for creative activities. Moreover, Lacks's principal, Vernon Mitchell, testified at trial, as he did at the school board hearing, that he informed Lacks that the use of profanity by the students was not permitted in the student newspaper, one form of creative activity. Mitchell told Lacks: "There is no way I would allow profanity in the newspaper."

In fact, Lacks received more notice than has been required in other cases. In *Bethel School District No. 403 v. Fraser*, a student was disciplined for using sexually suggestive language in a speech before a high school assembly. Before the student gave the speech, he told some of his teachers what he was going to say, and he was told that the speech was "inappropriate and that he probably should not deliver it" and that giving the speech could have "severe consequences." The Court rejected the student's argument that his due process rights had been violated because he had not received sufficient notice that delivery of the speech would result in discipline: "Given the school's need to be able to impose disciplinary sanctions for a wide range of unanticipated conduct disruptive of the educational process, the school disciplinary rules need not be as detailed as a criminal code which imposes criminal sanctions." In the present case, not only did Lacks admit that she was familiar with the school district's disciplinary rules and understood her obligation to enforce them, her principal also testified that he told her that the rules applied to one form of student creative activity. Therefore, as a matter of law, Lacks had sufficient notice that under the board's rules, she was not to permit profanity in her classroom. Perhaps the jury did not believe the principal's testimony about the warning he gave Lacks. Even so, the policy against profanity was explicit. Lacks well knew what the plays were like before she allowed the students to perform them. In acting as she did, she took the risk that the board would enforce the policy as written. Under the circumstances, the notice given was fair and constitutionally sufficient.

We also hold, as a matter of law, that the school board had a legitimate academic interest in prohibiting profanity by students in their creative writing. The Supreme Court has written that public education " 'must inculcate the habits and manner of civility as values in themselves conducive to happiness and as indispensable to the practice of self-government in the community and the nation.' " "While students in public schools do not 'shed their constitutional rights to freedom of speech or expression at the schoolhouse gate,' students' First Amendment rights "in schools and classrooms must be balanced against the society's countervailing interest in teaching students the boundaries of socially appropriate behavior." Accordingly, the Supreme Court has held that "educators do not offend the First Amendment by exercising editorial control over the style and content of student speech in school-sponsored expressive activities so long as their actions are reasonably related to legitimate pedagogical concerns."

A flat prohibition on profanity in the classroom is reasonably related to the legitimate pedagogical concern of promoting generally acceptable social standards. The Supreme Court has told us that "schools must teach by example the shared values of a civilized social order." The school board itself, in its opinion terminating Lacks's employment with the school district, wrote that the purpose of the board's disciplinary policies is "to establish, to foster, and to reflect the norms and standards of the community it serves." Allowing one student to call another a [profanity] and a [prostitute] in front of the rest of the class, and allowing a student to read aloud a poem that describes sexual encounters in the most graphic detail, as the students did in Lacks's classroom, hardly promotes these shared social standards. We consider the matter too plain for argument.

As a matter of law, the school board had the right to establish and require the enforcement of a rule which prohibits classroom profanity in any context, and it provided Lacks with enough notice of its disciplinary policies. Therefore, the judgment in the plaintiff's favor on her First Amendment claim is reversed.

C

At trial, Lacks set out to prove her race discrimination case by "direct" evidence of discrimination under *Price Waterhouse v. Hopkins* rather than the indirect, burden-shifting method of *McDonnell Douglas Corp. v. Green*. The jury found that Lacks had proved by a preponderance of the evidence that race was a motivating factor in the school board's decision to terminate her, and that the school board did not prove by a preponderance of the evidence that it would have discharged Lacks regardless of her race. We reverse, and hold as a matter of law that race was not a motivating factor in the school board's decision to terminate Lacks. In reaching that conclusion, we are mindful that the evidence must be viewed in the light most favorable to the jury's verdict, and that all reasonable inferences in support of the verdict must be allowed.

. . . .

. . . Because Lacks has produced insufficient evidence that the school board's decision to terminate her was motivated by race, the judgment in Lacks's favor on her race discrimination claims cannot stand. On this record, the inference that the school board acted because of Lacks's race is wholly unreasonable. In our view, the extreme nature of the language used and the exhaustive hearing given Lacks by the board leave no room for anyone reasonably to conclude that Lacks was disciplined because of her race.

The judgment of the District Court is reversed, and the cause remanded with directions to dismiss the complaint with prejudice.

It is so ordered.

NOTES

1. Given the teacher's years of experience, was the penalty of dismissal too harsh?

2. For a similar result, *see Boring v. Buncombe County Bd. of Educ.*, 136 F.3d 364 [124 Educ. L. Rep. 56] (4th Cir.1998), *cert. denied*, 525 U.S. 813, 119 S.Ct. 47, 142 L.Ed.2d 36 (1998), wherein the Fourth Circuit upheld the transfer of an award-winning drama coach and teacher in North Carolina for directing a controversial play that some members of the community found objectionable.

3. The Eighth Circuit resolved another employment case arguably involving academic freedom in *Cowan v. Strafford R–VI School Dist.*, 140 F.3d 1153 [125 Educ. L. Rep. 613] (8th Cir.1998). The court affirmed an award of damages, but not reinstatement, in favor of a second-grade teacher whose contract was not renewed

where a board acted on its fear of the encroachment of New Ageism, when she presented each member of her second grade class with a "magic rock" and a letter telling them that it would help them in whatever they did. What do you think about this case?

[CASE NO. 72]   TEACHER DISMISSAL–EVALUATION PROCEDURES

ROBERTS v. HOUSTON INDEPENDENT SCHOOL DISTRICT

Court of Appeals of Texas, 1990.
788 S.W.2d 107 [60 Educ. L. Rep. 251].

■ EVANS, CHIEF JUSTICE.

This is an appeal from a judgment upholding a school district's administrative decision to terminate appellant's employment for inefficiency or incompetency in the performance of duties. The cause was submitted to the trial court on an agreed stipulation of facts and exhibits, and on appeal, only a question of law is presented for review.

The stipulation of facts shows that appellant, Verna Roberts, had a continuing teacher's contract with the Houston Independent School District (school district). On numerous occasions during school years 1982–1983 and 1983–1984, the school district's assessment team, composed of an associate superintendent and an instructional supervisor, evaluated appellant's teaching performance. These evaluations included both written assessments and videotaping of appellant's classroom performance. The evaluation team used videotapes so that the teacher could more easily follow and understand the evaluation team's observations and criticisms. Appellant objected to the use of videotaping in her classroom.

Both the written evaluations and videotapes revealed problems with appellant's teaching performance. Appellant was told of these problems, but according to the assessment team, she did not correct or improve her performance. Based on appellant's classroom performance, the assessment team recommended that the school district terminate her employment at the end of the 1983–84 school year. (Appellant's contract allowed for termination for inefficiency or incompetence in the performance of duties.) The deputy superintendent accepted this recommendation and, in turn, recommended termination to the general superintendent. The deputy superintendent and three members of the assessment team met with appellant and notified her of the recommendation and the reason for their recommendation. On March 9, 1984, the board of education authorized the general superintendent to notify appellant that it had proposed her employment be terminated at the end of the 1983–84 school year ...

Appellant then notified the school district of her desire to contest the proposed termination and asked for a public hearing, which was scheduled for June 2, 1984. About 45 days before the hearing, appellant and her attorney were notified of the date, time, place, and procedures to be used at the termination proceedings. Appellant and her attorney were later given a witness list, a description of the testimony to be provided at the hearing, and a copy of the exhibits to be used. Appellant was not, however, given a copy of the videotape exhibits. Appellant asked for copies of all videotapes made of her classroom performance, but the school district refused. The school district did make the tapes available for appellant's review and inspection at its administrative offices.

On June 2, 1984, the school board heard testimony from appellant's supervisors, and it reviewed approximately 100 documents offered as evidence of appellant's classroom performance. The school board also viewed a 30–minute videotape, which included excerpts from the five separate videotapes made of appellant's classroom performance. The five tapes were all used by the assessment team in its evaluation of appellant's classroom performance.

Appellant chose not to testify at the hearing, and she did not present any witnesses or evidence on her own behalf. She limited her presentation to the cross-examination of appellee's witnesses. The hearing lasted approximately six hours, and at the end of the hearing, the school board voted unanimously to terminate appellant's employment at the end of the 1983–84 school year.

In her first point of error, appellant claims the trial court's judgment is flawed, as a matter of law, because she was denied both procedural and substantive due process in the termination proceedings.

I. Procedural Due Process

Appellant, as the holder of a continuing contract with the school district, possessed a property interest in her continued employment. The state may not deprive a person of a property interest without due process of law. At the very least, the law requires that a public employee with a protected right in continued employment be given notice and an opportunity to reply prior to termination.

The record reflects that appellant did receive notice and had an opportunity to respond before the termination of her employment.

On February 29, 1984, the deputy superintendent and members of the assessment team met with appellant, and explained their recommendation that the school district terminate her employment at the end of the 1983–84 school year. On March 12, 1984, the general superintendent wrote to appellant, notifying her of the proposed termination of her employment. In that letter, the general superintendent discussed the sections of appellant's contract upon which the school district was basing the proposed termination, and he enumerated specific complaints about her teaching performance. The superintendent stated that appellant had 10 days after receipt of the letter to notify him of her desire to contest the proposed termination, and that she could obtain copies of the evaluation reports and memoranda "touching or concerning" her "fitness or conduct as a teacher."

Appellant also received notice of the time, date, and place of the termination hearing. The school district notified appellant of the witnesses and testimony it would be offering, and gave appellant an opportunity to cross-examine each school district witness and produce evidence on her own behalf.

Appellant's principal contention is that she did not have notice of the contents of the edited videotape. We reject this contention. Appellant was told she could view the unedited videotapes at the school district's offices during regular business hours at any time between May 17, 1984, and June 2, 1984. This was about 10 days before the hearing. Appellant had also previously reviewed the tapes with the members of her assessment team after each evaluation. Although appellant was not given an opportunity, before the hearing, to view the composite tape that had been edited from the five evaluation tapes, she was given ample opportunity to view the five videotapes from which the composite was made. She simply chose not to do so.

II.   Substantive Due Process

Appellant argues that the administrative hearing, which resulted in her termination, violated her right of due process because "of the nature of the evidence presented and the resulting inability of (appellant) to defend against the evidence as presented."

In evaluating a substantive due process claim, based on allegedly arbitrary state action in academic matters, a reviewing court must ascertain whether the state's action was "such a substantial departure from accepted academic norms as to demonstrate that the person or committee responsible did not actually exercise professional judgment." In a suit challenging an academic dismissal, the reviewing court must determine from the record whether there was "some rational academic basis for the decision." If there was a rational academic basis for the decision, the court may not override the state's action, even though the evidence may indicate such action was arbitrarily made.

Here, the school board listened to six hours of testimony and other evidence before deciding to terminate appellant's employment. The board reviewed appellant's teaching evaluations, listened to testimony of appellant's supervisors, and viewed a 30-minute composite videotape of appellant's teaching. Appellant was represented by her attorney during the hearing, she was given an opportunity to testify and to present witnesses on her own behalf, and she was allowed to cross-examine the witnesses called by the school district. Appellant could have even shown portions of the unedited videotapes, had she chosen to do so.

We conclude that the school board did not act arbitrarily or deviate from accepted academic norms in reaching its judgment to terminate appellant's employment.

Appellant further complains that the board saw the composite videotape without any showing that the tape was authentic, and that the tape was not made available to her for copying before the hearing.

Although an administrative proceeding must meet minimum requirements of due process, strict rules applicable to courts of law do not apply to such proceedings. In the absence of some showing that the school district acted arbitrarily in considering the composite videotape, or that the videotape falsely or inaccurately presented appellant's teaching performance, we can only conclude that the administrative proceedings complied with applicable substantive due process requirements.

We overrule appellant's first point of error.

In her second point of error, appellant contends that the trial court erred in granting a judgment for the school district because the termination proceedings violated her right of privacy. Under this point, appellant argues that she had an expectation of privacy in her classroom to be free from intrusion by videotaping, and that by videotaping her performance, over her objection, the school district violated her right of privacy as well as its own policy....

Appellant has not cited any authority, and we have found none, relating to her claim of "involuntary videotaping" of her performance as a teacher. Based on the record before us, we conclude that appellant has not demonstrated that she had a "reasonable expectation of privacy" in her public classroom. The record shows that appellant was videotaped in a public classroom, in full view of her students, faculty members, and administrators. At no point, did the school district attempt to record appellant's private affairs.

The activity of teaching in a public classroom does not fall within the expected zone of privacy. To fall within the "zone of privacy," the activity must be one about which the individual possesses a reasonable expectation of privacy in the activity.

The right of privacy has been defined as the right of an individual to be left alone, to live a life of seclusion, to be free from unwarranted publicity. There is no invasion of the right of privacy when one's movements are exposed to public views generally.

The second point of error is overruled.

Appellant contends, in her third point of error, that the school district violated its own policy against involuntary videotaping. Under this point, she refers to the school district's Administrative Procedure Guide, section 572.720, which provides:

No mechanical or electronic device shall be utilized to listen to or record the procedures unless requested or permitted by the teacher.

The school district responds to this argument by suggesting that a newer administrative procedure manual has repealed section 572.720, and that the new manual provides:

The Teacher Quality Assurance Program was adopted by the Board of Education on October 7, 1982, and amended on August 4, 1983. The adoption and amendment supercede all prior policies and procedures on teacher evaluation in effect and will repeal and replace any policies or procedures in conflict....

If videotaping is used ..., the principal is to make arrangements for the videotaping. The taping session period should be a minimum of one hour/class session with the teacher. Videotaping can provide the teacher with an opportunity to see herself as the assessment team does.

Appellant contends these two sections are not in conflict, and that the section first quoted effectively prohibits videotaping "unless requested or permitted by the teacher."

We agree with the school district's interpretation of its own administrative procedures. The language in the new section expressly authorizes the principal to make arrangements for videotaping, and the quoted section does not require that the teacher must request or give consent to the videotaping. We accordingly conclude that the videotaping of appellant did not violate any of the school district's policies or procedures.

The third point of error is overruled.

The judgment of the trial court is affirmed.

NOTES

1. Note that the teacher did not take advantage of the opportunity to again view the videotapes before the hearing. Further, she did not testify at the hearing or present witnesses or evidence on her behalf.

2. Is the use of videotaping classes a sound tool for evaluating teacher performance?

[CASE NO. 73]   TEACHER FREE SPEECH—LETTER WRITING

PICKERING v. BOARD OF EDUCATION OF TOWNSHIP HIGH SCHOOL DISTRICT 205

Supreme Court of the United States, 1968.
391 U.S. 563, 88 S.Ct. 1731, 20 L.Ed.2d 811.

■ Mr. Justice Marshall delivered the opinion of the Court.

Appellant Marvin L. Pickering, a teacher in Township High School District 205, Will County, Illinois, was dismissed from his position by the appellee Board of Education for sending a letter to a local newspaper in connection with a recently proposed tax increase that was critical of the way in which the Board and the district superintendent of schools had handled past proposals to raise new revenue for the schools. Appellant's dismissal resulted from a determination by the Board, after a full hearing, that the publication of the letter was "detrimental to the efficient operation and administration of the schools of the district" and hence, under the relevant Illinois statute, that "interests of the schools require[d] [his dismissal]." . . .

The letter constituted, basically, an attack on the school board's handling of the 1961 bond issue proposals and its subsequent allocation of financial resources between the schools' educational and athletic programs. It also charged the superintendent of schools with attempting to prevent teachers in the district from opposing or criticizing the proposed bond issue.

The Board dismissed Pickering for writing and publishing the letter. Pursuant to Illinois law, the Board was then required to hold a hearing on the dismissal. At the hearing the Board charged that numerous statements in the letter were false and that the publication of the statements unjustifiably impugned the "motives, honesty, integrity, truthfulness, responsibility and competence" of both the Board and the school administration. The

Board also charged that the false statements damaged the professional reputations of its members and of the school administrators, would be disruptive of faculty discipline, and would tend to foment "controversy, conflict and dissension" among teachers, administrators, the Board of Education, and the residents of the district. . . .

To the extent that the Illinois Supreme Court's opinion may be read to suggest that teachers may constitutionally be compelled to relinquish the First Amendment rights they would otherwise enjoy as citizens to comment on matters of public interest in connection with the operation of the public schools in which they work, it proceeds on a premise that has been unequivocally rejected in numerous prior decisions of this Court. . . . At the same time it cannot be gainsaid that the State has interests as an employer in regulating the speech of its employees that differ significantly from those it possesses in connection with regulation of the speech of the citizenry in general. The problem in any case is to arrive at a balance between the interests of the teacher, as a citizen, in commenting upon matters of public concern and the interest of the State, as an employer, in promoting the efficiency of the public services it performs through its employees.

. . . Because of the enormous variety of fact situations in which critical statements by teachers and other public employees may be thought by their superiors, against whom the statements are directed, to furnish grounds for dismissal, we do not deem it either appropriate or feasible to attempt to lay down a general standard against which all such statements may be judged. However, in the course of evaluating the conflicting claims of First Amendment protection and the need for orderly school administration in the context of this case, we shall indicate some of the general lines along which an analysis of the controlling interests should run.

An examination of the statements in appellant's letter objected to by the Board reveals that they, like the letter as a whole, consist essentially of criticism of the Board's allocation of school funds between educational and athletic programs, and of both the Board's and the superintendent's methods of informing, or preventing the informing of, the district's taxpayers of the real reasons why additional tax revenues were being sought for the schools. The statements are in no way directed towards any person with whom appellant would normally be in contact in the course of his daily work as a teacher. Thus no question of maintaining either discipline by immediate superiors or harmony among coworkers is presented here. Appellant's employment relationships with the Board and, to a somewhat lesser extent, with the superintendent are not the kind of close working relationships for which it can persuasively be claimed that personal loyalty and confidence are necessary to their proper functioning. . . .

We next consider the statements in appellant's letter which we agree to be false. The Board's original charges included allegations that the publication of the letter damaged the professional reputations of the Board and the superintendent and would foment controversy and conflict among the Board, teachers, administrators, and the residents of the district. However, no evidence to support these allegations was introduced at the hearing. So far as the record reveals, Pickering's letter was greeted by everyone but its main target, the Board, with massive apathy and total disbelief. The Board must, therefore, have decided, perhaps by analogy with the law of libel, that the statements were per se harmful to the operation of the schools.

However, the only way in which the Board could conclude, absent any evidence of the actual effect of the letter, that the statements contained therein were per se detrimental to the interest of the schools was to equate the Board members' own interests with that of the schools. Certainly an accusation that too much money is being spent on athletics by the administrators of the school system (which is precisely the import of that portion of appellant's letter containing the statements that we have found to be false) cannot reasonably be regarded as per se detrimental to the district's schools. Such an accusation reflects rather a difference of opinion between Pickering and the Board as to the preferable manner of operating the school system, a difference of opinion that clearly concerns an issue of general public interest.

In addition, the fact that particular illustrations of the Board's claimed undesirable emphasis on athletic programs are false would not normally have any necessary impact on the actual operation of the schools, beyond its tendency to anger the Board. For example, Pickering's letter was written after the defeat at the polls of the second proposed tax increase. It could, therefore, have had no effect on the ability of the school district to raise necessary revenue, since there was no showing that there was any proposal to increase taxes pending when the letter was written.

More importantly, the question whether a school system requires additional funds is a matter of legitimate public concern on which the judgment of the school administration, including the School Board, cannot, in a society that leaves such questions to popular vote, be taken as conclusive. On such a question free and open debate is vital to informed decision-making by the electorate. Teachers are, as a class, the members of a community most likely to have informed and definite opinions as to how funds allotted to the operation of the schools should be spent. Accordingly, it is essential that they be able to speak out freely on such questions without fear of retaliatory dismissal.

In addition, the amounts expended on athletics which Pickering reported erroneously were matters of public record on which his position as a teacher in the district did not qualify him to speak with any greater authority than any other taxpayer. The Board could easily have rebutted appellant's errors by publishing the accurate figures itself, either via a letter to the same newspaper or otherwise. We are thus not presented with a situation in which a teacher has carelessly made false statements about matters so closely related to the day-to-day operations of the schools that any harmful impact on the public would be difficult to counter because of the teacher's presumed greater access to the real facts. Accordingly, we have no occasion to consider at this time whether under such circumstances a school board could reasonably require that a teacher make substantial efforts to verify the accuracy of his charges before publishing them.

What we do have before us is a case in which a teacher has made erroneous public statements upon issues then currently the subject of public attention, which are critical of his ultimate employer but which are neither shown nor can be presumed to have in any way either impeded the teacher's proper performance of his daily duties in the classroom or to have interfered with the regular operation of the schools generally. In these circumstances we conclude that the interest of the school administration in limiting teachers' opportunities to contribute to public debate is not significantly greater than its interest in limiting a similar contribution by any member of the general public. . . .

In sum, we hold that, in a case such as this, absent proof of false statements knowingly or recklessly made by him, a teacher's exercise of his right to speak on issues of public importance may not furnish the basis for his dismissal from public employment. Since no such showing has been made in this case regarding appellant's letter, his dismissal for writing it cannot be upheld and the judgment of the Illinois Supreme Court must, accordingly, be reversed and the case remanded for further proceedings not inconsistent with this opinion. It is so ordered.

Judgment reversed and case remanded with directions.

NOTES

1.   At what point are teachers ethically free to criticize local school officials in the public press? How, if at all, do the duties of teachers differ from those of other citizens in this regard?

2.   In light of *Pickering*, the Court vacated, and remanded, judgments upholding the dismissals of teachers for criticisms of school authorities. On remand, the Court of Appeals of New York ruled in favor of a teacher, *Puentes v. Board of Educ. of Union Free School Dist. No. 21 of Town of Bethpage*, 302 N.Y.S.2d 824 (N.Y. 1969), while the Supreme Court of Alaska reinstated its original judgment, *Watts v. Seward School Bd.*, 454 P.2d 732 (Alaska 1969), *cert. denied*, 397 U.S. 921, 90 S.Ct. 899, 25 L.Ed.2d 101 (1970).

[CASE NO. 74]   LIMITS ON THE FREE SPEECH RIGHTS OF PUBLIC EMPLOYEES

GARCETTI v. CEBALLOS

Supreme Court of the United States, 2006.
547 U.S. 410, 126 S.Ct. 1951, 164 L.Ed.2d 689.

■ JUSTICE KENNEDY delivered the opinion of the Court.

It is well settled that "a State cannot condition public employment on a basis that infringes the employee's constitutionally protected interest in freedom of expression." The question presented by the instant case is whether the First Amendment protects a government employee from discipline based on speech made pursuant to the employee's official duties.

I

Respondent Richard Ceballos has been employed since 1989 as a deputy district attorney for the Los Angeles County District Attorney's

Office. During the period relevant to this case, Ceballos was a calendar deputy in the office's Pomona branch, and in this capacity he exercised certain supervisory responsibilities over other lawyers. In February 2000, a defense attorney contacted Ceballos about a pending criminal case. The defense attorney said there were inaccuracies in an affidavit used to obtain a critical search warrant. The attorney informed Ceballos that he had filed a motion to traverse, or challenge, the warrant, but he also wanted Ceballos to review the case. According to Ceballos, it was not unusual for defense attorneys to ask calendar deputies to investigate aspects of pending cases.

After examining the affidavit and visiting the location it described, Ceballos determined the affidavit contained serious misrepresentations. The affidavit called a long driveway what Ceballos thought should have been referred to as a separate roadway. Ceballos also questioned the affidavit's statement that tire tracks led from a stripped-down truck to the premises covered by the warrant. His doubts arose from his conclusion that the roadway's composition in some places made it difficult or impossible to leave visible tire tracks.

Ceballos spoke on the telephone to the warrant affiant, a deputy sheriff from the Los Angeles County Sheriff's Department, but he did not receive a satisfactory explanation for the perceived inaccuracies. He relayed his findings to his supervisors, petitioners Carol Najera and Frank Sundstedt, and followed up by preparing a disposition memorandum. The memo explained Ceballos' concerns and recommended dismissal of the case. On March 2, 2000, Ceballos submitted the memo to Sundstedt for his review. A few days later, Ceballos presented Sundstedt with another memo, this one describing a second telephone conversation between Ceballos and the warrant affiant.

Based on Ceballos' statements, a meeting was held to discuss the affidavit. Attendees included Ceballos, Sundstedt, and Najera, as well as the warrant affiant and other employees from the sheriff's department. The meeting allegedly became heated, with one lieutenant sharply criticizing Ceballos for his handling of the case.

Despite Ceballos' concerns, Sundstedt decided to proceed with the prosecution, pending disposition of the defense motion to traverse. The trial court held a hearing on the motion. Ceballos was called by the defense and recounted his observations about the affidavit, but the trial court rejected the challenge to the warrant.

Ceballos claims that in the aftermath of these events he was subjected to a series of retaliatory employment actions. The actions included reassignment from his calendar deputy position to a trial deputy position, transfer to another courthouse, and denial of a promotion. Ceballos initiated an employment grievance, but the grievance was denied based on a finding that he had not suffered any retaliation. Unsatisfied, Ceballos sued in the United States District Court for the Central District of California, asserting, as relevant here, a claim under Rev. Stat. § 1979, 42 U.S.C. § 1983. He alleged petitioners violated the First and Fourteenth Amendments by retaliating against him based on his memo of March 2.

Petitioners responded that no retaliatory actions were taken against Ceballos and that all the actions of which he complained were explained by legitimate reasons such as staffing needs. They further contended that, in any event, Ceballos' memo was not protected speech under the First Amendment. Petitioners moved for summary judgment, and the District Court granted their motion. Noting that Ceballos wrote his memo pursuant to his employment duties, the court concluded he was not entitled to First Amendment protection for the memo's contents. It held in the alternative that even if Ceballos' speech was constitutionally protected, petitioners had qualified immunity because the rights Ceballos asserted were not clearly established.

The Court of Appeals for the Ninth Circuit reversed, holding that "Ceballos's allegations of wrongdoing in the memorandum constitute protected speech under the First. In reaching its conclusion the court looked to the First Amendment analysis set forth in *Pickering v. Board of Ed. of Township High School Dist. 205, Will Cty.*, and Connick. *Connick* instructs courts to begin by considering whether the expressions in question were made by the speaker "as a citizen upon matters of public concern." The Court of Appeals determined that Ceballos' memo, which recited what he thought to be governmental misconduct, was "inherently a matter of public concern." The court did not, however, consider whether the speech was made in Ceballos' capacity as a citizen. . . .

. . .

We granted certiorari and we now reverse.

II

As the Court's decisions have noted, for many years "the unchallenged dogma was that a public employee had no right to object to conditions placed upon the terms of employment—including those which restricted the exercise of constitutional rights That dogma has been qualified in important respects. The Court has made clear that public employees do not surrender all their First Amendment rights by reason of their employment. Rather, the First Amendment protects a public employee's right, in certain circumstances, to speak as a citizen addressing matters of public concern.

Pickering provides a useful starting point in explaining the Court's doctrine. There the relevant speech was a teacher's letter to a local newspaper addressing issues including the funding policies of his school board. "The problem in any case," the Court stated, "is to arrive at a balance between the interests of the teacher, as a citizen, in commenting upon matters of public concern and the interest of the State, as an employer, in promoting the efficiency of the public services it performs through its employees." The Court found the teacher's speech "neither [was] shown nor can be presumed to have in any way either impeded the teacher's proper performance of his daily duties in the classroom or to have interfered with the regular operation of the schools generally." Thus, the Court concluded that the "interest of the school administration in limiting teachers' opportunities to contribute to public debate is not significantly greater than its interest in limiting a similar contribution by any member of the general public."

Pickering and the cases decided in its wake identify two inquiries to guide interpretation of the constitutional protections accorded to public employee speech. The first requires determining whether the employee spoke as a citizen on a matter of public concern. If the answer is no, the employee has no First Amendment cause of action based on his or her employer's reaction to the speech. If the answer is yes, then the possibility of a First Amendment claim arises. The question becomes whether the relevant government entity had an adequate justification for treating the employee differently from any other member of the general public. This consideration reflects the importance of the relationship between the speaker's expressions and employment. A government entity has broader discretion to restrict speech when it acts in its role as employer, but the restrictions it imposes must be directed at speech that has some potential to affect the entity's operations.

To be sure, conducting these inquiries sometimes has proved difficult. This is the necessary product of "the enormous variety of fact situations in which critical statements by teachers and other public employees may be thought by their superiors ... to furnish grounds for dismissal." The Court's overarching objectives, though, are evident.

When a citizen enters government service, the citizen by necessity must accept certain limitations on his or her freedom. Government employers, like private employers, need a significant degree of control over their employees' words and actions; without it, there would be little chance for the efficient provision of public services. Public employees, moreover, often occupy trusted positions in society. When they speak out, they can express views that contravene governmental policies or impair the proper performance of governmental functions.

At the same time, the Court has recognized that a citizen who works for the government is nonetheless a citizen. The First Amendment limits the ability of a public employer to leverage the employment relationship to restrict, incidentally or intentionally, the liberties employees enjoy in their capacities as private citizens. So long as employees are speaking as citizens about matters of public concern, they must face only those speech restrictions that are necessary for their employers to operate efficiently and effectively.

The Court's employee-speech jurisprudence protects, of course, the constitutional rights of public employees. Yet the First Amendment interests at stake extend beyond the individual speaker. The Court has acknowledged the importance of promoting the public's interest in receiving the well-informed views of government employees engaging in civic discussion. *Pickering* again provides an instructive example. The Court characterized its holding as rejecting the attempt of school administrators to "limi[t] teachers' opportunities to contribute to public debate." It also noted that teachers are "the members of a community most likely to have informed and definite opinions" about school expenditures. The Court's approach acknowledged the necessity for informed, vibrant dialogue in a democratic society. It suggested, in addition, that widespread costs may arise when dialogue is repressed. The Court's more recent cases have expressed similar concerns.

The Court's decisions, then, have sought both to promote the individual and societal interests that are served when employees speak as citizens on matters of public concern and to respect the needs of government employers attempting to perform their important public functions. Underlying our cases has been the premise that while the First Amendment invests public employees with certain rights, it does not empower them to "constitutionalize the employee grievance."

III

With these principles in mind we turn to the instant case. Respondent Ceballos believed the affidavit used to obtain a search warrant contained serious misrepresentations. He conveyed his opinion and recommendation in a memo to his supervisor. That Ceballos expressed his views inside his office, rather than publicly, is not dispositive. Employees in some cases may receive First Amendment protection for expressions made at work. Many citizens do much of their talking inside their respective workplaces, and it would not serve the goal of treating public employees like "any member of the general public" to hold that all speech within the office is automatically exposed to restriction.

The memo concerned the subject matter of Ceballos' employment, but this, too, is nondispositive. The First Amendment protects some expressions related to the speaker's job. As the Court noted in *Pickering*: "Teachers are, as a class, the members of a community most likely to have informed and definite opinions as to how funds allotted to the operation of the schools should be spent. Accordingly, it is essential that they be able to speak out freely on such questions without fear of retaliatory dismissal." The same is true of many other categories of public employees.

The controlling factor in Ceballos' case is that his expressions were made pursuant to his duties as a calendar deputy. That consideration—the fact that Ceballos spoke as a prosecutor fulfilling a responsibility to advise his supervisor about how best to proceed with a pending case—distinguishes Ceballos' case from those in which the First Amendment provides protection against discipline. We hold that when public employees make statements pursuant to their official duties, the employees are not speaking as citizens for First Amendment purposes, and the Constitution does not insulate their communications from employer discipline.

Ceballos wrote his disposition memo because that is part of what he, as a calendar deputy, was employed to do. It is immaterial whether he experienced some personal gratification from writing the memo; his First Amendment rights do not depend on his job satisfaction. The significant point is that the memo was written pursuant to Ceballos' official duties. Restricting speech that owes its existence to a public employee's professional responsibilities does not infringe any liberties the employee might have enjoyed as a private citizen. It simply reflects the exercise of employer control over what the employer itself has commissioned or created. Contrast, for example, the expressions made by the speaker in *Pickering*, whose letter to the newspaper had no official significance and bore similarities to letters submitted by numerous citizens every day.

Ceballos did not act as a citizen when he went about conducting his daily professional activities, such as supervising attorneys, investigating charges, and preparing filings. In the same way he did not speak as a citizen by writing a memo that addressed the proper disposition of a pending criminal case. When he went to work and performed the tasks he was paid to perform, Ceballos acted as a government employee. The fact that his duties sometimes required him to speak or write does not mean his supervisors were prohibited from evaluating his performance.

This result is consistent with our precedents' attention to the potential societal value of employee speech. Refusing to recognize First Amendment claims based on government employees' work product does not prevent them from participating in public debate. The employees retain the prospect of constitutional protection for their contributions to the civic discourse. This prospect of protection, however, does not invest them with a right to perform their jobs however they see fit.

Our holding likewise is supported by the emphasis of our precedents on affording government employers sufficient discretion to manage their operations. Employers have heightened interests in controlling speech made by an employee in his or her professional capacity. Official communications have official consequences, creating a need for substantive consistency and clarity. Supervisors must ensure that their employees' official communications are accurate, demonstrate sound judgment, and promote the employer's mission. Ceballos' memo is illustrative. It demanded the attention of his supervisors and led to a heated meeting with employees from the sheriff's department. If Ceballos' superiors thought his memo was inflammatory or Misguided, they had the authority to take proper corrective action.

Ceballos' proposed contrary rule, adopted by the Court of Appeals, would commit state and federal courts to a new, permanent, and intrusive role, mandating judicial oversight of communications between and among government employees and their superiors in the course of official business. This displacement of managerial discretion by judicial supervision finds no support in our precedents. When an employee speaks as a citizen addressing a matter of public concern, the First Amendment requires a delicate balancing of the competing interests surrounding the speech and its consequences. When, however, the employee is simply performing his or her job duties, there is no warrant for a similar degree of scrutiny. To hold otherwise would be to demand permanent judicial intervention in the conduct of governmental operations to a degree inconsistent with sound principles of federalism and the separation of powers.

The Court of Appeals based its holding in part on what it perceived as a doctrinal anomaly. The court suggested it would be inconsistent to compel public employers to tolerate certain employee speech made publicly but not speech made pursuant to an employee's assigned duties. This objection misconceives the theoretical underpinnings of our decisions. Employees who make public statements outside the course of performing their official duties retain some possibility of First Amendment protection because that is the kind of activity engaged in by citizens who do not work for the government. The same goes for writing a letter to a local newspaper or discussing politics with a co-worker. When a public employee speaks pursuant to employment responsibilities, however, there is no relevant analogue to speech by citizens who are not government employees.

The Court of Appeals' concern also is unfounded as a practical matter. The perceived anomaly, it should be noted, is limited in scope: It relates only to the expressions an employee makes pursuant to his or her official responsibilities, not to statements or complaints (such as those at issue in cases like *Pickering* and *Connick* that are made outside the duties of employment. If, moreover, a government employer is troubled by the perceived anomaly, it has the means at hand to avoid it. A public employer that wishes to encourage its employees to voice concerns privately retains the option of instituting internal policies and procedures that are receptive to employee criticism. Giving employees an internal forum for their speech will discourage them from concluding that the safest avenue of expression is to state their views in public.

Proper application of our precedents thus leads to the conclusion that the First Amendment does not prohibit managerial discipline based on an employee's expressions made pursuant to official responsibilities. Because Ceballos' memo falls into this category, his allegation of unconstitutional retaliation must fail.

Two final points warrant mentioning. First, as indicated above, the parties in this case do not dispute that Ceballos wrote his disposition memo pursuant to his employment duties. We thus have no occasion to articulate a comprehensive framework for defining the scope of an employee's duties in cases where there is room for serious debate. We reject, however, the suggestion that employers can restrict employees' rights by creating excessively broad job descriptions. The proper inquiry is a practical one. Formal job descriptions often bear little resemblance to the duties an employee actually is expected to perform, and the listing of a given task in an employee's written job description is neither necessary nor sufficient to demonstrate that conducting the task is within the scope of the employee's professional duties for First Amendment purposes.

Second, Justice SOUTER suggests today's decision may have important ramifications for academic freedom, at least as a constitutional value. There is some argument that expression related to academic scholarship or classroom instruction implicates additional constitutional interests that are not fully accounted for by this Court's customary employee-speech jurisprudence. We need not, and for that reason do not, decide whether the analysis we conduct today would apply in the same manner to a case involving speech related to scholarship or teaching.

IV

Exposing governmental inefficiency and misconduct is a matter of considerable significance. As the Court noted in *Connick,* public employers should, "as a matter of good judgment," be "receptive to constructive criticism offered by their employees." The dictates of sound judgment are reinforced by the powerful network of legislative enactments—such as whistle-blower protection laws and labor codes—available to those who seek to expose wrongdoing. Cases involving government attorneys implicate additional safeguards in the form of, for example, rules of conduct and constitutional obligations apart from the First Amendment. These imperatives, as well as obligations arising from any other applicable constitutional provisions and mandates of the criminal and civil laws, protect employees and provide checks on supervisors who would order unlawful or otherwise inappropriate actions.

We reject, however, the notion that the First Amendment shields from discipline the expressions employees make pursuant to their professional duties. Our precedents do not support the existence of a constitutional cause of action behind every statement a public employee makes in the course of doing his or her job.

The judgment of the Court of Appeals is reversed, and the case is remanded for proceedings consistent with this opinion.

It is so ordered.

NOTES

1.   What should happen to a teacher who presents a lesson that is pedagogically sound but contrary to the school board's established curriculum? If the board subjects the teacher to discipline, can the educator raise a successful claim of academic freedom? The court rejected the teacher's claim for academic freedom in *Evans–Marshall v. Board of Educ. of Tipp City Exempted Village School Dist.*, 624 F.3d 332 [261 Educ. L. Rep. 904] (6th Cir. 2010), *cert. denied*, ___ U.S. ___, 131 S.Ct. 3068, 180 L.Ed.2d 889 (2011).

2.   Should public school teachers have academic freedom of the type enjoyed by their colleagues in higher education?

[CASE NO. 75]   PROCEDURAL DUE PROCESS—DISMISSAL FOR CAUSE

CLEVELAND BOARD OF EDUCATION v. LOUDERMILL PARMA BOARD OF EDUCATION V. DONNELLY

Supreme Court of the United States, 1985.
470 U.S. 532, 105 S.Ct. 1487, 84 L.Ed.2d 494 [23 Educ. L. Rep. 473].

■ JUSTICE WHITE delivered the opinion of the Court.

In these cases we consider what pretermination process must be accorded a public employee who can be discharged only for cause.

I

In 1979 the Cleveland Board of Education . . . hired respondent James Loudermill as a security guard. On his job application, Loudermill stated that he had never been convicted of a felony. Eleven months later, as part of a routine examination of his employment records, the Board discovered that in fact Loudermill had been convicted of grand larceny in 1968. By letter dated November 3, 1980, the Board's Business Manager informed Loudermill that he had been dismissed because of his dishonesty in filling out the employment application. Loudermill was not afforded an opportunity to respond to the charge of dishonesty or to challenge his dismissal. On November 13, the Board adopted a resolution officially approving the discharge.

Under Ohio law, Loudermill was a "classified civil servant." Such employees can be terminated only for cause, and may obtain administrative review if discharged. pursuant to this provision, Loudermill filed an appeal with the Cleveland Civil Service Commission on November 12. The Commission appointed a referee, who held a hearing on January 29, 1981. Loudermill argued that he had thought that his 1968 larceny conviction was for a misdemeanor rather than a felony. The referee recommended reinstatement. On July 20, 1981, the full Commission heard argument and orally announced that it would uphold the dismissal. . . .

Although the Commission's decision was subject to judicial review in the state courts, Loudermill instead brought the present suit in the Federal District Court for the Northern District of Ohio. The complaint alleged that § 124.34 was unconstitutional on its face because it did not provide the employee an opportunity to respond to the charges against him prior to removal. As a result, discharged employees were deprived of liberty and property without due process. . . .

The other case before us arises on similar facts and followed a similar course. Respondent Richard Donnelly was a bus mechanic for the Parma Board of Education. In August 1977, Donnelly was fired because he had failed an eye examination. He was offered a chance to retake the examination but did not do so. Like Loudermill, Donnelly appealed to the Civil Service Commission. After a year of wrangling about the timeliness of his appeal, the Commission heard the case. It ordered Donnelly reinstated, though without backpay. In a complaint essentially identical to Loudermill's, Donnelly challenged the constitutionality of the dismissal procedures. . . .

II

Respondents' federal constitutional claim depends on their having had a property right in continued employment. *Board of Regents v. Roth*. If they did, the State could not deprive them of this property without due process.

Property interests are not created by the Constitution, "they are created and their dimensions are defined by existing rules or understandings that stem from an independent source such as state law. . . ." The Ohio statute plainly creates such an interest. Respondents were "classified civil service employees," entitled to retain their positions "during good behavior and efficient service," who could not be dismissed "except . . . for . . . misfeasance, malfeasance, or nonfeasance in office." The statute plainly supports the conclusion . . . that respondents possessed property rights in continued employment. . . .

The Parma Board argues, however, that the property right is defined by, and conditioned on, the legislature's choice of procedures for its deprivation. The Board stresses that in addition to specifying the grounds for termination, the statute sets out procedures by which termination may take place. The procedures were adhered to in these cases. According to petitioner, "[t]o require additional procedures would in effect expand the scope of the property interest itself." . . .

. . . More recently, however, the Court has clearly rejected [this argument]. In *Vitek v. Jones* we pointed out that "minimum [procedural] requirements [are] a matter of federal law, they are not diminished by the fact that the State may have specified its own procedures that it may deem adequate for determining the preconditions to adverse official action." This conclusion was reiterated in *Logan v. Zimmerman Brush Co.* where we reversed the lower court's holding that because the entitlement arose from a state statute, the legislature had the prerogative to define the procedures to be followed to protect that entitlement.

In light of these holdings, it is settled that the "bitter with the sweet" approach misconceives the constitutional guarantee. If a clearer holding is needed, we provide it today. The point is straightforward: the Due Process Clause provides that certain substantive rights—life, liberty, and property—cannot be deprived except pursuant to constitutionally adequate procedures. The categories of substance and procedure are distinct. Were the rule otherwise, the Clause would be reduced to a mere tautology. "Property" cannot be defined by the procedures provided for its deprivation any more than can life or liberty. The right to due process "is conferred, not by legislative grace, but by constitutional guarantee. While the legislature may elect not to confer a property interest in [public] employment, it may not constitutionally authorize the deprivation of such an interest, once conferred, without appropriate procedural safeguards."

In short, once it is determined that the Due Process Clause applies, "the question remains what process is due." The answer to that question is not to be found in the Ohio statute.

III

An essential principle of due process is that a deprivation of life, liberty, or property "be preceded by notice and opportunity for hearing appropriate to the nature of the case." . . . We have described "the root requirement" of the Due Process Clause as being "that an individual be given an opportunity for a hearing before he is deprived of any significant property interest." This principle requires "some kind of a hearing" prior to the discharge of an employee who has a constitutionally protected property interest in his employment. *Board of Regents v. Roth, Perry v. Sindermann.* . . . [T]his rule has been settled for some time now. Even decisions finding no constitutional violation in termination procedures have relied on the existence of some pretermination opportunity to respond. . . .

The need for some form of pretermination hearing, recognized in these cases, is evident from a balancing of the competing interests at stake. These are the private interests in retaining employment, the governmental interest in the expeditious removal of unsatisfactory employees and the avoidance of administrative burdens, and the risk of an erroneous termination.

First, the significance of the private interest in retaining employment cannot be gainsaid. We have frequently recognized the severity of depriving a person of the means of livelihood. While a fired worker may find employment elsewhere, doing so will take some time and is likely to be burdened by the questionable circumstances under which he left his previous job.

Second, some opportunity for the employee to present his side of the case is recurringly of obvious value in reaching an accurate decision. Dismissals for cause will often involve factual disputes. Even where the facts are clear, the appropriateness or necessity of the discharge may not be; in such cases, the only meaningful opportunity to invoke the discretion of the decisionmaker is likely to be before the termination takes effect. (This is not to say that where state conduct is entirely discretionary the Due Process Clause is brought into play. Nor is it to say that a person can insist on a hearing in order to argue that the decisionmaker should be lenient and depart from legal requirements. The point is that where there is an entitlement, a prior hearing facilitates the consideration of whether a permissible course of action is also an appropriate one.)

The cases before us illustrate these considerations. Both respondents had plausible arguments to make that might have prevented their discharge. The fact that the Commission saw fit to reinstate Donnelly suggests that an error might have been avoided had he been provided an opportunity to make his case to the Board. As for Loudermill, given the Commission's ruling we cannot say that the discharge was mistaken. Nonetheless, in light of the referee's recommendation, neither can we say that a fully informed decisionmaker might not have exercised its discretion and decided not to dismiss him, notwithstanding its authority to do so. In any event, the termination involved arguable issues, and the right to a hearing does not depend on a demonstration of certain success.

The governmental interest in immediate termination does not outweigh these interests. As we shall explain, affording the employee an opportunity to respond prior to termination would impose neither a significant administrative burden nor intolerable delays. Furthermore, the employer shares the employee's interest in avoiding disruption and erroneous decisions; and until the matter is settled, the employer would continue to receive the benefit of the employee's labors. It is preferable to keep a qualified employee on than to train a new one. A governmental employer also has an interest in keeping citizens usefully employed rather than taking the possibly erroneous and counterproductive step of forcing its employees onto the welfare rolls. Finally, in those situations where the employer perceives a significant hazard in keeping the employee on the job, it can avoid the problem by suspending with pay.

IV

The foregoing considerations indicate that the pretermination "hearing," though necessary, need not be elaborate. We have pointed out that "[t]he formality and procedural requisites for the hearing can vary, depending upon the importance of the interests involved and the nature of the subsequent proceedings." In general, "something less" than a full evidentiary hearing is sufficient prior to adverse administrative action. Under state law, respondents were later entitled to a full administrative hearing and judicial review. The only question is what steps were required before the termination took effect.

... Here, the pretermination hearing need not definitively resolve the propriety of the discharge. It should be an initial check against mistaken decisions—essentially, a determination of whether there are reasonable grounds to believe that the charges against the employee are true and support the proposed action.

The essential requirements of due process ... are notice and an opportunity to respond. The opportunity to present reasons, either in person or in writing, why proposed action should not be taken is a fundamental due process requirement. The tenured public employee is entitled to oral or written notice of the charges against him, an explanation of the employer's evidence, and an opportunity to present his side of the story. To require more than this prior to termination would intrude to an unwarranted extent on the government's interest in quickly removing an unsatisfactory employee.

V

Our holding rests in part on the provisions in Ohio law for a full post-termination hearing. In his cross-petition Loudermill asserts, as a separate constitutional violation, that his administrative proceedings took too long. The Court of Appeals held otherwise, and we agree. The Due Process Clause requires provision of a hearing "at a meaningful time." At some point, a delay in the post-termination hearing would become a constitutional violation. In the present case, however, the complaint merely recites the course of proceedings and concludes that the denial of a "speedy resolution" violated due process. This reveals nothing about the delay except that it stemmed in part from the thoroughness of the procedures. A 9–month adjudication is not, of course, unconstitutionally lengthy per se. Yet Loudermill offers no indication that his wait was unreasonably prolonged other than the fact that it took nine months. The chronology of the proceedings set out in the complaint, coupled with the assertion that nine months is too long to wait, does not state a claim of a constitutional deprivation.

VI

We conclude that all the process that is due is provided by a pretermination opportunity to respond, coupled with post-termination administrative procedures as provided by the Ohio statute. Because respondents allege in their complaints that they had no chance to respond, the District Court erred in dismissing for failure to state a claim. The judgment of the Court of Appeals is affirmed, and the case is remanded for further proceedings consistent with this opinion. So ordered.

NOTES

1. Compare the minimum requirements of constitutional procedural due process that must precede the dismissal of public employees with tenure (or property rights) with those of students who are subjected to short-term suspensions.

2. Would extensive post-termination procedures and remedies including reinstatement, back pay, and attorney fees, remedy pre-termination constitutional due process deficiencies? Here the Court did not give attention to post-termination procedures beyond noting their existence as an integral part of Loudermill's property right.

[CASE NO. 76]   TEACHER DISMISSAL FOR CLASSROOM PERFORMANCE

KNOX COUNTY BOARD OF EDUCATION v. WILLIS

Court of Appeals of Kentucky, 1966.
405 S.W.2d 952.

■ CLAY, COMMISSIONER.

Appellant, Knox County Board of Education, terminated appellee's teaching contract after a hearing upon charges brought under KRS 161.790. On appeal to the circuit court the action of the Board was reversed, from which judgment the Board appeals to this court.

The charges against appellee were for "inefficiency, incompetency and neglect of duty". The notice of charges with which appellee was served made specific reference to and included a copy of a "supervisor's report". This report criticized appellee's conduct of classes, her lack of control and discipline over her students, and the destruction of classroom furniture. At the hearing substantial evidence was introduced concerning the inadequacy of records kept by appellee, although this deficiency did not appear in the charges. The Board found that appellee (1) failed and refused to keep proper order in her classes; (2) allowed the children to damage and destroy furniture and to use improper language, and failed to take appropriate corrective and disciplinary measures; and (3) failed to keep proper records. On the basis of these findings, the Board terminated her contract.

The circuit court on appeal found these proceedings arbitrary in almost every respect.

The first ground of alleged arbitrariness was the failure of the Board to furnish appellee with rules and regulations governing procedure in the conduct of the hearing. Apparently the Board did not have such rules and regulations, as the trial court found. Our first question is whether, as appellee insists, the Board is without power to conduct, or acts arbitrarily in conducting, a hearing such as this without written rules of procedure.

We find nothing in the statutes which requires a board of education to adopt formal procedural rules for the conduct of a hearing. While KRS 160.290(2) provides that each board "shall make and adopt ... rules, regulations and by-laws" for the regulation and management of schools and the transaction of its business, we must construe this language sensibly to require such rules and regulations as are necessary and proper. Otherwise a school board could not legally perform any act without a pre-established written rule specifically pertaining to it. If we adopt appellee's theory, it would require each board to draft a comprehensive code of procedure for hearings on the termination of teachers' contracts, and if such code failed to cover a single phase of procedure sought to be invoked, the board could not proceed. We simply cannot construe this statute so unrealistically. The average school board would certainly lack the competency to draft such a code.

We believe that KRS 161.790(2), (3) adequately outlines the procedure required for such a hearing, although a board could adopt consistent supplementary rules. . . . a proper hearing of this nature simply requires "orderly procedure" and "fundamental fairness" and not "the esoteric formalities of a medieval jousting match". Within the scope of "fundamental fairness" we must recognize the necessity for procedural flexibility, particularly since these proceedings ordinarily must be conducted by laymen. As suggested in that case, under proper circumstances resort may be had to our Rules of Civil Procedure.

Appellee's plea for the requirement of technical rules of procedure is really an academic one. She makes no claim that the hearing was not a fair one, that she was denied any right to be fully heard, or that she was prejudiced by the manner in which the hearing was conducted. We find nothing illegal or arbitrary in the conduct of this hearing without written rules of procedure.

The trial court correctly found that the Board acted arbitrarily in sustaining the charges against appellee for failure to keep proper records. She was given no fair notice of this charge, as required by KRS 161.790(2). However, the Board sustained two other charges against her. If she was given adequate notice of these other charges and there was substantial evidence to support them, the Board's action may be upheld even though the charge of failing to keep records was not properly prosecuted.

The trial court found the Board acted arbitrarily in sustaining the charges against appellee which involved the failure to keep proper order in her classroom and the failure to take appropriate corrective and disciplinary measures against students who were guilty of flagrant misconduct. The basis of this determination was that the charges against appellee were not sufficiently specific, and the evidence did not support the findings.

The charges against appellee were for "inefficiency, incompetency and neglect of duty". We agree that these charges, appearing in the "Notice of Termination of Contract", were not sufficiently specific under KRS 161.790(2). However, the notice incorporates a "supervisor's report" wherein certain details are set forth. It is apparently appellee's contention that the details must appear in the formal charges and that an interoffice communication does not have sufficient formal dignity to constitute adequate charges. It is also contended by appellee, and the trial court found, that the "supervisor's report" was not sufficiently detailed.

It is our opinion that the formal charges against appellee, coupled with the facts stated in the "supervisor's report", gave appellee fair notice that the charges of inefficiency, incompetency and neglect were based upon the manner in which she conducted her classes, with particular emphasis upon her failure to maintain any sort of discipline. We cannot go along with appellee's argument that the "supervisor's report" cannot be considered as part and parcel of the charges. This report was incorporated in the formal notice just as an exhibit to a pleading. The informality of the report has no bearing on the adequacy of the charges since we are seeking fair notice to the teacher.

We are also disinclined to agree with the trial court that the "supervisor's report" did not contain sufficient detail. We are convinced that it did give appellee fair notice that the charges were based upon the method of conducting her classes, which resulted in the specified abnormal conditions.

There was ample evidence of intolerable conduct on the part of students in her classroom, and there was ample evidence of a neglect upon her part in controlling her classes and students. Such being the case, we cannot find that the Board acted arbitrarily in upholding these grounds as justification for terminating appellee's contract. It may be noted in passing that there is no claim that this proceeding was politically or otherwise motivated except in the interest of efficient school administration. . . .

The judgment is reversed, with directions to enter a judgment sustaining the action of the Knox County Board of Education.

NOTES

1. In *Tichenor v. Orleans Parish School Bd.*, 144 So.2d 603 (La. Ct. App. 1962), an appellate court in Louisiana held that a teacher who refused supervision may be discharged on the ground of incompetency and wilful neglect of duty. The court described incompetence a relative term meaning disqualification, inability, or incapacity.

2. The Supreme Court of Nebraska annulled a teacher's discharge because of inadequate notice of the charges where he had received a vague and conclusory letter, even though he had access to his personnel file. *Irwin v. Board of Educ. of School Dist. No. 25 of Holt County*, 340 N.W.2d 877 [14 Educ. L. Rep. 1102] (Neb.1983).

[CASE NO. 77]   REDUCTION–IN–FORCE—SELECTION OF POSITION

MARTINEK v. BELMORE–KLEMME COMMUNITY SCHOOL DISTRICT

Supreme Court of Iowa, 2009.
772 N.W.2d 758 [249 Educ. L. Rep. 390], rehearing denied.

■ BAKER, JUSTICE.

The plaintiff, Cynthia Martinek, appeals from the district court's ruling affirming the termination of her employment as a principal under Iowa Code section 279.24 (2007) by the defendant, Belmond–Klemme Community School District. Martinek claims that the district court erred in failing to reverse the school board's decision to terminate her contract because the school district failed to establish just cause for her termination as required under Iowa Code section 279.24. We find that the district court did not err in determining a preponderance of competent evidence in the record supported the Belmond–Klemme Community School District's termination of Martinek due to declining enrollment, budget concerns, and essential staff reductions.

I.   Background Facts and Proceedings.

In 1993, Dr. Cynthia Martinek was hired as the elementary school principal for the Belmond–Klemme Community School District (District). She held that position for thirteen years. Martinek has a bachelor's degree, a master's degree, and a doctorate degree in educational leadership. She also holds teaching and administrative licenses which certify her to serve as a superintendent, high school principal, and elementary school principal.

On July 21, 2005, Martinek entered into the contract at issue with the District. This contract stated that Martinek "agrees to serve as Elementary School (PK–6) Principal in the Belmond–Klemme Community School District for a two (2) year period commencing with the 2005–2006 school year . . . ."

On April 25, 2007, the District sent Martinek a notification, stating that it intended to terminate her employment at the end of the 2006–2007 school year, on June 30, 2007. As grounds for the termination, the District listed: (1) declining enrollment, (2) budgetary restrictions and problems, (3) reduction of position(s), and (4) realignment of school organization.

Pursuant to the realignment, Larry Frakes, the former 7–12 principal, became the superintendent and part-time elementary school principal, and David Sextro, the former superintendent, served as assistant superintendent, part-time elementary school principal, and construction supervisor for the new elementary school. Five days after terminating Martinek, the District hired administrator Roy Frakes to serve as 7–12 principal and activities director. Roy Frakes is the brother of Larry Frakes. The District claimed that the hiring of Roy Frakes was part of a plan to gradually reduce administrators, and that a portion of Sextro's salary was paid out of the construction fund and had no effect on the school's yearly budget. At the hearing in front of the administrative law judge (ALJ), Sextro testified that at the end of the 2007–2008 school year he would retire, leaving the district with only two administrators.

Martinek sent a letter to the Belmond–Klemme School District Board of Directors (Board) contesting the reasons for her termination and requested a hearing before an ALJ pursuant to Iowa Code section 279.24(5)(c). A hearing was conducted, after which the ALJ issued a proposed decision finding the District had shown by a preponderance of the evidence that "just cause" existed to terminate the continuing contract of Martinek. Martinek appealed the ALJ's decision to the Board, which adopted the ALJ's proposed decision as its own.

Thereafter, Martinek filed a notice of appeal with the district court. The district court concluded the District's decision to terminate Martinek's contract for just cause was supported by a preponderance of the evidence. In ruling in favor of the District, the trial court only addressed three of the reasons argued in support of Martinek's termination: (1) declining enrollment, (2) budgetary problems, and (3) reduction of staff. Martinek appealed the district court's judgment.

II.   Discussion and Analysis.

A.   Scope of Review. Both parties agree that Martinek's termination is governed by Iowa Code section 279.24. Section 279.24 governs terminations that occur at the conclusion of an administrator's contract term, while section 279.25 governs terminations that occur during the contract term.

As this court has explained, the court must follow the guidelines in Iowa Code section 279.24(6) when reviewing a school board's decision to terminate an administrator's contract. *Martinek v. Belmond–Klemme Cmty. Sch. Dist.*, (hereinafter *Martinek I*). This Code section states:

> The court shall reverse, modify, or grant any other appropriate relief from the school board's action ... if substantial rights of the administrator have been prejudiced because the school board's action is ... [u]nsupported by a preponderance of the evidence in the record made before the school board when that record is reviewed as a whole.

. . .

Martinek claims that none of the District's asserted grounds for her termination constitute a legitimate reason as contemplated by the Iowa Supreme Court and that these stated grounds are not supported by a preponderance of the evidence. She also asserts that the reasons given are not sufficient because the District's actions have not saved it any money. Five days after firing Martinek the District hired another administrator at a salary $16,000 higher than Martinek's.

We must therefore determine whether the District's stated grounds are legitimate under the statute and whether the Board's decision to uphold the termination of Martinek was supported by a preponderance of competent evidence in the record. The court is limited on review to the record that was before the Board. While a preponderance of competent evidence is a higher standard than substantial evidence, this is not de novo review. A preponderance of the evidence is the evidence "that is more convincing than opposing evidence" or "more likely true than not true." It is evidence superior in weight, influence, or force.

B.   Preponderance of Competent Evidence. Martinek was terminated on June 30, 2007. Her two-year contract expired at the end of the 2006–2007 school year. Iowa Code section 279.24 governs this controversy. This section reads: "The notice shall state the specific reasons to be used by the school board for considering termination which for all administrators except superintendents shall be for just cause."

In *Martinek I*, this court reiterated that, for the purposes of the nonrenewal provision of Iowa Code section 279.24, just cause " 'include [s] legitimate reasons relating to the district's personnel and budgetary requirements.' " The District claims Martinek was terminated because of: (1) declining enrollment, (2) budgetary restrictions and problems, (3) reduction of position(s), and (4) realignment of school organization. These alleged grounds for termination are clearly related to the District's personnel and budget needs. Thus, the only issue remaining is to determine whether the

Board's decision to terminate Martinek for these stated reasons is supported by a preponderance of competent evidence in the record.

In its ruling in favor of the District, the district court explicitly addressed only three of the reasons argued in support of Martinek's termination: (1) declining enrollment, (2) budgetary problems, and (3) reduction of staff....

1. *Declining enrollment.* The District asserts that it has experienced a dramatic decline in enrollment since 1999. In upholding Martinek's termination, the Board adopted the ALJ's findings of fact and conclusions of law. In his proposed decision, the ALJ stated:

> The Belmond–Klemme School District, like most districts in rural Iowa, has experienced significant declines in student enrollment over the last several decades. Specifically in this district, reductions have exceeded twenty-five percent over the past eight school years....
>
> ... The projections for the 2007–2008 school year indicate a district-wide reduction of fifteen more students.... Should the enrollment projections for 2007–2008 be substantially correct, this would reflect a loss of slightly over six percent in the past 3 years. Clearly enrollment decline, though slowing, continues to be a reality in the Belmond–Klemme School District.

A preponderance of competent evidence in the record supports these findings. The evidence shows that the Belmond–Klemme Community School District lost over 200 students since the 1999–2000 school year. The evidence also establishes that the District receives approximately $5,338 per enrolled student in state aid. Thus, in the ten-year span covered by these figures, the District lost approximately $1 million dollars in yearly income, a significant reduction for a small school district.

Martinek counters that the District's figures are flawed because they are calculated by data beyond the time period at issue in this case. She claims the District must establish declining enrollment during the term of her contract, namely the 2005–2006 and 2006–2007 school years. Courts are not constrained to the term of the administrator's contract when deciding whether there has been a decline in enrollment. We find the District showed a preponderance of competent evidence demonstrating enrollment has significantly declined from 1999 through 2007.

2. *Budgetary problems.* The District also alleges that it is experiencing significant budgetary problems. According to the Independent Auditor's Reports for the Belmond–Klemme Community School District from 2003 to 2006, the District's unreserved fund balance declined from $1,131,919.00 to $229,161.00. The District projected that by the end of 2007 this balance will have further declined to $71,750.00. The District's auditor testified that the unreserved fund balance is the amount of money the District would have if it were liquidated.

In addition, the record indicates the District's solvency ratio has shrunk from 25% in 2003 to 3.5% in 2006. The solvency ratio is a figure used by the Iowa Schools Cash Anticipation Program to determine a district's financial health. The District projected that at the end of 2007, this ratio would be 1.1%. This solvency ratio would put the District into the solvency alert category. The evidence shows that the State requires districts with weak solvency ratios to be "more conservative budgeting revenues in the next budget year and [have] more stringent cost controls."

Other evidence provided by the District further shows that in the 2005–2006 school year the District outspent its incoming revenue by $310,000. Both the AEA Director of Finance and the District's auditor testified that the District must reduce its expenditures if it hopes to have a balanced budget in the future, as it is only expected to receive $7,831 in new money from the state for the 2007–2008 school year.

The court finds the District has demonstrated by a preponderance of competent evidence that it is experiencing budgetary problems.

3. *Reduction and realignment of staff.* Finally, the District claims Martinek was terminated because of the need for a reduction in administrative staff. The District states that due to the drop in enrollment from the 1999–2000 school year to the 2007–2008 school year it needed to reduce staff. Since 1999–2000, it has reduced teaching staff from approximately 70 teachers to around 55 teachers today. In that same time period, the District did not reduce any administrative staff positions.

In response to the declining enrollment and budgetary concerns, the District decided to reduce the number of administrative staff. The Board determined the best way to reduce school administrators was to eliminate the elementary school principal and divide that position's duties between the superintendent and the high school principal. Martinek was the District's only elementary school principal, and, therefore, she was the administrator chosen for termination.

Martinek argues that the District's own actions undermine its claim that it needed to reduce administrative staff. Five days after firing Martinek the District hired administrator Roy Frakes to serve as 7–12 principal and activities director. The District counters that Frakes' hiring was part of its plan to restructure its administrators. Thus, even though the District hired a new administrator to serve as 7–12 principal and activities director, it cut back to 2.5 administrative staff. According to the District's plan, once Sextro (the former superintendent) retired, the district would employ Larry Frakes as district superintendent and elementary school principal and Roy Frakes as 7–12 principal and activities director, leaving the district with just two administrators.

A preponderance of competent evidence substantiates the District's strategy to gradually reduce administrative staff. If the termination decision is based on some set policy or criteria it cannot be challenged in court, unless the policy or criteria used are illegal or irrational such as race, religious preference, sex, or political persuasion or based on "some petty vendetta." The District's decision to terminate Martinek was based upon objective criteria. The District needed to reorganize its administrative staff. Of the three administrative positions in the District, the Board determined that the elementary school principal duties could be best divided between the two remaining administrators, and, therefore, that position was eliminated. Martinek was the only elementary school principal in the District.

Roy Frakes was hired for a different position–7–12 principal and activities director. The qualifications and duties of this position are different than those of an elementary school principal. Therefore, his hiring does not disprove the District's claim that it needed to reduce and reorganize its administrative staff.

The burden is on Martinek to prove her termination was for an improper purpose, and the District's stated grounds are a pretext. Before Martinek's initial termination notice in 2006, there is no evidence or allegation of any discord between Martinek and the District. Her employment file was not entered into the record, and the District has not listed any fault reasons for her termination. There is no allegation or evidence that the termination was for any improper purpose. In short, there is no evidence in the record that suggests Martinek's termination was because of illegal or irrational reasons or due to a petty vendetta.

Martinek points to the District's contemporaneous hiring of Roy Frakes as proof that the District is not experiencing financial problems or enrollment decline. While the timing of his hiring certainly raises suspicions, given the evidence, this court cannot say that the District did not use objective criteria in deciding to terminate Martinek and hire Roy Frakes.

"The board is an elective body free to exercise its own discretion in deciding which ... positions to terminate." Accordingly, we find the District presented a preponderance of competent evidence demonstrating the need to reduce administrative staff positions and has shown an objective basis for its decision to eliminate Martinek's position.

The District met its burden to establish just cause existed to terminate Martinek.

III. Disposition.

We hold the district court did not err in finding the Belmond–Klemme Community School District provided a preponderance of competent evidence demonstrating Martinek's termination was necessary due to declining enrollment, budgetary concerns, and essential staff reductions. The district court decision is affirmed.

AFFIRMED.

NOTES

1. Iowa, like other states, requires school boards to articulate the criteria to be used in reduction-in-force situations. Do you approve of the ones used in this case?

2. Do you agree with the outcome in this case?

[CASE NO. 78]   MEDICAL BENEFITS AND RETIREMENT PAY

IN RE FARMINGTON TEACHERS ASSOCIATION

Supreme Court of New Hampshire, 2009.
969 A.2d 422 [244 Educ. L. Rep. 149].

■ BRODERICK, C.J.

In this petition for a writ of certiorari, the Farmington Teachers Association, NEA New Hampshire (petitioner), seeks review of a ruling of the Board of Trustees (board) of the respondent New Hampshire Retirement System (NHRS) that certain payments made to eight retired public school teachers by the Farmington School District (school district) were not "earnable compensation" for purposes of calculating retirement benefits. We affirm.

I

The facts are not in dispute. Between 1996 and 2005, the petitioner, which represents the eight teachers, entered into a series of collective bargaining agreements with the school district. Each of these agreements contained Article IX, Section 9.9 (section 9.9) that provided:

> A professional who has reached the age of 55 may, upon notification to the business office by August 15 for the next school year, elect to have his/her fringe benefits counted as if they were salary. The member is responsible for reimbursing the district for the district's share of the increased social security tax, state retirement, and the like, on these additional monies. The member must retain membership in the health care plan and the dental plan for the school year.

In the 20022005 agreement the age was lowered to fifty.

All eight teachers filed an election with the school district under this provision and the amount of each teacher's employer-provided health insurance premium was added to each teacher's paycheck. The teachers paid federal income tax on the additional money. Either bi-weekly or in a lump sum at the end of the year, each teacher paid back to the school district the cost of the health insurance premium, both the employer and employee share of FICA and Medicaid taxes, and the employer and employee contributions to the NHRS attributable to the medical premium amount.

The NHRS became aware of section 9.9 in October 2003 when a former school district employee sent a copy to the NHRS and inquired about its legality. After investigation, the NHRS concluded that section 9.9 did not comply with RSA chapter 100–A. The NHRS subsequently provided the eight teachers with a "Notice of Earnable Compensation, Contribution and Pension Adjustment," advising them that the payments at issue did not qualify as "earnable compensation" and that adjustments had been made to their NHRS records.

The petitioner appealed this decision to the board and a three-day administrative hearing was held before a hearings examiner. The hearings examiner recommended that the board "uphold the NHRS administrative staff's decision that certain payments to teachers in Farmington that were treated 'as if they were salary' are not earnable compensation and direct the staff to seek recoupment of the amounts overpaid to the members." The board approved the hearings examiner's recommendations, but waived recoupment of the retirement allowance payments made to four of the teachers who had already retired. This petition for a writ of certiorari followed.

The petitioner raises three issues: (1) whether the NHRS was unreasonable in concluding that the negotiated agreement to have health insurance benefits counted "as if they were salary" does not fall under the statutory definition of "earnable compensation" pursuant to RSA 100–A:1, XVII; (2) whether it was an unsustainable exercise of discretion for the NHRS not to promulgate an amended rule to clarify the requirements under the definition of earnable compensation and then apply the amended rule prospectively; and (3) whether the NHRS was unjust and unreasonable in denying any further relief to the petitioners.

. . .

II

Under the NHRS, one of the benefits each eligible retiree receives is a fixed annual "retirement allowance." The dollar amount of a retired member's service retirement allowance is tied to his or her "average final compensation." A member's "average final compensation" is equal to the "average earnable compensation" in the member's three highest earning years of NHRS creditable service. During the period of time relevant to this appeal, "earnable compensation" was defined in pertinent part as:

> [T]he full base rate of compensation paid plus any overtime pay, holiday and vacation pay, sick pay, longevity or severance pay, cost of living bonus, additional pay for extracurricular and instructional activities or for other extra or special duty, and other compensation paid to the member by the employer, plus the fair market value of non-cash compensation such as meals or living quarters if subject to federal income tax.

Resolution of this petition requires statutory interpretation, which is a question of law that we review *de novo*. "We are the final arbiter of the intent of the legislature as expressed in the words of a statute considered as a whole." "When examining the language of a statute, we ascribe the plain and ordinary meaning to the words used." "We interpret legislative intent from the statute as written and will not consider what the legislature might have said or add language that the legislature did not see fit to include. We interpret a statute in the context of the overall statutory scheme and not in isolation."

The petitioner argues that the salary payments under section 9.9 fall within the language of RSA 100–A:1, XVII because the phrase "earnable compensation" is "very broad" in that it includes "other compensation paid to the member by the employer." We believe, however, that "compensation" under the statute does not include payment of the cash equivalent of a fringe benefit that must then be returned to the employer. Under the terms of section 9.9, the school district agreed to increase the amount of pay credited to the teachers by having their health insurance benefits "counted as if they were salary" and in return, the teachers agreed to retain their memberships in the school district's health plan and to subsequently reimburse the school district for the total amount of the increased pay. Thus, the teachers did not receive any additional salary but, rather, simply had their fringe benefits counted *as if* they were salary, to enhance their retirement pensions.

Pursuant to section 9.9, the teachers did not receive any actual increase in their annual compensation. Rather, they received an increase in the amount of their bi-weekly paychecks conditioned upon their agreement to repay the additional amounts to the school district by the end of the school year. Because the teachers were not authorized to keep any of the additional amounts, we conclude that the reimbursed payments do not constitute "earnable compensation" under RSA chapter 100–A. As the hearings examiner found, "After the election of section 9.9 treatment, a member's salary appeared to increase because the number on the face of the paycheck and on the W2 went up. However, that money was never paid to the member in the sense that the member could keep it and spend it however he or she pleased. All of the apparent pay increase had to be returned to the Farmington School District." For these reasons, we hold that the mechanism employed in section 9.9 does not fall under the statutory definition of "earnable compensation" pursuant to RSA 100–A:1, XVII, and that "other compensation paid to the member by the employer" does not include employer-provided health insurance premiums for which the employee must reimburse the employer.

III

The petitioner argues that pursuant to *Milette v. N.H. Retirement System,* the NHRS may not exclude the section 9.9 payments from earnable compensation without a properly promulgated rule. In *Milette,* the petitioner was entitled to severance pay upon her retirement, but the amount was not actually paid to her until a year after she retired. After the petitioner retired and her severance pay was not received for one year, the NHRS calculated her retirement award without including her severance pay in the calculation, resulting in an award substantially less than the petitioner expected. The board determined that the statute required payment of severance at termination or else it could not be included in the calculation of benefits. The issue before us was whether the petitioner's severance pay should be included in her "earnable compensation" for her last year of service pursuant to RSA 100–A:1, XVII.

We held that the statute contained "no reference to any requirement that the employee's severance pay be paid 'at termination,' or by any other deadline, in order to be included in the calculation of the employee's retirement benefits." Accordingly, because there was no time frame set forth in the statute for actual payment of such pay, the calculation of retirement benefits should take into account any severance pay whether received at retirement or some later date. The board argued that *New Hampshire Administrative Rules,* which requires the board to consider in its calculations severance paid "after separation from service" should be understood as requiring severance pay to be paid within the "customary and usual" time frame in order to be included in the calculation of retirement benefits. We concluded that "[n]othing in the plain language of the rule distinguishes a delay of several weeks from a delay of one year in the actual payment of severance pay." While we "would accord deference to an agency's interpretation of its own rule where there was some ambiguity or inconsistency in the rule," we would not permit an agency to "add or delete requirements—without properly promulgating an amended rule—

through the mere expedient of 'interpreting' a rule that is clear and unambiguous on its face."

The petitioner relies upon *Milette* to argue that because there is nothing on the face of the statute to limit or exclude the payments made to the teachers pursuant to section 9.9, the NHRS may not interpret the statute to exclude such payments "without properly promulgating an amended rule." We disagree. As discussed above, we affirm the board's determination that the section 9.9 payments do not qualify as "earnable compensation" as the term is used in RSA 100–A:1, XVII. In making this determination, the board did not add or delete requirements contained in the plain language of the statute. Because we hold that *Milette* does not require the promulgation of a rule under the circumstances presented, we need not address the petitioner's arguments against the retrospective application of an amended rule.

We likewise disagree with the petitioner that section 9.9 can be characterized as an insurance buy-back provision whereby salary payments are made in lieu of health insurance coverage. The school district already offers a separate buy-back provision, Policy #4234, for any employee who elects insurance coverage under a spouse's plan. Under the buy-back policy, any employee who elects not to receive medical and dental insurance through the school district receives a sum equivalent to twenty percent of the total premium the district would otherwise pay for that employee's health insurance coverage. The policy is "intended to relieve the District from paying unnecessary premiums while at the same time providing an attractive incentive to the employee." The employee may use these payments in any way he or she chooses. In contrast, under section 9.9, the teachers did not give up their health insurance benefits and were not "compensated" for any such loss. Rather, they were mandated to retain membership in the school district's health plan and to reimburse the school district for the full amount of the additional monies received.

IV

The final issue is whether the NHRS was unjust and unreasonable in denying "any further relief" to the teachers. Specifically, the petitioner argues that the teachers should be reimbursed for the contributions they made to the retirement system.

As to the four teachers who had not retired before the appeal to the board, the NHRS reimbursed the school district the amount of money the employees paid to cover the employer's share of the contribution to the retirement system. As to the four teachers who had retired, the board waived recoupment of the benefits received by them during the years that the NHRS was unaware of the section 9.9 payments. The board declined to refund retirement contributions to the four retired teachers, because

> [t]he [teachers] have all received pension benefits that they did not earn based on artificially inflated earnable compensation figures. The [teachers] have received total excess benefits that are 10 times the amount of their total excess contributions. The [teachers] have had any money collected from them in error returned to them in the form of

excess pension benefits. They would be unjustly enriched if their contributions were returned to them again.

We cannot conclude that the board in so deciding "arrived at a conclusion which cannot legally or reasonably be made, or abused its discretion or acted arbitrarily, unreasonably, or capriciously." Rather, the board has acted in furtherance of its "fiduciary obligation to manage the NHRS for the benefit of its members and beneficiaries" in accordance with the statute.

Affirmed.

NOTE

Should teachers and other public school employees have to make greater contributions to help fund their medical and retirement benefits?

CHAPTER 12

COMPULSORY ATTENDANCE, CURRICULUM, AND INSTRUCTIONAL ISSUES

INTRODUCTION

The nature of American public education has changed dramatically since the emergence of compulsory attendance laws in the mid-nineteenth century. As school systems continue to evolve to meet the needs of the students and communities they serve, a variety of legal issues have surfaced dealing with what can be broadly classified as their instructional programs or curricula, regardless of how expansively these terms are defined. In light of the array of emerging questions with regard to providing educational programming for students, this chapter examines legal topics under the broad umbrella of curricular and instructional issues.

COMPULSORY EDUCATION

IN GENERAL

In 1852, Massachusetts became the first jurisdiction in the United States to enact a compulsory attendance law.[1] When Mississippi adopted its compulsory attendance law in 1918, all existing jurisdictions at that time had such statutes in place. Previously, Tennessee in 1905, North Carolina in 1907, Virginia in 1908, Arkansas in 1909, Louisiana in 1910, Alabama and South Carolina in 1915, and Georgia in 1916 became the last states to enact compulsory attendance laws in the twentieth century.[2]

Courts generally uphold compulsory education statutes[3] against charges that they unreasonably infringe on constitutional liberties.[4] In

---

1. MASS. GEN. LAWS ANN. 76 § 1 (historical notes St.1852, c. 240, §§ 1, 2, 4).

2. MICHAEL S. KATZ, A HISTORY OF COMPULSORY ATTENDANCE LAWS 18 1976.

3. *See, e.g.,* ALA. CODE ANN. § 16–28–7; ALASKA STAT. ANN. § 14.30.010; CAL. EDUC. CODE § 48200; DEL. CODE ANN. tit. 14 § 2702; GA. CODE ANN. § 20-2-690.1; HAW. REV. STAT. ANN. § 302A–1132; 105 ILL. COMP. STAT. ANN. 5/26–1; KY. REV. STAT. ANN. § 159.010; LA. REV. STAT. ANN. § 17:221; MD. CODE ANN., EDUC. § 7–301; MASS. GEN. LAWS ch. 76, § 1; N.J. STAT. ANN. § 18A:38–25; N.Y. EDUC. LAW § 3205; OHIO REV. CODE ANN. § 3321.01; OKLA. STAT. ANN. tit. 70, § 10–105; 24 PA. CONSOL. STAT. ANN. § 13–1327; TEX. EDUC. CODE ANN. § 25.085; VT. STAT. ANN. tit. 16, § 1121; WIS. STAT. ANN. § 118.15.

permitting compulsory attendance laws to remain in effect along with exemptions, for example, for parents who wish to send their children to non-public schools or educate them at home, the courts recognize these statutes as a valid exercise of state police power[5] that is served by the creation of an enlightened citizenry.

Based on the concept of *in loco parentis*, literally "in the place of the parent," compulsory attendance laws rely on the common law presumption that parents voluntarily submit their children to the authority of school officials.[6] Yet, a question can be raised about the continuing viability of the presumed voluntary nature of *in loco parentis* in light of compulsory attendance laws, not to mention other school rules,[7] which require parents to send their children to school at the risk of punishment for noncompliance.[8]

An alternative rationale for compulsory attendance rests on another common law principle, *parens patriae*, literally "father of the country," under which legislatures can enact reasonable laws for the welfare of their residents. However, in *Wisconsin v. Yoder*,[9] discussed below, the Supreme Court rejected the applicability of *parens patriae* to compulsory attendance while upholding the general principle that the state has the authority to regulate education. Placing aside the dispute over the tension between the authority of state officials and parents vis-a-vis the education of children in the interest of addressing the practical issues associated with compulsory attendance laws, suffice it to say that the courts agree that parents[10] must ensure that their children are educated.

Whether parents meet their duty of sending their children to school, or whether students who are absent from school without justification should be classified as truant,[11] or entitled to an attorney to represent those who are truant at hearings over their status,[12] is a joint responsibility shared by

---

4. *Parr v. State*, 157 N.E. 555 (Ohio 1927); *Concerned Citizens for Neighborhood Schools v. Board of Educ. of Chattanooga*, 379 F.Supp. 1233 (E.D. Tenn.1974); *Mazanec v. North Judson–San Pierre School Corp.*, 614 F.Supp. 1152 [27 Educ. L. Rep. 140] (N.D. Ind.1985); *Brown v. District of Columbia*, 727 A.2d 865 [134 Educ. L. Rep. 206] (D.C.1999). *But see Wisconsin v. Yoder*, 406 U.S. 205, 92 S.Ct. 1526, 32 L.Ed.2d 15 (1972). [Case No. 79]

5. *Matter of Shannon B.*, 522 N.Y.S.2d 488 [43 Educ. L. Rep. 1068] (N.Y. 1987).

6. *State ex rel. Burpee v. Burton*, 45 Wis. 150 (Wis.1878).

7. *See, e.g., Baker v. Owen*, 395 F.Supp. 294 (M.D.N.C.1975), *aff'd*, 423 U.S. 907, 96 S.Ct. 210, 46 L.Ed.2d 137 (1975) (affirming that parental disapproval of corporal punishment did not preclude its being used on a child).

8. *See, e.g., State v. Jones*, 711 S.E.2d 791 (N.C. Ct. App. 2011) (affirming the conviction of parents for failing to send their daughter to school).

9. 406 U.S. 205, 92 S.Ct. 1526, 32 L.Ed.2d 15 (1972). [Case No. 79]

10. While recognizing that many laws speak of guardians along with parents, unless otherwise noted, this chapter uses the term parents to include both parents and guardians.

11. *See, e.g., G.N. v. State*, 833 N.E.2d 1071 [201 Educ. L. Rep. 681] (Ind. Ct. App. 2005) (upholding a student's conviction as truant where evidence proved that he violated the state's compulsory attendance law).

12. *See Bellevue School Dist. v. E.S.*, 257 P.3d 570 [269 Educ. L. Rep. 915] (Wash. 2011) (rejecting the claim that a student was entitled to an attorney at an initial hearing even though she could ultimately have been assigned to a program of home monitoring since it had yet to be determined whether she was truant).

school officials and the courts.[13] Where educational officials failed to prove that a mother committed an essential element of the crime of failing to send her daughter to school regularly because they did not demonstrate that she did so knowingly or purposefully, the Supreme Court of Missouri reversed her conviction for allegedly violating the state's compulsory attendance statute.[14] Similarly, in vacating her conviction for violating the state's compulsory attendance law, Maryland's highest court ruled that once a mother dropped her daughter off at school, educators had the duty to ensure that the child was present in all of her classes.[15] Further, an appellate panel in Florida vitiated a stepfather's being in indirect contempt of court insofar as a trial judge failed to inform him that he was charged with interfering with a truancy order requiring his stepdaughter to attend school every day.[16]

As state and local officials enforce compulsory education laws, their goal is to strike a balance between the rights of individuals and the state. In seeking to preserve this balance, there is a limit beyond which state officials may not go without violating the constitutional rights of parents and students. Since this is not an abstract issue, the judiciary has intervened in cases where parents, and students, claimed that public officials intruded into their personal rights.

EXEMPTIONS FROM COMPULSORY ATTENDANCE

Parents who choose not to send their children to public schools must provide them with equivalent instruction elsewhere either by having them educated in non-public schools or via home schooling. As with other areas involving compulsory attendance, the courts generally uphold statutes and regulations dealing with equivalent instruction.[17] The Supreme Court of Ohio made an exception to this rule in noting that the state's minimum standards were so pervasive and all-encompassing "that total compliance by a non-public school would have effectively eradicated the distinction between public and non-public education."[18] Subsequently, the Supreme Courts of Georgia[19] and Wisconsin[20] agreed that where laws and regulations

---

13. *See, e.g., In re C.M.T.*, 861 A.2d 348 [193 Educ. L. Rep. 805] (Pa. Super. Ct. 2004); *In re Commissioner of Social Servs. On Behalf of Leslie C.*, 614 N.Y.S.2d 855 (N.Y. Fam. Ct. 1994).

14. *State v. Self*, 155 S.W.3d 756 [195 Educ. L. Rep. 1019] (Mo. 2005).

15. *In re Gloria H.*, 979 A.2d 710 [249 Educ. L. Rep.247] (Md. Ct. App. 2009). *See also In re Jamol F.*, 878 N.Y.S.2d 581 [244 Educ. L. Rep. 305] (N.Y. Fam. Ct. 2009) (dismissing charges of educational neglect against a mother who detailed her efforts to ensure that her son would attend school).

16. *Ensign v. State*, 67 So.3d 353 [270 Educ. L. Rep. 929] (Fla. Dist. Ct. App. 2011).

17. *State v. Shaver*, 294 N.W.2d 883 (N.D.1980); *State ex rel. Douglas v. Faith Baptist Church of Louisville*, 301 N.W.2d 571 (Neb.1981), *appeal dismissed*, 454 U.S. 803, 102 S.Ct. 75, 70 L.Ed.2d 72 (1981); *New Life Baptist Church Acad. v. Town of East Longmeadow*, 885 F.2d 940 [56 Educ. L. Rep. 82] (1st Cir.1989), *cert. denied*, 494 U.S. 1066, 110 S.Ct. 1782, 108 L.Ed.2d 784 (1990).

18. *State v. Whisner*, 351 N.E.2d 750, 768 (Ohio 1976). *See also State ex rel. Nagle v. Olin*, 415 N.E.2d 279 (Ohio 1980).

19. *Roemhild v. State*, 308 S.E.2d 154 [14 Educ. L. Rep. 383] (Ga.1983).

20. *State v. Popanz*, 332 N.W.2d 750 [10 Educ. L. Rep. 789] (Wis.1983). [Case No. 80]

lacked sufficient clarity with regard to standards for non-public schools, they were unenforceable.

Non–Public Schools

The most basic constitutional limitation on compulsory education laws is that parents can satisfy them by means other than having their children attend public schools. The law allows this approach because the primary goal of compulsory attendance statutes is to ensure that students obtain a minimum level of education rather than focus on where they are educated. The Supreme Court first enunciated this principle in *Pierce v. Society of the Sisters of the Holy Names of Jesus and Mary (Pierce)*[21] in which it struck down a law from Oregon which would have required children, other than those needing what today would be described as special education, between the ages of eight and sixteen to attend public schools.

Pierce was filed by officials in two non-public schools, one religiously affiliated and the other a military academy, who sought to avoid having their schools forced out of business, relying on their property rights under the Fourteenth Amendment. Ruling in favor of the schools, the Supreme Court explained that state officials could "reasonably [ ] regulate all schools, to inspect, supervise, and examine them, their teachers and pupils."[22] In practice, other than health and safety code issues, educational officials typically impose fewer restrictions on non-public schools than on public schools.

In agreeing with the school officials' due process claim, the Supreme Court found that insofar as parents had the right to direct the upbringing of their children, they could satisfy the compulsory attendance law by sending their young to non-public schools. In this way, the Court acknowledged that "[t]he child is not the mere creature of the state; those who nurture him and direct his destiny have the right, coupled with the high duty, to recognize and prepare him for additional obligations."[23]

Less than two years after *Pierce*, in *Farrington v. Tokushige*,[24] the Supreme Court basically reaffirmed the principle that parents had the right to send their children to non-public schools as a means of satisfying compulsory attendance laws. In upholding the Ninth Circuit's earlier order, the Court rejected attempts by public officials to regulate foreign language schools in Hawaii, most of which were Japanese; the remaining schools provided instruction in Chinese or Korean. The Court rejected the claim of state officials that the schools did not serve the public interest. Instead, the Court concluded that the regulations, which included provisions requiring educators to obtain written permission from public officials in order to operate, limiting the schools' hours of instruction, specifying the topics of instruction and books that the schools could use, mandating that teachers know American history and institutions, and requiring teachers to read and

---

21.   268 U.S. 510, 45 S.Ct. 571, 69 L.Ed. 1070 (1925). [Case No. 81]

22.   *Id.* at 534.

23.   *Id.* at 535.

24.   273 U.S. 284, 47 S.Ct. 406, 71 L.Ed. 646 (1927).

write English, infringed on the rights of the parents and owners of the schools. The Court also thought that the regulations violated the due process provisions of the Fifth Amendment.

Wisconsin v. Yoder (Yoder)[25] represents the most significant exception to judicial support for compulsory attendance laws. In *Yoder,* the Supreme Court ruled in favor of Amish parents who challenged the denial of their request that their children be excused from formal public education beyond eighth grade. The parents argued that insofar as their children would have received all of the preparation they needed in their home communities, it was unnecessary for them to attend public high schools. Relying on the First Amendment's Free Exercise Clause, the Court agreed that the community's almost 300–year way of life would have been gravely endangered, if not destroyed, by requiring them to comply with the compulsory education law.

In *Yoder,* the Supreme Court reiterated that the state could impose reasonable regulations over basic education. Even so, in balancing the competing interests, the Court placed greater weight on the First Amendment and the interests of parents with respect to the religious upbringing of their children. The Court observed that insofar as the Amish way of life and religion were inseparable, requiring the children to attend public high schools may have destroyed their religious beliefs and those of their families. In a partial dissent, Justice Douglas questioned whether children had rights apart from their parents based on his fear that students could have been "harnessed" to the lifestyles of their parents without opportunities to express their own wishes.[26]

Following *Yoder,* it is clear that few, if any, members of other religions can meet its test for being excused from compulsory education requirements. Other than the Amish, courts consistently deny religion-based applications for exemptions to substantial or material parts of compulsory education requirements such as home schooling[27] and sex-AIDS education.[28]

Home Schooling

After a flurry of activity starting in the 1980s, home schooling is legal

---

25.   406 U.S. 205, 92 S.Ct. 1526, 32 L.Ed.2d 15 (1972). [Case No. 79]

26.   According to Justice Douglas:

It is the student's judgment, not his parents,' that is essential if we are to give full meaning to what we have said about the Bill of Rights and of the right of students to be masters of their own destiny. If he is harnessed to the Amish way of life by those in authority over him and if his education is truncated, his entire life may be stunted and deformed. The child, therefore, should be given an opportunity to be heard before the State gives the exemption which we honor today.

Id. at 245–46. (Douglas, dissenting in part).

27.   *Johnson v. Charles City Community Schools Bd. of Educ.*, 368 N.W.2d 74 [25 Educ. L. Rep. 524] (Iowa 1985), *cert. denied sub nom. Pruessner v. Benton*, 474 U.S. 1033, 106 S.Ct. 594, 88 L.Ed.2d 574 [29 Educ. L. Rep. 493] (1985).

28.   *See, e.g., Ware v. Valley Stream High School Dist.*, 551 N.Y.S.2d 167 [58 Educ. L. Rep. 1242] (N.Y. 1989) (affirming the denial of a board's motion for summary judgment where genuine issues of material fact existed over the burden that exposure to an AIDS curriculum would have had on the religious beliefs of students and their parents).

throughout the nation as more than thirty states have enacted explicit statutes on point.[29] The remaining jurisdictions make home schooling legal under laws dealing with alternative,[30] comparable,[31] equivalent,[32] or other[33] instruction (including tutors)[34] and/or private,[35] church,[36] or parochial[37] school exceptions. Yet, as reflected by a case from California, while an appellate court conceded that home schooling is permitted as an exemption under the state's compulsory attendance law as a "private full-time day school," rather than as a "private tutor" situation, the parental right to educate their children at home is not absolute.[38] Reversing an earlier judgment forbidding home schooling, and remanding for further consideration of the safety of the students involved, an appellate panel held that a state dependency court, typically known as a family court in other jurisdictions, had the authority to order parents to send their children to schools outside of the home if doing so was in the best interest of their safety when there was a history of actual abuse or neglect.

In an area that has become contentious in view of the growth of home schooling, courts address whether children are receiving equivalent instruction due to their lack of interaction with peers. An older case from New Jersey suggested that children who were home schooled did not receive an equivalent education,[39] but a later one expressly rejected the need to consider social development in evaluating the equivalency of instruction.[40] The court posited that while children need group activity to develop socially, it did not necessarily have to take place in school.

It is important to note that home schooling, wherein parents educate their own children, is not the same as home-bound instruction for students with disabilities.[41] After legislative and regulatory approval of home school-

---

29. See, e.g., ARK. CODE ANN. § 6–15–501; COL. REV. STAT. ANN. § 22–33–104.5; DEL. CODE ANN. tit. 14 § 2703; GA. CODE ANN. § 20–2–690 (c); LA. REV. STAT. ANN. tit. 17 § 236.1; ME. REV. STAT. ANN. 20–A, § 5001–A(3)(A)(3); MICH. COMP. LAWS ANN. § 380.1561(3)(f); N.J. STAT. ANN. § 18A: 38–25; OHIO REV. CODE ANN. § 3321.04(A)(2); PA. STAT. ANN. tit. 24 § 13–1327.1; UTAH CODE ANN. § 53A–11–102(1)(b)(ii); VA. CODE ANN. § 22.1–254.1.

30. S.D. CODIFIED LAWS ANN. § 13–27–3.

31. IDAHO CODE ANN. § 33–202.

32. CONN. GEN. STAT. ANN. § 10–184; NEV. REV. STAT. ANN. § 392.070; N.Y. EDUC. LAW § 3204(2).

33. IND. CODE ANN. §§ 20–8.1–3–17 ("... some other school which is taught in the English language.").

34. ALA. CODE § 16–28–1(2) (addressing church schools and tutors).

35. For statutes covering home schooling as private schools, see CAL. EDUC. CODE § 48222; ILL. COMP. STAT. ANN. 105 5/26–1; IOWA CODE ANN. §§ 299A.1 et seq. (competent private instruction); MASS GEN. LAWS ANN. Ch. 76 § 1; OKLA. STAT. ANN. tit. 70 § 10–105(A) (private or other schools); TEX. EDUC. CODE ANN. § 25.086 (private or parochial schools).

36. KY. REV. STAT. ANN. § 159.030(b) (private, parochial, or church day schools); NEB. REV. STAT. ANN. § 79–1701(2) (private, parochial, or denominational schools).

37. KAN. STAT. ANN. § 72–1111(a)(2) (private, denominational, or parochial schools providing instruction that is substantially equivalent to that in the public schools).

38. Jonathan L. v. Superior Court, 81 Cal.Rptr.3d 571 [235 Educ. L. Rep. 492] (Cal. Ct. App. 2008).

39. Stephens v. Bongart, 189 A. 131 (N.J. Juv. & Dom. Rel. Ct.1937); Knox v. O'Brien, 72 A.2d 389 (N.J. County Ct.1950).

40. State v. Massa, 231 A.2d 252 (N.J. County Ct.1967).

41. See 20 U.S.C.A. § 1401(26)(A).

ing, courts have addressed an array of issues such as teacher qualifications, curricular content, and state oversight. While most states lack explicit educational requirements for parents who home school their children, the Supreme Court of North Dakota decided that officials could have expected them to meet reasonable certification requirements.[42] On the other hand, the Supreme Court of Michigan indicated that teacher certification requirements violated the free exercise rights of parents since state officials failed to show that they were the least restrictive means of achieving the state's claimed interest.[43] According to the court, this approach violated the rights of parents who home schooled their children since the legislature did not require teachers in non-public schools to be certificated and permitted individuals who lacked state certification to serve as substitute teachers in public schools.

An emerging issue with regard to home schooling is where children are to be educated if their parents, especially those who are divorced, disagree. In such a case, the Supreme Court of New Hampshire affirmed an earlier order that when divorced parents who shared joint custody of their daughter were unable to agree on where she should have been educated, the mother lacked the right to home school the girl over her father's objections.[44] In its analysis, the court applied the "best interests of the child"[45] test in reasoning that the mother could not act unilaterally in placing the child. Earlier, an appellate court in Alabama affirmed an order in favor of a custodial mother who preferred that her child be educated in a regular school setting rather than via home schooling.[46]

Most jurisdictions do not require parents who home school their children to cover specified subject areas. Still, litigation has arisen over curricular content for children who are home schooled. For instance, the Sixth Circuit, in a case from Kentucky, affirmed that a statute requiring children who were home schooled to pass an equivalency examination in order to receive credit for a home study program did not violate the due process, equal protection, or free exercise rights of a student and/or his parents based on the commonwealth's desire to ensure that it had an educated citizenry.[47] Using the same kind of analysis, a federal trial court in Texas rejected a claim that requiring students from non-accredited or home schools to pass proficiency examinations at their own expense in

---

42. *State v. Anderson*, 427 N.W.2d 316 [48 Educ. L. Rep. 649] (N.D.1988), *cert. denied*, 488 U.S. 965, 109 S.Ct. 491, 102 L.Ed.2d 528 (1988).

43. *People v. DeJonge*, 501 N.W.2d 127 [83 Educ. L. Rep. 773] (Mich.1993).

44. *In re Kurowski*, 20 A.3d 306 [268 Educ. L. Rep. 257] (N.H. 2011).

45. An appellate court in Michigan remanded a dispute for further consideration where a divorced non-custodial father questioned whether it would be in his daughter's best interest to be home schooled; this action focused on only one of the family's children. *Parent v. Parent*, 762 N.W.2d 553 [242 Educ. L. Rep. 369] (Mich. Ct. App. 2009). On remand in an unpublished opinion, an appellate panel affirmed an order granting the father's motion that all of the family's children attend public schools. *Appeal after remand, Parent v. Parent*, 2011 WL 2021927 (Mich. Ct. App. 2011).

46. *Morgan v. Morgan*, 964 So.2d 24 (Ala. Civ. App. 2007).

47. *Vandiver v. Hardin County Bd. of Educ.*, 925 F.2d 927 [65 Educ. L. Rep. 1045] (6th Cir. 1991).

order to receive credit toward graduation violated the rights of the children to equal protection and free exercise of religion.[48]

On the related matter of oversight, courts recognize the right of public officials to ensure that students are progressing in school whether by means of standardized tests[49] or other measures such as portfolios[50] and annual reports.[51] Even so, both the Supreme Judicial Court of Massachusetts[52] and the Ninth Circuit[53] invalidated requirements designed to have subjected home schooling families to visitations from public officials in basically agreeing that such oversight was overly intrusive since the same information could have been obtained in other ways such as having parents submit written reports. At the same time, an appellate court in Massachusetts affirmed that when home schooling parents refused to provide educational officials with the bare essentials of the learning plan they created for their children or to permit evaluations of their educational attainment, officials had the right to proceed with having the children declared as being in need of protection and committed to the care of the Department of Social Services.[54]

In like fashion, an appellate panel in Missouri affirmed that while a trial court erred in its discussion of the length of a school term, state officials had the authority to take jurisdiction over an autistic or nearly autistic child.[55] The court agreed that the parents could have been charged with educational neglect since they failed to provide the required hours of instruction or to keep proper records of the child's work and progress. Later, the Third Circuit affirmed that Pennsylvania's reporting and reviewing requirements dealing with such matters as minimum days and hours of instruction in identified subjects and having educational personnel review their records, including student portfolios, did not violate the free exercise of religion rights of parents who home schooled their children.[56] The court explained that insofar as the statute, which was intended to ensure that children who were being home schooled were progressing academically, neither interfered with nor authorized interference with the parents' religious teachings or use of religious materials, it did not violate their rights to free exercise or their alleged right to direct the education of their children.

---

48. *Hubbard By and Through Hubbard v. Buffalo Indep. School Dist.*, 20 F.Supp.2d 1012 [130 Educ. L. Rep. 647] (W.D. Tex.1998).

49. *Murphy v. State of Ark.*, 852 F.2d 1039 [48 Educ. L. Rep. 159] (8th Cir.1988).

50. *Stobaugh v. Wallace*, 757 F.Supp. 653 [66 Educ. L. Rep. 245] (W.D. Pa.1990); *Battles v. Anne Arundel County Bd. of Educ.*, 904 F.Supp. 471 [105 Educ. L. Rep. 93] (D. Md.1995), *aff'd without reported opinion*, 95 F.3d 41 (4th Cir.1996).

51. *State v. Rivera*, 497 N.W.2d 878 [81 Educ. L. Rep. 1064] (Iowa 1993), *reh'g denied* (1993).

52. *Brunelle v. Lynn Pub. Schools*, 702 N.E.2d 1182 [130 Educ. L. Rep. 1322] (Mass.1998).

53. *Calabretta v. Floyd*, 189 F.3d 808 (9th Cir.1999).

54. *In re Ivan*, 717 N.E.2d 1020 [138 Educ. L. Rep. 511] (Mass. Ct. App.1999), *review denied*, 723 N.E.2d 33 (Mass.2000).

55. *In re J.B.*, 58 S.W.3d 575 [159 Educ. L. Rep. 356] (Mo. Ct. App.2001), *reh'g and transfer denied* (2001).

56. *Combs v. Homer–Center School Dist.*, 540 F.3d 231 [236 Educ. L. Rep. 117] (3d Cir. 2008).

HOME SCHOOLING, EXTRACURRICULAR ACTIVITIES, AND PART-TIME ATTENDANCE

Parents who practice home schooling have had limited success over whether their children can participate in extracurricular activities. West Virginia's highest court was of the opinion that rules of the state athletic association prohibiting students who were home schooled from taking part in interscholastic athletics did not violate their rights under the equal protection clause of the state constitution.[57] The court pointed out that insofar as participation in extracurricular activities, including interscholastic athletics, did not rise to the level of a fundamental or constitutional right, the rule was rationally related to a legitimate state purpose. The court identified two key reasons in justifying its position. First, the court maintained that the rule prevented parents from withdrawing their children who may have been struggling academically simply to maintain athletic eligibility. Second, the court thought that insofar as local boards received funding only for students who are actually enrolled in classes, and having to offer services to students who are home schooled would have strained their budgets, the rule protected the financial well-being of school systems.

Along the same line, home schooled students and their parents in Michigan unsuccessfully challenged a rule of the state athletic association that would have required them to attend school before becoming eligible to participate in interscholastic athletic programs. In affirming the denial of the plaintiffs' request to enjoin the rule, the court remarked that the home schooled students lacked a statutory right to participate in the athletic programs since they are not required elements of the school program.[58] The court added that the enrollment requirement did not violate the students' rights to either the free exercise of religion or equal protection. Earlier, an appellate court in New York affirmed that a home schooled student was ineligible to take part in a local school's interscholastic sports program pursuant to state regulation which conditioned eligibility on being regularly enrolled in school.[59] The court found that the regulation did not infringe on the student's rights to due process or equal protection.

Home schooling parents have also not had much success in seeking to enroll their children in public schools on part-time bases. In such a case, the Tenth Circuit affirmed that a policy of a school board in Oklahoma

---

57. *Jones v. West Va. State Bd. of Educ.*, 622 S.E.2d 289 [203 Educ. L. Rep. 862] (W. Va. 2005).

58. *Reid v. Kenowa Hills Pub. Schools*, 680 N.W.2d 62 [188 Educ. L. Rep. 438] (Mich. Ct. App. 2004).

59. *Bradstreet v. Sobol*, 650 N.Y.S.2d 402 [114 Educ. L. Rep. 927] (N.Y. App. Div. 1996). *See also Angstadt v. Midd–West School Dist.*, 377 F.3d 338 [190 Educ. L. Rep. 48] (3d Cir. 2004) (affirming that a student who in a cyber school had no right to participate in interscholastic basketball since she failed to establish the likelihood of success on the merits of the claim that she had a property interest to do so).

prohibiting part-time attendance did not violate a home schooled student's right to the free exercise of religion.[60] The court agreed that the board's action was rooted in a neutral policy of general application that neither prohibited her parents from home schooling her in accordance with their religion nor forced them to do anything contrary to those beliefs.[61]

MARRIAGE AND/OR PARENTHOOD

Students who are eligible to attend public schools cannot be excluded if they are married. In an older case illustrating this rule, where a young woman conceived a child out of wedlock but was married by the time she gave birth, she sought to return to school when her husband deserted her and the child. The Supreme Court of Kansas, while conceding that school officials could bar individuals who were "of a licentious or immoral character,"[62] observed that having a child out of wedlock failed to prove that the woman was of such character. In the same year, the Supreme Court of Mississippi invalidated a board resolution designed to prohibit married persons from attending public schools. In ordering the student's admission, the court commented that insofar as marriage is a domestic relationship "highly favored by law.... [as] refining and elevating, rather than demoralizing,"[63] there was no reason why she should have been excluded.

Courts have struck down prohibitions aimed at limiting the participation of married students in extracurricular activities. The first three federal trial courts to address the issue agreed, in rapid succession, and without citing each other, that eligibility for school-sponsored activities could not be made dependent on marital status.[64]

RESIDENCE FOR SCHOOL PURPOSES

State laws grant school-aged children who are district residents the right to attend school on tuition-free bases. The great weight of authority is that residence for school purposes does not necessarily mean that children must have legal domiciles in districts since domicile is a place where individuals intend to remain indefinitely.[65] The common law rule is that the legal domicile of minors is that of their parent(s) and that children are legally incapable of establishing their own domiciles absent special circumstances such as the death or legal separation of their parents.[66]

---

60. *Swanson By and Through Swanson v. Guthrie Indep. School Dist. No. I–L*, 135 F.3d 694 [123 Educ. L. Rep. 1087] (10th Cir. 1998).

61. *See also Thomas v. Allegany County Bd. of Educ.*, 443 A.2d 622 [3 Educ. L. Rep. 670] (Md. Ct. Spec. App. 1982) (rejecting parental claims that officials violated the rights of their children who attended non-public schools by prohibiting them from participating in a music program offered only to full-time public school students since state law did not entitle such students to be admitted to any part or portion of the public school system which they choose).

62. *Nutt v. Board of Educ. of City of Goodland*, 278 P. 1065, 1066 (Kan.1929).

63. *McLeod v. State ex rel. Colmer*, 122 So. 737, 738 (Miss.1929).

64. *Holt v. Shelton*, 341 F.Supp. 821 (M.D. Tenn.1972); *Davis v. Meek*, 344 F.Supp. 298 (N.D. Ohio 1972); *Moran v. School Dist. No. 7, Yellowstone County*, 350 F.Supp. 1180 (D. Mont.1972).

65. *State ex rel. Doe v. Kingery*, 203 S.E.2d 358 (W. Va.1974).

While residence refers to the place where children actually live, neither physical presence alone[67] nor residing in a district solely in order to attend public school[68] is a sufficient basis to establish residence for purposes of attending school on a tuition-free basis. Accordingly, one may have multiple residences, but it is only possible to have one domicile. In such a case, when a child moved from Illinois to attend school in North Carolina while living with an uncle, her attorney was unable to rebut the presumption that her domicile was the same as her mother's. An appellate court thus affirmed that insofar as the residency requirements were uniformly applied, school officials did not violate the child's rights to due process or equal protection in forbidding her from attending school without having to pay tuition.[69]

In *Plyler v. Doe* (*Plyler*),[70] the Supreme Court affirmed that under the Equal Protection Clause, Texas could not deny a free public school education to school-aged children whose parents were undocumented residents. In so doing, the Court invalidated a statute that would have deprived local boards of state funds for the education of children who were not legally admitted to the United States and that authorized officials to refuse to enroll these students. In applying the right to equal protection to the children, the Justices determined that the constitutionality of a classification depended on whether it could be viewed as fairly furthering a substantial state interest. The Court was of the view that the uniqueness of education distinguishes it from general forms of social welfare, thereby triggering the necessity for a state to support withholding it by more substantial justification than required by the usual rational relationship test. The Court also ascertained both that the state's reasons for the statute failed to meet this test and that although the children were innocent of the conduct of their parents, the law's impact severely punished them as long as they were in the United States.

More than a decade after *Plyler*, a federal trial court in California enjoined the implementation of Proposition 187, a voter initiative requiring state personnel, including educators, to verify the immigration status of persons with whom they came into contact.[71] While not addressing the education provisions directly, the Ninth Circuit upheld the injunction.[72] On partial reconsideration, the trial court, citing *Plyler*, specified that the

66. *See A.M.S. ex rel. A.D.S. v. Board of Educ. of City of Margate*, 976 A.2d 402 [247 Educ. L. Rep. 354] (N.J. Super. Ct. App. Div. 2009) (applying the common law rule in affirming that the child of a widowed member of the military was domiciled in New Jersey even though he spent most of his time in Pennsylvania with his grandparents while his father was on active duty).

67. *Catlin v. Sobol*, 93 F.3d 1112 [111 Educ. L. Rep. 1114] (2d Cir.1996), *on remand*, 988 F.Supp. 85 [124 Educ. L. Rep. 166] (N.D.N.Y.1997).

68. *Mina ex rel. Anghel v. Board of Educ. for Homewood–Flossmoor*, 809 N.E.2d 168 [188 Educ. L. Rep. 405] (Ill. App. Ct. 2004).

69. *Graham v. Mock*, 545 S.E.2d 263 [153 Educ. L. Rep. 796] (N.C. Ct. App. 2001), *appeal dismissed, review denied*, 550 S.E.2d 776 (N.C.2001).

70. 457 U.S. 202, 102 S.Ct. 2382, 72 L.Ed.2d 786 [4 Educ. L. Rep. 953] (1982), *reh'g denied*, 458 U.S. 1131, 103 S.Ct. 14, 73 L.Ed.2d 1401 (1982). [Case No. 82]

71. *League of United Latin American Citizens v. Wilson*, 908 F.Supp. 755 (C.D. Cal. 1995).

72. *Gregorio T. By and Through Jose T. v. Wilson*, 59 F.3d 1002 (9th Cir. 1995).

portion of the initiative that would have denied access to schools to students was invalid since states cannot deny basic public education to children due to their immigration status or that of their parents.[73] On reconsideration in part, the court confirmed its original judgment on the rights of students to attend school.[74]

In a second case from Texas, *Martinez v. Bynum*, the Supreme Court rejected a challenge to the constitutionality of a residency requirement that denied tuition-free admission to public schools to minors who lived apart from their parents if they were in districts primarily to obtain a free education. In affirming that the statute violated neither the Fourteenth Amendment nor interfered with the constitutional right of interstate travel, the Court held that "[a] bona fide residence requirement, appropriately defined and uniformly applied, furthers the substantial state interest in assuring that services provided for its residents are enjoyed only by residents."[75]

The conditions under which students who live in one district can attend classes in another under open-enrollment statutes vary from one jurisdiction to another. School officials may accept students from other districts on tuition bases as long as state laws permit them to do so.[76] Non-resident parents can be required to pay tuition under these circumstances[77] since children do not have a right to attend public schools for free once their families have moved.[78] In such a dispute, an appellate court in Ohio permitted a board's fraud claim against parents to proceed where officials sought to recover tuition from them because they used false documentation to enroll their children in a district within which they did not live.[79]

As reflected in a case from the Supreme Court of Vermont, educational officials must be careful when considering whether parents are district residents whose children are eligible for free tuition. In affirming that state officials mistakenly identified parents as eligible for tuition payments in a district that did not operate its own schools, the panel agreed that a trial court did not abuse its discretion in denying a school board's motion for relief from the judgment without a hearing since local officials failed to file a response to the initial finding that the parents were eligible for free tuition.[80] In Pennsylvania, an appellate court rejected a mother's claim that her daughters should have been eligible to attend school in a neighboring district where she owned a second home.[81] The court asserted that insofar

---

73. *League of United Latin American Citizens v. Wilson*, 908 F.Supp. 755 (C.D. Cal. 1995).

74. *League of United Latin American Citizens v. Wilson*, 997 F.Supp. 1244 (C.D. Cal. 1997).

75. 461 U.S. 321, 328, 103 S.Ct. 1838, 75 L.Ed.2d 879 [10 Educ. L. Rep. 11] (1983). [Case No. 83]

76. *Union Free High School Dist. No. 1, Town of Iron River v. Joint School Dist. No. 1 of Town of Maple*, 117 N.W.2d 273 (Wis. 1962).

77. *In re White*, 715 N.E.2d 203 [137 Educ. L. Rep. 361] (Ohio Ct. App. 1998).

78. *Dunbar v. Hamden Bd. of Educ.*, 267 F. Supp.2d 178 [179 Educ. L. Rep. 258] (D. Conn. 2003).

79. *Shaker Heights City School Dist. Bd. of Educ. v. Cloud*, 738 N.E.2d 473 [148 Educ. L. Rep. 1031] (Ohio Ct. App.2000).

80. *Sandgate School Dist. v. Cate*, 883 A.2d 774 [202 Educ. L. Rep. 215] (Vt. 2005).

81. *Paek v. Pen Argyl Area School Dist.*, 923 A.2d 563 [220 Educ. L. Rep. 726] (Pa. Commw. Ct. 2007).

as the family spent, on average, two nights a week in the district, the children were insufficiently present for the purposes of attending school there.

Absent state laws to the contrary, children living in orphanages, charitable homes, and/or who are adjudicated wards of the state are generally considered residents of the districts within which they reside.[82] Courts also agree that school boards cannot refuse to enroll homeless children whose shelters are located within their boundaries.[83] In Texas, a federal trial court was persuaded that a rational relationship existed between a statute and the state's legitimate objectives of preserving the financial integrity of school districts while not expecting taxpayers to pay for educating children who were wards of other states.[84] If courts appoint guardians with whom children live, boards must accept them on tuition-free bases.[85]

A case from Pennsylvania reveals that public officials can enforce statutes providing that children who live in institutions and whose expenses are paid for in whole or part by other jurisdictions are not entitled to tuition-free attendance in local public schools.[86] Along these same lines, an appellate court in Illinois contended that when a school board placed a student that it expelled in a residential facility, it remained obligated to pay for his tuition even though officials argued that he could not have attended classes if he had not been excluded from school.[87]

New York's highest court addressed the status of students who lived with their mother before they were evicted from their home. The court decreed that the district where the children previously lived with their mother, rather than the one in which they resided in a homeless shelter when they were placed in foster care, was their district of residence within the meaning of state law.[88] The court was of the opinion that the board in the district where they lived with their mother was responsible for the cost of educating the children after they were placed in a family home.

In Pennsylvania, an appellate court considered the rights of a student whose grandmother was his sole care giver and supported him as if he were

---

82. *Catlin v. Sobol*, 93 F.3d 1112 [111 Educ. L. Rep. 1114] (2d Cir.1996), *on remand*, 988 F.Supp. 85 [124 Educ. L. Rep. 166] (N.D.N.Y. 1997); *State ex rel. Bd. of Christian Serv. of Lutheran Minn. Conference v. School Bd. of Consol. School Dist. No. 3*, 287 N.W. 625 (Minn. 1939).

83. *See, e.g., Harrison v. Sobol*, 705 F.Supp. 870 [52 Educ. L. Rep. 91] (S.D.N.Y.1988); *Orozco ex rel. Arroyo v. Sobol*, 703 F.Supp. 1113 [51 Educ. L. Rep. 865] (S.D.N.Y.1989); *Lampkin v. District of Columbia*, 27 F.3d 605 [92 Educ. L. Rep. 811] (D.C. Cir.1994), *cert. denied*, 513 U.S. 1016, 115 S.Ct. 578, 130 L.Ed.2d 493 (1994), *on remand*, 879 F.Supp. 116 [99 Educ. L. Rep. 137] (D.D.C.1995), *injunction terminated*, 886 F.Supp. 56 [100 Educ. L. Rep. 1031] (D.D.C. 1995).

84. *East Texas Guidance & Achievement Ctr. v. Brockette*, 431 F.Supp. 231 (E.D. Tex. 1977).

85. *University Ctr. v. Ann Arbor Pub. Schools*, 191 N.W.2d 302 (Mich. 1971).

86. *Steven M. v. Gilhool*, 700 F.Supp. 261 [50 Educ. L. Rep. 785] (E.D. Pa. 1988).

87. *Carbondale Community High School Dist. No. 165 v. Herrin Community Unit School Dist. No. 4*, 708 N.E.2d 844 [134 Educ. L. Rep. 538] (Ill. App. Ct. 1999).

88. *Longwood Cent. School Dist. v. Springs Union Free School Dist.*, 774 N.Y.S.2d 857 [187 Educ. L. Rep. 205] (N.Y. 2004).

her own child. The court concluded that insofar as the student lived with his grandmother all of his life, except for brief periods when he resided with his parents, who were not married to each other, he was entitled to attend school in the district where she lived free of charge.[89]

VACCINATIONS

In apparently the earliest published case involving vaccinations, albeit not in a school setting, the Supreme Court of Vermont upheld a community's right to have residents vaccinated against infectious diseases.[90] The court ruled that a local town council could impose a tax to help defray the cost of inoculating residents against smallpox even though there were no reported cases of the disease in the area.

In the first reported school case, more than sixty years after the dispute from Vermont, the Supreme Court of Pennsylvania upheld the right of school officials to exclude children who were not vaccinated against smallpox.[91] The court decided that even absent express legislation granting them the authority to do so, officials could exclude children from school who were not vaccinated in order to protect the public welfare.[92] Since vaccination requirements as a condition of attending school have been subject to a fair amount of controversy, this section highlights the cases that have been litigated.

In the first of two relevant older cases, the Supreme Court, in *Jacobson v. Commonwealth of Massachusetts*,[93] maintained that a statute empowering local authorities to require everyone to be vaccinated was constitutional. Although acknowledging the importance of individual liberty in seeking to avoid vaccinations, the Court thought that under the social compact theory, communities have the right to protect themselves against epidemics and diseases that might challenge the general welfare. Later, in refusing to hear an appeal in a case from Texas, in *Zucht v. King*,[94] the Court let stand a judgment that parents lacked a constitutional right to have their child attend school without being vaccinated. In rejecting the parental claim that a local ordinance requiring vaccinations infringed on their rights, the Court wrote that states have the authority to empower municipalities to enact ordinances protecting the general welfare.

Courts uniformly uphold statutes requiring or authorizing educators to adopt vaccination policies, typically for smallpox and diphtheria.[95] When

---

89. *Velazquez ex rel. Speaks–Velazquez v. East Stroudsburg Area School Dist.*, 949 A.2d 354 [233 Educ. L. Rep. 382] (Pa. Cmwlth. Ct. 2008), *appeal denied*, 964 A.2d 896 (Pa. 2009).

90. *Hazen v. Strong*, 2 Vt. 427 (Vt. 1830).

91. *Duffield v. School District of Williamsport*, 29 A. 742 (Pa. 1894).

92. For another early case, *see Viemeister v. White*, 179 N.Y. 235 (N.Y. 1904) (upholding a student's exclusion for not being vaccinated against smallpox).

93. 197 U.S. 11, 25 S.Ct. 358, 49 L.Ed. 643 (1905).

94. 260 U.S. 174, 43 S.Ct. 24, 67 L.Ed. 194 (1922).

95. *Board of Educ. of Mt. Lakes v. Maas*, 152 A.2d 394 (N.J. Super. Ct. App. Div. 1959); *McCartney v. Austin*, 298 N.Y.S.2d 26 (N.Y. App. Div. 1969); *Syska v. Montgomery County Bd. of Educ.*, 415 A.2d 301 (Md. Ct. Spec. App. 1980), *cert. denied*, 288 Md. 744 (Md. 1980), *appeal*

children who are not vaccinated are barred from schools, the remedies against parents are normally fines and threats of imprisonment. In one instance, the Supreme Court of Arkansas upheld an order removing a child from parental custody since their refusal to cooperate deprived a child of his right to an education.[96]

Where statutes provide for exceptions from compulsory vaccination requirements, parents have had more success. For example, the federal trial court in New Hampshire invalidated a provision that school officials may excuse a child for religious reasons at their discretion as unconstitutionally vague due to the lack of criteria guiding their actions.[97] Also, the Eighth Circuit reviewed a consolidated appeal which relied on the Establishment Clause in striking down a statute from Arkansas invalidating a religious-beliefs exemption mandating immunization of school children against Hepatitis B but which otherwise upheld, after severance, the underlying immunization requirement.[98] The court dismissed the appeal as moot since the legislature broadened the exemption to encompass philosophical and religious objections.[99]

Two federal trial courts in New York rejected parental requests for exemptions under a state law that excuses persons whose opposition to immunization stems from genuine and sincere religious beliefs where their objections were medical, not religious[100] and where their refusal to vaccinate their daughters was not based on genuine and sincere religious beliefs.[101] Yet, in a third case from New York, a mother who was a member of a religious congregation which opposed the introduction of foreign materials into the human body was granted a religious exemption from the state's immunization requirement. Even though educators were convinced that the mother's sincerely held religious beliefs were based on a personal philosophy rather than a legitimate religion, a federal trial court denied a board's motion to dismiss her claim since she established the likelihood of success on the merits because her views appeared to be religious in nature as opposed to merely philosophical or scientific.[102]

When parents seeking religious exemptions comply with statutory requirements, courts rule in their favor,[103] even if they are not required to

---

dismissed, 450 U.S. 961, 101 S.Ct. 1475, 67 L.Ed.2d 610 (1981); *Workman v. Mingo County Bd. of Educ.*, 419 Fed.Appx. 348 [268 Educ. L. Rep. 744] (4th Cir. 2011).

96. *Cude v. State of Ark.*, 377 S.W.2d 816 (Ark.1964).

97. *Avard v. Dupuis*, 376 F.Supp. 479 (D.N.H.1974).

98. The earlier cases were *McCarthy v. Boozman*, 212 F. Supp.2d 945 [168 Educ. L. Rep. 258] (W.D. Ark. 2002) and *Boone v. Boozman*, 217 F. Supp.2d 938 [169 Educ. L. Rep. 247] (E.D. Ark. 2002), *appeal dismissed sub nom. McCarthy v. Ozark School Dist.*, 359 F.3d 1029 [185 Educ. L. Rep. 453] (8th Cir. 2004).

99. *McCarthy v. Ozark School Dist.*, 359 F.3d 1029 [185 Educ. L. Rep. 453] (8th Cir. 2004).

100. *Farina v. Board of Educ. of City of N.Y.*, 116 F.Supp.2d 503 [148 Educ. L. Rep. 168] (S.D.N.Y. 2000).

101. *Caviezel v. Great Neck Pub. Schools*, 701 F.Supp.2d 414 [258 Educ. L. Rep. 555] (E.D.N.Y. 2010).

102. *Turner v. Liverpool Cent. School*, 186 F. Supp.2d 187, 188–89 [162 Educ. L. Rep. 256] (N.D.N.Y. 2002).

103. *In re LePage*, 18 P.3d 1177 [151 Educ. L. Rep. 605] (Wyo.2001); *Jones v. State, Dep't of Health*, 18 P.3d 1189 [151 Educ. L. Rep. 610] (Wyo. 2001).

substantiate the religious bases for their requests.[104] In a case where there was no dispute over the sincerity of a family's religious beliefs, a federal trial court in New York directed educational officials to permit a student to continue participating on his school's lacrosse team even though he had not received a tetanus shot.[105] The court reasoned that this was appropriate since the student played for years without the shot and there was no justification for treating him differently than those who had yet to receive vaccinations due to religious objections but were permitted to attend school.

FEDERAL STATUTES IMPACTING ON EDUCATION

Pursuant to the Tenth Amendment, education is a reserved power of states. Even so, since the enactment of the Elementary and Secondary Education Act in 1965, the federal government has adopted a more active role in public schooling. This section addresses two key federal statutes impacting on education, the Family Educational Rights and Privacy Act and the No Child Left Behind Act.

THE FAMILY EDUCATIONAL RIGHTS AND PRIVACY ACT

The Family Educational Rights and Privacy Act (FERPA),[106] also known as the Buckley Amendment, after its primary sponsor, New York Senator James Buckley, covers all educational institutions receiving federal financial assistance, most notably public schools. FERPA created two major obligations for educational institutions that receive funds administered by the United States Department of Education (DOE). First, FERPA assures eligible students, typically those over the age of eighteen, and parents of dependent children access to their educational records. Second, FERPA protects the confidentiality of these records by prohibiting their disclosure without prior consent of parents or eligible students, subject to two major exceptions. The first permits school officials to reveal "directory information"[107] about students, unless they, or their parents, object to the release of some or all of the information.[108] The second allows limited disclosure to

---

104. *Department of Health v. Curry*, 722 So.2d 874 [131 Educ. L. Rep. 870] (Fla. Dist. Ct. App. 1998), *review dismissed*, 729 So.2d 390 [134 Educ. L. Rep. 401] (Fla. 1999), *review denied*, 735 So.2d 1284 (Fla. 1999).

105. *Hadley v. Rush Henrietta Cent. School Dist.*, 409 F. Supp. 2d 164 [206 Educ. L. Rep. 609] (W.D.N.Y. 2006).

106. 20 U.S.C.A. § 1232g. Portions of this statute are in the Appendix.

107. Directory information includes "the student's name, address, telephone listing, date and place of birth, major field of study, participation in officially recognized activities and sports, weight and height of members of athletic teams, dates of attendance, degrees and awards received, and the most recent previous educational agency or institution attended by the student." 20 U.S.C.A. § 1232g(a)(5)(A).

108. 20 U.S.C.A. §§ 1232g(a)(5)(A), (B) identifies the content of "directory information" and the notice which must be given to students, and parents of students under eighteen and who have not graduated from high school, about the directory information to be revealed and the right to object to release.

entities[109] such as the juvenile justice system[110] and accrediting agencies[111] or, under specified circumstances, in response to subpoenas[112] or in emergencies "to protect the health or safety of the student or other persons."[113]

FERPA defines "education records" as "records, files, documents and other materials which . . . contain information directly related to a student and [which] are maintained by an educational . . . agency or institution or by a person acting for such . . . agency or institution."[114] FERPA excludes "records of instructional . . . personnel . . . which are in the sole possession of the maker . . . and which are not accessible or revealed to any other person except a substitute."[115]

Restrictions on access to student files notwithstanding, FERPA allows nine exceptions for when parties do not need prior permission to review educational records. First, school staff with legitimate educational interests can access student records.[116] Second, officials representing schools to which students applied for admission can access their records as long as parents and/or eligible students receive proper notice that the information has been sent to the receiving institutions.[117] Third, authorized representatives of specified federal, state, and local officials who are authorized to do so by state law can view student records for law enforcement purposes.[118] Fourth, persons who evaluate student eligibility for financial aid can review their educational records.[119] Fifth, members of organizations conducting studies on behalf of educational agencies or institutions developing predictive tests or administering aid programs and improving instruction can view records as long as they do not release personal information about students.[120] Sixth, individuals acting in the course of their duties for accrediting organizations can review student records.[121] Seventh, parents of dependent children can access student records.[122] Eighth, in emergency situations, persons who protect the health and safety of students or other persons can view records.[123] Ninth, written permission is unnecessary if student records are subpoenaed or otherwise sought via judicial orders

---

109. For a complete list of exceptions, see 20 U.S.C.A. §§ 1232g(b)(1)(A)–(J).

110. 20 U.S.C.A. § 1232g(b)(1)(E)(ii).

111. 20 U.S.C.A. § 1232g(b)(1)(G).

112. 20 U.S.C. § 1232g(a)(2)(B). See Baker v. Mitchell–Waters, 826 N.E.2d 894 [197 Educ. L. Rep. 777] (Ohio Ct. App. 2005) (affirming that FERPA and the equivalent state statute did not exempt documents from discovery where parents claimed that school officials were verbally and physically abusive to their son).

113. 20 U.S.C.A. § 1232g(b)(1)(I).

114. 20 U.S.C.A. § 1232g(a)(4)(A).

115. 20 U.S.C.A. § 1232g(a)(4)(B)(1).

116. 20 U.S.C.A. § 1232g(b)(1)(A).

117. 20 U.S.C.A. § 1232g(b)(1)(B).

118. 20 U.S.C.A. §§ 1232g(b)(1)(C), (E).

119. 20 U.S.C.A. § 1232g(b)(1)(D).

120. 20 U.S.C.A. § 1232g(b)(1)(F).

121. 20 U.S.C.A. § 1232g(b)(1)(G).

122. 20 U.S.C.A. § 1232g(b)(1)(H).

123. 20 U.S.C.A. § 1232g(b)(1)(I).

except that school board officials must notify parents and/or eligible students in advance of their intent to comply.[124]

Insofar as the DOE is responsible for enforcing FERPA, complaints must be filed with its Family Policy Compliance Office.[125] Parents and/or eligible students have enforcement rights and are entitled to "an opportunity for a hearing ... to challenge the content of ... education records."[126] As important as FERPA is with regard to student records, the Supreme Court did not address its first two cases on the law until more than twenty-five years after it went into effect.

In *Owasso Independent School District v. Falvo (Falvo)*,[127] a mother in Oklahoma challenged a school board's permitting the use of peer grading, whereby children grade the papers of their classmates before calling the scores out to their teachers. The Supreme Court noted that insofar as peer-grading does not turn the student papers into educational records covered by FERPA, the board did not violate the law by permitting teachers to use the practice over the mother's objection. In allowing school officials to permit teachers to continue using peer grading, the Court proceeded on the assumption that injured parties could file private causes of action under FERPA, a position that it explicitly rejected in the next case.

At issue in *Gonzaga University v. Doe (Gonzaga)*,[128] handed down four months after *Falvo*, was the claim of an undergraduate male student who alleged that university administrators violated his rights when, in the face of apparently unsubstantiated accusations of sexual misconduct involving a female, they released his records to state officials without his knowledge or consent. The male was then denied certification as a public school teacher. The Supreme Court observed that although the student's records were disclosed impermissibly, he did not have a private cause of action under section 1983 since his sole avenue of redress was to file a complaint with the DOE. As a result of these two cases, especially *Gonzaga*, it is unlikely that school systems will face much litigation under FERPA since the Justices essentially repudiated its position in *Falvo* by interpreting the law as not intending to create individually enforceable rights. Subsequently, a state appellate panel[129] and a federal trial court in New York[130] agreed that FERPA does not permit aggrieved plaintiffs to initiate individual claims to recover damages.

---

124. 20 U.S.C.A. §§ 1232g(b)(1)(J), 1232g(b)(2)(B). For an interesting case arising under the latter provision, *see Ragusa v. Malverne Union Free School Dist.*, 549 F. Supp.2d 288 [233 Educ. L. Rep. 236] (E.D.N.Y. 2008) (granting a high school teacher access to records when she filed suit claiming that officials transferred a disproportionate number of students with disabilities into her classes).

125. 20 U.S.C.A. §§ 1232g(f), (g).

126. 20 U.S.C.A. § 1232g(a)(2).

127. 534 U.S. 426, 122 S.Ct. 934, 151 L.Ed.2d 896 [161 Educ. L. Rep. 33] (2002). [Case No. 84]

128. 536 U.S. 273, 122 S.Ct. 2268, 153 L.Ed.2d 309 [165 Educ. L. Rep. 458] (2002).

129. *Goins v. Rome City School Dist.*, 811 N.Y.S.2d 520 [207 Educ. L. Rep. 292] (N.Y. App. Div. 2006). For the same outcome, albeit in higher education, *see Zona v. Clark Univ.*, 436 F.Supp.2d 287 [211 Educ. L. Rep. 218] (D. Mass. 2006).

130. *Simpson ex rel. Simpson v. Uniondale Union Free School Dist.*, 702 F. Supp.2d 122 [258 Educ. L. Rep. 613] (E.D. N.Y. 2010).

A case from the Supreme Court of Washington put an interesting twist on the meaning of student records. The court held that a videotape from a school bus surveillance camera was subject to disclosure under state law because it did not contain any personal information relating to students.[131] In another case involving FERPA, the Supreme Court of Montana ruled that school officials could not deny a request for student records under FERPA because it does not forbid the release of their disciplinary records.[132]

In New York, a father unsuccessfully filed suit alleging that school officials violated FERPA by entering his son's artwork in a contest without his knowledge. Since the child had a certificate of participation that he had brought home to his parents, a federal trial court dismissed all of the claims against the board and various school officials.[133]

No Child Left Behind Act

Disputes over the future of the controversial No Child Left Behind Act (NCLB) rage as this book heads to press. Amid debate over the NCLB's accountability provisions, as noted below, the President and United States Secretary of Education have granted waivers to these key provisions.

The NCLB was enacted in 2002 as the Strengthening and Improvement of Elementary and Secondary Schools,[134] part of the re-authorization of the Elementary and Secondary Education Act (ESEA). The ESEA, which became law in 1965, as the then most extensive federal education statute, created a pool of federal funds to be used to provide, or withhold, support for states based on whether they complied with its provisions and those of the Civil Rights Act of 1964.

At its core, the NCLB is designed to create a framework to improve the performance of elementary and secondary schools. Key elements in the NCLB are intended to make school systems accountable for student achievement, particularly by imposing standards for adequate yearly progress for students and districts; requiring school systems to rely on effective research based teaching methods; improving academic achievement among students who are economically disadvantaged; assisting in preparing, training, and recruiting highly qualified teachers; and affording parents better choices while creating innovative educational programs, especially if local school systems are unresponsive to their needs. Based on the extensive nature of the NCLB, this section provides an overview of the Act as it impacts curricular issues.

The NCLB is divided into nine subchapters, down from the ESEA's earlier fourteen. The law retains many of its original provisions such as

---

131. *Lindeman v. Kelso School Dist. No. 458*, 172 P.3d 329 [227 Educ. L. Rep. 334] (Wash. 2007).

132. *Board of Trustees, Cut Bank Pub. Schools v. Cut Bank Pioneer Press*, 160 P.3d 482 [220 Educ. L. Rep. 903] (Mont. 2007).

133. *Simpson ex rel. Simpson v. Uniondale Union Free School Dist.*, 702 F.Supp.2d 122 [258 Educ. L. Rep. 613] (E.D.N.Y. 2010).

134. 20 U.S.C.A. §§ 6301 *et seq.* Portions of the NCLB are in the Appendix.

Title (or Chapter) I, now Subchapter I, Improving the Academic Achievement of the Disadvantaged, perhaps the best known part of the ESEA.[135] Subchapter I requires local educational agencies (LEAs), typically school boards that receive federal financial assistance, to take steps to improve academic achievement among students who are economically disadvantaged. Subchapter I is divided into subparts which are designed to provide basic requirements such as remedial programs for specifically identified children from low income families. Other key subparts cover allocations; grants for improving reading skills; education for migratory children; prevention and intervention programs for children and youth who are neglected, delinquent, and/or at-risk; national assessment of Subchapter I; comprehensive school reform; advanced placement programs; and school dropout prevention. The Supreme Court's decision in *Agostini v. Felton*,[136] which removed earlier barriers to the contrary, now permits the on-site delivery of Title I services to students who attend religiously affiliated nonpublic schools.

Subchapter II, Preparing, Training, and Recruiting High Quality Teachers and Principals, sections that go to the heart of the NCLB, contain some of the Act's most controversial and far-reaching provisions.[137] The major parts of this subchapter address teacher and principal training-recruiting funds; mathematics and science partnerships; innovations for teacher quality; and programs to enhance education through technology.

Subchapter III, Language Instruction for Limited English Proficient and Immigrant Students, directs school officials to provide improved language instruction for children in need of such programs.[138] Subchapter IV, 21st Century Schools, is divided into two major parts: the first concerns safe and drug-free schools and communities while the second focuses on 21st Century Community Learning Centers.[139]

Subchapter V, Promoting Informed Parental Choice and Innovative Programs, covers innovative programs; charter schools; assistance for magnet schools; and providing funds for improving education.[140] Among the initiatives identified under funding are partnerships in character education; gifted and talented programs; star schools; foreign language assistance; physical education; excellence in economic education; grants to improve the mental health of children; combating domestic violence; and the Women's Educational Equity Act. These programs are intended to afford parents better choices while creating innovative educational offerings, especially if LEAs are unresponsive to their needs and those of their children.

Subchapter VI, Flexibility and Accountability, is divided into three key sections: improving academic achievement, rural education initiatives, and

---

135. 20 U.S.C.A. §§ 6301 *et seq.*

136. 521 U.S. 203, 117 S.Ct. 1997, 138 L.Ed.2d 391 [119 Educ. L. Rep. 29] (1997). [Case No. 11]

137. 20 U.S.C.A. §§ 6601 *et seq.*

138. 20 U.S.C.A. §§ 6801 *et seq.*

139. 20 U.S.C.A. §§ 7101 *et seq.*

140. 20 U.S.C.A. §§ 7201 *et seq.*

general provisions.[141] Subchapter VII, Indian, Native Hawaiian, and Alaska Native Education, supports the educational efforts of states, LEAs, and post-secondary institutions that serve the target populations.[142] Subchapter VIII, Impact Aid, offers financial aid to LEAs experiencing substantial and continuing financial burdens due to the federal government's acquisition of real property.[143] This section is designed to provide education for children who live, and whose parents are employed, on federal property; whose parents are in the military and live in low-rent housing; are part of heavy concentrations of children whose parents are federal employees but do not live on federal property; experience sudden and substantial increases or decreases in enrollments due to military realignments; and/or need special help with capital expenditures for construction projects.

Subchapter IX, General Provisions, largely contains what can best be described as boilerplate language.[144] This section reviews definitions; flexibility in the use of administrative and other funds; program coordination; waivers; uniform provisions including such topics as participation by students and teachers in non-public schools; complaint processes for the participation of non-public schools; uniform provisions; and evaluations.

ACCOUNTABILITY

In seeking to make states and LEAs more accountable for student progress, the NCLB requires states to develop challenging academic standards for students. Under this section, state officials must create challenging academic content standards in academic subjects that "(I) specify what children are expected to know and be able to do; (II) contain coherent and rigorous content; and (III) encourage the teaching of advanced skills."[145] Challenging student academic achievement standards are those "(I) . . . aligned with the State's academic content standards; (II) describe two levels of high achievement (proficient and advanced) that determine how well children are mastering the material in the State academic content standards; and (III) describe a third level of achievement (basic) to provide complete information about the progress of the lower-achieving children toward mastering the proficient and advanced levels of achievement."[146]

Accountability systems for students in regular education must be based on challenging state standards in reading and mathematics. This requires annual testing of all students in grades three through eight, and once in grades nine through twelve, that began in the 2005–2006 academic year,[147] along with annual statewide progress objectives ensuring that "not later than 12 years after the end of the 2001–2002 school year,"[148] or the 2013–

141. 20 U.S.C.A. §§ 7301 *et seq.*

142. 20 U.S.C.A. §§ 7401 *et seq.*

143. 20 U.S.C.A. §§ 7701 *et seq.*

144. 20 U.S.C.A. §§ 7801 *et seq.*

145. 20 U.S.C.A. § 6311(b)(1)(D)(i).

146. 20 U.S.C.A. § 6311(b)(1)(D)(ii).

147. 20 U.S.C.A. § 6311(a)(1)(C).

148. 20 U.S.C.A. § 6311(b)(2)(F).

2014 school year, that all groups of students will meet or exceed their state's level of academic achievement. However, as noted, States may now petition for waivers from this requirement.[149] Even though ninety-five percent of students with disabilities must participate in annual assessments based on state standards, the NCLB does permit the use of alternative assessments for such measures.[150]

A key element of accountability deals with whether school systems have achieved adequate yearly progress (AYP). States must define AYP "in a manner that (i) applies the same high standards of academic achievement to all public elementary school and secondary school students in the State; (ii) is statistically valid and reliable; (iii) results in continuous and substantial academic improvement for all students; (iv) measures the progress of public elementary schools, secondary schools, and local educational agencies and the State based primarily on the academic assessments described in paragraph (3); (v) includes separate measurable annual objectives for continuous and substantial improvement"[151] for students who attend public elementary and secondary schools; who are economically disadvantaged; are from major racial and ethnic groups; are disabled; and/or are of limited English proficiency.[152]

As to analyses of student outcomes, the NCLB makes an exception since states are not required to disaggregate data for students who were recently identified if the number of children in a category is insufficient to yield statistically reliable information or the results would reveal personally identifiable information about students. Finally, the NCLB permits states, at their discretion, to include other academic indicators for public school students, measured separately for each group described above such as achievement on additional state or locally administered assessments; decreases in grade-to-grade retention rates; attendance rates; and changes in the percentages of students completing gifted and talented, advanced placement, and college preparatory courses.[153]

If LEAs or individual schools fail to meet their AYP goals, significant accountability measures come into play. If schools fail to meet their goals for two consecutive years, officials must develop comprehensive plans with support from their states and/or LEAs.[154] Title I schools serving children who are most at-risk and that fail to reach AYP for two consecutive years have three options. First, and most draconian, parents can transfer their children to other schools within their systems.[155] This option, which has yet to be applied, could create considerable legal challenges, especially where teachers and other staff are tenured. Second, officials must notify parents

---

149. The primary document that the White House released on September 23, 2011 can be found at http://www.ed.gov/esea/flexibility. On the same day, the White House released a Fact Sheet with additional information; this is located at http://www.whitehouse.gov/the-press-office/ 2011/09/23/fact-sheet-bringing-flexibility-and-focus-education-law

150.   20 U.S.C.A. § 1412(a)(16)(A), 20 U.S.C.A. § 6311(b)(1)(I)(ii).

151.   20 U.S.C.A. § 6311(b)(2)(C) (capitalization of State in original).

152.   20 U.S.C.A. § 6311(b)(2)(C)(v)(I)(II).

153.   20 U.S.C.A. § 6311(b)(2)(C)(vii).

154.   20 U.S.C.A. §§ 6316(b)(1)(A), (c)(4).

155.   20 U.S.C.A. § 6316(b)(5)(A).

that their children are entitled to state-approved supplemental educational services such as after school or weekend tutoring;[156] these services can also be provided by private contractors. Parental notice must not only explain what the effect of and reasons why schools have been identified as failing but must also be in a language that, to the extent practicable, they can readily understand while offering them the opportunity to participate in addressing the academic issues that caused the schools to be identified as needing improvement.[157]

Third, educators must continue to provide schools that failed to achieve AYP with technical assistance[158] while taking corrective action[159] such as school restructuring,[160] meaning that if schools fail to improve after a full year of remedial action, local educational officials can again inform parents of their right to transfer their children to other schools, continue to provide supplemental services, or prepare to make arrangements for alternative governance.[161] Under the alternative governance provisions, schools can reopen as public charter schools; replace all or most of their staff (including principals); permit private management companies to take over operations; allow their state education agencies to operate schools; or develop other forms of major restructuring.

CURRICULUM

ESTABLISHMENT OF THE ELEMENTS

All jurisdictions have statutory and regulatory guidelines related to what must be taught as part of public school curricula and, in some instances, how subjects should be taught along with prohibitions against covering specified topics such as those advancing religious views.[162] Except for constitutional restraints, since legislatures have plenary power over public school curricula, they can require schools to teach that which is "plainly essential to good citizenship" while prohibiting that which is "manifestly inimical to the public welfare."[163] State officials may, and to differing degrees do, delegate curricular powers to local school boards. Local boards must thus deal with the innumerable aspects of school programs not specifically covered by state law.

---

156. 20 U.S.C.A. § 6316(b)(5)(B).

157. 20 U.S.C.A. § 6316(b)(6).

158. 20 U.S.C.A. § 6316(b)(5)(C).

159. 20 U.S.C.A. § 6316(b)(7).

160. 20 U.S.C.A. §§ 6316(b)(8)(A)(i)–(iii).

161. 20 U.S.C.A. § 6316(b)(8)(B).

162. *See, e.g., School Dist. of Abington Twp. v. Schempp,* 374 U.S. 203, 83 S.Ct. 1560, 10 L.Ed.2d 844 (1963) (striking down prayer and Bible reading in public schools) [Case No. 4]; *Epperson v. Arkansas,* 393 U.S. 97, 89 S.Ct. 266, 21 L.Ed.2d 228 (1968) (invalidating statutes that prohibited the teaching of evolution). [Case No. 6]

163. *Pierce v. Society of the Sisters of the Holy Names of Jesus and Mary,* 268 U.S. 510, 534, 45 S.Ct. 571, 69 L.Ed. 1070 (1925). [Case No. 81]

In *Meyer v. Nebraska*, the Supreme Court invalidated a prohibition against providing foreign language instruction in grades lower than the ninth under which a teacher in a non-public school was convicted of teaching German. The Court rejected the statute's purported goal of promoting civic development by "inhibiting training and education of the immature in foreign tongues and ideals before they could learn English and acquire American ideals, and 'that the English language should be and become the mother tongue of all children reared in this state.' "[164] In pointing out that the statute limited the rights of modern language teachers to teach, of students to gain knowledge, and of parents to control the education of their children, the Justices emphasized that there was no showing of harm that the state had the right to prevent. The Court added that absent an emergency, nothing rendered the knowledge of a language other than English so clearly harmful as warranting its prohibition. While conceding that it did not question the state's power over the curriculum in public schools, the thrust of the Court's analysis involved the constitutional right to pursue an occupation not contrary to the public interest.[165]

In *Pierce v. Society of the Sisters (Pierce)*,[166] discussed earlier, the Supreme Court held that "[t]he child is not the mere creature of the state; those who nurture him and direct his destiny have the right, coupled with the high duty, to recognize and prepare him for additional obligations."[167] In deciding that the parents in *Pierce* had the right to send their children to non-public schools as a means of satisfying Oregon's compulsory attendance statute, the Court emphasized that state officials, acting in and through local school boards, may not "unreasonably interfere with the liberty of parents and guardians to direct the upbringing and education of children under their control."[168] The Court reached a similar outcome in *Farrington v. Tokushige*,[169] also reviewed earlier in this chapter.

As important as the parental right to direct the upbringing of their children is, including the ability to withdraw them from public schools,[170] lower federal courts have sent a different message in this regard once parents place their children in public schools. To this end, the Sixth Circuit, joining other courts,[171] noted that "[w]hile parents may have a fundamental right to decide *whether* to send their child to a public school,

---

164.   262 U.S. 390, 401, 43 S.Ct. 625, 67 L.Ed. 1042 (1923).

165.   On the same day, in the companion case of *Bartels v. Iowa*, 262 U.S. 404, 43 S.Ct. 628, 67 L.Ed. 1047 (1923), the Supreme Court invalidated similar laws from Iowa and Ohio.

166.   268 U.S. 510, 534, 45 S.Ct. 571, 69 L.Ed. 1070 (1925). [Case No. 81]

167.   *Id.* at 535.

168.   *Id.* at 534–35.

169.   273 U.S. 284, 47 S.Ct. 406, 71 L.Ed. 646 (1927).

170.   While the Supreme Court has never precisely defined the contours of parental rights, it has suggested that they are not absolute. *See Lehr v. Robertson*, 463 U.S. 248, 103 S.Ct. 2985, 77 L.Ed.2d 614 (1983) (affirming that the state did not violate the rights of an unmarried father who failed to establish a substantial relationship with his child or to notify the putative father registry).

171.   *See, e.g., Dempsey v. Alston*, 966 A.2d 1 [242 Educ. L. Rep. 256] (N.J. Super. Ct. App. Div. 2009), *certification denied*, 973 A.2d 386 (N.J. 2009) (observing that "in certain circumstances the parental right to control the upbringing of a child must give way to a school's ability to control curriculum and the school environment.") (Internal citations omitted).

they do not have a fundamental right generally to direct *how* a public school teaches their child."[172]

The power of local school boards to offer courses and programs[173] beyond those mandated by state law or with which parents disagree rests on their implied, rather than plenary or inherent, powers. The implied power of boards was established beginning with the so-called "Kalamazoo case," in which the Supreme Court of Michigan, absent express legislative authority, declared that a local board had the power to operate a high school.[174]

Most cases support the general rule that local school boards have discretion to supplement courses required by state-level authorities.[175] Perhaps in no other sphere of school operations have the courts more liberally interpreted implied powers of local boards than in curricular matters, not only with regard to individual elements but also as to methods of carrying out both specific and general mandates.

In the face of a challenge to the establishment and operation of a non-graded program in an elementary school, an appellate court in Michigan later maintained that a local board's discretionary power was sufficiently broad to justify its action.[176] The court emphasized that insofar as the state board, in exercising its general supervision over public education, had not prohibited local boards from creating non-graded schools, officials could act as they saw fit. In support of its position, the court cited a case from the Supreme Court of Michigan which upheld the discretionary authority of local boards to establish half-day sessions and to offer subjects on a compressed schedule due to the lack of funds.[177]

Community residents cannot compel school boards to offer courses of instruction[178] or use specific books since these choices lay within their discretion absent state directives to the contrary as long as they do not deprive students of their constitutional rights.[179] Likewise, absent proof that materials or books are sectarian or subversive, citizens cannot require boards to remove them from curricula[180] or modify content to suit their wishes.[181]

---

172. *Blau v. Fort Thomas Pub. School Dist.*, 401 F.3d 381, 395–96 [196 Educ. L. Rep. 118] (6th Cir. 2005) (emphasis in original).

173. *Wake Cares v. Wake County Bd. of Educ.*, 675 S.E.2d 345 (N.C. 2009) (affirming that a local board was not obligated to procure parental consent in requiring students to attend year-round calendar schools because it thought that this was the best way to serve children).

174. *Stuart v. School Dist. No. 1 of Village of Kalamazoo*, 30 Mich. 69 (Mich. 1874).

175. *See, e.g., State ex rel. Andrews v. Webber*, 8 N.E. 708 (Ind.1886); *State Tax Comm'n v. Board of Educ. of Holton*, 73 P.2d 49 (Kan. 1937).

176. *Schwan v. Board of Educ. of Lansing School Dist.*, 183 N.W.2d 594 (Mich. Ct. App. 1970).

177. *Welling v. Board of Educ. for Livonia School Dist.*, 171 N.W.2d 545 (Mich. 1969).

178. *Wright v. Houston Indep. School Dist.*, 486 F.2d 137 (5th Cir.1973); *Mercer v. Michigan State Bd. of Educ.*, 379 F.Supp. 580 (E.D. Mich. 1974), *aff'd*, 419 U.S. 1081, 95 S.Ct. 673, 42 L.Ed.2d 678 (1974).

179. *See, e.g., Presidents Council, Dist. 25 v. Community School Bd. No. 25*, 457 F.2d 289 (2d Cir. 1972), *cert. denied*, 409 U.S. 998, 93 S.Ct. 308, 34 L.Ed.2d 260 (1972); *Board of Educ., Island Trees Union Free School Dist. No. 26 v. Pico*, 457 U.S. 853, 857, 102 S.Ct. 2799, 73 L.Ed.2d 435 [4 Educ. L. Rep. 1013] (1982).

180. *See, e.g., Rosenberg v. Board of Educ. of City of N.Y.*, 92 N.Y.S.2d 344 (N.Y. 1949); *Todd v. Rochester Community Schools*, 200 N.W.2d 90 (Mich. Ct. App. 1972); *Williams v.*

When states specify courses of study, local school boards must provide adequate financial resources to support them properly.[182] Still, electives must be curtailed if necessary to operate required programs. While boards cannot eliminate state-mandated courses,[183] they have implied power to drop electives, even if they have been offered over long periods of time since the courts recognize that local officials have the authority to meet changing educational conditions by creating new courses and rearranging curricula.[184] Since boards cannot be required to offer courses simply because they may be available elsewhere, officials do not violate student rights by refusing to offer electives.[185]

METHODS AND MATERIALS

Almost all jurisdictions have laws addressing teaching methodology. Even so, most prescriptions are general and suggestive rather than specific and exclusive. In general, curricular content and teaching methodology are essentially local, rather than state, responsibilities. When disputes arise over teaching methodologies, courts generally accept the authority of local school boards and the expertise of educational officials as to pedagogical techniques.[186]

At common law, there was no question as to the legal rights of states to prescribe textbooks.[187] The statutory trend has been to delegate more and more power over textbook selection to local officials.[188] Selection of supplementary books and instructional materials is generally subject to the same rules. Since school officials are free to select textbooks independent of the wishes of teachers, they need not accept recommendations of faculty

Board of Educ. of County of Kanawha, 388 F.Supp. 93 (S.D. W. Va.1975), *aff'd*, 530 F.2d 972 (4th Cir. 1975); *Grove v. Mead School Dist. No. 354*, 753 F.2d 1528 [22 Educ. L. Rep. 1141] (9th Cir. 1985), *cert. denied*, 474 U.S. 826, 106 S.Ct. 85, 88 L.Ed.2d 70 (1985).

181. *See Myers v. Loudoun County School Bd.*, 500 F. Supp.2d 539 [223 Educ. L. Rep. 786] (E.D. Va. 2007) (rejecting a father's request that officials accommodate his views on what he alleged was his school board's endorsement of religious-based patriotism in a policy calling for the daily recitation of the Pledge of Allegiance).

182. *See, e.g., Talbot v. Board of Educ. of N.Y.*, 14 N.Y.S.2d 340 (N.Y.1939); *Durant v. State of Mich.*, 650 N.W.2d 380 [169 Educ. L. Rep. 389] (Mich. Ct. App. 2002), *appeal denied*, 654 N.W.2d 329 (Mich. 2002), *reconsideration denied*, 658 N.W.2d 484 (Mich. 2003).

183. *Jones v. Board of Trustees of Culver City School Dist.*, 47 P.2d 804 (Cal. Ct. App. 1935).

184. *Jones v. Holes*, 6 A.2d 102 (Pa.1939).

185. *Board of Educ. of Okay Indep. School Dist. v. Carroll*, 513 P.2d 872 (Okla. 1973); *Zykan v. Warsaw Community School Corp.*, 631 F.2d 1300 (7th Cir. 1980).

186. *See, e.g., Boring v. Buncombe County Bd. of Educ.*, 136 F.3d 364 [124 Educ. L. Rep. 56] (4th Cir. 1998), *cert. denied*, 525 U.S. 813, 119 S.Ct. 47, 142 L.Ed.2d 36 (1998); *Lacks v. Ferguson Reorganized School Dist. R–2*, 147 F.3d 718 [127 Educ. L. Rep. 568] (8th Cir. 1998), *suggestion for reh'g en banc denied*, 154 F.3d 904 (8th Cir.1998), *cert. denied*, 526 U.S. 1012, 119 S.Ct. 1158, 143 L.Ed.2d 223 (1999).

187. *Leeper v. State of Tenn.*, 53 S.W. 962 (Tenn. 1899).

188. *See, e.g.,* KY. REV. STAT. ANN. § 160.345(g) (granting authority for textbook selection to school based decision-making councils). ("The school council shall determine which textbooks, instructional materials, and student support services shall be provided in the school.").

committees.[189] While courts do not often review disputes over the selection of textbooks, when they do, they typically defer to the choices of board officials rather than teachers[190] or parents.[191]

If anything, the courts are more likely to review disputes over the removal of material than the failure of educators to include items,[192] especially since the constitutional rights at issue more closely involve students (and their parents) than teachers.[193] In *Board of Education, Island Trees Union Free School District No. 26 v. Pico*,[194] the Supreme Court reviewed the rights of students and their parents in New Yorkto question a board's removal of books from a school library that officials found to be unacceptable. In a plurality, the Court remanded the dispute for a more specific review as to why officials removed the books since the trial court failed to address the issue adequately in granting the board's motion for summary judgment. Four of the five Justices supporting the remand agreed that removing the books would have been unconstitutional if the decisive factor was that the board sought to ban ideas with which it disagreed. These Justices also agreed that the board could remove books if they were convinced that they were "pervasively vulgar" or did not meet standards of "educational suitability." In addition, the Third Circuit affirmed that school officials in Delaware did not violate the First Amendment rights of students by rejecting their selection for a school play.[195]

One of the more extensive disputes on books used in public schools arose in Alabama. In stating that the books passed Establishment Clause analysis, the Eleventh Circuit rejected a parental claim that the use of forty-four state-approved books in history, social studies, and home economics amounted to the teaching of secular humanism.[196] The Sixth,[197]

---

189. *Minarcini v. Strongsville City School Dist.*, 541 F.2d 577 (6th Cir. 1976).

190. *Monteiro v. Tempe Union High School Dist.*, 158 F.3d 1022 (9th Cir. 1998).

191. *Porter v. Seattle School Dist. No. 1*, 248 P.3d 1111 [265 Educ. L. Rep. 786] (Wash. Ct. App. 2011) (rejecting a challenges to a mathematics book that officials selected because they were convinced that it would help teachers to overcome achievement gaps between high and low performing students).

192. *Pratt v. Independent School Dist. No. 831, Forest Lake, Minn.*, 670 F.2d 771 [2 Educ. L. Rep. 990] (8th Cir. 1982).

193. *Johnson v. Stuart*, 702 F.2d 193 [9 Educ. L. Rep. 1148] (9th Cir. 1983).

194. 457 U.S. 853, 102 S.Ct. 2799, 73 L.Ed.2d 435 [4 Educ. L. Rep. 1013] (1982).

195. *Seyfried v. Walton*, 668 F.2d 214 [2 Educ. L. Rep. 379] (3d Cir.1981). [Case No. 85] For a case filed by a teacher, *see Boring v. Buncombe County Bd. of Educ.*, 136 F.3d 364 [124 Educ. L. Rep. 56] (4th Cir. 1998), *cert. denied*, 525 U.S. 813, 119 S.Ct. 47, 142 L.Ed.2d 36 (1998) (upholding the transfer of an award-winning drama coach and teacher for directing a controversial play that some members of the community found objectionable).

196. *Smith v. Board of School Commr's of Mobile County*, 827 F.2d 684 [41 Educ. L. Rep. 452] (11th Cir. 1987).

197. For another lengthy battle of this type, *see Mozert v. Hawkins County Pub. Schools*, 579 F.Supp. 1051 [16 Educ. L. Rep. 473] (E.D. Tenn. 1984), *rev'd*, 765 F.2d 75 [25 Educ. L. Rep. 1063] (6th Cir. 1985), *on remand*, 647 F.Supp. 1194 [36 Educ. L. Rep. 90] (E.D. Tenn. 1986), *rev'd*, 827 F.2d 1058 [41 Educ. L. Rep. 473] (6th Cir. 1987), *cert. denied*, 484 U.S. 1066, 108 S.Ct. 1029, 98 L.Ed.2d 993 [44 Educ. L. Rep. 1000] (1988).

Seventh,[198] and Ninth[199] Circuits also rejected parental challenges that reading materials impermissibly burdened students' rights to free exercise of religion. The courts essentially concurred that where none of the books or materials were antagonistic toward religion or its place in culture and values, local officials had the authority to formulate the content of school curricula.

In Florida, even though state officials approved a book for use in a humanities course, a local school board voted to discontinue its adoption after parents complained about vulgarity and sexual subject matter in two of the selections. As a result, other parents sought to prevent the removal, claiming that doing so would have violated their First Amendment rights, emphasizing that the course was elective rather than required and that the disputed selections were not required readings. The Eleventh Circuit affirmed that insofar as the book was part of the curriculum, the board could control its content and that of the library where it was kept.[200] Subsequently, parents in Arkansas charged that school officials violated the First and Fourteenth Amendments when they required students to obtain parental permission before accessing books from the popular *Harry Potter* series in a school library. In granting the parents' motion for summary judgment on the ground that the educators violated the students' First Amendment right to receive information, the court awarded them court costs.[201]

The flip side deals with teacher rights. The Tenth Circuit affirmed that school officials in Colorado did not violate a teacher's rights in restricting his indirect use of the Bible in a fifth-grade class. The teacher frequently read his Bible silently as students sat at their desks reading books of their choice. The Bible was always on the teacher's desk and he displayed a wall poster with the message "You have only to open your eyes to see the hand of God." The court also upheld the removal of two books about the Bible and life of Jesus from the teacher's classroom library of "about 239 books of varying content that [he] had compiled over his nineteen-years of teaching,"[202] while permitting works on Buddhism, Greek gods and goddesses, and Indian religions to remain in the collection. The court discerned that while the teacher's practices violated the Establishment Clause, the principal should not have removed the Bible from the school library. On the other hand, when a teacher sued his school board claiming that officials directed him to refrain from teaching about non-Christian religions in response to parental complaints about his doing so, the federal trial court in Maine denied its motion for summary judgment.[203] The court reasoned that in light of remaining issues of fact as to whether restrictions on the curriculum were motivated by officials' desire to respond to parental requests to eliminate references to non-Christian religions, the dispute had

198. *Fleischfresser v. Directors of School Dist. 200*, 15 F.3d 680 [89 Educ. L. Rep. 429] (7th Cir. 1994).

199. *Brown v. Woodland Joint Unified School Dist.*, 27 F.3d 1373 [92 Educ. L. Rep. 828] (9th Cir. 1994).

200. *Virgil v. School Bd. of Columbia County, Fla.*, 862 F.2d 1517 [50 Educ. L. Rep. 718] (11th Cir. 1989).

201. *Counts v. Cedarville School Dist.*, 295 F. Supp.2d 996 [184 Educ. L. Rep. 305] (W.D. Ark. 2003).

202. *Roberts v. Madigan*, 921 F.2d 1047, 1049 [64 Educ. L. Rep. 1038] (10th Cir. 1990), *cert. denied*, 505 U.S. 1218, 112 S.Ct. 3025, 120 L.Ed.2d 896 (1992).

203. *Cole v. Maine School Admin. Dist. No. 1*, 350 F. Supp.2d 143 [195 Educ. L. Rep. 130] (D. Me. 2004).

to proceed to a trial on the merits over whether they violated the teacher's First Amendment rights.

As to testing, where parents and teachers enjoined a planned city-wide examination that they claimed was compromised due to cheating, the Court of Appeals of New York reversed in favor of the board. The court indicated that insofar as such educational matters as test selection and use are subject to the discretion of school officials, they are inappropriate for judicial resolution.[204] The court wrote that its involvement would have placed the judiciary in the role of displacing, or at least overseeing, officials charged with the school system's management. An appellate court in Washington applied the same analysis in affirming that school personnel could not be charged for allegedly failing to meet the instructional criteria established by a state basic education statute.[205]

In a case from New York with a unique factual setting, an appellate court affirmed that a student could not retake an admissions test for a specialized high school based on his claim that he did not do well on it due to noise in the examination room.[206] The court agreed that the student's request was moot insofar as the relief that he sought in the form of taking the test over could not have been granted since it had already been administered.

BILINGUAL-BICULTURAL STUDIES

In *Lau v. Nichols* (*Lau*),[207] a case involving bilingual education, the Supreme Court acknowledged that a class of non-English speaking students of Chinese origin in San Francisco was entitled to relief from the school board's policy of providing special English instruction for only about 1,000 of the over 2,800 eligible children. In rejecting the board's claim that it lacked the funds to implement a program, the Court responded that students who neither understand English nor received specialized instruction were effectively precluded from obtaining a meaningful education. The Court did not resolve the dispute on equal protection grounds, instead relying on Title VI of the Civil Rights Act of 1964 (Title VI), which bars discrimination under federally assisted programs on a ground of "race, color, or national origin."[208] According to the Court, federal guidelines required instruction for correction of language deficiencies and the board contractually agreed to abide by them in order to receive federal funds. The Court expressly refused to take a stance on what educational techniques educators should have used.

Two years after *Lau*, the Tenth Circuit reached a virtually identical result in a case involving students with Spanish-surnames who lived in

204. *James v. Board of Educ. of City of N.Y.*, 397 N.Y.S.2d 934 (N.Y. 1977).

205. *Camer v. Seattle School Dist. No. 1*, 762 P.2d 356 [49 Educ. L. Rep. 819] (Wash. Ct. App. 1988), *review denied*, 1989 WL 661505 (Wash.1989), *cert. denied*, 493 U.S. 873, 110 S.Ct. 204, 107 L.Ed.2d 157 (1989).

206. *Tessler v. Board of Educ. of City of N.Y.*, 854 N.Y.S.2d 66 [230 Educ. L. Rep. 706] (N.Y. App. Div. 2008).

207. 414 U.S. 563, 94 S.Ct. 786, 39 L.Ed.2d 1 (1974).

208. 42 U.S.C.A. §§ 2000d *et seq.*

New Mexico.[209] In recognizing that many students spoke Spanish at home and were growing up in a culture that was alien to the environment they faced in school, the court ordered officials to implement a bilingual education program. The following year, the same court rejected the notion that students had a constitutional right to bilingual-bicultural education.[210] On remand, the federal trial court in Colorado ordered the board to initiate a bilingual-bicultural program for students who spoke predominately Spanish. The Tenth Circuit reversed, observing that bilingual education is not a substitute for desegregation since Spanish-speaking students were constitutionally entitled to a non-segregated education that afforded them the opportunity to acquire English proficiency.

The Ninth Circuit later affirmed that neither Title VI nor the Equal Educational Opportunities Act of 1974 (EEOA)[211] conferred a right to bilingual-bicultural education.[212] The court remarked that a remedy designed to cure language deficiencies of non-English-speaking students in Arizona met legal requirements even though there was no bar to a school board's instituting the bilingual-bicultural program advocated by the plaintiffs. However, in the same year, a federal trial court in New York, contending that an English as a Second Language Program was deficient, directed school officials to provide instruction that complied with *Lau* for children who were of Puerto Rican ancestry.[213]

Two state cases dealt with a different aspect of bilingual and bicultural studies. In the first, an appellate court in North Carolina affirmed that parents could not prevent their children from attending school since their board failed to provide instruction in their heritage and culture.[214] The court rejected the argument that a deep-rooted conviction for Indian heritage was on a constitutional plane equal to religious beliefs. In another dispute over heritage, a mother with Indian ancestry in New York withdrew her child from school because she objected to some comments that her daughter's teacher made about Indians. An appellate court affirmed that the mother lacked a sufficient reason for refusing to comply with the state's compulsory education law when officials refused to meet her demands to institute curricular programs on the problems of Indians and to create a steering committee to implement a policy against racism in any form.[215]

In the first of two cases from Illinois, the Seventh Circuit was satisfied that Spanish-speaking students who were identified as being of limited English proficiency could enforce the EEOA in a class action suit against the state board of education.[216] On remand, a federal trial court responded that the class was entitled to certification. In another dispute from Illinois

---

209. *Serna v. Portales Mun. Schools,* 499 F.2d 1147 (10th Cir.1974).

210. *Keyes v. School Dist. No. 1, Denver, Colo.,* 521 F.2d 465 (10th Cir. 1975).

211. 20 U.S.C.A. § 1703(f).

212. *Guadalupe Org. v. Tempe Elementary School Dist.,* 587 F.2d 1022 (9th Cir.1978).

213. *Rios v. Read,* 480 F.Supp. 14 (E.D.N.Y.1978).

214. *Matter of McMillan,* 226 S.E.2d 693 (N.C. Ct. App.1976).

215. *Matter of Baum,* 401 N.Y.S.2d 514 (N.Y. App. Div.1978), *appeal denied,* 407 N.Y.S.2d 1026 (N.Y. 1978).

216. *Gomez v. Illinois State Bd. of Educ.,* 811 F.2d 1030 [37 Educ. L. Rep. 1073] (7th Cir. 1987), *on remand,* 117 F.R.D. 394 [42 Educ. L. Rep. 1211] (N.D. Ill. 1987).

involving minority and other students with limited English proficiency, a federal trial court rejected a school board's motion to dismiss a class action suit claiming that it failed to address the needs of these children by eliminating existing language barriers.[217] The court permitted the case to proceed since it agreed that the plaintiffs demonstrated the existence of language barriers and that the board failed to take appropriate action to overcome these barriers.

The Ninth Circuit, in a long-running dispute, affirmed that the Arizona Superintendent of Public Instruction was not entitled to a modification of an order placing the state in civil contempt for failing to provide adequate funding for English Language Learners programs in a school district in violation of the EEOA.[218] The court rejected the state's argument that a change in circumstances did not warrant such relief since the students continued to need extra help, at additional cost to the local board. The court also rejected the state's claim that its compliance with NCLB benchmarks automatically met the requirements of the EEOA.

On further review, in *Horne v. Flores*,[219] the Supreme Court reversed and remanded with instructions for the lower courts to consider whether four factors warranted relief: a transition from bilingual classes to structured English immersion, compliance with the NCLB, structural and management improvements, and an increase in overall education funding. The Court noted that research indicates that there is documented support for the idea that structured English immersion is more effective than bilingual education. On remand, the Ninth Circuit returned the case to the federal trial court, directing it to comply with the Supreme Court's opinion.[220]

In a long-running case from Texas, the Fifth Circuit remanded a dispute over whether a program helped overcome language barriers among students who were Spanish-speaking based on allegations that officials impeded their equal participation in a school system's instructional programs. The court declared that the program had to be evaluated on such criteria as whether it was based on an arguably sound educational theory, was reasonably calculated to implement the theory, and was a good faith effort consistent with local circumstances and resources.[221] Twenty-eight years later, the Fifth Circuit affirmed that absent evidence to support a finding that the actions of school officials contributed to the achievement gap between children of limited English proficiency and those who were proficient, they did not violate the EEOA.[222]

The Eighth Circuit, in a case from Minnesota, affirmed that a school board did not discriminate against students in an alternative school on the

---

217. *Leslie v. Board of Educ. for Ill. School Dist. U–46*, 379 F. Supp.2d 952 [201 Educ. L. Rep. 151] (N.D. Ill. 2005).

218. *Flores v. Arizona*, 516 F.3d 1140 [229 Educ. L. Rep. 427] (9th Cir.2008), *amended on denial of reh'g and reh'g en banc* (2008), *cert. granted sub nom. Horne v. Flores*, 555 U.S. 1092, 129 S.Ct. 893, 172 L.Ed.2d 768 (2009).

219. *Horne v. Flores*, 557 U.S. 433, 129 S.Ct. 2579, 174 L.Ed.2d 406 [245 Educ. L. Rep. 572] (2009).

220. *Flores v. Arizona*, 577 F.3d 1014 (9th Cir. 2009).

221. *United States v. State of Texas*, 680 F.2d 356 [5 Educ. L. Rep. 141] (5th Cir. 1982).

222. *United States v. State of Texas*, 601 F.3d 354 [255 Educ. L. Rep. 564] (5th Cir. 2010).

basis of national origin in violation of the EEOA when it delayed special education testing for English Language Learners for three years.[223] The court pointed out that insofar as the board's action impacted all students who had limited English proficiency, it did not violate the plaintiffs' rights to equal protection.[224]

A dispute from Pennsylvania may presage future litigation under the NCLB.[225] An appellate court affirmed that it was not practicable for the Commonwealth's Department of Education to provide native language testing.[226] The court specified that insofar as native language testing is not mandatory under the NCLB and should be provided only to the extent that it is practicable, the Department did not violate the law especially since officials were trying to determine which of the 125 native languages that are spoken in the commonwealth could feasibly be used in testing. In like fashion, an appellate court in California affirmed that offering standardized tests in English did not violate the NCLB because the Act does not require the testing of children of limited English proficiency in their primary languages.[227]

REQUIRED ELEMENTS

Controversies over whether subjects or activities can be required consider what officials can do if parents direct their children not to comply. In these cases, it is important to examine the nature of both the activities and the punishments, if any, and how to balance them with the parental right to guide the upbringing of their children, especially if they conflict with the rights of states to require the study of subjects essential to citizenship. Under common law, the courts tended to give parents the benefit of the doubt in matters unlikely to have an adverse impact on curricula or their children.

In an older case, where a father's objection to his daughter's studying rhetoric led to her being able to take a grammar class, he challenged officials for expelling her after he ordered her to discontinue studying the subject. The Supreme Court of Nebraska entered a judgment in favor of the father, directing officials to re-admit the child without her having to study rhetoric.[228] In another case, parents instructed their daughter not to attend a required domestic science class for females because they thought that she could have used the time spent traveling to the class more profitably in private music lessons. When officials expelled the child for not taking the

---

223. *Mumid v. Abraham Lincoln High School,* 618 F.3d 789 [260 Educ. L. Rep. 587] (8th Cir. 2010), *cert. denied,* ___ U.S. ___, 131 S.Ct. 1478, 179 L.Ed.2d 303 (2011).

224. For a novel case involving the EEOA, *see Lopez v. Bay Shore Union Free School Dist.,* 668 F.Supp.2d 406 [253 Educ. L. Rep. 302] (E.D.N.Y. 2009) (rejecting a claim that the failure of school officials to communicate with a student's mother in Spanish led to his being suspended in violation of the EEOA).

225. 20 U.S.C.A. § 6301. Portions of the NCLB are in the Appendix.

226. *Reading School Dist. v. Department of Educ.,* 855 A.2d 166 [191 Educ. L. Rep. 341] (Pa. Cmwlth. Ct. 2004), *appeal denied,* 877 A.2d 463 (Pa. 2005).

227. *Coachella Valley Unified School Dist. v. State,* 98 Cal.Rptr.3d 9 [247 Educ. L. Rep. 381] (Cal. Ct. App. 2009), *reh'g denied* (2009).

228. *State ex rel. Sheibley v. School–Dist. No. 1,* 48 N.W. 393 (Neb. 1891).

course, the Supreme Court of Nebraska ordered her reinstatement, explaining that the parental request was reasonable.[229] The court observed that if the parents wished to have their daughter study music, they had the right to have her do so.

If curricular requirements violate the constitutional rights of students and/or parents, school board officials lack the authority to require children to take specific courses. Of course, children cannot be expelled or suspended due to such refusals. In an older case from California, where a board included dancing as part of its physical education curriculum, the father of two students challenged the denial of their request that his children be excused from participating and their resulting expulsions. Entering a judgment in favor of the father, an appellate court was of the view that if a regulation was unduly burdensome or violated the fundamental right of a person or set of persons, it must be set aside as unconstitutional.[230]

Courts are now more willing to impose limits on the power of parents who seek to select what their children may study in school.[231] This is especially true where religious claims are tenuous, where secular reasons are weak, or where parents or children pressure others to follow their lead in seeking to be excused.[232] Even as educators try to accommodate minor parental requests, they are not required to make major curricular adjustments. The Sixth Circuit reviewed this issue at length where parents sought to have their children placed in a core reading program other than the one used in the local schools.[233] The program, which was coordinated with other subjects, contained books containing ideas with which the parents disagreed, largely on religious grounds. The court decided that students and their parents lacked a right not to be exposed to ideas in public schools as long as the positions they objected to were not promoted and children were neither obligated to affirm nor disaffirm their agreement with the ideas.

In a dispute over curricular content, a federal trial court in California dismissed claims filed by a group of parents and a former substitute teacher challenging "diversity education."[234] In granting the defendants' motion to dismiss, the court ruled that the plaintiffs lacked standing due to their inability to allege a concrete and particular injury that they suffered due to the inclusion of the material in school curricula.

Sexuality Education

A controversial topic in schools deals with objections, religious and secular, to sexuality and AIDS education. For instance, the First Circuit affirmed that a school board in Connecticut did not violate a father's Free

---

229. *State ex rel. Kelley v. Ferguson*, 144 N.W. 1039 (Neb. 1914).

230. *Hardwick v. Board of School Trustees of Fruitridge*, 205 P. 49 (Cal. Ct. App. 1921).

231. *Muka v. Cornell*, 368 N.Y.S.2d 874 (N.Y. App. Div. 1975).

232. *Davis v. Page*, 385 F.Supp. 395 (D.N.H. 1974).

233. *Mozert v. Hawkins County Bd. of Educ.*, 827 F.2d 1058 [41 Educ. L. Rep. 473] (6th Cir. 1987), *cert. denied*, 484 U.S. 1066, 108 S.Ct. 1029, 98 L.Ed.2d 993 (1988).

234. *Preskar v. United States*, 248 F.R.D. 576 [231 Educ. L. Rep. 304] (E.D. Cal. 2008), *report and recommendation adopted*, 2008 WL 802925 (E.D. Cal. 2008).

Exercise Clause rights in rejecting his request to excuse his son from a mandatory health education course that included lessons on family life, physical growth and development, and AIDS, and assigning him a failing grade for refusing to do so.[235]

In a case from Kentucky, students and their parents unsuccessfully challenged the denial of their request to be excused from a significant portion of diversity training, a large part of which was devoted to issues of sexual orientation and gender harassment, because they believed that homosexuality is sinful. After the Sixth Circuit initially reversed in favor of the sole remaining student,[236] an en banc panel vacated and superseded its order.[237] The court affirmed an earlier grant of summary judgment in favor of the board since the student failed to demonstrate how a favorable judgment might have redressed what it described as his purported injury and that he lacked standing to claim that the policy chilled his right to free speech.

The federal trial court in Maryland, in an unpublished order, temporarily enjoined the adoption of a proposed curriculum on human sexuality that opponents claimed endorsed a homosexual lifestyle in part on the basis that it violated the Establishment Clause.[238] Deciding that the curriculum presented only one view on the subject, to the exclusion of others, and criticized specific Christian faiths, the court determined that it threatened the First Amendment rights of students and their parents. After the parties reached a settlement agreement, critics of the curriculum filed suit in state court. In another unpublished opinion, the court upheld an order of the State Board of Education. Rejecting the argument that the curricular content on human sexuality was inaccurate on a variety of points, the court concluded that nothing in the record demonstrated that the Board's action was arbitrary, unreasonable, or illegal.[239]

In the first of four Circuit court cases revealing how issues involving sexuality can cause controversy, parents in Massachusetts challenged a highly explicit sex-education program that was presented to high school students. In upholding the authority of local officials over curricular content, the First Circuit pointed out that the parental right to direct the upbringing and education of their children does not encompass a broad-based right to restrict flow of information in public schools even though educators failed to comply with a commonwealth statute that required them to provide the parents with notice prior to offering the program.[240]

The Ninth Circuit affirmed a school board in California's motion for summary judgment in a suit filed by parents of first, third, and fifth grade

235. *Leebaert v. Harrington*, 332 F.3d 134 [177 Educ. L. Rep. 901] (2d Cir. 2003).

236. *Morrison v. Board of Educ. of Boyd County*, 507 F.3d 494 (6th Cir. 2007).

237. *Morrison v. Board of Educ. of Boyd County*, 521 F.3d 602 [231 Educ. L. Rep. 527] (6th Cir. 2008), *cert. denied*, 555 U.S. 1171, 129 S.Ct. 1318, 173 L.Ed.2d 586 (2009).

238. *Citizens for a Responsible Curriculum v. Montgomery County Pub. Schools*, 2005 WL 1075634 (D. Md. 2005).

239. *Citizens for a Responsible Curriculum v. Montgomery County Pub. Schools*, 2008 WL 4107114 (Md. Cir. Ct. 2008).

240. *Brown v. Hot, Sexy and Safer Productions*, 68 F.3d 525 [104 Educ. L. Rep. 106] (1st Cir.1995), *cert. denied*, 516 U.S. 1159, 116 S.Ct. 1044, 134 L.Ed.2d 191 (1996).

students against educators who distributed a sexually explicit survey to their children. The court posited both that parents had neither a fundamental due process right to be exclusive providers of information on sexual matters for their children nor due process or privacy rights to override public school officials as to the information to which students can be exposed.[241] The court agreed that including the questions about sexual topics in the survey was rationally related to the board's legitimate interest in effective education and mental welfare of children.

Shortly thereafter, the Third Circuit reached a similar result in affirming a grant of summary judgment in favor of a school board in New Jersey where parents objected to the use of a voluntary, anonymous survey designed to gather information about drug and alcohol use, sexual activity, experiences of physical violence, attempts at suicide, personal associations and relationships (including parental relationships), and views on matters of public interest from district students in grades seven to twelve.[242] The court agreed that officials neither violated the privacy rights of students nor the rights of parents to make important decisions about the care and control of their children.

In another case from Massachusetts, the First Circuit affirmed a grant of summary judgment in favor of a school committee and various officials in a dispute over the inclusion of material about same-sex marriage in a curriculum.[243] Relying in part on *Yoder* in rejecting the claims of two sets of parents of elementary school children, the court noted that educational officials did not significantly limit either their parental rights to due process or free exercise of religion in having teachers use books that portrayed diverse families, including ones in which both parents were of the same gender.

GRADUATION REQUIREMENTS

Setting graduation requirements for students rests within the powers of state education officials and, to the extent that it is expressly or impliedly delegated, to local school boards. As long as requirements are reasonable, students can be denied diplomas if they are unable to or refuse to meet curricular standards.

School officials have the authority to evaluate whether students completed the requisite courses and have the qualifications to earn diplomas. As illustrated in the following cases, once students have met the standards, issuance of diplomas is a mandatory or ministerial act.

The Supreme Court of Iowa affirmed that while a student could not be denied a diploma for refusing to wear a cap-and-gown at a graduation ceremony, he could be denied the privilege of participating in the event.[244]

---

241. *Fields v. Palmdale School Dist.*, 427 F.3d 1197 [203 Educ. L. Rep. 44] (9th Cir. 2005), *opinion amended on denial of reh'g*, 447 F.3d 1187 [209 Educ. L. Rep. 77] (9th Cir. 2006), *cert. denied*, 549 U.S. 1089, 127 S.Ct. 725, 166 L.Ed.2d 583 [215 Educ. L. Rep. 33] (2006).

242. *C.N. v. Ridgewood Bd. of Educ.*, 430 F.3d 159 [203 Educ. L. Rep. 468] (3d Cir. 2005).

243. *Parker v. Hurley*, 514 F.3d 87 [229 Educ. L. Rep. 328] (1st Cir. 2008), *cert. denied*, 555 U.S. 815, 129 S.Ct. 56, 172 L.Ed.2d 24 [237 Educ. L. Rep. 586] (2008).

244. *Valentine v. Independent School Dist.*, 183 N.W. 434 (Iowa 1921). *See also Bear v. Fleming*, 714 F.Supp.2d 972 [260 Educ. L. Rep. 779] (D.S.D. 2010) (denying a student's

The Supreme Court of Kansas asserted that a student who was accused of cheating on a final examination could not be denied a diploma since officials failed to prove that he had done so.[245] An appellate court in Missouri explained that a student could not be refused a certificate of attainment based on his failure to pay a fee for the support of the high school since it was convinced that the board exceeded its authority in setting this requirement.[246] Fifty years later, when a local board required students to attend class for eight semesters in order to qualify for diplomas, a student who left school after a disciplinary incident eight weeks before the end of his third year re-entered at the beginning of the next year with the credits he earned toward graduation. When officials denied the student a diploma due to the eight-semester rule, the same court agreed that it was unreasonable, especially since the superintendent's testimony showed that it would have been unnecessary for the student to earn additional credits, pass any courses, or attend any number of classes.[247] The court rejected the eight-semester rule as no more than an exercise in futility that would not have been of benefit to either the board or the student.

A federal trial court in Texas denied a high school student's request for a preliminary injunction that would have allowed him to deliver the valedictory address at his graduation ceremony.[248] The court was satisfied that officials met the minimal requirements of due process when they met with the student on at least two occasions, notifying him that his failure to exhibit good conduct at the alternative education center because he "hacked" into the school's computer system resulted in his being denied the opportunity to make the valedictory address.

In the face of school reform issues dealing with accountability for student performance, especially as are likely to emerge under the NCLB,[249] it is worth recalling that state and local school officials have the authority to require children to pass competency, or proficiency, tests before receiving their diplomas as long as they have had fair opportunities to learn the material. This question first emerged in higher education in the Supreme Court's judgment in *Board of Curators of University of Missouri v. Horowitz*,[250] a dispute over whether a medical student could be dismissed during her final year of course work for failing to meet academic standards. All nine Justices agreed, albeit on different grounds, that the student received procedural due process through warnings and chances to demonstrate improvement. Five of the Justices thought that there were distinct differences between excluding students for disciplinary and academic reasons.

request to enjoin a board policy that required him to wear a cap-and-gown over his Native American clothing since the board had a legitimate interest in honoring its graduates while preserving class unity).

245. *Ryan v. Board of Educ.*, 257 P. 945 (Kan. 1927).

246. *State ex rel. Roberts v. Wilson*, 297 S.W. 419 (Mo. Ct. App. 1927).

247. *State ex rel. Sageser v. Ledbetter*, 559 S.W.2d 230 (Mo. Ct. App. 1977). [Case No. 86]

248. *Khan v. Fort Bend Independent School Dist.*, 561 F. Supp.2d 760 [235 Educ. L. Rep. 353] (S.D. Tex. 2008).

249. *See* 20 U.S.C.A. § 6301 (Statement of Purpose, discussing the need for testing). This section of the statute is in the Appendix.

250. 435 U.S. 78, 98 S.Ct. 948, 55 L.Ed.2d 124 (1978).

The leading case on competency testing in elementary and secondary schools arose in Florida, where the then Fifth, now Eleventh, Circuit initially refused to allow the use of such an examination on the basis that it was fundamentally unfair since the students had not been exposed to the material on which they were being tested.[251] The court rejected the thirteen-month notice period that officials provided as insufficient to permit the students to prepare for the examination. Once it agreed that the test was valid for instructional purposes, students received sufficient notice, and there was no link between the disproportionate number of African American students who failed it and the effects of past discrimination in the schools, the court permitted officials to use the examination.[252]

Three cases from Texas reveal the extent to which the judiciary is split over the use of competency tests as preconditions for high school graduation. First, a federal trial court agreed that graduation was reserved for students who met all of the requirements.[253] The next year, a state appellate court vacated an injunction that would have permitted students who met all of the requirements other than passing the state competency examination from participating in a graduation ceremony.[254] The court maintained that this was a matter for educational officials, not the judiciary. In the same year, though, a second federal trial court in Texas disagreed.[255] The court permitted students who passed all of their required courses but failed the state's competency test to take part in graduation ceremonies in commenting that officials were prohibited from imposing new criteria on students without providing adequate notice and a sufficient nexus between the test and the curriculum. In granting the students' request for a preliminary injunction permitting them to participate in the ceremony, the court also directed school officials to grant them their diplomas.[256]

The Supreme Judicial Court of Massachusetts has since refused to enjoin a regulation requiring students to pass the tenth-grade English language arts and mathematics sections of the Massachusetts Comprehensive Assessment System (MCAS) examination as a prerequisite to graduation before the other sections of the MCAS were phased in.[257] The court affirmed that officials at the commonwealth's board of education could exercise their discretion by requiring students to prove their competence in English and arithmetic before being tested on competence in science,

---

251. *Debra P. v. Turlington,* 644 F.2d 397 (5th Cir. 1981), *reh'g denied,* 654 F.2d 1079 (5th Cir. 1981).

252. *Debra P. v. Turlington,* 730 F.2d 1405 [16 Educ. L. Rep. 1120] (11th Cir. 1984).

253. *Williams v. Austin Indep. School Dist.,* 796 F.Supp. 251 [77 Educ. L. Rep. 111] (W.D. Tex. 1992).

254. *Edgewood Indep. School Dist. v. Paiz,* 856 S.W.2d 269 [84 Educ. L. Rep. 556] (Tex. Ct. App. 1993).

255. *Crump v. Gilmer Indep. School Dist.,* 797 F.Supp. 552 [77 Educ. L. Rep. 205] (E.D. Tex. 1992).

256. Chapter 15 reviews the related issue of competency testing of students with disabilities.

257. *Student No. 9 v. Board of Educ.,* 802 N.E.2d 105 [184 Educ. L. Rep. 553] (Mass. 2004).

history, and other areas. The court subsequently upheld the use of the MCAS in the face of a challenge from a different group of students.[258]

Turning to disciplinary matters in relation to academic performance, appellate courts in Pennsylvania agreed that where one student sold a controlled substance on the morning of graduation[259] and another was suspended for a variety of offenses but completed course work as part of a home tutoring program,[260] they could not be denied diplomas. In both instances, the courts were convinced that insofar as the students met all of their graduation requirements, officials could not deny them their diplomas.

On another matter, increasing numbers of school boards have required students to engage in some forms of community service before graduation. The Second,[261] Third,[262] and Fourth[263] Circuits rejected claims that school officials forced students to engage in involuntary servitude outlawed by the Thirteenth Amendment.

A final case with regard to graduation ceremonies involved scheduling. The Second Circuit rejected the claim of a student in New York that having a high school graduation ceremony take place on a Saturday violated his right to the free exercise of religion. The court reiterated that as long as attendance at the ceremony was not a prerequisite for receiving a diploma, school officials were free to schedule graduation ceremonies when they saw fit.[264]

CLASSIFICATION AND ASSIGNMENT OF STUDENTS

In General

School boards clearly have the power to classify students. Even so, since procedures are sometimes challenged as arbitrary, the courts must resolve the legality of classification methods. As highlighted by an older case from the Supreme Court of Ohio, disputes in this regard often involve the recurring question of whether matters are educational or legal. At issue was a parental request that a student skip from fifth to seventh grade. The plaintiffs argued that insofar as the child was tutored during the summer

---

258. *Hancock v. Commissioner of Educ.*, 822 N.E.2d 1134 [195 Educ. L. Rep. 591] (Mass. 2005).

259. *Shuman v. Cumberland Valley School Dist. Bd. of Directors*, 536 A.2d 490 [44 Educ. L. Rep. 399] (Pa. Cmwlth. Ct. 1988), *appeal denied*, 593 A.2d 428 (Pa. 1991).

260. *Ream v. Centennial School Dist.*, 765 A.2d 1195 [150 Educ. L. Rep. 773] (Pa. Cmwlth. Ct. 2001), *appeal denied*, 782 A.2d 551 (Pa. 2001).

261. *Immediato v. Rye Neck School Dist.*, 73 F.3d 454 [106 Educ. L. Rep. 85] (2d Cir. 1996), *cert. denied*, 519 U.S. 813, 117 S.Ct. 60, 136 L.Ed.2d 22 (1996).

262. *Steirer v. Bethlehem Area School Dist.*, 987 F.2d 989 [81 Educ. L. Rep. 734] (3d Cir. 1993), *cert. denied*, 510 U.S. 824, 114 S.Ct. 85, 126 L.Ed.2d 53 (1993), *abrogated by Troster v. Pennsylvania State Dept. of Corr.*, 65 F.3d 1086, 1091 (3d Cir. 1995).

263. *Herndon by Herndon v. Chapel Hill–Carrboro City Bd. of Educ.*, 89 F.3d 174 [110 Educ. L. Rep. 1037] (4th Cir.1996), *cert. denied*, 519 U.S. 1111, 117 S.Ct. 949, 136 L.Ed.2d 837 (1997).

264. *Smith by Smith v. Board of Educ., N. Babylon Union Free School Dist.*, 844 F.2d 90 [46 Educ. L. Rep. 518] (2d Cir. 1988).

he made progress qualifying him for the higher grade.[265] On further review of an order granting the request, the court indicated that the trial judge erred since such questions are within the authority of educational officials, not the judiciary.

Other disputes have arisen over the assignments of students to kindergarten classes. A parent in New York unsuccessfully argued that insofar as public kindergarten was optional and his five-year-old had a state right to attend public school, the child should have been placed in first grade. An appellate court agreed with the father that his son had a right to attend school but affirmed that once kindergarten was established, whether he was assigned to it or to first grade was subject to criteria established by the local school board.[266] At the same time, an appellate court in Pennsylvania affirmed that where kindergarten was optional, a child who was below the requisite age for admission had neither a constitutionally protected right to attend kindergarten nor to a formal hearing before school officials acted.[267] Other courts consistently upheld statutes basing admission to public schools solely on age.[268]

As far-ranging as the authority of school boards may be, their rules must not have discriminatory effects. For example, where seven-year-olds who did not attend kindergarten in their district were automatically registered in first grade, an appellate court invalidated the requirement that they had to pass a readiness test for children who attended kindergarten.[269] In a different situation, the Supreme Court of Kansas was of the opinion that a board had the implied authority to require graduates of nonpublic schools to take an entrance examination before attending public high schools.[270] Almost three-quarters of a century later, the Sixth Circuit upheld an almost identical provision for those transferring from home study situations in Kentucky.[271] Previously, a court in New York approved the use of a placement test for a child who attended a private kindergarten.[272] However, where a statute permitted, but did not require, local boards to assess the readiness of children to attend school prior to the statutory starting date, an appellate court in Illinois reasoned that a board was not obligated to continue doing so.[273]

Requirements for progressing from one grade to the next are generally not subject to judicial review. The Fourth Circuit affirmed that the courts

---

265. *Board of Educ. of Sycamore v. State ex rel. Wickham*, 88 N.E. 412 (Ohio 1909).

266. *Isquith v. Levitt*, 137 N.Y.S.2d 497 (N.Y. App. Div. 1955).

267. *Goldsmith v. Lower Moreland School Dist.*, 461 A.2d 1341 [12 Educ. L. Rep. 431] (Pa. Cmwlth. Ct. 1983).

268. *See, e.g., Hammond v. Marx*, 406 F.Supp. 853 (D. Me.1975); *Wright v. Ector County Indep. School Dist.*, 867 S.W.2d 863 [88 Educ. L. Rep. 859] (Tex. Ct. App. 1993).

269. *Morgan v. Board of Educ., Trico Community Unit School Dist. No. 176*, 317 N.E.2d 393 (Ill. App. Ct. 1974).

270. *Creyhon v. Board of Educ.*, 163 P. 145 (Kan. 1917).

271. *Vandiver v. Hardin County Bd. of Educ.*, 925 F.2d 927 [65 Educ. L. Rep. 1045] (6th Cir. 1991).

272. *Silverberg v. Board of Educ. of Union Free School Dist. No. 18*, 303 N.Y.S.2d 816 (N.Y. 1969).

273. *Morrison v. Chicago Bd. of Educ.*, 544 N.E.2d 1099 [56 Educ. L. Rep. 524] (Ill. App. Ct. 1989).

should not intervene where school officials refused to promote students who failed reading-level tests.[274] The court accepted the evaluations of educators that even though the second-grade students in Virginia were capable of reading at the third-grade level, they should not have been promoted until they mastered the requisite skills. In like manner, the Eleventh Circuit affirmed that school officials in Alabama could initiate a new policy of refusing to promote students who performed unsatisfactorily.[275] Further, the Ninth Circuit rejected a challenge filed by a father who was unhappy with the grade of "C" that his daughter received in her physical education class.[276] The court posited that insofar as the poor grade was due to the student's lack of cooperation rather than improper racial bias or personal animus on the part of the teacher, his claim was without merit.

Courts also reviewed controversies involving specialized offerings. The Fifth Circuit affirmed that a student in Georgia lacked a federal claim over his inability to enroll in a course of study since school officials did not violate a specific state mandate.[277] Another student failed in his challenge to being denied readmission to a special program in automobile mechanics that was conducted at an area vocational-technical school after he was involved in a theft of automobile parts from a different location. The Eighth Circuit affirmed that officials in Missouri could deny a student's request for admission since participation was conditioned both on good citizenship and their interest in protecting the integrity of off-campus programs.[278]

Evaluation of students' academic progress has led to increasing amounts of litigation. The courts generally agree that attendance can be a factor affecting final course grades.[279] The Supreme Court of Connecticut issued an extensive order which responded to an array of arguments in permitting a student to be denied academic credit due to excessive absences.[280] The Supreme Court of Missouri reached the same result even though it determined that a student had the right to a hearing before officials could impose a penalty.[281] The essential educational consideration that courts accept is that presence in class adds a dimension to subject matter learning while affording many less-tangible benefits such as interactions with teachers and peers. An appellate court in Michigan, although not believing that the matter was of constitutional significance, stated that even if it were, the case from Connecticut provided persuasive precedent in

---

274. *Sandlin v. Johnson*, 643 F.2d 1027 (4th Cir. 1981).

275. *Bester v. Tuscaloosa City Bd. of Educ.*, 722 F.2d 1514 [15 Educ. L. Rep. 118] (11th Cir. 1984).

276. *Hurd v. Hansen*, 230 Fed.Appx. 692 [222 Educ. L. Rep. 125] (9th Cir. 2007).

277. *Arundar v. DeKalb County School Dist.*, 620 F.2d 493 (5th Cir. 1980).

278. *Felton v. Fayette School Dist.*, 875 F.2d 191 [53 Educ. L. Rep. 850] (8th Cir. 1989).

279. *See, e.g., Knight v. Board of Educ. of Tri–Point Community Unit School Dist. No. 6J*, 348 N.E.2d 299 (Ill. App. Ct. 1976).

280. *Campbell v. Board of Educ. of Town of New Milford*, 475 A.2d 289 [17 Educ. L. Rep. 840] (Conn. 1984). [Case No. 87]

281. *State ex rel. Yarber v. McHenry*, 915 S.W.2d 325 [107 Educ. L. Rep. 361] (Mo. 1995).

a like situation.[282]

In recognizing that board officials have wide discretion in student assignments, courts generally do not substitute their judgments for those of educators.[283] In fact, even if schools are more conveniently located for children, courts do not necessarily agree that this is determinative of a right to attend a particular school.[284] In a typical case, parents wished to have their children continue to attend the school nearest their homes when the local board rearranged assignments based on having to reduce over-crowded conditions at a high school and the need for additional classroom space in the school from which the students were to be moved to remedy the overflow. The Supreme Court of Michigan agreed that it would not substitute its judgment for that of a board.[285] The Supreme Court of Mississippi extended this rationale in affirming that a child does not have a right to attend the same school as a sibling as long as officials did not act arbitrarily and capriciously in denying such a request.[286]

At issue in one case was a school board's revision of attendance zones and reassigning students where race was not involved. The parents' main objection focused on a safety factor because even though the village had yet to erect a proposed school building, the board did not change reassignment plans for students. In upholding the board's plan, the Court of Appeals of New York agreed that it had a rational basis since it relied on the report of a citizens' advisory committee, board members personally visited class-rooms, conducted safety discussions with village officials, and walked the proposed routes.[287] According to the court, requiring a quasi-judicial hear-ing every time boards revise school attendance lines would have posed serious problems for educators. The Supreme Court of Washington applied the same kind of rationale when the school board in Seattle created a plan for busing to remedy de facto segregation.[288] Ten years later the Supreme Court struck down a statute of the same kind adopted by a statewide referendum that was designed to prevent student assignments to remedy de facto segregation in *Washington v. Seattle School District No. 1*.[289] Key to the Court's analysis was that insofar as state law permitted local boards to make all assignments except those for race-connected purposes, it violated the Equal Protection Clause.

---

282. *Slocum v. Holton Bd. of Educ.*, 429 N.W.2d 607 [49 Educ. L. Rep. 740] (Mich. Ct. App. 1988).

283. *State ex rel. Lewis v. Board of Educ. of Wilmington School Dist.*, 28 N.E.2d 496 (Ohio 1940). *But see Bartlett v. Board of Trustees of White Pine County School Dist.*, 550 P.2d 416 (Nev.1976) (rejecting a board plan to close a school).

284. *Bernstein v. Board of Educ. of Prince George's County*, 226 A.2d 243 (Md.1967); *Lillbask ex rel. Mauclaire v. Sergi*, 193 F. Supp.2d 503 [163 Educ. L. Rep. 767] (D. Conn. 2002).

285. *Hiers v. Brownell*, 136 N.W.2d 10 (Mich. 1965). For a more recent case with the same outcome, *see Clay v. Harrison Hills City School Dist. Bd. of Educ.*, 723 N.E.2d 1149 [141 Educ. L. Rep. 1164] (Ohio Com. Pl. 1999).

286. *Pascagoula Mun. Separate School Dist. v. Barton*, 776 So.2d 683 [151 Educ. L. Rep. 334] (Miss. 2001).

287. *Older v. Board of Educ. of Union Free School Dist. No. 1, Town of Mamaroneck*, 318 N.Y.S.2d 129 (N.Y. 1971).

288. *Citizens Against Mandatory Bussing v. Palmason*, 495 P.2d 657 (Wash. 1972).

289. 458 U.S. 457, 102 S.Ct. 3187, 73 L.Ed.2d 896 [5 Educ. L. Rep. 58] (1982).

The authority of school board officials to make assignments, combined with students' lack of a vested right to attend particular schools aside, this does not mean that courts never review these kinds of controversies. Parents of a high school student who studied Latin during her first year, was a member of the band, generally received high grades, and expected to go to a college that had an entrance requirement of a minimum of two units in two foreign languages or three units in Latin challenged her proposed reassignment to a school that had neither Latin nor a band. State law provided that when assignments were completed, officials could make changes if they were in the best interests of students and did not interfere with the administration of the schools. Since the board refused to reassign the student to her original school, the Supreme Court of North Carolina, observing that the law placed its emphasis on the welfare of students and the effect on the school to which reassignment was requested, directed the board to reassign the pupil to her original school.[290]

Ability Grouping

Parents and interest groups questioned school board policies for ability grouping, or tracking, of students in public schools, alleging that doing so violated federally protected rights. This issue first arose in the context of a challenge to policies and practices in the Washington, D.C., public school system. The plaintiffs succeeded in demonstrating that tracking deprived African American and poor children of their rights to equal educational opportunities. It appears that based on examinations that the students took relatively early in their school careers, officials assigned them to curricular tracks designed to prepare them for different types of jobs. In remarking that the absence of compensatory education made it almost impossible for children who were originally on one track to move to higher ones, the federal trial court struck down the practice as discriminatory. Raising general questions about the tests as a measure of ability, the court barred any system of ability grouping, which, through its failure to include and implement the concept of compensatory education, did not bring the great majority of children into the mainstream of public education.[291]

One objection that opponents to achievement tests typically raise is that they have a disparate impact on minority students. In order to prevail on disparate impact claims, plaintiffs must demonstrate that facially neutral practices have disproportionate effects. If plaintiffs succeed, the burden shifts to school boards to provide substantial legitimate justifications for their practices. Plaintiffs then have the chance to show either that the practices are pretexts for discrimination or to proffer equally effective practices that would result in less racial disproportionality in achieving their legitimate educational goals.[292]

---

290. *In re Hayes*, 135 S.E.2d 645 (N.C. 1964).

291. *Hobson v. Hansen*, 269 F.Supp. 401 (D.D.C.1967), *aff'd sub nom. Smuck v. Hobson*, 408 F.2d 175 (D.C. Cir. 1969).

292. *Quarles v. Oxford Mun. Separate School Dist.*, 868 F.2d 750 [52 Educ. L. Rep. 38] (5th Cir. 1989).

The use of I.Q. tests as a primary determinant in placing students who are mentally retarded has been challenged with differing results. Federal trial courts, in disputes arising in San Francisco[293] and Chicago,[294] reached opposite conclusions as to whether specified tests were culturally biased. As discussed in Chapter 15, the Individuals with Disabilities Act requires educators to use multiple measures in evaluating students with special needs.[295]

Gifted Education

The only applicable federal law, the Jacob K. Javits Gifted and Talented Act, which was incorporated into the No Child Left Behind Act,[296] does not afford federal statutory rights to specialized programs because even though it encourages local school boards to create programs, it does not provide funds to do so. States, of course, are free to offer programs for children who are gifted and talented.

Insofar as state and local officials have the authority to classify students as gifted, they may rely on I.Q. tests as a criterion for use in their identification.[297] If programs for the gifted can accommodate limited numbers of students, officials can use lotteries to select from among qualified applicants.[298] Amid disputes over the rights of gifted children, courts have reached mixed results with regard to programs for qualified students.

The Supreme Court of Pennsylvania unanimously affirmed that pursuant to a commonwealth statute and regulations requiring an Individualized Education Program (IEP) for each gifted student, a child had the right to gifted education.[299] Further, an appellate court in Pennsylvania affirmed that a school board was required to provide an education sufficient to confer a benefit on a gifted student that was tailored to his unique needs pursuant to his IEP.[300] Yet, another appellate panel in Pennsylvania clarified that this the law did not include requiring a board to provide children with individual tutors or exclusive programs exceeding existing, regular, and special, curricular offerings.[301]

---

293. *Larry P. v. Riles*, 495 F.Supp. 926 (N.D.Cal.1979), *aff'd in part*, 793 F.2d 969 (9th Cir. 1984) (striking tests down).

294. *Parents in Action on Special Educ. v. Hannon*, 506 F.Supp. 831 (N.D. Ill. 1980) (upholding the validity of tests).

295. *See* 20 U.S.C.A. § 1414(b)(2)(B) (specifying that no single procedure can be the sole criterion for determining eligibility or placement of students with special needs).

296. 20 U.S.C.A. § 7253. States often follow an approach such as the one used in Ohio which requires school board officials to identify, but not serve, students who are gifted. Oнio Rev. Code Ann. § 3324.04.

297. *Student Roe v. Commonwealth of Pa.*, 638 F.Supp. 929 [33 Educ. L. Rep. 1132] (E.D. Pa. 1986), *aff'd*, 813 F.2d 398 [38 Educ. L. Rep. 111] (3d Cir.1987), *cert. denied*, 483 U.S. 1021, 107 S.Ct. 3265, 97 L.Ed.2d 764 [39 Educ. L. Rep. 998] (1987).

298. *Bennett v. City School Dist. of New Rochelle*, 497 N.Y.S.2d 72 [29 Educ. L. Rep. 728] (N.Y. App. Div.1985).

299. *Centennial School Dist. v. Commonwealth, Dep't of Educ.*, 539 A.2d 785 [46 Educ. L. Rep. 278] (Pa.1988).

300. *York Suburban School Dist. v. S.P.*, 872 A.2d 1285 [197 Educ. L. Rep. 653] (Pa. Cmwlth. Ct. 2005).

301. *Abington School Dist. v. B.G.*, 6 A.3d 624 [261 Educ. L. Rep. 671] (Pa. Cmwlth. Ct. 2010).

A case from the Supreme Court of Connecticut is more typical of the treatment of children who are gifted.[302] The court unanimously affirmed that the state constitution did not confer the right to special educational programming on a student who was gifted. The court ruled that the legislature's failure to mandate a program for a child who is gifted did not violate his rights under the equal rights or equal protection provisions of the state constitution.

SEX

A contentious issue involves assignments of students based on sex. In an early case, the federal trial court in Massachusetts directed officials at the Boston Latin School to use the same admissions standards when evaluating the applications of males and females.[303] The court reasoned that officials violated the equal protection rights of female students not only because they attended classes in a smaller building but also since some of the young women who were excluded had higher scores on the entrance examination than males who were admitted.

Where the board in San Francisco operated a prestigious academic high school, in order to attract equal numbers of males and females, admissions criteria required females to have higher grades than males. In the face of a challenge, the Ninth Circuit directed officials to discontinue the practice of differential admissions requirements.[304] The court ascertained that board officials did not present any evidence that a balance of the sexes furthered the goal of better academic education.

A female in Philadelphia filed suit seeking to enter the city's only all-male high school rather than its only all-female high school. Enrollment at the schools was voluntary, the standards at both were high, and the schools were of like size and prestige. After a federal trial court ordered the board to admit the female, the Third Circuit reversed in its favor.[305] The court relied on the fact that attendance at either single sex-school was voluntary and the facilities were equal. An equally divided Supreme Court summarily affirmed in favor of the board in *Vorchheimer v. School District of Philadelphia.*[306]

Parents in New York City unsuccessfully challenged their school board's transforming its only all-girl public high school into a co-educational facility. A federal trial court declared that insofar as Title IX did not require officials to create all-female schools, the change did not deprive their daughters of the right to equal educational opportunities.[307]

---

302. *Broadley v. Board of Educ. of City of Meriden*, 639 A.2d 502 [90 Educ. L. Rep. 265] (Conn. 1994).

303. *Bray v. Lee*, 337 F.Supp. 934 (D. Mass. 1972).

304. *Berkelman v. San Francisco Unified School Dist.*, 501 F.2d 1264 (9th Cir.1974).

305. *Vorchheimer v. School Dist. of Philadelphia*, 532 F.2d 880 (3d Cir. 1976).

306. 430 U.S. 703, 97 S.Ct. 1671, 51 L.Ed.2d 750 (1977).

307. *Jones on Behalf of Michele v. Board of Educ. of City School Dist. of City of N.Y.*, 632 F.Supp. 1319 [32 Educ. L. Rep. 141] (E.D.N.Y. 1986).

When demographics revealed that its student population was predominately African American, the board in Detroit sought to open all-black male academies in an attempt to remedy educational and social difficulties that young black males experienced. After the mother of a female tried to enroll her daughter in one of the schools, a federal trial court in Michigan refused to let the schools open as planned.[308] Relying on *Mississippi University for Women v. Hogan*,[309] wherein the Supreme Court affirmed that excluding an individual from a public institution solely due to sex violated equal protection, the court was of the view that the rationale for founding the all-male academies was insufficient to override the female's rights.

In *United States v. Commonwealth of Virginia*,[310] a dispute from higher education, the Supreme Court concluded that due to the inability of officials at the Virginia Military Institute to justify the policy of excluding women, it violated their rights to equal protection. While rejecting the idea that programs can be designed for only one gender, the Court left the door open to the possibility that single-sex schools can be constitutional as long as they provide equal educational opportunities for females and males.[311]

In a related concern dealing with gender, litigation continued over the right of pregnant students to become members of the National Honor Society (NHS). The Ninth Circuit affirmed an award of attorney fees in favor of a pregnant, unmarried student in Arizona who was not living with the child's father and was excluded from the NHS.[312] The court upheld the award of attorney fees even though the amount exceeded the statutory cap since it was convinced that educators acted in bad faith in excluding the student. Similarly, a federal trial court in Kentucky granted a preliminary injunction to unmarried high school students who were excluded from the NHS after becoming pregnant and having children.[313] The court was satisfied that the students showed the strong likelihood of success on the merits of their claims and that they would have suffered irreparable injury if it did not grant the requested relief.

USE OF RACE IN ADMISSIONS DECISIONS

The use of race as an admissions criterion first surfaced in *Regents of University of California v. Bakke (Bakke)*.[314] Even though it was set in higher education, *Bakke* became the bellwether in suits involving race conscious admissions plans, also commonly referred to as affirmative ac-

---

308. *Garrett v. Board of Educ. of School Dist. of City of Detroit*, 775 F.Supp. 1004 [70 Educ. L. Rep. 1101] (E.D. Mich. 1991).

309. 458 U.S. 718, 102 S.Ct. 3331, 73 L.Ed.2d 1090 [5 Educ. L. Rep. 103] (1982).

310. 518 U.S. 515, 116 S.Ct. 2264, 135 L.Ed.2d 735 (1996), *on remand*, 96 F.3d 114 (4th Cir. 1996).

311. *See also Faulkner v. Jones*, 51 F.3d 440 [99 Educ. L. Rep. 99] (4th Cir.1995), *stay denied*, 66 F.3d 661 (4th Cir. 1995), *cert. dismissed*, 516 U.S. 910, 116 S.Ct. 331, 133 L.Ed.2d 202 [105 Educ. L. Rep. 395] (1995), *cert. denied*, 516 U.S. 938, 116 S.Ct. 352, 133 L.Ed.2d 248 [105 Educ. L. Rep. 396] (1995) (involving the Citadel).

312. *Cazares v. Barber*, 959 F.2d 753 [73 Educ. L. Rep. 931] (9th Cir. 1992).

313. *Chipman v. Grant County School Dist.*, 30 F. Supp.2d 975 [131 Educ. L. Rep. 994] (E.D. Ky.1998).

314. 438 U.S. 265, 98 S.Ct. 2733, 57 L.Ed.2d 750 (1978).

tion. In *Bakke*, the Supreme Court held that while the admissions program at issue, which set aside seats for minority applicants, was unacceptable, the use of race as a factor in admissions decisions was not per se impermissible. *Bakke* opened the door to a steady stream of litigation on the use of race in admissions to educational institutions.

In addition to terminating judicial oversight of school desegregation efforts in Denver, the federal trial court in Colorado reviewed a state constitutional provision which prohibited the use of race in school assignments. In rejecting the school board's claim that it had the right to place children as officials saw fit, the court posited that the state constitution forbade educators from making student transportation assignments pursuant to preconceived plans to achieve racial balancing in schools.[315] When the school board announced that it had no intention of carrying out the planned policy, the Tenth Circuit dismissed the appeal as moot.[316]

Parents challenged the admissions policy of the Boston Latin School because it took race and ethnicity into consideration. The First Circuit invalidated the policy in rejecting the notion that it was meant to remedy the vestiges of past discrimination. The court pointed out that insofar as diversity was not a compelling interest, educational officials had to admit a white student because the policy violated her right to equal protection.[317] Along the same line, in a case from Maryland, the Fourth Circuit found in favor of the parents of a first-grade student who questioned the constitutionality of a policy at a magnet school that used race and ethnicity as factors in considering whether students could transfer into the program.[318] The court directed officials to admit the child to the magnet school in determining that the use of race as a factor in the transfer policy violated equal protection because it was insufficiently narrowly tailored to achieve the goal of a diversified student body.

On the other hand, the Ninth Circuit upheld a policy from California that included race and ethnicity as criteria in admitting students to a university's laboratory school.[319] The court affirmed that in light of the state's compelling interest in providing effective education in urban schools, the use of race was narrowly tailored to achieve this goal.

The Supreme Court's most recent pronouncements on race-conscious affirmative action plans in higher education were companion cases from the University of Michigan. In *Grutter v. Bollinger (Grutter)*,[320] the Court upheld the university's affirmative action admissions policy in its law school. The Court discerned that insofar as diversity is a compelling governmental interest, officials could use race as a factor in admissions

315. *Keyes v. Congress of Hispanic Educators*, 902 F.Supp. 1274 [104 Educ. L. Rep. 1067] (D. Colo. 1995), *appeal dismissed*, 119 F.3d 1437 [120 Educ. L. Rep. 158] (10th Cir. 1997).

316. *Keyes v. School Dist. No. 1, Denver, Colo.*, 119 F.3d 1437 [120 Educ. L. Rep. 158] (10th Cir. 1997).

317. *Wessmann v. Gittens*, 160 F.3d 790 [130 Educ. L. Rep. 1009] (1st Cir. 1998).

318. *Eisenberg v. Montgomery County Pub. Schools*, 197 F.3d 123 [140 Educ. L. Rep. 88] (4th Cir. 1999), *cert. denied*, 529 U.S. 1019, 120 S.Ct. 1420, 146 L.Ed.2d 312 (2000).

319. *Hunter ex rel. Brandt v. Regents of the Univ. of Cal.*, 190 F.3d 1061 [138 Educ. L. Rep. 127] (9th Cir. 1999), *cert. denied*, 531 U.S. 877, 121 S.Ct. 186, 148 L.Ed.2d 128 (2000).

320. 539 U.S. 306, 123 S.Ct. 2325, 156 L.Ed.2d 304 [177 Educ. L. Rep. 801] (2003).

decisions since the criteria were sufficiently narrowly tailored to achieve the compelling state interest of having a racially diverse student body. In *Gratz v. Bollinger* (*Gratz*),[321] the Court struck down the university's reliance on a point system in admissions to undergraduate programs since its use of race was insufficiently narrowly tailored to achieve its goal of a diverse student body.[322] Not surprisingly, in the aftermath of these cases courts continue to reach mixed results on the use of race in admissions in K–12 schools. Three of the four circuit courts that considered race as a criterion agreed that educators acted with compelling state interests.

In a case from Louisiana initially involving a consent decree, a magnet school, and a court-ordered desegregation plan, the Fifth Circuit noted that a race-based admissions policy was not narrowly tailored enough to remedy the present effects of past segregation.[323] While not citing either *Grutter* or *Gratz*, the court asserted that the plan was unacceptable absent evidence that officials considered any race-neutral means of selecting students that might arguably have increased participation by African Americans. The court was not convinced that the quota system complied with the dictates of the consent decree.

The first of three cases to uphold the use of race involved a challenge by parents in Louisville, Kentucky, who questioned the use of a district-wide, race-conscious school choice plan. The Sixth Circuit affirmed that insofar as the plan was narrowly tailored to achieve the compelling goal of preserving the presence of minority students in each school as a means of successfully implementing racial integration, it was acceptable.[324] At the same time, parents in Massachusetts whose children were denied transfers on race-conscious criteria filed a discrimination claim against school officials. An en banc First Circuit affirmed that insofar as the plan was sufficiently narrowly tailored to meet the school committee's compelling interest in achieving the benefits of educational diversity, it was constitutional.[325] Following the case from Washington that reached the Supreme Court, and which is discussed in the following two paragraphs, the First Circuit refused to reconsider its judgment on the basis that absent a connection between the two suits there was no equitable basis on which to do so.[326]

---

321. 539 U.S. 244, 123 S.Ct. 2411, 156 L.Ed.2d 257 [177 Educ. L. Rep. 851] (2003).

322. In a related development, a federal trial court in Michigan held that an amendment to the state constitution prohibiting discrimination against or granting preferential treatment to any individual or group on basis of race, sex, color, ethnicity, or national origin neither discriminated against nor violated the equal protection rights of minorities when applied to public colleges and universities. *Coalition to Defend Affirmative Action v. Regents of Univ. of Mich.*, 539 F.Supp.2d 924 [231 Educ. L. Rep. 115] (E.D. Mich. 2008).

323. *Cavalier ex rel. Cavalier v. Caddo Parish School Bd.*, 403 F.3d 246 [196 Educ. L. Rep. 765] (5th Cir. 2005).

324. *McFarland ex rel. McFarland v. Jefferson County Pub. Schools*, 416 F.3d 513 (6th Cir. 2005), *reh'g and reh'g en banc denied* (2005).

325. *Comfort v. Lynn School Comm.*, 418 F.3d 1 [200 Educ. L. Rep. 541] (1st Cir. 2005), *cert. denied*, 546 U.S. 1061, 126 S.Ct. 798, 163 L.Ed.2d 627 (2005). On remand the federal trial court in Massachusetts denied the parents' request for relief from the final judgment, thereby dismissing their claim. *Comfort ex rel. Neumyer v. Lynn School Comm.*, 541 F.Supp.2d 429 [231 Educ. L. Rep. 739] (D. Mass. 2008).

326. *Comfort v. Lynn School Comm.*, 560 F.3d 22 [242 Educ. L. Rep. 659] (1st Cir. 2009).

A procedurally complex case from Washington state, which began prior to *Grutter* and *Gratz,* involved a parental challenge to the "open choice" assignment plans of their school boards. The parents claimed that the plan, which used race as a tiebreaker in assigning students to oversubscribed high schools, violated the Equal Protection Clause and state laws. After a federal trial court granted the board's motion for summary judgment,[327] the Ninth Circuit reversed in favor of the parents[328] but withdrew its opinion when it agreed to conduct a rehearing.[329] The court also certified the question to the Supreme Court of Washington as to whether use of a racial tiebreaker in making high school assignments violated a state law against discrimination or granting preferential treatment to individuals or groups due to race, color, ethnicity, or national origin in public schools.[330] The Supreme Court of Washington maintained that while racial diversity in education is a compelling interest, the board's use of race as a tiebreaker was not narrowly tailored to further such an interest. In conforming with the judgment of the Supreme Court of Washington, the Ninth Circuit reversed and remanded in favor of the parents with instructions to enjoin the plan.[331] The court was persuaded that the racial integration tiebreaker violated a state law which prohibited the preferential use of race in public schools. Subsequently, an en banc panel of the Ninth Circuit, relying on *Gratz* and *Grutter,* explained that the plan did not violate equal protection since its use of race was sufficiently narrowly tailored to achieve the compelling state interest of avoiding racial isolation while increasing diversity.[332]

On further review in *Parents Involved In Community Schools v. Seattle School District Number 1,*[333] a divided Supreme Court struck down plans from Seattle, Washington, and Louisville, Kentucky. In invalidating both programs, the Court observed that Seattle had never operated racially segregated schools nor has it ever been subject to a court-ordered desegregation order while Louisville's schools had been declared unitary and released from judicial supervision in 2000. The Court essentially concluded that school officials in both districts failed to demonstrate that the use of racial classifications in the student assignment plans was necessary to achieve their stated goal of racial diversity and that they failed to consider alternative approaches adequately.

---

327. *Parents Involved in Community Schools v. Seattle School Dist. No. 1,* 137 F.Supp.2d 1224 [153 Educ. L. Rep. 267] (W.D. Wash. 2001).

328. *Parents Involved in Community Schools v. Seattle School Dist., No. 1,* 285 F.3d 1236 [163 Educ. L. Rep. 572] (9th Cir. 2002).

329. *Parents Involved In Community Schools v. Seattle School Dist., No. 1,* 294 F.3d 1084 [167 Educ. L. Rep. 38] (9th Cir. 2002).

330. *Parents Involved in Community Schools v. Seattle School Dist. No. 1,* 294 F.3d 1085 [166 Educ. L. Rep. 511] (9th Cir. 2002).

331. *Parents Involved in Community Schools v. Seattle School Dist. No. 1,* 377 F.3d 949 [190 Educ. L. Rep. 79] (9th Cir. 2004).

332. *Parents Involved in Community Schools v. Seattle School Dist. No. 1,* 426 F.3d 1162 [202 Educ. L. Rep. 549] (9th Cir. 2005).

333. 551 U.S. 701, 127 S.Ct. 2738, 168 L.Ed.2d 508 [220 Educ. L. Rep. 84] (2007). [Case No. 88]

In another case involving race and ethnicity, a non-native Hawaiian student challenged a private school, its charitable trust, and trustees claiming that its race-conscious admissions policy of accepting only students of native Hawaiian ancestry was unconstitutional. The Ninth Circuit initially agreed with the plaintiff that insofar as the policy did not constitute a valid affirmative action plan that might have supplied legitimate nondiscriminatory reason for its actions, it violated Section 1981, but an en banc panel reversed in favor of the school.[334] The panel later remarked that insofar as the policy remedied the manifest imbalance in educational achievement between native Hawaiians and other ethnic groups, and educational opportunities were available for non-native Hawaiians, it passed constitutional muster.[335]

FEES

State constitutions typically require their legislatures to establish systems of free public schools. Even so, disputes arise over whether local boards can charge fees. A case from the Supreme Court of Arkansas illustrates the general rule that students and/or their parents cannot be charged registration fees in order to keep public schools open for a full term.[336] Further, the Supreme Court of Mississippi specified that boards may not indirectly violate the spirit of the constitutional provision that a state must operate a system of free public schools by charging athletic, library, and other such fees as a condition to being admitted to schools.[337] Since the courts have reached mixed results with regard to such items as transportation, textbooks, course materials, and summer programs, each of these is addressed separately.

Transportation

Absent express statutory directives, and as reflected in a case from Louisiana,[338] most states do not charge fees for transporting students to and from school. If boards discontinue transportation for students in public schools, parents whose children attend non-public schools cannot claim such a right for their children.[339] In addition, courts typically uphold requirements that children, regardless of whether they attend public or non-public schools, must live within specified limits in order to qualify for

---

334. *Doe v. Kamehameha Schools/Bernice Pauahi Bishop Estate*, 416 F.3d 1025 [200 Educ. L. Rep. 53] (9th Cir. 2005), *rev'd in part*, 470 F.3d 827 [214 Educ. L. Rep. 926] (9th Cir. 2006).

335. *Doe v. Kamehameha Schools/Bernice Pauahi Bishop Estate*, 470 F.3d 827 [214 Educ. L. Rep. 926] (9th Cir. 2006), *cert. dismissed*, 550 U.S. 931, 127 S.Ct. 2160, 167 L.Ed.2d 887 [219 Educ. L. Rep. 59] (2007).

336. *Dowell v. School Dist. No. 1, Boone County*, 250 S.W.2d 127 (Ark.1952). *See also Morris v. Vandiver*, 145 So. 228 (Miss. 1933).

337. *Morris v. Vandiver*, 145 So. 228 (Miss. 1933).

338. *Moreau v. Avoyelles Parish School Bd.*, 897 So.2d 875, 883 [197 Educ. L. Rep. 463] (La. Ct. App. 2005), *writs denied*, 904 So.2d 704, 705 (La. 2005) ("the concept of free education in Louisiana includes as a *primary* element the transportation to and from school.") (emphasis in original).

339. *Crowe ex rel. Crowe v. School Dist. of Pittsburgh*, 805 A.2d 691 [169 Educ. L. Rep. 314] (Pa. Cmwlth. Ct. 2002).

free transportation.[340] Even if statutes permit school boards to provide free transportation or pay the allowance for students, they have no duty to reimburse parents for the cost of transportation if their children make their own way to school.[341]

As reflected in its only case on transportation fees, *Kadrmas v. Dickinson Public Schools (Kadrmas)*,[342] the Supreme Court affirmed that North Dakota had the authority to permit such charges. The Court upheld a statute that allowed school boards to charge fees for transportation that did not exceed their actual estimated costs. According to the Court, the law did not violate equal protection because it not only encouraged local boards to provide bus service as a legitimate state purpose but was a rational way to avoid undermining its objective by means of a rule requiring the use of general revenues to subsidize an optional service that would have aided a minority of families. In treating transportation as different from fees for tuition and other items, some courts permitted these fees in agreeing that transportation is not at the heart of the obligation of states to provide students with a free public education.[343]

Textbooks

As important as textbooks are, courts disagree on whether all students in public schools are entitled to use them for free. The highest courts in Georgia,[344] Idaho,[345] Michigan,[346] Ohio,[347] and West Virginia,[348] agreed that students cannot be charged fees for textbooks. The Supreme Court of Michigan, citing the case from Idaho, thought that insofar as textbooks are necessary elements of school activities, officials should have provided them for students at no cost. The court in West Virginia, conceding that insofar as books and supplies are an essential part of free public schools, was of the opinion that denying them to students who cannot pay for them would have been akin to prohibiting them from attending school. The court added that a board cannot purchase books and sell them to students, even at wholesale prices, unless it is specially authorized to do so by statute.

---

340. *See, e.g., Quasti v. North Penn Sch. Dist.*, 907 A.2d 42 [213 Educ. L. Rep. 231] (Pa. Cmwlth. Ct. 2006).

341. *State ex rel. Fick v. Miller*, 584 N.W.2d 809 [129 Educ. L. Rep. 800] (Neb.1998).

342. 487 U.S. 450, 108 S.Ct. 2481, 101 L.Ed.2d 399 [47 Educ. L. Rep. 383] (1988).

343. *See, e.g., Salazar v. Eastin*, 39 Cal.Rptr.2d 21 [97 Educ. L. Rep. 1139] (Cal. 1995); *Arcadia Unified School Dist. v. State Dep't of Educ.*, 5 Cal.Rptr.2d 545 [72 Educ. L. Rep. 1137] (Cal.1992); *Sutton v. Cadillac Area Pub. Schools*, 323 N.W.2d 582 [6 Educ. L. Rep. 187] (Mich. Ct. App. 1982).

344. *Mathis v. Gordy*, 47 S.E. 171 (Ga. 1904).

345. *Paulson v. Minidoka County School Dist. No. 331*, 463 P.2d 935 (Idaho 1970).

346. *Bond v. Public Schools of Ann Arbor School Dist.*, 178 N.W.2d 484 (Mich.1970).

347. *State ex rel. Massie v. Gahanna–Jefferson Pub. Schools Bd. of Educ.*, 669 N.E.2d 839 [112 Educ. L. Rep. 421] (Ohio 1996) (permitting the board to charge a fee for materials used in the course of instruction with the exception of necessary textbooks).

348. *Randolph County Bd. of Educ. v. Adams*, 467 S.E.2d 150 [107 Educ. L. Rep. 324] (W. Va. 1995).

In cases reaching the opposite outcome, the Supreme Courts in Arizona,[349] Colorado,[350] Illinois,[351] North Dakota,[352] and Wisconsin,[353] along with an appellate court in Indiana,[354] upheld book fees. Even where state law permitted a textbook fee to be charged, a federal trial court in Indiana held that suspending a student for failing to pay it violated his right to equal protection.[355]

Course Materials and Other Fees

In a trilogy of cases, the Supreme Court of Illinois upheld charges for clean towels where the use of the service was optional,[356] a mandatory fee for a wide variety of supplies and materials such as workbooks that students used and kept,[357] and a lunchroom supervision fee for students who lived nearby but chose to eat their lunches in the lunchroom.[358] The Supreme Court of North Carolina upheld charging fees for purchasing supplementary supplies and materials for use by or on behalf of students whose parents were able to pay for them as long as local boards provided them with notice.[359] Conversely, the Supreme Court of Montana prohibited officials from charging fees in connection with activities that were reasonably related to recognized academic and educational goals of the school system.[360]

The Supreme Court of Ohio reasoned that statutes authorizing fees are to be strictly construed. The court thus invalidated a fee for "paper products, copier materials, and other necessary consumable educational supply items" as not covered by the phrase "any materials used in a course of instruction."[361] The court later clarified its rationale in acknowledging that school boards could charge instructional fees for classroom materials such as consumable non-food instructional supplies including paper, paste, pencils, paint, and other expenditures for items that teachers used to aid in

---

349. *Carpio v. Tucson High School Dist. No. 1 of Pima County*, 524 P.2d 948 (Ariz.1974), *cert. denied*, 420 U.S. 982, 95 S.Ct. 1412, 43 L.Ed.2d 664 (1975).

350. *Marshall v. School Dist. RE No. 3 Morgan County*, 553 P.2d 784 (Colo. 1976).

351. *Hamer v. Board of Educ. of School Dist. No. 109*, 265 N.E.2d 616 (Ill. 1970).

352. *Cardiff v. Bismarck Pub. School Dist.*, 263 N.W.2d 105 (N.D. 1978).

353. *Board of Educ. v. Sinclair*, 222 N.W.2d 143 (Wis. 1974).

354. *Chandler v. South Bend Community School Corp.*, 312 N.E.2d 915 (Ind. Ct. App. 1974). *But see Nagy v. Evansville–Vanderburgh School Corp.*, 844 N.E.2d 481, 484 [207 Educ. L. Rep. 311] (Ind. 2006) (striking down a mandatory student services fee), *on subsequent appeal*, 870 N.E.2d 12 [221 Educ. L. Rep. 845] (Ind. Ct. App. 2007) (reversing the denial of the parents' request for attorney fees), *transfer denied*, 891 N.E.2d 35 (Ind. 2008). [Case No. 89]

355. *Carder v. Michigan City School Corp.*, 552 F.Supp. 869 [8 Educ. L. Rep. 318] (N.D. Ind. 1982).

356. *Hamer v. Board of Educ. of School Dist. No. 109, Lake County*, 292 N.E.2d 569 (Ill. App. Ct. 1973).

357. *Beck v. Board of Educ. of Harlem Consol. School Dist. No. 122*, 344 N.E.2d 440 (Ill. 1976).

358. *Ambroiggio v. Board of Educ. of School Dist. No. 44*, 427 N.E.2d 1027 [1 Educ. L. Rep. 337] (Ill. App. Ct. 1981).

359. *Sneed v. Greensboro City Bd. of Educ.*, 264 S.E.2d 106 (N.C. 1980).

360. *Granger v. Cascade County School Dist. No. 1*, 499 P.2d 780 (Mont. 1972).

361. *Association for the Defense of Washington Local School Dist. v. Kiger*, 537 N.E.2d 1292, 1292 [53 Educ. L. Rep. 676] (Ohio 1989).

their instruction of students.[362] More recently, the Supreme Court of Indiana upheld a similar ban. The court struck down the twenty-dollar mandatory service fee that a local board imposed on students in grades K–12 in an attempt to balance its budget. The court viewed the fee as a violation of the state constitutional requirement that schools operate in a manner "wherein tuition shall be without charge, and equally open to all."[363] The court suggested that insofar as extracurricular activities and/or other services exceed the scope of the basic education mandated by the state constitution, the board could charge a fee for participation in these activities.

Elective Courses and Summer School

The Supreme Courts of Montana[364] and New Mexico[365] agreed that students can be charged fees for taking elective classes. Yet, the Supreme Court of California disagreed in contending that doing so violated the state constitutional guarantee to a free public school education.[366] In specifically addressing extracurricular sports[367] and music, the court observed that educational activities must be offered free to all, regardless of whether they are not for credit or extracurricular.[368] In a related concern, since extracurricular activities may tax the budgets of school systems, an appellate court in New York affirmed that where a board operated under a contingency budget, it was not required to fund interschool athletics, field trips, and other extracurricular activities.[369]

Disputes over specific programs have led to mixed results. The Supreme Judicial Court of Massachusetts[370] and an appellate court in California[371] agreed that where school boards offered driver's education, it had to be free of charge. Appellate courts in Illinois,[372] New Jersey[373] and New

---

362. *State ex rel. Massie v. Gahanna–Jefferson Pub. Schools Bd. of Educ.*, 669 N.E.2d 839 [112 Educ. L. Rep. 421] (Ohio 1996).

363. *Nagy v. Evansville–Vanderburgh School Corp.*, 844 N.E.2d 481, 484 [207 Educ. L. Rep. 311] (Ind. 2006) (citing Article I, section 8 of the state constitution), *on subsequent appeal*, 870 N.E.2d 12 [221 Educ. L. Rep. 845] (Ind. Ct. App. 2007) (reversing the denial of the parents' request for attorney fees), *transfer denied*, 891 N.E.2d 35 (Ind. 2008). [Case No. 89]

364. *Granger v. Cascade County School Dist. No. 1*, 499 P.2d 780 (Mont.1972).

365. *Norton v. Board of Educ. of School Dist. No. 16, Hobbs Mun. Schools*, 553 P.2d 1277 (N.M. 1976).

366. *Hartzell v. Connell*, 201 Cal.Rptr. 601 [17 Educ. L. Rep. 241] (Cal.1984).

367. For an early case striking down a fee for athletic privileges, *see Morris v. Vandiver*, 145 So. 228 (Miss. 1933).

368. *Attorney General v. East Jackson Pub. Schools*, 372 N.W.2d 638 [27 Educ. L. Rep. 304] (Mich. Ct. App. 1985) (upholding a fee for participation in interscholastic athletics).

369. *Polmanteer v. Bobo*, 794 N.Y.S.2d 171 [197 Educ. L. Rep. 726] (N.Y. App. Div. 2005).

370. *Johnson v. School Comm. of Brockton*, 358 N.E.2d 820 (Mass. 1977).

371. *California Ass'n for Safety Educ. v. Brown*, 36 Cal.Rptr.2d 404 [95 Educ. L. Rep. 1026] (Ct. App. 1994), *review denied* (1995).

372. *Sherman v. Township High School Dist. 214*, 937 N.E.2d 286 [261 Educ. L. Rep. 1054] (Ill. App. Ct. 2010), *reh'g denied* (2010), *appeal denied*, 943 N.E.2d 1109 (2011).

373. *Parsippany–Troy Hills Educ. Ass'n v. Board of Educ. of Parsippany–Troy Hills Twp.*, 457 A.2d 15 [9 Educ. L. Rep. 941] (N.J. Super. App. Div.1983), *certification denied*, 468 A.2d 182 (N.J. 1983).

York[374] disagreed, writing that absent statutory directives to the contrary, boards could charge fees for such elective courses.

Courts in California and South Carolina reached different results on fees for summer school programs. The former decided that a school board was powerless to charge fees unless the legislature authorized it to do so.[375] The latter disagreed in positing that insofar as a summer program was not included in the state constitutional provision for free public schools even though the classes could have been credited toward graduation, a board could assess fees.[376]

INTERSCHOLASTIC ACTIVITIES

In General

School boards are free to join and agree to abide by the rules of state or regional interscholastic activities organizations. Even though associations are voluntary, privately governed bodies, since most are intertwined with states, courts treat them as state actors.[377] Courts typically inquire into matters such as equal protection and due process which would not otherwise apply to private groups.

Courts generally agree that interscholastic associations can enforce rules against individual schools or boards. For example, the Supreme Court of Ohio refused to intervene in a dispute over the suspension of a team from competition since officials violated a provision governing the recruitment of football players.[378] The Supreme Court of Pennsylvania, citing this case, refused to grant relief where the athletic association placed a high school on probation when spectators fought after one of its football games.[379] The Third Circuit also rejected the claim of a student from Pennsylvania that a league unconstitutionally deprived him of the opportunity to play in post-season games because his team was suspended for rules violations.[380]

Association rules must meet constitutional standards. As such, the federal trial court in South Dakota invalidated a rule that hampered small-school debate teams by classifying schools by enrollment as a violation of equal protection.[381] More recently, an appellate court in New York upheld a rule of the state athletic association that divided schools with football

---

374. *Messina v. Sobol*, 553 N.Y.S.2d 529 [59 Educ. L. Rep. 868] (N.Y. App. Div.1990), *appeal dismissed*, 560 N.Y.S.2d 129 (N.Y. 1990).

375. *California Teachers Ass'n v. Board of Educ. of Glendale*, 167 Cal.Rptr. 429 (Cal. Ct. App. 1980).

376. *Washington v. Salisbury*, 306 S.E.2d 600 [13 Educ. L. Rep. 545] (S.C. 1983).

377. *See Brentwood Acad. v. Tennessee Secondary School Athletic Ass'n*, 531 U.S. 288, 121 S.Ct. 924, 148 L.Ed.2d 807 [151 Educ. L. Rep. 18] (2001). [Case No. 21]

378. *State ex rel. Ohio High School Athletic Ass'n v. Judges of Court of Common Pleas of Stark County*, 181 N.E.2d 261 (Ohio 1962).

379. *School Dist. of Harrisburg v. Pennsylvania Interscholastic Athletic Ass'n*, 309 A.2d 353 (Pa. 1973).

380. *Moreland v. Western Pa. Interscholastic Athletic League*, 572 F.2d 121 (3d Cir. 1978).

381. *Baltic Indep. School Dist. v. South Dakota High School Activities Ass'n*, 362 F.Supp. 780 (D.S.D. 1973).

teams into classes based on size because its action was not arbitrary and capricious.[382]

Student participation in interscholastic sports and other extracurricular activities is a privilege rather than a constitutionally protected civil right.[383] This means that school officials can institute rules that place greater responsibilities on participants than on their peers who do not take part in these activities.

There is a strong presumption in favor of rules designed to protect the educational value and integrity of interscholastic sports as well as the health and welfare of student-athletes. To this end, courts uphold rules as long as they are supported by rational bases. Where the father of a student-athlete in Alabama allegedly struck a referee in the face, an appellate court upheld the team's being placed on probation and forbidding it from playing whenever the father was present at a game.[384] Also, the Supreme Court of Oklahoma upheld the two-game suspension that prohibited a student-athlete from competing in football playoff games after he took part in an on-field fight in which he kicked at an opposing player's helmet.[385] The court agreed that there was no evidence suggesting that officials acted in anything other than good faith in conjunction with the rule of law when a referee who was positioned to see the play reacted immediately to the student-athlete's action.

The constitution does not require school officials to grant exceptions for students who wish to participate in extracurricular activities. As long as rules are reasonable, it is not the function of the courts to rewrite or administer them so as to provide for exceptions. The Supreme Court of North Dakota echoed this sentiment in refusing to grant an exception to transfer rules for students who changed schools primarily for academic reasons.[386] Moreover, although offering its opinion that it appeared to be harsh, the Supreme Court of Georgia upheld a rule stipulating that eligibility was for eight consecutive semesters or four consecutive years from when students first entered ninth grade.[387] In this case, the student dropped out of school for a little over a year because he had been forced to work due to his mother's illness.

Courts do not uphold rules if they are enforced arbitrarily or are not sufficiently narrowly tailored to achieve their goals.[388] Where a student-

382. *Suburban Scholastic Council v. Section 2 of N.Y. State Pub. High School Athletic Ass'n*, 803 N.Y.S.2d 270 [203 Educ. L. Rep. 334] (N.Y. App. Div. 2005).

383. *See, e.g., Albach v. Odle*, 531 F.2d 983 (10th Cir.1976) [Case No. 90]; *Palmer v. Merluzzi*, 868 F.2d 90 [51 Educ. L. Rep. 1196] (3d Cir.1989) [Case No. 93]; *Pirschel v. Sorrell*, 2 F.Supp.2d 930 [127 Educ. L. Rep. 124] (E.D. Ky.1998); *Florida High School Athletic Ass'n v. Melbourne Cent. Catholic High School*, 867 So.2d 1281 [186 Educ. L. Rep. 1025] (Fla. Dist. Ct. App. 2004); *Taylor v. Enumclaw School Dist.*, 133 P.3d 492 [208 Educ. L. Rep. 647] (Wash. Ct. App. 2006).

384. *Marshall v. Alabama High School Athletic Ass'n*, 717 So.2d 404 [129 Educ. L. Rep. 881] (Ala. Civ. App. 1998).

385. *Brown ex rel. Brown v. Oklahoma Secondary School Activities Ass'n*, 125 P.3d 1219 [205 Educ. L. Rep. 898] (Okla. 2005).

386. *Crandall v. North Dakota High School Activities Ass'n*, 261 N.W.2d 921 (N.D.1978).

387. *Smith v. Crim*, 240 S.E.2d 884 (Ga. 1977).

388. *See Trefelner ex rel. Trefelner v. Burrell School Dist.*, 655 F.Supp.2d 581 [251 Educ. L. Rep. 233] (W.D. Pa. 2009) (striking down a policy requiring students to be enrolled in the

athlete in Indiana moved from the custody of one parent to another due to their divorce, the Seventh Circuit overturned the league's rendering him ineligible to participate since the official responsible for eligibility changed his mind on three separate occasions with regard to the student.[389] In another case from Indiana, an appellate court agreed with a student-athlete that the denial of his request for a hardship exception to the transfer rule was arbitrary and capricious.[390] The court pointed out that in view of evidence that a family's financial circumstances changed following the divorce of the student's parents, through no fault of his own and without athletic motivation, he should have been permitted to retain his eligibility.

A dispute from Illinois presented a novel set of facts involving parents and interscholastic sports. The Seventh Circuit affirmed that school officials did not violate the free speech rights of parents for allegedly retaliating against them over comments that they made about their daughter's softball coach.[391] The court viewed the parents' complaints, that the board failed to respond to their written requests to meet, that they were not allowed to videotape games from the field, that they were not asked to serve as ticket takers, announcers, or boosters during the season, and that they were not informed of the correct time of an awards ceremony as such minor events that they could have happened to many softball families in high schools during the season.

Another dispute broadly involving the free speech rights of parents and an athletic program arose in Virginia. A federal trial court granted a school board's motion for summary judgment when officials refused to print an advertisement that a father, who was engaged in an on going dispute with it, sought to publish in opposition to what he described as "civil religion" in an athletic program.[392] The court agreed that the board could exclude the advertisement because the names of the Web sites that the father sought to include in it detailing his opposition to what he described as "civil religion" could be rejected as vulgar.[393]

Transfer Rules and Interscholastic Sports

The major issues in the realm of athletics include transfers, residency and age requirements, longevity rules, academic qualifications, and gender equity. Student-athletes who transfer from one school system to another must generally have letters explaining that they are not doing so exclusive-

---

districts within which they lived in order to be eligible to participate in extracurricular activities since it was narrowly tailored to achieve a compelling governmental interest).

389. *Crane by Crane v. Indiana High School Athletic Ass'n*, 975 F.2d 1315 [77 Educ. L. Rep. 722] (7th Cir. 1992).

390. *Indiana High School Athletic Ass'n v. Durham*, 748 N.E.2d 404 [154 Educ. L. Rep. 279] (Ind. Ct. App. 2001).

391. *Springer v. Durflinger*, 518 F.3d 479 [230 Educ. L. Rep. 525] (7th Cir. 2008).

392. *Myers v. Loudoun County School Bd.*, 500 F. Supp. 2d 539 [223 Educ. L. Rep. 786] (E.D. Va. 2007).

393. Previously, the Fourth Circuit affirmed the rejection of the father's argument that the daily recital of the pledge in school forced his children to worship a secular state, *Myers v. Loudoun County Pub. Schools*, 418 F.3d 395 [200 Educ. L. Rep. 581] (4th Cir. 2005).

ly for athletic purposes.[394] Students who transfer for athletic reasons,[395] such as where a player changed schools because of her dissatisfaction with her coach,[396] must ordinarily sit out a season of competition. However, students who transfer due to legitimate changes of residence such as where families relocate,[397] or where one switched to a Catholic school after converting to that faith,[398] are generally eligible immediately.

Where a rule rendered African American students in formerly segregated school districts in Arkansas reluctant to transfer, a federal trial court struck it down.[399] In another formerly segregated district, a federal trial court in Alabama rejected the claims of African American high school student-athletes who challenged a board policy requiring all students who transferred under a majority to minority program to sit out a year of interscholastic athletics.[400] The court thought that the policy's goal was to address the compelling problem of illegal recruiting and to revive schools in largely African American areas. The court maintained that any purported knowledge on the part of board members that the policy would have had a disparate impact on the students was insufficient to prove intent to discriminate based on race, especially given the board's clear intent to benefit predominately African American schools.

A case from California demonstrated the overlap between transfer and residency rules. When a student transferred from a religious to a public school because her father was unable to pay tuition due to his health problems, she sought to play varsity soccer even though she previously played basketball. Both schools were located in the same public school system and the family lived in the same home continuously. Once the student qualified for the team, she and her father successfully challenged her being rendered ineligible. After the plaintiffs obtained a temporary restraining order allowing the student to participate, an appellate court affirmed that it was appropriate since the actions of athletic officials were arbitrary and capricious.[401] The court also awarded attorney fees to the plaintiffs. On the other hand, where a student moved to live with his grandparents, an appellate court in Ohio decided that the state athletic association acted within its authority in declaring him ineligible because he was not entitled to an exemption under the circumstances.[402]

---

394. *See, e.g., Sutterby v. Zimar*, 594 N.Y.S.2d 607 [81 Educ. L. Rep. 508] (N.Y. 1993).

395. *Revesz ex rel. Revesz v. Pennsylvania Interscholastic Athletic Ass'n*, 798 A.2d 830 [165 Educ. L. Rep. 694] (Pa. Cmwlth. Ct. 2002).

396. *Indiana High School Athletic Ass'n v. Watson*, 938 N.E.2d 672 [262 Educ. L Rep. 608] (Ind. 2010).

397. *Indiana High School Athletic Ass'n v. Wideman*, 688 N.E.2d 413 [122 Educ. L. Rep. 1268] (Ind. Ct. App. 1997).

398. *Robbins by Robbins v. Indiana High School Athletic Ass'n*, 941 F.Supp. 786 [113 Educ. L. Rep. 1240] (S.D. Ind. 1996).

399. *Rogers v. Board of Educ.*, 281 F.Supp. 39 (E.D. Ark. 1968).

400. *Young By and Through Young v. Montgomery County Ala. Bd. of Educ.*, 922 F.Supp. 544 [109 Educ. L. Rep. 202] (M.D. Ala. 1996).

401. *Zuehlsdorf v. Simi Valley Unified School Dist.*, 55 Cal.Rptr.3d 467 [216 Educ. L. Rep. 561] (Cal. Ct. App. 2007), *review denied* (2007).

402. *Ulliman v. Ohio High School Athletic Ass'n*, 919 N.E.2d 763 [252 Educ. L. Rep. 462] (Ohio Ct. App. 2009).

Eligibility Rules and Interscholastic Sports

The Fifth Circuit rejected claims that a rule which required a student in Texas to reside in a district for a year before participating in interscholastic events burdened his right to travel and freedom of family association.[403] The same court previously rejected a claim that a student's losing a year of eligibility because he participated in an athletic camp infringed on parental rights.[404] The Supreme Court of Florida upheld a rule for postseason play that reduced each team's player limit below that allowed for regular season play.[405] The Supreme Court of New Hampshire refused to overrule an adjudication of the state athletic association that a student was ineligible to run in a special event because he failed to qualify in the preliminary despite his claim that he did not qualify because he had been fouled.[406]

When the two criteria overlap, courts reach comparable results in upholding eligibility requirements based on age[407] and longevity in the sense that students are typically limited to eight semesters of eligibility in interscholastic sports.[408] Most courts are unwilling to make exceptions for eligibility based on age for students with disabilities.[409]

The courts uniformly uphold academic eligibility requirements in extracurricular activities.[410] The courts reach these results regardless of whether rules come from legislatures,[411] state boards of education,[412] or

403. *Niles v. University Interscholastic League*, 715 F.2d 1027 [13 Educ. L. Rep. 257] (5th Cir.1983), *cert. denied*, 465 U.S. 1028, 104 S.Ct. 1289, 79 L.Ed.2d 691 (1984).

404. *Kite v. Marshall*, 661 F.2d 1027 [1 Educ. L. Rep. 44] (5th Cir.1981), *reh'g denied sub nom. Lackner v. Marshall*, 666 F.2d 591 (5th Cir. 1981), *cert. denied sub nom. Kite v. Marshall*, 457 U.S. 1120, 102 S.Ct. 2934, 73 L.Ed.2d 1333 (1982). [Case No. 91]

405. *The Florida High School Activities Ass'n v. Thomas*, 434 So.2d 306 [12 Educ. L. Rep. 1022] (Fla. 1983).

406. *Snow v. New Hampshire Interscholastic Athletic Ass'n*, 449 A.2d 1223 [6 Educ. L. Rep. 736] (N.H. 1982).

407. *Sandison v. Michigan High School Athletic Ass'n*, 64 F.3d 1026 [103 Educ. L. Rep. 56] (6th Cir. 1995). *But see Baisden v. West Virginia Secondary Schools Activities Com'n*, 568 S.E.2d 32 [168 Educ. L. Rep. 950] (W. Va. 2002) (prohibiting a nineteen-year-old with a learning disability from playing football).

408. *See, e.g., McPherson v. Michigan High School Athletic Ass'n*, 119 F.3d 453 [120 Educ. L. Rep. 96] (6th Cir. 1997); *Indiana High School Athletic Ass'n. v. Reyes*, 694 N.E.2d 249 [125 Educ. L. Rep. 848] (Ind. 1997).

409. *See, e.g., Pottgen v. Missouri State High School Activities Ass'n*, 40 F.3d 926 [95 Educ. L. Rep. 867] (8th Cir. 1994); *Washington v. Indiana High School Athletic Ass'n*, 181 F.3d 840 [136 Educ. L. Rep. 713] (7th Cir.1999), *cert. denied*, 528 U.S. 1046, 120 S.Ct. 579, 145 L.Ed.2d 482 (1999); *Cruz ex rel. Cruz v. Pennsylvania Interscholastic Athletic Ass'n*, 157 F. Supp.2d 485 [156 Educ. L. Rep. 633] (E.D. Pa. 2001). *But see University Interscholastic League v. Buchanan*, 848 S.W.2d 298 [81 Educ. L. Rep. 1145] (Tex. Ct. App. 1993), *reh'g overruled* (1993) (affirming an injunction permitting nineteen-year-olds with learning disabilities to participate in interscholastic sports).

410. *State ex rel. Bartmess v. Board of Trustees of School Dist. No. 1*, 726 P.2d 801 [35 Educ. L. Rep. 564] (Mont. 1986).

411. *Spring Branch Indep. School Dist. v. Stamos*, 695 S.W.2d 556 [27 Educ. L. Rep. 605] (Tex.1985), *appeal dismissed*, 475 U.S. 1001, 106 S.Ct. 1170, 89 L.Ed.2d 290 [30 Educ. L. Rep. 662] (1986) [Case No. 92]. *See also Texas Educ. Agency v. Dallas Indep. School Dist.*, 797 S.W.2d 367 [63 Educ. L. Rep. 670] (Tex. Ct. App. 1990) (dismissing a claim over an ineligible player as moot since the season was over).

local school boards.[413] Disputes over the controversial practice of "no pass, no play," even though upheld, have dissipated.

An interesting case that overlaps with academic eligibility and residency may portend issues to come. The Third Circuit affirmed the dismissal of a federal trial court's refusal to grant an injunction to a student at a cyber school who sought to participate in a junior varsity basketball program at a school in the district within which she and her parents lived.[414] The court agreed that the board did not act unreasonably since its rules were consistent with Pennsylvania statutes and officials did not violate the student's due process rights because she lacked a property interest in participating in extracurricular activities.

Gender Equity and Interscholastic Sports

Following a significant amount of litigation on gender equity in sports, it is settled law that the denial of equitable opportunities for female student-athletes violates Title IX.[415] In an older case from Minnesota, the Eighth Circuit noted that eligibility to participate in a non-contact sport cannot be based on sex.[416] The court found that where there were no teams for females in tennis, skiing, and running, and females were qualified to compete with males in those non-contact sports, a rule of the state interscholastic athletic league barring mixed athletics was unenforceable.

The first court to lift restrictions against females who wished to participate in contact sports was in Pennsylvania. An appellate court, referring to the equal rights amendment in the commonwealth's constitution, struck down a bylaw of the interscholastic athletic association which barred females from competing or practicing with boys in any athletic activity as facially unconstitutional.[417] In the same year, the Supreme Court of Washington, relying in part on the case from Pennsylvania, and an almost identical provision in its state constitution, invalidated sex barriers in contact sports.[418] Additionally, the Sixth Circuit, although stopping short of ordering co-educational teams in contact sports in Ohio, declared that a rule against such participation was unacceptable because it was more restrictive than Title IX required.[419]

Massachusetts' highest court, in applying strict scrutiny, was of the opinion that officials acted inappropriately in barring boys from girls'

---

412. *Bailey v. Truby*, 321 S.E.2d 302 [20 Educ. L. Rep. 980] (W. Va. 1984).

413. *Thompson v. Fayette County Pub. Schools*, 786 S.W.2d 879 [59 Educ. L. Rep. 1197] (Ky. Ct. App. 1990).

414. *Angstadt v. Midd–West School Dist.*, 377 F.3d 338 [190 Educ. L. Rep. 48] (3d Cir. 2004).

415. *See, e.g., Cohen v. Brown Univ.*, 101 F.3d 155 (1st Cir. 1996), *cert. denied*, 520 U.S. 1186, 117 S.Ct. 1469, 137 L.Ed.2d 682 (1997).

416. *Brenden v. Independent School Dist. 742*, 477 F.2d 1292 (8th Cir. 1973).

417. *Commonwealth by Packel v. Pennsylvania Interscholastic Athletic Ass'n*, 334 A.2d 839 (Pa. Cmwlth. Ct. 1975).

418. *Darrin v. Gould*, 540 P.2d 882 (Wash. 1975).

419. *Yellow Springs Exempted Village School Dist. Bd. of Ed. v. Ohio High School Athletic Ass'n*, 647 F.2d 651 (6th Cir. 1981).

teams.[420] Conversely, where there was no equal rights amendment in the state constitution, the Supreme Court of Rhode Island, applying intermediate scrutiny, asserted that a lower standard of scrutiny should have been applied to evaluate whether a state association rule violated the state constitution.[421] In remanding, the court observed that promoting safety and the preservation of interscholastic competition for males and females were important governmental interests. Still, courts disagree over whether school officials can permit a female volleyball team and exclude males from participating.[422]

Where there are no teams for females in sports that are offered for males only, school officials have three choices: discontinue teams;[423] field separate teams by sex with substantial equality in funding, coaching, officiating and opportunities to play; or permit both sexes to compete for positions on the same teams. Where there is only one team, females have been able to participate in baseball,[424] football,[425] soccer,[426] swimming,[427] tennis,[428] and wrestling.[429]

---

420. *Attorney General v. Massachusetts Interscholastic Athletic Ass'n*, 393 N.E.2d 284 (Mass. 1979).

421. *Kleczek v. Rhode Island Interscholastic League*, 612 A.2d 734 [77 Educ. L. Rep. 349] (R.I. 1992).

422. *Compare Gomes v. Rhode Island Interscholastic League*, 469 F.Supp. 659 (D.R.I. 1979), *vacated as moot* (due to the end of the season and the student's graduation), 604 F.2d 733 (1st Cir. 1979) (permitting participation in volleyball) with *Clark v. Arizona Interscholastic Ass'n*, 695 F.2d 1126 [8 Educ. L. Rep. 246] (9th Cir. 1982), *cert. denied*, 464 U.S. 818, 104 S.Ct. 79, 78 L.Ed.2d 90 (1983) (denying participation in volleyball) and *Kleczek on Behalf of Kleczek v. Rhode Island Interscholastic League*, 768 F.Supp. 951 [69 Educ. L. Rep. 366] (D.R.I. 1991) (denying participation in field hockey).

423. Male student-athletes have unsuccessfully sought to prevent their teams from being disbanded as institutions seek to comply with Title IX. *See Horner v. Kentucky High School Athletic Ass'n*, 206 F.3d 685 [142 Educ. L. Rep. 728] (6th Cir. 2000), *cert. denied*, 531 U.S. 824, 121 S.Ct. 69, 148 L.Ed.2d 34 (2000) (upholding the discontinuation of men's swimming while keeping the women's team). *See also, e.g., Harper v. Board of Regents, Ill. State Univ.*, 198 F.3d 633, [140 Educ. L. Rep. 509] (7th Cir. 1999), *cert. denied*, 530 U.S. 1284, 120 S.Ct. 2762, 147 L.Ed.2d 1022 (2000) (involving soccer and wrestling); *Chalenor v. University of N.D.*, 142 F.Supp.2d 1154 [154 Educ. L. Rep. 813] (D.N.D. 2000) (involving wrestling); *Miami Univ. Wrestling Club v. Miami Univ.*, 302 F.3d 608 [169 Educ. L. Rep. 50] (6th Cir. 2002) (involving soccer, tennis, and wrestling); *National Wrestling Coaches Ass'n v. Department of Educ.*, 366 F.3d 930 [187 Educ. L. Rep. 405] (D.C. Cir. 2004), *reh'g and reh'g en banc denied*, 383 F.3d 1047 (D.C. Cir. 2004), *cert. denied*, 545 U.S. 1104, 125 S.Ct. 2537, 162 L.Ed.2d 274 (2005) (involving wrestling).

424. *Israel by Israel v. West Virginia Secondary Schools Activities Comm'n*, 388 S.E.2d 480 [58 Educ. L. Rep. 795] (W. Va. 1989) (positing that insofar as baseball and softball are sufficiently different, it was a denial of equal protection to prohibit a female from playing baseball).

425. *Force v. Pierce City R–VI School Dist.*, 570 F.Supp. 1020 [13 Educ. L. Rep. 959] (W.D. Mo. 1983); *Lantz by Lantz v. Ambach*, 620 F.Supp. 663 [28 Educ. L. Rep. 783] (S.D.N.Y. 1985); *Balsley by Balsley v. North Hunterdon Reg'l School Dist. Bd. of Educ.*, 568 A.2d 895 [58 Educ. L. Rep. 675] (N.J. 1990).

426. *Hoover v. Meiklejohn*, 430 F.Supp. 164 (D. Colo. 1977); *Libby by Libby v. Illinois High School Ass'n*, 921 F.2d 96 [64 Educ. L. Rep. 708] (7th Cir. 1990).

427. *Leffel v. Wisconsin Interscholastic Athletic Ass'n*, 444 F.Supp. 1117 (E.D. Wis. 1978).

428. *Leffel v. Wisconsin Interscholastic Athletic Ass'n*, 444 F.Supp. 1117 (E.D. Wis. 1978).

429. *Saint v. Nebraska School Activities Ass'n*, 684 F.Supp. 626 [46 Educ. L. Rep. 960] (D. Neb. 1988).

Title IX and its regulations occupy a central role as to nondiscrimination in athletic activities. Consistent with their usual approach, and as highlighted by a dispute from Pennsylvania, courts avoid addressing constitutional questions if they can resolve disputes statutorily such as under Title IX.[430]

Title IX's goal of gender equity applies to reductions in options due to financial factors as well as to additional opportunities for the under-represented sex.[431] In such a case, the Fourth Circuit affirmed that a federal trial court in Virginia did not abuse its discretion in refusing to enjoin Title IX regulations that imposed gender equality in federally financed programs even though doing so led to the termination of teams for both women and men since balancing the harms did not favor its granting such a request.[432]

Courts have reached mixed results over the constitutionality of different seasons for females and males. The Supreme Court of Minnesota ruled that where limited athletic facilities made it necessary to schedule male and female high school teams in tennis and swimming during separate seasons and neither schedule was substantially better than the other, officials did not violate the females' rights to equal protection.[433] Six years later, the Ninth Circuit affirmed that insofar as it was unnecessary to align the basketball and volleyball seasons with the national norm, school officials in Montana did not violate the equal protection rights of females.[434]

West Virginia's highest court, relying on the equal protection clause in the state constitution, reached a different result in holding that having the girls' basketball season scheduled outside of the traditional season was impermissible.[435] The Second Circuit also affirmed that when two school boards in New York scheduled girls' soccer in the spring, they violated the rights of female student-athletes by preventing them from participating in the state soccer play-offs.[436] According to the court, the boards were unable to demonstrate either that the disadvantages that the girls' soccer teams faced were offset by comparable advantages to scheduling or that their actions were justified by nondiscriminatory factors. Further, in a suit from Michigan, the Sixth Circuit affirmed that the state athletic association's use of differential scheduling of girls' high school sports disadvantaged

---

430. *Williams v. School Dist. of Bethlehem, Pa.*, 998 F.2d 168 [84 Educ. L. Rep. 629] (3d Cir. 1993), *cert. denied*, 510 U.S. 1043, 114 S.Ct. 689, 126 L.Ed.2d 656 (1994).

431. *Cohen v. Brown Univ.*, 879 F.Supp. 185 [99 Educ. L. Rep. 149] (D.R.I.1995), *aff'd in part, rev'd in part*, 101 F.3d 155 [114 Educ. L. Rep. 394] (1st Cir.1996), *cert. denied*, 520 U.S. 1186, 117 S.Ct. 1469, 137 L.Ed.2d 682 (1997).

432. *Equity in Athletics v. Department of Educ.*, 504 F. Supp.2d 88 [224 Educ. L. Rep. 707] (W.D. Va. 2007), *aff'd*, 2008 WL 4104235 (4th Cir. 2008), *cert. denied*, ___ U.S. ___, 129 S.Ct. 1613, 173 L.Ed.2d 993 (2009).

433. *Striebel v. Minnesota State High School League*, 321 N.W.2d 400 [5 Educ. L. Rep. 245] (Minn. 1982).

434. *Ridgeway v. Montana High School Ass'n*, 858 F.2d 579 [49 Educ. L. Rep. 495] (9th Cir. 1988).

435. *State ex rel. Lambert by Lambert v. West Virginia State Bd. of Educ.*, 447 S.E.2d 901 [93 Educ. L. Rep. 1031] (W. Va. 1994).

436. *McCormick v. School Dist. of Mamaroneck*, 370 F.3d 275 [188 Educ. L. Rep. 62] (2d Cir. 2004).

female student-athletes in comparison to their male counterparts, in violation of their rights to equal protection.[437] On further review, the Supreme Court vacated[438] in light of its judgment in *Rancho Palos Verdes v. Abrams*,[439] in which it found that an individual was unable to file suit under section 1983 since the statute at issue provided a remedy. On remand, the Sixth Circuit affirmed that insofar as the athletic association was a state actor for the purposes of whether it violated the equal protection and Title IX rights of the students, their claims could proceed.[440]

In a related issue, a federal trial court in Florida ordered a school board to correct discrepancies with regard to equipment and supplies, game and practice times, schedules, and locker room facilities in its boys' baseball and girls' softball programs.[441] The court added that Title IX requires educators to administer athletic programs equitably. More recently, the federal trial court in Minnesota refused to dismiss the Title IX portion of a claim against the Office of Civil Rights (OCR) over its allowing the state athletic association to schedule ice hockey play-offs at a facility that was unequal to the one available for men.[442] In rejecting OCR's motion to dismiss, the court held that it was subject to a private cause of action since the claim accused officials of acting in a way that violated Title IX and fostered discrimination.

[CASE NO. 79]   THE AMISH EXCEPTION AND COMPULSORY EDUCATION

WISCONSIN v. YODER

Supreme Court of the United States, 1972.
406 U.S. 205, 92 S.Ct. 1526, 32 L.Ed.2d 15.

■ MR. CHIEF JUSTICE BURGER delivered the opinion of the Court.

On petition of the State of Wisconsin, we granted the writ of certiorari in this case to review a decision of the Wisconsin Supreme Court holding that respondents' convictions for violating the State's compulsory school-attendance law were invalid under the Free Exercise Clause of the First Amendment to the United States Constitution made applicable to the States by the Fourteenth Amendment. For the reasons hereafter stated we affirm the judgment of the Supreme Court of Wisconsin.

Respondents Jonas Yoder and Adin Yutzy are members of the Old Order Amish Religion, and respondent Wallace Miller is a member of the

---

437. *Communities for Equity v. Michigan High School Athletic Ass'n*, 377 F.3d 504 [190 Educ. L. Rep. 67] (6th Cir. 2004), *rehearing en banc denied* (2004).

438. *Michigan High School Athletic Ass'n v. Communities for Equity*, 544 U.S. 1012, 125 S.Ct. 1973, 161 L.Ed.2d 845 (2005).

439. 544 U.S. 113, 125 S.Ct. 1453, 161 L.Ed.2d 316 (2005).

440. *Communities for Equity v. Michigan High School Athletic Ass'n*, 459 F.3d 676 [212 Educ. L. Rep. 56] (6th Cir. 2006), *rehearing and rehearing en banc denied* (2006), *cert. denied*, 549 U.S. 1322, 127 S.Ct. 1912, 167 L.Ed.2d 566 (2007).

441. *Landow v. School Bd. of Brevard County*, 132 F. Supp.2d 958 [151 Educ. L. Rep. 909] (M.D. Fla. 2000).

442. *Cobb v. United States Dep't of Educ. Office for Civil Rights*, 487 F. Supp.2d 1049 [221 Educ. L. Rep. 138] (D. Minn. 2007).

Conservative Amish Mennonite Church. They and their families are residents of Green County, Wisconsin. Wisconsin's compulsory school attendance law required them to cause their children to attend public or private school until reaching age 16 but the respondents declined to send their children, ages 14 and 15, to public school after completing the eighth grade. The children were not enrolled in any private school, or within any recognized exception to the compulsory attendance law, and they are conceded to be subject to the Wisconsin statute.

On complaint of the school district administrator for the public schools, respondents were charged, tried, and convicted of violating the compulsory attendance law in Green County Court and were fined the sum of $5 each. . . .

In support of their position, respondents presented as expert witnesses scholars on religion and education whose testimony is uncontradicted. They expressed their opinions on the relationship of the Amish belief concerning school attendance to the more general tenets of their religion, and described the impact that compulsory high school attendance could have on the continued survival of Amish communities as they exist in the United States today. . . .

A related feature of Old Order Amish communities is their devotion to a life in harmony with nature and the soil, as exemplified by the simple life of the early Christian era which continued in America during much of our early national life. Amish beliefs require members of the community to make their living by farming or closely related activities. Broadly speaking, the Old Order Amish religion pervades and determines the entire mode of life of its adherents. . . .

Amish objection to formal education beyond the eighth grade is firmly grounded in these central religious concepts. They object to the high school and higher education generally because the values it teaches are in marked variance with Amish values and the Amish way of life; they view secondary school education as an impermissible exposure of their children to a "worldly" influence in conflict with their beliefs. The high school tends to emphasize intellectual and scientific accomplishments, self-distinction, competitiveness, worldly success, and social life with other students. Amish society emphasizes informal learning-through-doing, a life of "goodness," rather than a life of intellect, wisdom, rather than technical knowledge, community welfare rather than competition, and separation, rather than integration with contemporary worldly society. . . .

I

There is no doubt as to the power of a State, having a high responsibility for education of its citizens, to impose reasonable regulations for the control and duration of basic education. Providing public schools ranks at the very apex of the function of a State. Yet even this paramount responsibility was, in *Pierce,* made to yield to the right of parents to provide an equivalent education in a privately operated system. There the Court held that Oregon's statute compelling attendance in a public school from age eight to age 16 unreasonably interfered with the interest of parents in directing the rearing of their offspring including their education in church-operated schools. As that case suggests, the values of parental direction of the religious upbringing and education of their children in their early and formative years have a high place in our society. Thus, a State's interest in universal education, however highly we rank it, is not totally free from a balancing process when it impinges on other fundamental rights and interests, such as those specifically protected by the Free Exercise Clause of the First Amendment and the traditional interest of parents with respect to the religious upbringing of their children so long as they, in the words of *Pierce*, "prepare [them] for additional obligations."

It follows that in order for Wisconsin to compel school attendance beyond the eighth grade against a claim that such attendance interferes with the practice of a legitimate religious belief, it must appear either that the State does not deny the free exercise of religious belief by its requirement, or that there is a state interest of sufficient magnitude to override the interest claiming protection under the Free Exercise Clause. Long before there was general acknowledgment of the need for universal formal education, the Religion Clauses had specifically and firmly fixed the right to free exercise of religious beliefs, and buttressing this fundamental right was an equally firm, even if less explicit, prohibition against the establishment of any religion by government. The values underlying these two provisions relating to religion have been zealously protected, sometimes even at the expense of other interests of admittedly high social importance. The invalidation of financial aid to parochial schools by government grants for a salary subsidy for teachers is but one example of the extent to which courts have gone in this regard, notwithstanding that such aid programs were legislatively determined to be in the public interest and the service of sound educational policy by States and by Congress....

The essence of all that has been said and written on the subject is that only those interests of the highest order and those not otherwise served can overbalance legitimate claims to the free exercise of religion. We can accept it as settled, therefore, that however strong the State's interest in universal compulsory education, it is by no means absolute to the exclusion or subordination of all other interests.

II

We come then to the quality of the claims of the respondents concerning the alleged encroachment of Wisconsin's compulsory school attendance statute on their rights and the rights of their children to the free exercise of the religious beliefs they and their forbears [sic] have adhered to for almost three centuries. In evaluating those claims we must be careful to determine whether the Amish religious faith and their mode of life are, as they claim, inseparable and interdependent. A way of life, however virtuous and admirable, may not be interposed as a barrier to reasonable state regulation of education if it is based on purely secular considerations; to have the protection of the Religion Clauses, the claims must be rooted in religious belief. Although a determination of what is a "religious" belief or practice entitled to constitutional protection may present a most delicate question, the very concept of ordered liberty precludes allowing every person to make his own standards on matters of conduct in which society as a whole has important interests. . . .

Giving no weight to such secular considerations, however, we see that the record in this case abundantly supports the claim that the traditional way of life of the Amish is not merely a matter of personal preference, but one of deep religious conviction, shared by an organized group, and intimately related to daily living. . . .

In sum, the unchallenged testimony of acknowledged experts in education and religious history, almost 300 years of consistent practice, and strong evidence of a sustained faith pervading and regulating respondents' entire mode of life support the claim that enforcement of the State's requirement of compulsory formal education after the eighth grade would gravely endanger if not destroy the free exercise of respondents' religious beliefs.

III

. . .

The State advances two primary arguments in support of its system of compulsory education. It notes, as Thomas Jefferson pointed out early in our history, that some degree of education is necessary to prepare citizens to participate effectively and intelligently in our open political system if we are to preserve freedom and independence. Further, education prepares individuals to be self-reliant and self-sufficient participants in society. We accept these propositions.

However, the evidence adduced by the Amish in this case is persuasively to the effect that an additional one or two years of formal high school for Amish children in place of their long established program of informal vocational education would do little to serve those interests. Respondents' experts testified at trial, without challenge, that the value of all education must be assessed in terms of its capacity to prepare the child for life. It is one thing to say that compulsory education for a year or two beyond the eighth grade may be necessary when its goal is the preparation of the child for life in modern society as the majority live, but it is quite another if the goal of education be viewed as the preparation of the child for life in the separated agrarian community that is the keystone of the Amish faith.

The State attacks respondents' position as one fostering "ignorance" from which the child must be protected by the State. No one can question the State's duty to protect children from ignorance but this argument does not square with the facts disclosed in the record. Whatever their idiosyncrasies as seen by the majority, this record strongly shows that the Amish community has been a highly successful social unit within our society even if apart from the conventional "mainstream." Its members are productive and very law-abiding members of society; they reject public welfare in any of its usual modern forms. The Congress itself recognized their self-sufficiency by authorizing exemption of such groups as the Amish from the obligation to pay social security taxes. . . .

The State, however, supports its interest in providing an additional one or two years of compulsory high school education to Amish children because of the possibility that some such children will choose to leave the Amish community, and that if this occurs they will be ill-equipped for life. The State argues that if Amish children leave their church they should not be in the position of making their way in the world without the education available in the one or two additional years the State requires. However, on this record, that argument is highly speculative. There is no specific evidence of the loss of Amish adherents by attrition, nor is there any showing that upon leaving the Amish community Amish children, with their practical agricultural training and habits of industry and self-reliance, would become burdens on society because of educational shortcomings. Indeed, this argument of the State appears to rest primarily on the State's mistaken assumption, already noted, that the Amish do not provide any education for their children beyond the eighth grade, but allow them to grow in "ignorance." To the contrary, not only do the Amish accept the necessity for formal schooling through the eighth grade level, but continue to provide what has been characterized by the undisputed testimony of expert educators as an "ideal" vocational education for their children in the adolescent years. . . .

The requirement for compulsory education beyond the eighth grade is a relatively recent development in our history. Less than 60 years ago, the educational requirements of almost all of the States were satisfied by completion of the elementary grades, at least where the child was regularly and lawfully employed. The independence and successful social functioning of the Amish community for a period approaching almost three centuries and more than 200 years in this country is strong evidence that there is at best a speculative gain, in terms of meeting the duties of citizenship, from an additional one or two years of compulsory formal education. Against this background it would require a more particularized showing from the State on this point to justify the severe interference with religious freedom such additional compulsory attendance would entail.

We should also note that compulsory education and child labor laws find their historical origin in common humanitarian instincts, and that the age limits of both laws have been coordinated to achieve their related objectives. . . .

IV

. . .

Contrary to the suggestion of the dissenting opinion of Mr. Justice Douglas, our holding today in no degree depends on the assertion of the religious interest of the child as contrasted with that of the parents. It is the parents who are subject to prosecution here for failing to cause their children to attend school, and it is their right of free exercise, not that of their children, that must determine Wisconsin's power to impose criminal penalties on the parent. The dissent argues that a child who expresses a desire to attend public high school in conflict with the wishes of his parent should not be prevented from doing so. There is no reason for the Court to consider that point since it is not an issue in the case. The children are not parties to this litigation. The State has at no point tried this case on the theory that respondents were preventing their children from attending school against their expressed desires, and indeed the record is to the contrary. The State's position from the outset has been that it is empowered to apply its compulsory attendance law to Amish parents in the same manner as to other parents—that is, without regard to the wishes of the child. That is the claim we reject today. . . .

V

For the reasons stated we hold, with the Supreme Court of Wisconsin, that the First and Fourteenth Amendments prevent the State from compelling respondents to cause their children to attend formal high school to age 16. Our disposition of this case, however, in no way alters our recognition of the obvious fact that courts are not school boards or legislatures, and are ill-equipped to determine the "necessity" of discrete aspects of a State's program of compulsory education. This should suggest that courts must move with great circumspection in performing the sensitive and delicate task of weighing a State's legitimate social concern when faced with religious claims for exemption from generally applicable educational requirements. It cannot be over-emphasized that we are not dealing with a way of life and mode of education by a group claiming to have recently discovered some "progressive" or more enlightened process for rearing children for modern life.

Aided by a history of three centuries as an identifiable religious sect and a long history as a successful and self-sufficient segment of American society, the Amish in this case have convincingly demonstrated the sincerity of their religious beliefs, the interrelationship of belief with their mode of life, the vital role which belief and daily conduct play in the continued survival of Old Order Amish communities and their religious organization, and the hazards presented by the State's enforcement of a statute generally valid as to others. Beyond this, they have carried the even more difficult burden of demonstrating the adequacy of their alternative mode of continuing informal vocational education in terms of precisely those overall interests that the State advances in support of its program of compulsory high school education. In light of this convincing showing, one which probably few other religious groups or sects could make, and weighing the minimal difference between what the State would require and what the Amish already accept, it was incumbent on the State to show with more particularity how its admittedly strong interest in compulsory education would be adversely affected by granting an exemption to the Amish.

Nothing we hold is intended to undermine the general applicability of the State's compulsory school attendance statutes or to limit the power of the State to promulgate reasonable standards that, while not impairing the free exercise of religion, provide for continuing agricultural vocational education under parental and church guidance by the Old Order Amish or others similarly situated. The States have had a long history of amicable and effective relationships with church-sponsored schools, and there is no basis for assuming that, in this related context, reasonable standards cannot be established concerning the content of the continuing vocational education of Amish children under parental guidance, provided always that state regulations are not inconsistent with what we have said in this opinion.

Affirmed.

NOTES

1.   The Supreme Court noted that the Amish faith pervaded and directed the entire lives of its believers, whom it described as productive and law-abiding citizens. Might the Court have reached the same result if the religion was less pervasive and/or if its members created social problems?

2.   Would the Court have reached the same result in *Yoder* today? Consider your answer in light of *Employment Div., Dep't of Human Res. of Or. v. Smith*, 494 U.S. 872, 886, n. 3, 110 S.Ct. 1595, 108 L.Ed.2d 876 (1990) *reh'g denied*, 496 U.S. 913, 110 S.Ct. 2605, 110 L.Ed.2d 285 (1990); *on remand*, 799 P.2d 148 (Or. 1990) where, in upholding the dismissal of two Native American drug counselors for ingesting peyote as part of a religious ritual on the basis the Court ruled that "generally applicable, religion-neutral laws that have the effect of burdening a particular religious practice need not be justified by a compelling government interest."

3.   Justice Douglas expressed concern that no one asked the children whether they wished to maintain the Amish lifestyle of their parents. In light of this, what can, or should, be done to accommodate the wishes of students under these circumstances? Should children who do not wish to follow the lifestyles of their parents be emancipated? If so, who should pay for the living costs of such emancipated minors?

4.   Although home schooling proponents often cite *Yoder* for support, the courts are unreceptive. For example, in *Johnson v. Charles City Community Schools Bd. of Educ.*, 368 N.W.2d 74 [25 Educ. L. Rep. 524] (Iowa 1985), *cert. denied sub nom. Pruessner v. Benton*, 474 U.S. 1033, 106 S.Ct. 594, 88 L.Ed.2d 574 [29 Educ. L. Rep. 493] (1985), the Supreme Court of Iowa rejected a home schooling advocate's reliance on *Yoder*. The court ruled that unlike the Amish, who have preserved their way of life for hundreds of years, the plaintiffs operated a home school for only five years by the time it heard the case.

[CASE NO. 80]   CONSTITUTIONALITY OF COMPULSORY EDUCATION STATUTE

STATE v. POPANZ

Supreme Court of Wisconsin, 1983.
332 N.W.2d 750 [10 Educ. L. Rep. 789].

■ ABRAHAMSON, JUSTICE.

This is an appeal from a judgment of conviction of ... Lawrence C. Popanz on two counts of violating Wisconsin's compulsory school attendance law, [which] requires a person having control of a child who is between the ages of 6 and 18 years to cause the child to attend public or private school regularly....

The issue presented on certification is whether the phrase "private school" as used in sec. 118.15(1)(a) is impermissibly vague and sec. 118.15(1)(a) as applied to prosecutions involving "private schools" violates the fourteenth amendment to the United States Constitution and art. I, sec. 8, of the Wisconsin constitution....

There is no simple litmus-paper test to determine whether a criminal statute is void for vagueness. The principles underlying the void for vagueness doctrine ... stem from concepts of procedural due process. Due process requires that the law set forth fair notice of the conduct prohibited or required and proper standards for enforcement of the law and adjudication....

A criminal statute must be sufficiently definite to give a person of ordinary intelligence who seeks to avoid its penalties fair notice of conduct required or prohibited. "Vague laws may trap the innocent by not providing fair warning."

A criminal statute must also provide standards for those who enforce the laws and those who adjudicate guilt. A statute should be sufficiently definite to allow law enforcement officers, judges, and juries to apply the terms of the law objectively to a defendant's conduct in order to determine guilt without having to create or apply their own standards. The danger posed by a vague law is that officials charged with enforcing the law may apply it arbitrarily or the law may be so unclear that a trial court cannot properly instruct the jury as to the applicable law....

Like this defendant, we have searched the statutes, administrative rules and regulations and official Department of Public Instruction writings for a definition of "private school" or criteria which an entity must meet to be classified as a "private school" for purposes of sec. 118.15(1)(a). We have found neither a definition nor prescribed criteria. Nor does the phrase "private school" have a well-settled meaning in common parlance or in decisions of this court which could be used for purposes of applying sec. 118.15(1)(a). We therefore decline to adopt the definition of "private school" proposed by the court of appeals or by the State Superintendent of Public Instruction in an amicus brief....

We are not convinced that these definitions are the only ones a citizen, an administrator, or a court using dictionary definitions, court decisions and the statutes could deduce. In any event the legislature or its delegated agent should define the phrase "private school"; citizens or the courts should not have to guess at its meaning.

Since there is no definition of "private school," as that term is used in sec. 118.15(1)(a), the determination of what constitutes a "private school" apparently rests solely in the discretion of the school attendance officer of the district.... The record shows that in this school district a person seeking to comply with sec. 118.15(1)(a) apparently must consult the district school administrator to find out what that administrator considers a "private school" and must comply with the procedure set forth by that particular administrator to have a school classified as a private school....

The lack of definition of "private school" delegates the basic policy matter, the determination of whether or not children are attending a private school, to local school officials whose decisions may rest on *ad hoc* and subjective standards. Sec. 118.15(1)(a) thus poses the danger of arbitrary and discriminatory enforcement, contrary to the basic values underlying the principles of due process.

The persons who must obey the law should not have to guess at what the phrase "private school" means. They should have some objective standards to guide them in their attempts to "steer between lawful and unlawful conduct." Furthermore, standards cannot lie only in the minds of persons whose duty it is to enforce the laws. We must conclude that the statute fails to provide fair notice to those who would seek to obey it and also lacks sufficient standards for proper enforcement.

The Department of Public Instruction, recognizing that there are no standards for determining what constitutes a "private school" under sec. 118.15(1)(a), suggests that the school attendance officer file a charge under that section if he or she "felt the attendance was not at a 'private school,'" leaving the final determination of what constitutes a "private school" to the courts.... We do not think that sec. 118.15(1)(a) or any other statutes or any rules equip the courts to define "private school" or to instruct a jury on what constitutes a private school. Defining the contours of laws subjecting a violator to criminal penalty is a legislative, not a judicial, function. The legislature, not the courts, should clarify sec. 118.15(1)(a).

We hold that sec. 118.15(1)(a) is void for vagueness insofar as it fails to define "private school." The court of appeals' decision in *State v. White* ... is hereby overruled....

Judgment of the circuit court reversed; cause remanded with directions to dismiss the complaint.

NOTES

1. The court refused to approve a definition of "private school" despite requests from the state department of education in an amicus brief and the intermediate appellate court. Should it have done so?

2. Did the court exercise appropriate judicial restraint?

[CASE NO. 81] COMPULSORY EDUCATION, PARENTAL RIGHTS, AND NON–PUBLIC SCHOOLS

PIERCE v. SOCIETY OF THE SISTERS OF THE HOLY NAMES OF JESUS AND MARY

Supreme Court of the United States, 1925.
268 U.S. 510, 45 S.Ct. 571, 69 L.Ed. 1070.

■ MR. JUSTICE MCREYNOLDS delivered the opinion of the Court.

These appeals are from decrees, based upon undenied allegations, which granted preliminary orders restraining appellants from threatening or attempting to enforce the Compulsory Education Act ... under the initiative provision of her Constitution by the voters of Oregon. They present the same points of law; there are no controverted questions of fact. Rights said to be guaranteed by the federal Constitution were specially set up, and appropriate prayers asked for their protection.

The challenged act ... requires every parent, guardian, or other person having control or charge or custody of a child between 8 and 16 years to send him "to a public school for the period of time a public school shall be held during the current year" in the district where the child resides; and failure so to do is declared a misdemeanor. There are exemptions—not specially important here—for children who are not normal, or who have completed the eighth grade, or whose parents or private teachers reside at considerable distances from any public school, or who hold special permits from the county superintendent. The manifest purpose is to compel general attendance at public schools by normal children ... who have not completed the eight[h] grade. And without doubt enforcement of the statute would seriously impair, perhaps destroy, the profitable features of appellees' business and greatly diminish the value of their property.

Appellee the Society of Sisters is an Oregon corporation, organized in 1880, with power to care for orphans, educate and instruct the youth, establish and maintain academies or schools, and acquire necessary real and personal property. It has long devoted its property and effort to the secular and religious education and care of children, and has acquired the valuable good will of many parents and guardians. It conducts interdependent primary and high schools and junior colleges, and maintains orphanages for the custody and control of children between 8 and 16. In its primary schools many children between those ages are taught the subjects usually pursued in Oregon public schools during the first eight years. Systematic religious instruction and moral training according to the tenets of the Roman Catholic Church are also regularly provided. All courses of study, both temporal and religious, contemplate continuity of training under appellee's charge; the primary schools are essential to the system and the most profitable. It owns valuable buildings, especially constructed and equipped for school purposes. The business is remunerative—the annual income from primary schools exceeds $30,000—and the successful conduct of this requires long time contracts with teachers and parents. The Compulsory Education Act of 1922 has already caused the withdrawal from its schools of children who would otherwise continue, and their income has steadily declined. The appellants, public officers, have proclaimed their purpose strictly to enforce the statute.

After setting out the above facts, the Society's bill alleges that the enactment conflicts with the right of parents to choose schools where their children will receive appropriate mental and religious training, the right of the child to influence the parents' choice of a school, the right of schools and teachers therein to engage in a useful business or profession, and is accordingly repugnant to the Constitution and void. And, further, that unless enforcement of the measure is enjoined the corporation's business and property will suffer irreparable injury.

Appellee Hill Military Academy is a private corporation organized in 1908 under the laws of Oregon, engaged in owning, operating, and conducting for profit an elementary, college preparatory, and military training school for boys between the ages of 5 and 21 years. The average attendance is 100, and the annual fees received for each student amount to some $800. The elementary department is divided into eight grades, as in the public schools; the college preparatory department has four grades, similar to those of the public high schools; the courses of study conform to the requirements of the state board of education.... The business and incident good will are very valuable. In order to conduct its affairs, long time contracts must be made for supplies, equipment, teachers, and pupils. Appellants, law officers of the state and county, have publicly announced that the Act ... is valid and have declared their intention to enforce it. By reason of the statute and threat of enforcement appellee's business is being destroyed and its property depreciated; parents and guardians are refusing to make contracts for the future instruction of their sons, and some are being withdrawn.

The Academy's bill states the foregoing facts and then alleges that the challenged act contravenes the corporation's rights guaranteed by the Fourteenth Amendment and that unless appellants are restrained from proclaiming its validity and threatening to enforce it irreparable injury will result. The prayer is for an appropriate injunction.

No answer was interposed in either cause, and after proper notices they were heard by three judges on motions for preliminary injunctions upon the specifically alleged facts. The court ruled that the Fourteenth Amendment guaranteed appellees against the deprivation of their property without due process of law consequent upon the unlawful interference by appellants with the free choice of patrons, present and prospective. It declared the right to conduct schools was property and that parents and guardians, as a part of their liberty, might direct the education of children by selecting reputable teachers and places. Also, that appellees' schools were not unfit or harmful to the public, and that enforcement of the challenged statute would unlawfully deprive them of patronage and thereby destroy appellees' business and property. Finally, that the threats to enforce the act would continue to cause irreparable injury; and the suits were not premature.

No question is raised concerning the power of the state reasonably to regulate all schools, to inspect, supervise and examine them, their teachers and pupils; to require that all children of proper age attend some school, that teachers shall be of good moral character and patriotic disposition, that certain studies plainly essential to good citizenship must be taught, and that nothing be taught which is manifestly inimical to the public welfare.

The inevitable practical result of enforcing the act under consideration would be destruction of appellees' primary schools, and perhaps all other private primary schools for normal children within the state of Oregon. Appellees are engaged in a kind of undertaking not inherently harmful, but long regarded as useful and meritorious. Certainly there is nothing in the present records to indicate that they have failed to discharge their obligations to patrons, students, or the state. And there are no peculiar circumstances or present emergencies which demand extraordinary measures relative to primary education.

Under the doctrine of *Meyer v. Nebraska*, we think it entirely plain that the Act of 1922 unreasonably interferes with the liberty of parents and guardians to direct the upbringing and education of children under their control. As often heretofore pointed out, rights guaranteed by the Constitution may not be abridged by legislation which has no reasonable relation to some purpose within the competency of the state. The fundamental theory of liberty upon which all governments in this Union repose excludes any general power of the state to standardize its children by forcing them to accept instruction from public teachers only. The child is not the mere creature of the state; those who nurture him and direct his destiny have the right, coupled with the high duty, to recognize and prepare him for additional obligations.

Appellees are corporations, and therefore, it is said, they cannot claim for themselves the liberty which the Fourteenth Amendment guarantees. Accepted in the proper sense, this is true. But they have business and property for which they claim protection. These are threatened with destruction through the unwarranted compulsion which appellants are exercising over present and prospective patrons of their schools. And this court has gone very far to protect against loss threatened by such action. . . .

Generally, it is entirely true, as urged by counsel, that no person in any business has such an interest in possible customers as to enable him to restrain exercise of proper power of the state upon the ground that he will be deprived of patronage. But the injunctions here sought are not against the exercise of any proper power. Appellees asked protection against arbitrary, unreasonable, and unlawful interference with their patrons and the consequent destruction of their business and property. . . .

The suits were not premature. The injury to appellees was present and very real, not a mere possibility in the remote future. If no relief had been possible prior to the effective date of the act, the injury would have become irreparable. Prevention of impending injury by unlawful action is a well-recognized function of courts of equity.

The decrees below are affirmed.

NOTES

1. *Pierce* has been described as a kind of Magna Carta for non-public schools. Is this an accurate description?

2. Following *Pierce*, state level public school officials have granted great deference to educational leaders in religiously-affiliated non-public schools when it comes to curricular decision making. Should state officials exercise greater control over curriculum-related matters in non-public schools?

3. Is the Supreme Court's assertion that "[t]he child is not the mere creature of the state; those who nurture him and direct his destiny have the right, coupled with the high duty, to recognize and prepare him for additional obligations" 268 U.S. 510 at 535, 45 S.Ct. 571 at 573 of its opinion still true today? Put another way, do, or should, educators defer to parents in concerns over curricular content?

[CASE NO. 82]   EDUCATIONAL RIGHTS OF STUDENTS LACKING
DOCUMENTATION

PLYLER v. DOE

Supreme Court of the United States, 1982.
457 U.S. 202, 102 S.Ct. 2382, 72 L.Ed.2d 786 [4 Educ. L. Rep. 953].

■ JUSTICE BRENNAN delivered the opinion of the Court.

The question presented by these cases is whether, consistent with the
Equal Protection Clause of the Fourteenth Amendment, Texas may deny to
undocumented school-age children the free public education that it provides
to children who are citizens of the United States or legally admitted aliens.

I

. . .

In May 1975, the Texas Legislature revised its education laws to
withhold from local school districts any state funds for the education of
children who were not "legally admitted" into the United States. The 1975
revision also authorized local school districts to deny enrollment in their
public schools to children not "legally admitted" to the country. These
cases involve constitutional challenges to those provisions.

No. 80–1538

Plyler v. Doe

This is a class action, filed in the United States District Court for the
Eastern District of Texas in September 1977, on behalf of certain school-
age children of Mexican origin residing in Smith County, Tex., who could
not establish that they had been legally admitted into the United States.
The action complained of the exclusion of plaintiff children from the public
schools of the Tyler Independent School District. The Superintendent and
members of the Board of Trustees of the School District were named as
defendants; the State of Texas intervened as a party-defendant. After
certifying a class consisting of all undocumented school-age children of
Mexican origin residing within the School District, the District Court
preliminarily enjoined defendants from denying a free education to members of the plaintiff class. In December 1977, the court conducted an
extensive hearing on plaintiffs' motion for permanent injunctive relief.

In considering this motion, the District Court made extensive findings
of fact. The court found that neither § 21.031 nor the School District policy
implementing it had "either the purpose or effect of keeping illegal aliens
out of the State of Texas." Respecting defendants' further claim that
§ 21.031 was simply a financial measure designed to avoid a drain on the
State's fisc, the court recognized that the increases in population resulting
from the immigration of Mexican nationals into the United States had
created problems for the public schools of the State, and that these
problems were exacerbated by the special educational needs of immigrant
Mexican children. The court noted, however, that the increase in school
enrollment was primarily attributable to the admission of children who

were legal residents. It also found that while the "exclusion of all undocumented children from the public schools in Texas would eventually result in economies at some level," funding from both the State and Federal Governments was based primarily on the number of children enrolled. In net effect then, barring undocumented children from the schools would save money, but it would "not necessarily" improve "the quality of education." The court further observed that the impact of § 21.031 was borne primarily by a very small subclass of illegal aliens, "entire families who have migrated illegally and—for all practical purposes—permanently to the United States." Finally, the court noted that under current laws and practices "the illegal alien of today may well be the legal alien of tomorrow," and that without an education, these undocumented children, "[a]lready disadvantaged as a result of poverty, lack of English-speaking ability, and undeniable racial prejudices, . . . will become permanently locked into the lowest socio-economic class."

The District Court held that illegal aliens were entitled to the protection of the Equal Protection Clause of the Fourteenth Amendment, and that § 21.031 violated that Clause. . . . The District Court also concluded that the Texas statute violated the Supremacy Clause.

The Court of Appeals for the Fifth Circuit upheld the District Court's injunction. The Court of Appeals held that the District Court had erred in finding the Texas statute pre-empted by federal law. With respect to equal protection, however, the Court of Appeals affirmed in all essential respects the analysis of the District Court, concluding that 21.031 was "constitutionally infirm regardless of whether it was tested using the mere rational basis standard or some more stringent test." We noted probable jurisdiction.

No. 80–1934

In re Alien Children Education Litigation

During 1978 and 1979, suits challenging the constitutionality of § 21.031 and various local practices undertaken on the authority of that provision were filed in the United States District Courts for the Southern, Western, and Northern Districts of Texas. Each suit named the State of Texas and the Texas Education Agency as defendants, along with local officials. In November 1979, the Judicial Panel on Multidistrict Litigation, on motion of the State, consolidated the claims against the state officials into a single action to be heard in the District Court for the Southern District of Texas. A hearing was conducted in February and March 1980. In July 1980, the court entered an opinion and order holding that § 21.031 violated the Equal Protection Clause of the Fourteenth Amendment. The court held that "the absolute deprivation of education should trigger strict judicial scrutiny, particularly when the absolute deprivation is the result of complete inability to pay for the desired benefit." The court determined that the State's concern for fiscal integrity was not a compelling state interest, that exclusion of these children had not been shown to be necessary to improve education within the State, and that the educational needs of the children statutorily excluded were not different from the needs of children not excluded. The court therefore concluded that § 21.031 was not carefully tailored to advance the asserted state interest in an acceptable manner. While appeal of the District Court's decision was pending, the Court of Appeals rendered its decision in No. 80–1538. Apparently on the strength of that opinion, the Court of Appeals . . . summarily affirmed the decision of the Southern District. We noted probable jurisdiction and consolidated this case with No. 80–1538 for briefing and argument.

II

The Fourteenth Amendment provides that "[n]o State shall . . . deprive any person of life, liberty, or property, without due process of law; nor deny to *any person within its jurisdiction* the equal protection of the laws." (Emphasis added.) Appellants argue at the outset that undocumented aliens, because of their immigration status, are not "persons within the jurisdiction" of the State of Texas, and that they therefore have no right to the equal protection of Texas law. We reject this argument. Whatever his status under the immigration laws, an alien is surely a "person" in any ordinary sense of that term. Aliens, even aliens whose presence in this country is unlawful, have long been recognized as "persons" guaranteed due process of law by the Fifth and Fourteenth Amendments. Indeed, we have clearly held that the Fifth Amendment protects aliens whose presence in this country is unlawful from invidious discrimination by the Federal Government.

Appellants seek to distinguish our prior cases, emphasizing that the Equal Protection Clause directs a State to afford its protection to persons *within its jurisdiction* while the Due Process Clauses of the Fifth and Fourteenth Amendments contain no such assertedly limiting phrase. In appellants' view, persons who have entered the United States illegally are not "within the jurisdiction" of a State even if they are present within a State's boundaries and subject to its laws. Neither our cases nor the logic of the Fourteenth Amendment supports that constricting construction of the phrase "within its jurisdiction." We have never suggested that the class of persons who might avail themselves of the equal protection guarantee is less than coextensive with that entitled to due process. To the contrary, we have recognized that both provisions were fashioned to protect an identical class of persons, and to reach every exercise of state authority.

In concluding that "all persons within the territory of the United States," including aliens unlawfully present, may invoke the Fifth and Sixth Amendments to challenge actions of the Federal Government, we reasoned from the understanding that the Fourteenth Amendment was designed to afford its protection to all within the boundaries of a State. Our cases applying the Equal Protection Clause reflect the same territorial theme . . .

There is simply no support for appellants' suggestion that "due process" is somehow of greater stature than "equal protection" and therefore available to a larger class of persons. To the contrary, each aspect of the Fourteenth Amendment reflects an elementary limitation on state power. To permit a State to employ the phrase "within its jurisdiction" in order to identify subclasses of persons whom it would define as beyond its jurisdiction, thereby relieving itself of the obligation to assure that its laws are designed and applied equally to those persons, would undermine the principal purpose for which the Equal Protection Clause was incorporated in the Fourteenth Amendment. The Equal Protection Clause was intended to work nothing less than the abolition of all caste-based and invidious class-based legislation. That objective is fundamentally at odds with the power the State asserts here to classify persons subject to its laws as nonetheless excepted from its protection.

Although the congressional debate concerning § 1 of the Fourteenth Amendment was limited, that debate clearly confirms the understanding that the phrase "within its jurisdiction" was intended in a broad sense to offer the guarantee of equal protection to all within a State's boundaries, and to all upon whom the State would impose the obligations of its laws. Indeed, it appears from those debates that Congress, by using the phrase "person within its jurisdiction," sought expressly to ensure that the equal protection of the laws was provided to the alien population....

Use of the phrase "within its jurisdiction" thus does not detract from, but rather confirms, the understanding that the protection of the Fourteenth Amendment extends to anyone, citizen or stranger, who *is* subject to the laws of a State, and reaches into every corner of a State's territory. That a person's initial entry into a State, or into the United States, was unlawful, and that he may for that reason be expelled, cannot negate the simple fact of his presence within the State's territorial perimeter. Given such presence, he is subject to the full range of obligations imposed by the State's civil and criminal laws. And until he leaves the jurisdiction—either voluntarily, or involuntarily in accordance with the Constitution and laws of the United States—he is entitled to the equal protection of the laws that a State may choose to establish.

Our conclusion that the illegal aliens who are plaintiffs in these cases may claim the benefit of the Fourteenth Amendment's guarantee of equal protection only begins the inquiry. The more difficult question is whether the Equal Protection Clause has been violated by the refusal of the State of Texas to reimburse local school boards for the education of children who cannot demonstrate that their presence within the United States is lawful, or by the imposition by those school boards of the burden of tuition on those children. It is to this question that we now turn.

III

The Equal Protection Clause directs that "all persons similarly circumstanced shall be treated alike." But so too, "[t]he Constitution does not require things which are different in fact or opinion to be treated in law as though they were the same." The initial discretion to determine what is "different" and what is "the same" resides in the legislatures of the States. A legislature must have substantial latitude to establish classifications that roughly approximate the nature of the problem perceived, that accommodate competing concerns both public and private, and that account for limitations on the practical ability of the State to remedy every ill. In applying the Equal Protection Clause to most forms of state action, we thus seek only the assurance that the classification at issue bears some fair relationship to a legitimate public purpose.

But we would not be faithful to our obligations under the Fourteenth Amendment if we applied so deferential a standard to every classification. The Equal Protection Clause was intended as a restriction on state legislative action inconsistent with elemental constitutional premises. Thus we have treated as presumptively invidious those classifications that disadvantage a "suspect class," or that impinge upon the exercise of a "fundamental right." With respect to such classifications, it is appropriate to enforce the mandate of equal protection by requiring the State to demonstrate that its classification has been precisely tailored to serve a compelling governmental interest. In addition, we have recognized that certain forms of legislative classification, while not facially invidious, nonetheless give rise to recurring constitutional difficulties; in these limited circumstances we have sought the assurance that the classification reflects a reasoned judgment consistent with the ideal of equal protection by inquiring whether it may fairly be viewed as furthering a substantial interest of the State. We turn to a consideration of the standard appropriate for the evaluation of § 21.031.

A

Sheer incapability or lax enforcement of the laws barring entry into this country, coupled with the failure to establish an effective bar to the employment of undocumented aliens, has resulted in the creation of a substantial "shadow population" of illegal migrants—numbering in the millions—within our borders. This situation raises the specter of a permanent caste of undocumented resident aliens, encouraged by some to remain here as a source of cheap labor, but nevertheless denied the benefits that our society makes available to citizens and lawful residents. The existence of such an underclass presents most difficult problems for a Nation that prides itself on adherence to principles of equality under law.

The children who are plaintiffs in these cases are special members of this underclass. Persuasive arguments support the view that a State may withhold its beneficence from those whose very presence within the United States is the product of their own unlawful conduct. These arguments do not apply with the same force to classifications imposing disabilities on the minor children of such illegal entrants. At the least, those who elect to enter our territory by stealth and in violation of our law should be prepared to bear the consequences, including, but not limited to, deportation. But the children of those illegal entrants are not comparably situated. Their "parents have the ability to conform their conduct to societal norms," and presumably the ability to remove themselves from the State's jurisdiction; but the children who are plaintiffs in these cases "can affect neither their parents' conduct nor their own status." Even if the State found it expedient to control the conduct of adults by acting against their children, legislation directing the onus of a parent's misconduct against his children does not comport with fundamental conceptions of justice....

Of course, undocumented status is not irrelevant to any proper legislative goal. Nor is undocumented status an absolutely immutable characteristic since it is the product of conscious, indeed unlawful, action. But § 21.031 is directed against children, and imposes its discriminatory burden on the basis of a legal characteristic over which children can have little control. It is thus difficult to conceive of a rational justification for penalizing these children for their presence within the United States. Yet that appears to be precisely the effect of § 21.031.

Public education is not a "right" granted to individuals by the Constitution. But neither is it merely some governmental "benefit" indistinguishable from other forms of social welfare legislation. Both the importance of education in maintaining our basic institutions, and the lasting impact of its deprivation on the life of the child, mark the distinction. The "American people have always regarded education and [the] acquisition of knowledge as matters of supreme importance." We have recognized "the public schools as a most vital civic institution for the preservation of a democratic system of government" and as the primary vehicle for transmitting "the values on which our society rests." "[A]s ... pointed out early in our history, ... some degree of education is necessary to prepare citizens to participate effectively and intelligently in our open political system if we are to preserve freedom and independence." And these historic "perceptions of the public schools as inculcating fundamental values necessary to the maintenance of a democratic political system have been confirmed by the observations of social scientists." In addition, education provides the basic tools by which individuals might lead economically productive lives to the benefit of us all. In sum, education has a fundamental role in maintaining the fabric of our society. We cannot ignore the significant social costs borne by our Nation when select groups are denied the means to absorb the values and skills upon which our social order rests.

In addition to the pivotal role of education in sustaining our political and cultural heritage, denial of education to some isolated group of children poses an affront to one of the goals of the Equal Protection Clause: the abolition of governmental barriers presenting unreasonable obstacles to advancement on the basis of individual merit. Paradoxically, by depriving the children of any disfavored group of an education, we foreclose the means by which that group might raise the level of esteem in which it is held by the majority. But more directly, "education prepares individuals to be self-reliant and self-sufficient participants in society." Illiteracy is an enduring disability. The inability to read and write will handicap the individual deprived of a basic education each and every day of his life. The inestimable toll of that deprivation on the social economic, intellectual, and psychological well-being of the individual, and the obstacle it poses to individual achievement, make it most difficult to reconcile the cost or the principle of a status-based denial of basic education with the framework of equality embodied in the Equal Protection Clause....

B

These well-settled principles allow us to determine the proper level of deference to be afforded § 21.031. Undocumented aliens cannot be treated as a suspect class because their presence in this country in violation of federal law is not a "constitutional irrelevancy." Nor is education a fundamental right; a State need not justify by compelling necessity every variation in the manner in which education is provided to its population. But more is involved in these cases than the abstract question whether

§ 21.031 discriminates against a suspect class, or whether education is a fundamental right. Section 21.031 imposes a lifetime hardship on a discrete class of children not accountable for their disabling status. The stigma of illiteracy will mark them for the rest of their lives. By denying these children a basic education, we deny them the ability to live within the structure of our civic institutions, and foreclose any realistic possibility that they will contribute in even the smallest way to the progress of our Nation. In determining the rationality of § 21.031, we may appropriately take into account its costs to the Nation and to the innocent children who are its victims. In light of these countervailing costs, the discrimination contained in § 21.031 can hardly be considered rational unless it furthers some substantial goal of the State.

IV

It is the State's principal argument, and apparently the view of the dissenting Justices, that the undocumented status of these children *vel non* establishes a sufficient rational basis for denying them benefits that a State might choose to afford other residents. The State notes that while other aliens are admitted "on an equality of legal privileges with all citizens under non-discriminatory laws," the asserted right of these children to an education can claim no implicit congressional imprimatur. Indeed, in the State's view, Congress' apparent disapproval of the presence of these children within the United States, and the evasion of the federal regulatory program that is the mark of undocumented status, provides authority for its decision to impose upon them special disabilities. Faced with an equal protection challenge respecting the treatment of aliens, we agree that the courts must be attentive to congressional policy; the exercise of congressional power might well affect the State's prerogatives to afford differential treatment to a particular class of aliens. But we are unable to find in the congressional immigration scheme any statement of policy that might weigh significantly in arriving at an equal protection balance concerning the State's authority to deprive these children of an education.

The Constitution grants Congress the power to "establish an uniform Rule of Naturalization." Drawing upon this power, upon its plenary authority with respect to foreign relations and international commerce, and upon the inherent power of a sovereign to close its borders, Congress has developed a complex scheme governing admission to our Nation and status within our borders. The obvious need for delicate policy judgments has counseled the Judicial Branch to avoid intrusion into this field. But this traditional caution does not persuade us that unusual deference must be shown the classification embodied in § 21.031. The States enjoy no power with respect to the classification of aliens. This power is "committed to the political branches of the Federal Government." Although it is "a routine and normally legitimate part" of the business of the Federal Government to classify on the basis of alien status and to "take into account the character of the relationship between the alien and this country," only rarely are such matters relevant to legislation by a State. . . .

To be sure, like all persons who have entered the United States unlawfully, these children are subject to deportation. But there is no assurance that a child subject to deportation will ever be deported. An illegal entrant might be granted federal permission to continue to reside in this country, or even to become a citizen. In light of the discretionary federal power to grant relief from deportation, a State cannot realistically determine that any particular undocumented child will in fact be deported until after deportation proceedings have been completed. It would of course be most difficult for the State to justify a denial of education to a child enjoying an inchoate federal permission to remain.

We are reluctant to impute to Congress the intention to withhold from these children, for so long as they are present in this country through no fault of their own, access to a basic education. In other contexts, undocumented status, coupled with some articulable federal policy, might enhance state authority with respect to the treatment of undocumented aliens. But in the area of special constitutional sensitivity presented by these cases, and in the absence of any contrary indication fairly discernible in the present legislative record, we perceive no national policy that supports the State in denying these children an elementary education. The State may borrow the federal classification. But to justify its use as a criterion for its own discriminatory policy, the State must demonstrate that the classification is reasonably adapted to "the purposes for which the state desires to use it." We therefore turn to the state objectives that are said to support § 21.031.

V

Appellants argue that the classification at issue furthers an interest in the "preservation of the state's limited resources for the education of its lawful residents." Of course, a concern for the preservation of resources standing alone can hardly justify the classification used in allocating those resources. The State must do more than justify its classification with a concise expression of an intention to discriminate. Apart from the asserted state prerogative to act against undocumented children solely on the basis of their undocumented status—an asserted prerogative that carries only minimal force in the circumstances of these cases—we discern three colorable state interests that might support § 21.031.

First, appellants appear to suggest that the State may seek to protect itself from an influx of illegal immigrants. While a State might have an interest in mitigating the potentially harsh economic effects of sudden shifts in population, § 21.031 hardly offers an effective method of dealing with an urgent demographic or economic problem. There is no evidence in the record suggesting that illegal entrants impose any significant burden on the State's economy. To the contrary, the available evidence suggests that illegal aliens underutilize public services, while contributing their labor to the local economy and tax money to the state fisc. The dominant incentive for illegal entry into the State of Texas is the availability of employment; few if any illegal immigrants come to this country, or presumably to the State of Texas, in order to avail themselves of a free education. Thus, even making the doubtful assumption that the net impact of illegal aliens on the economy of the State is negative, we think it clear that "[c]harging tuition to undocumented children constitutes a ludicrously ineffectual attempt to stem the tide of illegal immigration," at least when compared with the alternative of prohibiting the employment of illegal aliens.

Second, while it is apparent that a State may "not . . . reduce expenditures for education by barring [some arbitrarily chosen class of] children from its schools," appellants suggest that undocumented children are appropriately singled out for exclusion because of the special burdens they impose on the State's ability to provide high-quality public education. But the record in no way supports the claim that exclusion of undocumented children is likely to improve the overall quality of education in the State. As the District Court in No. 80–1934 noted, the State failed to offer any "credible supporting evidence that a proportionately small diminution of the funds spent on each child [which might result from devoting some state funds to the education of the excluded group] will have a grave impact on the quality of education." And, after reviewing the State's school financing mechanism, the District Court in No. 80–1538 concluded that barring undocumented children from local schools would not necessarily improve the quality of education provided in those schools. Of course, even if improvement in the quality of education were a likely result of barring some *number* of children from the schools of the State, the State must support its selection of *this* group as the appropriate target for exclusion. In terms of educational cost and need, however, undocumented children are "basically indistinguishable" from legally resident alien children.

Finally, appellants suggest that undocumented children are appropriately singled out because their unlawful presence within the United States renders them less likely than other children to remain within the boundaries of the State, and to put their education to productive social or political use within the State. Even assuming that such an interest is legitimate, it is an interest that is most difficult to quantify. The State has no assurance that any child, citizen or not, will employ the education provided by the State within the confines of the State's borders. In any event, the record is clear that many of the undocumented children disabled by this classification will remain in this country indefinitely, and that some will become lawful residents or citizens of the United States. It is difficult to understand precisely what the State hopes to achieve by promoting the creation and perpetuation of a subclass of illiterates within our boundaries, surely adding to the problems and costs of unemployment, welfare, and crime. It is thus clear that whatever savings might be achieved by denying these children an education, they are wholly insubstantial in light of the costs involved to these children, the State, and the Nation.

VI

If the State is to deny a discrete group of innocent children the free public education that it offers to other children residing within its borders, that denial must be justified by a showing that it furthers some substantial state interest. No such showing was made here. Accordingly, the judgment of the Court of Appeals in each of these cases is

Affirmed.

NOTES

1. What do you think about the Court's position that the parents of the students at issue already paid taxes in a variety of forms? Is this sound judicial reasoning?

2. In light of issues surrounding immigration, do you think that the Court would reach the same result today?

[CASE NO. 83] CONSTITUTIONALITY OF RESIDENCE REQUIREMENT FOR TUITION–FREE ADMISSION TO PUBLIC SCHOOLS

MARTINEZ v. BYNUM

Supreme Court of the United States, 1983.
461 U.S. 321, 103 S.Ct. 1838, 75 L.Ed.2d 879 [10 Educ. L. Rep. 11].

■ JUSTICE POWELL delivered the opinion of the Court.

This case involves a facial challenge to the constitutionality of the Texas residency requirement governing minors who wish to attend public free schools while living apart from their parents or guardians.

I

Roberto Morales was born in 1969 in McAllen, Texas, and is thus a United States citizen by birth. His parents are Mexican citizens who reside in Reynosa, Mexico. He left Reynosa in 1977 and returned to McAllen to live with his sister, petitioner Oralia Martinez, for the primary purpose of attending school in the McAllen Independent School District. Although Martinez is now Morales's custodian, she is not—and does not desire to become—his guardian. As a result, Morales is not entitled to tuition-free admission to the McAllen schools. . . .

II

This Court frequently has considered constitutional challenges to residence requirements. On several occasions the Court has invalidated requirements that condition receipt of a benefit on a minimum period of residence within a jurisdiction, but it always has been careful to distinguish such durational residence requirements from bona fide residence requirements. In *Shapiro v. Thompson*, for example, the Court invalidated one-year durational residence requirements that applicants for public assistance benefits were required to satisfy despite the fact that they otherwise had "met the test for residence in their jurisdictions." . . .

We specifically have approved bona fide residence requirements in the field of public education. The Connecticut statute before us in *Vlandis v. Kline*, for example, was unconstitutional because it created an irrebuttable presumption of nonresidency for state university students whose legal addresses were outside of the State before they applied for admission. The statute violated the Due Process Clause because it in effect classified some bona fide state residents as nonresidents for tuition purposes. . . .

A bona fide residence requirement, appropriately defined and uniformly applied, furthers the substantial state interest in assuring that services provided for its residents are enjoyed only by residents. Such a requirement with respect to attendance in public free schools does not violate the Equal Protection Clause of the Fourteenth Amendment. It does not burden or penalize the constitutional right of interstate travel, for any person is free to move to a State and to establish residence there. A bona fide residence requirement simply requires that the person does establish residence before demanding the services that are restricted to residents.

There is a further, independent justification for local residence requirements in the public-school context.... The provision of primary and secondary education, of course, is one of the most important functions of local government. Absent residence requirements, there can be little doubt that the proper planning and operation of the schools would suffer significantly. The State thus has a substantial interest in imposing bona fide residence requirements to maintain the quality of local public schools.

III

The central question we must decide here is whether § 21.031(d) is a bona fide residence requirement. Although the meaning may vary according to context, "residence" generally requires both physical presence and an intention to remain.... This classic two-part definition of residence has been recognized as a minimum standard in a wide range of contexts time and time again....

Section 21.031 is far more generous than this traditional standard. It compels a school district to permit a child such as Morales to attend school without paying tuition if he has a bona fide intention to remain in the school district indefinitely, for he then would have a reason for being there other than his desire to attend school: his intention to make his home in the district. Thus § 21.031 grants the benefits of residency to all who satisfy the traditional requirements. The statute goes further and extends these benefits to many children even if they (or their families) do not intend to remain in the district indefinitely. As long as the child is not living in the district for the sole purpose of attending school, he satisfies the statutory test. For example, if a person comes to Texas to work for a year, his children will be eligible for tuition-free admission to the public schools.... In short, § 21.031 grants the benefits of residency to everyone who satisfies the traditional residence definition and to some who legitimately could be classified as nonresidents. Since there is no indication that this extension of the traditional definition has any impermissible basis, we certainly cannot say that § 21.031(d) violates the Constitution.

IV

The Constitution permits a State to restrict eligibility for tuition-free education to its bona fide residents. We hold that § 21.031 is a bona fide residence requirement that satisfies constitutional standards. The judgment of the Court of Appeals accordingly is affirmed.

NOTES

1. Can you reconcile the holdings in *Plyler* and *Martinez*?

2. The Texas statute in *Martinez* parallels the general commonlaw view.

3. Insofar as education is a state function, why should a child who resides in the state not be able to attend any public school in the state tuition-free? Should school boards in "better" districts advertise for out-of-district students as long as their parents are willing to pay tuition?

[CASE NO. 84] PEER GRADING AND STUDENT RECORDS

OWASSO INDEPENDENT SCHOOL DISTRICT NO. I–011 v. FALVO

Supreme Court of the United States, 2002.
534 U.S. 426, 122 S.Ct. 934, 151 L.Ed.2d 896 [161 Educ. L. Rep. 33].

■ JUSTICE KENNEDY delivered the opinion of the Court.

Teachers sometimes ask students to score each other's tests, papers, and assignments as the teacher explains the correct answers to the entire class. Respondent contends this practice, which the parties refer to as peer grading, violates the Family Educational Rights and Privacy Act of 1974 (FERPA or Act). We took this case to resolve the issue.

I

Under FERPA, schools and educational agencies receiving federal financial assistance must comply with certain conditions. § 1232g(a)(3). One condition specified in the Act is that sensitive information about students may not be released without parental consent. The Act states that federal funds are to be withheld from school districts that have "a policy or practice of permitting the release of education records (or personally identifiable information contained therein ...) of students without the written consent of their parents." § 1232g(b)(1). The phrase "education records" is defined, under the Act, as "records, files, documents, and other materials" containing information directly related to a student, which "are maintained by an educational agency or institution or by a person acting for such agency or institution." § 1232g(a)(4)(A). The definition of education records contains an exception for "records of instructional, supervisory, and administrative personnel ... which are in the sole possession of the maker thereof and which are not accessible or revealed to any other person except a substitute." § 1232g(a)(4)(B)(i). The precise question for us is whether peer-graded classroom work and assignments are education records.

Three of respondent Kristja J. Falvo's children are enrolled in Owasso Independent School District No. I–011, in a suburb of Tulsa, Oklahoma. The children's teachers, like many teachers in this country, use peer grading. In a typical case the students exchange papers with each other and score them according to the teacher's instructions, then return the work to the student who prepared it. The teacher may ask the students to report their own scores. In this case it appears the student could either call out the score or walk to the teacher's desk and reveal it in confidence, though by that stage, of course, the score was known at least to the one other student who did the grading. Both the grading and the system of calling out the scores are in contention here.

Respondent claimed the peer grading embarrassed her children. She asked the school district to adopt a uniform policy banning peer grading and requiring teachers either to grade assignments themselves or at least to forbid students from grading papers other than their own. The school district declined to do so, and respondent brought a class action. . . . against the school district, Superintendent Dale Johnson, Assistant Superintendent Lynn Johnson, and Principal Rick Thomas (petitioners). Respondent alleged the school district's grading policy violated FERPA and other laws not relevant here. The United States District Court for the Northern District of Oklahoma granted summary judgment in favor of the school district's position. The court held that grades put on papers by another student are not, at that stage, records "maintained by an educational agency or institution or by a person acting for such agency or institution," 20 U.S.C.[A.] § 1232g(a)(4)(A), and thus do not constitute "education records" under the Act. On this reasoning it ruled that peer grading does not violate FERPA.

The Court of Appeals for the Tenth Circuit reversed. . . . [it] held that peer grading violates the Act. The grades marked by students on each other's work, it held, are education records protected by the statute, so the very act of grading was an impermissible release of the information to the student grader.

We granted certiorari to decide whether peer grading violates FERPA. Finding no violation of the Act, we reverse.

II

At the outset, we note it is an open question whether FERPA provides private parties, like respondent, with a cause of action enforceable under § 1983. We have granted certiorari on this issue in another case. The parties, furthermore, did not contest the § 1983 issue before the Court of Appeals. That court raised the issue *sua sponte,* and petitioners did not seek certiorari on the question. We need not resolve the question here as it is our practice "to decide cases on the grounds raised and considered in the Court of Appeals and included in the question on which we granted certiorari." In these circumstances we assume, but without so deciding or expressing an opinion on the question, that private parties may sue an educational agency under § 1983 to enforce the provisions of FERPA here at issue. Though we leave open the § 1983 question, the Court has subject-matter jurisdiction because respondent's federal claim is not so "completely devoid of merit as not to involve a federal controversy." With these preliminary observations concluded, we turn to the merits.

The parties appear to agree that if an assignment becomes an education record the moment a peer grades it, then the grading, or at least the practice of asking students to call out their grades in class, would be an impermissible release of the records under § 1232g(b)(1). without deciding the point, we assume for the purposes of our analysis that they are correct. The parties disagree, however, whether peer-graded assignments constitute education records at all. The papers do contain information directly related to a student, but they are records under the Act only when and if they "are maintained by an educational agency or institution or by a person acting for such agency or institution." § 1232g(a)(4)(A).

Petitioners, supported by the United States as amicus curiae, contend the definition covers only institutional records—namely, those materials retained in a permanent file as a matter of course. They argue that records "maintained by an educational agency or institution" generally would include final course grades, student grade point averages, standardized test scores, attendance records, counseling records, and records of disciplinary actions—but not student homework or classroom work. Respondent, adopting the reasoning of the Court of Appeals, contends student-graded assignments fall within the definition of education records. That definition contains an exception for "records of instructional, supervisory, and administrative personnel ... which are in the sole possession of the maker thereof and which are not accessible or revealed to any other person except a substitute." § 1232g(a)(4)(B)(i). The Court of Appeals reasoned that if grade books are not education records, then it would have been unnecessary for Congress to enact the exception. Grade books and the grades within, the court concluded, are "maintained" by a teacher and so are covered by FERPA. The court recognized that teachers do not maintain the grades on individual student assignments until they have recorded the result in the grade books. It reasoned, however, that if Congress forbids teachers to disclose students' grades once written in a grade book, it makes no sense to permit the disclosure immediately beforehand. The court thus held that student graders maintain the grades until they are reported to the teacher.

The Court of Appeals' logic does not withstand scrutiny. ...

Two statutory indicators tell us that the Court of Appeals erred in concluding that an assignment satisfies the definition of education records as soon as it is graded by another student. First, the student papers are not, at that stage, "maintained" within the meaning of § 1232g(a)(4)(A). The ordinary meaning of the word "maintain" is "to keep in existence or continuance; preserve; retain." ... Even assuming the teacher's grade book is an education record—a point the parties contest and one we do not decide here—the score on a student-graded assignment is not "contained therein," § 1232g(b)(1), until the teacher records it. The teacher does not maintain the grade while students correct their peers' assignments or call out their own marks. Nor do the student graders maintain the grades within the meaning of § 1232g(a)(4)(A). The word "maintain" suggests FERPA records will be kept in a filing cabinet in a records room at the school or on a permanent secure database, perhaps even after the student is no longer enrolled. The student graders only handle assignments for a few moments as the teacher calls out the answers. It is fanciful to say they maintain the papers in the same way the registrar maintains a student's folder in a permanent file.

The Court of Appeals was further mistaken in concluding that each student grader is "a person acting for" an educational institution for purposes of § 1232g(a)(4)(A). The phrase "acting for" connotes agents of the school, such as teachers, administrators, and other school employees. Just as it does not accord with our usual understanding to say students are "acting for" an educational institution when they follow their teacher's direction to take a quiz, it is equally awkward to say students are "acting for" an educational institution when they follow their teacher's direction to score it. Correcting a classmate's work can be as much a part of the assignment as taking the test itself. It is a way to teach material again in a new context, and it helps show students how to assist and respect fellow pupils. By explaining the answers to the class as the students correct the papers, the teacher not only reinforces the lesson but also discovers whether the students have understood the material and are ready to move on. We do not think FERPA prohibits these educational techniques. We also must not lose sight of the fact that the phrase "by a person acting for [an educational] institution" modifies "maintain." Even if one were to agree students are acting for the teacher when they correct the assignment, that is different from saying they are acting for the educational institution in maintaining it.

Other sections of the statute support our interpretation. FERPA, for example, requires educational institutions to "maintain a record, kept with the education records of each student." § 1232g(b)(4)(A). This record must list those who have requested access to a student's education records and their reasons for doing so. The record of access "shall be available only to parents, [and] to the school official and his assistants who are responsible for the custody of such records."

Under the Court of Appeals' broad interpretation of education records, every teacher would have an obligation to keep a separate record of access for each student's assignments. Indeed, by that court's logic, even students who grade their own papers would bear the burden of maintaining records of access until they turned in the assignments. We doubt Congress would have imposed such a weighty administrative burden on every teacher, and certainly it would not have extended the mandate to students.

Also, FERPA requires "a record" of access for each pupil. This single record must be kept "with the education records." This suggests Congress contemplated that education records would be kept in one place with a single record of access. By describing a "school official" and "his assistants" as the personnel responsible for the custody of the records, FERPA implies that education records are institutional records kept by a single central custodian, such as a registrar, not individual assignments handled by many student graders in their separate classrooms.

FERPA also requires recipients of federal funds to provide parents with a hearing at which they may contest the accuracy of their child's education records. The hearings must be conducted "in accordance with regulations of the Secretary,'' which in turn require adjudication by a disinterested official and the opportunity for parents to be represented by an attorney. It is doubtful Congress would have provided parents with this elaborate procedural machinery to challenge the accuracy of the grade on every spelling test and art project the child completes.

Respondent's construction of the term "education records" to cover student homework or classroom work would impose substantial burdens on teachers across the country. It would force all instructors to take time, which otherwise could be spent teaching and in preparation, to correct an assortment of daily student assignments. Respondent's view would make it much more difficult for teachers to give students immediate guidance. The interpretation respondent urges would force teachers to abandon other customary practices, such as group grading of team assignments. Indeed, the logical consequences of respondent's view are all but unbounded. At argument, counsel for respondent seemed to agree that if a teacher in any of the thousands of covered classrooms in the Nation puts a happy face, a gold star, or a disapproving remark on a classroom assignment, federal law does not allow other students to see it.

We doubt Congress meant to intervene in this drastic fashion with traditional state functions. Under the Court of Appeals' interpretation of FERPA, the federal power would exercise minute control over specific teaching methods and instructional dynamics in classrooms throughout the country. The Congress is not likely to have mandated this result, and we do not interpret the statute to require it.

For these reasons, even assuming a teacher's grade book is an education record, the Court of Appeals erred, for in all events the grades on students' papers would not be covered under FERPA at least until the teacher has collected them and recorded them in his or her grade book. We limit our holding to this narrow point, and do not decide the broader question whether the grades on individual student assignments, once they are turned in to teachers, are protected by the Act.

The judgment of the Court of Appeals is reversed, and the case is remanded for further proceedings consistent with this opinion.

It is so ordered.

NOTES

1. Justice Scalia concurred with the Court's judgment that papers graded by peers were not educational records within the meaning of FERPA. However, he wrote separately because he was concerned that the Court's suggestion that the term educational record only included those documents maintained in a central repository at a school was unnecessary to resolve the dispute. Do you agree with Justice Scalia?

2. What do you think of the practice of peer-grading? Is it useful?

[CASE NO. 85] POWER OF SCHOOL AUTHORITIES TO CHOOSE
SPRING PLAY

SEYFRIED v. WALTON

United States Court of Appeals, Third Circuit, 1981.
668 F.2d 214 [2 Educ. L. Rep. 379].

■ ALDISERT, CIRCUIT JUDGE.

The question presented is whether a public school superintendent's
decision to cancel a high school dramatic production because of its sexual
theme violated the students' first amendment right of expression. Plaintiffs, parents of three students in the play, sued the school district, the
school board, and the district superintendent, seeking compensatory and
equitable relief under 42 U.S.C.[A.] § 1983. The district court, sitting
without a jury, held that the school superintendent's decision to cancel the
production as inappropriate for school sponsorship was no different from
other administrative decisions involving allocation of educational resources
and that the cancellation did not offend the students' first amendment
rights. We accept the reasoning given by the district court and we will
affirm. . . .

I.

. . . Caesar Rodney High School, located in Dover, Delaware, sponsors
autumn and spring theatrical productions each year. In December 1980, the
director of the spring production, an English teacher at the school, selected
the musical "Pippin" for presentation the following spring. Because the
play contained certain sexually explicit scenes, the director consulted the
assistant principal before reaching a final decision. After the director edited
the script, she and the assistant principal agreed that the revised scenes,
although still sexually suggestive, were appropriate for a high school
production.

In March 1981, shortly after rehearsals for the spring production had
begun, the father of a "Pippin" cast member complained to his brother, the
president of the school board, that the play mocked religion. The board
president directed the district superintendent to look into the matter. After
reviewing the edited script, the superintendent determined that the play
did not mock religion, but that it was inappropriate for a public high school
because of its sexual content. He directed the principal to stop production
of the play. After hearing the views of interested parents, the school board
refused to overturn the superintendent's decision. As a result, the school
did not present a spring play in 1981.

Parents of three members of the "Pippin" cast and crew then filed a
civil rights action under 42 U.S.C.[A.] § 1983, claiming that the students'
first amendment rights of expression had been unconstitutionally abridged.
After a two-day trial, the district court entered judgment in favor of the
defendants. Plaintiffs appeal.

II.

Appellants' principal contention is that the students of the "Pippin"
cast and crew had a first amendment right to produce the play. Although

we agree that, in general, dramatic expression is "speech" for purposes of the first amendment, we also agree with the district court that the decision to cancel the production of "Pippin" in these circumstances did not infringe on the students' constitutional rights.

In his well reasoned opinion, Judge Stapleton noted that a school community "exists for a specialized purpose—the education of young people," including the communication of both knowledge and social values. The first amendment, he concluded, must therefore be "applied in light of the special characteristics of the school environment...."

We believe that the district court properly distinguished student newspapers and other "non-program related expressions of student opinion" from school-sponsored theatrical productions. The critical factor in this case is the relationship of the play to the school curriculum. As found by the district court, both the staff and the administration view the spring production at Caesar Rodney as "an integral part of the school's educational program." Participation in the play, though voluntary, was considered a part of the curriculum in the theater arts.... Viewed in this light, the selection of the artistic work to be given as the spring production does not differ in principle from the selection of course curriculum, a process which courts have traditionally left to the expertise of educators. Just as a student has no First Amendment right to study a particular aspect or period of history in his or her senior history course, he or she has no First Amendment right to participate in the production of a particular dramatic work or version thereof.

The district court also noted the likelihood that the school's sponsorship of a play would be viewed as an endorsement of the ideas it contained. A school has an important interest in avoiding the impression that it has endorsed a viewpoint at variance with its educational program. The district court cautioned that administrators may not so chill the school's atmosphere for student and teacher expression that they cast "a pall of orthodoxy" over the school community, but it found no such danger here. The court found that no student was prohibited from expressing his views on any subject; no student was prohibited from reading the script, an unedited version of which remains in the school library; and no one was punished or reprimanded for any expression of ideas. In light of these facts, the court could find no reasonable threat of a chilling effect on the free exchange of ideas within the school community. These findings are amply supported by the record.

We agree with the district court that those responsible for directing a school's educational program must be allowed to decide how its limited resources can be best used to achieve the goals of educating and socializing its students. "Limitations of time and resources ... dictate that choices be made.... [S]ince the objective of the process is the 'inculcation of both knowledge and social values' in young people, these decisions as to what will be taught will necessarily involve an acceptance or preference of some values over others."

Because of the burden of responsibility given to school administrators, courts are reluctant to interfere with the operation of our school systems. . . .

By and large, public education in our Nation is committed to the control of state and local authorities. Courts do not and cannot intervene in the resolution of conflicts which arise in the daily operation of school systems and which do not directly and sharply implicate basic constitutional values.

We agree with the district court that the conflict here does not "directly and sharply implicate" the first amendment rights of the students. We hold, therefore, that the court properly entered judgment for the defendants.

NOTES

1.   The superintendent overruled the dramatic arts teacher's decision to produce "Pippin." The teacher did not challenge this action. Could she have? If so, on what grounds?

2.   Could the superintendent's involvement be characterized as censorship? Would your answer be different if the superintendent, rather than the teacher, was the one who was supposed to select the play?

3.   As a result of this controversy, there was no spring play. Who gained and who lost?

[CASE NO. 86]   POWER OF BOARD TO ESTABLISH GRADUATION REQUIREMENTS

STATE EX REL. SAGESER v. LEDBETTER

Missouri Court of Appeals, 1977.
559 S.W.2d 230.

■ Stone, Presiding Judge.

In this proceeding . . . relator Ronnie Sageser (hereinafter Ronnie) sought a writ of mandamus to compel . . . the members of the board of education of the Sarcoxie R–2 School District (hereinafter collectively referred to as the board), W.D. Ledbetter, the superintendent of schools for that district, and Jess Bair, the principal of Sarcoxie High School at the time of suit, to execute and deliver to relator Ronnie a diploma evidencing his graduation from that school. . . .

[For "showing disrespect" to a teacher, Ronnie had been suspended by the former principal Smith during his junior year.]

Either the next day by relator Ronnie's account, or "about five days later" according to principal Smith, the latter called Ronnie's home and requested that he report to the principal's office. Upon trial, principal Smith recalled that, when Ronnie did report, "his attitude [was] that of indifference toward returning to school and behaving"—in short, that "his attitude hadn't improved," so Smith told Ronnie "to go home until his attitude improved." Ronnie's recollection was that, in the course of this meeting, principal Smith had exclaimed, "You don't even know what you are doing here, do you" and, when Ronnie agreed and answered "No," the principal "just said, '[w]hy don't you just check out your books and go home.'" Although the principal declared that Ronnie's check-out and withdrawal were voluntary and without compulsion by any school official, certain portions of the principal's testimony cast doubt upon that characterization of Ronnie's withdrawal. (E.g., when asked on cross-examination "[d]id you instruct Ronald Sageser to check out of school," principal Smith responded "I don't remember whether I did or didn't"; and, in one entry book, Ronnie's name was listed with the comment "dropped 4/1/74.") But, regardless of whether the principal's above-quoted utterances to Ronnie constituted a mere suggestion, an admonition or a command, Ronnie did "go home" after having completed a "checkout form" obtainable only from the principal or upon his authorization. This "checkout form" was dated April 1, 1974, which was approximately eight weeks prior to the last day of the 1973–74 school year.

Ronnie reentered Sarcoxie High School in September 1974, was listed as a senior, continued in school through the 1974–75 academic year, and (with his academic credits from the three previous years) earned the twenty units of credit required for graduation. However, he was denied a diploma (so superintendent Ledbetter declared) because he had not completed "eight semesters of attending" as prescribed "in the policy that is made by the Board of Education" (hereinafter the eight-semester requirement).

When Ronnie's parents learned that he would not graduate with his class, one of the parents attended a meeting of the board of education and requested that the board waive the eight-semester requirement and give Ronnie's diploma to him, but the board refused to do so. However, acknowledging that Ronnie had satisfied all other requirements for graduation, superintendent Ledbetter declared that, if Ronnie would *enroll* for "[e]xactly the amount of time that was lacking from the time he dropped out [April 1, 1974] until the end of school which, I believe, [was] eight weeks, give or take a day or two," he would receive his diploma.

Since the Sarcoxie eight-semester requirement hatched this controversy, it becomes both appropriate and necessary to note the evidence concerning its origin, meaning and prior enforcement. We observe initially that the eight-semester requirement was *not* imposed or ordained by statute, but was a requirement for graduation formulated and prescribed by the Sarcoxie Board of Education (so superintendent Ledbetter declared) pursuant to a *recommendation* nestling in a footnote to the last sentence of paragraph 17, "High School Graduation Requirements," in the *Handbook for Classification and Accreditation of Public School Districts in Missouri* (1973) published by the Missouri State Board of Education, that sentence and footnote reading as follows:

> "The local board of education may require more than 20 units, adopt specific course requirements, and/or specify the number of semesters of attendance ... required for graduation from their local school district."

"... Eight semesters of attendance after grade eight are *recommended.*" (All emphasis herein is ours.)

Inasmuch as the proper disposition of this appeal does not involve or depend upon the wisdom vel non of this recommendation, the acceptance of which mandatorily herded all high school students, without regard to ability, aptitude, ambition, intellect, motivation, performance or prior scholastic record, onto the same conveyor belt geared to the pace of the mediocre or average student, we eschew comment concerning its adoption by the Sarcoxie board. . . .

Respondents' position in this proceeding (as *initially* stated by superintendent Ledbetter) was that, by reason of Ronnie's absence during approximately the last eight weeks of his Junior school year, he did not satisfy the four-year requirement and will not be entitled to receive a diploma until he does. Thus, Ledbetter initially declared that relator Ronnie would be required to attend Sarcoxie High School for "exactly" the additional number of school days that he missed in his Junior year from his suspension or "checkout" on April 1, 1974, to the end of that school year. However, Ledbetter subsequently conceded not only that the eight-semester requirement did *not* demand or necessitate any *attendance* but also that relator Ronnie already had earned the twenty units of credit which constituted and satisfied the "measure of academic achievement" required for graduation, from which it followed that it would not be necessary for Ronnie to earn any additional units of credit, pass any courses in which he might be enrolled, or for that matter even attend any classes. Thus, it becomes plain that the additional requirement of *enrollment* for eight weeks imposed by the school authorities would do no more than work an exercise in futility which would benefit neither the school district nor relator Ronnie and thus would fly in the teeth of the commonsense maxim that the law does not require the doing of a useless thing.

Although the foregoing is dispositive of this appeal, the earnest presentations of counsel move us to note other record evidence pointing to and supporting the same conclusion. . . . Supt. Ledbetter conceded that, during the three years prior to trial of this proceeding, four girls, identified by name in the transcript, had been graduated with a diploma although they had not *attended* eight semesters. One of those four girls who had become pregnant, had missed the last few weeks of the 1973–74 school year, but had graduated with her class in 1975. Relator Ronnie likewise had missed the last few weeks of the 1973–74 school year, but contrawise had been denied graduation with the 1975 class.

Although respondents assert that mandamus is inappropriate, the transcript establishes that relator had satisfied all academic requirements for graduation and that respondents rely solely, albeit mistakenly, on the eight-semester requirement to justify and support their denial of a diploma to relator Ronnie. Within reasonable limits a school board may determine graduation requirements but where, as here, a rule is applied or enforced unreasonably, capriciously, arbitrarily or inequitably to deny a diploma to a qualified candidate, mandamus is an appropriate remedy. . . .

The judgment of the circuit court making the alternative writ of mandamus permanent should be and is affirmed.

NOTES

1. What do you think of the behavior of the superintendent and former principal?

2. Should there be a required minimum period of attendance for high school graduation? Should graduation be based on the completion of a fixed number of courses? Should graduation be based on passing tests?

[CASE NO. 87]   BOARD POWER TO INCLUDE ATTENDANCE IN DETERMINING COURSE GRADES

CAMPBELL v. BOARD OF EDUCATION OF THE TOWN OF NEW MILFORD

Supreme Court of Connecticut, 1984.
475 A.2d 289 [17 Educ. L. Rep. 840].

■ PETERS, ASSOCIATE JUSTICE.

This case concerns the validity of the policy of a local school board that imposes academic sanctions for nonattendance upon high school students. In a class action brought by the named plaintiff, John A. Campbell, for himself and others similarly situated, the plaintiff class sought injunctive and declaratory relief, mandamus, and compensatory damages from the named defendant, the New Milford board of education, and others. The plaintiff claimed that the defendants' policy was ultra vires in light of governing state statutes, and unconstitutional in light of operative provisions of the Connecticut constitution and the United States constitution. The trial court rendered judgment for the defendants and the plaintiff has appealed.

The underlying facts are undisputed. The New Milford attendance policy, set out in an annually distributed student handbook, provides two sets of academic sanctions for students who are absent from school. Course credit is withheld from any student who, without receiving an administrative waiver, is absent from any year-long course for more than twenty-four class periods. In the calculation of the twenty-four maximum absences, all class absences are included except absences on school-sponsored activities or essential administrative business. In addition to the twenty-four absence limit, the course grade of any student whose absence from school is unapproved is subject to a five-point reduction for each unapproved absence after the first. In any one marking period, the grade may not, however, be reduced to a grade lower than 50, which is a failing grade. The grade reduction for unexcused absences is, like the twenty-four maximum absence policy, subject to administrative waiver. The policy of the school board entails extensive opportunities for counseling after a student's first confirmed unapproved absence from a class and thereafter.

The stated purpose of the attendance policy is educational rather than disciplinary. A student's disciplinary suspension from school, for reasons unrelated to attendance, is considered an approved rather than an unapproved absence. Such an absence cannot result in the diminution of a class grade although it may be counted, unless waived, as part of the twenty-four maximum absences for class credit. A student's absence from school, whether approved or unapproved, is not a ground for suspension or expulsion.

A student's report card lists, for each course, grades for each marking period, a final examination grade, a final grade, the amount of credit awarded, and the number of approved and unapproved absences. The report card conspicuously bears the following legend: "A circled grade indicates that the grade was reduced due to unapproved absences." In the case of the named plaintiff, his report card indicated grade reductions by the circling of grades in each of his academic courses, with the result that in three of the courses his final grade was lowered from passing to failing. In a fourth course, Architectural Drafting II, where the plaintiff's final grade was passing despite an indicated reduction for unapproved absences, the report card assigned him no credit because of a total of thirty-eight absences, thirty-one of which were approved and seven of which were unapproved. Any report card thus discloses, on its face, those grades which are affected by the enforcement of the attendance policy. . . .

I

The plaintiff's first argument on appeal is that the defendant school board's policy is invalid because it conflicts with a number of state statutes. This argument is twofold, that the attendance policy is ultra vires because it exceeds the authority conferred upon local school boards by state law and that the policy is preempted by state statutes with which it is inconsistent. We find neither argument persuasive.

The authority of local boards of education derives from their role as agents of the state. "[T]he furnishing of education for the general public, required by article eighth, § 1, of the Connecticut constitution, is by its very nature a state function and duty." This responsibility has been delegated to local boards which, as "agencies of the state in charge of education in the town . . . possess only such powers as are granted to them by the General Statutes expressly or by necessary implication." . . .

. . . The authority to adopt uniform rules concerning irregularity of attendance is necessarily implied in the conjunction of statutory provisions authorizing local implementation of the educational mission of the state. Significantly, § 10–220 expressly charges local boards with responsibility for the oversight of the school attendance of children from the ages of seven to sixteen made mandatory by § 10–184. Furthermore, the plaintiff's concession that school teachers, upon the instruction of local school boards, may properly consider class participation in the assignment of grades, logically implies the existence of an educational nexus between classroom presence and grading. If local school boards can delegate to others the authority to impose academic sanctions for nonattendance, the decision to adopt uniform school-wide rules for such sanctions can hardly be deemed ultra vires.

None of the out-of-state cases upon which the plaintiff relies compels the conclusion that school-wide academic sanctions for nonattendance should generally be adjudged to be ultra vires. It may well be improper to reduce a student's grade for nonattendance as an additional punishment for unrelated conduct leading to a suspension from class; but this school board's program does not permit such double punishment. It would indubitably be unlawful to apply a nonattendance program in an unreasonable, capricious, arbitrary or inequitable manner; but no such allegation has been factually demonstrated. It would finally be troublesome to bar a truant student from further class attendance and from taking a final examination; but the defendant board's program neither removes such a student from class nor excuses further compliance with the state's compulsory education law. In short, the plaintiff has cited no authority for his claim that attendance rules promulgated by local school boards, if carefully drafted and fairly applied, are to be deemed per se ultra vires. Our own research has likewise revealed no such caselaw. We agree that such regulations fall within the authority granted to local school boards by the statutes of this state.

In the alternative, the plaintiff maintains that the defendant school board's attendance policy is preempted by state statutes governing school attendance. . . .

The defendant school board's reply . . . calls upon us to recognize a distinction between sanctions which are disciplinary in nature and sanctions which relate to academic requirements. The question is not whether we concur in the judgment of the defendant board of education that "[l]earning experiences that occur in the classroom are . . . essential components of the learning process" or that "[t]ime lost from class tends to be irretrievable in terms of opportunity for instructional interaction." The policy decision that academic credentials should reflect more than the product of quizzes, examinations, papers and classroom participation nonetheless constitutes an academic judgment about academic requirements. We agree with the defendants' characterization of their policy. . . .

II

Even if the defendant school board's attendance policy is authorized by the relevant state statutes, the plaintiff class asserts that the policy cannot pass constitutional muster. The plaintiff relies on provisions of our state and federal constitutions to raise three different constitutional claims: a right to substantive due process, a right to procedural due process, and a right to equal protection of the laws. The trial court, upon consideration of these claims, found no infringement of the plaintiff's constitutional rights. We agree.

A

The plaintiff's challenge to the New Milford attendance policy as violative of the requirements of substantive due process claims infringement of students' fundamental rights to public education, of students' liberty interests in their academic reputation and of students' property interests in grades reflecting academic achievement. . . .

Of these substantive due process claims, the most serious is the charge of impairment of a fundamental right, because, if such an impairment were properly before us, the validity of the questioned governmental regulation would require strict scrutiny to determine whether the regulation was compellingly justified and narrowly drafted. We must therefore decide the applicability of the fundamental rights guaranteed by article eighth, § 1, to a school board's policy of imposing uniform school-wide academic sanctions for nonattendance. . . . This school board policy, which is neither disciplinary nor an infringement of equal educational opportunity, does not jeopardize any fundamental rights under our state constitution.

The standard by which the plaintiff's remaining substantive due process claims must be measured is therefore the more usual rational basis test. In order to succeed on these claims, the plaintiff bears the heavy burden of proving that the challenged policy has no reasonable relationship to any legitimate state purpose and that the plaintiff class has suffered a specific injury as a result of the policy's enforcement. The plaintiff has established neither the legal nor the factual predicate for meeting this burden of proof.

The plaintiff argues that it is unconstitutionally arbitrary and capricious for the defendant school board to require student grades to reflect more than academic achievement. With respect to the plaintiff's liberty interest, we can find no factual impairment of whatever rights the plaintiff might possibly assert. Inspection of the report card of the named plaintiff discloses the relationship between his academic performance and the reduction in his grades and class credit that resulted from application of the attendance policy. The plaintiff has failed to show how a student's reputation could be injured by a report card in this form. With respect to the plaintiff's property interest, we find it difficult to understand how a uniform school-wide policy that links class grades with attendance can be on its face more arbitrary, as a constitutional matter, than are similar judgments by individual teachers who may justifiably, according to the plaintiff, adjust classroom grades to reflect classroom participation. Furthermore, the trial court made no findings of fact that application of the attendance policy was arbitrary or capricious in the only two specific cases about which evidence was adduced at trial. On this record, the plaintiff class has not proven infringement of its liberty or property interest in a fair grading system.

The plaintiff argues finally that impermissible vagueness in the waiver provisions that ameliorate the potential rigor of the defendant board's attendance policy requires the conclusion that the policy is substantively unconstitutional. The policy of grade reduction is subject to waiver for "outstanding performance," and denial of class credit may be waived in extenuating circumstances calling for "special consideration." These provisions for waiver are unconstitutional, according to the plaintiff, because they permit school administrators to exercise unbridled discretion and hence invite arbitrary action. It is, however, by no means clear that provisions for waiver, which necessarily depend upon the equities of particular circumstances, require the same degree of precision as must accompany the imposition of sanctions in the first instance. Significantly, the plaintiff's challenge for vagueness does not contest any part of the attendance policy other than its provisions of waiver. In any case, the plaintiff class has again failed to make the factual showing necessary to prove that it has suffered a constitutional injury. The record contains no findings that any member of the class in fact misunderstood the waiver policy or was deprived of a waiver because of ambiguity in its statement. The plaintiff's claim of unconstitutional vagueness therefore cannot succeed.

B

The plaintiff also claims a deprivation of procedural due process. The plaintiff maintains that the New Milford attendance policy fails to provide constitutionally mandated basic procedural safeguards because students are not given notice of the dates of their alleged absences and are not afforded the opportunity to contest the imposition of an academic penalty, either at an internal hearing or before the board of education. These omissions, according to the plaintiff, jeopardize accurate and fair application of the defendants' policy.

Before we can consider this claim on its merits, we must clarify the standards that govern procedural fairness in a school setting. We have already held that the defendants' policy is academic rather than disciplinary in intent and effect, and that the policy impairs no fundamental rights. The Supreme Court of the United States has recently determined that flexible standards of procedural due process call for "far less stringent procedural requirements in the case of an academic dismissal" than for a dismissal based on disciplinary reasons. *Board of Curators of the University of Missouri v. Horowitz.* That court found it compelling that academic evaluations of a student necessarily depend upon professional judgments that are "more subjective and evaluative than the typical factual questions presented in the average disciplinary decision." For similar reasons, it is appropriate for this court to defer to the policy judgments of the academic administrators who formulated the defendant school board's attendance program. Such deferral does not of course obviate the fundamental requirements of procedural due process that a student must be given adequate notice of the program, and a meaningful timely opportunity to be heard. It does, however, mean that notice and hearings need not take any one particular form in order to pass constitutional muster.

In this case, the plaintiff does not argue that students at New Milford High School were not provided with sufficient notice of the existent attendance policy or of the academic sanctions that would ensue from recurrent class absences. The plaintiff asserts only that students had inadequate opportunities to contest whether absences had occurred, whether they were excused or unexcused, or whether they should be waived. The defendants introduced evidence to the contrary. In the absence of express findings by the trial court, we must conclude that the plaintiff class has not met the requirement that the challenged attendance program must be shown to have adversely affected a constitutionally protected right under the facts of this particular case rather than of some possible or hypothetical facts not proven to exist.

C

The plaintiff's final constitutional claim invokes the equal protection provisions of article first, § 20, of the Connecticut constitution and the fourteenth amendment to the United States constitution. The plaintiff urges us to hold that because the defendant board's attendance policy permits waiver of grade reductions for unexcused absences, the policy creates two unequal classes of students: students who are denied a waiver and students who are granted a waiver. In part the plaintiff's argument depends upon the assertion that the defendants' classification, because it allegedly affects a fundamental right to education, must meet the test of strict scrutiny. That assertion we have rejected, supra. Even if the applicable test is whether the waiver provision bears a reasonable relationship to legitimate governmental ends, the plaintiff argues that the waiver provision is constitutionally flawed because it ties eligibility for waiver to a student's "outstanding performance for the latter portion of the marking period." It is irrational, and a violation of equal protection, according to the plaintiff, to waive grade reduction for students who do "outstanding" work and to impose such sanctions on students whose work is, because of academic difficulties unrelated to class absence, only average.

The defendants offer several answers to this argument. Factually, they deny the premise that the waiver provision favors students on account of their ability rather than on account of their effort, since work may be considered "outstanding" in light of a particular student's past performance. Legally, they note that the waiver provision imports a reasonable element of flexibility into the assessment of a student's total classroom performance. Finally, they remind us that a district-wide policy is more likely to assure equality of treatment for all students than is a policy administered on an ad-hoc basis by individual classroom teachers. We find the defendants' arguments persuasive and therefore reject the plaintiff's equal protection claim.

There is no error.

NOTES

1. What do you think about the quality of the plaintiff's arguments and the evidence used to support his position?

2. How, if at all, should "approved" and "unapproved" absences be handled differently as regards academics? Where should absences caused by suspension fit?

[CASE NO. 88] USE OF RACE IN ADMISSIONS DECISIONS

PARENTS INVOLVED IN COMMUNITY SCHOOLS v. SEATTLE SCHOOL DISTRICT NO. 1

Supreme Court of the United States, 2007.
555 U.S. 701, 127 S.Ct. 2738, 168 L.Ed.2d 508 [220 Educ. L. Rep. 84].

■ CHIEF JUSTICE ROBERTS announced the judgment of the Court....

The school districts in these cases voluntarily adopted student assignment plans that rely upon race to determine which public schools certain children may attend. The Seattle school district classifies children as white or nonwhite; the Jefferson County school district as black or "other." In Seattle, this racial classification is used to allocate slots in oversubscribed high schools. In Jefferson County, it is used to make certain elementary school assignments and to rule on transfer requests. In each case, the school district relies upon an individual student's race in assigning that student to a particular school, so that the racial balance at the school falls within a predetermined range based on the racial composition of the school district as a whole. Parents of students denied assignment to particular schools under these plans solely because of their race brought suit, contending that allocating children to different public schools on the basis of race violated the Fourteenth Amendment guarantee of equal protection. The Courts of Appeals below upheld the plans. We granted certiorari, and now reverse.

I

Both cases present the same underlying legal question-whether a public school that had not operated legally segregated schools or has been found to be unitary may choose to classify students by race and rely upon that classification in making school assignments. Although we examine the plans under the same legal framework, the specifics of the two plans, and the circumstances surrounding their adoption, are in some respects quite different.

A

Seattle School District No. 1 operates 10 regular public high schools. In 1998, it adopted the plan at issue in this case for assigning students to these schools. The plan allows incoming ninth graders to choose from among any of the district's high schools, ranking however many schools they wish in order of preference.

Some schools are more popular than others. If too many students list the same school as their first choice, the district employs a series of "tiebreakers" to determine who will fill the open slots at the oversubscribed school. The first tiebreaker selects for admission students who have a sibling currently enrolled in the chosen school. The next tiebreaker depends upon the racial composition of the particular school and the race of the individual student. In the district's public schools approximately 41 percent of enrolled students are white; the remaining 59 percent, comprising all other racial groups, are classified by Seattle for assignment purposes as nonwhite. If an oversubscribed school is not within 10 percentage points of the district's overall white/nonwhite racial balance, it is what the district calls "integration positive," and the district employs a tiebreaker that selects for assignment students whose race "will serve to bring the school into balance." If it is still necessary to select students for the school after using the racial tiebreaker, the next tiebreaker is the geographic proximity of the school to the student's residence.

Seattle has never operated segregated schools-legally separate schools for students of different races-nor has it ever been subject to court-ordered desegregation. It nonetheless employs the racial tiebreaker in an attempt to address the effects of racially identifiable housing patterns on school assignments. Most white students live in the northern part of Seattle, most students of other racial backgrounds in the southern part. Four of Seattle's high schools are located in the north ... and five in the south.... One school ... is more or less in the center of Seattle.

For the 2000–2001 school year, five of these schools were oversubscribed ... so much so that 82 percent of incoming ninth graders ranked one of these schools as their first choice. Three of the oversubscribed schools were "integration positive" because the school's white enrollment the previous school year was greater than 51 percent.... Thus, more nonwhite students (107, 27, and 82, respectively) who selected one of these three schools as a top choice received placement at the school than would have been the case had race not been considered, and proximity been the next tiebreaker. [The] Franklin [school] was "integration positive" because its nonwhite enrollment the previous school year was greater than 69 percent; 89 more white students were assigned to Franklin by operation of the racial tiebreaker in the 2000–2001 school year than otherwise would have been. Garfield was the only oversubscribed school whose composition during the 1999–2000 school year was within the racial guidelines, although in previous years Garfield's enrollment had been predominantly nonwhite, and the racial tiebreaker had been used to give preference to white students.

Petitioner Parents Involved in Community Schools (Parents Involved) is a nonprofit corporation comprising the parents of children who have been or may be denied assignment to their chosen high school in the district because of their race. The concerns of Parents Involved are illustrated by Jill Kurfirst, who sought to enroll her ninth-grade son, Andy Meeks, in Ballard High School's special Biotechnology Career Academy. Andy suffered from attention deficit hyperactivity disorder and dyslexia, but had made good progress with hands-on instruction, and his mother and middle school teachers thought that the smaller biotechnology program held the most promise for his continued success. Andy was accepted into this selective program but, because of the racial tiebreaker, was denied assignment to Ballard High School. Parents Involved commenced this suit in the Western District of Washington....

The District Court granted summary judgment to the school district.... The Ninth Circuit initially reversed based on its interpretation of the Washington Civil Rights Act and enjoined the district's use of the integration tiebreaker. Upon realizing that the litigation would not be resolved in time for assignment decisions for the 2002–2003 school year, the Ninth Circuit withdrew its opinion, vacated the injunction, and ... certified the state-law question to the Washington Supreme Court.

The Washington Supreme Court determined that the State Civil Rights Act bars only preferential treatment programs "where race or gender is used by government to select a less qualified applicant over a more qualified applicant," and not "[p]rograms which are racially neutral, such as the [district's] open choice plan." The state court returned the case to the Ninth Circuit for further proceedings.

A panel of the Ninth Circuit then again reversed the District Court, this time ruling on the federal constitutional question. The panel determined that while achieving racial diversity and avoiding racial isolation are compelling government interests Seattle's use of the racial tiebreaker was not narrowly tailored to achieve these interests The Ninth Circuit granted rehearing en banc and overruled the panel decision, affirming the District Court's determination that Seattle's plan was narrowly tailored to serve a compelling government interest, We granted certiorari.

B

Jefferson County Public Schools operates the public school system in metropolitan Louisville, Kentucky. In 1973 a federal court found that Jefferson County had maintained a segregated school system, [the Supreme Court] vacated and remanded, reinstated with modifications, and in 1975 the District Court entered a desegregation decree. Jefferson County operated under this decree until 2000, when the District Court dissolved the decree after finding that the district had achieved unitary status by eliminating "[t]o the greatest extent practicable" the vestiges of its prior policy of segregation.

In 2001, after the decree had been dissolved, Jefferson County adopted the voluntary student assignment plan at issue in this case. Approximately 34 percent of the district's 97,000 students are black; most of the remaining 66 percent are white. The plan requires all nonmagnet schools to maintain a minimum black enrollment of 15 percent, and a maximum black enrollment of 50 percent.

At the elementary school level, based on his or her address, each student is designated a "resides" school to which students within a specific geographic area are assigned; elementary resides schools are "grouped into clusters in order to facilitate integration." The district assigns students to nonmagnet schools in one of two ways: Parents of kindergartners, first-graders, and students new to the district may submit an application indicating a first and second choice among the schools within their cluster; students who do not submit such an application are assigned within the cluster by the district. "Decisions to assign students to schools within each cluster are based on available space within the schools and the racial guidelines in the District's current student assignment plan." If a school has reached the "extremes of the racial guidelines," a student whose race would contribute to the school's racial imbalance will not be assigned there. After assignment, students at all grade levels are permitted to apply to transfer between nonmagnet schools in the district. Transfers may be requested for any number of reasons, and may be denied because of lack of available space or on the basis of the racial guidelines.

When petitioner Crystal Meredith moved into the school district in August 2002, she sought to enroll her son, Joshua McDonald, in kindergarten for the 2002–2003 school year. His resides school was only a mile from his new home, but it had no available space-assignments had been made in May, and the class was full. Jefferson County assigned Joshua to another elementary school in his cluster, Young Elementary. This school was 10 miles from home, and Meredith sought to transfer Joshua to a school in a different cluster, Bloom Elementary, which-like his resides school-was only a mile from home. Space was available at Bloom, and intercluster transfers are allowed, but Joshua's transfer was nonetheless denied because, in the words of Jefferson County, "[t]he transfer would have an adverse effect on desegregation compliance" of Young.

Meredith brought suit in the Western District of Kentucky, alleging violations of the Equal Protection Clause of the Fourteenth Amendment. The District Court found that Jefferson County had asserted a compelling interest in maintaining racially diverse schools, and that the assignment plan was (in all relevant respects) narrowly tailored to serve that compelling interest. The Sixth Circuit affirmed in a *per curiam* opinion relying upon the reasoning of the District Court, concluding that a written opinion "would serve no useful purpose." We granted certiorari.

II

As a threshold matter, we must assure ourselves of our jurisdiction. . . .

III

A

It is well established that when the government distributes burdens or benefits on the basis of individual racial classifications, that action is reviewed under strict scrutiny. As the Court recently reaffirmed, " 'racial classifications are simply too pernicious to permit any but the most exact connection between justification and classification.' " In order to satisfy this searching standard of review, the school districts must demonstrate that the use of individual racial classifications in the assignment plans here under review is "narrowly tailored" to achieve a "compelling" government interest.

Without attempting in these cases to set forth all the interests a school district might assert, it suffices to note that our prior cases, in evaluating the use of racial classifications in the school context, have recognized two interests that qualify as compelling. The first is the compelling interest of remedying the effects of past intentional discrimination. Yet the Seattle public schools have not shown that they were ever segregated by law, and were not subject to court-ordered desegregation decrees. The Jefferson County public schools were previously segregated by law and were subject to a desegregation decree entered in 1975. In 2000, the District Court that entered that decree dissolved it. . . .

. . .

The second government interest we have recognized as compelling for purposes of strict scrutiny is the interest in diversity in higher education upheld in *Grutter*. The specific interest found compelling in *Grutter* was student body diversity "in the context of higher education." The diversity interest was not focused on race alone but encompassed "all factors that may contribute to student body diversity." . . .

. . .

The entire gist of the analysis in *Grutter* was that the admissions program at issue there focused on each applicant as an individual, and not simply as a member of a particular racial group. The classification of applicants by race upheld in *Grutter* was only as part of a "highly individualized, holistic review." As the Court explained, "[t]he importance of this individualized consideration in the context of a race-conscious admissions program is paramount." The point of the narrow tailoring analysis in which the *Grutter* Court engaged was to ensure that the use of racial classifications was indeed part of a broader assessment of diversity, and not simply an effort to achieve racial balance, which the Court explained would be "patently unconstitutional."

In the present cases, by contrast, race is not considered as part of a broader effort to achieve "exposure to widely diverse people, cultures, ideas, and viewpoints;" race, for some students, is determinative standing alone. The districts argue that other factors, such as student preferences, affect assignment decisions under their plans, but under each plan when race comes into play, it is decisive by itself. It is not simply one factor weighed with others in reaching a decision, as in *Grutter*; it is *the* factor. Like the University of Michigan undergraduate plan struck down in *Gratz*, the plans here "do not provide for a meaningful individualized review of applicants" but instead rely on racial classifications in a "nonindividualized, mechanical" way.

Even when it comes to race, the plans here employ only a limited notion of diversity, viewing race exclusively in white/nonwhite terms in Seattle and black/"other" terms in Jefferson County. The Seattle "Board Statement Reaffirming Diversity Rationale" speaks of the "inherent educational value" in "[p]roviding students the opportunity to attend schools with diverse student enrollment." But under the Seattle plan, a school with 50 percent Asian–American students and 50 percent white students but no African–American, Native–American, or Latino students would qualify as balanced, while a school with 30 percent Asian–American, 25 percent African–American, 25 percent Latino, and 20 percent white students would not. It is hard to understand how a plan that could allow these results can be viewed as being concerned with achieving enrollment that is " 'broadly diverse.' "

Prior to *Grutter,* the courts of appeals rejected as unconstitutional attempts to implement race-based assignment plans-such as the plans at issue here-in primary and secondary schools. After *Grutter,* however, the two Courts of Appeals in these cases, and one other, found that race-based assignments were permissible at the elementary and secondary level, largely in reliance on that case.

In upholding the admissions plan in *Grutter,* though, this Court relied upon considerations unique to institutions of higher education, noting that in light of "the expansive freedoms of speech and thought associated with the university environment, universities occupy a special niche in our constitutional tradition." The Court explained that "[c]ontext matters" in applying strict scrutiny, and repeatedly noted that it was addressing the use of race "in the context of higher education." The Court in *Grutter* expressly articulated key limitations on its holding-defining a specific type of broad-based diversity and noting the unique context of higher education-but these limitations were largely disregarded by the lower courts in extending *Grutter* to uphold race-based assignments in elementary and secondary schools. The present cases are not governed by *Grutter*.

B

Perhaps recognizing that reliance on *Grutter* cannot sustain their plans, both school districts assert additional interests, distinct from the interest upheld in *Grutter*, to justify their race-based assignments. In briefing and argument before this Court, Seattle contends that its use of race helps to reduce racial concentration in schools and to ensure that racially concentrated housing patterns do not prevent nonwhite students from having access to the most desirable schools. Jefferson County has articulated a similar goal, phrasing its interest in terms of educating its students "in a racially integrated environment." Each school district argues that educational and broader socialization benefits flow from a racially diverse learning environment, and each contends that because the diversity they seek is racial diversity—not the broader diversity at issue in *Grutter*—it makes sense to promote that interest directly by relying on race alone.

The parties and their *amici* dispute whether racial diversity in schools in fact has a marked impact on test scores and other objective yardsticks or achieves intangible socialization benefits. The debate is not one we need to resolve, however, because it is clear that the racial classifications employed by the districts are not narrowly tailored to the goal of achieving the educational and social benefits asserted to flow from racial diversity. In design and operation, the plans are directed only to racial balance, pure and simple, an objective this Court has repeatedly condemned as illegitimate.

The plans are tied to each district's specific racial demographics, rather than to any pedagogic concept of the level of diversity needed to obtain the asserted educational benefits. In Seattle, the district seeks white enrollment of between 31 and 51 percent (within 10 percent of "the district white average" of 41 percent), and nonwhite enrollment of between 49 and 69 percent (within 10 percent of "the district minority average" of 59 percent). In Jefferson County, by contrast, the district seeks black enrollment of no less than 15 or more than 50 percent, a range designed to be "equally above and below Black student enrollment systemwide," based on the objective of achieving at "all schools ... an African–American enrollment equivalent to the average district-wide African–American enrollment" of 34 percent. In Seattle, then, the benefits of racial diversity require enrollment of at least 31 percent white students; in Jefferson County, at least 50 percent. There must be at least 15 percent nonwhite students under Jefferson County's plan; in Seattle, more than three times that figure. This comparison makes clear that the racial demographics in each district—whatever they happen to be—drive the required "diversity" numbers. The plans here are not tailored to achieving a degree of diversity necessary to realize the asserted educational benefits; instead the plans are tailored, in the words of Seattle's Manager of Enrollment Planning, Technical Support, and Demographics, to "the goal established by the school board of attaining a level of diversity within the schools that approximates the district's overall demographics.''

The districts offer no evidence that the level of racial diversity necessary to achieve the asserted educational benefits happens to coincide with the racial demographics of the respective school districts—or rather the white/nonwhite or black/"other" balance of the districts, since that is the only diversity addressed by the plans. . . .

In fact, in each case the extreme measure of relying on race in assignments is unnecessary to achieve the stated goals, even as defined by the districts. . . .

In *Grutter,* the number of minority students the school sought to admit was an undefined "meaningful number" necessary to achieve a genuinely diverse student body. Although the matter was the subject of disagreement on the Court, the majority concluded that the law school did not count back from its applicant pool to arrive at the "meaningful number" it regarded as necessary to diversify its student body. Here the racial balance the districts seek is a defined range set solely by reference to the demographics of the respective school districts.

This working backward to achieve a particular type of racial balance, rather than working forward from some demonstration of the level of diversity that provides the purported benefits, is a fatal flaw under our existing precedent. We have many times over reaffirmed that "[r]acial balance is not to be achieved for its own sake." *Grutter* itself reiterated that "outright racial balancing" is "patently unconstitutional."

Accepting racial balancing as a compelling state interest would justify the imposition of racial proportionality throughout American society, contrary to our repeated recognition that "[a]t the heart of the Constitution's guarantee of equal protection lies the simple command that the Government must treat citizens as individuals, not as simply components of a racial, religious, sexual or national class." Allowing racial balancing as a compelling end in itself would "effectively assur[e] that race will always be relevant in American life, and that the 'ultimate goal' of 'eliminating entirely from governmental decisionmaking such irrelevant factors as a human being's race' will never be achieved." An interest "linked to nothing other than proportional representation of various races . . . would support indefinite use of racial classifications, employed first to obtain the appropriate mixture of racial views and then to ensure that the [program] continues to reflect that mixture."

The validity of our concern that racial balancing has "no logical stopping point," is demonstrated here by the degree to which the districts tie their racial guidelines to their demographics. As the districts' demographics shift, so too will their definition of racial diversity.

. . .

The principle that racial balancing is not permitted is one of substance, not semantics. Racial balancing is not transformed from "patently unconstitutional" to a compelling state interest simply by relabeling it "racial diversity." While the school districts use various verbal formulations to describe the interest they seek to promote-racial diversity, avoidance of racial isolation, racial integration-they offer no definition of the interest that suggests it differs from racial balance.

. . .

C

The districts assert, as they must, that the way in which they have employed individual racial classifications is necessary to achieve their stated ends. The minimal effect these classifications have on student assignments, however, suggests that other means would be effective.

. . .

While we do not suggest that *greater* use of race would be preferable, the minimal impact of the districts' racial classifications on school enrollment casts doubt on the necessity of using racial classifications. In *Grutter,* the consideration of race was viewed as indispensable in more than tripling minority representation at the law school-from 4 to 14.5 percent. Here the most Jefferson County itself claims is that "because the guidelines provide a firm definition of the Board's goal of racially integrated schools, they 'provide administrators with the authority to facilitate, negotiate and collaborate with principals and staff to maintain schools within the 15–50% range.' " Classifying and assigning schoolchildren according to a binary conception of race is an extreme approach in light of our precedents and our Nation's history of using race in public schools, and requires more than such an amorphous end to justify it.

The districts have also failed to show that they considered methods other than explicit racial classifications to achieve their stated goals. Narrow tailoring requires "serious, good faith consideration of workable race-neutral alternatives," and yet in Seattle several alternative assignment plans-many of which would not have used express racial classifications-were rejected with little or no consideration. Jefferson County has failed to present any evidence that it considered alternatives, even though the district already claims that its goals are achieved primarily through means other than the racial classifications.

IV

Justice BREYER's dissent takes a different approach to these cases, one that fails to ground the result it would reach in law. Instead, it selectively relies on inapplicable precedent and even dicta while dismissing contrary holdings, alters and misapplies our well-established legal framework for assessing equal protection challenges to express racial classifications, and greatly exaggerates the consequences of today's decision.

To begin with, Justice BREYER seeks to justify the plans at issue under our precedents recognizing the compelling interest in remedying past intentional discrimination. Not even the school districts go this far, and for good reason. The distinction between segregation by state action and racial imbalance caused by other factors has been central to our jurisprudence in this area for generations. The dissent elides this distinction between *de jure* and *de facto* segregation, casually intimates that Seattle's school attendance patterns reflect illegal segregation and fails to credit the judicial determination-under the most rigorous standard-that Jefferson County had eliminated the vestiges of prior segregation. The dissent thus alters in fundamental ways not only the facts presented here but the established law.

. . .

At the same time it relies on inapplicable desegregation cases, misstatements of admitted dicta, and other noncontrolling pronouncements, Justice BREYER's dissent candidly dismisses the significance of this Court's repeated *holdings* that all racial classifications must be reviewed under strict scrutiny, arguing that a different standard of review should be applied because the districts use race for beneficent rather than malicious purposes.

This Court has recently reiterated, however, that " 'all racial classifications [imposed by government] . . . must be analyzed by a reviewing court under strict scrutiny.' " Justice BREYER nonetheless relies on the good intentions and motives of the school districts, stating that he has found "no case that . . . repudiated this constitutional asymmetry between that which seeks to exclude and that which seeks to include members of minority races." We have found many. Our cases clearly reject the argument that motives affect the strict scrutiny analysis.

This argument that different rules should govern racial classifications designed to include rather than exclude is not new; it has been repeatedly pressed in the past and has been repeatedly rejected.

The reasons for rejecting a motives test for racial classifications are clear enough. "The Court's emphasis on 'benign racial classifications' suggests confidence in its ability to distinguish good from harmful governmental uses of racial criteria. History should teach greater humility.... '[B]enign' carries with it no independent meaning, but reflects only acceptance of the current generation's conclusion that a politically acceptable burden, imposed on particular citizens on the basis of race, is reasonable."

. . .

. . .

If the need for the racial classifications embraced by the school districts is unclear, even on the districts' own terms, the costs are undeniable. "[D]istinctions between citizens solely because of their ancestry are by their very nature odious to a free people whose institutions are founded upon the doctrine of equality." Government action dividing us by race is inherently suspect because such classifications promote "notions of racial inferiority and lead to a politics of racial hostility," "reinforce the belief, held by too many for too much of our history, that individuals should be judged by the color of their skin" and "endorse race-based reasoning and the conception of a Nation divided into racial blocs, thus contributing to an escalation of racial hostility and conflict." As the Court explained in *Rice v. Cayetano*, "[o]ne of the principal reasons race is treated as a forbidden classification is that it demeans the dignity and worth of a person to be judged by ancestry instead of by his or her own merit and essential qualities."

All this is true enough in the contexts in which these statements were made-government contracting, voting districts, allocation of broadcast licenses, and electing state officers-but when it comes to using race to assign children to schools, history will be heard. In *Brown v. Board of Education* (*Brown I*), we held that segregation deprived black children of equal educational opportunities regardless of whether school facilities and other tangible factors were equal, because government classification and separation on grounds of race themselves denoted inferiority. It was not the inequality of the facilities but the fact of legally separating children on the basis of race on which the Court relied to find a constitutional violation in 1954. The next Term, we accordingly stated that "full compliance" with *Brown I* required school districts "to achieve a system of determining admission to the public schools on a nonracial basis."

The parties and their *amici* debate which side is more faithful to the heritage of *Brown,* but the position of the plaintiffs in *Brown* was spelled out in their brief and could not have been clearer: "[T]he Fourteenth Amendment prevents states from according differential treatment to American children on the basis of their color or race." What do the racial classifications at issue here do, if not accord differential treatment on the basis of race? As counsel who appeared before this Court for the plaintiffs in *Brown* put it: "We have one fundamental contention which we will seek to develop in the course of this argument, and that contention is that no State has any authority under the equal-protection clause of the Fourteenth Amendment to use race as a factor in affording educational opportunities among its citizens." There is no ambiguity in that statement. And it was that position that prevailed in this Court, which emphasized in its remedial opinion that what was "[a]t stake is the personal interest of the plaintiffs in admission to public schools as soon as practicable on a nondiscriminatory basis," and what was required was "determining admission to the public schools on a nonracial basis." What do the racial classifications do in these cases, if not determine admission to a public school on a racial basis?

Before *Brown,* schoolchildren were told where they could and could not go to school based on the color of their skin. The school districts in these cases have not carried the heavy burden of demonstrating that we should allow this once again—even for very different reasons. For schools that never segregated on the basis of race, such as Seattle, or that have removed the vestiges of past segregation, such as Jefferson County, the way "to achieve a system of determining admission to the public schools on a nonracial basis" is to stop assigning students on a racial basis. The way to stop discrimination on the basis of race is to stop discriminating on the basis of race.

The judgments of the Courts of Appeals for the Sixth and Ninth Circuits are reversed, and the cases are remanded for further proceedings.

It is so ordered.

NOTES

1. In *Grutter v. Bollinger,* 539 U.S. 306, 343, 123 S.Ct. 2325, 2347, 156 L.Ed.2d 304 [177 Educ. L. Rep. 801] (2003), in upholding the University of Michigan's affirmative action admissions policy in its law school, the Court suggested that "[w]e expect that 25 years from now, the use of racial preferences will no longer be necessary to further the interest approved today." What do you think about this statement?

2. Should race play a role in admissions decisions?

[CASE NO. 89]   SCHOOL FEES UNACCEPTABLE

NAGY EX REL. NAGY v. EVANSVILLE– VANDERBURGH SCHOOL CORP.

Supreme Court of Indiana, 2006.
844 N.E.2d 481 [207 Educ. L. Rep. 311].

■ RUCKER, JUSTICE.

The question presented is whether the mandatory $20 student services fee imposed on students enrolled in a school corporation violates Article 8, Section 1 of the Indiana Constitution. We conclude it does.

I.   Facts and Procedural History

The facts of this case are largely undisputed. For the 2002–2003 school year, the Evansville–Vanderburgh School Corporation ("EVSC") imposed a $20 student services fee on all students in grades Kindergarten through Twelve. EVSC acknowledges that the fee was imposed as an attempt to balance its budget, which had a $2.3 million deficit in 2002 and a predicted $5.5 million deficit for 2003. The fee, along with state funds and local property tax receipts, was deposited in EVSC's general fund and was used to pay for, among other things, a coordinator of student services, nurses, media specialists, alternative education, elementary school counselors, a police liaison program, and activities such as athletics, drama, and music. The $20 fee is charged to every student including students who qualify for the free or reduced school lunches and textbook programs. If the fee is not paid, a notice is sent to the student's parents notifying them that if payment is not received by a date certain the matter would be referred to a law firm for collection and attorney fees of up to $100 would be charged to the parent regardless of whether legal action is taken.

Frank Nagy and Sonja Brackett are residents of Evansville whose children are enrolled in public schools under EVSC's jurisdiction. EVSC charged Nagy and Brackett a $20 fee for each of their children enrolled for the 2002–2003 academic year. The Brackett children qualify for the reduced or free school lunch and textbook programs.

In October 2002, on behalf of himself and others similarly situated, Nagy filed a class action complaint seeking declaratory and injunctive relief. The complaint was later amended to add Sonja Brackett. Among other things the complaint alleged that the imposition of the fee violated

Article 8, Section 1 of the Indiana Constitution, as well as the due process clause of Fourteenth Amendment to the United States Constitution. EVSC responded with a motion to dismiss the Fourteenth Amendment due process claim, which the trial court initially granted. In the meantime the parties filed cross-motions for summary judgment. After conducting a hearing the trial court reconsidered its earlier ruling and granted summary judgment in favor of Brackett, on grounds that a fee imposed upon students who qualify for the reduced or free school lunch and textbook programs violated the due process clause of the Fourteenth Amendment. However, the trial court granted summary judgment in favor of EVSC on Plaintiffs' Indiana Constitutional claim. The Plaintiffs appealed and EVSC cross-appealed.

In a divided opinion, the Court of Appeals reversed the judgment of the trial court, holding that the $20 fee violates Article 8, Section 1 of the Indiana Constitution because it is used to pay for what amounts to tuition. Because the court found the fee in violation of the Indiana Constitution, it did not reach the federal due process claim. We agree that the student services fee is inconsistent with Article 8, Section 1, but for reasons slightly different than those expressed by the Court of Appeals. Having previously granted transfer, we now reverse the judgment of the trial court.

II. Discussion

A. Rules of Constitutional Construction

Article 8, Section 1 [of the Indiana Constitution] provides: "Knowledge and learning, generally diffused throughout a community, being essential to the preservation of a free government; it shall be the duty of the General Assembly to encourage, by all suitable means, moral, intellectual, scientific, and agricultural improvement; and to provide, by law, for a general and uniform system of Common Schools, wherein tuition shall be without charge, and equally open to all." Generally, questions arising under the Indiana Constitution are to be resolved by examining the language of the text in the context of the history surrounding its drafting and ratification, the purpose and structure of our Constitution, and case law interpreting the specific provisions. . . .

B. Context of the Historical Development of Common Schools

Exploring the framers' understanding of tuition and its application to the case before us, the Court of Appeals set forth the historical framework of Article 8, Section 1. The Court determined that "the evil to be addressed by what became Article 8 of our Constitution was a lack of education and the subsequent problem of illiteracy among Indiana's citizens." From this, the Court held "that, to have any forceful meaning at all, Article 8, Section 1 must be interpreted to mean that not only must Indiana public schools not charge for 'tuition' in the sense of the services of a teacher or instruction, but also must not charge for those functions and services which are by their very nature essential to teaching or 'tuition.' " Accordingly the Court of Appeals determined that imposition of the $20 student services fee at issue in this case runs afoul of Article 8, Section 1. The Court also called into question the continued validity of Indiana's public textbook scheme.

We are of the view that the holding expressed by our colleagues sweeps a little too broadly. The idea that tuition includes "those functions and services which are by their very nature essential to teaching" is certainly descriptive of what is meant by a "free" school system.

Indeed a number of jurisdictions contain provisions in their state constitutions for free public schools. However, unlike constitutions in a number of states, the framers of Indiana's constitution were careful not to provide for a free school system. Rather, at most the framers provided that tuition would be free, or more precisely "tuition shall be without charge." This is a subtle distinction, but a significant one that we believe the framers made intentionally. A free public school system implies a level of educational subsidization that the framers at least did not endorse and at most rejected outright.

1.   The Free Common School Debate

. . .

In apparent response to the efforts of the free common school movement supporters, the General Assembly called for a convention, to be held in Indianapolis, for the purpose of " 'consulting and devising the best course to be pursued to promote common school education' " in Indiana. The convention's delegates recommended that, "(1) additional [school] funds should be provided by a general tax; (2) [the schools] should be free, 'perfectly free, as the dew of heaven, to rich and poor, without the least recognition of pauperism or charity'; (3) they should be made as good as any other schools in the State; (4) a suitable standard of qualification should be erected for teachers . . .; [and] (5) there should be provided a superintendent of free common schools." An address of the arguments emerging from the convention was produced and a thousand copies were printed and distributed across the State of Indiana.

. . .

The 1848–49 General Assembly responded to the referendum with a legislative enactment to "increase and extend the benefits of the common schools." Although the new act addressed aspects of school funding, it stopped far short of establishing free schools. It was in this environment—a lively and sometimes acrimonious public debate over the establishment of free common schools and a referendum vote of 56% in support of free common schools—that the framers of Indiana's second constitution assembled at Indianapolis on October 7, 1850.

2.   The Constitutional Convention

Drafted in 1816, Indiana's first constitution provided the following provisions concerning education. . . .

. . . . The second constitutional convention consisted of 150 delegates. . . . On October 14, 1850, a ten-person Committee on Education was formed. To that committee was referred, among other things, the educational provision of the 1816 Constitution. On December 11, 1850 the committee reported the results of its deliberations to the full convention. . . . The proposed section was read a first time and passed to a second reading.

At the time of the second reading, on January 27, 1851, committee member James R.M. Bryant of Warren County noted a discrepancy between the proposed text and the intended proposal of the committee. . . . The delegates agreed with Bryant's motion to remove the clause from the provision, and the revised section was set for a third reading.

On January 28, 1851, Bryant reminded the convention delegates of recent developments in Indiana education and corresponding legislative responses. . . . After a third and final reading on January 30, the provision passed without further discussion . . . on February 7, Article 8, Section 1 had been slightly modified from "shall be gratis" to "shall be without charge," which apparently reflected a change from a Latin phrase to its English equivalent. The full text read as follows:

> Sec. 1. Knowledge and learning generally diffused throughout a community, being essential to the preservation of a free government, it shall be the duty of the General Assembly to encourage, by all suitable means, moral, intellectual, scientific, and agricultural improvement; and to provide by law for a general and uniform system of Common Schools, wherein tuition shall be without charge, and equally open to all.

Ultimately the delegates completed their work on February 10, 1851. After ratification by the voters, the Constitution took effect November 1, 1851.

C. *Application of Section 1 to the School Activity Fee*

Despite delegate Bryant's comments that the committee did not intend to insert anything that would have the effect of preventing or postponing "the establishment of *free* schools" (emphasis added), the text of the provision itself was far short of such a declaration. Rather than completely subsidizing education, which would fall within the meaning of a "free school" system, the framers pursued a more modest, and perhaps less controversial, route: a uniform statewide system of public schools that would be supported by taxation. Indeed the term "common school" was widely understood to mean "public school." In fact, "[t]he original common schools in America were not 'free,' since parents had to pay tuition in the form of 'rate bills.'" The rate bill was a fee charged to parents for sending their children to public school. The rate bill was abolished in Indiana in 1852, shortly after the 1851 constitution was ratified.

We observe that other than arguments concerning the funding of public schools there is nothing in the *Journal [of the Constitution,* a history] or [Record of the] *Debates* of the second constitutional convention concerning what the framers meant by the use of the term "tuition." However this is not surprising in that the historical record suggests that the term was neither technical nor particularly controversial. For example a period dictionary defines tuition as:

1. Guardianship; superintending care over a young person; the particular watch and care of a tutor or guardian over his pupil or ward.

2. *More especially,* instruction; the act or business of teaching the various branches of learning. We place our children under the preceptors of academies for *tuition.* [*This is now the common acceptation of the word.*]

3. The money paid for instruction. In our colleges, the *tuition* is from thirty to forty dollars a year. [emphasis in original]

The common understanding of the term "tuition" by those who framed the constitution as well as those who ratified it would have been consistent with the forgoing definition.

Arguing that tuition contemplates only fees for instruction, EVSC insists that "[e]xpenses incidental to credited, academic instruction such as heat, light, facility maintenance, non-instructional salaries/stipend do not fall within the commonly understood definition of 'tuition.'" EVSC suggests that other than legislatively-mandated curriculum requirements all other educationally related expenses may be assessed against students and their parents.

We agree in principle with EVSC's understanding of tuition as the term is used in Article 8, Section 1. . . . However the analysis does not end there. It is certainly the case that at the time the 1851 constitution was adopted the expenses associated with a public education were modest by today's standards, consisting primarily of school buildings—usually one-room schoolhouses—their maintenance, desks, textbooks, supplies, and teacher salaries. By the express terms of the Constitution, "tuition shall be without charge." Obviously tuition was to be subsidized through public funding sources. But to suppose that all remaining educational expense would be placed on the shoulders of parents whose children were attending public schools loses sight of the entire free school movement debate—a central and key element of which was that public schools would be operated largely at public expense. Indeed within three years of the Constitution's ratification this court noted that "the evils of the old system which were intended to be avoided by the new constitution—[were] inequality in education, inequality of taxation, lack of uniformity in schools, and a shrinking from legislative responsibilities. . . ."

It is of course true that what constitutes a public education has dramatically expanded over these several decades. We doubt for example that the framers could have had in their contemplation such cost items as computer labs, athletic departments, and media specialists. But it is equally true that determining the components of a public education is left within the authority of the legislative branch of government. Article 8, Section 1 imperatively places upon the legislature, "by all suitable means . . . to provide, by law, for a general and uniform system of Common Schools." But this imperative leaves to that branch considerable discretion in determining what will and what will not come within the meaning of a public education system. "The duty rests on the legislature to adopt the best [school] system that can be framed; but they, and not the courts, are to judge what is the best system. There is this limitation on the legislative power: the system must be 'a general and uniform one,' and tuition must be free and open to all; but the extent of this limitation is this, and nothing more."

Consistent with its constitutional mandate, the Indiana General Assembly has enacted a body of law directed at providing a general and uniform system of public schools. It is detailed, comprehensive, and includes among other things provisions for revenue and funding sources, curriculum requirements, and an assortment of special programs and projects. In addition, the legislature has delegated to the State Board of Education the authority to adopt rules concerning several matters, including "the distribution of funds and revenues appropriated for the support of schools in the state" and has authorized the State Board to "[e]stablish the educational goals of the state, developing standards and objectives for local school corporations." Under this grant of authority the State Board of Education has promulgated numerous rules outlining those components of education in Indiana that are a part of "public" education. They too are detailed and comprehensive.

Where the legislature—or through delegation of its authority the State Board—has identified programs, activities, projects, services or curricula that it either mandates or permits school corporations to undertake, the legislature has made a policy decision regarding exactly what qualifies as a part of a uniform system of public education commanded by Article 8, Section 1 and thus what qualifies for funding at public expense. And of course the legislature has the authority to place appropriate conditions or limitations on any such funding. However, absent specific statutory authority, fees or charges for what are otherwise public education cost items cannot be levied directly or indirectly against students or their parents. Only programs, activities, projects, services or curricula that are outside of or expand upon those identified by the legislature—what we understand to be "extracurricular"—may be considered as not a part of a publicly-funded education. And thus a reasonable fee may be assessed, but only against those students who participate in or take advantage of them.

In this case the $20 fee that EVSC imposes on all students is deposited into its general fund and is used to offset the costs of such things as: a coordinator of student services, nurses, media specialists, alternative education, elementary school counselors, a drama program, a music program, speech and debate programs, academic academies, athletic programs, and a police liaison program. But either the legislature or the State Board has already determined that all such items are part and parcel of a public school education and by extension qualify for public funding. For example public schools are required to provide student assistance services and to employ a qualified coordinator, provide health services and employ at least one registered nurse, and have a media program and employ a licensed media specialist. A school corporation is authorized to establish an alternative education program. Elementary schools must have a school counselor for every six hundred students enrolled in grades one through six in the school corporation. Public schools are encouraged to develop comprehensive plans to improve arts education, which includes programs in drama and music and are permitted to offer speech and debate as a part their language arts area of study. As for the "academic academies" the record shows these are after-school enrichment programs most of which "deal with the same type of information that's worked in through the school day," and we have already recognized that "athletics are an integral part of this constitutionally-mandated process of education." . . .

In essence, the very programs, services, and activities for which EVSC charges a fee already are a part of a publicly-funded education in the state of Indiana. However, this conclusion does not preclude EVSC from offering programs, services or activities that are outside of or expand upon those deemed by the legislature or State Board as part of a public education. The Indiana Constitution does not prohibit EVSC from charging individual students for their participation in such extracurriculars or for their consumption of such services. However the mandatory fee EVSC imposed generally on all students, whether the student avails herself of a service or participates in a program or activity or not, becomes a charge for attending a public school and obtaining a public education. Such a charge contravenes the "Common Schools" mandate as the term is used in Article 8, Section 1 and is therefore unconstitutional.

Conclusion

We reverse the judgment of the trial court and remand this cause for further proceedings.

NOTES

1.   On remand, an intermediate appellate court granted the parents' request for attorney fees as the prevailing party. *Nagy v. Evansville–Vanderburgh School Corp.*, 870 N.E.2d 12 [221 Educ. L. Rep. 845] (Ind. Ct. App. 2007), *transfer denied*, 891 N.E.2d 35 (Ind. 2008).

2.   The court suggested that school boards can charge fees for interscholastic and other activities. Is it fair to charge fees for these activities?

[CASE NO. 90]   ELIGIBILITY REQUIREMENT FOR INTERSCHOLASTIC ATHLETICS

ALBACH v. ODLE

United States Court of Appeals, Tenth Circuit, 1976.
531 F.2d 983.

■ Per Curiam.

This appeal seeks to test the application of transfer rules adopted by the New Mexico Activities Association. The rules automatically bar from interscholastic high school athletic competition for one year any student who transfers from his home district to a boarding school or from a boarding school to his home district. . . .

The trial court dismissed the complaint on various grounds, one of which was that it failed to raise a substantial federal question. We affirm.

Controlling precedent is found in *Oklahoma High School Athletic Ass'n v. Bray*, where this court stated. . . .

The court held that if Bray had not voluntarily dismissed the action, the trial court would have been compelled to dismiss for lack of a substantial federal question. Appellant's allegations are virtually identical with those noted above.

Appellant cites numerous cases in support of the contention that high school athletic regulations must survive constitutional scrutiny. The cases are distinguished by the fact that, in the context of athletic regulations, clearly defined constitutional principles are at issue. The supervision and regulation of high school athletic programs remain within the discretion of appropriate state boards, and are not within federal cognizance under 42 U.S.C.[A.] § 1983 unless the regulations deny an athlete a constitutionally protected right or classify him or her on a suspect basis.

Appellant also argues that *Goss v. Lopez* somehow negates our decision in *Bray*. We disagree. *Goss* recognizes a student's entitlement to a public education as a property interest which is constitutionally protected. A ten-day suspension from school without a hearing was found to violate a student's right to due process under the Fourteenth Amendment. But it is necessary to note that in framing the property interest the Court in *Goss* speaks in terms of the "educational process." The educational process is a broad and comprehensive concept with a variable and indefinite meaning. It is not limited to classroom attendance but includes innumerable separate components, such as participation in athletic activity and membership in school clubs and social groups, which combine to provide an atmosphere of intellectual and moral advancement. We do not read *Goss* to establish a property interest subject to constitutional protection in each of these separate components.

Affirmed.

NOTE

Are eligibility rules for interscholastic athletics too restrictive?

[CASE NO. 91] CONSTITUTIONALITY OF ELIGIBILITY REQUIREMENT FOR INTERSCHOLASTIC ATHLETICS—PARENT RIGHTS

KITE v. MARSHALL

United States Court of Appeals, Fifth Circuit, 1981.
661 F.2d 1027 [1 Educ. L. Rep. 44].

■ POLITZ, CIRCUIT JUDGE:

These consolidated actions challenge the validity of Section 21 of Article VIII of the Constitution and Contest Rules of the University Interscholastic League (UIL) of Texas. The challenged section suspends for one year the varsity athletics eligibility of any high school student who attends certain training camps. The district court enjoined the enforcement of section 21 and subsequently declared the rule unconstitutional as applied. We reverse.

UIL is a voluntary, non-profit association of public schools below collegiate rank in the State of Texas.... Its stated objective is "to foster among the public schools of Texas interschool competitions as an aid in the preparation for citizenship." In pursuit of this goal, UIL promulgates rules and regulations governing various aspects of competition in speech, journalism, literary and academic contests, drama, music and athletics. Although a private organization, UIL's functioning constitutes state action subject to the limitations of the fourteenth amendment to the Constitution. We must determine whether section 21 violates either the due process or equal protection clause of that amendment.

The district court found section 21 to be constitutionally infirm because it infringed protected parental authority in the child-rearing arena. Appellees exhort us to affirm the trial court's conclusions, principally relying on the "family choice doctrine" which has its genesis in *Prince v. Massachusetts*, *Pierce v. Society of Sisters*, and *Meyer v. Nebraska*. We cannot accept the invitation.

The *Meyer* and *Pierce* decisions are based on the premise that the state has no power to "standardize its children," or to "foster a homogeneous people," by foreclosing the opportunity of individuals "to heed the music of different drummers." ...

Appellees cite as controlling precedent a line of Supreme Court decisions which purportedly recognize the existence of a "private realm of family life which the state cannot enter," absent compelling reasons. Uncertainty abounds, not only as to the constitutional spring from which this family privacy right flows, but also as to its definition and character.

Recent decisions by the Supreme Court declaring that parents have no constitutional right to educate their children in private segregated academies, *Runyon v. McCrary*, or to demand approval before the administration of corporal punishment in school, *Ingraham v. Wright*, ... clearly signal that parental authority falls short of being constitutionally absolute. Confronted with these situations which, at first blush, appear to rest at the heart of parental decision making, the Supreme Court refrained from clothing parental judgment with a constitutional mantle.

The instant case presents a similar inquiry. Reduced to essentials, the legal questions posed are: (1) whether parents possess a fundamental right to send their children to summer athletic camps; and (2) whether the children have a constitutional right to attend such activities. As is frequently the case, in the very postulation of the questions the answer lies. A negative response to both questions is mandated. This case implicates no fundamental constitutional right.

The determination that no fundamental right to participate in summer athletic camp exists establishes the level of scrutiny to which we must subject section 21. The regulation will pass constitutional muster if it is found to have a rational basis.

Due Process

The UIL contends that its rules are designed to make competition among its 1,142 member schools as fair and equitable as possible. The UIL program, including the athletics component, is only a part of the overall educational process. Several reasons are advanced in support of section 21, including the need to control over-zealous coaches, parents and communities, the achieving of a competitive balance between those who can afford to attend summer camp and those who cannot, the avoidance of various excessive pressures on students, and the abrogation of the use of camps as recruiting mechanisms.

It cannot be argued seriously that section 21 is wholly arbitrary and totally without value in the promotion of a legitimate state objective. We do not evaluate the ultimate wisdom, *vel non,* of section 21, or the sagacity of its methodology. The school authorities have concluded that section 21 serves the purpose of making interscholastic athletics fairer and more competitive. We are not prepared to say that section 21 bears no meaningful relationship to the achievement of that ideal. The due process clause of the fourteenth amendment has not been offended.

Equal Protection

Traditionally, the equal protection analysis has been performed against the backdrop of the standards of strict scrutiny and minimum rationality. To withstand strict scrutiny, a statute must necessarily relate to a compelling state interest. The rational basis test requires only that the legislation or regulation under challenge rationally promote a legitimate governmental objective.

A state action viewed under the rational basis banner is presumed to be valid. In such a situation, "the burden is not upon the state to establish the rationality of its restriction, but is upon the challenger to show that the restriction is wholly arbitrary." Accordingly, only when a demonstration is made that the classification contained in the regulation is wholly arbitrary or does not teleologically relate to a permissible governmental objective is the equal protection clause violated. When "the classification created by the regulatory scheme neither trammels fundamental rights or interests nor burdens an inherently suspect class, equal protection analysis requires that the classification be rationally related to a legitimate state interest."

In view of the Supreme Court's prevailing opinions ... we believe that the minimum rationality test provides the guide for our equal protection evaluation.

Admittedly section 21 operates to treat student-athletes who attend summer athletic camps differently from those students who do not. The former lose eligibility in all varsity sports for the next year. But the categorization is not premised on impermissible, suspect grounds. Nor does the classification impinge upon the exercise of fundamental rights. The rule seeks to achieve a balance in interscholastic athletics. It is not unconstitutional.

The judgment of the district court, in these consolidated cases, is reversed.

NOTE

Suppose the parents sent their son to a summer drama school. Could school officials have enforced a ban on his trying out for the school play?

[CASE NO. 92]   STATE POWER TO SET ACADEMIC REQUIREMENTS FOR EXTRACURRICULAR ACTIVITIES

SPRING BRANCH I.S.D. v. STAMOS

Supreme Court of Texas, 1985.
695 S.W.2d 556 [27 Educ. L. Rep. 605].

■ RAY, JUSTICE.

This is a direct appeal brought by the Attorney General, representing the Texas Education Agency, and others, seeking immediate appellate review of an order of the trial court which held unconstitutional, and enjoined enforcement of, a provision of the Texas Education Code.... We hold that the statutory provision is not unconstitutional and reverse the judgment of the trial court.

Chris Stamos and others brought this suit on behalf of Nicky Stamos and others, seeking a permanent injunction against enforcement of the Texas "no pass, no play" rule by the Spring Branch and Alief Independent School Districts. The Texas Education Agency and the University Inter-scholastic League intervened. The district court issued a temporary re-straining order and later, after a hearing, a temporary injunction enjoining all parties from enforcing the rule. This court issued an order staying the district court's order and setting the cause for expedited review.

THE "NO PASS, NO PLAY" RULE

The Second Called Session of the 68th Legislature adopted a package of educational reforms known as "H.B. 72." A major provision of these educational reforms was the so-called "no pass, no play" rule, which generally requires that students maintain a "70" average in all classes to be eligible for participation in extracurricular activities. The rule is incorpo-rated in section 21.920 of the Texas Education Code and provides as follows:

§ 21.920.   Extracurricular Activities

(a) The State Board of Education by rule shall limit participation in and practice for extracurricular activities during the school day and the school week. The rules shall, to the extent possible, preserve the school day for academic activities without interruption for extracurric-ular activities. In scheduling those activities and practices, a district must comply with the rules of the board.

(b) A student, other than a mentally retarded student, enrolled in a school district in this state shall be suspended from participation in any extracurricular activity sponsored or sanctioned by the school district during the grade reporting period after a grade reporting period in which the student received a grade lower than the equivalent of 70 on a scale of 100 in any academic class. The campus principal may remove this suspension if the class is an identified honors or advanced class. A student may not be suspended under this subsection during the period in which school is recessed for the summer or during the initial grade reporting period of a regular school term on the basis of grades received in the final grade reporting period of the preceding regular school term.

. . .

ISSUES RAISED

The sole issue before this court is the constitutionality of the no pass, no play rule. The district court held the rule unconstitutional on the grounds that it violated equal protection and due process guarantees. The burden is on the party attacking the constitutionality of an act of the legislature. There is a presumption in favor of the constitutionality of an act of the legislature.

This court has long recognized the important role education plays in the maintenance of our democratic society. Article VII of the Texas Constitution "discloses a well-considered purpose on the part of those who framed it to bring about the establishment and maintenance of a comprehensive system of public education, consisting of a general public free school system and a system of higher education." Section 1 of article VII of the Constitution establishes a mandatory duty upon the legislature to make suitable provision for the support and maintenance of public free schools. The Constitution leaves to the legislature alone the determination of which methods, restrictions, and regulations are necessary and appropriate to carry out this duty, so long as that determination is not so arbitrary as to violate the constitutional rights of Texas' citizens.

Equal Protection

Stamos challenges the constitutionality of the "no pass, no play" rule on the ground that it violates the equal protection clause of the Texas Constitution. The first determination this court must make in the context of equal protection analysis is the appropriate standard of review. When the classification created by a state regulatory scheme neither infringes upon fundamental rights or interests nor burdens an inherently suspect class, equal protection analysis requires that the classification be rationally related to a legitimate state interest. Therefore, we must first determine whether the rule burdens an inherently suspect class or infringes upon fundamental rights or interests.

The no pass, no play rule classifies students based upon their achievement levels in their academic courses. We hold that those students who fail to maintain a minimum level of proficiency in all of their courses do not constitute the type of discrete, insular minority necessary to constitute a "suspect" class. Thus, the rule does not burden an inherently "suspect" class. . . .

Stamos also argues that the rule is subject to strict scrutiny under equal protection analysis because it impinges upon a fundamental right, i.e., the right to participate in extracurricular activities. We note that the overwhelming majority of jurisdictions have held that a student's right to participation in extracurricular activities does *not* constitute a fundamental right.

Stamos cites the case of *Bell v. Lone Oak Independent School District* for the proposition that students have a fundamental right to participate in extracurricular activities. In *Bell,* a school regulation prohibited married students from participating in extracurricular activities. Because the regulation impinged upon the fundamental right of marriage, the court of appeals held the regulation subject to strict scrutiny and struck it down because the school district had shown no compelling interest to support its enforcement. The presence of a fundamental right (marriage) distinguishes *Bell* from the present cause.

Fundamental rights have their genesis in the express and implied protections of personal liberty recognized in federal and state constitutions. A student's "right" to participate in extracurricular activities does not rise to the same level as the right to free speech or free exercise of religion, both of which have long been recognized as fundamental rights under our state and federal constitutions. We adopt the majority rule and hold that a student's right to participate in extracurricular activities *per se* does *not* rise to the level of a fundamental right under our constitution.

Because the no pass, no play rule neither infringes upon fundamental rights nor burdens an inherently suspect class, we hold that it is *not* subject to "strict" or heightened equal protection scrutiny....

The no pass, no play rule distinguishes students based upon whether they maintain a satisfactory minimum level of performance in each of their classes. Students who fail to maintain a minimum proficiency in all of their classes are ineligible for participation in school-sponsored extracurricular activities for the following six-week period, with no carry over from one school year to the next. The rule provides a strong incentive for students wishing to participate in extracurricular activities to maintain minimum levels of performance in all of their classes. In view of the rule's objective to promote improved classroom performance by students, we find the rule rationally related to the legitimate state interest in providing a quality education to Texas' public school students....

The distinctions recognized in the rule for mentally retarded students and students enrolled in honors or advanced courses likewise do not render the rule violative of the equal protection guarantees of the Texas Constitution. While the statute itself does not deprive students of their right to equal protection of the law, we recognize that the discretion given to school principals in the rule's provision dealing with honors or advanced courses may well give rise to arbitrary or discriminatory application violative of equal protection principles. We are faced with no allegations of discriminatory application of the rule's honors exception in the present case.

Procedural Due Process

We begin our analysis of the due process arguments in this cause by recognizing that the strictures of due process apply only to the threatened deprivation of liberty and property interests deserving the protection of the federal and state constitutions. The federal courts have made it clear that the federal constitution's due process guarantees do not protect a student's interest in participating in extracurricular activities. We must, then, examine our state constitution to determine whether its due process guarantees extend to a student's desire to participate in school-sponsored extracurricular activities.

A property or liberty interest must find its origin in some aspect of state law. Nothing in either our state constitution or statutes entitles students to an absolute right to participation in extracurricular activities. We are in agreement, therefore, with the overwhelming majority of jurisdictions that students do not possess a constitutionally protected interest in their participation in extracurricular activities. Therefore, the strictures of procedural due process do *not* apply to the determination by a campus principal, pursuant to section 21.920(b) of the Texas Education Code, as to whether a student who fails an identified honors or advanced course shall be permitted to participate in extracurricular activities.

Substantive Due Process

Stamos cites *Spann v. City of Dallas* to support his argument that the rule violates principles of fundamental fairness and notions of substantive due process by giving school principals discretion to determine whether students who fail honors or advanced courses may participate in extracurricular activities. In *Spann,* this court declared void a city ordinance that required persons seeking to construct commercial buildings within residential areas to first obtain the consent of both neighboring residents and the city building inspector. There, we found that the ordinance provided no standards for builders or building inspectors with regard to the proper design for such buildings. By leaving the approval for such buildings "subject to the arbitrary discretion of the inspector," the ordinance violated the would-be builders' property right to use their property as they saw fit. This court emphasized that the ordinance in *Spann* infringed upon well-recognized property rights by permitting wholly arbitrary limitations upon the uses which owners could make of their property.

In the present case, appellees liken the school principals' unfettered discretion in determining both which classes shall constitute "advanced" or "honors" courses and whether students failing such classes may participate in extracurricular activities to the building inspectors' unfettered discretion over approving commercial building plans. *Spann* is distinguishable for the obvious reason that a recognized property interest was affected by the Dallas ordinance. As stated previously, students have no constitutionally protected interest in participation in extracurricular activities. Because no constitutionally protected interest is implicated by this delegation of authority to school principals, no violation of due process, substantive or procedural, results therefrom.

We do not agree with Stamos' argument that a school principal's exercise of discretion pursuant to the "honors" exception to the rule is shielded from all review. Arbitrary, capricious, or discriminatory exercise of a school principal's discretion pursuant to subsection 21.920(b) of the Texas

Education Code may well give rise to claims based upon equal protection grounds. Accreditation audits of schools and school districts may also afford relief against improper utilization of the "honors" exception. We also note there are no findings of fact before us that any of the student-plaintiffs received failing grades in honors or advanced courses. . . .

Accordingly, we reverse the district court's judgment with regard to the constitutionality of section 21.920 of the Texas Education Code and dissolve the temporary injunction ordered by the district court.

NOTES

1.   West Virginia's highest court upheld a similar rule that was promulgated under the general supervisory powers of the state board of education. *Bailey v. Truby*, 321 S.E.2d 302 [20 Educ. L. Rep. 980] (W. Va.1984). The court rejected an argument that the rule infringed on the powers of county boards since they could not diminish the state board's constitutional power to pursue academic excellence. The court responded that county boards could set higher standards than their state counterpart.

2.   Parents and others challenged a local board policy that required a 2.0 grade point average in five of six classes in order for student-athletes to remain eligible to participate in extracurricular activities. An appellate court affirmed that the policy was reasonably designed to minimize outside activities which distract from academic matters while offering incentive so that student-athletes could earn grades that would help them to retain eligibility. *Thompson v. Fayette County Pub. Schools*, 786 S.W.2d 879 [59 Educ. L. Rep. 1197] (Ky. Ct. App.1990).

CHAPTER 13

STUDENT RIGHTS: DUE PROCESS, DISCIPLINE, AND SEXUAL HARASSMENT

INTRODUCTION

The Supreme Court's 1969 ruling in *Tinker v. Des Moines Independent Community School District* (*Tinker*)[1] was a watershed moment in the important area of student rights. *Tinker* stands out because it was the first time that the Justices recognized the First Amendment free speech rights of public school students. Six years later, in *Goss v. Lopez*,[2] the Justices further enhanced student rights by setting the parameters for dealing with disciplinary suspensions. Shortly thereafter, though, the Court refused to prohibit corporal punishment in *Ingraham v. Wright*.[3] The Court next enunciated rules for student searches in *New Jersey v. T.L.O.*,[4] later clarifying them as to strip searches in *Safford Unified School District No. 1 v. Redding*.[5] Although these cases are addressed in Chapter 14, it is worth noting that the Court limited student expressive activity in *Bethel School District No. 403 v. Fraser*,[6] *Hazelwood School District v. Kuhlmeier*,[7] and eventually *Morse v. Frederick*.[8]

The Justices also took the important step of permitting litigation aimed at eradicating sexual harassment by teachers in schools starting with *Franklin v. Gwinnett County Public Schools*.[9] The Supreme Court next clarified the circumstances under which school boards can be liable for

---

1. 393 U.S. 503, 89 S.Ct. 733, 21 L.Ed.2d 731 (1969). [Case No. 102]

2. 419 U.S. 565, 95 S.Ct. 729, 42 L.Ed.2d 725 (1975). [Case No. 94]

3. 430 U.S. 651, 97 S.Ct. 1401, 51 L.Ed.2d 711 (1977). [Case No. 95]

4. 469 U.S. 325, 105 S.Ct. 733, 83 L.Ed.2d 720 [21 Educ. L. Rep. 1122] (1985). [Case No. 96]

5. 557 U.S. 364, 129 S.Ct. 2633, 174 L.Ed.2d 354 [245 Educ. L. Rep. 626] (2009). [Case No. 97]

6. 478 U.S. 675, 106 S.Ct. 3159, 92 L.Ed.2d 549 [32 Educ. L. Rep. 1243] (1986). [Case No. 104]

7. 484 U.S. 260, 108 S.Ct. 562, 98 L.Ed.2d 592 [43 Educ. L. Rep. 515] (1988). [Case No. 105]

8. 551 U.S. 393, 127 S.Ct. 2618, 168 L.Ed.2d 290 [220 Educ. L. Rep. 50] (2007). [Case No. 106]

9. 503 U.S. 60, 112 S.Ct. 1028, 117 L.Ed.2d 208 [72 Educ. L. Rep. 32] (1992), *on remand*, 969 F.2d 1022 [76 Educ. L. Rep. 396] (11th Cir. 1992). [Case No. 99]

teacher sexual harassment in *Gebser v. Lago Vista Independent School District*,[10] and addressed peer-to-peer sexual harassment in *Davis v. Monroe County Board of Education*.[11] Finally, the Court upheld drug testing of students in *Vernonia School District 47J v. Acton*[12] and *Board of Education of Independent School District No. 92 of Pottawatomie v. Earls*.[13] In light of the significant legal questions that these and other important topics present, this chapter focuses on student rights in the areas of due process, discipline, and sexual harassment.

STUDENT RIGHTS AND SCHOOL RULES

IN GENERAL

Courts grant school officials broad discretion to ensure safe and orderly learning environments. School boards have the authority to adopt reasonable policies and procedures regulating student conduct. Since courts can, as noted in Chapter 1, only respond to real cases or controversies, rather than act in advisory capacities, a vast amount of litigation highlights the general proposition that even though the judiciary generally defers to educators, whether rules are enforceable depends on the fact-specific analysis of case law.

Since school board policies on student discipline and/or codes of conduct are presumptively valid, the burden of showing that they are unreasonable rests on students and their parents. The closer that rules encroach on the constitutional rights of students, the greater the need for justification by school officials since, even in light of the broad discretion that educators enjoy, pupils do not shed their constitutional rights at the schoolhouse gate.

If school rules involving discipline and safety infringe on the fundamental rights of students such as freedom from unreasonable searches, the burden of proof shifts to educators to demonstrate that rules are justified by a compelling need. Under these circumstances, courts have invalidated rules that are not rationally related to legitimate educational objectives, are too vague as to what they forbid, or are over-broad insofar as they cover constitutionally protected activities along with those that may be restricted.[14] As the severity of punishments increases, courts take closer looks at rules and their procedures.

---

10.   524 U.S. 274, 118 S.Ct. 1989, 141 L.Ed.2d 277 [125 Educ. L. Rep. 1055] (1998). [Case No. 100]

11.   526 U.S. 629, 119 S.Ct. 1661, 143 L.Ed.2d 839 [134 Educ. L. Rep. 477] (1999), *on remand*, 206 F.3d 1377 [143 Educ. L. Rep. 724] (11th Cir. 2000). [Case No. 101]

12.   515 U.S. 646, 115 S.Ct. 2386, 132 L.Ed.2d 564 [101 Educ. L. Rep. 37] (1995), *on remand*, 66 F.3d 217 [103 Educ. L. Rep. 608] (9th Cir. 1995).

13.   536 U.S. 822, 122 S.Ct. 2559, 153 L.Ed.2d 735 [166 Educ. L. Rep. 79] (2002), *on remand*, 300 F.3d 1222 [168 Educ. L. Rep. 581] (10th Cir. 2002). [Case No. 98]

14.   *See, e.g., Saxe v. State College Area School Dist.*, 240 F.3d 200 [151 Educ. L. Rep. 86] (3d Cir. 2001) (invalidating an anti-harassment policy as over-broad).

Whether all rules are written is immaterial if offenses such as cheating are punishable under general norms of school behavior. Since courts concede that educators cannot develop written rules for all possible student infractions, they typically defer to the authority of educators as long as they impose discipline that meets the requirements of due process.

When students know,[15] or reasonably ought to know, school rules and punishments are appropriate to their offenses,[16] regardless of whether misbehavior occurs in schools or away from schools, courts are unlikely to intervene on their behalf as long as educators treat similarly situated individuals similarly and provide them with the requisite level of due process.[17] While students have a right to know what conduct is prohibited, school rules need not meet the stringent criteria that courts apply in criminal cases.[18] Additionally, when school officials question students about their misbehavior in schools, courts agree that they are not entitled to receive *Miranda*[19] warnings from educators,[20] school resource officers,[21] or law enforcement officers who are in schools regularly and are assigned duties beyond those of ordinary officers[22] about their Fifth Amendment right against self-incrimination.[23]

When distinguishing between educators and police officials, the Supreme Court of Pennsylvania observed that insofar as school police officers who interrogated a juvenile about the break-in and vandalism of a classroom were law enforcement officers, they violated his rights by not providing him with a *Miranda* warning.[24] Subsequently, an appellate court in Georgia affirmed that where a police officer participated in the questioning of a student as part of a robbery investigation, and the school's assistant principal acted as an agent of the police, the plaintiff was entitled to a *Miranda* warning because he was in custody when he was interviewed about his actions.[25]

In *J.D.B. v. North Carolina (J.D.B.)*,[26] the Supreme Court entered the fray over the *Miranda* rights of students who are questioned by police

---

15. *Martinez v. School Dist. No. 60*, 852 P.2d 1275 [83 Educ. L. Rep. 454] (Colo. Ct. App. 1992).

16. *Kolesnick By and Through Shaw v. Omaha Pub. School Dist.*, 558 N.W.2d 807 [115 Educ. L. Rep. 1054] (Neb. 1997).

17. *Goss v. Lopez*, 419 U.S. 565, 95 S.Ct. 729, 42 L.Ed.2d 725 (1975). [Case No. 94]

18. *Wiemerslage Through Wiemerslage v. Maine Twp. High School Dist. 207*, 29 F.3d 1149 [93 Educ. L. Rep. 64] (7th Cir.1994).

19. *See Miranda v. Arizona*, 384 U.S. 436, 86 S.Ct. 1602, 16 L.Ed.2d 694 (1966) (requiring police to advise detainees of their right against self-incrimination).

20. *State v. Schloegel*, 769 N.W.2d 130 [246 Educ. L. Rep. 1003] (Wis. Ct. App. 2009); *In re Tateana R.*, 883 N.Y.S.2d 476 [247 Educ. L. Rep. 416] (N.Y. App. Div. 2009).

21. *See, e.g., State v. J.H.*, 898 So.2d 240 [197 Educ. L. Rep. 941] (Fla. Dist. Ct. App. 2005).

22. *R.D.S. v. State*, 245 S.W.3d 356 [230 Educ. L. Rep. 834] (Tenn. 2008).

23. *See, e.g., J.D. v. Commonwealth*, 591 S.E.2d 721 [184 Educ. L. Rep. 1049] (Va. Ct. App. 2004); *Commonwealth v. Ira I.*, 791 N.E.2d 894 [178 Educ. L. Rep. 491] (Mass.2003); *Bills by Bills v. Homer Consol. School Dist. No. 33–C*, 959 F.Supp. 507 [117 Educ. L. Rep. 1064] (N.D. Ill.1997); *Pollnow v. Glennon*, 757 F.2d 496 [23 Educ. L. Rep. 1219] (2d Cir. 1985).

24. *In re R.H.*, 791 A.2d 331 [162 Educ. L. Rep. 453] (Pa. 2002).

25. *In re T.A.G.*, 663 S.E.2d 392 [234 Educ. L. Rep. 423] (Ga. Ct. App. 2008).

26. ___ U.S. ___, 131 S.Ct. 2394, 180 L.Ed.2d 310 (2011).

officials. The Court ruled that when students who are in custodial school settings are questioned by the police over their possible involvement in criminal activity, then the police must take their ages into consideration when evaluating whether to provide them with *Miranda* warnings. A closely divided Court invalidated the adjudication of delinquency involving a middle school student who was questioned about a series of home break-ins, remanding for further consideration as to whether he was in police custody when he was questioned.

Shortly thereafter, the Supreme Court of Alaska relied in part on *J.D.B* in invalidating a state trooper's interrogation of a fifteen-year-old student.[27] The court decided that the student was in police custody for the purposes of *Miranda* when he was questioned about a series of crimes, including murder, even though the interrogations were not in a school building.

OUT-OF-SCHOOL CONDUCT

The authority of school officials to discipline students for their off-campus misconduct has led to a substantial amount of litigation with most courts deferring to educators as long as rules satisfy due process.[28] Clearly, educators can regulate student conduct that violates school rules even if it occurs at extracurricular activities such as football games.[29] It is, of course, more difficult to enforce conduct rules outside of school due to potential conflicts with the rights of parents and attenuated connections between student behavior and the educational process. As discussed in Chapter 14 under the heading of "Student Free Speech and Technology," courts reach mixed results in this emerging area.

The oldest reported case involving student discipline for off-premises behavior occurred in 1859 when a high school student, in the presence of friends, insulted his teacher as he walked by, calling him by the name "old Jack Seaver." After the teacher whipped the student in school the following day, he unsuccessfully challenged the educator's ability to do so. The Supreme Court of Vermont upheld the imposition of discipline since the student's behavior had ". . . a direct and immediate tendency to injure the school and bring the master's authority into contempt."[30]

Another older case, from Connecticut's highest court, explained the true test of educators' ability to punish students for infractions that occur away from campus as ". . . not the time or place of the offense, but its effect upon the morale and efficiency of the school."[31] The court upheld a male's being subjected to corporal punishment for annoying young female students who were on their way home from school. More than fifty years later, the Supreme Court of Wyoming upheld the punishment of a student

---

27. *Kalmakoff v. State*, 257 P.3d 108 [269 Educ. L. Rep. 881] (Alaska 2011).

28. *But see Packer v. Board of Educ. of Thomaston*, 717 A.2d 117 [129 Educ. L. Rep. 400] (Conn. 1998) (affirming the reinstatement of a student who was expelled from both school and extracurricular activities for possessing marijuana off of school grounds after hours where the rule was unconstitutionally vague because it did not provide adequate notice).

29. *Fuller ex rel. Fuller v. Decatur Pub. School Bd. of Educ. School Dist. 61*, 251 F.3d 662 [154 Educ. L. Rep. 127] (7th Cir. 2001).

30. *Lander v. Seaver*, 32 Vt. 114, *120 [WESTLAW designation at 1859 WL 5454] (Vt. 1859).

31. *O'Rourke v. Walker*, 128 A. 25, 26 (Conn. 1925).

for harassing a school bus driver who was en route to school with his passengers.[32] In another case, where out-of-school conduct was a continuation of misbehavior that started in school, the highest court in Massachusetts upheld the authority of officials to expel a student for assaulting a peer.[33]

Courts typically uphold rules preventing drug use and/or alcohol consumption, regardless of whether infractions occur on campus, especially by student-athletes, but not exclusively limited to them,[34] on two grounds. First, since taking part in extracurricular activities is a privilege rather than a right,[35] educators can impose higher disciplinary standards on students who participate in these activities than on those who do not take part in such programs. Second, officials can base rules on health and safety concerns. In either case, educators can suspend or dismiss students who violate team or activity rules regardless of whether parents approve of the behavior of their children. For example, the Eighth Circuit affirmed that officials did not violate the rights of two cheerleaders from Missouri who received ten-day out-of-school suspensions for consuming alcohol at the house of a third student before they performed at a school football jamboree.[36] The court held that even though the cheerleading advisor failed to follow board policy in investigating the allegation of the students' misconduct, neither she nor the board violated their rights since they received due process before being suspended.

As noted, rules cannot be too broad such as where one forbade student-athletes from being in cars where beer was being transported.[37] Yet, presence at events where alcohol is being consumed can provide the justification for student-athletes' being declared ineligible[38] as can drinking alcohol at school-sponsored events.[39] Moreover, rules must be applied equally to males and females[40] and when school officials dismiss players from teams, they must rely on sufficient evidence[41] and fair processes.[42]

---

32. *Clements v. Board of Trustees of Sheridan County School Dist. No. 2, in Sheridan County*, 585 P.2d 197 (Wyo. 1978).

33. *Nicholas B. v. School Comm. of Worcester*, 587 N.E.2d 211 [72 Educ. L. Rep. 1006] (Mass. 1992).

34. *See, e.g., Haas v. West Shore School Dist.*, 915 A.2d 1254 [216 Educ. L. Rep. 543] (Pa. Cmwlth. Ct. 2007) (upholding a student's expulsion for drinking alcohol on campus during school hours).

35. *Braesch v. DePasquale*, 265 N.W.2d 842 (Neb. 1978), *cert. denied*, 439 U.S. 1068, 99 S.Ct. 836, 59 L.Ed.2d 34 (1979); *Palmer v. Merluzzi*, 868 F.2d 90 [51 Educ. L. Rep. 1196] (3d Cir. 1989) [Case No. 93]; *Lowery v. Euverard*, 497 F.3d 584 [223 Educ. L. Rep. 575] (6th Cir. 2007), *cert. denied*, 555 U.S. 825, 129 S.Ct. 159, 172 L.Ed.2d 42 (2008); *Mather v. Loveland City School Dist. Bd. of Educ.*, 908 N.E.2d 1039 [245 Educ. L. Rep. 997] (Ohio Ct. App. 2009).

36. *Jennings v. Wentzville R–IV School Dist.*, 397 F.3d 1118 [195 Educ. L. Rep. 461] (8th Cir. 2005).

37. *Bunger v. Iowa High School Athletic Ass'n*, 197 N.W.2d 555 (Iowa 1972).

38. *Clements v. Board of Educ. of Decatur Pub. School Dist. No. 61*, 478 N.E.2d 1209 [25 Educ. L. Rep. 866] (Ill. App. Ct.1985); *Bush v. Dassel–Cokato Bd. of Educ.*, 745 F.Supp. 562 [63 Educ. L. Rep. 145] (D. Minn. 1990).

39. *Katchak v. Glasgow Indep. School Sys.*, 690 F.Supp. 580 [48 Educ. L. Rep. 533] (W.D. Ky. 1988).

40. *Schultzen v. Woodbury Cent. Community School Dist.*, 187 F. Supp.2d 1099 [162 Educ. L. Rep. 766] (N.D. Iowa 2002) (holding that a female student-athlete could not be punished more harshly than males for the same offense of smoking in violation of athletic training rules).

41. *Butler v. Oak Creek–Franklin School Dist.*, 172 F. Supp.2d 1102 [159 Educ. L. Rep. 166] (E.D. Wis. 2001).

42. *Id.*

Students can be punished for off-campus activities that threaten the health or safety of those in school. Courts have upheld sanctions for such off-campus misbehavior as drug sales,[43] possession of tobacco[44] or drugs[45] on school sponsored trips, and aggravated assaults.[46] An appellate court in Illinois upheld a high school football player's being barred from playing after he violated his school's zero tolerance policy by being picked up by the police, in front of a convenience store, at 3:00 A.M. since he displayed obvious signs of intoxication.[47] Also, the Seventh Circuit upheld the expulsions of student spectators in Illinois who took part in a fight at a high school football game.[48]

ZERO TOLERANCE POLICIES

Faced with ongoing difficulties associated with student substance abuse and violence in schools, boards have adopted zero tolerance policies in attempts to remedy, if not eliminate, these problems. When reviewing zero tolerance policies, courts look to ensure that school officials acted with discretion in disciplining students.

Courts have reached mixed results as to students who have had knives in schools. When school officials in Tennessee discovered a hunting knife in the glove compartment of a student's car, but it did not belong to him, the Sixth Circuit ruled that his proposed expulsion for possession of a weapon, pursuant to a zero tolerance policy under which students could have been disciplined for not knowingly possessing weapons, was invalid because it was not rationally related to a legitimate state interest.[49] Similarly, an appellate court in Pennsylvania affirmed that educators exceeded their authority when they sought to expel a seventh-grade student for a year because he found a Swiss Army knife in a school hallway but did not turn it

---

43. *Howard v. Colonial School Dist.*, 621 A.2d 362 [81 Educ. L. Rep. 878] (Del. Super. Ct. 1992), *aff'd without published opinion*, 615 A.2d 531 (Del. 1992).

44. *Ette ex rel. Ette v. Linn–Mar Community School Dist.*, 656 N.W.2d 62 [173 Educ. L. Rep. 662] (Iowa 2002) (sending an eighth-grade student home from a band trip for possessing cigarettes).

45. *Commonwealth v. Considine*, 860 N.E.2d 673 [215 Educ. L. Rep. 1058] (Mass. 2007) (involving non-public school students); *Rhodes v. Guarricino*, 54 F. Supp.2d 186 [137 Educ. L. Rep. 258] (S.D.N.Y. 1999) (involving public school students).

46. *Pollnow v. Glennon*, 594 F.Supp. 220 [20 Educ. L. Rep. 880] (S.D.N.Y.1984), *aff'd*, 757 F.2d 496 [23 Educ. L. Rep. 1219] (2d Cir. 1985).

47. *Jordan ex rel. Edwards v. O'Fallon Twp. High School Dist. No. 203 Bd. of Educ.*, 706 N.E.2d 137 [133 Educ. L. Rep. 214] (Ill. App. Ct. 1999).

48. *Fuller ex rel. Fuller v. Decatur Pub. School Bd. of Educ. School Dist. 61*, 251 F.3d 662 [154 Educ. L. Rep. 127] (7th Cir. 2001).

49. *Seal v. Morgan*, 229 F.3d 567 [148 Educ. L. Rep. 34] (6th Cir. 2000).

in immediately.[50] The court pointed out that the policy ignored the clear legislative intent that zero tolerance policies should not be applied blindly. Conversely, the Fourth Circuit affirmed that educators could suspend a student who had a knife in his locker even though he took it from a suicidal schoolmate.[51] The court was satisfied that officials provided the student with due process before he was suspended.

The Eleventh Circuit affirmed that a school board in Florida's zero tolerance policy as applied to school-related violent crime did not render it liable for constitutional violations when police arrested and strip searched a student who distributed anonymous pamphlets in which the author wondered about what might have happened if he shot the principal, teachers, or other students.[52] The court refused to impose liability on school officials for the actions of the police. In another case from Florida involving a zero tolerance policy, an appellate court refused to intervene on behalf of a student who was suspended for bringing a gun to school.[53] The court dismissed the claim because it lacked jurisdiction pursuant to state law. Previously, the federal trial court in South Dakota upheld a student's being disciplined for violating her school's zero tolerance policy with regard to the use of profanity.[54]

PUNISHMENTS

GENERALLY

Courts realize that educators need to use their discretion when disciplining students who break school rules.[55] If disciplinary policies and procedures satisfy due process, courts usually uphold the actions of educators as long as they are not arbitrary, capricious, or unreasonable. Courts have long taken the sex, age, and size as well as the mental, emotional, and physical conditions of students and the nature of their offenses into consideration when reviewing penalties.[56] In an illustrative case, when a student received a ten-day suspension for using inappropriate and disre-

---

50. *Lyons v. Penn Hills School Dist.*, 723 A.2d 1073 [132 Educ. L. Rep. 490] (Pa. Cmwlth. Ct. 1999). *See also Colvin ex rel. Colvin v. Lowndes County, Miss. School Dist.*, 114 F. Supp.2d 504 [147 Educ. L. Rep. 601] (N.D. Miss. 1999) (overturning the expulsion of a student with a disability for bringing a Swiss Army knife to school but otherwise agreeing that a school board had the authority to enact such a rule).

51. *Ratner v. Loudoun County Pub. Schools*, 16 Fed.Appx. 140 (4th Cir.2001), *cert. denied*, 534 U.S. 1114, 122 S.Ct. 922, 151 L.Ed.2d 886 (2002).

52. *Cuesta v. School Bd. of Miami–Dade County*, 285 F.3d 962 [163 Educ. L. Rep. 101] (11th Cir. 2002).

53. *D.K. ex rel. Kennedy v. District School Bd. Indian River County*, 981 So.2d 667 [233 Educ. L. Rep. 1006] (Fla. Dist. Ct. App. 2008).

54. *Anderson v. Milbank School Dist. 25–4*, 197 F.R.D. 682 (D.S.D. 2000).

55. *Spacek v. Charles*, 928 S.W.2d 88 [112 Educ. L. Rep. 525] (Tex. Ct. App. 1996).

56. *Berry v. Arnold School Dist.*, 137 S.W.2d 256 (Ark.1940); *Holman By and Through Holman v. Wheeler*, 677 P.2d 645 [16 Educ. L. Rep. 658] (Okla.1983), *superseded by statute on other grounds as stated in Leding v. Pittsburg County Dist. Ct.*, 928 P.2d 957 (Okla. Ct. App. 1996).

spectful language to school officials, a federal trial court in Michigan rejected his claim that the educators violated his rights to due process because he missed his graduation ceremony and other senior events.[57] The court reasoned that insofar as the student received all of the process he was due and the punishment was rationally related to his offense, his claim was without merit.

In reviewing disciplinary actions, courts consider whether punishments involve the denial of the right to attend school or privileges such as participation in extracurricular activities. While courts expect educators to provide students with greater due process protections when they seek to deny them the right to attend school, they cannot arbitrarily or capriciously exclude students from extracurricular activities. Even so, school officials can impose higher standards, such as drug testing,[58] as a condition for participation in extracurricular activities.

Courts ordinarily do not review student conduct rules with the same scrutiny as they use in criminal cases. For instance, in *Wood v. Strickland*, involving the attempted expulsion of students in Arkansas for consuming alcoholic beverages at school or school-sponsored activities, the Supreme Court asserted that the federal judiciary is not supposed to "supplant the interpretation of [a] regulation of those officers who adopted it and are entrusted with its enforcement."[59] In *Board of Education of Rogers, Arkansas v. McCluskey*, a brief per curiam judgment upholding the suspensions of students who were intoxicated at school, the Court was of the view that "a school board's interpretation of its rules [may be] so extreme as to be a violation of due process,"[60] a situation that was not present in the case at bar.

In a dispute from Illinois, the Seventh Circuit decided that educators who expelled a student for six weeks for public indecency and possession of pornography when he was photographed in a shower following wrestling practice did not violate his right to substantive due process.[61] The court thought that even though officials exercised what it described as questionable judgment in excluding the student, they did not violate his rights since he received a hearing and the punishment did not rise to the level of conscience shocking.

---

57. *Posthumus v. Board of Educ. of Mona Shores Pub. Schools*, 380 F.Supp.2d 891 [201 Educ. L. Rep. 184] (W.D. Mich. 2005) (also rejecting the student's claim that his speech was entitled to First Amendment protection).

58. *See, e.g., Vernonia School Dist. 47J v. Acton*, 515 U.S. 646, 115 S.Ct. 2386, 132 L.Ed.2d 564 [101 Educ. L. Rep. 37] (1995), *on remand*, 66 F.3d 217 [103 Educ. L. Rep. 608] (9th Cir. 1995); *Board of Educ. of Indep. School Dist. No. 92 of Pottawatomie v. Earls*, 536 U.S. 822, 122 S.Ct. 2559, 153 L.Ed.2d 735 [166 Educ. L. Rep. 79] (2002), *on remand*, 300 F.3d 1222 [168 Educ. L. Rep. 581] (10th Cir. 2002). [Case No. 98]

59. 420 U.S. 308, 325, 95 S.Ct. 992, 43 L.Ed.2d 214 (1975), *reh'g denied*, 421 U.S. 921, 95 S.Ct. 1589, 43 L.Ed.2d 790 (1975), *on remand sub nom. Strickland v. Inlow*, 519 F.2d 744 (8th Cir. 1975). [Case No. 40]

60. 458 U.S. 966, 970, 102 S.Ct. 3469, 73 L.Ed.2d 1273 [5 Educ. L. Rep. 136] (1982), *reh'g denied*, 458 U.S. 1132, 103 S.Ct. 16, 73 L.Ed.2d 1402 (1982), *on remand*, 688 F.2d 596 (8th Cir. 1982).

61. *Tun v. Whitticker*, 398 F.3d 899 [195 Educ. L. Rep. 479] (7th Cir. 2005).

As to the common practice of verbal warnings, in an older case, an appellate court in Illinois reiterated the rule that teachers can verbally chastise students as long as they do not make disparaging remarks that are malicious or wanton.[62] The Third[63] and Eighth[64] Circuits echoed this sentiment in affirming that teachers did not violate the rights of students where their actions failed to rise to the level required to support claims that they violated their substantive due process rights by engaging in conscience shocking behavior.

Among the many cases dealing with punishments, courts refused to overturn such penalties as receiving a grade of zero for the first offense of plagiarism on an assignment;[65] having to clean a toilet with one's bare hands;[66] being expelled for bringing a weapon to school;[67] being named a ward of the court for bringing a knife to school;[68] being dismissed from a marching band for missing a performance;[69] being seated at an isolated desk due to disruptive behavior;[70] being suspended for turning in an assignment which expressed the desire to blow up the school;[71] and being expelled from a private school for being rude to the principal.[72] Courts have upheld adjudications of juvenile delinquency against students for making obscene remarks to a teacher;[73] threatening a teacher;[74] being disruptive at school;[75] bringing a plastic toy gun to school;[76] making a false fire alarm report at school;[77] violating a statute against the possession of a weapon at school by bringing a paintball gun and markers to school;[78] and threatening to blow a counselor's brains out with a shotgun.[79]

---

62. *Wexell v. Scott*, 276 N.E.2d 735 (Ill. App. Ct. 1971).

63. *S.M. ex rel. L.G. v. Lakeland School Dist.*, 33 Fed.Appx. 635 [164 Educ. L. Rep. 83] (3d Cir. 2002).

64. *Costello v. Mitchell Pub. School Dist. 79*, 266 F.3d 916 [157 Educ. L. Rep. 520] (8th Cir. 2001).

65. *Zellman ex rel. M.Z. v. Independent School Dist. No. 2758*, 594 N.W.2d 216 [134 Educ. L. Rep. 1017] (Minn. Ct. App. 1999).

66. *Harris v. Robinson*, 273 F.3d 927 [159 Educ. L. Rep. 533] (10th Cir. 2001).

67. *J.M. v. Webster County Bd. of Educ.*, 534 S.E.2d 50 [147 Educ. L. Rep. 351] (W. Va. 2000).

68. *In re Randy G.*, 110 Cal.Rptr.2d 516 [155 Educ. L. Rep. 1292] (Cal. 2001).

69. *Mazevski v. Horseheads Cent. School Dist.*, 950 F.Supp. 69 [115 Educ. L. Rep. 885] (W.D. N.Y. 1997).

70. *Cole by Cole v. Greenfield–Cent. Community Schools*, 657 F.Supp. 56 [39 Educ. L. Rep. 76] (S.D. Ind. 1986).

71. *Cuff ex rel. B.C. v. Valley Cent. School Dist.*, 714 F.Supp.2d 462 [260 Educ. L. Rep. 730] (S.D.N.Y. 2010).

72. *Allen v. Harlem Int'l Community School*, 862 N.Y.S.2d 696 [235 Educ. L. Rep. 541] (N.Y. App. Term 2008).

73. *In Interest of D.A.D.*, 481 S.E.2d 262 [116 Educ. L. Rep. 449] (Ga. Ct. App. 1997).

74. *In re J.H.*, 797 A.2d 260 [165 Educ. L. Rep. 254] (Pa. Super. Ct. 2002).

75. *In re D.H.* 663 S.E.2d 139 [234 Educ. L. Rep. 420] (Ga. 2008); *M.C. v. State*, 695 So.2d 477 [119 Educ. L. Rep. 296] (Fla. Dist. Ct. App.1997), *review denied*, 700 So.2d 686 (Fla. 1997).

76. *In re B.N.S.*, 641 S.E.2d 411 [216 Educ. L. Rep. 970] (N.C. Ct. App. 2007).

77. *In re C.R.K.*, 56 S.W.3d 288 [158 Educ. L. Rep. 475] (Tex. Ct. App. 2001).

78. *In re M.H.M.*, 864 A.2d 1251 [195 Educ. L. Rep. 238] (Pa. Super. Ct. 2004), *appeal denied*, 880 A.2d 1239 (Pa. 2005).

79. *Andrews v. State*, 930 A.2d 846 [223 Educ. L. Rep. 883] (Del. 2007).

West Virginia's highest court reversed an order of the state's Human Rights Commission which posited that a teacher committed racial discrimination when she punished a student who committed a variety of in-class related offenses including tardiness and rudeness.[80] The court declared both that the Commission's order was clearly erroneous in light of the many misrepresentations in its findings of fact, which served as the basis of its adjudication, and that the student failed to produce sufficient evidence to prove that the teacher's attempts to discipline her were more than likely due to her race. The court concluded that discipline imposed on minority students in public schools does not alone equate to racial discrimination.

Other courts invalidated a variety of penalties as too harsh. For example, courts refused to uphold such penalties as a conviction for disorderly conduct where a student threatened to shoot up a school since no one took him seriously and there were no weapons in his home;[81] assault for throwing a partially eaten apple at a teacher;[82] adjudication as a juvenile delinquent for having a butter knife in a locker since it was incapable of being used as a deadly weapon;[83] and repeatedly using insulting and vulgar language to address a teacher.[84]

CORPORAL PUNISHMENT

At common law, teachers have the right to administer reasonable corporal punishment.[85] In fact, absent growing statutory prohibitions against corporal punishment[86] that render it illegal in more than half of the states, educators may employ the practice even against parental wishes[87] as long as local board policies authorize its use.[88] Unless they are contrary to

---

80. *Cobb v. West Va. Human Rights Comm'n*, 619 S.E.2d 274 [202 Educ. L. Rep. 373] (W. Va. 2005).

81. *State v. McCooey*, 802 A.2d 1216 [167 Educ. L. Rep. 814] (N.H. 2002).

82. *In re Gavin T.*, 77 Cal.Rptr.2d 701 [128 Educ. L. Rep. 313] (Cal. Ct. App. 1998).

83. *In re Melanie H.*, 706 A.2d 621 [124 Educ. L. Rep. 608] (Md. Ct. App. 1998).

84. *In re Nickolas S.*, 245 P.3d 446 [263 Educ. L. Rep. 419] (Ariz. 2011).

85. For an early case dealing with corporal punishment, *see State v. Mizner*, 50 Iowa 145 (Iowa 1878) (rejecting its use on a student whose father asked that she be excused from algebra class due to health concerns, stipulating that the appropriate penalty should have been expulsion).

86. *See, e.g.*, CAL. EDUC. CODE § 49000; IOWA CODE ANN. § 280.21; MICH. COMP. LAWS ANN. § 380.1312; NEB. REV. STAT. ANN. § 79–295, N.D. CENT. CODE 15.1–19–02 UTAH CODE ANN. § 53A–11–802; VA. CODE ANN. § 22.1–279.1; WASH. REV. CODE ANN. § 28A.150.300; W. VA. CODE ANN. § 18A–5–1; WIS. STAT. ANN. § 118.31. Other states explicitly give local boards the option of prohibiting corporal punishment. *See, e.g.*, FLA. STAT. ANN. § 1006.07; N.M. STAT. ANN. § 22–5–4.3; OHIO REV. CODE ANN. § 3319.41.

87. *Baker v. Owen*, 395 F.Supp. 294 (M.D.N.C.1975), *aff'd*, 423 U.S. 907, 96 S.Ct. 210, 46 L.Ed.2d 137 (1975) (affirming that parental disapproval of corporal punishment did not preclude its use on a child). *See also Setliff v. Rapides Parish School Bd.*, 888 So.2d 1156 [194 Educ. L. Rep. 755] (La. Ct. App. 2004), *writ denied*, 896 So.2d 1011 (2005) (refusing to find a board and principal liable for injuries a student allegedly sustained in connection with the use of corporal punishment where state law expressly authorized its use under specified conditions and the child subjected educators to a relatively long standing and continual pattern of misbehavior).

88. *Ware v. Estes*, 328 F.Supp. 657 (N.D. Tex.1971), *aff'd*, 458 F.2d 1360 (5th Cir.1972), *cert. denied*, 409 U.S. 1027, 93 S.Ct. 463, 34 L.Ed.2d 321 (1972).

state regulations, local board policies generally control.[89] The use of unreasonable corporal punishment or behavior that violates board policy or state law can serve as cause for dismissing teachers.[90]

In its only case on the merits of the practice, *Ingraham v. Wright*,[91] the Supreme Court refused to treat corporal punishment as per se unconstitutional. Ruling that the Eighth Amendment's prohibition against cruel and unusual punishments was designed to protect those guilty of crimes and was inapplicable to paddling students in order to preserve discipline, the Court rejected an analogy between children and inmates. In noting that most jurisdictions addressing corporal punishment at that time permitted its use, and that professional and public opinion was divided on the practice, the Court refused to strike it down as unconstitutional.

Turning to fact-specific cases, the Fourth,[92] Tenth,[93] and Eleventh[94] Circuits, as well as federal trial courts,[95] agreed that students can proceed with substantive due process claims where punishments are "... so brutal, demeaning, and harmful as literally to shock the conscience of a court."[96] In such a case, the Fourth Circuit affirmed the denial of a wrestling coach's claim for qualified immunity where a student sued him and other school officials after the coach encouraged members of his team to beat the plaintiff repeatedly.[97] On two occasions, though, the Fifth Circuit disagreed, maintaining that state statutory and common law provisions offered better redress in the way of damages and possible criminal liability rather than vitiate the use of corporal punishment.[98] As revealed in the preceding cases, most litigation involving corporal punishment has been resolved in favor of teachers based on the presumption of correctness which complaining students and parents were unable to overcome.[99]

---

89. *McKinney v. Greene*, 379 So.2d 69 (La. Ct. App. 1979), *writ denied*, 379 So.2d 69 (La. Ct. App. 1979).

90. *See, e.g., Bott v. Board of Educ., Deposit Cent. School Dist.*, 392 N.Y.S.2d 274 (N.Y. 1977); *Tucker v. Board of Educ., Community School Dist. No. 10*, 604 N.Y.S.2d 506 [87 Educ. L. Rep. 565] (N.Y. 1993); *Galbreath v. Board of Educ.*, 111 F.3d 123 (2d Cir. 1997), *cert. denied*, 522 U.S. 1001, 118 S.Ct. 571, 139 L.Ed.2d 410 (1997); *Madison v. Houston Indep. School Dist.*, 47 F. Supp.2d 825 [135 Educ. L. Rep. 535] (S.D. Tex. 1999), *aff'd without published opinion*, 207 F.3d 658 [143 Educ. L. Rep. 726] (5th Cir. 2000); *McPherson v. New York City Dep't of Educ.*, 457 F.3d 211 [211 Educ. L. Rep. 584] (2d Cir. 2006).

91. 430 U.S. 651, 97 S.Ct. 1401, 51 L.Ed.2d 711 (1977). [Case No. 95]

92. *Hall v. Tawney*, 621 F.2d 607 (4th Cir. 1980).

93. *Garcia v. Miera*, 817 F.2d 650 [39 Educ. L. Rep. 33] (10th Cir.1987), *cert. denied*, 485 U.S. 959, 108 S.Ct. 1220, 99 L.Ed.2d 421 [45 Educ. L. Rep. 486] (1988).

94. *Neal v. Fulton County Bd. of Educ.*, 229 F.3d 1069 [148 Educ. L. Rep. 86] (11th Cir.2000), *reh'g en banc denied*, 244 F.3d 143 (11th Cir. 2000).

95. *See, e.g., Nicol v. Auburn–Washburn USD 437*, 231 F. Supp.2d 1107 (D. Kan. 2002).

96. *Hall v. Tawney*, 621 F.2d 607, 613 (4th Cir. 1980).

97. *Meeker v. Edmundson*, 415 F.3d 317 [200 Educ. L. Rep. 16] (4th Cir. 2005).

98. *Cunningham v. Beavers*, 858 F.2d 269 [49 Educ. L. Rep. 490] (5th Cir.1988), *cert. denied*, 489 U.S. 1067, 109 S.Ct. 1343, 103 L.Ed.2d 812 (1989); *Moore v. Willis Indep. School Dist.*, 233 F.3d 871 [149 Educ. L. Rep. 337] (5th Cir.2000), *reh'g en banc denied*, 248 F.3d 1145 (5th Cir.2001).

99. *See also Fox v. Cleveland*, 169 F. Supp.2d 977 [158 Educ. L. Rep. 638] (W.D. Ark. 2001); *Campbell v. Gahanna–Jefferson Bd. of Educ.*, 717 N.E.2d 347 [137 Educ. L. Rep. 1104] (Ohio Ct. App. 1998); *Burnham v. Stevens*, 734 So.2d 256 [135 Educ. L. Rep. 1129] (Miss. Ct. App. 1999).

As illustrated by cases from the Second,[100] Third,[101] Sixth,[102] Seventh,[103] and Eleventh[104] Circuits, there are times when teachers can use force to discipline students, including those who are disruptive. In the case from the Seventh Circuit, the court specified that when a teacher in Illinois grabbed a student by her wrist and elbow to escort her from a classroom, he did not violate her rights to substantive due process amounting to corporal punishment. The Eleventh Circuit, in a dispute from Georgia, affirmed that a teacher did not violate a student's right to substantive due process when she administered corporal punishment on an unruly student since her use of force was not excessive. The court added that the teacher was entitled to official immunity from the student's state law claims of battery and intentional infliction of emotional distress. Courts agreed that teachers did not commit corporal punishment where they paddled a child on the buttocks;[105] restrained a child with Asperger's Syndrome;[106] grabbed the arm of a student who was attempting to retrieve a shirt and pulled him toward a door;[107] grabbed and twisted a child's wrist in an effort to compel her to turn over a twenty-dollar bill she found on the floor;[108] and grasped a student in an attempt to preserve discipline.[109]

SUSPENSION AND EXPULSION

Suspension and expulsion are the most serious penalties that school officials can impose on students. Allowing for variations in terminology from one jurisdiction to another, suspensions generally refer to temporary exclusions for set periods or until students satisfy specific conditions while expulsions are permanent removals from school. On a related point, whether students are entitled to educational services during expulsions varies from one jurisdiction to the next.[110] As discussed in greater detail below,

---

100. *Smith ex rel. Smith v. Half Hollow Hills Cent. School Dist.*, 298 F.3d 168 [167 Educ. L. Rep. 619] (2d Cir. 2002).

101. *Gottlieb ex rel. Calabria v. Laurel Highlands School Dist.*, 272 F.3d 168 [159 Educ. L. Rep. 16] (3d Cir. 2001).

102. *Nolan v. Memphis City Schools*, 589 F.3d 257 [251 Educ. L. Rep. 533] (6th Cir. 2009).

103. *Wallace by Wallace v. Batavia School Dist. 101*, 68 F.3d 1010 [104 Educ. L. Rep. 132] (7th Cir. 1995).

104. *T.W. ex rel. Wilson v. School Bd. of Seminole County, Fla.*, 610 F.3d 588 [258 Educ. L. Rep. 481] (11th Cir. 2010).

105. *Fox v. Cleveland*, 169 F. Supp.2d 977 [158 Educ. L. Rep. 638] (W.D. Ark. 2001).

106. *Brown ex rel. Brown v. Ramsey*, 121 F. Supp.2d 911 [149 Educ. L. Rep. 392] (E.D. Va. 2000), *aff'd without published opinion*, 10 Fed.Appx. 131 (4th Cir. 2001).

107. *Widdoes v. Detroit Pub. Schools*, 619 N.W.2d 12 [148 Educ. L. Rep. 1039] (Mich. Ct. App. 2000), *appeal denied*, 625 N.W.2d 785 (Mich. 2001).

108. *Bisignano v. Harrison Cent. School Dist.*, 113 F. Supp.2d 591 [147 Educ. L. Rep. 529] (S.D.N.Y. 2000).

109. *Young v. St. Landry Parish School Bd.*, 759 So.2d 800 (La. Ct. App.1999), *writ denied*, 756 So.2d 1144 (La. 2000).

110. *See, e.g., Madison Metropolitan School Dist. v. Circuit Court for Dane County*, 800 N.W.2d 442 [269 Educ. L. Rep. 802] (Wis. 2011) (affirming that school officials could refuse to

the elements of due process depend to a significant extent on the length of the exclusions being considered.

DUE PROCESS AND PUNISHMENTS

Courts generally defer to educators who use reasonable forms of discipline and can justify their actions.[111] Cases often hinge on whether officials provided students with adequate procedural due process. While due process does not require educators to afford students all of the safeguards that are present in criminal,[112] or, for that matter, civil,[113] proceedings, essential elements depend on the circumstances and seriousness of potential punishments. At the very least, students who are subject to significant disciplinary penalties are entitled to notice and opportunities to respond in the presence of fair and impartial third-party decision makers.[114]

The Fifth Circuit provided the earliest guidelines, albeit from higher education, as to required notice and hearings prior to long-term exclusions in a case where a student faced expulsion from a public college for non-academic reasons.[115] The court was of the opinion that notice should contain a statement of the specific charges and grounds which, if proven, would justify an expulsion. The court also ascertained that insofar as assessing misconduct depends on gathering facts that can be easily colored by witnesses, a fair and impartial third-party decision maker must hear both sides in considerable detail. Expressly rejecting any requirement of "... a full-dress judicial hearing, with the right to cross-examine witnesses,"[116] the court commented that "the rudiments of an adversary proceeding ... [require that] ... student[s] should be given the names of the witnesses against him and an oral or written report on the facts to which each witness testifies. [They] should also be given the opportunity to present ... [their] own defense against the charges and to produce either oral testimony or written affidavits of witnesses in [their] behalf."[117] The Fifth Circuit later applied these criteria in striking down a high school student's thirty-day suspension since he had not received any sort of

provide educational services to a juvenile who was expelled and adjudicated delinquent for possession of marijuana with the intent to deliver drugs).

111. *See In re Expulsion of N.Y.B.*, 750 N.W.2d 318 [232 Educ. L. Rep. 933] (Minn. Ct. App. 2008) (remanding a board's expulsion of a student for a calendar year for further consideration where it was unclear whether officials provided sufficient detail justifying their action).

112. *See, e.g., Brewer by Dreyfus v. Austin Indep. School Dist.*, 779 F.2d 260 [29 Educ. L. Rep. 56] (5th Cir. 1985).

113. *Colquitt v. Rich Twp. High School Dist. No. 227*, 699 N.E.2d 1109 [129 Educ. L. Rep. 733] (Ill. App. Ct. 1998).

114. *See, e.g., In re Z.K.*, 695 N.W.2d 656 [197 Educ. L. Rep. 820] (Minn. Ct. App. 2005) (overturning the expulsion of middle school students for shooting another juvenile with a BB gun because insofar as they were not advised that state law afforded them the right to free or low-cost legal assistance, their waivers of their right to a hearing before the school board were not knowing and intelligent).

115. *Dixon v. Alabama State Bd. of Educ.*, 294 F.2d 150 (5th Cir.1961), *cert. denied*, 368 U.S. 930, 82 S.Ct. 368, 7 L.Ed.2d 193 (1961).

116. *Id.* at 159.

117. *Id.*

hearing.[118] In a related development, the Seventh Circuit rejected the argument that students were entitled to the names of witnesses and information about their testimony[119] while the Second Circuit indicated that witnesses were not essential where the credibility of evidence was not at issue.[120] However, the Ninth Circuit affirmed that educators had to produce witnesses for cross-examination before students who committed a variety of disciplinary infractions could be expelled.[121]

In *Goss v. Lopez (Goss)*,[122] the Supreme Court set out the minimum constitutional requirements when dealing with suspensions of ten days or less. In a dispute from Ohio, students who did not receive a hearing challenged their suspensions for allegedly disruptive conduct. Ruling in favor of the students, the Court mandated that due process requires that they be given "oral or written notice of the charges against [them] and, if [they] den[y] them, an explanation of the evidence the authorities have and an opportunity to present [their] side of the story."[123] The Court determined that there is no need for a delay between school officials' giving students notice and the time of their hearings, acknowledging that in most cases disciplinarians may well have informally discussed alleged acts of misconduct with them shortly after they occurred.[124]

The *Goss* Court explained that if the presence of students constitutes threats of disruption, they may be removed immediately with the due process requirements to be fulfilled as soon as practicable. The Court expressly rejected the notion that students should be represented by counsel, be able to present witnesses, and be able to confront and cross-examine witnesses when facing short-term exclusions.[125] The Court observed that "[l]onger suspensions or expulsions for the remainder of the school term, or permanently, may require more formal procedures . . . [and that] in unusual situations, although involving only a short suspension, something more than the rudimentary procedures will be required."[126] States have followed the Court's suggestion and developed statutory guidelines when students are subject to long-term suspensions and/or expulsions.

Two years after *Goss*, in upholding the constitutionality of corporal punishment in *Ingraham v. Wright*,[127] the Supreme Court addressed proce-

118.   *Williams v. Dade County School Bd.*, 441 F.2d 299 (5th Cir.1971).

119.   *Linwood v. Board of Educ. of City of Peoria, School Dist. No. 150, Ill.*, 463 F.2d 763 (7th Cir.1972), *cert. denied*, 409 U.S. 1027, 93 S.Ct. 475, 34 L.Ed.2d 320 (1972).

120.   *Winnick v. Manning*, 460 F.2d 545 (2d Cir. 1972).

121.   *Black Coalition v. Portland School Dist. No. 1*, 484 F.2d 1040 (9th Cir. 1973).

122.   419 U.S. 565, 95 S.Ct. 729, 42 L.Ed.2d 725 (1975). [Case No. 94]

123.   *Id.* at 581.

124.   *Smith on Behalf of Smith v. Severn*, 129 F.3d 419 [122 Educ. L. Rep. 106] (7th Cir.1997).

125.   *See In re Gault*, 387 U.S. 1, 87 S.Ct. 1428, 18 L.Ed.2d 527 (1967) (stating that a fifteen-year-old who was committed to a facility for juvenile delinquents had the right to notice of charges, to counsel, to confront and cross-examine witnesses, and to the privilege against self-incrimination).

126.   *Goss v. Lopez*, 419 U.S. 565, 584, 95 S.Ct. 729, 42 L.Ed.2d 725 (1975). [Case No. 94]

127.   430 U.S. 651, 97 S.Ct. 1401, 51 L.Ed.2d 711 (1977). [Case No. 95]

dural due process. In recognizing that corporal punishment implicates a constitutionally protected liberty interest, the Court was satisfied that common law remedies afforded adequate due process. Refusing to impose a right to extra procedural safeguards, citing impracticability and cost as factors outweighing any incremental benefit, the Court rejected the argument that corporal punishment deprived the students of property rights because their schooling was not interrupted and state courts could have set procedural, and substantive, restrictions on its use.[128]

In the wake of *Goss*, federal trial courts began to apply its procedural requirements to student disciplinary transfers[129] and three-day suspensions.[130] The courts agreed that where the property interests of students were involved, they were of sufficient magnitude to qualify for the minimal constitutional due process protections. A federal trial court in Texas reached the same result where a student received a three-day suspension for taking allegedly compromising photographs of the principal's car while it was parked in front of a female teacher's house.[131] More recently, the Fifth Circuit upheld a student's suspension for less than ten days, agreeing that officials did not violate his rights to due process in light of his role in an attack on his school's computer network.[132]

In cases involving criminal misconduct, the Fifth[133] and Eleventh[134] Circuits determined that insofar as students who were transferred to alternative schools within their districts did not suffer the losses of property interests, they lacked rights to hearings. On the other hand, the Sixth Circuit remanded a dispute where a student was transferred due to criminal misbehavior for consideration of whether the failure of officials to afford him a hearing violated his rights.[135]

The argument that more extensive processes are necessary if disciplinary penalties indirectly lead to academic sanctions is not necessarily persuasive. In such a case, an appellate court in Illinois refused to intervene where a student's missing examinations due to a three-day suspension led to a grade reduction since its timing was not intended to make it a more onerous penalty.[136] The Seventh Circuit reached a similar outcome where a three-day suspension delayed a student's graduation.[137] In the first of three

---

128. *Smith v. West Va. State Bd. of Educ.*, 295 S.E.2d 680 [6 Educ. L. Rep. 1138] (W. Va. 1982).

129. *Everett v. Marcase*, 426 F.Supp. 397 (E.D. Pa. 1977).

130. *Hillman v. Elliott*, 436 F.Supp. 812 (W.D. Va. 1977).

131. *Riggan v. Midland Indep. School Dist.*, 86 F. Supp.2d 647 [142 Educ. L. Rep. 836] (W.D. Tex. 2000).

132. *Harris ex rel. Harris v. Pontotoc County School Dist.*, 635 F.3d 685 [265 Educ. L. Rep. 908] (5th Cir. 2011)

133. *Nevares v. San Marcos Consol. Indep. School Dist.*, 111 F.3d 25 [117 Educ. L. Rep. 470] (5th Cir. 1997).

134. *C.B. By and Through Breeding v. Driscoll*, 82 F.3d 383 [108 Educ. L. Rep. 1126] (11th Cir. 1996), *reh'g and suggestion for reh'g en banc denied*, 99 F.3d 1157 (11th Cir. 1996).

135. *Buchanan v. City of Bolivar, Tenn.*, 99 F.3d 1352 [114 Educ. L. Rep. 25] (6th Cir. 1996).

136. *Donaldson v. Board of Educ., Danville School Dist. No. 118*, 424 N.E.2d 737 (Ill. App. Ct. 1981).

137. *Lamb v. Panhandle Community Unit School Dist. No. 2*, 826 F.2d 526 (7th Cir. 1987).

cases from Pennsylvania, an appellate court found that a student whose suspension overlapped with graduation by one day lacked a constitutionally protected property right to attend the ceremony since it was only symbolic and not an essential component of his education.[138] Where school officials who caught a student selling drugs expelled him from school on the morning that he was due to graduate, an appellate court directed them to issue him a diploma because he completed all of the academic requirements for graduation.[139] Further, where a student was suspended for a variety of offenses but completed her course work, examinations, and the requirements necessary for graduation, an appellate court affirmed that she could not be denied her high school diploma.[140]

Courts disagree as to the precise requirements of procedural due process in connection with penalties that are more severe than the ten-day suspension involved in *Goss*. The lodestar is the elusive criterion of fairness. As such, most jurisdictions rely on the Supreme Court's perspective as set forth in *Mathews v. Eldridge*, that "[d]ue process is flexible and calls for such procedural protections as the particular situation demands."[141] For instance, where a student in Georgia received a nine-day suspension for fighting, screaming obscenities, and refusing to cooperate with and assaulting faculty members in connection with her possession of look-alike drugs at school, the Eleventh Circuit affirmed that educators met the requirements of due process when her mother participated in a telephone call with them on the day that the incident occurred.[142]

DUE PROCESS HEARINGS

Courts do not expect students to receive full judicial proceedings.[143] Even so, students facing expulsions are entitled to notice informing them of the time and place of some form of hearings.[144] School officials should also inform students of the charges and the nature of the evidence that they face[145] but not necessarily to pre-hearing notice of particular code or rule infractions. In specific cases, courts upheld expulsions where one student and his parents received repeated warnings that he faced expulsion for

---

138. *Mifflin County School Dist. v. Stewart*, 503 A.2d 1012 [30 Educ. L. Rep. 403] (Pa. Cmwlth. Ct. 1986).

139. *Shuman v. Cumberland Valley School Dist. Bd. of Directors*, 536 A.2d 490 [44 Educ. L. Rep. 399] (Pa. Cmwlth. Ct. 1988), *appeal denied*, 593 A.2d 428 (Pa. 1991).

140. *Ream v. Centennial School Dist.*, 765 A.2d 1195 [150 Educ. L. Rep. 773] (Pa. Cmwlth. Ct. 2001), *appeal denied*, 782 A.2d 551 (Pa. 2001).

141. 424 U.S. 319, 334, 96 S.Ct. 893, 47 L.Ed.2d 18 (1976).

142. *C.B. By and Through Breeding v. Driscoll*, 82 F.3d 383 [108 Educ. L. Rep. 1126] (11th Cir. 1996), *reh'g and suggestion for reh'g en banc denied*, 99 F.3d 1157 (11th Cir. 1996).

143. *See, e.g., Boykins v. Fairfield Bd. of Educ.*, 492 F.2d 697 (5th Cir.1974), *cert. denied*, 420 U.S. 962, 95 S.Ct. 1350, 43 L.Ed.2d 438 (1975); *Newsome v. Batavia Local School Dist.*, 842 F.2d 920 (6th Cir. 1988); *Smith ex rel. Smith v. Seligman Unified School Dist. No. 40 of Yavapai County, Ariz.*, 664 F.Supp.2d 1070 [252 Educ. L. Rep. 769] (D. Ariz. 2009).

144. *Bivins v. Albuquerque Pub. Schools*, 899 F.Supp. 556 [104 Educ. L. Rep. 195] (D.N.M.1995); *Donovan v. Ritchie*, 68 F.3d 14 [104 Educ. L. Rep. 80] (1st Cir. 1995); *Hammock ex rel. Hammock v. Keys*, 93 F. Supp.2d 1222 [143 Educ. L. Rep. 915] (S.D. Ala. 2000).

145. *C.B. By and Through Breeding v. Driscoll*, 82 F.3d 383 [108 Educ. L. Rep. 1126] (11th Cir. 1996).

possession of marijuana[146] and another was arrested and charged with two counts of illegal sales of controlled substances.[147] Both courts agreed that the students were expelled after hearings that were presided over by fair and impartial third-party decision makers who based their actions on the contents of the records.[148]

Other courts decided that students are not entitled to have their own attorneys present as trial counsel,[149] or at public expense if they can obtain their own pro bono lawyers,[150] to know the identity of[151] and/or to confront witnesses,[152] especially where there may be clear and serious danger to student witnesses.[153] Even so, a dispute arose where a state statute afforded students and their parents due process rights including notice, an opportunity to respond, the right to be represented by counsel, as well as to present evidence and question witnesses during their expulsion proceedings. When the student and his parents chose neither to have an attorney present during his initial hearing nor to exercise his statutory right to present evidence or question witnesses, the Supreme Court of South Carolina rejected their claim that officials violated his rights to procedural due process.[154]

As reflected by a case from the Sixth Circuit, there is a delicate balance between the rights of the accused to confront witnesses and the danger to accusers. The court noted that the necessity of protecting student witnesses from reprisal and ostracism generally outweighs the value to the truth-seeking process of allowing them to cross-examine their accusers.[155] In addition, hearsay evidence that was used in hearings has withstood judicial scrutiny where allowing police or school officials to testify protected student witnesses.[156]

---

146. *L.Q.A. By and Through Arrington v. Eberhart*, 920 F.Supp. 1208 [108 Educ. L. Rep. 680] (M.D. Ala. 1996), *aff'd without reported opinion*, 111 F.3d 897 (11th Cir. 1997). *See also South Gibson School Bd. v. Sollman*, 768 N.E.2d 437 [165 Educ. L. Rep. 316] (Ind. 2002).

147. *Rossi v. West Haven Bd. of Educ.*, 359 F. Supp.2d 178 [196 Educ. L. Rep. 522] (D. Conn. 2005).

148. *Newsome v. Batavia Local School Dist.*, 842 F.2d 920 [45 Educ. L. Rep. 1037] (6th Cir. 1988); *Ruef v. Jordan*, 605 N.Y.S.2d 530 [88 Educ. L. Rep. 198] (N.Y. App. Div. 1993).

149. *See, e.g., Osteen v. Henley*, 13 F.3d 221 [88 Educ. L. Rep. 939] (7th Cir. 1993); *Newsome v. Batavia Local School Dist.*, 842 F.2d 920 [45 Educ. L. Rep. 1037] (6th Cir. 1988); *Lake Central School Corp. v. Scartozzi*, 759 N.E.2d 1185 [160 Educ. L. Rep. 231] (Ind. Ct. App. 2001).

150. *In re Expulsion of N.Y.B.*, 750 N.W.2d 318 [232 Educ. L. Rep. 933] (Minn. Ct. App. 2008).

151. *Brewer by Dreyfus v. Austin Indep. School Dist.*, 779 F.2d 260 [29 Educ. L. Rep. 56] (5th Cir. 1985); *Paredes by Koppenhoefer v. Curtis*, 864 F.2d 426 [51 Educ. L. Rep. 20] (6th Cir. 1988); *Snyder on Behalf of Snyder v. Farnsworth*, 896 F.Supp. 96 [103 Educ. L. Rep. 230] (N.D.N.Y. 1995); *Coplin v. Conejo Valley Unified School Dist.*, 903 F.Supp. 1377 [104 Educ. L. Rep. 1204] (C.D. Cal. 1995), *aff'd in an unpublished opinion*, 116 F.3d 483 (9th Cir. 1997).

152. *Scanlon v. Las Cruces Pub. Schools*, 172 P.3d 185 [227 Educ. L. Rep. 326] (N.M. Ct. App. 2007); *Newsome v. Batavia Local School Dist.*, 842 F.2d 920 [45 Educ. L. Rep. 1037] (6th Cir. 1988).

153. *Dillon v. Pulaski County Special School Dist.*, 468 F.Supp. 54 (E.D. Ark. 1978), *aff'd*, 594 F.2d 699 (8th Cir. 1979); *John A. v. San Bernardino City Unified School Dist.*, 187 Cal.Rptr. 472 [7 Educ. L. Rep. 1059] (Cal. 1982).

154. *Stinney v. Sumter School Dist. 17*, 707 S.E.2d 397 [266 Educ. L. Rep. 515] (S.C. 2011).

155. *Newsome v. Batavia Local School Dist.*, 842 F.2d 920 [45 Educ. L. Rep. 1037] (6th Cir. 1988).

156. *E.K. v. Stamford Bd. of Educ.*, 557 F. Supp.2d 272 [234 Educ. L. Rep. 859] (D. Conn. 2008).

Other courts agreed that students lack rights to hearing officers who are not school employees[157] or, as noted earlier, to *Miranda* warnings when questioned by educational officials. Conversely, some courts granted students the right to have an attorney present;[158] to cross-examine witnesses;[159] to the presence of an impartial, non-school, third-party decision maker;[160] and to obtain a redacted copy of disciplinary records.[161]

In a case addressing various elements of due process, the Eighth Circuit affirmed that a middle school student in Arkansas failed to prove that educators violated his procedural due process rights when he was expelled due to an altercation with a teacher and principal. The court wrote that officials did not violate the student's rights because they fully informed his mother of the grounds for his expulsion and he received a hearing at which he was represented by counsel who had a full opportunity to examine and cross-examine witnesses.[162] The court pointed out that even though educators violated board rules by not supplying the student's attorney with the remarks of two witnesses in advance of the hearing, this did not amount to a constitutional violation.[163]

According to an older federal case from Illinois, students facing long-term suspensions or expulsions did not have a right to stenographic or mechanical recordings of proceedings.[164] Almost thirty years hence, an appellate court in the same state denied a student's request for a verbatim transcript of his expulsion hearing.[165] Along the same line, the federal trial court in Massachusetts agreed that a student who was excluded from school for disruptive behavior was not entitled to make a stenographic or mechanical recording of his expulsion hearing.[166] Almost twenty years later, the highest court of Massachusetts was of the view that when students request that testimony given at closed hearings be recorded electronically, it must be honored.[167]

Many challenges to disciplinary actions question whether school officials fully complied with statutory provisions or board policies. If infrac-

---

157. *John A. v. San Bernardino City Unified School Dist.*, 187 Cal.Rptr. 472 [7 Educ. L. Rep. 1059] (Cal. 1982).

158. *Givens v. Poe*, 346 F.Supp. 202 (W.D.N.C.1972); *Gonzales v. McEuen*, 435 F.Supp. 460 (C.D. Cal. 1977).

159. *Colquitt v. Rich Twp. High School Dist. No. 227*, 699 N.E.2d 1109 [129 Educ. L. Rep. 733] (Ill. App. Ct. 1998).

160. *Gonzales v. McEuen*, 435 F.Supp. 460 (C.D. Cal.1977).

161. *Graham v. West Babylon Union Free School Dist.*, 692 N.Y.S.2d 460 [136 Educ. L. Rep. 1012] (N.Y. App. Div. 1999).

162. *London v. Directors of DeWitt Pub. Schools*, 194 F.3d 873 [139 Ed. L. Rep. 145] (8th Cir. 1999).

163. *See also West v. Derby Unified School Dist. No. 260*, 206 F.3d 1358 [143 Educ. L. Rep. 43] (10th Cir.2000), *cert. denied*, 531 U.S. 825, 121 S.Ct. 71, 148 L.Ed.2d 35 (2000) (involving a student's three-day suspension for drawing a Confederate Flag).

164. *Whitfield v. Simpson*, 312 F.Supp. 889 (E.D. Ill. 1970).

165. *Colquitt v. Rich Twp. High School Dist. No. 227*, 699 N.E.2d 1109 [129 Educ. L. Rep. 733] (Ill. App. Ct. 1998).

166. *Pierce v. School Comm. of New Bedford*, 322 F.Supp. 957 (D. Mass. 1971).

167. *Nicholas B. v. School Comm. of Worcester*, 587 N.E.2d 211 [72 Educ. L. Rep. 1006] (Mass. 1992).

tions are minor and officials have not violated the rights of students, courts tend not to overturn the punishments. In an illustrative case, where a student did not receive the necessary written notice, but knew of the rules and charges, the Supreme Court of Vermont refused to invalidate his expulsion.[168] Earlier, where a student in Mississippi admitted that he brought a switchblade to school in violation of board policy, the Fifth Circuit affirmed that it was unnecessary for all witnesses and their testimony to have been identified before the hearing.[169] Additionally, where officials in Minnesota may not have provided a precise rationale for a contemplated three-day suspension of students who distributed an unofficial newspaper in school containing vulgarity, but the evidence against them was so overwhelming that a second hearing would not have altered the outcome, the Eighth Circuit reasoned that officials did not violate their rights to due process.[170] In a case with a different slant, where a state regulation stipulated that school officials could not impose long-term suspensions without first trying other forms of punishment, an appellate court in Washington set aside a student's lengthy exclusion for one incident of drinking champagne.[171]

A case from Illinois brought together a variety of elements dealing with due process hearings. The Seventh Circuit affirmed the denial of an injunction where a student faced a two-semester expulsion for participating in a verbal confrontation between two street gangs in his school's cafeteria in violation of a rule against belonging to "Subversive Organizations."[172] The court acknowledged that while the student had a hearing, he claimed that he was denied the opportunity to cross-examine witnesses even though the record demonstrated that he never asked to do so; he received only a written summary of the hearing officer's report rather than a verbatim transcript of the hearing; and he alleged that his parents did not receive the assistance of a Spanish language interpreter even though his father asked questions in English at the hearing. The court maintained that although other circuits viewed *Goss* as providing a starting point for due-process analysis when students face expulsions, it was unnecessary to balance the plaintiff's rights against those of others in the school since he received all of the process he was due.

THE FOURTH AMENDMENT

SEARCHES OF STUDENTS AND THEIR PROPERTY

The spread of violence, coupled with the presence of contraband such as weapons and drugs in schools, has led to litigation over the extent to

---

168. *Rutz v. Essex Junction Prudential Comm.*, 457 A.2d 1368 [10 Educ. L. Rep. 207] (Vt. 1983).

169. *McClain v. Lafayette County Bd. of Educ.*, 673 F.2d 106 [3 Educ. L. Rep. 298] (5th Cir. 1982), *reh'g denied*, 687 F.2d 121 [6 Educ. L. Rep. 346] (5th Cir. 1982).

170. *Bystrom By and Through Bystrom v. Fridley High School*, 686 F.Supp. 1387 [47 Educ. L. Rep. 905] (D. Minn.1987), *aff'd without reported opinion*, 855 F.2d 855 [48 Educ. L. Rep. 1144] (8th Cir. 1988).

171. *Quinlan v. University Place School Dist. 83*, 660 P.2d 329 [9 Educ. L. Rep. 1090] (Wash. Ct. App. 1983).

172. *Coronado v. Valleyview Pub. School Dist. 365–U*, 537 F.3d 791 [235 Educ. L. Rep. 780] (7th Cir. 2008).

which educators can search students and their property in attempts to maintain schools as safe and orderly learning environments. According to the Fourth Amendment, "[t]he right of the people to be secure in their persons, houses, papers, and effects, against unreasonable searches and seizures, shall not be violated...." This clause and the one following it, which pertains to search warrants, have been invoked in almost innumerable criminal cases but did not play much of a role in schools until the 1970s.

In an early case, an appellate court in California upheld a search based on an odor emanating from a student's locker.[173] Two additional early cases, from federal trial courts in Pennsylvania[174] and New York,[175] rejected the use of in-school strip searches for missing property. Other early cases involved the use of sniff dogs in schools as the Tenth Circuit, in a case from New Mexico,[176] and a federal trial court in Indiana[177] upheld their use while a federal trial court in Texas disagreed.[178] Moreover, the Fifth Circuit reached mixed results in a case from Texas, permitting the use of dogs in searches of student-owned cars and their lockers but not the students themselves.[179]

The Supreme Court first addressed the Fourth Amendment in a school setting in *New Jersey v. T.L.O. (T.L.O.)*.[180] When a fourteen-year-old, first-year high school student, identified as T.L.O., and a friend were accused of violating school rules by smoking cigarettes in a lavatory, the latter, who admitted to smoking, was not brought to the office for a search. Since T.L.O. denied smoking and claimed that she did not smoke at all, the teacher who confronted her brought her to the assistant principal's office. On opening T.L.O.'s purse, since the assistant principal saw her cigarettes "in plain view," a term of art borrowed from criminal law, he removed them and accused her of lying. Continuing with the search, the assistant principal discovered cigarette rolling papers, a small amount of marijuana, a pipe, a number of plastic bags, a substantial quantity of one-dollar bills, an index card that appeared to be a list of students who owed T.L.O. money, and two letters that implicated her in dealing marijuana.

---

173. *People v. Lanthier*, 97 Cal.Rptr. 297 (Cal. 1971).

174. *Potts v. Wright*, 357 F.Supp. 215 (E.D. Pa. 1973).

175. *Bellnier v. Lund*, 438 F.Supp. 47 (N.D.N.Y. 1977).

176. *Zamora v. Pomeroy*, 639 F.2d 662 (10th Cir. 1981).

177. *Doe v. Renfrow*, 475 F.Supp. 1012 (N.D. Ind.1979), *rev'd in part on other grounds*, 631 F.2d 91 (7th Cir.1980) *(per curiam)*, *cert. denied*, 451 U.S. 1022, 101 S.Ct. 3015, 69 L.Ed.2d 395 (1981).

178. *Jones v. Latexo Indep. School Dist.*, 499 F.Supp. 223 (E.D. Tex.1980).

179. *Horton v. Goose Creek Indep. School Dist.*, 690 F.2d 470 [6 Educ. L. Rep. 950] (5th Cir. 1982), *cert. denied*, 463 U.S. 1207, 103 S.Ct. 3536, 77 L.Ed.2d 1387 (1983).

180. 469 U.S. 325, 105 S.Ct. 733, 83 L.Ed.2d 720 [21 Educ. L. Rep. 1122] (1985). [Case No. 96]

Once T.L.O. confessed to selling marijuana at her high school, a trial court refused to suppress the evidence, adjudicated her delinquent, and sentenced her to a year on probation.[181] An appellate court affirmed the denial of the motion to suppress the search of T.L.O.'s purse but vacated and remanded the case since neither the record nor the findings and conclusions below were sufficient to evaluate whether she knowingly and voluntarily waived her Fifth Amendment rights before confessing.[182] The Supreme Court of New Jersey decreed that the search of T.L.O.'s purse violated the Fourth Amendment.[183]

On further review in *New Jersey v. T.L.O.*, the Supreme Court reversed in favor of the State of New Jersey. Positing that the Fourth Amendment's prohibition against unreasonable searches and seizures applies in public schools, the Court devised a two-part test to evaluate the legality of searches by school officials: "[f]irst, one must consider 'whether the . . . action was justified at its inception;' second, one must determine whether the search as actually conducted 'was reasonably related in scope to the circumstances which justified the interference in the first place.' "[184] The Court added that "a search will be permissible in its scope when the measures adopted are reasonably related to the objectives of the search and not excessively intrusive in light of the age and sex of the student and the nature of the infraction."[185]

The Supreme Court clarified that a search is justified at its inception "when there are reasonable grounds for suspecting that the search will turn up evidence that the student has violated or is violating either the law or the rules of the school."[186] A subjective measure based on specific facts that must be more than a mere hunch,[187] reasonable suspicion is significantly less than the probable cause standard that applies to the police. Since school, also known as administrative, searches are designed to ensure school safety where there are generally large numbers of young people and relatively few adults present, educators need only articulable justification in order to proceed.[188] In such a case, an appellate court in Indiana upheld a search of a student's backpack by an assistant principal and a school security officer who was wearing a police uniform that led to the discovery of marijuana based on their ability to articulate their determination that he

---

181. *In re T.L.O.*, 428 A.2d 1327 (N.J. Juv. & Dom. Rel. Ct. 1980).

182. *In re T.L.O.*, 448 A.2d 493 (N.J. Super. Ct. App. Div. 1982).

183. *In re T.L.O.*, 463 A.2d 934 [12 Educ. L. Rep. 1184] (N.J. 1983).

184. *New Jersey v. T.L.O.*, 469 U.S. 325, 341, 105 S.Ct. 733, 83 L.Ed.2d 720 [21 Educ. L. Rep. 1122] (1985). [Case No. 96]

185. *Id.* at 342.

186. *Id.*

187. *R.S.M. v. State*, 911 So.2d 283 [202 Educ. L. Rep. 440] (Fla. Dist. Ct. App. 2005) (declaring that a school official's hunch that something was wrong did not constitute reasonable suspicion justifying a search).

188. For a related issue, *see Greene v. Camreta*, 588 F.3d 1011 [251 Educ. L. Rep. 67] (9th Cir. 2009) (refusing to apply the reasonable suspicion standard to a social worker and deputy sheriff during an in-school investigation of child abuse but granting their motions for qualified immunity since the law was unclear in this area).

was under the influence of drugs in light of the results of an evaluation test they required him to undergo.[189]

A related concern in addressing the totality of circumstances is that school officials may have to depend on the reliability of witnesses in considering whether to search. In assessing the sufficiency of cause to conduct searches, courts consider such factors as the source(s) of information, students' records, the seriousness and prevalence of problems, and the urgency of making searches without delays.

Courts have upheld searches based on information supplied by students,[190] parents,[191] school employees,[192] and the police.[193] In an illustrative case, an appellate court in New York affirmed that a search was reasonable when a student's book bag made a metallic thud when he placed it on a cabinet.[194] Also, a federal trial court in New York rejected the claim of a sixth-grade student who alleged that officials violated his Fourth Amendment rights by forcing him to undergo psychological testing after he wrote and read a story to classmates in which named fellow students were murdered or sexually assaulted.[195] In granting the school board's motion for dismissal, the court thought that officials voiced a legitimate concern that the student might have committed violent acts.

When searches are based on anonymous tips, not all courts agree about their constitutionality. For example, state appellate courts in Texas[196] and Illinois[197] rejected such searches. On the flip side, an appellate court in California affirmed that the search of a student's backpack was permissible after a school's campus security officer received an anonymous telephone call reporting that it contained a knife.[198] The court upheld the search because the student admitted to having the knife without reference to the reliability of the anonymous telephone call. More recently, an appellate court in Ohio upheld an assistant principal's search of a student based on an anonymous tip that a police officer received that a pupil may have been in possession of drugs as reasonable at its inception in light of the school's

---

189. *State v. C.D.*, 947 N.E.2d 1018 (Ind. Ct. App. 2011). For a like result, *see State v. E.K.P.*, 255 P.3d 870 (Wash. Ct. App. 2011).

190. *See, e.g., Wofford v. Evans*, 390 F.3d 318 [193 Educ. L. Rep. 701] (4th Cir. 2004); *In re L.A.*, 21 P.3d 952 [152 Educ. L. Rep. 804] (Kan. 2001); *Commonwealth v. Snyder*, 597 N.E.2d 1363 [76 Educ. L. Rep. 843] (Mass. 1992).

191. *United States v. Aguilera*, 287 F. Supp.2d 1204 [183 Educ. L. Rep. 137] (E.D. Cal. 2003); *In re Joseph G.*, 38 Cal.Rptr.2d 902 [97 Educ. L. Rep. 1109] (Cal. Ct. App. 1995).

192. *Cornfield v. Consolidated High School Dist. No. 230*, 991 F.2d 1316 [82 Educ. L. Rep. 379] (7th Cir. 1993).

193. *In re D.E.M.*, 727 A.2d 570 [133 Educ. L. Rep. 990] (Pa. Super. Ct. 1999).

194. *Matter of Gregory M.*, 606 N.Y.S.2d 579 [88 Educ. L. Rep. 1127] (N.Y. 1993).

195. *D.F. ex rel. Finkle v. Board of Educ. of Syosset Cent. School Dist.*, 386 F. Supp.2d 119 [203 Educ. L. Rep. 160] (E.D.N.Y. 2005), *aff'd*, 180 Fed.Appx. 232 (2d Cir. 2006), *cert. denied*, 549 U.S. 1179, 127 S.Ct. 1170 166 L.Ed.2d 993 [216 Educ. L. Rep. 36] (2007).

196. *In re K.C.B.*, 141 S.W.3d 303 [191 Educ. L. Rep. 892] (Tex. Ct. App. 2004).

197. *People v. Kline*, 824 N.E.2d 295 (Ill. App. Ct. 2005), *appeal denied*, 833 N.E.2d 6 (Ill. 2005).

198. *In re Cody S.*, 16 Cal.Rptr.3d 653 [190 Educ. L. Rep. 436] (Cal. Ct. App. 2004).

zero tolerance policy requiring officials to act on all tips regardless of their source.[199]

Recognizing that different types of searches involve varying levels of intrusiveness, courts generally uphold searches of students' cars in school parking lots,[200] lockers,[201] and backpacks[202] for routine administrative purposes connected with the general welfare of schools. However, in a dispute from Florida that did not ultimately reach the merits of the case, *Howlett v. Rose*,[203] the Supreme Court addressed whether a school board and educators could assert sovereign immunity as a defense when they searched a student's car on school premises. When educators discovered liquor in his car, they suspended the student from class for five days. The Court found that the defendants could not rely on a sovereign immunity defense in the state case because it would have been unavailable had the dispute been litigated in a federal forum.

The Eighth Circuit determined that a school board policy in Arkansas, which permitted random, suspicionless searches of students and their belongings, violated the Fourth Amendment. Acting pursuant to the policy, officials ordered members of a seventh-grade class to empty their pockets and place all of their belongings, including backpacks and purses, on their desks. When the search uncovered marijuana in a student's purse, she was subject to criminal prosecution. Relying on the three part *Acton–Earls* test, discussed below, rather than *T.L.O.*, the court contended that insofar as the policy failed to demonstrate the required "special needs" that would have permitted the search to proceed, school officials violated the student's rights because their actions were not justified by individualized suspicion.[204]

Police/School Security Personnel Searches

As reflected by a case from New Mexico, when police officers enter schools, they must act based on the more stringent standard of probable cause.[205] The federal trial court invalidated the actions of officers who entered a school, searched, handcuffed, and arrested a student even though he was not suspected of having committed any crime. In addition, the court

---

199. *In re K.K.*, 950 N.E.2d 198 (Ohio Ct. App. 2011), *appeal not allowed*, 947 N.E.2d 683 (Ohio 2011), *reconsideration denied*, 951 N.E.2d 1049 (Ohio 2011).

200. *See, e.g., State v. Best*, 987 A.2d 605 [252 Educ. L. Rep. 908] (N.J. 2010); *State v. Schloegel*, 769 N.W.2d 130 [246 Educ. L. Rep. 1003] (Wis. Ct. App. 2009); *Hill v. Sharber*, 544 F. Supp.2d 670 [232 Educ. L. Rep. 200] (M.D. Tenn. 2008).

201. *Zamora v. Pomeroy*, 639 F.2d 662 (10th Cir. 1981); *Commonwealth v. Carey*, 554 N.E.2d 1199 [60 Educ. L. Rep. 920] (Mass. 1990); *In Interest of Isiah B.*, 500 N.W.2d 637 [83 Educ. L. Rep. 419] (Wis. 1993), *cert. denied*, 510 U.S. 884, 114 S.Ct. 231, 126 L.Ed.2d 186 (1993); *Commonwealth v. Cass*, 709 A.2d 350 [125 Educ. L. Rep. 705] (Pa. 1998), *cert. denied*, 525 U.S. 833, 119 S.Ct. 89, 142 L.Ed.2d 70 (1998); *In re F.B.*, 726 A.2d 361 [133 Educ. L. Rep. 528] (Pa. 1999), *cert. denied sub nom. F.B. v. Pennsylvania*, 528 U.S. 1060, 120 S.Ct. 613, 145 L.Ed.2d 508 (1999).

202. *Vassallo v. Lando*, 591 F. Supp.2d 172 [241 Educ. L. Rep. 95] (E.D.N.Y. 2008); *In re F.B.*, 726 A.2d 361 [133 Educ. L. Rep. 528] (Pa.1999), *cert. denied sub nom. F.B. v. Pennsylvania*, 528 U.S. 1060, 120 S.Ct. 613, 145 L.Ed.2d 508 (1999).

203. 496 U.S. 356, 110 S.Ct. 2430, 110 L.Ed.2d 332 [60 Educ. L. Rep. 358] (1990).

204. *Doe v. Little Rock School Dist.*, 380 F.3d 349 [191 Educ. L. Rep. 608] (8th Cir. 2004).

205. *Pacheco v. Hopmeier*, 770 F.Supp.2d 1174 [268 Educ. L. Rep. 845] (D.N.M. 2011).

rejected the principal's motion for qualified immunity due to his involvement in the incident since, at a minimum, it thought that he should have known that he needed reasonable suspicion to allow a related search of the student to proceed. Earlier, an appellate court in Georgia held that police searches in schools are subject to the more stringent standard of probable cause. When a law enforcement officer searched a student, albeit at the request of the school's principal, the court affirmed that it was invalid because the officer lacked probable cause.[206]

On the other hand, the Supreme Court of Tennessee decided that when a law enforcement officer who was regularly assigned to a school assumed duties beyond those ordinarily associated with her job such that she also could have been considered a school official, she was subject to the reasonable suspicion standard.[207] At issue was an incident wherein the search of the vehicle of a student who appeared to be intoxicated led to the discovery of marijuana.[208] In dicta, the court suggested that if the officer had not been associated with the school system, she would have been subject to the probable cause standard.[209]

Two appellate courts in Florida reached differing results in searches by school security personnel based on whether their actions were justified by reasonable suspicion. The first court affirmed an adjudication of delinquency where a school security officer's search of a student led to the discovery that he had a gun because it was rooted in reasonable suspicion.[210] Shortly thereafter, the second court suppressed the use of evidence against a student in a judicial proceeding since the search was not based on reasonable suspicion.[211]

After a vice principal's check of a locker uncovered a large amount of marijuana, the student unsuccessfully sought to suppress the evidence. The Supreme Judicial Court of Massachusetts affirmed that insofar as a memorandum between the police and school officials containing guidelines for reporting criminal behavior did not make educators police agents, the vice principal was not acting as an agent of law enforcement.[212] In addition, the court contended that the vice principal met the more stringent standard of probable cause to search the juvenile for drugs largely due to the strong smell of marijuana emanating from his person. Similarly, an appellate court in North Carolina affirmed that a deputy sheriff who acted in conjunction

---

206. *State v. K.L.M.*, 628 S.E.2d 651 [208 Educ. L. Rep. 654] (Ga. Ct. App. 2006), *cert. denied* (2006).

207. *R.D.S. v. State*, 245 S.W.3d 356 [230 Educ. L. Rep. 834] (Tenn. 2008).

208. *See also People v. Dilworth*, 661 N.E.2d 310 [107 Educ. L. Rep. 226] (Ill. 1996), *cert. denied*, 517 U.S. 1197, 116 S.Ct. 1692, 134 L.Ed.2d 793 (1996).

209. For another case upholding a police search on campus in an attempt to locate a student's identification as reasonable because it was justified at its inception, *see D.L. v. State*, 877 N.E.2d 500 [227 Educ. L. Rep. 908] (Ind. Ct. App. 2007), *transfer denied sub nom. In re D.L.*, 891 N.E.2d 39 (Ind. 2008).

210. *M.D. v. State*, 65 So.3d 563 [269 Educ. L. Rep. 991] (Fla. Dist. Ct. App. 2011), *reh'g denied* (2011). For an earlier case reaching the same outcome, albeit involving marijuana, *see R.B. v. State*, 975 So.2d 546 [230 Educ. L. Rep. 957] (Fla. Dist. Ct. App. 2008), *review denied*, 987 So.2d 1210 (Fla. 2008) (Table).

211. *C.A. v. State*, 977 So.2d 684 [231 Educ. L. Rep. 468] (Fla. Dist. Ct. App. 2008).

212. *Commonwealth v. Lawrence L.*, 792 N.E.2d 109 [178 Educ. L. Rep. 919] (Mass. 2003).

with school officials did not violate the Fourth Amendment.[213] The court maintained that the search, which took place in a school's weight room, was appropriate because the deputy had reasonable suspicion insofar as he smelled the strong odor of marijuana when the student walked past him in the hall. The court concluded that the search, which was limited to a pat down that included having the student empty his pockets, was reasonably related to the objective of preserving a drug-free educational environment and was not excessively intrusive in light of his age, gender, and the nature of the suspicion.

Juveniles who were charged with assault and battery as well as assault and battery with a dangerous weapon succeeded in having their statements to an assistant principal suppressed and the case dismissed without prejudice because officials failed to comply with discovery orders. On appeal, the Supreme Judicial Court of Massachusetts reversed in remarking that the failure of the prosecutors to provide the juveniles with statements taken by the assistant principal did not warrant the dismissal of the charges.[214] The court was of the opinion that insofar as the assistant principal was not acting as an agent of the state when he questioned the students, and they were not in his custody, their comments were admissible because they were voluntary.

When a security aide detained a student in Connecticut for questioning over possible drug use in school, the federal trial court granted the aide's motion for summary judgment in the student's suit which claimed that she was subjected to an illegal seizure.[215] The court posited that in light of the aide's desire to keep the school drug free, he was entitled to a grant of summary judgment that essentially dismissed the student's claim.

The Supreme Court of Oregon upheld a warrantless search that school officials conducted on a student before calling the police to report that he possessed illegal drugs.[216] The court was satisfied that in light of the need to maintain a safe and orderly learning environment, educational officials could search the student based on reasonable suspicion.

Off–Campus Searches

Rules applicable to school searches can extend to off-campus activities. For example, the Eighth Circuit affirmed that after a student from Minnesota who was on a field trip was seen opening a bottle of juice with a knife, he could be expelled for possession of an illegal weapon when a search revealed that he was carrying a baton resembling the kind used by police officers.[217] The court ascertained that even though the student was searched by both police officers and school officials, reasonable suspicion,

---

213. *In re S.W.*, 614 S.E.2d 424 [199 Educ. L. Rep. 451] (N.C. Ct. App. 2005), *review denied*, 623 S.E.2d 42 (N.C. 2005).

214. *Commonwealth v. Ira I.*, 791 N.E.2d 894 [178 Educ. L. Rep. 491] (Mass. 2003).

215. *DeFelice v. Warner*, 511 F. Supp.2d 241 [225 Educ. L. Rep. 563] (D. Conn. 2007).

216. *State ex rel. Juvenile Dep't of Clackamas County v. M.A.D.*, 233 P.3d 437 [257 Educ. L. Rep. 1080] (Or. 2010).

217. *Shade v. City of Farmington*, 309 F.3d 1054 [170 Educ. L. Rep. 529] (8th Cir. 2002).

rather than probable cause, was the appropriate standard.[218] Other courts upheld off-campus searches where officials had reasonable suspicion that students violated either school rules[219] or the law.[220]

Metal Detectors

In order to avoid having school personnel search, or help search, students, many school boards adopted the use of metal detectors since they are highly reliable and minimally intrusive. Conceding that individualized reasonable suspicion is not required, courts generally uphold the use of metal detectors,[221] including those that are hand-held and used in random searches.[222]

A dispute arose in Illinois when a student who entered a school was about to leave just as he saw that a metal detector was present. Before the student could leave, he responded to a police officer's command directing him to pass through the metal detector by informing the officer that he was carrying a gun. An appellate court affirmed that insofar as the seizure of the gun was not based on reasonable suspicion, it was inadmissible when he was charged with the unlawful use of a weapon.[223]

Video Cameras

In a case from Tennessee, the Sixth Circuit addressed the constitutionality of video surveillance equipment that officials installed in a boys' middle school locker room in an attempt to improve security. The court affirmed that the use of cameras was an unreasonable search since students had a clearly established right to privacy.[224] The court also rejected motions for qualified immunity entered on behalf of the principal and assistant principal but granted them in favor of school board members and

---

218. For cases applying reasonable suspicion in searches by school security personnel, *see People v. Dilworth*, 661 N.E.2d 310 [107 Educ. L. Rep. 226] (Ill. 1996), *cert. denied*, 517 U.S. 1197, 116 S.Ct. 1692, 134 L.Ed.2d 793 (1996); *In re Patrick Y.*, 746 A.2d 405 [142 Educ. L. Rep. 401] (Md. 2000); *T.S. v. State*, 863 N.E.2d 362 [217 Educ. L. Rep. 924] (Ind. Ct. App. 2007), *transfer denied, In re T.S.*, 869 N.E.2d 461 (Ind. 2007).

219. *See, e.g., Rhodes v. Guarricino*, 54 F. Supp.2d 186 [137 Educ. L. Rep. 258] (S.D.N.Y. 1999); *Juran v. Independence or Cent. School Dist.*, 898 F.Supp. 728 [103 Educ. L. Rep. 1068] (D. Or. 1995).

220. *See, e.g., Commonwealth v. Williams*, 749 A.2d 957 [143 Educ. L. Rep. 951] (Pa. Super. Ct. 2000), *appeal denied*, 764 A.2d 1069 (Pa. 2001); *People v. McKinney*, 655 N.E.2d 40 [103 Educ. L. Rep. 798] (Ill. App. Ct. 1995), *appeal denied*, 660 N.E.2d 1276 (Ill. 1995).

221. *Thompson v. Carthage School Dist.*, 87 F.3d 979 [110 Educ. L. Rep. 602] (8th Cir. 1996); *In re F.B.*, 726 A.2d 361 [133 Educ. L. Rep. 528] (Pa. 1999), *cert. denied sub nom. F.B. v. Pennsylvania*, 528 U.S. 1060, 120 S.Ct. 613, 145 L.Ed.2d 508 (1999); *Latasha W. v. People*, 70 Cal.Rptr.2d 886 [123 Educ. L. Rep. 277] (Cal. Ct. App. 1998); *People v. Pruitt*, 662 N.E.2d 540 [108 Educ. L. Rep. 329] (Ill. App. Ct. 1996), *appeal denied*, 667 N.E.2d 1061 (Ill. 1996); *People v. Dukes*, 580 N.Y.S.2d 850 (N.Y. Crim. Ct. 1992).

222. *State v. J.A.*, 679 So.2d 316 [112 Educ. L. Rep. 1107] (Fla. Dist. Ct. App. 1996), *reh'g denied* (1996), *review denied*, 689 So.2d 1069 (Fla. 1997), *cert. denied*, 522 U.S. 831, 118 S.Ct. 98, 139 L.Ed.2d 53 (1997).

223. *People v. Parker*, 672 N.E.2d 813 [114 Educ. L. Rep. 920] (Ill. App. Ct. 1996).

224. *Brannum v. Overton County School Bd.*, 516 F.3d 489 [229 Educ. L. Rep. 402] (6th Cir. 2008).

the superintendent because they neither approved the use of the cameras nor were aware that they were being used.[225]

On the other hand, an appellate court in North Carolina affirmed an earlier order refusing to suppress evidence obtained via cameras that led to a student's being adjudicated delinquent for possession of marijuana at school with the intent to distribute.[226] As an assistant principal and police officer watched on a monitoring camera that was posted in a hallway, they saw two males enter a bathroom while one stood guard outside. After the assistant principal told the officer that the situation looked strange, they entered the bathroom, searched the student, and discovered that he had marijuana in his pocket. The court agreed that this search was valid because it was based on reasonable suspicion.

Sniff Dogs

Many school boards have relied on trained dogs to sniff, or detect, the presence of contraband in educational settings. Most courts uphold the use of sniff dogs.

In early cases, a federal trial court in Indiana, in a classroom search,[227] and the Fifth Circuit, in a search of a car in a school parking lot in Texas,[228] rejected challenges to the use of sniff dogs. The courts agreed that having dogs sniff students were not searches within the meaning of the Fourth Amendment. Previously, the Tenth Circuit, in a case from New Mexico, upheld the use of sniff dogs in exploratory searches of student lockers.[229]

The Supreme Courts of Pennsylvania and Indiana, along with federal trial courts in Texas, Alabama, and Tennessee upheld the use of sniff dogs. In the case from Pennsylvania, the court judged that the use of a sniff dog in a general search of 2,000 lockers that led to the discovery of drugs and drug paraphernalia in a student's locker was permissible.[230] The court specified that the search was constitutional because it was a minimally intrusive invasion of the student's limited privacy interests in his locker, officials forewarned pupils of the possibility of a search which followed stringent guidelines in which its date and time were set weeks in advance, its scope was predetermined, and the drug dog was used to limit its

---

225. In an earlier case involving video cameras, the Ninth Circuit affirmed that a school board in Montana was not liable where males videotaped females as they undressed in a student locker room because officials lacked actual knowledge of their actions. *Harry A. v. Duncan*, 234 Fed.Appx. 463 [223 Educ. L. Rep. 626] (9th Cir. 2007).

226. *In re D.L.D.*, 694 S.E.2d 395 [257 Educ. L. Rep. 1096] (N.C. Ct. App. 2010).

227. *Doe v. Renfrow*, 475 F.Supp. 1012 (N.D. Ind.1979), *rev'd in part on other grounds*, 631 F.2d 91 (7th Cir.1980), *rehearing denied*, 635 F.2d 582 (7th Cir. 1980), *cert. denied*, 451 U.S. 1022, 101 S.Ct. 3015, 69 L.Ed.2d 395 (1981).

228. *Jennings v. Joshua Indep. School Dist.*, 869 F.2d 870 [52 Educ. L. Rep. 488] (5th Cir. 1989), *opinion amended and superseded*, 877 F.2d 313 [54 Educ. L. Rep. 1107] (5th Cir.1989), *cert. denied*, 496 U.S. 935, 110 S.Ct. 3212, 110 L.Ed.2d 660 (1990), *appeal after remand*, 948 F.2d 194 [71 Educ. L. Rep. 36] (5th Cir. 1991), *reh'g denied*, 952 F.2d 402 (5th Cir. 1992), *cert. denied*, 504 U.S. 956, 112 S.Ct. 2303, 119 L.Ed.2d 226 (1992).

229. *Zamora v. Pomeroy*, 639 F.2d 662 (10th Cir. 1981).

230. *Commonwealth v. Cass*, 709 A.2d 350 [125 Educ. L. Rep. 705] (Pa. 1998), *cert. denied*, 525 U.S. 833, 119 S.Ct. 89, 142 L.Ed.2d 70 (1998).

intrusiveness. The Supreme Court of Indiana affirmed that when officials used a sniff dog in a search for drugs but instead discovered a firearm in an unoccupied car in the school's parking lot, their actions were legal.[231] The court was of the view that insofar as educators did not need reasonable suspicion of criminal activity in order to proceed, there was no reason to suppress the evidence where the student was charged with felony possession of a firearm on school property.

In a case from Texas, a sniff dog alerted officials to a possible rule violation involving illegal narcotics or alcohol in a student's truck that was parked at school. Even though the search failed to discover drugs, the court remarked that the student could be suspended since educators uncovered a machete in the toolbox of his truck in violation of a school rule prohibiting students from possessing illegal weapons.[232] In like fashion, a federal trial court in Alabama was convinced that where a dog detected the odor of narcotics in a car in a school's parking lot, but none were discovered, a student could be placed in an alternative educational setting since officials uncovered an exacto knife and a large pocket knife in violation of rules against weapons.[233]

A federal trial court in Tennessee refused to suppress evidence where a student was disciplined under a zero tolerance policy after a random sweep by a sniff dog in a school parking lot led to the discovery that he had alcohol in a duffel bag inside of his vehicle.[234] The court observed that insofar as the drug dog that alerted the police to search the car was properly trained and possessed the requisite indicia of reliability, the search was constitutional. In an interesting twist in cases involving sniffing, a federal trial court in Virginia decided,[235] and another in Texas added in dicta,[236] that when educators, rather than dogs, sniffed the hands of children, they did perform searches.

The federal trial court in New Hampshire rejected a challenge to the use of sniff dogs to search a school with a history of drug problems.[237] While the search was carried out, students were instructed to leave all of their belongings in the school and report to the football field at which time they were informed that officials were conducting a safety check of the building. In addition to refusing to treat the use of the dogs in school as a search within the meaning of the Fourth Amendment, the court declined interpreting the actions of educators who directed the students to the football field as an impermissible seizure.

---

231. *Myers v. State*, 839 N.E.2d 1154 [204 Educ. L. Rep. 718] (Ind. 2005), *cert. denied*, 547 U.S. 1148, 126 S.Ct. 2295, 164 L.Ed.2d 814 [209 Educ. L. Rep. 30] (2006).

232. *Bundick v. Bay City Indep. School Dist.*, 140 F. Supp.2d 735 [154 Educ. L. Rep. 183] (S.D. Tex. 2001).

233. *Marner v. Eufaula City School Bd.*, 204 F. Supp.2d 1318 [166 Educ. L. Rep. 224] (M.D. Ala. 2002).

234. *Hill v. Sharber*, 544 F. Supp.2d 670 [232 Educ. L. Rep. 200] (M.D. Tenn. 2008).

235. *Burnham v. West*, 681 F.Supp. 1160 [46 Educ. L. Rep. 168] (E.D. Va. 1987), *order supplemented*, 681 F.Supp. 1169 (E.D. Va. 1988).

236. *Jones v. Latexo Indep. School Dist.*, 499 F.Supp. 223 (E.D. Tex. 1980).

237. *Doran v. Contoocook Valley School Dist.*, 616 F. Supp.2d 184 [245 Educ. L. Rep.682] (D.N.H. 2009).

An appellate court in Texas rejected a challenge from a student who was adjudicated delinquent after the use of a sniff dog led to the discovery of marijuana in her back pack.[238] The court affirmed that insofar as the student and her classmates were in a school hallway while the dog was in their classroom sniffing for drugs, the search was legal because the dog sniffed only the belongings and not the people.

On the other hand, the Fifth Circuit invalidated the use of a sniff dog to search students in Texas in declaring both that school officials lacked individualized reasonable suspicion and that having the canines place their noses directly on students was particularly intimidating and invasive of their privacy.[239] In the same opinion, the court wrote that a sniff search of student lockers and cars was permissible because insofar as they were only sniffing inanimate objects, the sole legal inquiry was about their record of reliability.[240] Subsequently, the Ninth Circuit expanded the Fifth Circuit's rationale in affirming that stationing a sniff dog at classroom doors in California, in close proximity to students, violated their rights to privacy.[241] At the same time, the court upheld the dismissal of a student's damages claim for lack of standing since he no longer attended the school where the search occurred or any other school in the district.

STRIP SEARCHES

An even more intrusive form of searches involves strip searches. In perhaps the earliest case, a federal trial court in Pennsylvania indicated that school officials and a city police chief were not entitled to the dismissal of Fourth Amendment claims filed by eight junior high school students who were strip searched in an unsuccessful attempt to locate a classmate's missing ring.[242] In another early case, a federal trial court in New York believed that individualized suspicion was necessary where school officials wished to strip search fifth-grade students in an attempt to locate three dollars that were reported missing.[243]

Following *T.L.O.*, the majority,[244] but not all,[245] courts struck down strip searches for personal items rather than drugs or other contraband. In

---

238. *In re D.H.*, 306 S.W.3d 955 [256 Educ. L. Rep. 455] (Tex. Ct. App. 2010).

239. *See also Jones v. Latexo Indep. School Dist.*, 499 F.Supp. 223 (E.D. Tex. 1980).

240. *Horton v. Goose Creek Indep. School Dist.*, 690 F.2d 470 [6 Educ. L. Rep. 950] (5th Cir.1982), *cert. denied*, 463 U.S. 1207, 103 S.Ct. 3536, 77 L.Ed.2d 1387 (1983). *See also Commonwealth v. Cass*, 709 A.2d 350 [125 Educ. L. Rep. 705] (Pa. 1998), *cert. denied*, 525 U.S. 833, 119 S.Ct. 89, 142 L.Ed.2d 70 (1998).

241. *B.C. v. Plumas Unified School Dist.*, 192 F.3d 1260 [138 Educ. L. Rep. 1003] (9th Cir. 1999).

242. *Potts v. Wright*, 357 F.Supp. 215 (E.D. Pa. 1973).

243. *Bellnier v. Lund*, 438 F.Supp. 47 (N.D.N.Y. 1977).

244. *See, e.g., State ex rel. Galford v. Mark Anthony B.*, 433 S.E.2d 41 [84 Educ. L. Rep. 1138] (W. Va. 1993); *Kennedy v. Dexter Consol. Schools*, 10 P.3d 115 [148 Educ. L. Rep. 1047] (N.M. 2000); *Thomas ex rel. Thomas v. Roberts*, 261 F.3d 1160 [156 Educ. L. Rep. 508] (11th Cir. 2001); *Bell v. Marseilles Elementary School*, 160 F. Supp.2d 883 [156 Educ. L. Rep. 1066] (N.D. Ill. 2001).

245. *Williams ex rel. Williams v. Ellington*, 936 F.2d 881 [68 Educ. L. Rep. 302] (6th Cir. 1991); *Cornfield by Lewis v. Consolidated High School Dist. No. 230*, 991 F.2d 1316 [82 Educ. L. Rep. 379] (7th Cir. 1993); *Jenkins by Hall v. Talladega City Bd. of Educ.*, 115 F.3d 821 [118

one case, the Seventh Circuit upheld a strip search of a student in Illinois when looking for drugs even though his mother refused to consent to a pat down and he became visibly agitated when searched.[246] The court affirmed that insofar as there was reasonable suspicion, educators met both prongs of the *T.L.O.* test.

In a case from Connecticut, after educators searched a student's bag and discovered that she possessed cigarettes in violation of school rules, but not the marijuana that they sought, they asked her mother to come to school to strip search her for marijuana. Even though the search did not lead to the discovery of marijuana or other illegal substances, the federal trial court granted the board's motion to dismiss the student's claim that officials violated her Fourth Amendment rights since it judged that educators met both parts of the *T.L.O.* test. On further review, the Second Circuit reversed in favor of the student.[247] The court explained that insofar as officials failed to investigate the matter before permitting the search, it was unjustified as overly intrusive since the discovery of cigarettes in the student's purse alone failed to give rise to suspicion that she was carrying marijuana in her underwear.[248]

Most,[249] but not all, courts[250] refused to impose personal liability on educators for unreasonable strip searches since case law did not clearly establish that their actions were unconstitutional. In such a case, the Eleventh Circuit affirmed that while a strip search of elementary school students in Georgia, in an attempt to locate twenty-six dollars that were missing, was unreasonable, officials were not liable for the searches under the theory of inadequate training or supervision, and the board was not faced with situations that were so much alike that there was a need for such training.[251] In a case from Texas, the Fifth Circuit affirmed an order refusing to impose liability on officials who searched a student with Down Syndrome after she was sexually assaulted in a boy's bathroom.[252] The

---

Educ. L. Rep. 867] (11th Cir. 1997), *cert. denied sub nom. Jenkins by Hall v. Herring*, 522 U.S. 966, 118 S.Ct. 412, 139 L.Ed.2d 315 (1997); *Cuesta v. School Bd. of Miami–Dade County*, 285 F.3d 962 [163 Educ. L. Rep. 101] (11th Cir. 2002).

246. Of course, consent for a search must be voluntary. *See Lopera v. Town of Coventry*, 640 F.3d 388 [267 Educ. L. Rep. 476] (1st Cir. 2011) (affirming that a visiting coach had *in loco parentis* authority to consent to a search of his players and that he was not coerced to do so where items were discovered missing in the home team's locker room).

247. *Phaneuf v. Cipriano*, 330 F. Supp.2d 74 [191 Educ. L. Rep. 752] (D. Conn. 2004).

248. *Phaneuf v. Fraikin*, 448 F.3d 591 [209 Educ. L. Rep. 624] (2d Cir. 2006), *on remand sub nom. Phaneuf v. Cipriano*, 2007 WL 274535 (D. Conn. 2007), *vacated in part on reconsideration*, 2007 WL 926890 (D. Conn. 2007) (vacating and dismissing state law causes of action).

249. *See, e.g., Williams ex rel. Williams v. Ellington*, 936 F.2d 881 [68 Educ. L. Rep. 302] (6th Cir. 1991); *Jenkins v. Talladega City Bd. of Educ.*, 115 F.3d 821 [118 Educ. L. Rep. 867] (11th Cir. 1997), *cert. denied sub nom. Jenkins by Hall v. Herring*, 522 U.S. 966, 118 S.Ct. 412, 139 L.Ed.2d 315 (1997).

250. *See, e.g., Kennedy v. Dexter Consol. Schools*, 10 P.3d 115 [148 Educ. L. Rep. 1047] (N.M. 2000); *Bell v. Marseilles Elementary School*, 160 F. Supp.2d 883 [156 Educ. L. Rep. 1066] (N.D. Ill. 2001); *Fewless v. Board of Educ.*, 208 F. Supp.2d 806 [167 Educ. L. Rep. 153] (W.D. Mich. 2002).

251. *Thomas ex rel. Thomas v. Roberts*, 261 F.3d 1160 [156 Educ. L. Rep. 508] (11th Cir. 2001).

252. *Teague ex rel. C.R.T. v. Texas City Indep. School Dist.*, 386 F. Supp.2d 893 [203 Educ. L. Rep. 205] (S.D. Tex. 2005), *aff'd*, 185 Fed.Appx. 355 [213 Educ. L. Rep. 167] (5th Cir. 2006).

court discerned that the board could not be liable because the search was not the result of an official custom or policy.

The Supreme Court of Kentucky refused to impose liability on educators who had middle school students in a physical education class drop their shorts below their knees and raise their shirts above their breasts, exposing their underwear in a fruitless search for a student's missing pair of shorts.[253] Also, the Sixth Circuit refused to impose liability on educators in Michigan who conducted an unsuccessful search for missing money since the law was not clearly established when they acted.[254] The facts showed that officials told a physical education teacher and a male teacher to strip search about twenty males by ordering them to lower their pants and underwear while removing their shirts and directed two female teachers to strip search at least five girls by having them pull up their shirts and pull down their pants while standing in a circle.[255]

It took a case from Arizona to get the Supreme Court involved in the fray over strip searches. In *Safford Unified School District No. 1* v. *Redding*,[256] an assistant principal ordered a school nurse and an administrative assistant to strip search a middle school student in an attempt to locate ibuprofen. Relying on *T.L.O.*, the Supreme Court affirmed that the search was unconstitutional because the assistant principal's level of suspicion did not match the degree of intrusion insofar as he was looking for what he knew were over-the-counter medications. The Court explained that no matter how much the presence of these pills in school violated board policy, the educator had no reason to suspect either that the student was distributing large amounts of drugs in school or that she was hiding painkillers in her underwear. The Court explained that such an intrusive search could not have been based on general possibilities where there was no evidence that students in the school had pills in their underwear. The Court added that absent evidence that the student posed a threat to her peers due to the power or quantity of the drugs or that she was hiding pills in her underwear, the search was unreasonable. At the same time, the Court was satisfied that the assistant principal was entitled to a grant of qualified immunity because the law with regard to strip searches was unclear at that time that he ordered the search.

In a post-*Redding* case from Kentucky, the Sixth Circuit affirmed that school officials who strip searched students for money, a credit card, and other items of value were not entitled to qualified immunity.[257] The court

---

253. *Lamb v. Holmes*, 162 S.W.3d 902 [198 Educ. L. Rep. 755] (Ky. 2005).

254. *Beard v. Whitmore*, 402 F.3d 598 [196 Educ. L. Rep. 438] (6th Cir. 2005), *reh'g and reh'g en banc denied* (2005).

255. *But see H.Y. ex rel. K.Y. v. Russell County Bd. of Educ.*, 490 F. Supp.2d 1174 (M.D. Ala. 2007) (finding that a pat down search of students was neither excessively intrusive nor violated their rights to privacy but that strip searches in school restrooms, where children were asked to lower their pants and lift up their shirts, were impermissible in light of the small amount of missing money).

256. 557 U.S. 364, 129 S.Ct. 2633, 174 L.Ed.2d 354 [245 Educ. L. Rep. 626] (2009). [Case No 96]

257. *Knisley v. Pike County Joint Vocational School Dist.*, 604 F.3d 977 [256 Educ. L. Rep. 535] (6th Cir. 2010), *cert. denied*, ___ U.S. ___, 131 S.Ct. 498, 178 L.Ed.2d 290 (2010).

explained that clearly established case law put the school board and its employees on notice that such a search was unconstitutional.

DRUG TESTING

Three years after *T.L.O.*, a dispute from Indiana became the first case directly addressing drug testing of student-athletes. After five baseball players tested positive for marijuana, their school board implemented a random drug testing policy for student-athletes and cheerleaders. The Seventh Circuit affirmed the validity of testing on the grounds that it was reasonable under the Fourth Amendment and that school officials instituted sufficient safeguards to protect student privacy.[258] The court found that insofar as student-athletes and cheerleaders gained enhanced prestige in the community, it was not unreasonable to require them to submit to drug testing.

The Supreme Court revisited the Fourth Amendment a decade after *T.L.O.* in considering mass suspicionless drug testing of student-athletes in *Vernonia School District 47J v. Acton (Acton)*.[259] The Court also addressed the question of individualized suspicion that it left unanswered in *T.L.O.* Acting in response to increased drug use among students, a school board in Oregon, following up on parental concerns, instituted a drug testing policy for student-athletes both because they were leaders of the drug culture and there were at least two incidents wherein student-athletes were injured due to the effects of drugs. The policy, which included elaborate safeguards to protect the privacy rights of the student-athletes, required individuals who wished to try out for interscholastic sports to submit to urinalysis drug testing.

When a seventh-grade student was suspended from interscholastic athletics because he and his parents refused to sign a consent form for drug testing, they challenged his exclusion, claiming that educators violated his rights under the Fourth Amendment and the state constitution absent evidence that he ever used drugs. After a federal trial court upheld the policy, the Ninth Circuit struck it down as unconstitutional.[260] When the school board appealed, the Supreme Court vacated and remanded in its favor.

In *Acton*, the Supreme Court applied a three-part balancing test in affirming the policy's constitutionality. First, the Court held that students have a lesser expectation of privacy than ordinary citizens. The Justices ruled that student-athletes in particular experience diminished privacy rights not only because they are subject to physical examinations before becoming eligible to play but also because they dress in open areas of locker rooms. Second, the Court posited that the urinalysis testing was minimally intrusive since it was coupled with safeguards that allowed little encroach-

258. *Schaill by Kross v. Tippecanoe County School Corp.*, 864 F.2d 1309 [51 Educ. L. Rep. 92] (7th Cir. 1988).

259. 515 U.S. 646, 115 S.Ct. 2386, 132 L.Ed.2d 564 [101 Educ. L. Rep. 37] (1995), *on remand*, 66 F.3d 217 [103 Educ. L. Rep. 608] (9th Cir. 1995).

260. *Acton v. Vernonia School Dist. 47J*, 23 F.3d 1514 [91 Educ. L. Rep. 495] (9th Cir. 1994).

ment on the students' privacy. Third, given the perception of increased drug use, the Court agreed with school officials and parents that there was a significant need for the policy. On remand, the Ninth Circuit affirmed "that the Oregon Supreme Court would not offer greater protection under the provisions of the Oregon Constitution in this case."[261]

Following *Acton*, the circuits remained divided over suspicionless testing of students involved in extracurricular activities including sports.[262] For instance, the Seventh Circuit twice upheld suspicionless drug testing even though it had reservations about doing so, suggesting that but for being bound by the precedent from its first case, it would have reached a different result in the latter.[263] Yet, the same court invalidated drug and alcohol testing of students who were suspended for three days or more for fighting absent a nexus between use of the banned substances and violent behavior.[264] The next year, the Eighth Circuit originally upheld random testing but vacated its judgment as moot when the student moved out of the district.[265]

The Tenth Circuit, in a case from Oklahoma that eventually made its way to the Supreme Court, struck down random drug testing as unconstitutional, thereby highlighting how the split between the circuits left educators without clear guidelines.[266] In a case not involving a student-athlete, the Third Circuit affirmed that educators did not violate the rights of a high school student who was suspected of being on drugs when, pursuant to board policy, she was subjected to urinalysis testing.[267] Even though the student tested negative for drugs, the court affirmed that officials did not violate her Fourth Amendment rights since testing was reasonably related to their objective of evaluating whether she used drugs. The court noted that while officials might have relied on less invasive means, such as testing the student's breath or saliva, rather than her urine, the test was not excessively intrusive.

A school board in Oklahoma adopted a student activities drug testing policy which required all middle and high school students to consent to urinalysis testing for drugs in order to participate in extracurricular activities. In practice, the policy applied only to students who took part in competitive extracurricular activities sanctioned by the state's secondary

---

261. *Acton v. Vernonia School Dist. 47J*, 66 F.3d 217, 218 [103 Educ. L. Rep. 608] (9th Cir. 1995).

262. The Supreme Court of Colorado prohibited random testing of members of a school band, including those who participated for academic credit, since they had greater expectations of privacy under the state constitution. *Trinidad School Dist. No. 1 v. Lopez*, 963 P.2d 1095 [129 Educ. L. Rep. 812] (Colo. 1998).

263. *Todd v. Rush County Schools*, 133 F.3d 984 [125 Educ. L. Rep. 18] (7th Cir.1998), *cert. denied*, 525 U.S. 824, 119 S.Ct. 68, 142 L.Ed.2d 53 (1998); *Joy v. Penn–Harris–Madison School Corp.*, 212 F.3d 1052 [144 Educ. L. Rep. 866] (7th Cir. 2000).

264. *Willis v. Anderson Community School Corp.*, 158 F.3d 415 [130 Educ. L. Rep. 89] (7th Cir. 1998), *cert. denied*, 526 U.S. 1019 119 S.Ct. 1254, 143 L.Ed.2d 351 (1999).

265. *Miller ex rel. Miller v. Wilkes*, 172 F.3d 574 [133 Educ. L. Rep. 765] (8th Cir. 1999).

266. *Earls ex rel. Earls v. Board of Educ. of Tecumseh Pub. School Dist.*, 242 F.3d 1264 [151 Educ. L. Rep. 752] (10th Cir. 2001), *cert. granted*, 534 U.S. 1015, 122 S.Ct. 509, 151 L.Ed.2d 418 [158 Educ. L. Rep. 544] (2001).

267. *Hedges v. Musco*, 204 F.3d 109 [141 Educ. L. Rep. 1020] (3d Cir. 2000).

schools activities association. Students and their parents filed suit alleging that the policy violated the Fourth Amendment since it failed to identify a special need to test participants in extracurricular activities, to address a proven problem, or to offer any benefits to students or their school.

Relying on *Acton*, a federal trial court granted the board's motion for summary judgment, but the Tenth Circuit entered a judgment in favor of the students. On further review in *Board of Education of Independent School District No. 92 of Pottawatomie v. Earls (Earls)*,[268] the Supreme Court reversed in favor of the board. As an initial matter, the Court pointed out that the students who were tested in *Earls* were not in regular classrooms and that results were not turned over to the police. This suggests that *Acton* and *Earls* are limited to the narrow range of disputes involving students in extracurricular activities.

Before applying *Acton*, the Supreme Court asserted that it relied on a fact-specific balancing of the intrusion on the Fourth Amendment rights of students against the promotion of legitimate governmental *qua* school interests. The Justices first considered the nature of the students' alleged privacy interest, reasoning that they are not only limited due to the need of officials to preserve discipline and safety but also that individuals who take part in extracurricular activities voluntarily subject themselves to greater intrusions on their privacy than their non-participating peers. The Court was satisfied that given the limited privacy expectations of the students who were affected by the policy, it was constitutional.

Turning to the character of the intrusion, the Supreme Court reviewed key elements of the policy, recognizing that it included procedures that were virtually identical to those in *Acton*. If anything, the Justices stated that this policy afforded even more protection since faculty members stood outside of closed restroom stalls, unlike *Acton* where males stood at urinals, and produced samples which were poured into different vials before being sent for testing. The Court also determined that the results were kept in separate confidential student files that were released on a need-to-know basis and were not turned over to law enforcement officials. The Court added that test results did not lead to the imposition of disciplinary or academic sanctions but only resulted in varying degrees of the loss of the privilege of participating in extracurricular activities. The Court was thus persuaded that insofar as the urine samples were collected in a minimally intrusive manner, and the test results had limited uses, the invasion into the students' privacy was not constitutionally significant.

As to the third part of the test, the nature and immediacy of the board's concerns and the policy's efficacy in meeting them, the Supreme Court recounted how it acknowledged the importance of governmental interest in preventing drug use, a problem that had not abated since *Acton*. In so doing, the Justices rejected the students' claims that drug use was not a problem at the school by relying on evidence to the contrary from board officials. The Court wrote that it did not require schools to have particularized or pervasive drug problems before permitting educators to conduct

---

268.   536 U.S. 822, 122 S.Ct. 2559, 153 L.Ed.2d 735 [166 Educ. L. Rep. 79] (2002), *on remand*, 300 F.3d 1222 [168 Educ. L. Rep. 581] (10th Cir. 2002). [Case No. 98]

suspicionless testing. Aware of the nationwide epidemic of drug use and the effectiveness of testing, the Court rejected the students' argument that testing had to be based on individualized suspicion since this would have been less intrusive. Even in conceding that drug testing was a reasonably effective means of addressing the board's legitimate concerns in preventing, deterring, and detecting drug use, in addressing the policy, the Court "express[ed] no opinion as to its wisdom."[269]

Following *Earls*, courts continue to uphold drug testing of student-athletes. In one such case, a federal trial court in Pennsylvania rejected claims by a member of a swim team that his being subjected to testing violated his Fourth Amendment rights.[270] The court thought that the coach's suspicions that the student was using drugs, coupled with evidence of his drug use and the potential harm that he would have faced if the coach failed to intervene, rendered the compulsory drug testing reasonable.

As controversies continue with regard to testing, a case from the Supreme Court of Indiana illustrates the trend that the judiciary generally upholds testing for alcohol and drugs but not for other substances. The court largely upheld a policy permitting random testing of students who participated in athletics, extracurricular, and co-curricular activities as well as those who wished to drive to and from school for alcohol and other non-tobacco-related drugs because it merely barred individuals from participating in privileged activities in which they were portrayed as role models. In pointing out that the policy was based on officials' valid interest in deterring student drug abuse, the court decided that it did not violate the unreasonable searches and seizures clause in the state constitution.[271] The court also declared that educators could not subject students to nicotine testing due to their negligible interest in this regard.[272] A year earlier, a federal trial court in Texas invalidated a drug testing policy which officials sought to apply to all students in junior and senior high school for the duration of the academic year as unreasonable.[273] The court struck the policy down as unacceptable because even though the method of testing imposed a low level of intrusion on students' rights to privacy, there was no compelling interest to outweigh their privacy interests. The court emphasized the fact that drug use in the school was actually lower than in other schools in the state.

The Supreme Court of Washington struck down a board policy of random drug and alcohol testing for students who participated in interscholastic athletics.[274] Although the board instituted the policy in response to

---

269. *Id.* at 838.

270. *Dominic J. v. Wyoming Valley West High School*, 362 F. Supp.2d 560 [197 Educ. L. Rep. 154] (M.D. Pa. 2005).

271. *Linke v. Northwestern School Corp.*, 763 N.E.2d 972 [162 Educ. L. Rep. 525] (Ind. 2002).

272. *See also Penn–Harris–Madison School Corp. v. Joy*, 768 N.E.2d 940 [165 Educ. L. Rep. 323] (Ind. Ct. App. 2002).

273. *Tannahill ex rel. Tannahill v. Lockney Indep. School Dist.*, 133 F.Supp.2d 919 [152 Educ. L. Rep. 549] (N.D. Tex. 2001).

274. *York v. Wahkiakum School Dist. No. 200*, 178 P.3d 995 [230 Educ. L. Rep. 425] (Wash. 2008).

persistent problems with drugs and alcohol, the court interpreted the state constitution as providing students with greater privacy protection than its federal counterpart. Conversely, the Supreme Court of Wyoming upheld a board policy requiring random drug and alcohol testing of all students in grades seven-to-twelve who wished to take part in extracurricular activities.[275] The court affirmed that in light of potential problems with substance abuse in schools and that testing was a search within the meaning of the state constitution, the policy was constitutional even though the board did not have to prove that its actions would achieve a specific level of success in deterring students from using drugs and/ or alcohol.

SEXUAL HARASSMENT

A long-term problem that has generated a large amount of litigation deals with sexual harassment of students by teachers and peers in cases filed under Title IX of the Education Amendments of 1972 (Title IX), a statute that was initially enacted to ensure gender equity in intercollegiate sports. According to the relevant portion of Title IX, "[n]o person in the United States shall, on the basis of sex, be excluded from participation in, be denied the benefits of, or be subjected to discrimination under any education program or activity receiving Federal financial assistance."[276]

The expansion of Title IX to cover educational disputes involving sexual harassment traces its origins to *Cannon v. University of Chicago* (*Cannon*).[277] In *Cannon*, a female applicant to two private medical schools filed suit under Title IX alleging that insofar as the institutions received federal financial assistance, they were liable for discrimination because she was denied admission due to her gender. After a federal trial court and the Seventh Circuit denied the applicant's claim on the basis that Title IX did not provide for a private cause of action, the Supreme Court reversed in her favor. The Court reasoned that insofar as the applicant was a member of the class that Title IX was designed to protect and its legislative history evidenced an intent to permit a private cause of action, such a remedy was consistent with the statute's approach because discrimination due to sex was a concern for the federal government. The Court thus concluded that the plaintiff had an implied cause of action for monetary damages under Title IX.[278] Still, more than a decade would pass before the federal courts applied Title IX to fight sexual harassment in schools.

After *Cannon*, the Supreme Court examined three cases dealing with sexual harassment in school settings while lower federal and state courts

---

275. *Hageman v. Goshen County School Dist. No. 1*, 256 P.3d 487 [269 Educ. L. Rep. 345] (Wyo. 2011).

276. 20 U.S.C.A. § 1681. Portions of this statute are in the Appendix.

277. 441 U.S. 677, 99 S.Ct. 1946, 60 L.Ed.2d 560 (1979).

278. *See also Meritor v. Vinson*, 477 U.S. 57, 106 S.Ct. 2399, 91 L.Ed.2d 49 (1986), *on remand sub nom. Vinson v. Taylor*, 801 F.2d 1436 (D.C. Cir.1986) (although decided under Title VII because it involved an employee who was subjected to sexual harassment in the workplace, this remains a significant decision in the fight against sexual harassment).

continue to resolve a large number of disputes. The first two cases involved situations where teachers engaged in inappropriate sexual misconduct with students while the third dealt with peer-to-peer sexual harassment.

SEXUAL HARASSMENT INVOLVING TEACHERS AND STUDENTS

The facts in *Franklin v. Gwinnett County Public Schools (Franklin)*[279] revealed egregious disregard for a student's well-being. A female high school sophomore in Georgia alleged that she and one of her male teachers developed a "special" friendship. The teacher conducted private meetings with the student, authorized her late entry to classes, and engaged her in sexually oriented conversations. On one occasion, after the two argued in the school parking lot, the teacher forcibly kissed the student on the mouth. During this time, the student's boyfriend personally notified the school's band director about the teacher's conduct, and at least one other student who told an assistant principal about it was admonished for doing so. Other female students informed a teacher and a guidance counselor that the teacher made sexual remarks to them. Even as officials were apparently unwilling to investigate the teacher's behavior, his conduct worsened to the point that he engaged the student in three acts of what the Supreme Court described as "coercive intercourse"[280] at school. When the principal was informed of the sexual activity, administrators discouraged the student from pursuing her complaint due to the negative publicity that it might have generated. In addition, the band director spoke with the student's boyfriend in an attempt to dissuade her from acting on her complaint. Shortly after officials began an inquiry into the student's complaints, they closed their investigation when the teacher agreed to resign at the end of the academic year; the band director voluntarily retired.

After unsuccessfully filing a complaint with the Federal Office of Civil Rights (OCR), an unreported federal trial court opinion rejected the student's Title IX damages claim. The Eleventh Circuit affirmed the dismissal of the student's complaint.[281]

In *Franklin*, a unanimous Supreme Court, relying in part on *Cannon*, expanded the scope of Title IX by applying it to sexual harassment in a school setting for the first time. Reversing in favor of the student, the Justices interpreted Title IX as implying a private right of action. The Court explained that insofar as nothing in congressional intent in enacting Title IX prevented individuals, students, or others, from bringing suits for monetary damages for harassment, the student was free to pursue this remedy since precluding her from doing so would have left her without any other legal recourse.

The second case involving teacher-student sexual harassment arose in Texas after an eighth-grade student joined a book-discussion club at the

---

279.   503 U.S. 60, 112 S.Ct. 1028, 117 L.Ed.2d 208 [72 Educ. L. Rep. 32] (1992), *on remand*, 969 F.2d 1022 [76 Educ. L. Rep. 396] (11th Cir. 1992). [Case No. 99]

280.   *Id.* at 63.

281.   *Franklin v. Gwinnett County Pub. Schools*, 911 F.2d 617 [62 Educ. L. Rep. 453] (11th Cir. 1990).

high school she ultimately attended. The dispute arose when the teacher in charge made sexually suggestive comments, eventually directing his more inappropriate remarks at the student. The teacher eventually initiated sexual contact with the student when he visited her home on the pretext of giving her a book, culminating in their regularly engaging in sexual relations. None of the sexual encounters took place on school property. The student did not complain at that time both because she was uncertain about how she should have behaved and since she wished to continue having the same teacher.

After more than a year passed, when parents of other students complained about the teacher's behavior, the principal warned him to be careful about what he said and informed the school guidance counselor about the incident but failed to notify the superintendent who also served as the district's Title IX coordinator. When a police officer happened to discover the teacher and student having sex, he was arrested. Unlike in *Franklin*, the school board promptly terminated the teacher's employment and the Texas Education Agency revoked his teaching license. The student and her mother filed suit in a federal trial court, seeking monetary damages under Title IX for the teacher's sexual harassment. On further review of a trial court's granting the board's motion for summary judgment, the Fifth Circuit affirmed that it was not vicariously liable under Title IX for the teacher's sexual misconduct pursuant to common law agency theory.[282]

In *Gebser v. Lago Vista Independent School District (Gebser)*,[283] the Supreme Court affirmed that a board could not be liable under Title IX for a teacher's misconduct unless an official who, at a minimum, has the authority to institute corrective measures, has actual notice of, and is deliberately indifferent to, a teacher's sexual misconduct. The Court found that insofar as the board behaved appropriately under the circumstances since officials acted promptly and decisively in punishing the teacher, the student and her mother could not proceed with their claim.

The Eighth Circuit, in an illustrative case, rejected the claim of a student in Nebraska that her school board was liable under Title IX when she had a homosexual relationship with a teacher.[284] The court contended that the board was not at fault since the student failed to make the necessary showing that officials acted with deliberate indifference after being informed about the teacher's behavior. Previously, the Supreme Court of Alabama affirmed that even though Title IX would support a claim for same-sex sexual harassment where a male teacher-coach harassed and abused a male student over a four-year period, the facts did not support the underlying charge.[285]

---

282. *Doe v. Lago Vista Indep. School Dist.*, 106 F.3d 1223 [125 Educ. L. Rep. 1074] (5th Cir. 1997).

283. 524 U.S. 274, 118 S.Ct. 1989, 141 L.Ed.2d 277 [125 Educ. L. Rep. 1055] (1998). [Case No. 100]

284. *Kinman v. Omaha Pub. School Dist.*, 171 F.3d 607 [133 Educ. L. Rep. 418] (8th Cir.1999).

285. *H.M. v. Jefferson County Bd. of Educ.*, 719 So.2d 793 [130 Educ. L. Rep. 952] (Ala. 1998).

In a case from Georgia, the Eleventh Circuit affirmed that a school board was not liable under Title IX where a male student failed to prove that school officials acted with deliberate indifference to reports that he engaged in a sexual relationship with a female teacher.[286] The panel ascertained that the trial court incorrectly applied the stricter Title IX standard that governs cases of student-on-student harassment. Focusing instead on the teacher-on-student standard enunciated in *Gebser*, the court clarified that insofar as officials unsuccessfully warned the teacher to end the relationship, they had not acted with deliberate indifference because they responded appropriately to allegations about the relationship even though they were unable to prevent additional abuse.

PEER-TO-PEER SEXUAL HARASSMENT

Davis v. Monroe County Board of Education (Davis)[287] involved a female fifth-grade student in Georgia who was subjected to a prolonged pattern of sexual harassment by a male classmate. Over five months, the male engaged in inappropriate behavior, including trying to touch the female's breasts and genital area along with verbal requests for sexual relations. Even though the student and her parents reported the male's behavior and repeatedly asked for help, officials failed to intervene. Due to the male's behavior, the female's grades suffered since she was unable to concentrate on school work; her father also discovered that she had written a suicide note. In addition, there was evidence that the plaintiff was not the only target of the male's behavior. The harassment did not stop until the male pled guilty to charges of sexual battery.

The student and her parents filed suit against the board of education under Title IX, seeking monetary damages and injunctive relief for peer-to-peer sexual harassment. A federal trial court granted the board's motion to dismiss for failure to state a claim upon which relief can be granted and the Eleventh Circuit affirmed.[288]

In *Davis,* the Supreme Court reversed in favor of the female and her parents.[289] The Justices began by clarifying that damages are limited "to circumstances wherein the recipient exercises substantial control over both the harasser and the context in which the known harassment occurs."[290] The Court decided that school boards, as recipients of federal financial

---

286. *Sauls v. Pierce County School Dist.*, 399 F.3d 1279 [195 Educ. L. Rep. 767] (11th Cir. 2005).

287. 526 U.S. 629, 119 S.Ct. 1661, 143 L.Ed.2d 839 [134 Educ. L. Rep. 477] (1999), *on remand*, 206 F.3d 1377 [143 Educ. L. Rep. 724] (11th Cir. 2000). [Case No. 101]

288. *Davis v. Monroe County Bd. of Educ.*, 74 F.3d 1186 [106 Educ. L. Rep. 486] (11th Cir. 1996), *reh'g en banc granted, opinion vacated*, 91 F.3d 1418 [111 Educ. L. Rep. 1107] (11th Cir. 1996), *on reh'g*, 120 F.3d 1390 [120 Educ. L. Rep. 390] (11th Cir. 1997).

289. For an earlier case holding a board liable for peer-to-peer harassment, *see Oona R.-S.-by Kate S. v. McCaffrey*, 143 F.3d 473 [126 Educ. L. Rep. 589] (9th Cir. 1998). *But see Rowinsky v. Bryan Indep. School Dist.*, 80 F.3d 1006 [108 Educ. L. Rep. 502] (5th Cir.1996), *cert. denied*, 519 U.S. 861, 117 S.Ct. 165, 136 L.Ed.2d 108 (1996) (denying relief in a case of peer-to-peer sexual harassment).

290. *Davis v. Monroe County Bd. of Educ.*, 526 U.S. 629, 646, 119 S.Ct. 1661, 143 L.Ed.2d 839 [134 Educ. L. Rep. 477] (1999), *on remand*, 206 F.3d 1377 [143 Educ. L. Rep. 724] (11th Cir. 2000). [Case No. 101]

assistance, "are properly held liable in damages only when they are deliberately indifferent to sexual harassment, of which they have actual knowledge, that is so severe, pervasive, and objectively offensive that it can be said to deprive the victims of access to the educational opportunities or benefits provided by the school."[291] The Court stressed that while boards may be accountable if officials are deliberately indifferent, this does not mean that they can avoid liability only by eliminating actionable peer-harassment claims or by taking specified disciplinary steps.

In rejecting the dissent's argument that the majority placed too much of a burden on school officials, the Supreme Court responded that the standard is flexible enough to account for the level of authority that they must apply while also protecting them from potential liability in disciplining students who sexually harass peers. The Court conceded that while it remains to be seen whether the female could have proved that board officials acted with deliberate indifference, she may have been able to demonstrate that administrators subjected her to discrimination by failing to respond to her complaints for five months.

LATER DEVELOPMENTS

Litigation involving sexual harassment in the schools continues at a brisk pace, especially when educators engage in sexual relationships with students.[292] Courts continue to refuse to dismiss claims, awarding damages to students for sexual harassment and/or forms of misconduct under Title IX for harassment by peers[293] and school employees,[294] or where school officials failed to supervise students to prevent such behavior in school settings when they agree that educators could have prevented the misconduct.[295] When they found that educators behaved responsibly, courts refused to impose liability on boards for harassment and/or misconduct by peers[296] and school employees,[297] especially absent evidence that officials acted with deliberate indifference to staff misconduct.[298]

---

291. *Id.* at 650.

292. *See, e.g., Baumgardt v. Wausau School Dist. Bd. of Educ.*, 475 F. Supp.2d 800 [218 Educ. L. Rep. 286] (W.D. Wis. 2007) (refusing to dismiss Title IX charges against a coach and officials who knew that he had a sexual relationship with a student-athlete and even booked an adjoining room for her when the team was on a road trip).

293. *See, e.g., Doe v. Brimfield Grade School*, 552 F. Supp.2d 816 [233 Educ. L. Rep. 684] (C.D. Ill. 2008) (involving same sex sexual harassment); *Bruning v. Carroll Comm. School Dist.*, 486 F. Supp.2d 892 [220 Educ. L Rep. 584] (N.D. Iowa 2007); *Vance v. Spencer County Pub. School Dist.*, 231 F.3d 253 [148 Educ. L. Rep. 616] (6th Cir. 2000).

294. *See, e.g., Baynard v. Malone*, 268 F.3d 228 [158 Educ. L. Rep. 19] (4th Cir. 2001).

295. *Vaughn v. Orleans Parish School Bd.*, 802 So.2d 967 [160 Educ. L. Rep. 973] (La. Ct. App. 2001), *writ of error denied*, 818 So.2d 773 (La. 2002).

296. *See, e.g., Sanches v. Carrollton–Farmers Branch Indep. School Dist.*, 647 F.3d 156 [270 Educ. L. Rep. 417] (5th Cir. 2011); *Rost ex rel. K.C. v. Steamboat Springs RE–2 School Dist.*, 511 F.3d 1114 [228 Educ. L. Rep. 632] (10th Cir. 2008); *Wilson ex rel. Adams v. Cahokia School Dist. No. 187*, 470 F. Supp. 2d 897 [217 Educ. L. Rep. 218] (S.D. Ill. 2007); *Hawkins v. Sarasota County School Bd.*, 322 F.3d 1279 [174 Educ. L. Rep. 678] (11th Cir. 2003).

297. *See, e.g., Craig v. Lima City Schools Bd. of Educ.*, 384 F. Supp.2d 1136 [202 Educ. L. Rep. 172] (N.D. Ohio 2005); *Johnson v. Elk Lake School Dist.*, 283 F.3d 138 [162 Educ. L. Rep. 679] (3d Cir. 2002); *P.H. v. School Dist. of Kansas City, Mo.*, 265 F.3d 653 [157 Educ. L. Rep. 42] (8th Cir. 2001); *Hartley v. Parnell*, 193 F.3d 1263 [139 Educ. L. Rep. 95] (11th Cir. 1999).

298. *See, e.g., Doe v. Flaherty*, 623 F.3d 577 [261 Educ. L. Rep. 552] (8th Cir. 2010); *Williams ex rel. Hart v. Paint Valley Local School Dist.*, 400 F.3d 360 [196 Educ. L. Rep. 27]

In the first of two cases from Illinois with like results, the Seventh Circuit affirmed an order refusing to dismiss Title IX claims involving sexual impropriety. The court agreed that a principal was not entitled to a grant of summary judgment where her refusal to investigate charges that a teacher sexually molested his students could have been interpreted as her attempting to cover up the male's actions.[299] Similarly, a federal trial court in Illinois refused to grant motions for summary judgment entered by a teacher and an array of officials when parents filed a variety of claims including allegations that he sexually abused their children and used a school computer to access pornography.[300] The court was satisfied that insofar as material issues of fact remained about what officials knew about the teacher's behavior as to Title IX liability precluded granting their motions for summary judgment. Earlier, a federal trial court in Arkansas rejected a school board's motion for summary judgment in a dispute where parents of a student who was mentally disabled was raped while in a locker room.[301] The court rebuffed the board's motion due to the existence of material facts over whether officials were deliberately indifferent to past incidents of inappropriate physical contact with the student who attacked the victim and whether they played an active role in creating the dangers that the student encountered.

A case with an interesting set of facts arose in Massachusetts where the First Circuit affirmed that a school committee was not liable for peer-to-peer sexual harassment when a child in kindergarten alleged that a third-grader on her bus subjected her to inappropriate sexual contact. The court agreed that officials did not act with deliberate indifference to the plight of the younger child since educators completed an immediate and thorough investigation that failed to turn up evidence of wrongdoing by the third-grader and the girl's accusations lacked credibility. On appeal, without considering the merits of the constitutional claims or the adequacy of the pleadings in *Fitzgerald v. Barnstable School Committee*,[302] a unanimous Supreme Court reversed in favor of the plaintiffs. The court decided that Title IX does not preclude a claim for unconstitutional gender discrimination in schools under section 1983.

In California, a federal trial court refused to grant a motion for summary judgment filed by two school boards that jointly operated a

(6th Cir. 2005); *Doe v. City of Roseville*, 296 F.3d 431 [167 Educ. L. Rep. 115] (6th Cir. 2002), *cert. denied*, 537 U.S. 1232, 123 S.Ct. 1357, 155 L.Ed.2d 196 (2003); *Sauls v. Pierce County School Dist.*, 399 F.3d 1279 [195 Educ. L. Rep. 767] (11th Cir. 2005); *Davis ex rel. Doe v. DeKalb County School Dist.*, 233 F.3d 1367 [149 Educ. L. Rep. 376] (11th Cir.2000), *cert. denied*, 532 U.S. 1066, 121 S.Ct. 2217, 150 L.Ed.2d 210 (2001); *Doe ex rel. Doe v. Dallas Indep. School Dist.*, 220 F.3d 380 [146 Educ. L. Rep. 80] (5th Cir.2000).

299. *T.E. v. Grindle*, 599 F.3d 583 [255 Educ. L. Rep. 30] (7th Cir. 2010).

300. *Doe 20 v. Board of Educ. of Community Unit School Dist. No. 5*, 680 F.Supp.2d 957 [255 Educ. L. Rep. 159] (C.D. Ill. 2010).

301. *Finch v. Texarkana School Dist. No. 7 of Miller County*, 557 F. Supp.2d 976 [234 Educ. L. Rep. 907] (W.D. Ark. 2008).

302. 555 U.S. 246, 129 S.Ct. 788, 172 L.Ed.2d 582 (2009).

football camp when a participant alleged that he was harassed by same-sex peers.[303] The court denied the motion by the board since material questions of fact existed as to whether coaches and other officials provided adequate supervision in a situation where they exercised substantial control over the players and operations at the camp.

One of the key related issues in sexual harassment cases concerns who is an appropriate person to have actual notice of harassment for the purpose of alleging that school boards and educators violated Title IX. In a dispute from South Dakota, a high school student unsuccessfully sued the board after one of her male teachers was fired for having subjected her to sexual advances.[304] The Eighth Circuit affirmed that although other teachers admitted having suspicions about the male's behavior, since they were not the appropriate persons for purposes of Title IX's actual knowledge requirement, the board was not liable.[305] Further, as evidenced by a second case from the Eighth Circuit, where a principal lacked actual knowledge of an inappropriate relationship between a teacher and student in Arkansas, the board was not liable under Title IX's deliberate indifference standard.[306]

A case with a twist due to the role of technology in sexual harassment arose in Indiana. A federal trial court refused to dismiss Title IX, equal protection, and intentional infliction of emotional distress claims against a teacher-tennis coach who harassed a female student by continually sending her instant messages from his personal computer.[307] The student did not block the teacher's messages because she feared that she might have suffered negative consequences. Even though the student did not read all of the messages or suffer any adverse consequences, the court denied the teacher's motion for summary judgment since questions of fact remained about whether his actions were sufficiently egregious to create a hostile environment, whether the harassment was due to her sex or because of a personal attraction, and whether he acted under color of state law in sending the messages.

In a case with what can only be described as a novel defense in the face of a teacher's sexual misconduct, which was premised on negligent supervision rather than Title IX, the Supreme Court of Washington rejected the notion that insofar as a middle school student voluntarily participated in a sexual relationship with one of her teachers, she was partially at fault.[308] In a case of first impression, the court ruled that insofar as the thirteen-year-old minor lacked the capacity to consent to sexual relations, she was under

---

303. *Roe ex rel. Callahan v. Gustine Unified School Dist.*, 678 F. Supp. 2d 1008 [254 Educ. L. Rep. 774] (E.D. Cal. 2009).

304. *Plamp v. Mitchell School Dist. No.17–2*, 565 F.3d 450 [244 Educ. L. Rep. 514] (8th Cir. 2009).

305. *See also Bostic v. Smyrna School Dist.*, 418 F.3d 355 [200 Educ. L. Rep. 573] (3d Cir. 2005).

306. *Doe v. Flaherty*, 623 F.3d 577 [261 Educ. L. Rep. 552] (8th Cir. 2010).

307. *Chivers v. Central Noble Community Schools*, 423 F. Supp. 2d 835 [208 Educ. L. Rep. 481] (N.D. Ind. 2006).

308. *Christensen v. Royal School Dist. No. 160*, 124 P.3d 283 [204 Educ. L. Rep. 385] (Wash. 2005).

no duty to protect herself from the abuse. Similarly, a federal trial court in Pennsylvania rejected a teacher's defense that he had not engaged in sexual misconduct during a ten-month long relationship with a female student because she lacked the legal capacity to welcome his sexual advances.[309]

A case from Michigan wherein a student was harassed by peers who not only used language questioning his sexuality but sexually assaulted him in a locker room serves as a segue to the next section on sexual orientation even though the courts did not identify this as the issue at bar. Reversing an earlier grant of summary judgment in favor of the school board and educators, the Sixth Circuit decided that the case should proceed to trial since genuine issues of material fact remained as to whether educators were deliberately indifferent to the reported incidents of student-on-student sexual harassment.[310] On remand, the federal trial court granted the board's motion for judgment as a matter of law after a jury returned a verdict in favor of the student.[311] The court explained that insofar as the harassment was not due to the student's sex, sexual orientation, or perceived sexual orientation and officials were not deliberately indifferent to his treatment, the jury verdict that the alleged actions violated Title IX was against the great weight of the evidence.

SEXUAL ORIENTATION

The first reported case dealing with harassment of students based on their sexual orientations arose in Wisconsin. The Seventh Circuit ruled that a student who was gay could proceed with his equal protection claims against school officials who failed to protect him from harassment by peers due to his sexual preference.[312]

When a student in Kansas claimed that officials were deliberately indifferent to his being sexually harassed by peers, the federal trial court rejected the school board's motion to dismiss in acknowledging that same-sex, student-on-student sexual harassment was actionable under Title IX.[313] After a jury entered a verdict in favor of the student, the board unsuccessfully filed a motion for a judgment as a matter of law. The court wrote that when viewing the evidence in a light most favorable to the plaintiff, it was sufficient for the jury to have returned a verdict in his favor where school officials acted with deliberate indifference to his plight.[314]

Former students in California, who were, or were perceived by others as being, lesbian, gay, and/or bisexual, sued school officials alleging that

---

309. *Chancellor v. Pottsgrove School Dist.*, 501 F. Supp.2d 695 [224 Educ. L. Rep. 76] (E.D. Pa. 2007).

310. *Patterson v. Hudson Area Schools*, 551 F.3d 438 [240 Educ. L. Rep. 20] (6th Cir. 2009), *reh'g and reh'g banc denied* (2009), *cert. denied*, ___ U.S. ___, 130 S.Ct. 299, 175 L.Ed.2d 136 (2009).

311. *Patterson v. Hudson Area Schools*, 724 F.Supp.2d 682 [261 Educ. L. Rep. 957] (E.D. Mich. 2010).

312. *Nabozny v. Podlesny*, 92 F.3d 446 [111 Educ. L. Rep. 740] (7th Cir. 1996).

313. *Theno v. Tonganoxie Unified School Dist. No. 464*, 377 F. Supp.2d 952 [200 Educ. L. Rep. 658] (D. Kan. 2005).

314. *Theno v. Tonganoxie Unified School Dist. No. 464*, 394 F. Supp.2d 1299 [204 Educ. L. Rep. 230] (D. Kan. 2005).

their failure to respond to complaints of student-on-student anti-homosexual harassment denied them their rights to equal protection under the Fourteenth Amendment rather than under Title IX. In affirming the denial of the officials' motion for summary judgment, the Ninth Circuit explained that at the time of the alleged incidents, the students' right to be free from intentional discrimination on the basis of sexual orientation was clearly established.[315]

In a second case from California, a federal trial court rejected a student's claim that school officials violated her rights to equal protection, free speech, and privacy when they disciplined her for inappropriate public displays of affection with a female despite being warned repeatedly to stop doing so.[316] In granting the defendants' motion for summary judgment, the court noted that the plaintiff lacked an equal protection claim since she was treated no differently from peers who were heterosexual and that her speech was not protected because it was inconsistent with the school's basic educational mission. The court found that school officials did not violate the student's reasonable expectation of privacy in notifying her parents because her right was outweighed by a state law requiring principals to inform parents when their children are disciplined.

The first of two cases that arose in New Jersey saw parents file suit on behalf of their son under the Individuals with Disabilities Education Act, claiming that he was bullied by other students, in part because of his lack of athleticism, physique, and perceived femininity. The Third Circuit held that school officials failed to provide the student with a free appropriate public education.[317] The court concluded that insofar as school officials failed to offer substantial reasons for not crediting witnesses who testified on behalf of the student at a due process hearing, they had to reimburse his parents for the cost associated with their unilaterally placing him in a public school in a neighboring district.

Where a mother filed a complaint with New Jersey's Division of Civil Rights (DCR), alleging that school officials violated the Law Against Discrimination due to her son's having been repeatedly subjected to harassment by peers at school on account of his perceived sexual orientation, the DCR agreed that insofar as the response of educators was inadequate, he was entitled to damages for emotional distress. On further review, the Supreme Court of New Jersey affirmed that in light of evidence establishing that officials did not effectively respond to two assaults on the student based on his perceived sexual orientation, the law explicitly recognizes a cause of action for peer-to-peer sexual orientation harassment independent of Title IX.[318] On the other hand, the Third Circuit affirmed the rejection of claims by parents from Pennsylvania who alleged that school officials were deliberately indifferent to harassment that their son experienced in light of

---

315. *Flores v. Morgan Hill Unified School Dist.*, 324 F.3d 1130 [175 Educ. L. Rep. 79] (9th Cir. 2003).

316. *Nguon v. Wolf*, 517 F. Supp.2d 1177 [226 Educ. L. Rep. 872] (C.D. Cal. 2007).

317. *Shore Reg'l High School Bd. of Educ. v. P.S. ex rel. P.S.*, 381 F.3d 194 [191 Educ. L. Rep. 641] (3d Cir. 2004).

318. *L.W. ex rel. L.G. v. Toms River Reg'l Schools Bd. of Educ.*, 915 A.2d 535 [216 Educ. L. Rep. 524] (N.J. 2007).

his effeminate characteristics.[319] The court rejected the argument that officials acted with deliberate indifference where they responded to each complaint by taking steps that they hoped would address, and eliminate, the harassment.

A student in Michigan who was openly gay sued his school board under Title IX and section 1983 alleging that officials violated his right to equal protection in failing to do enough to combat the peer-to-peer sexual harassment he encountered at school. The court denied the board's motion for summary judgment since issues of fact remained over whether the charges demonstrated that the behavior the student was subjected to was severe, pervasive, and objectively offensive enough to constitute a Title IX violation.[320] At the same time, the court granted the board's motion as to the section 1983 claim since it did not think that the actions of school officials deprived the student of a constitutionally protected federal right. In a like case from Indiana, a federal trial court refused to grant a board's motion for summary judgment where peers subjected an eighth-grade student to homophobic harassment and bullying due to his perceived sexual orientation.[321]

Conversely, the federal trial court in Connecticut granted a school board's motion for summary judgment when the parents of a nine-year-old filed suit under Title IX and other laws alleging that officials failed to respond adequately after peers called their son "gay" for asking a classmate if he loved him and expressing his love for the other child.[322] The court rejected the parents' claim that their son was subjected to a sexually hostile educational environment or that he was treated differently from other students due to his perceived sexual orientation in light of evidence that officials intervened on his behalf and punished those who harassed the child.

[CASE NO. 93]   DISCIPLINARY RULES FOR STUDENT–ATHLETES

PALMER v. MERLUZZI

United States Court of Appeals, Third Circuit, 1989.
868 F.2d 90 [51 Educ. L. Rep. 1196].

■ STAPLETON, CIRCUIT JUDGE.

This is an appeal from a summary judgment in favor of the defendants, Peter Merluzzi, Superintendent of Schools for the Hunterdon Central High School District, and the Hunterdon Central Board of Education. Plaintiff Dan Palmer, a student and football player at Hunterdon, claims that his Constitutional rights to due process and equal protection were violated

---

319. *Doe v. Bellefonte Area School Dist.*, 106 Fed.Appx. 798 [192 Educ. L. Rep. 386] (3d Cir. 2004).

320. *Martin v. Swartz Creek Community Schools*, 419 F. Supp. 2d 967 [207 Educ. L. Rep. 947] (E.D. Mich. 2006).

321. *Seiwert v. Spencer–Owen Comm. School Corp.*, 497 F. Supp.2d 942 [223 Educ. L. Rep. 654] (S.D. Ind. 2007).

322. *Levarge v. Preston Bd. of Educ.*, 552 F. Supp.2d 248 [233 Educ. L. Rep. 660] (D. Conn. 2008).

when Superintendent Merluzzi suspended him from playing interscholastic football for sixty days. We will affirm.

I

In September of 1986, Dan Palmer was a senior at Hunterdon Central High School and a starting wide receiver on the high school's football team. He was also enrolled in a high school course called "Careers in Broadcasting Technology." On the evening of September 28, 1986, in order to fill a course requirement, Palmer and three other students were assigned, without faculty supervision, to the school radio station, which is located on the school premises. The next morning, beer stains and a marijuana pipe were discovered at the radio station. Later that day, Palmer, school disciplinarian Dr. Grimm, and Mr. Buckley, Palmer's former football coach, met in Mr. Buckley's office and Palmer was questioned about this discovery. During that meeting, Palmer admitted that the evening before he had smoked marijuana and consumed beer at the radio station.

On September 30, 1986, Dr. Grimm sent Mr. and Mrs. Palmer a letter advising them that their son had been assigned a ten-day out-of-school suspension effective from September 30, 1986 to October 13, 1986. The letter asked the Palmers to call Dr. Grimm if they had additional questions and suggested that they and their son consider counseling. The Palmers took no action to contest the ten-day suspension.

After Dr. Grimm's meeting with Palmer, Superintendent Merluzzi conferred about the appropriateness of additional discipline with Dr. Grimm, Mr. Buckley, assistant principal Dr. Myers, Mr. Kleber, the faculty director of the radio station, and Palmer's current football Coach, Mr. Meert. Suspension from extra-curricular activities was discussed and all except Dr. Grimm agreed that such a step was appropriate. No specific number of days for such a suspension was discussed, however.

Thereafter, Merluzzi made telephone calls to two drug-counseling agencies. These agencies suggested sixty days as an average time for the rehabilitation of someone with a minor drug problem, and Merluzzi ultimately decided that sixty days would be an appropriate period for the students concerned to ponder their actions. All students who were involved in the incident at the radio station received the same punishment.

On October 13, on the eve of the expiration of the ten-day suspension, the Board of Education met. Palmer's father, James Palmer, hearing "rumors" concerning the possible imposition of additional sanctions on his son, attended the meeting and spoke with Merluzzi shortly before it started. Merluzzi confirmed that he was inclined to impose a sixty-day extra-curricular suspension, but told James Palmer that he could raise the issue with the Board. James Palmer was accorded half an hour in closed session to present his views; he argued that the additional suspension would adversely affect his son's chances of playing football in college and would also reduce his chances of being awarded college scholarships. The Board declined to intervene and, after the meeting, Merluzzi informed all concerned parents that he was definitely going to impose the sixty-day extra-curricular suspension.

Subsequent to the imposition of the sixty day extra-curricular suspension, Palmer appealed to the New Jersey State Commissioner of Education for a review of the actions of the defendants. On October 20, 1986, an evidentiary hearing was conducted before Administrative Law Judge Bruce R. Campbell. Judge Campbell found that the "ten-day out-of-school suspension was procedurally faultless and consistent with announced policy." With respect to the sixty-day football suspension, however, he concluded that Palmer had been denied procedural due process ... because Palmer was not given notice of the proposed sixty-day suspension and afforded a hearing thereon....

On appeal, the Commissioner of Education affirmed the ALJ's finding that "the actions of the Board's agents in suspending [Palmer] from school for 10 days in all respects comports with the due process requirements set forth in *Goss v. Lopez*." The commissioner did not, however, accept the ALJ's conclusion that "the decision to increase the penalty imposed on [Palmer] ... rises to the level of *requiring* that the Board provide to him an additional due process proceeding ..." (emphasis in original). In the course of reaching this conclusion, the commissioner noted that Palmer "could not or should not have been unaware of the fact that his role as a member of the football team, as well as his status as a student in the school, was in jeopardy when he decided to take the actions he did."

The district court granted summary judgment to the defendants, holding that for purposes of due process analysis, Palmer had no property or liberty interest in participating in the school's football program.

II

Resolution of this appeal does not require that we address the issue found dispositive by the ALJ and the district court—whether procedural due process is required whenever a public school student in New Jersey faces or receives for a breach of discipline solely a suspension from participation in his or her school's athletic program. Palmer did not commit an offense for which athletic suspension was the only potential sanction or the only sanction in fact imposed. Here there was a single proceeding on a single charge that resulted in two sanctions being imposed, a ten-day suspension from school and a sixty-day suspension from athletics. The ultimate issue before us is whether the process received by Palmer in that single proceeding was appropriate given the fact that he faced, and ultimately received, both of those sanctions. We conclude that it was.

The threshold issue is whether the interests that could be adversely affected in the proceeding against Palmer were such that the due process clause was implicated. The answer seems clear. In *Goss v. Lopez* the Supreme Court concluded that due process was required when a student faced a ten-day scholastic suspension. *A fortiori,* due process is required when a student faces a ten-day academic suspension *and* a sixty-day athletic suspension.

Having concluded that "some process" was due, we turn to the issue of how much was due. We know from *Goss* what process would have been due if only a ten-day academic suspension had been at stake. After balancing the competing interests involved, the Court decided that the student must be given "oral or written notice of the charges against him and, if he denies them, an explanation of the evidence the authorities have and an opportunity to present his side of the story." The Court continued, stating that "[t]here need be no delay between the time 'notice' is given and the time of the hearing.... We hold only that ... the student first be told what he is accused of doing and what the basis of the accusation is." The Court also stopped short of requiring that the student be given "the opportunity to secure counsel, to confront and cross-examine witnesses supporting the charge, or to call his own witnesses to verify his version of the incident." As long as the student "at least ha[s] the opportunity to characterize his conduct and put it in what he deems the proper context" due process has been satisfied.

Palmer received the process required by *Goss*. The day after the incident at the radio station, in an informal hearing with Dr. Grimm and Mr. Buckley, he was advised of what had been found in the radio station and thus of the character of the offense being investigated. He then admitted his participation in the smoking of marijuana and the drinking of beer at the station. Palmer's involvement in the activities of that evening has never been disputed. During the conference, Palmer had the opportunity to put the events of the prior evening into what he perceived to be their proper context and could have argued for leniency had he so chosen.

Palmer does not argue before us that the hearing afforded him did not comport with the kind of informal hearing contemplated by *Goss*. Moreover, Palmer acknowledges that due process would not have been violated if only the ten-day suspension from school had been imposed. Rather, Palmer's argument is that a second notice and a second hearing were required because at the time of his conference with Dr. Grimm, he did not have adequate notice that a sixty-day athletic suspension might be imposed upon him.

We find this argument unpersuasive. The notice required by *Goss* is notice of "what [the student] is accused of doing and what the basis of the accusation is." We have been cited to no authority, and we know of none, suggesting that the *notice of the charge and supporting evidence* in a *Goss* situation must include a statement of the *penalties* that could be imposed in the course of the proceeding. We decline to adopt such a requirement in a situation like the one before us, in which the possible sanctions are knowable from previously published materials or are obvious from the circumstances.

In this case, Palmer was advised at the outset that he was suspected of consuming alcohol and a drug on school property. The Student Handbook, which was applicable to all students, specified that "alcohol and/or drug use" would, if a first offense, result in "10 days suspension" from school. The Interscholastic Athletic Program policy statement, which was applicable to Palmer and other students participating in that program, warned that "no student may participate who has not demonstrated good citizenship and responsibility." Based on these provisions, the nature of the offense, and common sense, we, like the New Jersey Commissioner of

Education, are confident that Palmer must have realized from the outset that his football eligibility, as well as his status as a student, was at stake. Accordingly, we hold that Palmer's interview with Dr. Grimm and Mr. Buckley provided just as meaningful an opportunity to argue against the athletic suspension as against the scholastic suspension.

Having concluded that Palmer received the process contemplated by *Goss,* we turn to the issue of whether more than that process was required in this case because Palmer faced not only a ten-day suspension from school but a football suspension as well. As Palmer stresses, the Court in *Goss* expressly noted that it was addressing itself solely to the procedure that must be provided in connection with a "short suspension, not exceeding 10 days," and that "longer suspensions or expulsions for the remainder of the school term, or permanently, may require more formal procedures." Palmer urges, as we understand it, that his interest in avoiding an erroneous deprivation of his participation in the football program for sixty days was sufficiently great that before any decision was made concerning the sanction for his misconduct, he should have been given express notice of the fact that his football eligibility was in jeopardy and that he should have been given the opportunity to secure the advice of an attorney before presenting his defense. Although we acknowledge that the sixty-day football suspension had a substantial impact on Palmer, determination of the amount of process due in a given situation involves a balancing of interests and we conclude that, when the balance is struck, the procedure prescribed in *Goss* was sufficient under the circumstances of this case.

Due process is a flexible concept and the process due in any situation is to be determined by weighing (1) the private interests at stake, (2) the governmental interests at stake, and (3) the fairness and reliability of the existing procedures and the probable value, if any, of additional procedural safeguards. In *Goss,* the Court described the student's interest as one in avoiding "unfair or mistaken exclusion from the educational process with all its unfortunate consequences." Those consequences include not only the loss of the benefit of the educational process but also potential damage to "the students' standing with their fellow students and their teachers" and potential "interfer[ence] with later opportunities for higher education and employment."

From the school's and the public's point of view, *Goss* recognized the need for maintaining order and discipline in our schools without prohibitive costs and in a manner that will contribute to, rather than disrupt, the educational process. As we have noted, the Court concluded that an informal hearing process would reconcile the private and governmental interests and that requiring representation by counsel, cross-examination, and other, more formal procedural safeguards would not sufficiently increase the reliability and fairness of the process to warrant the additional expense and disruption of the educational process.

We accept for present purposes Palmer's contention that, while called an extra-curricular activity, the school's football program is an integral part of its educational program. Nevertheless, it is but one part of that program and in terms of lost educational benefit, the loss occasioned by a football suspension is far less than that occasioned by a suspension from school for a comparable period of time. In terms of the student's standing with teachers and peers, we believe the potential loss is likely to be a function of the nature of the offense rather than the penalty; it is therefore unlikely to be affected by the fact that the sanction includes an athletic as well as a school suspension. As a general proposition, we believe the same can be said for the potential for interference with later opportunities for higher education and employment. Indeed, Palmer does not argue otherwise. The loss that he emphasizes is the possible loss of the opportunity to play college football. Although we acknowledge that the loss of the opportunity to impress college scouts with one's senior year play can have a significant adverse effect on one's chances for a college football career, we believe it would be unduly disruptive of a school's educational process to require one disciplinary process for football players and similarly situated athletes and another disciplinary process for other students.

Since the governmental interest at stake here is the same as that in *Goss,* since the incremental efficacy of the process proposed over the process afforded is not materially different than the one in that case, and since we find the student's interest to be only slightly greater, we conclude that the process required by *Goss* was sufficient in the circumstances presented by this case.

III

Palmer also contends that his suspension violated his right to equal protection under the Fourteenth Amendment. Since participation in extracurricular activities is not a fundamental right under the Constitution and since Palmer's suspension was not based on a suspect classification, we must examine Palmer's argument under the "rational relationship test." We conclude that the disciplinary actions taken by the school were rationally related to a valid state interest. The State has very strong interests in preserving a drug-free environment in its schools and in discouraging drug use by its students. We are unwilling to say that the sanctions imposed on Palmer were not reasonably designed to serve those legitimate interests.

IV

Since Palmer's suspensions from school and participation in interscholastic football did not violate any right secured by the Constitution, we will affirm the judgment of the district court.

NOTES

1. What do you think about the fact that the student and his parents did not contest his ten-day exclusion from school?

2. Is it fair to hold student-athletes to higher standards of conduct?

3. Was the punishment in this case fair?

[CASE NO. 94] PROCEDURAL DUE PROCESS FOR SHORT–TERM SUSPENSIONS

GOSS v. LOPEZ

Supreme Court of the United States, 1975.
419 U.S. 565, 95 S.Ct. 729, 42 L.Ed.2d 725.

■ MR. JUSTICE WHITE delivered the opinion of the Court.

This appeal by various administrators of the Columbus, Ohio, Public School System (CPSS) challenges the judgment of a three-judge federal court, declaring that appellees—various high school students in the CPSS—were denied due process of law contrary to the command of the Fourteenth Amendment in that they were temporarily suspended from their high schools without a hearing either prior to suspension or within a reasonable time thereafter, and enjoining the administrators to remove all references to such suspensions from the students' records.

I

Ohio law, Rev. Code Ann. § 3313.64, provides for free education to all children between the ages of six and 21. Section 3313.66 of the Code empowers the principal of an Ohio public school to suspend a pupil for misconduct for up to 10 days or to expel him. In either case, he must notify the student's parents within 24 hours and state the reasons for his action. A pupil who is expelled, or his parents, may appeal the decision to the Board of Education and in connection therewith shall be permitted to be heard at the board meeting. The Board may reinstate in pupil following the hearing. No similar procedure is provided in section 3313.66 or any other provision of state law for a suspended student. Aside from a regulation tracking the statute, at the time of the imposition of the suspensions in this case the CPSS itself had not issued any written procedure applicable to suspensions. Nor, so far as the record reflects, had any of the individual high schools involved in this case. Each, however, had formally or informally described the conduct for which suspension could be imposed.

The nine named appellees, each of whom alleged that he or she had been suspended from public high school in Columbus for up to 10 days without a hearing pursuant to section 3313.66, filed an action under 42 U.S.C.[A.] § 1983 against the Columbus Board of Education and various administrators of the CPSS. The complaint sought a declaration that section 3313.66 was unconstitutional in that it permitted public school administrators to deprive plaintiffs of their rights to an education without a hearing of any kind, in violation of the procedural due process component of the Fourteenth Amendment. It also sought to enjoin the public school officials from issuing future suspensions pursuant to section 3313.66 and to require them to remove references to the past suspensions from the records of the students in question.

The proof below established that the suspensions arose out of a period of widespread student unrest in the CPSS during February and March 1971. Six of the named plaintiffs, Rudolph Sutton, Tyrone Washington,

Susan Cooper, Deborah Fox, Clarence Byars, and Bruce Harris, were students at the Marion–Franklin High School and were each suspended for 10 days on account of disruptive or disobedient conduct committed in the presence of the school administrator who ordered the suspension. One of these, Tyrone Washington, was among a group of students demonstrating in the school auditorium while a class was being conducted there. He was ordered by the school principal to leave, refused to do so, and was suspended. Rudolph Sutton, in the presence of the principal, physically attacked a police officer who was attempting to remove Tyrone Washington from the auditorium. He was immediately suspended. The other four Marion–Franklin students were suspended for similar conduct. None was given a hearing to determine the operative facts underlying the suspension, but each, together with his or her parents, was offered the opportunity to attend a conference, subsequent to the effective date of the suspension, to discuss the student's future.

Two named plaintiffs, Dwight Lopez and Betty Crome, were students at the Central High School and McGuffey Junior High School, respectively. The former was suspended in connection with a disturbance in the lunch-room which involved some physical damage to school property. Lopez testified that at least 75 other students were suspended from his school on the same day. He also testified below that he was not a party to the destructive conduct but was instead an innocent bystander. Because no one from the school testified with regard to this incident, there is no evidence in the record indicating the official basis for concluding otherwise. Lopez never had a hearing.

Betty Crome was present at a demonstration at a high school other than the one she was attending. There she was arrested together with others, taken to the police station, and released without being formally charged. Before she went to school on the following day, she was notified that she had been suspended for a 10–day period. Because no one from the school testified with respect to this incident, the record does not disclose how the McGuffey Junior High School principal went about making the decision to suspend Crome, nor does it disclose on what information the decision was based. It is clear from the record that no hearing was ever held. There was no testimony with respect to the suspension of the ninth named plaintiff, Carl Smith. The school files were also silent as to his suspension, although as to some, but not all, of the other named plaintiffs the files contained either direct references to their suspensions or copies of letters sent to their parents advising them of the suspension.

On the basis of this evidence, the three-judge court declared that plaintiffs were denied due process of law because they were "suspended without hearing prior to suspension or within a reasonable time thereafter," and that Ohio Rev.Code Ann. section 3313.66 and regulations issued pursuant thereto were unconstitutional in permitting such suspensions. It was ordered that all references to plaintiffs' suspensions be removed from school files.

Although not imposing upon the Ohio school administrators any particular disciplinary procedures and leaving ... the District Court declared that there were 'minimum requirements of notice and a hearing prior to suspension, except in emergency situations.' In explication, the court stated that relevant case authority would: (1) permit '(i)mmediate removal of a student whose conduct disrupts the academic atmosphere of the school, endangers fellow students, teachers or school officials, or damages property'; (2) require notice of suspension proceedings to be sent to the students' parents within 24 hours of the decision to conduct them; and (3) require a hearing to be held, with the student present, within 72 hours of his removal. Finally, the court stated that, with respect to the nature of the hearing, the relevant cases required that statements in support of the charge be produced, that the student and others be permitted to make statements in defense or mitigation, and that the school need not permit attendance by counsel.

The defendant school administrators have appealed the three-judge court's decision.... We affirm.

II

At the outset, appellants contend that because there is no constitutional right to an education at public expense, the Due Process Clause does not protect against expulsions from the public school system. This position misconceives the nature of the issue and is refuted by prior decisions. The Fourteenth Amendment forbids the State to deprive any person of life, liberty or property without due process of law. Protected interests in property are normally "not created by the Constitution. Rather, they are created and their dimensions are defined" by an independent source such as state statutes or rules entitling the citizen to certain benefits.

Accordingly, a state employee who under state law, or rules promulgated by state officials, has a legitimate claim of entitlement to continued employment absent sufficient cause for discharge may demand the procedural protections of due process. So may welfare recipients who have statutory rights to welfare as long as they maintain the specified qualifications....

Here, on the basis of state law, appellees plainly had legitimate claims of entitlement to a public education. Ohio Rev.Code §§ 3313.48 and 3313.64 direct local authorities to provide a free education to all residents between six and 21 years of age, and a compulsory attendance law requires attendance for a school year of not less than 32 weeks. It is true that § 3313.66 of the code permits school principals to suspend students for up to two weeks; but suspensions may not be imposed without any grounds whatsoever. All of the schools had their own rules specifying the grounds for expulsion or suspension. Having chosen to extend the right to an education to people of appellees' class generally, Ohio may not withdraw that right on grounds of misconduct absent fundamentally fair procedures to determine whether the misconduct has occurred.

Although Ohio may not be constitutionally obligated to establish and maintain a public school system, it has nevertheless done so and has required its children to attend. Those young people do not "shed their constitutional rights" at the schoolhouse door. "The Fourteenth Amendment, as now applied to the States, protects the citizen against the State itself and all of its creatures—Boards of Education not excepted." The authority possessed by the State to prescribe and enforce standards of conduct in its schools, although concededly very broad, must be exercised consistently with constitutional safeguards. Among other things, the State is constrained to recognize a student's legitimate entitlement to a public education as a property interest which is protected by the Due Process Clause and which may not be taken away for misconduct without adherence to the minimum procedures required by that clause.

The Due Process Clause also forbids arbitrary deprivations of liberty. "Where a person's good name, reputation, honor, or integrity is at stake because of what the government is doing to him," the minimal requirements of the clause must be satisfied. School authorities here suspended appellees from school for periods of up to 10 days based on charges of misconduct. If sustained and recorded, those charges could seriously damage the students' standing with their fellow pupils and their teachers as well as interfere with later opportunities for higher education and employment. It is apparent that the claimed right of the State to determine unilaterally and without process whether that misconduct has occurred immediately collides with the requirements of the Constitution.

Appellants proceed to argue that even if there is a right to a public education protected by the Due Process Clause generally, the clause comes into play only when the State subjects a student to a "severe detriment or grievous loss." The loss of 10 days, it is said, is neither severe nor grievous and the Due Process Clause is therefore of no relevance. Appellee's argument is again refuted by our prior decisions; for in determining "whether due process requirements apply in the first place, we must look not to the 'weight' but to the *nature* of the interest at stake." *Board of Regents v. Roth.* The Court's view has been that as long as a property deprivation is not *de minimis,* its gravity is irrelevant to the question whether account must be taken of the Due Process Clause. A 10–day suspension from school is not *de minimis* in our view and may not be imposed in complete disregard of the Due Process Clause.

... Neither the property interest in educational benefits temporarily denied nor the liberty interest in reputation, which is also implicated, is so insubstantial that suspensions may constitutionally be imposed by any procedure the school chooses, no matter how arbitrary.

III

"Once it is determined that due process applies, the question remains what process is due."

. . .

There are certain bench marks to guide us.... *Mullane v. Central Hanover Trust Co.,* a case often invoked by later opinions, said that "[m]any controversies have raged about the cryptic and abstract words of the Due Process Clause but there can be no doubt that at a minimum they require that deprivation of life, liberty or property by adjudication be preceded by notice and opportunity for hearing appropriate to the nature of the case." ... "The fundamental requisite of due process of law is the opportunity to be heard," a right that "has little reality or worth unless one is informed that the matter is pending and can choose for himself whether to ... contest." At the very minimum, therefore, students facing suspension and the consequent interference with a protected property interest must be given *some* kind of notice and afforded *some* kind of hearing....

It also appears from our cases that the timing and content of the notice and the nature of the hearing will depend on appropriate accommodation of the competing interests involved. The student's interest is to avoid unfair or mistaken exclusion from the educational process, with all of its unfortunate consequences. The Due Process Clause will not shield him from suspensions properly imposed, but it disserves both his interest and the interest of the State if his suspension is in fact unwarranted. The concern would be mostly academic if the disciplinary process were a totally accurate, unerring process, never mistaken and never unfair. Unfortunately, that is not the case, and no one suggests that it is. Disciplinarians, although proceeding in utmost good faith, frequently act on the reports and advice of others; and the controlling facts and the nature of the conduct under challenge are often disputed. The risk of error is not at all trivial, and it should be guarded against if that may be done without prohibitive cost or interference with the educational process.

The difficulty is that our schools are vast and complex. Some modicum of discipline and order is essential if the educational function is to be performed. Events calling for discipline are frequent occurrences and sometimes require immediate, effective action. Suspension is considered not only to be a necessary tool to maintain order but a valuable educational device. The prospect of imposing elaborate hearing requirements in every suspension case is viewed with great concern, and many school authorities may well prefer the untrammeled power to act unilaterally, unhampered by rules about notice and hearing. But it would be a strange disciplinary system in an educational institution if no communication was sought by the disciplinarian with the student in an effort to inform him of his defalcation and to let him tell his side of the story in order to make sure that an injustice is not done....

We do not believe that school authorities must be totally free from notice and hearing requirements if their schools are to operate with acceptable efficiency. Students facing temporary suspension have interests qualifying for protection of the Due Process Clause, and due process requires, in connection with a suspension of 10 days or less, that the student be given oral or written notice of the charges against him and, if he denies them, an explanation of the evidence the authorities have and an opportunity to present his side of the story. The clause requires at least these rudimentary precautions against unfair or mistaken findings of misconduct and arbitrary exclusion from school.

There need be no delay between the time "notice" is given and the time of the hearing. In the great majority of cases the disciplinarian may informally discuss the alleged misconduct with the student minutes after it has occurred. We hold only that, in being given an opportunity to explain his version of the facts at this discussion, the student first be told what he is accused of doing and what the basis of the accusation is. Lower courts which have addressed the question of the *nature* of the procedures required in short suspension cases have reached the same conclusion. Since the hearing may occur almost immediately following the misconduct, it follows that as a general rule notice and hearing should precede removal of the student from school. We agree with the District Court, however, that there are recurring situations in which prior notice and hearing cannot be insisted upon. Students whose presence poses a continuing danger to persons or property or an ongoing threat of disrupting the academic process may be immediately removed from school. In such cases, the necessary notice and rudimentary hearing should follow as soon as practicable, as the District Court indicated. . . .

We stop short of construing the Due Process Clause to require, countrywide, that hearings in connection with short suspensions must afford the student the opportunity to secure counsel, to confront and cross-examine witnesses supporting the charge or to call his own witnesses to verify his version of the incident. Brief disciplinary suspensions are almost countless. To impose in each such case even truncated trial type procedures might well overwhelm administrative facilities in many places and, by diverting resources, cost more than it would save in educational effectiveness. Moreover, further formalizing the suspension process and escalating its formality and adversary nature may not only make it too costly as a regular disciplinary tool but also destroy its effectiveness as part of the teaching process.

On the other hand, requiring effective notice and informal hearing permitting the student to give his version of the events will provide a meaningful hedge against erroneous action. At least the disciplinarian will be alerted to the existence of disputes about facts and arguments about cause and effect. He may then determine himself to summon the accuser, permit cross-examination and allow the student to present his own witnesses. In more difficult cases, he may permit counsel. In any event, his discretion will be more informed and we think the risk of error substantially reduced.

Requiring that there be at least an informal give-and-take between student and disciplinarian, preferably prior to the suspension, will add little to the factfinding function where the disciplinarian has himself witnessed the conduct forming the basis for the charge. But things are not always as they seem to be, and the student will at least have the opportunity to characterize his conduct and put it in what he deems the proper context.

We should also make it clear that we have addressed ourselves solely to the short suspension, not exceeding 10 days. Longer suspensions or expulsions for the remainder of the school term, or permanently, may require more formal procedures. Nor do we put aside the possibility that in unusual situations, although involving only a short suspension, something more than the rudimentary procedures will be required.

IV

The District Court found each of the suspensions involved here to have occurred without a hearing, either before or after the suspension, and that each suspension was therefore invalid and the statute unconstitutional insofar as it permits such suspensions without notice or hearing. Accordingly, the judgment is

Affirmed.

NOTES

1. *Goss* applies only to suspensions of up to ten-days. What are the possible consequences of having a ten-day suspension noted on the permanent record cards of students?

2. Has *Goss* opened avenues for judicial intervention that have had a negative impact on the daily operations of schools?

[CASE NO. 95]   CORPORAL PUNISHMENT IN PUBLIC SCHOOLS

INGRAHAM v. WRIGHT

Supreme Court of the United States, 1977.
430 U.S. 651, 97 S.Ct. 1401, 51 L.Ed.2d 711.

■ MR. JUSTICE POWELL delivered the opinion of the Court.

This case presents questions concerning the use of corporal punishment in public schools: first, whether the paddling of students as a means of maintaining school discipline constitutes cruel and unusual punishment in violation of the Eighth Amendment; and second, to the extent that paddling is constitutionally permissible, whether the Due Process Clause of the Fourteenth Amendment requires prior notice and an opportunity to be heard.

I

. . .

Petitioners' evidence may be summarized briefly. In the 1970–1971 school year many of the 237 schools in Dade County used corporal punishment as a means of maintaining discipline pursuant to Florida legislation and a local school board regulation. The statute then in effect authorized limited corporal punishment by negative inference, proscribing punishment which was "degrading or unduly severe" or which was inflicted without prior consultation with the principal or the teacher in charge of the school. The regulation . . . contained explicit directions and limitations. . . .

. . . Petitioners focused on Drew Junior High School, the school in which both Ingraham and Andrews were enrolled in the fall of 1970. In an apparent reference to Drew, the District Court found that "[t]he instances of punishment which could be characterized as severe, accepting the students' testimony as credible, took place in one junior high school." The evidence, consisting mainly of the testimony of 16 students, suggests that the regime at Drew was exceptionally harsh. The testimony of Ingraham and Andrews, in support of their individual claims for damages, is illustrative. Because he was slow to respond to his teacher's instructions, Ingraham was subjected to more than 20 licks with a paddle while being held over a table in the principal's office. The paddling was so severe that he suffered a hematoma requiring medical attention and keeping him out of school for several days. Andrews was paddled several times for minor infractions. On two occasions he was struck on his arms, once depriving him of the full use of his arm for a week.

The District Court made no findings on the credibility of the students' testimony. Rather, assuming their testimony to be credible, the court found no constitutional basis for relief. . . .

A panel of the Court of Appeals voted to reverse. . . . Upon rehearing, the en banc court rejected these conclusions and affirmed the judgment of the District Court. . . .

II

In addressing the scope of the Eighth Amendment's prohibition on cruel and unusual punishment this Court has found it useful to refer to "[t]raditional common law concepts," and to the "attitude[s] which our society has traditionally taken." So too, in defining the requirements of procedural due process under the Fifth and Fourteenth Amendments, the Court has been attuned to what "has always been the law of the land," and to "traditional ideas of fair procedure." We therefore begin by examining the way in which our traditions and our laws have responded to the use of corporal punishment in public schools.

The use of corporal punishment in this country as a means of disciplining school children dates back to the colonial period. It has survived the transformation of primary and secondary education from the colonials' reliance on optional private arrangements to our present system of compulsory education and dependence on public schools. Despite the general abandonment of corporal punishment as a means of punishing criminal offenders, the practice continues to play a role in the public education of school children in most parts of the country. Professional and public opinion is sharply divided on the practice, and has been for more than a century. Yet we can discern no trend toward its elimination.

At common law a single principle has governed the use of corporal punishment since before the American Revolution: teachers may impose reasonable but not excessive force to discipline a child. . . . The basic doctrine has not changed. The prevalent rule in this country today privileges such force as a teacher or administrator "reasonably believes to be necessary for [the child's] proper control, training, or education." . . . To the extent that the force is excessive or unreasonable, the educator in virtually all States is subject to possible civil and criminal liability.

Although the early cases viewed the authority of the teacher as deriving from the parents, the concept of parental delegation has been replaced by the view—more consonant with compulsory education laws—that the State itself may impose such corporal punishment as is reasonably necessary "for the proper education of the child and for the maintenance of group discipline." ... All of the circumstances are to be taken into account in determining whether the punishment is reasonable in a particular case. Among the most important considerations are the seriousness of the offense, the attitude and past behavior of the child, the nature and severity of the punishment, the age and strength of the child, and the availability of less severe but equally effective means of discipline....

Of the 23 States that have addressed the problem through legislation, 21 have authorized the moderate use of corporal punishment in public schools. Of these States only a few have elaborated on the common law test of reasonableness, typically providing for approval or notification of the child's parent, or for infliction of punishment only by the principal or in the presence of an adult witness. Only two States, Massachusetts and New Jersey, have prohibited all corporal punishment in their public schools. Where the legislatures have not acted, the state courts have uniformly preserved the common law rule permitting teachers to use reasonable force in disciplining children in their charge.

Against this background of historical and contemporary approval of reasonable corporal punishment, we turn to the constitutional questions before us.

III

The Eighth Amendment provides, "Excessive bail shall not be required, nor excessive fines imposed, nor cruel and unusual punishments inflicted." Bail, fines and punishment traditionally have been associated with the criminal process, and by subjecting the three to parallel limitations the text of the Amendment suggests an intention to limit the power of those entrusted with the criminal law function of government. An examination of the history of the Amendment and the decisions of this Court construing the proscription against cruel and unusual punishment confirms that it was designed to protect those convicted of crimes. We adhere to this longstanding limitation and hold that the Eighth Amendment does not apply to the paddling of children as a means of maintaining discipline in public schools.

A

The history of the Eighth Amendment is well known. The text was taken, almost verbatim, from a provision of the Virginia Declaration of Rights of 1776, which in turn derived from the English Bill of Rights of 1689. The English version, adopted after the accession of William and Mary, was intended to curb the excesses of English judges under the reign of James II....

. . .

B

In light of this history, it is not surprising to find that every decision of this Court considering whether a punishment is "cruel and unusual" within the meaning of the Eighth and Fourteenth Amendments has dealt with a criminal punishment....

In the few cases where the Court has had occasion to confront claims that impositions outside the criminal process constituted cruel and unusual punishment, it has had no difficulty finding the Eighth Amendment inapplicable....

C

Petitioners acknowledge that the original design of the Cruel and Unusual Punishments Clause was to limit criminal punishments, but urge nonetheless that the prohibition should be extended to ban the paddling of school children. Observing that the Framers of the Eighth Amendment could not have envisioned our present system of public and compulsory education, with its opportunities for noncriminal punishments, petitioners contend that extension of the prohibition against cruel punishments is necessary lest we afford greater protection to criminals than to schoolchildren. It would be anomalous, they say, if schoolchildren could be beaten without constitutional redress, while hardened criminals suffering the same beatings at the hands of their jailors might have a valid claim under the Eighth Amendment. Whatever force this logic may have in other settings, we find it an inadequate basis for wrenching the Eighth Amendment from its historical context and extending it to traditional disciplinary practices in the public schools.

The prisoner and the schoolchild stand in wholly different circumstances, separated by the harsh facts of criminal conviction and incarceration....

The schoolchild has little need for the protection of the Eighth Amendment. Though attendance may not always be voluntary, the public school remains an open institution. Except perhaps when very young, the child is not physically restrained from leaving school during school hours; and at the end of the school day, the child is invariably free to return home. Even while at school, the child brings with him the support of family and friends and is rarely apart from teachers and other pupils who may witness and protest any instances of mistreatment.

The openness of the public school and its supervision by the community afford significant safeguards against the kinds of abuses from which the Eighth Amendment protects the prisoner. In virtually every community where corporal punishment is permitted in the schools, these safeguards are reinforced by the legal constraints of the common law. Public school teachers and administrators are privileged at common law to inflict only such corporal punishment as is reasonably necessary for the proper education and discipline of the child; any punishment going beyond the privilege may result in both civil and criminal liability.... As long as the schools are open to public scrutiny, there is no reason to believe that the common law constraints will not effectively remedy and deter excesses such as those alleged in this case.

We conclude that when public school teachers or administrators impose disciplinary corporal punishment, the Eighth Amendment is inapplicable. The pertinent constitutional question is whether the imposition is consonant with the requirements of due process.

IV

The Fourteenth Amendment prohibits any State deprivation of life, liberty or property without due process of law. Application of this prohibition requires the familiar two-stage analysis: we must first ask whether the asserted individual interests are encompassed within the Fourteenth Amendment's protection of "life, liberty or property"; if protected interests are implicated, we then must decide what procedures constitute "due process of law." Following that analysis here, we find that corporal punishment in public school implicates a constitutionally protected liberty interest, but we hold that the traditional common law remedies are fully adequate to afford due process.

A

"[T]he range of interests protected by procedural due process is not infinite." . . .

. . . Among the historic liberties . . . protected was a right to be free from, and to obtain judicial relief for, unjustified intrusions on personal security.

While the contours of this historic liberty interest in the context of our federal system of government have not been defined precisely, they always have been thought to encompass freedom from bodily restraint and punishment. It is fundamental that the state cannot hold and physically punish an individual except in accordance with due process of law.

This constitutionally protected liberty interest is at stake in this case. There is, of course a *de minimis* level of imposition with which the Constitution is not concerned. But at least where school authorities, acting under color of state law, deliberately decide to punish a child for misconduct by restraining the child and inflicting appreciable physical pain, we hold that Fourteenth Amendment liberty interests are implicated.

B

"[T]he question remains what process is due." Were it not for the common law privilege permitting teachers, to inflict reasonable corporal punishment on children in their care, and the availability of the traditional remedies for abuse, the case for requiring advance procedural safeguards would be strong indeed. But here we deal with a punishment—paddling— within that tradition, and the question is whether the common law remedies are adequate to afford due process.

. . . Whether in this case the common law remedies for excessive corporal punishment constitute due process of law must turn on an analysis of the competing interests at stake, viewed against the background of "history, reason, [and] the past course of decisions." The analysis requires consideration of three distinct factors: "first, the private interest that will be affected . . . , second, the risk of an erroneous deprivation of such interest . . . and the probable value, if any, of additional or substitute procedural safeguards; and, finally, the [state] interest, including the function involved and the fiscal and administrative burdens that the additional or substitute procedural requirement would entail."

1

Because it is rooted in history, the child's liberty interest in avoiding corporal punishment while in the care of public school authorities is subject to historical limitations. . . .

The concept that reasonable corporal punishment in school is justifiable continues to be recognized in the laws of most States. . . . It represents "the balance struck by this country," between the child's interest in personal security and the traditional view that some limited corporal punishment may be necessary in the course of a child's education. Under that longstanding accommodation of interests, there can be no deprivation of substantive rights as long as disciplinary corporal punishment is within the limits of the common law privilege.

This is not to say that the child's interest in procedural safeguards is insubstantial. The school disciplinary process is not "a totally accurate, unerring process, never mistaken and never unfair. . . ." In any deliberate infliction of corporal punishment on a child who is restrained for that purpose, there is some risk that the intrusion on the child's liberty will be unjustified and therefore unlawful. In these circumstances the child has a strong interest in procedural safeguards that minimize the risk of wrongful punishment and provide for the resolution of disputed questions of justification.

We turn now to a consideration of the safeguards that are available under applicable Florida law.

2

Florida has continued to recognize, and indeed has strengthened by statute, the common law right of a child not to be subjected to excessive corporal punishment in school. Under Florida law the teacher and principal of the school decide in the first instance whether corporal punishment is reasonably necessary under the circumstances in order to discipline a child who has misbehaved. But they must exercise prudence and restraint. For Florida has preserved the traditional judicial proceedings for determining whether the punishment was justified. If the punishment inflicted is later found to have been excessive—not reasonably believed at the time to be necessary for the child's discipline or training—the school authorities inflicting it may be held liable in damages to the child and, if malice is shown, they may be subject to criminal penalties.

Although students have testified in this case to specific instances of abuse, there is every reason to believe that such mistreatment is an aberration. The uncontradicted evidence suggests that corporal punishment in the Dade County schools was, "[w]ith the exception of a few cases, . . . unremarkable in physical severity." Moreover, because paddlings are usually inflicted in response to conduct directly observed by teachers in their presence, the risk that a child will be paddled without cause is typically insignificant. In the ordinary case, a disciplinary paddling neither threatens seriously to violate any substantive rights nor condemns the child "to suffer grievous loss of any kind."

In those cases where severe punishment is contemplated, the available civil and criminal sanctions for abuse—considered in light of the openness of the school environment—afford significant protection against unjustified corporal punishment. Teachers and school authorities are unlikely to inflict corporal punishment unnecessarily or excessively when a possible consequence of doing so is the institution of civil or criminal proceedings against them. . . .

3

But even if the need for advance procedural safeguards were clear, the question would remain whether the incremental benefit could justify the cost. Acceptance of petitioners' claims would work a transformation in the law governing corporal punishment in Florida and most other States. Given the impracticability of formulating a rule of procedural due process that varies with the severity of the particular imposition, the prior hearing petitioners seek would have to precede *any* paddling, however moderate or trivial.

Such a universal constitutional requirement would significantly burden the use of corporal punishment as a disciplinary measure. Hearings—even informal hearings—require time, personnel, and a diversion of attention from normal school pursuits. . . .

Elimination or curtailment of corporal punishment would be welcomed by many as a societal advance. But when such a policy choice may result from this Court's determination of an asserted right to due process, rather than from the normal processes of community debate and legislative action, the societal costs cannot be dismissed as insubstantial. . . .

. . . In view of the low incidence of abuse, the openness of our schools, and the common law safeguards that already exist, the risk of error that may result in violation of a schoolchild's substantive rights can only be regarded as minimal. Imposing additional administrative safeguards as a constitutional requirement might reduce that risk marginally, but would also entail a significant intrusion into an area of primary educational responsibility. We conclude that the Due Process Clause does not require notice and a hearing prior to the imposition of corporal punishment in the public schools, as that practice is authorized and limited by the common law.

. . .

V

Petitioners cannot prevail on either of the theories before us in this case. The Eighth Amendment's prohibition against cruel and unusual punishment is inapplicable to school paddlings, and the Fourteenth Amendment's requirement of procedural due process is satisfied by Florida's preservation of common-law constraints and remedies. We therefore agree with the Court of Appeals that petitioners' evidence affords no basis for injunctive relief, and that petitioners cannot recover damages on the basis of any Eighth Amendment or procedural due process violation.

Affirmed.

NOTES

1.   In *Baker v. Owens*, 395 F.Supp. 294 (M.D.N.C.1975), *aff'd*, 423 U.S. 907, 96 S.Ct. 210, 46 L.Ed.2d 137 (1975), the Supreme Court summarily affirmed that school officials have the right to administer corporal punishment as they see fit, regardless of whether parents agree. What does this do to the presumed voluntary nature of state officials acting *in loco parentis*?

2.   The efficacy of corporal punishment has long been debated. To what extent is corporal punishment a legislative, rather than a judicial, concern? To what extent is it an educational, rather than a legal, concern?

[CASE NO. 96]   STUDENT SEARCHES

NEW JERSEY v. T.L.O.

Supreme Court of the United States, 1985.
469 U.S. 325, 105 S.Ct. 733, 83 L.Ed.2d 720 [21 Educ. L. Rep. 1122].

■ JUSTICE WHITE delivered the opinion of the Court.

We granted certiorari in this case to examine the appropriateness of the exclusionary rule as a remedy for searches carried out in violation of the Fourth Amendment by public school authorities. Our consideration of the proper application of the Fourth Amendment to the public schools, however, has led us to conclude that the search that gave rise to the case now before us did not violate the Fourth Amendment. Accordingly, we here address only the questions of the proper standard for assessing the legality of searches conducted by public school officials and the application of that standard to the facts of this case.

I

On March 7, 1980, a teacher at Piscataway High School in Middlesex County, N.J., discovered two girls smoking in a lavatory. One of the two girls was the respondent T.L.O., who at that time was a 14–year–old high school freshman. Because smoking in the lavatory was a violation of a school rule, the teacher took the two girls to the Principal's office, where they met with Assistant Vice Principal Theodore Choplick. In response to questioning by Mr. Choplick, T.L.O.'s companion admitted that she had violated the rule. T.L.O., however, denied that she had been smoking in the lavatory and claimed that she did not smoke at all.

Mr. Choplick asked T.L.O. to come into his private office and demanded to see her purse. Opening the purse, he found a pack of cigarettes, which he removed from the purse and held before T.L.O. as he accused her of having lied to him. As he reached into the purse for the cigarettes, Mr. Choplick also noticed a package of cigarette rolling papers. In his experience, possession of rolling papers by high school students was closely associated with the use of marihuana [sic]. Suspecting that a closer examination of the purse might yield further evidence of drug use, Mr. Choplick proceeded to search the purse thoroughly. The search revealed a small amount of marihuana, a pipe, a number of empty plastic bags, a substantial quantity of money in one-dollar bills, an index card that appeared to be a list of students who owed T.L.O. money, and two letters that implicated T.L.O. in marihuana dealing.

Mr. Choplick notified T.L.O.'s mother and the police, and turned the evidence of drug dealing over to the police. At the request of the police, T.L.O.'s mother took her daughter to police headquarters, where T.L.O. confessed that she had been selling marihuana at the high school. On the basis of the confession and the evidence seized by Mr. Choplick, the State brought delinquency charges against T.L.O.... Contending that Mr. Choplick's search of her purse violated the Fourth Amendment, T.L.O. moved to suppress the evidence found in her purse as well her confession, which, she argued, was tainted by the allegedly unlawful search....

II

In determining whether the search at issue in this case violated the Fourth Amendment, we are faced initially with the question whether that Amendment's prohibition on unreasonable searches and seizures applies to searches conducted by public school officials. We hold that it does.

It is now beyond dispute that "the Federal Constitution, by virtue of the Fourteenth Amendment, prohibits unreasonable searches and seizures by state officers." Equally indisputable is the proposition that the Fourteenth Amendment protects the rights of students against encroachment by public school officials....

... We have held school officials subject to the commands of the First Amendment, see *Tinker v. Des Moines Independent Community School District,* and the Due Process Clause of the Fourteenth Amendment. More generally, the Court has recognized that "the concept of parental delegation" as a source of school authority is not entirely "consonant with compulsory education laws." *Ingraham v. Wright.* Today's public school officials do not merely exercise authority voluntarily conferred on them by individual parents; rather, they act in furtherance of publicly mandated educational and disciplinary policies. In carrying out searches and other disciplinary functions pursuant to such policies, school officials act as representatives of the State, not merely as surrogates for the parents, and they cannot claim the parents' immunity from the strictures of the Fourth Amendment.

III

To hold that the Fourth Amendment applies to searches conducted by school authorities is only to begin the inquiry into the standards governing such searches. Although the underlying command of the Fourth Amendment is always that searches and seizures be reasonable, what is reasonable depends on the context within which a search takes place. The determination of the standard of reasonableness governing any specific class of searches requires "balancing the need to search against the invasion which the search entails." On one side of the balance are arrayed the individual's legitimate expectations of privacy and personal security; on the other, the government's need for effective methods to deal with breaches of public order.

We have recognized that even a limited search of the person is a substantial invasion of privacy. We have also recognized that searches of closed items of personal luggage are intrusions on protected privacy interests, for "the Fourth Amendment provides protection to the owner of every container that conceals its contents from plain view." A search of a child's person or of a closed purse or other bag carried on her person, no less than a similar search carried out on an adult, is undoubtedly a severe violation of subjective expectations of privacy.

Of course, the Fourth Amendment does not protect subjective expectations of privacy that are unreasonable or otherwise "illegitimate." To receive the protection of the Fourth Amendment, an expectation of privacy must be one that society is "prepared to recognize as legitimate." . . .

. . . In short, schoolchildren may find it necessary to carry with them a variety of legitimate, noncontraband items, and there is no reason to conclude that they have necessarily waived all rights to privacy in such items merely by bringing them onto school grounds.

Against the child's interest in privacy must be set the substantial interest of teachers and administrators in maintaining discipline in the classroom and on school grounds. . . .

How, then, should we strike the balance between the schoolchild's legitimate expectations of privacy and the school's equally legitimate need to maintain an environment in which learning can take place? It is evident that the school setting requires some easing of the restrictions to which searches by public authorities are ordinarily subject. The warrant requirement, in particular, is unsuited to the school environment: requiring a teacher to obtain a warrant before searching a child suspected of an infraction of school rules (or of the criminal law) would unduly interfere with the maintenance of the swift and informal disciplinary procedures needed in the schools. . . . [W]e hold today that school officials need not obtain a warrant before searching a student who is under their authority.

The school setting also requires some modification of the level of suspicion of illicit activity needed to justify a search. Ordinarily, a search—even one that may permissibly be carried out without a warrant—must be based upon "probable cause" to believe that a violation of the law has occurred. However, "probable cause" is not an irreducible requirement of a valid search. The fundamental command of the Fourth Amendment is that searches and seizures be reasonable. . . .

We join the majority of courts that have examined this issue in concluding that the accommodation of the privacy interests of schoolchildren with the substantial need of teachers and administrators for freedom to maintain order in the schools does not require strict adherence to the requirement that searches be based on probable cause to believe that the subject of the search has violated or is violating the law. Rather, the legality of a search of a student should depend simply on the reasonableness, under all the circumstances, of the search. Determining the reasonableness of any search involves a twofold inquiry: first, one must consider "whether the . . . action was justified at its inception"; second, one must determine whether the search as actually conducted "was reasonably related in scope to the circumstances which justified the interference in the first place." Under ordinary circumstances, a search of a student by a teacher or other school official will be "justified at its inception" when there are reasonable grounds for suspecting that the search will turn up evidence that the student has violated or is violating either the law or the rules of the school. Such a search will be permissible in its scope when the measures adopted are reasonably related to the objectives of the search and not excessively intrusive in light of the age and sex of the student and the nature of the infraction.

This standard will, we trust, neither unduly burden the efforts of school authorities to maintain order in their schools nor authorize unrestrained intrusions upon the privacy of schoolchildren. By focusing attention on the question of reasonableness, the standard will spare teachers and school administrators the necessity of schooling themselves in the niceties of probable cause and permit them to regulate their conduct according to the dictates of reason and common sense. At the same time, the reasonableness standard should ensure that the interests of students will be invaded no more than is necessary to achieve the legitimate end of preserving order in the schools.

IV

There remains the question of the legality of the search in this case.... Our review of the facts surrounding the search leads us to conclude that the search was in no sense unreasonable for Fourth Amendment purposes.

The incident that gave rise to this case actually involved two separate searches, with the first—the search for cigarettes—providing the suspicion that gave rise to the second—the search for marihuana. Although it is the fruits of the second search that are at issue here, the validity of the search for marihuana must depend on the reasonableness of the initial search for cigarettes, as there would have been no reason to suspect that T.L.O. possessed marihuana had the first search not taken place. Accordingly, it is to the search for cigarettes that we first turn our attention....

... T.L.O. had been accused of smoking, and had denied the accusation in the strongest possible terms when she stated that she did not smoke at all. Surely it cannot be said that under these circumstances, T.L.O.'s possession of cigarettes would be irrelevant to the charges against her or to her response to those charges. T.L.O.'s possession of cigarettes, once it was discovered, would both corroborate the report that she had been smoking and undermine the credibility of her defense to the charge of smoking. To be sure, the discovery of the cigarettes would not prove that T.L.O. had been smoking in the lavatory; nor would it, strictly speaking, necessarily be inconsistent with her claim that she did not smoke at all. But it is universally recognized that evidence, to be relevant to an inquiry, need not conclusively prove the ultimate fact in issue, but only have "any tendency to make the existence of any fact that is of consequence to the determination of the action more probable or less probable than it would be without the evidence." The relevance of T.L.O.'s possession of cigarettes to the question whether she had been smoking and to the credibility of her denial that she smoked supplied the necessary "nexus" between the item searched for and the infraction under investigation. . . .

Our conclusion that Mr. Choplick's decision to open T.L.O.'s purse was reasonable brings us to the question of the further search for marihuana once the pack of cigarettes was located. The suspicion upon which the search for marihuana was founded was provided when Mr. Choplick observed a package of rolling papers in the purse as he removed the pack of cigarettes. . . . The discovery of the rolling papers concededly gave rise to a reasonable suspicion that T.L.O. was carrying marihuana as well as cigarettes in her purse. This suspicion justified further exploration of T.L.O.'s purse, which turned up more evidence of drug-related activities: a pipe, a number of plastic bags of the type commonly used to store marihuana, a small quantity of marihuana, and a fairly substantial amount of money. Under these circumstances, it was not unreasonable to extend the search to a separate zippered compartment of the purse; and when a search of that compartment revealed an index card containing a list of "people who owe me money" as well as two letters, the inference that T.L.O. was involved in marihuana trafficking was substantial enough to justify Mr. Choplick in examining the letters to determine whether they contained any further evidence. In short, we cannot conclude that the search for marihuana was unreasonable in any respect. Accordingly, the judgment of the Supreme Court of New Jersey is

Reversed.

NOTES

1.   In footnote 5, 469 U.S. 325 at 338, 105 S.Ct. 733 at 741, the Supreme Court stated that it was addressing ". . . whether a school child has a legitimate expectation of privacy in lockers, desks, or other school property provided for the storage of school supplies." How far should the privacy rights of students in school extend?

2.   In footnote 8, 469 U.S. 325 at 342, 105 S.Ct. 733 at 743, the Court wrote that it did ". . . not decide whether individualized suspicion is an essential element of the reasonableness standard we adopt for searches by school authorities." Should the Court have considered this issue? Would its doing so have altered the result?

[CASE NO. 97]   STUDENT STRIP SEARCHES

SAFFORD UNIFIED SCHOOL DISTRICT #1 v. REDDING

Supreme Court of the United States, 2009.
557 U.S. 364, 129 S.Ct. 2633, 174 L.Ed.2d 354 [245 Educ. L. Rep. 626].

■ JUSTICE SOUTER delivered the opinion of the Court.

The issue here is whether a 13-year-old student's Fourth Amendment right was violated when she was subjected to a search of her bra and underpants by school officials acting on reasonable suspicion that she had brought forbidden prescription and over-the-counter drugs to school. Because there were no reasons to suspect the drugs presented a danger or were concealed in her underwear, we hold that the search did violate the Constitution, but because there is reason to question the clarity with which the right was established, the official who ordered the unconstitutional search is entitled to qualified immunity from liability.

I

The events immediately prior to the search in question began in 13–year–old Savana Redding's math class at Safford Middle School one October day in 2003. The assistant principal of the school, Kerry Wilson, came into the room and asked Savana to go to his office. There, he showed her a day planner, unzipped and open flat on his desk, in which there were several knives, lighters, a permanent marker, and a cigarette. Wilson asked Savana whether the planner was hers; she said it was, but that a few days before she had lent it to her friend, Marissa Glines. Savana stated that none of the items in the planner belonged to her.

Wilson then showed Savana four white prescription-strength ibuprofen 400–mg pills, and one over-the-counter blue naproxen 200–mg pill, all used for pain and inflammation but banned under school rules without advance permission. He asked Savana if she knew anything about the pills. Savana answered that she did not. Wilson then told Savana that he had received a report that she was giving these pills to fellow students; Savana denied it and agreed to let Wilson search her belongings. Helen Romero, an administrative assistant, came into the office, and together with Wilson they searched Savana's backpack, finding nothing.

At that point, Wilson instructed Romero to take Savana to the school nurse's office to search her clothes for pills. Romero and the nurse, Peggy Schwallier, asked Savana to remove her jacket, socks, and shoes, leaving her in stretch pants and a T-shirt (both without pockets), which she was then asked to remove. Finally, Savana was told to pull her bra out and to the side and shake it, and to pull out the elastic on her underpants, thus exposing her breasts and pelvic area to some degree. No pills were found.

Savana's mother filed suit against Safford Unified School District #1, Wilson, Romero, and Schwallier for conducting a strip search in violation of Savana's Fourth Amendment rights. The individuals (hereinafter petitioners) moved for summary judgment, raising a defense of qualified immunity. The District Court for the District of Arizona granted the motion on the ground that there was no Fourth Amendment violation, and a panel of the Ninth Circuit affirmed.

A closely divided Circuit sitting en banc, however, reversed. Following the two-step protocol for evaluating claims of qualified immunity, the Ninth Circuit held that the strip search was unjustified under the Fourth Amendment test for searches of children by school officials set out in *New Jersey v. T.L.O.*. The Circuit then applied the test for qualified immunity, and found that Savana's right was clearly established at the time of the search: " '[t]hese notions of personal privacy are "clearly established" in that they inhere in all of us, particularly middle school teenagers, and are inherent in the privacy component of the Fourth Amendment's proscription against unreasonable searches.' " The upshot was reversal of summary judgment as to Wilson, while affirming the judgments in favor of Schwallier, the school nurse, and Romero, the administrative assistant, since they had not acted as independent decisionmakers.

We granted certiorari and now affirm in part, reverse in part, and remand.

II

The Fourth Amendment "right of the people to be secure in their persons . . . against unreasonable searches and seizures" generally requires a law enforcement officer to have probable cause for conducting a search. "Probable cause exists where 'the facts and circumstances within [an officer's] knowledge and of which [he] had reasonably trustworthy information [are] sufficient in themselves to warrant a man of reasonable caution in the belief that' an offense has been or is being committed" and that evidence bearing on that offense will be found in the place to be searched.

In *T.L.O.*, we recognized that the school setting "requires some modification of the level of suspicion of illicit activity needed to justify a search" and held that for searches by school officials "a careful balancing of governmental and private interests suggests that the public interest is best served by a Fourth Amendment standard of reasonableness that stops short of probable cause." We have thus applied a standard of reasonable suspicion to determine the legality of a school administrator's search of a student and have held that a school search "will be permissible in its scope when the measures adopted are reasonably related to the objectives of the search and not excessively intrusive in light of the age and sex of the student and the nature of the infraction."

A number of our cases on probable cause have an implicit bearing on the reliable knowledge element of reasonable suspicion, as we have attempted to flesh out the knowledge component by looking to the degree to which known facts imply prohibited conduct, the specificity of the information received, and the reliability of its source. At the end of the day, however, we have realized that these factors cannot rigidly control and we have come back to saying that the standards are "fluid concepts that take their substantive content from the particular contexts" in which they are being assessed.

Perhaps the best that can be said generally about the required knowledge component of probable cause for a law enforcement officer's evidence search is that it raise a "fair probability" or a "substantial chance" of discovering evidence of criminal activity. The lesser standard for school searches could as readily be described as a moderate chance of finding evidence of wrongdoing.

III

A

In this case, the school's policies strictly prohibit the nonmedical use, possession,or sale of any drug on school grounds, including " '[a]ny prescription or over-the-counter drug, except those for which permission to use in school has been granted pursuant to Board policy.' " A week before Savana was searched, another student, Jordan Romero (no relation of the school's administrative assistant), told the principal and Assistant Principal Wilson that "certain students were bringing drugs and weapons on campus," and that he had been sick after taking some pills that "he got from a classmate." On the morning of October 8, the same boy handed Wilson a white pill that he said Marissa Glines had given him. He told Wilson that students were planning to take the pills at lunch.

Wilson learned from Peggy Schwallier, the school nurse, that the pill was Ibuprofen 400 mg, available only by prescription. Wilson then called Marissa out of class. Outside the classroom, Marissa's teacher handed Wilson the day planner, found within Marissa's reach, containing various contraband items. Wilson escorted Marissa back to his office.

In the presence of Helen Romero, Wilson requested Marissa to turn out her pockets and open her wallet. Marissa produced a blue pill, several white ones, and a razor blade. Wilson asked where the blue pill came from, and Marissa answered, " 'I guess it slipped in when *she* gave me the IBU 400s.' " when Wilson asked whom she meant, Marissa replied, " 'Savana Redding.' " Wilson then enquired about the day planner and its contents; Marissa denied knowing anything about them. Wilson did not ask Marissa any followup questions to determine whether there was any likelihood that Savana presently had pills: neither asking when Marissa received the pills from Savana nor where Savana might be hiding them.

Schwallier did not immediately recognize the blue pill, but information provided through a poison control hotline indicated that the pill was a 200–mg dose of an anti-inflammatory drug, generically called naproxen, available over the counter. At Wilson's direction, Marissa was then subjected to a search of her bra and underpants by Romero and Schwallier, as Savana was later on. The search revealed no additional pills.

It was at this juncture that Wilson called Savana into his office and showed her the day planner. Their conversation established that Savana and Marissa were on friendly terms: while she denied knowledge of the contraband, Savana admitted that the day planner was hers and that she had lent it to Marissa. Wilson had other reports of their friendship from staff members, who had identified Savana and Marissa as part of an unusually rowdy group at the school's opening dance in August, during which alcohol and cigarettes were found in the girls' bathroom. Wilson had reason to connect the girls with this contraband, for Wilson knew that Jordan Romero had told the principal that before the dance, he had been at a party at Savana's house where alcohol was served. Marissa's statement that the pills came from Savana was thus sufficiently plausible to warrant suspicion that Savana was involved in pill distribution.

This suspicion of Wilson's was enough to justify a search of Savana's backpack and outer clothing. If a student is reasonably suspected of giving out contraband pills, she is reasonably suspected of carrying them on her person and in the carryall that has become an item of student uniform in most places today. If Wilson's reasonable suspicion of pill distribution were not understood to support searches of outer clothes and backpack, it would not justify any search worth making. And the look into Savana's bag, in her presence and in the relative privacy of Wilson's office, was not excessively intrusive, any more than Romero's subsequent search of her outer clothing.

B

Here it is that the parties part company, with Savana's claim that extending the search at Wilson's behest to the point of making her pull out her underwear was constitutionally unreasonable. The exact label for this final step in the intrusion is not important, though strip search is a fair way to speak of it. Romero and Schwallier directed Savana to remove her clothes down to her underwear, and then "pull out" her bra and the elastic band on her underpants. Although Romero and Schwallier stated that they did not see anything when Savana followed their instructions, we would not define strip search and its Fourth Amendment consequences in a way that would guarantee litigation about who was looking and how much was seen. The very fact of Savana's pulling her underwear away from her body in the presence of the two officials who were able to see her necessarily exposed her breasts and pelvic area to some degree, and both subjective and reasonable societal expectations of personal privacy support the treatment of such a search as categorically distinct, requiring distinct elements of justification on the part of school authorities for going beyond a search of outer clothing and belongings.

Savana's subjective expectation of privacy against such a search is inherent in her account of it as embarrassing, frightening, and humiliating. The reasonableness of her expectation (required by the Fourth Amendment standard) is indicated by the consistent experiences of other young people similarly searched, whose adolescent vulnerability intensifies the patent intrusiveness of the exposure. The common reaction of these adolescents simply registers the obviously different meaning of a search exposing the body from the experience of nakedness or near undress in other school circumstances. Changing for gym is getting ready for play; exposing for a search is responding to an accusation reserved for suspected wrongdoers and fairly understood as so degrading that a number of communities have decided that strip searches in schools are never reasonable and have banned them no matter what the facts may be.

The indignity of the search does not, of course, outlaw it, but it does implicate the rule of reasonableness as stated in *T.L.O.*, that "the search as actually conducted [be] reasonably related in scope to the circumstances which justified the interference in the first place." The scope will be permissible, that is, when it is "not excessively intrusive in light of the age and sex of the student and the nature of the infraction."

Here, the content of the suspicion failed to match the degree of intrusion. Wilson knew beforehand that the pills were prescription-strength ibuprofen and over-the-counter naproxen, common pain relievers equivalent to two Advil, or one Aleve. He must have been aware of the nature and limited threat of the specific drugs he was searching for, and while just about anything can be taken in quantities that will do real harm, Wilson had no reason to suspect that large amounts of the drugs were being passed around, or that individual students were receiving great numbers of pills.

Nor could Wilson have suspected that Savana was hiding common painkillers in her underwear. Petitioners suggest, as a truth universally acknowledged, that "students ... hid[e] contraband in or under their clothing" and cite a smattering of cases of students with contraband in their underwear. But when the categorically extreme intrusiveness of a search down to the body of an adolescent requires some justification in suspected facts, general background possibilities fall short; a reasonable search that extensive calls for suspicion that it will pay off. But nondangerous school contraband does not raise the specter of stashes in intimate places, and there is no evidence in the record of any general practice among Safford Middle School students of hiding that sort of thing in underwear; neither Jordan nor Marissa suggested to Wilson that Savana was doing that, and the preceding search of Marissa that Wilson ordered yielded nothing. Wilson never even determined when Marissa had received the pills from Savana; if it had been a few days before, that would weigh heavily against any reasonable conclusion that Savana presently had the pills on her person, much less in her underwear.

In sum, what was missing from the suspected facts that pointed to Savana was any indication of danger to the students from the power of the drugs or their quantity, and any reason to suppose that Savana was carrying pills in her underwear. We think that the combination of these deficiencies was fatal to finding the search reasonable.

In so holding, we mean to cast no ill reflection on the assistant principal, for the record raises no doubt that his motive throughout was to eliminate drugs from his school and protect students from what Jordan Romero had gone through. Parents are known to overreact to protect their children from danger, and a school official with responsibility for safety may tend to do the same. The difference is that the Fourth Amendment places limits on the official, even with the high degree of deference that courts must pay to the educator's professional judgment.

We do mean, though, to make it clear that the *T.L.O.* concern to limit a school search to reasonable scope requires the support of reasonable suspicion of danger or of resort to underwear for hiding evidence of wrongdoing before a search can reasonably make the quantum leap from outer clothes and backpacks to exposure of intimate parts. The meaning of such a search, and the degradation its subject may reasonably feel, place a search that intrusive in a category of its own demanding its own specific suspicions.

IV

A school official searching a student is "entitled to qualified immunity where clearly established law does not show that the search violated the Fourth Amendment." To be established clearly, however, there is no need that "the very action in question [have] previously been held unlawful." The unconstitutionality of outrageous conduct obviously will be unconstitutional, this being the reason, as Judge Posner has said, that "[t]he easiest cases don't even arise." But even as to action less than an outrage, "officials can still be on notice that their conduct violates established law ... in novel factual circumstances."

T.L.O. directed school officials to limit the intrusiveness of a search, "in light of the age and sex of the student and the nature of the infraction" and as we have just said at some length, the intrusiveness of the strip search here cannot be seen as justifiably related to the circumstances. But we realize that the lower courts have reached divergent conclusions regarding how the *T.L.O.* standard applies to such searches.

A number of judges have read *T.L.O.* as the en banc minority of the Ninth Circuit did here. The Sixth Circuit upheld a strip search of a high school student for a drug, without any suspicion that drugs were hidden next to her body. . . .

We think these differences of opinion from our own are substantial enough to require immunity for the school officials in this case. We would not suggest that entitlement to qualified immunity is the guaranteed product of disuniform views of the law in the other federal, or state, courts, and the fact that a single judge, or even a group of judges, disagrees about the contours of a right does not automatically render the law unclear if we have been clear. That said, however, the cases viewing school strip searches differently from the way we see them are numerous enough, with well-reasoned majority and dissenting opinions, to counsel doubt that we were sufficiently clear in the prior statement of law. We conclude that qualified immunity is warranted.

V

The strip search of Savana Redding was unreasonable and a violation of the Fourth Amendment, but petitioners Wilson, Romero, and Schwallier are nevertheless protected from liability through qualified immunity.

It is so ordered.

NOTES

1. While the Court's analysis in *Redding* invalidated this search, it seemed to leave the door open to strip searches that are not as intrusive. Should officials be able to proceed with strip searches in any circumstances?

2. Justice Stevens, joined by Justice Ginsburg who also authored a separate dissent, agreed with the Court that the search was unconstitutional but would have imposed liability on the assistant principal. Would this have been fair?

[CASE NO. 98]   DRUG TESTING OF STUDENT–ATHLETES

**BOARD OF EDUCATION OF INDEPENDENT SCHOOL DISTRICT NO. 92 OF POTTAWATOMIE COUNTY
v. EARLS**

Supreme Court of the United States, 2002.
536 U.S. 822, 122 S.Ct. 2559, 153 L.Ed.2d 735 [166 Educ. L. Rep. 79].

■ Justice Thomas delivered the opinion of the Court.

The Student Activities Drug Testing Policy implemented by the Board of Education of Independent School District No. 92 of Pottawatomie County (School District) requires all students who participate in competitive extra-curricular activities to submit to drug testing. Because this Policy reasonably serves the School District's important interest in detecting and preventing drug use among its students, we hold that it is constitutional.

I

The city of Tecumseh, Oklahoma, is a rural community located approximately 40 miles southeast of Oklahoma City. The School District administers all Tecumseh public schools. In the fall of 1998, the School District adopted the Student Activities Drug Testing Policy (Policy), which requires all middle and high school students to consent to drug testing in order to participate in any extra-curricular activity. In practice, the Policy has been applied only to competitive extra-curricular activities sanctioned by the Oklahoma Secondary Schools Activities Association, such as the Academic Team, Future Farmers of America, Future Homemakers of America, band, choir, pom-pom, cheerleading, and athletics. Under the Policy, students are required to take a drug test before participating in an extra-curricular activity, must submit to random drug testing while participating in that activity, and must agree to be tested at any time upon reasonable suspicion. The urinalysis tests are designed to detect only the use of illegal drugs, including amphetamines, marijuana, cocaine, opiates, and barbituates, not medical conditions or the presence of authorized prescription medications.

At the time of their suit, both respondents attended Tecumseh High School. Respondent Lindsay Earls was a member of the show choir, the marching band, the Academic Team, and the National Honor Society. Respondent Daniel James sought to participate in the Academic Team. Together with their parents, Earls and James brought a 42 U.S.C.[A.] § 1983 action against the School District, challenging the Policy both on its face and as applied to their participation in extra-curricular activities. They alleged that the Policy violates the Fourth Amendment as incorporated by the Fourteenth Amendment and requested injunctive and declarative relief. They also argued that the School District failed to identify a special need for testing students who participate in extra-curricular activities, and that the "Drug Testing Policy neither addresses a proven problem nor promises to bring any benefit to students or the school."

Applying the principles articulated in *Vernonia School Dist. 47J v. Acton*, in which we upheld the suspicionless drug testing of school athletes, the United States District Court for the Western District of Oklahoma rejected respondents' claim that the Policy was unconstitutional and granted summary judgment to the School District. The court noted that "special needs" exist in the public school context and that, although the School District did "not show a drug problem of epidemic proportions," there was a history of drug abuse starting in 1970 that presented "legitimate cause for concern." The District Court also held that the Policy was effective because "[i]t can scarcely be disputed that the drug problem among the student body is effectively addressed by making sure that the large number of students participating in competitive, extra-curricular activities do not use drugs."

The United States Court of Appeals for the Tenth Circuit reversed, holding that the Policy violated the Fourth Amendment. ... We granted certiorari and now reverse.

II

The Fourth Amendment to the United States Constitution protects "[t]he right of the people to be secure in their persons, houses, papers, and effects, against unreasonable searches and seizures." Searches by public school officials, such as the collection of urine samples, implicate Fourth Amendment interests. We must therefore review the School District's Policy for "reasonableness," which is the touchstone of the constitutionality of a governmental search.

In the criminal context, reasonableness usually requires a showing of probable cause. The probable-cause standard, however, "is peculiarly related to criminal investigations" and may be unsuited to determining the reasonableness of administrative searches where the "Government seeks to *prevent* the development of hazardous conditions." The Court has also held that a warrant and finding of probable cause are unnecessary in the public school context because such requirements " 'would unduly interfere with the maintenance of the swift and informal disciplinary procedures [that are] needed.' "

Given that the School District's Policy is not in any way related to the conduct of criminal investigations, respondents do not contend that the School District requires probable cause before testing students for drug use. Respondents instead argue that drug testing must be based at least on some level of individualized suspicion. It is true that we generally determine the reasonableness of a search by balancing the nature of the intrusion on the individual's privacy against the promotion of legitimate governmental interests. But we have long held that "the Fourth Amendment imposes no irreducible requirement of [individualized] suspicion." "[I]n certain limited circumstances, the Government's need to discover such latent or hidden conditions, or to prevent their development, is sufficiently compelling to justify the intrusion on privacy entailed by conducting such searches without any measure of individualized suspicion." Therefore, in the context of safety and administrative regulations, a search unsupported by probable cause may be reasonable "when 'special needs, beyond the normal need for law enforcement, make the warrant and probable-cause requirement impracticable.' "

Significantly, this Court has previously held that "special needs" inhere in the public school context. While schoolchildren do not shed their constitutional rights when they enter the schoolhouse, "Fourth Amendment rights ... are different in public schools than elsewhere; the 'reasonableness' inquiry cannot disregard the schools' custodial and tutelary responsibility for children." In particular, a finding of individualized suspicion may not be necessary when a school conducts drug testing.

In *Vernonia*, this Court held that the suspicionless drug testing of athletes was constitutional. The Court, however, did not simply authorize all school drug testing, but rather conducted a fact-specific balancing of the intrusion on the children's Fourth Amendment rights against the promotion of legitimate governmental interests. Applying the principles of *Vernonia* to the somewhat different facts of this case, we conclude that Tecumseh's Policy is also constitutional.

A

We first consider the nature of the privacy interest allegedly compromised by the drug testing. As in *Vernonia*, the context of the public school environment serves as the backdrop for the analysis of the privacy interest at stake and the reasonableness of the drug testing policy in general. . . .

A student's privacy interest is limited in a public school environment where the State is responsible for maintaining discipline, health, and safety. Schoolchildren are routinely required to submit to physical examinations and vaccinations against disease. Securing order in the school environment sometimes requires that students be subjected to greater controls than those appropriate for adults . . .

Respondents argue that because children participating in nonathletic extra-curricular activities are not subject to regular physicals and communal undress, they have a stronger expectation of privacy than the athletes tested in *Vernonia*. This distinction, however, was not essential to our decision in *Vernonia*, which depended primarily upon the school's custodial responsibility and authority.

In any event, students who participate in competitive extra-curricular activities voluntarily subject themselves to many of the same intrusions on their privacy as do athletes. Some of these clubs and activities require occasional off-campus travel and communal undress. All of them have their own rules and requirements for participating students that do not apply to the student body as a whole. For example, each of the competitive extra-curricular activities governed by the Policy must abide by the rules of the Oklahoma Secondary Schools Activities Association, and a faculty sponsor monitors the students for compliance with the various rules dictated by the clubs and activities. This regulation of extra-curricular activities further diminishes the expectation of privacy among schoolchildren. We therefore conclude that the students affected by this Policy have a limited expectation of privacy.

B

Next, we consider the character of the intrusion imposed by the Policy. Urination is "an excretory function traditionally shielded by great privacy." But the "degree of intrusion" on one's privacy caused by collecting a urine sample "depends upon the manner in which production of the urine sample is monitored."

Under the Policy, a faculty monitor waits outside the closed restroom stall for the student to produce a sample and must "listen for the normal sounds of urination in order to guard against tampered specimens and to insure an accurate chain of custody." The monitor then pours the sample into two bottles that are sealed and placed into a mailing pouch along with a consent form signed by the student. This procedure is virtually identical to that reviewed in *Vernonia*, except that it additionally protects privacy by allowing male students to produce their samples behind a closed stall. Given that we considered the method of collection in *Vernonia* a "negligible" intrusion, the method here is even less problematic.

In addition, the Policy clearly requires that the test results be kept in confidential files separate from a student's other educational records and released to school personnel only on a "need to know" basis. Respondents nonetheless contend that the intrusion on students' privacy is significant because the Policy fails to protect effectively against the disclosure of confidential information and, specifically, that the school "has been careless in protecting that information: for example, the Choir teacher looked at students' prescription drug lists and left them where other students could see them." But the choir teacher is someone with a "need to know," because during off-campus trips she needs to know what medications are taken by her students. Even before the Policy was enacted the choir teacher had access to this information. In any event, there is no allegation that any other student did see such information. This one example of alleged carelessness hardly increases the character of the intrusion.

Moreover, the test results are not turned over to any law enforcement authority. Nor do the test results here lead to the imposition of discipline or have any academic consequences. Rather, the only consequence of a failed drug test is to limit the student's privilege of participating in extracurricular activities. Indeed, a student may test positive for drugs twice and still be allowed to participate in extra-curricular activities. After the first positive test, the school contacts the student's parent or guardian for a meeting. The student may continue to participate in the activity if within five days of the meeting the student shows proof of receiving drug counseling and submits to a second drug test in two weeks. For the second positive test, the student is suspended from participation in all extra-curricular activities for 14 days, must complete four hours of substance abuse counseling, and must submit to monthly drug tests. Only after a third positive test will the student be suspended from participating in any extra-curricular activity for the remainder of the school year, or 88 school days, whichever is longer.

Given the minimally intrusive nature of the sample collection and the limited uses to which the test results are put, we conclude that the invasion of students' privacy is not significant.

C

Finally, this Court must consider the nature and immediacy of the government's concerns and the efficacy of the Policy in meeting them. This Court has already articulated in detail the importance of the governmental concern in preventing drug use by schoolchildren. The drug abuse problem among our Nation's youth has hardly abated since *Vernonia* was decided in 1995. In fact, evidence suggests that it has only grown worse. As in *Vernonia*, "the necessity for the State to act is magnified by the fact that this evil is being visited not just upon individuals at large, but upon children for whom it has undertaken a special responsibility of care and direction." The health and safety risks identified in *Vernonia* apply with equal force to Tecumseh's children. Indeed, the nationwide drug epidemic makes the war against drugs a pressing concern in every school.

Additionally, the School District in this case has presented specific evidence of drug use at Tecumseh schools. Teachers testified that they had seen students who appeared to be under the influence of drugs and that they had heard students speaking openly about using drugs. A drug dog found marijuana cigarettes near the school parking lot. Police officers once found drugs or drug paraphernalia in a car driven by a Future Farmers of America member. And the school board president reported that people in the community were calling the board to discuss the "drug situation." We decline to second-guess the finding of the District Court that "[v]iewing the evidence as a whole, it cannot be reasonably disputed that the [board] was faced with a 'drug problem' when it adopted the Policy."

Respondents consider the proffered evidence insufficient and argue that there is no "real and immediate interest" to justify a policy of drug testing nonathletes. We have recognized, however, that "[a] demonstrated problem of drug abuse ... [is] not in all cases necessary to the validity of a testing regime," but that some showing does "shore up an assertion of special need for a suspicionless general search program." The School District has provided sufficient evidence to shore up the need for its drug testing program.

Furthermore, this Court has not required a particularized or pervasive drug problem before allowing the government to conduct suspicionless drug testing. For instance, in *Von Raab* the Court upheld the drug testing of customs officials on a purely preventive basis, without any documented history of drug use by such officials. In response to the lack of evidence relating to drug use, the Court noted generally that "drug abuse is one of the most serious problems confronting our society today," and that programs to prevent and detect drug use among customs officials could not be deemed unreasonable. Likewise, the need to prevent and deter the substantial harm of childhood drug use provides the necessary immediacy for a school testing policy. Indeed, it would make little sense to require a school district to wait for a substantial portion of its students to begin using drugs before it was allowed to institute a drug testing program designed to deter drug use.

Given the nationwide epidemic of drug use, and the evidence of increased drug use in Tecumseh schools, it was entirely reasonable for the School District to enact this particular drug testing policy. We reject the Court of Appeals' novel test that "any district seeking to impose a random suspicionless drug testing policy as a condition to participation in a school activity must demonstrate that there is some identifiable drug abuse problem among a sufficient number of those subject to the testing, such that testing that group of students will actually redress its drug problem." Among other problems, it would be difficult to administer such a test. As we cannot articulate a threshold level of drug use that would suffice to justify a drug testing program for schoolchildren, we refuse to fashion what would in effect be a constitutional quantum of drug use necessary to show a "drug problem."

Respondents also argue that the testing of nonathletes does not impli-cate any safety concerns, and that safety is a "crucial factor" in applying the special needs framework. They contend that there must be "surpassing safety interests," or "extraordinary safety and national security hazards," in order to override the usual protections of the Fourth Amendment. Respondents are correct that safety factors into the special needs analysis, but the safety interest furthered by drug testing is undoubtedly substantial for all children, athletes and nonathletes alike. We know all too well that drug use carries a variety of health risks for children, including death from overdose.

We also reject respondents' argument that drug testing must presump-tively be based upon an individualized reasonable suspicion of wrongdoing because such a testing regime would be less intrusive. In this context, the Fourth Amendment does not require a finding of individualized suspicion and we decline to impose such a requirement on schools attempting to prevent and detect drug use by students. Moreover, we question whether testing based on individualized suspicion in fact would be less intrusive. Such a regime would place an additional burden on public school teachers who are already tasked with the difficult job of maintaining order and discipline. A program of individualized suspicion might unfairly target members of unpopular groups. The fear of lawsuits resulting from such targeted searches may chill enforcement of the program, rendering it ineffective in combating drug use. In any case, this Court has repeatedly stated that reasonableness under the Fourth Amendment does not require employing the least intrusive means, because "[t]he logic of such elaborate less-restrictive-alternative arguments could raise insuperable barriers to the exercise of virtually all search-and-seizure powers."

Finally, we find that testing students who participate in extra-curricu-lar activities is a reasonably effective means of addressing the School District's legitimate concerns in preventing, deterring, and detecting drug use. While in *Vernonia* there might have been a closer fit between the testing of athletes and the trial court's finding that the drug problem was "fueled by the 'role model' effect of athletes' drug use," such a finding was not essential to the holding. *Vernonia* did not require the school to test the group of students most likely to use drugs, but rather considered the constitutionality of the program in the context of the public school's custodial responsibilities. Evaluating the Policy in this context, we conclude that the drug testing of Tecumseh students who participate in extra-curricular activities effectively serves the School District's interest in protecting the safety and health of its students.

III

Within the limits of the Fourth Amendment, local school boards must assess the desirability of drug testing schoolchildren. In upholding the constitutionality of the Policy, we express no opinion as to its wisdom. Rather, we hold only that Tecumseh's Policy is a reasonable means of furthering the School District's important interest in preventing and deter-ring drug use among its schoolchildren. Accordingly, we reverse the judg-ment of the Court of Appeals.

It is so ordered.

NOTES

1. As in *Acton*, the focus of the policy here was rehabilitative or therapeutic rather than punitive. If the policy focused on punishment would, or should, the Supreme Court have reached a different result?

2. In *Earls*, the Court lowered the bar with regard to the nature and immediacy of the governmental concern, making it easier for school officials to submit student-athletes to drug testing. Should educators be able to test students in other activities such as newspapers and school clubs?

3. Should students or school systems be required to pay what can be the considerable cost of mandatory drug testing? What if students cannot afford to pay?

[CASE NO. 99]   BOARD LIABILITY FOR SEXUAL HARASSMENT BY SCHOOL STAFF

FRANKLIN v. GWINNETT COUNTY PUBLIC SCHOOLS

Supreme Court of the United States, 1992.
503 U.S. 60, 112 S.Ct. 1028, 117 L.Ed.2d 208 [72 Educ. L. Rep. 32].

■ JUSTICE WHITE delivered the opinion of the Court.

This case presents the question whether the implied right of action under Title IX of the Education Amendments of 1972, (Title IX), which this Court recognized in *Cannon v. University of Chicago*, supports a claim for monetary damages.

I

Petitioner Christine Franklin was a student at North Gwinnett High School in Gwinnett County, Georgia, between September 1985 and August 1989. Respondent Gwinnett County School District operates the high school and receives federal funds. According to the complaint ... Franklin was subjected to continual sexual harassment beginning in the autumn of her tenth grade year (1986) from Andrew Hill, a sports coach and teacher employed by the district. Among other allegations, Franklin avers that Hill engaged her in sexually oriented conversations in which he asked about her sexual experiences with her boyfriend and whether she would consider having sexual intercourse with an older man, that Hill forcibly kissed her on the mouth in the school parking lot; that he telephoned her at her home and asked if she would meet him socially; and that, on three occasions in her junior year, Hill interrupted a class, requested that the teacher excuse Franklin, and took her to a private office where he subjected her to coercive intercourse. The complaint further alleges that though they became aware of and investigated Hill's sexual harassment of Franklin and other female students, teachers and administrators took no action to halt it and discouraged Franklin from pressing charges against Hill. On April 14, 1988, Hill resigned on the condition that all matters pending against him be dropped. The school thereupon closed its investigation.

In this action, the District Court dismissed the complaint on the ground that Title IX does not authorize an award of damages. The Court of Appeals affirmed....

Because this opinion conflicts with a decision of the Court of Appeals for the Third Circuit, we granted certiorari. We reverse.

II

In *Cannon v. University of Chicago*, the Court held that Title IX is enforceable through an implied right of action. We have no occasion here to reconsider that decision. Rather, in this case we must decide what remedies are available in a suit brought pursuant to this implied right. As we have often stated, the question of what remedies are available under a statute that provides a private right of action is "analytically distinct" from the issue of whether such a right exists in the first place. Thus, although we examine the text and history of a statute to determine whether Congress intended to create a right of action, we presume the availability of all appropriate remedies unless Congress has expressly indicated otherwise. This principle has deep roots in our jurisprudence.

A

"[W]here legal rights have been invaded, and a federal statute provides for a general right to sue for such invasion, federal courts may use any available remedy to make good the wrong done." The Court explained this longstanding rule as jurisdictional and upheld the exercise of the federal courts' power to award appropriate relief so long as a cause of action existed under the Constitution or laws of the United States.

The *Bell* Court's reliance on this rule was hardly revolutionary. From the earliest years of the Republic, the Court has recognized the power of the Judiciary to award appropriate remedies to redress injuries actionable in federal court, although it did not always distinguish clearly between a right to bring suit and a remedy available under such a right. In *Marbury v. Madison,* for example, Chief Justice Marshall observed that our Government "has been emphatically termed a government of laws, and not of men. It will certainly cease to deserve this high appellation, if the laws furnish no remedy for the violation of a vested legal right."....

B

Respondents and the United States as *amicus curiae,* however, maintain that whatever the traditional presumption may have been when the Court decided *Bell v. Hood,* it has disappeared in succeeding decades. We do not agree.... That a statute does not authorize the remedy at issue "in so many words is no more significant than the fact that it does not in terms authorize execution to issue on a judgment."....

The United States contends that the traditional presumption in favor of all appropriate relief was abandoned by the Court in *Davis v. Passman,* and that the *Bell v. Hood* rule was limited to actions claiming constitutional violations. The United States quotes language in *Davis* to the effect that "the question of who may enforce a *statutory* right is fundamentally different from the question of who may enforce a right that is protected by the Constitution." The Government's position, however, mirrors the very misunderstanding over the difference between a cause of action and the relief afforded under it that sparked the confusion we attempted to clarify in *Davis.* Whether Congress may limit the class of persons who have a right of action under Title IX is irrelevant to the issue in this lawsuit. To reiterate, "the question whether a litigant has a 'cause of action' is analytically distinct and prior to the question of what relief, if any, a litigant may be entitled to receive." *Davis,* therefore, did nothing to interrupt the long line of cases in which the Court has held that if a right of action exists to enforce a federal right and Congress is silent on the question of remedies, a federal court may order any appropriate relief.

... The general rule, therefore, is that absent clear direction to the contrary by Congress, the federal courts have the power to award any appropriate relief in a cognizable cause of action brought pursuant to a federal statute.

III

We now address whether Congress intended to limit application of this general principle in the enforcement of Title IX. Because the cause of action was inferred by the Court in *Cannon,* the usual recourse to statutory text and legislative history in the period prior to that decision necessarily will not enlighten our analysis. Respondents and the United States fundamentally misunderstand the nature of the inquiry, therefore, by needlessly dedicating large portions of their briefs to discussions of how the text and legislative intent behind Title IX are "silent" on the issue of available remedies. Since the Court in *Cannon* concluded that this statute supported no express right of action, it is hardly surprising that Congress also said nothing about the applicable remedies for an implied right of action.

During the period prior to the decision in *Cannon,* the inquiry in any event is *not* " 'basically a matter of statutory construction,' " as the United States asserts. Rather, in determining Congress' intent to limit application of the traditional presumption in favor of all appropriate relief, we evaluate the state of the law when the Legislature passed Title IX. In the years before and after Congress enacted this statute, the Court "follow[ed] a common-law tradition [and] regarded the denial of a remedy as the exception rather than the rule." As we outlined in Part II, this has been the prevailing presumption in our federal courts since at least the early 19th century. In *Cannon,* the majority upheld an implied right of action in part because in the decade immediately preceding enactment of Title IX in 1972, this Court had found implied rights of action in six cases. In three of those cases, the Court had approved a damages remedy. Wholly apart from the wisdom of the *Cannon* holding, therefore, the same contextual approach used to justify an implied right of action more than amply demonstrates the lack of any legislative intent to abandon the traditional presumption in favor of all available remedies.

In the years after the announcement of *Cannon,* on the other hand, a more traditional method of statutory analysis is possible, because Congress was legislating with full cognizance of that decision. Our reading of the two amendments to Title IX enacted after *Cannon* leads us to conclude that

Congress did not intend to limit the remedies available in a suit brought under Title IX. In the Rehabilitation Act Amendments of 1986, Congress abrogated the States' Eleventh Amendment immunity under Title IX, Title VI, § 504 of the Rehabilitation Act of 1973, and the Age Discrimination Act of 1975. This statute cannot be read except as a validation of *Cannon*'s holding. A subsection of the 1986 law provides that in a suit against a State, "remedies (including remedies both at law and in equity) are available for such a violation to the same extent as such remedies are available for such a violation in the suit against any public or private entity other than a State." While it is true that this saving clause says nothing about the nature of those other available remedies, absent any contrary indication in the text or history of the statute, we presume Congress enacted this statute with the prevailing traditional rule in mind.

In addition to the Rehabilitation Act Amendments of 1986, Congress also enacted the Civil Rights Restoration Act of 1987. Without in any way altering the existing rights of action and the corresponding remedies permissible under Title IX, Title VI, § 504 of the Rehabilitation Act, and the Age Discrimination Act, Congress broadened the coverage of these antidiscrimination provisions in this legislation.... We cannot say, therefore, that Congress has limited the remedies available to a complainant in a suit brought under Title IX.

IV

Respondents and the United States nevertheless suggest three reasons why we should not apply the traditional presumption in favor of appropriate relief in this case.

A

First, respondents argue that an award of damages violates separation of powers principles because it unduly expands the federal courts' power into a sphere properly reserved to the Executive and Legislative Branches. In making this argument, respondents misconceive the difference between a cause of action and a remedy. Unlike the finding of a cause of action, which authorizes a court to hear a case or controversy, the discretion to award appropriate relief involves no such increase in judicial power. Federal courts cannot reach out to award remedies when the Constitution or laws of the United States do not support a cause of action. Indeed, properly understood, respondents' position invites us to *abdicate* our historic judicial authority to award appropriate relief in cases brought in our court system. It is well to recall that such authority historically has been thought necessary to provide an important safeguard against abuses of legislative and executive power, as well as to ensure an independent Judiciary. Moreover, selective abdication of the sort advocated here would harm separation of powers principles in another way, by giving judges the power to render inutile causes of action authorized by Congress through a decision that *no* remedy is available.

B

Next, consistent with the Court of Appeals' reasoning, respondents and the United States contend that the normal presumption in favor of all appropriate remedies should not apply because Title IX was enacted pursuant to Congress' Spending Clause power. In *Pennhurst State School and Hospital v. Halderman,* the Court observed that remedies were limited under such Spending Clause statutes when the alleged violation was *unintentional.* Respondents and the United States maintain that this presumption should apply equally to *intentional* violations. We disagree. The point of not permitting monetary damages for an unintentional violation is that the receiving entity of federal funds lacks notice that it will be liable for a monetary award. This notice problem does not arise in a case such as this, in which intentional discrimination is alleged. Unquestionably, Title IX placed on the Gwinnett County Public Schools the duty not to discriminate on the basis of sex, and "when a supervisor sexually harasses a subordinate because of the subordinate's sex, that supervisor 'discriminate[s]' on the basis of sex." We believe the same rule should apply when a teacher sexually harasses and abuses a student. Congress surely did not intend for federal moneys to be expended to support the intentional actions it sought by statute to proscribe. . . .

C

Finally, the United States asserts that the remedies permissible under Title IX should nevertheless be limited to backpay and prospective relief. In addition to diverging from our traditional approach to deciding what remedies are available for violation of a federal right, this position conflicts with sound logic. First, both remedies are equitable in nature, and it is axiomatic that a court should determine the adequacy of a remedy in law before resorting to equitable relief. Under the ordinary convention, the proper inquiry would be whether monetary damages provided an adequate remedy, and if not, whether equitable relief would be appropriate. Moreover, in this case the equitable remedies suggested by respondent and the Federal Government are clearly inadequate. Backpay does nothing for petitioner, because she was a student when the alleged discrimination occurred. Similarly, because Hill—the person she claims subjected her to sexual harassment—no longer teaches at the school and she herself no longer attends a school in the Gwinnett system, prospective relief accords her no remedy at all. The Government's answer that administrative action helps other similarly situated students in effect acknowledges that its approach would leave petitioner remediless.

V

In sum, we conclude that a damages remedy is available for an action brought to enforce Title IX. The judgment of the Court of Appeals, therefore, is reversed, and the case is remanded for further proceedings consistent with this opinion.

So ordered.

NOTES

1.   There were no dissents in *Franklin.* Even so, Justice Scalia's concurrence was joined by Chief Justice Rehnquist and Justice Thomas.

2. School officials have universally adopted policies against sexual harassment. What specific provisions should policies contain?

[CASE NO. 100] BOARD NON–LIABILITY FOR SEXUAL HARASSMENT BY SCHOOL STAFF

GEBSER v. LAGO VISTA INDEPENDENT SCHOOL DISTRICT

Supreme Court of the United States, 1998.
524 U.S. 274, 118 S.Ct. 1989, 141 L.Ed.2d 277 [125 Educ. L. Rep. 1055].

■ JUSTICE O'CONNOR delivered the opinion of the Court.

The question in this case is when a school district may be held liable in damages in an implied right of action under Title IX of the Education Amendments of 1972 (Title IX), for the sexual harassment of a student by one of the district's teachers. We conclude that damages may not be recovered in those circumstances unless an official of the school district who at a minimum has authority to institute corrective measures on the district's behalf has actual notice of, and is deliberately indifferent to, the teacher's misconduct.

I

In the spring of 1991, when petitioner Alida Star Gebser was an eighth-grade student at a middle school in respondent Lago Vista Independent School District (Lago Vista), she joined a high school book discussion group led by Frank Waldrop, a teacher at Lago Vista's high school. Lago Vista received federal funds at all pertinent times. During the book discussion sessions, Waldrop often made sexually suggestive comments to the students. Gebser entered high school in the fall and was assigned to classes taught by Waldrop in both semesters. Waldrop continued to make inappropriate remarks to the students, and he began to direct more of his suggestive comments toward Gebser, including during the substantial amount of time that the two were alone in his classroom. He initiated sexual contact with Gebser in the spring, when, while visiting her home ostensibly to give her a book, he kissed and fondled her. The two had sexual intercourse on a number of occasions during the remainder of the school year. Their relationship continued through the summer and into the following school year, and they often had intercourse during class time, although never on school property.

Gebser did not report the relationship to school officials, testifying that while she realized Waldrop's conduct was improper, she was uncertain how to react and she wanted to continue having him as a teacher. In October 1992, the parents of two other students complained to the high school principal about Waldrop's comments in class. The principal arranged a meeting, at which, according to the principal, Waldrop indicated that he did not believe he had made offensive remarks but apologized to the parents and said it would not happen again. The principal also advised Waldrop to be careful about his classroom comments and told the school guidance counselor about the meeting, but he did not report the parents' complaint to Lago Vista's superintendent, who was the district's Title IX coordinator.

A couple of months later, in January 1993, a police officer discovered Waldrop and Gebser engaging in sexual intercourse and arrested Waldrop. Lago Vista terminated his employment, and subsequently, the Texas Education Agency revoked his teaching license. During this time, the district had not promulgated or distributed an official grievance procedure for lodging sexual harassment complaints; nor had it issued a formal anti-harassment policy.

Gebser and her mother filed suit against Lago Vista and Waldrop in state court in November 1993, raising claims against the school district under Title IX, 42 U.S.C.[A.] § 1983, and state negligence law, and claims against Waldrop primarily under state law. They sought compensatory and punitive damages from both defendants. After the case was removed, the United States District Court for the Western District of Texas granted summary judgment in favor of Lago Vista on all claims, and remanded the allegations against Waldrop to state court.

. . .

Petitioners appealed only on the Title IX claim. The Court of Appeals for the Fifth Circuit affirmed. . . .

. . . We granted certiorari to address the issue and we now affirm.

II

Title IX provides in pertinent part: "No person . . . shall, on the basis of sex, be excluded from participation in, be denied the benefits of, or be subjected to discrimination under any education program or activity receiving Federal financial assistance." The express statutory means of enforcement is administrative: The statute directs federal agencies that distribute education funding to establish requirements to effectuate the nondiscrimination mandate, and permits the agencies to enforce those requirements through "any . . . means authorized by law," including ultimately the termination of federal funding. The Court held in *Cannon v. University of Chicago* that Title IX is also enforceable through an implied private right of action, a conclusion we do not revisit here. We subsequently established in *Franklin v. Gwinnett County Public Schools* that monetary damages are available in the implied private action.

In *Franklin*, a high school student alleged that a teacher had sexually abused her on repeated occasions and that teachers and school administrators knew about the harassment but took no action, even to the point of dissuading her from initiating charges. The lower courts dismissed Franklin's complaint against the school district on the ground that the implied right of action under Title IX, as a categorical matter, does not encompass recovery in damages. We reversed the lower courts' blanket rule, concluding that Title IX supports a private action for damages, at least "in a case such as this, in which intentional discrimination is alleged." *Franklin* thereby establishes that a school district can be held liable in damages in cases involving a teacher's sexual harassment of a student; the decision, however, does not purport to define the contours of that liability.

We face that issue squarely in this case. Petitioners, joined by the United States as amicus curiae, would invoke standards used by the Courts of Appeals in Title VII cases involving a supervisor's sexual harassment of an employee in the workplace. In support of that approach, they point to a passage in *Franklin* in which we stated: "Unquestionably, Title IX placed on the Gwinnett County Public Schools the duty not to discriminate on the basis of sex, and 'when a supervisor sexually harasses a subordinate because of the subordinate's sex, that supervisor "discriminate[s]" on the basis of sex.' We believe the same rule should apply when a teacher sexually harasses and abuses a student.' " ... *Meritor Savings Bank, FSB v. Vinson* directs courts to look to common law agency principles when assessing an employer's liability under Title VII for sexual harassment of an employee by a supervisor. Petitioners and the United States submit that, in light of *Franklin's* comparison of teacher-student harassment with supervisor-employee harassment, agency principles should likewise apply in Title IX actions.

Specifically, they advance two possible standards under which Lago Vista would be liable for Waldrop's conduct. First, relying on a 1997 "Policy Guidance" issued by the Department of Education, they would hold a school district liable in damages under Title IX where a teacher is " 'aided in carrying out the sexual harassment of students by his or her position of authority with the institution,' " irrespective of whether school district officials had any knowledge of the harassment and irrespective of their response upon becoming aware. That rule is an expression of respondeat superior liability, i.e., vicarious or imputed liability, under which recovery in damages against a school district would generally follow whenever a teacher's authority over a student facilitates the harassment. Second, petitioners and the United States submit that a school district should at a minimum be liable for damages based on a theory of constructive notice, i.e., where the district knew or "should have known" about harassment but failed to uncover and eliminate it. Both standards would allow a damages recovery in a broader range of situations than the rule adopted by the Court of Appeals, which hinges on actual knowledge by a school official with authority to end the harassment.

Whether educational institutions can be said to violate Title IX based solely on principles of respondeat superior or constructive notice was not resolved by *Franklin's* citation of *Meritor*. That reference to *Meritor* was made with regard to the general proposition that sexual harassment can constitute discrimination on the basis of sex under Title IX, an issue not in dispute here. In fact, the school district's liability in *Franklin* did not necessarily turn on principles of imputed liability or constructive notice, as there was evidence that school officials knew about the harassment but took no action to stop it. Moreover, *Meritor's* rationale for concluding that agency principles guide the liability inquiry under Title VII rests on an aspect of that statute not found in Title IX: Title VII, in which the prohibition against employment discrimination runs against "an employer," Title IX contains no comparable reference to an educational institution's "agents," and so does not expressly call for application of agency principles.

In this case, moreover, petitioners seek not just to establish a Title IX violation but to recover damages based on theories of respondeat superior and constructive notice. It is that aspect of their action, in our view, that is most critical to resolving the case. Unlike Title IX, Title VII contains an express cause of action and specifically provides for relief in the form of monetary damages. Congress therefore has directly addressed the subject of damages relief under Title VII and has set out the particular situations in which damages are available as well as the maximum amounts recoverable. With respect to Title IX, however, the private right of action is judicially implied and there is thus no legislative expression of the scope of available remedies, including when it is appropriate to award monetary damages. In addition, although the general presumption that courts can award any appropriate relief in an established cause of action, coupled with Congress' abrogation of the States' Eleventh Amendment immunity under Title IX, led us to conclude in *Franklin* that Title IX recognizes a damages remedy, we did so in response to lower court decisions holding that Title IX does not support damages relief at all. We made no effort in *Franklin* to delimit the circumstances in which a damages remedy should lie.

III

Because the private right of action under Title IX is judicially implied, we have a measure of latitude to shape a sensible remedial scheme that best comports with the statute. That endeavor inherently entails a degree of speculation, since it addresses an issue on which Congress has not specifically spoken. To guide the analysis, we generally examine the relevant statute to ensure that we do not fashion the scope of an implied right in a manner at odds with the statutory structure and purpose.

Those considerations, we think, are pertinent not only to the scope of the implied right, but also to the scope of the available remedies. We suggested as much in *Franklin*, where we recognized "the general rule that all appropriate relief is available in an action brought to vindicate a federal right," but indicated that the rule must be reconciled with congressional purpose. The "general rule," that is, "yields where necessary to carry out the intent of Congress or to avoid frustrating the purposes of the statute involved."

Applying those principles here, we conclude that it would "frustrate the purposes" of Title IX to permit a damages recovery against a school district for a teacher's sexual harassment of a student based on principles of respondeat superior or constructive notice, i.e., without actual notice to a school district official. Because Congress did not expressly create a private right of action under Title IX, the statutory text does not shed light on Congress' intent with respect to the scope of available remedies. Instead, "we attempt to infer how the [1972] Congress would have addressed the issue had the . . . action been included as an express provision in the" statute.

As a general matter, it does not appear that Congress contemplated unlimited recovery in damages against a funding recipient where the recipient is unaware of discrimination in its programs. When Title IX was enacted in 1972, the principal civil rights statutes containing an express right of action did not provide for recovery of monetary damages at all, instead allowing only injunctive and equitable relief. It was not until 1991 that Congress made damages available under Title VII, and even then, Congress carefully limited the amount recoverable in any individual case, calibrating the maximum recovery to the size of the employer. Adopting petitioners' position would amount, then, to allowing unlimited recovery of damages under Title IX where Congress has not spoken on the subject of either the right or the remedy, and in the face of evidence that when Congress expressly considered both in Title VII it restricted the amount of damages available.

Congress enacted Title IX in 1972 with two principal objectives in mind: "[T]o avoid the use of federal resources to support discriminatory practices" and "to provide individual citizens effective protection against those practices." The statute was modeled after Title VI of the Civil Rights Act of 1964 which is parallel to Title IX except that it prohibits race discrimination, not sex discrimination, and applies in all programs receiving federal funds, not only in education programs. The two statutes operate in the same manner, conditioning an offer of federal funding on a promise by the recipient not to discriminate, in what amounts essentially to a contract between the Government and the recipient of funds.

That contractual framework distinguishes Title IX from Title VII, which is framed in terms not of a condition but of an outright prohibition. Title VII applies to all employers without regard to federal funding and aims broadly to "eradicat[e] discrimination throughout the economy." Thus, whereas Title VII aims centrally to compensate victims of discrimination, Title IX focuses more on "protecting" individuals from discriminatory practices carried out by recipients of federal funds. That might explain why, when the Court first recognized the implied right under Title IX in Cannon, the opinion referred to injunctive or equitable relief in a private action, but not to a damages remedy.

Title IX's contractual nature has implications for our construction of the scope of available remedies. When Congress attaches conditions to the award of federal funds under its spending power, as it has in Title IX and Title VI, we examine closely the propriety of private actions holding the recipient liable in monetary damages for noncompliance with the condition.

. . . If a school district's liability for a teacher's sexual harassment rests on principles of constructive notice or respondeat superior, it will likewise be the case that the recipient of funds was unaware of the discrimination. It is sensible to assume that Congress did not envision a recipient's liability in damages in that situation.

Most significantly, Title IX contains important clues that Congress did not intend to allow recovery in damages where liability rests solely on principles of vicarious liability or constructive notice. Title IX's express means of enforcement—by administrative agencies—operates on an assumption of actual notice to officials of the funding recipient. The statute entitles agencies who disburse education funding to enforce their rules implementing the nondiscrimination mandate through proceedings to suspend or terminate funding or through "other means authorized by law." Significantly, however, an agency may not initiate enforcement proceedings until it "has advised the appropriate person or persons of the failure to comply with the requirement and has determined that compliance cannot be secured by voluntary means." The administrative regulations implement that obligation, requiring resolution of compliance issues "by informal means whenever possible," and prohibiting commencement of enforcement proceedings until the agency has determined that voluntary compliance is unobtainable and "the recipient ... has been notified of its failure to comply and of the action to be taken to effect compliance."

In the event of a violation, a funding recipient may be required to take "such remedial action as [is] deem[ed] necessary to overcome the effects of [the] discrimination." While agencies have conditioned continued funding on providing equitable relief to the victim, the regulations do not appear to contemplate a condition ordering payment of monetary damages, and there is no indication that payment of damages has been demanded as a condition of finding a recipient to be in compliance with the statute. In *Franklin*, for instance, the Department of Education found a violation of Title IX but determined that the school district came into compliance by virtue of the offending teacher's resignation and the district's institution of a grievance procedure for sexual harassment complaints.

Presumably, a central purpose of requiring notice of the violation "of the appropriate person" and an opportunity for voluntary compliance before administrative enforcement proceedings can commence is to avoid diverting education funding from beneficial uses where a recipient was unaware of discrimination in its programs and is willing to institute prompt corrective measures. The scope of private damages relief proposed by petitioners is at odds with that basic objective. When a teacher's sexual harassment is imputed to a school district or when a school district is deemed to have "constructively" known of the teacher's harassment, by assumption the district had no actual knowledge of the teacher's conduct. Nor, of course, did the district have an opportunity to take action to end the harassment or to limit further harassment.

It would be unsound, we think, for a statute's express system of enforcement to require notice to the recipient and an opportunity to come into voluntary compliance while a judicially implied system of enforcement permits substantial liability without regard to the recipient's knowledge or its corrective actions upon receiving notice. Moreover, an award of damages in a particular case might well exceed a recipient's level of federal funding. Where a statute's express enforcement scheme hinges its most severe sanction on notice and unsuccessful efforts to obtain compliance, we cannot attribute to Congress the intention to have implied an enforcement scheme that allows imposition of greater liability without comparable conditions.

IV

Because the express remedial scheme under Title IX is predicated upon notice to an "appropriate person" and an opportunity to rectify any violation, we conclude, in the absence of further direction from Congress, that the implied damages remedy should be fashioned along the same lines. An "appropriate person" under § 1682 is, at a minimum, an official of the recipient entity with authority to take corrective action to end the discrimination. Consequently, in cases like this one that do not involve official policy of the recipient entity, we hold that a damages remedy will not lie under Title IX unless an official who at a minimum has authority to address the alleged discrimination and to institute corrective measures on the recipient's behalf has actual knowledge of discrimination in the recipient's programs and fails adequately to respond.

We think, moreover, that the response must amount to deliberate indifference to discrimination. The administrative enforcement scheme presupposes that an official who is advised of a Title IX violation refuses to take action to bring the recipient into compliance. The premise, in other words, is an official decision by the recipient not to remedy the violation. That framework finds a rough parallel in the standard of deliberate indifference. Under a lower standard, there would be a risk that the recipient would be liable in damages not for its own official decision but instead for its employees' independent actions. Comparable considerations led to our adoption of a deliberate indifference standard for claims under § 1983 alleging that a municipality's actions in failing to prevent a deprivation of federal rights was the cause of the violation.

Applying the framework to this case is fairly straightforward, as petitioners do not contend they can prevail under an actual notice standard. The only official alleged to have had information about Waldrop's misconduct is the high school principal. That information, however, consisted of a complaint from parents of other students charging only that Waldrop had made inappropriate comments during class, which was plainly insufficient to alert the principal to the possibility that Waldrop was involved in a sexual relationship with a student. Lago Vista, moreover, terminated Waldrop's employment upon learning of his relationship with Gebser.... Where a school district's liability rests on actual notice principles, however, the knowledge of the wrongdoer himself is not pertinent to the analysis.

Petitioners focus primarily on Lago Vista's asserted failure to promulgate and publicize an effective policy and grievance procedure for sexual harassment claims. They point to Department of Education regulations requiring each funding recipient to "adopt and publish grievance procedures providing for prompt and equitable resolution" of discrimination complaints, and to notify students and others that "it does not discriminate on the basis of sex in the educational programs or activities which it operates," Lago Vista's alleged failure to comply with the regulations, however, does not establish the requisite actual notice and deliberate indifference. And in any event, the failure to promulgate a grievance procedure does not itself constitute "discrimination" under Title IX. Of course, the Department of Education could enforce the requirement administratively: Agencies generally have authority to promulgate and enforce requirements that effectuate the statute's nondiscrimination mandate, even if those requirements do not purport to represent a definition of discrimination under the statute. We have never held, however, that the implied private right of action under Title IX allows recovery in damages for violation of those sorts of administrative requirements.

V

The number of reported cases involving sexual harassment of students in schools confirms that harassment unfortunately is an all too common aspect of the educational experience. No one questions that a student suffers extraordinary harm when subjected to sexual harassment and abuse by a teacher, and that the teacher's conduct is reprehensible and undermines the basic purposes of the educational system. The issue in this case, however, is whether the independent misconduct of a teacher is attributable to the school district that employs him under a specific federal statute designed primarily to prevent recipients of federal financial assistance from using the funds in a discriminatory manner. Our decision does not affect any right of recovery that an individual may have against a school district as a matter of state law or against the teacher in his individual capacity under state law or under 42 U.S.C.[A.] § 1983. Until Congress speaks directly on the subject, however, we will not hold a school district liable in damages under Title IX for a teacher's sexual harassment of a student absent actual notice and deliberate indifference. We therefore affirm the judgment of the Court of Appeals.

It is so ordered.

NOTES

1. Do you agree with the outcome in this case?

2. Is there anything that school officials and/or parents could have done to have prevented this kind of situation from occurring?

[CASE NO. 101]   PEER-TO-PEER SEXUAL HARASSMENT

DAVIS v. MONROE COUNTY BOARD OF EDUCATION

Supreme Court of the United States, 1999.
526 U.S. 629, 119 S.Ct. 1661, 143 L.Ed.2d 839 [134 Educ. L. Rep. 477].

■ JUSTICE O'CONNOR delivered the opinion of the Court.

Petitioner brought suit against the Monroe County Board of Education and other defendants, alleging that her fifth-grade daughter had been the victim of sexual harassment by another student in her class. Among petitioner's claims was a claim for monetary and injunctive relief under Title IX. . . . The District Court dismissed petitioner's Title IX claim on the ground that "student-on-student," or peer, harassment provides no ground for a private cause of action under the statute. The . . . Eleventh Circuit, sitting en banc, affirmed. We consider here whether a private damages action may lie against the school board in cases of student-on-student harassment. We conclude that it may, but only where the funding recipient acts with deliberate indifference to known acts of harassment in its programs or activities. Moreover, we conclude that such an action will lie only for harassment that is so severe, pervasive, and objectively offensive that it effectively bars the victim's access to an educational opportunity or benefit.

I

A

Petitioner's minor daughter, LaShonda, was allegedly the victim of a prolonged pattern of sexual harassment by one of her fifth-grade classmates at Hubbard Elementary School, a public school in Monroe County, Georgia. According to petitioner's complaint, the harassment began in December 1992, when the classmate, G.F., attempted to touch LaShonda's breasts and genital area and made vulgar statements such as " 'I want to get in bed with you' " and " 'I want to feel your boobs.' " Similar conduct allegedly occurred on or about January 4 and January 20, 1993. LaShonda reported each of these incidents to her mother and to her classroom teacher, Diane Fort. Petitioner, in turn, also contacted Fort, who allegedly assured petitioner that the school principal, Bill Querry, had been informed of the incidents. Petitioner contends that, notwithstanding these reports, no disciplinary action was taken against G.F.

G.F.'s conduct allegedly continued for many months. In early February, G.F. purportedly placed a door stop in his pants and proceeded to act in a sexually suggestive manner toward LaShonda during physical education class. LaShonda reported G.F.'s behavior to her physical education teacher, Whit Maples. Approximately one week later, G.F. again allegedly engaged in harassing behavior, this time while under the supervision of another classroom teacher, Joyce Pippin. Again, LaShonda allegedly reported the incident to the teacher, and again petitioner contacted the teacher to follow up.

Petitioner alleges that G.F. once more directed sexually harassing conduct toward LaShonda in physical education class in early March, and that LaShonda reported the incident to both Maples and Pippen. In mid-April 1993, G.F. allegedly rubbed his body against LaShonda in the school hallway in what LaShonda considered a sexually suggestive manner, and LaShonda again reported the matter to Fort.

The string of incidents finally ended in mid-May, when G.F. was charged with, and pleaded guilty to, sexual battery for his misconduct. The complaint alleges that LaShonda had suffered during the months of harassment, however; specifically, her previously high grades allegedly dropped as she became unable to concentrate on her studies, and, in April 1993, her father discovered that she had written a suicide note. The complaint further alleges that, at one point, LaShonda told petitioner that she " 'didn't know how much longer she could keep [G.F.] off her.' "

Nor was LaShonda G.F.'s only victim; it is alleged that other girls in the class fell prey to G.F.'s conduct. At one point, in fact, a group composed of LaShonda and other female students tried to speak with Principal Querry about G.F.'s behavior. According to the complaint, however, a teacher denied the students' request with the statement, " 'If [Querry] wants you, he'll call you.' "

Petitioner alleges that no disciplinary action was taken in response to G.F.'s behavior toward LaShonda. In addition to her conversations with Fort and Pippen, petitioner alleges that she spoke with Principal Querry in mid-May 1993. When petitioner inquired as to what action the school intended to take against G.F., Querry simply stated, " 'I guess I'll have to threaten him a little bit harder.' " Yet, petitioner alleges, at no point during the many months of his reported misconduct was G.F. disciplined for harassment. Indeed, Querry allegedly asked petitioner why LaShonda " 'was the only one complaining.' "

Nor, according to the complaint, was any effort made to separate G.F. and LaShonda. On the contrary, notwithstanding LaShonda's frequent complaints, only after more than three months of reported harassment was she even permitted to change her classroom seat so that she was no longer seated next to G.F. Moreover, petitioner alleges that, at the time of the events in question, the Monroe County Board of Education (Board) had not instructed its personnel on how to respond to peer sexual harassment and had not established a policy on the issue.

B

On May 4, 1994, petitioner filed suit in the United States District Court for the Middle District of Georgia against the Board, Charles Dumas, the school district's superintendent, and Principal Querry. The complaint alleged that the Board is a recipient of federal funding for purposes of Title IX, that "[t]he persistent sexual advances and harassment by the student G.F. upon [LaShonda] interfered with her ability to attend school and perform her studies and activities," and that "[t]he deliberate indifference by Defendants to the unwelcome sexual advances of a student upon LaShonda created an intimidating, hostile, offensive and abus[ive] school environment in violation of Title IX." The complaint sought compensatory and punitive damages, attorney's fees, and injunctive relief.

The defendants (all respondents here) moved to dismiss petitioner's complaint under Federal Rule of Civil Procedure 12(b)(6) for failure to state a claim upon which relief could be granted, and the District Court granted respondents' motion. With regard to petitioner's claims under Title IX, the court dismissed the claims against individual defendants on the ground that only federally funded educational institutions are subject to liability in private causes of action under Title IX. As for the Board, the court concluded that Title IX provided no basis for liability absent an allegation "that the Board or an employee of the Board had any role in the harassment."

Petitioner appealed the District Court's decision dismissing her Title IX claim against the Board, and a panel of the Court of Appeals for the Eleventh Circuit reversed. . . . The Eleventh Circuit panel recognized that petitioner sought to state a claim based on school "officials' failure to take action to stop the offensive acts of those over whom the officials exercised control," and the court concluded that petitioner had alleged facts sufficient to support a claim for hostile environment sexual harassment on this theory.

The Eleventh Circuit granted the Board's motion for rehearing en banc and affirmed the District Court's decision to dismiss petitioner's Title IX claim against the Board.

Writing in dissent, four judges urged that the statute, by declining to identify the perpetrator of discrimination, encompasses misconduct by third parties. . . .

We granted *certiorari*, in order to resolve a conflict in the Circuits over whether, and under what circumstances, a recipient of federal educational funds can be liable in a private damages action arising from student-on-student sexual harassment. . . . We now reverse.

II

. . .

Congress authorized an administrative enforcement scheme for Title IX. Federal departments or agencies with the authority to provide financial assistance are entrusted to promulgate rules, regulations, and orders to enforce the objectives of § 1681, and these departments or agencies may rely on "any . . . means authorized by law," including the termination of funding to give effect to the statute's restrictions.

There is no dispute here that the Board is a recipient of federal education funding for Title IX purposes. Nor do respondents support an argument that student-on-student harassment cannot rise to the level of "discrimination" for purposes of Title IX. Rather, at issue here is the question whether a recipient of federal education funding may be liable for damages under Title IX under any circumstances for discrimination in the form of student-on-student sexual harassment.

A

Petitioner urges that Title IX's plain language compels the conclusion that the statute is intended to bar recipients of federal funding from permitting this form of discrimination in their programs or activities. She emphasizes that the statute prohibits a student from being "subjected to discrimination under any education program or activity receiving Federal financial assistance." It is Title IX's "unmistakable focus on the benefited class," rather than the perpetrator, that, in petitioner's view, compels the conclusion that the statute works to protect students from the discriminatory misconduct of their peers.

Here, however, we are asked to do more than define the scope of the behavior that Title IX proscribes. We must determine whether a district's failure to respond to student-on-student harassment in its schools can support a private suit for money damages. This Court has indeed recognized an implied private right of action under Title IX, and we have held that money damages are available in such suits. Because we have repeatedly treated Title IX as legislation enacted pursuant to Congress' authority under the Spending Clause, however, private damages actions are available only where recipients of federal funding had adequate notice that they could be liable for the conduct at issue. When Congress acts pursuant to its spending power, it generates legislation "much in the nature of a contract: in return for federal funds, the States agree to comply with federally imposed conditions." . . .

. . . [R]espondents urge that Title IX provides no notice that recipients of federal educational funds could be liable in damages for harm arising from student-on-student harassment. Respondents contend, specifically, that the statute only proscribes misconduct by grant recipients, not third parties. Respondents argue, moreover, that it would be contrary to the very purpose of Spending Clause legislation to impose liability on a funding recipient for the misconduct of third parties, over whom recipients exercise little control.

We agree with respondents that a recipient of federal funds may be liable in damages under Title IX only for its own misconduct. The recipient itself must "exclud[e] [persons] from participation in, . . . den[y] [persons] the benefits of, or . . . subjec[t] [persons] to discrimination under" its "program[s] or activit[ies]" in order to be liable under Title IX. The Government's enforcement power may only be exercised against the funding recipient, and we have not extended damages liability under Title IX to parties outside the scope of this power. . . .

We disagree with respondents' assertion, however, that petitioner seeks to hold the Board liable for G.F.'s actions instead of its own. Here, petitioner attempts to hold the Board liable for its own decision to remain idle in the face of known student-on-student harassment in its schools. In *Gebser*, we concluded that a recipient of federal education funds may be liable in damages under Title IX where it is deliberately indifferent to known acts of sexual harassment by a teacher. In that case, a teacher had entered into a sexual relationship with an eighth-grade student, and the student sought damages under Title IX for the teacher's misconduct. We recognized that the scope of liability in private damages actions under Title IX is circumscribed by *Pennhurst's* requirement that funding recipients have notice of their potential liability. . . . in *Gebser* we once again required "that 'the receiving entity of federal funds [have] notice that it will be liable for a monetary award'" before subjecting it to damages liability. We also recognized, however, that this limitation on private damages actions is not a bar to liability where a funding recipient intentionally violates the statute. In particular, we concluded that *Pennhurst* does not bar a private damages action under Title IX where the funding recipient engages in intentional conduct that violates the clear terms of the statute.

Accordingly, we rejected the use of agency principles to impute liability to the district for the misconduct of its teachers. Likewise, we declined the invitation to impose liability under what amounted to a negligence standard—holding the district liable for its failure to react to teacher-student harassment of which it knew or should have known. Rather, we concluded that the district could be liable for damages only where the district itself intentionally acted in clear violation of Title IX by remaining deliberately indifferent to acts of teacher-student harassment of which it had actual knowledge. Contrary to the dissent's suggestion, the misconduct of the teacher in *Gebser* was not "treated as the grant recipient's actions." Liability arose, rather, from "an official decision by the recipient not to remedy the violation." By employing the "deliberate indifference" theory already used to establish municipal liability . . . we concluded in *Gebser* that recipients could be liable in damages only where their own deliberate indifference effectively "cause[d]" the discrimination. The high standard imposed in *Gebser* sought to eliminate any "risk that the recipient would be liable in damages not for its own official decision but instead for its employees' independent actions."

Gebser thus established that a recipient intentionally violates Title IX, and is subject to a private damages action, where the recipient is deliberately indifferent to known acts of teacher-student discrimination. Indeed, whether viewed as "discrimination" or "subject[ing]" students to discrimination, Title IX "[u]nquestionably ... placed on [the Board] the duty not" to permit teacher-student harassment in its schools and recipients violate Title IX's plain terms when they remain deliberately indifferent to this form of misconduct.

We consider here whether the misconduct identified in *Gebser*-deliberate indifference to known acts of harassment—amounts to an intentional violation of Title IX, capable of supporting a private damages action, when the harasser is a student rather than a teacher. We conclude that, in certain limited circumstances, it does. As an initial matter, in *Gebser* we expressly rejected the use of agency principles in the Title IX context, noting the textual differences between Title IX and Title VII. Additionally, the regulatory scheme surrounding Title IX has long provided funding recipients with notice that they may be liable for their failure to respond to the discriminatory acts of certain nonagents. The Department of Education requires recipients to monitor third parties for discrimination in specified circumstances and to refrain from particular forms of interaction with outside entities that are known to discriminate.

The common law, too, has put schools on notice that they may be held responsible under state law for their failure to protect students from the tortious acts of third parties. In fact, state courts routinely uphold claims alleging that schools have been negligent in failing to protect their students from the torts of their peers.

This is not to say that the identity of the harasser is irrelevant. On the contrary, both the "deliberate indifference" standard and the language of Title IX narrowly circumscribe the set of parties whose known acts of sexual harassment can trigger some duty to respond on the part of funding recipients. Deliberate indifference makes sense as a theory of direct liability under Title IX only where the funding recipient has some control over the alleged harassment. A recipient cannot be directly liable for its indifference where it lacks the authority to take remedial action.

The language of Title IX itself—particularly when viewed in conjunction with the requirement that the recipient have notice of Title IX's prohibitions to be liable for damages—also cabins the range of misconduct that the statute proscribes. The statute's plain language confines the scope of prohibited conduct based on the recipient's degree of control over the harasser and the environment in which the harassment occurs. If a funding recipient does not engage in harassment directly, it may not be liable for damages unless its deliberate indifference "subject[s]" its students to harassment. That is, the deliberate indifference must, at a minimum, "cause [students] to undergo" harassment or "make them liable or vulnerable" to it. Moreover, because the harassment must occur "under" "the operations of" a funding recipient, the harassment must take place in a context subject to the school district's control.

These factors combine to limit a recipient's damages liability to circumstances wherein the recipient exercises substantial control over both the harasser and the context in which the known harassment occurs. Only then can the recipient be said to "expose" its students to harassment or "cause" them to undergo it "under" the recipient's programs. We agree with the dissent that these conditions are satisfied most easily and most obviously when the offender is an agent of the recipient. We rejected the use of agency analysis in *Gebser*, however, and we disagree that the term "under" somehow imports an agency requirement into Title IX. As noted above, the theory in *Gebser* was that the recipient was directly liable for its deliberate indifference to discrimination. Liability in that case did not arise because the "teacher's actions [were] treated" as those of the funding recipient; the district was directly liable for its own failure to act. The terms "subjec[t]" and "under" impose limits, but nothing about these terms requires the use of agency principles.

Where, as here, the misconduct occurs during school hours and on school grounds—the bulk of G.F.'s misconduct, in fact, took place in the classroom—the misconduct is taking place "under" an "operation" of the funding recipient. In these circumstances, the recipient retains substantial control over the context in which the harassment occurs. More importantly, however, in this setting the Board exercises significant control over the harasser. We have observed, for example, "that the nature of [the State's] power [over public school children] is custodial and tutelary, permitting a degree of supervision and control that could not be exercised over free adults." On more than one occasion, this Court has recognized the importance of school officials' "comprehensive authority ..., consistent with fundamental constitutional safeguards, to prescribe and control conduct in the schools." The common law, too, recognizes the school's disciplinary authority. We thus conclude that recipients of federal funding may be liable for "subject[ing]" their students to discrimination where the recipient is deliberately indifferent to known acts of student-on-student sexual harassment and the harasser is under the school's disciplinary authority.

At the time of the events in question here, in fact, school attorneys and administrators were being told that student-on-student harassment could trigger liability under Title IX. In March 1993, even as the events alleged in petitioner's complaint were unfolding, the National School Boards Association issued a publication, for use by "school attorneys and administrators in understanding the law regarding sexual harassment of employees and students," which observed that districts could be liable under Title IX for their failure to respond to student-on-student harassment. Drawing on Equal Employment Opportunity Commission guidelines interpreting Title VII, the publication informed districts that, "if [a] school district has constructive notice of severe and repeated acts of sexual harassment by fellow students, that may form the basis of a [T]itle IX claim." The publication even correctly anticipated a form of *Gebser's* actual notice requirement: "It is unlikely that courts will hold a school district liable for sexual harassment by students against students in the absence of actual knowledge or notice to district employees." . . .

Likewise, although they were promulgated too late to contribute to the Board's notice of proscribed misconduct, the Department of Education's Office for Civil Rights (OCR) has recently adopted policy guidelines providing that student-on-student harassment falls within the scope of Title IX's proscriptions.

We stress that our conclusion here—that recipients may be liable for their deliberate indifference to known acts of peer sexual harassment—does not mean that recipients can avoid liability only by purging their schools of actionable peer harassment or that administrators must engage in particular disciplinary action. We thus disagree with respondents' contention that, if Title IX provides a cause of action for student-on-student harassment, "nothing short of expulsion of every student accused of misconduct involving sexual overtones would protect school systems from liability or damages." Likewise, the dissent erroneously imagines that victims of peer harassment now have a Title IX right to make particular remedial demands. In fact, as we have previously noted, courts should refrain from second-guessing the disciplinary decisions made by school administrators.

School administrators will continue to enjoy the flexibility they require so long as funding recipients are deemed "deliberately indifferent" to acts of student-on-student harassment only where the recipient's response to the harassment or lack thereof is clearly unreasonable in light of the known circumstances. The dissent consistently mischaracterizes this standard to require funding recipients to "remedy" peer harassment, and to "ensur[e] that . . . students conform their conduct to" certain rules. Title IX imposes no such requirements. On the contrary, the recipient must merely respond to known peer harassment in a manner that is not clearly unreasonable. This is not a mere "reasonableness" standard, as the dissent assumes. In an appropriate case, there is no reason why courts, on a motion to dismiss, for summary judgment, or for a directed verdict, could not identify a response as not "clearly unreasonable" as a matter of law.

Like the dissent, we acknowledge that school administrators shoulder substantial burdens as a result of legal constraints on their disciplinary authority. To the extent that these restrictions arise from federal statutes, Congress can review these burdens with attention to the difficult position in which such legislation may place our Nation's schools. We believe, however, that the standard set out here is sufficiently flexible to account both for the level of disciplinary authority available to the school and for the potential liability arising from certain forms of disciplinary action. . . .

While it remains to be seen whether petitioner can show that the Board's response to reports of G.F.'s misconduct was clearly unreasonable in light of the known circumstances, petitioner may be able to show that the Board "subject[ed]" LaShonda to discrimination by failing to respond in any way over a period of five months to complaints of G.F.'s in-school misconduct from LaShonda and other female students.

B

The requirement that recipients receive adequate notice of Title IX's proscriptions also bears on the proper definition of "discrimination" in the context of a private damages action. We have elsewhere concluded that sexual harassment is a form of discrimination for Title IX purposes and that Title IX proscribes harassment with sufficient clarity to satisfy *Pennhurst's* notice requirement and serve as a basis for a damages action. Having previously determined that "sexual harassment" is "discrimination" in the school context under Title IX, we are constrained to conclude that student-on-student sexual harassment, if sufficiently severe, can likewise rise to the level of discrimination actionable under the statute. The statute's other prohibitions, moreover, help give content to the term "discrimination" in this context. Students are not only protected from discrimination, but also specifically shielded from being "excluded from participation in" or "denied the benefits of" any "education program or activity receiving Federal financial assistance." § 1681(a). The statute makes clear that, whatever else it prohibits, students must not be denied access to educational benefits and opportunities on the basis of gender. We thus conclude that funding recipients are properly held liable in damages only where they are deliberately indifferent to sexual harassment, of which they have actual knowledge, that is so severe, pervasive, and objectively offensive that it can be said to deprive the victims of access to the educational opportunities or benefits provided by the school.

The most obvious example of student-on-student sexual harassment capable of triggering a damages claim would thus involve the overt, physical deprivation of access to school resources. Consider, for example, a case in which male students physically threaten their female peers every day, successfully preventing the female students from using a particular school resource—an athletic field or a computer lab, for instance. District administrators are well aware of the daily ritual, yet they deliberately ignore requests for aid from the female students wishing to use the resource. The district's knowing refusal to take any action in response to such behavior would fly in the face of Title IX's core principles, and such deliberate indifference may appropriately be subject to claims for monetary damages. It is not necessary, however, to show physical exclusion to demonstrate that students have been deprived by the actions of another student or students of an educational opportunity on the basis of sex. Rather, a plaintiff must establish sexual harassment of students that is so severe, pervasive, and objectively offensive, and that so undermines and detracts from the victims' educational experience, that the victim-students are effectively denied equal access to an institution's resources and opportunities.

Whether gender-oriented conduct rises to the level of actionable "harassment" thus "depends on a constellation of surrounding circumstances, expectations, and relationships," including, but not limited to, the ages of the harasser and the victim and the number of individuals involved. Courts, moreover, must bear in mind that schools are unlike the adult workplace and that children may regularly interact in a manner that would be unacceptable among adults. Indeed, at least early on, students are still learning how to interact appropriately with their peers. It is thus under-standable that, in the school setting, students often engage in insults, banter, teasing, shoving, pushing, and gender-specific conduct that is upsetting to the students subjected to it. Damages are not available for simple acts of teasing and name-calling among school children, however, even where these comments target differences in gender.

Rather, in the context of student-on-student harassment, damages are available only where the behavior is so severe, pervasive, and objectively offensive that it denies its victims the equal access to education that Title IX is designed to protect.

The dissent fails to appreciate these very real limitations on a funding recipient's liability under Title IX. . . .

Moreover, the provision that the discrimination occur "under any education program or activity" suggests that the behavior be serious enough to have the systemic effect of denying the victim equal access to an educational program or activity. Although, in theory, a single instance of sufficiently severe one-on-one peer harassment could be said to have such an effect, we think it unlikely that Congress would have thought such behavior sufficient to rise to this level in light of the inevitability of student misconduct and the amount of litigation that would be invited by entertaining claims of official indifference to a single instance of one-on-one peer harassment.

By limiting private damages actions to cases having a systemic effect on educational programs or activities, we reconcile the general principle that Title IX prohibits official indifference to known peer sexual harassment with the practical realities of responding to student behavior, realities that Congress could not have meant to be ignored. Even the dissent suggests that Title IX liability may arise when a funding recipient remains indifferent to severe, gender-based mistreatment played out on a "widespread level" among students.

. . .

C

Applying this standard to the facts at issue here, we conclude that the Eleventh Circuit erred in dismissing petitioner's complaint. Petitioner alleges that her daughter was the victim of repeated acts of sexual harassment by G.F. over a 5–month period, and there are allegations in support of the conclusion that G.F.'s misconduct was severe, pervasive, and objectively offensive. The harassment was not only verbal; it included numerous acts of objectively offensive touching, and, indeed, G.F. ultimately pleaded guilty to criminal sexual misconduct. Moreover, the complaint alleges that there were multiple victims who were sufficiently disturbed by G.F.'s misconduct to seek an audience with the school principal. Further, petitioner contends that the harassment had a concrete, negative effect on her daughter's ability to receive an education. The complaint also suggests that petitioner may be able to show both actual knowledge and deliberate indifference on the part of the Board, which made no effort whatsoever either to investigate or to put an end to the harassment.

On this complaint, we cannot say "beyond doubt that [petitioner] can prove no set of facts in support of [her] claim which would entitle [her] to relief." Accordingly, the judgment of the United States Court of Appeals for the Eleventh Circuit is reversed, and the case is remanded for further proceedings consistent with this opinion.

It is so ordered.

NOTES

1.   In dissent, Justice Kennedy feared that the Supreme Court's ruling would have left school boards susceptible to an avalanche of costly liability. While his concerns have apparently not been borne out, were they well-founded?

2.   What can, or should, school officials do to eliminate peer-to-peer sexual harassment?

CHAPTER 14

STUDENT RIGHTS: FREE SPEECH

INTRODUCTION

Tinker v. Des Moines Independent Community School District Tinker[1] is a landmark case. *Tinker* stands out both as the initial case in which the Supreme Court recognized the First Amendment rights of public school students and as the high point with regard to its protecting their rights to speech and expression. In its three subsequent cases on student expressive activity, *Bethel School District No. 403 v. Fraser*,[2] *Hazelwood School District v. Kuhlmeier*,[3] and *Morse v. Frederick*,[4] the Justices trimmed the protections they enunciated in *Tinker*. In light of the significant legal questions associated with student free speech and expression in its many forms, this chapter focuses on this important topic.

CONTROLS OVER STUDENT FREE SPEECH-EXPRESSIVE ACTIVITIES

Over time, the Supreme Court created essentially two standards addressing state-imposed limits on free speech. In *Schenck v. United States*, a dispute involving national security in the wake of World War I, the Court maintained, in often quoted, or paraphrased, language that "[t]he most stringent protection of free speech would not protect a man in falsely shouting fire in a theatre and causing a panic."[5] In so doing, the Court enunciated the clear and present danger test, noting that "[t]he question . . . is whether the words used are in such circumstances and are of such a nature as to create a clear and present danger. . . ."[6] Under this test, the mere possibility of disruption is insufficient to limit free speech. Rather, speech cannot be limited absent an explicit concern that serious harm may follow to the public welfare.

---

1. 393 U.S. 503, 89 S.Ct. 733, 21 L.Ed.2d 731 (1969). [Case No. 102]

2. 478 U.S. 675, 106 S.Ct. 3159, 92 L.Ed.2d 549 [32 Educ. L. Rep. 1243] (1986). [Case No. 104]

3. 484 U.S. 260, 108 S.Ct. 562, 98 L.Ed.2d 592 [43 Educ. L. Rep. 515] (1988). [Case No. 105]

4. 551 U.S. 393, 127 S.Ct. 2618, 168 L.Ed.2d 290 [220 Educ. L. Rep. 50] (2007), *on remand*, 499 F.3d 926 (2007). [Case No. 106]

5. 249 U.S. 47, 52, 39 S.Ct. 247, 63 L.Ed. 470 (1919).

6. *Id.*

Conceding that the clear and present danger test was not entirely appropriate for use in educational settings, the Supreme Court created a different measure for schools. In *Tinker v. Des Moines Independent Community School District*,[7] discussed in more detail below, the Court determined that educators could limit student free speech only if it causes material and substantial disruptions in school settings.

Prior to *Tinker v. Des Moines Independent Community School District*, courts deferred to the ability of school officials to control disruptive student expressive activity. In an early case, an appellate court in California upheld a student's expulsion for refusing to apologize after he made critical statements about a school facility during a speech at a school gathering.[8]

Two cases reaching different results involved the intersection of student expressive free speech and the ability of school officials to discipline unacceptable behavior. When all but one member of a high school basketball team in Oregon signed a petition asking their coach to resign because he treated his players poorly, they challenged their suspensions for refusing to board a bus to an away game. After a federal trial court granted the defendants' motion for summary judgment, the Ninth Circuit partially reversed in favor of the players.[9] The court ruled that the students' speech was protected because it could not reasonably have led officials to forecast substantial disruption of, or material interference with, a school activity. Still, in remanding, the court affirmed that even if the players' refusal to board the bus were treated as expressive, but unprotected, conduct, they could have been suspended for creating a substantial disruption to a school-sponsored activity. The court concluded that school officials lacked the authority to enforce the permanent suspensions since doing so could have been interpreted as a form of retaliation that would have led other student-athletes to refrain from complaining about abusive coaches if it meant that they would be unable to remain on their teams. Conversely, the Sixth Circuit held that a football coach in Tennessee did not violate the free speech rights of players he dismissed from the team after learning that they circulated a petition denouncing him and refusing to apologize for doing so.[10] Recognizing that the players lacked a right to play football and that their behavior threatened a substantial disruption to the team, the court found that the coach and school officials did not violate their rights to free speech.

As reflected in the ensuing discussion, courts have examined a wide range of issues involving student expression whether dealing with symbolic speech, such as dress, which is entitled to greater protection as a form of pure speech, or the spoken and/or written word, both of which have less protection. As to the former, in a non-school case establishing useful guidelines, the Supreme Court identified two factors to be considered in evaluating whether speech-related conduct qualifies as symbolic expression

---

7. 393 U.S. 503, 89 S.Ct. 733, 21 L.Ed.2d 731 (1969). [Case No. 102]

8. *Wooster v. Sunderland*, 148 P. 959 (Cal. Ct. App. 1915).

9. *Pinard v. Clatskanie School Dist. 6J*, 467 F.3d 755 [213 Educ. L. Rep. 952] (9th Cir. 2006).

10. *Lowery v. Euverard*, 497 F.3d 584 [223 Educ. L Rep. 575] (6th Cir. 2007), *cert. denied*, 555 U.S. 825, 129 S.Ct. 159, 172 L.Ed.2d 42 (2008).

afforded constitutional protection: whether the expression is intended to convey a particularized message and whether the message will be understood by recipients.[11] Even with such guidelines, the Seventh Circuit aptly remarked that "[m]any aspects of the law with respect to students' speech . . . are difficult to understand and apply."[12] While it can be difficult making clear distinctions in all cases and there can be a fair amount of overlapping between and among these issues, this section examines cases involving student expressive activities.

POLITICAL EXPRESSION

Tinker v. Des Moines Independent Community School District (*Tinker*)[13] was litigated during the social upheaval of the 1960s. In *Tinker* the Court invalidated a two-day-old board policy from Iowa which sought to prohibit students from wearing black armbands to school in protest of American activity in Vietnam.

Acknowledging that "[i]t can hardly be argued that either students or teachers shed their constitutional rights to freedom of speech or expression at the schoolhouse gate,"[14] the Supreme Court sought a middle ground to balance the rights of students against the needs of educators to preserve order and discipline. As an initial matter, the Court viewed the dispute as involving "direct, primary First Amendment rights akin to 'pure speech' [that did not concern] . . . speech or action that intrudes upon the work of the school or the rights of other students."[15] According to the Court, in order to prohibit students from expressing particular points of view, school officials had to be able to show that their actions were motivated by "more than a desire to avoid the discomfort and unpleasantness that always accompany an unpopular viewpoint. Certainly where there is no finding and no showing that engaging in the forbidden conduct would 'materially and substantially interfere with the requirements of appropriate discipline in the operation of the school,' the prohibition cannot be sustained."[16]

In the first of many post-*Tinker* cases to review the imposition of penalties against students who wore clothing with symbolic messages, the Sixth Circuit upheld a ban in a school in Ohio where there were serious racial tensions.[17] In refusing to disturb the forty-year-old rule applicable to emblems and other insignia unrelated to school activities, and which was originally intended to reduce divisions created within the student body by fraternities and sororities, the court relied on evidence that students

---

11. *Spence v. Washington*, 418 U.S. 405, 94 S.Ct. 2727, 41 L.Ed.2d 842 (1974).

12. *Hosty v. Carter*, 412 F.3d 731, 739 [199 Educ. L. Rep. 91] (7th Cir. 2005), *cert. denied*, 546 U.S. 1169, 126 S.Ct. 1330, 164 L.Ed.2d 47 (2006) (finding that a dean was entitled to qualified immunity in a case from higher education over the contents of a student newspaper).

13. 393 U.S. 503, 89 S.Ct. 733, 21 L.Ed.2d 731 (1969). [Case No. 102]

14. *Id.* at 506.

15. *Id.* at 508–509.

16. *Id.* at 509 citing *Burnside v. Byars*, 363 F.2d 744, 749 (5th Cir. 1966) (internal citations omitted).

17. *Guzick v. Drebus*, 431 F.2d 594 (6th Cir.1970), *cert. denied*, 401 U.S. 948, 91 S.Ct. 941, 28 L.Ed.2d 231 (1971). [Case No. 103]

increasingly attempted to wear buttons and badges expressing racially inflammatory messages that led to disruptions. Referring to the rule, which was enforced uniformly, the court agreed that it was acceptable since it served the goal of meaningful integration. Not long thereafter, the Fifth Circuit invalidated a directive designed to prevent students from wearing black armbands to school in connection with a protest over events in Vietnam[18] since officials were unaware of any potential disruptions and none actually occurred.[19]

The courts have considered a wide array of cases involving student speech in schools. In Oregon, for example, litigation transpired when students challenged their suspensions for refusing to stop carrying signs and wearing buttons to school referring to replacement teachers hired as substitutes for striking faculty members as "scabs." The Ninth Circuit was convinced that school officials violated the students' rights to wear the buttons since along with not being vulgar, there were no disruptions and none were reasonably forecast.[20] In like fashion, the federal trial court in New Jersey enjoined school officials from preventing fifth-grade students who wished to wear buttons to school that featured a picture of members of the Hitler Youth in protest against the board's mandatory uniform policy.[21] The court decided that officials lacked the authority to forbid the students from wearing the buttons absent evidence that their doing so would have materially and substantially disrupted the school's work and discipline.

Where school officials could reasonably forecast the occurrence of serious disturbances, courts entered judgments in their favor. In perhaps the earliest case on point, the Sixth Circuit upheld the suspension of a student who refused to stop wearing symbolic expression in the form of a Confederate Flag as a sleeve patch in a recently integrated racially tense school.[22] As evidenced by a later case from the Sixth Circuit,[23] courts continue to uphold prohibitions against such symbols. The court affirmed a ban against clothing depicting the Confederate Flag at school as constitutional since educators offered the reasonable forecast that allowing it to be worn would have disrupted schoolwork and discipline in light of racial tensions there, that the ban did not constitute viewpoint discrimination, and that the prohibition against clothing displaying racially divisive symbols did not violate the rights of students to equal protection.

---

18. *Butts v. Dallas Indep. School Dist.*, 436 F.2d 728 (5th Cir. 1971).

19. For a more recent case involving black armbands, *see Lowry v. Watson Chapel School Dist.*, 540 F.3d 752 [236 Educ. L. Rep. 158] (8th Cir. 2008) (where students wore black armbands to school voicing their opposition to the implementation of a dress code policy).

20. *Chandler v. McMinnville School Dist.*, 978 F.2d 524 [78 Educ. L. Rep. 282] (9th Cir. 1992). *But see Smith ex rel. Lanham v. Greene County School Dist.*, 100 F.Supp.2d 1354 [145 Educ. L. Rep. 368] (M.D. Ga. 2000) (rejecting a claim that educators violated a student's rights when he was disciplined for failing to comply with the school's dress code policy).

21. *DePinto v. Bayonne Bd. of Educ.*, 514 F. Supp.2d 633 [225 Educ. L. Rep. 896] (D.N.J. 2007).

22. *Melton v. Young*, 465 F.2d 1332 (6th Cir.1972), *cert. denied*, 411 U.S. 951, 93 S.Ct. 1926, 36 L.Ed.2d 414 (1973).

23. *Barr v. Lafon*, 538 F.3d 554 [236 Educ. L. Rep. 41] (6th Cir. 2008), *reh'g en banc denied*, 553 F.3d 463 (6th Cir. 2009), *cert. denied*, ___ U.S. ___, 130 S.Ct. 63, 175 L.Ed.2d 24 [249 Educ. L. Rep. 582] (2009).

In a variation on a theme, the Fourth Circuit upheld the suspensions of students in Virginia who violated school rules by wearing depictions of "Johnny Reb," a caricature of an emblematic Confederate soldier and former cartoon symbol of their high school after officials banned its use due to complaints from African American pupils and their parents.[24] The Eighth Circuit reached the same outcome when it allowed officials in Missouri to ban such t-shirts because the school had a history of racial tensions.[25]

Judicial differences emerged over students who wore expressive clothing as a subset of political speech apart from dress code issues.[26] The first of three cases that are conceptually related to the previous discussions involving the Confederate Flag arose in the Sixth Circuit. The court found that officials in Kentucky violated the rights of students who were suspended for ignoring their school's dress code by wearing t-shirts to a concert which depicted Confederate Flags as a form of their southern heritage because doing so constituted protected First Amendment speech.[27] The t-shirts also had the picture of a country music singer on the front and the phrase "Southern Thunder" on the back, through which they intended to commemorate the birthday of the singer's father, another famous country singer. Similarly, the Third Circuit observed that students in New Jersey could enjoin their school board's racial harassment policy on the basis that its preventing them from wearing t-shirts displaying depictions of a comedian known for "redneck" humor, a derogatory term for Southerners, violated their First Amendment rights to freedom of expression.[28] The court judged that insofar as educators were unable to demonstrate how the shirts would have caused disruptions, they could not prevent the students from wearing them to school. Additionally, a federal trial court in West Virginia granted a high school student's request for a preliminary injunction after he was disciplined for wearing a t-shirt and belt buckle displaying the Confederate Flag, purportedly in commemoration of his Southern heritage.[29] Since the court indicated that the part of the school's policy prohibiting "items displaying the Rebel flag" under the "racist language and/or symbols or graphics" was unconstitutional over-broad, it was unenforceable.

Along with conflicts over whether students can wear representations of the Confederate Flag on t-shirts, four circuit courts upheld policies banning its presence in other forms. Acting in response to racial tension, coupled

---

24. *Crosby v. Holsinger*, 852 F.2d 801 [48 Educ. L. Rep. 156] (4th Cir.1988).

25. *B.W.A. v. Farmington R–7 School Dist.*, 554 F.3d 734 [241 Educ. L. Rep. 41] (8th Cir. 2009).

26. *See also Hardwick ex rel. Hardwick v. Heyward*, 674 F.Supp.2d 725 [254 Educ. L. Rep. 104] (D.S.C. 2009), *appeal dismissed*, 404 Fed.Appx. 765 (4th Cir. 2010) (upholding a policy preventing students from wearing clothing displaying images of the Confederate flag because their doing so might have caused a substantial disruption).

27. *Castorina ex rel. Rewt v. Madison County School Bd.*, 246 F.3d 536 [152 Educ. L. Rep. 524] (6th Cir. 2001).

28. *Sypniewski v. Warren Hills Reg'l Bd. of Educ.*, 307 F.3d 243 [170 Educ. L. Rep. 83] (3d Cir.2002), *cert. denied*, 538 U.S. 1033, 123 S.Ct. 2077, 155 L.Ed.2d 1062 [176 Educ. L. Rep. 542] (2003).

29. *Bragg v. Swanson*, 371 F. Supp.2d 814 [199 Educ. L. Rep. 162] (S.D. W. Va. 2005).

with recommendations from a task force of parents, teachers, and community members, a school board in Kansas adopted a Racial Harassment and Intimidation Policy. When a middle school student, who had been informed of the policy, drew and displayed a Confederate Flag, he and his father challenged his three-day suspension. The Tenth Circuit affirmed that the policy neither violated the student's right to free speech nor was it overbroad or unconstitutionally vague.[30] The Eleventh Circuit reached the same outcome in two different cases from Florida, agreeing that bans against displaying the Confederate Flag on various forms of clothing in schools were not unconstitutional since they were designed to promote racial harmony.[31] The Fifth Circuit affirmed that officials did not violate the rights of two female students in Texas who challenged a policy under which they were sent home from school for carrying purses with large images of the Confederate Flag.[32] Based on evidence of racial tension involving the Confederate Flag imagery, the court agreed that officials could apply the *Tinker* standard to avoid a disruption. Finally, the Sixth Circuit affirmed a ban against a student in Tennessee's attempt to wear a Confederate Flag shirt and belt buckle to school even though board policy against displaying racial and gang symbols did not specifically impose such a rule.[33] The court was satisfied that officials articulated a reasonable forecast of material substantial disruption if the student wore the items to school.

Two cases involved pictures of President George W. Bush and student t-shirts. The first case arose in Michigan where a high school student wore a t-shirt displaying a photograph of the President with the caption "International Terrorist" without any problems until lunch, at which time school officials directed him to turn it inside-out for the rest of the day or leave school. After the student contacted his father and left school, the principal called him and told him he was not allowed to wear the shirt to school.[34] A federal trial court enjoined the principal from prohibiting the student from wearing the shirt because it constituted symbolic speech protected by the First Amendment and that he intended to convey a particularized message understood by its viewers. In rejecting the claim of school officials that this censorship was required because the shirt might have offended Iraqi students at the school, the court posited that insofar as educators failed to demonstrate the likelihood that wearing it would have caused a substantial disruption, their actions were unacceptable.

---

30.   *West v. Derby Unified School Dist. No. 260*, 206 F.3d 1358 [143 Educ. L. Rep. 43] (10th Cir.2000), *cert. denied*, 531 U.S. 825, 121 S.Ct. 71, 148 L.Ed.2d 35 (2000).

31.   *Denno v. School Bd. of Volusia County, Fla.*, 218 F.3d 1267 [145 Educ. L. Rep. 942] (11th Cir.2000), *reh'g and suggestion for reh'g en banc denied*, 235 F.3d 1347 (11th Cir. 2000), *cert. denied*, 531 U.S. 958, 121 S.Ct. 382, 148 L.Ed.2d 295 (2000); *Scott v. School Bd. of Alachua County*, 324 F.3d 1246 [175 Educ. L. Rep. 88] (11th Cir.2003), *cert. denied*, 540 U.S. 824, 124 S.Ct. 156, 157 L.Ed.2d 46 [182 Educ. L. Rep. 32] (2003).

32.   *A.M. ex rel. McAllum v. Cash*, 585 F.3d 214 [250 Educ. L. Rep. 56] (5th Cir. 2009).

33.   *Defoe ex rel. Defoe v. Spiva*, 625 F.3d 324 [262 Educ. L. Rep. 53] (6th Cir. 2010), *reh'g denied*, ___ F.3d ___, 2011 WL 1007948 (6th Cir. 2011), *cert. denied*, ___ U.S. ___, 132 S.Ct. 399, 181 L.Ed.2d 255 (2011).

34.   *Barber ex rel. Barber v. Dearborn Pub. Schools*, 286 F. Supp.2d 847 [183 Educ. L. Rep. 79] (E.D. Mich. 2003).

In Vermont, another federal trial court distinguished the two cases. Educators informed a middle school student who wore a t-shirt critical of President Bush and his alleged illegal drug use that he could wear the shirt only if he taped over portions that violated the school's dress code since it contained images depicting drugs and alcohol. When the student was sent home for the day for refusing to tape over the offending portions, he and his parents challenged his being disciplined. Although explaining that the student was not entitled to an injunction to prohibit officials from disciplining him for wearing the shirt, the court directed educators to expunge his record of any disciplinary actions because their initial act of censorship violated the First Amendment.[35] In addressing the differences between the cases, the court declared that educators could require the student to cover specific images on the t-shirt not because they were critical of the President but since they acted pursuant to a neutral policy against wearing clothing bearing images of drugs and alcohol. On further review, the Second Circuit vacated and remanded in favor of the student.[36] Finding that the policy violated the student's right to free speech because the images were not "plainly offensive" under *Bethel School District No. 403 v. Fraser*,[37] discussed below, or likely to cause a disruption under *Tinker*, the court ordered officials to expunge his record of the disciplinary action.

A case from Texas involved a dispute over how students could dress in protesting federal immigration policy. A federal trial court granted a superintendent's motion for summary judgment when students filed suit alleging that officials violated their rights to free speech in preventing them from wearing t-shirts with the message "We Are Not Criminals" as a form of protest against immigration policies.[38] Noting that other students at the school were going to wear t-shirts reading "Border Patrol" to antagonize the Hispanic protestors, the court recognized that officials had the duty to prevent the situation from developing into a material and substantial interference with the school's work and the rights of others in the school community.[39]

In the first of four cases involving attitudes toward homosexuality, the Seventh Circuit ruled that a school board in Illinois could not prevent students from wearing t-shirts with the message "Be Happy, Not Gay" because there was no reason to think that their doing so would have created a substantial disruption under the standard.[40] Following multiple

---

35. *Guiles ex rel. Lucas v. Marineau*, 349 F. Supp.2d 871 [194 Educ. L. Rep. 880] (D. Vt. 2004).

36. *Guiles ex rel. Guiles v. Marineau*, 461 F.3d 320 [212 Educ. L. Rep. 143] (2d Cir. 2006).

37. 478 U.S. 675, 106 S.Ct. 3159, 92 L.Ed.2d 549 [32 Educ. L. Rep. 1243] (1986). [Case No. 104]

38. *Madrid v. Anthony*, 510 F. Supp.2d 425 [225 Educ. L. Rep. 491] (S.D. Tex. 2007).

39. For an interesting, though not directly related, case, *see Garcia v. Montenegro*, 547 F. Supp.2d 738 [233 Educ. L. Rep. 146] (W.D. Tex. 2008), *aff'd*, 326 Fed.Appx. 312 (5th Cir. 2009) (affirming a school board's motion for summary judgment based on qualified immunity where an attendance clerk in another district expressed his support for a student walkout over proposed changes in federal immigration policy).

40. *Nuxoll ex rel. Nuxoll v. Indian Prairie School Dist. #204*, 523 F.3d 668 [231 Educ. L. Rep. 618] (7th Cir. 2008).

rounds of litigation, the court affirmed an award of nominal monetary damages to the students.[41]

Previously, the federal trial court in Minnesota enjoined a principal from preventing a student from wearing a sweatshirt emblazoned with the message "Straight Pride" to school.[42] The court was of the opinion that insofar as the student and his parents demonstrated the strong likelihood of success on the merits of their claim that the principal acted unreasonably, they were entitled to the injunction. In a case of the same kind, a federal trial court in Ohio granted a middle school student's request for an injunction, holding that educators violated his free speech rights when they tried to prohibit him from wearing a t-shirt that expressed his religious convictions in a message reading "Homosexuality is a sin!"[43] The shirt also proclaimed that "Islam is a lie!" and "Abortion is murder!" The court rejected the argument that school officials had the authority to restrict the student's message as plainly offensive speech. Instead, the court pointed out that the student could wear the t-shirt because officials failed to prove that it caused a material disruption of school activities, there was a reasonable likelihood that it might have caused such a disruption, or that it invaded the rights of others.[44] In like analysis, a federal trial court in Florida forbade officials in a public high school from preventing students from wearing or displaying t-shirts, armbands, stickers, or buttons conveying messages and symbols advocating the acceptance of and fair treatment for persons who are homosexual.[45] The court emphasized that educators could not limit student expression because it did not create a substantial disruption under *Tinker*.

Conversely, a dispute arose in California when school officials suspended a student for wearing a t-shirt displaying the religious message that "Homosexuality is shameful." The Ninth Circuit affirmed that officials did not violate the student's rights to freedom of speech and religion because they had the authority to prevent him from wearing the t-shirt insofar as it was inconsistent with the school's basic educational mission that included teaching tolerance and civic responsibility.[46] After the Supreme Court vacated the Ninth Circuit's judgment as moot,[47] a federal trial court in

---

41. *Zamecnik v. Indian Prairie School Dist. No. 204*, 636 F.3d 874 [266 Educ. L. Rep. 62] (7th Cir. 2011).

42. *Chambers v. Babbitt*, 145 F. Supp.2d 1068 [155 Educ. L. Rep. 252] (D. Minn. 2001).

43. *Nixon v. Northern Local School Dist. Bd. of Educ.*, 383 F. Supp.2d 965 [201 Educ. L. Rep. 904] (S.D. Ohio 2005).

44. In another case dealing with abortion and student speech, albeit not dress, a federal trial court in Virginia granted a high school student's request for an injunction when officials sought to prevent him from distributing literature supporting his position on the ground that the board policy failed under both the *Tinker* disruption standard and forum analysis. *Raker v. Frederick County Pub. Schools*, 470 F. Supp.2d 634 [217 Educ. L. Rep. 190] (W.D. Va. 2007).

45. *Gillman v. School Bd. for Holmes County, Fla.*, 567 F. Supp.2d 1359 [236 Educ. L. Rep. 763] (N.D. Fla. 2008).

46. *Harper ex rel. Harper v. Poway Unified School Dist.*, 345 F. Supp.2d 1096 [194 Educ. L. Rep. 208] (S.D. Cal. 2004), *aff'd*, 445 F.3d 1166 [208 Educ. L. Rep. 164] (9th Cir. 2006), *reh'g en banc denied*, 455 F.3d 1052 (9th Cir. 2006).

47. *Harper ex rel. Harper v. Poway Unified School Dist.*, *motion to expedite consideration denied*, 549 U.S. 1050, 127 S.Ct. 708, 166 L.Ed.2d 511 (2006), *cert. granted, vacated*, 549 U.S. 1262, 127 S.Ct. 1484, 167 L.Ed.2d 225 (2007), *on remand*, 485 F.3d 1052 (9th Cir. 2007).

California rejected the request of the plaintiff's sister's to reconsider the ban against the t-shirt.[48]

Students seeking to form clubs for peers who are gay and those who are not, in a different form of expression, experienced mixed success under the Equal Access Act. In relevant part, the Act stipulates that "[i]t shall be unlawful for any public secondary school which ... has a limited open forum to deny equal access or a fair opportunity to, or discriminate against, any students who wish to conduct a meeting ... on the basis of the religious, political, philosophical, or other content of the speech at such meetings."[49]

In the first of three related cases from Utah, high school students with a gay-positive perspective challenged a board policy denying them an opportunity to meet at school during non-instructional time and to have access to school facilities. The federal trial court interpreted the policy as violating the group's Equal Access Act rights since it denied the students the chance to meet when another non-curriculum-related student group was permitted to do so.[50] The same court later remarked that insofar as the plaintiffs failed to demonstrate how the policy had a disparate impact on their viewpoint, it did not have to examine the actual motives of board members regarding their allegations.[51] In the third case, the court reviewed the standards governing access to the limited forum that the board created for curriculum-related student clubs at the high school when a club sought to examine the impact, experience, and contributions of gays and lesbians in history and current events.[52] The court granted the club's request for a preliminary injunction since there was substantial likelihood that it would succeed on the merits of its First Amendment claim that the school official who was responsible for evaluating their application misapplied the appropriate standards or added a new one. Subsequently, the Eighth Circuit,[53] along with federal trial courts in Florida,[54] Indiana,[55] and Kentucky,[56]

---

48. *Harper v. Poway Unified School Dist.*, 545 F. Supp.2d 1072 [232 Educ. L. Rep. 755] (S.D. Cal. 2007).

49. 20 U.S.C.A. § 4071(a). Portions of this statute are in the Appendix.

50. *East High Gay/Straight Alliance v. Board of Educ.*, 81 F. Supp.2d 1166 [141 Educ. L. Rep. 776] (D. Utah 1999).

51. *East High Gay/Straight Alliance v. Board of Educ.*, 81 F. Supp.2d 1199 [141 Educ. L. Rep. 809] (D. Utah 1999).

52. *East High School Prism Club v. Seidel*, 95 F. Supp.2d 1239 [144 Educ. L. Rep. 260] (D. Utah 2000).

53. *Straights and Gays for Equality v. Osseo Area Schools–Dist. No. 279*, 540 F.3d 911 [236 Educ. L. Rep. 173] (8th Cir. 2008).

54. *Gay–Straight Alliance of Yulee High School v. School Bd. of Nassau County*, 602 F. Supp.2d 1233 [243 Educ. L. Rep. 301] (M.D. Fla. 2009); *Gonzalez v. School Bd. of Okeechobee County*, 571 F.Supp.2d 1257 [237 Educ. L. Rep. 291] (S.D. Fla. 2008). For the history of this case, *see Gay–Straight Alliance of Okeechobee High School v. School Bd. of Okeechobee County*, 483 F. Supp.2d 1224 [219 Educ. L. Rep. 728] (S.D. Fla. 2007).

55. *Franklin Central Gay/Straight Alliance v. Franklin Twp. Community School Corp.*, 2002 WL 32097530 (S.D. Ind. 2002), *reconsideration denied*, 2002 WL 31921332 (S.D. Ind. 2002).

56. *Boyd County High School Gay Straight Alliance v. Board of Educ. of Boyd County, Ky.*, 258 F. Supp.2d 667 [177 Educ. L. Rep. 211] (E.D. Ky. 2003). This case spawned litigation in which a student sought to be excluded from diversity training which focused on diversity and equity issues including discussion of anti-gay harassment.

agreed that school officials could not deny Gay/Straight Alliance clubs the opportunity to use school facilities under the Equal Access Act.

On the other hand, a federal trial court in Texas upheld a school board's rejection of a gay-straight student association's requests that members be permitted to post and distribute fliers about it at a high school, to use the school's public address system for announcements, and to be recognized as a student group that had the right to meet on campus.[57] The court maintained that school officials' investigation of the association's Web site, which led to the discovery that it posted sexually explicit material, was reasonable and nondiscriminatory for the purposes of the First Amendment. Since the Equal Access Act includes exceptions for avoiding disruption and preserving order in schools to protect student well-being, the court thought educators acted lawfully in denying the association's requests. In addition, a Gay/Straight Alliance Club in Colorado failed to procure a preliminary injunction ordering officials to recognize the group.[58] In an unreported opinion, the federal trial court concluded that the school's policy of officially recognizing only "curricular" clubs did not violate the Equal Access Act.

In a dispute over political free speech not involving clothing, students in Massachusetts filed suit when educators removed posters advertising the creation of the "Conservative Club" since their materials included a Web site containing a video about Islam displaying graphic videos of beheadings.[59] Since issues of fact remained over whether the videos would have materially and substantially interfered with the work of the school or impinged on the rights of other students, the federal trial court largely rejected the officials' motion for summary judgment.

INAPPROPRIATE STUDENT EXPRESSION

Seventeen years after *Tinker,* the Supreme Court revisited the limits of student expression in a dispute from Washington wherein a student delivered a nominating speech at a school assembly prior to elections for the student council. The speech included elaborate, graphic, and explicit sexual metaphors that caused a substantial disruption. Ignoring warnings from two teachers not to deliver the speech, the student received a three-day suspension and had his name removed from the list of possible speakers at his graduation. Even so, the student was elected by a write-in vote to serve as a speaker.

On further review of a judgment in favor of the student, in *Bethel School District No. 403 v. Fraser (Fraser),*[60] the Supreme Court reversed in favor of the school board. The Court reasoned that officials could discipline

---

57. *Caudillo v. Lubbock Indep. School Dist.,* 311 F. Supp.2d 550 [187 Educ. L. Rep. 564] (N.D. Tex. 2004).

58. *Palmer High School Gay/Straight Alliance v. Colorado Springs School Dist. No. 11,* 2005 WL 3244049 (D. Colo. 2005).

59. *Bowler v. Town of Hudson,* 514 F. Supp.2d 168 [225 Educ. L. Rep. 837] (D. Mass. 2007).

60. 478 U.S. 675, 106 S.Ct. 3159, 92 L.Ed.2d 549 [32 Educ. L. Rep. 1243] (1986). [Case No. 104]

the student for violating school rules because he delivered the speech after being advised not to do so. In its analysis, the Court distinguished the speech from *Tinker* where the armbands were a passive, nondisruptive expression of a political position, rather than a lewd and obscene speech totally lacking in any political viewpoint, incident to a student election that was delivered to an unsuspecting captive audience. Acknowledging the duty of educators to inculcate habits and manners of civility while teaching students the boundaries of socially appropriate behavior, the Court asserted that "[t]he determination of what manner of speech in the classroom or in school assembly is inappropriate properly rests with the school board."[61]

Four years later, the Sixth Circuit affirmed that officials in Tennessee could discipline a student for delivering a speech that was disrespectful of school authorities or disruptive of instructional activities.[62] The court wrote that where the candidate for the presidency of a student council made discourteous and rude remarks at an election assembly, his speech was not entitled to First Amendment protection.

In a different context, when a secretary overheard a student utter an expletive in school, the federal trial court in South Dakota upheld her suspension even though it did not create a disturbance because she violated a rule of which she was aware.[63] Previously, a federal trial court in Indiana, in upholding a student's suspension for uttering an obscenity, regardless of whether she was merely repeating and returning words directed at her since her clearly disruptive speech was heard by ninety students in a cafeteria, rejected her claim that school officials violated her right to freedom of speech.[64]

Most recently, in *Morse v. Frederick* (*Morse*),[65] the Supreme Court clarified the free speech rights of students at school-supervised events. *Morse* arose when a principal suspended a student who was at a parade near his school watching the Olympic Torch as it passed through Juneau, Alaska. The principal allowed students and staff who supervised the event to leave class to watch the relay as an approved social event. After the principal suspended a student for displaying a large banner which read "BONG HiTS [sic] 4 JESUS," because she interpreted it as advocating illegal drug use, the federal trial court granted the school board's motion for summary judgment, but the Ninth Circuit reversed in favor of the student.

Reversing in favor of the board, a closely divided Supreme Court began by rejecting the student's claim that he was not engaged in school speech. Explaining that the principal's interpretation of the banner was reasonable, the Court relied on its three previous cases involving student expression, *Tinker*, *Fraser*, and *Hazelwood*, in engaging in a two-part analysis. First,

---

61. *Id.* at 683.

62. *Poling v. Murphy*, 872 F.2d 757 [53 Educ. L. Rep. 37] (6th Cir.1989), *cert. denied*, 493 U.S. 1021, 110 S.Ct. 723, 107 L.Ed.2d 742 (1990).

63. *Anderson v. Milbank School Dist. 25–4*, 197 F.R.D. 682 (D.S.D. 2000).

64. *Heller v. Hodgin*, 928 F.Supp. 789 [110 Educ. L. Rep. 694] (S.D. Ind. 1996).

65. 551 U.S. 393, 127 S.Ct. 2618, 168 L.Ed.2d 290 [220 Educ. L. Rep. 50] (2007), *on remand*, 499 F.3d 926 (2007).

the Court noted that the free speech rights of students must be viewed in light of the "special characteristics" of the school environment. Second, the Court found that *Tinker* is neither absolute nor the only basis on which it could restrict student speech. Conceding that its Fourth Amendment jurisprudence understood the important, and perhaps even compelling, interest of educators to deter student drug use, the Court agreed that the principal acted properly in disciplining the plaintiff for displaying the banner. In rejecting the board's argument that the principal could have banned the banner under *Fraser's* "plainly offensive" standard as granting educators too much authority, the Court decided that the principal acted out of the legitimate concern of preventing the student from promoting illegal drug use.

In addition to the spoken word, as reflected by a case from the Eleventh Circuit, students can be disciplined for inappropriate non-political speech that might incite violence. The court affirmed that educators in Florida could discipline a student under a zero-tolerance policy for distributing anonymous pamphlets containing an essay wondering what might have happened if the author had shot the school's principal and others.[66] At the same time, the court agreed that school officials were not liable for the student's having been strip searched and arrested since the board did not have a custom permitting such a practice.

Two years later, in Louisiana, a high school student was suspended for bringing his brother's drawing to school which depicted a public school soaked in gasoline targeted by a missile and students pointing guns at the principal; it also included racial and obscene expletives. Officials searched the student's book bag and, after discovering a box cutter along with references to drugs, sex, death, and gangs, expelled him from school. The student sued the board on a variety of charges, most notably for violations of his First Amendment rights. In affirming a grant of summary judgment in favor of the defendants, the Fifth Circuit agreed that the drawing was not entitled to protection because in light of the unsettled nature of the relevant First Amendment law, the contours of the student's rights were not so clearly established that the principal's actions could have been categorized as objectively unreasonable.[67]

When dealing with threats, whether real or fictional in student writings, all but the first of the following seven cases upheld the rights of educators to discipline students for inappropriate musings. A student challenged his being adjudicated delinquent for making a criminal threat after he handed a classmate three sheets of "dark poetry," which included one that read, "I am Dark, Destructive, and Dangerous. I slap on my face of happiness but inside I am evil. For I can be the next kid to bring guns to kill students at school."[68] The Supreme Court of California posited that insofar as the student had both a plausible First Amendment defense, and since the poem was ambiguous, the circumstances of its dissemination were

---

66. *Cuesta v. School Bd. of Miami–Dade County*, 285 F.3d 962 [163 Educ. L. Rep. 101] (11th Cir. 2002).

67. *Porter v. Ascension Parish School Bd.*, 393 F.3d 608 [194 Educ. L. Rep. 497] (5th Cir. 2004), *cert. denied*, 544 U.S. 1062, 125 S.Ct. 2530, 161 L.Ed.2d 1112 (2005).

68. *In re George T.*, 16 Cal.Rptr.3d 61, 64 [190 Educ. L. Rep. 550] (Cal. 2004).

such that school officials failed to establish that it presented a criminal threat.

The Second Circuit affirmed that a principal in New York did not violate the rights of a middle school student he removed from class and placed in an in-school suspension room as a result of an essay that he wrote.[69] In his essay, which he submitted to his teacher but never presented in class or shared with peers, the student described getting drunk, smoking, using drugs, and ending with his taking cyanide plus shooting himself in the head in front of his friends. The court agreed that insofar as the principal's precautionary action was designed to ensure that the student's ambiguous written expression did not lead to disruption or violence, he did not act in retaliation for the child's exercising of his right to free speech. Previously, a federal trial court in New York dismissed the claims of a fifth-grader's parents against a principal and others when their son was suspended for five days for turning in an assignment in which he expressed his desire to blow up his school.[70] The court rejected the parents' arguments that their son's assignment was entitled to First Amendment protection and that his suspension was unconstitutionally severe.

In a case from Texas, the Fifth Circuit held that officials did not violate the free speech rights of a student who was transferred to an alternative educational setting for writing entries in his personal journal referring to a "Columbine" style attack at his school.[71] In light of the direct threat that the student's speech presented to the physical safety of the school population, the court rejected his claim that the contents were fictional, instead finding that his writings were not entitled to First Amendment protection.

The Eighth Circuit affirmed that educators in Minnesota did not violate the First Amendment rights of a high school student who wrote three disturbing essays, the first two of which his teacher considered to be simply offensive due to graphic representations of sexual activity and blood, the last of which described a student's shooting a teacher to death and committing suicide.[72] In response to the essays, officials suspended the student and had him placed in protective custody for a psychological examination before allowing him to return to class. Since it was satisfied that the third essay constituted a true threat that was not entitled to First Amendment protection in light of the educators' reasonable concern that the student was at risk, the court indicated that they had not violated his rights when he was taken into protective custody pursuant to state law.

Earlier, the Ninth Circuit affirmed that educators in Washington did not violate a high school student's First Amendment rights in expelling him on an emergency basis after showing his teacher a poem he wrote, which was filled with imagery of violent death, suicide, and the shooting of peers, even if it was protected speech.[73] Still, since the court added that officials

---

69. *Cox v. Warwick Valley Cent. School Dist.*, 654 F.3d 267 (2d Cir. 2011).

70. *Cuff ex rel. B.C. v. Valley Cent. School Dist.*, 559 F. Supp.2d 415 [235 Educ. L. Rep. 102] (S.D.N.Y. 2008).

71. *Ponce v. Socorro*, 508 F.3d 765 [227 Educ. L. Rep. 561] (5th Cir. 2007).

72. *Riehm v. Engelking*, 538 F.3d 952 [236 Educ. L. Rep. 65] (8th Cir. 2008).

73. *LaVine v. Blaine School Dist.*, 257 F.3d 981 [155 Educ. L. Rep. 1019] (9th Cir.2001), *reconsideration en banc denied*, 279 F.3d 719 (9th Cir. 2002), *cert. denied*, 536 U.S. 959, 122 S.Ct. 2663, 153 L.Ed.2d 837 (2002).

violated the student's rights by placing, and keeping, documentation about the incident in his file after the perceived threat subsided, it directed them to remove those materials from his record.

Finally, the Eleventh Circuit affirmed that school officials in Georgia did not violate a student's First Amendment rights when she was suspended for writing a story about shooting her mathematics teacher.[74] The court agreed that the student's actions were likely to have caused a material and substantial disruption to the school environment.

A case from Missouri concerned a different kind of speech. A high school student and his parents unsuccessfully sued their school board, alleging that his being disqualified as a candidate for student body president for the unauthorized distribution of condoms attached to stickers bearing his campaign slogan violated his First Amendment right to free speech. The Eighth Circuit affirmed that the election was a school-sponsored event over which officials had the authority to restrict even protected student expression that materially and substantially interfered with school discipline.[75]

In Ohio, a federal trial cout rejected a male student's free speech claim when school officials disciplined him for writing a sexually related message in the yearbook of a female friend.[76] Relying in part on *Fraser*, the court reiterated the right of officials to prevent students from engaging in vulgar or offensive speech, including sexual innuendo.

PUBLICATIONS

Courts have applied *Tinker* in cases involving student publications in school-sponsored, curricular-related activities. Consistent with *Tinker's* rationale, courts agree that while student expressive activities are entitled to First Amendment protection and that their content is not subject to the unrestricted will of school officials, educators need not permit all forms of student expression. Controversies in this area fall under two overlapping headings: school-sponsored curriculum-related publications and student-sponsored underground publications.

School–Sponsored/Curriculum Related

The first post-*Tinker* federal case to address attempted expulsions occurred in Illinois where high school students produced an off-campus newspaper but distributed it in school. The content of the newspaper was critical of school policies and officials. Reinstating the students, even in conceding that it contained stories that were disrespectful toward authority, the Seventh Circuit ruled that the expulsions were unjustified since the newspaper neither forecast, nor led to, disruptions in school.[77]

---

74. *Boim v. Fulton County School Dist.*, 494 F.3d 978 [223 Educ. L. Rep. 109] (11th Cir. 2007).

75. *Henerey ex rel. Henerey v. City of St. Charles*, 200 F.3d 1128 [141 Educ. L. Rep. 95] (8th Cir. 1999).

76. *Doe v. DePalma*, 163 F. Supp.2d 870 [157 Educ. L. Rep. 628] (S.D. Ohio 2000).

77. *Scoville v. Board of Educ. of Joliet Twp. High School Dist. 204*, 425 F.2d 10 (7th Cir.1970), *cert. denied*, 400 U.S. 826, 91 S.Ct. 51, 27 L.Ed.2d 55 (1970).

In another early case, the Second Circuit upheld a ban preventing staff members of a high school newspaper in New York from distributing a questionnaire on sexual attitudes and habits where educators feared that doing so might have inflicted emotional harm on some students. Emphasizing that the issue was neither a ban against the distribution of sex-related information nor an attempt to restrict the expression of student views, the court decreed that the First Amendment did not include the "right to importune others to respond to questions when there is reason to believe that such importuning may result in harmful consequences."[78]

Hazelwood School District v. Kuhlmeier (Hazelwood)[79] is the Supreme Court's only case involving school-sponsored publications. *Hazelwood* arose when a principal in Missouri deleted two articles, one on teenage pregnancy, the other about the divorce of a student's father, from a newspaper that was written and edited by members of a journalism class that was part of the school's curriculum. The Court recognized that the newspaper was neither an open forum nor made one by past practice. As such, the Court noted that the principal acted reasonably in light of the possible identification of unnamed pregnant students, references to sexual activity and birth control in the first article that were inappropriate for some younger readers, and a student's unilateral criticism of her father in the second article.

The Supreme Court distinguished *Hazelwood* from *Tinker* since the issue was not so much the right of students to speak as it was the duty of educators not to promote particular student speech. The latter area concerns the authority of educators over school-sponsored publications, theatrical productions, and other expressive activities that could reasonably be perceived to bear a school's imprimatur.

As part of its analysis, and as discussed in Chapter 6,[80] the Supreme Court reviewed the three different types of fora that it delineated for free speech. Under the first category, governmental power to regulate expression is most restricted on public properties that are traditional public fora such as parks, streets, and sidewalks. The government may "exclude a speaker from a traditional public forum 'only when the exclusion is necessary to serve a compelling state interest and the exclusion is narrowly drawn to achieve that interest.' "[81] Narrowly tailored content-neutral regulations as to time, place, and manner of expression can be enforced, but only if the governmental interest is significant and alternative channels of communication are open.

---

78. *Trachtman v. Anker*, 563 F.2d 512, 520 (2d Cir.1977), *cert. denied*, 435 U.S. 925, 98 S.Ct. 1491, 55 L.Ed.2d 519 (1978).

79. 484 U.S. 260, 108 S.Ct. 562, 98 L.Ed.2d 592 [43 Educ. L. Rep. 515] (1988). [Case No. 105]

80. *See* Chapter 6, notes 119–125 and accompanying text for a similar discussion.

81. *Arkansas Educ. Television Comm'n v. Forbes*, 523 U.S. 666, 677, 118 S.Ct. 1633, 140 L.Ed.2d 875 (1998) (quoting *Cornelius v. NAACP Legal Def. & Educ. Fund*, 473 U.S. 788, 800, 105 S.Ct. 3439, 87 L.Ed.2d 567 (1985)).

The same standard that applies in public fora govern designated public fora, public property that the state has opened for public use as places for expressive activity.[82] The government can create such fora either by express policy or by substantial practice. In limited public fora, First Amendment protections provided to traditional public fora apply, but only to entities of a character similar to those the government admits to the fora. The government is not indefinitely bound to retain the open nature of limited fora.

A non-public forum, the third category of public property, such as classrooms,[83] "is not by tradition or designation a forum for public communication."[84] As such, non-public fora are subject to less rigorous scrutiny than traditional open or designated public fora. In these settings, the government qua school boards and educational officials can enforce regulations to reserve fora for their intended purposes, communicative or otherwise, but they "must be 'reasonable in light of the purpose served by the forum.' "[85] Limitations cannot be intended to suppress expression since public officials oppose viewpoints.[86] During the day, schools are generally non-public fora. Once the day is over, the type of fora that schools become depends on board policies and practices.

In key language mirroring the rational relations test used in equal protection analysis, the Supreme Court explained that "educators do not offend the First Amendment by exercising editorial control over the style and content of student speech in school-sponsored expressive activities so long as their actions are reasonably related to legitimate pedagogical concerns."[87]

Following *Hazelwood,* a student editor in California was successful in his claim that school officials violated his free speech rights in refusing to print his editorial that was critical of immigration. Pointing out that officials had not disciplined the student and that the superintendent had not even read the editorial, the court relied on *Tinker, Fraser,* and *Hazelwood* in observing that they violated his constitutional and statutory rights to freedom of speech. The court added that "[a]lthough 'Immigration' communicates [the student's] viewpoint in a disrespectful and unsophisticated manner, it contains no direct provocation or racial epithets. We

---

82. *Arkansas Educ. Television Comm'n v. Forbes, Id.*

83. *See, e.g., Walz ex rel. Walz v. Egg Harbor Twp. Bd. of Educ.,* 342 F.3d 271 [180 Educ. L. Rep. 115] (3d Cir. 2003), *cert. denied,* 541 U.S. 936, 124 S.Ct. 1658, 158 L.Ed.2d 356 (2004).

84. *Perry Educ. Ass'n v. Perry Local Educators' Ass'n,* 460 U.S. 37, 46, 103 S.Ct. 948, 74 L.Ed.2d 794 [9 Educ. L. Rep. 23] (1983).

85. *Good News Club v. Milford Cent. School,* 533 U.S. 98, 106–107, 121 S.Ct. 2093, 150 L.Ed.2d 151 [154 Educ. L. Rep. 45] (2001) [Case No 13] (quoting *Cornelius v. NAACP Legal Defense and Educ. Fund,* 473 U.S. 788, 806, 105 S.Ct. 3439, 87 L.Ed.2d 567 (1985)); *Arkansas Educ. Television Comm'n v. Forbes,* 523 U.S. 666, 682, 118 S.Ct. 1633, 140 L.Ed.2d 875 (1998); *Rosenberger v. Rector and Visitors of Univ. of Va.,* 515 U.S. 819, 829, 115 S.Ct. 2510, 132 L.Ed.2d 700 [101 Educ. L. Rep. 552] (1995); *Lamb's Chapel v. Center Moriches Union Free School Dist.,* 508 U.S. 384, 392–93, 113 S.Ct. 2141, 124 L.Ed.2d 352 [83 Educ. L. Rep. 30] (1993), *on remand,* 17 F.3d 1425 [89 Educ. L. Rep. 783] (2d Cir. 1994). [Case No. 38]

86. *See, e.g., Cornelius v. NAACP Legal Defense and Educ. Fund,* 473 U.S. 788, 105 S.Ct. 3439, 87 L.Ed.2d 567 (1985).

87. *Id.* at 273.

conclude that 'Immigration' was not inciting speech that the [board] was authorized to prohibit"[88] under the law.[89]

The Second Circuit affirmed that educational officials in New York did not violate the rights of students when they refused to print a cartoon depicting stick figures in sexual positions in the high school's newspaper.[90] Noting both that the newspaper was a limited open forum and that the cartoon was lewd, the court agreed that officials did not violate the rights of the plaintiffs insofar as their actions were reasonably related to the legitimate pedagogical concern that the cartoons would have undermined their concerted efforts to stress the seriousness of sexual relations involving students.

A related concern arises over advertisements in student newspapers. In the first reported case on this topic, a federal trial court in New York decreed that insofar as a school newspaper published articles questioning American policy in Vietnam, there was no logical reason to forbid it from printing a paid advertisement on the same topic.[91] After *Hazelwood*, questions of advertising raise issues over whether school-sponsored publications constitute an open forum for expression by students and/or the public or whether they bear the imprimatur of schools so that access may be more limited.

The Ninth Circuit, relying on *Hazelwood*, affirmed that insofar as the student publications at issue were not open fora, and officials in Nevada did not create limited-purpose fora by opening them up for advertisers of lawful goods and services, educators could apply reasonable editorial control over the content of a student newspaper and exclude advertisements from a wide range of organizations, including, as here, a group that focused on family planning.[92] A similar action arose in Massachusetts when student editors refused to modify their school newspaper and yearbook policy under which they agreed to refrain from publishing political or advocacy advertising, including those for candidates for student government.[93] The First Circuit affirmed that school officials were not liable for refusing to run advertisements promoting sexual abstinence since the student policy did not involve state action.

---

88. *Smith v. Novato Unified School Dist.*, 59 Cal.Rptr.3d 508, 521 [220 Educ. L. Rep. 292] (Cal. Ct. App. 2007), *review denied* (2007), *cert. denied*, 552 U.S. 1184, 128 S.Ct. 1256, 170 L.Ed.2d 67 (2008).

89. For another dispute over immigration, *see Corales v. Bennett*, 567 F.3d 554 [244 Educ. L. Rep. 1045] (9th Cir. 2009) (affirming that an assistant principal did not violate the free speech and expression rights of middle school students for disciplining them for leaving campus without permission to attend a protest on immigration policy).

90. *R.O. ex rel. Ochshorn v. Ithaca City School Dist.*, 645 F.3d 533 [269 Educ. L. Rep. 464] (2d Cir. 2011), *cert. denied*, ___ U.S. ___, 132 S.Ct. 422, 181 L.Ed.2d 261 (2011).

91. *Zucker v. Panitz*, 299 F.Supp. 102 (S.D.N.Y.1969).

92. *Planned Parenthood of S. Nev. v. Clark County School Dist.*, 941 F.2d 817 [69 Educ. L. Rep. 252] (9th Cir. 1991).

93. *Yeo v. Town of Lexington*, 131 F.3d 241 [122 Educ. L. Rep. 924] (1st Cir.1997), *cert. denied*, 524 U.S. 904, 118 S.Ct. 2060, 141 L.Ed.2d 138 (1998).

Underground Activities and School Distribution Policies

Along with school-sponsored publications, whether curricular or extra-curricular, students have developed their own underground publications that have led to litigation. Absent reasonable forecasts of material and/or substantial disruption, courts have permitted educators to impose reasonable time, manner, and place restrictions on the distribution of materials while preventing them from disciplining students who operated within these guidelines. In a case that is instructive on the importance of such limits, the Supreme Court upheld an anti-noise ordinance designed to prohibit persons who were on grounds adjacent to buildings in which schools were in session from wilfully making noises that disturbed the peace. According to the Court, "[t]he crucial question is whether the manner of expression is basically incompatible with the normal activity of a particular place at a particular time."[94]

When students in New York produced and distributed an off-campus paper containing a vulgar satire about the school community, the Second Circuit refused to allow educators to punish its creators.[95] In dicta, the court suggested that while there are circumstances under which school officials can deem specific publications unacceptable, this was not the case in the dispute at bar because the students diligently labored to insure that the publication was printed outside of school even though copies were sold on school grounds. Conversely, the Eighth Circuit upheld disciplining of students in Minnesota who circulated an unofficial newspaper containing vulgar and indecent language while indirectly encouraging violence against teachers because it led to a material disruption in school.[96]

The Second Circuit, in a case from Connecticut, discussed the extent to which educators can exercise prior restraint on publications that are distributed at schools.[97] The court upheld, but modified, an order invalidating a board rule requiring officials to grant prior approval for all such materials. The court held that in order for a rule requiring prior submission of material for distribution to be valid, it must prescribe a definite, brief period within which the review is to be completed along with identifying to whom and how it is to be submitted for clearance. In like fashion, the Ninth Circuit, in a case from Washington, expressing doubts that a constitutionally sound pre-distribution policy could be effectively established, struck down a plan that would have required approval for all non-school-sponsored materials.[98] The court invalidated the policy because it was overbroad.

---

94. *Grayned v. City of Rockford*, 408 U.S. 104, 116, 92 S.Ct. 2294, 33 L.Ed.2d 222 (1972).

95. *Thomas v. Board of Educ., Granville Cent. School Dist.*, 607 F.2d 1043 (2d Cir. 1979), *cert. denied*, 444 U.S. 1081, 100 S.Ct. 1034, 62 L.Ed.2d 765 (1980).

96. *Bystrom By and Through Bystrom v. Fridley High School*, 686 F.Supp. 1387 [47 Educ. L. Rep. 905] (D. Minn. 1987), *aff'd without reported opinion*, 855 F.2d 855 [48 Educ. L. Rep. 1144] (8th Cir. 1988).

97. *Eisner v. Stamford Bd. of Educ.*, 440 F.2d 803 (2d Cir. 1971).

98. *Burch v. Barker*, 861 F.2d 1149 [50 Educ. L. Rep. 339] (9th Cir. 1988).

STUDENT FREE SPEECH AND TECHNOLOGY

The Internet

As technology plays an increasingly larger role in schools, the litigation discussed below reflects how courts are reaching markedly different outcomes on the extent to which educational officials can punish students when their actions violate school rules, particularly when they raise claims that their being disciplined violates their First Amendment rights to free speech.

Where material issues of fact remained as to the motives of educational officials, a federal trial court in Ohio denied a school board's motion for summary judgment in a dispute over the expulsion of a middle school student for using school computers, during class hours, to access a Web site he created on his own computer, on his own time, at home, containing insulting graphics and remarks about three classmates.[99] The court asserted that while the conduct code's catch-all phrase was invalid on its face, its remaining sections were not unconstitutionally vague and that officials did not chill the student's First Amendment rights to expression. Federal trial courts in Missouri[100] and Michigan[101] reached the same outcomes in rejecting the arguments of school officials that material on Web sites disrupted school activities in a way which permitted them to discipline students.

In the first of three relatively early cases from Pennsylvania, a federal trial court granted a motion for summary judgment in favor of parents who challenged officials for disciplining their son because of postings he made on a Web site message board.[102] The court agreed that provisions in a school handbook relating to student discipline, responsibility and technology were vague and over-broad especially since they did not geographically limit the authority of educators to discipline expression that occurred on school premises or at school-related activities. In a case that went even further, another federal trial court specified that educators exceeded their authority in attempting to suspend a student for writing a letter ridiculing his school's athletic director and e-mailing it to friends from his home computer.[103] The court pointed out that even though the message was lewd and vulgar, since the student created it away from school and did not bring it to campus, officials could not discipline absent evidence that it would have caused a substantial disruption. Conversely, a student unsuccessfully fought his expulsion for creating a Web site, on his own computer while at home, that contained derogatory remarks about his algebra teacher and asking for collections to pay a hit man to kill her. The board expelled the student for violating his school's code of conduct by threatening, harassing, and showing disrespect to the teacher. The Supreme Court of Pennsylvania affirmed that insofar as the student's messages substantially disrupted school activities, educators did not violate his First Amendment rights.[104]

---

99. *Coy v. Board of Educ.*, 205 F. Supp.2d 791 [166 Educ. L. Rep. 535] (N.D. Ohio 2002).

100. *Beussink ex rel. Beussink v. Woodland R–IV School Dist.*, 30 F. Supp.2d 1175 [131 Educ. L. Rep. 1000] (E.D. Mo.1998).

101. *Mahaffey ex rel. Mahaffey v. Aldrich*, 236 F. Supp.2d 779 (E.D. Mich. 2002).

102. *Flaherty v. Keystone Oaks School Dist.*, 247 F. Supp.2d 698 [175 Educ. L. Rep. 188] (W.D. Pa. 2003).

103. *Killion v. Franklin Reg'l School Dist.*, 136 F. Supp.2d 446 [153 Educ. L. Rep. 90] (W.D. Pa. 2001).

104. *J.S. v. Bethlehem Area School Dist.*, 807 A.2d 847 [170 Educ. L. Rep. 302] (Pa. 2002).

A case from Connecticut made two trips to the Second Circuit over whether school officials in Connecticut violated a student's free speech or equal protection rights.[105] The dispute arose after officials denied the plaintiff the opportunity to run for office on the student council because she posted a vulgar blog about them on a Web site independent of the school and wore a homemade t-shirt to a school assembly protesting their actions. On further review after being remanded, the court explained that officials were entitled to qualified immunity and that they had not selectively disciplined the student.[106] The court observed that even if officials mistakenly thought that their actions were justified by the potential disruption that might have ensued if they allowed the student to wear the t-shirt, it was a reasonable error. The court suggested that it would have forgiven such an error since the student's supporters were upset by her being denied the opportunity to run for office and her most recent post on her blog demonstrated her willingness to incite confrontation with them.

In a case involving MySpace,[107] the Supreme Court of Indiana invalidated a student's being adjudicated delinquent for posting vulgar remarks about her school's policy of prohibiting bodily piercings since she engaged in protected free speech by criticizing a governmental action with which she disagreed. The court found that there was insufficient evidence proving that the student had the requisite intent to harass, annoy, or alarm her former middle school principal.[108]

Lower courts remain divided over whether postings by students that are either threatening or critical of educators are protected free speech. Some permit school officials to punish students who post such critical material on the Internet[109] while others prevent them from doing so.[110]

The Fourth Circuit affirmed that officials in West Virginia did not violate a student's First Amendment rights when he was suspended for creating and posting to a Web page ridiculing a classmate.[111] The court agreed that once the expression reached school it would create a disruption.[112] Similarly, the Eighth Circuit upheld the suspension of a high school student in Missouri who used instant messaging to communicate with a friend about his desire to bring weapons to school to harm others.[113] The

---

105. *Doninger v. Niehoff*, 527 F.3d 41 [233 Educ. L. Rep. 30] (2d Cir. 2008).

106. *Doninger v. Niehoff*, 642 F.3d 334 [268 Educ. L. Rep. 643] (2d Cir. 2011), *cert. denied*, ___ U.S. ___, 132 S.Ct. 499, 181 L.Ed.2d 346 (2011).

107. For an interesting, albeit non-school, case involving MySpace, *see Doe v. MySpace*, 528 F.3d 413 (5th Cir. 2008), *cert. denied*, ___ U.S. ___, 129 S.Ct. 600, 172 L.Ed.2d 456 (2008) (where the mother of a thirteen-year-old who misrepresented her age unsuccessfully filed suit after her daughter was sexually assaulted by a nineteen-year-old that she met on the Internet on the basis that company officials had no duty to protect her daughter).

108. *A.B. v. State*, 885 N.E.2d 1223 [231 Educ. L. Rep. 921] (Ind. 2008).

109. *See, e.g., Barnett v. Tipton County Bd. of Educ.*, 601 F. Supp.2d 980 [243 Educ. L. Rep.269] (W.D. Tenn. 2009).

110. *Evans v. Bayer*, 684 F. Supp.2d 1365 [255 Educ. L. Rep. 728] (S.D. Fla. 2010).

111. *See also In re Keelin B.*, 27 A.3d 689 (N.H. 2011) (affirming both that school officials could suspend a student for sending e-mails containing sexually explicit language to a principal and teacher under the name of a peer and that the thirty-four days exclusion was excessive).

112. *Kowalski v. Berkeley County Schools*, 652 F.3d 565 (4th Cir. 2011). [Case No. 107]

113. *D.J.M. ex rel. D.M. v. Hannibal Pub. School Dist. No. 60*, 647 F.3d 754 [270 Educ. L. Rep. 465] (8th Cir. 2011).

court affirmed that insofar as the messages constituted "true threats," they were not entitled to protection under the First Amendment. Earlier, the Second Circuit reached a similar outcome in upholding a grant of summary judgment in favor of officials in New York who suspended a student for creating an instant messaging icon depicting the shooting of his teacher.[114] Although refusing to address whether the icon was a true threat, the court relied on the *Tinker* standard in deciding that although the conduct occurred off campus, officials could discipline the student because his actions could have materially and substantially interfered with school activities.

On the other hand, in two cases from Pennsylvania involving MySpace that it resolved on the same day, the Third Circuit reached the opposite result. An en banc panel affirmed that school officials violated the First Amendment rights of a student who was suspended after using his grandmother's home computer to create a fake internet profile of his principal.[115] The court maintained that officials lacked the authority to punish students for expressive conduct occurring outside of school that they considered to be lewd and offensive. In the second case, the court agreed that officials violated the rights of an eighth-grader who used her home computer to create a fake profile of her principal, insinuating, among other things, that he was a sex addict and a pedophile.[116] The court was convinced that insofar as the student took specific steps to try to keep the profile "private" so only her friends could access it and it was so outrageous as to not be taken seriously, educators violated her rights because they could not reasonably have forecast the substantial disruption of, or material interference with, school activities due to the posting.

In the first of two cases involving imaginative student use of technology, a federal trial court in Washington denied a student's motion for a temporary restraining order when he was suspended for secretly making a videotape of one of his high school teachers and posting it on You Tube.[117] In rejecting the student's First Amendment claim, the court noted that insofar as he was disciplined for his actions in secretly taping the teacher rather than for expressing his opinion, officials could punish him for his inappropriate behavior because he violated a board policy on the use of electronic equipment in school. Conversely, a student challenged her two-day suspension for posting a video clip of peers insulting a classmate on You Tube. In granting the student's motion for summary judgment, essentially rescinding her suspension, a federal trial court in California indicated that insofar as the incident occurred in a local restaurant rather than at school, and did not result in a substantial disruption or risk thereof to the

---

114. *Wisniewski v. Board of Educ. Weedsport Cent. School Dist.*, 494 F.3d 34 [223 Educ. L. Rep. 34] (2d Cir. 2007), *cert. denied*, 552 U.S. 1296, 128 S.Ct. 1741, 170 L.Ed.2d 540 (2008).

115. *Layshock ex rel. Layshock v. Hermitage School Dist.*, 650 F.3d 205 (3d Cir. 2011). [Case No. 108]

116. *J.S. ex rel. Snyder v. Blue Mountain School Dist.*, 650 F.3d 915 (3d Cir. 2011).

117. *Requa v. Kent School Dist. No. 415*, 492 F. Supp.2d 1272 [222 Educ. L. Rep. 178] (W.D. Wash. 2007).

educational environment under *Tinker*, officials lacked the authority to punish the student for her actions.[118]

An interesting application of school discipline and technology, albeit in a non-public school, was at issue when the Supreme Court of Alabama affirmed a grant of summary judgment in favor of officials who expelled female ninth-grade students for taking nude photographs of themselves and e-mailing them to male friends, a practice known as sexting.[119] In rejecting the students' claims, which included breach of contract, invasion of privacy, and due process violations, the court explained that they failed to produce evidence supporting their allegations.[120]

A public school case involving sexting arose in Pennsylvania where a district attorney offered high school students the opportunity to write apologies for their behavior rather than face criminal charges with potentially lengthy sentences.[121] The Third Circuit affirmed that the district attorney exceeded his authority in trying to require the students to compose the essays since this violated their First Amendment rights to be free from compelled speech.[122]

In different kinds of application involving discipline and technology, the Fifth Circuit upheld the suspension of a student in Mississippi for not more than ten days because he invaded his school's computer systems.[123] The court was satisfied that insofar as officials offered the student multiple opportunities to respond to the accusations that he was responsible for service attacks on his school's computer networks, they did not violate his rights to due process. Earlier, an appellate court in Pennsylvania reached the same result in affirming a student's expulsion for the remainder of a semester for "hacking" into his district's computer system.[124]

A novel dispute involving technology occurred in Virginia when high school students unsuccessfully filed a copyright infringement claim against the company that owned and operated a system, used by over 7,000 educational institutions around the world, to evaluate the originality of work in order to detect plagiarism. The students, who were required to submit their written school assignments on the system, sued the company because it saves files in an archive against which it compares written materials. On appeal, in the most relevant part of its order, the Fourth Circuit affirmed that the actions of company officials did not undermine

---

118. *J.C. ex rel. R.C. v. Beverly Hills Unified School Dist.*, 711 F. Supp.2d 1094 [260 Educ. L. Rep. 212] (C.D. Cal. 2010).

119. *S.B. v. Saint James School*, 959 So.2d 72 [222 Educ. L. Rep. 444] (Ala. 2006).

120. *See also Lawrence ex rel. Lawrence v. St. Augustine High School*, 955 So.2d 183 [220 Educ. L. Rep. 429] (La. Ct. App. 2007) (refusing to intervene where a check of a student's home Internet account provided evidence that he was involved in plagiarism at his non-public school).

121. *Miller v. Mitchell*, 598 F.3d 139 (3d Cir. 2010).

122. *See also State v. Canal*, 773 N.W.2d 528 (Iowa 2009) (affirming the criminal conviction of an eighteen-year-old senior for sending two pictures, including one of his genitals, to a fourteen-year-old female who attended his high school).

123. *Harris ex rel. Harris v. Pontotoc County School Dist.*, 635 F.3d 685 [265 Educ. L. Rep. 908] (5th Cir. 2011).

124. *M.T. for A.T. v. Central York School Dist.*, 937 A.2d 538 [228 Educ. L. Rep. 342] (Pa. Cmwlth. Ct. 2007), *appeal denied*, 951 A.2d 1168 (Pa. 2008).

the rights of the students since the use of the papers was unrelated to any creative component.[125] The court added that any harm the students may have suffered was not the kind of injury that the copyright law was designed to protect against.

Cell Phones

As widespread as the use of cell phones has become, it is surprising that there have been relatively few reported cases involving related disputes over their presence in schools.[126]

Perhaps the most notable of the three reported cases, the first two of which were resolved in favor of school boards, occurred in New York City. An appellate court affirmed that a school board policy banning the use of cell phones was a nonjusticiable controversy since it did not implicate any discrete issues of law.[127] The policy does allow principals to grant permission for students to bring cell phones into schools for documented medical reasons.

A year earlier, when school officials in Tennessee confiscated a middle school student's cell phone because it rang in class and subjected her to a one-day, in-school suspension, the Sixth Circuit rejected her claims that they acted inappropriately.[128] In conceding the authority of educational officials to enforce school rules, the court concluded that they did not violate the student's due process property interest in public education because she was allowed to remain in school and complete her class work.

On the other hand, when educational officials in Pennsylvania confiscated a high school student's cell phone, called classmates listed in his phone number directory, accessed his text messages and voice mail, and engaged in an instant messaging conversation with his brother without identifying themselves, he and his parents filed a variety of claims. In largely rejecting the defendants' motion for dismissal, the court held that if the student could prove that educators called his friends on the phone, their actions constituted an unconstitutional search.[129] The court asserted that the student presented actionable claims for an unreasonable search and seizure against the board and officials in their individual capacities for false light invasion of privacy and negligence. The court permitted the parents to proceed with their separate claims for negligence and punitive damages.

---

125. *A.V. ex rel. Vanderhye v. iParadigms, LLC*, 562 F.3d 630 (4th Cir. 2009).

126. For a novel case, albeit one not involving speech, see *A.W. ex rel. Wilson v. Fairfax County School Bd.*, 548 F. Supp.2d 219 [233 Educ. L. Rep. 166] (E.D. Va. 2008) (permitting officials to discipline a student with Asperger's Syndrome for sexually harassing a classmate by using his cell phone to take pictures up her skirt without her knowledge).

127. *Price v. New York City Bd. of Educ.*, 855 N.Y.S.2d 530 [231 Educ. L. Rep. 856] (N.Y. App. Div. 2008).

128. *Laney v. Farley*, 501 F.3d 577 [225 Educ. L. Rep. 93] (6th Cir. 2007).

129. *Klump v. Nazareth Area School Dist.*, 425 F. Supp.2d 622 [209 Educ. L. Rep. 82] (E.D. Pa. 2006).

DRESS CODES AND GROOMING

Dress Codes

Amid evolving judicial and social perspectives on student dress and grooming, two early cases reflected the attitudes of the times. In a case cited in *Tinker*, the Supreme Court of Arkansas upheld a school board rule prohibiting "[t]he wearing of transparent hosiery, low-necked dresses, or any style of clothing tending toward immodesty in dress, or the use of face paint or cosmetics."[130] Eight years later, the Supreme Court of North Dakota applied an analogous rationale in refusing to disturb a rule against wearing metal heel plates since doing so damaged school floors and was noisy.[131]

If dress codes are narrowly drawn to cover specific activities, much of the judicial disagreement dissolves. Courts continue to uphold dress code policies as long as they are rationally related to legitimate pedagogical concerns in support of schools' educational missions[132] and are neither vague nor over-broad.[133]

A federal trial court in Arkansas upheld a mandatory school uniform policy in the face of a protest by students who wore black armbands to school voicing their opposition to its being implemented.[134] In allowing students to be suspended for wearing the armbands as a form of protest, the court rejected the argument that the policy was not unconstitutionally over-broad. The court declared that the policy was acceptable since it was adopted pursuant to state legislative findings that uniforms furthered governmental interests in rendering student socioeconomic disparities less obvious, advancing learning rather than having students focus on how peers were dressed, and helping to improve security while not limiting particular viewpoints in merely regulating the types of clothes that students could wear to school. On further review of a jury verdict in favor of students, the Eighth Circuit affirmed in their behalf.[135] The court decreed that the board's voluntarily amending its policy in an unspecified manner did not render the case moot, that officials violated the students' rights to free speech, and that they were entitled to attorney fees in an amount equal to about one half of the expenses they incurred even though they had only been awarded nominal damages.

Disputes involving political expression and clothing discussed earlier aside, courts reach mixed results on the appropriateness of limits on student dress, most notably t-shirts displaying questionable, but non-

---

130. *Pugsley v. Sellmeyer*, 250 S.W. 538, 538 (Ark. 1923).

131. *Stromberg v. French*, 236 N.W. 477 (N.D. 1931).

132. *Blau v. Fort Thomas Pub. School Dist.*, 401 F.3d 381 [196 Educ. L. Rep. 118] (6th Cir. 2005); *Dempsey v. Alston*, 966 A.2d 1 [242 Educ. L. Rep. 256] (N.J. Super. Ct. App. Div. 2009), *certification denied*, 973 A.2d 386 (N.J. 2009).

133. *See, e.g.*, *Canady v. Bossier Parish School Bd.*, 240 F.3d 437 [151 Educ. L. Rep. 110] (5th Cir. 2001); *Littlefield v. Forney Ind. School Dist.*, 268 F.3d 275 [158 Educ. L. Rep. 36] (5th Cir. 2001); *Long v. Board of Educ. of Jefferson County, Ky.*, 121 F. Supp.2d 621 [149 Educ. L. Rep. 157] (W.D.Ky.2000), *aff'd*, 21 Fed.Appx. 252 [160 Educ. L. Rep. 392] (6th Cir. 2001).

134. *Lowry v. Watson Chapel School Dist.*, 508 F. Supp.2d 713 [225 Educ. L. Rep. 394] (E.D. Ark. 2007).

135. *Lowry v. Watson Chapel School Dist.*, 540 F.3d 752 [236 Educ. L. Rep. 158] (8th Cir. 2008), *cert. denied*, 555 U.S. 1212, 129 S.Ct. 1526, 173 L.Ed.2d 656 [242 Educ. L. Rep. 22] (2009).

disruptive, messages. For example, the Supreme Judicial Court of Massachusetts allowed students to wear t-shirts with arguably vulgar, lewd, and/or offensive messages such as "Coed Naked Band: Do It To the Rhythm" as long as their doing so did not cause disruptions at school.[136] On the other hand, the Sixth Circuit affirmed that officials did not act unreasonably in prohibiting a student from wearing t-shirts containing symbols and words promoting values contrary to the school's educational mission.[137] The court was of the opinion that one t-shirt was offensive because it mocked Jesus while the others featured a singer who encouraged destructive conduct and demoralizing values along with promoting drug use.

As highlighted by a case from a federal trial court in Georgia, the judiciary defers to educators in evaluating the appropriateness of student dress that is not offensive or vulgar.[138] The court upheld a student's three-day suspension in determining that even though his having worn a t-shirt to school that contained the message "Even adults lie" on front may have been a factor in his being excluded, educators did not violate his free speech rights and the school's dress code was not over-broad. Earlier, a federal trial court in Oklahoma enjoined school officials from preventing students from wearing t-shirts with the message "The best of the night's adventures are reserved for people with nothing planned."[139] In acknowledging limits between school officials and student expression, the court rejected the board's claim that insofar as this was a phrase taken from an advertisement for a company that sells rum, it violated its policy against wearing t-shirts that advertise alcoholic beverages because the message was open to many possible interpretations, was not disruptive, and did not otherwise violate the dress code.

When public school students in an eighth-grade gifted program submitted a design for their official class t-shirt depicting a child with a physical disability with the word "Gifties" on the back, administrators disapproved of its design and forbade them from wearing them or the unofficial versions that they created. After students who wore the t-shirts were punished, officials lifted the ban. Students filed suit claiming that they were subjected to continued reprimands, detentions, and suspensions for frivolous reasons amounting, in effect, to retaliation. The Seventh Circuit affirmed the denial of the students' claims that the t-shirt design was a protected expression of their individuality. The court bluntly wrote that "the picture and the few words imprinted on the ... [t]-shirt are no more expressive of an idea or opinion that the First Amendment might be thought to protect than a

---

136. *Pyle By and Through Pyle v. South Hadley School Comm.*, 861 F.Supp. 157, 158 [94 Educ. L. Rep. 729] (D. Mass.1994), *question certified by*, 55 F.3d 20 [100 Educ. L. Rep. 579] (1st Cir. 1995), *question certified to state court*, 667 N.E.2d 869 [111 Educ. L. Rep. 481] (Mass. 1996).

137. *Boroff v. Van Wert City Bd. of Educ.*, 220 F.3d 465 [146 Educ. L. Rep. 629] (6th Cir. 2000), *cert. denied*, 532 U.S. 920, 121 S.Ct. 1355, 149 L.Ed.2d 286 (2001).

138. *Smith ex rel. Lanham v. Greene County School Dist.*, 100 F. Supp.2d 1354 [145 Educ. L. Rep. 368] (M.D. Ga. 2000).

139. *McIntire v. Bethel School, Indep. School Dist. No. 3*, 804 F.Supp. 1415, 1418 [78 Educ. L. Rep. 828] (W.D. Okla. 1992).

young child's talentless infantile drawing which [the] design successfully mimics."[140]

The father of a middle school student in Virginia sought to enjoin part of a dress code that prohibited messages on clothing, jewelry, and personal belongings related to weapons. The Fourth Circuit maintained that the trial court abused its discretion in believing that the father failed the test for obtaining a preliminary injunction.[141] The court pointed out that the father demonstrated a strong likelihood of success on his claim that the policy was over-broad absent evidence that clothing worn by students with messages related to weapons ever substantially disrupted the school or interfered with the rights of others.

A case arose in Texas where a student and his parents unsuccessfully disputed his high school's dress code which banned all shirts with printed messages other than small logos on shirts and principal-approved shirts promoting school clubs, organizations, athletic teams, or school spirit; the policy did allow students to wear political buttons and pins. In applying intermediate scrutiny, the Fifth Circuit affirmed that the policy, which was no more strict than necessary, did not violate the student's free speech rights because it was designed "to maintain an orderly and safe learning environment, increase the focus on instruction, promote safety and life-long learning, and encourage professional and responsible dress for all students."[142]

In the first of three cases involving dress requirements and religious issues, an atheist mother in New Jersey unsuccessfully filed an equal protection challenge to her school board's mandatory dress code policy which would have permitted an exemption for students based on their sincerely held religious beliefs.[143] The Third Circuit affirmed that the exemption was acceptable because it was rationally drawn to advance the school board's legitimate interest in accommodating the right of students to the free exercise of religion without undermining the pedagogical goals of the uniform policy.

The Ninth Circuit affirmed an order in favor of a school board from Nevada upholding a mandatory dress code under which officials refused to make allowances for students who wished to wear religious items.[144] The court agreed that the policy did not violate the dress, speech, free exercise, or due process rights of students since the part of the code requiring students to wear clothing devoid of all messages other than occasional

---

140. *Brandt v. City of Chicago*, 480 F.3d 460, 465–466 [217 Educ. L. Rep. 123] (7th Cir. 2007), *reh'g and reh'g en banc denied* (7th Cir. 2007), *cert. denied*, 552 U.S. 976, 128 S.Ct. 441, 169 L.Ed.2d 308 [225 Educ. L. Rep. 52] (2007).

141. *Newsom ex rel. Newsom v. Albemarle County*, 354 F.3d 249 [184 Educ. L. Rep. 24] (4th Cir. 2003).

142. *Palmer ex rel. Palmer v. Waxahachie Indep. School Dist.*, 579 F.3d 502, 510 [248 Educ. L. Rep. 579] (5th Cir. 2009), *cert. denied*, ___ U.S. ___, 130 S.Ct. 1055, 175 L.Ed.2d 883 (2010) (the t-shirts the student sought to wear expressed his support for the Presidential candidacy of John Edwards).

143. *Wilkins v. Penns Grove–Carneys Point*, 123 Fed.Appx. 493 [196 Educ. L. Rep. 449] (3d Cir. 2005).

144. *Jacobs v. Clark County School Dist.*, 526 F.3d 419 [232 Educ. L. Rep. 578] (9th Cir. 2008).

displays of the school logo was a viewpoint neutral rule that was justified due to health and safety concerns.[145] Further, the federal trial court in South Dakota denied a student's motion for summary judgment in his suit alleging that officials violated his right to free speech when they directed him to wear a cap-and-gown over his Native American dress.[146] Although conceding that the student's desire to wear his traditional clothing was a form of expressive activity protected by the First Amendment, being required to wear the cap-and-gown did not violate his rights because insofar as the graduation was a school-sponsored event, the board had a legitimate interest in preserving class unity while honoring its graduates.

When clothing or items of dress signify affiliations that can have a potentially detrimental impact on school discipline, disputes arise over whether they can be banned. After students wore rosaries to school as necklaces, a federal trial court in Texas was convinced that educators violated their First Amendment right to pure speech by asking them to remove the rosaries because they are a form of religious expression.[147] The court concluded that the dress code's prohibition of gang-related apparel was unconstitutionally vague because officials could not demonstrate that wearing rosaries would have caused actual or anticipated disruptions. In another case involving a religious symbol, after a high school student in Iowa had a small tattoo of a cross on her hand removed via laser surgery rather than be disciplined for violating a board policy against gang symbols, the Eighth Circuit voided the policy for vagueness since it did not adequately define the term "gang symbols."[148]

An appellate court in New Mexico affirmed that a dress code did not violate the First Amendment because it was reasonably related to school officials' interest in reducing distractions caused by clothing and increased campus security, among other goals.[149] Similarly, a federal trial court in West Virginia refused to intervene where a student was suspended for ten days for wearing a t-shirt demonstrating support for a peer who had been expelled from school due to his having been charged with attempted murder and armed robbery.[150] Rejecting the student's free speech claim, the court held that insofar as there was widespread concern about gang presence at the school, he could be disciplined even if the display on his shirt was passive and peaceful because it could have caused a disruption. Earlier, a federal trial court in Illinois upheld a board's authority to forbid male students from wearing earrings connected with gang membership even though females were permitted to wear such ornamentations.[151]

---

145. *Jacobs v. Clark County School Dist.*, 526 F.3d 419 [232 Educ. L. Rep. 578] (9th Cir. 2008).

146. *Bear v. Fleming*, 714 F.Supp.2d 972 [260 Educ. L. Rep. 779] (D.S.D. 2010).

147. *Chalifoux v. New Caney Indep. School Dist.*, 976 F.Supp. 659 [121 Educ. L. Rep. 751] (S.D. Tex. 1997).

148. *Stephenson v. Davenport Community School Dist.*, 110 F.3d 1303 [117 Educ. L. Rep. 443] (8th Cir. 1997).

149. *Phoenix Elem. School Dist. No. 1 v. Green*, 943 P.2d 836 [120 Educ. L. Rep. 1170] (Ariz. Ct. App. 1997).

150. *Brown ex rel. Brown v. Cabell County Bd. of Educ.*, 714 F.Supp.2d 587 [260 Educ. L. Rep. 767] (S.D.W.Va. 2010).

151. *Olesen v. Board of Educ. of School Dist. No. 228*, 676 F.Supp. 820 [44 Educ. L. Rep. 205] (N.D. Ill. 1987).

Turning to earrings specifically, an appellate court in Louisiana affirmed that educators could prohibit a male elementary school student, but not females, from wearing them since a school rule advanced the legitimate educational objective of inspiring discipline and a positive learning environment.[152] To date, the only two reported cases addressing body piercings, both of which arose in Kentucky and were resolved by the Sixth Circuit, upheld dress code policies that included prohibitions against body piercings other than earrings.[153] The rules against body piercings were not at the heart of either case.[154]

The federal trial court in New Mexico rejected a high school student's challenge to his dress code's prohibition against wearing "sagging" pants as a violation of his First Amendment expressive rights.[155] The court noted that wearing "sagging" pants was not a form of speech. In like manner, the federal trial court in Maryland indicated that a policy prohibiting students from wearing hats to school did not violate the First Amendment speech rights of a young woman who wanted to wear a head wrap to celebrate her cultural heritage.[156] The court declared that the rule was permissible since it was content-neutral and furthered the important governmental interest of providing a safe, respectful school environment that was conducive to learning. Also, a state court from Connecticut rejected a challenge filed by students who were expelled for violating a school's dress code policy.[157] The court was of the view that insofar as the policy of prohibiting students from wearing blue jeans was rationally related to the school board's goal of reducing disruption, taunting, theft, and loss of attention to course work, it did not violate their First Amendment rights to free expression.[158]

Student Grooming

Courts have reached mixed results as to grooming and hair-length for males as some permitted restrictions[159] to remain in effect while others

---

152. *Jones v. W.T. Henning Elementary School*, 721 So.2d 530 [131 Educ. L. Rep. 330] (La. Ct. App. 1998).

153. *See Blau v. Fort Thomas Pub. School Dist.*, 401 F.3d 381 [196 Educ. L. Rep. 118] (6th Cir. 2005); *Long v. Board of Educ. of Jefferson County, Ky.*, 121 F. Supp.2d 621 [149 Educ. L. Rep. 157] (W.D. Ky. 2000), *aff'd*, 21 Fed.Appx. 252 [160 Educ. L. Rep. 392] (6th Cir. 2001).

154. For an unreported case rejecting a challenge to a policy that limited body piercing to any place other than the ears during the school day, *see Bar–Navon v. School Bd. of Brevard County, Fla.*, 2007 WL 3284322 (M.D. Fla. 2007), *aff'd*, 290 Fed.Appx. 273 (11th Cir. 2008).

155. *Bivens v. Albuquerque Pub. Schools*, 899 F.Supp. 556 [104 Educ. L. Rep. 195] (D.N.M. 1995).

156. *Isaacs v. Board of Educ. of Howard County*, 40 F. Supp.2d 335 [134 Educ. L. Rep. 166] (D. Md. 1999).

157. *Byars v. City of Waterbury*, 795 A.2d 630 [164 Educ. L. Rep. 311] (Conn. Super. Ct. 2001).

158. *See also Bannister v. Paradis*, 316 F.Supp. 185 (D.N.H. 1970) (upholding a ban against blue jeans); *Fowler v. Williamson*, 251 S.E.2d 889 (N.C. Ct. App. 1979) (upholding a ban against wearing jeans to a graduation ceremony).

159. *Gfell v. Rickelman*, 441 F.2d 444 (6th Cir. 1971); *Freeman v. Flake*, 448 F.2d 258 (10th Cir. 1971), *cert. denied*, 405 U.S. 1032, 92 S.Ct. 1292, 31 L.Ed.2d 489 (1972); *Karr v. Schmidt*, 460 F.2d 609 (5th Cir. 1972), *cert. denied*, 409 U.S. 989, 93 S.Ct. 307, 34 L.Ed.2d 256 (1972); *Sherling v. Townley*, 464 F.2d 587 (5th Cir. 1972); *Zeller v. Donegal School Dist. Bd. of*

refused to allow limitations to stand.[160] In a case involving student-athletes, the Eleventh Circuit upheld a policy from Alabama requiring basketball and football players to be clean-shaven.[161] The court was satisfied that the policy was acceptable since it was rationally aimed at presenting the school in a favorable light, not at improving performance. Subsequently, in two separate cases, the Supreme Court of Texas agreed that school officials could set hair-length restrictions for males.[162]

A case involving grooming in a non-public school exemplifies the general rule. The Supreme Court of Rhode Island, reversing an earlier order to the contrary, reasoned that school officials could enforce a policy limiting the hair length of male students.[163] The court posited that insofar as the rule did not violate public policy, it was an enforceable provision of the school's educational contract with students.

[CASE NO. 102] STUDENT RIGHTS TO POLITICAL FREE SPEECH IN SCHOOLS, I

TINKER v. DES MOINES INDEPENDENT COMMUNITY SCHOOL DISTRICT

Supreme Court of the United States, 1969.
393 U.S. 503, 89 S.Ct. 733, 21 L.Ed.2d 731.

■ MR. JUSTICE FORTAS delivered the opinion of the Court.

Petitioner John F. Tinker, 15 years old, and petitioner Christopher Eckhardt, 16 years old, attended high schools in Des Moines. Petitioner Mary Beth Tinker, John's sister, was a 13–year–old student in junior high school.

In December 1965, a group of adults and students in Des Moines, Iowa, held a meeting at the Eckhardt home. The group determined to publicize their objections to the hostilities in Vietnam and their support for a truce by wearing black armbands during the holiday season and by fasting on December 16 and New Year's Eve. Petitioners and their parents had previously engaged in similar activities, and they decided to participate in the program.

The principals of the Des Moines schools became aware of the plan to wear armbands. On December 14, 1965, they met and adopted a policy that any student wearing an armband to school would be asked to remove it, and if he refused he would be suspended until he returned without the

Educ., 517 F.2d 600 (3d Cir. 1975); *Canady v. Bossier Parish School Bd.*, 240 F.3d 437 [151 Educ. L. Rep. 110] (5th Cir. 2001).

160. *Richards v. Thurston*, 424 F.2d 1281 (1st Cir. 1970); *Bishop v. Colaw*, 450 F.2d 1069 (8th Cir. 1971); *Massie v. Henry*, 455 F.2d 779 (4th Cir. 1972); *Arnold v. Carpenter*, 459 F.2d 939 (7th Cir. 1972); *Breese v. Smith,* 501 P.2d 159 (Alaska 1972).

161. *Davenport by Davenport v. Randolph County Bd. of Educ.*, 730 F.2d 1395 [16 Educ. L. Rep. 1116] (11th Cir. 1984).

162. *Barber v. Colorado Indep. School Dist.*, 901 S.W.2d 447 [101 Educ. L. Rep. 1241] (Tex. 1995); *Board of Trustees of Bastrop Indep. School Dist. v. Toungate*, 958 S.W.2d 365 [123 Educ. L. Rep. 392] (Tex. 1997), *reh'g of cause overruled* (Tex. 1998).

163. *Gorman v. St. Raphael Academy*, 853 A.2d 28 [189 Educ. L. Rep. 784] (R.I. 2004).

armband. Petitioners were aware of the regulation that the school authorities adopted.

On December 16, Mary Beth and Christopher wore black armbands to their schools. John Tinker wore his armband the next day. They were all sent home and suspended from school until they would come back without their armbands. They did not return to school until after the planned period for wearing armbands had expired—that is, until after New Year's Day. . . .

First Amendment rights, applied in light of the special characteristics of the school environment, are available to teachers and students. It can hardly be argued that either students or teachers shed their constitutional rights to freedom of speech or expression at the schoolhouse gate. This has been the unmistakable holding of this Court for almost 50 years. . . .

. . . On the other hand, the Court has repeatedly emphasized the need for affirming the comprehensive authority of the States and of school officials, consistent with fundamental constitutional safeguards, to prescribe and control conduct in the schools. . . .

The problem presented by the present case does not relate to regulation of the length of skirts or the type of clothing, to hair style or deportment. It does not concern aggressive, disruptive action or even group demonstrations. Our problem involves direct, primary First Amendment rights akin to "pure speech."

The school officials banned and sought to punish petitioners for a silent, passive, expression of opinion, unaccompanied by any disorder or disturbance on the part of petitioners. There is here no evidence whatever of petitioners' interference, actual or nascent, with the school's work or of collision with the rights of other students to be secure and to be let alone. Accordingly, this case does not concern speech or action that intrudes upon the work of the school or the rights of other students.

Only a few of the 18,000 students in the school system wore the black armbands. Only five students were suspended for wearing them. There is no indication that the work of the school or any class was disrupted. Outside the classrooms, a few students made hostile remarks to the children wearing armbands, but there were no threats or acts of violence on school premises.

The District Court concluded that the action of the school authorities was reasonable because it was based upon their fear of a disturbance from the wearing of the armbands. But, in our system, undifferentiated fear or apprehension of disturbance is not enough to overcome the right to freedom of expression. Any departure from absolute regimentation may cause trouble. Any variation from the majority's opinion may inspire fear. Any word spoken, in class, in the lunchroom or on the campus, that deviates from the views of another person, may start an argument or cause a disturbance. But our Constitution says we must take this risk; and our history says that it is this sort of hazardous freedom—this kind of openness—that is the basis of our national strength and of the independence and vigor of Americans who grow up and live in this relatively permissive, often disputatious society.

In order for the State in the person of school officials to justify prohibition of a particular expression of opinion, it must be able to show that its action was caused by something more than a mere desire to avoid the discomfort and unpleasantness that always accompany an unpopular viewpoint. Certainly where there is no finding and no showing that the exercise of the forbidden right would "materially and substantially interfere with the requirements of appropriate discipline in the operation of the school," the prohibition cannot be sustained.

In the present case, the District Court made no such finding, and our independent examination of the record fails to yield evidence that the school authorities had reason to anticipate that the wearing of the armbands would substantially interfere with the work of the school or impinge upon the rights of other students. Even an official memorandum prepared after the suspension that listed the reasons for the ban on wearing the armbands made no reference to the anticipation of such disruption.

On the contrary, the action of the school authorities appears to have been based upon an urgent wish to avoid the controversy which might result from the expression, even by the silent symbol of armbands, of opposition to this Nation's part in the conflagration in Vietnam. It is revealing, in this respect, that the meeting at which the school principals decided to issue the contested regulation was called in response to a student's statement to the journalism teacher in one of the schools that he wanted to write an article on Vietnam and have it published in the school paper.

It is also relevant that the school authorities did not purport to prohibit the wearing of all symbols of political or controversial significance. The record shows that students in some of the schools wore buttons relating to national political campaigns, and some even wore the Iron Cross, traditionally a symbol of nazism. The order prohibiting the wearing of armbands did not extend to these. Instead, a particular symbol—black armbands worn to exhibit opposition to this Nation's involvement in Vietnam—was singled out for prohibition. Clearly, the prohibition of expression of one particular opinion, at least without evidence that it is necessary to avoid material and substantial interference with school work or discipline, is not constitutionally permissible....

... The principal use to which the schools are dedicated is to accommodate students during prescribed hours for the purpose of certain types of activities. Among those activities is personal intercommunication among the students. This is not only an inevitable part of the process of attending school. It is also an important part of the educational process. A student's rights therefore, do not embrace merely the classroom hours. When he is in the cafeteria, or on the playing field, or on the campus during the authorized hours, he may express his opinions, even on controversial subjects like the conflict in Vietnam, if he does so "[without] materially and substantially interfering with ... appropriate discipline in the operation of the school" and without colliding with the rights of others. But conduct by the student, in class or out of it, which for any reason—whether it stems from time, place, or type of behavior—materially disrupts classwork or involves substantial disorder or invasion of the rights of others is, of course, not immunized by the constitutional guaranty of freedom of speech.

Under our Constitution, free speech is not a right that is given only to be so circumscribed that it exists in principle but not in fact. Freedom of expression would not truly exist if the right could be exercised only in an area that a benevolent government has provided as a safe haven for crackpots. The Constitution says that Congress (and the States) may not abridge the right to free speech. This provision means what it says. We properly read it to permit reasonable regulation of speech-connected activities in carefully restricted circumstances. But we do not confine the permissible exercise of First Amendment rights to a telephone booth or the four corners of a pamphlet, or to supervised and ordained discussion in a school classroom.

If a regulation were adopted by school officials forbidding discussion of the Vietnam conflict, or the expression by any student of opposition to it anywhere on school property except as part of a prescribed classroom exercise, it would be obvious that the regulation would violate the constitutional rights of students, at least if it could not be justified by a showing that the students' activities would materially and substantially disrupt the work and discipline of the school. . . . In the circumstances of the present case, the prohibition of the silent passive "witness of the armbands," as one of the children called it, is no less offensive to the constitution's guaranties.

As we have discussed the record does not demonstrate any facts which might reasonably have led school authorities to forecast substantial disruption of or material interference with school activities, and no disturbances or disorders on the school premises in fact occurred. . . .

Reversed and remanded.

NOTES

1. Both school officials and students cite *Tinker* almost ritualistically in student discipline cases since it establishes general guidelines applicable to many different situations.

2. The Supreme Court placed the burden of showing that student behavior might lead to a forecast of material and/or substantial disruption on school officials. To what extent should school officials be permitted to adopt preventive rules and when should they be required to wait for disruptions to occur before being able to act?

[CASE NO. 103]   STUDENT RIGHTS TO POLITICAL FREE SPEECH
IN SCHOOLS, II

GUZICK v. DREBUS

United States Court of Appeals, Sixth Circuit, 1970.
431 F.2d 594.

■ O'SULLIVAN, SENIOR CIRCUIT JUDGE.

Plaintiff–Appellant, Thomas Guzick, Jr.—prosecuting this action by his father and next friend, Thomas Guzick—appeals from dismissal of his complaint in the United States District Court for the Northern District of Ohio, Eastern Division. Plaintiff's complaint sought an injunction and other relief against defendant Drebus, the principal of Shaw High School in East Cleveland, Ohio, as well as against the Superintendent and Board of Education for the schools of said city. Plaintiff also asked for declaratory relief and damages.

The complaint charged that Thomas Guzick, Jr., a seventeen year old, eleventh grade student at Shaw High School, had been denied the right of free speech guaranteed to him by the United States Constitution's First Amendment. He asserted that this right had been denied him when he was suspended for refusing to remove, while in the classrooms and the school premises, a button which solicited participation in an anti-war demonstration that was to take place in Chicago on April 5. The legend of the button was:

"April 5 Chicago GI—Civilian Anti–War Demonstration Student Mobilization Committee"

. . .

On March 11, 1969, young Guzick and another student Havens, appeared at the office of defendant Drebus, principal of the high school, bringing with them a supply of pamphlets which advocated attendance at the same planned Chicago anti-war demonstration as was identified by the button. The boys were denied permission to distribute the pamphlets, and were also told to remove the buttons which both were then wearing. Guzick said that his lawyer, counsel for him in this litigation, told him that a United States Supreme Court decision entitled him to wear the button in school. Principal Drebus directed that he remove it and desist from wearing it in the school. Being told by Guzick that he would not obey, the principal suspended him and advised that such suspension would continue until Guzick obeyed. The other young man complied, and returned to school. Guzick did not, and has made no effort to return to school. This lawsuit promptly followed on March 17. . . .

The District Judge denied plaintiff's application for a preliminary injunction, and after a plenary evidentiary hearing, which was concluded on March 26, 1969, the complaint was dismissed. . . .

We affirm.

Plaintiff insists that the facts of this case bring it within the rule of *Tinker v. Des Moines Independent Community School District.* We are at once aware that unless *Tinker* can be distinguished, reversal is required. We consider that the facts of this case clearly provide such distinction.

The rule applied to appellant Guzick was of long standing—forbidding all wearing of buttons, badges, scarves and other means whereby the wearers identify themselves as supporters of a cause or bearing messages unrelated to their education. Such things as support the high school athletic teams or advertise a school play are not forbidden, The rule had its genesis in the days when fraternities were competing for the favor of the students and it has been uniformly enforced. The rule has continued as one of universal application and usefulness. While controversial buttons appeared from time to time, they were required to be removed as soon as the school authorities could get to them.

. . .

From the total evidence, including that of educators, school administrators and others having special relevant qualifications, the District Judge concluded that abrogation of the rule would inevitably result in collisions and disruptions which would seriously subvert Shaw High School as a place of education for its students, black and white.

1.   The Rule of *Tinker*.

Contrasting with the admitted long standing and uniform enforcement of Shaw's no symbol rule, the majority opinion in *Tinker* was careful to point out,

> "It is also relevant that the school authorities [in *Tinker*] did not purport to prohibit the wearing of all symbols of political or controversial significance...."

The armband demonstration in *Tinker* was a one time affair, with a date for its ending fixed in its original plan. Plaintiff here argues that Shaw's no symbol rule should be abrogated to accommodate his wish to be relieved from obeying it....

Further distinguishing *Tinker* from our case are their respective settings. No potential racial collisions were background to *Tinker,* whereas here the changing racial composition of Shaw High from all white to 70% black, made the no symbol rule of even greater good than had characterized its original adoption. In our view, school authorities should not be faulted for adhering to a relatively non-oppressive rule that will indeed serve our ultimate goal of meaningful integration of our public schools....

2.   Shaw High School's need for its Rule.

In *Tinker* the Court concluded that a regulation forbidding expressions opposing the Vietnam conflict anywhere on school property would violate the students' constitutional rights,

> "at least *if it could not be justified* by a showing that the students' activities would materially and substantially disrupt the work and discipline of the school." (Emphasis supplied.) ...

The District Judge was of the view that the situation at Shaw was "incendiary." The evidence justified such a view.

"The Court has concluded that if all buttons were permitted at Shaw High, many students would seek to wear buttons conveying an inflammatory or provocative message or which would be considered as an insult or affront to certain of the other students. Such buttons have been worn at Shaw High School in the past. One button of this nature, for example, contained the message 'Happy Easter, Dr. King.' This button caused a fight last year in the school cafeteria at Shaw. Other buttons, such as 'Black Power,' 'Say it loud, Black and Proud,' and buttons depicting a black mailed fist have been worn at Shaw and would likely be worn again, if permitted. These buttons would add to the already incendiary situation and would undoubtedly provoke further fighting among the students and lead to a material and substantial disruption of the educational process at Shaw High."

Further distinction from *Tinker* is provided by the long standing and *universal application* of Shaw's rule....

The District Judge here points out that for school authorities to allow some buttons and not others would create an unbearable burden of selection and enforcement....

In our view, the potentiality and the imminence of the admitted rebelliousness in the Shaw students support the wisdom of the no-symbol rule. Surely those charged with providing a place and atmosphere for educating young Americans should not have to fashion their disciplinary rules only after good order has been at least once demolished.

3. Conclusion.

We will not attempt extensive review of the many great decisions which have forbidden abridgment of free speech. We have been thrilled by their beautiful and impassioned language. They are part of our American heritage. None of these masterpieces, however, were composed or uttered to support the wearing of buttons in high school classrooms. We are not persuaded that enforcement of such a rule as Shaw High School's no-symbol proscription would have excited like judicial classics. Denying Shaw High School the right to enforce this small disciplinary rule could, and most likely would, impair the rights of its students to an education and the rights of its teachers to fulfill their responsibilities....

. . .

The complaint's contention that Guzick was denied equal protection of the law is not argued to this Court; neither is it now asserted that he was denied due process of law in the method by which the relevant discipline was imposed.

Judgment affirmed.

NOTES

1. Can you distinguish *Guzick* from *Tinker*?

2. Could *Tinker* have been resolved differently if the board prohibited all controversial symbols rather than only black armbands? How does the concept of invalidity for being overly-broad square with *Guzick*?

[CASE NO. 104]   BOARD POWER TO DISCIPLINE A STUDENT FOR
VULGAR SPEECH

BETHEL SCHOOL DISTRICT NO. 403 v. FRASER

Supreme Court of the United States, 1986.
478 U.S. 675, 106 S.Ct. 3159, 92 L.Ed.2d 549 [32 Educ. L Rep. 1243].

■ CHIEF JUSTICE BURGER delivered the opinion of the Court.

We granted certiorari to decide whether the First Amendment prevents
a school district from disciplining a high school student for giving a lewd
speech at a school assembly.

I

A

On April 26, 1983, respondent Matthew N. Fraser, a student at Bethel
High School in Bethel, Washington, delivered a speech nominating a fellow
student for student elective office. Approximately 600 high school students,
many of whom were 14–year–olds, attended the assembly. Students were
required to attend the assembly or to report to the study hall. The
assembly was part of a school-sponsored educational program in self-
government. Students who elected not to attend the assembly were required to report to study hall. During the entire speech, Fraser referred to
his candidate in terms of an elaborate, graphic, and explicit sexual metaphor.

Two of Fraser's teachers, with whom he discussed the contents of his
speech in advance, informed him that the speech was ''inappropriate and
that he probably should not deliver it'' and that his delivery of the speech
might have ''severe consequences.''

During Fraser's delivery of the speech, a school counselor observed the
reaction of students to the speech. Some students hooted and yelled; some
by gestures graphically simulated the sexual activities pointedly alluded to
in respondent's speech. Other students appeared to be bewildered and
embarrassed by the speech. One teacher reported that on the day following
the speech, she found it necessary to forgo a portion of the scheduled class
lesson in order to discuss the speech with the class.

A Bethel High School disciplinary rule prohibiting the use of obscene
language in the school provides:

''Conduct which materially and substantially interferes with the educational process is prohibited, including the use of obscene, profane
language or gestures.''

The morning after the assembly, the Assistant Principal called Fraser into
her office and notified him that the school considered his speech to have
been a violation of this rule. Fraser was presented with copies of five letters
submitted by teachers, describing his conduct at the assembly; he was given
a chance to explain his conduct, and he admitted to having given the speech
described and that he deliberately used sexual innuendo in the speech.
Fraser was then informed that he would be suspended for three days, and

that his name would be removed from the list of candidates for graduation speaker at the school's commencement exercises.

Fraser sought review of this disciplinary action through the School District's grievance procedures. The hearing officer determined that the speech given by respondent was "indecent, lewd, and offensive to the modesty and decency of many of the students and faculty in attendance at the assembly." The examiner determined that the speech fell within the ordinary meaning of "obscene," as used in the disruptive-conduct rule, and affirmed the discipline in its entirety. Fraser served two days of his suspension, and was allowed to return to school on the third day.

B

... Respondent alleged a violation of his First Amendment right to freedom of speech and sought both injunctive relief and monetary damages under 42 U.S.C.[A] § 1983.... The District Court awarded respondent $278 in damages, $12,750 in litigation costs and attorney's fees, and enjoined the School District from preventing respondent from speaking at the commencement ceremonies. Respondent, who had been elected graduation speaker by a write-in vote of his classmates, delivered a speech at the commencement ceremonies on June 8, 1983.

The Court of Appeals for the Ninth Circuit affirmed the judgment of the District Court....

... We reverse.

II

This Court acknowledged in *Tinker v. Des Moines Independent Community School Dist.*, that students do not "shed their constitutional rights to freedom of speech or expression at the schoolhouse gate." The Court of Appeals read that case as precluding any discipline of Fraser for indecent speech and lewd conduct in the school assembly. That court appears to have proceeded on the theory that the use of lewd and obscene speech in order to make what the speaker considered to be a point in a nominating speech for a fellow student was essentially the same as the wearing of an armband in *Tinker* as a form of protest or the expression of a political position.

The marked distinction between the political "message" of the armbands in *Tinker* and the sexual content of respondent's speech in this case seems to have been given little weight by the Court of Appeals. In upholding the students' right to engage in a nondisruptive, passive expression of a political viewpoint in *Tinker,* this Court was careful to note that the case did "not concern speech or action that intrudes upon the work of the schools or the rights of other students."

It is against this background that we turn to consider the level of First Amendment protection accorded to Fraser's utterances and actions before an official high school assembly attended by 600 students.

III

The role and purpose of the American public school system was well described by two historians, saying "public education must prepare pupils for citizenship in the Republic.... It must inculcate the habits and manners of civility as values in themselves conducive to happiness and as indispensable to the practice of self-government in the community and the nation." In *Ambach v. Norwick* we echoed the essence of this statement of the objectives of public education as the "inculcat[ion of] fundamental values necessary to the maintenance of a democratic political system."

These fundamental values of "habits and manners of civility" essential to a democratic society must, of course, include tolerance of divergent political and religious views, even when the views expressed may be unpopular. But these "fundamental values" must also take into account consideration of the sensibilities of others, and, in the case of a school, the sensibilities of fellow students. The undoubted freedom to advocate unpopular and controversial views in schools and classrooms must be balanced against the society's countervailing interest in teaching students the boundaries of socially appropriate behaviour. Even the most heated political discourse in a democratic society requires consideration for the personal sensibilities of the other participants and audiences.

In our Nation's legislative halls, where some of the most vigorous political debates in our society are carried on, there are rules prohibiting the use of expressions offensive to other participants in the debate.... Can it be that what is proscribed in the halls of Congress is beyond the reach of school officials to regulate?

The First Amendment guarantees wide freedom in matters of adult public discourse. A sharply divided Court upheld the right to express an antidraft viewpoint in a public place, albeit in terms highly offensive to most citizens. It does not follow, however, that simply because the use of an offensive form of expression may not be prohibited to adults making what the speaker considers a political point, that the same latitude must be permitted to children in a public school. In *New Jersey v. T.L.O.* we reaffirmed that the constitutional rights of students in public school are not automatically coextensive with the rights of adults in other settings....

Surely it is a highly appropriate function of public school education to prohibit the use of vulgar and offensive terms in public discourse. Indeed, the "fundamental values necessary to the maintenance of a democratic political system" disfavor the use of terms of debate highly offensive or highly threatening to others. Nothing in the Constitution prohibits the states from insisting that certain modes of expression are inappropriate and subject to sanctions. The inculcation of these values is truly the "work of the schools." The determination of what manner of speech in the classroom or in school assembly is inappropriate properly rests with the school board.

The process of educating our youth for citizenship in public schools is not confined to books, the curriculum, and the civics class; schools must teach by example the shared values of a civilized social order. Consciously or otherwise, teachers—and indeed the older students—demonstrate the appropriate form of civil discourse and political expression by their conduct and deportment in and out of class. Inescapably, like parents, they are role models. The schools, as instruments of the state, may determine that the essential lessons of civil, mature conduct cannot be conveyed in a school that tolerates lewd, indecent, or offensive speech and conduct such as that indulged in by this confused boy.

The pervasive sexual innuendo in Fraser's speech was plainly offensive to both teachers and students—indeed to any mature person. By glorifying male sexuality, and in its verbal content, the speech was acutely insulting to teenage girl students. The speech could well be seriously damaging to its less mature audience, many of whom were only 14 years old and on the threshold of awareness of human sexuality. Some students were reported as bewildered by the speech and the reaction of mimicry it provoked.

This Court's First Amendment jurisprudence has acknowledged limitations on the otherwise absolute interest of the speaker in reaching an unlimited audience where the speech is sexually explicit and the audience may include children. In *Ginsberg v. New York*, this Court upheld a New York statute banning the sale of sexually oriented material to minors, even though the material in question was entitled to First Amendment protection with respect to adults. And in addressing the question whether the First Amendment places any limit on the authority of public schools to remove books from a public school library, all Members of the Court, otherwise sharply divided, acknowledged that the school board has the authority to remove books that are vulgar. These cases recognize the obvious concern on the part of parents, and school authorities acting in loco parentis to protect children—especially in a captive audience—from exposure to sexually explicit, indecent, or lewd speech.

We have also recognized an interest in protecting minors from exposure to vulgar and offensive spoken language. . . .

We hold that petitioner School District acted entirely within its permissible authority in imposing sanctions upon Fraser in response to his offensively lewd and indecent speech. Unlike the sanctions imposed on the students wearing armbands in *Tinker,* the penalties imposed in this case were unrelated to any political viewpoint. The First Amendment does not prevent the school officials from determining that to permit a vulgar and lewd speech such as respondent's would undermine the school's basic educational mission. A high school assembly or classroom is no place for a sexually explicit monologue directed towards an unsuspecting audience of teenage students. Accordingly, it was perfectly appropriate for the school to disassociate itself to make the point to the pupils that vulgar speech and lewd conduct is wholly inconsistent with the "fundamental values" of public school education. . . .

IV

Respondent contends that the circumstances of his suspension violated due process because he had no way of knowing that the delivery of the speech in question would subject him to disciplinary sanctions. This argument is wholly without merit. We have recognized that "maintaining security and order in the schools requires a certain degree of flexibility in school disciplinary procedures, and we have respected the value of preserving the informality of the student-teacher relationship." Given the school's need to be able to impose disciplinary sanctions for a wide range of unanticipated conduct disruptive of the educational process, the school disciplinary rules need not be as detailed as a criminal code which imposes criminal sanctions. Two days' suspension from school does not rise to the level of a penal sanction calling for the full panoply of procedural due process protections applicable to a criminal prosecution. The school disciplinary rule proscribing "obscene" language and the prespeech admonitions of teachers gave adequate warning to Fraser that his lewd speech could subject him to sanctions.

The judgment of the Court of Appeals for the Ninth Circuit is

Reversed.

NOTES

1. Justice Brennan concurred in the judgment, but wrote "... separately to express my understanding of the breadth of the Court's holding," *Bethel School Dist. No. 403 v. Fraser*, at 688, which he placed in the framework of prior Supreme Court opinions. His concurrence repeated parts of the speech:

> Respondent gave the following speech at a high school assembly in support of a candidate for student government office:

> I know a man who is firm-he's firm in his pants, he's firm in his shirt, his character is firm-but most ... of all, his belief in you, the students of Bethel, is firm. Jeff Kuhlman is a man who takes his point and pounds it in. If necessary, he'll take an issue and nail it to the wall. He doesn't attack things in spurts-he drives hard, pushing and pushing until finally-he succeeds. Jeff is a man who will go to the very end—even the climax, for each and every one of you. So vote for Jeff for A.S.B. vice-president—he'll never come between you and the best our high school can be. *Id.* at 687.

In light of the contents of the speech, do you think that the punishment was appropriate?

2. The Supreme Court never defined vulgar or lewd, relying on a kind of "I know it when I see it" standard, consistent with Justice Stewart's concurrence in *Jacobellis v. State of Ohio*, 378 U.S. 184, 197, 84 S.Ct. 1676, 12 L.Ed.2d 793 (1964) a case dealing with "... hard-core-pornography. I shall not today attempt further to define the kinds of material I understand to be embraced within that shorthand description; and perhaps I could never succeed in intelligibly doing so. But I know it when I see it, and the motion picture involved in this case is not that."

3. Should the student have been subjected to the same punishment if he had not mentioned the contents of his speech to teachers? Should a student be punished for delivering such a speech at a school-sponsored "Comedy Club" on a Saturday night that members of the audience had to purchase tickets to attend?

[CASE NO. 105]   REGULATING THE CONTENT OF A NEWSPAPER
PRODUCED BY A JOURNALISM CLASS

HAZELWOOD SCHOOL DISTRICT v. KUHLMEIER

Supreme Court of the United States, 1988.
484 U.S. 260, 108 S.Ct. 562, 98 L.Ed.2d 592 [43 Educ. L. Rep. 515].

■ JUSTICE WHITE delivered the opinion of the Court.

This case concerns the extent to which educators may exercise editorial
control over the contents of a high school newspaper produced as part of
the school's journalism curriculum.

I

Petitioners are the Hazelwood School District in St. Louis County,
Missouri; various school officials; Robert Eugene Reynolds, the principal of
Hazelwood East High School, and Howard Emerson, a teacher in the school
district. Respondents are three former Hazelwood East students who were
staff members of Spectrum, the school newspaper. They contend that
school officials violated their First Amendment rights by deleting two pages
of articles from the May 13, 1983, issue of Spectrum.

Spectrum was written and edited by the Journalism II class at Hazelwood East. The newspaper was published every three weeks or so during
the 1982–1983 school year. More than 4,500 copies of the newspaper were
distributed during that year to students, school personnel, and members of
the community.

The Board of Education allocated funds from its annual budget for the
printing of Spectrum. These funds were supplemented by proceeds from
sales of the newspaper. The printing expenses during the 1982–1983 school
year totaled $4,668.50; revenue from sales was $1,166.84. The other costs
associated with the newspaper—such as supplies, textbooks, and a portion
of the journalism teacher's salary—were borne entirely by the Board.

The Journalism II course was taught by Robert Stergos for most of the
1982–1983 academic year. Stergos left Hazelwood East to take a job in
private industry on April 29, 1983, when the May 13 edition of Spectrum
was nearing completion, and petitioner Emerson took his place as newspaper adviser for the remaining weeks of the term.

The practice at Hazelwood East during the spring 1983 semester was
for the journalism teacher to submit page proofs of each Spectrum issue to
Principal Reynolds for his review prior to publication. On May 10, Emerson
delivered the proofs of the May 13 edition to Reynolds, who objected to two
of the articles scheduled to appear in that edition. One of the stories
described three Hazelwood East students' experiences with pregnancy; the
other discussed the impact of divorce on students at the school.

Reynolds was concerned that, although the pregnancy story used false
names "to keep the identity of these girls a secret," the pregnant students
still might be identifiable from the text. He also believed that the article's
references to sexual activity and birth control were inappropriate for some

of the younger students at the school. In addition, Reynolds was concerned that a student identified by name in the divorce story had complained that her father "wasn't spending enough time with my mom, my sister and I" prior to the divorce, "was always out of town on business or out late playing cards with the guys," and "always argued about everything" with her mother. Reynolds believed that the student's parents should have been given an opportunity to respond to these remarks or to consent to their publication. He was unaware that Emerson had deleted the student's name from the final version of the article.

Reynolds believed that there was no time to make the necessary changes in the stories before the scheduled press run and that the newspaper would not appear before the end of the school year if printing were delayed to any significant extent. He concluded that his only options under the circumstances were to publish a four-page newspaper instead of the planned six-page newspaper, eliminating the two pages on which the offending stories appeared, or to publish no newspaper at all. Accordingly, he directed Emerson to withhold from publication the two pages containing the stories on pregnancy and divorce. He informed his superiors of the decision, and they concurred.

Respondents subsequently commenced this action. . . .

II

Students in the public schools do not "shed their constitutional rights to freedom of speech or expression at the schoolhouse gate." They cannot be punished merely for expressing their personal views on the school premises—whether "in the cafeteria, or on the playing field, or on the campus during the authorized hours"—unless school authorities have reason to believe that such expression will "substantially interfere with the work of the school or impinge upon the rights of other students."

We have nonetheless recognized that the First Amendment rights of students in the public schools "are not automatically coextensive with the rights of adults in other settings," and must be "applied in light of the special characteristics of the school environment." A school need not tolerate student speech that is inconsistent with its "basic educational mission," even though the government could not censor similar speech outside the school. Accordingly, we held in *Bethel School District No. 403 v. Fraser* that a student could be disciplined for having delivered a speech that was "sexually explicit" but not legally obscene at an official school assembly, because the school was entitled to "disassociate itself" from the speech in a manner that would demonstrate to others that such vulgarity is "wholly inconsistent with the 'fundamental values' of public school education." We thus recognized that "[t]he determination of what manner of speech in the classroom or in school assembly is inappropriate properly rests with the school board," rather than with the federal courts. It is in this context that respondents' First Amendment claims must be considered.

A

We deal first with the question whether Spectrum may appropriately be characterized as a forum for public expression. The public schools do not possess all of the attributes of streets, parks, and other traditional public forums that "time out of mind, have been used for purposes of assembly, communicating thoughts between citizens, and discussing public questions." Hence, school facilities may be deemed to be public forums only if school authorities have "by policy or by practice" opened those facilities "for indiscriminate use by the general public," or by some segment of the public, such as student organizations. If the facilities have instead been reserved for other intended purposes, "communicative or otherwise," then no public forum has been created, and school officials may impose reasonable restrictions on the speech of students, teachers, and other members of the school community. "The government does not create a public forum by inaction or by permitting limited discourse, but only by intentionally opening a nontraditional forum for public discourse."

The policy of school officials toward Spectrum was reflected in Hazelwood School Board Policy 348.51 and the Hazelwood East Curriculum Guide. Board Policy 348.51 provided that "[s]chool sponsored publications are developed within the adopted curriculum and its educational implications in regular classroom activities." The Hazelwood East Curriculum Guide described the Journalism II course as a "laboratory situation in which the students publish the school newspaper applying skills they have learned in Journalism I." The lessons that were to be learned from the Journalism II course, according to the Curriculum Guide, included development of journalistic skills under deadline pressure, "the legal, moral, and ethical restrictions imposed upon journalists within the school community," and "responsibility and acceptance of criticism for articles of opinion." Journalism II was taught by a faculty member during regular class hours. Students received grades and academic credit for their performance in the course.

School officials did not deviate in practice from their policy that production of Spectrum was to be part of the educational curriculum and a "regular classroom activit[y]." The District Court found that Robert Stergos, the journalism teacher during most of the 1982–1983 school year, "both had the authority to exercise and in fact exercised a great deal of control over Spectrum." For example, Stergos selected the editors of the newspaper, scheduled publication dates, decided the number of pages for each issue, assigned story ideas to class members, advised students on the development of their stories, reviewed the use of quotations, edited stories, selected and edited the letters to the editor, and dealt with the printing company. Many of these decisions were made without consultation with the Journalism II students. The District Court thus found it "clear that Mr. Stergos was the final authority with respect to almost every aspect of the production and publication of Spectrum, including its content." Moreover, after each Spectrum issue had been finally approved by Stergos or his successor, the issue still had to be reviewed by Principal Reynolds prior to publication. Respondents' assertion that they had believed that they could publish "practically anything" in Spectrum was therefore dismissed by the District Court as simply "not credible." These factual findings are amply supported by the record, and were not rejected as clearly erroneous by the Court of Appeals.

... School officials did not evince either "by policy or by practice" any intent to open the pages of Spectrum to "indiscriminate use" by its student reporters and editors, or by the student body generally. Instead, they "reserve[d] the forum for its intended purpos[e]" as a supervised learning experience for journalism students. Accordingly, school officials were entitled to regulate the contents of Spectrum in any reasonable manner. It is this standard, rather than our decision in *Tinker v. Des Moines Independent Community School Dist.,* that governs this case.

B

The question whether the First Amendment requires a school to tolerate particular student speech—the question that we addressed in *Tinker*—is different from the question whether the First Amendment requires a school affirmatively to promote particular student speech. The former question addresses educators' ability to silence a student's personal expression that happens to occur on the school premises. The latter question concerns educators' authority over school-sponsored publications, theatrical productions, and other expressive activities that students, parents, and members of the public might reasonably perceive to bear the imprimatur of the school. These activities may fairly be characterized as part of the school curriculum, whether or not they occur in a traditional classroom setting, so long as they are supervised by faculty members and designed to impart particular knowledge or skills to student participants and audiences.

Educators are entitled to exercise greater control over this second form of student expression to assure that participants learn whatever lessons the activity is designed to teach, that readers or listeners are not exposed to material that may be inappropriate for their level of maturity, and that the views of the individual speaker are not erroneously attributed to the school. Hence, a school may in its capacity as publisher of a school newspaper or producer of a school play "disassociate itself" not only from speech that would "substantially interfere with [its] work ... or impinge upon the rights of other students," but also from speech that is, for example, ungrammatical, poorly written, inadequately researched, biased or prejudiced, vulgar or profane, or unsuitable for immature audiences. A school must be able to set high standards for the student speech that is disseminated under its auspices—standards that may be higher than those demanded by some newspaper publishers or theatrical producers in the "real" world—and may refuse to disseminate student speech that does not meet those standards. In addition, a school must be able to take into account the emotional maturity of the intended audience in determining whether to disseminate student speech on potentially sensitive topics, which might range from the existence of Santa Clause in an elementary school setting to the particulars of teenage sexual activity in a high school setting. A school must also retain the authority to refuse to sponsor student speech that might reasonably be perceived to advocate drug or alcohol use, irresponsible sex, or conduct otherwise inconsistent with "the shared values of a civilized social order," or to associate the school with any position other than neutrality on matters of political controversy. Otherwise, the schools would be unduly constrained from fulfilling their role as "a principal instrument in awakening the child to cultural values, in preparing him for later professional training, and in helping him to adjust normally to his environment."

Accordingly, we conclude that the standard articulated in *Tinker* for determining when a school may punish student expression need not also be the standard for determining when a school may refuse to lend its name and resources to the dissemination of student expression. Instead, we hold that educators do not offend the First Amendment by exercising editorial control over the style and content of student speech in school-sponsored expressive activities so long as their actions are reasonably related to legitimate pedagogical concerns.

This standard is consistent with our oft-expressed view that the education of the Nation's youth is primarily the responsibility of parents, teachers, and state and local school officials, and not of federal judges. It is only when the decision to censor a school-sponsored publication, theatrical production, or other vehicle of student expression has no valid educational purpose that the First Amendment is so "directly and sharply implicate[d]" as to require judicial intervention to protect students' constitutional rights.

III

We also conclude that Principal Reynolds acted reasonably in requiring the deletion from the May 13 issue of Spectrum of the pregnancy article, the divorce article, and the remaining articles that were to appear on the same pages of the newspaper.

The initial paragraph of the pregnancy article declared that "[a]ll names have been changed to keep the identity of these girls a secret." The principal concluded that the students' anonymity was not adequately protected, however, given the other identifying information in the article and the small number of pregnant students at the school. Indeed, a teacher at the school credibly testified that she could positively identify at least one of the girls and possibly all three. It is likely that many students at Hazelwood East would have been at least as successful in identifying the girls. Reynolds therefore could reasonably have feared that the article violated whatever pledge of anonymity had been given to the pregnant students. In addition, he could reasonably have been concerned that the article was not sufficiently sensitive to the privacy interests of the students' boyfriends and parents, who were discussed in the article but who were given no opportunity to consent to its publication or to offer a response. The article did not contain graphic accounts of sexual activity. The girls did comment in the article, however, concerning their sexual histories and their use or nonuse of birth control. It was not unreasonable for the principal to have concluded that such frank talk was inappropriate in a school-sponsored publication distributed to 14–year–old freshmen and presumably taken home to be read by students' even younger brothers and sisters.

The student who was quoted by name in the version of the divorce article seen by Principal Reynolds made comments sharply critical of her father. The principal could reasonably have concluded that an individual publicly identified as an inattentive parent—indeed, as one who chose "playing cards with the guys" over home and family—was entitled to an opportunity to defend himself as a matter of journalistic fairness. These concerns were shared by both of Spectrum's faculty advisers for the 1982–1983 school year, who testified that they would not have allowed the article to be printed without deletion of the student's name.

Principal Reynolds testified credibly at trial that, at the time that he reviewed the proofs of the May 13 issue during an extended telephone conversation with Emerson, he believed that there was no time to make any changes in the articles, and that the newspaper had to be printed immediately or not at all. It is true that Reynolds did not verify whether the necessary modifications could still have been made in the articles, and that Emerson did not volunteer the information that printing could be delayed until the changes were made. We nonetheless agree with the District Court that the decision to excise the two pages containing the problematic articles was reasonable given the particular circumstances of this case. These circumstances included the very recent replacement of Stergos by Emerson, who may not have been entirely familiar with Spectrum editorial and production procedures, and the pressure felt by Reynolds to make an immediate decision so that students would not be deprived of the newspaper altogether.

In sum, we cannot reject as unreasonable Principal Reynolds' conclusion that neither the pregnancy article nor the divorce article was suitable for publication in Spectrum. Reynolds could reasonably have concluded that the students who had written and edited these articles had not sufficiently mastered those portions of the Journalism II curriculum that pertained to the treatment of controversial issues and personal attacks, the need to protect the privacy of individuals whose most intimate concerns are to be revealed in the newspaper, and "the legal, moral, and ethical restrictions imposed upon journalists within [a] school community" that includes adolescent subjects and readers. Finally, we conclude that the principal's decision to delete two pages of Spectrum, rather than to delete only the offending articles or to require that they be modified, was reasonable under the circumstances as he understood them. Accordingly, no violation of First Amendment rights occurred.

The judgment of the Court of Appeals for the Eighth Circuit is therefore

Reversed.

NOTES

1. The Court suggested that it is unnecessary to have specific written policies covering prepublication controls over school-sponsored publications since doing so could unduly constrain the ability of teachers to educate. Is this reasonable? Should boards adopt such policies?

2. From an educational viewpoint, were both issues equally as problematic? Would, or should, the result be the same today? Would it be the same in all locations?

3. In an interesting, albeit non-publication case, a federal trial court in Missouri ruled that a superintendent could prevent a school marching band from playing the song "White Rabbit" because it was used to promote illegal drug use. *McCann v. Fort Zumwalt School Dist.*, 50 F. Supp.2d 918 [136 Educ. L. Rep. 390] (E.D. Mo. 1999).

[CASE NO. 106] LIMITING STUDENT SPEECH RELATED TO DRUGS

MORSE v. FREDERICK

Supreme Court of the United States, 2007.
551 U.S. 393, 127 S.Ct. 2618, 168 L.Ed.2d 290 [220 Educ. L. Rep. 50].

■ CHIEF JUSTICE ROBERTS delivered the opinion of the Court.

At a school-sanctioned and school-supervised event, a high school principal saw some of her students unfurl a large banner conveying a message she reasonably regarded as promoting illegal drug use. Consistent with established school policy prohibiting such messages at school events, the principal directed the students to take down the banner. One student—among those who had brought the banner to the event—refused to do so. The principal confiscated the banner and later suspended the student. The Ninth Circuit held that the principal's actions violated the First Amendment, and that the student could sue the principal for damages.

Our cases make clear that students do not "shed their constitutional rights to freedom of speech or expression at the schoolhouse gate." At the same time, we have held that "the constitutional rights of students in public school are not automatically coextensive with the rights of adults in other settings," and that the rights of students "must be 'applied in light of the special characteristics of the school environment.'" Consistent with these principles, we hold that schools may take steps to safeguard those entrusted to their care from speech that can reasonably be regarded as encouraging illegal drug use. We conclude that the school officials in this case did not violate the First Amendment by confiscating the pro-drug banner and suspending the student responsible for it.

I

On January 24, 2002, the Olympic Torch Relay passed through Juneau, Alaska, on its way to the winter games in Salt Lake City, Utah. The torchbearers were to proceed along a street in front of Juneau–Douglas High School (JDHS) while school was in session. Petitioner Deborah Morse, the school principal, decided to permit staff and students to participate in the Torch Relay as an approved social event or class trip. Students were allowed to leave class to observe the relay from either side of the street. Teachers and administrative officials monitored the students' actions.

Respondent Joseph Frederick, a JDHS senior, was late to school that day. When he arrived, he joined his friends (all but one of whom were JDHS students) across the street from the school to watch the event. Not all the students waited patiently. Some became rambunctious, throwing plastic cola bottles and snowballs and scuffling with their classmates. As the torchbearers and camera crews passed by, Frederick and his friends unfurled a 14–foot banner bearing the phrase: "BONG HiTS 4 JESUS." The large banner was easily readable by the students on the other side of the street.

Principal Morse immediately crossed the street and demanded that the banner be taken down. Everyone but Frederick complied. Morse confiscated the banner and told Frederick to report to her office, where she suspended him for 10 days. Morse later explained that she told Frederick to take the banner down because she thought it encouraged illegal drug use, in violation of established school policy. Juneau School Board Policy No. 5520 states: "The Board specifically prohibits any assembly or public expression that ... advocates the use of substances that are illegal to minors...." In addition, Juneau School Board Policy No. 5850 subjects "[p]upils who participate in approved social events and class trips" to the same student conduct rules that apply during the regular school program.

Frederick administratively appealed his suspension, but the Juneau School District Superintendent upheld it, limiting it to time served (8 days). In a memorandum setting forth his reasons, the superintendent determined that Frederick had displayed his banner "in the midst of his fellow students, during school hours, at a school-sanctioned activity." He further explained that Frederick "was not disciplined because the principal of the school 'disagreed' with his message, but because his speech appeared to advocate the use of illegal drugs."

. . .

Relying on our decision in [Bethel School District No. 403 v.] Fraser, the superintendent concluded that the principal's actions were permissible because Frederick's banner was "speech or action that intrudes upon the work of the schools." The Juneau School District Board of Education upheld the suspension.

Frederick then filed suit under 42 U.S.C.[A.] § 1983, alleging that the school board and Morse had violated his First Amendment rights. He sought declaratory and injunctive relief, unspecified compensatory damages, punitive damages, and attorney's fees. The District Court granted summary judgment for the school board and Morse, ruling that they were entitled to qualified immunity and that they had not infringed Frederick's First Amendment rights. The court found that Morse reasonably interpreted the banner as promoting illegal drug use—a message that "directly contravened the Board's policies relating to drug abuse prevention." Under the circumstances, the court held that "Morse had the authority, if not the obligation, to stop such messages at a school-sanctioned activity."

The Ninth Circuit reversed. Deciding that Frederick acted during a "school-authorized activit[y]," and "proceed[ing] on the basis that the banner expressed a positive sentiment about marijuana use," the court nonetheless found a violation of Frederick's First Amendment rights because the school punished Frederick without demonstrating that his speech gave rise to a "risk of substantial disruption." The court further concluded that Frederick's right to display his banner was so "clearly established" that a reasonable principal in Morse's position would have understood that her actions were unconstitutional, and that Morse was therefore not entitled to qualified immunity.

We granted certiorari on two questions: whether Frederick had a First Amendment right to wield his banner, and, if so, whether that right was so clearly established that the principal may be held liable for damages. We resolve the first question against Frederick, and therefore have no occasion to reach the second.

II

At the outset, we reject Frederick's argument that this is not a school speech case-as has every other authority to address the question. The event occurred during normal school hours. It was sanctioned by Principal Morse "as an approved social event or class trip" and the school district's rules expressly provide that pupils in "approved social events and class trips are subject to district rules for student conduct." Teachers and administrators were interspersed among the students and charged with supervising them. The high school band and cheerleaders performed. Frederick, standing among other JDHS students across the street from the school, directed his banner toward the school, making it plainly visible to most students. Under these circumstances, we agree with the superintendent that Frederick cannot "stand in the midst of his fellow students, during school hours, at a school-sanctioned activity and claim he is not at school." There is some uncertainty at the outer boundaries as to when courts should apply school-speech precedents, but not on these facts.

III

The message on Frederick's banner is cryptic. It is no doubt offensive to some, perhaps amusing to others. To still others, it probably means nothing at all. Frederick himself claimed "that the words were just non-sense meant to attract television cameras." But Principal Morse thought the banner would be interpreted by those viewing it as promoting illegal drug use, and that interpretation is plainly a reasonable one.

As Morse later explained in a declaration, when she saw the sign, she thought that "the reference to a 'bong hit' would be widely understood by high school students and others as referring to smoking marijuana." She further believed that "display of the banner would be construed by students, District personnel, parents and others witnessing the display of the banner, as advocating or promoting illegal drug use"—in violation of school policy.

We agree with Morse. At least two interpretations of the words on the banner demonstrate that the sign advocated the use of illegal drugs. First, the phrase could be interpreted as an imperative: "[Take] bong hits . . ."— a message equivalent, as Morse explained in her declaration, to "smoke marijuana" or "use an illegal drug." Alternatively, the phrase could be viewed as celebrating drug use—"bong hits [are a good thing]," or "[we take] bong hits"—and we discern no meaningful distinction between celebrating illegal drug use in the midst of fellow students and outright advocacy or promotion.

The pro-drug interpretation of the banner gains further plausibility given the paucity of alternative meanings the banner might bear. The best Frederick can come up with is that the banner is "meaningless and funny." The dissent similarly refers to the sign's message as "curious," "ambiguous," "nonsense," "ridiculous," "obscure," "silly," "quixotic," and "stupid." Gibberish is surely a possible interpretation of the words on the banner, but it is not the only one, and dismissing the banner as meaningless ignores its undeniable reference to illegal drugs.

The dissent mentions Frederick's "credible and uncontradicted explanation for the message—he just wanted to get on television." But that is a description of Frederick's *motive* for displaying the banner; it is not an interpretation of what the banner says. The *way* Frederick was going to fulfill his ambition of appearing on television was by unfurling a pro-drug banner at a school event, in the presence of teachers and fellow students.

Elsewhere in its opinion, the dissent emphasizes the importance of political speech and the need to foster "national debate about a serious issue," as if to suggest that the banner is political speech. But not even Frederick argues that the banner conveys any sort of political or religious message. Contrary to the dissent's suggestion, this is plainly not a case about political debate over the criminalization of drug use or possession.

IV

The question thus becomes whether a principal may, consistent with the First Amendment, restrict student speech at a school event, when that speech is reasonably viewed as promoting illegal drug use. We hold that she may.

In *Tinker,* this Court made clear that "First Amendment rights, applied in light of the special characteristics of the school environment, are available to teachers and students." *Tinker* involved a group of high school students who decided to wear black armbands to protest the Vietnam War. School officials learned of the plan and then adopted a policy prohibiting students from wearing armbands. When several students nonetheless wore armbands to school, they were suspended. The students sued, claiming that their First Amendment rights had been violated, and this Court agreed.

Tinker held that student expression may not be suppressed unless school officials reasonably conclude that it will "materially and substantially disrupt the work and discipline of the school." The essential facts of *Tinker* are quite stark, implicating concerns at the heart of the First Amendment. The students sought to engage in political speech, using the armbands to express their "disapproval of the Vietnam hostilities and their advocacy of a truce, to make their views known, and, by their example, to influence others to adopt them." Political speech, of course, is "at the core of what the First Amendment is designed to protect." The only interest the Court discerned underlying the school's actions was the "mere desire to avoid the discomfort and unpleasantness that always accompany an unpopular viewpoint," or "an urgent wish to avoid the controversy which might result from the expression." That interest was not enough to justify banning "a silent, passive expression of opinion, unaccompanied by any disorder or disturbance."

This Court's next student speech case was *Fraser*. Matthew Fraser was suspended for delivering a speech before a high school assembly in which he employed what this Court called "an elaborate, graphic, and explicit sexual metaphor." Analyzing the case under *Tinker*, the District Court and Court of Appeals found no disruption, and therefore no basis for disciplining Fraser. This Court reversed, holding that the "School District acted entirely within its permissible authority in imposing sanctions upon Fraser in response to his offensively lewd and indecent speech."

The mode of analysis employed in *Fraser* is not entirely clear . . . .

We need not resolve this debate to decide this case. For present purposes, it is enough to distill from *Fraser* two basic principles. First, *Fraser's* holding demonstrates that "the constitutional rights of students in public school are not automatically coextensive with the rights of adults in other settings." Had Fraser delivered the same speech in a public forum outside the school context, it would have been protected. In school, however, Fraser's First Amendment rights were circumscribed "in light of the special characteristics of the school environment." Second, *Fraser* established that the mode of analysis set forth in *Tinker* is not absolute. Whatever approach *Fraser* employed, it certainly did not conduct the "substantial disruption" analysis prescribed by *Tinker*.

Our most recent student speech case, [*Hazelwood School District v.*] *Kuhlmeier*, concerned "expressive activities that students, parents, and members of the public might reasonably perceive to bear the imprimatur of the school." Staff members of a high school newspaper sued their school when it chose not to publish two of their articles. The Court of Appeals analyzed the case under *Tinker*, ruling in favor of the students because it found no evidence of material disruption to classwork or school discipline. This Court reversed, holding that "educators do not offend the First Amendment by exercising editorial control over the style and content of student speech in school-sponsored expressive activities so long as their actions are reasonably related to legitimate pedagogical concerns."

Kuhlmeier does not control this case because no one would reasonably believe that Frederick's banner bore the school's imprimatur. The case is nevertheless instructive because it confirms both principles cited above. *Kuhlmeier* acknowledged that schools may regulate some speech "even though the government could not censor similar speech outside the school." And, like *Fraser*, it confirms that the rule of *Tinker* is not the only basis for restricting student speech.

Drawing on the principles applied in our student speech cases, we have held in the Fourth Amendment context that "while children assuredly do not 'shed their constitutional rights . . . at the schoolhouse gate,' . . . the nature of those rights is what is appropriate for children in school." In particular, "the school setting requires some easing of the restrictions to which searches by public authorities are ordinarily subject."

Even more to the point, these cases also recognize that deterring drug use by schoolchildren is an "important-indeed, perhaps compelling" interest. Drug abuse can cause severe and permanent damage to the health and well-being of young people: "School years are the time when the physical, psychological, and addictive effects of drugs are most severe. Maturing nervous systems are more critically impaired by intoxicants than mature ones are; childhood losses in learning are lifelong and profound; children grow chemically dependent more quickly than adults, and their record of recovery is depressingly poor. And of course the effects of a drug-infested school are visited not just upon the users, but upon the entire student body and faculty, as the educational process is disrupted."

Just five years ago, we wrote: "The drug abuse problem among our Nation's youth has hardly abated since *Vernonia* was decided in 1995. In fact, evidence suggests that it has only grown worse."

The problem remains serious today. About half of American 12th graders have used an illicit drug, as have more than a third of 10th graders and about one-fifth of 8th graders. Nearly one in four 12th graders has used an illicit drug in the past month. Some 25% of high schoolers say that they have been offered, sold, or given an illegal drug on school property within the past year.

Congress has declared that part of a school's job is educating students about the dangers of illegal drug use. It has provided billions of dollars to support state and local drug-prevention programs, and required that schools receiving federal funds under the Safe and Drug–Free Schools and Communities Act of 1994 certify that their drug prevention programs "convey a clear and consistent message that . . . the illegal use of drugs [is] wrong and harmful."

Thousands of school boards throughout the country—including JDHS—have adopted policies aimed at effectuating this message. Those school boards know that peer pressure is perhaps "the single most important factor leading schoolchildren to take drugs," and that students are more likely to use drugs when the norms in school appear to tolerate such behavior. Student speech celebrating illegal drug use at a school event, in the presence of school administrators and teachers, thus poses a particular challenge for school officials working to protect those entrusted to their care from the dangers of drug abuse.

The "special characteristics of the school environment" and the governmental interest in stopping student drug abuse—reflected in the policies of Congress and myriad school boards, including JDHS—allow schools to restrict student expression that they reasonably regard as promoting illegal drug use. *Tinker* warned that schools may not prohibit student speech because of "undifferentiated fear or apprehension of disturbance" or "a mere desire to avoid the discomfort and unpleasantness that always accompany an unpopular viewpoint." The danger here is far more serious and palpable. The particular concern to prevent student drug abuse at issue here, embodied in established school policy, extends well beyond an abstract desire to avoid controversy.

Petitioners urge us to adopt the broader rule that Frederick's speech is proscribable because it is plainly "offensive" as that term is used in *Fraser*. We think this stretches *Fraser* too far; that case should not be read to encompass any speech that could fit under some definition of "offensive." After all, much political and religious speech might be perceived as offensive to some. The concern here is not that Frederick's speech was offensive, but that it was reasonably viewed as promoting illegal drug use.

Although accusing this decision of doing "serious violence to the First Amendment" by authorizing "viewpoint discrimination," the dissent concludes that "it might well be appropriate to tolerate some targeted viewpoint discrimination in this unique setting" Nor do we understand the dissent to take the position that schools are required to tolerate student advocacy of illegal drug use at school events, even if that advocacy falls short of inviting "imminent" lawless action. And even the dissent recognizes that the issues here are close enough that the principal should not be held liable in damages, but should instead enjoy qualified immunity for her actions. Stripped of rhetorical flourishes, then, the debate between the dissent and this opinion is less about constitutional first principles than about whether Frederick's banner constitutes promotion of illegal drug use. We have explained our view that it does. The dissent's contrary view on that relatively narrow question hardly justifies sounding the First Amendment bugle.

* * *

School principals have a difficult job, and a vitally important one. When Frederick suddenly and unexpectedly unfurled his banner, Morse had to decide to act—or not act—on the spot. It was reasonable for her to conclude that the banner promoted illegal drug use—in violation of established school policy—and that failing to act would send a powerful message to the students in her charge, including Frederick, about how serious the school was about the dangers of illegal drug use. The First Amendment does not require schools to tolerate at school events student expression that contributes to those dangers.

The judgment of the United States Court of Appeals for the Ninth Circuit is reversed, and the case is remanded for further proceedings consistent with this opinion.

It is so ordered.

NOTES

1. Justice Alito, joined by Justice Kennedy, in a concurrence that received a fair amount of attention, agreed with restricting speech advocating illegal drug use but would have gone no further, refusing to extend such a ban to, for example, political or social issues. Is this an apt reading of *Morse*?

2. In a dissent joined by Justices Ginsburg and Souter, Justice Stevens maintained that "I find it hard to believe the Court would support punishing [the student] for flying a 'WINE SiPS 4 JESUS' banner—which could quite reasonably be construed either as a protected religious message or as a pro-alcohol message— the breathtaking sweep of its opinion suggests it would." Is this a fair comparison

with the principal's interpreting the original sign as supporting the use of illegal drugs? *Morse*, 551 U.S. 393 at 446, 127 S.Ct. 2618 at 2650.

[CASE NO. 107]   STUDENT PUNISHED FOR AN INTERNET POSTING

KOWALSKI v. BERKELEY COUNTY SCHOOLS

United States Court of Appeals, Fourth Circuit, 2011.
652 F.3d 565.

■ NIEMEYER, CIRCUIT JUDGE:

When Kara Kowalski was a senior at Musselman High School in Berkeley County, West Virginia, school administrators suspended her from school for five days for creating and posting to a MySpace.com Web page called "S.A.S.H.," which Kowalski claims stood for "Students Against Sluts Herpes" and which was largely dedicated to ridiculing a fellow student. Kowalski commenced this action, under 42 U.S.C. § 1983, against the Berkeley County School District and five of its officers, contending that in disciplining her, the defendants violated her free speech and due process rights under the First and Fourteenth Amendments. She alleges, among other things, that the School District was not justified in regulating her speech because it did not occur during a "school-related activity," but rather was "private out-of-school speech."

The district court entered summary judgment in favor of the defendants, concluding that they were authorized to punish Kowalski because her webpage was "created for the purpose of inviting others to indulge in disruptive and hateful conduct," which caused an "in-school disruption."

Reviewing the summary judgment record *de novo*, we conclude that in the circumstances of this case, the School District's imposition of sanctions was permissible. Kowalski used the Internet to orchestrate a targeted attack on a classmate, and did so in a manner that was sufficiently connected to the school environment as to implicate the School District's recognized authority to discipline speech which "materially and substantially interfere[es] with the requirements of appropriate discipline in the operation of the school and collid[es] with the rights of others." Accordingly, we affirm.

I

On December 1, 2005, Kara Kowalski, who was then a 12th grade student at Musselman High School in the Berkeley County School District, returned home from school and, using her home computer, created a discussion group webpage on MySpace.com with the heading "S.A.S.H." Under the webpage's title, she posted the statement, "No No Herpes, We don't want no herpes." Kowalski claimed in her deposition that "S.A.S.H." was an acronym for "Students Against Sluts Herpes," but a classmate, Ray Parsons, stated that it was an acronym for "Students Against Shay's Herpes," referring to another Musselman High School Student, Shay N., who was the main subject of discussion on the webpage.

After creating the group, Kowalski invited approximately 100 people on her MySpace "friends" list to join the group. MySpace discussion groups allow registered users to post and respond to text, comments, and photographs in an interactive fashion. Approximately two dozen Musselman High School students responded and ultimately joined the group. Kowalski later explained that she had hoped that the group would "make other students actively aware of STDs," which were a "hot topic" at her school.

Ray Parsons responded to the MySpace invitation at 3:40 p.m. and was the first to join the group, doing so from a school computer during an after hours class at Musselman High School. Parsons uploaded a photograph of himself and a friend holding their noses while displaying a sign that read, "Shay Has Herpes," referring to Shay N. The record of the webpage shows that Kowalski promptly responded, stating, "Ray you are soo funny!=)" It shows that shortly thereafter, she posted another response to the photograph, stating that it was "the best picture [I]'ve seen on myspace so far!!!!" Several other students posted similar replies. Parsons also uploaded to the "S.A.S.H." webpage two additional photographs of Shay N., which he edited. In the first, he had drawn red dots on Shay N.'s face to simulate herpes and added a sign near her pelvic region, that read, "Warning: Enter at your own risk." In the second photograph, he captioned Shay N.'s face with a sign that read, "portrait of a whore."

The commentary posted on the "S.A.S.H." webpage mostly focused on Shay N. The first five comments were posted by other Musselman High School students and ridiculed the pictures of Shay N. One student stated that "shay knows about the sign" and then stated, "wait til she sees the page lol." (The abbreviation "lol" means "laugh out loud" or "laughing out loud.") The next comment replied, "Haha ... screw" her and repeatedly stated, "This is great." After expressing her approval of the postings, this student noted the "Shay has herpes sign" and stated, "Kara sent me a few interesting pics ... Would you be interested in seeing them Ray?" One student posted, "Kara= My Hero," and another said, "your so awesome kara ... i never thought u would mastermind a group that hates [someone] tho, lol." A few of the posts assumed that Kowalski had posted the photographs of Shay N., but Parsons later clarified that it was he who had posted the photographs.

A few hours after the photographs and comments had been posted to the MySpace.com page, Shay N.'s father called Parsons on the telephone and expressed his anger over the photographs. Parsons then called Kowalski, who unsuccessfully attempted to delete the "S.A.S.H." group and to remove the photographs. Unable to do so, she renamed the group "Students Against Angry People."

The next morning, Shay N.'s parents, together with Shay, went to Musselman High School and filed a harassment complaint with Vice Principal Becky Harden regarding the discussion group, and they provided Harden with a printout of the "S.A.S.H." webpage. Shay thereafter left the school with her parents, as she did not want to attend classes that day, feeling uncomfortable about sitting in class with students who had posted comments about her on the MySpace webpage.

After receiving Shay N.'s complaint, Principal Ronald Stephens contacted the central school board office to determine whether the issue was one that should be addressed with school discipline. A school board official indicated that discipline was appropriate. Principal Stephens then conducted an investigation into the matter, during which he and Vice Principal Harden interviewed the students who had joined the "S.A.S.H." group to determine who posted the photographs and comments. As part of the investigation, Principal Stephens and Vice Principal Harden questioned Parsons, who admitted that he had posted the photographs. Vice Principal Harden met with Kowalski, who admitted that she had created the "S.A.S.H." group but denied that she posted any of the photographs or disparaging remarks.

School administrators concluded that Kowalski had created a "hate Web site," in violation of the school policy against "harassment, bullying, and intimidation." For punishment, they suspended Kowalski from school for 10 days and issued her a 90day "social suspension," which prevented her from attending school events in which she was not a direct participant. Kowalski was also prevented from crowning the next "Queen of Charm" in that year's Charm Review, having been elected "Queen" herself the previous year. In addition, she was not allowed to participate on the cheerleading squad for the remainder of the year. After Kowalski's father asked school administrators to reduce or revoke the suspension, Assistant Superintendent Rick Deuell reduced Kowalski's out-of-school suspension to 5 days, but retained the 90day social suspension.

Kowalski claims that, as a result of her punishment, she became socially isolated from her peers and received cold treatment from teachers and administrators. She stated that she became depressed and began taking prescription medication for her depression.

Kowalski acknowledged that at the beginning of each school year, including her senior year, she had received a Student Handbook which included the School District's Harassment, Bullying, and Intimidation Policy, as well as the Student Code of Conduct. The Harassment, Bullying, and Intimidation Policy prohibited "any form of . . . sexual . . . harassment . . . or any bullying or intimidation by any student . . . during any school-related activity or during any education-sponsored event, whether in a building or other property owned, use[d] or operated by the Berkeley Board of Education." The Policy defined "Bullying, Harassment and/or Intimidation" as "any intentional gesture, or any intentional written, verbal or physical act that"

1.   A reasonable person under the circumstances should know will have the effect of:

a.   Harming a student or staff member; [. . . sic]

2.   Is sufficiently inappropriate, severe, persistent, or pervasive that it creates an intimidating, threatening or abusive educational environment for a student.

The policy also provided that violators would be suspended and that disciplinary actions could be appealed.

The Student Code of Conduct provided, "All students enrolled in Berkeley County public schools shall behave in a safe manner that promotes a school environment that is nurturing, orderly, safe, and conducive to learning and personal-social development." It also committed students to "help create an atmosphere free from bullying, intimidation and harassment" and to "treat others with respect" and "demonstrate compassion and caring." The Code classified "Bullying/Harassment/Intimidation" as a "Level III Violation" with possible consequences including an out-of-school suspension up to 10 days; signing a behavioral contract; being denied participation in class and/or school activities; and a social suspension of up to one semester. Before punishing a student under the Student Code of Conduct, a principal was required to "immediately undertake or authorize an investigation" of the incident and complaint, including "personal interviews with the complain[an]t, the individual(s) against whom the complaint is filed, and others who may have knowledge of the alleged incident(s) or circumstances giving rise to the complaint."

The school administrators' meetings with Kowalski and the other students involved in the "S.A.S.H." webpage were intended to fulfill the procedures described in the Student Handbook.

Kowalski commenced this action in November 2007 against the Berkeley County School District, Superintendent Manny Arvon (in his official capacity), Principal Ronald Stephens (in his official and individual capacities), Vice Principal Becky Harden (in her official and individual capacities), cheerleading coach Buffy Ashcraft (in her official and individual capacities), and Assistant Superintendent Rick Deuell (in his official capacity), alleging free speech violations under the First Amendment, due process violations under the Fifth Amendment (which Kowalski has acknowledged should have been under the Fourteenth Amendment), cruel and unusual punishment under the Eighth Amendment, and equal protection violations under the Fourteenth Amendment. The complaint also alleged violations of corresponding provisions of the West Virginia Constitution and a state law claim for intentional or negligent infliction of emotional distress. In addition to damages, Kowalski sought a declaratory judgment that the School District's harassment policy was unconstitutionally vague or overbroad and an injunction requiring the school to expunge any record of her discipline.

On the defendants' motion to dismiss the complaint, the district court dismissed Kowalski's free speech claim for lack of standing, concluding that she failed to allege that she had been disciplined under the School District's policy for engaging in speech protected by the First Amendment. In a later ruling denying Kowalski's motion for reconsideration, however, the district court recognized that Kowalski had engaged in speech. Nonetheless, it held that Kowalski lacked standing because her injury would "not be redressed by a favorable decision." Despite this ruling, the district court revisited the merits of Kowalski's free speech claim when it denied her subsequent motion for reconsideration and again when it considered the defendants' motion for summary judgment on Kowalski's remaining claims. In ruling on the summary judgment motion, the court concluded that "the defendants could legitimately take action for [Kowalski's] vulgar and offensive speech and her encouragement of other students to follow suit." The district court also dismissed Kowalski's cruel and unusual punishment claim.

In granting summary judgment to the defendants, in addition to ruling against Kowalski on her free speech claim, the district court denied Kowalski's due process claim, concluding (1) that Kowalski was on notice that she could be punished for her off-campus behavior and (2) that she was provided with an opportunity to be heard prior to her suspension. The court also denied Kowalski's state law claims and her equal protection claim, with regard to which she had failed to produce any evidence. Finally, the court denied Kowalski's motion for reconsideration.

Kowalski appealed the district court's rulings on her free speech and due process claims under the U.S. Constitution and her state law claim for intentional or negligent infliction of emotional distress. At oral argument, she stipulated that we should treat the district court's judgment as granting summary judgment (rather than a motion to dismiss) on the issues appealed. We review the district court's rulings de novo.

II

Kowalski contends first that the school administrators violated her free speech rights under the First Amendment by punishing her for speech that occurred outside the school. She argues that because this case involved "off-campus, non-school related speech," school administrators had no power to discipline her. As she asserts, "The [Supreme] Court has been consistently careful to limit intrusions on students' rights to conduct taking place on school property, at school functions, or while engaged in school-sponsored or school-sanctioned activity." She maintains that "no Supreme Court case addressing student speech has held that a school may punish students for speech away from school—indeed every Supreme Court case addressing student speech has taken pains to emphasize that, were the speech in question to occur away from school, it would be protected."

The Berkeley County School District and its administrators contend that school officials "may regulate off-campus behavior insofar as the off-campus behavior creates a foreseeable risk of reaching school property and causing a substantial disruption to the work and discipline of the school," citing *Doninger v. Niehoff*. Relying on *Doninger*, the defendants note that Kowalski created a Web-page that singled out Shay N. for harassment, bullying and intimidation; that it was foreseeable that the off-campus conduct would reach the school; and that it was foreseeable that the off-campus conduct would "create a substantial disruption in the school."

The question thus presented is whether Kowalski's activity fell within the outer boundaries of the high school's legitimate interest in maintaining order in the school and protecting the well-being and educational rights of its students.

The First Amendment prohibits Congress and, through the Fourteenth Amendment, the States from "abridging the freedom of speech." It is a "bedrock principle" of the First Amendment that "the government may not prohibit the expression of an idea simply because society finds the idea itself offensive or disagreeable."

While students retain significant First Amendment rights in the school context, their rights are not coextensive with those of adults. Because of the "special characteristics" of the school environment, school administrators have some latitude in regulating student speech to further educational objectives. Thus in *Tinker,* the Court held that student speech, consisting of wearing armbands in political protest against the Vietnam War, was protected because it did not " 'materially and substantially interfer[e] with the requirements of appropriate discipline in the operation of the school' [or] collid[e] with the rights of others," and thus did not "materially disrupt[ ] classwork or involve[ ] substantial disorder or invasion of the rights of others," Student speech also may be regulated if it is otherwise "vulgar and lewd." Finally, the Supreme Court has held that school administrators are free to regulate and punish student speech that encourages the use of illegal drugs.

Although the Supreme Court has not dealt specifically with a factual circumstance where student speech targeted classmates for verbal abuse, in *Tinker* it recognized the need for regulation of speech that interfered with the school's work and discipline, describing that interference as speech that "disrupts classwork," creates "substantial disorder," or "collid[es] with" or "inva[des]" "the rights of others."

In *Tinker,* the Court pointed out at length how wearing black armbands in protest against the Vietnam War was passive and did not create "disorder or disturbance" and therefore did not interfere with the school's work or collide with other students' rights "to be secure and to be let alone." Of course, a mere desire to avoid "discomfort and unpleasantness" was an insufficient basis to regulate the speech; there had to be disruption in the sense that the speech "would materially and substantially interfere with the requirements of appropriate discipline in the operation of the school." The Court amplified the nature of the disruption it had in mind when it stated:

> [C]onduct by [a] student, in class or out of it, which for any reason— whether it stems from time, place, or type of behavior—materially disrupts classwork or involves substantial disorder or invasion of the rights of others is, of course, not immunized by the constitutional guarantee of freedom of speech.

The *Tinker* Court referred to this amplified statement of its test later in its opinion in shorthand when it concluded that the regulation of armbands "would violate the constitutional rights of students, at least if it could not be justified by a showing that the students' activities would materially and substantially disrupt *the work and discipline of the school.*" (emphasis added). Because, in *Tinker,* the students' wearing of the armbands "neither interrupted school activities nor sought to intrude in the school affairs or the lives of others," there was "no interference with work and no disorder" to justify regulation of the speech.

Thus, the language of *Tinker* supports the conclusion that public schools have a "compelling interest" in regulating speech that interferes with or disrupts the work and discipline of the school, including discipline for student harassment and bullying.

According to a federal government initiative, student-on-student bullying is a "major concern" in schools across the country and can cause victims to become depressed and anxious, to be afraid to go to school, and to have thoughts of suicide. Just as schools have a responsibility to provide a safe environment for students free from messages advocating illegal drug use, schools have a duty to protect their students from harassment and bullying in the school environment,. Far from being a situation where school authorities "suppress speech on political and social issues based on disagreement with the viewpoint expressed," school administrators must be able to prevent and punish harassment and bullying in order to provide a safe school environment conducive to learning.

We are confident that Kowalski's speech caused the interference and disruption described in *Tinker* as being immune from First Amendment protection. The "S.A.S.H." webpage functioned as a platform for Kowalski and her friends to direct verbal attacks towards classmate Shay N. The webpage contained comments accusing Shay N. of having herpes and being a "slut," as well as photographs reinforcing those defamatory accusations by depicting a sign across her pelvic area, which stated, "Warning: Enter at your own risk" and labeling her portrait as that of a "whore." One student's posting dismissed any concern for Shay N.'s reaction with a comment that said, "screw her." This is not the conduct and speech that our educational system is required to tolerate, as schools attempt to educate students about "habits and manners of civility" or the "fundamental values necessary to the maintenance of a democratic political system."

While Kowalski does not seriously dispute the harassing character of the speech on the "S.A.S.H." webpage, she argues mainly that her conduct took place at home after school and that the forum she created was therefore subject to the full protection of the First Amendment. This argument, however, raises the metaphysical question of where her speech occurred when she used the Internet as the medium. Kowalski indeed pushed her computer's keys in her home, but she knew that the electronic response would be, as it in fact was, published beyond her home and could reasonably be expected to reach the school or impact the school environment. She also knew that the dialogue would and did take place among Musselman High School students whom she invited to join the "S.A.S.H." group and that the fallout from her conduct and the speech within the group would be felt in the school itself. Indeed, the group's name was "*Students* Against Sluts Herpes" and a vast majority of its members were Musselman students. As one commentator on the Web-page observed, "wait til [Shay N.] sees the page lol." Moreover, as Kowalski could anticipate, Shay N. and her parents took the attack as having been made in the school context, as they went to the high school to lodge their complaint.

There is surely a limit to the scope of a high school's interest in the order, safety, and well-being of its students when the speech at issue originates outside the schoolhouse gate. But we need not fully define that limit here, as we are satisfied that the nexus of Kowalski's speech to Musselman High School's pedagogical interests was sufficiently strong to justify the action taken by school officials in carrying out their role as the trustees of the student body's well-being.

Of course, had Kowalski created the "S.A.S.H." group during school hours, using a school-provided computer and Internet connection, this case would be more clear-cut, as the question of where speech that was transmitted by the Internet "occurred" would not come into play. To be sure, a court could determine that speech originating outside of the schoolhouse gate but directed at persons in school and received by and acted on by them was in fact in-school speech. In that case, because it was determined to be in-school speech, its regulation would be permissible not only under *Tinker* but also, as vulgar and lewd in-school speech, under *Fraser*. *But cf. Layshock v. Hermitage Sch. Dist.* (en banc) (holding that a school could not punish a student for online speech merely because the speech was vulgar and reached the school) [This case is next]. We need not resolve, however, whether this was in-school speech and therefore whether *Fraser* could apply because the School District was authorized by *Tinker* to discipline Kowalski, regardless of where her speech originated, because the speech was materially and substantially disruptive in that it "interfer[ed] . . . with the schools' work [and] colli[ded] with the rights of other students to be secure and to be let alone."

Given the targeted, defamatory nature of Kowalski's speech, aimed at a fellow classmate, it created "actual or nascent" substantial disorder and disruption in the school. First, the creation of the "S.A.S.H." group forced Shay N. to miss school in order to avoid further abuse. Moreover, had the school not intervened, the potential for continuing and more serious harassment of Shay N. as well as other students was real. Experience suggests that unpunished misbehavior can have a snowballing effect, in some cases resulting in "copycat" efforts by other students or in retaliation for the initial harassment.

Other courts have similarly concluded that school administrators' authority to regulate student speech extends, in the appropriate circumstances, to speech that does not originate at the school itself, so long as the speech eventually makes its way to the school in a meaningful way. For example, . . . in *Doninger*, the Second Circuit concluded, after a student applied for a preliminary injunction in a factual circumstance not unlike the one at hand, that a school could discipline a student for an out-of-school blog post that included vulgar language and misleading information about school administrators, as long as it was reasonably foreseeable that the post would reach the school and create a substantial disruption there. The court explained, "a student may be disciplined for expressive conduct, even conduct occurring off school grounds, when this conduct would foreseeably create a risk of substantial disruption within the school environment, at least when it was similarly foreseeable that the off-campus expression might also reach campus."

Thus, even though Kowalski was not physically at the school when she operated her computer to create the webpage and form the "S.A.S.H." MySpace group and to post comments there, other circuits have applied *Tinker* to such circumstances. To be sure, it was foreseeable in this case that Kowalski's conduct would reach the school via computers, smartphones, and other electronic devices, given that most of the "S.A.S.H." group's members and the target of the group's harassment were Musselman High School students. Indeed, the "S.A.S.H." webpage did make its way into the school and was accessed first by Musselman student Ray Parsons at 3:40 p.m., from a school computer during an after hours class. Furthermore, as we have noted, it created a reasonably foreseeable substantial disruption there.

At bottom, we conclude that the school was authorized to discipline Kowalski because her speech interfered with the work and discipline of the school.

III

Kowalski next contends that she was denied due process because she "was afforded neither adequate notice nor a meaningful opportunity to be heard before she was deprived of her right to an education and her right to free speech." She argues that "no language" in the Harassment, Bullying and Intimidation Policy puts students on notice that they "could be subjected to discipline at school for behavior outside of school" and that the school "did not provide the due process required by [its] own policy."

The defendants contend that Kowalski acknowledged receiving copies of the Student Handbook at the beginning of each school year and that the Student Handbook put Kowalski on notice of the Harassment, Bullying and Intimidation Policy, as well as the Student Code of Conduct, both of which prohibit harassment and bullying. They argue, moreover, that "it was reasonably foreseeable [to Kowalski] that [her] chat room could, and in fact did, reach the school premises and cause a substantial disruption" there. The defendants also assert that Kowalski was told about Shay N.'s complaint and allowed to respond before being punished and that "an appeal process was available, and used on her behalf."

While schools are required to provide students with some level of due process, " 'maintaining security and order in the schools requires a certain degree of flexibility in school disciplinary procedures, and we have respected the value of preserving the informality of the student-teacher relationship.' " Moreover, schools require this flexibility because they "need ... to control such a wide range of disruptive behavior." In other words, "the school disciplinary rules need not be as detailed as a criminal code which imposes criminal sanctions."

We are satisfied that the Musselman High School Harassment, Bullying and Intimidation Policy, in conjunction with the Student Code of Conduct, adequately put Kowalski on notice of the type of behavior that could be punished by school authorities. The Policy prohibits "any form of racial, sexual, religious/ethnic and disability harassment or violence or any bullying or intimidation by any student ... during any school-related activity or during any school-sponsored event," and the separate Student Code of Conduct "sets the requirements for the conduct of students in Berkeley County Schools in order to assure a nurturing and orderly, safe, drug-free, violence and harassment-free learning environment that supports student academic achievement and personal-social development." The Code provides explicitly that "a student will not bully/intimidate or harass another student."

Although the prohibitions against harassment and bullying applied in a "school-related" context, both the Harassment, Bullying and Intimidation Policy and the Student Code of Conduct applied when conduct could adversely affect the school environment. Thus, while the prohibited conduct had to be related to the school, this is not to say that volatile conduct was only punishable if it physically originated in a school building or during the school day. Rather, the prohibitions are designed to regulate student behavior that would *affect* the school's learning environment. Because the Internet-based bullying and harassment in this case could reasonably be expected to interfere with the rights of a student at Musselman High School and thus disrupt the school learning environment, Kowalski was indeed on notice that Mussel-man High School administrators could regulate and punish the conduct at issue here.

With respect to Kowalski's claim that she did not receive an adequate opportunity to be heard, due process in this context only requires, "in connection with a suspension of 10 days or less, that the student be given oral or written notice of the charges against [her] and, if [she] denies them, an explanation of the evidence the authorities have and an opportunity to present [her] side of the story." Here, these requirements were satisfied. Vice Principal Harden called Kowalski into her office, informed her of the harassment and bullying charge, discussed the "S.A.S.H." group with her, and, after Kowalski acknowledged her role, imposed a 10–day suspension. Because Kowalski admitted her conduct, the administrators were not required to provide a more extensive opportunity to allow her to justify her conduct.

Kowalski's argument that school administrators did not follow their own policies was not demonstrated in the record and also has no legal merit. Violations of state laws or school procedures "are insufficient by themselves to implicate the interests that trigger a [federal] due process claim."

IV

Finally, Kowalski challenges the district court's dismissal of her claim for intentional or negligent infliction of emotional distress. . . . Finding no error in the court's analysis of these claims, we affirm the district court's dismissal of them.

V

Kowalski's role in the "S.A.S.H." webpage, which was used to ridicule and demean a fellow student, was particularly mean-spirited and hateful. The webpage called on classmates, in a pack, to target Shay N., knowing that it would be hurtful and damaging to her ability to sit with other students in class at Musselman High School and have a suitable learning experience. . . .

Kowalski asserts that the protections of free speech and due process somehow insulate her activities from school discipline because her activity was not sufficiently school-related to be subject to school discipline. Yet, every aspect of the webpage's design and implementation was school-related. Kowalski designed the Web site for "students," perhaps even against Shay N.; she sent it to students inviting them to join; and those who joined were mostly students, with Kowalski encouraging the commentary. The victim understood the attack as school-related, filing her complaint with school authorities. Ray Parsons, who provided the vulgar and lewd—indeed, defamatory—photographs understood that the object of the attack was Shay N., and he participated from a school computer during class, to the cheering of Kowalski and her fellow classmates, whom she invited to the affair.

Rather than respond constructively to the school's efforts to bring order and provide a lesson following the incident, Kowalski has rejected those efforts and sued school authorities for damages and other relief. Regretfully, she yet fails to see that such harassment and bullying is inappropriate and hurtful and that it must be taken seriously by school administrators in order to preserve an appropriate pedagogical environment. Indeed, school administrators *are* becoming increasingly alarmed by the phenomenon, and the events in this case are but one example of such bullying and school administrators' efforts to contain it. Suffice it to hold here that, where such speech has a sufficient nexus with the school, the Constitution is not written to hinder school administrators' good faith efforts to address the problem.

The judgment of the district court is

AFFIRMED.

NOTES

1. Do you agree with the outcome of this case?

2. Should it matter if student Internet postings originate on their home computers and then make their way on to school computers?

[CASE NO. 108]   SCHOOL OFFICIALS VIOLATED STUDENT'S RIGHTS OVER AN FOR INTERNET POSTING

LAYSHOCK EX REL. LAYSHOCK v. HERMITAGE SCHOOL DISTRICT

United States Court of Appeals, Third Circuit, 2011.
650 F.3d 205.

■ McKEE, CHIEF JUDGE.

We are asked to determine if a school district can punish a student for expressive conduct that originated outside of the schoolhouse, did not disturb the school environment and was not related to any school sponsored event. We hold that, under these circumstances, the First Amendment prohibits the school from reaching beyond the schoolyard to impose what might otherwise be appropriate discipline.

It all began when Justin Layshock used his grandmother's computer to access a popular social networking internet Web site where he created a fake internet "profile" of his Hickory High School Principal, Eric Trosch. His parents filed this action under 42 U.S.C. § 1983, after the School

District punished Justin for that conduct. The suit alleges, *inter alia,* that the School District's punishment transcended Justin's First Amendment right of expression. The district court granted summary judgment in favor of Justin on his First Amendment claim. We originally affirmed the district court. Thereafter, we entered an order vacating that opinion and granting rehearing en banc. For the reasons that follow, we once again affirm the district court's holding that the school district's response to Justin's conduct transcended the protection of free expression guaranteed by the First Amendment.

I. FACTUAL BACKGROUND

In December of 2005, Justin Layshock was a seventeen-year old senior at Hickory High School, which is part of the Hermitage School District in Hermitage, Pennsylvania. Sometime between December 10th and 14th, 2005, while Justin was at his grandmother's house during non-school hours, he used her computer to create what he would later refer to as a "parody profile" of his Principal, Eric Trosch. The only school resource that was even arguably involved in creating the profile was a photograph of Trosch that Justin copied from the School District's Web site. Justin copied that picture with a simple "cut and paste" operation using the computer's internet browser and mouse. Justin created the profile on "MySpace." MySpace is a popular social-networking Web site that "allows its members to create online profiles, which are individual Web pages on which members post photographs, videos, and information about their lives and interests."

Justin created the profile by giving bogus answers to survey questions taken from various templates that were designed to assist in creating a profile. The survey included questions about favorite shoes, weaknesses, fears, one's idea of a "perfect pizza," bedtime, etc. All of Justin's answers were based on a theme of "big," because Trosch is apparently a large man. For example, Justin answered "tell me about yourself" questions as follows:

Birthday: too drunk to remember

Are you a health freak: big steroid freak

In the past month have you smoked: big blunt

In the past month have you been on pills: big pills

In the past month have you gone Skinny Dipping . . .

In the past month have you Stolen Anything: big keg

Ever been drunk: big number of times

Ever been called a Tease: . . .

Ever been Beaten up: . . .

Ever Shoplifted: big bag of kmart

Number of Drugs I have taken: big

Under "Interests," Justin listed: "Transgender, Appreciators of Alcoholic Beverages." Justin also listed "Steroids International" as a club Trosch belonged to.

Justin afforded access to the profile to other students in the School
District by listing them as "friends" on the MySpace Web site, thus
allowing them to view the profile. Not surprisingly, word of the profile
"spread like wildfire" and soon reached most, if not all, of Hickory High's
student body.

During mid-December 2005, three other students also posted unflattering profiles of Trosch on MySpace. Each of those profiles was more vulgar
and more offensive than Justin's. Trosch first learned about one of the
other profiles from his daughter, who was in eleventh grade. On Monday,
December 12, 2005, Trosch told his Co–Principal, Chris Gill, and the
District Superintendent, Karen Ionta, about this other profile and asked
the Technology Director, Frank Gingras, to disable it. However, despite the
administration's best efforts, students found ways to access the profiles.
Trosch discovered Justin's profile on Thursday evening, December 15th,
and a fourth profile on Sunday, December 18th.

Trosch believed all of the profiles were "degrading," "demeaning,"
"demoralizing," and "shocking." He was also concerned about his reputation and complained to the local police. Although he was not concerned for
his safety, he was interested in pressing charges against those responsible
for the bogus profiles, and he discussed whether the first profile he
discovered might constitute harassment, defamation, or slander. However,
no criminal charges were ever filed against Justin or any of the other
student authors of profiles.

On December 15th, Justin used a computer in his Spanish classroom to
access his MySpace profile of Trosch. He also showed it to other classmates,
although he did not acknowledge his authorship. After viewing the profile,
the students logged off of MySpace. Justin again attempted to access the
profile from school on December 16th, purportedly to delete it. School
district administrators were unaware of Justin's in-school attempts to
access MySpace until their investigation the following week. Teacher Craig
Antush glimpsed the profile in his computer lab class and told the students
who were congregating around a computer and giggling to shut it down.

The School District administrators were not able to totally block
students from visiting the MySpace Web page at school because Gingras,
the Technology Coordinator, was on vacation on December 16th. However,
the school was able to control students' computer access by limiting the
students' use of computers to computer labs or the library where internet
access could be supervised. School officials continued to limit computer use
from December 16th until December 21st, which was the last day of school
before Christmas recess. Computer programming classes were also cancelled.

According to the district court, the School District's investigation
revealed how many students had accessed MySpace before access to the site
at school was disabled, but the school could not determine how many
students actually accessed any of the Trosch profiles, or which Trosch
profiles had been viewed while a student was on the MySpace Web site.

School District officials first learned that Justin might have created
one of the Trosch profiles on December 21. On that day, Justin and his

mother were summoned to a meeting with Superintendent Ionta and Co–Principal Gill. During that meeting, Justin admitted creating a profile, but no disciplinary action was then taken against him. After the meeting, without prompting from anyone, Justin went to Trosch's office and apologized for creating the profile.

Justin's parents were understandably upset over Justin's behavior. They discussed the matter with him, expressed their extreme disappointment, "grounded" him, and prohibited him from using their home computer.

On January 3, 2006, the school district sent a letter to Justin and his parents giving them notice of an informal hearing that was to be held. The letter read, in pertinent part, as follows:

> Justin admitted prior to the informal hearing that he created a profile about Mr. Trosch.
>
> This infraction is a violation of the Hermitage School District Discipline Code: Disruption of the normal school process; Disrespect; Harassment of a school administrator via computer/internet with remarks that have demeaning implications; Gross misbehavior; Obscene, vulgar and profane language; Computer Policy violations (use of school pictures without authorization).
>
> The School District subsequently found Justin guilty of all of those charges.

In addition to a ten-day, out-of-school suspension, Justin's punishment consisted of (1) being placed in the Alternative Education Program (the "ACE" program) at the high school for the remainder of the 2005–2006 school year; (2) being banned from all extracurricular activities, including Academic Games and foreign-language tutoring; and (3) not being allowed to participate in his graduation ceremony. The Layshocks were also informed that the School District was considering expelling Justin. Ironically, Justin, who created the least vulgar and offensive profile, and who was the only student to apologize for his behavior, was also the only student punished for the MySpace profiles.

II. DISTRICT COURT PROCEEDINGS

The Layshocks initiated this action on January 27, 2006, by filing a three count complaint pursuant to 42 U.S.C. § 1983 individually, and on Justin's behalf, against the Hermitage School District, Karen Ionta, Eric Trosch, and Chris Gill, in their official and individual capacities (hereinafter collectively referred to as the "School District" or "District"). The Layshocks also filed a motion for a temporary restraining order and/or preliminary injunction. Count I of the complaint alleged that the District's punishment of Justin violated his rights under the First Amendment. Count II alleged that the District's policies and rules were unconstitutionally vague and/or overbroad, both on their face and as applied to Justin. Count III alleged that the District's punishment of Justin interfered with, and continued to interfere with, their right as parents to determine how to best raise, nurture, discipline and educate their child in violation of their rights under the Due Process Clause of the Fourteenth Amendment.

The district court denied the request for a temporary restraining order and the Layshocks withdrew their motion for a preliminary injunction pursuant to the district court's efforts at mediation. On March 31, 2006, the district court denied the District's motion to dismiss the Layshocks' claims. The court ruled that the parents may assert a claim for a violation of their own due process right to "raise, nurture, discipline and educate their children" based on a school district's punishment of their child for speech the child uttered in the family home.

After discovery, both sides moved for summary judgment, and the court thereafter entered summary judgment in favor of Justin and against the School District only on the First Amendment claim. The court concluded that a jury trial was necessary to determine compensatory damages and attorneys' fees.

Thereafter, the district court denied the District's motion for entry of judgment . . . or, in the alternative, for the issuance of a certificate of appealability. . . .

The parties subsequently filed a joint motion in which they stipulated to damages and requested entry of final judgment while preserving all appellate issues pertaining to liability. The district court then entered a consent judgment, and the School District appealed the district court's grant of summary judgment in favor of Justin on his First Amendment claim.

III. SUMMARY JUDGMENT

"Summary judgment is proper when the pleadings, depositions, answers to interrogatories, and admissions on file, together with the affidavits, if any, show that there is no genuine issue as to any material fact and that the moving party is entitled to judgment as a matter of law." In ruling on a motion for summary judgment, the district court must view the facts in the light most favorable to the non-moving party. However, "the mere existence of *some* alleged factual dispute between the parties will not defeat an otherwise properly supported motion for summary judgment." "As our review of a grant of summary judgment is plenary, we operate under the same legal standards as the District Court."

IV. DISCUSSION

1. The First Amendment's Application in Public Schools.

In the landmark case of *Tinker v. Des Moines Indep. Cmty. Sch. Dist.* (1969), a group of high school students decided to wear black arm bands to school to protest the war in Vietnam. . . . the Supreme Court . . . held that student expression may not be suppressed unless school officials reasonably conclude that it will "materially and substantially disrupt the work and discipline of the school." The Court concluded that the students were doing nothing more than engaging in political speech, and wearing armbands to express their disapproval of the Vietnam hostilities and "their advocacy of a truce, to make their views known, and, by their example, to influence others to adopt them." . . . In one of its most famous passages, the Court explained:

First Amendment rights, applied in light of the special characteristics of the school environment, are available to teachers and students. It can hardly be argued that either students or teachers shed their constitutional rights to freedom of speech or expression at the schoolhouse gate.

Thus, although the Court concluded that the First Amendment did reach inside the "schoolhouse gate," it also recognized that the unique nature of the school environment had to be part of any First Amendment inquiry. . . .

The Court next addressed the scope of the First Amendment in the context of student speech in Bethel School District No. 403 v. Fraser (1986). There, the Court upheld the school's suspension of a high school student for delivering a nominating speech at a school assembly using "an elaborate, graphic, and explicit sexual metaphor." The Court explained:

> The schools, as instruments of the state, may determine that the essential lessons of civil, mature conduct cannot be conveyed in a school that tolerates lewd, indecent, or offensive speech and conduct such as that indulged in by [Fraser].

The Court concluded that the school could punish Fraser for his offensive nominating speech during a school assembly because the First Amendment does not prevent schools from encouraging the "fundamental values of 'habits and manners of civility'" by "insisting that certain modes of expression are inappropriate and subject to sanctions." Thus, "[t]he determination of what manner of speech in the classroom or in school assembly is inappropriate properly rests with the school board."

Similarly, in *Hazelwood School District. v. Kuhlmeier* (1988), the Court held that a principal's deletion of student articles on teen pregnancy from a school-sponsored newspaper did not violate the First Amendment. The Court distinguished *Tinker* by noting that because the school had not opened the newspaper up as a public forum, the school could "exercis[e] editorial control over the style and content of student speech in school-sponsored expressive activities so long as [its] actions are reasonably related to legitimate pedagogical concerns.". . .

The extent to which First Amendment protections apply in the public school context was most recently addressed in *Morse v. Frederick* (2007). There, "[a]t a school-sanctioned and school-supervised event, a high school principal [Morse] saw some of her students unfurl a large banner conveying a message she reasonably regarded as promoting illegal drug use." The banner read: "BONG HiTS 4 JESUS." "Consistent with established school policy prohibiting such messages at school events, [Morse] directed the students to take down the banner." Frederick, one of the students who brought the banner to the event, refused to remove it, and Morse "confiscated the banner and later suspended [Frederick]." Frederick sued Morse and the school district pursuant to 42 U.S.C. § 1983, alleging a violation of his First Amendment right of expression. The district court granted summary judgment to the school district and Morse, holding that they were entitled to qualified immunity and that they had not infringed Frederick's

First Amendment rights. The Court of Appeals for the Ninth Circuit reversed.

The Supreme Court granted certiorari to determine "whether Frederick had a First Amendment right to wield his banner, and, if so, whether that right was so clearly established that the principal may be held liable for damages." The Court "resolve[d] the first question against Frederick," and, therefore, did not have to reach the second. The Court explained that its Fourth Amendment jurisprudence recognized that "deterring drug use by school children is an important—indeed, perhaps compelling interest." The "special characteristics of the school environment, and the governmental interest in stopping student drug abuse allow schools to restrict student expression that they reasonably regard as promoting such abuse." Thus, "a principal may, consistent with the First Amendment, restrict student speech at a school event, when that speech is reasonably viewed as promoting illegal drug use". . . .

It is against this legal backdrop that we must determine whether the District's actions here violated Justin's First Amendment rights.

At the outset, it is important to note that the district court found that the District could not "establish[ ] a sufficient nexus between Justin's speech and a substantial disruption of the school environment[,]" and the School District does not challenge that finding on appeal. Therefore, the School District is not arguing that it could properly punish Justin under the *Tinker* exception for student speech that causes a material and substantial disruption of the school environment. Rather, the District's argument is twofold:

> [A] sufficient nexus exists between Justin's creation and distribution of the vulgar and defamatory profile of Principal Trosch and the School District to permit the School District to regulate this conduct. The "speech" initially began on-campus: Justin entered school property, the School District Web site, and misappropriated a picture of the Principal. The "speech" was aimed at the School District community and the Principal and was accessed on campus by Justin. It was reasonably foreseeable that the profile would come to the attention of the School District and the Principal.

2.   Justin's "Entry" Onto the District's Web site.

The School District's attempt to forge a nexus between the School and Justin's profile by relying upon his "entering" the District's Web site to "take" the District's photo of Trosch is unpersuasive at best. The argument equates Justin's act of signing onto a Web site with the kind of trespass he would have committed had he broken into the principal's office or a teacher's desk; and we reject it.

We find the reasoning in *Thomas v. Board of Educ.* far more persuasive. *Thomas* involved a group of students who were suspended for producing "a satirical publication addressed to the school community." . . . "Some of the initial preparation for publication occurred after school hours in the classroom" of a teacher whom the students consulted "for advice on isolated questions of grammar and content." In addition, "an occasional article was composed or typed within the school building, always after classes," and the finished magazine was stored in a "classroom closet" with the classroom teacher's permission.

However, the students were very careful to distribute the periodical only after school and off campus, and the vast majority of their work on the publication was done "in their homes, off campus and after school hours." The school principal learned of the magazine when a teacher confiscated a copy from another student on campus, and "following consultation with the Board of Education," the principal imposed penalties that included a five-day suspension of the students involved. The punishment was based on the students' publication of "an allegedly 'morally offensive, indecent, and obscene,' tabloid."

The students sued the school board and other school officials under 42 U.S.C. § 1983. They sought "injunctive and declaratory relief from alleged deprivations of their First and Fourteenth Amendment rights." The district court denied the students' request for injunctive relief. . . .

The Court of Appeals for the Second Circuit concluded that the students' conduct was not sufficiently related to the school to justify the school's exercise of authority. . . .

The court reached that conclusion even though the students actually stored the offending publication inside a classroom and did some minimal amount of work on the periodical in school using school resources. Here, the relationship between Justin's conduct and the school is far more attenuated than in *Thomas*. We agree with the analysis in *Thomas*. Accordingly, because the School District concedes that Justin's profile did not cause disruption in the school, we do not think that the First Amendment can tolerate the School District stretching its authority into Justin's grandmother's home and reaching Justin while he is sitting at her computer after school in order to punish him for the expressive conduct that he engaged in there.

We realize, of course, that it is now well established that *Tinker*'s "schoolhouse gate" is not constructed solely of the bricks and mortar surrounding the "school yard." Nevertheless, the concept of the school yard is not without boundaries and the reach of school authorities is not without limits. In *Morse*, the Court held that the First Amendment does not prevent a principal from "restrict[ing] student speech *at a school event,* when that speech is reasonably viewed as promoting illegal drug use." (emphasis added). Nevertheless, with regard to expressive conduct that occurs outside of the school context, the Court, referring to its earlier decision in *Fraser*, was careful to note that "[h]ad Fraser delivered the same speech in a public forum outside the school context, it would have been protected."

It would be an unseemly and dangerous precedent to allow the state, in the guise of school authorities, to reach into a child's home and control his/her actions there to the same extent that it can control that child when he/she participates in school sponsored activities. Allowing the District to punish Justin for conduct he engaged in while at his grandmother's house using his grandmother's computer would create just such a precedent, and we therefore conclude that the district court correctly ruled that the District's response to Justin's expressive conduct violated the First Amendment guarantee of free expression.

3. The District Cannot Punish Justin Merely Because His Speech Reached Inside the School.

As noted above, the School District also claims that Justin's speech can be treated as "on-campus" speech because it "was aimed at the School District community and the Principal and was accessed on campus by Justin [and] [i]t was reasonably foreseeable that the profile would come to the attention of the School District and the Principal."

The district court held that the School District's punishment of Justin was not appropriate under *Fraser* because "[t]here is no evidence that Justin engaged in any lewd or profane speech while in school." It also held that Justin's punishment was not appropriate under *Tinker* because the School District did "not establish[ ] a sufficient nexus between Justin's speech and a substantial disruption of the school environment."

The School District does not dispute the district court's finding that its punishment of Justin was not appropriate under *Tinker;* it rests its argument on the Supreme Court's analysis in *Fraser*. In the School District's view, Justin's speech—his MySpace profile of Trosch—was unquestionably vulgar, lewd and offensive, and therefore not shielded by the First Amendment because it ended up inside the school community. Similarly, the School District argues that under our decision in Saxe, there is no First Amendment protection for lewd, vulgar, indecent or plainly offensive speech in schools.

The District rests this argument primarily on three cases which it claims allow it to respond to a student's vulgar speech when that speech is posted on the internet. The District cites *J.S. v. Bethlehem Area Sch. Dist.* (2002); *Wisniewski v. Bd. of Educ. of Weedsport Cent. Sch. Dist.* (2d Cir.2007); and *Doninger v. Niehoff* (2d Cir.2008). However, as we will explain, each of those cases involved off campus expressive conduct that resulted in a substantial disruption of the school, and the courts allowed the schools to respond to the substantial disruption that the student's out of school conduct caused.

In *J.S.*, an eighth grade student created a threatening Web site aimed at his algebra teacher that went so far as to explain "[w]hy Should She Die," and requested money "to help pay for the hitman." The site frightened several students and parents and the algebra teacher was so badly frightened that she ended up having to take medical leave from her teaching responsibilities. As a result of her inability to return to teaching, "three substitute teachers were required to be utilized which disrupted the educational process of the students." "In sum, the Web site created disorder and significantly and adversely impacted the delivery of instruction." The Supreme Court of Pennsylvania concluded that the resulting disruption of instruction and the educational environment allowed the school to punish the student for his expressive conduct even though the student created the Web site from his home.

Similarly, the school suspended the student in *Wisniewski,* for creating an image on the internet from his home computer that depicted a pistol firing a bullet at a teacher's head with dots representing splattered blood above the head. The words: "Kill Mr. VanderMolen" were printed beneath the drawing. VanderMolen was the student's English teacher. The student created the image a couple of weeks after his class was instructed that threats would not be tolerated at the school, and would be treated as acts of violence. The court of appeals affirmed the district court's grant of summary judgment in favor of the school district in a suit alleging a violation of the First Amendment based on the school's suspension of the student for the out-of-school conduct. The court reasoned that "[t]he fact that [the student's] creation and transmission of the icon occurred away from school property [did] not necessarily insulate him from school discipline." The court reasoned that "even if [the student's] transmission of an [image] depicting and calling for the killing of his teacher could be viewed as an expression of opinion within the meaning of *Tinker,*" it was not protected by the First Amendment because "it cross[ed] the boundary of protected speech and pose[d] a reasonably foreseeable risk [of] materially and substantially disrupting the work and discipline of the school."

Finally, in *Doninger,* a student, who was a class officer, posted a message on her publicly accessible web log or "blog" that resulted in school authorities not allowing her to participate in an election for class office. In her message, she complained about a school activity that was cancelled . . . and encouraged others to contact the central office. . . ." When the principal learned of the student's posting, she prohibited her from running for senior class secretary "because [the student's] conduct had failed to display the civility and good citizenship expected of class officers." The student and her parents then sought injunctive relief in the form of a court order allowing her to run for class office. The court of appeals affirmed the district court's denial of relief because the student's out of school expressive conduct "created a foreseeable risk of substantial disruption to the work and discipline of the school." "[The student] herself testified that . . . students were 'all riled up' and that a sit-in was threatened." Accordingly, the court of appeals held that the student's mother "failed to show clearly that [the student's] First Amendment rights were violated when she was disqualified from running" for class office.

However, for our purposes, it is particularly important to note that the court in *Doninger* was careful to explain that it "[had] no occasion to consider whether a different, more serious consequence than disqualification from student office would raise constitutional concerns." Of course, Justin's consequences were more serious; he was suspended. Moreover, in citing *Doninger,* we do not suggest that we agree with that court's conclusion that the student's out of school expressive conduct was not protected by the First Amendment there. Rather, we cite *Doninger* only to respond to the School District's contention that that case supports its actions against Justin.

As noted earlier, the District's January 3, 2006, letter to the Layshocks advising them of Justin's suspension reads, in relevant part, that it was punishing Justin because "Justin admitted prior to the informal hearing that he created a profile about Mr. Trosch." Although the letter also mentions disruption, we have taken care to stress that the District does not now challenge the district court's finding that Justin's conduct did not result in any substantial disruption. Moreover, when pressed at oral argument, counsel for the School District conceded that the District was relying solely on the fact that Justin created the profile of Trosch, and not arguing that it created any substantial disruption in the school. However, as noted above, *Fraser* does not allow the School District to punish Justin for expressive conduct which occurred outside of the school context. Moreover, we have found no authority that would support punishment for creating such a profile unless it results in foreseeable and substantial disruption of school.

We believe the cases relied upon by the School District stand for nothing more than the rather unremarkable proposition that schools may punish expressive conduct that occurs outside of school, as if it occurred inside the "schoolhouse gate," under certain very limited circumstances, none of which are present here.

As the court of appeals explained in *Thomas:* "[O]ur willingness to defer to the schoolmaster's expertise in administering school discipline rests, in large measure, upon the supposition that the arm of authority does not reach beyond the schoolhouse gate." We need not now define the precise parameters of when the arm of authority can reach beyond the schoolhouse gate because, as we noted earlier, the district court found that Justin's conduct did not disrupt the school, and the District does not appeal that finding. Thus, we need only hold that Justin's use of the District's Web site does not constitute entering the school, and that the District is not empowered to punish his out of school expressive conduct under the circumstances here.

Based on those two conclusions, we will affirm the district court's grant of summary judgment to Justin Layshock on his First Amendment claim.

NOTES

1. Can you reconcile the outcomes in this case and the previous one?

2. Is it possible to develop a policy for student use of the Internet and social media that could survive a challenge for being over-broad?

CHAPTER 15

STUDENTS WITH DISABILITIES

INTRODUCTION

The educational rights of students with disabilities are governed primarily by two[1] federal statutes: Section 504 of the Rehabilitation Act (Section 504)[2] and the Individuals with Disabilities Education Act (IDEA).[3] Prior to the enactment of these laws, many states overlooked the educational needs of children with disabilities.[4]

Two federal class action suits provided a major impetus for the development of the law of special education. In *Pennsylvania Association for Retarded Children v. Pennsylvania (PARC)*,[5] a federal trial court, in a consent decree, enunciated many of the principles that would be included in the IDEA. In *PARC*, the parties agreed that children who were mentally retarded or those who were thought to have been so could neither have been denied admission to public schools nor subjected to changes in their educational placements unless their parents received procedural due process and that placements in regular school classrooms were preferable to those in more restrictive settings. The court also ruled that all children can learn in school settings while ordering educators to provide those who were mentally retarded with placements affording them a free appropriate public education along with programs meeting their individualized needs.

Mills v. Board of Education of the District of Columbia (Mills)[6] addressed the merits of a case in which the parents of seven named exceptional children filed suit in the federal trial court in Washington, D.C., on behalf of perhaps as many as 18,000 students with disabilities who were not receiving programs of specialized education. Most of the children, who

---

1. A third law, the Americans with Disabilities Act (ADA), 42 U.S.C.A. §§ 12101 *et seq.*, as modified by the ADA Amendments Act of 2008, PL 110–325, 122 Stat. 3553 (2008), extends similar protections to individuals in the private sector. Insofar as the ADA's provisions impacting public education are nearly identical to those of Section 504, and cases interpreting both statutes are compatible, this chapter does not cover the ADA separately.

2. 29 U.S.C.A. § 794(a). This statute is in the Appendix.

3. 20 U.S.C.A. §§ 1400 *et seq.* Portions of this statute are in the Appendix.

4. For apparently the earliest reported case involving a student with a disability, *see Watson v. City of Cambridge*, 32 N.E. 864 (Mass. 1893) (upholding a student's exclusion for being "weak-minded"). *See also State v. Board of Educ. of City of Antigo*, 172 N.W. 153 (Wis. 1919) (affirming the exclusion of a student whose paralysis caused him to speak hesitatingly and drool uncontrollably even though he had the academic ability to benefit from school because "his physical condition and ailment produce[d] a depressing and nauseating effect upon the teachers and school children.").

5. 334 F.Supp. 1257 (E.D. Pa. 1971), 343 F.Supp. 279 (E.D. Pa. 1972).

6. 348 F.Supp. 866 (D.D.C. 1972).

were minorities, were classified as having behavioral problems or mentally retarded, emotionally disturbed, and/or hyperactive. The court rejected the claim of officials that the school board lacked resources for all of its students, deciding that it had to spend its funds equitably so that all children would have been educated in a manner consistent with their individualized needs and abilities. The court decreed that the board could not deny services to children with disabilities or exclude them from school without providing them and their parents with due process. The court ordered the board to provide due process safeguards before any children were excluded from school, reassigned, or had special education services terminated while outlining elaborate due process procedures that essentially formed the foundation for the due process safeguards that were included in the IDEA.

In light of the developments spurred on by *PARC* and *Mills*, this chapter examines the major elements of Section 504 and the IDEA along with key cases from the vast amount of litigation they have generated.

SECTION 504 OF THE REHABILITATION ACT OF 1973

Section 504 of the Rehabilitation Act of 1973, which traces its origins to the wake of World War I, at which time the United States government sought to provide vocational rehabilitation to injured soldiers, is the first federal law addressing the needs of the disabled.[7] According to Section 504, in language close to that in Title VI of the Civil Rights Act of 1964[8] and Title IX of the Educational Amendments of 1972,[9] "[n]o otherwise qualified individual with a disability in the United States ... shall, solely by reason of her or his disability, be excluded from the participation in, be denied the benefits of, or be subjected to discrimination under any program or activity receiving [f]ederal financial assistance...."[10]

There are at least eight initial major differences between Section 504 and the IDEA. First, while Section 504 applies to school systems receiving federal financial assistance, a broadly construed concept,[11] whether in the form of money, books, or free lunches, they do not receive additional funds under its provisions as do the boards that serve children who qualify for IDEA services.[12] Second, Section 504 protects individuals under the broader notion of impairment rather than the IDEA's reliance on the statutorily

---

7. RICHARD K. SCOTCH. FROM GOOD WILL TO CIVIL RIGHTS: TRANSFORMING FEDERAL DISABILITY POLICY (2001).

8. 42 U.S.C.A. §§ 2000 *et seq.* Portions of this statute are in the Appendix.

9. 20 U.S.C.A. § 1681. Portions of this statute are in the Appendix.

10. 29 U.S.C.A. § 794(a).

11. *See, e.g., Bob Jones Univ. v. United States,* 461 U.S. 574, 103 S.Ct. 2017, 76 L.Ed.2d 157 [10 Educ. L. Rep. 918] (1983) (affirming the denial of tax-exempt status to a private university because of its racially discriminatory admissions policy).

12. Since costs issues associated with special education have long been contentious, the revised IDEA set the goal of achieving its initial 1975 promise of funding forty percent of the national average of per-pupil spending by 2011. 20 U.S.C.A. §§ 1411(a)(2)(A)(ii), (h)(7)(B)(I).

defined, and delineated, disabilities. Third, Section 504 has no age limitations while the IDEA covers students from the ages of three to twenty-one or younger if they complete high school. Fourth, while Section 504 covers students, employees, and others, including parents, in schools, the IDEA is limited to students; even so, this chapter focuses on the rights of students. Chapter 9 examines the rights of employees with impairments.

Fifth, while the IDEA places an affirmative obligation on states, through local school boards, to identify, assess, and serve students with disabilities,[13] including those whose parents placed them in private schools,[14] individuals seeking the protections of Section 504 must request accommodations from school officials and may be required to submit proof that they are qualified in the event that there is a difference of opinion. Sixth, the IDEA includes much more extensive due process protections than Section 504, including the requirement that school officials provide written Individualized Education Programs for students who are covered by the IDEA. Seventh, unlike the IDEA, Section 504 does not explicitly require parental consent when providing accommodations for students. Eighth, unlike the IDEA's zero-reject approach, school officials can rely on Section 504's three defenses to avoid being charged with noncompliance.

A regulation enacted to Section 504 defines an eligible individual as one "who (i) has a physical or mental impairment which substantially limits one or more of such person's major life activities, (ii) has a record of such an impairment, or (iii) is regarded as having such an impairment."[15] In order to have "a record of impairment," individuals must have a history of, or been identified as having, a mental or physical impairment that substantially limits one or more major life activities, including learning and working.[16] Once students are identified as having impairments, school officials must consider whether they are "otherwise qualified."

In order to be "otherwise qualified," children must be "(i) of an age during which nonhandicapped persons are provided such services, (ii) of any age during which it is mandatory under state law to provide such services to handicapped persons, or (iii) [one] to whom a state is required to provide a free appropriate public education [under the IDEA]."[17] Persons who are "otherwise qualified,"[18] meaning that they are eligible to participate in programs or activities despite the existence of impairments, must be permitted to do so in such activities as long as they can be provided with "reasonable accommodations."[19]

---

13.   20 U.S.C.A. § 1412(a)(3).

14.   20 U.S.C.A. § 1412(a)(10)(A)(ii)(I).

15.   34 C.F.R. § 104.3(j)(1).

16.   34 C.F.R. § 104.3(j)(2)(ii) ("Major life activities means functions such as caring for one's self, performing manual tasks, walking, seeing, hearing, speaking, breathing, learning, and working.").

17.   34 C.F.R. § 104.3(l)(2).

18.   The Supreme Court examined "otherwise qualified" in *Southeastern Community College v. Davis*, 442 U.S. 397, 410, 99 S.Ct. 2361, 60 L.Ed.2d 980 (1979) [Case No. 109]. The Court modified its analysis in *Alexander v. Choate*, 469 U.S. 287, 105 S.Ct. 712, 83 L.Ed.2d 661 (1985) by adding that qualified individuals are capable of participating in programs or activities if reasonable accommodations are available.

19.   *See Ohio Civil Rights Comm'n v. Case Western Reserve Univ.*, 666 N.E.2d 1376 [110 Educ. L. Rep. 1202] (Ohio 1996) (denying a blind student admission to a medical school

Once officials determine that children are "otherwise qualified" to receive assistance under Section 504, they must decide what accommodations they are willing to provide. Even though Section 504 and its regulations do not explicitly require educational officials to develop written agreements resembling the Individualized Education Programs mandated under the IDEA, it is not uncommon for them to do so. These written agreements, commonly referred to as Section 504 service plans, typically include demographic and other relevant information about children such as their impairments, the names of individuals who participated in developing the plans, copies of reports and data that were relied on in putting plans together, a description of the accommodations that school officials are willing to make, and information about how often and where the services are to be provided.

Reasonable accommodations may involve minor adjustments such as permitting a child to be accompanied by a service dog[20] or having a hearing interpreter.[21] The federal trial court in Minnesota denied a school board's motion for summary judgment in a dispute over whether Section 504 required its officials to train staff at a day care center it operated to provide glucagon injections for a child with Type I diabetes.[22] The court posited that questions of fact remained over the reasonableness and burdensomeness of the request from the child's parents. Typical academic modifications include allowing students more time to complete tests or assignments, having tutors, modifying their class schedules, and/or permitting them to use computers to record answers on examinations. In modifying facilities, officials do not have to make every room and/or area of buildings accessible since it should be enough to bring services to children in areas of schools that have been adapted for their use.

Section 504 prohibits discrimination by requiring educators to make individualized modifications for students who are "otherwise qualified." To this end, officials must offer benefits and/or services that are comparable to those available to students who are not disabled. As such, children who are covered by Section 504 must receive comparable materials, teacher quality, length of school term, and daily hours of instruction. These programs should not be separate from those available to students who are not disabled unless segregation is essential for them to be effective. While school officials are not prohibited from offering separate programs for students under Section 504, children cannot be required to attend such

---

because the accommodations she sought were not reasonable). *See also Hunt v. St. Peter School*, 963 F.Supp. 843 [118 Educ. L. Rep. 663] (W.D. Mo. 1997) (refusing to provide a scent-free environment for a student who was not otherwise qualified because she could not safely attend school without such a modification).

20. *Sullivan v. Vallejo City Unified School Dist.*, 731 F.Supp. 947 [59 Educ. L. Rep. 73] (E.D. Cal.1990). *But see Cave v. East Meadow Union Free School Dist.*, 514 F.3d 240 [229 Educ. L. Rep. 349] (2d Cir. 2008), *on remand*, 2008 WL 268282 (E.D.N.Y. 2008) (denying a request for an order to allow a student to bring a service dog to school since he was accommodated satisfactorily and his parents failed to exhaust administrative remedies before filing suit).

21. *Jones v. Illinois Dep't of Rehab. Servs.*, 689 F.2d 724 [6 Educ. L. Rep. 927] (7th Cir.1982).

22. *AP ex rel. Peterson v. Anoka–Hennepin Indep. School Dist. No. 11*, 538 F. Supp.2d 1125 [230 Educ. L. Rep. 627] (D. Minn. 2008).

classes unless it is not possible to serve them adequately in such settings.[23] If programs are offered separately, facilities must be comparable.[24]

Even if children appear to be "otherwise qualified" under Section 504, school officials can rely on one of three defenses to avoid being charged with noncompliance. This represents another major difference between Section 504 and the IDEA since the latter does not recognize defenses. First, officials can be excused from making accommodations that would result in "a fundamental alteration in the nature of [a] program."[25] The second defense allows officials to avoid making modifications that would impose "undue financial burden[s]"[26] on institutions. The third defense is that "otherwise qualified" students can be excluded from programs if their presence creates a substantial risk of injury to themselves or others.[27] For example, a child with a significant visual impairment could possibly be excluded from a biology laboratory class that involves the use of scalpels for fear of becoming injured. In order to comply with Section 504, officials would likely have to offer a reasonable accommodation such as providing a computer-assisted program to meet an instructional goal that is consistent with what would have been achieved in the laboratory.

In order to guarantee that an appropriate education is made available to all students, Section 504's regulations include due process requirements for evaluation that are similar to, but are not as extensive as, those under the IDEA. Among these requirements, Section 504 directs school officials to file assurances of compliance that their programs are nondiscriminatory,[28] take voluntary remedial actions if they have violated the law so as to overcome the effects of conditions that resulted in limiting the participation of individuals with disabilities,[29] complete self-evaluations to ensure that they comply with Section 504,[30] designate a staff member as compliance coordinator,[31] and adopt grievance procedures[32] even though neither the law nor an accompanying regulation specify what steps such a process should follow. Section 504 also requires recipients of federal financial aid to provide notice to students, parents, employees, and others that they do not discriminate on the basis of disability.[33]

Parties that are dissatisfied with regard to the delivery of educational services under Section 504[34] can file complaints with the Office of Civil

---

23. 34 C.F.R. § 104.4(b)(3).

24. 34 C.F.R. § 104.34(c).

25. *Southeastern Community College v. Davis*, 442 U.S. 397, 410, 99 S.Ct. 2361, 60 L.Ed.2d 980 (1979) [Case No. 109]; *Alexander v. Choate*, 469 U.S. 287, 105 S.Ct. 712, 83 L.Ed.2d 661 (1985).

26. *Davis, id.* at 412.

27. *See School Bd. of Nassau County v. Arline*, 480 U.S. 273, 287–88, 107 S.Ct. 1123, 94 L.Ed.2d 307 [37 Educ. L. Rep. 448] (1987). [Case No. 55]

28. 34 C.F.R. § 104.5.

29. 34 C.F.R. §§ 104.6(a), (b).

30. 34 C.F.R. § 104.6(c).

31. 34 C.F.R. § 104.7(a).

32. 34 C.F.R. § 104.7(b).

33. 34 C.F.R. § 104.8.

34. 7 C.F.R. § 2.300(a)(1)(vi).

Rights, which is responsible for enforcing the law, within 180 days[35] of when alleged infractions occurred. In another difference with the IDEA, Section 504's regulations do not require aggrieved parties to exhaust administrative remedies via due process hearing before filing suits in federal courts. In one such case, a federal trial court in New York rejected a school board's motion for summary judgment where there was evidence that officials acted with deliberate indifference to the pervasive, severe disability harassment that a child suffered at the hands of peers.[36] The Sixth Circuit reached the opposite result in affirming that officials at a model laboratory middle school located on the campus of a university in Kentucky were not liable for disability-based peer-to-peer harassment under Section 504.[37] The court agreed that insofar as officials met with and disciplined offending students in addition to communicating with their parents, they did not demonstrate deliberate indifference that could have rendered them liable.

INDIVIDUALS WITH DISABILITIES EDUCATION ACT

GENERALLY

Initially enacted in 1975 as the Education for All Handicapped Children Act,[38] the IDEA was revised in 1986, 1990, 1997, and 2004; the 2004 version of the IDEA became fully effective on July 1, 2005.[39] As noted. a pre-condition of receiving federal funds[40] under the IDEA and its regulations affirmatively obligates states, through local educational agencies or school boards, to identify, evaluate, and serve all children with disabilities,[41] including those in private schools,[42] regardless of the severity of their needs.

Insofar as the child find provisions are included as a related service in the IDEA's regulations, many school systems screen pre-school children[43] to

---

35. 34 C.F.R. § 100.7(b).

36. *K.M. ex rel. D.G. v. Hyde Park Cent. School Dist.*, 381 F. Supp.2d 343 [201 Educ. L. Rep. 510] (S.D.N.Y. 2005). *But see Werth v. Board of Directors of Pub. Schools of City of Milwaukee*, 472 F. Supp.2d 1113 [217 Educ. L. Rep. 415] (E.D. Wis. 2007) (denying such a claim).

37. *S.S. v. Eastern Ky. Univ.*, 532 F.3d 445 [234 Educ. L. Rep. 612] (6th Cir. 2008).

38. The IDEA is still sometimes referred to as P.L. 94–142, indicating that it was the one hundred and forty-second piece of legislation introduced during the Ninety–Fourth Congress. For the sake of consistency, this chapter refers to the law as the IDEA, which incorporated the changes in the Individuals with Disabilities Education Improvement Act of 2004, even for cases that were resolved before the statute's 1990 reauthorization and name change.

39. For the sake of consistency, this chapter refers to the most recent re-authorization of the IDEA as the 2004 version of the law.

40. *Fayette County Bd. of Educ. v. M.R.D. ex rel. K.D.*, 158 S.W.3d 195 [197 Educ. L. Rep. 413] (Ky. 2005).

41. *See Carmel Cent. School Dist. v. V.P. ex rel. G.P.*, 373 F. Supp.2d 402 [199 Educ. L. Rep. 666] (S.D.N.Y. 2005) (reiterating the rule that only children classified as disabled are entitled to special education services from their public school boards under the IDEA).

42. 34 C.F.R. § 300.129.

assist in the early identification of students with disabilities.[44] A significant change in the 2004 version of the IDEA requires public school officials not only to identify children who attend private schools in the districts where they attend classes,[45] rather than within which they live,[46] but also to provide child find activities for these students that are comparable to those used in public schools.[47] Public school officials must also report the number of children from private schools who are evaluated, identified as having disabilities, and served to personnel at state education agencies.[48]

School boards can meet their child find responsibilities, in part, by distributing information about the process for obtaining evaluations for special education. For example, the Third Circuit affirmed that a school board in Pennsylvania satisfied the IDEA's child find activities by placing annual notices in local newspapers, on its Web site, on public access television as well as by placing posters and pamphlets in public and private school buildings along with including notices to parents in their annual tax bills.[49]

Another noteworthy change associated with identifying children in need of special education services requires state officials to develop policies and procedures to prevent the over-identification or disproportionate representation of students by race and ethnicity.[50] This part of the law directs educators to record the number of students from minority groups who are in special education classes and to provide early intervention services for children in groups deemed to be over-represented. In a case interpreting this provision, a federal trial court in Pennsylvania rejected the request of parents who sought class certification based on their claim that their school board practiced systematic and intentional racial segregation against African American students with learning disabilities.[51] The court ruled both that the proposed class of students was too broad and that any such claim had to be filed by individuals rather than by members of a group.

In order to be covered by the IDEA, children must meet four requirements. First, students must be between the ages of three and twenty-one;[52] students are treated as being twenty-one until the end of the academic

---

43.   20 U.S.C.A. §§ 1412(3)(A), 1412(a)(10)(a).

44.   *See, e.g., Independent School Dist. No. 709 v. Bonney,* 705 N.W.2d 209 [202 Educ. L. Rep. 828] (Minn. Ct. App. 2005) (affirming that school officials violated the IDEA and state law in not providing services for pre-school children with disabilities).

45.   20 U.S.C.A. § 1412(a)(10)(A)(I).

46.   *But see District of Columbia v. Abramson,* 493 F. Supp.2d 80 [222 Educ. L. Rep. 207] (D.D.C. 2007) (holding that the IDEA does not prevent parents from asking for evaluations in the districts where children live and that nothing relieves boards of their duty to carry out such requests).

47.   20 U.S.C.A. § 1412(a)(10)(A)(ii)(I).

48.   20 U.S.C.A. § 1412(a)(10)(A)(ii).

49.   *P.P. ex rel. Michael P. v. West Chester Area Sch. Dist.,* 585 F.3d 727 [250 Educ. L. Rep. 517] (3d Cir. 2009).

50.   20 U.S.C.A. §§ 1412(a)(24), 1418(d)(1)(A)(B).

51.   *Blunt v. Lower Merion School Dist.,* 262 F.R.D. 481 [251 Educ. L. Rep. 775] (E.D. Pa. 2009).

52.   20 U.S.C.A. § 1412(a)(1)(A). The IDEA also addresses the needs of children aged three through nine who are "(I) experiencing developmental delays, as defined by the State and as

years in which they reach the statutory age limit.[53] Second, children must have specifically identified disabilities.[54] Third, students must be in need of special education,[55] meaning that they need a "free appropriate public education"[56] (FAPE) in the least restrictive environments where their education is directed by the contents of their Individualized Education Programs (IEP).[57] Fourth, children must be in need of related services.[58]

The IDEA includes extensive due process protections safeguarding the rights of children[59] and their parents.[60] Among these protections, parents must be informed before consenting to initial evaluations[61] which must occur within sixty days of when educational officials received consent to conduct them,[62] and/or placements of their children[63] and have the right to take part in developing IEPs that direct the education of their children.[64]

Pursuant to the IDEA, state and local officials are not required to develop IEPs for students if their parents either refuse to consent to the receipt of special education services or fail to respond to requests to provide their consent.[65] This section of the IDEA adds that if parents do not consent to initial evaluations or fail to respond to requests to provide consent, officials can still pursue initial evaluations by utilizing the procedures described in the IDEA's due process provisions unless doing so would be inconsistent with state law relating to parental consent.[66] The First[67]

---

measured by appropriate diagnostic instruments and procedures, in 1 [sic] or more of the following areas: physical development; cognitive development; communication development; social or emotional development; or adaptive development." 20 U.S.C.A. § 1401(3)(B)(I).

53. *C.T. ex rel. M.T. v. Verona Bd. of Educ.*, 464 F. Supp.2d 383 [215 Educ. L. Rep. 874] (D.N.J. 2006).

54. 20 U.S.C.A. § 1401(3)(A)(I). This section reads:

The term "child with a disability" means a child—

(I) with mental retardation, hearing impairments (including deafness), speech or language impairments, visual impairments (including blindness), serious emotional disturbance (referred to in this chapter as "emotional disturbance"), orthopedic impairments, autism, traumatic brain injury, other health impairments, or specific learning disabilities....

55. 20 U.S.C.A. § 1401(3)(A)(ii).

56. 20 U.S.C.A. § 1401(9).

57. 20 U.S.C.A. §§ 1401(11), 1414(d).

58. 20 U.S.C.A. § 1401(3)(A)(ii).

59. 20 U.S.C.A. § 1415.

60. The IDEA's expanded definition of parent covers natural, adoptive, or foster parents, guardians, and individuals acting in the place of natural or adoptive parents (including grandparents, stepparents, or other relatives) with whom children live, or individuals who are legally responsible for a child's welfare. 20 U.S.C.A. § 1401(23).

61. 20 U.S.C.A. § 1414(a)(1)(D)(i)(I) (in performing initial evaluations, no single procedure can be the sole criterion for determining eligibility or placement of students with special needs), 20 U.S.C.A. § 1414(b)(2)(B)

62. 20 U.S.C.A. § 1414(a)(1)(C)(i)(I).

63. 20 U.S.C.A. § 1414(a)(1)(D)(I). *Gill v. Columbia 93 School Dist.*, 217 F.3d 1027 [145 Educ. L. Rep. 894] (8th Cir.2000), *reh'g and reh'g en banc denied* (2000).

64. 20 U.S.C.A. § 1414(d)(1)(B)(i).

65. 20 U.S.C.A. §§ 1414(a)(1)(D)(ii)(II), (III).

66. 20 U.S.C.A. § 1414(a)(1)(D)(ii)(I).

67. *C.G. and B.S. v. Five Town Community School Dist.*, 513 F.3d 279 [229 Educ. L. Rep. 18] (1st Cir. 2008) (affirming that where parents obstructed the IEP process, there was no reason to disturb a school board's having placed their child in a public non-residential school).

and Seventh[68] Circuits agreed that boards cannot be liable for failing to provide services to students with disabilities if their parents refuse to cooperate in the IEP process. Earlier, the Fourth Circuit reached the same outcome.[69] Further, in a case from New York involving home schooling, a federal trial court overturned the results of a due process hearing in favor of a school board in noting that insofar as the parents refused to consent to services, there was no reason for the dispute to have proceeded.[70]

Once students are placed in special education settings, school officials must notify parents before trying to change their placements.[71] Parents may be entitled to independent evaluations at public expense if they disagree with school board evaluations[72] or if officials fail either to evaluate their children entirely[73] or in a timely manner.[74] Parents who successfully challenge the assessments of their children can be reimbursed for the costs of doing so.[75] If hearing officers or courts determine that board evaluations were appropriate, parents are not entitled to further testing at public expense.[76]

The IDEA[77] and its accompanying regulations,[78] supplemented by the Family Educational Rights and Privacy Act (FERPA)[79] and its regulations,[80] protect the confidentiality of information used in the evaluation, placement, and education of students with disabilities.[81] While FERPA is

---

68. *Hjortness v. Neenah Joint School Dist.*, 498 F.3d 655 [224 Educ. L. Rep. 41] (7th Cir. 2007) (withdrawn from bound volume), *amended and superseded, petition for reh'g en banc denied*, 508 F.3d 851 (7th Cir. 2007) (affirming that a board was not liable where parents refused to cooperate in formulating a second IEP for their son), *cert. denied*, 554 U.S. 930, 128 S.Ct. 2962, 171 L.Ed.2d 906 [233 Educ. L. Rep. 522] (2008).

69. *MM ex rel. DM v. School Dist. of Greenville County*, 303 F.3d 523 [169 Educ. L. Rep. 59] (4th Cir. 2002) (finding that parents who refused to participate in its formulation could not render school officials liable for failing to have an IEP completed and signed since their inability to do so was caused by their own lack of cooperation).

70. *Durkee v. Livonia Cent. School Dist.*, 487 F. Supp.2d 313 [221 Educ. L. Rep. 129] (W.D.N.Y. 2007).

71. 20 U.S.C.A. § 1415(b)(3)(A).

72. 20 U.S.C.A. § 1415(b)(1).

73. *N.B. v. Hellgate Elementary School Dist., ex rel. Bd. of Directors, Missoula County, Mont.*, 541 F.3d 1202 [236 Educ. L. Rep. 603] (9th Cir. 2008) (affirming that a board's failure to evaluate a student in all areas of his suspected disability, including whether he was autistic, was a procedural error denying him a FAPE).

74. *Idea Public Charter School v. District of Columbia*, 374 F. Supp.2d 158 [199 Educ. L. Rep. 754] (D.D.C. 2005). *But see Herbin ex rel. Herbin v. District of Columbia*, 362 F. Supp.2d 254 [197 Educ. L. Rep. 142] (D.D.C. 2005) (rejecting a claim that a four-month delay in assessing a child violated the IDEA where current evaluations existed and educators were unable to determine why the request was necessary).

75. *A.S. ex rel. S. v. Norwalk Bd. of Educ.*, 183 F. Supp.2d 534 [161 Educ. L. Rep. 827] (D. Conn. 2002).

76. 34 C.F.R. § 300.502(b). *See also Lauren W. ex rel. Jean W. v. DeFlaminis*, 480 F.3d 259 [217 Educ. L. Rep. 96] (3d Cir. 2007); *P.R. v. Woodmore Local School Dist.*, 481 F. Supp.2d 860 [219 Educ. L. Rep. 654] (N.D. Ohio 2007), *aff'd*, 256 Fed.Appx. 751 [230 Educ. L. Rep. 190] (6th Cir. 2007).

77. 20 U.S.C.A. § 1417(c).

78. 34 C.F.R. §§ 300.610 *et seq.*

79. 29 U.S.C.A. § 1232g.

80. 34 C.F.R. §§ 99.1 *et seq.*

81. 20 U.S.C.A. § 1417(c).

examined in some detail in Chapter 12, it is worth noting that the IDEA has made an important clarification concerning the transfer of parental rights to students who have achieved the age of majority. Pursuant to this part of the law, when children with disabilities who are not adjudicated incompetent under state law achieve the age of majority, school officials must notify them and their parents that the parental rights of access have been transferred to their children.[82] A special rule applies to students who are not adjudicated incompetent but lack the ability to provide informed consent with respect to their educational programming. In such situations, officials must establish procedures for appointing their parents, or if they are not available, other appropriate persons, to represent students' educational interests throughout their remaining period of eligibility under the IDEA.[83]

INDIVIDUALIZED EDUCATION PROGRAMS

Individualized Education Programs must provide students with disabilities with more than trivial advancement[84] and must be developed by teams identified by various names depending on state law. IEPs must describe students' current levels of educational performance, annual goals and short-term objectives, the specific services that they will receive, the extent to which they can take part in general education, the date services are to begin and how long they will be offered, and criteria to evaluate whether they are achieving their goals.[85] At the same time, IEPs must discuss, on a "case-by-case basis"[86] how students' disabilities affect their ability to be involved in and progress in inclusive settings as well as necessary modifications to allow them to take part in the general curriculum,[87] possibly including participation in extracurricular activities that may be appropriate to advance their educational needs.[88]

IEPs must detail the related services students need to benefit from their programming.[89] A new provision in the 2004 version of the IDEA

---

82. 20 U.S.C.A. § 1415(m)(1).

83. 20 U.S.C.A. § 1415(m)(2).

84. *D.F. ex rel. N.F. v. Ramapo Cent. School Dist.*, 430 F.3d 595 [203 Educ. L. Rep. 500] (2d Cir. 2005).

85. 20 U.S.C.A. § 1414(d)(1)(A). *See also, e.g., Mackey v. Board of Educ. for Arlington Cent. School Dist.*, 373 F. Supp.2d 292 [199 Educ. L. Rep. 655] (S.D.N.Y. 2005) (reiterating the IDEA's general provisions concerning IEPs).

86. *C.B. ex rel. B.B. v. Special School Dist. No. 1, Minneapolis, Minn.*, 636 F.3d 981, 989 [266 Educ. L. Rep. 71] (8th Cir. 2011).

87. For a case on measuring the progress of a student with a disability, *see Claudia C–B v. Board of Trustees of Pioneer Valley Performing Arts Charter School*, 539 F. Supp.2d 474 [231 Educ. L. Rep. 89] (D. Mass. 2008) (rejecting a parental claim that officials should have modified a school's grading system to accommodate their son since they allegedly received insufficient input on his progress to decide whether they should have requested that he be provided with additional assistance; the child had been evaluated under a competency-based system affording his teachers flexibility in considering whether he mastered the subject matter, through the use of tests, discussions, or other methods and simply passed or failed him without awarding letter or numerical grades).

88. *Independent School Dist. No. 12 v. Minnesota Dep't of Educ.*, 788 N.W.2d 907 [260 Educ. L. Rep. 409] (Minn. 2010), *cert. denied*, ___ U.S. ___, 131 S.Ct. 1556, 179 L.Ed.2d 309 (2011).

specifies that IEP teams are no longer required to develop benchmarks and short-term objectives for children with disabilities other than for those who take alternate assessments aligned to alternate achievement standards.[90]

When assessments are completed, and children are identified as being in need of IEPs, school officials must convene IEP meetings within thirty calendar days.[91] However, in a case from California, the Ninth Circuit agreed that school officials who failed to meet this deadline did not violate a student's right to a FAPE because they would have been unable to assess his need adequately during this time frame.[92]

Teams must include a child's parents who have the right to participate actively in the development of the IEP;[93] at least one regular education teacher if the child is, or will be, participating, in regular education;[94] at least one special education teacher or, if appropriate, one of the child's special education providers; a representative of the school board who is qualified to provide, or supervise, the delivery of special education, knowledgeable about general education, the board's resources, and evaluation procedures; a person who can interpret the instructional implications of evaluation results; others, at the discretion of parents or boards, who are knowledgeable or have special expertise about the student; and, when appropriate, the child.[95] Nothing prevents school officials from bringing draft IEPs to meetings.[96] If a student attends a private school, then a representative of the school should be present at IEP conferences.[97]

The language of the IDEA notwithstanding, courts disagree on who should be present at IEP meetings. A federal trial court in New York ruled that an IEP team without a teacher who taught, or would be teaching, a student denied him a FAPE.[98] Conversely, another federal trial court in

---

89. 20 U.S.C.A. § 1414(d)(1)(A)(i)(IV).

90. 20 U.S.C.A. § 1414(d)(1)(A)(I).

91. 34 C.F.R. § 300.323(c)(1).

92. *A.M. ex rel. Marshall v. Monrovia Unified School Dist.*, 627 F.3d 773 [263 Educ. L. Rep. 44] (9th Cir. 2010).

93. *Fort Osage R–1 School Dist. v. Sims ex rel. B.S.*, 641 F.3d 996 [268 Educ. L. Rep. 78] (8th Cir. 2011) (noting that teams must consider parental concerns in developing IEPs).

94. *See Matrejek v. Brewster Cent. School Dist.*, 293 Fed.Appx. 20 [239 Educ. L. Rep. 344] (2d Cir. 2008) (although rejecting a parental placement as unilateral, acknowledging that a hearing officer struck down an earlier version of an IEP as deficient since the IEP team failed to include teachers who either taught the student or would be teaching a program appropriate for the child). *But see L.R. v. Manheim Twp. School Dist.*, 540 F. Supp.2d 603 [231 Educ. L. Rep. 197] (E.D. Pa. 2008) (holding that while a board's failure to include a regular education teacher on a student's IEP team violated the IDEA's procedural requirement, her absence did not deprive the child of a FAPE).

95. 20 U.S.C.A. § 1414(d)(1)(B); 34 C.F.R. § 300.321(a).

96. *See, e.g., Board of Educ. of Twp. High School Dist. No. 211 v. Ross*, 486 F.3d 267 [220 Educ. L. Rep. 482] (7th Cir. 2007) (affirming that even though educators brought a draft IEP to a meeting, their doing so did not deprive parents of their participation rights). *But see D.B. ex rel. H.B. v. Gloucester Twp. School Dist.*, 751 F.Supp.2d 764 [265 Educ. L. Rep. 719] (D.N.J. 2010) (declaring that board officials who predetermined a child's IEP denied her parents the opportunity to engage in meaningful participation in its development).

97. 34 C.F.R. § 300.325(a)(2).

98. *Matrejek v. Brewster Cent. School Dist.*, 293 Fed.Appx. 20 [239 Educ. L. Rep. 344] (2d Cir. 2008). *But see A.H. ex rel. J.H. v. Department of Educ.*, 394 Fed.Appx 718 [263 Educ. L.

New York refused to invalidate an IEP where a child's regular education teacher was not present at his IEP meeting since he was not going to be placed in a regular educational setting.[99] Similarly, the Ninth Circuit agreed that a board did not violate a child's right to a FAPE by failing to place a teacher who instructed him on his IEP team since the IDEA grants officials discretion as to their membership.[100]

Prior to the enactment of the 2004 version of the IDEA, federal appellate courts disagreed over whether regular education teachers should attend IEP meetings. On the one hand, the Ninth Circuit found that the failure of a school board in Washington to include a regular education teacher on a child's IEP team was a significant violation of the IDEA since he was going to spend time in a regular education setting.[101] Yet, the Fourth Circuit[102] thought it unnecessary for a board in North Carolina to have a regular education teacher at an IEP meeting since the child was not being considered for a placement in regular education.[103]

Once IEPs are developed, officials must implement them "[a]s soon as possible."[104] IEPs must be reviewed at least annually[105] and re-evaluated at least once every three years unless parents and local school officials agree that re-evaluations are unnecessary.[106] The 2004 IDEA includes three significant changes with regard to IEPs. First, the IDEA no longer specifies the need for benchmarks and short-term objectives for children with disabilities other than those who take alternate assessments aligned to alternate achievement standards.[107] Second, the IDEA allows up to fifteen states to pilot comprehensive multi-year IEPs as long as they do not exceed three years and are designed to coincide with natural transition points in a child's education.[108] Third, teams can make minor changes to IEPs by means of conference calls or letters.[109]

Rep. 56] (2d Cir. 2010) (ruling that even though a child's special education teacher was not present at an IEP meeting, the IEP could remain in effect because it was substantively adequate).

99. *W.T. and K.T. ex rel. J.T. v. Board of Educ. of School Dist. of N.Y.C.*, 716 F. Supp. 2d 270 (S.D.N.Y. 2010).

100. *R.B., ex rel. F.B. v. Napa Valley Unified School Dist.*, 496 F.3d 932 [223 Educ. L. Rep. 559] (9th Cir. 2007).

101. *M.L. v. Federal Way School Dist.*, 394 F.3d 634 [194 Educ. L. Rep. 811] (9th Cir. 2005), *cert. denied*, 545 U.S. 1128, 125 S.Ct. 2941, 162 L.Ed.2d 867 (2005). *See also Werner v. Clarkstown Cent. School Dist.*, 363 F. Supp.2d 656 [197 Educ. L. Rep. 244] (S.D.N.Y. 2005) (positing that a board failed to comply with the IDEA's procedural requirements by not including a representative from its recommended therapeutic placement at a child's IEP meeting).

102. *Cone v. Randolph County Schools*, 103 Fed.Appx. 731 (4th Cir. 2004), *cert. denied*, 543 U.S. 1124, 125 S.Ct. 1077, 160 L.Ed.2d 1075 (2005).

103. *See also Johnson ex rel. Johnson v. Olathe District Schools Unified School Dist. No. 233, Special Servs. Div.*, 316 F. Supp.2d 960 [188 Educ. L. Rep. 307] (D. Kan. 2003) (stating that a board did not violate the IDEA by failing to include a regular education teacher on a child's IEP team since he was not going to spend any time in a regular educational class).

104. 34 C.F.R. § 300.323(c)(2).

105. 20 U.S.C.A. § 1414(d)(4).

106. 20 U.S.C.A. § 1414(a)(2)(B)(ii).

107. 20 U.S.C.A. § 1414(d)(1)(A)(I).

108. 20 U.S.C.A. § 1414(d)(5)(A).

109. 20 U.S.C.A. § 1414(f).

Two related changes accompany the proposed three-year IEP provision. The first seeks to reduce the significant amount of paperwork associated with the delivery of special education services;[110] this allows up to fifteen states to pilot paperwork-reduction plans to reduce the burden on teachers, administrators, and related service providers.[111] The second complements the paperwork reduction provisions by directing the Secretary of Education to develop model forms for IEPs, individualized family service plans, the IDEA's procedural safeguards, and its prior written notice provisions no later than when the IDEA's final regulations were promulgated.[112]

As children near graduation or begin to "age out" of special education, educators must develop individualized transition services plans to promote their movement to post-school activities.[113] To this end, federal trial courts in Massachusetts[114] and Texas[115] agreed that the failure of school boards to develop appropriate transition plans for students violated their rights to a FAPE. In a related matter, the First Circuit affirmed that transition plans need not be stand-alone components of IEPs.[116]

In a case from California, the Ninth Circuit addressed the crucial question of the circumstances under which school boards can be liable for failing to implement IEPs. Ruling in favor of the board in a dispute involving an autistic child, the court explained that educational officials were not at fault because the alleged variation in how they implemented the student's IEP did not amount to a material failure to carry out its terms[117] since the IDEA does not necessarily require strict compliance with their terms.[118]

A novel question arose in Ohio as to whether parents could tape record an IEP meeting. A federal trial court rejected a parental request to tape record the meeting since the IDEA neither creates such a right nor did they articulate a good reason for wanting to do so.[119]

FREE APPROPRIATE PUBLIC EDUCATION

The IDEA entitles children to instruction, at no cost to their parents, that is specially designed to meet their unique needs.[120] If parents have

---

110.   20 U.S.C.A. § 1408(2)(A).

111.   20 U.S.C.A. § 1414(d)(5)(B)(i).

112.   20 U.S.C.A. § 1417(e).

113.   20 U.S.C.A. § 1414(d)(1)(A)(VII)(ii); 20 U.S.C.A. § 1401(30). *Browell v. Lemahieu*, 127 F. Supp.2d 1117 [150 Educ. L. Rep. 732] (D. Haw. 2000).

114.   *Dracut School Comm. v. Bureau of Special Educ. Appeals of Mass. Dep't of Elementary and Secondary Educ.*, 737 F. Supp. 2d 35 [263 Educ. L. Rep. 625] (D. Mass. 2010).

115.   *Klein Indep. School Dist. v. Hovem*, 745 F. Supp. 2d 700 [265 Educ. L. Rep. 55] (S.D. Tex. 2010).

116.   *Lessard v. Wilton Lyndeborough Coop. School Dist.*, 518 F.3d 18 [230 Educ. L. Rep. 485] (1st Cir. 2008).

117.   *Van Duyn ex rel. van Duyn v. Baker School Dist.*, 502 F.3d 811 [225 Educ. L. Rep. 136] (9th Cir. 2007).

118.   *See also Catalan v. District of Columbia*, 478 F. Supp.2d 73 [218 Educ. L. Rep. 477] (D.D.C. 2007) (deciding that a school board's inability to comply strictly with an IEP was excusable since the student was often too tired to continue his therapy).

119.   *Horen v. Board of Educ. of Toledo Pub. Sch. Dist.*, 655 F. Supp.2d 794 [251 Educ. L. Rep. 252] (N.D. Ohio 2009).

insurance, they can be asked to file claims to help defray costs.[121] However, this does not permit school officials to refuse to provide services if parents are unwilling, or unable, to bill their insurance carriers.

Insofar as neither the IDEA nor its regulations included a definition of "appropriate," it was necessary to seek judicial intervention. In *Board of Education of the Hendrick Hudson Central School District v. Rowley* (*Rowley*),[122] its first case involving the IDEA, the Supreme Court interpreted "appropriate" as providing a floor of opportunities rather than as a vehicle to maximize a child's potential.[123] In *Rowley*, parents of a kindergarten student in New York who was hearing impaired challenged their school board's refusal to provide their daughter with a sign-language interpreter. After a hearing officer and lower federal courts agreed that officials had to provide the child with an interpreter since an appropriate education was one that would have allowed her to achieve at about the same level as her peers who were not disabled, the Court reversed in favor of the board.

The Supreme Court, acknowledging that the child earned passing marks and advanced academically without the sign-language interpreter, reasoned that an "appropriate" education was one that met the IDEA's procedures and was "sufficient to confer some educational benefit"[124] on her by providing "a basic floor of opportunity."[125] In being convinced that the child received "some educational benefit" without the sign-language interpreter, the Court concluded that she was not entitled to one even though she might have achieved at a higher level if officials provided her with such assistance.

Rowley's interpreting the IDEA as having set a minimum level of appropriateness does not prevent states from setting higher standards. Courts have upheld higher state requirements in California,[126] Michigan,[127]

120.   20 U.S.C.A. § 1401(29).

121.   34 C.F.R. §§ 300.154(d)–(g).

122.   458 U.S. 176, 102 S.Ct. 3034, 73 L.Ed.2d 690 [5 Educ. L. Rep. 34] (1982) [Case No. 110]. *See also Todd v. Duneland School Corp.*, 299 F.3d 899 [168 Educ. L. Rep. 67] (7th Cir. 2002).

123.   *See Mr. and Mrs. C. v. Maine School Admin. Dist. No. 6*, 538 F. Supp.2d 298 [230 Educ. L. Rep. 599] (D. Me. 2008) (deciding that the IDEA's definition of a FAPE does not require school officials to maximize the potential of students with disabilities).

124.   *Rowley*, 458 U.S. 176 at 200. *See Thompson R2–J School Dist. v. Luke P., ex rel. Jeff P.*, 540 F.3d 1143 [236 Educ. L. Rep. 179] (10th Cir. 2008), *cert. denied*, 555 U.S. 1173, 129 S.Ct. 1356, 173 L.Ed.2d 590 (2009) (ruling that this standard does not require educators to prepare students to be independently self-sufficient).

125.   *Fayette County Bd. of Educ. v. M.R.D. ex rel. K.D.*, 158 S.W.3d 195, 202 [197 Educ. L. Rep. 413] (Ky. 2005) (denying a parental request for reimbursement for a unilateral private school placement in citing to *Rowley*).

126.   *Pink v. Mt. Diablo Unified School Dist.*, 738 F.Supp. 345 [61 Educ. L. Rep. 120] (N.D. Cal. 1990).

127.   *Barwacz v. Michigan Dep't of Educ.*, 681 F.Supp. 427 [46 Educ. L. Rep. 98] (W.D. Mich. 1988).

Missouri,[128] New Jersey,[129] and North Carolina.[130] Some of these courts recognized that the higher state standards replaced the federal requirements since the IDEA expects special education programs to meet "the standards of the state educational agency."[131] At least one state, West Virginia, specifies that "no state rule, policy or standard under this article or any county board rule, policy or standard governing special education may exceed the requirements of federal law or regulation."[132] Further, the federal trial court in Massachusetts noted that after having set a higher standard of appropriateness than federal law for students with disabilities, in 2002 officials amended commonwealth statutes to conform to the more basic IDEA standard.[133]

Courts have interpreted *Rowley's* "some educational benefit" criterion as requiring more than minimal growth,[134] adding that it must be meaningful[135] or appreciable.[136] In this regard, the Eleventh Circuit maintained that in order to meet the *Rowley* standard, student gains must be measurable.[137]

Under the *Rowley* standard, the services school officials provide for students with disabilities must be reasonably calculated to enable them to receive educational benefits under their IEPs. In such a case, the Eighth Circuit affirmed that insofar as a student's attention deficit and hyperactivity disorder (ADHD) adversely impacted his educational performance, he was entitled to an IEP because he met the IDEA's requirements as being "other health impaired."[138] Conversely, the federal trial court in Hawaii rejected a proposed IEP for a student with ADHD because it was not convinced that it was reasonably calculated to enable him to receive educational benefits insofar as officials failed to take his progress report into account in developing the IEP.[139] Earlier, the Eighth Circuit ruled that a student with Ehlers–Danlos Syndrome was not entitled to an IEP because

---

128. *Lagares v. Camdenton R–III School Dist.*, 68 S.W.3d 518 [162 Educ. L. Rep. 1003] (Mo. Ct. App. 2001).

129. *Geis v. Board of Educ. of Parsippany–Troy Hills*, 774 F.2d 575 [27 Educ. L. Rep. 1093] (3d Cir. 1985).

130. *CM ex rel. JM v. Board of Educ. of Henderson County*, 85 F. Supp.2d 574 [142 Educ. L. Rep. 299] (W.D.N.C.1999), *aff'd in part, rev'd and remanded in part*, 241 F.3d 374 [151 Educ. L. Rep. 157] (4th Cir.2001), *on remand*, 184 F. Supp.2d 466 [162 Educ. L. Rep. 126] (W.D.N.C.2002).

131. 20 U.S.C.A. § 1401(a)(9)(B).

132. W. VA. CODE ANN. § 18–20–5(3).

133. *Wanham v. Everett Pub. Schools*, 550 F. Supp.2d 152 [233 Educ. L. Rep. 573] (D. Mass. 2008).

134. *Hall v. Vance County Bd. of Educ.*, 774 F.2d 629 [27 Educ. L. Rep. 1107] (4th Cir.1985); *Carter v. Florence County School Dist. Four*, 950 F.2d 156 [71 Educ. L. Rep. 633] (4th Cir. 1991), *aff'd on other grounds*, 510 U.S. 7, 114 S.Ct. 361, 126 L.Ed.2d 284 [86 Educ. L. Rep. 41] (1993); *County School Bd. of Henrico County, Va. v. Z.P. ex rel. R.P.*, 399 F.3d 298 [195 Educ. L. Rep. 715] (4th Cir. 2005).

135. *Samuel Tyler W. ex rel. Harvey W. v. Northwest Indep. School Dist.*, 202 F. Supp.2d 557 [165 Educ. L. Rep. 572] (N.D. Tex. 2002).

136. *Chris C. v. Gwinnett County School Dist.*, 780 F.Supp. 804 [72 Educ. L. Rep. 146] (N.D. Ga. 1991).

137. *JSK v. Hendry County School Bd.*, 941 F.2d 1563 [69 Educ. L. Rep. 689] (11th Cir.1991).

138. *Hansen ex rel. J.H. v. Republic R–III School Dist.*, 632 F.3d 1024 [265 Educ. L. Rep. 9] (8th Cir. 2011), *reh'g and reh'g en banc denied* (2011).

139. *Marc M. ex rel. Aidan M. v. Department of Educ., Hawaii*, 762 F.Supp.2d 1235 [267 Educ. L. Rep. 189] (D. Haw. 2011).

it did not adversely impact his educational performance.[140] Even so, under the IDEA's so-called "zero-reject" approach, illustrated by a seminal case from the First Circuit,[141] all eligible children must be served regardless of the severity of their disabilities.

Requiring school officials to provide students with disabilities with a "public education" is closely aligned with the fact that it must be free, meaning at public expense, even if children are not educated in public schools. This notion is highlighted in the ensuing discussions of the continuum of placements and on the rights of students who attend private schools. Concerns over its demise notwithstanding, the Ninth Circuit reiterated that the *Rowley* standard is alive and well because Congress has made no attempt to change the Supreme Court's holding.[142]

LEAST RESTRICTIVE ENVIRONMENT

Students with disabilities must be educated in the least restrictive environment.[143] In carrying out this requirement, school officials must provide a continuum of alternative placements[144] from least to most restrictive. The first four options, which are typically in a child's home school, are full inclusion in a regular class, inclusion in a regular class with help such as a teacher's aide,[145] partial inclusion with an aide plus some time in a resource room, and a self-contained placement in a resource room.[146] The final, more restrictive, options are special day schools, hospital or homebound instruction, and residential placements.[147] In addition, the IDEA forbids educational officials from requiring parents to obtain prescriptions for their children for substances such as Ritalin under the Controlled Substances Act as a condition of attending school, being evaluated, or receiving special education services.[148]

Two federal appellate courts agreed that educators must review a variety of factors when considering the restrictiveness of the environment

---

140. *Marshall Joint School Dist. No. 2 v. C.D. ex rel. Brian D.*, 616 F.3d 632 [260 Educ. L. Rep. 46] (7th Cir. 2010), *reh'g and reh'g en banc denied* (2010).

141. *Timothy W. v. Rochester, N.H., School Dist.*, 875 F.2d 954 [54 Educ. L. Rep.74] (1st Cir.1989), *cert. denied*, 493 U.S. 983, 110 S.Ct. 519, 107 L.Ed.2d 520 (1989). [Case No. 111]

142. *J.L., M.L., K.L. v. Mercer Island School Dist.*, 592 F.3d 938 [252 Educ. L. Rep. 591] (9th Cir. 2010).

143. 20 U.S.C.A. §§ 1406(b)(2), 1412(a)(5).

144. 34 C.F.R. § 300.115(a).

145. *A.B. ex rel. D.B. v. Lawson*, 354 F.3d 315 [184 Educ. L. Rep. 37] (4th Cir. 2004).

146. *Lt. T.B. ex rel. N.B. v. Warwick School Comm.*, 361 F.3d 80 [186 Educ. L. Rep. 15] (1st Cir. 2004).

147. 34 C.F.R. § 300.115(b)(1).

148. 20 U.S.C.A. § 1412(a)(25). For some of the earlier litigation over Ritalin, *see, e.g.*, *DeBord v. Board of Educ. of the Ferguson–Florissant School Dist.*, 126 F.3d 1102 (8th Cir. 1997), *cert. denied*, 523 U.S. 1073, 118 S.Ct. 1514, 140 L.Ed.2d 667 (1998); *Davis v. Francis Howell School Dist.*, 138 F.3d 754 [124 Educ. L. Rep. 840] (8th Cir. 1998) (agreeing that school officials did not violate Section 504 or the IDEA in refusing to administer Ritalin to unruly students). *See also Valerie J. v. Derry Co-op. School Dist.*, 771 F.Supp. 483 [69 Educ. L. Rep. 1067] (D.N.H. 1991), *clarifying order*, 771 F.Supp. 492 (D.N.H. 1991) (indicating that officials could not require a student to take Ritalin to control his behavior since they failed to comply with an order calling for it to be administered based on a physician's prescription and with parental consent).

within which children are to be educated. In a case from New Jersey, the Third Circuit announced a two-part test, which initially appeared in a dispute from the Fifth Circuit,[149] for assessing compliance with the IDEA's least restrictive environment mandate.[150] The first element considers whether education in regular classes, with the use of supplementary aids and services, can be achieved satisfactorily. Under the second part of the test, if placements outside of regular classrooms are necessary, educators must consider whether children are mainstreamed, now referred to as full inclusion, as much as possible.

In the second case, a dispute from California, the Ninth Circuit expanded the existing criteria, stipulating that IEP teams had to take four factors into account in placing students: the educational benefits of placing children in regular classrooms; the nonacademic benefits of such placements; the effect that the presence of students with disabilities would have on teachers and other children in classes; and the costs of inclusionary placements.[151] In a suit dealing with cost, the federal trial court in Utah pointed out that if officials are considering two different programs, either one of which offers an appropriate education, they can take expense into account when making placement decisions.[152]

The IDEA's goal of full inclusion aside, not all students with disabilities must be placed in regular education classes.[153] Courts have approved more restrictive placements where students could not function in regular classes, even with supplementary aids and services[154] or inclusion was unsuccessful.[155] In a case from Connecticut, the Second Circuit affirmed a grant of summary judgment in favor of a school board since officials ensured that he spent enough time with peers who were not disabled; the trial court acknowledged that increasing a child's time with peers who were not disabled from sixty-three percent to seventy-four percent each week of the school year met the IDEA's inclusion mandate.[156] Also, a federal trial

---

149. *See Daniel R.R. v. State Bd. of Educ.*, 874 F.2d 1036 [53 Educ. L. Rep. 824] (5th Cir.1989). *See also Greer v. Rome City School Dist.*, 967 F.2d 470 [76 Educ. L. Rep. 26] (11th Cir.1992), *reh'g denied*, 974 F.2d 173 (11th Cir. 1992).

150. *Oberti v. Board of Educ. of the Borough of Clementon School Dist.*, 995 F.2d 1204 [83 Educ. L. Rep. 1009] (3d Cir. 1993).

151. *Sacramento City Unified School Dist., Bd. of Educ. v. Rachel H.*, 14 F.3d 1398 [89 Educ. L. Rep. 57] (9th Cir.1994), *cert. denied*, 512 U.S. 1207, 114 S.Ct. 2679, 129 L.Ed.2d 813 (1994).

152. *L.B. and J.B. v. Nebo School Dist.*, 214 F. Supp.2d 1172 [168 Educ. L. Rep. 771] (D. Utah 2002), *aff'd in part, rev'd in part, on other grounds*, 379 F.3d 966 [191 Educ. L. Rep. 92] (10th Cir. 2004).

153. *See e.g., J.P. ex rel. Peterson v. County School Bd. of Hanover County, Va.*, 516 F.3d 254 [229 Educ. L. Rep. 391] (4th Cir. 2008) (rejecting a private school placement for a child with autism); *C.G. ex rel. A.S. v. Five Town Community School Dist.*, 513 F.3d 279 [229 Educ. L. Rep. 18] (1st Cir. 2008) (affirming a non-residential public school placement for a child with an emotional disability).

154. *Clyde K. v. Puyallup School Dist. No. 3*, 35 F.3d 1396 [94 Educ. L. Rep. 707] (9th Cir. 1994); *Capistrano Unified School Dist. v. Wartenberg*, 59 F.3d 884 [101 Educ. L. Rep. 640] (9th Cir. 1995).

155. *Beth B. v. Van Clay*, 282 F.3d 493 [162 Educ. L. Rep. 47] (7th Cir.2002), *cert. denied*, 537 U.S. 948, 123 S.Ct. 412, 154 L.Ed.2d 292 (2002); *School Dist. of Wisconsin Dells v. Z.S. ex rel. Littlegeorge*, 295 F.3d 671 [167 Educ. L. Rep. 40] (7th Cir. 2002).

156. *P. ex rel. Mr. and Mrs. P. v. Newington Bd. of Educ.*, 512 F. Supp.2d 89 [225 Educ. L. Rep. 639] (D. Conn. 2007), *aff'd*, 546 F.3d 111 [238 Educ. L. Rep. 517] (2d Cir. 2008).

court in Pennsylvania refused to order a school board to provide an inclusive setting in a private extended year summer art program for a student with autism.[157] The court explained that inclusion is not mandatory during the summer since the board was not obligated to provide extended school year programs for students who were not disabled.

PRIVATE SCHOOL AND RESIDENTIAL PLACEMENTS

Officials may have to place children in private settings if school boards lack appropriate options[158] such as when students have low incidence disabilities and there are not enough other children with the same needs in systems to warrant the development of programs.[159] At the same time, courts may order residential placements for students with severe, profound, or multiple disabilities if they need twenty-four hour programming or consistency between school and home.[160] Residential placements may also be made if children have significant behavioral disorders,[161] district-operated programs failed,[162] or need total immersion in educational environments in order to progress.[163] Boards are not required to provide residential placements designed to permit children to reach their full potential.[164]

If children need residential placements solely for educational reasons, school boards must pay for their entire costs.[165] However, if placements are made because students have, for instance, medical[166] or psychological[167] needs, boards may only be required to pay for the educational costs of residential placements.[168] Who must pay when parents unilaterally place

---

157. *Travis G. v. New Hope–Solebury School Dist.*, 544 F. Supp.2d 435 [232 Educ. L. Rep. 165] (E.D. Pa. 2008).

158. 20 U.S.C.A. § 1412(a)(10)(B). *See, e.g., Reid ex rel. Reid v. District of Columbia*, 401 F.3d 516 [196 Educ. L. Rep. 402] (D.C. Cir. 2005); *Casey K. ex rel. Norman K. v. St. Anne Community High School Dist. No. 302*, 400 F.3d 508 [196 Educ. L. Rep. 38] (7th Cir. 2005), *cert. denied*, 546 U.S. 821, 126 S.Ct. 354, 163 L.Ed.2d 63 [202 Educ. L. Rep. 29] (2005).

159. *See, e.g., Colin K. v. Schmidt*, 715 F.2d 1 [13 Educ. L. Rep. 221] (1st Cir. 1983).

160. *Gladys J. v. Pearland Indep. School Dist.*, 520 F.Supp. 869 (S.D. Tex. 1981).

161. *Chris D. v. Montgomery County Bd. of Educ.*, 743 F.Supp. 1524 [62 Educ. L. Rep. 1001] (M.D. Ala. 1990).

162. *Linda E. ex rel. S.E. v. Bristol Warren Reg'l School Dist.*, 758 F.Supp.2d 75 [266 Educ. L. Rep. 718] (D.R.I. 2010).

163. *Abrahamson v. Hershman*, 701 F.2d 223 [9 Educ. L. Rep. 837] (1st Cir. 1983).

164. *Johnson ex rel. Johnson v. Olathe Dist. Schools Unified School Dist. No. 233, Special Servs. Div.*, 316 F. Supp.2d 960 [188 Educ. L. Rep. 307] (D. Kan. 2003).

165. 34 C.F.R. § 300.104. *Abrahamson v. Hershman*, 701 F.2d 223 [9 Educ. L. Rep. 837] (1st Cir. 1983); *Mrs. B. v. Milford Bd. of Educ.*, 103 F.3d 1114 [115 Educ. L. Rep. 324] (2d Cir. 1997); *Knable ex rel. Knable v. Bexley City School Dist.*, 238 F.3d 755 [150 Educ. L. Rep. 628] (6th Cir.2001), *cert. denied*, 533 U.S. 950, 121 S.Ct. 2593, 150 L.Ed.2d 752 (2001).

166. *Clovis Unified School Dist. v. California Office of Admin. Hearings*, 903 F.2d 635 [60 Educ. L. Rep. 728] (9th Cir. 1990).

167. *Gladstone School Dist. v. AM*, 105 F.3d 664 (9th Cir.1996).

168. *But see Lamoine School Comm. v. Ms. Z. ex rel. N.S.*, 353 F. Supp.2d 18 [195 Educ. L. Rep. 511] (D. Me. 2005) (remarking that a board could not avoid responsibility for the costs of a residential placement simply because it addressed a student's physical, emotional, psychological, or behavioral concerns rather than/or in addition to his educational problems since these issues were intertwined).

their children in private schools is discussed below under the heading "Tuition Reimbursement."

STUDENTS IN RELIGIOUSLY AFFILIATED PRIVATE SCHOOLS

As revealed in Chapter 2, there has been a great deal of litigation over the boundaries of state aid to students who attend religiously affiliated private schools.[169] As with so many other areas, the delivery of special education services is no exception.

In *Zobrest v. Catalina Foothills School District*,[170] the Supreme Court reasoned that the Establishment Clause did not prevent a school board in Arizona from providing the on-site delivery of the services of a sign-language interpreter for a student who attended a Roman Catholic high school. The Court noted that insofar as the interpreter was essentially a conduit through whom information passed, the on-site delivery of this service was constitutionally acceptable. Four years later, in *Agostini v. Felton*,[171] the Court largely eliminated barriers against the on-site delivery of services to students who attended religiously affiliated private schools as long as appropriate safeguards were in place. While the 1997 modifications of the IDEA adopted a similar perspective, its regulations restricted the amount of services that children can receive in their religiously affiliated private schools, thereby effectively minimizing *Zobrest's* impact as to the on-site delivery of special education services in religiously affiliated private schools.

Students whose parents voluntarily enroll them in private schools are entitled to some level of special education services even if it is unequal to what they would have received had they stayed in public schools. This means that school officials must budget only a proportionate share of their federal IDEA funds to serve children whose parents place them in private schools.[172] For example, the federal trial court in Delaware refused, as a matter of law, to order a local board to provide a full-time sign-language interpreter for a deaf student whose parents placed him in a religiously affiliated private school in noting that the requested aid would have cost significantly more than its entire allotment for students in private schools.[173]

The IDEA affords public school officials, in consultation with representatives from private schools, the authority to select which students from private schools will be served, what services they will receive, and how they will be delivered.[174] Even so, an appellate court in Minnesota affirmed that school officials violated a state shared-time statute when they sought to

---

169. For the sake of consistency, this section describes schools that are religiously affiliated as private with the language used in the IDEA.

170. 509 U.S. 1, 113 S.Ct. 2462, 125 L.Ed.2d 1 [83 Educ. L. Rep. 930] (1993).

171. 521 U.S. 203, 117 S.Ct. 1997, 138 L.Ed.2d 391 [119 Educ. L. Rep. 29] (1997). [Case No. 11]

172. 20 U.S.C.A. § 1412(a)(10)(A)(i).

173. *Board of Educ. of Appoquinimink School Dist. v. Johnson*, 543 F. Supp.2d 351 [231 Educ. L. Rep. 794] (D. Del. 2008), *stay denied*, 2008 WL 5043472 (D. Del. 2008).

174. 20 U.S.C.A. § 1412(a)(10)(A)(iii).

deny services to children with disabilities who were enrolled in private schools.[175]

State and local educational agencies can supplement federal funds in providing special education services to children whose parents place them in private schools. At the same time, public agencies can offer services to these students either directly or by contract with other agencies or organizations as long as local school boards maintain control of funds and ownership of equipment or materials purchased with public funds.[176] Of course, public school personnel can continue to conduct diagnostic tests on-site in private schools to evaluate whether children are eligible for services in programs that are supported by public funds.[177]

The IDEA permits, but does not require,[178] public school officials to provide the on-site delivery of special education services for students with disabilities whose parents placed them in "private, including religious, schools, to the extent consistent with the law,"[179] as long as appropriate safeguards are in place to avoid excessive entanglement with religious institutions. If services are not offered on-site and students must be transported to locations to receive them, boards must provide transportation.[180] Under this provision, the cost of transportation may be included in calculating the minimum amount of federal funds that school boards must spend on students in private schools. School boards need not transport children between their homes and religious schools since they must only do so between sites during the school day.

Students in private schools are entitled to receive services from personnel who meet the same standards as educators in public schools[181] even though they may receive a different amount from their peers in public schools.[182] In fact, since children in private schools have no right to the same amount of aid as if they were enrolled in public schools, they lack entitlements to IEPs. Instead of IEPs, officials must develop services plans describing the aid to be offered to students in private schools.[183] Services plans must meet IEP content requirements along with being developed, reviewed, and revised in a manner consistent with the IEP process.[184] The IDEA's procedural safeguards are inapplicable to complaints that boards

---

175. *Independent School Dist. No. 281 v. Minnesota Dep't of Educ.*, 743 N.W.2d 315 [228 Educ. L. Rep. 458] (Minn. Ct. App. 2008).

176. 20 U.S.C.A. § 612(a)(10)(A)(I). This establishes the rule that federal funds can supplement, not supplant, local funds. *See State of Washington v. United States Dep't of Educ.*, 905 F.2d 274 [60 Educ. L. Rep. 1118] (9th Cir. 1990).

177. *See Meek v. Pittenger*, 421 U.S. 349, 95 S.Ct. 1753, 44 L.Ed.2d 217 (1975); *Wolman v. Walter*, 433 U.S. 229, 97 S.Ct. 2593, 53 L.Ed.2d 714 (1977).

178. *Cefalu on Behalf of Cefalu v. East Baton Rouge Parish School Bd.*, 117 F.3d 231 [119 Educ. L. Rep. 338] (5th Cir.1997); *Russman v. Board of Educ. of City of Watervliet*, 150 F.3d 219 [128 Educ. L. Rep. 576] (2d Cir. 1998), *on remand*, 92 F. Supp.2d 95 [143 Educ. L. Rep. 784] (N.D. N.Y.2000), *vacated*, 260 F.3d 114 [156 Educ. L. Rep. 70] (2d Cir. 2001).

179. 20 U.S.C.A. § 1412(a)(10)(A)(i)(III).

180. 34 C.F.R. § 300.139(b).

181. 34 C.F.R. § 300.138(a)(1).

182. 34 C.F.R. § 300.138(a)(2).

183. 34 C.F.R. § 300.138(b).

184. 34 C.F.R. § 300.138(b)(2)(ii).

failed to deliver services to students in private schools other than with regard to the IDEA's child find provisions.[185]

The IDEA limits the amount of money that school boards must spend to provide services to students in private schools. The total is restricted to a proportionate amount of the federal funds boards receive based on the number of students in private schools in relation to the overall number of children in districts.[186] Boards are not prohibited from using state or local funds to offer more than the IDEA requires since the regulation only sets a minimum amount that they must spend on children who attend religiously affiliated private schools. As reviewed earlier, a change in the IDEA's child find provision requires school board officials both to identify children who attend private schools in the districts where they attend classes rather than within which they live and to employ child find activities for students in private schools comparable to those used for their peers in the public schools.[187]

Officials cannot use IDEA funds to help finance existing instructional programs in the private schools that students with disabilities attend.[188] The regulations do allow boards to employ public school personnel in private schools as long as they are not supplanting services normally provided by those institutions.[189] Additionally, equipment purchased with IDEA funds can only be used on-site in private schools for the benefit of students with disabilities.[190]

The net result is that while children in religious schools are entitled to receive some special education services, funding restrictions limit what they can receive and the locations where they can attend school. In such a case, a federal trial court in New York granted a board's motion for summary judgment, essentially rejecting a unilateral parental placement of their son in a religiously affiliated non-public school as inappropriate.[191]

EXTENDED SCHOOL YEAR PROGRAMS

Children with disabilities who need educational programming extending beyond regular school years are entitled to placements at public expense.[192] The Fifth[193] and Tenth[194] Circuits interpreted the IDEA as

---

185. 34 C.F.R. § 300.140(a). *Gary S. v. Manchester School Dist.*, 374 F.3d 15 [189 Educ. L. Rep. 494] (1st Cir. 2004), *cert. denied*, 543 U.S. 988, 125 S.Ct. 505, 160 L.Ed.2d 373 (2004).

186. 20 U.S.C.A. § 1412(a)(10)(A)(i)(I). *Fowler v. Unified School Dist.*, 128 F.3d 1431 [122 Educ. L. Rep. 391] (10th Cir. 1997).

187. 20 U.S.C.A. § 1412(a)(10)(A)(ii).

188. 34 C.F.R. § 300.141(a).

189. 34 C.F.R. § 300.142.

190. 34 C.F.R. § 300.144.

191. *J.G. ex rel. N.G. v. Kiryas Joel Union Free School Dist.*, 777 F.Supp.2d 606 [270 Educ. L. Rep. 135] (S.D.N.Y. 2011).

192. 20 U.S.C.A. § 1412(a)(1), 34 C.F.R. § 300.106.

193. *Alamo Heights Indep. School Dist. v. State Bd. of Educ.*, 790 F.2d 1153 [32 Educ. L. Rep. 445] (5th Cir.1986). *See also J.W. v. Contoocook Valley School Dist.*, 154 F. Supp.2d 217 [156 Educ. L. Rep. 224] (D.N.H. 2001).

194. *Johnson By and Through Johnson v. Independent School Dist. No. 4 of Bixby, Tulsa County, Okla.*, 921 F.2d 1022 [64 Educ. L. Rep. 1027] (10th Cir.1990), *cert. denied*, 500 U.S. 905, 111 S.Ct. 1685, 114 L.Ed.2d 79 (1991).

meaning that children are entitled to extended year programs when they regress and the time it takes to regain, often addressed as regression-recoupment, lost skills interferes with their overall progress toward attaining IEP goals and objectives. The Fourth[195] and Seventh[196] Circuits disagreed, recognizing that if regression is minimal, extended school year programs are not required.[197] The Fifth Circuit subsequently decided that a student was not entitled to extended year services in his residential placement.[198] The court was of the view that the child's parents were unable to establish the need for what they sought where school officials developed an appropriate IEP for him in an inclusive setting offering educational support and assistive-technology adaptations.

In a dispute over extended year programming from Pennsylvania, a federal trial court rejected a request from parents to place their son with autism in a private art program during the summer.[199] The court ruled that insofar as the student received all of the compensatory education to which he would otherwise have been entitled before his interim IEP was implemented, he lacked a right to the placement since such inclusion cannot be required during summer breaks especially because officials provided him with many more hours of service than were called for in his IEP.

MINIMUM-COMPETENCY TESTS

Minimum-competency tests may be used either as graduation requirements to assure that students receiving diplomas have acquired specified knowledge bases or to identify children who have not achieved competency in basic skills and may require remedial instruction. Since the IDEA requires students with disabilities to participate in some form of state assessments,[200] the accountability provisions of the No Child Left Behind Act, which requires local school systems to make adequate yearly progress,[201] may have a major impact on the delivery of special education services.

States may require students with disabilities to pass competency tests before earning high school diplomas as long as these examinations satisfy three guidelines. First, tests must be valid, reliable measures of what students have been taught.[202] Second, since educators must afford students

---

195. *MM ex rel. DM v. School Dist. of Greenville County*, 303 F.3d 523 [169 Educ. L. Rep. 59] (4th Cir. 2002).

196. *Anderson v. Thompson*, 658 F.2d 1205 (7th Cir.1981); *Todd v. Duneland School Corp.*, 299 F.3d 899 [168 Educ. L. Rep. 67] (7th Cir. 2002).

197. *See also Moser v. Bret Harte Union High School Dist.*, 366 F. Supp.2d 944 [198 Educ. L. Rep. 171] (E.D. Cal. 2005) (asserting that under federal law, regression-recoupment is not the standard for the availability of extended year services).

198. *Kenton County School Dist. v. Hunt*, 384 F.3d 269 [192 Educ. L. Rep. 55] (6th Cir. 2004).

199. *Travis G. v. New Hope–Solebury School Dist.*, 544 F. Supp.2d 435 [232 Educ. L. Rep. 165] (E.D. Pa. 2008).

200. 20 U.S.C.A. § 1412(a)(16).

201. 20 U.S.C.A. §§ 6301, 6311, 6312, 6316.

202. *Debra P. v. Turlington*, 730 F.2d 1405 [16 Educ. L. Rep. 1120] (11th Cir. 1984); *Anderson v. Banks*, 520 F.Supp. 472 (S.D. Ga.1981), *modified*, 540 F.Supp. 761 [4 Educ. L.

with disabilities and their parents sufficient notice that they must pass competency tests in order to receive diplomas,[203] IEPs should specify areas in need of additional instruction. Third, consistent with the non-discrimination standards in the IDEA's evaluation procedures, tests cannot be racially, linguistically, or ethnically discriminatory.[204]

Parents of children with disabilities are responsible for working with the members of their IEP teams in formulating IEPs for their children.[205] Accordingly, school officials should make parents aware of the general content of tests, where and how they are to be administered, and the purposes for which results are to be used.

RELATED SERVICES

Children with disabilities are entitled to related, or supportive, services to help them benefit from special education.[206] As reflected by a case from Connecticut, though, a student with serious behavioral problems who did not need services in order to make academic progress lacked an entitlement to a twenty-four hour crisis plan, respite care for his family, and an in-home mentor.[207] Moreover, the term "related services" does not include surgically implanted medical devices or their replacements[208] such as cochlear implant mapping.[209]

Transportation, including such specialized equipment as adapted buses, lifts, and ramps, is the most common related service. An ongoing question concerns where children who are entitled to transportation must be dropped off after school. While the Fifth Circuit pointed out that a child

Rep. 1127] (S.D. Ga.1982), *appeal dismissed sub. nom. Johnson v. Sikes*, 730 F.2d 644 [16 Educ. L. Rep. 1085] (11th Cir. 1984).

203. *Debra P., id.* (striking down a thirteen-month notice period). *But see Anderson v. Banks*, 520 F.Supp. 472 (S.D. Ga.1981), *modified*, 540 F.Supp. 761 [4 Educ. L. Rep. 1127] (S.D. Ga. 1982) (treating notice of twenty-four months as sufficient).

204. 20 U.S.C.A. § 1414(b)(3).

205. 20 U.S.C.A. § 1414(d)(1)(B)(i).

206. The IDEA, 20 U.S.C.A. § 1401(26)(A), defines related services as (26) Related services

(A) In general

The term "related services" means transportation, and such developmental, corrective, and other supportive services (including speech-language pathology and audiology services, interpreting services, psychological services, physical and occupational therapy, recreation, including therapeutic recreation, social work services, school nurse services designed to enable a child with a disability to receive a free appropriate public education as described in the individualized education program of the child, counseling services, including rehabilitation counseling, orientation and mobility services, and medical services, except that such medical services shall be for diagnostic and evaluation purposes only) as may be required to assist a child with a disability to benefit from special education, and includes the early identification and assessment of disabling conditions in children.

(B) Exception

The term does not include a medical device that is surgically implanted, or the replacement of such device.

207. *M.K. ex rel. Mrs. K. v. Sergi*, 554 F. Supp.2d 201 [233 Educ. L. Rep. 751] (D. Conn. 2008).

208. 20 U.S.C.A. § 1401(26)(B).

209. *Petit v. United States Dep't of Educ.*, 756 F.Supp.2d 11 [266 Educ. L. Rep. 206] (D.D.C. 2010).

is entitled to transportation to the home of a caretaker, even if that person lived outside of a district's attendance boundaries,[210] the Eighth Circuit reached the opposite result, maintaining that a child was not entitled to be dropped off at a day care center that was outside of his school's attendance area.[211]

The Supreme Court first addressed the issue of related services in *Irving Independent School District v. Tatro*,[212] observing that procedures such as catheterizations that can be performed by school nurses or trained lay persons are required related services under the IDEA. In *Cedar Rapids Community School District v. Garret F.*[213] the Court interpreted the IDEA as requiring a board to provide, and pay for, regardless of cost, a full-time nurse while a student was in school since his medical condition needed constant monitoring.

Perhaps the most controversial aspect of related services is the distinction between medical and school health services. Procedures that must be performed by licensed physicians are exempted medical services. Evaluating this distinction can be complicated since many students with significant medical needs require twenty-four-hour nursing services that fall somewhere on the continuum between school health services and medical services.

An ususual case arose in Ohio over a medical service where the mother of a special education student withdrew her daughter from school in a dispute over whether staff members would administer the child's insulin injections. A local newspaper then published a letter the mother wrote criticizing school officials before contacting the Federal Office of Civil Rights and Department of Education with her complaint. The mother, joined by another mother with some of the same kinds of grievances, sued the superintendent and board after a school nurse allegedly made false reports of medical neglect to the Department of Children Services. The Sixth Circuit affirmed that the superintendent did not violate the privacy or substantive due process rights of the mothers to direct the upbringing of their children for purportedly having the nurse make the report to Children Services.[214] However, the court reversed in rejecting the superintendent's motion for summary judgment since questions of fact remained over whether he retaliated against the first mother, but not the second, for exercising her First Amendment rights.

---

210.   *Alamo Heights Indep. School Dist. v. State Bd. of Educ.*, 790 F.2d 1153 [32 Educ. L. Rep. 445] (5th Cir. 1986).

211.   *Fick ex rel. Fick v. Sioux Falls School Dist. 49–5*, 337 F.3d 968 [179 Educ. L. Rep. 144] (8th Cir. 2003), *reh'g and reh'g en banc denied* (2003).

212.   468 U.S. 883, 104 S.Ct. 3371, 82 L.Ed.2d 664 [18 Educ. L. Rep. 138] (1984).

213.   526 U.S. 66, 119 S.Ct. 992, 143 L.Ed.2d 154 [132 Educ. L. Rep. 40] (1999). [Case No. 112]

214.   *Jenkins v. Rock Hill Local School Dist.*, 513 F.3d 580 [229 Educ. L. Rep. 40] (6th Cir. 2008), *cert. denied*, 553 U.S. 1033, 128 S.Ct. 2445, 171 L.Ed.2d 232 (2008).

ASSISTIVE TECHNOLOGY

The definitions of assistive technology devices[215] or services,[216] were first included in the IDEA in 1990 and expanded in its 1997 amendments and regulations. Yet, assistive technology is not included in the definitions of special education or related services. Assistive technology fits within the definitions of special education as specially designed instruction and related services as developmental, corrective, or supportive services. Instead of including assistive technology within either of these definitions, Congress made assistive technology a separate category. Assistive technology can thus be considered to be either a special education service, a related service, or a supplementary aid or service. Regardless of which rubric they are covered by, school boards must provide students with disabilities with supplementary aids and services designed to allow them to be educated in the least restrictive environment.[217]

Assistive technology devices are any items, pieces of equipment, or product systems used to increase, maintain, or improve the functional capabilities of students with disabilities.[218] These devices may include commercially available, modified, or customized equipment. Assistive technology services include "selecting, designing, fitting, customizing, adapting, applying, maintaining, repairing, or replacing assistive technology devices."[219]

If assistive technology is mandatory to provide children with the services identified in their IEPs,[220] teams must consider whether students need these items in order to ensure that their placements are appropriate.[221] Despite this language, the IDEA fails to include provisions directing IEP teams to document their discussions of students' assistive technology needs or to justify whether they were required. If IEP teams believe that students need school-provided assistive technology devices in their homes, then children are entitled to have them there.[222] In one of the few cases on point, a federal trial court in Illinois granted a school board's motion for summary judgment, finding that it met the needs of a student with disabilities by providing him with both an assistive technology evaluation and then affording him access to calculators, computers, and books on tape to meet his needs.[223]

Turning to one particular item, if students with hearing impairments, including deafness, wear hearing aids to school, educators must ensure that they are functioning properly.[224] At the same time, students with disabili-

---

215. 20 U.S.C.A. § 1401(1).

216. 20 U.S.C.A. § 1401(2).

217. *Oberti v. Board of Educ. of the Borough of Clementon School Dist.*, 995 F.2d 1204 [83 Educ. L. Rep. 1009] (3d Cir. 1993).

218. 20 U.S.C.A. § 1401(1).

219. 20 U.S.C.A. § 1401(2)(c).

220. 34 C.F.R. § 300.105(a).

221. 34 C.F.R. § 300.324(a)(2)(v).

222. 34 C.F.R. § 300.105(b).

223. *Jaccari J. v. Board of Educ. of the City of Chicago, Dist. No. 299*, 690 F. Supp. 2d 687 [256 Educ. L. Rep. 785] (N.D. Ill. 2010).

224. 34 C.F.R. § 300.113(a).

ties are entitled to access general technology that is available to peers who are not disabled. Of course, if students require accommodations in order to use general technology, they must be provided.

In a case from New York, the Second Circuit ruled that a student whose learning disability affected his ability in mathematics could not use a more advanced calculator in a class where the evidence demonstrated that he was capable of passing the course with the assistance of a less advanced calculator.[225] The court commented that not permitting the student to use the calculator was consistent with the educational goals of the curriculum for the course and that his own lack of effort contributed to his failing grade.

DISCIPLINE

As important as the topic of disciplining students with disabilities is, the IDEA did not address it until 1997. The IDEA now permits school officials to discipline students as long as they follow procedures designed to protect the rights of children.[226] Early case law agreed that while students with disabilities could not be expelled for misconduct that were manifestations of their disabilities, they could have been excluded if no such relationship was present.[227]

Honig v. Doe (Honig)[228] is the Supreme Court's only case involving discipline and special education. In a dispute over whether educators in California could exclude two students with disabilities from school, the Court addressed three issues. First, the Court affirmed that the case was moot with regard to one of the students because he was already over the age of twenty-one. Second, in refusing to write a dangerousness exception into the statute, the Court affirmed that the IDEA's stay-put provisions prohibit educators from unilaterally excluding students with disabilities from school for dangerous or disruptive actions that are manifestations of their disabilities during the pendency of review proceedings. The Court added that officials could impose normal, non-placement-changing procedures, including temporary suspensions for up to ten school days, for students who posed immediate threats to school safety. The Justices conceded that if educators and parents agreed, students could be given interim placements as proceedings progressed. If this approach failed, the Court acknowledged that officials could file suit for injunctive relief to remove children. Third, an equally divided Court affirmed that state-level

225. *Sherman v. Mamaroneck Union Free School Dist.*, 340 F.3d 87 [179 Educ. L. Rep. 617] (2d Cir. 2003).

226. *LIH ex rel. LH v. New York City Bd. of Educ.*, 103 F. Supp.2d 658 [145 Educ. L. Rep. 1031] (E.D.N.Y. 2000).

227. *See, e.g., Stuart v. Nappi*, 443 F.Supp. 1235 (D. Conn.1978); *S–1 v. Turlington*, 635 F.2d 342 (5th Cir.1981), *cert. denied*, 454 U.S. 1030, 102 S.Ct. 566, 70 L.Ed.2d 473 (1981), *abrogated by Honig v. Doe*, 484 U.S. 305, 108 S.Ct. 592, 98 L.Ed.2d 686 [43 Educ. L. Rep. 857] (1988); *School Bd. of Prince William County, Va. v. Malone*, 762 F.2d 1210 [25 Educ. L. Rep. 141] (4th Cir. 1985).

228. 484 U.S. 305, 108 S.Ct. 592, 98 L.Ed.2d 686 [43 Educ. L. Rep. 857] (1988). [Case No. 113]

officials can be compelled to provide services directly to students with disabilities when local boards fail to do so.

Honig's failure to resolve all of the legal issues surrounding disciplining students with disabilities led to additional litigation and eventual legislative action.[229] Congress sought to clarify unanswered questions by creating specific procedures as part of the IDEA's 1997 Amendments.[230] The IDEA now affords educators the authority to suspend special education students for not more than ten school days as long as the same kinds of sanctions apply to children who are not disabled.[231]

The IDEA's regulations specify that a series of removals resulting in a pattern of exclusions cumulatively having children with disabilities out of school for more than ten school days may be considered changes in placements.[232] The regulations stipulate that if students are suspended for misbehavior substantially similar to past actions that have been identified as manifestations of their disabilities, then this constitutes changes in placements.[233] In making such judgments, the regulations direct school officials to consider the length of each removal, the total amount of time that children have been out of school, and the proximity of the removals to one another in evaluating whether changes in placements occurred.[234]

Educators can remove students with disabilities from school for separate, but dissimilar, acts of misconduct for more than ten cumulative days in a school year.[235] After students with disabilities are removed from school for ten days in the same school year, during any later removals, educators must provide them with educational services.[236] As exemplified by a case from Minnesota, though, where parents refused to consent to a change of placement for their daughter as a result of her disciplinary suspension, the Eighth Circuit ruled that educators did not violate the IDEA's stay-put provisions in continuing to exclude her for misbehaving in ways presenting dangers to herself, other students, and school staff.[237]

School officials have increased authority when dealing with students with disabilities who possess weapons or drugs at school.[238] Under an expanded definition of a dangerous weapon, the IDEA incorporates language from another federal statute such that it now includes instruments,

---

229. *Hayes Through Hayes v. Unified School Dist. No. 377*, 877 F.2d 809 [54 Educ. L. Rep. 450] (10th Cir.1989); *Hacienda La Puente Unified School Dist. of Los Angeles v. Honig*, 976 F.2d 487 [77 Educ. L. Rep. 1117] (9th Cir. 1992); *Light v. Parkway C–2 School Dist.*, 41 F.3d 1223 [96 Educ. L. Rep. 98] (8th Cir.1994), *reh'g and suggestion for reh'g en banc denied* (1995), *cert. denied*, 515 U.S. 1132, 115 S.Ct. 2557, 132 L.Ed.2d 811 (1995).

230. 20 U.S.C.A. §§ 1415(i), (j), (k), (*l*).

231. 20 U.S.C.A. § 1415(k)(1)(B).

232. 34 C.F.R. § 300.536(a)(1).

233. 34 C.F.R. § 300.536(a)(2).

234. 34 C.F.R. § 300.536(a)(2)(iii).

235. 34 C.F.R. § 300.530(b)(1).

236. 34 C.F.R. § 300.536(b)(2).

237. *M.M. ex rel. L.R. v. Special School Dist. No. 1*, 512 F.3d 455 [228 Educ. L. Rep. 684] (8th Cir. 2008), *reh'g and reh'g en banc denied* (2008), *cert. denied*, 555 U.S. 979, 129 S.Ct. 452, 172 L.Ed.2d 343 (2008).

238. 20 U.S.C.A. §§ 1415(k)(7)(A), (B).

devices, materials, and substances capable of inflicting harm in addition to firearms, but does not include small pocket knives.[239] The IDEA defines illegal drugs as controlled substances but excludes those that may be legally prescribed by physicians.[240]

Pursuant to provisions dealing with the immediate removal of students with disabilities, school officials may unilaterally transfer students to interim alternative placements for up to forty-five school days for carrying or possessing weapons[241] or for knowing possession, use, sale, or solicitation of drugs[242] on school property or at school functions as long as this sanction applies under like circumstances for peers who are not disabled.[243] In a case focusing more on procedural than substantive issues, the Eighth Circuit ruled that officials in South Dakota did not violate the rights of a student with disabilities who was placed in an alternative educational setting for thirty-eight days when he was suspended for fighting and bringing a pocket knife to school.[244] The court explained that insofar as the board lacked the authority to reverse the decision of the IEP team acting in conjunction with the student's mother in placing him in the alternative setting, it did not violate his right to due process in refusing to conduct a hearing.

In an important addition in the 2004 version of the IDEA, students who have inflicted serious bodily injury on other persons while at school, on school premises, or at school functions can be placed in alternative educational settings.[245] In defining "serious bodily injury," the IDEA relies on another federal law which defines the term as one involving a substantial risk of death, extreme physical pain, protracted and obvious disfigurement, or protracted loss or impairment of the function of a bodily member, organ, or mental faculty.[246]

Under the IDEA's interim alternative placement provisions, school officials must permit students to continue to progress in general educational curricula where they still receive necessary services outlined in their IEPs.[247] Educators must also provide students with services and modifications designed to prevent the misbehaviors from recurring.[248]

When students are moved to alternative placements for more than ten school days,[249] educators must conduct functional behavioral assessments (FBAs) and implement behavioral intervention plans (BIPs) if they are not

---

239. 18 U.S.C.A. § 930(g)(2).

240. 20 U.S.C.A. § 1415(k)(7)(B). For the list of controlled substances, *see* 21 U.S.C.A. § 812(c).

241. 20 U.S.C.A. § 1415(k)(1)(G)(i).

242. 20 U.S.C.A. § 1415(k)(1)(G)(ii).

243. 20 U.S.C.A. § 1415(k)(1)(C).

244. *Doe ex rel. Doe v. Todd County School Dist.*, 625 F.3d 459 [262 Educ. L. Rep. 85] (8th Cir. 2011), *cert. denied*, ___ U.S. ___, 132 S.Ct. 367, ___ L.Ed.2d ___ (2011).

245. 20 U.S.C.A. § 1415(k)(1)(G)(iii).

246. 18 U.S.C.A. § 1365(h)(3).

247. 20 U.S.C.A. § 1415(k)(1)(D)(i).

248. 20 U.S.C.A. § 1415(k)(1)(D)(ii).

249. 20 U.S.C.A. § 1415(k)(1)(D)(ii).

already in place.[250] If plans were in place when children misbehaved, IEP teams must review them and their implementation in order to make any necessary modifications.[251] If parents disagree with alternative placements and request hearings, consistent with the IDEA's stay-put provision, children must remain in their alternative settings.[252] Once the forty-five day periods expire, officials must return students to their former settings even if hearings on school board proposals to change their placements are pending unless parents and educators agree otherwise.[253]

Educators must complete FBAs and BIPs if they interpret disciplinary infractions as manifestations of students' disabilities.[254] As important as FBAs and BIPs can be, and as prescriptive as the IDEA and its regulations typically are, neither addresses their content or form. Further, there is scant case law on point.[255] In a case from New York involving both a FBA and a BIP, a federal trial court decided that a school board did not have to include one in a student's IEP because her classroom teacher would be able to address the child's behavior sufficiently.[256] The court added that even assuming that the child's actions interfered with her learning, her IEP team developed, and included, strategies in her IEP to address her behavior.

A case involving discipline of a four-year-old with an IEP but not a BIP arose in Alabama. A federal trial court rejected a mother's claims that educators violated her son's substantive and procedural due process rights when his teacher placed him in a toddler chair with a velcro seat belt strapped on his waist and feet as he sat facing the corner in an unsupervised hallway so he could calm down.[257] The court was satisfied that the teacher's behavior was a *de minimis* deprivation of the child's rights not implicating procedural due process since he had been kicking her and other children coupled with the fact that the teacher anticipated the arrival of his mother to pick him up within ten minutes.

The IDEA includes definitions and procedures to evaluate whether, on "case-by-case determinations,"[258] misconduct is related to students' disabilities.[259] The IDEA defines a manifestation as conduct caused by or having a direct and substantial relationship to students' disabilities or as the direct result of the failure of school officials to implement IEPs properly. In

---

250. 20 U.S.C.A. § 1415(k)(1)(D)(ii); 34 C.F.R. § 300.530(d)(ii).

251. 34 C.F.R. § 300.530(f)(1)(ii).

252. 20 U.S.C.A. § 1415(k)(4)(A). *See J.S., ex rel. Duck v. Isle of Wight County School Bd.*, 368 F. Supp.2d 522 [198 Educ. L. Rep. 587] (E.D. Va. 2005) (rejecting a mother's claim that officials violated her son's rights by suspending him and placing him in an alternative school due to accusations of a sexual nature by a female student).

253. 20 U.S.C.A. § 1415(k)(4)(A).

254. 20 U.S.C.A. § 1415(k)(1)(F)(I).

255. *See, e.g., School Bd. of Indep. School Dist. No. 11 v. Renollett*, 440 F.3d 1007 [207 Educ. L. Rep. 36] (8th Cir. 2006) (explaining that a BIP need not be in writing).

256. *E. Z.–L. ex rel. R.L. v. New York City Dep't of Educ.*, 763 F.Supp.2d 584 [267 Educ. L. Rep. 201] (S.D.N.Y. 2011).

257. *D.D. ex rel. Davis v. Chilton County Bd. of Educ.*, 701 F.Supp.2d 1236 [258 Educ. L. Rep. 596] (M.D. Ala. 2010).

258. 20 U.S.C.A. § 1415(k)(1)(A).

259. 20 U.S.C.A. § 1415(k).

reviewing whether placements are inappropriate, relevant members of IEP teams should gather and use the same standards they applied in prospectively evaluating whether proposed placements were appropriate.[260] If teams interpret misconduct as either manifestations of students' disabilities or as results of improperly implemented IEPs, children may not be expelled or suspended for more than ten days and school officials must reconsider their current placements.[261] In rendering manifestation determinations, teams must consider all relevant information, including evaluations and diagnostic results as well as student observations.[262]

As with other aspects related to special education, manifestation determinations are subject to the IDEA's administrative appeals process. The 2004 amendments require school officials to expedite hearings incident to manifestation determinations. More specifically, hearings must occur within twenty school days of the dates on which they were requested and hearing officers must render decisions within ten days of hearings.[263] If parents contest manifestation determinations, then educators must postpone long-term suspensions or expulsions until hearings have been completed; still, students may remain in interim alternative educational settings.[264] In addition to leaving children in their then current, or pendent, placements, hearing officers may issue change in placement orders.[265] In a case from New York, the Second Circuit ruled that while a student could challenge whether his being placed in an interim alternative setting denied him the opportunity to take part in extracurricular activities, he lacked a right to return to a regular school setting while his situation was under review.[266]

Two cases from Virginia highlight the principle that if the inappropriate actions of students are not manifestations of their disabilities, then they may be disciplined in the same manner as peers who are not disabled. In the first dispute, a student with Asperger's Syndrome who was already on probation filed suit after a manifestation determination review found that insofar as his behavior was unrelated to his condition, he could be suspended and reassigned to another school for sexually harassing a classmate by using his cell phone to take pictures up her skirt without her knowledge.[267] Rejecting the student's claim that he was disciplined due to his disability, and granting the school board's motion to dismiss, the court required him to exhaust administrative remedies under the IDEA before initiating litigation.[268] In the second case, another federal trial court rejected the claim of a

---

260. 20 U.S.C.A. § 1415(k)(1)(E)(I).

261. 20 U.S.C.A. § 1415(k)(1)(C).

262. 20 U.S.C.A. § 1415(k)(1)(E)(i).

263. 20 U.S.C.A. § 1415(k)(4)(B).

264. 20 U.S.C.A. § 1415(k)(4)(A).

265. 20 U.S.C.A. § 1415(k)(3)(B).

266. *Coleman v. Newburgh Enlarged City School Dist.*, 503 F.3d 198 [225 Educ. L. Rep. 168] (2d Cir. 2007).

267. *A.W. ex rel. Wilson v. Fairfax County School Bd.*, 548 F. Supp.2d 219 [233 Educ. L. Rep. 166] (E.D. Va. 2008).

268. *See also Farrin v. Maine School Admin. Dist. No. 59*, 165 F. Supp.2d 37 [157 Educ. L. Rep. 709] (D. Me. 2001) (refusing to order the reinstatement of a student who was expelled for

student with emotional disabilities that he was improperly disciplined for his role in a paintball shooting incident at his school. Where the record revealed that the student drove his car, with friends inside of the vehicle, past the school and shot paintballs at the building at least twice, the court rebuffed his assertion that his misbehavior was a manifestation of his disability.[269]

The IDEA clarified whether school officials can discontinue services for children who are properly expelled for misconduct that is not disability-related. In codifying a federal policy directing officials to provide services for a student who was excluded for misbehavior unrelated to his disability, the IDEA essentially repudiated a case from Virginia wherein the Fourth Circuit rejected the notion that such a requirement existed.[270] The IDEA now requires boards to provide appropriate educational placements for all students with disabilities including those who have been expelled from school.[271] As such, even if students are expelled for disciplinary infractions unrelated to their disabilities, they must be provided with services allowing them to progress toward achieving their IEP goals.[272]

Prior to the adoption of the statute's 1997 revisions, courts disagreed over the treatment of students who were not yet assessed for special education but claimed to have been covered by the IDEA. Officials must now provide the IDEA's protections to students if they knew that children were disabled before they misbehaved.[273] As a case from Connecticut illustrates, officials are considered to be on notice if parents request evaluations.[274] Educators may also be considered to be on notice in light of students' prior behavioral and academic performances and the concerns of teachers about their performances.[275] An exception exists if educators already conducted evaluations and concluded that students were not disabled or if parents refused to grant their permission for evaluations or declined offered special education services.[276]

If parents request evaluations when students are subject to disciplinary sanctions, they must be conducted in an expedited manner.[277] Consistent with the IDEA's stay-put provision, until expedited evaluations are completed, students must remain in the placements deemed appropriate by

---

violating his school's drug policy since his pupil evaluation team decided that his misbehavior was unrelated to his learning disability).

269. *Fitzgerald v. Fairfax County School Bd.*, 556 F. Supp.2d 543 [234 Educ. L. Rep. 830] (E.D. Va. 2008).

270. *Commonwealth of Va., Dep't of Educ. v. Riley*, 106 F.3d 559 [116 Educ. L. Rep. 40] (4th Cir. 1997).

271. 20 U.S.C.A. §§ 1412(a)(1)(A), 1415(k)(1)(D)(i).

272. 34 C.F.R. § 300.530(d)(i).

273. 20 U.S.C.A. § 1415(k)(8).

274. *J.C. v. Regional School Dist. No. 10*, 115 F. Supp.2d 297 [147 Educ. L. Rep. 935] (D. Conn. 2000), *rev'd on other grounds*, 278 F.3d 119 [161 Educ. L. Rep. 68] (2d Cir. 2002).

275. 20 U.S.C.A. § 1415(k)(5)(B).

276. 20 U.S.C.A. § 1415(k)(5)(C). For such a case, *see M.G. v. Crisfield*, 547 F. Supp.2d 399 [233 Educ. L. Rep. 109] (D.N.J. 2008) (rejecting a parental claim that school officials inappropriately suspended their son since they consistently refused to have him identified and served under the IDEA).

277. 20 U.S.C.A. § 1415(k)(5)(D)(ii).

educators.[278] If evaluation teams have reason to believe that children are disabled, they must provide students with special education services.[279] In a case reaching mixed results, a federal trial court in Mississippi decided that while officials violated the IDEA by failing to provide a testing procedure to evaluate whether a student who was expelled for bringing a Swiss Army knife to school had a disability, they did not contravene the statute's stay-put provision in excluding him from school.[280]

The IDEA's discipline provisions do not prohibit school officials from reporting student crimes to the proper authorities or impeding law enforcement and judicial authorities from carrying out their duties.[281] If officials do report crimes, they must make copies of students' special education and disciplinary records available to appropriate authorities.[282]

DISPUTE RESOLUTION

"The IDEA favors prompt resolution of disputes"[283] over the education of students with disabilities because Congress realized the need to help children who may be at formative stages in their development. Consistent with the previous sentence, in 2004, Congress presented new findings in the IDEA that "[p]arents and schools should be given expanded opportunities to resolve their disagreements in positive and constructive ways," and that "[t]eachers, schools, local educational agencies, and States should be relieved of irrelevant and unnecessary paperwork burdens that do not lead to improved educational outcomes."[284] Parents who disagree with any of the actions of IEP teams or school officials about the placements of their children may request mediation in lieu of adversarial proceedings.[285] Insofar as mediation is voluntary, it may not be used to deny or delay parental requests for administrative hearings.

Parents may request due process hearings, which must be presided over by fair and impartial third-party decision makers,[286] if they are dissatisfied with any aspect of the education of their children.[287] Parents have requested due process hearings in situations such as where school

---

278.   20 U.S.C.A. § 1415(k)(5)(D)(ii).

279.   *Id.*

280.   *Colvin ex rel. Colvin v. Lowndes County, Miss. School Dist.*, 114 F. Supp.2d 504 [147 Educ. L. Rep. 601] (N.D. Miss. 1999).

281.   20 U.S.C.A. § 1415(k)(6)(A). *Commonwealth v. Nathaniel N.*, 764 N.E.2d 883 [162 Educ. L. Rep. 951] (Mass. App. Ct. 2002) (affirming that a juvenile court proceeding did not constitute a change in placement even when it took place due to a student's misconduct at school).

282.   20 U.S.C.A. § 1415(k)(6)(B).

283.   *Sanders v. Santa Fe Pub. Schools*, 383 F. Supp.2d 1305, 1311 [201 Educ. L. Rep. 931] (D.N.M. 2004). *But see Herbin ex rel. Herbin v. District of Columbia*, 362 F. Supp.2d 254 [197 Educ. L. Rep. 142] (D.D.C. 2005) (permitting a four-month delay in responding to a request for a reevaluation).

284.   20 U.S.C.A. §§ 1400(c)(8), (9).

285.   20 U.S.C.A. § 1415(e).

286.   20 U.S.C.A. § 1415(e)(2)(B).

287.   20 U.S.C.A. § 1415(f).

officials refused to assess whether their child had a disability,[288] where they disagreed with the findings and recommendations that school officials offered,[289] and where they were dissatisfied with the content or implementation of their child's IEP.[290] Boards may request due process hearings if parents refuse to consent to evaluations of their children.[291]

In an important preliminary concerning dispute resolution, the Supreme Court resolved the split between the circuits in addressing the question of who bears the burden of proof in challenges to the contents of IEPs in due process hearings. In *Schaffer ex rel. Schaffer v. Weast*,[292] the Court affirmed an order of the Fourth Circuit placing the burden of proof on the parties challenging IEPs.[293] In rejecting the claim that parents who questioned their son's IEP were at a disadvantage due to a lack of knowledge, the Court found they had significant due process protections available to make sure that this was not so. The Court emphasized that while the question was not before it, states could have, as some already had, overridden what it described as the default position by placing this burden of proof on school boards. On remand, the Fourth Circuit affirmed that the IEP was reasonably calculated to provide educational benefit and met the child's educational needs.[294]

As to the dispute resolution process, depending on state law, either state or local school boards may conduct due process hearings.[295] In states with two-tiered systems, if local boards conduct initial hearings, either party can appeal to the state.[296]

In an important addition, the IDEA now includes a two-year limitations period during which parties can request due process hearings.[297] If state laws set different limitations periods, then those time frames prevail.[298] Moreover, the IDEA stipulates that the federal statute of limitations is to be stayed if parents can show that school officials misrepresented

---

288. *Hacienda La Puente Unified School Dist. of Los Angeles v. Honig*, 976 F.2d 487 [77 Educ. L. Rep. 1117] (9th Cir.1992).

289. *Dong v. Board of Educ.*, 197 F.3d 793 [140 Educ. L. Rep. 116] (6th Cir. 1999).

290. *Kuszewski v. Chippewa Valley Schools*, 117 F. Supp.2d 646 [148 Educ. L. Rep. 745] (E.D. Mich. 2000).

291. *Yates v. Charles County Bd. of Educ.*, 212 F. Supp.2d 470 [168 Educ. L. Rep. 238] (D. Md. 2002).

292. 546 U.S. 49, 126 S.Ct. 528, 163 L.Ed.2d 387 [203 Educ. L. Rep. 29] (2005). [Case No. 114]

293. For the earlier opinion, *see* 377 F.3d 449 (4th Cir. 2004).

294. *Schaffer ex rel. Schaffer v. Weast*, 554 F.3d 470 [241 Educ. L. Rep. 30] (4th Cir. 2009).

295. 20 U.S.C.A. § 1415(f)(1)(A).

296. 20 U.S.C.A. § 1415(g).

297. 20 U.S.C.A. § 1415(f)(3)(C).

298. *See, e.g., D.C. and A.C. v. Klein Indep. School Dist.*, 711 F. Supp. 2d 739 [260 Educ. L. Rep. 176] (S.D. Tex. 2010) (rejecting a parental wish for a due process hearing as time-barred under a state law requiring requests to be made within one year of the date complainants knew or should have known about the alleged actions giving rise to requests; the parents asked for the hearing fourteen months after an IEP was developed). *But see Anchorage School Dist. v. D.S. and C.S.*, 688 F. Supp. 2d 883 [256 Educ. L. Rep. 298] (D. Alaska 2009) (applying the IDEA's two-year statute of limitations rather than the state's one-year time frame where board officials incorrectly notified the parents that the two-year statute of limitations applied).

attempts at resolving disagreements or if they withheld pertinent information from the parents.[299]

As a matter of first impression, the Third Circuit applied an interesting twist to the application of the IDEA's statute of limitations. The court held that insofar as counterclaims are not actions within the meaning of the law because they are reactive rather than proactive, the IDEA's statute of limitations was inapplicable.[300] As such, the court allowed the counterclaim of a school board in Pennsylvania, challenging an award of compensatory services in favor of a student with disabilities, to proceed. The Third Circuit, in another case from Pennsylvania, later decided that the IDEA's two-year statute of limitations applied to claims that developed before it became effective, ignoring the seven-month gap between when the facts giving rise to a parental complaint occurred and when they initiated their action.[301]

Hearing officers, typically selected pursuant to state law, must be impartial,[302] meaning that they cannot be employees of the states or school boards involved in educating students or have personal or professional interests in the outcomes of disputes.[303] A federal trial court in New York rejected a parental claim of bias where a hearing officer cohabited with an employee of the state department of education absent evidence that his living arrangements created a personal interest in the outcome of the dispute warranting his disqualification.[304] Conversely, a federal trial court in Indiana refused to dismiss a claim that a hearing officer was biased due to a conflict of interest because he taught a workshop for school administrators at a local university;[305] in dicta the court reiterated that individuals who otherwise qualify as hearing officers are not considered state or board employees solely by virtue of being paid to serve in this capacity.[306] Public agencies must keep lists of hearing officers along with explanations of their qualifications.[307] As to an important legal issue, a federal trial court in New York[308] reiterated the general rule[309] that hearing officers who exercise

---

299. 20 U.S.C.A. § 1415(f)(3)(D).

300. *Jonathan H. v. The Souderton Area School Dist.*, 562 F.3d 527 (3d Cir. 2009).

301. *Steven I. v. Central Bucks School Dist.*, 618 F.3d 411 [260 Educ. L. Rep. 573] (3d Cir. 2010), *cert. denied,* ___ U.S. ___, 131 S.Ct. 1507, 179 L.Ed.2d 307 (2011).

302. *But see A.B. ex rel. Susan B. v. Montgomery County Intermediate Unit*, 409 Fed.Appx. 602 [266 Educ. L. Rep. 634] (2011) (affirming that a due process hearing officer did not have to disclose his former working relationship with a school's attorney or his current working relationship with counsel's wife in a dispute involving a child who was hearing impaired).

303. 20 U.S.C.A. § 1415(f)(3)(A). This section also delineates the qualities that hearing officers should possess. Although some states specify that hearing officers should be attorneys, this is not a requirement under federal law.

304. *W.T. and K.T. ex rel. J.T. v. Board of Educ. of School Dist. of N.Y. City*, 716 F. Supp. 2d 270 (S.D.N.Y. 2010).

305. *H.H. ex rel. Hough v. Indiana Bd. of Special Educ. Appeals*, 501 F. Supp.2d 1188 [224 Educ. L. Rep. 131] (N.D. Ind. 2007).

306. 34 C.F.R. § 300.511(c)(2).

307. 34 C.F.R. § 300.511(c)(3).

308. *B.J.S. ex rel N.S. v. State Educ. Dep't/ Univ. of the State of N.Y.*, 699 F. Supp.2d 586 [258 Educ. L. Rep. 140] (W.D.N.Y. 2010).

309. *See, e.g., M.O. ex rel. C.O. and L.O. v. Indiana Dep't of Educ.*, 635 F. Supp.2d 847 [248 Educ. L. Rep. 392] (N.D. Ind. 2009); *Independent School Dist. No. 283, St. Louis Park v.*

quasi-judicial powers are entitled to the same absolute immunity as judicial officials when they act in their official capacities.

Within fifteen-days of receiving parental requests for due process hearings,[310] school officials must meet with them in mandatory resolution sessions to discuss their disagreements.[311] If the parties are able to resolve their differences, they must execute legally binding agreements enforceable in state courts or in federal trial courts.[312] The parties may void their agreements within three business days of their being executed.[313]

If parents and school officials are unable to resolve their differences within thirty-days, then the due process time lines come into play.[314] Under these provisions, hearing officers must render final decisions based on the record[315] within forty-five days after the expiration of the thirty-day period,[316] but can grant specific extensions of these time frames at the request of either party.[317] The orders of hearing officers are final unless one of the parties appeals.[318] In jurisdictions with two-tiered due process hearing systems, officials must ensure that final judgments are reached within thirty days of when requests for reviews are made.[319]

In preparing for hearings, both parties must make full disclosures of all evaluations completed to date and recommendations they intend to rely on at least five business days in advance.[320] If parties fail to provide this information, hearing officers can prevent them from introducing the relevant evaluations or recommendations at hearings without the consent of the other parties.[321]

Whether hearings are open to the public is a parental choice.[322] In a case from Missouri dealing with judicial proceedings where a student with a disability brought a loaded handgun to school, the Eighth Circuit noted that strong public policy favors the protection of the privacy of minors when sensitive matters are concerned. In rejecting a newspaper's attempt to cover a judicial hearing, the court affirmed that IDEA proceedings can be

---

S.D. ex rel. J.D. and N.D., 948 F.Supp. 860 [115 Educ. L. Rep. 747 (D. Minn. 1995), *aff'd on other grounds*, 88 F.3d 556 [110 Educ. L. Rep. 987 (8th Cir. 1996).

310. 20 U.S.C.A. § 1415(f)(1)(B).

311. *See D.D. ex rel. Davis v. District of Columbia*, 470 F. Supp.2d 1 [217 Educ. L. Rep. 166] (D.D.C. 2007) (holding that while it was unable to award attorney fees incident to a resolution session, the IDEA did not forbid the parties from discussing the recovery of fees).

312. 20 U.S.C.A. § 1415(f)(1)(B)(iii).

313. 20 U.S.C.A. § 1415(f)(1)(B)(iv).

314. 20 U.S.C.A. § 1415(f)(1)(B)(ii).

315. 20 U.S.C.A. §§ 1415(f)(3)(E)(i), (ii).

316. 34 C.F.R. § 300.515(a).

317. 34 C.F.R. § 300.515(c). See *Lake Washington School Dist. No. 414 v. Office of Superintendent of Pub. Instr.*, 634 F.3d 1065 [265 Educ. L. Rep. 889] (9th Cir. 2011) (affirming that a local board lacked standing to challenge a continuance beyond the statutory limit granted by an administrative law judge).

318. 20 U.S.C.A. § 1415(i)(1)(A).

319. 34 C.F.R. § 300.515(b).

320. 20 U.S.C.A. § 1415(f)(2)(A).

321. 20 U.S.C.A. § 1415(f)(2)(B).

322. 34 C.F.R. § 300.512(c)(2).

closed to the public.[323] The court added that the IDEA restricts the release of student information without parental consent.

As quasi-judicial proceedings, the parties involved in due process hearings have the right to be accompanied and advised by counsel and by individuals with special knowledge or training with respect to the problems of children with disabilities;[324] the right to present evidence and confront, cross-examine, and compel the attendance of witnesses;[325] the right to written, or, at the option of the parents, electronic verbatim records of such hearings;[326] and the right to written, or, at the option of the parents, electronic findings of fact and final adjudications.[327]

Parties displeased by the results of administrative proceedings may appeal to state or federal courts within ninety days[328] or the appropriate state time limitations[329] but, before doing so, must first exhaust all administrative remedies unless it is futile to do so.[330] The burden of proving futility rests on the party raising such a claim.[331]

As illustrated by a case from the Second Circuit, where school officials failed to notify parents in New York of their procedural rights, they were not required to exhaust administrative remedies.[332] Two years later, the Seventh Circuit reasoned that where a student's alleged injuries for physical and emotional harm were non-educational ones for which the IDEA did not provide remedies, exhaustion was unnecessary.[333] However, the Second Circuit ruled that a student with disabilities in New York who was subject to an exclusion from school was not entitled to recover attorney fees in his claim against educational officials because he failed to exhaust administrative remedies before filing suit.[334] While administrative or judicial actions are pending, the IDEA's stay-put provisions require that unless school

---

323. *Webster Groves School Dist. v. Pulitzer Publishing Co.*, 898 F.2d 1371 [59 Educ. L. Rep. 630] (8th Cir. 1990).

324. 20 U.S.C.A. § 1415(h)(1).

325. 20 U.S.C.A. § 1415(h)(2).

326. 20 U.S.C.A. § 1415(h)(3). *See Stringer v. St. James R–1 School Dist.*, 446 F.3d 799 [208 Educ. L. Rep. 725] (8th Cir. 2006) (affirming that a school board's failure to comply with the IDEA's requirement of providing a mother with an audio recording of a hearing was a harmless error since she received a written verbatim record of the record from a certified court reporter and never alleged that it was inaccurate).

327. 20 U.S.C.A. § 1415(h)(4).

328. 20 U.S.C.A. § 1415(i)(2)(B).

329. 20 U.S.C.A. § 1415(i)(2)(B).

330. For cases upholding the exhaustion requirement, *see, e.g., TC v. Valley Cent. School Dist.*, 777 F.Supp.2d 577 (S.D.N.Y. 2011); *B.I. v. Montgomery County Bd. of Educ.*, 750 F.Supp.2d 1280 [265 Educ. L. Rep. 641] (M.D. Ala. 2010); *Kutasi v. Las Virgenes Unified School Dist.*, 494 F.3d 1162 [223 Educ. L. Rep. 117] (9th Cir. 2007).

331. *Piazza v. Florida Union Free School Dist.*, 777 F.Supp.2d 669 [270 Educ. L. Rep. 189] (S.D.N.Y. 2011).

332. *Weixel v. Board of Educ. of the City of N.Y.*, 287 F.3d 138 [163 Educ. L. Rep. 640] (2d Cir. 2002).

333. *McCormick v. Waukegan School Dist. No. 60*, 374 F.3d 564 [189 Educ. L. Rep. 518] (7th Cir. 2004). *See also Blanchard v. Morton School Dist.*, 420 F.3d 918 [201 Educ. L. Rep. 106] (9th Cir. 2005); *Polera v. Board of Educ. of the Newburgh Enlarged City School Dist.*, 288 F.3d 478 [164 Educ. L. Rep. 573] (2d Cir. 2002).

334. *Coleman v. Newburgh Enlarged City School Dist.*, 503 F.3d 198 [225 Educ. L. Rep. 168] (2d Cir. 2007).

officials and parents agree[335] or officials obtain either orders from hearing officers[336] or judicial decrees[337] granting them permission to change their placements, students must remain in their then current settings.

Courts have the authority to review the record of administrative proceedings, hear additional evidence,[338] and grant such relief as they deem appropriate based on the preponderance of evidence standard.[339] Even so, in *Rowley* the Supreme Court has advised judges not to substitute their views of proper educational decisionmaking for that of school authorities. To this end, in *Rowley* the Court declared that: "[w]e ... have cautioned that courts lack the 'specialized knowledge and experience' necessary to resolve 'persistent and difficult questions of educational policy.' ... Therefore, once a court determines that the requirements of the Act have been met, questions of methodology are for resolution by the States."[340]

As extensive as it is, the IDEA is not the exclusive avenue through which parents can enforce the rights of their children. According to the IDEA, its provisions cannot be interpreted as limiting or restricting the rights, procedures, and remedies available under the Constitution, Section 504, or other federal laws protecting the rights of students with disabilities.[341]

REMEDIES

As indicated, once parents take school boards to courts in disputes over the placements of their children, the judiciary has the power to award relief that they deem appropriate.[342] Courts can provide monetary damages, tuition reimbursement, compensatory services, and attorney fees.

Damages

Courts generally have not imposed monetary damages on school officials in their individual[343] or official[344] capacities for failing to provide a

---

335. 20 U.S.C.A. § 1415(j).

336. 20 U.S.C.A. § 1415(k)(2).

337. *Honig v. Doe*, 484 U.S. 305, 108 S.Ct. 592, 98 L.Ed.2d 686 [43 Educ. L. Rep. 857] (1988).

338. 20 U.S.C.A. §§ 1415(i)(2)(C)(i), (ii). *School Bd. of Collier County, Fla. v. K.C.*, 285 F.3d 977 [163 Educ. L. Rep. 111] (11th Cir. 2002); *A.S. v. Trumbull Bd. of Educ.*, 359 F. Supp.2d 102 [196 Educ. L. Rep. 518] (D. Conn. 2005).

339. 20 U.S.C.A. § 1415(i)(2)(C)(iii). For discussion of this standard, *see, e.g., Kruelle v. New Castle County School Dist.*, 642 F.2d 687 (3d Cir. 1981); *Independent School Dist. No. 283 v. S.D. by J.D.*, 88 F.3d 556 [110 Educ. L. Rep. 987] (8th Cir. 1996); *Evanston Community Consol. School Dist. Number 65 v. Michael M.*, 356 F.3d 798 [184 Educ. L. Rep. 692] (7th Cir. 2004); *Lamoine School Comm. v. Ms. Z. ex rel. N.S.*, 353 F. Supp.2d 18 [195 Educ. L. Rep. 511] (D. Me. 2005).

340. 458 U.S. 176, 208, 102 S.Ct. 3034, 3052, 73 L.Ed.2d 690 [5 Educ. L. Rep. 34] (1982) [Case No. 110].

341. 20 U.S.C.A. § 1415(*l*).

342. 20 U.S.C.A. § 1415(i)(2)(C)(iii).

343. *See, e.g., Taylor v. Altoona Area School Dist.*, 513 F. Supp.2d 540 [225 Educ. L. Rep. 778] (W.D. Pa. 2007); *L.M.P. ex rel. E.P. v. School Bd. of Broward County*, 516 F. Supp.2d 1305 [226 Educ. L. Rep. 784] (S.D. Fla. 2007) (cases involving the IDEA).

344. *See, e.g., Bradley v. Arkansas Dep't of Educ.*, 301 F.3d 952 [168 Educ. L. Rep. 646] (8th Cir.2002); *Mark H. v. Lemahieu*, 513 F.3d 922 [229 Educ. L. Rep. 53] (9th Cir. 2008) (cases involving the IDEA).

FAPE or services for students with disabilities,[345] especially if remedies are available under the IDEA.[346] Moreover, courts have refused to impose punitive damages on educators or boards for failing in this regard.[347]

Courts have not awarded general damages for "pain and suffering"[348] in disputes over special education. Even so, recent litigation suggests that this may be changing. As evidence of this possible shift in judicial thinking, the Ninth Circuit decided that monetary damages may be available under Section 504[349] if parents can show that educators engaged in intentional discrimination or egregiously disregarded the rights of their children. Other courts agreed that officials can be liable if they acted with deliberate indifference to the needs of children.[350]

Tuition Reimbursement

Parents who disagree with the placements of their children may enroll them in private schools and attempt to recover the costs of tuition.[351] In *School Committee of the Town of Burlington v. Department of Education, Commonwealth of Massachusetts*,[352] the Supreme Court pointed out that parents are entitled to tuition reimbursement if they can show that officials failed to offer appropriate placements and their chosen placements are appropriate.[353] The Court posited that awarding reimbursement requires boards to pay retroactively for costs that they should have absorbed from the beginning. In another aspect of the issue, in *Florence County School District Four v. Carter*,[354] the Court held that parents are entitled to reimbursements for expenses such as tuition[355] even if their chosen place-

345. *See Taylor v. Altoona Area School Dist.*, 513 F. Supp.2d 540 [225 Educ. L. Rep. 778] (W.D. Pa. 2007) (denying damages against individual defendants under Section 504).

346. *See, e.g., D. A. v. Houston Indep. School Dist.*, 629 F.3d 450 [264 Educ. L. Rep. 50] (5th Cir. 2010).

347. *See, e.g., Chambers v. School Dist. of Philadelphia Bd. of Educ.*, 587 F.3d 176 [250 Educ. L. Rep. 884] (3d Cir. 2009).

348. *See, e.g., Ft. Zumwalt School Dist. v. Missouri State Bd. of Educ.*, 865 F.Supp. 604 [95 Educ. L. Rep. 253] (E.D. Mo.1994).

349. In remanding such a case for reconsideration, the Ninth Circuit ruled that obtaining relief under the IDEA did not preclude parents from seeking damages under Section 504 where they claimed that school officials in Hawaii violated both statutes in denying their daughter with autism a FAPE. *Mark H. v. Lemahieu*, 513 F.3d 922 [229 Educ. L. Rep. 53] (9th Cir. 2008).

350. *Butler v. South Glens Falls Central School Dist.*, 106 F. Supp.2d 414 [146 Educ. L. Rep. 701] (N.D.N.Y. 2000); *Patricia N. v. Lemahieu*, 141 F. Supp.2d 1243 [154 Educ. L. Rep. 532] (D. Haw. 2001).

351. 20 U.S.C.A. § 1412(a)(10)(C)(ii).

352. 471 U.S. 359, 105 S.Ct. 1996, 85 L.Ed.2d 385 [23 Educ. L. Rep. 1189] (1985).

353. *See Werner v. Clarkstown Cent. School Dist.*, 363 F. Supp.2d 656 [197 Educ. L. Rep. 244] (S.D.N.Y. 2005) (reasoning that while a school board failed to comply with the IDEA's procedural requirements, since parents were unable to show that their chosen placement in a private school was appropriate, they were not entitled to reimbursement).

354. 510 U.S. 7, 114 S.Ct. 361, 126 L.Ed.2d 284 [86 Educ. L. Rep. 41] (1993).

355. *Jennifer D. ex rel. Travis D. v. New York City Dep't of Educ.*, 550 F. Supp.2d 420 [233 Educ. L. Rep. 588] (S.D.N.Y. 2008) (involving a placement in a special program at a religiously affiliated non-public school).

ments are not in state-approved facilities as long as they place their children in otherwise appropriate settings.[356] Still, in a case from Maine, the First Circuit affirmed that parents can be denied reimbursements for educational expenses for unilaterally placing their children in private schools if they unreasonably delay making their requests.[357]

When parents placed their children in private schools without availing themselves of the IDEA's procedures in public school settings, federal courts disagreed over whether they do so at their own financial risk since, as noted in the previous paragraph, they are not entitled to reimbursements if board officials can show that they offered, and could provide, appropriate placements.[358] In two separate cases, the First Circuit[359] agreed that parents were not entitled to tuition reimbursement where they failed to apprise officials that they were changing the placements of their children and did not afford them opportunities to re-evaluate the students. The Third Circuit[360] and the federal trial court in Maryland[361] reached similar outcomes. On the other hand, the Second Circuit twice,[362] joined by the Eleventh Circuit,[363] refused to interpret the IDEA as precluding parents from receiving reimbursement for private placements without first enrolling their children in public schools.

In an attempt to resolve this split, the Supreme Court agreed to hear an appeal. Only ten days after hearing oral arguments, the Court issued a one line opinion in *Board of Education of the City School District of the City of New York v. Tom F. ex rel. Gilbert F (Tom. F.)* that "[t]he judgment is affirmed by an equally divided Court."[364] The Court added without further explanation that "Justice Kennedy took no part in the decision of this case."[365] Since *Tom F.* is a plurality, it remains precedent only in the Second Circuit. As reflected by a case from New Jersey, the federal trial court ruled that parents did not have to first accept an IEP for their son in order to remain eligible for reimbursement of tuition costs after unilaterally placing him in a private school.[366]

---

356. *See, e.g., Lauren W. ex rel. Jean W. v. DeFlaminis,* 480 F.3d 259 [217 Educ. L. Rep. 96] (3d Cir. 2007); *N.G. v. District of Columbia,* 556 F. Supp.2d 11 [234 Educ. L. Rep. 660] (D.D.C. 2008).

357. *School Union No. 37 v. Ms. C.,* 518 F.3d 31 [230 Educ. L. Rep. 498] (1st Cir. 2008).

358. *Z.W. ex rel. G. and J.W. v. Smith,* 210 Fed.Appx. 282 [217 Educ. L. Rep. 816] (4th Cir. 2006).

359. *Greenland School Dist. v. Amy N.,* 358 F.3d 150 [185 Educ. L. Rep. 73] (1st Cir. 2004), 557 U.S. 230, 129 S.Ct. 2484, 174 L.Ed.2d 168 [245 Educ. L. Rep. 551] (2009); *Ms. M. ex rel. K.M. v. Portland School Comm.,* 360 F.3d 267 [185 Educ. L. Rep. 819] (1st Cir. 2004).

360. *Marissa F. ex rel. Mark and Lavinia F. v. William Penn School Dist.,* 199 Fed.Appx. 151 [215 Educ. L. Rep. 259] (3d Cir. 2006).

361. *Baltimore City Bd. of Sch. Comm'rs v. Taylorch,* 395 F. Supp.2d 246 [204 Educ. L. Rep. 244] (D. Md. 2005).

362. *Frank G. v. Board of Educ. of Hyde Park,* 459 F.3d 356 [212 Educ. L Rep. 35] (2d Cir. 2006), *cert. denied,* 552 U.S. 985, 128 S.Ct. 436, 169 L.Ed.2d 325 (2007); *Board of Educ. of the City School Dist. of the City of N.Y. v. Tom F.,* 193 Fed.Appx. 26 (2d Cir. 2006), *cert. granted,* 549 U.S. 1251, 127 S.Ct. 1393, 167 L.Ed.2d 158 (2007).

363. *M.M. ex rel. C.M. v. School Board of Miami–Dade County,* 437 F.3d 1085 (11th Cir. 2006).

364. 552 U.S. 1, 128 S.Ct. 1, 169 L.Ed.2d 1 [225 Educ. L. Rep. 44] (2007).

365. *Id.*

Litigation continued over whether parents could unilaterally place their children in private schools and seek reimbursement. The Ninth Circuit subsequently determined that the parents of a student in Oregon who had not previously received special education services were eligible for tuition reimbursement since it was appropriate relief even though his parents placed him there unilaterally.[367] On further review in *Forest Grove School District v. T.A.*,[368] the Supreme Court resolved the judicial split in deciding that the parents were entitled to reimbursement for the tuition they spent in placing their son in the private setting even though he had not first received special education in a public school. Yet, on remand after the federal trial court in Oregon denied the parental request for tuition reimbursement,[369] the Ninth Circuit affirmed that the equities did not require the board to reimburse them for cost of tuition at the private school.[370]

Courts continue to award tuition reimbursement for parents when school boards fail to provide meaningful education benefits[371] or a FAPE to children,[372] if IEPs are inadequate,[373] and if officials fail to address a child's progress when developing a new IEP.[374] However, where parents in Delaware refused to cooperate in the formulation of their son's IEP, the Third Circuit affirmed that they were ineligible to receive tuition reimbursement after placing him in a private school.[375]

Compensatory Services

Tuition reimbursement is unlikely to help parents who cannot place their children in private schools because they cannot afford to pay for tuition. If parents lack the funds to make unilateral placements, their

---

366. *D.L. ex rel J.L. v. Springfield Bd. of Educ.*, 536 F. Supp.2d 534 [230 Educ. L. Rep. 221] (D.N.J. 2008).

367. *Forest Grove v. T.A.*, 523 F.3d 1078 [231 Educ. L. Rep. 657] (9th Cir. 2008), *cert. granted*, 555 U.S. 1130, 129 S.Ct. 987, 173 L.Ed.2d 171 (2009).

368. 557 U.S. 230, 129 S.Ct. 2484, 174 L.Ed.2d 168 [245 Educ. L. Rep. 551] (2009).

369. *Forest Grove School Dist. v. T.A.*, 675 F. Supp.2d 1063 [254 Educ. L. Rep. 174] (D. Or. 2009).

370. *Forest Grove School Dist. v. T.A.*, 638 F.3d 1234 [267 Educ. L. Rep. 22] (9th Cir. 2011).

371. *Board of Educ. of City School Dist. of Cincinnati v. Wilhelmy*, 689 F. Supp. 2d 970 [256 Educ. L. Rep. 677] (S.D. Ohio 2010); *D.B. v. Bedford County School Bd.*, 708 F. Supp. 2d 564 [259 Educ. L. Rep. 608] (W.D. Va. 2010).

372. *C.B. ex rel. Baquerizo v. Garden Grove Unified School Dist.*, 635 F.3d 1155 [265 Educ. L. Rep. 917] (9th Cir. 2011); *C.B. ex rel. B.B. v. Special School Dist. No. 1, Minneapolis, Minn.*, 636 F.3d 981 [266 Educ. L. Rep. 71] (8th Cir. 2011); *Sudbury Pub. Schools v. Massachusetts Dep't of Elementary and Secondary Educ.*, 762 F.Supp.2d 254 [267 Educ. L. Rep. 142] (D. Mass. 2010).

373. *A.D. and M.D. ex rel. E.D. v. Board of Educ. of City of N.Y.*, 690 F. Supp.2d 193 [256 Educ. L. Rep. 746] (S.D.N.Y. 2010); *M.H. and E.K. ex rel. P.H. v. New York City Dep't of Educ.*, 712 F. Supp. 2d 125 [260 Educ. L. Rep. 639] (S.D.N.Y. 2010); *R.B. and H.Z. ex rel. C.Z. v. New York City Dep't of Educ.*, 713 F. Supp. 2d 235 [260 Educ. L. Rep. 689] (S.D.N.Y. 2010).

374. *E.S. v. Katonah–Lewisboro School Dist.*, 742 F. Supp. 2d 417 [264 Educ. L. Rep. 724] (S.D.N.Y. 2010).

375. *C.H. v. Cape Henlopen School Dist.*, 606 F.3d 59 [257 Educ. L. Rep. 39] (3d Cir. 2010).

children may have to remain in inappropriate settings while disputes work their way through administrative and legal proceedings. If this occurs, courts can award extra educational services and prospective relief to compensate parents, and their children, for the loss of appropriate educational services. Needless to say, compensatory services must be implemented in a timely manner.[376]

The courts observed that compensatory services, like reimbursements, are designed to offer relief for the failure of school board officials to provide children with appropriate educations.[377] The rationale for awards of compensatory services is that appropriate remedies should be available to all parents regardless of whether they can afford to pay for alternate educational placements while litigation is pending. Compensatory services are ordinarily awarded for the time that children were denied services[378] even if they passed the IDEA's age limit.[379]

As with tuition reimbursement, compensatory services can be awarded only if hearing officers or courts agree that school officials failed to provide appropriate placements. In such a case, the Eighth Circuit affirmed that parents in Missouri were entitled to compensatory services for their son after officials improperly ended homebound services and left him without programming.[380] The federal trial court in Massachusetts adopted a different approach in concluding that where a school committee provided all of the programming a child was due under his IEP, he was not entitled to compensatory services.[381] Moreover, a federal trial court in Pennsylvania granted a parental request for compensatory services where officials did not identify their daughter, a child with multiple disabilities, as a candidate for special education and related services.[382]

In a dispute from Georgia, the Eleventh Circuit affirmed that an eighteen-year-old student who read at a third grade level due to his learning disabilities was entitled to compensatory services where school officials failed either to evaluate his progress for more than five years or to

---

376. *Board of Educ. of City of Chicago v. Illinois State Bd. of Educ.*, 741 F. Supp. 2d 920 [264 Educ. L. Rep. 271] (N.D. Ill. 2010) (indicating that under state law services had to be provided within ten days).

377. *Burr by Burr v. Ambach*, 863 F.2d 1071 [50 Educ. L. Rep. 964] (2d Cir.1988), *vacated and remanded sub nom. Sobol v. Burr*, 492 U.S. 902, 109 S.Ct. 3209, 106 L.Ed.2d 560 [54 Educ. L. Rep. 410] (1989), *re-aff'd on remand*, 888 F.2d 258 [56 Educ. L. Rep. 1126] (2d Cir.1989), *cert. denied*, 494 U.S. 1005, 110 S.Ct. 1298, 108 L.Ed.2d 475 (1990); *Blackman v. District of Columbia*, 374 F. Supp.2d 168 [199 Educ. L. Rep. 764] (D.D.C. 2005).

378. *Todd D. by Robert D. v. Andrews*, 933 F.2d 1576 [67 Educ. L. Rep. 1065] (11th Cir.1991), *reh'g denied*, 943 F.2d 1316 (11th Cir.1991); *Birmingham v. Omaha School Dist.*, 298 F.3d 731 [167 Educ. L. Rep. 632] (8th Cir.2002).

379. *Pihl v. Massachusetts Dep't of Educ.*, 9 F.3d 184 [87 Educ. L. Rep. 341] (1st Cir.1993); *Jones v. Schneider*, 896 F.Supp. 488 [103 Educ. L. Rep. 700] (D.V.I. 1995).

380. *Hale ex rel. Hale v. Poplar Bluffs R–I School Dist.*, 280 F.3d 831 [161 Educ. L. Rep. 778] (8th Cir. 2002).

381. *Shawsheen Valley Reg'l Vocational Technical School Dist. School Comm. v. Commonwealth of Mass. Bureau of Special Educ. App.*, 367 F. Supp.2d 44 [198 Educ. L. Rep. 217] (D. Mass. 2005).

382. *Heather D. v. Northampton Area School Dist.*, 511 F. Supp.2d 549 [225 Educ. L. Rep. 571] (E.D. Pa. 2007).

implement his IEP in a timely fashion.[383] The panel agreed that in light of the actions of officials, the trial court did not abuse its discretion in awarding the student a placement in a private school for about five years or until he graduated high school, whichever came first. The court explained that such a placement would have put the student in a situation he would have been in but for the way in which officials violated the IDEA and was reasonably calculated to provide him with the educational benefits he would have received had he been placed properly at the outset. In a case reaching a different outcome, the Tenth Circuit affirmed the denial of compensatory services to a student in New Mexico in rejecting her claim based on equitable considerations.[384] The court asserted that insofar as the student dropped out of school and demonstrated her unwillingness to return, she would have received the services she sought simply by re-enrolling in school.

ATTORNEY FEES

Parents who succeeded in court against their school boards had reasonable expectations of being reimbursed for the significant legal expenses they incurred in protecting the educational rights of their children.[385] Parents argued that they achieved little when they prevailed but were left with significant legal bills.[386] As such, parents are entitled to representation and legal fees, but must be represented by attorneys[387] rather than lay advocates.[388] In at least one case where parents prevailed in a dispute with their board and managed to avoid having their child assessed for special education, though, a federal trial court in New York refused their request for attorney fees on the ground that their child was not a student with a disability.[389] Further, the Fifth Circuit, in a case from Texas, vacated an earlier award in favor of a mother whose son had not yet been determined as qualified to receive services under the IDEA.[390] The court ruled that the mother was not entitled to receive attorney fees since its reading of the

---

383. *Draper v. Atlanta Indep. School Sys.*, 518 F.3d 1275 [230 Educ. L. Rep. 545] (11th Cir. 2008).

384. *Garcia v. Board of Educ. of Albuquerque Pub. Schools*, 520 F.3d 1116 [231 Educ. L. Rep. 25] (10th Cir. 2008).

385. *See, e.g., Bucher v. District of Columbia*, 777 F.Supp.2d 69 [270 Educ. L. Rep. 86] (D.D.C. 2011) (finding that attorney fees of $300 and $350 per hour, depending on when they were billed, were reasonable).

386. *See, e.g., J.P. ex rel. Peterson v. County School Bd. of Hanover County, Va.*, 516 F.3d 254 [229 Educ. L. Rep. 391] (4th Cir. 2008) (although reversing an earlier order in their favor, the court pointed out that parents incurred attorney fees and costs in excess of $180,000); *B.W. v. New York City Dep't of Educ.*, 716 F. Supp.2d 336 [261 Educ. L. Rep. 267] (S.D.N.Y. 2010) (granting attorney fees of $18,642.50).

387. 20 U.S.C.A. § 1415(h)(1).

388. *See In re Arons*, 756 A.2d 867 [146 Educ. L. Rep. 763] (Del. 2000), *cert. denied sub nom. Arons v. Office of Disciplinary Counsel of Sup. Ct. of Del.*, 532 U.S. 1065, 121 S.Ct. 2215, 150 L.Ed.2d 208 (2001).

389. *Durkee v. Livonia Cent. School Dist.*, 487 F. Supp.2d 318 [221 Educ. L. Rep. 134] (W.D.N.Y. 2007).

390. *T.B. ex rel. Debbra B. v. Bryan Indep. School Dist.*, 628 F.3d 240 [263 Educ. L. Rep. 490] (5th Cir. 2010) (involving a child with ADHD).

plain language of the IDEA made it clear that her son had to be receiving services before she could recover such costs.

Initially, in *Smith v. Robinson*,[391] the Supreme Court refused to permit parents of children with disabilities to recover legal expenses from their school boards even if they prevailed. Unhappy with this result, Congress amended the IDEA by passing the Handicapped Children's Protection Act (HCPA).[392] The HCPA grants courts the ability to award attorney fees to prevailing parents[393] in actions or proceedings against their boards under the IDEA.[394] Awards must be based on a variety of factors[395] including the prevailing rates in the areas in which cases were litigated[396] and are subject to review to ensure that trial courts did not abuse their discretion.[397]

Courts have denied parental requests for attorney fees where they rejected settlement offers and failed to obtain more favorable judicial relief;[398] they reached settlements without resorting to due process hearings;[399] they reached settlements pursuant to the IDEA's complaint resolution procedures;[400] attorney fees were excessive;[401] the time billed for legal services was excessive[402] or vague;[403] and a student's dropping out of school without having availed herself of the relief offered rendered the litigation wasteful since it failed to contribute to her welfare.[404]

---

391. 468 U.S. 992, 104 S.Ct. 3457, 82 L.Ed.2d 746 [18 Educ. L. Rep. 148] (1984).

392. 20 U.S.C.A. §§ 1415(i)(3)(B), (C). For limitations on attorney fees, *see* 20 U.S.C.A. §§ 1415(i)(3)(D)–(G).

393. *See, e.g., Gary G. v. El Paso Indep. School Dist.*, 632 F.3d 201 [264 Educ. L. Rep. 686] (5th Cir. 2011); *Birmingham v. Omaha School Dist.*, 298 F.3d 731 [167 Educ. L. Rep. 632] (8th Cir.2002).

394. For a different look at the ability to recover attorney fees, *see Brown v. Barbara Jordan P.C.S.*, 539 F. Supp.2d 436 [231 Educ. L. Rep. 85] (D.D.C. 2008) (holding that a local statutory cap on attorney fees only applied to schools operated by the board of education, not charter schools).

395. For a list of factors that courts take into consideration when setting attorney fees, *see Board of Educ. of Frederick County v. I.S. ex rel. Summers*, 358 F. Supp.2d 462 [196 Educ. L. Rep. 487] (D. Md. 2005).

396. 20 U.S.C.A. § 1415(i)(3)(B). *Angela L. v. Pasadena Indep. School Dist.*, 918 F.2d 1188 [64 Educ. L. Rep. 350] (5th Cir. 1990).

397. *A.R. ex rel. R.V. v. New York City Dep't of Educ.*, 407 F.3d 65 [197 Educ. L. Rep. 525] (2d Cir. 2005).

398. 20 U.S.C.A. § 1415(i)(3)(D)(I). *Mr. L. & Mrs. L. on Behalf of Matthew L. v. Woonsocket Educ. Dep't*, 793 F.Supp. 41 [76 Educ. L. Rep. 398] (D.R.I.1992); *Dell v. Board of Educ.*, 918 F.Supp. 212 [108 Educ. L. Rep. 139] (N.D. Ill.1995).

399. *See, e.g., P.O. ex rel. L.T. v. Greenwich Bd. of Educ.*, 210 F. Supp.2d 76 [167 Educ. L. Rep. 743] (D. Conn.2002).

400. *Vultaggio ex rel. Vultaggio v. Board of Educ., Smithtown Cent. School Dist.*, 343 F.3d 598 [180 Educ. L. Rep. 528] (2d Cir. 2003).

401. *Holmes v. Millcreek Twp. School Dist.*, 205 F.3d 583 [142 Educ. L. Rep. 667] (3d Cir.2000); *S.W. ex rel. N.W. v. Board of Educ. of City of N.Y. (Dist. Two)*, 407 F.3d 65 [197 Educ. L. Rep. 525] (2d Cir. 2005).

402. *Cavanaugh ex rel. Cavanaugh v. Cardinal Local School Dist.*, 409 F.3d 753 [198 Educ. L. Rep. 443] (6th Cir. 2005), *reh'g denied* (2005), *abrogated by Winkelman v. Parma City School Dist.*, 550 U.S. 516, 127 S.Ct. 1994, 167 L.Ed.2d 904 [219 Educ. L. Rep. 39] (2007); *Sabatini v. Corning–Painted Post Area School Dist.*, 190 F. Supp.2d 509 (W.D.N.Y. 2001).

403. *C.C. ex rel. Mrs. D. v. Granby Bd. of Educ.*, 453 F. Supp.2d 569 [214 Educ. L. Rep. 231] (D. Conn. 2006).

404. *E.M. v. Marriott Hospitality Pub. Chartered High School*, 541 F. Supp.2d 395 [231 Educ. L. Rep. 728] (D.D.C. 2008).

The courts disagree over whether parents who are attorneys are entitled to fees when they represent their children. Although some courts permit attorney parents to recover fees,[405] most refuse[406] to do so. In a factually unique situation, the Ninth Circuit permitted prevailing parents in California to recover attorney fees even though they received legal representation from the child's paternal grandmother.[407] The court explained that even though she was obviously related to the child, the grandmother was neither his legal guardian nor was she acting in the place of his parents when she served as the family lawyer.

The school board in the nation's capital unsuccessfully sought to recover attorney fees from the lawyer who brought an administrative complaint against it on behalf of a student with special needs.[408] The Circuit Court for the District of Columbia rejected the board's request for fees since it was not the prevailing party insofar as the case was rendered moot due to actions by school officials.

As with other issues related to non-public schools under the IDEA, the rules for attorney fees are different. In such a case, the Sixth Circuit affirmed that insofar as a private school in Ohio was not a proper party in a parental action challenging their son's expulsion from the school, it was ineligible to receive attorney fees.[409]

The Eighth Circuit went so far as to reduce fees to a mother in Minnesota it identified as "overly litigious."[410] In two cases from Illinois, federal trial courts reduced attorney fees as excessive where a lawyer had eight similar entries for work performed on the same day amounting to two hours over records requests to various institutions[411] and where a lawyer had duplicative billing plus inadequate documentation of travel time associated with the case.[412]

In what may turn out to be one of the more significant additions in the 2004 version of the IDEA, the law permits school boards to seek reimbursement of their legal expenses when parents file complaints that are later found to be frivolous, unreasonable, or without foundation or when litigation was continued after it clearly became frivolous, unreasonable, or

---

405. *Matthew V. v. Dekalb County School Sys.*, 244 F. Supp.2d 1331 [174 Educ. L. Rep. 731] (N.D. Ga. 2003) (noting that while an attorney-parent could recover fees pursuant to the IDEA, his son was not the prevailing party in an administrative action).

406. *See, e.g., Pardini v. Allegheny Intermediate Unit*, 524 F.3d 419 [232 Educ. L. Rep. 37] (3d Cir. 2008); *Woodside v. School Dist. of Philadelphia Bd. of Educ.*, 248 F.3d 129 [153 Educ. L. Rep. 525] (3d Cir. 2001); *Erickson v. Board of Educ. of Baltimore County*, 162 F.3d 289 [131 Educ. L. Rep. 31] (4th Cir.1998), *opinion amended and superseded*, 165 F.3d 260 [131 Educ. L. Rep. 928] (4th Cir.1998), *cert. denied*, 526 U.S. 1159, 119 S.Ct. 2049, 144 L.Ed.2d 216 (1999).

407. *Weissburg v. Lancaster School Dist.*, 591 F.3d 1255 [252 Educ. L. Rep. 578] (9th Cir. 2010).

408. *District of Columbia v. Ijeabuonwu*, 642 F.3d 1191 [268 Educ. L. Rep. 698] (D.C. Cir. 2011).

409. *Children's Ctr. for Developmental Enrichment v. Machle*, 612 F.3d 518 [259 Educ. L. Rep. 30] (6th Cir. 2010), *reh'g and reh'g en banc denied* (2010).

410. *Independent School Dist. No. 623, Roseville, Minn. v. Digre*, 893 F.2d 987, 992 [58 Educ. L. Rep. 92] (8th Cir. 1990).

411. *Benito M. v. Board of Educ. of City of Chicago, Dist. 299*, 544 F.Supp.2d 713 [232 Educ. L. Rep. 222] (N.D. Ill. 2008).

412. *Ryan M. v. Board of Educ. of City of Chicago, Dist. 299*, 731 F. Supp. 2d 776 [263 Educ. L. Rep. 85] (N.D. Ill. 2010).

without foundation.[413] This change permits boards to recover costs from attorneys who file suit on behalf of parents if their actions are premised on improper purposes, cause unnecessary delays, or needlessly increase the cost of litigation.[414]

As reflected by cases from California[415] and the District of Columbia,[416] courts are beginning to grant board requests for reimbursements from lawyers in these kinds of cases while another court in California, relying on the Federal Rules of Civil Procedure, imposed sanctions on a school board.[417] In a case from Arizona, though, the Ninth Circuit denied the request of parents of a child with autism to sanction a board and its attorney absent evidence that they acted recklessly or in bad faith in addressing the rights of their son.[418]

The status of attorney fees under the catalyst theory, pursuant to which courts have awarded fees if litigation, or the threat of a suit or administrative actions, motivated school board officials to grant parental requests, is now in doubt.[419] The viability of the catalyst theory is uncertain in light of a non-school case, *Buckhannon Board & Care Home v. West Virginia Department of Health and Human Resources (Buckhannon)*.[420] In *Buckhannon*, the Supreme Court rejected the catalyst theory in acknowledging that prevailing parties must succeed in court by obtaining judgments on the merits or consent decrees. Federal courts have since reached mixed results over this question. The First,[421] Second,[422] and Third[423] Circuits and at least two federal trial courts[424] denied requests for attorney

---

413. 20 U.S.C.A. § 1415(i)(3)(B)(i)(II).

414. 20 U.S.C.A. § 1415(i)(3)(B)(i)(III).

415. *K.S. ex rel. P.S. v. Fremont Unified School Dist.*, 545 F. Supp.2d 995 [232 Educ. L. Rep. 738] (N.D. Cal. 2008) (upholding an administrative law judge's imposition of unnamed sanctions against the attorney who represented parents in their unsuccessful challenge to their daughter's IEP).

416. *See, e.g., Bridges Pub. Charter Sch. v. Barrie*, 709 F. Supp. 2d 94 [259 Educ. L. Rep. 654] (D.D.C. 2010) (involving a charter school). However, in three other cases the same court conceded that the board was the prevailing party but refused to award attorney fees because the parental claims were not sanctionable insofar as they were neither frivolous nor unreasonable; *see District of Columbia v. Nahass*, 699 F. Supp. 2d 175 [258 Educ. L. Rep. 112] (D.D.C. 2010); *District of Columbia v. West*, 699 F. Supp. 2d 273 [258 Educ. L. Rep. 131] (D.D.C. 2010); *District of Columbia v. Barrie*, 741 F. Supp. 2d 250 [264 Educ. L. Rep. 253] (D.D.C. 2010).

417. *Moser v. Bret Harte Union High School Dist.*, 366 F. Supp.2d 944 [198 Educ. L. Rep. 171] (E.D. Cal. 2005).

418. *R.P. ex rel. C.P. v. Prescott Unified School Dist.*, 631 F.3d 1117 [264 Educ. L. Rep. 618] (9th Cir. 2011).

419. *See, e.g., Daniel S. v. Scranton School Dist.*, 230 F.3d 90 [149 Educ. L. Rep. 17] (3d Cir. 2000); *Doucet ex rel. Doucet v. Chilton County Bd. of Educ.*, 65 F. Supp.2d 1249 [139 Educ. L. Rep. 375] (M.D. Ala. 1999).

420. 532 U.S. 598, 121 S.Ct. 1835, 149 L.Ed.2d 855 (2001).

421. *Doe v. Boston Pub. Schools*, 358 F.3d 20 [185 Educ. L. Rep. 62] (1st Cir. 2004).

422. *J.C. v. Regional School Dist. 10, Bd. of Educ.*, 278 F.3d 119 [161 Educ. L. Rep. 68] (2d Cir. 2002).

423. *John T. ex rel. Paul T. v. Delaware County Intermediate Unit*, 318 F.3d 545 [173 Educ. L. Rep. 442] (3d Cir. 2003); *J.O. ex rel. C.O. v. Orange Twp. Bd. of Educ.*, 287 F.3d 267 [164 Educ. L. Rep. 44] (3d Cir. 2002).

424. *J.S. v. Ramapo Cent. School Dist.*, 165 F. Supp.2d 570 [157 Educ. L. Rep. 728] (S.D.N.Y. 2001); *P.O. ex rel. L.T. v. Greenwich Bd. of Educ.*, 210 F. Supp.2d 76 [167 Educ. L. Rep. 743] (D. Conn. 2002).

fees based on settlement agreements. Conversely, since the District of Columbia Circuit,[425] federal trial courts in California,[426] the District of Columbia,[427] Massachusetts,[428] and New York[429] distinguished the disputes that they resolved from *Buckhannon*, they granted requests for attorney fees.

Expert Witness Fees

Courts initially disagreed over whether parents may recover fees for expert witnesses under the IDEA. While the Circuit Court for the District of Columbia refused to award such fees to parents,[430] the Second Circuit, in a case from New York, reached the opposite result in affirming an order that treated the IDEA's fee shifting provision as covering the costs of expert witnesses who assisted parents in obtaining services for their son.[431] On further review in *Arlington Central School District v. Murphy*,[432] the Supreme Court reversed in interpreting the IDEA as not permitting parents to be reimbursed for the services of expert witnesses or consultants who assisted them in their disagreements with school boards. In refusing to revise the statute, even though it left parents without recourse insofar as they could recover fees from attorneys but not costs associated with expert witnesses and consultants, the Court reasoned that insofar as Congress was unwilling to modify the IDEA despite requests for it to make such a change, it was not its job to do so.[433]

PRO SE PARENTS

Another issue that arose with some regularity, but which led to a judicial split was whether non-attorney parents could act *pro se*, literally, "to appear on one's own behalf," in cases over whether school officials provided their children with disabilities with FAPEs. On the one hand, the First Circuit[434] and a federal trial court in California[435] ruled that there

---

425. *Goldring v. District of Columbia*, 416 F.3d 70 [200 Educ. L. Rep. 25] (D.C. Cir. 2005), *cert. denied*, 548 U.S. 924, 126 S.Ct. 2985, 165 L.Ed.2d 986 (2006) (granting attorney, but not expert witness, fees for an administrative proceeding).

426. *Ostby v. Oxnard Union High*, 209 F. Supp.2d 1035 [167 Educ. L. Rep. 732] (C.D. Cal. 2002).

427. *Johnson v. District of Columbia*, 190 F. Supp.2d 34 [163 Educ. L. Rep. 366] (D.D.C. 2002).

428. *Doe v. Boston Pub. Schools*, 550 F. Supp.2d 170 [233 Educ. L. Rep. 583] (D. Mass. 2008).

429. *D.M. ex rel. G.M. v. Board of Educ., Center Moriches Union Free School Dist.*, 296 F. Supp.2d 400 [184 Educ. L. Rep. 762] (E.D.N.Y. 2003).

430. *Goldring v. District of Columbia*, 416 F.3d 70 [200 Educ. L. Rep. 25] (D.C. Cir. 2005), *cert. denied*, 548 U.S. 924, 126 S.Ct. 2985, 165 L.Ed.2d 986 (2006).

431. *Murphy v. Arlington Cent. School Dist. Bd. of Educ.*, 402 F.3d 332 [196 Educ. L. Rep. 415] (2d Cir. 2005), *cert. granted in part*, 546 U.S. 1085, 126 S.Ct. 978, 163 L.Ed.2d 721 (2006).

432. 548 U.S. 291, 126 S.Ct. 2455, 165 L.Ed.2d 526 (2006).

433. For cases following this precedent, *see Friendship Edison Pub. Charter School v. Nesbitt*, 704 F. Supp. 2d 50 [259 Educ. L. Rep. 46] (D.D.C. 2010); *Fisher v. District of Columbia*, 517 F.3d 570 [230 Educ. L. Rep. 154] (D.C. Cir. 2008); *A.W. v. East Orange Bd. of Educ.*, 248 Fed.Appx. 363 [228 Educ. L. Rep. 91] (3d Cir. 2007) (involving a *pro se* parent).

434. *Maroni v. Pemi–Baker Reg'l School Dist.*, 346 F.3d 247 [181 Educ. L. Rep. 357] (1st Cir. 2003).

were no limits on the ability of parents to act on behalf of their children or themselves in judicial proceedings. On the other hand, the Third,[436] Seventh,[437] and Eleventh[438] Circuits permitted parents to act *pro se* on their own interests, not those of their children, in judicial actions. The Second[439] and Sixth Circuits,[440] joined by a federal trial court in Oregon[441] agreed that non-attorney parents lacked the ability to initiate judicial actions on behalf of themselves or their children.

In resolving the split in *Winkelman v. Parma City School District*,[442] the Supreme Court, in a case from Ohio, reversed a judgment of the Sixth Circuit. The Court held that insofar as non-attorney parents have rights separate and apart from those of their children, they can proceed *pro se* in judicial actions challenging the IEPs of their children. Not long thereafter, in denying a request for attorney fees for educational advocates and parents, the federal trial court in the District of Columbia explained that they filed suit under the same limitations as parents who file *pro se* actions.[443] Further, the Ninth Circuit initially dismissed a *pro se* mother's appeal over the sufficiency of her daughter's IEP since she was not an aggrieved party due to the fact that she had not suffered an injury-in-fact because any harm that she might have suffered was speculative in nature.[444] On rehearing, in an unpublished order, the court again dismissed in finding that insofar as the parties entered a settlement agreement, the mother had not suffered an injury-in-fact.[445]

FINANCIAL CONSIDERATIONS

Aware of the need to provide assistance for state and local school officials as they pay for the costs associated with the delivery of special

---

435. *D.K. ex rel. Kumetz–Coleman v. Huntington Beach Union High School Dist.*, 428 F. Supp.2d 1088 [210 Educ. L. Rep. 194] (C.D. Cal. 2006).

436. *Collinsgru v. Palmyra Bd. of Educ.*, 161 F.3d 225 [130 Educ. L. Rep. 1054] (3d Cir. 1998), abrogated by *Winkelman v. Parma City School Dist.*, 550 U.S. 516, 127 S.Ct. 1994, 167 L.Ed.2d 904 [219 Educ. L. Rep. 39] (2007).

437. *Navin v. Park Ridge School Dist.*, 270 F.3d 1147, 1149 [158 Educ. L. Rep. 576] (7th Cir. 2001), *on remand*, 2002 WL 774300 (N.D. Ill. 2002), *aff'd*, 49 Fed.Appx. 69 (7th Cir. 2002).

438. *Devine v. Indian River County School Bd.*, 121 F.3d 576 [120 Educ. L. Rep. 436] (11th Cir. 1997).

439. *Fauconier v. Committee on Special Educ.*, 2003 WL 21345549 (S.D.N.Y. 2003), *aff'd*, 112 Fed.Appx. 85 [193 Educ. L. Rep. 136] (2d Cir. 2004).

440. *Cavanaugh ex rel. Cavanaugh v. Cardinal Local School Dist.*, 409 F.3d 753 [198 Educ. L. Rep. 443] (6th Cir. 2005); *Winkelman v. Parma City School Dist.*, 411 F. Supp.2d 722 (N.D. Ohio 2005), 150 Fed.Appx. 406 [204 Educ. L. Rep. 31] (6th Cir. 2005), *cert. granted*, 549 U.S. 990, 127 S.Ct. 467, 166 L.Ed.2d 333 (2006), *abrogated by Winkelman v. Parma City School Dist.*, 550 U.S. 516, 127 S.Ct. 1994, 167 L.Ed.2d 904 [219 Educ. L. Rep. 39] (2007).

441. *C.O. v. Portland Pub. Schools*, 406 F. Supp.2d 1157 [206 Educ. L. Rep. 156] (D. Or. 2005).

442. 550 U.S. 516, 127 S.Ct. 1994, 167 L.Ed.2d 904 [219 Educ. L. Rep. 39] (2007). [Case No. 115]

443. *Bowman v. District of Columbia*, 496 F. Supp.2d 160 [223 Educ. L. Rep. 210] (D.D.C. 2007).

444. *Levina v. San Luis Coastal Unified School Dist.*, 514 F.3d 866 [229 Educ. L. Rep. 361] (9th Cir. 2007), *reh'g granted, opinion withdrawn*, 523 F.3d 992 (9th Cir. 2008).

445. *Levina v. San Luis Coastal Unified School Dist.*, 275 Fed.Appx. 625 [234 Educ. L. Rep. 67] (9th Cir. 2008).

education services, the IDEA has set the goal of achieving its initial 1975 promise of funding forty percent of the national average of per-pupil spending by 2011.[446] While these provisions are not mandatory, the IDEA has increased the authorized levels for funding the excess costs associated with educating students with disabilities by about $2.3 billion each year.[447] Even though the federal government assists in paying for the delivery of special education services, since the amount of federal IDEA money is inadequate, educators in Massachusetts,[448] New Hampshire,[449] and Washington[450] unsuccessfully challenged the law as an unfunded federal mandate.

In a related financial matter, given the high cost of caring for some children, such as those who are medically fragile,[451] the IDEA authorizes officials to use IDEA funds to establish and maintain "risk pools" to aid local school systems in providing high-cost services or for the unexpected enrollments of students with disabilities.[452] The IDEA also permits boards to allocate unused funds to be placed in a pool for the next fiscal year.[453]

[CASE NO. 109]   ELIGIBILITY UNDER SECTION 504 OF THE REHABILITATION ACT

SOUTHEASTERN COMMUNITY COLLEGE v. DAVIS

Supreme Court of the United States, 1979.
442 U.S. 397, 99 S.Ct. 2361, 60 L.Ed.2d 980.

■ JUSTICE POWELL delivered the opinion of the Court.

This case presents a matter of first impression for this Court: Whether § 504 of the Rehabilitation Act of 1973, which prohibits discrimination against an "otherwise qualified handicapped individual" in federally funded programs "solely by reason of his handicap," forbids professional schools from imposing physical qualifications for admission to their clinical training programs.

I

Respondent, who suffers from a serious hearing disability, seeks to be trained as a registered nurse. During the 1973–1974 academic year she was enrolled in the College Parallel program of Southeastern Community College, a state institution that receives federal funds. Respondent hoped to progress to Southeastern's Associate Degree Nursing program, completion

---

446.   20 U.S.C.A. § 1411(a)(2)(A)(ii).

447.   For the specific projected amounts of aid, *see* 20 U.S.C.A. § 1411(h)(7)(B)(i).

448.   *City of Worcester v. The Governor*, 625 N.E.2d 1337 [88 Educ. L. Rep. 227] (Mass. 1994).

449.   *Nashua School Dist. v. State*, 667 A.2d 1036 [105 Educ. L. Rep. 578] (N.H. 1995).

450.   *School Districts' Alliance for Adequate Funding of Special Educ. v. State*, 244 P.3d 1 [262 Educ. L. Rep. 1004] (Wash. 2010).

451.   *See, e.g., Timothy W. v. Rochester, N.H., School Dist.*, 875 F.2d 954 [54 Educ. L. Rep.74] (1st Cir.1989), *cert. denied*, 493 U.S. 983, 110 S.Ct. 519, 107 L.Ed.2d 520 (1989). [Case No. 111]

452.   20 U.S.C.A. § 1411(e)(3).

453.   *Id.*

of which would make her eligible for state certification as a registered nurse. In the course of her application to the nursing program, she was interviewed by a member of the nursing faculty. It became apparent that respondent had difficulty understanding questions asked, and on inquiry she acknowledged a history of hearing problems and dependence on a hearing aid. She was advised to consult an audiologist.

On the basis of an examination at Duke University Medical Center, respondent was diagnosed as having a "bilateral, sensori-neural hearing loss." A change in her hearing aid was recommended, as a result of which it was expected that she would be able to detect sounds "almost as well as a person would who has normal hearing." But this improvement would not mean that she could discriminate among sounds sufficiently to understand normal spoken speech. Her lipreading skills would remain necessary for effective communication. . . .

Southeastern next consulted Mary McRee, Executive Director of the North Carolina Board of Nursing. On the basis of the audiologist's report, McRee recommended that respondent not be admitted to the nursing program. In McRee's view, respondent's hearing disability made it unsafe for her to practice as a nurse. In addition, it would be impossible for respondent to participate safely in the normal clinical training program, and those modifications that would be necessary to enable safe participation would prevent her from realizing the benefits of the program: "To adjust patient learning experiences in keeping with [respondent's] hearing limitations could, in fact, be the same as denying her full learning to meet the objectives of your nursing programs."

After respondent was notified that she was not qualified for nursing study because of her hearing disability, she requested reconsideration of the decision. . . . Upon further deliberation, the staff voted to deny respondent admission.

Respondent then filed suit in the United States District Court for the Eastern District of North Carolina, alleging both a violation of § 504 of the Rehabilitation Act of 1973 and a denial of equal protection and due process. After a bench trial, the District Court entered judgment in favor of Southeastern . . .

. . . the District Court concluded that respondent was not an "otherwise qualified handicapped individual" protected against discrimination by § 504. In its view, "[o]therwise qualified, can only be read to mean otherwise able to function sufficiently in the position sought in spite of the handicap, if proper training and facilities are suitable and available." Because respondent's disability would prevent her from functioning "sufficiently" in Southeastern's nursing program, the court held that the decision to exclude her was not discriminatory within the meaning of § 504.

On appeal, the Court of Appeals for the Fourth Circuit reversed. It did not dispute the District Court's findings of fact, but held that the court had misconstrued § 504. . . . the appellate court believed that § 504 required Southeastern to "reconsider plaintiff's application for admission to the nursing program without regard to her hearing ability." It concluded that the District Court had erred in taking respondent's handicap into account in determining whether she was "otherwise qualified" for the program, rather than confining its inquiry to her "academic and technical qualifications."

Because of the importance of this issue to the many institutions covered by § 504, we granted *certiorari*. We now reverse.

II

... this is the first case in which this Court has been called upon to interpret § 504. It is elementary that "[t]he starting point in every case involving construction of a statute is the language itself." Section 504 by its terms does not compel educational institutions to disregard the disabilities of handicapped individuals or to make substantial modifications in their programs to allow disabled persons to participate. Instead, it requires only that an "otherwise qualified handicapped individual" not be excluded from participation in a federally funded program "solely by reason of his handicap," indicating only that mere possession of a handicap is not a permissible ground for assuming an inability to function in a particular context.

The court below, however, believed that the "otherwise qualified" persons protected by § 504 include those who would be able to meet the requirements of a particular program in every respect except as to limitations imposed by their handicap. Taken literally, this holding would prevent an institution from taking into account any limitation resulting from the handicap, however disabling. It assumes, in effect, that a person need not meet legitimate physical requirements in order to be "otherwise qualified." We think the understanding of the District Court is closer to the plain meaning of the statutory language. An otherwise qualified person is one who is able to meet all of a program's requirements in spite of his handicap.

The regulations promulgated by the Department of HEW to interpret § 504 reinforce, rather than contradict, this conclusion. According to these regulations, a "[q]ualified handicapped person" is, "[w]ith respect to post-secondary and vocational education services, a handicapped person who meets the academic and technical standards requisite to admission or participation in the [school's] education program or activity...."

A ... note emphasizes that legitimate physical qualifications may be essential to participation in particular programs. We think it clear, therefore, that HEW interprets the "other" qualifications which a handicapped person may be required to meet as including necessary physical qualifications.

III

The remaining question is whether the physical qualifications Southeastern demanded of respondent might not be necessary for participation in its nursing program. It is not open to dispute that, as Southeastern's Associate Degree Nursing program currently is constituted, the ability to understand speech without reliance on lipreading is necessary for patient safety during the clinical phase of the program. As the District Court found, this ability also is indispensable for many of the functions that a registered nurse performs.

Respondent contends nevertheless that § 504, properly interpreted, compels Southeastern to undertake affirmative action that would dispense with the need for effective oral communication. First, it is suggested that respondent can be given individual supervision by faculty members whenever she attends patients directly. Moreover, certain required courses might be dispensed with altogether for respondent. It is not necessary, she argues, that Southeastern train her to undertake all the tasks a registered nurse is licensed to perform. Rather, it is sufficient to make § 504 applicable if respondent might be able to perform satisfactorily some of the duties of a registered nurse or to hold some of the positions available to a registered nurse.

Respondent finds support for this argument in portions of the HEW regulations discussed above. In particular, a provision applicable to postsecondary educational programs requires covered institutions to make "modifications" in their programs to accommodate handicapped persons, and to provide "auxiliary aids" such as sign-language interpreters. Respondent argues that this regulation imposes an obligation to ensure full participation in covered programs by handicapped individuals and, in particular, requires Southeastern to make the kind of adjustments that would be necessary to permit her safe participation in the nursing program.

We note first that on the present record it appears unlikely respondent could benefit from any affirmative action that the regulation reasonably could be interpreted as requiring. [A federal regulation], for example, explicitly excludes "devices or services of a personal nature" from the kinds of auxiliary aids a school must provide a handicapped individual. Yet the only evidence in the record indicates that nothing less than close, individual attention by a nursing instructor would be sufficient to ensure patient safety if respondent took part in the clinical phase of the nursing program. Furthermore, it also is reasonably clear that [the regulation] does not encompass the kind of curricular changes that would be necessary to accommodate respondent in the nursing program. In light of respondent's inability to function in clinical courses without close supervision, Southeastern, with prudence, could allow her to take only academic classes. Whatever benefits respondent might realize from such a course of study, she would not receive even a rough equivalent of the training a nursing program normally gives. Such a fundamental alteration in the nature of a program is far more than the "modification" the regulation requires.

Moreover, an interpretation of the regulations that required the extensive modifications necessary to include respondent in the nursing program would raise grave doubts about their validity. If these regulations were to require substantial adjustments in existing programs beyond those necessary to eliminate discrimination against otherwise qualified individuals, they would do more than clarify the meaning of § 504. Instead, they would constitute an unauthorized extension of the obligations imposed by that statute.

The language and structure of the Rehabilitation Act of 1973 reflect a recognition by Congress of the distinction between the evenhanded treatment of qualified handicapped persons and affirmative efforts to overcome the disabilities caused by handicaps. Section 501(b), governing the employment of handicapped individuals by the Federal Government, requires each federal agency to submit "an affirmative action program plan for the hiring, placement, and advancement of handicapped individuals. . . ." These plans "shall include a description of the extent to which and methods whereby the special needs of handicapped employees are being met." Similarly, § 503(a), governing hiring by federal contractors, requires employers to "take affirmative action to employ and advance in employment qualified handicapped individuals. . . ."

Under § 501(c) of the Act, by contrast, state agencies such as Southeastern are only "encourage[d] . . . to adopt and implement such policies and procedures." Section 504 does not refer at all to affirmative action, and except as it applies to federal employers it does not provide for implementation by administrative action. A comparison of these provisions demonstrates that Congress understood accommodation of the needs of handicapped individuals may require affirmative action and knew how to provide for it in those instances where it wished to do so.

Although an agency's interpretation of the statute under which it operates is entitled to some deference, "this deference is constrained by our obligation to honor the clear meaning of a statute, as revealed by its language, purpose, and history." Here, neither the language, purpose, nor history of § 504 reveals an intent to impose an affirmative-action obligation on all recipients of federal funds. Accordingly, we hold that even if HEW has attempted to create such an obligation itself, it lacks the authority to do so.

IV

We do not suggest that the line between a lawful refusal to extend affirmative action and illegal discrimination against handicapped persons always will be clear. It is possible to envision situations where an insistence on continuing past requirements and practices might arbitrarily deprive genuinely qualified handicapped persons of the opportunity to participate in a covered program. Technological advances can be expected to enhance opportunities to rehabilitate the handicapped or otherwise to qualify them for some useful employment. Such advances also may enable attainment of these goals without imposing undue financial and administrative burdens upon a State. Thus, situations may arise where a refusal to modify an existing program might become unreasonable and discriminatory. Identification of those instances where a refusal to accommodate the needs of a disabled person amounts to discrimination against the handicapped continues to be an important responsibility of HEW.

In this case, however, it is clear that Southeastern's unwillingness to make major adjustments in its nursing program does not constitute such discrimination. The uncontroverted testimony of several members of Southeastern's staff and faculty established that the purpose of its program was to train persons who could serve the nursing profession in all customary ways. This type of purpose, far from reflecting any animus against handicapped individuals is shared by many if not most of the institutions that train persons to render professional service. It is undisputed that respondent could not participate in Southeastern's nursing program unless the standards were substantially lowered. Section 504 imposes no requirement upon an educational institution to lower or to effect substantial modifications of standards to accommodate a handicapped person.

Respondent's argument misses the point. Southeastern's program, structured to train persons who will be able to perform all normal roles of a registered nurse, represents a legitimate academic policy, and is accepted by the State. In effect, it seeks to ensure that no graduate will pose a danger to the public in any professional role in which he or she might be cast. Even if the licensing requirements of North Carolina or some other State are less demanding, nothing in the Act requires an educational institution to lower its standards.

One may admire respondent's desire and determination to overcome her handicap, and there well may be various other types of service for which she can qualify. In this case, however, we hold that there was no violation of § 504 when Southeastern concluded that respondent did not qualify for admission to its program. Nothing in the language or history of § 504 reflects an intention to limit the freedom of an educational institution to require reasonable physical qualifications for admission to a clinical training program. Nor has there been any showing in this case that any action short of a substantial change in Southeastern's program would render unreasonable the qualifications it imposed.

V

Accordingly, we reverse the judgment of the court below, and remand for proceedings consistent with this opinion.

So ordered.

NOTES

1. An argument can be made that if parents were fully aware of the parameters of Section 504, then schools would have to operate differently. Do you agree? Would this be beneficial?

2. Since Section 504 applies to anyone in school buildings, a federal trial court in New York directed educators to provide a sign language interpreter for deaf parents of hearing students in order to enable them to participate in school conferences. *Rothschild v. Grottenthaler*, 725 F.Supp. 776 [57 Educ. L. Rep. 832] (S.D.N.Y. 1989).

[CASE NO. 110]   INTERPRETING APPROPRIATENESS UNDER THE
IDEA

**BOARD OF EDUCATION OF THE HENDRICK HUDSON
CENTRAL SCHOOL DISTRICT v. ROWLEY**

Supreme Court of the United States, 1982.
458 U.S. 176, 102 S.Ct. 3034, 73 L.Ed.2d 690 [5 Educ. L. Rep. 34].

■ JUSTICE REHNQUIST delivered the opinion of the Court.

This case presents a question of statutory interpretation. Petitioners
contend that the Court of Appeals and the District Court misconstrued the
requirements imposed by Congress upon States which receive federal funds
under the Education of the Handicapped Act. We agree and reverse the
judgment of the Court of Appeals.

I

. . .

The Education of the Handicapped Act (Act) provides federal money to
assist state and local agencies in educating handicapped children, and
conditions such funding upon a State's compliance with extensive goals and
procedures. The Act represents an ambitious federal effort to promote the
education of handicapped children, and was passed in response to Congress'
perception that a majority of handicapped children in the United States
"were either totally excluded from schools or [were] sitting idly in regular
classrooms awaiting the time when they were old enough to 'drop out.' "
. . .

. . . The Act broadly defines "handicapped children" to include "mentally retarded, hard of hearing, deaf, speech impaired, visually handicapped,
seriously emotionally disturbed, orthopedically impaired, [and] other health
impaired children, [and] children with specific learning disabilities."

The "free appropriate public education" required by the Act is tailored
to the unique needs of the handicapped child by means of an "individualized educational program" (IEP).... The IEP, which is prepared at a
meeting between a qualified representative of the Local or regional educational agencies must review, and where appropriate revise, each child's
IEP at least annually.

. . . although the Act leaves to the States the primary responsibility for
developing and executing educational programs for handicapped children, it
imposes significant requirements to be followed in the discharge of that
responsibility. Compliance is assured by provisions permitting the withholding of federal funds upon determination that a participating state or
local agency has failed to satisfy the requirements of the Act, and by the
provision for judicial review....

II

This case arose in connection with the education of Amy Rowley, a deaf
student at the Furnace Woods School in the Hendrick Hudson Central

School District, Peekskill, N.Y. Amy has minimal residual hearing and is an excellent lipreader. During the year before she began attending Furnace Woods, a meeting between her parents and school administrators resulted in a decision to place her in a regular kindergarten class in order to determine what supplemental services would be necessary to her education. Several members of the school administration prepared for Amy's arrival by attending a course in sign-language interpretation, and a teletype machine was installed in the principal's office to facilitate communication with her parents who are also deaf. At the end of the trial period it was determined that Amy should remain in the kindergarten class, but that she should be provided with an FM hearing aid which would amplify words spoken into a wireless receiver by the teacher or fellow students during certain classroom activities. Amy successfully completed her kindergarten year.

As required by the Act, an IEP was prepared for Amy during the fall of her first-grade year. The IEP provided that Amy should be educated in a regular classroom at Furnace Woods, should continue to use the FM hearing aid, and should receive instruction from a tutor for the deaf for one hour each day and from a speech therapist for three hours each week. The Rowleys agreed with parts of the IEP, but insisted that Amy also be provided a qualified sign-language interpreter in all her academic classes in lieu of the assistance proposed in other parts of the IEP. Such an interpreter had been placed in Amy's kindergarten class for a 2–week experimental period, but the interpreter had reported that Amy did not need his services at that time. The school administrators likewise concluded that Amy did not need such an interpreter in her first-grade classroom. . . .

When their request for an interpreter was denied, the Rowleys demanded and received a hearing before an independent examiner. After receiving evidence from both sides, the examiner agreed with the administrators' determination that an interpreter was not necessary because "Amy was achieving educationally, academically, and socially" without such assistance. The examiner's decision was affirmed on appeal by the New York Commissioner of Education on the basis of substantial evidence in the record. . . . the Rowleys then brought an action in the United States District Court for the Southern District of New York, claiming that the administrators' denial of the sign-language interpreter constituted a denial of the "free appropriate public education" guaranteed by the Act.

The District Court found that Amy "is a remarkably well-adjusted child" who interacts and communicates well with her classmates and has "developed an extraordinary rapport" with her teachers. It also found that "she performs better than the average child in her class and is advancing easily from grade to grade," but "that she understands considerably less of what goes on in class than she could if she were not deaf" and thus "is not learning as much, or performing as well academically, as she would without her handicap," This disparity between Amy's achievement and her potential led the court to decide that she was not receiving a "free appropriate public education," which the court defined as "an opportunity to achieve [her] full potential commensurate with the opportunity provided to other children." According to the District Court, such a standard "requires that the potential of the handicapped child be measured and compared to his or her performance, and that the resulting differential or 'shortfall' be compared to the shortfall experienced by nonhandicapped children" ...

A divided panel of the United States Court of Appeals for the Second Circuit affirmed ...

We granted certiorari to review the lower courts' interpretation of the Act. Such review requires us to consider two questions: What is meant by the Act's requirement of a "free appropriate public education"? And what is the role of state and federal courts in exercising the review granted by 20 U.S.C.[A.] § 1415? We consider these questions separately.

III

A

This is the first case in which this Court has been called upon to interpret any provision of the Act. As noted previously, the District Court and the Court of Appeals concluded that "[t]he Act itself does not define 'appropriate education,'" but leaves "to the courts and the hearing officers" the responsibility of "giv[ing] content to the requirement of an 'appropriate education.'" Petitioners contend that the definition of the phrase "free appropriate public education" used by the courts below overlooks the definition of that phrase actually found in the Act. Respondents agree that the Act defines "free appropriate public education," but contend that the statutory definition is not "functional" and thus "offers judges no guidance in their consideration of controversies involving 'the identification, evaluation, or educational placement of the child or the provision of a free appropriate public education.'" The United States, appearing as amicus curiae on behalf of respondents, states that "[a]lthough the Act includes definitions of a 'free appropriate public education' and other related terms, the statutory definitions do not adequately explain what is meant by 'appropriate.'"

We are loath to conclude that Congress failed to offer any assistance in defining the meaning of the principal substantive phrase used in the Act. It is beyond dispute that, contrary to the conclusions of the courts below, the Act does expressly define "free appropriate public education":

> The term 'free appropriate public education' means *special education* and *related services* which (A) have been provided at public expense, under public supervision and direction, and without charge, (B) meet the standards of the State educational agency, (C) include an appropriate preschool, elementary, or secondary school education in the State involved, and (D) are provided in conformity with the individualized education program required under section 1414(a)(5) of this title.

"Special education," as referred to in this definition, means "specially designed instruction, at no cost to parents or guardians, to meet the unique needs of a handicapped child, including classroom instruction, instruction in physical education, home instruction, and instruction in hospitals and institutions." "Related services" are defined as "transportation, and such developmental, corrective, and other supportive services ... as may be required to assist a handicapped child to benefit from special education."

Like many statutory definitions, this one tends toward the cryptic rather than the comprehensive, but that is scarcely a reason for abandoning the quest for legislative intent. Whether or not the definition is a "functional" one, as respondents contend it is not, it is the principal tool which Congress has given us for parsing the critical phrase of the Act. We think more must be made of it than either respondents or the United States seems willing to admit.

According to the definitions contained in the Act, a "free appropriate public education" consists of educational instruction specially designed to meet the unique needs of the handicapped child, supported by such services as are necessary to permit the child "to benefit" from the instruction. . . . the definition also requires that such instruction and services be provided at public expense and under public supervision, meet the State's educational standards, approximate the grade levels used in the State's regular education, and comport with the child's IEP. Thus, if personalized instruction is being provided with sufficient supportive services to permit the child to benefit from the instruction, and the other items on the definitional checklist are satisfied, the child is receiving a "free appropriate public education" as defined by the Act. . . .

Noticeably absent from the language of the statute is any substantive standard prescribing the level of education to be accorded handicapped children. Certainly the language of the statute contains no requirement like the one imposed by the lower courts—that States maximize the potential of handicapped children "commensurate with the opportunity provided to other children." That standard was expounded by the District Court without reference to the statutory definitions or even to the legislative history of the Act. Although we find the statutory definition of "free appropriate public education" to be helpful in our interpretation of the Act, there remains the question of whether the legislative history indicates a congressional intent that such education meet some additional substantive standard. For an answer, we turn to that history.

B

(i)

As suggested in Part I, federal support for education of the handicapped is a fairly recent development. Before passage of the Act some States had passed laws to improve the educational services afforded handicapped children, but many of these children were excluded completely from any form of public education or were left to fend for themselves in classrooms designed for education of their nonhandicapped peers . . .

This concern, stressed repeatedly throughout the legislative history, confirms the impression conveyed by the language of the statute: By passing the Act, Congress sought primarily to make public education available to handicapped children. But in seeking to provide such access to public education, Congress did not impose upon the States any greater substantive educational standard than would be necessary to make such access meaningful. Indeed, Congress expressly "recognize[d] that in many instances the process of providing special education and related services to handicapped children is not guaranteed to produce any particular outcome." Thus, the intent of the Act was more to open the door of public education to handicapped children on appropriate terms than to guarantee any particular level of education once inside.

Both the House and the Senate Reports attribute the impetus for the Act and its predecessors to two federal-court judgments rendered in 1971 and 1972. . . . The first case, (PARC), was a suit on behalf of retarded children challenging the constitutionality of a Pennsylvania statute which acted to exclude them from public education and training. The case ended in a consent decree which enjoined the State from "deny[ing] to any mentally retarded child *access* to a free public program of education and training."

PARC was followed by *Mills v. Board of Education of District of Columbia*, a case in which the plaintiff handicapped children had been excluded from the District of Columbia public schools. The court's judgment . . . provided that "no [handicapped] child eligible for a publicly supported education in the District of Columbia public schools shall be excluded from a regular school assignment by a Rule, policy, or practice of the Board of Education of the District of Columbia or its agents unless such child is provided (a) adequate alternative educational services suited to the child's needs, which may include special education or tuition grants, and (b) a constitutionally adequate prior hearing and periodic review of the child's status, progress, and the *adequacy* of any educational alternative."

Mills and *PARC* both held that handicapped children must be given access to an adequate, publicly supported education. Neither case purports to require any particular substantive level of education. Rather, like the language of the Act, the cases set forth extensive procedures to be followed in formulating personalized educational programs for handicapped children. The fact that both *PARC* and *Mills* are discussed at length in the legislative Reports suggests that the principles which they established are the principles which, to a significant extent, guided the drafters of the Act. . . .

It is evident from the legislative history that the characterization of handicapped children as "served" referred to children who were receiving some form of specialized educational services from the States, and that the characterization of children as "unserved" referred to those who were receiving no specialized educational services. . . .

(ii)

Respondents contend that "the goal of the Act is to provide each handicapped child with an equal educational opportunity." We think, however, that the requirement that a State provide specialized educational services to handicapped children generates no additional requirement that the services so provided be sufficient to maximize each child's potential "commensurate with the opportunity provided other children." Respondents and the United States correctly note that Congress sought "to provide assistance to the States in carrying out their responsibilities under . . . the Constitution of the United States to provide equal protection of the laws." But we do not think that such statements imply a congressional intent to achieve strict equality of opportunity or services.

The educational opportunities provided by our public school systems undoubtedly differ from student to student, depending upon a myriad of factors that might affect a particular student's ability to assimilate information presented in the classroom. The requirement that States provide "equal" educational opportunities would thus seem to present an entirely unworkable standard requiring impossible measurements and comparisons. Similarly, furnishing handicapped children with only such services as are available to nonhandicapped children would in all probability fall short of the statutory requirement of "free appropriate public education"; to require, on the other hand, the furnishing of every special service necessary to maximize each handicapped child's potential is, we think, further than Congress intended to go. Thus to speak in terms of "equal" services in one instance gives less than what is required by the Act and in another instance more. The theme of the Act is "free appropriate public education," a phrase which is too complex to be captured by the word "equal" whether one is speaking of opportunities or services.

The legislative conception of the requirements of equal protection was undoubtedly informed by the two District Court decisions referred to above. But cases such as *Mills* and *PARC* held simply that handicapped children may not be excluded entirely from public education. . . .

. . . To the extent that Congress might have looked further than these cases which are mentioned in the legislative history, at the time of enactment of the Act this Court had held at least twice that the Equal Protection Clause of the Fourteenth Amendment does not require States to expend equal financial resources on the education of each child.

In explaining the need for federal legislation, the House Report noted that "no congressional legislation has required a precise guarantee for handicapped children, i.e. a basic floor of opportunity that would bring into compliance all school districts with the constitutional right of equal protection with respect to handicapped children." Assuming that the Act was designed to fill the need identified in the House Report—that is, to provide a "basic floor of opportunity" consistent with equal protection—neither the Act nor its history persuasively demonstrates that Congress thought that equal protection required anything more than equal access. Therefore, Congress' desire to provide specialized educational services, even in furtherance of "equality," cannot be read as imposing any particular substantive educational standard upon the States.

The District Court and the Court of Appeals thus erred when they held that the Act requires New York to maximize the potential of each handicapped child commensurate with the opportunity provided nonhandicapped children. Desirable though that goal might be, it is not the standard that Congress imposed upon States which receive funding under the Act. Rather, Congress sought primarily to identify and evaluate handicapped children, and to provide them with access to a free public education.

(iii)

Implicit in the congressional purpose of providing access to a "free appropriate public education" is the requirement that the education to which access is provided be sufficient to confer some educational benefit upon the handicapped child. It would do little good for Congress to spend millions of dollars in providing access to a public education only to have the handicapped child receive no benefit from that education. The statutory definition of "free appropriate public education," in addition to requiring that States provide each child with "specially designed instruction," expressly requires the provision of "such . . . supportive services . . . as may be required to assist a handicapped child to benefit from special education." We therefore conclude that the "basic floor of opportunity" provided by the Act consists of access to specialized instruction and related services which are individually designed to provide educational benefit to the handicapped child.

The determination of when handicapped children are receiving sufficient educational benefits to satisfy the requirements of the Act presents a more difficult problem. The Act requires participating States to educate a wide spectrum of handicapped children, from the marginally hearing-impaired to the profoundly retarded and palsied. It is clear that the benefits obtainable by children at one end of the spectrum will differ dramatically from those obtainable by children at the other end, with infinite variations in between. One child may have little difficulty competing successfully in an academic setting with nonhandicapped children while another child may encounter great difficulty in acquiring even the most basic of self-maintenance skills. We do not attempt today to establish any one test for determining the adequacy of educational benefits conferred upon all children covered by the Act. Because in this case we are presented with a handicapped child who is receiving substantial specialized instruction and related services, and who is performing above average in the regular classrooms of a public school system, we confine our analysis to that situation.

The Act requires participating States to educate handicapped children with nonhandicapped children whenever possible. When that "mainstreaming" preference of the Act has been met and a child is being educated in the regular classrooms of a public school system, the system itself monitors the educational progress of the child. Regular examinations are administered, grades are awarded, and yearly advancement to higher grade levels is permitted for those children who attain an adequate knowledge of the course material. The grading and advancement system thus constitutes an important factor in determining educational benefit. Children who graduate from our public school systems are considered by our society to have been "educated" at least to the grade level they have completed, and access to an "education" for handicapped children is precisely what Congress sought to provide in the Act.

C

When the language of the Act and its legislative history are considered together, the requirements imposed by Congress become tolerably clear.

Insofar as a State is required to provide a handicapped child with a "free appropriate public education," we hold that it satisfies this requirement by providing personalized instruction with sufficient support services to permit the child to benefit educationally from that instruction. Such instruction and services must be provided at public expense, must meet the State's educational standards, must approximate the grade levels used in the State's regular education, and must comport with the child's IEP. In addition, the IEP, and therefore the personalized instruction, should be formulated in accordance with the requirements of the Act and, if the child is being educated in the regular classrooms of the public education system, should be reasonably calculated to enable the child to achieve passing marks and advance from grade to grade.

In defending the decisions of the District Court and the Court of Appeals, respondents and the United States rely upon isolated statements in the legislative history concerning the achievement of maximum potential as support for their contention that Congress intended to impose greater substantive requirements than we have found. These statements, however, are too thin a reed on which to base an interpretation of the Act which disregards both its language and the balance of its legislative history. . . . As already demonstrated, the Act and its history impose no requirements on the States like those imposed by the District Court and the Court of Appeals. A fortiori Congress has not done so unambiguously, as required in the valid exercise of its spending power.

IV

A

As mentioned in Part I, the Act permits "[a]ny party aggrieved by the findings and decision" of the state administrative hearings "to bring a civil action" in "any State court of competent jurisdiction or in a district court of the United States without regard to the amount in controversy." The complaint, and therefore the civil action, may concern "any matter relating to the identification, evaluation, or educational placement of the child, or the provision of a free appropriate public education to such child." In reviewing the complaint, the Act provides that a court "shall receive the record of the [state] administrative proceedings, shall hear additional evidence at the request of a party, and, basing its decision on the preponderance of the evidence, shall grant such relief as the court determines is appropriate."

The parties disagree sharply over the meaning of these provisions, petitioners contending that courts are given only limited authority to review for state compliance with the Act's procedural requirements and no power to review the substance of the state program, and respondents contending that the Act requires courts to exercise de novo review over state educational decisions and policies. We find petitioners' contention unpersuasive, for Congress expressly rejected provisions that would have so severely restricted the role of reviewing courts. In substituting the current language of the statute for language that would have made state administrative findings conclusive if supported by substantial evidence, the Conference Committee explained that courts were to make "independent decision[s] based on a preponderance of the evidence."

But although we find that this grant of authority is broader than claimed by petitioners, we think the fact that it is found in § 1415, which is entitled "Procedural safeguards," is not without significance. When the elaborate and highly specific procedural safeguards embodied in § 1415 are contrasted with the general and somewhat imprecise substantive admonitions contained in the Act, we think that the importance Congress attached to these procedural safeguards cannot be gainsaid. It seems to us no exaggeration to say that Congress placed every bit as much emphasis upon compliance with procedures giving parents and guardians a large measure of participation at every stage of the administrative process as it did upon the measurement of the resulting IEP against a substantive standard. We think that the congressional emphasis upon full participation of concerned parties throughout the development of the IEP, as well as the requirements that state and local plans be submitted to the Secretary for approval, demonstrates the legislative conviction that adequate compliance with the procedures prescribed would in most cases assure much if not all of what Congress wished in the way of substantive content in an IEP.

Thus the provision that a reviewing court base its decision on the "preponderance of the evidence" is by no means an invitation to the courts to substitute their own notions of sound educational policy for those of the school authorities which they review. The very importance which Congress has attached to compliance with certain procedures in the preparation of an IEP would be frustrated if a court were permitted simply to set state decisions at nought. The fact that § 1415(e) requires that the reviewing court "receive the records of the [state] administrative proceedings" carries with it the implied requirement that due weight shall be given to these proceedings. And we find nothing in the Act to suggest that merely because Congress was rather sketchy in establishing substantive requirements, as opposed to procedural requirements for the preparation of an IEP, it intended that reviewing courts should have a free hand to impose substantive standards of review which cannot be derived from the Act itself. In short, the statutory authorization to grant "such relief as the court determines is appropriate" cannot be read without reference to the obligations, largely procedural in nature, which are imposed upon recipient States by Congress.

Therefore, a court's inquiry in suits brought under § 1415(e)(2) is twofold. First, has the State complied with the procedures set forth in the Act? And second, is the individualized educational program developed through the Act's procedures reasonably calculated to enable the child to receive educational benefits? If these requirements are met, the State has complied with the obligations imposed by Congress and the courts can require no more.

B

In assuring that the requirements of the Act have been met, courts must be careful to avoid imposing their view of preferable educational methods upon the States. The primary responsibility for formulating the education to be accorded a handicapped child, and for choosing the educational method most suitable to the child's needs, was left by the Act to state and local educational agencies in cooperation with the parents or guardian of the child. The Act expressly charges States with the responsibility of "acquiring and disseminating to teachers and administrators of programs for handicapped children significant information derived from educational research, demonstration, and similar projects, and [of] adopting, where appropriate, promising educational practices and materials." In the face of such a clear statutory directive, it seems highly unlikely that Congress intended courts to overturn a State's choice of appropriate educational theories in a proceeding conducted pursuant to § 1415(e)(2).

We previously have cautioned that courts lack the "specialized knowledge and experience" necessary to resolve "persistent and difficult questions of educational policy." We think that Congress shared that view when it passed the Act. As already demonstrated, Congress' intention was not that the Act displace the primacy of States in the field of education, but that States receive funds to assist them in extending their educational systems to the handicapped. Therefore, once a court determines that the requirements of the Act have been met, questions of methodology are for resolution by the States.

V

Entrusting a child's education to state and local agencies does not leave the child without protection. Congress sought to protect individual children by providing for parental involvement in the development of state plans and policies and in the formulation of the child's individual educational program. . . .

VI

Applying these principles to the facts of this case, we conclude that the Court of Appeals erred in affirming the decision of the District Court. Neither the District Court nor the Court of Appeals found that petitioners had failed to comply with the procedures of the Act, and the findings of neither court would support a conclusion that Amy's educational program failed to comply with the substantive requirements of the Act. On the contrary, the District Court found that the "evidence firmly establishes that Amy is receiving an 'adequate' education, since she performs better than the average child in her class and is advancing easily from grade to grade." In light of this finding, and of the fact that Amy was receiving personalized instruction and related services calculated by the Furnace Woods school administrators to meet her educational needs, the lower courts should not have concluded that the Act requires the provision of a sign-language interpreter. Accordingly, the decision of the Court of Appeals is reversed, and the case is remanded for further proceedings consistent with this opinion.

So ordered.

NOTES

1. *Rowley* sets a fairly low standard. The dissent interpreted Congressional intent in enacting the IDEA as providing children with disabilities with educational opportunities commensurate with those of their peers who are not disabled. How might such an interpretation have changed the face of special education? Regular education?

2. The Supreme Court has been reluctant to re-examine the issues it addressed in *Rowley*. Should the Court reconsider the meaning of an appropriate education? Should Congress?

[CASE NO. 111] "ZERO REJECT" FOR STUDENTS WITH DISABILITIES

TIMOTHY W. v. ROCHESTER, NEW HAMPSHIRE, SCHOOL DISTRICT

United States Court of Appeals, First Circuit, 1989.
875 F.2d 954 [54 Educ. L. Rep. 74].

■ BOWNES, CIRCUIT JUDGE.

Plaintiff-appellant Timothy W. appeals an order of the district court which held that under the Education for All Handicapped Children Act, a handicapped child is not eligible for special education if he cannot benefit from that education, and that Timothy W., a severely retarded and multiply handicapped child was not eligible under that standard. We reverse.

I. BACKGROUND

Timothy W. was born two months prematurely on December 8, 1975 with severe respiratory problems, and shortly thereafter experienced an intracranial hemorrhage, subdural effusions, seizures, hydrocephalus, and meningitis. As a result, Timothy is multiply handicapped and profoundly mentally retarded. He suffers from complex developmental disabilities, spastic quadriplegia, cerebral palsy, seizure disorder and cortical blindness. His mother attempted to obtain appropriate services for him, and while he did receive some services from the Rochester Child Development Center, he did not receive any educational program from the Rochester School District when he became of school age.

On February 19, 1980, the Rochester School District convened a meeting to decide if Timothy was considered educationally handicapped under the state and federal statutes.... The school district adjourned without making a finding. In a meeting on March 7, 1980, the school district decided that Timothy was not educationally handicapped—that since his handicap was so severe he was not "capable of benefitting" from an education, and therefore was not entitled to one. During 1981 and 1982, the school district did not provide Timothy with any educational program.

In May, 1982, the New Hampshire Department of Education reviewed the Rochester School District's special education programs and made a finding of non-compliance, stating that the school district was not allowed to use "capable of benefitting" as a criterion for eligibility. No action was taken in response to this finding until one year later, on June 20, 1983, when the school district met to discuss Timothy's case.... The school district, however, continued its refusal to provide Timothy with any educational program or services.

In response to a letter from Timothy's attorney, on January 17, 1984, the school district's placement team met.... The placement team recommended that Timothy be placed at the Child Development Center so that he could be provided with a special education program. The Rochester School Board, however, refused to authorize the placement team's recommendation to provide educational services for Timothy, contending that it still needed more information....

On April 24, 1984, Timothy filed a complaint with the New Hampshire Department of Education requesting that he be placed in an educational program immediately. On October 9, 1984, the Department of Education issued an order requiring the school district to place him, within five days, in an educational program, until the appeals process on the issue of whether Timothy was educationally handicapped was completed. The school district, however, refused to make any such educational placement. On October 31, 1984, the school district filed an appeal of the order. There was also a meeting on November 8, 1984, in which the Rochester School Board reviewed Timothy's case and concluded he was not eligible for special education.

On November 17, 1984, Timothy filed a complaint in the United States District Court, pursuant to 42 U.S.C.[A.] § 1983, alleging that his rights under the Education for All Handicapped Children Act the corresponding New Hampshire state law (RSA 186–C), § 504 of the Rehabilitation Act of 1973 and the equal protection and due process clauses of the United States and New Hampshire Constitutions, had been violated by the Rochester School District. The complaint sought preliminary and permanent injunctions directing the school district to provide him with special education, and $175,000 in damages.

A hearing was held in the district court on December 21, 1984.... On January 3, 1985, the district court denied Timothy's motion for a preliminary injunction, and on January 8, stated it would abstain on the damage claim pending exhaustion of the state administrative procedures....

In September, 1986, Timothy again requested a special education program. In October, 1986, the school district continued to refuse to provide him with such a program, claiming it still needed more information....

On May 20, 1987, the district court found that Timothy had not exhausted his state administrative remedies before the New Hampshire Department of Education, and precluded pretrial discovery until this had been done. On September 15, 1987, the hearing officer in the administrative hearings ruled that Timothy's capacity to benefit was not a legally permissible standard for determining his eligibility to receive a public education, and that the Rochester School District must provide him with an education. The Rochester School District, on November 12, 1987, appealed this decision to the United States District Court by filing a counterclaim, and on March 29, 1988, moved for summary judgment. Timothy filed a cross motion for summary judgment....

On July 15, 1988, the district court rendered its opinion entitled "Order on Motion for Judgment on the Pleadings or in the Alternative, Summary Judgment." ... The court made rulings of law and findings of fact. It first ruled that "under EAHCA [the Education for All Handicapped Children Act], an initial determination as to the child's ability to benefit from special education, must be made in order for a handicapped child to qualify for education under the Act." After noting that the New Hampshire statute (RSA) was intended to implement the EAHCA, the court held: "Under New Hampshire law, an initial decision must be made concerning the ability of a handicapped child to benefit from special education before an entitlement to the education can exist." The court then reviewed the materials, reports and testimony and found that "Timothy W. is not capable of benefitting from special education.... As a result, the defendant [school district] is not obligated to provide special education under either EAHCA [the federal statute] or RSA 186–C [the New Hampshire statute]." Timothy W. has appealed this order....

The primary issue is whether the district court erred in its rulings of law. Since we find that it did, we do not review its findings of fact.

II. THE LANGUAGE OF THE ACT

A. The Plain Meaning of the Act Mandates a Public Education for All Handicapped Children

The Education for All Handicapped Children Act, [hereinafter the Act], was enacted in 1975 to ensure that handicapped children receive an education which is appropriate to their unique needs. In assessing the plain meaning of the Act, we first look to its title: The Education for All Handicapped Children Act. The Congressional Findings section of the Act states that there were eight million handicapped children, that more than half of them did not receive appropriate educational services, and that one million were excluded entirely from the public school system. Given these grim statistics, Congress concluded that "State and local educational agencies have a responsibility to provide education for all handicapped children...." The Act's stated purpose was "to assure that *all* handicapped children have available to them ... a free appropriate public education which emphasizes special education and related services designed to meet their unique needs, ... [and] to assist states and localities to provide for the education of all handicapped children...."

. . .

The language of the Act could not be more unequivocal. The statute is permeated with the words "*all* handicapped children" whenever it refers to the target population. It never speaks of any exceptions for severely handicapped children. Indeed, as indicated *supra*, the Act gives priority to the most severely handicapped. Nor is there any language whatsoever which requires as a prerequisite to being covered by the Act, that a handicapped child must demonstrate that he or she will "benefit" from the educational program. Rather, the Act speaks of the state's responsibility to design a special education and related services program that will meet the unique "needs" of all handicapped children. The language of the Act in its entirety makes clear that a "zero-reject" policy is at the core of the Act, and that no child, regardless of the severity of his or her handicap, is to ever again be subjected to the deplorable state of affairs which existed at the time of the Act's passage, in which millions of handicapped children received inadequate education or none at all. In summary, the Act mandates an appropriate public education for all handicapped children, regardless of the level of achievement that such children might attain.

B.   Timothy W.: A Handicapped Child Entitled to An Appropriate Education

Given that the Act's language mandates that all handicapped children are entitled to a free appropriate education, we must next inquire if Timothy W. is a handicapped child, and if he is, what constitutes an appropriate education to meet his unique needs.

(1) *Handicapped children:*

. . .

There is no question that Timothy W. fits within the Act's definition of a handicapped child: he is multiply handicapped and profoundly mentally retarded. He has been described as suffering from severe spasticity, cerebral palsy, brain damage, joint contractures, cortical blindness, is not ambulatory, and is quadriplegic.

. . .

The record shows that Timothy W. is a severely handicapped and profoundly retarded child in need of special education and related services. Much of the expert testimony was to the effect that he is aware of his surrounding environment, makes or attempts to make purposeful movements, responds to tactile stimulation, responds to his mother's voice and touch, recognizes familiar voices, responds to noises, and parts his lips when spoon fed. The record contains testimony that Timothy W.'s needs include sensory stimulation, physical therapy, improved head control, socialization, consistency in responding to sound sources, and partial participation in eating. The educational consultants who drafted Timothy's individualized education program recommended that Timothy's special education program should include goals and objectives in the areas of motor control, communication, socialization, daily living skills, and recreation. The special education and related services that have been recommended to meet Timothy W.'s needs fit well within the statutory and regulatory definitions of the Act.

We conclude that the Act's language dictates the holding that Timothy W. is a handicapped child who is in need of special education and related services because of his handicaps. He must, therefore, according to the Act, be provided with such an educational program. There is nothing in the Act's language which even remotely supports the district court's conclusion that "under [the Act], an initial determination as to a child's ability to benefit from special education, must be made in order for a handicapped child to qualify for education under the Act." The language of the Act is directly to the contrary: a school district has a duty to provide an educational program for every handicapped child in the district, regardless of the severity of the handicap.

III. LEGISLATIVE HISTORY

An examination of the legislative history reveals that Congress intended the Act to provide a public education for all handicapped children, without exception; that the most severely handicapped were in fact to be given priority attention; and that an educational benefit was neither guaranteed nor required as a prerequisite for a child to receive such education. These factors were central, and were repeated over and over again, in the more than three years of congressional hearings and debates, which culminated in passage of the 1975 Act.

A. Education For All Handicapped Children

The Act was a response to tomes of testimony and evidence that handicapped children were being systematically excluded from education outright, or were receiving grossly inadequate education. The Office of Education provided Congress with a report documenting that there were eight million handicapped children, and that more than four million of them were not receiving an appropriate education, including almost two million who were receiving *no* education at all. . . .

The record is replete with statements by legislators that the Act was in response to this deplorable state of affairs. . . .

Moreover, the legislative history is unambiguous that the primary purpose of the Act was to remedy the then current state of affairs, and provide a public education for *all* handicapped children. . . .

. . .

B. Priority For The Most Severely Handicapped

Not only did Congress intend that all handicapped children be educated, it expressly indicated its intent that the most severely handicapped be given priority. This resolve was reiterated over and over again in the floor debates and congressional reports, as well as in the final legislation. . . .

. . .

This priority reflected congressional acceptance of the thesis that early educational intervention was very important for severely handicapped children. . . .

If the order of the district court denying Timothy W. the benefits of the Act were to be implemented, he would be classified by the Act as in even greater need for receiving educational services than a severely multi-handicapped child receiving inadequate education. He would be in the *highest priority*—as a child who was not receiving any education at all.

C. Guarantees of Educational Benefit Are Not A Requirement For Child Eligibility

In mandating a public education for all handicapped children, Congress explicitly faced the issue of the possibility of the non-educability of the most severely handicapped. The Senate Report stated, "The Committee recognizes that in many instances the process of providing special education and related services to handicapped children is not guaranteed to produce any particular outcome." The report continued: "The Committee has deleted the language of the bill as introduced which required objective criteria and evaluation procedures by which to assure that the short term instructional goals were met."

Thus, the district court's major holding, that proof of an educational benefit is a prerequisite before a handicapped child is entitled to a public education, is specifically belied, not only by the statutory language, but by the legislative history as well. We have not found in the Act's voluminous legislative history, nor has the school district directed our attention to, a single affirmative averment to support a benefit/eligibility requirement. But there is explicit evidence of a contrary congressional intent, that *no* guarantee of any particular educational outcome is required for a child to be eligible for public education.

We sum up. In the more than three years of legislative history leading to passage of the 1975 Act ... the Congressional intention is unequivocal: Public education is to be provided to all handicapped children, unconditionally and without exception. It encompasses a universal right, and is not predicated upon any type of guarantees that the child will benefit from the special education and services before he or she is considered eligible to receive such education. Congress explicitly recognized the particular plight and special needs of the severely handicapped, and rather than excluding them from the Act's coverage, gave them priority status. The district court's holding is directly contradicted by the Act's legislative history, as well as the statutory language.

D. Subsequent Amendments to the Act

In the 14 years since passage of the Act, it has been amended four times. Congress thus has had ample opportunity to clarify any language originally used, or to make any modifications that it chose. Congress has not only repeatedly reaffirmed the original intent of the Act, to educate all handicapped children regardless of the severity of their handicap, and to give priority attention to the most severely handicapped, it has in fact *expanded* the provisions covering the most severely handicapped children. Most significantly, Congress has never intimated that a benefit/eligibility requirement was to be instituted....

In summary, the Congressional reaffirmation of its intent to educate all handicapped children could not be any clearer. It was unequivocal at the time of passage of the Act in 1975, and it has been equally unequivocal during the intervening years. The school district's attempt in the instant case to "roll back" the entire thrust of this legislation completely ignores the overwhelming congressional consensus on this issue.

IV.   CASE LAW

A.   Cases Relied on in the Act

In its deliberations over the Act, Congress relied heavily on two landmark cases, *Pennsylvania Association for Retarded Children v. Commonwealth of Pennsylvania (PARC)*, and *Mills v. Board of Education of the District of Columbia*, which established the principle that exclusion from public education of any handicapped child is unconstitutional.... The Consent Agreement for the case, approved by the court, concluded that "Pennsylvania may not deny any mentally retarded child access to a free public program of education and training." In *Mills*, the court held that denying handicapped children a public education was violative of the constitutional guarantees of equal protection and due process. It ordered that the District of Columbia "shall provide to each child of school age a free and suitable publicly-supported education regardless of the degree of the child's mental, physical or emotional disability or impairment."

B.   All Handicapped Children are Entitled to a Public Education

Subsequent to the enactment of the Act, the courts have continued to embrace the principle that all handicapped children are entitled to a public education, and have consistently interpreted the Act as embodying this principle....

. . .

C.   Education is Broadly Defined

The courts have also made it clear that education for the severely handicapped under the Act is to be broadly defined. In Battle, the court stated that under the Act, the concept of education is necessarily broad with respect to severely and profoundly handicapped children, and "[w]here basic self help and social skills such as toilet training, dressing, feeding and communication are lacking, formal education begins at that point." ...

In the instant case, the district court's conclusion that education must be measured by the acquirement of traditional "cognitive skills" has no basis whatsoever in the 14 years of case law since the passage of the Act. All other courts have consistently held that education under the Act encompasses a wide spectrum of training, and that for the severely handicapped it may include the most elemental of life skills.

D.   Proof of Benefit is Not Required

The district court relied heavily on *Board of Education of Hendrick Hudson Central School District v. Rowley* in concluding that as a matter of law a child is not entitled to a public education unless he or she can benefit from it. The district court, however, has misconstrued Rowley....

Rowley focused on the *level* of services and the quality of programs that a *state* must provide, not the criteria for *access* to those programs. The Court's use of "benefit" in *Rowley* was a substantive limitation placed on the state's choice of an educational program; it was not a license for the state to exclude certain handicapped children. In ruling that a state was not required to provide the maximum benefit possible, the Court was *not* saying that there must be proof that a child will benefit before the state is obligated to provide any education at all. Indeed, the Court in *Rowley* explicitly acknowledged Congress' intent to ensure public education to all handicapped children without regard to the level of achievement that they might attain. . . .

Rowley simply does not lend support to the district court's finding of a benefit/eligibility standard in the Act. As the Court explained, while the Act does not require a school to maximize a child's potential for learning, it does provide a "basic floor of opportunity" for the handicapped, consisting of "access to specialized instruction and related services." Nowhere does the Court imply that such a "floor" contains a trap door for the severely handicapped. Indeed, *Rowley* explicitly states: "[t]he Act requires special educational services for children 'regardless of the severity of their handicap,'" and "[t]he Act requires participating States to educate a wide spectrum of handicapped children, from the marginally hearing-impaired to the profoundly retarded and palsied." . . .

And most recently, the Supreme Court, in *Honig v. Doe*, has made it quite clear that it will not rewrite the language of the Act to include exceptions which are not there. . . .

The district court in the instant case, is, as far as we know, the only court in the 14 years subsequent to passage of the Act, to hold that a handicapped child was not entitled to a public education under the Act because he could not benefit from the education. This holding is contrary to the language of the Act, its legislative history, and the case law.

V. CONCLUSION

The statutory language of the Act, its legislative history, and the case law construing it, mandate that all handicapped children, regardless of the severity of their handicap, are entitled to a public education. The district court erred in requiring a benefit/eligibility test as a prerequisite to implicating the Act. School districts cannot avoid the provisions of the Act by returning to the practices that were widespread prior to the Act's passage, and which indeed were the impetus for the Act's passage, of unilaterally excluding certain handicapped children from a public education on the ground that they are uneducable.

The law explicitly recognizes that education for the severely handicapped is to be broadly defined, to include not only traditional academic skills, but also basic functional life skills, and that educational methodologies in these areas are not static, but are constantly evolving and improving. It is the school district's responsibility to avail itself of these new approaches in providing an education program geared to each child's individual needs. The only question for the school district to determine, in conjunction with the child's parents, is what constitutes an appropriate individualized education program (IEP) for the handicapped child. We emphasize that the phrase "appropriate individualized education program" cannot be interpreted, as the school district has done, to mean "no educational program."

We agree with the district court that the Special Education Act of New Hampshire, ... implements the federal statute. ...

The judgment of the district court is reversed, judgment shall issue for Timothy W. The case is remanded to the district court which shall retain jurisdiction until a suitable IEP for Timothy W. is effectuated by the school district. Timothy W. is entitled to an interim special educational placement until a final IEP is developed and agreed upon by the parties. The district court shall also determine the question of damages.

Costs are assessed against the school district.

NOTES

1. What do you think about the change in the IDEA authorizing state officials to use IDEA funds to establish and maintain "risk pools" to aid local school systems in providing high-cost services of students with disabilities? 20 U.S.C.A. § 1411(e)(3).

2. Should boards be responsible for all of the costs associated with the placement of children such as Timothy W. even if education makes up only a small component of their IEPs?

[CASE NO. 112]   NURSING SERVICES UNDER THE IDEA

CEDAR RAPIDS COMMUNITY SCHOOL DISTRICT v. GARRET F.

Supreme Court of the United States, 1999.
526 U.S. 66, 119 S.Ct. 992, 143 L.Ed.2d 154 [132 Educ. L. Rep. 40].

■ JUSTICE STEVENS delivered the opinion of the Court.

The Individuals with Disabilities Education Act (IDEA) ... was enacted, in part, "to assure that all children with disabilities have available to them ... a free appropriate public education which emphasizes special education and related services designed to meet their unique needs." Consistent with this purpose, the IDEA authorizes federal financial assistance to States that agree to provide disabled children with special education and "related services." The question presented in this case is whether the definition of "related services" in § 1401(a)(17) requires a public school district in a participating State to provide a ventilator-dependent student with certain nursing services during school hours.

I

Respondent Garret F. is a friendly, creative, and intelligent young man. When Garret was four years old, his spinal column was severed in a motorcycle accident. Though paralyzed from the neck down, his mental capacities were unaffected. He is able to speak, to control his motorized wheelchair through use of a puff and suck straw, and to operate a computer with a device that responds to head movements. Garret is currently a student in the Cedar Rapids Community School District (District), he attends regular classes in a typical school program, and his academic performance has been a success. Garret is, however, ventilator dependent, and therefore requires a responsible individual nearby to attend to certain physical needs while he is in school.

During Garret's early years at school his family provided for his physical care during the school day. When he was in kindergarten, his 18–year–old aunt attended him; in the next four years, his family used settlement proceeds they received after the accident, their insurance, and other resources to employ a licensed practical nurse. In 1993, Garret's mother requested the District to accept financial responsibility for the health care services that Garret requires during the schoolday. The District denied the request, believing that it was not legally obligated to provide continuous one-on-one nursing services.

Relying on both the IDEA and Iowa law, Garret's mother requested a hearing before the Iowa Department of Education. An Administrative Law Judge (ALJ) received extensive evidence concerning Garret's special needs, the District's treatment of other disabled students, and the assistance provided to other ventilator-dependent children in other parts of the country. In his 47–page report, the ALJ found that the District has about 17,500 students, of whom approximately 2,200 need some form of special education or special services. Although Garret is the only ventilator-dependent student in the District, most of the health care services that he needs are already provided for some other students. "The primary difference between Garret's situation and that of other students is his dependency on his ventilator for life support." The ALJ noted that the parties disagreed over the training or licensure required for the care and supervision of such students, and that those providing such care in other parts of the country ranged from nonlicensed personnel to registered nurses. However, the District did not contend that only a licensed physician could provide the services in question.

The ALJ explained that federal law requires that children with a variety of health impairments be provided with "special education and related services" when their disabilities adversely affect their academic performance, and that such children should be educated to the maximum extent appropriate with children who are not disabled. In addition, the ALJ explained that applicable federal regulations distinguish between "school health services," which are provided by a "qualified school nurse or other qualified person," and "medical services," which are provided by a licensed physician. The District must provide the former, but need not provide the latter (except, of course, those "medical services" that are for diagnostic or evaluation purposes). According to the ALJ, the distinction in the regulations does not just depend on "the title of the person providing the service"; instead, the "medical services" exclusion is limited to services that are "in the special training, knowledge, and judgment of a physician to carry out." The ALJ thus concluded that the IDEA required the District to bear financial responsibility for all of the services in dispute, including continuous nursing services.

The District challenged the ALJ's decision in Federal District Court, but that court approved the ALJ's IDEA ruling and granted summary judgment against the District. The Court of Appeals affirmed. It noted that, as a recipient of federal funds under the IDEA, Iowa has a statutory duty to provide all disabled children a "free appropriate public education," which includes "related services." The Court of Appeals read our opinion in *Irving Independent School Dist. v. Tatro*, to provide a two-step analysis of the "related services" definition in § 1401(a)(17)—asking first, whether the requested services are included within the phrase "supportive services"; and second, whether the services are excluded as "medical services." The Court of Appeals succinctly answered both questions in Garret's favor. The Court found the first step plainly satisfied, since Garret cannot attend school unless the requested services are available during the school day. As to the second step, the court reasoned that *Tatro* "established a bright-line test: the services of a physician (other than for diagnostic and evaluation purposes) are subject to the medical services exclusion, but services that can be provided in the school setting by a nurse or qualified layperson are not."

In its petition for *certiorari*, the District challenged only the second step of the Court of Appeals' analysis. The District pointed out that some federal courts have not asked whether the requested health services must be delivered by a physician, but instead have applied a multifactor test that considers, generally speaking, the nature and extent of the services at issue. We granted the District's petition to resolve this conflict.

II

The District contends that § 1401(a)(17) does not require it to provide Garret with "continuous one-on-one nursing services" during the schoolday, even though Garret cannot remain in school without such care. However, the IDEA's definition of "related services," our decision in *Irving Independent School District v. Tatro* and the overall statutory scheme all support the decision of the Court of Appeals.

The text of the "related services" definition broadly encompasses those supportive services that "may be required to assist a child with a disability to benefit from special education." As we have already noted, the District does not challenge the Court of Appeals' conclusion that the in-school services at issue are within the covered category of "supportive services." As a general matter, services that enable a disabled child to remain in school during the day provide the student with "the meaningful access to education that Congress envisioned."

This general definition of "related services" is illuminated by a parenthetical phrase listing examples of particular services that are included within the statute's coverage. "[M]edical services" are enumerated in this list, but such services are limited to those that are "for diagnostic and evaluation purposes." The statute does not contain a more specific definition of the "medical services" that are excepted from the coverage of § 1401(a)(17).

The scope of the "medical services" exclusion is not a matter of first impression in this Court. In *Tatro* we concluded that the Secretary of Education had reasonably determined that the term "medical services" referred only to services that must be performed by a physician, and not to school health services. Accordingly, we held that a specific form of health care (clean intermittent catheterization) that is often, though not always, performed by a nurse is not an excluded medical service. We referenced the likely cost of the services and the competence of school staff as justifications for drawing a line between physician and other services, but our endorsement of that line was unmistakable. It is thus settled that the phrase "medical services" in § 1401(a)(17) does not embrace all forms of care that might loosely be described as "medical" in other contexts, such as a claim for an income tax deduction.

The District does not ask us to define the term so broadly. Indeed, the District does not argue that any of the items of care that Garret needs, considered individually, could be excluded from the scope of 20 U.S.C.[A.] § 1401(a)(17). It could not make such an argument, considering that one of the services Garret needs (catheterization) was at issue in *Tatro,* and the others may be provided competently by a school nurse or other trained personnel. As the ALJ concluded, most of the requested services are already provided by the District to other students, and the in-school care necessitated by Garret's ventilator dependency does not demand the training, knowledge, and judgment of a licensed physician. While more extensive, the in-school services Garret needs are no more "medical" than was the care sought in *Tatro.*

Instead, the District points to the combined and continuous character of the required care, and proposes a test under which the outcome in any particular case would "depend upon a series of factors, such as [1] whether the care is continuous or intermittent, [2] whether existing school health personnel can provide the service, [3] the cost of the service, and [4] the potential consequences if the service is not properly performed."

The District's multifactored test is not supported by any recognized source of legal authority. The proposed factors can be found in neither the text of the statute nor the regulations that we upheld in *Tatro.* Moreover, the District offers no explanation why these characteristics make one service any more "medical" than another. The continuous character of certain services associated with Garret's ventilator dependency has no apparent relationship to "medical" services, much less a relationship of equivalence. Continuous services may be more costly and may require additional school personnel, but they are not thereby more "medical." Whatever its imperfections, a rule that limits the medical services exemption to physician services is unquestionably a reasonable and generally workable interpretation of the statute. Absent an elaboration of the statutory terms plainly more convincing than that which we reviewed in *Tatro,* there is no good reason to depart from settled law.

Finally, the District raises broader concerns about the financial burden that it must bear to provide the services that Garret needs to stay in school. The problem for the District in providing these services is not that its staff cannot be trained to deliver them; the problem, the District contends, is that the existing school health staff cannot meet all of their responsibilities and provide for Garret at the same time. Through its multifactor test, the District seeks to establish a kind of undue-burden exemption primarily based on the cost of the requested services. The first two factors can be seen as examples of cost-based distinctions: Intermittent care is often less expensive than continuous care, and the use of existing personnel is cheaper than hiring additional employees. The third factor-the cost of the service-would then encompass the first two. The relevance of the fourth factor is likewise related to cost because extra care may be necessary if potential consequences are especially serious.

The District may have legitimate financial concerns, but our role in this dispute is to interpret existing law. Defining "related services" in a manner that *accommodates* the cost concerns Congress may have had is altogether different from using cost *itself* as the definition. Given that § 1401(a)(17) does not employ cost in its definition of "related services" or excluded "medical services," accepting the District's cost-based standard as the sole test for determining the scope of the provision would require us to engage in judicial lawmaking without any guidance from Congress. It would also create some tension with the purposes of the IDEA. The statute may not require public schools to maximize the potential of disabled students commensurate with the opportunities provided to other children and the potential financial burdens imposed on participating States may be relevant to arriving at a sensible construction of the IDEA. But Congress intended "to open the door of public education" to all qualified children and "require[d] participating States to educate handicapped children with non-handicapped children whenever possible."

This case is about whether meaningful access to the public schools will be assured, not the level of education that a school must finance once access is attained. It is undisputed that the services at issue must be provided if Garret is to remain in school. Under the statute, our precedent, and the purposes of the IDEA, the District must fund such "related services" in order to help guarantee that students like Garret are integrated into the public schools.

The judgment of the Court of Appeals is accordingly

Affirmed.

NOTES

1. The dissent argued that insofar as *Tatro* could not be "squared with the text of IDEA," the Supreme Court should not have applied it in *Garret F.* The dissent added that even assuming the Court was correct in *Tatro*, its unwarranted extension ignored the constitutionally-mandated rules of construction applicable to legislation enacted pursuant to Congress' spending power. Do you agree?

2. Should cost ever into discussions about serving students with special needs?

[CASE NO. 113]   DISCIPLINING STUDENTS WITH DISABILITIES

HONIG v. DOE

Supreme Court of the United States, 1988.
484 U.S. 305, 108 S.Ct. 592, 98 L.Ed.2d 686 [43 Educ. L. Rep. 857].

■ JUSTICE BRENNAN delivered the opinion of the Court.

As a condition of federal financial assistance, the Education of the Handicapped Act requires States to ensure a "free appropriate public education" for all disabled children within their jurisdictions. In aid of this goal, the Act establishes a comprehensive system of procedural safeguards designed to ensure parental participation in decisions concerning the education of their disabled children and to provide administrative and judicial review of any decisions with which those parents disagree. Among these safeguards is the so-called "stay-put" provision, which directs that a disabled child "shall remain in [his or her] then current educational placement" pending completion of any review proceedings, unless the parents and state or local educational agencies otherwise agree. Today we must decide whether, in the face of this statutory proscription, state or local school authorities may nevertheless unilaterally exclude disabled children from the classroom for dangerous or disruptive conduct growing out of their disabilities. In addition, we are called upon to decide whether a district court may, in the exercise of its equitable powers, order a State to provide educational services directly to a disabled child when the local agency fails to do so.

I

. . .

The present dispute grows out of the efforts of certain officials of the San Francisco Unified School District (SFUSD) to expel two emotionally disturbed children from school indefinitely for violent and disruptive conduct related to their disabilities. In November 1980, respondent John Doe assaulted another student at the Louise Lombard School, a developmental center for disabled children. Doe's April 1980 IEP identified him as a socially and physically awkward 17–year–old who experienced considerable difficulty controlling his impulses and anger. Among the goals set out in his IEP was "[i]mprovement in [his] ability to relate to [his] peers [and to] cope with frustrating situations without resorting to aggressive acts." Frustrating situations, however, were an unfortunately prominent feature of Doe's school career: physical abnormalities, speech difficulties, and poor grooming habits had made him the target of teasing and ridicule as early as the first grade; his 1980 IEP reflected his continuing difficulties with peers, noting that his social skills had deteriorated and that he could tolerate only minor frustration before exploding.

On November 6, 1980, Doe responded to the taunts of a fellow student in precisely the explosive manner anticipated by his IEP: he choked the student with sufficient force to leave abrasions on the child's neck, and kicked out a school window while being escorted to the principal's office afterwards. Doe admitted his misconduct and the school subsequently suspended him for five days. Thereafter, his principal referred the matter to the SFUSD Student Placement Committee (SPC or Committee) with the recommendation that Doe be expelled. On the day the suspension was to end, the SPC notified Doe's mother that it was proposing to exclude her child permanently from SFUSD and was therefore extending his suspension until such time as the expulsion proceedings were completed. The Committee further advised her that she was entitled to attend the November 25 hearing at which it planned to discuss the proposed expulsion.

After unsuccessfully protesting these actions by letter, Doe brought this suit.... Alleging that the suspension and proposed expulsion violated the EHA, he sought a temporary restraining order canceling the SPC hearing and requiring school officials to convene an IEP meeting. The District Judge granted the requested injunctive relief and further ordered defendants to provide home tutoring for Doe on an interim basis; shortly thereafter, she issued a preliminary injunction directing defendants to return Doe to his then current educational placement at Louise Lombard School pending completion of the IEP review process. Doe reentered school on December 15, 5 1/2 weeks, and 24 school-days, after his initial suspension.

Respondent Jack Smith was identified as an emotionally disturbed child by the time he entered the second grade in 1976. School records prepared that year indicated that he was unable "to control verbal or physical outburst[s]" and exhibited a "[s]evere disturbance in relationships with peers and adults." Further evaluations subsequently revealed that he had been physically and emotionally abused as an infant and young child and that, despite above average intelligence, he experienced academic and social difficulties as a result of extreme hyperactivity and low self-esteem. Of particular concern was Smith's propensity for verbal hostility; one evaluator noted that the child reacted to stress by "attempt[ing] to cover his feelings of low self worth through aggressive behavior[,] ... primarily verbal provocations."

Based on these evaluations, SFUSD placed Smith in a learning center for emotionally disturbed children. His grandparents, however, believed that his needs would be better served in the public school setting and, in September 1979, the school district acceded to their requests and enrolled him at A.P. Giannini Middle School. His February 1980 IEP recommended placement in a Learning Disability Group, stressing the need for close supervision and a highly structured environment. Like earlier evaluations, the February 1980 IEP noted that Smith was easily distracted, impulsive, and anxious; it therefore proposed a half-day schedule and suggested that the placement be undertaken on a trial basis.

At the beginning of the next school year, Smith was assigned to a full-day program; almost immediately thereafter he began misbehaving. School officials met twice with his grandparents in October 1980 to discuss returning him to a half-day program; although the grandparents agreed to the reduction, they apparently were never apprised of their right to challenge the decision through EHA procedures. The school officials also warned them that if the child continued his disruptive behavior—which included stealing, extorting money from fellow students, and making sexual comments to female classmates—they would seek to expel him. On November 14, they made good on this threat, suspending Smith for five days after he made further lewd comments. His principal referred the matter to the SPC, which recommended exclusion from SFUSD. As it did in John Doe's case, the Committee scheduled a hearing and extended the suspension indefinitely pending a final disposition in the matter. On November 28, Smith's counsel protested these actions on grounds essentially identical to those raised by Doe, and the SPC agreed to cancel the hearing and to return Smith to a half-day program at A.P. Giannini or to provide home tutoring. Smith's grandparents chose the latter option and the school began home instruction on December 10; on January 6, 1981, an IEP team convened to discuss alternative placements.

After learning of Doe's action, Smith sought and obtained leave to intervene in the suit. The District Court subsequently entered summary judgment in favor of respondents on their EHA claims and issued a permanent injunction. In a series of decisions, the District Judge found that the proposed expulsions and indefinite suspensions of respondents for conduct attributable to their disabilities deprived them of their congressionally mandated right to a free appropriate public education, as well as their right to have that education provided in accordance with the procedures set out in the EHA. The District Judge therefore permanently enjoined ... any disciplinary action other than a 2– or 5–day suspension against any disabled child for disability-related misconduct, or from effecting any other change in the educational placement of any such child without parental consent pending completion of any EHA proceedings. In addition, the judge barred the State from authorizing unilateral placement changes and directed it to establish an EHA compliance-monitoring system or, alternatively, to enact guidelines governing local school responses to disability-related misconduct. Finally, the judge ordered the State to provide services directly to disabled children when, in any individual case, the State determined that the local educational agency was unable or unwilling to do so.

... the Ninth Circuit affirmed the orders with slight modifications. Agreeing with the District Court that an indefinite suspension in aid of expulsion constitutes a prohibited "change in placement" under § 1415(e)(3), the Court of Appeals held that the stay-put provision admitted of no "dangerousness" exception and that the statute therefore rendered invalid those provisions of the California Education Code permitting the indefinite suspension or expulsion of disabled children for misconduct arising out of their disabilities. The court concluded, however, that fixed suspensions of up to 30 schooldays did not fall within the reach of § 1415(e)(3), and therefore upheld recent amendments to the state Education Code authorizing such suspensions. Lastly, the court affirmed that portion of the injunction requiring the State to provide services directly to a disabled child when the local educational agency fails to do so.

Petitioner Bill Honig, California Superintendent of Public Instruction, sought review in this Court, claiming that the Court of Appeals' construction of the stay-put provision conflicted with that of several other Courts of Appeals which had recognized a dangerousness exception and that the direct services ruling placed an intolerable burden on the State. We granted certiorari to resolve these questions and now affirm.

II

At the outset, we address the suggestion, raised for the first time during oral argument, that this case is moot. Under Article III of the Constitution this Court may only adjudicate actual, ongoing controversies. That the dispute between the parties was very much alive when suit was filed, or at the time the Court of Appeals rendered its judgment, cannot substitute for the actual case or controversy that an exercise of this Court's jurisdiction requires. In the present case, we have jurisdiction if there is a reasonable likelihood that respondents will again suffer the deprivation of EHA-mandated rights that gave rise to this suit. We believe that, at least with respect to respondent Smith, such a possibility does in fact exist and that the case therefore remains justiciable.

Respondent John Doe is now 24 years old and, accordingly, is no longer entitled to the protections and benefits of the EHA, which limits eligibility to disabled children between the ages of 3 and 21.... and thus the case is moot as to him. Respondent Jack Smith, however, is currently 20 and has not yet completed high school. Although at present he is not faced with any proposed expulsion or suspension proceedings, and indeed no longer even resides within the SFUSD, he remains a resident of California and is entitled to a "free appropriate public education" within that State. His claims under the EHA, therefore, are not moot if the conduct he originally complained of is " 'capable of repetition, yet evading review.' " Given Smith's continued eligibility for educational services under the EHA, the nature of his disability, and petitioner's insistence that all local school districts retain residual authority to exclude disabled children for dangerous conduct, we have little difficulty concluding that there is a "reasonable expectation," that Smith would once again be subjected to a unilateral "change in placement" for conduct growing out of his disabilities were it not for the statewide injunctive relief issued below.

Our cases reveal that ... we generally have been unwilling to assume that the party seeking relief will repeat the type of misconduct that would once again place him or her at risk of that injury. No such reluctance, however, is warranted here. It is respondent Smith's very inability to conform his conduct to socially acceptable norms that renders him "handicapped" within the meaning of the EHA. As noted above, the record is replete with evidence that Smith is unable to govern his aggressive, impulsive behavior—indeed, his notice of suspension acknowledged that "Jack's actions seem beyond his control." In the absence of any suggestion that respondent has overcome his earlier difficulties, it is certainly reasonable to expect, based on his prior history of behavioral problems, that he will again engage in classroom misconduct. Nor is it reasonable to suppose that Smith's future educational placement will so perfectly suit his emotional and academic needs that further disruptions on his part are improbable....

We think it equally probable that, should he do so, respondent will again be subjected to the same unilateral school action for which he initially sought relief. In this regard, it matters not that Smith no longer resides within the SFUSD. While the actions of SFUSD officials first gave rise to this litigation, the District Judge expressly found that the lack of a state policy governing local school responses to disability-related misconduct had led to, and would continue to result in, EHA violations, and she therefore enjoined the state defendant from authorizing, among other things, unilateral placement changes. She of course also issued injunctions directed at the local defendants, but they did not seek review of those orders in this Court. Only petitioner, the State Superintendent of Public Instruction, has invoked our jurisdiction, and he now urges us to hold that local school districts retain unilateral authority under the EHA to suspend or otherwise remove disabled children for dangerous conduct. Given these representations, we have every reason to believe that were it not for the injunction barring petitioner from authorizing such unilateral action, respondent would be faced with a real and substantial threat of such action in any California school district in which he enrolled. Certainly, if the SFUSD's past practice of unilateral exclusions was at odds with state policy and the practice of local school districts generally, petitioner would not now stand before us seeking to defend the right of all local school districts to engage in such aberrant behavior.

We have previously noted that administrative and judicial review under the EHA is often "ponderous," and this case, which has taken seven years to reach us, amply confirms that observation. For obvious reasons, the misconduct of an emotionally disturbed or otherwise disabled child who has not yet reached adolescence typically will not pose such a serious threat to the well-being of other students that school officials can only ensure classroom safety by excluding the child. Yet, the adolescent student improperly disciplined for misconduct that does pose such a threat will often be finished with school or otherwise ineligible for EHA protections by the time review can be had in this Court. Because we believe that respondent Smith has demonstrated both "a sufficient likelihood that he will again be wronged in a similar way," and that any resulting claim he may have for relief will surely evade our review, we turn to the merits of his case.

III

The language of § 1415(e)(3) is unequivocal. It states plainly that during the pendency of any proceedings initiated under the Act, unless the state or local educational agency and the parents or guardian of a disabled child otherwise agree, "the child *shall* remain in the then current educational placement." (emphasis added). Faced with this clear directive, petitioner asks us to read a "dangerousness" exception into the stay-put provision on the basis of either of two essentially inconsistent assumptions: first, that Congress thought the residual authority of school officials to exclude dangerous students from the classroom too obvious for comment; or second, that Congress inadvertently failed to provide such authority and this Court must therefore remedy the oversight. Because we cannot accept either premise, we decline petitioner's invitation to rewrite the statute.

Petitioner's arguments proceed, he suggests, from a simple, common-sense proposition: Congress could not have intended the stay-put provision to be read literally, for such a construction leads to the clearly unintended, and untenable, result that school districts must return violent or dangerous students to school while the often lengthy EHA proceedings run their course. We think it clear, however, that Congress very much meant to strip schools of the *unilateral* authority they had traditionally employed to exclude disabled students, particularly emotionally disturbed students, from school. In so doing, Congress did not leave school administrators powerless to deal with dangerous students; it did, however, deny school officials their former right to "self-help," and directed that in the future the removal of disabled students could be accomplished only with the permission of the parents or, as a last resort, the courts.

As noted above, Congress passed the EHA after finding that school systems across the country had excluded one out of every eight disabled children from classes. In drafting the law, Congress was largely guided by the recent decisions in *Mills v. Board of Education of District of Columbia* and *PARC*, both of which involved the exclusion of hard-to-handle disabled students. . . .

Congress attacked such exclusionary practices in a variety of ways. It required participating States to educate *all* disabled children, regardless of the severity of their disabilities, and included within the definition of "handicapped" those children with serious emotional disturbances. It further provided for meaningful parental participation in all aspects of a child's educational placement, and barred schools, through the stay-put provision, from changing that placement over the parent's objection until all review proceedings were completed. Recognizing that those proceedings might prove long and tedious, the Act's drafters did not intend to operate inflexibly and they therefore allowed for interim placements where parents and school officials are able to agree on one. Conspicuously absent from § 1415(e)(3), however, is any emergency exception for dangerous students. This absence is all the more telling in light of the injunctive decree issued in *PARC,* which permitted school officials unilaterally to remove students in " 'extraordinary circumstances.' " Given the lack of any similar exception in *Mills,* and the close attention Congress devoted to these "landmark" decisions, we can only conclude that the omission was intentional; we are therefore not at liberty to engraft onto the statute an exception Congress chose not to create.

Our conclusion that § 1415(e)(3) means what it says does not leave educators hamstrung. The Department of Education has observed that, "[w]hile the [child's] placement may not be changed [during any complaint proceeding], this does not preclude the agency from using its normal procedures for dealing with children who are endangering themselves or others." Such procedures may include the use of study carrels, timeouts, detention, or the restriction of privileges. More drastically, where a student poses an immediate threat to the safety of others, officials may temporarily suspend him or her for up to 10 schooldays. This authority, which respondent in no way disputes, not only ensures that school administrators can protect the safety of others by promptly removing the most dangerous of students, it also provides a "cooling down" period during which officials can initiate IEP review and seek to persuade the child's parents to agree to an interim placement. And in those cases in which the parents of a truly dangerous child adamantly refuse to permit any change in placement, the 10–day respite gives school officials an opportunity to invoke the aid of the courts under, which empowers courts to grant any appropriate relief.

Petitioner contends, however, that the availability of judicial relief is more illusory than real, because a party seeking review under § 1415(e)(2) must exhaust time-consuming administrative remedies, and because under the Court of Appeals' construction of § 1415(e)(3), courts are as bound by the stay-put provision's "automatic injunction," as are schools. It is true that judicial review is normally not available under § 1415(e)(2) until all administrative proceedings are completed, but as we have previously noted, parents may bypass the administrative process where exhaustion would be futile or inadequate. While many of the EHA's procedural safeguards protect the rights of parents and children, schools can and do seek redress through the administrative review process, and we have no reason to believe that Congress meant to require schools alone to exhaust in all cases, no matter how exigent the circumstances. The burden in such cases, of course, rests with the school to demonstrate the futility or inadequacy of administrative review, but nothing in § 1415(e)(2) suggests that schools are completely barred from attempting to make such a showing. Nor do we think that § 1415(e)(3) operates to limit the equitable powers of district courts such that they cannot, in appropriate cases, temporarily enjoin a dangerous disabled child from attending school. As the EHA's legislative history makes clear, one of the evils Congress sought to remedy was the unilateral exclusion of disabled children by *schools*, not courts, and one of the purposes of § 1415(e)(3), therefore, was "to prevent *school* officials from removing a child from the regular public school classroom over the parents' objection pending completion of the review proceedings." The stay-put provision in no way purports to limit or pre-empt the authority conferred on courts by § 1415(e)(2); indeed, it says nothing whatever about judicial power.

In short, then, we believe that school officials are entitled to seek injunctive relief under § 1415(e)(2) in appropriate cases. In any such action, § 1415(e)(3) effectively creates a presumption in favor of the child's current educational placement which school officials can overcome only by showing that maintaining the child in his or her current placement is substantially likely to result in injury either to himself or herself, or to others. In the present case, we are satisfied that the District Court, in enjoining the state and local defendants from indefinitely suspending respondent or otherwise unilaterally altering his then current placement, properly balanced respondent's interest in receiving a free appropriate public education in accordance with the procedures and requirements of the EHA against the interests of the state and local school officials in maintaining a safe learning environment for all their students.

IV

We believe the courts below properly construed and applied § 1415(e)(3), except insofar as the Court of Appeals held that a suspension in excess of 10 schooldays does not constitute a "change in placement." We therefore affirm the Court of Appeals' judgment on this issue as modified herein. Because we are equally divided on the question whether a court may order a State to provide services directly to a disabled child where the local agency has failed to do so, we affirm the Court of Appeals' judgment on this issue as well.

Affirmed.

NOTES

1.   Without addressing the merits of the case, the dissent thought that the entire case should have been rendered moot since the students were no longer in school. What do you think?

2.   What can, or should, school officials do to protect the educational and safety rights of other children when students with disabilities are disruptive in class?

[CASE NO. 114]   BURDEN OF PROOF AT DUE PROCESS HEARINGS

SCHAFFER EX REL. SCHAFFER v. WEAST

Supreme Court of the United States, 2005.
546 U.S. 49, 126 S.Ct. 528, 163 L.Ed.2d 387 [203 Educ. L. Rep. 29].

■ JUSTICE O'CONNOR delivered the opinion of the Court.

The Individuals with Disabilities Education Act (IDEA or Act) is a Spending Clause statute that seeks to ensure that "all children with disabilities have available to them a free appropriate public education." Under IDEA, school districts must create an "individualized education program" (IEP) for each disabled child. If parents believe their child's IEP is inappropriate, they may request an "impartial due process hearing." The Act is silent, however, as to which party bears the burden of persuasion at such a hearing. We hold that the burden lies, as it typically does, on the party seeking relief.

I

A

Congress first passed IDEA as part of the Education of the Handicapped Act in 1970 and amended it substantially in the Education for All Handicapped Children Act of 1975....

IDEA is "frequently described as a model of 'cooperative federalism.' " It "leaves to the States the primary responsibility for developing and executing educational programs for handicapped children, [but] imposes significant requirements to be followed in the discharge of that responsibility. For example, the Act mandates cooperation and reporting between state and federal educational authorities." Participating States must certify to the Secretary of Education that they have "policies and procedures" that will effectively meet the Act's conditions. (Unless otherwise noted, [the Court applied] ... the pre-2004 version of the statute because this is the version that was in effect during the proceedings below. We note, however, that nothing in the recent 2004 amendments appears to materially affect the rule announced here.) State educational agencies, in turn, must ensure that local schools and teachers are meeting the State's educational standards. Local educational agencies (school boards or other administrative bodies) can receive IDEA funds only if they certify to a state educational agency that they are acting in accordance with the State's policies and procedures.

The core of the statute, however, is the cooperative process that it establishes between parents and schools. The central vehicle for this collaboration is the IEP process. State educational authorities must identify and evaluate disabled children, develop an IEP for each one, and review every IEP at least once a year. Each IEP must include an assessment of the child's current educational performance, must articulate measurable educational goals, and must specify the nature of the special services that the school will provide.

Parents and guardians play a significant role in the IEP process. They must be informed about and consent to evaluations of their child under the Act. Parents are included as members of "IEP teams." They have the right to examine any records relating to their child, and to obtain an "independent educational evaluation of the[ir] child." They must be given written prior notice of any changes in an IEP, and be notified in writing of the procedural safeguards available to them under the Act. If parents believe that an IEP is not appropriate, they may seek an administrative "impartial due process hearing." School districts may also seek such hearings, as Congress clarified in the 2004 amendments. They may do so, for example, if they wish to change an existing IEP but the parents do not consent, or if parents refuse to allow their child to be evaluated. As a practical matter, it appears that most hearing requests come from parents rather than schools.

Although state authorities have limited discretion to determine who conducts the hearings, and responsibility generally for establishing fair hearing procedures, Congress has chosen to legislate the central components of due process hearings. It has imposed minimal pleading standards, requiring parties to file complaints setting forth "a description of the nature of the problem" and "a proposed resolution of the problem to the extent known and available at the time." At the hearing, all parties may be accompanied by counsel, and may "present evidence and confront, cross-examine, and compel the attendance of witnesses." After the hearing, any aggrieved party may bring a civil action in state or federal court. Prevailing parents may also recover attorney's fees. Congress has never explicitly stated, however, which party should bear the burden of proof at IDEA hearings.

B

This case concerns the educational services that were due, under IDEA, to petitioner Brian Schaffer. Brian suffers from learning disabilities and speech-language impairments. From prekindergarten through seventh grade he attended a private school and struggled academically. In 1997, school officials informed Brian's mother that he needed a school that could better accommodate his needs. Brian's parents contacted respondent Montgomery County Public Schools System (MCPS) seeking a placement for him for the following school year.

MCPS evaluated Brian and convened an IEP team. The committee generated an initial IEP offering Brian a place in either of two MCPS middle schools. Brian's parents were not satisfied with the arrangement, believing that Brian needed smaller classes and more intensive services. The Schaffers thus enrolled Brian in another private school, and initiated a due process hearing challenging the IEP and seeking compensation for the cost of Brian's subsequent private education.

In Maryland, IEP hearings are conducted by administrative law judges (ALJs). After a 3–day hearing, the ALJ deemed the evidence close, held that the parents bore the burden of persuasion, and ruled in favor of the school district. The parents brought a civil action challenging the result. The United States District Court for the District of Maryland reversed and remanded, after concluding that the burden of persuasion is on the school district. Around the same time, MCPS offered Brian a placement in a high school with a special learning center. Brian's parents accepted, and Brian was educated in that program until he graduated from high school. The suit remained alive, however, because the parents sought compensation for the private school tuition and related expenses.

Respondents appealed to the ... Fourth Circuit. While the appeal was pending, the ALJ reconsidered the case, deemed the evidence truly in "equipoise," and ruled in favor of the parents. The Fourth Circuit vacated and remanded the appeal so that it could consider the burden of proof issue along with the merits on a later appeal. The District Court reaffirmed its ruling that the school district has the burden of proof. On appeal, a divided panel of the Fourth Circuit reversed. Judge Michael, writing for the majority, concluded that petitioners offered no persuasive reason to "depart from the normal rule of allocating the burden to the party seeking relief." We granted *certiorari*, to resolve the following question: At an administrative hearing assessing the appropriateness of an IEP, which party bears the burden of persuasion?

II

A

The term "burden of proof" is one of the "slipperiest member[s] of the family of legal terms." Part of the confusion surrounding the term arises from the fact that historically, the concept encompassed two distinct burdens: the "burden of persuasion," *i.e.,* which party loses if the evidence is closely balanced, and the "burden of production," *i.e.,* which party bears the obligation to come forward with the evidence at different points in the proceeding. We note at the outset that this case concerns only the burden of persuasion, as the parties agree, and when we speak of burden of proof in this opinion, it is this to which we refer.

When we are determining the burden of proof under a statutory cause of action, the touchstone of our inquiry is, of course, the statute. The plain text of IDEA is silent on the allocation of the burden of persuasion. We therefore begin with the ordinary default rule that plaintiffs bear the risk of failing to prove their claims.

Thus, we have usually assumed without comment that plaintiffs bear the burden of persuasion regarding the essential aspects of their claims. For example, Title VII of the Civil Rights Act of 1964, does not directly state that plaintiffs bear the "ultimate" burden of persuasion, but we have so concluded. In numerous other areas, we have presumed or held that the default rule applies. . . .

The ordinary default rule, of course, admits of exceptions. For example, the burden of persuasion as to certain elements of a plaintiff's claim may be shifted to defendants, when such elements can fairly be characterized as affirmative defenses or exemptions. Under some circumstances this Court has even placed the burden of persuasion over an entire claim on the defendant. But while the normal default rule does not solve all cases, it certainly solves most of them. Decisions that place the *entire* burden of persuasion on the opposing party at the *outset* of a proceeding—as petitioners urge us to do here—are extremely rare. Absent some reason to believe that Congress intended otherwise, therefore, we will conclude that the burden of persuasion lies where it usually falls, upon the party seeking relief.

B

Petitioners contend first that a close reading of IDEA's text compels a conclusion in their favor. They urge that we should interpret the statutory words "due process" in light of their constitutional meaning, and apply the balancing test established by *Mathews v. Eldridge*. Even assuming that the Act incorporates constitutional due process doctrine, *Eldridge* is no help to petitioners, because "[o]utside the criminal law area, where special concerns attend, the locus of the burden of persuasion is normally not an issue of federal constitutional moment."

Petitioners next contend that we should take instruction from the lower court opinions of *Mills v. Board of Education* and *Pennsylvania Association for Retarded Children v. Commonwealth* (hereinafter *PARC*). IDEA's drafters were admittedly guided "to a significant extent" by these two landmark cases. As the court below noted, however, the fact that Congress "took a number of the procedural safeguards from *PARC* and *Mills* and wrote them directly into the Act" does not allow us to "conclude that Congress intended to adopt the ideas that it failed to write into the text of the statute."

Petitioners also urge that putting the burden of persuasion on school districts will further IDEA's purposes because it will help ensure that children receive a free appropriate public education. In truth, however, very few cases will be in evidentiary equipoise. Assigning the burden of persuasion to school districts might encourage schools to put more resources into preparing IEPs and presenting their evidence. But IDEA is silent about whether marginal dollars should be allocated to litigation and administrative expenditures or to educational services. Moreover, there is reason to believe that a great deal is already spent on the administration of the Act.

Litigating a due process complaint is an expensive affair, costing schools approximately $8,000–to–$12,000 per hearing. Congress has also repeatedly amended the Act in order to reduce its administrative and litigation-related costs. For example, in 1997 Congress mandated that States offer mediation for IDEA disputes. In 2004, Congress added a mandatory "resolution session" prior to any due process hearing. It also made new findings that "[p]arents and schools should be given expanded opportunities to resolve their disagreements in positive and constructive ways," and that "[t]eachers, schools, local educational agencies, and States should be relieved of irrelevant and unnecessary paperwork burdens that do not lead to improved educational outcomes."

Petitioners in effect ask this Court to assume that every IEP is invalid until the school district demonstrates that it is not. The Act does not support this conclusion. IDEA relies heavily upon the expertise of school districts to meet its goals. It also includes a so-called "stay-put" provision, which requires a child to remain in his or her "then-current educational placement" during the pendency of an IDEA hearing. Congress could have required that a child be given the educational placement that a parent requested during a dispute, but it did no such thing. Congress appears to have presumed instead that, if the Act's procedural requirements are respected, parents will prevail when they have legitimate grievances.

Petitioners' most plausible argument is that "[t]he ordinary rule, based on considerations of fairness, does not place the burden upon a litigant of establishing facts peculiarly within the knowledge of his adversary." But this "rule is far from being universal, and has many qualifications upon its application." School districts have a "natural advantage" in information and expertise, but Congress addressed this when it obliged schools to safeguard the procedural rights of parents and to share information with them. As noted above, parents have the right to review all records that the school possesses in relation to their child. They also have the right to an "independent educational evaluation of the[ir] child." The regulations clarify this entitlement by providing that a "parent has the right to an independent educational evaluation at public expense if the parent disagrees with an evaluation obtained by the public agency." IDEA thus ensures parents access to an expert who can evaluate all the materials that the school must make available, and who can give an independent opinion. They are not left to challenge the government without a realistic opportunity to access the necessary evidence, or without an expert with the firepower to match the opposition.

Additionally, in 2004, Congress added provisions requiring school districts to answer the subject matter of a complaint in writing, and to provide parents with the reasoning behind the disputed action, details about the other options considered and rejected by the IEP team, and a description of all evaluations, reports, and other factors that the school used in coming to its decision. Prior to a hearing, the parties must disclose evaluations and recommendations that they intend to rely upon. IDEA hearings are deliberately informal and intended to give ALJs the flexibility that they need to ensure that each side can fairly present its evidence. IDEA, in fact, requires state authorities to organize hearings in a way that guarantees parents and children the procedural protections of the Act. Finally, and perhaps most importantly, parents may recover attorney's fees if they prevail. These protections ensure that the school bears no unique informational advantage.

III

Finally, respondents and several States urge us to decide that States may, if they wish, override the default rule and put the burden always on the school district. Several States have laws or regulations purporting to do so, at least under some circumstances. . . . Because no such law or regulation exists in Maryland, we need not decide this issue today. Justice BREYER contends that the allocation of the burden ought to be left *entirely* up to the States. But neither party made this argument before this Court or the courts below. We therefore decline to address it.

We hold no more than we must to resolve the case at hand: The burden of proof in an administrative hearing challenging an IEP is properly placed upon the party seeking relief. In this case, that party is Brian, as represented by his parents. But the rule applies with equal effect to school districts: If they seek to challenge an IEP, they will in turn bear the burden of persuasion before an ALJ. The judgment of the United States Court of Appeals for the Fourth Circuit is, therefore, affirmed.

It is so ordered.

THE CHIEF JUSTICE took no part in the consideration or decision of this case.

NOTES

1. Is this outcome fair to parents (and their children)?

2. Should individual states be free to set their own burdens of proof?

[CASE NO. 115]   PARENTAL RIGHTS UNDER THE IDEA

WINKELMAN v. PARMA CITY SCHOOL DISTRICT

Supreme Court of the United States, 2007.
550 U.S. 516, 127 S.Ct. 1994, 167 L.Ed.2d 904 [219 Educ. L. Rep. 39].

■ JUSTICE KENNEDY delivered the opinion of the Court.

Some four years ago, Mr. and Mrs. Winkelman, parents of five children, became involved in lengthy administrative and legal proceedings. They had sought review related to concerns they had over whether their youngest child, 6–year–old Jacob, would progress well at Pleasant Valley Elementary School, which is part of the Parma City School District in Parma, Ohio.

Jacob has autism spectrum disorder and is covered by the Individuals with Disabilities Education Act (Act or IDEA). His parents worked with the school district to develop an individualized education program (IEP), as required by the Act. All concede that Jacob's parents had the statutory right to contribute to this process and, when agreement could not be reached, to participate in administrative proceedings including what the Act refers to as an "impartial due process hearing."

The disagreement at the center of the current dispute concerns the procedures to be followed when parents and their child, dissatisfied with the outcome of the due process hearing, seek further review in a United States District Court. The question is whether parents, either on their own behalf or as representatives of the child, may proceed in court unrepresented by counsel though they are not trained or licensed as attorneys. Resolution of this issue requires us to examine and explain the provisions of IDEA to determine if it accords to parents rights of their own that can be vindicated in court proceedings, or alternatively, whether the Act allows them, in their status as parents, to represent their child in court proceedings.

I

Respondent Parma City School District, a participant in IDEA's educational spending program, accepts federal funds for assistance in the education of children with disabilities. As a condition of receiving funds, it must comply with IDEA's mandates. IDEA requires that the school district provide Jacob with a "free appropriate public education," which must operate in accordance with the IEP that Jacob's parents, along with school officials and other individuals, develop as members of Jacob's "IEP Team."

The school district proposed an IEP for the 2003–2004 school year that would have placed Jacob at a public elementary school. Regarding this IEP as deficient under IDEA, Jacob's nonlawyer parents availed themselves of the administrative review provided by IDEA. They filed a complaint alleging respondent had failed to provide Jacob with a free appropriate public education; they appealed the hearing officer's rejection of the claims in this complaint to a state-level review officer; and after losing that appeal they filed, on their own behalf and on behalf of Jacob, a complaint. . . . In reliance upon 20 U.S.C.[A.] § 1415(i)(2) they challenged the administrative decision. . . . The Winkelmans' complaint sought reversal of the administrative decision, reimbursement for private-school expenditures and attorney's fees already incurred, and, it appears, declaratory relief.

The District Court granted respondent's motion for judgment on the pleadings, finding it had provided Jacob with a free appropriate public education. Petitioners, proceeding without counsel, filed an appeal with the Court of Appeals for the Sixth Circuit. Relying on its recent decision in *Cavanaugh v. Cardinal Local School Dist.*, the Court of Appeals entered an order dismissing the Winkelmans' appeal unless they obtained counsel to represent Jacob. In *Cavanaugh* the Court of Appeals had rejected the proposition that IDEA allows nonlawyer parents raising IDEA claims to proceed *pro se* in federal court. . . .

Petitioners sought review in this Court. In light of the disagreement among the Courts of Appeals as to whether a nonlawyer parent of a child with a disability may prosecute IDEA actions *pro se* in federal court, we granted certiorari.

II

Our resolution of this case turns upon the significance of IDEA's interlocking statutory provisions. Petitioners' primary theory is that the Act makes parents real parties in interest to IDEA actions, not "mer[e] guardians of their children's rights." If correct, this allows Mr. and Mrs. Winkelman back into court, for there is no question that a party may represent his or her own interests in federal court without the aid of counsel. Petitioners cannot cite a specific provision in IDEA mandating in direct and explicit terms that parents have the status of real parties in interest. They instead base their argument on a comprehensive reading of IDEA. Taken as a whole, they contend, the Act leads to the necessary conclusion that parents have independent, enforceable rights. Respondent, accusing petitioners of "knit[ting] together various provisions pulled from the crevices of the statute" to support these claims reads the text of IDEA to mean that any redressable rights under the Act belong only to children.

We agree that the text of IDEA resolves the question presented. We recognize, in addition, that a proper interpretation of the Act requires a consideration of the entire statutory scheme. Turning to the current version of IDEA, which the parties agree governs this case, we begin with an overview of the relevant statutory provisions.

A

The goals of IDEA include "ensur[ing] that all children with disabilities have available to them a free appropriate public education" and "ensur[ing] that the rights of children with disabilities and parents of such children are protected." To this end, the Act includes provisions governing four areas of particular relevance to the Winkelmans' claim: procedures to be followed when developing a child's IEP; criteria governing the sufficiency of an education provided to a child; mechanisms for review that must be made available when there are objections to the IEP or to other aspects of IDEA proceedings; and the requirement in certain circumstances that States reimburse parents for various expenses....

IDEA requires school districts to develop an IEP for each child with a disability with parents playing "a significant role" in this process. Parents serve as members of the team that develops the IEP....

The Act defines a "free appropriate public education" pursuant to an IEP to be an educational instruction "specially designed ... to meet the unique needs of a child with a disability," coupled with any additional " 'related services' " that are "required to assist a child with a disability to benefit from [that instruction]." ...

When a party objects to the adequacy of the education provided, the construction of the IEP, or some related matter, IDEA provides procedural recourse: It requires that a State provide "[a]n opportunity for any party to present a complaint ... with respect to any matter relating to the identification, evaluation, or educational placement of the child, or the provision of a free appropriate public education to such child." By presenting a complaint a party is able to pursue a process of review that, as relevant, begins with a preliminary meeting "where the parents of the child discuss their

complaint" and the local educational agency "is provided the opportunity
to [reach a resolution]." If the agency "has not resolved the complaint to
the satisfaction of the parents within 30 days," the parents may request an
"impartial due process hearing," which must be conducted either by the
local educational agency or by the state educational agency and where a
hearing officer will resolve issues raised in the complaint.

IDEA sets standards the States must follow in conducting these
hearings. Among other things, it indicates that the hearing officer's decision "shall be made on substantive grounds based on a determination of
whether the child received a free appropriate public education," and that,
"[i]n matters alleging a procedural violation," the officer may find a child
"did not receive a free appropriate public education" only if the violation

> (I) impeded the child's right to a free appropriate public edu-
> cation;

> (II) significantly impeded the parents' opportunity to participate
> in the decisionmaking process regarding the provision of a free appro-
> priate public education to the parents' child; or

> (III) caused   a   deprivation   of   educational   benefits.
> §§ 1415(f)(3)(E)(i)–(ii).

If the local educational agency, rather than the state educational
agency, conducts this hearing, then "any party aggrieved by the findings
and decision rendered in such a hearing may appeal such findings and
decision to the State educational agency." Once the state educational
agency has reached its decision, an aggrieved party may commence suit in
federal court: "Any party aggrieved by the findings and decision made [by
the hearing officer] shall have the right to bring a civil action with respect
to the complaint."

IDEA, finally, provides for at least two means of cost recovery that
inform our analysis. First, in certain circumstances it allows a court or
hearing officer to require a state agency "to reimburse the parents [of a
child with a disability] for the cost of [private school] enrollment if the
court or hearing officer finds that the agency had not made a free
appropriate public education available to the child." Second, it sets forth
rules governing when and to what extent a court may award attorney's
fees. . . .

B

Petitioners construe these various provisions to accord parents independent, enforceable rights under IDEA. We agree. The parents enjoy
enforceable rights at the administrative stage, and it would be inconsistent
with the statutory scheme to bar them from continuing to assert these
rights in federal court.

The statute sets forth procedures for resolving disputes in a manner
that, in the Act's express terms, contemplates parents will be the parties
bringing the administrative complaints. In ... A wide range of review is
available: . . . . The statute then grants "[a]ny party aggrieved by the

findings and decision made [by the hearing officer] . . . the right to bring a civil action with respect to the complaint.''

Nothing in these interlocking provisions excludes a parent who has exercised his or her own rights from statutory protection the moment the administrative proceedings end. Put another way, the Act does not *sub silentio* or by implication bar parents from seeking to vindicate the rights accorded to them once the time comes to file a civil action. Through its provisions for expansive review and extensive parental involvement, the statute leads to just the opposite result.

Respondent, resisting this line of analysis, asks us to read these provisions as contemplating parental involvement only to the extent parents represent their child's interests. In respondent's view IDEA accords parents nothing more than "collateral tools related to the child's underlying substantive rights-not freestanding or independently enforceable rights.''

This interpretation, though, is foreclosed by provisions of the statute. IDEA defines one of its purposes as seeking "to ensure that the rights of children with disabilities and parents of such children are protected.'' The word "rights'' in the quoted language refers to the rights of parents as well as the rights of the child; otherwise the grammatical structure would make no sense.

Further provisions confirm this view. IDEA mandates that educational agencies establish procedures "to ensure that children with disabilities and their parents are guaranteed procedural safeguards with respect to the provision of a free appropriate public education.'' It presumes parents have rights of their own when it defines how States might provide for the transfer of the "rights accorded to parents'' by IDEA and it prohibits the raising of certain challenges "[n]otwithstanding any other individual right of action that a parent or student may maintain under [the relevant provisions of IDEA].'' To adopt respondent's reading of the statute would require an interpretation of these statutory provisions (and others) far too strained to be correct.

Defending its countertextual reading of the statute, respondent cites a decision by a Court of Appeals concluding that the Act's "references to parents are best understood as accommodations to the fact of the child's incapacity.'' This, according to respondent, requires us to interpret all references to parents' rights as referring in implicit terms to the child's rights-which, under this view, are the only enforceable rights accorded by IDEA. Even if we were inclined to ignore the plain text of the statute in considering this theory, we disagree that the sole purpose driving IDEA's involvement of parents is to facilitate vindication of a child's rights. It is not a novel proposition to say that parents have a recognized legal interest in the education and upbringing of their child. There is no necessary bar or obstacle in the law, then, to finding an intention by Congress to grant parents a stake in the entitlements created by IDEA. Without question a parent of a child with a disability has a particular and personal interest in fulfilling "our national policy of ensuring equality of opportunity, full participation, independent living, and economic self-sufficiency for individuals with disabilities.''

We therefore find no reason to read into the plain language of the statute an implicit rejection of the notion that Congress would accord parents independent, enforceable rights concerning the education of their children. We instead interpret the statute's references to parents' rights to mean what they say: that IDEA includes provisions conveying rights to parents as well as to children.

A variation on respondent's argument has persuaded some Courts of Appeals. The argument is that while a parent can be a "party aggrieved" for aspects of the hearing officer's findings and decision, he or she cannot be a "party aggrieved" with respect to all IDEA-based challenges. Under this view the causes of action available to a parent might relate, for example, to various procedural mandates. The argument supporting this conclusion proceeds as follows: Because a "party aggrieved" is, by definition, entitled to a remedy, and parents are, under IDEA, only entitled to certain procedures and reimbursements as remedies, a parent cannot be a "party aggrieved" with regard to any claim not implicating these limited matters.

This argument is contradicted by the statutory provisions we have recited. True, there are provisions in IDEA stating parents are entitled to certain procedural protections and reimbursements; but the statute prevents us from placing too much weight on the implications to be drawn when other entitlements are accorded in less clear language. We find little support for the inference that parents are excluded by implication whenever a child is mentioned, and vice versa. Without more, then, the language in IDEA confirming that parents enjoy particular procedural and reimbursement-related rights does not resolve whether they are also entitled to enforce IDEA's other mandates, including the one most fundamental to the Act: the provision of a free appropriate public education to a child with a disability.

We consider the statutory structure. The IEP proceedings entitle parents to participate not only in the implementation of IDEA's procedures but also in the substantive formulation of their child's educational program. . . . The IEP, in turn, sets the boundaries of the central entitlement provided by IDEA: It defines a " 'free appropriate public education' " for that parent's child.

The statute also empowers parents to bring challenges based on a broad range of issues. . . . To resolve these challenges a hearing officer must make a decision based on whether the child "received a free appropriate public education." When this hearing has been conducted by a local educational agency rather than a state educational agency, "any party aggrieved by the findings and decision rendered in such a hearing may appeal such findings and decision" to the state educational agency. Judicial review follows, authorized by a broadly worded provision phrased in the same terms used to describe the prior stage of review: "[a]ny party aggrieved" may bring "a civil action."

These provisions confirm that IDEA, through its text and structure, creates in parents an independent stake not only in the procedures and costs implicated by this process but also in the substantive decisions to be made. We therefore conclude that IDEA does not differentiate, through isolated references to various procedures and remedies, between the rights accorded to children and the rights accorded to parents. As a consequence, a parent may be a "party aggrieved" for purposes of § 1415(i)(2) with regard to "any matter" implicating these rights. The status of parents as parties is not limited to matters that relate to procedure and cost recovery. To find otherwise would be inconsistent with the collaborative framework and expansive system of review established by the Act.

Our conclusion is confirmed by noting the incongruous results that would follow were we to accept the proposition that parents' IDEA rights are limited to certain nonsubstantive matters. The statute's procedural and reimbursement-related rights are intertwined with the substantive adequacy of the education provided to a child and it is difficult to disentangle the provisions in order to conclude that some rights adhere to both parent and child while others do not. Were we nevertheless to recognize a distinction of this sort it would impose upon parties a confusing and onerous legal regime, one worsened by the absence of any express guidance in IDEA concerning how a court might in practice differentiate between these matters. It is, in addition, out of accord with the statute's design to interpret the Act to require that parents prove the substantive inadequacy of their child's education as a predicate for obtaining, for example, reimbursement under § 1412(a)(10)(C)(ii), yet to prevent them from obtaining a judgment mandating that the school district provide their child with an educational program demonstrated to be an appropriate one. The adequacy of the educational program is, after all, the central issue in the litigation. The provisions of IDEA do not set forth these distinctions, and we decline to infer them.

The bifurcated regime suggested by the courts that have employed it, moreover, leaves some parents without a remedy. The statute requires, in express terms, that States provide a child with a free appropriate public education "at public expense," including specially designed instruction "at no cost to parents." Parents may seek to enforce this mandate through the federal courts, we conclude, because among the rights they enjoy is the right to a free appropriate public education for their child. Under the countervailing view, which would make a parent's ability to enforce IDEA dependant on certain procedural and reimbursement-related rights, a parent whose disabled child has not received a free appropriate public education would have recourse in the federal courts only under two circumstances: when the parent happens to have some claim related to the procedures employed; and when he or she is able to incur, and has in fact incurred, expenses creating a right to reimbursement. Otherwise the adequacy of the child's education would not be regarded as relevant to any cause of action the parent might bring; and, as a result, only the child could vindicate the right accorded by IDEA to a free appropriate public education.

The potential for injustice in this result is apparent. What is more, we find nothing in the statute to indicate that when Congress required States to provide adequate instruction to a child "at no cost to parents," it intended that only some parents would be able to enforce that mandate. The statute instead takes pains to "ensure that the rights of children with disabilities and parents of such children are protected."

We conclude IDEA grants parents independent, enforceable rights. These rights, which are not limited to certain procedural and reimbursement-related matters, encompass the entitlement to a free appropriate public education for the parents' child.

C

Respondent contends, though, that even under the reasoning we have now explained petitioners cannot prevail without overcoming a further difficulty. Citing our opinion in *Arlington Central School Dist. Bd. of Ed. v. Murphy,* respondent argues that statutes passed pursuant to the Spending Clause, such as IDEA, must provide " 'clear notice' " before they can burden a State with some new condition, obligation, or liability. Respondent contends that because IDEA is, at best, ambiguous as to whether it accords parents independent rights, it has failed to provide clear notice of this condition to the States.

Respondent's reliance on *Arlington* is misplaced. In *Arlington* we addressed whether IDEA required States to reimburse experts' fees to prevailing parties in IDEA actions. "[W]hen Congress attaches conditions to a State's acceptance of federal funds," we explained, "the conditions must be set out 'unambiguously.' " The question to be answered in *Arlington,* therefore, was whether IDEA "furnishes clear notice regarding the liability at issue." We found it did not.

The instant case presents a different issue, one that does not invoke the same rule. Our determination that IDEA grants to parents independent, enforceable rights does not impose any substantive condition or obligation on States they would not otherwise be required by law to observe. The basic measure of monetary recovery, moreover, is not expanded by recognizing that some rights repose in both the parent and the child. Were we considering a statute other than the one before us, the Spending Clause argument might have more force: A determination by the Court that some distinct class of people has independent, enforceable rights might result in a change to the States' statutory obligations. But that is not the case here.

Respondent argues our ruling will, as a practical matter, increase costs borne by the States as they are forced to defend against suits unconstrained by attorneys trained in the law and the rules of ethics. Effects such as these do not suffice to invoke the concerns under the Spending Clause. Furthermore, IDEA does afford relief for the States in certain cases. The Act empowers courts to award attorney's fees to a prevailing educational agency whenever a parent has presented a "complaint or subsequent cause of action . . . for any improper purpose, such as to harass, to cause unnecessary delay, or to needlessly increase the cost of litigation."

This provision allows some relief when a party has proceeded in violation of these standards.

III

The Court of Appeals erred when it dismissed the Winkelmans' appeal for lack of counsel. Parents enjoy rights under IDEA; and they are, as a result, entitled to prosecute IDEA claims on their own behalf. The decision by Congress to grant parents these rights was consistent with the purpose of IDEA and fully in accord with our social and legal traditions. It is beyond dispute that the relationship between a parent and child is sufficient to support a legally cognizable interest in the education of one's child; and, what is more, Congress has found that "the education of children with disabilities can be made more effective by . . . strengthening the role and responsibility of parents and ensuring that families of such children have meaningful opportunities to participate in the education of their children at school and at home."

In light of our holding we need not reach petitioners' alternative argument, which concerns whether IDEA entitles parents to litigate their child's claims *pro se*.

The judgment of the Court of Appeals is reversed, and the case is remanded for further proceedings consistent with this opinion.

It is so ordered.

NOTES

1. Could *Winkelman* have parents seeking further appeals because they poorly represented their cases? Should parents who represented themselves be allowed to raise such claims? Who should bear the costs of these appeals?

2. What might happen if students disagree with their parents over the content of their IEPs? Is it possible that students, and their parents, let alone school officials, could each have different points of view, and attorneys, in disputes over the appropriateness of IEPs?

CHAPTER 16

SCHOOL DESEGREGATION

INTRODUCTION

Brown v. Board of Education, Topeka (Brown I),[1] is the Supreme Court's most significant case involving K–12 education, one of its most important decisions ever.[2] In *Brown I*, the Court struck down de jure segregation, based on law, as opposed to de facto segregation, based on the facts, because it deprived students who were African American of their rights to equal educational opportunities in violation of the Equal Protection Clause of the Fourteenth Amendment.[3] In addition to initiating the litigation on school desegregation that is discussed in this chapter, *Brown I* served as the catalyst leading to fundamental changes in American society.

BROWN V. BOARD OF EDUCATION

"Separate but equal" entered the national legal consciousness in *Plessy v. Ferguson (Plessy)*,[4] a case from Louisiana wherein the Supreme Court, in an eight-to-one judgment, upheld racial discrimination in public railway accommodations. In *Plessy* the Court affirmed the constitutionality of a criminal statute under which the plaintiff, who "was seven-eighths Caucasian and one-eighth African [American] ... the mixture of [which] was not discernible in [him],"[5] was fined for taking a seat in a railway car reserved for whites. The concept traces its origins to an earlier case wherein the Supreme Judicial Court of Massachusetts upheld "separate but equal" in denying a student who was African American the opportunity to attend a school for white children that was closer to her home than the school that

---

1. 347 U.S. 483, 74 S.Ct. 686, 98 L.Ed. 873 (1954). [Case No. 116]

2. A case can be made that the Supreme Court's decision in *Marbury v. Madison*, 5 U.S. (1 Cranch) 137, 2 L. Ed. 60 (1803), wherein the Justices asserted their authority to review actions of the other branches of government rivals *Brown* in significance since it gave the Court the power to engage in judicial review.

3. On the same day that it announced its judgment in *Brown I*, the Court struck down segregation in the public schools of Washington, D.C., reasoning that the practice violated the Due Process Clause of the Fifth Amendment, which applies to the federal government. *Bolling v. Sharpe*, 347 U.S. 497, 74 S.Ct. 693, 98 L.Ed. 884 (1954).

4. 163 U.S. 537, 16 S.Ct. 1138, 41 L.Ed. 256 (1896). Justice Harlan's dissent presaged the Court's opinion in *Brown I*.

5. *Id.* at 541.

she was assigned to attend.[6]

Three years after *Plessy*, in *Cumming v. County Board of Education*,[7] the Supreme Court went even further in upholding laws that established separate schools for whites in Georgia where officials failed to provide comparable schools for children who were African American.[8] The Court feared that enjoining the enforcement of the law would have disadvantaged the white children without providing any advantage to the students who were African American. The Court explicitly extended "separate but equal" to K–12 education in *Gong Lum v. Rice*,[9] a dispute from Mississippi in which it permitted officials to exclude a student of Chinese descent from a public school for white children.

By the time *Brown I* reached the Supreme Court, proponents of equal educational opportunities had begun to make judicial headway in the fight against racial segregation. In *Sweatt v. Painter*[10] and *McLaurin v. Oklahoma State Regents for Higher Education*,[11] the Court repudiated inter and intra institution segregation, respectively, in higher education.[12] In both of these cases the Court emphasized the importance of "intangible factors" in connection with equal educational opportunities. Even so, the Court did not focus on psychological considerations until *Brown I*. Relying in part on the precedent set in these cases, the National Association for the Advancement of Colored People, led by its chief counsel and future Supreme Court Justice Thurgood Marshall, challenged racial segregation in K–12 schools.

Brown I, a class action suit from Kansas, challenged a state law that permitted the exclusion of students who were African American from schools attended by children who were white. *Brown I* also questioned state constitutions and statutes from Delaware, South Carolina, and Virginia that required racially segregated schools.

Unable to reach a decision during its 1952–53 Term, the Supreme Court reheard oral arguments in *Brown I* in December of 1953. The Court handed down its monumental ruling on May 17, 1954. In its analysis, the Court acknowledged that "[t]oday, education is perhaps the most impor-

---

6. *Roberts v. City of Boston*, 59 Mass. (5 Cush.) 198 (1850).

7. 175 U.S. 528, 20 S.Ct. 197, 44 L.Ed. 262 (1899). The opinion was written by Justice Harlan, the sole dissenter in *Plessy*.

8. *See also Berea College v. Kentucky*, 211 U.S. 45, 29 S.Ct. 33, 53 L.Ed. 81 (1908) (upholding a criminal conviction against a private college for teaching African Americans and whites together).

9. 275 U.S. 78, 48 S.Ct. 91, 72 L.Ed. 172 (1927).

10. 339 U.S. 629, 70 S.Ct. 848, 94 L.Ed. 1114 (1950).

11. 339 U.S. 637, 70 S.Ct. 851, 94 L.Ed. 1149 (1950).

12. Previously, the Court was critical of racial segregation in higher education in *State of Missouri ex rel. Gaines v. Canada*, 305 U.S. 337, 59 S.Ct. 232, 83 L.Ed. 208 (1938), *reh'g denied*, 305 U.S. 676, 59 S.Ct. 356, 83 L.Ed. 437 (1939), *mandate conformed to*, 131 S.W.2d 217 (Mo. 1939) (holding that denying a student who was African American admission to a public law school violated the Equal Protection Clause) and *Sipuel v. Board of Regents of Univ. of Okla.*, 332 U.S. 631, 68 S.Ct. 299, 92 L.Ed. 247 (1948), *mandate denied sub nom. Fisher v. Hurst*, 333 U.S. 147, 68 S.Ct. 389, 92 L.Ed. 604 (1948) (although ruling that the state had to integrate a public university or provide a separate facility for African Americans in conformity with the Equal Protection Clause, the Court was satisfied that officials did not violate its order by creating a separate facility in which three faculty members taught the plaintiff rather than allow her to study with white students).

tant function of state and local governments. Compulsory school attendance laws and the great expenditures for education both demonstrate our recognition of the importance of education to our democratic society."[13]

Writing for a unanimous Court, Chief Justice Earl Warren then framed the issue as: "[d]oes segregation of children in public schools solely on the basis of race, even though the physical facilities and other "tangible" factors may be equal, deprive the children of the minority group of equal educational opportunities?[14] The Court answered, "[w]e believe that it does."[15] Relying, in part, on data from the social sciences, in evidence presented by psychologist Dr. Kenneth B. Clark, who testified about the deleterious effect that segregation had on children who were African American,[16] the Court held "that in the field of public education the doctrine of 'separate but equal' has no place. Separate educational facilities are inherently unequal."[17]

As important as *Brown I* was, it was limited to ending segregation. Thus, the Supreme Court conducted further oral arguments to consider remedies. The following year, in *Brown v. Board of Education, Topeka, II* (*Brown II*), the Court directed school officials to act "with all deliberate speed"[18] in implementing its mandate to provide equal educational opportunities for all children regardless of race. While recognizing that additional time might have been necessary to bring about change, the Court set the burden of proof on the need for more time on school boards acting in the public interest and consistent with good faith compliance as soon as practicable. In addition, *Brown II* placed primary responsibility on educational officials to take initial steps to desegregate schools while ordering lower courts to retain their jurisdiction and to evaluate whether the actions of school boards constituted good faith implementation of its dictates.

DELINEATION OF THE CONSTITUTIONAL MANDATE

Brown I and *II* met with less than universal acclaim in many parts of the United States. In *Cooper v. Aaron*,[19] its first post-*Brown* desegregation case, the Supreme Court made it clear that a governor and legislature could not refuse to implement its mandate. A year after President Eisenhower dispatched federal troops to Little Rock, Arkansas, to enforce a desegregation order, the local board sought to postpone the effective date of its plan due to turmoil and hostilities, a situation encouraged by state officials.[20]

---

13.   347 U.S. 483, 493, 74 S.Ct. 686, 98 L.Ed. 873 (1954). [Case No. 116]

14.   *Id.*

15.   *Id.*

16.   *Id.* at 495, note 11.

17.   *Id.* at 495.

18.   349 U.S. 294, 301, 75 S.Ct. 753, 99 L.Ed. 1083 (1955). [Case No. 117]

19.   358 U.S. 1, 78 S.Ct. 1401, 3 L.Ed.2d 5 (1958).

20.   Little Rock, Arkansas, achieved unitary status in 2009. *Little Rock School Dist. v. North Little Rock School Dist.*, 561 F.3d 746 [243 Educ. L. Rep. 14] (8th Cir. 2009).

While expressing some sympathy for the board, the Court rejected its request for a postponement, reminding officials that constitutional rights "are not to be sacrificed or yielded to the violence and disorder which have followed upon the actions of the Governor and Legislature."[21]

The Supreme Court did not address another case involving school desegregation until it reviewed a dispute from Knoxville, Tennessee, five years later. In *Goss v. Board of Education*[22] the Court invalidated a program designed to permit students to request transfers back to their original schools when, after re-zoning, they would have been in racial minorities. The Court rejected the plan, which was based solely on racial factors, due to its concern that this approach would have brought back racial segregation.[23]

Ten years after *Brown I*, in *Griffin v. County School Board of Prince Edward County* (*Griffin*), the Supreme Court declared that "[t]he time for mere 'deliberate speed' had run out."[24] The Justices invalidated a plan designed to close public schools in a county in Virginia while the commonwealth contributed to the support of private segregated white schools. Noting that the plan would have denied African American students the right to equal protection, the Court pointed out that they were entitled to immediate relief.

The next year, in *Rogers v. Paul*,[25] the Supreme Court ruled in favor of students in Arkansas who were African American in their challenge to a plan that would have desegregated only one grade per year. The Justices determined that while full implementation of a desegregation plan was pending, students were entitled to immediate transfers to schools from which they were excluded due to their races and which had programs offering more extensive course offerings.

In *Green v. County School Board of New Kent County* (*Green*)[26] the Supreme Court considered freedom-of-choice plans for the first time. Realizing that little progress had been made in breaking down a dual or segregated system in Virginia since *Brown I*, the Court explained that the school board bore the burden of developing a realistic desegregation plan. While not expressly striking the plan down, the Justices thought that if other reasonably available remedies such as zoning could have been used to achieve quicker and more effective conversions to unitary or desegregated status, freedom-of-choice plans were unacceptable. In its rationale, the Court enunciated the six so-called *Green* factors that continue to be a key measure in evaluating whether dual systems have achieved unitary status.

21. 358 U.S. 1, 16, 78 S.Ct. 1401, 1409, 3 L.Ed.2d 5 (1958).

22. 373 U.S. 683, 83 S.Ct. 1405, 10 L.Ed.2d 632 (1963).

23. *See also McNeese v. Board of Educ., Community Unit School Dist. 187*, 373 U.S. 668, 83 S.Ct. 1433, 10 L.Ed.2d 622 (1963) (positing that an aggrieved party did not have to exhaust administrative remedies in state court before turning to the federal courts for relief).

24. 377 U.S. 218, 234, 84 S.Ct. 1226, 12 L.Ed.2d 256 (1964).

25. 382 U.S. 198, 86 S.Ct. 358, 15 L.Ed.2d 265 (1965).

26. 391 U.S. 430, 88 S.Ct. 1689, 20 L.Ed.2d 716 (1968).

These factors address the composition of a student body, faculty, staff, transportation, extracurricular activities, and facilities.[27]

Dissatisfied with the slow pace of implementing desegregation, in *Alexander v. Holmes County Board of Education* (*Alexander*), the first case under then recently appointed Chief Justice Warren Burger, the Supreme Court discarded the "all deliberate speed" standard. Instead, the Court asserted that "the obligation of every school district [is] to terminate dual school systems at once and to operate now and hereafter only unitary schools."[28] Reversing judgments that granted time extensions to school boards in Mississippi, the Court found that dual systems immediately had to give way to unitary districts while objections and amendments to court-ordered plans could be heard only after systems achieved unitary status.

REMEDIES FOR DE JURE SEGREGATION

The immediate impact of the Supreme Court's declaration in *Alexander* led to a multitude of lower court orders for desegregating dual systems. To the extent that the lower courts called for a variety of arrangements, inconsistencies appeared over precisely what was constitutionally required and by what techniques desegregation could be achieved. The Court addressed these issues in *Swann v. Charlotte–Mecklenburg Board of Education* (*Swann*),[29] delineating the responsibilities of school officials in desegregating a dual school system.

Swann is noteworthy for two reasons. First, *Swann* was the Supreme Court's last unanimous judgment in a major school desegregation case. Second, *Swann* is the first case in which the Court examined the use of busing to achieve school desegregation. *Swann* involved a federal trial court in North Carolina's approval, and the Fourth Circuit's modification, of a plan creating restructured attendance zones that relied on busing to bring about a greater racial balance in the schools. Conceding that it could not establish rigid guidelines for busing, the Court noted that if assigning children to neighborhood schools did not effectively dismantle segregated schools, a federal trial court could employ busing to implement an equitable solution.

As part of its analysis in *Swann*, the Supreme Court discussed matters that it had not reviewed extensively. As to school construction, the Court maintained that in devising remedies for de jure segregation, officials and the courts had to ensure that future construction and abandonment is not used to perpetuate or re-establish dual systems. Turning to one-race schools, the Court observed that where a proposed plan for conversion from

27. For cases applying these factors, *see, e,g., Robinson v. Shelby County Bd. of Educ.*, 566 F.3d 642 [244 Educ. L. Rep.934] (6th Cir. 2009); *Smiley v. Blevins*, 626 F. Supp.2d 659 [247 Educ. L. Rep.177] (S.D. Tex. 2009); *United States v. Alamance–Burlington Bd. of Educ.*, 640 F. Supp.2d 670 [249 Educ. L. Rep.232] (M.D.N.C. 2009).

28. 396 U.S. 19, 20, 90 S.Ct. 29, 24 L.Ed.2d 19 (1969).

29. 402 U.S. 1, 91 S.Ct. 1267, 28 L.Ed.2d 554 (1971). [Case No. 118]

a dual to a unitary system considered the continued existence of some schools that were all or predominately of one race, officials had to have proven that such assignments were genuinely nondiscriminatory. The Justices added that while it is unnecessary for every school in a district to reflect a system's racial composition as a whole, a federal trial court may apply a racial ratio or quota as a starting point in shaping a remedy since so-called "racially neutral" assignment plans are insufficient to counteract the continuing effects of past segregation. Looking to the future, the Court indicated that boards did not have to make annual adjustments in the racial compositions of student bodies once they ended segregation.

The Supreme Court handed down two similar judgments on the same day in refusing to permit city school districts to be carved out of segregated county systems since doing so would have slowed down their shifts to unitary status. The difference was that in *Wright v. City Council of Emporia*[30] the motivation for change came from city officials in Virginia, while in *United States v. Scotland Neck City Board of Education*[31] the impetus came from the legislature in North Carolina.

Another novel issue before the Supreme Court was the scope and authority of the federal judiciary in remedying de jure segregation. The Court addressed whether adjacent districts that were heavily populated by whites could have been required to participate in remedies where de jure segregated systems contained such high percentages of students who were African American that meaningful racial mixing could not have taken place. In *Milliken v. Bradley* (*Milliken I*),[32] the first major defeat for supporters of school desegregation since *Brown I*, the Court rejected such a remedy absent proof that the state or surrounding districts were involved in discriminatory acts.

Milliken I involved a federal trial court's order which called for a multi-district, area-wide remedy that would have required fifty-three sub-urban districts to participate in the process of desegregating schools in Detroit, Michigan. The trial court contended that insofar as Detroit's schools were already segregated and proposed remedies would have exacerbated the situation, it had to go beyond district boundaries in crafting a remedy. A closely divided Supreme Court reversed in believing that the inter-district remedy was inappropriate.[33] The Court remarked that absent evidence that they were segregated or that their boundaries were created in order to promote segregation, the suburban boards were not accountable, especially since they did not even have a chance to present their case or to participate in developing the proposed remedy.

---

30.   407 U.S. 451, 92 S.Ct. 2196, 33 L.Ed.2d 51 (1972).

31.   407 U.S. 484, 92 S.Ct. 2214, 33 L.Ed.2d 75 (1972).

32.   418 U.S. 717, 94 S.Ct. 3112, 41 L.Ed.2d 1069 (1974). [Case No. 119]

33.   Despite *Milliken I*, later cases permitted inter-district remedies. *See, e.g., Newburg Area Council v. Board of Educ. of Jefferson County, Ky.*, 510 F.2d 1358 (6th Cir.1974), *cert. denied*, 421 U.S. 931, 95 S. Ct. 1658, 44 L. Ed.2d 88 (1975); *United States v. Board of School Commr's of the City of Indianapolis*, 503 F.2d 68 (7th Cir.1974), *cert. denied*, 421 U.S. 929, 95 S.Ct. 1655, 44 L.Ed.2d 86 (1975); *Hoots v. Commonwealth of Pa.*, 672 F.2d 1107 [3 Educ. L. Rep. 244] (3d Cir.1982), *cert. denied sub nom. Swissvale Area School Dist. v. Hoots*, 459 U.S. 824, 103 S.Ct. 55, 74 L.Ed.2d 60 (1982), *reh'g denied*, 459 U.S. 1058, 103 S.Ct. 476, 74 L.Ed.2d 624 (1982).

On remand in *Milliken I*, a federal trial court's proposed remedy created student assignment and remedial plans for the Detroit schools while directing the state to share equally in their cost. In *Milliken v. Bradley II*,[34] the Court affirmed that the remedy was appropriate since the trial court based its judgment on substantial evidence aimed at eradicating the vestiges of de jure segregation. In affording a measure of vindication for supporters of school desegregation, the Court concluded that the lower court acted within its jurisdiction in ordering prospective relief and requiring the state to share fiscal responsibility for implementing the remedy.[35]

The Supreme Court first addressed de facto segregation in *Keyes v. School District No. 1, Denver, Colorado (Keyes)*.[36] In K*eyes*, the Court was of the view that the actions of school officials may have the effect of creating de jure segregation. As such, the case is addressed here rather than under de facto segregation. *Keyes* was also the first case in which the Court specified that another minority group, students who were Mexican American, should be placed in the same category as children who were African American since both suffered from the effects of segregated schools.

In *Keyes*, the Supreme Court affirmed earlier findings of de jure segregation in one section of Denver that were caused by the school board's establishment of school sites and attendance zones which created and maintained segregated schools, thereby, in effect, creating a spatial presumption when defining segregation. Even though the schools were not segregated by law or the state constitution, the Court was convinced that the board's actions led to the creation of a core of inner-city schools to serve minority students that were inferior to those educating children in predominately white schools in the rest of the city. Based on its recognition that the board's action gave rise to a prima facie case of intentional discrimination, the Court shifted the burden to school officials to prove that they had not deliberately created segregated schools.

Resolved three years after *Keyes*, *Pasadena City Board of Education v. Spangler*[37] was the Supreme Court's first desegregation case from California. The Court stated that once a school district achieved unitary status, its board was not obligated to make annual readjustments in attendance zones to reflect demographic changes in population.

In the subsequent round of litigation the Supreme Court examined remedies for de jure segregation, beginning with a dispute over questions of proof and the function of the federal judiciary. The Sixth Circuit, having twice invalidated a remedy as inadequate, upheld an extensive system-wide

---

34. 433 U.S. 267, 97 S.Ct. 2749, 53 L.Ed.2d 745 (1977). [Case No. 120]

35. The Court reached a like result with regard to a state's duty to pay for a remedy in *Missouri v. Jenkins III*, 515 U.S. 70, 115 S.Ct. 2038, 132 L.Ed.2d 63 [100 Educ. L. Rep. 506] (1995), *appeal after remand, Jenkins v. Missouri*, 103 F.3d 731 [115 Educ. L. Rep. 302] (8th Cir.1997). *See also United States v. Board of School Commr's of City of Indianapolis*, 677 F.2d 1185 [4 Educ. L. Rep. 447] (7th Cir.1982), *cert. denied sub nom. Orr v. Board of School Commr's of City of Indianapolis*, 459 U.S. 1086, 103 S.Ct. 568, 74 L.Ed.2d 931 (1982) (placing the entire burden of paying for an inter-district remedy on the state where it was solely responsible for the violations).

36. 413 U.S. 189, 93 S.Ct. 2686, 37 L.Ed.2d 548 (1973). [Case No. 121]

37. 427 U.S. 424, 96 S.Ct. 2697, 49 L.Ed.2d 599 (1976).

busing plan for Dayton, Ohio. However, in *Dayton Board of Education v. Brinkman*,[38] the Court vacated and remanded in writing that where the board's actions did not have a system-wide effect, the judicial remedy had to be narrowly tailored to apply only to schools that were adversely impacted by the board's actions. On remand, the Sixth Circuit held that a system-wide remedy was warranted. In *Dayton Board of Education v. Brinkman (Dayton II)*,[39] the Court affirmed that where board actions at least partially contributed to the district's being segregated, officials had to act to rid the entire system of discrimination.[40]

On the same day that the Supreme Court resolved *Dayton II*, it considered a second case from Ohio in which a federal trial court and the Sixth Circuit agreed on a system-wide remedy. In *Columbus Board of Education v. Penick*,[41] the Court affirmed that in light of proof of the long-standing intentional segregation imposed by the local board, a system-wide remedy was appropriate. According to the Court, local officials preserved a segregated system by assigning teachers who were African American only to schools with predominantly African American student bodies, manipulating attendance zones, and making site selections for new schools that had the foreseeable and anticipated effect of preserving racial separation in schools.

In *Missouri v. Jenkins (Jenkins II)*,[42] the Supreme Court examined the financing of desegregation remedies. After lower federal courts essentially agreed that Kansas City and the State of Missouri had to finance a desegregation order, the local board claimed that it was unable to raise its share of the funds without violating state school finance and taxing laws. The Court affirmed that while the federal judiciary cannot impose tax increases, it can require boards to levy property taxes at rates adequate to fund desegregation remedies and can enjoin the operation of statutes that prevented the board from complying with its order. The Court relied on the need to enforce the Equal Protection Clause and *Griffin* wherein it posited that if public schools were closed in one county to avoid desegregation, courts could require a county legislative body to levy taxes to preserve a desegregated district. *Jenkins II* was the last Supreme Court victory for proponents of school desegregation.

The Supreme Court next examined when officials in a formerly unitary system did enough to remedy segregation. In a dispute involving a more than twenty-year-old desegregation decree,[43] *Board of Education of Okla-*

---

38.   433 U.S. 406, 97 S.Ct. 2766, 53 L.Ed.2d 851 (1977).

39.   443 U.S. 526, 99 S.Ct. 2971, 61 L.Ed.2d 720 (1979).

40.   The court-ordered remedy for busing in Dayton, the last school system in Ohio operating under such an order, terminated in April 2002. Scott Elliott, *Desegregation Busing Ends; Pact Avoids Court Hearing*, DAYTON DAILY NEWS, April 16, 2002, at A1.

41.   443 U.S. 449, 99 S.Ct. 2941, 61 L.Ed.2d 666 (1979).

42.   495 U.S. 33, 110 S.Ct. 1651, 109 L.Ed.2d 31 [59 Educ. L. Rep. 298] (1990), *subsequent appeal, Jenkins v. Missouri*, 949 F.2d 1052 [71 Educ. L. Rep. 409] (8th Cir.1991). The Court refused to hear an appeal in an earlier iteration of this case, *cert. denied, Missouri v. Jenkins I*, 484 U.S. 816, 108 S.Ct. 70, 98 L.Ed.2d 34 [42 Educ. L. Rep. 34] (1987).

43.   For the earlier litigation, *see Dowell v. Board of Educ. of Oklahoma City Pub. Schools*, 396 U.S. 269, 90 S.Ct. 415, 24 L.Ed.2d 414 (1969) (holding that a federal trial court's approval of the board's plan for furthering desegregation of selected city schools by revising attendance

homa City Public Schools v. Dowell,[44] the Court decided that insofar as desegregation orders are not meant to operate in perpetuity, the judiciary had to consider whether local boards acted in good faith in eliminating the vestiges of past discrimination as far as practicable.[45] The Court acknowledged that in addressing whether a board remedied the vestiges of past discrimination, a court had to take the six *Green* factors into consideration.

A year later the Supreme Court addressed another question of first impression over whether judicial supervision of a desegregation order can be achieved incrementally. In *Freeman v. Pitts*,[46] the Justices, relying on a federal trial court in Georgia's application of the *Green* factors, remanded for further consideration. The Court declared that insofar as equity required the adjustment of remedies in a feasible and practical manner that returned control of school systems to regular educational officials, federal trial courts can relinquish control over desegregation plans incrementally as long as they are content that boards made good faith commitments to comply with their orders.[47]

In *Missouri v. Jenkins III (Jenkins III)*,[48] the Supreme Court revisited the ongoing litigation in Kansas City, Missouri. This time the Court thought lower federal courts exceeded their discretion in mandating a costly desegregation remedy. The trial court had ordered the state to pay for both across-the-board salary increases for virtually all personnel and quality education programs including the creation of a comprehensive magnet school[49] and a capital improvements plan, at a total cost of more than $1.3 billion dollars, since student achievement was still at or below national norms on many grade levels.[50]

---

boundaries was not inappropriate prior to consideration and adoption of a comprehensive plan for complete desegregation of the district).

44. 498 U.S. 237, 111 S.Ct. 630, 112 L.Ed.2d 715 [64 Educ. L. Rep. 628] (1991), *on remand*, 778 F.Supp. 1144 [71 Educ. L. Rep. 741] (W.D. Okla.1991), *aff'd sub nom. Dowell v. Board of Educ. of Oklahoma City Pub. Schools*, 8 F.3d 1501 [87 Educ. L. Rep. 67] (10th Cir.1993). [Case No. 122]

45. *See also, e.g., Anderson v. School Bd. of Madison County*, 517 F.3d 292 [230 Educ. L. Rep. 139] (5th Cir. 2008); *Manning v. School Bd. of Hillsborough County*, 244 F.3d 927 [152 Educ. L. Rep. 51],*cert. denied*, 534 U.S. 824, 122 S.Ct. 61, 151 L.Ed.2d 28 (2001); *People Who Care v. Rockford Bd. of Educ. School Dist. No. 205*, 246 F.3d 1073 [152 Educ. L. Rep. 543] (7th Cir. 2001); *Lockett v. Board of Educ. of Muscogee County School Dist.*, 111 F.3d 839 [117 Educ. L. Rep. 487] (11th Cir.1997), *reh'g en banc denied*, 121 F.3d 724 (11th Cir.1997).

46. 503 U.S. 467, 112 S.Ct. 1430, 118 L.Ed.2d 108 [72 Educ. L. Rep. 717] (1992), *on remand*, 979 F.2d 1472 [78 Educ. L. Rep. 696] (11th Cir.1992), *on remand*, 942 F.Supp. 1449 [114 Educ. L. Rep. 178] (N.D. Ga.1996), *aff'd*, 118 F.3d 727 [119 Educ. L. Rep. 844] (11th Cir.1997). [Case No. 123]

47. *See also Belk v. Charlotte–Mecklenburg Bd. of Educ.*, 269 F.3d 305 [158 Educ. L. Rep. 86] (4th Cir.2001), *cert. denied sub nom. Capacchione v. Charlotte–Mecklenburg Bd. of Educ.*, 535 U.S. 986, 122 S.Ct. 1537, 152 L.Ed.2d 465 (2002); *Holton v. City of Thomasville School Dist.*, 425 F.3d 1325 [202 Educ. L. Rep. 54] (11th Cir. 2005).

48. 515 U.S. 70, 115 S.Ct. 2038, 132 L.Ed.2d 63 [100 Educ. L. Rep. 506] (1995). [Case No. 124]

49. For another case involving magnet schools, *see Hernandez v. Board of Educ. of Stockton Unified School Dist.*, 25 Cal.Rptr.3d 1 [195 Educ. L. Rep. 919] (Cal. Ct. App. 2004) (affirming that state funding for magnet schools did not violate the state constitutional prohibition against racial discrimination in education for two years since the district achieved unitary status).

50. In a related dispute, *Jenkins v. Kansas City Missouri School Dist.*, 516 F.3d 1074 [229 Educ. L. Rep. 414] (8th Cir. 2008), *reh'g and reh'g en banc denied* (2008), the Eighth Circuit

The gap since *Jenkins III*, the longest time period within which the Supreme Court has not addressed a K–12 school desegregation case since *Brown I*, illustrates its disengagement in this important arena.[51] Moreover, as evidence of ongoing disputes, the Department of Justice's Fiscal Year 2011 Performance Budget for its Civil Rights Division reports that it continues "to monitor 308 school districts currently covered by desegregation orders in cases in which the United States is a party"[52] even as federal courts continue to release some,[53] but not all,[54] school systems from judicial oversight.

TEACHER DESEGREGATION

The Supreme Court did not address faculty desegregation until more than a decade after *Brown I*. When the desegregation plan for Richmond, Virginia, failed to contain a provision for faculty assignments, the Fourth Circuit refused to treat this omission as a reason to reject the proposed remedy. The lower court asserted that after it eliminated all direct discrimination in student assignments, it could examine the effect of teacher assignments on schools. In *Bradley v. School Board, City of Richmond (Bradley)*,[55] the Court noted that the case should have been remanded for hearings over the claim that staff racial assignments affected students. The Justices ascertained that there was no merit to the suggestion that the relationship between faculty allocations on an alleged racial basis and the adequacy of desegregation plans was entirely speculative. In refusing to postpone proposed hearings, the Court reasoned that it had to act because more than a decade passed since it called for the desegregation of public school facilities "with all deliberate speed."

affirmed that the state could not be required to use funds designed to desegregate public schools for a charter school. For another case involving a charter school, *see Cleveland v. Union Parish School Bd.*, 570 F.Supp.2d 858 [237 Educ. L. Rep. 220] (W.D. La. 2008) (refusing to allow a charter school to open because it would have undermined a desegregation decree by promoting resegregation).

51. Insofar as the school systems in Seattle, Washington, and Louisville, Kentucky, were not operating under judicially mandated desegregation remedies when their race-conscious admissions plans were challenged, *Parents Involved in Community Schools v. Seattle School Dist. No. 1*, 551 U.S. 701, 127 S.Ct. 2738, 168 L.Ed.2d 508 [220 Educ. L. Rep. 84] (2007). [Case No. 88], is not treated as a desegregation case.

52. U.S. Department of Justice, FY 2011 Performance Budget, Civil Rights Division, Congressional Submission, http://www.justice.gov/jmd/2011justification/pdf/fy11–crt-justification.pdf at 14

53. *See, e.g., Anderson v. School Bd. of Madison County*, 517 F.3d 292 [230 Educ. L. Rep. 139] (5th Cir. 2008) (affirming the termination of a desegregation order that had been in effect since 1969); *Robinson v. Shelby County Bd. of Educ.*, 566 F.3d 642 [244 Educ. L. Rep. 934 (6th Cir. 2009) (terminating a plan that was implemented in 1965); *United States v. Alamance–Burlington Bd. of Educ.*, 640 F.Supp.2d 670 [249 Educ. L. Rep. 232] (M.D.N.C. 2009) (dissolving an order that had been in place since 1971); *Smiley v. Blevins*, 626 F.Supp.2d 659 [247 Educ. L. Rep. 177] (S.D. Tex. 2009) (terminating a plan that was implemented in 1961).

54. For a case where the Ninth Circuit denied a motion for unitary status, *see Fisher v. Tucson Unified School Dist.*, 652 F.3d 1131 (9th Cir. 2011) (holding that officials who adopted a desegregation plan promising future improvements failed to demonstrate past good faith).

55. 382 U.S. 103, 86 S.Ct. 224, 15 L.Ed.2d 187 (1965).

Following *Bradley*, progress in desegregation of school faculties continued at a slower pace than for students. The lack of a clear test to apply for faculty desegregation made it difficult for lower federal courts to formulate decrees to help prevent delays. In *United States v. Montgomery County Board of Education*,[56] the Supreme Court upheld a plan under which the goal for faculty desegregation was that each school in a district in Alabama would have approximately the same ratio of African American and white teachers as existed in the system as a whole.

A year later, the Fifth Circuit, in an appeal of cases from states throughout the Southeast, *Singleton v. Jackson Municipal Separate School District*, (*Singleton*),[57] adopted the ratio concept as a guide for integrating teaching staffs in the so-called *Singleton* criteria. The Fifth Circuit later explained that at the time of its initial judgment, the trial court should have insisted on immediate steps to assure that the composition of the faculty in each school reflected the district-wide racial ratio of faculty members and that all teachers accept reassignment as a condition of continued employment.[58] In the latter case, the trial court accepted the slow pace of faculty change predicated on the board's claim that a more rapid pace would have caused "white flight" among the faculty. The Fifth Circuit retorted that the fear of faculty resistance to desegregation measures, like the fear of community resistance, could not be the basis for failing to adopt the plan most likely to achieve a unitary system.

Other legal issues impacting teachers in the desegregation process arose over the non-retention of many African Americans. In states lacking tenure laws, judicial review was the only effective remedy available to teachers. The courts took the history of racial discrimination and the failure of many public school systems to desegregate into account in light of the suddenly disproportionate reduction in the ranks of teachers who were African American. This increase gave rise to an inference of discrimination, thereby placing the burden of proof on boards to justify their actions by setting up objective employment standards for teacher hiring and retention.

In a case from North Carolina in which the Fourth Circuit first enunciated the principle of equal treatment, white teachers who wished to be retained were able to keep their jobs while sixteen out of twenty-four African American teachers who worked the previous year were not re-hired.[59] The court pointed out that African American teachers who were no longer needed due to a reduction of enrollment by minority students in their schools were entitled to hiring preferences over new candidates as long as this arrangement was used for white teachers.[60]

---

56.   395 U.S. 225, 89 S.Ct. 1670, 23 L.Ed.2d 263 (1969).

57.   419 F.2d 1211 (5th Cir.1969), *cert. denied*, 396 U.S. 1032, 90 S.Ct. 612, 24 L.Ed.2d 530 (1970).

58.   *United States v. DeSoto Parish School Bd.*, 574 F.2d 804 (5th Cir. 1978), *cert. denied*, 439 U.S. 982, 99 S.Ct. 571, 58 L.Ed.2d 653 (1978).

59.   *Chambers v. Hendersonville City Bd. of Educ.*, 364 F.2d 189 (4th Cir. 1966).

60.   *North Carolina Teachers Ass'n v. Asheboro City Bd. of Educ.*, 393 F.2d 736 (4th Cir. 1968).

Courts in states where de jure segregation was the norm followed the Fourth Circuit's lead. For example, the Fifth Circuit, in applying the *Singleton* criteria, pointed out that the objective and reasonable non-discriminatory standards which applied in cases of dismissal or demotion had to have been developed prior to a staff reduction.[61] The court was of the opinion that no staff vacancy could have been filled through recruitment of a person of a race, color, or national origin different from that of the individual who was dismissed or demoted until each qualified displaced staff member was offered an opportunity to fill the vacancy. Conversely, the Fifth Circuit thought that the criteria applicable to dismissal or demotion during a staff reduction due to desegregation was inapplicable to personnel actions which occurred when there was no reduction, even if a school system was still in the desegregation process.[62]

The Fifth Circuit, in a series of cases, added that reductions invoking the *Singleton* criteria should be measured by appropriate subclasses such as high school teachers and/or principals, rather than by overall figures.[63] As to demotions, since the court was concerned that responsibility is the central value to be protected,[64] individuals could have been considered to have been demoted even though they received salary increases.[65] Yet, where a principal was named an administrative assistant to a superintendent, the court did not treat this as a demotion despite the change of title.[66] Finally, where a demotion was at issue, the court observed that the *Singleton* criteria placed the burden of proof on a plaintiff to show that there was, in fact, a demotion.[67]

Cases involving non-retention of individual teachers who were African American led to important results. In a dispute from North Carolina, a school board chose not to renew the contract of an African American teacher with thirteen years of experience and a masters degree even though the African American principal in her African American school recommended that she be rehired. When the superintendent notified the principal that the teaching staff at the school was to be reduced for the next year because, under a newly instituted freedom-of-choice plan, the number of African American students transferring to formerly all-white schools reduced enrollment, he did not provide instructions on how to reduce staff. Once the teacher was informed that she was not going to retain her position, the superintendent suggested that she apply for a job at other schools in the county. When the female was unable to procure employment in any of the schools, a federal trial court deferred to the board's choosing not to rehire the teacher.[68] On appeal, a unanimous en banc panel of the Fourth Circuit reversed in favor of the teacher, maintaining that she was

---

61. *Singleton v. Jackson Mun. Separate School Dist.*, 419 F.2d 1211 (5th Cir.1969), *cert. denied*, 396 U.S. 1032, 90 S.Ct. 612, 24 L.Ed.2d 530 (1970).

62. *Wright v. Houston Indep. School Dist.*, 569 F.2d 1383 (5th Cir. 1978).

63. *Pickens v. Okolona Mun. Separate School Dist.*, 527 F.2d 358 (5th Cir. 1976).

64. *Lee v. Russell County Bd. of Educ.*, 563 F.2d 1159 (5th Cir. 1977).

65. *Lee v. Macon County Bd. of Educ.*, 453 F.2d 1104 (5th Cir. 1971).

66. *Lee v. Macon County Bd. of Educ.*, 470 F.2d 958 (5th Cir. 1972).

67. *Lee v. Pickens County School Sys.*, 563 F.2d 143 (5th Cir. 1977).

68. *Wall v. Stanly County Bd. of Educ.*, 259 F.Supp. 238 (M.D.N.C.1966).

entitled to the opportunity to be considered objectively for re-employment with the burden of justifying a failure to rehire placed on the board.[69]

Desegregating a teaching staff was clearly an essential element in correcting de jure segregation of students. As such, court orders were premised on the rights of students and were not confined to actions necessary to vindicate the rights of teachers who were African American. The First Circuit made this point when it upheld a desegregation order in a dispute from Boston.[70] The court wrote that insofar as the school system had not achieved unitary status with regard to hiring faculty and administrative staff, officials had a continuing duty to reach set hiring goals for minority candidates.[71] The Third Circuit agreed in principle in rejecting a suit by four white teachers from Pennsylvania who sought to invalidate a racial ratio for staff assignments in a district after commonwealth officials released it from a requirement that was imposed as a condition of eligibility for federal funds.[72] The next year, the Sixth Circuit affirmed the ongoing use of the same kind of faculty teacher assignment policy, rejecting a challenge from teachers who claimed that it violated equal protection and conflicted with their collective bargaining contract.[73] The court determined that the plan was substantially related to the important governmental objective of achieving a racially integrated faculty throughout the district and did not conflict with the bargaining contract. The court was satisfied that involuntary transfers and denials of requests for voluntary transfers had a race-neutral impact.

The Supreme Court refused to hear an appeal in a case from New York involving a plan approved by the Second Circuit for preserving elements of a teacher desegregation program that required hiring of minority teachers and considering seniority rights of majority teachers during a period of layoffs due to fiscal problems and declining enrollments.[74] The court rejected claims that state law or collective bargaining contracts could prevail over the constitutional mandate to eliminate vestiges of de jure segregation from an urban system that were being perpetuated in its teaching staff. The court upheld a percentage layoff plan but struck down one of its aspects as needlessly harsh in its treatment of recall rights of laid-off probationary and permanent teachers.

In *Wygant v. Jackson Board of Education (Wygant)*,[75] the Supreme

---

69. *Wall v. Stanly County Bd. of Educ.*, 378 F.2d 275 (4th Cir.1967).

70. *Morgan v. Kerrigan*, 509 F.2d 599 (1st Cir.1975). *See also Morgan v. Kerrigan*, 509 F.2d 580 (1st Cir.1974), *cert. denied*, 421 U.S. 963, 95 S.Ct. 1950, 44 L.Ed.2d 449 (1975).

71. *Morgan v. Burke*, 926 F.2d 86 [65 Educ. L. Rep. 1075] (1st Cir.), *cert. denied sub nom. Boston Teachers Union Local 66 v. Morgan*, 503 U.S. 983, 112 S.Ct. 1664, 118 L.Ed.2d 386 (1992).

72. *Kromnick v. School Dist. of Philadelphia*, 739 F.2d 894 [19 Educ. L. Rep. 52] (3d Cir. 1984), *cert. denied*, 469 U.S. 1107, 105 S.Ct. 782, 83 L.Ed.2d 777 [21 Educ. L. Rep. 1157] (1985).

73. *Jacobson v. Cincinnati Bd. of Educ.*, 961 F.2d 100 [74 Educ. L. Rep. 51] (6th Cir.1992), *cert. denied*, 506 U.S. 830, 113 S.Ct. 94, 121 L.Ed.2d 55 (1992).

74. *Arthur v. Nyquist*, 712 F.2d 816 [12 Educ. L. Rep. 663] (2d Cir.1983), *cert. denied*, 467 U.S. 1259, 104 S.Ct. 3555, 82 L.Ed.2d 856 [19 Educ. L. Rep. 23] (1984).

75. *Wygant v. Jackson Bd. of Educ.*, 476 U.S. 267, 106 S.Ct. 1842, 90 L.Ed.2d 260 [32 Educ. L. Rep. 20] (1986), *reh'g denied*, 478 U.S. 1014, 106 S.Ct. 3320, 92 L.Ed.2d 728 [35 Educ. L. Rep. 20] (1986).

Court invalidated a plan from Michigan that was reached through collective bargaining to cover layoffs even though there was no discrimination prior to its implementation. Under the provision, the seniority basis for layoffs was to be adjusted so that at no time would there be a greater percent of minority personnel whose contracts were terminated than the current percent of minority staff who were employed when a reduction-in-force (RIF) went into effect. This approach led to layoffs of white teachers who were senior to African Americans who were retained. A plurality of the Court vitiated the plan as violating equal protection. According to the plurality, while layoffs placed the entire burden of achieving racial equality on particular individuals, hiring goals were a less intrusive means of accomplishing similar purposes since the burden that had to be borne by innocent individuals was diffused to a considerable extent among society generally.[76]

The Second Circuit applied *Wygant* in rejecting a RIF plan that would have removed only white teachers in Connecticut.[77] The court emphasized that even though a RIF plan had to have been narrowly tailored, a proportional layoff scheme could have been developed where an earlier consent decree failed to address layoffs. Instead, the court held that the bargaining agreement spoke in terms of preserving gains made, suggesting that laying off teachers from only one race in an effort to remedy past injustices was an impermissible means toward reaching a legitimate end. The panel directed the trial court to consider whether there was a strong rationale for ruling that hiring practices contributed to creating a segregated school system before crafting such a remedy.

Another case involving RIF was days away from oral argument before the Supreme Court when the parties reached a settlement.[78] At issue was a dispute from New Jersey wherein a school board, mistakenly acting on its belief that its affirmative action program required it to terminate the contract of a white, rather than African American, teacher based solely on race, dismissed the white woman even though the two had virtually identical credentials. An en banc Third Circuit affirmed that insofar as the board's plan, which was adopted to promote racial diversity rather than remedying discrimination or the effects of past discrimination, trammeled the rights of non-minorities, it was unconstitutional.[79]

DE FACTO SEGREGATION

DEFINITION AND SCOPE

---

76. For another case where a plaintiff prevailed in challenging a race-based policy in conjunction with a RIF, *see Cunico v. Pueblo School Dist. No. 60*, 917 F.2d 431 [63 Educ. L. Rep. 713] (10th Cir. 1990).

77. *Crumpton v. Bridgeport Educ. Ass'n*, 993 F.2d 1023 [83 Educ. L. Rep. 63] (2d Cir. 1993).

78. Mark Walsh, *N.J. District Settles Case on Race Bias: Action Heads off High Court Review*, EDUCATION WEEK, Nov. 26, 1997, at 1, 22.

79. *Taxman v. Board of Educ. of the Twp. of Piscataway*, 91 F.3d 1547 [111 Educ. L. Rep. 696] (3d Cir.1996), *cert. granted*, 521 U.S. 1117, 117 S.Ct. 2506, 138 L.Ed.2d 1010 [122 Educ. L. Rep. 389] (1997), *cert. dismissed*, 522 U.S. 1010, 118 S.Ct. 595, 139 L.Ed.2d 431 [122 Educ. L. Rep. 570] (1997).

De facto, as opposed to de jure, segregation occurs when, without governmental action or inaction, a substantial majority of students in schools are of the same racial or ethnic minority. Since *Brown I* and *II* began a line of cases focused on de jure segregation in public schools, de facto segregation remained ripe for judicial review.

Outside of the South, some local educational officials gerrymandered attendance zones and/or took other steps to contribute to keeping large concentrations of African Americans in segregated schools. Remedying such actions came under *Brown II's* auspices since the segregation in question came about due to governmental action. Thus, although often referred to as de facto, such actions were really covert de jure segregation.

An early leading case of "false de facto" segregation came from New York where the Second Circuit held that a school board realigned attendance boundaries and, until about ten years earlier, permitted transfers of white, but not African American, students within the area of a school where more than ninety percent of the student body was African American.[80] The court viewed the purpose and effect of the board's approach as being designed to produce a substantially segregated school in violation of the Fourteenth Amendment as a form of de jure segregation.

Courts agreed that "false de facto" segregation had to be corrected. For instance, a federal trial court in California indicated that school board action, and inaction, caused a pattern of racial imbalance involving students and staff.[81] The court realized that board officials redrew attendance zone lines from time to time while adhering to policies calling for neighborhood schools and opposing forced cross-town busing even as staff-assignment policies created racial imbalances. When ordered to submit a plan to remedy the situation, the board complied and parents unsuccessfully petitioned the Ninth Circuit.[82] When the board sought to avoid having to implement the plan due to changed circumstances, most notably, alleged "white flight," the Ninth Circuit again denied relief.[83]

In a like case from Michigan, the Sixth Circuit recognized that school officials purposefully segregated students who were African American over a long period of time.[84] Even though officials tried to alleviate racial imbalances, since the court discerned that they were inadequate it approved a remedial plan that included busing to cure the effects of years of segregation. On appeal, the court rejected the argument of the board's attorney that the plan would have required it to expend large sums of

---

80. *Taylor v. Board of Educ. of City School Dist. of New Rochelle*, 294 F.2d 36 (2d Cir.1961), *cert. denied*, 368 U.S. 940, 82 S.Ct. 382, 7 L.Ed.2d 339 (1961).

81. *Spangler v. Pasadena City Bd. of Educ.*, 311 F.Supp. 501 (C.D. Cal.1970).

82. *Spangler v. Pasadena City Bd. of Educ.*, 427 F.2d 1352 (9th Cir.1970), *cert. denied*, 402 U.S. 943, 91 S.Ct. 1607, 29 L.Ed.2d 111 (1971).

83. *Spangler v. Pasadena City Bd. of Educ.*, 519 F.2d 430 (9th Cir.1975).

84. *Davis v. School Dist. of City of Pontiac*, 443 F.2d 573 (6th Cir.1971), *cert. denied*, 404 U.S. 913, 92 S.Ct. 233, 30 L.Ed.2d 186 (1971).

money that might not have been available. In upholding the remedial plan, the court asserted that failing to implement the plan would have done no more than reaffirm the previous inadequate policies. A year earlier, the Seventh Circuit, in a case from Illinois, became the first court to call for busing as a partial remedy in a school desegregation case over school zoning, student transfers, and transportation.[85]

The Supreme Court finally addressed de facto segregation in *Keyes v. School District No. 1, Denver, Colorado*,[86] discussed earlier, although it conceded that the actions of school board officials may have the effect of creating de jure segregation. More recently, in a multifaceted case from Illinois involving children who were minorities and of limited English proficiency, a federal trial court rejected a board's motion to dismiss a class action suit claiming that it denied the students the right to equal educational opportunities.[87] The court commented that the allegations that the board evidenced a discriminatory intent in implementing its redistricting plan that not only closed neighborhood schools in minority areas but also had racially disparate effects, including undue transportation burdens and insufficient services and educational opportunities for students of limited English proficiency, were sufficient to state a claim that educators violated their rights to equal protection.

A long-running desegregation case from Chicago involved students who are racial and ethnic minorities as well as children who are English Language Learners.[88] A federal trial court in Illinois released Chicago's public schools from judicial oversight because it was satisfied that officials met the *Green* factors, thereby entitling the board to an order that the district achieved unitary status.[89]

DUTY TO CORRECT

A basic question relevant to de facto segregation is whether educators had to act to correct racial imbalances that developed through housing patterns and the uniform application of school zoning and student-transfer policies.[90] While five circuit courts responded that boards were not required to do so,[91] this did not mean that unequal facilities, programs, and/or staffs

---

85. *United States v. School Dist. 151 of Cook County, Ill.*, 432 F.2d 1147 (7th Cir.1970), *cert. denied*, 402 U.S. 943, 91 S.Ct. 1610, 29 L.Ed.2d 111 (1971).

86. 413 U.S. 189, 93 S.Ct. 2686, 37 L.Ed.2d 548 (1973). [Case No. 121]

87. *Leslie v. Board of Educ. for Ill. School Dist. U–46*, 379 F. Supp.2d 952 [201 Educ. L. Rep. 151] (N.D. Ill. 2005).

88. For the first of more than forty opinions in this dispute, *see Johnson v. Board of Educ. of City of Chicago*, 604 F.2d 504 (7th Cir. 1979).

89. *United States v. Board of Educ. of the City of Chicago*, 663 F. Supp.2d 649 [252 Educ. L. Rep. 688] (N.D. Ill. 2009).

90. For the latest iteration in long-term litigation involving housing inequities in the context of school desegregation, *see United States v. Yonkers Board of Educ.*, 30 F. Supp.2d 650 [131 Educ. L. Rep. 990] (S.D.N.Y. 1998).

91. *See Bell v. School City of Gary, Ind.*, 324 F.2d 209 (7th Cir.1963), *cert. denied*, 377 U.S. 924, 84 S.Ct. 1223, 12 L.Ed.2d 216 (1964); *Downs v. Board of Educ.*, 336 F.2d 988 (10th Cir.1964), *cert. denied*, 380 U.S. 914, 85 S.Ct. 898, 13 L.Ed.2d 800 (1965); *Springfield School*

were permitted to remain in predominantly minority schools. Faced with such situations, tangible school deficiencies required boards to enact positive corrective measures, not on the ground of racial balance per se, but on the basis of general equality of educational opportunity. The judicial attitude in this regard seemed to have been to remedy reasonably correctable educational inequalities but not to have required racial mixing per se.[92]

One of the lengthiest and most comprehensive cases in the history of urban school desegregation arose in Washington, D.C., where the federal trial court ordered extensive changes ranging from school zoning patterns and teacher segregation to tracking while targeting financial inequities as an underlying cause in denying equal educational opportunities to all students.[93] In a key aspect of this case, the court struck down the tracking system of ability grouping primarily because educators placed students by relying on questionable early-testing procedures that made it difficult to change tracks.[94] When the board chose not to appeal and refused to allow the superintendent to do so, he resigned, and, joined by a member of the board, challenged the trial court's order as a form of judicial interference in the administration of the schools. The District of Columbia Circuit Court affirmed most of the initial order including the abolition of tracking.[95] However, rather than affirm the entire decree, the court remanded so that a newly elected board, replacing the appointed one, would not have been unduly restricted in creating new programs.

In a case from New Jersey, the federal trial court rejected a claim that state educational officials failed to do enough to remedy racial imbalances in the schools.[96] The court decreed that insofar as the degeneration of the state's unitary system of public education that led to the creation of an extreme racial imbalance was beyond the scope of its jurisdiction, the complaint failed to present a claim for which relief could have been granted. On further review in *Spencer v. Kugler*,[97] the Supreme Court upheld a plan that, although not segregative in intent, resulted in de facto segregation.

The Supreme Court of California found that school boards had a state constitutional duty to enact reasonably feasible steps to alleviate segregation regardless of whether it was de jure or de facto.[98] The court explained

Comm. v. Barksdale, 348 F.2d 261 (1st Cir. 1965); *Offerman v. Nitkowski*, 378 F.2d 22 (2d Cir. 1967); *Deal v. Cincinnati Bd. of Educ.*, 369 F.2d 55 (6th Cir.1966), *cert. denied*, 389 U.S. 847, 88 S.Ct. 39, 19 L.Ed.2d 114 (1967).

92. *Deal v. Cincinnati Bd. of Educ.*, 369 F.2d 55 (6th Cir. 1966), *cert. denied*, 389 U.S. 847, 88 S.Ct. 39, 19 L.Ed.2d 114 (1967).

93. *Hobson v. Hansen*, 269 F.Supp. 401 (D.D.C. 1967).

94. A federal trial court, on remand in a long-running case, ruled that where vestiges of segregation remained in a district with regard to academic tracking, special education, and programs for students who have limited English proficiency, the state would have to assist in helping to implement remedies. *United States Yonkers Branch–NAACP v. Yonkers Board of Education*, 123 F.Supp.2d 694 [149 Educ. L. Rep. 721] (S.D.N.Y. 2000).

95. *Smuck v. Hobson*, 408 F.2d 175 (D.C. Cir. 1969).

96. *Spencer v. Kugler*, 326 F.Supp. 1235 (D.N.J. 1971).

97. 404 U.S. 1027, 92 S.Ct. 707, 30 L.Ed.2d 723 (1972).

98. *Crawford v. Board of Educ. of City of Los Angeles*, 130 Cal. Rptr. 724 (Cal. 1976).

that the judiciary's function is to evaluate whether boards initiated courses of action to alleviate the effects of segregation and made reasonable progress toward this goal. The court ascertained that if such were not the case, judicial intervention was warranted to protect the rights of minority children. The court indicated that the student population in each school in districts need not reflect the racial composition of systems as a whole since its duty was to eliminate imbalances in those schools in which the minority enrollment was so disproportionate as to isolate the children in them from integrated educational experiences.

In a later iteration of the same case from California, voters approved a state constitutional amendment prohibiting state courts from ordering mandatory pupil assignments or transportation unless the federal judiciary would have done so to remedy a federal constitutional violation. When this amendment was subjected to an equal protection challenge in *Crawford v. Board of Education of the City of Los Angeles*,[99] the Supreme Court rejected the claim that once a state does more than the Fourteenth Amendment requires, it may never recede. The Justices decided that the Fourteenth Amendment did not embody a racial classification and neither declared nor implied that persons be treated differently on account of race. The Court reasoned that it only forbade state courts from ordering pupil school assignments or transportation plans absent a Fourteenth Amendment violation. The Court added that it could not infer a discriminatory motive as the reason why almost sixty-nine percent of the electorate voted in favor of the amendment.

The Seventh Circuit rejected the argument that a school board's failure to comply with a law from Illinois directing it to eliminate de facto segregation created a conclusive presumption of segregative intent.[100] The court stated that the board's failure to correct de facto segregation was insufficient to establish segregative intent, especially where the law provided that a board could, under some conditions, assert that existing attendance boundaries need not be revised.

POWER TO CORRECT

Another basic question was whether school officials could have taken steps to correct racial imbalances that developed due to housing patterns coupled with the uniform application of school zoning and student transfer policies. Courts responded that officials had a duty to remedy such imbalances. The Supreme Court included dicta to this effect in *Swann* and endorsed it in *Washington v. Seattle School District No. 1*.[101] The main challenges in these cases came from individuals who argued that race could not have been considered for any purpose and that the United States Constitution was colorblind for all purposes, a contention that has been rejected in its absolute form. Constitutionality depends on the purpose of looking at race as a factor since the courts interpret the Constitution as

---

99.   458 U.S. 527, 102 S.Ct. 3211, 73 L.Ed.2d 948 [5 Educ. L. Rep. 82] (1982).

100.   *Coates v. Illinois State Bd. of Educ.*, 559 F.2d 445 (7th Cir.1977).

101.   458 U.S. 457, 102 S.Ct. 3187, 73 L.Ed.2d 896 [5 Educ. L. Rep. 58] (1982).

preventing the invidious use of race to disadvantage persons or racial groups. If the courts ignored race completely, they would not only have made it virtually impossible to dismantle dual school systems but would also have defeated *Brown's* mandate by precluding attempts to prevent or correct de facto segregation. As discussed in Chapter 12, courts have allowed school officials to take race into account in student assignment policies as long as their actions are sufficiently narrowly tailored to meet a compelling governmental interest such as diversity.[102]

The Supreme Court of Washington discussed many of the arguments against busing to achieve racial balances in school systems experiencing de facto segregation.[103] Residents in Seattle who opposed mandatory busing enjoined the school board from implementing its plan for a year. The court dissolved the injunction in acknowledging that a system of voluntary student transfers failed to accomplish its objective of creating desegregated schools. The court specified that the board developed the plan with the help of experts and others who conducted hearings where all were urged to express their opinions. Interestingly, the plaintiffs who sought the delay had not submitted a plan. The court rejected the call for a referendum, responding that students lacked the right to attend the schools closest to their homes in pointing out that in a city the size of Seattle, neighborhood boundaries meant little in day-to-day life. The court thus refused to invalidate the board's plan for equalizing educational opportunities for all students because some parents feared that their children would have been disadvantaged by attending schools outside of their immediate neighborhoods. The court also rejected the theory that parents had the right to select specific public schools for their children. As discussed below, in *Washington v. Seattle School District No. 1*,[104] the Supreme Court invalidated the initiative as unconstitutional.

Parents of white students filed most of the suits challenging local board policies designed to correct racial imbalances. Yet, parents of African American children initiated early suits claiming that they were forced to absorb all or most of the inconveniences of reassignments. In such a dispute from California, a federal trial court struck down a board's plan when officials closed an apparently suitable school for students who were African Americans and transferred them to schools where the majority of students were white.[105] The court invalidated the plan in observing that insofar as it was neither absolutely nor reasonably necessary, it had to consider the fairly obvious fact that it placed the burden of desegregation entirely on one racial group, namely African Americans.

On the other hand, the Second Circuit determined that a school board in Connecticut did not deny children who were African American and

---

102. *See, e.g., Comfort v. Lynn School Comm.*, 418 F.3d 1 [200 Educ. L. Rep. 541] (1st Cir. 2005), *cert. denied*, 546 U.S. 1061, 126 S.Ct. 798, 163 L.Ed.2d 627 (2005), *on remand, sub nom. Comfort ex rel. Neumyer v. Lynn School Comm.*, 541 F. Supp.2d 429 [231 Educ. L. Rep. 739] (D. Mass. 2008) (denying a request for relief from the final judgment, thus dismissing the claim).

103. *Citizens Against Mandatory Bussing v. Palmason*, 495 P.2d 657 (Wash.1972).

104. 458 U.S. 457, 102 S.Ct. 3187, 73 L.Ed.2d 896 [5 Educ. L. Rep. 58] (1982).

105. *Brice v. Landis*, 314 F.Supp. 974 (N. D. Cal. 1969).

Puerto Rican equal protection by busing them to schools in white neighborhoods without concurrently operating schools in African American neighborhoods and cross-busing white children.[106] The court was satisfied that insofar as the board voluntarily adopted the plan absent a history of de jure segregation, officials had no duty to act. The court noted not only that the board's good faith attempt to improve education of children in some neighborhoods by transferring them to other schools did not infringe any rights but also that all neighborhoods had to be treated the same unless distinctions emerged due to improper purposes.

Legislatures have created state-level commissions to deal with issues of discrimination and human relations. The ability of commissions to order corrective measures to remedy de facto segregation in school systems depended on their enabling statutes. For example, the Supreme Court of Pennsylvania remarked that a commission had the authority to order local school boards to end discriminatory practices and draw up plans for eliminating de facto segregation in some schools.[107] The court added that the commission did not have to find that boards intentionally fostered and maintained segregation before invoking its authority since it only had to decide whether imbalances were present. The court subsequently conceded that the commission could have adopted a mathematical definition of de facto segregation.[108] Conversely, the Supreme Court of Kansas pointed out that a state commission lacked the power to order a local board to reassign teachers in order to produce a better racial balance on its staff.[109]

POWER TO PREVENT CORRECTION

Federal courts in New York and Michigan struck down state laws aimed at preventing correction of de facto segregation while such statutes were given innocuous meanings in attempts to preserve a law's constitutionality in California prior to the Supreme Court's doing so. After the legislature in New York enacted a law prohibiting student assignments for balancing purposes except by elected school boards, a federal trial court struck it down.[110] The court pointed out that the statute was unconstitutional because it created a single exception to the broad supervisory powers that the state commissioner of education exercised over local boards. The court concluded that insofar as the statute established a purely racial classification by treating educational matters involving race differently from other issues involving schooling and it made dealing with racial imbalances in the public schools more difficult, it was unconstitutional.

When the school board in Detroit voluntarily adopted a plan to provide a better balance between African American and white high school students,

---

106. *Norwalk Core v. Norwalk Bd. of Educ.*, 423 F.2d 121 (2d Cir. 1970)

107. *Pennsylvania Human Relations Comm'n v. Chester School Dist.*, 233 A.2d 290 (Pa. 1967).

108. *Pennsylvania Human Relations Comm'n v. Uniontown Area School Dist.*, 313 A.2d 156 (Pa. 1973).

109. *Londerholm v. Unified School Dist. No. 500*, 430 P.2d 188 (Kan.1967)

110. *Lee v. Nyquist*, 318 F.Supp. 710 (W.D.N.Y.1970),
aff'd, 402 U.S. 935, 91 S.Ct. 1618, 29 L.Ed.2d 105 (1971).

the state legislature attempted to counterbalance this by enacting an open-enrollment policy granting preference to students living near each school. The law was limited to "first class" school districts, of which Detroit was the only one. The Sixth Circuit invalidated the act as unconstitutional because it obstructed lawful steps to protect Fourteenth Amendment rights.[111] Even in expressing no opinion as to whether the board was obligated to adopt all or any part of its plan, the court distinguished this case from one of its earlier judgments[112] on the basis that this board acted on its own while in the previous action the plaintiffs sought to force it to act. In a second case from Michigan to reach the Sixth Circuit, after a board adopted a plan to correct de facto segregation, voters recalled all of the members who voted for the plan. The plaintiffs then challenged the new board's stated intention of rescinding the plan at the end of the school year. The Sixth Circuit affirmed an injunction preventing the new board from rescinding the plan since doing so would have had the effect of reassigning students to their previously segregated schools.[113]

In California, plaintiffs challenged a statute designed to prevent school boards from transporting students without written parental consent. The state's highest court, upholding the law, treated it as not interfering with a board's power over assigning students to schools in order to improve racial balances.[114] The court interpreted the law in light of its literal meaning that students were not required to use any school transportation. The court feared that any other interpretation would have rendered the statute unconstitutional since it could not have been upheld if it granted governmental support to a system of de facto segregation.

After unsuccessful attempts to block busing as a remedy for de facto segregation in Seattle, voters endorsed a measure that would have prevented local boards from requiring students to attend schools other than one of the two closest to their homes and from using a number of assignment methods such as redefining attendance zones and pairing schools. Expressly accepting the analytical approach of a federal trial court, in *Washington v. Seattle School District No. 1*,[115] the Supreme Court invalidated the initiative. The Court ruled that insofar as the voter initiative impermissibly classified individuals based on race and sought to end busing to achieve racial integration, it violated the equal protection rights of minority students. The Court posited that although state officials could have made all student assignments, they could not have delegated the matter to local boards with race-conscious strings attached.

PROOF OF INTENT TO DISCRIMINATE

Whether governmental actions which had disproportionately adverse effects on African Americans, singly or as a class, were racially motivated presents a significant issue because, depending on the answer, courts applied the law of de jure or de facto segregation. In the pre-*Brown* South,

---

111.   *Bradley v. Milliken*, 433 F.2d 897 (6th Cir.1970).

112.   *Deal v. Cincinnati Bd. of Educ.*, 369 F.2d 55 (6th Cir. 1966), *cert. denied*, 389 U.S. 847, 88 S.Ct. 39, 19 L.Ed.2d 114 (1967).

113.   *National Ass'n for the Advancement of Colored People, Lansing Branch v. Lansing Bd. of Educ.*, 485 F.2d 569 (6th Cir. 1973).

114.   *San Francisco Unified School Dist. v. Johnson*, 92 Cal.Rptr. 309 (Cal. 1971).

115.   458 U.S. 457, 102 S.Ct. 3187, 73 L.Ed.2d 896 [5 Educ. L. Rep. 58] (1982).

district-wide segregation was typically based on codified state law. As such, since the question of intent was academic, courts relied on district-wide remedies for de jure segregation. On the other hand, outside of the South, since segregation was typically de facto rather than de jure, plaintiffs had to prove segregative intent before the federal courts would intervene, with the scope of remedies depending on the extent of the violations.

The essential Supreme Court case with regard to segregative intent is *Keyes.* Even so, in litigation in other fields, the Justices offered guidelines designed to clarify what evidence may have been probative as to discriminatory intent. The Court's most extensive elaboration of this topic was in *Village of Arlington Heights v. Metropolitan Housing Development Corporation (Arlington Heights),*[116] a non-school case from Illinois wherein it upheld a zoning ordinance dealing with low-cost housing. Although conceding that the elements were not exhaustive, the Court enunciated six factors for assessing whether official action had a discriminatory intent. These factors address an action's impact, its historical background, the sequence of events leading up to it, departures from normal procedural sequences, departures from the weighting usually given operative factors, and its legislative or administrative history.

Amid the many cases citing *Arlington Heights,* some courts treated discriminatory intent as a ground for imposing liability in school settings.[117] If plaintiffs establish prima facie cases of purposeful segregation by relying on factors such as those enunciated in *Arlington Heights,* school boards can rebut the presumptions by presenting evidence that their actions or inactions were consistent with racially neutral policies reasonably associated with acceptable educational practices. In order to support claims of constitutional violations, plaintiffs must show more than that they experienced disparate impacts. In such a case, the Supreme Court ruled that a plaintiff must provide evidence that a decision maker "selected or reaffirmed a particular course of action at least in part 'because of,' not merely 'in spite of,' its adverse effects."[118] In a footnote, the Court explained that "[t]his is not to say that the inevitability or foreseeability of consequences of a neutral rule has no bearing upon the existence of discriminatory intent."[119]

[CASE NO. 116]   ELIMINATING RACIAL SEGREGATION IN PUBLIC SCHOOLS

BROWN v. BOARD OF EDUCATION OF TOPEKA (I)

Supreme Court of the United States, 1954.
347 U.S. 483, 74 S.Ct. 686, 98 L.Ed. 873.

■ MR. CHIEF JUSTICE WARREN delivered the opinion of the Court.

These cases come to us from the States of Kansas, South Carolina, Virginia, and Delaware. They are premised on different facts and different

---

116.   429 U.S. 252, 97 S.Ct. 555, 50 L.Ed.2d 450 (1977).

117.   *See, e.g., Arthur v. Nyquist,* 573 F.2d 134 (2d Cir. 1978), *cert. denied,* 439 U.S. 860, 99 S.Ct. 179, 58 L.Ed.2d 169 (1978); *National Ass'n for the Advancement of Colored People v. Lansing Bd. of Educ.,* 559 F.2d 1042 (6th Cir. 1977), *cert. denied,* 434 U.S. 997, 98 S.Ct. 635, 54 L.Ed.2d 491 (1977).

118.   *Personnel Adm'r of Mass. v. Feeney,* 442 U.S. 256, 99 S.Ct. 2282, 60 L.Ed.2d 870 (1979).

119.   *Id.* at 279, note 25.

local conditions, but a common legal question justifies their consideration together in this consolidated opinion.

In each of the cases, minors of the Negro race, through their legal representatives, seek the aid of the courts in obtaining admission to the public schools of their community on a nonsegregated basis. In each instance, they have been denied admission to schools attended by white children under laws requiring or permitting segregation according to race. This segregation was alleged to deprive the plaintiffs of the equal protection of the laws under the Fourteenth Amendment. In each of the cases other than the Delaware case, a three-judge federal district court denied relief to the plaintiffs on the so-called "separate but equal" doctrine announced by this Court in *Plessy v. Ferguson*. Under that doctrine, equality of treatment is accorded when the races are provided substantially equal facilities, even though these facilities be separate. In the Delaware case, the Supreme Court of Delaware adhered to that doctrine, but ordered that the plaintiffs be admitted to the white schools because of their superiority to the Negro schools.

The plaintiffs contend that segregated public schools are not "equal" and cannot be made "equal," and that hence they are deprived of the equal protection of the laws. Because of the obvious importance of the question presented, the Court took jurisdiction. Argument was heard in the 1952 Term, and reargument was heard this Term on certain questions propounded by the Court. . . .

In the first cases in this Court constructing the Fourteenth Amendment, decided shortly after its adoption, the Court interpreted it as proscribing all state-imposed discriminations against the Negro race. The doctrine of "separate but equal" did not make its appearance in this Court until 1896 in the case of *Plessy v. Ferguson*, involving not education but transportation. American courts have since labored with the doctrine for over half a century. In this Court, there have been six cases involving the "separate but equal" doctrine in the field of public education. In *Cumming v. Board of Education of Richmond County*, and *Gong Lum v. Rice*, the validity of the doctrine itself was not challenged. In more recent cases, all on the graduate school level, inequality was found in that specific benefits enjoyed by white students were denied to Negro students of the same educational qualifications. (*State of Missouri ex rel. Gaines v. Canada*; *Sipuel v. Board of Regents of University of Oklahoma*; *Sweatt v. Painter*; *McLaurin v. Oklahoma State Regents*). In none of these cases was it necessary to re-examine the doctrine to grant relief to the Negro plaintiff. And in *Sweatt v. Painter*, the Court expressly reserved decision on the question whether *Plessy v. Ferguson* should be held inapplicable to public education.

In the instant cases, that question is directly presented. Here, unlike *Sweatt v. Painter*, there are findings below that the Negro and white schools involved have been equalized, or are being equalized, with respect to buildings, curricula, qualifications and salaries of teachers, and other "tangible" factors. Our decision, therefore, cannot turn on merely a comparison of these tangible factors in the Negro and white schools involved in each of the cases. We must look instead to the effect of segregation itself on public education.

In approaching this problem, we cannot turn the clock back to 1868 when the Amendment was adopted, or even to 1896 when *Plessy v. Ferguson* was written. We must consider public education in the light of its full development and its present place in American life throughout the Nation. Only in this way can it be determined if segregation in public schools deprives these plaintiffs of the equal protection of the laws.

Today, education is perhaps the most important function of state and local governments. Compulsory school attendance laws and the great expenditures for education both demonstrate our recognition of the importance of education to our democratic society. It is required in the performance of our most basic public responsibilities, even service in the armed forces. It is the very foundation of good citizenship. Today it is a principal instrument in awakening the child to cultural values, in preparing him for later professional training, and in helping him to adjust normally to his environment. In these days, it is doubtful that any child may reasonably be expected to succeed in life if he is denied the opportunity of an education. Such an opportunity, where the state has undertaken to provide it, is a right which must be made available to all on equal terms.

We come then to the question presented: Does segregation of children in public schools solely on the basis of race, even though the physical facilities and other "tangible" factors may be equal, deprive the children of the minority group of equal educational opportunities? We believe that it does.

In *Sweatt v. Painter*, in finding that a segregated law school for Negroes could not provide them equal educational opportunities, this Court relied in large part on "those qualities which are incapable of objective measurement but which make for greatness in a law school." In *McLaurin v. Oklahoma State Regents*, the Court, in requiring that a Negro admitted to a white graduate school be treated like all other students, again resorted to intangible considerations: ". . . his ability to study, to engage in discussions and exchange views with other students, and, in general, to learn his profession." Such considerations apply with added force to children in grade and high schools. To separate them from others of similar age and qualifications solely because of their race generates a feeling of inferiority as to their status in the community that may affect their hearts and minds in a way unlikely ever to be undone. The effect of this separation on their educational opportunities was well stated by a finding in the Kansas case by a court which nevertheless felt compelled to rule against the Negro plaintiffs:

"Segregation of white and colored children in public schools has a detrimental effect upon the colored children. The impact is greater when it has the sanction of the law; for the policy of separating the races is usually interpreted as denoting the inferiority of the Negro group. A sense of inferiority affects the motivation of a child to learn. Segregation with the sanction of law, therefore, has a tendency to [retard] the educational and mental development of Negro children and to deprive them of some of the benefits they would receive in a racial[ly] integrated school system."

Whatever may have been the extent of psychological knowledge at the time of *Plessy v. Ferguson*, this finding is amply supported by modern authority. Any language in *Plessy v. Ferguson* contrary to this finding is rejected.

We conclude that in the field of public education the doctrine of "separate but equal" has no place. Separate educational facilities are inherently unequal. Therefore, we hold that the plaintiffs and others similarly situated for whom the actions have been brought are, by reason of the segregation complained of, deprived of the equal protection of the laws guaranteed by the Fourteenth Amendment. This disposition makes unnecessary any discussion whether such segregation also violates the Due Process Clause of the Fourteenth Amendment.

Because these are class actions, because of the wide applicability of this decision, and because of the great variety of local conditions, the formulation of decrees in these cases presents problems of considerable complexity. On reargument, the consideration of appropriate relief was necessarily subordinated to the primary question—the constitutionality of segregation in public education. We have now announced that such segregation is a denial of the equal protection of the laws. In order that we may have the full assistance of the parties in formulating decrees, the cases will be restored to the docket, and the parties are requested to present further argument on Questions 4 and 5 previously propounded by the Court for the reargument this Term. The Attorney General of the United States is again invited to participate. The Attorneys General of the states requiring or permitting segregation in public education will also be permitted to appear as *amici curiae* upon request to do so by September 15, 1954, and submission of briefs by October 1, 1954.

It is so ordered.

NOTES

1. The Supreme Court does not often render unanimous judgments in cases dealing with significant matters of social policy. Clearly, the Justices were aware of the importance of a single statement in this situation. Would an 8–1 ruling have had the same impact?

2. The Court called for an end to segregated schooling in *Brown I* and its progeny. Yet, the Court never affirmatively ordered school systems to integrate. What do you think about this distinction?

[CASE NO. 117] REMEDIES FOR SEGREGATION

BROWN v. BOARD OF EDUCATION OF TOPEKA (II)

Supreme Court of the United States, 1955.
349 U.S. 294, 75 S.Ct. 753, 99 L.Ed. 1083.

■ MR. CHIEF JUSTICE WARREN delivered the opinion of the Court.

These cases were decided on May 17, 1954. The opinions of that date, declaring the fundamental principle that racial discrimination in public education is unconstitutional, are incorporated herein by reference. All provisions of federal, state, or local law requiring or permitting such discrimination must yield to this principle. There remains for consideration the manner in which relief is to be accorded.

Because these cases arose under different local conditions and their disposition will involve a variety of local problems, we requested further argument on the question of relief. In view of the nationwide importance of the decision, we invited the Attorney General of the United States and the Attorneys General of all states requiring or permitting racial discrimination in public education to present their views on that question. The parties, the United States, and the States of Florida, North Carolina, Arkansas, Oklahoma, Maryland, and Texas filed briefs and participated in the oral argument.

These presentations were informative and helpful to the Court in its consideration of the complexities arising from the transition to a system of public education freed of racial discrimination. The presentations also demonstrated that substantial steps to eliminate racial discrimination in public schools have already been taken, not only in some of the communities in which these cases arose, but in some of the states appearing as *amici curiae,* and in other states as well. Substantial progress has been made in the District of Columbia, and in the communities in Kansas and Delaware involved in this litigation. The defendants in the cases coming to us from South Carolina and Virginia are awaiting the decision of this Court concerning relief.

Full implementation of these constitutional principles may require solution of varied local school problems. School authorities have the primary responsibility for elucidating, assessing, and solving these problems; courts will have to consider whether the action of school authorities constitutes good faith implementation of the governing constitutional principles. Because of their proximity to local conditions and the possible need for further hearings, the courts which originally heard these cases can best perform this judicial appraisal. Accordingly, we believe it appropriate to remand the cases to those courts.

In fashioning and effectuating the decrees, the courts will be guided by equitable principles. Traditionally, equity has been characterized by a practical flexibility in shaping its remedies and by a facility for adjusting and reconciling public and private needs. These cases call for the exercise of these traditional attributes of equity power. At stake is the personal interest of the plaintiffs in admission to public schools as soon as practicable on a nondiscriminatory basis. To effectuate this interest may call for elimination of a variety of obstacles in making the transition to school systems operated in accordance with the constitutional principles set forth in our May 17, 1954, decision. Courts of equity may properly take into account the public interest in the elimination of such obstacles in a systematic and effective manner. But it should go without saying that the vitality of these constitutional principles cannot be allowed to yield simply because of disagreement with them.

While giving weight to these public and private considerations, the courts will require that the defendants make a prompt and reasonable start toward full compliance with our May 17, 1954, ruling. Once such a start has been made, the courts may find that additional time is necessary to carry out the ruling in an effective manner. The burden rests upon the defendants to establish that such time is necessary in the public interest and is consistent with good faith compliance at the earliest practicable date. To that end, the courts may consider problems related to administration, arising from the physical condition of the school plant, the school transportation system, personnel, revision of school districts and attendance areas into compact units to achieve a system of determining admission to the public schools on a nonracial basis, and revision of local laws and regulations which may be necessary in solving the foregoing problems. They will also consider the adequacy of any plans the defendants may propose to meet these problems and to effectuate a transition to a racially nondiscriminatory school system. During this period of transition, the courts will retain jurisdiction of these cases.

The judgments below, except that in the Delaware case, are accordingly reversed and remanded to the District Courts to take such proceedings and enter such orders and decrees consistent with this opinion as are necessary and proper to admit to public schools on a racially nondiscriminatory basis with all deliberate speed the parties to these cases. The judgment in the Delaware case—ordering the immediate admission of the plaintiffs to schools previously attended only by white children—is affirmed on the basis of the principles stated in our May 17, 1954, opinion, but the case is remanded to the Supreme Court of Delaware for such further proceedings as that court may deem necessary in the light of this opinion.

It is so ordered.

NOTES

1. Was the Supreme Court's use of the phrase "with all deliberate speed" a mistake? Considering the realities of the situation existing in the South at that time, did the Court have alternatives?

2. Was it realistic for the Court to expect locally-elected school boards to be effective in eliminating racial segregation?

3. The Court placed the burden of establishing time frames for compliance on local boards acting under judicial supervision. Since education is a state function, can you think of reasons why the Court did not place the responsibility on state officials?

[CASE NO. 118]   GUIDELINES FOR ELIMINATING RACIAL
SEGREGATION

SWANN v. CHARLOTTE–MECKLENBURG
BOARD OF EDUCATION

Supreme Court of the United States, 1971.
402 U.S. 1, 91 S.Ct. 1267, 28 L.Ed.2d 554.

■ Mr. Chief Justice Burger delivered the opinion of the Court.

We granted certiorari in this case to review important issues as to the
duties of school authorities and the scope of powers of federal courts under
this Court's mandates to eliminate racially separate public schools established and maintained by state action.

This case and those argued with it arose in states having a long history
of maintaining two sets of schools in a single school system deliberately
operated to carry out a governmental policy to separate pupils in schools
solely on the basis of race. That was what *Brown v. Board of Education* was
all about. These cases present us with the problem of defining in more
precise terms than heretofore the scope of the duty of school authorities
and district courts in implementing *Brown I* and the mandate to eliminate
dual systems and establish unitary systems at once. . . .

I

The Charlotte–Mecklenburg school system, the 43d largest in the
Nation, encompasses the city of Charlotte and surrounding Mecklenburg
County, North Carolina. The area is large—550 square miles—spanning
roughly 22 miles east-west and 36 miles north-south. During the 1968–1969
school year the system served more than 84,000 pupils in 107 schools.
Approximately 71% of the pupils were found to be white and 29% Negro. As
of June 1969 there were approximately 24,000 Negro students in the
system, of whom 21,000 attended schools within the city of Charlotte. Two-
thirds of those 21,000—approximately 14,000 Negro students—attended 21
schools which were either totally Negro or more than 99% Negro. . . .

II

Nearly 17 years ago this Court held, in explicit terms, that state-
imposed segregation by race in public schools denies equal protection of the
laws. At no time has the Court deviated in the slightest degree from that
holding or its constitutional underpinnings. . . .

Over the 16 years since *Brown II,* many difficulties were encountered
in implementation of the basic constitutional requirement that the State
not discriminate between public school children on the basis of their race.
Nothing in our national experience prior to 1955 prepared anyone for
dealing with changes and adjustments of the magnitude and complexity
encountered since then. Deliberate resistance of some to the Court's
mandates has impeded the good-faith efforts of others to bring school
systems into compliance. The detail and nature of these dilatory tactics
have been noted frequently by this Court and other courts.

By the time the Court considered *Green v. County School Board* in 1968, very little progress had been made in many areas where dual school systems had historically been maintained by operation of state laws. In *Green,* the Court was confronted with a record of a freedom-of-choice program that the District Court had found to operate in fact to preserve a dual system more than a decade after *Brown II.* While acknowledging that a freedom-of-choice concept could be a valid remedial measure in some circumstances, its failure to be effective in *Green* required that

> The burden on a school board today is to come forward with a plan that promises realistically to work *now* ... until it is clear that state-imposed segregation has been completely removed.

This was plain language, yet the 1969 Term of Court brought fresh evidence of the dilatory tactics of many school authorities. *Alexander v. Holmes County Bd. of Educ.* restated the basic obligation asserted in *Griffin v. County School Board* and *Green,* that the remedy must be implemented *forthwith.*

> The problems encountered by the district courts and courts of appeals make plain that we should now try to amplify guidelines, however incomplete and imperfect, for the assistance of school authorities and courts. The failure of local authorities to meet their constitutional obligations aggravated the massive problem of converting from the state-enforced discrimination of racially separate school systems....

III

The objective today remains to eliminate from the public schools all vestiges of state-imposed segregation....

If school authorities fail in their affirmative obligations under these holdings, judicial authority may be invoked. Once a right and a violation have been shown, the scope of a district court's equitable powers to remedy past wrongs is broad, for breadth and flexibility are inherent in equitable remedies....

School authorities are traditionally charged with broad power to formulate and implement educational policy and might well conclude, for example, that in order to prepare students to live in a pluralistic society each school should have a prescribed ratio of Negro to white students reflecting the proportion for the district as a whole. To do this as an educational policy is within the broad discretionary powers of school authorities; absent a finding of a constitutional violation, however, that would not be within the authority of a federal court. As with any equity case, the nature of the violation determines the scope of the remedy. In default by the school authorities of their obligation to proffer acceptable remedies, a district court has broad power to fashion a remedy that will assure a unitary school system.

The school authorities argue that the equity powers of federal district courts have been limited by Title IV of the Civil Rights Act of 1964. The language and the history of Title IV shows that it was not enacted to limit but to define the role of the Federal Government in the implementation of the *Brown I* decision. It authorizes the Commissioner of Education to provide technical assistance to local boards in the preparation of desegregation plans, to arrange "training institutes" for school personnel involved in desegregation efforts, and to make grants directly to schools to ease the transition to unitary systems. It also authorizes the Attorney General, in specified circumstances, to initiate federal desegregation suits. Section 2000c(b) defines "desegregation" as it is used in Title IV:

'Desegregation' means the assignment of students to public schools and within such schools without regard to their race, color, religion, or national origin, but 'desegregation' shall not mean the assignment of students to public schools in order to overcome racial imbalance.

Section 2000c–6, authorizing the Attorney General to institute federal suits, contains the following proviso:

nothing herein shall empower any official or court of the United States to issue any order seeking to achieve a racial balance in any school by requiring the transportation of pupils or students from one school to another or one school district to another in order to achieve such racial balance, or otherwise enlarge the existing power of the court to insure compliance with constitutional standards.

On their face, the sections quoted support only to insure that the provisions of Title IV of the Civil Rights Act of 1964 will not be read as granting new powers. The proviso in § 2000c–6 is in terms designed to foreclose any interpretation of the Act as expanding the *existing* powers of federal courts to enforce the Equal Protection Clause. There is no suggestion of an intention to restrict those powers or withdraw from courts their historic equitable remedial powers. The legislative history of Title IV indicates that Congress was concerned that the Act might be read as creating a right of action under the Fourteenth Amendment in the situation of so-called "de facto segregation," where racial imbalance exists in the schools but with no showing that this was brought about by discriminatory action of state authorities. In short, there is nothing in the Act which provides us material assistance in answering the question of remedy for state-imposed segregation in violation of *Brown I*. The basis of our decision must be the prohibition of the Fourteenth Amendment that no State shall "deny to any person within its jurisdiction the equal protection of the laws."

IV

We turn now to the problem of defining with more particularity the responsibilities of school authorities in desegregating a state-enforced dual school system in light of the Equal Protection Clause. Although the several related cases before us are primarily concerned with problems of student assignment, it may be helpful to begin with a brief discussion of other aspects of the process.

In *Green,* we pointed out that existing policy and practice with regard to faculty, staff, transportation, extracurricular activities, and facilities were among the most important indicia of a segregated system. Independent of student assignment, where it is possible to identify a "white school" or a "Negro school" simply by reference to the racial composition of teachers and staff, the quality of school buildings and equipment, or the organization of sports activities, a *prima facie* case of violation of substantive constitutional rights under the Equal Protection Clause is shown.

When a system has been dual in these respects, the first remedial responsibility of school authorities is to eliminate invidious racial distinctions. With respect to such matters as transportation, supporting personnel, and extracurricular activities, no more than this may be necessary. Similar corrective action must be taken with regard to the maintenance of buildings and the distribution of equipment. In these areas, normal administrative practice should produce schools of like quality, facilities, and staffs. Something more must be said, however, as to faculty assignment and new school construction.

In the companion *Davis* case, the Mobile school board has argued that the Constitution requires that teachers be assigned on a "color blind" basis. It also argues that the Constitution prohibits district courts from using their equity power to order assignment of teachers to achieve a particular degree of faculty desegregation. We reject that contention.

. . .

The construction of new schools and the closing of old ones is one of the most important functions of local school authorities and also one of the most complex. They must decide questions of location and capacity in light of population growth, finances, land values, site availability, through an almost endless list of factors to be considered. The result of this will be a decision which when combined with one technique or another of student assignment, will determine the racial composition of the student body in each school in the system. Over the long run, the consequences of the choices will be far reaching. People gravitate toward school facilities, just as schools are located in response to the needs of people. The location of schools may thus influence the patterns of residential development of a metropolitan area and have important impact on composition of inner city neighborhoods.

In the past, choices in this respect have been used as a potent weapon for creating or maintaining a state-segregated school system. In addition to the classic pattern of building schools specifically intended for Negro or white students, school authorities have sometimes, since *Brown,* closed schools which appeared likely to become racially mixed through changes in neighborhood residential patterns. This was sometimes accompanied by building new schools in the areas of white suburban expansion farthest from Negro population centers in order to maintain the separation of the races with a minimum departure from the formal principles of "neighborhood zoning." Such a policy does more than simply influence the short-run composition of the student body of a new school. It may well promote segregated residential patterns which, when combined with "neighborhood zoning," further lock the school system into the mold of separation of the races. Upon a proper showing a district court may consider this in fashioning a remedy. . . .

V

The central issue in this case is that of student assignment, and there are essentially four problem areas:

(1) to what extent racial balance or racial quotas may be used as an implement in a remedial order to correct a previously segregated system;

(2) whether every all-Negro and all-white school must be eliminated as an indispensable part of a remedial process of desegregation;

(3) what are the limits, if any, on the rearrangement of school districts and attendance zones, as a remedial measure; and

(4) what are the limits, if any, on the use of transportation facilities to correct state-enforced racial school segregation.

(1) Racial Balances or Racial Quotas.

. . .

We are concerned in these cases with the elimination of the discrimination inherent in the dual school systems, not with myriad factors of human existence which can cause discrimination in a multitude of ways on racial, religious, or ethnic grounds. The target of the cases from *Brown I* to the present was the dual school system. The elimination of racial discrimination in public schools is a large task and one that should not be retarded by efforts to achieve broader purposes lying beyond the jurisdiction of school authorities. One vehicle can carry only a limited amount of baggage. It would not serve the important objective of *Brown I* to seek to use school desegregation cases for purposes beyond their scope, although desegregation of schools ultimately will have impact on other forms of discrimination. We do not reach in this case the question whether a showing that school segregation is a consequence of other types of state action, without any discriminatory action by the school authorities, is a constitutional violation requiring remedial action by a school desegregation decree. This case does not present that question and we therefore do not decide it.

Our objective in dealing with the issues presented by these cases is to see that school authorities exclude no pupil of a racial minority from any school, directly or indirectly, on account of race; it does not and cannot embrace all the problems of racial prejudice, even when those problems contribute to disproportionate racial concentrations in some schools....

... If we were to read the holding of the District Court to require, as a matter of substantive constitutional right, any particular degree of racial balance or mixing, that approach would be disapproved and we would be obliged to reverse. The constitutional command to desegregate schools does not mean that every school in every community must always reflect the racial composition of the school system as a whole....

We see therefore that the use made of mathematical ratios was no more than a starting point in the process of shaping a remedy, rather than an inflexible requirement. From that starting point the District Court proceeded to frame a decree that was within its discretionary powers, an equitable remedy for the particular circumstances. As we said in *Green,* a school authority's remedial plan or a district court's remedial decree is to be judged by its effectiveness. Awareness of the racial composition of the whole school system is likely to be a useful starting point in shaping a remedy to correct past constitutional violations. In sum, the very limited use made of mathematical ratios was within the equitable remedial discretion of the District Court.

(2) One–Race Schools.

The record in this case reveals the familiar phenomenon that in metropolitan areas minority groups are often found concentrated in one part of the city. In some circumstances certain schools may remain all or largely of one race until new schools can be provided or neighborhood patterns change. Schools all or predominantly of one race in a district of mixed population will require close scrutiny to determine that school assignments are not part of state-enforced segregation.

In light of the above, it should be clear that the existence of some small number of one-race, or virtually one-race, schools within a district is not in and of itself the mark of a system which still practices segregation by law. The district judge or school authorities should make every effort to achieve the greatest possible degree of actual desegregation and will thus necessarily be concerned with the elimination of one-race schools. No *per se* rule can adequately embrace all the difficulties of reconciling the competing interests involved; but in a system with a history of segregation the need for remedial criteria of sufficient specificity to assure a school authority's compliance with its constitutional duty warrants a presumption against schools that are substantially disproportionate in their racial composition. Where the school authority's proposed plan for conversion from a dual to a unitary system contemplates the continued existence of some schools that are all or predominately of one race, they have the burden of showing that such school assignments are genuinely nondiscriminatory. The court should scrutinize such schools, and the burden upon the school authorities will be to satisfy the court that their racial composition is not the result of present or past discriminatory action. . . .

(3) Remedial Altering of Attendance Zones.

The maps submitted in these cases graphically demonstrate that one of the principal tools employed by school planners and by courts to break up the dual school system has been a frank—and sometimes drastic—gerrymandering of school districts and attendance zones. An additional step was pairing, "clustering," or "grouping" of schools with attendance assignments made deliberately to accomplish the transfer of Negro students out of formerly segregated Negro schools and transfer of white students to formerly all-Negro schools. More often than not, these zones are neither compact nor contiguous; indeed they may be on opposite ends of the city. As an interim corrective measure, this cannot be said to be beyond the broad remedial powers of a court. . . .

No fixed or even substantially fixed guidelines can be established as to how far a court can go, but it must be recognized that there are limits. The objective is to dismantle the dual school system. "Racially neutral" assign-ment plans proposed by school authorities to a district court may be inadequate; such plans may fail to counteract the continuing effects of past school segregation resulting from discriminatory location of school sites or distortion of school size in order to achieve or maintain an artificial racial separation. When school authorities present a district court with a "loaded game board," affirmative action in the form of remedial altering of attend-ance zones is proper to achieve truly nondiscriminatory assignments. In short, an assignment plan is not acceptable simply because it appears to be neutral.

In this area, we must of necessity rely to a large extent, as this Court has for more than 16 years, on the informed judgment of the district courts in the first instance and on courts of appeals.

We hold that the pairing and grouping of non-contiguous school zones is a permissible tool and such action is to be considered in light of the objectives sought....

(4) Transportation of Students.

The scope of permissible transportation of students as an implement of a remedial decree has never been defined by this Court and by the very nature of the problem it cannot be defined with precision. No rigid guidelines as to student transportation can be given for application to the infinite variety of problems presented in thousands of situations. Bus transportation has been an integral part of the public education system for years, and was perhaps the single most important factor in the transition from the one-room schoolhouse to the consolidated school. Eighteen million of the nation's public school children, approximately 39% were transported to their schools by bus in 1969–1970 in all parts of the country.

The importance of bus transportation as a normal and accepted tool of educational policy is readily discernible in this and the companion case. The Charlotte school authorities did not purport to assign students on the basis of geographically drawn zones until 1965 and then they allowed almost unlimited transfer privileges. The District Court's conclusion that assign-ment of children to the school nearest their home serving their grade would not produce an effective dismantling of the dual system is supported by the record.

Thus the remedial techniques used in the District Court's order were within that court's power to provide equitable relief; implementation of the decree is well within the capacity of the school authority.

The decree provided that the buses used to implement the plan would operate on direct routes. Students would be picked up at schools near their homes and transported to the schools they were to attend. The trips for elementary school pupils average about seven miles and the District Court found that they would take "not over 35 minutes at the most." This system compares favorably with the transportation plan previously operated in Charlotte under which each day 23,600 students on all grade levels were transported an average of 15 miles one way for an average trip requiring over an hour. In these circumstances, we find no basis for holding that the local school authorities may not be required to employ bus transportation as one tool of school desegregation. Desegregation plans cannot be limited to the walk-in school.

An objection to transportation of students may have validity when the time or distance of travel is so great as to risk either the health of the children or significantly impinge on the educational process. . . .

VI

The Court of Appeals, searching for a term to define the equitable remedial power of the district courts, used the term "reasonableness." In *Green,* this Court used the term "feasible" and by implication, "workable," "effective," and "realistic" in the mandate to develop "a plan that promises realistically to work, and . . . to work *now.*" On the facts of this case, we are unable to conclude that the order of the District Court is not reasonable, feasible and workable. However, in seeking to define the scope of remedial power or the limits on remedial power of courts in an area as sensitive as we deal with here, words are poor instruments to convey the sense of basic fairness inherent in equity. Substance, not semantics, must govern, and we have sought to suggest the nature of limitations without frustrating the appropriate scope of equity.

At some point, these school authorities and others like them should have achieved full compliance with this Court's decision in *Brown I.* The systems will then be "unitary" in the sense required by our decisions in *Green* and *Alexander.*

It does not follow that the communities served by such systems will remain demographically stable, for in a growing, mobile society, few will do so. Neither school authorities nor district courts are constitutionally required to make year-by-year adjustments of the racial composition of student bodies once the affirmative duty to desegregate has been accomplished and racial discrimination through official action is eliminated from the system. This does not mean that federal courts are without power to deal with future problems; but in the absence of a showing that either the school authorities or some other agency of the State has deliberately attempted to fix or alter demographic patterns to affect the racial composition of the schools, further intervention by a district court should not be necessary.

For the reasons herein set forth, the judgment of the Court of Appeals is affirmed as to those parts in which it affirmed the judgment of the District Court. The order of the District Court, dated August 7, 1970, is also affirmed. It is so ordered.

Judgment of Court of Appeals affirmed in part; order of District Court affirmed.

NOTES

1. In a companion case, the Justices reversed a judgment from the Supreme Court of Georgia for having erroneously interpreted the busing provisions in the Civil Rights Act of 1964. *McDaniel v. Barresi,* 402 U.S. 39, 91 S.Ct. 1287, 28 L.Ed.2d

582 (1971). In another case, the Court partially reversed the order of a federal trial court in Alabama because it gave inadequate consideration to the possible use of bus transportation and split zoning to remedy segregation. *Davis v. Board of School Commr's of Mobile County*, 402 U.S. 33, 91 S.Ct. 1289, 28 L.Ed.2d 577 (1971).

2.   The Fourth Circuit, in *Belk v. Charlotte–Mecklenburg Bd. of Educ.*, 269 F.3d 305 [158 Educ. L. Rep. 86] (4th Cir.2001), *cert. denied sub nom. Capacchione v. Charlotte–Mecklenburg Bd. of Educ.*, 535 U.S. 986, 122 S.Ct. 1537, 152 L.Ed.2d 465 (2002), ended judicial oversight in Charlotte–Mecklenburg when it was satisfied that the district achieved unitary status because it met all of the *Green* factors.

[CASE NO. 119]   THE STATUS OF INTER–DISTRICT DESEGREGATION REMEDIES

MILLIKEN v. BRADLEY (I)

Supreme Court of the United States, 1974.
418 U.S. 717, 94 S.Ct. 3112, 41 L.Ed.2d 1069.

■ Mr. CHIEF JUSTICE BURGER delivered the opinion of the Court.

We granted certiorari in these consolidated cases to determine whether a federal court may impose a multidistrict, areawide remedy to a single district *de jure* segregation problem absent any finding that the other included school districts have failed to operate unitary school systems within their districts, absent any claim or finding that the boundary lines of any affected school district were established with the purpose of fostering racial segregation in public schools, absent any finding that the included districts committed acts which effected segregation within the other districts, and absent a meaningful opportunity for the included neighboring school districts to present evidence or be heard on the propriety of a multidistrict remedy or on the question of constitutional violations by those neighboring districts.

I

. . .

The District Court found that the Detroit Board of Education created and maintained optional attendance zones within Detroit neighborhoods undergoing racial transition and between high school attendance areas of opposite predominant racial compositions. These zones, the court found, had the "natural, probable, foreseeable and actual effect" of allowing White pupils to escape identifiably Negro schools. Similarly, the District Court found that Detroit school attendance zones had been drawn along north-south boundary lines despite the Detroit Board's awareness that drawing boundary lines in an east-west direction would result in significantly greater desegregation. . . .

The District Court found that in the operation of its school transportation program, which was designed to relieve overcrowding, the Detroit Board had admittedly bused Negro Detroit pupils to predominantly Negro schools which were beyond or away from closer White schools with available space. This practice was found to have continued in recent years

despite the Detroit Board's avowed policy, adopted in 1967, of utilizing transportation to increase desegregation. . . .

With respect to the Detroit Board of Education's practices in school construction, the District Court found that Detroit school construction generally tended to have segregative effect with the great majority of schools being built in either overwhelmingly all-Negro or all-white neighborhoods so that the new schools opened as predominantly one race schools. . . .

The District Court also found that the State of Michigan had committed several constitutional violations with respect to the exercise of its general responsibility for, and supervision of, public education. The State, for example, was found to have failed, until the 1971 Session of the Michigan Legislature, to provide authorization or funds for the transportation of pupils within Detroit regardless of their poverty or distance from the school to which they were assigned; during this same period the State provided many neighboring, mostly White, suburban districts the full range of state supported transportation. . . .

Turning to the question of an appropriate remedy for these several constitutional violations, the District Court . . . proceeded to order the Detroit Board of Education to submit desegregation plans limited to the segregation problems found to be existing within the city of Detroit. At the same time, however, the state defendants were directed to submit desegregation plans encompassing the three-county metropolitan area despite the fact that the school districts of these three counties were not parties to the action and despite the fact that there had been no claim that these outlying counties, encompassing some 85 separate school districts, had committed constitutional violations. . . .

. . . [Eventually] the court designated 53 of the 85 suburban school districts plus Detroit as the "desegregation area" and appointed a panel to prepare and submit "an effective desegregation plan" for the Detroit schools [276,000 students] that would encompass the entire desegregation area [503,000 additional students]. . . .

The Court of Appeals . . . agreed with the District Court that "any less comprehensive a solution than a metropolitan area plan would result in an all black school system immediately surrounded by practically all white suburban school systems, with an overwhelming white majority population in the total metropolitan area." The court went on to state that it could "[not] see how such segregation can be any less harmful to the minority students than if the same result were accomplished within one school district."

Accordingly, the Court of Appeals concluded that "the only feasible desegregation plan involves the crossing of the boundary lines between the Detroit School District and adjacent or nearby school districts for the limited purpose of providing an effective desegregation plan." It reasoned that such a plan would be appropriate because of the State's violations, and could be implemented because of the State's authority to control local school districts. . . .

II

Proceeding from these basic principles [from prior desegregation cases], we first note that in the District Court the complainants sought a remedy aimed at the *condition* alleged to offend the Constitution—the segregation within the Detroit City School District. . . . Thereafter, however, the District Court abruptly rejected the proposed Detroit-only plans on the ground that "while it would provide a racial mix more in keeping with the Black–White proportions of the student population, [it] would accentuate the racial identifiability of the [Detroit] district as a Black school system, and would not accomplish desegregation." . . . Consequently, the court reasoned, it was imperative to "look beyond the limits of the Detroit school district for a solution to the problem of segregation in the Detroit schools . . ." since "[s]chool district lines are simply matters of political convenience and may not be used to deny constitutional rights." Accordingly, the District Court proceeded to redefine the relevant area to include areas of predominantly White pupil population in order to ensure that "upon implementation, no school, grade or classroom [would be] substantially disproportionate to the overall racial composition" of the entire metropolitan area. . . .

Viewing the record as a whole, it seems clear that the District Court and the Court of Appeals shifted the primary focus from a Detroit remedy to the metropolitan area only because of their conclusion that total desegregation of Detroit would not produce the racial balance which they perceived as desirable. Both courts proceeded on an assumption that the Detroit schools could not be truly desegregated—in their view of what constituted desegregation—unless the racial composition of the student body of each school substantially reflected the racial composition of the population of the metropolitan area as a whole. The metropolitan area was then defined as Detroit plus 53 of the outlying school districts. . . .

Here the District Court's approach to what constituted "actual desegregation" raises the fundamental question . . . as to the circumstances in which a federal court may order desegregation relief that embraces more than a single school district. The court's analytical starting point was its conclusion that school district lines are no more than arbitrary lines on a map "drawn for political convenience." Boundary lines may be bridged where there has been a constitutional violation calling for interdistrict relief, but, the notion that school district lines may be casually ignored or treated as a mere administrative convenience is contrary to the history of public education in our country. No single tradition in public education is more deeply rooted than local control over the operation of schools; local autonomy has long been thought essential both to the maintenance of community concern and support for public schools and to quality of the educational process. . . .

The Michigan educational structure involved in this case, in common with most States, provides for a large measure of local control and a review of the scope and character of these local powers indicates the extent to which the inter-district remedy approved by the two courts could disrupt and alter the structure of public education in Michigan. The metropolitan remedy would require, in effect, consolidation of 54 independent school districts historically administered as separate units into a vast new super school district.... Entirely apart from the logistical and other serious problems attending large-scale transportation of students, the consolidation would give rise to an array of other problems in financing and operating this new school system....

It may be suggested that all of these vital operational problems are yet to be resolved by the District Court.... But it is obvious from the scope of the inter-district remedy itself that absent a complete restructuring of the laws of Michigan relating to school districts the District Court will become first, a *de facto* "legislative authority" to resolve these complex questions, and then the "school superintendent" for the entire area. This is a task which few, if any, judges are qualified to perform and one which would deprive the people of control of schools through their elected representatives.

Of course, no state law is above the Constitution. School district lines and the present laws with respect to local control, are not sacrosanct and if they conflict with the Fourteenth Amendment federal courts have a duty to prescribe appropriate remedies.... But our prior holdings have been confined to violations and remedies within a single school district. We therefore turn to address, for the first time, the validity of a remedy mandating cross-district or inter-district consolidation to remedy a condition of segregation found to exist in only one district.

The controlling principle consistently expounded in our holdings is that the scope of the remedy is determined by the nature and extent of the constitutional violation. Before the boundaries of separate and autonomous school districts may be set aside by consolidating the separate units for remedial purposes or by imposing a cross-district remedy, it must first be shown that there has been a constitutional violation within one district that produces a significant segregative effect in another district. Specifically it must be shown that racially discriminatory acts of the state or local school districts, or of a single school district have been a substantial cause of inter-district segregation. Thus an inter-district remedy might be in order where the racially discriminatory acts of one or more school districts caused racial segregation in an adjacent district, or where district lines have been deliberately drawn on the basis of race. In such circumstances an inter-district remedy would be appropriate to eliminate the inter-district segregation directly caused by the constitutional violation. Conversely, without an inter-district violation and inter-district effect, there is no constitutional wrong calling for an inter-district remedy.

The record before us, voluminous as it is, contains evidence of *de jure* segregated conditions only in the Detroit schools; indeed, that was the theory on which the litigation was initially based and on which the District Court took evidence....

The constitutional right of the Negro respondents residing in Detroit is to attend a unitary school system in that district. Unless petitioners drew the district lines in a discriminatory fashion, or arranged for White students residing in the Detroit district to attend schools in Oakland and

Macomb Counties, they were under no constitutional duty to make provisions for Negro students to do so. . . .

III

We recognize that the six-volume record presently under consideration contains language and some specific incidental findings thought by the District Court to afford a basis for interdistrict relief. However, these comparatively isolated findings and brief comments concern only one possible inter-district violation and are found in the context of a proceeding that, as the District Court conceded, included no proofs of segregation practiced by any of the 85 suburban school districts surrounding Detroit. . . .

IV

. . .

We conclude that the relief ordered by the District Court and affirmed by the Court of Appeals was based upon an erroneous standard and was unsupported by record evidence that acts of the outlying districts affected the discrimination found to exist in the schools of Detroit. Accordingly, the judgment of the Court of Appeals is reversed and the case is remanded for further proceedings consistent with this opinion leading to prompt formulation of a decree directed to eliminating the segregation found to exist in Detroit city schools, a remedy which has been delayed since 1970.

Reversed and remanded.

NOTES

1.   The Supreme Court emphasized the need for local control in education. The dissent believed that insofar as the state is responsible for education, officials had the duty to use all available resources to correct segregation regardless of where it occurred. What, if any, is the relationship between control of the schools and segregation?

2.   What do you think about the Court's discussion of the lack of evidence of segregation outside of Detroit, coupled with the fact that the other school systems were not allowed to be heard, on the appropriateness of the proposed multi-district remedy?

[CASE NO. 120]   THE FEDERAL COURTS AND INTRA–DISTRICT REMEDIES FOR SEGREGATION

MILLIKEN v. BRADLEY (II)

Supreme Court of the United States, 1977.
433 U.S. 267, 97 S.Ct. 2749, 53 L.Ed.2d 745.

■ MR. CHIEF JUSTICE BURGER delivered the opinion of the Court.

We granted certiorari in this case to consider two questions concerning the remedial powers of federal district courts in school desegregation cases, namely, whether a District Court can, as part of a desegregation decree, order compensatory or remedial educational programs for schoolchildren who have been subjected to past acts of *de jure* segregation, and whether, consistent with the Eleventh Amendment, a federal court can require state officials found responsible for constitutional violations to bear part of the costs of those programs.

Due to the intervening death of Judge Stephen J. Roth, who had presided over the litigation from the outset, the case on remand was reassigned to Judge Robert E. DeMascio [who] promptly ordered respondent Bradley and the Detroit Board to submit desegregation plans limited to the Detroit school system. On April 1, 1975, both parties submitted their proposed plans. . . .

In addition to student reassignments, the Board's plan called for implementation of 13 remedial or compensatory programs, referred to in the record as "educational components." These compensatory programs, which were proposed in addition to the plan's provisions for magnet schools and vocational high schools, included three of the four components at issue in this case—in-service training for teachers and administrators, guidance and counseling programs, and revised testing procedures. Pursuant to the District Court's direction, the State Department of Education on April 21, 1975, submitted a critique of the Detroit Board's desegregation plan; in its report, the Department opined that, although "[i]t is possible that none of the thirteen 'quality education' components is essential . . . to correct the constitutional violation . . .", eight of the 13 proposed programs nonetheless deserved special consideration in the desegregation setting. . . .

After receiving the State Board's critique, the District Court conducted extensive hearings on the two plans over a two-month period. Substantial testimony was adduced with respect to the proposed educational components, including testimony by petitioners' expert witnesses. Based on this evidence and on reports of court-appointed experts, the District Court on August 11, 1975, approved, in principle, the Detroit Board's inclusion of remedial and compensatory educational components in the desegregation plan. . . .

The District Court expressly found that the two components of testing and counseling, as then administered in Detroit's schools, were infected with the discriminatory bias of a segregated school system. . . . The District Court also found that, to make desegregation work, it was necessary to include remedial reading programs and in-service training for teachers and administrators. . . .

Having established these general principles, the District Court formulated several "remedial guidelines" to govern the Detroit Board's development of a final plan. Declining "to substitute its authority for the authority of elected state and local officials to decide which educational components are beneficial to the school community," the District Judge laid down the following guidelines with respect to each of the four educational components at issue here [dealing with reading, in-service training, testing, and counseling and career guidance, and]:

Nine months later, on May 11, 1976, the District Court entered its final order. Emphasizing that it had "been careful to order only what is essential for a school district undergoing desegregation," the court ordered the Detroit Board and the state defendants to institute comprehensive programs as to the four educational components by the start of the September 1976 school term. The cost of these four programs, the court concluded, was to be equally borne by the Detroit School Board and the State. To carry out this cost-sharing, the court directed the local board to calculate its highest budget allocation in any prior year for the several educational programs and, from that base, any excess cost attributable to the desegregation plan was to be paid equally by the two groups of defendants responsible for prior constitutional violations, *i.e.*, the Detroit Board and the state defendants. . . .

This Court has not previously addressed directly the question whether federal courts can order remedial education programs as part of a school desegregation decree. However, the general principles governing our resolution of this issue are well settled by the prior decisions of this Court. In the first case concerning federal courts' remedial powers in eliminating *de jure* school segregation, the Court laid down the basic rule which governs to this day: "In fashioning and effectuating the [desegregation] decrees, the courts will be guided by equitable principles."

Application of those "equitable principles," we have held, requires federal courts to focus upon three factors. In the first place, like other equitable remedies, the nature of the desegregation remedy is to be determined by the nature and scope of the constitutional violation. The remedy must therefore be related to "the *condition* alleged to offend the Constitution. . . ." *Milliken I.* Second, the decree must indeed be *remedial* in nature, that is, it must be designed as nearly as possible "to restore the victims of discriminatory conduct to the position they would have occupied in the absence of such conduct." Third, the federal courts in devising a remedy must take into account the interests of state and local authorities in managing their own affairs, consistent with the Constitution. In *Brown II* the Court squarely held that "[s]chool authorities have the *primary* responsibility for elucidating, assessing, and solving these problems. . . ." If, however, "school authorities fail in their affirmative obligations . . . judicial authority may be invoked." Once invoked, "the scope of a district court's equitable powers to remedy past wrongs is broad, for breadth and flexibility are inherent in equitable remedies."

In challenging the order before us, petitioners do not specifically question that the District Court's mandated programs are designed, as nearly as practicable, to restore the schoolchildren of Detroit to a position they would have enjoyed absent constitutional violations by state and local officials. And, petitioners do not contend, nor could they, that the prerogatives of the Detroit School Board have been abrogated by the decree, since of course the Detroit School Board itself proposed incorporation of these programs in the first place. Petitioners' sole contention is that, under *Swann,* the District Court's order exceeds the scope of the constitutional violation. Invoking our holding in *Milliken I* petitioners claim that, since the constitutional violation found by the District Court was the unlawful segregation of students on the basis of race, the court's decree must be limited to remedying unlawful pupil assignments. This contention misconceives the principle petitioners seek to invoke, and we reject their argument.

The well-settled principle that the nature and scope of the remedy are to be determined by the violation means simply that federal court decrees must directly address and relate to the constitutional violation itself. Because of this inherent limitation upon federal judicial authority, federal court decrees exceed appropriate limits if they are aimed at eliminating a condition that does not violate the Constitution or does not flow from such a violation, or if they are imposed upon governmental units that were neither involved in nor affected by the constitutional violation, as in *Milliken I.* But where, as here, a constitutional violation has been found, the remedy does not "exceed" the violation if the remedy is tailored to cure the "*condition* that offends the Constitution."

The "condition" offending the Constitution is Detroit's *de jure* segregated school system, which was so pervasively and persistently segregated that the District Court found that the need for the educational components flowed directly from constitutional violations by both state and local officials. These specific educational remedies, although normally left to the discretion of the elected school board and professional educators, were deemed necessary to restore the victims of discriminatory conduct to the position they would have enjoyed in terms of education had these four components been provided in a nondiscriminatory manner in a school system free from pervasive *de jure* racial segregation.

. . .

. . . in *Swann* we reaffirmed the principle that "existing policy and practice with regard to faculty, staff, transportation, extracurricular activities, and facilities were among the most important indicia of a segregated system." In a word, discriminatory student assignment policies can themselves manifest and breed other inequalities built into a dual system founded on racial discrimination. Federal courts need not, and cannot, close their eyes to inequalities, shown by the record, which flow from a long-standing segregated system.

In light of the mandate of *Brown I* and *Brown II,* federal courts have, over the years, often required the inclusion of remedial programs in desegregation plans to overcome the inequalities inherent in dual school systems. . . .

. . . On this record . . . we are bound to conclude that the decree before us was aptly tailored to remedy the consequences of the constitutional violation. Children who have been thus educationally and culturally set apart from the larger community will inevitably acquire habits of speech, conduct, and attitudes reflecting their cultural isolation. They are likely to acquire speech habits, for example, which vary from the environment in which they must ultimately function and compete, if they are to enter and be a part of that community. This is not peculiar to race; in this setting, it can affect any children who, as a group, are isolated by force of law from the mainstream.

Pupil assignment alone does not automatically remedy the impact of previous, unlawful educational isolation; the consequences linger and can be dealt with only by independent measures....

The decree to share the future costs of educational components in this case fits squarely within the prospective-compliance exception.... That exception ... permits federal courts to enjoin state officials to conform their conduct to requirements of federal law, notwithstanding a direct and substantial impact on the state treasury. The order challenged here does no more than that. The decree requires state officials, held responsible for unconstitutional conduct, in findings which are not challenged, to eliminate a *de jure* segregated school system. More precisely, the burden of state officials is that set forth in *Swann*—to take the necessary steps "to eliminate from the public schools all vestiges of state-imposed segregation." The educational components, which the District Court ordered into effect *prospectively,* are plainly designed to wipe out continuing conditions of inequality produced by the inherently unequal dual school system long maintained by Detroit.... We therefore hold that such prospective relief is not barred by the Eleventh Amendment.

Finally, there is no merit to petitioners' claims that the relief ordered here violates the Tenth Amendment and general principles of federalism.

The judgment of the Court of Appeals is therefore

Affirmed

NOTES

1. Lower federal courts frequently ordered specific remedies other than busing or different student assignment techniques in attempting to correct the effects of de jure segregation. This was the first time the Supreme Court considered remedies other than student or teacher reassignments.

2. Do you agree with the trial court's guidelines? Did the trial court, despite its disclaimer, substitute its authority for that of state and local education officials in deciding which programs were beneficial to the school community?

[CASE NO. 121]   STANDARDS APPLICABLE TO DE FACTO SEGREGATION

KEYES v. SCHOOL DISTRICT NO. 1, DENVER, COLORADO

Supreme Court of the United States, 1973.
413 U.S. 189, 93 S.Ct. 2686, 37 L.Ed.2d 548.

■ Mr. Justice Brennan delivered the opinion of the Court.

This school desegregation case concerns the Denver, Colorado, school system. That system has never been operated under a constitutional or statutory provision that mandated or permitted racial segregation in public education. Rather, the gravamen of this action ... is that respondent School Board alone, by use of various techniques such as the manipulation of student attendance zones, schoolsite selection and a neighborhood school policy, created or maintained racially or ethnically (or both racially and ethnically) segregated schools throughout the school district, entitling petitioners to a decree directing desegregation of the entire school district. . . .

I

Before turning to the primary question we decide today, a word must be said about the . . . method of defining a "segregated" school. Denver is a tri-ethnic, as distinguished from a bi-racial, community. The over-all racial and ethnic composition of the Denver public schools is 66% Anglo, 14% Negro, and 20% Hispano. . . . What is or is not a segregated school will necessarily depend on the facts of each particular case. In addition to the racial and ethnic composition of a school's student body, other factors, such as the racial and ethnic composition of faculty and staff and the community and administration attitudes toward the school must be taken into consideration. . . .

. . . [T]hough of different origins Negroes and Hispanos in Denver suffer identical discrimination in treatment when compared with the treatment afforded Anglo students. In that circumstance, we think petitioners are entitled to have schools with a combined predominance of Negroes and Hispanos included in the category of "segregated" schools.

II

. . . Petitioners proved that for almost a decade after 1960 respondent School Board had engaged in an unconstitutional policy of deliberate racial segregation in the Park Hill schools. Indeed, the District Court found that "[b]etween 1960 and 1969 the Board's policies with respect to these northeast Denver schools show an undeviating purpose to isolate Negro students" in segregated schools "while preserving the Anglo character of [other] schools." This finding did not relate to an insubstantial or trivial fragment of the school system. On the contrary, respondent School Board was found guilty of following a deliberate segregation policy at schools attended, in 1969, by 37.69% of Denver's total Negro school population, including one-fourth of the Negro elementary pupils, over two-thirds of the Negro junior high pupils, and over two-fifths of the Negro high school pupils. In addition, there was uncontroverted evidence that teachers and staff had for years been assigned on the basis of a minority teacher to a minority school throughout the school system. Respondent argues, however, that a finding of state-imposed segregation as to a substantial portion of the school system can be viewed in isolation from the rest of the district, and that even if state-imposed segregation does exist in a substantial part of the Denver school system, it does not follow that the District Court could predicate on that fact a finding that the entire school system is a dual system. We do not agree. We have never suggested that plaintiffs in school desegregation cases must bear the burden of proving the elements of *de jure* segregation as to each and every school or each and every student within the school system. Rather, we have held that where plaintiffs prove that a current condition of segregated schooling exists within a school district where a dual system was compelled or authorized by statute at the time of our decision in *Brown I,* the State automatically assumes an affirmative duty "to effectuate a transition to a racially nondiscriminatory school system," that is, to eliminate from the public schools within their school system "all vestiges of state-imposed segregation."

This is not a case, however, where a statutory dual system has ever existed. Nevertheless, where plaintiffs prove that the school authorities have carried out a systematic program of segregation affecting a substantial portion of the students, schools, teachers, and facilities within the school system, it is only common sense to conclude that there exists a predicate for a finding of the existence of a dual school system. Several considerations support this conclusion. First, it is obvious that a practice of concentrating Negroes in certain schools by structuring attendance zones or designating "feeder" schools on the basis of race has the reciprocal effect of keeping other nearby schools predominantly white. Similarly, the practice of building a school—such as the Barrett Elementary School in this case—to a certain size and in a certain location, "with conscious knowledge that it would be a segregated school," has a substantial reciprocal effect on the racial composition of other nearby schools. So also, the use of mobile classrooms, the drafting of student transfer policies, the transportation of students, and the assignment of faculty and staff, on racially identifiable bases, have the clear effect of earmarking schools according to their racial composition, and this, in turn, together with the elements of student assignment and school construction, may have a profound reciprocal effect on the racial composition of residential neighborhoods within a metropolitan area, thereby causing further racial concentration within the schools. . . .

In short, common sense dictates the conclusion that racially inspired school board actions have an impact beyond the particular schools that are the subjects of those actions. This is not to say, of course, that there can never be a case in which the geographical structure of, or the natural boundaries within, a school district may have the effect of dividing the district into separate, identifiable and unrelated units. Such a determination is essentially a question of fact to be resolved by the trial court in the first instance, but such cases must be rare. In the absence of such a determination, proof of state-imposed segregation in a substantial portion of the district will suffice to support a finding by the trial court of the existence of a dual system. Of course, where that finding is made, as in cases involving statutory dual systems, the school authorities have an affirmative duty "to effectuate a transition to a racially nondiscriminatory school system."

III

. . .

On the question of segregative intent, petitioners presented evidence tending to show that the Board, through its actions over a period of years, intentionally created and maintained the segregated character of the core city schools. Respondents countered this evidence by arguing that the segregation in these schools is the result of a racially neutral "neighborhood school policy" and that the acts of which petitioners complain are explicable within the bounds of that policy. . . .

... Plainly, a finding of intentional segregation as to a portion of a school system is not devoid of probative value in assessing the school authorities' intent with respect to other parts of the same school system. On the contrary where, as here, the case involves one school board, a finding of intentional segregation on its part in one portion of a school system is highly relevant to the issue of the board's intent with respect to the other segregated schools in the system. This is merely an application of the well-settled evidentiary principle that "the prior doing of other similar acts, whether clearly a part of a scheme or not, is useful as reducing the possibility that the act in question was done with innocent intent." ...

... [W]e hold that a finding of intentionally segregative school board actions in a meaningful portion of a school system, as in this case, creates a presumption that other segregated schooling within the system is not adventitious. It establishes, in other words, a prima facie case of unlawful segregative design on the part of school authorities, and shifts to those authorities the burden of proving that other segregated schools within the system are not also the result of intentionally segregative actions. This is true even if it is determined that different areas of the school district should be viewed independently of each other because, even in that situation, there is high probability that where school authorities have effectuated an intentionally segregative policy in a meaningful portion of the school system, similar impermissible considerations have motivated their actions in other areas of the system. We emphasize that the differentiating factor between *de jure* segregation and so-called *de facto* segregation ... is *purpose* or *intent* to segregate. Where school authorities have been found to have practiced purposeful segregation in part of a school system, they may be expected to oppose system-wide desegregation, as did the respondents in this case, on the ground that their purposefully segregative actions were isolated and individual events, thus leaving plaintiffs with the burden of proving otherwise. But at that point where an intentionally segregative policy is practiced in a meaningful or significant segment of a school system, as in this case, the school authorities cannot be heard to argue that plaintiffs have proved only "isolated and individual" unlawfully segregative actions. In that circumstance, it is both fair and reasonable to require that the school authorities bear the burden of showing that their actions as to other segregated schools within the system were not also motivated by segregative intent. . . .

Thus, respondent School Board having been found to have practiced deliberate racial segregation in schools attended by over one-third of the Negro school population, that crucial finding establishes a prima facie case of intentional segregation in the core city schools. In such case, respondent's neighborhood school policy is not to be determinative "simply because it appears to be neutral."

IV

In summary, the District Court on remand, *first,* will afford respondent School Board the opportunity to prove its contention that the Park Hill area is a separate, identifiable and unrelated section of the school district that should be treated as isolated from the rest of the district. If respondent

School Board fails to prove that contention, the District Court, *second,* will determine whether respondent School Board's conduct over almost a decade after 1960 in carrying out a policy of deliberate racial segregation in the Park Hill schools constitutes the entire school system a dual school system. If the District Court determines that the Denver school system is a dual school system, respondent School Board has the affirmative duty to desegregate the entire system "root and branch." If the District Court determines, however, that the Denver school system is not a dual school system by reason of the Board's actions in Park Hill, the court, *third,* will afford respondent School Board the opportunity to rebut petitioners' prima facie case of intentional segregation in the core city schools raised by the finding of intentional segregation in the Park Hill schools. There, the Board's burden is to show that its policies and practices with respect to schoolsite location, school size, school renovations and additions, student-attendance zones, student assignment and transfer options, mobile class-room units, transportation of students, assignment of faculty and staff, etc., considered together and premised on the Board's so-called "neighborhood school" concept, either were not taken in effectuation of a policy to create or maintain segregation in the core city schools, or, if unsuccessful in that effort, were not factors in causing the existing condition of segregation in these schools. Considerations of "fairness" and "policy" demand no less in light of the Board's intentionally segregative actions. If respondent Board fails to rebut petitioners' prima facie case, the District Court must, as in the case of Park Hill, decree all-out desegregation of the core city schools.

The judgment of the Court of Appeals is modified to vacate instead of reverse the parts of the Final Decree that concern the core city schools, and the case is remanded to the District Court for further proceedings consistent with this opinion

Modified and remanded.

It is so ordered.

NOTES

1. Note the indicia in the last paragraph for determining what makes a school segregated.

2. Denver failed to achieve unitary status until twenty-two-years later. *Keyes v. Congress of Hispanic Educators,* 902 F.Supp. 1274 [104 Educ. L. Rep. 1067] (D. Colo. 1995), *appeal dismissed sub nom. Keyes v. School Dist. No. 1, Denver, Colo.,* 119 F.3d 1437 [120 Educ. L. Rep. 158] (10th Cir. 1997).

[CASE NO. 122] DESEGREGATION ORDERS NOT MEANT TO OPERATE IN PERPETUITY

BOARD OF EDUCATION OF OKLAHOMA CITY PUBLIC SCHOOLS, INDEPENDENT SCHOOL DISTRICT NO. 89 v. DOWELL

Supreme Court of the United States, 1991.
498 U.S. 237, 111 S.Ct. 630, 112 L.Ed.2d 715 [64 Educ. L. Rep. 628].

■ CHIEF JUSTICE REHNQUIST delivered the opinion of the Court.

Petitioner Board of Education of Oklahoma City sought dissolution of a decree entered by the District Court imposing a school desegregation plan. The District Court granted relief over the objection of respondents Robert L. Dowell, black students and their parents. The Court of Appeals for the Tenth Circuit reversed, holding that the Board would be entitled to such relief only upon " '[n]othing less than a clear showing of grievous wrong evoked by new and unforeseen conditions....' " We hold that the Court of Appeals' test is more stringent than is required either by our cases dealing with injunctions or by the Equal Protection Clause....

I

This school desegregation litigation began almost 30 years ago. In 1961, respondents, black students and their parents, sued petitioners, the Board of Education of Oklahoma City (Board), to end *de jure* segregation in the public schools. In 1963, the District Court found that Oklahoma City had intentionally segregated both schools and housing in the past, and that Oklahoma City was operating a "dual" school system—one that was intentionally segregated by race. In 1965, the District Court found that the School Board's attempt to desegregate by using neighborhood zoning failed to remedy past segregation because residential segregation resulted in one-race schools. Residential segregation had once been state imposed, and it lingered due to discrimination by some realtors and financial institutions. The District Court found that school segregation had caused some housing segregation. In 1972, finding that previous efforts had not been successful at eliminating state imposed segregation, the District Court ordered the Board to adopt the "Finger Plan," under which kindergarteners would be assigned to neighborhood schools unless their parents opted otherwise; children in grades 1–4 would attend formerly all white schools, and thus black children would be bused to those schools; children in grade 5 would attend formerly all black schools, and thus white children would be bused to those schools; students in the upper grades would be bused to various areas in order to maintain integrated schools; and in integrated neighborhoods there would be stand-alone schools for all grades.

In 1977, after complying with the desegregation decree for five years, the Board made a "Motion to Close Case." The District Court held that "... Jurisdiction in this case is terminated ipso facto subject only to final disposition of any case now pending on appeal." This unpublished order was not appealed.

In 1984, the School Board faced demographic changes that led to greater burdens on young black children. As more and more neighborhoods became integrated, more stand-alone schools were established, and young black students had to be bused farther from their inner-city homes to outlying white areas. In an effort to alleviate this burden and to increase parental involvement, the Board adopted the Student Reassignment Plan (SRP), which relied on neighborhood assignments for students in grades K–4 beginning in the 1985–1986 school year. Busing continued for students in grades 5–12. Any student could transfer from a school where he or she was in the majority to a school where he or she would be in the minority. Faculty and staff integration was retained, and an "equity officer" was appointed.

In 1985, respondents filed a "Motion to Reopen the Case," contending that the School District had not achieved "unitary" status and that the SRP was a return to segregation. Under the SRP, 11 of 64 elementary schools would be greater than 90% black, 22 would be greater than 90% white plus other minorities, and 31 would be racially mixed. The District Court refused to reopen the case, holding that its 1977 finding of unitariness was *res judicata* as to those who were then parties to the action, and that the district remained unitary. The District Court found that the School Board, administration, faculty, support staff, and student body were integrated, and transportation, extracurricular activities and facilities within the district were equal and nondiscriminatory. Because unitariness had been achieved, the District Court concluded that court-ordered desegregation must end.

The Court of Appeals for the Tenth Circuit reversed....

On remand, the District Court found that demographic changes made the Finger Plan unworkable, that the Board had done nothing for 25 years to promote residential segregation, and that the school district had bused students for more than a decade in good-faith compliance with the court's orders. The District Court found that present residential segregation was the result of private decisionmaking and economics, and that it was too attenuated to be a vestige of former school segregation. It also found that the district had maintained its unitary status, and that the neighborhood assignment plan was not designed with discriminatory intent. The court concluded that the previous injunctive decree should be vacated and the school district returned to local control.

The Court of Appeals again reversed, holding that " 'an injunction takes on a life of its own and becomes an edict quite independent of the law it is meant to effectuate.' " ... it held that a desegregation decree remains in effect until a school district can show "grievous wrong evoked by new and unforseen conditions" and "dramatic changes in conditions unforseen at the time of the decree that ... impose extreme and unexpectedly oppressive hardships on the obligor." Given that a number of schools would return to being primarily one-race schools under the SRP, circumstances in Oklahoma City had not changed enough to justify modification of the decree. The Court of Appeals held that, despite the unitary finding, the

Board had the " 'affirmative duty ... not to take any action that would impede the process of disestablishing the dual system and its effects.' "

We granted the Board's petition for certiorari to resolve a conflict between the standard laid down by the Court of Appeals in this case and that laid down in *Spangler v. Pasadena City Board of Education* and *Riddick v. School Bd. of City of Norfolk*. We now reverse....

II

We must first consider whether respondents may contest the District Court's 1987 order dissolving the injunction which had imposed the desegregation decree. Respondents did not appeal from the District Court's 1977 order finding that the school system had achieved unitary status, and petitioner contends that the 1977 order bars respondents from contesting the 1987 order. We disagree, for the 1977 order did not dissolve the desegregation decree, and the District Court's unitariness finding was too ambiguous to bar respondents from challenging later action by the Board.

The lower courts have been inconsistent in their use of the term "unitary." Some have used it to identify a school district that has completely remedied all vestiges of past discrimination. Under that interpretation of the word, a unitary school district is one that has met the mandate of *Brown v. Board of Education*. Other courts, however, have used "unitary" to describe any school district that has currently desegregated student assignments, whether or not that status is solely the result of a court-imposed desegregation plan. In other words, such a school district could be called unitary and nevertheless still contain vestiges of past discrimination. That there is such confusion is evident in *Georgia State Conference of Branches of NAACP v. Georgia*, where the Court of Appeals drew a distinction between a "unitary school district" and a district that has achieved "unitary status." The court explained that a school district that has not operated segregated schools ... "for a period of several years" is unitary, but that a school district cannot be said to have achieved "unitary status" unless it "has eliminated the vestiges of its prior discrimination and has been adjudicated as such through the proper judicial procedures."

We think it is a mistake to treat words such as "dual" and "unitary" as if they were actually found in the Constitution. The constitutional command of the Fourteenth Amendment is that "[n]o State shall ... deny to any person ... the equal protection of the laws." Courts have used the terms "dual" to denote a school system which has engaged in intentional segregation of students by race, and "unitary" to describe a school system which has been brought into compliance with the command of the Constitution. We are not sure how useful it is to define these terms more precisely, or to create subclasses within them. But there is no doubt that the differences in usage described above do exist. The District Court's 1977 order is unclear with respect to what it meant by unitary and the necessary result of that finding. We therefore decline to overturn the conclusion of the Court of Appeals that while the 1977 order of the District Court did bind the parties as to the unitary character of the district, it did not finally terminate the Oklahoma City school litigation. In *Pasadena City Board of Education v. Spangler*, we held that a school board is entitled to a rather precise statement of its obligations under a desegregation decree. If such a decree is to be terminated or dissolved, respondents as well as the school board are entitled to a like statement from the court.

III

The Court of Appeals relied upon language from this Court's decision in *United States v. Swift and Co.*, for the proposition that a desegregation decree could not be lifted or modified absent a showing of "grievous wrong evoked by new and unforeseen conditions." It also held that "compliance alone cannot become the basis for modifying or dissolving an injunction." We hold that its reliance was mistaken.

. . .

. . . . In the present case, a finding by the District Court that the Oklahoma City School District was being operated in compliance with the commands of the Equal Protection Clause of the Fourteenth Amendment, and that it was unlikely that the school board would return to its former ways, would be a finding that the purposes of the desegregation litigation had been fully achieved. No additional showing of "grievous wrong evoked by new and unforeseen conditions" is required of the school board.

In *Milliken v. Bradley [II]*, we said:

> "[F]ederal-court decrees must directly address and relate to the constitutional violation itself. Because of this inherent limitation upon federal judicial authority, federal-court decrees exceed appropriate limits if they are aimed at eliminating a condition that does not violate the Constitution or does not flow from such a violation. . . ."

From the very first, federal supervision of local school systems was intended as a temporary measure to remedy past discrimination. *Brown* considered the "complexities arising from the transition to a system of public education freed of racial discrimination" in holding that the implementation of desegregation was to proceed "with all deliberate speed." *Green* also spoke of the "transition to a unitary, nonracial system of public education."

Considerations based on the allocation of powers within our federal system, we think, support our view that quoted language from *Swift* does not provide the proper standard to apply to injunctions entered in school desegregation cases. Such decrees, unlike the one in *Swift*, are not intended to operate in perpetuity. Local control over the education of children allows citizens to participate in decisionmaking, and allows innovation so that school programs can fit local needs. The legal justification for displacement of local authority by an injunctive decree in a school desegregation case is a violation of the Constitution by the local authorities. Dissolving a desegregation decree after the local authorities have operated in compliance with it for a reasonable period of time properly recognizes that "necessary concern for the important values of local control of public school systems dictates that a federal court's regulatory control of such systems not extend beyond the time required to remedy the effects of past intentional discrimination."

The Court of Appeals, as noted, relied for its statement that "compliance alone cannot become the basis for modifying or dissolving an injunction" on our decision in *United States v. W.T. Grant Co.* That case, however, did not involve the dissolution of an injunction, but the question of whether an injunction should be issued in the first place. This Court observed that a promise to comply with the law on the part of a wrongdoer did not divest a district court of its power to enjoin the wrongful conduct in which the defendant had previously engaged.

A district court need not accept at face value the profession of a school board which has intentionally discriminated that it will cease to do so in the future. But in deciding whether to modify or dissolve a desegregation decree, a school board's compliance with previous court orders is obviously relevant. In this case the original finding of *de jure* segregation was entered in 1961, the injunctive decree from which the Board seeks relief was entered in 1972, and the Board complied with the decree in good faith until 1985. Not only do the personnel of school boards change over time, but the same passage of time enables the District Court to observe the good faith of the school board in complying with the decree. The test espoused by the Court of Appeals would condemn a school district, once governed by a board which intentionally discriminated, to judicial tutelage for the indefinite future. Neither the principles governing the entry and dissolution of injunctive decrees, nor the commands of the Equal Protection Clause of the Fourteenth Amendment, require any such Draconian result.

Petitioner urges that we reinstate the decision of the District Court terminating the injunction, but we think that the preferable course is to remand the case to that court so that it may decide, in accordance with this opinion, whether the Board made a sufficient showing of constitutional compliance as of 1985, when the SRP was adopted, to allow the injunction to be dissolved. The District Court should address itself to whether the Board had complied in good faith with the desegregation decree since it was entered, and whether the vestiges of past discrimination had been eliminated to the extent practicable.

In considering whether the vestiges of *de jure* segregation had been eliminated as far as practicable, the District Court should look not only at student assignments, but "to every facet of school operations—faculty, staff, transportation, extra-curricular activities and facilities."

After the District Court decides whether the Board was entitled to have the decree terminated, it should proceed to decide respondent's challenge to the SRP. A school district which has been released from an injunction imposing a desegregation plan no longer requires court authorization for the promulgation of policies and rules regulating matters such as assignment of students and the like, but it of course remains subject to the mandate of the Equal Protection Clause of the Fourteenth Amendment. If the Board was entitled to have the decree terminated as of 1985, the District Court should then evaluate the Board's decision to implement the SRP under appropriate equal protection principles.

The judgment of the Court of Appeals is reversed, and the case is remanded to the District Court for further proceedings consistent with this opinion.

It is so ordered.

NOTE

1. Many school desegregation cases experienced multiple rounds of litigation. Since this is the case, do you think that the Supreme Court was signaling that it was no longer concerned with school desegregation?

2. What should the role of the federal judiciary be in school desegregation cases?

[CASE NO. 123] INCREMENTAL TERMINATION OF JUDICIAL OVERSIGHT OF DESEGREGATION PLANS

FREEMAN v. PITTS

Supreme Court of the United States, 1992.
503 U.S. 467, 112 S.Ct. 1430, 118 L.Ed.2d 108 [72 Educ. L. Rep. 717].

■ JUSTICE KENNEDY delivered the opinion of the Court.

DeKalb County, Georgia, is a major suburban area of Atlanta. This case involves a court-ordered desegregation decree for the DeKalb County School System (DCSS). DCSS now serves some 73,000 students in kindergarten through high school and is the 32nd largest elementary and secondary school system in the Nation.

DCSS has been subject to the supervision and jurisdiction of the United States District Court for the Northern District of Georgia since 1969, when it was ordered to dismantle its dual school system. In 1986, petitioners filed a motion for final dismissal.... We now [hold] that a district court is permitted to withdraw judicial supervision with respect to discrete categories in which the school district has achieved compliance with a court-ordered desegregation plan. A district court need not retain active control over every aspect of school administration until a school district has demonstrated unitary status in all facets of its system.

I

A

For decades before our decision in *Brown v. Board of Education* (*Brown I*) and our mandate in *Brown v. Board of Education* (*Brown II*), which ordered school districts to desegregate with "all deliberate speed," DCSS was segregated by law. DCSS's initial response to the mandate of *Brown II* was an all too familiar one. Interpreting "all deliberate speed" as giving latitude to delay steps to desegregate, DCSS took no positive action toward desegregation until the 1966–1967 school year, when it did nothing more than adopt a freedom of choice transfer plan. Some black students chose to attend former *de jure* white schools, but the plan had no significant effect on the former *de jure* black schools.

In 1968 we decided *Green v. New Kent County School Bd.* We held that adoption of a freedom of choice plan does not, by itself, satisfy a school district's mandatory responsibility to eliminate all vestiges of a dual system. *Green* was a turning point in our law in a further respect.... We said that the obligation of school districts once segregated by law was to come forward with a plan that "promises realistically to work, and promises realistically to work *now*." The case before us requires an understanding and assessment of how DCSS responded to the directives set forth in *Green*.

Within two months of our ruling in *Green*, respondents, who are black school children and their parents, instituted this class action in the United States District Court for the Northern District of Georgia. After the suit was filed, DCSS voluntarily began working with the Department of Health, Education and Welfare to devise a comprehensive and final plan of desegregation. The District Court in June 1969 entered a consent order approving the proposed plan, which was to be implemented in the 1969–1970 school year. The order abolished the freedom of choice plan and adopted a neighborhood school attendance plan that had been proposed by the DCSS and accepted by the Department of Health, Education and Welfare subject to a minor modification. Under the plan all of the former *de jure* black schools were closed and their students were reassigned among the remaining neighborhood schools. The District Court retained jurisdiction.

Between 1969 and 1986 respondents sought only infrequent and limited judicial intervention into the affairs of DCSS. . . .

In 1986 petitioners filed a motion for final dismissal of the litigation. They sought a declaration that DCSS had satisfied its duty to eliminate the dual education system, that is to say a declaration that the school system had achieved unitary status. The District Court approached the question whether DCSS had achieved unitary status by asking whether DCSS was unitary with respect to each of the factors identified in *Green*. The court considered an additional factor that is not named in *Green*: the quality of education being offered to the white and black student populations.

The District Court found DCSS to be "an innovative school system that has travelled the often long road to unitary status almost to its end," noting that "the court has continually been impressed by the successes of the DCSS and its dedication to providing a quality education for all students within that system." It found that DCSS is a unitary system with regard to student assignments, transportation, physical facilities, and extracurricular activities, and ruled that it would order no further relief in those areas. The District Court stopped short of dismissing the case, however, because it found that DCSS was not unitary in every respect. The court said that vestiges of the dual system remain in the areas of teacher and principal assignments, resource allocation, and quality of education. DCSS was ordered to take measures to address the remaining problems.

B

Proper resolution of any desegregation case turns on a careful assessment of its facts. Here, as in most cases where the issue is the degree of compliance with a school desegregation decree, a critical beginning point is the degree of racial imbalance in the school district, that is to say a comparison of the proportion of majority to minority students in individual schools with the proportions of the races in the district as a whole. This inquiry is fundamental, for under the former *de jure* regimes racial exclusion was both the means and the end of a policy motivated by disparagement of or hostility towards the disfavored race. In accord with this principle, the District Court began its analysis with an assessment of the current racial mix in the schools throughout DCSS and the explanation for the racial imbalance it found. . . .

In the extensive record that comprises this case, one fact predominates: remarkable changes in the racial composition of the county presented DCSS and the District Court with a student population in 1986 far different from the one they set out to integrate in 1969. Between 1950 and 1985, DeKalb County grew from 70,000 to 450,000 in total population, but most of the gross increase in student enrollment had occurred by 1969, the relevant starting date for our purposes. Although the public school population experienced only modest changes between 1969 and 1986 (remaining in the low 70,000's), a striking change occurred in the racial proportions of the student population. The school system that the District Court ordered desegregated in 1969 had 5.6% black students; by 1986 the percentage of black students was 47%.

To compound the difficulty of working with these radical demographic changes, the northern and southern parts of the county experienced much different growth patterns. The District Court found that "[a]s the result of these demographic shifts, the population of the northern half of DeKalb County is now predominantly white and the southern half of DeKalb County is predominantly black." In 1970, there were 7,615 nonwhites living in the northern part of DeKalb County and 11,508 nonwhites in the southern part of the county. By 1980, there were 15,365 nonwhites living in the northern part of the county, and 87,583 nonwhites in the southern part. Most of the growth in the nonwhite population in the southern portion of the county was due to the migration of black persons from the city of Atlanta. Between 1975 and 1980 alone, approximately 64,000 black citizens moved into southern DeKalb County, most of them coming from Atlanta. During the same period, approximately 37,000 white citizens moved out of southern DeKalb County to the surrounding counties.

. . .

The demographic changes that occurred during the course of the desegregation order are an essential foundation for the District Court's analysis of the current racial mix of DCSS. As the District Court observed, the demographic shifts have had "an immense effect on the racial compositions of the DeKalb County schools." From 1976 to 1986, enrollment in elementary schools declined overall by 15%, while black enrollment in elementary schools increased by 86%. During the same period, overall high school enrollment declined by 16%, while black enrollment in high school increased by 119%. These effects were even more pronounced in the southern portion of DeKalb County. . . .

Respondents argued in the District Court that this racial imbalance in student assignment was a vestige of the dual system, rather than a product of independent demographic forces. In addition to the statistical evidence that the ratio of black students to white students in individual schools varied to a significant degree from the system-wide average, respondents contended that DCSS had not used all available desegregative tools in order to achieve racial balancing....

Although the District Court found that DCSS was desegregated for at least a short period under the court-ordered plan of 1969, it did not base its finding that DCSS had achieved unitary status with respect to student assignment on that circumstance alone. Recognizing that "[t]he achievement of unitary status in the area of student assignment cannot be hedged on the attainment of such status for a brief moment," the District Court examined the interaction between DCSS policy and demographic shifts in DeKalb County.

The District Court noted that DCSS had taken specific steps to combat the effects of demographics on the racial mix of the schools. Under the 1969 order, a biracial committee had reviewed all proposed changes in the boundary lines of school attendance zones. Since the original desegregation order, there had been about 170 such changes. It was found that only three had a partial segregative effect....

The District Court also noted that DCSS, on its own initiative, ... [had taken some steps to promote more balanced student assignments]....

Having found no constitutional violation with respect to student assignment, the District Court next considered the other *Green* factors, beginning with faculty and staff assignments.... [It ordered more to be done to integrate teachers and to disperse black administrators throughout the system.] ...

. . .

Despite its finding that there was no intentional violation, the District Court found that DCSS had not achieved unitary status with respect to quality of education because teachers in schools with disproportionately high percentages of white students tended to be better educated and have more experience than their counterparts in schools with disproportionately high percentages of black students, and because per pupil expenditures in majority white schools exceeded per pupil expenditures in majority black schools. From these findings, the District Court ordered DCSS to equalize spending and remedy the other problems.

The final *Green* factors considered by the District Court were: (1) physical facilities, (2) transportation, and (3) extracurricular activities....

In accordance with its factfinding, the District Court held that it would order no further relief in the areas of student assignment, transportation, physical facilities and extracurricular activities. The District Court, however, did order DCSS to establish a system to balance teacher and principal assignments and to equalize per pupil expenditures throughout DCSS. Having found that blacks were represented on the school board and throughout DCSS administration, the District Court abolished the biracial committee as no longer necessary.

Both parties appealed to the United States Court of Appeals for the Eleventh Circuit.... [which held that the board had to satisfy all six *Green* factors at the same time in order to achieve unitary status].

II

Two principal questions are presented. The first is whether a district court may relinquish its supervision and control over those aspects of a school system in which there has been compliance with a desegregation decree if other aspects of the system remain in noncompliance. As we answer this question in the affirmative, the second question is whether the Court of Appeals erred in reversing the District Court's order providing for incremental withdrawal of supervision in all the circumstances of this case.

A

The duty and responsibility of a school district once segregated by law is to take all steps necessary to eliminate the vestiges of the unconstitutional *de jure* system. This is required in order to insure that the principal wrong of the *de jure* system, the injuries and stigma inflicted upon the race disfavored by the violation, is no longer present. . . .

The concept of unitariness has been a helpful one in defining the scope of the district courts' authority, for it conveys the central idea that a school district that was once a dual system must be examined in all of its facets, both when a remedy is ordered and in the later phases of desegregation when the question is whether the district courts' remedial control ought to be modified, lessened, or withdrawn. But, as we explained last term in *Board of Education of Oklahoma City v. Dowell,* the term "unitary" is not a precise concept:

> "[I]t is a mistake to treat words such as 'dual' and 'unitary' as if they were actually found in the Constitution. . . . Courts have used the term 'dual' to denote a school system which has engaged in intentional segregation of students by race, and 'unitary' to describe a school system which has been brought into compliance with the command of the Constitution. We are not sure how useful it is to define these terms more precisely, or to create subclasses within them."

It follows that we must be cautious not to attribute to the term a utility it does not have. The term "unitary" does not confine the discretion and authority of the District Court in a way that departs from traditional equitable principles.

That the term "unitary" does not have fixed meaning or content is not inconsistent with the principles that control the exercise of equitable power. The essence of a court's equity power lies in its inherent capacity to adjust remedies in a feasible and practical way to eliminate the conditions or redress the injuries caused by unlawful action. Equitable remedies must be flexible if these underlying principles are to be enforced with fairness and precision. . . .

. . . A federal court in a school desegregation case has the discretion to order an incremental or partial withdrawal of its supervision and control. This discretion derives both from the constitutional authority which justified its intervention in the first instance and its ultimate objectives in formulating the decree. The authority of the court is invoked at the outset to remedy particular constitutional violations. In construing the remedial authority of the district courts, we have been guided by the principles that "judicial powers may be exercised only on the basis of a constitutional violation," and that "the nature of the violation determines the scope of the remedy." A remedy is justifiable only insofar as it advances the ultimate objective of alleviating the initial constitutional violation.

We have said that the court's end purpose must be to remedy the violation and in addition to restore state and local authorities to the control of a school system that is operating in compliance with the Constitution.... Partial relinquishment of judicial control, where justified by the facts of the case, can be an important and significant step in fulfilling the district court's duty to return the operations and control of schools to local authorities....

We hold that, in the course of supervising desegregation plans, federal courts have the authority to relinquish supervision and control of school districts in incremental stages, before full compliance has been achieved in every area of school operations. While retaining jurisdiction over the case, the court may determine that it will not order further remedies in areas where the school district is in compliance with the decree. That is to say, upon a finding that a school system subject to a court-supervised desegregation plan is in compliance in some but not all areas, the court in appropriate cases may return control to the school system in those areas where compliance has been achieved, limiting further judicial supervision to operations that are not yet in full compliance with the court decree. In particular, the district court may determine that it will not order further remedies in the area of student assignments where racial imbalance is not traceable, in a proximate way, to constitutional violations.

A court's discretion to order the incremental withdrawal of its supervision in a school desegregation case must be exercised in a manner consistent with the purposes and objectives of its equitable power. Among the factors which must inform the sound discretion of the court in ordering partial withdrawal are the following: whether there has been full and satisfactory compliance with the decree in those aspects of the system where supervision is to be withdrawn; whether retention of judicial control is necessary or practicable to achieve compliance with the decree in other facets of the school system; and whether the school district has demonstrated, to the public and to the parents and students of the once disfavored race, its good faith commitment to the whole of the court's decree and to those provisions of the law and the Constitution that were the predicate for judicial intervention in the first instance.

In considering these factors a court should give particular attention to the school system's record of compliance. A school system is better positioned to demonstrate its good-faith commitment to a constitutional course of action when its policies form a consistent pattern of lawful conduct directed to eliminating earlier violations....

B

We reach now the question whether the Court of Appeals erred in prohibiting the District Court from returning to DCSS partial control over some of its affairs. We decide that the Court of Appeals did err in holding that, as a matter of law, the District Court had no discretion to permit DCSS to regain control over student assignment, transportation, physical facilities, and extracurricular activities, while retaining court supervision over the areas of faculty and administrative assignments and the quality of education, where full compliance had not been demonstrated.

It was an appropriate exercise of its discretion for the District Court to address the elements of a unitary system discussed in *Green,* to inquire whether other elements ought to be identified, and to determine whether minority students were being disadvantaged in ways that required the formulation of new and further remedies to insure full compliance with the court's decree. Both parties agreed that quality of education was a legitimate inquiry in determining DCSS' compliance with the desegregation decree, and the trial court found it workable to consider the point in connection with its findings on resource allocation. . . . The District Court's approach illustrates that the *Green* factors need not be a rigid framework. . . .

That there was racial imbalance in student attendance zones was not tantamount to a showing that the school district was in noncompliance with the decree or with its duties under the law. Racial balance is not to be achieved for its own sake. It is to be pursued when racial imbalance has been caused by a constitutional violation. Once the racial imbalance due to the *de jure* violation has been remedied, the school district is under no duty to remedy imbalance that is caused by demographic factors. . . . If the unlawful *de jure* policy of a school system has been the cause of the racial imbalance in student attendance, that condition must be remedied. The school district bears the burden of showing that any current imbalance is not traceable, in a proximate way, to the prior violation.

The findings of the District Court that the population changes which occurred in DeKalb County were not caused by the policies of the school district, but rather by independent factors, are consistent with the mobility that is a distinct characteristic of our society. . . .

The requirement that the school district show its good faith commitment to the entirety of a desegregation plan so that parents, students and the public have assurance against further injuries or stigma also should be a subject for more specific findings. We stated in [*Board of Educ. of Oklahoma City v.*] *Dowell* that the good faith compliance of the district with the court order over a reasonable period of time is a factor to be considered in deciding whether or not jurisdiction could be relinquished. A history of good-faith compliance is evidence that any current racial imbalance is not the product of a new *de jure* violation, and enables the district court to accept the school board's representation that it has accepted the principle of racial equality and will not suffer intentional discrimination in the future. . . .

. . .

The judgment is reversed, and the case is remanded to the Court of Appeals. It should determine what issues are open for its further consideration in light of the previous briefs and arguments of the parties and in light of the principles set forth in this opinion. Thereupon it should order further proceedings as necessary or order an appropriate remand to the District Court.

Each party is to bear its own costs.

It is so ordered.

NOTES

1. What do you think about the Supreme Court's repeated emphasis on the element of good-faith compliance? Can it really be measured?

2. The Court placed the burden of showing that any current imbalance in student attendance patterns is not the result of earlier de jure segregation on local school boards. Was this fair? Was it appropriate?

3. Can a school system truly be desegregated if elements of segregation remain?

[CASE NO. 124]   LIMITS ON JUDICIAL AUTHORITY IN SCHOOL DESEGREGATION LITIGATION

MISSOURI v. JENKINS (III)

Supreme Court of the United States, 1995.
515 U.S. 70, 115 S.Ct. 2038, 132 L.Ed.2d 63 [100 Educ. L. Rep. 506].

■ Chief Justice Rehnquist delivered the opinion of the Court.

As this school desegregation litigation enters its 18th year, we are called upon again to review the decisions of the lower courts. In this case, the State of Missouri has challenged the District Court's order of salary increases for virtually all instructional and noninstructional staff within the Kansas City, Missouri, School District (KCMSD) and the District Court's order requiring the State to continue to fund remedial "quality education" programs because student achievement levels were still "at or below national norms at many grade levels."

I

A general overview of this litigation is necessary for proper resolution of the issues upon which we granted certiorari. This case has been before the same United States District Judge since 1977. . . . Plaintiffs alleged that the State, the surrounding suburban school districts (SSD's), and various federal agencies had caused and perpetuated a system of racial segregation in the schools of the Kansas City metropolitan area. The District Court realigned the KCMSD as a nominal defendant and certified as a class, present and future KCMSD students. The KCMSD brought a cross-claim against the State for its failure to eliminate the vestiges of its prior dual school system.

After a trial that lasted 7 1/2 months, the District Court dismissed the case against the federal defendants and the SSD's, but determined that the State and the KCMSD were liable for an intradistrict violation, i.e., they had operated a segregated school system within the KCMSD. The District Court determined that prior to 1954 "Missouri mandated segregated schools for black and white children." Furthermore, the KCMSD and the

State had failed in their affirmative obligations to eliminate the vestiges of the State's dual school system within the KCMSD.

In June 1985, the District Court issued its first remedial order and established as its goal the "elimination of all vestiges of state imposed segregation." The District Court determined that "[s]egregation ha[d] caused a system wide reduction in student achievement in the schools of the KCMSD." The District Court made no particularized findings regarding the extent that student achievement had been reduced or what portion of that reduction was attributable to segregation. . . .

The District Court, pursuant to plans submitted by the KCMSD and the State, ordered a wide range of quality education programs for all students attending the KCMSD. . . .

The KCMSD was awarded an AAA rating in the 1987–1988 school year, and there is no dispute that since that time it has " 'maintained and greatly exceeded AAA requirements.' " The total cost for these quality education programs has exceeded $220 million.

The District Court also set out to desegregate the KCMSD but believed that "[t]o accomplish desegregation within the boundary lines of a school district whose enrollment remains 68.3% black is a difficult task." Because it had found no interdistrict violation, the District Court could not order mandatory interdistrict redistribution of students between the KCMSD and the surrounding SSD's. The District Court refused to order additional mandatory student reassignments because they would "increase the instability of the KCMSD and reduce the potential for desegregation." . . .

In November 1986, the District Court approved a comprehensive magnet school and capital improvements plan and held the State and the KCMSD jointly and severally liable for its funding. Under the District Court's plan, every senior high school, every middle school, and one-half of the elementary schools were converted into magnet schools. The District Court adopted the magnet-school program to "provide a greater educational opportunity to all KCMSD students" and because it believed "that the proposed magnet plan [was] so attractive that it would draw non-minority students from the private schools who have abandoned or avoided the KCMSD, and draw in additional non-minority students from the suburbs. . . ." Since its inception, the magnet-school program has operated at a cost, including magnet transportation, in excess of $448 million . . .

In June 1985, the District Court ordered substantial capital improvements to combat the deterioration of the KCMSD's facilities. . . . [it] dismissed as "irrelevant" the "State's argument that the present condition of the facilities [was] not traceable to unlawful segregation." Instead, the District Court focused on its responsibility to "remed[y] the vestiges of segregation" and to "implemen[t] a desegregation plan which w[ould] maintain and attract non-minority enrollment." The initial phase of the capital-improvements plan cost $37 million. The District Court also required the KCMSD to present further capital-improvements proposals "in order to bring its facilities to a point comparable with the facilities in neighboring suburban school districts." In November 1986, the District Court approved further capital improvements in order to remove the vestiges of racial segregation and "to ... attract non-minority students back to the KCMSD."

In September 1987, the District Court adopted, for the most part, KCMSD's long-range capital-improvements plan at a cost in excess of $187 million. The plan called for the renovation of approximately 55 schools, the closure of 18 facilities, and the construction of 17 new schools.... As of 1990, the District Court had ordered $260 million in capital improvements. Since then, the total cost of capital improvements ordered has soared to over $540 million.

As part of its desegregation plan, the District Court has ordered salary assistance ... only for teachers within the KCMSD. Since that time, however, the District Court has ordered salary assistance to all but three of the approximately 5,000 KCMSD employees. The total cost of this component of the desegregation remedy since 1987 is over $200 million.

The District Court's desegregation plan has been described as the most ambitious and expensive remedial program in the history of school desegregation. The annual cost per pupil at the KCMSD far exceeds that of the neighboring SSD's or of any school district in Missouri. Nevertheless, the KCMSD, which has pursued a "friendly adversary" relationship with the plaintiffs, has continued to propose ever more expensive programs. As a result, the desegregation costs have escalated and now are approaching an annual cost of $200 million. These massive expenditures have financed high schools in which every classroom will have air conditioning, an alarm system, and 15 microcomputers; a 2,000–square–foot planetarium; green houses and vivariums; a 25–acre farm with an air-conditioned meeting room for 104 people; a Model United Nations wired for language translation; broadcast capable radio and television studios with an editing and animation lab; a temperature controlled art gallery; movie editing and screening rooms; a 3,500–square–foot dust-free diesel mechanics room; 1,875–square–foot elementary school animal rooms for use in a zoo project; swimming pools; and numerous other facilities. Not surprisingly, the cost of this remedial plan has "far exceeded KCMSD's budget, or for that matter, its authority to tax." The State ... has borne the brunt of these costs.

II

With this background, we turn to the present controversy. First, the State has challenged the District Court's requirement that it fund salary increases for KCMSD instructional and noninstructional staff. The State claimed that funding for salaries was beyond the scope of the District Court's remedial authority. Second, the State has challenged the District Court's order requiring it to continue to fund the remedial quality education programs for the 1992–1993 school year.

The District Court rejected the State's arguments....

The Court of Appeals for the Eighth Circuit affirmed.... [and later] denied rehearing en banc, with five judges dissenting....

Because of the importance of the issues, we granted certiorari to consider the following: (1) whether the District Court exceeded its constitutional authority when it granted salary increases to virtually all instructional and noninstructional employees of the KCMSD, and (2) whether the District Court properly relied upon the fact that student achievement test scores had failed to rise to some unspecified level when it declined to find that the State had achieved partial unitary status as to the quality education programs.

III

Respondents argue that the State may no longer challenge the District Court's remedy, and in any event, the propriety of the remedy is not before the Court. We disagree on both counts. In *Jenkins II*, we granted certiorari to review the manner in which the District Court had funded this desegregation remedy. Because we had denied *certiorari* on the State's challenge to review the scope of the remedial order, we resisted the State's efforts to challenge the scope of the remedy. Thus, we neither "approv[ed]" nor "disapprov[ed] the Court of Appeals' conclusion that the District Court's remedy was proper."

Here, however, the State has challenged the District Court's approval of across-the-board salary increases for instructional and noninstructional employees as an action beyond its remedial authority. An analysis of the permissible scope of the District Court's remedial authority is necessary for a proper determination of whether the order of salary increases is beyond the District Court's remedial authority and thus, it is an issue subsidiary to our ultimate inquiry. Given that the District Court's basis for its salary order was grounded in "improving the desegregative attractiveness of the KCMSD" we must consider the propriety of that reliance in order to resolve properly the State's challenge to that order. We conclude that a challenge to the scope of the District Court's remedy is fairly included in the question presented.

. . .

In short, the State has challenged the scope of the District Court's remedial authority. . . . there is no unfairness or imprudence in deciding issues that have been passed upon below, are properly before us, and have been briefed by the parties. We turn to the questions presented.

. . .

In the first place, like other equitable remedies, the nature of the desegregation remedy is to be determined by the nature and scope of the constitutional violation. The remedy must therefore be related to "the condition alleged to offend the Constitution. . . ." Second, the decree must indeed be remedial in nature, that is, it must be designed as nearly as possible "to restore the victims of discriminatory conduct to the position they would have occupied in the absence of such conduct." Third, the federal courts in devising a remedy must take into account the interests of state and local authorities in managing their own affairs, consistent with the Constitution.

We added that the "principle that the nature and scope of the remedy are to be determined by the violation means simply that federal-court decrees must directly address and relate to the constitutional violation itself." In applying these principles, we have identified "student assignments, . . . 'faculty, staff, transportation, extracurricular activities and facilities' " as the most important indicia of a racially segregated school system.

Because "federal supervision of local school systems was intended as a temporary measure to remedy past discrimination" we also have considered the showing that must be made by a school district operating under a desegregation order for complete or partial relief from that order. In Freeman, we stated that

> [a]mong the factors which must inform the sound discretion of the court in ordering partial withdrawal are the following: [1] whether there has been full and satisfactory compliance with the decree in those aspects of the system where supervision is to be withdrawn; [2] whether retention of judicial control is necessary or practicable to achieve compliance with the decree in other facets of the school system; and [3] whether the school district has demonstrated, to the public and to the parents and students of the once disfavored race, its good-faith commitment to the whole of the courts' decree and to those provisions of the law and the Constitution that were the predicate for judicial intervention in the first instance.

The ultimate inquiry is " 'whether the [constitutional violator] ha[s] complied in good faith with the desegregation decree since it was entered, and whether the vestiges of past discrimination ha[ve] been eliminated to the extent practicable.' "

Proper analysis of the District Court's orders challenged here, then, must rest upon their serving as proper means to the end of restoring the victims of discriminatory conduct to the position they would have occupied in the absence of that conduct and their eventual restoration of "state and local authorities to the control of a school system that is operating in compliance with the Constitution."

The State argues that the order approving salary increases is beyond the District Court's authority because it was crafted to serve an "interdistrict goal," in spite of the fact that the constitutional violation in this case is "intradistrict" in nature. . . .

. . . this case involved no interdistrict constitutional violation that would support interdistrict relief. Thus, the proper response by the District Court should have been to eliminate to the extent practicable the vestiges of prior de jure segregation within the KCMSD: a systemwide reduction in student achievement and the existence of 25 racially identifiable schools with a population of over 90% black students.

The District Court and Court of Appeals, however, have felt that because the KCMSD's enrollment remained 68.3% black, a purely intradistrict remedy would be insufficient. But, as noted in Milliken I we have rejected the suggestion "that schools which have a majority of Negro students are not 'desegregated' whatever the racial makeup of the school district's population and however neutrally the district lines have been drawn and administered."

Instead of seeking to remove the racial identity of the various schools within the KCMSD, the District Court has set out on a program to create a school district that was equal to or superior to the surrounding SSD's. Its remedy has focused on "desegregative attractiveness," coupled with "suburban comparability...."

The purpose of desegregative attractiveness has been not only to remedy the system-wide reduction in student achievement, but also to attract nonminority students not presently enrolled in the KCMSD. This remedy has included an elaborate program of capital improvements, course enrichment, and extracurricular enhancement not simply in the formerly identifiable black schools, but in schools throughout the district. The District Court's remedial orders have converted every senior high school, every middle school, and one-half of the elementary schools in the KCMSD into "magnet" schools. The District Court's remedial order has all but made the KCMSD itself into a magnet district.

. . .

The District Court's remedial plan in this case, however, is not designed solely to redistribute the students within the KCMSD in order to eliminate racially identifiable schools within the KCMSD. Instead, its purpose is to attract nonminority students from outside the KCMSD schools. But this interdistrict goal is beyond the scope of the intradistrict violation identified by the District Court. In effect, the District Court has devised a remedy to accomplish indirectly what it admittedly lacks the remedial authority to mandate directly: the interdistrict transfer of students.

. . .

Respondents argue that the District Court's reliance upon desegregative attractiveness is justified in light of the District Court's statement that segregation has "led to 'white flight' from the KCMSD to suburban districts." The lower courts' "findings" as to "white flight" are both inconsistent internally and inconsistent with the typical supposition, bolstered here by the record evidence, that "white flight" may result from desegregation, not de jure segregation. The United States, as amicus curiae, argues that the District Court's finding that "de jure segregation in the KCMSD caused white students to leave the system ... is not inconsistent with the district court's earlier conclusion that the suburban districts did nothing to cause this 'white flight' and therefore could not be included in a mandatory interdistrict remedy." But the District Court's earlier findings, affirmed by the Court of Appeals, were not so limited....

In *Freeman*, we stated that "[t]he vestiges of segregation that are the concern of the law in a school case may be subtle and intangible but nonetheless they must be so real that they have a causal link to the de jure violation being remedied." The record here does not support the District Court's reliance on "white flight" as a justification for a permissible expansion of its intradistrict remedial authority through its pursuit of desegregative attractiveness.

. . .

The District Court's pursuit of "desegregative attractiveness" cannot be reconciled with our cases placing limitations on a district court's remedial authority. It is certainly theoretically possible that the greater the expenditure per pupil within the KCMSD, the more likely it is that some unknowable number of nonminority students not presently attending schools in the KCMSD will choose to enroll in those schools. Under this reasoning, however, every increased expenditure, whether it be for teachers, noninstructional employees, books, or buildings, will make the KCMSD in some way more attractive, and thereby perhaps induce nonminority students to enroll in its schools. But this rationale is not susceptible to any objective limitation. This case provides numerous examples demonstrating the limitless authority of the District Court operating under this rationale. In short, desegregative attractiveness has been used "as the hook on which to hang numerous policy choices about improving the quality of education in general within the KCMSD."

Nor are there limits to the duration of the District Court's involvement. The expenditures per pupil in the KCMSD currently far exceed those in the neighboring SSD's. Sixteen years after this litigation began, the District Court recognized that the KCMSD has yet to offer a viable method of financing the "wonderful school system being built." Each additional program ordered by the District Court—and financed by the State—to increase the "desegregative attractiveness" of the school district makes the KCMSD more and more dependent on additional funding from the State; in turn, the greater the KCMSD's dependence on state funding, the greater its reliance on continued supervision by the District Court. But our cases recognize that local autonomy of school districts is a vital national tradition and that a district court must strive to restore state and local authorities to the control of a school system operating in compliance with the Constitution.

The District Court's pursuit of the goal of "desegregative attractiveness" results in so many imponderables and is so far removed from the task of eliminating the racial identifiability of the schools within the KCMSD that we believe it is beyond the admittedly broad discretion of the District Court. In this posture, we conclude that the District Court's order of salary increases, which was "grounded in remedying the vestiges of segregation by improving the desegregative attractiveness of the KCMSD" is simply too far removed from an acceptable implementation of a permissible means to remedy previous legally mandated segregation.

Similar considerations lead us to conclude that the District Court's order requiring the State to continue to fund the quality education programs because student achievement levels were still "at or below national norms at many grade levels" cannot be sustained. The State does not seek from this Court a declaration of partial unitary status with respect to the quality education programs. It challenges the requirement of indefinite funding of a quality education program until national norms are met, based on the assumption that while a mandate for significant educational improvement, both in teaching and in facilities, may have been justified originally, its indefinite extension is not.

Our review in this respect is needlessly complicated because the District Court made no findings in its order approving continued funding of the quality education programs. . . .

But this clearly is not the appropriate test to be applied in deciding whether a previously segregated district has achieved partially unitary status. The basic task of the District Court is to decide whether the reduction in achievement by minority students attributable to prior de jure segregation has been remedied to the extent practicable. Under our precedents, the State and the KCMSD are "entitled to a rather precise statement of [their] obligations under a desegregation decree." Although the District Court has determined that "[s]egregation has caused a system wide reduction in achievement in the schools of the KCMSD" it never has identified the incremental effect that segregation has had on minority student achievement or the specific goals of the quality education programs.

In reconsidering this order, the District Court should apply our three-part test from *Freeman v. Pitts*. The District Court should consider that the State's role with respect to the quality education programs has been limited to the funding, not the implementation, of those programs. As all the parties agree that improved achievement on test scores is not necessarily required for the State to achieve partial unitary status as to the quality education programs, the District Court should sharply limit, if not dispense with, its reliance on this factor. Just as demographic changes independent of de jure segregation will affect the racial composition of student assignments, so too will numerous external factors beyond the control of the KCMSD and the State affect minority student achievement. So long as these external factors are not the result of segregation, they do not figure in the remedial calculus. Insistence upon academic goals unrelated to the effects of legal segregation unwarrantably postpones the day when the KCMSD will be able to operate on its own.

The District Court also should consider that many goals of its quality education plan already have been attained: the KCMSD now is equipped with "facilities and opportunities not available anywhere else in the country." KCMSD schools received an AAA rating eight years ago, and the present remedial programs have been in place for seven years. It may be that in education, just as it may be in economics, a "rising tide lifts all boats," but the remedial quality education program should be tailored to remedy the injuries suffered by the victims of prior de jure segregation. . . .

On remand, the District Court must bear in mind that its end purpose is not only "to remedy the violation" to the extent practicable, but also "to restore state and local authorities to the control of a school system that is operating in compliance with the Constitution."

The judgment of the Court of Appeals is reversed.

It is so ordered.

NOTES

1. Note how the composition of the Supreme Court influences the outcome of cases. The four dissenters in *Jenkins II*, Chief Justice Rehnquist and Justices

Kennedy, O'Connor, and Scalia, were joined by Justice Thomas who was not on the bench in 1990, in creating the majority in this case.

2. The Court was clearly concerned with the cost of implementing the desegregation order in this case. Is such a concern justified?

APPENDIX

SELECTED PROVISIONS OF THE UNITED STATES CONSTITUTION

Article I

Section 1. All legislative Powers herein granted shall be vested in a Congress of the United States....

Section 8. The Congress shall have Power To.... provide for the ... general Welfare of the United States;....

Section 10. No State shall ... pass any ... law impairing the obligation of contracts....

Article II

Section 1. The executive Power shall be vested in a President of the United States of America.

Article III

Section 1. The judicial Power of the United States shall be vested in one supreme Court and in such inferior Courts as the Congress may from time to time ordain and establish.

Article VI

Section 2: This Constitution, and the Laws of the United States which shall be made in Pursuance thereof; and all Treaties made, or which shall be made, under the Authority of the United States, shall be the supreme Law of the Land; and the Judges in every State shall be bound thereby, any Thing in the Constitution or Laws of any State to the Contrary notwithstanding.

Amendment 1

Congress shall make no law respecting an establishment of religion, or prohibiting the free exercise thereof; or abridging the freedom of speech, or of the press; or the right of the people peaceably to assemble, and to petition the Government for a redress of grievances.

Amendment 4

The right of the people to be secure in their persons, houses, papers, and effects, against unreasonable searches and seizures, shall not be violated, and no warrants shall issue, but upon probable cause, supported by oath or affirmation, and particularly describing the place to be searched, and the persons or things to be seized.

Amendment 5

No person ... shall be compelled in any criminal case to be a witness against himself, nor be deprived of life, liberty, or property, without due process of law; nor shall private property be taken for public use, without just compensation.

Amendment 8

Excessive bail shall not be required, nor excessive fines imposed, nor cruel and unusual punishments inflicted.

Amendment 10

The powers not delegated to the United States by the Constitution, nor prohibited by it to the States, are reserved to the States respectively, or to the people.

Amendment 11

The judicial power of the United States shall not be construed to extend to any suit in law or equity, commenced or prosecuted against one of the United States by citizens of another State, or by citizens or subjects of any foreign State.

Amendment 14

Section 1. All persons born or naturalized in the United States, and subject to the jurisdiction thereof, are citizens of the United States and of the State wherein they reside. No State shall make or enforce any law which shall abridge the privileges or immunities of citizens of the United States; nor shall any State deprive any person of life, liberty, or property, without due process of law; nor deny to any person within its jurisdiction the equal protection of the laws.

Selected Federal Statutory Provisions Applicable to Schools

Family Educational Rights and Privacy Act

20 U.S.C.A. § 1232g

(a) Conditions for availability of funds to educational agencies or institutions; inspection and review of education records; specific information to be made available; procedure for access to education records; reasonableness of time for such access; hearings; written explanations by parents; definitions

(1)(A) No funds shall be made available under any applicable program to any educational agency or institution which has a policy of denying, or which effectively prevents, the parents of students who are or have been in attendance at a school of such agency or at such institution, as the case may be, the right to inspect and review the education records of their children. If any material or document in the education record of a student includes information on more than one student, the parents of one of such students shall have the right to inspect and review only such part of such material or document as relates to such student or to be informed of the specific information contained in such part of such material. Each educational agency or institution shall establish appropriate procedures for the granting of a request by parents for access to the education records of their children within a reasonable period of time, but in no case more than forty-five days after the request has been made.

(B) No funds under any applicable program shall be made available to any State educational agency (whether or not that agency is an educational agency or institution under this section) that has a policy of denying, or effectively prevents, the parents of students the right to inspect and review the education records maintained by the State educational agency on their children who are or have been in attendance at any school of an educational agency or institution that is subject to the provisions of this section.

(C) The first sentence of subparagraph (A) shall not operate to make available to students in institutions of postsecondary education the following materials:

(i) financial records of the parents of the student or any information contained therein;

(ii) confidential letters and statements of recommendation, which were placed in the education records prior to January 1, 1975, if such letters or statements are not used for purposes other than those for which they were specifically intended;

(iii) if the student has signed a waiver of the student's right of access under this subsection in accordance with subparagraph (D), confidential recommendations—

(I) respecting admission to any educational agency or institution,

(II) respecting an application for employment, and

(III) respecting the receipt of an honor or honorary recognition.

(D) A student or a person applying for admission may waive his right of access to confidential statements described in clause (iii) of subparagraph (C), except that such waiver shall apply to recommendations only if (i) the student is, upon request, notified of the names of all persons making confidential recommendations and (ii) such recommendations are used solely for the purpose for which they were specifically intended. Such waivers may not be required as a condition for admission to, receipt of financial aid from, or receipt of any other services or benefits from such agency or institution.

(2) No funds shall be made available under any applicable program to any educational agency or institution unless the parents of students who are or have been in attendance at a school of such agency or at such institution are provided an opportunity for a hearing by such agency or institution, in accordance with regulations of the Secretary, to challenge the content of such student's education records, in order to insure that the records are not inaccurate, misleading, or otherwise in violation of the privacy rights of students, and to provide an opportunity for the correction or deletion of any such inaccurate, misleading or otherwise inappropriate data contained therein and to insert into such records a written explanation of the parents respecting the content of such records.

(3) For the purposes of this section the term "educational agency or institution" means any public or private agency or institution which is the recipient of funds under any applicable program.

(4)(A) For the purposes of this section, the term "education records" means, except as may be provided otherwise in subparagraph (B), those records, files, documents, and other materials which—

(i) contain information directly related to a student; and

(ii) are maintained by an educational agency or institution or by a person acting for such agency or institution.

(B) The term "education records" does not include—

(i) records of instructional, supervisory, and administrative personnel and educational personnel ancillary thereto which are in the sole possession of the maker thereof and which are not accessible or revealed to any other person except a substitute;

(ii) records maintained by a law enforcement unit of the educational agency or institution that were created by that law enforcement unit for the purpose of law enforcement;

(iii) in the case of persons who are employed by an educational agency or institution but who are not in attendance at such agency or institution, records made and maintained in the normal course of business which relate exclusively to such person in that person's capacity as an employee and are not available for use for any other purpose; or

(iv) records on a student who is eighteen years of age or older, or is attending an institution of postsecondary education, which are made or maintained by a physician, psychiatrist, psychologist, or other recognized professional or paraprofessional acting in his professional or paraprofessional capacity, or assisting in that capacity, and which are made, maintained, or used only in connection with the provision of treatment to the student, and are not available to anyone other than persons providing such treatment, except that such records can be personally reviewed by a physician or other appropriate professional of the student's choice.

(5)(A) For the purposes of this section the term "directory information" relating to a student includes the following: the student's name, address, telephone listing, date and place of birth, major field of study, participation in officially recognized activities and sports, weight and height of members of athletic teams, dates of attendance, degrees and awards received, and the most recent previous educational agency or institution attended by the student.

(B) Any educational agency or institution making public directory information shall give public notice of the categories of information which it has designated as such information with respect to each student attending the institution or agency and shall allow a reasonable period of time after such notice has been given for a parent to inform the institution or agency that any or all of the information designated should not be released without the parent's prior consent.

(6) For the purposes of this section, the term "student" includes any person with respect to whom an educational agency or institution maintains education records or personally identifiable information, but does not include a person who has not been in attendance at such agency or institution.

(b) Release of education records; parental consent requirement; exceptions; compliance with judicial orders and subpoenas; audit and evaluation of federally-supported education programs; recordkeeping

(1) No funds shall be made available under any applicable program to any educational agency or institution which has a policy or practice of permitting the release of education records (or personally identifiable information contained therein other than directory information, as defined in paragraph (5) of subsection (a) of this section) of students without the written consent of their parents to any individual, agency, or organization, other than to the following—

(A) other school officials, including teachers within the educational institution or local educational agency, who have been determined by such agency or institution to have legitimate educational interests, including the educational interests of the child for whom consent would otherwise be required;

(B) officials of other schools or school systems in which the student seeks or intends to enroll, upon condition that the student's parents be notified of the transfer, receive a copy of the record if desired, and have an opportunity for a hearing to challenge the content of the record;

(C)(i) authorized representatives of (I) the Comptroller General of the United States, (II) the Secretary, or (III) State educational authorities, under the conditions set forth in paragraph (3), or (ii) authorized representatives of the Attorney General for law enforcement purposes under the same conditions as apply to the Secretary under paragraph (3);

(D) in connection with a student's application for, or receipt of, financial aid;

(E) State and local officials or authorities to whom such information is specifically allowed to be reported or disclosed pursuant to State statute adopted—

   (i) before November 19, 1974 . . .

   (ii) after November 19, 1974, if—
      (I) the allowed reporting or disclosure concerns the juvenile justice system and such system's ability to effectively serve, prior to adjudication, the student whose records are released; and
      (II) the officials and authorities to whom such information is disclosed certify in writing to the educational agency or institution that the information will not be disclosed to any other party except as provided under State law without the prior written consent of the parent of the student.

(F) organizations conducting studies for, or on behalf of, educational agencies or institutions for the purpose of developing, validating, or administering predictive tests, administering student aid programs, and improving instruction, if such studies are conducted in such a manner as will not permit the personal identification of students and their parents by persons other than representatives of such organizations and such information will be destroyed when no longer needed for the purpose for which it is conducted;

(G) accrediting organizations in order to carry out their accrediting functions;

(H) parents of a dependent student of such parents, as defined in section 152 of Title 26;

(I) subject to regulations of the Secretary, in connection with an emergency, appropriate persons if the knowledge of such information is necessary to protect the health or safety of the student or other persons; and

(J)(i) the entity or persons designated in a Federal grand jury subpoena, in which case the court shall order, for good cause shown, the educational agency or institution (and any officer, director, employee, agent, or attorney for such agency or institution) on which the subpoena is served, to not disclose to any person the existence or contents of the subpoena or any information furnished to the grand jury in response to the subpoena; and

(ii) the entity or persons designated in any other subpoena issued for a law enforcement purpose, in which case the court or other issuing agency may order, for good cause shown, the educational agency or institution (and any officer, director, employee, agent, or attorney for such agency or institution) on which the subpoena is served, to not disclose to any person the existence or contents of the subpoena or any information furnished in response to the subpoena. . . .

Individuals with Disabilities Education Act

20 U.S.C.A. §§ 1400 *et seq.*

§ 1401 Definitions

Except as otherwise provided, in this chapter:

(3) Child with a disability

(A) In general

The term "child with a disability" means a child—

(i) with mental retardation, hearing impairments (including deafness), speech or language impairments, visual impairments (including blindness), serious emotional disturbance (referred to in this chapter as "emotional disturbance"), orthopedic impairments, autism, traumatic brain injury, other health impairments, or specific learning disabilities; and

(ii) who, by reason thereof, needs special education and related services.

(B) Child aged 3 through 9

The term "child with a disability" for a child aged 3 through 9 (or any subset of that age range, including ages 3 through 5), may, at the discretion of the State and the local educational agency, include a child—

(i) experiencing developmental delays, as defined by the State and as measured by appropriate diagnostic instruments and procedures, in 1 or more of the following areas: physical development; cognitive development; communication development; social or emotional development; or adaptive development; and

(ii) who, by reason thereof, needs special education and related services.

(9) Free appropriate public education

The term "free appropriate public education" means special education and related services that—

(A) have been provided at public expense, under public supervision and direction, and without charge;

(B) meet the standards of the State educational agency;

(C) include an appropriate preschool, elementary school, or secondary school education in the State involved; and

(D) are provided in conformity with the individualized education program required under section 1414(d) of this title.

(10) Highly qualified

(A) In general

For any special education teacher, the term "highly qualified" has the meaning given the term in section 9101 of the Elementary and Secondary Education Act of 1965 [20 U.S.C.A. § 7801], except that such term also—

(i) includes the requirements described in subparagraph (B); and

(ii) includes the option for teachers to meet the requirements of section 9101 of such Act by meeting the requirements of subparagraph (C) or (D).

(B) Requirements for special education teachers

When used with respect to any public elementary school or secondary school special education teacher teaching in a State, such term means that—

(i) the teacher has obtained full State certification as a special education teacher (including certification obtained through alternative routes to certification), or passed the State special education teacher licensing examination, and holds a license to teach in the State as a special education teacher, except that when used with respect to any teacher teaching in a public charter school, the term means that the teacher meets the requirements set forth in the State's public charter school law;

(ii) the teacher has not had special education certification or licensure requirements waived on an emergency, temporary, or provisional basis; and

(iii) the teacher holds at least a bachelor's degree.

(C) Special education teachers teaching to alternate achievement standards

When used with respect to a special education teacher who teaches core academic subjects exclusively to children who are assessed against alternate achievement standards established under the regulations promulgated under section 1111(b)(1) of the Elementary and Secondary Education Act of 1965 [20 U.S.C.A. § 6311(b)(1)], such term means the teacher, whether new or not new to the profession, may either—

(i) meet the applicable requirements of section 9101 of such Act for any elementary, middle, or secondary school teacher who is new or not new to the profession; or

(ii) meet the requirements of subparagraph (B) or (C) of section 9101(23) of such Act as applied to an elementary school teacher, or, in the case of instruction above the elementary level, has subject matter knowledge appropriate to the level of instruction being provided, as determined by the State, needed to effectively teach to those standards.

(D) Special education teachers teaching multiple subjects

When used with respect to a special education teacher who teaches 2 or more core academic subjects exclusively to children with disabilities, such term means that the teacher may either—

(i) meet the applicable requirements of section 9101 of the Elementary and Secondary Education Act of 1965 [20 U.S.C.A. § 7801] for any elementary, middle, or secondary school teacher who is new or not new to the profession;

(ii) in the case of a teacher who is not new to the profession, demonstrate competence in all the core academic subjects in which the teacher teaches in the same manner as is required for an elementary, middle, or secondary school teacher who is not new to the profession under section 9101(23)(C)(ii) of such Act [20 U.S.C.A. § 7801(23)(C)(ii)], which may include a single, high objective uniform State standard of evaluation covering multiple subjects; or

(iii) in the case of a new special education teacher who teaches multiple subjects and who is highly qualified in mathematics, language arts, or science, demonstrate competence in the other core academic subjects in which the teacher teaches in the same manner as is required for an elementary, middle, or secondary school teacher under section 9101(23)(C)(ii) of such Act [20 U.S.C.A. § 7801(23)(C)(ii)], which may include a single, high objective uniform State standard of evaluation covering multiple subjects, not later than 2 years after the date of employment.

(14) Individualized education program; IEP

The term "individualized education program" or "IEP" means a written statement for each child with a disability that is developed, reviewed, and revised in accordance with section 1414(d) of this title.

(23) Parent

The term "parent" means—

(A) a natural, adoptive, or foster parent of a child (unless a foster parent is prohibited by State law from serving as a parent);

(B) a guardian (but not the State if the child is a ward of the State);

(C) an individual acting in the place of a natural or adoptive parent (including a grandparent, stepparent, or other relative) with whom the child lives, or an individual who is legally responsible for the child's welfare; or

(D) except as used in sections 1415(b)(2) of this title and 1439(a)(5) of this title, an individual assigned under either of those sections to be a surrogate parent.

(26) Related services

(A) In general

The term "related services" means transportation, and such developmental, corrective, and other supportive services (including speech-language pathology and audiology services, interpreting services, psychological services, physical and occupational therapy, recreation, including therapeutic recreation, social work services, school nurse services designed to enable a child with a disability to receive a free appropriate public education as described in the individualized education program of the child, counseling services, including rehabilitation counseling, orientation and mobility services, and medical services, except that such medical services shall be for diagnostic and evaluation purposes only) as may be required to assist a child with a disability to benefit from special education, and includes the early identification and assessment of disabling conditions in children.

(B) Exception

The term does not include a medical device that is surgically implanted, or the replacement of such device.

(29) Special education

The term "special education" means specially designed instruction, at no cost to parents, to meet the unique needs of a child with a disability, including—

(A) instruction conducted in the classroom, in the home, in hospitals and institutions, and in other settings; and

(B) instruction in physical education.

(30) Specific learning disability

(A) In general

The term "specific learning disability" means a disorder in 1 or more of the basic psychological processes involved in understanding or in using language, spoken or written, which disorder may manifest itself in the imperfect ability to listen, think, speak, read, write, spell, or do mathematical calculations.

(B) Disorders included

Such term includes such conditions as perceptual disabilities, brain injury, minimal brain dysfunction, dyslexia, and developmental aphasia.

(C) Disorders not included

Such term does not include a learning problem that is primarily the result of visual, hearing, or motor disabilities, of mental retardation, of emotional disturbance, or of environmental, cultural, or economic disadvantage.

Title IX of Education Amendments of 1972

20 U.S.C.A. § 1681

(a) Prohibition against discrimination; exceptions

No person in the United States shall, on the basis of sex, be excluded from participation in, be denied the benefits of, or be subjected to discrimination under any education program or activity receiving Federal financial assistance, except that:

(1) Classes of educational institutions subject to prohibition

in regard to admissions to educational institutions, this section shall apply only to institutions of vocational education, professional education, and graduate higher education, and to public institutions of undergraduate higher education;

(2) Educational institutions commencing planned change in admissions

in regard to admissions to educational institutions, this section shall not apply (A) for one year from June 23, 1972, nor for six years after June 23, 1972, in the case of an educational institution which has begun the process of changing from being an institution which admits only students of one sex to being an institution which admits students of both sexes, but only if it is carrying out a plan for such a change which is approved by the Secretary of Education or (B) for seven years from the date an educational institution begins the process of changing from being an institution which admits only students of only one sex to being an institution which admits students of both sexes, but only if it is carrying out a plan for such a change which is approved by the Secretary of Education, whichever is the later;

(3) Educational institutions of religious organizations with contrary religious tenets

this section shall not apply to an educational institution which is controlled by a religious organization if the application of this subsection would not be consistent with the religious tenets of such organization;

(4) Educational institutions training individuals for military services or merchant marine

this section shall not apply to an educational institution whose primary purpose is the training of individuals for the military services of the United States, or the merchant marine;

(5) Public educational institutions with traditional and continuing admissions policy

in regard to admissions this section shall not apply to any public institution of undergraduate higher education which is an institution that traditionally and continually from its establishment has had a policy of admitting only students of one sex;

(6) Social fraternities or sororities; voluntary youth service organizations

this section shall not apply to membership practices—

(A) of a social fraternity or social sorority which is exempt from taxation under section 501(a) of Title 26, the active membership of which consists primarily of students in attendance at an institution of higher education, or

(B) of the Young Men's Christian Association, Young Women's Christian Association, Girl Scouts, Boy Scouts, Camp Fire Girls, and voluntary youth service organizations which are so exempt, the membership of which has traditionally been limited to persons of one sex and principally to persons of less than nineteen years of age;

(7) Boy or Girl conferences

this section shall not apply to—

(A) any program or activity of the American Legion undertaken in connection with the organization or operation of any Boys State conference, Boys Nation conference, Girls State conference, or Girls Nation conference; or

(B) any program or activity of any secondary school or educational institution specifically for—

(i) the promotion of any Boys State conference, Boys Nation conference, Girls State conference, or Girls Nation conference; or

(ii) the selection of students to attend any such conference;

(8) Father-son or mother-daughter activities at educational institutions

this section shall not preclude father-son or mother-daughter activities at an educational institution, but if such activities are provided for students of one sex, opportunities for reasonably comparable activities shall be provided for students of the other sex; and

(9) Institution of higher education scholarship awards in "beauty" pageants

this section shall not apply with respect to any scholarship or other financial assistance awarded by an institution of higher education to any individual because such individual has received such award in any pageant in which the attainment of such award is based upon a combination of factors related to the personal appearance, poise, and talent of such individual and in which participation is limited to individuals of one sex only, so long as such pageant is in compliance with other nondiscrimination provisions of Federal law.

(b) Preferential or disparate treatment because of imbalance in participation or receipt of Federal benefits; statistical evidence of imbalance

Nothing contained in subsection (a) of this section shall be interpreted to require any educational institution to grant preferential or disparate treatment to the members of one sex on account of an imbalance which may exist with respect to the total number or percentage of persons of that sex participating in or receiving the benefits of any federally supported program or activity, in comparison with the total number or percentage of persons of that sex in any community, State, section, or other area: Provided, That this subsection shall not be construed to prevent the consideration in any hearing or proceeding under this chapter of statistical evidence tending to show that such an imbalance exists with respect to the participation in, or receipt of the benefits of, any such program or activity by the members of one sex.

(c) "Educational institution" defined

For purposes of this chapter an educational institution means any public or private preschool, elementary, or secondary school, or any institution of vocational, professional, or higher education, except that in the case of an educational institution composed of more than one school, college, or department which are administratively separate units, such term means each such school, college, or department.

Equal Access Act

20 U.S.C.A. § 4071

Denial of equal access prohibited

(a) Restriction of limited open forum on basis of religious, political, philosophical, or other speech content prohibited

It shall be unlawful for any public secondary school which receives Federal financial assistance and which has a limited open forum to deny equal access or a fair opportunity to, or discriminate against, any students who wish to conduct a meeting within that limited open forum on the basis of the religious, political, philosophical, or other content of the speech at such meetings.

(b) "Limited open forum" defined

A public secondary school has a limited open forum whenever such school grants an offering to or opportunity for one or more noncurriculum related student groups to meet on school premises during noninstructional time.

(c) Fair opportunity criteria

Schools shall be deemed to offer a fair opportunity to students who wish to conduct a meeting within its limited open forum if such school uniformly provides that—

(1) the meeting is voluntary and student-initiated;

(2) there is no sponsorship of the meeting by the school, the government, or its agents or employees;

(3) employees or agents of the school or government are present at religious meetings only in a nonparticipatory capacity;

(4) the meeting does not materially and substantially interfere with the orderly conduct of educational activities within the school; and

(5) nonschool persons may not direct, conduct, control, or regularly attend activities of student groups.

(d) Construction of subchapter with respect to certain rights

Nothing in this subchapter shall be construed to authorize the United States or any State or political subdivision thereof—

(1) to influence the form or content of any prayer or other religious activity;

(2) to require any person to participate in prayer or other religious activity;

(3) to expend public funds beyond the incidental cost of providing the space for student-initiated meetings;

(4) to compel any school agent or employee to attend a school meeting if the content of the speech at the meeting is contrary to the beliefs of the agent or employee;

(5) to sanction meetings that are otherwise unlawful;

(6) to limit the rights of groups of students which are not of a specified numerical size; or

(7) to abridge the constitutional rights of any person.

(e) Federal financial assistance to schools unaffected

Notwithstanding the availability of any other remedy under the Constitution or the laws of the United States, nothing in this subchapter shall be construed to authorize the United States to deny or withhold Federal financial assistance to any school.

(f) Authority of schools with respect to order, discipline, well-being, and attendance concerns

Nothing in this subchapter shall be construed to limit the authority of the school, its agents or employees, to maintain order and discipline on school premises, to protect the well-being of students and faculty, and to assure that attendance of students at meetings is voluntary.

No Child Left Behind Act

20 U.S.C.A. § 6301

Strengthening and Improvement of Elementary and Secondary Schools

Subchapter I. Improving The Academic Achievement of the Disadvantaged

Statement of purpose

The purpose of this subchapter is to ensure that all children have a fair, equal, and significant opportunity to obtain a high-quality education and reach, at a minimum, proficiency on challenging state academic achievement standards and state academic assessments. This purpose can be accomplished by

(1) ensuring that high-quality academic assessments, accountability systems, teacher preparation and training, curriculum, and instructional materials are aligned with challenging State academic standards so that students, teachers, parents, and administrators can measure progress against common expectations for student academic achievement;

(2) meeting the educational needs of low-achieving children in our Nation's highest-poverty schools, limited English proficient children, migratory children, children with disabilities, Indian children, neglected or delinquent children, and young children in need of reading assistance;

(3) Closing the achievement gap between high and low-performing children, especially the achievement gaps between minority and nonminority students, and between disadvantaged children and their more advantaged peers;

(4) holding schools, local educational agencies, and States accountable for improving the academic achievement of all students, and identifying and turning around low-performing schools that have failed to provide a high-quality education to their students, while providing alternatives to students in such schools to enable the students to receive a high-quality education;

(5) distributing and targeting resources sufficiently to make a difference to local educational agencies and schools where needs are greatest;

(6) improving and strengthening accountability, teaching, and learning by using State assessment systems designed to ensure that students are meeting challenging State academic achievement and content standards and increasing achievement overall, but especially for the disadvantaged;

(7) providing greater decisionmaking authority and flexibility to schools and teachers in exchange for greater responsibility for student performance;

(8) providing children an enriched and accelerated educational program, including the use of schoolwide programs or additional services that increase the amount and quality of instructional time;

(9) promoting schoolwide reform and ensuring the access of children to effective, scientifically based instructional strategies and challenging academic content;

(10) significantly elevating the quality of instruction by providing staff in participating schools with substantial opportunities for professional development;

(11) coordinating services under all parts of this title with each other, with other educational services, and, to the extent feasible, with other agencies providing services to youth, children, and families; and

(12) affording parents substantial and meaningful opportunities to participate in the education of their children.

20 U.S.C.A. § 7801

(19) Exemplary teacher

The term "exemplary teacher" means a teacher who—

(A) is a highly qualified teacher such as a master teacher;

(B) has been teaching for at least 5 years in a public or private school or institution of higher education;

(C) is recommended to be an exemplary teacher by administrators and other teachers who are knowledgeable about the individual's performance;

(D) is currently teaching and based in a public school; and

(E) assists other teachers in improving instructional strategies, improves the skills of other teachers, performs teacher mentoring, develops curricula, and offers other professional development.

(23) Highly qualified

The term "highly qualified"—

(A) when used with respect to any public elementary school or secondary school teacher teaching in a State, means that—

(i) the teacher has obtained full State certification as a teacher (including certification obtained through alternative routes to certification) or passed the State teacher licensing examination, and holds a license to teach in such State, except that when used with respect to any teacher teaching in a public charter school, the term means that the teacher meets the requirements set forth in the State's public charter school law; and

(ii) the teacher has not had certification or licensure requirements waived on an emergency, temporary, or provisional basis;

(B) when used with respect to—

(i) an elementary school teacher who is new to the profession, means that the teacher—

(I) holds at least a bachelor's degree; and

(II) has demonstrated, by passing a rigorous State test, subject knowledge and teaching skills in reading, writing, mathematics, and other areas of the basic elementary school curriculum (which may consist of passing a State-required certification or licensing test or tests in reading, writing, mathematics, and other areas of the basic elementary school curriculum); or

(ii) a middle or secondary school teacher who is new to the profession, means that the teacher holds at least a bachelor's degree and has demonstrated a high level of competency in each of the academic subjects in which the teacher teaches by—

(I) passing a rigorous State academic subject test in each of the academic subjects in which the teacher teaches (which may consist of a passing level of performance on a State-required certification or licensing test or tests in each of the academic subjects in which the teacher teaches); or

(II) successful completion, in each of the academic subjects in which the teacher teaches, of an academic major, a graduate degree, coursework equivalent to an undergraduate academic major, or advanced certification or credentialing; and

(C) when used with respect to an elementary, middle, or secondary school teacher who is not new to the profession, means that the teacher holds at least a bachelor's degree and—

(i) has met the applicable standard in clause (i) or (ii) of subparagraph (B), which includes an option for a test; or

(ii) demonstrates competence in all the academic subjects in which the teacher teaches based on a high objective uniform State standard of evaluation that—

(I) is set by the State for both grade appropriate academic subject matter knowledge and teaching skills;

(II) is aligned with challenging State academic content and student academic achievement standards and developed in consultation with core content specialists, teachers, principals, and school administrators;

(III) provides objective, coherent information about the teacher's attainment of core content knowledge in the academic subjects in which a teacher teaches;

(IV) is applied uniformly to all teachers in the same academic subject and the same grade level throughout the State;

(V) takes into consideration, but not be based primarily on, the time the teacher has been teaching in the academic subject;

(VI) is made available to the public upon request; and

(VII) may involve multiple, objective measures of teacher competency.

Age Discrimination in Employment Act

29 U.S.C.A. § 623

Prohibition of age discrimination

(a) Employer practices

It shall be unlawful for an employer—

(1) to fail or refuse to hire or to discharge any individual or otherwise discriminate against any individual with respect to his compensation, terms, conditions, or privileges of employment, because of such individual's age;

(2) to limit, segregate, or classify his employees in any way which would deprive or tend to deprive any individual of employment opportunities or otherwise adversely affect his status as an employee, because of such individual's age; or

(3) to reduce the wage rate of any employee in order to comply with this chapter.

(c) Labor organization practices

It shall be unlawful for a labor organization—

(1) to exclude or to expel from its membership, or otherwise to discriminate against, any individual because of his age;

(2) to limit, segregate, or classify its membership, or to classify or fail or refuse to refer for employment any individual, in any way which would deprive or tend to deprive any individual of employment opportunities, or would limit such employment opportunities or otherwise adversely affect his status as an employee or as an applicant for employment, because of such individual's age;

(3) to cause or attempt to cause an employer to discriminate against an individual in violation of this section.

(f) Lawful practices; age an occupational qualification; other reasonable factors; laws of foreign workplace; seniority system; employee benefit plans; discharge or discipline for good cause

It shall not be unlawful for an employer, employment agency, or labor organization—

(1) to take any action otherwise prohibited under subsections (a), (b), (c), or (e) of this section where age is a bona fide occupational qualification reasonably necessary to the normal operation of the particular business, or where the differentiation is based on reasonable factors other than age, or where such practices involve an employee in a workplace in a foreign country, and compliance with such subsections would cause such employer, or a corporation controlled by such employer, to violate the laws of the country in which such workplace is located;

(2) to take any action otherwise prohibited under subsection (a), (b), (c), or (e) of this section—

(A) to observe the terms of a bona fide seniority system that is not intended to evade the purposes of this chapter, except that no such seniority system shall require or permit the involuntary retirement of any individual specified by section 631(a) of this title because of the age of such individual; or

(B) to observe the terms of a bona fide employee benefit plan—

(i) where, for each benefit or benefit package, the actual amount of payment made or cost incurred on behalf of an older worker is no less than that made or incurred on behalf of a younger worker, as permissible under section 1625.10, title 29, Code of Federal Regulations (as in effect on June 22, 1989); or

(ii) that is a voluntary early retirement incentive plan consistent with the relevant purpose or purposes of this chapter.

Notwithstanding clause (i) or (ii) of subparagraph (B), no such employee benefit plan or voluntary early retirement incentive plan shall excuse the failure to hire any individual, and no such employee benefit plan shall require or permit the involuntary retirement of any individual specified by section 631(a) of this title, because of the age of such individual. An employer, employment agency, or labor organization acting under subparagraph (A), or under clause (i) or (ii) of subparagraph (B), shall have the burden of proving that such actions are lawful in any civil enforcement proceeding brought under this chapter; or

(3) to discharge or otherwise discipline an individual for good cause.

Section 504 of the Rehabilitation Act

29 U.S.C.A. § 794(a)

No otherwise qualified individual with a disability in the United States, as defined in section 705(20) of this title, shall, solely by reason of her or his disability, be excluded from the participation in, be denied the benefits of, or be subjected to discrimination under any program or activity receiving Federal financial assistance or under any program or activity conducted by any Executive agency or by the United States Postal Service. The head of each such agency shall promulgate such regulations as may be necessary to carry out the amendments to this section made by the Rehabilitation, Comprehensive Services, and Developmental Disabilities Act of 1978. Copies of any proposed regulation shall be submitted to appropriate authorizing committees of the Congress, and such regulation may take effect no earlier than the thirtieth day after the date on which such regulation is so submitted to such committees.

Section 1981 (Civil Rights Act of 1866)

42 U.S.C.A. § 1981

§ 1981. Equal rights under the law

(a) Statement of equal rights

All persons within the jurisdiction of the United States shall have the same right in every State and Territory to make and enforce contracts, to sue, be parties, give evidence, and to the full and equal benefit of all laws and proceedings for the security of persons and property as is enjoyed by white citizens, and shall be subject to like punishment, pains, penalties, taxes, licenses, and exactions of every kind, and to no other.

(b) "Make and enforce contracts" defined

For purposes of this section, the term "make and enforce contracts" includes the making, performance, modification, and termination of contracts, and the enjoyment of all benefits, privileges, terms, and conditions of the contractual relationship.

(c) Protection against impairment

The rights protected by this section are protected against impairment by nongovernmental discrimination and impairment under color of State law.

Section 1983 (Civil Rights Act of 1871)

42 U.S.C.A. § 1983

Every person who, under color of any statute, ordinance, regulation, custom, or usage, of any State or Territory or the District of Columbia, subjects, or causes to be subjected, any citizen of the United States or other person within the jurisdiction thereof to the deprivation of any rights, privileges, or immunities secured by the Constitution and laws, shall be liable to the party injured in an action at law, suit in equity, or other proper proceeding for redress, except that in any action brought against a judicial officer for an act or omission taken in such officer's judicial capacity, injunctive relief shall not be granted unless a declaratory decree was violated or declaratory relief was unavailable. For the purposes of this section, any Act of Congress applicable exclusively to the District of Columbia shall be considered to be a statute of the District of Columbia.

Title VI of Civil Rights Act of 1964

42 U.S.C.A. § 2000d

No person in the United States shall, on the ground of race, color or national origin, be excluded from participation in, be denied the benefits of, or be subjected to discrimination under any program or activity receiving Federal financial assistance.

Title VII of Civil Rights Act of 1964

42 U.S.C.A. § 2000e–2(a)

(a) Employer practices

It shall be an unlawful employment practice for an employer—

(1) to fail or refuse to hire or to discharge any individual, or otherwise to discriminate against any individual with respect to his compensation, terms, conditions, or privileges of employment, because of such individual's race, color, religion, sex, or national origin; or

(2) to limit, segregate, or classify his employees or applicants for employment in any way which would deprive or tend to deprive any individual of employment opportunities or otherwise adversely affect his status as an employee, because of such individual's race, color, religion, sex, or national origin.

(c) Labor organization practices

It shall be an unlawful employment practice for a labor organization—

(1) to exclude or to expel from its membership, or otherwise to discriminate against, any individual because of his race, color, religion, sex, or national origin;

(2) to limit, segregate, or classify its membership or applicants for membership, or to classify or fail or refuse to refer for employment any individual, in any way which would deprive or tend to deprive any individual of employment opportunities, or would limit such employment opportunities or otherwise adversely affect his status as an employee or as an applicant for employment, because of such individual's race, color, religion, sex, or national origin; or

(3) to cause or attempt to cause an employer to discriminate against an individual in violation of this section.

(m) Impermissible consideration of race, color, religion, sex, or national origin in employment practices

Except as otherwise provided in this subchapter, an unlawful employment practice is established when the complaining party demonstrates that race, color, religion, sex, or national origin was a motivating factor for any employment practice, even though other factors also motivated the practice.

GLOSSARY

Action. A lawsuit.

Ad litem. Literally, "for the suit;" for the purposes of a particular suit.

Ad valorem. According to value; refers to a tax imposed on the value of property.

Affidavit. A written statement made under oath.

Agent. One authorized to act in behalf of another.

Amicus curiae. Literally, "friend of the court;" refers to briefs submitted by individuals or organizations that are not parties to litigation but are interested in its outcome.

Appellant. Party bringing an action in a higher court.

Appellee. Party against whom an action is brought in a higher court.

Arguendo. Literally, "in arguing;" for the sake of argument something is assumed to be true.

Assault. An immediate threat or attempt to inflict bodily injury where a victim has reason to believe that an injury may be inflicted.

Battery. Unconsented to physical touching.

Bequest. Gift of personal property by a will.

Bona fide. Literally, "in good faith."

Case at bar. The case presently being decided by a court.

Caveat. Literally, "let one beware;" a warning.

Certiorari. Literally, "to be informed of;" a proceeding in which a higher court reviews a decision of an inferior court.

Class action. A suit brought by one or more persons on behalf of all persons similarly situated as to their complaint and proposed remedy.

Collateral. Indirect; not directly connected to the matter at hand.

Color of law. Acting as if one has the appearance of a legal right or authority to act.

Complainant. One initiating a suit; a plaintiff.

Consent decree. A judgment agreed on by the parties and approved by a court. Insofar as a consent decree it is not the result of a judicial determination, but is subject to continued judicial supervision, it is of limited precedential value.

Cy pres. Literally, "as near as possible." This doctrine can be invoked by a court when the purpose of a charitable trust cannot be fulfilled literally.

Damages. Awards to parties which have been injured by the wrongful act or acts of others. Compensatory, or legal, damages are designed to redress wrongs and place injured parties in the financial position that they would have been in but for the injuries. Equitable damages, as reflected in injunctions or mandamus orders, direct parties to act, or refrain from performing, specified acts. Under limited circumstances, damages can be punitive or exemplary to punish wrongdoers and to serve as deterrents.

Declaratory judgment. A judgment establishing the rights of the parties or deciding a point of law without an order for any action.

De facto. Literally, "in fact."

Defendant. The party against whom an action is brought.

De jure. Literally, "by action of law."

De minimis. Literally, "concerning something minimal;" something so insignificant as to be unworthy of judicial attention.

Demurrer. A response to the effect that, even if facts asserted by the plaintiff are true, there is no cause of action.

De novo. Literally, "concerning the new thing;" a judicial proceeding at which all that transpired at prior proceedings is ignored.

Deposition. A statement of a witness under oath, obtained before trial, in oral question and answer format with cross-examination as if it were offered in court.

Devise. A gift of real estate by a will.

Dicta, **short for** *obiter dictum.* Literally, "a remark by the way;" a gratuitous statement in a judicial opinion that is not necessary to the resolution of a cases. Dicta is persuasive precedent.

Directory. Involving no invalidating consequence if disregarded.

Duress. Unlawful pressure to do what one ordinarily would not do.

En banc. Literally, "in the bench;" an order or opinion by all of the judges in a court.

Enjoin. To direct a party to maintain the status quo either by doing or refraining from doing a specific act; the writ is called an injunction.

Equity. Concept of fairness or justice whereby a court is empowered to remedy a situation where rights are being violated but existing law does not cover the situation.

Estoppel. A bar precluding one from making an assertion because of a prior act.

Et alia, et al. Literally, "and others."

Et sequitur, et seq. Literally, "and those following."

Ex officio. Literally, "by authority of the office."

Ex parte. Literally, "on one side;" a proceeding at which only one party appears.

Express. Directly set forth in words.

Expunge. Obliterate; physically remove, as from a record.

Ex relatione, ex rel. Literally, "on the information;" a proceeding initiated, typically by the state, on behalf of one who provides the information.

Face. What the words alone mean, without amplification or specific application; usually expressed as "on its face" or "facially."

Guilty. Legally responsible in a criminal matter.

Holding. A court's ruling or decision on a question at bar.

In camera. Literally, "in chambers;" a hearing before a judge in the judge's chambers that is not open to the public.

Infra. Literally, "below."

Injunction. See "enjoin."

In loco parentis. Literally, "in place of the parent;" having some of the rights and duties of a parent.

Instant case. The case presently before a court.

Inter alia. Literally, "among other things."

Interrogatory. A written examination before trial, usually in question and answer format.

Inter se, inter sese. Literally, "among or between themselves."

Ipso facto. Literally, "in and of itself."

Judgment. Final judicial determination.

Laches. Unreasonable delay in bringing a legal action to assert a right and which may result in prejudice to party.

Liable. Legally responsible in a civil matter.

Libel. Written defamation.

Malfeasance. Acting with an unlawful or evil intent.

Malice. Improper motive; intentionally committing a wrongful act without justification.

Mandamus. Literally, "we command;" a writ directing a public official to execute a non-discretionary duty.

Material. Important.

Merits. The factual issues raised, as distinguished from procedural issues; the substance of a case rather than procedural matters.

Ministerial. Not involving discretion as to whether or how an act is to be performed; this is an administrative, rather than a policymaking, function.

Misfeasance. Improperly committing a lawful act.

Mitigation. Diminution of a penalty imposed by law, as with damages for breach of contract which are reduced in amount by circumstances not barring a cause of action but only affecting the extent of an injury.

Modus operandi. Literally, "method of operating."

Moot case. No longer a live case or controversy; a case in which a judgment would be abstract with no practical effect.

Nexus. Connection.

Nonfeasance. Failing to perform a legal duty.

Novation. Substitution of a new obligation for an old one.

Nunc pro tunc. Literally, "now for then;" these are acts that are permitted to be done after the time that they should have been done and given retroactive effect.

Opinion. Reasoning to explain a court's judgment. The opinion of the court is the rationale accepted by a majority of participating judges; it authoritatively enunciates the law of a case. Views of individual judges who agree with a court's judgment, but not its full rationale, may appear in concurring opinions; views of judges who disagree are in dissenting opinions.

Parens patriae. Literally, "parent of the country;" the concept of the state's guardianship over persons, such as minors, who are unable to direct their own affairs.

Parol Evidence. Verbal evidence.

Pendent jurisdiction. Doctrine whereby federal courts under limited conditions can decide matters of state law as well as federal matters involved in a single suit.

Per curiam. Literally, "by the court;" an opinion with no identification of the author.

Per se. Literally, "in and of itself."

Petitioner. Party bringing a case before a court; the appellant in an appellate case.

Plaintiff. The party instituting a legal action.

Plenary. Full power or authority.

Police power. The inherent power of government to impose restrictions in order to provide for health, safety, and welfare of its constituents.

Prayer. A request for relief.

Preempt. Take control of; preclude actions by others.

Prima facie. Literally, "on the first appearance, on its face;" evidence supporting a conclusion unless it is rebutted.

Pro forma. Literally, "as a matter of form;" not carefully considered.

Pro Se. Literally, "for the self;" a suit wherein one acts as one's own attorney.

Quantum meruit. Literally, "as much as its deserved;" reasonable value of goods furnished or services rendered.

Quasi. Literally, "as if."

Quid pro quo. Literally, "this for that;" something done in exchange for an act of another.

Quo warranto. Literally, "by what authority;" a writ to test a claim to a public office.

Ratio decidendi. Literally, "the reason for a decision;" the opposite of dicta, it sets forth a court's rationale.

Reductio ad absurdum. Literally, "reduction to the absurd;" an interpretation which would lead to results clearly illogical or not intended.

Remand. To send a case back to the court from which it was appealed for further action.

Res judicata. Literally, "a thing decided;" the final outcome in a case.

Respondent. Party against whom a legal action is brought; the appellee in an appellate case.

Reverter. A provision whereby one who transfers property retains the right to reclaim the property under specified conditions.

Scienter. Literally, "knowingly."

Slander. Oral defamation.

Stare decisis. Literally, "to abide by;" the doctrine of precedent whereby prior judicial decisions are followed under similar facts.

Status quo. Literally, "state in which;" the positions and relationships existing at a specific point in time.

Sua sponte. Literally, "of one's own will." Voluntarily; without necessity or prompting.

Sub judice. Literally, "under or before a judge or court;" a matter being considered by a court.

Summary. Immediate; without a full proceeding.

Supra. Literally, "above, preceding."

Tort. A civil wrong not involving contracts.

Ultra vires. Literally, "beyond the powers;" outside the legal power of an individual or body.

Vacate. To annul.

Vel non. Literally, "or not."

Vested. Fixed; accrued; not subject to any contingency.

Void. Having no legal force or effect.

Waiver. Voluntary and intentional relinquishment of a known right.

INDEX

†